Architectural
GRAPHIC
Standards

JOHN WILEY & SONS, INC.

New York · Chichester · Weinheim · Brisbane · Singapore · Toronto

RAMSEY/SLEEPER

Architectural GRAPHIC Standards

Ninth Edition

1998 Cumulative Supplement

JOHN RAY HOKE, JR., FAIA
EDITOR IN CHIEF

THE AMERICAN INSTITUTE OF ARCHITECTS

SUBSCRIPTION NOTICE

Architectural Graphic Standards is updated on a periodic basis to reflect important changes in the subject matter. If you purchased this product directly from John Wiley & Sons, Inc., we have already recorded your subscription for this update service

If, however, you purchased this product from a bookstore and wish to receive future updates or editions billed separately with a 15-day examination review, please send your name, company name (if applicable), address, and the title of this product to:

Supplement Department
John Wiley & Sons, Inc.
One Wiley Drive
Somerset, NJ 08875
1-(800)-225-5945

This book is printed on acid-free paper. ∞

The drawings, tables, data, and other information in this book have been obtained from many sources, including government organizations, trade associations, suppliers of building materials, and professional architects or architecture firms. The American Institute of Architects (AIA), the Architectural Graphic Standards Task Force of the AIA, and the publisher have made every reasonable effort to make this reference work accurate and authoritative, but do not warrant, and assume no liability for, the accuracy or completeness of the text or its fitness for any particular purpose. It is the responsibility of users to apply their professional knowledge in the use of information contained in this book, to consult the original sources for additional information when appropriate, and, if they themselves are not professional architects, to consult an architect when appropriate.

ISBN 0-471-29553-1

Printed in the United States of America.
10 9 8 7 6 5 4 3 2 1

CONTENTS

The following pages supplement sixteen of the
twenty chapters in the ninth edition of
Architectural Graphic Standards.

PUBLISHER'S NOTE

As publisher of Ramsey/Sleeper's *Architectural Graphic Standards* since 1932, John Wiley & Sons, Inc., is deeply committed to providing the design community with current, reliable information resources. We have witnessed landmark changes in the field, from the integration of the computer in the design office to new zoning and building code regulations that govern the industry. Several years ago, our readers encouraged us to provide more frequent updates to keep them apprised of these important changes. In response to these requests and our own assessment of the field, we developed the supplement program for *Architectural Graphic Standards*. The intent of the program is to provide design professionals with essential new information annually—Information that otherwise would remain inaccessible until the publication of the new edition.

The *1998 Architectural Graphic Standards Supplement* is the fourth supplement published since the release of the ninth edition in 1994. We will continue to review and update the ninth edition through annual supplementation until the tenth edition of *Architectural Graphic Standards* is launched.

The *1998 Supplement* contains important new information and standards concerning acoustics, parking, sitework, special construction, HVAC systems, athletic facilities, and retail stores. We have also included a complete index that integrates material from the ninth edition with material from the cumulative supplement.

We are proud to publish the *1998 Architectural Graphic Standards Supplement* and welcome your comments and suggestions for future updates.

ROBERT C. GARBER
Publisher
John Wiley & Sons, Inc.

FOREWORD

We at the American Institute of Architects are committed to providing our members—whether sole practitioners or those in small, medium, or large firms—with superior tools, skills, and resources to enhance and promote the value of the architecture profession. This commitment must be the fundamental purpose of any association, and it is the key to the AIA's growth.

Most of all, the AIA is about "knowledge"—about creating it and sharing it, and thereby adding to our members' competitive advantage. Among the many resources available, *Architectural Graphic Standards* stands alone as a visual compendium of architectural knowledge. It is the "bible," an old friend, and a source of cutting-edge technology wrapped in one package. Architects young and old rely on *AGS* as an indispensable professional reference.

The joint venture between the AIA and publishing partner John Wiley & Sons, Inc., has yielded four major editions of *AGS*. The ninth edition appeared in 1994. This volume is the fourth cumulative supplement to that edition.

America's architects have been well served by the Institute in this core publication, which encourages AIA members to share their knowledge of practice and design. *Architectural Graphic Standards* is one of our profession's greatest assets and one of the Institute's brightest stars.

MARK HURWITZ, Ph.D., CAE
Chief Executive Officer
The American Institute of Architects

PREFACE

The American Institute of Architects and John Wiley & Sons, Inc., are delighted to offer the fourth supplement to the ninth edition of *Architectural Graphic Standards*. For many architects, this annual supplement of 100 new pages has become a useful companion to the main edition. Our mission for the supplement program is to provide architects and other members of the building team with current design data and to keep them abreast of the rapidly changing construction industry.

The book features a comprehensive index, which covers the entire ninth edition as well as the supplement pages. This combined index should save time in cross-referencing and should better integrate the supplement with the main edition.

It is our intention with this and future supplements to build on whole *AGS* chapters rather than to revise or produce isolated pages. This approach should bring more balance and editorial coordination to the tenth edition, scheduled for publication in March 2000.

At John Wiley & Sons, Inc., I would like to thank Joel Stein, editorial director; Amanda Miller, senior editor; Robert J. Fletcher IV, associate production director; Meg Day, associate marketing director; and Anthony Lewandowski, CAD graphic consultant, all of whom contribute their vast talent and craftsmanship to making these supplements the very best source of technical information available to design professionals. The fine work of Automated Composition Service Inc., of Lancaster, Pennsylvania, is also greatly appreciated.

At the AIA, I am delighted with the dedication of our gifted professionals. My special thanks go to consulting editor Richard J.

Vitullo, AIA, for his good work in researching and developing these pages. Our fantastic editorial team consisted of Janet Rumbarger, managing editor, and Pamela James Blumgart, copy editor. I am very fortunate to have them as my associates.

As always, our greatest debt is to the AIA firms, members, and other contributors for their tremendous efforts on this book. Their valuable service and dedication to excellence is apparent on every page. I would also like to thank Mark W. Hurwitz, Ph.D., CAE, chief executive officer, and Fred DeLuca, Hon. AIA, senior vice president, for their trust and support of this important AIA program.

On a more personal note. I have dedicated this supplement to the memory of W. Bradford Wiley (1911-1998), Chairman, Emeritus at Wiley, for his many years of support and interest in *AGS*. Brad began his career at Wiley about the same time the first edition was published in 1932, and he always considered this book to be John Wiley's flagship publication. I had the privilege to consider Brad a friend, and I will always be indebted to this publishing giant.

The American Institute of Architects and John Wiley & Sons, Inc., hope you will keep alive Ramsey and Sleeper's vision of *Architectural Graphic Standards* as a publication with no limit on what might be included in future volumes. We are always glad to hear readers' ideas about how the AIA can improve this book.

JOHN RAY HOKE, JR., FAIA
Editor in Chief

Architectural
GRAPHIC
Standards

GENERAL

According to the theory of plate tectonics, the earth's crust is divided into constantly moving plates. Earthquakes occur when, as a result of slowly accumulating pressure, the ground slips abruptly along a geological fault plane on or near a plate boundary. The resulting waves of vibration within the earth create ground motions at the surface, which, in turn, induce movement within buildings. The frequency, magnitude, and duration of the ground motion, physical characteristics of the building, and geology of a site determine how these forces affect a building.

DESIGN JUDGMENT

In an earthquake, buildings designed to the minimum levels required by model codes often sustain damage. Early discussions with an owner should explore the need to limit property loss in an earthquake and the desirability of attempting to ensure continued building operation immediately afterward. To achieve these results, it may be necessary to make design decisions more carefully tuned to the seismic conditions of a site than code requires.

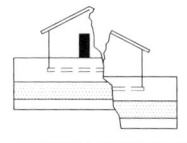  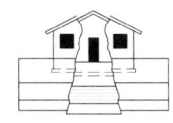 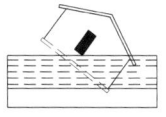

GROUND RUPTURE   GROUND SHAKING   DIFFERENTIAL SUBSIDENCE   LIQUEFACTION

MAIN CAUSES OF FOUNDATION FAILURE

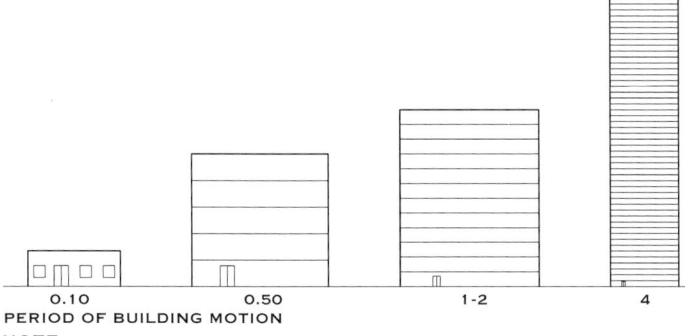 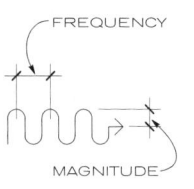

| 0.10 | 0.50 | 1-2 | 4 |

PERIOD OF BUILDING MOTION

FREQUENCY

MAGNITUDE

SEISMIC GROUND MOTION

NOTE

The relationship between the period of ground motion and the period of building motion is of great importance. Fundamental periods of motion in structures range from 0.1 second for a one-story building to 4.0 seconds or more for a high-rise building. Ground generally vibrates for a period of between 0.5 and 1.0 second. If the period of ground motion and the natural period of motion in a building coincide, the building may resonate and the loads will be increased. Theoretically, one part of the seismic design problem is to "tune" the building so that its own period of motion falls outside the estimated range of ground motion frequency. In practice, this tuning is very seldom carried out. Rather, architects rely on increased load effects required by the applicable code to take care of the problem.

FUNDAMENTAL PERIODS

SEISMIC ACCELERATION FOR LOW BUILDINGS EXPRESSED AS A PERCENTAGE OF GRAVITY

William W. Stewart, FAIA; Stewart-Schaberg Architects; Clayton, Missouri
Map courtesy of the U.S. Geological Survey, National Seismic Hazard Mapping Project (June 1996)

SEISMIC CODES

The seismic requirements in the Uniform Building Code have historically been based on Recommended Lateral Force Requirements, generally referred to as "The Blue Book," an earthquake design manual developed by the Structural Engineers Association of California. The seismic requirements in the National Building Code and the Standard Building Code are based on FEMA 222, the National Earthquake Hazards Reduction Program Recommended Provisions for Seismic Regulations for New Buildings. Since the Blue Book and the NEHRP provisions incorporate the expertise of many of the same engineers, and since the anticipated International Building Code will encourage convergence of the requirements, the seismic code development community intends to make the two codes similar.

The following information is based on the requirements expected to appear in the 1997 NEHRP provisions and in subsequent issues of all model codes. Detached one- and two-family dwellings will be exempt from seismic regulations in areas other than those with high seismicity. Seismic codes are constantly evolving, and architects should always consult the relevant code before beginning a project.

A recent, significant change in the seismic codes is the elimination of seismic zones as a basis for establishing design acceleration. Seismic maps have been redrawn (completely for the first time since 1976) to show building response periods as a percentage of gravity.

The map below, based on a building response period of 0.2 second, gives accelerations to be used for low buildings. A similar map based on a building response of 1.0 second is proposed for taller buildings. Before determining what level of ground shaking applies to a project, an architect must find out what type of earth the building will be built on. The maps are based on buildings built on soft rock, but ground motion increases as the soil becomes softer.

TERMS

The seismic community has an extensive set of terms with which to describe common conditions in the field. Following is a short list of these terms and their definitions:

BASE SHEAR (static analysis): calculated total shear force acting at the base of a structure, used in codes as a static representation of lateral earthquake forces; also referred to as "equivalent lateral force."

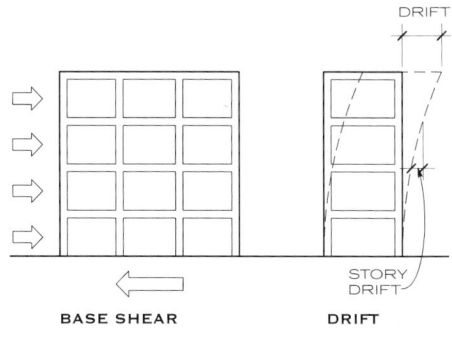

DRIFT

STORY DRIFT

BASE SHEAR   DRIFT

BASE SHEAR AND DRIFT

DESIGN EARTHQUAKE: earthquake ground motion for which a building is designed.

DRIFT: lateral deflection of a building or structure. Story drift is the relative movement between adjacent floors.

DUCTILITY: the ability of a structural frame to bend but not break. Its ductility is a major factor in establishing the ability of a building to withstand large earthquakes. Ductile materials (steel in particular) fail only after permanent deformation has taken place. Good ductility requires special detailing of the joints.

DYNAMIC ANALYSIS: a structural analysis based on the vibration motion of a building. Dynamic analysis is time-consuming and normally reserved for complex projects.

FORCES, IN-PLANE: forces exerted parallel to a wall or frame.

FORCES, OUT-OF-PLANE: forces exerted perpendicular to a wall or frame.

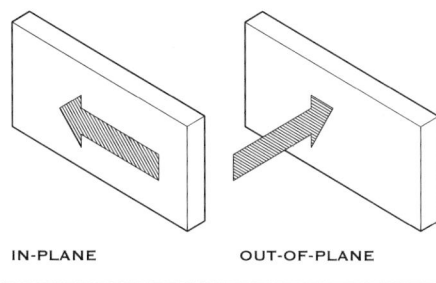

IN-PLANE   OUT-OF-PLANE

FORCE DIAGRAMS

MAXIMUM CONSIDERED EARTHQUAKE: the greatest ground shaking expected to occur during an earthquake at a site. These values are somewhat higher than those of the design earthquake, particularly in areas where seismic events are very infrequent. The code maps are based on earthquakes of this magnitude.

RE-ENTRANT CORNER: The inside building corner of an L-, H-, X-, or T-shaped plan.

GENERAL

Each building and site lies within a broader context of regional seismicity, localized geology, community vulnerability, and adjacent structures and land uses. Siting decisions, therefore, can have a significant impact on the overall seismic performance of a structure. This page focuses on the following criteria for siting a building:

1. Avoid unstable sites.
2. Avoid nonengineered fill.
3. Avoid or design for sites that can subside or liquefy.
4. Avoid building over surface faulting.
5. Avoid adjacent hazardous buildings.
6. Prevent battering from adjacent buildings.
7. Create safe areas of refuge when redeveloping older buildings.

Decisions on appropriate land uses for a specific site, separation from active ground faulting, site stability, and separation from adjacent buildings are critical to performance. Although many of these factors have traditionally been considered city planning issues, the designer must also incorporate them into the architectural development of a seismically resistant building.

SEISMIC ZONATION TO REDUCE RISK

RELATIVE RISK OF SITE	LAND USE
Low	High-density commercial/retail
	High occupancy and assembly
	Essential services (fire stations, hospitals, emergency operations centers, etc.)
	Hazardous industrial processes
Medium	Medium- and low-density residential
	Low-rise commercial/retail
	Industrial uses
High	Very low-density residential
	Nonhazardous industrial
	Recreation
	Public open space
	Public rights-of-way

NOTE

Land uses should reflect the relative risk of the location.

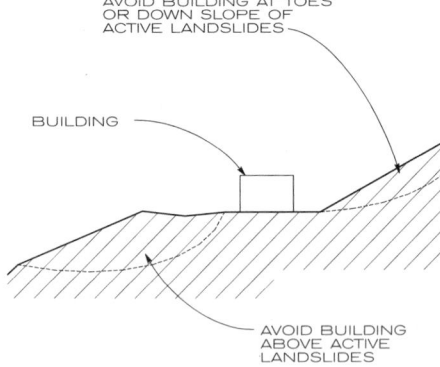

SITE SECTION

NOTE

On sloping sites, earthquakes can trigger landslides. Also, alluvium and unconsolidated soils can increase the violence and duration of ground shaking. In areas of young soil deposits, design for greater ground shaking. For example, during the 1989 Loma Prieta earthquake, ground shaking in San Francisco's marina district, on nonengineered fill, was more than twice as violent and lasted more than twice as long as ground shaking on adjacent bedrock sites.

UNSTABLE SITES

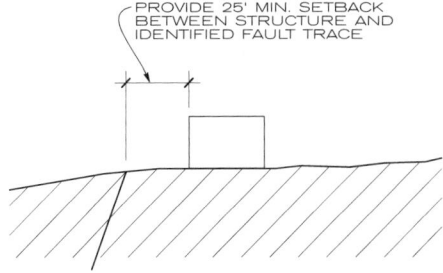

SITE SECTION

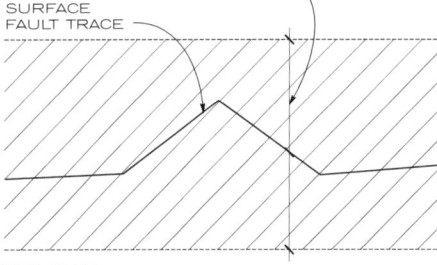

SITE PLAN

NOTE

Within a fault zone, trench to determine the exact location of the fault trace. Development within a fault zone should be restricted to low-density land uses, open space, and other low-occupancy activities.

SURFACE FAULTING

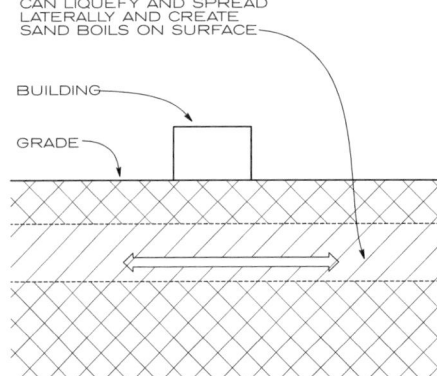

SITE SECTION (BEFORE LIQUEFACTION)

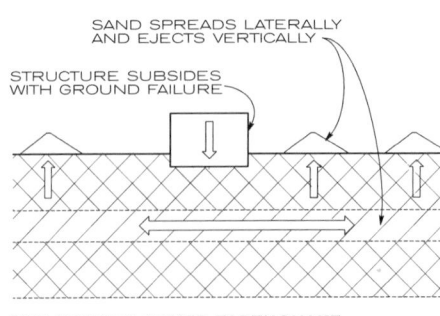

SITE SECTION (AFTER EARTHQUAKE AND LIQUEFACTION)

NOTE

Avoid sites subject to liquefaction (water saturated sandy soils), design foundation systems to withstand ground failure, drain water from the site, and change the composition of the soil and compact the site.

SUBSIDENCE OR LIQUEFACTION

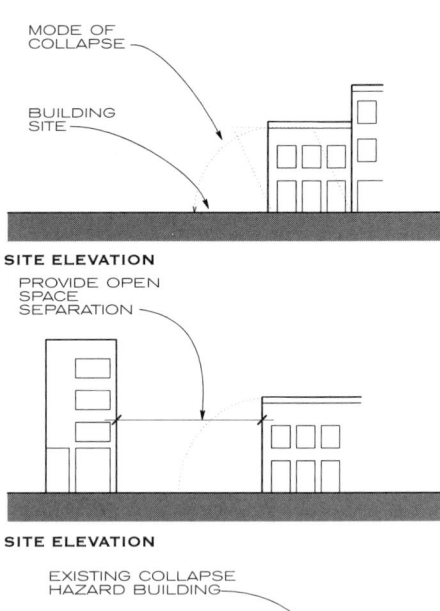

SITE ELEVATION

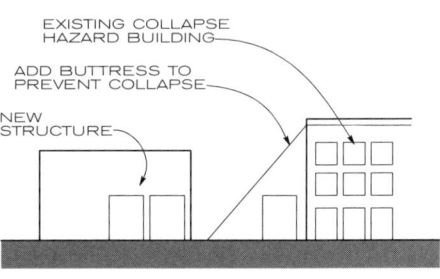

SITE ELEVATION

ADJACENT HAZARDOUS BUILDINGS

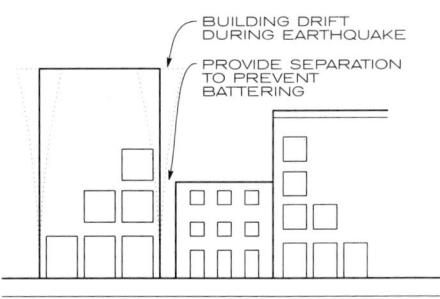

BATTERING FROM ADJACENT BUILDINGS

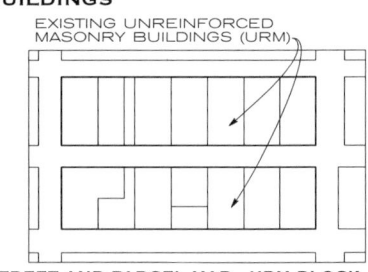

STREET AND PARCEL MAP—URM BLOCK

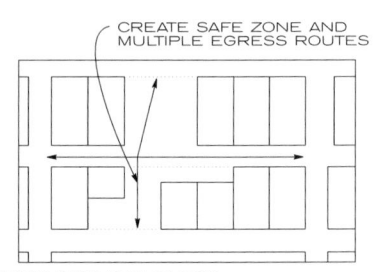

REVITALIZED URM BLOCK

SAFE AREAS OF REFUGE IN OLDER BUILDINGS

Richard Eisner, FAIA; Governor's Office of Emergency Services; Oakland, California

Building Configuration for Seismic Areas

LOAD PATHS

A load path is the path seismic forces take from the roof to the foundation of a structure. Typically the load travels from the diaphragms through connections to the vertical lateral force-resisting elements and on to the foundation by way of additional connections. This path should be direct and uninterrupted. Seismic design begins with, and codes require, the establishment of a continuous load path.

The seismic-resistant framing system selected for a structure must meet both architectural and seismic design requirements. Although most buildings can be made seismic resistant, some architectural configurations interrupt the load path or otherwise interfere with the seismic design process. Inappropriate design choices increase construction cost and make the seismic restraint system less effective. The examples on this page contrast configurations that probably would cause problems in areas with high levels of seismicity with variations that should avoid these problems.

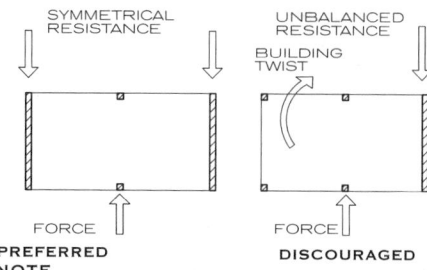

PREFERRED **DISCOURAGED**

NOTE

The lateral force resisting system for a symmetrical building is much easier to design than that for an asymmetrical building. Because the source of an earthquake cannot be known, symmetry in both directions should be considered.

TORSION IN PLAN

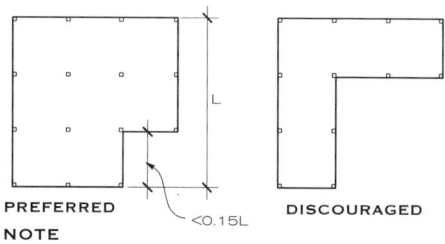

PREFERRED **DISCOURAGED**

NOTE

This is a variation of the symmetry issue. When the notch gets too big, the building tends to tear at the inside corner.

RE-ENTRANT CORNERS

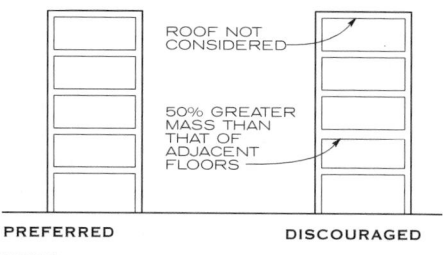

PREFERRED **DISCOURAGED**

NOTE

While all floors do not have to be the same, it is important that no floor has too much more mass than those adjacent.

MASS IRREGULARITY

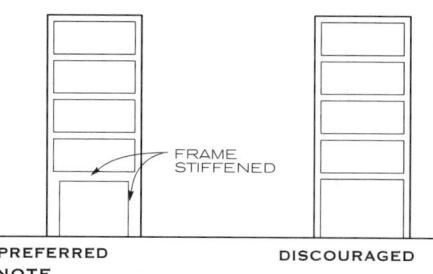

PREFERRED **DISCOURAGED**

NOTE

When a taller (inherently weaker) first floor is desired, anticipate using much heavier first floor framing to equalize the stiffness with that of the floors above.

SOFT STORY

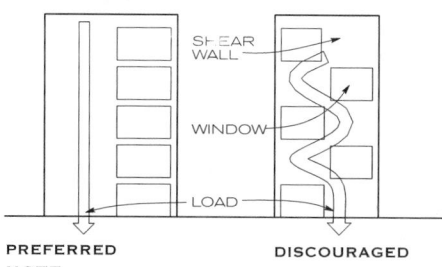

PREFERRED **DISCOURAGED**

NOTE

Although both drawings illustrate shear walls in the same plane, one arrangement is discouraged because the load path is not direct enough.

IN-PLANE DISCONTINUITY

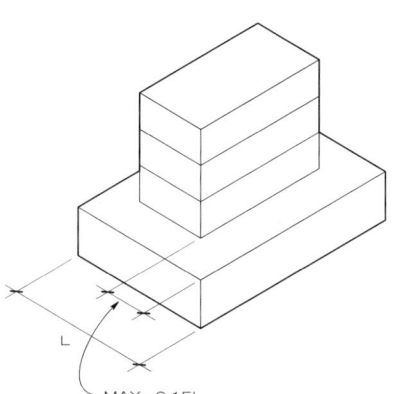

PREFERRED

NOTE

The base should not be too much larger than the tower above.

VERTICAL GEOMETRY IRREGULARITY

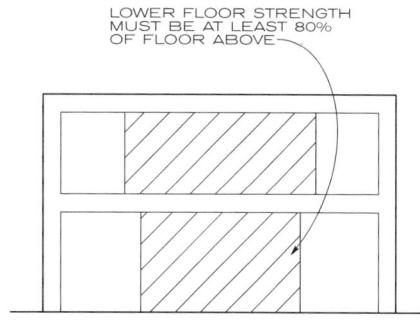

PREFERRED

NOTE

While it is best to have uniform stiffness, some variation is acceptable.

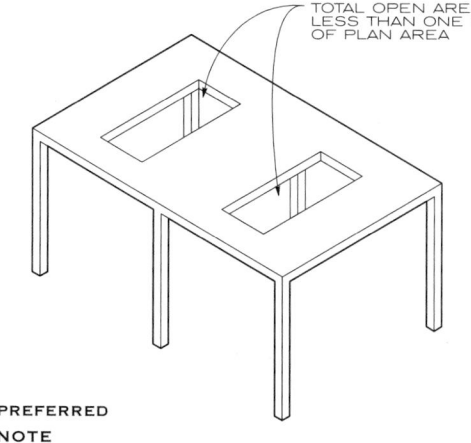

PREFERRED

NOTE

Horizontal diaphragms (floors and roofs) can more readily transfer earthquake loads to the vertical force resisting

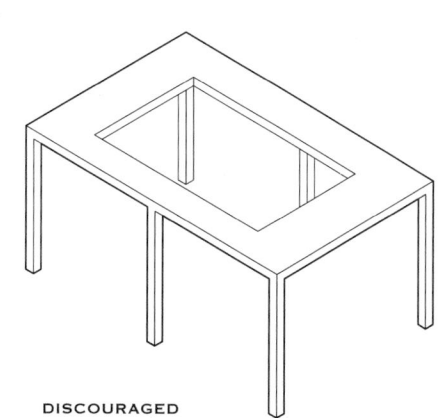

DISCOURAGED

system when the size and number of holes in the diaphragm are limited.

DIAPHRAGM DISCONTINUITIES

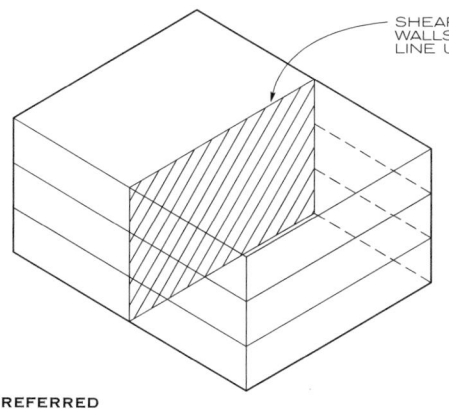

PREFERRED

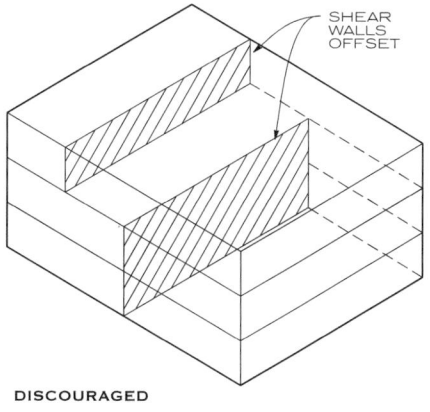

DISCOURAGED

OUT-OF-PLANE VERTICAL OFFSETS

William W. Stewart, FAIA; Stewart-Schaberg Architects; Clayton, Missouri

ESTABLISHING SEISMIC FORCES

The equivalent lateral force procedure is the most common method of establishing seismic design forces. In it, the seismic load, V (base shear), is determined by multiplying the weight of the building by a factor C_s ($V=C_sW$). The value of C_s depends on the size of the design earthquake, the type of soil, and the response modification factor (a variable corresponding to the type of lateral force resisting system used). This force is applied at the base of the structure then distributed throughout the building according to the mass and strength of the structure.

DESIGN FOR RESISTING SEISMIC FORCES

Shear walls are load-bearing or nonload-bearing walls that resist seismic forces acting in the plane of the wall. Shear wall design is simpler and more cost-effective than other lateral force resisting systems; however, the architectural design must be able to accommodate the locations of these walls and the small number of openings they permit.

Diaphragms are horizontal or nearly horizontal structural elements (usually a floor or roof) designed to transmit lateral forces to the vertical elements of a seismic resisting system. Diaphragms must be rigid enough and the connections strong enough to transfer the entire load to the lateral force resisting system.

Tall, narrow structures tend to tip over before they slide, while short structures slide rather than tip. Earthquake waves rock buildings, increasing overturning loads, and can act in any direction. Thus, resistance to overturning is best achieved at a building's perimeter rather than at its core.

Building foundations must be designed to resist the lateral forces transmitted through the earth and the forces transmitted from the lateral load resisting system to the earth. In general, softer soils amplify the effects of an earthquake.

BUILDING FRAMES

Braced frames depend on diagonal braces to resist lateral forces. Although cost-effective, most braces limit the number of openings possible in a wall. Eccentric bracing is a configuration that allows for more openings than are normally achievable. K-bracing used to be a common variation of X-bracing, but it was discovered that the forces at the intersection are very great, making the connection difficult.

A moment frame is one in which members and joints are able to resist lateral forces along the axis of the members as well as by bending. It is an alternative to solid shear walls that allows for openness and design flexibility.

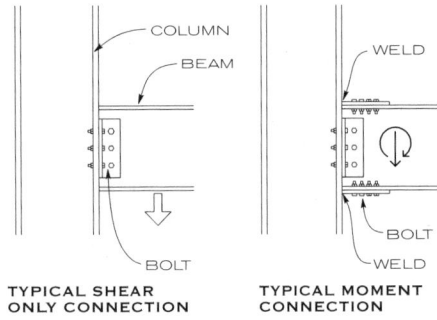

TYPICAL SHEAR ONLY CONNECTION   **TYPICAL MOMENT CONNECTION**

CONNECTIONS

WOOD CONNECTIONS

Connections are an important element of the lateral force resisting framing system. Wood connections come in a variety of types, many of which are not appropriate for seismic or wind loading conditions. End grain nailing performs poorly and should be avoided, and toe nailing as the sole means of attachment is inadequate. Positive connections using appropriate fasteners are necessary to establish a continuous load path. Shear walls must be fastened securely to the foundation. Diaphragms should be properly attached to the lateral force resisting system. Connector design and detailing should include proper use of connectors to achieve required load capacity and code compliance. Adequate size and placing of nails is necessary to minimize splitting and optimize the load carrying ability of the frame. (See AGS pages on wood seismic design and structural wood fasteners for details.)

William W. Stewart, FAIA; Stewart-Schaberg Architects; Clayton, Missouri

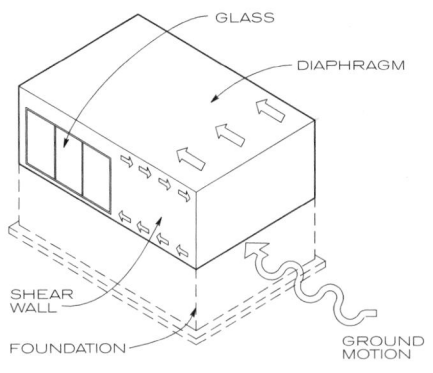

SHEAR WALLS AND DIAPHRAGMS

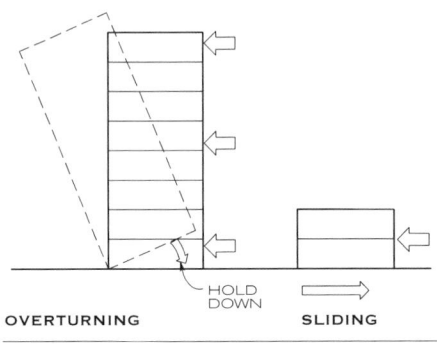

OVERTURNING   **SLIDING**

OVERTURNING AND SLIDING

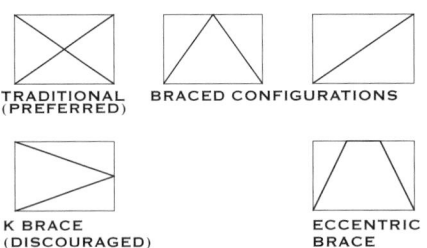

TRADITIONAL (PREFERRED)   **BRACED CONFIGURATIONS**

K BRACE (DISCOURAGED)   **ECCENTRIC BRACE**

BRACED FRAMES

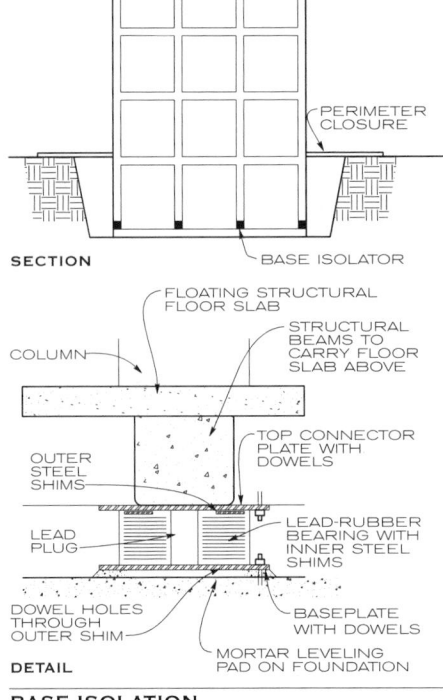

SECTION

DETAIL

BASE ISOLATION

ANCHORAGE

Anchors are either cast-in-place or drilled in after placement of the concrete. When anchors can be precisely located before the concrete is poured, cast-in-place anchors are typically used. Post-installed anchors are usually employed when anchor locations cannot be predetermined with accuracy. Spacing between anchors, the distance to the edge of the concrete, embedment depth, stiffness characteristics, and the type of loading (e.g., dead, live, dynamic, seismic) all must be considered. For structural elements that require seismic design, only anchors tested under dynamic loading should be used. The preferred anchor types for seismic performance include cast-in-place bolts and inserts. Acceptable post-installed anchors are undercut anchors, heavy-duty sleeve (torque-controlled expansion) anchors, and chemical anchors. J-bolts and L-bolts cannot be counted on to resist much uplift.

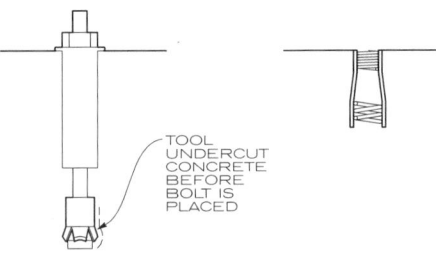

UNDERCUT POST-INSTALLED ANCHOR   **THREADED CAST-IN-PLACE ANCHOR**

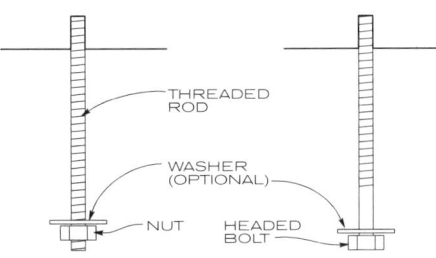

HEADED CAST-IN-PLACE ANCHORS

ANCHORAGE

BASE ISOLATION

Base isolation is a major seismic design innovation. Analogous to the suspension of an automobile, isolators separate the building from ground motion. Base isolation is most cost-effective for buildings in areas of high seismicity, buildings that must have an irregular shape, large historic buildings, and buildings that must remain in operation immediately after an earthquake.

When using base isolation, it is important to ensure that the isolators are the only place where the building touches the surrounding earth. This is normally accomplished by positioning the building in a large scooped out area and connecting it to the surrounding ground with flexible "bridges." The base isolators are usually located in a sub-basement dedicated to their use.

A recent variation of base isolation is offered by a family of devices that absorb or dissipate energy and change the response of a structure to seismic activity. These systems appear most useful for improving existing structures without the need for an entirely new structural system.

REFERENCES

AIA/ACSA Council on Architectural Research. Buildings at Risk: Seismic Design Basics for Practicing Architects.

Ceilings and Interior Systems Construction Association. Recommendations for Direct-Hung Acoustical Tile and Lay-in Panel Ceilings. 5700 Old Orchard Rd., Skokie, IL 60077.

National Earthquake Hazards Reduction Program (NEHRP). Recommended Provisions for Seismic Regulations for New Buildings, 1994 ed. Part 1, "Provisions" (FEMA-222A); part 2, "Commentary" (FEMA-223A).

——. Handbook for the Seismic Evaluation of Existing Buildings (FEMA-178) and Handbook of Techniques for the Seismic Rehabilitation of Existing Buildings (FEMA-172).

——. Non-Technical Explanation of the 1994 NEHRP Recommended Provisions (FEMA-99).

GENERAL

When detailing architectural and mechanical elements for seismic resistance, the architect's primary concerns are to minimize falling hazards and to maintain a normal egress route. Features such as masonry chimneys, parapets, light fixtures, suspended mechanical equipment, large duct-work, and heavy pipes are potential falling hazards. Cabinets and bookcases can block exits if they fall. An additional concern for architects designing for earthquake-prone areas is the need for a building to remain in operation after an earthquake.

Many resources that offer detailed solutions for seismic design only address areas with high seismic activity. However, no single detail is appropriate for all areas. This page is meant to guide architects through the philosophy of seismic design. Readers should use the references listed to develop the right solution for a particular site.

To determine seismic forces on architectural components, an importance factor (I) is introduced into the force equation. I is either 1.0 or 1.5. If the component is essential or might create a hazardous condition when falling or breaking, there is a 50% increase in the design load. The lateral force = $1.6\ S_{aS}\ IW$. W is the weight of the part. S_{aS} is the spectral acceleration. In reality the force decreases as the location (height) of the component within the building is lowered. A more complicated formula is available if it is necessary to reduce the loads.

SEISMIC DESIGN CATEGORY FOR STRUCTURES

	SEISMIC USE GROUP		
VALUE OF S_{aS}	I	II	III
$S_{aS} \leq 0.167\ g$	A	A	A
$0.167\ g \leq S_{aS} < 0.33\ g$	B	B	C
$0.33\ g \leq S_{aS} < 0.50\ g$	C	C	D
$0.50\ g \leq S_{aS} < 1.0\ g$	D	D	D
$1.0\ g \leq S_{aS}$	E	E	F

NOTES

1. g—weight of object being analyzed; S_{aS}—spectral response acceleration
2. Seismic use group classification is assigned to each building depending on the importance of maintaining function or protecting occupant safety. Buildings in seismic use group III are those that are required to function for post earthquake recovery. Seismic use group II buildings are buildings with relatively large occupant loads. Any remaining buildings fall into group I. The level of seismic detailing is expressed by letters A through F and is based on the relationship between the seismic use group and the level of design ground motion. This level of detailing is known as the seismic design category.

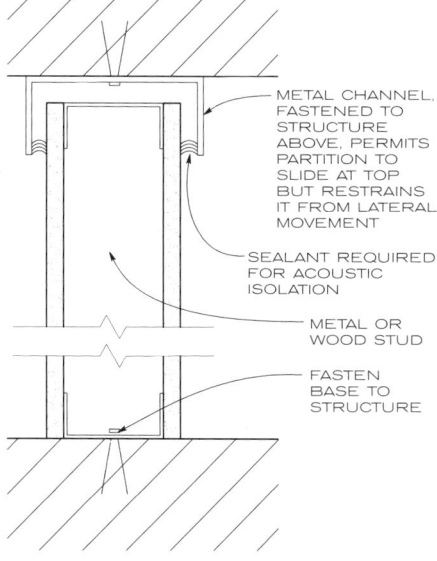

NOTE

This detail must be checked for acceptability when the partition is fire-rated. Partitions that extend to the structure above usually perform well if consideration has been given to potential building racking (i.e., being forced out of plumb).

PARTITION DETAIL FOR SEISMIC AREAS

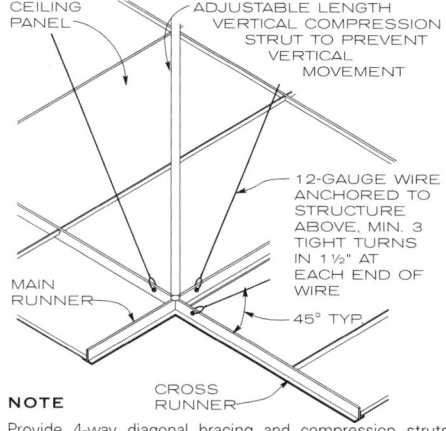

NOTE

Provide 4-way diagonal bracing and compression struts approximately every 12 ft each way.

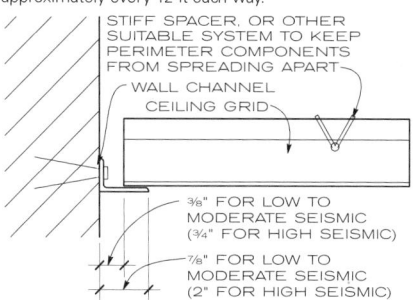

WALL ATTACHMENT DETAIL
NOTE

For ceiling grids, pull-out capacity at the joints is a key to good seismic performance. Vertical (compression) struts prevent failure from wave-like or galloping motion. Solutions for all levels of seismic activity are addressed in the Ceilings and Interior Systems Construction Association standards.

CEILING DETAILS FOR SEISMIC AREAS

LIGHT FIXTURES

There are two ways to handle light fixtures that could shake free from the ceiling grid and create a falling hazard. One is to suspend the light fixture from the structure above with two to four wires (if two wires, they should be in opposite corners). The second method (not used in areas with high seismicity) is to brace the ceiling and clip the light fixtures to the grid. Pendant-mounted fixtures should be designed so they cannot swing and hit other building components.

EXTERIOR CLADDING

Exterior cladding must be secured to the building to prevent it from falling. Heavier veneers require more anchorage. When cladding is anchored to the structural frame, consideration must be given to how movement of the frame will affect movement in the cladding. A major concern is the difference in movement between floors and/or floor and roof (story drift), which is addressed with connections that permit the cladding to move independently of the structural frame. Commonly used are push-pull connections, caulked joints, slip joints, and covers that collapse.

SPRINKLER SYSTEMS

To brace sprinkler systems, architects must address three main problems: the falling hazard of heavy mains, separation of the mains at the joints (property loss is critical here), and breaking of the pipes where the heads pass through the ceiling. The latter problem is solved by enlarging the hole (with up to 1 in. clearance) and covering it with a large escutcheon plate. An alternative is to detail a swing joint in the sprinkler drop that will provide 1 in. movement in all directions. Another solution is to detail the grid and sprinkler drops as one integral unit. (See NFPA 13 for information on sprinkler bracing.)

WATER HEATERS

When a water heater overturns, a gas line can rupture. Depending on the level of seismicity, the common solution for residential water heaters is to use a flexible gas connection and/or a simple steel strap wrapped around the tank and securely anchored to a stud or solid wall.

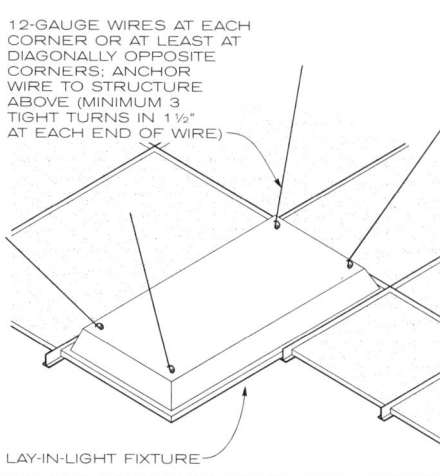

LIGHTING FIXTURE DETAIL FOR SEISMIC AREAS

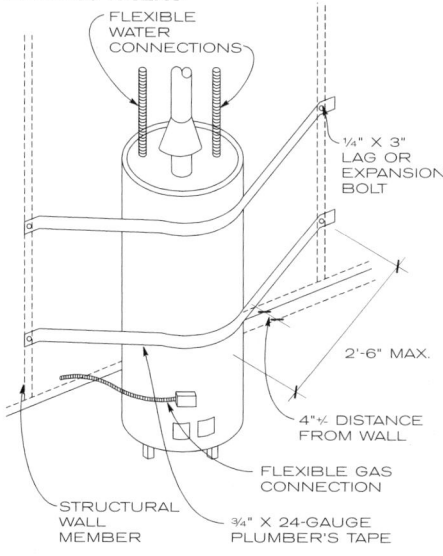

NOTE

Fill space between water heater and wall with 2x blocking with cushioned face.

WATER HEATER SEISMIC REINFORCING

SHELVING AND CABINETS

Shelves and racks can overturn during seismic activity, injuring building occupants or blocking exits. The hazard increases with the occupancy density and the height of the equipment. Fixtures should be bolted onto heavy-gauge studs above their center of gravity.

ELEVATORS

Traction elevators cause the most concern in regard to seismic activity. The main problem is that the counterweights may come loose and strike the cab. Current elevator standards address this problem, but older elevators may need to be upgraded.

HVAC, ELECTRICAL, AND PLUMBING COMPONENTS

HVAC equipment is often heavy, with large inertial forces; securely attaching such equipment greatly reduces damage. Piping systems generally perform well during seismic activity but are vulnerable at equipment connections.

Heavy electrical equipment such as switchgear, transformers, and batteries are the parts of the electrical system most vulnerable to seismic activity. Emergency systems depend on electrical power for fuel or control and so may fail even though the equipment remains functional.

Plumbing distribution systems are relatively flexible and can withstand a fair amount of shaking. Piping and equipment should be anchored so it will move with the structure, limiting differential movement at the joints.

William W. Stewart, FAIA; Stewart-Schaberg Architects; Clayton, Missouri

GENERAL

The greatest hazard in major earthquakes stems from older buildings that were designed under early seismic codes or before such codes were introduced. Seismic rehabilitation (or seismic retrofit) refers to design and construction intended to improve the seismic performance of an existing building.

Some cities have established seismic rehabilitation programs to reduce the risk caused by unreinforced masonry (URM) buildings, which are particularly hazardous in earthquakes. The City of Los Angeles, for example, passed an URM ordinance in 1981 that required all of the 8000 URM buildings in the city to be strengthened or demolished. San Francisco has a similar ordinance. Many buildings also have been voluntarily rehabilitated.

REHABILITATION PROCESS

The first steps in rehabilitation are to identify the seismic deficiencies and determine a method of rehabilitation. Other steps involve budgeting, preparing contract documents, and selecting a contractor.

EVALUATION PROCEDURES

Two procedures exist for evaluating buildings for seismic rehabilitation. The first, called rapid visual screening (RVS), is used to assess the rehabilitation needs of a number of buildings: a whole city, a few city blocks, a college campus, etc. RVS involves surveying the exterior of a building and recording its major features in a way that allows it to be rated for possible seismic risk. The evaluation takes about 30 minutes per building. The intent is not to provide a definitive seismic rating but rather to indicate which buildings should undergo a more detailed evaluation. This procedure is described in Federal Emergency Management Agency (FEMA) Publication 154.

The second, more detailed seismic evaluation process is described in FEMA Publication 178. The evaluation begins with collecting information about a structure and classifying it according to one of fifteen model building types. This qualitative investigation determines whether the building exhibits any of the defined life-threatening performance characteristics that similar structures have demonstrated in previous earthquakes. If such characteristics are identified, a detailed evaluation is recommended and permissible capacity/demand ratios are suggested. Although the detailed procedure generally takes several days to complete, it provides an evaluation of the building's threat to life and a list of the particular structural and nonstructural features that must be addressed.

Another aspect of the evaluation is establishing the benefit-cost ratio for seismic rehabilitation. FEMA Publication 227 describes such a procedure and provides computer software to perform the evaluation.

HAZARDOUS BUILDING TYPES

Any building may be hazardous in an earthquake if it is not designed according to seismic codes and, perhaps more significant, the designer does not understand or have experience with seismic design. Many old buildings, designed before seismic codes existed, are well designed seismically and have stood the test of time. Other, newer buildings are unsafe because they were designed according to an obsolete code and without an understanding of seismic design issues.

A number of typical building types have been identified as hazardous because of their generally poor performance in earthquakes:

1. URMs: bearing wall buildings with unreinforced masonry walls, usually brick.
2. Nonductile concrete frame: typical of buildings constructed in the United States before about 1975, when new codes came into effect that recognized the problems caused by underreinforced concrete frame structures subject to brittle failure. (Ductility refers to the ability of structures, usually steel structures, to deform greatly under load without collapsing.)
3. Concrete or steel frame with unreinforced masonry walls (often hollow tile): popular for buildings constructed from the early 20th century until World War II.
4. Precast concrete tilt-up construction: common industrial building type that relies on the exterior concrete walls to act as shear walls against earthquake forces. Unless correctly detailed, the roofs are likely to pull away from the walls and collapse during earthquakes.

REHABILITATION STRATEGIES

Although the unique characteristics of each building must be considered when devising a rehabilitation strategy, some fundamental concepts have been developed from experience:

1. Add strength.
2. Alter building stiffness.
3. Create structural continuity.
4. Add structural containment.
5. Rationalize existing capacity.
6. Isolate the building from the ground.
7. Add energy-dissipating details.

In addition to purely structural issues, architectural concerns influence rehabilitation design. For historic buildings, rehabilitation measures must be devised that respect the original architecture, and the addition of external strengthening components is not an option. For other buildings this may not be a concern, and affordable cost, safety, and preservation of building function may be the paramount objectives.

FEMA publication 172 provides conceptual design guidance on methods of rehabilitating all 15 model building types described in FEMA 178.

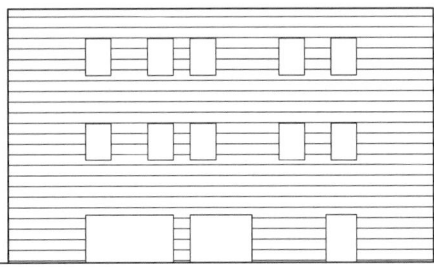

**UNREINFORCED MASONRY
BEARING WALL**

NONDUCTILE CONCRETE FRAME

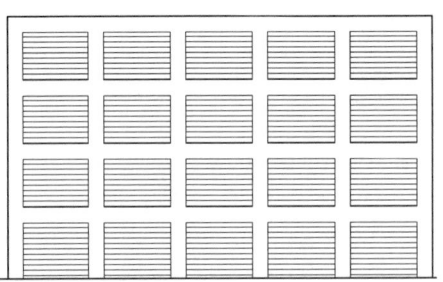

**CONCRETE FRAME WITH
UNREINFORCED MASONRY INFILL**

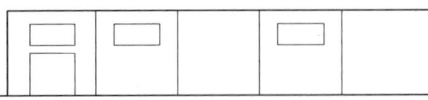

PRECAST CONCRETE TILT-UP

HAZARDOUS STRUCTURAL TYPES

CODES AND REGULATIONS

At present a general code for seismic rehabilitation of buildings does not exist. For URM buildings, the City of Los Angeles Section 88 Code may be appropriate; for certain types of historic URM buildings, the Uniform Code for Building Conservation may be used. Following the Northridge earthquake, Los Angeles developed criteria for rehabilitating tilt-up buildings and nonductile reinforced concrete frame buildings.

The Building Seismic Safety Council/National Earthquake Hazard Reduction Program is developing the first comprehensive criteria (available about 1998) for the rehabilitation of all building types in any geographic region.

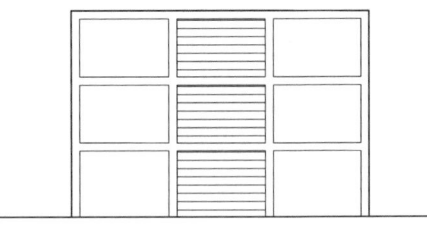

**ADD REINFORCED INFILL WALLS TO
INCREASE STRENGTH AND STIFFNESS**

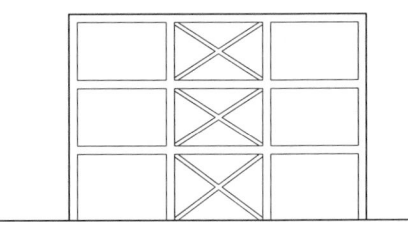

ADD BRACING TO INCREASE STIFFNESS

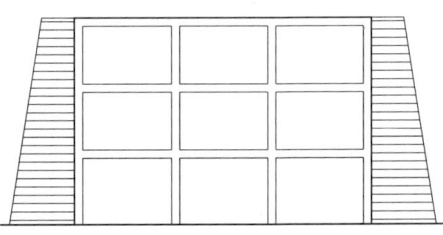

ADD BUTTRESSES FOR CONTAINMENT

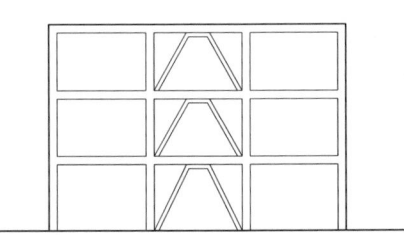

**ADD ENERGY DISSIPATING BRACES TO
REDUCE DRIFT AND INCREASE DAMPING**

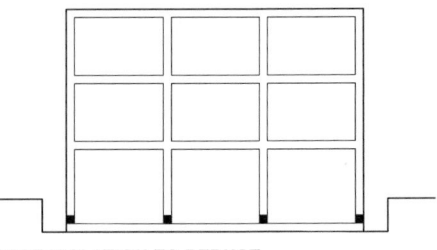

**BASE ISOLATION TO REDUCE
RESPONSE AND AID DAMAGE CONTROL**

REHABILITATING A CONCRETE FRAME

Christopher Arnold, FAIA, RIBA, Building Systems Development, Inc.; Palo Alto, California

GENERAL

Empirical rules and formulas for the design of masonry structures resulted from the long history of masonry use and thus predate engineering and analysis. Empirical design is a method of sizing and proportioning masonry elements that depends on centering gravity loads over bearing walls, neglecting the effect of steel reinforcing.

For most masonry work, empirical design is conservative. It is generally appropriate for smaller buildings with interior masonry partitions and stiff floors, as well as buildings in lower seismic exposure areas and walls not part of the lateral resisting system (even when other walls are engineered). Buildings that are in higher exposure areas or have walls that are part of the lateral resistance system require engineering design that conforms to local codes.

There are specific limits on masonry as to height, wind or other horizontal loads, and seismic loads. In many cases, design for wind and industry recommendations for crack control due to shrinkage or expansion may govern building reinforcement in areas with lower seismic activity.

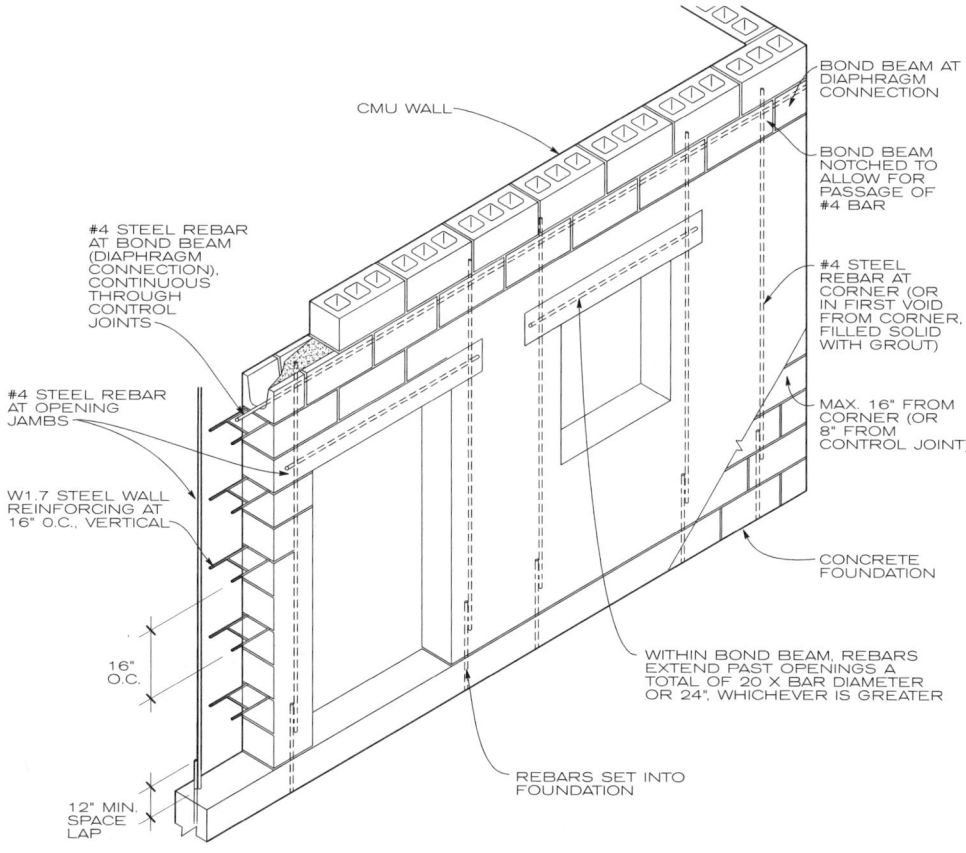

BOND BEAM AT DIAPHRAGM CONNECTION

BOND BEAM NOTCHED TO ALLOW FOR PASSAGE OF #4 BAR

CMU WALL

#4 STEEL REBAR AT BOND BEAM (DIAPHRAGM CONNECTION), CONTINUOUS THROUGH CONTROL JOINTS

#4 STEEL REBAR AT CORNER (OR IN FIRST VOID FROM CORNER, FILLED SOLID WITH GROUT)

#4 STEEL REBAR AT OPENING JAMBS

MAX. 16" FROM CORNER (OR 8" FROM CONTROL JOINT)

W1.7 STEEL WALL REINFORCING AT 16" O.C., VERTICAL

16" O.C.

CONCRETE FOUNDATION

WITHIN BOND BEAM, REBARS EXTEND PAST OPENINGS A TOTAL OF 20 X BAR DIAMETER OR 24", WHICHEVER IS GREATER

12" MIN. SPACE LAP

REBARS SET INTO FOUNDATION

NOTE

Standard construction practice for masonry crack control requires W1.7 at 16 in. o.c., which would cover seismic requirements as well. W1.7 steel reinforcement at 8 in. o.c. should be used in parapet locations.

WALL REINFORCING FOR MASONRY WALL (EMPIRICAL DESIGN FOR MODERATE SEISMIC AREAS)

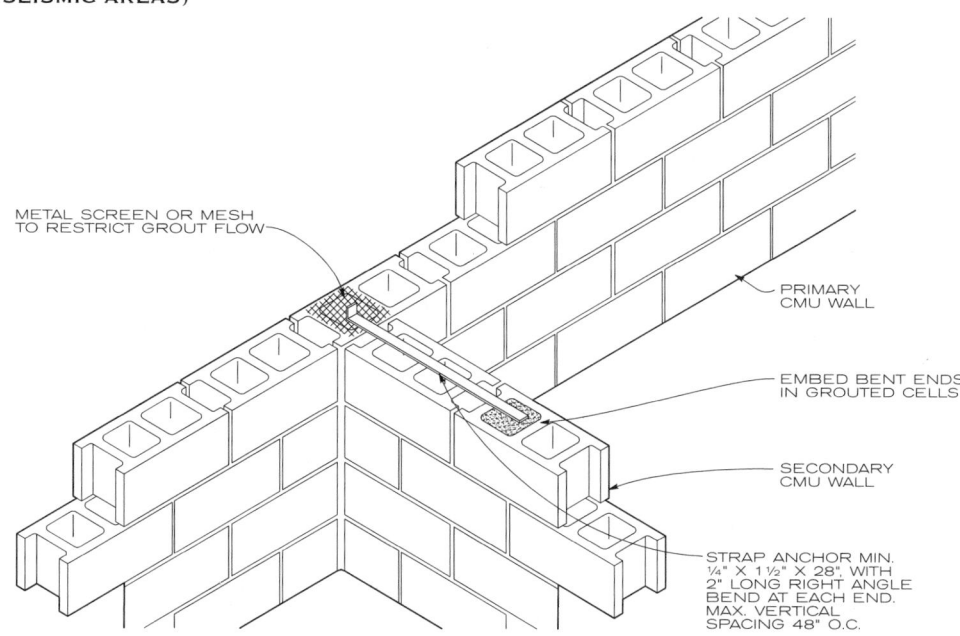

METAL SCREEN OR MESH TO RESTRICT GROUT FLOW

PRIMARY CMU WALL

EMBED BENT ENDS IN GROUTED CELLS

SECONDARY CMU WALL

STRAP ANCHOR MIN. ¼" X 1½" X 28", WITH 2" LONG RIGHT ANGLE BEND AT EACH END. MAX. VERTICAL SPACING 48" O.C.

INTERSECTING WALL DETAIL

Edgar Glock, Masonry Institute of St. Louis; St. Louis, Missouri

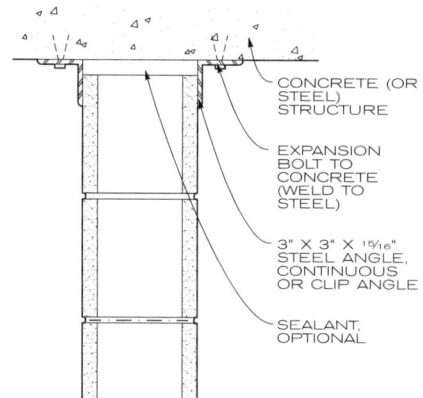

CONCRETE (OR STEEL) STRUCTURE

EXPANSION BOLT TO CONCRETE (WELD TO STEEL)

3" X 3" X 15/16" STEEL ANGLE, CONTINUOUS OR CLIP ANGLE

SEALANT, OPTIONAL

NOTE

This detail allows transfer of out-of-plane forces but isolates in-plane forces from the structure.

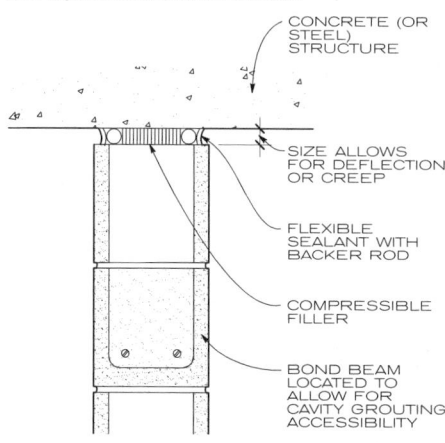

CONCRETE (OR STEEL) STRUCTURE

SIZE ALLOWS FOR DEFLECTION OR CREEP

FLEXIBLE SEALANT WITH BACKER ROD

COMPRESSIBLE FILLER

BOND BEAM LOCATED TO ALLOW FOR CAVITY GROUTING ACCESSIBILITY

NONBEARING WALL ISOLATION DETAILS

SHEAR WALL SPACING RATIO—EMPIRICAL DESIGN

Bearing walls	Solid units	l / t < 20
	Fully grouted	l / t < 20
	Others	l / t < 18
Nonbearing walls	Exterior	l / t < 18
	Interior	l / t < 36

l—wall length; t—wall thickness

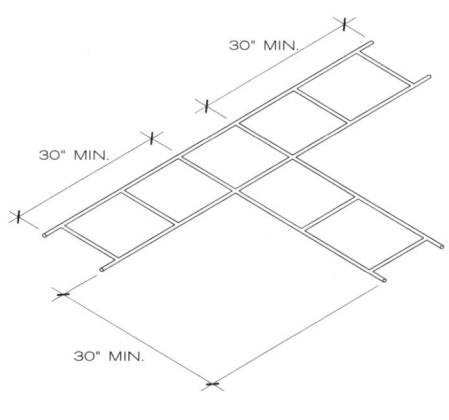

30" MIN.

30" MIN.

30" MIN.

NOTE

Preformed, hot-dipped galvanized tees (W1.7 wire at 8 in. o.c., vertical for bearing; 16 in. o.c. for nonbearing) are used for reinforcing intersecting walls.

INTERSECTING WALL REINFORCING

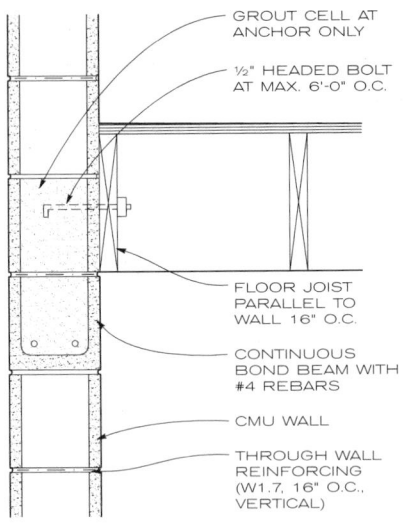

NOTE

Anchors should also be placed at cross-bracing for joists.

DIAPHRAGM CONNECTION FOR WOOD JOIST/RAFTER PARALLEL TO WALL

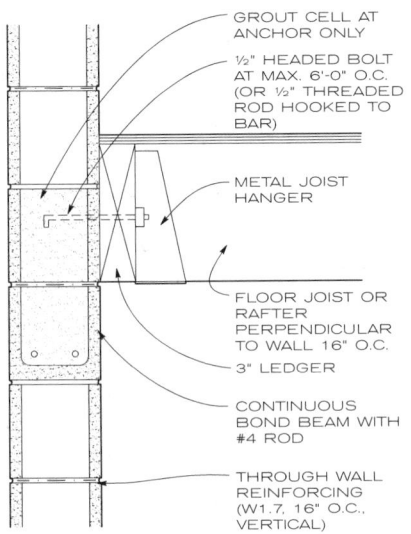

DIAPHRAGM CONNECTION FOR WOOD JOIST/RAFTER PERPENDICULAR TO WALL

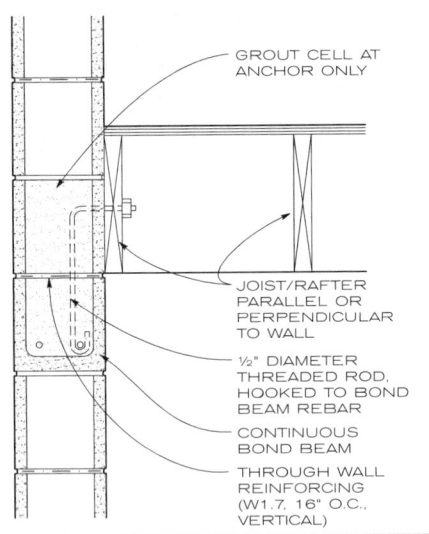

ALTERNATE DIAPHRAGM CONNECTION FOR WOOD JOIST/RAFTER

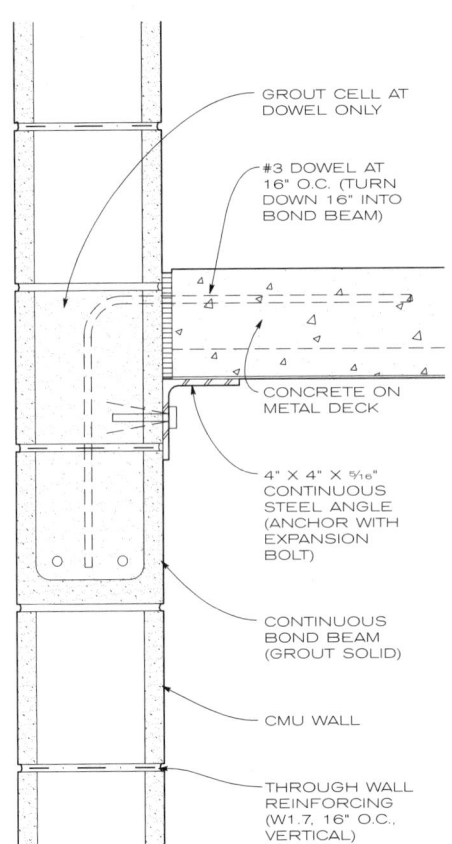

DIAPHRAGM CONNECTION FOR STEEL JOISTS PARALLEL TO WALL

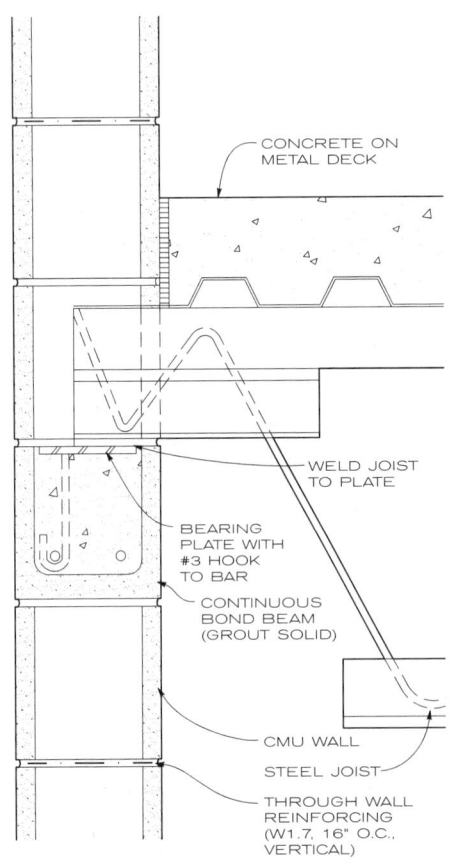

DIAPHRAGM CONNECTION FOR STEEL JOISTS PERPENDICULAR TO WALL

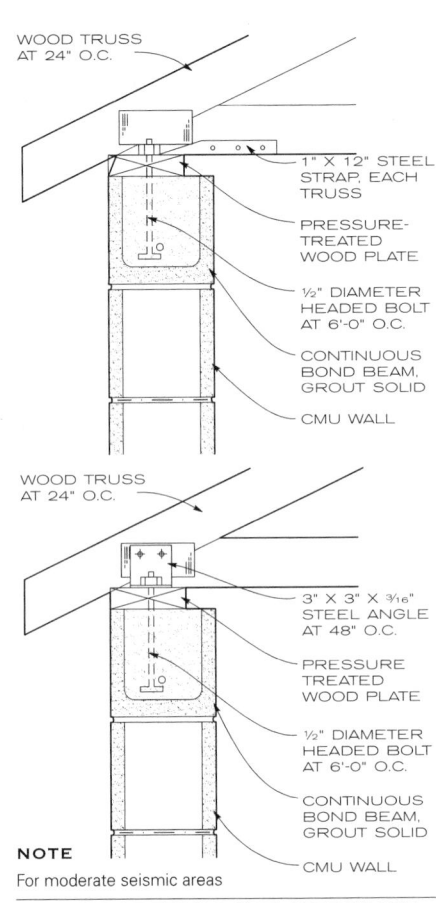

NOTE

For moderate seismic areas

ROOF TIE DETAILS FOR MODERATE SEISMIC AREAS

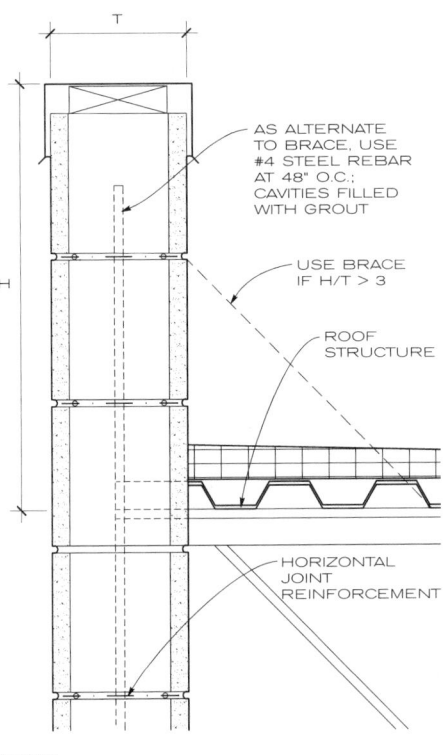

NOTE

Empirical design for masonry parapets should be used only in areas with low seismicity. Engineering analysis is required when the height-to-thickness ratio of three-to-one is exceeded and in areas of higher seismicity.

MASONRY PARAPET DETAIL FOR SEISMIC AREAS

Edgar Glock, Masonry Institute of St. Louis; St. Louis, Missouri

1   SEISMIC DESIGN

GENERAL

Wood frame structures with a variety of solid wood and engineered wood products can be designed to resist seismic forces using many of the same principles used to resist wind forces. Wind-resistant design involves resolving loads assumed to be applied to the structure in one direction for a short time (monotonic loads). Wind load can induce shear that is both perpendicular and parallel with the structure, resulting in an overturning motion as well as uplift on the structure. Seismic loads, on the other hand, are cyclical, moving in different directions over a short period.

Seismic loading conditions on conventional construction are referenced in four main sources, which also provide information about the capacity of various materials: American Society of Civil Engineers 7-95, Section A9.9.10; the Building Code, Section 2326; the Standard Building Code, Sections 2308.2.2 and 2310; and the National Building Code, Section 2305.8. In general, these provisions are limited to buildings with bearing walls not exceeding 10 ft in height and gravity dead loads not exceeding 15 psf for floors and exterior walls and 10 psf for floors and partitions. Sheathing for braced walls must be at least 48 in. wide over studs spaced not more than 24 in. o.c.

Wood construction standards for all seismic areas include the following: wall anchorage must use a minimum of t o.c., maximum. Walls must be capped with double top plates, Uniform with end joints offset by at least 4 ft. Bottom plates must be 1¹/₂ in. thick (2 in. nominal) and at least the width of the studs.

Forces must be transferred from the roof and floor(s) to braced walls and from the braced walls in upper stories to the braced walls in the story below, then into the foundation. Transfer must be accomplished with toe nails using three 8d nails per joist or rafter where not more than 2 ft o.c. or with metal framing devices capable of transmitting the lateral force. Roof to wall connections must be made at the exterior walls when the building is 50 ft or less in length. A combination of exterior and interior bearing walls is necessary when the building length exceeds 50 ft.

Connections designed for both lateral and vertical (uplift or overturning) loads must be used in conventional wood frame structures designed for seismic areas. Traditional nailing schedules are often adequate to handle lateral forces. Vertical forces can be addressed by lapping structural sheathing and/or strapping the roof, walls, and floors together at appropriate intervals. In addition, the overturning loads in walls must be restrained by anchoring the ends of the shear panels (whether traditional or perforated) to the structural wall below.

Nontraditional materials such as LVL, I joists, and structural composite lumber can be used in seismic design; the capacities and applicable connection types of these products are available from the manufacturers.

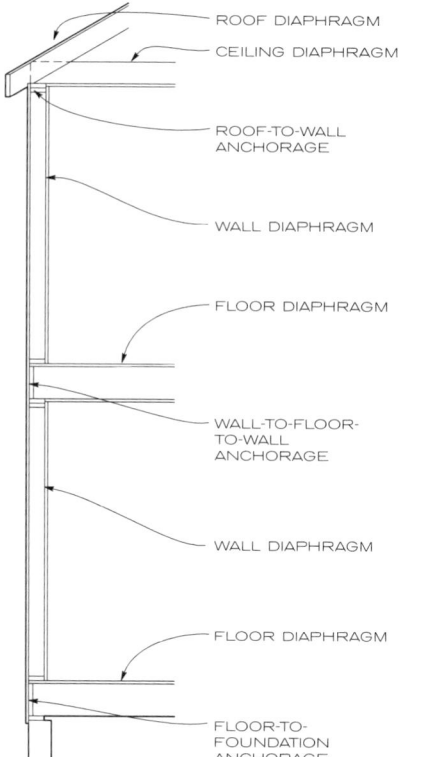

TYPICAL WALL SECTION FOR CONVENTIONAL WOOD FRAMING

NOTES

1. Diaphragms (the roof, floor(s), and shear panels in walls) must be designed to resist forces created by the dead load mass of the structure and applied seismic loads. In wood frame construction, a diaphragm is typically a structural "panel" made of a skin (sheathing) stretched over and fastened to ribs (wood members such as 2x4s). The resulting construction is stiff and strong enough to transmit forces to resisting systems such as the foundation. Connections must be designed to transfer lateral forces and restrain overturning motion. Lateral forces can be either perpendicular or parallel to the structure. The load from each part of a building that is created as the building shifts from the movement of the earth must be transferred to adjoining elements (roof sheathing to rafters to top plates to wall sheathing and studs to bottom plates to floor sheathing and framing and so on, until the lowest level of floor framing, from which the load moves to the foundation; in slab-on-grade construction, the load moves finally from the wall sheathing and studs to the bottom plates).

2. The roof diaphragm comprises roof sheathing, roof framing (rafters, top chord of truss, etc.), and blocking.

3. The ceiling diaphragm comprises ceiling finish material (for example, gypsum wallboard) and ceiling framing (joists, lower chord of trusses, etc).

4. Roof-to-wall anchorage consists of hold-down anchors to resist uplift forces and nailing to resist shear forces.

5. The wall diaphragm comprises wall sheathing, wall framing, and sheathing fasteners.

6. The floor diaphragm comprises floor sheathing, floor framing (joists, trusses, etc.), blocking, etc.

7. Wall-to-floor-to-wall anchorage consists of hold-down anchors and shear connectors (for example, nails).

8. Floor-to-foundation anchorage consists of hold-down anchors to resist overturning forces and anchor bolts (¹/₂ in. diameter at 6 ft o.c.) to resist shear forces.

SPACING FOR BLOCKED DIAPHRAGM*

BOUNDARY PANELS (IN.)	OTHER PANELS (IN.)	CAPACITIES (LB/FT)
6	6	320
4	6	425
2¹/₂	4	640
2	3	730

*¹⁵/₃₂-in. panel sheathing; 10d nails into 2X framing (Douglas fir, larch, southern pine).

BRACED WALL SPACING

SEISMIC PERFORMANCE CATEGORY	DISTANCE BETWEEN BRACED WALLS	MAXIMUM NUMBER OF STORIES
A	35 ft	3
B	35 ft	3
C	25 ft	2
D	25 ft	1*

*Two stories for detached one- and two-family dwellings

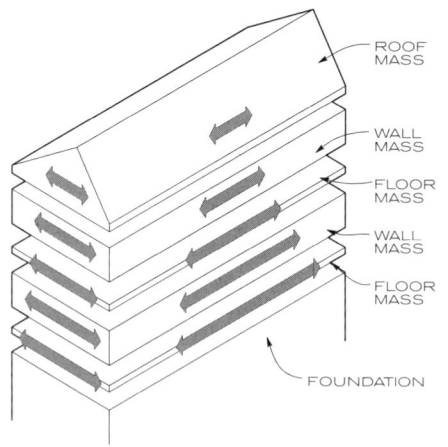

NOTE

Each diaphragm in a building must resist the seismic effects in both directions of all the mass above it as well as of its own mass. The seismic loads caused by the roof mass must be transferred to the wall, and the wall must be designed to resist both the effect of the mass of the roof and the mass of the wall. These combined loads must then be transferred to the floor below, which must be designed to resist the effect of both its mass and the load applied by the wall above. In turn, walls below must resist these loads, until the force reaches the foundation, which must be able to resist the combined loads from the rest of the building.

SEISMIC LOAD TRANSFER

NOTES

1. Use ¹⁵/₃₂ in. sheathing for the outside of shear panels, with 10d nails in 2x framing.

2. Capacities are based on structural I panels of Douglas fir, larch, or southern pine. For additional thicknesses or alternative wood species, consult the American Plywood Association.

3. The aspect ratio (the ratio of the longer dimension to the shorter) of a floor or roof diaphragm is limited to $L_2/L_1 \leq 4$. Openings in the diaphragm are limited to either 12 ft or half the length of the diaphragm, whichever is smaller.

FLOOR AND ROOF DIAPHRAGM

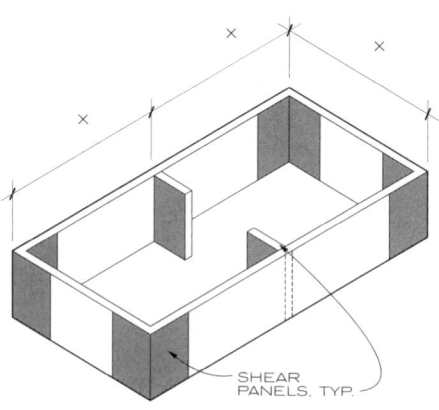

NOTE

The bracing element is typically a shear panel that is anchored against both shear and overturning.

BRACED WALL SPACING

David S. Collins, FAIA; American Forest & Paper Association; Cincinnati, Ohio

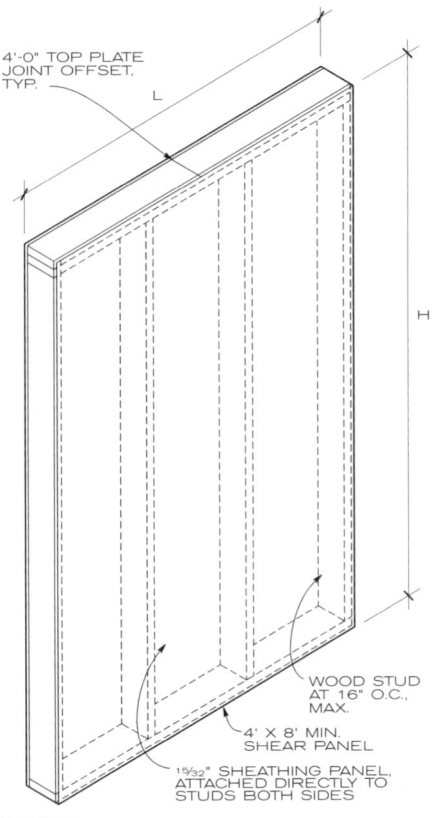

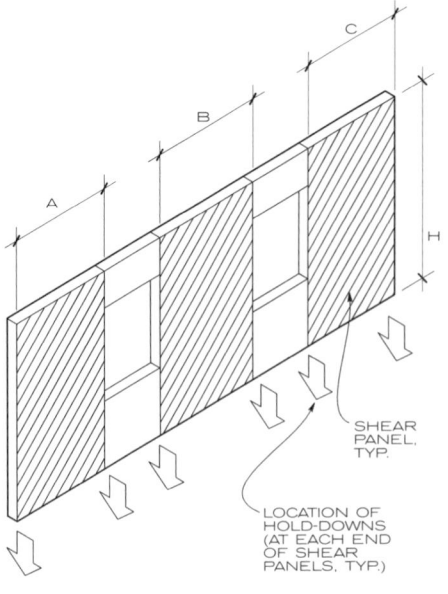

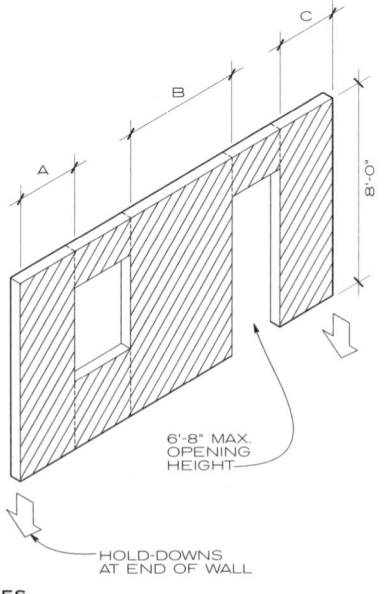

NOTES

1. Shear panels that consist of framing members and sheathing panel(s) or diagonal sheathing members provide the principal lateral resistance to shear loads. Sheathing panels are made of plywood and OSB (for structural panels), gypsum sheathing, or fiberboard. Diagonal wood sheathing boards or strapping can also be used. The shear capacity of the material depends on the quality of the framing and sheathing materials and on the connections. Building codes require a minimum aspect ratio of $H/L \leq 2$ or $3\frac{1}{2}$ for the panel. Sheathing both sides with the same material doubles the capacity of the shear panel. Tests have shown that sheathing each side with a different material adds capacity, although this concept is not accepted by all codes.

2. Use 10d nails at all edges and in field (center area) as follows: for edge nailing, 6 in. o.c. for 280 lb/lin. ft; 4 in. o.c. for 430 lb/lin. ft; 3 in. o.c. for 550 lb/lin. ft; 2 in. o.c. for 730 lb/lin. ft; and 12 in. o.c. for field nailing.

3. This drawing is based on use of structural I panels of Douglas fir, larch, or southern pine. For additional thicknesses or alternative wood species, consult the American Plywood Association.

WOOD WALL SHEAR PANEL

NOTES

1. In traditional shear wall design, parts of the wall that are sheathed from top to bottom without openings are considered individually as shear panels. Hold-down anchors are required at both ends of each of these panels. Each segment must be restrained against the overturning motion and the shear to which it will be exposed.

2. The capacity of a traditional shear wall is the sum of the capacities of the individual shear wall segments, which are determined by multiplying the length of each segment by the capacity of the sheathing (lb/lin. ft). Example: Use $^{15}/_{32}$ in. sheathing for the outside of the shear panel, with 10d nails spaced 6 in. o.c. for 280 lb/lin. ft. The capacity of this shear wall would be equal to 280 × (A + B + C); 280 × H = uplift (hold-down capacity).

TRADITIONAL SHEAR WALLS

NOTES

1. For perforated shear walls, the whole wall is considered as a single shear panel without regard to wall openings. Hold-down anchors are required only at the ends of the wall. To determine the capacity of the wall, the lengths of the full-height sheathed areas are added together and the sum multiplied by the capacity of the sheathing.

2. Perforated shear walls may require higher capacity sheathing than traditional shear walls to compensate for the lack of intermediate hold-down anchors.

3. The sheathed walls above and below the openings in a perforated shear wall increase the capacity of the wall. The capacity of the shear wall must be adjusted by a factor derived from two variables: the maximum opening height and the percentage of full-height sheathing on the shear panel. In the following example, a factor of 0.49 is applied. The Wood Frame Construction Manual gives more examples. Example: Use $^{15}/_{32}$ in. sheathing for the outside of the shear panel, with 10d nails spaced 6 in. o.c. for 280 lb/lin. ft. Shear = 280 × (A + B + C) × 0.49; 280 × 8 = 2240 lb uplift (hold-down capacity).

PERFORATED SHEAR WALLS

MINIMUM LENGTH OF BRACED WALL

STORY	SHEATHING TYPE*	LOW RISK			HIGH RISK
Top or only	G-P	8'-0"	12'-0"	16'-0"	20'-0"
	SW	4'-0"	8'-0"	8'-0"	12'-0"
Story below top	G-P	12'-0"	16'-0"	20'-0"	—
	SW	8'-0"	8'-0"	12'-0"	29'-0"
Bottom of 3 stories	G-P	16'-0"	—	—	—
	SW	8'-0"	Not permitted as conventional		

*G-P—gypsum; SW—structural wood

LUMBER DESIGN VALUES FOR SEISMIC CONDITIONS

DESIGN VALUE*	2 x 8	ADJUSTMENT FACTORS			ADJUSTED DESIGN VALUE (PSI)
		SIZE	REPETITIVE MEMBER 1.15	LOAD 1.6	
F_b	Douglas fir-larch no. 2; 875 psi	1.2 F_b=1050	1210	1930	1930
	SPF no. 1/no. 2; 875 psi	1.2 F_b=1050	1210	1930	1930
	Southern pine no. 2; 1200 psi	--	1380	2210	2210
F_v	Douglas fir-larch no. 2; 95 psi	--	--	150	150
	SPF no. 1/no.2; 70 psi	--	--	110	110
	Southern pine no. 2; 90 psi	--	--	145	145
$F_{c_\perp}$	Douglas fir-larch no. 2; 625 psi	--	--	--	625
	SPF no. 1/no. 2; 425 psi	--	--	--	425
	Southern pine no. 2; 565 psi	--	--	--	565
$F_{c_\parallel}$	Douglas fir-larch no. 2; 1300 psi	1.05 $F_{c_\parallel}$=1560	--	2185	2185
	SPF no. 1/no. 2; 1100 psi	1.05 $F_{c_\parallel}$=1320	--	1850	1850
	Southern pine no. 2; 1550 psi	--	--	2480	2480

*Additional design values for other species and grades of lumber can be obtained from the Supplement to the AF&PA National Design Specification.

NOTE

Design values for traditional solid wood products and connections are available in the American Forest and Paper Association's National Design Specification. The values published for wood products must be adjusted by various factors, including size (except for southern pine), to determine the appropriate design values for a particular application. Repetitive members, consisting of three members spaced not more than 2 ft o.c. and sharing a load, must be increased by a factor of 1.15, while the adjustment for seismic and wind conditions is a factor of 1.6. These factors are applicable only to solid wood products and glued laminated timbers. Connections have similar adjustment factors.

David S. Collins, FAIA; American Forest & Paper Association; Cincinnati, Ohio

1 **SEISMIC DESIGN**

GENERAL

Lighting design involves selecting lighting fixtures (luminaires) and determining their locations and control devices to realize the desired effects. Basic lighting designs are fairly generic and require but a modest level of effort to achieve a workable result. Attractive and/or complex lighting designs, on the other hand, can require significantly more design work and detail in specifying products and locations. Typical steps in the process are these:

1. Establish project criteria: Determine the quantity and quality of illumination, color of light, and luminaire type (style, appearance) wanted. Check applicable codes and standards, and find out the cost and power limits.
2. Create design concepts: Select the types of luminaires to be used, outline desired controls, and propose locations. Test cost and power budgets.
3. Refine the design: Make calculations and adjustments, sketch details, draft specifications, and coordinate mechanical and structural work.
4. Prepare working drawings: Draw lighting plans, make fixture schedules, and plan layout and circuit controls. Determine emergency, life safety, and egress lighting.

As with all creative processes, it is not unusual to repeat steps until an acceptable result is achieved. With increasing enforcement of energy codes, traditional designs (especially those using incandescent lighting) will not meet energy code requirements. Reiterations involving different light sources or luminaires will often be necessary.

SETTING DESIGN CRITERIA

Lighting design requires the definition of the following criteria for each application: quantity of illumination, quality of illumination, color of light, and suitable luminaire styles.

QUANTITY OF ILLUMINATION

Standards for illumination are set by the Illuminating Engineering Society of North America (IESNA). Illumination is generally measured in the horizontal plane 30 in. above the floor. The units of illumination are footcandles (lumens per square foot) and lux (lumens per square meter). IESNA-recommended levels are summarized on the following page (Lighting and Lighting Systems)—more detailed and specific information is given in the IESNA Lighting Handbook and in other IESNA publications.

Specific lighting levels may be set by codes, such as life safety codes and health codes. For instance, NFPA 101 (National Fire Protection Association Life Safety Standard) recommends an average illumination of 1 footcandle (10 lux) along a path of emergency egress with an emergency power source. Some owners establish their own lighting level requirements for specific areas.

Choosing lighting levels involves thoughtful application of IESNA recommendations to meet the goals of the project. Too much light will lead to excessive energy use and failure to meet energy code limits. Use of high lighting levels (more than 200 footcandles) is rare and usually is associated with special purpose lighting systems like surgical lights.

The IESNA recommends exterior lighting levels for specific applications such as street lighting, sports lighting, and parking lot lighting. Although the IESNA makes some recommendations for exterior lighting applications that are more artistic, such as building facades or statuary, most of these are left to the designer's discretion.

The uniformity of lighting levels is also subject to IESNA recommendations. For interior lighting, IESNA generally recommends the following ratios of illumination for comfort:

1. Task proper: 100%.
2. Immediate surround: 33-100%.
3. Distant surround: 10-100%.

When light is designed to maintain these relationships, the human eye continually adapts to the light level and responds quickly to visual stimulus. However, visual interest is caused by contrast in which ratios between task and surround might be 100:1 or even greater. This is one of the greatest paradoxes of lighting design: The most appealing visual scenes are often uncomfortable.

James Robert Benya, PE, FIES, IALD, Pacific Lightworks; Portland, Oregon
Robert Sardinsky, Rising Sun Enterprises; Basalt, Colorado

LIGHT SOURCE SELECTION GUIDE

	APPLICATIONS
LAMP CCT[1] (KELVINS OR K)	
<2500	Bulk industrial and security (HPS) lighting
2700–3000	Low light levels in most spaces (<10 FC); general residential lighting; hotels, fine dining and family restaurants, theme parks
2950–3200	Display lighting for retail and galleries; feature lighting
3500–4100	General lighting in offices, schools, stores, industry, medicine; display lighting; sports lighting
4100–5000	Special application lighting when color discrimination is very important; not commonly used for general lighting
5000–7500	Special application lighting when color discrimination is critical; uncommon for general lighting
MINIMUM LAMP CRI[2]	
<50	Noncritical industrial, storage, and security lighting
50–70	Industrial and general illumination when color is not important
70–79	Most office, retail, school, medical, and other work and recreational spaces
80–89	Retail, work, and residential spaces when color quality is important
90–100	Retail and work spaces when color rendering is critical

[1] CCT—correlated color temperature

[2] CRI—color rendering index

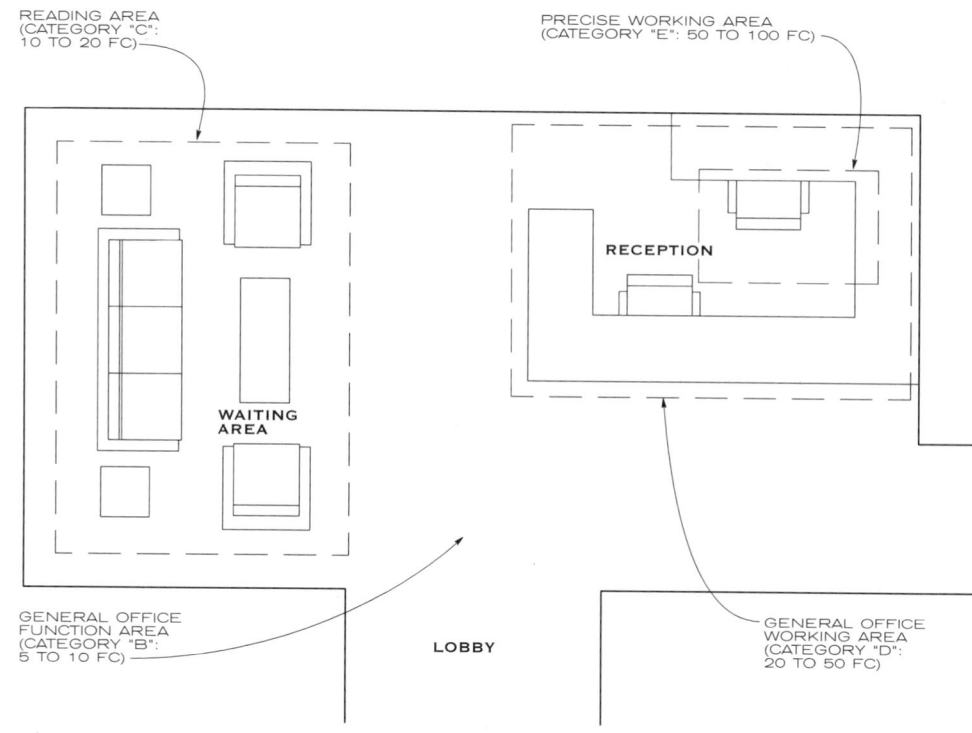

READING AREA (CATEGORY "C": 10 TO 20 FC)

PRECISE WORKING AREA (CATEGORY "E": 50 TO 100 FC)

RECEPTION

WAITING AREA

GENERAL OFFICE FUNCTION AREA (CATEGORY "B": 5 TO 10 FC)

LOBBY

GENERAL OFFICE WORKING AREA (CATEGORY "D": 20 TO 50 FC)

NOTE

In this example, choosing the proper amount of light in each area not only meets visual needs but consumes only the minimum necessary energy. Use the high end of the light level ranges for older people, where finishes are especially dark, or where the work is particularly important or requires great speed.

LIGHTING LEVELS FOR TYPICAL OFFICE RECEPTION AREA

QUALITY OF ILLUMINATION

Quality of illumination remains largely an aesthetic issue. However, a number of specific quality issues can be addressed objectively:

1. Eliminate flicker: Light sources should minimize or eliminate flicker caused by AC power or other influences.
2. Eliminate or minimize glare: Shield lamps from view. Minimize very bright and very dark surfaces. Illuminate walls and ceilings.
3. Use light sources with good color rendering: Halogen, high CRI (color rendering index) full size and compact fluorescent, and high CRI metal halide and white HPS lamps should be used whenever possible.

COLOR OF LIGHT

Both the correlated color temperature (CCT) and color rendering index (CRI) for light sources should be used in choosing light sources. In general, try to match CCT when mixing sources, such as halogen and fluorescent.

SUITABLE LUMINAIRE STYLES

Many design problems have reasonably obvious solutions determined by a combination of budget, energy code, and industry standards. For instance, most office lighting designs utilize recessed troffers because they are cost-effective and energy-efficient and they meet the standard expectations of owners and tenants. Choices among troffers require further consideration, although at that point style is a lesser issue.

Some situations call for uncommon or creative designs. In these cases, the distribution of the luminaire and its physical appearance become critical. In particular, luminaires that enhance the architecture are desired for residences, hotels, restaurants, and other nonwork spaces. Decorative styles range from contemporary to very traditional; lamp options may permit a choice between incandescent and more energy-efficient light sources, such as compact fluorescent or low watt high-intensity discharge (HID) luminaires. In fact, energy-efficient decorative lighting fixtures, both interior and exterior, are one of the fastest growing parts of the lighting fixture industry as the market for attractive luminaires that comply with energy codes grows.

GENERAL

Most buildings are equipped with electric lighting systems for interior uses. Early in the history of lighting, illumination systems were designed for minimum use of interior space at night. Today, however, electric illumination systems generally are designed to be used in place of natural light.

FUNCTIONS OF LIGHTING

Light is one of many tools available to help in space design. In the beginning of any project, it is wise to recall the functions of lighting and to be certain each has been examined.

1. Performance of tasks: Lighting to perform work, whether it is reading, assembling parts, or seeing a blackboard, is referred to as task lighting. Visual work is a primary reason for providing lighting.

2. Enhancement of space and structure: It is only through the presence of light that spatial volume, planes, ornament, and color are revealed. For centuries, structural systems evolved partly in response to aesthetic as well as functional desires for light of a certain quality. The progress from bearing wall to curtain wall was driven by the push of newly discovered technologies (both in materials and in technique), by evolving cultural desires for certain spatial characteristics, and by a desire to admit light of a particular quality. These developments are reflected in the Gothic church window, the baroque oculus, and the Bauhaus wall of glass. With the advent of electric lighting systems, this connection of structure to light was no longer entirely necessary, but most architects continue to pay homage to this historical tie.

3. Focusing attention: The quality of light in a space profoundly affects people's perception of that space. The timing and the direction of an individual's gaze are often a function of the varying quality and distribution of light through the space. Lighting draws attention to points of interest and helps guide the user of a space.

4. Provision of security: Lighting can enhance visibility and thereby engender a sense of security. Lighting can also be used to illuminate hazards, such as a changing floor plane or moving objects.

BASIC LIGHTING TERMS

LUMINAIRE: a structure that holds an electric lamp and its socket, wiring, and auxiliaries, such as ballasts.

PORTABLE LUMINAIRE (LAMP): a luminaire equipped with a cord and plug and designed to be moved from space to space.

LIGHTING FIXTURE: a luminaire that is permanently attached ("hard wired") to a building.

LIGHTING SYSTEM: the lighting fixtures in a building, sometimes including portable lights, subdivided into smaller systems (e.g., the lighting system in a room or all luminaires of a particular type in a room or building).

ILLUMINANCE: the measure of light striking a surface, in footcandles (lumens per square meter). Illuminance can be measured and predicted using calculations; also illumination.

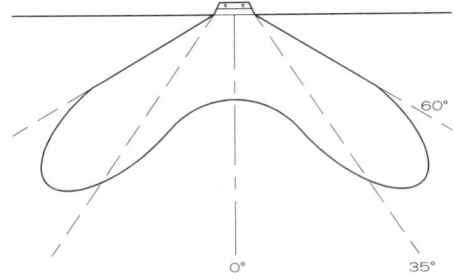

NOTE

Fixture manufacturers have developed luminaires (mostly fluorescent) that produce a light distribution that tends to reduce direct glare and veiling reflections if used in large, uniform arrays and typical open office geometries. This distribution pattern is called batwing.

LUMINAIRE LIGHT DISTRIBUTION PATTERN

ILLUMINANCE VALUES FOR VARIOUS INDOOR ACTIVITIES

TYPES OF ACTIVITY	ILLUMINANCE CATEGORY	RANGES OF ILLUMINANCE		REFERENCE WORK PLANE
		LUX	FOOTCANDLES	
Public spaces with dark surroundings	A	20-30-50	2-3-5	General lighting throughout spaces
Simple orientation for short, temporary visits	B	50-75-100	5-7.5-10	
Working spaces used only occasionally for visual tasks	C	100-150-200	10-15-20	
Performance of visual tasks of high contrast or large size	D	200-300-500	20-30-50	Illuminance on task
Performance of visual tasks of medium contrast or small size	E	500-750-1000	50-75-100	
Performance of visual tasks of low contrast or small size	F	1000-1500-2000	100-150-200	
Performance of visual tasks of low contrast and very small size over a prolonged period	G	2000-3000-5000	200-300-500	Illuminance on task, provided by a combination of general and local (supplementary) lighting
Performance of very prolonged and exacting visual tasks	H	5000-7500-10000	500-750-1000	
Performance of very special visual tasks of extremely low contrast and small size	I	10000-15000-20000	1000-1500-2000	

NOTE

Standards for lighting and illumination in North America are established by the Illuminating Engineering Society of North America. IESNA recommendations are summarized in the IESNA Lighting Handbook, 8th edition, from which this table is taken.

LAMP: the electric bulb or tube within a luminaire.

PHOTOMETRY: the measure of light, especially with respect to a luminaire.

PHOTOMETRIC REPORT: a written report that describes the manner in which light is emitted from a luminaire, presented in an industry standard format.

ENERGY EFFICIENCY: the measure of how a lighting system compares to standards, in the context of building size and function.

LUMEN METHOD

Lighting design involves determining how many luminaires are needed for a particular application and where to locate them. The most accurate means of determining illumination performance is by computer; a number of point-by-point lighting programs are available with DXF and DWG interfaces and other features. (See the annual computer issue of Lighting Design and Application, an IESNA publication, for a current list of commercially available programs.) It is also possible to estimate illumination results from a proposed lighting design using the lumen method and photometric report(s) from candidate luminaires.

The lumen method, also known as the zonal cavity system, is a calculation method that can be used to determine the horizontal illuminance that will result from a proposed lighting fixture selection and layout or the number of fixtures required by a proposed fixture selection and its horizontal illuminance value.

The lumen method is based on the definition of average footcandles over an area. The method modifies the fundamental equation of 1 fc = 1 lumen/sq ft to account for room size and proportion; reflectance from walls, ceiling, and floors; fixture efficiency; and reduction in output over time due to dirt accumulation, deterioration of reflecting surfaces, and reduction of lumen output.

The lumen method requires the following information:

1. Room dimensions (to compute wall area and floor area)
2. Height of fixtures above work plane
3. Reflectance levels of major surfaces (ceiling, walls, floor)
4. An estimate of the light loss factor (LLF)
5. Initial lamp lumens
6. A target illuminance level

The coefficient of utilization (CU) is the percentage of total lamp lumens that reaches the work plane. As such, it has nothing to do with the intensity of the fixture but rather with the efficiency of the fixture (lumens emitted from the fixture divided by lamp lumens and the direction of the lamp output—this direction of output is graphically represented by the candlepower distribution curve). For purposes of this procedure, the plane of interest is invariably a horizontal plane (typically either the floor or desk level), therefore a fixture that throws the greatest percentage of its lumens downward will have a higher CU (room cavity ratio and reflectance values being equal) than one that distributes light in any other direction. A higher CU is not necessarily a virtue; it only ranks fixtures according to their ability to provide horizontal illuminance.

The lumen method/zonal cavity system is limited by the following:

1. It is based on a single number, average value.
2. It assumes a uniform array of lighting fixtures.
3. It assumes all room surfaces have a matte (lambertian) finish.
4. It assumes the room is devoid of obstruction, at least down to the level of the work plane.

The light loss factor (LLF) is used to calculate the illuminance of a lighting system at a specific point in time under given conditions. It incorporates variations from test conditions in temperature and voltage, dirt accumulation on lighting fixtures and room surfaces, lamp lumen output depreciation, maintenance procedures (mainly frequency of cleaning), and atmospheric conditions. The LLF is also known as the maintenance factor.

To use a CU table, assumptions must first be made about the reflectance of major room surfaces. Then the room cavity ratio (RCR) can be determined according to one of the following formulas:

For rectangular rooms: RCR = [5 × H(L + W)] / (L × W), in which H is the cavity height

For odd-shaped rooms: RCR = 2.5 wall area/floor area

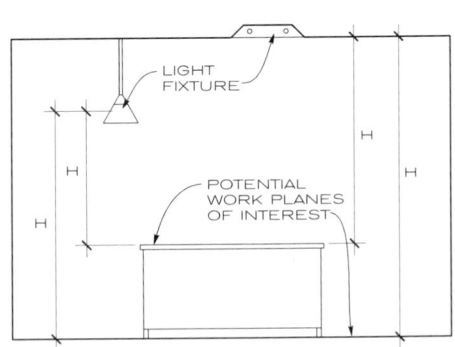

NOTE

Any one of these dimensions may be the cavity height (H), which is the distance from the light fixture to the work plane of interest.

CAVITY HEIGHT DIAGRAM

James Robert Benya, PE, FIES, IALD, Pacific Lightworks; Portland, Oregon
Robert Sardinsky, Rising Sun Enterprises; Basalt, Colorado
Robert Prouse, IALD, IES; H.M. Brandston & Partners, Inc.; New York, New York

GENERAL

Lighting can be designed both to use minimum energy and to realize environmental benefits such as reduced air and groundwater pollution. Electric light sources more efficacious than traditional incandescent lamps have been developed to meet most lighting needs. The key to achieving efficient design is knowing how and when to choose efficient sources, luminaires, and controls.

CODES

The U.S. Energy Policy Act of 1992 requires states to develop codes that require efficiency in lighting design. Each code must meet or exceed the requirements of ASHRAE/IES 90.1-1989. In 1996, although in many states compliance was mandatory and enforced, some states had yet to adopt such a code, while others had not yet begun enforcement. For federal government buildings, a version of 90.1 with more stringent values was in force. Progress toward regulating energy efficiency in Canada was similar.

All codes presently calculate allowed watts based on building type and area. Codes generally determine allowed interior lighting watts in one of three ways—room by room, by area (groups of rooms), or for the entire building:

1. Room by room: Determine the specific use of each room and its net area. Multiply the area of each room by the allowed power density (watts/sq ft) adjusted for the room cavity ratio (RCR). Add the wattage for all rooms together.
2. Area: Determine the use of major portions of a building or renovation and the gross lighted area of each. Multiply the gross lighted area by the allowed power density (watts/sq ft) for each group of rooms by type. Add the figures for all areas together.
3. Whole building: Determine the building type and the gross lighted area for the entire building. Multiply the gross lighted area by the allowed power density (watts/sq ft) for the entire building by type.

To find the total allowed watts for the interior of a building, start with the total wattage as determined by one of the three methods above. Then subtract "credit" watts for lighting controlled by advanced automatic devices such as daylighting or motion sensing and add other allowed watts, if any.

An allowed lighting load can also be determined by using a building energy simulation program like DOE-2. However, because the program's algorithm is based on the same power density assumptions as the allowed amount given above, it is unlikely the value for lighting determined in this manner will be significantly different.

Exterior lighting is governed less than interior lighting, and under some codes it may not be governed at all. As well, energy codes in general do not regulate lighting watts in dwelling units.

ADDITIONAL CODE REQUIREMENTS

In addition to limiting lighting power in a building, lighting energy codes also have other requirements. These vary by state but may include the following:

1. Mandatory use of readily accessible switching in all enclosed spaces. (Exceptions are allowed for spaces in which this would be unsafe.)
2. Use of multilamp or electronic fluorescent ballasts whenever possible.
3. Separate switching for daylighted and nondaylighted spaces in building interiors.
4. Ability through switching or dimming to adjust lighting levels in a space exceeding 100 sq ft and 100 watts.
5. Automatic shutoff controls for lights in spaces in larger buildings (usually larger than 5000 sq ft).
6. Automatic shutoff controls for exterior lights.

LIGHTING CONTROLS IN ENERGY-EFFICIENCT APPLICATIONS

While most energy codes require switching for all spaces, some switch types control energy use better through automatic switching and/or dimming. "Control credits" are often offered by codes that permit the designer to reduce the watts of all lights connected to certain automatic devices; this arrangement allows the design to employ more lighting watts and still comply with the energy code.

COMPLIANCE STRATEGY

To realize design compliance with local energy codes without significant redesign, observe the following process:

1. Choose a general lighting system that uses one of these sources: fluorescent T-8 with electronic ballasts, high-wattage compact fluorescent with electronic ballast, or metal halide or HPS (high-pressure sodium).
2. Make certain the luminaire and room are reasonably efficient. Use direct lighting for tasks whenever possible, and make room finishes light, especially ceilings.
3. Design to just barely meet IESNA recommendations for each space.
4. For downlighting, wallwashing, and other traditional incandescent applications, use compact fluorescent or HID (high-intensity discharge) sources.
5. Minimize the amount of track lighting by using recessed fixtures or monopoints when possible.
6. Use incandescent and halogen sources sparingly, confining them to necessary decorative lighting.
7. Add advanced controls such as motion sensors and daylighting dimming. These allow the reduction of actual lighting watts and can help bring a design into compliance with energy efficiency requirements.

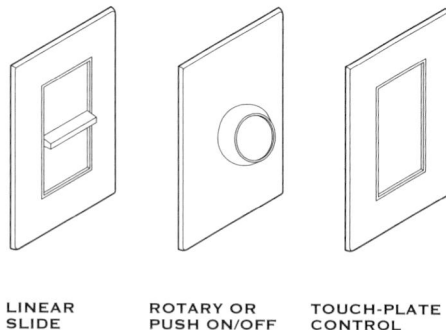

LINEAR   ROTARY OR   TOUCH-PLATE
SLIDE   PUSH ON/OFF   CONTROL
CONTROL   CONTROL

DIMMING CONTROL DEVICES

TRADEOFFS

Energy codes do not regulate lighting design or the amount of lighting in a particular space. For instance, a designer could slightly reduce the lighting loads throughout an office building by using efficient lighting equipment. With the energy saved, an important space like the main lobby could be illuminated in a less efficient manner, such as with incandescent chandeliers, and the project would still comply with the energy code.

Tradeoffs are allowed among interior spaces in the same building, but they are not allowed between interior and exterior lighting. In addition, tradeoffs are not allowed between buildings, even if they are owned by the same company and stand on the same site.

ENERGY-EFFICIENT LIGHTING CONTROLS

DEVICE OR METHOD	OPERATION	TYPICAL CREDIT*
Time clock (with manual override readily accessible)	Turns lights on and off at scheduled times	0-10%
Dimmer	Reduces lighting power by manual adjustment	0%
Motion sensor	Turns lights on and off based on space use	15% (>250 sq ft) to 30% (<250 sq ft)
Daylighting controls	Reduces interior lighting power based on amount of daylight in space	20% (stepped) to 30% (continuous dimming)
Scene preset dimming	Reduces average power by dimming combinations of lighting systems	10-20%
Tuning	Reduces lighting power by hidden adjustment	10-15%
Lumen maintenance	Reduces interior lighting power based on age of lamps and cleanliness of space	10-15%
Combined systems	Combinations of the above are not directly additive	Up to 45%

*The credit offered varies from code to code and may not be available everywhere.

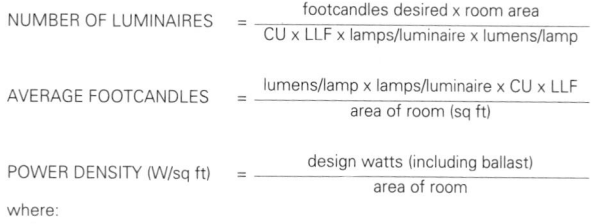

$$\text{NUMBER OF LUMINAIRES} = \frac{\text{footcandles desired} \times \text{room area}}{\text{CU} \times \text{LLF} \times \text{lamps/luminaire} \times \text{lumens/lamp}}$$

$$\text{AVERAGE FOOTCANDLES} = \frac{\text{lumens/lamp} \times \text{lamps/luminaire} \times \text{CU} \times \text{LLF}}{\text{area of room (sq ft)}}$$

$$\text{POWER DENSITY (W/sq ft)} = \frac{\text{design watts (including ballast)}}{\text{area of room}}$$

where:
  CU = coefficient of utilization (percentage of light that actually reaches task)
  LLF = light loss factor (time-dependent depreciation factors)

NOTE

See manufacturer's photometric tables or the Lighting Handbook of the Illuminating Engineering Society for tables of values for CU, LLF, lumens/lamps, etc

$$\text{NUMBER OF FIXTURES} = \frac{50 \times 25 \times 40}{0.67 \times 0.7 \times 4 \times 2850} = 9.35 \text{ luminaires (use 9 or 10)}$$

$$\text{POWER DENSITY (W/sq ft)} = \frac{9 \times 111}{25 \times 40} \text{ or } \frac{10 \times 111}{25 \times 40} = \begin{array}{l} 0.999 \text{ W/sq ft (9 luminaires) or} \\ 1.111 \text{ W/sq ft (10 luminaires)} \end{array}$$

TYPICAL EXAMPLES

Room size 25 x 40 ft; ceiling height 9 ft; illumination level 50 footcandles (IESNA category 10); 2 x 4 ft. recessed troffers with four 32-watt T8 lamps (2850 lm) each.

CU = 0.67 (plastic lens)
Electronic ballast input watts = 111
LLF = .70

FORMULAS FOR AVERAGE LIGHTING CALCULATIONS

James Robert Benya, PE, FIES, IALD, Pacific Lightworks; Portland, Oregon
Robert Sardinsky, Rising Sun Enterprises; Basalt, Colorado

DETERMINING THE EFFECT OF PARTITIONS ON LIGHTING LEVELS

The illumination that reaches a desk top in a direct lighting system is a combination of light arriving directly from the lighting fixture and indirectly via reflectance from various room surfaces. A partition not only interferes with this indirect component of light but can drastically reduce the potential direct component.

Consider the example shown in the accompanying diagrams. In diagram "A," the workstation is contained within 42 inch high panels. Extending "sightlines" (as if the desk top could "see" the ceiling) from the center of the station out to the ceiling over the top of the panels, it can be seen that in a 10 by 10 ft workstation, a ceiling area of 4,225 sq ft (65 x 65 ft) has the potential for contributing light to the workstation. If the lighting fixtures are installed 8 ft apart, there would be an average of 66 fixtures [4,225 sq ft ÷ (8 x 8 ft)] that could contribute light directly to the desk top.

If the same 10 x 10 ft workstation had partitions 60 in. tall, the projected lines would enclose a ceiling area of 676 sq ft (26 x 26 ft). This area would include only ten or eleven fixtures [676 sq ft ÷ (8 x 8 ft)]. This 80% decrease in the number of lighting fixtures that could possibly contribute light directly to the desk top does not translate into an 80% drop in light levels at the desk top. However, it will cause a significant decrease, the amount of which is influenced by factors such as the distribution pattern of the lighting fixtures and the finishes of the partitions.

Clearly, task lighting is important to consider when partitions are more than 42 in. high.

LIGHTING CALCULATIONS FOR SPACES WITH PARTITIONS

A rough approximation of the magnitude of the effect of partition height on lighting levels can be calculated using the following technique. (However, do not use this technique for totally direct lighting systems unless several luminaires directly contribute light to the cubicle.)

1. Use the coefficient of utilization (CU) table for the fixture to calculate the average illuminance at the top of the partitions. Use the distance from the luminaires to the top of the partitions as the cavity height, and use actual reflectance values except for the floor; use "0" for the floor cavity reflectance.
2. Determine the transfer coefficient of a virtual ceiling luminaire: Use the distance from the top of the partition to the desk top as the cavity height. Use the cubicle's partition reflectance as the wall reflectance, and use the effective ceiling cavity reflectance of the actual ceiling cavity above the top of the partitions. Use the table below to find the transfer coefficient.
3. Multiply the illuminance from the first step (at the top of the partitions) by the transfer coefficient to find the approximate average illuminance at the desk top.

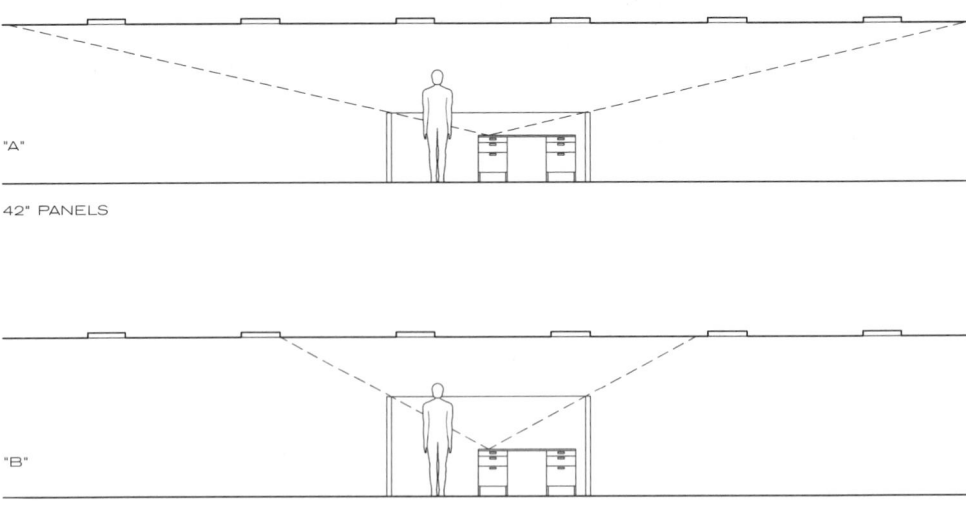

"A"

42" PANELS

"B"

60" PANELS

PANEL HEIGHT COMPARISON

TRANSFER COEFFICIENTS

CEILING	80			50		
WALLS	50	30	10	50	30	10
RCR*						
0	1.19	1.19	1.19	1.11	1.11	1.11
1	1.03	0.98	0.94	0.96	0.93	0.89
2	0.89	0.81	0.75	0.83	0.78	0.73
3	0.77	0.69	0.62	0.73	0.66	0.60
4	0.68	0.59	0.52	0.64	0.57	0.51
5	0.61	0.51	0.45	0.58	0.50	0.44
6	0.55	0.45	0.39	0.52	0.44	0.38
7	0.49	0.40	0.34	0.47	0.39	0.34
8	0.45	0.36	0.30	0.43	0.35	0.30
9	0.41	0.33	0.27	0.39	0.32	0.27
10	0.38	0.30	0.25	0.36	0.29	0.24

*RCR—room cavity ratio

James Robert Benya, PE, FIES, IALD, Pacific Lightworks; Portland, Oregon
Robert Sardinsky, Rising Sun Enterprises; Basalt, Colorado

LIGHTING CONTROL CHOICES

Energy codes require readily accessible switching for all electric lights. The National Electric Code requires switching at specific locations in houses. Traditional switches meet these requirements. Other lighting controls choices are discussed here:

SWITCHING

Standard toggle switches are the most commonly used lighting switches. Three-way and four-way switches permit control from several locations. Choices include standard toggle switches and the more modern "decora" or paddle switches. Electronic touch switches are also becoming more common.

DIMMING

Manual dimming is popular in homes and many other spaces. To dim fluorescent lighting, use modern high frequency electronic dimming ballast systems. An energy credit may be available for using manual dimming under some conditions.

SCENE DIMMING

Scene dimming or multichannel preset dimming systems are increasingly being used for spaces with four or more independent dimming channels, such as restaurants, custom-built houses, and boardrooms. Scene dimming systems are like modern theatrical dimming in that there is a cross-fade between scenes, which are combinations of preset dim light levels.

TIME SCHEDULING

Lighting controls that use clocks to switch lights on and off on predictable schedules are the most commonly used form of automatic lighting controls. Some energy codes require automatic controls of this type as a minimum standard. Controls may vary from individual "time clock" switches to programmable timers and large-scale energy management systems.

OCCUPANCY SENSING

Motion sensors can be used to control lights according to space occupancy. Passive infrared sensors are the most commonly used; ultrasonic sensors are also popular and work better in spaces with partitions. Sensors have sensitivity and timeout adjustments. Choose wallbox sensors with internal switches or dimmers for small rooms, ceiling-mounted sensors with remote relays for larger rooms. Multiple sensors can be used in the same room to ensure coverage.

Energy credits for using motion sensor systems are fairly substantial, as these systems save quite a bit of energy in most applications.

DAYLIGHTING AND RELATED CONTROLS

Daylighting systems use dimming or switching to reduce interior lighting when adequate daylight is present. In buildings with windows near the work area, savings can be significant, and most codes permit a substantial controls credit for daylighting.

Lumen-maintenance controls allow lighting to be dimmed automatically when it is new and, through photoelectric sensing, to be increased gradually as lamps age and luminaires get dirty. The equipment for these controls is similar to that for daylighting, and most systems do both.

Adaptation compensation controls (the opposite of daylighting) increase interior light as exterior light increases. Tunnels are classic applications for adaptation compensation, but the same principles can be used to save energy in supermarkets.

DEMAND MANAGEMENT

Lighting can be dimmed 10-20% with little effect on productivity but a profound impact on overall building load. By sensing incoming electric service for peaks, lighting can be dimmed when other building systems are peaking in load. The result is a "flattening" of the energy use curve, which lowers electric energy cost.

APPLICATIONS FOR LIGHTING CONTROLS

Office buildings, schools	Motion sensors in private offices, classrooms, and conference rooms
	Time scheduling systems for open office areas, corridors, halls, and lobbies
	Motion sensors in toilet rooms and storage
	Daylighting in areas adjacent to windows or skylights
	Combined systems (e.g., motion and daylighting) wherever logical
Retail	Time scheduling for store windows, general and display lighting
	Motion sensing for storage and dressing rooms
	Daylighting and lumen maintenance near skylights
	Adaptation compensation for general lighting
Industrial, institutional	Time scheduling in most areas
	Daylighting near windows and skylights
	Motion sensing in restrooms, little used storage areas
Outdoor	Choices include photoelectric switches, motion sensors, time switches, and manual switches

GENERAL

A luminaire is any device that includes a lampholder, a means of electrification, and a support. Lighting fixtures are luminaires that are permanently attached to a building. Luminaires are characterized by the manner in which light is distributed. Luminaire types are identified in the chart below.

LUMINAIRE TYPES

TYPE	LIGHT DISTRIBUTION
Direct	Emits light downward. Most recessed lighting types, including downlights and troffers, are direct luminaires.
Indirect	Emits light upward, so it bounces from a ceiling into the space below. Many styles of suspended luminaires, sconces, and some portable lamps provide indirect lighting.
Diffuse	Emits light in all directions uniformly. This type includes most bare lamps, globes, and chandeliers and some table and floor lamps.
Direct/indirect	Emits light upward and downward but not to the side. Many types of suspended luminaires, and some table and floor lamps, offer this type of lighting. These luminaires can offer mostly direct or mostly indirect lighting.
Asymmetric	For special applications. For instance, asymmetric uplights are indirect luminaires with a stronger distribution in one direction, such as away from a wall. Wall-washers are a form of direct luminaire with stronger distribution to one side to light a wall.
Adjustable	Usually, direct luminaires that can be adjusted to throw light in directions other than down. Examples are track lights, floodlights, and accent lights.

CHOOSING LUMINAIRES

DIRECT luminaires tend to be more efficient because they distribute light directly onto the task area. They generally create dark ceilings and upper walls, which can be dramatic but can create discomfort from the high contrast.

INDIRECT luminaires generally create comfortable low-contrast soft light, which psychologically enlarges space. They tend to be less efficient for task lighting.

DIFFUSE luminaires create broad general light that often is considered glaring due to the lack of side shielding. They are generally chosen for ornamental reasons or for utilitarian applications.

DIRECT/INDIRECT luminaires are often a good compromise between the efficiency of direct lighting and the comfort of indirect lighting.

James Robert Benya, PE, FIES, IALD, Pacific Lightworks; Portland, Oregon
Robert Sardinsky, Rising Sun Enterprises; Basalt, Colorado

LUMINAIRE STYLES

Downlights and troffers are discussed below; commercial fluorescent fixtures, indirect and direct/indirect lighting systems, architectural lighting fixtures, and decorative lighting are discussed on the following page.

DOWNLIGHTS

Downlights are often called "cans" or "tophats." They are principally used for general illumination in a wide range of residential and commercial applications, especially in lobbies, halls, corridors, stores, and other finished spaces. Downlights can be equipped with incandescent, halogen, low-voltage, compact fluorescent, or HID (high-intensity discharge) lamps. There are several major types, which accommodate varying source types, ceiling heights, plenum heights, room types, and beamspreads. These include the following:

OPEN CONE: the cone of this type of downlight shields the lamp and develops a beam pattern.

OPEN BAFFLE: ridged baffles shield the lamp and minimize glare.

OPEN ELLIPSOIDAL: an elliptical reflector allows a small aperture only; this beamspread is highly efficient.

LENSED (prismatic or fresnel): generally used outdoors or in wet locations, the lens protects and seals the lamp compartment of this type of downlight.

DIFFUSER: a diffuser distributes light broadly, which is especially useful in closets and showers.

ADJUSTABLE: adjustable downlights can be used as a downlight or as an accent light.

PULLDOWN: this feature allows the light to be used as a downlight or an accent light and permits a wide aim.

DOWNLIGHT RATINGS

Choice of a downlight depends on the applications for which it is listed. The primary rating types are these:

THERMALLY PROTECTED (T) downlights are suitable for all applications except direct concrete pour.

INSULATION-PROTECTED (IP) downlights are used when the fixture may come in contact with insulation. They are designed to prevent fixture overheating.

INSULATED CEILING (IC) fixtures are used when the fixture is intended to be in contact with insulation.

AIRTIGHT INSULATED CEILING (AIC) downlights are for applications in which the fixture is in contact with insulation and air leaks in the ceiling must be prevented.

DAMP LOCATION fixtures can be exposed to moist air but not to direct water spray or rain.

WET LOCATION fixtures can be exposed to direct water spray or rain.

SPA OR SHOWER fixtures are designed to be used in a shower stall or over a spa.

CONCRETE-POUR fixtures are designed to be installed in direct contact with concrete.

EMERGENCY fixtures are equipped with a backup battery to produce light for at least 90 minutes during a power outage (generally available only for compact fluorescent luminaires).

TROFFERS

Troffers are widely used in offices, stores, schools, and other commercial and institutional facilities for general lighting in work and sales areas. They are the most common type of fluorescent luminaire.

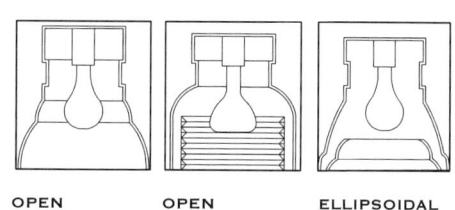

OPEN CONE   OPEN BAFFLE   ELLIPSOIDAL

DOWNLIGHTS

LENSED troffers use a plastic lens to refract light and distribute it in the desired area. The lens cuts off light distribution to minimize glare and protects lamps from breaking in food preparation and service areas. Lenses can contain internal RFI shields for use in hospital operating and laboratory rooms. Lens troffers equipped with highly polished internal reflectors offer very high efficiency.

PARABOLIC troffers have parabolically shaped aluminum or plastic louvers that shield the lamp to improve visual comfort. These troffers offer sharp cutoff, which makes some of them suitable for use in computer work spaces. "Parabolics" generally refer to deep-cell louvers 6 in. or larger across; "paracubes" are shallower troffers with smaller cells. Larger cells are more efficient, but smaller cells make it easier to hide the lamps.

Fixtures meeting IESNA recommendations for computer work spaces are generally identified.

Most troffers are recessed and designed to be laid into acoustic tile ceilings, with the fixture face matching the size of the tile. The most common troffer sizes are 2 x 4 ft, although 2 x 2 ft and 1 x 4 ft are also readily available. Other sizes exist, often to match a specific ceiling (such as 20 x 60 in. fixtures for a 5-ft ceiling grid system). Different mounting types are made, including the following identified by the National Electrical Manufacturers Association:

NEMA "G": for fixtures in a standard exposed inverted T grid.

NEMA "F": for fixtures furnished with a flange and designed to be installed in an opening in plaster or wallboard.

NEMA "SS": for fixtures in a screw-slot inverted T grid.

NEMA "NFSG": for fixtures in a narrow face slot T grid.

NEMA "Z": for fixtures in a concealed Z spline ceiling.

NEMA "MT": for fixtures in a metal pan ceiling system.

Some recessed troffers are also designed to interface with the building HVAC system: "Heat extraction" troffers have vents in the top of the fixture to allow return air to be pulled into the troffer, past the lamps, and into the ceiling plenum. "Air-handling fixtures" have slots around the lens or louvers to supply air to a room (by means of a special boot that can transfer air to the supply air system) or to remove it (by connection to a return duct).

Troffers can also be equipped with emergency battery packs to power some or all of the lamps during a power outage or emergency condition.

TROFFER RATINGS

Most troffers are rated for standard dry indoor applications and must not touch insulation. Some special types include

1. Gasketed: can be damp or even wet rated.
2. Fire-rated: can maintain up to one hour ceiling rating in certain rated ceilings.
3. Vandal-resistant: equipped with vandal-resistant lens.
4. RFI: lens troffers that are shielded from radio frequencies.
5. Specially gasketed: rated for clean room applications.

Troffers can be equipped with most fluorescent technologies, including dimming, magnetic or electronic ballasts, and T-12 or T-8 lamps. Special troffers are made for ceiling systems like the linear metal slat system (4 in. wide). Recessed troffer depth varies from $3\frac{1}{2}$ to more than 7 in., so troffers must be coordinated with other elements above the ceiling.

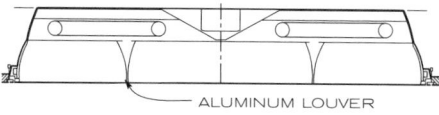

ALUMINUM LOUVER

PARABOLIC LOUVERED

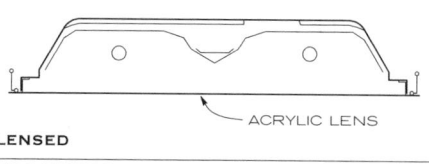

ACRYLIC LENS

LENSED

TROFFERS

LUMINAIRE STYLES

Downlights and troffers are discussed on the previous page, where the subject of lighting equipment is introduced.

COMMERCIAL FLUORESCENT FIXTURES

Several types of fluorescent direct luminaires appropriate for general and utility lighting are employed as commercial fixtures. Most utilize wraparound lenses or diffusers in which the lamp is surrounded by the lens; either way, the lamp is hidden from direct view while radiating light downward and to the sides. Commercial luminaires are among the lowest cost lighting fixtures and are typically used for general and utility lighting in modest projects.

COMMERCIAL RATINGS

Most commercial fixtures are rated for dry locations. Some have damp labels. Most can be equipped with a battery pack for emergency power.

INDUSTRIAL LIGHTING FIXTURES

These fixtures generally have a utilitarian or functional appearance. Fluorescent industrials have strip lights and open fixtures with simple reflectors that are designed to be surface-mounted or hung by chains or rods. HID (high-intensity discharge) industrials include high bay downlights and low bay downlights. Industrial fixtures are used in factories and warehouses and increasingly in schools and retail stores where a less-finished appearance is desired.

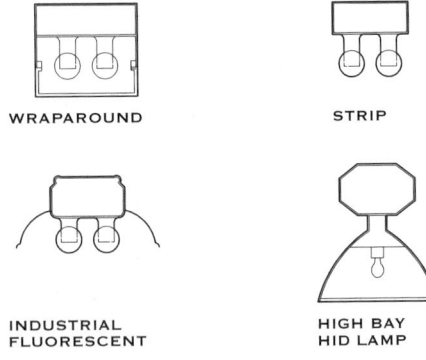

WRAPAROUND   STRIP

INDUSTRIAL FLUORESCENT   HIGH BAY HID LAMP

COMMERCIAL AND INDUSTRIAL FIXTURES

CHANDELIER   PENDANT

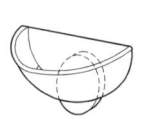

TRADITIONAL SCONCE   CONTEMPORARY SCONCE

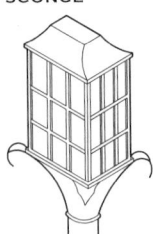

TRADITIONAL LANTERN   CONTEMPORARY CLOSE-TO-CEILING

DECORATIVE FIXTURES

INDUSTRIAL RATINGS

Most industrial fixtures are listed for dry locations. Some have finishes such as glass or porcelain that resist corrosion caused by airborne gases or particles; others are made of aluminum or plastic. Certain fixtures are specifically designed for demanding environmental applications ranging from wet or saltwater marine luminaires to explosionproof products for use in petrochemical plants, grain storage, and other unusual locations.

INDIRECT AND DIRECT/INDIRECT LIGHTING SYSTEMS

Most indirect and direct-indirect lighting systems are designed to illuminate offices and similar finished spaces. In almost all cases, the ceiling should be finished in white paint or white acoustical tile, as the reflectance of the ceiling plane is critical.

Indirect lighting systems only produce uplight. Generally they should be mounted at least 15-18 in. below the ceiling; longer suspension lengths can improve uniformity but potentially will decrease efficiency. To maintain adequate clearance, ceilings should be at least 9 ft high.

Direct/indirect lighting systems are intended to produce some indirect lighting for its comfort and balance and some direct lighting for efficient production of task lighting. Similar suspension length and ceiling height considerations apply. The percentage of uplight to downlight varies; generally the higher the ceiling, the greater the downlight percentage should be.

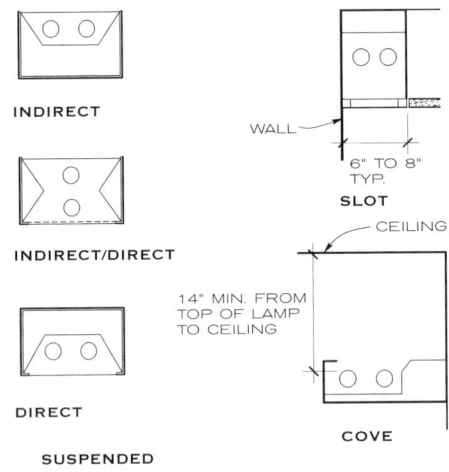

INDIRECT

WALL

6" TO 8" TYP.

SLOT

INDIRECT/DIRECT

CEILING

14" MIN. FROM TOP OF LAMP TO CEILING

DIRECT

COVE

SUSPENDED

INDIRECT, DIRECT/INDIRECT, AND DIRECT LUMINAIRES

ROUND 4" TO 9" DIAMETER (UP, DOWN, OR UP/DOWN)

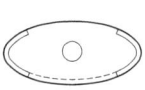

OVOID (UP, DOWN, OR UP/DOWN)

ELONGATED OCTAGON (UP, DOWN, OR UP/DOWN)

RACETRACK OVAL (UP, DOWN, OR UP/DOWN)

"V" OR WEDGE (UP ONLY)

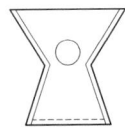

OPTIMAL FOR USE WITH VIDEO DISPLAY TERMINAL (UP/DOWN)

SUSPENDED LIGHTING SHAPES

INDIRECT AND DIRECT/INDIRECT LIGHTING SYSTEM RATINGS

Almost all indirect and direct/indirect luminaires are intended for dry, relatively clean indoor locations. Many of these systems are designed to meet IESNA recommendations for lighting computer workspaces and are rated as complying with either IESNA /ANSI RP-1-1993 or IESNA RP-24-1989. These ratings are based on ceiling brightness and uniformity criteria.

ARCHITECTURAL LIGHTING FIXTURES

Like downlights, architectural lighting fixtures are functional and inconspicuous rather than decorative. They are used to illuminate architectural shapes and forms.

WALLWASHERS come in several types. Eyelid wallwashers essentially are downlights with an eyelid-shaped shield on the room side. Recessed lens wallwashers resemble downlights but use an angled lens to throw light more to one side. Surface and semi-recessed lens and open wallwashers, which throw light onto an adjacent wall, generally work best; they can also be mounted to track. Downlight wallwashers are designed to illuminate rather than scallop an adjacent wall, although the light they provide is not good enough for display purposes.

WALL GRAZING FIXTURES, sometimes called "wall slots," are used to illuminate walls in lobbies, corridors, and core areas. They are especially suited for textured or polished surfaces.

ACCENT FIXTURES focus light on art and building surfaces. Recessed accent lights appear as downlights but internally permit rotation and elevation of the light beam. Eyeballs and pulldown accents resemble downlights that cannot be adjusted. Track lighting systems are specifically designed for accent lighting of art and retail displays, with easy relocation of lampholders along the track.

COVE LIGHTS provide uplighting from coves or other architectural elements more efficiently than strip lights and without socket shadows.

TASK LIGHTS are specifically designed to illuminate a desk area while minimizing veiling reflections.

DECORATIVE LIGHTING

Lighting is the "jewelry of architecture" and, in many building types, plays a significant role in building style, period, or motif.

CHANDELIERS are ornate luminaires that generally comprise many small incandescent lamps to simulate the effect of candle flames. Chandeliers are hung from the ceiling and are used for general illumination in dining rooms, foyers, and other formal spaces.

PENDANTS are also ceiling-hung decorative fixtures. In general, the term is used for luminaires that are less formal than chandeliers, such as those used in offices or restaurants. Most pendant luminaires also use incandescent lamps, although modern variations are available with HID and fluorescent sources.

CLOSE-TO-CEILING luminaires are similar to pendants but are mounted close to the ceiling to allow use in rooms with conventional ceiling heights.

SCONCES are ornate or decorative wall-mounted luminaires. Often they match an adjacent chandelier; in other cases, they are the sole decorative lighting element. Sconces generally exhibit the widest range of styles, from crystal sconces with flame-tip lamps to modern designs.

LAMPS are traditional portable luminaires generally used for table or floor mounting. Torchères are floor lamps designed for uplighting. Most portable lighting uses incandescent or halogen sources, although compact fluorescent options should be considered for commercial and hospitality applications.

LANTERNS are outdoor luminaires mounted to ceilings, walls posts, or poles.

DECORATIVE LIGHTING RATINGS

Lanterns are generally rated with wet labels. Most other decorative fixtures are rated for dry indoor use, although a few sconces also have damp or wet labels.

James Robert Benya, PE, FIES, IALD, Pacific Lightworks; Portland, Oregon
Robert Sardinsky, Rising Sun Enterprises; Basalt, Colorado

ILLUMINATION CRITERIA

The lighting levels given are average figures:

1. Typical offices: 40–60 fc (400–600 lux) in an empty room.
2. Offices, mostly computer work: 20–40 fc (200–400 lux) in an empty room with task lighting as needed.
3. Offices, traditional paper tasks: 40–60 fc (400–600 lux) in an empty room with task lighting at work locations to provide 60-120 fc (600-1200 lux) for specific tasks.
4. Conference and meeting rooms: 30–50 fc (300–500 lux) in an empty room.
5. Lobbies and hallways: 10–20 fc (100–200 lux) in an empty room.

OTHER RECOMMENDED CRITERIA

VISUAL COMFORT PROBABILITY (VCP): This figure is only useful for comparing direct (troffer) lighting systems. A minimum of 70 is recommended. (Note that high VCP does not guarantee visual comfort.)

CCT and CRI: Correlated color temperatures (CCT) and the color rendering index (CRI) suitable for common office uses are shown in the accompanying table.

LIGHTING POWER DENSITY: Approximate design targets using T8 lamps and electronic high frequency ballasts (not including task lights) are shown in the accompanying table.

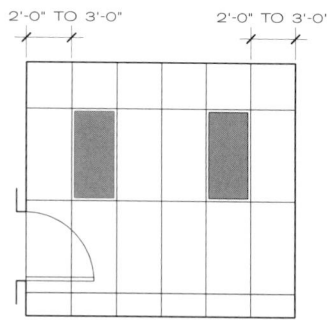

REFLECTED CEILING PLAN
NOTE

In this 10 x 10 ft office, two fixtures produce 50–60 fc on the work area at 1.18 watts/sq ft.

In small offices, maximize comfort and efficiency by having fixtures straddle the work area. Avoid placing a single overhead fixture. Partial symmetry is better than checkerboard or other asymmetrical layouts. Maintain approximately 2-3 ft from fixtures to side walls. Lensed fixtures and indirect lighting systems work best in small rooms.

SMALL OFFICE LIGHTING LAYOUT

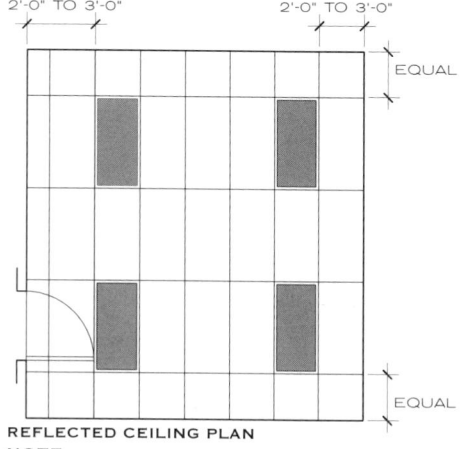

REFLECTED CEILING PLAN
NOTE

In this 14 x 16 ft room, four two-lamp fixtures produce 25–35 fc uniformly at 1.08 watts/sq ft. If higher lighting levels are needed, as in a mailroom, use three-lamp fixtures. In meeting rooms, consider adding task lights such as downlights or wall-wash luminaires.

In larger offices and work rooms, arrange fixtures as symmetrically as possible. Vary the spacing if necessary, for example, from the standard 8 x 8 ft to 6 x 8 or 10 x 8 ft. Keep the long sides of fixtures within 2–3 ft of the wall.

LARGE OFFICE LIGHTING LAYOUT

DESIGN CONSIDERATIONS

LENSED SYSTEMS provide good basic light at the lowest cost, are the easiest to install, and tend to be the most efficient. Most are not suitable for computer work in large open rooms.

PARABOLIC LOUVERED SYSTEMS are more attractive and better for larger rooms where computer work is undertaken. Walls should not be too dark.

INDIRECT LIGHTING SYSTEMS, which provide a comfortable light, must be properly spaced to avoid light stripes on the ceiling. They require ceilings taller than 8 ft and generally require the use of task and/or accent lighting.

DIRECT/INDIRECT LIGHTING SYSTEMS must be properly spaced as well, but they offer a good balance between comfort and efficiency. They require ceilings taller than 8 ft and tend to be more complex and costly than other lighting systems.

Choose luminaires carefully, taking manufacturer's recommendations into account.

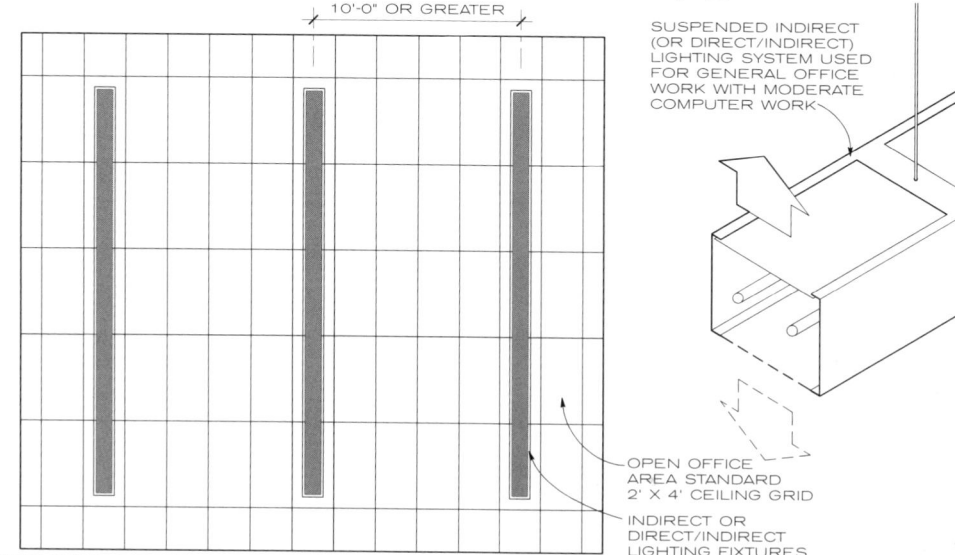

REFLECTED CEILING PLAN
NOTE

Using two lamps in every fixture, this layout produces 30-50 fc in an empty room at 1.22 watts/sq ft. Using one lamp, the design produces 15–30 fc at 0.6 watts/sq ft. The spacing between rows can be made wider. At 12 ft, the design delivers around 20–40 fc. Suspension length is critical.

SUSPENDED INDIRECT AND DIRECT/INDIRECT SYSTEMS

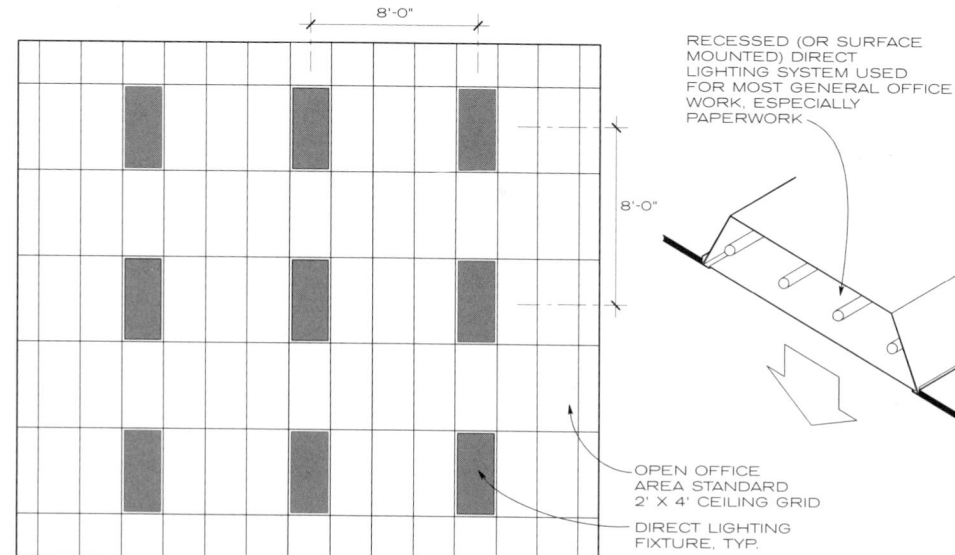

REFLECTED CEILING PLAN
NOTE

This layout produces 30–50 fc in an empty room using two F32T8 lamps in a lensed or parabolic luminaire at 0.92 watts/sq ft. With three lamps, it produces 50–75 fc at 1.38 watts/sq ft. Increasing horizontal spacing to 10 ft with three lamps produces 40–60 fc at 1.22 watts/sq ft. Also consider 2 x 2 fixtures with two F32T8/U or four F17T8.

GENERAL DIRECT LIGHTING SYSTEMS

LIGHTING CRITERIA FOR OFFICES

OFFICE TYPE	CCT[1]	CRI[2]
Most office space	3500 or 4100K	>70 CRI
Executive office	3000 or 3500K	>70 CRI
Medical/dental office	3500 or 4100K	>80 CRI
Art/graphics, dental operatory	5000K	>90 CRI

	LIGHTING POWER DENSITY
General office space	0.8–1.2 watts/sq ft
Executive office	1.1–1.4 watts/sq ft
Medical/dental office	1.0–1.8 watts/sq ft
Drafting/accounting space	1.4–2.0 watts/sq ft
Meeting rooms	1.0–1.6 watts/sq ft
Lobbies and hallways	0.4–0.8 watts/sq ft

[1]CCT—correlated color temperature
[2]CRI—color rendering index

James Robert Benya, PE, FIES, IALD, Pacific Lightworks; Portland, Oregon
Robert Sardinsky, Rising Sun Enterprises; Basalt, Colorado

CORRIDOR LIGHTING

In office buildings, corridors require reasonably uniform illumination with minimum glare. Using ordinary troffers is tempting but generally creates too much light beneath the fixtures and not enough evenly distributed light.

Downlighting is easy but tends to create deep shadows and cavelike spaces. Mixing downlights and other lighting sources, such as sconces or wallwashers, creates a more attractive design with a better balance of brightness among walls, ceiling, and floor.

Wall lighting is an alternative to downlights and sconces for use in corridors. It enhances art and graphics and can reveal wall textures, such as those of stone and brick. Grazing lights can highlight polished or shiny surfaces such as granite or wood.

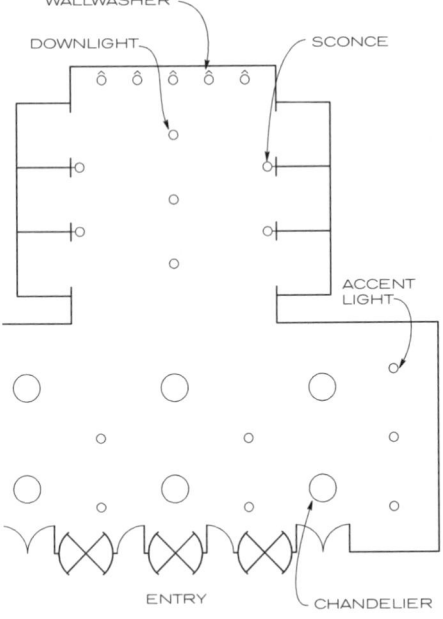

PLAN

NOTE

Fluorescent pendants and sconces produce general light. Compact fluorescent downlights and wallwashers and halogen art accent fixtures provide more specialized lighting that showcases the architecture and artwork and creates an atmosphere.

MAIN AND ELEVATOR LOBBIES

LOBBY LIGHTING

Lobbies offer a primary opportunity for use of creative or decorative lighting. Pendants, ceiling fixtures, and sconces are the primary lighting systems, supplemented by downlights, wallwashers, and other architectural light sources. To most easily meet energy code requirements, use fluorescent, compact fluorescent, and/or low wattage HID (high-intensity discharge) lamps instead of incandescent.

Main lobbies are a most important venue for ornamental and decorative lighting design. Wall lighting is especially useful for providing a sense of spaciousness and cheerfulness. Art objects such as paintings or sculpture may require accent lighting.

Architectural and decorative lighting sources are generally used in combination in lobbies. Incandescent and halogen lamps are often preferred for specific luminaire types, such as art display lights. However, whenever possible, use of more efficacious lighting sources such as fluorescent or HID fixtures is recommended.

LIGHTING FOR CONFERENCE AND MEETING ROOMS

A combination of lighting systems works best in meeting rooms. Uplights from sconces or pendants produce general, ambient light. Downlights illuminate the table. Wallwashers light presentation or art walls. Although the potential combined lighting power is high, preset control systems minimize simultaneous use.

James Robert Benya, PE, FIES, IALD, Pacific Lightworks; Portland, Oregon
Robert Sardinsky, Rising Sun Enterprises; Basalt, Colorado

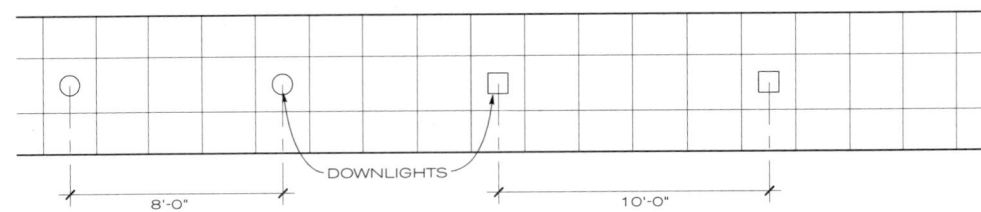

NOTE

In this scheme, each round downlight uses 26 watts of compact fluorescent light (either two 13-watt lamps or one 28-watt lamp). Square downlights use two 16-18-watt lamps. Designs produce 10–20 footcandles (fc) at 0.6–0.7 watts/sq ft.

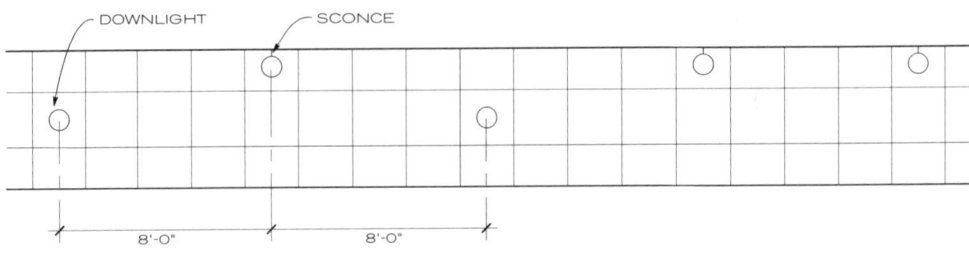

NOTE

In this arrangement, sconce quantity can be minimized by maintaining a nominal 8-ft either-or spacing. Sconces and downlights each have two 13-watt lamps or one 26-watt lamp. Designs produce 10–15 fc at 0.6–0.7 watts/sq ft.

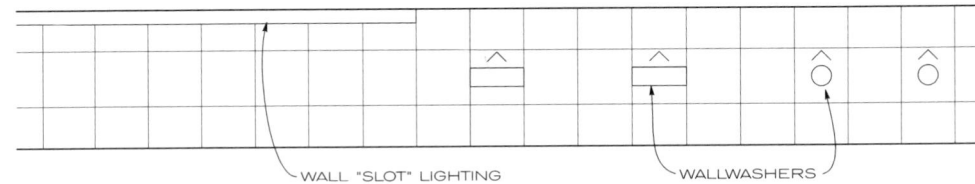

NOTE

Although asymmetric, lighting one wall of a hall or corridor can both provide effective light and be an attractive element, potentially highlighting art or graphics. A wall slot (shown at left) is best for textured or polished surfaces and creates a floating ceiling; wallwashers (right) are better for lighting art or graphics. While footcandles are about the same as in the two schemes above, power use increases to 1.2–1.5 watts/sq ft to illuminate vertical surfaces.

REFLECTED CEILING PLANS FOR CORRIDOR LIGHTING

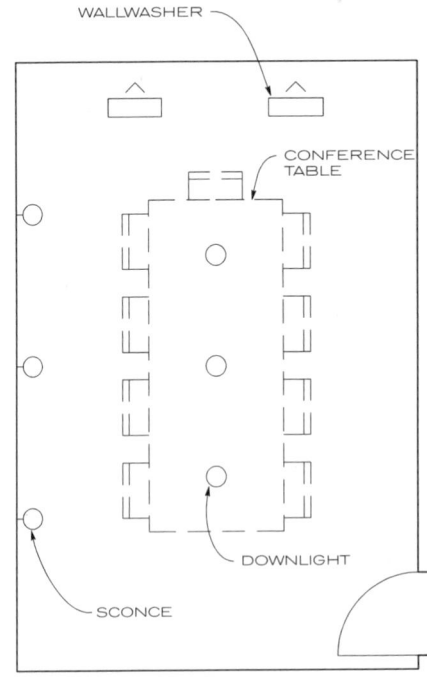

NOTES

1. The lighting load total in this plan of 2.75 watts/sq ft (5.25 watts/sq ft for halogen lamps) is not often reached because, in most cases, not all fixtures are used simultaneously.

2. Wallwashers produce vertical illumination at 30 footcandles (fc) on one short wall, using about .5 watts/sq ft with fluorescent lamps and 1.5 watts/sq ft with halogen lamps.

3. Downlights produce direct light at 10–15 fc that is concentrated downward, usually onto the table surface in a conference room. Compact fluorescent fixtures require 0.5 watts/sq ft, while halogen fixtures require about 1.25 watts/sq ft. The ability to the dim lights is a requirement for most conference rooms.

4. Sconces produce indirect light at approximately 10–15 footcandles. Compact fluorescent lamps require 1 watt/sq ft to light a room, while halogen lamps require 2.5 watts/sq ft.

5. Incandescent and halogen light sources are often used in board and other meeting rooms. When a building houses a number of conference rooms, it is best to use fluorescent sources to avoid overspending in the overall building energy budget.

AVERAGE CONFERENCE ROOM LIGHTING PLAN

SPECIAL LIGHTING ISSUES FOR OFFICES

Lighting for computer use, task lighting, and wall lighting are among the specialized lighting issues in office design.

COMPUTER LIGHTING

Lighting for computer workspaces is becoming increasingly specialized. There are four distinct approaches to this sort of design:

1. Parabolic troffers optimized for computer spaces: By meeting specific cutoff and distribution specifications, some parabolic and small-cell louvered direct lighting fixtures provide lighting acceptable for concentrated computer workspace applications. These lighting systems are generally fairly efficient but tend to create spaces with dark upper walls and ceilings.
2. Indirect suspended lighting: Indirect lighting systems that illuminate ceilings uniformly are also considered good for computer workspaces. General indirect lighting tends to be comfortable but bland. Supplemental task lighting is usually necessary.
3. Direct/indirect lighting: Some direct/indirect lighting systems have been optimized for illuminating computer workspaces, providing the advantages of the two lighting systems just described. The greatest disadvantage of these direct/indirect systems is cost.
4. Intensive CADD workspaces: CADD workspaces are the most demanding of all computer workspaces. Neither parabolic nor indirect lighting, even if optimized for computer workspaces, is acceptable. Task-only lighting systems or very low levels of general light are needed. The unusual requirements of these spaces are often resolved by creating a cavelike space and letting employees manipulate lighting levels and types with switches and dimmers.

TASK LIGHTING

For use under cabinets or shelves, continuous fluorescent task lights are generally the best choice. Good task lights offer the ability to dim or alter the distribution of light to minimize veiling reflections.

Table lamps and task lights produce localized task illumination using a portable luminaire. The area of influence is small but proper location can achieve a successful result. Use compact fluorescent lamps whenever possible.

WALL LIGHTING

Office spaces generally require supplemental wall lighting to compensate for the lack of wall lighting provided by most general lighting systems. Wall grazing and wallwashing are two methods used to accomplish this lighting task.

FINAL TOUCHES

Many offices are furnished with partition-style systems furniture. In this case, best results are obtained by coordinating lighting and furniture plans. Try to use fluorescent lamps of consistent color.

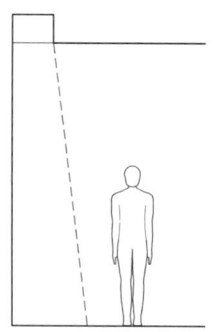

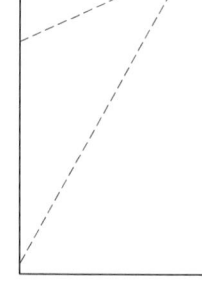

WALL SLOT LIGHTING   **WALLWASHER LIGHTING**

NOTE

A grazing light such as a wall slot is appropriate for illuminating interior core walls in open office spaces, but wallwashers or sconces can be used as well. Wall slot lighting accentuates the wall texture and enhances polished surfaces. Wallwashers accentuate wall pigment and work best for ordinary wall finishes with artwork hanging on them.

WALL LIGHTING

James Robert Benya, PE, FIES, IALD, Pacific Lightworks; Portland, Oregon
Robert Sardinsky, Rising Sun Enterprises; Basalt, Colorado

ILLUMINATION CRITERIA FOR COMMERCIAL SPACES

The lighting levels given are average figures for these commercial spaces:

1. Grocery store, general light: 70–90 footcandles (fc), or 700–900 lux, in an empty room, which will result in average center-of-aisle illumination of 50 fc.
2. Wholesale merchandise: 30–50 fc (300–500 lux) in an empty room with display lighting added as needed. For spaces with warehouse-style shelving, use 30-50 fc in aisles but take shelving into account.
3. General merchandise: 40–60 fc (400–600 lux) in an empty room with display lighting added at key locations to provide 70–100 fc (700–1000 lux) for secondary merchandise displays and 150–300 fc (1500–3000 lux) for primary displays.
4. Boutique and specialty retail stores: 20–30 fc (200–300 lux) in an empty room for general lighting. Display lighting is added throughout to provide 70–100 fc for most merchandise and 150–300 fc (1500–3000 lux) for primary displays.
5. Back-of-house storage and stock areas: 10–20 fc (100–200 lux) in an empty room.

OTHER RECOMMENDED CRITERIA

The correlated color temperature (CCT) and color rendering index (CRI) measurements for light can be used to help specify lighting fixtures:

Wholesale and grocery	3500 or 4100K > 70 CRI
Boutique/specialty	3000 or 3500K > 80 CRI
General merchandise	3500 or 4100K > 70 CRI
Jewelry, art	3000 or 5000K > 90 CRI

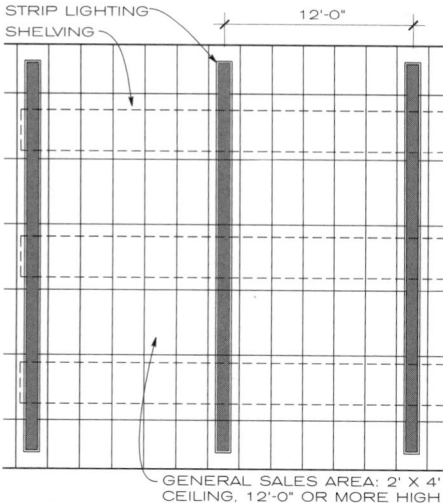

STRIP LIGHTS/STRIP TROUGH LIGHTS

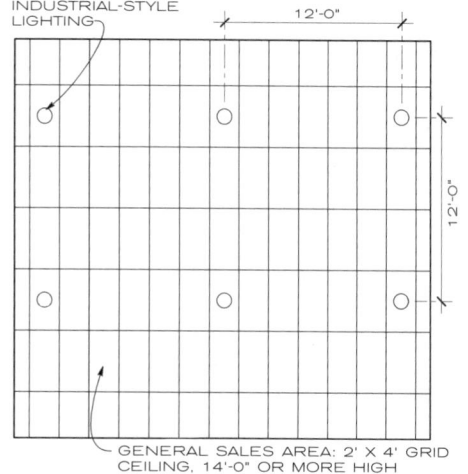

INDUSTRIAL-STYLE LIGHTING

REFLECTED CEILING PLANS FOR WHOLESALE, GROCERY, AND MERCHANDISE STORES

Lighting power density: Listed below are approximate design targets for whole stores, including back of house. These targets are based on HID (high-intensity discharge) systems of T8/compact fluorescent lamps and electronic high-frequency ballasts, including display lights.

Grocery	1.4–2.0 watts/sq ft
Wholesale	1.0–1.4 watts/sq ft
General merchandise	1.2–1.8 watts/sq ft
Department store	2.0–3.0 watts/sq ft
Specialty retail	1.8–3.5 watts/sq ft
Jewelry, china	2.5–4.5 watts/sq ft

DESIGN OPTIONS FOR GENERAL COMMERCIAL LIGHTING

FLUORESCENT STRIP LIGHTS AND LENS TROFFERS provide basic light for the lowest cost and are the easiest to install. They tend to be the most efficient, as well, but appear budget-minded.

HID INDUSTRIAL-STYLE FIXTURES also provide good basic light at low cost but appear budget-conscious. They can be used to create a warehouse motif in a retail outlet.

PARABOLIC LOUVERED SYSTEMS appear more expensive and suggest higher quality merchandise. They should be used in conjunction with valances and/or other perimeter and display lighting.

SUSPENDED DIRECT, DIRECT/INDIRECT, AND INDIRECT SYSTEMS require ceilings taller than 8 ft. These lighting types play a major role in the appearance and style of a space and are generally chosen to reinforce a specific marketing motif.

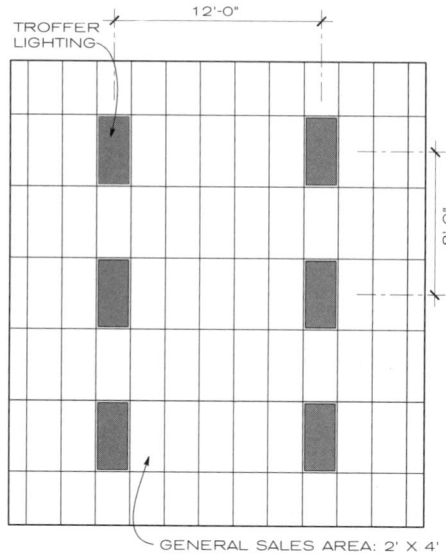

TROFFER LIGHTING

NOTES

1. Strip lights and strip trough lights are common in large retail grocery stores and many mass merchandise stores. The layout illustrated (above left) produces 60–80 fc in an empty room using two F96T8 lamps in a strip light or open trough in continuous rows at 1.15 watts/sq ft. Lights usually run perpendicular to shelving to allow rearrangement, but parallel lighting is preferable when shelves are fixed.
2. Industrial-style lights are commonly used for lighting warehouse-style discount stores. The layout shown at left produces 30–40 fc in an empty room using one 100-watt metal halide lamp in an industrial-style luminaire at 0.85 watts/sq ft. Using a 150-watt metal halide lamp, the lighting level is about 40–60 fc at 1.27 watts/sq ft.
3. Troffers in lay-in ceilings are common in the discount retail industry and serve as general purpose lighting for hardware and general merchandise. The layout above produces 60–70 fc in an empty room using four F32T8 lamps in a lensed or parabolic luminaire at 1.15 watts/sq ft. With high light level ballasts, this arrangement produces 80–100 fc at 1.58 watts/sq ft.

DESIGN OPTIONS FOR DISPLAY LIGHTING

TRACK LIGHTING is the most popular and commonly used display lighting system. Use halogen, fluorescent, or high-intensity discharge (HID) display luminaires.

RECESSED DISPLAY LIGHTS are not as flexible as track lights but can be concealed better. This category includes adjustable accent lights and wallwashers. Sources include halogen, low-wattage HID, and compact fluorescent.

DISPLAY MONOPOINT LIGHTS are adjustable lights installed at fixed locations.

VALANCE LIGHTING is used for clothing and other displays in which a niche is created. Full-sized fluorescent lamps work best for the application.

DISPLAY CASE LIGHTING is similar to valance lighting except the light is built into the display cases to illuminate the task. Fluorescent, compact fluorescent, or low voltage incandescent or tungsten halogen lamps are used. Fiber-optic lighting systems may be useful in certain situations.

Among these options, track lighting offers the greatest versatility and the lowest installed cost. However, most energy codes count track light wattage by the foot rather than by the fixture. This makes it advisable to use other display lighting methods whenever possible so track lights can be used where really needed.

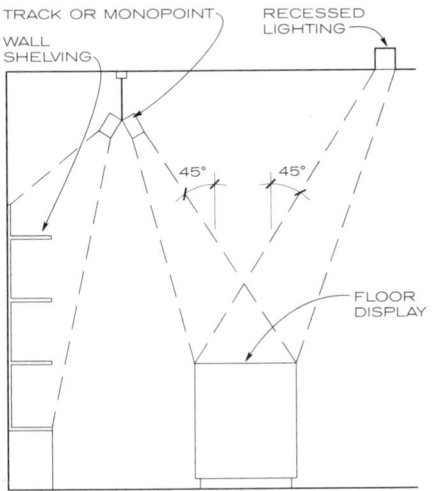

NOTE
The maximum angle of elevation for lighting is 45° except when walls are being lighted.

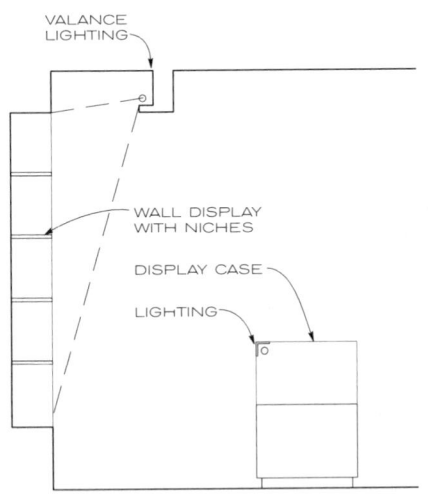

NOTE
Use wallwashers or accent lighting for walls and shelves, track lights or monopoints for floor displays, and valances in wall niches. Display case lighting is suitable for many applications, from jewelry cases to meat and produce counters.

TYPICAL DISPLAY LIGHTING

James Robert Benya, PE, FIES, IALD, Pacific Lightworks; Portland, Oregon
Robert Sardinsky, Rising Sun Enterprises; Basalt, Colorado

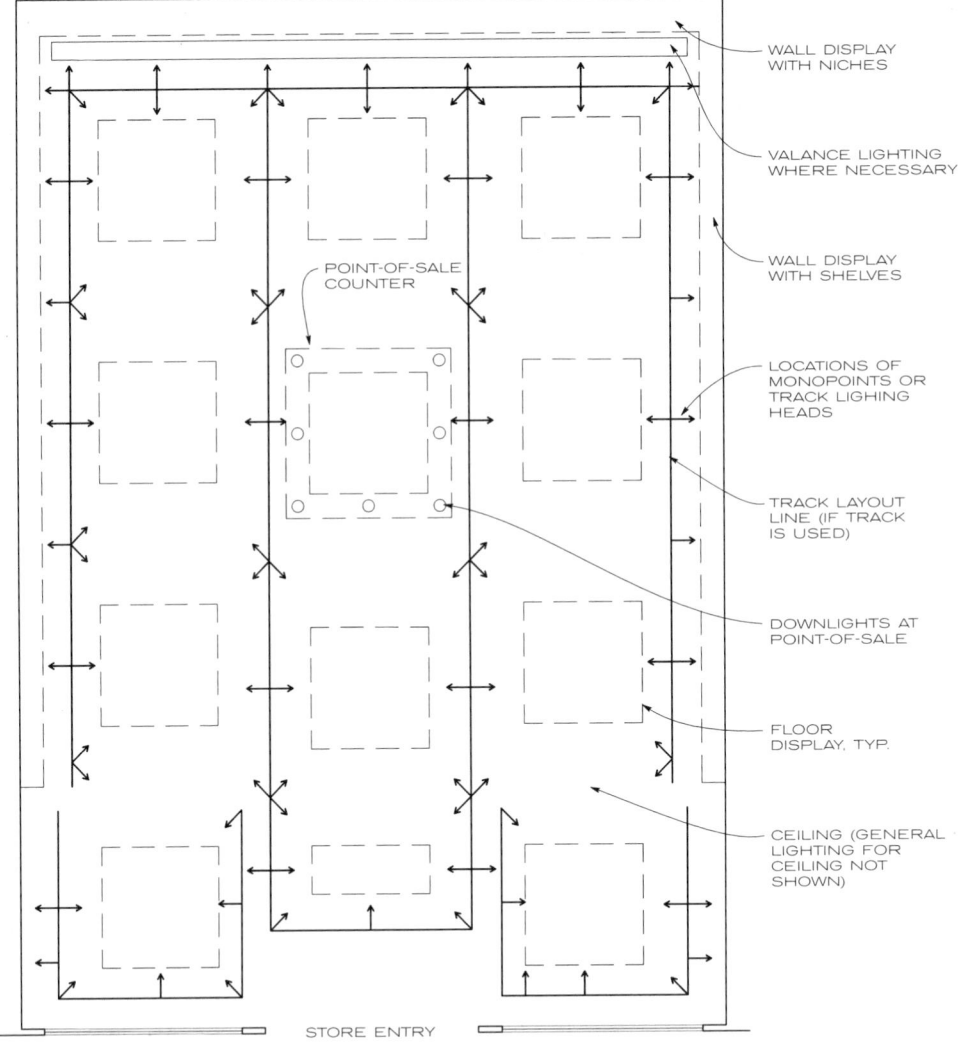

REFLECTED CEILING PLAN

LAYOUT OF DISPLAY LIGHTING

DRESSING ROOMS
Good lighting helps sell clothing. For higher quality stores, provide attractive light with diffuse illumination of the customer; avoid downlights and track lighting. In lower cost and trendy stores, place the emphasis on fixture style and survivability.

STORE WINDOWS
Use high-wattage track lighting and/or low-voltage accent lighting. Run track vertically along the window sides, across the top of the window, and possibly along the bottom of the window as well. Provide outlets for portable lighting inside the window.

OTHER SPECIFIC APPLICATIONS
Use high color rendering or special purpose fluorescent lamps for meat cases, fabrics, and similar demanding merchandise. For fine jewelry, consider high color rendering index, high color temperature fluorescent lamps and/or blue-filtered halogen lamps to achieve 4100-5000K.

DISPLAY LIGHTING FOR STORES

LIGHT SOURCE	ADVANTAGES	DISADVANTAGES	APPLICATIONS
Tungsten halogen (for greatest energy efficiency use halogen infrared reflecting [HIR] lamps)	Low cost, ready availability, excellent color, excellent beam control, dimmability, availability in wide range of sizes/wattages	Not energy-efficient, short lamp life	Recessed accent lights, track and monopoints, wallwashers of all types, portable lighting, low voltage lighting, showcase lighting, downlights
Full-size fluorescent lamps (primarily T8)	Low cost, ready availability, very good color, dimmability, energy efficiency, long lamp life	Very poor beam control, care required when used in cold environments	Valance lights, showcase lights, some types of wallwashers
Compact fluorescent (including high power T-5 twin tube)	Low cost, ready availability, very good color, dimmability, energy efficiency, long lamp life	Poor beam control, care required when used in cold environments	Wallwashers of all types, some types of floodlights, downlights
Compact hid (low-wattage metal halide and white high-pressure sodium are main choices)	Energy efficiency, very good beam control, long lamp life, good to very good color	High cost, not dimmable, limited range of sizes and wattages	Recessed accent lights, track and monopoints, wallwashers of all types, portable lighting, downlights

ILLUMINATION CRITERIA

The lighting levels given are average figures:

1. Classrooms with traditional paper tasks: 40–60 footcandles (400–600 lux) in an empty room.
2. Classrooms with mostly computer work: an average of 20–40 footcandles (200–400 lux) in an empty room with task lighting as needed.
3. Art, music, industrial, mechanics, and laboratory classrooms: 50–70 footcandles (500–700 lux) in an empty room, with task lighting as needed.
4. Lecture halls: 20–40 footcandles (fc) task illumination dimmable to 5 fc with cutoff for video/film presentation.
5. Hallways, commons (not including work spaces): 10–20 footcandles (100–200 lux) in an empty room.
6. Libraries: in active stacks, 20 footcandles minimum vertical illumination; for reading rooms, card files, and catalogs, 50–70 fc in an empty room; computer files and computer study/carrell areas, 20–40 fc in an empty room.
7. Gymnasiums: general illumination of 50 footcandles (500 lux) throughout; signficantly higher levels may be required for high school or college sports that will be televised.
8. Typical administrative offices: 40–60 footcandles (400–600 lux) in an empty room.

OTHER RECOMMENDED CRITERIA

Visual comfort probability (VCP) is useful only for comparing direct (troffer) lighting systems. A minimum of 70 is recommended. (Note that a high VCP does not guarantee visual comfort.)

The correlated color temperature (CCT) and color rendering index (CRI) measurements for light can be used to help specify lighting fixtures:

Most classrooms	3500 or 4100K > 70 CRI
Commons, lunchrooms	3000 or 3500K > 70 CRI
Medical/dental classes	3500 or 4100K > 80 CRI
Art/graphics classes	4100–5000K > 80 CRI

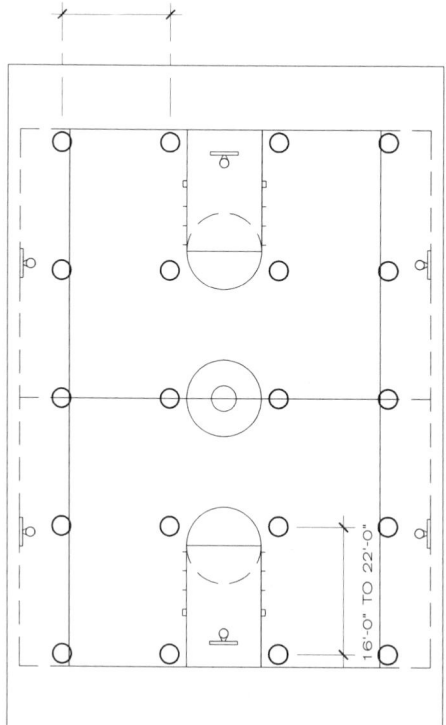

16'-0" TO 22'-0"

16'-0" TO 22'-0"

REFLECTED CEILING PLAN

NOTE

In a 10,000 sq ft gymnasium, average lighting would be 40–50 footcandles at 0.95 watts/sq ft provided by 400-watt metal halide fixtures.

GYMNASIUM LIGHTING

Lighting power density: Listed are approximate design targets using T8 lamps and electronic high-frequency ballasts or high-intensity discharge (HID) systems (not including task lights):

Classrooms	0.8–1.2 W/sq ft
Lecture halls	1.2–2.0 W/sq ft
Arts and industrial education	1.2–1.8 W/sq ft
Gymnasiums (primary-secondary)	1.2–1.6 W/sq ft
Commons and hallways	0.4–0.8 W/sq ft

DESIGN OPTIONS

More information about these lighting systems is available in the section on lighting for offices.

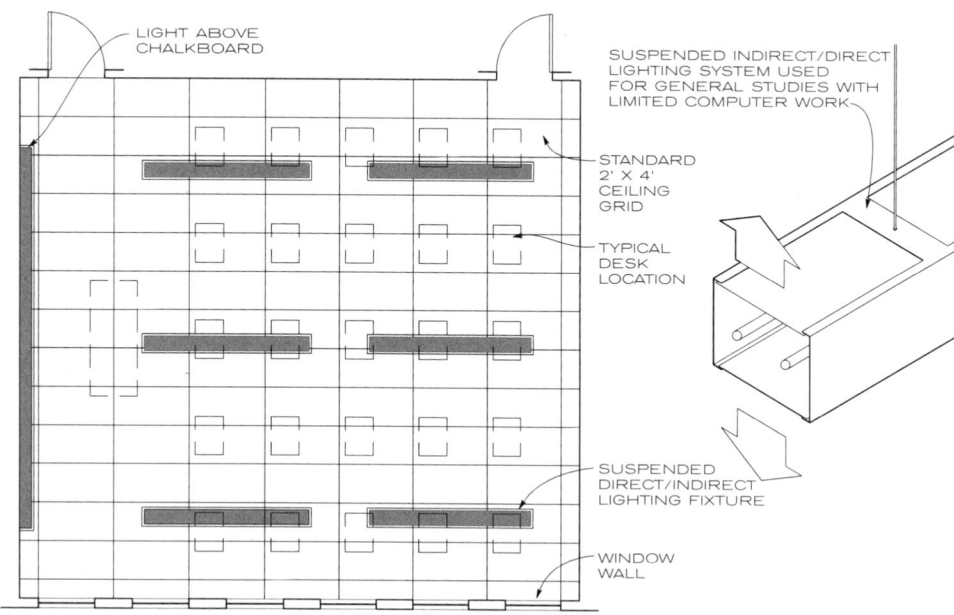

LIGHT ABOVE CHALKBOARD

SUSPENDED INDIRECT/DIRECT LIGHTING SYSTEM USED FOR GENERAL STUDIES WITH LIMITED COMPUTER WORK

STANDARD 2' X 4' CEILING GRID

TYPICAL DESK LOCATION

SUSPENDED DIRECT/INDIRECT LIGHTING FIXTURE

WINDOW WALL

REFLECTED CEILING PLAN

NOTE

A layout with four F32T8 lamps and an electronic ballast in each suspended classroom fixture produces 40–50 fc in the seating area and 20–30 vertical fc on the chalkboard at 0.97 watts/sq ft. The direct/indirect fixtures are designed for traditional classrooms. An indirect lighting system might be used in a computer classroom.

SUSPENDED DIRECT/INDIRECT LIGHTING SYSTEMS

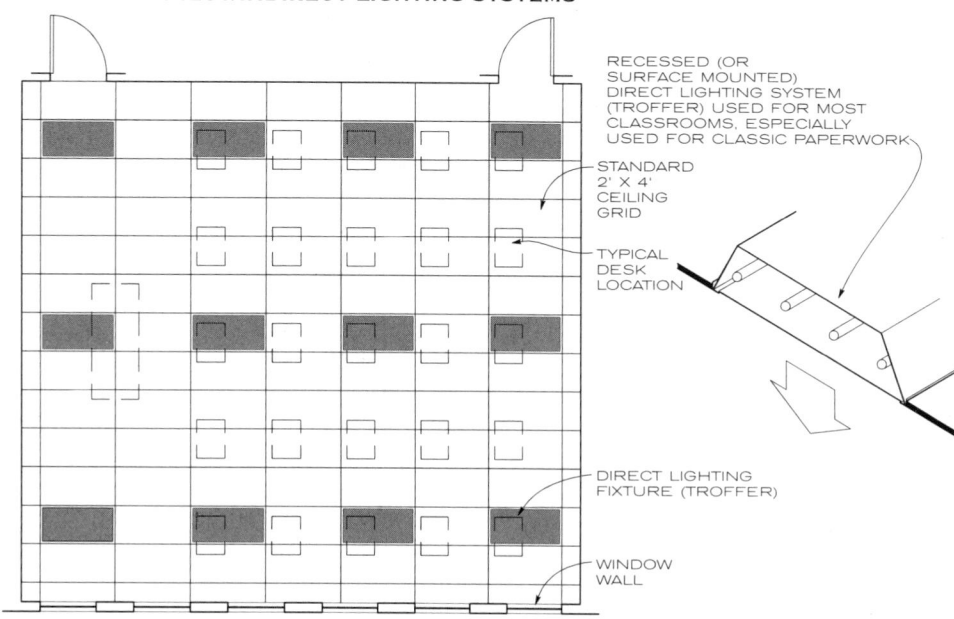

RECESSED (OR SURFACE MOUNTED) DIRECT LIGHTING SYSTEM (TROFFER) USED FOR MOST CLASSROOMS, ESPECIALLY USED FOR CLASSIC PAPERWORK

STANDARD 2' X 4' CEILING GRID

TYPICAL DESK LOCATION

DIRECT LIGHTING FIXTURE (TROFFER)

WINDOW WALL

REFLECTED CEILING PLAN

NOTE

This layout, suitable for traditional classrooms, produces 50–60 fc in an empty room using three F32T8 lamps in a lensed or parabolic luminaire at 1.29 watts/sq ft. With a low light level ballast, it can also produce 40–50 fc at 1.09 watts/sq ft.

For computer classrooms, use computer-optimized parabolics and dimming.

CLASSROOM WITH TROFFERS

TROFFER SYSTEMS, lensed or parabolic, provide good, acceptable light at low cost and are commonly used in schools. Recessed lighting minimizes vandalism and is efficient.

SUSPENDED DIRECT/INDIRECT and INDIRECT SYSTEMS are favored for better lighting comfort and are suited for spaces with ceilings higher than 9 ft.

INDUSTRIAL-STYLE LIGHTING SYSTEMS are often used in industrial education, arts, gymnasium, and other spaces requiring plentiful, inexpensive, durable lighting. If using HID sources, provide quartz auxiliary lamps on some fixtures or an independent instant-on lighting system.

Choose luminaires carefully, considering manufacturer's recommendations.

James Robert Benya, PE, FIES, IALD, Pacific Lightworks; Portland, Oregon
Robert Sardinsky, Rising Sun Enterprises; Basalt, Colorado

DESIGN OPTIONS

INDUSTRIAL HID DOWNLIGHT SYSTEMS provide good acceptable light at low cost and thus are frequently used in industrial spaces. High-bay downlights are specifically suited for mounting heights greater than 20 ft. Low-bay downlights generally have lower wattage and are best for mounting heights less than 20 ft. Aluminum reflectors and prismatic glass or acrylic reflectors direct most light downward, although some light is directed upward in certain luminaires. Special aisle-lighters and other types are available.

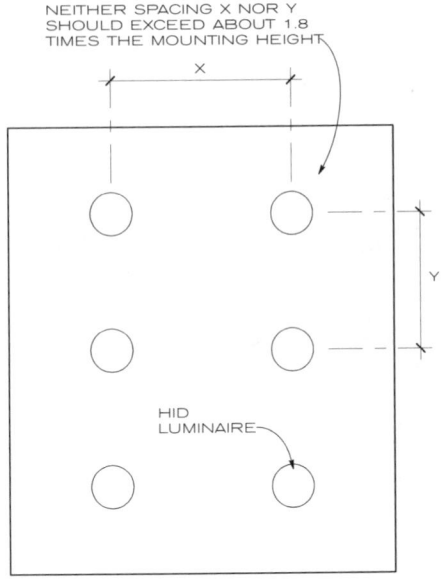

NEITHER SPACING X NOR Y SHOULD EXCEED ABOUT 1.8 TIMES THE MOUNTING HEIGHT

HID LUMINAIRE

REFLECTED CEILING PLAN

NOTE

A low-bay layout using HID lighting requires the fewest luminaires. HPS offers the longest lamp life and lowest maintenance costs. Metal halide lighting is preferred for visibility and color rendering.

HID LOW-BAY LAYOUT

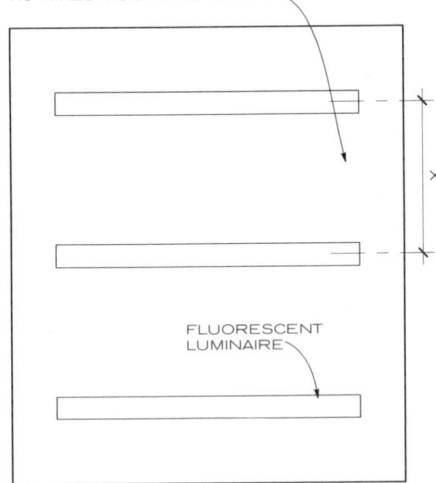

ROWS SHOULD BE SPACED (X) UP TO ABOUT 1.5 TIMES THE MOUNTING HEIGHT WITH GAPS UP TO ABOUT 1.0 TIMES MOUNTING HEIGHT

FLUORESCENT LUMINAIRE

REFLECTED CEILING PLAN

NOTE

Fluorescent luminaires offer superior color and flicker-free operation with electronic ballasts. No warmup time, instant restriking, and long lamp life are other advantages of this lighting type.

FLUORESCENT LOW-BAY LAYOUT

FLUORESCENT SYSTEMS are useful for mounting heights up to about 20 ft. They require more fixtures than HID systems but provide more uniform light with softer shadows; use electronic ballasts to eliminate stroboscopy. Fluorescent systems make good task lights for work stations.

SPECIAL APPLICATION LUMINAIRES come in hundreds of different types, each optimized for a specific job, work station, environment, or hazard. Examples include explosion-proof, vapor-tight, and paint booth luminaires.

Choose luminaires for specific applications carefully, taking into account manufacturer recommendations.

ILLUMINATION CRITERIA

The lighting levels given are average figures:

1. Industrial manufacturing—general: 30-50 footcandles (300-500 lux) in an empty room with task lighting as needed.
2. Industrial manufacturing—assembly and rough inspection: 50-70 footcandles (500-700 lux) in an empty room.
3. Industrial manufacturing—fine assembly and moderate inspection: 50-70 footcandles (500-700 lux) in an empty room with task lighting as needed to achieve 100-200 footcandles (fc) depending on type of work.
4. Industrial manufacturing--specialized: refer to the IESNA Lighting Handbook.
5. Lunchrooms and break areas: 20-30 fc (200-300 lux) in an empty room.
6. Hallways and circulation areas (excluding work spaces): 10-20 footcandles (100-200 lux) in an empty room.
7. Warehouses: with high stacks, 20 footcandles minimum vertical illumination on stacks; for general use, 20-40 fc in an empty room.
8. Storage areas: general illumination of 5-10 footcandles (50 to 100 lux).

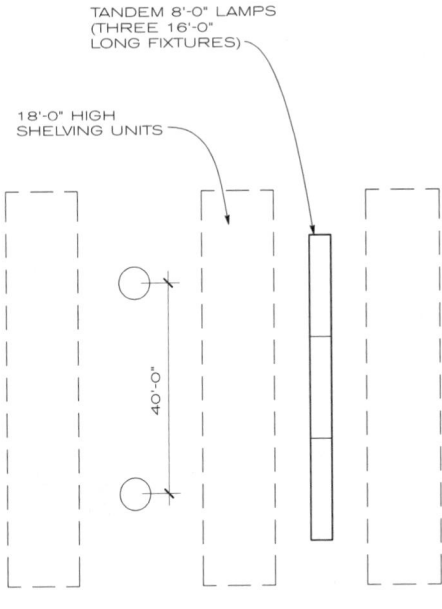

TANDEM 8'-0" LAMPS (THREE 16'-0" LONG FIXTURES)

18'-0" HIGH SHELVING UNITS

40'-0"

DOWNLIGHTS

REFLECTED CEILING PLAN

NOTE

In the left aisle shown, two 250-watt HPS aisle lighter downlights illuminate the shelving units at 0.6 W/sq ft. In the right aisle, the task is performed by fluorescent F96T8/HO lamps at 0.5 W/sq ft. The fixture mounting height is about 18 ft above finished floor.

ACTIVE AISLE LIGHTING FOR WAREHOUSES

James Robert Benya, PE, FIES, IALD, Pacific Lightworks; Portland, Oregon
Robert Sardinsky, Rising Sun Enterprises; Basalt, Colorado

OTHER RECOMMENDED CRITERIA

ATMOSPHERE/ENVIRONMENT: The amount and type of dirt and other airborne particles present in an application can affect luminaire selection. For spaces where hazardous, corrosive, or explosive vapors or dust are present, special lighting equipment is generally required.

SAFETY: Backup quartz auxiliary lamps are needed for high-intensity discharge (HID) systems. Where rotating machinery is used, take precautions to prevent strobosopic problems by using fluorescent lighting systems or rotating phases of power.

CCT and CRI: Correlated color temperatures (CCT) and the color rendering index (CRI) suitable for industrial uses are listed here:

Heavy industry, storage	2100 to 5000K >20 CRI
Most industrial	3000 to 5000K >50 CRI
Most warehouse	2100 to 5000K >20 CRI
Precise assembly	4100 to 5000K >70 CRI

LIGHTING POWER DENSITY: Listed are approximate design targets using HID systems or T8 lamps and electronic high-frequency ballasts (not including task lights):

Warehouse	0.2–0.5 W/sq ft
Light industrial	0.8–1.2 W/sq ft
Precision industrial and inspection areas	1.2–1.8 W/sq ft
Storage areas	0.1–0.3 W/sq ft
Lunchrooms and hallways	0.6–1.0 W/sq ft

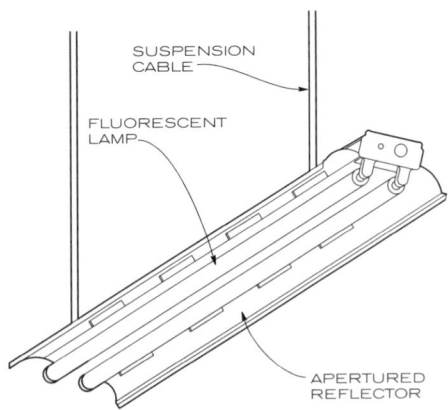

SUSPENSION CABLE

FLUORESCENT LAMP

APERTURED REFLECTOR

FLUORESCENT DOWNLIGHTING

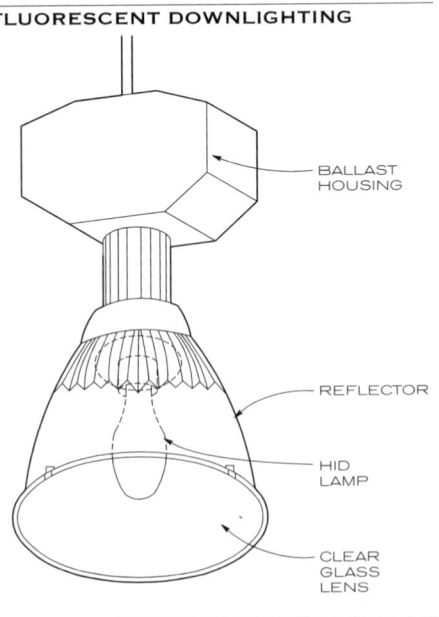

BALLAST HOUSING

REFLECTOR

HID LAMP

CLEAR GLASS LENS

HID DOWNLIGHTING

GENERAL

Outdoor lighting systems include a wide variety of lighting types used to illuminate buildings, parking areas, roads, landscapes, signs, and other outdoor areas.

STREET AND ROADWAY LIGHTING

Four significantly different lighting systems are used to illuminate roads and streets (and often large parking lots). All employ high-intensity discharge (HID) lamps:

1. Standard roadway lights, called cobraheads, are usually mounted to a mast arm and suspended over the roadway at mounting heights of 25–40 ft.
2. Sharp cutoff roadway lights, called shoeboxes, are specifically designed to minimize light pollution and trespass. They are typically mounted between 20 and 40 ft.
3. Traditionally shaped post lights often have a particular theme or design. They are usually less than 25 ft high.
4. High mast lights consist of multiple high-wattage lamps atop poles 60–120 ft high.

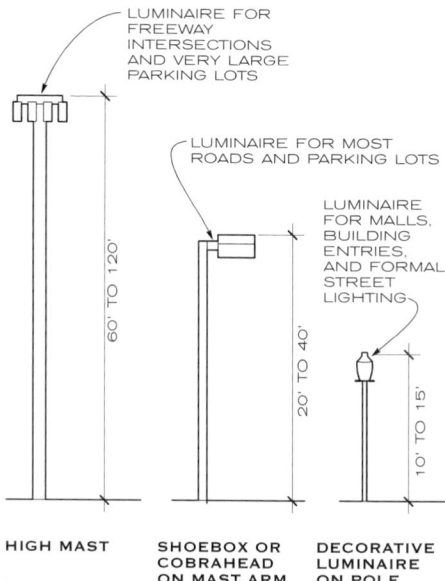

LUMINAIRE FOR FREEWAY INTERSECTIONS AND VERY LARGE PARKING LOTS

LUMINAIRE FOR MOST ROADS AND PARKING LOTS

LUMINAIRE FOR MALLS, BUILDING ENTRIES, AND FORMAL STREET LIGHTING

60' TO 120'

20' TO 40'

10' TO 15'

HIGH MAST   **SHOEBOX OR COBRAHEAD ON MAST ARM**   **DECORATIVE LUMINAIRE ON POLE**

STREET AND ROADWAY LIGHTING

LAYOUT OF STREET AND PARKING LOT LIGHTING. Most luminaires for street and parking lighting are categorized according to the lighting patterns they create on the ground. Types I–V are described in the accompanying chart.

Computer point-by-point calculations are recommended. However, it is possible to lay out roadway and parking lot lighting using isolux curves (similar to those illustrated), making sure the overlapping footcandle lines achieve at least 25% of the intended average footcandle level.

AREA FLOODLIGHTING

Floodlighting is used to illuminate exterior fields, lots, yards, docks, and other similar areas. Special care is often needed to minimize light trespass and light pollution.

Floodlights are described by their light distribution. The National Electrical Manufacturers Association (NEMA) developed a system in which floodlight beams are measured in degrees of vertical and horizontal distribution, then rated from 1 (very narrow field angle) to 7 (very wide field angle).

GENERAL PURPOSE FLOODLIGHTS are usually made in rectangular boxes and typically have wide distributions (5V x 6H or 6V x 7H). Applications include work yards, general security and sports lighting, and building floodlighting. Lamps are usually HID from very low wattage (35 W) to 1,000 watts, but some floodlights use compact fluorescent and halogen lamps.

SPORTS LIGHTS are designed to throw narrow to medium wide beams (NEMA 2H x 2V to NEMA 4H x 4V). Most sports lights are round with standard 400-1500 watt HID lamps mounted in an axial position to create a round beam. Some advanced designs use special double-ended metal halide lamps (1500-2000 watts) for more precise optical control with less trespass.

James Robert Benya, PE, FIES, IALD, Pacific Lightworks; Portland, Oregon
Robert Sardinsky, Rising Sun Enterprises; Basalt, Colorado

SHARP CUTOFF FLOODLIGHTS resemble shoebox parking lot luminaires with characteristics of Type IV distribution. These luminaires are designed to be elevated slightly in front to throw light farther. Sharp cutoff floods are especially good for car lots and sports lighting near residential districts where light trespass must be avoided.

LIGHT TRESPASS AND POLLUTION

LIGHT TRESPASS occurs when outdoor night lighting encroaches onto adjacent properties. Trespassing light is often annoying and can be quite offensive. Some cities have ordinances designed to prevent light trespass, although few of these are competently written.

LIGHT POLLUTION occurs when light is emitted upwards into the night sky. It both wastes energy and causes light pollution, a condition in which the upward light strikes dirt and airborne pollution and obscures the view of the night sky. Some municipalities and counties with important observatories have developed lighting ordinances that regulate light sources, cutoff, and hours of operation in an attempt to make astronomy more possible.

Both light trespass and light pollution can be minimized or prevented by using sharp cutoff equipment and careful design practices. For street and roadway lighting, this means using shoebox luminaires, including decorative luminaires that employ shoebox-style optics. For floodlighting, this means using sharp cutoff floodlights and special sports lights equipped with louvers and visors to prevent upward light. These high-performance lights require careful layout to meet design criteria.

LUMINAIRES FOR STREET AND PARKING LIGHTING

CATEGORY	USE
Type I	Roads and streets where the luminaire is mounted in the median or suspended over the road center. Spacing is 6–7 MH.*
Type II	Roads and streets where the luminaire is mounted above the road but to the side. Spacing is 5–6 MH.*
Type III	Roads and streets where the luminaire is to the side and not above the road; also used for parking lots. Spacing is 4–5 MH.*
Type IV	Parking lots and service areas requiring a forward throw distribution.
Type V	Parking lots. Spacing is 3–4 MH.*

*MH—multiples of mounting height.

OTHER COMMON TYPES OF EXTERIOR LIGHTING

Exterior luminaires are designed specifically for many outdoor lighting applications. Some of the more common types are described in the accompanying chart.

Choose outdoor lighting with consideration for the elements and for the threat of vandalism or other damage. Some luminaires are composed of plastics or composite materials to resist damage and corrosion. Also keep in mind temperature extremes and the minimum starting temperatures of the lamp and ballast.

LIGHTING INFORMATION SOURCES

The best general purpose reference document for lighting information is the IESNA Lighting Handbook, published by the Illuminating Engineering Society of North America in New York. IESNA Recommended Practices provide in-depth information on specific applications, for example, office lighting, roadway lighting, and residential lighting.

Additional information on new and evolving lighting technologies is available from Advanced Lighting Guidelines, a publication of the U.S. Department of Energy from Battele Pacific Northwest National Labs, and from Specifier Reports, published by the Lighting Research Center at Rensselaer Polytechnic Institute, Troy, New York.

Additional information on design and applications can be found in a number of textbooks on the subject of architectural lighting design, landscape lighting, and related topics. Popular lighting industry publications offering current projects and industry news include Lighting Design and Application, Architectural Lighting, Lighting Dimensions, and Architectural Record Lighting Supplement.

COMMON EXTERIOR LIGHTING TYPES

TYPE	USE
Bollards	Walkway and pathway lighting. A typical bollard is 42–48 in. high and uses a lamp ranging from about 35-watt to 100-watt HID (high-intensity discharge).
Step lights	Walkway and stairway lighting from adjacent retaining walls. The light is mounted at or below the rail height
Well lights, direct burial lights	Illumination of trees and structures from below. These are concealed uplights.
Landscape lights	Includes a wide variety of low-level lights, such as path, planter bed, and wallwash lights and uplights in several styles. For residential landscapes, most lighting systems are low voltage (12V typically) for ease of wiring and safety.
Parking garage lights	Parking garages. These are a unique type of HID luminaire designed specifically for the low concrete ceilings of garages. They typically are 100- to 175-watt fixtures.
Sign lights	Illumination of signs. These are designed to be mounted below and in front of a sign and to illuminate upwards evenly.

ILLUMINATION CRITERIA

The lighting levels given here are average figures.

1. Parking lots with pedestrian cross-traffic: from 0.8 fc in places with low activity to 3.6 fc in places with a high level of activity; uniformity of 4:1.
2. Parking lots with minimum pedestrian cross-traffic: from 0.5 fc and uniformity of 4:1 in places of low activity to 2.0 fc with uniformity of 3:1 in places of high activity.
3. Sidewalks and bikeways: from 0.2 fc with 10:1 uniformity in residential areas to 1.0 fc with 4:1 uniformity in commercial areas.
4. Building entrances: from 1.0 fc near inactive entrances to 5.0 fc at active entrances.
5. Outdoor industrial areas: 0.2 fc for storage and dump areas; 2.0 to 5.0 fc for active loading, unloading, and rough work areas; 10 to 20 fc for work areas such as passenger loading, gas pumps, and railroad hump areas.
6. Outdoor sports: from 5 fc for recreational sport areas to 150 fc for major league baseball. Refer to the IESNA Lighting Handbook for more information.

OTHER RECOMMENDED CRITERIA

COLOR OF LIGHT: White light sources like metal halide, fluorescent, and compact fluorescent luminaires are recommended for sports, most applications involving pedestrians, and situations that require color discrimination. Light sources that provide poor color, such as high-pressure sodium fixtures, may be better suited for security lighting. Tungsten sources, including halogen fixtures, offer excellent color rendition but poor energy efficiency and short life.

SURVIVABILITY: Choose fixtures that are physically strong and resistant to vandals and the weather and environment.

STARTING AND OPERATING TEMPERATURE: Fixtures should be able to start and operate at the lowest expected temperature on a site. Minimum starting temperatures for common sources are shown in the accompanying table.

LIGHT TRESPASS: Minimize the light shining onto adjacent properties by using sharp cutoff lighting. Maximum mounting height for a fixture is a function of the cutoff angle.

LIGHT POLLUTION: Minimize light pollution by preventing stray upward light. Use cutoff luminaires.

DESIGN CONSIDERATIONS FOR PARKING AREAS

Poles between 12 ft and 40 ft high are most commonly used for parking areas because they provide good acceptable light at low cost. Pole spacing is generally about 4 times the mounting height; optimum pole heights are 15–20 ft for spacing along every aisle and 30–40 ft for spacing along every other aisle.

High mast poles higher than 40 ft (up to 100 ft) can be used to light large parking areas economically. Poles must be equipped with lowering devices for servicing luminaires.

Floodlights mounted onto buildings are often a low-cost alternative to mounting poles. To minimize light trespass, the farthest distance from the building to the edge of the lot or illuminated area is about 5 times the mounting height.

DESIGN FOR WALKWAYS

Walkways away from a building are usually illuminated by the parking lot lighting system. But near the building (or in areas like a park when there is no parking lot nearby) other lighting should be added. Consider these options:

1. Short "pedestrian" poles: similar to parking lot luminaires, these poles are 8–15 ft high and use lower wattage lamps. Spacing is 4–6 times the mounting height.
2. Low level "bollards": these are typically 42–48 in. high. Spacing is about 4 times the height of the bollards.
3. Step lights recessed into retaining walls.
4. Building-mounted wall brackets (wallpacks).

Keep in mind the overhang of adjacent buildings. Canopies and soffits can serve as locations for recessed lighting to illuminate walks near the building foundation.

MINIMUM STARTING TEMPERATURES

COMMON LIGHT SOURCES	MINIMUM TEMPERATURE
Tungsten (incandescent, halogen)	No limit
MH, MV HID Lamps	-20°F
HPS lamps	-40°F
Fluorescent HO	-20°F
Fluorescent T12/T8	0°F*
Compact fluorescent amalgam (26-32-42 w)	-10°F*
Standard compact fluorescent	32°F

*These temperatures are with specific low temperature ballast; with standard ballast, the temperature may be as high as 50°F.

NOTE

In a parking area, typical spacing of 17-ft fixtures is about 68 ft across by 60–70 ft across. Sides of buildings are good places to mount lights to illuminate side drives. Bollards are used near visitor parking to "dress up" the entry.

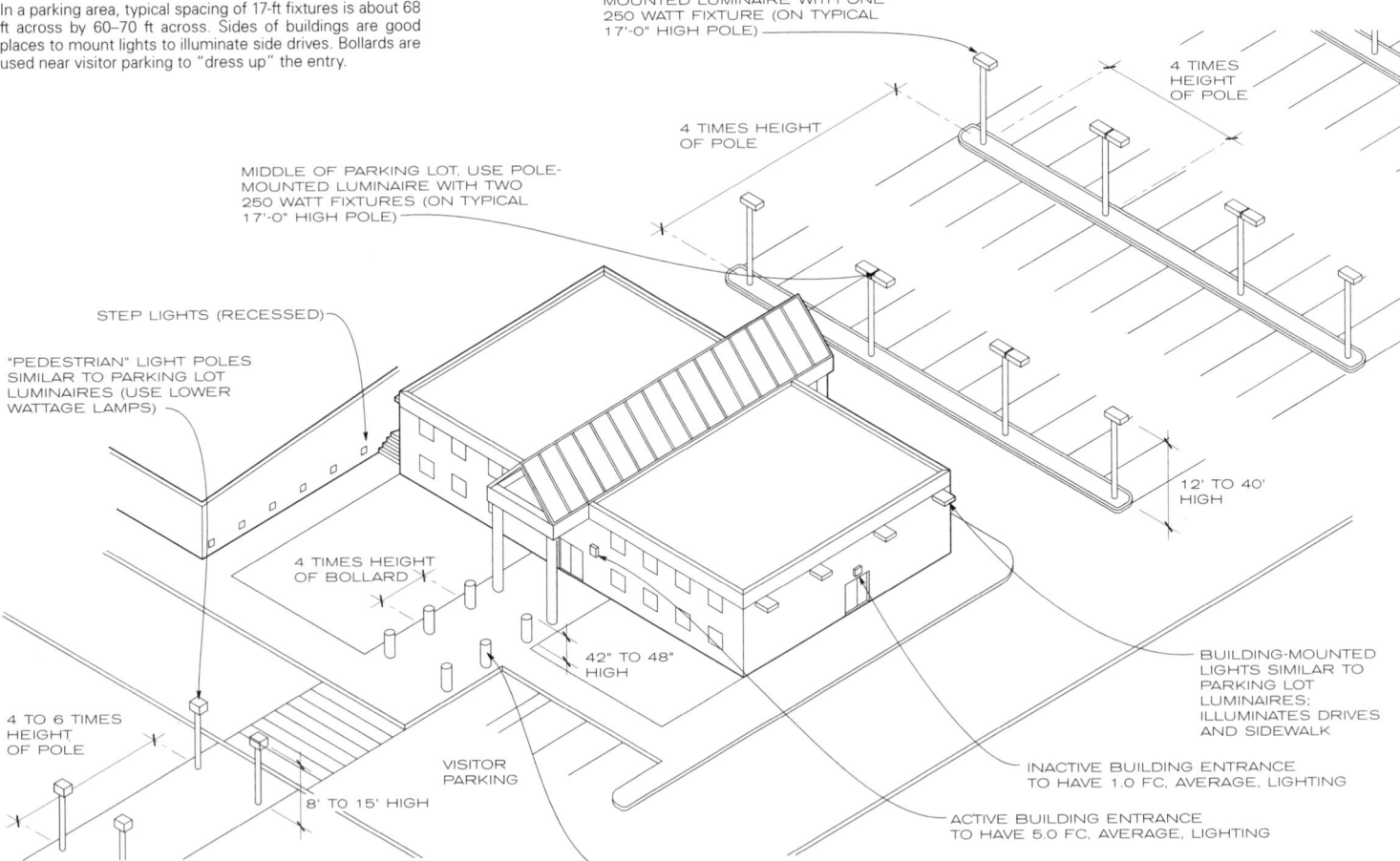

PERIMETER OF PARKING LOT, USE POLE-MOUNTED LUMINAIRE WITH ONE 250 WATT FIXTURE (ON TYPICAL 17'-0" HIGH POLE)

4 TIMES HEIGHT OF POLE

4 TIMES HEIGHT OF POLE

MIDDLE OF PARKING LOT, USE POLE-MOUNTED LUMINAIRE WITH TWO 250 WATT FIXTURES (ON TYPICAL 17'-0" HIGH POLE)

STEP LIGHTS (RECESSED)

"PEDESTRIAN" LIGHT POLES SIMILAR TO PARKING LOT LUMINAIRES (USE LOWER WATTAGE LAMPS)

12' TO 40' HIGH

4 TIMES HEIGHT OF BOLLARD

42" TO 48" HIGH

4 TO 6 TIMES HEIGHT OF POLE

8' TO 15' HIGH

VISITOR PARKING

BUILDING-MOUNTED LIGHTS SIMILAR TO PARKING LOT LUMINAIRES; ILLUMINATES DRIVES AND SIDEWALK

INACTIVE BUILDING ENTRANCE TO HAVE 1.0 FC, AVERAGE, LIGHTING

ACTIVE BUILDING ENTRANCE TO HAVE 5.0 FC, AVERAGE, LIGHTING

LIGHTS IN BOLLARDS ILLUMINATE WALKS NEAR ENTRY AND HELP SIGNIFY "ENTRANCE"

DRIVES AND PARKING AREAS NEAR A BUILDING

James Robert Benya, PE, FIES, IALD, Pacific Lightworks; Portland, Oregon
Robert Sardinsky, Rising Sun Enterprises; Basalt, Colorado

GENERAL

Sound is energy produced by a vibrating object or surface and transmitted as a wave through an elastic medium. Such a medium may be air (airborne sound) or any solid common building material, such as steel, concrete, wood, piping, gypsum board, etc. (structure-borne sound). A sound wave has amplitude and frequency.

The amplitude of sound waves is measured in decibels (dB). The decibel scale is a logarithmic scale based on the logarithm of the ratio of a sound pressure to a reference sound pressure (the threshold of audibility). The values of a logarithmic scale, such as the decibel levels of two noise sources, cannot be added directly. Instead, use the simplified method described in the table immediately below:

Difference between sound levels (in dB)	0–1	2–3	4–9	>10
Add this number to higher sound level	3	2	1	0

For example, 90 dB + 20 dB = 90 dB; 60 dB + 60 dB = 63 dB.

The frequency of sound waves is measured in Hertz (Hz, also known as cycles per second) and grouped into octaves (an octave band is labeled by its geometric center frequency). An octave band covers the range from one frequency (Hz) to twice that frequency (f to 2f). The range of human hearing covers the frequencies from 20 to 16,000 Hz. Human hearing is most acute in the 1000 to 4000 Hz octave bands.

The human ear discriminates against low frequencies in a manner matched by the A-weighting filter of a sound level meter, measured in dBA, or A-weighted decibels. This is the most universally accepted single number rating for human response to sound.

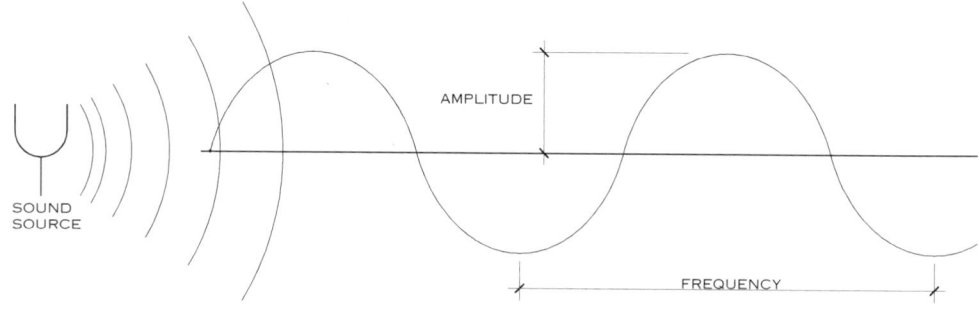

SOUND AND FREQUENCY

FREQUENCY

RANGE OF OCTAVE (Hz)	OCTAVE BAND CENTER FREQUENCY (Hz)
22–44	31.5
44–88	63
88–175	125
175–350	250
350–700	500
700–1400	1000
1400–2800	2000
2800–5600	4000
5600–11,200	8000

SUBJECTIVE REACTIONS TO CHANGE IN SOUND LEVEL

CHANGE IN SOUND LEVEL*	CHANGE IN APPARENT LOUDNESS
1 to 2	Imperceptible
3	Barely perceptible
5 or 6	Clearly noticeable
10	Significant change—twice as loud (or half as loud)
20	Dramatic change—four times as loud (or a quarter as loud)

*Measured in decibels (plus or minus)

FREQUENCY OF COMMON SOUNDS

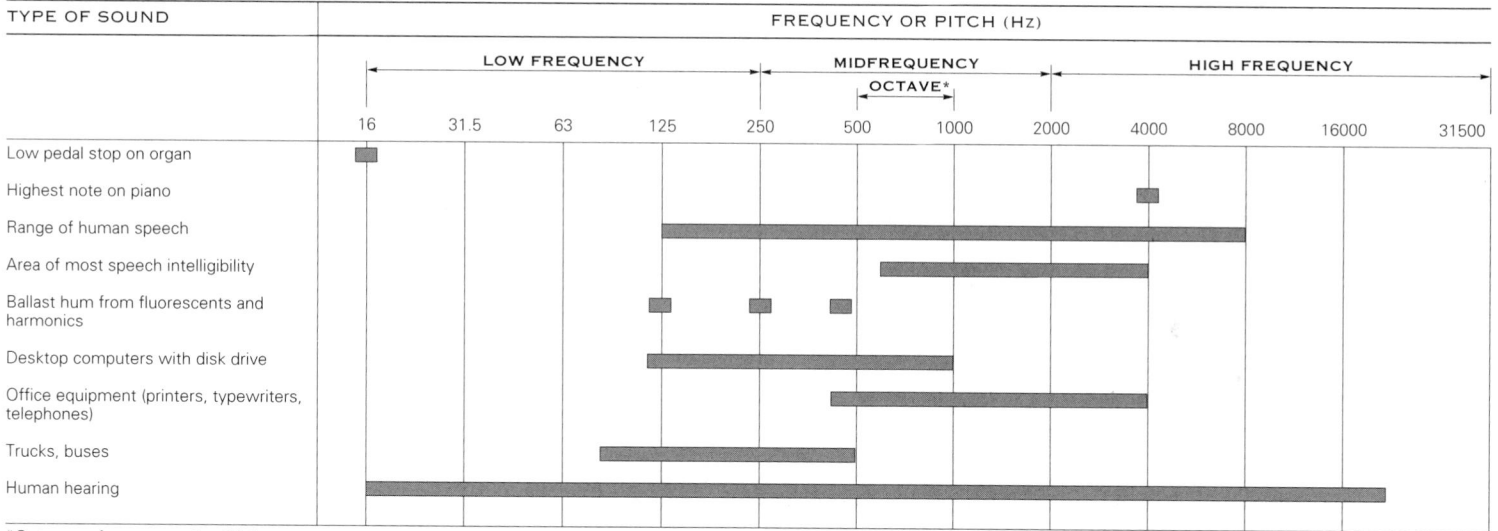

*Octave—a frequency ratio of 2:1

TYPICAL SOUND LEVELS

SOUND LEVEL (dBA)	SUBJECTIVE EVALUATIONS	ENVIRONMENT	
		OUTDOOR	INDOOR
140	Deafening	Near jet engine and artillery fire	—
130	Threshold of pain	Jet aircraft departure (within 500 ft)	—
120	Threshold of feeling	Elevated train	Hard-rock band
110		Jet flyover at 1000 ft	Inside propeller plane
100	Very loud	Power mower, motorcycle at 25 ft, auto horn at 10 ft	Crowd noise in arena
90		Propeller plane flyover at 1000 ft, noisy urban street	Full symphony or band, food blender, noisy factory
80	Moderately loud	Diesel truck at 40 mph at 50 ft	Inside auto at high speed, garbage disposal, dishwasher
70	Loud	Heavy urban traffic	Face-to-face conversation, vacuum cleaner, electric typewriter
60	Moderate	Air-conditioning condenser at 15 ft, near freeway auto traffic	General office
50	Quiet	Large transformer at 100 ft	Large public lobby, atrium
40		Bird calls	Private office, soft radio music in apartment
30	Very quiet	Quiet residential neighborhood	Bedroom, average residence without stereo
20		Rustling leaves	Quiet theater, whisper
10	Just audible	Still night in rural area	Recording studio
0	Threshold of hearing	—	—

Carl Rosenberg, AIA; Acentech, Inc.; Cambridge, Massachusetts

GENERAL

All materials and surfaces absorb some sound greater than 0% and less than 100%. The percentage of incident sound energy that is absorbed by a material, divided by 100, equals the coefficient of absorption, designated α, which ranges from 0 to .99. The coefficient varies as a function of frequency, Hz.

Any material can be tested in a proper laboratory to determine its α values, as per ASTM C423. Some tests give values greater than 1.0, but this is an anomaly caused by the testing procedure; such values should be corrected to be not more than 1.0, since no material can absorb more than 100% of the incident energy that strikes its surface.

SOUND ENERGY ABSORPTION MECHANISMS

There are three mechanisms by which sound energy is absorbed or dissipated as it strikes a surface. In all cases, sound energy is converted to heat, although never enough heat to be felt.

POROUS ABSORPTION entails the use of soft, porous, "fuzzy" materials like glass fiber, mineral wool, and carpet. The pressure fluctuations of a sound wave in air cause the fibers of such materials to move, and the friction of the fibers dissipates the sound energy.

TYPICAL VALUES FOR POROUS ABSORPTION

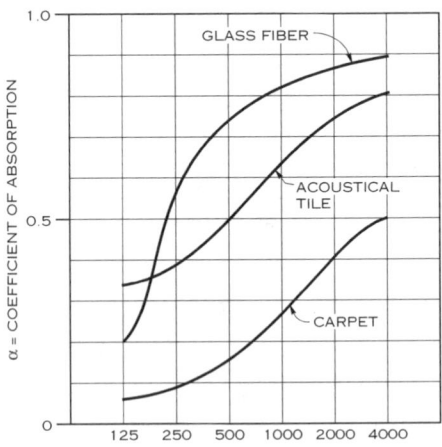

PANEL ABSORPTION involves installation of thin lightweight panels like gypsum board, glass, and plywood. Sound waves cause panels to vibrate. Sound absorption for a panel is greatest at that resonant frequency.

TYPICAL VALUES FOR PANEL ABSORPTION

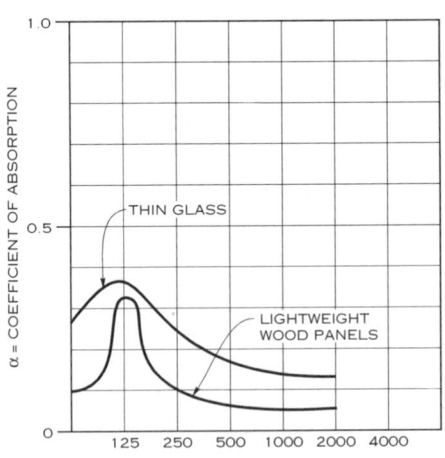

CAVITY ABSORPTION entails the movement of air pressure fluctuations across the narrow neck of an enclosed air cavity, such as a space behind a perforated panel or a slotted concrete masonry unit, also called a Helmholtz resonator. The natural frequency at which the resonator most efficiently absorbs sound is related to the volume of the cavity, the size of the neck opening, and the presence of any insulation in the cavity.

NOISE REDUCTION COEFFICIENT

The noise reduction coefficient (NRC) is the arithmetic average of the absorption coefficients, α, at four designated frequencies: 250 Hz, 500 Hz, 1,000 Hz, and 2,000 Hz. These frequencies have been selected because they represent the middle range of most representative sound sources pertinent to architectural applications. Because the NRC value is meant to be only a general indication of a material's efficiency at absorbing sound, it is rounded off to the nearest .05 value and often represented as a .10 range (for example, .50 to .60). NRC ratings can never be less than 0 or greater than 1.00. The following formula can be used to compute the NRC for a particular application:

$$NRC = (\alpha250 + \alpha500 + \alpha1000 + \alpha2000)/4$$

SAMPLE DERIVATION OF NRC

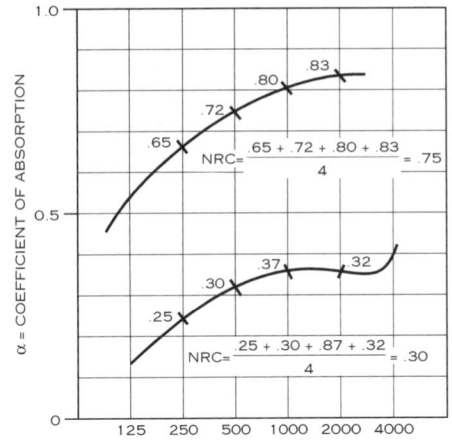

$$NRC = \frac{.65 + .72 + .80 + .83}{4} = .75$$

$$NRC = \frac{.25 + .30 + .87 + .32}{4} = .30$$

SOUND-ABSORBING COEFFICIENTS FOR VARIOUS MATERIALS

The sound-absorbing coefficients for a given material may vary depending on the thickness of the material, how it is supported or mounted, the depth of the air space behind the material, and the facing in front of the material. In general, thicker porous materials absorb more sound; the air space behind a material will increase the absorption efficiency, especially at low frequencies; and thin facings degrade high frequency absorption.

MOUNTING ASSEMBLIES

For consistency in comparing test results, there are set standards for the mounting assembly used in testing absorbent materials. These mounting conditions should be reported along with any and all test data so that the data accurately reflect field conditions. Mounting types A, D, and E are typical for standard sound-absorbing materials. A numerical suffix is used to specify the mounting depth in millimeters; for example, E-400 indicates mounting type E with a 400 mm airspace (a typical 16 in. plenum) as specified by ASTM E795. Mounting types are specified by ASTM E795.

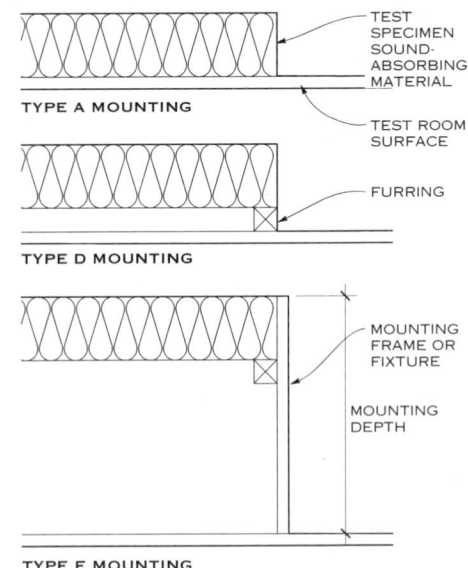

TYPICAL MOUNTING TYPES

ACOUSTICAL PERFORMANCE PER MOUNTING ASSEMBLY

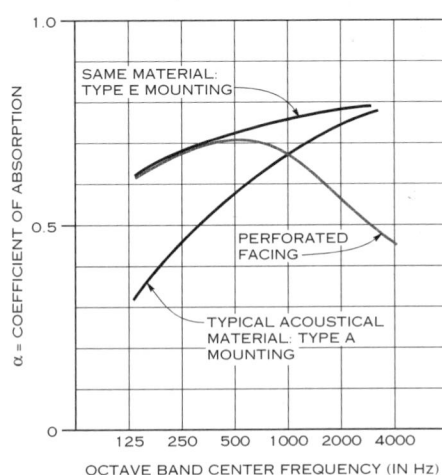

NOTE

Acoustical performance varies with mounting assembly and facing.

SOUND-ABSORBING COEFFICIENTS FOR VARIOUS MATERIALS

TYPICAL DATA/MATERIAL	125 Hz	250 Hz	500 Hz	1000 Hz	2000 Hz	4000 Hz	NRC
Marble	.01	.01	.01	.01	.02	.02	.00
Gypsum board, 1/2 in.	.29	.10	.05	.04	.07	.09	.05
Wood, 1 in. thick, with air space behind	.19	.14	.09	.06	.06	.05	.10
Heavy carpet on concrete	.02	.06	.14	.37	.60	.65	.30
Acoustical tile, surface-mounted	.34	.28	.45	.66	.74	.77	.55
Acoustical tile, suspended	.43	.38	.53	.77	.87	.77	.65
Acoustical tile, painted (est.)	.35	.35	.45	.50	.50	.45	.45
Audience area, empty, hard seats	.15	.19	.22	.39	.38	.30	.30
Audience area, occupied, upholstered seats	.39	.57	.80	.94	.92	.87	.80
Glass fiber, 1 in.	.04	.21	.73	.99	.99	.90	.75
Glass fiber, 4 in.	.77	.99	.99	.99	.99	.99	.95
Thin fabric, stretched tight to wall	.03	.04	.11	.17	.24	.35	.15
Thick fabric, bunched 4 in. from wall	.14	.35	.55	.72	.70	.65	.60

NOTE

This table gives representative absorption coefficients at various frequencies for some typical materials. To determine values not provided here, refer to manufacturer's data or extrapolate from similar constructions. All materials have some absorption values that can be determined from proper test reports.

Carl Rosenberg, AIA; Acentech, Inc.; Cambridge, Massachusetts

1   ACOUSTICAL DESIGN

GENERAL

The total sound absorbing units (a) provided by a given material are a function of the absorptive properties (α) and surface area (S) of that material as defined by the formula

$$a = S\alpha$$

in which a = sabins (units of sound absorption), S = surface area (measured in sq m or sq ft), and α = the coefficient of absorption.

The total sabins in a room can be determined by adding together the sabins of all the surfaces, which vary as a function of frequency. Since most materials absorb more high-frequency sound waves than low-frequency ones, it is typical to find more sabins in a room at high frequencies than at low frequencies.

In general, sound energy that is not absorbed will be reflected, thus surfaces with low coefficients of absorption can be used to encourage sound reflection when appropriate.

PROPERTIES OF SOUND

The sound properties distance and time are described here:

DISTANCE

Outdoors, sound drops off 6 dB each time the distance from a source is doubled (Inverse Square Law). Indoors, the reflecting sound energy in a room reaches a constant level as a function of the sound absorbing units (sabins) in the room. The noise level in a room can be reduced by adding more absorption, as shown in this formula:

$$\text{Noise reduction (NR)} = 10 \log a2/a1$$

TIME

Outdoors, sound ceases when the source stops. Indoors, sound energy lingers and this decay is called reverberation. The reverberation time (RT) is defined as the length of time, in seconds, it takes for sound to decay by 60 dB. Reverberation time is directly proportional to the volume of a space and inversely proportional to the units of absorption (sabins) in it, as expressed in this formula

$$RT = KV/a$$

in which RT = reverberation time in seconds, K = .161 (if volume is in m^3) or .049 (if volume is in cu ft), V = volume in m^3 or cu ft, and a = total absorption in sabins (metric or English units).

Shorter reverberation times greatly enhance speech intelligibility and are imperative in listening environments for people with hearing impairments and for rooms with live microphones for teleconferencing.

SOUND ABSORPTION

Sound-absorptive materials (such as acoustic tile, glass fiber, wall panels, carpet, curtains, etc.) can be added to a room in order to control or reduce noise levels or shorten reverberation time. Noise control is especially helpful when the noise sources are distributed around a room, as in a gymnasium, classroom, or cafeteria.

While sound-absorptive materials can be added to any surface in a room, the greatest area available for coverage is usually the ceiling. Because many soft porous materials are fragile, they should not be located on surfaces that are susceptible to abuse. For these reasons, sound-absorptive materials are often installed on ceilings.

See the accompanying chart for guidelines on the use of sound absorption treatments.

GUIDELINES FOR USE OF SOUND ABSORPTION

ROOM TYPE	TREATMENT
Classrooms, corridors and lobbies, patient rooms, laboratories, shops, factories, libraries, private and open plan offices, restaurants	Ceiling or equivalent area; add additional wall treatment if room is quite high
Boardrooms, teleconferencing rooms, gymnasiums, arenas, recreational spaces, meeting and conference rooms	Ceiling or equivalent area; add wall treatments for further noise reduction and reverberation control and eliminate flutter or echo
Auditoriums, churches, etc. (list)	Special considerations and complex applications

Carl Rosenberg, AIA; Acentech, Inc.; Cambridge, Massachusetts

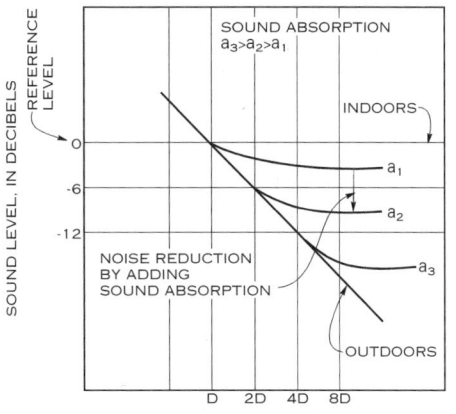

SOUND OVER DISTANCE

NOTE

The more sound absorption (sabins) inside a room, the lower the noise levels (approaching the drop-off with distance outdoors).

PROPERTIES OF SOUND

AVERAGE COEFFICIENT OF ABSORPTION

One measure of the quality of sound in a room is the average coefficient of absorption (or average noise reduction coefficient–NRC) for all surfaces combined, as determined by this formula:

$$\bar{\alpha} = a/S$$

in which $\bar{\alpha}$ = the average coefficient (at a given frequency or average NRC), a = the total sabins (sound absorbing units), and S = the total surface area in the room (metric or English units; be consistent).

As determined by using the average coefficient of absorption, the quality of sound in a room can be evaluated as .1, .2, or .3. A room with an average coefficient of .1 is rather "live," loud, and uncomfortably noisy; one with an average coefficient of .2 is comfortable, with well-controlled noise; and one with .3 is rather "dead," suitable for spaces in which the emphasis will be on amplified sound, electronic playback, or a live microphone for teleconferencing.

CALCULATION OF AVERAGE COEFFICIENT OF ABSORPTION

(Sample at 1000 Hz)

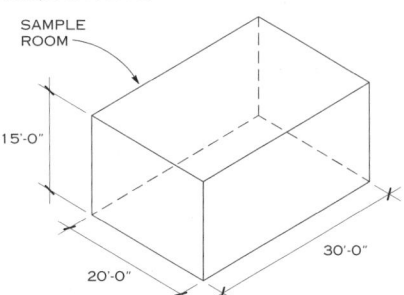

SAMPLE ROOM

15'-0"
20'-0"
30'-0"

The volume of this sample room is 9000 cu ft (l x w x h).

SAMPLE CALCULATION 1

SURFACE	MATERIAL	AREA (SQ FT)	α	a
Floor	Carpet	600 sq ft	.37	222
Ceiling	Gypsum board	600 sq ft	.01	6
All 4 walls	Gypsum board	1500 sq ft	.01	15
Total	—	2700 sq ft	—	243

The reverberation time for the sample room with a gypsum board ceiling is calculated as follows:

$$RT = .049V/a = .049 \times 9000 \text{ cu ft}/243 = 1.8 \text{ sec}$$

SAMPLE CALCULATION 2

SURFACE	MATERIAL	AREA (SQ FT)	α	a
Floor	Carpet	600 sq ft	.37	222
Ceiling	Acoustical tile	600 sq ft	.77	462
All 4 walls	Gypsum board	1500 sq ft	.01	15
Total	—	2700 sq ft	—	699

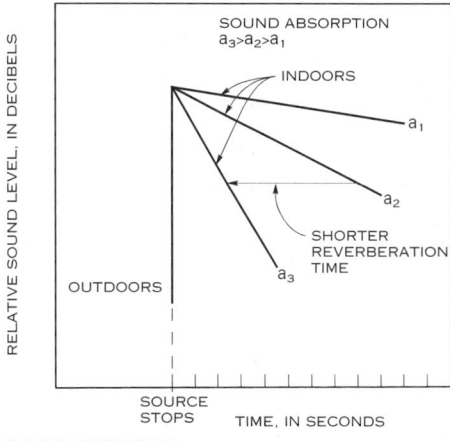

SOUND OVER TIME

NOTE

The more sound absorption (sabins) inside a room, the shorter the reverberation time.

The reverberation time for the sample room with an acoustical tile ceiling is calculated as follows:

$$RT = .049V/a = .049 \times 9000 \text{ cu ft}/699 = .63 \text{ sec}$$

The average coefficient of absorption (α) in the sample room changes significantly from sample 1 to sample 2. The room with a gypsum board ceiling is rather live and noisy, while the room with an acoustical tile ceiling is comfortable, with well-controlled noise. The calculations that show this follow:

Before: $\bar{\alpha} = a/S = 243/2700 = .09$

After: $\bar{\alpha} = a/S = 699/2700 = .26$

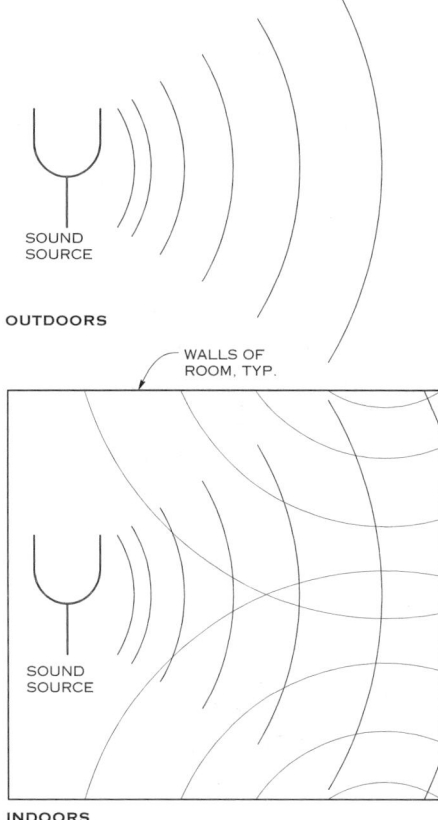

SOUND SOURCE

OUTDOORS

WALLS OF ROOM, TYP.

SOUND SOURCE

INDOORS

NOTE

Outdoors, sound waves expand spherically, becoming more dispersed (i.e., quieter) over distance and time. Indoors, sound waves reflect off surrounding surfaces, building up energy so sound drops off less quickly over distance or time.

SOUND PATTERNS

GENERAL

The property of a material or construction system that blocks the transfer of sound energy from one side to another is transmission loss (TL), which is measured in decibels (dB). Specifically, TL is the attenuation of airborne sound transmission through a construction during laboratory testing according to ASTM E90. Transmission loss values range from 0 to 70 or 80 (or higher). A high TL value indicates a better ability to block sound; that is, more sound energy is "lost" as the sound wave travels through the material.

Sound transmission class (STC) is a single number rating system designed to combine TL values from many frequencies. STC values for site-built construction range from 10 (practically no isolation, e.g., an open doorway) to 65 or 70 (such high performance is only achieved with special construction techniques). Average construction might provide noise reduction in the range of STC 30 to 60.

It is very difficult to measure the STC performance of a single wall or door in the field because of the number of flanking paths and nonstandard conditions. Field performance is measured with noise isolation class (NIC) ratings, which cover effects from all sound transfer paths between rooms.

DERIVATION AND USE OF THE STC CURVE

To determine the STC rating for a particular construction, the STC curve shown in the accompanying figure is applied over the transmission loss (TL) curve for a laboratory test of the construction. The STC curve is then manipulated in accordance with prescribed rules to obtain the highest possible rating. The procedure states that the TL curve cannot be more than 8 dB less than the STC curve in any one-third octave band, nor can the TL curve be more than a total of 32 dB less than the STC curve (average of 2 dB for each of 16 one-third octave band frequencies). Any values from the TL curve that are above the STC curve are of no benefit in the rating. The object is to move the STC curve up as high as possible and to read the STC rating number from the point where the STC curve at 500 Hz crosses the TL curve.

The STC curve has three segments: the first segment, from 125 to 400 Hz, rises at the rate of 9 dB per octave (3 dB per one-third octave); the second segment, from 400 to 1250 Hz, rises at the rate of 2 dB per octave (1 dB per one-third octave); and the third segment, from 1250 to 4000 Hz, flat.

TRANSMISSION LOSS

Design of construction and materials for high transmission loss builds on three principles:

MASS: Lightweight materials do not block sound. Sound transmission through walls, floors, and ceilings varies with the frequency of sound, the weight (or mass) and stiffness of the construction, and the cavity absorption. Theoretically, the transmission loss increases at the rate of 6 dB per doubling of the surface weight of the construction. A single solid panel behaves less well than the mass law would predict, since the mass law assumes a homogeneous, infinitely resilient material/wall.

SEPARATION: Improved TL performance without an undue increase in mass can be achieved by separation of materials. A true double wall with separate unconnected elements performs better than the mass law predicts for a single wall of

the same weight. The transmission loss tends to increase about 5 dB for each doubling of the airspace between wythes (minimum effective space is approximately 2 in.). Resilient attachment of surface skins to studs or structural surfaces provides a similar benefit, as do separate wythes.

ABSORPTION: Use of soft, resilient, absorptive materials in the cavity between wythes, particularly for lightweight staggered or double stud construction, increases transmission loss significantly. Viscoelastic (somewhat resilient but not fully elastic) materials, such as certain insulation boards, dampen or restrict the vibration of rigid panels such as gypsum board and plywood, increasing transmission loss somewhat. Follow manufacturer-recommended installation details.

NOISE REDUCTION

Noise reduction (NR) depends on the properties of a room and is the actual difference in sound pressure level between

two spaces. It is the amount of sound blocked by all intervening sound paths between rooms, including the common wall but also the floor, ceiling, outside path, doors, etc.

Noise reduction also depends on the relative size of a room. If the noise source is in a small room next to a large receiving room, the noise reduction will be greater than the TL performance of the wall alone because the sound radiating from the common wall between office and gym is dissipated in such a large space. On the other hand, if the noise source is in a large room next to a small one (as from a gym to an office next door), the noise reduction will be far less than the TL of the wall alone because the common wall, which radiates sound, is such a large part of the surface of the smaller room. An adjustment for this ratio, plus the contribution of the absorptive finishes in the receiving room, enters into the calculation of actual noise reduction between adjacent spaces.

GRAPHIC TECHNIQUE TO DETERMINE COMPOSITE TRANSMISSION LOSS
(COMBINING TWO DIFFERENT CONSTRUCTION ELEMENTS)

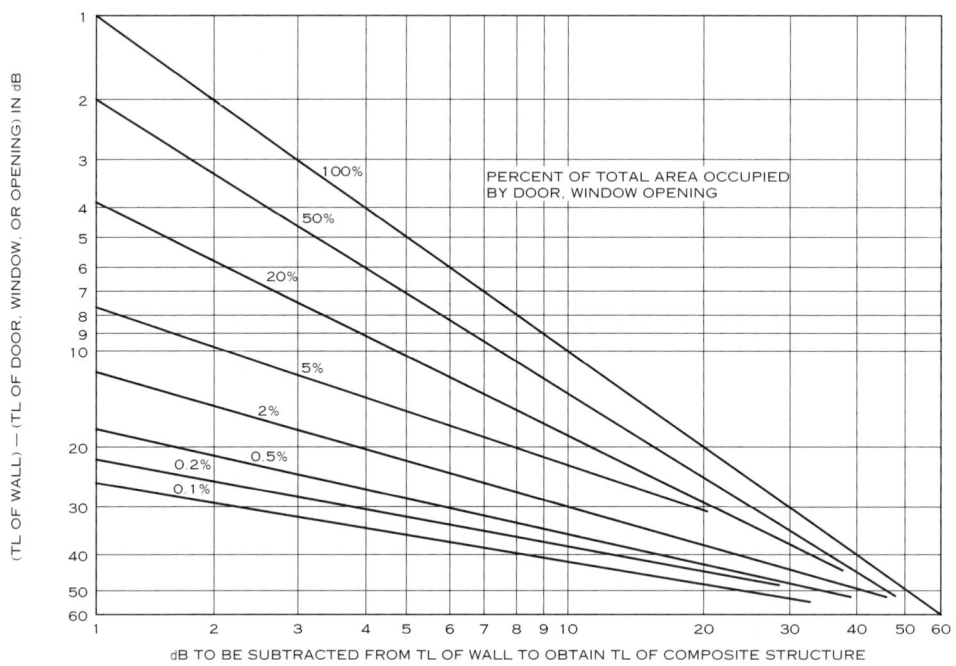

NOTES

1. When a wall or surface of a room is made up of two or more different structures (e.g., a window in an outside wall or a door in an office), the TL performance (or STC) of the composite construction should be evaluated by

combining the TL (or STC) values of the components of the wall alone, in accordance with the chart above.

2. Note that small gaps and cracks such as the perimeter of an ungasketed door can dramatically degrade the performance of a high TL construction.

BENEFIT OF AIRSPACE IN IMPROVING TRANSMISSION LOSS (TL)

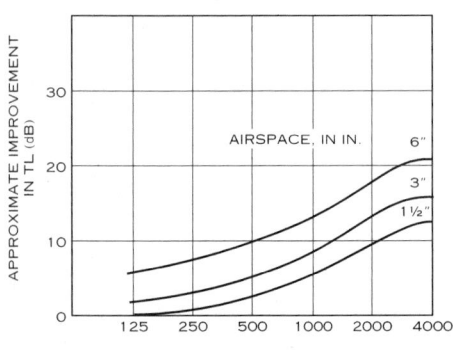

NOTE

If two layers of dense material are separated by an airspace (rather than being continuous), they create two independent walls. The improvement in transmission loss depends on the size of the airspace and the frequency of sound., Avoid ties between layers in all double wall construction. The graph above indicates the approximate improvement in TL when a wall of a given weight is split into two separate walls.

SOUND TRANSMISSION CLASS (STC) RATING CURVE

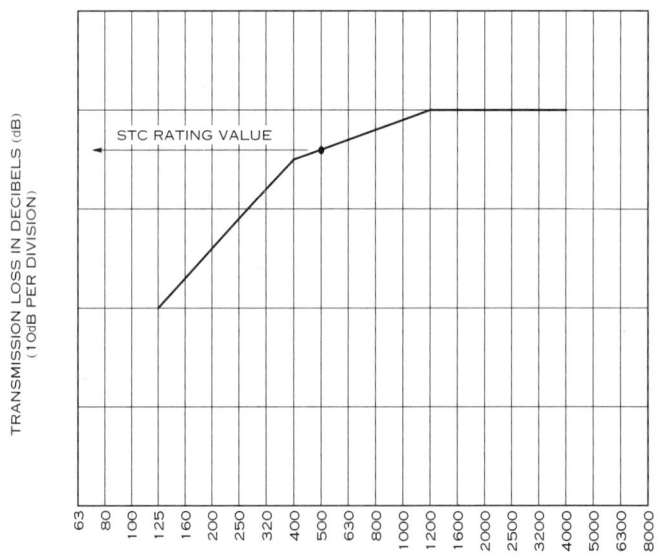

Carl Rosenberg, AIA; Acentech, Inc.; Cambridge, Massachusetts

1   **ACOUSTICAL DESIGN**

SOUND ISOLATION CRITERIA

SOURCE ROOM OCCUPANCY	RECEIVER ROOM ADJACENT	SOUND ISOLATION REQUIREMENT (MIN.) FOR ALL PATHS BETWEEN SOURCE AND RECEIVER
Executive areas, doctors' suites, personnel offices, large conference rooms; confidential privacy requirements	Adjacent offices and related spaces	STC 50-55
Normal offices, regular conference rooms for group meetings; normal privacy requirements	Adjacent offices and similar activities	STC 45-50
Large general business offices, drafting areas, banking floors	Corridors, lobbies, data processing; similar activities	STC 40-45
Shop and laboratory offices in manufacturing laboratory or test areas; normal privacy	Adjacent offices; test areas, corridors	STC 40-45
Mechanical equipment rooms	Any spaces	STC 50-60+[1]
Multifamily dwellings	Neighbors (separate occupancy)	
Bedrooms	Bedrooms	STC 48-55[2]
	Bathrooms	STC 52-58[2]
	Kitchens	STC 52-58[2]
	Living rooms	STC 52-57[2]
	Corridors	STC 52-58[2]
Living Rooms	Living Rooms	STC 48-55[2]
	Bathrooms	STC 50-57[2]
	Kitchens	STC 48-50[2]
School buildings	Adjacent classrooms	STC 50
Classrooms	Laboratories	STC 50
	Corridors	STC 45
Large music or drama area	Adjacent music or drama area	STC 60[3]
Music practice rooms	Music practice rooms	STC 55[3]
Interior occupied spaces	Exterior of building	STC 35-60[4]
Theaters, concert halls, lecture halls, radio and TV studios	Any and all adjacent	Use qualified acoustical consultants to assist in the design of construction details for these critical occupancies

[1] Use acoustical consultants when designing mechanical equipment rooms to house equipment other than that used for air handling (e.g., chillers, pumps, and compressors) and heavy manufacturing areas that house equipment that generates noise at or above OSHA allowable levels or generates high vibration levels.

[2] Ratings depend on nighttime, exterior background levels and other factors directly related to the location of a building. Grades I, II, and III are discussed in "Guide to Airborne, Impact, and Structureborne Noise Control in Multifamily Dwellings," HUD TS-24 (1974).

[3] The STC ratings shown are guidelines only. These spaces typically require double layer construction with resilient connections between layers or, preferably, structurally independent "room-within-a-room" construction. The level of continuous background noise, such as that provided by the HVAC system or an electronic masking system, has a significant impact on the quality of construction selected and must be coordinated with the other design parameters.

[4] Ratings depend on the nature of the exterior background noise—its level, spectrum shape, and constancy—as well as the client's budget and thermal considerations. Use qualified acoustical consultants for analysis of high noise outdoor environments such as airports, highways (especially those with heavy truck traffic), and industrial facilities.

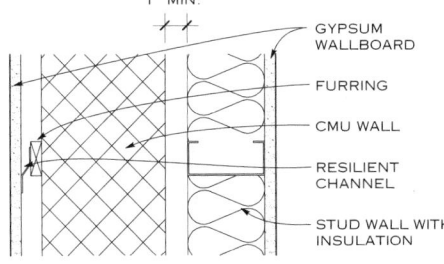

DOUBLE STUD WALL

(Labels: 1" MIN.; SEPARATE WOOD OR METAL STUD WALLS ON SEPARATE FLOOR PLATES OR TRACKS; AVOID BACK-TO-BACK WALL OUTLETS; BATT INSULATION, 3" THICK MIN.; 2 LAYERS GYPSUM WALLBOARD)

DOUBLE WALL—CMU AND STUD

(Labels: 1" MIN.; GYPSUM WALLBOARD; FURRING; CMU WALL; RESILIENT CHANNEL; STUD WALL WITH INSULATION)

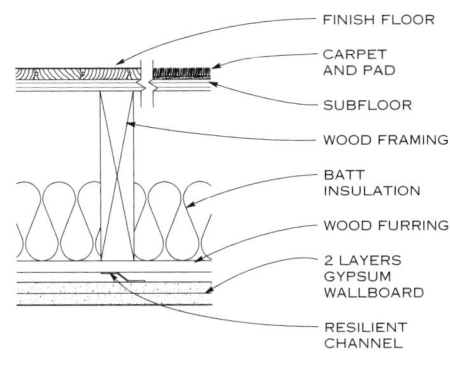

FLOOR/CEILING CONSTRUCTION—CONCRETE

(Labels: CMU WALL; ISOLATION BOARD; 4" FLOATED CONCRETE FLOOR; PLYWOOD; NEOPRENE SPRING OR GLASS FIBER ISOLATOR; STRUCTURAL FLOOR; RESILIENT HANGER; FRAMING CHANNELS; INSULATION; 2 LAYERS GYPSUM WALLBOARD)

FLOOR/CEILING CONSTRUCTION—WOOD

(Labels: FINISH FLOOR; CARPET AND PAD; SUBFLOOR; WOOD FRAMING; BATT INSULATION; WOOD FURRING; 2 LAYERS GYPSUM WALLBOARD; RESILIENT CHANNEL)

TYPICAL HIGH SOUND ISOLATION CONSTRUCTION

Carl Rosenberg, AIA; Acentech, Inc.; Cambridge, Massachusetts

GENERAL

One of the most common goals in the design of sound isolation construction is achievement of acoustical privacy from a neighbor. This privacy is a function of whether the signal from the neighbor is audible and intelligible above the ordinary background noise level in the environment.

Privacy index = noise reduction + background noise

Noise reduction is measured as a field performance where it is evaluated and given an STC value. Background sound levels from steady mechanical heating and ventilating systems, a constant part of our environment, are measured in accordance with ASHRAE standards by a set of uniform curves called noise criteria (NC) ratings. These NC curves are constantly refined, so check the latest ASHRAE guides.

Normal privacy, in which you are aware of a neighbor's activity but not overly distracted by it, can usually be achieved with a privacy index of 68 or higher. Confidential privacy, in which you are aware of the neighbor, usually requires a privacy index of 75 or higher.

A quiet environment with little or no natural background sound (from HVAC systems) between neighbors requires a higher degree of sound separation construction to achieve the same privacy as that in a noisier environment with louder background sound.

IMPACT NOISE DESIGN CRITERIA

Floors are subject to impact or structure-borne sound transmission noises such as footfalls, dropped objects, and scraping furniture. Parallel to development of laboratory sound transmission class (STC) ratings for partition constructions is the development of an impact insulation class (IIC). This is a single-number rating system used to evaluate the effectiveness of floor construction in preventing impact sound transmission to spaces beneath the floor. The current IIC rating method is similar to the STC rating.

Testing for IIC ratings is a complex procedure using a standard tapping machine. Because the machine is portable, it cannot simulate the weight of a person walking across a floor. Therefore, the creak or boom footsteps cause in a timber floor cannot be reflected in the single-figure impact rating produced from the tapping machine. The correlation between tapping machine tests in the laboratory and field performance of floors under typical conditions may vary greatly, depending on the construction of the floor and the nature of the impact.

Often the greatest annoyance caused by footfall noise is the low-frequency sound energy it generates, which is beyond the frequency range of standardized tests. Sometimes this sound energy is near or at the resonant frequency of the building structure.

Whenever possible, to stifle unwanted sounds use carpet with padding on floors in residential buildings and resilient, suspended ceilings with cavity insulation. For especially critical situations, such as pedestrian bridges or tunnels, hire an acoustical consultant.

Slamming doors or cabinet drawers are other sources of impact noise. If possible, bureaus should not be placed directly against a wall. Door closers or stops can be added to cushion the impact of energy from a door so it is not imparted directly into the structure. Common sense arrangements can help minimize problems in multifamily dwellings. For example, kitchen cabinets should not be placed on the other side of a common wall from a neighbor's bedroom.

CONSTRUCTION NOTES

1. Edge attachment and junction of walls, partitions, floors, and ceiling can cause large differences in transmission loss (TL) performance. The transverse waves set up in continuous, stiff, lightweight walls or floors can carry sound a long distance from the source to other parts of the structure with little attenuation. Curtain walls, thin concrete floors on bar joists, and wood framed structures are particularly subject to this weakness.

2. Properly designed discontinuities such as interrupted floor slab/toppings are helpful in reducing structural flanking.

3. A resilient (airtight) joint between exterior wall and partition or partition and floor can appreciably improve TL.

4. Continuous pipes, conduits, or ducts can act as transmission paths from room to room. Care must be taken to isolate such services from the structure.

GENERAL

Mechanical system noise, as a major component of acoustics in modern buildings, must be addressed in developing mechanical design and acoustical goals.

Background sound levels from mechanical systems are measured and evaluated by means of noise criteria (NC) ratings as well as by actual A-weighted decibel levels. The noise criteria curves provide a convenient way of defining the ambient noise level in terms of octave band sound pressure levels. The NC curves consist of a family of curves that relate the spectrum of a noise to the environment being specified. Higher noise levels are permitted at lower frequencies since the ear is less sensitive to noise at these levels. The complete octave band frequency of an acceptable ambient noise level can be specified with one NC number.

Mechanical equipment creates noise and vibration from the rotation of the equipment motor. Four aspects of the noise and vibration to be addressed are described here:

MACHINE NOISE: Sound isolation requirements for the walls and floors of a mechanical equipment room depend on the type of equipment to be housed and the sensitivity of adjacent spaces. Chillers can be extremely loud, requiring double walls and extra thick floor slabs. Air-handling units may only require regular wall construction, perhaps STC 50 systems. Major secondary sound paths are duct penetrations, open curbs under rooftop units, and doors; all potential sound paths must be controlled.

FAN NOISE: Rotation of the fan motor and the fan itself generates noise, which is transmitted along the duct path (both supply and return) to the listening space. Typical fan noise control elements include package silencers (inserted into a straight run of duct, often at the wall of the mechanical equipment room) and internal acoustical duct lining (glass fibers adhered to the duct walls). The degree of fan noise attenuation can be determined by calculations based on the size and sound power levels of the fan, the length and configuration of duct runs, the attenuation of the duct systems, the number and type of diffusers, and the room finishes in the listening space.

AIR NOISE: Movement of air through a duct generates turbulence, which creates noise. For sensitive spaces and quiet noise levels, the airflow must be at low velocity (hence the need for large ducts) with smooth inlet and outflow conditions. For extremely quiet noise levels, air velocities at diffusers or terminal devices may need to be below 400 fpm. Volume dampers to control flow for such spaces are critical; keep dampers 10 ft from diffusers, and avoid opposed blade dampers at diffusers. A simple duct layout that provides even distribution of air to all diffusers in a room can eliminate many problems (see preferred duct layout below).

VIBRATION ISOLATION: Rotating equipment generates vibration, which can travel through a structure and be radiated as noise in a distant location. Vibration isolation may entail use of neoprene pads, spring isolators, or inertia bases, depending on the size and power of the rotating equipment, the proximity of sensitive spaces, and the stiffness of the supporting structure. Piping attached to rotating equipment, especially chilled water piping, must also be isolated from the structure to prevent transmission of sound energy. The effectiveness of a vibration isolator depends on the static deflection of the isolator under load; lower frequency mechanical equipment rotation requires greater static deflection isolation to be effective.

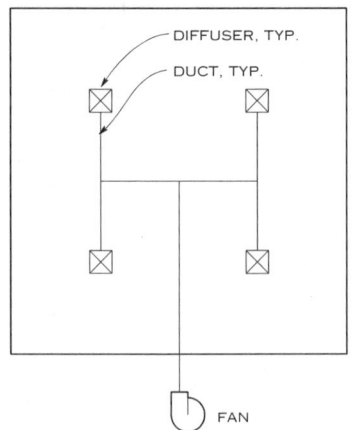

NOTE

All diffusers are equidistant from the fan. The system is self-balancing. The duct layout does not need volume dampers.

PREFERRED DUCT LAYOUT

Doug Sturz; Acentech, Inc.; Cambridge, Massachusetts

1   ACOUSTICAL DESIGN

RECOMMENDED BACKGROUND NOISE CRITERIA FOR TYPICAL OCCUPANCIES

TYPE OF SPACE	USES	NC RATING RANGE	A-WEIGHTED DECIBELS
Sensitive listening spaces	Broadcast and recording studios, concert halls	NC-15 to NC-20	25 dBA
Performance spaces	Theaters, churches (no amplification), video and teleconferencing (live microphone)	NC-20 to NC-25	30 dBA
General presentation spaces	Large conference rooms, small auditoriums, orchestral rehearsal rooms, movie theaters, courtrooms, meeting and banquet rooms, executive offices	NC-25 to NC-30	35 dBA
Quiet areas	Offices, small conference rooms, classrooms, private residences, hospitals, hotels, libraries	NC-30 to NC-35	40 dBA
Public spaces	Restaurants, lobbies, open plan offices and clinics	NC-35 to NC-40	45 dBA
Service and support spaces	Computer equipment rooms, public circulation areas, arenas, convention floors	NC-40 to NC-45	50 dBA

NOISE CRITERIA SOUND PRESSURE LEVEL TABLE*

NC CURVE	SOUND PRESSURE LEVEL (DB)							
	63 Hz	125 Hz	250 Hz	500 Hz	1000 Hz	2000 Hz	4000 Hz	8000 Hz
NC-70	83	79	75	72	71	70	69	68
NC-65	80	75	71	68	66	64	63	62
NC-60	77	71	67	63	61	59	58	57
NC-55	74	67	62	58	56	54	53	52
NC-50	71	64	58	54	51	49	48	47
NC-45	67	60	54	49	46	44	43	42
NC-40	64	57	50	45	41	39	38	37
NC-35	60	52	45	40	36	34	33	32
NC-30	57	48	41	36	31	29	28	27
NC-25	54	44	37	31	27	24	22	21
NC-20	50	41	33	26	22	19	17	16
NC-15	47	36	29	22	17	14	12	11

*For convenience in using noise criteria data, the table lists the sound pressure level (SPL) in decibels for each NC curve.

NOISE CRITERIA CURVES

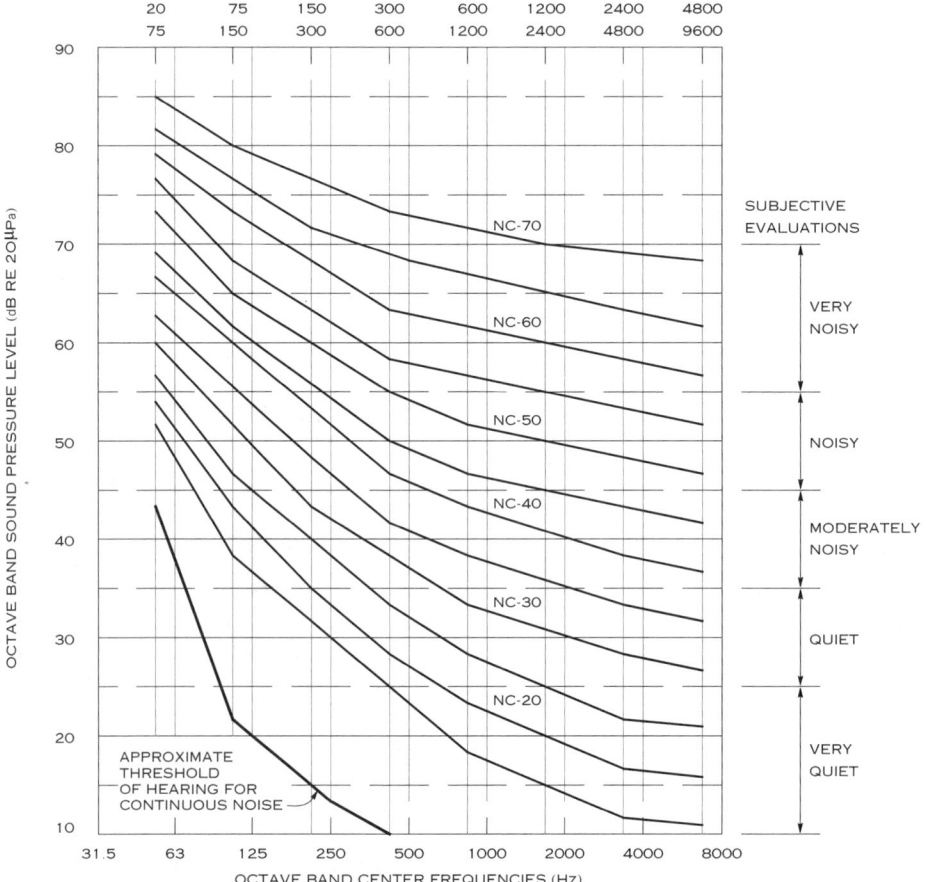

GENERAL

Performance spaces are rooms in which good hearing conditions are particularly critical to the use of the space and exchange of aural information. Such spaces include classrooms, lecture halls, recital halls, theaters, cinemas, concert halls, churches and synagogues. Critical design of a performance space may require assistance from an acoustical consultant, but the primary tools at the architect's direction are outlined here:

LOUDNESS

Audience and performers should be in the same space, and any sound generated by a speaker or musician should be projected efficiently to the audience and captured within the space. The "sending end" of the room (i.e., the stage) should be acoustically hard. Walls near the performer should be angled or splayed to enhance projection and prevent "flutter echoes" at the stage. Walls and ceilings where the audience sits should be hard so they can reflect sound, unless absorptive treatment is needed to eliminate problematic reflections or focusing or to reduce reverberation time (RT) for particular program needs.

QUIET

Good hearing environments should maximize the signal-to-noise ratio; in other words, in addition to the desired signal being well projected (see loudness), unwanted noise should be eliminated. To accomplish this requires very low background sound levels (NC-20 perhaps) from mechanical equipment. Sound lock vestibules eliminate intrusive noise from a lobby and allow latecomers to enter without acoustical interference to the show, and carpeted aisles help reduce footfall noise. Noise from exterior environmental sources should also be considered. Avoid lightweight roofs, which will transmit rain noise.

SPACIOUSNESS

Because of the lateral configuration of our ears, sound signals that are slightly different in each ear allow the listener to hear an acoustical quality called spaciousness, which is usually highly desired, especially for classical music. This sense of spaciousness can be enhanced if the distribution of sound through a large hall is diffused, and the ear literally hears reflections from many facets of the side and rear walls. This diffusion can be enhanced by protrusions and angled surfaces on the side walls.

REVERBERATION TIME (RT)

Refer to the accompanying charts on optimum reverberation times and preferred volume/seat ratios. Room volume and area of absorption can be calculated to predict RT. The biggest design factor affecting RT is ceiling height. The relationship between the volume of a hall and the number of seats is often a good approximation of sound quality in the room.

In wide halls with high ceilings, seats in the center of the orchestra often suffer from lack of early reflections. Reflecting canopies or arrays over the front rows can bring reflected sound to these seating areas, which otherwise may suffer from poor articulation. Often, seating at the rear of the balcony does not experience this problem, and these seats have excellent acoustics.

PREFERRED VOLUME/SEAT RATIOS

VOLUME/SEAT		SOUND QUALITY OF SPACE
CU FT	M³	
Less than 200	Less than 6	Quite dead, suitable for speech and cinema
300 to 350	8 to 10	Good for music
Greater than 500	Greater than 14	Good for organ music only, too reverberant for speech

ARTICULATION

Much of the clarity of sound that audiences need for speech intelligibility and clear musical attacks comes from the sound reflected off hard surfaces that reaches listeners within 50 to 80 milliseconds of the direct sound (which always reaches the listener first). To enhance articulation of acoustics in a hall, the design must ensure there are enough surfaces to reduce the time gap between the initial (direct) sound and these early reflections; the initial time delay gap should be less than 50 milliseconds. Sound travels 1120 ft/second (in SI units, 333 m/second), so the initial time delay gap for prime seating locations should not exceed 50 ft (13 m).

OTHER FACTORS

Following are several other features to be considered when designing performance spaces.

FOCUSING

Focusing concentrates sound waves in one area, causing "hot spots" where the sound is louder or unnatural in quality. Concave surfaces either in plan or section can present major focusing problems if they are not identified and treated.

SEATS

The largest area of sound-absorbing surface in a performance hall is the seating. If the seats are made of a sound-reflecting material (wood, vinyl, plastic, etc.), their absorptive properties will change dramatically when they are occupied, since a person introduces about 5 sabins for each seat, which significantly affects reverberation time. Use of upholstered seats or pew cushions makes the RT similar whether the seats are empty or fully occupied and will never make the empty hall RT more dead than it would be when fully occupied.

BALCONIES

Balconies bring additional persons into a given volume and create more intimacy between audience and performer. However, seating under a balcony can be cut off from the main volume of sound if the balcony overhang is too great. A reasonable rule of thumb is that the overhang depth should not exceed the height of the opening (greater ratios are acceptable where live music is not part of the program).

ORCHESTRA PIT

The surface over the orchestra pit should be angled to project sound out to the audience but diffuse so that some energy is reflected back to the performers on stage. The front wall of the orchestra pit should be a hard surface so the front rows of the audience do not hear direct sound and so that more energy is reflected back to the performers on stage. Also, both the front and back walls may need to be treated with movable curtains to vary and control the degree of sound reflected off these surfaces.

SOUND SYSTEM

Electronic sound systems may be used for amplification (making the source louder for a big hall), for playback or recorded material, or for both. Depending on the source, the loudspeakers used to distribute the sound should be located at the center slightly in front of the speaker (for speech amplification) or on the left and right sides (for musical stereo playback or amplification of the orchestra pit). Additional loudspeakers may be needed under a balcony or at the rear of the hall to cover the upper balconies. Special effects loudspeakers are added around the hall as needed. The sound control location must be well placed within the audience area covered by the loudspeakers. Additional transmitters using infrared signals or FM radio signals can be used to meet ADA requirements.

OPTIMUM REVERBERATION TIMES AT MIDFREQUENCIES (500–1000 HZ) FOR PERFORMANCE SPACES

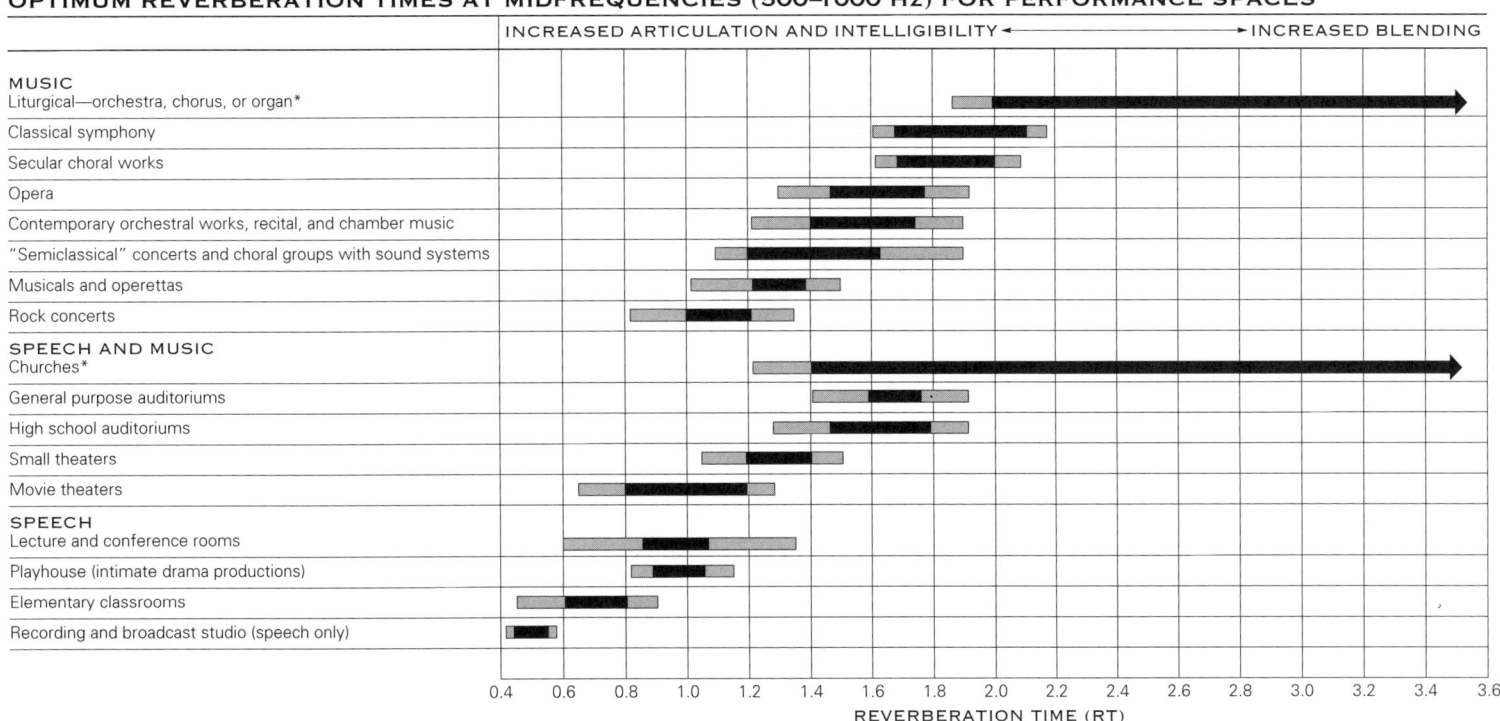

INCREASED ARTICULATION AND INTELLIGIBILITY ◄———————► INCREASED BLENDING

MUSIC
Liturgical—orchestra, chorus, or organ*
Classical symphony
Secular choral works
Opera
Contemporary orchestral works, recital, and chamber music
"Semiclassical" concerts and choral groups with sound systems
Musicals and operettas
Rock concerts

SPEECH AND MUSIC
Churches*
General purpose auditoriums
High school auditoriums
Small theaters
Movie theaters

SPEECH
Lecture and conference rooms
Playhouse (intimate drama productions)
Elementary classrooms
Recording and broadcast studio (speech only)

0.4 0.6 0.8 1.0 1.2 1.4 1.6 1.8 2.0 2.2 2.4 2.6 2.8 3.0 3.2 3.4 3.6
REVERBERATION TIME (RT)

*May go up to 8 seconds in reverberation time

NOTE

The breadth of RT range for each room type is a function of the room volume: the larger the room volume, the closer to the longer end of the range and vice versa.

Carl Rosenberg, AIA; Acentech, Inc.; Cambridge, Massachusetts

GENERAL

Open plan offices can provide great flexibility in office arrangements and work flow. However, because workstations or cubicles do not have full-height partitions, noise can be a major problem in such offices. The extent to which speech is distracting depends on the degree to which it is intelligible. An overheard conversation can be annoying or distracting, while an inaudible murmur is not. When designing open plan offices, the need for communication between workstations should be evaluated in light of work functions and practical separation.

Speech intelligibility and acoustics in an open plan office can be rated in terms of an articulation index (AI), which is a measure of the ratio between a signal (a neighbor's voice or intrusive noise) and steady background noise (ambient noise from mechanical equipment, traffic, or electronic sound masking). AI values range from near 0 (very low signal and relatively high noise; no intelligibility or good speech privacy) to 1.0 (very high signal and low noise; excellent communication or no speech privacy). When communication is desired (e.g., in classrooms or teleconference rooms), it is preferable to have a high AI so people can hear well. In an office, however, it is preferable to have a low AI so people can be freed from distraction and will be better able to concentrate. Average noise requirements for various office functions are shown in the accompanying chart.

ARTICULATION INDEX (AI) FOR OPEN PLAN OFFICES

AI VALUE	NOISE REQUIREMENTS	
>.65	Good communication	Necessary when communication is desirable (conference rooms, classrooms, auditoriums, etc.)
.35	Freedom from distraction	Reasonable work conditions not requiring heavy concentration or speech privacy; hear and understand neighboring conversations
.20	Normal speech privacy	Occasional intelligibility from a neighbor's conversation; work patterns not interrrupted
<.05	Confidential speech privacy	Aware of neighbor's conversation but it is not intelligible

DESIGN CONSIDERATIONS

Low AI ratings for open plan office spaces can be achieved in three primary ways: by blocking sound, by covering (masking) sound, and by absorbing sound.

BLOCKING SOUND

Partial-height barriers or partitions are necessary to block direct sound transmission between workstations. The barriers must be high enough and wide enough to interrupt the line of sight between a source and a receiver; hence, the first 4 ft or so of barrier height do not help speech privacy at all. Barrier heights of 5 ft are a minimum requirement for acoustical separation, and heights of 6 ft are typical for normal privacy. The barrier should be able to block sound at least as well as the path for sound traveling over the barrier, which means a minimum laboratory sound transmission class value of 24. Barriers or screens should extend to the floor or leave only an inch or so open at the bottom. There should be no open gaps between adjacent panels. Barriers may need to have sound-absorbing facings to reduce reflections to the next workstation.

COVERING SOUND

The character and level of background sound is perhaps the most important acoustical design consideration for an open plan office. A modest level of background or ambient sound will cover, or mask, annoying, intrusive sounds. The masking sound must be pleasant and neutral with an even tonal spectrum (like the sound of a comfortable ventilation system) that drops off at the high end of the frequency range. There should be no pure tones or annoying characteristics (like the hum of a fluorescent light ballast).

BACKGROUND SOUND LEVEL FOR OPEN PLAN OFFICES

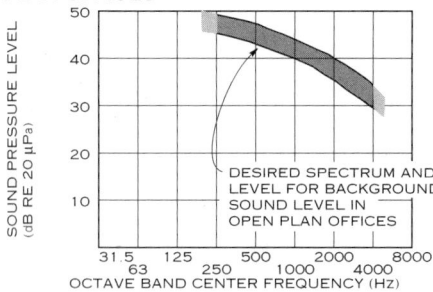

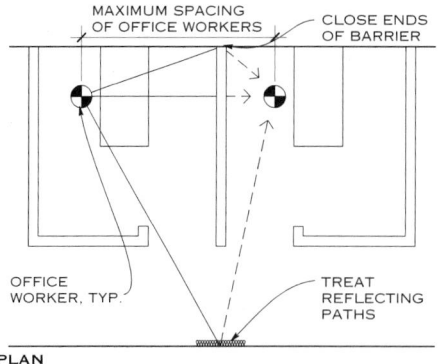

PLAN

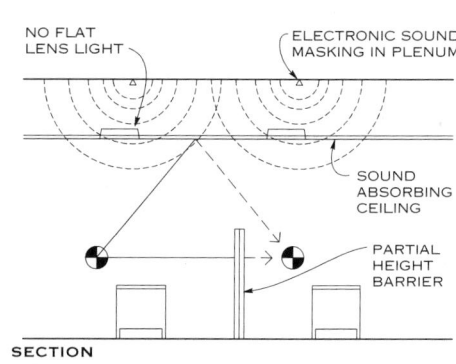

SECTION

ARCHITECTURAL SOLUTIONS FOR SOUND CONTROL IN OPEN OFFICES

The sound should be evenly distributed throughout the office so no areas are louder than others. In addition, the sound should not vary in the open plan area by more than 3 decibels in any octave band. Masking sound should be neither too loud nor too quiet, perhaps between 45 and 50 dBA. It should be loud enough to cover intrusive noises but never loud enough to be distracting in itself. Conference rooms and private offices, which require lower levels of background noise, should have plenum treatments so they are shielded from direct exposure to the masking sound.

Normal air conditioning and ventilation could generate enough background noise to mask sound between offices, but this sound source is not well designed for this purpose. Most office buildings use variable volume air distribution, so noise from the HVAC system may be erratic and uneven in distribution and change over time and season. The preferred solution is to install an electronic sound masking system.

Sound masking systems comprise a noise generator, an equalizer to shape the sound spectrum properly, amplifiers, and loudspeakers hidden above an accessible acoustical tile ceiling. Such systems generate a broadband, pleasant sounding, evenly distributed masking noise. The sound in the plenum filters down through the ceiling and provides an even blanket of sound that will mask the intrusive noise from a neighbor. Avoid untreated sound leaks in the ceiling such as openings for return air; these become noticeable "hot spots" and draw unwanted attention to the sound from the ceiling. Masking sound from two channels can improve spatial uniformity. Ceiling height and plenum conditions (fireproofing, beams, ducts, etc.) will determine loudspeaker spacing and location. Electronic sound masking should be professionally designed and installed.

ABSORBING SOUND

The ceiling in an open plan office is the most important surface to treat with highly efficient sound-absorbing material. Glass-fiber ceiling panels often have NRC values of .85 or higher and are the preferred material for open plan spaces. Regular mineral-fiber acoustical panels have typical NRC values of about .55-.65. Hard sound-reflective materials such as exposed structure or gypsum board will dramatically reduce privacy and raise annoying sound levels in an office. Most ceiling tile manufacturers provide extensive NRC data for their products and have special products with high absorptive performance for use in open plan spaces. Materials must also be selected for their ability to reflect light.

Most sound-absorbing materials are measured in a reverberation chamber in accordance with ASTM C 423 to determine their random incidence sound-absorption coefficients (α) and from these data, manufacturers typically report the noise reduction coefficient (NRC). The NRC value is a good first approximation of the ability of a material to absorb sound from the human speech range. For office acoustics, however, a more useful value is the ability of a material to absorb sound at an incident angle of 40-60° from a flat ceiling and at frequencies weighted to reflect the relative contribution to speech intelligibility. Therefore, a more effective tool for evaluating the effectiveness of ceiling materials for sound absorption is the speech absorption coefficient (SAC), which can be calculated from standard sound absorption coefficients as follows:

$$SAC = \Sigma (0.06\alpha_{250} + 0.15\alpha_{500} + 0.24\alpha_{1000} + 0.32\alpha_{2000} + 0.23\alpha_{4000})$$

OTHER FACTORS

Arrange offices so that entrances are offset, and eliminate direct line of sight or an open view through doorways from one workstation to another. Workstations should be 8-10 ft apart so voice levels are adequately reduced over distance. Higher ceilings can help reduce noise transfer. Light fixtures in the ceiling plane should not have hard lenses or be placed directly above a partition because the fixture can then act as a mirror for sound across the barrier. Absorptive material may be necessary on some barriers or reflecting surfaces (e.g., walls, file cabinets).

Carpet helps reduce footfall and impact noise and is a great benefit in open offices. Finally, voice levels should be kept to a minimum; even the best acoustical treatments cannot prevent disturbances caused by loud voices.

All the factors outlined in the paragraphs above are interrelated. For example, doubling the distance between adjacent workstations will reduce a nearby conversation by 5 dBA, while raising the height of a 5-ft barrier to 6 ft may reduce the sound path over the top by 3 dBA. Changing from a mineral-fiber acoustical ceiling tile to a glass-fiber ceiling tile may reduce reflected noise by 5 dBA. Adding sound masking may change the ambient level by 10-20 dBA.

An acoustics consultant can evaluate proposed layouts and materials as part of the design process. The acoustical outcome of a design should be analyzed before construction. As a rough initial guideline, offices in which freedom from distraction is the only criterion will require highly efficient sound-absorbing ceilings and an electronic background masking sound at levels between 45 and 50 dBA. For normal speech privacy, these conditions should be augmented by keeping workstations 8-10 ft apart and adding partial-height barriers at least 5 ft high, with increased attention to office layout and reflecting sound paths. Confidential privacy requires higher partitions and more attention to related details and is extremely difficult to achieve in an open plan.

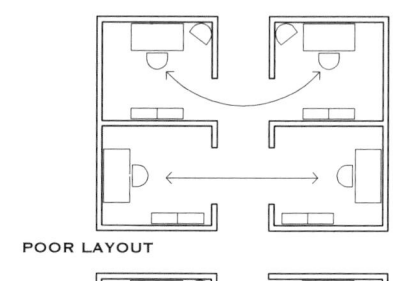

POOR LAYOUT

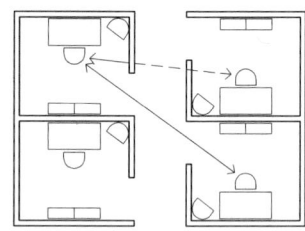

FAIR LAYOUT

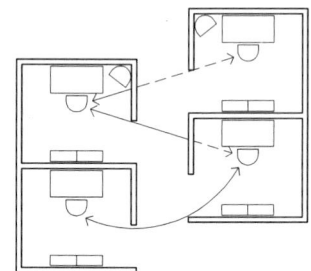

PREFERRED LAYOUT

OPEN OFFICE CONFIGURATIONS

Christopher Savereid; Acentech, Inc.; Cambridge, Massachusetts

GENERAL

Sound systems are used primarily to provide better listening conditions through sound amplification that increases the loudness of a sound source. Secondary uses of sound systems include recording and playback of audio signals, distribution of audio signals to remote locations, and satisfaction of ADA requirements for provision of assistive listening systems for hearing-impaired individuals.

Sound systems are recommended in all places of assembly, including auditoriums, churches, classrooms, and lecture halls with more than 60 seats; large conference rooms; courtrooms; legislative chambers; and sports arenas, particularly if these facilities will be used by inexperienced speakers. Sound amplification systems should not be used as a substitute for good room acoustical design. The sound system equipment chosen, its location in a space, and the reproduction quality it provides depend on the acoustical properties of that space.

Sound amplification systems should be used when one or more of the following conditions occur: (1) the room volume exceeds 50,000 cu ft; (2) the distance between source and farthest receiver exceeds 50 ft indoors and 25 ft outdoors; (3) the receiver is located beyond 70° horizontally from the source; (4) the room reverberation time exceeds 1.5 sec; and (5) the ambient noise levels are greater than NC-40 indoors or 55 dBA outdoors.

TYPES OF SOUND SYSTEMS

Sound systems are designed to serve a wide variety of functions, program types, and spaces. The primary functions are voice and music reinforcement, assistive listening, paging and emergency announcements, sound masking, and audio recording/playback.

VOICE AND MUSIC REINFORCEMENT

Voice and music reinforcement systems amplify the spoken word or a music program. Voice reinforcement systems are used in virtually all places of public assembly, but use of music reinforcement systems is usually restricted to auditoriums, amphitheaters, arenas, and churches. Loudspeaker locations are dictated by ceiling height and stage layout. Spaces with ceiling heights greater than 25 ft normally have a large "central cluster" loudspeaker system located above and forward of the stage. Low-ceiling spaces, such as classrooms or under balconies in a theater, normally have small (4- or 8-in. diameter) ceiling-mounted loudspeakers in a "distributed" speaker layout. Music reinforcement typically uses large loudspeakers located on either side of the stage, either set on the floor or hung from the building structure.

ASSISTIVE LISTENING

Assistive listening systems provide localized sound reinforcement to listeners who have difficulty hearing the program. These systems are used to comply with ADA requirements. An electrical output from the sound system is routed to a transmitter, either FM or infrared, which radiates a modulated audio signal that is picked up by a receiver carried by the listener. A small in-the-ear headset is connected to the receiver.

PAGING AND EMERGENCY ANNOUNCEMENTS

Paging and emergency announcement systems distribute voice or alarm signals. Codes may require that emergency announcement systems be dedicated, use equipment certified by Underwriters Laboratories (UL), or be capable of operating from emergency power sources. The audio program is transmitted via a distributed ceiling loudspeaker system in a 70.7-volt configuration.

SOUND MASKING

Sound masking systems radiate pink noise, the frequency content of which is adjusted to make speech less intelligible, thus increasing speech privacy. These systems are commonly used in open office environments, where partial-height workstations may make speech privacy difficult to achieve. Loudspeakers in a 70.7-volt configuration are located in the ceiling plenum, and the sound radiates through the ceiling tile into the space below. Precision adjustment and tuning of sound masking systems is crucial to their acceptance by employees.

AUDIO RECORDING/PLAYBACK

Audio media recording/playback systems provide for amplification of sources such as audiotape or compact disc (CD). These systems can function as an element of a larger sound system or they can stand alone. Recording systems use electrical output from the sound system to record the program content to cassette tape or digital audiotape (DAT). Reproducing systems amplify sound from signal storage media, such as cassette tape, DAT, CD, digital video disc (DVD), tape carts, message repeaters, or from a distant origin, such as radio or TV transmissions.

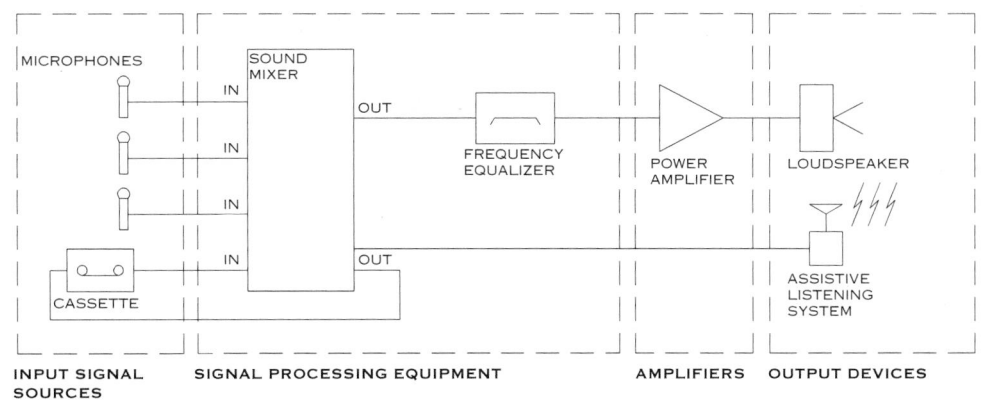

INPUT SIGNAL SOURCES   SIGNAL PROCESSING EQUIPMENT   AMPLIFIERS   OUTPUT DEVICES

BASIC SOUND AMPLIFICATION SYSTEM

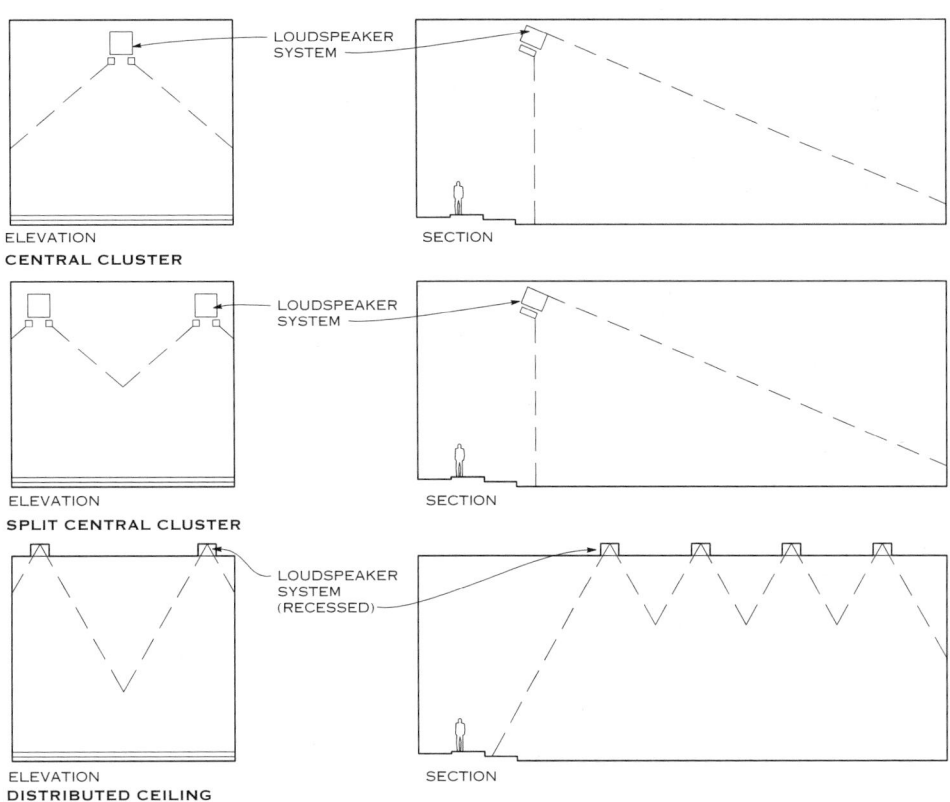

ELEVATION   SECTION
CENTRAL CLUSTER

ELEVATION   SECTION
SPLIT CENTRAL CLUSTER

ELEVATION   SECTION
DISTRIBUTED CEILING

LOUDSPEAKER SYSTEM TYPES

LOUDSPEAKER INSTALLATIONS

To provide good sound coverage, loudspeakers must be properly integrated into the architectural design of a space. Most spaces have an optimum loudspeaker configuration that should be examined before exploring other options. Loudspeakers can be recessed behind architectural elements, assuming a suitably large opening with acoustically transparent grille cloth is provided.

The major loudspeaker installations include central cluster, split cluster, and distributed ceiling types.

CENTRAL CLUSTER LOUDSPEAKER

The central cluster loudspeaker system is located just forward of center stage and elevated a minimum of 20 ft above floor level. Separate low frequency and mid/high frequency loudspeaker components, either individual horn systems or multiway loudspeakers, are used. Listeners must have line-of-sight relationships to loudspeakers in order to receive good sound coverage.

Central cluster systems are not recommended for spaces with ceiling heights less than 20 ft due to sound level differences between the front and rear of the space. Advantages include low cost and naturalness of reproduction because of the inability of the ear to localize sound in the vertical plane.

SPLIT CENTRAL CLUSTER LOUDSPEAKER

The split central cluster loudspeaker system is similar in design and operational concepts to the central cluster system, but separate loudspeaker clusters are located at stage right and stage left locations, as might occur in a church with a separate pulpit and lectern or in a music reinforcement system. Each loudspeaker cluster is designed to cover the entire listener seating area. When the talker is at the stage right location, only that loudspeaker operates, likewise for the stage left location. This system provides greater source localization than the central cluster system since it uses the ability of the ear to localize sound in the horizontal plane.

DISTRIBUTED CEILING LOUDSPEAKER

Distributed ceiling loudspeaker systems use 4-, 8-, or 12-in. diameter, full-range, transformer-coupled cone loudspeakers, typically in a 70.7-volt configuration installed in the ceiling plane. These systems are normally used in spaces with a ceiling height less than 20 ft. The size of the loudspeaker depends on the ceiling height and whether the system will be used for voice or music reproduction. In spaces where the unamplified source to receiver distance exceeds 30 ft, it is often necessary to electrically delay the signal to the loudspeaker so the listener hears the unamplified sound first, followed in several milliseconds by the sound from the amplified ceiling loudspeaker. The signal processing technique of this system type helps to preserve source localization.

Neil Thompson Shade; Acoustical Design Collaborative, Ltd.; Falls Church, Virginia

SOUND SYSTEM ELEMENTS

Sound systems comprise input signal sources, signal processing equipment to alter the properties of the signal, amplifiers to increase weak signal levels, and loudspeakers to convert electrical signals to acoustical signals.

MICROPHONES

A microphone is a transducer that converts sound waves into electrical AC voltage corresponding to the acoustical characteristics of the source. Microphones can be classified by type, transducer element, or polar pattern. The major microphone types are thin profile lectern, performer's handheld, boundary layer, and lavaliere.

LINE LEVEL SOURCES

Line level signal sources include audio formats such as magnetic tape, audio and optical discs, video, telephonic devices, and radio. These sources are classified as recorded audio (magnetic tape, audio discs, and optical discs) or real-time audio (videoconferencing, telephone, and radio).

SOUND MIXERS

Sound mixers combine the electrical output of microphone and line level sources into a composite output signal for distribution to other components of the sound system. Sound mixers are classified as manually operated or automatic hands-off types. Manually operated mixers require placement in the same sound field the audience experiences so the operator can properly adjust the sound system. Automatic microphone mixers control turning on/off of microphones, adjusting gain, and routing of signals.

SIGNAL PROCESSING

Signal processing equipment provides the means for altering the frequency, magnitude, delay time, and distribution of audio signals received from the mixer. Signal processing equipment includes frequency equalizers, crossovers, signal delay lines, and distribution amplifiers. These items can be discrete components, or computer-controlled digital signal processing (DSP) can be used to execute their functions.

AMPLIFIERS

Amplifiers increase the voltage of the audio signals received from the signal processing devices and distribute the stronger signal to the loudspeakers. Amplifiers are configured as either low impedance output for driving 4, 8, or 16 ohm loudspeakers or as 25, 70.7, or 100 constant voltage output driving transformer-coupled loudspeakers.

LOUDSPEAKERS

Loudspeakers convert electrical AC voltage into sound waves. Sound reinforcement loudspeakers have either full-range cone drivers, commonly used for ceiling distributed systems, or multiway loudspeaker systems with separate low frequency and mid/high frequency drivers. Typically, mid/high frequency systems use compression drivers connected to a horn system to provide controlled directional sound coverage output.

INFRASTRUCTURE

Sound system equipment is normally installed in standard 19-in. wide equipment rack enclosures. Signal cables are routed from these enclosures to audio wall plates that connect to input and output devices. Normally, metal conduit is used to minimize signal interference and to protect cables.

ELECTRICAL POWER REQUIREMENTS

Sound systems should have dedicated power circuits separate from other building electrical services. The major electrical power load comes from the amplifiers, which can easily exceed the power requirements of all other sound system components by a factor of 100. When computer-controlled sound systems are used, provide electrical power surge protection and a source of uninterruptible power.

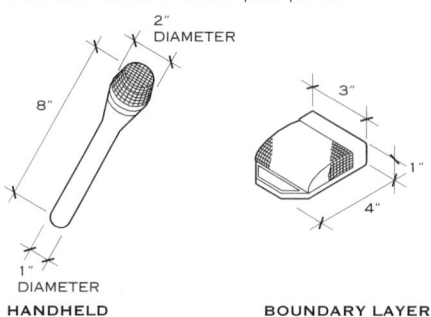

HANDHELD PERFORMER'S MICROPHONE

BOUNDARY LAYER MICROPHONE

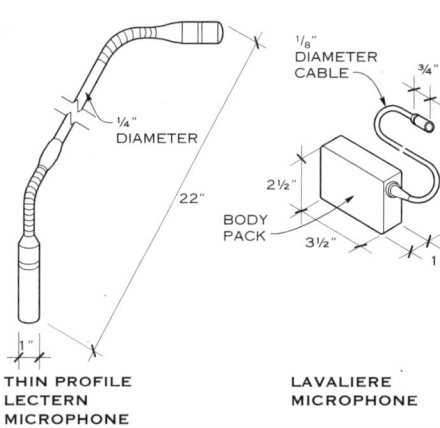

THIN PROFILE LECTERN MICROPHONE

LAVALIERE MICROPHONE

MICROPHONE TYPES

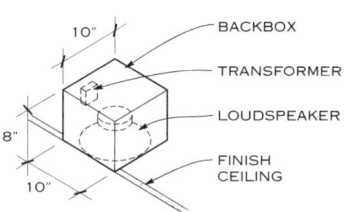

FULL-RANGE CEILING LOUDSPEAKER

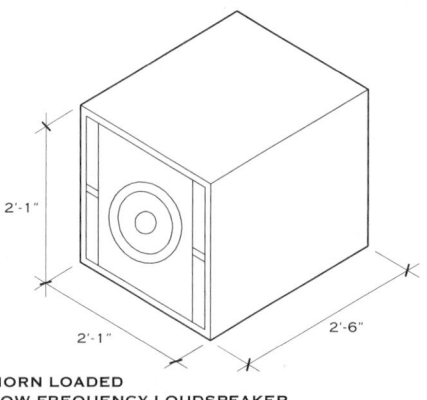

HORN LOADED LOW-FREQUENCY LOUDSPEAKER

LOUDSPEAKERS

AUDIO EQUIPMENT ROOMS

Equipment rack enclosures are often housed in a dedicated audio equipment room. In this case, clearance should be left around the enclosures to permit maintenance work. When power amplifiers create a large sensible heat load, audio equipment rooms may require forced air cooling.

Locate audio equipment rooms as close as possible to the microphones and loudspeakers to minimize cable length. Often a separate equipment room is required so the power amplifiers can be located close to the loudspeakers.

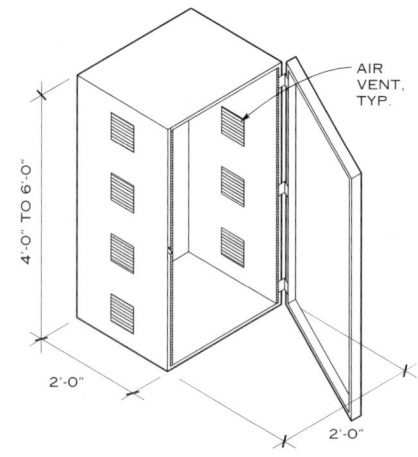

AUDIO EQUIPMENT RACK

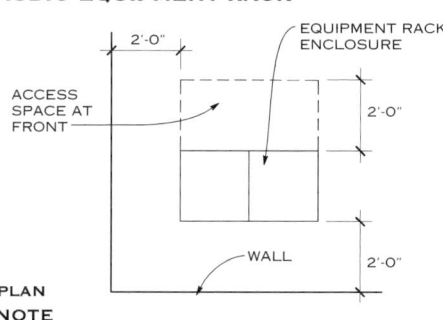

PLAN

NOTE

Plan for space at each side, in front of, and behind equipment rack enclosures to allow for maintenance and access.

AUDIO EQUIPMENT ROOM

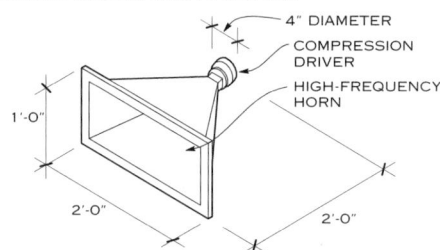

COMPRESSION DRIVER WITH HORN

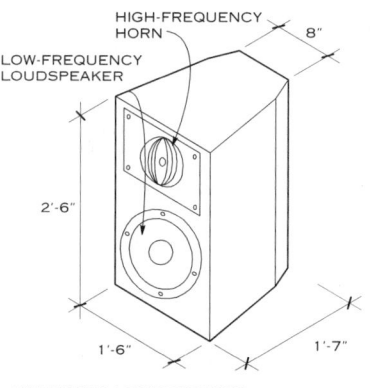

MULTIWAY LOUDSPEAKER

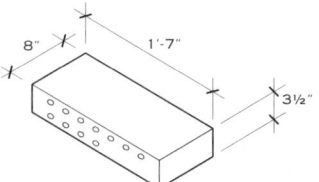

AUTOMATIC MICROPHONE MIXER

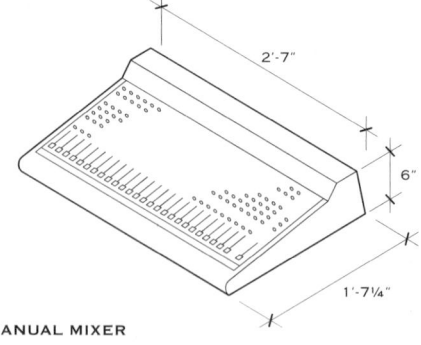

MANUAL MIXER

SOUND MIXERS

Neil Thompson Shade; Acoustical Design Collaborative, Ltd.; Falls Church, Virginia

1 ACOUSTICAL DESIGN

GENERAL

Crimes such as vandalism, terrorism, burglary, shoplifting, employee theft, assault, and espionage endanger lives and threaten the built environment. Despite this, security as a design consideration has often been inadequately addressed and poorly funded. Now, however, in many jurisdictions police authorities require security plan reviews as part of the building permit process in the same way they review life safety and fire prevention plans.

Security design is more than bars on windows, a security guard booth, a camera, or a wall. Security involves the systematic integration of design, technology, and operation for the protection of three critical assets—people, information, and property. Protection of these assets is a concern in all building types and should be considered throughout the design and construction process, from programming, schematic design, design development, preparation of construction documents, and bidding, through construction.

The most efficient, least expensive way to provide security is during the design process. Architects called on to address security and crime concerns must be able to determine security requirements, know security technology, and understand the architectural implications of security needs.

Designing without security in mind can lead to expensive retrofitting, which may require more security personnel than security equipment designed in from the start. As well, installation of retrofit security equipment can distort key building design elements and inhibit building function. Most important, planning without security can lead to successful claims against owners, architects, and building managers.

The process of designing security into architecture is known as crime prevention through environmental design (CPTED). It involves designing the built environment to reduce the opportunity for and fear of stranger-to-stranger predatory crime. This approach to security design recognizes the intended use of space in a building and is different from traditional crime prevention practice, which focuses on denying access to a crime target with barrier techniques such as locks, alarms, fences, and gates. CPTED takes advantage of opportunities for natural access control, surveillance, and territorial reinforcement. It is possible for natural and normal uses of the environment to meet the same security goals as physical and technical protection methods.

CPTED strategies are implemented by

1. ELECTRONIC METHODS: mechanical security products, target-hardening techniques, locks, alarms, CCTV, gadgets
2. ARCHITECTURAL METHODS: architectural design and layout, site planning and landscaping, signage, circulation control
3. ORGANIZATIONAL METHODS: manpower, police, security guards, receptionists, doormen, and business block watches

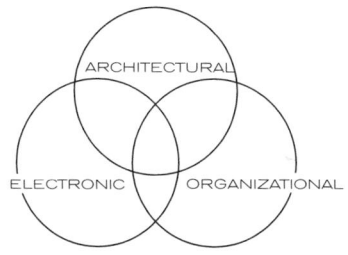

CPTED STRATEGIES

CPTED CONCEPTS

Concepts involved in crime prevention through environmental design are described below.

DEFENSIBLE SPACE

Oscar Newman coined the expression "defensible space" as a term for a range of mechanisms, real and symbolic barriers, strongly defined areas of influence, and improved opportunities for surveillance that combine to bring the environment under the control of its residents.

NATURAL ACCESS CONTROL

Natural access control involves decreasing opportunities for crime by denying access to crime targets and creating a perception of risk in offenders. It is accomplished by designing streets, sidewalks, building entrances, and neighborhood gateways to mark public routes and by using structural elements to discourage access to private areas.

Randall I. Atlas, Ph.D., AIA, CPP; Atlas Safety & Security Design, Inc.; Miami, Florida

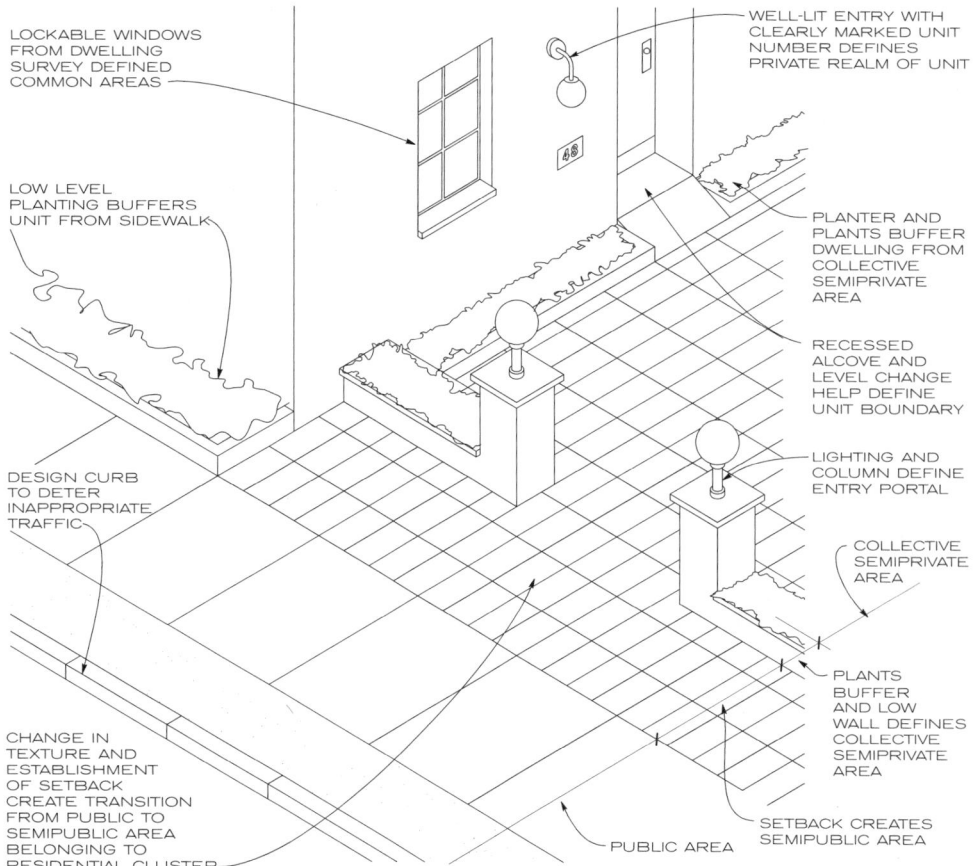

LOCKABLE WINDOWS FROM DWELLING SURVEY DEFINED COMMON AREAS

LOW LEVEL PLANTING BUFFERS UNIT FROM SIDEWALK

DESIGN CURB TO DETER INAPPROPRIATE TRAFFIC

CHANGE IN TEXTURE AND ESTABLISHMENT OF SETBACK CREATE TRANSITION FROM PUBLIC TO SEMIPUBLIC AREA BELONGING TO RESIDENTIAL CLUSTER

WELL-LIT ENTRY WITH CLEARLY MARKED UNIT NUMBER DEFINES PRIVATE REALM OF UNIT

PLANTER AND PLANTS BUFFER DWELLING FROM COLLECTIVE SEMIPRIVATE AREA

RECESSED ALCOVE AND LEVEL CHANGE HELP DEFINE UNIT BOUNDARY

LIGHTING AND COLUMN DEFINE ENTRY PORTAL

COLLECTIVE SEMIPRIVATE AREA

PLANTS BUFFER AND LOW WALL DEFINES COLLECTIVE SEMIPRIVATE AREA

SETBACK CREATES SEMIPUBLIC AREA

PUBLIC AREA

SECURITY LAYERING OF SPACES

NATURAL SURVEILLANCE

A design concept intended to make intruders easily observable, natural surveillance is promoted by features that maximize visibility of people, parking areas, and building entrances. Examples are doors and windows that look onto streets and parking areas, pedestrian-friendly sidewalks and streets, front porches, and adequate nighttime lighting.

TERRITORIAL REINFORCEMENT

Physical design can create or extend a sphere of influence. In this setting, users develop a sense of territorial control, while potential offenders perceive this control and are discouraged from their criminal intentions. Territorial reinforcement is promoted by features that define property lines and distinguish private spaces from public spaces such as landscape plantings, pavement design, gateway treatments, and fences.

MANAGEMENT AND MAINTENANCE

Operational and management concepts that maintain buildings and facilities in good working order and that maintain a standard of care consistent with national and local standards contribute to the security effort. Equipment and materials used in a facility should be designed or selected with safety and security in mind.

LEGITIMATE ACTIVITY SUPPORT

Legitimate activity for a space or building is encouraged through use of natural surveillance and lighting and architectural design that clearly defines the purpose of the structure or space. Crime prevention and design strategies can discourage illegal activity and protect a property from chronic problem activity.

ADA AND BUILDING SECURITY

The Americans with Disabilities Act of 1990 (ADA) affects architecture, life safety design, and building security technology dramatically. Sample regulations are listed below. For specifics, please see the act itself.

1. Instructions for access control card readers must be provided in braille for the visually disabled.

2. Door hardware, such as handles, pulls, latches, locks, and other operating devices, must be shaped so they are easy to grasp with one hand. Lever, push-type, and U-shaped mechanisms are acceptable, knobs are not.

3. Elevators must have visual signals to indicate when each call is registered and answered. Elevator doors must remain open for at least 3 seconds.

4. Regulations require counters to be 28 to 34 in. off the floor.

5. Alarm systems for evacuation must provide warnings for the blind, deaf, and nonambulatory staff of the building. Announcements must be louder than 15 dB but not exceed 120 dB for 30 seconds. Visual alarms must flash and be tied into the emergency power circuit. Fire alarms should also incorporate visual strobes to alert individuals who are hearing impaired.

6. ATM controls must be at least 15 to 54 in. high and have operating instructions in braille. Night deposit mechanisms must not require a tight grasp (no knobs).

7. Security vestibules must be accessible to individuals in wheelchairs. A maneuvering clearance of at least 4 ft must be provided.

Areas affected by ADA requirements for building security include vaults, safety deposit box rooms, front desk counters, security desk and information counters, control rooms, life safety equipment, safe-refuge areas, turnstiles and security screening checkpoints, all door and locking hardware, and access control devices.

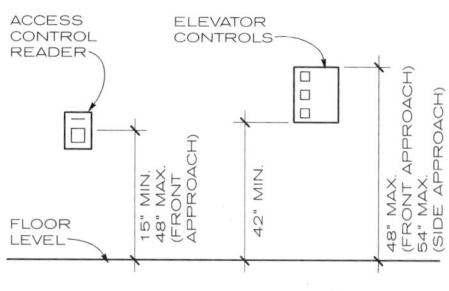

ACCESS CONTROL READER

ELEVATOR CONTROLS

FLOOR LEVEL

15" MIN. 48" MAX (FRONT APPROACH)

42" MIN.

48" MAX (FRONT APPROACH) 54" MAX (SIDE APPROACH)

SECURITY CONTROLS FOR ADA

PROJECT-RELATED SECURITY EVALUATION

Security needs for an architectural project should be determined early, preferably as part of the programming and needs definition stage. Surveys of similar existing operations and interviews with personnel at these sites can help identify security concerns.

Once a client, owner, or security consultant has identified the security objectives of a project, the architect must ensure the design supports these objectives. Basic decisions about circulation, access, building materials, fenestration, and other design features can support or thwart overall security aims. The architect's role is to incorporate the basic security requirements and programmatic objectives into the project.

PROJECT DESCRIPTION

The first step in determining site-related security requirements is to identify the location, building type, style of operation, and economic aspects of the project. Security levels (high-low) can be defined by determining which areas, items of equipment, buildings, and activities and personnel are most sensitive or vulnerable.

SITE SELECTION AND EVALUATION FOR THREATS AND VULNERABILITY

Security objectives should be considered when choosing a site. For example, crowded sites can make it difficult to provide an adequate buffer around the perimeter or to control and check on-site circulation

Once a site has been selected, the crime prevention through environmental design (CPTED) and security analysis process can identify measures to overcome any security deficiencies. The architect should consider conditions on and off the site, including topography; vegetation; adjacent land uses; circulation patterns; sightlines; potential areas for refuge or concealment; existing lighting conditions; and the types and locations of utilities, including their vulnerability to tampering or sabotage.

Steps for determining the threats to and vulnerability of a project and site are outlined here:

1. Identify a mission statement for the project.
   a. Identify the assets to be protected.
   b. Determine what is to be protected according to the categories of people, property, and information.
   c. Determine the replacement value of the information and property to be protected.
2. Determine how critical security is to the design of the project.
   a. Analyze the mission of the project.
   b. Determine present posture/operation positions.
   c. Determine the ease with which the property and information to be protected could be replaced.
   d. Analyze the value of what is to be protected.

3. Determine the threats to the project.
   a. Consider threats from sabotage, espionage, terrorism, street crime, disgruntled employees, workplace violence, among others.
   b. Consider the value of the assets to be protected, the objectives of potential aggressors, the perceived deterrence of security measures, and the risk level at the site.
4. Determine what modes of attack may threaten the project. Among those to be considered are these:
   a. Covert entry
   b. Insider alone
   c. Insider with others
   d. Bombing
   e. Surveillance
   f. Demonstrations
   g. Aerial attack
   h. Standoff attack
   i. Theft, burglary, robbery
   j. Destruction
   k. Contamination
   l. Unauthorized entry
5. Determine the severity of the potential attacks. Which of the following would the perpetrators be most likely to use?
   a. Tools
   b. Weapons
   c. Explosives
6. Determine the vulnerability of the site, considering the state of the following security measures at the site:
   a. Security force capabilities
   b. Penetration delay
   c. Detection capabilities
   d. Assessment capabilities
   e. Access controls
   f. Procedural controls
   g. Mission requirements
7. Identify the constraints that will affect what security measures are implemented:
   a. Financial
   b. Operational
8. Determine the protection required for the project:
   a. Where is security critical?
      1) At the outer perimeter?
      2) At the inner perimeter?
      3) At the asset?
   b. What security measures will be implemented?
      1) Barrier/delay
      2) Detection
      3) Assessment
      4) Access control
      5) Command and control
      6) Manpower
      7) Security procedures

SECURITY LAYERING

Once the risks, threats, and vulnerabilities of a project have been assessed, analyze the security measures that could be used for the project. The choices fall into three classifi-

cations: organizational (people strategies), electronic (technology and hardware), and architectural (design and circulation patterns). These classifications should be considered for each level of defense or security layer:

1. First level—outer perimeter and site
2. Second level—building exterior
3. Third level—interior control and point security

In defensible space, these security layers are defined as public, semipublic, semiprivate, and private spaces.

LIGHTING FOR SECURITY

Security lighting does not prevent or stop crime, but it can help owners protect people and property. Good pedestrian lighting offers the natural surveillance people need to feel comfortable walking ahead or across a parking lot to their cars. Lighting can prevent surprises from jump-out criminals or give pedestrians the opportunity to request assistance, to turn and go another way, or to retreat.

Security lighting goals should be to achieve a uniform, consistent level of light on both pedestrian and vehicular paths of travel. Lighting is critical for the illumination of street and building names and numbers for effective response by police, fire, and emergency personnel. Design lighting to avoid light intrusion into residential settings.

The quality of lighting may be an important security feature. True-color, full spectrum light rendition can help with identification of vehicles and persons. Car lots and gas stations are examples of building types where metal halide luminaires are used for full spectrum light rendition.

NOTES

1. Proper beam control saves a system from glare, loss of light energy, and light intrusion.
2. Fixtures should be installed to cast a light pattern over a broad horizontal area rather than a tall vertical area.
3. Light surfaces reflect light more efficiently than dark surfaces.
4. Keep in mind the line of sight between the location of a light fixture and objects that may cast a shadow. Careful placement will avoid dark corners behind doors, trashcans, and other features.

RECOMMENDED LIGHTING LEVELS (IN LUMENS) BY BUILDING TYPE

	COMMERCIAL	INDUSTRIAL	RESIDENTIAL
Entrances	10	5	5
Interiors	30–100	30	10
Bathrooms	30	30	30
Elevators and stairs	20	20	20
Public spaces	30	30	—
Private spaces	20	20	20
Self-parking	1.0	1.0	1.0
Attendant parking	2.0	2.0	2.0
Sidewalks	0.9	0.6	0.2

VAULT

THIRD LEVEL: INTERIOR CONTROL AND POINT SECURITY

SECOND LEVEL: BUILDING EXTERIOR

FIRST LEVEL: OUTER PERIMETER

CLASSIFICATIONS FOR VARIOUS LEVELS OF DEFENSE

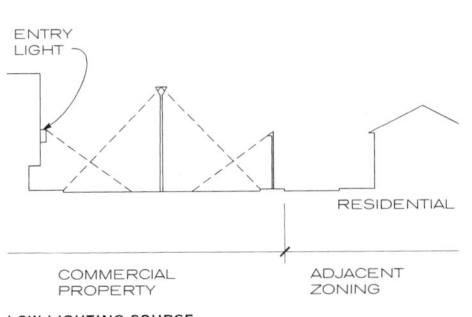

ENTRY LIGHT
RESIDENTIAL
COMMERCIAL PROPERTY
ADJACENT ZONING
LOW LIGHTING SOURCE

LIGHT SOURCE
ENTRY LIGHT
PARKING
RESIDENTIAL
COMMERCIAL PROPERTY
ADJACENT ZONING
TALL LIGHTING SOURCE

SECURITY LIGHTING FOR COMMERCIAL PROPERTY

Randall I. Atlas, Ph.D., AIA, CPP; Atlas Safety & Security Design, Inc.; Miami, Florida

1   BUILDING SECURITY

A SYSTEMS APPROACH
TO SECURITY

An interdependent arrangement of security barriers, technology systems, and security response capabilities yields a responsive and complete security delivery system.

The physical security process primarily consists of fences, building walls, inner walls and doors, and safes and vaults.

The proliferation of electronic security devices and systems, coupled with rapid and substantial advances in the capabilities of these systems, has resulted in a wide array of choices in security technology. To choose effectively among these, architects must gain a basic understanding of the principles and applications of crime prevention through environmental design (CPTED), security design, and operational security.

Use of alarmed surveillance systems can greatly reduce property loss. Reports have shown that even when actual breaking and entering incidents have increased, the amount of property stolen has decreased. This is due in part to the use of alarms, perimeter protection, and intrusion detection systems. However, integrated systems—those that employ the proper procedures, equipment, and people in combination—are the most effective.

In general, the security response capabilities at a particular facility depend on the efforts of the on-site security team. However, architects must design buildings that permit security staff to respond efficiently to incidents requiring their action.

SENSOR SECURITY SYSTEMS

Sensor security systems are commonly designed to protect perimeters or to monitor interior space.

PERIMETER SENSOR SYSTEMS may include the following features: continuous line of detection, in-depth protection, complementary sensors, alarm combination, priority schemes, clear zone, site specific system, sensor configuration, tamper protection, self-test compatibility, suitability for physical and environmental conditions, integration with video system, and integration with barrier delay.

Physical and environmental conditions that affect exterior sensors include topography, vegetation, wildlife, background noise, climate and weather, and soil and pavement.

The conceptual design stage of a perimeter sensor system involves identifying targets, defining threats, establishing security requirements, and developing basic security features.

The final design stage requires defining the clear zone surface, determining sensor locations, completing system engineering and specifications, locating perimeter fencing, and designing power and signal distribution.

Tasks in the construction stage include procuring materials, performing surveys, installing conduit and wiring, applying surface material, and installing outer fences and sensors.

Operation tasks are maintenance, testing, training, and documentation.

INTERIOR DETECTION SYSTEMS offer in-depth protection, detect intruders in time for adequate response, detect tampering, and are able to self-test. As well, they must be properly installed (no loose mountings, wiring in conduits, sensors in proper location for detection).

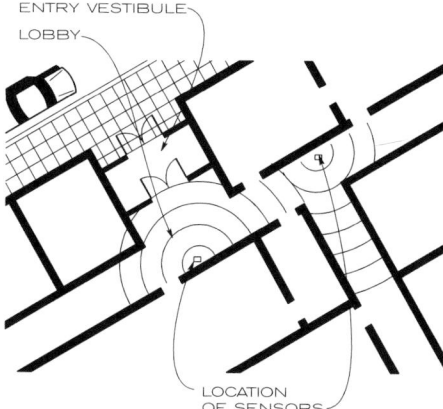

SAMPLE LAYOUT OF INTERIOR SENSORS

Randall I. Atlas, Ph.D., AIA, CPP; Atlas Safety & Security Design, Inc.; Miami, Florida

TYPES OF SENSORS
AND CONDITIONS OF USE

ULTRASONIC MOTION DETECTORS are used when air turbulence is low and when there are external noise sources that could affect a motion detector that radiated energy outside of the protected area. Use low frequency detectors if audible noise is not objectionable.

MICROWAVE MOTION DETECTORS are used when air turbulence is present in the protected room and when there are no potential false alarm sources outside of the room and in the field of the detector.

PASSIVE INFRARED DETECTORS are used when air turbulence is present in an area or point to be protected. Temperature changes do not affect this type of device, but abrupt changes in light level may cause false alarms.

DETECTORS FOR ROOM BOUNDARIES are used when detectors are needed to give the earliest possible warning of an intrusion. They are used only in conjunction with space detectors for the interior of a room; vibration detectors, acoustic detectors, break beams, and breakwires are suggested.

MULTIPLE SPACE DETECTORS are used jointly when detectors are not affected in the same measure by external noise sources and when false alarm rates can be reduced drastically while still maintaining a reasonable probability of detection.

Multiple space detectors are used singly when one type of detector can protect one part of a room and another detector can protect another part of a room because external noise sources are specifically located.

VIBRATION DETECTORS are used when air turbulence, acoustical noises, and motion outside the room are present. These devices are best suited to protect room boundaries from penetration by drilling or hammering.

ACOUSTIC DETECTORS are used when light air turbulence, vibration, and motion are present outside the room. These devices are most effective in protecting room boundaries from penetration by drilling or hammering.

THERMAL DETECTORS are used to detect temperature rises in small enclosures such as vaults when an intruder uses a torch or burning bar to gain entrance. This device would normally be used in a system that includes other types of intrusion detectors.

ENVIRONMENTAL EFFECTS ON SENSORS

Environmental conditions that affect interior sensors include the electromagnetic energy, nuclear radiation, acoustic energy, thermal energy, optical effects, seismic phenomena, and meteorological conditions.

ACCESS CONTROL SYSTEMS

The following statements describe features of a good access control system:

1. They cannot be bypassed.
2. They allow observation by a protective force guard.
3. They protect the guard.
4. They block passage until access and material control procedures have been performed.
5. They provide secondary inspection of those who cannot pass the automated inspection.
6. They accommodate peak loads.
7. They accommodate vehicles and people.
8. They perform access and material control.
9. They are under surveillance by a central alarm station.
10. They are designed for both entry and exist.

CARD TECHNOLOGIES

BAR CODE cards have a series of vertical or horizontal stripes and spaces printed in a manner that represents coded data. The spaces between the stripes are read optically by a photodetector cell.

EMBOSSED CARDS exhibit pattern codes that are raised or indented in the card's surface and read by their relative position in the card reader.

HOLLERITH CARDS have a pattern of small holes punched into the card that presents specific data to the card reader. This card can be read optically or mechanically. The optical reader depends on the light patterns passing through the holes, while the mechanical reader uses electric reed, brush, or switch contacts to read the coded patterns.

INFRARED CARDS depend on encoding information with varying density patterns that are read by infrared detectors. The patterns are optically detected and not visible to the human eye.

MAGNETIC SLUG CARDS have magnetic slugs or metal pieces embedded or layered in them; they are read by magnetic sensing devices. Also known as shim cards, they are generally limited to a single code, making them most suitable for parking operations.

MAGNETIC STRIPE CARDS have stripes or layers of a magnetic material embedded between layers or on a card's surface in vertical columns or horizontal rows. Areas or patterns on this magnetic material can be magnetized in coded patterns and read by magnetic sensing devices.

OPTICAL MEMORY CARDS depend on varied transparency densities arranged in rows, columns, or spots. These patterns are read by a system of light sources and photodetectors.

PROXIMITY CARDS incorporate embedded or laminated RF circuits that utilize electrically tuned circuits that resonate when activated by a transmitter sweeping through the RF range. A receiver picks up the resonating frequency and activates the code deciphering system. Unlike other access cards, the proximity card can be worn or carried and detected at various ranges depending on the design capabilities of the system.

SMART CARDS contain an onboard computer chip and a power supply, normally a lithium battery capable of storing up to six pages of text.

WATERMARK MAGNETIC CARDS contain small oxide particles physically oriented into zones of varying widths. The particles are set while the iron oxide slurry is still fluid; the binary structure spacing of this computer-generated pattern is then oven-cured to create an unalterable 10- or 12-digit code number but leaving another layer of the magnetic stripe available for encoding soft conventional data.

WIEGAND CARDS utilize magnetically embedded unstable ferromagnetic wires formed in a permanently tensioned helical twist. The wiegand card reader uses a magnetic coil that picks up the flux reversal characteristics of the wires and converts them to binary pulses.

VIDEO SURVEILLANCE SYSTEMS

The major components of a video system are the camera, lens, and mount; lighting system; transmission system; synchronization system; video switching equipment; video recorder; video monitor; and video controller.

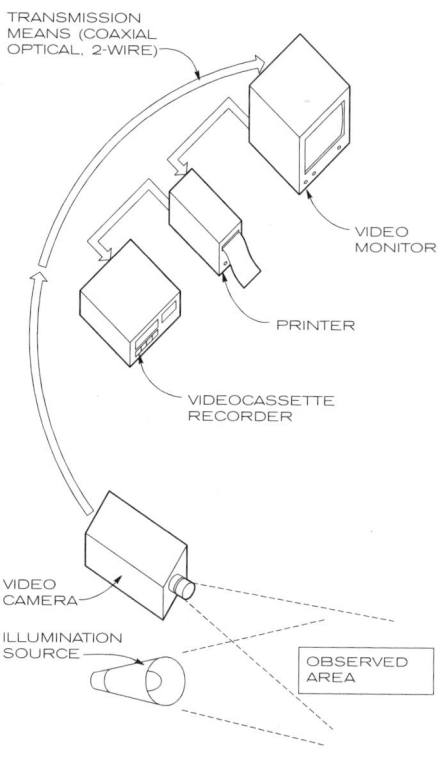

MAJOR COMPONENTS OF A VIDEO SECURITY SYSTEM

GENERAL

Basic security design strategies for building perimeters, interiors, lobbies, stairwells, loading docks, and roofs are outlined here. Also given are specific strategies for practicing crime prevention through environmental design (CPTED) and for addressing the need for bomb resistance.

BUILDING PERIMETER

1. Reduce the number of stairwells that exit to the outside.
2. Make the exit through the lobby whenever possible.
3. Entries should funnel people toward the control point.
4. Don't place any entries behind the control point.
5. Define public vs. private areas.
6. Project the image of a secure building.

INTERNAL AREAS

1. Place occupant services within protected floor space.
2. Control access to critical operation areas.
3. Provide buffer/reception zones in executive areas.
4. Provide multiple paths of entry/exit for executives.
5. Consider creating safe havens in senior executive offices.

BUILDING LOBBY

1. Position the control point between the entry and access to other floors.
2. Move flow past control point.
3. Place restrooms in public areas.
4. Make it possible to secure the lobby level.

COMMON STAIRWELLS

1. Designate stairways for emergency use only whenever possible.
2. Prevent access to floors from the garage and public areas.
3. Place stairs so they exit into the lobby.
4. Use internal stairwells for floor-to-floor transit.

LOADING DOCKS

1. Restrict access to authorized personnel.
2. Control access from the dock into the building.
3. Provide comfort area for drivers on the dock.
4. Make it possible to close off the dock.
5. Place dumpsters within controlled dock area.
6. Give vehicle staging a separate area.

ROOFS

1. Minimize entry points onto the roof.
2. Minimize entry via skylights by using multiple mullions. Solid or fixed diffusers in the light well can also prevent access.
3. Protect roof equipment, such as HVAC cooling towers, from vandalism with roof enclosures with lockable louvered doors spaced far enough from the equipment to allow proper ventilation.
4. Restrict the height of parapets to allow for surveillance from the ground.

ENVIRONMENTAL SECURITY STRATEGIES

1. Establish a physical boundary separating public from private property.
2. Design vehicular and pedestrian traffic patterns to maximize natural surveillance of arrivals and departures.
3. Clearly indicate primary and secondary entrances for employees, as well as a primary entrance for visitors.
4. Ensure that visitors will be processed at the main reception area before they proceed to secondary areas of the facility.
5. Erect physical barriers to separate public reception from private office areas.
6. Establish physical and electronic control over exterior and interior access points.
7. Compartmentalize and electronically control access to critical areas such as computer rooms, executive areas, power and telephone closets, and other restricted areas.
8. Physically separate shipping and receiving areas.
9. Restrict access to inventory storage areas.

10. Limit the number of facility exit doors based on operational necessity and fire loading regulations.
11. Clearly mark site entrances with signs that indicate visitor and vendor processing points.
12. Establish physical control over loading docks, equipment sheds, boiler rooms, and trashbins.
13. Provide adequate lighting and surveillance of employee and visitor parking lots.
14. If possible, separate employee and visitor parking.
15. Provide tenants with the means to control their own office areas.
16. Provide reception personnel with a means of covertly signaling duress situations.
17. Establish a uniform means of identification and access for multitenant sites.
18. Utilize primary and secondary authentication methods for access to highly sensitive areas.
19. Clearly delineate employee, visitor, vendor, and contractor status on badges along with the locations and times they are allowed access.
20. Design floor layout plans with security in mind.

STRATEGIES FOR BOMB RESISTANCE

Key defensive architectural design considerations for bomb resistance are listed here:

1. Establish a secured perimeter around the building as far from the building as possible.
2. Use poured-in-place reinforced concrete for all framing, including slabs, walls, columns, and roofs.
3. Roof and base slabs should be at least 8 in. thick, exterior walls 12 in. thick, and columns spaced no more than 30 ft apart.
4. Use seismic detailing at connection points.
5. Reinforce floor slabs and roofs using a two-way reinforcing scheme.
6. Design windows that comprise no more than 15% of the wall area between supporting columns.
7. Reduce the flying glass hazard by using a plastic mylar coating on the inside face of the windows.
8. Install specially designed blast curtains inside the windows to catch pieces of glass, while permitting the air-blast pressure to pass through the curtain.

9. Design artistically pleasing concrete barriers as planters or works of art and position them near curbs at a distance from the building.
10. Design buildings in a simple geometric rectangular layout to minimize the defraction effect when blast waves bounce off U-shaped or L-shaped buildings and cause additional damage.
11. Drastically reduce or eliminate ornamentation on buildings that could easily break away and endanger building occupants or pedestrians at street level. All external cladding should be of lightweight materials to minimize damage if they become flying objects after an explosion.

PARKING GARAGES

NATURAL ACCESS CONTROL

1. Garages should be attended or monitored openly with cameras and sound monitors marked with signs.
2. Place all pedestrian entrances adjacent to vehicle entrances.
3. Stairwells should be visible, without solid walls.
4. Place elevators close to the main entrance so the entire interior of the elevator is in view when the doors are open.
5. Elevators must not have permanent stop buttons.
6. Design the ground floor to provide a view of the garage; use wire mesh or stretch cable.
7. Limit access to no more than two designated, monitored entrances.

NATURAL SURVEILLANCE

1. All elevators should be monitored by cameras and sound or clear materials should be used for the entire car.
2. Replace retaining walls with stretch cable railings for maximum visibility.
3. Parking areas and driving lanes should be well lighted.

MANAGEMENT

1. Prohibit free access to adjacent buildings without direct monitoring.
2. Designate public and private parking spaces.
3. Operate during hours similar to those of local businesses.
4. Secure the garage when it is closed.

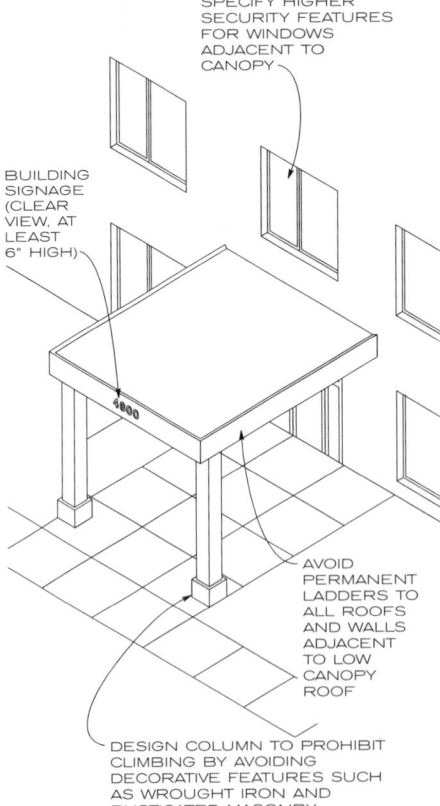

SPECIFY HIGHER SECURITY FEATURES FOR WINDOWS ADJACENT TO CANOPY

BUILDING SIGNAGE (CLEAR VIEW, AT LEAST 6" HIGH)

AVOID PERMANENT LADDERS TO ALL ROOFS AND WALLS ADJACENT TO LOW CANOPY ROOF

DESIGN COLUMN TO PROHIBIT CLIMBING BY AVOIDING DECORATIVE FEATURES SUCH AS WROUGHT IRON AND RUSTICATED MASONRY

ROOF AND CANOPY DESIGN

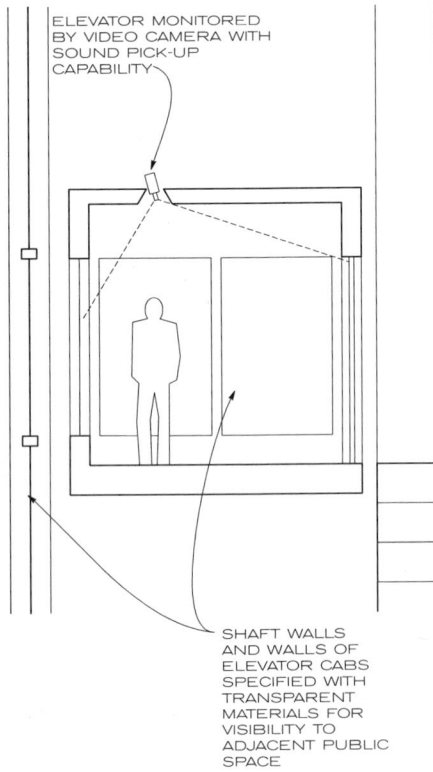

ELEVATOR MONITORED BY VIDEO CAMERA WITH SOUND PICK-UP CAPABILITY

SHAFT WALLS AND WALLS OF ELEVATOR CABS SPECIFIED WITH TRANSPARENT MATERIALS FOR VISIBILITY TO ADJACENT PUBLIC SPACE

ELEVATORS

Randall I. Atlas, Ph.D., AIA, CPP; Atlas Safety & Security Design, Inc.; Miami, Florida

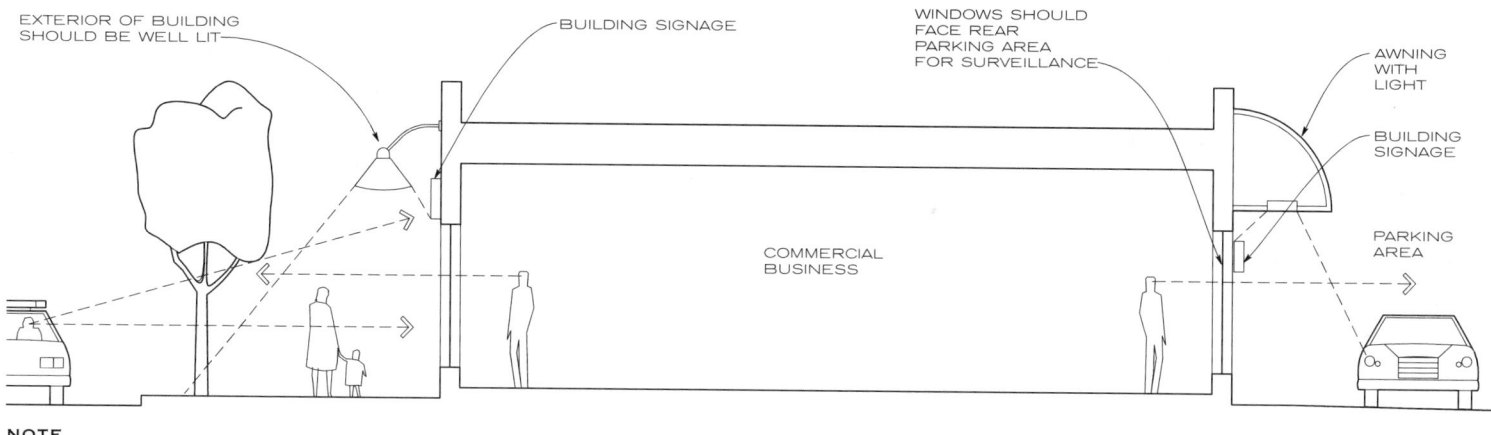

EXTERIOR OF BUILDING SHOULD BE WELL LIT

BUILDING SIGNAGE

WINDOWS SHOULD FACE REAR PARKING AREA FOR SURVEILLANCE

AWNING WITH LIGHT

BUILDING SIGNAGE

PARKING AREA

COMMERCIAL BUSINESS

NOTE

Clear visibility should be maintained from store to sidewalk, street, parking areas, and passing vehicles. Window signs should cover no more than 15% of any window area.

NATURAL SURVEILLANCE FOR COMMERCIAL PROPERTY

COMMERCIAL SECURITY

Designing safe stores and malls is critical to ensuring strong business draw and retention. Commercial security measures and design must protect the patrons, property, and business information of a business.

COMMERCIAL STOREFRONTS

NATURAL ACCESS CONTROL

1. Locate cash registers in the front of the store near the main entrance.
2. Clearly mark public paths.
3. Signs should direct patrons to parking and entrances.
4. There should be no easy access to the roof.
5. Shops with rear parking lots should have rear entrances.

NATURAL SURVEILLANCE

1. Plan for good visibility: Windows should face rear parking lots. Signs in windows should cover no more than 15% of the window area. Interior shelving and displays should be no higher than five feet. Unobstructed views should be available from the store to the street, sidewalk, parking areas, and passing vehicles.
2. The building exterior should be well-lighted.
3. Loading areas should not create hiding places.
4. Drainage retention areas should be visual amenities, a landscaped pond or smaller waterway rather than a fenced area, but to be secure they should be visible from nearby buildings and streets.
5. All entrances should be under visual surveillance or monitored electronically.

TERRITORIAL REINFORCEMENT

1. Where possible, mark property boundaries with hedges, low fences, or gates.
2. Distinguish private areas from public spaces.
3. Identify shops with wall signs for those parking in the rear.
4. Specify awnings over rear doors and windows.

COMMERCIAL SHOPPING MALL

NATURAL ACCESS CONTROL

1. Use signs to mark public entrances clearly.
2. Clearly mark sidewalks and public areas with special paving and/or landscaping.
3. Separate loading zones from public parking zones; designate limited delivery hours.
4. The parking garage should provide no exterior access to adjacent rooftops.

NATURAL SURVEILLANCE

1. Make restroom doors visible from main pedestrian areas and keep them away from outside exits.
2. Parking areas should be well lighted. Use high-intensity lighting in parking garages to minimize hiding places. In addition, all levels of the parking garage should be visible from the street or ground floor.
3. Loading areas should not create dead-end alleys or blind spots.

TERRITORIAL REINFORCEMENT

1. Define property perimeters with landscaping, post-and-pillar fencing, and gates.
2. Keep the number of entrances as low as possible and make them obvious and celebrated.

MANAGEMENT

1. Assign close-in parking for nighttime employees.
2. Help business associations work together to promote shopper and business safety.

COMMERCIAL DRIVE-THROUGHS

NATURAL SURVEILLANCE

1. Locate ATMs in front of banks facing main roads or as a drive-through in the drive-in teller lanes.
2. Place the ordering station for a restaurant within sight of the restaurant interior.

OFFICE BUILDINGS

Office building security focuses on the safety and security of people, goods, and services. Office building security can assume a high or low profile based on the type and number of building users.

NATURAL ACCESS CONTROL

1. Clearly define public entrances with walkways and signs.
2. Accentuate building entrances with architectural elements, lighting, and landscaping and/or paving stones.

NATURAL SURVEILLANCE

1. Place restrooms where they can be observed from nearby offices.
2. All exterior doors and hallways should be well-lighted, as well as all parking areas and walkways.
3. Dumpsters should not create blind spots or hiding places.
4. Windows and exterior doors should be visible from the street or to neighbors.
5. All four facades should have windows.
6. Do not obstruct windows with signs.

7. Windows and doors should have views into hallways--including peepholes and vision panels.
8. Assign parking spaces to each employee and visitor.
9. Parking areas should be visible from the windows; side parking areas should be visible from the street.
10. Keep shrubbery below 3 ft and tree branches at least 10 ft above the ground for good visibility.

TERRITORIAL REINFORCEMENT

1. Define the perimeter with landscaping or fencing.
2. Design fences to permit visibility from the street.
3. Make exerior private areas easily distinguishable from public areas.
4. Position a security and/or a reception area to screen all entrances.

INDUSTRIAL BUILDINGS

Industrial enterprises need to protect the assets in their facilities. Special security consideration must be given to receiving and outgoing areas to reduce theft. Individual building tenants should have security technology availability for continuous monitoring and supervision of their space.

NATURAL ACCESS CONTROL

1. Avoid creating dead-end spaces.
2. Make site entrances easy to secure.
3. Control entrances to parking areas with fences, gates, or an attendant's booth.
4. Parking should be assigned by shifts and planned so late workers have the close-in spaces.
5. Restrict access to railroad tracks.
6. Plan storage yards for vehicular access by patrol car.
7. Avoid access to roofs via dumpster, loading docks, poles, stacked items, etc.
8. Delivery entrances should be separate, well-marked, and monitored.
9. Place employee entrances close to employee parking and work areas.
10. Separate nighttime parking areas from service entrances.
11. Avoid providing access from one part of the building into other areas.

NATURAL SURVEILLANCE

1. All entrances should be well-lighted, well-defined, and visible to public and patrol vehicles.
2. Parking areas should be visible to patrol cars, pedestrians, parking attendants, and/or building personnel.
3. Position the parking attendant for maximum visibility of the property.
4. Give reception areas a view of parking areas.
5. Use walls only when necessary.
6. Blind alleys, storage yards, and other out-ot-the-way places should not offer hiding places.

Randall I. Atlas, Ph.D., AIA, CPP; Atlas Safety & Security Design, Inc.; Miami, Florida

GENERAL

Designing CPTED (crime prevention through environmental design) and security features into residential buildings and neighborhoods can reduce opportunities for and vulnerability to criminal behavior and help create a sense of community. The goal in residential design is to create safe dwelling places through limited access to properties, good surveillance, and a sense of ownership and responsibility.

SINGLE-FAMILY DWELLINGS

NATURAL ACCESS CONTROL AND SURVEILLANCE

1. Use walkways and landscaping to direct visitors to the proper entrance and away from private areas.
2. All doorways that open to the outside as well as sidewalks and all areas of the yard should be well-lighted.
3. Make the front door at least partially visible from the street and clearly visible from the driveway.
4. Windows on all sides of the house should provide full views of the property. The driveway should be visible from the front or back door and from at least one window.
5. Properly maintained landscaping should provide good views to and from the house.

TERRITORIAL REINFORCEMENT

1. Front porches or stoops create a transitional area between the street and the house.
2. Define property lines and private areas with plantings, pavement treatments, or fences.
3. The street address should be clearly visible from the street with numbers a minimum of 5 in. high and made of nonreflective material.

SUBDIVISIONS

NATURAL ACCESS CONTROL

1. Limit access to the subdivision without completely disconnecting it from neighboring areas. However, try to design streets to discourage cut-through traffic.
2. Paving treatments, plantings and architectural design features such as columned gateways can guide visitors away from private areas.
3. Locate walkways where they can direct pedestrian traffic and remain unobscured.

NATURAL SURVEILLANCE

1. Landscaping should not create blind spots or hiding places.
2. Locate open green spaces and recreational areas so they can be observed from nearby houses.
3. Use pedestrian-scale street lighting in areas with high pedestrian traffic.

TERRITORIAL REINFORCEMENT

1. Design lots, streets, and houses to encourage interaction between neighbors.
2. Accent entrances with changes in street elevation, different paving materials, and other design features.
3. Clearly identify residences with street address numbers that are a minimum of 5 in. high and well-lighted at night.
4. Property lines should be defined with post-and-pillar fencing, gates, and plantings to direct pedestrian traffic.
5. All parking should be assigned.

MULTIFAMILY DWELLINGS

NATURAL ACCESS CONTROL

1. Balcony railings should never be made of a solid, opaque material or be more than 42 in. high.
2. Define parking lot entrances with curbs, landscaping, and/or architectural design or a guard booth; block dead-end areas with a fence or gate.
3. Hallways should be well-lighted, and elevators and stairs should be centrally located.
4. Common building entrances should have locks that automatically lock when the door closes.
5. Limit access to the building to no more than two points. No more than four units should share the same entrance.

NATURAL SURVEILLANCE

1. Make exterior doors visible to the street or neighbors, and ensure they are well-lighted.
2. All four building facades should have windows. Site buildings so the windows and doors of one unit are visible from those of other units.

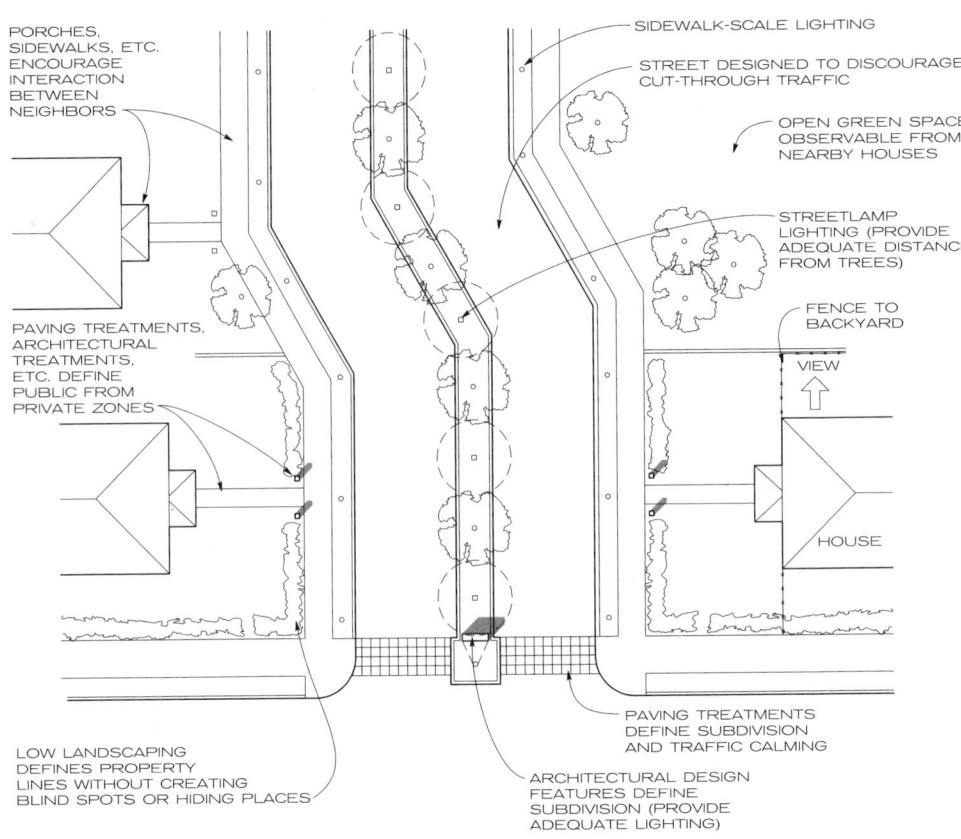

PORCHES, SIDEWALKS, ETC. ENCOURAGE INTERACTION BETWEEN NEIGHBORS

PAVING TREATMENTS, ARCHITECTURAL TREATMENTS, ETC. DEFINE PUBLIC FROM PRIVATE ZONES

LOW LANDSCAPING DEFINES PROPERTY LINES WITHOUT CREATING BLIND SPOTS OR HIDING PLACES

SIDEWALK-SCALE LIGHTING

STREET DESIGNED TO DISCOURAGE CUT-THROUGH TRAFFIC

OPEN GREEN SPACE OBSERVABLE FROM NEARBY HOUSES

STREETLAMP LIGHTING (PROVIDE ADEQUATE DISTANCE FROM TREES)

FENCE TO BACKYARD

VIEW

HOUSE

PAVING TREATMENTS DEFINE SUBDIVISION AND TRAFFIC CALMING

ARCHITECTURAL DESIGN FEATURES DEFINE SUBDIVISION (PROVIDE ADEQUATE LIGHTING)

CRIME PREVENTION THROUGH ENVIRONMENTAL DESIGN—PLANNING FOR SUBDIVISIONS

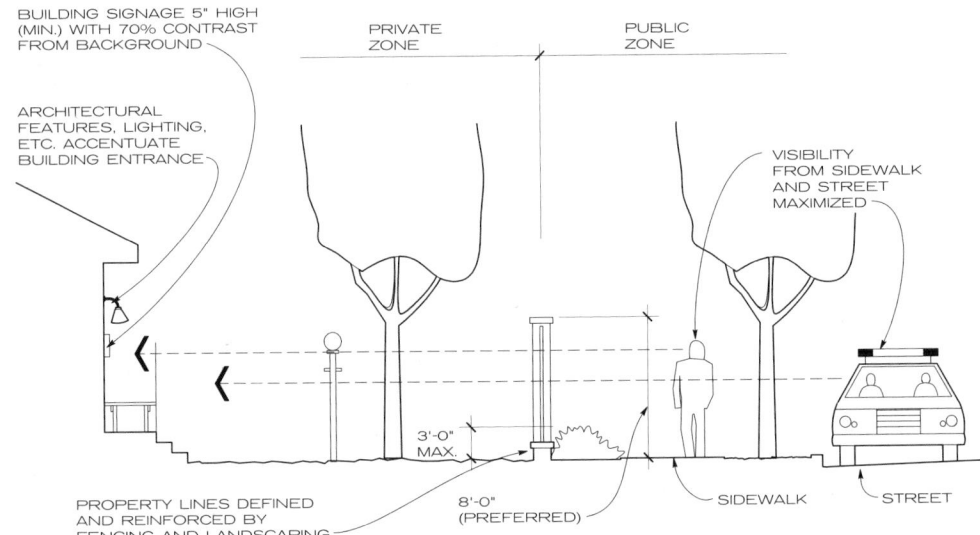

BUILDING SIGNAGE 5" HIGH (MIN.) WITH 70% CONTRAST FROM BACKGROUND

ARCHITECTURAL FEATURES, LIGHTING, ETC. ACCENTUATE BUILDING ENTRANCE

PROPERTY LINES DEFINED AND REINFORCED BY FENCING AND LANDSCAPING

PRIVATE ZONE

PUBLIC ZONE

VISIBILITY FROM SIDEWALK AND STREET MAXIMIZED

3'-0" MAX.

8'-0" (PREFERRED)

SIDEWALK

STREET

CRIME PREVENTION THROUGH ENVIRONMENTAL DESIGN—PLANNING FOR RESIDENTIAL PROPERTY

3. Assign parking spaces to each unit and locate them next to the unit. Designate special parking spaces for visitors.
4. Parking areas and walkways should be well-lighted.
5. Recreation areas should be visible from a multitude of windows and doors.
6. Dumpsters should not create blind spots or hiding places.
7. Elevators and stairwells should be clearly visible from windows and doors. In addition, they should be well-lighted and open to view—not hidden behind solid walls.
8. Shrubbery should be no more than 3 ft high for clear visibility and tree canopies not lower than 8 ft 6 in.

TERRITORIAL REINFORCEMENT

1. Define property lines with landscaping or post-and-pillar fencing, but keep shrubbery and fences low to allow visibility from the street.
2. Accent building entrances with architectural elements and lighting and/or landscape features.
4. Doorknobs should be 40 in. from window panes.
5. Clearly identify all buildings and residential units with well-lighted address numbers a minimum of 5 in. high.
6. Common doorways should have windows and be key-controlled by residents.
7. Locate mailboxes next to the appropriate residences.

Randall I. Atlas, Ph.D., AIA, CPP; Atlas Safety & Security Design, Inc.; Miami, Florida

DESIGN GUIDELINES

Each commercial development project will have its own set of requirements. This outline is intended as an overview of the subjects the architect, engineer, and owner should consider when planning a small to medium commercial development.

LOCAL PLANNING REGULATIONS

As with all new projects, the designer should research the laws, codes, and ordinances that govern development in the jurisdiction. This may include municipal, township, county, state, and federal regulations as they pertain to land and building development.

ZONING

Confirm that the zoning classification of the property permits the intended use. For example, to build a warehouse the tract of land would have to be zoned for industrial use. The zoning classification also determines what level of development is allowed on a particular tract of land.

BUILDING CODES

The architect should find out what relevant codes/laws require in regard to life safety, welfare, and accessibility. These requirements should provide minimum criteria by which to measure the design and construction of a project. The intended use and type of construction will dictate allowable heights and areas.

Codes vary around the country, so architects must consult the local government for all applicable codes/laws and local amendments. Pertinent laws include the BOCA, UBC, SBCC, NFPA, ASHRAE, ANSI, and the ADA universal accessibility law.

ENVIRONMENTAL ANALYSIS

Environmental issues such as wetlands preservation, potential groundwater contamination, and preservation of native flora and fauna should be considered. Local groups can provide information regarding local environmental issues.

GEOTECHNICAL ANALYSIS

A geotechnical engineer should be retained at the inception of a project to provide a thorough subsurface investigation of the property. The key information provided by such a survey includes the following:

1. Soil quality/type: Soils are described, ranging from their composition to drainage.
2. Bearing capacity: A variety of field and/or laboratory testing, considered in conjunction with anticipated structural dead loads, goes into analyzing how a planned building will react to the soil conditions on a site. Settlement is one issue to be considered here.
3. Foundation recommendations: The geotechnical engineer uses analytical data about the soil quality/type and the bearing capacity of the soil to make recommendations regarding the most efficient/cost-effective foundation system.

LOT COVERAGE

Zoning laws regulate the amount of physical construction that can occur on a given piece of land. Physical construction covers buildings and paved, impervious surfaces (e.g., sidewalks, blacktop). Another measure affecting the allowable building footprint is building setback, the distance that must exist between a structure and the property line. Building setbacks are typically described in terms of front, rear, and side yards; rights-of-way; and property easements. Local municipal ordinances describe required setbacks, which vary based on location and intended use.

PROPERTY SURVEY

Property surveys verify the property boundaries, street lines, contours, pertinent landmarks, rights-of-way, and easements (construction restrictions) of a piece of property.

DRAINAGE EASEMENT

When properties share a common storm water basin, local authorities can hold easements to allow for storm water drainage across multiple properties. Drainage easements are not required when individual property owners are responsible for storm water management.

MAXIMUM BUILDING HEIGHT

The maximum height buildings on a particular site can reach is usually defined in terms of both stories and feet above the finished grade. These criteria are set by local ordinance and building code.

PARKING REQUIREMENTS

Parking requirements typically are a function of intended use and building size (e.g., one space per 250 sq ft of building area). In suburban office park planning, this is commonly the governing factor when maximizing buildable area on small and constricted sites.

UTILITIES

The architect must determine which utilities are required, which are available, how site access will be designed, and where the utility lines will enter the building. Utilities include water, sewer, gas, electric, and telephone.

BUILDING ENTRANCE

Public exposure, topography, orientation, and parking should be considered in designing and siting the main entrance. To maximize a building's presence on the site and help orient users, the main entrance should be obvious and easily visible. Site topography and the intended use of the building will determine orientation of the entrance, with consideration of sun angles and views. The main entrance should be readily recognizable from the main parking area.

TRAFFIC SURVEY

A typical traffic survey analyzes traffic patterns, densities, generators, and peak periods. This information is used to determine the guidelines/procedures required to provide safe and effective flows of vehicular and pedestrian traffic. Local governing agencies determine the scope and extent of survey required.

SERVICE ACCESS

Architects must consider vehicular service access to both the site and the building. Site design and building orientation must allow for maneuverability of service, delivery, and sanitary vehicles.

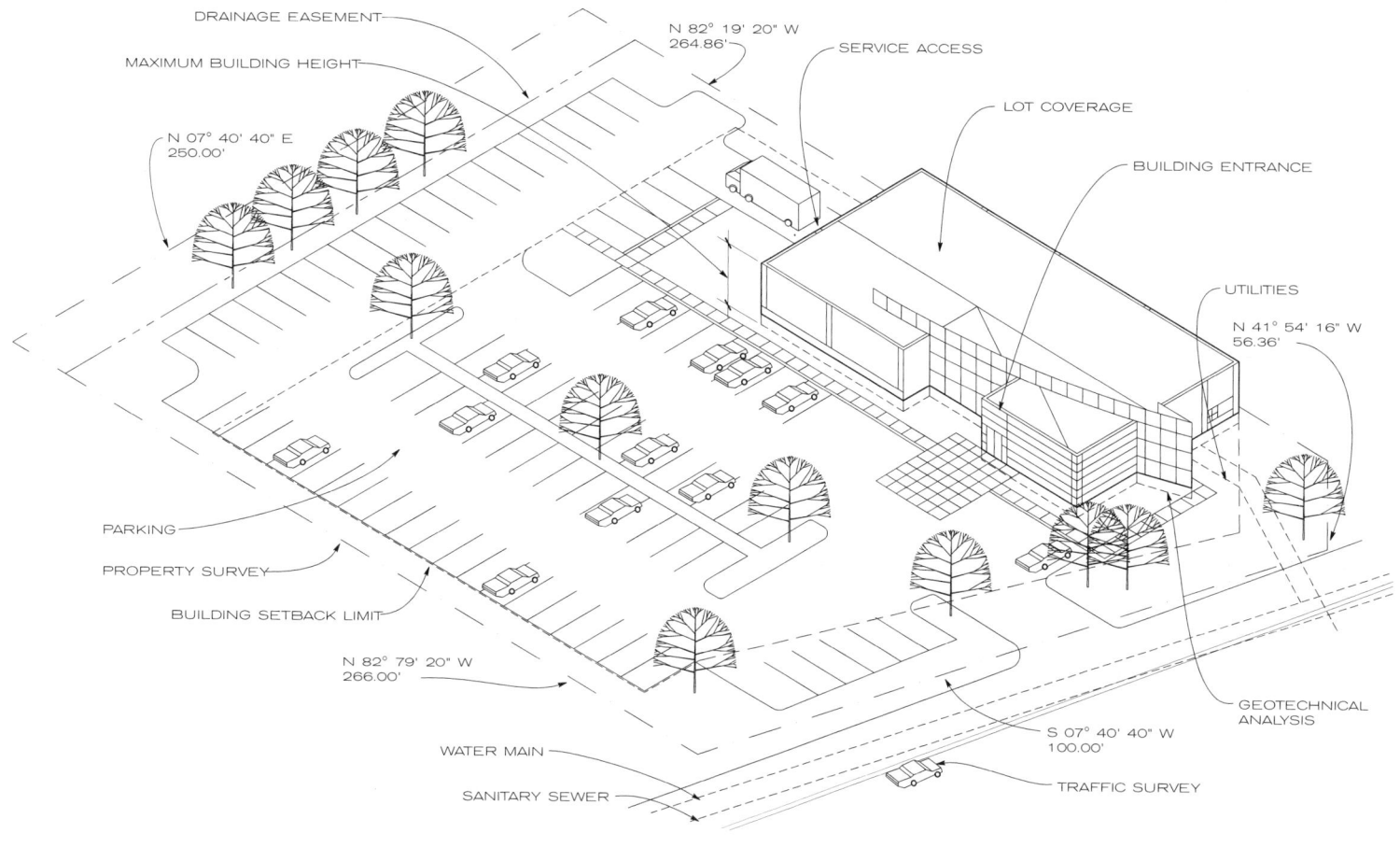

SITE DEVELOPMENT DIAGRAM

Greenfield Architects, Ltd.; Lancaster, Pennsylvania

SITE, COMMUNITY, AND URBAN PLANNING   1

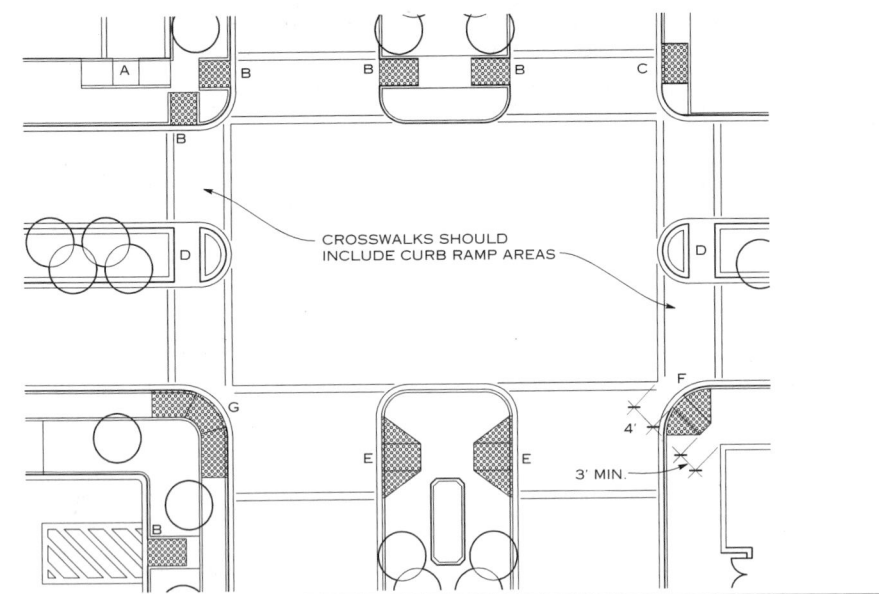

CROSSWALKS SHOULD INCLUDE CURB RAMP AREAS

4'

3' MIN.

DESIGN CONSIDERATIONS

1. Design storm drain systems to shed water away from curb ramps.
2. The dimensions shown are for new construction. For alterations when these dimensions are impractical, review the Americans with Disabilities Act Accessibility Guidelines (ADAAG) for less strict dimensions.
3. The ADAAG requirement for detectable warnings was suspended by the Architectural and Transportation Barriers Compliance Board, pending revision of the detectable warning detail. Many states continue to require detectable warnings at locations shown on this page but the details specified vary.

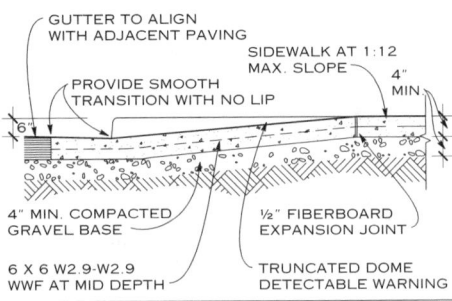

GUTTER TO ALIGN WITH ADJACENT PAVING
PROVIDE SMOOTH TRANSITION WITH NO LIP
SIDEWALK AT 1:12 MAX. SLOPE
4" MIN
6"
4" MIN. COMPACTED GRAVEL BASE
6 X 6 W2.9-W2.9 WWF AT MID DEPTH
½" FIBERBOARD EXPANSION JOINT
TRUNCATED DOME DETECTABLE WARNING

ACCESSIBLE CURB RAMP PLAN

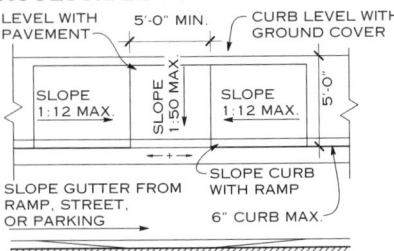

LEVEL WITH PAVEMENT
5'-0" MIN.
CURB LEVEL WITH GROUND COVER
SLOPE 1:12 MAX.
SLOPE 1:50 MAX
SLOPE 1:12 MAX.
5'-0"
SLOPE GUTTER FROM RAMP, STREET, OR PARKING
SLOPE CURB WITH RAMP
6" CURB MAX.

TYPE A

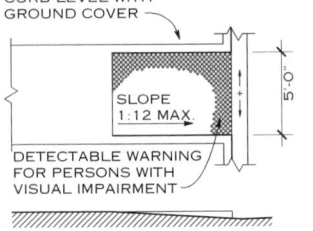

CURB LEVEL WITH GROUND COVER
SLOPE 1:12 MAX.
5'-0"
DETECTABLE WARNING FOR PERSONS WITH VISUAL IMPAIRMENT

TYPE B

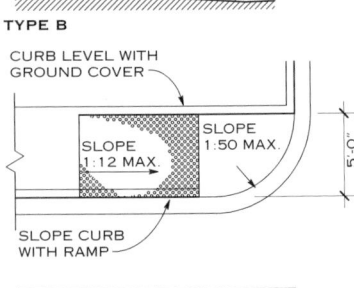

CURB LEVEL WITH GROUND COVER
SLOPE 1:12 MAX.
SLOPE 1:50 MAX.
5'-0"
SLOPE CURB WITH RAMP

TYPE C

LEVEL WITH ROADWAY
5'-0"
4'-0" MIN.

TYPE D

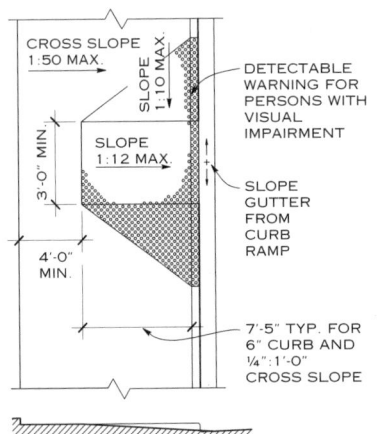

CROSS SLOPE 1:50 MAX.
SLOPE 1:10 MAX.
DETECTABLE WARNING FOR PERSONS WITH VISUAL IMPAIRMENT
3'-0" MIN.
SLOPE 1:12 MAX.
SLOPE GUTTER FROM CURB RAMP
4'-0" MIN.
7'-5" TYP. FOR 6" CURB AND ¼":1'-0" CROSS SLOPE

TYPE E

CURB RAMP SECTION

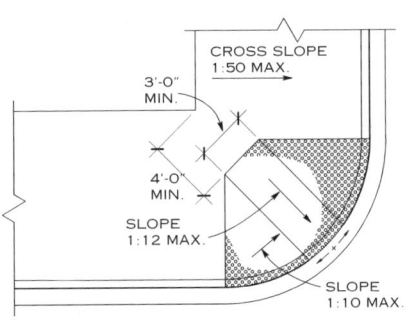

CROSS SLOPE 1:50 MAX.
3'-0" MIN.
4'-0" MIN.
SLOPE 1:12 MAX.
SLOPE 1:10 MAX.

NOTE

If the 4 ft 0 in. minimum dimension cannot be met for type F, the 1:10 slope becomes 1:12 maximum.

TYPE F

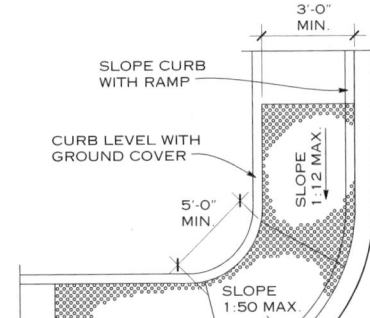

3'-0" MIN.
SLOPE CURB WITH RAMP
CURB LEVEL WITH GROUND COVER
SLOPE 1:12 MAX.
5'-0" MIN.
SLOPE 1:50 MAX.

TYPE G

CURB RAMP TYPES

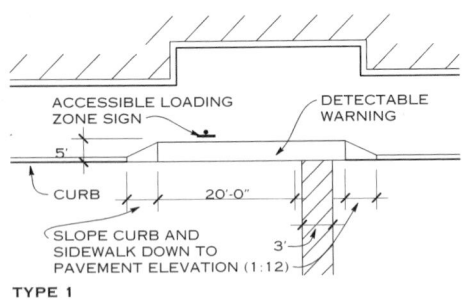

ACCESSIBLE LOADING ZONE SIGN
DETECTABLE WARNING
5'
CURB
20'-0"
SLOPE CURB AND SIDEWALK DOWN TO PAVEMENT ELEVATION (1:12)
3'

TYPE 1

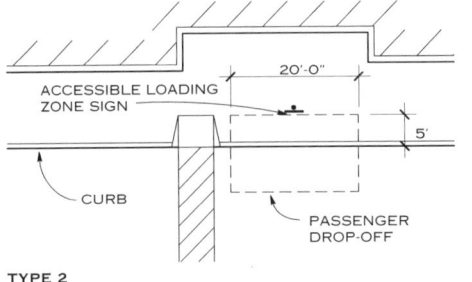

20'-0"
ACCESSIBLE LOADING ZONE SIGN
5'
CURB
PASSENGER DROP-OFF

TYPE 2

ACCESSIBLE PASSENGER LOADING ZONE

NOTE

If passenger loading zones are provided, at least one must be accessible, with a 5 ft wide x 20 ft long access aisle. The surface slopes of the vehicle standing space and the access aisle must not exceed 1:50 (2%). The path of travel to and from a vehicle standing stall must have a minimum vehicular clearance of 9 ft 6 in. If there are curbs between the vehicle standing space and the access aisle, a curb ramp must be provided.

Mary S. Smith, P.E.; Walker Parking Consultants/Engineers, Inc.; Indianapolis, Indiana
Mark J. Mazz, AIA; CEA, Inc.; Hyattsville, Maryland

GENERAL

In setting design parameters, the designer assumes that all vehicles present are "design vehicles." Design vehicles are selected to represent approximately the 85th percentile vehicle in a range from smallest to largest. In the recent past, small or compact car stalls were often separated from large or standard stalls in parking designs. However, a decline in smaller car sales and the increasing use of light trucks, vans, and utility vehicles (LTVUs) for personal transportation have made small-car-only stalls ineffective as a design tool. Therefore, while small car and large car design vehicles—as well as a composite encompassing both small and large—have been given here for reference, parking design must be based on a composite passenger vehicle that includes not only cars but light trucks, vans, and sport/utility vehicles.

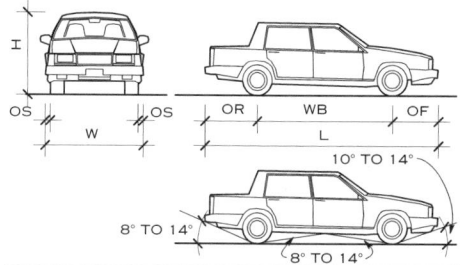

PASSENGER CAR

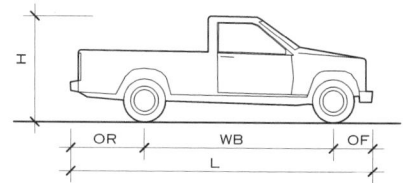

LIGHT TRUCK

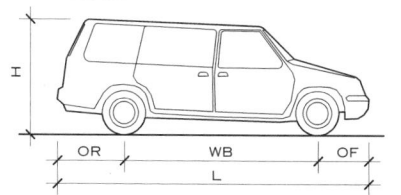

VAN

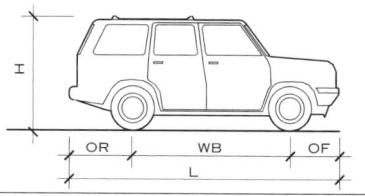

SPORT/UTILITY

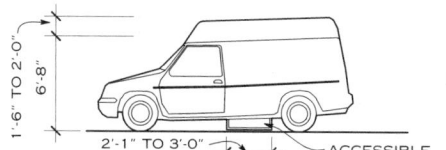

WHEELCHAIR LIFT VAN

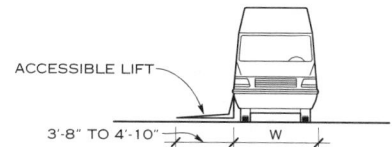

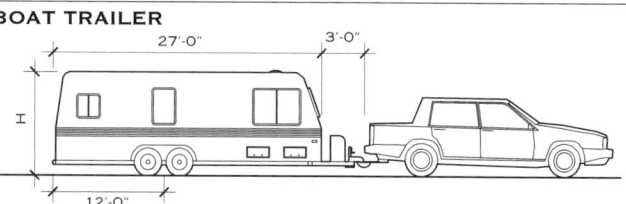

BOAT TRAILER

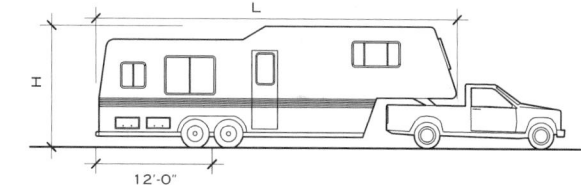

RV—CONVENTIONAL TRAILER

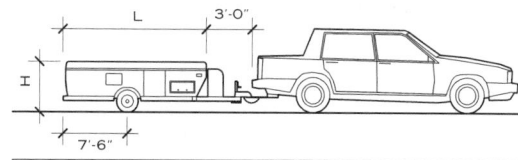

RV—FIFTH WHEEL (PICKUP-BASE)

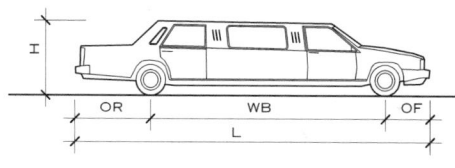

RV—FOLDING TRAILER

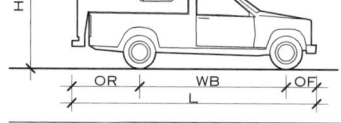

SLIDE-IN CAMPER

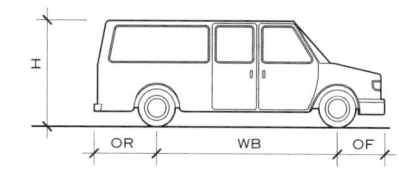

SHUTTLE VAN

STRETCH LIMOUSINE

DESIGN VEHICLE DIMENSIONS

VEHICLE	LENGTH (L)	WIDTH (W)	HEIGHT (H)	WHEELBASE (WB)	OVERHANG FRONT (OF)	OVERHANG REAR (OR)	GROSS WEIGHT
	(FT-IN.)						(LB)
Small car[1]	15-0	5-7	4-8	8-6	2-0	4-6	2850
Composite passenger vehicle[2]	16-9	6-4	6-10	9-5	3-0	4-4	6000
Light truck	17-9	6-6	6-0	11-0	2-9	4-0	8600
Van	16-9	6-3	6-10	10-0	2-9	4-0	4600
Sport/utility vehicle	16-0	6-4	6-2	9-4	3-0	3-8	6000
Wheelchair lift van (personal use)	17-8	6-8	8-0	11-6	2-6	3-8	6000
Boat trailer	20-0	8-0	6-0	See detail	3-0	8-0	4000
RV—conventional trailer	27-0	7-0	9-0	See detail	3-0	12-0	5000
RV—fifth wheel (pickup-based)	34-0	8-6	12-0	8-0	22-0	12-2	3500
RV—folding trailer	16-0	7-6	5-0	–	8-6	7-6	1500
Slide-in pickup camper	18-11	10-0	7-3	–	–	–	2900
Stretch limousine	24-6	6-0	5-0	15-6	4-0	5-0	9000
Shuttle van (11 passengers)	20-0	6-6	6-10	11-6	3-0	5-6	11,000

[1] Small car classes 5 through 7 per Parking Consultants Council (PCC).

[2] A composite passenger vehicle is a design vehicle that encompasses passenger cars, light trucks, vans, and sport/utility vehicles. It is the vehicle for which a parking facility should be designed.

Mary S. Smith, P.E.; Walker Parking Consultants/Engineers, Inc.; Indianapolis, Indiana

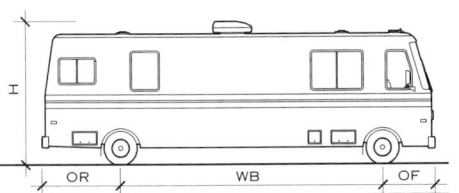

CLASS A MOTOR HOME

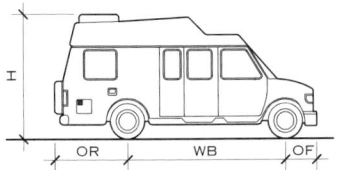

CLASS B MOTOR HOME

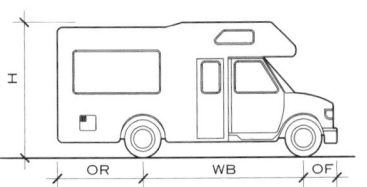

CLASS C MOTOR HOME

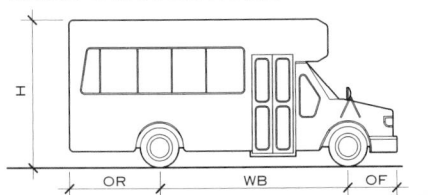

PARATRANSIT/SHUTTLE BUS

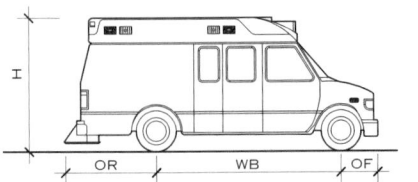

AMBULANCE VAN

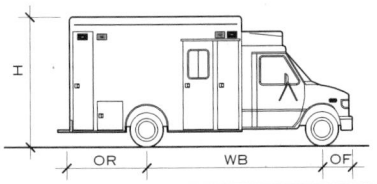

PARAMEDIC UNIT

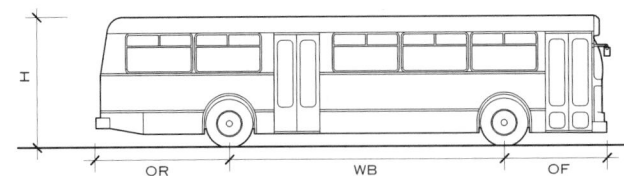

INTERCITY/CHARTER BUS

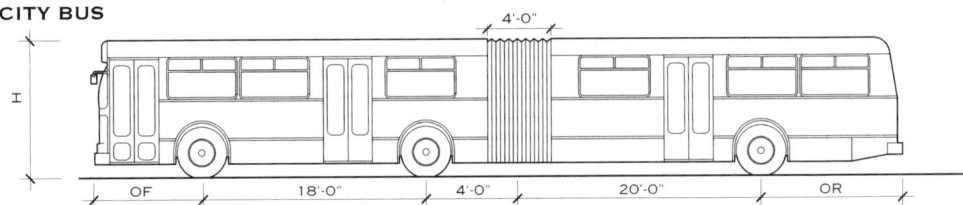

CITY BUS

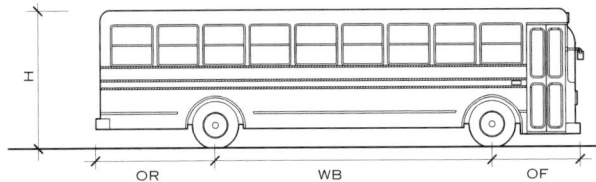

ARTICULATED BUS

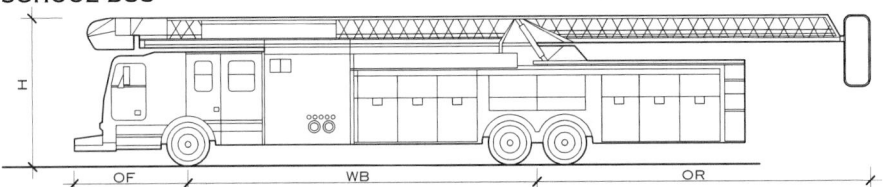

SCHOOL BUS

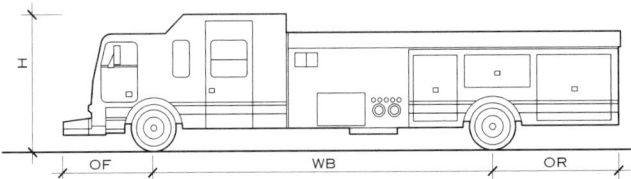

FIRE TRUCK—AERIAL

FIRE TRUCK—PUMPER

DESIGN VEHICLE DIMENSIONS

VEHICLE	LENGTH (L)	WIDTH (W)	HEIGHT (H)	WHEELBASE (WB)	OVERHANG FRONT (OF)	OVERHANG REAR (OR)	GROSS WEIGHT
	(FT-IN.)						(LB)
Class A motor home (self-contained)	30-0	8-0	11-0	20-0	4-0	6-0	17,000
Class B motor home (van conversion)	20-0	6-8	8-6	11-6	2-6	6-0	9000
Class C motor home (van cutaway)	19-0	7-6	9-0	11-0	2-6	5-6	11,000
Paratransit/shuttle bus (20 passengers)	25-0	6-10	8-9	11-6	3-0	5-6	11,000
Intercity/charter bus	40-0	8-6	11-6	20-6	9-0	10-6	47,000
City bus*	40-0	8-6	11-2	25-0	7-0	8-0	47,000
Articulated bus*	60-0	8-6	10-4	See detail	8-6	9-6	50,000
School bus	40-0	8-0	10-0	22-0	8-0	10-0	47,000
Ambulance van	19-10	6-8	9-6	11-6	2-8	5-8	9400
Paramedic unit	22-6	7-8	9-6	13-2	2-8	7-0	11,500
Fire truck—pumper	31-0	8-0	9-8	18-8	5-0	7-5	35,000
Fire truck—aerial	45-9	8-0	10-2	20-3	6-2	19-4	52,000

*Generally in conformance with standards of the American Association of State Highway and Transportation Officials (AASHTO).

Mary S. Smith, P.E.; Walker Parking Consultants/Engineers, Inc.; Indianapolis, Indiana

1 AUTOMOBILES, ROADS, AND PARKING

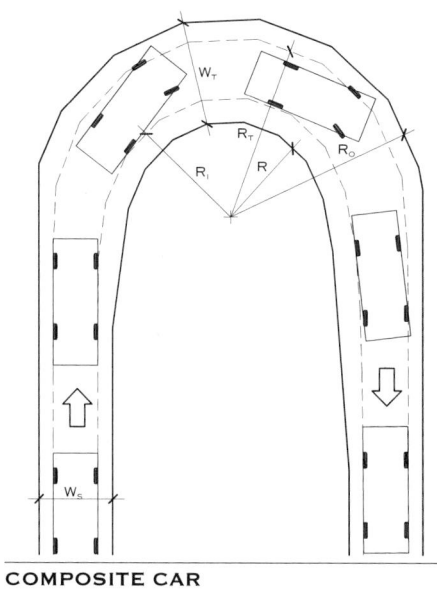

COMPOSITE CAR

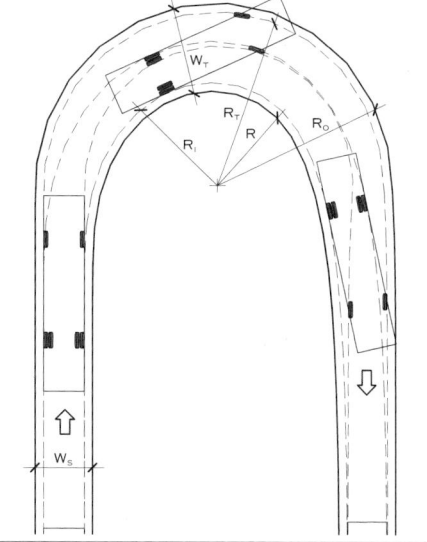

INTERCITY BUS

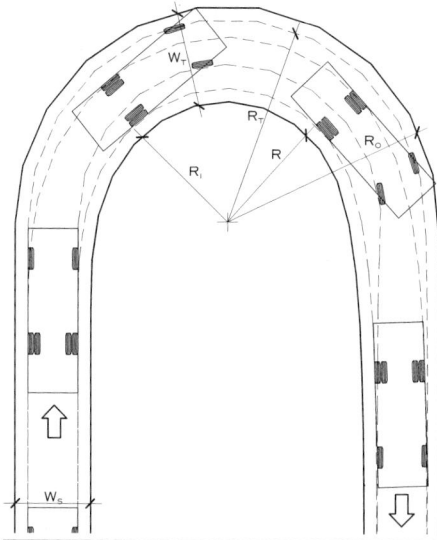

GARBAGE TRUCK

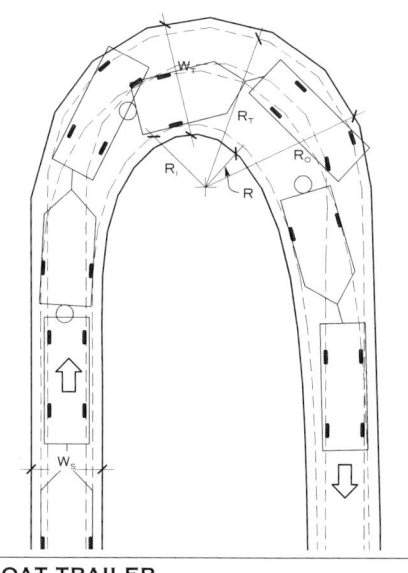

BOAT TRAILER

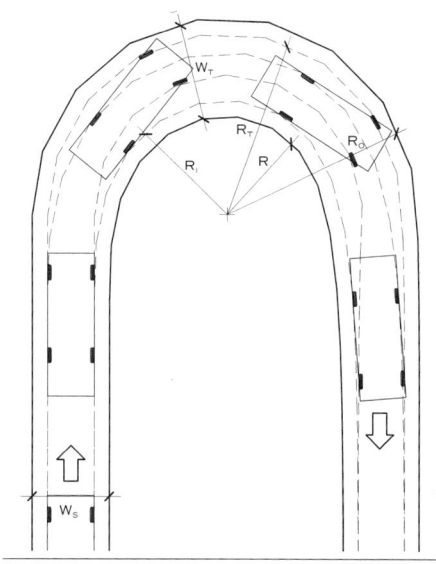

AMBULANCE VAN

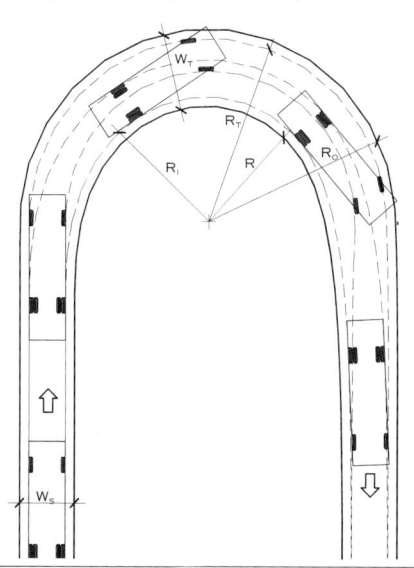

FIRE TRUCK—PUMPER

MINIMUM TURNING RADIUS FOR DESIGN VEHICLES (FT-IN.)

VEHICLE TYPE	MIN. TURNING RADIUS (R_T)	OUTSIDE FRONT RADIUS (R_O)	INSIDE REAR RADIUS (R_I)	STRAIGHT LANE WIDTH (W_S)	CURVED LANE WIDTH (W_T)	INSIDE CURB RADIUS (R)	TANGENT LENGTH (T)
Composite private vehicle	24-0	26-0	15-6	10-0	13-6	12-6	24-7
Wheelchair lift van	24-9	26-8	16-7	10-0	12-6	14-0	24-4
Boat trailer	24-0	24-11	8-5	11-0	16-11	6-10	60-9
RV trailer	23-10	25-4	5-7	11-0	18-4	4-1	83-3
Motor home	39-7	42-8	27-6	11-0	19-0	23-0	41-2
Stretch limousine	32-7	34-10	23-8	11-0	14-6	20-2	34-1
Shuttle van	24-10	26-11	16-5	11-0	13-6	13-4	29-7
Paratransit/shuttle bus	25-2	26-11	16-6	11-0	13-6	13-4	29-4
Intercity bus	35-3	36-10	23-5	12-0	17-10	18-7	60-0
City bus	42-0	46-6	24-0	12-0	27-0	21-0	60-0
Articulated bus	38-0	43-0	14-0	12-0	22-0	11-0	62-0
School bus	41-9	43-6	28-7	12-0	17-8	25-3	56-4
Garbage truck	31-0	33-4	20-8	12-0	14-6	18-6	38-0
Ambulance van	24-9	27-2	16-7	11-0	13-5	13-5	29-0
Paramedic unit	28-5	30-10	18-8	12-0	15-1	15-6	33-0
Fire truck–pumper	38-11	41-0	27-7	12-0	16-4	24-4	44-0

Source: American Association of State Highway and Transportation Officials (AASHTO).

NOTES

1. Minimum turn radii at less than 10 mph.
2. Obstructions (columns, walls, light poles, etc.) should be held a minimum of 6 in. (2 ft preferred) from the edge of the lane given above. See details on the AGS page on driveways and roadways.

Mary S. Smith, P.E.; Walker Parking Consultants/Engineers, Inc.; Indianapolis, Indiana

GENERAL

Public streets and highways are designed to accommodate a variety of vehicles, up to and including semitrailer trucks. When private driveways and roadways will only serve passenger vehicles, it may be appropriate to use smaller dimensions in some instances. Nonetheless, be certain private roads are wide enough to allow passage of fire and emergency vehicles.

The "level of service" approach employed by traffic engineers can be used as a tool for adapting designs to the specific needs of users. Level of service (LOS) A, which is the most comfortable, allows vehicle movement with little or no constraint. As the level of service decreases, from A to D, the comfort level decreases. LOS D is the minimum dimension for safe maneuvering of a vehicle at low speed.

The level of service selected for a particular application should reflect the needs of the users and of the owner of a property. Make adjustments according to the local vehicle size and mix and any concerns particular to the location.

COMPARISON OF LEVELS OF SERVICE

LEVEL OF SERVICE	LOS D	LOS A
Type of users	Familiar, young adults	Unfamiliar, elderly
Length of stay	Long-term	Short-term
Turnover	Less than 2 per day	More than 5 per day
Type of generator	Industrial	Retail
Location	Urban	Rural
Image	Spec office	Corporate headquarters
Percent small cars	High	Low
Percent light trucks, vans, and utility vehicles	Low	High

RECOMMENDED DESIGN PARAMETERS FOR VEHICULAR CIRCULATION[1]

	DRAWING KEY	LOS D	LOS C	LOS B	LOS A
Lane width, straight	W_S				
One lane[2]		10'-0"	10'-6"	11'-0"	11'-6"
Multiple lanes		9'-0"	9'-6"	10'-0"	10'-6"
Clearance to obstructions[3]	C	0'-6"	1'-0"	1'-6"	2'-0"
Radius, turning (outside front wheel)	R_T	24'-0"	30'-0"	36'-0"	42'-0"
Lane width, turning[4,5]	W_T				
One lane		13'-6"	13'-6"	13'-6"	13'-6"
Each additional lane		12'-0"	12'-0"	12'-0"	12'-0"
Circular helix[4,6]					
Single-threaded[7]					
Outside diameter	D_O	60'-0"	74'-0"	88'-0"	102'-0"
Inside diameter[8]	D_I	24'-0"	36'-0"	48'-0"	60'-0"
Double-threaded[9]					
Outside diameter	D_O	80'-0"	95'-0"	110'-0"	125'-0"
Inside diameter[9]	D_I	44'-0"	57'-0"	70'-0"	83'-0"
Express ramp slope	S	16%	14%	12%	10%
Transition length	L_T	10'-0"	11'-0"	12'-0"	13'-0"
Gated/controlled width[10]	W_G	8'-9"	9'-0"	9'-3"	9'-6"

Source: Mary S. Smith, *Parking Structures: Planning, Design, Maintenance and Repair*, 2d ed. (Chapman and Hall, 1996).

[1] The design parameters recommended are for design speeds ranging from 10 mph (LOS D) to 25 mph (LOS A). Additional dimensions for parking access aisles and turning bays are provided on the AGS page on parking design parameters.

[2] For all levels of service, use a 15-ft lane to make room for passing a broken-down vehicle.

[3] The clearance given is from the edge of a lane to a wall, column, parked vehicle, or other obstruction, as cited in American Association of State Highway and Transportation Officials, *A Policy on Geometric Design of Highways and Streets* (1990) [ASHTO 1990], figure 111-25.

[4] The dimensions given for LOS D are from AASHTO 1990 figure 111-23, except the clearance cited in that figure has been reduced to 2 ft, per figure 111-25.

[5] For all levels of service, use a 20-ft lane to allow room to pass a broken-down vehicle, per AASHTO 1990 figure 111-23.

[6] The diameters given measure from outside face to outside face of the walls (6-in. walls assumed).

[7] Turning radii/lane width increased 3 ft because of multiple Turns.

[8] Decrease 3 ft 6 in. to provide 20-ft lane in order to leave room to pass broken-down vehicles.

[9] Ramp slope, minimum lane width, and clearance to walls control dimensions for double-threaded helix.

[10] The dimensions given assume a straight approach to lane; check turns into lanes with template.

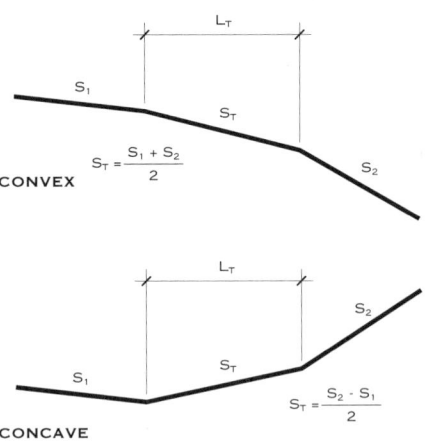

$$S_T = \frac{S_1 + S_2}{2}$$

CONVEX

$$S_T = \frac{S_2 - S_1}{2}$$

CONCAVE

TRANSITION SLOPES

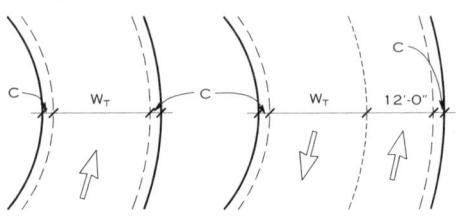

ONE-WAY **TWO-WAY**

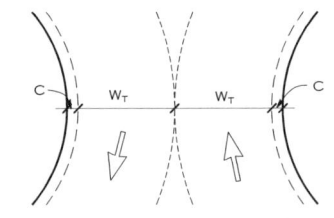

NONCONCENTRIC TWO-WAY

LANE WIDTH (TURNING)

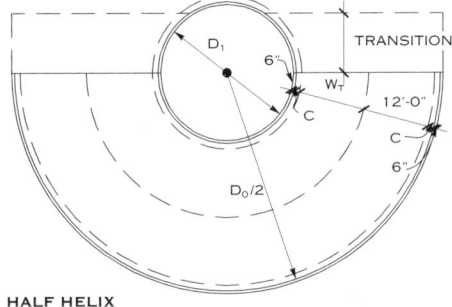

HALF HELIX

FULL HELIX

CIRCULAR HELIX (TURNING)

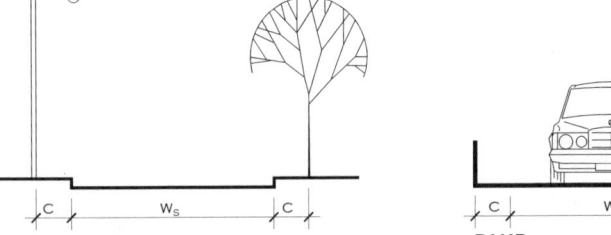

ROADWAY

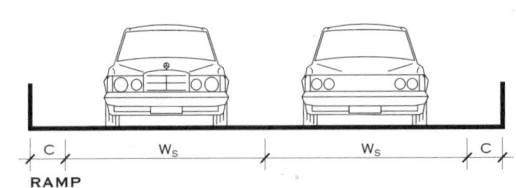

RAMP

ROADWAY AND RAMP WIDTHS

Mary S. Smith, P.E.; Walker Parking Consultants/Engineers, Inc.; Indianapolis, Indiana

GENERAL

Vehicle dimensions are shown on the AGS page on design vehicles. The U-shaped drive shown here illustrates a procedure for developing any drive configuration, given the design vehicle and its turning radii (R). The tangent (T_G) dimension is an approximate minimum required for transition from one turn direction to another.

NOTE

For R_C, R_I, R_O, W_S, W_T, and T_G, see the AGS page on vehicle turning radii. For L, OR, and W, see the AGS page on design vehicles.

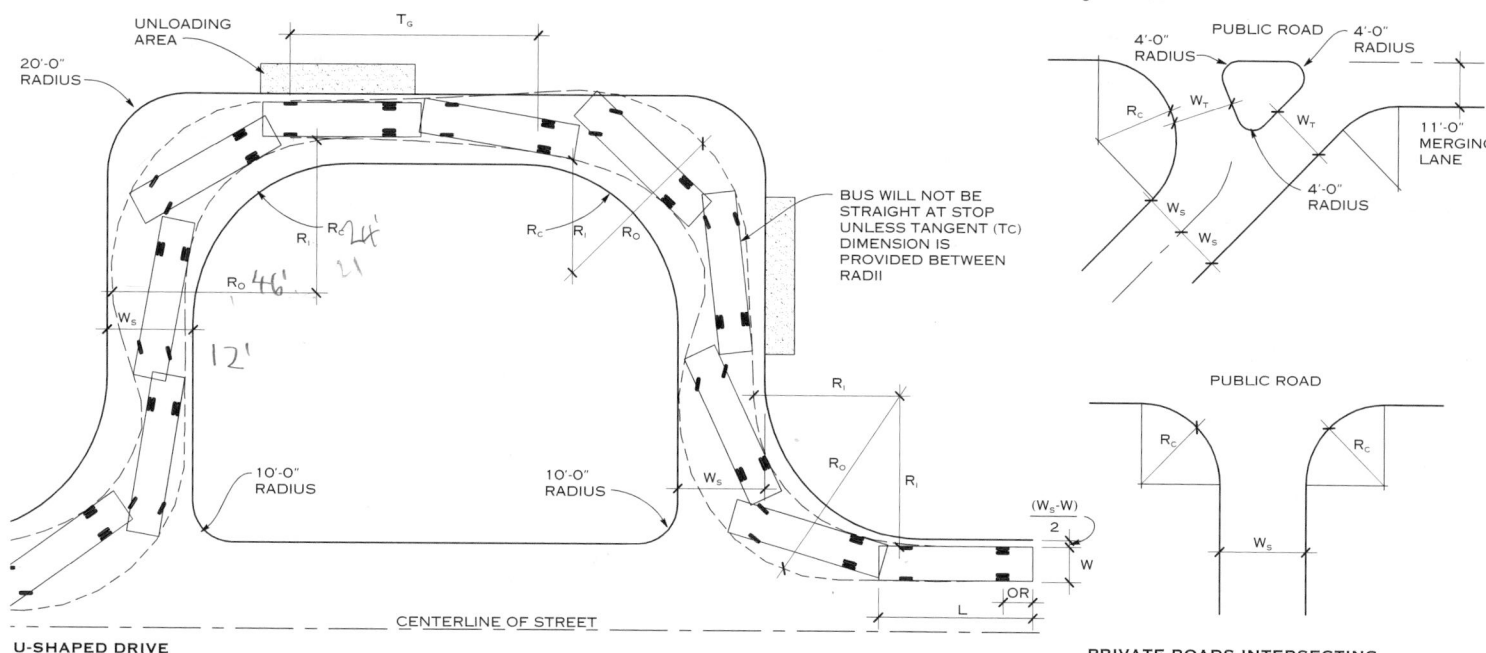

U-SHAPED DRIVE

PRIVATE ROADS INTERSECTING PUBLIC ROADS

INTERSECTIONS AND DRIVES

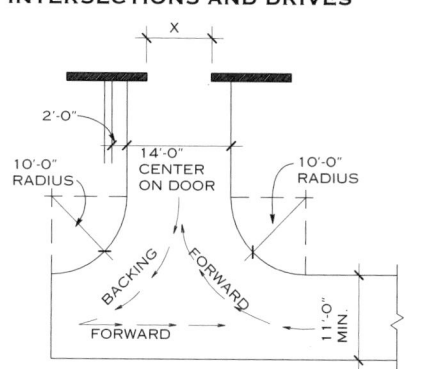

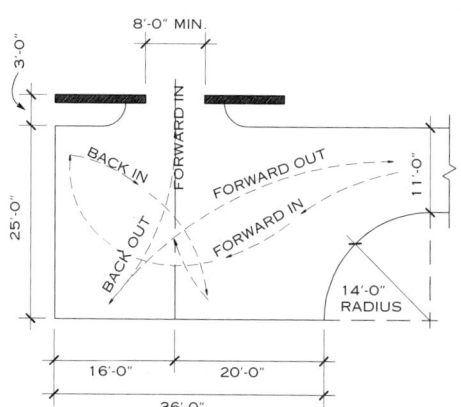

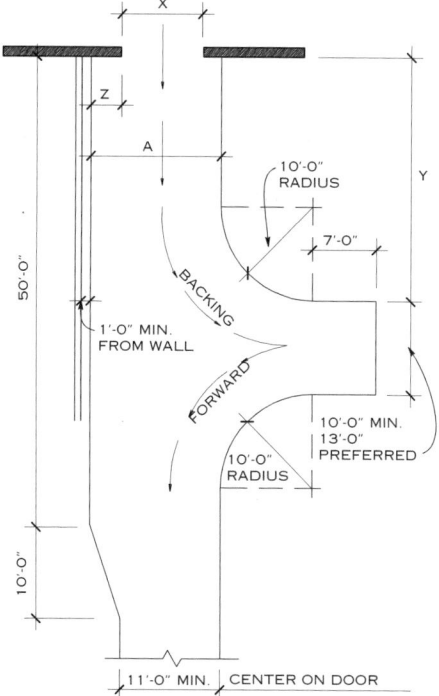

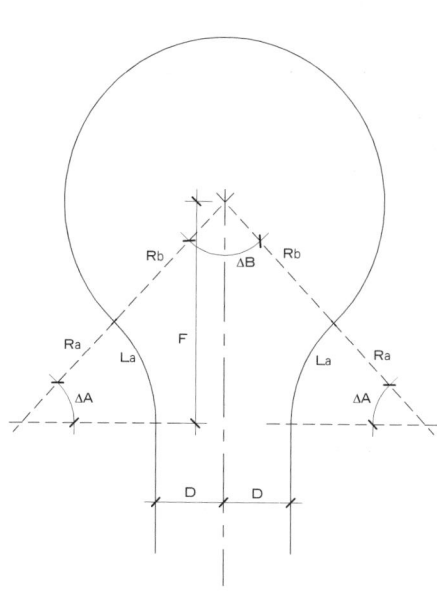

NOTE

Use this three-maneuver entrance for single car garages only when space limitations demand it. The drawing is based on dimensions for a large car.

PRIVATE DRIVEWAYS TO RESIDENTIAL GARAGES

SPACE REQUIREMENTS FOR DRIVEWAY LAYOUTS (FT-IN.)

90° IN–BACK OUT (1 CAR)

X	8-9	9-0	10-0	11-0	12-0
Y	25-0	24-6	23-8	23-0	22-0

STRAIGHT IN–BACK OUT

X	9-0	10-0	12-0	16-0
Y	26-0	25-0	23-6	24-0
Z	3-4	3-1	2-0	3-0
A	14-4	14-5	14-8	20-0

CUL-DE-SAC DIMENSIONS

	SMALL	LARGE
D	16'-0"	22'-0"
F	50'-11"	87'-3"
ΔA	46.71°	35.58°
ΔB	273.42°	251.15°
Ra	32'-0"	100'-0"
Rb	38'-0"	50'-0"
La	26'-1"	61'-8"
Lb	181'-4"	219'-2"

NOTE

The R values for vehicles intended to use these culs-de-sac should not exceed Rb.

CULS-DE-SAC

Mary S. Smith, P.E.; Walker Parking Consultants/Engineers, Inc.; Indianapolis, Indiana

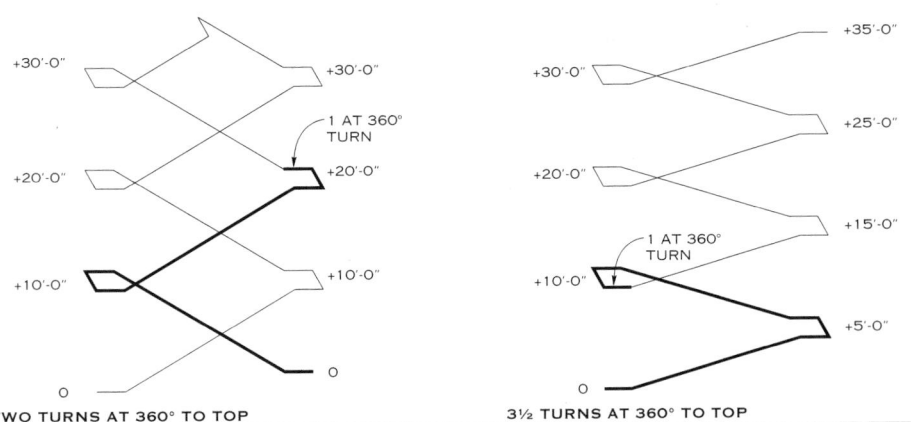

TWO TURNS AT 360° TO TOP

3½ TURNS AT 360° TO TOP

TURNS IN PATH OF TRAVEL

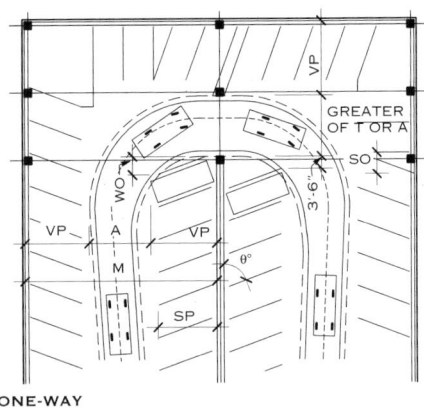

ONE-WAY

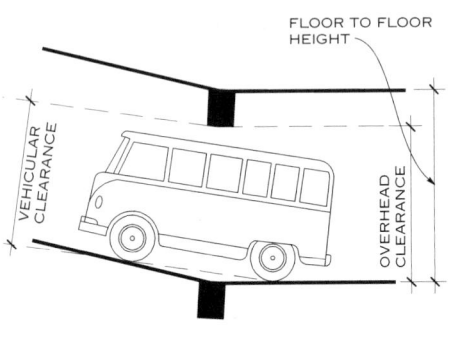

CLEARANCES FOR VEHICLES

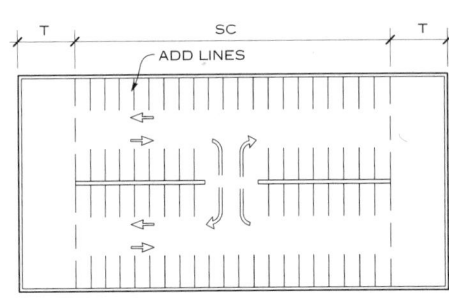

NOTE

If the bay run is greater than the "small car" dimension, provide a short circuit to help traffic flow.

SHORT CIRCUIT IN LONG BAY

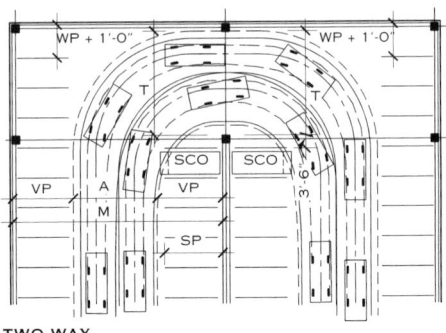

TWO-WAY

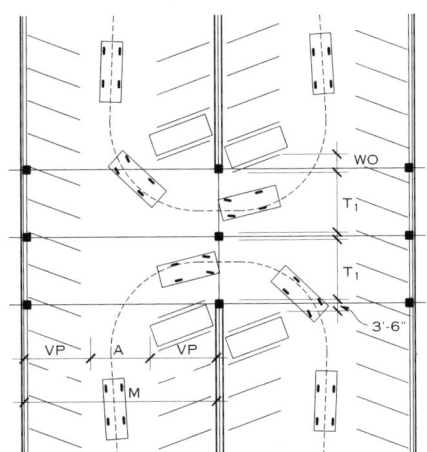

NONCONCENTRIC

TURNING BAYS

RECOMMENDED DESIGN PARAMETERS FOR WAYFINDING AND USER-FRIENDLINESS IN PARKING FACILITIES

DESIGN STANDARD FOR	LEVEL OF SERVICE (LOS)			
	D	C	B	A
Maximum walking distance				
Within parking facilities				
Surface lot	1400'-0"	1050'-0"	700'-0"	350'-0"
Structure	1200'-0"	900'-0"	600'-0"	300'-0"
From parking to destination				
Climate-controlled	5200'-0"	3800'-0"	2400'-0"	1000'-0"
Outdoors, covered	2000'-0"	1500'-0"	1000'-0"	500'-0"
Outdoors, uncovered	1600'-0"	1200'-0"	800'-0"	400'-0"
Height from floor-to-floor[1]				
Long span, posttensioned	9'-6"	10'-6"	11'-6"	12'-6"
Long span, precast	10'-6"	11'-6"	12'-6"	13'-6"
Percentage of parking spaces on flat floors	0%	30%	60%	90%
Parking ramp slope	6.5%	6%	5.5%	5%
Number of 360° turns to top	7	5.5	4	2.5
Short circuit in long run (SC)[2]	400'-0"	350'-0"	300'-0"	250'-0"
Travel distance to crossover[3]	750'-0"	600'-0"	450'-0"	300'-0"
Number of spaces searched or compartment				
Angled	1600	1200	800	400
Perpendicular	1000	750	500	250
Radius, turning (R$_T$)[4]	24'-0"	26'-0"	28'-0"	30'-0"
Turning bays, clear (T)[5]				
One lane	14'-6"	15'-9"	17'-0"	18'-3"
Two lanes, concentric[6]	26'-6"	28'-0"	29'-6"	31'-0"
Two lanes, nonconcentric	29'-0"	31'-6"	34'-0"	36'-6"

Source: Mary S. Smith, *Parking Structures: Planning, Design, Maintenance, and Repair*, 2d ed. (Chapman & Hall, 1996).

[1] Minimum vertical clearance for van accessibility is 8 ft 2 in., which requires minimum floor-to-floor heights per LOS C.

[2] A short circuit in a long run is used to shorten the exit path.

[3] In one-way designs, it is necessary to continue on the inbound travel path before connection to the outbound path.

[4] Due to lower design speeds, the turning radius in parking areas is less than that required for through-circulation elements.

[5] Clear between face of columns, curbs, or obstructions; check clearance at back of parking stalls with turning template.

[6] If flow is largely in one direction, the turning bay for a two-lane, concentric design can be reduced by 3 ft.

KEY TO DRAWINGS

ABBREVIATION	TERM
θ	Angle of park
A	Aisle width
M	Module
SC	Short circuit
SCO	Small car only space
SO	Stripe offset
SP	Stripe protection
T	Turning bay
VP	Vehicle projection
WO	Wall offset
WP	Width projection

Mary S. Smith, P.E.; Walker Parking Consultants/Engineers, Inc.; Indianapolis, Indiana

PARKING SPACE DIMENSIONS (FT-IN.)[1]

ALL LEVELS OF SERVICE

ANGLE OF PARK	VEHICLE PROJECTION	WALL OFFSET	OVERHANG	STRIPE OFFSET
45	17-1	10-7	1-9	16-3
50	17-8	9-4	1-11	13-8
55	18-1	8-2	2-1	11-5
60	18-5	7-1	2-2	9-5
65	18-7	6-0	2-3	7-7
70	18-8	4-11	2-4	5-11
75	18-7	3-10	2-5	4-4
90	17-6	1-0	2-6	0-0

LEVEL OF SERVICE A

ANGLE OF PARK	STALL PROJECTION	MODULE	AISLE	INTERLOCK
0	8-9	31-6	14-0[2]	0-0
0	8-9	42-6	25-0[3]	0-0
45	12-4	49-0	14-10	3-1
50	11-5	50-6	15-2	2-10
55	10-8	51-9	15-7	2-6
60	10-1	53-4	16-6	2-2
65	9-8	54-6	17-4	1-10
70	9-4	55-9	18-5	1-6
75	9-1	57-0	19-10	1-2
90	8-9	61-0	26-0	0-0

LEVEL OF SERVICE B

ANGLE OF PARK	STALL PROJECTION	MODULE	AISLE	INTERLOCK
0	8-6	30-0	13-0[2]	0-0
0	8-6	40-0	23-0[3]	0-0
45	12-0	48-0	13-10	3-0
50	11-1	49-6	14-2	2-9
55	10-5	50-9	14-7	2-5
60	9-10	52-4	15-6	2-2
65	9-5	53-6	16-4	1-10
70	9-1	54-9	17-5	1-5
75	8-10	56-0	18-10	1-1
90	8-6	60-0	25-0	0-0

LEVEL OF SERVICE C

ANGLE OF PARK	STALL PROJECTION	MODULE	AISLE	INTERLOCK
0	8-3	28-6	12-0[2]	0-0
0	8-3	37-6	21-0[3]	0-0
45	11-8	47-0	12-10	2-11
50	10-9	48-6	13-2	2-8
55	10-1	49-9	13-7	2-4
60	9-6	51-4	14-6	2-1
65	9-1	52-6	15-4	1-9
70	8-9	53-9	16-5	1-5
75	8-6	55-0	17-10	1-1
90	8-3	59-0	24-0	0-0

LEVEL OF SERVICE D

ANGLE OF PARK	STALL PROJECTION	MODULE	AISLE	INTERLOCK
0	8-0	27-0	11-0[2]	0-0
0	8-0	35-0	19-0[3]	0-0
45	11-4	46-0	11-10	2-10
50	10-5	47-6	12-2	2-7
55	9-9	48-9	12-7	2-4
60	9-3	50-4	13-6	2-0
65	8-10	51-6	14-4	1-8
70	8-6	52-9	15-5	1-4
75	8-3	54-0	16-10	1-0
90	8-0	58-0	23-0	0-0

[1] All dimensions are rounded to the nearest inch.

[2] These are minimum aisle widths for one-way traffic at each level of service.

[3] Figures given are widths for two-way traffic.

Mary S. Smith, P.E.; Walker Parking Consultants/Engineers, Inc.; Indianapolis, Indiana

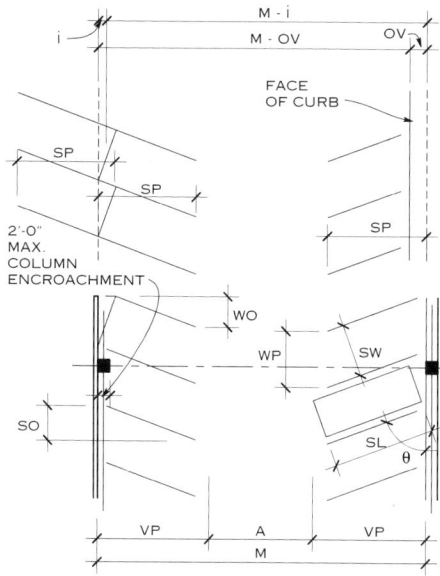

KEY

θ = angle of park	SO = stripe offset
A = aisle width	SP = stripe projection
i = interlock reduction	SW = stall width
OV = overhang	VP = vehicle projection
M = module	WO = wall offset
SL = stall length	WP = stall projection

BASIC LAYOUT DIMENSIONS

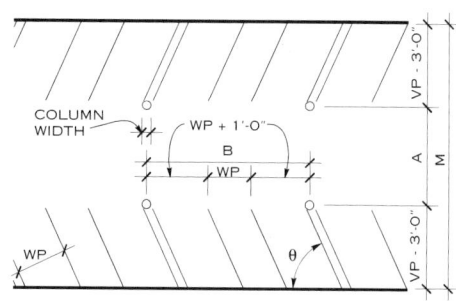

NOTE

Stalls adjacent to columns must be wider to provide the same level of service of turn.

SHORT SPAN CONSTRUCTION DETAILS

NOTES

1. Parking stalls for a design vehicle 6 ft 4 in. wide and 16 ft 9 in. long should have a stripe projection of 16 ft 3 in. and parallel stall length of 20 ft 9 in.

2. Small-car-only stalls (7 ft 5 in. wide by 15 ft long) should only be used at constrained locations or in remnants of space. The number of these stalls should not exceed 10% of total parking capacity at a site.

3. Angles between 76 and 89° are not recommended for one-way design because these angles permit drivers of smaller cars to back out and exit the wrong way.

4. Angled parking is not recommended for use with two-way aisles as drivers often attempt to make a U-turn into stalls on the other side of the aisle.

5. Add 1 ft to the module for surface parking bays without curbs or other parking guides (frequent poles or columns or walls) in areas with frequent heavy snowfall.

6. To maintain the same level of service (LOS), reduce the module (M) by 3 in. for each additional inch in stall width (SW) while maintaining minimum aisle width (see footnotes 2 and 3 to accompanying chart). For example,

    8 ft 9 in. @ 90° on 61-ft module = LOS A

    9 ft 0 in. @ 90° on 60-ft 3-in. module = LOS A

7. Columns and light poles may protrude into a parking module a combined maximum of 2 ft as long as they do not affect more than 25% of the stalls in that bay. For example, a 2-ft encroachment by a column on one side of the aisle or 1 ft each from columns on both sides is permissible.

GENERAL

The information on this page conforms to the Americans with Disabilities Act Accessibility Guidelines for Buildings and Facilities (36 CFR 1191, July 26, 1991), also known as ADAAG, and Bulletin No. 6: Parking (February 1994), both issued by the Architectural and Transportation Barriers Compliance Board. State and local requirements may differ, but ADA requires that designs conform to the higher requirement.

NOTES

1. Accessible parking stalls should be 8 ft wide with an adjacent 5-ft access aisle. No special clearance is required for these stalls.

2. Van-accessible stalls should be 8 ft wide with an adjacent 8-ft access aisle accessible from the passenger side of the vehicle. (Backing into 90° stalls from a two-way aisle is an acceptable method of achieving this.) Vehicular clearance along the path of travel to and from a van-accessible stall should be 8 ft 2 in. In parking structures, van-accessible stalls may be grouped on a single level.

3. It is permissible for all required accessible stalls to conform with Universal Parking Design guidelines. Because in this arrangement, vans may use any accessible stall, universal stalls must have 8 ft 2 in. vehicle clearance.

4. Access aisles should be delineated separately from parking spaces. Access aisles must be at the same level as parking stalls (not above, at sidewalk height). Required curb ramps should not be located in access aisles. Two spaces may share a single access aisle (except when van stalls require passenger-side access in one-way designs).

5. Parking spaces and access aisles should be level with surface slopes not exceeding 1:50 (2%) in any direction.

6. The stalls required for a specific facility may be relocated to another location if equivalent or greater accessibility in terms of distance, cost, and convenience is ensured.

7. Accessible stalls in the numbers shown in the accompanying table must be included in parking facilities leased or 100% reserved for employees. However, they need not be reserved for accessible parking (i.e., they need not be marked with signs) until or unless an employee with a disability needs the stall in that location.

8. Provide an accessible route from accessible parking stalls to the destination. This should make it possible for persons in wheelchairs to travel without rolling down parking aisles past more than one parked vehicle (other than their own). Crossing a parking aisle at 90° is preferable to rolling down a parking aisle.

9. Signs should be provided at accessible stalls to reserve the spaces for individuals with disabilities; pavement markings alone are not acceptable. Signs need not be provided for every accessible stall if they clearly delineate the accessible parking spaces.

REQUIRED MINIMUM NUMBER OF ACCESSIBLE PARKING SPACES

TOTAL PARKING SPACES IN LOT	TOTAL ACCESSIBLE SPACES REQUIRED	VAN-ACCESSIBLE SPACES
1–25	1	1
26–50	2	1
51–75	3	1
76–100	4	1
101–150	5	1
151–200	6	1
201–300	7	1
301–400	8	2
401–500	9	2
501–1000	2% of total	1 for every 8 accessible spaces
1001 and over	20 plus 1 for each 100 spaces over 1000	1 for every 8 accessible spaces

NOTES

1. At facilities providing outpatient medical care and other services, 10% of the parking spaces serving visitors and patients must be accessible.

2. At facilities specializing in treatment or services for persons with mobility impairments, 20% of the spaces provided for visitors and patients must be accessible.

3. The information in this table does not apply to valet parking facilities, but such facilities must have an accessible loading zone. One or more self-park van-accessible stalls is recommended for patrons with specially equipped driving controls.

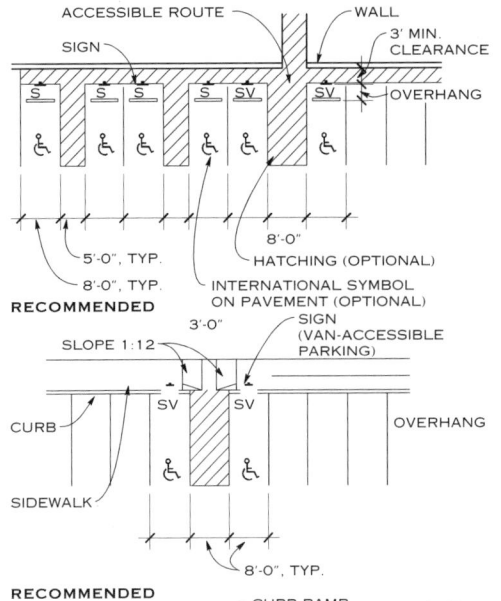

RECOMMENDED

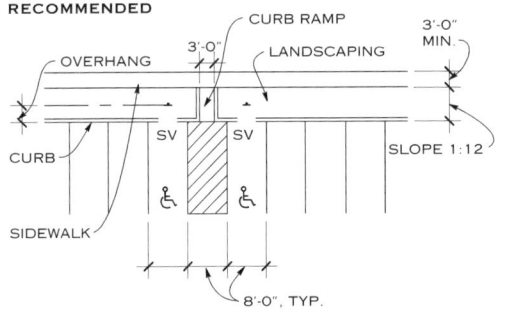

RECOMMENDED

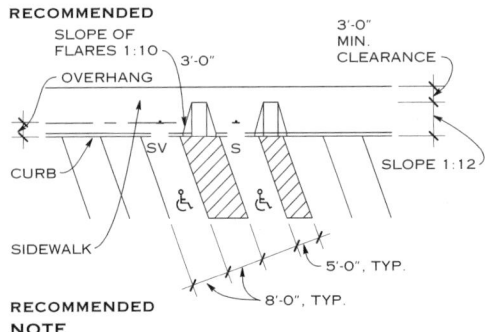

RECOMMENDED

RECOMMENDED

NOTE
S—accessible parking sign; SV—van-accessible parking sign.

ACCESSIBLE PARKING LAYOUTS

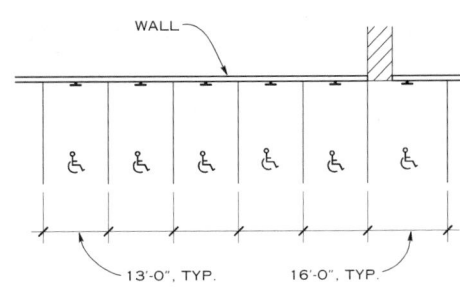

NONCOMPLIANT (ACCESS AISLE NOT MARKED)

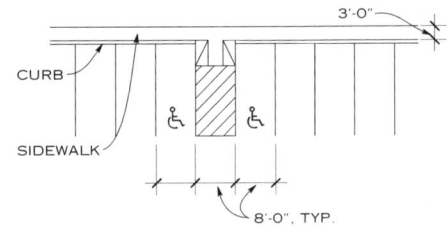

NONCOMPLIANT (RAMP IN ACCESS AISLE)

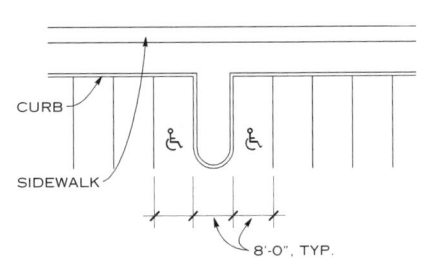

NONCOMPLIANT (ACCESS AISLE NOT AT SAME LEVEL AS STALL)

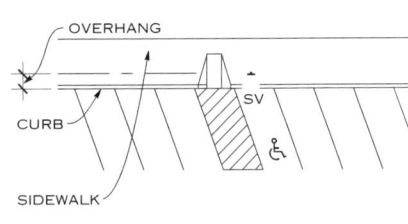

NONCOMPLIANT (ACCESS AISLE ON WRONG SIDE FOR VAN)

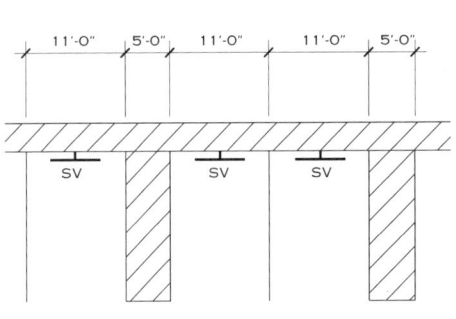

NOTE
SV—van-accessible parking sign. (All universal spaces are van-accessible.)

UNIVERSAL PARKING DESIGN

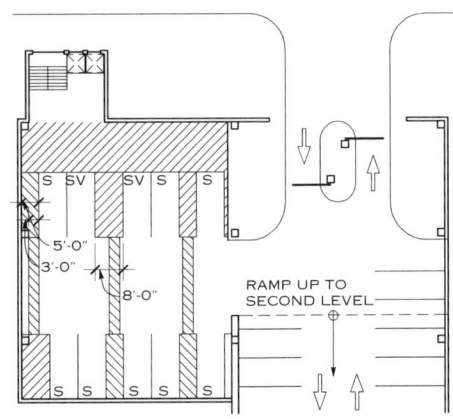

ACCESSIBLE PARKING IN DEDICATED BAY

Mary S. Smith, P.E.; Walker Parking Consultants/Engineers, Inc.; Indianapolis, Indiana

1 AUTOMOBILES, ROADS, AND PARKING

GENERAL

ADAAG (Americans with Disabilities Act Accessibility Guidelines for Buildings and Facilities, 36 CFR 1191, July 26, 1991) requires all cashier booths in new construction (and in alterations that result in the removal of existing islands) to be accessible "to and through" the door. This mandate is found under the requirements for employee work areas or stations. A booth can meet this requirement if it is recessed in the pavement so the interior floor is at the same elevation as the driving lane. An accessible cashier booth can also have a curb ramp and appropriate latch-side clearance for the rear swinging door.

ADAAG recommends—but does not require—that at least one booth be a fully accessible workstation (have a 5-ft diameter wheelchair turning space, adjustable counter, accessible controls, etc.). A booth can meet this requirement with accessible doors on both sides, which allows T turning movements.

KEY TO DRAWINGS

TERM	ABBREVIATION	SYMBOL
Autogate	AG	
Ticket dispenser	TD	
Card reader	CR	
"Lot full" sign	LFS	
Detector loop	—	
Bollard	—	

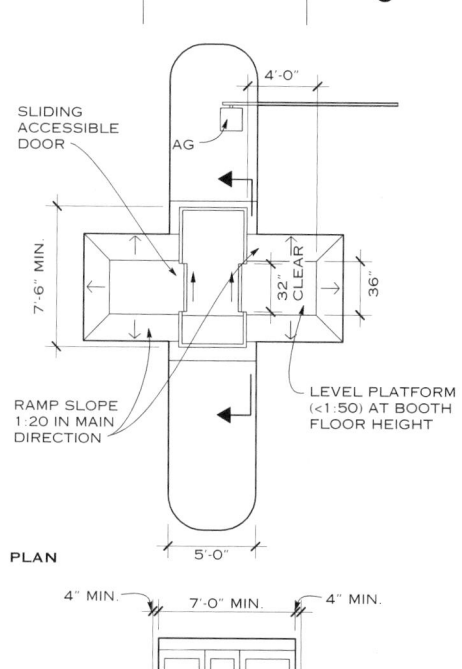

PLAN

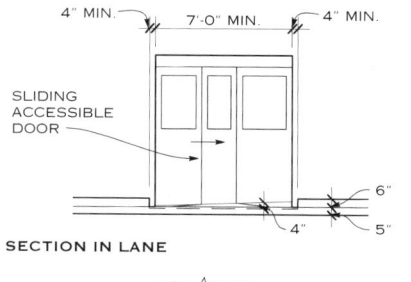

SECTION IN LANE

SECTION AT BOOTH

EXIT WITH ACCESSIBLE CASHIER BOOTH

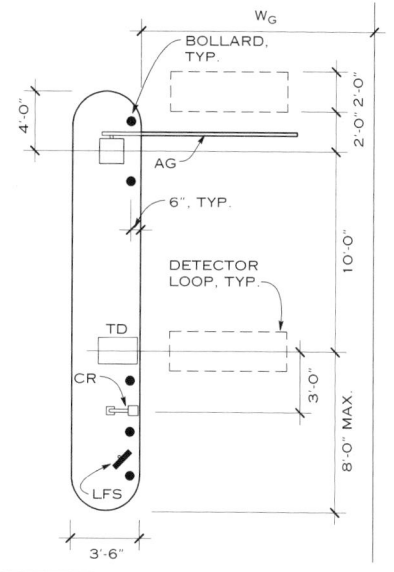

ENTRANCE WITH TICKET DISPENSER

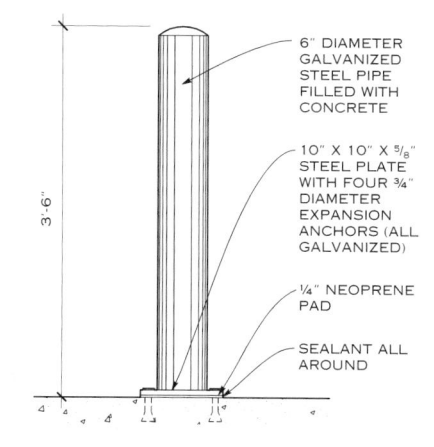

NOTE
Place bollards so they are plumb.

PIPE BOLLARD

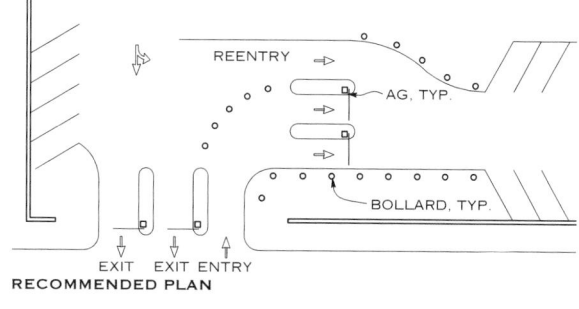

RECOMMENDED PLAN

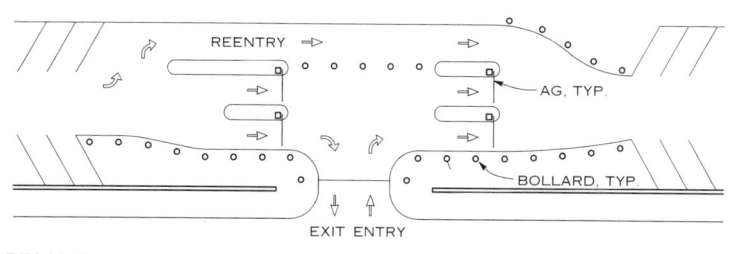

RECOMMENDED PLAN

PARKING LOT ENTRY CONFIGURATIONS

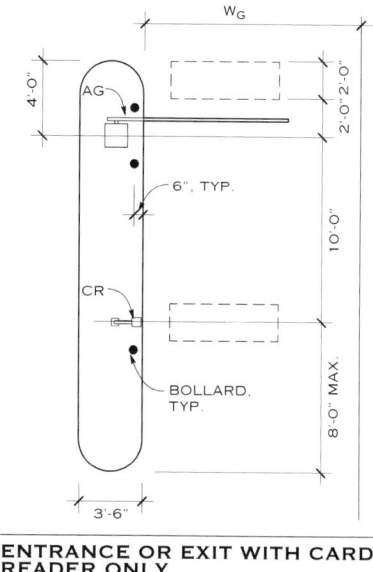

ENTRANCE OR EXIT WITH CARD READER ONLY

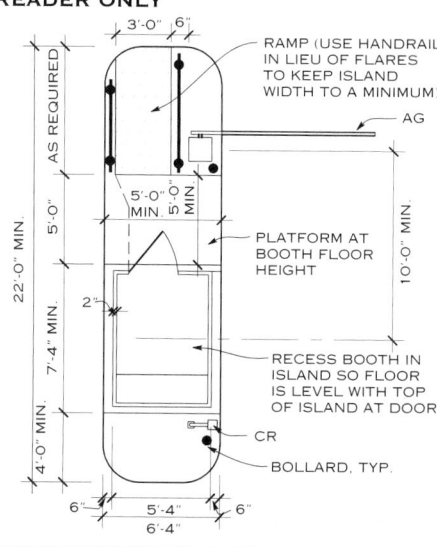

EXIT WITH ACCESSIBLE CASHIER BOOTH AND CARD READER

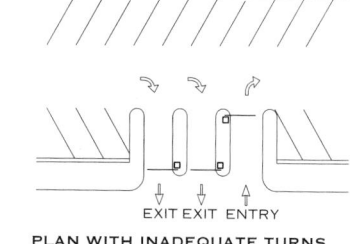

PLAN WITH INADEQUATE TURNS

Mary S. Smith, P.E.; Walker Parking Consultants/Engineers, Inc.; Indianapolis, Indiana

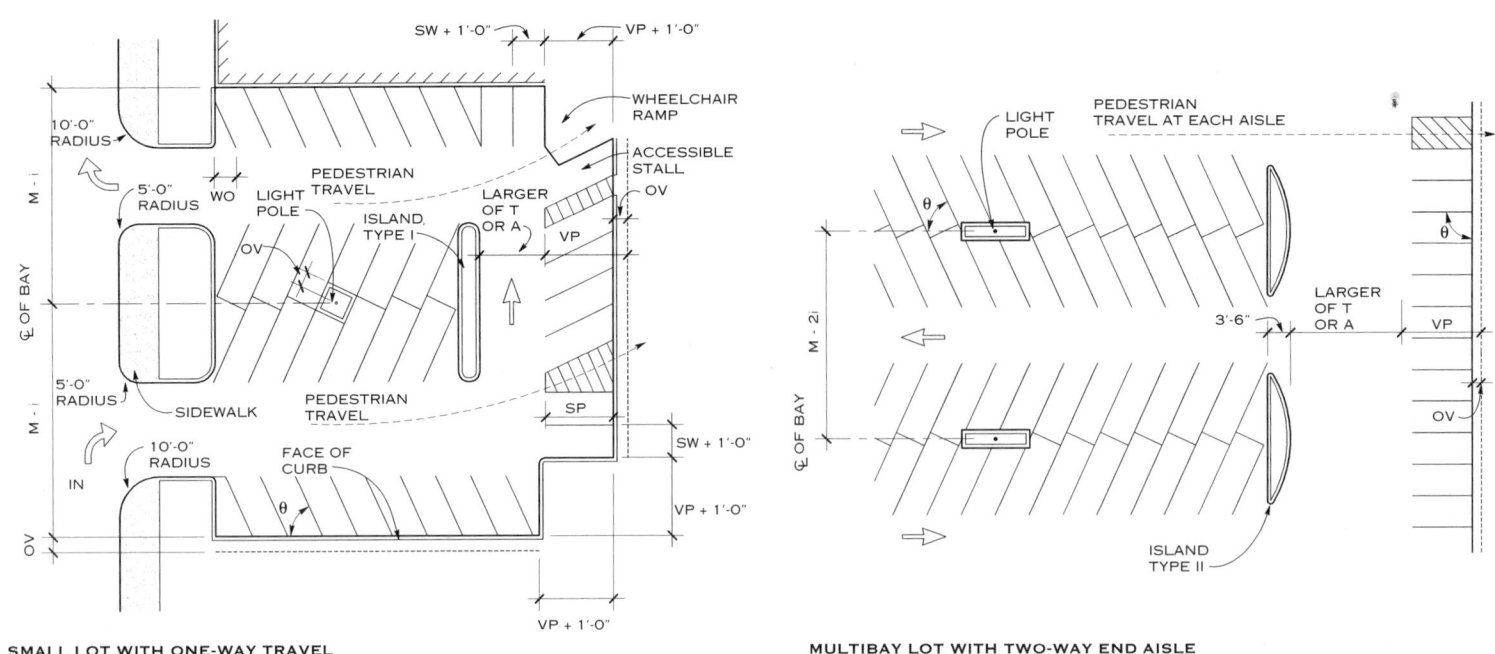

SMALL LOT WITH ONE-WAY TRAVEL

MULTIBAY LOT WITH TWO-WAY END AISLE

LOT DESIGNS WITH ISLANDS

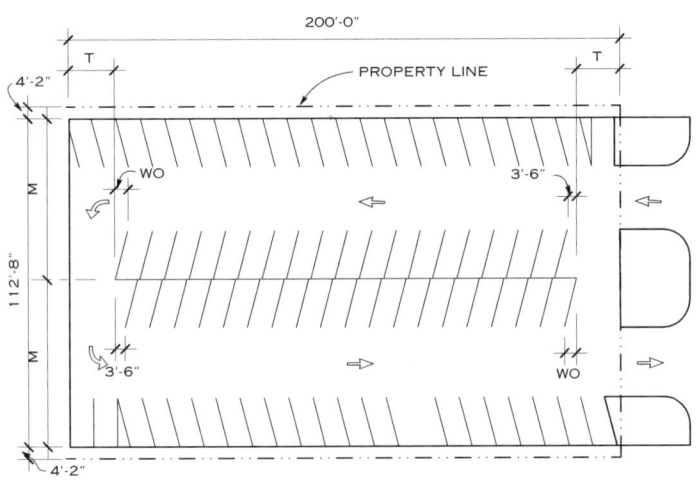

ANGLED PARKING

NOTES

1. GPA = 200 ft x 56.33 ft x 2 = 22,532 sq ft
2. Capacity = 80 vehicles
3. Efficiency = 22,532 sq ft/80 vehicles = 281.7 sq ft/space

90° PARKING

NOTES

1. GPA = 200 ft x 60.5 ft x 2 = 24,200 sq ft
2. Capacity = 80 vehicles
3. Efficiency = 24,200 sq ft/80 vehicles = 302.5 sq ft/space

SMALL LOT DESIGNS

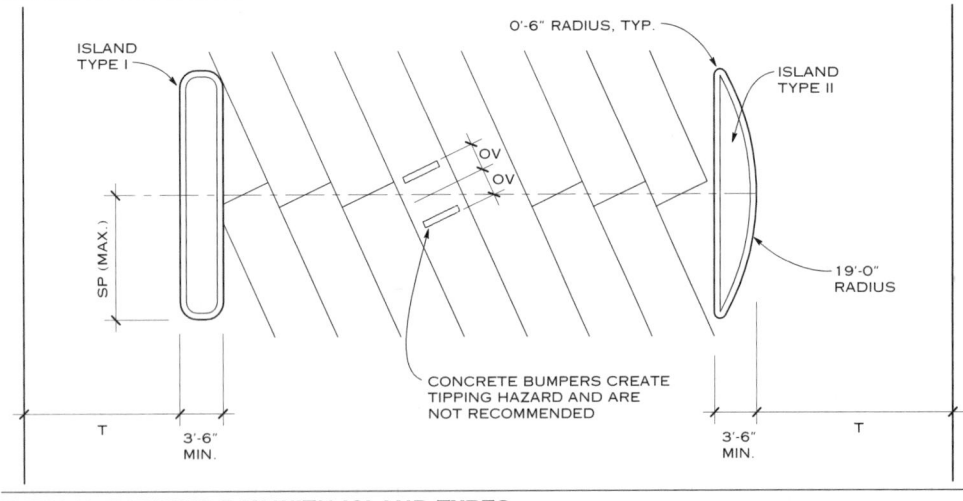

TYPICAL PARKING BAY WITH ISLAND TYPES

KEY TO DRAWINGS

ABBREVIATION	TERM
θ	Angle of park
A	Aisle width
i	Interlock reduction
GPA	Gross parking area
M	Module
OV	Overhang
R	Radius
SP	Stripe protection
SW	Stall width
T	Turning bay
VP	Vehicle projection
WO	Wall offset

Mary S. Smith, P.E.; Walker Parking Consultants/Engineers, Inc.; Indianapolis, Indiana

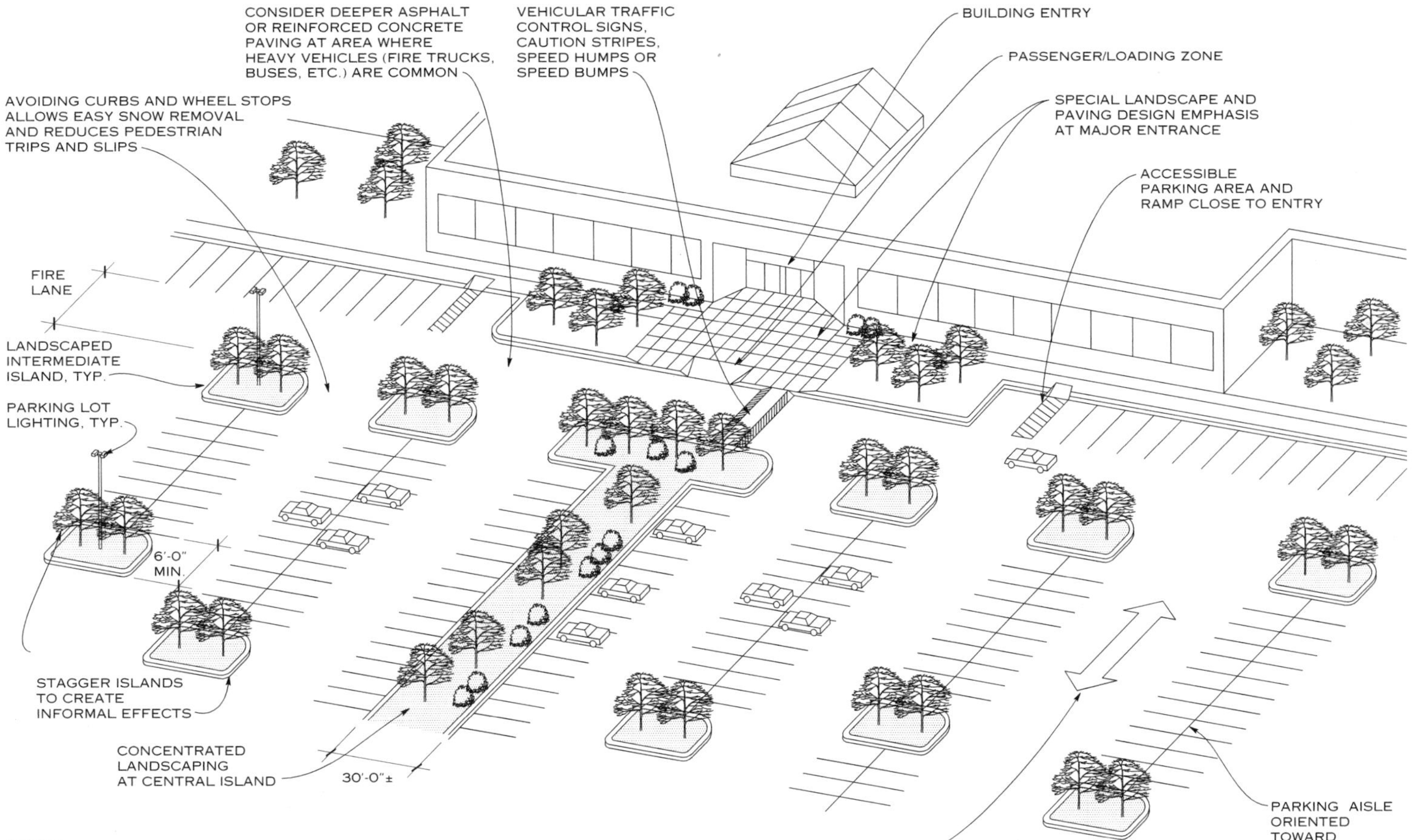

CONSIDER DEEPER ASPHALT OR REINFORCED CONCRETE PAVING AT AREA WHERE HEAVY VEHICLES (FIRE TRUCKS, BUSES, ETC.) ARE COMMON

VEHICULAR TRAFFIC CONTROL SIGNS, CAUTION STRIPES, SPEED HUMPS OR SPEED BUMPS

BUILDING ENTRY

PASSENGER/LOADING ZONE

SPECIAL LANDSCAPE AND PAVING DESIGN EMPHASIS AT MAJOR ENTRANCE

ACCESSIBLE PARKING AREA AND RAMP CLOSE TO ENTRY

AVOIDING CURBS AND WHEEL STOPS ALLOWS EASY SNOW REMOVAL AND REDUCES PEDESTRIAN TRIPS AND SLIPS

FIRE LANE

LANDSCAPED INTERMEDIATE ISLAND, TYP.

PARKING LOT LIGHTING, TYP.

6'-0" MIN.

STAGGER ISLANDS TO CREATE INFORMAL EFFECTS

CONCENTRATED LANDSCAPING AT CENTRAL ISLAND

30'-0"±

PARKING AISLE ORIENTED TOWARD DESTINATION (BUILDING ENTRY)

TRAFFIC FLOW

NOTE

Confirm requirements for fire lanes adjacent to buildings. Consult local codes.

COMMERCIAL PARKING ARRANGEMENT

NOTES ON DESIGN GUIDELINES

1. Determine an efficient means of laying out the parking lot (see vehicle and parking space dimension data on other AGS pages on parking). A smaller paved area costs less to build and maintain, offers a shorter walking distance from car to building, lessens water runoff problems, and leaves more space for site landscaping.

2. Provide safe and coherent site circulation routes.

3. Provide access for fire rescue and mass transit vehicles. Consult local requirements.

4. Parking lots should offer direct and easy access for people walking between their vehicles and the building entrances. Pedestrians usually walk in the aisles behind parked vehicles; aisles perpendicular to the building face allow pedestrians to walk to and from the building without squeezing between parked cars. Walking areas should be graded to prevent standing water.

5. Accessible design is now mandatory, requiring designated parking spaces and curb ramps near building entrances. See AGS page on accessible curb ramps and passenger loading.

LANDSCAPING

Plants in parking areas can help relieve the visually overwhelming scale of large parking lots. To maximize the effect of landscaping, consider the screening capabilities of plants. Low branching, densely foliated trees and shrubs can soften the visual impact of large parking areas. High branching canopy trees do not create a visual screen at eye level but do provide shade. When possible, create islands large enough to accommodate a mixture of canopy trees, flowering trees, evergreen trees, shrubs, and flowers. Consider using evergreens, and avoid plants that drop fruit or sap.

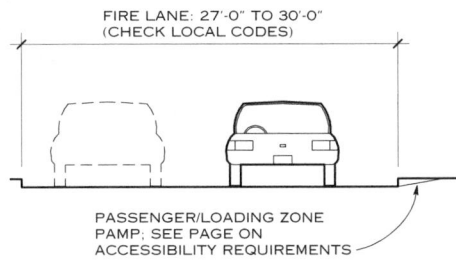

FIRE LANE: 27'-0" TO 30'-0" (CHECK LOCAL CODES)

PASSENGER/LOADING ZONE RAMP; SEE PAGE ON ACCESSIBILITY REQUIREMENTS

FIRE LANE

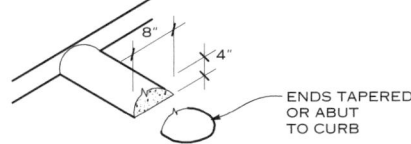

8"

4"

ENDS TAPERED OR ABUT TO CURB

SPEED BUMP

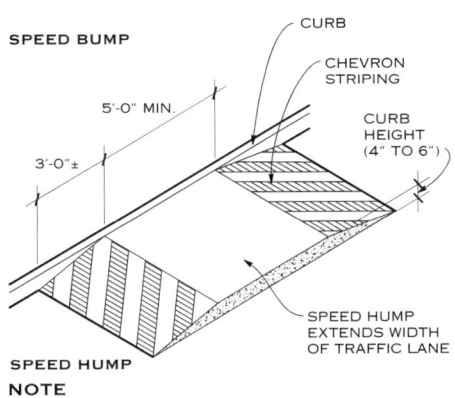

CURB

CHEVRON STRIPING

CURB HEIGHT (4" TO 6")

5'-0" MIN.

3'-0"±

SPEED HUMP EXTENDS WIDTH OF TRAFFIC LANE

SPEED HUMP

NOTE

Use of a speed hump eliminates the need for an accessible curb ramp.

SPEED CONTROL DEVICES

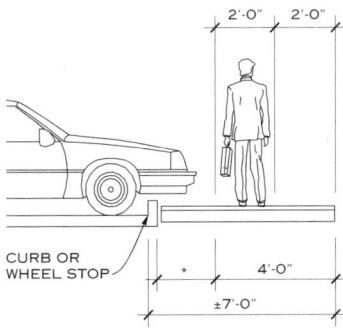

2'-0"   2'-0"

CURB OR WHEEL STOP

4'-0"

*

±7'-0"

AT SIDEWALKS

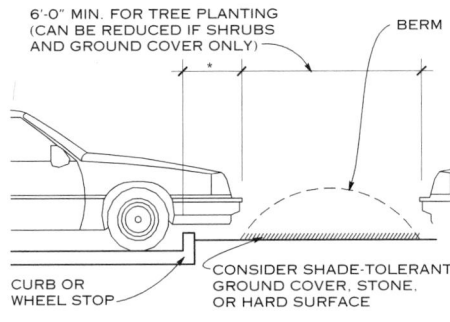

6'-0" MIN. FOR TREE PLANTING (CAN BE REDUCED IF SHRUBS AND GROUND COVER ONLY)

BERM

*

CURB OR WHEEL STOP

CONSIDER SHADE-TOLERANT GROUND COVER, STONE, OR HARD SURFACE

AT PLANTING AREAS AND BERMS

*See the AGS pages on design vehicle dimensions for perpendicular dimension of overhang; adjust for angled parking.

AUTOMOBILE OVERHANG REQUIREMENTS

Mary S. Smith, P.E.; Walker Parking Consultants/Engineers, Inc.; Indianapolis, Indiana

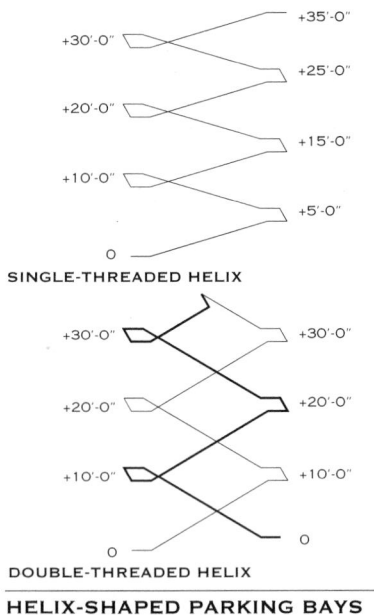

SINGLE-THREADED HELIX

DOUBLE-THREADED HELIX

HELIX-SHAPED PARKING BAYS

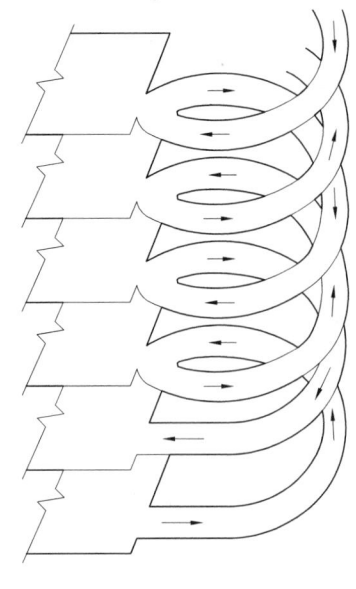

DOUBLE-THREADED CIRCULAR HELIX

NOTES

1. Floor-to-floor circulation in a parking structure is typically provided either by parking ramps or express ramps (those without parking) or a combination of both.

2. Almost all ramp systems are based on helical patterns, whether a fully circular express helix or a combination of straight runs and turning bays at the end.

3. The two fundamental helical patterns are the single-threaded helix, which rises one full floor in each 360° of revolution, and the double-threaded helix, which rises two floors with each complete revolution.

4. Express helices can be either single threaded or double threaded. Parking ramps can also be configured in single- and double-threaded patterns.

5. On a site that can accommodate two parking modules in width but is short (less than 200 ft), a single-threaded helix can be used only with two-way traffic flow and 90° parking.

6. Application of a two-bay single-threaded helix arrangement may be limited by the desirable number of turns, spaces passed, etc. of the selected level of service and/or by flow capacity considerations.

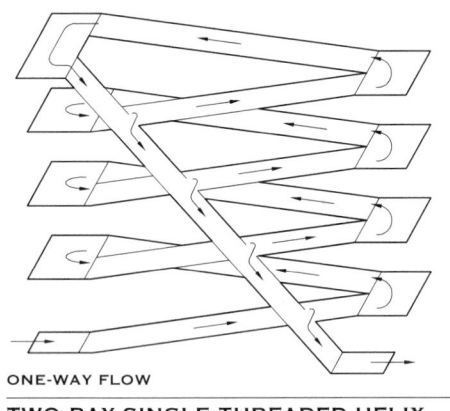

ONE-WAY FLOW

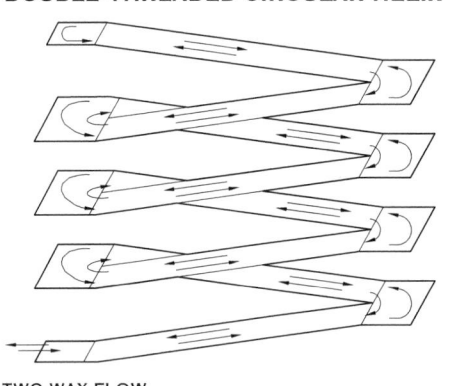

TWO-WAY FLOW

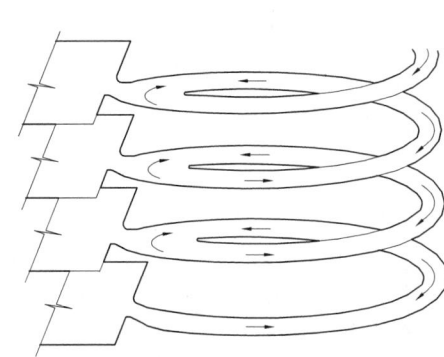

CIRCULAR FLOW

TWO-BAY SINGLE-THREADED HELIX

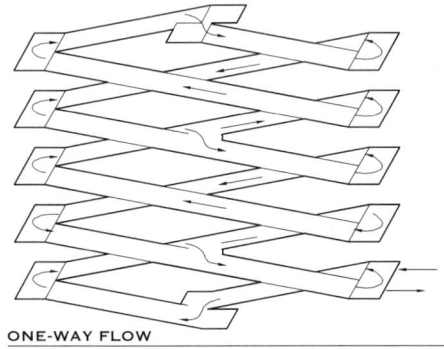

ONE-WAY FLOW

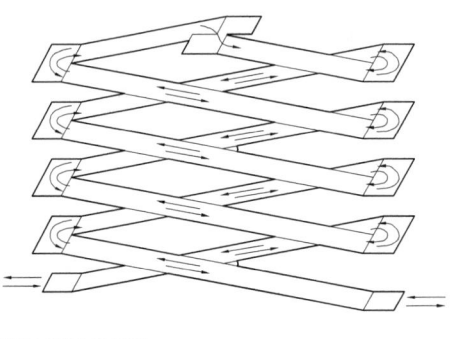

TWO-WAY FLOW

NOTES

1. The two-bay double-threaded helix can be taller and accommodate more spaces than the two-bay single-threaded model; however, it requires a longer site (typically more than 200 ft in length). Because this design may offer less desirable wayfinding and user-friendliness to unfamiliar users, it is most often used for predominantly employee parking.

2. A two-bay double-threaded helix may have either one-way or two-way traffic flow. The former has one up and one down route, while the latter provides two up routes and two down ones.

TWO-BAY DOUBLE-THREADED HELIX

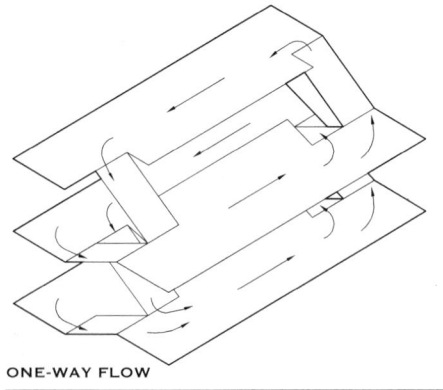

ONE-WAY FLOW

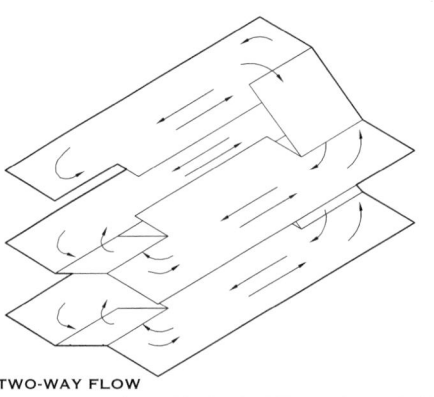

TWO-WAY FLOW

NOTES

1. The split-level design is a modification of the single-threaded helix in which the parking bays are flattened and speed ramps are used to accomplish a vertical rise. Split-level parking structures may have either two-way or one-way traffic flow.

2. Although they provide a level facade, split-level parking structures have a number of disadvantages. The main ones are loss of stalls (compared to a typical two-bay single-threaded helix), difficult design for turns and speed ramp, and poor efficiency (the square footage of parking area per stall is too high).

SPLIT LEVEL

Mary S. Smith, P.E., Walker Parking Consultants/Engineers, Inc.; Indianapolis, Indiana
William T. Mahan, AIA; Santa Barbara, California

1 AUTOMOBILES, ROADS, AND PARKING

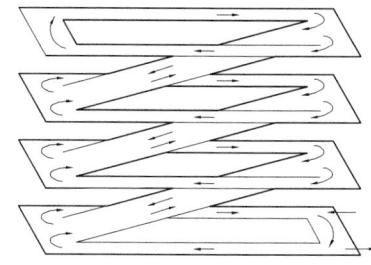

THREE-BAY SIDE-BY-SIDE

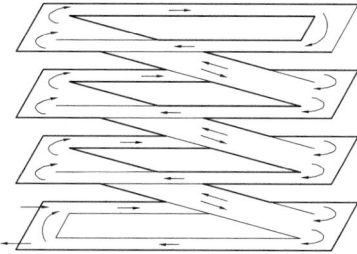

FOUR-BAY SIDE-BY-SIDE

NOTES

1. On wider sites, a combination of sloped parking bays and flat bays in single-threaded patterns can provide level facades with superior wayfinding and user-friendliness. These facilities may be limited primarily by height (too much height yields an excessive number of turns) or flow capacity (the number of spaces passed on the path of travel).

2. On longer sites, single-threaded helices can be combined in a camelback helix to provide one-way traffic flow. This one-way flow offers better wayfinding for unfamiliar users than a double-threaded helix. However, because there are more turning bays, the efficiency (sq ft/parking space) of the garage will be affected.

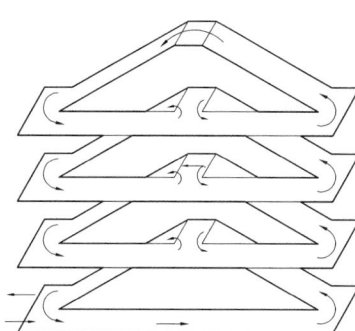

END-TO-END

CAMELBACK

SINGLE-THREADED HELIX COMBINATIONS

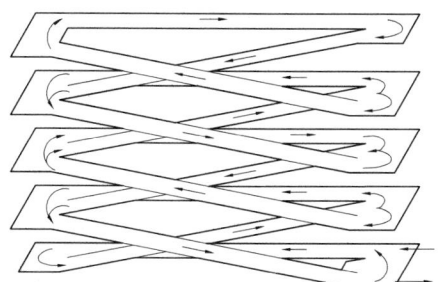

THREE-BAY DOUBLE-THREADED HELIX

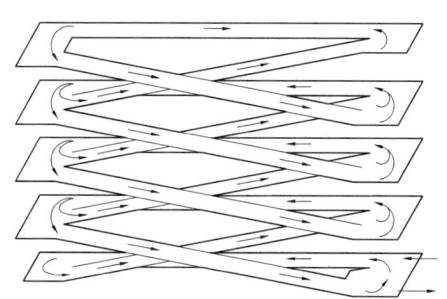

THREE-BAY SINGLE-THREADED
INTERLOCKED HELIX

NOTES

1. Traffic can be routed in either a single-threaded or double-threaded pattern on the same configuration of flat and sloped parking bays.

2. The three-bay double-threaded helix option provides quicker vertical circulation and better flow capacity. However, because the flow is different on every other floor, making it confusing for unfamiliar users, this design works best for employee parking.

3. The interlocked helix offers better wayfinding (because it has the same flow pattern on every floor) but reduced flow capacity. The flow capacity is especially low during periods of high turnover because inbound and outbound traffic must merge at every floor.

COMBINATION SLOPED AND FLAT BAYS

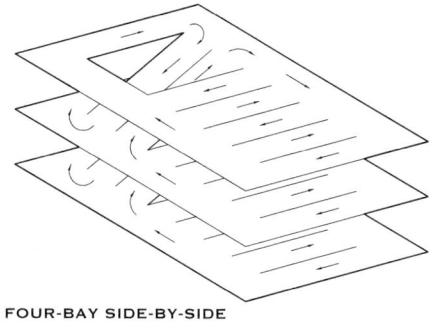

FOUR-BAY SIDE-BY-SIDE
WITH SIDE FLAT BAYS

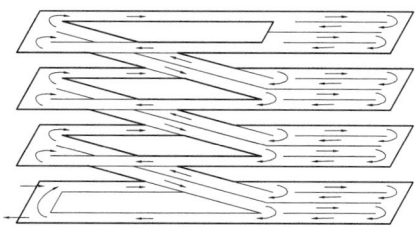

FOUR-BAY SIDE-BY-SIDE
HELIX WITH END FLAT BAYS

NOTES

1. As a parking structure footprint becomes wider, it is generally preferable to add flat parking bays and keep the floor-to-floor circulation at the far end of the structure. Similarly, when a parking structure is longer than needed for floor-to-floor circulation, keep the ramps at one end and add flat areas close to the ultimate destination of those using the facility.

2. Totally flat floor parking combined with express ramps yields the best combination of wayfinding, user-friendliness, and security. Express ramps may be designed to require traffic to circulate through the floors or to allow vehicles to pass directly from floor to floor. The latter arrangement provides the greatest flow capacity and ease of access in very large structures (those with more than 2000 parking spaces).

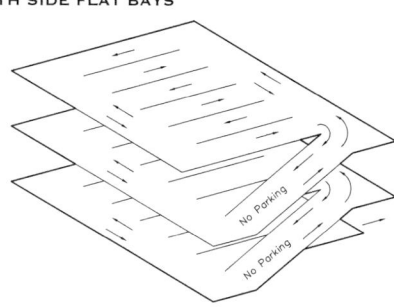

SINGLE-THREADED EXTERIOR EXPRESS RAMPS

FLAT FLOOR WITH EXPRESS RAMP

FLAT FLOOR PARKING

Mary S. Smith, P.E.; Walker Parking Consultants/Engineers, Inc.; Indianapolis, Indiana

AUTOMOBILES, ROADS, AND PARKING

1

DESIGN VEHICLE DIMENSIONS

VEHICLE TYPE	LENGTH (L)	WIDTH (W)	HEIGHT (H)	WHEELBASE (WB)	OVERHANG FRONT (OF)	OVERHANG REAR (OR)	GROSS WEIGHT
Trash truck	25'-5"	7'-11"	10'-0"	13'-2"	4'-8"	7'-7"	20,000 lb
Single unit truck*	30'-0"	8'-6"		20'	4'-0"	6'-0"	20,000 lb
WB-40 truck*	50'-0"	8'-6"	see table below	13'/23'/4'	4'-0"	6'-0"	80,000 lb
WB-50 truck*	60'-0"	8'-6"		16'/4'/26'/4	3'-0"	2'-0"	80,000 lb
WB-60 truck*	65'-0"	8'-6"		10'/20'/10'/18'	2'-0"	5'-0"	80,000 lb

*Generally in conformance with AASHTO, *A Policy on Geometric Design of Highways and Streets* (1990).

MAXIMUM ALLOWABLE HEIGHT AND WIDTH (FT-IN.)

VEHICLE HEIGHT		VEHICLE WIDTH	
TOTAL HEIGHT	STATE	TOTAL WIDTH	STATE
13-6	In all states except those listed below	8-6	In all states except those listed below
13-0	CO	8-0	DC, GA, IL, KY, LA, MI, MD, MO, NC, PA, WV
14-0	AK, CA, HI, ID, KS, MT, NM, NV, ND, OR, UT, WA, WY		
14-6	NB	9-0	HI

NOTE

Width is 8 ft 0 in. or 8 ft 6 in. according to state regulations.

Length and area restrictions vary by state and locale. Verify exact dimensions and restrictions.

MINIMUM TURNING RADIUS FOR DESIGN VEHICLES (FT-IN.)

VEHICLE TYPE	MIN. TURNING RADIUS (R_T)	OUTSIDE FRONT RADIUS (R_O)	INSIDE REAR RADIUS (R_I)	STRAIGHT LANE WIDTH (W_S)	CURVED LANE WIDTH (W_T)	INSIDE CURB RADIUS (R_C)	TANGENT LENGTH (T)
Trash truck	31-0	33-1	21-2	12-0	14-11	18-4	38-0
Single unit truck	42-0	44-0	28-0	12-0	20-0	25-0	40-10
WB-40 truck	40-0	41-6	19-0	12-0	25-0	16-0	67-1
WB-50 truck	45-0	46-0	19-0	12-0	30-0	16-0	116-8
WB-60 truck	45-0	45-6	22-0	12-0	27-0	19-0	65-0

NOTES

1. Minimum turn radii at less than 10 mph.
2. Obstructions (columns, walls, light poles, etc.) should be held a minimum of 6 in. (2 ft preferred) from the edge of the lane given above. See details on the AGS page on driveways and roadways.

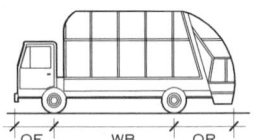

TRASH TRUCK

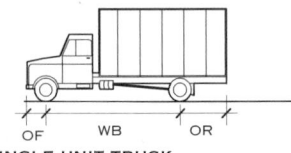

SINGLE-UNIT TRUCK

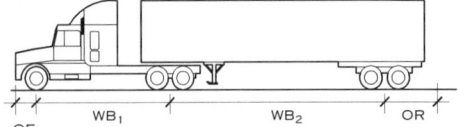

TRACTOR AND SEMITRAILER

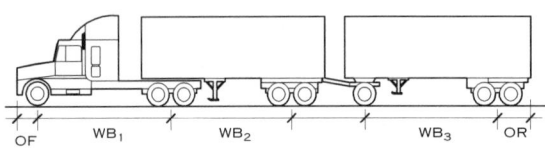

TRACTOR AND DOUBLE SEMITRAILER

TRUCK TYPES

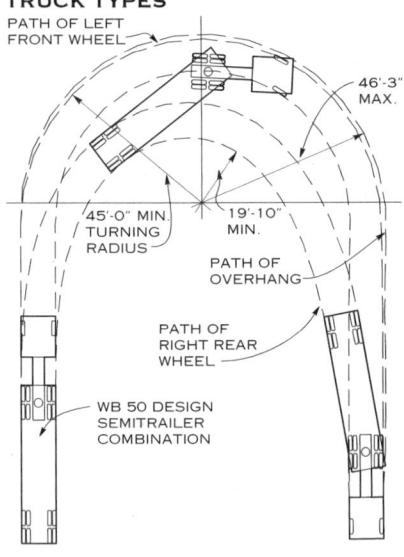

PATH OF LEFT FRONT WHEEL

46'-3" MAX.

45'-0" MIN. TURNING RADIUS

19'-10" MIN.

PATH OF OVERHANG

PATH OF RIGHT REAR WHEEL

WB 50 DESIGN SEMITRAILER COMBINATION

WB-50 SEMITRAILER DESIGN VEHICLE

PATH OF LEFT FRONT WHEEL

43'-11" MIN.

42'-0" MIN. TURNING RADIUS

28'-5" MIN.

PATH OF OVERHANG

PATH OF RIGHT REAR WHEEL

SINGLE-UNIT TRUCK DESIGN VEHICLE

TURNING RADIUS

MAXIMUM ALLOWABLE LENGTH (FT-IN.)

SEMITRAILER AND TRACTOR

UNIT	EACH TRAILER	STATE
55-0	48-0	DC
60-0	45-0	HI
60-0	53-0	DE, GA
60-0	—	MO, NC, OR, WV
65-0	48-0	ME, NY, VT, WI
65-0	53-0	IL, KY
65-0	—	CA, LA, NM, VA
70-0	57-4	CO
75-0	48-0	ID
75-0	53-0	AK, MN, ND
92-0	53-0	UT
—	48-0	CT, FL, MA, NV
—	48-6	RI
—	50-0	MI, MS, TN
—	53-0	MD, MS, MT, NB, NH, NJ, IN, IA, OH, OK, PA, SC, SD, WA
—	53-6	AR
—	57-6	AZ
—	59-0	TX
—	59-6	KS
—	60-0	WY

DOUBLE SEMITRAILER AND TRACTOR

UNIT	EACH TRAILER	STATE
59-0	28-6	MI
60-0	29-0	DE
61-0	—	UT, WA
65-0	28-0	MD, MO
65-0	28-6	AR, IL
65-0	—	NB, NM, NY
70-0	28-0	OK
70-0	28-6	CO
75-0	28-0	ND, ID
75-0	28-6	CA, MN
75-0	—	AK, OR
80-0	28-6	SD
—	28-0	CT, DC, FL, GA, MA, NH, NJ
—	28-6	AZ, IN, IA, KS, MT, NV, OH, RI
—	30-0	MS
—	—	WY

STRAIGHT BODY TRUCKS

UNIT	STATE
40-0	In all states, except those listed below
35-0	NC[1], SC[1]
42-0	IL
42-6	KS
45-0	CT, HI, ID, KY, OK, ME, SD, TX, UT
50-0	ND
55-0	MT
60-0	GA, WY
65-0	VT

TRIPLE SEMITRAILER AND TRACTOR[2]

UNIT	STATE
75-0	ID
85-0	AK
Each trailer 28-0	MO
Each trailer 28-6	AZ, CO, OH, MT, IN, SD
Each trailer 29-0	OK
105-0	OR, UT
110-0	ND
119-0	KS

[1] Two axles—35 ft; three axles—40 ft
[2] Maximum allowable length not permitted, except in those states listed.

William T. Mahan, AIA; Santa Barbara, California
Mary S. Smith, P.E.; Walker Parking Consultants/Engineers, Inc.; Indianapolis, Indiana

1   TRUCKS, TRAINS, AND BOATS

GENERAL

Embankment stabilization is required when steep slopes are subject to erosion from stormwater runoff or flowing streams. Erosion can damage the site and pollute waterways with sediment.

The need for mechanical stabilization can be reduced through careful site gradings that divert or slow the velocity of runoff. Avoid disturbing stable, natural stream banks. Check with regulatory agencies before planning to grade stream banks, wetlands, or floodplains.

Numerous proprietary products are available for stream bank stabilization and erosion control; consult manufacturers.

NOTES

1. Control erosion during construction with silt fences, straw bales, sediment ponds, and seeding and mulching. Follow local and state guidelines and regulations.
2. Line channels with erosion-resistant material (sod, stone riprap, erosion-control blanket). Channel dimensions and lining should be designed for expected runoff.
3. At the bottom of the slope drain channel, the flow should be conveyed to a storm sewer, detention pond, constructed wetland, or other control method that meets regulations.

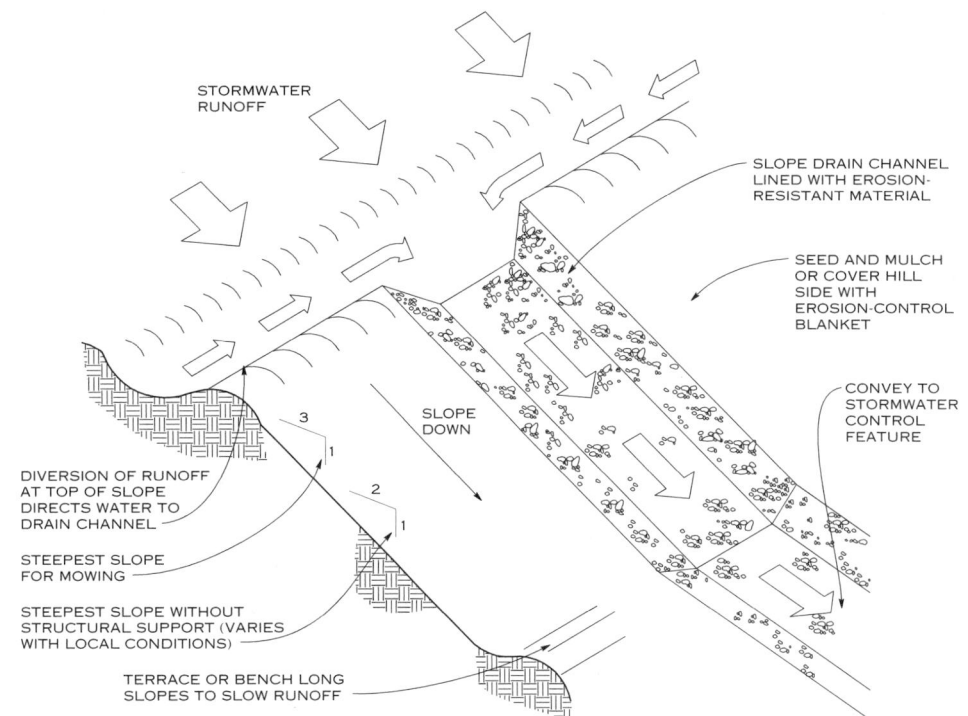

STORMWATER RUNOFF

SLOPE DRAIN CHANNEL LINED WITH EROSION-RESISTANT MATERIAL

SEED AND MULCH OR COVER HILL SIDE WITH EROSION-CONTROL BLANKET

CONVEY TO STORMWATER CONTROL FEATURE

SLOPE DOWN

3 1
2 1

DIVERSION OF RUNOFF AT TOP OF SLOPE DIRECTS WATER TO DRAIN CHANNEL

STEEPEST SLOPE FOR MOWING

STEEPEST SLOPE WITHOUT STRUCTURAL SUPPORT (VARIES WITH LOCAL CONDITIONS)

TERRACE OR BENCH LONG SLOPES TO SLOW RUNOFF

GRADING AND EROSION CONTROL

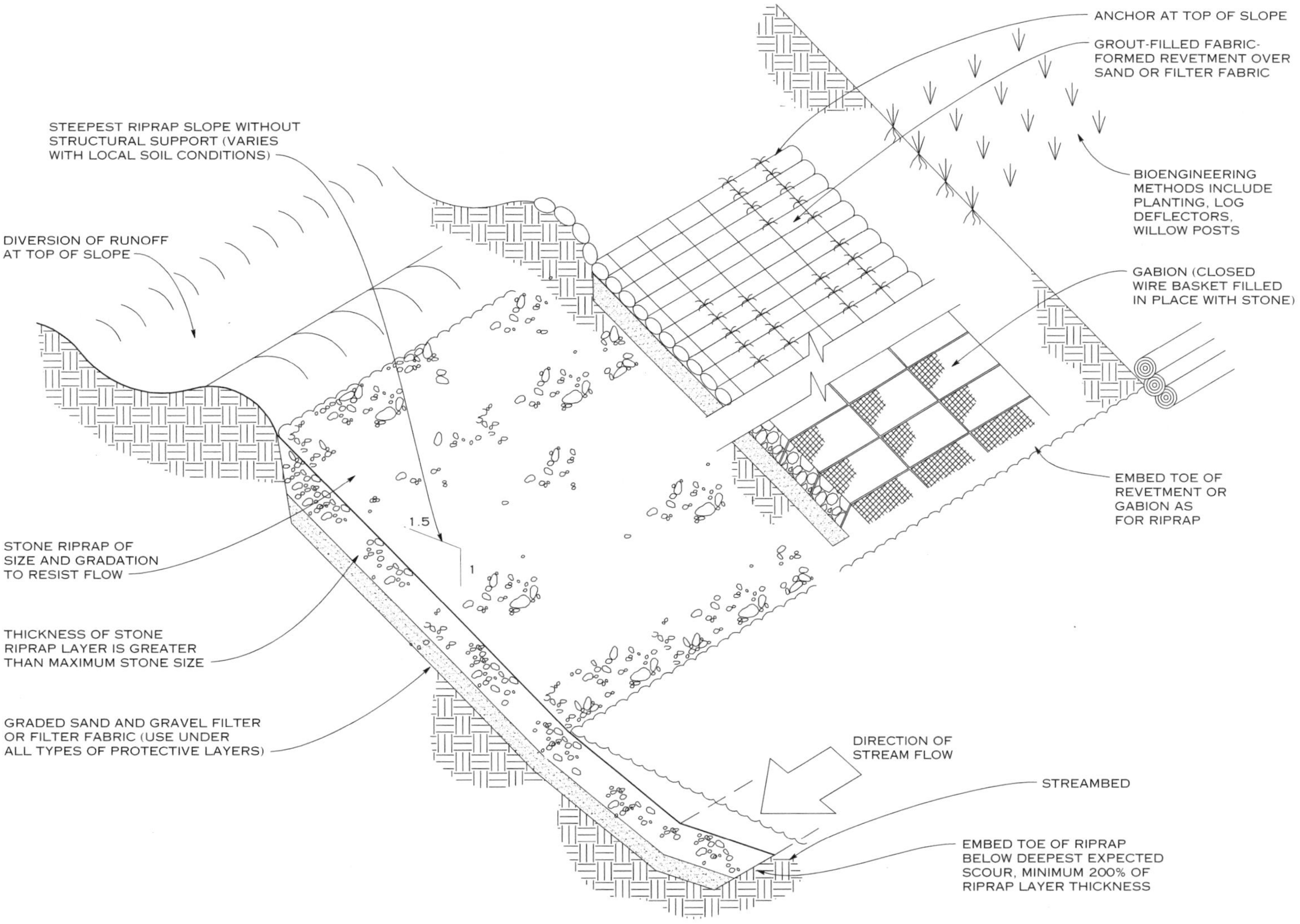

ANCHOR AT TOP OF SLOPE

GROUT-FILLED FABRIC-FORMED REVETMENT OVER SAND OR FILTER FABRIC

BIOENGINEERING METHODS INCLUDE PLANTING, LOG DEFLECTORS, WILLOW POSTS

GABION (CLOSED WIRE BASKET FILLED IN PLACE WITH STONE)

EMBED TOE OF REVETMENT OR GABION AS FOR RIPRAP

STEEPEST RIPRAP SLOPE WITHOUT STRUCTURAL SUPPORT (VARIES WITH LOCAL SOIL CONDITIONS)

DIVERSION OF RUNOFF AT TOP OF SLOPE

1.5
1

STONE RIPRAP OF SIZE AND GRADATION TO RESIST FLOW

THICKNESS OF STONE RIPRAP LAYER IS GREATER THAN MAXIMUM STONE SIZE

GRADED SAND AND GRAVEL FILTER OR FILTER FABRIC (USE UNDER ALL TYPES OF PROTECTIVE LAYERS)

DIRECTION OF STREAM FLOW

STREAMBED

EMBED TOE OF RIPRAP BELOW DEEPEST EXPECTED SCOUR, MINIMUM 200% OF RIPRAP LAYER THICKNESS

STREAM BANK STABILIZATION

James E. Sekela, P.E.; Pittsburgh, Pennsylvania

GENERAL

Retaining walls are designed and constructed to resist the thrust of the soil, which can cause the wall to fail by overturning, sliding, or settling. In stone walls, resistance to soil thrust can be helped by battering the stonework (that is, recessing or sloping the masonry back in successive courses).

Garden-type retaining walls, usually no higher than 4 ft, are made from small building units of stone, masonry, or wood. For higher walls, reinforced concrete is more commonly used. Terracing may be built with walls of wood, stone, brick, or concrete.

Walls less than 2 ft high do not require drains or weep holes. Pressure-treated wood is recommended for any design in which wood is in contact with the ground. Redwood may be substituted if desired.

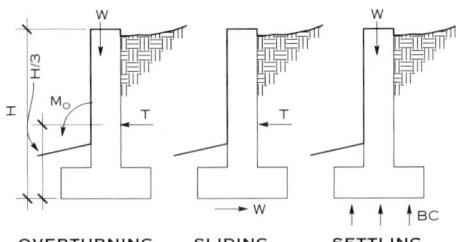

OVERTURNING   **SLIDING**   **SETTLING**

NOTES

1. H = height of wall, A = area of footing, W = composite weight of wall; T = lateral thrust of soil on wall; d = width of base of wall; M_O = overturning moment of a retaining wall; M_R = resisting moment; w = lateral force on wall in psf; BC = bearing capacity of soil.

2. The overturning moment of a retaining wall (equal to T x H/3) is resisted by the resisting moment of the wall. For symmetrical sections, the resisting moment equals W x d/2. Using a safety factor of 2, $M_R \geq 2 \times M_O$ (assume 33° angle of repose of soil).

3. The lateral (sliding) thrust of soil on a wall must be resisted. The resisting force is the weight of the wall multiplied by the coefficient of soil friction. Using a safety factor of 1.5, W ≥ 1.5T, where T = (w x H2)/2.

4. The bearing capacity of the soil must resist vertical forces (settling)—the weight of the wall plus any soil bearing on the base plus any vertical component of the soil thrust for a wall with any surcharge. Using a safety factor of 1.5, BC ≥ 1.5W/A.

FORCES RESISTED BY RETAINING WALLS

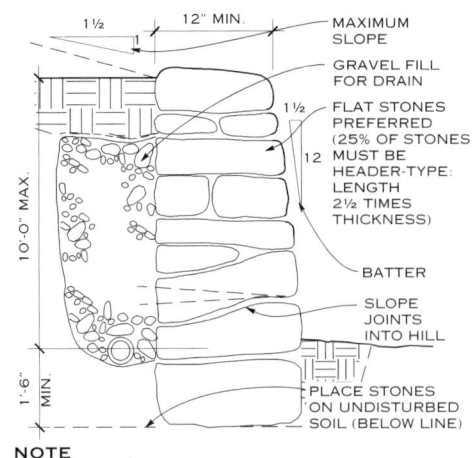

NOTE

Stagger vertical joints from course to course 6 in. min. horizontally. The thickness of the wall at any point should not be less than half the distance from that point to the top of the wall.

DRY STONE WALL

BRICK ROWLOCK
FILTER FABRIC
GRAVEL FILL FOR DRAIN
FACE BRICK (OMIT ONE VERTICAL JOINT AT 4'-0" O.C. FOR WEEPS)
BRICK ROWLOCK OVER 4" X 16" REINFORCED CONCRETE PAD (ACTS AS MOWING STRIP)
8" X 8" CONCRETE FOOTING WITH TWO #3 REBARS, SET BELOW FROST LINE

BRICK WALL

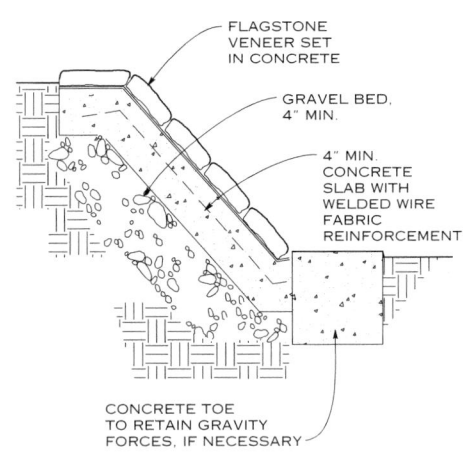

FLAGSTONE VENEER SET IN CONCRETE
GRAVEL BED, 4" MIN.
4" MIN. CONCRETE SLAB WITH WELDED WIRE FABRIC REINFORCEMENT
CONCRETE TOE TO RETAIN GRAVITY FORCES, IF NECESSARY

STONE BANK

STONE OR BRICK COPING
GALVANIZED WALL TIE
GRAVEL FILL FOR DRAIN
4" STONE OR BRICK VENEER
WEEP HOLES AT 4'-0" O.C., TYP.
12" CMU
FROST LINE
24" X 8" CONCRETE FOOTING

STONE/BRICK VENEER WALL

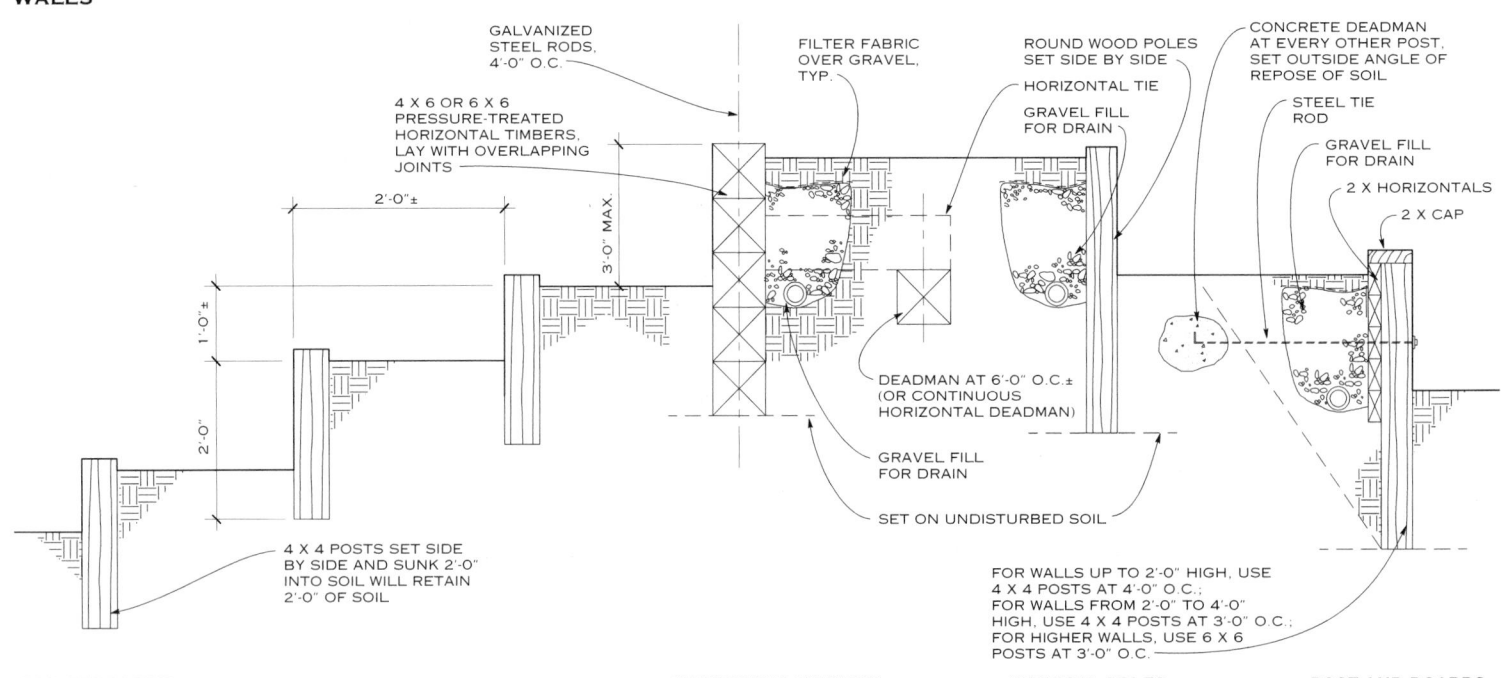

GALVANIZED STEEL RODS, 4'-0" O.C.

4 X 6 OR 6 X 6 PRESSURE-TREATED HORIZONTAL TIMBERS, LAY WITH OVERLAPPING JOINTS

FILTER FABRIC OVER GRAVEL, TYP.

ROUND WOOD POLES SET SIDE BY SIDE
HORIZONTAL TIE
GRAVEL FILL FOR DRAIN

CONCRETE DEADMAN AT EVERY OTHER POST, SET OUTSIDE ANGLE OF REPOSE OF SOIL
STEEL TIE ROD
GRAVEL FILL FOR DRAIN
2 X HORIZONTALS
2 X CAP

DEADMAN AT 6'-0" O.C.± (OR CONTINUOUS HORIZONTAL DEADMAN)

GRAVEL FILL FOR DRAIN

SET ON UNDISTURBED SOIL

4 X 4 POSTS SET SIDE BY SIDE AND SUNK 2'-0" INTO SOIL WILL RETAIN 2'-0" OF SOIL

FOR WALLS UP TO 2'-0" HIGH, USE 4 X 4 POSTS AT 4'-0" O.C.; FOR WALLS FROM 2'-0" TO 4'-0" HIGH, USE 4 X 4 POSTS AT 3'-0" O.C.; FOR HIGHER WALLS, USE 6 X 6 POSTS AT 3'-0" O.C.

SOIL TERRACING   **HORIZONTAL TIMBERS**   **VERTICAL POLES**   **POST AND BOARDS**

NOTE

A structural engineer should be consulted for the final design.

WOOD RETAINING WALL

Donald Neubauer, P. E.; Neubauer Consulting Engineers; Potomac, Maryland

 RETAINING WALLS

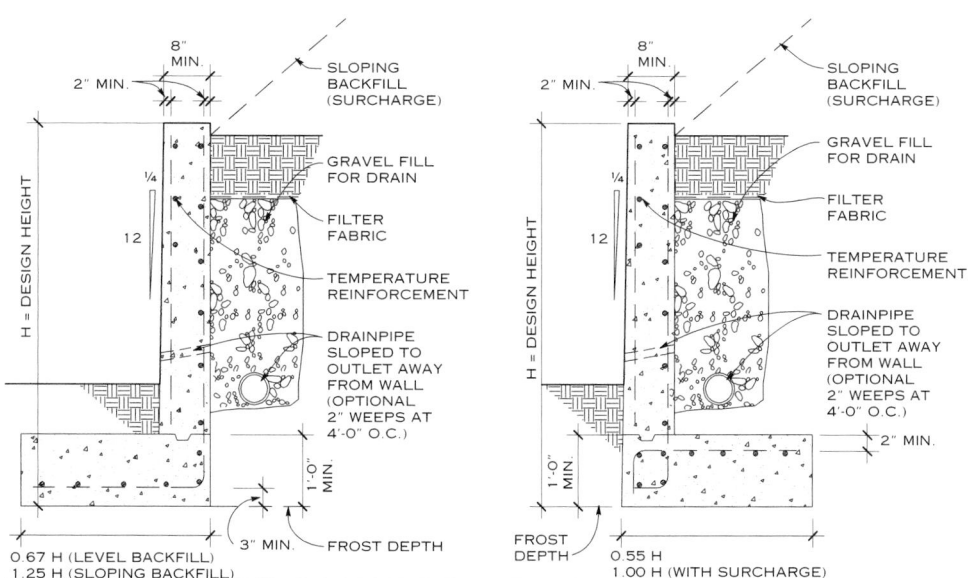

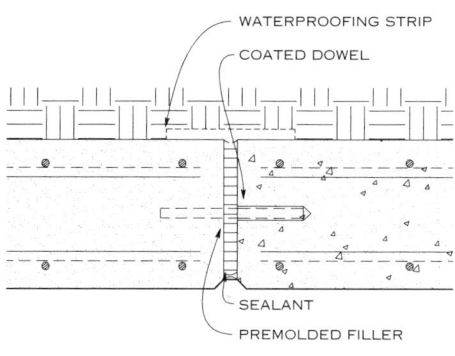

VERTICAL EXPANSION JOINT

L-TYPE RETAINING WALLS

0.67 H (LEVEL BACKFILL)
1.25 H (SLOPING BACKFILL)

0.55 H
1.00 H (WITH SURCHARGE)

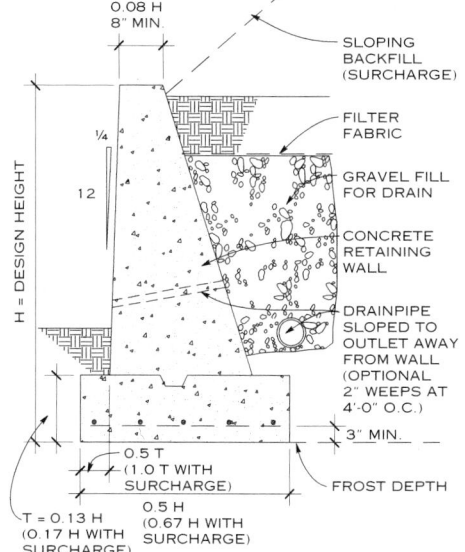

GRAVITY RETAINING WALL

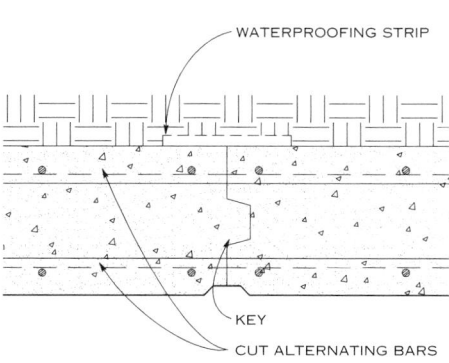

VERTICAL CONTROL JOINT

RETAINING WALL JOINTS

NOTES

1. Provide control and/or construction joints in concrete retaining walls about every 25 ft. Every fourth control and/or construction joint should be an expansion joint. Coated dowels should be used if average wall height on either side of a joint is different.
2. Consult with a structural engineer for final design of all concrete retaining walls.
3. Concrete keys may be required below retaining wall footing to prevent sliding in high walls and those built on moist clay.
4. T = the lateral thrust of the soil on the wall in the drawing of a gravity retaining wall.

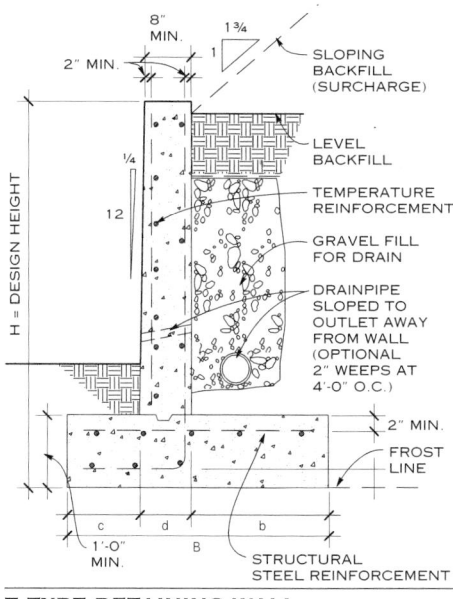

T-TYPE RETAINING WALL

PRELIMINARY DIMENSIONS FOR CONCRETE RETAINING WALLS

APPROXIMATE CONCRETE DIMENSIONS (FT-IN.)

BACKFILL SLOPING DIA. = 29° 45' (1¾:1)					BACKFILL LEVEL—NO SURCHARGE				
HEIGHT OF WALL (H)	WIDTH OF BASE (B)	WIDTH OF WALL (a)	HEEL (b)	TOE (c)	HEIGHT OF WALL (H)	WIDTH OF BASE (B)	WIDTH OF WALL (a)	HEEL (b)	TOE (c)
3-0	2-8	0-9	1-5	0-6	3-0	2-1	0-8	1-0	0-5
4-0	3-5	0-9	2-0	0-8	4-0	2-8	0-8	1-7	0-5
5-0	4-6	0-10	2-6	1-2	5-0	3-3	0-8	2-2	0-5
6-0	5-4	0-10	2-11	1-7	6-0	3-9	0-8	2-5	0-8
7-0	6-3	0-10	3-5	2-0	7-0	4-2	0-8	2-6	1-0
8-0	7-0	1-0	3-8	2-4	8-0	4-8	1-0	2-8	1-0
9-0	7-6	1-0	4-2	2-4	9-0	5-2	1-0	3-2	1-0
10-0	8-6	1-0	4-9	2-9	10-0	5-9	1-0	3-7	1-2
11-0	11-0	1-1	7-2	2-9	11-0	6-7	1-1	4-1	1-5
12-0	12-0	1-2	7-10	3-0	12-0	7-3	1-2	4-7	1-6
13-0	13-0	1-4	8-5	3-3	13-0	7-10	1-2	5-0	1-8
14-0	14-0	1-5	9-1	3-6	14-0	8-5	1-3	5-5	1-9
15-0	15-0	1-6	9-9	3-9	15-0	9-0	1-4	5-9	1-11
16-0	16-0	1-7	10-5	4-0	16-0	9-7	1-5	6-2	2-0
17-0	17-0	1-8	11-1	4-3	17-0	10-3	1-6	6-7	2-2
18-0	18-0	1-10	11-8	4-6	18-0	10-10	1-6	7-1	2-3
19-0	19-0	1-11	12-4	4-9	19-0	11-5	1-7	7-5	2-5
20-0	20-0	2-0	13-0	5-0	20-0	12-0	1-8	7-10	2-6
21-0	21-0	2-2	13-7	5-3	21-0	12-7	1-9	8-2	2-8
22-0	22-0	2-4	14-4	5-4	22-0	13-3	1-11	8-7	2-9

Donald Neubauer, P.E.; Neubauer Consulting Engineers; Potomac, Maryland

NOTES

1. Materials and construction practices for concrete masonry retaining walls should comply with "Building Code Requirements for Concrete Masonry Structures (ACI 531)."

2. Use fine grout when grout space is less than 3 in. in the least dimension. Use coarse grout when the least dimension of the grout space is 3 in. or more.

3. Steel reinforcement bars should be clean, free from harmful rust, and in compliance with applicable ASTM standards for deformed bars and steel wire.

4. Alternate vertical bars may be stopped at the mid height of the wall. Vertical reinforcement is usually secured in place after the masonry work has been completed and before grouting.

5. Designs shown are based on an assumed soil weight (vertical pressure) of 100 pcf. Horizontal pressure is based on an equivalent fluid weight for the soil of 45 pcf.

6. The walls illustrated are designed with a safety factor against overturning of not less than 2 and a safety factor against horizontal sliding of not less than 1.5. Computations in the table for wall heights are based on level backfill. One method of providing for additional loads from sloping backfill or surface loads is to consider them as additional depth of soil. In other words, an extra load of 300 psf can be treated as 3 ft of extra soil weighing 100 psf.

7. The top of masonry retaining walls should be capped or otherwise protected to prevent water from entering unfilled hollow cells and spaces. If bond beams are used, steel is placed in the beams as the wall is constructed. However, horizontal joint reinforcement may be placed in each joint (8 in. o.c.) and the bond beams omitted.

8. Allow 24 hrs for masonry to set before grouting. Pour grout in 4 ft layers, with one hour between each pour. Break long walls into panels 20 to 30 ft long with vertical control joints. Allow seven days for finished walls to set before backfilling. Prevent water from accumulating behind walls by means of 4 in. diameter weep holes spaced 5 to 10 ft apart (with screen and graded stone) or by a continuous drain with felt-covered open joints combined with waterproofing.

9. When backfill height exceeds 6 ft, provide a key under the footing base to resist the tendency of the wall to slide horizontally.

10. Heavy equipment used in backfilling should not come closer to the top of the wall than a distance equal to the wall height.

11. A structural engineer should be consulted for the final design.

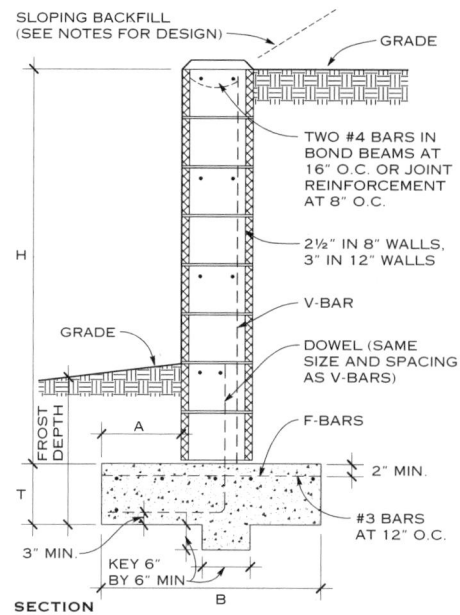

SECTION

DIMENSIONS AND REINFORCEMENT FOR CMU RETAINING WALLS

WALL	H	B	T	A	V-BARS	F-BARS
8"	3'-4"	2'-4"	9"	8"	#3 @ 32"	#3 @ 27"
	4'-0"	2'-9"	9"	10"	#4 @ 32"	#3 @ 27"
	4'-8"	3'-4"	10"	12"	#5 @ 32"	#3 @ 27"
	5'-4"	3'-8"	10"	14"	#4 @ 16"	#4 @ 30"
	6'-0"	4'-2"	12"	16"	#6 @ 24"	#4 @ 25"
12"	5'-4"	3'-8"	10"	14"	#4 @ 24"	#3 @ 25"
	6'-0"	4'-2"	12"	15"	#4 @ 16"	#4 @ 30"
	6'-8"	4'-6"	12"	16"	#6 @ 24"	#4 @ 22"
	7'-4"	4'-10"	12"	18"	#5 @ 16"	#5 @ 26"
	8'-0"	5'-4"	12"	20"	#7 @ 24"	#5 @ 21"
	8'-8"	5'-10"	14"	22"	#6 @ 8"	#6 @ 26"
	9'-4"	6'-2"	14"	24"	#8 @ 8"	#6 @ 21"

TYPICAL CANTILEVER RETAINING WALL

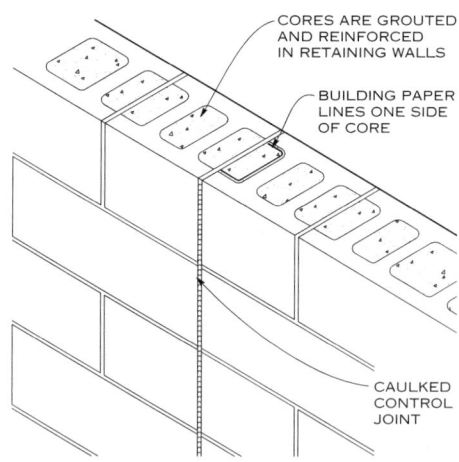

NOTE

Long retaining walls should be broken with vertical control joints into panels 20 to 30 ft long. These panels must be designed to resist shear and other lateral forces while permitting longitudinal movement.

SHEAR-RESISTING CONTROL JOINT

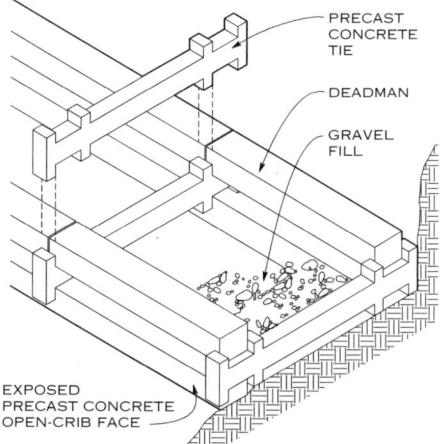

DETAIL

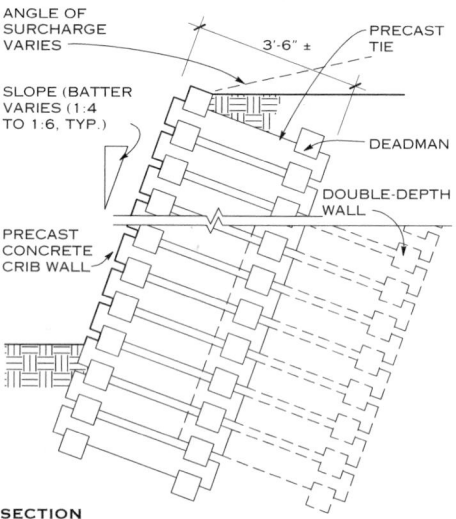

SECTION

NOTE

For retaining walls taller than a certain height, double- or triple-depth walls may be needed. Fill composition varies from crushed stone to granular soil, according to conditions. Consult a structural engineer.

PRECAST CONCRETE CRIB WALL SYSTEM

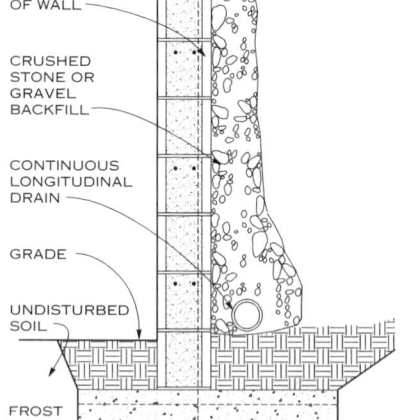

WITH IMPERMEABLE BACKFILL

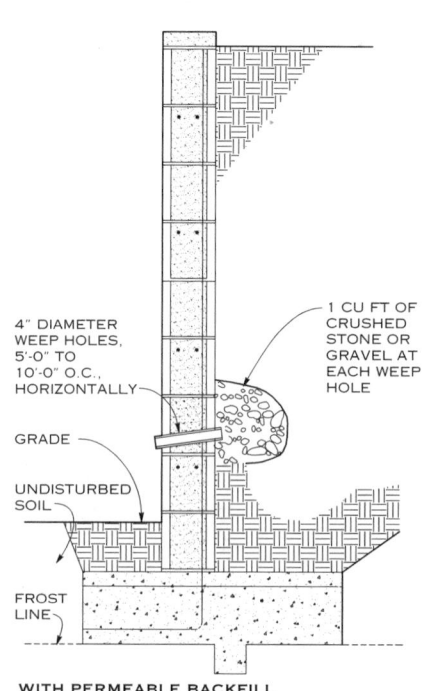

WITH PERMEABLE BACKFILL

DRAINAGE DETAILS FOR RETAINING WALLS

Donald Neubauer, P.E.; Neubauer Consulting Engineers; Potomac, Maryland

 RETAINING WALLS

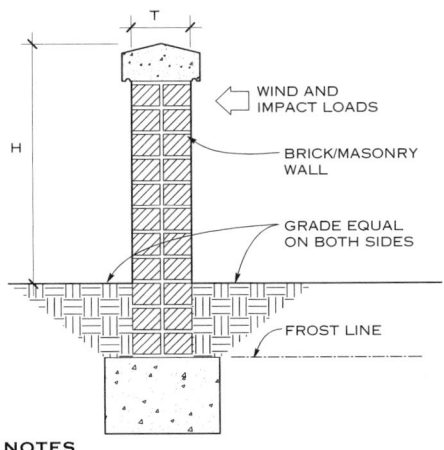

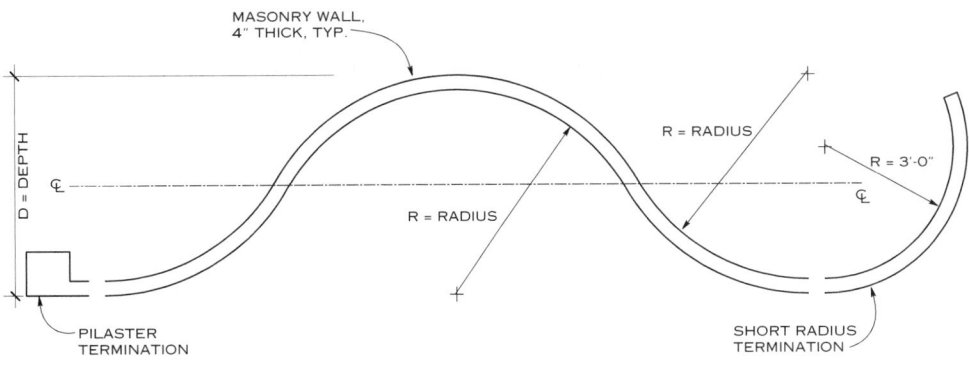

NOTES

1. Design straight garden walls (without piers) with sufficient thickness to provide lateral stability.
2. To resist 10 psf wind pressure, the height above grade (H) and thickness (T) should relate as follows: $H \leq .75T^2$ (H and T are in inches).

NOTES

1. The radius of curvature (R) of a 4-in. thick serpentine wall should be no more than twice the height of the wall above finished grade.
2. The depth (D) of curvature of a serpentine wall should be no less than half the height of the wall above grade (max. height = 5 ft 0 in., typical).

3. The running bond brick pattern is best for serpentine walls.
4. No reinforcing steel is used in this type of wall.
5. Serpentine walls are not recommended for use in seismic areas.

STRAIGHT GARDEN WALLS

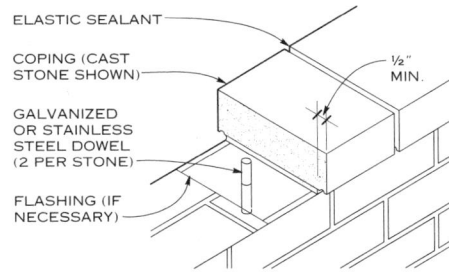

STONE

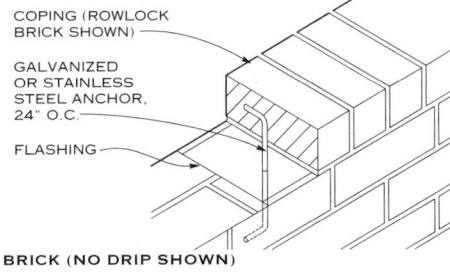

BRICK (NO DRIP SHOWN)

NOTE

In general, through-wall flashing should be used immediately under the coping of garden walls. However, this decision depends on several factors, including the type of coping used, the number of joints used, and the climatic conditions of the area (whether there is high or low precipitation and the number of freezing and thawing cycles).

COPING DETAILS

REQUIRED EMBEDMENT FOR PIER FOUNDATION*

WALL SPAN (FT)	WIND LOAD (10 PSF)			WIND LOAD (15 PSF)			WIND LOAD (20 PSF)		
	WALL HEIGHT (FT)								
	4	6	8	4	6	8	4	6	8
8	2'-0"	2'-3"	2'-9"	2'-3"	2'-6"	3'-0"	2'-3"	2'-9"	3'-0"
10	2'-0"	2'-6"	2'-9"	2'-3"	2'-9"	3'-3"	2'-6"	3'-0"	3'-3"
12	2'-3"	2'-6"	3'-0"	2'-3"	3'-0"	3'-3"	2'-6"	3'-3"	3'-6"
14	2'-3"	2'-9"	3'-0"	2'-6"	3'-0"	3'-3"	2'-9"	3'-3"	3'-9"
16	2'-3"	2'-9"	3'-0"	2'-6"	3'-3"	3'-6"	2'-9"	3'-3"	4'-0"

*For wall sizes shown within heavy lines, a 24-in. diameter foundation is required. All other values have been obtained using an 18-in. diameter foundation.

NOTE

To figure the vertical spacing and size of reinforcing steel required for panel walls, consider the probable wind load and the wall span between piers. Consult a structural engineer for assistance.

Dennis Carmichael; EDAW, Inc.; Alexandria, Virginia

SERPENTINE GARDEN WALLS

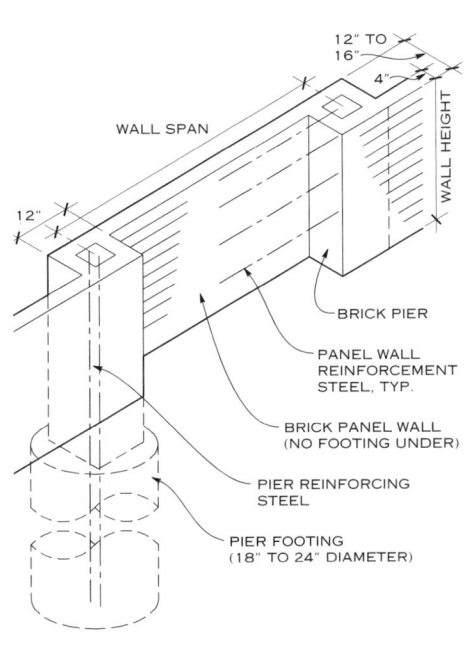

PIER-AND-PANEL SYSTEM

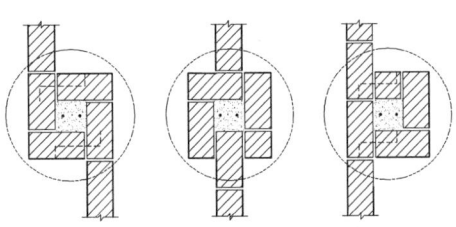

PIER TYPES

NOTE

The pier-and-panel wall is composed of a series of relatively thin (4-in. thick) reinforced brick masonry panels, which are braced intermittently with masonry piers. This wall is relatively easy to build and is economical because of the narrowness of the panels. It is also easily adapted to varying terrain conditions.

PIER-AND-PANEL GARDEN WALLS

BRICK

TERRA-COTTA

CAST STONE/CONCRETE

NOTES

1. Copings and caps prevent water from entering the inner wall from above by shedding water to the sides, where it is thrown clear of the wall, usually by means of a drip edge.
2. Anchor coping as necessary. If the coping material is different from the wall material, compare their thermal and moisture expansion characteristics and make provisions for differential movement.

COPING TYPES FOR WALLS

PIER REINFORCING STEEL*

WALL SPAN (FT)	WIND LOAD (10 PSF)			WIND LOAD (15 PSF)			WIND LOAD (20 PSF)		
	WALL HEIGHT (FT)								
	4	6	8	4	6	8	4	6	8
8	2#3	2#4	2#5	2#3	2#5	2#6	2#4	2#5	2#5
10	2#3	2#4	2#5	2#4	2#5	2#7	2#4	2#6	2#6
12	2#3	2#5	2#6	2#4	2#6	2#6	2#4	2#6	2#7
14	2#3	2#5	2#6	2#4	2#6	2#6	2#5	2#6	2#7
16	2#4	2#5	2#7	2#4	2#6	2#7	2#5	2#6	2#7

*For wall sizes shown within heavy lines, 12 × 16 in. piers are required. All other values have been obtained with 12 × 12 in. piers.

FREESTANDING GARDEN WALLS

Freestanding garden walls provide a physical or visual barrier to outdoor areas. Walls higher than eye level (approximately 5 ft 6 in.) provide both a physical and visual barrier; typically they are situated near and designed to blend with an adjacent architectural structure. Walls designed under eye level provide a sense of partial enclosure while maintaining a view, which is sometimes framed by the wall design.

Design factors that should be addressed when designing freestanding garden walls include these:

1. Quality and durability of materials (unit material, mortar, and reinforcement) and detailing when exposed over time to rain, wind, sun, thermal movement, and degradation
2. Appearance of both sides of the wall
3. Foundation design
4. Adjacent plantings

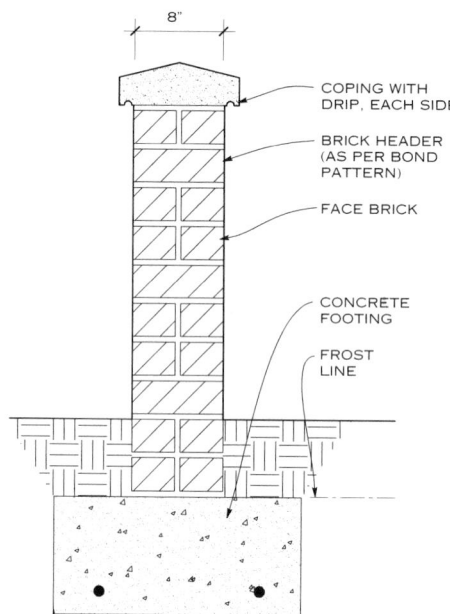

COPING WITH DRIP, EACH SIDE

BRICK HEADER (AS PER BOND PATTERN)

FACE BRICK

CONCRETE FOOTING

FROST LINE

8"

SOLID MASONRY

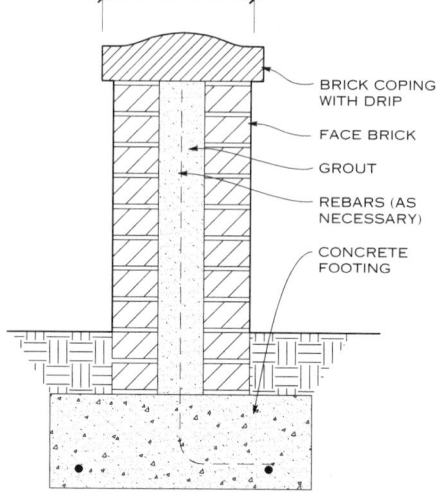

BRICK COPING WITH DRIP

FACE BRICK

GROUT

REBARS (AS NECESSARY)

CONCRETE FOOTING

12"

GROUTED REINFORCED MASONRY

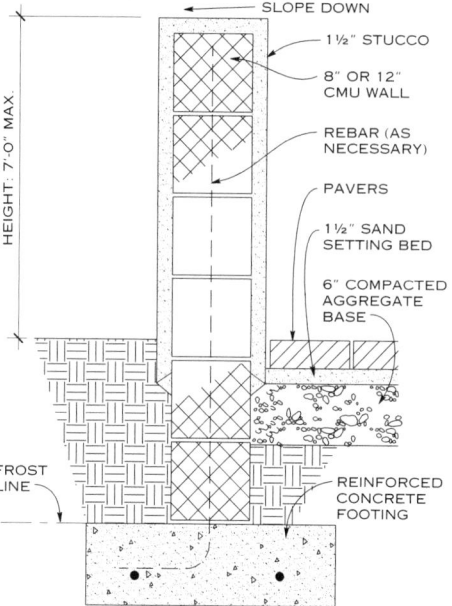

SLOPE DOWN

1½" STUCCO

8" OR 12" CMU WALL

REBAR (AS NECESSARY)

PAVERS

1½" SAND SETTING BED

6" COMPACTED AGGREGATE BASE

FROST LINE

REINFORCED CONCRETE FOOTING

HEIGHT: 7'-0" MAX.

STUCCO OVER CMU

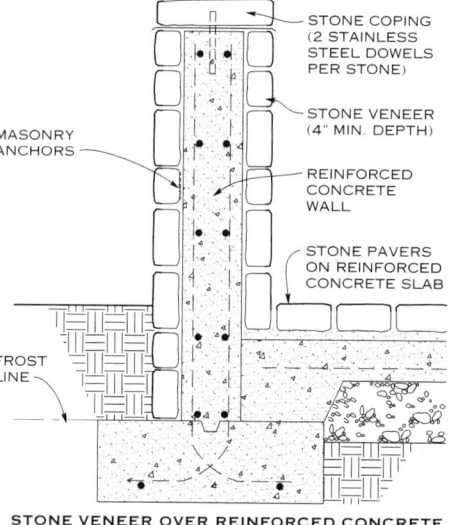

SLOPE DOWN

STONE COPING (2 STAINLESS STEEL DOWELS PER STONE)

STONE VENEER (4" MIN. DEPTH)

MASONRY ANCHORS

REINFORCED CONCRETE WALL

STONE PAVERS ON REINFORCED CONCRETE SLAB

FROST LINE

STONE VENEER OVER REINFORCED CONCRETE

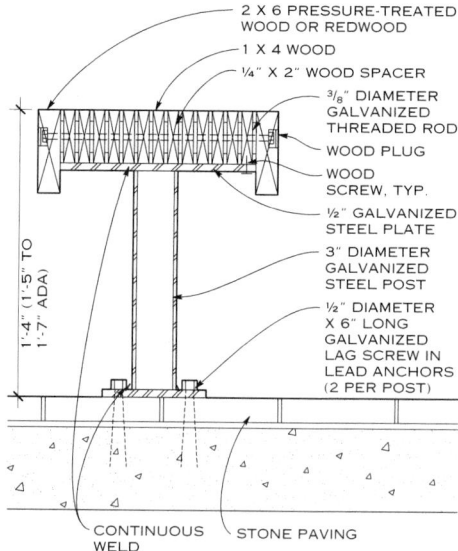

2 X 6 PRESSURE-TREATED WOOD OR REDWOOD

1 X 4 WOOD

¼" X 2" WOOD SPACER

³⁄₈" DIAMETER GALVANIZED THREADED ROD

WOOD PLUG

WOOD SCREW, TYP.

½" GALVANIZED STEEL PLATE

3" DIAMETER GALVANIZED STEEL POST

½" DIAMETER X 6" LONG GALVANIZED LAG SCREW IN LEAD ANCHORS (2 PER POST)

CONTINUOUS WELD

STONE PAVING

1'-4" (1'-5" TO 1'-7" ADA)

WOOD SITE BENCH

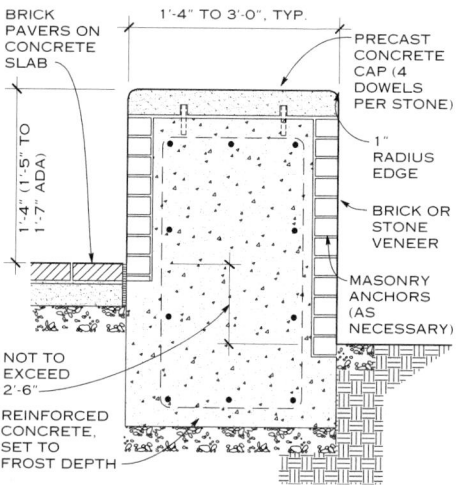

BRICK PAVERS ON CONCRETE SLAB

PRECAST CONCRETE CAP (4 DOWELS PER STONE)

1" RADIUS EDGE

BRICK OR STONE VENEER

MASONRY ANCHORS (AS NECESSARY)

NOT TO EXCEED 2'-6"

REINFORCED CONCRETE, SET TO FROST DEPTH

1'-4" (1'-5" TO 1'-7" ADA)

1'-4" TO 3'-0", TYP.

BRICK VENEER SEAT WALL

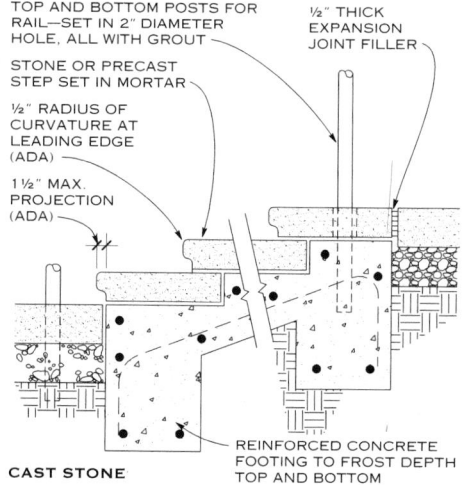

TOP AND BOTTOM POSTS FOR RAIL—SET IN 2" DIAMETER HOLE, ALL WITH GROUT

STONE OR PRECAST STEP SET IN MORTAR

½" RADIUS OF CURVATURE AT LEADING EDGE (ADA)

1½" MAX. PROJECTION (ADA)

½" THICK EXPANSION JOINT FILLER

REINFORCED CONCRETE FOOTING TO FROST DEPTH TOP AND BOTTOM

CAST STONE

NOTES

1. Provide handrails on both sides of all stairs along accessible routes.

2. Step surfaces should be sloped so water will not accumulate on the walking surface.

3. These details are for reference only. Consult ADAAG for tread and handrail requirements for specific applications and BOCA for riser-to-tread ratios.

FREESTANDING MASONRY GARDEN WALLS

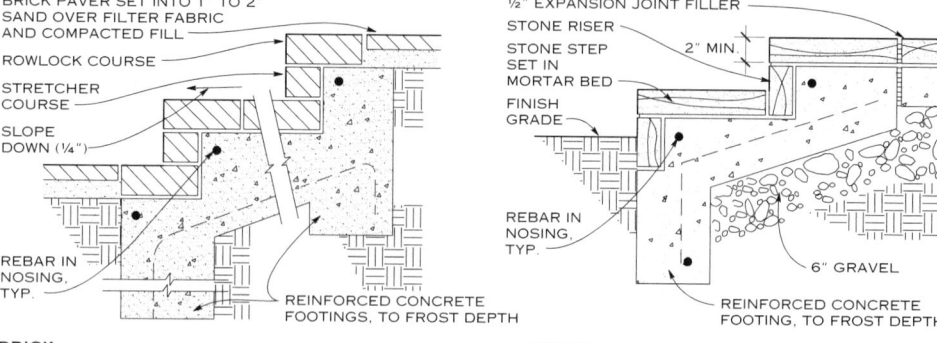

BRICK PAVER SET INTO 1" TO 2" SAND OVER FILTER FABRIC AND COMPACTED FILL

ROWLOCK COURSE

STRETCHER COURSE

SLOPE DOWN (¼")

REBAR IN NOSING, TYP.

REINFORCED CONCRETE FOOTINGS, TO FROST DEPTH

BRICK

½" EXPANSION JOINT FILLER

STONE RISER

STONE STEP SET IN MORTAR BED

FINISH GRADE

2" MIN.

REBAR IN NOSING, TYP.

6" GRAVEL

REINFORCED CONCRETE FOOTING, TO FROST DEPTH

STONE

MASONRY SITE STEPS

Dennis Carmichael; EDAW, Inc.; Alexandria, Virginia

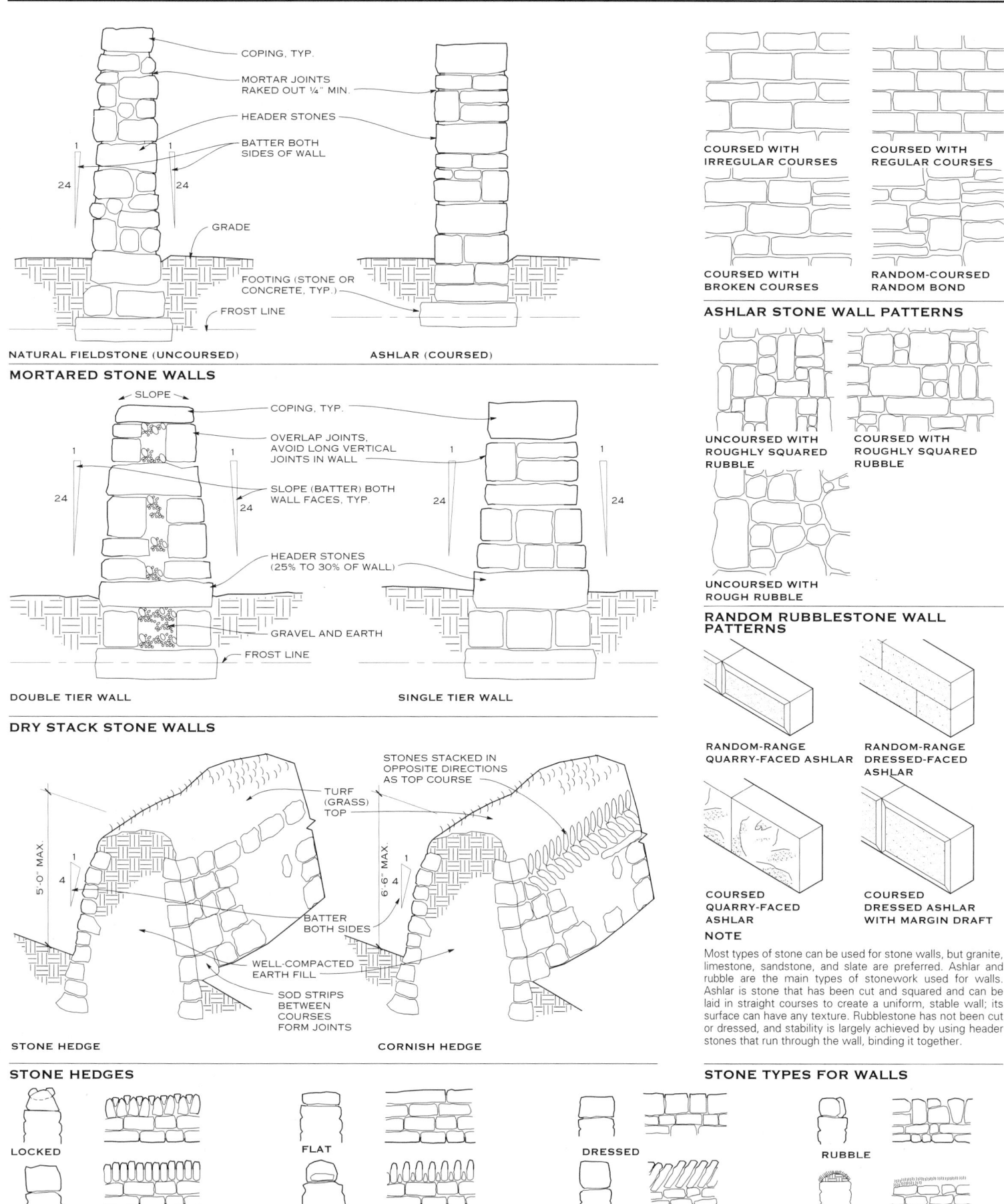

MORTARED STONE WALLS

COPING, TYP.

MORTAR JOINTS RAKED OUT ¼" MIN.

HEADER STONES

BATTER BOTH SIDES OF WALL

24 24

GRADE

FOOTING (STONE OR CONCRETE, TYP.)

FROST LINE

NATURAL FIELDSTONE (UNCOURSED)

ASHLAR (COURSED)

DRY STACK STONE WALLS

SLOPE

COPING, TYP.

OVERLAP JOINTS, AVOID LONG VERTICAL JOINTS IN WALL

SLOPE (BATTER) BOTH WALL FACES, TYP.

HEADER STONES (25% TO 30% OF WALL)

GRAVEL AND EARTH

FROST LINE

DOUBLE TIER WALL

SINGLE TIER WALL

STONE HEDGES

STONES STACKED IN OPPOSITE DIRECTIONS AS TOP COURSE

TURF (GRASS) TOP

5'-0" MAX.

6'-6" MAX.

BATTER BOTH SIDES

WELL-COMPACTED EARTH FILL

SOD STRIPS BETWEEN COURSES FORM JOINTS

STONE HEDGE

CORNISH HEDGE

STONE WALL COPINGS

LOCKED

ROWLOCK

FLAT

BUCK AND DOE

DRESSED

TILTED

RUBBLE

TURF/GRASS

COURSED WITH IRREGULAR COURSES

COURSED WITH REGULAR COURSES

COURSED WITH BROKEN COURSES

RANDOM-COURSED RANDOM BOND

ASHLAR STONE WALL PATTERNS

UNCOURSED WITH ROUGHLY SQUARED RUBBLE

COURSED WITH ROUGHLY SQUARED RUBBLE

UNCOURSED WITH ROUGH RUBBLE

RANDOM RUBBLESTONE WALL PATTERNS

RANDOM-RANGE QUARRY-FACED ASHLAR

RANDOM-RANGE DRESSED-FACED ASHLAR

COURSED QUARRY-FACED ASHLAR

COURSED DRESSED ASHLAR WITH MARGIN DRAFT

NOTE

Most types of stone can be used for stone walls, but granite, limestone, sandstone, and slate are preferred. Ashlar and rubble are the main types of stonework used for walls. Ashlar is stone that has been cut and squared and can be laid in straight courses to create a uniform, stable wall; its surface can have any texture. Rubblestone has not been cut or dressed, and stability is largely achieved by using header stones that run through the wall, binding it together.

STONE TYPES FOR WALLS

Dennis Carmichael; EDAW, Inc.; Alexandria, Virginia

GENERAL

Unit paving assemblies are principally used for applications such as shopping plazas, building entrances, walkways, patios, residential driveways, and residential parking areas. However, they may be used for streets with heavy vehicular traffic and for industrial floors or other special conditions. Consult with a landscape architect or engineer for appropriate design guidelines.

NOTES

1. Paver units are selected according to color, texture, abrasion resistance, and resistance to weathering. The texture of the unit affects slip resistance--the coarser the

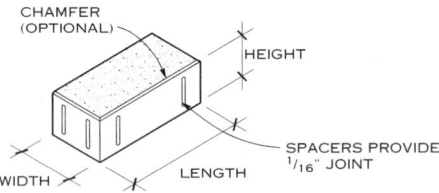

RECTANGULAR

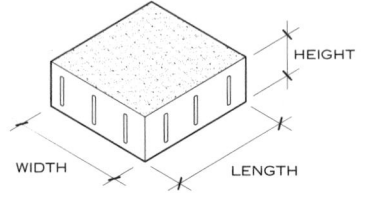

SQUARE

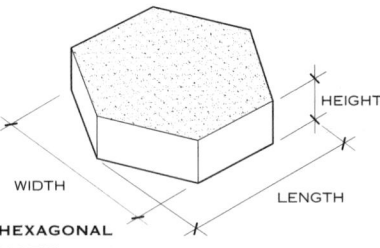

HEXAGONAL

NOTE

Rectangular, square, and hexagonal pavers are available in both brick and concrete.

TYPICAL PAVER SHAPES

TYPICAL PAVER SIZES IN IN. (MM)

RECTANGULAR*		SQUARE	HEXAGONAL	
W	L	W & L	W	L
4 (100)	8 (200)	4 (100)	6 (150)	6 (150)
3 5/8 (92)	7 5/8 (194)	6 (150)	8 (200)	8 (200)
3 1/2 (89)	7 1/2 (190)	8 (200)	12 (300)	12 (300)
7 5/8 (194)	7 5/8 (194)	12 (300)		
8 (200)	8 (200)	16 (400)		

*Check with manufacturer for availability of chamfers.

NOTE

The height of pavers varies with the manufacturer and application but is usually 1 1/4 (32), 2 1/4 (57), 2 5/8 (67), or 2 3/4 (70).

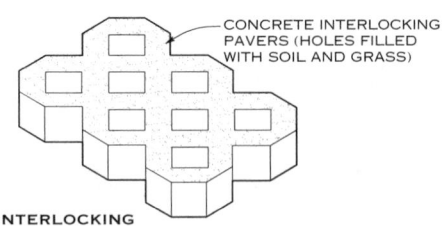

INTERLOCKING

NOTES

1. Voids may be filled with grass, ground cover, or gravel.
2. Grass pavers may be used to control erosion.

GRASS PAVER TYPES

texture, the better the slip resistance. Abrasion resistance refers to the wear and tear an assembly is subjected to under normal use. According to ASTM C902, "Standard Specification for Pedestrian and Light Traffic Paving Brick," an abrasion index classification determines the type of unit required for an intended exposure. A dense, hard-burned extruded brick with 8000 psi compressive strength that conforms to ASTM C902, Class SX, Type 1, resists both abrasion and weathering and is adequate for most heavy-traffic exterior applications. Molded brick with 4000 psi compressive strength that conforms to ASTM C902, Class SX, Type 2, is adequate for most exterior pedestrian applications. If materials other than brick are used for paving, consult the manufacturer to learn which products are suitable for use as pavers in a particular application.

2. Assess potential traffic loads when planning unit paving installations. Heavy vehicular loads require a rigid or semirigid continuous base, while a flexible base and flexible paving are suitable for light vehicular loads (residential-type). Use either base type for pedestrian traffic. Choose a bond pattern based on expected traffic patterns; traffic should travel perpendicular to the long dimension of the paving unit. For vehicular areas, use a gravel subbase

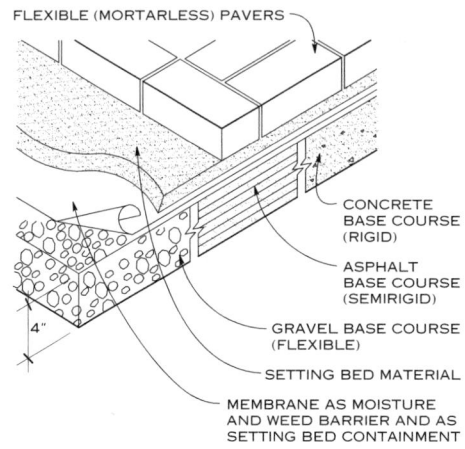

FLEXIBLE (MORTARLESS) PAVER

NOTES

1. Unit paving assemblies are classified according to the type of base supporting the paver, either rigid (mortared) or flexible (mortarless). Base types are a reinforced or unreinforced concrete slab on grade that accepts either rigid or flexible pavers (rigid); asphalt or bituminous concrete that accepts flexible pavers only (semirigid continuous); a compacted gravel, sand, or sand-cement mixture that accepts flexible pavers only (flexible); and suspended diaphragm or structural floor and roof assemblies, which vary by design and accept either rigid or flexible pavers.

2. Setting bed (cushion) material, placed between base and paving surface, functions as a leveling layer to help refine the finished grade and compensate for irregularities in the base and paver unit surfaces. Setting bed material can be a 1- or 2-in. layer of sand, pea gravel, stone screenings, roofing felt, asphalt (7% asphalt, 93% sand with a neoprene tack coat), or mortar. Sand for setting beds, bases, joints, and mortar should conform to ASTM C144, "Aggregate for Masonry Mortar." Use mortar setting or leveling beds only in conjunction with concrete and asphalt bases; the thickness of the bed may vary from 1/2 to 2 in.

PAVER ASSEMBLY TYPES

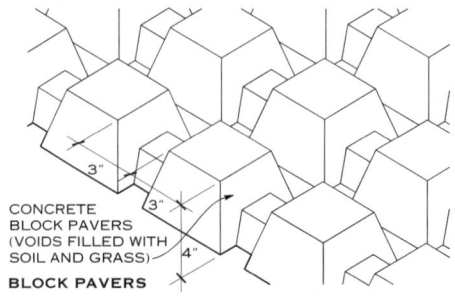

BLOCK PAVERS

3. Grass rings are available with close ring spacing for pedestrian use or with wide ring spacing for vehicular use.

(minimum 6 in. crushed gravel) compacted to 95% and paver sizes 8 in. square or smaller. Consult an engineer to accurately define paver sizes, shapes, gravel depth, concrete base depth, and concrete reinforcement requirements.

3. Proper subgrade preparation of areas to be paved is important. Remove all vegetation and organic material, and consider the location of existing or proposed underground utilities and storm drainage, as well as user convenience.

4. Plan for surface and subsurface drainage. Slope paving away from buildings, retaining walls, etc. at 1/8 to 1/4 in. per foot. Rigid paving always requires adequate surface drainage, with the long dimension of the mortar joints running parallel to the direction of runoff. Flexible paving requires both surface and subsurface drainage.

5. To prevent horizontal movement of flexible (mortarless) paving assemblies, use a curb of brick soldier coursing set in concrete, landscape timbers, or other edging material.

6. There are three major types of unit paver joint material: mortar, grout (portland cement and sand without hydrated lime), and a dry mixture of grout.

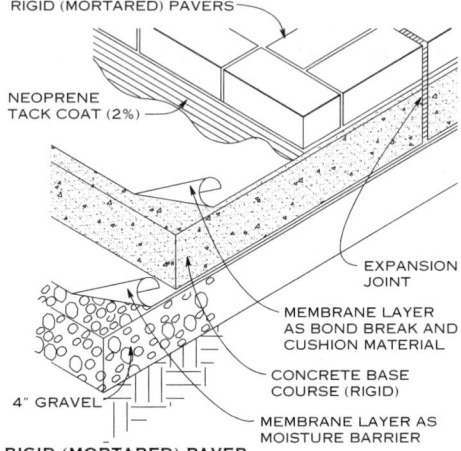

RIGID (MORTARED) PAVER

3. Membranes are installed in unit paving assemblies for several purposes: to control the passage of moisture, reduce weed growth, prevent the sand course from filtering into lower courses, and as a bond break. Consider using bond breaks between rigid paving and rigid bases to accommodate differential movement. Membranes are of sheet or liquid material that can resist moisture, rot, and decay. Sheet material includes asphalt roofing felt, polyethylene film, vinyl, neoprene, or rubber. Liquid types are asphalt, modified urethane, or polyurethane bitumen; these are preferred for irregular surfaces.

4. Use base materials, including gravel, concrete, and asphalt, for support, drainage, and/or ground swell protection. For maximum drainage efficiency and to prevent upward capillary action, specify clean, washed gravel.

5. Expansion joints can alleviate thermal and moisture movement, especially in rigid or mortared assemblies. Expansion joints are generally located parallel or adjacent to curbs and edgings, at right angle turns, around interruptions (e.g., manhole cover assemblies), at set distances in long runs of masonry, and where dissimilar materials meet.

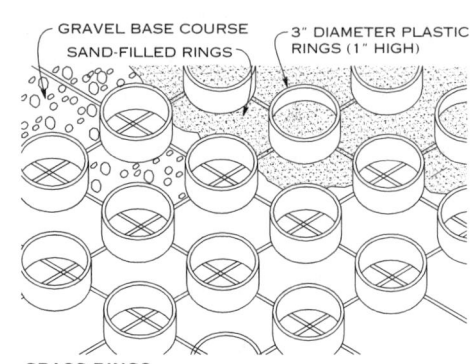

GRASS RINGS

Dennis Carmichael; EDAW, Inc.; Alexandria, Virginia

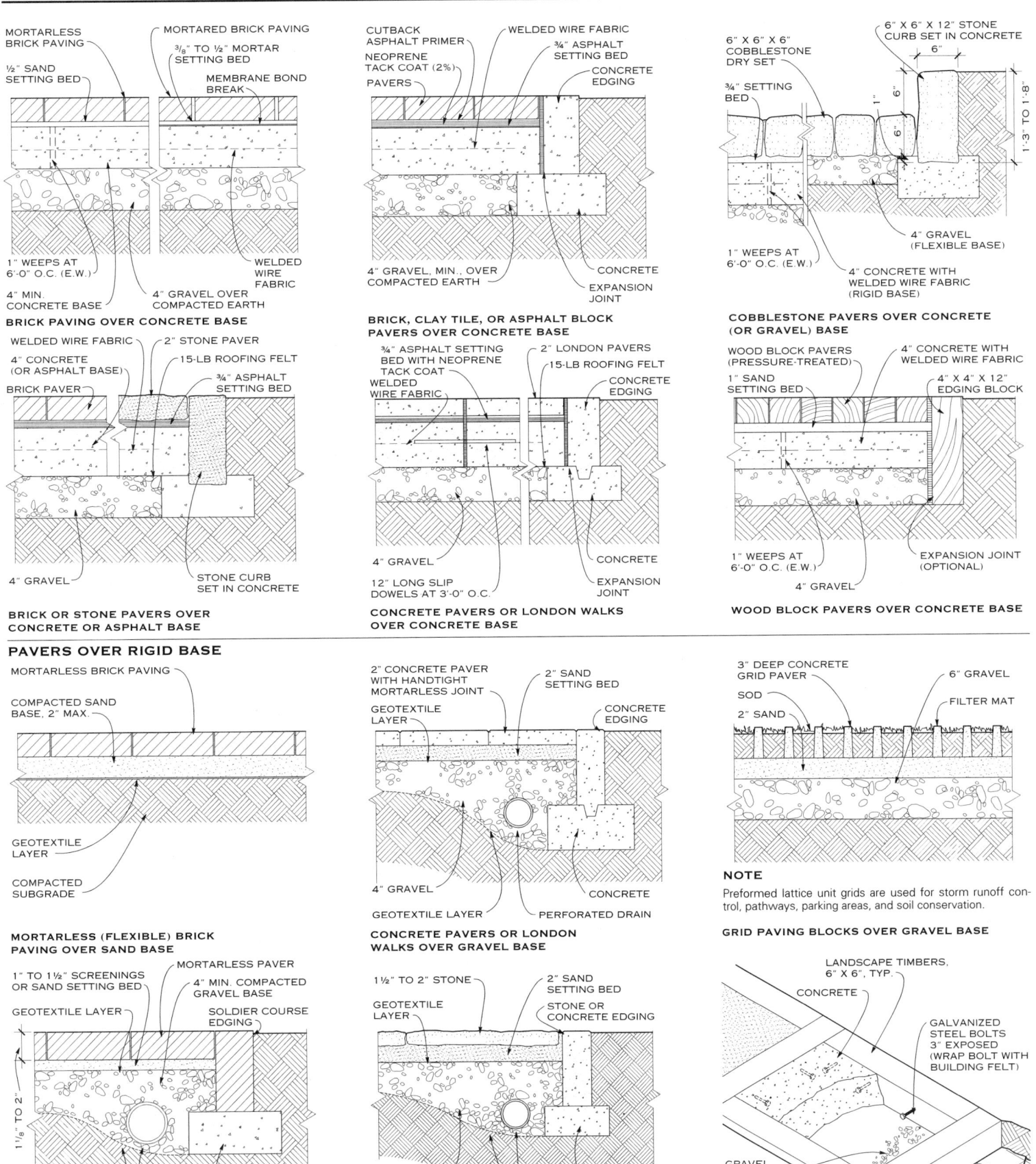

MORTARLESS BRICK PAVING
½" SAND SETTING BED
1" WEEPS AT 6'-0" O.C. (E.W.)
4" MIN. CONCRETE BASE
MORTARED BRICK PAVING
⅜" TO ½" MORTAR SETTING BED
MEMBRANE BOND BREAK
4" GRAVEL OVER COMPACTED EARTH
WELDED WIRE FABRIC

BRICK PAVING OVER CONCRETE BASE

CUTBACK ASPHALT PRIMER
NEOPRENE TACK COAT (2%)
PAVERS
WELDED WIRE FABRIC
¾" ASPHALT SETTING BED
CONCRETE EDGING
4" GRAVEL, MIN., OVER COMPACTED EARTH
CONCRETE
EXPANSION JOINT

BRICK, CLAY TILE, OR ASPHALT BLOCK PAVERS OVER CONCRETE BASE

6" X 6" X 6" COBBLESTONE DRY SET
¾" SETTING BED
6" X 6" X 12" STONE CURB SET IN CONCRETE
6"
1"
6"
6"
1'-3" TO 1'-8"
4" GRAVEL (FLEXIBLE BASE)
1" WEEPS AT 6'-0" O.C. (E.W.)
4" CONCRETE WITH WELDED WIRE FABRIC (RIGID BASE)

COBBLESTONE PAVERS OVER CONCRETE (OR GRAVEL) BASE

WELDED WIRE FABRIC
4" CONCRETE (OR ASPHALT BASE)
BRICK PAVER
2" STONE PAVER
15-LB ROOFING FELT
¾" ASPHALT SETTING BED
4" GRAVEL
STONE CURB SET IN CONCRETE

BRICK OR STONE PAVERS OVER CONCRETE OR ASPHALT BASE

¾" ASPHALT SETTING BED WITH NEOPRENE TACK COAT
WELDED WIRE FABRIC
2" LONDON PAVERS
15-LB ROOFING FELT
CONCRETE EDGING
4" GRAVEL
12" LONG SLIP DOWELS AT 3'-0" O.C.
CONCRETE
EXPANSION JOINT

CONCRETE PAVERS OR LONDON WALKS OVER CONCRETE BASE

WOOD BLOCK PAVERS (PRESSURE-TREATED)
1" SAND SETTING BED
4" CONCRETE WITH WELDED WIRE FABRIC
4" X 4" X 12" EDGING BLOCK
1" WEEPS AT 6'-0" O.C. (E.W.)
4" GRAVEL
EXPANSION JOINT (OPTIONAL)

WOOD BLOCK PAVERS OVER CONCRETE BASE

PAVERS OVER RIGID BASE

MORTARLESS BRICK PAVING
COMPACTED SAND BASE, 2" MAX.
GEOTEXTILE LAYER
COMPACTED SUBGRADE

MORTARLESS (FLEXIBLE) BRICK PAVING OVER SAND BASE

2" CONCRETE PAVER WITH HANDTIGHT MORTARLESS JOINT
GEOTEXTILE LAYER
2" SAND SETTING BED
CONCRETE EDGING
4" GRAVEL
GEOTEXTILE LAYER
CONCRETE
PERFORATED DRAIN

CONCRETE PAVERS OR LONDON WALKS OVER GRAVEL BASE

3" DEEP CONCRETE GRID PAVER
SOD
2" SAND
6" GRAVEL
FILTER MAT

NOTE

Preformed lattice unit grids are used for storm runoff control, pathways, parking areas, and soil conservation.

GRID PAVING BLOCKS OVER GRAVEL BASE

1" TO 1½" SCREENINGS OR SAND SETTING BED
GEOTEXTILE LAYER
1⅛" TO 2"
MORTARLESS PAVER
4" MIN. COMPACTED GRAVEL BASE
SOLDIER COURSE EDGING
GEOTEXTILE LAYER
PERFORATED DRAIN
CONCRETE

BRICK, CLAY TILE, OR ASPHALT BLOCK PAVERS OVER GRAVEL BASE

1½" TO 2" STONE
GEOTEXTILE LAYER
2" SAND SETTING BED
STONE OR CONCRETE EDGING
4" GRAVEL
GEOTEXTILE LAYER
PERFORATED DRAIN
CONCRETE

CUT STONE PAVERS OVER SAND AND GRAVEL BASE

LANDSCAPE TIMBERS, 6" X 6", TYP.
CONCRETE
GALVANIZED STEEL BOLTS 3" EXPOSED (WRAP BOLT WITH BUILDING FELT)
GRAVEL BASE
3'-0", TYP.

CONCRETE AND TIMBER SITE-FORMED PAVER WALK

PAVERS OVER FLEXIBLE BASE

Dennis Carmichael; EDAW, Inc.; Alexandria, Virginia
Charles A. Szoradi, AIA; Washington. D.C.

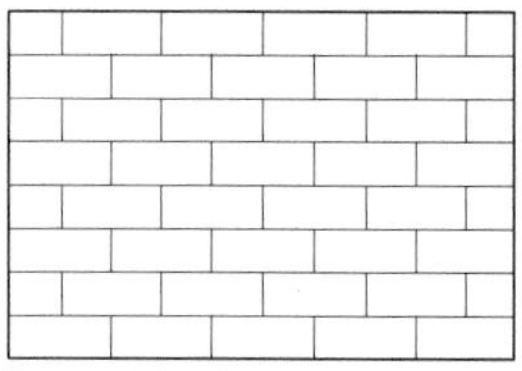

RUNNING BOND

OFFSET BOND

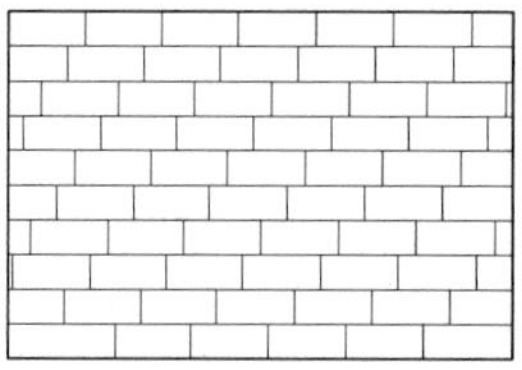

OFFSET BOND

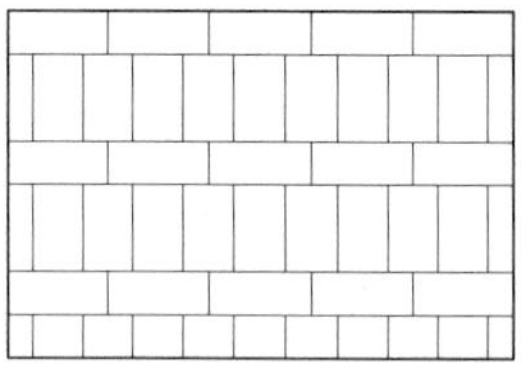

MIXED RUNNING AND STACK BOND

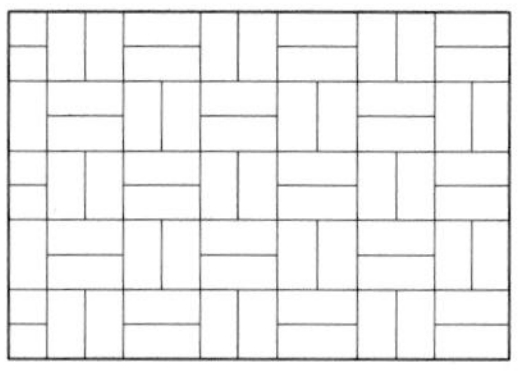

BASKET WEAVE

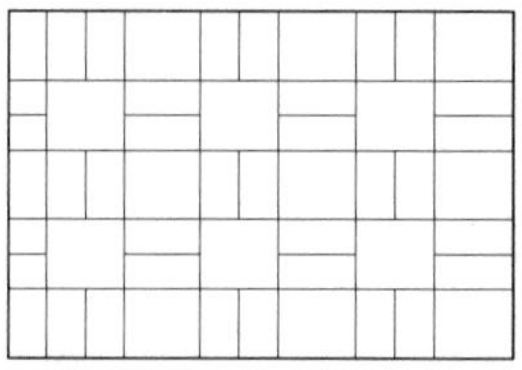

BASKET WEAVE

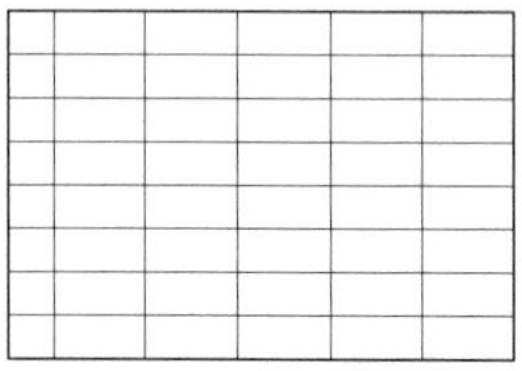

STACK BOND

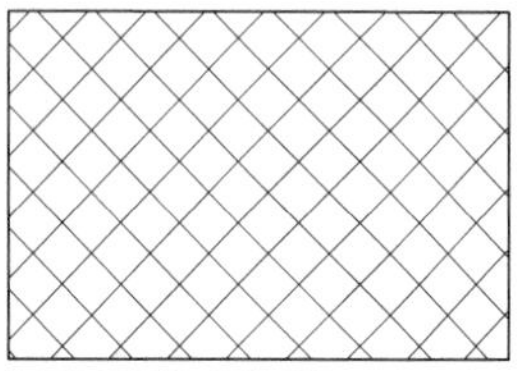

DIAGONAL STACK

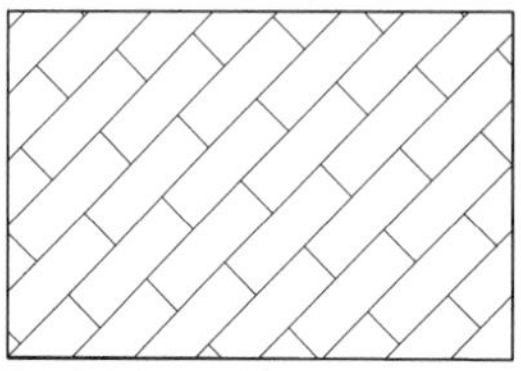

DIAGONAL BOND

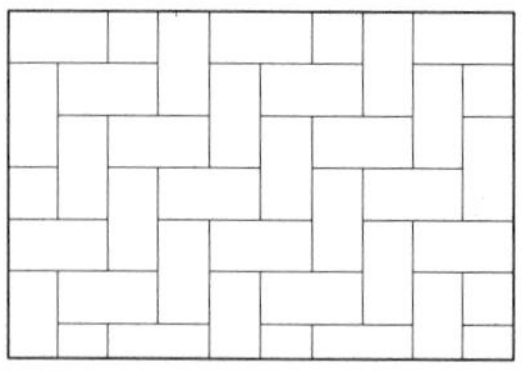

HERRINGBONE

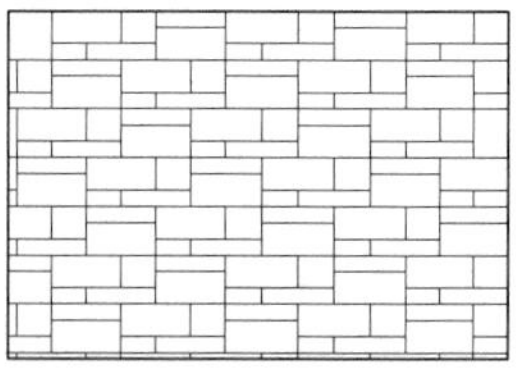

PATTERNED ASHLAR

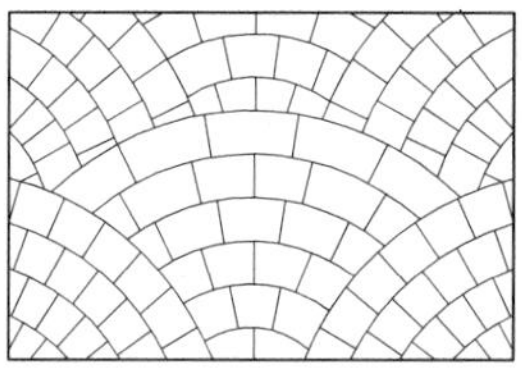

ROMAN COBBLE

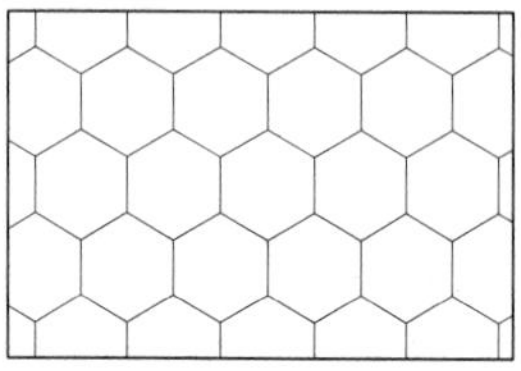

HEXAGON

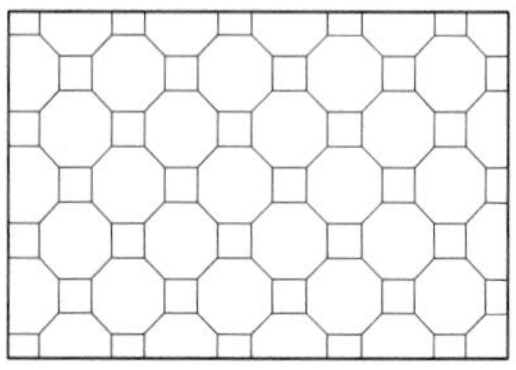

BASKET WEAVE OR PARQUET

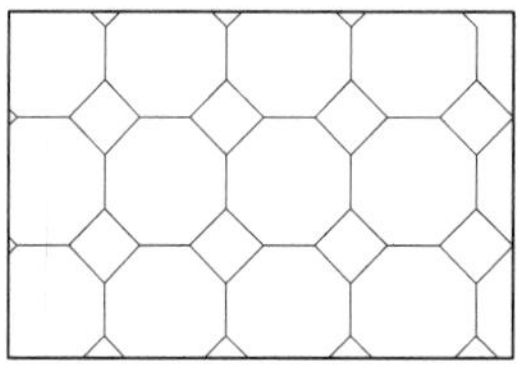

OCTAGON AND DOT

UNIT PAVERS

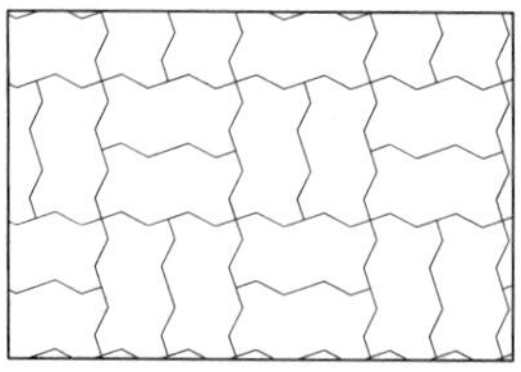

BASKET WEAVE

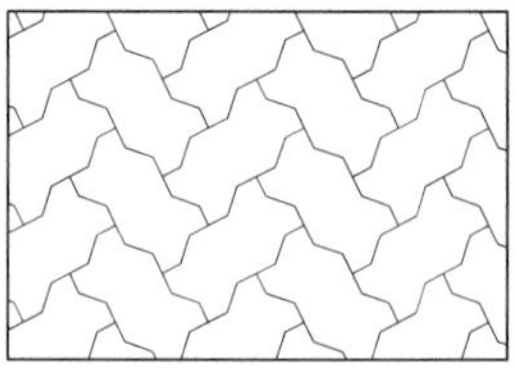

HERRINGBONE

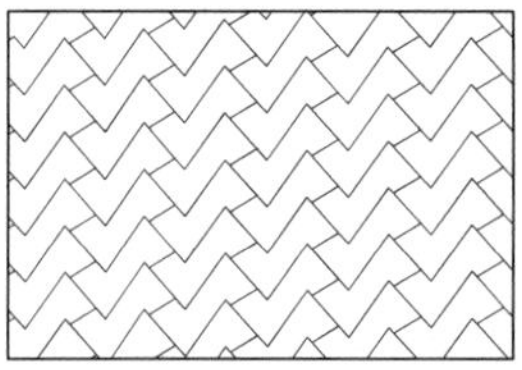

DIAGONAL RUNNING BOND

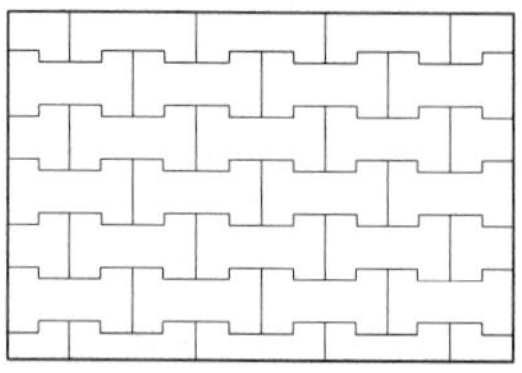

RUNNING BOND

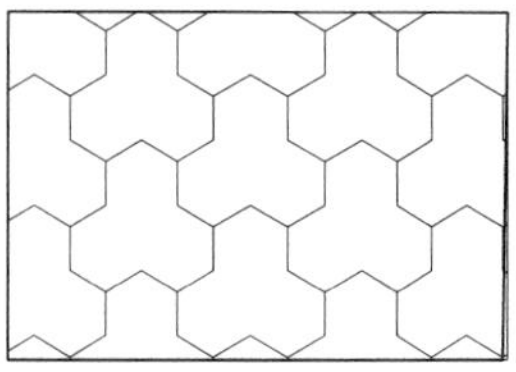

COMBINED HEXAGON

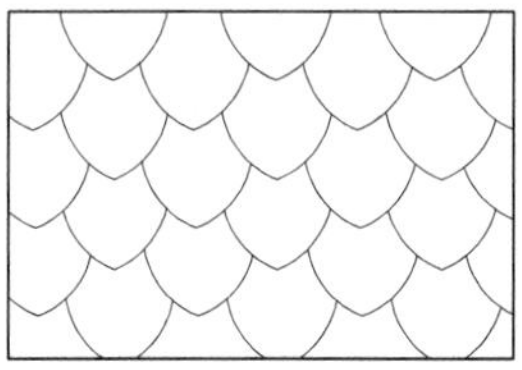

CATHEDRAL

INTERLOCKING UNIT PAVERS

Dennis Carmichael; EDAW, Inc.; Alexandria, Virginia

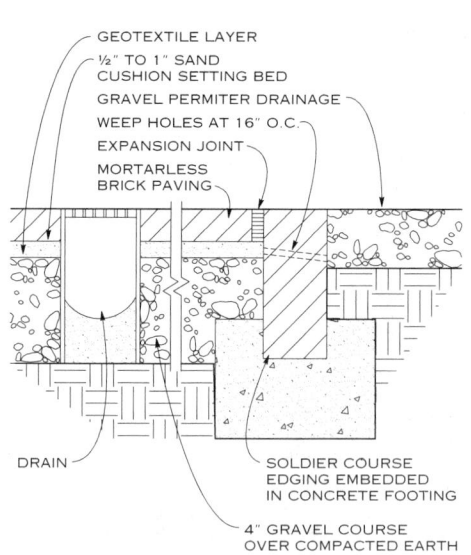

GEOTEXTILE LAYER
½" TO 1" SAND CUSHION SETTING BED
GRAVEL PERMITER DRAINAGE
WEEP HOLES AT 16" O.C.
EXPANSION JOINT
MORTARLESS BRICK PAVING

DRAIN

SOLDIER COURSE EDGING EMBEDDED IN CONCRETE FOOTING

4" GRAVEL COURSE OVER COMPACTED EARTH

EDGE DRAINAGE AT FLEXIBLE PAVING

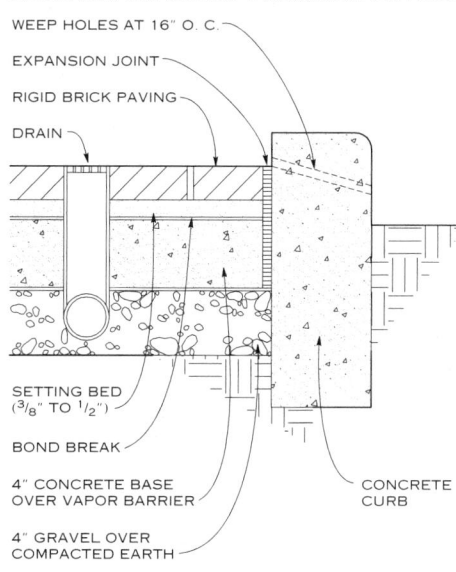

WEEP HOLES AT 16" O. C.

EXPANSION JOINT

RIGID BRICK PAVING

DRAIN

SETTING BED ($\frac{3}{8}$" TO $\frac{1}{2}$")

BOND BREAK

4" CONCRETE BASE OVER VAPOR BARRIER

4" GRAVEL OVER COMPACTED EARTH

CONCRETE CURB

EDGE DRAINAGE AT RIGID PAVING

NOTES

1. Drainpipes may be omitted at well-drained areas.
2. Provide positive outflow for drainpipes.
3. Do not use unsatisfactory soil (expanding organic).
4. Satisfactory soil must be compacted to 95%.
5. Handtight paving joints are preferred over mortar joints. However, when mortar joints are required and freezing and thawing are frequent, use latex-modified mortar.
6. Concrete footing for edging should be 10 to 14 in. wide and 6 to 8 in. deep. It is preferable to place the bottom of the footing at freezing depth. If the freezing depth is deeper than the bottom of the footing, provide 4 in. of gravel below the footing.
7. Interlocking pavers are available in concrete, hydraulically pressed concrete, asphalt, and brick in different weight classifications, compressive strengths, surface textures, finishes, and colors. Consult local suppliers for availability.
8. Subject to the manufacturer's recommendations and local code requirements, interlocking concrete pavers may be used in areas subject to heavy vehicle loads at speeds of 30 to 40 mph.
9. Concrete interlocking paver sizes are based on metric dimensions.
10. When paver shape permits, the herringbone pattern is recommended for paving subject to vehicular traffic.
11. Continuous curb or other edge restraint is required to anchor pavers in applications subject to vehicular traffic.

TYPES OF WATER SUPPLY

Water supply systems commonly employed for residential use are public water supply systems (mains); wells; cisterns/rainwater catchments; natural springs; natural waterways (ponds, lakes, streams, rivers); and distillation.

GENERAL NOTES

1. All water supply systems should be inspected, tested, and approved by local or state authorities, as required, before operation.

2. Flush newly installed systems with fresh water, disinfect to remove contaminants, and perform bacteriological and chemical tests as required. Repeat testing on a regular basis, biennially or as recommended by health authorities.

3. Surface contamination can extend to depths of 20 ft (or greater, depending on soil material). Seal casing/piping joints and voids surrounding the piping to prevent contamination seepage.

4. Depending on the source, groundwater is generally cleaner and more pure than surface water. The ultimate use of the water (for toilet or laundry, irrigation, watering farm animals, human drinking and bathing) determines purity requirements. Consider disinfection and filtration systems to remove harmful bacteria and excessive impurities and minerals that affect water taste or quality.

5. "Graywater" (water retrieved from bathing, laundry, or kitchen sources) can easily be filtered, stored, and recycled for nonpotable uses such as toilets, car washing, or irrigation. In addition, it can be processed through natural biological systems and returned to potable uses.

WELLS

Well details given here are generally from the *Manual of Individual Water Supply Systems* prepared by the Environmental Protection Agency's Office of Drinking Water (1982).

WELL LOCATION: Wells should be located at least 100 ft from (septic tank) sewage disposal. Check local codes.

CAPACITY OF WELL, PUMP, AND PRESSURE TANK: After drilling, test capacity for at least 4 hrs at a constant yield and drawdown. Determine minimum acceptable well capacity from the chart on this page titled "Determining Recommended Pump Capacity," then add a factor of safety and usage, preferably 100%. Use the same chart to determine the required pump capacity. The capacity of the pressure tank is figured by multiplying the pumping rate by 5 or 10 (42 gal minimum).

If a well does not have a pump capacity shown in the chart on this page, provide a smaller well pump and storage tank followed by a circulating pump and pressure tank.

DISINFECTION: Wells and associated piping should be disinfected before they are put into operation.

TYPES OF WELL PUMPING SYSTEMS: Pumping systems used for wells include a centrifugal pump with a motor aboveground and below the water level in the well; a jet pump, which has both pump and motor aboveground; and direct and reciprocating pumps in the well with a motor aboveground. (An artesian well is one in which the power of the water pressure elevates a column of water above the original water level without pumps.)

CISTERNS

Cisterns are man-made collection reservoirs (usually covered to stop evaporation) that store rainwater collected from roofs or paved areas called catchments. Cisterns are made of steel, polyethylene, concrete, and other chemically inert materials.

TYPES OF WELLS

TYPE	DEPTH	DIAM.	REMARKS
Dug	To 50 ft	3–20 ft	"Wishing well" type; masonry lining; can absorb surface contamination; susceptible to periodic dry spells
Bored	To 100 ft	2–30 in.	Bored with augers; vitrified tile or steel pipe casing; seal joints to 20-ft depth to prevent surface contamination
Driven	To 50 ft	1–2 in.	Driven by well-points; coupled pipe section casing; quick and cheap but shallow depth
Drilled	To 1000 ft	4–24 in.	Drilled by percussion or rotary bit; plastic or steel casing installed after full depth is drilled; expensive, large machinery required but greatest depths/water availability and constancy

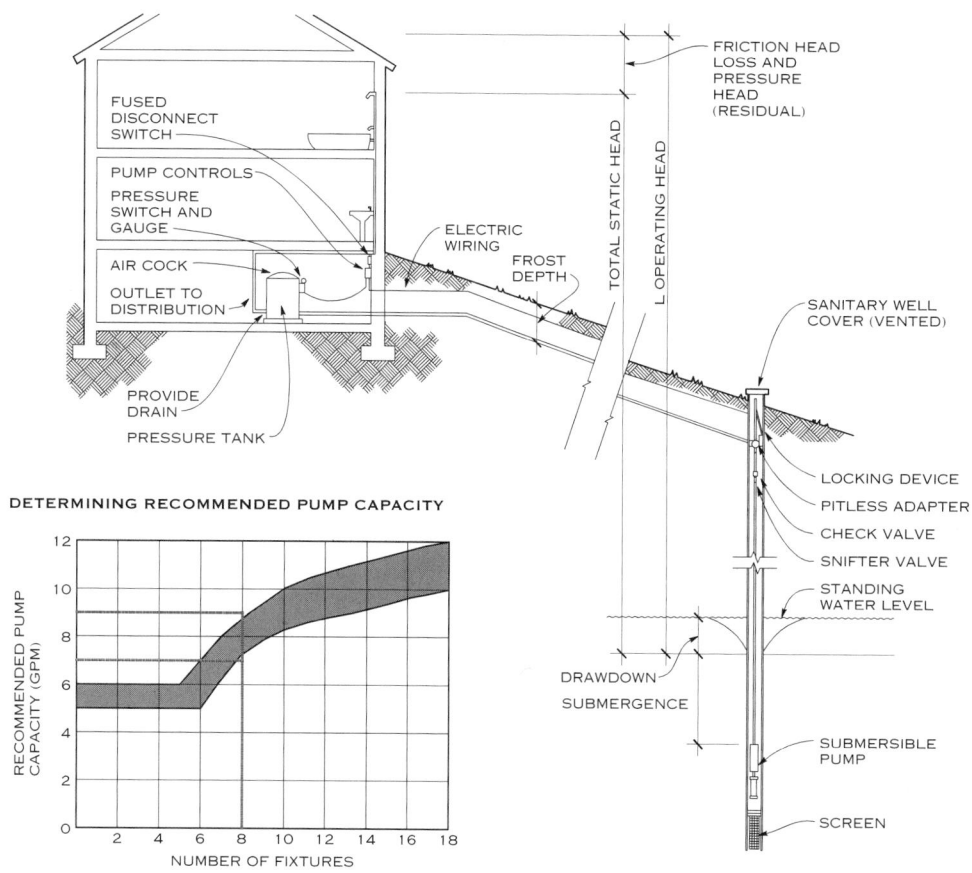

DETERMINING RECOMMENDED PUMP CAPACITY

TYPICAL DRILLED WELL AND DOMESTIC WATER DISTRIBUTION

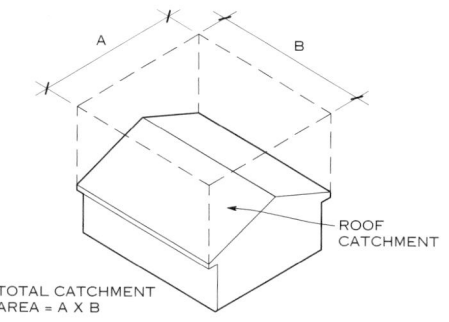

TOTAL CATCHMENT
AREA = A X B

ROOF CATCHMENT CALCULATION FOR CISTERN DESIGN

Nonresistive materials are used for catchment areas and drainpipes. Water from cisterns may be used for emergencies only or for garden watering, cleaning, toilet flushing, bathing, laundry, dishwashing, or other, nonpotable uses.

Major factors used to estimate cistern capacity are amount of rainfall in the catchment area, effective collections surface, storage capacity, user water consumption per day, longest dry period for the region, and availability of other sources of water for emergencies. Basically, cistern size comes down to the relationship between how fast the tank is emptied and how fast it is filled and how much of a buffer is required. For residential use, consumption ranges from 30–50 gal/person/day. Water is produced at a rate between 0.4 and 0.6 gal/sq ft of catchment area per in. of rain. Consult local meteorological records and codes to determine cistern design.

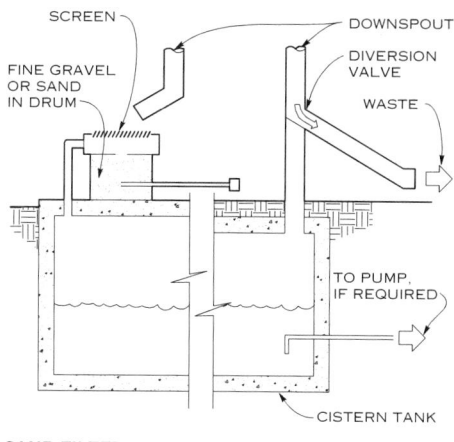

SAND FILTER   DIVERSION VALVE

CISTERN TYPES FOR WATER PURIFICATION

NOTES ON CISTERNS

1. Locate cisterns as close as practical to the ultimate point of use and away from potential flooding to avoid contamination.

2. Screen inlet and outlet piping to prevent the entrance of debris, insects, or animals.

3. Provide sump, drainage, and lockable access for annual cleaning and disinfection of the storage tank.

CAPACITIES OF TANKS AND CISTERNS (GALLONS)

DEPTH (FT)	SQUARE TANK SIZES			ROUND TANK SIZES (DIAM.)			
	8 FT	10 FT	12 FT	8 FT	10 FT	12 FT	14 FT
4	1920	3000	4320	1500	2350	3380	4610
6	2880	4500	6480	2250	3520	5070	6920
8	3840	6000	8640	3000	4700	6760	9220
10	4790	7500	10,800	3760	5870	8460	11,520
12	5748	8976	12,960	4510	7040	10,150	13,830

Daniel F. C. Hayes, AIA; Washington, D.C.

GENERAL

Subsurface drainage systems are very different engineering designs than surface drainage systems. Surface drainage systems intercept and collect storm water runoff and convey it away from a building and site with the use of large inlets and storm drains. Subsurface drainage systems typically are smaller in size and capacity, designed to intercept the slower underground flows of a natural groundwater table, underground stream, or infiltration of soils from surface sources. Surface and subsurface systems typically require discharge either through a pumping station or by gravity drainage to an adequate outfall.

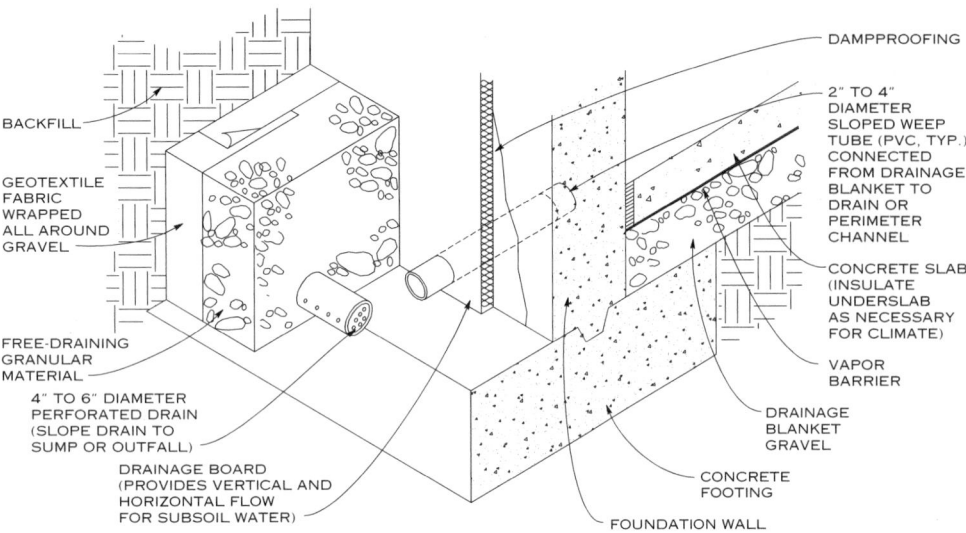
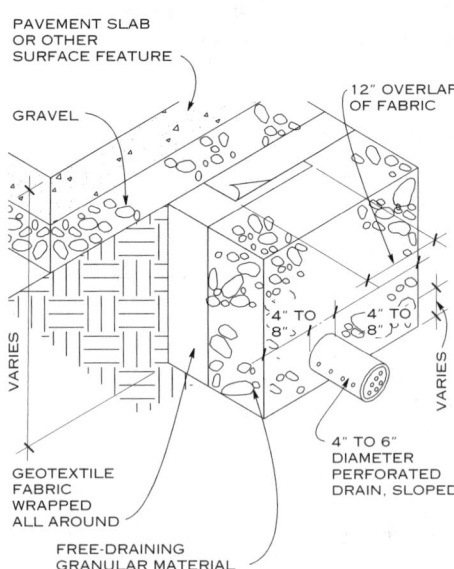

TYPICAL PERIMETER FOOTING DRAIN

NOTES

1. The depth of a drain determines how much subsurface water levels will be reduced.
2. When a perforated drain is used, install it with the holes facing down.
3. When used to intercept hillside seepage, the bottom of a trench should be cut a minimum of 6 in. into underlying impervious material.

TYPICAL SUBSURFACE DRAIN

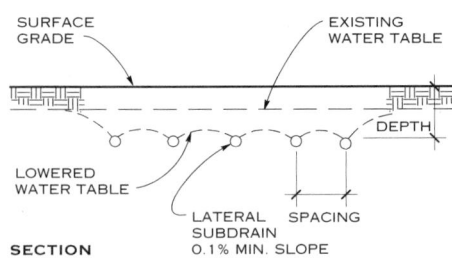

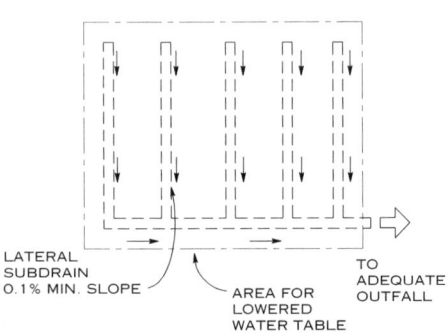

PLAN
NOTES

1. Subsoil drainage systems are laid out to meet the needs of a site. A grid, parallel lines, or random pattern at low points in the topography is used to collect subsurface water.
2. Depth and spacing of subsoil drainage pipes depend on soil conditions. Geotechnical design may be required to ensure effective operation of a subsoil drainage system.

UNDER-SITE SUBSOIL DRAINAGE

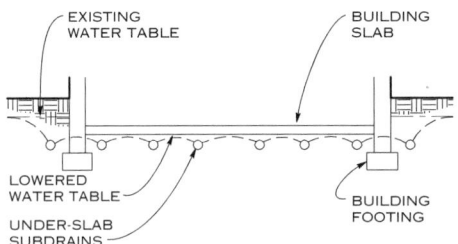

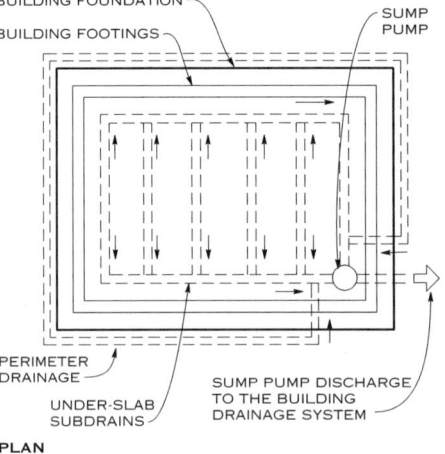

PLAN

UNDER-BUILDING SUBSOIL DRAINAGE

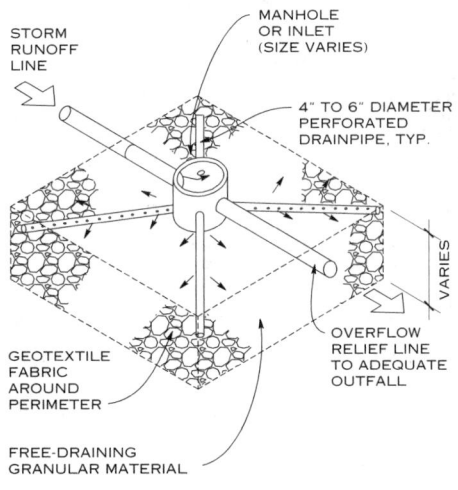

NOTE

Dry wells provide an underground disposal system for surface runoff, but their effectiveness is in direct proportion to the porosity of surrounding soils, and they are efficient only for draining small areas. High rainfall runoff rates cannot be absorbed at the rather low percolation rates of most soils, so the difference is stored temporarily in a dry well. Efficiency is reduced during extended periods of wet weather, when receiving soils are saturated and the well is refilled before it drains completely.

DRY WELL

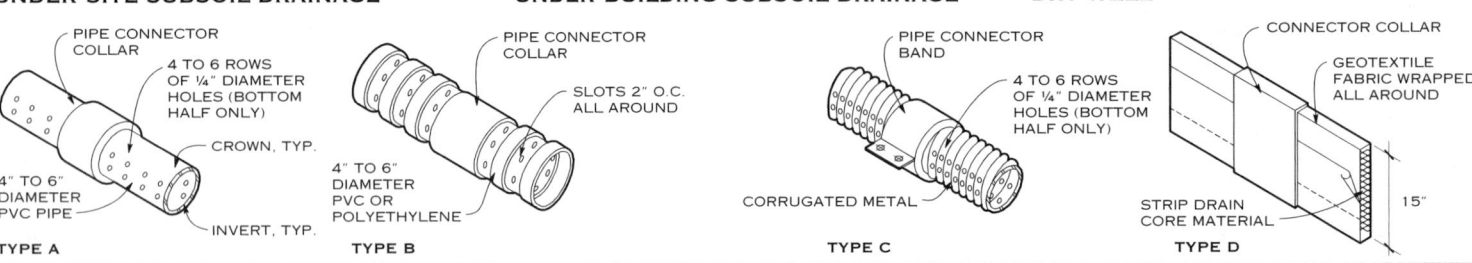

SUBSURFACE DRAINPIPES

Joseph P. Mensch, P.E.; Wiles Mensch Corporation; Reston, Virginia
Kurt N. Pronske, P.E.; Reston, Virginia
Harold C. Munger, FAIA; Munger Munger + Associates Architects; Toledo, Ohio

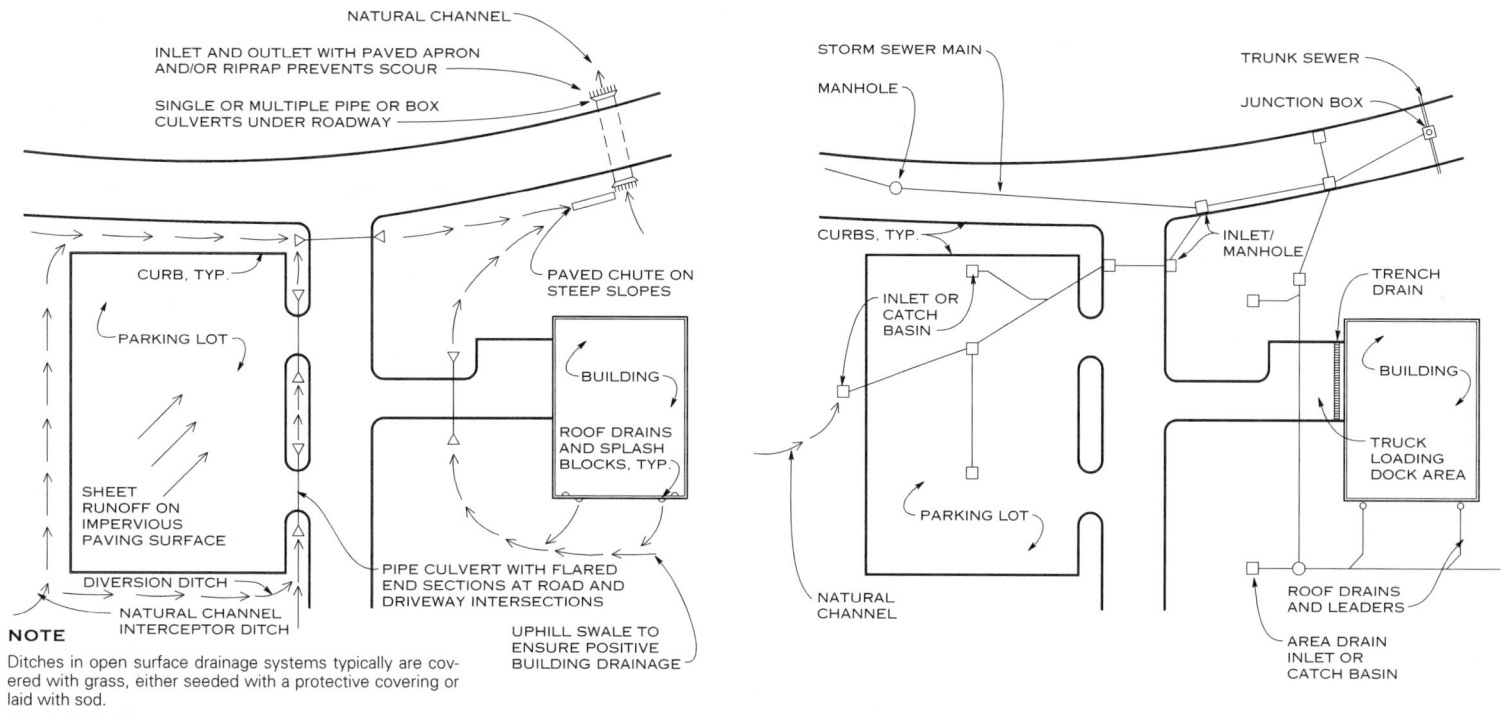

NOTE

Ditches in open surface drainage systems typically are covered with grass, either seeded with a protective covering or laid with sod.

OPEN SYSTEM

CLOSED SYSTEM

SURFACE DRAINAGE SYSTEM TYPES (IMPERVIOUS PAVING)

GENERAL

Surface drainage systems are designed to collect and dispose of rainfall runoff to prevent the flow of water from damaging building structures (through foundation leakage), site structures, and the surface grade (through erosion). The two basic types of surface drainage are the open system and the closed system.

The open system, which utilizes a ditch/swale and culvert, is used in less densely populated, more open areas where the flow of water above grade can be accommodated fairly easily. The closed system, which utilizes pipes, an inlet/catch basin, and manholes, is used in more urban, populated areas, where land must be used efficiently and water brought below the surface quickly to avoid interference with human activity. The two systems are commonly combined where terrain, human density, and land uses dictate.

A pervious or porous paving system is often used for parking and other hard site surfaces. This drainage system allows water to percolate through the paved surface into the soil, similar to the way the land would naturally absorb water.

NOTES

1. All slopes, grates, swales, and other drainage features must be laid out according to the ADA, without restricting accessible routes for persons with disabilities.

2. Lay out grades so runoff can safely flow away from buildings. If drains become blocked, backed-up water should not accumulate around the foundation.

3. An open system, or one in which water is kept on top of the surface as long as possible, is generally more economical than a closed system.

4. Consider the effect of ice forming on the surface when determining slopes for vehicles and pedestrians.

5. Consult local codes on such criteria as intensity and duration of rainstorms and allowable runoff for the locality.

6. Formulas given on this page are meant for approximation only. Consult a qualified engineer or landscape architect to design a site-specific system.

RUNOFF VELOCITY

VELOCITIES (Channel)	MIN. (ft/sec)	MAX. (ft/sec)
Grass—athletic field	0.5	2
Walks—long.	0.5	12*
Walks—transverse	1	4
Streets—long.	0.5	20
Parking	1	5
Channels—grass swale	1	8
Channels—paved swale	0.5	12

*8.3% maximum for handicapped access

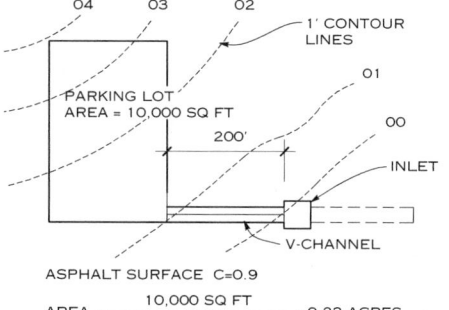

ASPHALT SURFACE C=0.9

$$AREA = \frac{10,000 \text{ SQ FT}}{43,560 \text{ SQ FT/ACRE}} = 0.23 \text{ ACRES}$$

NOTE

Following is a simplified method for calculating the approximate runoff of areas less than 100 acres:

Q = C x I x A
  Q = flow (cu ft/sec)
  C = surface runoff value (see table)
  I = intensity (in./hr; obtain from local codes)
  A = area of site (acres)

For example, assume the local code requires I = 5 in./hr:

Q = C x I x A
Q = 0.9 x 5 x 0.23
Q = 1.04 cu ft/sec
Q = approximate volume of water per second entering the V-channel from the parking lot

CALCULATION OF RUNOFF

SURFACE RUNOFF VALUES (C)

SURFACE	VALUE
Roofs	0.95–1.00
Pavement	0.90–1.00
Roads	0.30–0.90
Bare soil—sand	0.20–0.40
Bare soil—clay	0.30–0.75
Grass	0.15–0.60
Commercial development	0.60–0.75
High-density residential development	0.50–0.65
Low-density residential development	0.30–0.55

NOTE

All values are approximate.

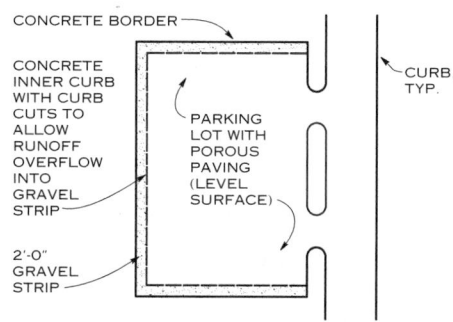

POROUS PAVING SYSTEM

POROUS PAVING MATERIALS

The two principal types of porous paving are a monolithic surfacing material and unit pavers. Monolithic porous paving is stone aggregate bound with asphalt or portland cement. The aggregate must be sorted to exclude the "fines" or sand-sized particles that normally fill the voids between larger pieces. Without the fines, the paving material allows water to run through it. Generally, porous asphalt and concrete are both strong enough for parking and roadway surfaces and pedestrian uses. Precast unit pavers, with shapes that allow water to flow through them, can also give surface stability for parking or driveways. Paver types are available for exposed placement or for burial just below the surface. In the latter case, the soil-pea gravel or vegetation in the pavers is exposed and can help percolate precipitation into the ground.

To reduce runoff and increase water absorption, porous paving must be underlaid with a bed of unbound aggregate. The unbound aggregate acts as a structural support and forms a reservoir to hold precipitation until it can percolate into the soil. Use of porous paving may permit use of a significantly smaller and simpler storm drainage system.

SLOPES

DESCRIPTION	MIN. %	MAX. %	REC. %
Grass—mowed	1	25	1.5–10
Grass—athletic field	0.5	2	1
Walks—long.	0.5	12*	1.5
Walks—transverse	1	4	1–2
Streets—long.	0.5	20	1–10
Parking	1	5	2–3
Channels—grass swale	1	8	1.5–2
Channels—paved swale	0.5	12	4–6

*8.3% maximum for handicapped access

Pearse O'Doherty, ASLA; Graham Landscape Architecture; Annapolis, Maryland

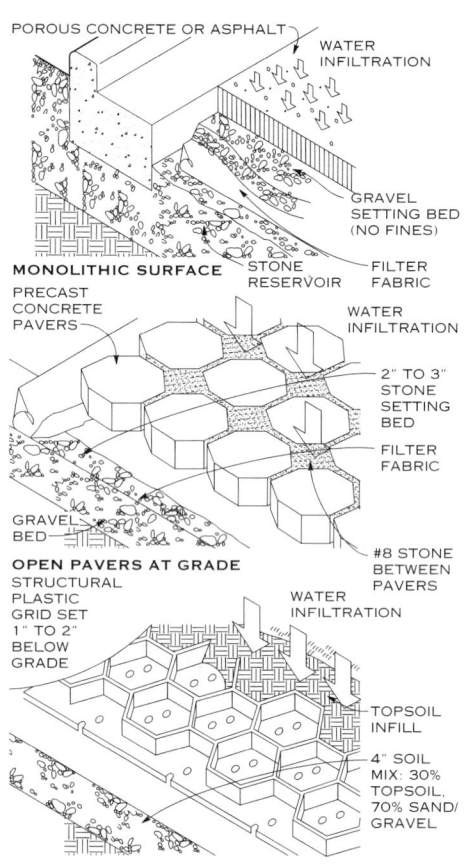

MONOLITHIC SURFACE

POROUS CONCRETE OR ASPHALT
WATER INFILTRATION
GRAVEL SETTING BED (NO FINES)
STONE RESERVOIR
FILTER FABRIC

OPEN PAVERS AT GRADE

PRECAST CONCRETE PAVERS
WATER INFILTRATION
2" TO 3" STONE SETTING BED
FILTER FABRIC
GRAVEL BED
#8 STONE BETWEEN PAVERS

STRUCTURAL GRID/PAVERS BELOW GRADE

STRUCTURAL PLASTIC GRID SET 1" TO 2" BELOW GRADE
WATER INFILTRATION
TOPSOIL INFILL
4" SOIL MIX: 30% TOPSOIL, 70% SAND/GRAVEL

POROUS PAVING TYPES

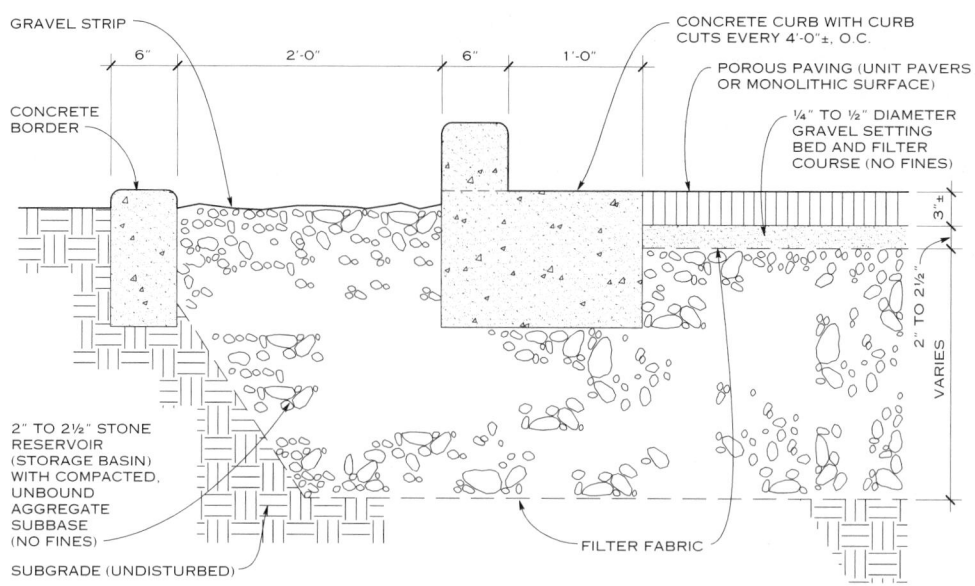

GRAVEL STRIP
CONCRETE BORDER
CONCRETE CURB WITH CURB CUTS EVERY 4'-0"± O.C.
POROUS PAVING (UNIT PAVERS OR MONOLITHIC SURFACE)
¼" TO ½" DIAMETER GRAVEL SETTING BED AND FILTER COURSE (NO FINES)
6" 2'-0" 6" 1'-0"
3"±
2" TO 2½"
VARIES
2" TO 2½" STONE RESERVOIR (STORAGE BASIN) WITH COMPACTED, UNBOUND AGGREGATE SUBBASE (NO FINES)
SUBGRADE (UNDISTURBED)
FILTER FABRIC

POROUS PAVING AND STONE RESERVOIR DETAIL

NOTES ON POROUS PAVING

1. Soils around porous paving installations must have a minimum percolation rate of about ½ in./hr and should not be more than about 30% clay. On sites where the slope is greater than 3%, terracing the paved areas allows the bottom of each reservoir to remain level.

2. Proper specification and supervision are important in the installation of porous paving materials. Soil under the reservoir must not be unduly compacted during construction.

3. Porous concrete can withstand heavier loads than porous asphalt. Because it does not soften in hot weather and may be more susceptible to freeze-thaw damage, it is better suited to warmer climates. Additives may be introduced to improve cold climate performance.

4. Porous asphalt has good freeze-thaw resistance but is best suited for areas in which traffic is limited, such as employee parking.

5. While clogging of monolithic porous paving is generally not a problem, recommended maintenance may include use of a hydrovac once or twice a year, as well as the prompt removal of leaves and windblown sand.

6. The reservoir below porous paving has no fixed depth but is designed according to the slope of the site, the soil percolation rate, and the size of the design storm. Consult a civil engineer or landscape architect.

METHOD FOR SIZING CHANNELS

Channels and pipes for handling water runoff may be sized by determining the flow of water (Q) with the formula Q = Va. V is the velocity of the runoff water in ft/sec as determined by the Manning formula, and "a" is the cross-sectional area of water given in square feet. For a given Q, adjust the channel or pipe shape, size, and/or slope to obtain the desired velocity (one that will not erode earth, grass ditches, or other features).

The Manning formula is $V = 1.486/n \times r^{0.67} \times S^{0.5}$, in which n = values relating to surface characteristics of channels (see table), r = hydraulic radius (see table), and S = slope (the drop in ft/length).

For example, assume a 200-ft concrete V-channel for which

W = 2 ft
h = 0.5 ft
S = 0.005 (1 ft/200 ft)
r = 0.37 (calculated using V-channel properties)
$V = (1.486/0.015) \times 0.25^{0.67} \times 0.005^{0.5}$
= 2.6 ft/sec (see runoff velocity table on first AGS surface drainage page).

To check flow, follow these steps:

Q = Va ("a" from channel properties)
= 2.6 × 0.5 = 1.3 cu ft/sec.

Use the formula for calculating runoff (Q = C × I × A; given on the first AGS surface drainage page) to determine the flow required for a site; compare it to the capacity of a channel sized according to the Manning formula to determine whether the channel design is satisfactory.

n VALUES FOR MANNING FORMULA

CHANNEL SURFACE	n
Cast iron	0.012
Corrugated steel	0.032
Clay tile	0.014
Cement grout	0.013
Concrete	0.015
Earth ditch	0.023
Cut rock channel	0.033
Winding channel	0.025

HYDRAULIC PROPERTIES OF TYPICAL CHANNEL SECTIONS

TYPE SECTION	WIDTH (W)	BASE (b)	DEPTH (d)	AREA (a)	WETTED PERIMETER (P)	HYDRAULIC RADIUS (r)
RECTANGULAR	b or $\frac{a}{d}$	W or $\frac{a}{d}$	$\frac{a}{b}$	wd	W + 2d	$\dfrac{d}{1 + \frac{2d}{W}}$
TRIANGULAR	2e	—	$\frac{a}{e}$	ed	$e\sqrt{e^2 + d^2}$	$\dfrac{ed}{2\sqrt{e^2 + d^2}}$
TRIANGULAR (curb and gutter)	$\frac{2a}{d}$	—	$\frac{2a}{W}$	$\frac{Wd}{2}$	$d + \sqrt{d^2 + W^2}$	$\dfrac{2Wd}{d + \sqrt{W^2 + W^2}}$
TRAPEZOIDAL (even sides)	b + 2e	W − 2e	$\frac{a}{b + e}$	d(b + e)	$b + 2\sqrt{e^2 + d^2}$	$\dfrac{d(b + e)}{b + 2\sqrt{e^2 + d^2}}$
PARABOLIC	$\frac{a}{0.67d}$	—	$\frac{a}{0.67W}$	0.67 Wd	$W + \left(\frac{8d^2}{3W}\right)$	$\dfrac{a}{W + \left(\frac{8d^2}{3W}\right)}$

NOTE

0.3–0.5 ft recommended for freeboard (F).

Pearse O'Doherty, ASLA; Graham Landscape Architecture; Annapolis, Maryland

GENERAL

The grate design chosen for a particular application depends on the priorities assigned to each of the functions listed below. Local conditions may require inclusion of some or all of the performance features in a design.

CAPACITY: Interception of storm water is generally considered the most important function a grate can perform. The geometry and size of the openings affect this ability. Consult a civil engineer or hydrologist for individual grate capacities.

SCREENING OF LARGE DEBRIS: An inlet grate must act as a strainer to prevent harmful debris from entering sewer lines. A well-designed grate prevents objects such as branches, sticks, sheets of semirigid material, and chunks of wood, which can easily pass by large curb openings (such as open-throat type), from entering the catch basin.

PASSING OF SMALL DEBRIS: Organic material such as grass clippings, leaves, small stones, or twigs may be permitted to pass into the catch basin as they are not a hazard in sewer lines. Provide grate openings wide enough, long enough, or of special design to pass this debris and still meet requirements for roadway-safe grates.

STRENGTH: Inlet grates placed in roadways must be designed to withstand heavy traffic loads. The most generally accepted specifications for highway loading criteria come from the American Association of State Highway and Transportation Officials (AASHTO).

PERMANENCY: An inlet grate should be designed to match or exceed the expected life of the installation. Steel, aluminum, and cast iron are generally accepted materials for inlet grates, although other materials such as brass, chrome, and structural polyethylene are used in special applications.

BICYCLE SAFETY: Grates can be made safer for bicycle and pedestrian traffic through attention to design and installation. Options include diagonal bars set at a 45° angle; slotted grates, provided the slots are $1^1/_4$ to $2^1/_4$ in. wide and a maximum of 9 in. long and the transverse (cross) bars are spaced so a bicycle wheel cannot drop lower than about 1 in.; and bars transverse to the direction of traffic and storm water flow and slanted to conduct water into the catch basin. Grate design does not ensure safe usage; attention must be paid to usage patterns of probable users. Consult traffic engineers and local codes for more information.

Consider clogging hazards and the geometry of flow-through efficiency when designing for bicycle safety. Use of vane-shaped or sloped bars, rather than conventional vertical bars, may improve the capacity of a grate to pass storm water. Grates with these types of bars are safe for bicycles; consult manufacturers. Do not allow gutter slopes to be substantially swaled into the curb, which could create a pocket in the roadway affecting the safety of bicycles and other traffic.

GRATE SIZING

Most grates are oversized to prevent buildup of water; see manufacturers' catalogs for free area. The following formula for sizing grates is based on a given allowable depth of water over the grate.

$$Q = .66 \, CA \, (64.4 \, d)^{0.5}$$

where A = free area (sq ft)
  d = allowable depth of water above grate (ft)
  C = orifice coefficient (0.6 for square edges, 0.8 for round)
  .66 = clogging factor

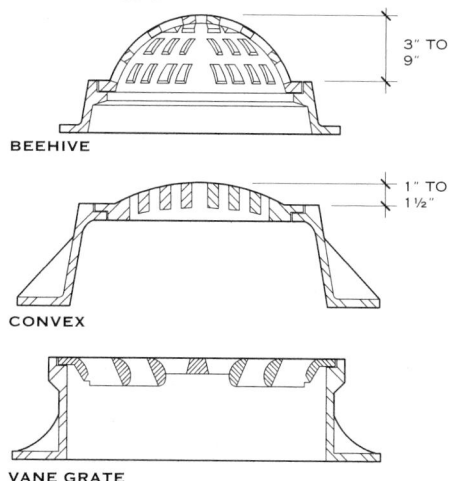

BEEHIVE   3" TO 9"

CONVEX   1" TO 1½"

VANE GRATE

MISCELLANEOUS GRATE DESIGNS

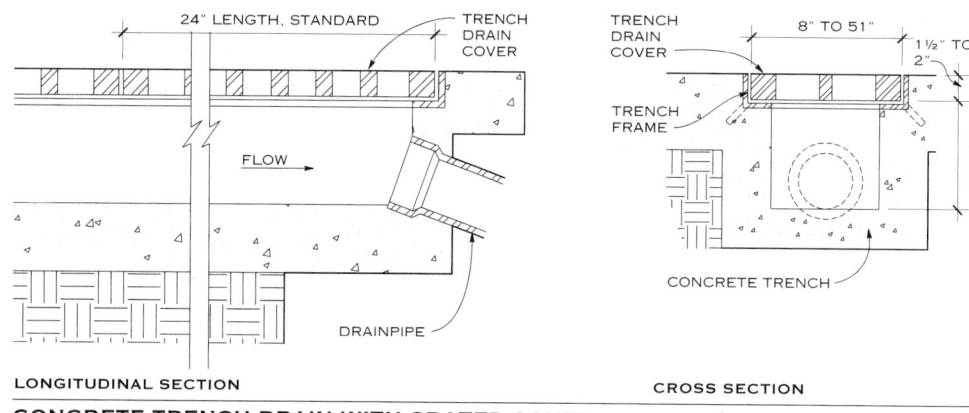

LONGITUDINAL SECTION   CROSS SECTION

CONCRETE TRENCH DRAIN WITH GRATED COVER

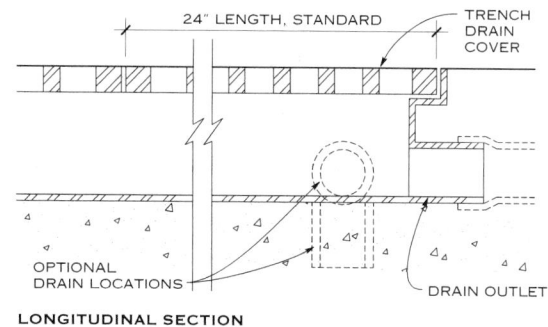

LONGITUDINAL SECTION   CROSS SECTION

METAL TRENCH DRAIN ASSEMBLY

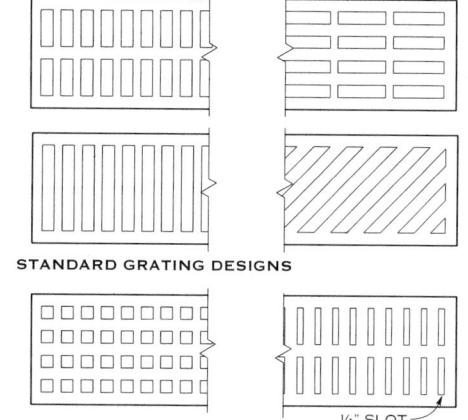

STANDARD GRATING DESIGNS

¼" SLOT

GRATINGS FOR HEAVY PEDESTRIAN TRAFFIC

GRATING DESIGN TYPES

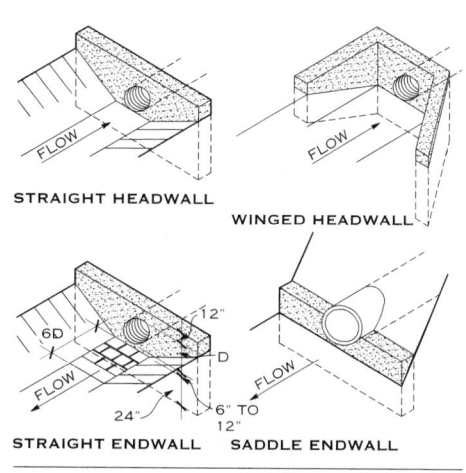

STRAIGHT HEADWALL   WINGED HEADWALL

STRAIGHT ENDWALL   SADDLE ENDWALL

HEADWALLS AND ENDWALLS

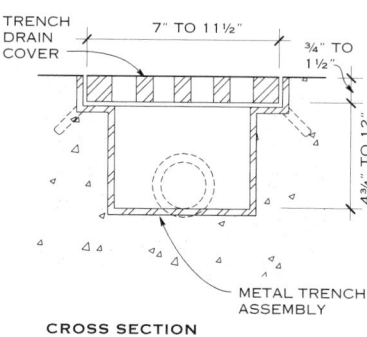

LIGHT-DUTY TRENCH DRAINS

CONCEALED DRAIN

MISCELLANEOUS DRAINS

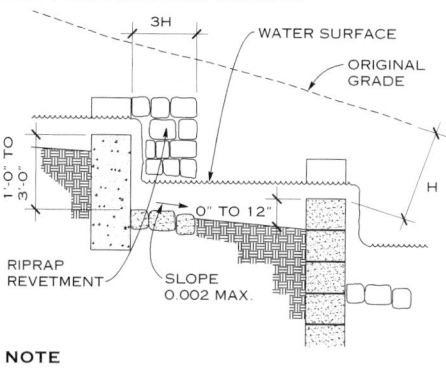

NOTE

Use check dams where channel slope and velocity will cause erosion.

CHECK DAMS

Pearse O'Doherty, ASLA; Graham Landscape Architecure; Annapolis, Maryland

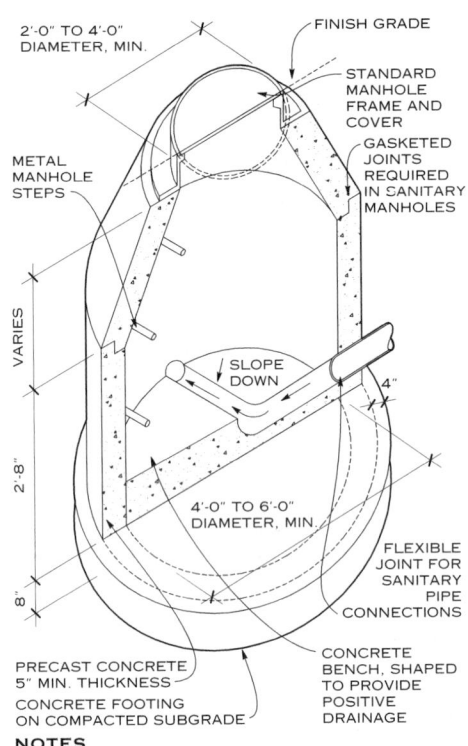

2'-0" TO 4'-0" DIAMETER, MIN.

FINISH GRADE

STANDARD MANHOLE FRAME AND COVER

GASKETED JOINTS REQUIRED IN SANITARY MANHOLES

METAL MANHOLE STEPS

VARIES

SLOPE DOWN

4"

2'-8"

4'-0" TO 6'-0" DIAMETER, MIN.

FLEXIBLE JOINT FOR SANITARY PIPE CONNECTIONS

8"

PRECAST CONCRETE 5" MIN. THICKNESS

CONCRETE FOOTING ON COMPACTED SUBGRADE

CONCRETE BENCH, SHAPED TO PROVIDE POSITIVE DRAINAGE

NOTES

1. Parging may be omitted in construction of storm sewer manholes.
2. Wall thickness on precast concrete manholes increases with depths greater than 12 ft.
3. Brick walls 8 in. thick may be used for manholes up to 12 ft deep. For that part of the manhole deeper than 12 ft, brick-and-block walls should be 12 in. thick. Manholes greater than 12 ft deep should have a base 12 in. thick.

COMBINED OR SANITARY SEWER MANHOLE

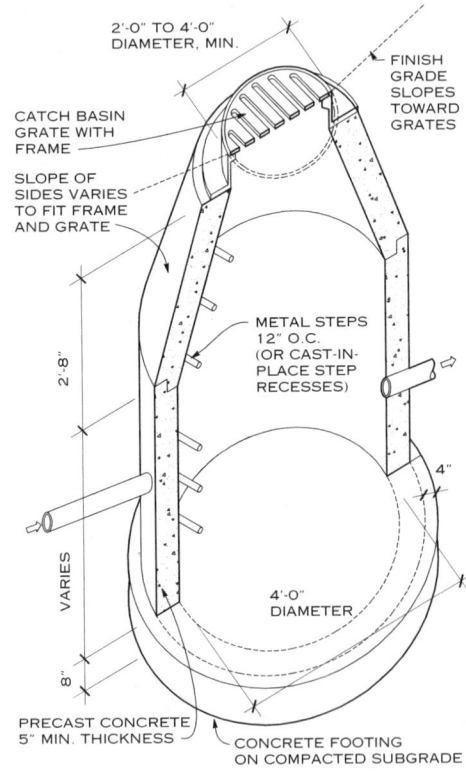

2'-0" TO 4'-0" DIAMETER, MIN.

FINISH GRADE SLOPES TOWARD GRATES

CATCH BASIN GRATE WITH FRAME

SLOPE OF SIDES VARIES TO FIT FRAME AND GRATE

METAL STEPS 12" O.C. (OR CAST-IN-PLACE STEP RECESSES)

2'-8"

VARIES

4"

4'-0" DIAMETER

8"

PRECAST CONCRETE 5" MIN. THICKNESS

CONCRETE FOOTING ON COMPACTED SUBGRADE

NOTE

A pipe trap or hood is required for connections to combination sewers.

CATCH BASIN

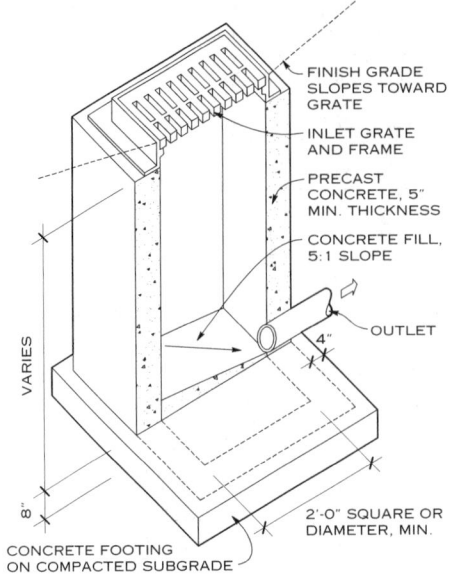

FINISH GRADE SLOPES TOWARD GRATE

INLET GRATE AND FRAME

PRECAST CONCRETE, 5" MIN. THICKNESS

CONCRETE FILL, 5:1 SLOPE

4"   OUTLET

VARIES

8"

2'-0" SQUARE OR DIAMETER, MIN.

CONCRETE FOOTING ON COMPACTED SUBGRADE

INLET

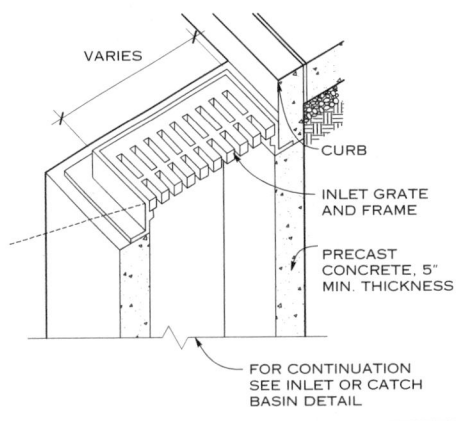

VARIES

CURB

INLET GRATE AND FRAME

PRECAST CONCRETE, 5" MIN. THICKNESS

FOR CONTINUATION SEE INLET OR CATCH BASIN DETAIL

GUTTER INLET

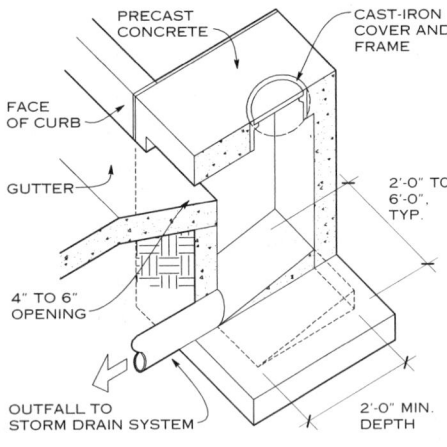

PRECAST CONCRETE

CAST-IRON COVER AND FRAME

FACE OF CURB

GUTTER

2'-0" TO 6'-0", TYP.

4" TO 6" OPENING

OUTFALL TO STORM DRAIN SYSTEM

2'-0" MIN. DEPTH

CURB INLET

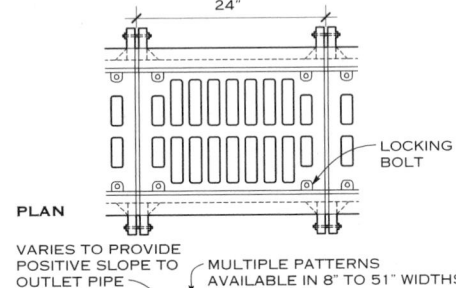

24"

PLAN

LOCKING BOLT

VARIES TO PROVIDE POSITIVE SLOPE TO OUTLET PIPE

MULTIPLE PATTERNS AVAILABLE IN 8" TO 51" WIDTHS

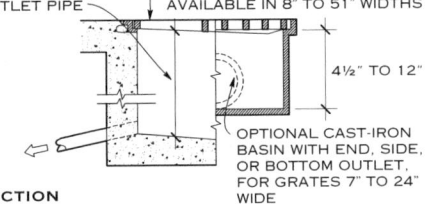

4½" TO 12"

OPTIONAL CAST-IRON BASIN WITH END, SIDE, OR BOTTOM OUTLET, FOR GRATES 7" TO 24" WIDE

SECTION

NOTE

Grates without bolts are available.

TRENCH DRAIN

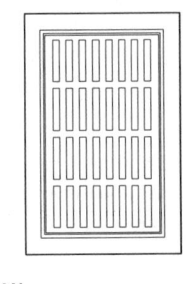

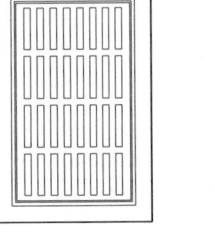

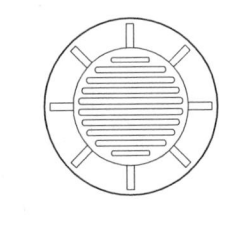

PLAN   PLAN

21" TO 60" (SOME PATTERNS CAN BE INSTALLED AS DOUBLE UNITS)

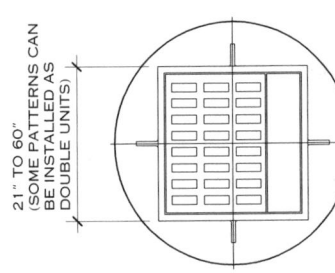

PLAN

2¼"   VARIES   2¼"

8" X 8" TO 36" X 36"

SECTION

FINISH GRADE

28" TO 62"

VARIES

SECTION

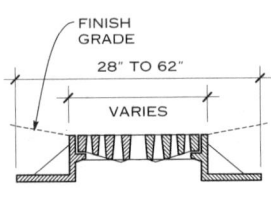

ALTERNATIVE SHAPES AVAILABLE TO MATCH CURB SECTIONS; CURBS ADJUSTABLE FROM 3" TO 9"

19" TO 36"

11" TO 24"

5" TO 8"

6" TO 9"

2" R

4" TO 8"

SECTION

NOTES

1. Frames and grates are available in many standard shapes and sizes. Constructed of cast or ductile iron, aluminum, and bronze, they are made for light- or heavy-duty loading conditions. Common shapes include round, rectangular, square, and linear. In addition, grates may be flat, concave, or convex. Consult manufacturers' catalogs for the full range of available castings.

2. Locate drainage structures with grated openings on or beyond the periphery of traveled ways to minimize contact with pedestrian or vehicular traffic. Grates that may come into contact with feet or narrow wheels must be constructed to prevent penetration by heels, crutch and cane tips, and slim tires but still have sufficient openings to pass the expected runoff.

TYPICAL FRAMES AND GRATES

Joseph P. Mensch, P.E.; Wiles Mensch Corporation; Reston, Virginia
Kurt N. Pronske, P.E.; Reston, Virginia

GENERAL

Natural filtration devices in the environment retain and treat pollutants such as sediment, fertilizer, pesticides, and air pollutants before they can enter water bodies. Increasing development, however, compromises the ability of the landscape to prevent water resource contamination. Typically, when land is developed, trees that formerly intercepted rainfall and pollutants are felled; natural depressions that temporarily ponded water are graded, soil is compacted; and the thick leaf-litter humus layer of the forest floor, which had absorbed rainfall, is scraped off or erodes.

Once a site has been developed, it can no longer store as much water, and rainfall is immediately transformed into runoff and transported to rivers, lakes, wetlands, or other surface water systems. Once construction is complete and some vegetation has returned to the site, expansive impervious surfaces such as rooftops and parking lots prevent most runoff from percolating into the soil. Instead, it must be directed off site by a surface drainage system of curbs, culverts, gutters, and storm sewers.

Measures for managing pollutants include methods of construction and land development that replace natural pollution filtration pathways (e.g., forests, wetlands) with similar filtering mechanisms. Water detention systems retain water, provide for percolation to groundwater, and filter pollutants out of water runoff. These systems comprise detention basins, constructed wetlands, and other temporary and permanent erosion control measures.

When choosing appropriate runoff control measures for a site, consider the following factors: the sensitivity of the local ecosystem; slope of the site; depth of the water table; proximity to bedrock, foundations, and wells; land consumption; land use restrictions; high sediment input; and thermal impacts to downstream areas.

NATURAL WETLAND SYSTEMS

Wetlands naturally detain and filter water. Scattered throughout the United States, from tropical areas to tundra, they form in depressions in the landscape where the water table is near or at the surface of the soil. They may be as small as a tabletop or span tens of thousands of acres. There is no single, correct, ecologically sound definition for wetlands, primarily because of their diversity. These systems are an important part of the ecosystem because they produce food and timber, purify drinking water, absorb and store floodwater, suppress storm surges, and help maintain biodiversity. Water is supplied to a wetland either by surface sources (e.g., streams or rivers) or by groundwater.

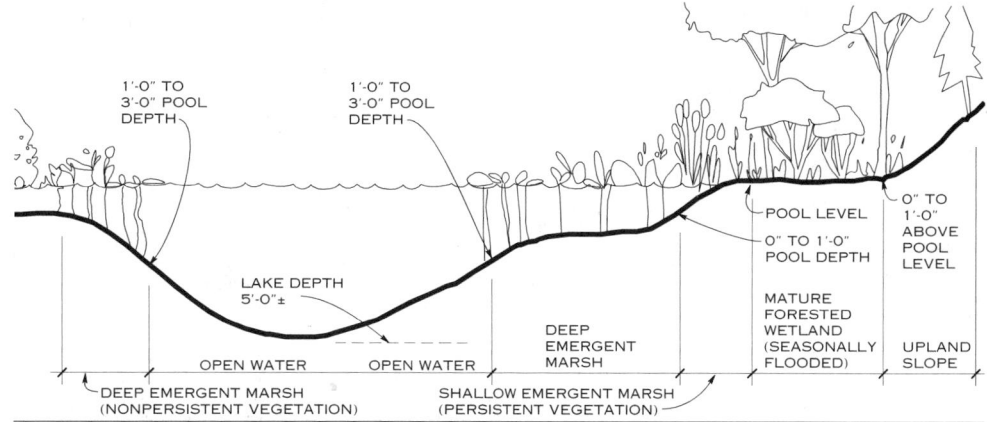

CROSS-SECTION OF NATURAL FRESHWATER, NONTIDAL WETLANDS

The sensitivity of wetlands determines appropriate buffer distances between them and developed areas. Buffers, which may range from 30 to 300 ft or more, should respond to the effect runoff may have on the wetland ecosystem. (Consult a wetlands scientist to formulate buffer distances.)

In general, four wetland sensitivity issues should be taken into account: hydrology—the wetland's source of water could be altered by development; vegetation—the plant species in a wetland have different levels of hardiness; ecological state—more pristine systems are more sensitive to development and runoff pollution; and animal species—for instance, nesting birds need greater buffer distances than wintering waterfowl.

ON-SITE RUNOFF CONTROL MEASURES

Architects can use several on-site measures to control runoff in development projects. One of the most commonly used is a simple open storage area for runoff. The configuration of such open systems varies, depending on the desired level of pollutant treatment. Typically called storage ponds, detention basins, or (when made to resemble a natural environment) a constructed storm water wetland, open systems generally operate more thoroughly with increased retention time.

Simple storage ponds are typically dry between storms after runoff has evaporated or infiltrated the groundwater. Dry ponds sometimes include a wet lower area for additional runoff retention. Wet ponds are permanently wet, allowing pollutants to settle to the bottom. Wet ponds that extend runoff retention time with control devices can remove a very high percentage of particulate pollutants.

Constructed storm water wetlands (engineered, shallow marshlike areas) retain runoff for long periods, allowing pollutants to settle out of the water column and providing biological, chemical, and physical processes for breaking down pollutants. Wetland vegetation slows the velocity of storm water, reducing erosion and allowing pollutants to settle. Many organic and inorganic compounds are removed from wetlands by the chemical processes of absorption, precipitation, and volatilization.

Constructed storm water wetlands can also filter excess nutrients such as nitrogen and phosphorus contained in runoff from gardens and septic tanks. To correctly size a wetland used for storm water runoff control, consider the total volume and velocity of water entering and leaving the system.

Potential advantages of using constructed storm water wetlands are that they have relatively low capital and operating costs, offer consistent compliance with permit requirements, and greatly reduce operational and maintenance costs.

COMPARATIVE ASSESSMENT OF THE EFFECTIVNESS OF URBAN BEST MANAGEMENT PRACTICES (BMPs)

URBAN BMP OPTIONS	POLLUTANT REMOVAL RELIABILITY	LONGEVITY*	APPLICABILITY TO MOST DEVELOPMENTS	WILDLIFE HABITAT POTENTIAL	ENVIRONMENTAL CONCERNS	COMPARATIVE COSTS	SPECIAL CONSIDERATIONS
Storm water wetlands	Moderate to high, depending on design	20+ years expected	Applicable to most sites if land is available	High	Stream warming, natural wetland alteration	Marginally higher than wet ponds	Recommended with design improvements and with the use of micropools and wetlands
Extended detention ponds	Moderate but not always reliable	20+ years but frequent clogging and short detention common	Widely applicable but requires at least 10 acres of drainage area	Moderate	Possible stream warming and habitat destruction	Lowest cost alternative in size range	Recommended with design improvements and with the use of micropools and wetlands
Wet ponds	Moderate to high	20+ years	Widely applicable but requires drainage area of more than 2 acres	Moderate to high	Possible stream warming, tropic shifts, habitat	Moderate to high compared to conventional	Recommended, with careful site evaluation
Multiple pond systems	Moderate to high (redundancy increases reliability)	20+ years	Widely applicable	Moderate to high	Selection of appropriate pond option minimizes overall environmental impact	Most expensive pond option	Recommended
Infiltration trenches	Presumed moderate	50% failure rate within 5 years	Highly restricted (soils, groundwater, slope, area, sediment input)	Low	Slight risk of groundwater contamination	Cost-effective on smaller sites, rehab costs can be considerable	Recommended with pretreatment and geotechnical evaluation
Infiltration basins	Presumed moderate, if working	60–100% failure within 5 years	Highly restricted (soils, groundwater, slope, area, sediment input)	Low to moderate	Slight risk of groundwater contamination	Construction cost moderate, but rehab cost high	Not widely recommended until longevity is improved
Porous pavement	High, if working	75% failure within 5 years	Extremely restricted (traffic, soils, groundwater, slope, area, sediment input)	Low	Possible groundwater impacts, uncontrolled runoff	Cost-effective compared to conventional asphalt when working properly	Recommended in highly restricted applications with careful construction and effective maintenance
Sand filters	Moderate to high	20+ years	Applicable for smaller developments	Low	Minor	Comparatively high construction costs and frequent maintenance	Recommended, with local demonstration
Grassed swales	Low to moderate but unreliable	20+ years	Low-density development and roads	Low	Minor	Low compared to curb and gutter	Recommended, with check-dams, as one part of a BMP system
Filter strips	Unreliable in urban settings	Unknown but may be limited	Restricted to low-density areas	Moderate if forested	Minor	Low	Recommended as one element of a BMP system
Water quality inlets	Presumed low	20+ years	Small, highly impervious catchments (less than 2 acres)	Low	Resuspension of hydrocarbon loadings, disposal of hydrocarbon and toxic residuals	High compared to trenches and sand filters	Not currently recommended as a primary BMP option

*Based on current designs and prevailing maintenance practices

NOTE

The variety of urban BMPs available to remove pollutants from urban runoff differs widely in performance, longevity, feasibility, cost, and environmental impact. As the matrix shows, storm water wetlands are an attractive BMP choice at many development sites.

Carrie Fischer, "Design for Wetlands Preservation," topic II.A.1 in *Environmental Resource Guide* (Washington, D.C.: The American Institute of Architects, 1992).
Thomas Schueler; Metropolitan Washington Council of Governments; Washington, D.C.

STORM WATER WETLANDS

Storm water wetlands can be defined as constructed systems explicitly designed to mitigate the effects of storm water quality and quantity on urban development. They temporarily store storm water runoff in shallow pools that create growing conditions suitable for emergent and riparian wetland plants. In combination, the runoff storage, complex microtopography, and emergent plants in the constructed wetland form an ideal matrix for the removal of urban pollutants.

Unlike natural wetlands, which often express the underlying groundwater level, storm water wetlands are dominated by surface runoff. Storm water wetlands can best be described as semitidal, in that they have a hydroperiod characterized by a cyclic pattern of inundation and subsequent drawdown, occurring 15-30 times a year, depending on rainfall and the imperviousness of the contributing watershed.

Storm water wetlands usually fall into one of four basic designs:

SHALLOW MARSH SYSTEM: The large surface area of a shallow marsh design demands a reliable groundwater supply or base flow to maintain sufficient water elevation to support emergent wetland plants. Shallow marsh systems take up a lot of space, requiring a sizable contributing watershed (often more than 25 acres) to support a shallow permanent pool.

POND/WETLAND SYSTEM: A pond/wetland design utilizes two separate cells for storm water treatment, a wet pond and a shallow marsh. The multiple functions of the latter are to trap sediments, reduce incoming runoff velocity, and remove pollutants. Pond/wetland systems consume less space than shallow marsh systems because the bulk of the treatment is provided by a deep pool rather than a shallow marsh.

EXTENDED DETENTION WETLAND: In extended detention wetlands, extra runoff storage is created by temporarily detaining runoff above the shallow marsh. This extended detention feature enables the wetland to occupy less space as temporary vertical storage partially substitutes for shallow marsh storage. A growing zone is created along the gentle side slopes of extended detention wetlands, from the normal pool level to the maximum extended detention water surface.

POCKET WETLANDS: Pocket wetlands are adapted to serve small sites (from one to ten acres). Because the drainage area is small, pocket wetlands usually do not have a reliable base flow, creating a widely fluctuating water level. In most cases, water levels in the wetland are supported by excavating down to the water table. In drier areas, a pocket wetland is supported only by storm water runoff, and during extended periods of dry weather it will have no shallow pool at all (only saturated soils). Due to their small size and fluctuat-

ing water levels, pocket wetlands often have low plant diversity and poor wildlife habitat value.

The selection of a particular wetland design usually depends on three factors: available space, contributing watershed area, and desired environmental function. However, storm water wetlands are not typically located within delineated natural wetland areas, which provide critical habitat and ecosystem services and are protected under local, state, and federal statutes. Storm water wetlands should also not be confused with constructed wetlands used to mitigate the permitted loss of natural wetlands under wetland protection regulations. The primary goal of wetland mitigation is to replicate the species diversity and ecological function of the lost natural wetland; whereas the more limited goal of storm water wetlands is to maximize pollutant removal and create generic wetland habitat.

Storm water wetlands are also distinguished from natural wetlands that receive storm water runoff as a consequence of upstream development. Although not intended for storm water treatment, wetlands influenced by storm water are common in urban settings. Storm water runoff that becomes a major component of the water balance of a natural wetland can severely alter the functional and structural qualities of the wetland. The end result is a storm water-influenced natural wetland that is more characteristic of a storm water wetland than a natural one.

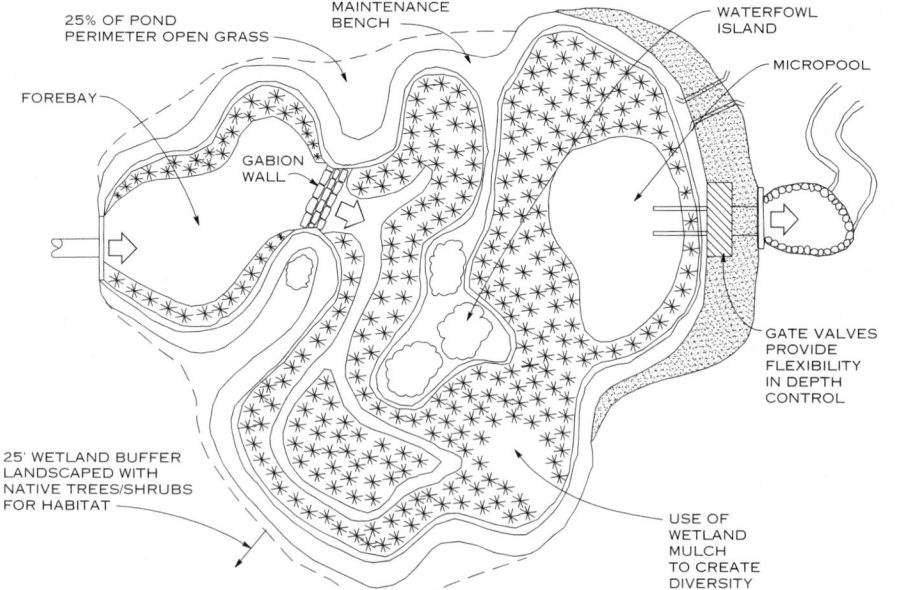

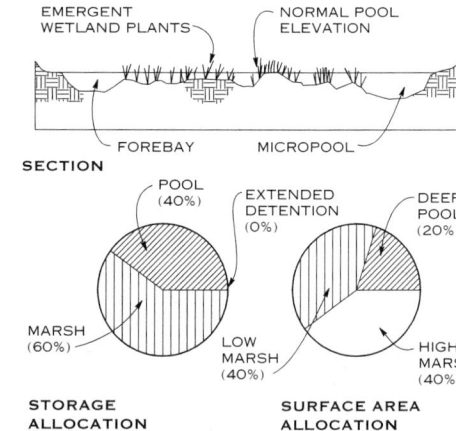

SECTION

NOTE

Most of the shallow marsh system is 0-18 in. deep, a depth that creates favorable conditions for the growth of emergent wetland plants. A deeper forebay is located at the major inlet, and a deep micropool is situated near the outlet.

SHALLOW MARSH SYSTEM

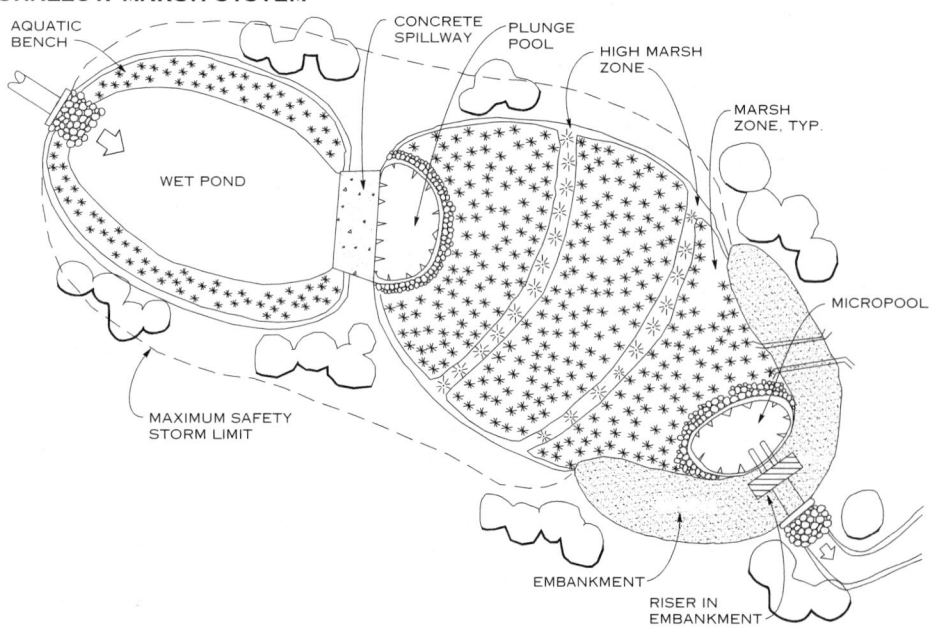

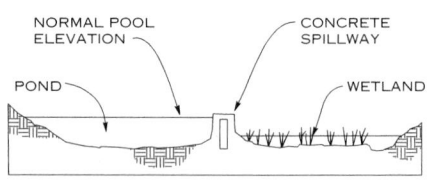

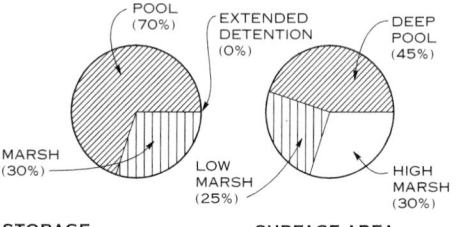

SECTION

NOTE

The pond/wetland system consists of a deep pond that leads to a shallow wetland. The pond removes pollutants and reduces the space required for the system.

POND/WETLAND SYSTEM

Pearse O'Doherty, ASLA; Graham Landscape Architecture; Annapolis, Maryland
Thomas Schueler; Metropolitan Washington Council of Governments; Washington, D.C.

COMPARATIVE ATTRIBUTES OF FOUR STORM WATER WETLAND DESIGNS

ATTRIBUTE	SHALLOW MARSH	POND/WETLAND	EXTENDED DETENTION WETLAND	POCKET WETLAND
Pollutant removal capability	Moderate; reliable removal of sediments and nutrients	Moderate to high; reliable removal of nutrients and sediment	Moderate; less reliable removal of nutrients	Moderate; can be subject to resuspension and groundwater displacement
Land consumption	High; shallow marsh storage consumes space	Moderate, as vertical pool substitutes for marsh storage	Moderate, as vertical extended detention substitutes for marsh storage	Moderate, but can be shoehorned into site
Water balance	Dry weather base flow normally recommended to maintain water elevations; groundwater not recommended as primary source of water supply to wetland			Water supply provided by excavation to groundwater
Wetland area/watershed area	Minimum ratio of .02	Minimum ratio of .01	Minimum ratio of .01	Minimum ratio of .01
Contributing watershed area	Drainage area of 25 acres or more, with dry weather Q*	Drainage area of 25 acres or more, with dry weather Q*	Minimum of 10 acres required for extended detention	1-10 acres
Deepwater cells	Forebay, channels, micropool	Pond, micropool	Forebay, micropool	Micropool, if possible
Outlet configuration	Reversed slope pipe extending from riser, withdrawn approximately 1 ft below normal pool; pipe and pond drain equipped with gate valve			Broad-crested weir with half-round trash rack and pond drain
Sediment cleanout cycle (approximate)	Cleanout of forebay every 2-5 yr	Cleanout of pond every 10 yr	Cleanout of forebay every 2-5 yr	Cleanout of wetland every 5-10 yr, on-site disposal and stockpile mulch
Native plant diversity	High, if complex microtopography is present	High, with sufficient wetland complexity and area	Moderate; fluctuating water levels impose physiological constraints	Low to moderate, due to small surface area and poor control of water levels
Wildlife habitat potential	High, with complexity and buffer	High, with buffer, attracts waterfowl	Moderate, with buffer	Low, due to small area and low diversity

*Q—coefficient of runoff

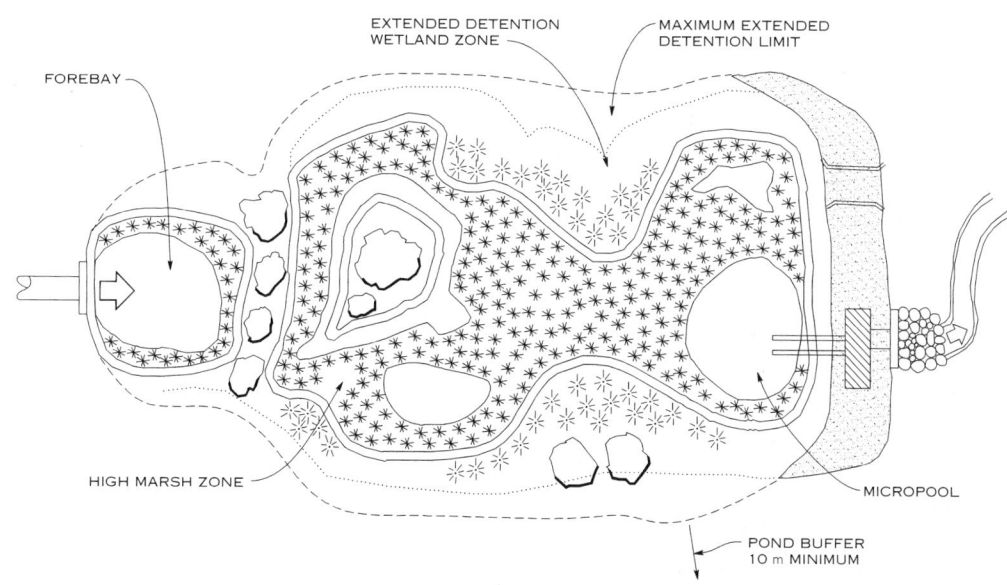

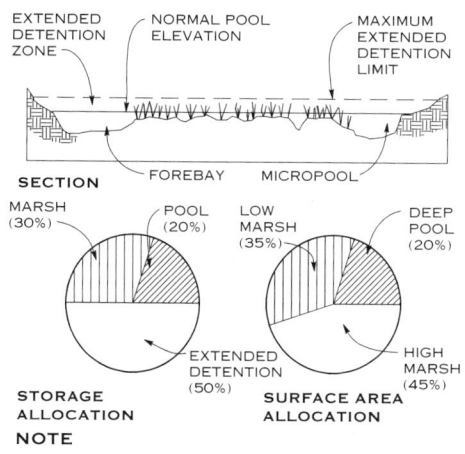

NOTE

The water level in an extended detention wetland can increase by as much as 3 ft after a storm, returning to normal levels within 24 hr. As much as half the total treatment volume can be provided as extended detention storage, which helps protect downstream channels from erosion and reduces the space needed for the wetland.

EXTENDED DETENTION WETLAND

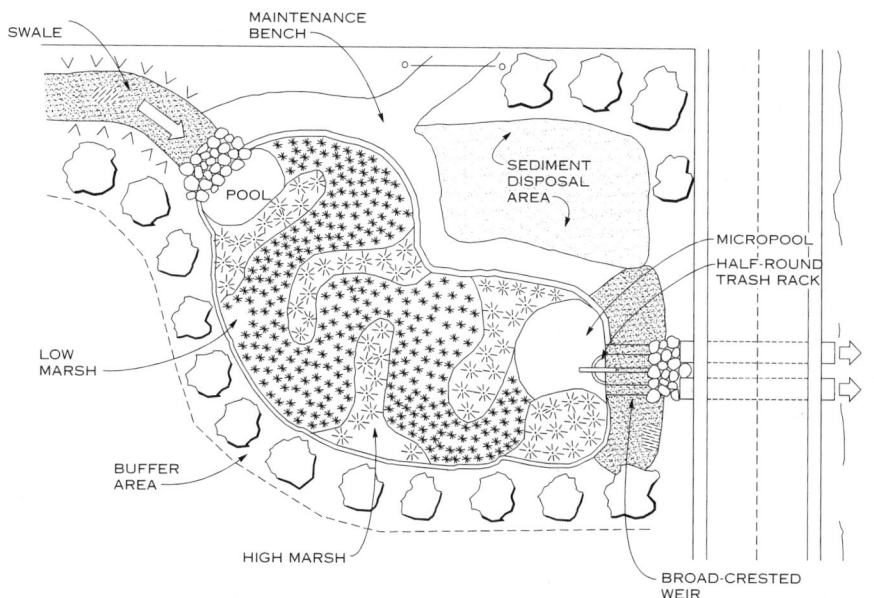

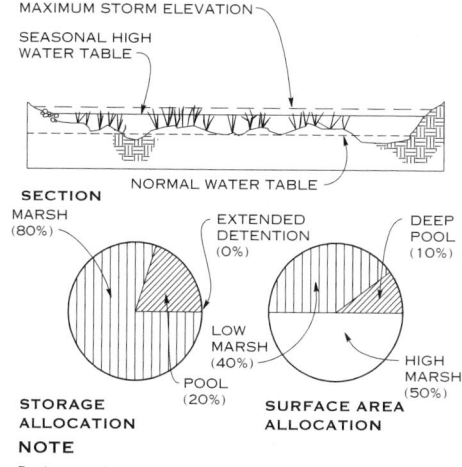

NOTE

Pocket wetlands are seldom more than a tenth of an acre and serve sites from 1-10 acres. They have no sediment forebay, and their size and unreliable water supply prevent them from offering all the benefits of other wetland designs. Despite many drawbacks, pocket wetlands may be an attractive alternative for smaller developments.

POCKET STORM WATER WETLAND

Pearse O'Doherty, ASLA; Graham Landscape Architecture; Annapolis, Maryland
Thomas Schueler; Metropolitan Washington Council of Governments; Washington, D.C.

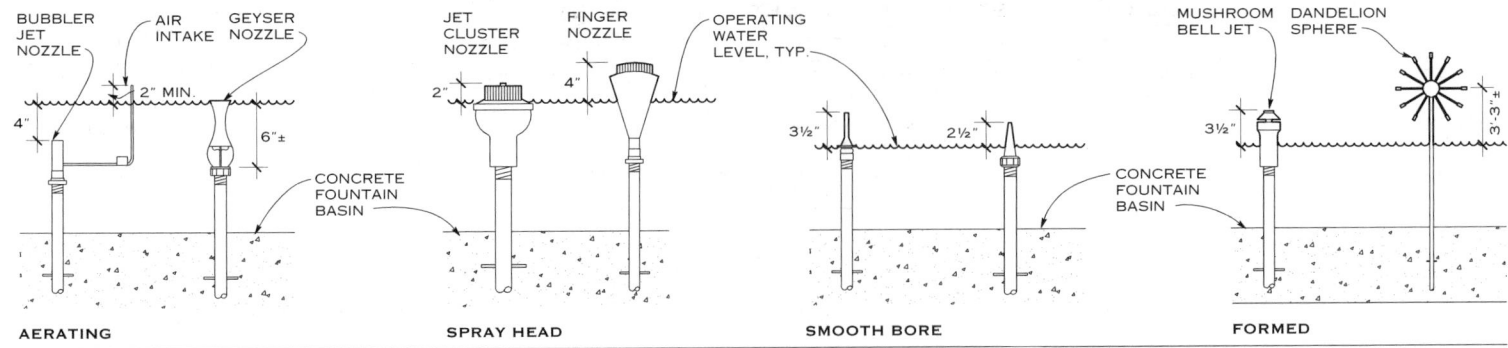

FOUNTAIN NOZZLE TYPES

AERATING   SPRAY HEAD   SMOOTH BORE   FORMED

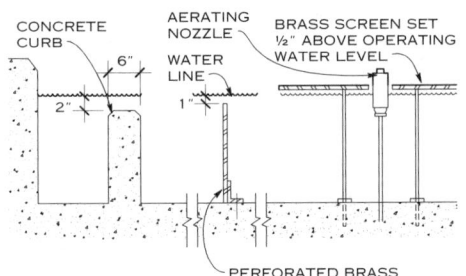

SURGE REDUCTION DEVICES

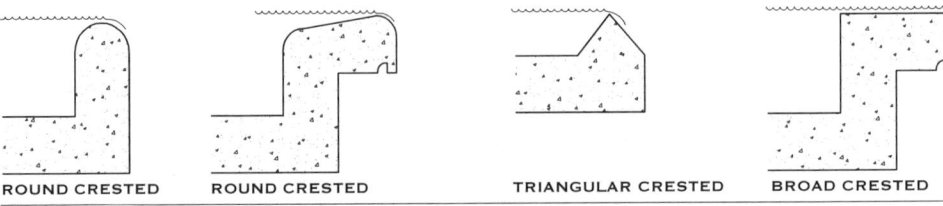

ROUND CRESTED   ROUND CRESTED   TRIANGULAR CRESTED   BROAD CRESTED

FOUNTAIN LIP SECTIONS

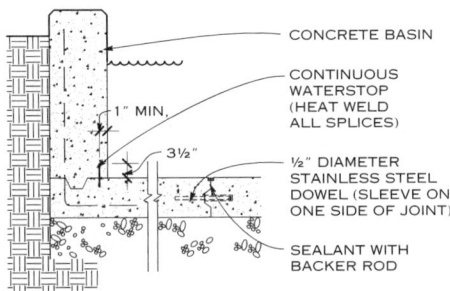

CONCRETE BASIN JOINT DETAILS

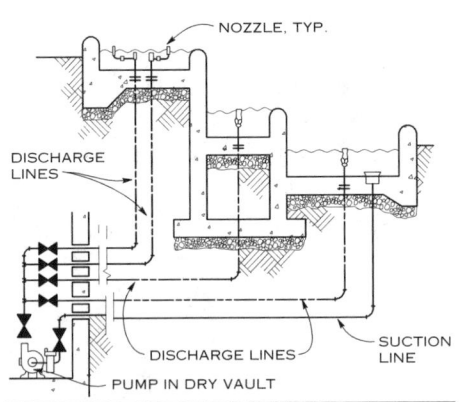

PIPE SCHEMATIC FOR DRY CENTRIFUGAL PUMP

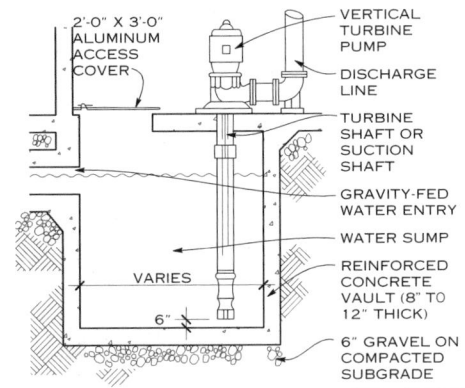

VERTICAL TURBINE PUMP

GENERAL

Materials used in fountain and pool design should be durable and resist damage caused by water, cracks, weather, stains, and freeze-thaw cycles. Suitable materials include stone, concrete, brick, tile, and metals such as copper, bronze, cast iron, and steel. Fiberglass, acrylic, and waterproof membranes such as PVC, EPDM, and butyl are commonly used.

OVERALL DESIGN CONSIDERATIONS

SCALE: Consider the size of the water feature in relation to its surroundings.

BASIN SIZING: For width, consider fountain height and prevailing winds. For depth, consider weight (1 cu ft water = 62.37 lb). Consider children playing near or in the pool. Allow space for lights, nozzles, and pumps. Local codes may classify basins of a certain depth as swimming pools. Nozzle spray may be cushioned to prevent excessive surge.

BOTTOM APPEARANCE: When clear water is maintained, bottom appearance is important. Enhance the bottom with patterns, colors, materials, three-dimensional objects, or textures. Dark bottoms increase reflectivity.

EDGES OR COPINGS: In designing the water's edge, consider the difference between the operating water level and the static water level. Loosely defined edges (as in a pond) make movement into the water possible both visually and physically. Clearly defined edges (as in a basin) use coping to delineate the water's edge.

LIPS AND WEIRS: A lip is an edge over which flowing water falls. A weir is a dam in the water that diverts the water flow or raises the water level. If volume and velocity are insufficient to break the surface tension, a reglet on the underside of the edge may overcome this problem.

WATER FORM FOR FOUNTAINS

STATIC WATER: Form and reflectivity are design considerations for water contained in pools and ponds.
FALLING WATER: The effect of falling water depends on water velocity and volume, the container surface, and the edge over or through which the water moves.

FLOWING WATER: The visual effect of a volume of flowing water can be changed by narrowing or widening a channel, placing objects in the path of the water, and changing the direction of the flow or the slope and roughness of the bottom and sides.

JETS: A pattern is created by forcing water into the air with a jet. Jet types include single orifice nozzles, tiered jets, aerated nozzles, and formed jets in a wide variety of forms, patterns, and types.

SURGE: A contrast between relatively quiet water and a surge (a wave or a splash) is made by quickly adding water, raising or lowering an object or moving it back and forth in the water, or introducing strong air currents to the water.

WATER EFFECTS SYSTEM

The water effects system comprises the pump, nozzles, and piping that move water through the fountain. The combination of nozzles, spray rings, eyeballs, pipes, weirs, and/or channels in a fountain or pool requires a pump system to generate water pressure, a suction line to bring water to the pump, and a discharge line to move water from the pump to the nozzles.

Fountain nozzles come in four basic types: aerating nozzles, spray heads, smooth-bore nozzles, and formed nozzles. Aerating nozzles (also known as bubbler jets, geyser nozzles, or foam nozzles) are characterized by white frothy water created by combining air and water. Spray heads are characterized by combinations of thin clear water jets coming from a distribution head in the shape of a fan or circle (suction or in-

line strainer required). Smooth-bore nozzles are characterized by a clear, thin solid stream jet of water that breaks up into small droplets as it reaches its maximum height or distance. Formed nozzles are typified by a thin sheet of water that originates in a jet of varied size and shape. The thinness of the sheet of water makes the tolerances in the jet very tight (suction or in-line strainer required).

Fountains are usually closed water systems, i.e., the pump continuously cycles the water in the basin to the nozzles and back to the basin again. The pumps used to generate water pressure and operate the water effects of a fountain are largely powered by electric motors. Three types of pumps are commonly used: submersible, dry centrifugal, and vertical turbine pumps.

Submersible pumps, used for low volume fountains, are among the simplest pumping systems. A watertight electric motor and pump are set under the water of the fountain basin. The pump is usually equipped with a motor of $1/20$ to 1 horsepower and moves a maximum of 100 gallons per minute (gpm). This type of pump requires fewer pipe penetrations in the basin wall than dry centrifugal or vertical turbine pumps.

Dry centrifugal pumps, most commonly used for larger water features, consist of an electric motor, a pump, a suction line, and a discharge line. This pump type ranges from $1/4$ to 100 horsepower.

Vertical turbine pumps, used in large water features, are able to move tremendous amounts of water. They require a pump and motor, a water sump located in an equipment vault, a gravity feed mechanism to fill the sump, and a discharge line. These pumps are more energy-efficient than those with suction lines, as gravity moves water to the pump. The electric motor is not submerged in water, making a watertight seal less important. Vertical turbine pumps can move up to 5000 gpm.

GENERAL

Selection criteria to use when choosing a fence for a particular application include the degree of privacy or openness and sense of enclosure desired; the aesthetic and stylistic nature of the materials and setting; cultural and historical precedents; and security issues. Consider, as well, materials and maintenance requirements; soil conditions at the site and the foundations and anchorage required; topography, climate, and wind conditions at the site; the effects a design will have on neighbors and adjacent natural features; the size of the property; and the permanence and cost of the structure.

Local zoning and building codes often regulate the height of a fence and its relationship to the property line. Fences should not obstruct traffic sight lines at intersections but should prevent access to potential danger (e.g., unattended children at swimming pools or pedestrians at a construction site).

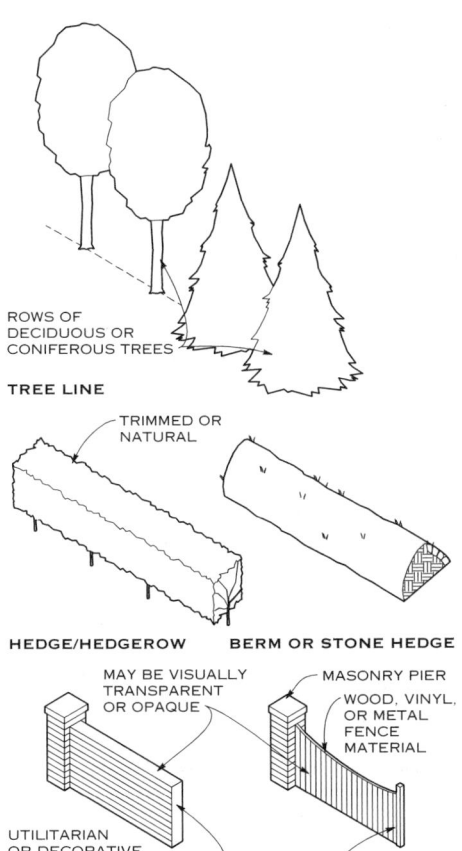

ROWS OF DECIDUOUS OR CONIFEROUS TREES

TREE LINE

TRIMMED OR NATURAL

HEDGE/HEDGEROW   **BERM OR STONE HEDGE**

MAY BE VISUALLY TRANSPARENT OR OPAQUE

MASONRY PIER

WOOD, VINYL, OR METAL FENCE MATERIAL

UTILITARIAN OR DECORATIVE STONE, BRICK, OR BLOCK

WOOD POST

MASONRY WALLS   **WOOD FENCES**

RETAINING WALL

NOTE

A retaining wall positioned to be invisible to the viewer (a "ha-ha") can prevent unwanted entry by outsiders.

RETAINING WALL AS FENCE

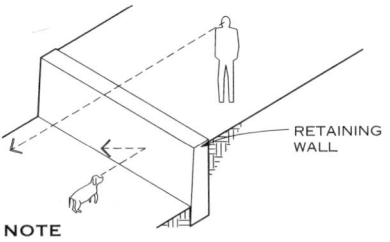

WOOD OR METAL

WROUGHT IRON, CHAIN LINK, OR WIRE

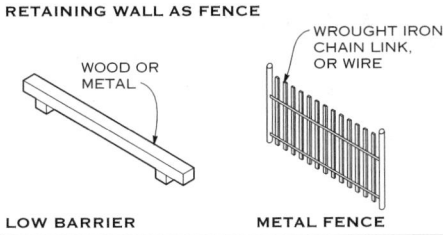

LOW BARRIER   **METAL FENCE**

PHYSICAL BARRIER TYPES

Daniel F. C. Hayes, AIA; Washington, D.C.

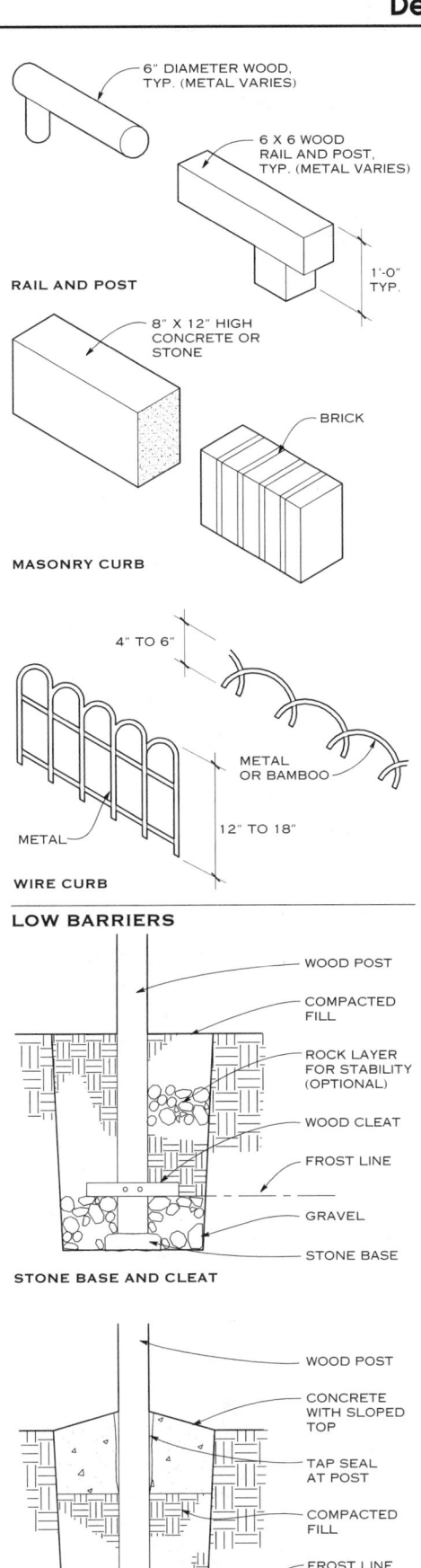

6" DIAMETER WOOD, TYP. (METAL VARIES)

6 X 6 WOOD RAIL AND POST, TYP. (METAL VARIES)

1'-0" TYP.

RAIL AND POST

8" X 12" HIGH CONCRETE OR STONE

BRICK

MASONRY CURB

4" TO 6"

METAL OR BAMBOO

METAL

12" TO 18"

WIRE CURB

LOW BARRIERS

WOOD POST

COMPACTED FILL

ROCK LAYER FOR STABILITY (OPTIONAL)

WOOD CLEAT

FROST LINE

GRAVEL

STONE BASE

STONE BASE AND CLEAT

WOOD POST

CONCRETE WITH SLOPED TOP

TAP SEAL AT POST

COMPACTED FILL

FROST LINE

GRAVEL

STONE BASE AND CONCRETE CAP

EMBEDDED POST DETAILS

STRAP HINGE

FENCE POST (4 X 4 OR 6 X 6, TYP.) WITH CAP

COMPRESSION BRACING

2 X 4 FRAME

GATE STYLE USUALLY CONSISTENT WITH ADJACENT FENCING

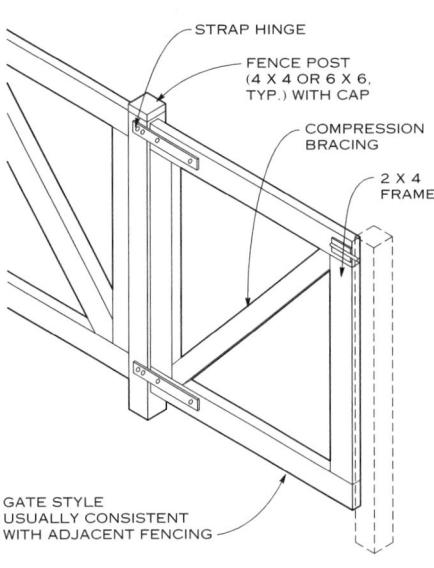

TYPICAL WOOD GATE

1" DRIP

1 X PRESSURE-TREATED WOOD CAP, 10° SLOPE, MIN.

ALUMINUM CAP

POST

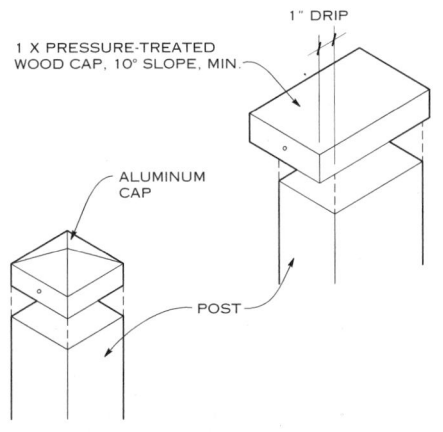

POST CAP DETAILS

NOTES

1. Gates permit personnel and vehicles to pass through barriers. Construction techniques and operation of gates are similar to door methods; refer to AGS chapter 8 for further information on these subjects.

2. Compression bracing extending from the upper extremity to the lower connection point of a gate is often required; tension can be modulated through rods and turnbuckles to prevent warpage and sagging. Large or heavy gates can be fitted with rollers or wheels to aid operation; metal tracks mounted in paving prevent uneven surface wear.

3. Hardware should be made of noncorrosive materials. Latches with internal padlock hasps or locking mechanisms are available for security protection.

WOOD POST

ELEVATED U-SHAPED GALVANIZED STEEL POST BASE

CONCRETE FOOTING (8" TO 12" DIAMETER, TYP.)

FROST LINE

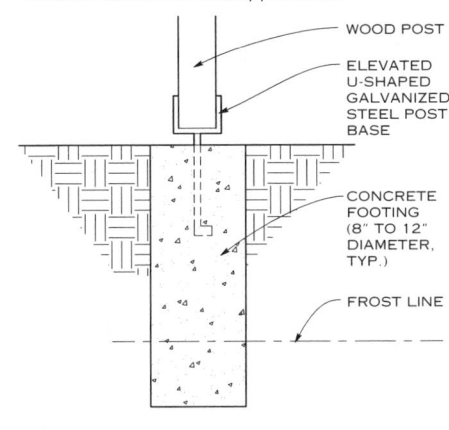

POST WITH CONCRETE FOOTING

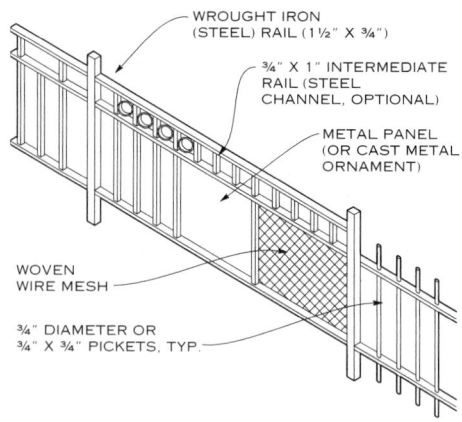

NOTE

Materials used for this type of fence are steel or aluminum in wrought or cast form.

METAL BAR

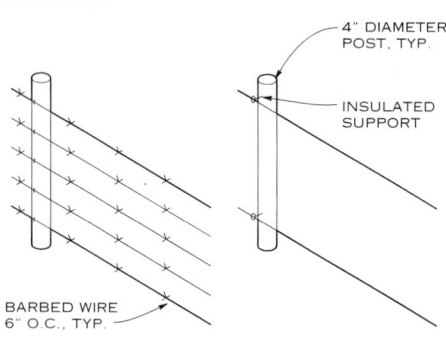

BARBED WIRE   **ELECTRIC WIRE**

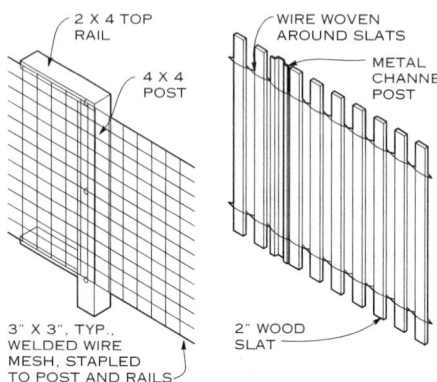

WELDED WIRE MESH   **SNOW FENCE**

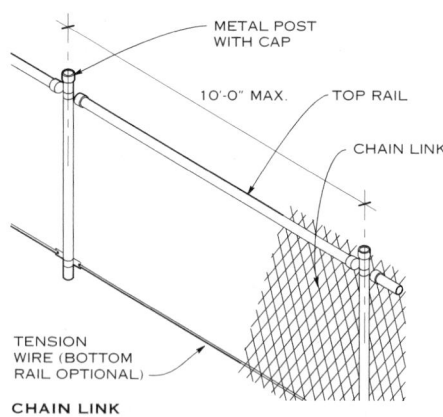

CHAIN LINK

METAL FENCE TYPES

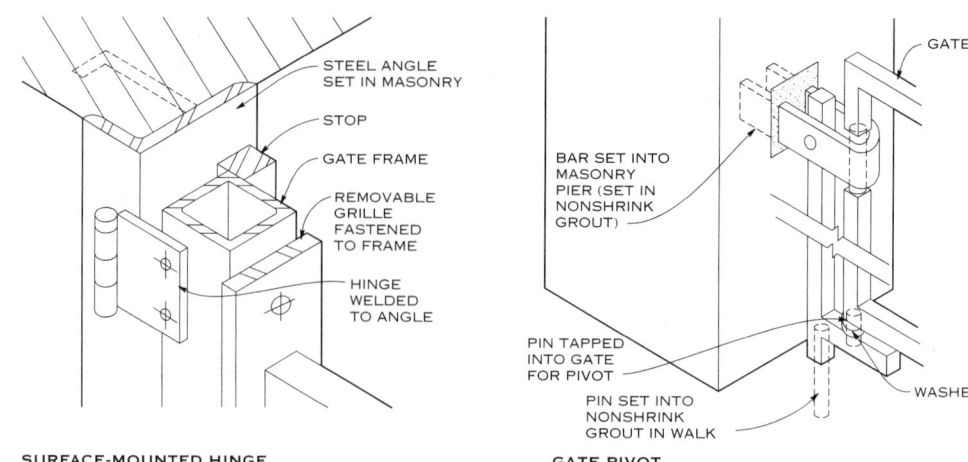

SURFACE-MOUNTED HINGE   **GATE PIVOT**

GATE DETAILS FOR WROUGHT IRON

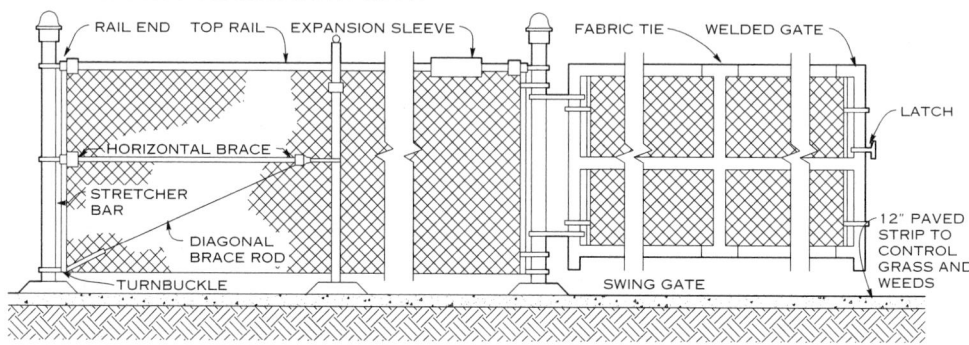

CORNER POST   LINE POST   GATEPOST

NOTE

For fences 5 ft and taller, a horizontal or diagonal brace, or both, is used for greater stability. Post spacing should be equidistant and should not exceed 10 ft o.c.

CHAIN-LINK FENCE AND GATE—ELEVATION

CHAIN-LINK FENCE MATERIALS

MATERIAL	SIZES AVAILABLE*
Wire gauge	Usually no. 11 or no. 9
	For especially rugged use, use no. 6
	For tennis courts, no. 11 is generally used
Wire mesh	Usually 2"
	For tennis courts, usually $1\frac{5}{8}$" or $1\frac{3}{4}$" of chain-link steel that has been coated with hot dip galvanizing after weaving
	Top and bottom selvage may be barbed or knuckled
Corner and end posts	For lawn fences, usually 2" outside diameter
	For estate fences, 2 in. for low, $2\frac{1}{2}$ in. for medium, and 3 in. outside diameter for heavy or high
	For tennis courts 3" outside diameter
Line or intermediate posts	For lawn fences, $1\frac{3}{8}$" or 2" outside diameter round
	For estate fences, etc., 2", $2\frac{1}{4}$", or $2\frac{1}{2}$" H or I sections
	For tennis courts, $2\frac{1}{2}$" round outside diameter or $2\frac{1}{4}$" H or I sections
Gateposts	Same or next size larger than corner posts; footings should be 3'-6" deep
Top rails	$1\frac{5}{8}$" outside diameter except some lawn fence may be $1\frac{3}{8}$" outside diameter
Middle rails	On 12'-0" fence, same as top rail
Gates	Single or double; any width desired
	Accessible routes require clear opening width of 32" min. and 18" latchside clearance; latches must be accessible
Post spacing	Line posts 10'-0" o.c.; 8'-0" o.c. may be used on heavy construction

*Sizes given are not standard but represent the average sizes used.

COATINGS

Protective coatings, such as zinc and aluminum, can be used on metal fencing. Also available are various decorative coatings, including vinyl bonding and organic coatings; these are available from most manufacturers.

VINYL-COATED WIRE FABRIC MESH

Vinyl-coated wire fabric mesh is suitable for residential, commercial, and industrial applications. The mesh comes in five sizes—1, $1\frac{1}{4}$, $1\frac{1}{2}$, $1\frac{3}{4}$, and 2 in.—and in four gauges—11, 9, 6, and 3.

SPECIAL FENCING

ORNAMENTAL: This fencing type uses vertical struts only; no chain-link fabric is required. Ornamental fencing is ideal for landscaping or as a barrier fence.

ELEPHANT FENCE: This fence can actually stop an elephant, hold back a rock slide, or bring a small truck to a halt. Its size is specified as gauge 3 with a 2 in. mesh.

SECURITY FENCE: This fabric is nonclimbable and cannot be penetrated by gun muzzles, knives, or other weapons. It is suitable as a security barrier for police stations, prisons, reformatories, hospitals, and mental institutions. Mesh sizes available are $\frac{3}{8}$ in. for maximum security, $\frac{1}{2}$ in. for high security, $\frac{5}{8}$ in. for super security, and 1 in. for standard security.

POST SIZES FOR HEAVY-DUTY GATES

ASA SCHEDULE 40 PIPE SIZES (IN.)	SWING GATE OPENINGS (FT)	
	SINGLE	DOUBLE
$2\frac{1}{2}$	Up to 6	Up to 12
$3\frac{1}{2}$	Over 6 to 18	Over 12 to 26
6	Over 13 to 18	Over 26 to 36
8	Over 18 to 32	Over 36 to 64

Daniel F. C. Hayes, AIA; Washington, D.C.

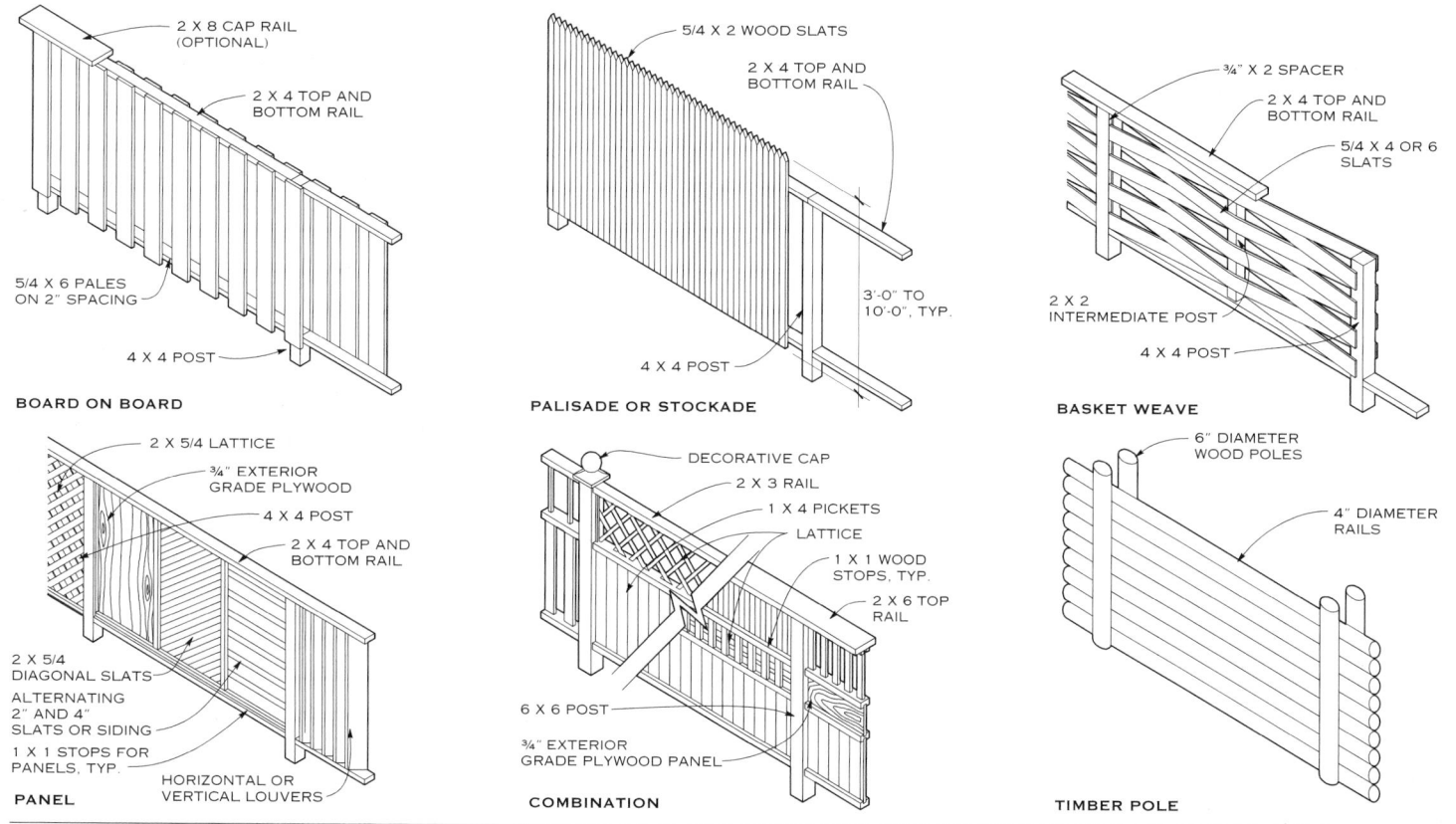

BOARD ON BOARD

- 2 X 8 CAP RAIL (OPTIONAL)
- 2 X 4 TOP AND BOTTOM RAIL
- 5/4 X 6 PALES ON 2" SPACING
- 4 X 4 POST

PALISADE OR STOCKADE

- 5/4 X 2 WOOD SLATS
- 2 X 4 TOP AND BOTTOM RAIL
- 3'-0" TO 10'-0", TYP.
- 4 X 4 POST

BASKET WEAVE

- ¾" X 2 SPACER
- 2 X 4 TOP AND BOTTOM RAIL
- 5/4 X 4 OR 6 SLATS
- 2 X 2 INTERMEDIATE POST
- 4 X 4 POST

PANEL

- 2 X 5/4 LATTICE
- ¾" EXTERIOR GRADE PLYWOOD
- 4 X 4 POST
- 2 X 4 TOP AND BOTTOM RAIL
- 2 X 5/4 DIAGONAL SLATS ALTERNATING 2" AND 4" SLATS OR SIDING
- 1 X 1 STOPS FOR PANELS, TYP.
- HORIZONTAL OR VERTICAL LOUVERS

COMBINATION

- DECORATIVE CAP
- 2 X 3 RAIL
- 1 X 4 PICKETS
- LATTICE
- 1 X 1 WOOD STOPS, TYP.
- 2 X 6 TOP RAIL
- 6 X 6 POST
- ¾" EXTERIOR GRADE PLYWOOD PANEL

TIMBER POLE

- 6" DIAMETER WOOD POLES
- 4" DIAMETER RAILS

WOOD PRIVACY FENCES

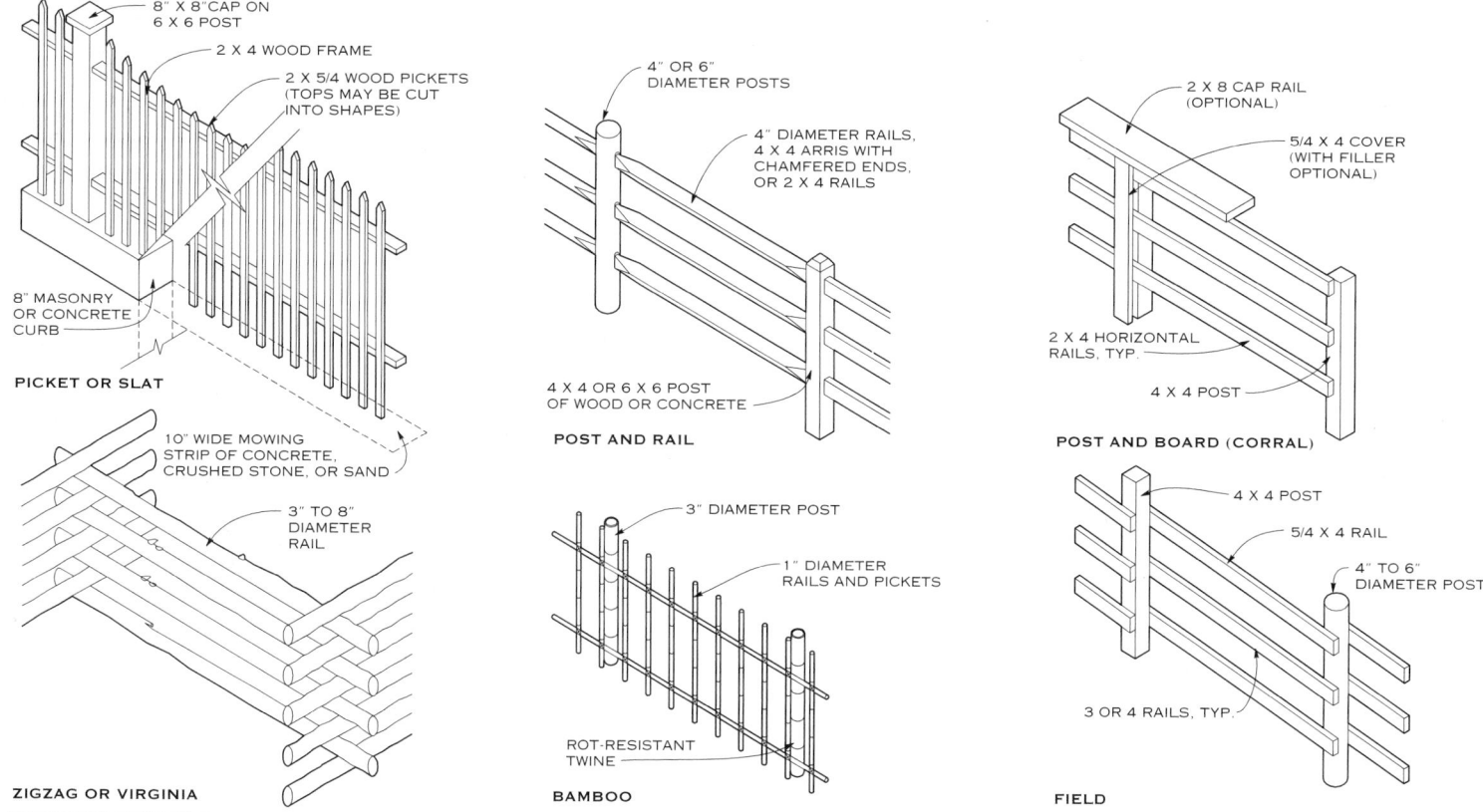

PICKET OR SLAT

- 8" X 8" CAP ON 6 X 6 POST
- 2 X 4 WOOD FRAME
- 2 X 5/4 WOOD PICKETS (TOPS MAY BE CUT INTO SHAPES)
- 8" MASONRY OR CONCRETE CURB
- 10" WIDE MOWING STRIP OF CONCRETE, CRUSHED STONE, OR SAND

ZIGZAG OR VIRGINIA

- 3" TO 8" DIAMETER RAIL

POST AND RAIL

- 4" OR 6" DIAMETER POSTS
- 4" DIAMETER RAILS, 4 X 4 ARRIS WITH CHAMFERED ENDS, OR 2 X 4 RAILS
- 4 X 4 OR 6 X 6 POST OF WOOD OR CONCRETE

BAMBOO

- 3" DIAMETER POST
- 1" DIAMETER RAILS AND PICKETS
- ROT-RESISTANT TWINE

POST AND BOARD (CORRAL)

- 2 X 8 CAP RAIL (OPTIONAL)
- 5/4 X 4 COVER (WITH FILLER OPTIONAL)
- 2 X 4 HORIZONTAL RAILS, TYP.
- 4 X 4 POST

FIELD

- 4 X 4 POST
- 5/4 X 4 RAIL
- 4" TO 6" DIAMETER POST
- 3 OR 4 RAILS, TYP.

WOOD BOUNDARY FENCES

NOTES

1. Untreated wood materials such as white oak or tamarack can last up to 10 years; cypress, redwood, and sassafras up to 15 years; red and white cedar up to 20 years; and black locust and osage orange up to 25 years. Weather and insect preservative treatments can extend the useful life to 25 to 30 years for most species. Verify life expectancies and compatibility with finishes and hardware with manufacturers.

2. Fasteners should be made of noncorrosive materials such as aluminum alloys or stainless steel; high quality hot-dipped galvanized steel is acceptable. Metal flanges, cleats, bolts, and screws are preferable to common nails.

3. Virgin or recycled plastic may be used as an alternative material for the fences illustrated on this page.

Daniel F. C. Hayes, AIA; Washington, D.C.

GENERAL

The physical environment of the site, the design needs of the project, and the design character of the trees are all factors that must be considered in selecting trees and preparing a landscape plan for a building.

Soil conditions (acidity, porosity) at the site, the amount and intensity of sunlight and precipitation, and the seasonal temperature range in the area create the physical environment in which trees must be able to survive. As well, consider how the location and topography of the site will direct the wind, resulting in cold winds and cooling breezes that can affect the health of trees.

Trees can be used to address the design needs of a project by directing pedestrian or vehicle movement, framing vistas, screening objectionable views, and defining and shaping exterior space. Trees can also be used to modify the microclimate of a site and to help conserve building energy use from heating, cooling, and lighting systems.

The design character of the trees themselves plays a part in which species are best suited for a particular application. The shape of a tree can be columnar, conical, spherical, or spreading, and the resulting height and mass will change over time as the tree matures. Some trees grow quickly and others more slowly, and their color and texture varies from coarse to medium to fine, affecting their character. The appearance of deciduous trees changes with the seasons, while the effect of an evergreen remains relatively constant.

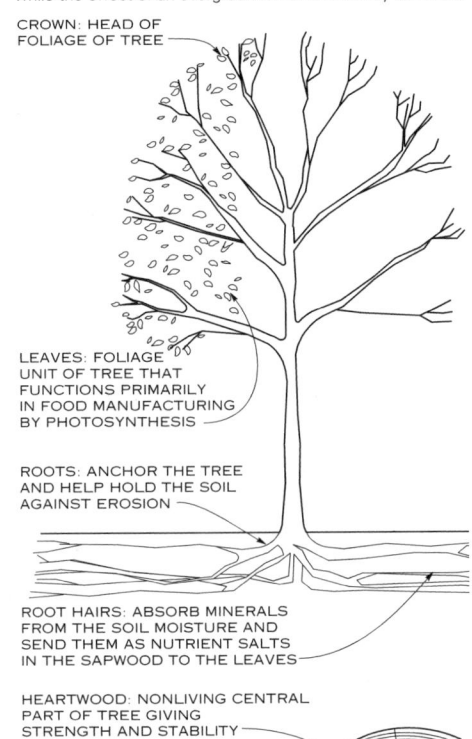

CROWN: HEAD OF FOLIAGE OF TREE

LEAVES: FOLIAGE UNIT OF TREE THAT FUNCTIONS PRIMARILY IN FOOD MANUFACTURING BY PHOTOSYNTHESIS

ROOTS: ANCHOR THE TREE AND HELP HOLD THE SOIL AGAINST EROSION

ROOT HAIRS: ABSORB MINERALS FROM THE SOIL MOISTURE AND SEND THEM AS NUTRIENT SALTS IN THE SAPWOOD TO THE LEAVES

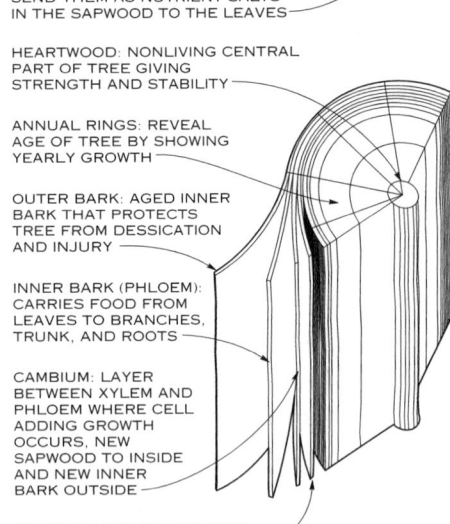

HEARTWOOD: NONLIVING CENTRAL PART OF TREE GIVING STRENGTH AND STABILITY

ANNUAL RINGS: REVEAL AGE OF TREE BY SHOWING YEARLY GROWTH

OUTER BARK: AGED INNER BARK THAT PROTECTS TREE FROM DESSICATION AND INJURY

INNER BARK (PHLOEM): CARRIES FOOD FROM LEAVES TO BRANCHES, TRUNK, AND ROOTS

CAMBIUM: LAYER BETWEEN XYLEM AND PHLOEM WHERE CELL ADDING GROWTH OCCURS, NEW SAPWOOD TO INSIDE AND NEW INNER BARK OUTSIDE

SAPWOOD (XYLEM): CARRIES NUTRIENTS AND WATER TO LEAVES FROM ROOTS

PHYSICAL CHARACTERISTICS OF TREES

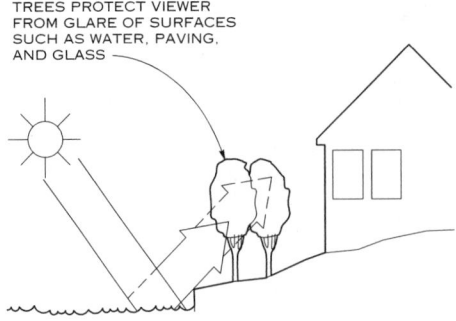

TREES PROTECT VIEWER FROM GLARE OF SURFACES SUCH AS WATER, PAVING, AND GLASS

NOTE

The vertical angle of the sun changes seasonally; therefore, the area of a building subject to the glare of reflected sunlight varies. Plants of various heights can screen sun (and artificial light) glare from adjacent surfaces.

GLARE PROTECTION

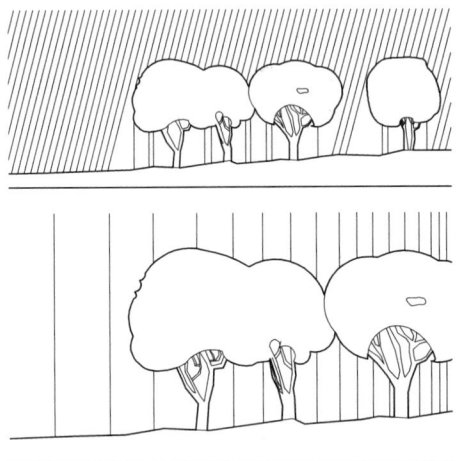

NOTE

Large masses of plants physically and chemically filter and deodorize the air, reducing air pollution. (Top) Particulate matter trapped on the leaves is washed to the ground during rainfall. Gaseous pollutants are assimilated by the leaves. (Bottom) Fragrant plants can mechanically mask fumes and odors. As well, these pollutants are chemically metabolized in the photosynthetic process.

AIR FILTRATION

CONSTANT WIND VELOCITY = 100%

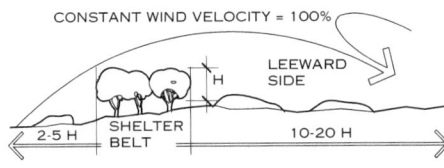

LEEWARD SIDE

H

SHELTER BELT

2-5 H   10-20 H

H = HEIGHT OF TREES

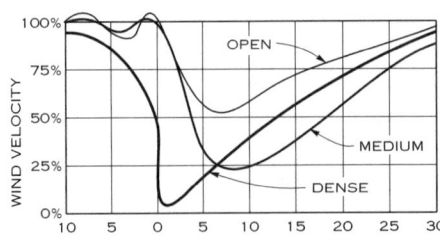

MULTIPLE OF SHELTER BELT HEIGHT

NOTE

Shelter belt wind protection reduces evaporation at ground level, increases relative humidity, lowers the temperature in summer and reduces heat loss in winter, and reduces blowing dust and drifting snow. The amount of protection afforded is directly related to the height and density of the shelter belt.

WIND PROTECTION

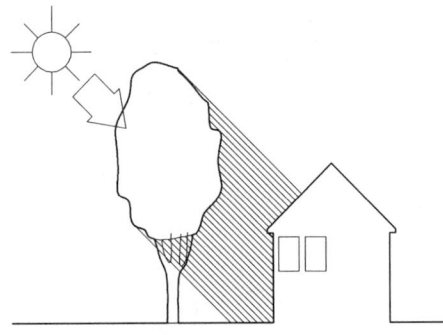

NOTE

In summer, trees obstruct or filter the strong radiation from the sun, cooling and protecting the area beneath them. In winter, evergreen trees still have this effect, while deciduous trees, having lost their leaves, do not.

SHADE PROVISION

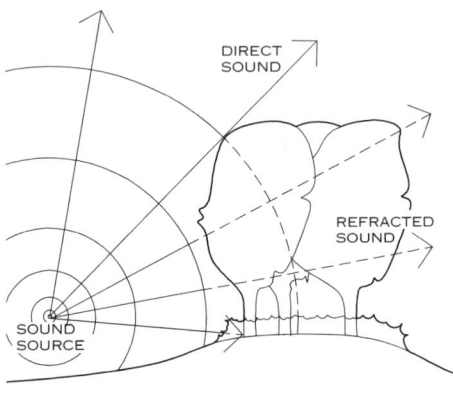

DIRECT SOUND

REFRACTED SOUND

SOUND SOURCE

NOTE

A combination of deciduous and evergreen trees and shrubs reduces sound more effectively than deciduous plants alone. Planting trees and shrubs on earth mounds increases the attenuating effects of a buffer belt.

SOUND ATTENUATION

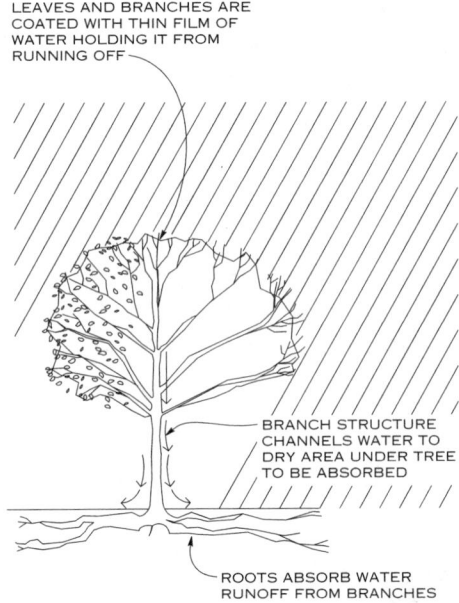

LEAVES AND BRANCHES ARE COATED WITH THIN FILM OF WATER HOLDING IT FROM RUNNING OFF

BRANCH STRUCTURE CHANNELS WATER TO DRY AREA UNDER TREE TO BE ABSORBED

ROOTS ABSORB WATER RUNOFF FROM BRANCHES

NOTE

Mature trees absorb or delay runoff from stormwater at a rate 4 to 5 times that of bare ground.

RUNOFF REDUCTION

James Urban, ASLA; James Urban Landscape Architecture; Annapolis, Maryland

2 LANDSCAPING

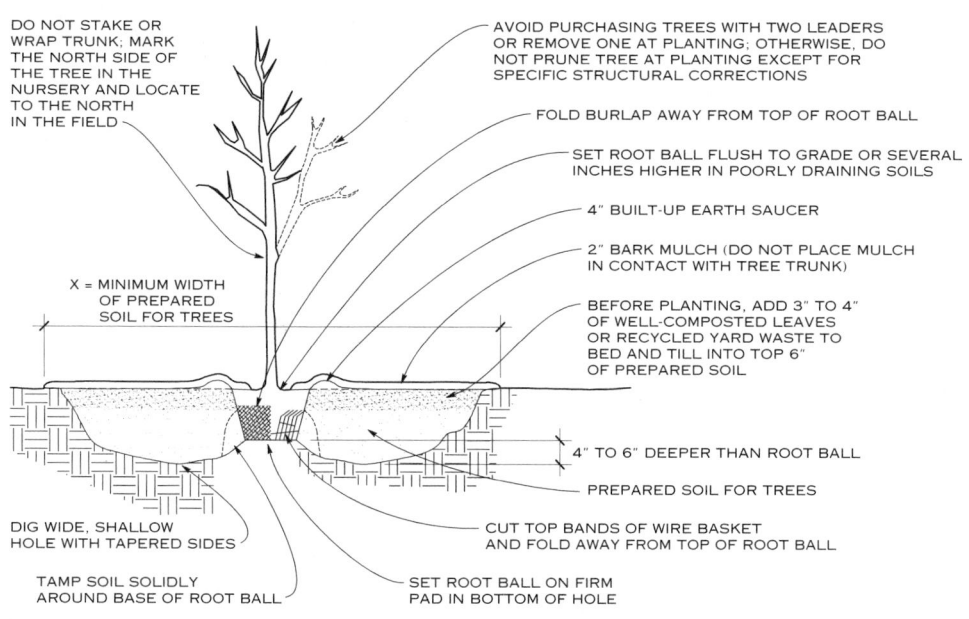

DO NOT STAKE OR WRAP TRUNK; MARK THE NORTH SIDE OF THE TREE IN THE NURSERY AND LOCATE TO THE NORTH IN THE FIELD

AVOID PURCHASING TREES WITH TWO LEADERS OR REMOVE ONE AT PLANTING; OTHERWISE, DO NOT PRUNE TREE AT PLANTING EXCEPT FOR SPECIFIC STRUCTURAL CORRECTIONS

FOLD BURLAP AWAY FROM TOP OF ROOT BALL

SET ROOT BALL FLUSH TO GRADE OR SEVERAL INCHES HIGHER IN POORLY DRAINING SOILS

4" BUILT-UP EARTH SAUCER

2" BARK MULCH (DO NOT PLACE MULCH IN CONTACT WITH TREE TRUNK)

BEFORE PLANTING, ADD 3" TO 4" OF WELL-COMPOSTED LEAVES OR RECYCLED YARD WASTE TO BED AND TILL INTO TOP 6" OF PREPARED SOIL

X = MINIMUM WIDTH OF PREPARED SOIL FOR TREES

4" TO 6" DEEPER THAN ROOT BALL

PREPARED SOIL FOR TREES

DIG WIDE, SHALLOW HOLE WITH TAPERED SIDES

CUT TOP BANDS OF WIRE BASKET AND FOLD AWAY FROM TOP OF ROOT BALL

TAMP SOIL SOLIDLY AROUND BASE OF ROOT BALL

SET ROOT BALL ON FIRM PAD IN BOTTOM OF HOLE

NOTES

1. For container-grown trees, use fingers or small hand tools to pull the roots out of the outer layer of potting soil; then cut or pull apart any roots circling the perimeter of the container.
2. Incorporate commercially prepared mycorrhiza spores in the soil immediately around the root ball at rates specified by the manufacturer.
3. During the design phase, confirm that water drains out of the soil; design alternative drainage systems as required.
4. Thoroughly soak the tree root ball and adjacent prepared soil several times during the first month after planting and regularly throughout the following two summers.
5. The planting process is similar for deciduous and evergreen trees.

TREE PLANTING DETAIL (BALLED AND BURLAPPED PLANTS)

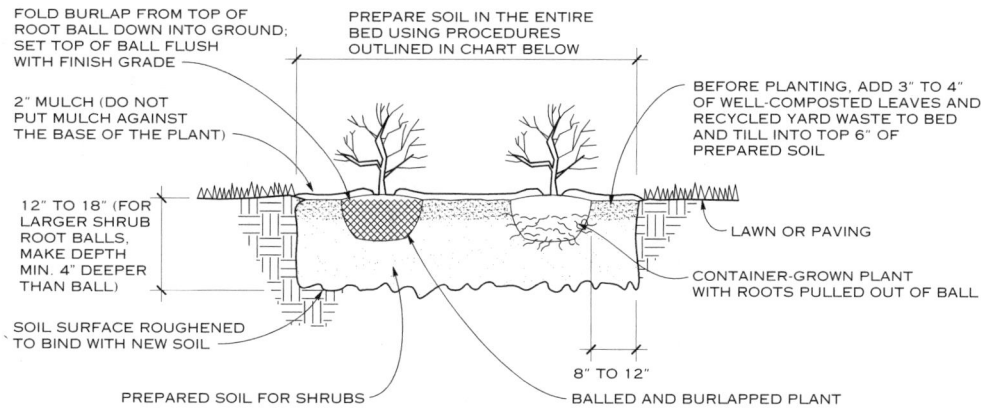

FOLD BURLAP FROM TOP OF ROOT BALL DOWN INTO GROUND; SET TOP OF BALL FLUSH WITH FINISH GRADE

PREPARE SOIL IN THE ENTIRE BED USING PROCEDURES OUTLINED IN CHART BELOW

BEFORE PLANTING, ADD 3" TO 4" OF WELL-COMPOSTED LEAVES AND RECYCLED YARD WASTE TO BED AND TILL INTO TOP 6" OF PREPARED SOIL

2" MULCH (DO NOT PUT MULCH AGAINST THE BASE OF THE PLANT)

12" TO 18" (FOR LARGER SHRUB ROOT BALLS, MAKE DEPTH MIN. 4" DEEPER THAN BALL)

LAWN OR PAVING

CONTAINER-GROWN PLANT WITH ROOTS PULLED OUT OF BALL

SOIL SURFACE ROUGHENED TO BIND WITH NEW SOIL

PREPARED SOIL FOR SHRUBS

8" TO 12"

BALLED AND BURLAPPED PLANT

NOTES

1. For container-grown shrubs, use fingers or small hand tools to pull the roots out of the outer layer of potting soil; then cut or pull apart any roots that circle the perimeter of the container.
2. Incorporate commercially prepared mycorrhiza spores in the soil immediately around the root ball at rates specified by the manufacturer.
3. Confirm that water drains out of the soil during the design phase; design alternative drainage systems as required.

SHRUB PLANTING DETAILS

SOIL IMPROVEMENT

The quality of soil available for planting varies widely from site to site, especially after construction activity has occurred. The nature of construction results in compaction, filling, contamination, and grading of the original soil on a site, rapidly making it useless for planting. Previous human activity at a site can also affect the ability of the soil to support plants.

During the design phase, assumptions must be made regarding the probable condition of the soil after construction is complete. The health of existing or remaining soil determines what types of soil preparation will be required and the volume of soil to be prepared. Conditions will vary from location to location within a project, and details must be condition-specific. For large projects or extreme conditions, it is useful to consult an expert experienced in modifying planting soils at urban sites.

NOTES

1. If site or design constraints prohibit use of the dimensions shown on this page, follow the guidelines for planting in urban areas.
2. Whenever possible, the soil improvement area should be connected from tree to tree.
3. Always test soil for pH and nutrient levels and adjust these as required.
4. Loosen soil with a backhoe or other large coarse-tilling equipment when possible. Tilling that produces large, coarse chunks of soil is preferable to tilling that results in fine grains uniform in texture.
5. The bottom of planting soil excavations should be rough to avoid matting of soil layers as new soil is added. It is preferable to till the first lift (2 to 3 in.) of planting soil into the subsoil.

STANDARD ROOT BALL SIZES FOR NURSERY-GROWN SHADE TREES

CALIPER* (IN.)	HEIGHT RANGE (FT-IN.)	MAX. HEIGHT (FT)	MIN. BALL DIA. (IN.)	MIN. BALL DEPTH (IN.)
$1/2$	5-6	8	12	9
$3/4$	6-8	10	14	$10\text{-}1/2$
1	8-10	11	16	12
$1\text{-}1/4$	8-10	12	18	$13\text{-}1/2$
$1\text{-}1/2$	10-12	14	20	$13\text{-}1/2$
$1\text{-}3/4$	10-12	14	22	$14\text{-}1/2$
2	12-14	16	24	16
$2\text{-}1/2$	12-14	16	28	$18\text{-}1/2$
3	14-16	18	32	$19\text{-}1/2$
$3\text{-}1/2$	14-16	18	38	23
4	16-18	22	42	25
5	18-20	26	54	$32\text{-}1/2$

*Up to and including the 4-in. caliper size, the caliper measurement indicates the diameter of the trunk 6 in. above ground level. For larger sizes, the caliper measurement is taken 12 in. above ground level.

NOTES

1. See American Standard for Nursery Stock, ANSI Z60.1, for complete list of nursery standards for other types and sizes of trees and shrubs.
2. See International Society of Arboriculture's "Principles and Practices of Planting Trees and Shrubs," 1997.

GENERAL RANGE OF SOIL MODIFICATIONS AND VOLUMES FOR VARIOUS SOIL CONDITIONS

POSTCONSTRUCTION SOIL CONDITION	MIN. WIDTH PREPARED SOIL FOR TREES (X)	TYPE OF PREPARATION
Good soil (not previously graded or compacted, topsoil layer intact)	6 ft or twice the width of the root ball, whichever is greater	Loosen the existing soils to the widths and depths shown in details above.
Compacted soil (not previously graded, topsoil layer disturbed but not eliminated)	15 ft	Loosen the existing soils to the widths and depths shown in details above; add composted organic matter to bring the organic content up to 5% dry weight.
Graded subsoils and clean fills with clay content between 5 and 35%	20 ft	Minimum treatment: loosen existing soil to widths and depths shown, add composted organic matter to bring organic content up to 5% dry weight. Optimum treatment: remove top 8-10 in. or the existing material, loosen existing soils to the widths and depths shown, add 8-10 in. of loam topsoil.
Poor quality fills, heavy clay soils, soils contaminated with rubble or toxic material	20 ft	Remove existing soils to the widths and depths shown, replace with loam topsoil.

James Urban, ASLA; James Urban Landscape Architecture; Annapolis, Maryland
American Nursery & Landscape Association (formerly AAN); Washington, D.C.

CONSTRUCTION AROUND EXISTING TREES

Great care should be taken not to compact, cut, or fill the earth within the crown area of existing trees. Most tree roots are located in the top 6 to 18 in. of the soil and often spread considerably farther than the drip line of the tree. Compaction can cause severe root damage and reduce the movement of water and air through the soil. To avoid compacting the earth, do not operate equipment or store materials within the crown spread.

Before construction begins, inject the soil within the crown area of nearby mature trees with commercially prepared kelp-based fertilizer and mychorrhiza fungus developed to invigorate tree roots. Prune tree roots at the edge of the root save area, as roots pulled during grading can snap or split well into the root save area. Rot and disease that enters dying roots in compacted or filled areas can move into the tree if root pruning has not been carried out. Install tree protection fencing and silt protection at the limits of construction activity near trees.

During construction, apply additional water in the canopy area to compensate for any root loss beyond the crown spread. Have all mature trees inspected by a certified arborist before construction begins to identify any special problems. Remove all deadwood and treat all trees for existing insect and disease problems. When possible, begin fertilization and problem treatments at least one full growing season before construction.

Removal of significant portions of the crown will affect the health of a tree by reducing its ability to photosynthesize in proportion to the mass of its trunk. Younger, healthier trees withstand construction impacts better than older trees.

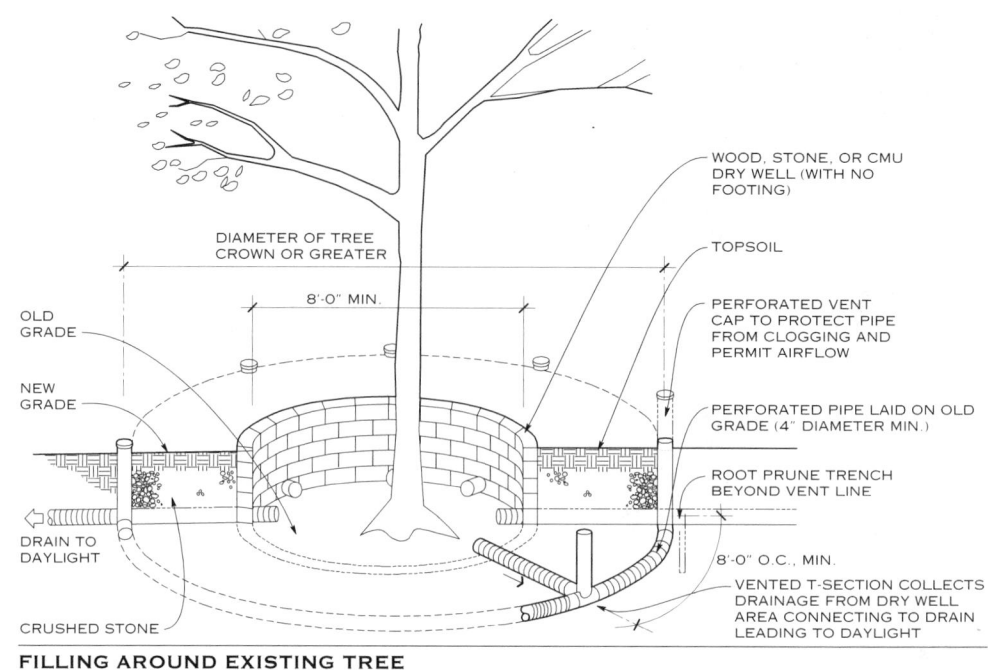

FILLING AROUND EXISTING TREE

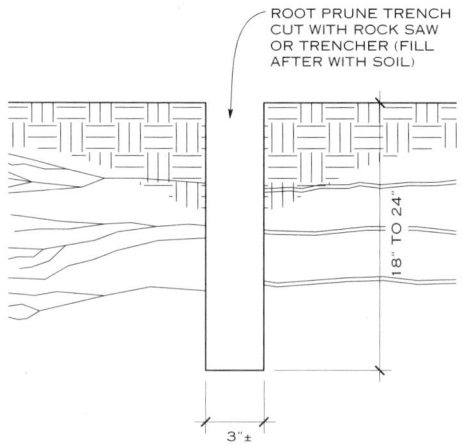

NOTE

A root prune trench severs roots with a clean cut, protecting remaining roots from cracking, rot, and disease.

ROOT PRUNE TRENCH

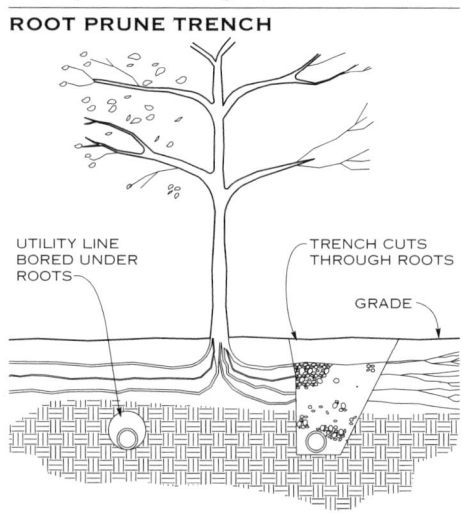

NOTE

Fewer roots are severed by tunneling under a tree than by digging a trench beside it.

UNDERGROUND UTILITY LINE NEAR EXISTING TREES

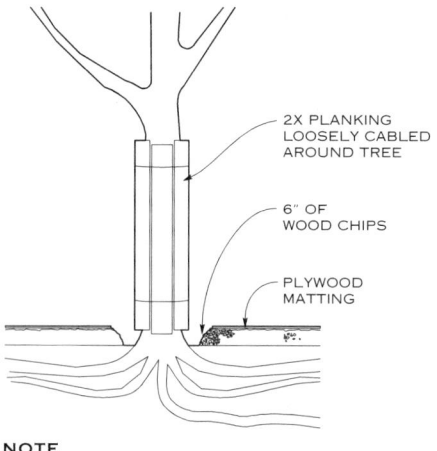

NOTE

If construction operations must take place within the crown spread area, install 6 in. of wood chips on top of the soil to protect it. Use plywood matting over mulch in areas where equipment must operate. Protect the trunk of the tree with planking loosely cabled around the tree to reduce scarring by equipment. Remove planking, matting, and mulch as soon as operations are finished.

TREE AND ROOT PROTECTION

NOTE

A barrier such as that illustrated can keep construction equipment and personnel from compacting the soil around tree roots.

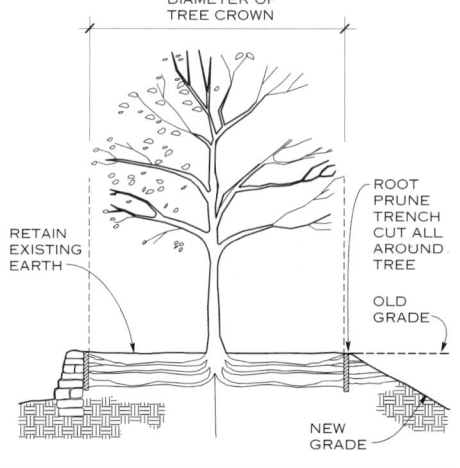

CUTTING GRADE AROUND EXISTING TREE

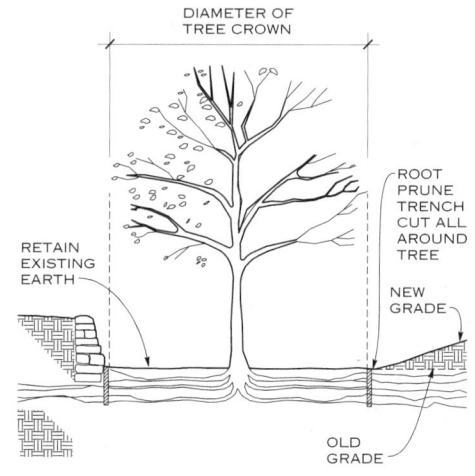

FILLING GRADE AROUND EXISTING TREE

James Urban, ASLA; James Urban Landscape Architecture; Annapolis, Maryland

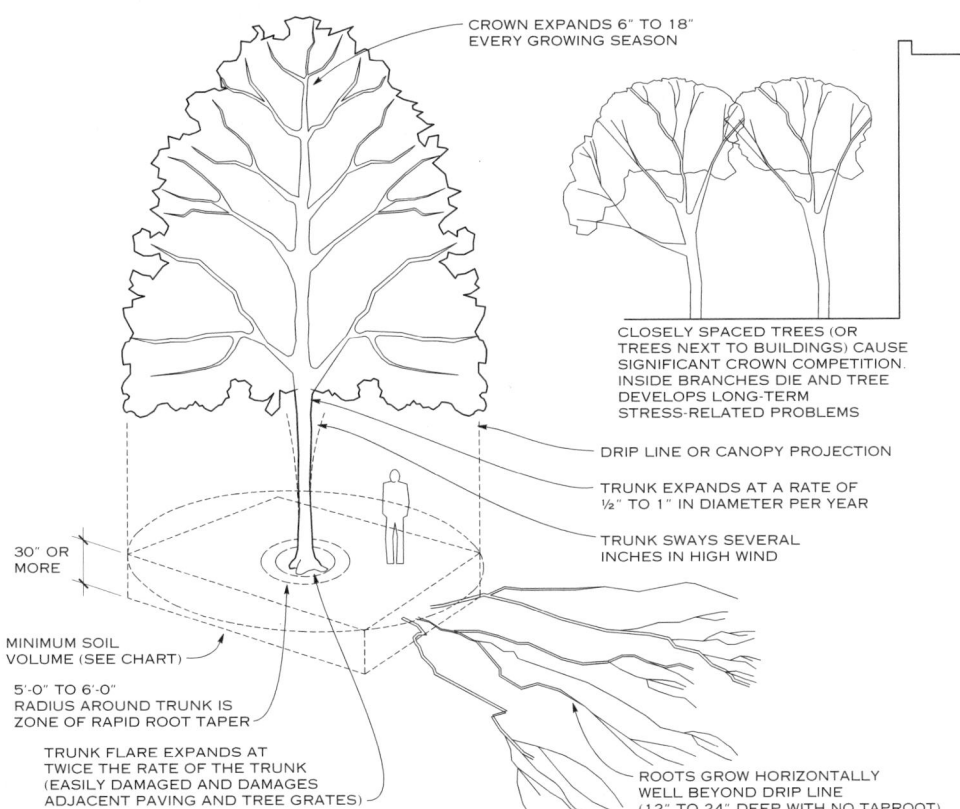

CROWN EXPANDS 6" TO 18" EVERY GROWING SEASON

CLOSELY SPACED TREES (OR TREES NEXT TO BUILDINGS) CAUSE SIGNIFICANT CROWN COMPETITION. INSIDE BRANCHES DIE AND TREE DEVELOPS LONG-TERM STRESS-RELATED PROBLEMS

DRIP LINE OR CANOPY PROJECTION

TRUNK EXPANDS AT A RATE OF ½" TO 1" IN DIAMETER PER YEAR

TRUNK SWAYS SEVERAL INCHES IN HIGH WIND

30" OR MORE

MINIMUM SOIL VOLUME (SEE CHART)

5'-0" TO 6'-0" RADIUS AROUND TRUNK IS ZONE OF RAPID ROOT TAPER

TRUNK FLARE EXPANDS AT TWICE THE RATE OF THE TRUNK (EASILY DAMAGED AND DAMAGES ADJACENT PAVING AND TREE GRATES)

ROOTS GROW HORIZONTALLY WELL BEYOND DRIP LINE (12" TO 24" DEEP WITH NO TAPROOT)

TREE STRUCTURE—PARTS AND GROWING CHARACTERISTICS

GENERAL

Areas of dense urban development leave little room for tree roots to develop. Large areas of pavement, competition with foundations and utilities for space below ground, and extensive soil compaction and disruption limit the amount of soil available for trees. When the area of ground around the tree open to the rain and sun is less than 400 to 500 sq ft per tree, the following design guidelines should be followed to encourage the growth of large healthy trees.

Five major parts of the tree structure must be accommodated in the design process:

CROWN GROWTH: The tree crown expands every growing season at a rate of 6 to 18 in. per year. Once the crown reaches a competing object such as a building or another tree canopy, the canopy growth in that area slows and then stops. Eventually the branches on that side of the tree die. As the canopy expansion potential is reduced, the overall growth rate and tree health are also reduced.

TRUNK GROWTH: The tree trunk expands about ½ to 1 in. per year. As the tree increases in size, the lower branches die and the trunk lengthens. Tree trunks move considerably in the wind, especially during the early years of development, and are damaged by close objects.

TRUNK FLARE: At the point where the trunk leaves the ground, most tree species develop a pronounced swelling or flare as the tree matures. This flare grows at more than twice the rate of the main trunk diameter and helps the tree remain structurally stable. Any hard object placed in this area, such as a tree grate or confining pavement, will either damage the tree or be moved by the tremendous force of this growth.

ZONE OF RAPID ROOT TAPER: Tree roots begin to form in the trunk flare and divide several times in the immediate area around the trunk. In this area, about 5 to 6 ft away from the trunk, the roots rapidly taper from about 6 in. in diameter to about 2 in. Most damage to adjacent paving occurs in this area immediately around the tree. Keeping the zone of rapid taper free of obstructions is important to long-term tree health. Once a tree is established, the zone of rapid taper is generally less susceptible to compaction damage than the rest of the root zone.

ROOT ZONE: Tree roots grow radially and horizontally from the trunk and occupy only the upper layers (12 to 24 in.) of the soil. Trees in all but the most well-drained soils do not have taproots. A relationship exists between the amount of tree canopy and the volume of root-supporting soil required (see the accompanying chart). This relationship is the most

critical factor in determining long-term tree health. Root-supporting soil is generally defined as soil with adequate drainage, low compaction, and sufficient organic and nutrient components to support the tree. The root zone must be protected from compaction both during and after construction. Root zones that are connected from tree to tree generally produce healthier trees than isolated root zones.

SOIL MODIFICATIONS

Thoroughly till organic matter into the top 6 to 12 in. of most planting soils to improve the soil's ability to retain water and nutrients. (Do not add organic matter to soil more than 12 in. deep.) Use composted bark, recycled yard waste, peat moss, or municipal processed sewage sludge. All products should be composted to a dark color and be free of pieces with identifiable leaf or wood structure. Recycled material should be tested for pH and certified free of toxic material by the supplier. Avoid material with a pH higher than 7.5.

Modify heavy clay or silt soils (more than 40% clay or silt) by adding composted pine bark (up to 30% by volume) and/or gypsum. Coarse sand may be used if enough is added to bring the sand content to more than 60% of the total mix. Improve drainage in heavy soils by planting on raised mounds or beds and including subsurface drainage lines.

Modify extremely sandy soils (more than 85% sand) by adding organic matter and/or dry, shredded clay loam up to 30% of the total mix.

SOIL VOLUME FOR TREES

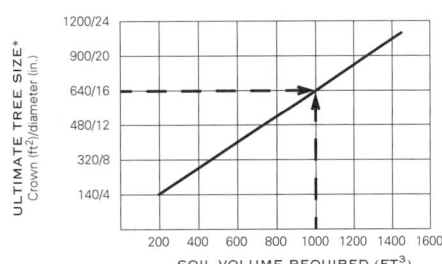

*The ultimate tree size is defined by the projected size of the crown and the diameter of the tree at breast height.

NOTE

For example, a 16-in. diameter tree requires 1000 cu ft of soil.

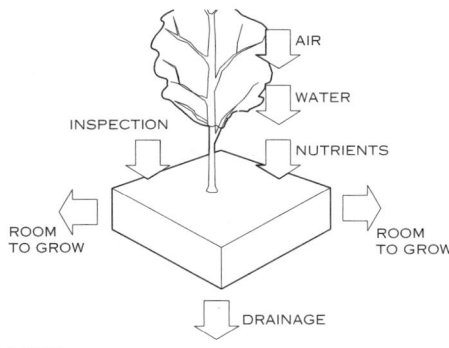

INSPECTION — AIR — WATER — NUTRIENTS

ROOM TO GROW — ROOM TO GROW

DRAINAGE

NOTE

Soil volume provided for trees in urban areas must be sufficient for long-term maintenance.

SOIL VOLUME—REQUIREMENTS FOR TREES

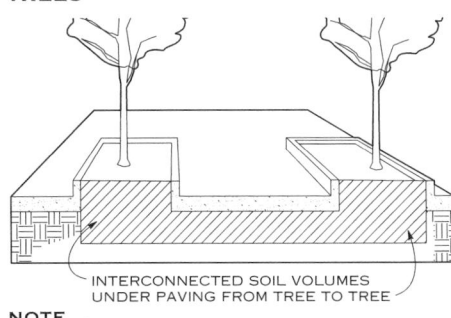

INTERCONNECTED SOIL VOLUMES UNDER PAVING FROM TREE TO TREE

NOTE

The interconnection of soil volumes from tree to tree has been observed to improve the health and vigor of trees.

SOIL VOLUME—INTERCONNECTION

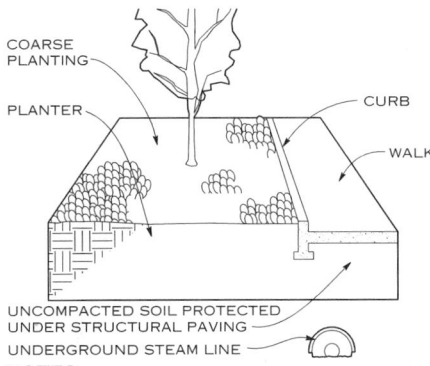

COARSE PLANTING

PLANTER

CURB

WALK

UNCOMPACTED SOIL PROTECTED UNDER STRUCTURAL PAVING

UNDERGROUND STEAM LINE

NOTES

1. Coarse plantings keep pedestrians out of planters.
2. Curbs protect planters from pedestrians and deicing salts.
3. Underground steam lines must be insulated or vented to protect planter soil.

SOIL PROTECTION FROM COMPACTION AND DEGRADATION

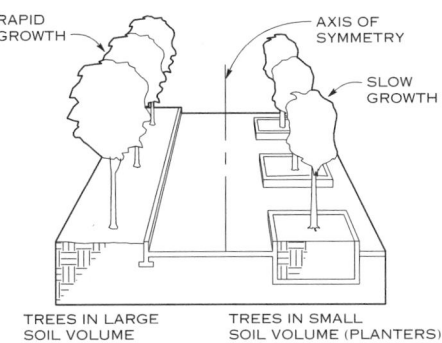

RAPID GROWTH

AXIS OF SYMMETRY

SLOW GROWTH

TREES IN LARGE SOIL VOLUME

TREES IN SMALL SOIL VOLUME (PLANTERS)

NOTE

If visually symmetrical tree planting is required, symmetrical soil volumes are also required to produce trees of similar crown size.

VISUALLY SYMMETRICAL TREES

James Urban, ASLA; James Urban Landscape Architecture; Annapolis, Maryland

GENERAL

Traditional urban designs in which trees are regularly spaced in small openings within paved areas generally result in poor tree performance. This is because such designs generally do not provide adequate soil for root growth and ignore the fact that trees must significantly increase trunk size every year. As well, competition for space, both at ground level and below, is intense in urban areas.

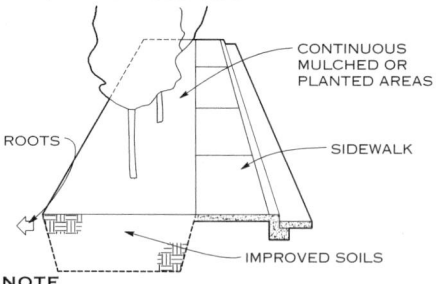

NOTE

Best design option: Planting trees between sidewalks and buildings creates the fewest conflicts between roots and paving by permitting rooting activity on adjacent property.

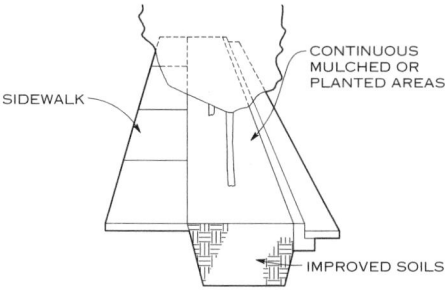

NOTE

Acceptable design option: Planting between curbs and sidewalks in a continuous unpaved planting bed provides good soil levels for trees but contributes to root/paving conflicts as trees mature.

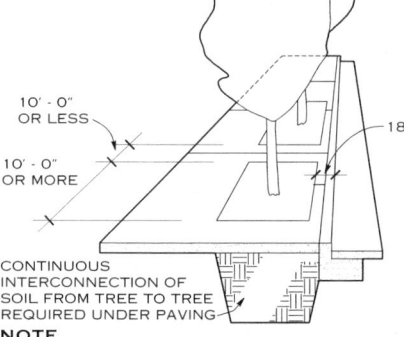

NOTE

Difficult design option: In highly developed areas with parking adjacent to the curb, planting in long narrow tree openings with an 18-in. wide walk along the curb accommodates pedestrians exiting cars. Root/paving conflicts are probable.

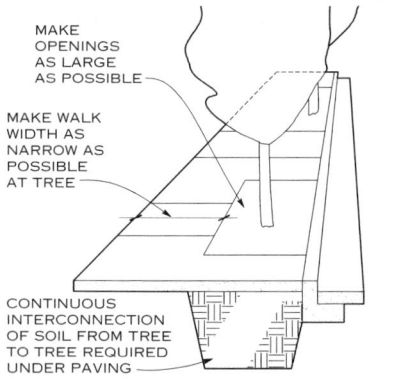

NOTE

Most difficult (and most expensive) design option: Tree openings are undersized for future trunk/root development. Severe root/paving conflicts are very likely.

SIDEWALK PLANTING OPTIONS

Although it is possible to design uncompacted soil volumes for trees under pavement, this is very expensive and the soil is never as efficient as that in open planting beds. Increasing trunk size can only be accommodated by using flexible materials that can change configuration over time. Urban designs that have flexible relationships between trees, paving, and planting beds and large areas of open planting soil offer the best opportunity for long-term tree health and lower maintenance costs.

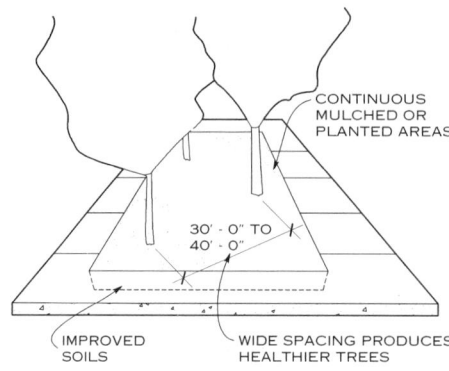

NOTE

Best design option: Separate planting and walking areas. Avoid small disconnected soil volumes to minimize root/paving conflicts.

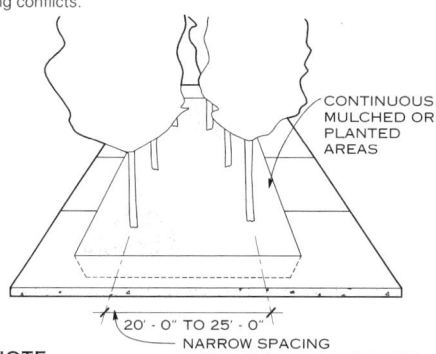

NOTE

Acceptable design option: Each tree has a smaller canopy with less yearly growth. More disease and insect problems are likely. Ground plantings eliminated by shade over time.

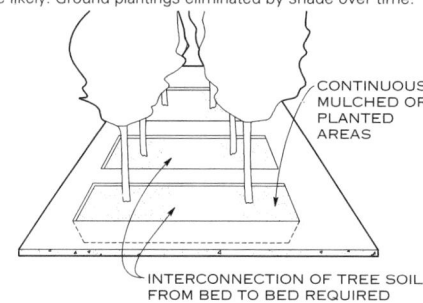

NOTE

Difficult design option: Shading, slow tree growth, and poor health are problems. Root/paving conflicts are likely.

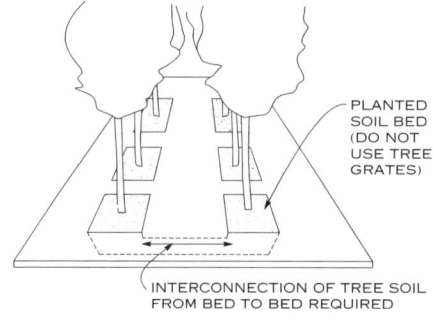

NOTE

Most difficult (and most expensive) design option: Slow tree growth and severe root/paving conflicts are to be expected.

PLAZA TREE PLANTING OPTIONS

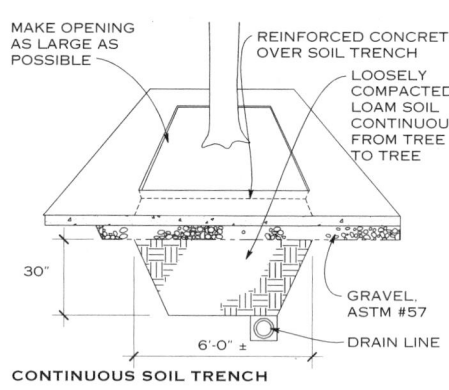

CONTINUOUS SOIL TRENCH
NOTE

A continuous soil trench provides very good soil but in limited quantity. Use in areas where adjacent backfill is compacted soils or fills.

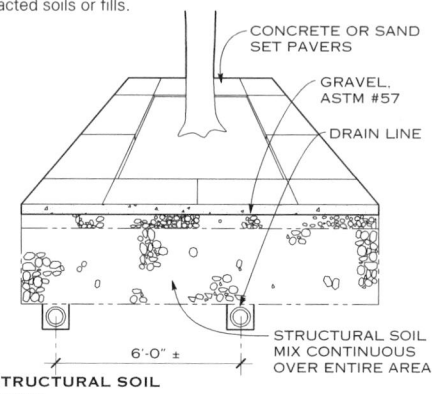

STRUCTURAL SOIL
NOTE

Structural planting soils replace subgrade material with a fill that can be compacted to meet normal engineering compaction requirements and still support root growth below the pavement. The principle is that when the gravel is compacted, the soil is not because the amount of soil in the mix is insufficient to fill all the voids. Hydrogel, a cross-linked potassium copolymer, is used to help bind the mixture during the mixing process. The soil mix includes ASHTO #4 gravel (100 lb calculated dry weight), shredded clay loam (15-18 lb), hydrogel (0.03 lb), and water ±10 (including the water calculated in the gravel and the soil). For further information, contact the Urban Horticulture Institute at Cornell University (Ithaca, NY).

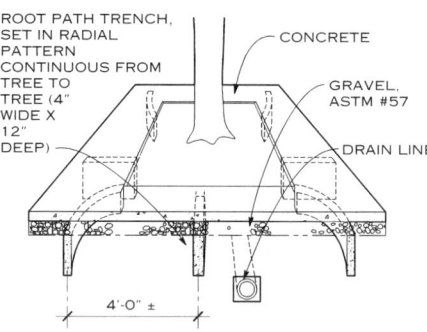

ROOT PATH TRENCH

NOTES

1. In urban areas where the pavement subgrade is compacted soil that is free from rubble, toxic, or poorly drained fills, a system of root paths can be installed to guide roots under the pavement, where they have room to grow. These roots grow deeper in the soil, causing fewer root/paving conflicts than roots left to exploit the normal minor weaknesses in paving and subgrades.

2. A root path trench is made by installing a length of strip drain material (a 12-in. wide x 1-in. thick plastic drain core wrapped in filter fabric) in a narrow trench and backfilling with loam topsoil. This allows air and water to flow more freely into the soil under the pavement. Install geotextile fabric and the gravel base material and then the paving.

3. Root paths cannot replace larger soil trenches or structural planting soil in areas in which existing soil conditions are extremely poor for root exploration.

TREE SOIL INTERCONNECTION OPTIONS UNDER PAVING

James Urban, ASLA; James Urban Landscape Architecture; Annapolis, Maryland

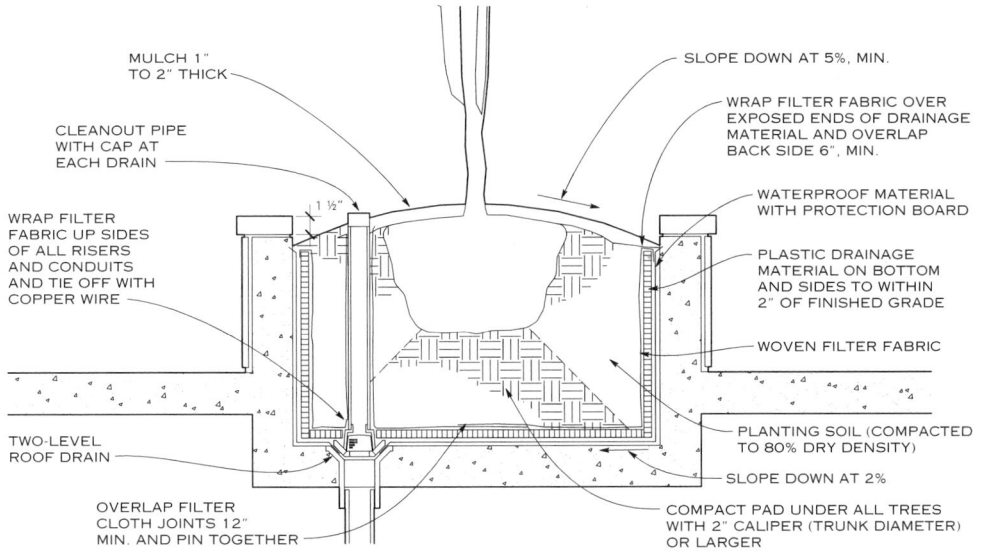

MULCH 1" TO 2" THICK

CLEANOUT PIPE WITH CAP AT EACH DRAIN

1 1/2"

WRAP FILTER FABRIC UP SIDES OF ALL RISERS AND CONDUITS AND TIE OFF WITH COPPER WIRE

TWO-LEVEL ROOF DRAIN

OVERLAP FILTER CLOTH JOINTS 12" MIN. AND PIN TOGETHER

SLOPE DOWN AT 5%, MIN.

WRAP FILTER FABRIC OVER EXPOSED ENDS OF DRAINAGE MATERIAL AND OVERLAP BACK SIDE 6", MIN.

WATERPROOF MATERIAL WITH PROTECTION BOARD

PLASTIC DRAINAGE MATERIAL ON BOTTOM AND SIDES TO WITHIN 2" OF FINISHED GRADE

WOVEN FILTER FABRIC

PLANTING SOIL (COMPACTED TO 80% DRY DENSITY)

SLOPE DOWN AT 2%

COMPACT PAD UNDER ALL TREES WITH 2" CALIPER (TRUNK DIAMETER) OR LARGER

ROOFTOP PLANTER

SELECTING PLANTS FOR ROOFTOP PLANTING

When choosing plants for a rooftop setting, consider the factors outlined below:

WIND TOLERANCE: Higher elevations and exposure to wind can cause defoliation and increase the transpiration rate of plants. High parapet walls with louvers can reduce wind velocity and provide shelter for plants.

HIGH EVAPORATION RATE: The drying effects of wind and sun on the soil in a planter reduce soil moisture rapidly. Irrigation, mulches, and moisture-holding soil additives (diatomaceous earth or organic matter) help reduce this moisture loss.

RAPID SOIL TEMPERATURE FLUCTUATION: The variation in conduction capacity of planter materials results in a broad range of soil temperatures in planters of different materials. Cold or heat can cause severe root damage in certain plant species. Proper drainage helps alleviate this condition.

TOPSOIL: Improve topsoil in planters to provide optimum growing conditions for the plants selected. A general formula calls for adding fertilizer (determined by soil testing) and one part peat moss to five parts sandy loam topsoil. More specific requirements for certain varieties of plants or grasses should be considered.

ROOT CAPACITY: Choose plant species carefully, considering their adaptation to the size of the plant bed. If species with shallow, fibrous roots are used instead of species with a coarse root system, consult with a nursery advisor. Consider the ultimate maturity of the plant species when sizing a planter.

PLANTING DETAILS

SOIL DEPTH: Minimum soil depth in a planter varies with the plant type: for large trees, the soil should be 36 in. deep or 6 in. deeper than the root ball; for small trees, 30 in. deep;

for shrubs, 24 in. deep; and for lawns, 12 in. deep (10 in. if irrigated).

SOIL VOLUME: To determine sufficient soil volume, see chart on Soil Volumes for Trees (on another AGS page in this section).

SOIL WEIGHT: The saturated weight of normal soil mix ranges from 100 to 120 pcf, depending on soil type and compaction rate. Soils can be made lighter by adding expanded shale or perlite. Soils lighter than 80 pcf cannot provide structure adequate to support trees.

DRAINAGE FABRIC: Plastic drainage material should be a minimum of 1/2 in. thick. Most drainage material comes with a filter fabric attached, but the overlap joints provided are not wide enough for the unconsolidated soils found in planters. A second layer of woven filter fabric, delivered in rolls greater than 10 ft in width, should be installed. Tuck the fabric over the exposed top of the drainage material to keep soil out of the drainage layer.

INSULATION: Most planters do not require insulation; however, in colder climates planters with small soil volumes located over heated structures may require insulation. Consult local sources for a list of cold-hardy plants.

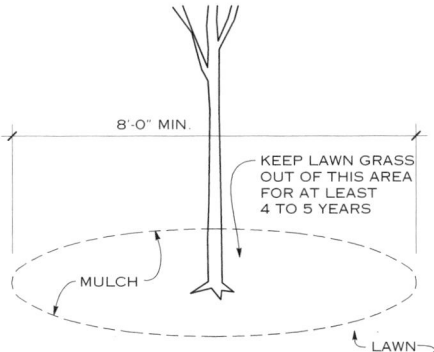

8'-0" MIN.

KEEP LAWN GRASS OUT OF THIS AREA FOR AT LEAST 4 TO 5 YEARS

MULCH

LAWN

NOTE

Young trees planted in lawn areas face substantial competition from the roots of grasses.

TREES PLANTED IN LAWNS

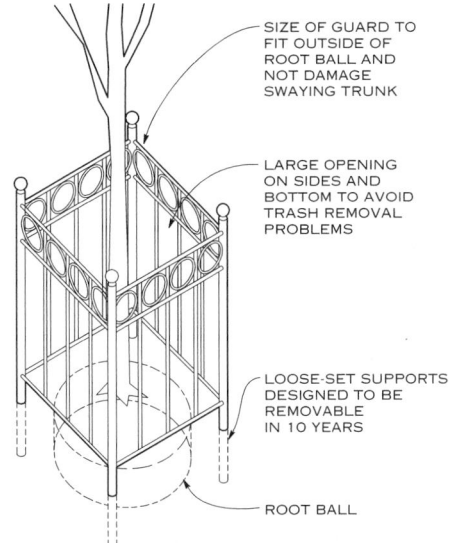

SIZE OF GUARD TO FIT OUTSIDE OF ROOT BALL AND NOT DAMAGE SWAYING TRUNK

LARGE OPENING ON SIDES AND BOTTOM TO AVOID TRASH REMOVAL PROBLEMS

LOOSE-SET SUPPORTS DESIGNED TO BE REMOVABLE IN 10 YEARS

ROOT BALL

NOTE

Tree guards can protect young trees from trunk damage caused by bicycles. If made too small, however (less than 30 in. in diameter), they can damage the tree as it grows and are difficult to remove. The high cost and potential harm to trees outweigh the minor protection tree guards afford a trunk. They should only be used in areas with particularly high traffic.

TREE GUARDS

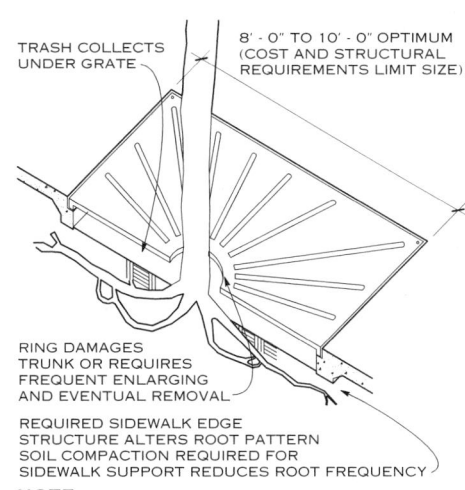

TRASH COLLECTS UNDER GRATE

8'-0" TO 10'-0" OPTIMUM (COST AND STRUCTURAL REQUIREMENTS LIMIT SIZE)

RING DAMAGES TRUNK OR REQUIRES FREQUENT ENLARGING AND EVENTUAL REMOVAL

REQUIRED SIDEWALK EDGE STRUCTURE ALTERS ROOT PATTERN SOIL COMPACTION REQUIRED FOR SIDEWALK SUPPORT REDUCES ROOT FREQUENCY

NOTE

Tree grates decorate the base of a tree but provide no significant benefit. Many aspects of tree grates can damage a tree or reduce its potential for growth.

TREE GRATES

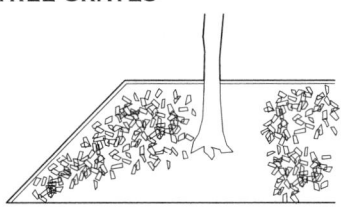

BARK MULCH

GROUND COVER PLANTS

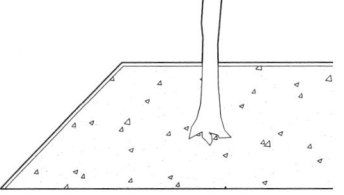

STONE DUST OR GRAVEL

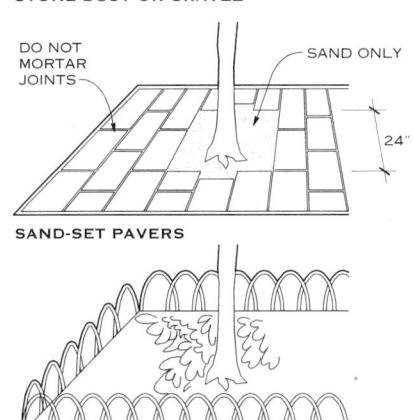

DO NOT MORTAR JOINTS

SAND ONLY

24"

SAND-SET PAVERS

LOW FENCE AND GROUND COVER

NOTE

Alternatives to tree grates (and guards) include softer, organic coverings that suit the purpose better, are less expensive, and require less maintenance over the life of the tree.

TREE BASE PROTECTION

James Urban, ASLA; James Urban Landscape Architecture; Annapolis, Maryland

GENERAL

Formwork costs are a substantial part of the total cost of putting concrete in place—anywhere from 35 to 60 percent. Thus, by developing design elements and details that simplify or standardize form requirements, the architect can help contain overall costs:

1. Reuse forms: This is crucial to economy of construction. The designer can facilitate form reuse by standardizing the dimensions of windows, columns, beams, and footings, using as few different sizes of each as possible. Where columns must change size, hold one dimension (e.g., width) constant, while varying the other (depth). This enables at least half of the form panels to be used many times. Repeat the same floor and column layout from bay to bay on each floor and from floor to floor. This improves labor productivity and permits reuse of many forms.

2. Use a preconstruction mockup: The architect and builder should agree on the location and desired appearance of architectural surfaces before any of the exposed concrete work begins. Specify a full-scale preconstruction mockup to help achieve this and to avoid postconstruction disagreements.

3. Handle forms in large panels: This also reduces construction costs. Wherever possible, make uninterrupted formed areas the same size. Increasing the size of such areas enables the builder to combine form panels into gangs for efficient crane use.

4. Simplify design details: Intricacies and irregularities cost more and often do not add proportionately to the aesthetic effect.

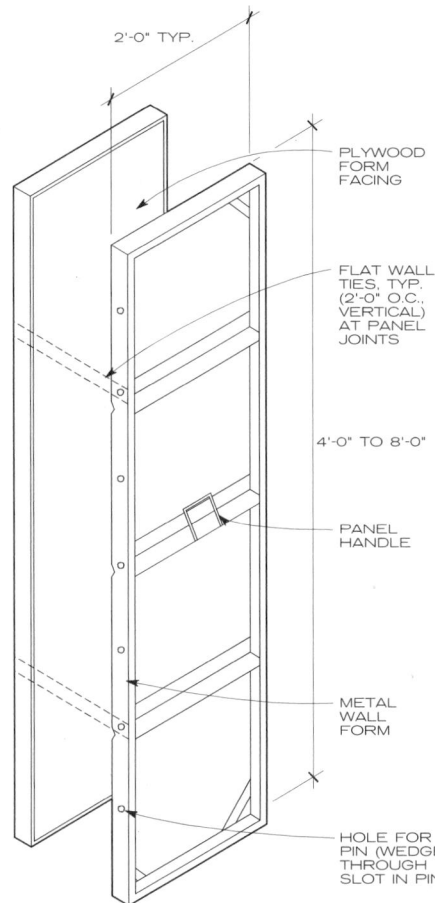

NOTES

1. Commonly made of steel-framed plywood, panels are also available in aluminum. Wall ties (typically flat ties) and wall forms are held together by slotted pins that run through adjoining holes. A wedge pushed down into the slot alongside the wall form tightens the joint. Service life can be extended by turning or replacing the plywood face.

2. Reusable plastic liners may be attached to inner surfaces to produce patterned concrete.

3. For maximum economy, panels can be assembled in large gangs and set in place by crane.

HAND-SET MANUFACTURED WALL FORMS

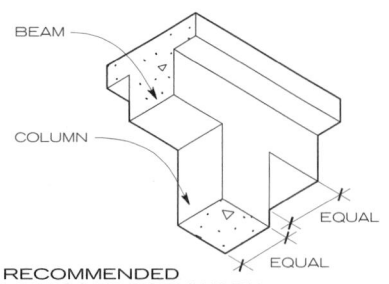

RECOMMENDED LOW-COST FORMWORK

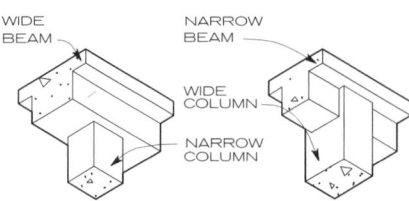

MID-COST FORMWORK   HIGH-COST FORMWORK

NOTE

In general, the least costly design to form has columns the same width or narrower than the beams they support, allowing the beam form to be erected in a continuous line. In mid-cost formwork design, the beam bottom forms are cut to fit around the column tops. In high-cost formwork design, the beam forms are fitted into pockets on both sides of the column forms.

BEAM-TO-COLUMN FORMWORK ECONOMIES

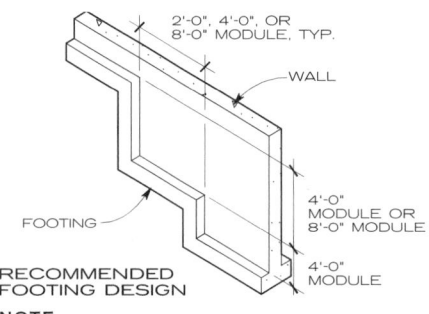

RECOMMENDED FOOTING DESIGN

NOTE

When stepped footings are required, use fewer steps and design them to standard lumber and plywood dimensions or modular divisions of these dimensions.

WALL FOOTINGS

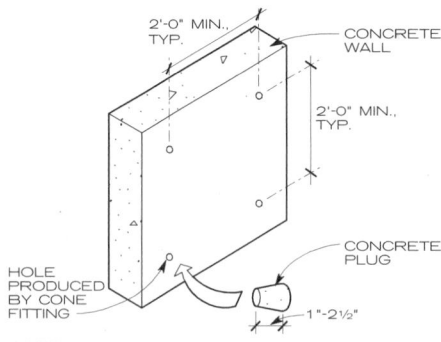

NOTE

Installing and removing ties and patching tie holes are some of the most labor-intensive operations in forming walls. Also, getting a durable, inconspicuous patch often proves difficult. Avoid this problem by specifying smooth cone fittings at the tie ends, then either leaving the resulting uniform tie holes exposed or plugging them with preformed concrete plugs and a bonding agent. Leave no exposed corrodible metal within $1\frac{1}{2}$ in. of concrete surface. Contractors may propose tie spacing wider than 2 ft o.c. to reduce the total number of ties to save money, but this calls for stronger ties and heavier form supports.

FORM TIE PATTERN

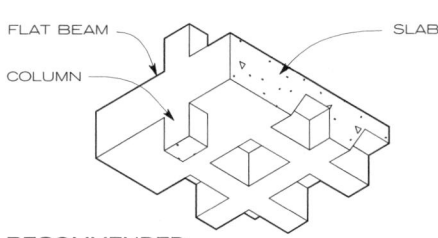

RECOMMENDED LOW-COST FORMWORK

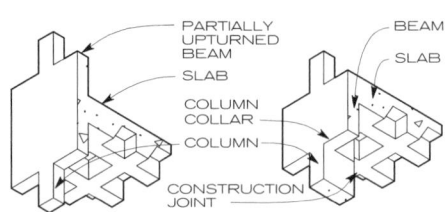

MID-COST FORMWORK   HIGH-COST FORMWORK

NOTE

Flat beams designed to be equal in depth to the floor assembly are the least costly, since they most efficiently accommodate flying form construction. Deeper, narrower beams cost more, but if deeper beams are needed, costs can be controlled by making the beam the same thickness as the column depth and at least partially upturned. The most costly option is a column thicker than the beam, since this requires a column collar with construction joint.

SPANDREL BEAM FORMWORK ECONOMIES

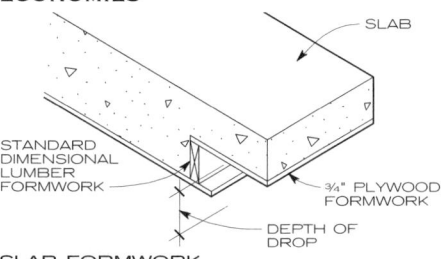

SLAB FORMWORK

NOTE

Adapting design elements to the modular sizes of formwork lumber and plywood and dimensioning parts of the structure to fit the modules can save the expense of custom formwork. For example, to save the waste and time of sawing and piecing together the edge form, make the depth of the drop in a slab equal to the actual size of standard lumber plus $\frac{3}{4}$ in. for the plywood's thickness.

STANDARD LUMBER FORMS

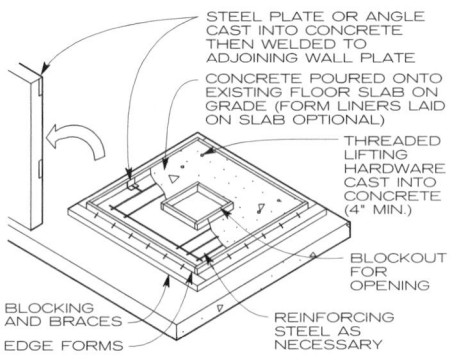

TILT-UP WALL FORMWORK

NOTE

In tilt-up construction, walls are cast on the completed floor slab, which must be level, smoothly finished, and treated with a bond-breaking agent to permit easy separation. The wall is then tilted or lifted into vertical position and fastened to the adjoining wall piece. This method reduces formwork and labor and eliminates transportation requirements that may limit panel size.

TILT-UP WALLS

Mary K. Hurd; Engineered Publications; Farmington Hills, Michigan

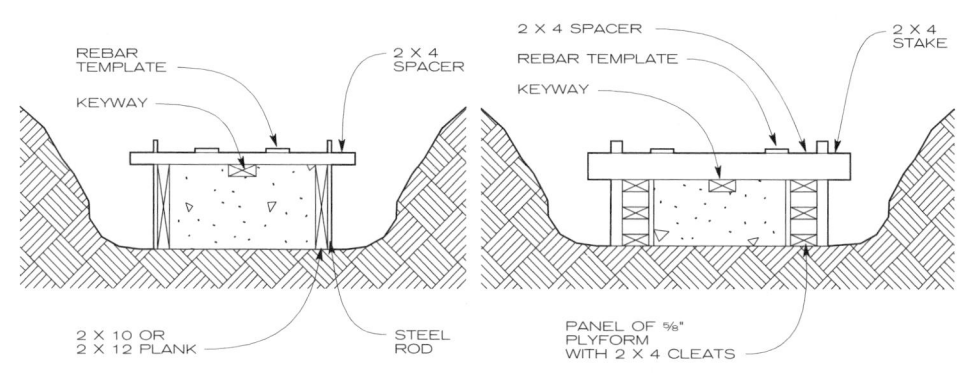

REBAR
TEMPLATE
KEYWAY
2 X 4
SPACER

2 X 10 OR
2 X 12 PLANK
STEEL
ROD

2 X 4 SPACER
REBAR TEMPLATE
KEYWAY
2 X 4
STAKE

PANEL OF ⅝"
PLYFORM
WITH 2 X 4 CLEATS

WALL FOOTINGS

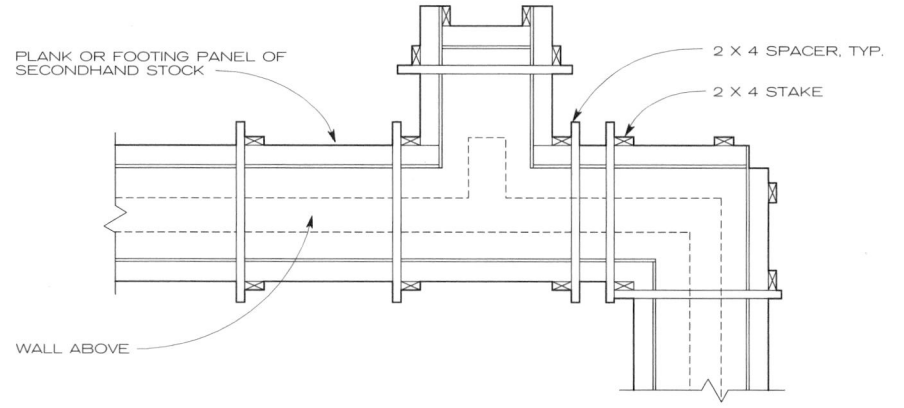

PLANK OR FOOTING PANEL OF
SECONDHAND STOCK

2 X 4 SPACER, TYP.

2 X 4 STAKE

WALL ABOVE

WALL FOOTING PLAN

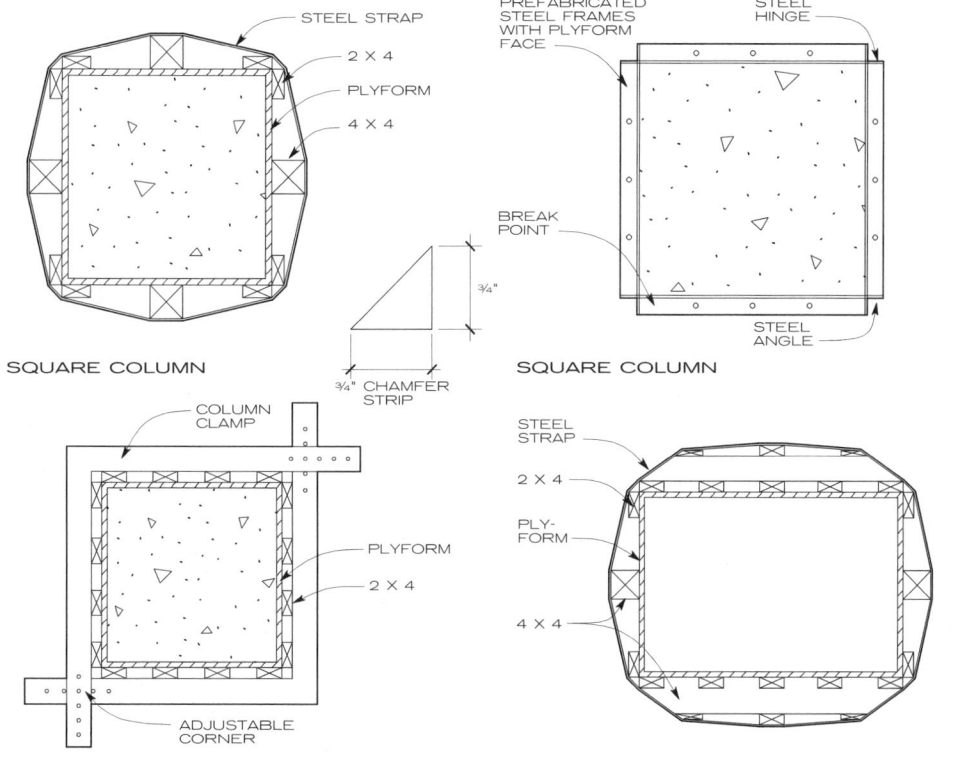

STEEL STRAP
2 X 4
PLYFORM
4 X 4

SQUARE COLUMN

PREFABRICATED
STEEL FRAMES
WITH PLYFORM
FACE

STEEL
HINGE

BREAK
POINT

¾"

¾" CHAMFER
STRIP

STEEL
ANGLE

SQUARE COLUMN

COLUMN
CLAMP

PLYFORM
2 X 4

ADJUSTABLE
CORNER

SQUARE COLUMN
NOTE

It is recommended that chamfer strips be used at all outside corners to reduce damage to concrete when forms are

STEEL
STRAP
2 X 4
PLY-
FORM
4 X 4

LARGE COLUMN PLAN

removed. Consult manufacturers' guides and catalogs for ideal materials, pour rate (ft/hr), and outside temperature (oF).

COLUMN PLANS

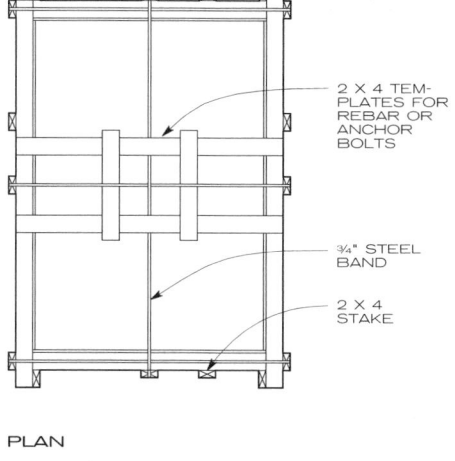

2 X 4
KICKER
2 X 4
BAND
SPACER

2 X 4 TEM-
PLATES FOR
REBAR OR
ANCHOR
BOLTS

¾" STEEL
BAND

2 X 4
STAKE

PLAN

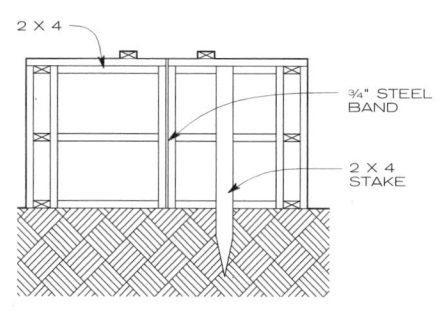

2 X 4

¾" STEEL
BAND

2 X 4
STAKE

ELEVATION
COLUMN FOOTINGS

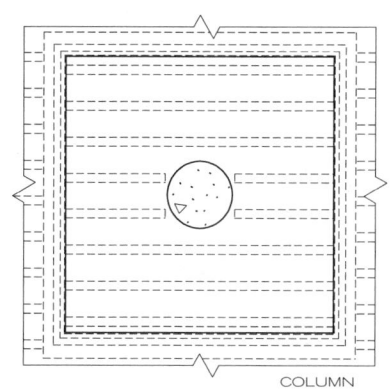

COLUMN

PLAN

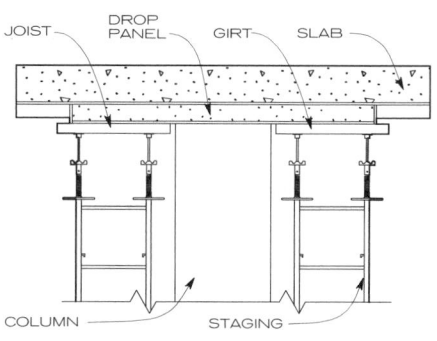

JOIST
DROP
PANEL
GIRT
SLAB

COLUMN
STAGING

SECTION
DROP PANELS AT COLUMN TOPS

Tucker Concrete Form Company; Stoughton, Massachusetts

CONCRETE FORMWORK   3

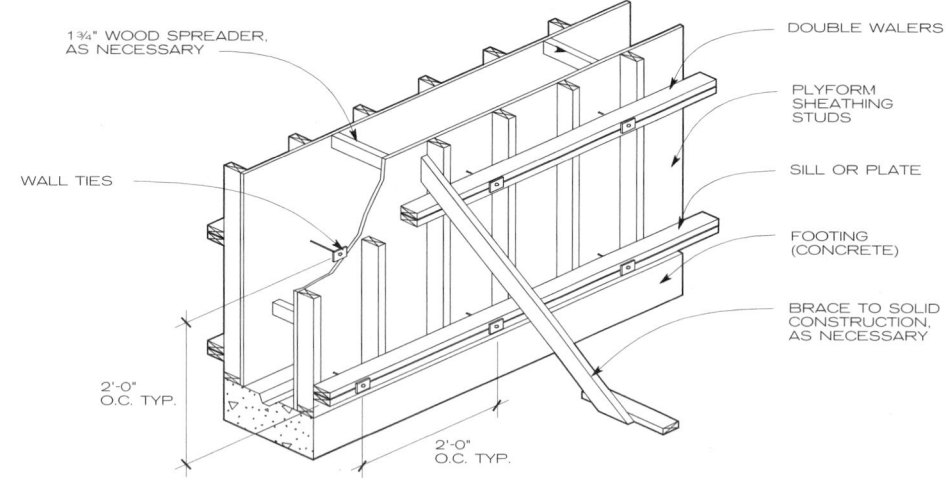

1¾" WOOD SPREADER, AS NECESSARY

WALL TIES

DOUBLE WALERS

PLYFORM SHEATHING STUDS

SILL OR PLATE

FOOTING (CONCRETE)

BRACE TO SOLID CONSTRUCTION, AS NECESSARY

2'-0" O.C. TYP.

2'-0" O.C. TYP.

TYPICAL SITE-BUILT WALL FORMWORK

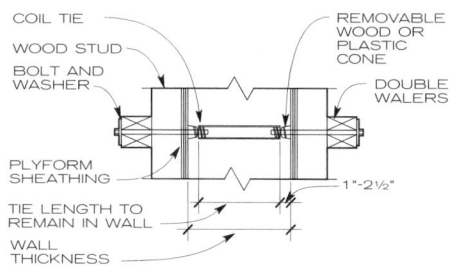

COIL TIE

WOOD STUD

BOLT AND WASHER

REMOVABLE WOOD OR PLASTIC CONE

DOUBLE WALERS

PLYFORM SHEATHING

TIE LENGTH TO REMAIN IN WALL

WALL THICKNESS

1"-2½"

SECTION AT WALL TIE

SITE-BUILT WALL FORMS

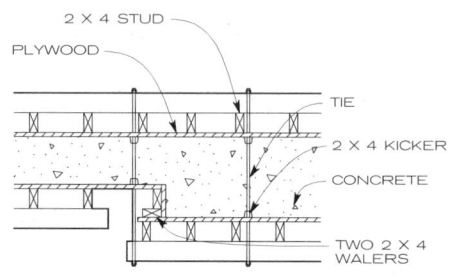

2 X 4 STUD

PLYWOOD

TIE

2 X 4 KICKER

CONCRETE

TWO 2 X 4 WALERS

TYPICAL CORNER

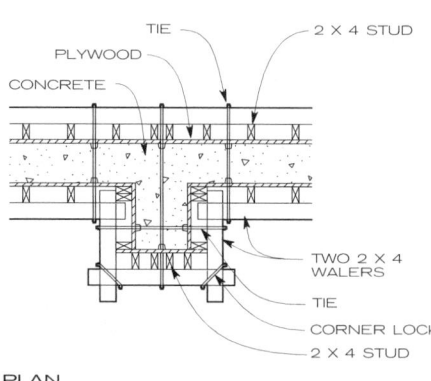

TIE

PLYWOOD

CONCRETE

TWO 2 X 4 WALERS

TIE

CORNER LOCK

2 X 4 STUD

2 X 4 STUD

PLAN

PILASTER

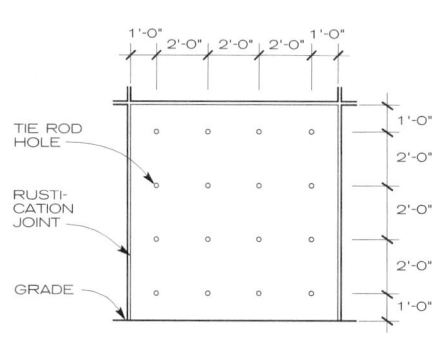

1'-0" 2'-0" 2'-0" 2'-0" 1'-0"

TIE ROD HOLE

RUSTI-CATION JOINT

GRADE

1'-0"

2'-0"

2'-0"

2'-0"

1'-0"

TYPICAL EXPOSED CONCRETE ELEVATION

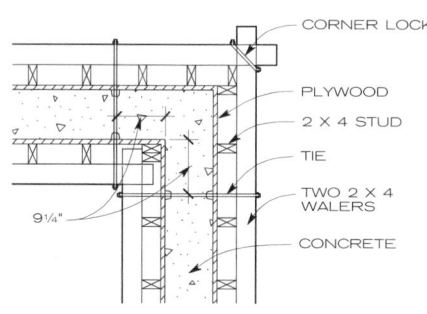

CORNER LOCK

PLYWOOD

2 X 4 STUD

TIE

TWO 2 X 4 WALERS

CONCRETE

9¼"

PLAN

TYPICAL WALL WITH OFFSET

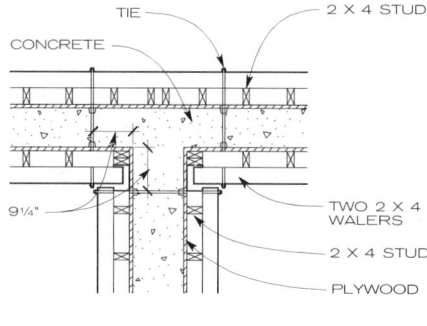

TIE

CONCRETE

9¼"

2 X 4 STUD

TWO 2 X 4 WALERS

2 X 4 STUD

PLYWOOD

PLAN

TYPICAL T WALL JUNCTION

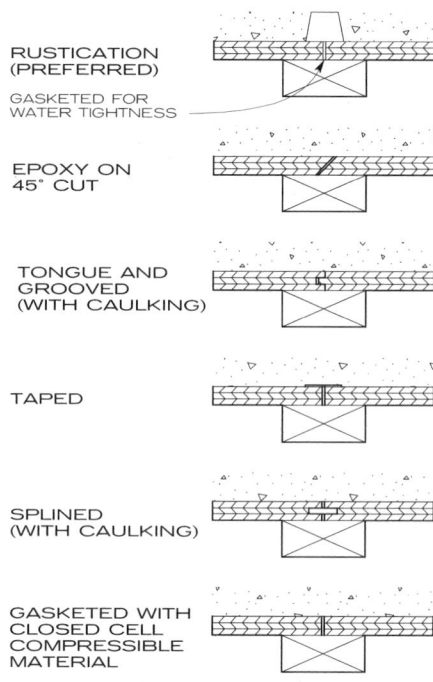

RUSTICATION (PREFERRED)

GASKETED FOR WATER TIGHTNESS

EPOXY ON 45° CUT

TONGUE AND GROOVED (WITH CAULKING)

TAPED

SPLINED (WITH CAULKING)

GASKETED WITH CLOSED CELL COMPRESSIBLE MATERIAL

FORM SHEATHING JOINT DETAILS

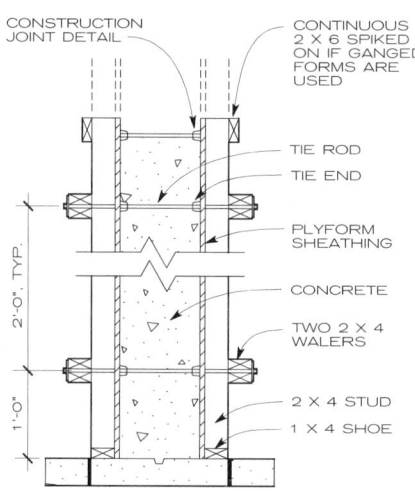

CONSTRUCTION JOINT DETAIL

CONTINUOUS 2 X 6 SPIKED ON IF GANGED FORMS ARE USED

TIE ROD

TIE END

PLYFORM SHEATHING

CONCRETE

TWO 2 X 4 WALERS

2 X 4 STUD

1 X 4 SHOE

2'-0" TYP.

1'-0"

NOTE

Verify size and spacing of components for each job. The combination of plyform sheathing, studs, walers, and ties must be chosen carefully to safely resist concrete pressure and limit deflection of the form face. Steel and aluminum studs and walers may be used in place of wood.

TYPICAL JOB-BUILT WALL SECTION

NOTES

1. The typical wood and plywood framing details shown must be modified as necessary to accommodate the lateral pressure of fresh concrete on the forms. Studs and walers of aluminum or steel are frequently used. Lateral pressure varies depending on the rate at which the form is filled, the temperature of the concrete, vibration procedures, and the type of admixtures used in the concrete.

2. Consult manufacturers' recommendations for safe working loads on ties. Consult the American Concrete Institute's *Formwork for Concrete* (SP-4) for detailed design recommendations.

3. A great variety of form ties are commercially available (see AGS page on concrete formwork hardware). For architectural surfaces exposed to weather, choose a tie that leaves no corrodible metal closer than 1½ in. from the concrete surface. Ties should be tight fitting and sealed as necessary to prevent leakage at holes in the forms.

4. Ties fitted with wood or plastic cones should leave depressions at least as deep as the surface diameter of the cone. The holes may be filled with recessed plugs or left unfilled if noncorroding ties are used.

5. Provide cleanout doors at the bottom of wall forms.

Tucker Concrete Form Company; Stoughton, Massachusetts
Mary K. Hurd; Engineered Publications; Farmington Hills, Michigan

3 **CONCRETE FORMWORK**

GENERAL NOTES

1. Scaffolding, steel shores, or wood posts may be used under stringers depending on loads and height requirements.

2. For flat slabs of flat plate forming, metal "flying forms" are commonly used.

3. Patented steel forms or fillers can be special ordered for unusual conditions; see manufacturers' catalogs. Fiber forms are also on the market in similar sizes. Plyform deck is required for forming.

4. Plyform is usually ⅝ in. minimum thickness, Exposure 1.

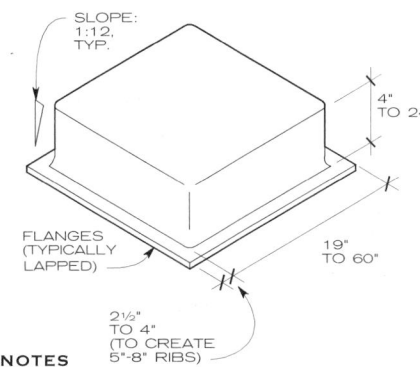

NOTES

1. Standard waffle slab forms are square for ease of use and economy. Dimensions vary slightly from manufacturer to manufacturer. Consult ANSI A48.2-1986 for complete dome form standards.

2. Forms are available in steel and lightweight fiberglass. Consult form manufacturer for options in material, textures, and dimensions.

TYPICAL DOME FORM FOR WAFFLE OR TWO-WAY SLAB

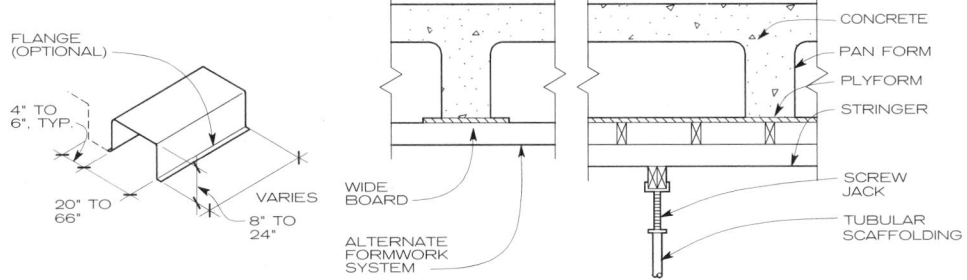

TYPICAL PAN FORM   **TYPICAL CENTERING**

NOTES

1. Forms are available in steel and lightweight fiberglass. Consult manufacturers for forms with different dimensions and rib-form variations. Typically three types are available: nail-down flange (simplest, but produces rough, nonarchitectural surface); slip-in type (based on nail-down form but with board insert for smooth appearance); and adjustable (without flanges; produces smooth rib).

2. Consult ANSI A48.1-1986 for complete pan form standards.

TYPICAL PAN FORM FOR ONE-WAY SLAB

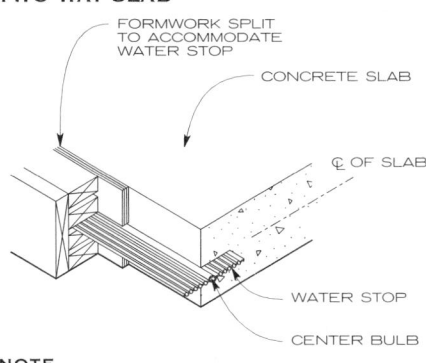

NOTE

Waterstops are flexible barriers used to prevent the passage of liquids and gasses under pressure through joints in concrete slabs. Waterstops are typically made of polyvinyl chloride, and their shapes vary according to application. If a center bulb is specified, it must remain unembedded in the center of the joint.

SLAB FORMWORK WITH WATER STOP

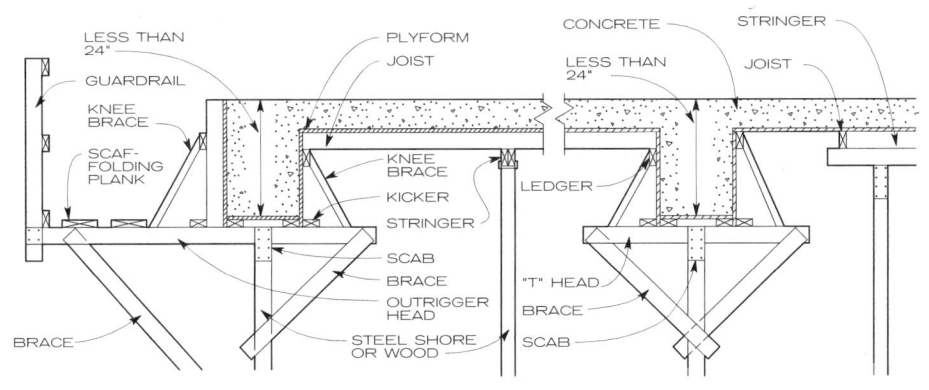

TYPICAL SLAB AND SHALLOW BEAM FORMING

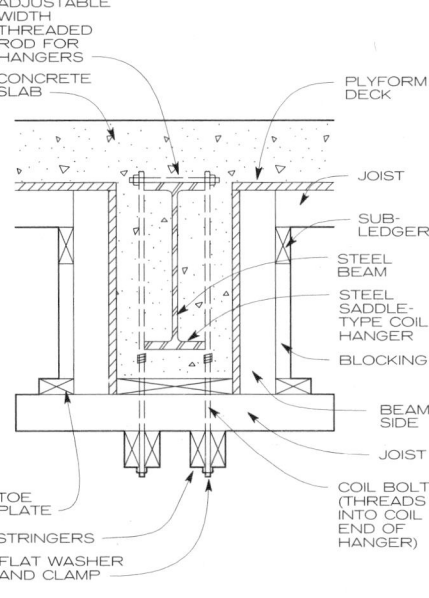

NOTE

This type of formwork is used to fireproof structural steel beams by wrapping them in concrete.

TYPICAL SUSPENDED FORM WITH COIL SADDLE-TYPE HANGERS

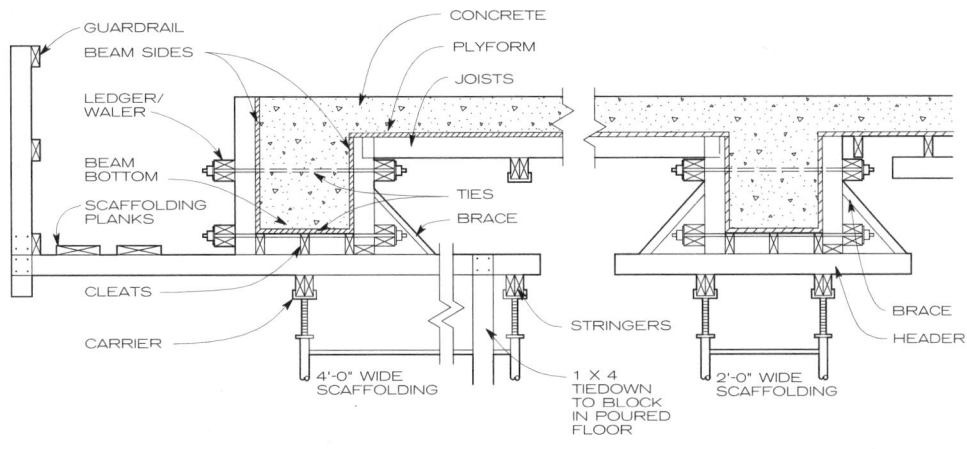

TYPICAL SLAB AND HEAVY BEAM FORMING

Tucker Concrete Form Company; Stoughton, Massachusetts

GENERAL

Concrete formwork hardware includes ties, anchors, hangers, and spacers used to hold forms and reinforcements in place against the forces of unhardened concrete and other loads applied during construction. Concrete ties are tensile units adapted to hold concrete forms together and may be classified by use or by load-carrying capacity. Classified by use are two main concrete tie types: "continuous single member," in which the entire tie rod extends through the wall and through both sides of the formwork (this can be a pull-out tie or a snap-off tie), and "internal disconnecting," in which the tensile unit has an inner part with threaded connections to removable external members. Classified by load-carrying capacity are light-duty (safe working loads of up to 3750 lb) and heavy-duty (loads of more than 3750 lb) concrete ties. Safe working load should be set at no more than half the tie's ultimate strength. Other hardware systems and configurations may be available; consult manufacturers for complete details.

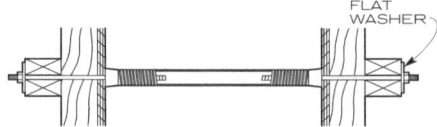

WALL SECTION

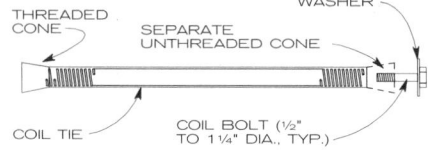

NOTE

Coil ties are medium- to heavy-duty ties fabricated to accept a threaded bolt, which passes through the formwork lumber.

COIL TIES

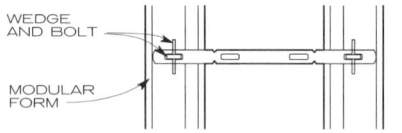

WALL SECTION

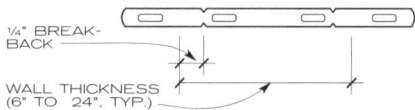

NOTE

Flat ties are light-duty ties used with a wedge and bolt to secure and space modular wall forms.

FLAT TIE

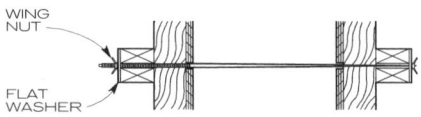

WALL SECTION

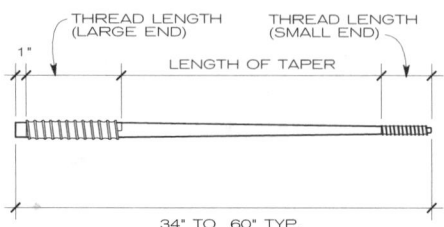

NOTE

Generally used for heavy-duty loads of up to 50,000 lb, the taper tie system is a versatile forming system whose parts are removed after the concrete sets and may be reused. Ties may be installed after forms are in place.

STEEL TAPER TIE

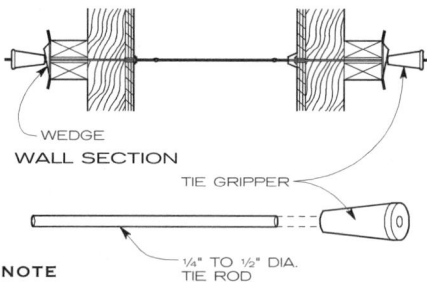

WALL SECTION

NOTE

Fiberglass form ties, straight rods secured with reusable external metal grippers, have safe working loads ranging from 2250 to 25,000 psi. The ties are readily broken off or cut at the concrete surface, then ground flush.

FIBERGLASS FORM TIE

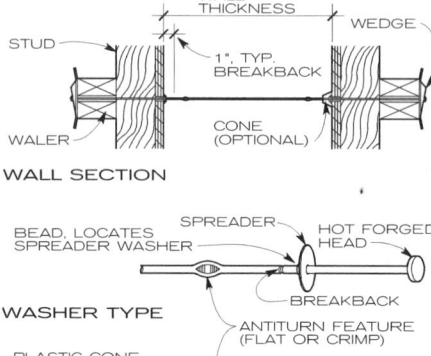

WALL SECTION

WASHER TYPE

CONE TYPE
NOTE

Snap ties are a type of through tie for light-duty use, fabricated so the exposed ends of the tie can be snapped off at the breakback (a notch in the rod). The antiturn device makes it easier to break off the exposed end.

SNAP TIES

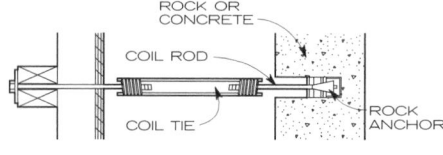

WALL SECTION

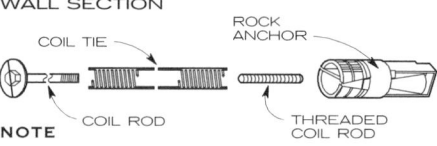

NOTE

Rock anchors are used with coil ties to facilitate one-side forming of walls.

ROCK ANCHOR

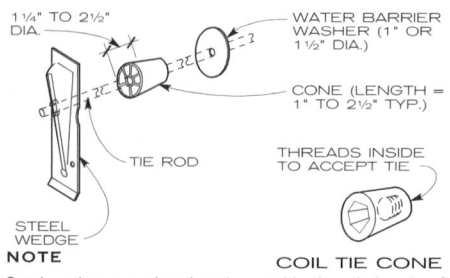

NOTE

Steel wedges are placed at the outside threaded ends of pull-out or snap tie rods, holding the formwork in place. Plastic or wood cones may be placed on the tie rod at the formwork wall surface, so that when the formwork is removed the tie rod ends are set back for subsequent finishing (with plugs, etc.).

TIE ROD ACCESSORIES

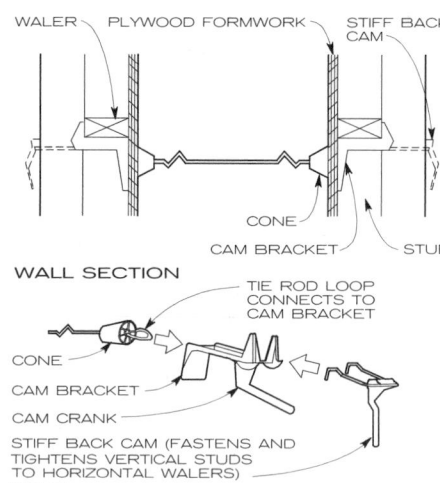

WALL SECTION

NOTE

This light-duty system is suitable for job-set forms.

CAM LOCK BRACKET/TIE SYSTEM

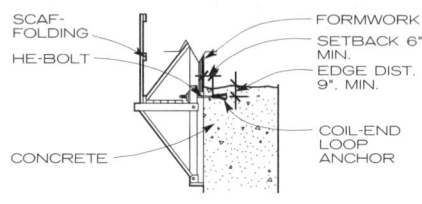

WALL SECTION

NOTE

The coil anchor is embedded near the top of a concrete lift to support the formwork of the succeeding lift. The reusable he-bolt is threaded into the coil.

HE-BOLT WITH COIL ANCHOR

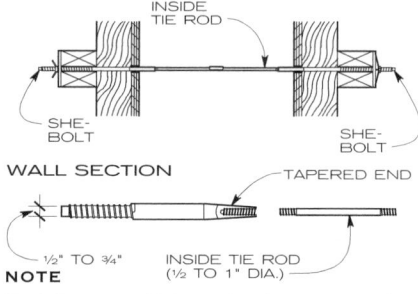

WALL SECTION

NOTE

She-bolts are reusable heavy-duty tie components threaded onto an internal tie rod permanently embedded in the concrete. They are typically used with crane-handled forms.

SHE-BOLT/TIE ROD

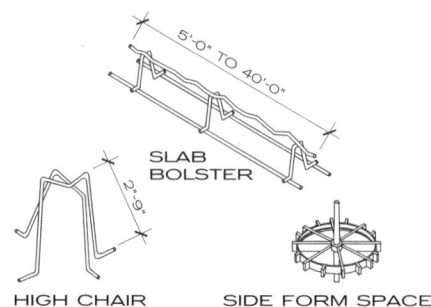

NOTE

Bar supports are used to maintain the reinforcement's design distance from the wall sides or slab bottom. They are typically made of stainless steel or epoxy- or plastic-coated steel.

REINFORCING BAR AND MESH SUPPORTS

Mary K. Hurd; Engineered Publications; Farmington Hills, Michigan

GENERAL

Steel reinforcement for concrete consists of reinforcing bars and welded wire fabric. Bars are manufactured by hot-roll process as round rods with lugs, or deformations, which inhibit longitudinal movement of the bar in the surrounding concrete. Bar sizes are indicated by numbers. For sizes #3 through #8, the numbers are the number of eighths of an inch in the nominal diameter of the bars. Numbers 9, 10, and 11 are round and correspond to the former 1 in., $1\frac{1}{8}$ in., and $1\frac{1}{4}$ in. square sizes. Sizes #14 and #18 correspond to the former $1\frac{1}{2}$ in. and 2 in. square sizes. The nominal diameter of a deformed bar is equal to the actual diameter of a plain bar with the same weight per foot as the deformed bar. Epoxy-coated, zinc-coated (galvanized), and stainless steel reinforcing bars are used when corrosion protection is needed; stainless steel also has nonmagnetic properties. In some instances, a fiber-reinforced plastic (FRP) rebar is used for highly specialized concrete reinforcement because of its high tensile strength and light weight, corrosion resistance, and dielectric (nonconductive) properties. FRP rebars are manufactured in the same sizes as steel rebars and also have deformations on the surface. Consult manufacturers for further information.

Welded wire fabric is used in thin slabs, shells, and other designs in which available space is too limited to give proper cover and clearance to deformed bars. Welded wire fabric, also called mesh, consists of cold drawn wire (smooth or deformed) in orthogonal patterns; it is resistance welded at all intersections.

Wire in the form of individual wire or groups of wires is used in the fabrication of prestressed concrete.

ASTM STANDARD REINFORCING BAR SIZES

ASTM SIZE DESIGNATION	AREA (SQ IN., ACTUAL)	WEIGHT (LB/FT, ACTUAL)	DIAMETER (IN., ACTUAL)
#18	4.00	13.600	2.257
#14	2.25	7.650	1.693
#11	1.56	5.313	1.410
#10	1.27	4.303	1.270
#9	1.00	3.400	1.128
#8	0.74	2.670	1.000
#7	0.60	2.044	0.875
#6	0.44	1.502	0.750
#5	0.31	1.043	0.625
#4	0.20	0.668	0.500
#3	0.11	0.376	0.375

NOTE

Metrication of reinforcing bars is being considered in the United States; as of October 1995, a decision had not been made about what metric rebar sizes would apply in the United States. Metrication may result in a reengineering of reinforced concrete structures using the new bar sizes.

SHRINKAGE AND TEMPERATURE REINFORCEMENT FOR STRUCTURAL CONCRETE

REINFORCEMENT		PERCENT OF CROSS-SECTIONAL AREA OF CONCRETE, ONE WAY
GRADE	TYPE	
40/50	Deformed bars	0.20
—	Welded wire fabric	0.18
60	Deformed bars	0.18

COMMON STOCK STYLES OF WELDED WIRE FABRIC

NEW DESIGNATION (W-NUMBER)	OLD DESIGNATION (WIRE GAUGE)	STEEL AREA (IN./SQ FT)		WEIGHT (LB/100 SQ FT)
		LONG.	TRANS.	
SHEETS AND ROLLS				
6 x 6 - W1.4 x W1.4	6 x 6 - 10 x 10	.028	.028	21
6 x 6 - W2.0 x W2.0	6 x 6 - 8 x 8	.040	.040	29
6 x 6 - W2.9 x W2.9	6 x 6 - 6 x 6	.058	.058	42
6 x 6 - W4.0 x W4.0	6 x 6 - 4 x 4	.080	.080	58
4 x 4 - W1.4 x W1.4	4 x 4 - 10 x 10	.042	.042	31
4 x 4 - W2.0 x W2.0	4 x 4 - 8 x 8	.060	.060	43
4 x 4 - W2.9 x W2.9	4 x 4 - 6 x 6	.087	.087	62
4 x 4 - W4.0 x W4.0	4 x 4 - 4 x 4	.120	.120	85

LONGITUDINAL WIRE   Spacing   Wire Size   LONGITUDINAL WIRE

TRANSVERSE WIRE   6 x 12   -   W16 x W8   TRANSVERSE WIRE

METHOD OF DESIGNATION FOR WELDED WIRE FABRIC

Concrete Reinforcing Steel Institute; Schaumburg, Illinois
Gordon B. Batson, P.E.; Potsdam, New York

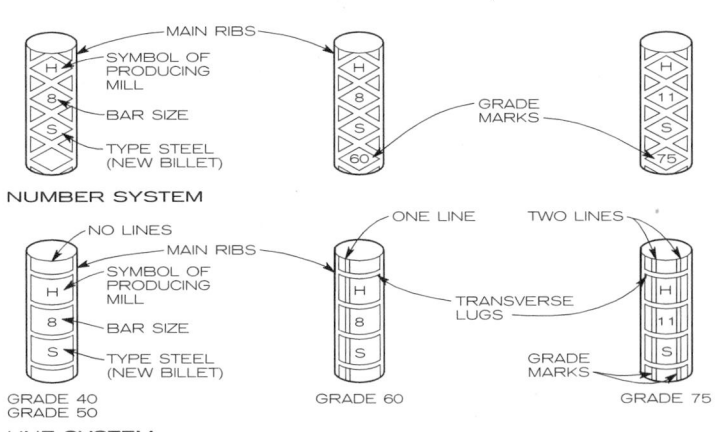

NUMBER SYSTEM

MAIN RIBS — SYMBOL OF PRODUCING MILL — BAR SIZE — TYPE STEEL (NEW BILLET) — GRADE MARKS

LINE SYSTEM

NO LINES — MAIN RIBS — SYMBOL OF PRODUCING MILL — BAR SIZE — TYPE STEEL (NEW BILLET) — ONE LINE — TWO LINES — TRANSVERSE LUGS — GRADE MARKS

GRADE 40 / GRADE 50   GRADE 60   GRADE 75

NOTE

Steel type grade marks: S—billet (A615), I—rail (A616), IR—rail meeting supplementary requirements, S1 (A616), A—axle (A617), W—low alloy (A706).

REINFORCING BAR GRADE MARK IDENTIFICATION

STANDARD STEEL WIRE SIZES AND GAUGES

PLAIN WIRE NUMBER	DEFORMED WIRE NUMBER	ASW GAUGE NUMBER	FRACTIONAL DIAMETER (IN.)	DECIMAL DIAMETER (IN.)	AREA (SQ IN.)	WEIGHT (LB/LIN. FT)
W20	D20	—	$\frac{1}{2}$	.505	.200	.680
—	—	$\frac{7}{0}$	$\frac{31}{64}$	.490	.189	.642
W18	D18	—	$\frac{15}{32}$	.479	.180	.612
—	—	$\frac{6}{0}$	$\frac{5}{32}$	.462	.168	.571
W16	D16	—	$\frac{29}{64}$	.451	.160	.544
—	—	$\frac{5}{0}$	$\frac{7}{16}$	.431	.146	.496
W14	D14	—	$\frac{13}{32}$	.422	.140	.476
—	—	$\frac{4}{0}$	$\frac{13}{32}$	.394	.122	.415
W12	D12	—	$\frac{25}{64}$	.391	.120	.408
W11	D11	—	$\frac{3}{8}$	.374	.110	.374
W10.5	—	—	$\frac{3}{8}$	.366	.105	.357
—	—	$\frac{3}{0}$	$\frac{23}{64}$	.363	.103	.350
W10	D10	—	$\frac{23}{64}$	.357	.100	.340
W9.5	—	—	$\frac{11}{32}$	.348	.095	.323
W9	D9	—	$\frac{11}{32}$	.338	.090	.306
—	—	$\frac{2}{0}$	$\frac{11}{32}$	.331	.086	.292
W8.5	—	—	$\frac{21}{64}$	.329	.085	.289
W8	D8	—	$\frac{21}{64}$	.319	.080	.272
W7.5	—	—	$\frac{5}{16}$	.309	.075	.255
—	—	$\frac{1}{0}$	$\frac{5}{16}$	.307	.074	.251
W7	D7	—	$\frac{19}{64}$	.299	.070	.238
W6.5	—	—	$\frac{19}{64}$	.288	.065	.221
—	—	1	$\frac{19}{64}$	.283	.063	.214
W6	D6	—	$\frac{9}{32}$	.276	.060	.204
W5.5	—	—	$\frac{17}{64}$	.265	.055	.187
—	—	2	$\frac{17}{64}$	.263	.054	.183
W5	D5	—	$\frac{1}{4}$	.252	.050	.170
—	—	3	$\frac{15}{64}$	.244	.047	.160
W4.5	—	—	$\frac{15}{64}$	.239	.045	.153
W4	D4	4	$\frac{7}{32}$	.226	.040	.136
W3.5	—	—	$\frac{7}{32}$	.211	.035	.119
—	—	5	$\frac{13}{64}$	.207	.034	.115
W3	—	—	$\frac{3}{16}+$	.195	.030	.102
W2.9	—	6	$\frac{3}{16}+$	.192	.029	.098
W2.5	—	7	$\frac{3}{16}$	.178	.025	.085
W2.1	—	8	$\frac{11}{64}$	.162	.021	.071
W2	—	—	$\frac{5}{32}$	.160	.020	.068
—	—	9	$\frac{5}{32}$	.148	.017	.058
W1.4	—	—	$\frac{9}{64}$	.124	.014	.048

REINFORCING BAR GRADES AND STRENGTHS

ASTM SPEC	MIN. YIELD STRENGTH (PSI)	MIN. TENSILE STRENGTH (PSI)	STEEL TYPE
Billet steel ASTM A 615			
Grade 40	40,000	70,000	S
Grade 60	60,000	90,000	
Grade 75	75,000	100,000	
Rail steel ASTM A 616			
Grade 50	50,000	80,000	R
Grade 60	60,000	90,000	
Axle steel ASTM A 617			
Grade 40	40,000	70,000	A
Grade 60	60,000	90,000	
Low-alloy ASTM A 706			
Grade 60	60,000	80,000	W
Deformed wire ASTM A 496			
Welded fabric	70,000	80,000	—
Plain wire ASTM A 82			
Welded fabric < W 1.2	56,000	70,000	—
Size ≥ W 1.2	65,000	75,000	

CAST-IN-PLACE CONCRETE

Concrete is basically a mixture of two components: aggregates and paste. The paste is composed of portland cement, water, and entrapped air or purposely entrained air. This paste binds the aggregates (sand, gravel, or crushed stone) into a rocklike mass as the paste hardens. (The term "portland cement" refers to a calcarious hydraulic cement produced by heating the oxides of silicon, calcium, aluminum, and iron.) Cement paste ordinarily constitutes about 25 to 40% of the total volume of concrete; of this, the absolute volume of cement is usually between 7 and 15%, water between 14 and 21%, and air content up to 8%.

Reinforced concrete consists of concrete and reinforcing steel. The concrete resists the compressive stresses and the reinforcing steel resists the tensile stresses. (See AGS pages on reinforcing bars and wire for a complete review of reinforcing steel.)

LIGHTWEIGHT CONCRETES

Normal-weight concrete contains regular sand, gravel, or crushed stone and has a dry density in the range of 130 to 155 lb/cubic ft (pcf).

Structural lightweight concrete is similar to normal-weight concrete except that it has a lower density, being made from lightweight aggregates (all-lightweight concrete) or with a combination of lightweight and normal-weight aggregates. Structural lightweight concrete has an air-dry density in the range of 85 to 115 pcf and a 28-day compressive strength in excess of 2500 lb/sq in. (psi). It is used primarily to reduce the dead-load weight in concrete members such as floors in high-rise buildings.

Aggregates for structural lightweight concrete include rotary kiln expanded clays, shales, and slates; sintering grate expanded shales and slates; pelletized or extruded fly ash; expanded slags; pumice; and scoria. These aggregates have densities ranging from 35 to 70 pcf compared to 75 to 110 pcf for normal-weight aggregates.

Moderate-strength lightweight concrete weighs about 50 to 120 pcf oven-dry and has a compressive strength of 1000 to 2500 psi. At lower densities, it is used as fill for thermal and sound insulation of floors, walls, and roofs and is referred to as "fill concrete." At higher densities, it is used in cast-in-place walls, floors, and roofs and precast wall and floor panels.

Low-density concrete, also called insulating concrete, is a lightweight concrete with an oven-dry unit weight of between 15 and 50 pcf, with a 28-day compressive strength between 100 and 1000 psi. Cast-in-place low-density concrete is used primarily for thermal and sound insulation, roof decks, fill for slab-on-grade subbases, leveling courses for floors and roofs, firewalls, etc.

For further discussion of lightweight concrete and other concrete information, consult *Design and Control of Concrete Mixtures*, 13th ed. (Portland Cement Association, Skokie, Ill.).

TYPES OF CEMENT

Five types of portland cement are manufactured to meet ASTM standards:

Type I is a general purpose cement for all uses. It is the most commonly used type.

Type II cement provides moderate protection from sulfate attack for concrete in drainage structures and a lower heat of hydration for concrete used in heavy retaining walls, piers, and abutments where heat buildup in the concrete can cause problems.

Type III cement achieves high strength at an early stage, after a week or less. It is used when rapid removal of forms is desired and in cold weather to reduce the time for controlled curing conditions.

Type IV cement has a low heat of hydration and is used for massive concrete structures such as gravity dams.

Type V cement is sulfate-resisting for use where the soil and groundwater have a high sulfate content.

Other cementitious materials, including fly ash, ground granulated blast furnace slag, and silica fume, are sometimes used in conjunction with portland cement. (Fly ash is a powdery residue resulting from combustion in coal-fired electric generating plants. It reacts chemically with calcium hydroxide produced by hydration to form cementitious compounds.) Depending on the application, these cementitious materials may be used to replace a portion of the cement or as a supplementary material. They are used to modify fresh or hardened concrete properties (for example, to increase the amount of fine aggregate in the concrete mixture to improve workability, to limit the initial heat of hydration of the concrete, or to produce high-strength, low-permeability concretes).

Adjusting mixture proportions is more complicated than simply replacing portland cement either by weight or volume. For example, silica fume mixes typically need a high-range water-reducing admixture to be workable and may have finishing characteristics different from those of conventional concretes. Mixtures with these cementitious materials require entrained air for durability, just as mixtures with only portland cement do. For concrete subjected to freezing and thawing and de-icers, the contents of ash, slag, and silica fume are limited to a specified percentage of the total cementitious materials because the scaling behavior of these concretes is not fully understood.

Although ASTM C150 specifies five cement types, all may not be available in a given market. Type II is routinely substituted for Type I. Type IV may be available only in quantities prohibitively large for most applications.

AGGREGATES

Normal-weight concrete (135 to 165 pcf) can contain both fine and coarse aggregates. The fine aggregate is generally sand particles less than $3/8$ in. in size. The coarse aggregate is crushed rock or gravel. Lightweight aggregate is manufactured from expanded shale, slate, clay, or slag, and the concrete weighs between 85 and 115 pcf. Recycled concrete, or crushed concrete, is a feasible source of aggregate and an economical alternative when other aggregates are scarce.

Normal-weight aggregates must meet ASTM Specification C33. Lightweight aggregates must meet ASTM Specification C330. The aggregate represents 60 to 80% of the concrete volume, and the gradation (range of particle sizes) affects the amount of cement and water required in the mix, physical properties during placing and finishing, and compressive strength. Aggregates should be clean, hard, strong, and free of surface materials.

ADMIXTURES

Admixtures are various compounds other than cement, water, and aggregate that are added to a mixture to modify the properties of fresh or hardened concrete. Refer to pages on concrete admixtures for more information.

CYLINDER TEST

A standard compression test is made by placing three layers of concrete in a cardboard cylinder 6 in. in diameter and 12 in. high. Each layer is tamped 25 times with a $5/8$ in. diameter steel rod. At the end of the test curing time, usually 7 to 28 days, the concrete cylinder is removed from its form and placed under increasing pressure. The load at which the cylinder breaks is registered on a gauge in pounds, and the strength of the concrete is calculated in lb/sq in.

A major problem with these tests is that the compressive strength—the most important characteristic of concrete—cannot be determined until after curing has begun. Thus deficient concrete occasionally must be removed several weeks after it was placed.

PLACING CONCRETE

Concrete should be placed as near its final position as possible, and it should not be moved horizontally in forms because the mortar may separate from the coarser material. Concrete should be placed in horizontal layers of uniform thickness, with each layer thoroughly consolidated before the next layer is positioned.

RECOMMENDED SLUMPS FOR VARIOUS CONSTRUCTION TYPES

CONCRETE CONSTRUCTION	MAXIMUM*	MINIMUM
Reinforced foundation walls and footings	3	1
Plain footings, caissons, and substructure walls	3	1
Beams and reinforced walls	4	1
Building columns	4	1
Pavement and slabs	3	1
Mass concrete	2	1

* May be increased by 1 in. for consolidation by hand methods such as rodding and spading.

Concrete can be consolidated either by hand tamping or by mechanical internal or external vibration. The frequency and amplitude of an internal vibrator should be appropriate for the plastic properties (stiffness or slump) and space in the forms to prevent segregation of the concrete during placing. External vibration can be accomplished by surface vibration for thin sections (slabs) for which internal vibration is not practical. Surface vibrators may be used directly on the surface of the slab or with plates attached to the concrete form stiffeners. External vibration must be sustained longer (1 to 2 minutes) than internal vibration (5 to 15 seconds) to achieve the same consolidation.

SLUMP TEST

The ASTM standard slump cone test is only for determining the consistency among batches of concrete of the same mix design; it should not be used to compare concrete made from different mix proportions. A slump test mold is a funnel-shaped sheet metal form. It is filled from the top in three layers, and at each level the concrete is tamped 25 times with a $5/8$ in. diameter rod. The mold is removed slowly, allowing the concrete to slump down from its original height. The difference between the top of the mold and the top of the molded concrete is the slump. There is no "right" slump consistency for all concrete work: It can vary from 1 in. to 6 in., depending on the specific requirements of the job. The accompanying table lists recommended slumps for various types of construction.

Workability is the ease or difficulty of placing, consolidating, and finishing the concrete. Concrete should be workable, but not so much so that it segregates or bleeds excessively before finishing.

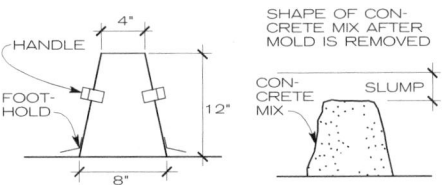

SLUMP TEST MOLD   SLUMP TEST

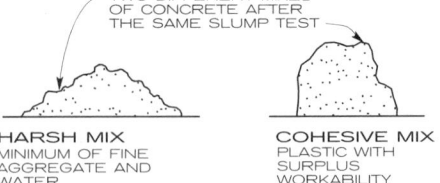

HARSH MIX
MINIMUM OF FINE AGGREGATE AND WATER

COHESIVE MIX
PLASTIC WITH SURPLUS WORKABILITY

SLUMP TEST

ACCEPTED MAXIMUM AGGREGATE SIZE FOR VARIOUS TYPES OF CONCRETE CONSTRUCTION[1]

MINIMUM DIMENSION OF SECTION OF CONCRETE TO BE POURED (IN.)	MAXIMUM SIZE OF AGGREGATE (SQUARE SCREEN OPENINGS)[2]		
	REINFORCED WALLS, BEAMS, AND COLUMNS	HEAVY REINFORCED CONCRETE SLABS	LIGHTLY REINFORCED OR PLAIN CONCRETE SLABS
5 or less (127 mm)	—	$3/4$ to $1 1/2$ in. (19-38 mm)	$3/4$ to $1 1/2$ in. (19-38 mm)
6–11 (152 to 279 mm)	$3/4$ to $1 1/2$ in. (19-38 mm)	$1 1/2$ in. (38 mm)	$1 1/2$ to 3 in. (38-76 mm)
12–29 (205 to 737 mm)	$1 1/2$ to 3 in. (38-76 mm)	3 in. (76 mm)	3 to 6 in. (76-152 mm)
30 or more (762 mm)	$1 1/2$ to 3 in. (38-76 mm)	3 in. (76 mm)	6 in. (152 mm)

[1] Aggregate size should always be checked in relation to the spacing of reinforcement rods, bars, etc., and to the size of reinforcing mesh.

[2] For pumping concrete, the aggregate size is controlled by the height of pumping, air entrainment, and reinforcement and mesh spacing.

Robert W. Shuldes, P.E.; Portland Cement Association; Skokie, Illinois

CAST-IN-PLACE CONCRETE

PROPERTIES OF CONCRETE

Concrete design strength generally is stated as a minimum compressive strength of concrete after 28 days of curing. The normal 28-day compressive strength for commercial ready-mix concrete is 3000 to 4000 psi; however, strengths of 5000 to 7000 psi generally are required for pre- or post-tensioned concrete. Concrete design strengths of 10,000 to 12,000 psi have been used for columns in high-rise buildings, and a design strength of 20,000 psi has been used for concrete columns confined in a steel tube or pipe.

Compressive strength depends primarily on the type of cement, the aggregate quality, and the water-cement ratio; the latter is the most important. The lower the water-cement ratio, the greater the compressive strength for workable mixes.

Concrete gains strength by hydration, a chemical reaction independent of drying, in which water, cement, and aggregate are mixed. Concrete does not require air to cure; it sets up under water (thus the term "hydraulic cement"). Concrete sets or becomes firm hours after it has been mixed, but curing, the process of attaining strength, takes considerably longer. For 28-day design strengths of less than 10,000 psi, most of the strength is achieved in a few days; approximately 50% is reached in three days; and 70% is reached in seven days. The remaining 30% is gained mostly during the last 21 days; but strength can continue to increase beyond the 28 days.

It can take from 56 to 90 days for concrete to achieve a design strength of greater than 12,000 psi. The cylinders used to test the compressive strength of this very high-strength concrete are usually 4 x 8 in. rather than 6 x 12 in. Making such strong concretes requires close coordination among the concrete mix vendor, contractor, and concrete inspection service.

CURING AND PROTECTION

Two physical conditions profoundly affect concrete's final compressive strength and curing: temperature and the rate at which water used in mixing is allowed to leave the concrete. If moisture for curing is adequate, concrete gains strength faster at higher temperatures. However, if the temperature is too high, long-term strengths may not develop properly. Excellent quality concrete can be made at lower temperatures, but it will take longer to reach a specified strength level, since the cement hydrates more slowly. Freezing concrete during curing greatly reduces its compressive strength and weather resistance.

Proper curing is essential to obtain design strength. Moisture, at temperatures above 50°F, must be available for hydration, but concrete must be protected against temperatures below 40°F during early curing. The longer water is in the concrete, the stronger it becomes.

Moisture conditions can be maintained by spreading wet burlap or mats, waterproof paper, or plastic sheets over the concrete; by placing plastic sheets on the ground before the slab is poured; by spraying liquid curing compound on the surface of fresh concrete; and by leaving the concrete in forms for a longer time.

HOT AND COLD WEATHER CONSTRUCTION

Additional precautions are needed in extreme weather to ensure proper curing of concrete. High temperatures accelerate hardening. More water is needed to maintain the mix consistency; more cement is required to prevent reduced strength from the additional water. Chilled water or ice reduces the temperature of the aggregates, and admixtures can retard the initial set.

Temperatures ranging from 75 to 90°F are considered hot weather construction conditions. Weather that is dry as well as hot is especially problematic for finishing newly placed concrete as it causes the concrete to dry too rapidly and crack. Special care in finishing and curing must be taken to achieve a good quality finish.

In cold weather concrete must be heated to above 40°F during placing and early curing (the first seven days). Protection against freezing may be necessary for up to two weeks. This is accomplished by covering the concrete with plastic sheets and heating the interior space with a portable heater. Concrete floors should be protected from carbon dioxide with specially vented heaters that conduct the exhaust away from the concrete. The time concrete must be protected can be reduced by using Type III and IIIA cement, by maintaining a low water-cement ratio, by using accelerator admixtures, and by steam curing. Never place concrete directly on frozen ground. Fresh concrete that has frozen during curing should be replaced because frozen concrete containing ice crystals has very little strength.

Robert W. Shuldes, P.E.; Portland Cement Association; Skokie, Illinois

PROPORTION OF STRUCTURAL ELEMENTS

Rules of thumb for approximating proportions of solid rectangular beams and slabs are one inch of depth for each foot of span, and beam width about two-thirds of the depth. The area of steel varies from 1 to 2% of the cross-sectional area of the beam and less than 1% for slabs. Columns usually have higher steel percentages than beams. The maximum for columns is 8% of the cross-sectional area; however, common range is 3 to 6%.

DEFLECTIONS

Deflection of a reinforced concrete member is affected by shrinkage, duration of sustained loads, and creep. Creep is the continuous deformation of the concrete due to sustained loads. Creep and shrinkage may double the initial (instantaneous) deflection in five years under sustained loads. The American Concrete Institute Building Requirements for Reinforced Concrete (ACI 318) set minimum length-to-depth ratios for concrete members (see the table om minimum thickness). When members meet or exceed these minimums, deflections usually are not a problem and do not need to be calculated.

SAMPLE CONCRETE MIXTURES[1]

MIXTURE CHARACTERISTICS	BUILDING INTERIOR	HIGH-STRENGTH INTERIOR COLUMN	POSTTENSIONED PARKING STRUCTURE
Compressive strength F'c (psi)	3500	8000	7500 [2]
Air content (percent)	1.5	2.0	6
Water-to-cement ratio	0.55	0.38 [3]	0.37 [3]
Max. aggregate size (in.)	1	$3/4$	$3/4$
Slump (in.)	3 to 4	3 to 5	6 to 8 [4]
Admixtures	0	Conventional water reducer	Air-refreshing agent and high-range water reducer[5]

MIX PROPORTIONS, LB/CU YD

Water	258	315	263
Cement	470	729	658
Other cementitious material	0	100 (fly ash)	53 (silica fume)
Fine aggregate	1190	1250	1200
Coarse aggregate	2100	1695	1660

[1] These mixtures are only examples to illustrate differences in proportioning. Local materials and experience should guide proportioning mixtures for specific projects.

[2] Structural requirements are about 5000 psi. Actual strength is higher due to early strength required for post-tensioning and durability limits on water–cementitious materials ratio.

[3] Calculated using all cementitious materials: cement, fly ash, silica fume, etc.

[4] Reduce slump for steep ramps.

[5] Use of silica fume typically increases dosing requirements of high-range water reducer by 50 to 100%.

MINIMUM THICKNESS (IN.) OF NONPRESTRESSED BEAMS AND ONE-WAY SLABS

	SIMPLY SUPPORTED	ONE END CONTINUOUS	BOTH ENDS CONTINUOUS	CANTILEVER
Solid one-way slabs	Span length/20	Span length/24	Span length/28	Span length/10
Beams or ribbed one-way slabs	Span length/16	Span length/18.5	Span length/21	Span length/8

NOTE

Span length is in inches. Values given are for members with normal weight concrete and Grade 60 reinforcement in construction that does not support or connect to partitions or other construction likely to be damaged by large deflection. See ACI 318 for more information.

MAXIMUM WATER–CEMENT RATIOS FOR VARIOUS EXPOSURES

EXPOSURE CONDITION	NORMAL WEIGHT CONCRETE, ABSOLUTE WATER-CEMENT RATIO BY WEIGHT
Concrete protected from exposure to freezing and thawing or application of de-icer chemicals	Water-cement ratio based on strength, workability, and finishing needs
Watertight concrete* In fresh water In sea water	0.50 0.45
Frost-resistant concrete* Thin sections; any section with less than 2 in. cover over reinforcement and any concrete exposed to de-icers All other structures	0.45 0.50
Exposure to sulfates* Moderate Severe	0.50 0.45

* Contain entrained air within the limits of the minimum thickness table.

FORMWORK

Forming costs can account for 30 to 50% of a concrete structure. Reusing forms saves money; it is cheaper, for example, to use one column size throughout a structure than it is to vary column sizes.

In sizing individual floor members, it is usually more economical to use wider girders that are as deep as the joists of beams they support than to use narrow, deeper girders. Using wall pilasters, lugs, and openings increases forming costs. Size all members for use of readily available standard forms rather than custom job-built forms.

SHORING

Floor framing forms are supported by temporary columns and bracing called shoring. Concrete must be cured for a certain time or reach a specified percentage of its design strength before shores and forms can be removed. Reshoring is normally required for several floors if the cycle time for formwork is to be minimized.

MAXIMUM PERMISSIBLE WATER–CEMENT RATIOS

SPECIFIED COMPRESSIVE STRENGTH F'c (PSI)[1]	MAXIMUM ABSOLUTE PERMISSIBLE WATER-CEMENT RATIO, BY WEIGHT	
	NON-AIR-ENTRAINED CONCRETE	AIR-ENTRAINED CONCRETE
2500	0.67	0.54
3000	0.58	0.46
3500	0.51	0.40
4000	0.44	0.35
4500	0.38	[2]
5000	[2]	[2]

[1] 28-day strength. For most materials, the water-cement ratios shown will provide average strengths greater than required.

[2] For strengths above 4500 psi (non-air-entrained concrete) and 4000 psi (air-entrained concrete), proportions should be established by the trial batch method.

NOTE

1000 psi = 7 MPa.

GENERAL

Admixtures are those ingredients in concrete other than portland cement, water, and aggregates that are added to the mixture immediately before or during mixing. Admixtures can be classified by function as follows: air-entraining admixtures; water-reducing admixtures; retarding admixtures; accelerating admixtures; superplasticizers; finely divided mineral admixtures; miscellaneous admixtures that aid workability, bonding, dampproofing, gas-forming, grouting (nonshrink), and coloring and help reduce permeability and inhibit corrosion.

Concrete should be workable, finishable, strong, durable, watertight, and wear-resistant. These qualities can usually be achieved by selecting suitable materials or by changing the mix proportions. Sometimes air-entraining admixtures are necessary, but in most cases admixtures can be forgone. No admixture can substitute for good concreting practice.

The major reasons for using admixtures are to reduce the cost of concrete construction; to achieve certain properties in concrete more effectively; to ensure the quality of concrete during mixing, transporting, placing, and curing in adverse weather conditions; and to overcome certain emergencies during concreting operations.

NOTES

1. The effectiveness of an admixture depends on such factors as type, brand, and amount of cement; water content; aggregate shape, gradation, and proportions; mixing time; slump; and concrete and air temperatures.
2. Trial mixtures should be made with the admixture and the job materials at temperatures and humidities anticipated on the job to ensure compatibility with other admixtures and job materials and to allow observation of how the properties of the fresh and hardened concrete are affected by local conditions.
3. The cost of using admixtures should be compared with the cost of changing the basic concrete mixture. Determine how using an admixture will affect the cost of transporting, placing, finishing, curing, and protecting the concrete.
4. Recommended total air contents for different exposure conditions are shown for different aggregate sizes in the table below.

TOTAL TARGET AIR CONTENT FOR CONCRETE[1]

NOMINAL MAXIMUM AGGREGATE SIZE (IN.)	AIR CONTENT (PERCENT)[2]		
	SEVERE EXPOSURE[3]	MODERATE EXPOSURE[3]	MILD EXPOSURE[3]
$^3/_8$	$7^1/_2$	6	$4^1/_2$
$^1/_2$	7	$5^1/_2$	4
$^3/_4$	6	5	$3^1/_2$
1	6	$4^1/_2$	3
$1^1/_2$	$5^1/_2$	$4^1/_2$	$2^1/_2$
$2^1/_2$	5	4	2
3	$4^1/_2$	$3^1/_2$	$1^1/_2$

[1] Experience shows that hardened concrete with the air contents specified in this table, as sampled and tested in the plastic state, performs satisfactorily. The air content of hardened concrete may be somewhat different.

[2] Project specifications often allow the air content of the delivered concrete to be within several percentage points of the table target values.

[3] Severe exposure is an environment in which concrete is exposed to wet freeze-thaw conditions, de-icers, or other aggressive agents. Moderate exposure is an environment in which concrete is exposed to freezing but will not be continually moist, not exposed to water for long periods before freezing, and will not be in contact with de-icers or aggressive chemicals. Mild exposure is an environment in which concrete is not exposed to freezing conditions, de-icers, or aggressive agents.

CONCRETE ADMIXTURES BY CLASSIFICATION

TYPE OF ADMIXTURE	DESIRED EFFECT	MATERIAL
Accelerators (ASTM C 494, Type C)	Accelerate setting and early-strength development	Calcium chloride (ASTM D 98); Triethanolamine, sodium thiocyanate, calcium formate, calcium nitrate, calcium nitrite
Air detrainers	Decrease air content	Tributyl phosphate, dibutyl phthalate, octyl alcohol, water-insoluble esters of carbonic and boric acid, silicones
Air-entraining admixtures (ASTM C 260)	Improve durability in environments of freeze-thaw, de-icers, sulfate, and alkali reactivity; Improve workability; segregation and bleeding are reduced or eliminated	Salts of wood resins (Vinsol resin); some synthetic detergents; salts of sulfonated lignin; salts of petroleum acids; salts of proteinaceous material; fatty and resinous acids and their salts; alkylbenzene sulfonates; salts of sulfonated hydrocarbons
Alkali-reactivity reducers	Reduce alkali-reactivity expansion	Pozzolans (fly ash, silica fume), blast-furnace slag, salts of lithium and barium, air entraining agents
Bonding admixtures	Increase bond strength	Rubber, polyvinyl chloride, polyvinyl acetate, acrylics, butadiene-styrene copolymers
Coloring agents	Colored concrete	Modified carbon black, iron oxide, phthalicyanine, umber, chromium oxide, titanium oxide, cobalt blue (ASTM C 979)
Corrosion inhibitors	Reduce steel corrosion activity in a chloride environment	Calcium nitrite, sodium nitrite, sodium benzoate, certain phosphates of fluosilicates, fluoaluminates
Dampproofing admixtures	Retard moisture penetration into dry concrete	Soaps of calcium or ammonium stearate or oleate; butyl stearate; petroleum products
Finely divided mineral admixtures		
Cementitious	Hydraulic properties; partial cement replacement	Ground granulated blast-furnace slag (ASTM C 989); natural cement; hydraulic hydrated lime (ASTM C 141)
Pozzolans	Pozzolanic activity; improve workability, plasticity, sulfate resistance; reduce alkali reactivity, permeability, heat of hydration; partial cement replacement; filler	Diatomaceous earth, opaline cherts, clays, shales, volcanic tuffs, pumicites (ASTM C 618, Class N); fly ash (ASTM C 618, Class F and C), silica fume
Pozzolanic and cementitious	Same as cementitious and pozzolan categories	High calcium fly ash (ASTM C 618, Class C); ground granulated blast-furnace slag (ASTM C 989)
Nominally inert	Improve workability; filler	Marble, dolomite, quartz, granite
Fungicides, germicides, and insecticides	Inhibit or control bacterial and fungal growth	Polyhalogenated phenols; dieldrin emulsions; copper compounds
Gas formers	Cause expansion before setting	Aluminum powder; resin soap and vegetable or animal glue; saponin; hydrolyzed protein
Grouting agents	Adjust grout properties for specific applications (i.e., non-shrink grout for setting steel on masonry or concrete, fill reglets and cracks)	See air-entrained admixtures, accelerators, retarders, workability agents
Permeability reducers	Decrease permeability	Silica fume; fly ash (ASTM C 618); ground slag (ASTM C 989); natural pozzolans; water reducers; latex
Pumping aides	Improve pumpability	Organic and synthetic polymers; organic flocculents; organic emulsions of paraffin, coal tar, asphalt, acrylics; bentonite and pyrogenic silicas; natural pozzolans (ASTM C 618, Class N); fly ash (ASTM C 618, Classes F and C); hydrated lime (ASTM C 141)
Retarders (ASTM C 494, Type B)	Retard setting time to offset effect of hot weather, to delay initial set for difficult placement, or for special finishing, such as exposed aggregate	Lignin; borax; sugar; tartaric acids and salts
Superplasticizers * (ASTM C 1017, Type 1)	Flowing concrete; reduce water-cement ratio	Sulfonated melamine formaldehyde condensates; sulfonated naphthalene formaldehyde condensates; lignosulfonates
Superplasticizer* and retarder (ASTM C 1017, Type 2)	Flowing concrete with retarded set; reduce water	See superplasticizers and water reducers
Water reducer (ASTM C 494, Type A)	Reduce water demand at least 5%	Lignosulfonates; hydroxylated carboxylic acids; carbohydrates (also tend to retard set so accelerator is often added)

* Superplasticizers are also referred to as high-range water reducers or plasticizers. These admixtures often meet both ASTM 494 and C 1017 specifications simultaneously.

Robert W. Shuldes, P.E.; Portland Cement Association; Skokie, Illinois

 CAST-IN-PLACE CONCRETE

GENERAL NOTES

1. The information presented on these pages is intended only as a preliminary design guide. All structural dimensions for slab thickness, beam and joint sizes, column sizes, etc., should be calculated and analyzed for each project condition by a licensed professional engineer.

2. Spans shown are approximate and are based on use of mild reinforcing steel. Spans may be increased 25 to 50% with the use of prestressing. For spans greater than 40 ft, consider posttensioning.

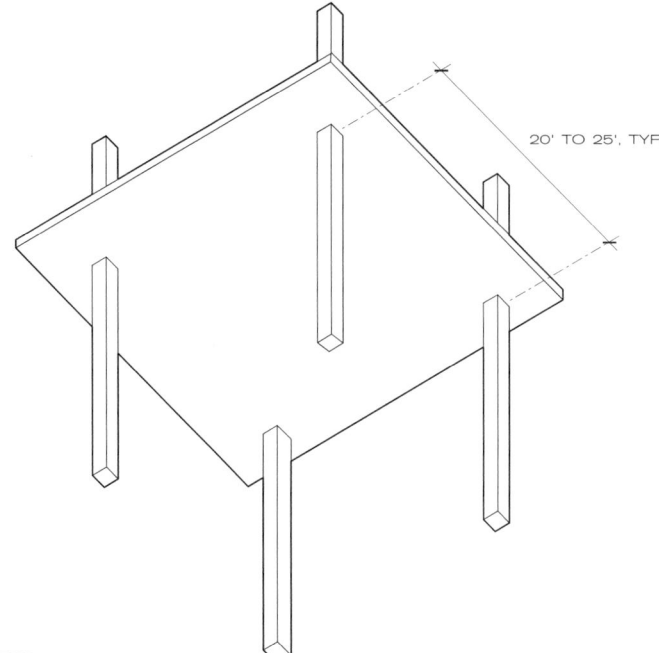

20' TO 25', TYP.

NOTES

1. Advantages: Inexpensive formwork; ceilings may be exposed; minimum thickness; fast erection; flexible column location.
2. Disadvantages: Excess concrete for longer spans; low shear capacity; greater deflections.
3. Appropriate building types: Hotels, motels, dormitories, condominiums, hospitals.
4. A flat plate is best for moderate spans because it is the most economical floor system and has the lowest structural thickness. Avoid penetrations for piping and ductwork through the slab near the columns. Spandrel beams may be necessary.

FLAT PLATE

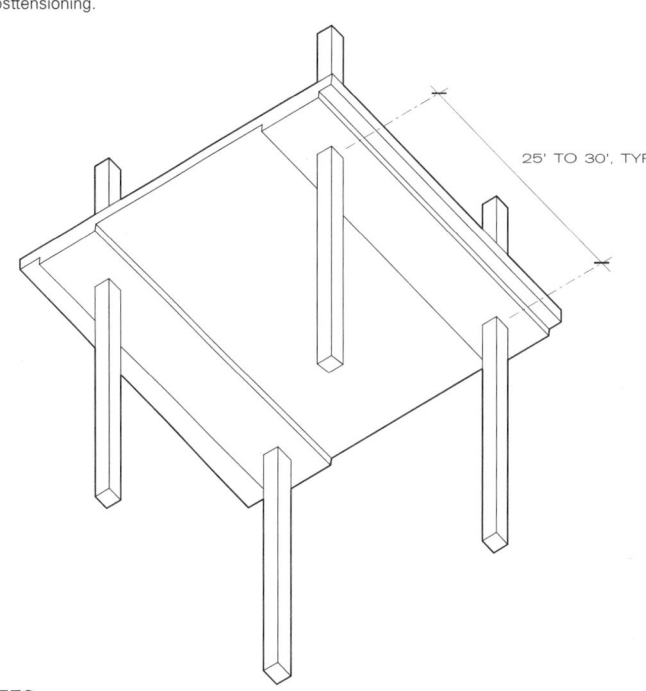

25' TO 30', TYP.

NOTES

1. Advantages: Longer spans than flat plate; typically posttensioned; minimum thickness.
2. Disadvantages: Must reuse formwork many times to be economical.
3. Appropriate building types: High-rise buildings; same use as flat plates if flying forms can be used more than 10 times.
4. A banded slab has most of the advantages of a flat plate but permits a longer span in one direction. It can resist greater lateral loads in the direction of the beams.

BANDED SLAB

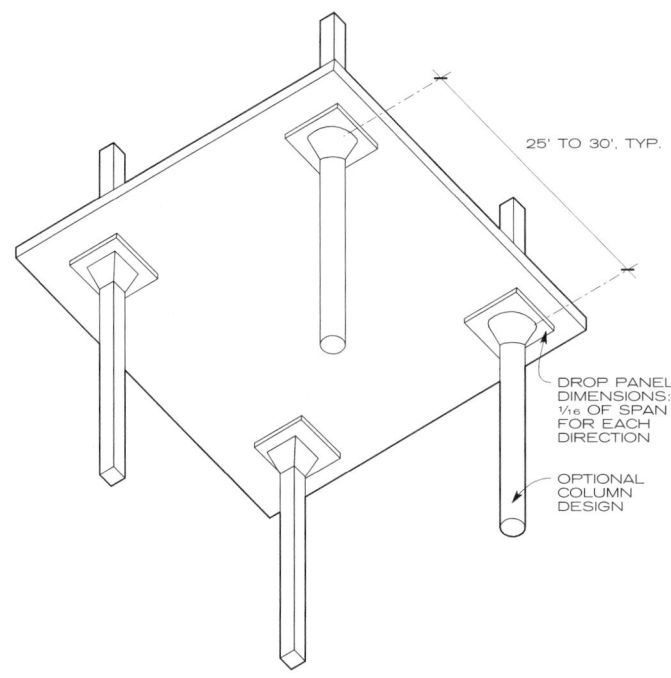

25' TO 30', TYP.

DROP PANEL DIMENSIONS: 1/16 OF SPAN FOR EACH DIRECTION

OPTIONAL COLUMN DESIGN

NOTES

1. Advantages: Economical for design loads greater than 150 psf.
2. Disadvantages: Formwork is costly.
3. Appropriate building types: Warehouses, industrial structures; parking structures
4. Flat slabs are most commonly used today for buildings supporting very heavy loads. When live load exceeds 150 lb per sq ft, this scheme is by far the most economical.

FLAT SLAB

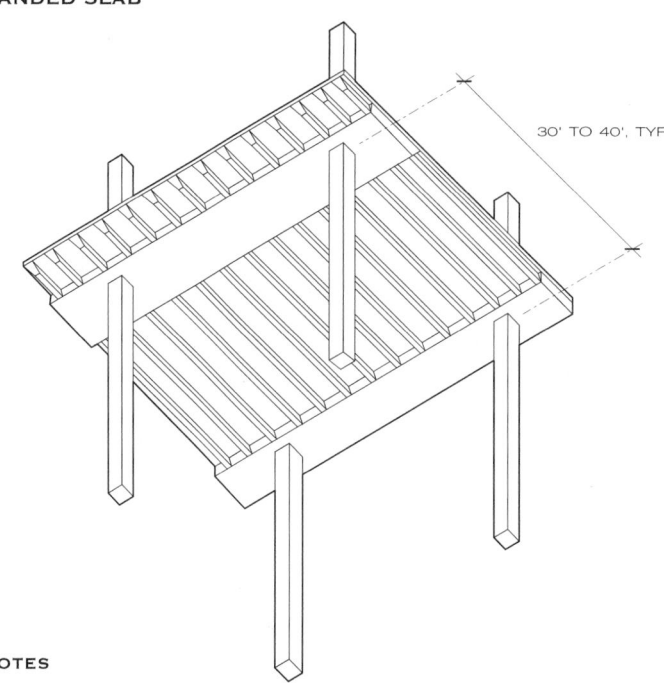

30' TO 40', TYP.

NOTES

1. Advantages: Minimum concrete and steel; minimum weight, hence reduced column and footing size; long spans in one direction; accommodates poke-through electrical systems.
2. Disadvantages: Unattractive for a ceiling; formwork may cost more than flat plate.
3. Appropriate building types: Schools, offices, churches, hospitals, public and institutional buildings, buildings with moderate loadings and spans.
4. This is the best scheme if slabs are too long for a flat plate and the structure is not exposed. The slab thickness between joints is determined by fire requirements. Joists are most economical if beams are the same depth as the joists. Orient joists in the same direction throughout the building and in the long direction of long rectangular bays.

JOIST SLAB

Russell S. Fling, P.E., Consulting Engineer; Columbus, Ohio

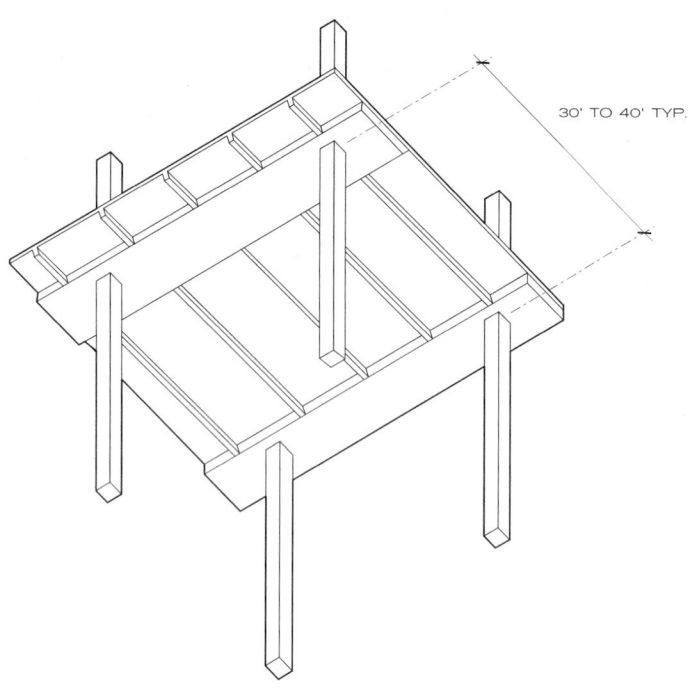

30' TO 40' TYP.

NOTES

1. Advantages: Uses less concrete than joist slab; lower rebar placing costs; joist space used for mechanical systems. Permits lights and equipment to be recessed between joists.
2. Disadvantages: Similar to joist slab; joists must be designed as beams; forms may require special order.
3. Appropriate building type: Same as for joist slabs, especially for longer fire ratings.
4. Ensure the availability of formwork before specifying skip joists. For larger projects, a skip joist slab should be less expensive than a joist slab, and it permits lights and equipment recessed between joinsts.

SKIP JOIST

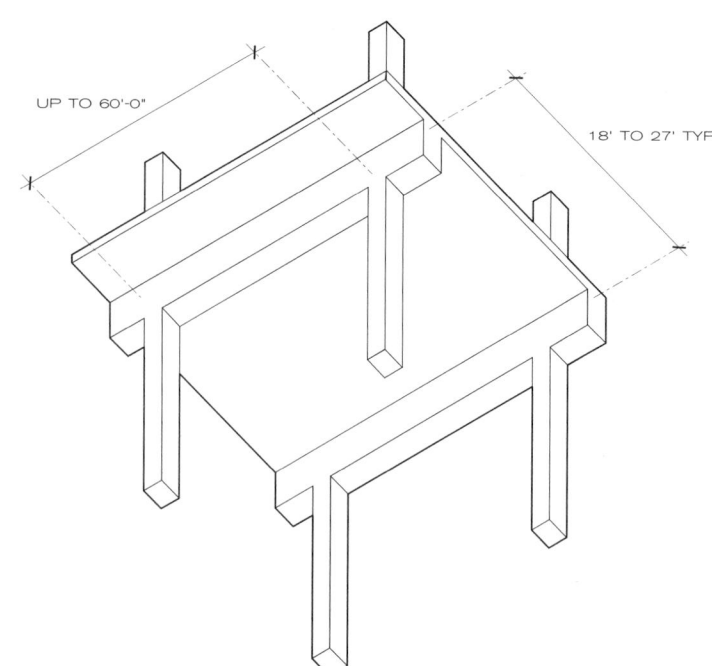

UP TO 60'-0"

18' TO 27' TYP.

NOTES

1. Advantages: Long span in one direction.
2. Disadvantages: Beams interfere with mechanical services; more expensive forms than flat plate.
3. Appropriate building types: Parking garages, especially with posttensioning.
4. This scheme is most favored for parking garages, but the long span of about 60 ft must be prestressed unless beams are quite deep. Shallow beams will deflect excessively.

ONE-WAY BEAM AND SLAB

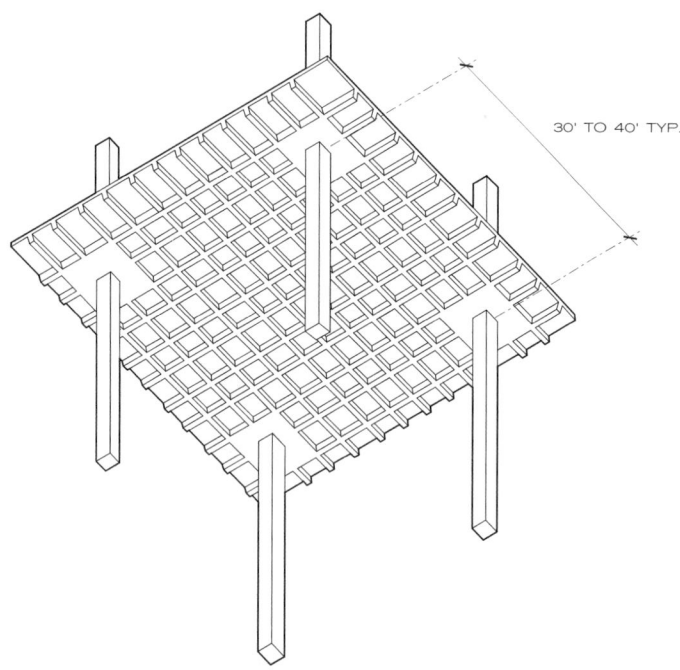

30' TO 40' TYP.

NOTES

1. Advantages: Longer two-way spans; attractive exposed ceilings; heavy load capacity.
2. Disadvantages: Formwork costs more and uses more concrete and steel than a joist slab.
3. Appropriate building types: Prominent buildings with exposed ceiling structure; same types as are suitable for flat slab but with longer spans.
4. Column spacing should be multiples of pan spacing to ensure uniformity of drop panels at each column. Drop panels can be diamond-shaped, square, or rectangular.

WAFFLE SLAB

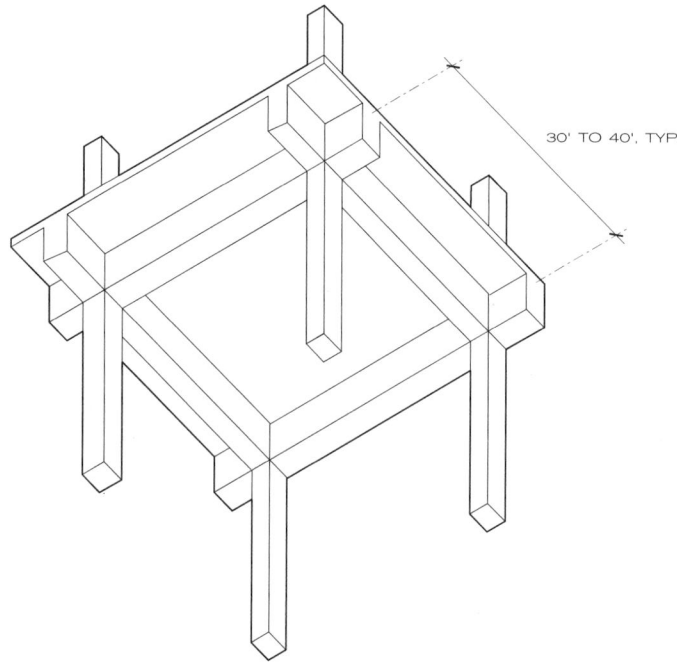

30' TO 40', TYP.

NOTES

1. Advantages: Long span in two directions; small deflection; can carry concentrated loads.
2. Disadvantages: Same as for one-way beams, only more so.
3. Appropriate building types: Portions of buildings in which two-way beam framing is needed for other reasons; industrial buildings with heavy concentrated loads.
4. The high cost of the formwork and structural interference with mechanical systems make this scheme unattractive unless heavy concentrated loads must be carried.

TWO-WAY SLAB AND BEAM

Russell S. Fling, P.E., Consulting Engineer; Columbus, Ohio

③ CAST-IN-PLACE CONCRETE

GENERAL

Architectural concrete and structural concrete are both made from portland cement, aggregate, and water, but they have entirely different concrete mix designs. A variety of architectural finishes and colors can be achieved by changing the mix of these three simple ingredients. The cost of production usually determines the limit of finish choices. There are three basic ways to change the appearance of a concrete surface finish:

MATERIAL VARIATION involves changing the size, shape, texture, and color of the coarse and fine aggregate, particularly in exposed aggregate concrete, and choosing white or gray cement.

MOLD OR FORM VARIATION involves changing the texture or pattern of the concrete surface by means of form design, form liners, or joint/edge treatments.

SURFACE TREATMENT involves treating or tooling the surface after the concrete has cured.

Design drawings for architectural concrete should show form details, including openings, joints (contraction, construction, and rustication), and other important specifics. Other factors that affect concrete surfaces are mixing and placing techniques, slump control, curing methods, and release agents.

NOTES

1. Choosing a placing technique (pumping vs. bottom drop or other bucket type) is an important step toward achieving a desired architectural concrete surface and finish. Evaluate whether architectural concrete forms can also be used for structural concrete. Verify that the vibrators used are of the proper size, frequency, and power.

2. Shop drawings should be carefully checked to determine form quality and steel reinforcement placement. Require approval of forms and finishes; field mockup is advised to evaluate the appearance of the concrete panel and the quality of workmanship.

3. Release agents are chemical treatments applied to the liner or face of the form that react with the cement to prevent it from sticking to the form. The safest way to select a release agent is to evaluate several products on a test panel under actual job conditions. The curing compound, used to retard or reduce evaporation of moisture from concrete or to extend curing time, is typically applied immediately after final finishing of the concrete surface. Consult manufacturers and the American Concrete Institute for more detailed information about the compatibility of these treatments and the form surface material or other finishes and surfaces to be applied to the concrete.

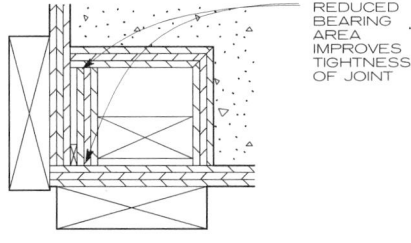

STANDARD JOINT DETAIL WITH MAX. BEARING AREA

REDUCED BEARING AREA IMPROVES TIGHTNESS OF JOINT

ARCHITECTURAL FEATURE AT CORNER

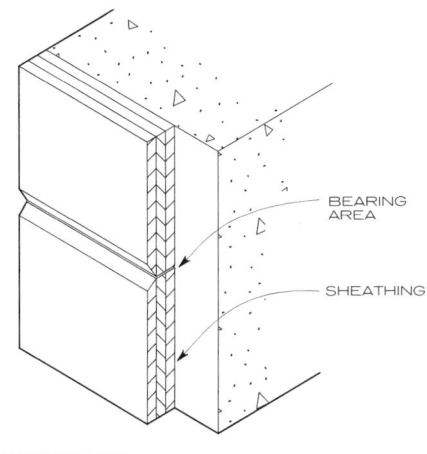

BEARING AREA

SHEATHING

HORIZONTAL FORMWORK JOINT

NOTE

A notch at the joint between two form members reduces the bearing area at the point of contact, improving the tightness of the joint. A non-notched joint is acceptable, but a notch is recommended.

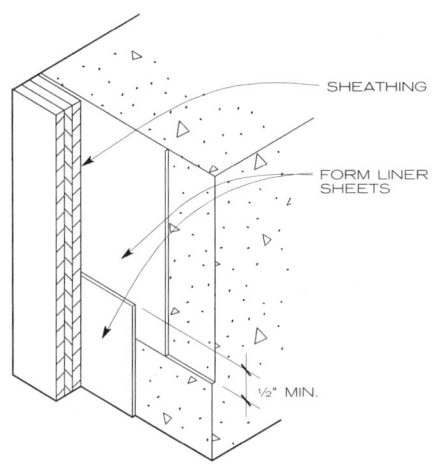

SHEATHING

FORM LINER SHEETS

½" MIN.

FORM LINER JOINT

NOTE

Placing the inner sheet above the outer sheet reduces shadows, particularly on smooth surfaces.

JOINTS IN FORMWORK

EXPOSURE METHODS FOR ARCHITECTURAL CONCRETE SURFACES

METHOD	FINISH EFFECT	COLOR SOURCE	FORM SURFACE	CRITICAL DETAILS
1. As cast	Remains as is after form removal, usually exhibits board marks or wood grain	Cement first influence, fine aggregate second influence	Smooth and textured	Slump = $2\frac{1}{2}$ to $3\frac{1}{2}$" Joinery of forms Proper release agent Point form joints to avoid marks
2. Abrasive blasted surfaces				
a. Brush blast	Uniform scour cleaning	Cement and fine aggregate have equal influence	All smooth	Scouring after 7 days Slump = $2\frac{1}{2}$ to $3\frac{1}{2}$"
b. Light blast	Blasted to expose fine and some coarse aggregate (sand blast, water blast, air blast, ice blast)	Fine aggregate primary, coarse aggregate and cement secondary	All smooth	10% more coarse aggregate Slump = $2\frac{1}{2}$ to $3\frac{1}{2}$" Blasting between 7 and 45 days Water and air blasting used where sand blasting prohibited 1500 PSI concrete compressive strength, min.
c. Medium exposed aggregate	Blasted to expose coarse aggregate (sand blast, water blast, air blast, ice blast)	Coarse aggregate	All smooth	Higher than normal coarse aggregate Slump = 2 to 3" Blast before 7 days
d. Heavy exposed aggregate	Blasted to expose coarse aggregate (sand blast, ice blast) 80% visible	Coarse aggregate	All smooth	Special mix coarse aggregate Slump = 0 to 2" Blast within 24 hours Use high-frequency vibrator
3. Chemical retardation of surface set	Chemicals expose aggregate Aggregate can be adhered to surface	Coarse aggregate and cement	All smooth, glass fiber best	Chemical grade determines etch depth Stripping scheduled to prevent long drying between stripping and washoff
4. Mechanically fractured surfaces, scaling, bush hammering, jack-hammering, tooling	Varied	Fine and coarse cement and aggregate	Textured	Aggregate particles $\frac{3}{8}$" for scaling and tooling $2\frac{1}{2}$" minimum concrete cover over reinforced steel 4000 PSI concrete compressive strength, minimum
5. Combination/fluted	Striated/abrasive blasted/irregular pattern Corrugated/abrasive Vertical rusticated/abrasive blasted Reeded and bush hammered Reeded and hammered Reeded and chiseled	The shallower the surface, the more influence fine aggregate and cement have	Wood or rubber strips, corrugated sheet metal, or glass fiber	Depends on type of finish desired Wood flute kerfed and nailed loosely
6. Grinding and polishing	Terrazzo-like finish	Aggregate and cement	All smooth	Surface blemishes should be patched 5000 PSI concrete compressive strength, minimum

D. Neil Rankins; RGA/Virginia; Richmond, Virginia

AGGREGATE

Aggregate is one of three components of concrete and greatly affects the final appearance of the concrete surface. Aggregate should be selected on the basis of color, hardness, size, shape, gradation, method of exposure, durability, availability, and cost. Aggregate hardness and density must be compatible with structural requirements and weathering conditions.

Sources for coarse and fine aggregates should be kept the same for an entire job to avoid variations in the final surface appearance, particularly in light-toned concrete. Following are the common types of aggregate available:

QUARTZ is available in clear, white, yellow, green, gray, and light pink or rose. Clear quartz is used as a sparkling surface to complement other colors and pigmented cements.

GRANITE is known for its durability and beauty and is available in shades of pink, red, gray, dark blue, black, and white. Traprock such as basalt can be used for gray, black, or green.

MARBLE probably offers the widest selection of colors–green, yellow, red, pink, gray, white, and black.

LIMESTONE is available in white and gray.

MISCELLANEOUS GRAVEL, after being washed and screened, can be used for brown and reddish-brown finishes. Yellow ochers, umbers, buff shades, and pure white are abundant in riverbed gravels. Check local supplies.

CERAMIC exhibits the most brilliant and varied colors when vitreous materials are used.

EXPANDED LIGHTWEIGHT SHALE may be used to produce reddish-brown, gray, or black aggregate. Porous and crushable, this shale produces a dull surface with soft colors. It should be tested for iron staining characteristics and must meet ASTM C 330.

RECYCLED CONCRETE aggregate is produced when old concrete is crushed. Primarily used in pavement work, this material generally has a higher absorbsion rate and lower density than conventional aggregate. It should be tested for durability, gradation, and other properties, as with any new aggregate source.

EXPOSED AGGREGATE

An exposed aggregate surface is a decorative finish for concrete work achieved by removing the surface cement to expose the aggregate. Aggregates suitable for exposure may vary from $^1/_4$ in. to a cobblestone more than 6 in. in diameter. The extent to which the pieces of aggregate are revealed is largely determined by their size. Size is generally selected on the basis of the distance from which it will be viewed and the appearance desired.

Aggregates with rough surfaces have better bonding properties than those with smoother surfaces; bind is important, particularly when small aggregate is used. For better weathering and appearance, the area of exposed cement matrix between pieces of aggregate should be minimal, which makes the color of cement in exposed aggregate concrete less important.

SUGGESTED VISIBILITY SCALE

AGGREGATE SIZE, IN. (MM)	DISTANCE AT WHICH TEXTURE IS VISIBLE, FT (M)
$^1/_4$–$^1/_2$ (6-13)	20–30 (6-9)
$^1/_2$–1 (13-25)	30–75 (9-23)
1–2 (25-50)	75–125 (23-38)
2–3 (50-75)	125–175 (38-53)

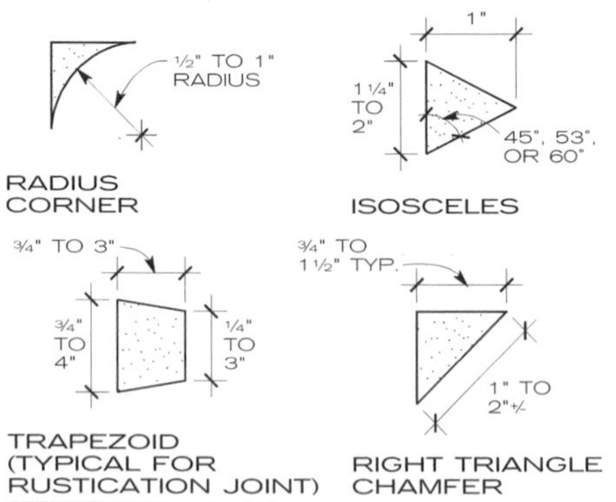

½" TO 1" RADIUS
RADIUS CORNER
1"
1 ¼" TO 2"
45°, 53°, OR 60°
ISOSCELES
¾" TO 3"
¾" TO 4"
¼" TO 3"
TRAPEZOID (TYPICAL FOR RUSTICATION JOINT)
¾" TO 1 ½" TYP.
1" TO 2"+/-
RIGHT TRIANGLE CHAMFER

MISCELLANEOUS CONCRETE JOINT/EDGE SHAPES

SURFACE TEXTURE/FORM LINER

Patterned forms and liners make it possible to simulate in concrete the textures of wood, brick, and stone at a lower cost. The texture and resulting shadow patterns conceal minor color variations or damage that would be conspicuous and unacceptable on a smooth surface. Use of rustication strips at joints in textured liners simplifies form assembly work.

NOTES

1. The choice of liner material may depend on whether the work is precast, cast-in-place, or tilt-up. Thin liners that work well for horizontal casting may wrinkle and sag in vertical forms, where sturdier liner materials are required. Form liners such as plastic foams can usually be used only once, while many elastomeric liners are good for 100 or more uses with reasonable care.
2. Reusable aluminum wall forms, textured with various patterns, can also be used; sections are held together with metal pins. Typical sizes are 3 x 8 ft and larger.
3. Making a preconstruction mock-up is helpful in choosing patterned liner materials. If built on site, the mock-up can be used as a reference standard for inspectors and workers. If ribbed liners are specified, the largest aggregate particle should be smaller than the rib.
4. Typical form liner materials are
   a. Plyform: Sandblasted, wire-brushed, or striated plyform can be used as form sheathing or as a liner inside other structurally adequate forms.
   b. Unfinished sheathing lumber: Used to produce rough, board-marked concrete, this lumber can be used as form sheathing or liner. Ammonia spray on wood will raise grain and accentuate the wood pattern.
   c. Rigid plastics: ABS, PVC, and high-impact polystyrene sheets can be molded or extruded to produce nearly any pattern or texture. Although typically supplied in sheets of 4 x 8 , 4 x 10, and 4 x 12 ft, they can be special ordered in lengths up to 30 ft or longer.
   d. Glass fiber-reinforced plastics (GFRP): These look much like other plastics but are stronger and more durable, particularly laminated GFRP. Extruded GFRP is less expensive (and less durable). Custom lengths up to 40 ft are available.
   e. Elastomeric plastics: These rubbery liners, typically polyurethane, are the most costly, but they are very strong and durable and flexible enough to accommodate finer details. Standard sheets in sizes up to 4 x 12 ft arer available, as are larger custom sheets. Typically attached to form sheathing with adhesive, they are sensitive to temperature change and may deform; consult manufacturers.
   f. Polystyrene foam: Single-use liners are used to produce unique patterns for specific jobs.
5. Joints in the forms and liners must be executed carefully and the liners handled properly to achieve high-quality workmanship. Check liners for compatibility with release agents and adhesives.

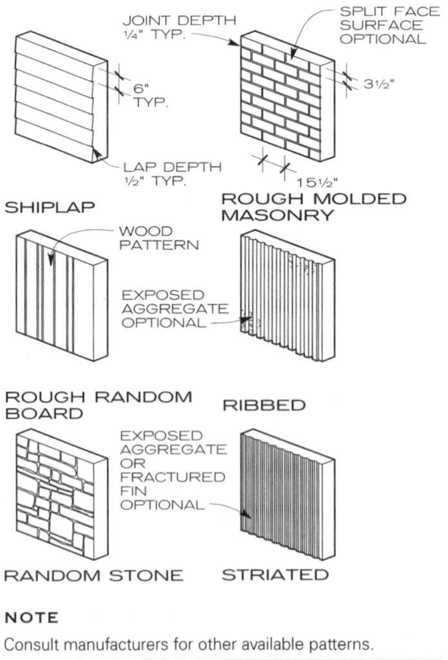

JOINT DEPTH ¼" TYP.
6" TYP.
LAP DEPTH ½" TYP.
SHIPLAP
SPLIT FACE SURFACE OPTIONAL
3½"
15½"
ROUGH MOLDED MASONRY
WOOD PATTERN
EXPOSED AGGREGATE OPTIONAL
ROUGH RANDOM BOARD
RIBBED
EXPOSED AGGREGATE OR FRACTURED FIN OPTIONAL
RANDOM STONE
STRIATED

NOTE

Consult manufacturers for other available patterns.

REUSABLE FORM LINER PATTERNS

INTEGRALLY COLORED CEMENT

Colored concrete can provide a cost-effective simulation of natural stone or other building materials. Two standard types of cement are available, offering different shades of color: standard gray portland cement and white cement. Integrally colored concrete is made by adding mineral oxide pigments to concrete mixes made with one of these two types. Fine aggregates should be selected carefully, since they can enhance the color effect. The amount of coloring material should not exceed 10% by weight of the cement; any excess pigment may reduce concrete strength, and strong colors can be achieved with less than 10% pigment. White cement is used when lighter, more delicate shades of concrete are desired, although it is more expensive; darker hues can be produced using gray cement.

NOTES

1. Variations in all components of the concrete mix make color formulas only approximate. After a basic color is selected, the exact shade may be determined by preparing a number of small panels, varying the ratio of pigment to cement, with aggregate playing a more important role in exposed aggregate mixes. To evaluate panels properly, store them for about five days under conditions similar to those on the construction site. Panels lighten as they dry.
2. Batching, mixing, placing, and curing practices must be uniform, and sources of ingredients must be constant throughout a job to maintain color uniformity. Avoid admixtures that contain calcium chloride, since it can cause discoloration. Clean forms and nonstaining release agents are vital. Consult pigment manufacturers' recommendations.
3. Pigments should meet the quality standards of ASTM C979. Finely ground iron oxides are the most widely used pigments for coloring concrete. Colors and their sources include blue (cobalt oxide), brown (brown iron oxide), buff (yellow iron oxide), green (chromium oxide), red (red iron oxide), gray/slate (black iron oxide).
4. Color-conditioning admixturesoffer integral color and have additives that improve workability, better disperse color and cement, and reduce color bleeding for improved uniformity. Consult manufacturers.

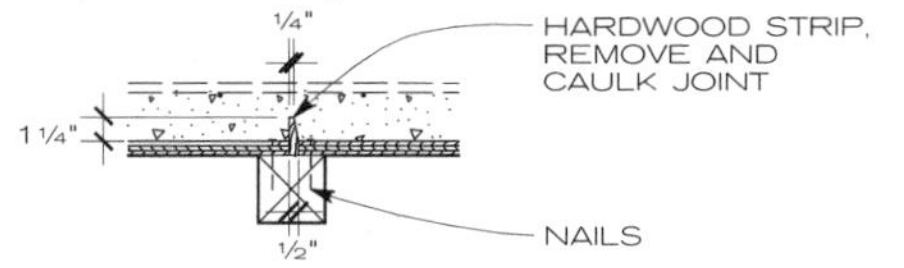

¼"
HARDWOOD STRIP, REMOVE AND CAULK JOINT
1 ¼"
NAILS
½"

WOOD FORM INSERT

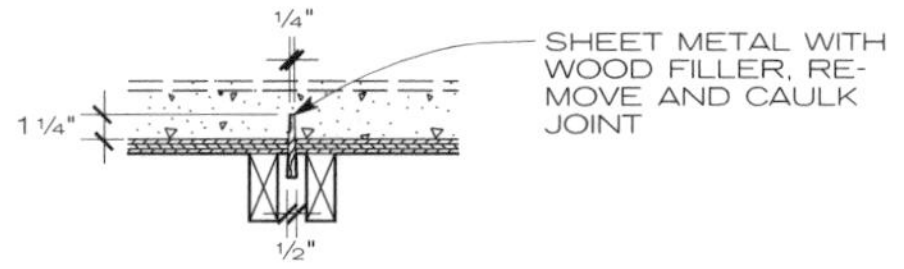

¼"
SHEET METAL WITH WOOD FILLER, REMOVE AND CAULK JOINT
1 ¼"
½"

SHEET METAL FORM INSERT

NOTE

In flat concrete work, a rotary saw may be used to make a contraction joint.

CONTRACTION JOINTS

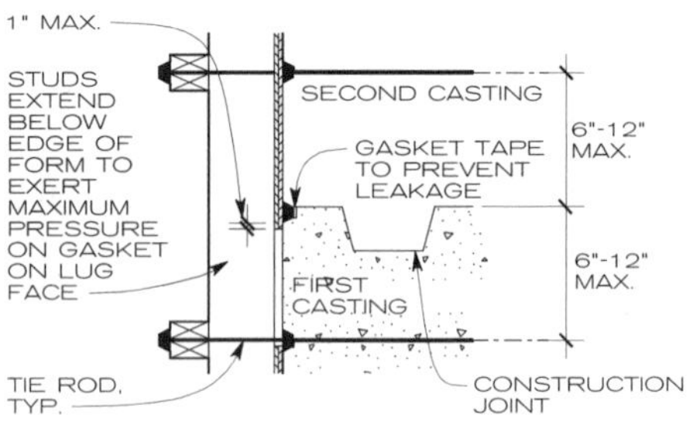

1" MAX.
STUDS EXTEND BELOW EDGE OF FORM TO EXERT MAXIMUM PRESSURE ON GASKET ON LUG FACE
SECOND CASTING
6"-12" MAX.
GASKET TAPE TO PREVENT LEAKAGE
6"-12" MAX.
FIRST CASTING
TIE ROD, TYP.
CONSTRUCTION JOINT

TYPICAL CONSTRUCTION JOINT

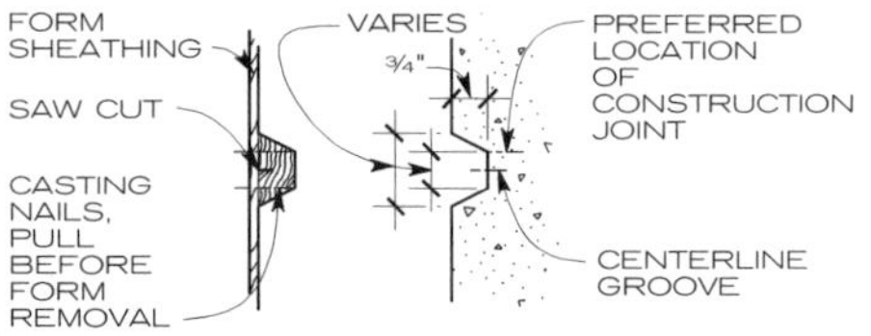

FORM SHEATHING
VARIES
¾"
PREFERRED LOCATION OF CONSTRUCTION JOINT
SAW CUT
CASTING NAILS, PULL BEFORE FORM REMOVAL
CENTERLINE GROOVE

RUSTICATION AT CONSTRUCTION JOINT

D. Neil Rankins; RGA/Virginia; Richmond, Virginia

CONCRETE REPAIR

Damage or deterioration of concrete can occur at any time during service life. Minor repairs may be required during initial construction, for example, filling form tie holes; patching lifting loops on precast concrete; or repairing broken edges on beams, walls, and columns. Distress may result from inadequate design or construction, or deterioration, natural effects, or exposure to aggregate chemicals. Most repairs improve appearance, blending adjacent surfaces by matching texture and color. The repair area should be permanently bonded to the adjacent concrete and sufficiently impermeable to liquid penetration to keep it from shrinking or cracking. Repairs should withstand freeze/thaw cycles as well as surrounding concrete does.

The American Concrete Institute defines generally acceptable architectural concrete surfaces as those with minimal color and texture variation and minimal surface defects when viewed at 20 ft. Most architectural concrete contains some irregularities, such as blowholes or bugholes. Criteria for acceptability should be defined in advance, but patches should match the surrounding area as much as possible.

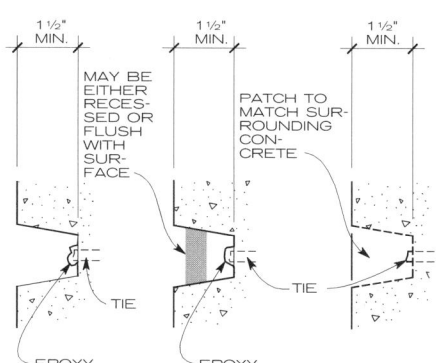

EPOXY OVER TIE   SOLID PLUG   PATCH

NOTE

Solid plugs may be made of precast mortar, plastic, or lead. Mortar of a drytamp consistency will be less likely to smear on surrounding concrete. If surrounding concrete is smooth, recess plug or patch.

TIE HOLE TREATMENT OPTIONS

REPAIR MATERIALS

Prepackaged cementitious and latex-modified cementitious repair materials are available, with formulations for thin or thicker repairs. Where aesthetics are important, use the same cement and aggregates as in the surrounding work. Most types of Portland cement are acceptable, but match the original type, if possible. Certain prepackaged mixes must conform to ASTM C 928. Aggregates should match the existing concrete aggregate, if possible. For exposed aggregate, matching the texture and color may require special mixtures. Any admixture used in concrete work can be used in repair mixtures. Bonding agents may be required for some repairs, especially thin ones; they are typically either cement-based, latex-based (ASTM C 1059), or epoxy-based (ASTM C 881). Acrylics, methyl methacrylates, and polymers are less expensive than epoxy bonding agents but are more likely to shrink. Repaired areas should be sealed or coated to the same specifications as the surrounding concrete work to protect against natural forces, corrosives, and chemicals.

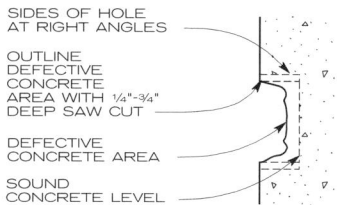

SIDES OF HOLE AT RIGHT ANGLES
OUTLINE DEFECTIVE CONCRETE AREA WITH 1/4"-3/4" DEEP SAW CUT
DEFECTIVE CONCRETE AREA
SOUND CONCRETE LEVEL

NOTE

Larger and thicker patches should be anchored mechanically to the surrounding concrete.

PATCHING OF DEFECTIVE CONCRETE SURFACES

GUIDELINES FOR PATCHING

1. Design patch mix to match original, with small amount of white cement; may eliminate coarse aggregate or hand-place it. Trial and error, the only reliable match method, should be performed on a mock-up first.
2. Remove defective concrete down to sound concrete; for exposed aggregate concrete, chip slightly deeper than maximum size of aggregate.
3. Clean area; saturate with water and apply bonding agent to base of hole and to water of patch mix.
4. Pack patch mix to density of original.
5. Place exposed aggregate by hand.
6. Bristle-brush after setup to match existing material.
7. Moist-cure to minimize shrinking.
8. Use form or finish to match original.

PROTECTIVE AND DECORATIVE COATINGS

Concrete surfaces may require a sealer or coating to protect against severe weather, chemicals, or abrasions; to prevent dusting of the surface layer; to harden the surface layer; or to add a decorative finish.

Sealers are usually clear and are expected to penetrate the surface without leaving a visible film. Coatings are clear or opaque and, while they may have some penetration, they leave a visible film on the surface. Sealers and coatings should allow vapor emission from the concrete but at the same time keep moisture from penetrating after curing.

Decorative coatings usually protect as well and are formulated in a wide selection of colors. Decorative coatings include water-based acrylic emulsion; elastomeric acrylic resin; liquid polymer stain; solvent-based acrylic stain; portland cement-based finish coating; and water-based acidic stain (a solution of metallic salts).

PROTECTIVE COATINGS AND SEALERS

FINISH	USE
Cementitious acrylic polymeric coating	Aesthetic treatment
2-component epoxy coating	Protects damp or underwater surfaces
Solvent-based aliphatic urethane coating	Resists graffiti, chemicals, abrasion
Epoxy coal tar-based coating	Waterproof, resists corrosion
Coal tar-modified epoxy resin coating	Nonskid waterproof surface membrane
Water-based epoxy coating	Chemical, abrasion resistance for interiors
Vinyl ester-based coating	High chemical resistance
Aliphatic urethane coating	Chemical, abrasion
Solvent-based acrylic methacrylate copolymer sealer	Reduces water penetration
Silane/siloxane sealer penetrating water repellent	Protects from deicers and freeze/thaw damage

NOTES

1. Floor-hardening agents are applied to reduce dusting and increase hardness slightly at the surface.
2. Consult a qualified specialist to determine the correct coating or sealer for a particular application.
3. There may be restrictions on the use of solvent-based coatings and sealers in some areas due to the presence of VOCs (volatile organic compounds).

CRACKING IN CONCRETE CONSTRUCTION

	SLABS ON GRADE					BEAMS, WALLS, COLUMNS, AND STRUCTURAL SLABS		
	SURFACE CRAZING	PLASTIC SHRINKAGE	EARLY CONCRETE VOLUME CHANGES	OTHER CRACKING		SETTLEMENT CRACKS		OTHER CRACKING
Cause	Shrinkage of cement paste at exposed concrete surfaces due to concrete mix, too-wet excessive bleeding, overtroweling surface, rapid drying of surface	Water at the concrete surface evaporates too rapidly due to job site conditions such as low humidity, high wind speeds, high concrete temperatures, high to moderate air temperatures	As concrete cools and hardens, concrete volume shrinks; cracking will occur if slab is restrained at any point	Subgrade settlement	Premature excessive loading on slab	Same as for slabs on grade; also, heavier amounts of reinforcement and nature of formed or shored construction	Flexible forms and insufficient vibration can increase likelihood	Subgrade or formwork settlement, early volume changes, construction overloads, errors in design and detailing
Effect	Unsightly cracking of surface layer although surface is probably sound	Parallel cracking, fairly wide at the exposed surface but shallow; doesn't typically extend to slab edge; crack spacing and length vary greatly	Random or regularly spaced cracks, usually passing completely through slab; during sawcutting of joints, crack may jump ahead of sawcut	Slab will bend and crack	Punch-through at edge by heavy equipment, etc.	Longitudinal cracks develop over reinforcement bars; can cause reinforcement bar corrosion		General cracking
Preventive measures	Reduce amount and rate of shrinkage at concrete surface by avoiding wet mixes, limiting bleeding by increasing sand or air content, limiting troweling/not troweling too early, curing as soon as possible	Reduce rate at which surface moisture evaporates by erecting windbreaks or building walls before slab, avoiding wet mixes, dampening subgrade before concrete pour, curing as soon as possible, avoiding vapor barrier under slab unless necessary	Not always preventable; careful joint design or reinforcement may help; other measures: tool or sawcut joints 1/4 of slab thickness, min., time sawcut according to concrete curing rate; locate contraction joints at column lines, min.; for unreinforced slabs, space joints at 24 to 36 times slab thickness, max.; posttension at slab; isolate slabs from adjoining structures with preformed joint filler or if continuity is required, increase slab reinforcement	Compact subgrade well	Generally, curing periods of 4 to 7 days, followed by 1 to 2 days of drying	Proper form design and sufficient vibration or revibration: use lowest possible slump, increase concrete cover		Consult with structural concrete engineer or consultant to prevent

NOTE

Expect some cracking in concrete construction. Generally, cracking is controlled with joints and reinforcement; however, not all cracks indicate errors or performance problems, and not all cracks need to be repaired.

Grant Halvorsen, S.E., P.E.; Wheaton, Illinois

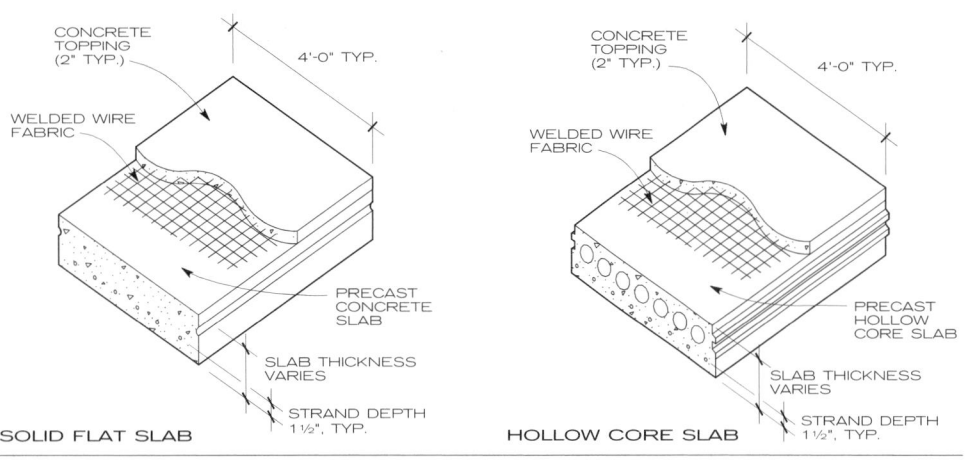

NOTES

1. Normal weight (150 pcf) or lightweight concrete (115 pcf) is used in standard slab construction. Topping concrete is usually normal weight concrete with a cylinder strength of 3000 psi. All units are prestressed with strand release when concrete strength is 3500 psi.

2. Strands are available in various sizes, strengths and placements according to individual manufacturers.

Strand designation code (SDC):
78 - S
— straight
— diameter of strands in sixteenths
— number of strands

3. Camber varies substantially depending on slab design, span, and loading. Nonstructural components attached to members may be affected by camber variations. Calculations of topping quantities should recognize camber variations.

4. Safe superimposed surface loads include a dead load of 10 psf for untopped concrete and 15 psf for topped concrete. The remainder is live load.

FLAT DECK MEMBERS

SAFE SUPERIMPOSED SERVICE LOADS (PSF) FOR SOLID FLAT SLABS (4-FT WIDTH, 5000 PSI)

SLAB THICKNESS (IN.) (150 PCF CONCRETE)	SLAB DESIGNATION	TOPPING THICKNESS (IN.)	SPAN (FT)																					
			10	11	12	13	14	15	16	17	18	19	20	21	22	23	24	25	26	27	28	29	30	31	32
4' — S.D.C. : 68-S	FS4	None	300	252	214	180	152	127	105	88	73	60	50	40	32									
	FS4+2	2				335	268	213	169	132	101	74	52	32										
6' — S.D.C. : 78-S	FS6	None					396	351	303	261	225	195	168	146	126	109	94	81	69	59	49	41	33	
	FS6+2	2								371	323	281	239	201	169	140	115	93	73	56	40		
8" — S.D.C. : 68-S	FS8	None								358	311	271	237	207	182	159	138	120	103	88	75	63	53	43	34
	FS8+2	2								395	344	301	264	231	199	167	140	115	94	74	57	41	

SAFE SUPERIMPOSED SERVICE LOADS (PSF) FOR 6- AND 8-IN. HOLLOW-CORE SLABS (4-FT WIDTH, 5000 PSI)

SLAB THICKNESS (IN.) (150 PCF CONCRETE)	SLAB DESIGNATION	TOPPING THICKNESS (IN.)	SPAN (FT)																					
			15	16	17	18	19	20	21	22	23	24	25	26	27	28	29	30	31	32	33	34	35	36	37
6" — S.D.C. : 78-S	4HC6	None	364	317	277	243	214	189	168	150	134	120	107	96	87	78	70	62							
	4HC6+2	2				382	335	294	260	231	205	181	157	137	119	102	88	75	63						
8" — S.D.C. : 88-S	4HC8	None	360	335	311	290	272	256	242	229	215	205	188	170	154	141	128	117	106	97	89	81	74	67	
	4HC8+2	2				346	325	306	286	271	252	227	205	186	168	152	138	124	111	98	86	76	66	56

SAFE SUPERIMPOSED SERVICE LOADS (PSF) FOR 10- AND 12-IN. HOLLOW-CORE SLABS (4-FT WIDTH, 5000 PSI)

SLAB THICKNESS (IN.) (150 PCF CONCRETE)	SLAB DESIGNATION	TOPPING THICKNESS (IN.)	SPAN (FT)																					
			20	21	22	23	24	25	26	27	28	29	30	31	32	33	34	35	36	37	38	39	40	41	42
10" — S.D.C. : 97-S	4HC10	None	298	278	264	248	237	223	214	203	193	179	164	150	138	126	116	106	98	90	82	75	69	63	57
	4HC10+2	2				295	278	265	250	239	226	218	201	184	168	154	138	124	111	98	87	77	67	58	49
12" — S.D.C. : 78-S	4HC12	None									194	185	177	169	162	155	148	142	137	131	126	121	120	112	104
	4HC12+2	2				280	264	249	236	223	212	201	195	185	177	169	161	154	147	141	135	129	126	116	107

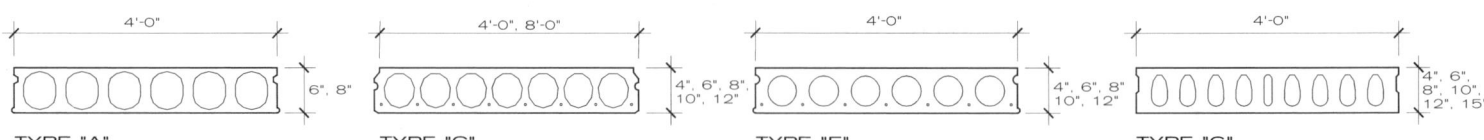

TYPE "A"   TYPE "C"   TYPE "E"   TYPE "G"

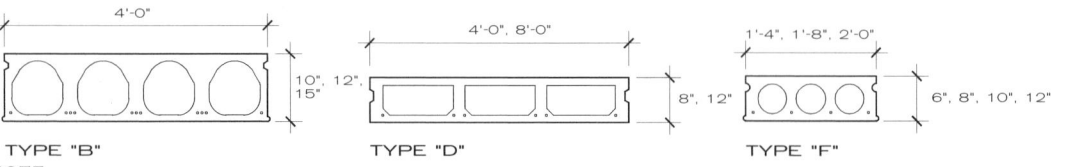

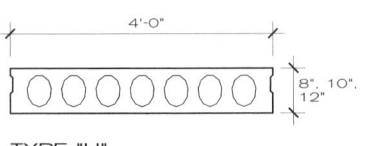

TYPE "B"   TYPE "D"   TYPE "F"   TYPE "H"

NOTE

All sections are not available from all producers; check availability with local manufacturers.

HOLLOW CORE SLAB TYPES

Sidney Freedman; Precast/Prestressed Concrete Institute; Chicago, Illinois

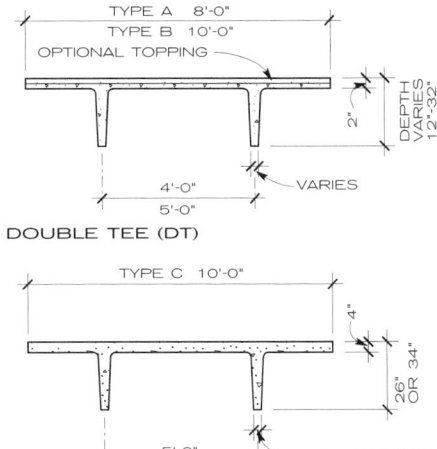

TYPE A   8'-0"
TYPE B   10'-0"
OPTIONAL TOPPING
2"
DEPTH VARIES 12"-32"
4'-0"
5'-0"
VARIES

DOUBLE TEE (DT)

TYPE C   10'-0"
4"
26" OR 34"
5'-0"
3¾" OR 4¾"

PRETOPPED DOUBLE TEE

NOTES

1. Safe loads shown indicate dead load of 10 psf for untopped members and 15 psf for topped members. Remainder is live load.
2. Contact manufacturers in the geographic area of the proposed structure to determine availability, exact dimensions, and load tables for various sections.
3. Check camber for its effect on nonstructural members (partitions, folding doors, etc.), which should be placed with adequate allowance for error. Calculations for topping quantities should also recognize camber variations.
4. Normal-weight concrete is assumed to be 150 lb/cu ft; lightweight concrete is assumed to be 115 lb/cu ft.

STEMMED DECK MEMBERS

APPROXIMATE MAXIMUM SPAN FOR STEMMED DECK SECTIONS

DECK TYPE	DEPTH (IN.)	CONCRETE WEIGHT	DESIGNATION	TOPPING DEPTH (IN.)	STRAND DESIGNATION	MAX. SPAN (FT)	SAFE LOAD (PSF)
A	12	Normal weight	8DT12	0	88 D1	44	32
			8DT12+2	2	68 D1	34	50
		Lightweight	8LDT12	0	68 D1	42	33
			8LDT12+2	2	68 D1	38	33
A	18	Normal weight	8DT18	0	108 D1	60	34
			8DT18+2	2	88 D1	48	47
		Lightweight	8LDT18	0	108 D1	64	34
			8LDT18+2	2	88 D1	52	39
A	24	Normal weight	8DT24	0	148 D1	74	45
			8DT24+2	2	128 D1	64	49
		Lightweight	8LDT24	0	148 D1	80	42
			8LDT24+2	2	108 D1	68	46
A	32	Normal weight	8DT32	0	228 D1	94	52
			8DT32+2	2	208 D1	80	72
		Lightweight	8LDT32	0	228 D1	100	50
			8LDT32+2	2	208 D1	86	65
B	32	Normal weight	10DT32	0	228 D1	88	53
			10DT32+2	2	208 D1	76	66
		Lightweight	10LDT32	0	228 D1	98	42
			10LDT32+2	2	208 D1	82	58
C	26	Normal weight	10DT26	0	148 D1	68	33
		Lightweight	10LDT26	0	148 D1	72	37
C	34	Normal weight	10DT34	0	228 D1	90	34
		Lightweight	10LDT34	0	228 D1	90	51

NOTE

Strand pattern designation:

```
          ┌─ Number of strands (20)
          │  ┌─ S = straight, D = depressed
      208 D1
          │  └─ Number of depression points
          └─ Diameter of strand in sixteenths
```

Topping concrete = 3000 psi

150 lb/cu ft lc = 5000 psi for normal or lightweight deck

SAFE SUPERIMPOSED SERVICE LOAD (PLF)* FOR PRECAST BEAM SECTIONS

TYPE	DESIG-NATION	NO. STRAND	H (IN.)	H1/H2 (IN.)	SPAN (FT)																	
					16	18	20	22	24	26	28	30	32	34	36	38	40	42	44	46	48	50
RECTANGULAR B = 12" OR 16"	12RB24	10	24		8884	6957	5578	4558	3782	3178	2699	2312	1996	1734	1514	1328	1170	1033				
	12RB32	13	32				8238	6859	5785	4933	4246	3683	3217	2826	2495	2213	1970	1760	1576	1415	1272	
	16RB24	13	24			9278	7439	6079	5044	4239	3600	3084	2662	2313	2020	1772	1560	1378	1220	1082	961	
	16RB32	18	32					9145	7713	6577	5661	4911	4289	3768	3327	2951	2627	2346	2010	1886	1697	
	16RB40	22	40								9010	7839	6867	6054	5365	4777	4271	3832	3449	3113	2817	
L - SHAPED 1'-0" / H1 / H2 / 1'-6"	18LB20	9	20	12/18	6675	5211	4164	3389	2800	2341	1978	1684	1444	1245	1080							
	18LB28	12	28	16/12			8387	6857	5694	4789	4071	3491	3017	2624	2295	2017	1781	1578	1402	1249	1114	995
	18LB36	16	36	24/12				9617	8117	6927	5966	5180	4529	3983	3521	3126	2787	2493	2236	2011	1813	
	18LB44	19	44	28/16						9039	7866	6893	6078	5389	4800	4293	3854	3471	3153	2838		
	18LB52	23	52	36/16								9798	8658	7694	6871	6162	5548	5012	4542	4127		
	18LB60	27	60	44/16											9292	8349	7532	6819	6193	5641		
INVERTED TEE 6" 1'-0" 6" / H1 / H2 / 2'-0"	24IT20	9	20	12/8	7078	5515	4404	3582	2957	2470	2084	1773	1518	1307	1130	980						
	24IT28	13	28	16/12			8874	7247	6013	5053	4292	3677	3175	2758	2409	2113	1861	1644	1456	1292	1147	1020
	24IT36	16	36	24/12				8594	7327	6305	5469	4776	4199	3710	3293	2934	2623	2352	2114	1904		
	24IT44	20	44	28/16						9554	8306	7272	6409	5680	5057	4520	4056	3650	3295	2981		
	24IT52	24	52	36/16								9164	8137	7261	6507	5853	5283	4786	4348			
	24IT60	28	60	44/16										9863	8857	7986	7226	6559	5970			

* Safe loads shown indicate 50% dead load and 50% live load; 800 psi top tension has been allowed, therefore additional top reinforcement is required.

Sidney Freedman; Precast/Prestressed Concrete Institute; Chicago, Illinois

PRECAST CONCRETE

3

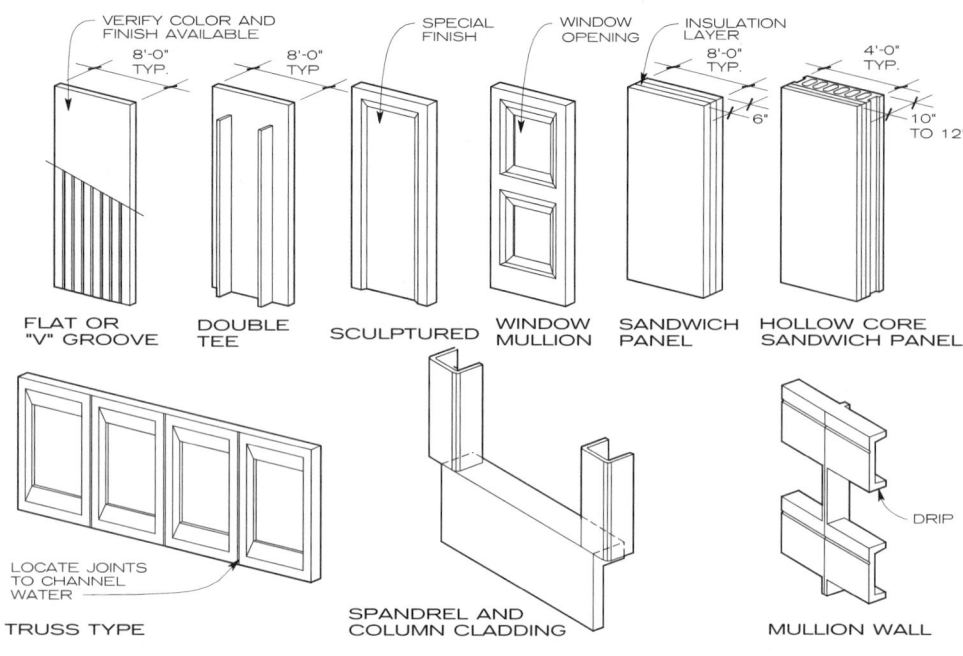

FLAT OR "V" GROOVE

DOUBLE TEE

SCULPTURED

WINDOW MULLION

SANDWICH PANEL

HOLLOW CORE SANDWICH PANEL

TRUSS TYPE

SPANDREL AND COLUMN CLADDING

MULLION WALL

PANEL VARIATIONS

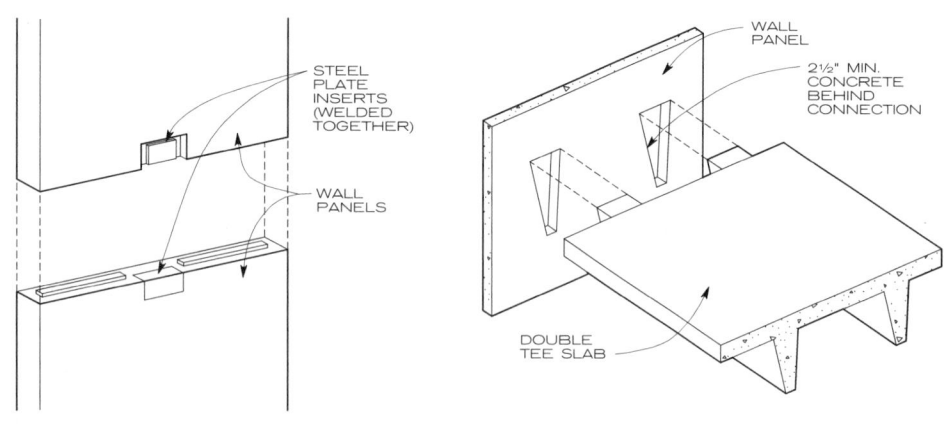

WALL PANEL TO WALL PANEL

NOTE

Pocket connection may be at top of panel.

SLAB-TO-WALL PANEL

BEARING PANEL CONDITIONS

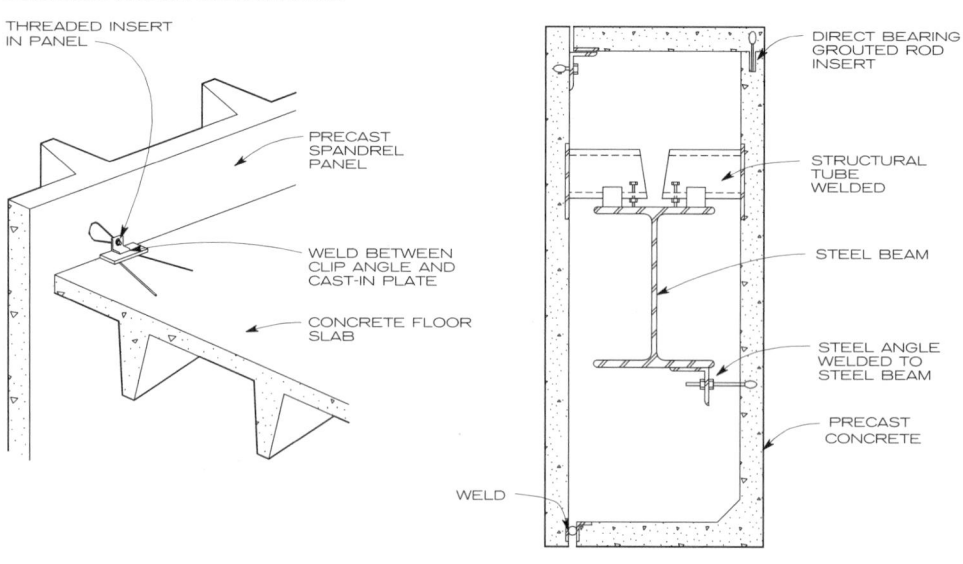

SPANDREL CONDITIONS

Sidney Freedman; Precast/Prestressed Concrete Institute; Chicago, Illinois

 PRECAST CONCRETE

WALL PANELS

Carefully distinguish between the more specialized architectural wall panel and the structural wall panel that is a derivative of floor systems. Always work with manufacturers early in the design process. Careful attention must be given to manufacturing and joint tolerance during design. Thoroughly examine joint sealants for adhesion and expected joint movement.

FINISHES

Form liner molds provide a wide variety of smooth and textured finishes. Finishes after casting but prior to hardening include exposed aggregate, broom, trowel, screed, float, or stippled. After hardening, finishes include acid-etched, sandblasted, honed, polished, and hammered rib.

COLORS

Select a color range, as complete uniformity cannot be guaranteed. White cement offers the best color uniformity; gray cement is subject to color variations even when supplied from one source. Pigments require high-quality manufacturing and curing standards. Fine aggregate color requires control of the mixture graduation; coarse aggregate color provides the best durability and appearance.

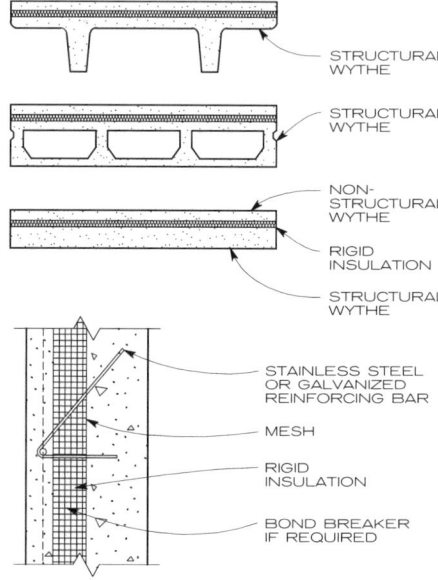

VERTICAL SECTION AT TIE

NOTE

Panel requires accurate location of ties and reinforcement and established concrete quality control.

SANDWICH WALL CONSTRUCTION

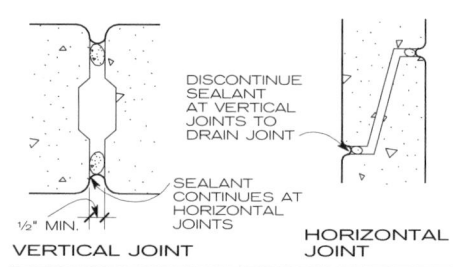

VERTICAL JOINT

HORIZONTAL JOINT

TWO-STAGE SEALANT JOINTS

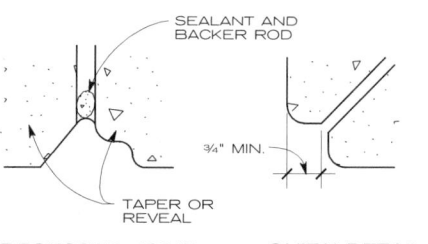

RECESSED JOINT

QUIRK DETAIL

JOINT DETAILS

GENERAL

Architectural precast concrete is subject to the same erection and manufacturing tolerances as other building materials. When such tolerances are considered in the design stage, the task of determining and specifying them is simpler. By requiring realistic tolerances, architects strengthen and simplify their standards for acceptance. Unrealistic, close tolerances are costly, particularly for custom-produced elements.

Tolerances set the limits of size and shape for precast concrete units. Three groups of tolerances should be established in precast concrete design: product (manufacturing) tolerances, erection tolerances, and interfacing tolerances. Product and erection tolerances usually do not cause site problems. Tolerances are most problematic at the interface of precast concrete and other building materials.

Tolerances should be established for the following reasons:

STRUCTURAL: To ensure that structural design properly accounts for factors sensitive to variations in dimensional control. Examples include eccentric loading condition, bearing areas, hardware and hardware anchorage locations, and locations of reinforcing or prestressing steel.

FEASIBILITY: To ensure acceptable performance of joints and interfacing materials in the finished structure.

VISUAL: To ensure that the variations will be controllable and result in a structure that is visually acceptable.

ECONOMIC: To ensure ease and speed of production and erection by having agreed-upon dimensions for precast concrete products.

LEGAL: To avoid encroaching on property lines and to establish a standard against which the work can be compared in event of a dispute.

CONTRACTUAL: To establish a known acceptability range and responsibility for developing, achieving, and maintaining mutually agreed-upon tolerances.

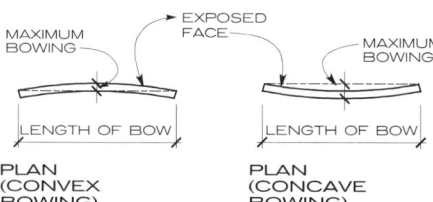

PLAN
(CONVEX
BOWING)

PLAN
(CONCAVE
BOWING)

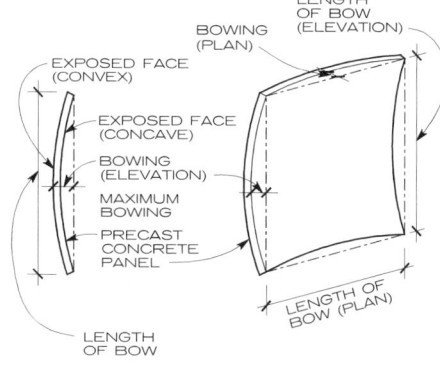

ELEVATION

PANEL BOWED IN
BOTH PLAN AND
ELEVATION

BOWING DEFINITIONS FOR PANELS

GUIDELINES FOR PANEL THICKNESS[1]

PANEL DIMENSIONS[2]	8 FT	10 FT	12 FT	16 FT	20 FT	24 FT	28 FT	32 FT
4 ft	3 in.	4 in.	4 in.	5 in.	5 in.	6 in.	6 in.	7 in.
6 ft	3 in.	4 in.	4 in.	5 in.	6 in.	6 in.	6 in.	7 in.
8 ft	4 in.	5 in.	5 in.	6 in.	6 in.	7 in.	7 in.	8 in.
10 ft	5 in.	5 in.	6 in.	6 in.	7 in.	7 in.	8 in.	8 in.

[1] This table should not be used for panel thickness selection.

[2] This table shows a relationship between overall flat panel dimensions and thicknesses below which suggested bowing and warpage tolerances should be reviewed and possibly increased. For ribbed panels, the equivalent thickness should be the overall thickness of such ribs if continuous from one end of the panel to the other.

PLAN

ELEVATION

A = Plan location from building grid datum ±$\frac{1}{2}$ in.[1]

A$_1$ = Plan location from centerline of steel ±$\frac{1}{2}$ in.[2]

B = Top elevation from nominal top elevation: exposed individual panel ±$\frac{1}{4}$ in.; nonexposed individual panel ±$\frac{1}{2}$ in.; exposed relative to adjacent panel $\frac{1}{4}$ in.; nonexposed relative to adjacent panel $\frac{1}{2}$ in.[1]

C = Support elevation from nominal elevation: maximum low $\frac{1}{2}$ in.; maximum high $\frac{1}{4}$ in.

D = Maximum plumb variation over height of structure or 100 ft, whichever is less 1 in.[1]

E = Plumb in any 10 ft of element height $\frac{1}{4}$ in.

F = Maximum jog in alignment of matching edges $\frac{1}{4}$ in.

G = Joint width (governs over joint taper) ±$\frac{1}{4}$ in.

H = Joint taper max. $\frac{3}{8}$ in.

H$_{10}$= Joint taper over 10 ft length $\frac{1}{4}$ in.

I = Max. jog in alignment of matching faces $\frac{1}{4}$ in.

J = Differential bowing or camber as erected between adjacent members of the same design $\frac{1}{4}$ in.

[1] For precast buildings taller than 100 ft, tolerances A and D can increase at the rate of $\frac{1}{8}$ in. per story to a maximum of 2 in.

[2] For precast concrete erected on a steel frame building, this tolerance takes precedence over tolerance on dimension A.

ERECTION TOLERANCES FOR WALL PANELS

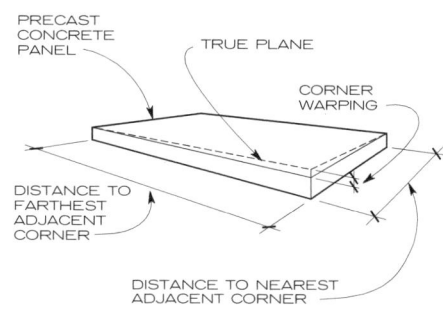

WARPING DEFINITIONS FOR PANELS

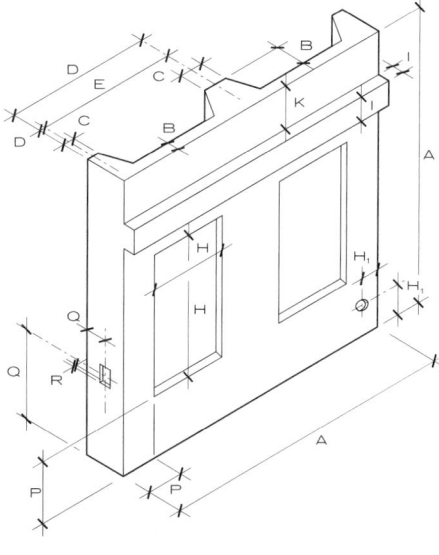

A = Overall length and width (measured at neutral axis of ribbed members): 10 ft or under ±$\frac{1}{8}$ in.; 10 to 20 ft +$\frac{1}{8}$ in., -$\frac{3}{16}$ in.; 20 to 40 ft ±$\frac{1}{4}$ in.; each additional 10 ft ±$\frac{1}{16}$ in. per 10 ft.

B = Total thickness or flange thickness -$\frac{1}{8}$ in., +$\frac{1}{4}$ in.

C = Rib thickness ±$\frac{1}{8}$ in.

D = Rib to edge of flange ±$\frac{1}{8}$ in.

E = Distance between ribs ±$\frac{1}{8}$ in.

F = Angular variation of plane of side mold ±$\frac{1}{32}$ in. per 3 in. of depth or ±$\frac{1}{16}$ in., whichever is greater.

G = Variation from square or designated skew (difference in length of the two diagonal measurements) ±$\frac{1}{8}$ in. per 6 ft of diagonal or ±$\frac{1}{2}$ in., whichever is greater.*

H = Length and width of blockouts and openings within one unit ±$\frac{1}{4}$ in.

H$_1$ = Location and dimensions of blockouts hidden from view and used for HVAC and utility penetrations ±$\frac{3}{4}$ in.

H$_2$ = Some types of window and equipment frames require more accurate types of openings. When this is the case, the minimum practical tolerance should be defined with input from the producer.

I = Dimensions of haunches ±$\frac{1}{4}$ in.

J = Haunch bearing surface deviation from specified plane ±$\frac{1}{8}$ in.

K = Difference in relative position of adjacent haunch bearing surfaces from specified relative position ±$\frac{1}{4}$ in.

L = Bowing ±L/360 max. 1 in.

M = Differential bowing between adjacent panels of the same design $\frac{1}{8}$ in.

N = Local smoothness $\frac{1}{4}$ in. in 10 ft. (does not apply to visually concealed surfaces.

O = Warping of distance from nearest adjacent corner $\frac{1}{16}$ in. per ft.

P = Location of window opening within panel ±$\frac{1}{4}$ in.

Q = Position of plates ±1 in.

R = Tipping and flushness of plates ±$\frac{1}{4}$ in.

* Applies both to panel and to major openings in the panel.

Position tolerance for cast-in items measured from datum line location as shown on approved erection drawings: weld plates ±1 in.; inserts ±$\frac{1}{2}$ in.; handling devices ±3 in.; reinforcing steel and welded wire fabric where position has structural implications or affects concrete cover ±$\frac{1}{4}$ in., otherwise ±$\frac{1}{2}$ in.; tendons ±$\frac{1}{8}$ in.; flashing reglets ±$\frac{1}{4}$ in.; flashing reglets at edge of panel ±$\frac{1}{8}$ in.; reglets for glazing gaskets ±$\frac{1}{16}$ in.; groove width for glazing gaskets ±$\frac{1}{16}$ in.; electrical outlets, hose bibs, etc. ±$\frac{1}{2}$ in.; haunches ±$\frac{1}{4}$ in.

TOLERANCES FOR PANELS, SPANDRELS, AND COLUMN COVERS

Sidney Freedman; Precast/Prestressed Concrete Institute; Chicago, Illinois

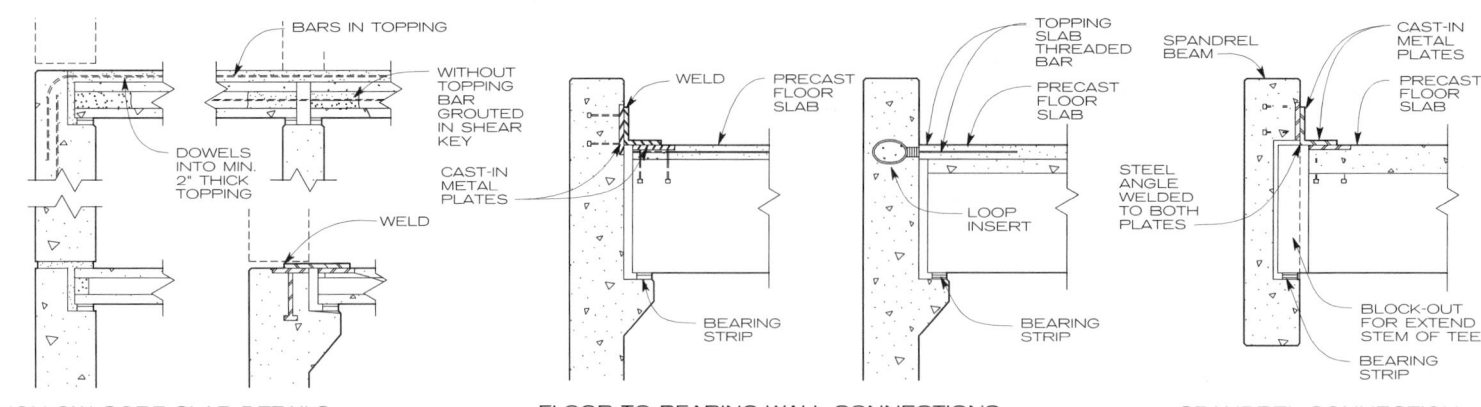

BARS IN TOPPING

WITHOUT TOPPING BAR GROUTED IN SHEAR KEY

DOWELS INTO MIN. 2" THICK TOPPING

CAST-IN METAL PLATES

WELD

WELD

TOPPING SLAB THREADED BAR

PRECAST FLOOR SLAB

PRECAST FLOOR SLAB

LOOP INSERT

BEARING STRIP

BEARING STRIP

SPANDREL BEAM

CAST-IN METAL PLATES

PRECAST FLOOR SLAB

STEEL ANGLE WELDED TO BOTH PLATES

BLOCK-OUT FOR EXTEND STEM OF TEE

BEARING STRIP

HOLLOW CORE SLAB DETAILS

FLOOR-TO-BEARING WALL CONNECTIONS

SPANDREL CONNECTION

FLOOR-TO-WALL CONNECTIONS

GENERAL

To fasten members to foundations, set them on shims, tighten nuts to level, then fill space with nonshrink grout.

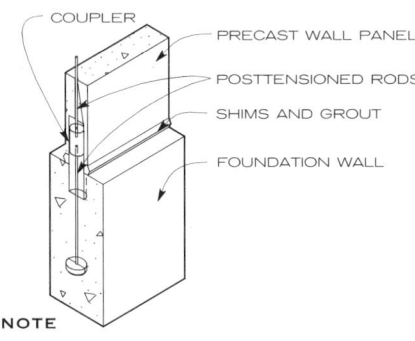

COUPLER

PRECAST WALL PANEL

POSTTENSIONED RODS

SHIMS AND GROUT

FOUNDATION WALL

NOTE

Vertical posttensioning can be used to resist uplift forces; moment resistance is achieved.

POSTTENSIONED WALL-TO-FOUNDATION CONNECTION

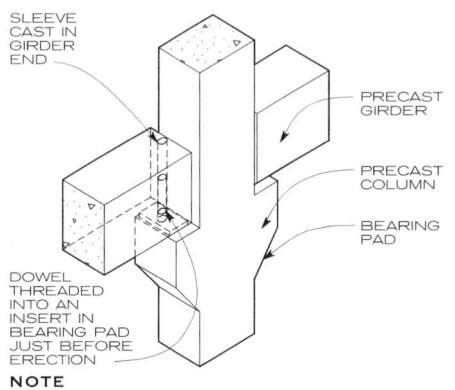

SLEEVE CAST IN GIRDER END

PRECAST GIRDER

PRECAST COLUMN

BEARING PAD

DOWEL THREADED INTO AN INSERT IN BEARING PAD JUST BEFORE ERECTION

NOTE

The girder sits on the bearing pad, which provides uniform bearing and accommodates small movements due to shrinkage, creep, and temperature changes.

DOWELED BEAM-TO-COLUMN CONNECTION

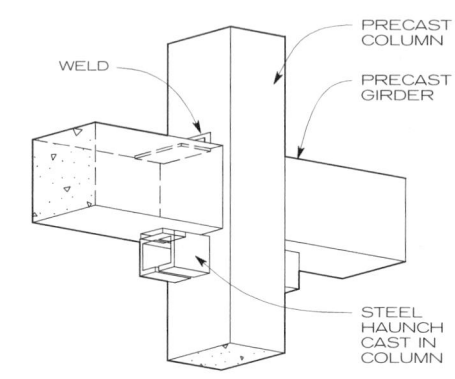

WELD

PRECAST COLUMN

PRECAST GIRDER

STEEL HAUNCH CAST IN COLUMN

NOTE

Steel haunches are smaller than concrete bearing pads, which is important if headroom is critical.

HAUNCHED BEAM-TO-COLUMN CONNECTION

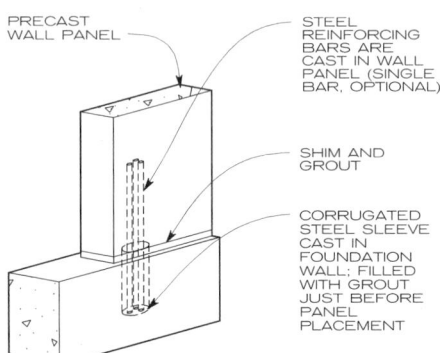

PRECAST WALL PANEL

STEEL REINFORCING BARS ARE CAST IN WALL PANEL (SINGLE BAR, OPTIONAL)

SHIM AND GROUT

CORRUGATED STEEL SLEEVE CAST IN FOUNDATION WALL; FILLED WITH GROUT JUST BEFORE PANEL PLACEMENT

GROUTED WALL-TO-FOUNDATION CONNECTION

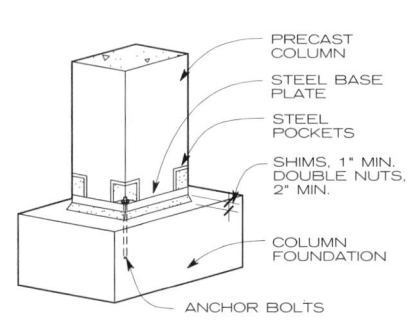

PRECAST COLUMN

STEEL BASE PLATE

STEEL POCKETS

SHIMS, 1" MIN. DOUBLE NUTS, 2" MIN.

COLUMN FOUNDATION

ANCHOR BOLTS

COLUMN–BASE CONNECTION

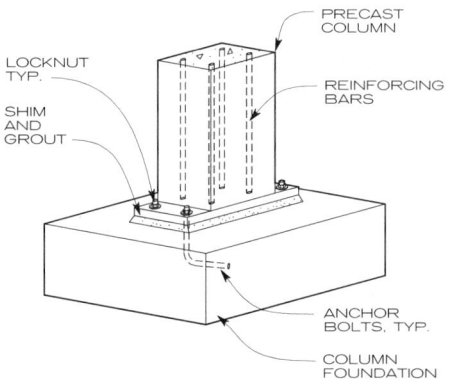

LOCKNUT TYP.

SHIM AND GROUT

PRECAST COLUMN

REINFORCING BARS

ANCHOR BOLTS, TYP.

COLUMN FOUNDATION

OVERSIZED BASE PLATE AT COLUMN–BASE CONNECTION

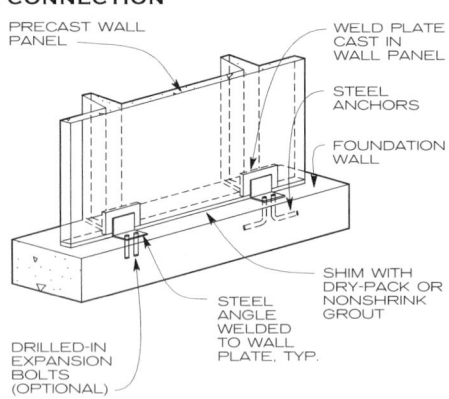

PRECAST WALL PANEL

WELD PLATE CAST IN WALL PANEL

STEEL ANCHORS

FOUNDATION WALL

DRILLED-IN EXPANSION BOLTS (OPTIONAL)

STEEL ANGLE WELDED TO WALL PLATE, TYP.

SHIM WITH DRY-PACK OR NONSHRINK GROUT

BOLTED WALL-TO-FOUNDATION CONNECTION

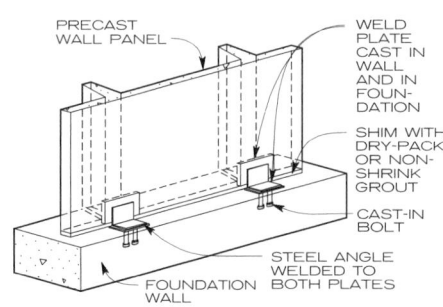

PRECAST WALL PANEL

WELD PLATE CAST IN WALL AND IN FOUNDATION

SHIM WITH DRY-PACK OR NON-SHRINK GROUT

CAST-IN BOLT

STEEL ANGLE WELDED TO BOTH PLATES

FOUNDATION WALL

NOTE

Two connections per panel are typical.

WELDED WALL-TO-FOUNDATION CONNECTION

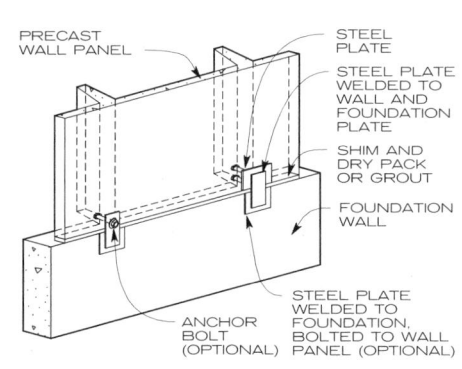

PRECAST WALL PANEL

STEEL PLATE

STEEL PLATE WELDED TO WALL AND FOUNDATION PLATE

SHIM AND DRY PACK OR GROUT

FOUNDATION WALL

ANCHOR BOLT (OPTIONAL)

STEEL PLATE WELDED TO FOUNDATION, BOLTED TO WALL PANEL (OPTIONAL)

WELDED PLATE-TO-FOUNDATION CONNECTION

Sidney Freedman; Precast/Prestressed Concrete Institute; Chicago, Illinois

PRECAST CONCRETE

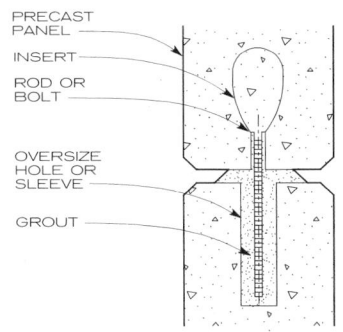

NOTE

Shim stacks occur at two points per panel adjacent to connection.

DIRECT BEARING CONNECTION

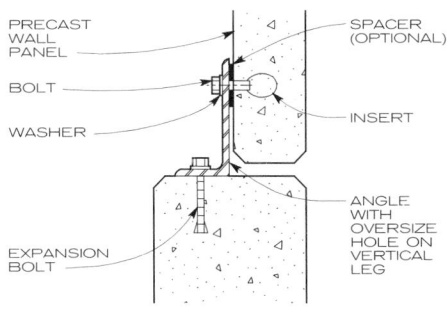

NOTE

Accommodates large tolerance with expansion bolts.

BOLTED TIE-BACK

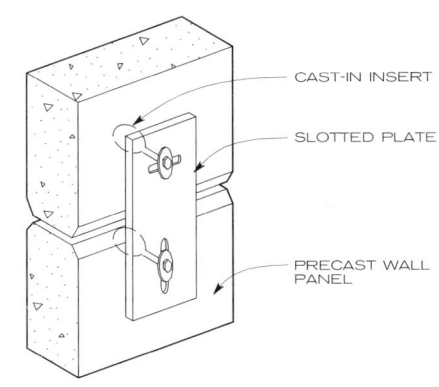

BOLTED ALIGNMENT

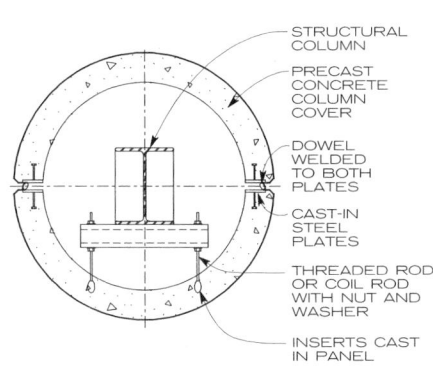

COLUMN COVER CONNECTION

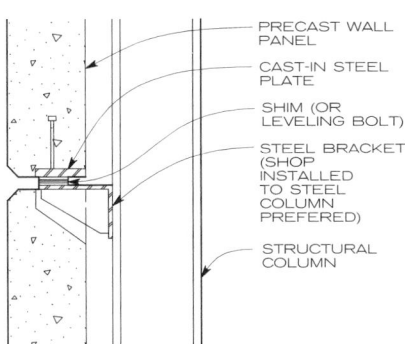

DIRECT BEARING CONNECTION

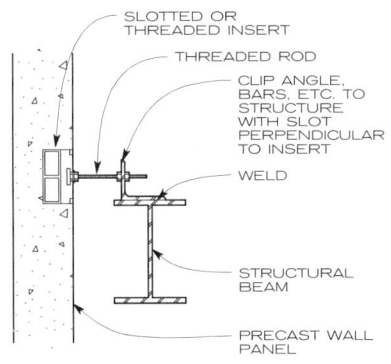

BOLTED TIE-BACK CONNECTION

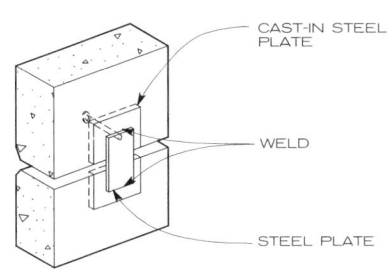

NOTES

1. Good shear transfer.
2. Rigid connection.
3. Possible volume change restraint problems.

WELDED ALIGNMENT

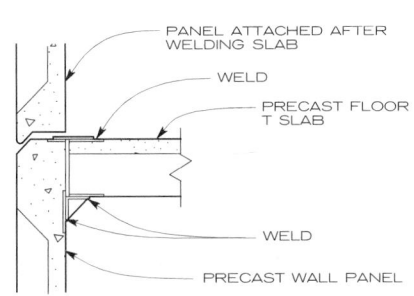

NOTES

1. Avoid use of this detail at both ends of slab to prevent excessive restraint.
2. Rotation of wall elements and effects on bracing wall connections and volume changes must be considered.

SLAB-TO-WALL CONNECTION

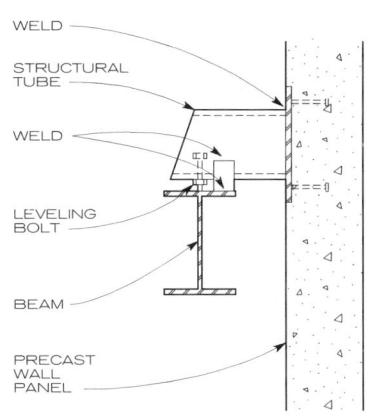

ECCENTRIC BEARING CONNECTION

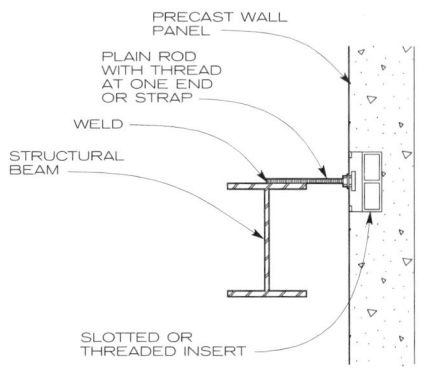

WELDED TIE-BACK CONNECTION

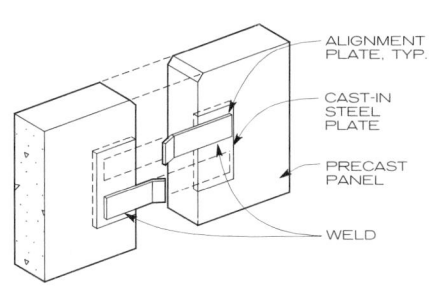

NOTE

Alignment plate is welded to one plate only to allow for possible volume change of panels.

WELDED ALIGNMENT

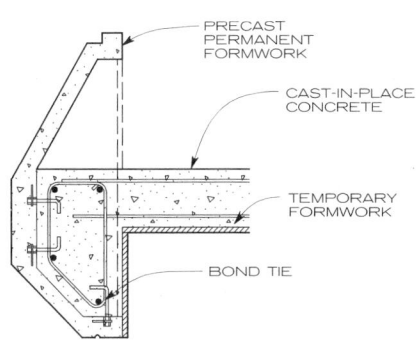

NOTE

One-piece spandrels may require support and restrict placement of concrete.

PRECAST PERMANENT FORMWORK

Sidney Freedman; Precast/Prestressed Concrete Institute; Chicago, Illinois

PRECAST CONCRETE   3

GENERAL

Tilt-up concrete construction is a fast, economical method of enclosing a building with durable, load-bearing walls. The wall panel units are formed and cast horizontally at the job site, on either the building slab floor or on a temporary casting slab. Since the panels do not have to be transported, there are fewer restrictions on panel size. Wood formwork is typically used to define the edges, reveals, details, and openings in the panel. Once the concrete has reached sufficient strength, the panels are lifted, or tilted up, by crane and placed on isolated or continuous foundations (usually grade beams). The panels are braced against the floor slab or a brace foundation until they are tied to the roof and floor system and become an integral part of the completed structure. Although tilt-up concrete construction is mainly restricted to buildings of one story, walls up to four stories tall have been cast and lifted into position.

DESIGN

Panel thickness varies from $5\frac{1}{2}$ to $11\frac{1}{4}$ in. depending on height, loads, span, depth of reveals, surface finish, local codes, and construction practices. Full-height panel widths of 20 ft and weights of 30,000 to 50,000 lb are typical. Spans of 30 ft are common for spandrel panels, as are cantilevers of 10 to 15 ft. Panels are designed structurally to resist lifting stresses, which frequently exceed in-place loads. Floor slab design must accommodate panel and crane loads.

FINISH

Most of the finishes used for factory precast concrete are possible in tilt-up construction. Panels can be cast either face down or face up, depending on desired finish and formwork methods. The face-down method, however, is usually easier to erect. Casting method, desired finish, and available aggregates affect concrete mix design. Control of the concrete mix design and placement of the concrete in the forms are more difficult than with factory-cast units. Discoloration occurs if cracks and joints in the casting are not sealed. Commonly used finishes are as follows:

1. Sandblasting (light, medium, or heavy exposure)
2. Fracture (similar to bushhammered)
3. Form liner (metal deck, plastic, fiberglass, EPS)
4. Paint (usually textured)
5. Brick or tile veneer
6. Aggregate (cast face down in sand bed)

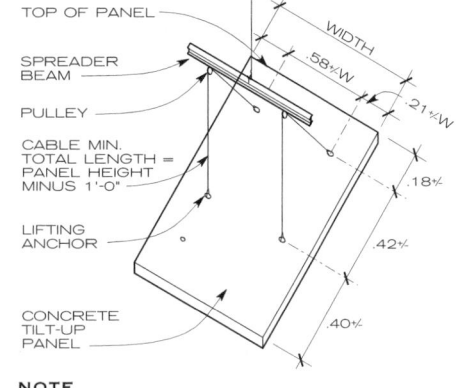

NOTE

The rigging and anchor configuration shown is the most common for tilt-up construction for plain panels without openings. Other configurations may be required depending on the size and shape of the panel; consult a tilt-up construction specialist.

TILT-UP PROCEDURE

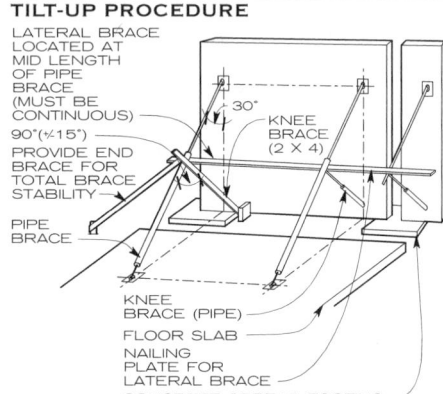

TEMPORARY CONSTRUCTION BRACING

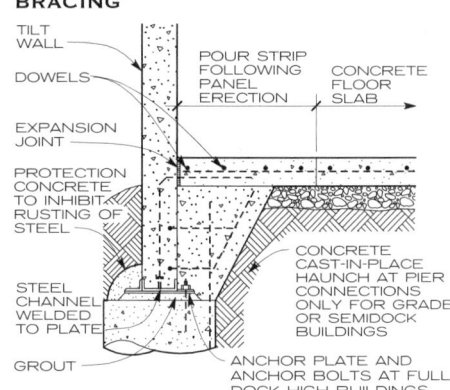

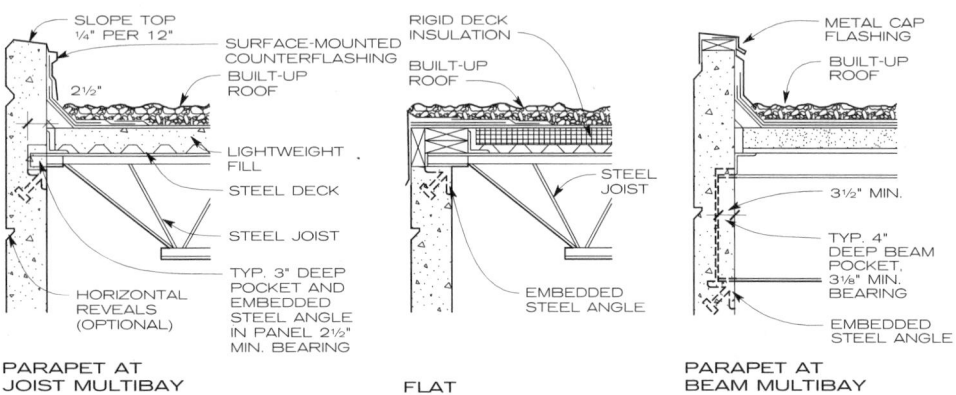

PANEL TYPES

PARAPET AT JOIST MULTIBAY

FLAT

PARAPET AT BEAM MULTIBAY

PIER CONNECTION (SECTION)

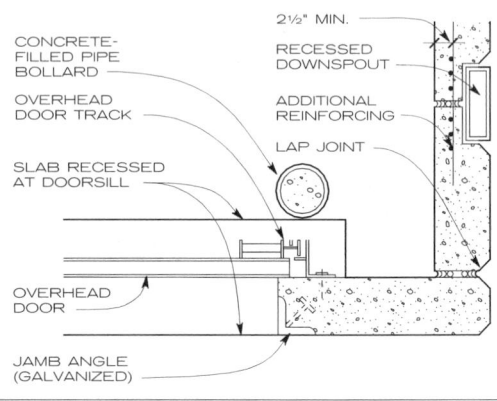

LOAD-BEARING PANEL CONNECTIONS AT ROOF (SECTIONS)

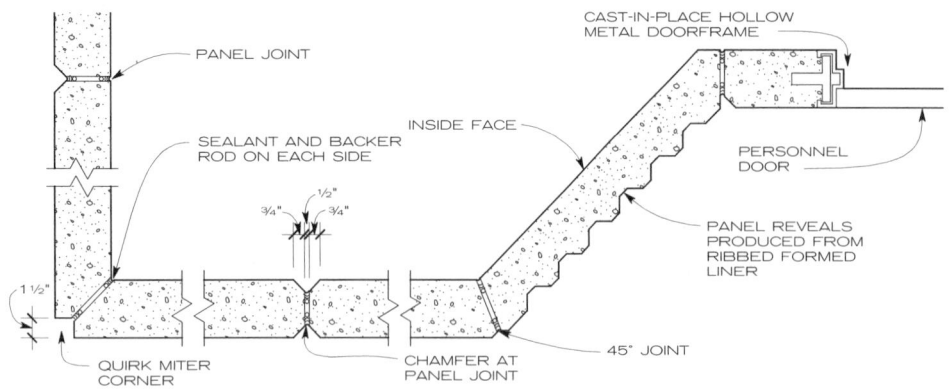

PANEL DETAILS (PLAN)

Haynes Whaley Associates, Structural Engineers; Houston, Texas
Robert P. Foley, P.E.; Con/Steel Tilt-up Systems; Dayton, Ohio

 PRECAST CONCRETE

PROPERTIES OF METALS

Basic metals and their alloys are classified in two broad categories, ferrous and nonferrous. Ferrous metals are mainly iron, and nonferrous metal alloys normally contain no iron.

FERROUS METALS

Iron, steel, and their alloys are usually the most cost-effective metal choices for structural applications.

Iron that contains no trace of carbon is soft, ductile, and easily worked, but it rusts in a relatively short time and is susceptible to corrosion by most acids.

The characteristics of the many types of cast iron vary widely among six basic groups: gray, malleable, ductile, white, compacted graphite, and high alloy iron. All cast irons have high compressive strengths, but tensile and yield strengths vary widely depending on basic type. Cast iron is relatively corrosion-resistant but cannot be hammered or beaten into shapes.

Gray irons are rather brittle because they have a high carbon and silicon content. Castings of gray iron possess excellent for damping (absorbing vibrations) and are produced in eight ASTM classes or grades with tensile-strength ratings from 20,000 to 60,000 psi. Applications include decorative shapes, such as fences and posts, gratings, and stair components, as well as utility uses such as manhole covers and fireplugs.

Malleable iron, which is more expensive than gray iron, has been used for decades in applications that require great toughness and high ductility. This low-carbon white iron is cast, reheated, and slowly cooled, or annealed, to improve its workability.

Ductile iron is made by adding magnesium to molten iron shortly before the metal is poured into molds. The magnesium alters the surface-tension mechanism of the molten iron and precipitates the carbon out as small spheres instead of flakes, which make the iron casting more ductile. Ductile iron is less brittle, stiffer, stronger, and more shock-resistant than gray iron. Ductile iron castings are more expensive than gray iron but usually less than malleable iron. Ductile iron is the fastest growing segment of the metal casting industry.

Ductile irons are produced in strength ratings from 55,000 to 130,000 psi. Ductile castings using a special austempering heat-treating process offer much higher tensile strengths, ranging from 125,000 to 230,000 psi. Called ADI castings, they rival or surpass certain alloy steel castings in tensile and yield strengths.

White iron castings, which are extremely hard and brittle, are used primarily in industrial machinery parts that experience high wear and require abrasion resistance.

The characteristics of compacted graphite iron fall between those of gray and ductile iron. The properties of this metal are so difficult to control during production that very few metal casters manufacture it.

High alloy irons are gray, ductile, or white irons with an alloy content of 3 to more than 30%. Their properties are significantly different from those of unalloyed irons.

Wrought iron or steel is relatively soft, corrosion- and fatigue-resistant, and machinable. It is easily worked, making it ideal for railings, grilles, fences, screens, and various types of ornamental work. It is commercially available in bars, rods, tubing, sheets, and plates.

Carbon steel is iron that contains low to medium amounts of carbon. A higher carbon content increases metal strength and hardness but reduces its ductility and weldability. The corrosion resistance of carbon steels is improved by galvanizing, which is a hot zinc dipping process, or applying an organic coating. Some architectural uses include structural shapes such as welded fabrications or castings, metal studs and joists, fasteners, wall grilles, and ceiling suspension grids.

High strength, low alloy (HSLA) steels have better corrosion resistance than carbon steels, and they are chosen when weight is a consideration and higher strength is specified. Low alloy steels are seldom used in exterior architectural applications that involve water runoff because adjacent materials could become stained with rust.

Typical elements used to modify steel include the following:

1. Aluminum for surface hardening.
2. Chromium for corrosion resistance.
3. Copper for atmospheric corrosion resistance.
4. Manganese in small amounts for additional hardening, in larger amounts for better wear resistance.
5. Molybdenum, combined with other metals such as chromium and nickel, to increase corrosion resistance and raise tensile strength without reducing ductility.
6. Nickel to increase tensile strength without reducing ductility; in high concentrations, nickel improves corrosion resistance.
7. Silicon to strengthen low alloy steels and improve oxidation resistance; larger amounts produce hard, brittle castings that are resistant to corrosive chemicals.
8. Sulfer for free machining, especially.
9. Titanium to prevent intergranular corrosion of stainless steels.
10. Tungsten, vanadium, and cobalt for hardness and corrosion resistance.

Stainless steels are at least 11.5% chromium. Nickel is added to boost atmospheric corrosion resistance; molybdenum is added when maximum corrosion resistance is needed, such as when iron will come into contact with sea water. Stainless steel is used in construction for flashing, coping, fasciae, wall panels, floor plates, gratings, handrails, hardware, fasteners, and anchors. Decorative shapes and statuary can be cast in stainless steel.

NONFERROUS METALS

Nonferrous metals and their alloys can be categorized into seven major groups for architectural applications: those based on aluminum, copper (pure copper, brasses, and bronzes), lead, zinc, tin, nickel, and magnesium. Another approach is to divide nonferrous alloys into two groups: heavy metals (copper-, zinc-, lead-, and nickel-based) and light metals (aluminum- and magnesium- based).

ALUMINUM

The nonferrous metal workhorse for architectural applications is aluminum. It has good forming and casting characteristics and offers good corrosion resistance. When exposed to air, aluminum does not oxidize progressively because a hard, thin oxide coating forms on the surface and seals the metal from its environment.

Aluminum and its alloys, numbering in the hundreds, are widely available in common commercial forms. Aluminum alloy sheets can be formed, drawn, stamped, or spun. Many wrought or cast aluminum alloys can be welded, brazed, or soldered, and aluminum surfaces readily accept a wide variety of finishes, both mechanical and chemical.

Although it is light in weight, commercially pure aluminum has a tensile strength of about 13,000 psi. Most aluminum alloys lose strength at elevated temperatures. At subzero temperatures, on the other hand, aluminum is stronger than at room temperature but no less ductile. Cold-working the metal may nearly double its tensile strength. Aluminum can be further strengthened by alloying it with elements such as manganese, silicon, copper, magnesium, zinc, or lithium. The manganese-based aluminum alloy 3003 is used for roofing, sheet metal, siding, and electrical conduit.

BRASS, COPPER, AND BRONZE

Good thermal and electrical conductivity, corrosion resistance, and easy forming and joining all make copper and its alloys useful in construction. However, copper and many of its alloys have relatively low strength-to-weight ratios, and their strength is even further reduced at elevated temperatures. These metals are offered in rod, plate, strip, sheet, and tube shapes; forgings; castings; and electrical wire.

These metals can be grouped according to composition in several general categories: copper, high-copper alloys, and many types of brass and bronze. Monel metal is a copper-nickel alloy that offers excellent corrosion resistance; it is often used for corrosion-resistant fasteners.

Bronze originally was a copper-tin alloy, but today there are aluminum bronzes, silicon bronzes, and leaded phosphor bronzes, among others. Phosphor bronze is a copper-tin-phosphorus alloy; and leaded phosphor bronze is composed of copper, lead, tin, and phosphorus.

Brass is copper with zinc as its principal alloying element. It is important to know that some brass alloys may be called bronzes even though they have little or no tin in them. Some common nonbronze brass alloys are commercial bronze (90% copper, 10% zinc), naval brass (60% copper, 29% zinc, and 1% tin), Muntz metal (60% copper, 40% zinc), and manganese bronze (58% copper, 39% zinc, and 1% tin and iron). When a metal is identified as bronze, the alloy cannot contain zinc or nickel; if it does, it is probably brass. Architectural brasses and bronzes are actually all brasses; they are used for doors, windows, door and window frames, railings, trim and grilles, and finish hardware. Muntz metal, also called malleable brass, is a bronze alloy resembling extruded architectural bronze in color. It is available in sheet and strip and is used in flat surfaces in architectural compositions in connection with extruded architectural bronze.

Copper-based alloys characteristically form adherent films that are relatively impervious to corrosion and protect the base metal from further attack. Certain alloy systems darken rather rapidly from brown to black outdoors. Under most outdoor weather conditions, however, copper surfaces, such as roofs or statuary, develop a blue-green patina. Lacquer coatings can help retain the original alloy color.

LEAD

An extremely dense metal, lead is corrosion-resistant and easily worked. Alloys are added to it to improve properties such as hardness and strength. Typical applications of lead include waterproofing, sound and vibration isolation, and radiation shielding. It can be combined with tin alloy to plate iron or steel, which is commonly called "terneplate." Care should be taken how and where lead is used because lead vapors and lead dust are toxic if ingested.

ZINC

Although it is corrosion-resistant in water and air, zinc is brittle and low in strength. Its major use is in galvanizing (dipping hot iron or steel in molten zinc), although zinc is also used to create sand-cast or die-cast components. Major building industry uses are roofing, flashing, nails, plumbing hardware, structural parts, and decorative shapes.

TIN

Key properties of tin are its low melting point (450° F), relative softness, good formability, and readiness to form alloys. Principal uses for tin are as a constituent of solder, a coating for steel (tinplate, terneplate), and an alloy with other metals that can be cast, rolled, extruded, or atomized. Tin is most popular as an alloy for copper, antimony, lead, bismuth, silver, and zinc. Pewter alloys contain 1 to 8% antimony and 0.5 to 3% copper. Alloy metal in tin solders ranges from 40% lead to no lead and 3.5% silver.

NICKEL

Whitish in color, nickel is used for plating other metals or as a base for chromium plating. Nickel polishes well and does not tarnish. It is also widely applied as an additive in iron and steel alloys as well as other metal alloys. Nickel-iron castings are more ductile and more resistant to corrosion than conventional cast iron. Adding nickel makes steel more resistant to impact.

CHROMIUM

A hard, steel-gray metal, chromium is commonly used to plate other metals, including iron, steel, brass, and bronze. Plated cast shapes can be brightly polished and do not tarnish. Several steel alloys, such as stainless plate, contain as much as 18% chromium. Chromium does not rust, which makes chromium alloys excellent for exterior uses.

MAGNESIUM

Lightest of all metals used in construction, pure magnesium is not strong enough for general structural functions. (For comparison, if a block of steel weighs 1,000 lb, equal volumes of aluminum and magnesium weigh 230 lb and 186 lb respectively.) Combining other metals such as aluminum with magnesium results in lightweight alloy materials used in ladders, furniture, hospital equipment, and wheels for automobiles.

Robert C. Rodgers, P.E.; Richmond Heights, Ohio

METAL CORROSION

Corrosion, which is caused by galvanic action, occurs between dissimilar metals or between metals and other material when sufficient moisture is present to carry an electrical current. The galvanic series shown in the table below is a useful indicator of corrosion susceptibility caused by galvanic action. The metals listed are arranged in order from the least noble (most reactive to corrosion) to the most noble (least reactive to corrosion). The farther apart two metals on the list are, the greater the deterioration of the less noble one will be if they come in contact under adverse conditions.

Metal deterioration also occurs when metals come in contact with chemically active materials, particularly when moisture is present. For example, aluminum corrodes when in direct contact with concrete or mortar, and steel corrodes when in contact with certain treated woods.

Pitting and concentration cell corrosion are other types of metal deterioration. Pitting takes place when particles or bubbles of gas are deposited on a metal surface. Oxygen deficiency under these deposits sets up anodic areas, which cause pitting. Concentration cell corrosion is similar to galvanic corrosion; the difference is in the electrolytes. Concentration cell corrosion can be produced by differences in ion concentration, oxygen concentration, or foreign matter adhering to the surface.

SHAPING AND FABRICATION OF METALS

Many different manufacturing processes are applied to metal to produce structural forms and shapes required in the construction and ornamentation of buildings.

Rolling hot or cold metal between pressurized rollers produces most of the readily available, standard construction material shapes. Baked enamel-coated aluminum is cold rolled to make siding and gutters.

In the extruding process, heated metal ingots or bars are pushed through a die orifice to produce a wide variety of simple and complex shapes. Sizes are limited only by the size or capacity of the die.

THE GALVANIC SERIES

Anode (least noble) +	Magnesium, magnesium alloys
	Zinc
	Aluminum 1100
	Cadmium
	Aluminum 2024-T4
	Steel or iron, cast iron
	Chromium iron (active)
	Ni-Resist
	Type 304, 316 stainless (active)
	Hastelloy "C"
	Lead, tin
Electric current flows from positive (+) to negative (−)	Nickel (Inconel) (active)
	Hastelloy "B"
	Brasses, copper, bronzes, copper-nickel alloys, monel
	Silver solder
	Nickel (Inconel) (passive)
	Chromium iron (passive)
	Type 304, 316 stainless (passive)
	Silver
	Titanium
Cathode (most noble) −	Graphite, gold, platinum

Casting is a process in which molten metal is poured into molds or forced into dies and allowed to solidify in the shape of the mold or die. The casting process is used with virtually all metals; however, surface quality and physical characteristics are greatly affected by the metal alloy and casting process selected. Almost all metals can be cast in sand molds. Only aluminum, zinc, and magnesium are ordinarily cast in metal dies in what is called either a die-casting or permanent-mold process. Round, hollow building products such as cast-iron pipe for plumbing and sewer applications are made by centrifugal casting machines.

In the drawing process, either hot or cold metal is pulled through dies that alter or reduce its cross-sectional shape to produce architectural product configurations. Common drawn products are sheets, tubes, pipes, rods, bars, and wires. Drawing can be used with all metals except iron.

Forging is hammering hot metal or pressing cold metal to a desired shape in dies of a harder metal. The process usually improves the strength and surface characteristics of the metal. Aluminum, copper, and steel can be forged.

Machining is used to finish areas of castings or forgings requiring highly precise fits or contours. Shapes can also be machined from heavy plate or solid blocks of metal.

Bending produces curved shapes in tubing, pipe, and extrusions.

Brake forming of metal plate or sheet metal is a process of successive pressings to achieve shapes with straight-line angles.

In the spinning process, ductile types of sheet metal (usually copper or aluminum) are shaped with tools while being spun on an axis.

Embossing and coining are stamped metal with textured or raised patterns.

Blanking is shearing, sawing, or cutting metal sheets with a punch press to achieve a desired configuration.

Perforating is punching or drilling holes through flat plate or sheet metal.

WEIGHTS OF METALS FOR BUILDINGS

MATERIAL	SPECIFIC GRAVITY	DENSITY	
		(LB/CU FT)	(LB/CU IN.)
Magnesium	1.76	110	0.064
Aluminum	2.77	173	0.100
Zinc	7.14	446	0.258
Cast iron	7.22	450	0.260
Wrought iron	7.70	480	0.278
Steel	7.85	490	0.283
Brass	8.47	529	0.306
Copper and bronze	8.92	556	0.322
Lead	11.35	708	0.410

TYPES AND PROPERTIES OF BRASS

NAME	ARCHITECTURAL BRONZE	COMMERCIAL BRONZE	MUNTZ METAL
Composition (%) Copper (Cu) Zinc (Zn) Lead (Pb)	56.5 41.25 2.25	90.0 10.0	60.0 40.0
Color	Bronze	Bronze	Light yellow
Cold workability	Very poor	Excellent	Fair
Machinability	Good	Poor	Good
Weldability	Poor	Gas, carbon arc, metal arc	Gas, carbon arc, metal arc, spot and seam welding for thin sheets
Hot workability (and soldering and polishing)	Very good	Very good	Very good
Other properties	Excellent forging and free-machining	Very ductile	High strength; low ductility

Piercing punches holes through metal without removing any of the metal.

Fusion welding is used to join metal pieces by melting filler metal (welding rod) and the adjacent edges briefly with a torch and then allowing the molten metal to solidify. Two common types of fusion welding are electric-arc and gas. Electric-arc or metallic-arc welding normally uses metal welding rods as electrodes in the welding tool.

Gas welding is also known as oxyacetylene welding because it uses a mixture of oxygen and acetylene to fuel the flames produced by the blowtorch. Oxyacetylene blowtorches are widely used in construction work to cut through metal structural beams and metal plates.

Soldering is a metal joining process that uses either hard or soft solder. The metal pieces being joined together do not melt as they do in the welding process because solders melt at much lower temperatures. Soft solders consist of tin with a high percentage of lead and melt at temperatures of 360° to 370°F. Hard solders are composed of tin and a low content of antimony or silver and melt at temperatures ranging from 430 to 460°F.

Brazing, which is sometimes called hard soldering, also joins two pieces of metal together by torch melting a filler rod material between them. The filler has a high content of copper and melts between 800 and 900°F.

MELTING TEMPERATURES OF METALS

BASE METAL	MELTING TEMPERATURES	
	DEGREES C	DEGREES F
Aluminum	660	1220
Antimony	631	1168
Cadmium	321	610
Chromium	1857	3375
Cobalt	1495	2723
Copper	1083	1981
Gold	1064	1947
Iron	1535	2795
Lead	328	622
Magnesium	649	1200
Manganese	1244	2271
Nickel	1453	2647
Silver	962	1764
Tin	232	450
Zinc	420	788
Zirconium	1852	3366

Robert C. Rodgers, P.E.; Richmond Heights, Ohio

 METAL MATERIALS, FINISHES, AND COATINGS

GENERAL

The finishes commonly used on architectural metals fall into three categories:

MECHANICAL FINISHES are the result of physically changing the surface of the metal through mechanical means: the forming process itself or a subsequent procedure performed either before or after the metal is fabricated into an end-use product.

CHEMICAL FINISHES are achieved by means of chemicals, which may or may not have a physical effect on the surface of the metal.

COATINGS are applied as finishes, either to the metal stock or the fabricated product. These coatings either change the metal itself, through a process of chemical or electrochemical conversion, or they are simply applied to the metal surface.

Application environments, service requirements, and aesthetics together determine which metal finish or coating is best to specify. Finishes are usually selected for both appearance and function: Chromium plating on metal bathroom water faucets and handles or baked enamel on sheet metal lighting fixtures, for example, must be attractive as well as functionally protective.

For structural and exterior metal building products, such as steel framing products, metal siding, and outdoor lighting fixtures, function and operating environments are more important criteria. From a design standpoint, it is important to recognize how various finishes and coatings resist wear, corrosion, and erosion. To choose the right coating or finish, architects must know which material or process is best suited for a specific application.

MECHANICAL FINISHES

AS-FABRICATED FINISHES are the texture and surface appearance given to a metal by the fabrication process.

BUFFED FINISHES are produced by successive polishing and buffing operations using fine abrasives, lubricants, and soft fabric wheels. Polishing and buffing improve edge and surface finishes and render many types of cast parts more durable, efficient, and safe.

PATTERNED FINISHES are available in various textures and designs. They are produced by passing an as-fabricated sheet between two matched-design rollers, embossing patterns on both sides of the sheet, or between a smooth roll and a design roll, embossing or coining on one side of the sheet only.

DIRECTIONAL TEXTURED FINISHES are produced by making tiny parallel scratches on the metal surface using a belt or wheel and fine abrasive, or by hand rubbing with steel wool. Metal treated this way has a smooth, satiny sheen.

PEENED FINISHES are achieved by firing a stream of small steel shot at a metal surface at high velocity. The primary aim of shot peening is increasing the fatigue strength of the component; the decorative finish is a by-product. Other nondirectional textured finishes are produced by blasting metal, under controlled conditions, with silica sand, glass beads, and aluminum oxide.

CHEMICAL FINISHES

CHEMICAL CLEANING cleans the metal surface without affecting it in any other way. This finish is achieved with chlorinated and hydrocarbon solvents and inhibited chemical cleaners or solvents (for aluminum and copper) and pickling, chlorinated, and alkaline solutions (for iron and steel).

ETCHED FINISHES produce a matte, frosted surface with varying degrees of roughness by treating the metal with an acid (sulfuric and nitric acid) or alkali solution.

The BRIGHT FINISH process, not used widely, involves chemical or electrolytic brightening of a metal surface, typically aluminum.

CONVERSION COATING is typically categorized as a chemical finish, but since a layer or coating is produced by a chemical reaction, it could be considered a coating as well. Conversion coatings typically prepare the surface of a metal for painting or for receiving another type of finish but are also used to produce a patina or statuary finish. A component is treated with a dilute solution of phosphoric acid or sulfuric acid and other chemicals that convert the surface of the metal to an integral, mildly protective layer of insoluble crystalline phosphate or sulphate or the like. Such coatings can be applied by either spray or immersion and provide temporary resistance to a mildly corrosive environment. They can be specified for gray, ductile, and malleable iron castings as well as steel castings, forgings, or weldments, such as railings and outdoor furniture.

COATINGS

ORGANIC COATINGS on metal can provide protection only or serve both protective and decorative functions. The former category includes primers or undercoats, pigmented topcoats in hidden areas, and clear finishes. Organic coatings serving double duty include pigmented coatings in visible areas, clear finishes used for gloss, and transparent or translucent clear finishes with dyes added.

Organic coatings usually fall under the general categories of paints, varnishes, enamels, lacquers, plastisols, organisols, and powders. Literally hundreds of different organic coating formulations offer an almost unlimited range of properties. Many organic coatings are applied with brushes and rollers, but dipping and spraying of paints account for most industrial and commercial building projects. Dipping is useful for coating complex metal parts, but spraying is used for most architectural applications. Spraying is fast and inexpensive, and new computer-controlled guns can follow even complex curvatures. Conventional spraying, however, has two disadvantages: For one thing, there is no easy, inexpensive way to collect and re-use the coating material. And when solvent-based paints are used, there is the added problem of meeting environmental restrictions.

ELECTRODEPOSITION, an increasingly popular alternative to spraying, is similar to electroplating, except that organic resins are deposited instead of metal. Electrodeposition is based on the principles of electrophoresis—the movement of charged particles in a liquid under the influence of an applied voltage.

Electrodeposition offers several advantages: The coating builds up to a uniform thickness without runs or sags; very little paint is wasted; low levels of volatile organic compounds (VOCs) are emitted; and coatings can be deposited even into deeply recessed areas of a complex shape. Electrodeposition also has disadvantages. Coating thickness is limited, and because only one coat can be applied this way, subsequent coats must be sprayed.

POWDER COATING is perhaps the best known environmentally acceptable painting process. Powder coatings offer several advantages. Because the paints are solventless, they are safer and "greener." In addition, the paints cost less and last a long time.

Powdered paints are formulated in much the same way as solvent-based paints, with the same pigments, fillers, and extenders, but are dry at room temperatures. Heat-reactive or "heat-latent" hardeners, catalysts, or cross-linkers are used as curing agents.

Powder coatings are either thermoplastic or thermosetting. As the term implies, thermoplastic coatings, which include vinyl, polyethylene, and certain polyesters, are melted by heat during application. Before such coatings are applied, the surface must be primed to ensure good adhesion. Thermosetting paints undergo a chemical change; they cannot be remelted by heat. The thermosets do not require a primer. Coating powders include epoxies, polyurethanes, acrylics, and polyesters.

COMPARATIVE APPLICABILITY OF VARIOUS FINISHES FOR ARCHITECTURAL APPLICATIONS

TYPE OF FINISH OR TREATMENT	METAL			
	ALUMINUM	COPPER ALLOYS	STAINLESS STEEL	CARBON STEEL AND IRON
MECHANICAL FINISHES				
As fabricated	Common to all of the metals (produced by hot rolling, extruding, or casting)			
Bright rolled	Commonly used (produced by cold rolling)			Not used
Directional grit textured	Commonly used (produced by polishing, buffing, hand rubbing, brushing, or cold rolling)			Rarely used
Nondirectional matte textured	Commonly used (produced by sand or shot blasting)			Rarely used
Bright polished	Commonly used (produced by polishing and buffing)			Not used
Patterned	Available in light sheet gauges of all metals			
CHEMICAL FINISHES				
Nonetch cleaning	Commonly used on all of the metals			
Matte finish	Etched finishes widely used	Seldom used	Not used	Not used
Bright finish	Limited uses	Rarely used	Not used	Not used
Conversion coatings	Widely used as pretreatment for painting	Widely used to provide added color variation	Not used	Widely used as pretreatment for painting
COATINGS				
Organic	Widely used	Opaque types rarely used: transparent types common	Sometimes used	Most important type of finish
Anodic	Most important type of finish	Not used	Not used	Not used
Vitreous	Widely used	Limited use	Not used	Widely used
Metallic	Rarely used	Limited use	Limited use	Widely used
Laminated	Substantial uses	Limited use	Not used	Substantial uses

NOTE

For more information, see the "Metal Finishes Manual for Architectural and Metal Products," published by the Architectural Metal Products Division of the National Association of Architectural Metal Manufacturers.

Robert C. Rodgers, P.E.; Richmond Heights, Ohio

GENERAL

The two most common methods of applying powdered finishes to metal are spraying and dipping, the same as those used for solvent-based paint. Electrostatic spraying is used to apply powder films from 1 to 5 mil thick. A mixture of air and powder moves from a hopper to a spray gun. The mixture is charged electrostatically as it passes through the spray gun, causing it to stick to any grounded metal object. Powder that falls to the floor is recycled.

For coatings thicker than 5 mil, fluidized-bed dipping is used. The powder is placed in a special tank into which air is blown, turning the powder into a fluid-like mass. Parts are dipped in the "fluid" and baked to cure the finish.

ANODIC COATINGS

Anodic oxides are widely used to protect aluminum and many of its alloys from corrosion. When the metal is anodized in one of a variety of acids, a protective oxide is formed on the surface. Depending on the acid, the oxide may range from thin and nonporous to thick and porous. Three types of anodizing are used for aluminum: chromic, sulfuric, and hardcoat.

CHROMIC ANODIZING results in a relatively soft coating and is the least used of the three types, but it does offer several advantages. It has excellent corrosion resistance, so rinsing is not as important. It is suitable for complex cast parts and offers a coating of the most consistently uniform thickness and the most enduring fatigue strength.

SULFURIC ANODIZING, the most widely used method, produces a harder coating than chromic anodizing, but it can be scratched. It offers a pleasing appearance and can be dyed in several colors. Corrosion resistance is good.

HARDCOAT ANODIZING produces a relatively thick, extremely hard coating that can be dyed in a range of colors. Corrosion resistance is good. Hardcoats are porous, making them suitable as a base for paints and adhesives.

Since all anodic processes produce porous aluminum-oxide coatings, sealing is usually desirable. The coating is immersed in hot water, the oxide is hydrated, and the pores swell shut. Several manufacturers claim that their sealing agents do the same thing through catalytic action at lower temperatures. Chromic- and sulfuric-anodized coatings nearly always are sealed, but hardcoats are not.

VITREOUS COATINGS are composed of inorganic glossy materials (glass). Porcelain enamels are the most commonly used vitreous coating for architectural applications. Although one of the hardest and most durable finishes, they are brittle. Deformation of metal surfaces can cause cracking and splitting. Porcelain enamel coatings come in a wide range of colors and finishes and are typically applied to steel and aluminum (bathtubs, sinks, column covers). Embossed patterns and textures may be applied by altering the metal backing surface or the coating itself.

HOT DIPPING of ferrous metal objects consists of immersing clean parts into a molten bath of the desired coating metal. In general, molten aluminum, lead, zinc, and some alloys can be applied as hot-dip coatings to irons. Each offers specific advantages. Hot-dip coatings are particularly suitable for intricately shaped cast ferrous items such as metal roofing components and nails and other fasteners.

METALLIC PLATING is done by either electrodeposition or electroplating.

In electrodeposition, an electrical current is carried across an electrolyte and an organic resin substance deposited on an electrode (the metal object being painted). In electroplating, the "substance" is a metal, such as chromium, in an electrolyte. Water usually serves as the solvent in the electrolyte. Although chromium is commonly used for plating, many metals can be deposited on the substrate.

Similarly, a wide range of plating quality is available. For example, a thin coating of zinc will protect a metal component from rust or corrosion for a short time. Chromium plating, on the other hand, protects longer and looks better.

Materials widely used to plate complex metal components include bronze, brass, chromium, cadmium, chromates, copper, lead, lead-tin, nickel, phosphates, silver, tin-nickel, and tin-zinc. Not all of these materials can be deposited on all metal substrates. For example, zinc electroplate can be used on steel but not on cast iron. Therefore, coating/substrate compatibility is a crucial consideration in matching coating performance to application requirements. Typical applications for plating include food servicing areas, plumbing fixtures, exterior metal, and architectural products.

LAMINATED COATINGS

Lamination involves bonding preformed plastic films to metals with adhesives. Laminated coatings provide finishes for products such as interior paneling, partitions, and exterior metalwork. Three types of plastic film are widely used: polyvinyl chloride (PVC), polyvinyl fluoride (PVF), and acrylic.

PVC films provide excellent stain and abrasion resistance. Available in five or six colors, these laminates may come with graining or embossing to simulate wood grain, leather, or fabric. Film thicknesses range from 0.004 in. to 0.041 in., but most common and most economical are those from 0.008 and 0.014 in.

PVF films are usually laminated in a thickness of 0.002 in. and have a smooth, medium gloss surface. Despite their thinness, they are very strong, tough, and weather resistant, making them particularly suited to exterior applications such as siding materials. Their color range is limited, but they resist staining and chemical damage well.

Acrylic films are low cost products that stand up well to weather and are widely used for exterior metalwork. They resist UV radiation and yellowing and retain their flexibility with aging. They are usually applied in a thickness of 0.003 in. and are reasonably priced.

REPRESENTATIVE ARCHITECTURAL USES AND COMPARATIVE PROPERTIES OF COATINGS

BINDER TYPE	TYPICAL USES[1]	COST	OUTDOOR LIFE (YEARS)	COLOR STABLE, EXTERIOR	GLOSS RETENTION, EXTERIOR	STAIN RESISTANCE	WEATHER RESISTANCE	ABRASION AND IMPACT RESISTANCE	FLEXIBILITY	WATER REDUCIBLE AVAILABLE	CLEAR AVAILABLE	WELDABLE AS PRIMER
Acrylics												
Solvent-reducible		M	10	yes	G	F	G	G	G	—	yes	yes[2]
Water-reducible:	Residential siding and similar products; cabinets and implements; clear topcoats											
air dried		M	5–10	yes	F	F	G	G	G	yes	yes	yes[2]
baked		M	15–20	yes	G–E	F	G–E	G	G	yes	yes	yes[2]
Alkyds	Exterior primers and enamels	L–M	5–9	no	G	F	F	F	F–G	yes	yes	yes[2]
Cellulose (acetate or butyrate)	Decorative high-gloss finishes	M	NA	yes	G	F	G	G	G	no	yes	no
Chlorinated rubber	Corrosion-resistant paints; swimming pool coatings; protection of dissimilar metals	M	10	yes	F	F	G	G	G	no	no	no
Chloro sulfonated polyethylene	Paints for piping, tanks, valves, etc.	VH	15	yes	NA	F	E	F–G	E	no	no	no
Epoxy	Moisture- and alkali-resistant coatings; nondecorative interior uses requiring high chemical resistance	H–VH	15–20	no	P	G	G–E	E	G	no	no	yes[2]
Fluorocarbons	High-performance exterior coatings; industrial siding; curtain walls	VH	20+	yes	E	E	E	E	G	no	no	no
Phenol formaldehyde	Chemical- and moisture-resistant coatings	M	10	no	F	F	G–E	G–E	G	no	yes	yes[2]
Polyester	Cabinets and furniture; ceiling tile; piping	H	15	some versions	G–E	G–E	G–E	G	G–E	yes	yes	no
Polyvinyl chloride	Residential siding; plastisols; industrial siding; curtain walls	H	15	yes	G	F	G–E	G–E	G–E	yes	no	yes[2]
Silicates (inorganic)	Corrosion-inhibitive primers; solvent-resistant coatings	H	NA	NA	NA	NA	NA	G	G	no	no	yes
Silicone-modified polymers	High-performance exterior coatings; industrial siding; curtain walls	H–VH	15–20	yes	G–E	G	G–E	G–E	G	yes	no	no
Urethane (aliphatic-cured)	Heavy-duty coatings for stain chemical, abrasion, and corrosion resistance	VH	20+	some versions	E	G–E	G–E	G–E	E	yes	yes	yes[2]

L–low; M–moderate; H–high; VH–very high; NA–not applicable or not available; P–poor; F–fair; G–good; E–excellent

[1] All coatings may be shop applied; all may be field applied except solvent reducible acrylics, baked acrylic, cellulose, and fluorocarbons.

[2] For light nonstructural welding only.

Robert C. Rodgers, P.E.; Richmond Heights, Ohio

 METAL MATERIALS, FINISHES, AND COATINGS

STRUCTURAL
ECONOMY OF STEEL FRAMING

The steel industry is in transition from a 36,000 psi (36 ksi) yield strength steel (ASTM A36) base to a 50,000 psi (50 ksi) yield strength steel (ASTM A 572 grade 50) base. The higher yield strength is currently the most common for structural members, while most connection materials, such as angles and plates, are of 36,000 psi yield strength.

The American Institute of Steel Construction *Manual of Steel Construction* maintains column and beam load tables for both 50,000 and 36,000 psi yield strengths.

Several grades of structural carbon steel are available, including "weathering steel," which offers improved atmospheric corrosion resistance. The table below lists the characteristics of the commonly specified structural carbon steels.

STRUCTURAL STEEL DATA

ASTM DESIGNATION	STRENGTH GRADES KSI	ATMOSPHERIC CORROSION RESISTANCE	REMARKS
A 36	36		Common in connecting elements
A 572	42, 50, 60, 65	Same as A36	Common in structural members
A 588	42, 46, 50*	4 times that of carbon steel	Most commonly specified "weathering steel"
A 242	42, 46, 50*	5 to 8 times that of carbon steel	Used exposed as "weathering steel"

* 50 ksi normally provided, but reduced for material thicker than 4 in. for A 588, ³/₄ in. for A 242.

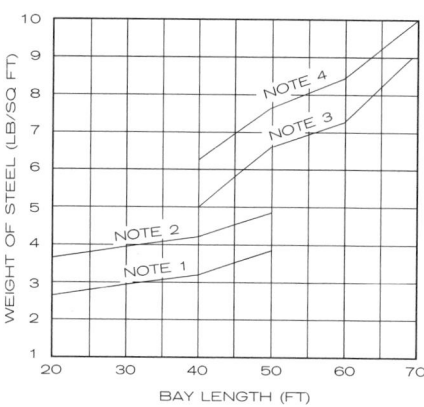

NOTES

1. The roof of a 15-ft high, one-story structure, H-series open-web joists on continuous A572 grade 50 girders (weight of A572 grade 50 columns included). Joist span equals 30 ft.

2. Same as note 1 except that joist span equals 45 ft.

3. Typical level of five-story garage, A572 grade 50 steel throughout (weight of columns included), bay width equals 20 ft.

4. Same as note 3 except that bay width equals 30 ft.

WEIGHT OF NONCOMPOSITE STRUCTURAL STEEL FLOOR OR ROOF

GENERAL NOTES

1. The weight of structural steel per square foot of floor area increases with bay size, as does the depth of the structure. Cost of structural steel may not rise as rapidly as the weight if the number of pieces to be fabricated and erected can be reduced. The improved space utilization afforded by larger bay sizes may be offset by increases in wall area and building volume necessary when structure depth is increased.

2. Steel frame economy can be improved by incorporating as many of the following into the layout and design of a structure as architectural requirements permit:

   a. Keep columns in line in both directions, and avoid offsets or omissions of columns.

   b. Design for maximum repetition of member sizes within each level and from floor to floor.

   c. Reduce the number of beams and girders per level to reduce fabrication and erection time and cost.

   d. Maximize the use of simple beam connections by bracing the structure at a limited number of moment-resisting bents or by the most efficient method, cross-bracing.

   e. Consider composite design and the effects of in-slab electric raceways or other discontinuities.

   f. Consider open-web steel joists, especially for large roofs of one-story structures and for floor framing in many applications.

3. An analysis of alternate framing schemes for a 20 x 40 ft interior bay appears in the table to the left.

4. One constant relationship illustrated in the alternate framing table is the decrease in girder depth when long beams and short girders are used. Steel for roofs or lightly loaded floors is generally the lightest when long beams and short girders are used. For heavier loadings, long girders and short filler beams should result in less steel weight. The most economical framing type (composite, noncomposite, continuous, simple spans, etc.) and arrangement must be determined for each structure, considering such factors as structure depth, building volume, wall area, mechanical system requirements, deflection or vibration limitations, and wind or seismic load interaction between floor systems and columns or shear walls.

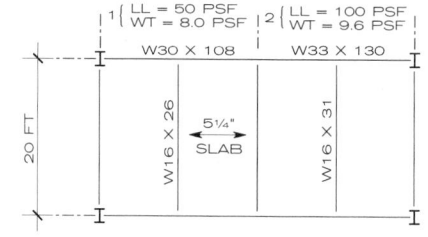

NONCOMPOSITE

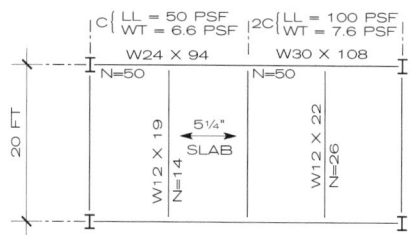

COMPOSITE

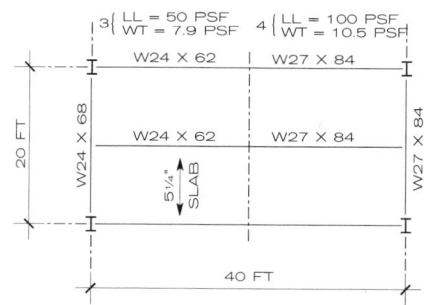

NONCOMPOSITE

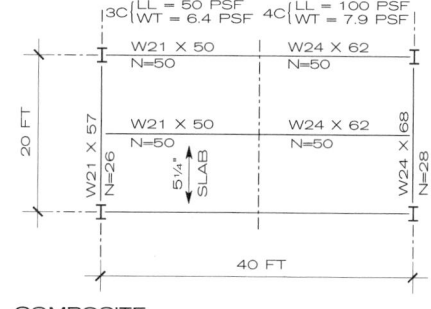

COMPOSITE

STEEL FRAMING LAYOUTS

ALTERNATE FRAMING

	SHORT BEAMS, LONG GIRDERS				LONG BEAMS, SHORT GIRDERS			
	LL = 50 PSF		LL = 100 PSF		LL = 100 PSF		LL = 100 PSF	
	1	1C	2	2C	3	3C	4	4C
Girder depth	30 in.	24 in.	33 in.	30 in.	24 in.	21 in.	27 in.	24 in.
Steel weight per bay (lb)	6400	5280	7680	6080	6320	5140	8400	6320
Weight ratio—Noncomposite: composite	1.21 : 1		1.26 : 1		1.23 : 1		1.33 :1	
Number of shear studs	0	106	0	154	0	126	0	128
Cost ratio (see note 5)	1.16 : 1		1.19 : 1		1.16 : 1		1.27 :1	

NOTES

1. Floor slab: 3¹/₄ in. lightweight concrete over 2 in. composite metal deck (5¹/₄ in. total thickness), all schemes. This provides a 2 hr fire rating without spraying the deck.

2. Additional dead load allowance for finishes, etc.: 30 psf, all schemes.

3. All steel ASTM A572 grade 50.

4. Shear studs: ³/₄ in. diameter x 3¹/₂ in. long. N=50 means 50 studs per beam.

5. The cost ratio between noncomposite and composite floor steel is approximately 95% of the weight ratio. The cost of studs accounts for the difference.

6. Vibration of floor beams should be analyzed.

American Institute of Steel Construction; Chicago, Illinois

SAFE TOTAL UNIFORMLY DISTRIBUTED LOAD (KIPS) FOR BEAMS LATERALLY SUPPORTED—ASTM A 572 GRADE 50 STEEL, ALLOWABLE STRESS DESIGN[1]

SPAN LENGTH (FT)	DEPTH[2] WEIGHT	W 6			W 8								W 10				W 10				W 12								W 14		M 14
		9	12	16	10	13	15	18	21	24	28	31	12	15	17	19	22	26	30	33	14	16	19	22	26	30	35	40	22	26	18
6		20	27	37	28	36	43	56	67	77	89	91	40	51	59	69	85	102	119	113	55	63	78	93	112	128	150		106	129	77
8		15	20	28	21	27	32	42	50	57	67	76	30	38	45	52	64	77	89	96	41	47	59	70	92	106	125	141	80	97	58
10		12	16	22	17	22	26	33	40	46	53	60	24	30	36	41	51	61	71	77	33	38	47	56	73	85	100	114	64	78	46
12		10	13	19	14	18	22	28	33	38	45	50	20	25	30	34	43	51	59	64	27	31	39	47	61	71	84	95	53	65	39
14		8.7	11	16	12	16	19	24	29	33	38	43	17	22	25	30	36	44	51	55	23	27	33	40	52	61	72	82	46	55	33
16					11	14	16	21	25	29	33	38	15	19	22	26	32	38	45	48	20	24	29	35	46	53	63	71	40	49	29
18					9	12	14	19	22	26	30	34	13	17	20	23	28	34	40	43	18	21	26	31	41	47	56	63	35	43	26
20					9	11	13	17	20	23	27	30	12	15	18	21	26	31	36	39	16	19	23	28	37	42	50	57	32	39	23
22													11	14	16	19	23	28	32	35	15	17	21	25	33	39	46	52	29	35	21
24													10	13	15	17	21	26	30	32	14	16	20	23	31	35	42	48	27	32	19

[1] For capacity of beams not shown see *AISC Manual of Steel Construction*, 2d ed. (load and resistance factor design) and 9th ed. (allowable stress design).

[2] Depth = steel designation (in.); weight = lb/ft; kip = 1000 lb.

NOTES

1. Consult structural engineer to verify lateral support.
2. Multiply loads by 1.5 to obtain approximate capacities for load and resistance factor design method.

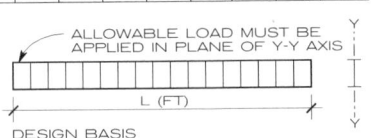

ALLOWABLE LOAD MUST BE APPLIED IN PLANE OF Y-Y AXIS

L (FT)

DESIGN BASIS

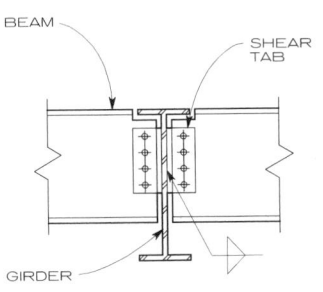

SHOP WELDED TAB FIELD HIGH STRENGTH BOLTED

SHEAR CONNECTION BEAM TO GIRDER

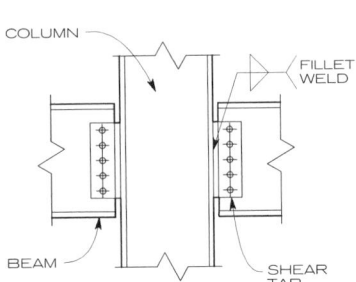

SHOP WELDED TAB FIELD HIGH STRENGTH BOLTED

NONMOMENT CONNECTION BEAM TO COLUMN FLANGE

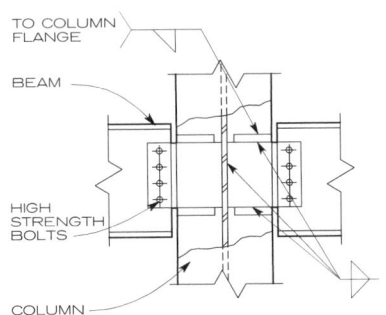

SHOP WEDED TAB TO COLUMN WEB AND PLATES FIELD H.S. BOLTED

NONMOMENT CONNECTION BEAM TO COLUMN WEB

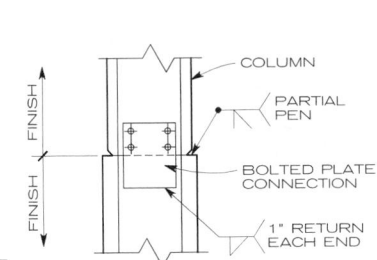

WEB-FIELD H.S. BOLTED FLANGE—PARTIAL PENETRATION

COLUMN SPLICE FLANGE AND WEB

CONNECTIONS AND SPLICES

SAFE TOTAL CONCENTRIC LOAD (KIPS) FOR COLUMNS—ASTM A 572 GRADE 50 STEEL (W SHAPES) AND ASTM A 500 STEEL (TS-SHAPES AND PIPE, 46 KSI), ALLOWABLE STRESS DESIGN *

DESIGNATION	**	6	7	8	9	10	11	12	13	14	15	16	17	18	19	20	22	24
W4	13	79	70	60	49	40	33	28	24	20	18	16						
W6	15	108	102	96	89	82	74	66	57	49	43	38	33	30	27	24	20	17
	20	145	137	129	121	112	102	92	81	70	61	54	47	42	38	34	28	24
	25	182	173	163	152	141	129	117	103	90	78	69	61	54	49	44	36	31
W8	24	178	170	161	152	142	132	121	109	97	85	74	66	59	53	48	39	33
	28	208	198	188	178	166	154	142	128	114	100	88	78	69	62	56	46	39
	31	241	234	226	217	208	199	189	179	168	156	145	132	119	107	97	80	67
Pipe 3", 3.5" O.D.	0.216	38	36	34	31	28	25	22	19	16	14	12	11	10	9			
	0.300	52	48	45	41	37	33	28	24	21	18	16	14	12	11			
	0.600	91	84	77	69	60	51	43	37	32	28	24	22					
Pipe 3.5", 4" O.D.	0.226	48	46	44	41	38	35	32	29	25	22	19	17	15	14	12	10	
	0.318	66	63	59	55	51	47	43	38	33	29	25	23	20	18	16		
Pipe 4", 4.5" O.D.	0.237	59	57	54	52	49	46	43	40	36	33	29	26	23	21	19	15	13
	0.337	81	78	75	71	67	63	59	54	49	44	39	35	31	28	25	21	17
	0.674	147	140	133	126	118	109	100	91	81	70	62	55	49	44	40	33	
Pipe 5", 5.563" O.D.	0.258	83	81	78	76	73	71	68	65	61	58	55	51	47	43	39	32	27
	0.375	118	114	111	107	103	99	95	91	86	81	76	70	65	59	54	44	37
	0.750	216	209	202	195	187	178	170	160	151	141	130	119	108	97	87	72	61
Pipe 6", 6.625" O.D.	0.280	110	108	106	103	101	98	95	92	89	86	82	79	75	71	67	59	51
	0.432	166	162	159	155	151	146	142	137	132	127	122	117	111	105	99	86	73
	0.864	306	299	292	284	275	266	257	247	237	227	216	205	193	181	168	142	119
TS 4 x 4	0.250	83	79	75	70	65	60	55	49	43	38	33	29	26	24	21	18	15
TS 5 x 5	0.250	111	108	104	100	96	92	87	82	77	72	66	60	54	49	44	36	31
TS 6 x 6	0.250	140	137	133	130	126	122	117	113	108	104	99	94	88	83	77	65	55
TS 5 x 3	0.250	76	70	64	58	51	43	36	31	28	23	20	18	16	15			
TS 6 x 4	0.250	107	103	98	92	87	81	75	68	61	54	48	42	38	34	30	25	21
TS 8 x 4	0.250	132	126	120	114	108	101	94	86	79	70	62	55	49	40	33		

* For additional columns and actual dimensions of tubing, see *AISC Manual of Steel Construction*, 2d ed. (load and resistance factor design) and 9th ed. (allowable stress design).

** Weight per ft for W columns. Wall thickness for tubing. kip = 1000 lb; K = effective length factor (verify with structural engineering consultant).

NOTE

Multiply loads by 1.5 to obtain approximate capacities for load and resistance factor design method.

American Institute of Steel Construction; Chicago, Illinois

STRUCTURAL METAL FRAMING

W SHAPES— DIMENSIONS FOR DETAILING

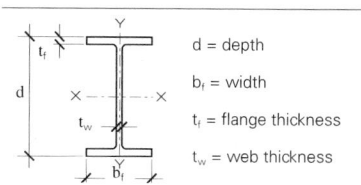

d = depth
b_f = width
t_f = flange thickness
t_w = web thickness

DESIG-NATION	DEPTH (IN.)	FLANGE WIDTH (IN.)	FLANGE THICKNESS (IN.)	WEB THICKNESS (IN.)
W36 x 300	36 3/4	16 5/8	1 11/16	15/16
x 280	36 1/2	16 5/8	1 9/16	7/8
x 260	36 1/4	16 1/2	1 7/16	13/16
x 245	36 1/8	16 1/2	1 3/8	13/16
x 230	35 7/8	16 1/2	1 1/4	3/4
W36 x 210	36 3/4	12 1/8	1 3/8	13/16
x 194	36 1/2	12 1/8	1 1/4	3/4
x 182	36 3/8	12 1/8	1 3/16	3/4
x 170	36 1/8	12	1 1/8	11/16
x 160	36	12	1	5/8
x 150	35 7/8	12	15/16	5/8
x 135	35 1/2	12	13/16	5/8
W33 x 241	34 1/8	15 7/8	1 3/8	13/16
x 221	33 7/8	15 3/4	1 1/4	3/4
x 201	33 5/8	15 3/4	1 1/8	11/16
W33 x 152	33 1/2	11 5/8	1 1/16	5/8
x 141	33 1/4	11 1/2	1	5/8
x 130	33 1/8	11 1/2	7/8	9/16
x 118	32 7/8	11 1/2	3/4	9/16
W30 x 211	31	15 1/8	1 5/16	3/4
x 191	30 5/8	15	1 3/16	11/16
x 173	30 1/2	15	1 1/16	5/8
W30 x 132	30 1/4	10 1/2	1	5/8
x 124	30 1/8	10 1/2	15/16	9/16
x 116	30	10 1/2	7/8	9/16
x 108	29 7/8	10 1/2	3/4	9/16
x 99	29 5/8	10 1/2	5/8	1/2
W27 x 178	27 3/4	14 1/8	1 3/16	3/4
x 161	27 5/8	14	1 1/16	11/16
x 146	27 3/8	14	1	5/8
W27 x 114	27 1/4	10 1/8	15/16	9/16
x 102	27 1/8	10	13/16	1/2
x 94	26 7/8	10	3/4	1/2
x 84	26 3/4	10	5/8	7/16
W24 x 162	25	13	1 1/4	11/16
x 146	24 3/4	12 7/8	1 1/16	5/8
x 131	24 1/2	12 7/8	15/16	5/8
x 117	24 1/4	12 3/4	7/8	9/16
x 104	24	12 3/4	3/4	1/2
W24 x 94	24 1/4	9 1/8	7/8	1/2
x 84	24 1/8	9	3/4	1/2
x 76	23 7/8	9	11/16	7/16
x 68	23 3/4	9	9/16	7/16
W24 x 62	23 3/4	7	9/16	7/16
x 55	23 5/8	7	1/2	3/8
W21 x 147	22	12 1/2	1 1/8	3/4
x 132	21 7/8	12 1/2	1 1/8	5/8
x 122	21 5/8	12 3/8	15/16	5/8
x 111	21 1/2	12 3/8	7/8	9/16
x 101	21 3/8	12 1/4	13/16	1/2
W21 x 93	21 5/8	8 3/8	15/16	9/16
x 83	21 3/8	8 3/8	13/16	1/2
x 73	21 1/4	8 1/4	3/4	7/16
x 68	21 1/8	8 1/4	11/16	7/16
x 62	21	8 1/4	5/8	3/8
W21 x 57	21	6 1/2	5/8	3/8
x 50	20 7/8	6 1/2	9/16	3/8
x 44	20 5/8	6 1/2	7/16	3/8
W18 x 119	19	11 1/4	1 1/16	5/8
x 106	18 3/4	11 1/4	15/16	9/16
x 97	18 5/8	11 1/8	7/8	9/16
x 86	18 3/8	11 1/8	3/4	1/2
x 76	18 1/4	11	11/16	7/16
W18 x 71	18 1/2	7 5/8	13/16	1/2
x 65	18 3/8	7 5/8	3/4	7/16
x 60	18 1/4	7 1/2	11/16	7/16
x 55	18 1/8	7 1/2	5/8	3/8
x 50	18	7 1/2	9/16	3/8
W18 x 46	18	6	5/8	3/8
x 40	17 7/8	6	1/2	5/16
x 35	17 3/4	6	7/16	5/16
W16 x 100	17	10 3/8	1	9/16
x 89	16 3/4	10 3/8	7/8	1/2
x 77	16 1/2	10 1/4	3/4	7/16
x 67	16 3/8	10 1/4	11/16	3/8
W16 x 57	16 3/8	7 1/8	11/16	7/16
x 50	16 1/4	7 1/8	5/8	3/8
x 45	16 1/8	7	9/16	3/8
x 40	16	7	1/2	5/16
x 36	15 7/8	7	7/16	5/16
W16 x 31	15 7/8	5 1/2	7/16	1/4
x 26	15 3/4	5 1/2	3/8	1/4
W14 x 730	22 3/8	17 7/8	4 15/16	3 1/16
x 665	21 5/8	17 5/8	4 1/2	2 13/16
x 605	20 7/8	17 3/8	4 3/16	2 5/8
x 550	20 1/4	17 1/4	3 13/16	2 3/8
x 500	19 5/8	17	3 1/2	2 3/16
x 455	19	16 7/8	3 3/16	2
W14 x 426	18 5/8	16 3/4	3 1/16	1 7/8
x 398	18 1/4	16 5/8	2 7/8	1 3/4
x 370	17 7/8	16 1/2	2 11/16	1 5/8
x 342	17 1/2	16 3/8	2 1/2	1 9/16
x 311	17 1/8	16 1/4	2 1/4	1 7/16
x 283	16 3/4	16 1/8	2 1/16	1 5/16
x 257	16 3/8	16	1 7/8	1 3/16
x 233	16	15 7/8	1 3/4	1 1/16
x 211	15 3/4	15 3/4	1 9/16	1
x 193	15 1/2	15 3/4	1 7/16	7/8
x 176	15 1/4	15 5/8	1 5/16	13/16
x 159	15	15 5/8	1 3/16	3/4
x 145	14 3/4	15 1/2	1 1/16	11/16
W14 x 132	14 5/8	14 3/4	1	5/8
x 120	14 1/2	14 5/8	15/16	9/16
x 109	14 3/8	14 5/8	7/8	1/2
x 99	14 1/8	14 5/8	3/4	1/2
x 90	14	14 1/2	11/16	7/16
W14 x 82	14 1/4	10 1/8	7/8	1/2
x 74	14 1/8	10 1/8	13/16	7/16
x 68	14	10	3/4	7/16
x 61	13 7/8	10	5/8	3/8
W14 x 53	13 7/8	8	11/16	3/8
x 48	13 3/4	8	5/8	5/16
x 43	13 5/8	8	1/2	5/16
W14 x 38	14 1/8	6 3/4	1/2	5/16
x 34	14	6 3/4	7/16	5/16
x 30	13 7/8	6 3/4	3/8	1/4
W14 x 26	13 7/8	5	7/16	1/4
x 22	13 3/4	5	5/16	1/4
W12 x 336	16 7/8	13 3/8	2 15/16	1 3/4
x 305	16 3/8	13 1/4	2 11/16	1 5/8
x 279	15 7/8	13 1/8	2 1/2	1 1/2
x 252	15 3/8	13	2 1/4	1 3/8
x 230	15	12 7/8	2 1/16	1 5/16
x 210	14 3/4	12 3/4	1 7/8	1 3/16
W12 x 190	14 3/8	12 5/8	1 3/4	1 1/16
x 170	14	12 5/8	1 9/16	15/16
x 152	13 3/4	12 1/2	1 3/8	7/8
x 136	13 3/8	12 3/8	1 1/4	13/16
x 120	13 1/8	12 3/8	1 1/8	11/16
x 106	12 7/8	12 1/4	1	5/8
x 96	12 3/4	12 1/8	7/8	9/16
x 87	12 1/2	12 1/8	13/16	1/2
x 79	12 3/8	12 1/8	3/4	1/2
x 72	12 1/4	12	11/16	7/16
x 65	12 1/4	12	5/8	3/8
W12 x 58	12 1/4	10	5/8	3/8
x 53	12	10	9/16	3/8
W12 x 50	12 1/4	8 1/8	5/8	3/8
x 45	12	8	9/16	5/16
x 40	12	8	1/2	5/16
W12 x 35	12 1/2	6 1/2	1/2	5/16
x 30	12 3/8	6 1/2	7/16	1/4
x 26	12 1/4	6 1/2	3/8	1/4
W12 x 22	12 1/4	4	7/16	1/4
x 19	12 1/8	4	3/8	1/4
x 16	12	4	1/4	1/4
x 14	11 7/8	4	1/4	3/16
W10 x 112	11 3/8	10 3/8	1 1/4	3/4
x 100	11 1/8	10 3/8	1 1/8	11/16
x 88	10 7/8	10 1/4	1	5/8
x 77	10 5/8	10 1/4	7/8	1/2
x 68	10 3/8	10 1/8	3/4	1/2
x 60	10 1/4	10 1/8	11/16	7/16
x 54	10 1/8	10	5/8	3/8
x 49	10	10	9/16	5/16
W10 x 45	10 1/8	8	5/8	3/8
x 39	9 7/8	8	1/2	5/16
x 33	9 3/4	8	7/16	5/16
W10 x 30	10 1/2	5 3/4	1/2	5/16
x 26	10 3/8	5 3/4	7/16	1/4
x 22	10 1/8	5 3/4	3/8	1/4
W10 x 19	10 1/4	4	3/8	1/4
x 17	10 1/8	4	5/16	1/4
x 15	10	4	1/4	1/4
x 12	9 7/8	4	3/16	3/16
W8 x 67	9	8 1/4	15/16	9/16
x 58	8 3/4	8 1/4	13/16	1/2
x 48	8 1/2	8 1/8	11/16	3/8
x 40	8 1/4	8 1/8	9/16	3/8
x 35	8 1/8	8	1/2	5/16
x 31	8	8	7/16	5/16

M SHAPES— DIMENSIONS FOR DETAILING

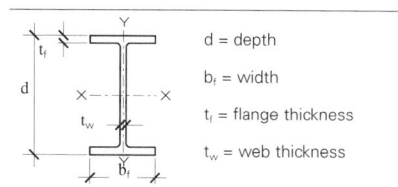

d = depth
b_f = width
t_f = flange thickness
t_w = web thickness

DESIG-NATION	DEPTH (IN.)	FLANGE WIDTH (IN.)	FLANGE THICKNESS (IN.)	WEB THICKNESS (IN.)
M14 x 18	14	4	1/4	3/16
M12 x 11.8	12	3 1/8	1/4	3/16
x 10.8	12	3 1/8	1/4	3/16
x 10	12	3 1/4	3/16	3/16
M10 x 9	10	2 3/4	3/16	3/16
x 8	10	2 3/4	3/16	3/16
x 7.5	10	2 3/4	3/16	3/16
M8 x 6.5	8	2 1/4	3/16	1/8
M6 x 4.4	6	1 7/8	3/16	1/8
M5 x 18.9	5	5	7/16	5/16

American Institute of Steel Construction; Chicago, Illinois

ANGLES — DIMENSIONS FOR DETAILING

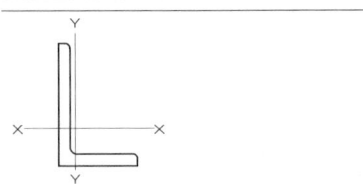

SIZE AND THICKNESS (IN.)		WEIGHT PER FT (LB)	SIZE AND THICKNESS (IN.)		WEIGHT PER FT (LB)
L8 x 8 x	$1\frac{1}{8}$	56.9	L4 x 4 x	$\frac{3}{4}$	18.5
	1	51.0		$\frac{5}{8}$	15.7
	$\frac{7}{8}$	45.0		$\frac{1}{2}$	12.8
	$\frac{3}{4}$	38.9		$\frac{7}{16}$	11.3
	$\frac{5}{8}$	32.7		$\frac{3}{8}$	9.8
	$\frac{9}{16}$	29.6		$\frac{5}{16}$	8.2
	$\frac{1}{2}$	26.4		$\frac{1}{4}$	6.6
L8 x 6 x	1	44.2	L4 x $3\frac{1}{2}$ x	$\frac{1}{2}$	11.9
	$\frac{7}{8}$	39.1		$\frac{7}{16}$	10.6
	$\frac{3}{4}$	33.8		$\frac{3}{8}$	9.1
	$\frac{5}{8}$	28.5		$\frac{5}{16}$	7.7
	$\frac{9}{16}$	25.7		$\frac{1}{4}$	6.2
	$\frac{1}{2}$	23.0	L4 x 3 x	$\frac{1}{2}$	11.1
	$\frac{7}{16}$	20.2		$\frac{7}{16}$	9.8
L8 x 4 x	1	37.4		$\frac{3}{8}$	8.5
	$\frac{3}{4}$	28.7		$\frac{5}{16}$	7.2
	$\frac{9}{16}$	21.9		$\frac{1}{4}$	5.8
	$\frac{1}{2}$	19.6	L$3\frac{1}{2}$ x $3\frac{1}{2}$ x	$\frac{1}{2}$	11.1
L7 x 4 x	$\frac{3}{4}$	26.2	x	$\frac{7}{16}$	9.8
	$\frac{5}{8}$	22.1		$\frac{3}{8}$	8.5
	$\frac{1}{2}$	17.9		$\frac{5}{16}$	7.2
	$\frac{3}{8}$	13.6		$\frac{1}{4}$	5.8
L6 x 6 x	1	37.4	L$3\frac{1}{2}$ x 3 x	$\frac{1}{2}$	10.2
	$\frac{7}{8}$	33.1		$\frac{7}{16}$	9.1
	$\frac{3}{4}$	28.7		$\frac{3}{8}$	7.9
	$\frac{5}{8}$	24.2		$\frac{5}{16}$	6.6
	$\frac{9}{16}$	21.9		$\frac{1}{4}$	5.4
	$\frac{1}{2}$	19.6	L$3\frac{1}{2}$ x $2\frac{1}{2}$ x	$\frac{1}{2}$	9.4
	$\frac{7}{16}$	17.2	x	$\frac{7}{8}$	8.3
	$\frac{3}{8}$	14.9		$\frac{3}{8}$	7.2
	$\frac{5}{16}$	12.4		$\frac{5}{16}$	6.1
L6 x 4 x	$\frac{7}{8}$	27.2		$\frac{1}{4}$	4.9
	$\frac{3}{4}$	23.6	L3 x 3 x	$\frac{1}{2}$	9.4
	$\frac{5}{8}$	20.0		$\frac{7}{16}$	8.3
	$\frac{9}{16}$	18.1		$\frac{3}{8}$	7.2
	$\frac{1}{2}$	16.2		$\frac{5}{16}$	6.1
	$\frac{7}{16}$	14.3		$\frac{1}{4}$	4.9
	$\frac{3}{8}$	12.3		$\frac{3}{16}$	3.71
	$\frac{5}{16}$	10.3	L3 x $2\frac{1}{2}$ x	$\frac{1}{2}$	8.5
L6 x $3\frac{1}{2}$ x	$\frac{1}{2}$	15.3		$\frac{7}{16}$	7.6
	$\frac{3}{8}$	11.7		$\frac{3}{8}$	6.6
	$\frac{5}{16}$	9.8		$\frac{5}{16}$	5.6
L5 x 5 x	$\frac{7}{8}$	27.2		$\frac{1}{4}$	4.5
	$\frac{3}{4}$	23.6		$\frac{3}{16}$	3.39
	$\frac{5}{8}$	20.0	L3 x 2 x	$\frac{1}{2}$	7.7
	$\frac{1}{2}$	16.2		$\frac{7}{16}$	6.8
	$\frac{7}{16}$	14.3		$\frac{3}{8}$	5.9
	$\frac{3}{8}$	12.3		$\frac{5}{16}$	5.0
	$\frac{5}{16}$	10.3		$\frac{1}{4}$	4.1
L5 x $3\frac{1}{2}$ x	$\frac{3}{4}$	19.8		$\frac{3}{16}$	3.07
	$\frac{5}{8}$	16.8	L$2\frac{1}{2}$ x $2\frac{1}{2}$ x	$\frac{1}{2}$	7.7
	$\frac{1}{2}$	13.6	x	$\frac{3}{8}$	5.9
	$\frac{7}{16}$	12.0		$\frac{5}{16}$	5.0
	$\frac{3}{8}$	10.4		$\frac{1}{4}$	4.1
	$\frac{5}{16}$	8.7		$\frac{3}{16}$	3.07
	$\frac{1}{4}$	7.0	L$2\frac{1}{2}$ x 2 x	$\frac{3}{8}$	5.3
L5 x 3 x	$\frac{5}{8}$	15.7		$\frac{5}{16}$	4.5
	$\frac{1}{2}$	12.8		$\frac{1}{4}$	3.62
	$\frac{7}{16}$	11.3		$\frac{3}{16}$	2.75
	$\frac{3}{8}$	9.8	L2 x 2 x	$\frac{3}{8}$	4.7
	$\frac{5}{16}$	8.2		$\frac{5}{16}$	3.92

MISCELLANEOUS CHANNELS— DIMENSIONS FOR DETAILING

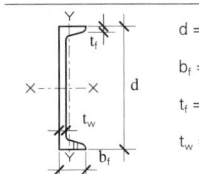

d = depth
b_f = width
t_f = flange thickness
t_w = web thickness

DESIGNATION	DEPTH (IN.)	FLANGE WIDTH (IN.)	FLANGE AVG. THICKNESS (IN.)	WEB THICKNESS (IN.)
MC 18 x 58	18	$4\frac{1}{4}$	$\frac{5}{8}$	$\frac{11}{16}$
x 51.9	18	$4\frac{1}{8}$	$\frac{5}{8}$	$\frac{5}{8}$
x 45.8	18	4	$\frac{5}{8}$	$\frac{1}{2}$
x 42.7	18	4	$\frac{5}{8}$	$\frac{7}{16}$
MC 13 x 50	13	$4\frac{3}{8}$	$\frac{5}{8}$	$\frac{13}{16}$
x 40	13	$4\frac{1}{4}$	$\frac{5}{8}$	$\frac{9}{16}$
x 35	13	$4\frac{1}{8}$	$\frac{5}{8}$	$\frac{7}{16}$
x 31.8	13	4	$\frac{5}{8}$	$\frac{3}{8}$
MC 12 x 50	12	$4\frac{1}{8}$	$\frac{11}{16}$	$\frac{13}{16}$
x 45	12	4	$\frac{11}{16}$	$\frac{11}{16}$
x 40	12	$3\frac{7}{8}$	$\frac{11}{16}$	$\frac{9}{16}$
x 35	12	$3\frac{3}{4}$	$\frac{11}{16}$	$\frac{7}{16}$
x 31	12	$3\frac{5}{8}$	$\frac{11}{16}$	$\frac{3}{8}$
MC 12 x 37	12	$3\frac{5}{8}$	$\frac{5}{8}$	$\frac{5}{8}$
x 32.9	12	$3\frac{1}{2}$	$\frac{5}{8}$	$\frac{1}{2}$
x 30.9	12	$3\frac{1}{2}$	$\frac{5}{8}$	$\frac{7}{16}$
MC 12 x 10.6	12	$1\frac{1}{2}$	$\frac{5}{16}$	$\frac{3}{16}$
MC 10 x 41.1	10	$4\frac{3}{8}$	$\frac{9}{16}$	$\frac{13}{16}$
x 33.6	10	$4\frac{1}{8}$	$\frac{9}{16}$	$\frac{9}{16}$
x 28.5	10	4	$\frac{9}{16}$	$\frac{7}{16}$
x 25	10	$3\frac{3}{8}$	$\frac{9}{16}$	$\frac{3}{8}$
x 22	10	$3\frac{3}{8}$	$\frac{9}{16}$	$\frac{5}{16}$
MC 10 x 8.4	10	$1\frac{1}{2}$	$\frac{1}{4}$	$\frac{3}{16}$
MC 10 x 6.5	10	$1\frac{1}{8}$	$\frac{3}{16}$	$\frac{1}{8}$
MC 9 x 25.4	9	$3\frac{1}{2}$	$\frac{7}{16}$	$\frac{9}{16}$
x 23.9	9	$3\frac{1}{2}$	$\frac{3}{8}$	$\frac{9}{16}$
MC 8 x 22.8	8	$3\frac{1}{2}$	$\frac{7}{16}$	$\frac{1}{2}$
x 21.4	8	$3\frac{1}{2}$	$\frac{3}{8}$	$\frac{1}{2}$
MC 8 x 20	8	3	$\frac{3}{8}$	$\frac{1}{2}$
x 18.7	8	3	$\frac{3}{8}$	$\frac{1}{2}$
MC 8 x 8.5	8	$1\frac{7}{8}$	$\frac{3}{16}$	$\frac{5}{16}$

HP SHAPES— DIMENSIONS FOR DETAILING

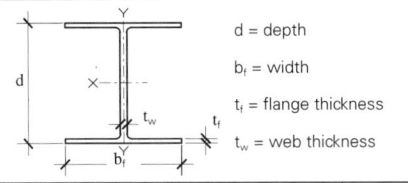

d = depth
b_f = width
t_f = flange thickness
t_w = web thickness

DESIGNATION	DEPTH (IN.)	FLANGE WIDTH (IN.)	FLANGE AVG. THICKNESS (IN.)	WEB THICKNESS (IN.)
HP 14 x 117	$14\frac{1}{4}$	$14\frac{7}{8}$	$\frac{13}{16}$	$\frac{13}{16}$
x 102	14	$14\frac{3}{4}$	$\frac{11}{16}$	$\frac{11}{16}$
x 89	$13\frac{7}{8}$	$14\frac{3}{4}$	$\frac{5}{8}$	$\frac{5}{8}$
x 73	$13\frac{5}{8}$	$14\frac{5}{8}$	$\frac{1}{2}$	$\frac{1}{2}$
HP 13 x 100	$13\frac{1}{8}$	$13\frac{1}{4}$	$\frac{3}{4}$	$\frac{3}{4}$
x 87	13	$13\frac{1}{8}$	$\frac{11}{16}$	$\frac{11}{16}$
x 73	$12\frac{3}{4}$	13	$\frac{9}{16}$	$\frac{9}{16}$
x 60	$12\frac{1}{2}$	$12\frac{7}{8}$	$\frac{7}{16}$	$\frac{7}{16}$
HP 12 x 84	$12\frac{1}{4}$	$12\frac{1}{4}$	$\frac{11}{16}$	$\frac{11}{16}$
x 74	$12\frac{1}{4}$	$12\frac{1}{4}$	$\frac{5}{8}$	$\frac{5}{8}$
x 63	12	$12\frac{1}{8}$	$\frac{1}{2}$	$\frac{1}{2}$
x 53	$11\frac{3}{4}$	12	$\frac{7}{16}$	$\frac{7}{16}$
HP 10 x 57	10	$10\frac{1}{4}$	$\frac{9}{16}$	$\frac{9}{16}$
x 42	$9\frac{3}{4}$	$10\frac{1}{8}$	$\frac{7}{16}$	$\frac{7}{16}$

S SHAPES— DIMENSIONS FOR DETAILING

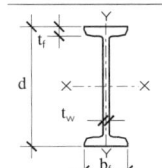

d = depth
b_f = width
t_f = flange thickness
t_w = web thickness

DESIGNATION	DEPTH D (IN.)	FLANGE WIDTH BF (IN.)	FLANGE AVG. THICKNESS TF (IN.)	WEB THICKNESS TW
S24 x 121	$24\frac{1}{2}$	8	$1\frac{1}{16}$	$\frac{13}{16}$
x 106	$24\frac{1}{2}$	$7\frac{7}{8}$	$1\frac{1}{16}$	$\frac{5}{8}$
S24 x 100	24	$7\frac{1}{4}$	$\frac{7}{8}$	$\frac{3}{4}$
x 90	24	$7\frac{1}{8}$	$\frac{7}{8}$	$\frac{5}{8}$
x 80	24	7	$\frac{7}{8}$	$\frac{1}{2}$
S20 x 96	$20\frac{1}{4}$	$7\frac{1}{4}$	$\frac{15}{16}$	$\frac{13}{16}$
x 86	$20\frac{1}{4}$	7	$\frac{15}{16}$	$\frac{11}{16}$
S20 x 75	20	$6\frac{3}{8}$	$\frac{13}{16}$	$\frac{5}{8}$
x 66	20	$6\frac{1}{4}$	$\frac{13}{16}$	$\frac{1}{2}$
S18 x 70	18	$6\frac{1}{4}$	$\frac{11}{16}$	$\frac{11}{16}$
x 54.7	18	6	$\frac{11}{16}$	$\frac{7}{16}$
S15 x 50	15	$5\frac{5}{8}$	$\frac{5}{8}$	$\frac{9}{16}$
x 42.9	15	$5\frac{1}{2}$	$\frac{5}{8}$	$\frac{7}{16}$
S12 x 50	12	$5\frac{1}{2}$	$\frac{11}{16}$	$\frac{11}{16}$
x 40.8	12	$5\frac{1}{4}$	$\frac{11}{16}$	$\frac{7}{16}$
S12 x 35	12	$5\frac{1}{8}$	$\frac{9}{16}$	$\frac{7}{16}$
x 31.8	12	5	$\frac{9}{16}$	$\frac{3}{8}$
S10 x 35	10	5	$\frac{1}{2}$	$\frac{5}{8}$
x 25.4	10	$4\frac{5}{8}$	$\frac{1}{2}$	$\frac{5}{16}$
S8 x 23	8	$4\frac{1}{8}$	$\frac{7}{16}$	$\frac{7}{16}$
x 18.4	8	4	$\frac{7}{16}$	$\frac{1}{4}$

AMERICAN STANDARD CHANNELS— DIMENSIONS FOR DETAILING

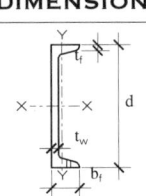

d = depth
b_f = width
t_f = flange thickness
t_w = web thickness

DESIGNATION	DEPTH (IN.)	FLANGE WIDTH (IN.)	FLANGE AVG. THICKNESS (IN.)	WEB THICKNESS (IN.)
C 15 x 50	15	$3\frac{3}{4}$	$\frac{5}{8}$	$\frac{11}{16}$
x 40	15	$3\frac{1}{2}$	$\frac{5}{8}$	$\frac{1}{2}$
x 33.9	15	$3\frac{3}{8}$	$\frac{5}{8}$	$\frac{3}{8}$
C 12 x 30	12	3	$\frac{1}{2}$	$\frac{1}{2}$
x 25	12	3	$\frac{1}{2}$	$\frac{3}{8}$
x 20.7	12	3	$\frac{1}{2}$	$\frac{5}{16}$
C 10 x 30	10	3	$\frac{7}{16}$	$\frac{11}{16}$
x 25	10	$2\frac{7}{8}$	$\frac{7}{16}$	$\frac{1}{2}$
x 20	10	$2\frac{3}{4}$	$\frac{7}{16}$	$\frac{3}{8}$
x 15.3	10	$2\frac{5}{8}$	$\frac{7}{16}$	$\frac{1}{4}$
C 9 x 20	9	$2\frac{5}{8}$	$\frac{7}{16}$	$\frac{7}{16}$
x 15	9	$2\frac{1}{2}$	$\frac{7}{16}$	$\frac{5}{16}$
x 13.4	9	$2\frac{3}{8}$	$\frac{7}{16}$	$\frac{1}{4}$
C 8 x 18.75	8	$2\frac{1}{2}$	$\frac{3}{8}$	$\frac{1}{2}$
x 13.75	8	$2\frac{3}{8}$	$\frac{3}{8}$	$\frac{5}{16}$
x 11.5	8	$2\frac{1}{4}$	$\frac{3}{8}$	$\frac{1}{4}$
C 7 x 14.75	7	$2\frac{1}{4}$	$\frac{3}{8}$	$\frac{7}{16}$
x 12.25	7	$2\frac{1}{4}$	$\frac{3}{8}$	$\frac{5}{16}$
x 9.8	7	$2\frac{1}{8}$	$\frac{3}{8}$	$\frac{3}{16}$
C 6 x 13	6	$2\frac{1}{8}$	$\frac{5}{16}$	$\frac{7}{16}$
x 10.5	6	2	$\frac{5}{16}$	$\frac{5}{16}$
x 8.2	6	$1\frac{7}{8}$	$\frac{5}{16}$	$\frac{3}{16}$
C 5 x 9	5	$1\frac{7}{8}$	$\frac{5}{16}$	$\frac{5}{16}$
x 6.7	5	$1\frac{3}{4}$	$\frac{5}{16}$	$\frac{3}{16}$

American Institute of Steel Construction; Chicago, Illinois

STRUCTURAL TEES CUT FROM W SHAPES— DIMENSIONS FOR DETAILING

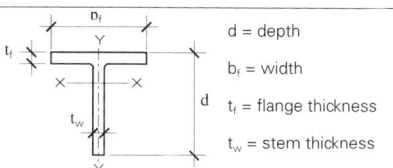

d = depth
b_f = width
t_f = flange thickness
t_w = stem thickness

DESIGNATION	DEPTH OF TEE (IN.)	FLANGE WIDTH (IN.)	FLANGE THICKNESS (IN.)	STEM THICKNESS (IN.)
WT 16.5 x 177	17 3/4	16 1/8	2 1/16	1 3/16
x 159	17 9/16	16	1 7/8	1 1/16
x 145.5	17 7/16	15 7/8	1 3/4	1
x 131.5	17 1/4	15 3/4	1 9/16	7/8
x 120.5	17 1/8	15 7/8	1 3/8	13/16
x 110.5	17	15 3/4	1 1/4	3/4
x 100.5	16 7/8	15 3/4	1 1/8	11/16
WT 16.5 x 84.5	16 15/16	11 1/2	1 1/4	11/16
x 76	16 3/4	11 5/8	1 1/16	5/8
x 70.5	16 5/8	11 1/2	15/16	5/8
x 65	16 1/2	11 1/2	7/8	9/16
x 59	16 3/8	11 1/2	3/4	9/16
WT 15 x 117.5	15 5/8	15	1 1/2	13/16
x 105.5	15 1/2	15 1/8	1 5/16	3/4
x 95.5	15 3/8	15	1 3/16	11/16
x 86.5	15 1/4	15	1 1/16	5/8
WT 15 x 74	15 5/16	10 1/2	1 3/16	5/8
x 66	15 1/8	10 1/2	1	5/8
x 62	15 1/8	10 1/2	15/16	9/16
x 58	15	10 1/2	7/8	9/16
x 54	14 7/8	10 1/2	3/4	9/16
x 49.5	14 7/8	10 1/2	11/16	1/2
WT 13.5 x 108.5	14 3/16	14 1/8	1 1/2	13/16
x 97	14 1/16	14	1 5/16	3/4
x 89	13 7/8	14 1/8	1 3/16	3/4
x 80.5	13 3/4	14	1 1/16	11/16
x 73	13 3/4	14	1	5/8
WT 13.5 x 64.5	13 13/16	10	1 1/8	5/8
x 57	13 5/8	10 1/8	15/16	9/16
x 51	13 1/2	10	13/16	1/2
x 47	13 1/2	10	3/4	1/2
x 42	13 3/8	10	5/8	7/16
WT 12 x 88	12 5/8	12 7/8	1 5/16	3/4
x 81	12 1/2	13	1 1/4	11/16
x 73	12 3/8	12 7/8	1 1/16	5/8
x 65.5	12 1/4	12 7/8	15/16	5/8
x 58.5	12 1/8	12 3/4	7/8	9/16
x 52	12	12 3/4	3/4	1/2
WT 12 x 51.5	12 1/4	9	1	9/16
x 47	12 1/8	9 1/8	7/8	1/2
x 42	12	9	3/4	1/2
x 38	12	9	11/16	7/16
x 34	11 7/8	9	9/16	7/16
WT 12 x 31	11 7/8	7	9/16	7/16
x 27.5	11 3/4	7	1/2	3/8
WT 10.5 x 83	11 1/4	12 3/8	1 3/8	3/4
x 73.5	11	12 1/2	1 1/8	3/4
x 66	10 7/8	12 1/2	1 1/16	5/8
x 61	10 7/8	12 3/8	15/16	5/8
x 55.5	10 3/4	12 3/8	7/8	9/16
x 50.5	10 5/8	12 1/4	13/16	1/2
WT 10.5 x 46.5	10 3/4	8 3/8	15/16	9/16
x 41.5	10 3/4	8 3/8	7/8	1/2
x 36.5	10 5/8	8 1/4	3/4	7/16
x 34	10 5/8	8 1/4	11/16	7/16
x 31	10 1/2	8 1/4	5/8	3/8
WT 10.5 x 28.5	10 1/2	6 1/2	5/8	3/8
x 25	10 3/8	6 1/2	9/16	3/8
x 22	10 3/8	6 1/2	7/16	3/8

DESIGNATION	DEPTH OF TEE (IN.)	FLANGE WIDTH (IN.)	FLANGE THICKNESS (IN.)	STEM THICKNESS (IN.)
WT 9 x 71.5	9 3/4	11 1/4	1 5/16	3/4
x 65	9 5/8	11 1/4	1 3/16	11/16
x 59.5	9 1/2	11 1/4	1 1/16	5/8
x 53	9 3/8	11 1/4	15/16	9/16
x 48.5	9 1/4	11 1/8	7/8	9/16
x 43	9 1/4	11 1/8	3/4	1/2
x 38	9 1/8	11	11/16	7/16
WT 9 x 35.5	9 1/4	7 5/8	13/16	1/2
x 32.5	9 1/8	7 5/8	3/4	7/16
x 30	9 1/8	7 1/2	11/16	7/16
x 27.5	9	7 1/2	5/8	3/8
x 25	9	7 1/2	9/16	3/8
WT 9 x 23	9	6	5/8	3/8
x 20	9	6	1/2	5/16
x 17.5	8 7/8	6	7/16	5/16
WT 8 x 50	8 1/2	10 3/8	1	9/16
x 44.5	8 3/8	10 3/8	7/8	1/2
x 38.5	8 1/4	10 1/4	3/4	7/16
x 33.5	8 1/8	10 1/4	11/16	3/8
WT 8 x 28.5	8 1/4	7 1/8	11/16	7/16
x 25	8 1/8	7 1/8	5/8	3/8
x 22.5	8 1/8	7	9/16	3/8
x 20	8	7	1/2	5/16
x 18	7 7/8	7	7/16	5/16
WT 8 x 15.5	8	5 1/2	7/16	1/4
x 13	7 7/8	5 1/2	3/8	1/4
WT 7 x 365	11 1/4	17 7/8	4 15/16	3 1/16
x 332.5	10 7/8	17 5/8	4 1/2	2 13/16
x 302.5	10 1/2	17 3/8	4 3/16	2 5/8
x 275	10 1/8	17 1/4	3 3/4	2 3/8
x 250	9 3/4	17	3 1/2	2 3/16
x 227.5	9 1/2	16 7/8	3 13/16	2
x 213	9 3/8	16 3/4	3 1/16	1 7/8
x 199	9 1/2	16 5/8	2 7/8	1 3/4
x 185	9	16 1/2	2 11/16	1 5/8
x 171	8 3/4	16 3/8	2 1/2	1 9/16
x 155.5	8 1/2	16 1/4	2 1/4	1 7/16
x 141.5	8 3/8	16 1/8	2 1/8	1 5/16
x 128.5	8 1/4	16	1 7/8	1 3/16
x 116.5	8	15 7/8	1 3/4	1 1/16
x 105.5	7 7/8	15 3/4	1 9/16	1
x 96.5	7 3/4	15 3/4	1 7/16	7/8
x 88	7 7/8	15 5/8	1 5/16	13/16
x 79.5	7 1/2	15 5/8	1 3/16	3/4
x 72.5	7 3/8	15 1/2	1 1/16	11/16
WT 7 x 66	7 3/8	14 3/4	1	5/8
x 60	7 1/4	14 5/8	15/16	9/16
x 54.5	7 1/8	14 5/8	7/8	1/2
x 49.5	7 1/8	14 5/8	3/4	1/2
x 45	7	14 1/2	11/16	7/16
WT 7 x 41	7 1/8	10 1/8	7/8	1/2
x 37	7 1/8	10 1/8	13/16	7/16
x 34	7	10	3/4	7/16
x 30.5	7	10	5/8	3/8
WT 7 x 26.5	7	8	11/16	3/8
x 24	6 7/8	8	5/8	5/16
x 21.5	6 7/8	8	1/2	5/16
WT 7 x 19	7	6 3/4	1/2	5/16
x 17	7	6 3/4	7/16	5/16
WT 7 x 13	7	5	7/16	1/4
x 11	6 7/8	5	5/16	1/4
WT 6 x 168	8 3/8	13 3/8	2 15/16	3/4
x 152.5	8 1/8	13 1/4	2 11/16	1 5/8
x 139.5	7 7/8	13 1/8	2 1/2	1 1/2
x 126	7 3/4	13	2 1/4	1 3/8
x 115	7 1/2	12 7/8	2 1/16	1 5/16
x 105	7 3/8	12 3/4	1 7/8	1 3/16
x 95	7 1/4	12 5/8	1 3/4	1 1/16
x 85	7	12 5/8	1 9/16	15/16

DESIGNATION	DEPTH OF TEE (IN.)	FLANGE WIDTH (IN.)	FLANGE THICKNESS (IN.)	STEM THICKNESS (IN.)
x 76	6 7/8	12 1/2	1 3/8	7/8
x 68	6 3/4	12 3/8	1 1/4	13/16
x 60	6 1/2	12 3/8	1 1/8	11/16
x 53	6 1/2	12 1/4	1	5/8
x 48	6 3/8	12 1/8	7/8	9/16
x 43.5	6 1/4	12 1/8	13/16	1/2
x 39.5	6 1/4	12 1/8	3/4	1/2
x 36	6 1/8	12	11/16	7/16
x 32.5	6	12	5/8	3/8
WT 6 x 29	6 1/8	10	5/8	3/8
x 26.5	6	10	9/16	3/8
WT 6 x 25	6 1/8	8 1/8	5/8	3/8
x 22.5	6	8	9/16	5/16
x 20	6	8	1/2	5/16
WT 6 x 17.5	6 1/4	6 1/2	1/2	5/16
x 15	6 1/8	6 1/2	7/16	1/4
x 13	6 1/8	6 1/2	3/8	1/4
WT 6 x 11	6 1/4	4	7/16	1/4
x 9.5	6 1/8	4	3/8	1/4
x 8	6	4	1/4	1/4
x 7	6	4	1/4	3/16
WT 5 x 56	5 5/8	10 3/8	1 1/4	3/4
x 50	5 1/2	10 3/8	1 1/8	11/16
x 44	5 3/8	10 1/4	1	5/8
x 38.5	5 1/4	10 1/4	7/8	1/2
x 34	5 1/4	10 1/4	3/4	1/2
x 30	5 1/8	10 1/4	11/16	7/16
x 27	5	10	5/8	3/8
x 24.5	5	10	9/16	5/16
WT 5 x 22.5	5	8	5/8	3/8
x 19.5	5	8	1/2	5/16
x 16.5	4 7/8	8	7/16	5/16
WT 5 x 15	5 1/4	5 1/2	1/2	5/16
x 13	5 1/4	5 3/4	7/16	1/4
x 11	5 1/8	5 3/4	3/8	1/4

STRUCTURAL TEES CUT FROM S SHAPES— DIMENSIONS FOR DETAILING

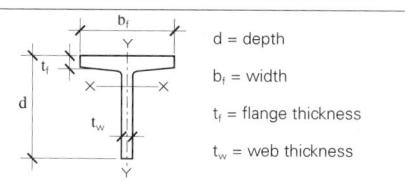

d = depth
b_f = width
t_f = flange thickness
t_w = web thickness

DESIGNATION	DEPTH OF TEE (IN.)	FLANGE WIDTH (IN.)	FLANGE THICKNESS (IN.)	STEM THICKNESS (IN.)
ST 10 x 48	10 1/8	7 1/4	15/16	13/16
x 43	10 1/8	7	15/16	11/16
ST 10 x 37.5	10	6 3/8	13/16	5/8
x 33	10	6 1/4	13/16	1/2
ST 9 x 35	9	6 1/4	11/16	11/16
x 27.35	9	6	11/16	7/16
ST 7.5 x 25	7 1/2	5 5/8	5/8	9/16
x 21.4	7 1/2	5 1/2	5/8	7/16
ST 6 x 25	6	5 1/2	11/16	11/16
x 20.4	6	5 1/4	11/16	7/16
ST 6 x 17.5	6	5 1/8	9/16	7/16
x 15.9	6	5	9/16	3/8
ST 5 x 17.5	5	5	1/2	5/8
x 12.7	5	4 5/8	1/2	5/16
ST 4 x 11.5	4	4 1/8	7/16	7/16
x 9.2	4	4 1/8	7/16	1/4
ST 3.5 x 10	3 1/2	3 7/8	3/8	7/16
x 7.65	3 1/2	3 5/8	3/8	1/4

American Institute of Steel Construction; Chicago, Illinois

GENERAL

A space frame is a three-dimensional truss with linear members that form a series of triangulated polyhedrons. It can be seen as a plane of constant depth that can sustain fairly long spans and varied configurations of shape.

NOTES

1. The prime attributes of space frame structural systems are their light weight; inherent rigidity; their wide variety of form, size, and span; and compatible interaction with other building support systems, primarily HVAC.

2. Most systems are designed for specific applications, and a structural engineer with space frame experience should always be consulted. Manufacturers can provide the full range of capabilities–loading, spans, shapes, specific details–for their products. Standardized systems in 4- and 5-ft modules are available.

3. Metal space frames are classified as noncombustible construction and can usually be exposed when 20 ft above the floor. However, an automatic fire extinguishing system or a rated ceiling may be required. Consult applicable building and fire codes.

4. The finishes commonly available are paint, thermoset polyester, galvanizing, stainless steel, or metal plating.

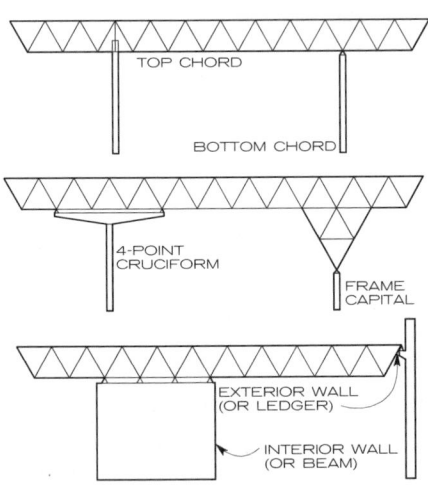

TOP CHORD

BOTTOM CHORD

4-POINT CRUCIFORM

FRAME CAPITAL

EXTERIOR WALL (OR LEDGER)

INTERIOR WALL (OR BEAM)

SUPPORT TYPES

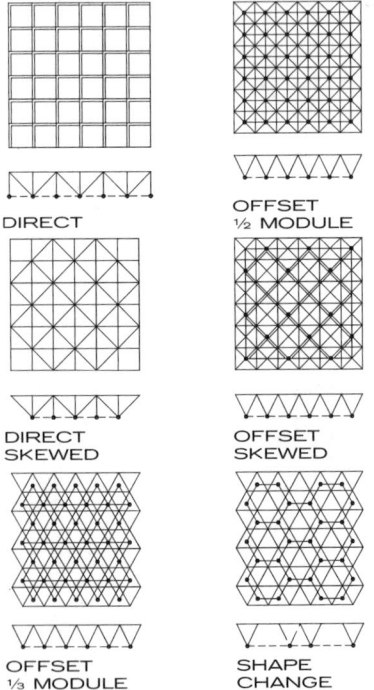

DIRECT

OFFSET ½ MODULE

DIRECT SKEWED

OFFSET SKEWED

OFFSET ⅓ MODULE

SHAPE CHANGE

NOTE

Many proprietary node systems are available for specific applications and budgets. Keep field connections to a minimum; welded connections often eliminate joint pieces.

COMMON PATTERNS

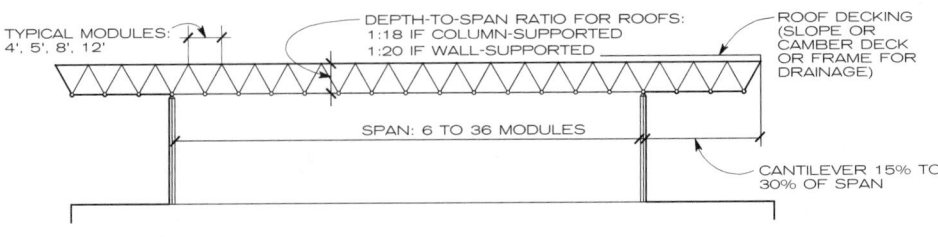

TYPICAL MODULES: 4', 5', 8', 12'

DEPTH-TO-SPAN RATIO FOR ROOFS:
1:18 IF COLUMN-SUPPORTED
1:20 IF WALL-SUPPORTED

ROOF DECKING (SLOPE OR CAMBER DECK OR FRAME FOR DRAINAGE.)

SPAN: 6 TO 36 MODULES

CANTILEVER 15% TO 30% OF SPAN

NOTE

Select a space frame module that is compatible with the building planning module in shape (e.g., a square module with orthogonal plan) and size (a multiple of the planning module); is consistent with the limitations of the interfacing systems (e.g., the maximum span of the roof deck or mullion spacing of the glazing system); and satisfies the spatial and aesthetic effects in scale and form.

MODULE SELECTION AND CHARACTERISTICS

NOTE

Square tubes or angles within their span range are often the most economical.

MEMBER SHAPES

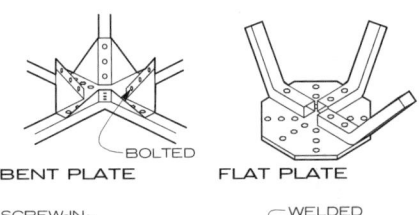

BENT PLATE   FLAT PLATE

BOLTED

SCREW-IN

WELDED

BOX SECTION OUTER CHORD

SCREW-IN

FOR DIRECT ATTACHMENT OF CLADDING OR GLAZING

FULL SPHERE   PARTIAL SPHERE

NOTE

Space frame supports are at panel joints only, not along members.

NODE CONNECTIONS

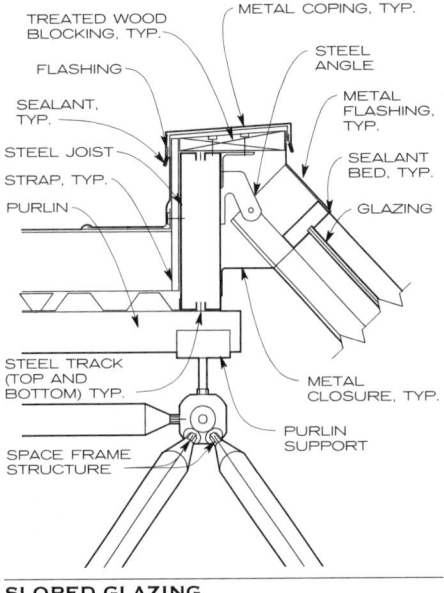

TREATED WOOD BLOCKING, TYP.

METAL COPING, TYP.

FLASHING

STEEL ANGLE

SEALANT, TYP.

METAL FLASHING, TYP.

STEEL JOIST

SEALANT BED, TYP.

STRAP, TYP.

PURLIN

GLAZING

STEEL TRACK (TOP AND BOTTOM) TYP.

METAL CLOSURE, TYP.

SPACE FRAME STRUCTURE

PURLIN SUPPORT

SLOPED GLAZING

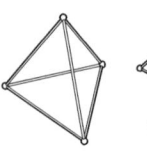 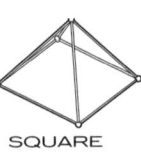 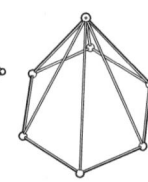

TETRAHEDRON   SQUARE   HEXAGONAL

GRID SHAPES

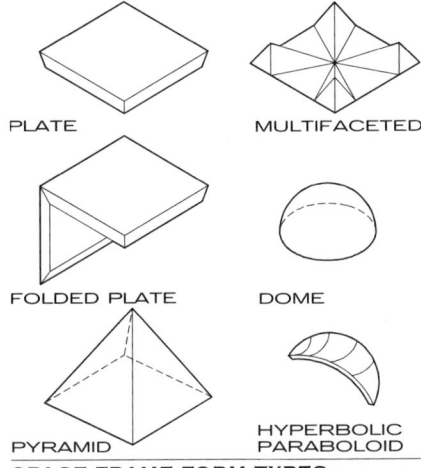

PLATE   MULTIFACETED

FOLDED PLATE   DOME

PYRAMID   HYPERBOLIC PARABOLOID

SPACE FRAME FORM TYPES

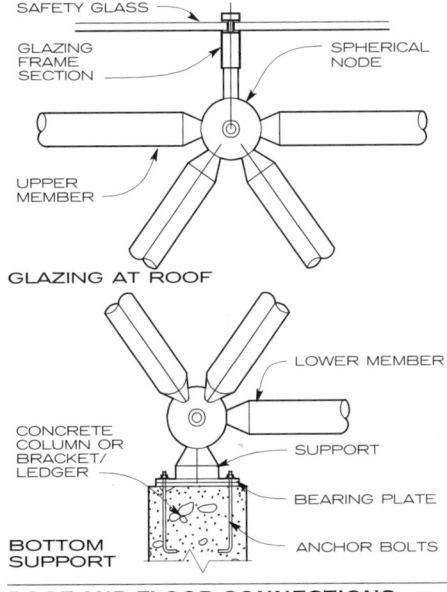

SAFETY GLASS

GLAZING FRAME SECTION

SPHERICAL NODE

UPPER MEMBER

GLAZING AT ROOF

LOWER MEMBER

CONCRETE COLUMN OR BRACKET/ LEDGER

SUPPORT

BEARING PLATE

ANCHOR BOLTS

BOTTOM SUPPORT

ROOF AND FLOOR CONNECTIONS

Severud Associates; New York, New York

PRELIMINARY JOIST SELECTION

The accompanying tables are not to be used for final joist design but are intended as an aid in selecting steel joists for preliminary design and planning. Determining the final design must be a separate and thorough process, involving a complete investigation of pertinent conditions; this page is not intended to support that effort. Consult a structural engineer.

An example of how to use the information presented here follows: Assume a particular clear span. By assuming a joist spacing and estimating the total load, a joist can immediately be selected from the table. Then proceed with preliminary design studies.

NOTES

1. Total safe load = live load + dead load. Dead load includes the weight of the joists. For dead loads and recommended live loads, see pages on weights of materials. Local codes will govern.
2. Span should not exceed a depth 24 times that of a nominal joist.
3. For more information, refer to the standard specifications and load tables adopted by the Steel Joist Institute.

NOTE

The following information applies to both open-web and long-span steel joists.

JOIST DESIGNATION:

```
25  K  10
```
— Chord
— K-Series
— Nominal depth (in.)

For greater economy, the K-series joist replaced the H-series joist in 1986.

ROOF CONSTRUCTION: Joists are usually covered with steel decking topped with either rigid insulation board or lightweight concrete fill and either a roof of built-up felt and gravel or single-ply roofing with ballast. Plywood, poured gypsum, or structural wood fiber deck systems can also be used with a built-up roof.

CEILINGS: Ceiling supports can be suspended from or mounted directly to the bottom chords of joists, although suspended systems are recommended because of dimensional variations in actual joist depths.

FLOOR CONSTRUCTION: Joists are usually covered by $2\frac{1}{2}$ to 3 in. of concrete on steel decking. Concrete thickness may be increased to accommodate electrical conduit or electrical/communications raceways. Precast concrete, gypsum planks, or plywood can also be used for the floor system.

VIBRATION: Objectionable vibrations can occur in open web joist and $2\frac{1}{2}$ in. concrete slab designs for open floor areas at spans between 20 and 40 ft, especially at 28 ft. When a floor area cannot have partitions, objectionable vibrations can be prevented or reduced by increasing slab thickness or modifying the joist span. Attention should also be given to support for framing beams, which can magnify a vibration problem when unsupported.

OPENINGS IN FLOOR OR ROOF SYSTEMS: Small openings between joists are framed with angles or channel supported on the adjoining two joists. Larger openings necessitating interruption of joists are framed with steel angle or channel headers spanning the two adjoining joists. The interrupted joists bear on the headers.

ROOF DRAINAGE: On level or near level roofs, especially those with parapet walls, roof drainage should be carefully considered. Roof insulation can be sloped, and joists can be sloped or obtained with top chords that slope in one or both directions. Overflow scuppers should be provided in parapet walls. If roof slope is less than $\frac{1}{4}$ in. per ft, the roof system should be investigated to ensure stability under ponding conditions.

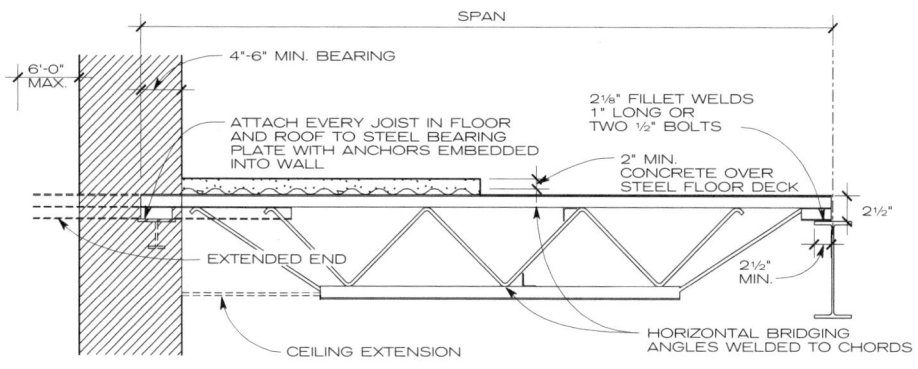

SECTION THROUGH JOIST BEARING

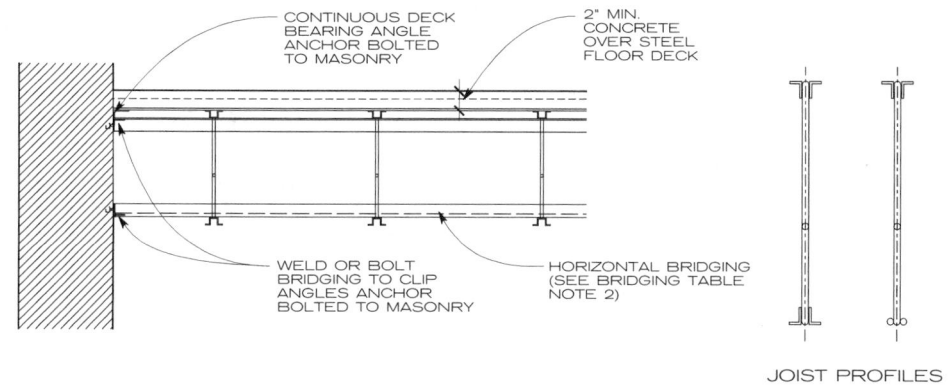

JOIST PROFILES

SECTION THROUGH JOISTS

SELECTED LOAD TABLES: K SERIES—TOTAL SAFE UNIFORMLY DISTRIBUTED LOAD (LB/FT)

JOIST DESIGNATION	SPAN (FT)											
	8	12	16	20	24	28	32	26	42[1]	48[1]	54[1]	60[1]
K SERIES = 30,000												
8K1	550	444	246									
10K1		550	313	199								
12K3		550	476	302	208							
14K4			550	428	295	216						
16K5			550	550	384	281	214[2]					
18K6				550	473	346	264	208[2]				
20K7				550	550	430	328	259				
22K9					550	550	436	344	252[2]			
24K9					550	550	478	377	276	211[2]		
26K10						550	549	486	356	272		
28K10						550	549	487	384	294	232[2]	
30K11							549	487	417	362	285[2]	231[2]
30K12							549	487	417	365	324[2]	262[2]

[1] All joists 40 ft or longer require a row of bolted bridging in place before hoisting lines are slackened.

[2] Where the designed joist span is equal to or greater than this span, the row of bridging nearest the midspan of the joist shall be installed as bolted diagonal bridging. Hoisting cables shall not be released until this bolted diagonal bridging is completely installed.

NUMBER OF ROWS OF BRIDGING

CHORD SIZE[1]	1 ROW[2]	2 ROWS[2]	3 ROWS[2]	4 ROWS[2]	5 ROWS[2]
#1	up to 16	16-24	24-28		
#2	up to 17	17-25	25-32		
#3	up to 18	18-28	28-28	38-40	
#4	up to 19	19-28	28-38	38-48	
#5	up to 19	19-29	29-39	39-50	50-52
#6	up to 19	19-29	29-39	39-51	51-56
#7	up to 20	20-33	33-45	45-58	58-60
#8	up to 20	20-33	33-45	45-58	58-60
#9	up to 20	20-33	33-46	46-59	59-60
#10	up to 20	20-37	37-51	51-60	
#11	up to 20	20-38	38-53	53-60	
#12	up to 20	20-39	39-53	53-60	

[1] Last digit(s) of joist designation shown in accompanying load table.

[2] Check maximum joist span for required midspan bolted diagonal bridging.

NOTE

Distances are clear span dimensions (ft).

Kenneth D. Franch, P.E., AIA; Aguirre, Inc.; Dallas, Texas

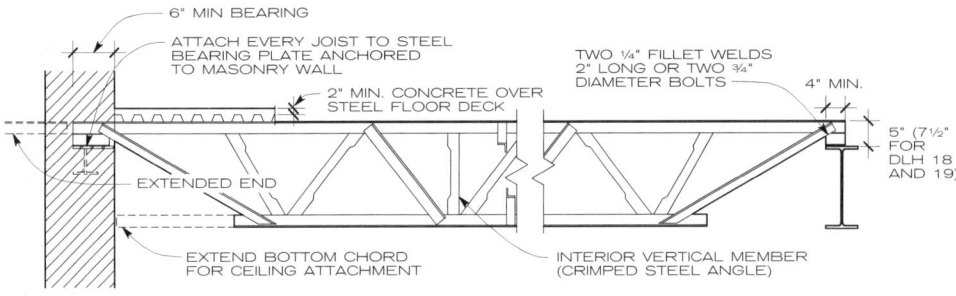

NOTE

Web member type depends on span and load characteristics.

SECTION THROUGH JOIST BEARING

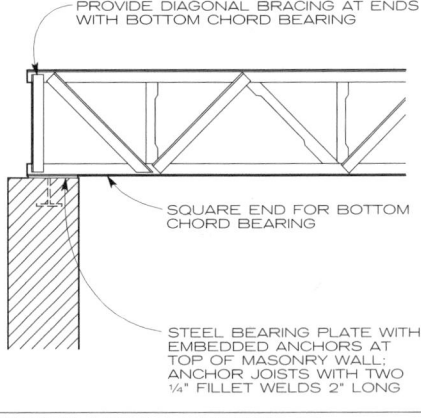

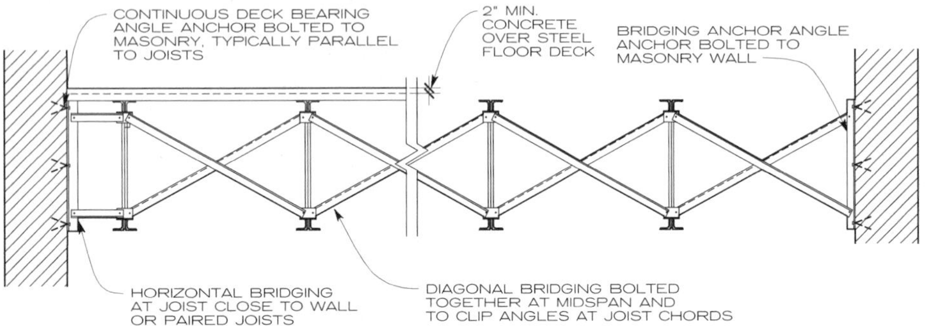

BOTTOM CHORD BEARING AT SQUARE END

SECTION THROUGH JOISTS

FIRE RESISTANCE RATING

TIME (HR)	FLOOR/CEILING ASSEMBLIES	TIME (HR)	ROOF/CEILING ASSEMBLIES
1	2½ in. reinforced concrete, listed ⅝ in. gypsum plaster on metal lath attached to bottom chord of joist	1	Built-up roofing on listed 1 in. wood with cement binder fiberboard over 1½ in. metal deck with listed ¾ in. gypsum plaster ceiling on metal lath attached to furring channels hung from joist
	2 in. reinforced concrete, listed ⅝ in. cement plaster over metal lath attached to bottom chord of joist		Built-up roofing on listed 1 in. wood fiberboard over 1½ in. metal deck with listed ¾ in. gypsum plaster ceiling on metal lath attached to furring channels supported from joist
2	2½ in. reinforced concrete, listed ¾ in. gypsum plaster on metal lath attached to bottom chord of joist	2	Built-up roofing on listed 1⅞ in. wood with cement binder fiberboard over 1½ in. gypsum plaster ceiling on metal lath attached to furring channels supported from joist
	2½ in. reinforced concrete, listed ⅝ in. type X wallboard attached to furring channels tied to bottom chord of joist		Built-up roofing on listed 1½ in. wood fiberboard over 1½ in. metal deck with listed ⅞ in. gypsum plaster ceiling on metal lath attached to furring channels supported from joist
	2½ in. reinforced concrete, listed ¾ in. wood fiber gypsum plaster over metal lath on channels secured to joist		Built-up roofing on listed 1 in. expanded perlite board over 1½ in. metal deck with listed ⅞ in. gypsum-vermiculite plaster on metal lath attached to runner channels supported from joist

NOTE

These are abbreviated assembly descriptions. Table 7-C of the Uniform Building Code gives complete descriptions.

Underwriters Laboratories and Factory Mutual provide additional system, material, and approval guidelines.

SELECTED LOAD TABLES: LH AND DLH SERIES—TOTAL SAFE UNIFORMLY DISTRIBUTED LOAD (LB/FT)

JOIST DESIGNATION		28	32	36	42	48	54	60	66	72	78	84	90	96
		CLEAR SPAN (FT)												
LH Series $f_t^2 = 30{,}000$ psi	18LH05	581	448	355										
	20LH06	723	560	444										
	24LH07			588	446	343								
	28LH09				639	499	401							
	32LH10						478	389						
	26LH11							451	378	322				
	40LH12								472	402	346			
	44LH13										423	369		
	48LH14											444	390	346

JOIST DESIGNATION		90	96	102	108	114	120	126	132	138	144			
DLH Series $f_t = 30{,}000$ psi	52DLH13	433	381	338										
	56DLH14			411	368									
	60DLH15				442	398	361							
	64DLH16					466	421	382						
	68DLH17						460	420						
	72DLH18							505	463	426				

NOTE

Number preceding letter is joist depth (32LH10 is 32 in. deep).

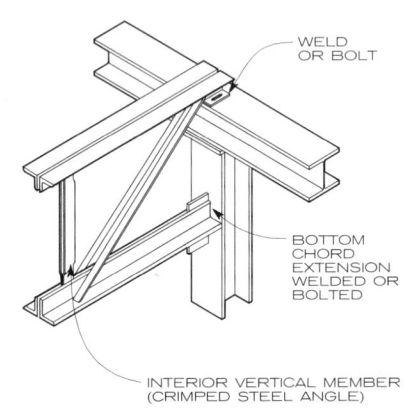

BOTTOM CHORD EXTENSION DETAIL

PRELIMINARY JOIST SELECTION

The accompanying tables should not be used for final joist design but are intended to speed selection of steel joists for preliminary design and planning.

Determining the final design must be a separate, thorough process, involving a complete investigation of pertinent conditions; this page is not to be used for that purpose. Consult a structural engineer.

An example of how to use the information presented here follows: Assume a particular clear span. By assuming a joist spacing and estimating the total load, a joist can immediately be selected from the table. Then proceed with preliminary design studies.

NOTES

1. Total safe load = live load + dead load. Dead load includes the weight of the joist. For dead loads and recommended live loads, see pages on weights of materials. Local codes will govern.
2. Span should not exceed 24 times the depth of a nominal joist for roofs, 20 times the depth of a nominal joist for floors.
3. For more information, refer to standard specifications and load tables adopted by the Steel Joist Institute.

LH AND DLH BRIDGING

BRIDGING SPACING (FT)

CHORD SIZE	MAXIMUM SPACING (FT)
02–04	11
05–06	12
07–08	13
09–10	14
11–14	16
15–17	21
18–19	26

NOTE

Welded horizontal bridging is used for typical joist spans. Check joist bridging requirements when joist spans require midspan bolted diagonal bridging. For spans of more than 60 ft, all bridging should be bolted diagonal bridging.

Charles M. Ault; Setter, Leach & Lindstrom, Architects & Engineers; Minneapolis, Minnesota

ALLOWABLE SPANS FOR SINGLE-SPAN FLOOR JOISTS

NOMINAL JOIST SIZE (WITH MIL THICKNESS)	10 PSF DEAD LOAD + 30 PSF LIVE LOAD SPACING O.C. (IN.)			10 PSF DEAD LOAD + 40 PSF LIVE LOAD SPACING O.C. (IN.)		
	12	16	24	12	16	24
2 x 6 x 33	11 ft 7 in.	10 ft 7 in.	9 ft 1 in.	10 ft 7 in.	9 ft 7 in.	8 ft 1 in.
2 x 6 x 43	12 ft 8 in.	11 ft 6 in.	10 ft 0 in.	11 ft 6 in.	10 ft 5 in.	9 ft 1 in.
2 x 6 x 54	13 ft 7 in.	12 ft 4 in.	10 ft 9 in.	12 ft 4 in.	11 ft 2 in.	9 ft 9 in.
2 x 6 x 68	14 ft 6 in.	13 ft 2 in.	11 ft 6 in.	13 ft 2 in.	12 ft 0 in.	10 ft 6 in.
2 x 6 x 97	16 ft 1 in.	14 ft 7 in.	12 ft 9 in.	14 ft 7 in.	13 ft 3 in.	11 ft 7 in.
2 x 8 x 33	15 ft 8 in.	13 ft 3 in.	8 ft 10 in.	14 ft 0 in.	10 ft 7 in.	7 ft 1 in.
2 x 8 x 43	17 ft 1 in.	15 ft 6 in.	13 ft 7 in.	15 ft 6 in.	14 ft 1 in.	12 ft 3 in.
2 x 8 x 54	18 ft 4 in.	16 ft 8 in.	14 ft 7 in.	16 ft 8 in.	15 ft 2 in.	13 ft 3 in.
2 x 8 x 68	19 ft 8 in.	17 ft 11 in.	15 ft 7 in.	17 ft 11 in.	16 ft 3 in.	14 ft 2 in.
2 x 8 x 97	21 ft 10 in.	19 ft 10 in.	17 ft 4 in.	19 ft 10 in.	18 ft 0 in.	15 ft 9 in.
2 x 10 x 43	20 ft 6 in.	18 ft 8 in.	15 ft 3 in.	18 ft 8 in.	16 ft 8 in.	13 ft 1 in.
2 x 10 x 54	22 ft 1 in.	20 ft 1 in.	17 ft 6 in.	20 ft 1 in.	18 ft 3 in.	15 ft 11 in.
2 x 10 x 68	23 ft 8 in.	21 ft 6 in.	18 ft 10 in.	21 ft 6 in.	19 ft 7 in.	17 ft 1 in.
2 x 10 x 97	26 ft 4 in.	23 ft 11 in.	20 ft 11 in.	23 ft 11 in.	21 ft 9 in.	19 ft 0 in.
2 x 12 x 43	23 ft 5 in.	20 ft 3 in.	14 ft 1 in.	20 ft 11 in.	16 ft 10 in.	11 ft 3 in.
2 x 12 x 54	25 ft 9 in.	23 ft 4 in.	19 ft 7 in.	23 ft 4 in.	21 ft 3 in.	17 ft 6 in.
2 x 12 x 68	27 ft 8 in.	25 ft 1 in.	21 ft 11 in.	25 ft 1 in.	22 ft 10 in.	19 ft 11 in.
2 x 12 x 97	30 ft 9 in.	27 ft 11 in.	24 ft 5 in.	27 ft 11 in.	25 ft 4 in.	22 ft 2 in.

SINGLE SPAN

SPAN

ALLOWABLE SPANS FOR MULTIPLE-SPAN FLOOR JOISTS

NOMINAL JOIST SIZE (WITH MIL THICKNESS)	10 PSF DEAD LOAD + 30 PSF LIVE LOAD SPACING O.C. (IN.)			10 PSF DEAD LOAD + 40 PSF LIVE LOAD SPACING O.C. (IN.)		
	12	16	24	12	16	24
2 x 6 x 33	12 ft 10 in.	10 ft 6 in.	7 ft 10 in.	11 ft 0 in.	9 ft 0 in.	6 ft 7 in.
2 x 6 x 43	15 ft 8 in.	13 ft 6 in.	11 ft 0 in.	14 ft 0 in.	12 ft 1 in.	9 ft 10 in.
2 x 6 x 54	17 ft 7 in.	15 ft 3 in.	12 ft 5 in.	15 ft 9 in.	13 ft 8 in.	11 ft 2 in.
2 x 6 x 68	19 ft 6 in.	17 ft 2 in.	14 ft 0 in.	17 ft 8 in.	15 ft 4 in.	12 ft 6 in.
2 x 6 x 97	21 ft 7 in.	19 ft 7 in.	16 ft 8 in.	19 ft7 in.	17 ft 10 in.	14 ft 11 in.
2 x 8 x 33	12 ft 9 in.	10 ft 2 in.	7 ft 1 in.	10 ft 9 in.	8 ft 6 in.	5 ft 8 in.
2 x 8 x 43	19 ft 5 in.	16 ft 8 in.	12 ft 6 in.	17 ft 5 in.	14 ft 3 in.	10 ft 8 in.
2 x 8 x 54	23 ft 0 in.	19 ft 11 in.	16 ft 3 in.	20 ft 6 in.	17 ft 9 in.	14 ft 6 in.
2 x 8 x 68	25 ft 10 in.	22 ft 5 in.	18 ft 3 in.	23 ft 2 in.	20 ft 0 in.	16 ft 4 in.
2 x 8 x 97	29 ft 4 in.	26 ft 7 in.	21 ft 11 in.	26 ft 7 in.	24 ft 0 in.	19 ft 7 in.
2 x 10 x 43	20 ft 3 in.	16 ft 5 in.	12 ft 1 in.	17 ft 3 in.	13 ft 11 in.	10 ft 2 in.
2 x 10 x 54	25 ft 6 in.	22 ft 1 in.	18 ft 0 in.	22 ft 10 in.	19 ft 9 in.	15 ft 6 in.
2 x 10 x 68	30 ft 6 in.	26 ft 5 in.	21 ft 7 in.	27 ft 4 in.	23 ft 8 in.	19 ft 3 in.
2 x 10 x 97	35 ft 4 in.	31 ft 9 in.	25 ft 11 in.	32 ft 1 in.	28 ft 5 in.	23 ft 2 in.
2 x 12 x 43	19 ft 8 in.	15 ft 9 in.	11 ft 3 in.	16 ft 7 in.	13 ft 3 in.	9 ft 0 in.
2 x 12 x 54	27 ft 8 in.	23 ft 9 in.	17 ft 10 in.	24 ft 9 in.	20 ft 4 in.	15 ft 2 in.
2 x 12 x 68	32 ft 7 in.	28 ft 3 in.	23 ft 0 in.	29 ft 2 in.	25 ft 3 in.	20 ft 7 in.
2 x 12 x 97	41 ft 3 in.	36 ft 7 in.	29 ft 10 in.	37 ft 5 in.	32 ft 9 in.	26 ft 9 in

NOTES

1. The tables above provide maximum joist spans, in feet and inches. For multiple spans, span is either to the right or left of the interior support.

2. Interior bearing supports for multiple span joists should consist of structural (bearing) walls or beams.

3. Bearing stiffeners should be installed at all support points and concentrated loads. End bearing stiffeners are not required for floor joists 54 mil or thicker, spanning 14 ft or less, for one-story houses (walls and roof only) in areas with maximum ground snow load of 30 psf or less.

4. Joists supporting a roof and single wall only may cantilever up to a maximum of 24 in. measured from the center-line of the bearing point, provided that bearing stiffeners are installed at the end of the cantilever and the bearing point and no punchouts are allowed in the cantilevered section. Hole reinforcements may be used to cover up holes.

5. Deflection criteria: L/480 for live loads: L/240 for total loads.

TWO EQUAL SPANS

SPAN   SPAN

American Iron and Steel Institute; Washington, D.C.

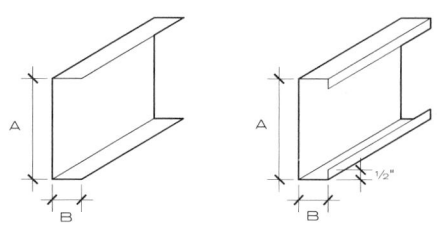

CHANNEL STUDS		C MEMBER	
A (IN.)	B (IN.)	A (IN.)	B (IN.)
2 1/2	1	3 1/2	1 5/8
3 1/4	1 3/8	5 1/2	
3 5/8		8	
4		10	
6		12	

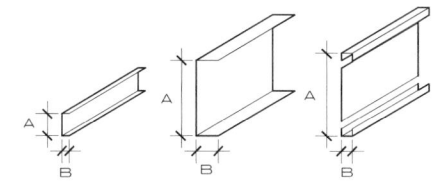

FURRING CHANNEL		C JOIST CLOSURE		NESTABLE JOIST	
A (IN.)	B (IN.)	A (IN.)	B (IN.)	A (IN.)	B (IN.)
3/4	1/2	5 1/2	1 1/4	7 1/4	1 3/4 in.
1 1/2	17/32	6		7 1/2	
		7 1/4		8	
		8		9 1/4	
		9 1/4		9 1/2	
		10		11 1/2	
		12		13 1/2	
		Normally available in all joist sizes			

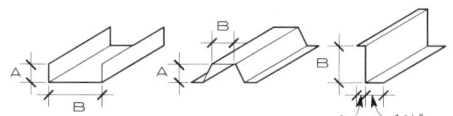

RUNNER CHANNEL		FURRING HAT CHANNEL		Z FURRING	
A (IN.)	B (IN.)	A (IN.)	B (IN.)	A (IN.)	B (IN.)
3/4	2 11/16	7/8	1 3/8	3/4	1
1	3 13/16	1 1/2	1 1/4		1 1/2
1 3/8	3 7/16				2
1 1/4	4 3/16				3
1 1/2	6 3/16				
1 3/4	8 3/16				
3 1/2					

NOTE

Members available in dimensions of 33 through 97 mil.

LIGHT-GAUGE FRAMING MEMBERS

COLD-FORMED STEEL—MINIMUM MATERIAL THICKNESS

Designation (mil)*	18	27	33	43	54	68	97
Minimum delivered uncoated thickness inches (mm)	0.018 (0.455)	0.027 (0.683)	0.033 (0.836)	0.043 (1.087)	0.054 (1.367)	0.068 (1.720)	0.097 (2.454)
Reference gauge number	25	22	20	18	16	14	12

* 1 mil = 1/1000 in.

CEILING JOISTS ALLOWABLE SPANS—SINGLE SPANS, WITHOUT ATTIC STORAGE

NOMINAL JOIST SIZE	UNBRACED SPACING (IN.)			MID-SPAN BRACING SPACING (IN.)			THIRD-POINT BRACING SPACING (IN.)		
	12	16	24	12	16	24	12	16	24
2 x 4 x 33	9 ft 10 in.	9 ft 2 in.	8 ft 3 in.	11 ft 4 in.	10 ft 4 in.	9 ft 0 in.	11 ft 4 in.	10 ft 4 in.	9 ft 0 in.
2 x 4 x 43	10 ft 8 in.	9 ft 11 in.	8 ft 10 in.	12 ft 4 in.	11 ft 2 in.	9 ft 9 in.	12 ft 4 in.	11 ft 2 in.	9 ft 9 in.
2 x 4 x 54	11 ft 7 in.	10 ft 8 in.	9 ft 6 in.	13 ft 2 in.	12 ft 0 in.	10 ft 6 in.	13 ft 2 in.	12 ft 0 in.	10 ft 6 in.
2 x 4 x 68	12 ft 8 in.	11 ft 7 in.	10 ft 4 in.	14 ft 1 in.	12 ft 8 in.	11 ft 2 in.	14 ft 1 in.	12 ft 8 in.	11 ft 2 in.
2 x 4 x 97	14 ft 11 in.	13 ft 7 in.	12 ft 1 in.	15 ft6 in.	14 ft 1 in.	12 ft 4 in.	15 ft 6 in.	14 ft 1 in.	12 ft 4 in.
2 x 6 x 33	11 ft 2 in.	10 ft 5 in.	9 ft 5 in.	15 ft 9 in.	14 ft 5 in.	10 ft 0 in.	16 ft 2 in.	14 ft 8 in.	10 ft 0 in.
2 x 6 x 43	12 ft 1 in.	11 ft 2 in.	10 ft 1 in.	16 ft 10 in.	15 ft 7 in.	13 ft 10 in.	17 ft 7 in.	15 ft 11 in.	13 ft 11 in.
2 x 6 x 54	13 ft 0 in.	12 ft 0 in.	10 ft 9 in.	17 ft 11 in.	16 ft 7 in.	14 ft 9 in.	18 ft 10 in.	17 ft 1 in.	14 ft 11 in.
2 x 6 x 68	14 ft 0 in.	12 ft 11 in.	11 ft 7 in.	19 ft 2 in.	17 ft 8 in.	15 ft 10 in.	20 ft 2 in.	18 ft 4 in.	16 ft 0 in.
2 x 6 x 97	16 ft 3 in.	14 ft 11 in.	13 ft 2 in.	21 ft 6 in.	19 ft 10 in.	17 ft 8 in.	22 ft 4 in.	20 ft 3 in.	17 ft 8 in.
2 x 8 x 33*	12 ft 7 in.	11 ft 8 in.	10 ft 6 in.	17 ft 8 in.	16 ft 5 in.	14 ft 9 in.	21 ft 5 in.	19 ft 5 in.	16 ft 7 in.
2 x 8 x 43	13 ft 6 in.	12 ft 6 in.	11 ft 3 in.	18 ft 10 in.	17 ft 6 in.	15 ft 10 in.	23 ft 0 in.	21 ft 2 in.	17 ft 9 in.
2 x 8 x 54	14 ft 4 in.	13 ft 4 in.	11 ft 11 in.	20 ft 0 in.	18 ft 7 in.	16 ft 9 in.	24 ft 4 in.	22 ft 7 in.	20 ft 0 in.
2 x 8 x 68	15 ft 5 in.	14 ft 3 in.	12 ft 9 in.	21 ft 3 in.	19 ft 8 in.	17 ft 8 in.	25 ft 9 in.	23 ft 11 in.	21 ft 4 in.
2 x 8 x 97	17 ft 8 in.	16 ft 2 in.	14 ft 5 in.	23 ft 8 in.	21 ft 10 in.	19 ft 6 in.	28 ft 4 in.	26 ft 3 in.	23 ft 6 in.
2 x 10 x 43*	14 ft 5 in.	13 ft 4 in.	12 ft 1 in.	20 ft 2 in.	18 ft 9 in.	16 ft 11 in.	24 ft 8 in.	22 ft 11 in.	20 ft 6 in.
2 x 10 x 54	15 ft 4 in.	14 ft 2 in.	12 ft 9 in.	21 ft 4 in.	19 ft 10 in.	17 ft 10 in.	26 ft 0 in.	24 ft 2 in.	21 ft 9 in.
2 x 10 x 68	16 ft 5 in.	15 ft 2 in.	13 ft 7 in.	22 ft 8 in.	21 ft 0 in.	18 ft 11 in.	27 ft 6 in.	25 ft 6 in.	23 ft 0 in.
2 x 10 x 97	18 ft 7 in.	17 ft 1 in.	15 ft 2 in.	25 ft 1 in.	23 ft 2 in.	20 ft 9 in.	30 ft 2 in.	27 ft 11 in.	25 ft 1 in.
2 x 12 x 43	15 ft 2 in.	14 ft 1 in.	12 ft 8 in.	21 ft 4 in.	19 ft 10 in.	17 ft 11 in.	26 ft 1 in.	24 ft 3 in.	21 ft 6 in.
2 x 12 x 54	16 ft 1 in.	15 ft 0 in.	13 ft 5 in.	22 ft 7 in.	20 ft 11 in.	18 ft 11 in.	27 ft 6 in.	25 ft 7 in.	23 ft 1 in.
2 x 12 x 68	17 ft 3 in.	15 ft 11 in.	14 ft 4 in.	23 ft 11 in.	22 ft 2 in.	19 ft 11 in.	29 ft 0 in.	27 ft 0 in.	24 ft 4 in.
2 x 12 x 97	19 ft 5 in.	17 ft 10 in.	15 ft 11 in.	26 ft 4 in.	24 ft 4 in.	21 ft 10 in.	31 ft 8 in.	29 ft 4 in.	26 ft 5 in.

* Bearing stiffeners shall be installed at all support points and concentrated loads.

CEILING JOISTS ALLOWABLE SPANS—SINGLE SPANS, WITH ATTIC STORAGE (20 PSF)

NOMINAL JOIST SIZE	UNBRACED SPACING (IN.)			MID-SPAN BRACING SPACING (IN.)			THIRD-POINT BRACING SPACING (IN.)		
	12	16	24	12	16	24	12	16	24
2 x 4 x 33	8 ft 8 in.	8 ft 0 in.	6 ft 0 in.	9 ft 7 in.	8 ft 8 in.	6 ft 0 in.	9 ft 7 in.	8 ft 8 in.	6 ft 0 in.
2 x 4 x 43	9 ft 4 in.	8 ft 8 in.	7 ft 8 in.	10 ft 5 in.	9 ft 5 in.	8 ft 3 in.	10 ft 5 in.	9 ft 5 in.	8 ft 3 in.
2 x 4 x 54	10 ft 0 in.	9 ft 3 in.	8 ft 3 in.	11 ft 2 in.	10 ft 1 in.	8 ft 10 in.	11 ft 2 in.	10 ft 1 in.	8 ft 10 in.
2 x 4 x 68	10 ft 11 in.	10 ft 0 in.	8 ft 11 in.	10 ft 11 in.	10 ft 0 in.	8 ft 11 in.	1 ft11 in.	10 ft 0 in.	8 ft 11 in.
2 x 4 x 97	12 ft 8 in.	11 ft 7 in.	10 ft3 in.	13 ft 1 in.	11 ft 11 in.	10 ft 5 in.	13 ft 1 in.	11 ft 11 in.	10 ft 5 in.
2 x 6 x 33*	9 ft 10 in.	9 ft 0 in.	6 ft 0 in.	12 ft 0 in.	9 ft 0 in.	6 ft 0 in.	12 ft 0 in.	9 ft 0 in.	6 ft 0 in.
2 x 6 x 43	10 ft 7 in.	9 ft 10 in.	8 ft 10 in.	14 ft 7 in.	13 ft 4 in.	11 ft 6 in.	14 ft 10 in.	13 ft 5 in.	11 ft 8 in.
2 x 6 x 54	11 ft 3 in.	10 ft 5 in.	9 ft 5 in.	15 ft 7 in.	14 ft 4 in.	12 ft 6 in.	15 ft 11 in.	14 ft 5 in.	12 ft 7 in.
2 x 6 x 68	12 ft 2 in.	11 ft 3 in.	10 ft 0 in.	16 ft 8 in.	15 ft 4 in.	13 ft 5 in.	17 ft 0 in.	15 ft 5 in.	13 ft 6 in.
2 x 6 x 97	13 ft 11 in.	12 ft 9 in.	11 ft 4 in.	18 ft 7 in.	17 ft 1 in.	14 ft 11 in.	18 ft 10 in.	17 ft 1 in.	14 ft 11 in.
2 x 8 x 33	11 ft 0 in.	10 ft 3 in.	9 ft 3 in.	15 ft 6 in.	14 ft 4 in.	12 ft 5 in.	17 ft 10 in.	15 ft 11 in.	13 ft 4 in.
2 x 8 x 43	11 ft 10 in.	10 ft 11 in.	9 ft 10 in.	16 ft 7 in.	15 ft 5 in.	10 ft 8 in.	19 ft 9 in.	16 ft 0 in.	10 ft 8 in.
2 x 8 x 54	12 ft 7 in.	11 ft 8 in.	10 ft 6 in.	17 ft 6 in.	16 ft 33 in.	14 ft 7 in.	21 ft 2 in.	19 ft 3 in.	16 ft 8 in.
2 x 8 x 68	13 ft 5 in.	12 ft 5 in.	11 ft 2 in.	18 ft 7 in.	17 ft 3 in.	15 ft 6 in.	22 ft 6 in.	20 ft 7 in.	18 ft 0 in.
2 x 8 x 97	15 ft 2 in.	13 ft 11 in.	12 ft 5 in.	20 ft 6 in.	18 ft 11 in.	17 ft 0 in.	24 ft 8 in.	22 ft 9 in.	20 ft 1 in.
2 x 10 x 43*	12 ft 7 in.	11 ft 9 in.	10 ft 7 in.	17 ft 9 in.	16 ft 6 in.	14 ft 10 in.	21 ft 7 in.	19 ft 10 in.	17 ft 1 in.
2 x 10 x 54	13 ft 5 in.	12 ft 52 in.	11 ft 2 in.	18 ft 9 in.	17 ft 5 in.	15 ft 8 in.	22 ft 10 in.	21 ft 1 in.	16 ft 9 in.
2 x 10 x 68	14 ft 3 in.	13 ft 3 in.	11 ft 10 in.	19 ft 10 in.	18 ft 5 in.	16 ft 7 in.	24 ft 1 in.	22 ft 4 in.	19 ft 11 in.
2 x 10 x 97	16 ft 0 in.	14 ft 9 in.	13 ft 2 in.	21 ft 9 in.	20 ft 2 in.	18 ft 1 in.	26 ft 3 in.	24 ft 4 in.	21 ft 10 in.
2 x 12 x 43	13 ft 4 in.	12 ft 5 in.	11 ft 2 in.	18 ft 9 in.	17 ft 5 in.	15 ft 8 in.	22 ft 9 in.	20 ft 9 in.	18 ft 0 in.
2 x 12 x 54	14 ft 1 in.	13 ft 1 in.	11 ft 9 in.	19 ft 9 in.	18 ft 5 in.	16 ft 7 in.	24 ft 2 in.	22 ft 5 in.	20 ft 1 in.
2 x 12 x 68	15 ft 0 in.	13 ft 11 in.	12 ft 6 in.	20 ft 11 in.	19 ft 5 in.	17 ft 6 in.	25 ft 6 in.	23 ft 8 in.	21 ft 3 in.
2 x 12 x 97	16 ft 9 in.	15 ft 5 in.	13 ft 10 in.	22 ft 11 in.	21 ft 2 in.	19 ft 0 in.	27 ft 8 in.	25 ft 8 in.	23 ft 1 in.

* Bearing stiffeners shall be installed at all support points and concentrated loads.

NOTES

1. The tables above provide the maximum ceiling joist span in feet and inches.
2. Deflection criteria: L/240 for total loads.
3. Ceiling dead load = 5 psf (0.24 kPa).
4. 1 in. = 25.4 mm, 1 ft = 304.8 mm, 1 psf = 48 Pa.

American Iron and Steel Institute; Washington, D.C.

COLD-FORMED METAL FRAMING

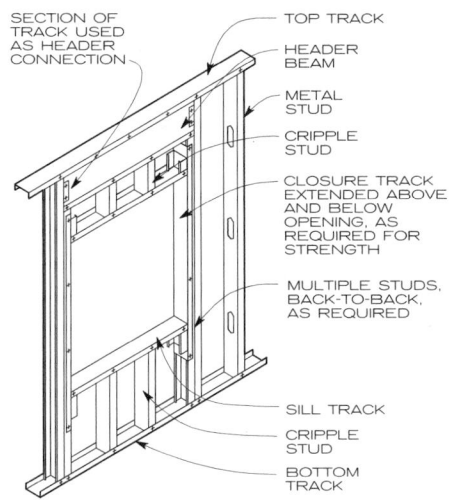

SECTION OF TRACK USED AS HEADER CONNECTION

TOP TRACK

HEADER BEAM

METAL STUD

CRIPPLE STUD

CLOSURE TRACK EXTENDED ABOVE AND BELOW OPENING, AS REQUIRED FOR STRENGTH

MULTIPLE STUDS, BACK-TO-BACK, AS REQUIRED

SILL TRACK

CRIPPLE STUD

BOTTOM TRACK

WINDOW OPENING

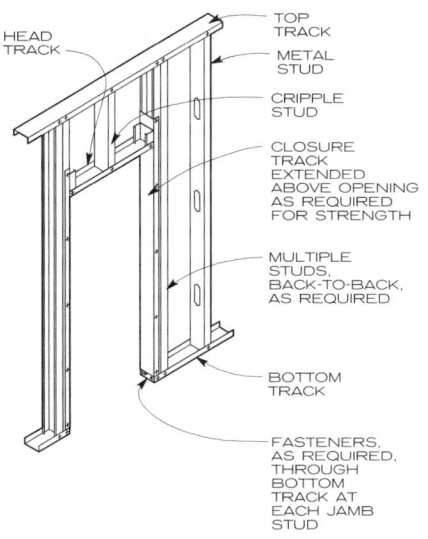

DOORJAMB

SECTION OF STUD AS REQUIRED TO STIFFEN TRACK

FASTENERS AS REQUIRED AT EACH JAMB STUD

TRACK

WEB STIFFENER AS REQUIRED

SOLID BLOCKING BETWEEN JOISTS AT DOORJAMB

JOIST TRACK

SHEATHING

JOIST

DOORJAMB BASE AT FLOOR FRAMING

HEAD TRACK

TOP TRACK

METAL STUD

CRIPPLE STUD

CLOSURE TRACK EXTENDED ABOVE OPENING AS REQUIRED FOR STRENGTH

MULTIPLE STUDS, BACK-TO-BACK, AS REQUIRED

BOTTOM TRACK

FASTENERS, AS REQUIRED, THROUGH BOTTOM TRACK AT EACH JAMB STUD

DOOR OPENING

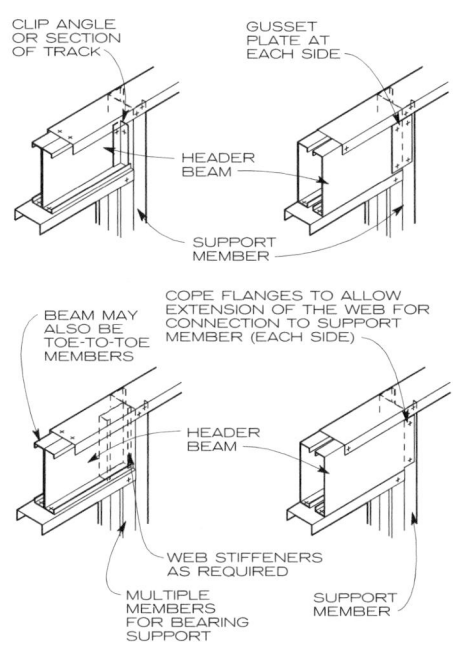

CLIP ANGLE OR SECTION OF TRACK

GUSSET PLATE AT EACH SIDE

HEADER BEAM

TOP TRACK

SUPPORT MEMBER

BEAM MAY ALSO BE TOE-TO-TOE MEMBERS

COPE FLANGES TO ALLOW EXTENSION OF THE WEB FOR CONNECTION TO SUPPORT MEMBER (EACH SIDE)

HEADER BEAM

WEB STIFFENERS AS REQUIRED

MULTIPLE MEMBERS FOR BEARING SUPPORT

SUPPORT MEMBER

HEADER BEAMS FOR WIDE OPENINGS

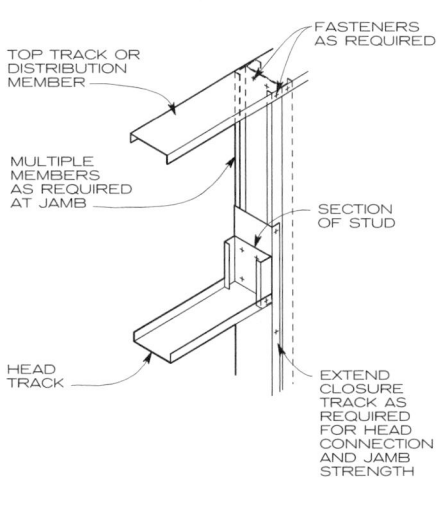

TOP TRACK OR DISTRIBUTION MEMBER

FASTENERS AS REQUIRED

MULTIPLE MEMBERS AS REQUIRED AT JAMB

SECTION OF STUD

HEAD TRACK

EXTEND CLOSURE TRACK AS REQUIRED FOR HEAD CONNECTION AND JAMB STRENGTH

NOTE

Detail may be applicable to larger openings in interior partitions. For nonaxial loads.

HEAD AT OPENING LESS THAN 4 FEET (LOAD-BEARING WALL)

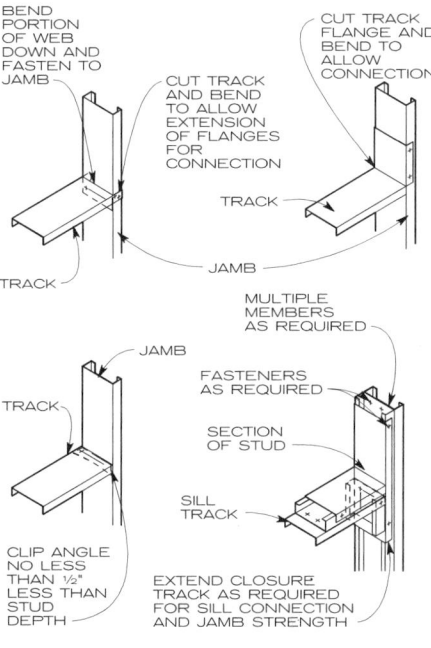

BEND PORTION OF WEB DOWN AND FASTEN TO JAMB

CUT TRACK AND BEND TO ALLOW EXTENSION OF FLANGES FOR CONNECTION

CUT TRACK FLANGE AND BEND TO ALLOW CONNECTION

TRACK

TRACK

JAMB

MULTIPLE MEMBERS AS REQUIRED

JAMB

TRACK

FASTENERS AS REQUIRED

SECTION OF STUD

SILL TRACK

CLIP ANGLE NO LESS THAN ½" LESS THAN STUD DEPTH

EXTEND CLOSURE TRACK AS REQUIRED FOR SILL CONNECTION AND JAMB STRENGTH

SILL CONNECTIONS AT JAMB

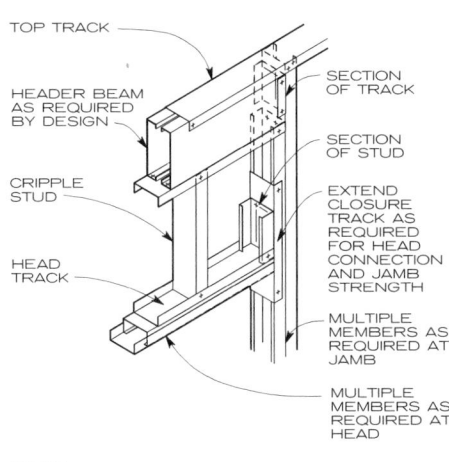

TOP TRACK

HEADER BEAM AS REQUIRED BY DESIGN

CRIPPLE STUD

HEAD TRACK

SECTION OF TRACK

SECTION OF STUD

EXTEND CLOSURE TRACK AS REQUIRED FOR HEAD CONNECTION AND JAMB STRENGTH

MULTIPLE MEMBERS AS REQUIRED AT JAMB

MULTIPLE MEMBERS AS REQUIRED AT HEAD

NOTE

For axial loads.

OPENING GREATER THAN OR EQUAL TO 4 FEET(LOAD-BEARING WALL)

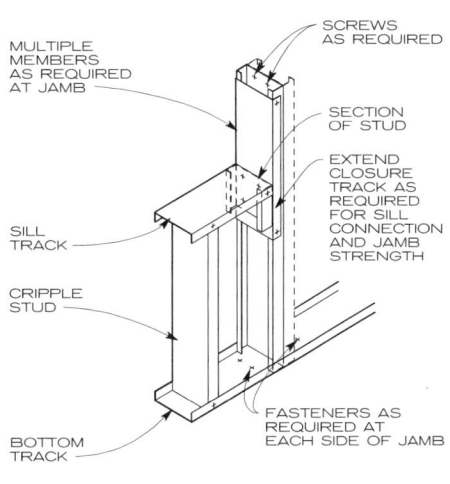

MULTIPLE MEMBERS AS REQUIRED AT JAMB

SCREWS AS REQUIRED

SECTION OF STUD

EXTEND CLOSURE TRACK AS REQUIRED FOR SILL CONNECTION AND JAMB STRENGTH

SILL TRACK

CRIPPLE STUD

BOTTOM TRACK

FASTENERS AS REQUIRED AT EACH SIDE OF JAMB

JAMB AND SILL AT OPENING LESS THAN 4 FEET

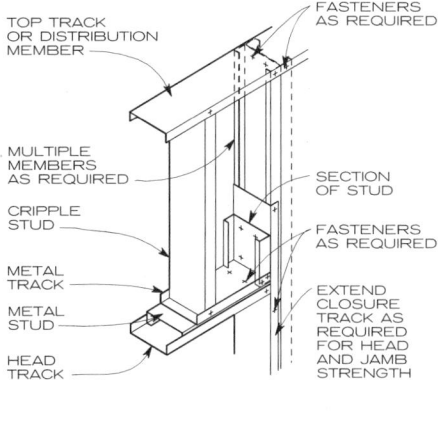

TOP TRACK OR DISTRIBUTION MEMBER

FASTENERS AS REQUIRED

MULTIPLE MEMBERS AS REQUIRED

CRIPPLE STUD

METAL TRACK

METAL STUD

HEAD TRACK

SECTION OF STUD

FASTENERS AS REQUIRED

EXTEND CLOSURE TRACK AS REQUIRED FOR HEAD AND JAMB STRENGTH

NOTE

For nonaxial loads.

OPENINGS GREATER THAN OR EQUAL TO 4 FEET(LOAD-BEARING WALL)

American Iron and Steel Institute; Washington, D.C.

COLD-FORMED METAL FRAMING   5

GENERAL

Lightweight steel framing is cold-formed, which means the components are manufactured by brake-forming and punching galvanized coil and sheet stock. Steel framing members consist of two basic types of components that are C-shaped in section: one type has $1/4$-in. flanges folded inward and the other has no flanges. Studs, joists, and rafters are made with flanges to stiffen them so they will more readily stand vertically. Components without flanges, called tracks, have unpunched solid webs. For added strength, tracks are sized slightly larger than the flanged members so the tracks will fit snugly inside them as sill or top plates or as part of posts or headers.

Steel framing is strong and versatile. The strength (and load-carrying capacity) of a member can be increased simply by increasing the thickness, or gauge, of the metal; the dimensions of the member, or the spacing, do not necessarily have to be increased. There is little limitation on the length of steel framing members; joists or studs may be fabricated in lengths up to 40 ft. If handled with care, steel framing is straight and consistent; also, it is not affected by moisture content.

Disadvantages of steel framing include lack of insulating qualities, difficulty in cutting compared to wood, and dangerously sharp edges. Consult the American Iron and Steel Institute (AISI) for further information.

BRACING

Buildings must be properly braced to resist racking under wind and seismic loads. Diagonal strap bracing is sloped to resist racking forces in tension and fastened by screws or welds to studs and plates. Properly spaced lateral steel bracing resists stud rotation and minor axis bending under wind, seismic, and axial loads; it is especially critical during construction, before sheathing or finishes are installed.

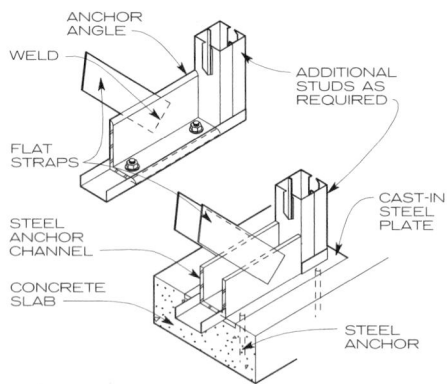

NOTE

The top detail is for one-to-two story buildings and the bottom detail for buildings greater than two stories. Steel channel, plate, and anchor size depend on applied uplift and horizontal shear forces.

DIAGONAL STABILITY BRACING ANCHORAGE DETAILS

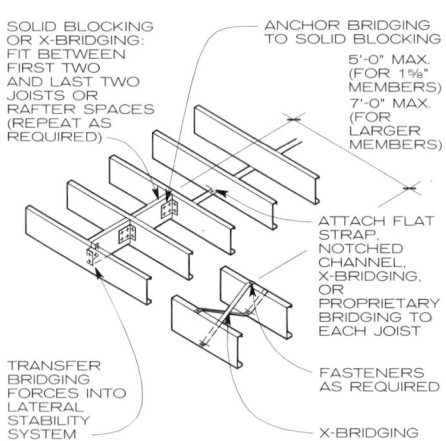

NOTE

If sheathing is not installed on members, bridging is required on both flanges.

JOIST OR RAFTER BRIDGING

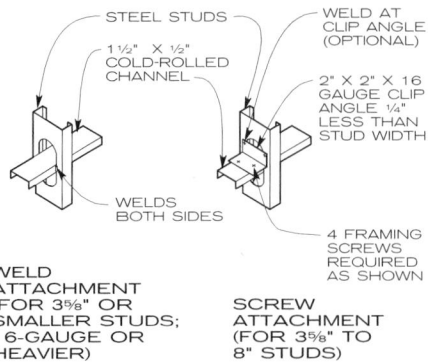

WELD ATTACHMENT (FOR 3⅝" OR SMALLER STUDS; 16-GAUGE OR HEAVIER)   SCREW ATTACHMENT (FOR 3⅝" TO 8" STUDS)

NOTE

Channels to be spaced as required by design.

LATERAL BRACING ATTACHMENT

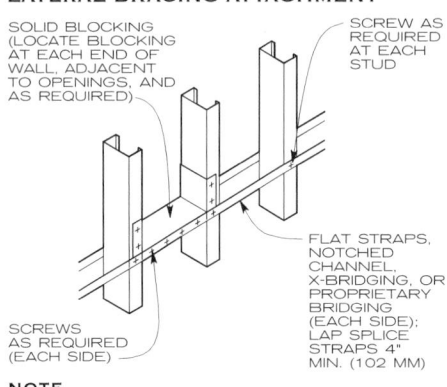

NOTE

Number of rows of bridging as required by design.

WALL BRIDGING

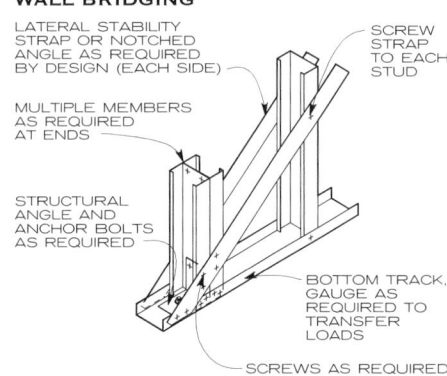

NOTE

Strap forces may require additional stiffening of the bottom track or structural angle.

DIAGONAL STABILITY BRACING ANCHORAGE

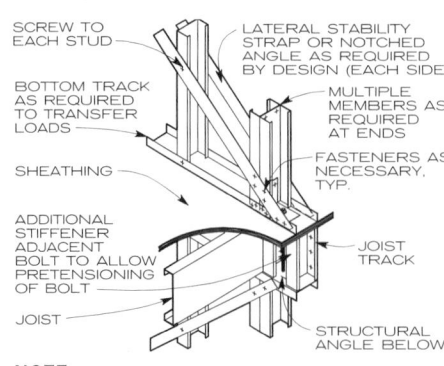

NOTE

Strap forces may require additional stiffening of top and bottom track or structural angle.

DIAGONAL STABILITY BRACING AT INTERMEDIATE FLOOR

LIMITING HEIGHT TABLES FOR INTERIOR PARTITIONS AND CHASE WALL PARTITIONS

STUD WIDTH	STUD SPAC-ING	ALLOW DEFL.	PARTITION ONE LAYER	PARTITION TWO LAYERS

LIMITING HEIGHT 18 MIL STEEL STUD ASSEMBLIES

STUD WIDTH	STUD SPAC-ING	ALLOW DEFL.	PARTITION ONE LAYER	PARTITION TWO LAYERS
1⅝"	16"	$1/120$	10' 9" d	10' 9" d
		$1/240$	9' 6" d	10' 6" d
	24"	$1/120$	8' 9" f	8' 9" f
		$1/240$	8' 3" f	8' 9" f
2½"	16"	$1/120$	14' 3" f	14' 3" f
		$1/240$	12' 6" d	13' 6" d
	24"	$1/120$	11' 6" f	11' 6" f
		$1/240$	10' 9" d	11' 6" f
3⅝"	16 "	$1/120$	18' 3" f	18' 3" f
		$1/240$	16' 0" d	17' 0" d
	24"	$1/120$	15' 0" f	15' 0" f
		$1/240$	14' 0" d	14' 9" d
4"	16"	$1/120$	19' 6" f	19' 6" f
		$1/240$	17' 3" d	18' 3" d
	24"	$1/120$	16' 0" f	16' 0" f
		$1/240$	15' 0" d	15' 0" d

33 MIL STEEL STUD ASSEMBLIES

STUD WIDTH	STUD SPAC-ING	ALLOW DEFL.	PARTITION ONE LAYER	PARTITION TWO LAYERS
2½"	16"	$1/120$	17' 9" d	18' 6" d
		$1/240$	14' 0" d	14' 9" d
	24"	$1/120$	15' 6" d	16' 3" f
		$1/240$	12' 3" d	13' 0" d
3⅝"	16"	$1/120$	23' 0" d	24' 0" d
		$1/240$	18' 3" d	19' 0" d
	24"	$1/120$	20' 0" d	20' 9" d
		$1/240$	16' 0" d	16' 6" d
4"	16"	$1/120$	24' 9" d	25' 9" d
		$1/240$	19' 6" d	20' 3" d
	24"	$1/120$	21' 6" d	22' 0" f
		$1/240$	17' 3" d	17' 9" d

LIMITING HEIGHT 18 MIL CHASE WALL PARTITIONS

STUD WIDTH	STUD SPAC-ING	ALLOW DEFL.	PARTITION ONE LAYER	PARTITION TWO LAYERS
1⅝"	16"	$1/120$	15' 3" f	15' 3" f
		$1/240$	13' 3" d	14' 6" d
	24"	$1/120$	12' 6" f	12' 6" f
		$1/240$	11' 6" d	12' 6" f
2½"	16"	$1/120$	90' 3" f	20' 3" f
		$1/240$	17' 6" d	19' 0"' d
	24"	$1/120$	16' 6" f	16' 6" f
		$1/240$	15' 6" d	16' 6" f
3⅝"	16"	$1/120$	25' 9" f	25' 9" f
		$1/240$	22' 9" d	24' 3" d
	24"	$1/120$	21' 0" d	21' 0" f
		$1/240$	19' 9" d	21' 0" f
2½" *	16"	$1/120$	24' 3" d	25' 9" d
		$1/240$	19' 3" d	20' 6" d
	24"	$1/120$	21' 3" d	22' 6" f
		$1/240$	17' 0" d	18' 0" d

* 33 mil chase wall partitions.

NOTE

Limiting height for $1/2$ or $5/8$ in. thick panels and 5 psf uniform load perpendicular to partition or furring. Use one-layer heights for unbalanced assemblies. Consult local code authority for limiting criteria (d—deflection, f—bending stress).

American Iron and Steel Institute; Washington, D.C.

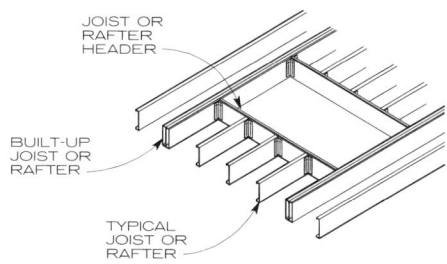

TYPICAL OPENING IN JOISTS/RAFTERS

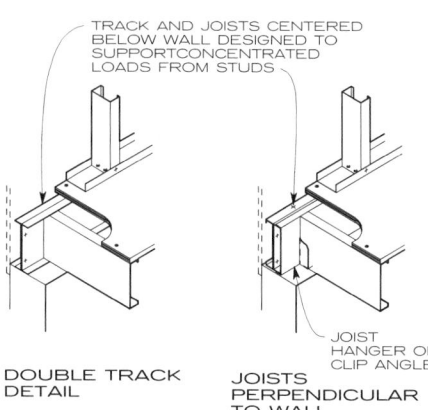

DOUBLE TRACK DETAIL

JOISTS PERPENDICULAR TO WALL

RIM JOIST DETAILS

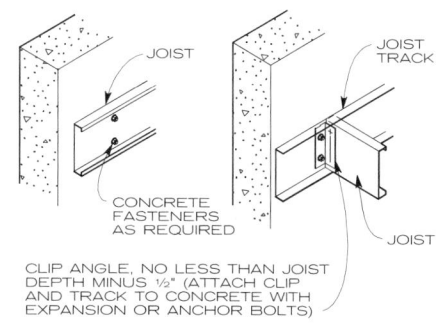

FLOOR JOISTS PARALLEL TO WALL

FLOOR JOIST SUPPORT AT WALL

NOTE

Provide solid blocking and bridging as required.

FLOOR JOISTS AT CONTINUOUS WALL

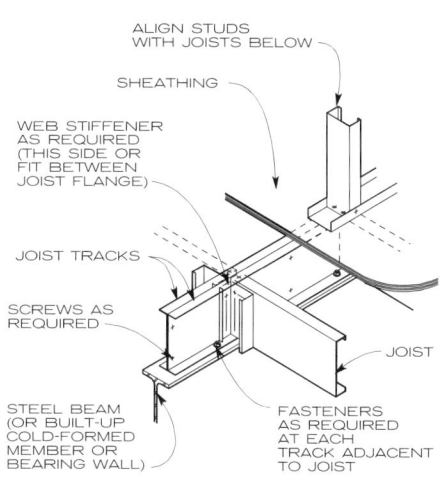

JOISTS SUPPORTED BY BEAM OR BEARING WALL

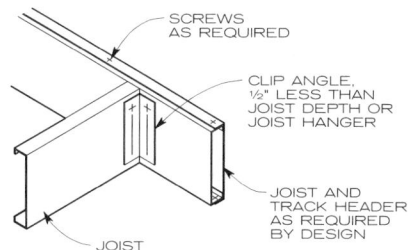

JOIST-TO-JOIST HEADER

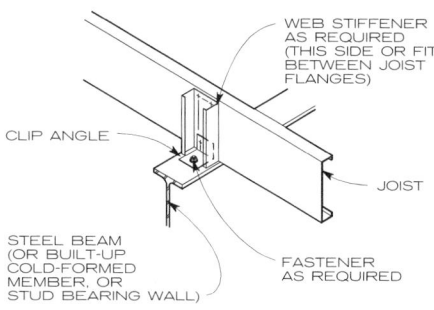

NOTES

1. Continuous bridging is required between each joist above a beam. Solid blocking in every other space may be used in lieu of bridging.

2. When a bearing wall is above, the studs must align with the joists below.

3. Web stiffeners are not required when continuous solid blocking is used.

JOISTS OVER BEAM OR BEARING WALL (CONTINUOUS SPAN)

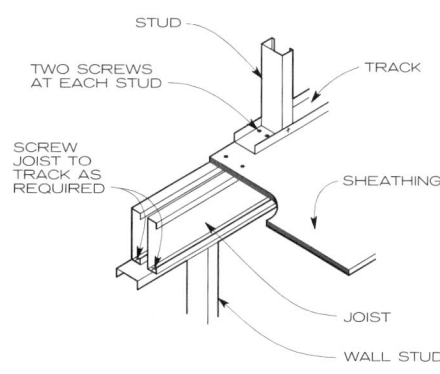

FLOOR JOISTS PARALLEL TO EXTERIOR WALL

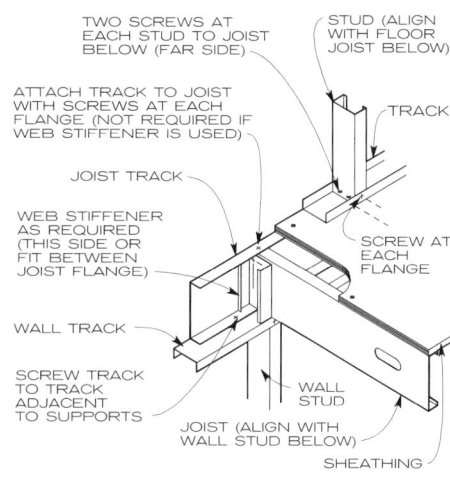

FLOOR FRAMING AT EXTERIOR WALL

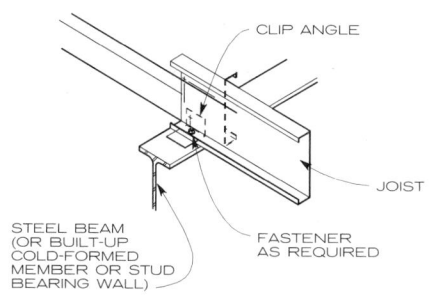

NOTES

1. Continuous bridging is required between each joist above a beam. Solid blocking in every other space may be used in lieu of bridging.

2. When a bearing wall is above, studs must align with joists below.

FLOOR JOISTS SUPPORTED BY BEAM OR BEARING WALL (OVERLAPPED)

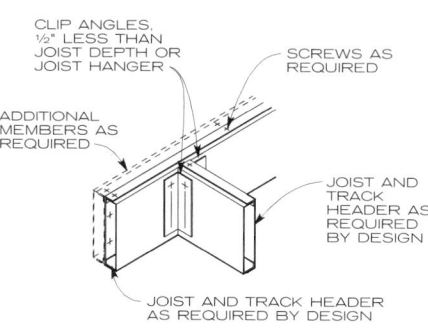

JOIST HEADER TO BUILT-UP JOISTS

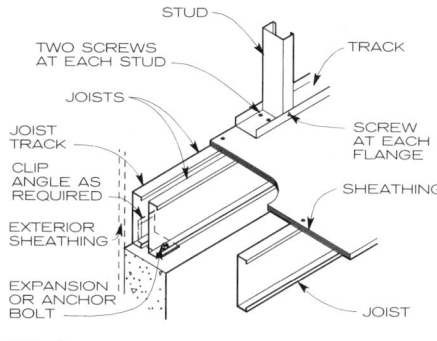

NOTE

Provide solid blocking and bridging as required.

FLOOR JOISTS PARALLEL TO FOUNDATION

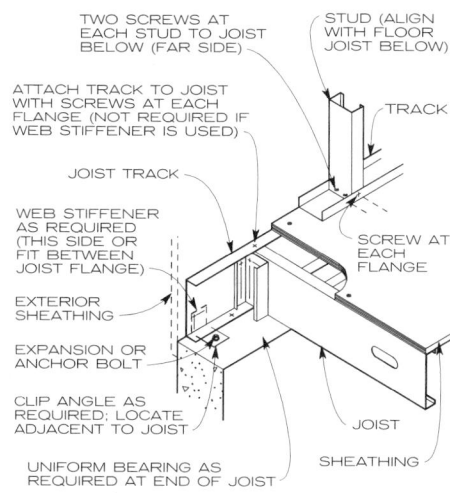

FLOOR JOISTS BEARING ON FOUNDATION

American Iron and Steel Institute; Washington, D.C.

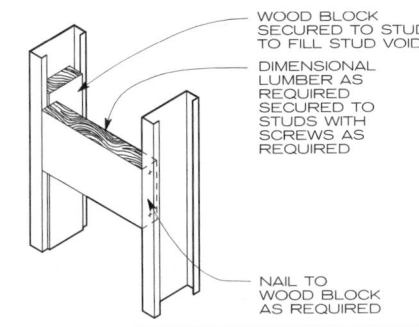

WOOD BLOCK SECURED TO STUD TO FILL STUD VOID

DIMENSIONAL LUMBER AS REQUIRED SECURED TO STUDS WITH SCREWS AS REQUIRED

NAIL TO WOOD BLOCK AS REQUIRED

HEAVY FIXTURE ATTACHMENT

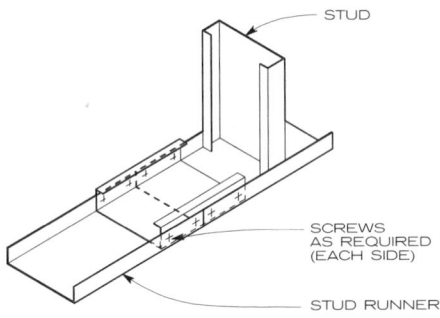

STUD

SCREWS AS REQUIRED (EACH SIDE)

STUD RUNNER

TOP AND BOTTOM TRACK SPLICE

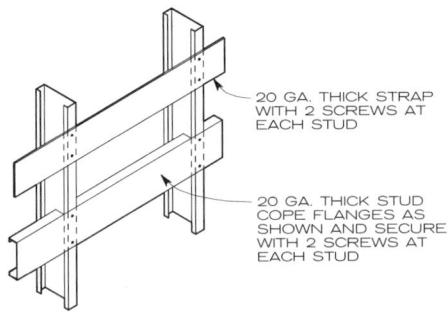

20 GA. THICK STRAP WITH 2 SCREWS AT EACH STUD

20 GA. THICK STUD COPE FLANGES AS SHOWN AND SECURE WITH 2 SCREWS AT EACH STUD

NOTE

Dimensional lumber may also be used for backing.

BACKING FOR CABINETS

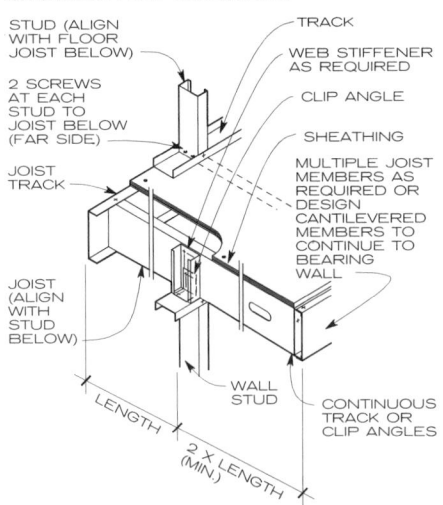

STUD (ALIGN WITH FLOOR JOIST BELOW)

TRACK

WEB STIFFENER AS REQUIRED

2 SCREWS AT EACH STUD TO JOIST BELOW (FAR SIDE)

CLIP ANGLE

SHEATHING

JOIST TRACK

MULTIPLE JOIST MEMBERS AS REQUIRED OR DESIGN CANTILEVERED MEMBERS TO CONTINUE TO BEARING WALL

JOIST (ALIGN WITH STUD BELOW)

WALL STUD

CONTINUOUS TRACK OR CLIP ANGLES

LENGTH

2 X LENGTH (MIN.)

NOTES

1. Provide continuous bridging between each joist at the lower wall.
2. Solid blocking in every other space may be used in lieu of bridging.
3. Where axial load-bearing members do not align vertically, provide top track distribution members at wall below.

FLOOR CANTILEVER

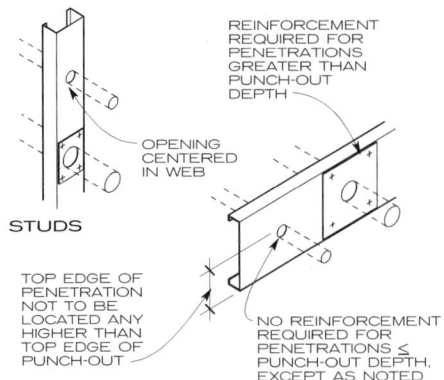

REINFORCEMENT REQUIRED FOR PENETRATIONS GREATER THAN PUNCH-OUT DEPTH

OPENING CENTERED IN WEB

STUDS

TOP EDGE OF PENETRATION NOT TO BE LOCATED ANY HIGHER THAN TOP EDGE OF PUNCH-OUT

NO REINFORCEMENT REQUIRED FOR PENETRATIONS ≤ PUNCH-OUT DEPTH, EXCEPT AS NOTED

JOISTS OR RAFTERS

NOTES

1. Do not notch or cut flanges.
2. Capacity verification by design is required for any openings located at concentrated loads and bearing ends.
3. For unpunched members, consult the manufacturer.

JOIST, STUD, OR RAFTER WEB PENETRATIONS

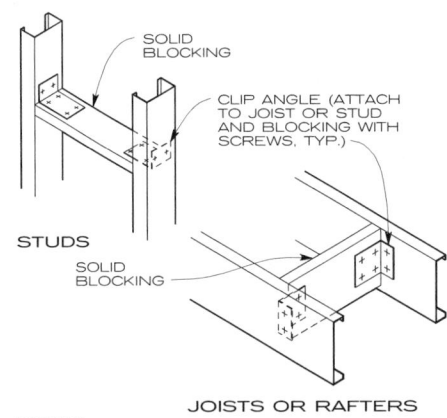

SOLID BLOCKING

CLIP ANGLE (ATTACH TO JOIST OR STUD AND BLOCKING WITH SCREWS, TYP.)

STUDS

SOLID BLOCKING

JOISTS OR RAFTERS

NOTES

1. Where blocking material thickness allows, notch and bend track 90 degrees for connection.
2. Where provisions are made for transfer of flange forces to solid blocking, blocking need not be in the full depth of the member.

SOLID BLOCKING

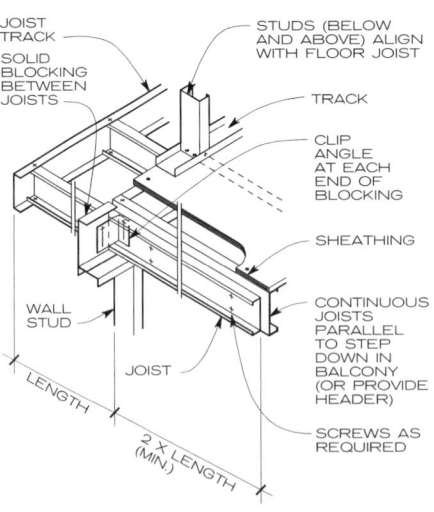

JOIST TRACK

SOLID BLOCKING BETWEEN JOISTS

STUDS (BELOW AND ABOVE) ALIGN WITH FLOOR JOIST

TRACK

CLIP ANGLE AT EACH END OF BLOCKING

SHEATHING

WALL STUD

JOIST

CONTINUOUS JOISTS PARALLEL TO STEP DOWN IN BALCONY (OR PROVIDE HEADER)

SCREWS AS REQUIRED

LENGTH

2 X LENGTH (MIN.)

NOTES

1. Balconies require special detailing and protection against moisture and thermal bridging.
2. Where axial load-bearing members do not align vertically, provide top track distribution members at wall below.

BALCONY WITH STEP DOWN

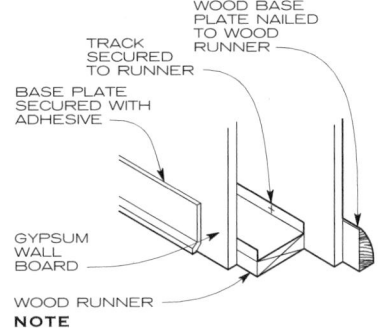

WOOD BASE PLATE NAILED TO WOOD RUNNER

TRACK SECURED TO RUNNER

BASE PLATE SECURED WITH ADHESIVE

GYPSUM WALL BOARD

WOOD RUNNER

NOTE

This detail is optional depending on contractor preference.

NAILABLE BASE PLATE

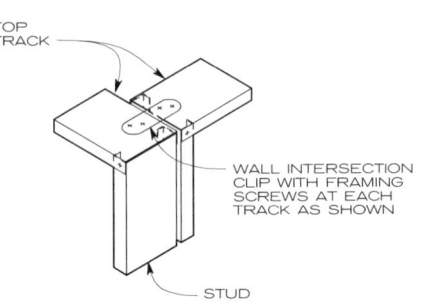

TOP TRACK

WALL INTERSECTION CLIP WITH FRAMING SCREWS AT EACH TRACK AS SHOWN

STUD

TOP PLATE INTERSECTION

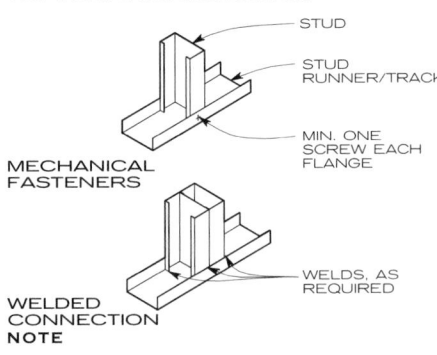

STUD

STUD RUNNER/TRACK

MIN. ONE SCREW EACH FLANGE

MECHANICAL FASTENERS

WELDS, AS REQUIRED

WELDED CONNECTION

NOTE

Load-bearing studs must be seated tight to track web.

STUD-TO-TRACK CONNECTION

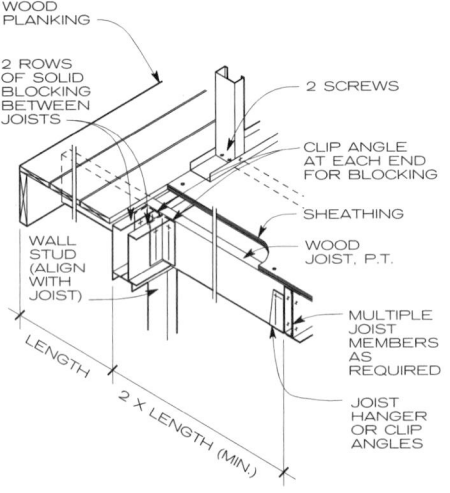

WOOD PLANKING

2 ROWS OF SOLID BLOCKING BETWEEN JOISTS

2 SCREWS

CLIP ANGLE AT EACH END FOR BLOCKING

SHEATHING

WALL STUD (ALIGN WITH JOIST)

WOOD JOIST, P.T.

MULTIPLE JOIST MEMBERS AS REQUIRED

JOIST HANGER OR CLIP ANGLES

LENGTH

2 X LENGTH (MIN.)

NOTES

1. Balconies require special detailing and protection against moisture and thermal bridging.
2. Where axial load-bearing members do not align vertically, provide top track distribution members at top of wall below.

WOOD DECK BALCONY

American Iron and Steel Institute; Washington, D.C.

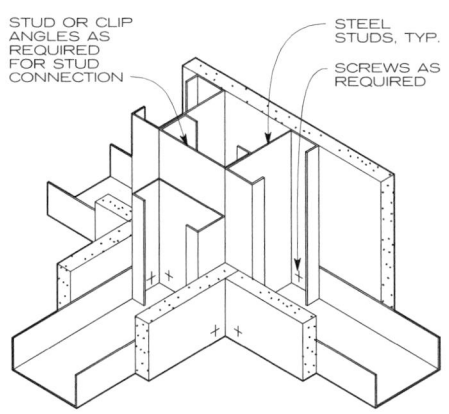

WALL INTERSECTION FRAMING

Labels: STUD OR CLIP ANGLES AS REQUIRED FOR STUD CONNECTION; STEEL STUDS, TYP.; SCREWS AS REQUIRED

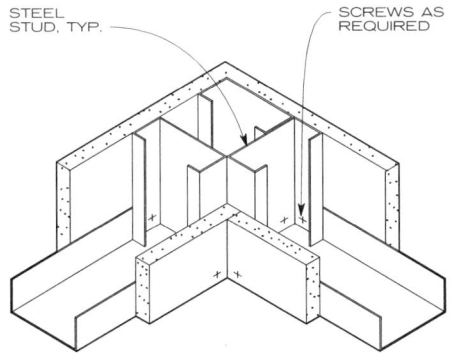

CORNER FRAMING

Labels: STEEL STUD, TYP.; SCREWS AS REQUIRED

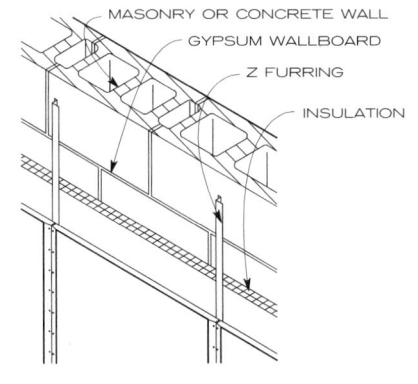

FURRING CHANNELS

Labels: MASONRY OR CONCRETE WALL; GYPSUM WALLBOARD; Z FURRING; INSULATION

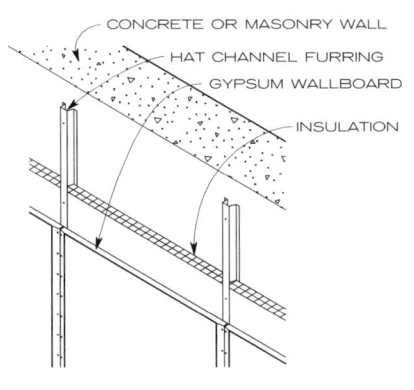

FURRING CHANNELS

Labels: CONCRETE OR MASONRY WALL; HAT CHANNEL FURRING; GYPSUM WALLBOARD; INSULATION

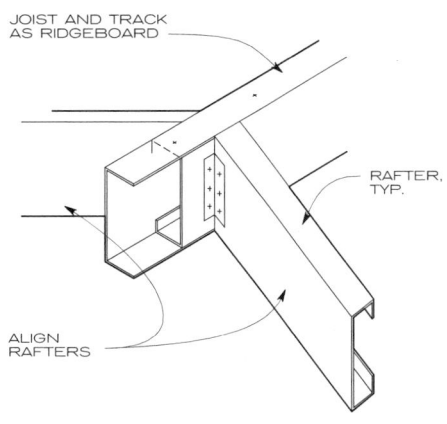

RIDGEBOARD

Labels: JOIST AND TRACK AS RIDGEBOARD; RAFTER, TYP.; ALIGN RAFTERS

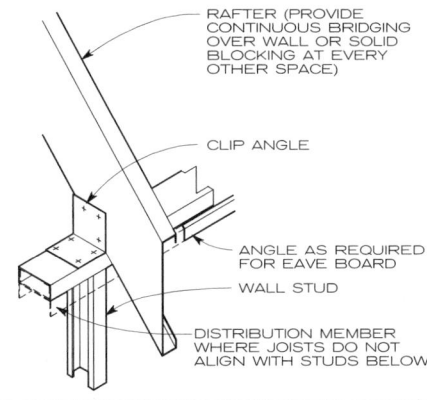

ROOF EAVE AT CATHEDRAL CEILING

Labels: RAFTER (PROVIDE CONTINUOUS BRIDGING OVER WALL OR SOLID BLOCKING AT EVERY OTHER SPACE); CLIP ANGLE; ANGLE AS REQUIRED FOR EAVE BOARD; WALL STUD; DISTRIBUTION MEMBER WHERE JOISTS DO NOT ALIGN WITH STUDS BELOW

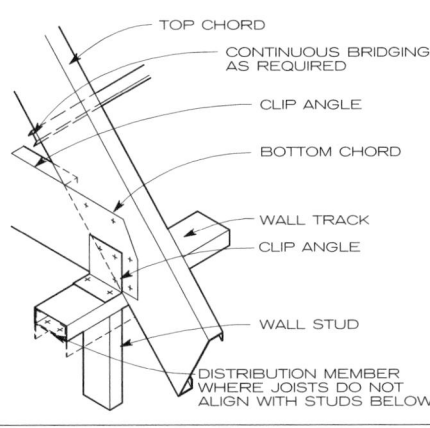

ROOF TRUSS EAVE DETAIL

Labels: TOP CHORD; CONTINUOUS BRIDGING AS REQUIRED; CLIP ANGLE; BOTTOM CHORD; WALL TRACK; CLIP ANGLE; WALL STUD; DISTRIBUTION MEMBER WHERE JOISTS DO NOT ALIGN WITH STUDS BELOW

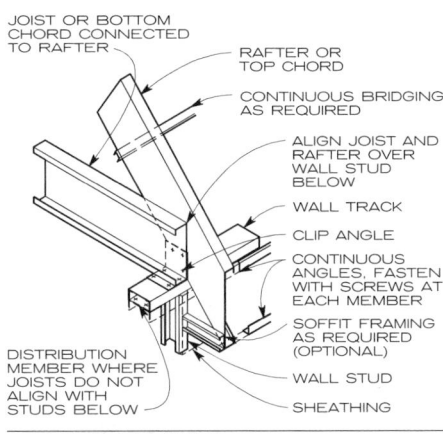

ROOF EAVE DETAIL

Labels: JOIST OR BOTTOM CHORD CONNECTED TO RAFTER; RAFTER OR TOP CHORD; CONTINUOUS BRIDGING AS REQUIRED; ALIGN JOIST AND RAFTER OVER WALL STUD BELOW; WALL TRACK; CLIP ANGLE; CONTINUOUS ANGLES, FASTEN WITH SCREWS AT EACH MEMBER; SOFFIT FRAMING AS REQUIRED (OPTIONAL); WALL STUD; SHEATHING; DISTRIBUTION MEMBER WHERE JOISTS DO NOT ALIGN WITH STUDS BELOW

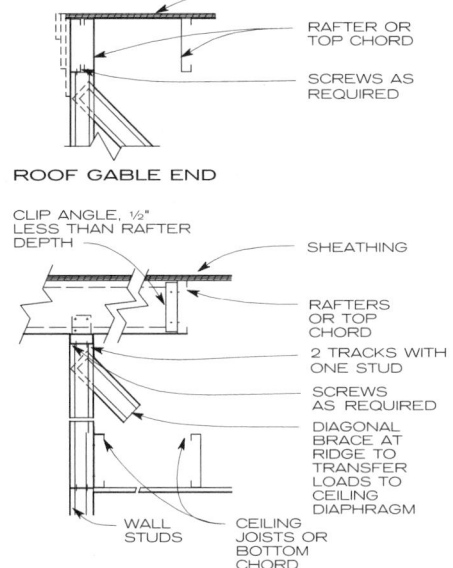

ROOF GABLE END

Labels: SHEATHING; RAFTER OR TOP CHORD; SCREWS AS REQUIRED

CANTILEVERED ROOF GABLE END

Labels: CLIP ANGLE, ½" LESS THAN RAFTER DEPTH; SHEATHING; RAFTERS OR TOP CHORD; 2 TRACKS WITH ONE STUD; SCREWS AS REQUIRED; DIAGONAL BRACE AT RIDGE TO TRANSFER LOADS TO CEILING DIAPHRAGM; WALL STUDS; CEILING JOISTS OR BOTTOM CHORD

NOTE

Provide bridging at ceiling joists and roof rafters and continuous bridging between rafters at wall.

ROOF END DETAILS

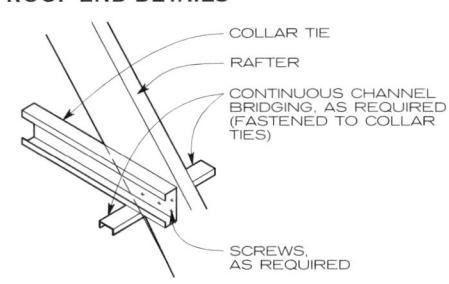

COLLAR TIE DETAIL

Labels: COLLAR TIE; RAFTER; CONTINUOUS CHANNEL BRIDGING, AS REQUIRED (FASTENED TO COLLAR TIES); SCREWS, AS REQUIRED

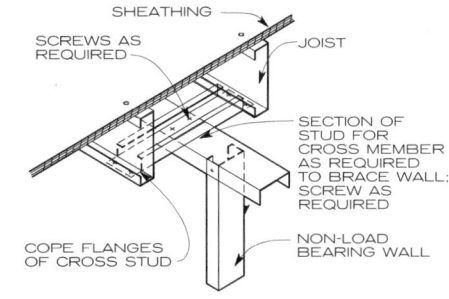

TOP OF NON-LOAD BEARING WALL PARALLEL TO JOISTS

Labels: SHEATHING; SCREWS AS REQUIRED; JOIST; SECTION OF STUD FOR CROSS MEMBER AS REQUIRED TO BRACE WALL; SCREW AS REQUIRED; COPE FLANGES OF CROSS STUD; NON-LOAD BEARING WALL

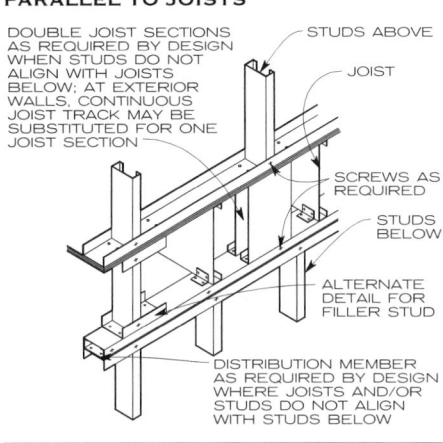

TOP TRACK DISTRIBUTION MEMBER

Labels: DOUBLE JOIST SECTIONS AS REQUIRED BY DESIGN WHEN STUDS DO NOT ALIGN WITH JOISTS BELOW; AT EXTERIOR WALLS, CONTINUOUS JOIST TRACK MAY BE SUBSTITUTED FOR ONE JOIST SECTION; STUDS ABOVE; JOIST; SCREWS AS REQUIRED; STUDS BELOW; ALTERNATE DETAIL FOR FILLER STUD; DISTRIBUTION MEMBER AS REQUIRED BY DESIGN WHERE JOISTS AND/OR STUDS DO NOT ALIGN WITH STUDS BELOW

American Iron and Steel Institute; Washington, D.C.

COLD-FORMED METAL FRAMING 5

GUIDELINES

1. Width of stair:
   a. Dwelling stairs: minimum 36 in. treads.
   b. Public exit stairs: minimum 44 in. treads.
   c. Rescue assistance area (ADA): 48 in. between hand-rails.
2. Treads:
   a. Dwellings: 9 in. minimum (nosing to nosing).
   b. Other (ADA): 11 in. minimum (nosing to nosing).
   c. Uniform width within one flight.
3. Risers:
   a. Dwellings: $8\frac{1}{4}$ in. maximum.
   b. Other (ADA): minimum 4 in., maximum 7 in.
   c. Uniform height within one flight.
4. Nosing: maximum $1\frac{1}{2}$ in. with 60° under nosing; maximum $\frac{1}{2}$ in. radius at edge.
5. Stair rails:
   a. Height in dwellings: 36 in.
   b. Height in exit stairs: 42 in.
   c. Rails should be arranged so that a sphere 4 in. in diameter cannot be passed through.

d. Rails should be arranged to discourage climbing.
e. Concentrated load nonconcurrently applied at the top rail shall be 200 lb per ft in vertical downward and horizontal direction. The test loads are applicable for railings with supports not more than 8 ft apart.
6. Handrails:
   a. Dwellings: on one side only, required.
   b. Other (ADA): required on both sides.
   c. Height: 34 to 38 in.
   d. Grip surface: $1\frac{1}{4}$ to $1\frac{1}{2}$ in.
   e. Clearance at wall: $1\frac{1}{2}$ in.
   f. Projecting or recessed.
   g. Extension at top of run: 12 in.
   h. Extension at bottom of run: 12 in. plus width of tread.
   i. When a guardrail more than 38 in. high is used, a separate handrail should be installed (ASTM).
   j. Nothing should interrupt the continuous sliding of hands.
7. Regulators and standards: building codes, ADA, ASTM, ANSI, NFPA, and OSHA.

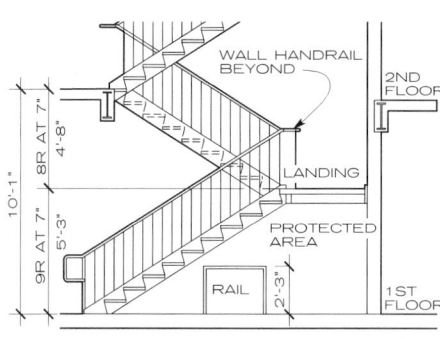

STAIR SECTION

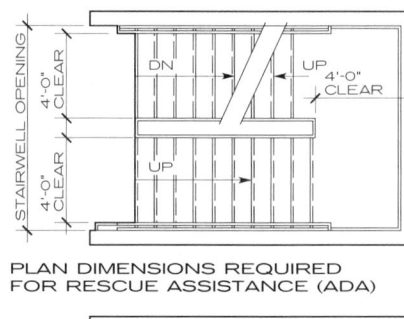

PLAN DIMENSIONS REQUIRED FOR RESCUE ASSISTANCE (ADA)

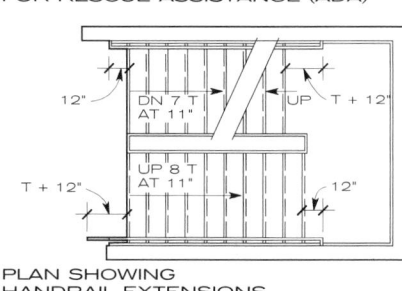

PLAN SHOWING HANDRAIL EXTENSIONS

STEEL STAIR RAILS

NOSING OF CLOSELY SPACED BARS, ANGLE ENDS

CHECKER PLATE NOSING, BAR END PLATES

NOSING OF ANGLE AND ABRASIVE STRIP AND BAR ENDS

FLOOR PLATE NOSING, BAR END PLATES

HEAVY FRONT AND BACK BEARING BARS AND BAR END PLATES

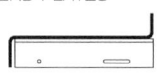

PLATE TYPE

TREADS

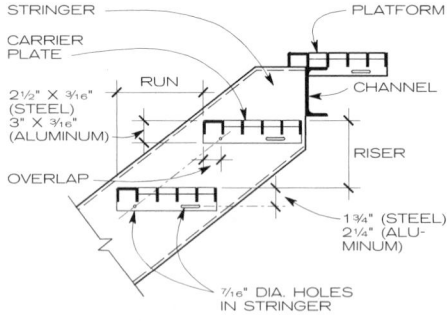

NOTE

This stair is not suitable for persons with disabilities.

INDUSTRIAL AND SERVICE STAIRS

PAN-TYPE STAIR CONSTRUCTION

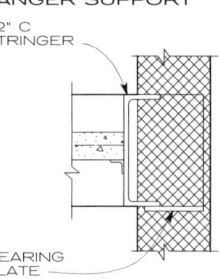

HANGER SUPPORT

BEARING SUPPORT

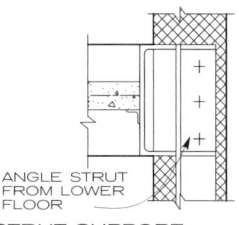

STRUT SUPPORT

Charles A. Szoradi, AIA; Washington, D.C.

 METAL FABRICATION

GENERAL NOTES

1. Materials for ladders and supports include galvanized steel and aluminum. Galvanized steel ladders are fastened to the wall with galvanized steel fasteners; aluminum ladders are fastened with stainless steel fasteners.

2. All fixed wall ladders must conform to OSHA/ANSI A14.3 standards. Also consult local codes for design requirements.

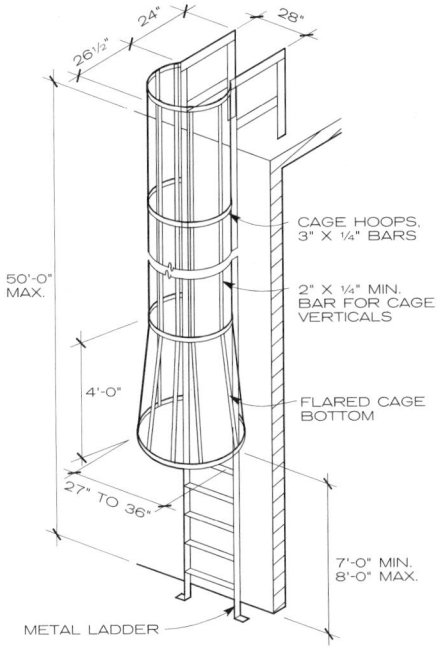

CAGE HOOPS, 3" X ¼" BARS
2" X ¼" MIN. BAR FOR CAGE VERTICALS
FLARED CAGE BOTTOM
50'-0" MAX.
4'-0"
24"
28"
26½"
27" TO 36"
7'-0" MIN. 8'-0" MAX.
METAL LADDER

NOTE

Cages should be used on ladders at hazardous locations or on short ladders at high locations.

FIXED VERTICAL LADDER (50 FEET OR LESS)

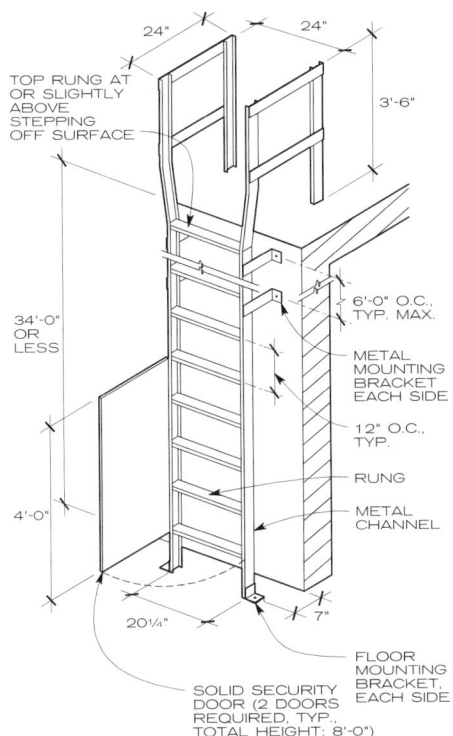

TOP RUNG AT OR SLIGHTLY ABOVE STEPPING OFF SURFACE
24"
24"
3'-6"
34'-0" OR LESS
4'-0"
6'-0" O.C., TYP. MAX.
METAL MOUNTING BRACKET EACH SIDE
12" O.C., TYP.
RUNG
METAL CHANNEL
20¼"
7"
FLOOR MOUNTING BRACKET, EACH SIDE
SOLID SECURITY DOOR (2 DOORS REQUIRED, TYP., TOTAL HEIGHT: 8'-0")

FIXED VERTICAL LADDER (UP TO 24 FEET)

Richard J. Vitullo, AIA; Oak Leaf Studio; Crownsville, Maryland

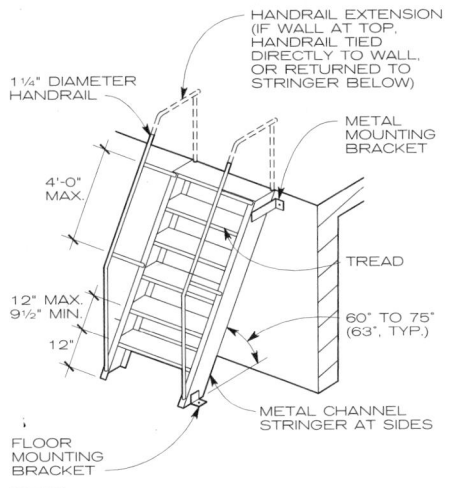

HANDRAIL EXTENSION (IF WALL AT TOP, HANDRAIL TIED DIRECTLY TO WALL, OR RETURNED TO STRINGER BELOW)
1¼" DIAMETER HANDRAIL
METAL MOUNTING BRACKET
TREAD
4'-0" MAX.
12" MAX. 9½" MIN.
12"
60" TO 75" (63", TYP.)
METAL CHANNEL STRINGER AT SIDES
FLOOR MOUNTING BRACKET

NOTE

The maximum rise between treads depends on exact ladder height and angle.

SHIP'S LADDER

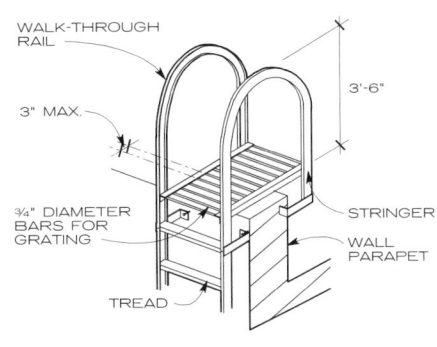

WALK-THROUGH RAIL
3" MAX.
3'-6"
STRINGER
¾" DIAMETER BARS FOR GRATING
WALL PARAPET
TREAD

ALTERNATE VERTICAL LADDER WALK THROUGH

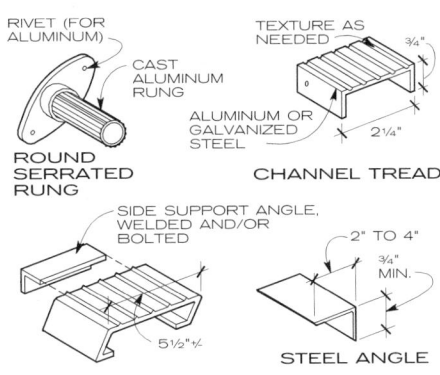

RIVET (FOR ALUMINUM)
CAST ALUMINUM RUNG
TEXTURE AS NEEDED
¾"
ALUMINUM OR GALVANIZED STEEL
2¼"
ROUND SERRATED RUNG
CHANNEL TREAD
SIDE SUPPORT ANGLE, WELDED AND/OR BOLTED
2" TO 4"
¾" MIN.
5½"+/-
SHIP'S LADDER TREAD
STEEL ANGLE

TREADS AND RUNGS

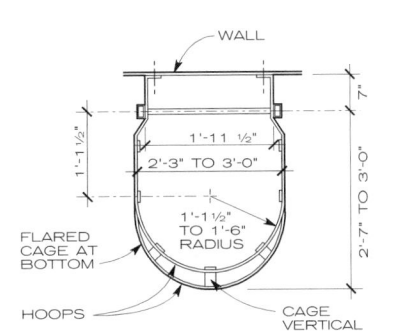

WALL
7"
1'-11½"
2'-3" TO 3'-0"
1'-1½"
1'-1½" TO 1'-6" RADIUS
2'-7" TO 3'-0"
FLARED CAGE AT BOTTOM
HOOPS
CAGE VERTICAL

SAFETY CAGE

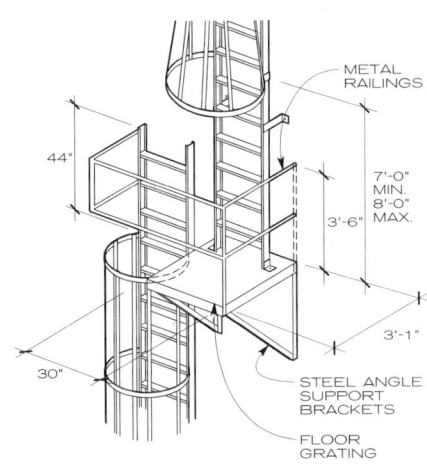

METAL RAILINGS
44"
7'-0" MIN. 8'-0" MAX.
3'-6"
30"
3'-1"
STEEL ANGLE SUPPORT BRACKETS
FLOOR GRATING

NOTE

Cages and rest platforms are required for climbing heights of more than 50 ft.

REST PLATFORM

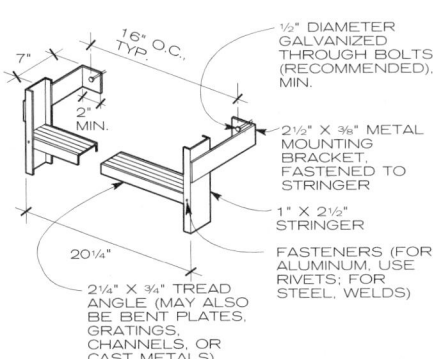

½" DIAMETER GALVANIZED THROUGH BOLTS (RECOMMENDED), MIN.
16" O.C., TYP.
7"
2" MIN.
2½" X ⅜" METAL MOUNTING BRACKET, FASTENED TO STRINGER
1" X 2½" STRINGER
20¼"
2¼" X ¾" TREAD ANGLE (MAY ALSO BE BENT PLATES, GRATINGS, CHANNELS, OR CAST METALS)
FASTENERS (FOR ALUMINUM, USE RIVETS; FOR STEEL, WELDS)

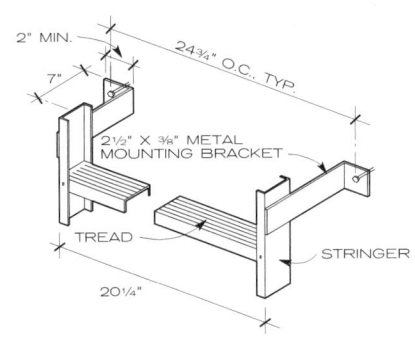

2" MIN.
7"
24¾" O.C., TYP.
2½" X ⅜" METAL MOUNTING BRACKET
TREAD
STRINGER
20¼"

SIDE RAIL MOUNTING BRACKET DETAILS

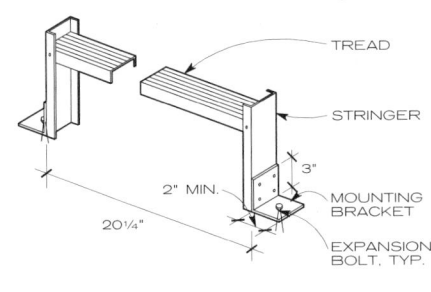

TREAD
STRINGER
2" MIN.
3"
MOUNTING BRACKET
EXPANSION BOLT, TYP.
20¼"

FLOOR-MOUNTING BRACKET DETAIL

GENERAL

Wrought iron is a commercial form of iron with a relatively soft and malleable fibrous structure. The term literally means "fashioned" or "formed" iron and is widely associated with ironwork details. ASTM A 186 defines wrought iron as iron with a carbon content between 0.03 and 0.05%, a material prevalent up to the 19th century. Iron with such a low carbon content is scarce today, so most fabricators use steels containing combinations of iron with a higher percentage of carbon for ornamental details. Low carbon steel or mild steel is the most desirable of these.

NOTES

1. Steel and iron are the metals most frequently used for ornamental structures. Other popular metals are aluminum (favored for its light weight and rust resistance), polished bronze, brass, and copper. Blacksmiths primarily produce custom work today; a smaller proportion of their work is restoration.

2. Working with iron is a craft not readily mastered by generalists; low bidders may not be qualified to deliver a high-quality product. Check references for similar types of jobs performed or jobs at similar costs. Consult the National Ornamental and Miscellaneous Metal Association (NOMMA) and the Artists-Blacksmiths Association of North America for more information on references and lists of blacksmith shops in the United States.

3. NOMMA publishes voluntary guidelines for joint finishes in ornamental work. They are Finish #1 (no evidence of a welded joint); Finish #2 (completely sanded joint, some undercutting and pinholes); Finish #3 (partially dressed weld with splatter removed); and Finish #4 (good quality, uniform undressed weld with minimal splatter).

TYPICAL SIZES AND WEIGHTS (LB PER FT) FOR SOLID IRON AND CARBON STEEL BARS

DIAMETER OR THICKNESS (IN.)		$^1/_8$	$^3/_{16}$	$^1/_4$	$^5/_{16}$	$^3/_8$	$^7/_{16}$	$^1/_2$	$^5/_8$	$^3/_4$	$^7/_8$	1	$1^1/_4$	$1^1/_2$
ROUNDS (DIAMETER IN.)		.042	.094	.167	.261	.376	.511	.668	1.04	1.50	2.04	2.67	4.17	6.01
Flat bars (width)	$^1/_8$ in.	0.053												
	$^3/_{16}$ in.	0.080	0.120											
	$^1/_4$ in.	0.106	0.160	0.213										
	$^5/_{16}$ in.	0.133	0.200	0.266	0.322									
	$^3/_8$ in.	0.159	0.239	0.399	0.398	0.478								
	$^7/_{16}$ in.	0.186	0.279	0.372	0.464	0.558	0.651							
	$^1/_2$ in.	0.212	0.319	0.425	0.531	0.637	0.744	0.850						
	$^5/_8$ in.	0.266	0.398	0.531	0.664	0.797	0.930	1.062	1.328					
	$^3/_4$ in.	0.319	0.478	0.637	0.797	0.956	1.116	1.275	1.594	1.912				
	$^7/_8$ in.	0.372	0.558	0.748	0.930	1.116	1.302	1.487	1.859	2.231	2.603			
	1 in.	0.425	0.637	0.850	1.062	1.275	1.487	1.700	2.125	2.550	2.975	3.400		
	$1^1/_4$ in.	0.531	0.797	1.062	1.328	1.594	1.859	2.125	2.656	3.187	3.719	4.250	5.312	
	$1^1/_2$ in.	0.638	0.956	1.275	1.594	1.913	2.231	2.550	3.188	3.825	4.463	5.100	6.375	7.650
	$1^3/_4$ in.	0.744	1.116	1.488	1.859	2.231	2.603	2.975	3.719	4.463	5.206	5.950	7.438	8.925
	2 in.	0.850	1.275	1.700	2.125	2.550	2.975	3.400	4.250	5.100	5.950	6.800	8.500	10.200
	$2^1/_2$ in.	1.063	1.594	2.125	2.656	3.188	3.719	4.250	5.313	6.375	7.438	8.500	10.625	12.750

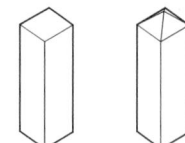 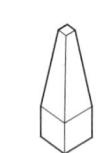 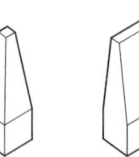    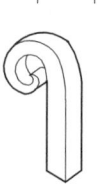

BAR ENDS

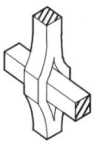 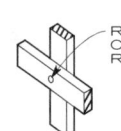  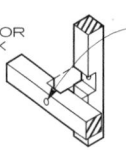

ROUND HEAD OR COUNTERSUNK RIVET

PIN MAY BE CUT, COUNTERSUNK, OR PEENED (HAMMERED)

INTERSECTING MEMBERS

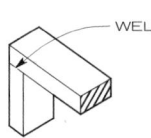 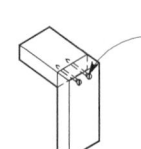  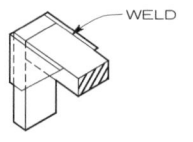

WELD

2 FLAT HEAD TAPPED SCREWS

WELD

CORNER CONDITIONS

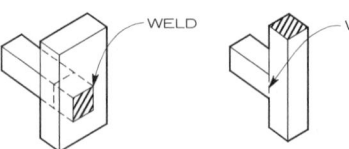 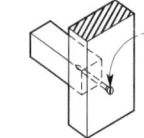  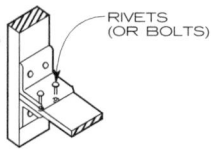

WELD

WELD

FLAT HEAD TAPPED SCREW

RIVETS (OR BOLTS)

EDGE CONDITIONS

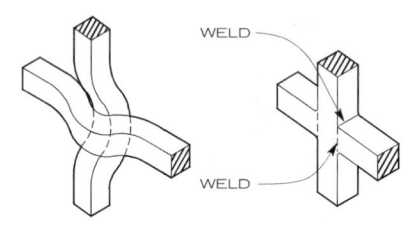

ORNAMENTAL GRILLE, TYP.

WELD

STEEL BAR SET INTO MASONRY

METAL PIN

STEEL ANGLE

EXPANSION BOLT

EXPANSION BOLTS, AS NECESSARY

METAL GRILLWORK INSTALLATION— DETAILS FOR MASONRY OPENINGS

WELD

WELD

CRIMPED AND WELDED MEMBERS

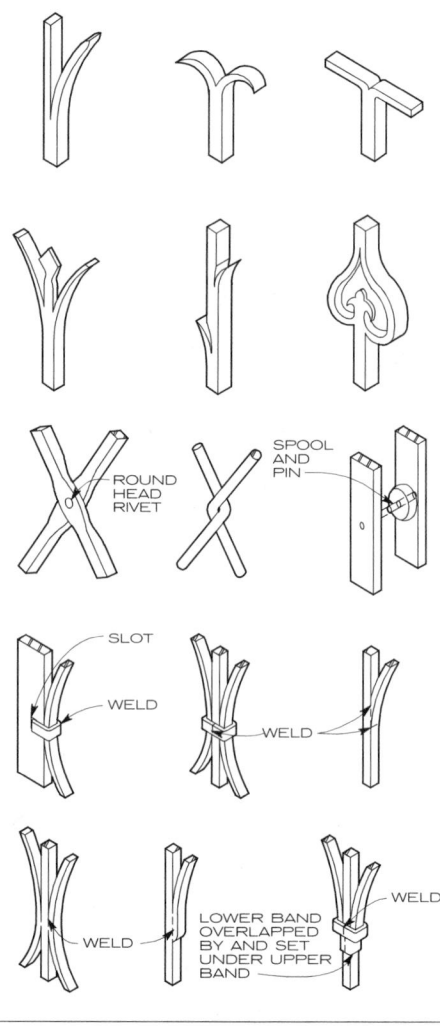

ROUND HEAD RIVET

SPOOL AND PIN

SLOT

WELD

WELD

WELD

WELD

LOWER BAND OVERLAPPED BY AND SET UNDER UPPER BAND

WELD

MISCELLANEOUS CONNECTIONS

Richard J. Vitullo, AIA; Oak Leaf Studio; Crownsville, Maryland

5 ORNAMENTAL METAL

GENERAL

Perforated metals were initially created to fulfill industrial needs such as minimizing the weight of a particular component or controlling the passage of fluids or gasses. As an architectural component, perforated metals can be used as control devices or simply as decoration. They can serve as sound suppression acoustical devices in ceilings, walls, and grilles; when incorporated into light fixtures, grilles, or ceiling and wall components, they can filter light and obscure views. Since perforated metals retain a great deal of their strength and also ventilate well, they are often employed in furniture and other designs. Because they can bend and interrupt wavelengths of many types, perforated metals are used to contain microwave radiation and the EMI/RFI radiation emitted by electrical devices.

NOTES

1. Metal is typically perforated with hole-punching machines, which work best on sheets .008 in. to 3/4 in. thick. Specialized equipment is available for thicker metal.

2. The intended use of the perforated metal sheet determines the size, shape, and pattern of the holes punched. The strength and stiffness required vary according to use. Since perforated materials can be used in different applications involving a wide range of geometries, materials, and loading conditions, design data are given in very general form.

3. The enormous number of perforating patterns possible with round holes, squares, slots, and other special perforations make it impractical to list every pattern combination. The numbered perforations listed by the Industrial Perforators Association (IPA) are considered standard.

4. For design and tolerances of perforated metals, consult the IPA.

5. Round holes from .020 in. to more than 6 in. in diameter make up the majority of all perforated metal sheets produced. This is because round holes can be produced with greater efficiency and less expense and are generally stronger than other hole shapes.

6. Nonstandard end patterns may require special dies. Unperforated borders may cause distortions of the finished sheet. Roller leveling may be used to correct some of these distortions but may not always work. To calculate the (round) holes per square inch:

$$\frac{\% \text{ Open area}}{78.54 \times D \times D}$$

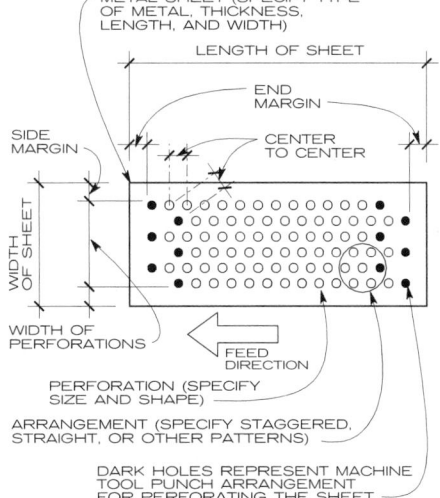

NOTE

Spacing can be specified as a center-to-center dimension, a percentage of open area, or holes per square inch.

TYPICAL TERMS FOR SPECIFYING PERFORATED METAL

ROUND HOLES

IPA NUMBERS	PERFORATIONS (IN.)	CENTERS (IN.)	HOLES PER SQ IN.	% OPEN AREA	LINE	S*/S, STRENGTH WIDTH DIRECTION	S*/S, STRENGTH LENGTH DIRECTION
100	.020		625	20	Staggered	.530	.465
101	.023		576	24	Straight		
102	.027		400	23	Straight		
103	.032		324	26	Straight		
104	.040		225	30	Straight		
105	.045		224	37	Straight		
106	1/16	1/8		23	Staggered	.500	.435
107	5/64	7/64		46	Staggered	.286	.225
108	5/64	1/8		36	Staggered	.375	.310
109	3/32	5/32		32	Staggered	.400	.334
110	3/32	3/16		23	Staggered	.500	.435
111	3/32	1/4		12	Staggered		
112	1/10	5/32		36	Staggered	.360	.296
113	1/8	3/16		40	Staggered	.333	.270
114	1/8	7/32		29	Staggered	.428	.363
115	1/8	1/4		23	Staggered	.500	.435
116	5/32	7/32		46	Staggered	.288	.225
117	5/32	1/4		36	Staggered	.375	.310
118	3/16	1/4		51	Staggered	.250	.192
119	3/16	5/16		33	Staggered	.400	.334
120	1/4	5/16		58	Staggered	.200	.147
121	1/4	3/8		40	Staggered	.333	.270
122	1/4	7/16		30	Staggered	.428	.363
123	1/4	1/2		23	Staggered	.500	.435
124	3/8	1/2		51	Staggered	.250	.192
125	3/8	9/16		40	Staggered	.333	.270
126	3/8	5/8		33	Staggered	.400	.334
127	7/16	5/8		45	Staggered	.300	.239
128	1/2	11/16		47	Staggered	.273	.214
129	9/16	3/4		51	Staggered	.250	.192
130	5/8	13/16		53	Staggered	.231	.175
131	3/4	1		51	Staggered	.250	.192

S* = yield strength of perforated material

S = yield strength of unperforated material (strength for 60° standard staggered pattern)

Length direction = parallel to straight row of holes

Width direction = direction of stagger

Industrial Perforators Association; Milwaukee, Wisconsin

CHECKLIST OF PERFORATING COST INFLUENCES

1. Material type: The least expensive material may not save money; a higher strength alloy may allow thickness to be reduced.

2. Material thickness: Thinner materials can be perforated easier and faster.

3. Hole shape and pattern: Round holes are the most economical; the 60×° staggered round hole pattern is the strongest, most versatile, and most common.

4. Hole size: Do not go below a 1-to-1 ratio of hole to size to sheet thickness; stay with a 2-to-1 ratio or larger if possible.

5. Bar size: Do not use bars with less than a 1-to-1 ratio with sheet thickness.

6. Center distance: This controls the feed rate and thus the conduction rate. If possible, choose a pattern with longer center distance.

7. Open areas: Extreme open area proportions tend to increase distortion; if possible, stay under 70 percent.

8. Margins: Keep side margins to a minimum to reduce distortion. Use standard unfinished end margins if possible.

9. Blank areas: Consider the die pattern when determining blank areas; consult the metal supplier.

10. Standardization: Specify standard hole patterns, material dimensions, and tolerances when possible. Before specifying a "special," ask the perforator what can be done with existing tooling.

11. Accept normal commercial burrs unless otherwise specified.

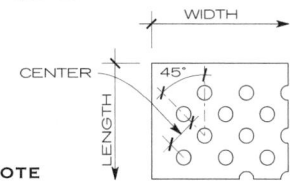

NOTE

This standard IPA option is stronger than straight row patterns but not as strong as a 60×° staggered arrangement. It is also not as versatile in providing compact hole spacing and high open areas as the 60×° arrangement.

45° STAGGERED ROUND HOLE PATTERN

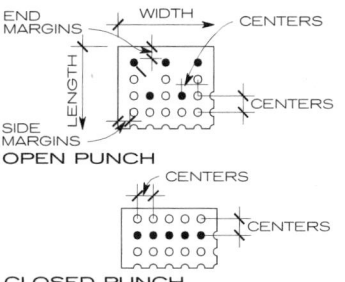

OPEN PUNCH

CLOSED PUNCH

NOTE

A straight line pattern of holes is weaker than a staggered arrangement and can stretch the material more. Dark holes in the drawings above indicate the punch patterns.

STRAIGHT LINE ROUND HOLE PATTERN

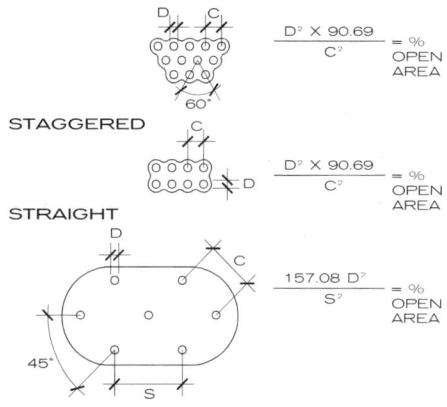

$$\frac{D^2 \times 90.69}{C^2} = \% \text{ OPEN AREA}$$

STAGGERED

$$\frac{D^2 \times 90.69}{C^2} = \% \text{ OPEN AREA}$$

STRAIGHT

$$\frac{157.08 \, D^2}{S^2} = \% \text{ OPEN AREA}$$

45° STAGGERED PATTERN (SPECIAL)

ROUND HOLE OPEN AREAS

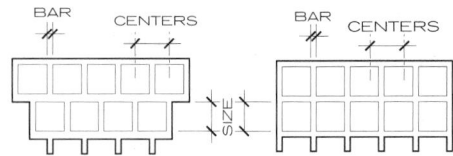

SQUARE
PERFORATIONS
STAGGERED

SQUARE
PERFORATIONS
STRAIGHT LINES

SQUARES

IPA NUMBER	PERFOR-ATIONS (IN.)	CENTERS (IN.)	OPEN AREA	LINE
200	$^2/_{10}$	$^1/_4$	64%	Straight
201	$^1/_4$	$^3/_8$		
202	$^3/_8$	$^1/_2$	56%	Straight
203	$^1/_2$	$^{11}/_{16}$	53%	Straight
204	$^3/_4$	1	56%	Straight
205	1	$1^1/_4$		Straight
206	1	$1^3/_8$		Straight

SQUARE HOLE OPEN AREAS

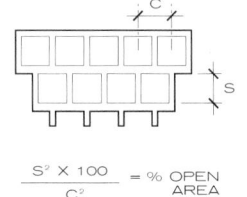

$$\frac{S^2 \times 100}{C^2} = \% \text{ OPEN AREA}$$

NOTE

Square holes, principally used for grilles and machine guards, offer optimal visibility and throughput. Typically punched in a straight line, in either straight or staggered patterns, square holes make for weaker perforated sheets than round hole patterns and are generally more expensive. Sharp corners make square hole tooling wear out faster than round hole tooling.

SQUARE HOLES

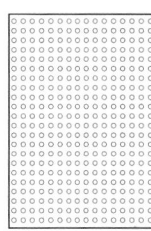

NO. 105, .045"
DIA., 37%
OPEN AREA

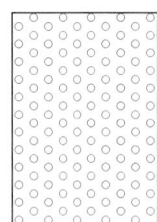

NO. 108, $^5/_{64}$"
DIA., 36%
OPEN AREA

NO. 120, $^1/_4$" DIA.,
58% OPEN AREA

NO. 200,
$^1/_8$", 64%
OPEN AREA

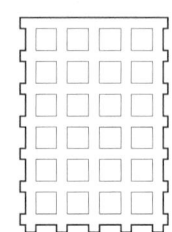

NO. 201, $^1/_4$"
OPENNING

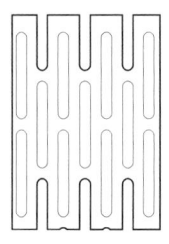

NO. 208, $^1/_8$" X 1"
OPENING, 43%
OPEN AREA

MISCELLANEOUS PERFORATION PATTERNS

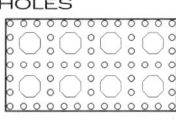

HEXAGONAL
HOLES

ROUND CANE

OCTAGONAL
CANE

GRECIAN

NOTE

A broad assortment of nonstandard hole shapes and patterns is available; consult metal perforator. Also available are indented holes, collared holes, and louvered holes.

MISCELLANEOUS NONSTANDARD PERFORATION PATTERNS

NOTE

These three types of slots are IPA standard types. Nonstandard square-end slots are also available. Consult manufacturers for other open area calculations for slots.

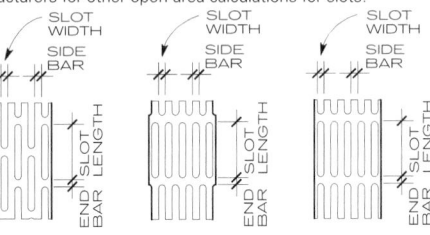

SLOTS
SIDE
STAGGER

SLOTS
END
STAGGER

SLOTS
STRAIGHT
LINES

SLOTS

IPA NUMBER	PERFORATIONS	OPEN AREA	LINE
207	$^1/_8$" x $^3/_4$"	41%	Side staggered
208	$^1/_8$" x 1"	43%	Side staggered

SLOTS

GAUGES AND WEIGHTS OF SHEET METALS*

	STEEL		GALVANIZED STEEL		LONG TERNE		STAINLESS-USS GAUGE			MONEL	
	USS GAUGE REV.		USS GAUGE		USS GAUGE			LB/SQ FT		USS GAUGE	
GAUGE	DECIMAL THICKNESS	LB/SQ FT	DECIMAL THICKNESS	LB/SQ FT	DECIMAL THICKNESS	LB/SQ FT	DECIMAL THICKNESS	CHROME ALLOY	CHROME NICKEL	DECIMAL THICKNESS	LB/SQ FT
32	.0100		.0130	.563			.0100	.418	.427		
31	.0110		.0140	.594			.0109	.450	.459		
30	.0120	.500	.0157	.656	.012	.518	.0125	.515	.525		
29	.0135	.563	.0172	.719	.014	.581	.0140	.579	.591		
28	.0149	.625	.0187	.781	.015	.643	.0156	.643	.656		
27	.0164	.688	.0202	.844	.017	.706	.0171	.708	.721		
26	.0179	.750	.0217	.906	.018	.768	.0187	.772	.787	.0187	.827
25	.0209	.875	.0247	1.031	.021	.893	.0218	.901	.918	.0218	.965
24	.0239	1.000	.0276	1.156	.024	1.018	.0250	1.030	1.050	.0250	1.148
23	.0269	1.125	.0306	1.281	.027	1.143	.0281	1.158	1.181	.0281	1.286
22	.0299	1.250	.0336	1.406	.030	1.268	.0312	1.287	1.312	.0312	1.424
21	.0329	1.375	.0366	1.531	.033	1.393	.0343	1.416	1.443	.0343	1.562
20	.0359	1.500	.0396	1.656	.036	1.518	.0375	1.545	1.575	.0375	1.700
19	.0418	1.750	.0456	1.906	.042	1.768	.0437	1.802	1.837	.0437	1.975
18	.0478	2.000	.0516	2.156	.048	2.018	.0500	2.060	2.100	.0500	2.297
17	.0538	2.250	.0575	2.406	.054	2.268	.0562	2.317	2.362	.0562	2.572
16	.0598	2.500	.0635	2.656	.060	2.518	.0625	2.575	2.625	.0625	2.848
15	.0673	2.812	.0710	2.969	.068	2.831	.0703	2.896	2.953	.0703	3.216
14	.0747	3.125	.0785	3.281	.075	3.143	.0781	3.218	3.281	.0781	3.583
13	.0897	3.750	.0934	3.906	.090	3.768	.0937	3.862	3.937	.0937	4.272
12	.1046	4.375	.1084	4.531	.105	4.393	.1093	4.506	4.593	.1093	5.007
11	.1196	5.000	.1233	5.156	.120	5.018	.1250	5.150	5.250	.1250	5.742
10	.1345	5.625	.1382	5.781	.135	5.643	.1406	5.793	5.906	.1406	6.431
9	.1494	6.250	.1532	6.406			.1562	6.437	6.562	.1562	7.166
8	.1644	6.875	.1681	7.031			.1718	7.081	7.218	.1718	7.855
7	.1793	7.500					.1875	7.590	7.752	.1875	8.590

*Gauges and weights have been computed subject to standard commercial tolerances.

Industrial Perforators Association; Milwaukee, Wisconsin

ORNAMENTAL METAL

GUIDE FOR SELECTING CARBON STEEL FOR PERFORATING APPLICATIONS

TYPE	DESCRIPTION	RECOMMENDED SIZE SHEETS			RECOMMENDED SIZE COILS		CARBON CONTENT	TYPICAL MECHANICAL PROPERTIES TENSILE PSI	YIELD, PSI	% ELONG. 2 IN.	HARD-NESS	APPROXIMATE RELATIVE COST (10-GA. H.R. STEEL = 100) SHEETS	COILS
		TH	W	L	TH	W							
HOT-ROLLED STEELS													
Commercial quality (SAE or ASI 1008; ASTM A 569)	A low-cost sheet steel with moderate drawing and forming qualities for use when finish is unimportant. For best perforating results specify pickled and oiled for removal of oxides.	7 to 16 ga.	up to 60 in.	up to 144 in.	7 to 16 ga.	up to 60 in.	0.10 max.	45,000 to 60,000	30,000 to 40,000	28 to 38	55 to 70	100 pickled and oiled-104	95 99
Drawing quality (SAE or AISI 1008; ASTM A 621)	This quality is intended for use when forming requirements are too severe for commercial quality. Pickling and oiling to remove oxides is recommended. In-stock availability is not as great as commercial quality.	7 to 16 ga.	up to 60 in.	up to 144 in.	7 to 16 ga.	up to 60 in.	0.10 max	45,000 to 60,000	30,000 to 40,000	28 to 38	55 to 70	103	98
High-strength, low alloy (USS Cor-Ten or equivalent; ASTM A 375)	Good formability because of low carbon content in combination with relatively high Yield and Tensile properties permit these steels to be used in lighter gauges to reduce weight in applications in which strength in important. Readily available.	7 to 16 ga.	up to 60 in.	up to 144 in.	11 to 14 ga.	up to 60 in.	0.12 max	70,000 min	50,000 min	22 min	80 to 90	132	126
Abrasion-resisting (C .35-.50; Mn 1.50-2.00; P .050 max.; S .055 max.; Si .15-.35)	High manganese content in combination with intermediate carbon greatly enhances resistance to abrasion; can improve part life 2 to 10 times. Moderate formability.	7 to 16 ga.	up to 60 in.	up to 144 in.	N.A.	N.A.	.35 to .50	100,000 to 120,000	55,000 to 70,000	10 to 20	210 to 225 (Bhn.)	118	N.A.
COLD-ROLLED STEELS													
Commercial quality (SAE or AISI 1008; ASTM A 366)	Cold rolled steels have improved surface finishes and tighter size tolerances than hot rolled steels. They are available in two classes: Class 1 is intended for exposed applications; Class 2 is for unexposed use. Three finishes can be specified: Matte is the standard finish. It is uniformly dull and suitable for painting. Commercial bright finish is a relatively bright, intermediate finish. Luster finish is smooth and bright and most suitable for plating. Because perforating alters surface appearance, surface preparation after perforating may be required before application of the final finish.	7 to 28 ga.	up to 60 in.	up to 18 ft	11 to 28 ga.	up to 60 in.	0.10 max	40,000 to 50,000	25,000 to 35,000	30 to 40	45 to 60	119 (16 ga.)	113
Drawing quality (ASTM A 619)	Recommended for use when forming requirements are too severe for commercial quality. Can be supplied (Class 1) free of fluting or stretcher straining when intended for use in a reasonably short time. Available in mill quantities.	7 to 28 ga.	up to 60 in.	up to 18 ft	11 to 28 ga.	up to 60 in.	0.10 max	40,000 to 50,000	20,000 to 30,000	38 to 40	40 to 50	125 (16 ga.)	120
Drawing quality special milled (ASTM A 620)	For use when the material must be free of surface disturbances without roller leveling immediately before use and essentially free from significant changes in mechanical properties over an extended period of time. Available in mill order quantities.	7 to 28 ga.	up to 60 in.	up to 18 ft	11 to 28 ga.	up to 60 in.	0.10 max	40,000 to 50,000	20,000 to 30,000	38 to 40	40 to 50	127 (16 ga.)	122
CORROSION-RESISTANT STEELS													
Galvanized (ASTM 525)	A versatile, low-cost, corrosion-resistant steel with a zinc coating applied in a continuous hot-dip process. Available in commercial, drawing, and other qualities.	10 to 20 ga.	up to 60 n.	up to 18 ft	12 to 28 ga.	up to 60 in.	0.10 max	45,000 to 55,000	35,000 to 45,000	25 to 35	50 to 65	147 (20 ga.)	145
Mill-bonderized galvanized	Galvanized sheet with a coating of mill-bonderized phosphate for immediate painting without flaking or peeling.	16 to 26 ga.	up to 60 in.	up to 18 ft	16 to 26 ga.	up to 60 in.	0.10 max	45,000 to 55,000	35,000 to 45,000	25 to 35	50 to 65	149 (20 ga.)	N.A.
Galvanealed (coating designation A 60)	Heat-treated galvanized sheet, dull gray without spangles with a rough texture well suited to painting. Can withstand temperatures to 750° without flaking. Less ductile than regular galvanized coating.	14 to 26 ga.	up to 48 in.	up to 18 ft	14 to 26 ga.	up to 48 in.	0.10 max	40,000 to 55,000	32,000 to 42,000	25 to 35	50 to 65	150 (20 ga.)	147
Electro-galvanized (ASTM A 591)	A thin zinc coating is applied to cold rolled steel by electroplating so as not to appreciably affect the weight-thickness relationship. Smooth, without spangles, it is recommended as an undercoat for painted finishes. Available in commercial and drawing qualities.	14 to 26 ga.	up to 60 in.	up to 18 ft	14 to 26 ga.	up to 60 in.	0.10 max	40,000 to 50,000	25,000 to 35,000	30 to 40	45 to 60	146 (20 ga.)	144
Aluminized, type 1 (ASTM 463)	Sheet steel coated on both sides with aluminum combines the properties of both metals. Type 1 is provided in two weights, regular and light, and is available in commercial and drawing qualities. If the heaviest Type 2 aluminized coating is desired, consult with a supplier or the steel manufacturer.	14 to 26 ga.	up to 60 in.	up to 18 ft	14 to 26 ga.	up to 60 in.	0.10 max	50,000 to 60,000	35,000 to 45,000	18 to 28	60 to 70	162 (20 ga.)	157

Industrial Perforators Association; Milwaukee, Wisconsin

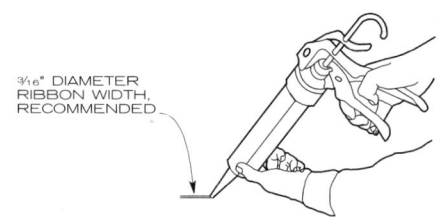

³⁄₁₆" DIAMETER RIBBON WIDTH, RECOMMENDED

ADHESIVE GUN

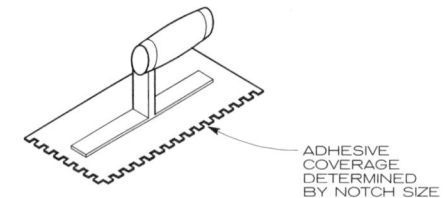

ADHESIVE COVERAGE DETERMINED BY NOTCH SIZE

NOTCHED TROWEL (TO SPREAD ADHESIVE OVER LARGE AREAS)

ADHESIVE APPLICATIONS

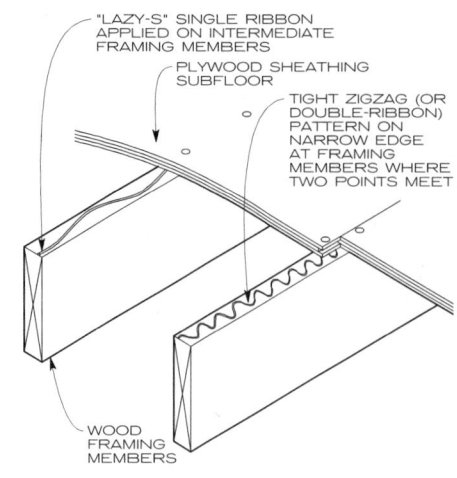

"LAZY-S" SINGLE RIBBON APPLIED ON INTERMEDIATE FRAMING MEMBERS

PLYWOOD SHEATHING SUBFLOOR

TIGHT ZIGZAG (OR DOUBLE-RIBBON) PATTERN ON NARROW EDGE AT FRAMING MEMBERS WHERE TWO POINTS MEET

WOOD FRAMING MEMBERS

WALL PANELING

GYPSUM BOARD

"LAZY-S" ON HORIZONTAL SURFACE OF FRAMING MEMBERS

ADHESIVE APPLIED IN PARALLEL RIBBONS 16" APART

CONTINUOUS RIBBON AROUND THE PERIMETER

NOTE

Adhesive is applied to one surface only.

RECOMMENDED ADHESIVE BEAD PATTERNS

ADHESIVES SUMMARY

CLASS	FORM	PROPERTIES	TYPICAL USES
Urea resin	Dry powders or liquids; may be blended with melamine or other resins	High strength under both wet and dry conditions; moderately durable under damp conditions; moderate to low resistance to temperatures above 120°F; white or tan color	Hardwood plywood for interior use and furniture; interior particleboard; flush doors; furniture core stock
Phenol resin*	Dry powders or liquids	High strength under both wet and dry conditions; very resistant to moisture and damp conditions; dark red in color	Primary adhesive for exterior softwood plywood and flakeboard
Resorcinol resin and phenol-resorcinol resins	Liquid; hardener supplied separately	High strength under both wet and dry conditions; very resistant to moisture and damp conditions; dark red color	Primary adhesive for laminated timbers and assembly joints to withstand severe service conditions
Polyvinyl acetate resin emulsions	Liquid; ready to use	Generally high strength in dry conditions; low resistance to moisture and elevated temperatures; joints tend to yield under continued stress; white or yellow color	Furniture assembly, flush doors, bonding of plastic laminates, architectural woodworking
Cross-linkable polyvinyl acetate resin emulsions	Similar to polyvinyl acetate resin emulsions but includes a resin capable of forming linkage	Improved resistance to moisture and elevated temperatures; improved long-term performance in moist or wet environment; color varies	Interior and exterior doors, molding and architectural woodworking
Contact adhesives	Typically an elastomer base in organic solvents or water emulsion	Initial joint strength develops immediately upon pressing, increases slowly over a period of weeks; dry strength generally lower than those of conventional woodworking glues; water resistance and resistance to severe conditions variable; color varies	For some nonstructural bonds; high-pressure decorative laminates to substrates. Useful for low-strength metal and some plastic bonding.
Mastics (elastomeric construction adhesives)	Puttylike consistency, synthetic or natural elastomer base, usually in organic solvents	Gap filling; develops strength slowly over several weeks; water resistance and resistance for severe conditions vary; color varies	Lumber and plywood to joists and studs; gypsum board; styrene and urethane foams
Thermoplastic synthetic resins (hot melts)	Solid chunks, pellets, ribbons, rods, or films; solvent-free	Rapid bonding; gap filling; lower strength than conventional woodworking adhesives; minimal penetration; moisture resistant; white to tan color	Edge banding of panels; films and paper overlays
Epoxy resins	Chemical polymers, usually in two parts, both liquid; completely reactive, no solvents	Good adhesion to metals, glass, certain plastics, and wood products; permanence in wood joints not adequately established; gap-filling	Used in combination with other resins for bonding metals, plastics, and materials other than wood; fabrication of cold-molded wood panels
Protein glues (casein and hide)	Dry powders or reconstituted liquid	Bonds extremely well to wood; moisture resistant	Interior applications; laminating beam

*Most types used in the U.S. are alkaline-catalyzed. The general statements refer to this type.

Data: Adapted from Table 100-G-12, *Architectural Woodwork Quality Standards* (6th ed., version 1.1, 1994)

GENERAL

Adhesives have been used for bonding wood for centuries, but until the 1930s they were limited to only a few naturally derived substances–those based on animal or vegetable proteins, gums, or resins. Stepped-up materials research efforts during World War II spurred the development of synthetic adhesives for bonding metals, concrete, glass, rubber, plastics, and wood.

Many of these synthetic adhesives are used to manufacture products such as plywood, oriented-strand board (OSB), and laminated timbers. They can also be used during construction to attach plywood subfloors to floor joists, adhere ceramic tiles to floors or walls, attach drywall, and the like. In addition to their structural use, adhesives also can be used to eliminate squeaks in floors and for some mechanical fastening.

Adhesives are composed of a base component, dispersion medium, and various additives that impart specific properties. The elastomeric base of a construction-type adhesive accounts for 30 to 50% of its weight. Depending on its intended application, this base is made of natural rubber (isoprene) or synthetic rubbers such as neoprene, butyl, polyurethane, polysulfide, nitrile, styrene-butadiene, or butadiene acrylonitrile. Additives include tackifiers, flow and extrusion modifiers, curing agents, antioxidants, and fillers. Together, the base and the additives are dispersed (or dissolved) in a liquid, typically an organic solvent or water.

Currently, most adhesives use organic solvents, but water-based adhesives are gaining in popularity because they do not emit harmful vapors, are easy to clean up, and can be discarded as regular trash. During the specification process, disposal of the containers from organic solvents must be considered. Many jurisdictions are enacting clean air statutes in which organic solvents are targeted as air pollutants. In addition, organic solvents can have adverse affects on the workers who apply them as well as future building occupants. One drawback to most water-based adhesives is that they tend only to resist water, while the solvent-based adhesives are waterproof.

CONSTRUCTION ADHESIVES

Construction adhesives are defined as elastomer-based extrudable mastics, which means that the main adhesive component is elastic and will continue to maintain some of its flexibility indefinitely. Mastics are a type of adhesive with high viscosity, or resistance to flow. A construction adhesive is a substance capable of holding materials together by surface attachment.

Adhesives used for building have been formulated to tolerate many of the often adverse conditions that exist at most job sites, such as extreme temperatures and temperature fluctuations. They are excellent for filling gaps, and thus work on both smooth and rough surfaces. Because they form bond lines up to ¼ in. thick, they can bridge gaps between ill-fitting pieces. The degree of adhesion depends on the surface conditions of the materials; ice, dirt, grease, or other contaminants will all have a negative effect.

Many of the characteristics of modern adhesives are described in the table. Note that most adhere to wood, but performance depends on careful consideration of physical and chemical compatibility of glue and wood, processing requirements, mechanical properties, and durability under design conditions.

Richard J. Vitullo, AIA; Oak Leaf Studio; Crownsville, Maryland

FASTENERS AND ADHESIVES

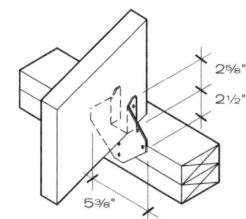

NOTE: For tying unnotched 2x rafters to top wall plates; for uplift and lateral load resistance.

TWO-SIDED RAFTER TIE

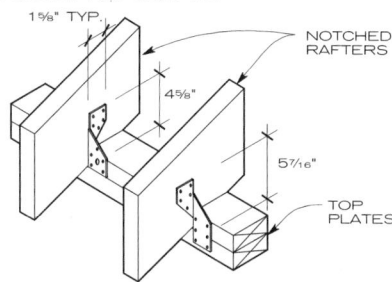

NOTE: Ties one or two top plates to notched rafters for tension cord connections.

ONE-SIDED RAFTER TIES

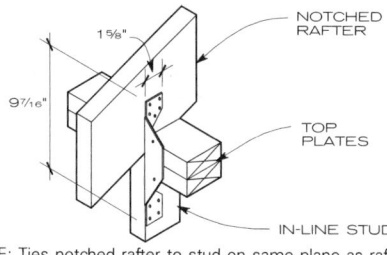

NOTE: Ties notched rafter to stud on same plane as rafter for tension load connection.

RAFTER-TO-STUD TIE

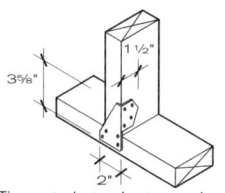

NOTE: Ties stud to bottom plate for tension load connection.

STUD TIE

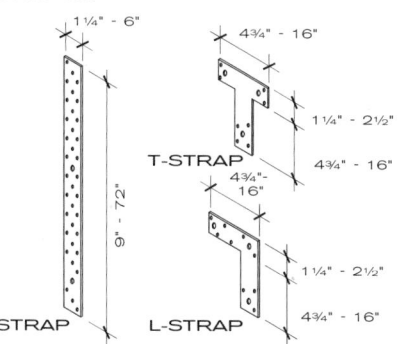

STRAP: For tying varied tension load connections, e.g., joists at ridge, wall-to-floor connections, etc.

T- AND L-STRAPS: For varied vertical to horizontal connections.

TIES

NOTES

1. For utmost rigidity, strength, and service, each type of fastener requires joint designs adapted to wood strength along and across the grain and to dimensional changes that may occur with variations in moisture content.

2. For forces such as wind uplift and lateral loads (wind and earthquake), the foundation, floor-to-floor, and roof connections are the main areas of concern, although, in varying degrees, all connections taken together will resist

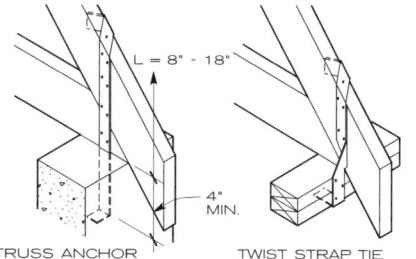

NOTE: Provides tension for wood-to-wood or wood-to-masonry connections for wood trusses and joists.

TRUSS ANCHORS

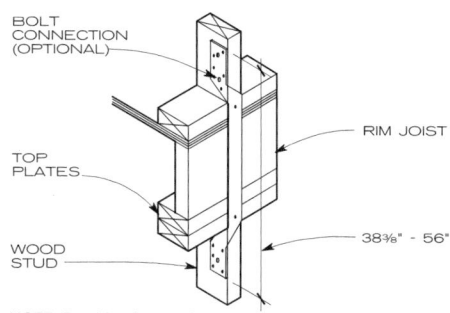

NOTE: Provides floor-to-floor tension connection; for nailed or bolted connections.

FLOOR TIE ANCHOR

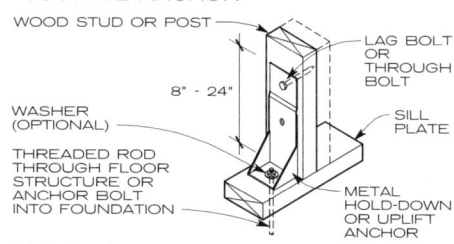

NOTE: Transfers tension loads between floors; ties studs/posts to foundation.

METAL HOLD-DOWN/UPLIFT ANCHOR

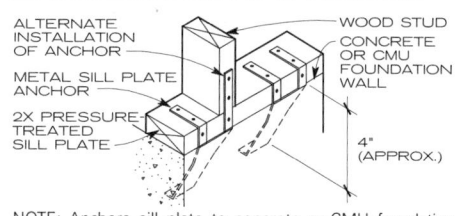

NOTE: Anchors sill plate to concrete or CMU foundation wall and/or studs.

SILL PLATE ANCHORS/SIDE INSTALLATION

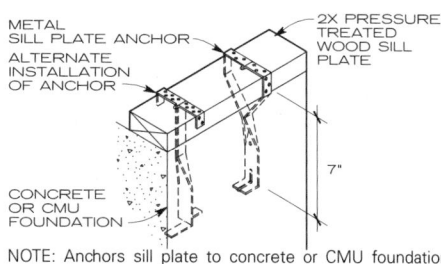

NOTE: Anchors sill plate to concrete or CMU foundation wall.

SILL PLATE ANCHORS/CENTERLINE INSTALLATION

ANCHORS

these forces. In some joints, the fastener or connector is the only resistor to the applied load.

3. Most fasteners used to join wood framing or to attach metal connectors to framing are made of steel, with a hot-dipped galvanized coating the most typical finish used. Stainless steel, or finishes such as a corrosion-resistant primer or a copolymer coating, can also be used. In the presence of moisture, metals used for nails

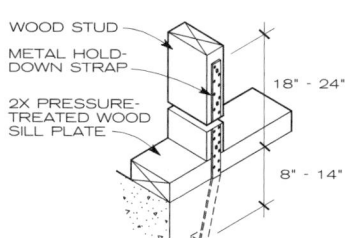

NOTE: Anchors sill plate and stud to concrete or CMU foundation wall.

METAL HOLD-DOWN/UPLIFT STRAP

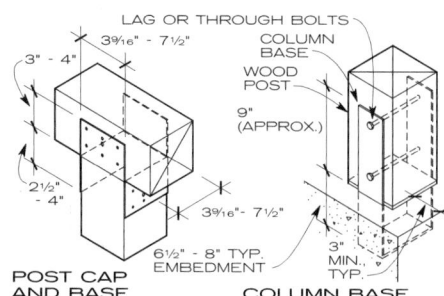

POST CAP/ BASE: For varied post cap or base connections.
COLUMN BASE: Attaches wood post to concrete embedment to resist high uplift loads.

COLUMN CAPS AND BASES

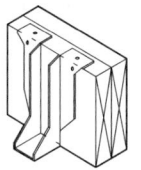 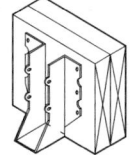

NOTE: Joist connector (in wide variety of sizes).

JOIST HANGERS

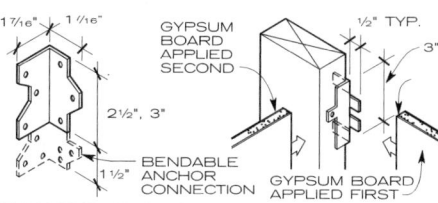

FRAMING ANCHOR: For varied wood-to-wood two-way connections; optional bendable extensions allow three-way connections.

BACK-UP CLIP: To provide back-up support for gypsum board in lieu of wood framing; can save wood material.

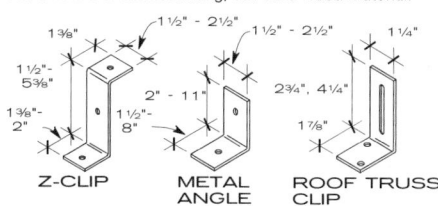

Z-CLIP: Secures 2x blocking between joists and/or trusses.
METAL ANGLE: Provides varied wood-to-wood or wood-to-concrete anchorage.
ROOF TRUSS CLIP: Provides alignment control between roof truss and nonbearing walls; slot permits load-induced truss movement.

VARIOUS CLIPS AND ANCHORS

and other fasteners may corrode when in contact with material treated with certain preservatives. Fasteners made of hot-dipped galvanized steel, copper, silicon bronze, and 304 and 316 stainless steel have performed well in wood treated with ammoniacal copper arsenate (ACA) and chromated copper arsenate (CCA), the most common preservatives for wood. Of course, provision should always be made to avoid galvanic action between dissimilar metals.

Richard J. Vitullo, AIA; Oak Leaf Studio; Crownsville, Maryland

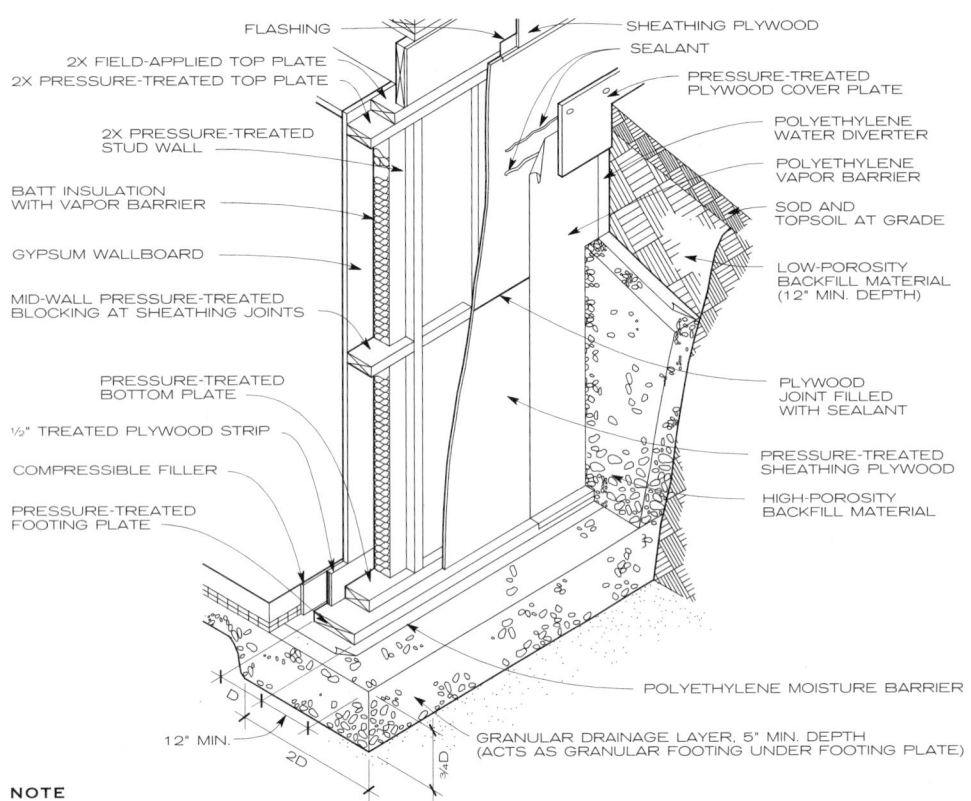

TYPICAL BASEMENT WALL

NOTE

1. Geotextile material may be used under and around drainage layers and backfill if soil conditions warrant.

2. Stud size and spacing vary with material grade and backfill depth. In general, 42 in. backfill requires 2 x 4 at 12 in. o.c., 64 in. requires 2 x 6 at 16 in. o.c., and 84 in. requires 2 x 6 at 12 in. o.c.

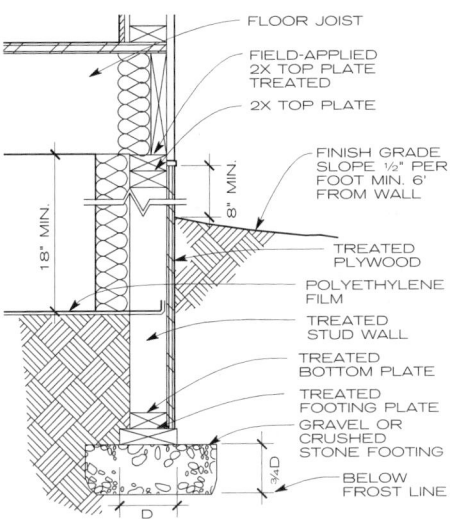

CRAWL SPACE WALL

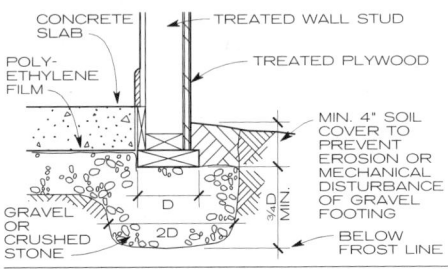

MINIMUM SOIL COVER ON SHALLOW FOOTINGS

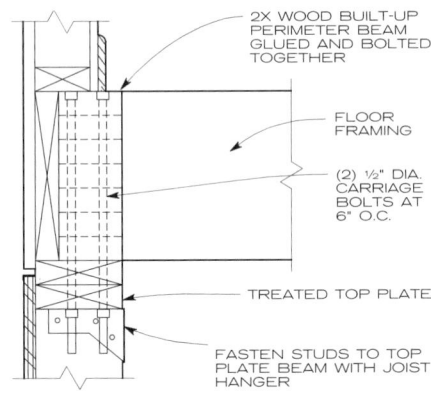

BUILT-UP PERIMETER BEAM AT STAIRS

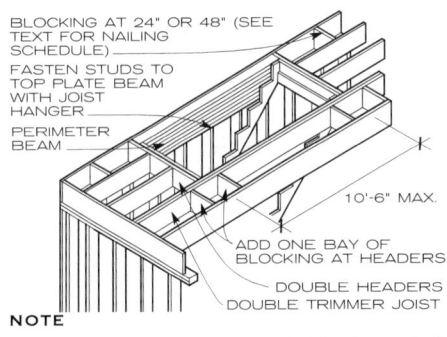

NOTE

For less than 48 in. backfill, use standard framing methods and fasten stairwell header to top plate with three 10d toenails.

STAIR OPENING AT PERIMETER WALL

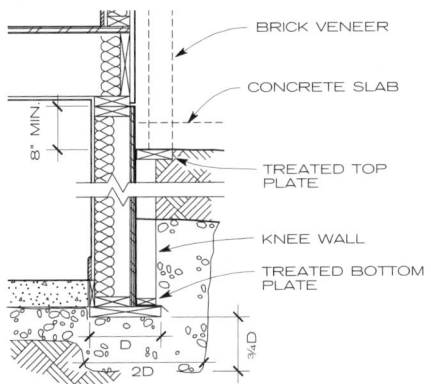

BASEMENT WALL WITH EXTERIOR KNEE WALL

INTRODUCTION

The construction of treated wood foundations is similar to the construction of standard wood light-frame walls except for two factors: (1) the wood used is pressure treated with wood preservatives, and (2) the extra loading and stress requirements caused by below-grade conditions must be accommodated in the design and detailing of the fasteners, connections, blocking, wall corners, and the like.

As with standard masonry or concrete foundation systems, treated wood foundations require a good drainage system in order to maintain dry basements and crawl spaces. However, the drainage system typically used with treated wood foundations is different from that used with masonry or concrete systems. The components of a drainage system suitable for use with a treated wood foundation are

1. A highly porous backfill material, which directs water down to a granular drainage layer.

2. A porous granular drainage layer under the entire foundation and floor system to collect and discharge water.

3. Positive discharge of water by means of a sump system designed for the soil type. This drainage system, developed for treated wood foundations, takes the place of the typical porous backfill over a perimeter drain tile.

NOTES

1. Characteristics of a treated wood foundation system:

   a. All framing is standard 2x construction.

   b. Can be erected in any weather and when site access for concrete or masonry is a problem.

   c. Deep wall cavities allow use of high R-value insulation without loss of interior space.

   d. Wiring and finishing are easily achieved.

2. Treated wood foundations are not appropriate for all sites. Selection of the proper foundation system for a project depends on site conditions, including soil types, drainage conditions, ground water, and other factors. Wet sites in low areas, especially areas with coarse-grained soil, should be avoided if a full basement is desired, although a crawl space-type foundation can be used in these cases. Consult a soils engineer to determine the viability of any foundation system.

3. Lumber and plywood used in treated wood foundations must be grade-stamped for foundation use and are typically pressure treated with chromated copper arsenate. Treated wood products used in foundation construction are required to contain more preservative than treated wood used in applications such as fencing and decking. Codes generally call for hot-dipped galvanized fasteners above grade and stainless steel fasteners below grade.

4. Avoid skin contact and prolonged or frequent inhalation of sawdust when handling or working with any pressure-treated wood product.

5. Consult applicable building codes and the American Forest & Paper Association's "Permanent Wood Foundation System—Design, Fabrication, Installation Manual" for requirements and design guidelines. In the early stages of a project, consult with the building code officials for the area or jurisdiction to assess their familiarity with and willingness to approve this type of system.

6. The vertical and horizontal edge-to-edge joints of all plywood panels used in these systems should be sealed with a suitable sealant. Consult the American Plywood Association Source List "Caulks and Adhesives for Permanent Wood Foundation System, Form H405" for a list of high-performance caulking compounds.

7. Correct materials and details of construction are very important for treated wood foundations. If the contractor to be used for the installation is unfamiliar with this foundation system, the design should include the use of prefabricated foundation panels. Most problems with treated wood foundations can be traced to improper installation by inexperienced workers.

8. Since this type of foundation system depends especially on the first floor deck to absorb and distribute any backfill loads, backfilling cannot occur until the first floor deck is complete.

Richard J. Vitullo, AIA; Oak Leaf Studio; Crownsville, Maryland
American Forest & Paper Association; Washington, D.C.

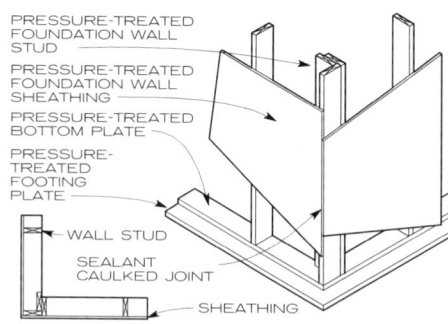

PRESSURE-TREATED FOUNDATION WALL STUD

PRESSURE-TREATED FOUNDATION WALL SHEATHING

PRESSURE-TREATED BOTTOM PLATE

PRESSURE-TREATED FOOTING PLATE

WALL STUD

SEALANT CAULKED JOINT

SHEATHING

NOTES

1. At an outside corner, soil pressures tend to force the wall sections together, making reinforcement unnecessary.
2. Three studs should be used at the corner to support interior finishes.

OUTSIDE CORNER DETAILS

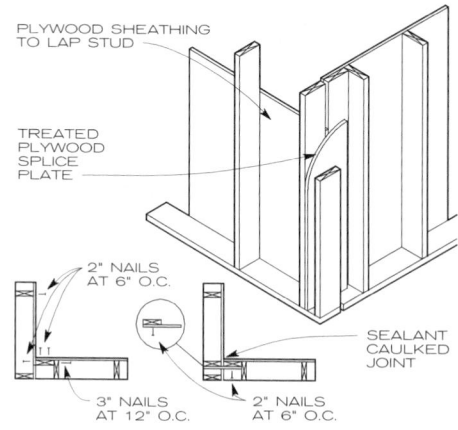

PLYWOOD SHEATHING TO LAP STUD

TREATED PLYWOOD SPLICE PLATE

2" NAILS AT 6" O.C.

SEALANT CAULKED JOINT

3" NAILS AT 12" O.C.

2" NAILS AT 6" O.C.

DETAIL 1

PLYWOOD SHEATHING LAPS STUD AND IS NAILED TO STUD FACE

FILLER PIECE TO SUPPORT SHEATHING

GALVANIZED STEEL STRAP

3½" NAILS AT 6" O.C.

DETAIL 2

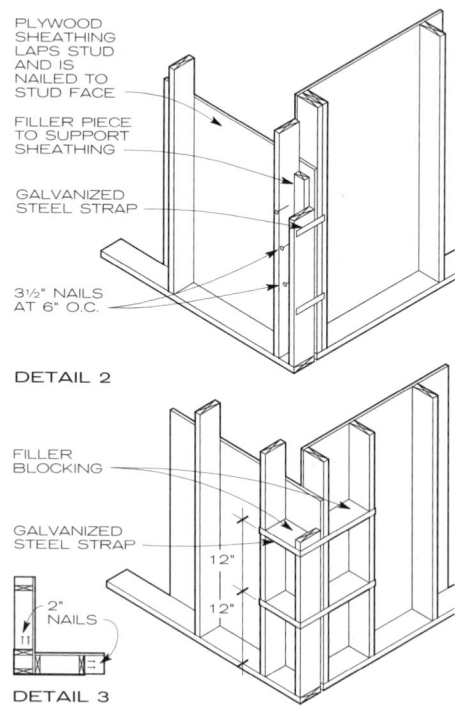

FILLER BLOCKING

GALVANIZED STEEL STRAP

12"

12"

2" NAILS

DETAIL 3

NOTES

1. At inside corners, soil pressures tend to force the wall panels apart, making additional structural reinforcement necessary.
2. Detail no. 1 provides the required additional reinforcement with a treated plywood splice plate and additional nailing below grade.

INSIDE CORNER DETAILS

Richard J. Vitullo, AIA; Oak Leaf Studio; Crownsville, Maryland
American Forest & Paper Association; Washington, D.C.

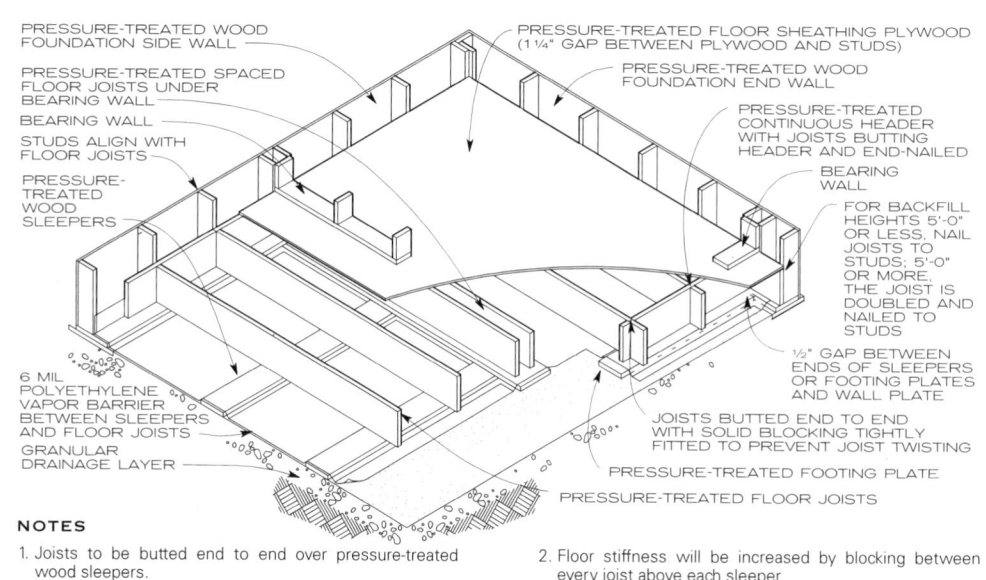

PRESSURE-TREATED WOOD FOUNDATION SIDE WALL

PRESSURE-TREATED SPACED FLOOR JOISTS UNDER BEARING WALL

BEARING WALL

STUDS ALIGN WITH FLOOR JOISTS

PRESSURE-TREATED WOOD SLEEPERS

6 MIL POLYETHYLENE VAPOR BARRIER BETWEEN SLEEPERS AND FLOOR JOISTS

GRANULAR DRAINAGE LAYER

PRESSURE-TREATED FLOOR SHEATHING PLYWOOD (1¼" GAP BETWEEN PLYWOOD AND STUDS)

PRESSURE-TREATED WOOD FOUNDATION END WALL

PRESSURE-TREATED CONTINUOUS HEADER WITH JOISTS BUTTING HEADER AND END-NAILED

BEARING WALL

FOR BACKFILL HEIGHTS 5'-0" OR LESS, NAIL JOISTS TO STUDS; 5'-0" OR MORE, THE JOIST IS DOUBLED AND NAILED TO STUDS

½" GAP BETWEEN ENDS OF SLEEPERS OR FOOTING PLATES AND WALL PLATE

JOISTS BUTTED END TO END WITH SOLID BLOCKING TIGHTLY FITTED TO PREVENT JOIST TWISTING

PRESSURE-TREATED FOOTING PLATE

PRESSURE-TREATED FLOOR JOISTS

NOTES

1. Joists to be butted end to end over pressure-treated wood sleepers.

2. Floor stiffness will be increased by blocking between every joist above each sleeper.

WOOD SLEEPER FLOOR SYSTEM

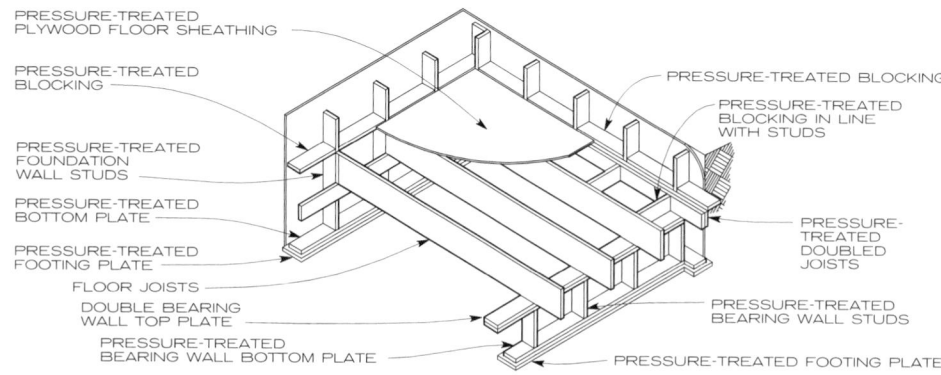

PRESSURE-TREATED PLYWOOD FLOOR SHEATHING

PRESSURE-TREATED BLOCKING

PRESSURE-TREATED FOUNDATION WALL STUDS

PRESSURE-TREATED BOTTOM PLATE

PRESSURE-TREATED FOOTING PLATE

FLOOR JOISTS

DOUBLE BEARING WALL TOP PLATE

PRESSURE-TREATED BEARING WALL BOTTOM PLATE

PRESSURE-TREATED BLOCKING

PRESSURE-TREATED BLOCKING IN LINE WITH STUDS

PRESSURE-TREATED DOUBLED JOISTS

PRESSURE-TREATED BEARING WALL STUDS

PRESSURE-TREATED FOOTING PLATE

SUSPENDED WOOD FLOOR

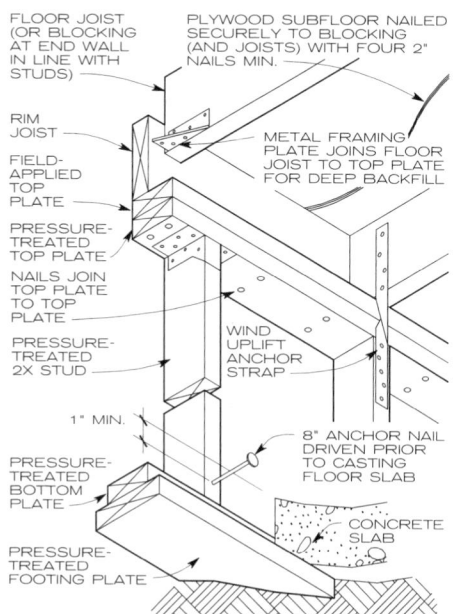

FLOOR JOIST (OR BLOCKING AT END WALL IN LINE WITH STUDS)

PLYWOOD SUBFLOOR NAILED SECURELY TO BLOCKING (AND JOISTS) WITH FOUR 2" NAILS MIN.

RIM JOIST

FIELD-APPLIED TOP PLATE

PRESSURE-TREATED TOP PLATE

NAILS JOIN TOP PLATE TO TOP PLATE

PRESSURE-TREATED 2X STUD

METAL FRAMING PLATE JOINS FLOOR JOIST TO TOP PLATE FOR DEEP BACKFILL

WIND UPLIFT ANCHOR STRAP

1" MIN.

8" ANCHOR NAIL DRIVEN PRIOR TO CASTING FLOOR SLAB

PRESSURE-TREATED BOTTOM PLATE

CONCRETE SLAB

PRESSURE-TREATED FOOTING PLATE

NOTES

1. Fasteners and connector plates transfer soil pressure thrust from wall sheathing and studs to floor system; type and amount of fasteners and connectors depend on height of backfill.

2. Wind uplift anchor straps and anchor nails spaced as required by code.

WALL ANCHORAGE DETAIL

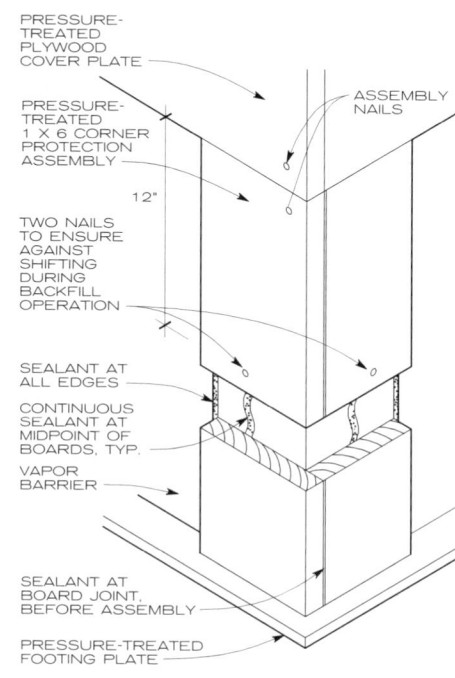

PRESSURE-TREATED PLYWOOD COVER PLATE

PRESSURE-TREATED 1 X 6 CORNER PROTECTION ASSEMBLY

ASSEMBLY NAILS

12"

TWO NAILS TO ENSURE AGAINST SHIFTING DURING BACKFILL OPERATION

SEALANT AT ALL EDGES

CONTINUOUS SEALANT AT MIDPOINT OF BOARDS, TYP.

VAPOR BARRIER

SEALANT AT BOARD JOINT, BEFORE ASSEMBLY

PRESSURE-TREATED FOOTING PLATE

OUTSIDE CORNER PROTECTION DETAIL

NOTE

All wood members within 18 in. of the ground should be bottom treated.

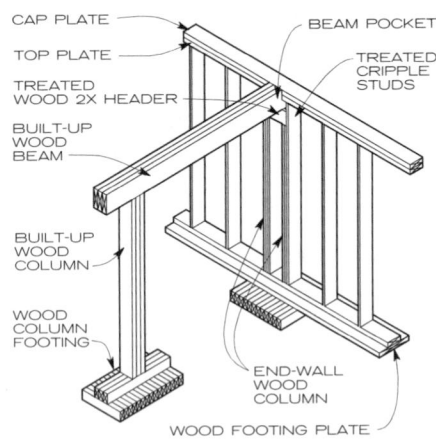

MAIN BEAMS AND COLUMNS

CAP PLATE
TOP PLATE
TREATED WOOD 2X HEADER
BUILT-UP WOOD BEAM
BUILT-UP WOOD COLUMN
WOOD COLUMN FOOTING
BEAM POCKET
TREATED CRIPPLE STUDS
END-WALL WOOD COLUMN
WOOD FOOTING PLATE

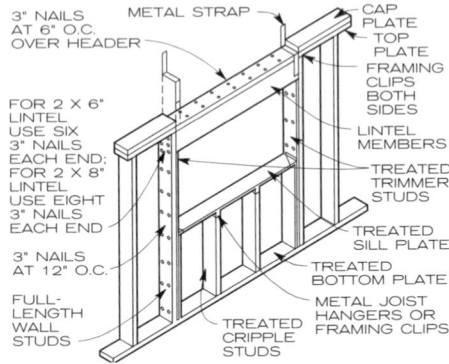

3" NAILS AT 6" O.C. OVER HEADER
METAL STRAP
CAP PLATE
TOP PLATE
FRAMING CLIPS BOTH SIDES
FOR 2 X 6" LINTEL USE SIX 3" NAILS EACH END; FOR 2 X 8" LINTEL USE EIGHT 3" NAILS EACH END
LINTEL MEMBERS
TREATED TRIMMER STUDS
3" NAILS AT 12" O.C.
TREATED SILL PLATE
TREATED BOTTOM PLATE
METAL JOIST HANGERS OR FRAMING CLIPS
FULL-LENGTH WALL STUDS
TREATED CRIPPLE STUDS

NOTES

1. For backfill heights up to 4 ft 6 in. and if width of opening is 4 ft 0 in. to 5 ft 6 in., use double sill plates and double full-length wall studs.

2. For backfill heights up to 4 ft 6 in. and if width of opening is 6 ft 0 in. to 9 ft 0 in., use triple sill plates and triple full-length wall studs.

3. For backfill heights of 48 in. or less, nailing and fastening can conform to the appropriate building code.

4. For backfill heights greater than 4 ft 6 in. or openings wider than 9 ft 0 in., contact engineer for design.

WINDOW FRAMING DETAIL

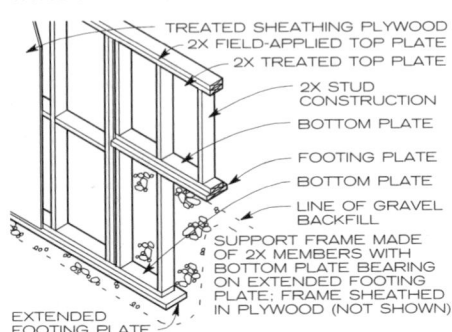

TREATED SHEATHING PLYWOOD
2X FIELD-APPLIED TOP PLATE
2X TREATED TOP PLATE
2X STUD CONSTRUCTION
BOTTOM PLATE
FOOTING PLATE
BOTTOM PLATE
LINE OF GRAVEL BACKFILL
SUPPORT FRAME MADE OF 2X MEMBERS WITH BOTTOM PLATE BEARING ON EXTENDED FOOTING PLATE; FRAME SHEATHED IN PLYWOOD (NOT SHOWN)
EXTENDED FOOTING PLATE

STEPPED FOOTING DETAIL

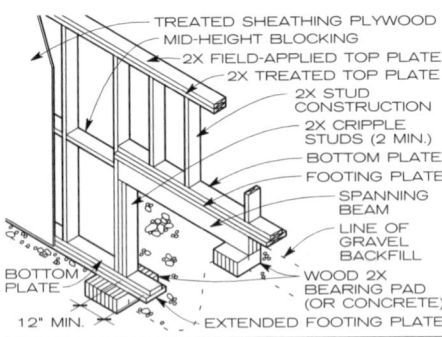

TREATED SHEATHING PLYWOOD
MID-HEIGHT BLOCKING
2X FIELD-APPLIED TOP PLATE
2X TREATED TOP PLATE
2X STUD CONSTRUCTION
2X CRIPPLE STUDS (2 MIN.)
BOTTOM PLATE
FOOTING PLATE
SPANNING BEAM
LINE OF GRAVEL BACKFILL
BOTTOM PLATE
WOOD 2X BEARING PAD (OR CONCRETE)
EXTENDED FOOTING PLATE
12" MIN.

SPANNING BEAM DETAIL

Richard J. Vitullo, AIA; Oak Leaf Studio; Crownsville, Maryland
American Forest & Paper Association; Washington, D.C.

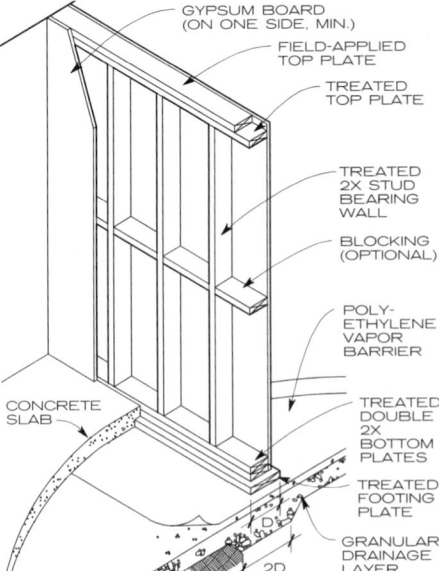

GYPSUM BOARD (ON ONE SIDE, MIN.)
FIELD-APPLIED TOP PLATE
TREATED TOP PLATE
TREATED 2X STUD BEARING WALL
BLOCKING (OPTIONAL)
POLY-ETHYLENE VAPOR BARRIER
CONCRETE SLAB
TREATED DOUBLE 2X BOTTOM PLATES
TREATED FOOTING PLATE
GRANULAR DRAINAGE LAYER
2D

BEARING WALL AT CONCRETE SLAB

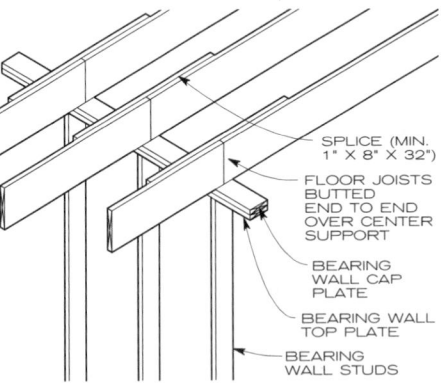

SPLICE (MIN. 1" X 8" X 32")
FLOOR JOISTS BUTTED END TO END OVER CENTER SUPPORT
BEARING WALL CAP PLATE
BEARING WALL TOP PLATE
BEARING WALL STUDS

INTERIOR BEARING WALL—FLOOR JOIST SUPPORT

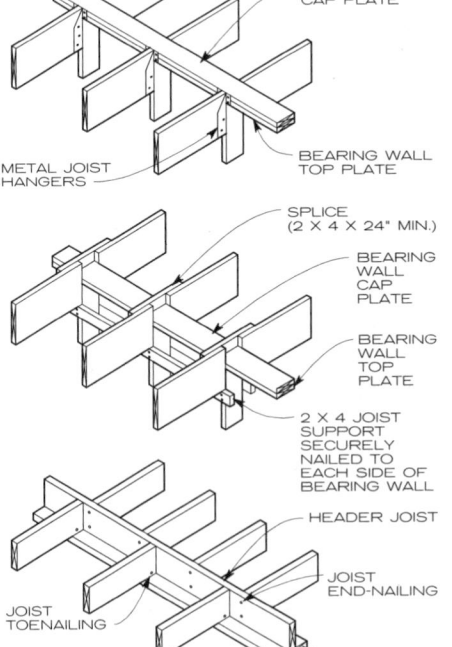

BEARING WALL CAP PLATE
METAL JOIST HANGERS
BEARING WALL TOP PLATE
SPLICE (2 X 4 X 24" MIN.)
BEARING WALL CAP PLATE
BEARING WALL TOP PLATE
2 X 4 JOIST SUPPORT SECURELY NAILED TO EACH SIDE OF BEARING WALL
HEADER JOIST
JOIST END-NAILING
JOIST TOENAILING
CAP PLATE

INTERIOR BEARING WALL—FLOOR JOIST SUPPORT (ALTERNATIVES)

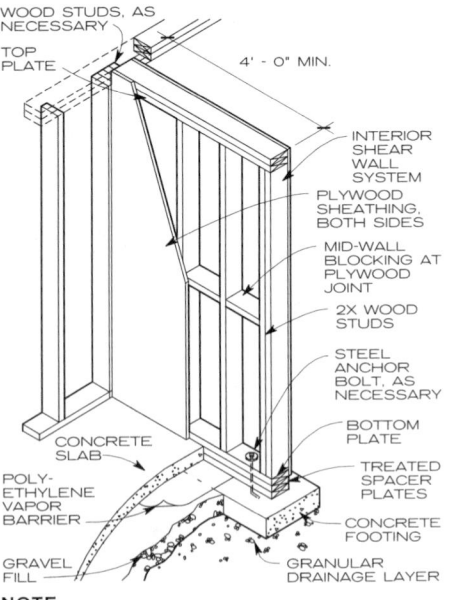

WOOD STUDS, AS NECESSARY
TOP PLATE
4' - 0" MIN.
INTERIOR SHEAR WALL SYSTEM
PLYWOOD SHEATHING, BOTH SIDES
MID-WALL BLOCKING AT PLYWOOD JOINT
2X WOOD STUDS
STEEL ANCHOR BOLT, AS NECESSARY
BOTTOM PLATE
TREATED SPACER PLATES
CONCRETE FOOTING
GRANULAR DRAINAGE LAYER
CONCRETE SLAB
POLY-ETHYLENE VAPOR BARRIER
GRAVEL FILL

NOTE

Interior shear wall material does not need to be treated with wood preservatives.

INTERIOR SHEAR WALL DETAIL

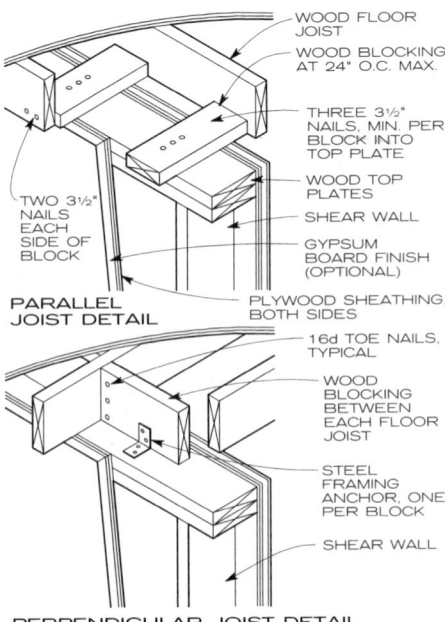

WOOD FLOOR JOIST
WOOD BLOCKING AT 24" O.C. MAX.
THREE 3½" NAILS, MIN. PER BLOCK INTO TOP PLATE
WOOD TOP PLATES
SHEAR WALL
GYPSUM BOARD FINISH (OPTIONAL)
PLYWOOD SHEATHING, BOTH SIDES
TWO 3½" NAILS EACH SIDE OF BLOCK

PARALLEL JOIST DETAIL

16d TOE NAILS, TYPICAL
WOOD BLOCKING BETWEEN EACH FLOOR JOIST
STEEL FRAMING ANCHOR, ONE PER BLOCK
SHEAR WALL

PERPENDICULAR JOIST DETAIL

SHEAR WALL ANCHORAGE

SHEAR WALLS AS RACKING RESISTANCE

Foundation walls may be subject to racking loads, which occur parallel to a wall and can cause shearing forces along the plane of the wall. Racking loads are caused by soil pressure and other lateral forces such as earthquake and wind. Walls, connections, and fasteners must be designed to resist these forces. Generally, soil pressure comes into play for backfill greater than 24 in. in height; check anticipated wind and earthquake forces to determine how best to accommodate them.

Check long shear walls or those with a length-to-width ratio greater than 2:1 for diaphragm deflection, particularly if the structure is built on a slope. The unequal heights of the backfill on a slope apply unequal loads to the end walls or walls parallel to the floor joist system. These walls, having received these loads by the diaphragm action of the floor system, then act as shear walls. Internal shear walls, accommodated within interior partitions, also may be needed.

The strength of a diaphragm or shear wall depends on careful nailing of the plywood to the structural members. Plywood joints should be staggered to increase stiffness.

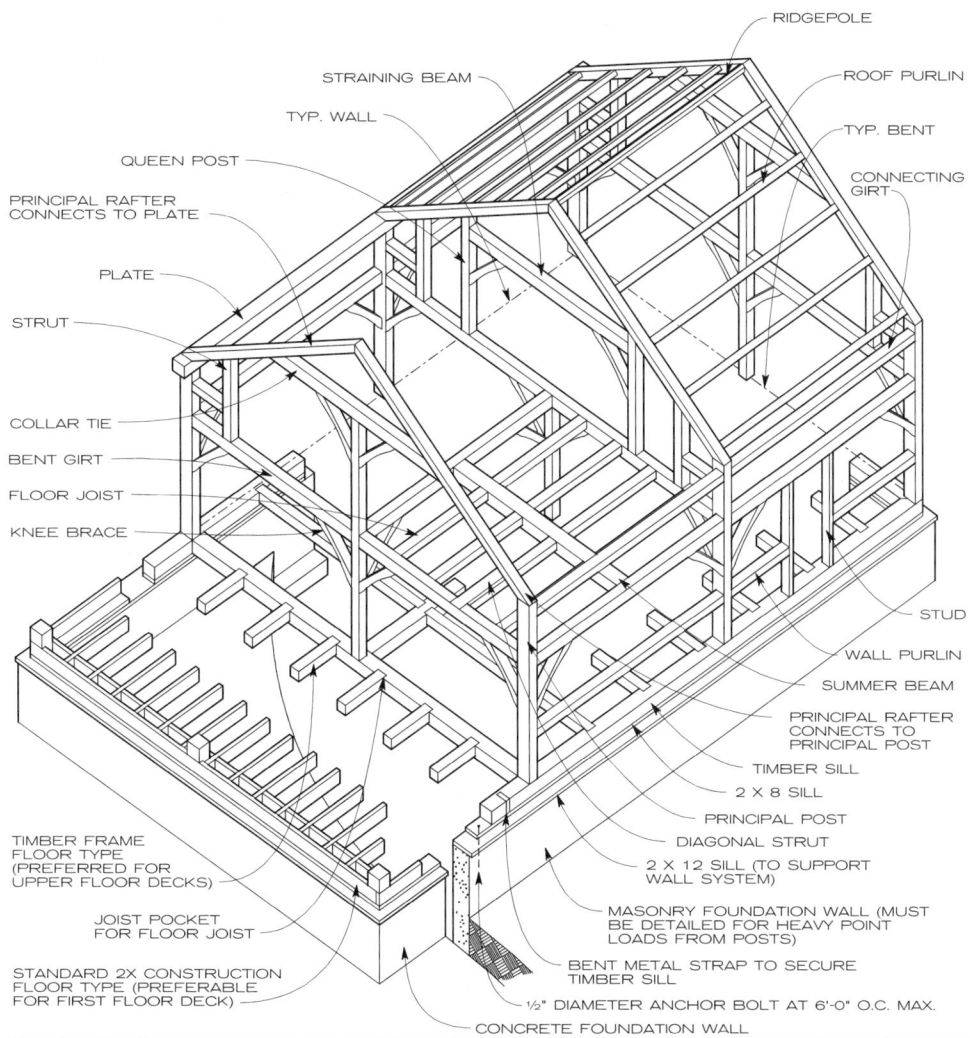

TYPICAL TIMBER FRAME (SHOWING TWO ROOF AND FLOOR TYPES)

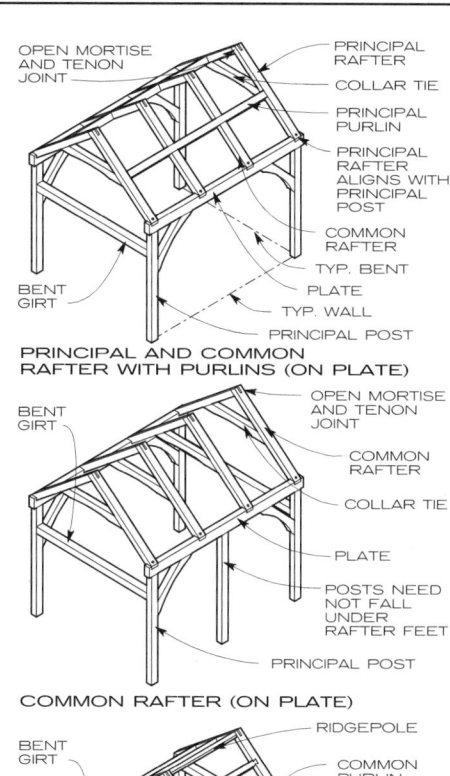

PRINCIPAL AND COMMON RAFTER WITH PURLINS (ON PLATE)

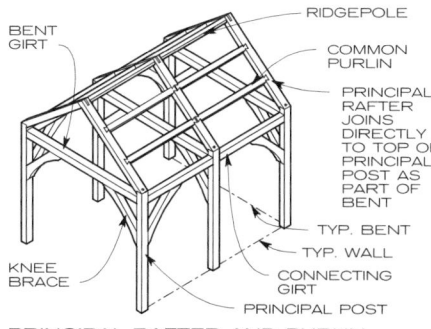

COMMON RAFTER (ON PLATE)

PRINCIPAL RAFTER AND PURLIN

TIMBER FRAME ROOF TYPES

GENERAL

Timber frame buildings are characterized by large, exposed timber structural members. The distinction between timber framing and other types of heavy timber construction is somewhat subjective, but in a true timber frame, the posts, beams, and braces are connected to one another with elegant, largely all-wood joints based on very old traditions. Sound timber frame construction requires high standards of design, engineering, and workmanship. It can be compared to the craftsmanship of cabinetmaking, rather than to conventional wood frame construction.

One of the reasons timber frame construction faded from popularity around 1900, after centuries of dominance, was the cost of its labor-intensive building methods. During the past twenty years, techniques have been developed that offset this drawback: the frame can be prefabricated in shops with heavy tools, and structural, insulated wall panels can be used to build the walls. Connection details in true timber frame construction are still rooted in the ancient wood-pegged, mortise-and-tenon joint. More modern wood connectors of steel can be used, depending on budget and aesthetics, but many would say the resulting structure would not be a true timber frame.

Typically, posts in timber-framed buildings are spaced in a grid, 8 to 16 ft apart. These relatively large posts support beams, girts, connectors, plates, and principal rafters. In turn, those members support rafters, purlins, summer beams, and joists, which are spaced at 2 to 6 ft centers. The relatively large timbers make timber frame construction inherently fire resistant, qualifying as Class IV construction under most building codes.

The walls and roof in a timber frame, freed of the task of supporting great loads, can be made of materials that need to function only as a rain screen and curtain walls. These materials are attached to the outside of the larger, structural members, enclosing the space while exposing the timbers to the interior and protecting the frame from deterioration.

Nonstructural foam-core panels with an exterior layer of wood sheathing, a foam core, and an interior drywall finish layer are extremely energy efficient and cost-effective for use in wall and roof construction in a timber frame. Sometimes it is preferable to use structural foam-core panels, with oriented-strand board (OSB) or plywood sheathing on both sides, as they better resist warping and lateral forces and provide a better nailing surface for attaching interior trim, cabinets, artwork, etc. These structural panels are typically installed outside a layer of gypsum board that is back-screwed to the inner OSB skin.

ANATOMY OF A TIMBER FRAME BUILDING

In the design process, the general layout of timbers is determined first, based on the rough program and layout of spaces. Once the wood species has been selected, each timber is sized individually. Next, the connection details, or joinery, and the embellishments and finishes are designed.

A typical timber frame can be divided into four major systems: walls, floors, roof, and bents. Walls, in the terminology of timber framing, are planar compositions of timbers parallel to the ridge. Bents run perpendicular to the walls and are often the primary preassembled sections of the building. Usually, bents include the principal structural posts of the frame and the major supporting rafters. The space between two bents is called a bay and is generally between 10 and 16 ft wide. If the roof structure is not included in the bent system, a large timber plate is set at the top of the bent or wall for the roof framing to rest on.

ROOF SYSTEMS

More than any other factor, the arrangement of timbers in the roof determines whether the walls or the bents will be the principal structural unit. Frames are often defined by the type of roof they support, since the roof is usually the most difficult aspect of the frame to design, detail, and erect. The choice of roof system most appropriate for a particular building depends on the shape and pitch of the roof, the loading, wood species, available timber length, floor plan, and personal aesthetic preferences.

NOTES

1. Wood shrinks considerably across the grain but very little along the grain, and all dimensions based on sections through plates and sills must account for this shrinkage. Bents that connect principal rafters directly to the posts and are not interrupted by plates will have negligible differential movement between roof and wall joints.

2. Timber systems that rely on full-length plates, sills, ridgepoles, or tie beams tend to require timbers of considerable length, which are scarce. These long lengths must be assembled from shorter members tied together with scarf joints. Since most sawmills cannot obtain timbers longer than 30 ft, it is important to consult with a structural engineer and local sawmill to determine the most practical dimensions for the timbers before the design is completed.

3. Depending on budget or aesthetic priorities, hybrid systems can be devised, such as timber frame walls with conventional roof framing or conventional stud walls with a timber frame roof. Consult a structural engineer about the design, detailing, and integration of these systems.

Richard J. Vitullo, AIA; Oak Leaf Studio; Crownsville, Maryland
Tedd Benson and Ben Brungraber, Ph.D., PE; Benson Woodworking Co., Inc.; Alstead, New Hampshire

ROUGH CARPENTRY

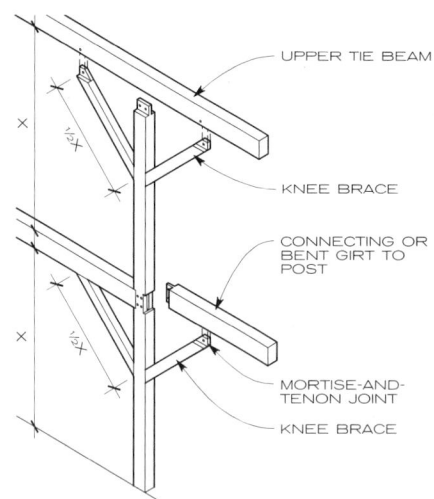

UPPER TIE BEAM

KNEE BRACE

CONNECTING OR BENT GIRT TO POST

MORTISE-AND-TENON JOINT

KNEE BRACE

NOTE

For basic structural rigidity within a timber frame, the knee brace is a critical component. It is typically used between the upper ends of vertical posts and horizontal beams, but may also be used at the base of a post or to brace an inclined member, such as a rafter. Rigidity in a frame can be achieved by using a few well-placed long braces or several shorter braces. Braces typically should not be shorter than half the length of the beam-to-beam span of the post.

KNEE BRACE

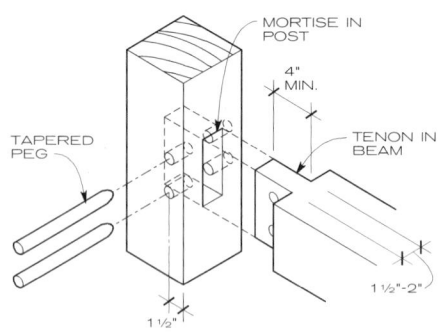

MORTISE IN POST

4" MIN.

TAPERED PEG

TENON IN BEAM

1 1/2"-2"

1 1/2"

NOTE

The basic mortise-and-tenon joint can be very effective in resisting both tension and compression forces. To increase tensile strength, increase the depth and thickness of the tenon and use additional pegs if the width and length of the tenon allow.

BASIC MORTISE-AND-TENON JOINT

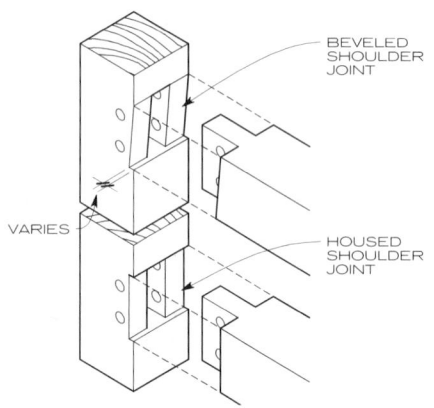

BEVELED SHOULDER JOINT

VARIES

HOUSED SHOULDER JOINT

NOTE

A beveled shoulder or housed joint is used to connect all load-bearing beams, such as bent and connecting girts and summer beams, to posts. Angled variations can be used when principal rafters join to posts or for diagonal braces. The depth of the shoulder depends on loading, torsion, other joinery in the area, and wood species.

SHOULDERED MORTISE-AND-TENON JOINTS

Richard J. Vitullo, AIA; Oak Leaf Studio; Crownsville, Maryland
Tedd Benson and Ben Brungraber, Ph.D., PE; Benson Woodworking Co., Inc.; Alstead, New Hampshire

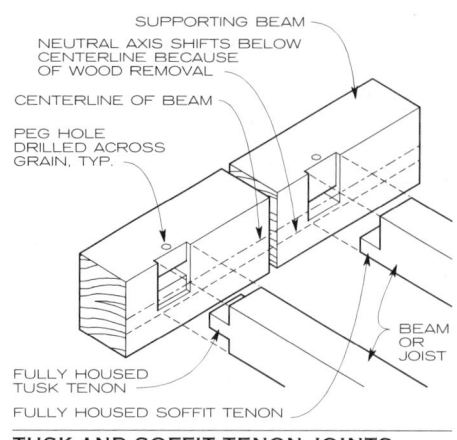

SUPPORTING BEAM

NEUTRAL AXIS SHIFTS BELOW CENTERLINE BECAUSE OF WOOD REMOVAL

CENTERLINE OF BEAM

PEG HOLE DRILLED ACROSS GRAIN, TYP.

BEAM OR JOIST

FULLY HOUSED TUSK TENON

FULLY HOUSED SOFFIT TENON

TUSK AND SOFFIT TENON JOINTS

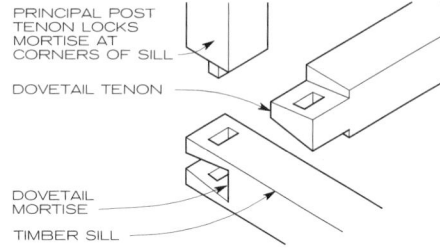

PRINCIPAL POST TENON LOCKS MORTISE AT CORNERS OF SILL

DOVETAIL TENON

DOVETAIL MORTISE

TIMBER SILL

DOVETAIL MORTISE AND TENON

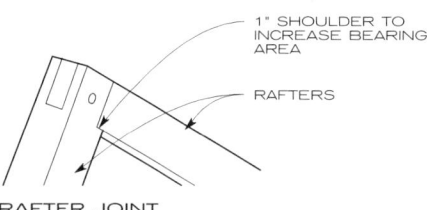

1" SHOULDER TO INCREASE BEARING AREA

RAFTERS

RAFTER JOINT

OPEN MORTISE-AND-TENON JOINTS

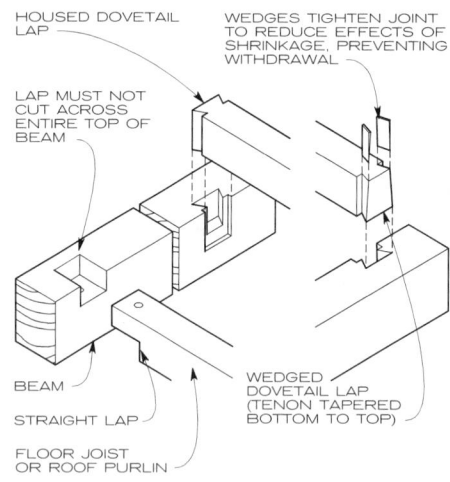

HOUSED DOVETAIL LAP

WEDGES TIGHTEN JOINT TO REDUCE EFFECTS OF SHRINKAGE, PREVENTING WITHDRAWAL

LAP MUST NOT CUT ACROSS ENTIRE TOP OF BEAM

BEAM

STRAIGHT LAP

FLOOR JOIST OR ROOF PURLIN

WEDGED DOVETAIL LAP (TENON TAPERED BOTTOM TO TOP)

LAP JOINTS

WOOD JOINERY

Most timber framing joints are variations on the mortise and tenon, in which a tongue on one timber is received by a slot in the other and locked with rounded pegs driven through holes drilled through both parts of the joint. The simplest version of this joint is used in compression situations or for situations with minimal loading. Knee braces and collar ties generally use an angled variation.

Spline joints are similar to a mortise and tenon, except that a third member, called a spline or "free tenon" (usually hardwood), is introduced to connect between mortised timbers and to serve as the tie. Spline joints are an effective way to achieve minimum end and edge distances without being dependent on the size and capacity of the receiving post or beam.

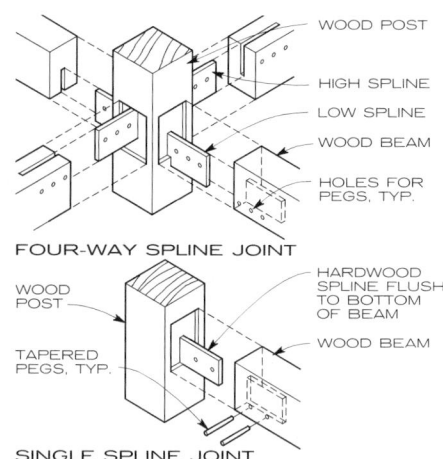

WOOD POST

HIGH SPLINE

LOW SPLINE

WOOD BEAM

HOLES FOR PEGS, TYP.

FOUR-WAY SPLINE JOINT

WOOD POST

TAPERED PEGS, TYP.

HARDWOOD SPLINE FLUSH TO BOTTOM OF BEAM

WOOD BEAM

SINGLE SPLINE JOINT
NOTE

Using through-splines made of hardwood leaves all the pegs loaded parallel to the grain, with plenty of available end-grain distance, and avoids loaded edges in the posts. Spline edges often are left prominent to achieve a decorative effect.

SPLINE JOINTS

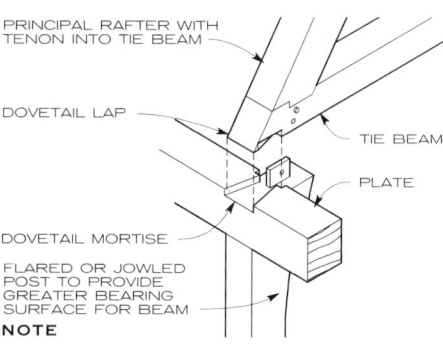

PRINCIPAL RAFTER WITH TENON INTO TIE BEAM

DOVETAIL LAP

TIE BEAM

PLATE

DOVETAIL MORTISE

FLARED OR JOWLED POST TO PROVIDE GREATER BEARING SURFACE FOR BEAM

NOTE

A tying joint is a combination of joints used to connect several members. The intersection of a principal post, a plate, a tie beam, and a rafter is known as a tying joint.

TYING JOINT

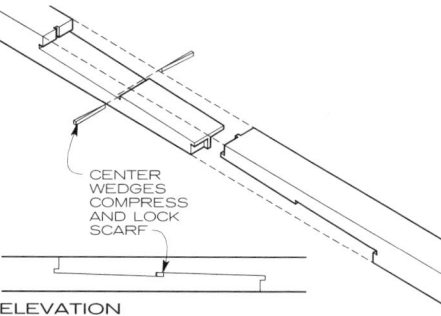

CENTER WEDGES COMPRESS AND LOCK SCARF

ELEVATION
NOTE

Scarf joints are lap joints used to splice two or more shorter timbers into one long timber. Although there are many variations, scarf joints are used primarily for plates and sills that demand long continuous timber.

SCARF JOINT

Lap joints, such as simple overlaps or dovetails, constitute the other broad category of joints used in timber frames. Scarfs, used to splice timbers along their length, are variations of the lap joint.

Joints are chosen on the basis of the tasks they are to fulfill, including locking the frame together, bearing weight, and transferring forces and building loads from one timber to another.

Compound joinery, such as where two timber valley rafters meet at a purlin, is one of the difficult aspects of timber framing. The complex geometry and the precision required demand master-level craftsmanship.

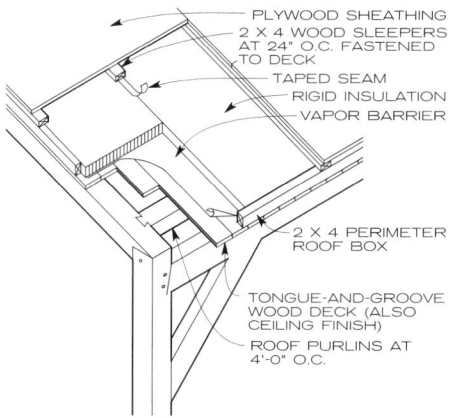

WOOD SLEEPERS AND TONGUE-AND-GROOVE CEILING ON ROOF PURLINS

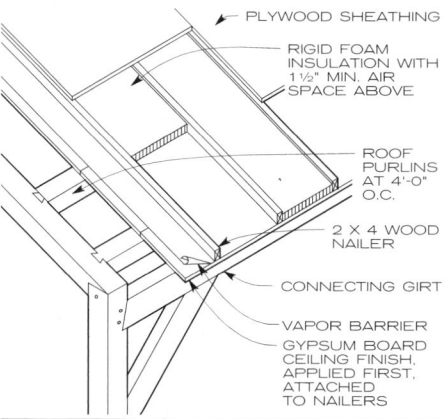

WOOD NAILERS ON ROOF PURLINS

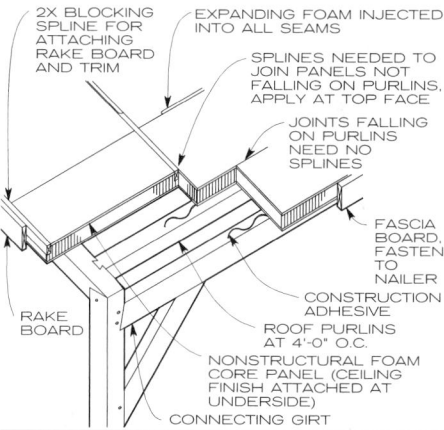

NONSTRUCTURAL FOAM CORE PANELS ON ROOF PURLINS

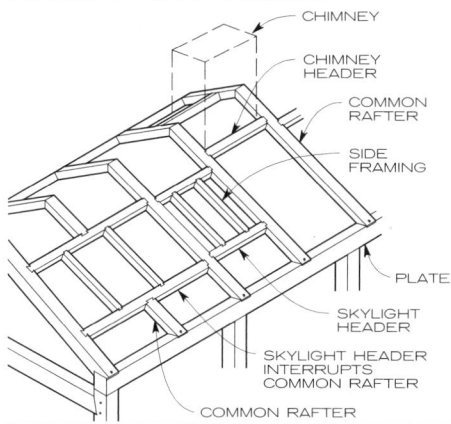

ROOF FRAMING HEADERS

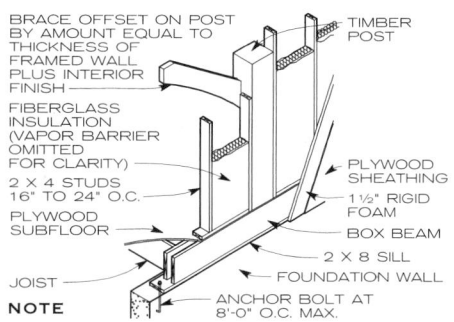

NOTE

This system reduces the exposure of the timber frame by partially concealing the frame in the wall system. It allows air infiltration due to shrinkage and movement and requires an exterior rigid foam insulation layer to minimize the potential for air movement and condensation.

INFILL WOOD STUD SYSTEM

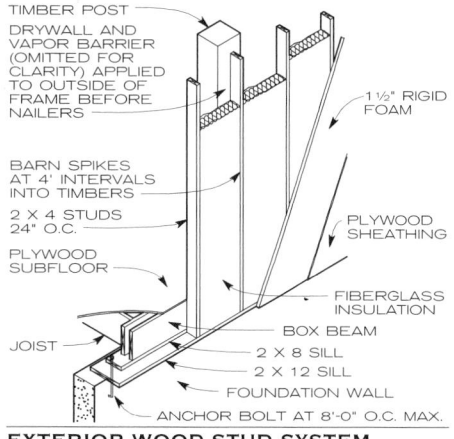

EXTERIOR WOOD STUD SYSTEM

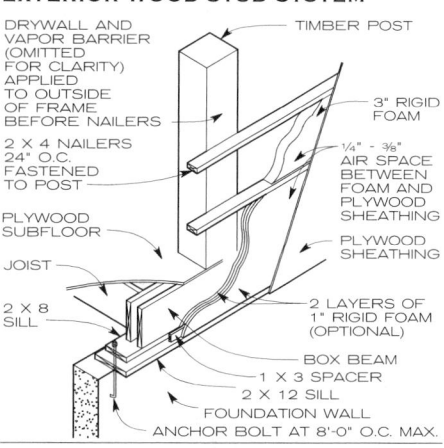

HORIZONTAL NAILER WALL SYSTEM

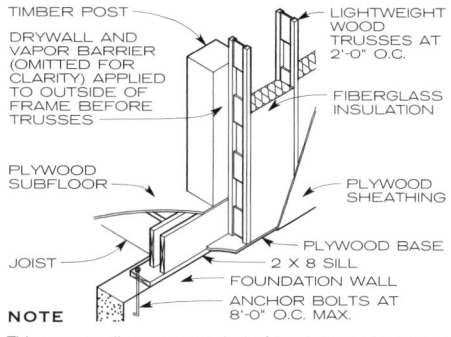

NOTE

This system allows a great deal of insulation to be packed into the nonstructural wall cavity between trusses. The foundation wall may be offset to the outside of the truss system (with pilasters added on the inside to support timber posts) to avoid the appearance of excess overhang.

EXTERIOR LIGHTWEIGHT WOOD TRUSS SYSTEM

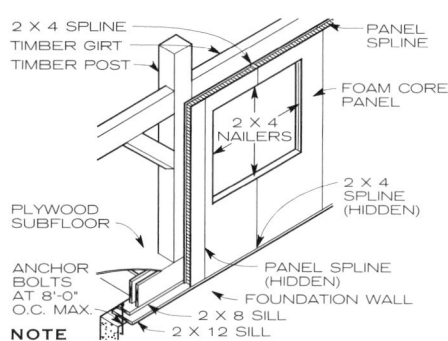

NOTE

Structural foam core panels (with wood sheathing on both sides of the foam core) may be needed at areas that may have excess stress or loading with interior finish attached to the frame before the panels are attached.

FOAM CORE PANEL WALL SYSTEM

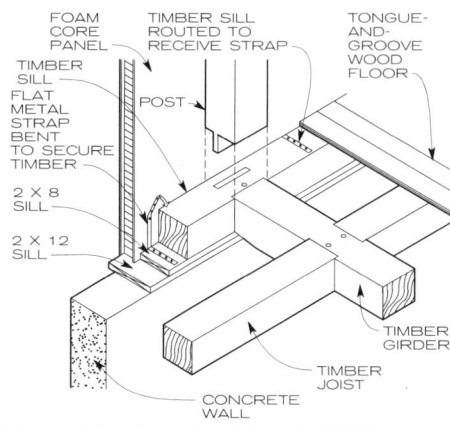

TIMBER SILL AND JOIST SYSTEM

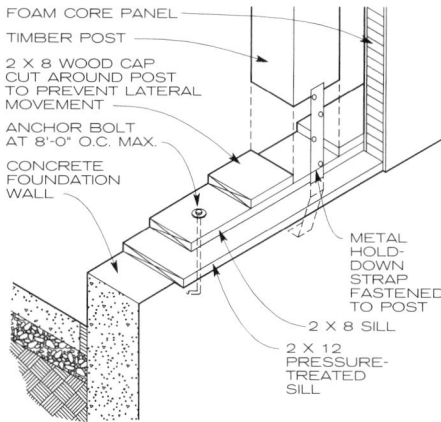

STANDARD 2X LUMBER SILL

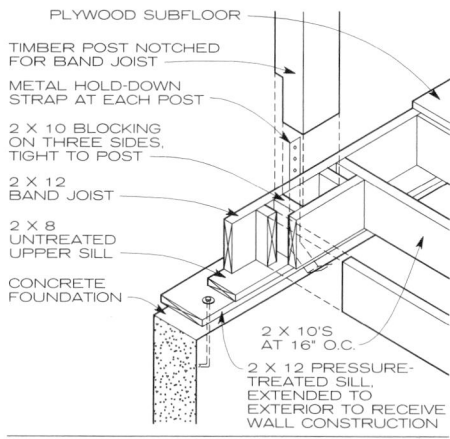

STICK FRAME SILL AND FLOOR DECK

Richard J. Vitullo, AIA; Oak Leaf Studio; Crownsville, Maryland
Tedd Benson and Ben Brungraber, Ph.D., PE; Benson Woodworking Co., Inc.; Alstead, New Hampshire

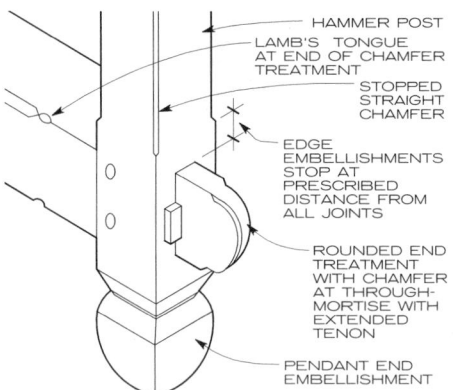

END AND EDGE EMBELLISHMENTS

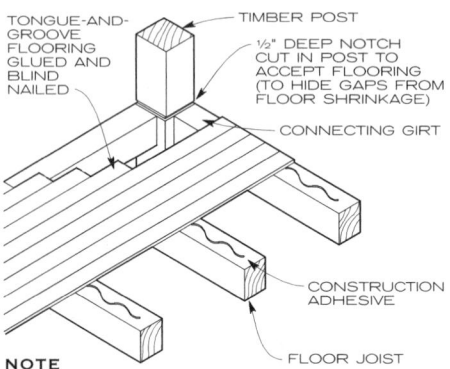

NOTE

Maintain ⅝ in. gap between flooring edge and wall for expansion and contraction.

STANDARD TONGUE-AND-GROOVE FLOOR

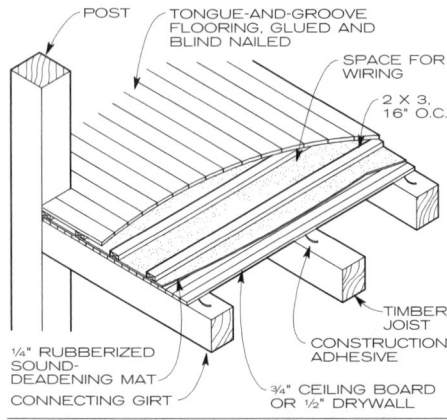

SOUND-RESISTANT FLOOR DETAIL

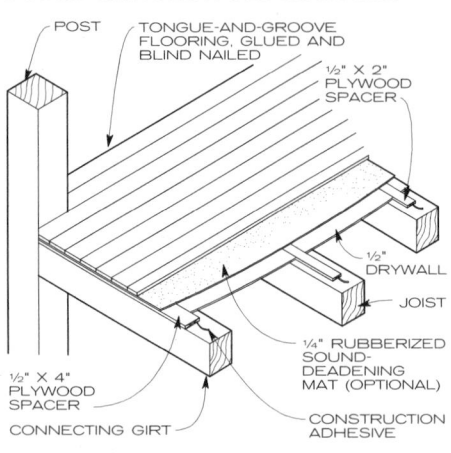

GYPSUM BOARD CEILING WITH SPACERS

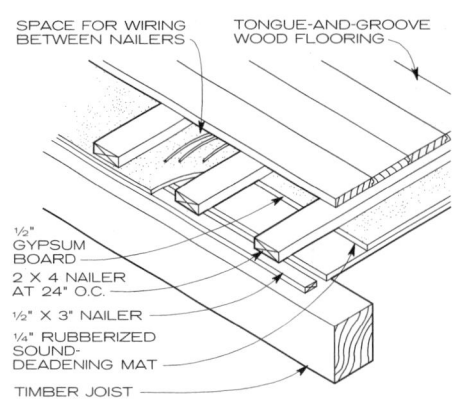

UNDER FLOOR SERVICE CHASE

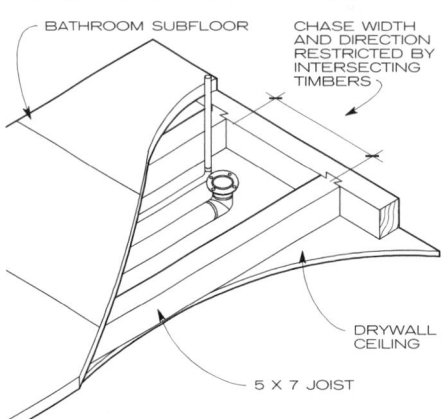

UNDER FLOOR SERVICE CHASE BETWEEN TIMBER JOISTS

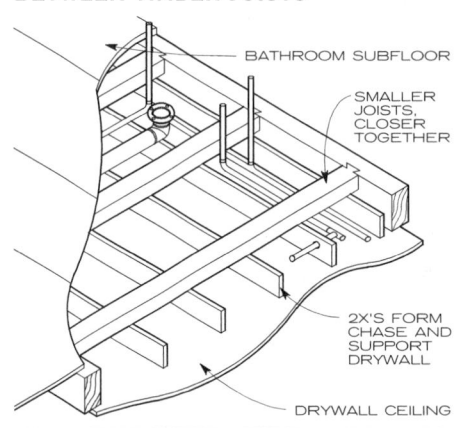

UNDER FLOOR SERVICE CHASE WITH DROPPED CEILING DETAIL

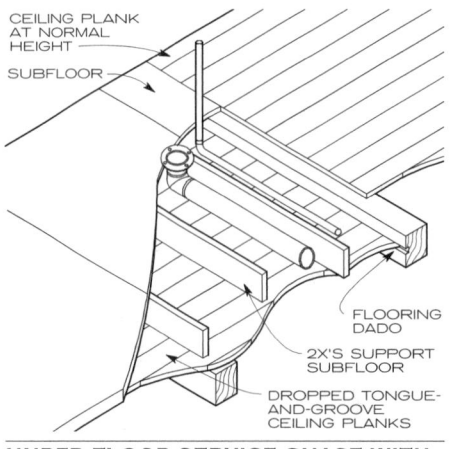

UNDER FLOOR SERVICE CHASE WITH DROPPED FLOOR DETAIL

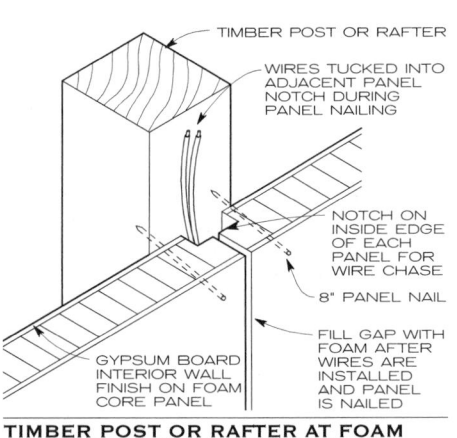

TIMBER POST OR RAFTER AT FOAM CORE PANEL WIRE CHASE DETAIL

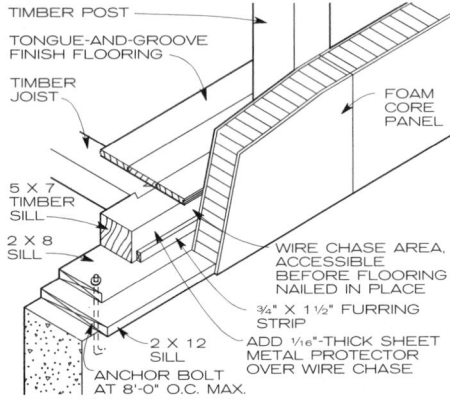

TIMBER-SILL WIRE CHASE DETAIL

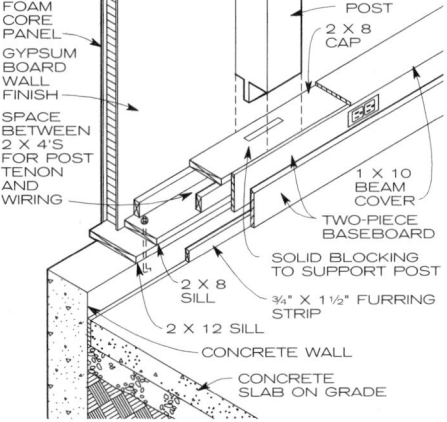

BOX BEAM SILL WIRE CHASE DETAIL

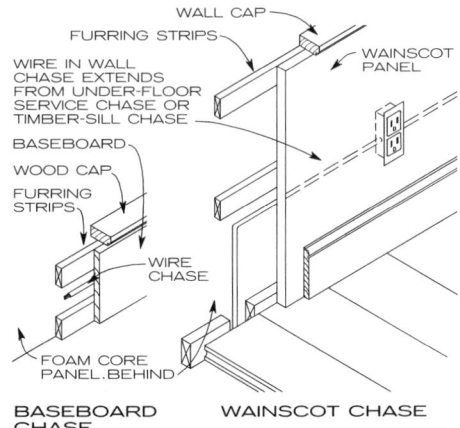

BASEBOARD CHASE   WAINSCOT CHASE

SURFACE-MOUNTED WIRE CHASES AT FOAM CORE PANEL

Richard J. Vitullo, AIA; Oak Leaf Studio; Crownsville, Maryland
Tedd Benson and Ben Brungraber, Ph.D., PE; Benson Woodworking Co., Inc.; Alstead, New Hampshire

 ROUGH CARPENTRY

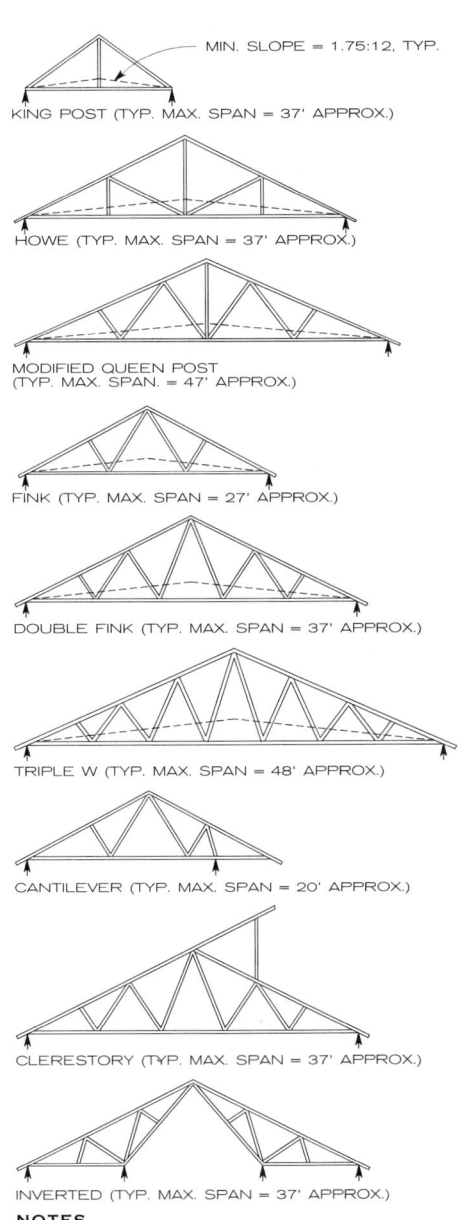

MIN. SLOPE = 1.75:12, TYP.

KING POST (TYP. MAX. SPAN = 37' APPROX.)

HOWE (TYP. MAX. SPAN = 37' APPROX.)

MODIFIED QUEEN POST
(TYP. MAX. SPAN. = 47' APPROX.)

FINK (TYP. MAX. SPAN = 27' APPROX.)

DOUBLE FINK (TYP. MAX. SPAN = 37' APPROX.)

TRIPLE W (TYP. MAX. SPAN = 48' APPROX.)

CANTILEVER (TYP. MAX. SPAN = 20' APPROX.)

CLERESTORY (TYP. MAX. SPAN = 37' APPROX.)

INVERTED (TYP. MAX. SPAN = 37' APPROX.)

NOTES

1. The average spacing for light trusses (trussed rafters) is 2 ft o.c. but varies up to 4 ft. The average combined dead and live loads is 45 lb per sq ft. Spans are usually between 20 and 32 ft but can be as much as 50 ft.

2. Early in the design process, consult an engineer or truss supplier for pre-engineered truss designs to establish the most economical and efficient truss proportions. The supplier may provide final truss engineering design.

3. Permanent and temporary erection bracing must be installed as specified to prevent failure of properly designed trusses.

4. Some locales require an engineer's stamp when prefab trusses are used. Check local codes.

5. Member forces in a truss rise rapidly as the lower chord is raised above the horizontal.

PITCHED CHORD TRUSSES

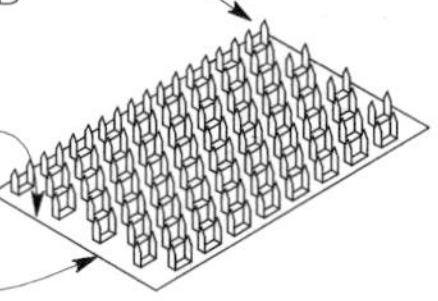

PLATE TOOTH PUNCHED THROUGH PLATE HAS PARTICULAR LENGTH, SHAPE, AND TWIST; ALL AFFECT WITHDRAWAL STRENGTH (TOOTH LATERAL RESISTANCE)

GAUGE NET AREA OF STRUCTURAL STEEL LEFT IN PLATE AFTER PUNCHED TEETH ARE FORMED; RESIDUAL STRENGTH OF THIS UNPUNCHED STEEL IS USED TO TRANSFER FORCES IN TRUSS JOINT

PLATE CONNECTOR PRESSED BY PNEUMATIC, HYDRAULIC, OR ROLLER PRESS INTO BOTH SIDES OF TRUSS

TYPICAL METAL PLATE CONNECTOR

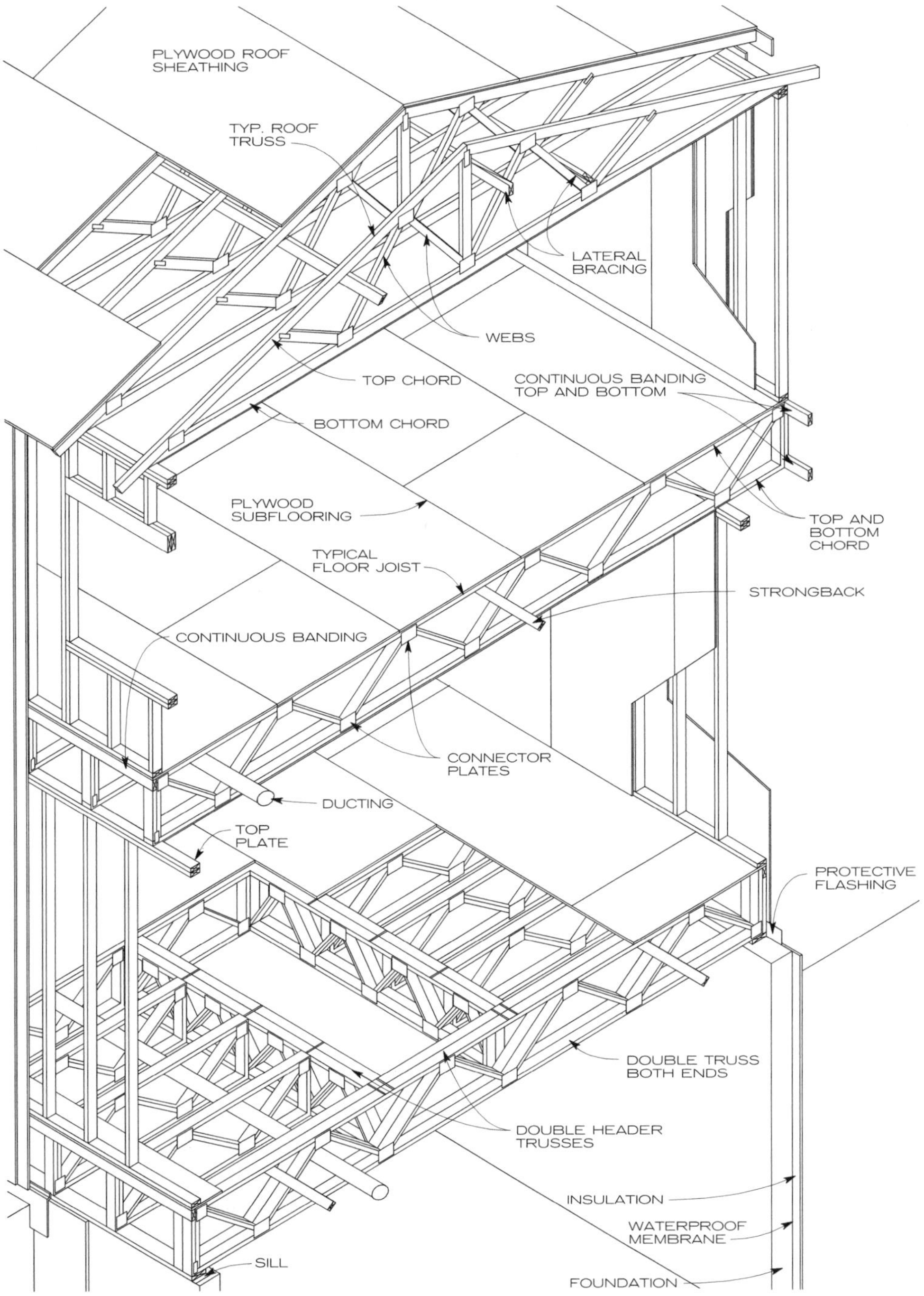

Richard J. Vitullo, AIA; Oak Leaf Studio; Crownsville, Maryland

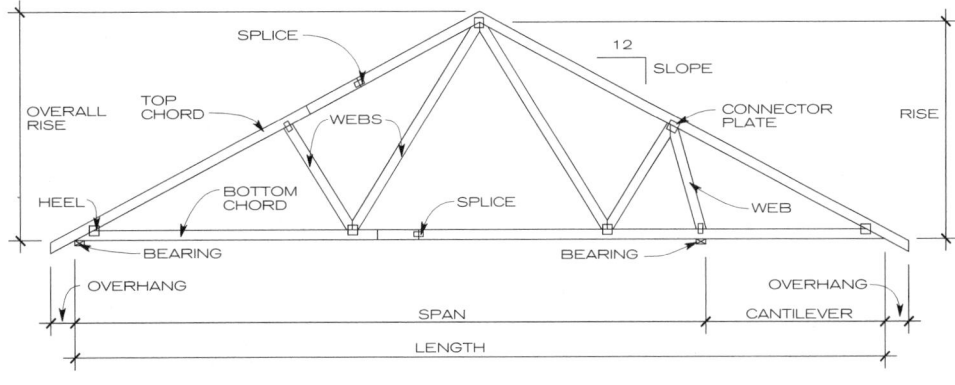

PLYWOOD ROOF SHEATHING

TYP. ROOF TRUSS

LATERAL BRACING

WEBS

TOP CHORD

CONTINUOUS BANDING TOP AND BOTTOM

BOTTOM CHORD

PLYWOOD SUBFLOORING

TOP AND BOTTOM CHORD

TYPICAL FLOOR JOIST

STRONGBACK

CONTINUOUS BANDING

CONNECTOR PLATES

DUCTING

TOP PLATE

PROTECTIVE FLASHING

DOUBLE TRUSS BOTH ENDS

DOUBLE HEADER TRUSSES

INSULATION

WATERPROOF MEMBRANE

FOUNDATION

SILL

TRUSS FRAMING

SPLICE

12
SLOPE

OVERALL RISE

TOP CHORD

WEBS

CONNECTOR PLATE

RISE

HEEL

BOTTOM CHORD

SPLICE

WEB

BEARING

BEARING

OVERHANG

SPAN

OVERHANG

CANTILEVER

LENGTH

TYPICAL PITCHED CHORD ROOF TRUSS

ROUGH CARPENTRY   6

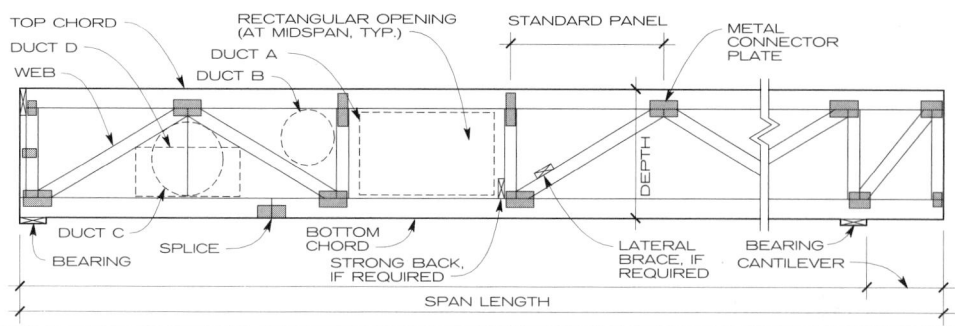

TYPICAL PARALLEL CHORD FLOOR AND ROOF TRUSS

DEPTH OF TRUSS AND SIZE OF DUCTWORK (IN.)

DEPTH	A	B	C	D		
10	6 1/2 x 22	5 1/2	5	3 x 25	4 x 15	5 x 9
12	8 1/2 x 22	6 1/2	7	5 x 20	6 x 14	7 x 7
14	10 1/2 x 22	7 1/2	9	6 x 23	7 x 16	8 x 11
16	12 1/2 x 22	9	11	7 x 22	8 x 18	9 x 14
18	14 1/2 x 22	10	12	8 x 24	9 x 20	10 x 16
20	16 1/2 x 22	11	14 1/2	8 x 28	9 x 24	10 x 21
22	18 1/2 x 22	12	16	8 x 30	10 x 25	12 x 19

NOTE: The relative ease of running electrical and mechanical components through framing is a major advantage of a truss roof system. Sizes given here are approximate; verify individual sizes carefully. Duct sizes are based on maximum panel sizes allowable by prior arrangement.

PARALLEL CHORD TRUSS—SPANS FOR PRELIMINARY DESIGN

	TRUSSED RAFTERS SPACING (C TO C)(IN.)—RESIDENTIAL LOADS								
	FLOORS			ROOFS					
	A. 55 PSF			B. 40 PSF		C. 55 PSF		C. 55 PSF*	
DEPTH (IN.)	12	16	24	16	24	16	24	16	24
12	23-6	21-0	17-1	24-0	21-4	21-11	18-2		
13	24-11	22-0	17-11						
14	26-4	22-11	18-8	27-5	23-3	24-5	19-10		
15	27-7	23-10	19-5						
16	28-7	24-9	20-1	30-3	25-0	26-4	21-4	31-10	27-10
18	30-6	26-4	21-5	32-11	26-9	28-1	22-9	35-1	30-7
20	32-4	27-11	22-8	34-8	28-0	29-7	23-11	38-1	33-1
22	34-0	26-9	23-11						
24	35-8	30-10	25-0	38-3	30-11	32-7	26-4	43-10	36-7
28				41-6	33-6	35-5	28-7	49-2	39-11
32				44-3	35-7	37-8	30-4	52-9	42-9
36				47-0	37-10	40-1	32-3	56-3	45-7
48								60-0	53-3

	TRUSSED RAFTERS SPACING (C TO C)(IN.)—COMMERCIAL FLOOR LOADS								
	D. 80 PSF			E. 100 PSF			F. 120 PSF		
DEPTH (IN.)	12	16	24	12	16	24	12	16	24
12	19-0	17-3	15-1	17-3	15-8	13-7	16-0	14-7	12-4
14	21-4	19-4	16-6	19-4	17-7	14-9	18-0	16-4	13-6
16	23-6	21-5	17-10	21-5	19-5	15-11	19-10	17-11	14-6
18	25-8	23-4	19-0	23-4	21-0	17-0	21-8	19-2	15-6
20	27-8	24-10	20-2	25-2	22-3	18-0	23-4	20-3	16-5
24	31-6	27-5	22-2	28-5	24-6	19-10	25-11	22-4	18-1
16*	27-7	25-1	21-11	25-1	22-9	19-11	23-2	21-2	18-5
24*	38-0	34-6	30-1	34-6	31-4	27-4	32-0	29-1	25-1
32*	47-1	42-9	36-1	42-9	38-10	32-3	39-8	36-1	29-5

LOAD	A (PSF)	B (PSF)	C (PSF)	D (PSF)	E (PSF)	F (PSF)
Top chord live load	40	20	35	60	80	100
Top chord dead load	10	10	10	10	10	10
Bottom chord dead load	5	10	10	10	10	10
TOTAL LOAD	55	40	55	80	100	120

* indicates a double-chorded truss, top and bottom.

NOTES

1. Spans are clear, inside to inside, for bottom chord bearing. Values shown would vary only slightly for a truss with top chord loading.
2. Designed deflection limit under total load is l/240 for roofs, l/360 for residential floors, and l/480 for commercial floors.
3. Spans should not exceed 24 in. x depth of truss.
4. Roof spans include a +15% short-term stress.
5. Spans shown are for only one type of lumber; in this case—#2 Southern pine, with an f_b value of 1550. Charts are available for other grades and species. Lumber and grades may be mixed in the same truss, but chord size must be identical. Repetitive member bending stress is used in this chart.

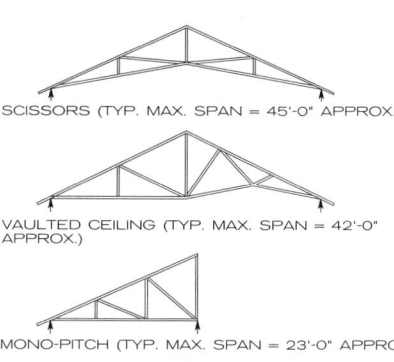

SCISSORS (TYP. MAX. SPAN = 45'-0" APPROX.)

VAULTED CEILING (TYP. MAX. SPAN = 42'-0" APPROX.)

MONO-PITCH (TYP. MAX. SPAN = 23'-0" APPROX.)

DUAL PITCH (TYP. MAX. SPAN =32'-0" APPROX.)

PITCHED WARREN (TYP. MAX. SPAN = 42'-0" APPROX.)

SCISSORED WARREN (TYP. MAX. SPAN = 42'-0" APPROX.)

BOWSTRING (TYP. MAX. SPAN = 30'-0" APPROX.)

PITCHED TRUSSES

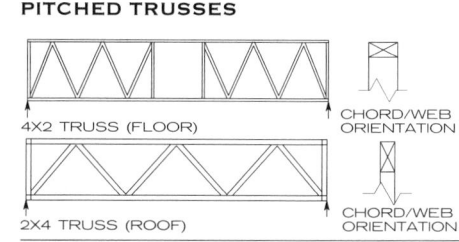

4X2 TRUSS (FLOOR)

CHORD/WEB ORIENTATION

2X4 TRUSS (ROOF)

CHORD/WEB ORIENTATION

PARALLEL TRUSSES

GENERAL

Metal plate-connected wood trusses have been used in building construction since 1953, when the metal connector plate was invented. These proprietary metal plates are available in a range of styles and tooth orientations. The metal plates are punched with barbs that grab onto the wood truss, thus reducing the hand nailing required to fabricate a structure. Plate size for a given truss is based on a combination of the tooth withdrawal strength of the plate, the tensile and shear strength of the steel, and the net sectional area of the lumber.

This system is primarily used for roofs with either pitched or parallel chord trusses. It is occasionally employed for floors with parallel chord trusses. Individual trusses are cut from 2 x 4 in. or 2 x 6 in. lumber and can be spaced 24 in. or 48 in. o.c. For typical residential construction, 24 in. o.c. is used. Exceptionally long spans are possible with metal plate-connected trusses, allowing the large, unencumbered interior spaces often required in commercial, agricultural, and other nonresidential building types.

Camber is designed for dead load only:
    Camber (in.) = Length (ft)/60

BRACING

Providing adequate bracing for trusses is essential, both during installation and in the overall roof design. Truss members must be held in place with supports that meet them at right angles. Truss chords and web members are placed in a vertical, plumb position and maintain that position, resisting applied design loads, throughout the life of the structure. Permanent bracing and anchorage are expected to be an integral part of construction, and strongbacks are often used for this purpose.

Movement by crane can damage trusses. Crane spreader bars are used to avoid this "out-of-plane" buckling. Special stiffening may be applied to trusses during erection.

Richard J. Vitullo, AIA; Oak Leaf Studio; Crownsville, Maryland

ROUGH CARPENTRY

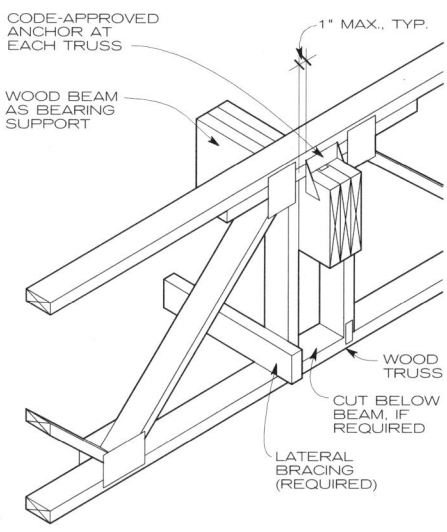

CODE-APPROVED ANCHOR AT EACH TRUSS

WOOD BEAM AS BEARING SUPPORT

1" MAX., TYP.

WOOD TRUSS

CUT BELOW BEAM, IF REQUIRED

LATERAL BRACING (REQUIRED)

TOP CHORD SUPPORT DETAIL AT WOOD BEAM

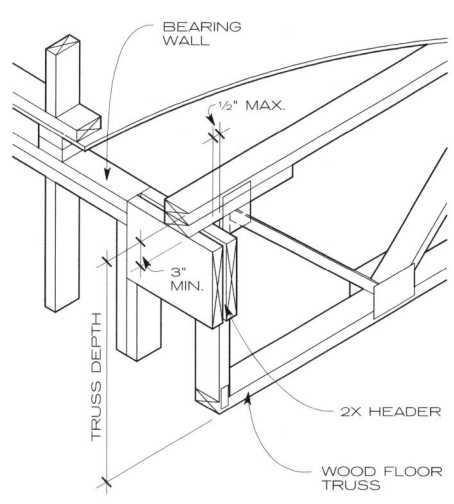

BEARING WALL

½" MAX.

3" MIN.

TRUSS DEPTH

2X HEADER

WOOD FLOOR TRUSS

TOP CHORD SUPPORT DETAIL AT EXTERIOR BEARING WALL

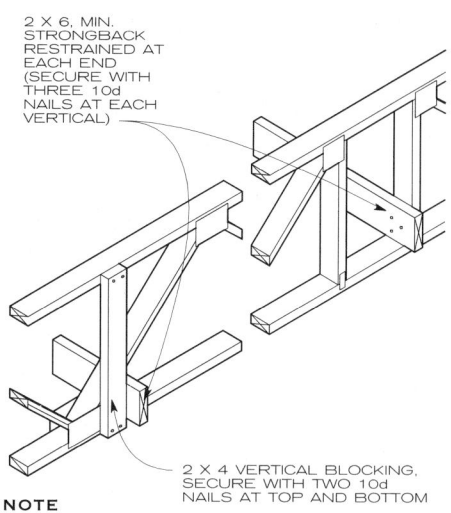

2 X 6, MIN. STRONGBACK RESTRAINED AT EACH END (SECURE WITH THREE 10d NAILS AT EACH VERTICAL)

2 X 4 VERTICAL BLOCKING, SECURE WITH TWO 10d NAILS AT TOP AND BOTTOM

NOTE

Locate strongbacks at maximum 10 ft o.c. at free-span trusses.

STRONGBACK DETAILS

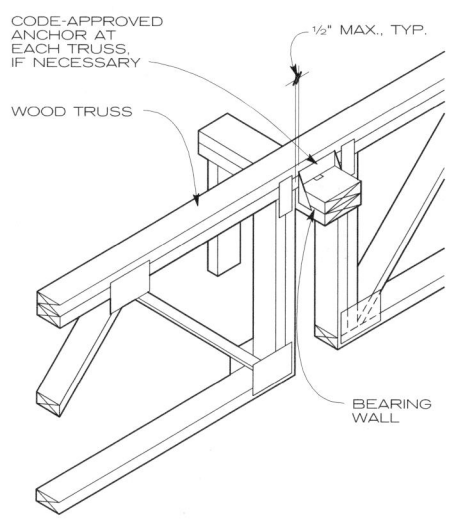

CODE-APPROVED ANCHOR AT EACH TRUSS, IF NECESSARY

½" MAX., TYP.

WOOD TRUSS

BEARING WALL

TOP CHORD SUPPORT DETAIL AT INTERIOR BEARING WALL

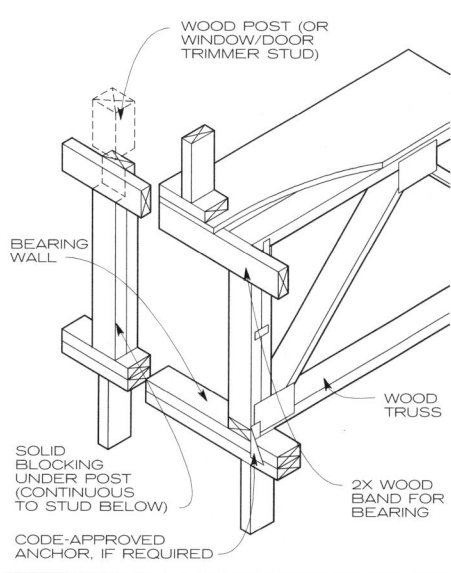

WOOD POST (OR WINDOW/DOOR TRIMMER STUD)

BEARING WALL

WOOD TRUSS

2X WOOD BAND FOR BEARING

SOLID BLOCKING UNDER POST (CONTINUOUS TO STUD BELOW)

CODE-APPROVED ANCHOR, IF REQUIRED

EXTERIOR WALL BEARING DETAIL

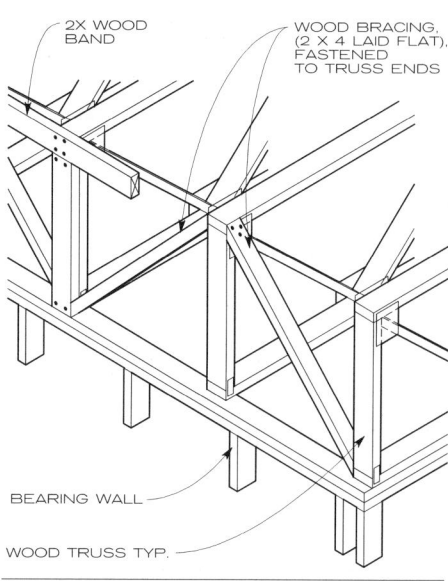

2X WOOD BAND

WOOD BRACING, (2 X 4 LAID FLAT), FASTENED TO TRUSS ENDS

BEARING WALL

WOOD TRUSS TYP.

DIAGONAL BRACING AT BEARING END

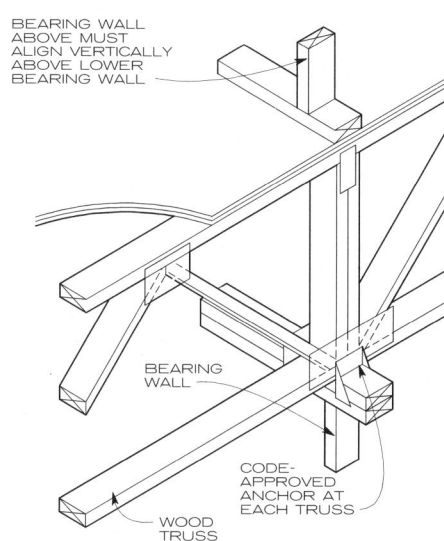

BEARING WALL ABOVE MUST ALIGN VERTICALLY ABOVE LOWER BEARING WALL

BEARING WALL

CODE-APPROVED ANCHOR AT EACH TRUSS

WOOD TRUSS

BOTTOM CHORD SUPPORT AT BEARING WALL

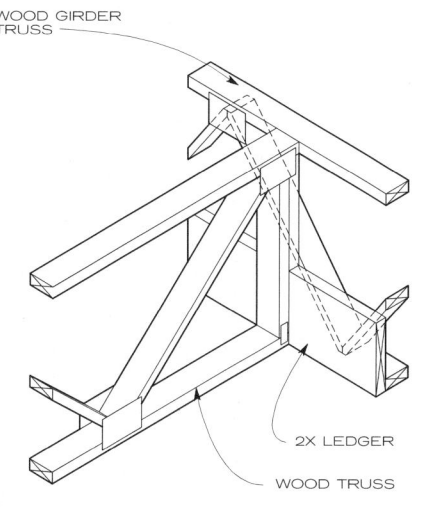

WOOD GIRDER TRUSS

2X LEDGER

WOOD TRUSS

LEDGER DETAIL

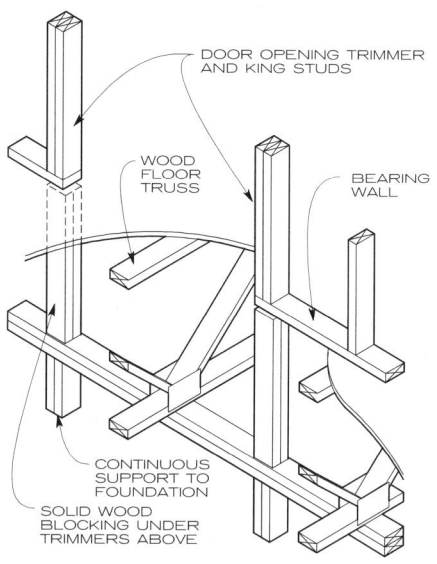

DOOR OPENING TRIMMER AND KING STUDS

WOOD FLOOR TRUSS

BEARING WALL

CONTINUOUS SUPPORT TO FOUNDATION

SOLID WOOD BLOCKING UNDER TRIMMERS ABOVE

BLOCKING DETAIL AT INTERIOR BEARING WALL

Richard J. Vitullo, AIA; Oak Leaf Studio; Crownsville, Maryland

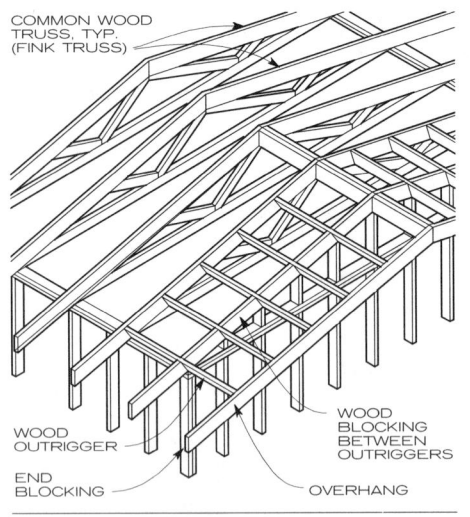

COMMON WOOD TRUSS, TYP. (FINK TRUSS)

WOOD BLOCKING BETWEEN OUTRIGGERS

WOOD OUTRIGGER

END BLOCKING

OVERHANG

GABLE ROOF OVERHANG DETAIL

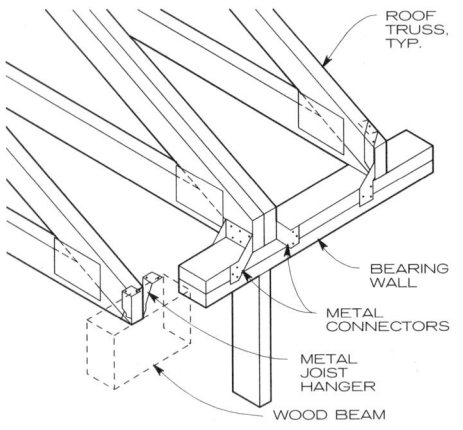

ROOF TRUSS, TYP.

BEARING WALL

METAL CONNECTORS

METAL JOIST HANGER

WOOD BEAM

END-BEARING ROOF TRUSS WITH METAL CONNECTORS

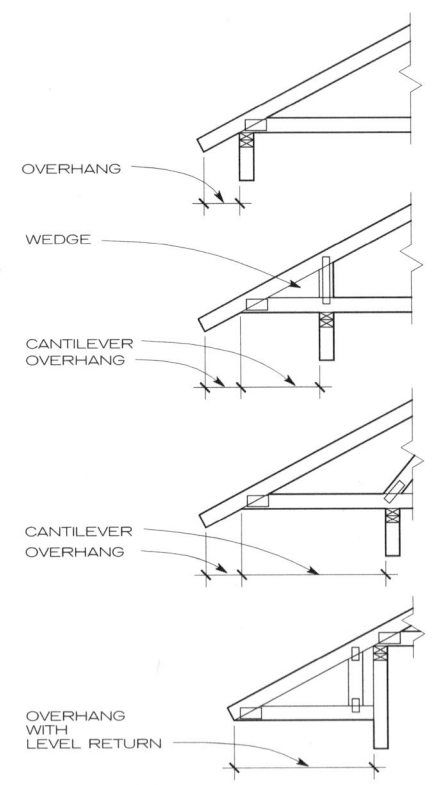

OVERHANG

WEDGE

CANTILEVER OVERHANG

CANTILEVER OVERHANG

OVERHANG WITH LEVEL RETURN

OVERHANG DETAILS

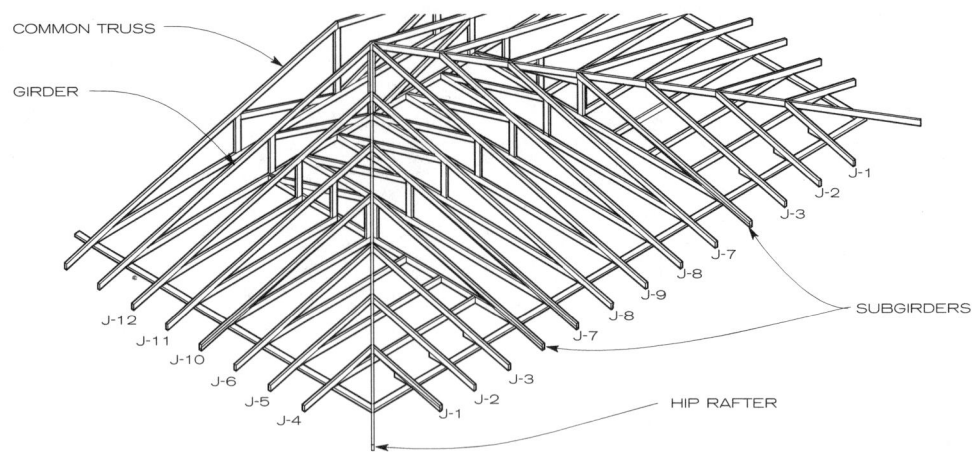

COMMON TRUSS

GIRDER

J-1
J-2
J-3
J-7
J-8
J-8
J-9
J-7
J-12
J-11
J-10
J-6
J-5
J-4
J-1
J-2
J-3

SUBGIRDERS

HIP RAFTER

JACK TRUSS SYSTEM

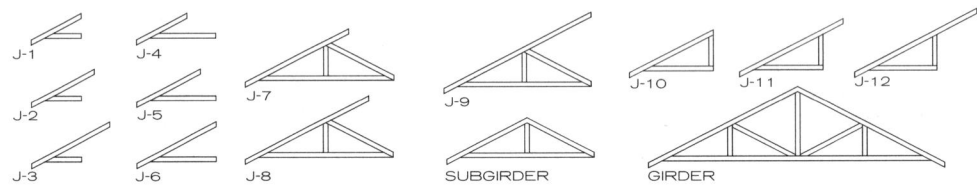

J-1
J-2
J-3
J-4
J-5
J-6
J-7
J-8
J-9
J-10
J-11
J-12
SUBGIRDER
GIRDER

JACK TRUSS COMPONENTS

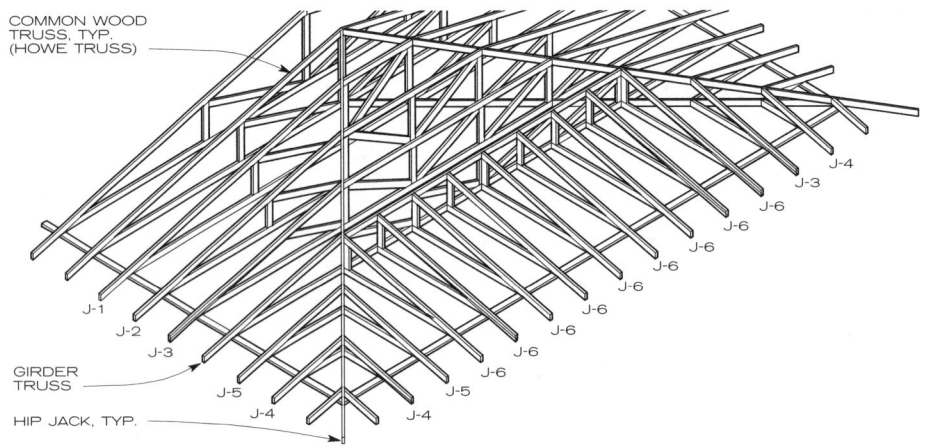

COMMON WOOD TRUSS, TYP. (HOWE TRUSS)

J-4
J-3
J-6
J-6
J-6
J-6
J-6
J-6
J-6
J-6
J-5
J-5
J-4
J-4
J-1
J-2
J-3

GIRDER TRUSS

HIP JACK, TYP.

STEP-DOWN TRUSS SYSTEM

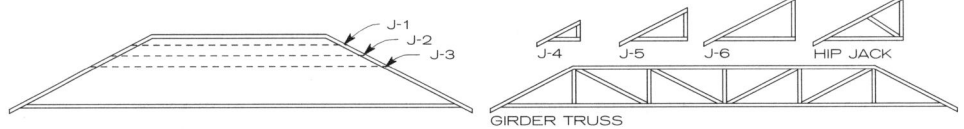

J-1
J-2
J-3
J-4
J-5
J-6
HIP JACK

GIRDER TRUSS

STEP-DOWN COMPONENTS

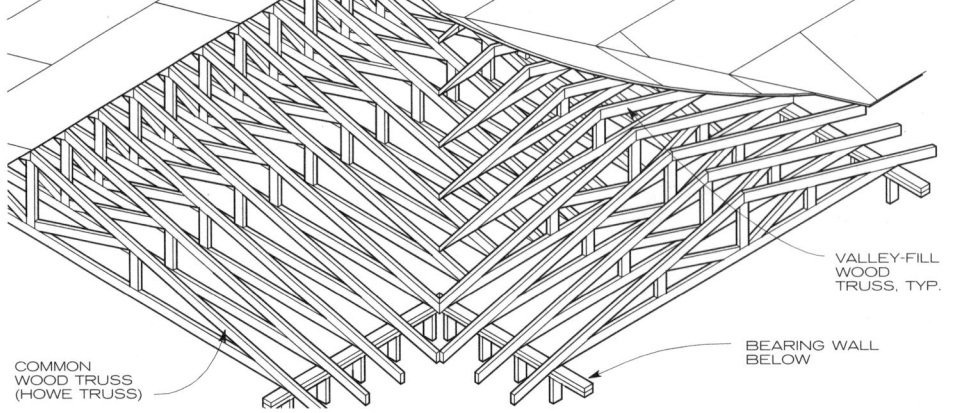

VALLEY-FILL WOOD TRUSS, TYP.

BEARING WALL BELOW

COMMON WOOD TRUSS (HOWE TRUSS)

ROOF INTERSECTION WITH VALLEY FILL

Richard J. Vitullo, AIA; Oak Leaf Studio; Crownsville, Maryland

 ROUGH CARPENTRY

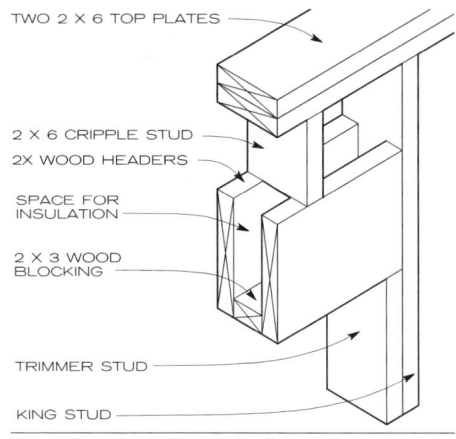

TWO 2 X 6 TOP PLATES
2 X 6 CRIPPLE STUD
2X WOOD HEADERS
SPACE FOR INSULATION
2 X 3 WOOD BLOCKING
TRIMMER STUD
KING STUD

2X6 BEARING WALL—HEADER DETAIL

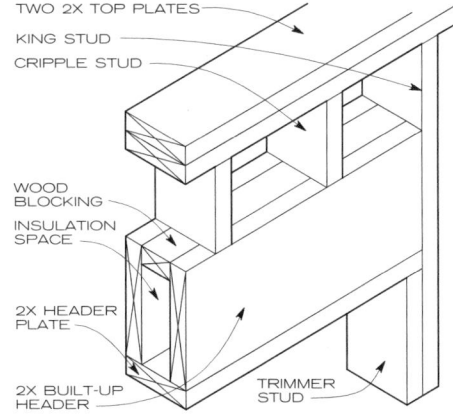

TWO 2X TOP PLATES
KING STUD
CRIPPLE STUD
WOOD BLOCKING
INSULATION SPACE
2X HEADER PLATE
2X BUILT-UP HEADER
TRIMMER STUD

2X BEARING WALL—HEADER DETAIL

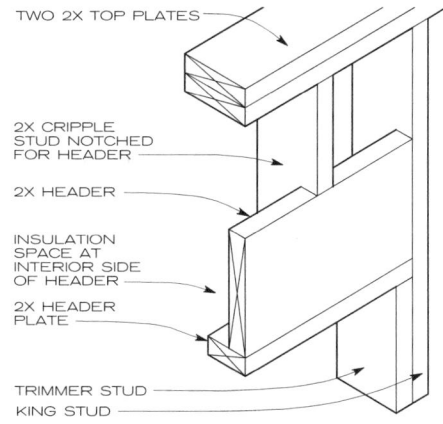

TWO 2X TOP PLATES
2X CRIPPLE STUD NOTCHED FOR HEADER
2X HEADER
INSULATION SPACE AT INTERIOR SIDE OF HEADER
2X HEADER PLATE
TRIMMER STUD
KING STUD

2X BEARING WALL—HEADER DETAIL

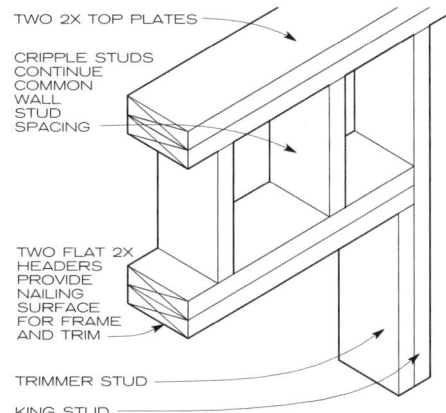

TWO 2X TOP PLATES
CRIPPLE STUDS CONTINUE COMMON WALL STUD SPACING
TWO FLAT 2X HEADERS PROVIDE NAILING SURFACE FOR FRAME AND TRIM
TRIMMER STUD
KING STUD

2X PARTITION WALL—HEADER DETAIL

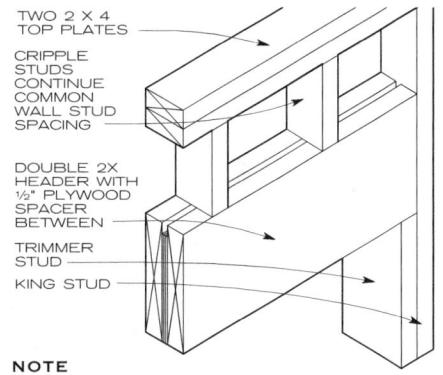

TWO 2 X 4 TOP PLATES
CRIPPLE STUDS CONTINUE COMMON WALL STUD SPACING
DOUBLE 2X HEADER WITH ½" PLYWOOD SPACER BETWEEN
TRIMMER STUD
KING STUD

NOTE

Provides maximum nailing surface on interior and exterior walls.

2X4 BEARING WALL—HEADER DETAIL

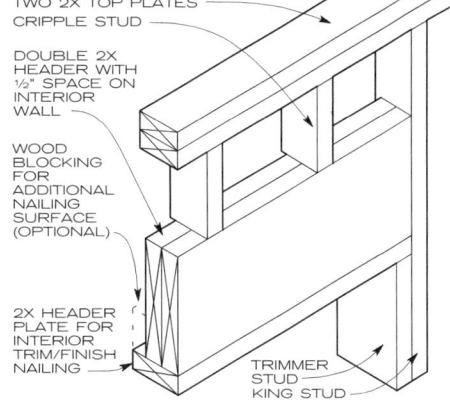

TWO 2X TOP PLATES
CRIPPLE STUD
DOUBLE 2X HEADER WITH ½" SPACE ON INTERIOR WALL
WOOD BLOCKING FOR ADDITIONAL NAILING SURFACE (OPTIONAL)
2X HEADER PLATE FOR INTERIOR TRIM/FINISH NAILING
TRIMMER STUD
KING STUD

2X BEARING WALL—HEADER DETAIL

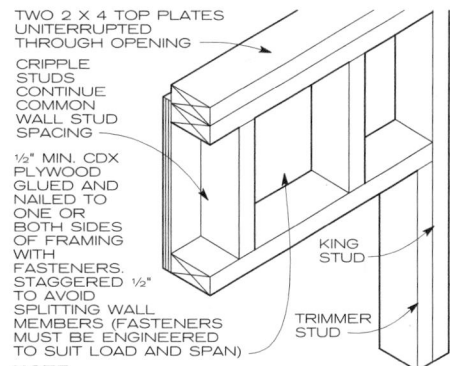

TWO 2 X 4 TOP PLATES UNITERRUPTED THROUGH OPENING
CRIPPLE STUDS CONTINUE COMMON WALL STUD SPACING
½" MIN. CDX PLYWOOD GLUED AND NAILED TO ONE OR BOTH SIDES OF FRAMING WITH FASTENERS. STAGGERED ½" TO AVOID SPLITTING WALL MEMBERS (FASTENERS MUST BE ENGINEERED TO SUIT LOAD AND SPAN)
KING STUD
TRIMMER STUD

NOTE

Interior plywood face must be smooth for finishing with gypsum board.

2X4 BEARING WALL—OPEN BOX PLYWOOD—HEADER DETAIL

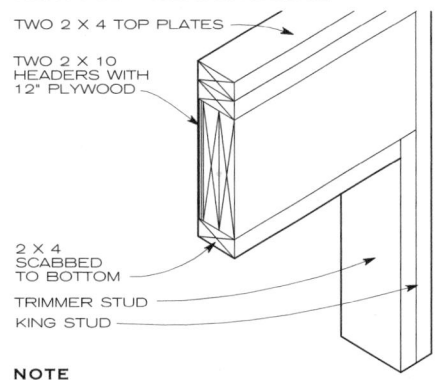

TWO 2 X 4 TOP PLATES
TWO 2 X 10 HEADERS WITH 12" PLYWOOD
2 X 4 SCABBED TO BOTTOM
TRIMMER STUD
KING STUD

NOTE

This detail eliminates cripple studs above opening.

2X BEARING WALL—HEADER DETAIL

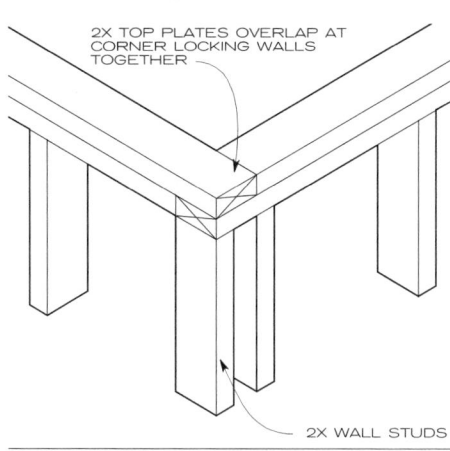

2X TOP PLATES OVERLAP AT CORNER LOCKING WALLS TOGETHER
2X WALL STUDS

TOP PLATE FRAMING DETAIL

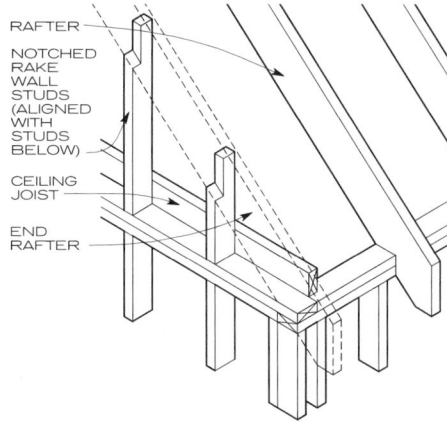

RAFTER
NOTCHED RAKE WALL STUDS (ALIGNED WITH STUDS BELOW)
CEILING JOIST
END RAFTER

RAKE WALL DETAIL—PLATFORM FRAMING

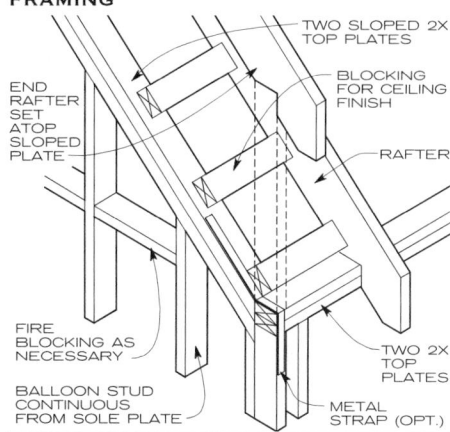

TWO SLOPED 2X TOP PLATES
BLOCKING FOR CEILING FINISH
END RAFTER SET ATOP SLOPED PLATE
RAFTER
FIRE BLOCKING AS NECESSARY
BALLOON STUD CONTINUOUS FROM SOLE PLATE
TWO 2X TOP PLATES
METAL STRAP (OPT.)

RAKE WALL DETAIL—BALLOON FRAMING

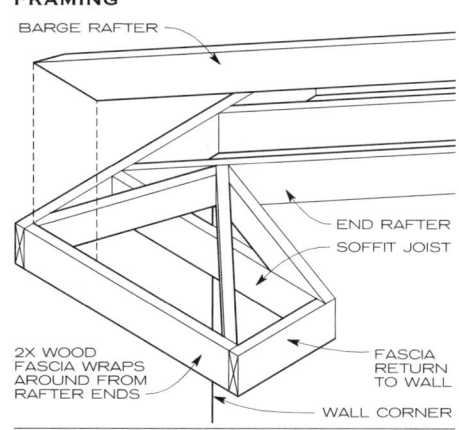

BARGE RAFTER
END RAFTER
SOFFIT JOIST
2X WOOD FASCIA WRAPS AROUND FROM RAFTER ENDS
FASCIA RETURN TO WALL
WALL CORNER

GREEK RETURN

Richard J. Vitullo, AIA; Oak Leaf Studio; Crownsville, Maryland

ROUGH CARPENTRY

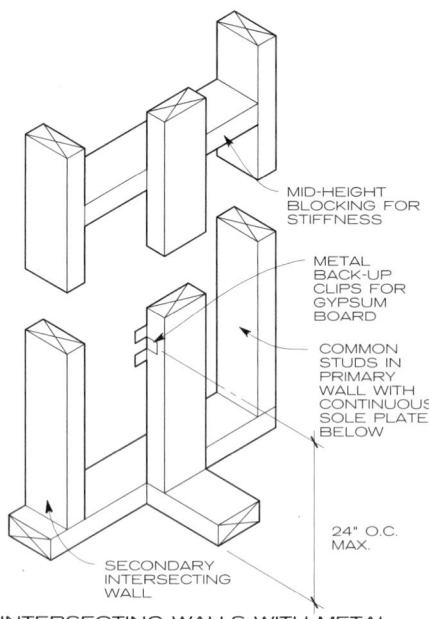

MID-HEIGHT BLOCKING FOR STIFFNESS

METAL BACK-UP CLIPS FOR GYPSUM BOARD

COMMON STUDS IN PRIMARY WALL WITH CONTINUOUS SOLE PLATE BELOW

24" O.C. MAX.

SECONDARY INTERSECTING WALL

INTERSECTING WALLS WITH METAL GYPSUM BOARD CLIPS

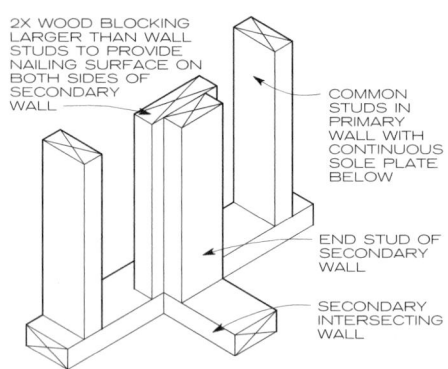

2X WOOD BLOCKING LARGER THAN WALL STUDS TO PROVIDE NAILING SURFACE ON BOTH SIDES OF SECONDARY WALL

COMMON STUDS IN PRIMARY WALL WITH CONTINUOUS SOLE PLATE BELOW

END STUD OF SECONDARY WALL

SECONDARY INTERSECTING WALL

INTERSECTING WALLS WITH BLOCKING

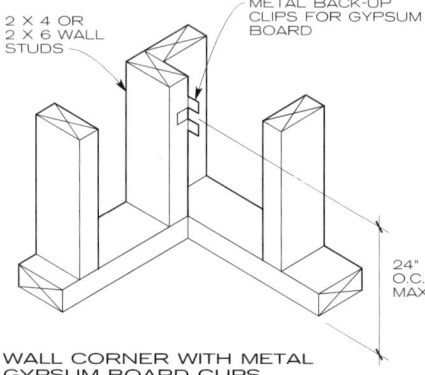

2 X 4 OR 2 X 6 WALL STUDS

METAL BACK-UP CLIPS FOR GYPSUM BOARD

24" O.C. MAX.

WALL CORNER WITH METAL GYPSUM BOARD CLIPS

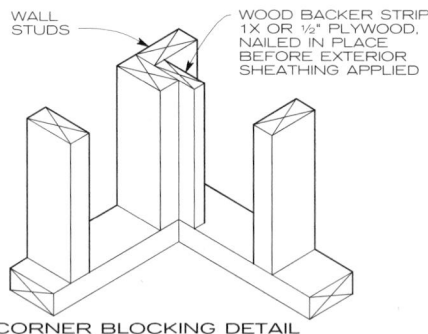

WALL STUDS

WOOD BACKER STRIP 1X OR ½" PLYWOOD, NAILED IN PLACE BEFORE EXTERIOR SHEATHING APPLIED

CORNER BLOCKING DETAIL
INSULATED WALL DETAILS

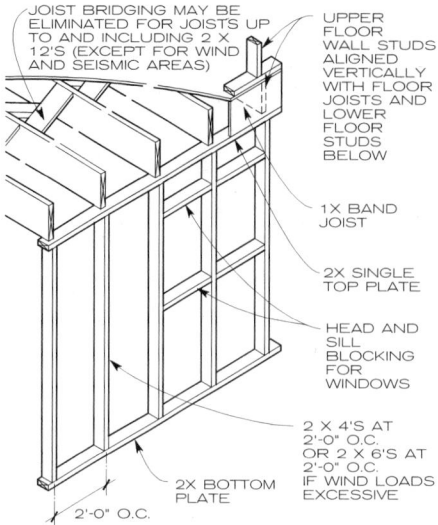

JOIST BRIDGING MAY BE ELIMINATED FOR JOISTS UP TO AND INCLUDING 2 X 12'S (EXCEPT FOR WIND AND SEISMIC AREAS)

UPPER FLOOR WALL STUDS ALIGNED VERTICALLY WITH FLOOR JOISTS AND LOWER FLOOR STUDS BELOW

1X BAND JOIST

2X SINGLE TOP PLATE

HEAD AND SILL BLOCKING FOR WINDOWS

2 X 4'S AT 2'-0" O.C. OR 2 X 6'S AT 2'-0" O.C. IF WIND LOADS EXCESSIVE

2X BOTTOM PLATE

2'-0" O.C.

IN-LINE FRAMING

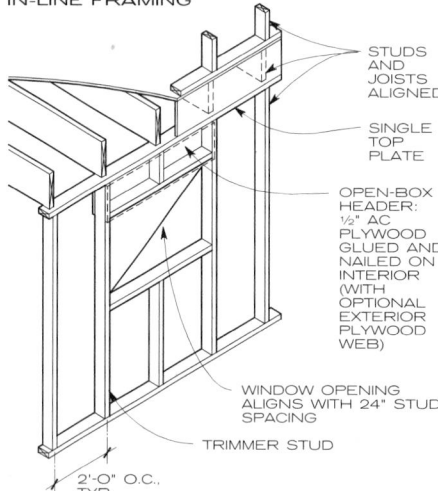

STUDS AND JOISTS ALIGNED

SINGLE TOP PLATE

OPEN-BOX HEADER: ½" AC PLYWOOD GLUED AND NAILED ON INTERIOR (WITH OPTIONAL EXTERIOR PLYWOOD WEB)

WINDOW OPENING ALIGNS WITH 24" STUD SPACING

TRIMMER STUD

2'-0" O.C., TYP.

IN-LINE FRAMING WITH WIDE OPENING

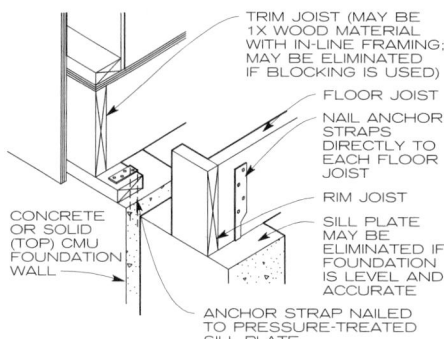

TRIM JOIST (MAY BE 1X WOOD MATERIAL WITH IN-LINE FRAMING; MAY BE ELIMINATED IF BLOCKING IS USED)

FLOOR JOIST

NAIL ANCHOR STRAPS DIRECTLY TO EACH FLOOR JOIST

RIM JOIST

SILL PLATE MAY BE ELIMINATED IF FOUNDATION IS LEVEL AND ACCURATE

CONCRETE OR SOLID (TOP) CMU FOUNDATION WALL

ANCHOR STRAP NAILED TO PRESSURE-TREATED SILL PLATE

REDUCED SILL PLATE AND RIM JOIST DETAILS

NOTES

1. Some framing details rely on techniques that reduce the amount of lumber in wood construction. Among these are in-line framing details and corner details with metal framing clips for gypsum board. These types of details were developed to conserve wood resources, reduce material cost and job-site waste, and enhance energy efficiency by reducing thermal bridging across wall systems and increasing insulation cavities. When wood levels are to be reduced, a structural engineer should first be consulted.

2. Gypsum board installed at inside corners with metal clips or wood backers does not get fastened to either. The sheet resting against the backer or clips is installed first so the second sheet (which is nailed to the stud) will lock the first sheet in place. The "floating joint" that results is recommended to reduce cracks in the corner.

REDUCED WOOD FRAMING DETAILS

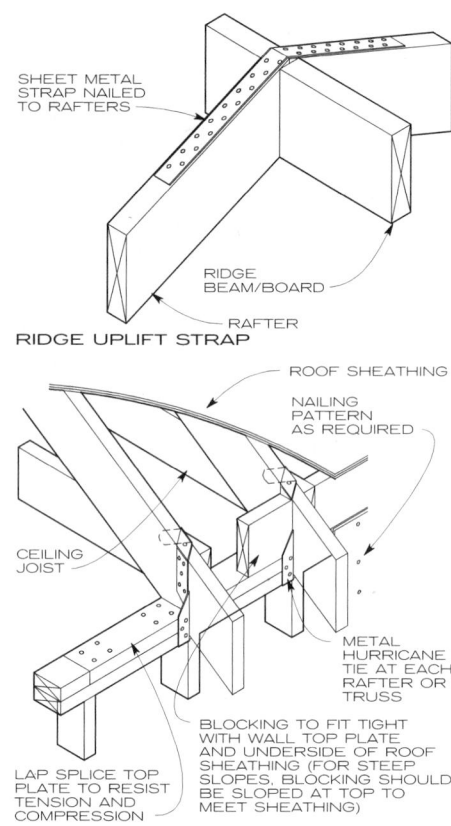

SHEET METAL STRAP NAILED TO RAFTERS

RIDGE BEAM/BOARD

RAFTER

RIDGE UPLIFT STRAP

ROOF SHEATHING

NAILING PATTERN AS REQUIRED

CEILING JOIST

METAL HURRICANE TIE AT EACH RAFTER OR TRUSS

BLOCKING TO FIT TIGHT WITH WALL TOP PLATE AND UNDERSIDE OF ROOF SHEATHING (FOR STEEP SLOPES, BLOCKING SHOULD BE SLOPED AT TOP TO MEET SHEATHING)

LAP SPLICE TOP PLATE TO RESIST TENSION AND COMPRESSION

ROOF DIAPHRAGM PERIMETER

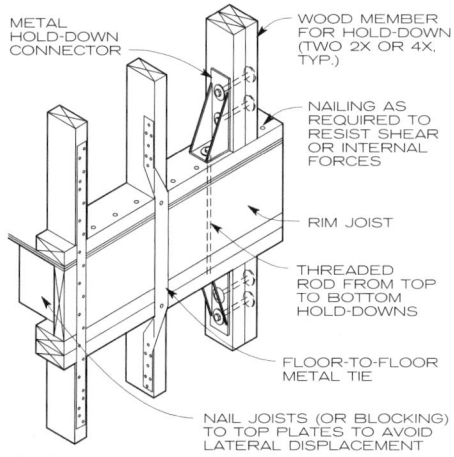

METAL HOLD-DOWN CONNECTOR

WOOD MEMBER FOR HOLD-DOWN (TWO 2X OR 4X, TYP.)

NAILING AS REQUIRED TO RESIST SHEAR OR INTERNAL FORCES

RIM JOIST

THREADED ROD FROM TOP TO BOTTOM HOLD-DOWNS

FLOOR-TO-FLOOR METAL TIE

NAIL JOISTS (OR BLOCKING) TO TOP PLATES TO AVOID LATERAL DISPLACEMENT

TIES BETWEEN FLOORS

NOTE

It is essential to provide a continuous path of resistance from roof to foundation in order to dissipate both lateral and uplift forces. Connections along this load path will guarantee uninterrupted resistance. Seismic and wind forces are transferred from the roof diaphragm to shear walls and through the walls into the ground at the foundation. Shear walls resist horizontal forces in the roof and floor diaphragms and so must be connected to them. It is important to apply wall sheathing to the full wall height, nailing it to the top plate, blocking, or rim joist and also to the mud sill or bottom plate. Shear wall height/width ratios are an important consideration; consult a structural engineer for their design. The details illustrated show several connection paths; for each specific design, a structural engineer familiar with seismic and wind resistant construction should be consulted. Many of the requirements for high wind situations apply to seismic loading as well, except in shear wall design.

Ties between floors: Wood members (studs) must be sized for the load-carrying capacity at the critical net section.

WIND AND SEISMIC CONNECTOR FRAMING

Richard J. Vitullo, AIA; Oak Leaf Studio; Crownsville, Maryland

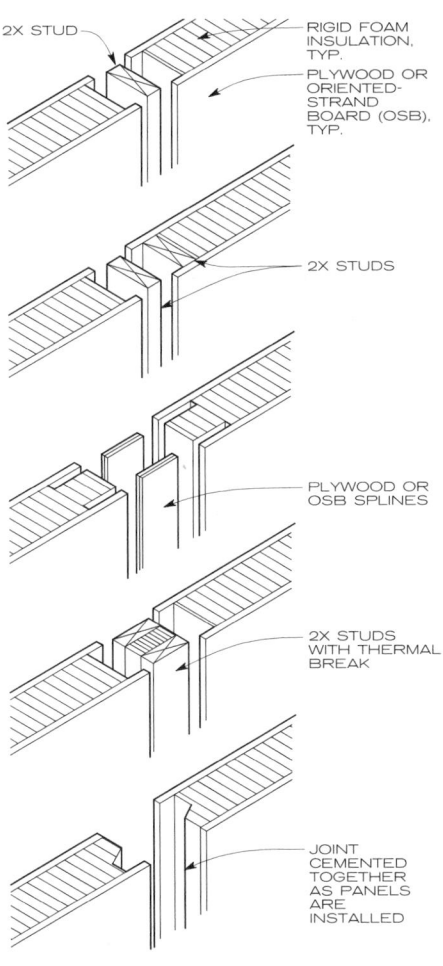

NOTE
Studs and splines are screwed (and usually glued) to panels from both sides. Consult manufacturer's specifications. Joints are typically sealed with expanding foam.

TYPICAL INTERMEDIATE PANEL SPLINE DETAILS

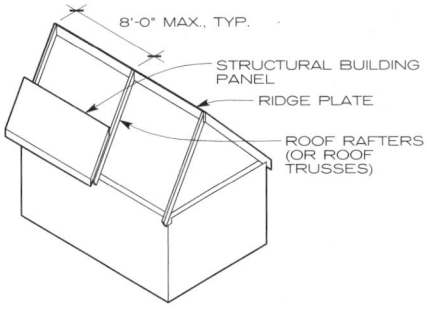

ROOF FRAMING WITH RAFTERS AND TRUSSES

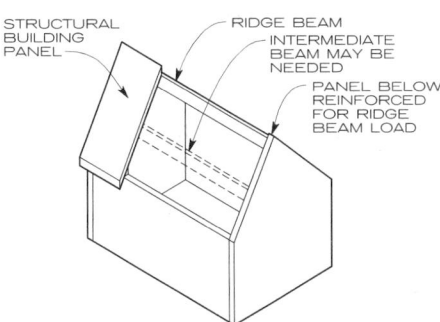

ROOF FRAMING WITH RIDGE BEAM

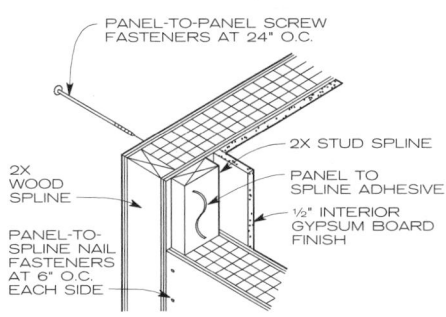

TYPICAL CORNER DETAIL

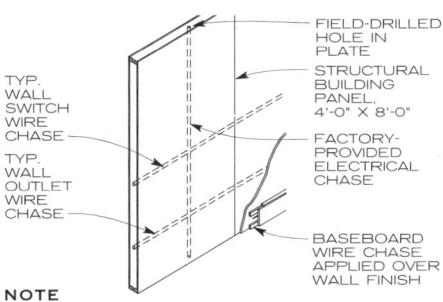

NOTE
Consult local codes for all electrical installations.

TYPICAL WIRE CHASE LOCATIONS IN PANELS

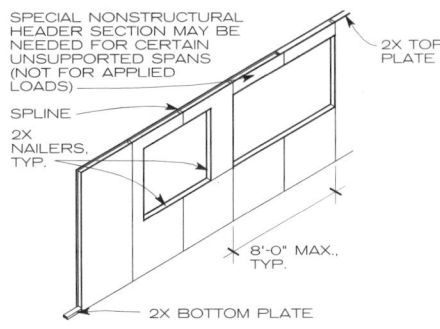

TYPICAL WINDOW DETAILS

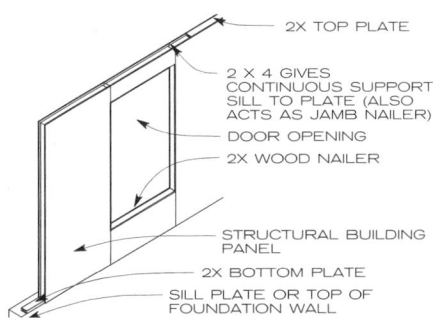

TYPICAL REINFORCED DOOR OPENING DETAIL

GENERAL

Structural building panels are factory-assembled composite panels ready for installation as a complete structural and/or insulating wall section. The material of each component of the panel system is very important when selecting a panel manufacturer. Components include the skin, foam core, adhesive, and optional exterior or interior finish. The application for which the panel is intended determines the materials used. Consult manufacturers for specifications.

Sizes vary from 4 by 8 ft panels weighing about 100 lb to 8 by 28 ft panels that must be installed using a crane.

PANEL TYPES

There are two main types of structural building panels—stress-skin panels and foam core panels:

STRESS-SKIN PANELS are manufactured by gluing and nailing plywood skins to both sides of a wood frame, resulting in a unit that performs like an I-beam. Stress-skin panels are not necessarily insulated.

STRUCTURAL FOAM CORE PANELS fall into two groups: sandwich panels and unfaced panels. Sandwich panels are rigid-foam panels faced with two structural-grade skins, usually made of oriented-strand board (OSB) or plywood. Depending on the application and the manufacturer, these foam core panels may or may not include framing members within the core. Unfaced structural foam core panels look like panels of stick-framing with rigid foam between the members instead of fiberglass batt insulation. Interior and exterior finishes are applied to these panels in the field.

The skins of structural building panels (like I-beam flanges) resist tension and compression, while the wood frame or core (like an I-beam web) resists shear and prevents buckling of the skins.

Richard J. Vitullo, AIA; Oak Leaf Studio; Crownsville, Maryland

All structural foam core panels are insulated with a core of expanded polystyrene (EPS), extruded polystyrene, or urethane foam, from $3\frac{1}{2}$ to $11\frac{1}{4}$ in. thick. Urethane panels are either glue-laminated like polystyrene or foamed in place (either in the factory or in the field). Urethane has an R-value of 6 or 7 per inch versus R-5 for extruded polystyrene and R-4 for EPS foam. Urethane is about twice as strong in compression as polystyrene and has a perm rating of less than one, which technically qualifies it as a vapor barrier. EPS has a perm rating of from 1 to 3 and may require a vapor barrier. EPS, however, is inert, nontoxic (if ingested), and resilient; it doesn't feed microorganisms and is generally cheaper than urethane. Consult manufacturers on CFC and formaldehyde content in the foam core and skin material as it varies among manufacturers. Regarding flammability of both foam core types, consult with the manufacturer about the individual product.

APPLICATIONS

In above-grade applications, the most common materials for exterior facings are plywood OSB or finish materials like T-111 plywood, tongue-and-groove pine, and other wood siding material. For below-grade situations, pressure-treated plywood skins and splines are used. Generally, structural building panels should not be used for plumbing walls, as the spaces needed for plumbing runs would compromise the insulation and structural integrity of the panel.

For roof applications it is best to use a vented structural foam panel, either integral or field-installed. Many asphalt-shingle manufacturers will not warrant their product when it is installed on unvented panels because of overheating, which accelerates deterioration.

CHARACTERISTICS

Using structural building panels generally enhances the speed of construction because the panels replace three different steps in standard construction: framing, sheathing, and insulation. Panel systems offer superior energy performance compared to a stick-frame house of similar cost and standard of construction. This is largely because the rigid insulation has higher R-values, there are fewer seams to seal, and conductive heat is not lost through air infiltration around the framing. Structural building panels also offer good resistance to lateral loads.

Panels can be susceptible to infestation by insects such as carpenter ants and termites, which eat through wood and tunnel through the foam core material, reducing insulation value and even compromising structural integrity. Use of termite shields, foam cores treated with insect repellent, and other strategies should be considered.

NOTES

1. Since structural building panels are a relatively new building system, code officials should be consulted early and often to prevent any misunderstandings or delays in the code approval process. Also, check with manufacturers to determine whether their product has received compliance approval with BOCA, ICBO, SBCCI, or HUD.

2. The seams are the part of a structural building panel system most prone to infiltration and weakness and most likely to show the results of expansion and contraction. Tight spline connections with sealant at all edges–top, bottom, and sides–can greatly increase thermal efficiency.

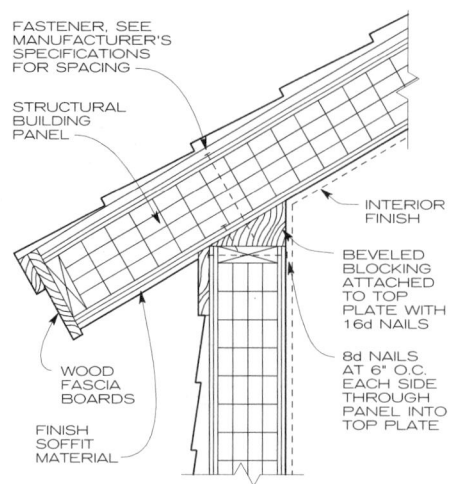

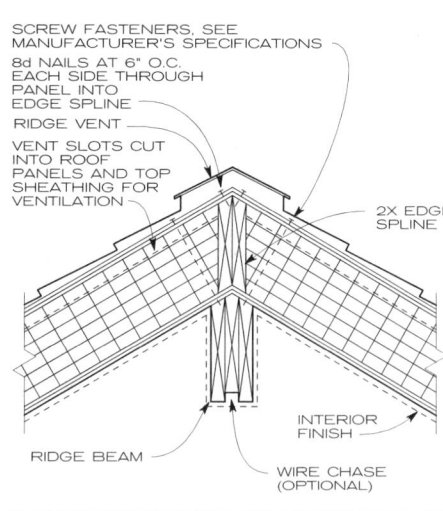

ROOF EAVE DETAIL WITH PANEL CEILING

ROOF EAVE DETAIL WITH SLOPED CEILING

PANEL AT RIDGE CONNECTION

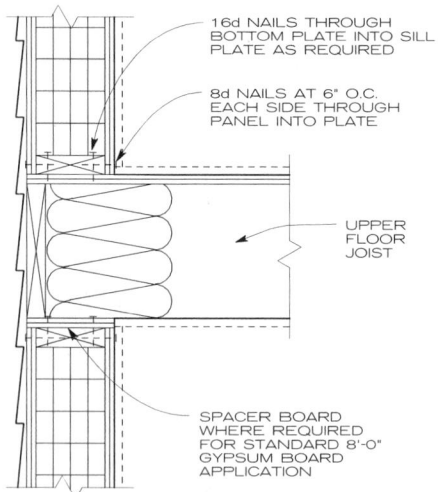

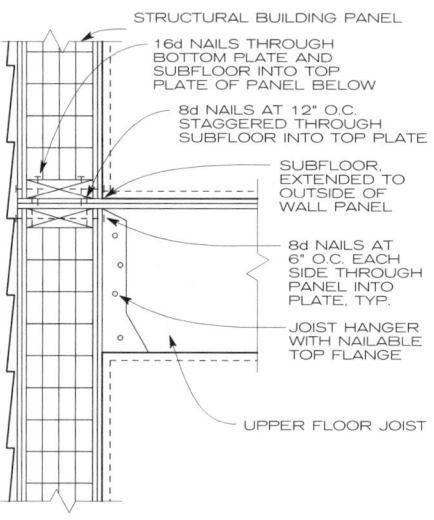

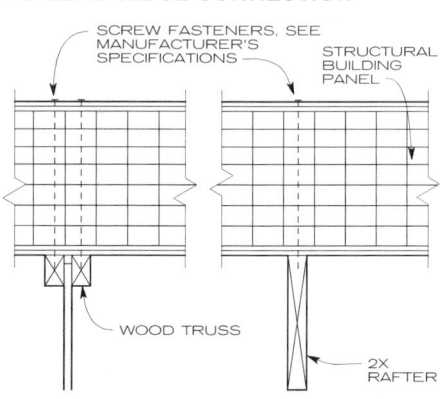

CONTINUOUS PANEL DETAIL AT ROOF

PANEL AT UPPER FLOOR CONNECTION WITH FLOOR JOIST BETWEEN

PANEL AT UPPER FLOOR CONNECTION WITH FLOOR JOIST ADJACENT

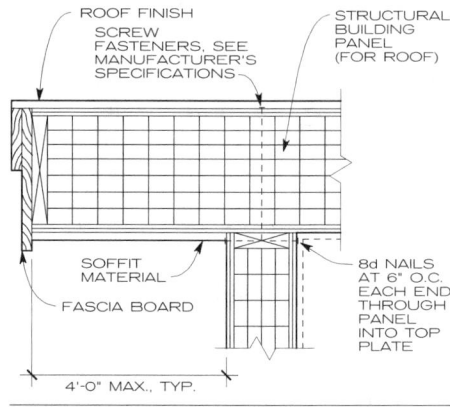

GABLE END OVERHANG AT ROOF PANEL DETAIL

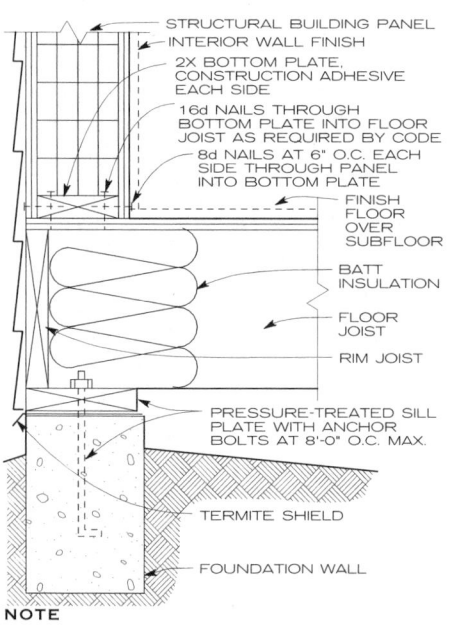

NOTE

Check perm rating of foam core insulation to determine whether additional vapor barrier is required. Consult local codes.

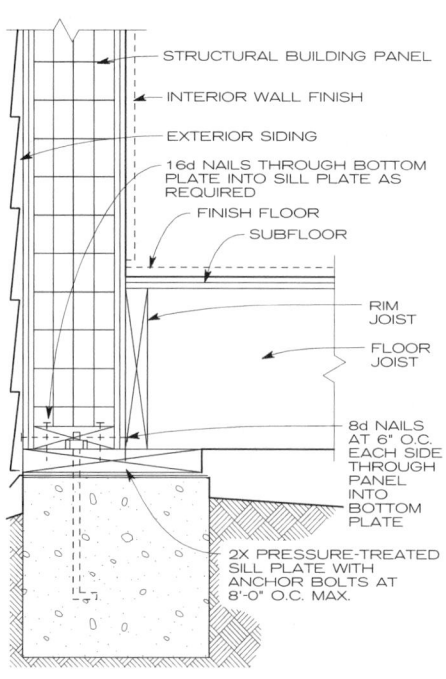

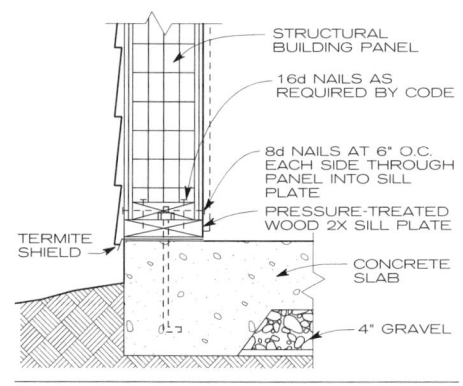

PANEL AT SILL WITH FLOOR JOIST BELOW CONNECTION

PANEL AT SILL CONNECTION WITH FLOOR JOIST ADJACENT

PANEL AT SILL ON SLAB-ON-GRADE

Richard J. Vitullo, AIA; Oak Leaf Studio; Crownsville, Maryland

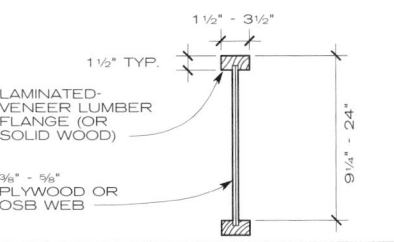

TYPICAL WOOD I-JOIST

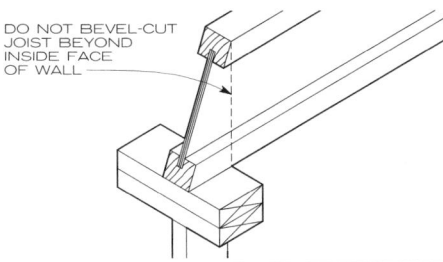

TYPICAL BEVEL-CUT JOIST

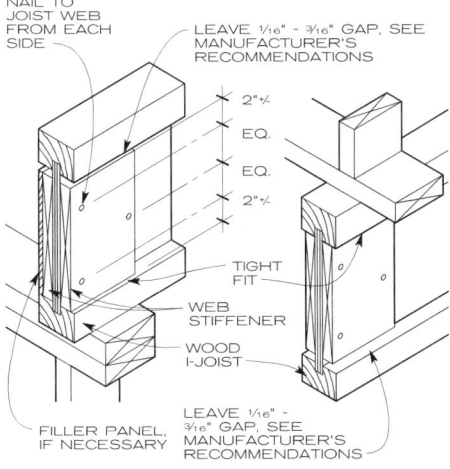

BEARING WALL BELOW   **BEARING WALL ABOVE**

WEB STIFFENER DETAILS

GENERAL

A wood I-joist is made of a web with top and bottom flanges. It is similar in shape and profile to the steel I-beam, but while the steel component is forged from a single ingot, the wood member is a composition. Plywood or oriented strand board (OSB) is used for the web of the wood I-joist, and either solid lumber or laminated-veneer lumber for the flanges. Many manufacturers produce wood I-joists under different trade names, and each differs in its dimensions, as well as span and deflection, loading, and performance characteristics. Consult manufacturers for details and performance criteria.

Compared to solid lumber, wood I-joists have both relative advantages and disadvantages:

ADVANTAGES

1. Easier to handle and lighter weight, with about 50% less wood material per joist than an equivalent solid wood member.
2. Makes efficient use of a natural resource—the I-joist can be made from second and third growth timber stands, with no need for old growth trees.
3. Available in lengths up to 60 ft, priced per linear foot.
4. Greatest strength when loaded parallel to plane of web.
5. A high degree of uniformity, with no crowns, checks, or loose knots.
6. Plumbing and HVAC can easily be run through web structure (based on the manufacturer's guidelines).
7. Starts with dry materials, so there is much less shrinkage than with solid lumber.
8. Wood I-joists can generally be set at wider on-center spacing, thus reducing installation time.

Richard J. Vitullo, AIA; Oak Leaf Studio; Crownsville, Maryland

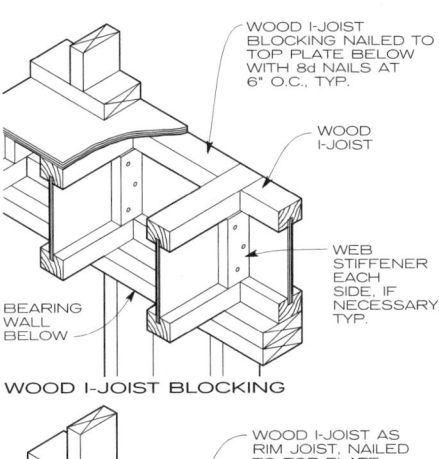

WOOD I-JOIST BLOCKING

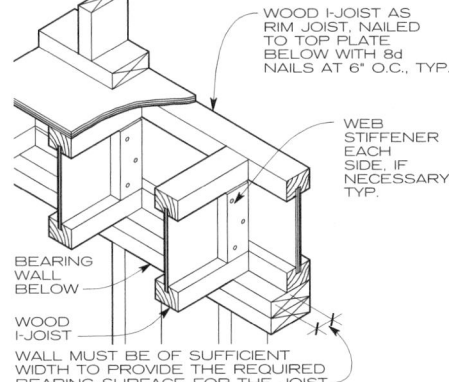

WOOD I-JOIST AS RIM JOIST

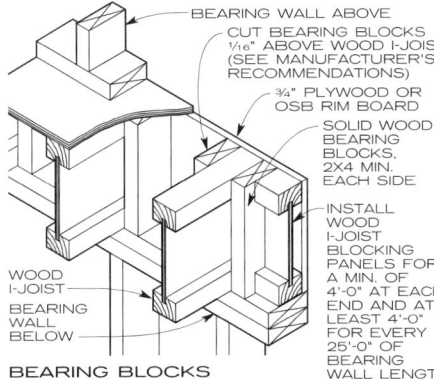

BEARING BLOCKS

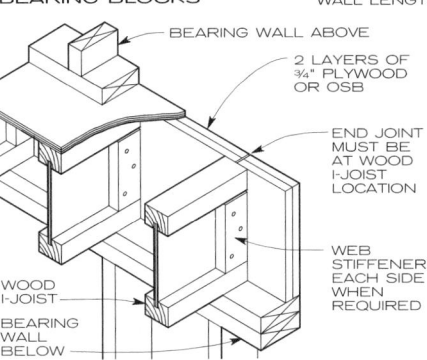

STANDARD 2X RIM JOIST

NOTE

Check building code for appropriate detail in areas of high lateral load.

STUD BEARING WALL DETAILS

DISADVANTAGES

1. Material costs are generally more (per linear foot) than for solid lumber (for standard residential floor joist dimensions and spans).
2. Contractors are less familiar with wood I-joists and can create problems by cutting holes into webs and weakening the member.

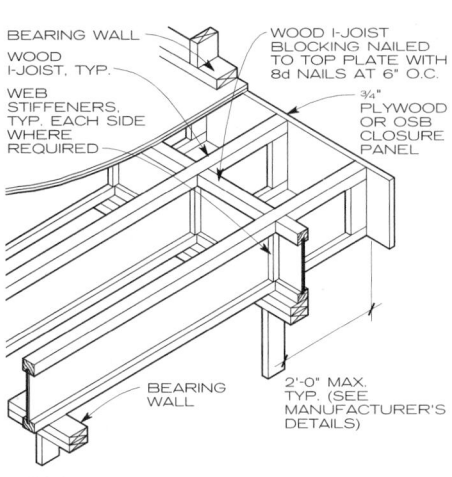

NOTE

Joist must be designed to carry the load-bearing wall.

LOAD-BEARING CANTILEVER DETAIL

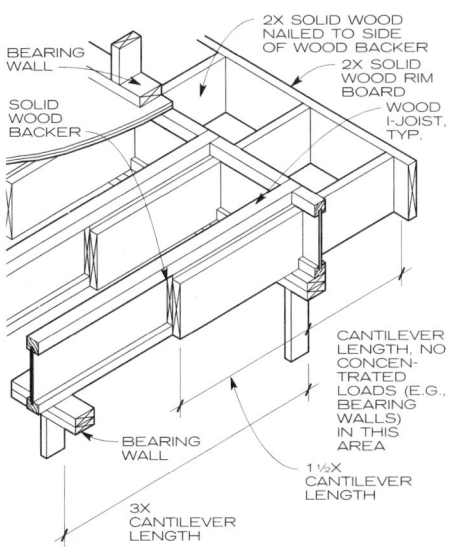

NON-LOAD-BEARING DROPPED CANTILEVER DETAIL

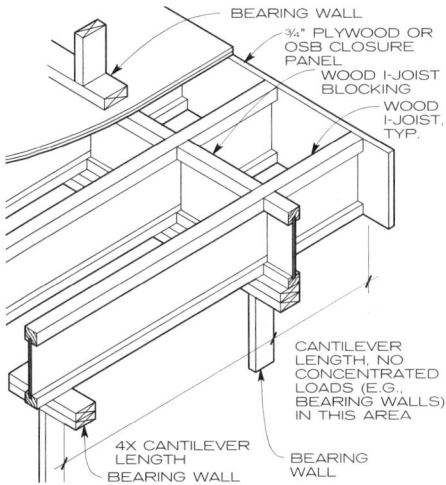

NON-LOAD-BEARING CANTILEVER DETAIL

CANTILEVER DETAILS

3. Less lateral stiffness than solid lumber.
4. Can be shifted by winds during construction due to light weight.
5. Some adhesives used in laminated-veneer components may pose indoor air-quality problems.

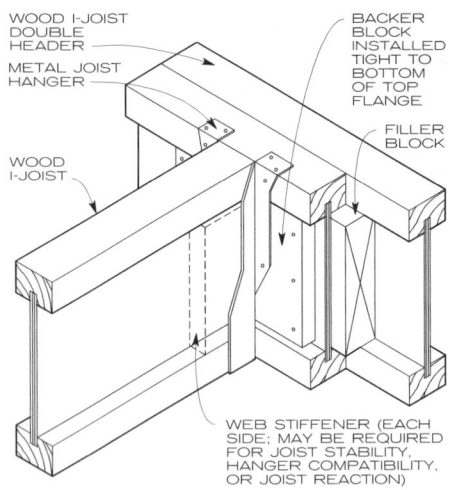

NOTE

Connection between joists must provide adequate load transfer between members.

WOOD I-JOIST CONNECTION TO WOOD I-JOIST HEADER

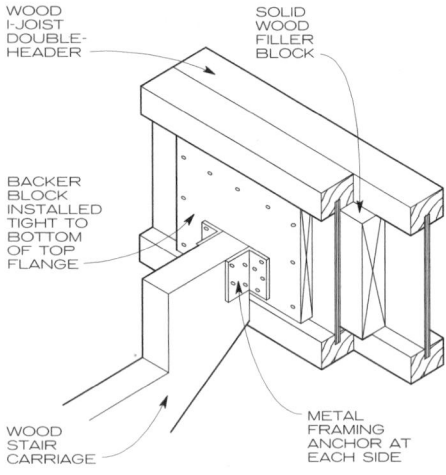

NOTE

Connection between joists must provide adequate load transfer between members.

STAIR CARRIAGE CONNECTION

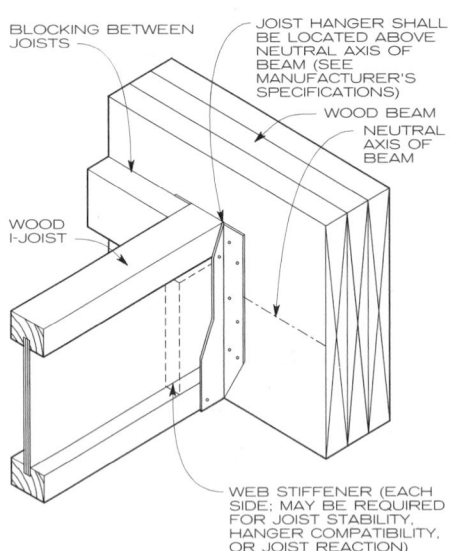

JOIST HANGER DETAIL

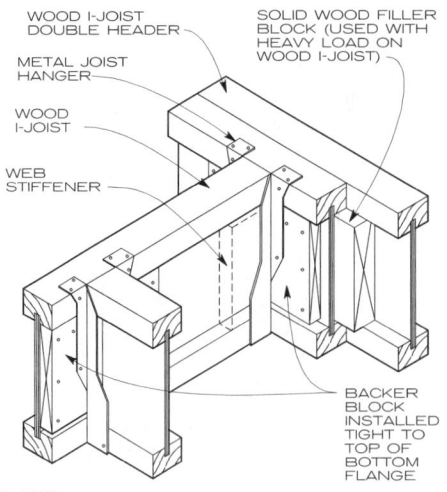

NOTE

Connection between joists must provide adequate load transfer between members.

WOOD I-JOIST CONNECTION TO WOOD I-JOIST HEADER (HEAVY LOAD)

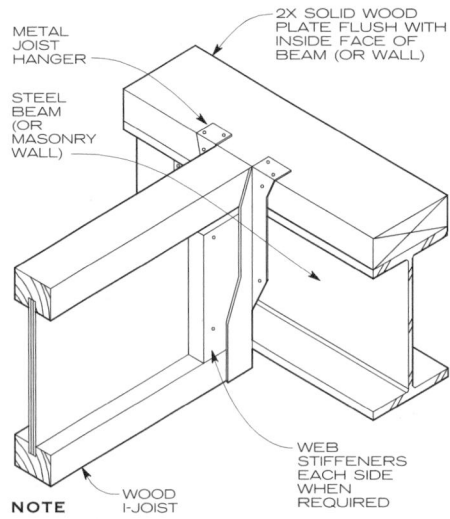

NOTE

Thicker wood plate over beam may be required; check hanger manufacturer's top flange nailing requirements.

WOOD I-JOIST SUPPORTED AT TOP OF BEAM (OR WALL)

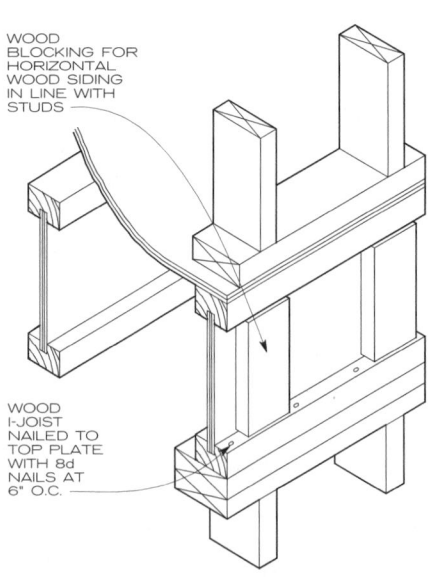

TYPICAL WOOD BLOCKING AT EXTERIOR WALL

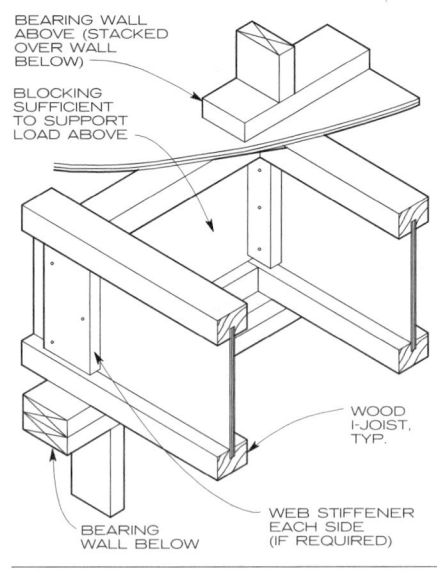

BEARING WALL ABOVE AND BELOW

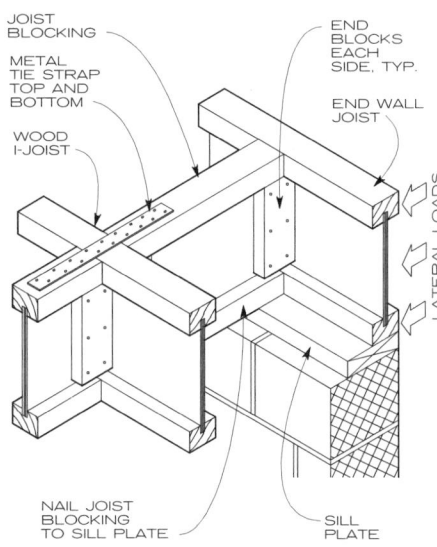

LATERAL LOAD BLOCKING AT END WALL

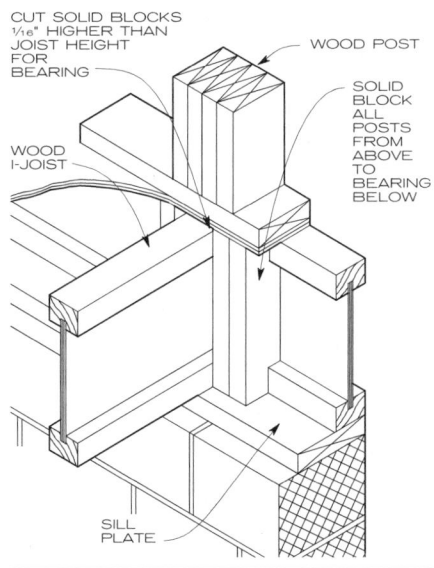

COLUMN LOAD TRANSFER

Richard J. Vitullo, AIA; Oak Leaf Studio; Crownsville, Maryland

 ROUGH CARPENTRY

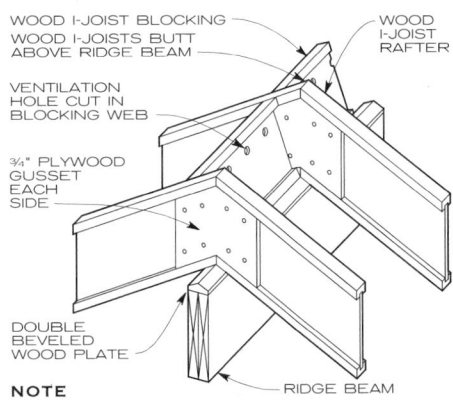

WOOD I-JOIST BLOCKING
WOOD I-JOISTS BUTT ABOVE RIDGE BEAM
VENTILATION HOLE CUT IN BLOCKING WEB
¾" PLYWOOD GUSSET EACH SIDE
WOOD I-JOIST RAFTER
DOUBLE BEVELED WOOD PLATE
RIDGE BEAM

NOTE
Uplift connections may be required.

WOOD I-JOIST RAFTER AT RIDGE BEAM DETAIL

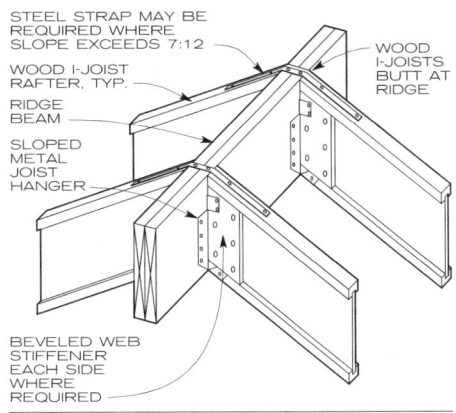

STEEL STRAP MAY BE REQUIRED WHERE SLOPE EXCEEDS 7:12
WOOD I-JOIST RAFTER, TYP.
RIDGE BEAM
SLOPED METAL JOIST HANGER
WOOD I-JOISTS BUTT AT RIDGE
BEVELED WEB STIFFENER EACH SIDE WHERE REQUIRED

WOOD I-JOIST RAFTER AT RIDGE BEAM DETAIL

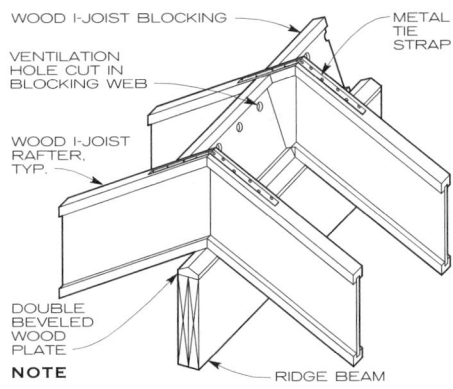

WOOD I-JOIST BLOCKING
VENTILATION HOLE CUT IN BLOCKING WEB
WOOD I-JOIST RAFTER, TYP.
METAL TIE STRAP
DOUBLE BEVELED WOOD PLATE
RIDGE BEAM

NOTE
Uplift connections may be required.

WOOD I-JOIST RAFTER AT RIDGE BEAM DETAIL

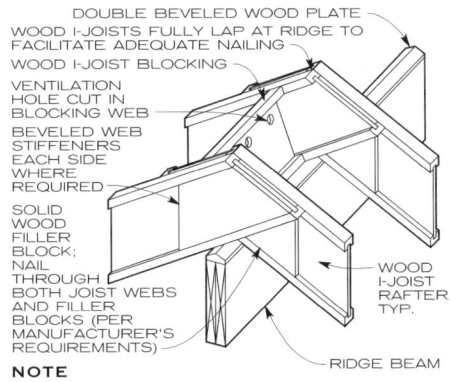

DOUBLE BEVELED WOOD PLATE
WOOD I-JOISTS FULLY LAP AT RIDGE TO FACILITATE ADEQUATE NAILING
WOOD I-JOIST BLOCKING
VENTILATION HOLE CUT IN BLOCKING WEB
BEVELED WEB STIFFENERS EACH SIDE WHERE REQUIRED
SOLID WOOD FILLER BLOCK; NAIL THROUGH BOTH JOIST WEBS AND FILLER BLOCKS (PER MANUFACTURER'S REQUIREMENTS)
WOOD I-JOIST RAFTER, TYP.
RIDGE BEAM

NOTE
Uplift connections may be required.

LAPPED WOOD I-JOIST RAFTER AT RIDGE BEAM

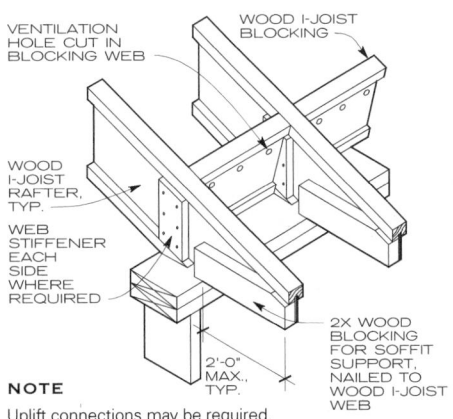

VENTILATION HOLE CUT IN BLOCKING WEB
WOOD I-JOIST BLOCKING
WOOD I-JOIST RAFTER, TYP.
WEB STIFFENER EACH SIDE WHERE REQUIRED
2'-0" MAX., TYP.
2X WOOD BLOCKING FOR SOFFIT SUPPORT, NAILED TO WOOD I-JOIST WEB

NOTE
Uplift connections may be required.

WOOD I-JOIST RAFTER AT OVERHANG

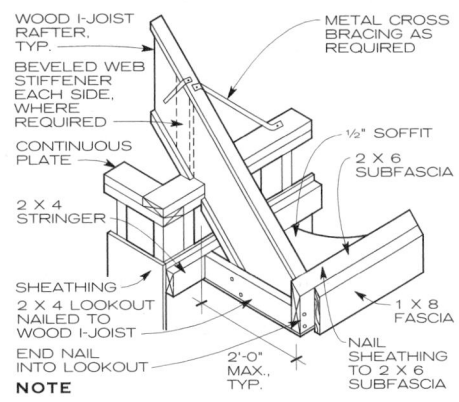

WOOD I-JOIST RAFTER, TYP.
BEVELED WEB STIFFENER EACH SIDE, WHERE REQUIRED
CONTINUOUS PLATE
2 X 4 STRINGER
SHEATHING
2 X 4 LOOKOUT NAILED TO WOOD I-JOIST
END NAIL INTO LOOKOUT
METAL CROSS BRACING AS REQUIRED
½" SOFFIT
2 X 6 SUBFASCIA
1 X 8 FASCIA
NAIL SHEATHING TO 2 X 6 SUBFASCIA
2'-0" MAX., TYP.

NOTE
Uplift connections may be required.

WOOD I-JOIST RAFTER AT OVERHANG

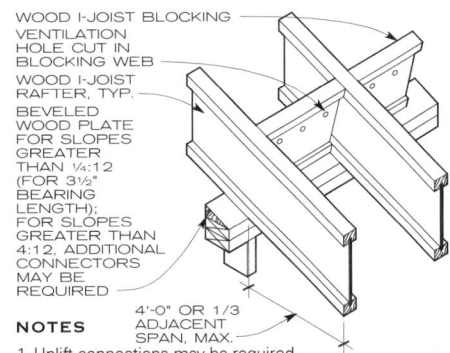

WOOD I-JOIST BLOCKING
VENTILATION HOLE CUT IN BLOCKING WEB
WOOD I-JOIST RAFTER, TYP.
BEVELED WOOD PLATE FOR SLOPES GREATER THAN ¼:12 (FOR 3½" BEARING LENGTH); FOR SLOPES GREATER THAN 4:12, ADDITIONAL CONNECTORS MAY BE REQUIRED
4'-0" OR ⅓ ADJACENT SPAN, MAX.

NOTES
1. Uplift connections may be required.
2. Special sloped seat-bearing metal connectors can be used in lieu of beveled wood plate in some sloped applications. See manufacturer's recommendations.

WOOD I-JOIST RAFTER AT OVERHANG

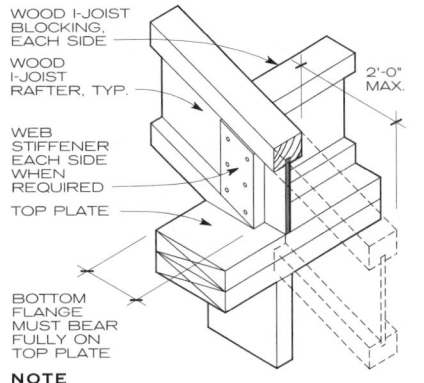

WOOD I-JOIST BLOCKING, EACH SIDE
WOOD I-JOIST RAFTER, TYP.
WEB STIFFENER EACH SIDE WHEN REQUIRED
TOP PLATE
BOTTOM FLANGE MUST BEAR FULLY ON TOP PLATE
2'-0" MAX.

NOTE
Uplift connections may be required.

TYPICAL BIRD'S MOUTH I-JOIST CUT DETAIL

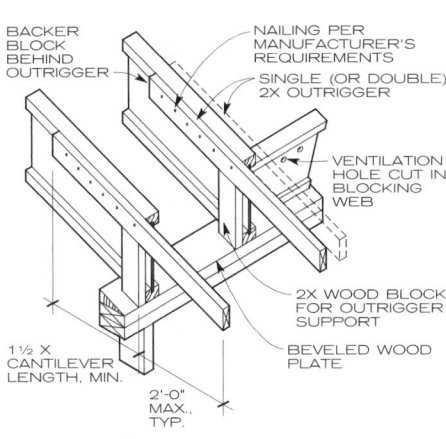

BACKER BLOCK BEHIND OUTRIGGER
NAILING PER MANUFACTURER'S REQUIREMENTS
SINGLE (OR DOUBLE) 2X OUTRIGGER
VENTILATION HOLE CUT IN BLOCKING WEB
2X WOOD BLOCK FOR OUTRIGGER SUPPORT
BEVELED WOOD PLATE
1½ X CANTILEVER LENGTH, MIN.
2'-0" MAX., TYP.

WOOD I-JOIST RAFTER WITH OUTRIGGER

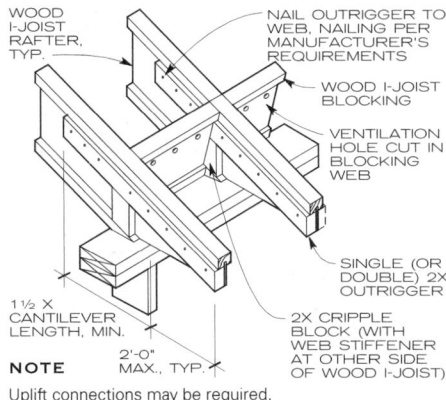

WOOD I-JOIST RAFTER, TYP.
NAIL OUTRIGGER TO WEB, NAILING PER MANUFACTURER'S REQUIREMENTS
WOOD I-JOIST BLOCKING
VENTILATION HOLE CUT IN BLOCKING WEB
SINGLE (OR DOUBLE) 2X OUTRIGGER
2X CRIPPLE BLOCK (WITH WEB STIFFENER AT OTHER SIDE OF WOOD I-JOIST)
1½ X CANTILEVER LENGTH, MIN.
2'-0" MAX., TYP.

NOTE
Uplift connections may be required.

WOOD I-JOIST RAFTER AT OUTRIGGER

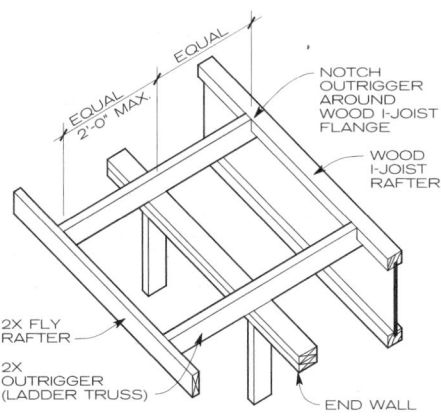

EQUAL EQUAL
2'-0" MAX.
NOTCH OUTRIGGER AROUND WOOD I-JOIST FLANGE
WOOD I-JOIST RAFTER
2X FLY RAFTER
2X OUTRIGGER (LADDER TRUSS)
END WALL

FLY RAFTER DETAIL

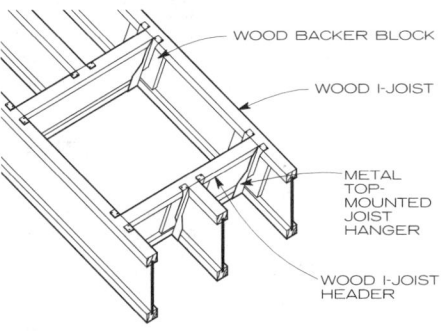

WOOD BACKER BLOCK
WOOD I-JOIST
METAL TOP-MOUNTED JOIST HANGER
WOOD I-JOIST HEADER

WOOD I-JOIST SKYLIGHT FRAMING DETAIL

NOTE
Check code and manufacturer's requirements for all ventilation hole sizes cut in blocking web.

Richard J. Vitullo, AIA; Oak Leaf Studio; Crownsville, Maryland

ROUGH CARPENTRY 6

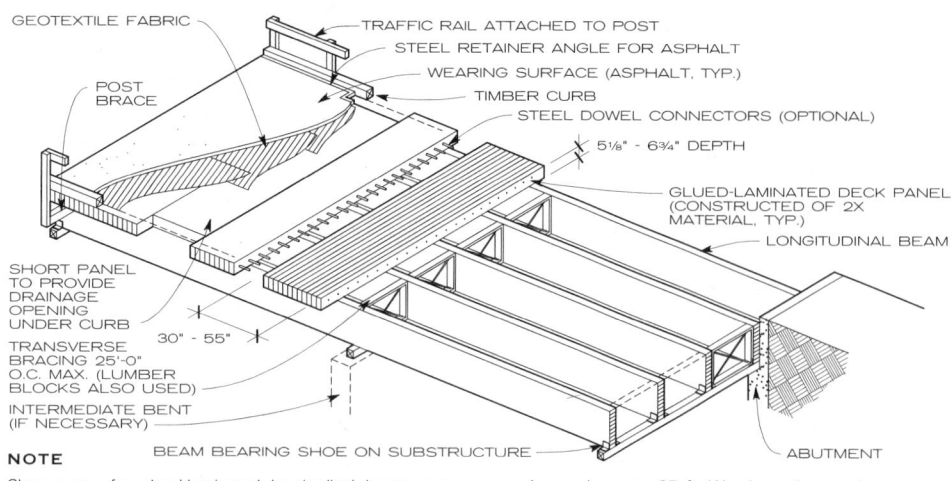

NOTE

Clear spans for glued-laminated longitudinal beams are from 20 to 100 ft. For sawn lumber beams, clear spans can be made up to 25 ft. Wood species used are generally Douglas fir-larch or Southern pine.

TYPICAL LONGITUDINAL BEAM BRIDGE

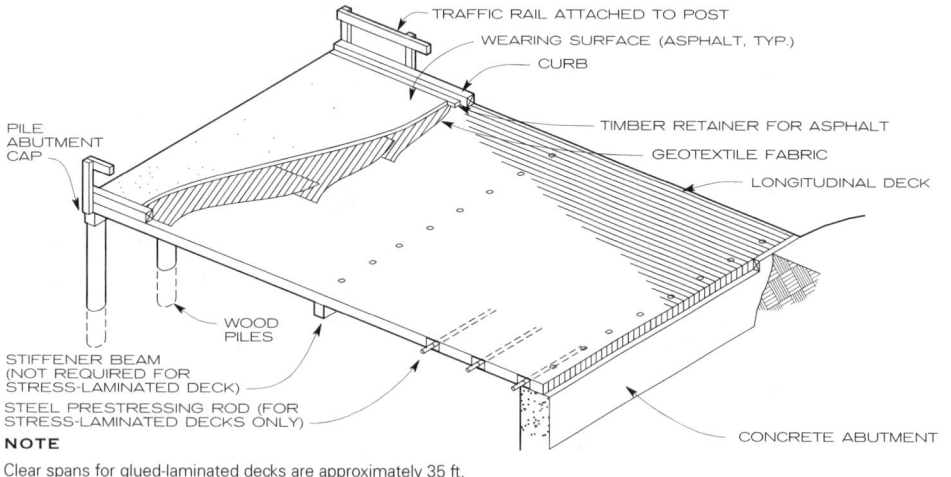

NOTE

Clear spans for glued-laminated decks are approximately 35 ft.

TYPICAL LONGITUDINAL DECK SUPERSTRUCTURE

CONTINUOUS WIDTH NAIL-LAMINATED DECK (SPANS TO 21 FT)

PANELIZED NAIL-LAMINATED DECK (SPANS TO 38 FT)

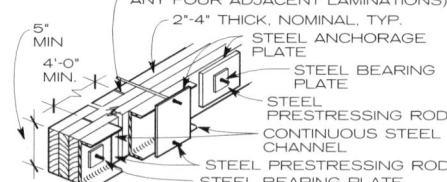

STRESS-LAMINATED DECK ANCHORAGE DETAILS

LONGITUDINAL DECK DETAILS

DECK (SPAN UP TO 24 FT)

BOX SECTION (SPAN UP TO 70 FT)

T-SECTION (SPAN UP TO 63 FT)

NOTE

T-section may be preferable over box section for long spans because of ease of inspection and maintenance.

TYPICAL STRESS-LAMINATED TIMBER SUPERSTRUCTURES

INTRODUCTION

Although wood was probably the first material used to construct a bridge, in the 20th century concrete and steel have became the major bridge construction materials. Wood is still widely used for short- and medium-span bridges. The strength, light weight, and energy absorption properties of timber make it a desirable material for bridge construction. Timber can carry short-term overloads without adverse effects. Large wood members are fire resistive, impervious to continuous freezing and thawing, and resist the harmful effects of de-icing agents.

In modern applications, the life of timber bridges is extended to forty years or longer through the use of preservative-treated wood, which requires little or no maintenance. The specifications and standards for the preservative treatment of wood maintained by the American Wood Preservers Association (AWPA) are the most widely used and comprehensive documents covering treatment procedures for sawn lumber, glued-laminated timber (glulam), piling, and poles used for timber bridges.

STRUCTURAL CHARACTERISTICS

All timber bridges consist of two basic components—the superstructure and the substructure. The superstructure is the framework of the bridge span and includes the deck, floor system, main supporting members, railings, and other incidental components. The five basic types of superstructure are beam, deck (slab), truss, arch, and suspension. The substructure is the portion of the bridge that transmits loads from the superstructure to the supporting rock or soil. Timber substructures include abutments and bents. Abutments support the two bridge ends, while bents provide intermediate support for multiple-span crossings.

TIMBER SUPERSTRUCTURES

LONGITUDINAL BEAM (in bridge design, the longitude is measured in the direction of traffic flow): The simplest and most common timber bridge superstructure, the longitudinal beam type consists of a deck system supported by a series of timber beams between two or more supports. Beams are constructed from logs, sawn lumber, glued-laminated timber (glulam), or laminated veneer lumber (LVL).

LONGITUDINAL DECK: Longitudinal deck or slab superstructures are constructed of glulam, nail-laminated sawn lumber, or stress-laminated lumber decks placed longitudinally between supports, with the wide dimension of the lamination vertical. In this type of superstructure, the deck is designed to resist all applied loads and deflection without additional supporting members or beams. Nonetheless, transverse distributor beams are usually attached to the underside of the deck to help distribute the load. Maximum clear spans are approximately 35 ft.

TRUSS: Trusses are structural frames consisting of straight members connected to form a series of triangles. Trusses can span distances of up to 250 ft. In bridge applications, a typical truss superstructure consists of two main trusses, a floor system, and bracing. This type is classified as a deck truss (in which the deck is at or above the level of the top chord) or a through truss (in which the deck is near the bottom chord). When the height of a through truss is insufficient for overhead bracing, it is called a half-through or pony truss. Timber trusses are constructed in many geometric configurations, but two of the most popular are the bow-string truss and parallel chord truss.

ARCH: Arches used in clear span timber bridge construction have glued-laminated timbers for the main members. This type of superstructure, called a glulam deck arch, probably best shows the versatility of glulam in bridge construction. The glulam arches are manufactured in segmental, circular, or parabolic shapes. Two basic arch types are used: the two-hinge arch (for short spans of 80 ft or less) and the three-hinge arch (for long spans of between 80 and 200 ft). The roadway for deck arch bridges is supported by glulam post bents connected to the arches with steel gusset plates. Use of this design is most practical when considerable height is required and when foundations can be constructed to resist horizontal end reactions. It is particularly suitable for deep crossings because long clear spans result in substantial substructure cost savings.

SUSPENSION: Timber suspension bridges consist of a timber deck structure suspended from flexible steel cables or chains supported by timber towers. This superstructure type is capable of spanning clear distances of more than 500 ft and is normally used only when span requirements make other bridge types impractical or when it is not feasible to use intermediate bents.

TIMBER SUBSTRUCTURES

ABUTMENTS: Abutments support the bridge ends and contain roadway embankment material. The simplest timber abutment is a sawn lumber or glulam spread footing placed directly on the surface of the embankment if foundation materials permit. Another type is the post abutment, in which the superstructure is supported on sawn lumber or glulam posts connected to a spread footing. Pile abutments may be used if soils cannot hold footings.

BENTS: Bents are intermediate supports between abutments used for multiple-span bridges. They are made from timber piles or sawn lumber frames, depending on height requirements and soil conditions.

GENERAL DESIGN CRITERIA

For design criteria and specifications for timber bridges, refer to the current edition of the American Association of State Highway and Transportation Officials (AASHTO) Standard Specifications for Highway Bridges and "Timber Bridges: Design, Construction, Inspection, and Maintenance," U.S. Department of Agriculture, August 1992.

Richard J. Vitullo, AIA; Oak Leaf Studio; Crownsville, Maryland
Michael A. Ritter, PE, Structural Engineer; Forest Products Lab, USDA; Madison, Wisconsin

 HEAVY TIMBER CONSTRUCTION

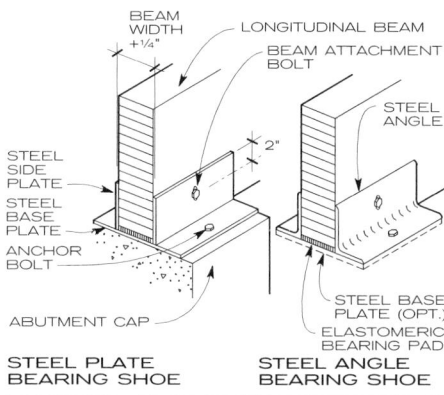

STEEL PLATE BEARING SHOE

STEEL ANGLE BEARING SHOE

TYPICAL BEARING SHOE DETAILS

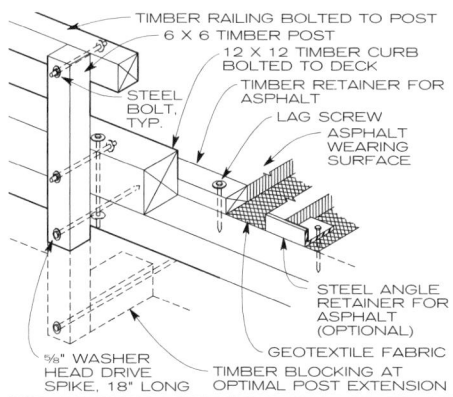

BRIDGE EDGE CONDITION

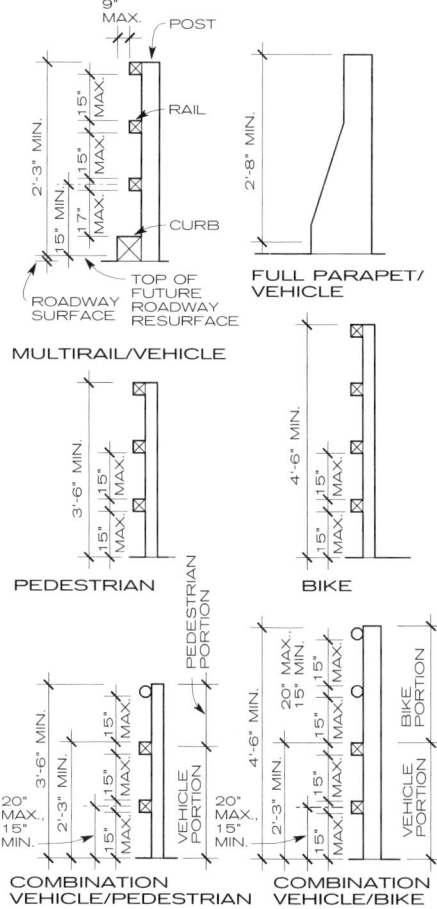

MULTIRAIL/VEHICLE

FULL PARAPET/ VEHICLE

PEDESTRIAN

BIKE

COMBINATION VEHICLE/PEDESTRIAN

COMBINATION VEHICLE/BIKE

TYPICAL RAIL SYSTEMS

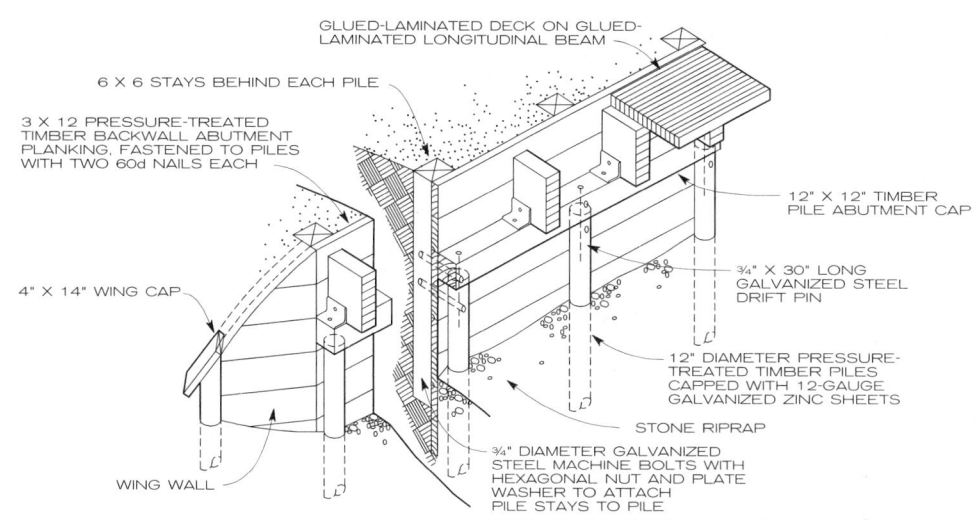

TYPICAL PILE ABUTMENT DETAIL

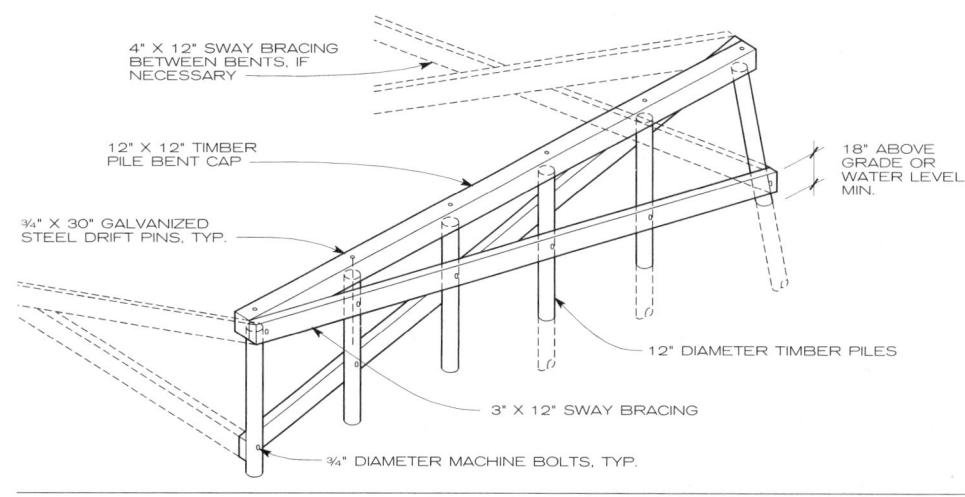

TYPICAL PILE BENT DETAIL

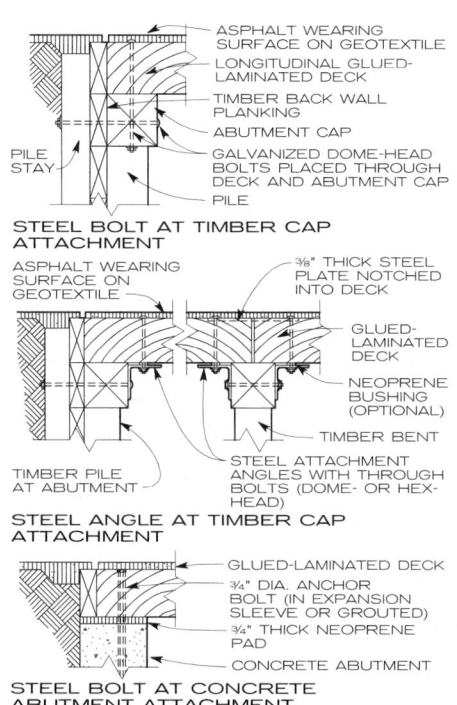

STEEL BOLT AT TIMBER CAP ATTACHMENT

STEEL ANGLE AT TIMBER CAP ATTACHMENT

STEEL BOLT AT CONCRETE ABUTMENT ATTACHMENT

TYPICAL LONGITUDINAL DECK ATTACHMENT DETAILS

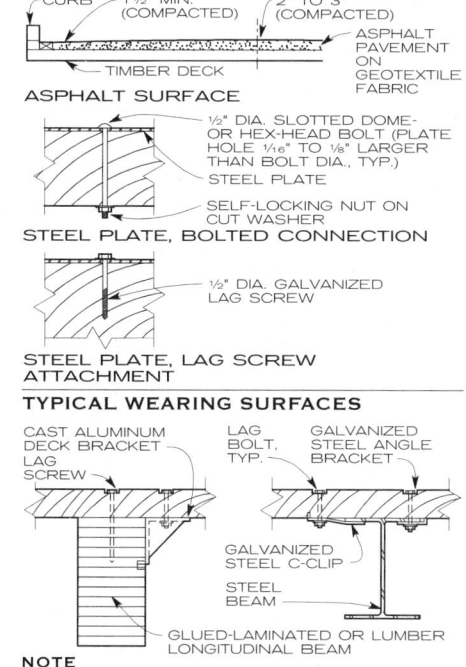

ASPHALT SURFACE

STEEL PLATE, BOLTED CONNECTION

STEEL PLATE, LAG SCREW ATTACHMENT

TYPICAL WEARING SURFACES

NOTE

Deck brackets include small teeth that firmly grip the deck and beam.

TYPICAL GLUED-LAMINATED DECK ATTACHMENT DETAILS

Richard J. Vitullo, AIA; Oak Leaf Studio; Crownsville, Maryland
Michael A. Ritter, PE, Structural Engineer; Forest Products Lab, USDA; Madison, Wisconsin

HEAVY TIMBER CONSTRUCTION

RELATIVE TREATABILITY OF SELECTED DOMESTIC SPECIES

HEARTWOOD LEAST DIFFICULT TO PENETRATE	HEARTWOOD MODERATELY DIFFICULT TO PENETRATE	HEARTWOOD DIFFICULT TO PENETRATE	HEARTWOOD VERY DIFFICULT TO PENETRATE
Bristlecone pine, pinyon pine, redwood	Bald cypress, California red fir, Douglas fir (coast), Eastern white pine, jack pine, loblolly pine, longleaf pine, ponderosa pine, red pine, shortleaf pine, sugar pine, Western hemlock	Eastern hemlock, Engelmann spruce, grand fir, lodgepole pine, noble fir, sitka spruce, Western larch, white fir, white spruce	Alpine fir, corkbark fir, Douglas fir (Rocky Mountain), Northern white cedar, tamarack, Western red cedar

RELATIVE HEARTWOOD DECAY RESISTANCE OF NATURALLY RESISTANT UNTREATED WOODS*

RESISTANT OR VERY RESISTANT	MODERATELY RESISTANT	SLIGHTLY OR NONRESISTANT
Bald cypress (old growth), cedar, white oak, redwood	Bald cypress (new growth), Douglas fir, Western larch, Eastern white pine, Southern yellow pine (longleaf, slash), tamarack	Pines other than longleaf, slash, and Eastern white, spruces, true firs

* Source: U.S. Forest Products Laboratory Wood Handbook

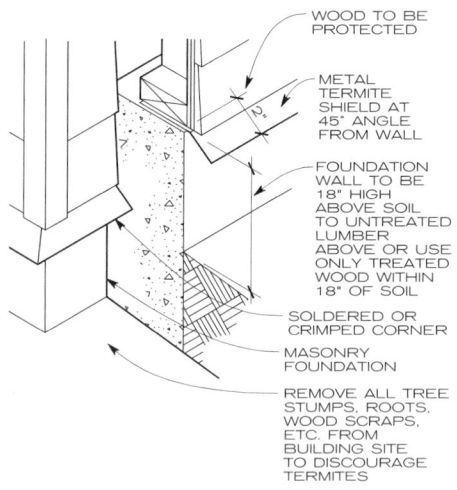

GENERAL

Wood may be destroyed by decay fungi; by insects like carpenter ants and termites; and by marine borers in saltwater exposures. Four conditions must exist before these organisms can destroy wood: (1) a free oxygen supply; (2) a moisture level in the wood above the fiber saturation point (20%); (3) a temperature in the range of 50 to 90°F; (4) the presence of a food source, in this case, the wood.

In most indoor environments, where moisture levels are generally low, wood will last for a very long time. In certain indoor environments, however, and in many exterior environments, wood cannot be kept dry or out of the proximity of moisture. Most building codes recognize this by requiring the use of pressure-treated wood or naturally resistant wood species where building components come into contact with concrete, masonry, or exposed soil. This requirement also covers floor joists and crawl space support members within 12 to 18 in. of exposed soil.

DECAY-RESISTANT WOOD

When specifying a wood that will resist decay, the choice is between naturally decay-resistant wood or wood treated with preservatives. The first requires use of the heartwood of naturally decay-resistant woods such as Western red cedar, bald cypress, redwood, and others that contain natural poisons called extractives, which are not palatable to decay-causing organisms. However, not all grades or species of these woods are suitable for some structural situations. Treating wood with preservatives is a process that impregnates wood with chemicals through a pressure-treatment process. Use of nonpressure treatments such as spraying, dipping, and brushing is mostly limited to field treatment of wood during construction or remedial treatment of existing wood in place.

PRESSURE-TREATED WOOD

There are two processes commonly used for pressure treating wood, the full cell and modified full cell processes. In both, the wood is placed in a large, cylindrical tank and the preservative forced under pressure into its cells.

In the modified full-cell process the preservative coats the walls of the wood cells and is absorbed when the process is finished the wood cell cavities are empty of preservatives. Most over-the-counter pressure-treated wood is treated with this process. In the full-cell process, a vacuum is introduced at the beginning to force the air out of the wood cell cavities, which then remain filled with preservative after treatment. The full-cell process is used in most creosote and pentachlorophenol treating for wood used in severe environments, including applications such as utility poles, railroad ties, saltwater piles, and timber bridges. Regardless of which process is used, the wood is generally dried to a 20% moisture content prior to treatment to promote maximum penetration of the preservative.

PENETRATION AND RETENTION OF PRESERVATIVES

Penetration and retention are the two measures that define the effectiveness of preservation methods. Penetration depends on the species of wood and the size of the lumber member being treated. Some species that resist preservative penetration, such as Douglas fir, are incised with small slits to make treatment more effective. Others, such as Southern yellow pine, are easily treated without incisions. While the sapwood of some species is readily penetrated, the heartwood of most resists penetration (although the

heartwood of all species naturally resists decay). While the penetration of preservatives is hard to determine without damaging the wood, retention of the preservative can be measured directly by weighing the wood, stated in terms of pounds (of the chemical retained) per cubic foot (pcf). Retention standards are set by the American Wood Preservers' Association and enforced through chemical analysis of treated wood by an independent third-party agency approved by the American Lumber Standard Committee (ALSC). A quality mark outlining pertinent information can be found on complying wood stock.

PRESERVATIVE TYPES

Three classes of preservatives are in use today: creosote, oil-borne (organic), and waterborne (inorganic).

CREOSOTE is a coal-tar product that is dissolved in a distilled solution or petroleum oil. It is an effective preservative in applications with extreme exposure to decay or insect attack (marine borers in saltwater environments, such as marine piles or bridge timbers). Wood treated with the full-cell process is more effective in these applications, but the creosote may bleed into the surroundings, causing contamination. Most utility poles, freshwater piles, and fenceposts are treated with the empty-cell process, which yields a clean, nonbleeding surface. Creosote-treated products cannot be painted, but epoxy shellac and coal-tar pitch are acceptable sealants. This type of preservative can last from thirty to sixty years. Clean air standards prohibit the use of creosote in many areas.

ORGANIC OIL-BORNE PRESERVATIVES are carried in organic solvents such as liquefied isobutane and are used to treat most softwoods and hardwoods. These preservatives include pentachlorophenol (penta), copper naphthenate, tributyl tinoxide (TBTO), and copper 8-quinolinolate.

Penta extends the service life of wood by twenty to forty years and is used to treat utility poles, fenceposts, and highway timbers. Tinted light to dark brown, penta-treated wood accepts adhesives and finishes reasonably well once the oil medium has evaporated. Polyurethane, shellac, varnish, and latex enamel are effective as sealants. Penta can migrate to the surface of wood, leach into the surrounding soil, and contaminate groundwater. Only slowly does it break down into biodegradable compounds..

Plywood and other wood treated with copper-8-quinolinate can be used in applications where food is harvested, transported, or stored. The chemical is dissolved in liquid petroleum gas or light hydrocarbon solvents so the surface is clean and free of solvent odor. Consult with the treatment company regarding applicable FDA and USDA acceptances.

INORGANIC WATERBORNE PRESERVATIVES are the most popular and commonly available types used for treating wood. They include chromated copper arsenate (CCA), ammoniacal copper arsenate (ACA), and ammoniacal copper zinc arsenate (ACZA). These preservatives are related chemically and have a lot in common. Chromium holds the other components in the wood and prevents leaching; ammonia helps carry copper, zinc, and arsenic deeper into the wood; arsenic guards against attack by termites and fungi. Southern yellow pine is usually treated with CCA, and Douglas fir and other western woods with ACA and ACZA. The various formulations of CCA vary in the amount of chromium, copper, and arsenic they contain. The oxide form of CCA, type C, is widely preferred for most construction. During the treatment process, CCA is water soluble, but air drying for a few days renders it insoluble. This is

TERMITE PROTECTION DETAILS

because the chromium reacts chemically with the wood, permanently bonding itself and the copper and arsenic to the cell walls, preventing leaching during its service life. CCA-treated wood can last up to forty years.

Another waterborne preservative is borax, which has promise due to its effectiveness against fungi and insects and its low-toxicity to people and animals. However, it leaches out when the wood gets wet.

FINISHING OF PRESERVATIVE-TREATED WOOD

Waterborne preservatives are recommended when clean, odorless, and paintable wood products are required. Wood treated with such preservatives may be used indoors if sawdust and construction debris are cleaned up. Painting wood treated with creosote or oil-borne pentachlorophenol is not recommended, as it is difficult to use, requiring extensive care and an aluminum-based paint. Paintable waterborne pentachlorophenol treatments are available. For certain interior applications in commercial, industrial, or farm buildings, creosote- or penta-treated wood may be used if exposed surfaces are sealed with two coats of urethane or epoxy paint or shellac. Guidelines for precautions in these cases are outlined in an EPA-approved consumer information sheet for each preservative treatment.

FASTENERS

CCA, ACA, and ACC are corrosive to uncoated metals. For aboveground construction, hot-dipped or hot-tumbled galvanized steel and stainless steel fasteners are recommended. Joist hangers and framing anchors should also be corrosion resistant. For below-grade construction, such as treated wood foundation systems, types 304 and 316 stainless steel Type H silicon bronze, ETP copper, and monel fasteners are required. Adhesives work well with CCA-treated wood. Phenolresorcinol, resorcinol, and melemineformaldehyde structural adhesives are used in glulam beams made from treated wood members. On job sites, use adhesives recommended for use with treated wood.

PRECAUTIONS FOR USE AND HANDLING

The chemical formulations used for preservative treatment of wood are registered with the EPA, which has approved guidelines for the use of pressure-treated wood to ensure safe handling and avoid environmental or other health hazards. Some guidelines for use and handling follow:

1. Dispose of treated wood by ordinary trash collection or burial. Treated wood should never be burned in open fires or in stoves, fireplaces, or residential boilers.

2. Avoid frequent inhalation of sawdust from treated wood. Whenever possible, sawing and machining of treated wood should be done outdoors.

3. Avoid frequent or prolonged skin contact with penta- or creosote-treated wood.

4. After handling treated wood products, wash exposed areas thoroughly before eating or drinking.

Richard J. Vitullo, AIA; Oak Leaf Studio; Crownsville, Maryland
American Plywood Association; Tacoma, Washington

 WOOD TREATMENT

SOUTHERN PINE PRESERVATIVE RETENTIONS AND APPLICABLE AWPA STANDARDS[1]

WOOD USES	APPLICATIONS		RETENTION ASSAY OF TREATED WOOD—LB/CU FT							
			WATERBORNE PRESERVATIVES[2]				CRESOTE AND OILBORNE PRESERVATIVES[3]			
			AMMONIACAL COPPER ARSENATE (ACA)	AMMONIACAL COPPER ZINC ARSENATE (ACZA)	CHROMATED COPPER ARSENATE (CCA)	AWPA STANDARDS	CREOSOTE	CREOSOTE-PETROLEUM	CREOSOTE SOLUTIONS	PENTA-CHLORO-PHENOL (PENTA)
LUMBER, TIMBERS, AND PLYWOOD	Aboveground		0.25	0.25	0.25	C2/C9	8[5]	8[5]	8[5]	0.40
	Soil and freshwater use		0.40	0.40	0.40	C2/C9	10[5]	10[5]	10[5]	0.50
	Permanent wood foundation (PWF)		0.60	0.60	0.60	C22	NR*	NR	NR	NR
	Saltwater use		2.5	2.5	2.5	C2/C9	25	NR	25	NR
PILES	Land or freshwater use and foundations		0.80	0.80	0.80	C3	12	12	12	0.60
	Marine One prevalent marine organism	Teredo only	2.5[4] and 1.5	2.5[4] and 1.5	2.5[4] and 1.5	C18	20	NR	20	NR
		Pholads only	NR	NR	NR	C18	20	NR	20	NR
		Limnoria tripunc-tata only	2.5[4] and 1.5	2.5[4] and 1.5	2.5[4] and 1.5	C18	NR	NR	NR	NR
	Marine Sphaeroma tere-brans or combination of pholads and limnoria tripunctata (use a dual treatment)	First treatment	1.0	1.0	1.0	C18	—	—	—	—
		Second treatment	—	—	—	C18	20	—	20	—
POLES	Utility	Normal	0.60	0.60	0.60	C4	7.5	7.5	7.5	0.38
		Severe service conditions (high incidence of decay and termite attack)	0.60	0.60	0.60	C4	9.0	9.0	9.0	0.45
	Building construction	Round	0.60	0.60	0.60	C23	9.0[5]	NR	NR	0.45
POSTS	Commercial-residential fence	Round, half-round, and quarter-round	0.40	0.40	0.40	C5	8[5]	8[5]	8[5]	0.40
		Sawn four sides	0.40	0.40	0.40	C2	10[5]	10[5]	10[5]	0.50
	Highway construction: Fence, guide, sign, and sight	Round, half-round, and quarter-round	0.40	0.40	0.40	C14	8	8	8	0.40
		Sawn four sides	0.40	0.40	0.40	C14	10	10	10	0.50
	Highway construction: Guardrail and spacer blocks	Round	0.50	0.50	0.50	C14	10	10	10	0.50
		Sawn four sides	0.50	0.50	0.50	C14	12	12	12	0.60

* NR = not recommended

[1] American Wood Preservers' Association (AWPA) Standards detail plant operating procedures for pressure treatment of wood. These standards include minimum vacuum, pressure, and penetration requirements and maximum steaming parameters. AWPA also details minimum retention requirements, sampling zones for assay and maximum redrying temperature allowances for each preservative, commodity, and wood species. For a copy of the AWPA standards booklet, write to the American Wood Preservers' Association, P.O. Box 286, Woodstock, MD 21163-0286. For other wood species, contact the relevant organization.

[2] ACA, ACZA, and CCA are the most commonly available waterborne preservatives. Ammoniacal copper quat (ACQ) is also approved by AWPA as a waterborne preservative for Southern pine, Western hemlock, Hem-fir, and Douglas fir as lumber, timbers, plywood, and fence-posts.

[3] Copper naphthenate is also approved by AWPA as an oil-borne preservative for specific wood species and applications excluding saltwater use.

[4] Assay retentions are based on two assay zones—0 to 0.5 in. and 0 to 2.0 in.

[5] Not recommended where cleanliness and freedom from odor are necessary.

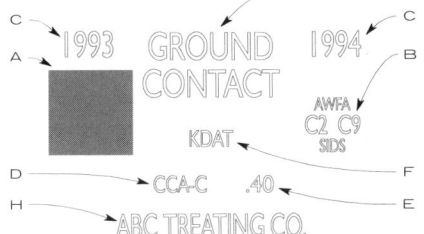

A: Trademark of inspection agency certified by the American Lumber Standard Committee (ALSC); contact the Southern Pine Council (SPC) or ALSC for a list of certified inspection agencies.
B: Applicable American Wood Preservers' Association (AWPA) standard
C: Year of treatment
D: Preservative used for treatment
E: Retention level
F: Dry or KDAT (kiln-dried after treatment), if applicable
G: Proper exposure conditions
H: Treating company and location

TYPICAL QUALITY MARK FOR TREATED LUMBER

Richard J. Vitullo, AIA; Oak Leaf Studio; Crownsville, Maryland
Southern Pine Council; Kenner, Louisiana
American Plywood Association; Tacoma, Washington

USE PRECAUTIONS FOR PRESSURE-TREATED WOOD[1]

APPLICATIONS	ORGANIC PRESERVATIVES		INORGANIC PRESERVATIVES
	CREOSOTE	PENTACHLORO-PHENOL	ARSENICALS
1. Skin contact applications	Okay[2]	Okay[2]	Okay
2. Residential interiors	No	No	Okay
3. For interior components of industrial and farm buildings that are in ground contact and subject to decay or insect attack (also see #5 below)	Okay[2]	Okay[2]	Okay
4. Laminated beams for commercial or industrial buildings	No	Okay[2]	Okay
5. Interiors of farm buildings when animals can crib (bite) or lick the treated wood	No	No	Okay
6. Agricultural farrowing or brooding facilities	No	No	Okay
7. Applications in which preservatives may become a component of food or animal feed, such as structures or containers for storing silage or food	No	No	No
8. Cutting boards or countertops for preparing food	No	No	No
9. Decks, patios, and walkways if surface is visibly clean and free from residues	Okay	Okay	Okay
10. Portions of beehives that may come into contact with honey	No	No	No
11. Applications in which treated wood can come into direct or indirect contact with drinking water for public or animal consumption	No[3]	No[3]	No[3]

[1] Based on EPA-approved consumer information sheets

[2] Must be painted with two coats of recommended sealer

[3] Okay for incidental contact such as bridges or docks

GENERAL

Building construction materials are tested for four criteria related to performance during a fire: fire resistance, flame spread, fuel contributed, and smoke developed. Fire resistance is the material's ability to resist burning while retaining its structural integrity. Flame spread measures the rate at which flames travel along the surface of a material. Fuel contributed is a measure of how much combustible matter a material furnishes to a fire. Smoke developed is a measure of the surface burning characteristics of a material.

How fire spreads through wood structures depends on the size and arrangement of wood members and the details that restrict or encourage air movement around them. Larger cross sections take longer to burn. As wood burns, it develops an outer layer of charcoal, which insulates the wood beneath and slows burning. This "char" layer proceeds through the burning wood at an average rate of $1\frac{1}{2}$ in. per hour. Various design strategies can be used to resist fire damage to a wood structure and its spread to adjacent areas, but the most important is to protect the wood members by means of coverings, coatings, or treatments.

FIRE-RETARDANT TREATMENT

Modern fire-retardant treatment (FRT) of wood consists of pressure treatment with aqueous solutions of various organic and inorganic chemicals, followed by kiln drying to reduce moisture content to 19% or less for lumber under 2 in. thick and 15% or less for plywood. All proprietary FRTs must conform to UL classifications. FRT wood is commonly used in plywood sheathing, roof trusses, rafters, floor joists, studs, staging, and shingles and shakes. Fire- retardant chemical combinations include zinc chloride, ammonium sulfates, borax or boric acid, and lesser amounts of sodium dichromate. Ammonium phosphates are no longer used because they cause rapid disintegration of wood.

Fire retardants work when fire-retardant chemicals react with the tars and gases normally produced by burning wood. The resultant carbon char acts as thermal insulation (greater than on untreated wood), slowing the rate of burning. Gases released from the FRT wood are diluted with carbon dioxide and water vapor, lessening the chance of flashover, in which wood gases are ignited by high temperatures and then explode.

FRT STANDARDS AND CLASSIFICATIONS

Interior fire retardants meet Class I ratings, which are required by code for vertical exit ways and special areas. Class II ratings are required for horizontal exit ways, but this rating is rarely reached with untreated wood. FRT lumber and plywood are recognized substitutes for noncombustible materials for insurance purposes. Many codes accept FRT wood products for a variety of applications.

Both the flame spread index and smoke-developed index give numerical scales for a material's fire classification. The flame spread index is the primary test for fire performance, according to ASTM E-84, which mandates a flame spread rating of 25 or less. In the Model Building Codes, flame spread ratings are classified as 0-25 (Class I or A), 26-75 (Class II or B), and 76-200 (Class III or C).

A smoke-developed index of 450 or less is permitted for FRT wood. The UL FR-S listing applies only to treated products with a UL-723 (ASTM E-84) flame and smoke classification not exceeding 25 in a 30-min. test. The classification applies to the species tested and does not pertain to the structures in which the materials are installed.

Fire retardants come in interior and exterior types. Interior fire retardants are used on wood trusses and studs; exterior retardants protect exterior lumber, siding, roof shakes and shingles, and scaffold planking. The latter type offers durable, nonleachable, long-term fire protection in outdoor or moist (relative humidity of 95% or greater) conditions.

Some codes count Class C or Class B FRT shingles and shakes as noncombustible materials. For wood exposed to the weather, specify exterior-type retardants that retain their protective properties under the standard rain test.

Interior Type A wood is appropriate for interior and weather-protected applications with less than 95% relative humidity. In rare instances, when relative humidity is less than 75%, Type B can be specified. Interior Type A is used when a wood with low hygroscopicity (the rate at which the chemical draws moisture from the air) is required.

FRT INTERIOR WOODWORK

Instead of solid lumber, it is often desirable to build members of treated cores clad with untreated veneers $\frac{1}{28}$ in. thick or less. Most codes discount this narrow finishing in determining the flame spread index of the wood, permit-

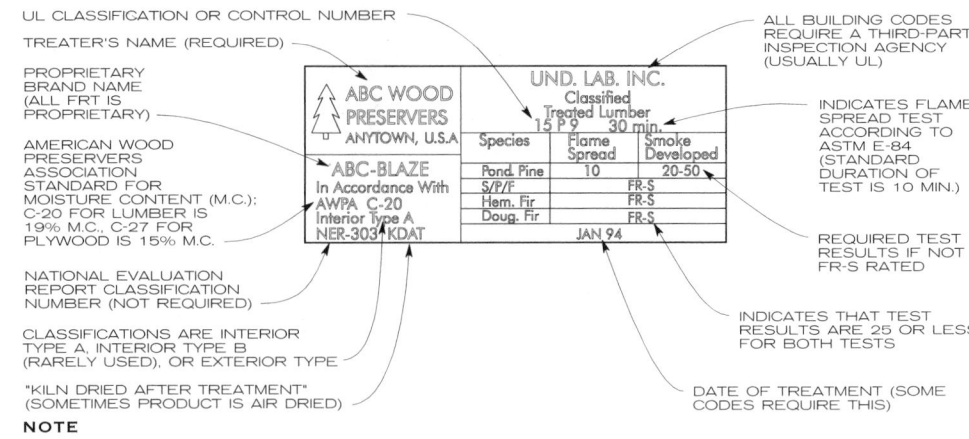

UL CLASSIFICATION OR CONTROL NUMBER

TREATER'S NAME (REQUIRED)

PROPRIETARY BRAND NAME (ALL FRT IS PROPRIETARY)

AMERICAN WOOD PRESERVERS ASSOCIATION STANDARD FOR MOISTURE CONTENT (M.C.); C-20 FOR LUMBER IS 19% M.C., C-27 FOR PLYWOOD IS 15% M.C.

NATIONAL EVALUATION REPORT CLASSIFICATION NUMBER (NOT REQUIRED)

CLASSIFICATIONS ARE INTERIOR TYPE A, INTERIOR TYPE B (RARELY USED), OR EXTERIOR TYPE

"KILN DRIED AFTER TREATMENT" (SOMETIMES PRODUCT IS AIR DRIED)

ALL BUILDING CODES REQUIRE A THIRD-PARTY INSPECTION AGENCY (USUALLY UL)

INDICATES FLAME SPREAD TEST ACCORDING TO ASTM E-84 (STANDARD DURATION OF TEST IS 10 MIN.)

REQUIRED TEST RESULTS IF NOT FR-S RATED

INDICATES THAT TEST RESULTS ARE 25 OR LESS FOR BOTH TESTS

DATE OF TREATMENT (SOME CODES REQUIRE THIS)

NOTE

Wood shakes and shingles are further classified as class B or C. Rather than stamp each piece, each bundle is tagged with an identification mark.

TYPICAL FIRE-RETARDANT TREATED WOOD IDENTIFICATION MARK

ting use of untreated wood in about 10% of the combined wall and ceiling surface area. Sizes and species currently being treated (flame spread index less than 25) include red oak and Western red cedar up to 4/4 and yellow poplar up to 8/4. Color and finishes are affected by FRTs.

FINISHING AND FINISHES

FRT lumber and plywood can be lightly sanded for cosmetic cleaning after treatment. Painting and staining are possible but not always successful, particularly transparent finishes. Test finishes for compatibility before application.

Treated lumber may be end cut, but ripping and extensive surfacing will normally void the UL label. To the extent possible, materials should be precut before treatment, otherwise a wood treater should be consulted. Treated plywood can be cut in either direction without loss of fire protection.

Intumescent coatings are sometimes used to reduce flammability of wood surfaces in both opaque and transparent finishes. Under high heat, these coatings expand or foam, creating an insulating effect that reduces flame spread.

Check local codes before specifying these coatings because they tend to be less durable, softer, and more hygroscopic than standard finishes.

NOTES

1. These standards apply to FRT wood: ASTM E-84, ASTM D-2898, ASTM D-3201, ASTM E-108, AWPA C-20, AWPA C-27, and ULI Building Materials Directory (current edition). For more information, contact the American Wood Preservers' Association (AWPA), American Wood Preservers' Institute, USDA Forest Service, Southern Forest Products Association, Western Wood Preservers Institute, and American Forest and Paper Association.

2. FRT wood has increased weight and decreased strength; consult a structural engineer and the wood treater for actual design values for structural applications.

3. FRT wood fasteners must be hot-dipped, zinc-coated galvanized stainless steel, silicon bronze, or copper; other materials deteriorate upon contact with FRT chemicals.

4. The smoke-developed index for the products listed in the flame spread index remained below 450, the limiting value used in most building codes.

FLAME SPREAD INDEX

MATERIAL[1]		ASTM E-84 FLAME SPREAD	SOURCE[2]
Lumber	Birch, yellow	105-110	UL
	Cedar, Western red	70	HPMA
	Douglas fir	70-100	UL
	Maple (flooring)	104	CWC
	Oak, red or white	100	UL
	Pine, Ponderosa	105-230[3]	UL
	Pine, Southern yellow	130-195	UL
	Poplar	170-185	UL
	Redwood	65	CRA
	Spruce, Northern	65	UL
Softwood plywood (Exterior glue)	Douglas fir, $\frac{1}{4}$"	118	CWC
	Douglas fir, $\frac{5}{8}$"	95	APA
	Southern pine, $\frac{1}{4}$"	95-110	APA
Hardwood plywood	Lauan, $\frac{1}{4}$"	150	HPMA
Particleboard	$\frac{1}{2}$" 47 lb/cu ft	156	NBS
	$\frac{5}{8}$" 44 lb/cu ft	153	NBS
Flakeboard	Red oak, $\frac{1}{2}$", 42-47 lb/cu ft (four types)	71-189	FPL
Shakes	Western red cedar, $\frac{1}{2}$"	69	HPMA
Shingles	Western red cedar, $\frac{1}{2}$"	49	HPMA

[1] Unless indicated, thickness of material is 1 in. nominal.

[2] Sources: APA—American Plywood Association; CRA— California Redwood Association; CWC—Canadian Wood Council; FPL—USDA Forest Products Laboratory; HPMA—Hardwood Plywood Manufacturers Associa-

FLAME SPREAD INDEX OF FACTORY-FINISHED PRODUCTS

MATERIAL			ASTM E-84 FLAME SPREAD[4]
Particleboard	$\frac{1}{32}$"	Factory finish printed	118-178
	$\frac{1}{2}$"	Paper overlay	175
	$\frac{5}{8}$"	Vinyl overlay	100
Medium-density fiberboard (MDF)	$\frac{3}{16}$"	Factory finish printed	167
Hardboard	$\frac{1}{8}$"	Factory finish printed	158-194
		Paper overlay	155-166
Flakeboard	Aromatic cedar, $\frac{3}{16}$"		156
Hardwood plywood	Aspen, $\frac{1}{4}$"	Factory finished	196
	Birch, $\frac{5}{32}$"	Factory finished	160-195
	Cherry, $\frac{1}{4}$"	Factory finished	160
	Hickory, $\frac{1}{4}$"	Factory finished	140
	Lauan, $\frac{1}{4}$"	Factory finish printed	99-141
	Maple, $\frac{1}{4}$"	Factory finished	155
	Oak, $\frac{1}{4}$"	Factory finished	125-185
	Pine, $\frac{1}{4}$"	Factory finished	120-140
	Walnut, $\frac{1}{4}$"	Factory finished	138-160

tion; NBS—National Bureau of Standards; UL—Underwriters Laboratories.

[3] Average of 18 tests was 154 with three values over 200.

[4] Hardwood Plywood Manufacturers Association test records

Richard J. Vitullo, AIA; Oak Leaf Studio; Crownsville, Maryland

WOOD TREATMENT

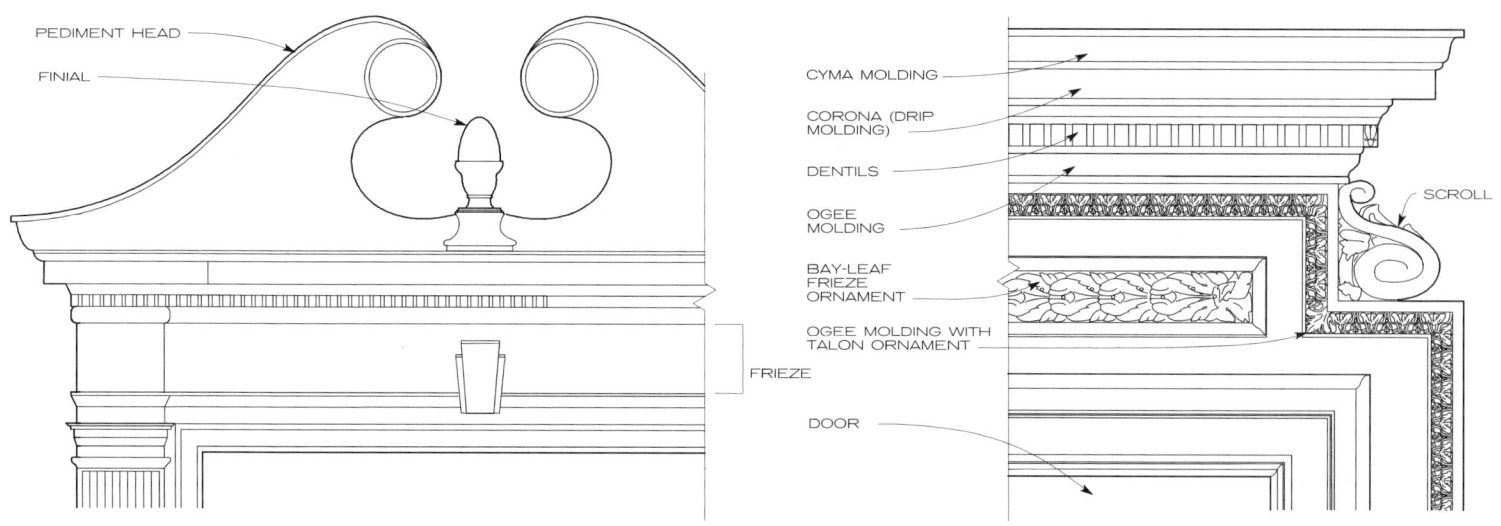

PEDIMENT HEAD

FINIAL

CYMA MOLDING

CORONA (DRIP MOLDING)

DENTILS

OGEE MOLDING

BAY-LEAF FRIEZE ORNAMENT

OGEE MOLDING WITH TALON ORNAMENT

SCROLL

FRIEZE

DOOR

OVERDOOR DETAILS

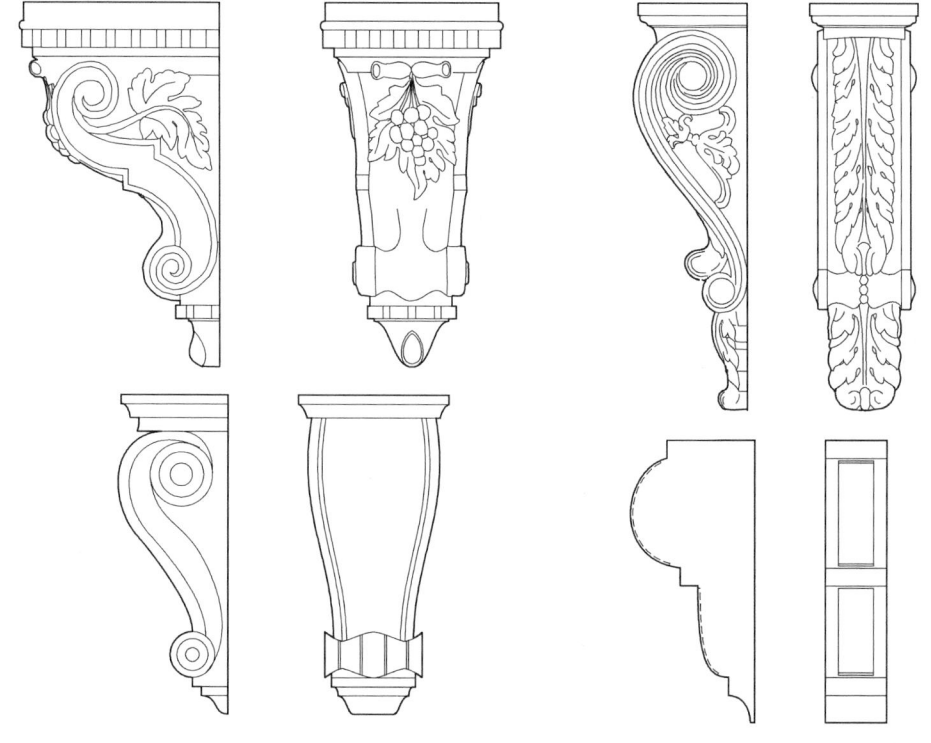

WOOD CORBEL (BRACKET)

CORNICE

FRIEZE WITH LEAF ORNAMENTS

ARCHITRAVE

PILASTER CAPITAL

FLUTED PILASTER

WOOD CORBELS

GENERAL

Woodwork is considered an ornament when it has a special or unique design that does not fall within the standard categories of architectural woodwork as defined by the Architectural Woodwork Institute.

Some typical uses for ornamental wood include pediment heads, mantels, ornamental grilles, fluted pilasters, cupolas, finials, medallions, corbels, balusters, posts, and columns. Within the classification of ornamental wood are combinations of flat or molded solid lumber, or cored lumber components with wood veneer faces with, or without, the addition of moldings. All joinings between ornamental members should be designed for functional as well as decorative purposes.

Wood ornamentation is an art that can take shape in an almost infinite number of forms and designs, limited only by the mechanical production constraints of woodworking shops. "Wood" ornaments can also be produced in larger quantities (in molds) with the synthetic material polyurethane. Once cured, the polyurethane can be painted and substituted for the wood ornaments.

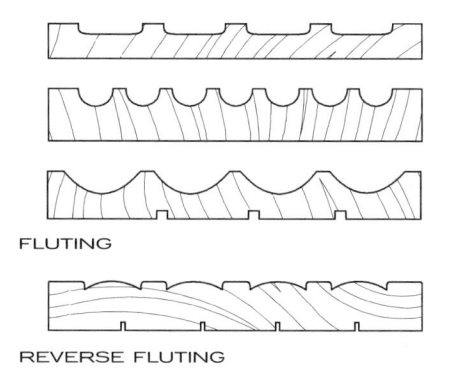

FLUTING

REVERSE FLUTING

FLUTING SECTIONS

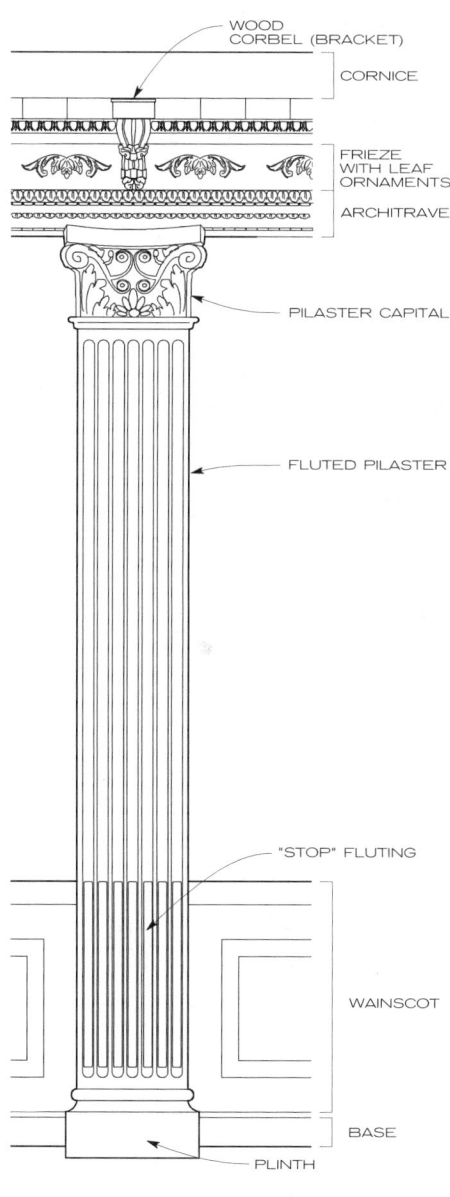

"STOP" FLUTING

WAINSCOT

BASE

PLINTH

ORNAMENTAL WOOD PILASTER

Richard J. Vitullo, AIA; Oak Leaf Studio; Crownsville, Maryland

FREIZE ORNAMENTS

MISCELLANEOUS ORNAMENTS

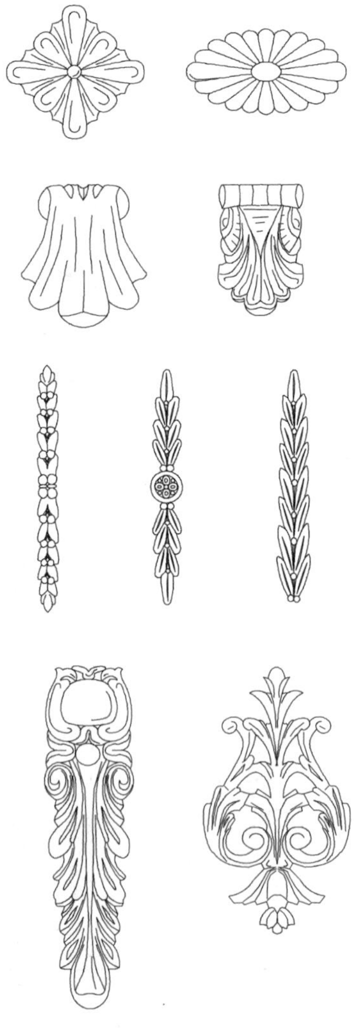

MISCELLANEOUS ORNAMENTS

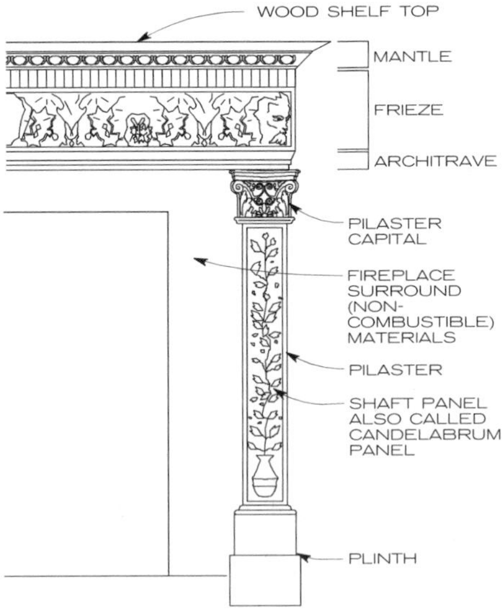

WOOD SHELF TOP

MANTLE

FRIEZE

ARCHITRAVE

PILASTER CAPITAL

FIREPLACE SURROUND (NON-COMBUSTIBLE) MATERIALS

PILASTER

SHAFT PANEL ALSO CALLED CANDELABRUM PANEL

PLINTH

FIREPLACE MANTEL

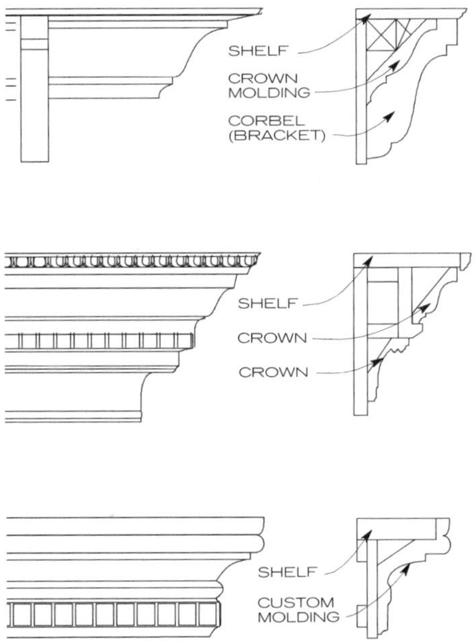

SHELF

CROWN MOLDING

CORBEL (BRACKET)

SHELF

CROWN

CROWN

SHELF

CUSTOM MOLDING

MANTELS

PINEAPPLE   ACORN   ACORN

FINIALS

Richard J. Vitullo, AIA; Oak Leaf Studio; Crownsville, Maryland

 ARCHITECTURAL WOODWORK

GENERAL

Interior trim is a generally decorative treatment applied after wall, floor, and ceiling finishes have been installed. It can be made of flat or molded wood from single pieces of wood or built-up pieces that give a more complex and decorative appearance. Interior trim conceals joints between different materials and blocks air infiltration through walls, which typically is greatest at material joints. Interior trim also frames wall and ceiling openings (door and window/skylight trim), defines planar edges (crown and base molding), and acts as a visual divider between dissimilar materials (chair rail).

The Architectural Woodwork Institute differentiates wood trim according to its length. Standing wood trim is trim that can be accommodated easily with single lengths of wood (depending on species), such as crown moldings, fascias, soffits, chair rails, baseboards, and shoe moldings. Running trim is usually made up of finger-jointed wood to achieve the lengths customarily needed for this type of trim.

NOTES

1. Blocking that receives moldings should be set plumb, level, true, and straight, with no distortion, and should be provided for full surface contact. Attach blocking to substrates with nails, screws, or bolts.

2. Woodwork should be stored in a dry, ventilated space. If this is not possible, seal the ends of all pieces as soon as possible. Moldings should be at optimum moisture content at the time of installation and should be allowed to acclimate to project conditions before installation.

3. Joints in adjacent and related members should be staggered. Cope at inside corners and miter at outside corners to produce tight-fitting joints with full surface contact throughout the length of the joint; use scarf joints (face mitered) for end-to-end joints in trim.

4. Blind nail where possible, and use finishing nails in exposed areas. Predrill as required to eliminate splitting; set exposed nail heads for filling.

5. Most flat trim like baseboards and casing has a ploughed or relieved back, which gives wide trim a degree of flexibility, allowing it to fit snugly against a wall surface.

6. The molding profiles illustrated are a small sampling of those available from most millwork shops. Custom profiles should be shown on drawings full size. Dimensions given are for typical stock molding profiles.

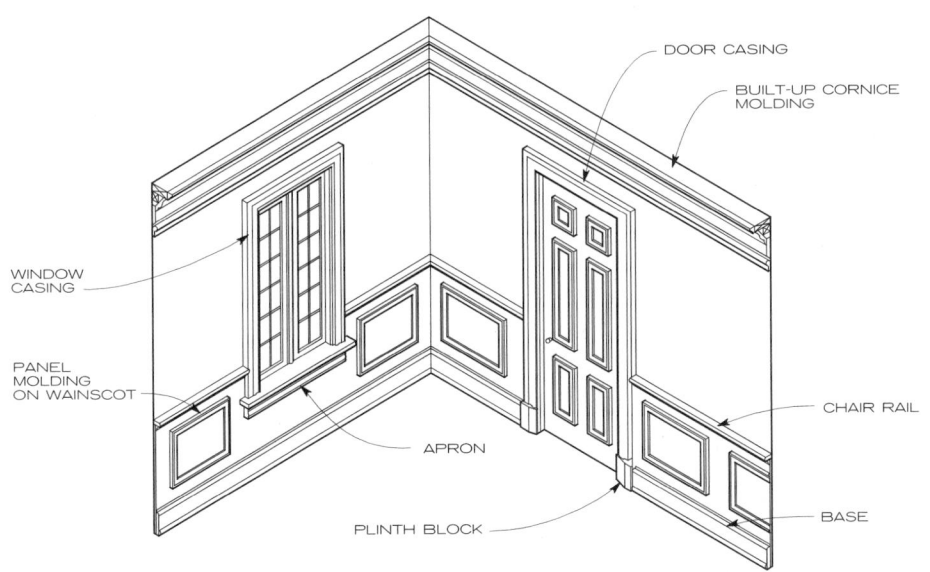

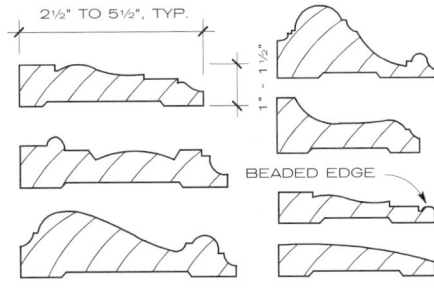

NOTE

Casings are used to finish the joint between the window or door head and side jambs and wall finish. Often a casing used at windows is also used as apron material, with the wide side toward the stool.

CASINGS

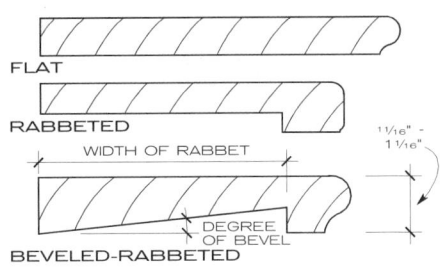

NOTE

Stools are used as interior caps on windowsills and receive casing from above and apron below. They are specified by width of rabbet and degree of bevel.

STOOLS

TYPICAL WOOD TRIM AND MOLDINGS

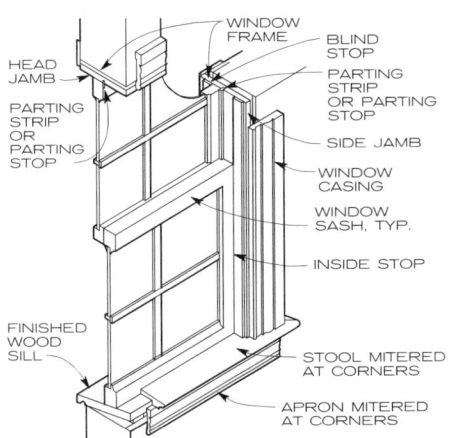

TYPICAL WINDOW TRIM

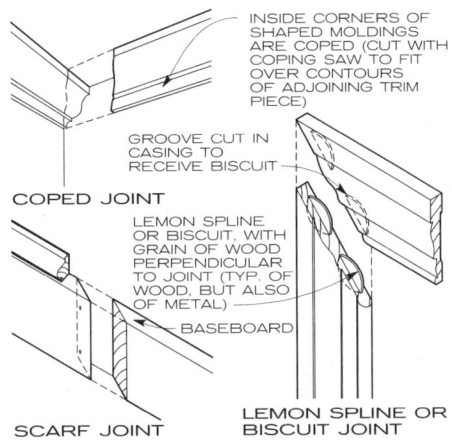

MOLDING CONNECTION DETAILS

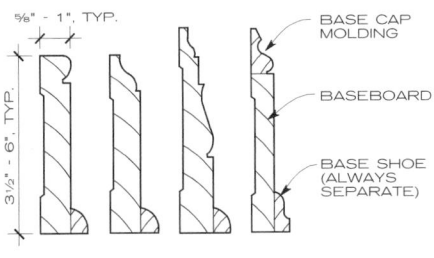

NOTE

Baseboards and base moldings are used at the juncture of wall and floor exclusively. Baseboard may be one piece (with integral base cap) or flat with optional base cap. Separate caps and shoes are flexible and facilitate a close fit to uneven wall and floor surfaces.

TYPICAL CORNICE TRIM

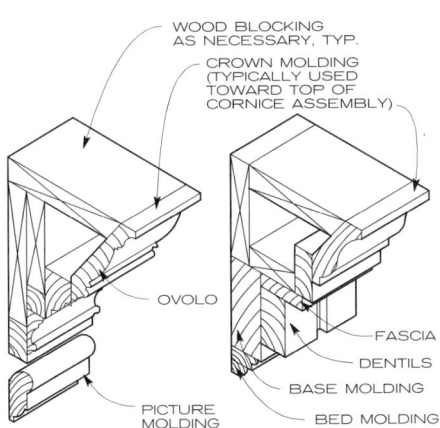

TYPICAL DOOR AND BASE TRIM

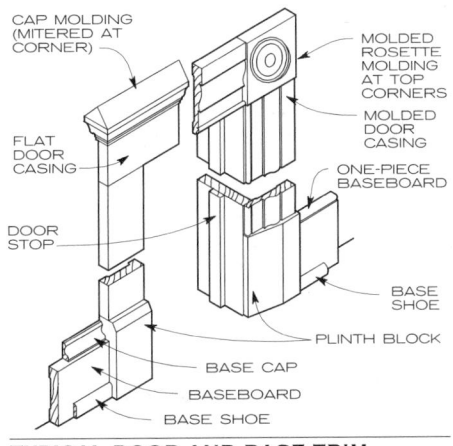

BASEBOARD AND BASE MOLDINGS

Richard J. Vitullo, AIA; Oak Leaf Studio; Crownsville, Maryland

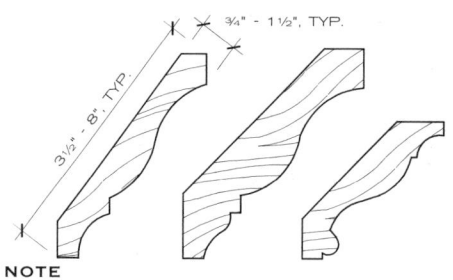

NOTE

Crown moldings are applied alone at the joint between wall and ceiling or together with other moldings in a built-up cornice, typically toward the top of the cornice assembly; measured edge to edge.

CROWN MOLDINGS

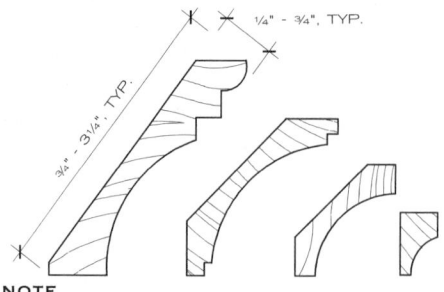

NOTE

Cove moldings are used at inside corners, such as wall-to-wall or ceiling-to-wall.

COVE MOLDINGS

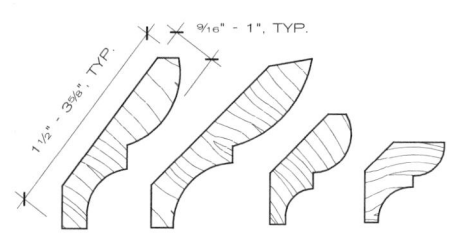

NOTE

Bed moldings are used at the bottom of built-up cornices and at other vertical-to-horizontal junctures.

BED MOLDINGS

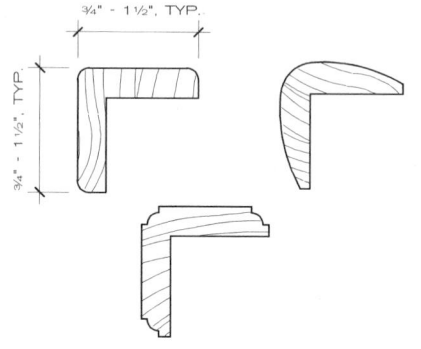

NOTE

This molding is used on outside corners.

CORNERS

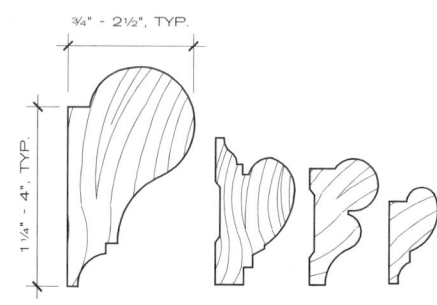

NOTE

Often integrated with cornices, picture moldings are used as continuous projecting supports for picture hooks. Custom-made hooks are available to fit these profiles.

PICTURE MOLDINGS

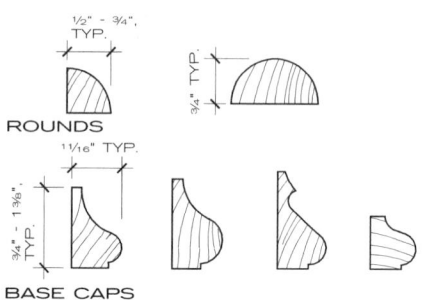

ROUNDS

BASE CAPS

NOTES

1. Half-rounds are used to conceal vertical and horizontal joints. Quarter-rounds are used at inside corners and as base shoe.

2. Base caps are applied at the top of the baseboard, flush against the wall.

BASE CAPS AND ROUNDS

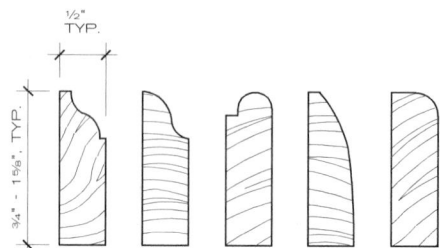

NOTE

Stops are used at jambs to guide windows and stop doors.

STOPS

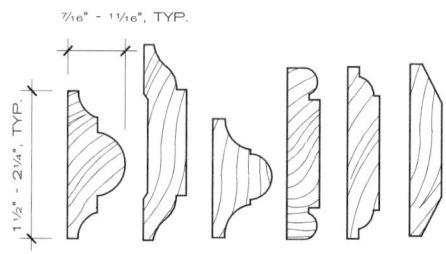

NOTE

These moldings are used in panels to conceal joints, over window jamb edges in a multiple-opening window, and as astragals at middle joints of double-leaf doors.

PANEL STRIPS, BATTENS, AND ASTRAGALS

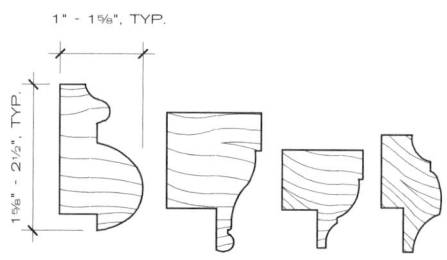

NOTE

Backbands are applied as trim at the outer edge of door jamb and head, among other uses.

BACKBANDS

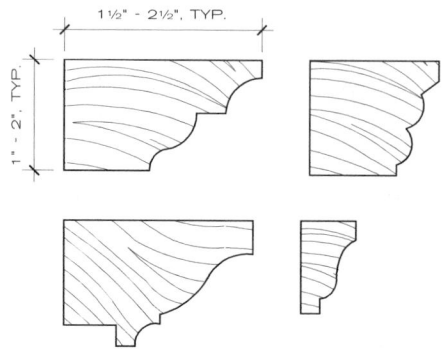

NOTE

Cap or rake moldings are used at head of door and window trim and at top of wainscots.

CAP OR RAKE MOLDINGS

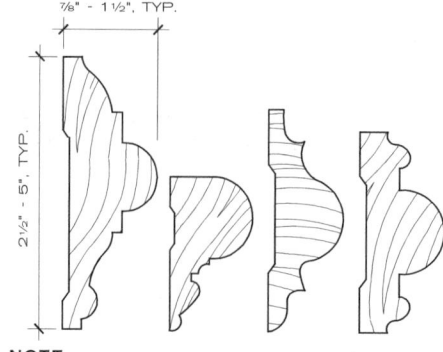

NOTE

Chair rails were originally meant to protect the wall surface from chair backs; applied typically $1/3$ up from the floor, either alone or atop wainscot paneling.

CHAIR RAILS

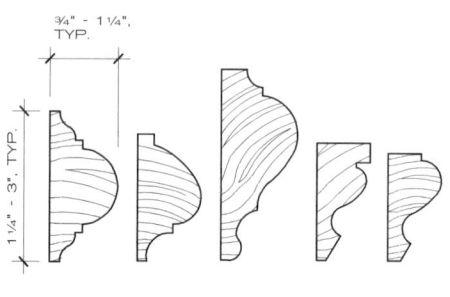

NOTE

Panel moldings are typically used as door and wainscot trim, mitered together and arranged in rectangles.

PANEL MOLDINGS

Richard J. Vitullo, AIA; Oak Leaf Studio; Crownsville, Maryland

 ARCHITECTURAL WOODWORK

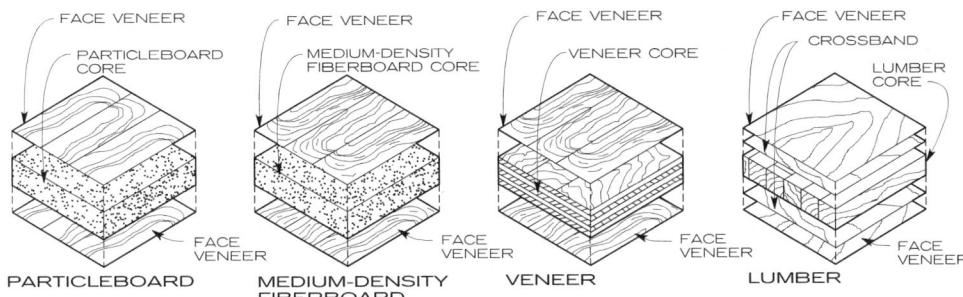

PARTICLEBOARD

MEDIUM-DENSITY FIBERBOARD

VENEER

LUMBER

HARDWOOD PLYWOOD CORE TYPES

GENERAL

Architectural wood panels are made from wood material that is cut or formed into sheet products that are referred to as the "panel core." These sheets are used alone (with or without a finish) or laminated together with other veneer products to make plywood. A great variety of panels are manufactured using different core materials and adhesives or binders and various forming techniques and surface treatments. The characteristics of the panels vary with these differences in material and construction.

PANEL CORE TYPES

Panel cores, which serve as the substrate for laminates and veneers on the outer surface, are classified by ingredients and methods of manufacture. The following types of panel cores are suitable for architectural use:

INDUSTRIAL GRADE PARTICLEBOARD CORE

This core type is made by using heat and pressure to bond together synthetic resin or binder and wood particles of various sizes. Employed in a wide variety of architectural woodwork applications, industrial grade particleboard is especially well suited as a substrate for high-quality veneers and decorative laminates. When used as panels without any surface layers, the product is called particleboard. When used with wood veneer on the surface, the panels are referred to as particle-core plywood. Particleboard core classified by density or weight per cubic ft falls into three categories:

1. Low density—less than 40 lb per cubic ft (640 kg per cubic meter)
2. Medium density—40 to 50 lb per cubic ft (640 to 800 kg per cubic meter)
3. High density—more than 50 lb per cubic ft (800 kg per cubic meter)

MOISTURE-RESISTANT PARTICLEBOARD CORE

Some medium-density industrial particleboard is bonded with phenolic resins, which makes it more resistant to swelling when exposed to moisture. Phenolic resins, unlike urea resins, do not emit significant quantities of formaldehyde. The most common grades are type 2-M-2 (M-2 exterior glue) and 2-M-3 (M-3 exterior glue).

FIRE-RETARDANT PARTICLEBOARD CORE

Medium-density industrial particleboard may be treated during manufacture to carry a UL Class 1 fire rating stamp (flame spread 20, smoke developed 25). This material can be used as substrate for paneling requiring a Class 1 rating.

MEDIUM-DENSITY FIBERBOARD (MDF) CORE

MDF is made from wood particles reduced to fibers in a moderate-pressure steam vessel, combined with resin, and bonded together under heat and pressure. The surface is flat, smooth, uniform, dense, and free of knots or grain pattern. MDF is useful as a substrate for paint, thin overlay materials, veneers, and decorative laminates. The homogeneous edge allows machining and paint finishes. MDF is one of the most stable mat-formed panel products and is widely used as an architectural panel.

MOISTURE-RESISTANT MDF CORE

Some MDF is bonded with an exterior resin to produce a highly water-resistant product.

VENEER CORE (PLYWOOD)

This panel product is made up of alternating layers of thin veneer and is commonly known as plywood. Adhesive is placed between the layers, and the panels are pressed until the adhesive is set; heat is often used to speed the cure. The two outside layers, often selected for species, grain, and appearance, are called the face veneers.

HARDBOARD CORE

Hardboard is made of interfelted fibers consolidated under heat and pressure to a density of 31 lb per cubic ft or more. Available with either one side (S1S) or two sides (S2S) smooth, hardboard is often used for casework backs, drawer bottoms, and divider panels. Architectural woodworkers typically use two types of hardboard core: standard (untempered) and tempered, which is standard hardboard that has been subjected to a curing treatment to increase its stiffness, hardness, and weight.

PLYWOOD TYPES

The term "plywood" means a panel product made of three or more layers (plies) of wood or wood products (veneers or overlays and/or core materials) that have been laminated into a single sheet (panel). Plywood falls into two groups according to materials and manufacturing:

HARDWOOD PLYWOOD panels are made from hardwood or decorative softwood veneers over a core material such as medium-density particleboard, medium-density fiberboard, or low-density lumber.

SOFTWOOD PLYWOOD panels are made with softwood face veneers and are seldom incorporated into finished architectural woodworking projects because of the instability of the core material and core voids.

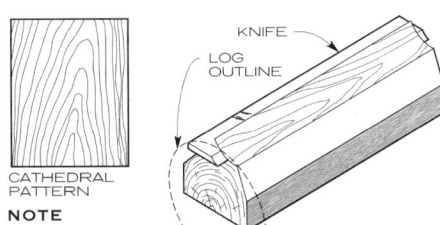

NOTE

This is the slicing method most often used to produce veneers for high-quality architectural woodworking. Slicing is done parallel to a line through the center of the log. A combination of cathedral and straight-grain patterns results, with a natural progression of pattern from leaf to leaf.

PLAIN-SLICED (FLAT-SLICED) VENEER

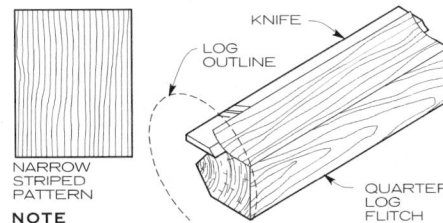

NOTE

Quarter slicing, roughly parallel to a radius line through the log segment, simulates the quarter-sawing process used with solid lumber. In many species the individual leaves are narrow as a result. A series of stripes is produced, varying in density and thickness among species. "Flake" is a characteristic of this slicing method in red and white oak.

QUARTER-SLICED VENEER

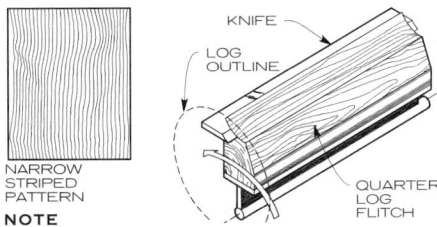

NOTE

Rift veneers are produced most often in red and white oak, rarely in other species. Note that rift veneers and rift-sawn solid lumber are produced so differently that a "match" between them is highly unlikely. In both cases the cutting is done slightly off the radius lines, minimizing the "flake" associated with quarter slicing.

RIFT-SLICED (RIFT-CUT) VENEER

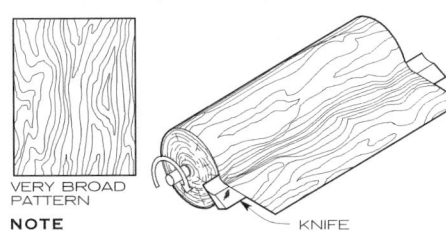

NOTE

To create rotary-cut veneers, the log is center mounted on a lathe and "peeled" along the path of the growth rings, like unwinding a roll of paper. This provides a bold, random appearance. Rotary-cut veneers vary in width, and matching at veneer joints is extremely difficult. Almost all softwood veneers are cut this way. Rotary-cut veneers are the least useful in fine architectural woodwork.

ROTARY-CUT VENEER

CHARACTERISTICS OF CORE MATERIAL PERFORMANCE

PANEL TYPE	FLATNESS	VISUAL EDGE QUALITY	SURFACE UNIFORMITY	DIMENSIONAL STABILITY	SCREW HOLDING	BENDING STRENGTH	AVAILABILITY
Industrial particleboard core (medium-density)	Excellent	Good	Excellent	Fair	Fair	Good	Ready
Medium-density fiberboard core (MDF)	Excellent	Excellent	Excellent	Fair	Good	Good	Ready
Veneer core–all hardwood	Fair	Good	Good	Excellent	Excellent	Excellent	Ready
Veneer core–all softwood	Fair	Good	Fair	Excellent	Excellent	Excellent	Ready
Lumber core–hardwood or softwood	Good	Good	Good	Good	Excellent	Excellent	Limited
Standard hardboard core	Excellent	Excellent	Excellent	Fair	Good	Good	Ready
Tempered hardboard core	Excellent	Good	Good	Good	Good	Good	Limited
Moisture-resistant particleboard core	Excellent	Good	Good	Fair	Fair	Good	Limited
Moisture-resistant MDF core	Excellent	Excellent	Good	Fair	Good	Good	Limited
Fire-resistant particleboard core	Excellent	Fair	Good	Fair	Fair	Good	Limited

NOTE

Characteristics of core material performance are influenced by the grade and thickness of the core and specific gravity of the core species. Visual edge quality is rated before treatment with edge bands or fillers and, for lumber core, assumes the use of "clear edge" grade. Surface uniformity is directly related to the performance of fine veneers placed over the surface. Dimensional stability is usually related to exposure to wide variations in relative humidity. Screw holding and bending strength are influenced by proper design and engineering.

Richard J. Vitullo, AIA; Oak Leaf Studio; Crownsville, Maryland
Architectural Woodwork Institute; Centreville, Virginia

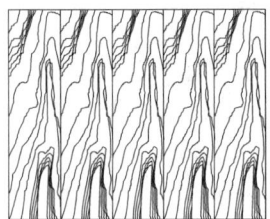

SLIP MATCH

BOOK MATCH

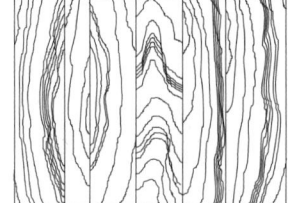

RANDOM MATCH

RUNNING MATCH

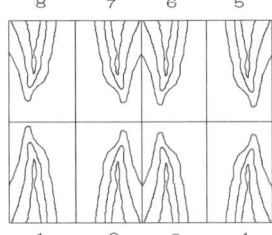

PANEL END MATCH

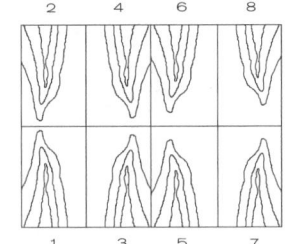

ARCHITECTURAL END MATCH

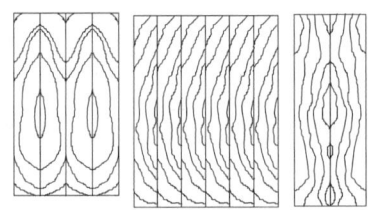

BALANCE AND CENTER MATCH

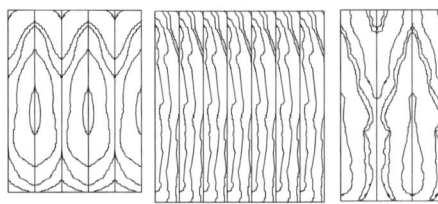

BALANCE MATCH

VENEER MATCH TYPES

GENERAL CHARACTERISTICS OF WOOD VENEER SPECIES

SPECIES		WIDTH TO (IN.)	LENGTH (FT)	FLITCH SIZE	COST[1]	AVAILABILITY
Mahogany	Plain sliced Honduras mahogany	18	12	Large	Moderate	Good
	Quartered Honduras mahogany	12	12	Large	High	Moderate
	Plain sliced African mahogany	18	12	Large	Moderate	Moderate
	Quartered African mahogany	12	12	Large	High	Good
Ash	Plain sliced American white ash	12	10	Medium	Moderate	Good
	Quartered American white ash	8	12	Small	High	Good
	Quartered or plain sliced European ash	6, 10	10	Medium	High	Limited
Anegre	Quartered or plain sliced anegre	6, 12	12	Large	High	Good
Avodire	Quartered avodire	10	10	Large	High	Limited
Cherry	Plain sliced American cherry	12	11	Medium	Moderate	Good
	Quartered American cherry	4	10	Very small	High	Moderate
Birch	Rotary cut birch (natural)	48	10	Large	Low	Good
	Rotary cut birch (select red or white)	36	10	Medium	Moderate	Moderate
	Plain sliced birch (natural)	10	10	Small	Moderate	Limited
	Plain sliced birch (select red or white)	5	10	Small	High	Limited
Butternut	Plain sliced butternut	12	10	Medium	High	Limited
Makore	Quartered or plain sliced makore	6, 12	12	Large	High	Good
Maple	Pl. sl. (half round) American maple	12	10	Medium	Moderate	Good[2]
	Rotary bird's-eye maple	20	10	Medium	Very high	Good
Oak	Plain sliced English brown oak	12	10	Medium	Very high	Limited
	Quartered English brown oak	10	10	Medium	Very high	Limited
	Plain sliced American red oak	16	12	Large	Moderate	Good
	Quartered American red oak	8	10	Small	Moderate	Good
	Rift sliced American red oak	10	10	Medium	Moderate	Good
	Comb grain rift American red oak	8	10	Small	Very high	Limited
	Plain sliced American white oak	16	12	Medium	Moderate	Good
	Quartered American white oak	8	10	Small	Moderate	Good
	Rift sliced American white oak	8	10	Medium	High	Good
	Comb grain rift American white oak	8	10	Small	Very high	Limited
Hickory or Pecan	Plain sliced American hickory or pecan	12	10	Small	Moderate	Good
Sapele	Quartered or plain sliced sapele	6, 12	12	Large	High	Good
Sycamore	Plain sliced English sycamore	10	10	Medium	Very high	Limited
	Quartered English sycamore	6	10	Medium	Very high	Limited
Teak	Plain sliced teak	16	12	Large	Very high	Limited[3]
	Quartered teak	12	12	Medium	Very high	Limited[3]
Walnut	Plain sliced American walnut	12	12	Medium	Moderate	Good
	Quarter sliced American walnut	6	10	Very small	High	Rare

[1]Cost reflects raw veneer costs weighted for waste or yield characteristics and degree of labor difficulty.

[2]Seasonal factors may affect availability.

[3]Availability of blond teak is very rare.

NOTE

When quartered or plain sliced are listed on the same line, the width dimensions are listed with quartered first and plain sliced second.

MATCHING BETWEEN ADJACENT VENEER LEAVES

It is possible to achieve certain visual effects by the manner in which the leaves are arranged. Rotary cut veneers are difficult to match, therefore most matching is done with sliced veneers. Matching of adjacent veneer leaves must be specified. Consult your AWI woodworker for choices.

BOOK MATCHING

Book matching is the most commonly used match in the industry. In it, every other piece of veneer is reversed so adjacent pieces (leaves) are "opened" like the pages of a book. Because the "tight" and "loose" faces alternate in adjacent leaves, they reflect light and accept stain differently. The veneer joints match, creating a symmetrical pattern that yields maximum continuity of grain.

SLIP MATCHING

Adjoining leaves are placed (slipped out) in sequence without being turned, thus all the same face sides are exposed. The grain figure repeats but joints do not show grain match. All faces have some light refraction.

END MATCHING

End matching is often used to extend the apparent length of available veneers for high wall panels and long conference tables. End matching occurs in two types:

ARCHITECTURAL END MATCH: Leaves are individually book or slip matched, alternating end-to-end and side-to-side. Architectural end matching yields the best continuous grain patterns for length as well as width.

PANEL END MATCH: Leaves are book or slip matched on panel subassemblies, with sequenced subassemblies end matched, resulting in some modest cost savings on projects where applicable. For most species, panel end matching yields a pleasing, blended appearance and grain continuity.

RANDOM MATCHING

Veneer leaves are placed next to each other in a random order and orientation, producing a casual board-by-board effect in many species. Conscious effort is made to mismatch the grain at joints.

RUNNING MATCHING

Each panel face is assembled from as many veneer leaves as necessary. This often results in an asymmetrical appearance, with some veneer leaves of unequal width.

BALANCE MATCHING

Each panel face is assembled from an odd or even number of veneer leaves of uniform width before edge trimming.

BALANCE AND CENTER MATCHING

Each panel face is assembled from an even number of veneer leaves of uniform width before edge trimming. Thus, there is a veneer joint in the center of the panel, producing horizontal symmetry.

Richard J. Vitullo, AIA; Oak Leaf Studio; Crownsville, Maryland
Architectural Woodwork Institute; Centreville, Virginia

8-PIECE SUNBURST

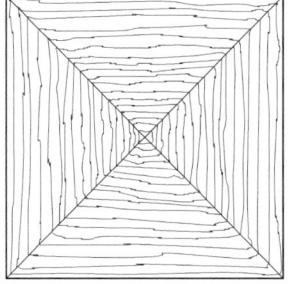
BOX MATCH

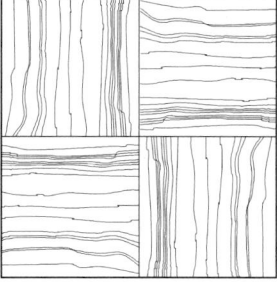
PARQUET MATCH

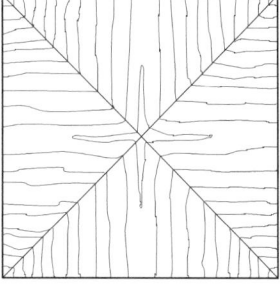
REVERSE OR END GRAIN BOX

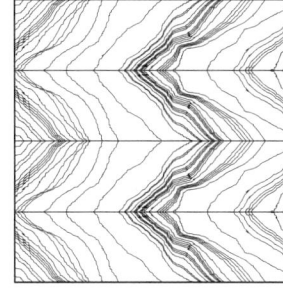
HERRINGBONE

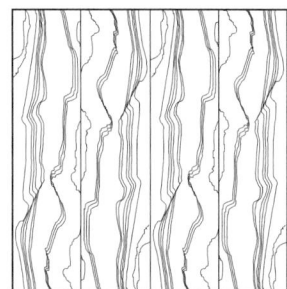
SWING MATCH

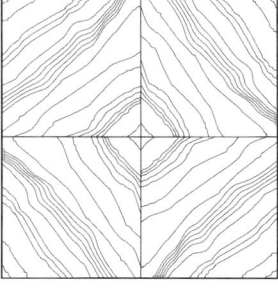
DIAMOND

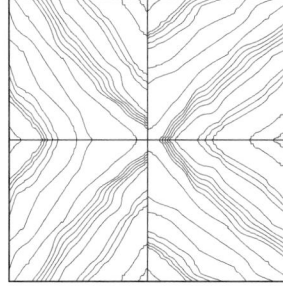
REVERSE DIAMOND

SKETCH FACE

NOTE

During specification, use both names and illustrations to define the desired effect, as names vary by region for these matching techniques.

SPECIAL WOOD VENEER MATCHING OPTIONS

COMMON FACE VENEER PATTERNS OF SELECTED COMMERCIAL SPECIES

PRIMARY COMMERCIAL HARDWOOD SPECIES	FACE VENEER PATTERNS[1]			
	PLAIN SLICED (FLAT CUT)	QUARTER CUT	RIFT CUT AND COMB GRAIN	ROTARY CUT
Ash	Yes	Yes	—	Yes
Birch	Yes	—	—	Yes
Cherry	Yes	Yes	—	Yes
Hickory	Yes	—	—	Yes
Lauan	—	Yes	—	Yes
Mahogany (African)	Yes	Yes	—	Yes
Mahogany (Honduras)	Yes	Yes	—	Yes
Maple	Yes	Yes	—	Yes
Meranti	—	Yes	—	Yes
Oak (red)	Yes	Yes	Yes	Yes
Oak (white)	Yes	Yes	Yes	Yes
Pecan	Yes	—	—	Yes
Walnut (black)	Yes	Yes	—	Yes
Yellow poplar	Yes	—	—	Yes
Typical methods of cutting[2]	Plain slicing or half-round on rotary lathe	Quarter slicing	Offset quarter on rotary lathe	Rotary lathe

[1] The headings above refer to the face veneer pattern, not to the method of cutting. Face veneer patterns other than those listed are obtainable by special order.

[2] The method of cutting for a given face veneer pattern shall be at mill option unless otherwise specified by the buyer in an explicit manner to avoid the possibility of misunderstanding. For example, plain-sliced veneer cut on a vertical slicer or plain-sliced veneer cut on a half-round rotary lathe could be specified.

Richard J. Vitullo, AIA; Oak Leaf Studio; Crownsville, Maryland
Architectural Woodwork Institute; Centreville, Virginia
Chart reprinted with permission from the Hardwood Plywood and Veneer Association

FACING MATERIAL TYPES

Wood product substrates are classified in two main facing material categories: decorative laminates/overlays and wood veneers.

DECORATIVE LAMINATES/OVERLAYS

This finish surface category can be broken down into the following broad groups:

HIGH-PRESSURE DECORATIVE LAMINATES are formed under heat and pressure from resin-impregnated kraft paper substrates with decorative plastic face materials and a clear protective top sheet. This assembly, commonly called plastic laminate, offers resistance to wear and many stains and chemicals. Common uses include casework exteriors, countertops, and wall paneling.

THERMALLY FUSED DECORATIVE PANELS are flat pressed from a thermoset polyester or melamine resin-impregnated web, and most have been prelaminated to industrial particleboard or medium-density fiberboard substrates when they arrive at the woodwork fabricator. Performance is similar to that of high-pressure decorative laminates. Common uses include casework interiors, furniture, shelving, display materials, and decorative paneling.

MEDIUM-DENSITY OVERLAYS are made from pressed resin-impregnated paper overlays and are highly resistant to moisture. They are available applied to cores suitable for both interior and exterior uses. The seamless panel face and uniform density offer a sound base for opaque finishes and paint.

VINYL FILMS, FOILS, AND LOW BASIS WEIGHT PAPERS are decorative facing materials that, although they have limited use in custom architectural woodworking, are suitable for some installations.

WOOD VENEERS

Wood veneers are produced in a variety of industry standard thicknesses. The slicing process is controlled by a number of variables, but the thickness of the veneer has little bearing on the quality of the end product.

There are two types of veneers, hardwood and softwood. Hardwood veneers are available in many domestic and imported wood species and are normally plain sliced, but certain species can be rift sliced, quarter sliced, or rotary cut. Softwood veneers are usually sliced from Douglas fir, but pine and other softwoods are available. Most softwood veneer is rotary cut, but plain-sliced and rift-sliced (vertical grain) softwoods can be obtained with a special order.

Most veneers are taken from large trees, but some are sliced from fast-growing trees, dyed, and reglued in molds to create "grain" patterns. The color of these reconstituted veneers is established during manufacture because the high percentage of glue line resists later staining.

The manner in which a log segment is cut with relation to the annual rings of the tree determines the appearance of the veneer. Individual pieces of veneer, referred to as "leaves," are kept in the order in which they were sliced for reference during installation. The group of leaves from one slicing is called a "flitch" and is identified by a number and the gross square feet it contains. The faces of the leaves with relation to their position in the log are identified as the "tight face" (toward the outside of the log) and the "loose face" (toward the inside or heart of the log).

NOTES

1. To achieve balanced construction, panel products should be absolutely symmetrical from the center line. Materials used on either side should contract and expand or exhibit moisture permeability at the same rate as the veneer.

2. In panel construction, the thinner the facing material, the less force it can generate to cause warping. The thicker the substrate, the more it can resist a warping movement or force.

3. Wood veneer standards: For hardwood plywood, the face veneer characteristics of the Hardwood Plywood and Veneer Association (HPVA) have generally been adapted for use. These face grades apply to custom architectural woodwork.

4. Flame spread factors: The fire rating of the core material determines the rating of the assembled panel. Fire-retardant veneered panels must have a fire-retardant core. Particleboard core is available with a Class I (Class A) rating, but MDF is not currently available with a fire rating. Existing building codes, except where locally amended, provide that facing materials $1/_{28}$ in. or thinner are not considered in determining the flame spread rating of the panel. For more information, refer to the Architectural Woodwork Institute guide "Fire Code Summary."

ARCHITECTURAL WOODWORK

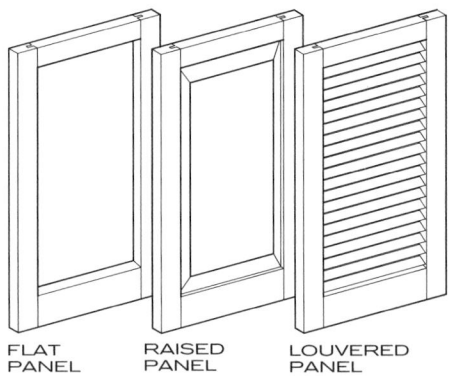

FLAT PANEL   RAISED PANEL   LOUVERED PANEL

SHUTTER TYPES

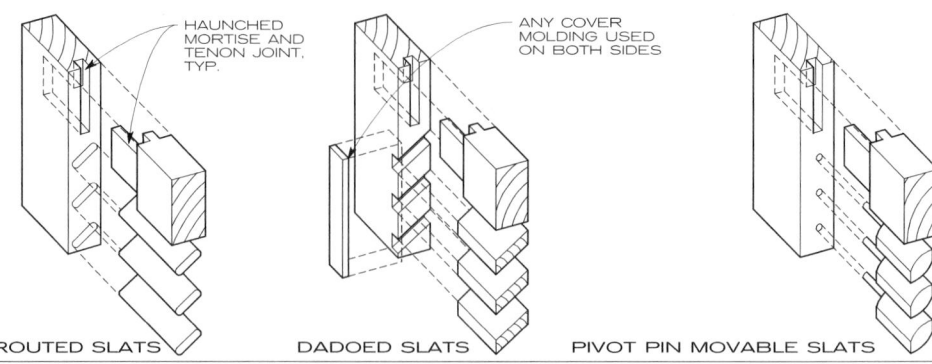

HAUNCHED MORTISE AND TENON JOINT, TYP.

ANY COVER MOLDING USED ON BOTH SIDES

ROUTED SLATS   DADOED SLATS   PIVOT PIN MOVABLE SLATS

LOUVER TYPES

SCREEN MATERIALS

WORKMAN-SHIP LEVEL	CUSTOM		PREMIUM		ECONOMY	
APPLIED FINISH	TRANSPARENT FINISH	OPAQUE FINISH	TRANSPARENT FINISH	OPAQUE FINISH	TRANSPARENT FINISH	OPAQUE FINISH
AWI lumber grade	II	II	II	II	II	II
Screen frame parts, any of the listed species unless otherwise specified	Ponderosa pine, sugar pine, Idaho white pine, northern white pine, mahogany, Douglas fir	Unless otherwise specified, same as transparent	Teak, South American mahogany, African mahogany	Unless otherwise specified, same as transparent	Any pine, fir, hemlock, larch	Unless otherwise specified, same as transparent
Wire cloth, any of the listed materials unless otherwise specified	Aluminum wire, bronze wire (18 x 14 mesh)		Bronze wire (18 x 14 mesh)		Nylon or fiberglass mesh	

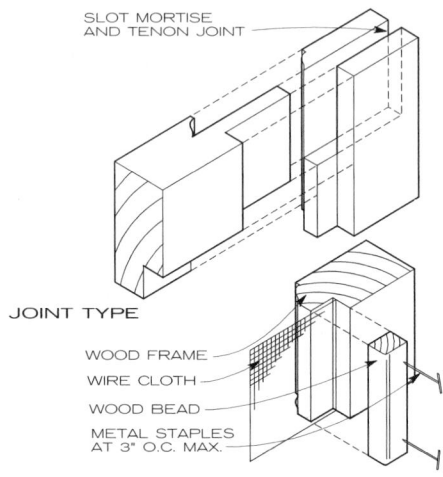

SLOT MORTISE AND TENON JOINT

JOINT TYPE

WOOD FRAME
WIRE CLOTH
WOOD BEAD
METAL STAPLES AT 3" O.C. MAX.

WIRE CLOTH INSTALLATION DETAIL

CUSTOM WORKMANSHIP GRADE SCREEN DETAILS

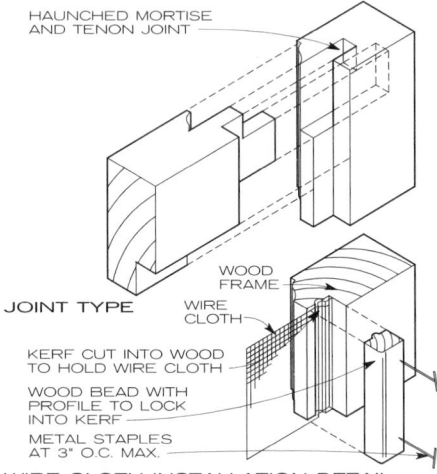

HAUNCHED MORTISE AND TENON JOINT

JOINT TYPE

WOOD FRAME
WIRE CLOTH
KERF CUT INTO WOOD TO HOLD WIRE CLOTH
WOOD BEAD WITH PROFILE TO LOCK INTO KERF
METAL STAPLES AT 3" O.C. MAX.

WIRE CLOTH INSTALLATION DETAIL

PREMIUM WORKMANSHIP GRADE SCREEN DETAILS

BLIND AND SHUTTER MATERIALS

MATERIALS		CUSTOM WORKMANSHIP		PREMIUM WORKMANSHIP		ECONOMY WORKMANSHIP	
		TRANSPARENT FINISH	OPAQUE FINISH	TRANSPARENT FINISH	OPAQUE FINISH	TRANSPARENT FINISH	OPAQUE FINISH
AWI grade lumber	Stiles, rails, slats and mullions; Applied moldings	II plus compatibility of color between veneer and lumber	II	I plus compatibility of grain and color between veneer and lumber	II	II with no selection for grain or color	II
	Flat panels	II permitted for panels less than 14 in. across the grain		not permitted		II permitted for panels in any dimension	
	Raised panels	II used to rim panel product centers and permitted for panels less than 14 in. across the grain		I used to rim panel product centers	II used to rim panel product centers	II permitted for panels in any dimension	
Panel products	Veneered stiles, rails, and mullions	particleboard or fiberboard (veneer only by direct specification)	particleboard or fiberboard recommended (veneer permitted)	particleboard or fiberboard (veneer only by direct specification)		not applicable	
	Flat and raised panel core	particleboard or fiberboard (veneer only by direct specification)	particleboard or fiberboard recommended (veneer permitted)	particleboard or fiberboard (veneer only by direct specification)		particleboard or fiberboard recommended (veneer permitted)	particleboard, fiberboard, or veneer
	Face: veneer grade for transparent finish and material for opaque finish	"A" face plus compatibility of color between veneer and lumber	"B" veneer, plain fiberboard, or medium-density overlay	"AA" face plus compatibility of grain and color between veneer and lumber	"A" veneer, plain fiberboard, or medium-density overlay	"B" face veneer	"B" veneer, plain fiberboard, or medium-density overlay
Minimum panel products thickness	Veneered stiles and rails	3/4" (19 mm)		3/4" (19 mm)		1/2" (13 mm)	
	Flat panels	1/2" (13 mm)		1/2" (13 mm)		1/4" (6 mm)	
	Raised panels	3/4" (19 mm)		3/4" (19 mm)		1/2" (13 mm)	

NOTES

1. For additional information, refer to Architectural Woodwork Quality Standards, 6th edition (version 1.1), 1994, Architectural Woodwork Institute (AWI).

2. Lumber grades indicated in the charts on this page are according to AWI quality standards:

   Grade I: Pieces are selected for uniform grain and color on exposed faces and edges.

   Grade II: Pieces are selected for uniform grain on exposed faces and edges.

   Grade III: No matching for grain or color is required.

3. AWI recognizes three levels of workmanship for wood screens, blinds, and shutters:

   CUSTOM GRADE: Most conventional architectural woodwork falls within this grade. High-quality workmanship, materials, and installation are required for work with this designation.

   PREMIUM GRADE: This specification requires careful oversight to guarantee the highest quality workmanship, materials, installation, and execution of design intent. It is typically reserved for special projects or project features.

   ECONOMY GRADE: This grade indicates the minimum expectations for quality, materials, and installation within the scope of AWI standards.

4. All exterior screens and shutters must be treated with a wood preservative in accordance with AWI Quality Standards, Section 100.

5. Pivot pins for use in damp or coastal areas must be manufactured of nylon, stainless steel, or brass.

6. Exterior grade panel products are recommended for blinds and shutters because once installed they are typically kept open, with one face constantly exposed to the sun and other weathering (and drying) conditions, while the other face is likely to retain moisture.

Richard J. Vitullo, AIA; Oak Leaf Studio; Crownsville, Maryland

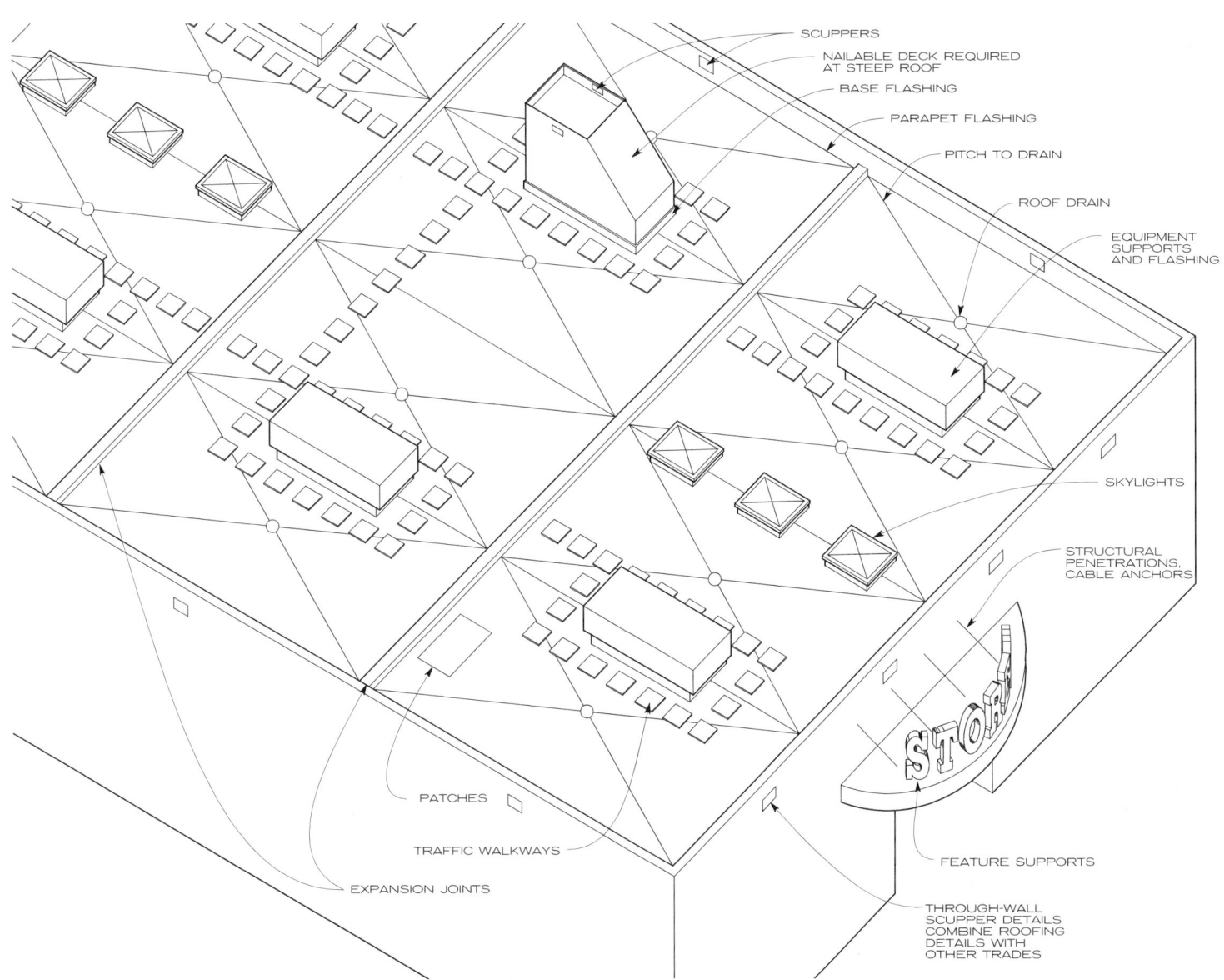

SCUPPERS

NAILABLE DECK REQUIRED
AT STEEP ROOF

BASE FLASHING

PARAPET FLASHING

PITCH TO DRAIN

ROOF DRAIN

EQUIPMENT
SUPPORTS
AND FLASHING

SKYLIGHTS

STRUCTURAL
PENETRATIONS,
CABLE ANCHORS

FEATURE SUPPORTS

THROUGH-WALL
SCUPPER DETAILS
COMBINE ROOFING
DETAILS WITH
OTHER TRADES

PATCHES

TRAFFIC WALKWAYS

EXPANSION JOINTS

LOW-SLOPE MEMBRANE ROOFING

MEMBRANE PRINCIPLES

The membrane is the weatherproofing component of a roof. All roof membranes serve at least three functions: waterproofing, reinforcement, and surfacing; some membrane materials can perform more than one of these roles. The waterproofing agent is the most important element within the roof membrane. In built-up and modified bitumen roofing, the waterproofing agent is bitumen. In single-ply roofing, the waterproofing agent is synthetic rubber or plastic.

REINFORCEMENT

Reinforcement stabilizes the roof membrane, holds the waterproofing agent in place, and provides tensile strength to the membrane. In built-up roofing, reinforcement is provided by organic or glass fiber roofing felts. In modified bitumen roofing, the reinforcement is generally glass fiber felt or polyester scrim, which is factory-fabricated into the finished sheet. Reinforcement for single-ply membranes, if required, consists of polyester and other woven fabrics.

SURFACING AND AGGREGATE

Most membranes require some type of wearing surface. Surfacing materials protect the waterproofing and reinforcement elements from the effects of sunlight and weather exposure and provide other properties, such as fire resistance, traffic protection, and reflectivity. Membranes may be field or factory surfaced with aggregates or other coatings. Gravel, slag, marble chips, or mineral granules are used as aggregates; asphalt and liquid coatings are used on smooth surfaced roofs.

ROOF MEMBRANE SELECTION

Low-slope roofing membranes are manufactured from a wide variety of materials. A conventional built-up roofing system is fabricated on site from bitumen and saturated felt plies. Factory-modified bitumen sheets are available, which improve the resistance of the system to various factors; these are installed in layers similar to built-up roofing. Single-sheet systems include elastomeric (EPDM) and plastomeric (PVC) roofing, both of which have improved resistance to chemical or other hazards. For unusually high traffic situations, protected (inverted) membrane roofing can protect the waterproof membrane with a top layer of insulation or other material.

Complex surfaces may require liquid or spray foam roofing for adequate waterproofing coverage. Manufactured low-slope metal panel systems are also used as roofing membranes. The roof membrane is produced by combining a number of components to form a waterproof barrier for the building. The characteristics of each component must be considered when specifying the roof system.

The roof membrane is subjected to the stresses of expansion and contraction, weathering from moisture and sunlight, abrasion from foot traffic, wind forces, and live and instantaneous loading factors. ASTM standards outline the minimum requirements for manufacturing materials used for moisture proofing.

Four factors must be given primary consideration in selecting the roofing system: the membrane material, slope of the roof, roof substrate on which the membrane will be installed, and method of attaching the roof membrane to the substrate. Other critical factors include proper design and installation of flashing, expansion joints, and roof penetrations. Regardless of the type of roof membrane, insulation, or roof deck, proper drainage of the roof system is the single most important design consideration for ensuring the performance of the roofing system. Premature failure of a roof system that is improperly drained is virtually assured.

Valerie Eickelberger; Rippeteau Architects, PC; Washington, D.C.
National Roofing Contractors Association; Rosemont, Illinois

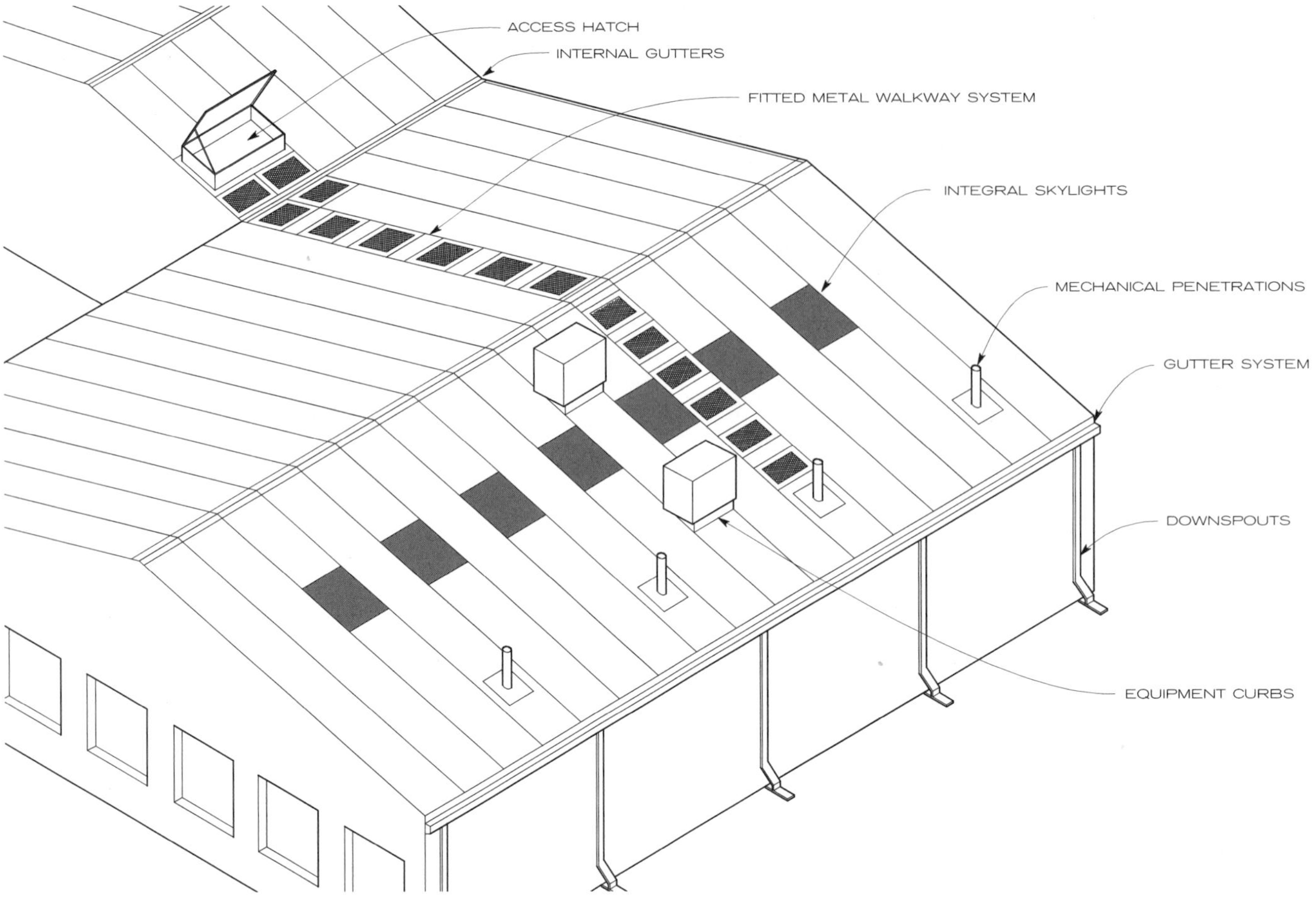

ACCESS HATCH

INTERNAL GUTTERS

FITTED METAL WALKWAY SYSTEM

INTEGRAL SKYLIGHTS

MECHANICAL PENETRATIONS

GUTTER SYSTEM

DOWNSPOUTS

EQUIPMENT CURBS

LOW-SLOPE MANUFACTURED METAL ROOFING

LOW-SLOPE ROOFING COMPONENTS

ROOF SUBSTRATE

The roof substrate (or deck) determines the membrane system to be selected for a building. The roof deck should provide positive drainage; this can be accomplished by sloping the structural deck, installing tapered board insulation, or installing insulating fill. Drains should be located at low points in the roof, not at columns or bearing walls. Some roof decks and insulation substrates require special precautions or may be unsuitable for use with certain roof membrane systems.

NAILABLE AND NON-NAILABLE DECKS

The roof deck may be nailable, non-nailable, or insulated. Nailable roof decks include those made of cement-wood fiber panels, lightweight insulating concrete, poured gypsum concrete, metal bound gypsum planks, and wood planks and plywood. Non-nailable roof decks include those made of precast concrete panels, prestressed concrete, reinforced concrete, steel, and thermosetting insulating fill. Many roof decks have at least one layer of insulation on the top side, which the fasteners must penetrate to reach the insulation substrate and the roof deck below.

In general, roof membranes are not fully attached directly onto a nailable deck surface. Rather, for nailable decks, the first layer of material (i.e., base sheet, slip sheet, insulation, or membrane base ply) generally is mechanically fastened to the deck. Non-nailable roof decks may require the installation of a base sheet or insulation separator, to be either spot or channel mopped in place before installation of a fully adhered single-ply or built-up roof membrane. Some roof membranes may be attached directly to a non-nailable roof deck.

FLASHING

Most roof leaks occur at points where the horizontal roof deck joins a vertical surface. Proper installation of composition (base) flashing and metal counterflashing can prevent leaks. Base flashing should be installed 8 to 14 in. above the finished roof surface and fastened to the base flashing at the top edge. Since the bending radius of present composition roofing materials is limited to 45 degrees, cant strips are installed between the roof and any vertical surface to protect the base flashing. Metal counterflashing must extend low enough to protect the top of the base flashing from wind-driven snow or rain. Varying expansion/contraction characteristics make it inadvisable to connect sheet metal to the roof membrane, which can tear or crack.

ROOF EXPANSION JOINTS

Roof expansion joints accommodate movement of the roof assembly that results from thermal expansion and contraction. These joints are also designed to prevent membrane splitting and ridging and to accommodate movement within the building itself. Roof expansion joints should be provided at expansion or contraction joints in the structural system, places where joints or the structural framing system change direction or material, intersections between the building and wings and additions, junctions where interior heating conditions change, and sites where movement between walls and roof deck may occur.

MECHANICAL EQUIPMENT AND PENETRATIONS

Mechanical equipment and piping on or through the roof should be curb-mounted with cant strips at the base of the curb and provision for attachment of base flashing. Two-piece metal counterflashing should be installed over the base flashing. Units using curbs with built-in metal base flashing flanges should not be used. Short pipe projections may be flashed into the membrane by using soft metal or lead flashing with integral flashing flanges stripped into the membrane, but pitch pockets should be avoided.

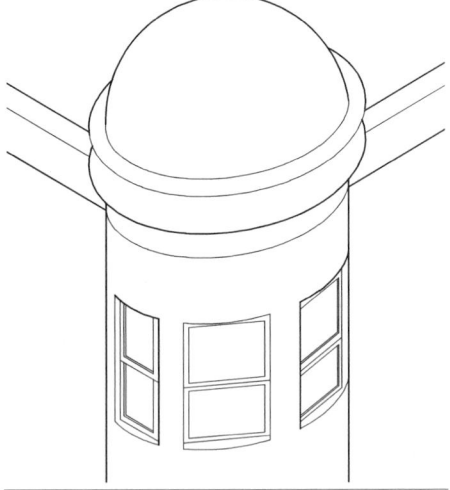

LIQUID MEMBRANE ROOFING AT DOME

COMPLEX SURFACES

Liquid or spray foam membranes may be used on complex or curved surfaces such as domes to provide moisture protection. These types of membranes are also commonly used for reroofing and for areas that would otherwise be difficult to waterproof. Liquid membranes consist of a liquid basecoat, reinforcing fabric, and a liquid topcoat. Spray foam membranes have a high insulating value and consist of foam sprayed on the deck surface and covered with a protective coating of aggregate or elastomeric material.

Valerie Eickelberger; Rippeteau Architects, PC; Washington, D.C.
National Roofing Contractors Association; Rosemont, Illinois

7 INTRODUCTION

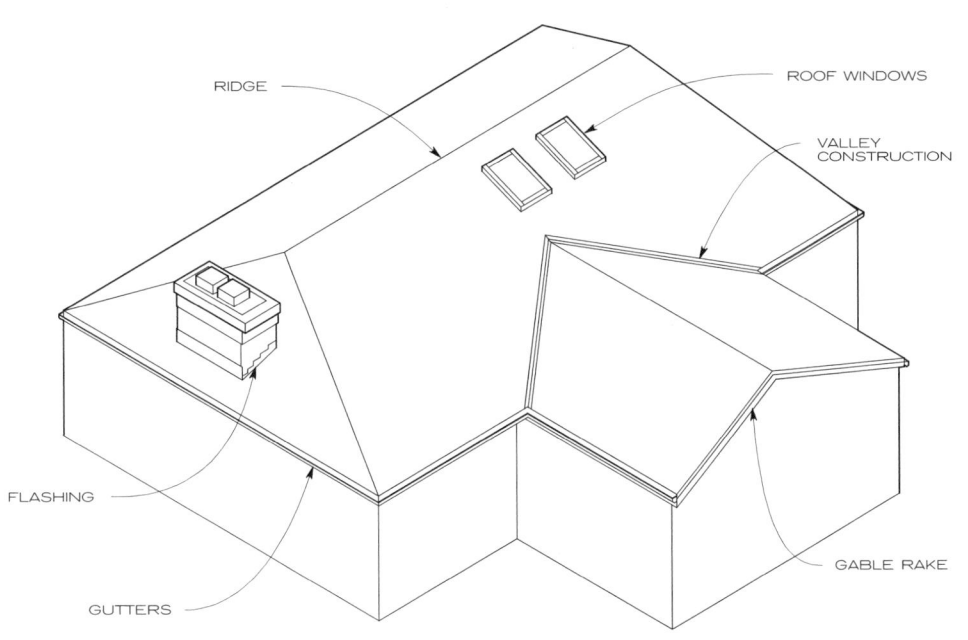

RIDGE

ROOF WINDOWS

VALLEY CONSTRUCTION

FLASHING

GUTTERS

GABLE RAKE

PITCHED ROOF WITH LOW SLOPE

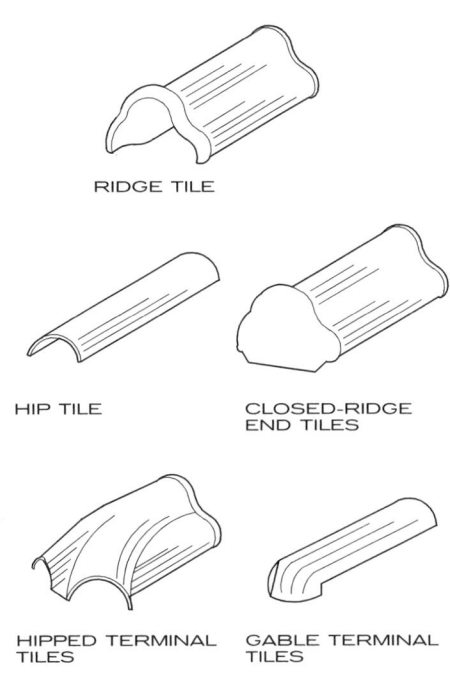

RIDGE TILE

HIP TILE

CLOSED-RIDGE END TILES

HIPPED TERMINAL TILES

GABLE TERMINAL TILES

SPECIAL TILES

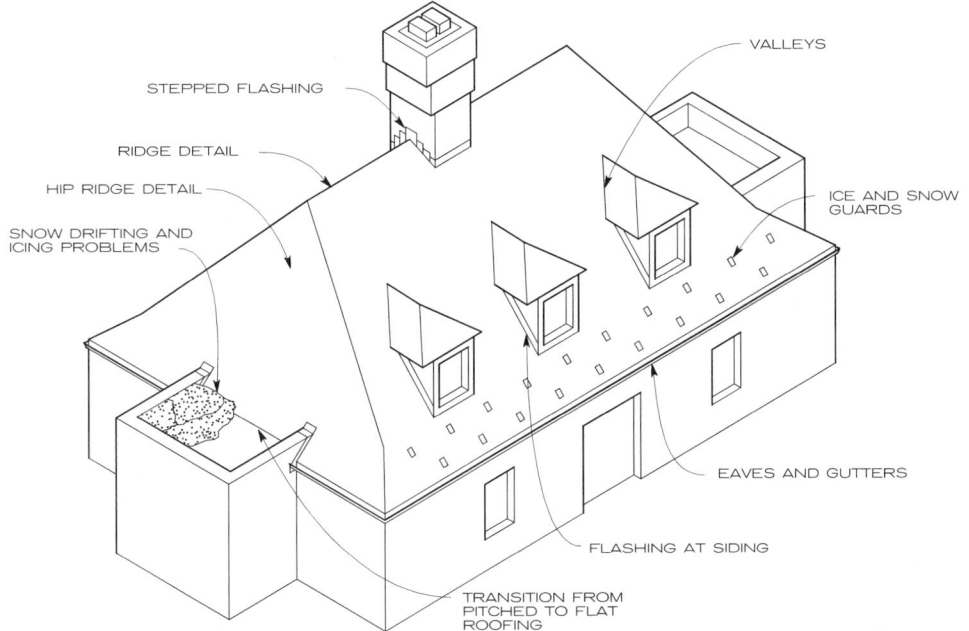

STEPPED FLASHING

RIDGE DETAIL

HIP RIDGE DETAIL

SNOW DRIFTING AND ICING PROBLEMS

VALLEYS

ICE AND SNOW GUARDS

EAVES AND GUTTERS

FLASHING AT SIDING

TRANSITION FROM PITCHED TO FLAT ROOFING

PITCHED ROOF WITH STEEP SLOPE

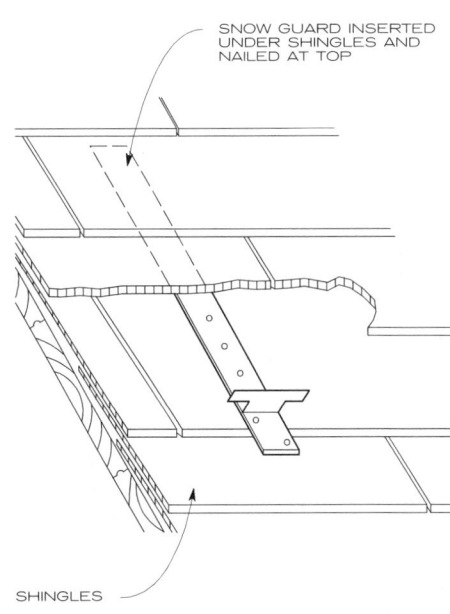

SNOW GUARD INSERTED UNDER SHINGLES AND NAILED AT TOP

SHINGLES

SNOW GUARD

STEEP ROOFING

Steep roofs have a slope that is generally 3 in. per ft or greater. Roofing materials suitable for steep roofs include asphalt rolls or shingles, clay and concrete tiles, composition roofing tiles, metal shingles or panels, wood shingles and shakes (split from logs), and slate. Steep roofs often have complicated roof intersections. Step flashing, crickets, and valleys keep moisture away from these intersections. Crickets are formed at an upward angle to prevent the accumulation of snow and ice and to deflect water. Where sloping roofs join at a downward angle, valleys concentrate water runoff and are highly vulnerable to leakage. Transitional details may be necessary to prevent snow and ice accumulation where roof surfaces join. Flashing should be installed at eaves wherever a possibility exists of ice forming along the eaves and causing a backup of water. Manufactured ice shields for eaves are also available. Damage to persons or property from sliding ice and snow may be prevented with snow guards.

TILE ROOF TYPES

Traditional types of roofing tile are made from clay, concrete, and metal. Contemporary tile roofing materials include composite materials, fiber cement, cement wood, and ceramic slate. Tile offers a wide range of design possibilities because of the large variety of types and shapes available, including roll tiles (barrel or mission tile), S shapes, flat tile, and ridge tiles of various shapes. Graduated tiles (tiles of diminishing widths) are required for round towers, circular bays, and porches. Tile manufacturers furnish graduated tiles in all popular shapes. Some manufacturers also offer special valley tile, manufactured in an angular or round form, and other special shapes for particular applications.

RESISTANCE TO WIND

If tiles are nailed too tightly, they lift up at the butt, allowing high winds to blow them off the roof or rainwater to be driven under them. Tiles should be nailed individually, and nails should be driven in until the nail head just clears the tile and the tile hangs on the nail. Building officials have designated some localities with high-wind conditions as wind hazard areas. In these areas, the nose ends of all eaves-course tiles should be secured with hurricane clips, which are available in different shapes to suit the type of roof sheathing used. Tiles should be laid with a 3 in. minimum headlap.

Valerie Eickelberger; Rippeteau Architects, PC; Washington, D.C.
National Roofing Contractors Association; Rosemont, Illinois

INTRODUCTION **7**

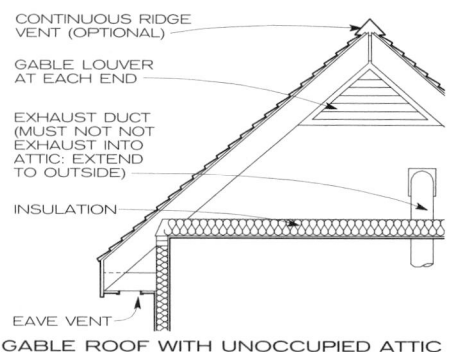

GABLE ROOF WITH UNOCCUPIED ATTIC

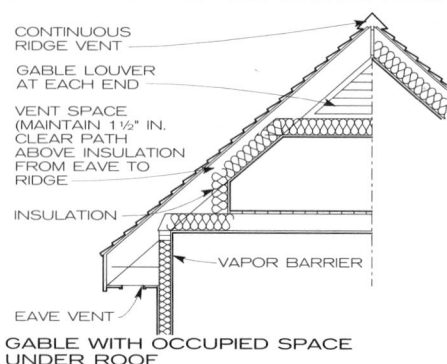

GABLE WITH OCCUPIED SPACE UNDER ROOF

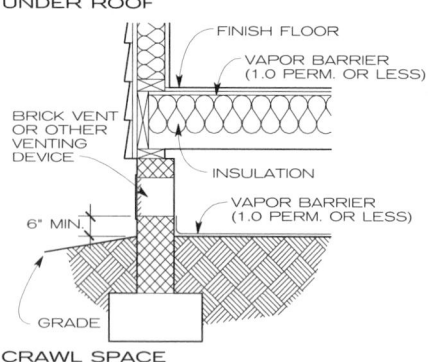

CRAWL SPACE

VENT APPLICATIONS

GENERAL

Attics and crawl spaces must be ventilated to remove moisture and water vapor that has entered the spaces from surrounding air or soil or that has been created by human activity. Generally, crawl spaces (and basements) require a greater amount of ventilation than an equivalent area of attic. The quantity of water vapor depends on the building type (e.g., residence, school, etc.), activity (e.g., bathroom, kitchen, etc.), air temperature, and relative humidity. If the temperature of the ventilated space falls below the dew point temperature, condensation will occur which will deteriorate insulation, framing, etc. This can be avoided by proper detailing to limit moisture infiltration and increase ventilation to remove it if it does enter the space.

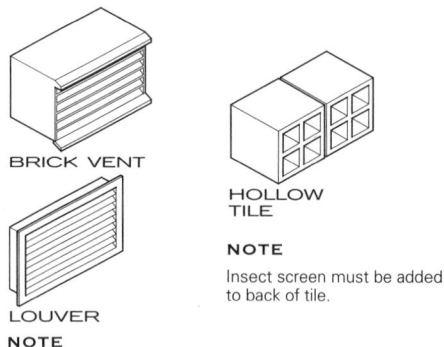

BRICK VENT

HOLLOW TILE

NOTE
Insect screen must be added to back of tile.

LOUVER

NOTE
Most vents for crawl spaces are set into unit masonry (and are sized accordingly) or concrete. Consult manufacturers. Metal louvers and vents have integral insect screens.

CRAWL SPACE VENTILATION MATERIALS

Richard J. Vitullo, AIA; Oak Leaf Studio; Crownsville, Maryland
Erik K. Beach; Rippeteau Architects, PC; Washington, D.C.

VENTILATION REQUIREMENTS TO PREVENT CONDENSATION

SPACE	DESCRIPTION		TOTAL NET AREA OF VENTILATION (A)	REMARKS
Joist/rafter (finish ceiling attached to underside of joists)	Flat		a = A/250. Uniformly distributed vents at eaves.	Vent each joist space at both ends. Maintain 1 1/2 in. minimum clear path above insulation for ventilation.
	Sloped		a = A/150. Uniformly distributed vents at eaves with a continuous ridge vent.	
Attic (unheated)	Gable		a = A/150. At least two louvers on opposite sides near ridge or one continuous ridge vent. Uniformly distributed vents at eaves.	Any combination of gable/hip louvers and/or ridge vents may be used to achieve required ventilation.
	Hip			Vent area may be reduced by inclusion of wind-driven or mechanical ventilators. Consult mechanical engineer.
Crawl space/basement			a = 2L/100 + A/300 Where L = crawl space/basement perimeter (linear feet)	Provide at least one opening per side, as high as possible in wall.

NOTES

1. A = area of space to be ventilated, in square feet.
2. The openings in insect screening should not exceed 1/4 in. (6 mm). The effective net area of ventilation is reduced by screening; consult manufacturers of screening materials for percentage of "free air" flow reduced by the amount of solid material in screening.

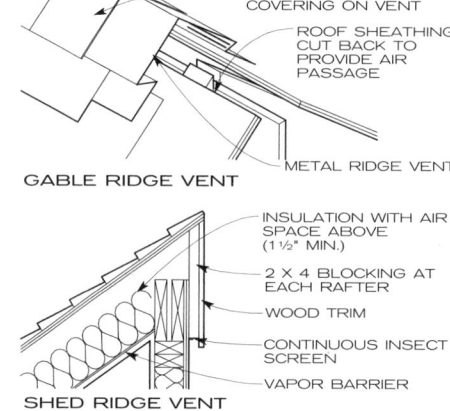

GABLE RIDGE VENT

SHED RIDGE VENT

RIDGE VENTS

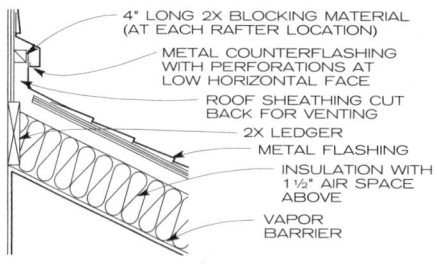

VENT FOR SHED ROOF AT WALL

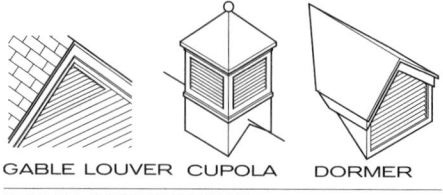

GABLE LOUVER   **CUPOLA**   **DORMER**

ROOF LOUVER TYPES

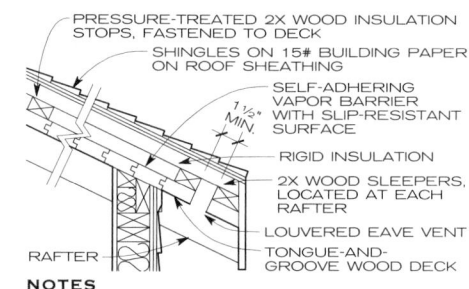

NOTES

1. Provide ridge vent to complete cavity ventilation detail.
2. Fasteners should be carefully selected and located to secure insulation, stops, sleepers, sheathing, etc. to structural tongue-and-groove deck.

INSULATED TONGUE-AND-GROOVE ROOF VENTILATION DETAIL

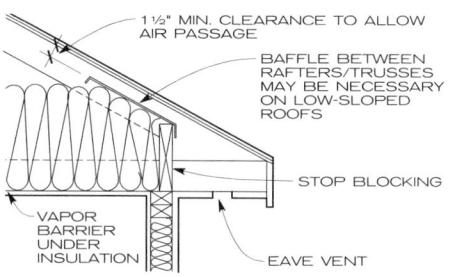

INSULATION BLOCKING AND BAFFLE

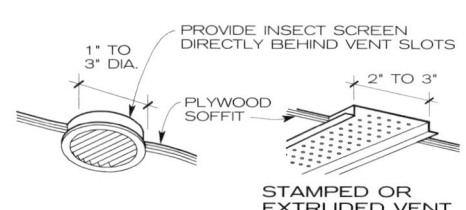

CIRCULAR VENTS   **STAMPED OR EXTRUDED VENT STRIPS**

EAVE VENTILATION TYPES

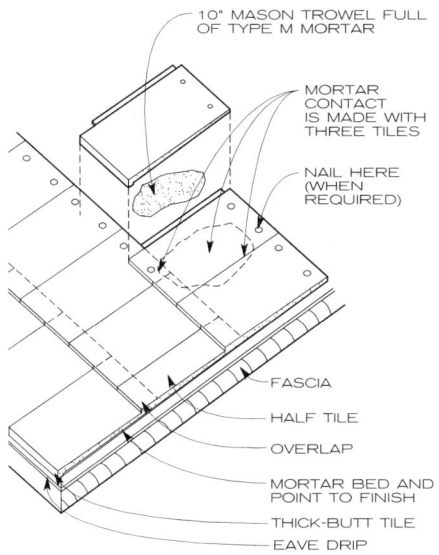

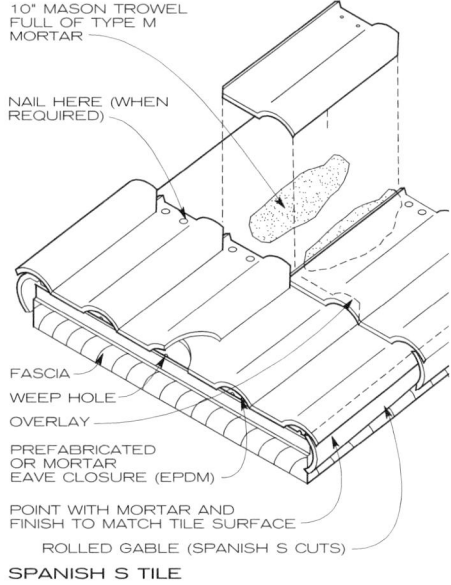

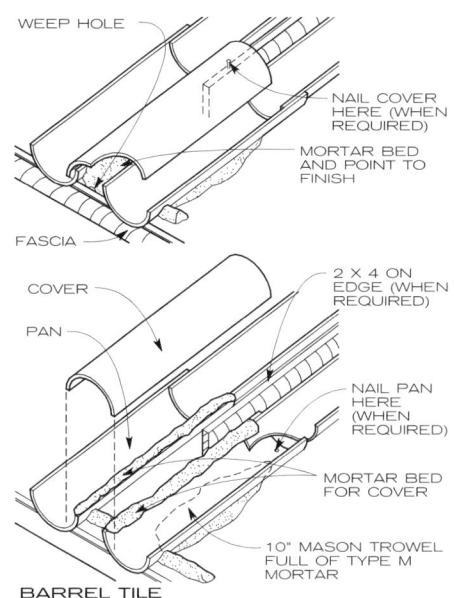

FLAT TILE
NOTE

Mortar contact is made with 3 tiles.

BARREL TILE

SPANISH S TILE

MORTAR AND TILE PLACEMENT

GENERAL

Concrete tile is manufactured by extruding a mixture of portland cement, sand, and water on individual molds under high pressure. The finish surface of the tile is covered with a cementitious material that has been colored with synthetic oxides. The tiles are cured to required strengths in chambers where humidity and temperature are controlled. Moisture absorption by concrete tiles can lead to structural roof problems, and particular care should be given to specifying the correct concrete tile for a given environment.

For both categories of concrete tile—roll or flat—it is important to adhere to minimum slope requirements as follows:

1. Roll tile and flat tile can be installed on roof decks with slopes of 4 in. per ft or more when at least one layer of 30-lb felt underlayment is applied horizontally and tiles are nailed or wired with a minimum 3 in. headlap. Use of spaced sheathing is not recommended.

2. Any concrete tile can be used on solid-sheathed roof decks with slopes less than 4 in. per ft as long as two or more layers of No. 30 or No. 40 asphalt-saturated (non-perforated) felt are set in hot asphalt or mastic to serve as the underlayment. A single layer of modified bitumen-coated roofing systems roll-good sheet with laps either torched or heat welded is acceptable. Vertical lath stringers with horizontal battens are installed over the underlayment, creating a supporting surface for the tile, which must be installed with at least 4 in. headlap. Do not use spaced sheathing.

3. Regardless of slope, in localities where the January mean temperature is less than 30°F, stricter minimum requirements apply. Refer to the National Roofing Contractors Association manual.

FLAT TILE

When using flat roof tiles, a metal eave-riser with weep holes should be installed at the eave line. During installation, adjust tile spacing to provide uniform exposure, with a minimum 3 in. headlap.

ROLL TILE

When using roll, or mission, tile, apply the first course above a metal bird-stop with weep holes. Fit the underside of the tile with specially formed eave closure strips, fastened inside the tile cover. The heads of all remaining tiles should be aligned with the horizontal guide lines. Adjust roll tile spacing to provide uniform exposure, with at least a 3 in. headlap. Jamming interlocking tiles together (side to side) will restrict movement and result in broken corners.

ROOF SLOPE

For roof slopes 5 in. in 12 and less, solid sheathing may be used with or without battens. Nailing is not required with battens, but every tile should be nailed if battens are not used. In either case, perimeter nailing is required for 3 ft or three courses, whichever is greater, from all eaves, rakes, ridges, hips, or valleys. (Do not nail into valley metal.)

For roof slopes between 5 and 7 in. in 12, nail every other tile over solid sheathing with battens and every tile if battens are not used. For slopes between 7 and 12 in. in 12, every other tile should be nailed over solid sheathing with battens. Perimeter nailing is required in all these situations.

For slopes 12 in. in 12 and greater, nail every tile over solid sheathing with battens; perimeter nailing is necessary.

TILES SET IN MORTAR

The practice of installing cement tiles with mortar over a built-up subroof evolved in high-wind and high-moisture areas of the southeastern United States. In this system, the built-up subroof provides the moisture barrier, and the tiles protect the subroof from solar ultraviolet rays, high winds, and external damage. This concrete tile system can also be used on low-slope roofs, but the minimum is 2 in. in 12. On slopes between 5 in. in 12 and 7 in. in 12, additional mechanical fastening is required for the first three courses of tile in areas subject to high winds. For roofs with steeper slopes, tile should be mechanically fastened.

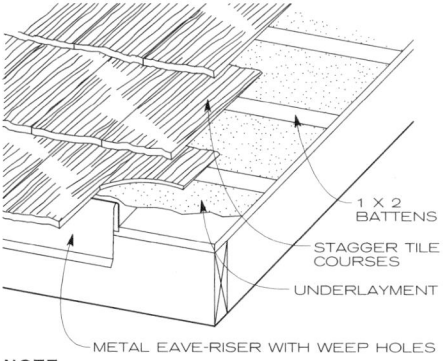

TYPICAL ROLL TILES

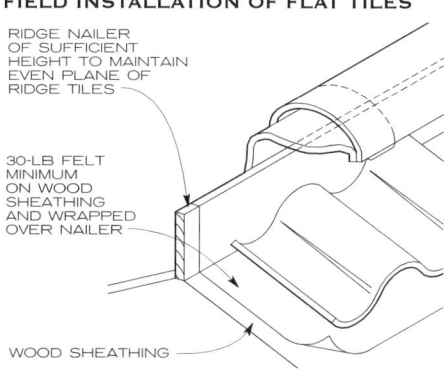

NOTE

This detail is for pitches 4:12 and greater.

FIELD INSTALLATION OF FLAT TILES

ATTACHMENT PROCEDURES FOR CONCRETE ROOF TILES

ROOF SLOPE	FIELD TILE NAILING		NAILING FOR PERIMETER TILE AND TILE ON CANTILEVERED AREAS[2]
	SOLID SHEATHING WITH BATTENS	SOLID SHEATHING WITHOUT BATTENS[1]	
3:12 to and including 5:12	Not required	Every tile	Every tile
Above 5:12 to less than 12:12	Every other tile	Every tile to 7:12	Every tile
12:12 and over	Every tile	N/A	Every tile

NOTES

1. For slopes exceeding 7:12, battens are required.

2. Perimeter nailing areas include three tile courses but not less than 36 inches from either side of hips or ridges and from edges of eaves and gable rakes. In special wind areas designated by the building official, additional fastenings may be required.

HIP AND RIDGE DETAIL

National Roofing Contractors Association; Rosemont, Illinois
Grace S. Lee; Rippeteau Architects, PC; Washington, D.C.

COMPOSITE ROOFING TILES

Fiber cement, cement wood, galvanized steel with acrylic coating, and ceramic slate roofing tiles are popular alternatives to clay or concrete roofing tiles. These composite tiles have been designed to be lighter, stronger, and easier to install than traditional, "natural" tiles. Their strength and combination of materials make them more fire retardant and wind resistant than conventional tiles.

FIBER CEMENT

Fiber cement tiles combine organic fiber with cement, silica, water, and other additives. The resulting product is a roof slate that is lightweight, strong, versatile, and easy to install. The tiles can be made in a variety of distinctive shapes, colors, and textures that mimic natural materials such as slate and patterned wood shingles. Fiber cement tiles resist deterioration and moisture penetration and are immune to pests and fungal growth. They are well-suited for coastal regions and other areas with high humidity.

Fiber cement tiles should be applied to nailable decks only. For plywood decks with rafters spaced 20 in. or less, the plywood should be at least $1/2$ in. thick. If rafters are spaced greater than 20 in., $5/8$ in. plywood is recommended. To fasten, use standard $1^1/_2$ in. galvanized 11-gauge flat-head roofing nails with a $3/8$ in. head. Flashing should be of a noncorrosive metal not lighter than 28 gauge.

CERAMIC SLATE

Ceramic slate tiles combine the look of natural slate with the fired-in strength and durability of ceramic tile. Such tiles have the thickness, texture, and appearance of older slate but at a fraction of the weight and cost. They are impervious to freeze-thaw cycles, fire, moisture, and efflorescence.

CEMENT WOOD TILES

Cement wood tiles are lightweight tiles that can be used for reroofing as well as for new construction. They have excellent impact resistance and are easily sawn and nailed. As a richly textured, composite product, cement wood tiles create an aesthetic similar to that of heavy cedar shakes yet provide the fire protection associated with cementitious products. Cement wood tiles, with their composite of portland cement and wood fiber, are long lasting. The portland cement is noncombustible and allows for Class A fire ratings, and the wood fibers provide excellent tensile strength and a light weight when compared to standard concrete tiles.

METAL ROOFING TILES

The advantage of metal roofing tiles over traditional clay or concrete tiles is that they are lightweight. They are easier to handle, quicker to install, and, because they require fewer building components, are less costly. Minimum recommended roof pitch for use of metal roofing tiles is a slope of 3 in 12. Roofs with shallower slopes require sealant in all side laps.

Metal roofing tiles usually come in sheets and have a base material of roll-formed 24- to 26-gauge prepainted galvanized or galvalume steel. A layer of crushed and graded stone granules is bonded to the steel panels with an acrylic resin formula and then a clear acrylic overglaze is applied. Slow oven curing completes the process, and the underside of the tile is protected with a final coat of polyester paint. Panels can be installed quickly and are secured to either wood or steel battens, creating a strong, weatherproof construction. The panels can be installed directly over existing roofs, unlike clay or concrete tiles, and are thus ideally suited for retrofitting roofs.

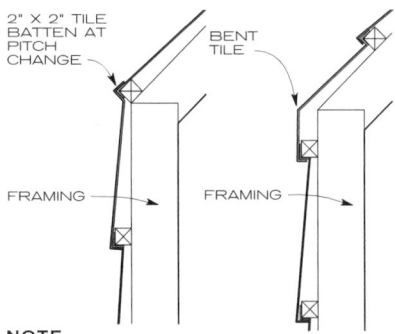

NOTE

When an equal number of full courses cannot be accommodated at the pitch change, a full panel can be bent to suit. When the roofline changes dramatically, install a batten at the pitch change.

METAL ROOFING AT PITCH CHANGE

Grace S. Lee; Rippeteau Architects, PC; Washington, D.C.

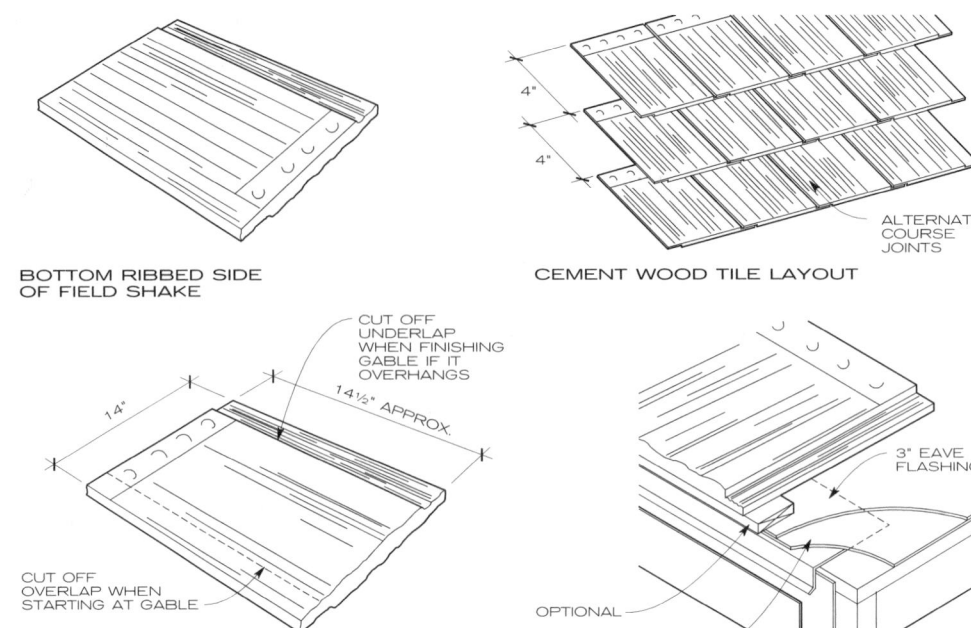

BOTTOM RIBBED SIDE OF FIELD SHAKE

CEMENT WOOD TILE LAYOUT

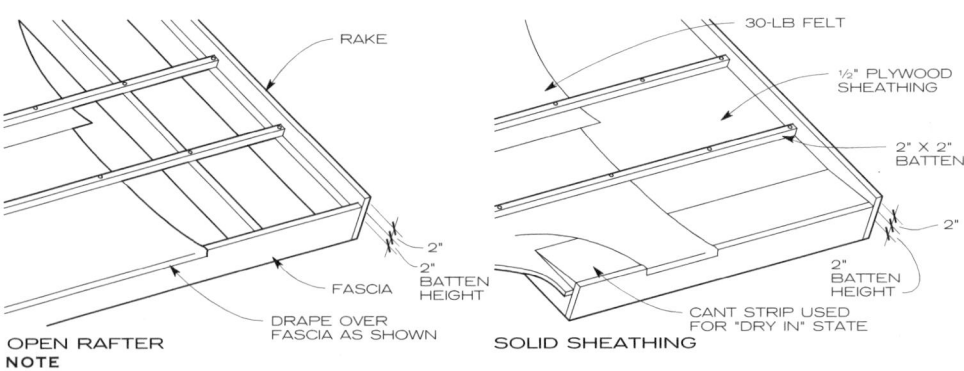

TOP SIDE OF FIELD SHAKE

EAVE DETAIL

CEMENT WOOD TILES

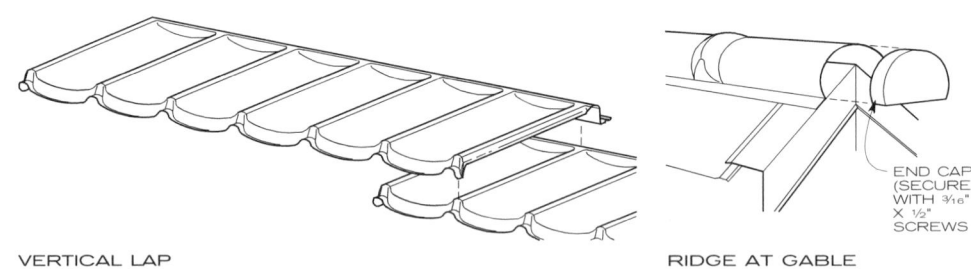

OPEN RAFTER

SOLID SHEATHING

NOTE

Metal roofing panels can be applied directly over solid plywood sheathing or over open rafters if a self-supporting underlayment is used.

METAL ROOFING TILE UNDERLAYMENT

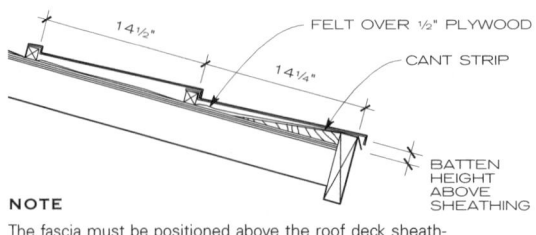

VERTICAL LAP

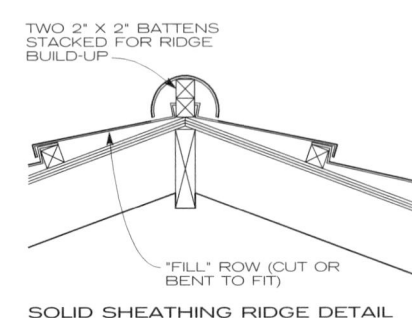

RIDGE AT GABLE

METAL ROOFING TILES

NOTE

The fascia must be positioned above the roof deck sheathing or rafters by the height of the batten. The fascia becomes the first panel batten.

SOLID SHEATHING AT EAVE

SOLID SHEATHING RIDGE DETAIL

METAL ROOFING DETAILS AT EAVE AND RIDGE

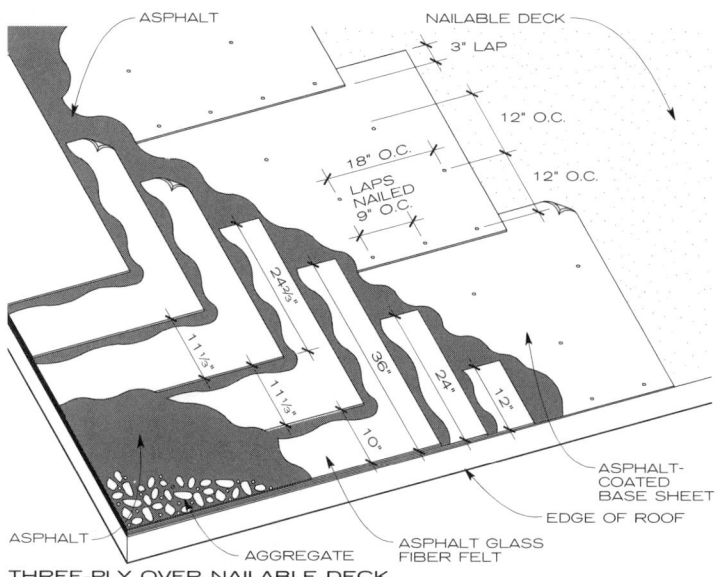

THREE-PLY OVER NAILABLE DECK

NOTES

1. If applied over sheathing panels, add rosin-sized sheathing paper between the deck and base sheet.

2. In lieu of asphalt, coal tar is an acceptable product.

AGGREGATE SURFACE BUILT-UP ROOFING

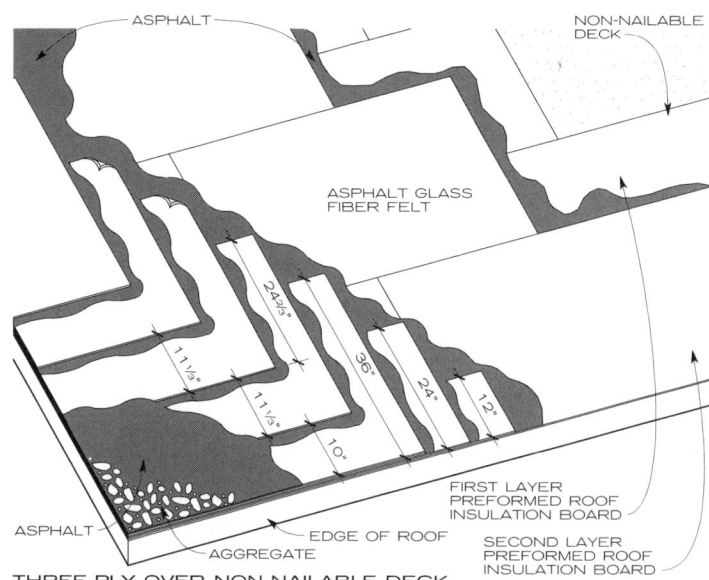

THREE-PLY OVER NON-NAILABLE DECK

NOTES

1. For a more conservative system, specify four plies rather than three.

2. In lieu of asphalt, coal tar is an acceptable product.

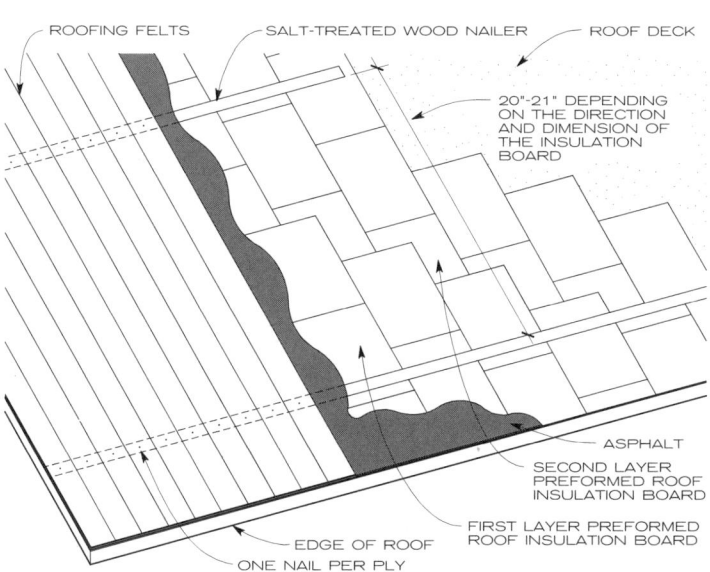

WOOD NAILER BACKNAILING SYSTEM

COAL TAR TYPES

ASTM D-450 TYPE NO.	KIND OF COAL TAR	SOFTENING POINT (°F)	
		MIN.	MAX.
I	Coal-tar pitch	126	140
II	Waterproofing pitch	106	126
III	Coal-tar bitumen	133	147

ASPHALT TYPES

TYPE	KIND OF ASPHALT	SOFTENING POINT (°F)		MAX. TEMP. (°F)
		MIN.	MAX.	
I	Dead level asphalt	151	135	475
II	Flat asphalt	176	158	500
III	Steep asphalt	205	185	525
IV	Special steep asphalt	225	210	525

GENERAL

A built-up roofing (BUR) system is composed of a base sheet attached to the roof substrate, two or more reinforcing felt ply sheets, and a surfaced cap sheet. Asphalt and coal tar are the bitumens used for built-up roofing. As the heated mopping bitumen fuses with the saturating bitumen in the roofing felts, the layers are welded together. Surfacings include aggregate, minerals, protective or reflective coatings, and smooth surface.

Four types of asphalt and two types of coal tar are presently used as bitumens in built-up roofing systems. The grade of asphalt used for BUR systems should be appropriate for the slope of the roof. Backnailing of felts is recommended for built-up roofing whenever the roof slope exceeds $1/2$ in. per ft. Aggregate-surfaced built-up roofing should not be used on slopes exceeding 3 in. per ft.

Reinforcing felts for BUR may be saturated, coated, or impregnated with bitumen and are manufactured from both organic and inorganic materials. Organic felts are manufactured from the fiber of paper, wood, or rags. Saturated felts are saturated with asphalt or coal tar bitumen. Impregnated roofing felts are generally lighter in weight and termed impregnated because their surface is not completely covered (coated) with asphalt. Saturated and coated roofing felts are generally factory coated on both sides and sur-

faced on one or both sides with fine mineral sand or other release agents to prevent adhesion inside the roll prior to application.

Prepared roofing materials are saturated and coated felts with talc, mica, sand, or ceramic granules incorporated into the weather surface of the felts, both to provide weather protection and for decorative purposes. Reinforced flashing membrane consists of a glass-fiber base felt that is laminated with cotton or glass-fiber fabric and coated with asphalt. Rosin-sized sheathing paper is a rosin-coated building paper generally used in built-up roofing to separate felts from wood plank roof decks.

TEMPERATURE

Proper application temperatures are vital to the creation of a quality roof membrane system. Temperatures that are too high can lead to incomplete coverage, voids, and a lack of waterproofing qualities. Temperatures that are too low can lead to poor adhesion, high expansion properties, and low tensile strength.

Bitumens can be heated at high temperatures for short periods of time without damage and must be heated at

high temperatures in order to achieve complete fusion and strong bonding of the plies. There is an optimum viscosity range and an optimum temperature range at the point of application that allow complete fusion, optimum wetting and mopping properties, and the desirable interply bitumen weight. The equiviscous temperature (EVT) is defined as the temperature at which the viscosity of roofing asphalt is 125 centistokes, plus or minus 25°F, at the mop bucket or felt layer immediately prior to application to the substrate. A centistoke is a unit that measures the kinematic viscosity.

Centistokes = [Dynamic Viscosity/Density] x Centipoise

The recommended EVT range for roofing asphalt, Types I, II, III, and IV, is the temperature at which a viscosity of 75 centipoise is attained, plus or minus 25°F. The recommended EVT range for coal tar products, types I and III, is the temperature at which a viscosity of 25 centipoise is attained, plus or minus 25°F. One consequence of a change in EVT from 125 centistokes to 75 centipoise, plus or minus 25°F, is the potential need to increase the temperature at which bitumen is heated in the kettle or tanker. Excessive and prolonged heating of asphalt and coal tar products may have a deleterious effect on the quality of the product.

National Roofing Contractors Association; Rosemont, Illinois
Valerie Eickelberger; Rippeteau Architects, PC; Washington, D.C.

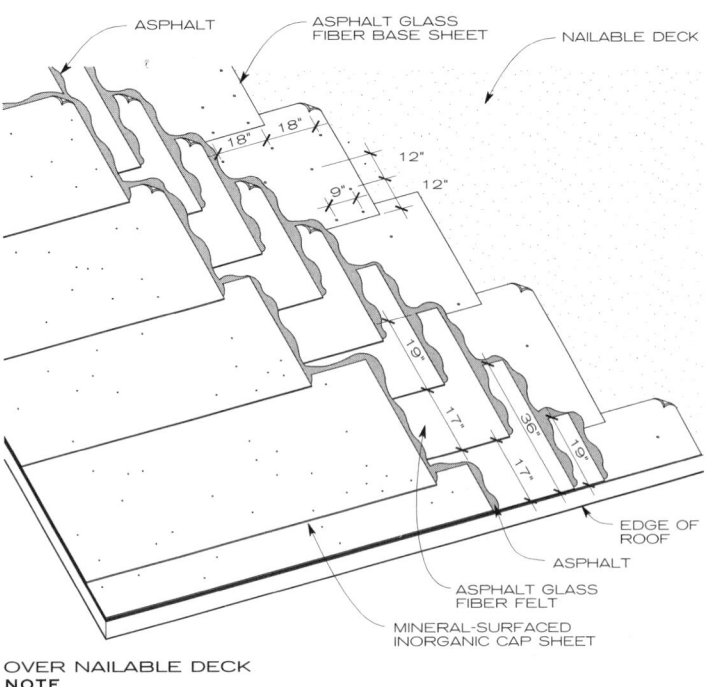

OVER NAILABLE DECK

NOTE

If applied over nailable deck sheathing panels, add a rosin-sized sheathing paper between the deck and base sheet.

MINERAL-SURFACED CAP SHEET BUILT-UP ROOFING

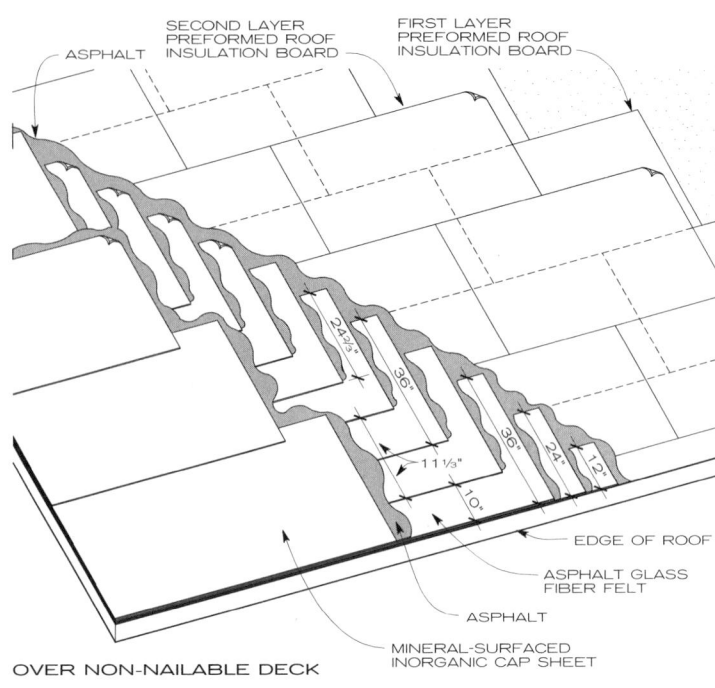

OVER NON-NAILABLE DECK

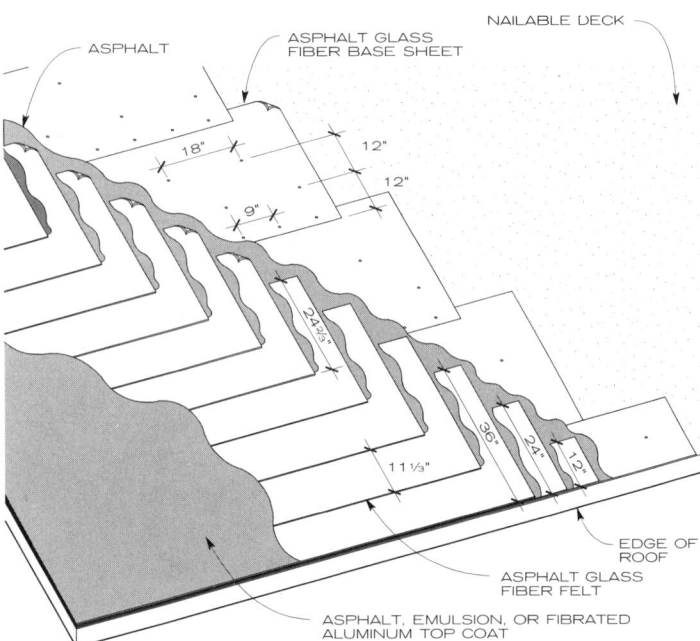

THREE-PLY OVER NAILABLE DECK

NOTE

If applied over sheathing panels, add a rosin-sized sheathing paper between the deck and base sheet.

SMOOTH SURFACE BUILT-UP ROOFING

THREE-PLY OVER NON-NAILABLE DECK

NOTE

For a more conservative system, specify four plies rather than three.

BUILT-UP ROOF SURFACING

Surfacing protects the bitumen and felts of a built-up roof from direct sunlight and weather exposure, and may provide other properties such as fire resistance or reflectivity. Surfacing types include aggregate, smooth surfacing, and mineral cap sheet.

AGGREGATE SURFACING

The aggregate in roofing serves as an opaque covering that improves the appearance and fire resistance of the roof and helps resist premature aging and damage from weather, temperature fluctuations, and ultraviolet rays. Aggregate also increases the wind uplift resistance of the roof membrane and permits much heavier pourings of bitumen than would otherwise be possible.

SMOOTH SURFACING

Built-up roof membranes may be left smooth, surfaced with a top coating of hot asphalt. Smooth surfacing should not be confused with a built-up membrane left unsurfaced (exposed felts). Smooth surfaced built-up roofing should be specified only in those circumstances where aggregate-surfaced built-up roofing is impractical, such as when the roof surface exceeds 3 in. per ft, where the proximity of an air-intake or exhaust equipment may cause loose aggregate, or where appropriate aggregate is not available.

MINERAL SURFACED (CAP SHEET)

Some areas of the country, particularly the far western and southern states, use mineral-surfaced cap sheets as the final surfacing for built-up roofing membranes. These specifications are similar to aggregate and smooth-surfaced specifications except that a final layer of prepared roofing material is installed on top of the multiply built-up roof assembly. This specification is not popular in colder climates, primarily because it requires phased construction of the final layer of roofing material.

National Roofing Contractors Association; Rosemont, Illinois
Valerie Eickelberger; Rippeteau Architects, PC; Washington, D.C.

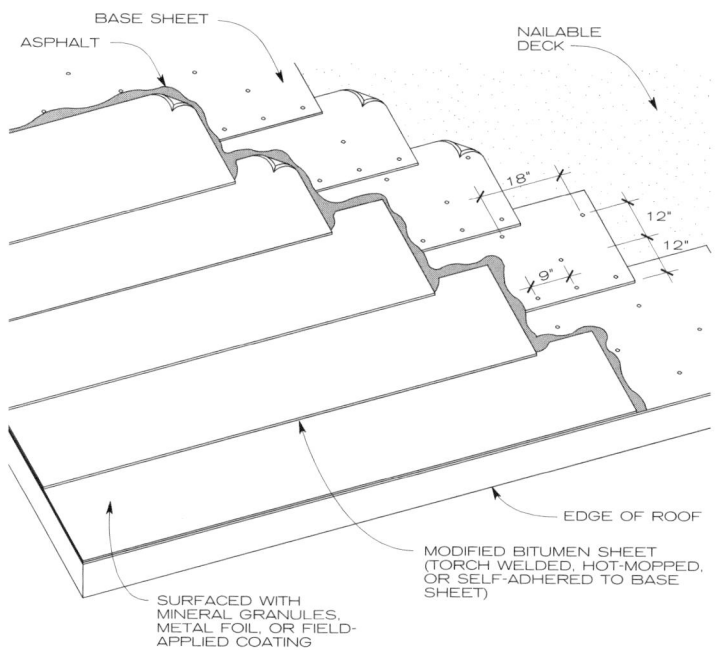

ASPHALT
BASE SHEET
NAILABLE DECK
18"
12"
12"
9"
EDGE OF ROOF
MODIFIED BITUMEN SHEET (TORCH WELDED, HOT-MOPPED, OR SELF-ADHERED TO BASE SHEET)
SURFACED WITH MINERAL GRANULES, METAL FOIL, OR FIELD-APPLIED COATING

TWO-PLY OVER NAILABLE DECK

NOTE

If applied over-sheathing panels when the cap sheet is hot-mopped, add a rosin-sized sheathing paper between the deck and base sheet.

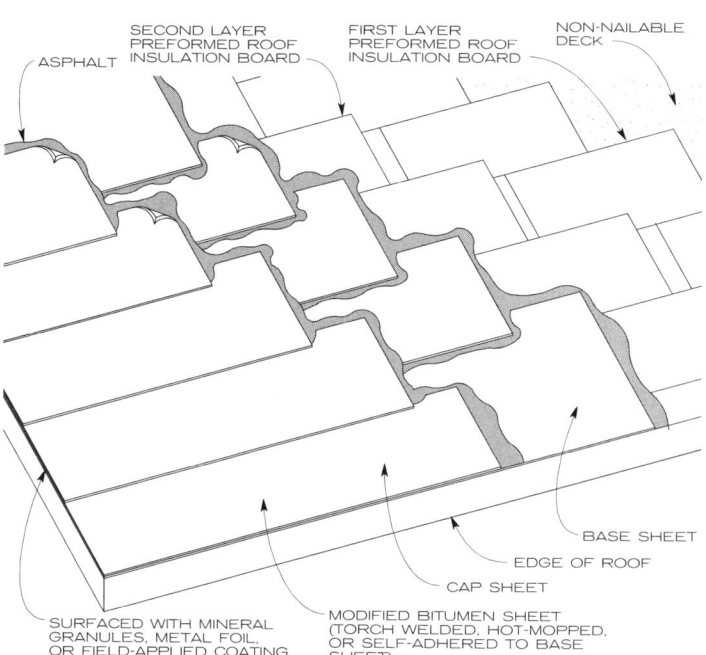

ASPHALT
SECOND LAYER PREFORMED ROOF INSULATION BOARD
FIRST LAYER PREFORMED ROOF INSULATION BOARD
NON-NAILABLE DECK
BASE SHEET
EDGE OF ROOF
CAP SHEET
MODIFIED BITUMEN SHEET (TORCH WELDED, HOT-MOPPED, OR SELF-ADHERED TO BASE SHEET)
SURFACED WITH MINERAL GRANULES, METAL FOIL, OR FIELD-APPLIED COATING

TWO-PLY OVER NON-NAILABLE DECK

TWO-PLY MODIFIED BITUMEN MEMBRANE

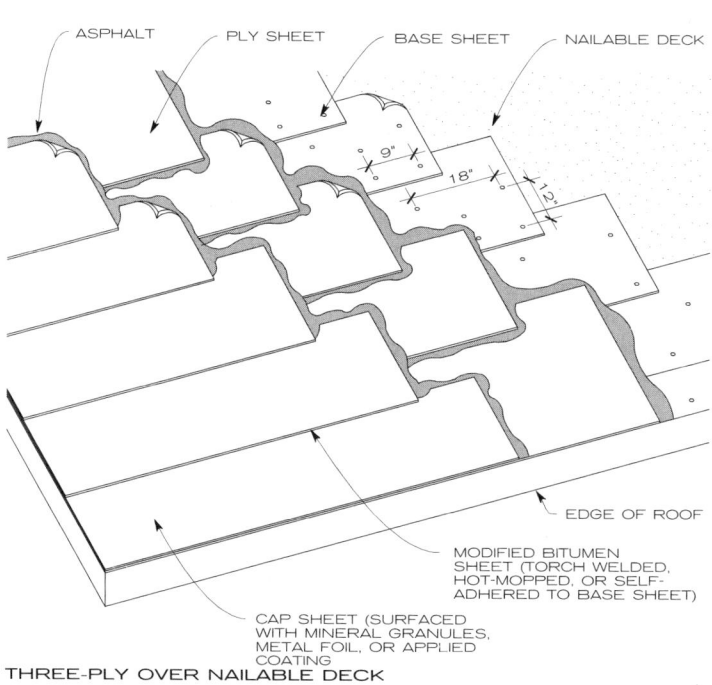

ASPHALT
PLY SHEET
BASE SHEET
NAILABLE DECK
9"
18"
12"
EDGE OF ROOF
MODIFIED BITUMEN SHEET (TORCH WELDED, HOT-MOPPED, OR SELF-ADHERED TO BASE SHEET)
CAP SHEET (SURFACED WITH MINERAL GRANULES, METAL FOIL, OR APPLIED COATING

THREE-PLY OVER NAILABLE DECK

ASPHALT
SECOND LAYER PREFORMED ROOF INSULATION BOARD
FIRST LAYER PREFORMED ROOF INSULATION BOARD
NON-NAILABLE DECK
BASE SHEET
PLY SHEET
EDGE OF ROOF
MODIFIED BITUMEN SHEET (TORCH WELDED, HOT-MOPPED, OR SELF-ADHERED TO BASE SHEET)
CAP SHEET (SURFACED WITH MINERAL GRANULES, METAL FOIL, OR FIELD-APPLIED COATING)

THREE-PLY OVER NON-NAILABLE DECK

NOTE

If applied over-sheathing panels when the cap sheet is hot-mopped, add a rosin-sized sheathing paper between the deck and base sheet.

THREE-PLY MODIFIED BITUMEN MEMBRANE

MODIFIED BITUMEN MEMBRANES

Polymer-modified bitumen membranes couple bitumen and polymers with various reinforcements to form a membrane system with improved properties. Modifiers include atactic polypropylene, styrene-butadiene-styrene, and styrene-butadiene-rubber. The modifying compounds impart improved flexibility, cohesive strength, toughness, and resistance to flow at high temperatures. The seams are sealed by torch welding or with hot asphalt. Thickness ranges from 40 to 160 mils.

For some systems a base sheet is fastened to the deck as an underlayment. In the hot-mopped system, the membrane is constructed similar to a built-up roof with hot asphalt mopped between the plies. Self-adhered sheets have a factory-applied asphalt-adhesive coating on the underside. The protective sheet is peeled away to stick the membrane to the roof deck. Torch-applied membrane systems have a factory-applied coating of modified asphalt on the underside of the sheet, which is melted with a propane torch to make the sheet adhere.

Reinforcing materials for polymer modified bitumen membranes include plastic film, polyester mat, glass fiber, felt or fabric, and metal foils, embedded within or laminated onto the modified bitumen sheet. Membranes may be surfaced with liquid coatings, metallic laminates, or ceramic or mineral granules to enhance resistance to weathering, ultraviolet rays, or fire or to improve appearance. Terminations at roof edges, parapets, and other flashings may be torch-applied, hot-mopped, or self-adhered. Laps are formed as the sheet is being applied.

National Roofing Contractors Association; Rosemont, Illinois
Valerie Eickelberger; Rippeteau Architects, PC; Washington, D.C.

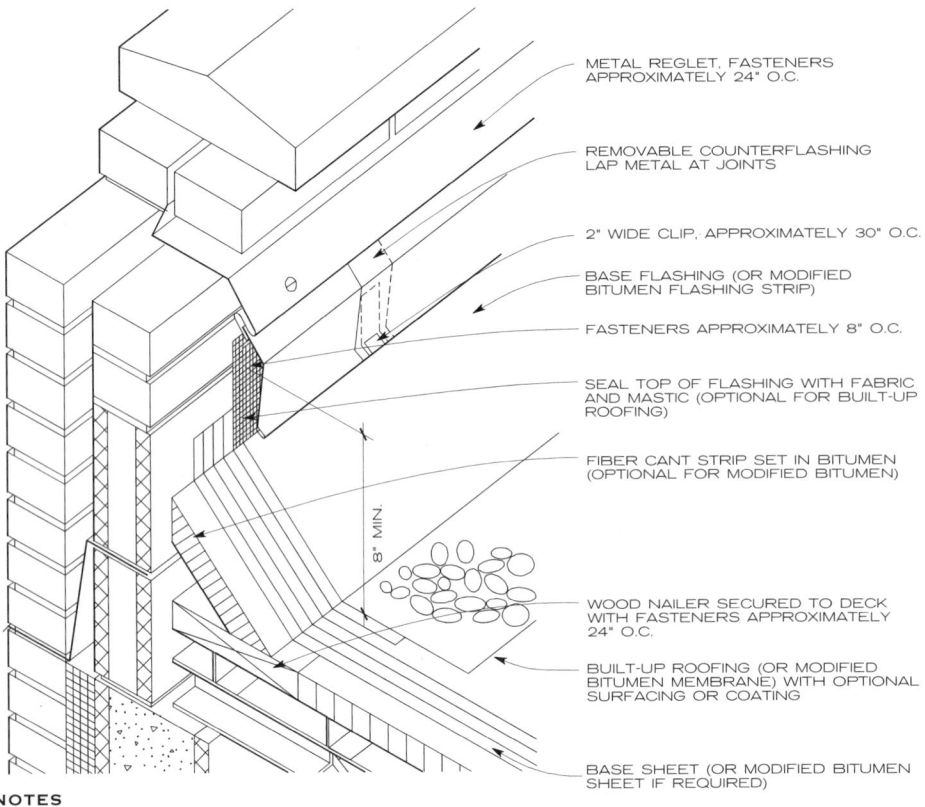

METAL REGLET, FASTENERS APPROXIMATELY 24" O.C.

REMOVABLE COUNTERFLASHING LAP METAL AT JOINTS

2" WIDE CLIP, APPROXIMATELY 30" O.C.

BASE FLASHING (OR MODIFIED BITUMEN FLASHING STRIP)

FASTENERS APPROXIMATELY 8" O.C.

SEAL TOP OF FLASHING WITH FABRIC AND MASTIC (OPTIONAL FOR BUILT-UP ROOFING)

FIBER CANT STRIP SET IN BITUMEN (OPTIONAL FOR MODIFIED BITUMEN)

8" MIN.

WOOD NAILER SECURED TO DECK WITH FASTENERS APPROXIMATELY 24" O.C.

BUILT-UP ROOFING (OR MODIFIED BITUMEN MEMBRANE) WITH OPTIONAL SURFACING OR COATING

BASE SHEET (OR MODIFIED BITUMEN SHEET IF REQUIRED)

NOTES

1. This detail should be used only when the deck is supported by the wall.

2. The joints in the two pieces of flashing should not be soldered. Breaks in soldered joints could channel water behind the flashing. Clips at the bottom of the flashing are not necessary on flashings of 6 in. or less.

BASE FLASHING FOR WALL-SUPPORTED DECK

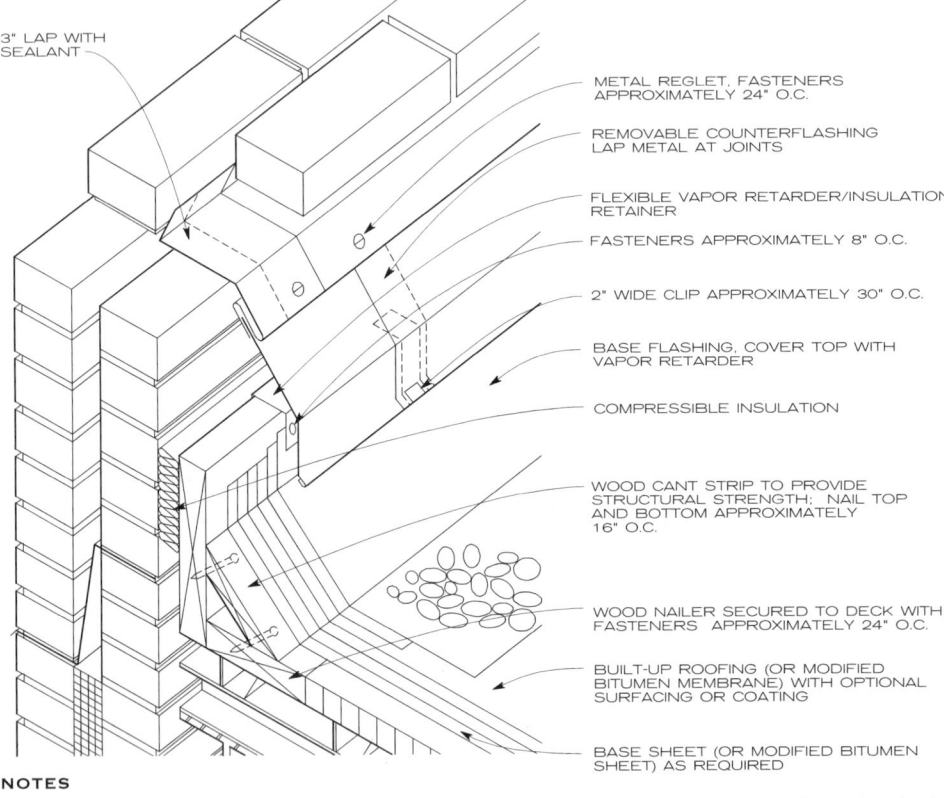

3" LAP WITH SEALANT

METAL REGLET, FASTENERS APPROXIMATELY 24" O.C.

REMOVABLE COUNTERFLASHING LAP METAL AT JOINTS

FLEXIBLE VAPOR RETARDER/INSULATION RETAINER

FASTENERS APPROXIMATELY 8" O.C.

2" WIDE CLIP APPROXIMATELY 30" O.C.

BASE FLASHING, COVER TOP WITH VAPOR RETARDER

COMPRESSIBLE INSULATION

WOOD CANT STRIP TO PROVIDE STRUCTURAL STRENGTH; NAIL TOP AND BOTTOM APPROXIMATELY 16" O.C.

WOOD NAILER SECURED TO DECK WITH FASTENERS APPROXIMATELY 24" O.C.

BUILT-UP ROOFING (OR MODIFIED BITUMEN MEMBRANE) WITH OPTIONAL SURFACING OR COATING

BASE SHEET (OR MODIFIED BITUMEN SHEET) AS REQUIRED

NOTES

1. This detail allows wall and deck to move independently.

2. This detail should be used where there is any possibility that differential movement will occur between the deck and a vertical surface, such as at a penthouse wall. The vertical wood member should be fastened to the deck only. This is one satisfactory method of joining the two-piece flashing system. Other methods may be used.

BASE FLASHING FOR NON-WALL-SUPPORTED DECK

National Roofing Contractors Association; Rosemont, Illinois
Valerie Eickelberger; Rippeteau Architects, PC; Washington, D.C.

GENERAL

In general, the details for installation of bitumen roofing, whether built-up roofing or modified bitumen roofing, are similar in many respects. Details for both types of roofing are included where applicable. The details show typical conditions that occur at bitumen roofs, such as roof edge conditions, piping penetrations, and equipment supports.

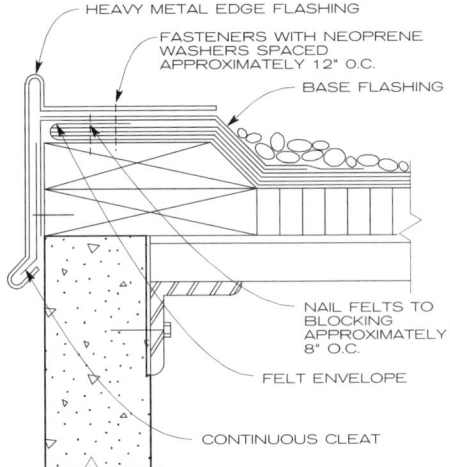

HEAVY METAL EDGE FLASHING

FASTENERS WITH NEOPRENE WASHERS SPACED APPROXIMATELY 12" O.C.

BASE FLASHING

NAIL FELTS TO BLOCKING APPROXIMATELY 8" O.C.

FELT ENVELOPE

CONTINUOUS CLEAT

HEAVY METAL ROOF EDGE

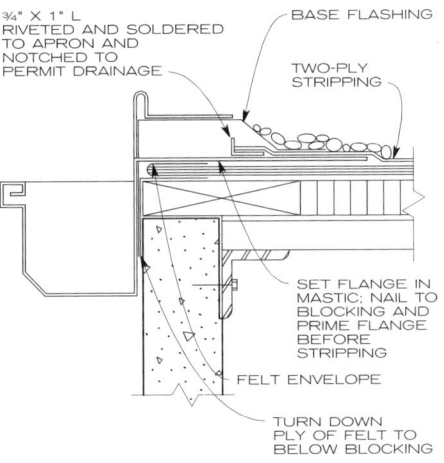

¾" X 1" L RIVETED AND SOLDERED TO APRON AND NOTCHED TO PERMIT DRAINAGE

BASE FLASHING

TWO-PLY STRIPPING

SET FLANGE IN MASTIC; NAIL TO BLOCKING AND PRIME FLANGE BEFORE STRIPPING

FELT ENVELOPE

TURN DOWN PLY OF FELT TO BELOW BLOCKING

SCUPPER THROUGH ROOF EDGE

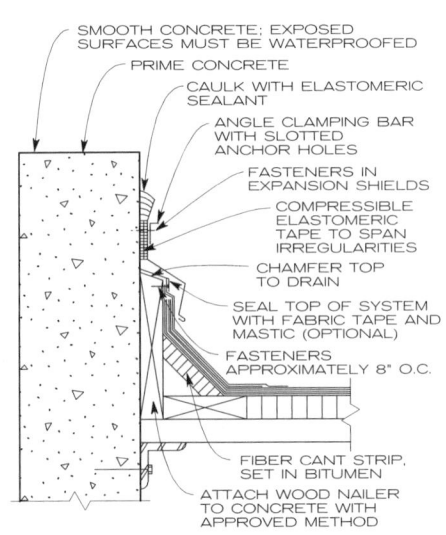

SMOOTH CONCRETE; EXPOSED SURFACES MUST BE WATERPROOFED

PRIME CONCRETE

CAULK WITH ELASTOMERIC SEALANT

ANGLE CLAMPING BAR WITH SLOTTED ANCHOR HOLES

FASTENERS IN EXPANSION SHIELDS

COMPRESSIBLE ELASTOMERIC TAPE TO SPAN IRREGULARITIES

CHAMFER TOP TO DRAIN

SEAL TOP OF SYSTEM WITH FABRIC TAPE AND MASTIC (OPTIONAL)

FASTENERS APPROXIMATELY 8" O.C.

FIBER CANT STRIP, SET IN BITUMEN

ATTACH WOOD NAILER TO CONCRETE WITH APPROVED METHOD

COUNTERFLASHING CONCRETE PARAPET

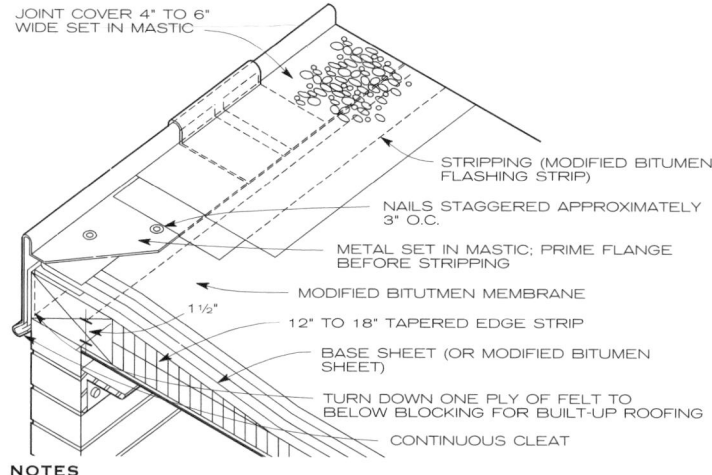

JOINT COVER 4" TO 6" WIDE SET IN MASTIC

STRIPPING (MODIFIED BITUMEN FLASHING STRIP)

NAILS STAGGERED APPROXIMATELY 3" O.C.

METAL SET IN MASTIC; PRIME FLANGE BEFORE STRIPPING

MODIFIED BITUTMEN MEMBRANE

12" TO 18" TAPERED EDGE STRIP

BASE SHEET (OR MODIFIED BITUMEN SHEET)

TURN DOWN ONE PLY OF FELT TO BELOW BLOCKING FOR BUILT-UP ROOFING

CONTINUOUS CLEAT

1½"

NOTES

1. Envelope shown is for coal tar pitch and low-slope asphalt.

2. Attach nailer to masonry wall.

3. This detail should be used only where the deck is supported by the outside wall.

4. This detail should be used with light-gauge metals, such as 16 oz. copper, 24-gauge galvanized metal, or 0.040 in. aluminum. A tapered edge strip is used to raise the gravel stop. Frequent nailing is necessary to control thermal movement.

5. Wood blocking may be slotted for venting where required.

GRAVEL STOP

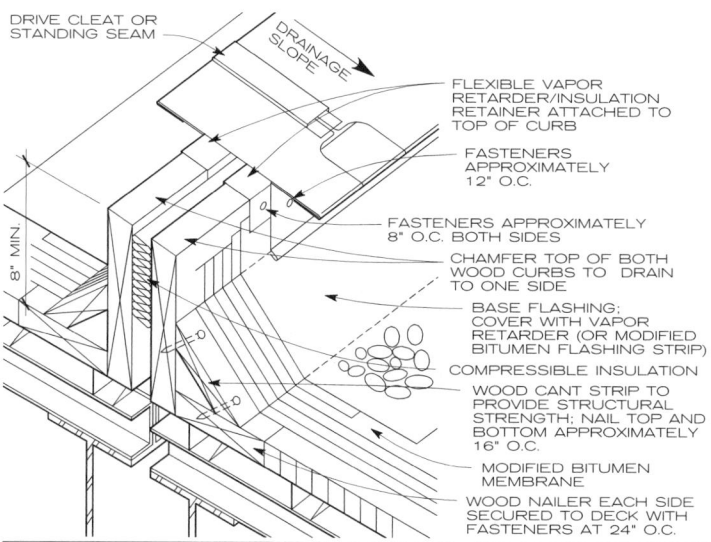

DRIVE CLEAT OR STANDING SEAM

DRAINAGE SLOPE

FLEXIBLE VAPOR RETARDER/INSULATION RETAINER ATTACHED TO TOP OF CURB

FASTENERS APPROXIMATELY 12" O.C.

FASTENERS APPROXIMATELY 8" O.C. BOTH SIDES

CHAMFER TOP OF BOTH WOOD CURBS TO DRAIN TO ONE SIDE

BASE FLASHING; COVER WITH VAPOR RETARDER (OR MODIFIED BITUMEN FLASHING STRIP)

COMPRESSIBLE INSULATION

WOOD CANT STRIP TO PROVIDE STRUCTURAL STRENGTH; NAIL TOP AND BOTTOM APPROXIMATELY 16" O.C.

MODIFIED BITUMEN MEMBRANE

WOOD NAILER EACH SIDE SECURED TO DECK WITH FASTENERS AT 24" O.C.

8" MIN.

EXPANSION JOINT

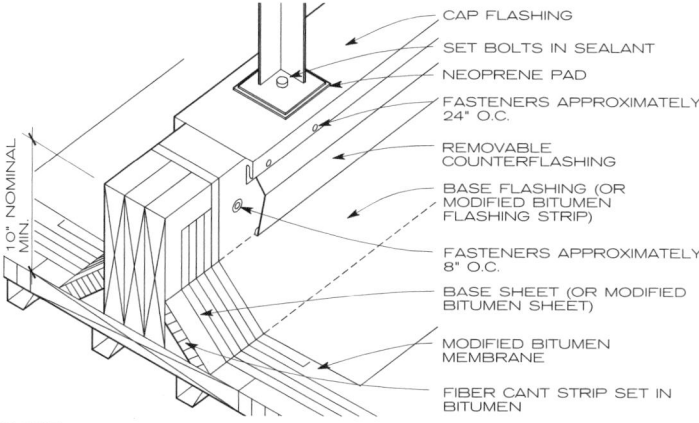

CAP FLASHING

SET BOLTS IN SEALANT

NEOPRENE PAD

FASTENERS APPROXIMATELY 24" O.C.

REMOVABLE COUNTERFLASHING

BASE FLASHING (OR MODIFIED BITUMEN FLASHING STRIP)

FASTENERS APPROXIMATELY 8" O.C.

BASE SHEET (OR MODIFIED BITUMEN SHEET)

MODIFIED BITUMEN MEMBRANE

FIBER CANT STRIP SET IN BITUMEN

10" NOMINAL MIN.

NOTE

This detail allows for roof maintenance around the equipment support. Continuous support is preferred in lightweight roof systems because equipment weight can be spread over two or more supporting members. Clearance must be provided for removal and replacement of roofing and flashing between parallel supports.

EQUIPMENT SUPPORT ON LIGHT ROOF DECK

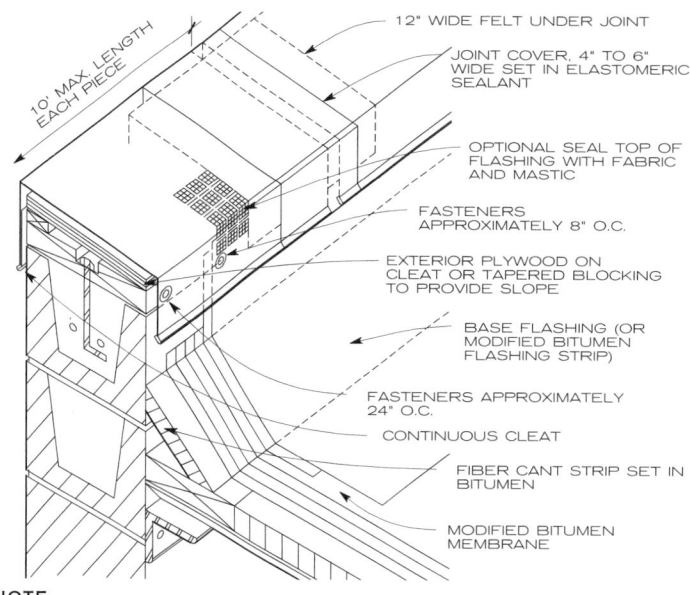

12" WIDE FELT UNDER JOINT

JOINT COVER, 4" TO 6" WIDE SET IN ELASTOMERIC SEALANT

OPTIONAL SEAL TOP OF FLASHING WITH FABRIC AND MASTIC

FASTENERS APPROXIMATELY 8" O.C.

EXTERIOR PLYWOOD ON CLEAT OR TAPERED BLOCKING TO PROVIDE SLOPE

BASE FLASHING (OR MODIFIED BITUMEN FLASHING STRIP)

FASTENERS APPROXIMATELY 24" O.C.

CONTINUOUS CLEAT

FIBER CANT STRIP SET IN BITUMEN

MODIFIED BITUMEN MEMBRANE

10' MAX. LENGTH EACH PIECE

NOTE

This detail should be used only when the deck is supported by the wall. An expansion joint detail should be used for a deck not supported by a wall.

LIGHT METAL PARAPET CAP

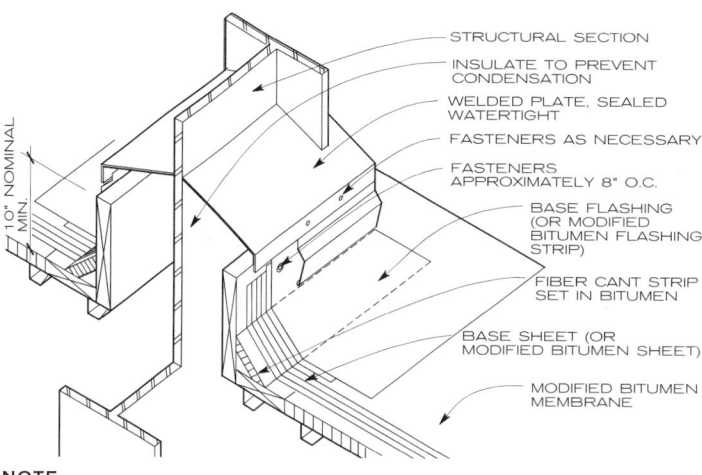

STRUCTURAL SECTION

INSULATE TO PREVENT CONDENSATION

WELDED PLATE, SEALED WATERTIGHT

FASTENERS AS NECESSARY

FASTENERS APPROXIMATELY 8" O.C.

BASE FLASHING (OR MODIFIED BITUMEN FLASHING STRIP)

FIBER CANT STRIP SET IN BITUMEN

BASE SHEET (OR MODIFIED BITUMEN SHEET)

MODIFIED BITUMEN MEMBRANE

10" NOMINAL MIN.

NOTE

This detail illustrates one method of eliminating pitch pockets. The curbed system allows for movement in the structural member without disturbing the roof system.

STRUCTURAL MEMBER THROUGH ROOF

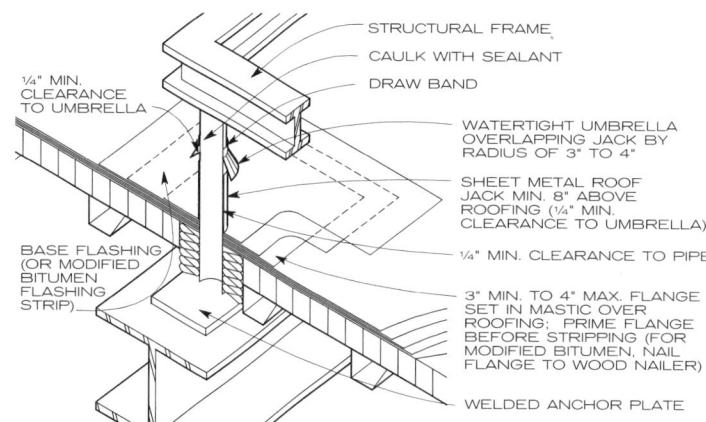

STRUCTURAL FRAME

CAULK WITH SEALANT

DRAW BAND

WATERTIGHT UMBRELLA OVERLAPPING JACK BY RADIUS OF 3" TO 4"

SHEET METAL ROOF JACK MIN. 8" ABOVE ROOFING (¼" MIN. CLEARANCE TO UMBRELLA)

¼" MIN. CLEARANCE TO PIPE

3" MIN. TO 4" MAX. FLANGE SET IN MASTIC OVER ROOFING; PRIME FLANGE BEFORE STRIPPING (FOR MODIFIED BITUMEN, NAIL FLANGE TO WOOD NAILER)

WELDED ANCHOR PLATE

¼" MIN. CLEARANCE TO UMBRELLA

BASE FLASHING (OR MODIFIED BITUMEN FLASHING STRIP)

NOTE

This detail depicts site-fabricated construction. Many manufacturers now offer prefabricated flashing pieces or permit the use of materials for flashing purposes other than those shown here. Proprietary designs vary widely; consult individual manufacturers about use.

INSULATED DECK STEEL FRAME SUPPORT

National Roofing Contractors Association; Rosemont, Illinois
Valerie Eickelberger; Rippeteau Architects, PC; Washington, D.C.

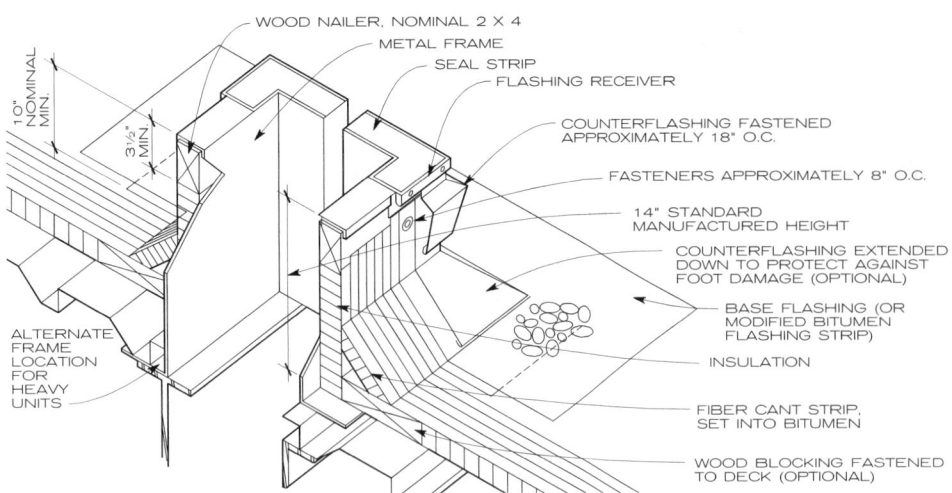

EQUIPMENT CURB

WOOD NAILER, NOMINAL 2 X 4
METAL FRAME
SEAL STRIP
FLASHING RECEIVER
COUNTERFLASHING FASTENED APPROXIMATELY 18" O.C.
FASTENERS APPROXIMATELY 8" O.C.
14" STANDARD MANUFACTURED HEIGHT
COUNTERFLASHING EXTENDED DOWN TO PROTECT AGAINST FOOT DAMAGE (OPTIONAL)
BASE FLASHING (OR MODIFIED BITUMEN FLASHING STRIP)
INSULATION
FIBER CANT STRIP, SET INTO BITUMEN
WOOD BLOCKING FASTENED TO DECK (OPTIONAL)
ALTERNATE FRAME LOCATION FOR HEAVY UNITS
1'0" NOMINAL MIN.
3 1/2" MIN

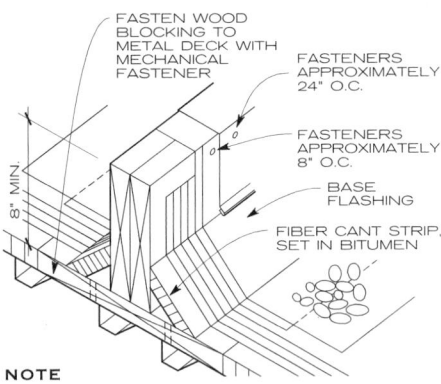

AREA DIVIDER

FASTEN WOOD BLOCKING TO METAL DECK WITH MECHANICAL FASTENER
FASTENERS APPROXIMATELY 24" O.C.
FASTENERS APPROXIMATELY 8" O.C.
BASE FLASHING
FIBER CANT STRIP, SET IN BITUMEN
8" MIN

NOTE

An area divider is designed simply as a raised double wood member attached to a properly flashed wood base plate that is anchored to the roof deck. Area dividers should be located between the roof's expansion joints at 150 to 200 ft intervals, depending upon climatic conditions and area practices. They should never restrict the flow of water.

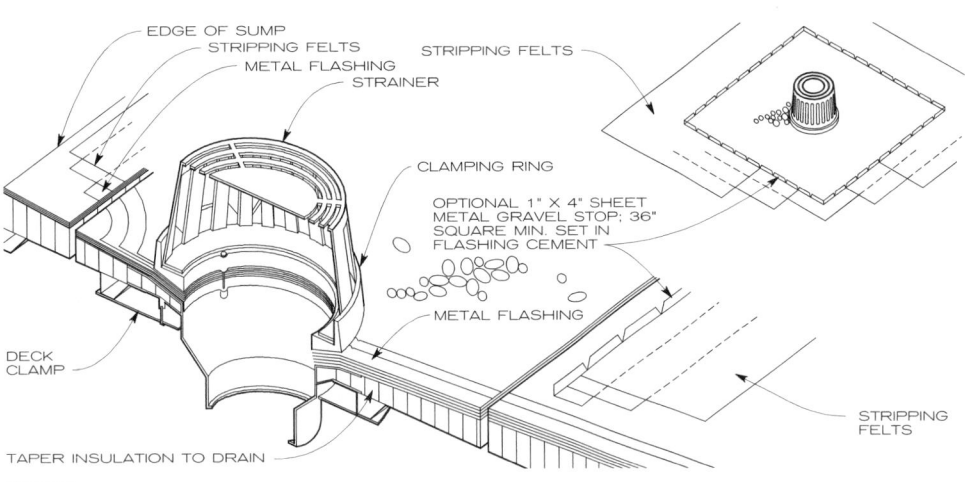

ROOF DRAIN

EDGE OF SUMP
STRIPPING FELTS
METAL FLASHING
STRAINER
STRIPPING FELTS
CLAMPING RING
OPTIONAL 1" X 4" SHEET METAL GRAVEL STOP; 36" SQUARE MIN. SET IN FLASHING CEMENT
METAL FLASHING
DECK CLAMP
TAPER INSULATION TO DRAIN
STRIPPING FELTS

NOTES

1. Minimum 30 in. square, 2 1/2 to 4 lb lead or 16 oz soft copper flashing set on finished roof felts set in mastic. Prime top surface before stripping.
2. Membrane plies, metal flashing, and flash-in plies extend under the clamping ring.
3. Stripping felts extend 4 in. and 6 in. beyond edge of flashing sheet, but not beyond edge of sump.
4. The use of metal deck sump pans is not recommended.

PIPE ROLLER SUPPORT

SET BOLTS IN ELASTOMERIC SEALANT
ADJUSTS VERTICALLY AND HORIZONTALLY

NOTE

This detail allows for expansion and contraction of pipes without roof damage.

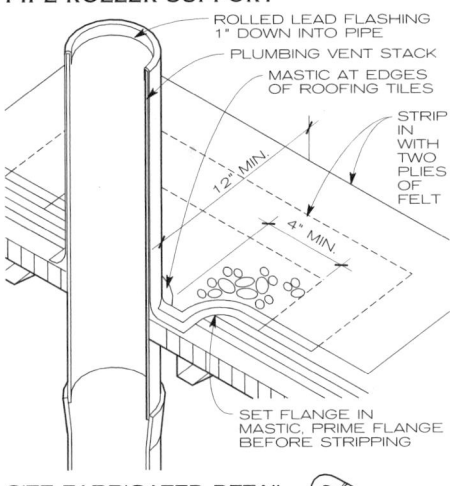

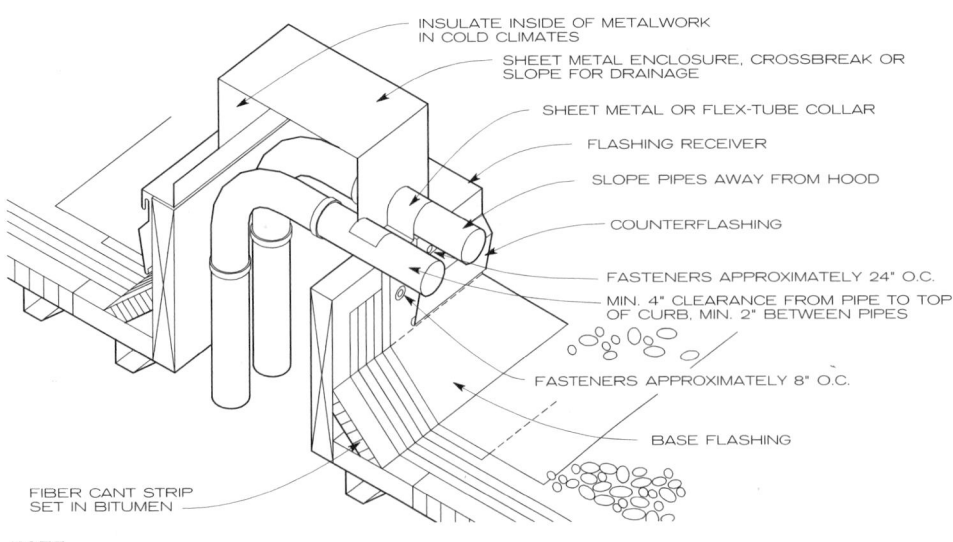

MULTIPLE PIPE PENETRATION

INSULATE INSIDE OF METALWORK IN COLD CLIMATES
SHEET METAL ENCLOSURE, CROSSBREAK OR SLOPE FOR DRAINAGE
SHEET METAL OR FLEX-TUBE COLLAR
FLASHING RECEIVER
SLOPE PIPES AWAY FROM HOOD
COUNTERFLASHING
FASTENERS APPROXIMATELY 24" O.C.
MIN. 4" CLEARANCE FROM PIPE TO TOP OF CURB, MIN. 2" BETWEEN PIPES
FASTENERS APPROXIMATELY 8" O.C.
BASE FLASHING
FIBER CANT STRIP SET IN BITUMEN

NOTE

This detail illustrates another method of eliminating pitch pockets and a satisfactory method of grouping piping that must come up above the roof surface.

ROLLED LEAD FLASHING 1" DOWN INTO PIPE
PLUMBING VENT STACK
MASTIC AT EDGES OF ROOFING TILES
STRIP IN WITH TWO PLIES OF FELT
SET FLANGE IN MASTIC, PRIME FLANGE BEFORE STRIPPING
12" MIN.
4" MIN.

SITE-FABRICATED DETAIL

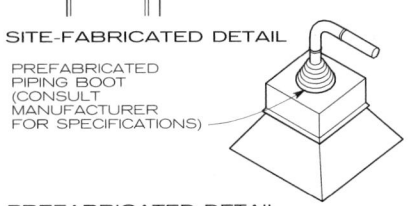

PREFABRICATED PIPING BOOT (CONSULT MANUFACTURER FOR SPECIFICATIONS)

PREFABRICATED DETAIL

NOTES

1. Sheet lead minimum of 2 1/2 lb per sq ft.
2. Minimum clearance of 12 in. from cant strips and other curbs or pipes.

SINGLE PIPE PENETRATION

National Roofing Contractors Association; Rosemont, Illinois
Valerie Eickelberger; Rippeteau Architects, PC; Washington, D.C.

7 **MEMBRANE ROOFING**

EPDM SINGLE-PLY ROOFING

Ethylene propylene diene monomer (EPDM) membranes are 30 to 60 mil thick, single-sheet roofing materials. They are available either nonreinforced or reinforced with fabric. Seams in the membrane are spliced and cemented. EPDM membranes are highly resistant to degradation from certain chemicals, ozone, and ultraviolet radiation and have excellent resilience, tensile strength, abrasion resistance, hardness, and weathering properties.

EPDM membranes may be laid loose, mechanically fastened, or fully adhered to either nailable or non-nailable decks. For loose-laid systems, ballast provides resistance against wind uplift forces. Some membranes require field application of surfacings or coatings to provide weather resistance, aesthetics, or other properties. Specifications for formulation and installation of EPDM membranes vary with the individual manufacturer.

Separation layers of asphalt-saturated organic felt or board-type roof insulation permit the membrane to move relative to the deck without abrasion. Membrane terminations at roof edges, parapets, and other flashings employ material identical to the roof membrane material shaped to conform to the substrate and area being flashed. Standards for EPDM membranes are maintained by ASTM and the Rubber Manufacturers Association.

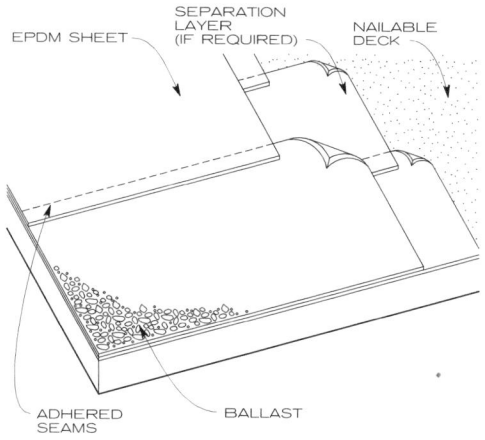

OVER NAILABLE DECK

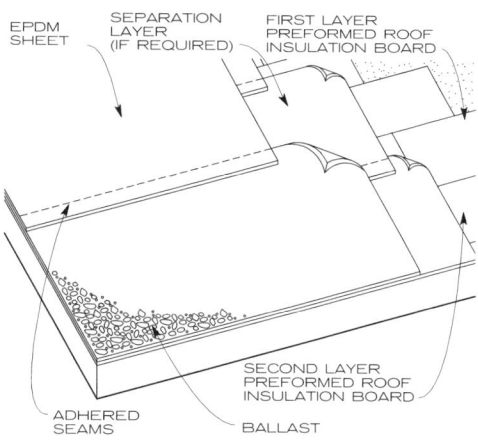

OVER NON-NAILABLE DECK

LOOSE-LAID EPDM ROOFING

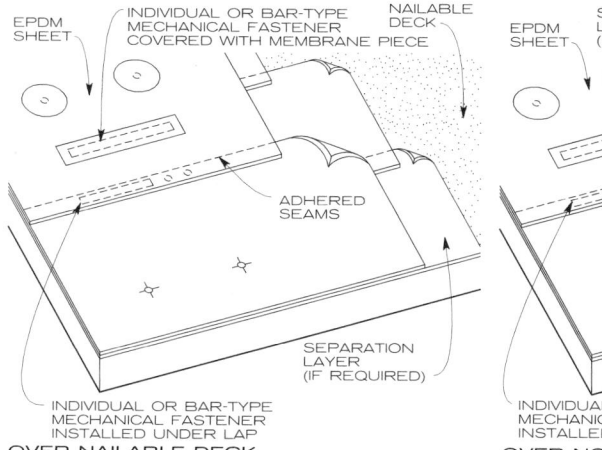

OVER NAILABLE DECK

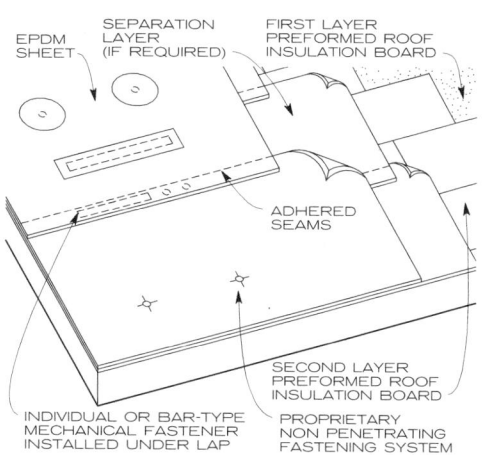

OVER NON-NAILABLE DECK

MECHANICALLY FASTENED EPDM ROOFING

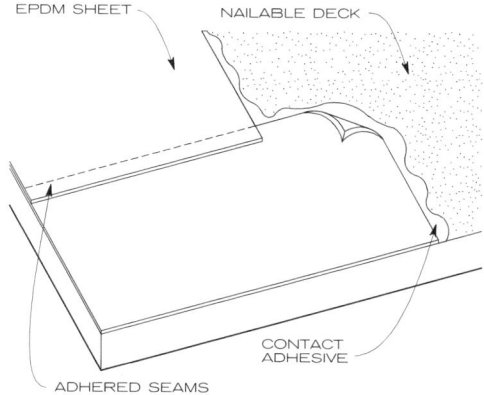

OVER NAILABLE DECK

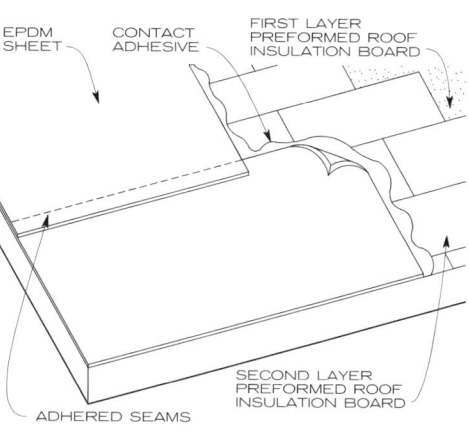

OVER NON-NAILABLE DECK

FULLY ADHERED EPDM ROOFING

National Roofing Contractors Association; Rosemont, Illinois
Valerie Eickelberger; Rippeteau Architects, PC; Washington, D.C.

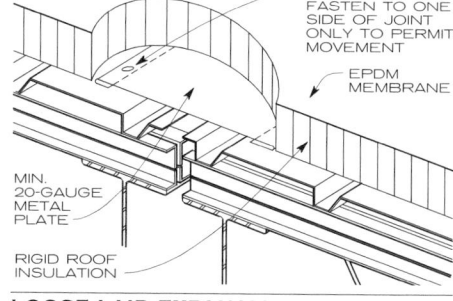

LOOSE-LAID EXPANSION JOINT

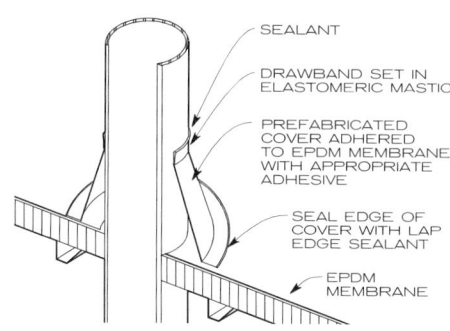

PREFABRICATED PIPE FLASHING

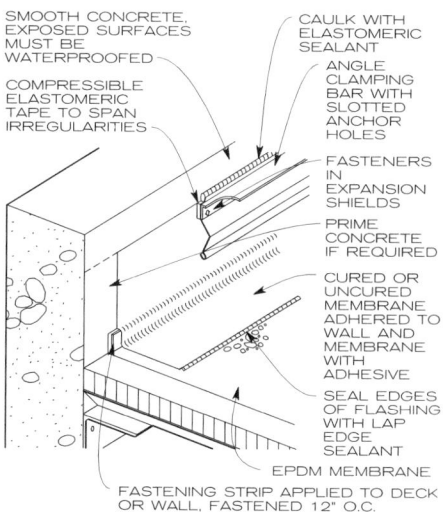

PARAPET COUNTERFLASHING

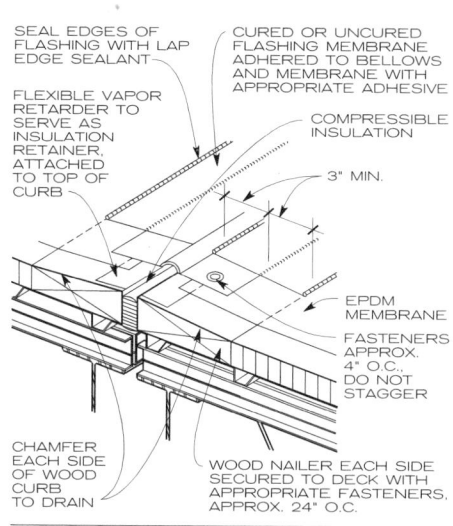

EXPANSION JOINT

SINGLE-PLY PVC ROOFING

Polyvinyl chloride (PVC) membranes may be nonreinforced or reinforced with glass fibers or polyester fabric 45 to 60 mils thick. Seams are formed by heat or chemical welding, and may require additional caulking. PVC membranes are resistant to bacterial growth, industrial chemical atmospheres, root penetration, and extreme weather conditions. PVC membranes have excellent fire resistance and seaming capabilities.

ASTM Standard D-4434 classes PVC materials into several types and classes depending upon the construction of the sheet material:

TYPE I: Unreinforced sheet
TYPE II, CLASS I: Unreinforced sheet containing fibers
TYPE II, CLASS II: Unreinforced sheet containing fabrics
TYPE III: Reinforced sheet containing fibers or fabrics

PVC membranes may be laid loose, mechanically fastened, or fully adhered to either nailable or non-nailable decks. For loose-laid systems, ballast provides resistance against wind uplift forces. Some PVC membranes have a factory-applied coating to provide weather resistance, aesthetics, or other properties to the membrane. Some membranes may require field application of surfacings or coatings to provide these properties.

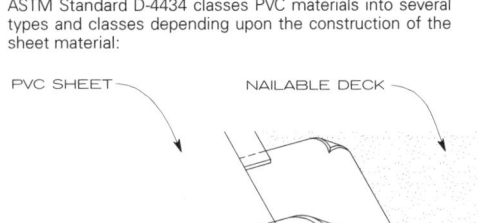
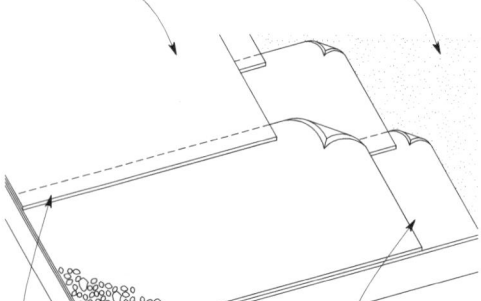
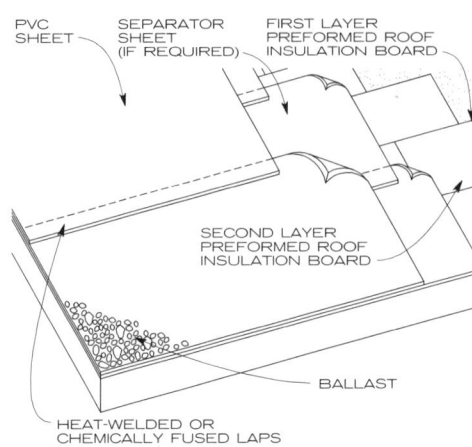

OVER NAILABLE DECK

OVER NON-NAILABLE DECK

LOOSE-LAID PVC ROOFING

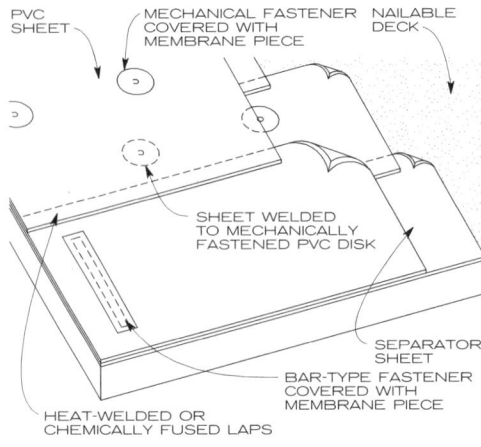

OVER NAILABLE DECK

OVER NON-NAILABLE DECK

MECHANICALLY FASTENED PVC ROOFING

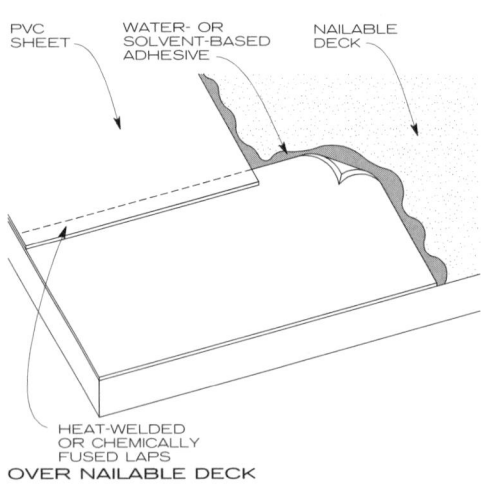

OVER NAILABLE DECK

OVER NON-NAILABLE DECK

FULLY ADHERED PVC ROOFING

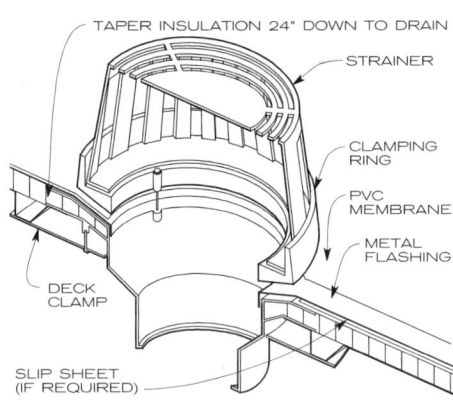

ROOF DRAIN

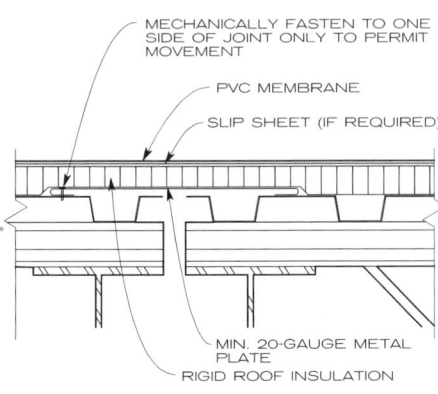

LOOSE-LAID EXPANSION JOINT

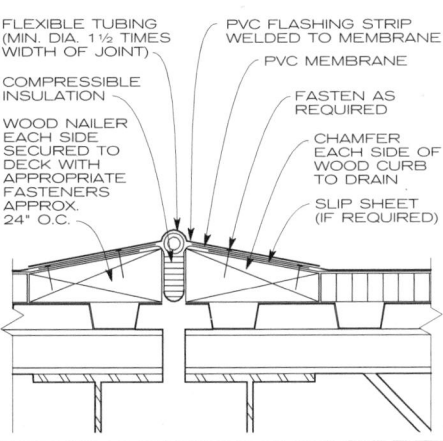

EXPANSION JOINT

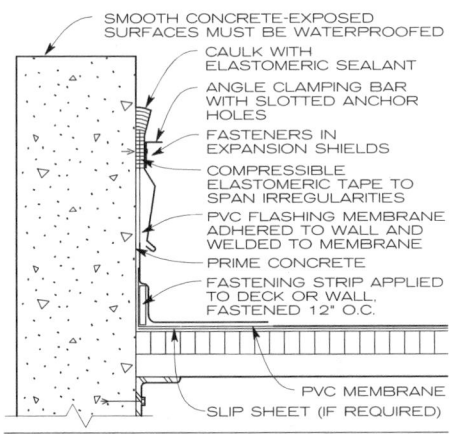

PARAPET COUNTERFLASHING

National Roofing Contractors Association; Rosemont, Illinois
Valerie Eickelberger; Rippeteau Architects, PC; Washington, D.C.

GENERAL

Liquid-applied roofing systems are systems primarily applied as liquids at ambient temperatures. Most of them have some sort of reinforcing fabric that is applied along with the liquid component. Liquid-applied roofing applied over existing roofs is not generally accepted as a "membrane" but as a coating.

Acrylic latex and urethane are the two main types of liquid-applied roofing. Acrylic latex refers to a family of products that use water-based polymers and cure by water evaporation. Liquid-applied urethane roof coatings are chemically cured to form an elastomeric membrane. Because these coatings are applied as liquids, installation is relatively simple, even for roofs with irregular geometries or multiple penetrations. For systems using a reinforcing fabric, a coating is applied to an acceptable surface. While the coating is still wet, a layer of polyester or fiberglass is laid into it followed by an additional layer of coating. Subsequent layers may be added as desired or necessary.

Liquid-applied roofing systems are appropriate for new construction but are most commonly used as enhancements or for repairs to existing roofs, including modified bitumen roofs and built-up roofs.

Advantages of liquid-applied roofing are that it conforms very well to irregular surfaces, is easily applied, and comes in various colors. However, it does cause marginal ponded water performance and is best used in sloped roof situations.

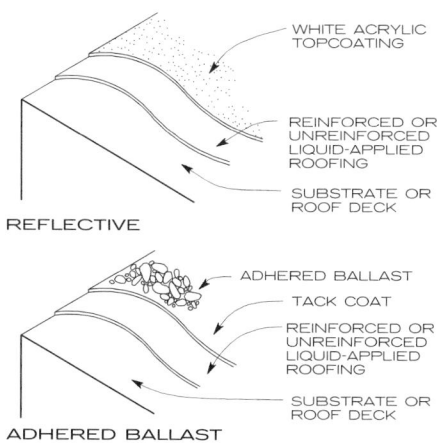

REFLECTIVE

ADHERED BALLAST

NOTE

Liquid-applied roofing systems may also be used under rigid insulation and ballast for further protection. Refer to "Protected Membrane Roofing" for further details.

LIQUID-APPLIED ROOFING SYSTEMS

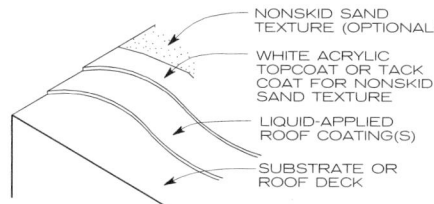

UNREINFORCED MEMBRANE

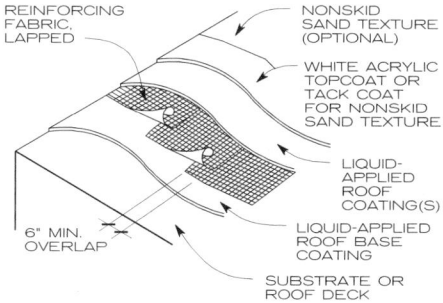

REINFORCED MEMBRANE
LIQUID-APPLIED MEMBRANE TYPES

Richard J. Vitullo, AIA; Oak Leaf Studio; Crownsville, Maryland
Rich Boon; The Roofing Industry Educational Institute; Englewood, Colorado

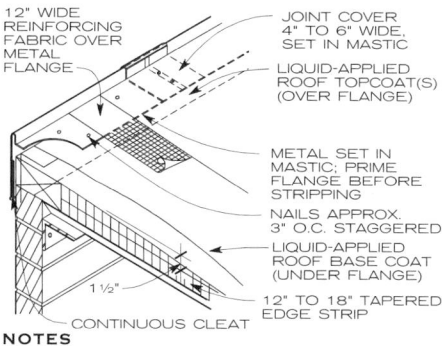

NOTES

1. Attach nailer to masonry wall. Refer to Factory Mutual data sheet # 1-49.
2. This detail should be used only when the deck is supported by the outside wall.
3. This detail should be used with light-gauge metals such as a 16-oz copper, 24-gauge galvanized metal, or 0.04-in. aluminum. A tapered edge strip is used to raise the gravel stop. Frequent nailing is necessary to control thermal movement.

GRAVEL STOP

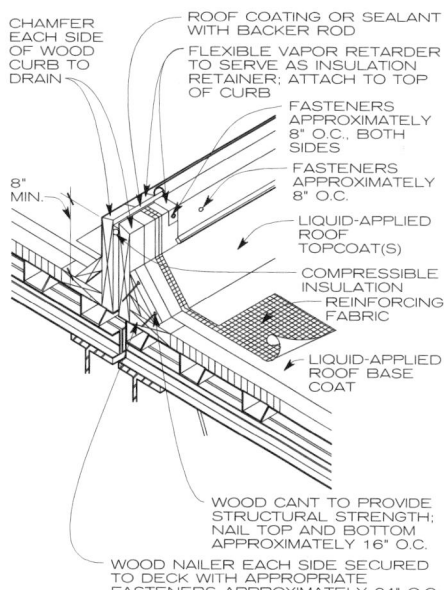

EXPANSION JOINT

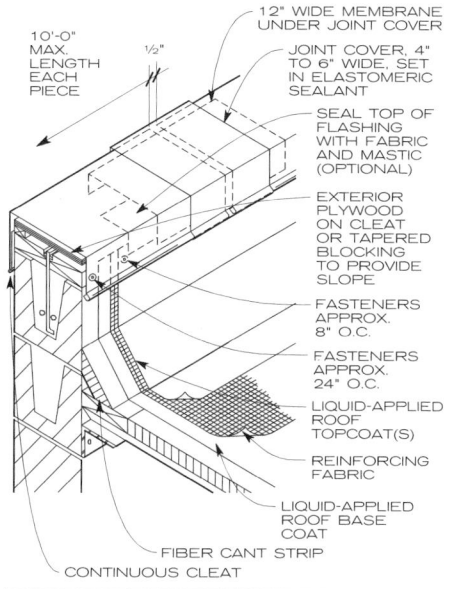

LIGHT METAL PARAPET CAP

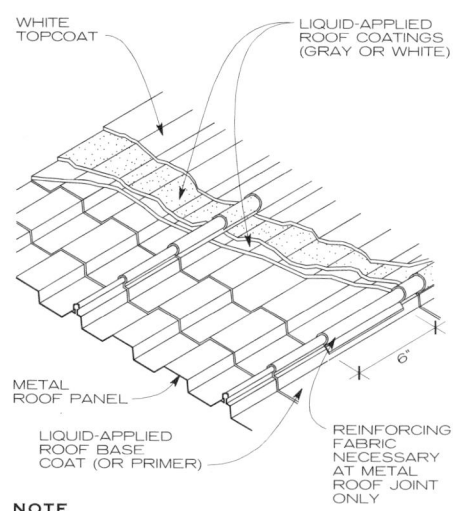

NOTE

Roof slope minimum is 1/4 in. in 12 or 2%; no maximum.

RETROFIT LIQUID-APPLIED ROOFING OVER EXISTING METAL ROOF

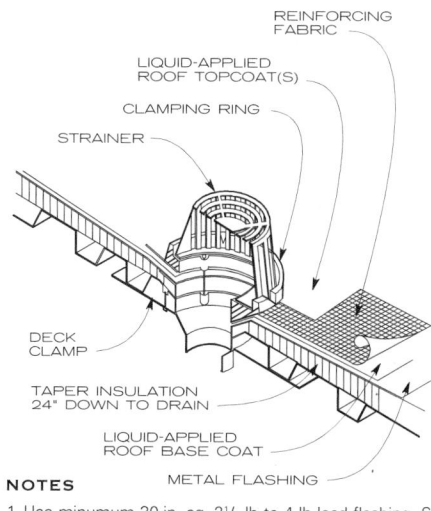

NOTES

1. Use minumum 30-in. sq, 2 1/2 lb to 4 lb lead flashing. Set in mastic. Prime top surface before stripping.
2. Liquid-applied roof coatings, reinforcing fabric, and metal flashing (optional) extend under clamping ring.

ROOF DRAIN

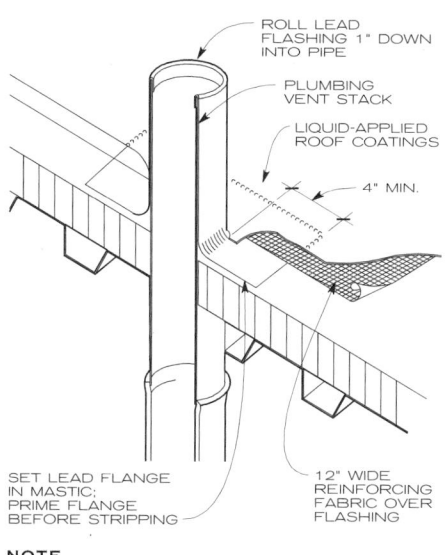

NOTE

Sheet lead minimum of 2 1/2 lb per sq ft.

SINGLE PIPE PENETRATION

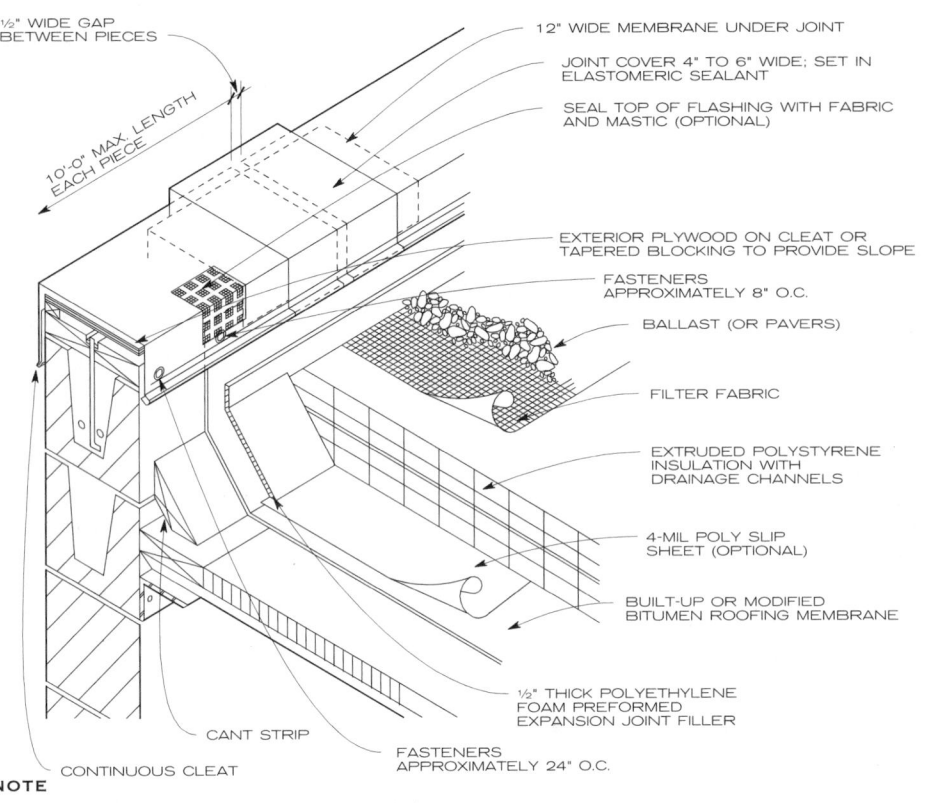

½" WIDE GAP BETWEEN PIECES

10'-0" MAX. LENGTH EACH PIECE

12" WIDE MEMBRANE UNDER JOINT

JOINT COVER 4" TO 6" WIDE; SET IN ELASTOMERIC SEALANT

SEAL TOP OF FLASHING WITH FABRIC AND MASTIC (OPTIONAL)

EXTERIOR PLYWOOD ON CLEAT OR TAPERED BLOCKING TO PROVIDE SLOPE

FASTENERS APPROXIMATELY 8" O.C.

BALLAST (OR PAVERS)

FILTER FABRIC

EXTRUDED POLYSTYRENE INSULATION WITH DRAINAGE CHANNELS

4-MIL POLY SLIP SHEET (OPTIONAL)

BUILT-UP OR MODIFIED BITUMEN ROOFING MEMBRANE

½" THICK POLYETHYLENE FOAM PREFORMED EXPANSION JOINT FILLER

CANT STRIP

FASTENERS APPROXIMATELY 24" O.C.

CONTINUOUS CLEAT

NOTE

Membrane may be built-up, modified bitumen, or single-ply. If thermoplastic membrane is specified, provide slip sheet between insulation and membrane.

LIGHT METAL PARAPET CAP AT BUILT-UP OR MODIFIED BITUMEN ROOF

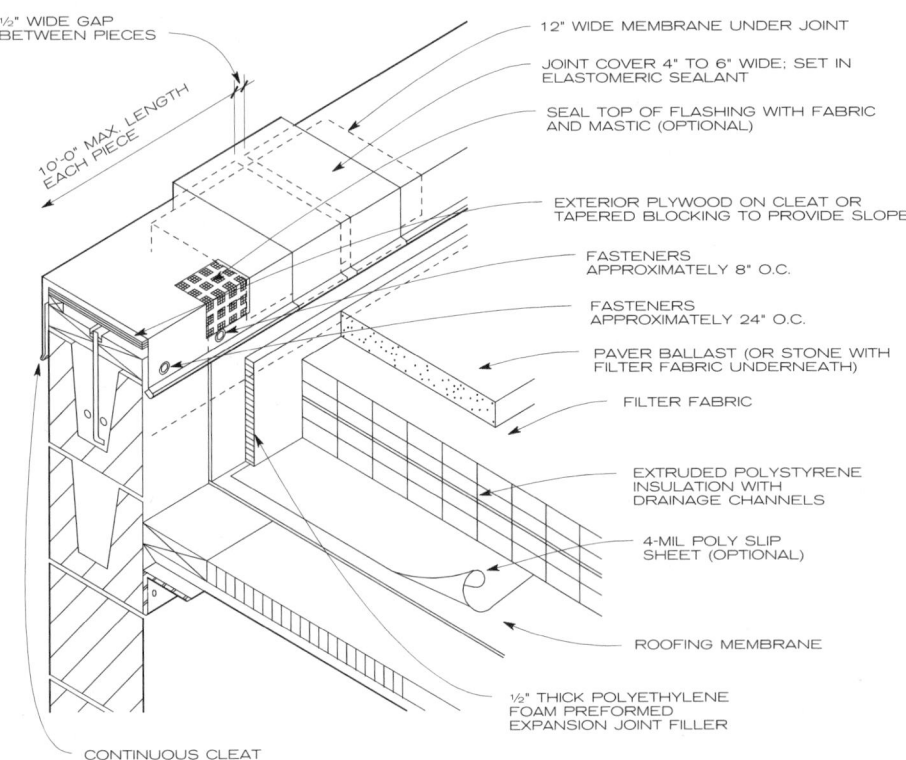

½" WIDE GAP BETWEEN PIECES

10'-0" MAX. LENGTH EACH PIECE

12" WIDE MEMBRANE UNDER JOINT

JOINT COVER 4" TO 6" WIDE; SET IN ELASTOMERIC SEALANT

SEAL TOP OF FLASHING WITH FABRIC AND MASTIC (OPTIONAL)

EXTERIOR PLYWOOD ON CLEAT OR TAPERED BLOCKING TO PROVIDE SLOPE

FASTENERS APPROXIMATELY 8" O.C.

FASTENERS APPROXIMATELY 24" O.C.

PAVER BALLAST (OR STONE WITH FILTER FABRIC UNDERNEATH)

FILTER FABRIC

EXTRUDED POLYSTYRENE INSULATION WITH DRAINAGE CHANNELS

4-MIL POLY SLIP SHEET (OPTIONAL)

ROOFING MEMBRANE

½" THICK POLYETHYLENE FOAM PREFORMED EXPANSION JOINT FILLER

CONTINUOUS CLEAT

NOTES

1. Membrane must be single-ply. If thermoplastic membrane is specified, provide slip sheet between insulation and membrane.

2. Set pavers on pedestals or specify that the top layer of insulation boards have ribs on the top side to facilitate drying.

LIGHT METAL PARAPET AT SINGLE-PLY ROOF

Richard J. Vitullo, AIA; Oak Leaf Studio; Crownsville, Maryland
Rich Boon; The Roofing Industry Educational Institute; Englewood, Colorado

GENERAL

In a typical roofing system, the waterproof membrane system (built-up, modified bitumen, or single-ply) is applied on top of the insulation, which lies on top of the substrate and/or structural deck. The membrane in this situation is exposed to temperature extremes and wear and tear from people walking or working on the roof. In a protected membrane roof (sometimes called the inverted or insulated roof membrane assembly, or IRMA), a layer of extruded polystyrene insulation board protects the membrane. Extruded polystyrene is the only material generally approved for this application because it does not absorb moisture. This roofing system is best used in extreme climates, where it is important to protect the membrane from the elements, or where the rooftop will receive heavy use (e.g., plaza or parking deck applications).

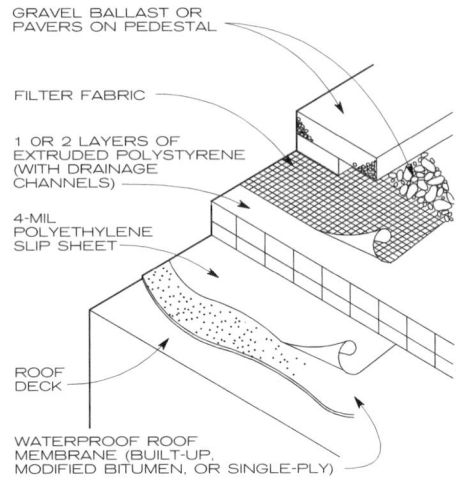

GRAVEL BALLAST OR PAVERS ON PEDESTAL

FILTER FABRIC

1 OR 2 LAYERS OF EXTRUDED POLYSTYRENE (WITH DRAINAGE CHANNELS)

4-MIL POLYETHYLENE SLIP SHEET

ROOF DECK

WATERPROOF ROOF MEMBRANE (BUILT-UP, MODIFIED BITUMEN, OR SINGLE-PLY)

NOTES

1. Ballast weight is a minimum of 10 lb per square foot.

2. Refer to ANSI/SPRI/RMA RP-4 for wind design guidance.

3. In lieu of aggregate or concrete ballast, proprietary insulation boards with concrete topping are available. These boards weigh between 4.5 lb per square foot and 10 lb per square foot, depending on the product selected.

TYPICAL PROTECTED MEMBRANE ROOF SYSTEM

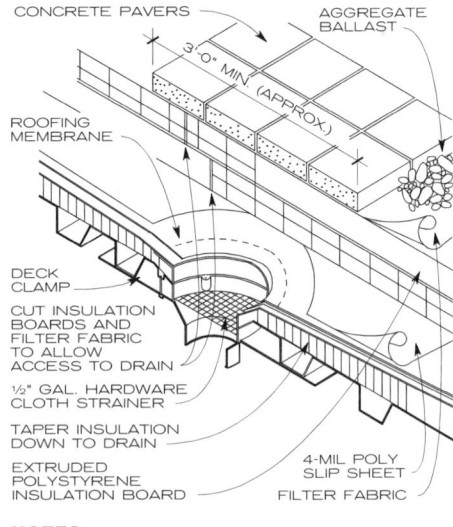

CONCRETE PAVERS

AGGREGATE BALLAST

3'-0" MIN (APPROX.)

ROOFING MEMBRANE

DECK CLAMP

CUT INSULATION BOARDS AND FILTER FABRIC TO ALLOW ACCESS TO DRAIN

½" GAL. HARDWARE CLOTH STRAINER

TAPER INSULATION DOWN TO DRAIN

EXTRUDED POLYSTYRENE INSULATION BOARD

4-MIL POLY SLIP SHEET

FILTER FABRIC

NOTES

1. Standard weight concrete pavers should be used to mark drain locations and to facilitate access to drains.

2. To facilitate placement of insulation boards, etc., the clamping ring and strainer are to be removed from metal drains. A ½ in. hardware cloth strainer should be laid at the bottom of the drain bowl.

3. For a thermoplastic membrane, use a 4-mil polyethylene slip sheet between the membrane and the insulation boards. Cut a hole in the sheet at the drain, approximately 2 in. larger than the diameter of the drain bowl.

ROOF DRAIN

GENERAL

Polyurethane foam roofing is spray-applied, seamless, and fully adhered. The foam is made by mixing isocyanate and resin components at a 1:1 ratio. Spray polyurethane foam is a closed-cell foam that provides good insulation and water resistance. These systems are used with a protective coating or stone ballast covering system, which protects the foam roofing from ultraviolet rays and mechanical damage.

These systems can be applied in varying thicknesses to eliminate ponding, to improve drainage, and to meet specified R-values (approximately R-6.25 per inch). Some advantages of spray foam systems are that they can be used over highly irregular surfaces, unusual geometries, or existing sloped metal systems. They are also inherently lightweight and offer good wind uplift resistance.

NOTES

1. Before spray polyurethane foam is applied, all surfaces must be clean, free of contaminants, securely fastened to the substrate, and completely dry. Moisture-sensitive indicators may be needed to detect any moisture within the existing roof assembly. Vapor retarders may be necessary; consult with the manufacturer to coordinate a specific roofing condition with foam application.

2. Most polyurethane foam manufacturers produce three seasonal grades: winter (fast), regular, and summer (slow).

3. If wind speed affects foam quality, use wind screens or discontinue spraying. The surface texture of sprayed foam can vary due to wind, equipment adjustment, spray technique, and characteristics of the system used. Foam that will be elastomeric coated should have a smooth texture resembling orange peel. For an aggregate covering, the texture should be no rougher than popcorn.

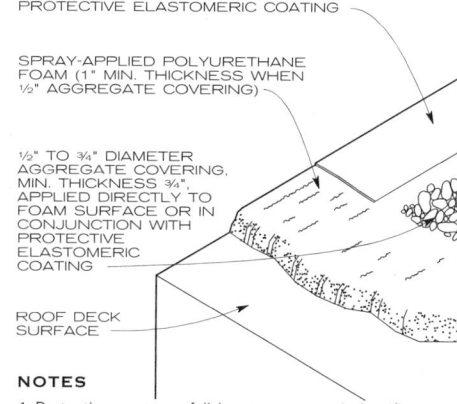

PROTECTIVE ELASTOMERIC COATING

SPRAY-APPLIED POLYURETHANE FOAM (1" MIN. THICKNESS WHEN ½" AGGREGATE COVERING)

½" TO ¾" DIAMETER AGGREGATE COVERING, MIN. THICKNESS ¾", APPLIED DIRECTLY TO FOAM SURFACE OR IN CONJUNCTION WITH PROTECTIVE ELASTOMERIC COATING

ROOF DECK SURFACE

NOTES

1. Protection systems fall into two general classifications, protective elastomeric coatings and aggregate. There are seven generic types of elastomeric protective coatings: acrylic, silicone, urethane, butyl, hypalon, neoprene, and modified asphalt. The physical properties of these coatings may vary, and the coating manufacturer should be consulted for recommendations on specific needs.

2. Granules may be applied to the wet uncured protective topcoat to enhance the resistance of the coating systems to UV or mechanical damage.

SPRAY-APPLIED POLYURETHANE FOAM ROOFING SYSTEM

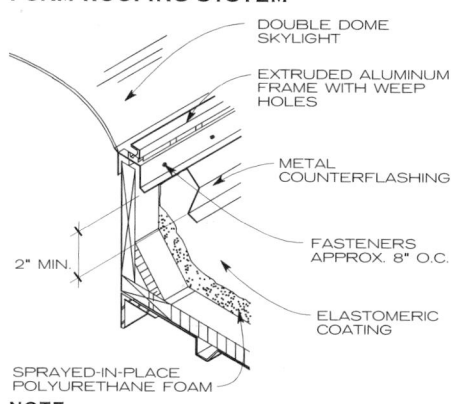

DOUBLE DOME SKYLIGHT

EXTRUDED ALUMINUM FRAME WITH WEEP HOLES

METAL COUNTERFLASHING

FASTENERS APPROX. 8" O.C.

ELASTOMERIC COATING

2" MIN.

SPRAYED-IN-PLACE POLYURETHANE FOAM

NOTE

On skylights, do not cover weep holes with polyurethane foam or coating.

SKYLIGHT, SCUTTLE, OR VENT CURB

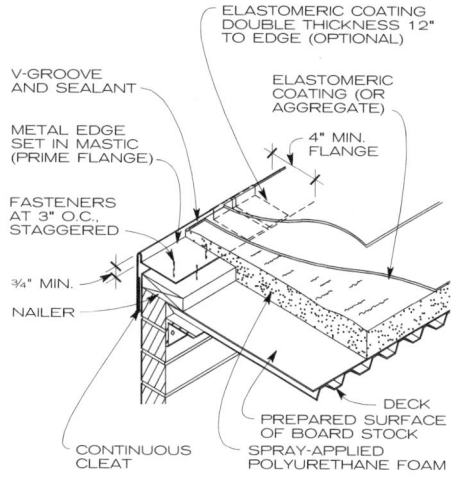

ELASTOMERIC COATING DOUBLE THICKNESS 12" TO EDGE (OPTIONAL)

V-GROOVE AND SEALANT

METAL EDGE SET IN MASTIC (PRIME FLANGE)

ELASTOMERIC COATING (OR AGGREGATE)

4" MIN. FLANGE

FASTENERS AT 3" O.C., STAGGERED

¾" MIN.

NAILER

CONTINUOUS CLEAT

DECK

PREPARED SURFACE OF BOARD STOCK

SPRAY-APPLIED POLYURETHANE FOAM

METAL ROOF EDGE

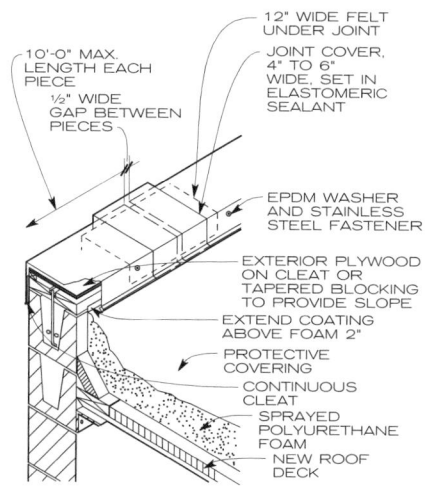

10'-0" MAX. LENGTH EACH PIECE

½" WIDE GAP BETWEEN PIECES

12" WIDE FELT UNDER JOINT

JOINT COVER, 4" TO 6" WIDE, SET IN ELASTOMERIC SEALANT

EPDM WASHER AND STAINLESS STEEL FASTENER

EXTERIOR PLYWOOD ON CLEAT OR TAPERED BLOCKING TO PROVIDE SLOPE

EXTEND COATING ABOVE FOAM 2"

PROTECTIVE COVERING

CONTINUOUS CLEAT

SPRAYED POLYURETHANE FOAM

NEW ROOF DECK

NOTE

This detail should be used only when the deck is supported by the wall. An expansion joint detail should be used for non-wall-supported decks.

LIGHT METAL PARAPET CAP

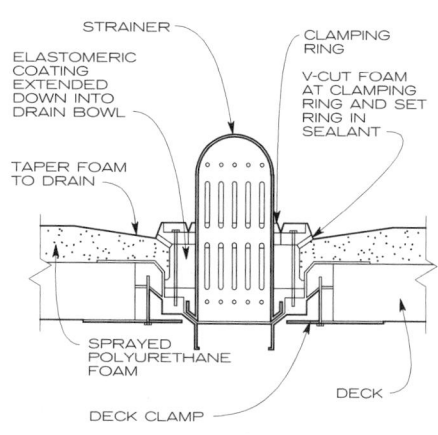

STRAINER

CLAMPING RING

ELASTOMERIC COATING EXTENDED DOWN INTO DRAIN BOWL

V-CUT FOAM AT CLAMPING RING AND SET RING IN SEALANT

TAPER FOAM TO DRAIN

SPRAYED POLYURETHANE FOAM

DECK CLAMP

DECK

NOTES

1. Remove clamping ring prior to foam application. Place protective covering over drain bowl opening to prevent overspray from filling bowl.

2. Taper foam toward drain bowl to provide positive drainage.

3. The use of metal deck sump pans is not recommended.

ROOF DRAIN

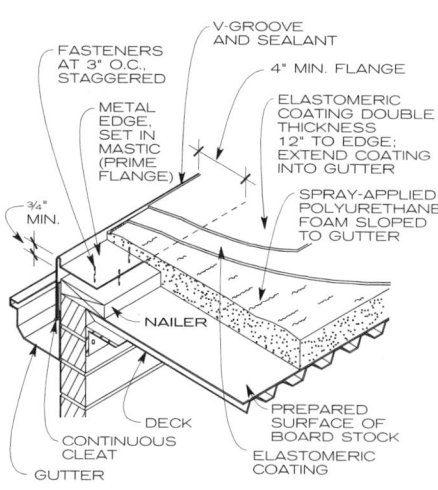

FASTENERS AT 3" O.C., STAGGERED

V-GROOVE AND SEALANT

4" MIN. FLANGE

METAL EDGE, SET IN MASTIC (PRIME FLANGE)

ELASTOMERIC COATING DOUBLE THICKNESS 12" TO EDGE; EXTEND COATING INTO GUTTER

SPRAY-APPLIED POLYURETHANE FOAM SLOPED TO GUTTER

¾" MIN.

NAILER

DECK

CONTINUOUS CLEAT

GUTTER

PREPARED SURFACE OF BOARD STOCK

ELASTOMERIC COATING

ROOF EDGE AT GUTTER

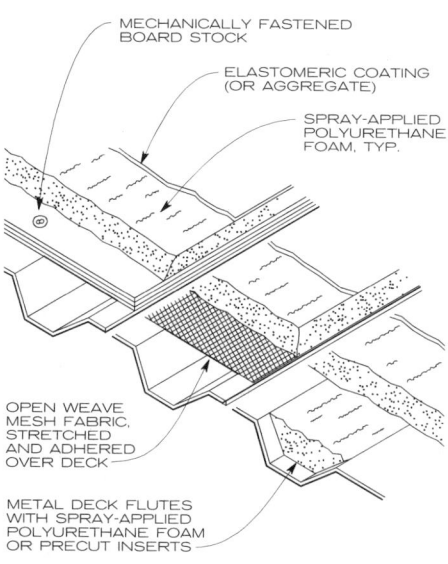

MECHANICALLY FASTENED BOARD STOCK

ELASTOMERIC COATING (OR AGGREGATE)

SPRAY-APPLIED POLYURETHANE FOAM, TYP.

OPEN WEAVE MESH FABRIC, STRETCHED AND ADHERED OVER DECK

METAL DECK FLUTES WITH SPRAY-APPLIED POLYURETHANE FOAM OR PRECUT INSERTS

METAL DECK DETAILS

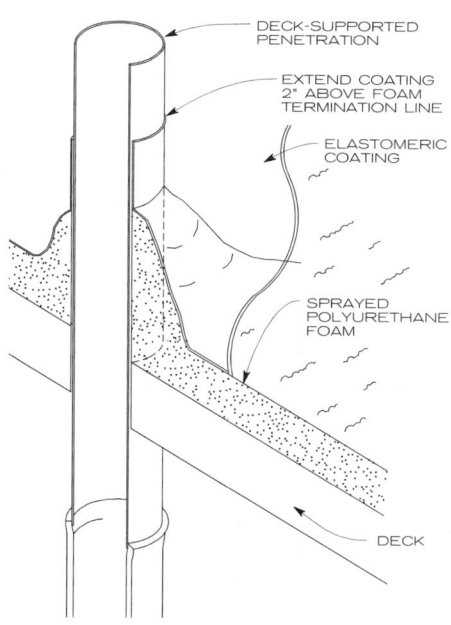

DECK-SUPPORTED PENETRATION

EXTEND COATING 2" ABOVE FOAM TERMINATION LINE

ELASTOMERIC COATING

SPRAYED POLYURETHANE FOAM

DECK

SINGLE PIPE PENETRATION

Richard J. Vitullo, AIA; Oak Leaf Studio; Crownsville, Maryland
Rich Boon; The Roofing Institute Educational Institute; Englewood, Colorado

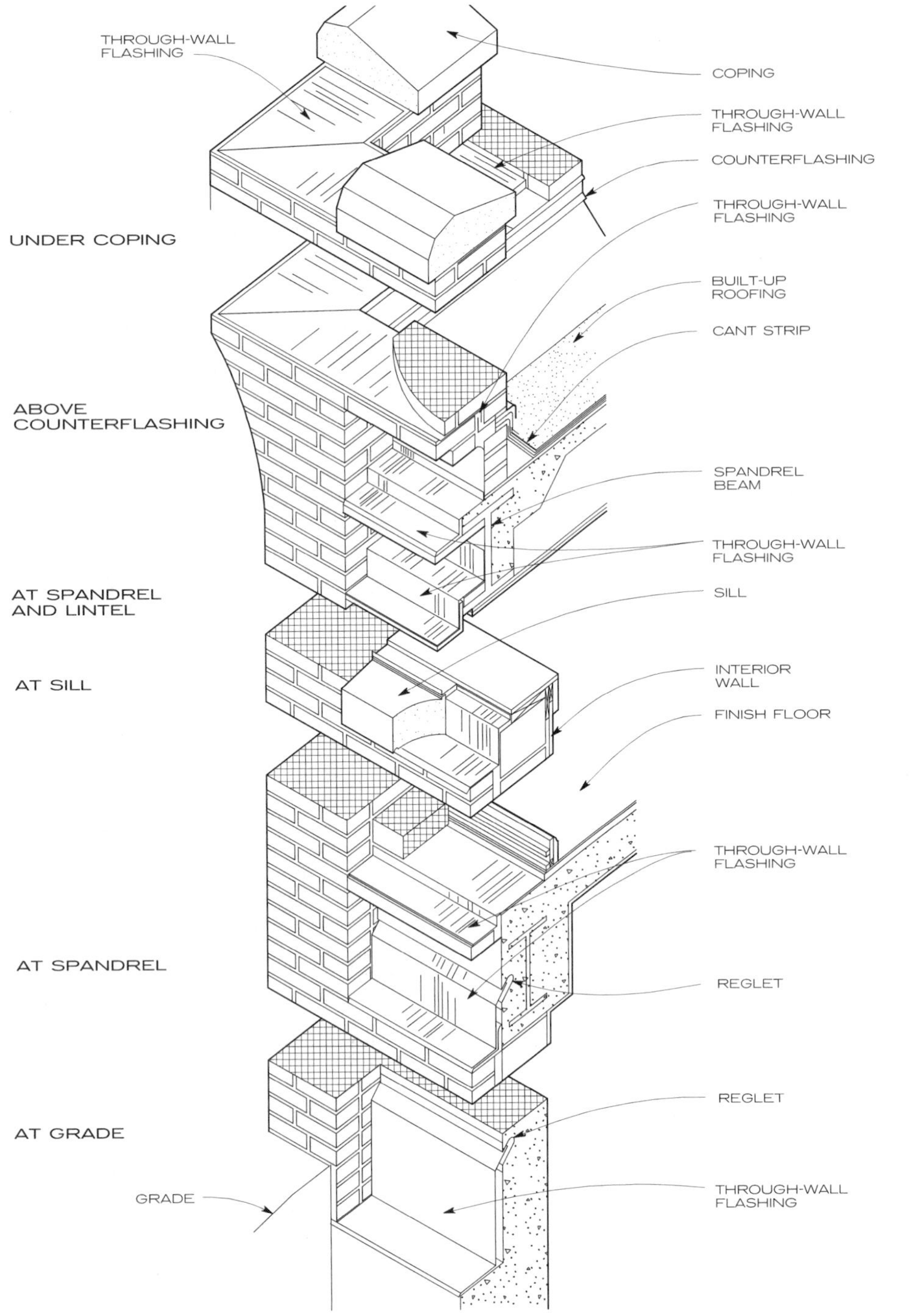

THROUGH-WALL
FLASHING

COPING

THROUGH-WALL
FLASHING

UNDER COPING

COUNTERFLASHING

THROUGH-WALL
FLASHING

BUILT-UP
ROOFING

ABOVE
COUNTERFLASHING

CANT STRIP

SPANDREL
BEAM

AT SPANDREL
AND LINTEL

THROUGH-WALL
FLASHING

SILL

AT SILL

INTERIOR
WALL

FINISH FLOOR

THROUGH-WALL
FLASHING

AT SPANDREL

REGLET

REGLET

AT GRADE

THROUGH-WALL
FLASHING

GRADE

THROUGH-WALL FLASHING INSTALLATION

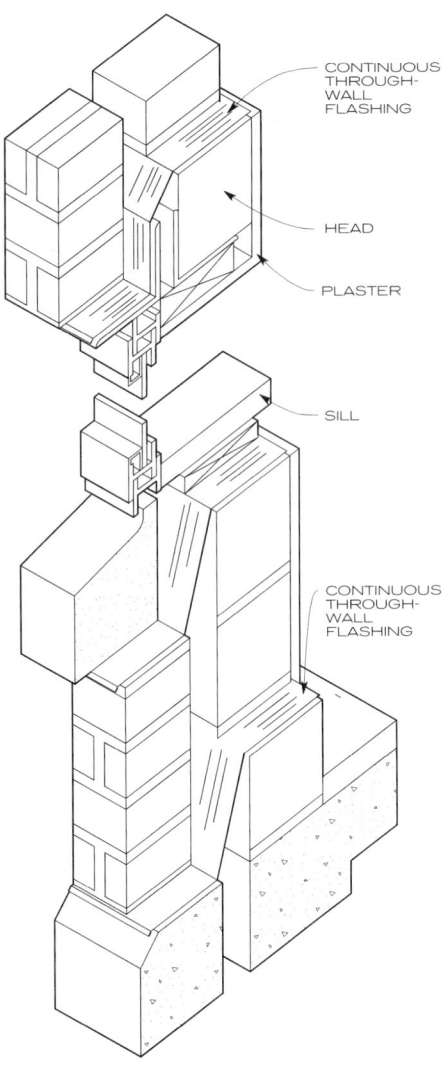

CONTINUOUS
THROUGH-WALL
FLASHING

HEAD

PLASTER

SILL

CONTINUOUS
THROUGH-WALL
FLASHING

THROUGH-WALL FLASHING AT CAVITY WALL

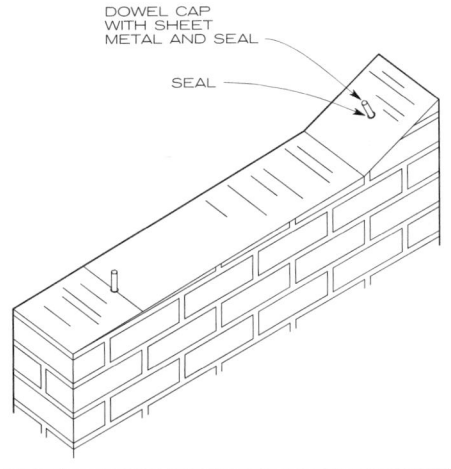

DOWEL CAP
WITH SHEET
METAL AND SEAL

SEAL

THROUGH-WALL FLASHING UNDER COPING

GENERAL

Modern building materials are often waterproof, but they are not permanently impervious to wind-driven moisture. Gradual shrinkage of some materials and the natural movement of buildings can eventually cause leaks. When moisture enters walls it tends to form pockets of water, which eventually drain into the interior of the building, sometimes by gravity, other times by capillary action. This water will damage interiors, deface exteriors, disintegrate mortar and masonry, and rust steel spandrels, lintels, etc.

Flashings should be used wherever there is any possibility of water entering a structure. Through-wall flashing is the most successful method of permanently preventing leaks, except in areas exposed to earthquakes, where through-wall flashing is not recommended. Through-wall flashing is

made of many different materials, including metals, plastics, and combinations of metals with paper, fabric, or rubber. Materials that are in contact must be compatible without deterioration.

Joints in flashings must be durable and waterproof and should usually lap 4 in. When the flashing is metal, joints should be soldered. Flashing should be extended to within $1/2$ in. of the exterior face. End- and edge-formed dams should be used where necessary to control drainage direction. Metal flashing that extends below grade is installed in reglets after the surface waterproofing has been applied below-grade.

SMACNA, Inc., from the SMACNA Architectural Sheet Metal Manual, 5th ed., with permission
Valerie Eickelberger; Rippeteau Architects, PC; Washington, D.C.

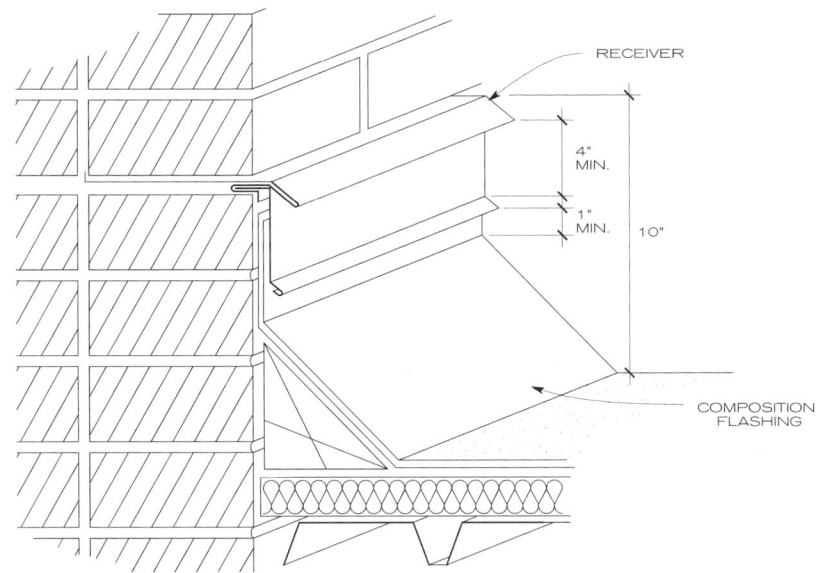

COUNTERFLASHING INSTALLATION

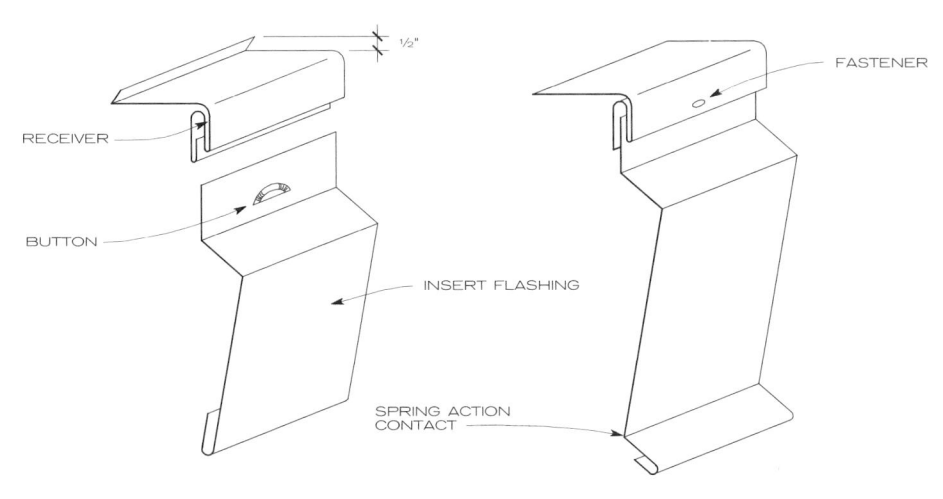

TWO-PIECE COUNTERFLASHING

GENERAL

Careful consideration must be given to flashing systems where a roof and wall meet. The base flashing system must keep water from entering the building and must allow for building movement. Counterflashing turns water away from a wall onto the roof or base flashing. The base flashing is usually inserted into a reglet, which must be capable of supporting the flashing. In high wind areas, clips can be specified for the lower edge of the counterflashing. Counterflashing that is removable is cost effective for the work installation sequence and for repair of roofing systems.

All membrane roofing should have removable counterflashing. Metal counterflashing should be used in conjunction with composition base flashing. Metal base flashings are used with shingle or metal roofs, but are not recommended for use with membrane roofing systems. A metal base flashing may be used over a composition flashing as a protective cover in locations where the base flashing may be abused by traffic. It is recommended that base flashings be applied over a cant and be extended up the wall a minimum of 10 in. above the roofline.

Receivers for counterflashing should be elevated 10 in. above the finished roof. Install metal counterflashing to cover a minimum of 4 in. of the base flashing. After the counterflashing is installed, the receiver is bent 45 degrees to provide a drip edge. The lower edge of metal counterflashing should be a minimum of 1 in. above a cant. The counterflashing is notched and lapped at inside corners and joints, and seamed at outside corners. The flashing receiver is notched and lapped 4 in. at corners and joints.

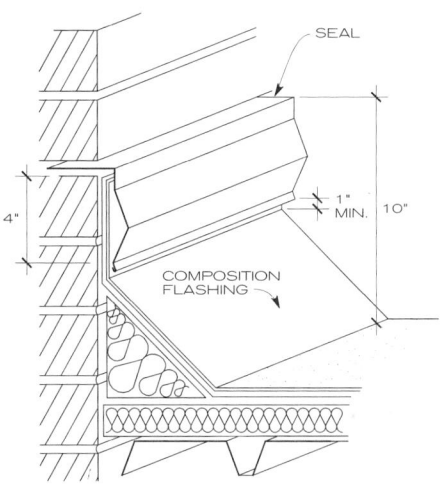

COUNTERFLASHING WITH RECEIVER

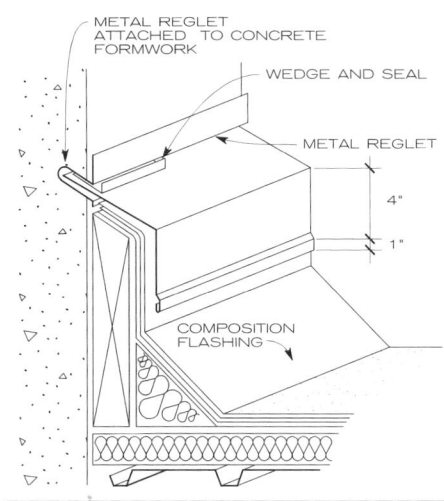

COUNTERFLASHING WITHOUT RECEIVER

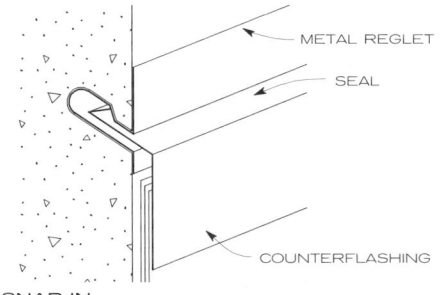

SNAP-IN

SPRING LOCKED

INSERT FLASHING DETAIL

SMACNA, Inc., from the SMACNA Architectural Sheet Metal Manual, 5th ed., with permission
Valerie Eickelberger; Rippeteau Architects, PC; Washington, D.C.

FLASHING AND SHEET METAL   7

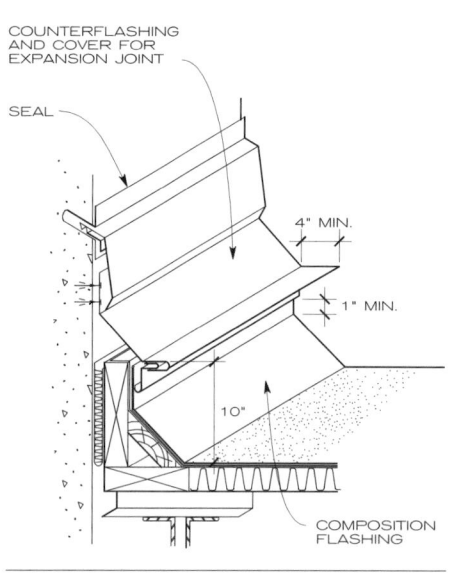

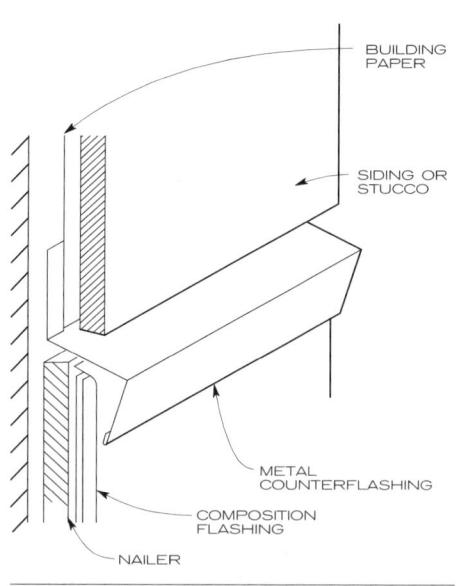

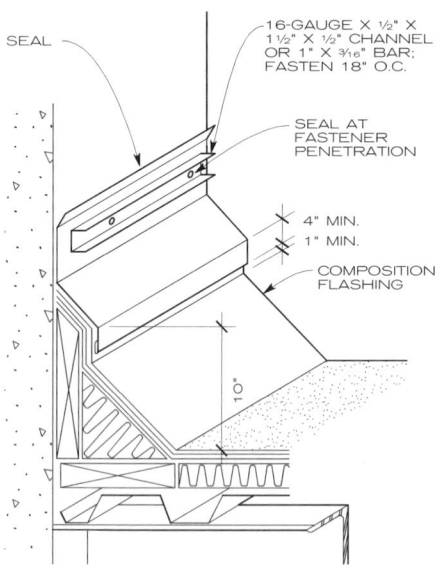

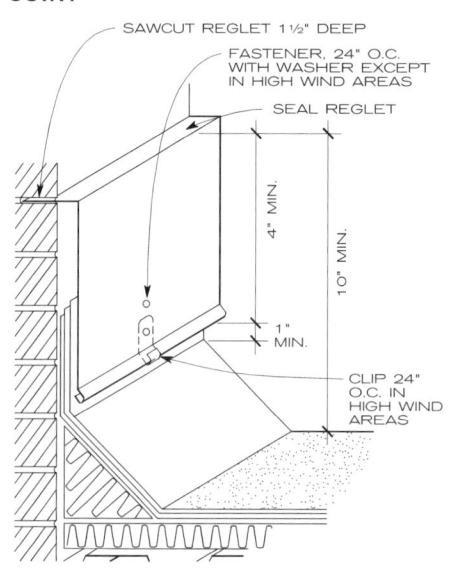

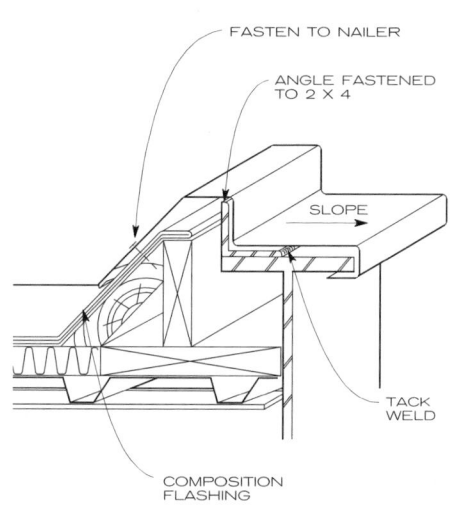

COUNTERFLASHING FOR CONCRETE

COUNTERFLASHING EXPANSION JOINT

COUNTERFLASHING FOR NONMASONRY WALL

COUNTERFLASHING AT EXISTING WALL

COUNTERFLASHING WITHOUT RECEIVER

COUNTERFLASHING OVER STRUCTURAL STEEL

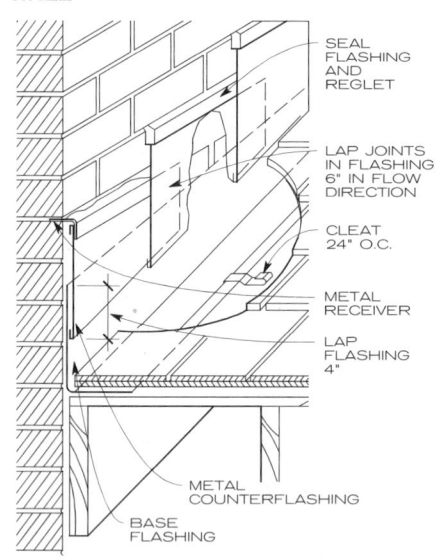

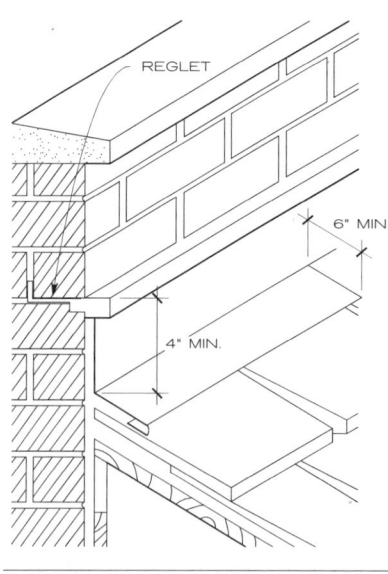

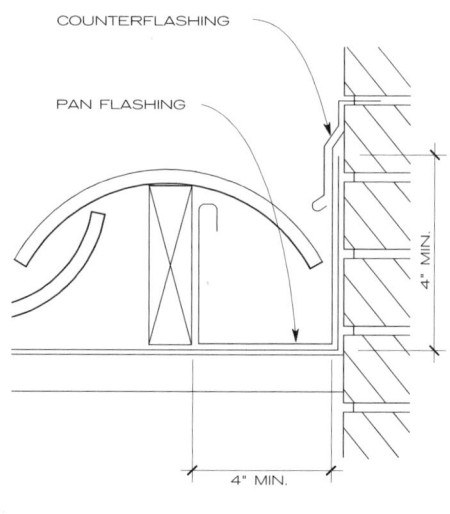

COUNTERFLASHING AT SLOPED ROOF

COUNTERFLASHING AT SLOPED ROOF

COUNTERFLASHING AT TILE ROOF

SMACNA, Inc., from the SMACNA Architectural Sheet Metal Manual, 5th ed., with permission
Valerie Eickelberger; Rippeteau Architects, PC; Washington, D.C.

7 **FLASHING AND SHEET METAL**

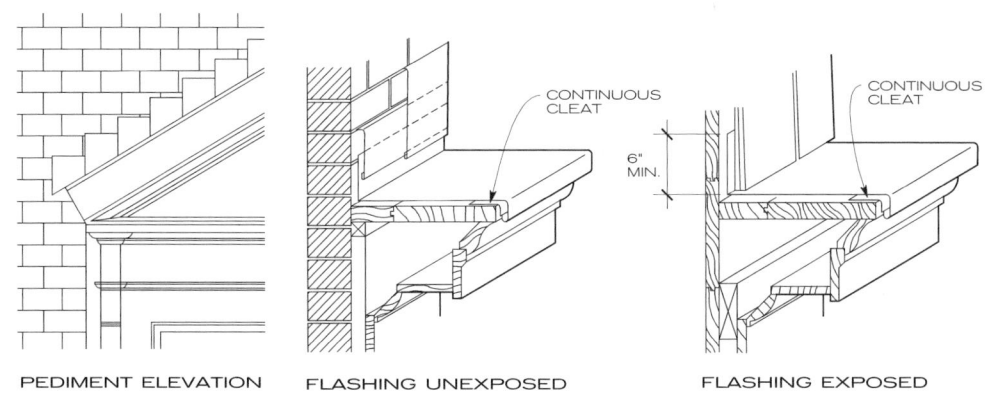

PEDIMENT ELEVATION   FLASHING UNEXPOSED   FLASHING EXPOSED

WOOD PEDIMENT LEDGE FLASHING

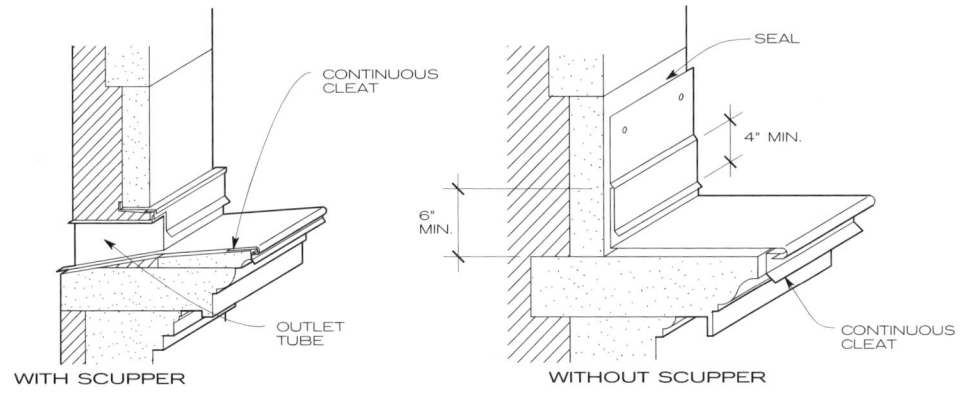

WITH SCUPPER   WITHOUT SCUPPER

STONE LEDGE FLASHING

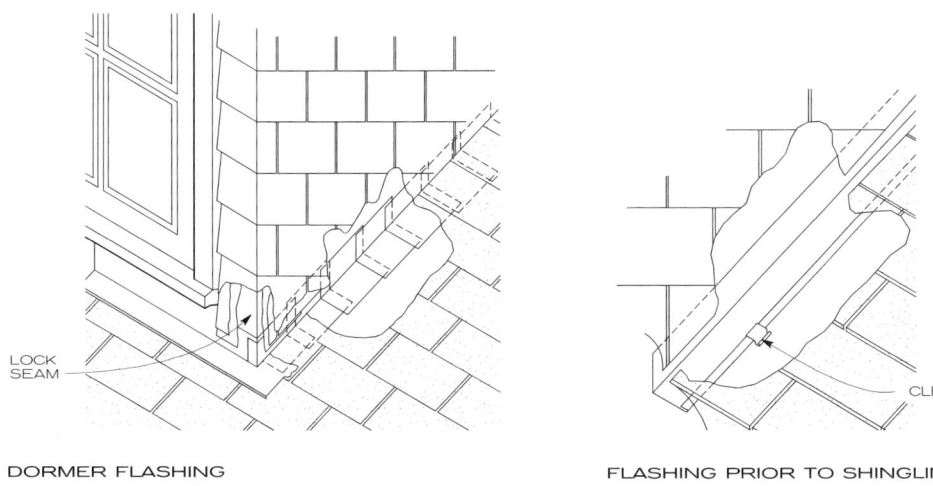

DORMER FLASHING   FLASHING PRIOR TO SHINGLING

DORMER FLASHING

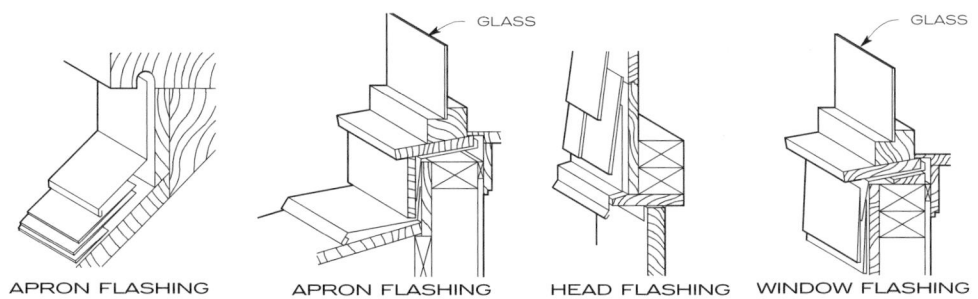

APRON FLASHING   APRON FLASHING   HEAD FLASHING   WINDOW FLASHING

DORMER FLASHING DETAILS

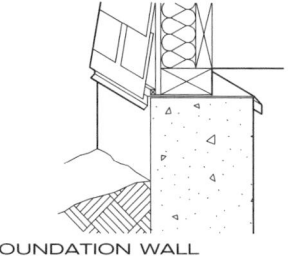

FOUNDATION WALL

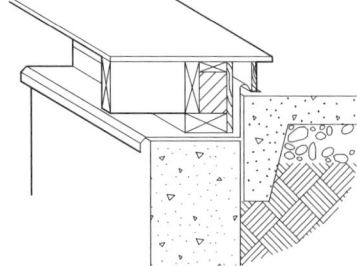

FOUNDATION WALL WITH PORCH FLOOR

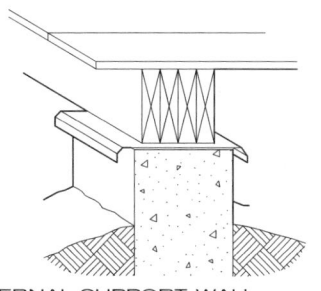

INTERNAL SUPPORT WALL

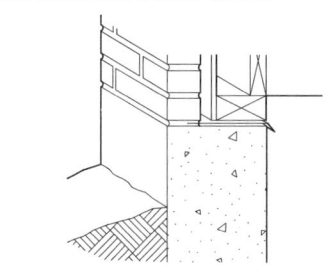

BRICK VENEER WALL

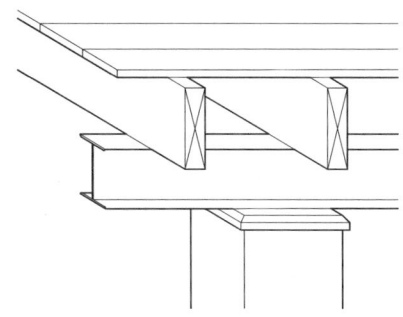

INTERNAL FLOOR SUPPORT

NOTES

1. Termite shields may be fabricated of copper or galvanized steel. Aluminum may be used except where masonry is above the termite shield.
2. Joints should be lapped $3/4$ in. and soldered or flat locked. Corners should be notched, filled, and soldered.

TERMITE SHIELDS

SMACNA, Inc., from the SMACNA Architectural Sheet Metal Manual, 5th ed., with permission
Valerie Eickelberger; Rippeteau Architects, PC; Washington, D.C.

FLASHING AND SHEET METAL   **7**

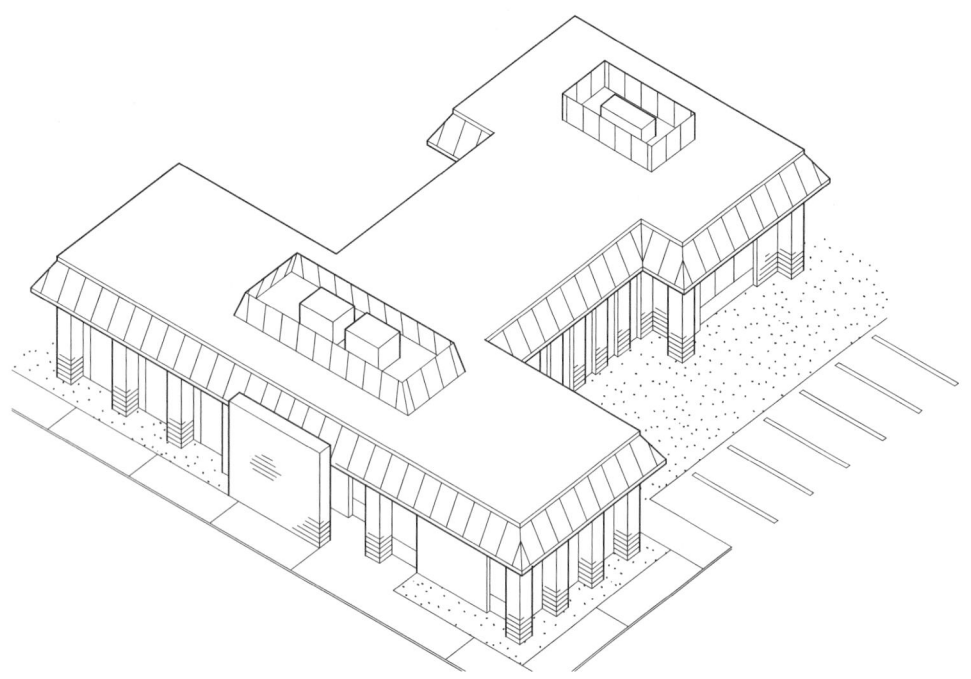

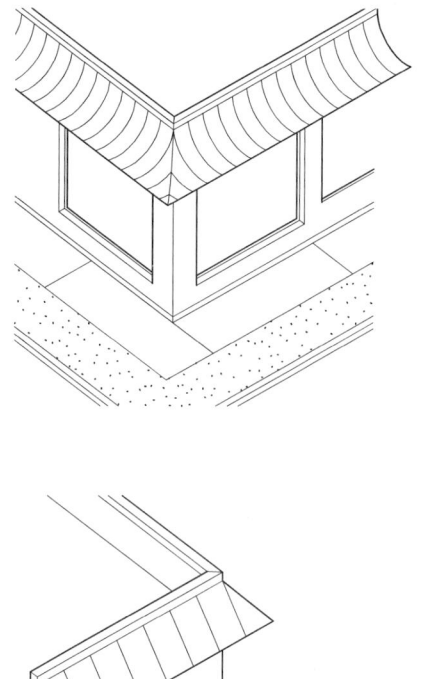

TYPICAL MANSARD ROOF

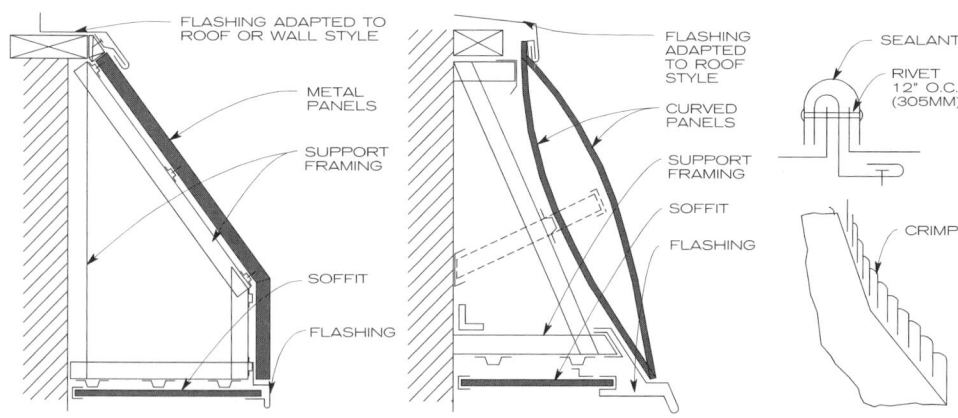

FLASHING ADAPTED TO ROOF OR WALL STYLE
METAL PANELS
SUPPORT FRAMING
SOFFIT
FLASHING

FLASHING ADAPTED TO ROOF STYLE
CURVED PANELS
SUPPORT FRAMING
SOFFIT
FLASHING

SEALANT
RIVET 12" O.C. (305MM)
CRIMP

SELF-SUPPORTING ROOF

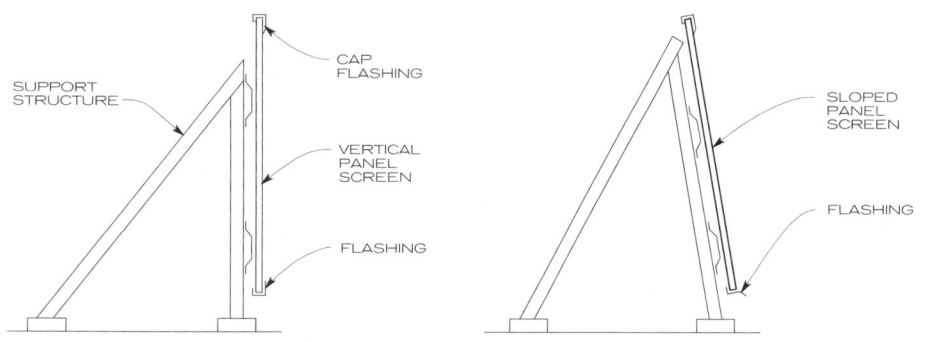

SUPPORT STRUCTURE
CAP FLASHING
VERTICAL PANEL SCREEN
FLASHING

SLOPED PANEL SCREEN
FLASHING

CONTINUOUSLY SUPPORTED ROOF

ORNAMENTAL ROOF CANOPY

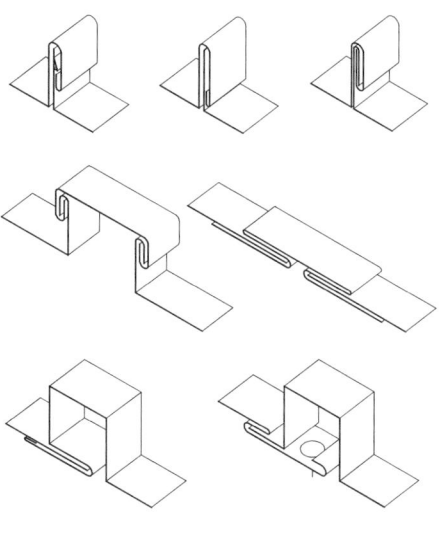

SEAM PROFILES

METAL MANSARD ROOFS

Metal mansard roofs are typically used on one-story commercial structures. Often they conceal rooftop equipment, using batten screens or louvered enclosures. Metal mansard roofs are also used for flat or curved ornamental roofs or canopies for the front of buildings.

Aluminum, copper, stainless steel, galvanized steel, or prefinished metals may be used for metal mansard roofs. The metal can be prefabricated for several styles of field connection using various seam configurations. Prefinished metals used in curved applications typically have a 15-ft

radius limit. Concave or convex panels normally have a 24-in. minimum radius for standing seams and a 72-in. minimum radius for batten seams. Soft metals are used when the metal must be stretched.

Metal mansard roofs may be continuously supported or self-supporting. Continuously supported roofs have a continuous sheathing substrate. Self-supporting roofs have structural framing with vertical and horizontal members located where needed for metal panel attachment. Mansard roofs require cap and sill flashing.

SMACNA, Inc., from the SMACNA Architectural Sheet Metal Manual, 5th ed., with permission
Valerie Eickelberger; Rippeteau Architects, PC; Washington, D.C.

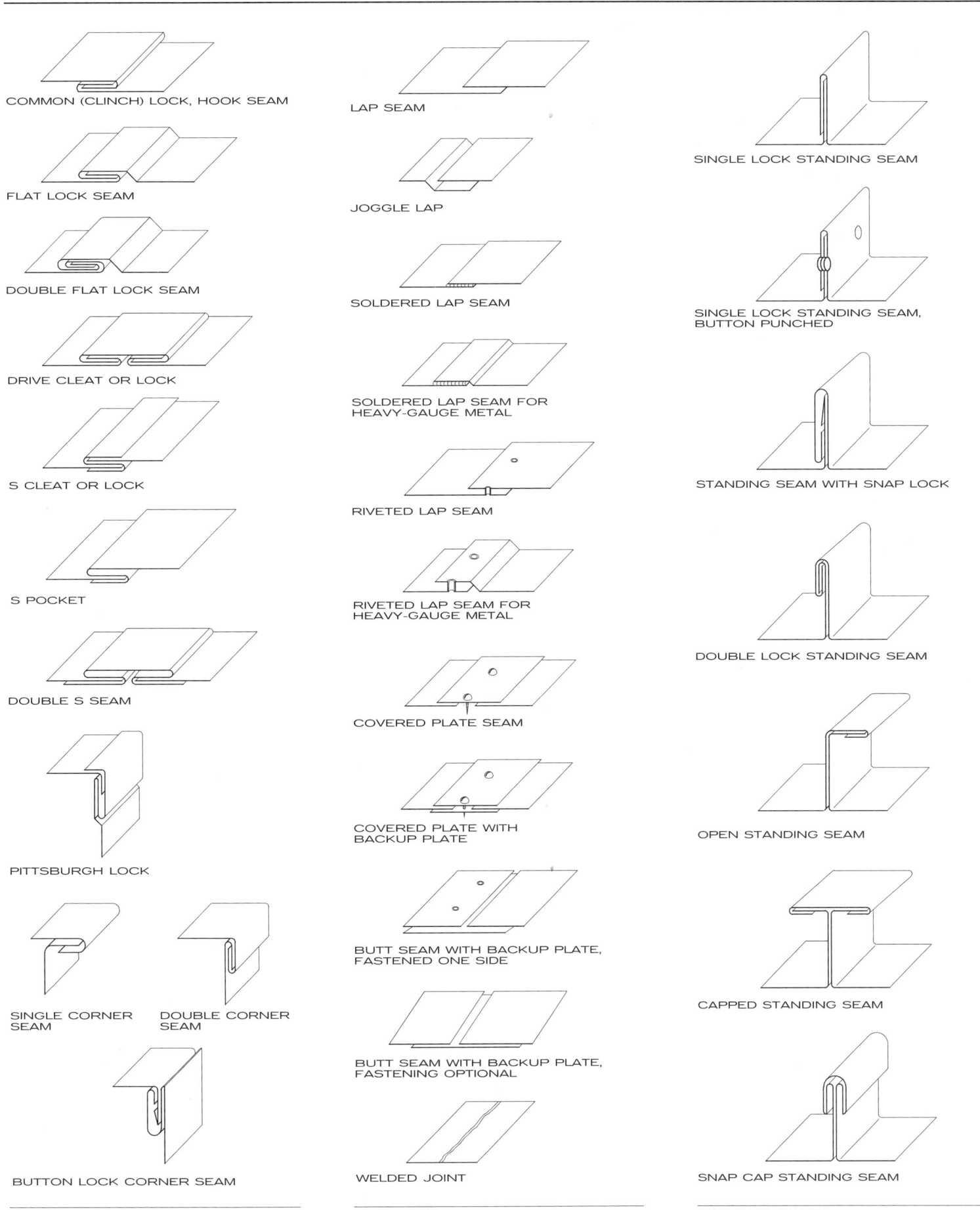

COMMON (CLINCH) LOCK, HOOK SEAM

FLAT LOCK SEAM

DOUBLE FLAT LOCK SEAM

DRIVE CLEAT OR LOCK

S CLEAT OR LOCK

S POCKET

DOUBLE S SEAM

PITTSBURGH LOCK

SINGLE CORNER SEAM

DOUBLE CORNER SEAM

BUTTON LOCK CORNER SEAM

LOCK SEAM

LAP SEAM

JOGGLE LAP

SOLDERED LAP SEAM

SOLDERED LAP SEAM FOR HEAVY-GAUGE METAL

RIVETED LAP SEAM

RIVETED LAP SEAM FOR HEAVY-GAUGE METAL

COVERED PLATE SEAM

COVERED PLATE WITH BACKUP PLATE

BUTT SEAM WITH BACKUP PLATE, FASTENED ONE SIDE

BUTT SEAM WITH BACKUP PLATE, FASTENING OPTIONAL

WELDED JOINT

FLAT SEAM

SINGLE LOCK STANDING SEAM

SINGLE LOCK STANDING SEAM, BUTTON PUNCHED

STANDING SEAM WITH SNAP LOCK

DOUBLE LOCK STANDING SEAM

OPEN STANDING SEAM

CAPPED STANDING SEAM

SNAP CAP STANDING SEAM

STANDING SEAM

SMACNA, Inc., from the SMACNA Architectural Sheet Metal Manual, 5th ed., with permission
Valerie Eickelberger; Rippeteau Architects, PC; Washington, D.C.

FLASHING AND SHEET METAL 7

GENERAL

Structural metal panels are used in roofing applications when removal of the existing roof membrane is too costly or undesirable. Metal panel roofs are durable, have good wind and fire resistance ratings, and require little maintenance. The panels are manufactured either from steel or aluminum and are mechanically seamed on the job site. Sealants in tape or gel form are used as a gasket between metal connections. The sealant, applied in the female corrugation to make the roof more weathertight, allows the panels to expand and contract independently of the insulation and structural systems.

Two-part clips concealed inside the standing seams accommodate thermal expansion and eliminate the need for fasteners in the flat parts of the panel. The top part of the clip holds the metal panel, while the base of the clip is fastened to the structural member. A slot between the two parts of the clips allows independent movement. The concealed clip also provides the attachment necessary for wind uplift ratings.

Structural metal roofs can be used with slopes as low as $1/4$ in. per ft but may also be used in a steep slope configuration. The panels are available in a wide variety of colors and typically have corrosion-resistant coatings.

Before adding the weight of structural metal roof panels to a building, it is important to verify the load-bearing capacity of the existing roof structure.

FLAT ROOF REMOVAL REQUIRES EXPENSE OF REMOVAL AND DISPOSAL OF EXISTING ROOF MEMBRANE

FAILED CAP FLASHING

INFILTRATION THROUGH PARAPET

PROBLEMATIC DRAINAGE LEAKS (FREEZING DRAINS, INTERNAL DRAINS)

SCUPPER LEAKS INTO WALL

EXISTING PROBLEMATIC FLAT ROOF

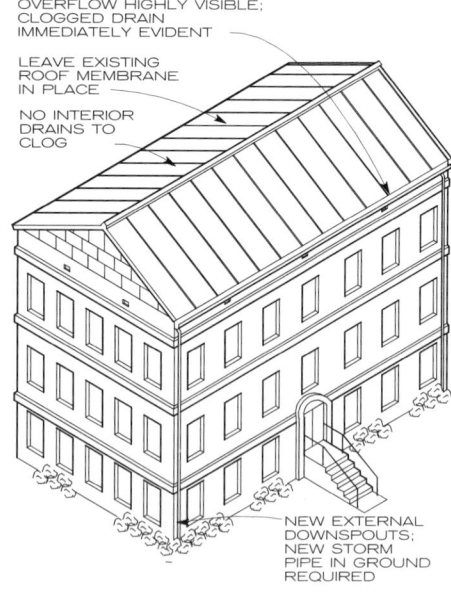

OVERFLOW HIGHLY VISIBLE; CLOGGED DRAIN IMMEDIATELY EVIDENT

LEAVE EXISTING ROOF MEMBRANE IN PLACE

NO INTERIOR DRAINS TO CLOG

NEW EXTERNAL DOWNSPOUTS; NEW STORM PIPE IN GROUND REQUIRED

RETROFIT WITH METAL PANEL ROOF

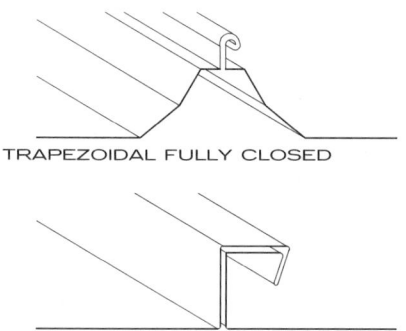

TRAPEZOIDAL FULLY CLOSED

VERTICAL PARTIALLY CLOSED

SEAM TYPES FOR METAL ROOFING PANELS

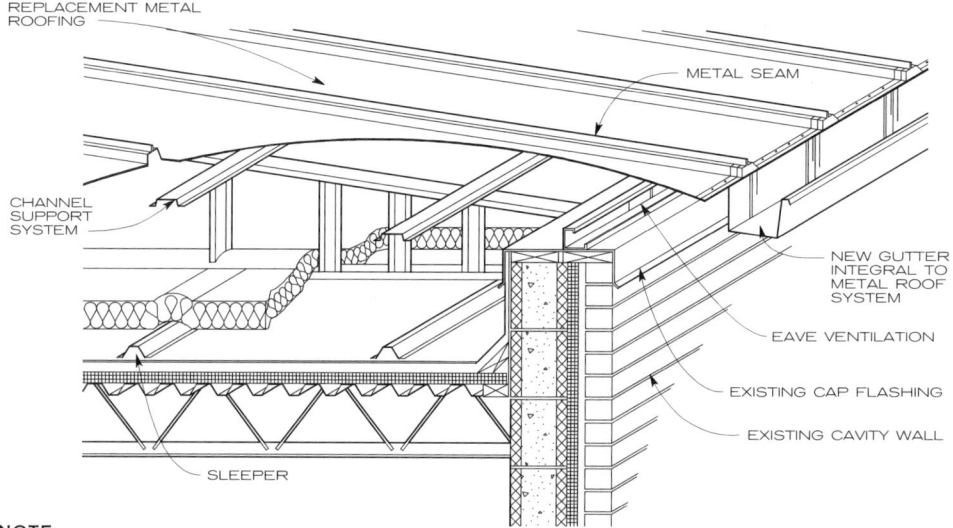

REPLACEMENT METAL ROOFING

METAL SEAM

CHANNEL SUPPORT SYSTEM

SLEEPER

NEW GUTTER INTEGRAL TO METAL ROOF SYSTEM

EAVE VENTILATION

EXISTING CAP FLASHING

EXISTING CAVITY WALL

NOTE

Design sleeper to distribute roof load adequately over the roof surface. Consider compressibility of insulation and condition of membrane. Provide bearing plates and hold-down clips as necessary.

BUILDING SECTION THROUGH ROOF SYSTEM

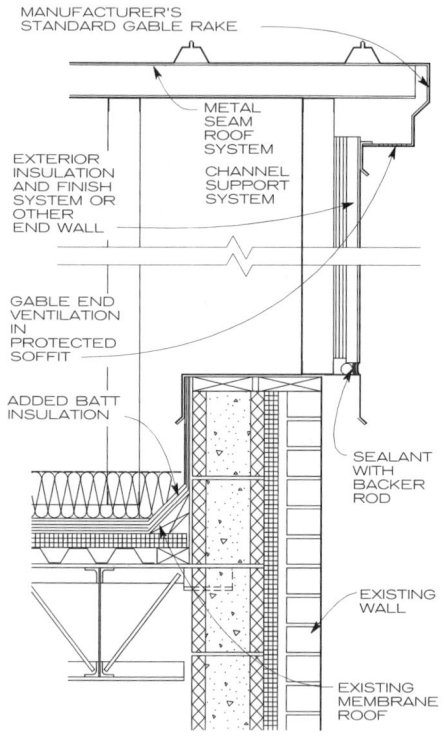

MANUFACTURER'S STANDARD GABLE RAKE

METAL SEAM ROOF SYSTEM

CHANNEL SUPPORT SYSTEM

EXTERIOR INSULATION AND FINISH SYSTEM OR OTHER END WALL

GABLE END VENTILATION IN PROTECTED SOFFIT

ADDED BATT INSULATION

SEALANT WITH BACKER ROD

EXISTING WALL

EXISTING MEMBRANE ROOF

GABLE END WALL

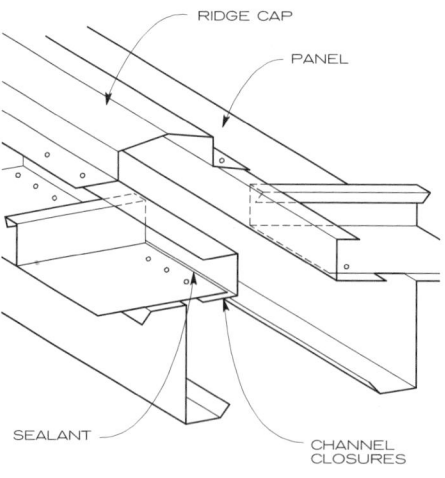

RIDGE CAP

PANEL

SEALANT

CHANNEL CLOSURES

RIDGE CAP FOR METAL ROOFING PANELS

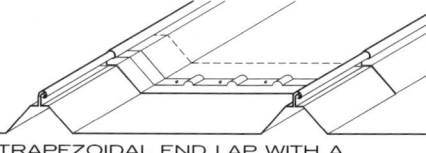

TRAPEZOIDAL END LAP WITH A TOP PANEL STRAP

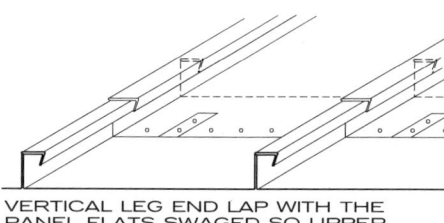

VERTICAL LEG END LAP WITH THE PANEL FLATS SWAGED SO UPPER PANEL FITS INTO LOWER

END LAPS FOR METAL ROOFING PANELS

Valerie Eickelberger; Rippeteau Architects, PC; Washington, D.C.
Paul Nimitz; PDN Associates; Blue Springs, Montana

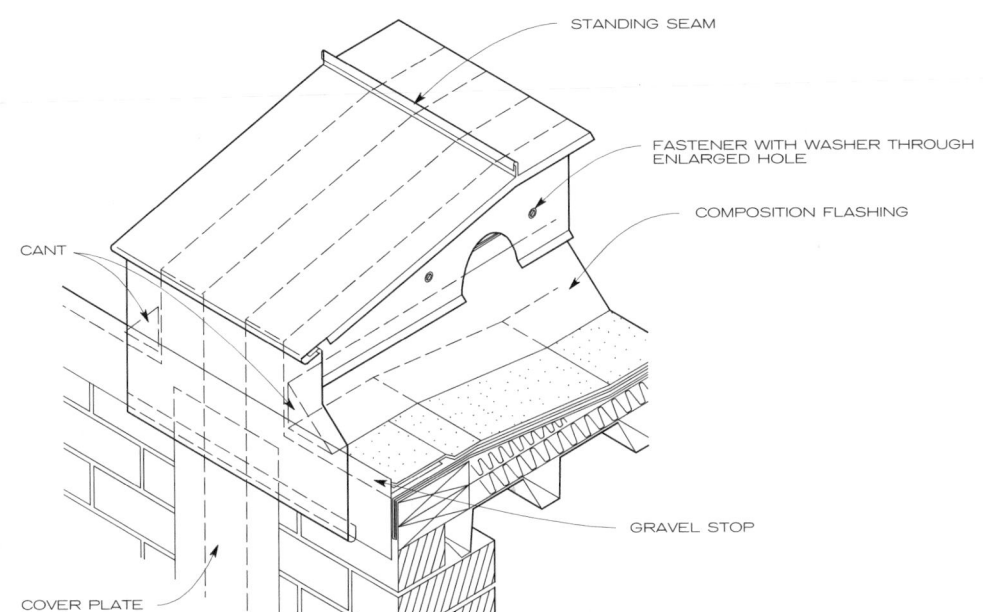

STANDING SEAM

FASTENER WITH WASHER THROUGH ENLARGED HOLE

COMPOSITION FLASHING

CANT

GRAVEL STOP

COVER PLATE

EXPANSION JOINT AT GRAVEL STOP

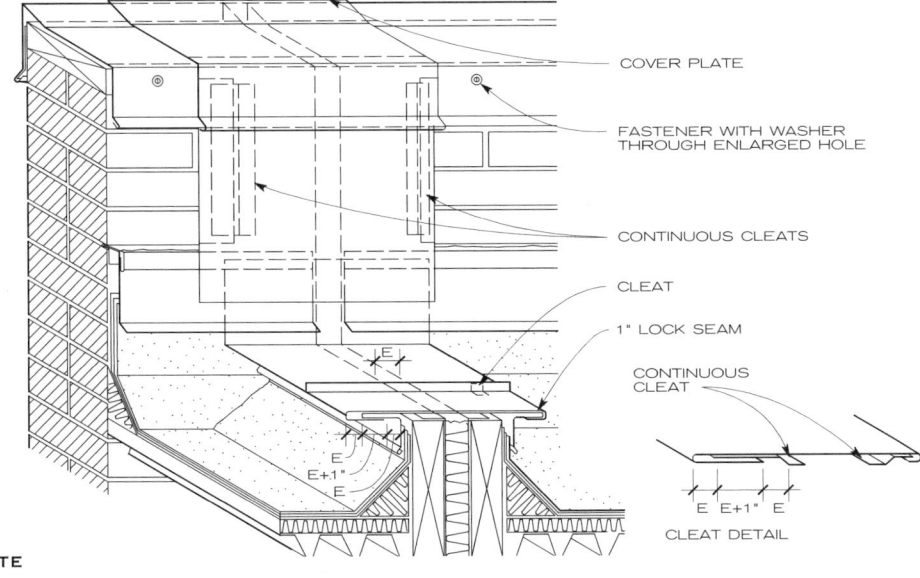

COVER PLATE

FASTENER WITH WASHER THROUGH ENLARGED HOLE

CONTINUOUS CLEATS

CLEAT

1" LOCK SEAM

E

E

$E+1"$

E

CONTINUOUS CLEAT

E $E+1"$ E

CLEAT DETAIL

NOTE

E = Maximum allowance for expansion.

EXPANSION JOINT AT PARAPET

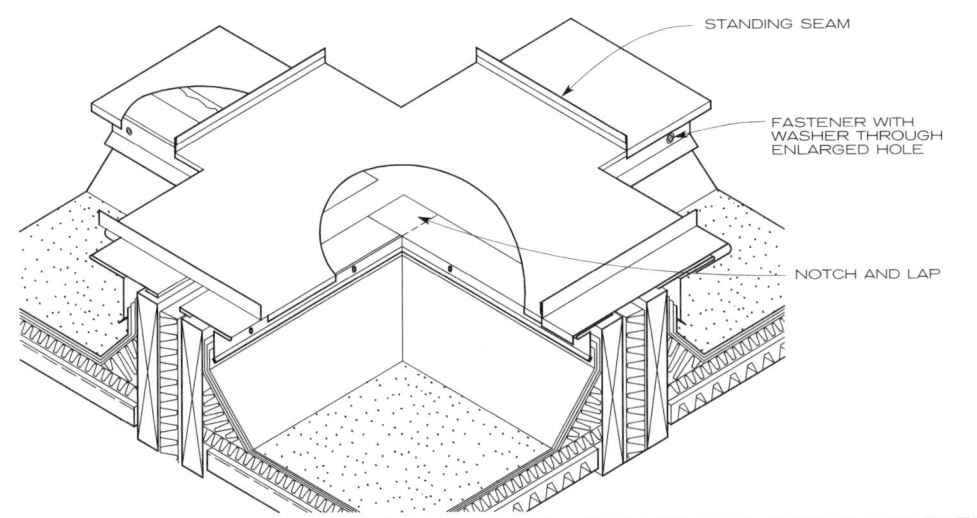

STANDING SEAM

FASTENER WITH WASHER THROUGH ENLARGED HOLE

NOTCH AND LAP

EXPANSION JOINT INTERSECTION

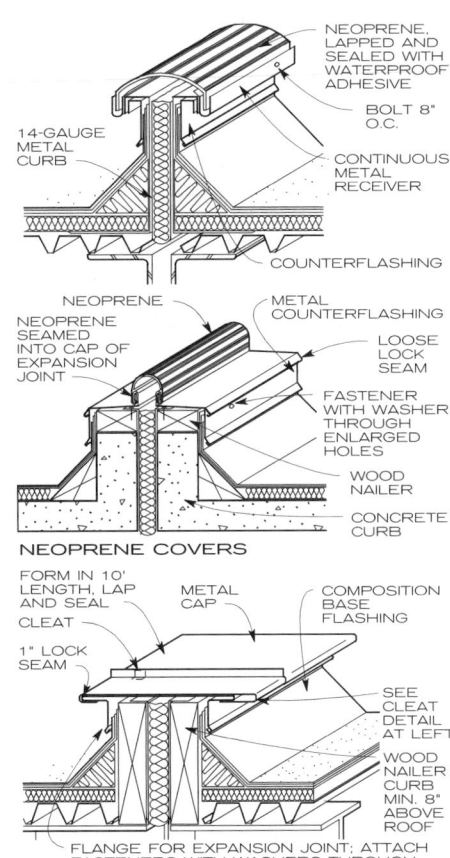

NEOPRENE, LAPPED AND SEALED WITH WATERPROOF ADHESIVE

14-GAUGE METAL CURB

BOLT 8" O.C.

CONTINUOUS METAL RECEIVER

COUNTERFLASHING

NEOPRENE

NEOPRENE SEAMED INTO CAP OF EXPANSION JOINT

METAL COUNTERFLASHING

LOOSE LOCK SEAM

FASTENER WITH WASHER THROUGH ENLARGED HOLES

WOOD NAILER

CONCRETE CURB

NEOPRENE COVERS

FORM IN 10' LENGTH, LAP AND SEAL

METAL CAP

COMPOSITION BASE FLASHING

CLEAT

1" LOCK SEAM

SEE CLEAT DETAIL AT LEFT

WOOD NAILER CURB MIN. 8" ABOVE ROOF

FLANGE FOR EXPANSION JOINT; ATTACH FASTENERS WITH WASHERS THROUGH SLOTTED HOLE 24" O.C.

METAL COVER

NOTES

1. The minimum recommended gauge for the expansion joint shown is 24-gauge stainless steel, 16 oz copper, 22-gauge galvanized steel, or 0.050 in. aluminum.

2. Expansion joints allow independent movement of the roof structure.

ROOF EXPANSION JOINT

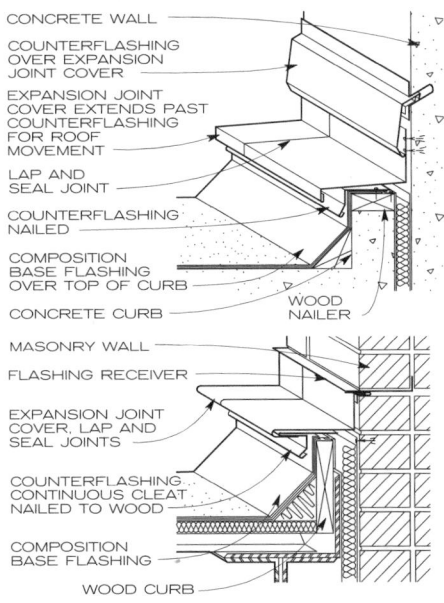

CONCRETE WALL

COUNTERFLASHING OVER EXPANSION JOINT COVER

EXPANSION JOINT COVER EXTENDS PAST COUNTERFLASHING FOR ROOF MOVEMENT

LAP AND SEAL JOINT

COUNTERFLASHING NAILED

COMPOSITION BASE FLASHING OVER TOP OF CURB

CONCRETE CURB

WOOD NAILER

MASONRY WALL

FLASHING RECEIVER

EXPANSION JOINT COVER, LAP AND SEAL JOINTS

COUNTERFLASHING CONTINUOUS CLEAT NAILED TO WOOD

COMPOSITION BASE FLASHING

WOOD CURB

NOTES

1. The minimum recommended gauge for the expansion joint shown is 24-gauge stainless steel, 16 oz copper, 22-gauge galvanized steel, or 0.050 in. aluminum.

2. Expansion joints allow independent movement of the roof structure.

ROOF-TO-WALL EXPANSION JOINT

SMACNA, Inc., from the SMACNA Architectural Sheet Metal Manual, 5th ed., with permission
Valerie Eickelberger; Rippeteau Architects, PC; Washington, D.C.

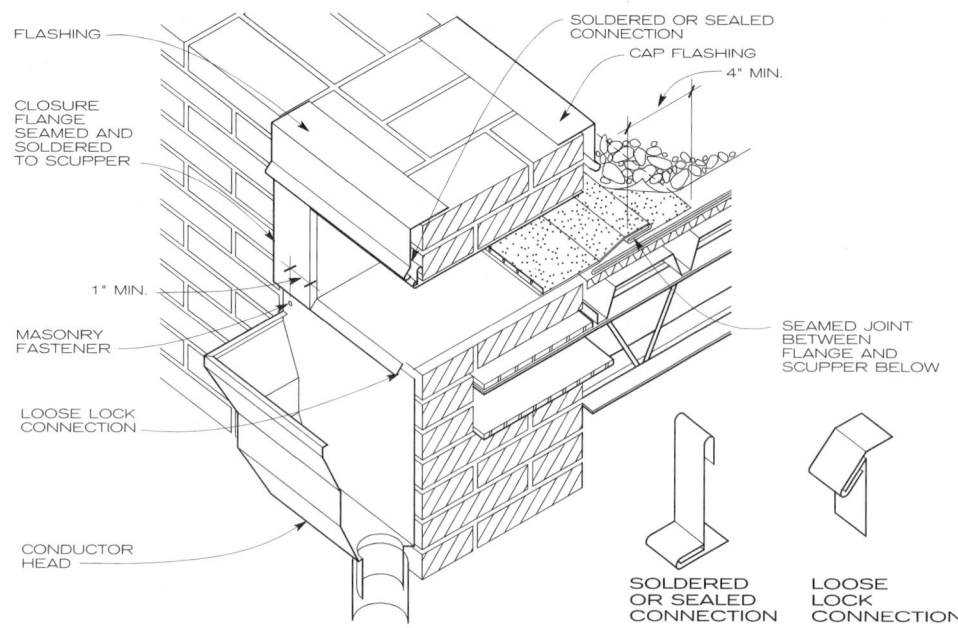

SCUPPER DETAIL AT PARAPET WALL (CONDUCTOR HEAD SIDE)

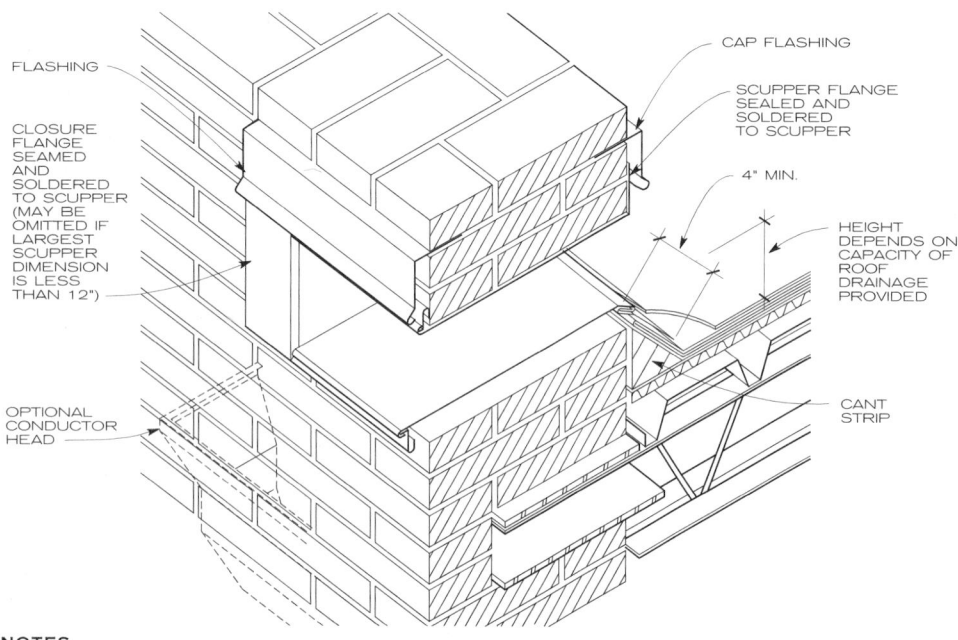

NOTES

1. Use overflow scuppers when roof is completely surrounded by parapets and drainage depends on scuppers or internal damage.

2. Precast concrete panels with scuppers do not need closure flanges on face; all penetrations should be seated.

OVERFLOW SCUPPER DETAIL AT PARAPET WALL

SCUPPER CAPACITY IN GPM*

HEAD (H)(IN.)	LENGTH (L) OF WEIR (IN.)									
	4	6	8	10	12	18	24	30	36	48
1	11.0	17.4	23.40	29.3	35.4	53.4	71.5	89.5	107.5	143.2
2	30.5	47.5	64.4	81.4	98.3	149.1	200.0	251.1	302.0	403.4
3	52.9	84.1	115.2	146.3	177.5	270.9	364.3	457.7	551.1	737.9
4	76.7	124.6	172.6	220.5	269.0	412.3	556.1	700.0	843.7	1133.3
6	123.3	211.4	299.4	387.5	475.5	739.7	1003.9	1268.1	1532.3	2060.7

*Based on the Francis formula: $Q = 3.33 (L - 0.2H) H^{1.5}$, in which

Q = Flow rate, cubic ft per second

L = Length of scupper opening, ft (should be 4 to 8 times H)

H = Head on scupper, ft (measured 6 ft back from opening)

1 GPM = 448.8 CFS

GENERAL

The size and number of scuppers should be carefully determined to control ponding on roofs. Rectangular shapes convey more water (per inch of water depth on the roof) than round shapes. The performance of rectangular shapes approximates that of a broad-crested weir. Standard equations for channel flow are based on test models larger than typical roof scuppers. While downspout sizes normally are based on draining a given area of roof, that flow rate may not pass through a scupper that has been sized to have a cross-sectional area equal to the downspout area.

SCUPPER SIZING PROCEDURES

1. Determine the head (H) in inches of water (typically 1 in. minimum by code) at a point 6 ft back from the scupper opening.

2. Determine the roof drainage area in sq ft (SF).

3. Using rainfall intensity in inches per hour (IPH) from a rainfall data table, determine discharge capacity in gallons per minute (GPM). GPM = SF of room area x IPH x 0.0104. The constant is 7.48 gallons per cubic foot divided by 12 inches per foot divided by 60 minutes per hour:

   GPM = (0.0104) IPH x SF

4. Using H and the GPM, find the aggregate scupper length (L) in the scupper capacity table (below).

5. Select enough individual scuppers to satisfy the total GPM requirement and locate them proportionately.

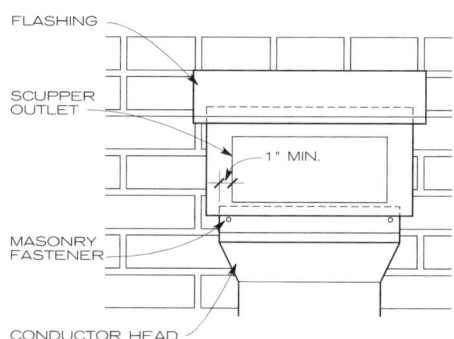

NOTE

Scupper assemblies from top to bottom (flashing to scupper outlet to conductor head) should be overlapped to ensure that water will be directed away from the wall.

SCUPPER ASSEMBLY ELEVATION

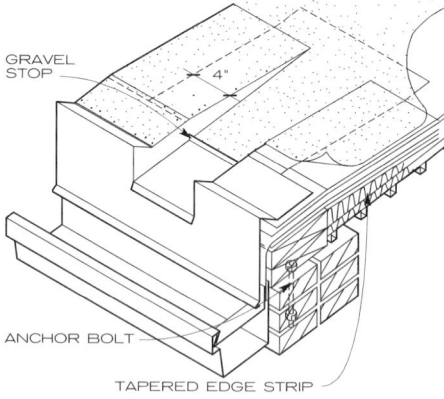

NOTE

Scuppers that empty into a gutter may be integrated with a roof edge. The scuppers are soldered into a formed gravel stop-fascia system. The suggested maximum scupper interval is 10 ft. The front rim of the gutter must be 1 in. below the back edge, and it should be below the nailers used to elevate the roof edge. The drip edge on the fascia should lap the back edge of the gutter a minimum of 1 in. The gutter must be free to move behind the fascia.

COMBINATION SCUPPER AND GUTTER

SMACNA, Inc., from the SMACNA Architectural Sheet Metal Manual, 5th ed., with permission
Grace S. Lee; Rippeteau Architects, PC; Washington, D.C.

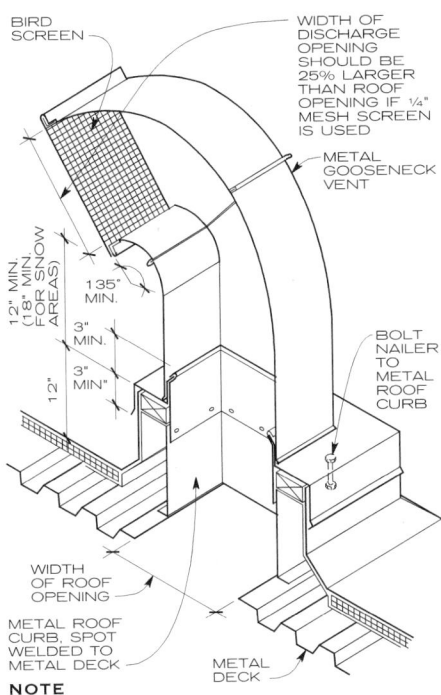

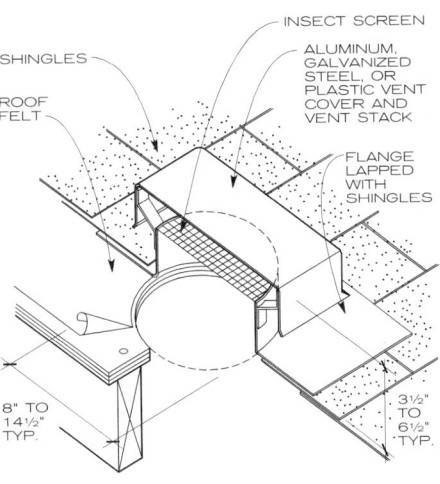

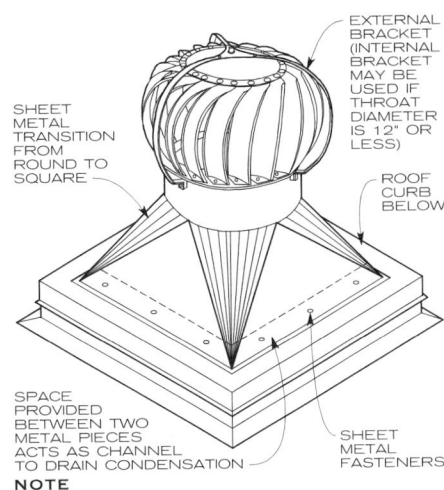

ROOF VENT IN SLOPED ROOF

NOTE

This ventilator may be used on a sloped roof.

ROTATING VENTILATOR

NOTE

This ventilator may be used for either intake or exhaust with gravity flow.

GOOSENECK GRAVITY VENTILATOR

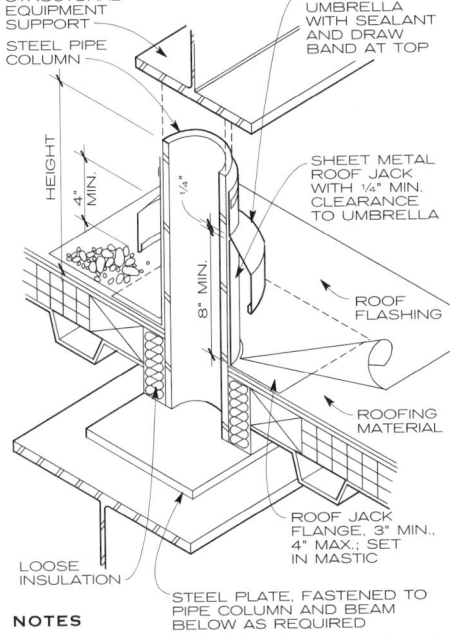

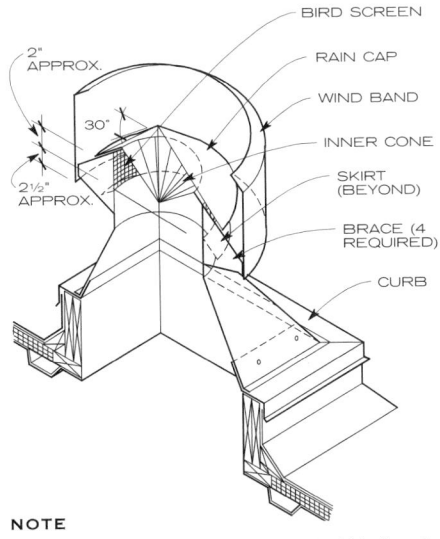

NOTE

All sloped partial or full conical shapes should be based on the same angle (generally 30º).

STATIONARY GRAVITY ROOF VENTILATOR

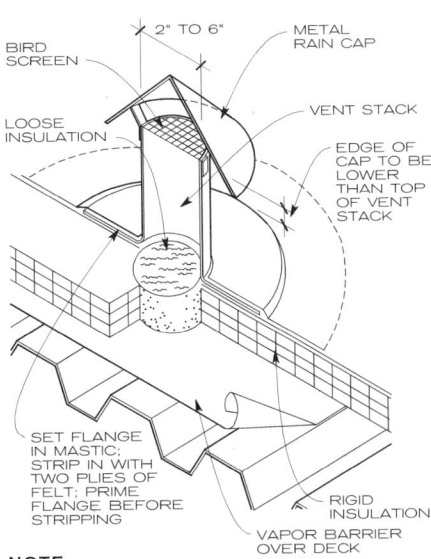

NOTE

This detail allows moisture due to leaks, faulty vapor barriers, or construction work to escape from the roof system.

ROOF RELIEF VENT

NOTES

1. This detail can be adapted for other uses, such as sign supports.
2. Many roofing manufacturers offer prefabricated flashing pieces or permit the use of materials other than those shown here for flashing. Specifications on these proprietary designs vary; consult the manufacturers.
3. For access to areas underneath equipment, vary pipe column height as shown in the accompanying chart.

COLUMN EQUIPMENT SUPPORT

PIPE COLUMN HEIGHT

EQUIPMENT WIDTH (IN.)	COLUMN HEIGHT (IN.)
Up to 24	14
25 to 36	18
37 to 48	24
49 to 60	30
61 and wider	48

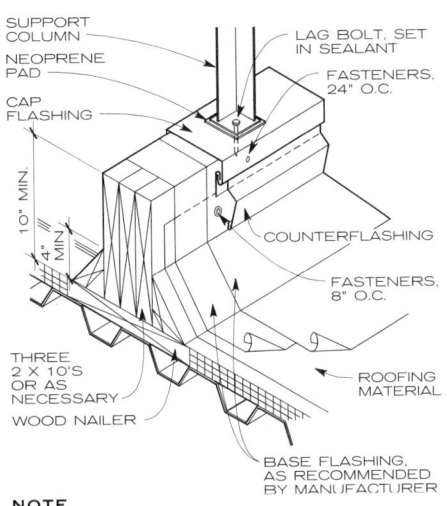

NOTE

This detail allows for roof maintenance around the equipment or sign. The continuous support, in contrast to the point load of a pipe column support, is preferred for lightweight roof systems. Clearance must be provided for removal and replacement of roofing and flashing between parallel supports.

CONTINUOUS EQUIPMENT SUPPORT CURB

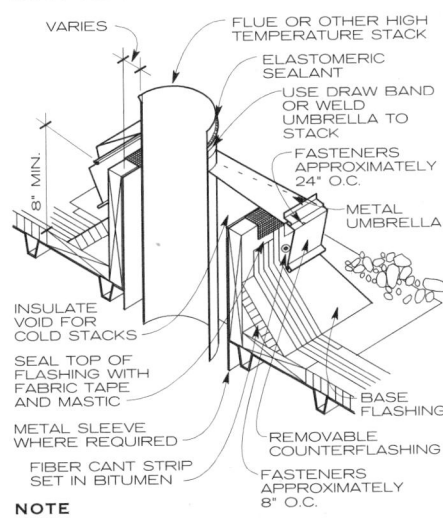

NOTE

This detail allows the opening to be completed before the stack is placed. The metal sleeve and the clearance necessary will depend on the temperature of the material handled by the stack.

FLUE STACK ROOF PENETRATION

Richard J. Vitullo, AIA; Oak Leaf Studio; Crownsville, Maryland

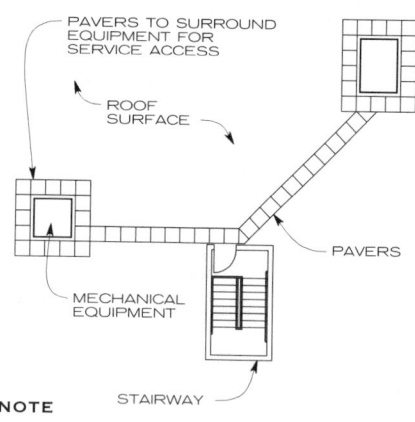

NOTE

Roof pavers provide a stable walking service on any flat roof surface and protect the roof membrane from wear and tear. Service walkways should follow the most direct route to equipment to avoid shortcuts by maintenance personnel. Consult mechanical engineer about access needed to mechanical equipment.

SERVICE WALKWAYS ON ROOFS

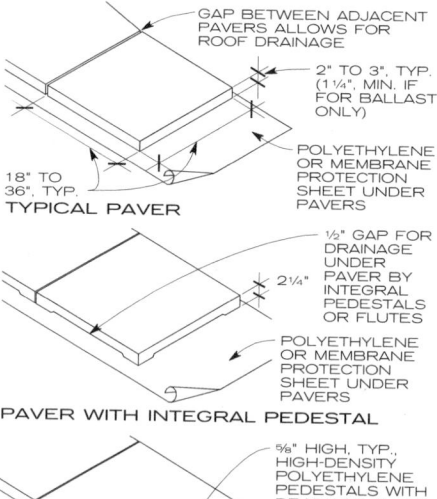

TYPICAL PAVER

PAVER WITH INTEGRAL PEDESTAL

PAVER ON SUPPORT PEDESTALS

NOTE

Ballast pavers are typically made from precast concrete with a non-skid texture on the surface.

BALLAST PAVERS

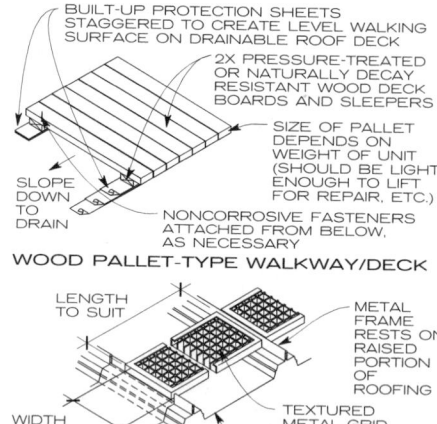

WOOD PALLET-TYPE WALKWAY/DECK

MISCELLANEOUS ROOF WALKING SURFACES

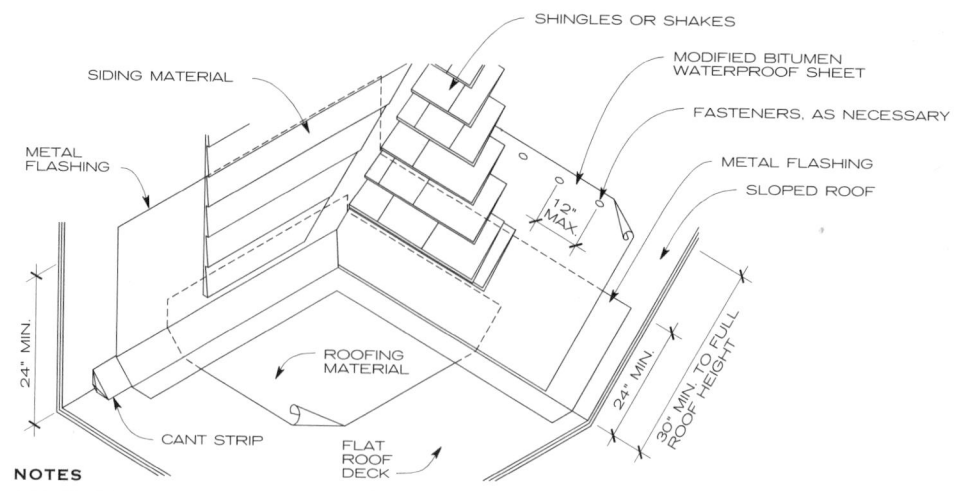

NOTES

1. Modified bitumen sheet specified to provide self-sealing around fastener.

2. Height of flashing and waterproof sheet depends on local snow probabilities and codes and on the roof slope.

WATERPROOFING AT ROOF TRANSITIONS

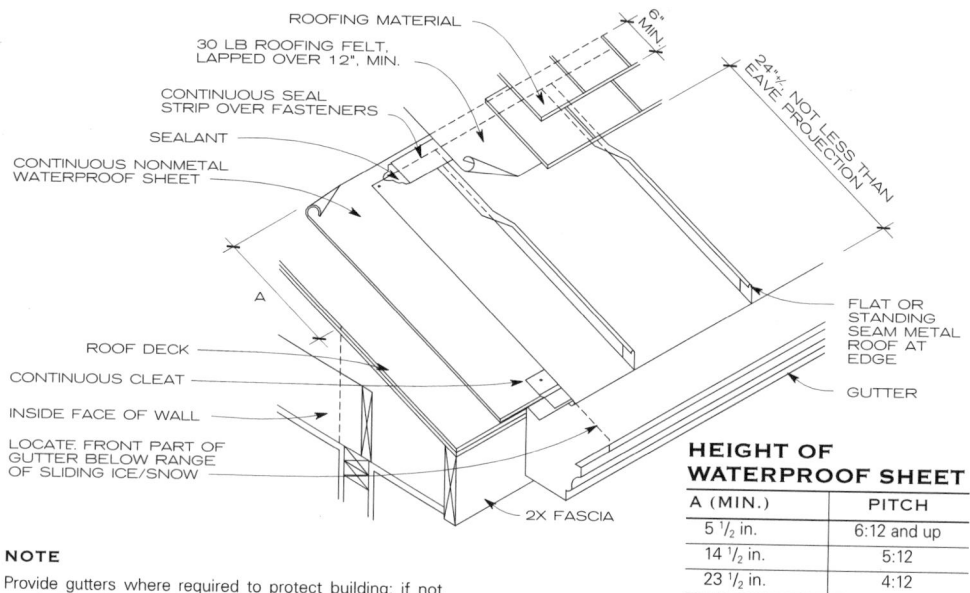

NOTE

Provide gutters where required to protect building; if not required, avoid gutters where icing is common.

HEIGHT OF WATERPROOF SHEET

A (MIN.)	PITCH
5 1/2 in.	6:12 and up
14 1/2 in.	5:12
23 1/2 in.	4:12
to ridge	3:12

ICE DAM DETAILING AT EAVE WITH GUTTER

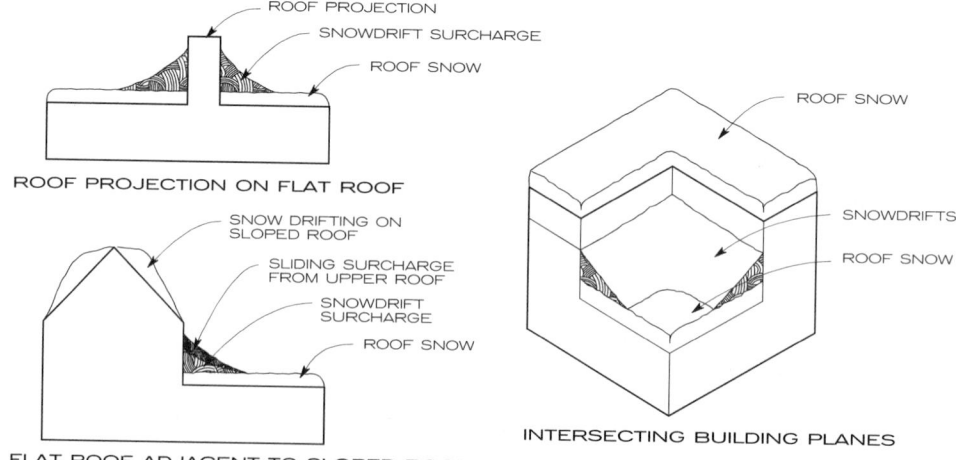

ROOF PROJECTION ON FLAT ROOF

FLAT ROOF ADJACENT TO SLOPED ROOF

INTERSECTING BUILDING PLANES

NOTES

1. Consult codes for projected local snow heights.

2. Snow accumulation on roofs is generally unequal due to wind action. The resulting unequal load distribution might be aggravated by unequal melting of accumulated snow.

SNOW TENDENCIES ON BUILDING SURFACES

Richard J. Vitullo, AIA; Oak Leaf Studio; Crownsville, Maryland

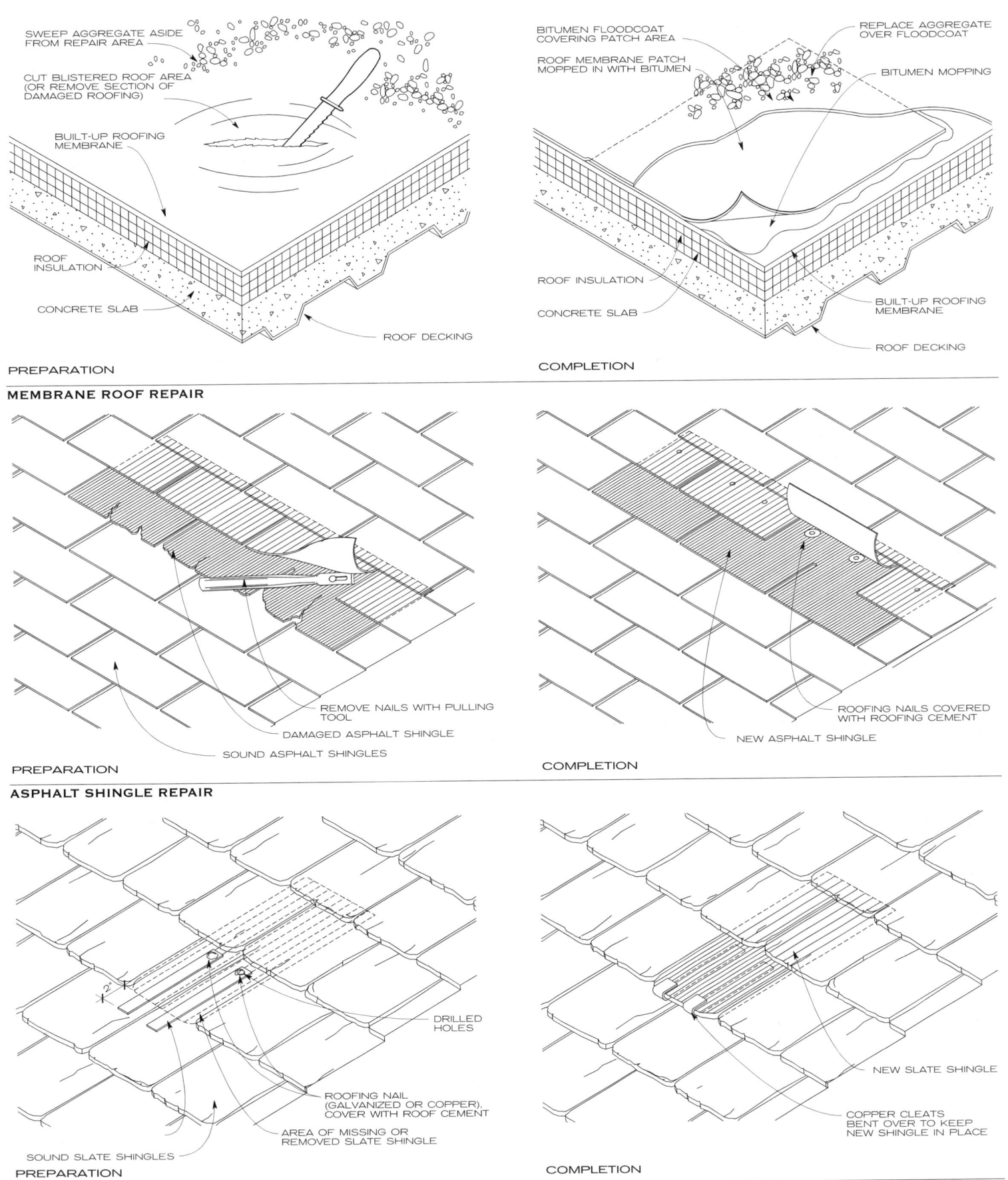

SWEEP AGGREGATE ASIDE FROM REPAIR AREA

CUT BLISTERED ROOF AREA (OR REMOVE SECTION OF DAMAGED ROOFING)

BUILT-UP ROOFING MEMBRANE

ROOF INSULATION

CONCRETE SLAB

ROOF DECKING

PREPARATION

BITUMEN FLOODCOAT COVERING PATCH AREA

ROOF MEMBRANE PATCH MOPPED IN WITH BITUMEN

REPLACE AGGREGATE OVER FLOODCOAT

BITUMEN MOPPING

ROOF INSULATION

CONCRETE SLAB

BUILT-UP ROOFING MEMBRANE

ROOF DECKING

COMPLETION

MEMBRANE ROOF REPAIR

REMOVE NAILS WITH PULLING TOOL

DAMAGED ASPHALT SHINGLE

SOUND ASPHALT SHINGLES

PREPARATION

ROOFING NAILS COVERED WITH ROOFING CEMENT

NEW ASPHALT SHINGLE

COMPLETION

ASPHALT SHINGLE REPAIR

2"

DRILLED HOLES

ROOFING NAIL (GALVANIZED OR COPPER), COVER WITH ROOF CEMENT

AREA OF MISSING OR REMOVED SLATE SHINGLE

SOUND SLATE SHINGLES

PREPARATION

NEW SLATE SHINGLE

COPPER CLEATS BENT OVER TO KEEP NEW SHINGLE IN PLACE

COMPLETION

SLATE SHINGLE REPAIR

Valerie Eickelberger; Rippeteau Architects, PC; Washington, D.C.

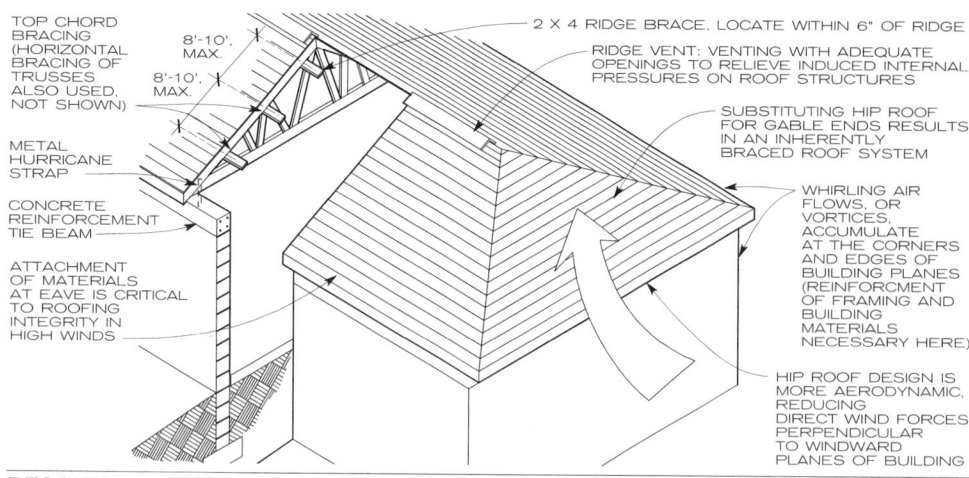

TOP CHORD BRACING (HORIZONTAL BRACING OF TRUSSES ALSO USED, NOT SHOWN)

8'-10' MAX.

8'-10' MAX.

METAL HURRICANE STRAP

CONCRETE REINFORCEMENT TIE BEAM

ATTACHMENT OF MATERIALS AT EAVE IS CRITICAL TO ROOFING INTEGRITY IN HIGH WINDS

2 X 4 RIDGE BRACE, LOCATE WITHIN 6" OF RIDGE

RIDGE VENT: VENTING WITH ADEQUATE OPENINGS TO RELIEVE INDUCED INTERNAL PRESSURES ON ROOF STRUCTURES

SUBSTITUTING HIP ROOF FOR GABLE ENDS RESULTS IN AN INHERENTLY BRACED ROOF SYSTEM

WHIRLING AIR FLOWS, OR VORTICES, ACCUMULATE AT THE CORNERS AND EDGES OF BUILDING PLANES (REINFORCMENT OF FRAMING AND BUILDING MATERIALS NECESSARY HERE)

HIP ROOF DESIGN IS MORE AERODYNAMIC, REDUCING DIRECT WIND FORCES PERPENDICULAR TO WINDWARD PLANES OF BUILDING

RECOMMENDED WOOD FRAME ROOF DESIGN

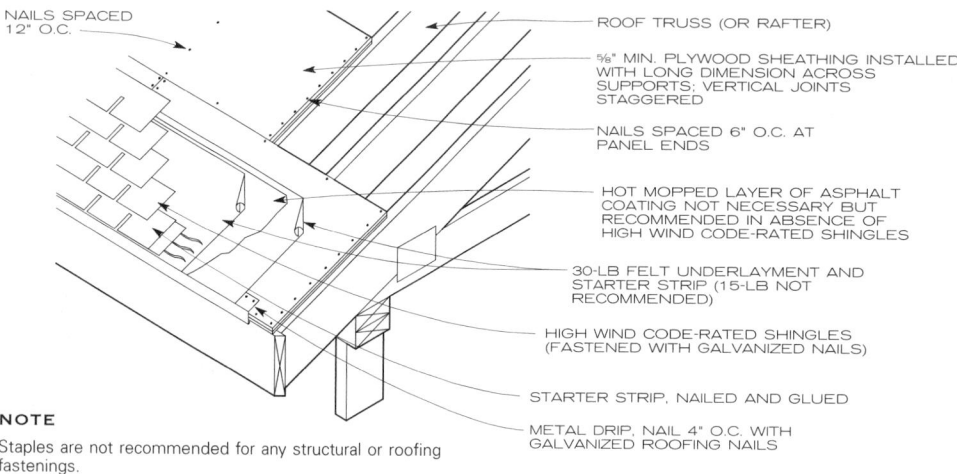

NAILS SPACED 12" O.C.

ROOF TRUSS (OR RAFTER)

⅝" MIN. PLYWOOD SHEATHING INSTALLED WITH LONG DIMENSION ACROSS SUPPORTS; VERTICAL JOINTS STAGGERED

NAILS SPACED 6" O.C. AT PANEL ENDS

HOT MOPPED LAYER OF ASPHALT COATING NOT NECESSARY BUT RECOMMENDED IN ABSENCE OF HIGH WIND CODE-RATED SHINGLES

30-LB FELT UNDERLAYMENT AND STARTER STRIP (15-LB NOT RECOMMENDED)

HIGH WIND CODE-RATED SHINGLES (FASTENED WITH GALVANIZED NAILS)

STARTER STRIP, NAILED AND GLUED

METAL DRIP, NAIL 4" O.C. WITH GALVANIZED ROOFING NAILS

NOTE

Staples are not recommended for any structural or roofing fastenings.

HIGH WIND RESISTANCE DETAIL—COMPOSITION AND ASPHALT SHINGLES

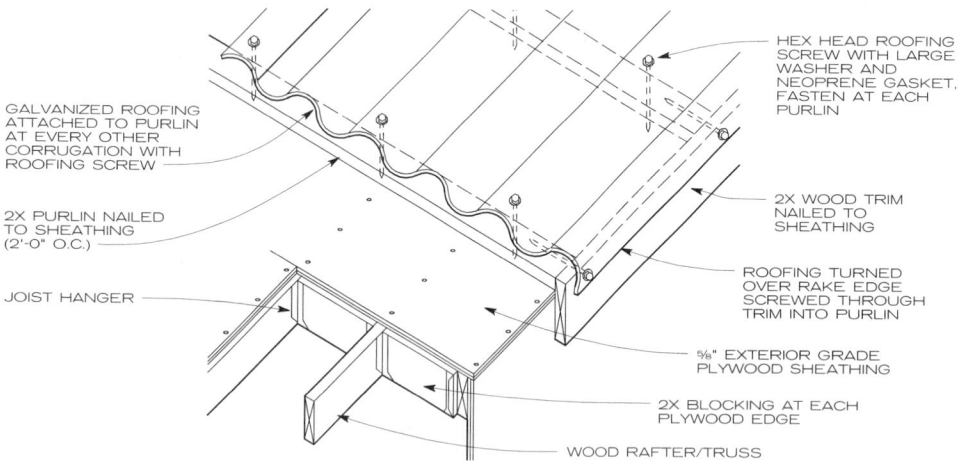

GALVANIZED ROOFING ATTACHED TO PURLIN AT EVERY OTHER CORRUGATION WITH ROOFING SCREW

2X PURLIN NAILED TO SHEATHING (2'-0" O.C.)

JOIST HANGER

HEX HEAD ROOFING SCREW WITH LARGE WASHER AND NEOPRENE GASKET, FASTEN AT EACH PURLIN

2X WOOD TRIM NAILED TO SHEATHING

ROOFING TURNED OVER RAKE EDGE SCREWED THROUGH TRIM INTO PURLIN

⅝" EXTERIOR GRADE PLYWOOD SHEATHING

2X BLOCKING AT EACH PLYWOOD EDGE

WOOD RAFTER/TRUSS

HIGH WIND RESISTANCE DETAIL—GALVANIZED METAL ROOFING

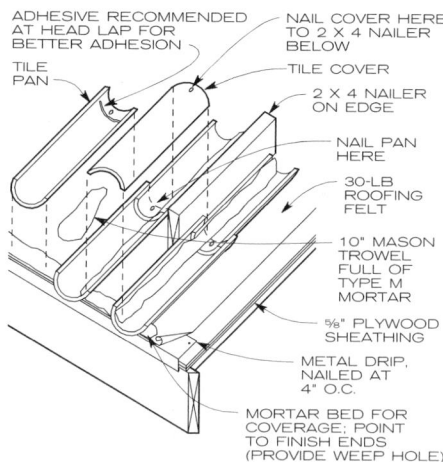

ADHESIVE RECOMMENDED AT HEAD LAP FOR BETTER ADHESION

TILE PAN

NAIL COVER HERE TO 2 X 4 NAILER BELOW

TILE COVER

2 X 4 NAILER ON EDGE

NAIL PAN HERE

30-LB ROOFING FELT

10" MASON TROWEL FULL OF TYPE M MORTAR

⅝" PLYWOOD SHEATHING

METAL DRIP, NAILED AT 4" O.C.

MORTAR BED FOR COVERAGE; POINT TO FINISH ENDS (PROVIDE WEEP HOLE)

HIGH WIND RESISTANCE DETAIL— BARREL TILE ROOFING

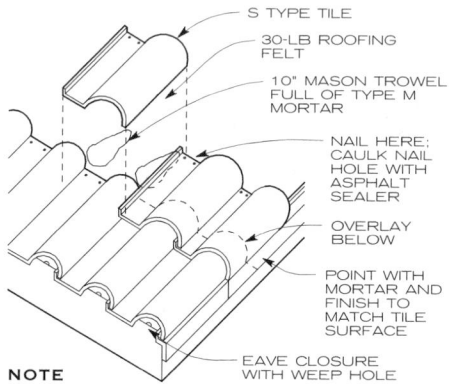

S TYPE TILE

30-LB ROOFING FELT

10" MASON TROWEL FULL OF TYPE M MORTAR

NAIL HERE; CAULK NAIL HOLE WITH ASPHALT SEALER

OVERLAY BELOW

POINT WITH MORTAR AND FINISH TO MATCH TILE SURFACE

EAVE CLOSURE WITH WEEP HOLE

NOTE

After tile roofs are laid up completely, traffic should not be allowed on roof and no work that creates vibration in framing or roof sheathing should be allowed for 72 hours, minimum (24 hours is needed to ensure proper set).

HIGH WIND RESISTANCE DETAIL— S TYPE TILE ROOFING

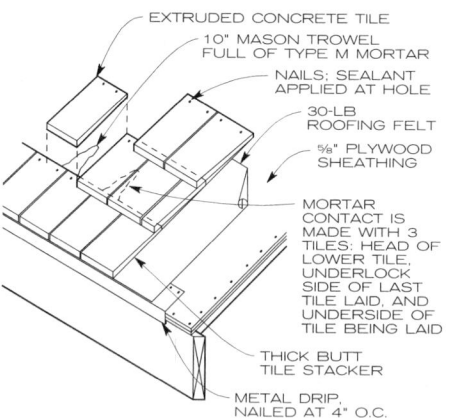

EXTRUDED CONCRETE TILE

10" MASON TROWEL FULL OF TYPE M MORTAR

NAILS; SEALANT APPLIED AT HOLE

30-LB ROOFING FELT

⅝" PLYWOOD SHEATHING

MORTAR CONTACT IS MADE WITH 3 TILES: HEAD OF LOWER TILE, UNDERLOCK SIDE OF LAST TILE LAID, AND UNDERSIDE OF TILE BEING LAID

THICK BUTT TILE STACKER

METAL DRIP, NAILED AT 4" O.C.

HIGH WIND RESISTANCE DETAIL— EXTRUDED CONCRETE

GENERAL

Roofing materials are particularly susceptible to damage from wind uplift and debris borne by high winds. Contributing to this problem is the use of inferior roofing materials and fasteners, substandard workmanship practices, and poor design choices for areas known for frequent or potentially severe high winds. Use of design practices that resist wind uplift and lateral forces can protect the total building system from damage due to high winds and/or hurricanes. Anchoring framing members to the foundation system, tying together all framing, and bracing members, particularly roof trusses, are practices that strengthen and brace the entire building. Only when that has been accomplished are good roofing design and details relevant.

Richard J. Vitullo, AIA; Oak Leaf Studio; Crownsville, Maryland

ROOFING FAILURES IN HIGH WIND

Some of the main reasons for roofing material failure caused by high winds are described here:

1. Roof sheathing—Inadequate reinforcement at the edges causes sheathing to separate from the roof truss or rafter. Wafer board, composite board, oriented strand board, or structural particleboard used as sheathing does not provide sufficient wind resistance.

2. Composition shingle and felt underlayment—Use of shingles, attachment adhesives, and/or fasteners not rated for high winds or fasteners used in insufficient numbers, locations, and/or orientation can lead to wind damage.

3. Extruded concrete or clay tile—Poor nailing and/or mortar connections and underlayment failure due to lack of bonding between the underlayment and mortar or mortar and tile can cause failure of the roof. As well, clay tile may shatter when hit with flying debris.

4. Sheet metal—Inadequately adhered and fastened eave flashing, drips, and metal gravel stops can cause failure.

GENERAL

Roof openings such as skylights, scuttles, and vents must be detailed with care, considering they will be exposed to the same external factors as the roof assembly itself. These factors include wind pressure—both positive and negative—which acts on the framing and/or glazing; rainwater penetration; live loads from snow and ice; dynamic loads from impact; daily cycles of thermal expansion and contraction; drainage of water and melting snow; and abuse from maintenance personnel. In addition, measures must be specified to keep people from falling through these openings.

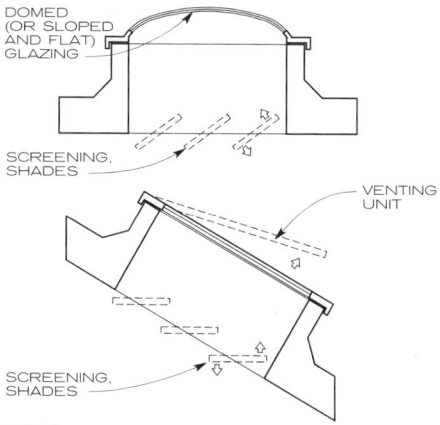

DOMED (OR SLOPED AND FLAT) GLAZING

SCREENING, SHADES

VENTING UNIT

SCREENING, SHADES

NOTE

In determining the desired form and size of the skylight unit/assembly, consideration should be given to

1. Environmental conditions, including orientation and winter and summer solar penetration angles at the site
2. Prevailing wind direction and patterns
3. Precipitation quantity and patterns
4. Adjacent topography and landscaping (shade trees, etc.)
5. Coordination with HVAC system
6. Use of shading, screening, or light reflecting/bouncing devices
7. Views desired relative to view obstructions, streetlights, etc.

SKYLIGHTS

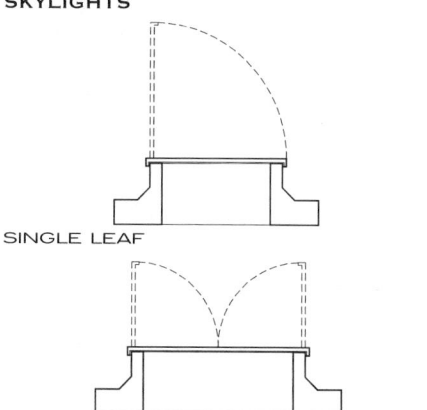

SINGLE LEAF

DOUBLE LEAF

SCUTTLES

SCUTTLES

Scuttles, often referred to as roof hatches, provide roof access for maintenance personnel using ladders, a built-in ship's ladder, or stairs; an emergency escape route in the event of a fire; and access for moving large equipment into or out of the building, possibly eliminating the need for extra-large doors in rooms and corridors below.

Scuttles come as preassembled units, often with integral curbs, and are usually made with spring-assisted openings. When glazing is introduced, scuttles can function as skylights as well. For use as smoke/fire vents, scuttles must have automatic opening capability.

If scuttles are to serve as a required means of egress, consult building codes for number, size, and location required; type of access permitted (ship's ladder, stair, etc.); and type of operation permitted (manual force required to open unit or powered opening).

Richard J. Vitullo, AIA; Oak Leaf Studio; Crownsville, Maryland

SKYLIGHTS

Skylights provide daylight to interior spaces and can reduce dependence on electrical lighting. In passive solar designs, skylights are used to admit direct solar radiation, enhancing space heating, and, when vented properly, to induce convective airflow, reducing cooling loads through natural ventilation.

Skylights are available as preassembled units, which are shipped to the site ready to be installed, or as framed assemblies of stock components, which arrive prefabricated for site assembly. Both fixed and hinged skylights are manufactured. The hinged variety can be opened manually or by remote control devices for venting. Frames are typically mounted on a built-up prefabricated or site-built curb, with integral counterflashing; they can be assembled with or without insulation.

Self-flashing skylight units are available with or without curbs. Those without curbs are intended only for pitched roof assemblies and are not recommended for roof assemblies with finished spaces below.

Framed skylight assemblies are custom designed by manufacturers to meet the necessary wind, roof, and dead loads of the assembly itself. When a skylight is pitched beyond a certain angle, it must be designed to resist environmental factors as does a curtain wall assembly. Roof drainage for rain- and storm water can limit skylight dimensions. Condensate gutters are needed in the body of the skylight assembly and around its perimeter.

FRAMING, GLAZING, AND GASKETS

The heart of a well-designed skylight unit or skylight framed assembly is the detailing of frames, glazing, and sealant systems. Thickness, size, and geometric profile of all glass and acrylic glazing materials should be carefully selected for compliance with building codes and manufacturers' recommendations. The following glazing materials are considered resistant to impact and breakage and are generally approved by codes (listed in descending order of cost):

1. Formed acrylic with mar-resistant finish
2. Formed acrylic
3. Polycarbonates
4. Flat acrylic
5. Laminated glass
6. Tempered glass
7. Clear polished wire glass
8. Textured obscure wire glass

Framed skylights require somewhat greater mullion widths when glazed with acrylics in order to accommodate the expansion and contraction characteristics of plastics. When glazed with glass, framed skylight mullions are spaced according to the standard glass widths: laminated glass (48 in., maximum), wire glass (60 in., maximum), and tempered glass (72 in., maximum). High-performance insulating glass is generally used in preassembled units (and sometimes framed assemblies) and provides important energy savings.

For economy, tinted acrylics should be limited to $1/4$ in. thickness. A combination fiberglass sheet and aluminum frame system with high insulating value and good light diffusion can be a cost-effective alternative. Domed acrylic glazing is almost self-cleaning, as the sloped shapes facilitate rain washing of the surface.

Frame systems must be engineered to carry the total resultant forces of the loads imposed on the skylight in accordance with all building codes. Framing, glazing, and gaskets also must be able to resist exposure to airborne pollutants. Frames with thermal breaks incorporated have better energy performance.

Finishes for aluminum frame components are available as mill finish, clear anodized, duranodic bronze or black, acrylic enamel, and fluorocarbon.

Gaskets are especially subject to degradation from solar ultraviolet rays. Excessive expansion and contraction of acrylic glazing can cause "rolling" of the gasket between metal framing. Small valleys created at the bottom of the sloped glazing and the horizontal glazing cap will hold water, which increases the chance of gasket breakdown and subsequent water infiltration.

SECURITY AND SAFETY

Frames or screens to protect glazing from impact, fire brands, or forced entry can be designed into the skylight system. To avoid forced entry, a framed skylight should include deterrents to disassembling the framing, removing the snap-on cover, and melting the glazing (acrylics can easily be burned with a torch). Metal security screens may be required.

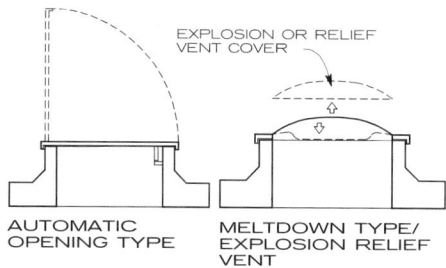

EXPLOSION OR RELIEF VENT COVER

AUTOMATIC OPENING TYPE

MELTDOWN TYPE/ EXPLOSION RELIEF VENT

FIRE AND SMOKE VENTS

FIRE AND SMOKE VENTING

In certain building types and occupancies, such as those with large expanses of unobstructed space, fire and smoke vents that open automatically with a fire-induced temperature increase are required. Roof vents are often required over stairs, elevator hoistways, high-hazard occupancy areas (to offer explosion relief), and in areas behind the proscenium in theaters. The vents permit smoke, heat, and volatile gases to escape, lower the temperature at floor level, and reduce water damage by limiting active sprinkler heads to those in the immediate area of the fire.

There are two basic types of fire and smoke vents, both commonly available with integral curbs and flashing:

1. Meltdown: plastic glazing that softens and drops out of the frame when exposed to high temperatures (unit must be replaced once exposed to fire).

2. Automatic opening: solid or glazed cover with springs held by a fusible link that melts when the temperature rises, releasing the springs and opening the vent.

Enough vents must be distributed over the entire roof area to ensure early venting of a fire, regardless of its location. The size and spacing of the vents must be determined for each building according to its size and use and the degree of hazard involved. When UL- or FM-listed vents are required, choice of size is generally limited to stock sizes. Venting is based on moving a specific number of cubic feet of air per minute through the vents. Consult building codes for required capacity, size, and spacing.

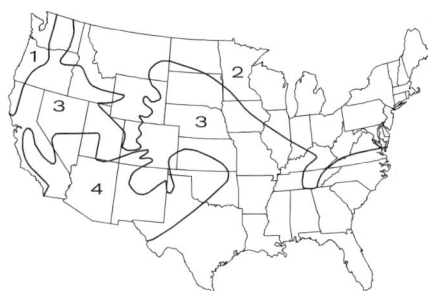

PERCENTAGE OF ROOF AREA REQUIRED FOR SKYLIGHTING

LIGHT ZONE	LIGHT DESIGN LEVELS (FC)		
	30	60	120
1	3.3	5.2	13.3
2	2.8	4.3	10.8
3	1.8	3.2	6.9
4	1.5	2.8	4.0

Typical roof vent area requirements are 0.67% roof area for low heat release occupancies, 1% roof area for moderate heat release occupancies, and 2% roof area for high heat release occupancies.

Generally, several small units satisfy the total venting area requirement better than a few larger ones (NFPA #204). Roof scuttles are available that may also serve as fire and smoke vents. Consider the spacing of vents relative to interior spaces and their uses, proximity to exits, and, if glazed, their role in daylighting.

Explosion relief vents are a type of fire and smoke vent that opens automatically when interior pressure rises above a predetermined level. Plastic glazed units deform under higher than normal air pressure and are released from their frame.

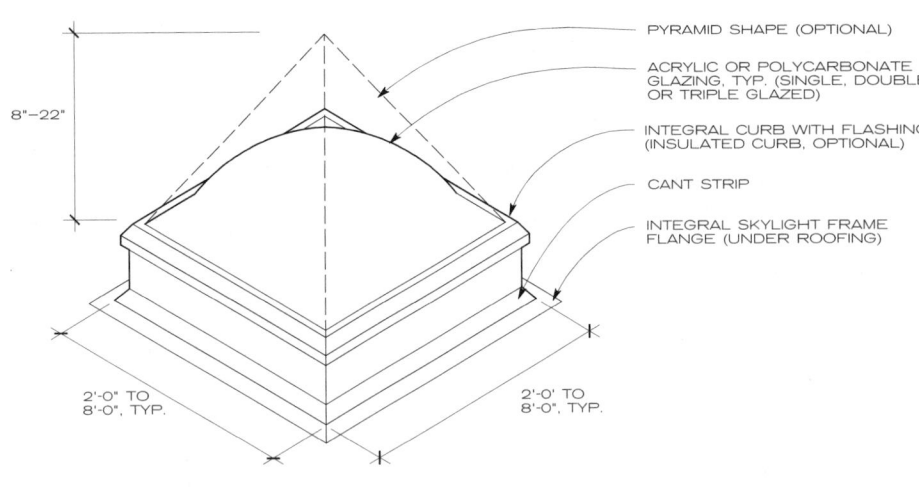

8"–22"

2'-0" TO 8'-0", TYP.   2'-0" TO 8'-0", TYP.

PYRAMID SHAPE (OPTIONAL)

ACRYLIC OR POLYCARBONATE GLAZING, TYP. (SINGLE, DOUBLE, OR TRIPLE GLAZED)

INTEGRAL CURB WITH FLASHING (INSULATED CURB, OPTIONAL)

CANT STRIP

INTEGRAL SKYLIGHT FRAME FLANGE (UNDER ROOFING)

NOTE
Glazing may be clear, tinted transparent, or white translucent.

DOME UNIT SKYLIGHT—FLAT ROOF

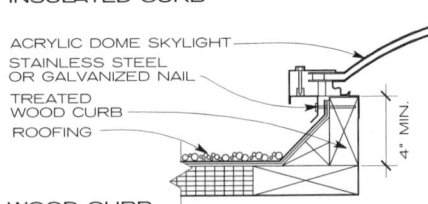

ACRYLIC PLASTIC DOME
PVC CAP
CONDENSATE GUTTER
BUTYL SEALANT
ALUMINUM RETAINING ANGLE
ALUMINUM CURB FRAME
NEOPRENE GASKET
ALUMINUM CURB
1" RIGID INSULATION
ROOFING

3"

INSULATED CURB

ACRYLIC DOME SKYLIGHT
STAINLESS STEEL OR GALVANIZED NAIL
TREATED WOOD CURB
ROOFING

4" MIN.

WOOD CURB

UNIT SKYLIGHT SECTION

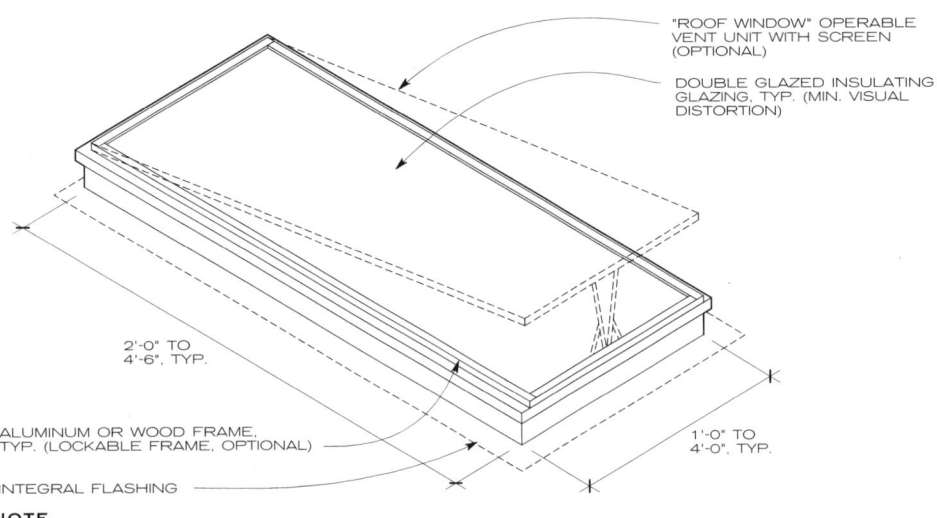

"ROOF WINDOW" OPERABLE VENT UNIT WITH SCREEN (OPTIONAL)

DOUBLE GLAZED INSULATING GLAZING, TYP. (MIN. VISUAL DISTORTION)

2'-0" TO 4'-6", TYP.

1'-0" TO 4'-0", TYP.

ALUMINUM OR WOOD FRAME, TYP. (LOCKABLE FRAME, OPTIONAL)

INTEGRAL FLASHING

NOTE
1. Clear and tinted transparent glass, typical; tempered, laminated, and wire glass available.
2. Manual and powered vent operation, venetian blinds, shades, and exterior awnings available. Consult manufacturer.

FLAT PANEL UNIT SKYLIGHT—SLOPED ROOF

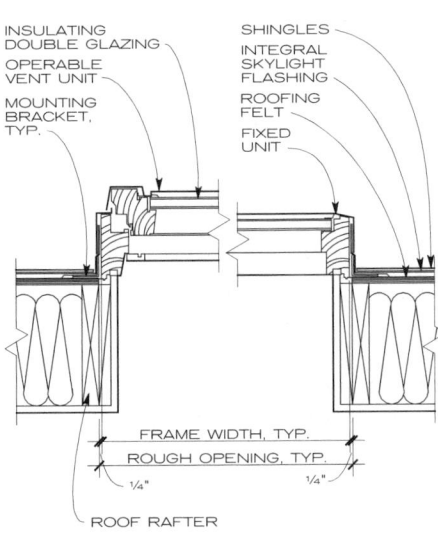

INSULATING DOUBLE GLAZING
OPERABLE VENT UNIT
MOUNTING BRACKET, TYP.

SHINGLES
INTEGRAL SKYLIGHT FLASHING
ROOFING FELT
FIXED UNIT

FRAME WIDTH, TYP.
ROUGH OPENING, TYP.
¼"   ¼"

ROOF RAFTER

FLAT PANEL UNIT SKYLIGHT SECTION

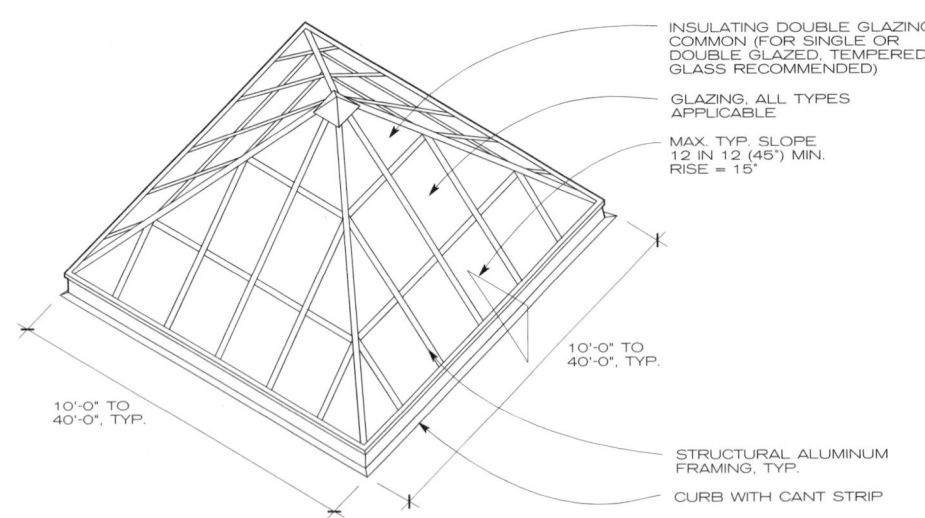

INSULATING DOUBLE GLAZING COMMON (FOR SINGLE OR DOUBLE GLAZED, TEMPERED GLASS RECOMMENDED)

GLAZING, ALL TYPES APPLICABLE

MAX. TYP. SLOPE 12 IN 12 (45°) MIN. RISE = 15°

10'-0" TO 40'-0", TYP.

10'-0" TO 40'-0", TYP.

STRUCTURAL ALUMINUM FRAMING, TYP.

CURB WITH CANT STRIP

PYRAMID FRAMED SKYLIGHT ASSEMBLY

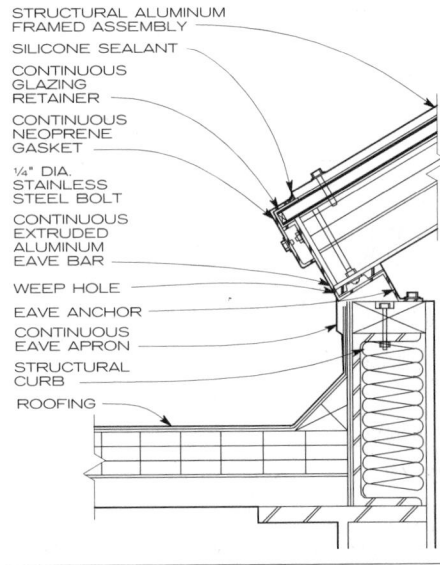

STRUCTURAL ALUMINUM FRAMED ASSEMBLY
SILICONE SEALANT
CONTINUOUS GLAZING RETAINER
CONTINUOUS NEOPRENE GASKET
¼" DIA. STAINLESS STEEL BOLT
CONTINUOUS EXTRUDED ALUMINUM EAVE BAR
WEEP HOLE
EAVE ANCHOR
CONTINUOUS EAVE APRON
STRUCTURAL CURB
ROOFING

CURB DETAIL AT SLOPED FRAMED ASSEMBLY

Richard J. Vitullo, AIA; Oak Leaf Studio; Crownsville, Maryland

7   SKYLIGHTS

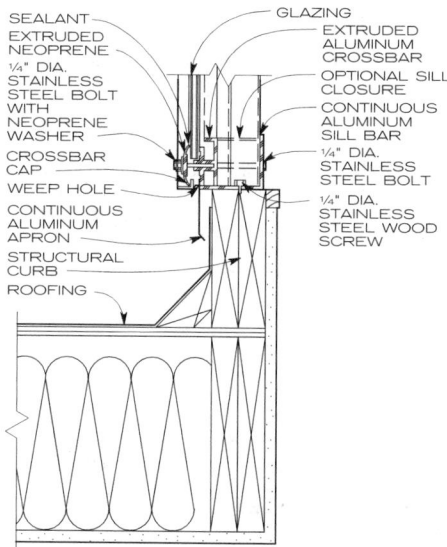

SEALANT
EXTRUDED NEOPRENE
¼" DIA. STAINLESS STEEL BOLT WITH NEOPRENE WASHER
CROSSBAR CAP
WEEP HOLE
CONTINUOUS ALUMINUM APRON
STRUCTURAL CURB
ROOFING

GLAZING
EXTRUDED ALUMINUM CROSSBAR
OPTIONAL SILL CLOSURE
CONTINUOUS ALUMINUM SILL BAR
¼" DIA. STAINLESS STEEL BOLT
¼" DIA. STAINLESS STEEL WOOD SCREW

VERTICAL FRAME CURB DETAIL (WOOD FRAME)

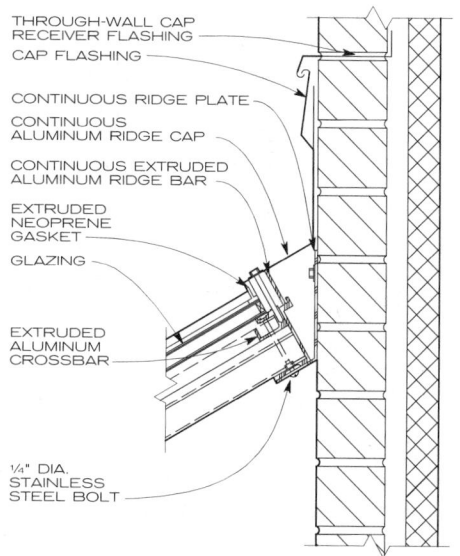

THROUGH-WALL CAP RECEIVER FLASHING
CAP FLASHING
CONTINUOUS RIDGE PLATE
CONTINUOUS ALUMINUM RIDGE CAP
CONTINUOUS EXTRUDED ALUMINUM RIDGE BAR
EXTRUDED NEOPRENE GASKET
GLAZING
EXTRUDED ALUMINUM CROSSBAR
¼" DIA. STAINLESS STEEL BOLT

SINGLE-PITCH BACK WALL DETAIL AT TOP (MASONRY WALL)

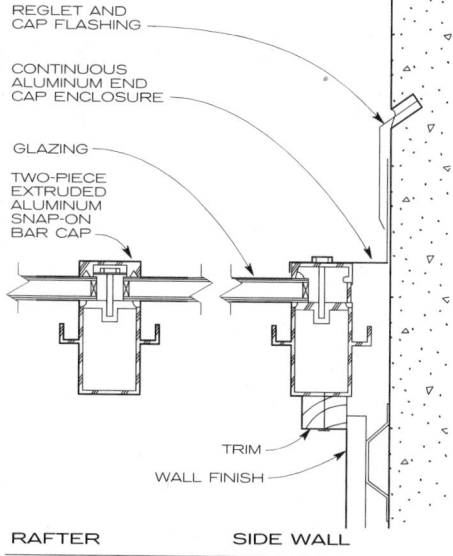

REGLET AND CAP FLASHING
CONTINUOUS ALUMINUM END CAP ENCLOSURE
GLAZING
TWO-PIECE EXTRUDED ALUMINUM SNAP-ON BAR CAP
TRIM
WALL FINISH

RAFTER   SIDE WALL

SINGLE-PITCH RAFTER AND SIDE WALL DETAIL (CONCRETE WALL)

Richard J. Vitullo, AIA; Oak Leaf Studio; Crownsville, Maryland

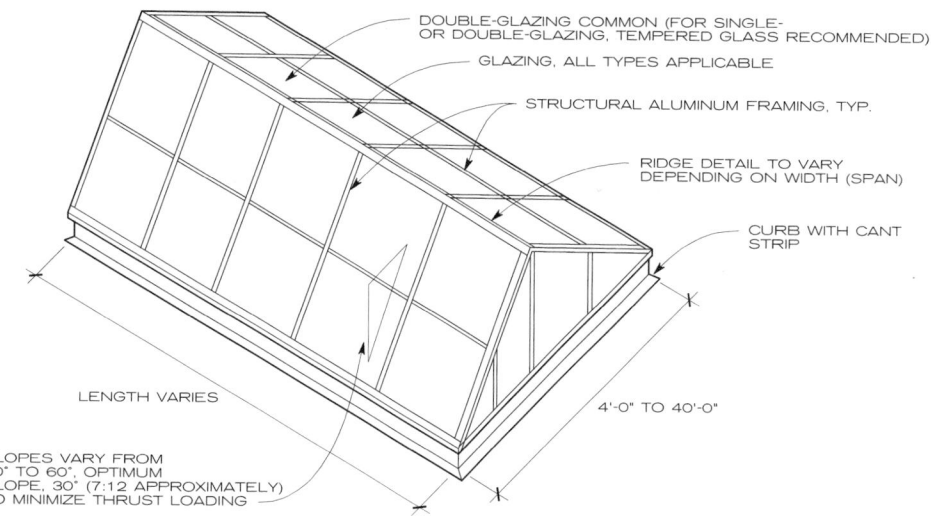

DOUBLE-GLAZING COMMON (FOR SINGLE- OR DOUBLE-GLAZING, TEMPERED GLASS RECOMMENDED)
GLAZING, ALL TYPES APPLICABLE
STRUCTURAL ALUMINUM FRAMING, TYP.
RIDGE DETAIL TO VARY DEPENDING ON WIDTH (SPAN)
CURB WITH CANT STRIP

LENGTH VARIES

4'-0" TO 40'-0"

SLOPES VARY FROM 10° TO 60°, OPTIMUM SLOPE, 30° (7:12 APPROXIMATELY) TO MINIMIZE THRUST LOADING

NOTE

Options for a pitched skylight include (1) integration of skylight with roof structure at ridge, slope of skylight to match slope of roof, no end glazing; (2) hip end glazing; and (3) vaulted framing; minimum rise is 22%.

DOUBLE-PITCH FRAMED SKYLIGHT ASSEMBLY

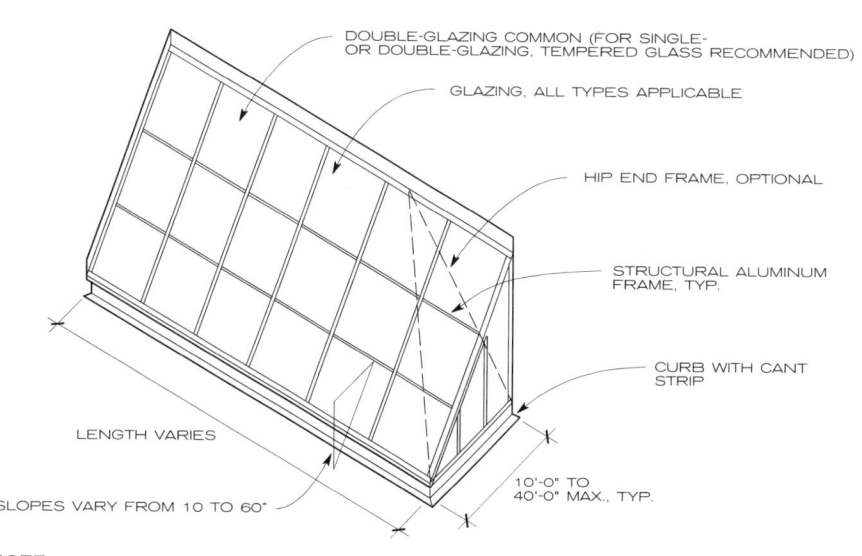

DOUBLE-GLAZING COMMON (FOR SINGLE- OR DOUBLE-GLAZING, TEMPERED GLASS RECOMMENDED)
GLAZING, ALL TYPES APPLICABLE
HIP END FRAME, OPTIONAL
STRUCTURAL ALUMINUM FRAME, TYP.
CURB WITH CANT STRIP

LENGTH VARIES

10'-0" TO 40'-0" MAX., TYP.

SLOPES VARY FROM 10 TO 60°

NOTE

Sloped aluminum frame may be segmented or curved.

SINGLE-PITCH FRAMED SKYLIGHT ASSEMBLY

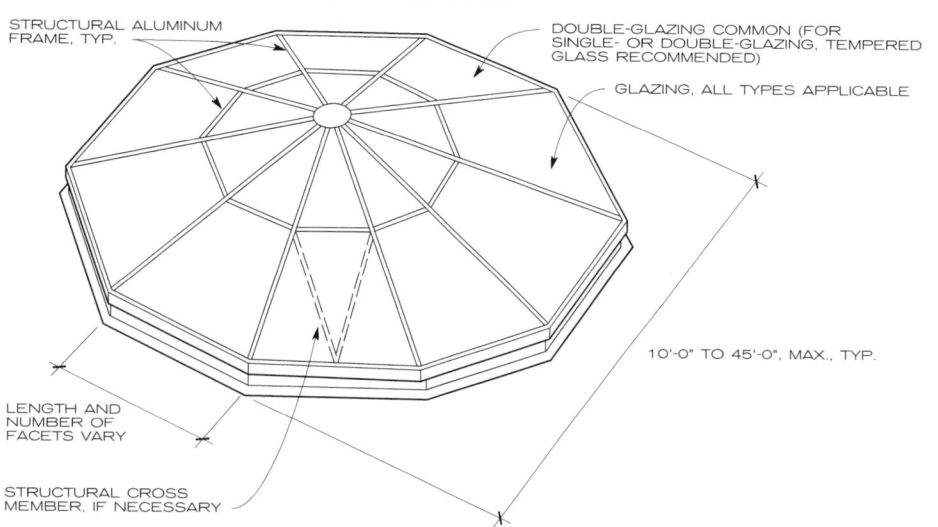

STRUCTURAL ALUMINUM FRAME, TYP.
DOUBLE-GLAZING COMMON (FOR SINGLE- OR DOUBLE-GLAZING, TEMPERED GLASS RECOMMENDED)
GLAZING, ALL TYPES APPLICABLE

10'-0" TO 45'-0", MAX., TYP.

LENGTH AND NUMBER OF FACETS VARY
STRUCTURAL CROSS MEMBER, IF NECESSARY

POLYGONAL FRAMED SKYLIGHT ASSEMBLY

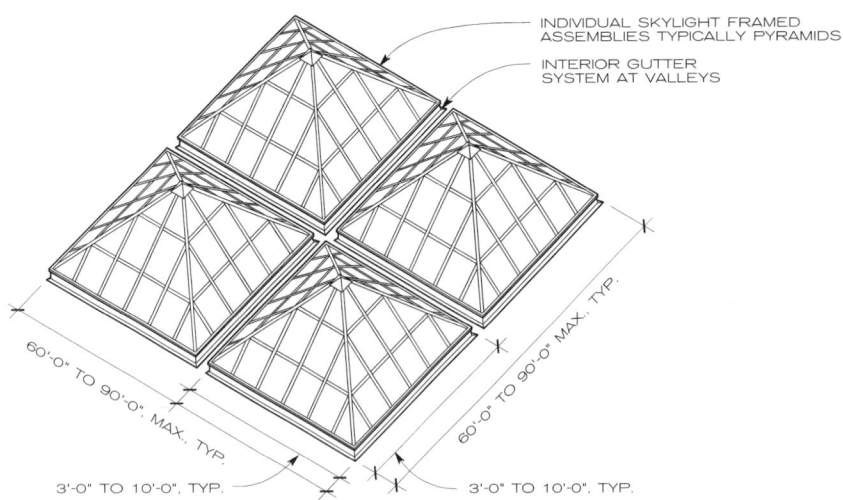

INDIVIDUAL SKYLIGHT FRAMED ASSEMBLIES TYPICALLY PYRAMIDS

INTERIOR GUTTER SYSTEM AT VALLEYS

60'-0" TO 90'-0" MAX., TYP.

60'-0" TO 90'-0" MAX. TYP.

3'-0" TO 10'-0", TYP.

3'-0" TO 10'-0", TYP.

NOTES

1. Individual skylights for unit skylights may be pyramids or domes for flat roofs or flat panels for sloped roofs.
2. The number of multiples of individual skylights depends only on the structural frame system below, although the larger the grid assembly, the more water runoff must be accommodated.

MULTIPLE-GRID SKYLIGHTS—UNIT AND FRAMED ASSEMBLIES

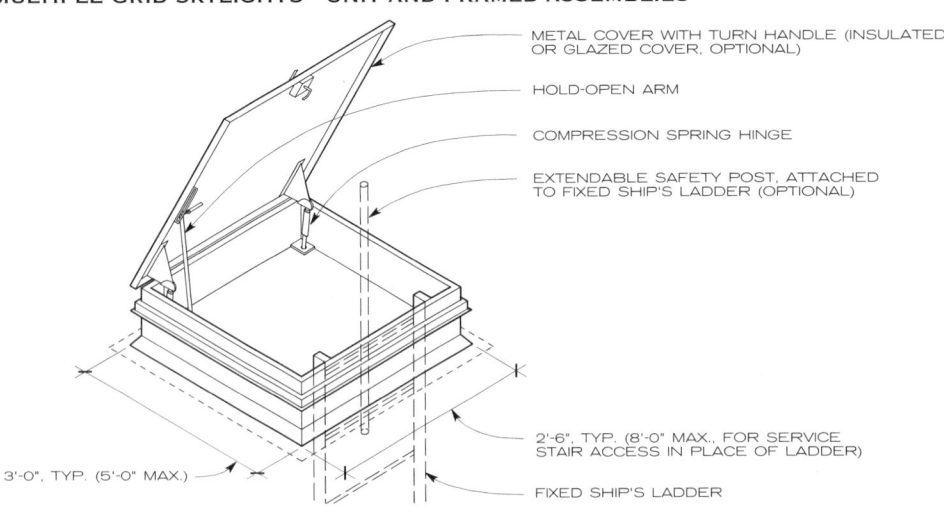

METAL COVER WITH TURN HANDLE (INSULATED OR GLAZED COVER, OPTIONAL)

HOLD-OPEN ARM

COMPRESSION SPRING HINGE

EXTENDABLE SAFETY POST, ATTACHED TO FIXED SHIP'S LADDER (OPTIONAL)

2'-6", TYP. (8'-0" MAX., FOR SERVICE STAIR ACCESS IN PLACE OF LADDER)

3'-0", TYP. (5'-0" MAX.)

FIXED SHIP'S LADDER

NOTE

Double leaf scuttles are typically specified for larger openings.

ROOF SCUTTLE

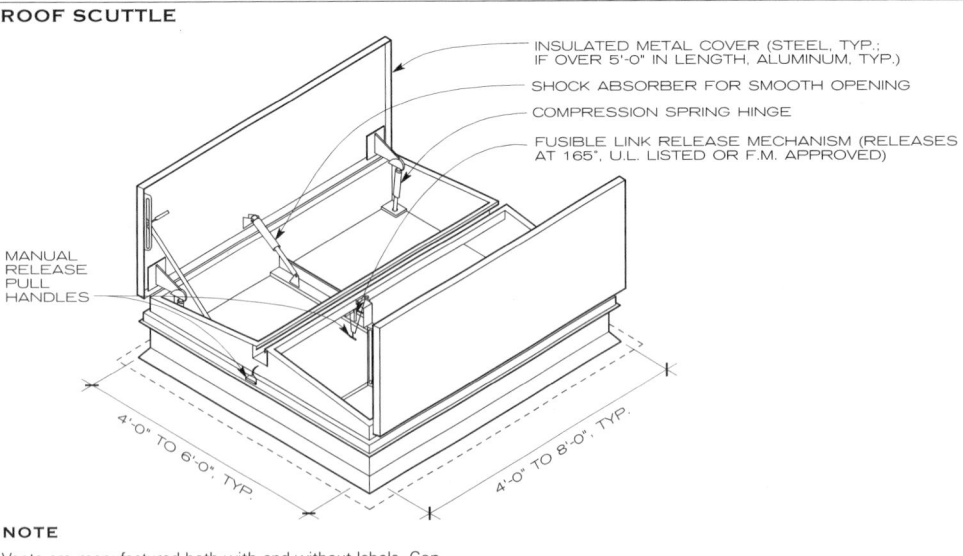

INSULATED METAL COVER (STEEL, TYP.; IF OVER 5'-0" IN LENGTH, ALUMINUM, TYP.)

SHOCK ABSORBER FOR SMOOTH OPENING

COMPRESSION SPRING HINGE

FUSIBLE LINK RELEASE MECHANISM (RELEASES AT 165°, U.L. LISTED OR F.M. APPROVED)

MANUAL RELEASE PULL HANDLES

4'-0" TO 6'-0", TYP.

4'-0" TO 8'-0", TYP.

NOTE

Vents are manufactured both with and without labels. Consult codes for vent requirements. Fire and smoke vents can be adapted for use as explosion vent.

FIRE AND SMOKE VENT

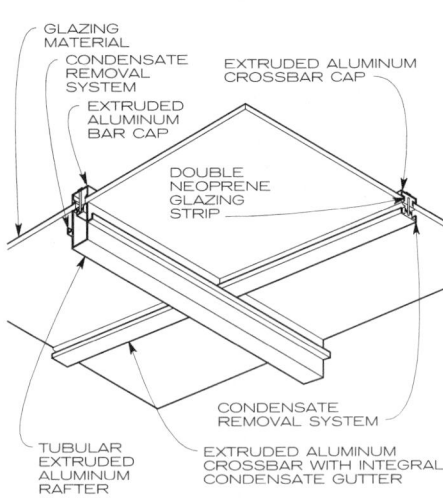

GLAZING MATERIAL

CONDENSATE REMOVAL SYSTEM

EXTRUDED ALUMINUM CROSSBAR CAP

EXTRUDED ALUMINUM BAR CAP

DOUBLE NEOPRENE GLAZING STRIP

CONDENSATE REMOVAL SYSTEM

TUBULAR EXTRUDED ALUMINUM RAFTER

EXTRUDED ALUMINUM CROSSBAR WITH INTEGRAL CONDENSATE GUTTER

TYPICAL TUBULAR ALUMINUM FRAME DETAIL

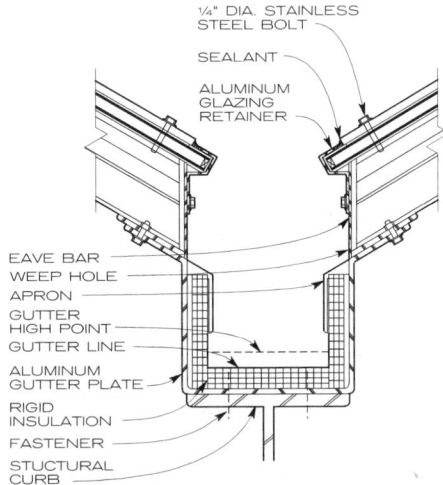

¼" DIA. STAINLESS STEEL BOLT

SEALANT

ALUMINUM GLAZING RETAINER

EAVE BAR

WEEP HOLE

APRON

GUTTER HIGH POINT

GUTTER LINE

ALUMINUM GUTTER PLATE

RIGID INSULATION

FASTENER

STUCTURAL CURB

NOTE

Structural gutter system available for multiple and grid network systems of ridge- and pyramid-type enclosures.

MULTIPLE GRID GUTTER SECTION DETAIL

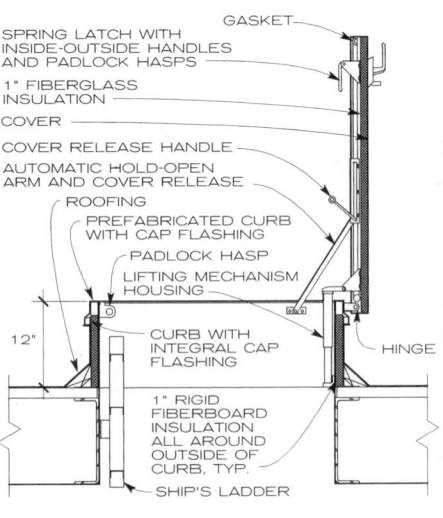

SPRING LATCH WITH INSIDE-OUTSIDE HANDLES AND PADLOCK HASPS

GASKET

1" FIBERGLASS INSULATION

COVER

COVER RELEASE HANDLE

AUTOMATIC HOLD-OPEN ARM AND COVER RELEASE

ROOFING

PREFABRICATED CURB WITH CAP FLASHING

PADLOCK HASP

LIFTING MECHANISM HOUSING

CURB WITH INTEGRAL CAP FLASHING

12"

HINGE

1" RIGID FIBERBOARD INSULATION ALL AROUND OUTSIDE OF CURB, TYP.

SHIP'S LADDER

NOTE

Fire and smoke vent section is similar in construction, hardware, and integration with roof assembly. Consult manufacturer for all additional hardware.

SCUTTLE SECTION DETAIL

Richard J. Vitullo, AIA; Oak Leaf Studio; Crownsville, Maryland

GENERAL

Fire-rated assemblies for door and window openings, used to protect against the spread of fire and smoke, consist of a fire-rated door or window with frame, hardware, and accessories, including gasketing. Each component is crucial to the overall performance of the assembly as a fire barrier. Choices to be made regarding the enclosure of openings in fire-rated walls include the following:

1. Fire-rated wall requirements
2. Size of opening
3. Means of egress
   a. Required size per occupancy
   b. Quantity and location
   c. Direction of egress flow and operation of enclosure
   d. Hardware requirements
   e. Window egress requirements
4. Materials and finishes
5. Security
6. Visibility and glazing

FIRE PROTECTION CRITERIA

NFPA 80, Standard for Fire Doors and Fire Windows, is a consensus standard that establishes minimum criteria for installing and maintaining assemblies and devices used to protect openings in walls, ceilings, and floors from the spread of fire and smoke. The degree of fire protection (in hours) required for a given opening is referenced in the model building codes (BOCA, SBCCI, and UBC) and the Life Safety Code (NFPA 101). Fire doors are classified by hourly references determined by testing done in accordance with NFPA 252, Standard Method of Fire Tests of Door Assemblies (also known as UL 10B). Further information is available in chapter 6, section 6 of the NFPA's Fire Protection Handbook.

TYPES OF OPENINGS

4-HR AND 3-HR OPENINGS (formerly class A): located in fire walls or in walls that divide a single building into fire areas.

$1\frac{1}{2}$-HR AND 1-HR OPENINGS (formerly class D and B, respectively): located in multistory vertical communication enclosures and in 2-hr rated partitions providing horizontal fire separations.

$\frac{3}{4}$-HR AND 20-MIN. OPENINGS (formerly class C, E): located in walls or partitions between rooms and corridors with a fire-resistance rating of one hour or less.

The hourly protection rating for openings depends on the use of the barrier, as in exit enclosures, vertical openings in buildings, building separation walls, corridor walls, smoke barriers, and hazardous locations. In most codes, class designations have been replaced by hour classifications.

TYPES OF FRAMES

Fire-rated doorframes can be assembled at the factory or in the field. Frames must be adequately anchored at the jambs and floor according to the manufacturer's specifications. Codes require doors to be installed in accordance with NFPA 80. Section 2-5, Frames, indicates only labeled frames are to be used.

LIGHT-GAUGE METAL FRAME: head and jamb members with or without transom panel made from aluminum (45-min. maximum rating) or light-gauge steel ($1\frac{1}{2}$-hr maximum rating); installed over finished wall.

PRESSED STEEL (HOLLOW METAL): head and jamb members with or without solid or glazed transoms or sidelights made from 18-gauge or heavier steel (3-hr. maximum rating); required for most metal doors.

DEFINITIONS

The following definitions are typically used in relation to fire-rated openings:

AUTOMATIC: providing a function without the necessity of human intervention.

FIRE BARRIER: a continuous membrane, either vertical or horizontal (for example, a wall, floor, or ceiling assembly), that is designed and constructed with a specified fire-resistance rating to limit the spread of fire and restrict the movement of smoke.

FIRE RESISTANCE: the property of materials or their assemblies that prevents or retards the passage of excessive heat, hot gas, or flames under conditions of use.

FIRE-RESISTANCE RATING: the time, in minutes or hours, that materials or assemblies have withstood fire exposure in accordance with the test procedure of NFPA 252.

LABELED: equipment or materials marked with the label, symbol, or other identifying mark of an organization concerned with product evaluation and acceptable to the local jurisdiction. This organization must periodically inspect production of labeled equipment, and the manufacturer, by labeling the product, indicates compliance in a specified manner with appropriate standards or performance.

NONCOMBUSTIBLE: a material that, in the form in which it is used and under the conditions anticipated, will not aid combustion or add appreciable heat to an ambient fire.

SELF-CLOSING: as applied to a fire door or other protective opening, self-closing means the door is normally closed and is equipped with an approved device that will ensure closure after the door has been opened.

SMOKE BARRIER: a continuous membrane, either vertical or horizontal, such as a wall, floor, or ceiling assembly, that is designed and constructed to restrict the movement of smoke. A smoke barrier may or may not have a fire-resistance rating.

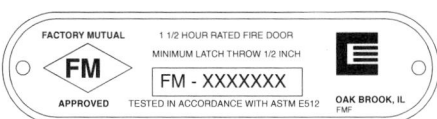

DOOR LABEL

FRAME LABEL

NOTE

Various agencies test and rate fire door and window units and assemblies. Manufacturers locate metal labels in accessible but concealed locations (the hinge edge of doors, for example); these labels must remain in place, unpainted, uncovered, and unaltered.

TESTING LABELS

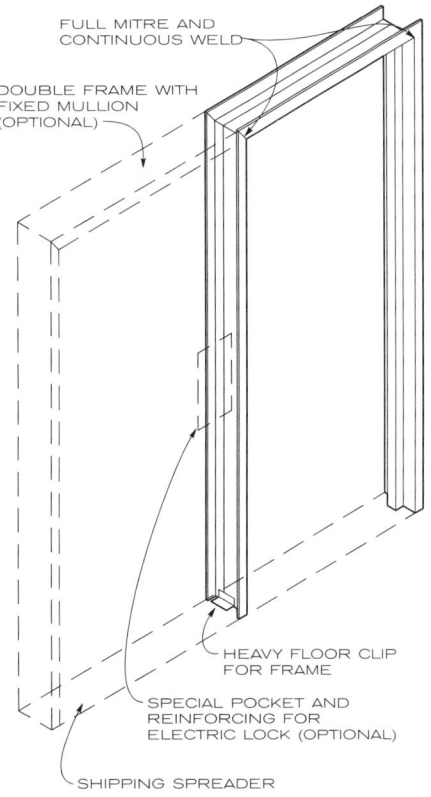

FULL MITRE AND CONTINUOUS WELD

DOUBLE FRAME WITH FIXED MULLION (OPTIONAL)

HEAVY FLOOR CLIP FOR FRAME

SPECIAL POCKET AND REINFORCING FOR ELECTRIC LOCK (OPTIONAL)

SHIPPING SPREADER

SECURITY FRAME REINFORCING FOR FIRE-RATED OPENINGS

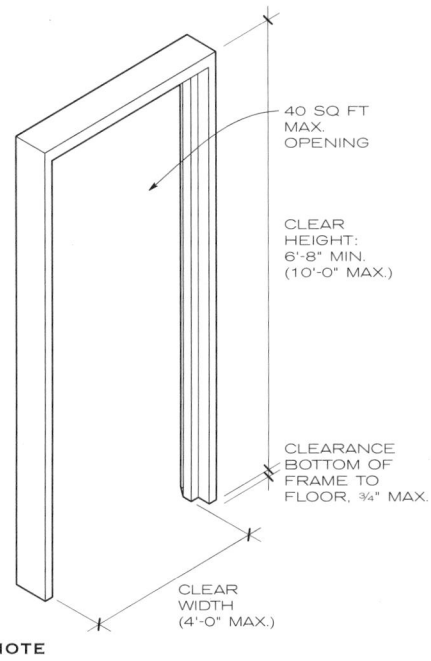

40 SQ FT MAX. OPENING

CLEAR HEIGHT: 6'-8" MIN. (10'-0" MAX.)

CLEARANCE BOTTOM OF FRAME TO FLOOR, ¾" MAX.

CLEAR WIDTH (4'-0" MAX.)

NOTE

The minimum width of each door opening must be sufficient for the occupant load it serves. Verify the following general guidelines for door width with local codes:

1. Dwelling units that are not required to be accessible or adaptable: $29\frac{3}{4}$ in.
2. Hospital and other medical facilities: 36 in.
3. Standard openings: 32 in.

DOOR OPENINGS FOR MEANS OF EGRESS

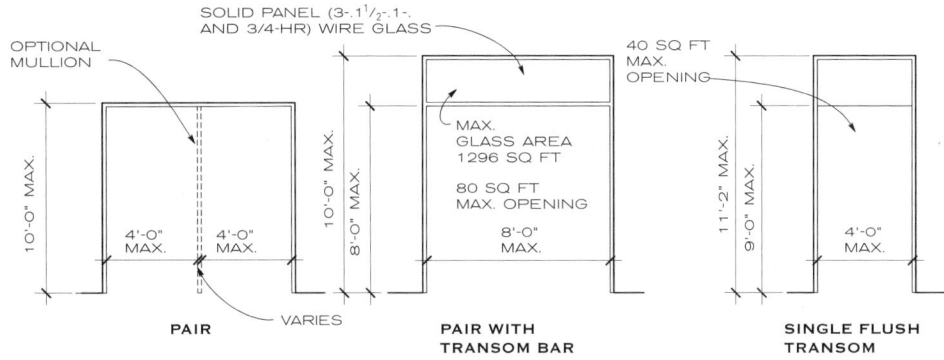

OPTIONAL MULLION

SOLID PANEL (3-.1½-.1-. AND 3/4-HR) WIRE GLASS

MAX. GLASS AREA 1296 SQ FT

80 SQ FT MAX. OPENING

40 SQ FT MAX. OPENING

10'-0" MAX.

4'-0" MAX.   4'-0" MAX.

VARIES

PAIR

10'-0" MAX.

8'-0" MAX.

8'-0" MAX.

PAIR WITH TRANSOM BAR

11'-2" MAX.

9'-0" MAX.

4'-0" MAX.

SINGLE FLUSH TRANSOM

FIRE-RATED STEEL FRAME ELEVATIONS

National Fire Protection Association; Quincy, Massachusetts
Daniel F. C. Hayes, AIA; Washington, D.C.

FIRE RATING AND SECURITY

8

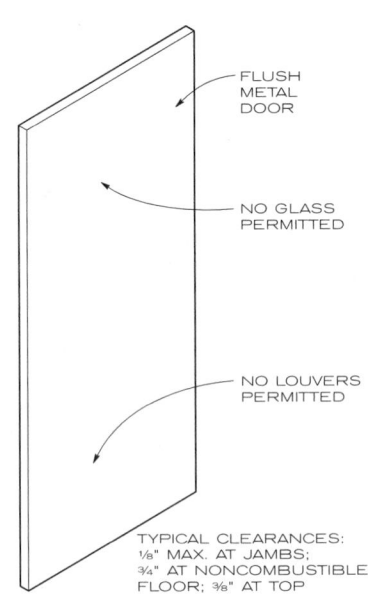

FLUSH METAL DOOR

NO GLASS PERMITTED

NO LOUVERS PERMITTED

TYPICAL CLEARANCES: ⅛" MAX. AT JAMBS; ¾" AT NONCOMBUSTIBLE FLOOR; ⅜" AT TOP

4-HOUR/3-HOUR CLASSIFICATION

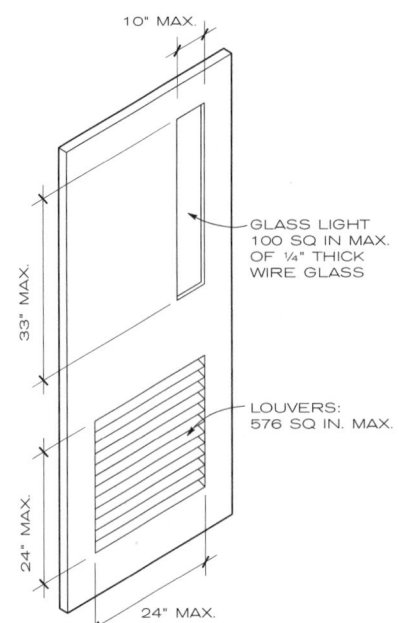

10" MAX.

GLASS LIGHT 100 SQ IN MAX. OF ¼" THICK WIRE GLASS

33" MAX.

LOUVERS: 576 SQ IN. MAX.

24" MAX.

24" MAX.

1½-HOUR/1-HOUR CLASSIFICATION

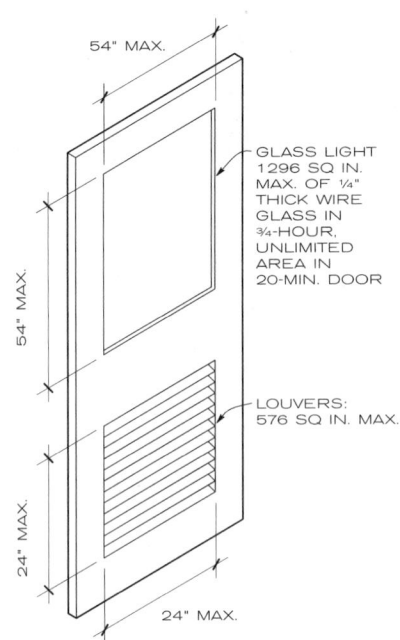

54" MAX.

GLASS LIGHT 1296 SQ IN. MAX. OF ¼" THICK WIRE GLASS IN ¾-HOUR, UNLIMITED AREA IN 20-MIN. DOOR

54" MAX.

LOUVERS: 576 SQ IN. MAX.

24" MAX.

24" MAX.

¾-HOUR/20-MIN. CLASSIFICATION

NOTES

1. All hinges or pivots must be steel. Two hinges are required on doors up to 5 ft in height; an additional hinge is required for each additional 2 ft 6 in. of door height or fraction thereof. The same requirement holds for pivots.

2. While wired glass ¼ in. thick is the most common material used for glass lights, other materials have been listed and approved for installation. Refer to the UL fire protection directory.

3. Consult all authorities with jurisdiction before installation of glass lights and louvers.

4. Fusible-link/automatic closing louvers are permitted in fire-rated doors with restrictions; they are not permitted in smoke-barrier doors.

FIRE-RATED DOOR CLASSIFICATIONS

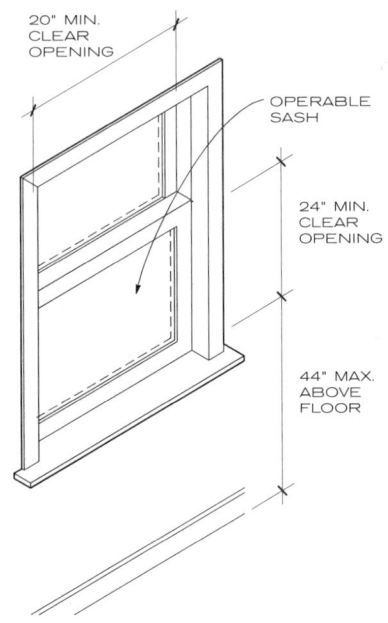

20" MIN. CLEAR OPENING

OPERABLE SASH

24" MIN. CLEAR OPENING

44" MAX. ABOVE FLOOR

NOTE

When required for egress, such as in sleeping areas in residences, windows must meet the following criteria:

1. Clear opening per sash must be a minimum of 5.7 sq ft.

2. Bars, grilles, or screens must be releasable from inside without use of tools or key.

3. Windows opening onto fire escapes have additional requirements; refer to codes.

4. Check with manufacturers for integral release hardware options for awning, casement, pivot, or other windows.

5. Double-hung window units with fully removable sash that do not require special tools, force, or knowledge to operate may offer greater flexibility in unit selection to meet size requirements for egress openings; verify with manufacturers and code officials.

WINDOW EGRESS REQUIREMENTS

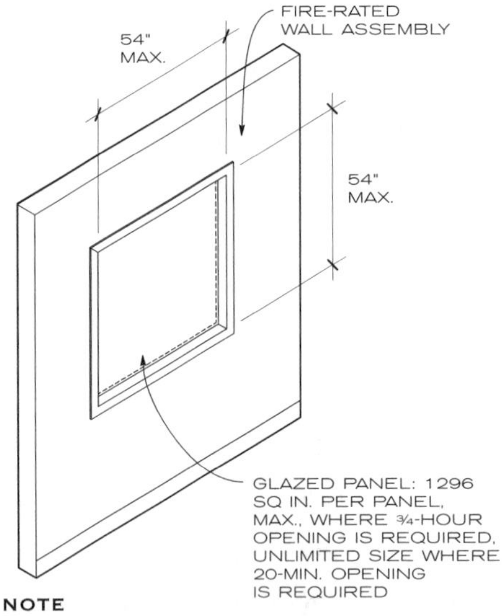

FIRE-RATED WALL ASSEMBLY

54" MAX.

54" MAX.

GLAZED PANEL: 1296 SQ IN. PER PANEL, MAX., WHERE ¾-HOUR OPENING IS REQUIRED, UNLIMITED SIZE WHERE 20-MIN. OPENING IS REQUIRED

NOTE

Glazed panel assemblies in fire-rated walls must conform to the size limitations indicated below and to wire glass and other approved material requirements. Multiple panels are permitted, but the aggregate area of all panels and openings must not exceed 25% of the wall surface. Refer to specific codes for details.

GLAZED PANEL REQUIREMENTS

MAXIMUM DOOR SIZES (HOLLOW METAL, ALL CLASSES*)

Single door	4 x 10 ft with labeled single-point or 3-point latching device
	4 x 8 ft with fire exit hardware
Pair of doors	8 x 10 ft active leaf with labeled single-point or 3-point latching device
	8 x 10 ft inactive leaf with labeled 2-point latching device or top and bottom bolts
	8 x 8 ft with fire exit hardware

*Wood door size requirements are similar.

CONSTRUCTION OF SWINGING FIRE DOORS

Outlined here are different types of swinging fire doors and notes about the hardware used with them.

TYPES OF DOORS

1. Composite fire doors: wood, steel, or plastic sheets bonded to and supported by a solid core material.

2. Hollow metal fire doors: flush or panel design with a steel face of not less than 20-gauge steel.

3. Metal-clad fire-doors: flush or panel design consisting of metal-covered wood cores or stiles and rails and insulated panels that are covered with steel of 24-gauge or lighter.

4. Sheet metal fire doors: 22-gauge or lighter steel of corrugated, flush sheet, or panel design.

5. Tin-clad fire doors: wood core with a terne plate or galvanized steel facing (30- or 24-gauge).

6. Wood core doors: wood, hardboard, or plastic face sheets bonded to a wood block or wood particleboard core material with untreated wood edges.

DOOR OPERATION

1. Doors that swing in the direction of egress are preferred for fire-rated doors.

2. Horizontal sliding and revolving doors are permitted with restrictions.

HARDWARE

1. Door hardware is provided by the builder independent of the assembly or furnished by the manufacturer with the door assembly. In either case, the manufacturer prepares the door and frame to receive hardware to ensure the integrity of the fire-rated assembly.

2. Fire doors are hung on steel ball-bearing hinges and must be self-closing. Labeled automatic latches and door closers can be self-operated or controlled by fail-safe devices that activate in a fire.

3. Pairs of doors require coordinators with astragals to ensure that both doors close.

4. Heads and jambs should be sealed with gaskets when smoke control is required.

5. Panic hardware may be required when space occupancy is greater than 100 people.

National Fire Protection Association; Quincy, Massachusetts

DEFINITIONS

BUCK: a subframe of wood or metal set in a wall or partition to support the finish frame of a door or window; also called door buck or rough buck.

CASING: the finished, often decorative framework around a door or window opening, especially that which is parallel to the surrounding surface and at right angles to the jamb; also called trim.

SUBCASING: finish frame components that support and guide the door or sash.

HEAD: horizontal members at top of door or window.

JAMB: vertical members at sides of door or window.

STOP: integral or applied member that prevents a door or window from swinging past its closed position, or members that guide horizontal or vertical sliding movement.

SILL: horizontal members at bottom of door or window.

THRESHOLD: applied wood, stone, or metal plate, usually weatherproof.

SADDLE: part of a threshold, usually bridging dissimilar flooring materials.

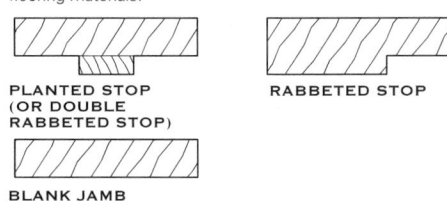

PLANTED STOP (OR DOUBLE RABBETED STOP)   **RABBETED STOP**

BLANK JAMB (FOR CASED OPENING)

FRAME AND STOP TYPES

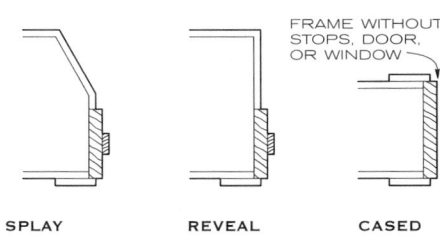

FRAME WITHOUT STOPS, DOOR, OR WINDOW

SPLAY   REVEAL   CASED

OPENING TYPES

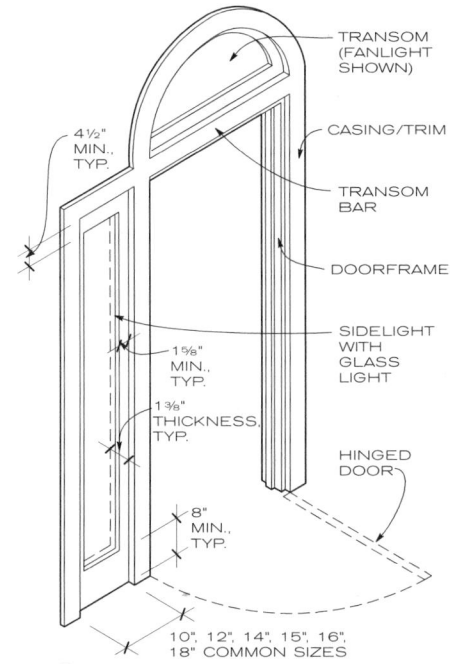

TRANSOM (FANLIGHT SHOWN)

CASING/TRIM

TRANSOM BAR

DOORFRAME

4½" MIN., TYP.

SIDELIGHT WITH GLASS LIGHT

1⅝" MIN., TYP.

1⅜" THICKNESS, TYP.

HINGED DOOR

8" MIN., TYP.

10", 12", 14", 15", 16", 18" COMMON SIZES

DOOR ACCESSORIES

Daniel F. C. Hayes, AIA; Washington, D.C.

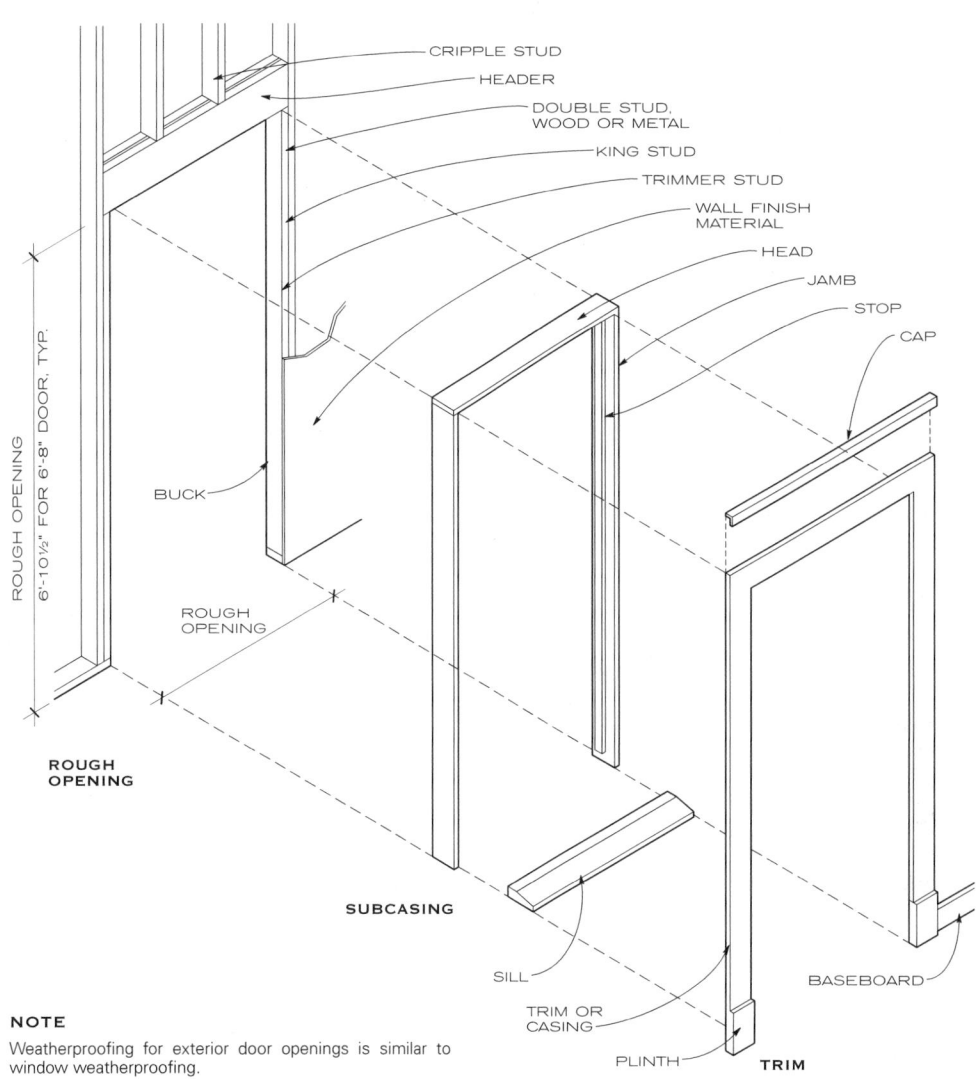

CRIPPLE STUD
HEADER
DOUBLE STUD, WOOD OR METAL
KING STUD
TRIMMER STUD
WALL FINISH MATERIAL
HEAD
JAMB
STOP
CAP

ROUGH OPENING 6'-10½" FOR 6'-8" DOOR, TYP.

BUCK

ROUGH OPENING

ROUGH OPENING

SUBCASING

SILL

TRIM OR CASING

PLINTH

TRIM

BASEBOARD

NOTE

Weatherproofing for exterior door openings is similar to window weatherproofing.

DOOR OPENING COMPONENTS

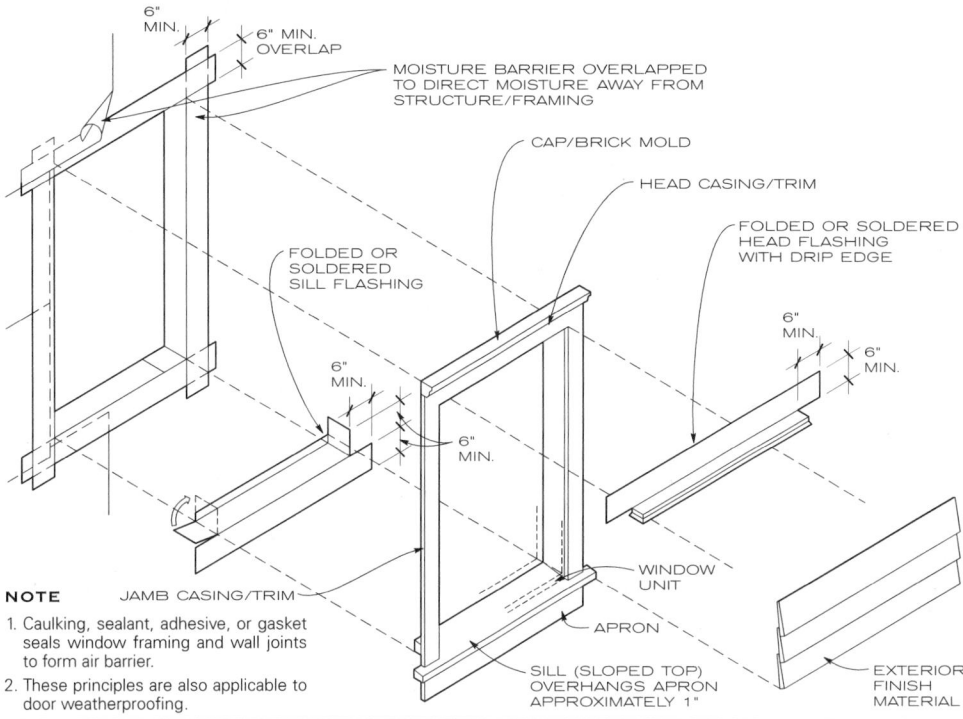

6" MIN.
6" MIN. OVERLAP

MOISTURE BARRIER OVERLAPPED TO DIRECT MOISTURE AWAY FROM STRUCTURE/FRAMING

CAP/BRICK MOLD

HEAD CASING/TRIM

FOLDED OR SOLDERED HEAD FLASHING WITH DRIP EDGE

FOLDED OR SOLDERED SILL FLASHING

6" MIN.

6" MIN.

6" MIN.

6" MIN.

WINDOW UNIT

JAMB CASING/TRIM

APRON

SILL (SLOPED TOP) OVERHANGS APRON APPROXIMATELY 1"

EXTERIOR FINISH MATERIAL

NOTE

1. Caulking, sealant, adhesive, or gasket seals window framing and wall joints to form air barrier.
2. These principles are also applicable to door weatherproofing.

WINDOW WEATHERPROOFING PRINCIPLES

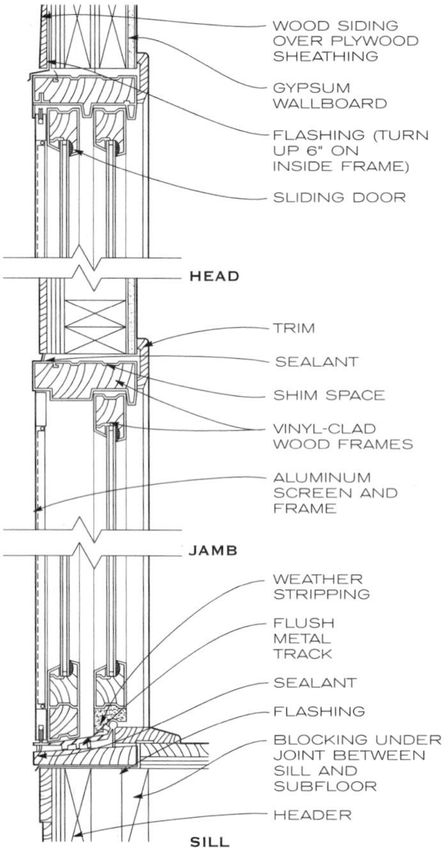

Sliding Door in Wood Frame

WOOD SIDING OVER PLYWOOD SHEATHING
GYPSUM WALLBOARD
FLASHING (TURN UP 6" ON INSIDE FRAME)
SLIDING DOOR

HEAD

TRIM
SEALANT
SHIM SPACE
VINYL-CLAD WOOD FRAMES
ALUMINUM SCREEN AND FRAME

JAMB

WEATHER STRIPPING
FLUSH METAL TRACK
SEALANT
FLASHING
BLOCKING UNDER JOINT BETWEEN SILL AND SUBFLOOR
HEADER

SILL

SLIDING DOOR IN WOOD FRAME

Interior Swing Door in Wood Frame

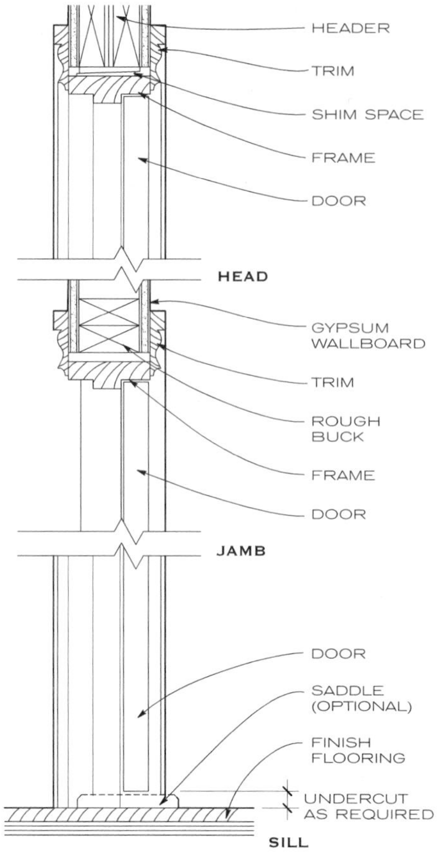

HEADER
TRIM
SHIM SPACE
FRAME
DOOR

HEAD

GYPSUM WALLBOARD
TRIM
ROUGH BUCK
FRAME
DOOR

JAMB

DOOR
SADDLE (OPTIONAL)
FINISH FLOORING
UNDERCUT AS REQUIRED

SILL

INTERIOR SWING DOOR IN WOOD FRAME

Exterior Swing Door in Wood Frame

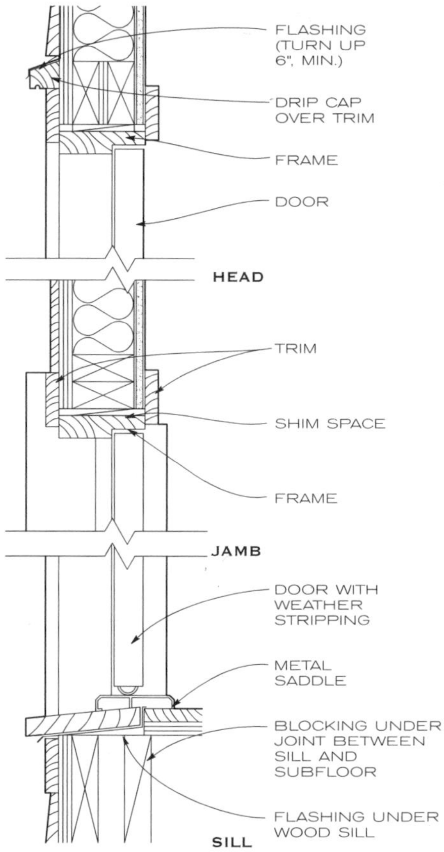

FLASHING (TURN UP 6", MIN.)
DRIP CAP OVER TRIM
FRAME
DOOR

HEAD

TRIM
SHIM SPACE
FRAME

JAMB

DOOR WITH WEATHER STRIPPING
METAL SADDLE
BLOCKING UNDER JOINT BETWEEN SILL AND SUBFLOOR
FLASHING UNDER WOOD SILL

SILL

EXTERIOR SWING DOOR IN WOOD FRAME

DOORFRAME DETAILS IN WOOD WALL CONSTRUCTION

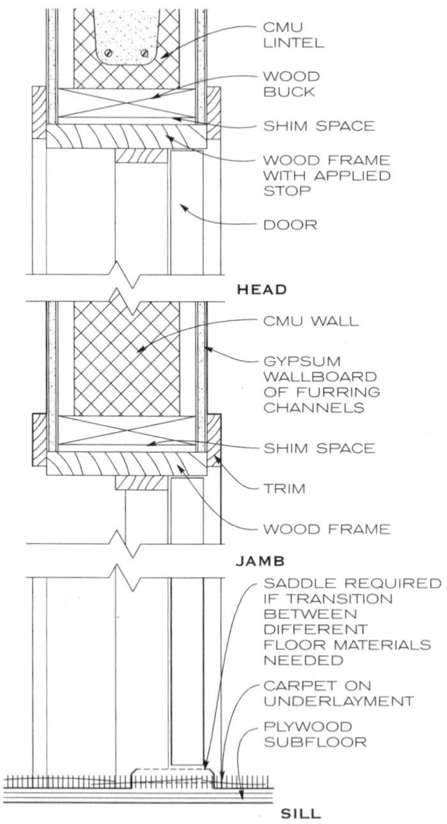

Interior Swing Door in Masonry Wall

CMU LINTEL
WOOD BUCK
SHIM SPACE
WOOD FRAME WITH APPLIED STOP
DOOR

HEAD

CMU WALL
GYPSUM WALLBOARD OF FURRING CHANNELS
SHIM SPACE
TRIM
WOOD FRAME

JAMB

SADDLE REQUIRED IF TRANSITION BETWEEN DIFFERENT FLOOR MATERIALS NEEDED
CARPET ON UNDERLAYMENT
PLYWOOD SUBFLOOR

SILL

INTERIOR SWING DOOR IN MASONRY WALL

Swing Door in Masonry Veneer

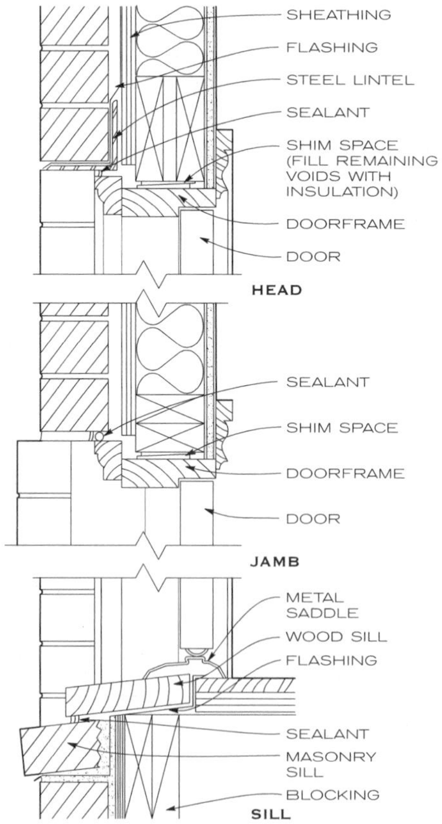

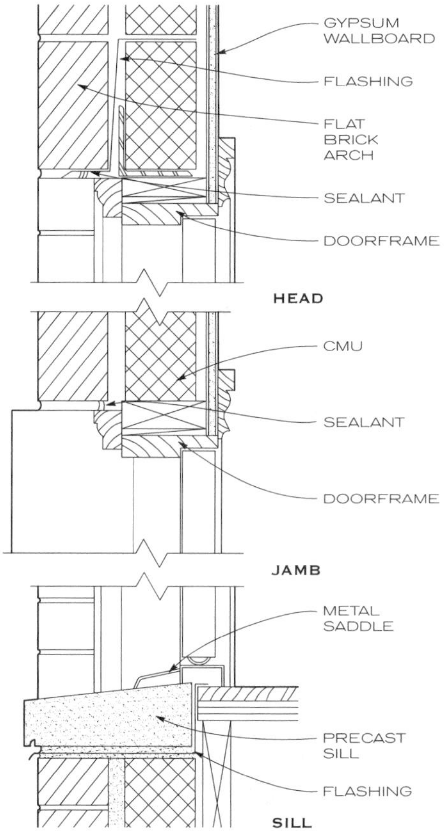

SHEATHING
FLASHING
STEEL LINTEL
SEALANT
SHIM SPACE (FILL REMAINING VOIDS WITH INSULATION)
DOORFRAME
DOOR

HEAD

SEALANT
SHIM SPACE
DOORFRAME
DOOR

JAMB

METAL SADDLE
WOOD SILL
FLASHING
SEALANT
MASONRY SILL
BLOCKING

SILL

SWING DOOR IN MASONRY VENEER

Swing Door in Solid Masonry

GYPSUM WALLBOARD
FLASHING
FLAT BRICK ARCH
SEALANT
DOORFRAME

HEAD

CMU
SEALANT
DOORFRAME

JAMB

METAL SADDLE
PRECAST SILL
FLASHING

SILL

SWING DOOR IN SOLID MASONRY

DOORFRAME DETAILS IN MASONRY WALL CONSTRUCTION

Daniel F. C. Hayes, AIA; Washington, D.C.
Richard J. Vitullo, AIA; Oak Leaf Studio; Crownsville, Maryland

DOOR AND WINDOW OPENINGS

MATERIALS

Hollow metal doorframes are available in various steel gauges according to where and how they will be used. Local codes and governing authorities establish minimum gauges, which should always be consulted. Some manufacturers make custom moldings for a specific design, as long as a sufficient quantity is required.

For security, the exterior moldings on exterior doors should be welded into the frame and exposed fasteners should be tamperproof.

TYPES OF FRAMES

Doorframes can be factory or field assembled. All frames must be adequately anchored at the jambs and floor according to the manufacturer's specifications.

LIGHT-GAUGE METAL FRAME: head and jamb members, with or without a transom panel, of aluminum (45 min. maximum rating) or light-gauge steel (1.5 hr maximum rating). Frame is installed over finished wall.

PRESSED STEEL (HOLLOW METAL): head and jamb members, with or without solid or glazed transoms or sidelights, of 18-gauge or heavier steel (3 hr maximum rating). This frame is required for most metal doors.

FINISHES

Hollow metal frames should receive at least one shop coat of rust-inhibitive primer before delivery to the job site. In very corrosive atmospheres, such as saltwater beach locations, is it advisable to have doors and frames hot dipped galvanized for additional protection.

Frames with factory-applied paint finishes in various colors are available from several manufacturers.

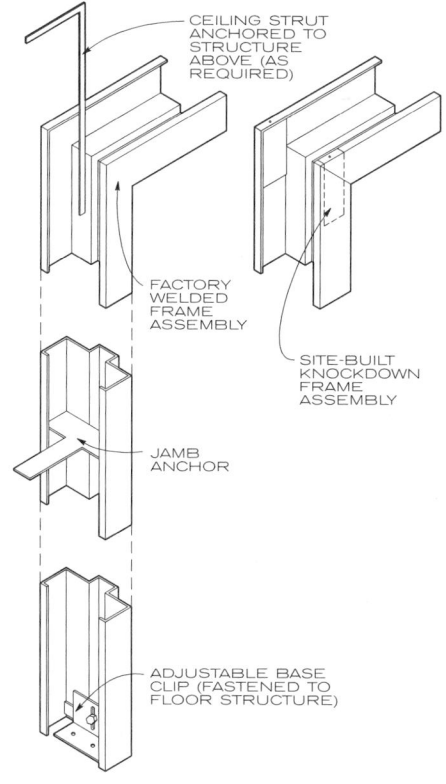

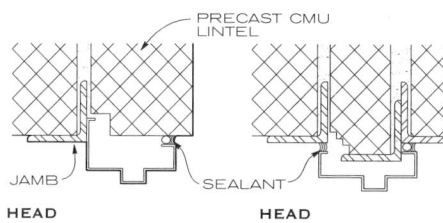

HOLLOW METAL FRAME COMPONENTS

HEAD (JAMB SIMILAR)   HEAD (JAMB SIMILAR)

WEATHERPROOF INSTALLATIONS

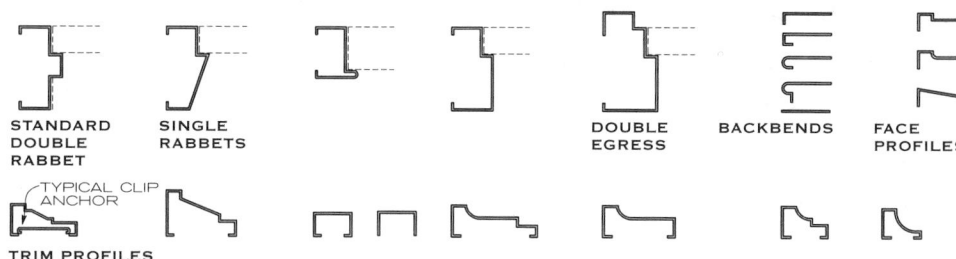

STANDARD DOUBLE RABBET   SINGLE RABBETS   DOUBLE EGRESS   BACKBENDS   FACE PROFILES

TYPICAL CLIP ANCHOR

TRIM PROFILES

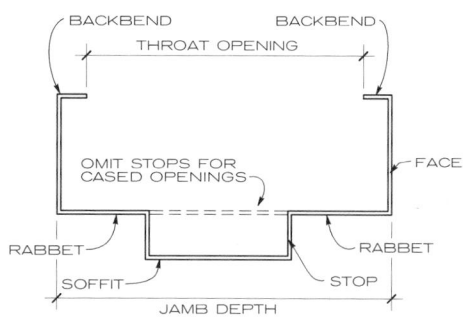

STANDARD DOUBLE RABBET
NOTE

Maximum gauge is 10; consult manufacturers for lighter gauges.

HOLLOW METAL FRAME PROFILES AND COMPONENTS

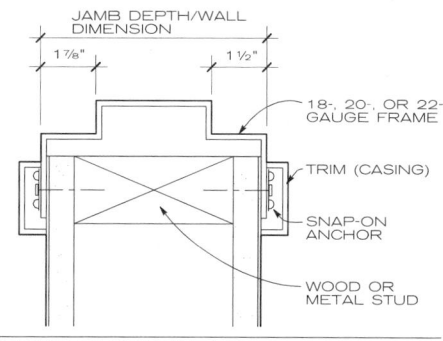

LIGHT-GAUGE FRAME

FRAME GAUGES

GRADE	DUTY	MINIMUM GAUGE
I	Standard	18
II	Heavy	16
III	Extra heavy	16

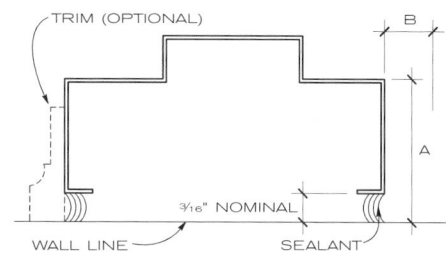

BUTT FRAME/FLUSH FRAME

NOTES

1. Use anchors appropriate for the type of wall construction; a minimum of three per jamb is required.
2. Grout frame with mortar or plaster as used in wall.
3. Caulk frame at wall.
4. Dimension A is minimum 3 in. in area of pull or knob hardware.
4. Trim may be used to cover joint at wall line.
5. Check dimension B on hinge side for door swing greater than 90°.

FRAME CONDITION AT WALL

VARIOUS STANDARD PROFILES

	JAMB DEPTH (IN.)								
	$2\frac{3}{4}$	3	$3\frac{3}{4}$	$4\frac{3}{4}$	$5\frac{1}{2}$	$5\frac{3}{4}$	$6\frac{3}{4}$	$7\frac{3}{4}$	$8\frac{3}{4}$
Rabbet*	Single rabbet only			$1\frac{15}{16}$ in. standard for $1\frac{3}{4}$ in. door					
Soffit*									
Rabbet*				$1\frac{9}{16}$ in. standard for $1\frac{3}{8}$ in. door					
Backbend	$\frac{1}{2}$	$\frac{7}{16}$	$\frac{1}{2}$	$\frac{1}{2}$	$\frac{3}{4}$	$\frac{1}{2}$	$\frac{1}{2}$	$\frac{1}{2}$	$\frac{1}{2}$
Throat	$1\frac{3}{4}$	$2\frac{1}{8}$	2	$3\frac{3}{4}$	4	$4\frac{3}{4}$	$5\frac{3}{4}$	$6\frac{3}{4}$	$7\frac{3}{4}$

* Omit stops for cased opening frames.

NOTES

1. Many other profiles are available; consult manufacturers' lists for dimensions and options.
2. Depths vary in $\frac{1}{8}$ in. increments to $12\frac{3}{4}$ in. maximum.
3. Standard stops are $\frac{5}{8}$ in. ($\frac{1}{2}$ in. minimum); standard faces are 2 in. (1 in. minimum).

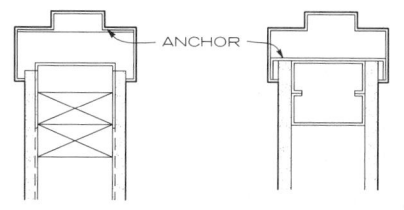

WOOD STUDS WITH PLASTER   METAL STUDS WITH GYPSUM BOARD

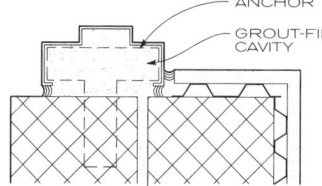

MASONRY WITH GYPSUM BOARD BUTTED TO FRAME

METAL FRAME INSTALLATIONS

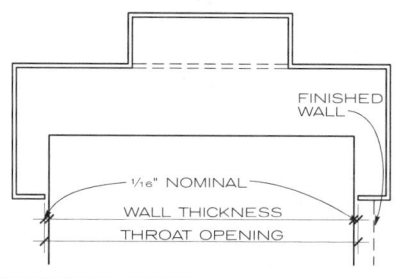

WRAPAROUND FRAME

NOTES

1. Basic wall dimension is less than throat opening dimension.
2. Use anchors appropriate for the type of wall construction; a minimum of three per jamb is required.
3. Fill frame with mortar or plaster as used in the wall.
4. Grout frame at masonry wall.
5. Backbend may vary as selected.

James W. G. Watson, AIA; Ronald A. Spahn and Associates; Cleveland Heights, Ohio
Daniel F. C. Hayes, AIA; Washington, D.C.

HOLLOW METAL DOORS

Hollow metal doors are available in steel gauges ranging from 20 to 12; which gauge to use depends on where and how a door will be used. Consult local codes and governing authorities for minimum gauges that may have been established. Some manufacturers will custom make doors to a specific design if an order is large enough.

For security, exterior moldings on exterior doors should be welded to the door and all exposed fasteners should be tamperproof.

FINISHES

Hollow metal doors should receive at least one shop coat of rust-inhibitive primer before delivery to the job site. In very corrosive atmospheres, such as saltwater beach locations, the doors and frames should be hot-dipped galvanized for additional protection.

Doors can be purchased from the manufacturer with factory-applied paint finishes in various colors.

FLUSH WOOD DOORS

CORE MATERIAL

SOLID CORE: wood block, single specie, maximum $2^1/_2$ in. width, surfaced two sides, no spaces or defects impairing strength or visible through hardwood veneer facing.

HOLLOW CORE: wood, wood derivative, or class A insulation board.

SPECIAL CORES

SOUND-INSULATING CORE: thicknesses of $1^3/_4$ and $2^1/_4$ in.; sound transmission class rating of 36 for $1^3/_4$ in. and 42 for $2^1/_4$ in. barrier faces separated by a void or damping compound to keep faces from vibrating in unison. Special stops, gaskets, and threshold devices may be required.

LEAD-LINED CORE: $^1/_{32}$ in. to $^1/_2$ in. continuous lead sheeting from edge to edge inside door construction; may be reinforced with lead bolts or glued. (See UL requirements.)

GROUNDED CORE: wire mesh at center of core, grounded with copper wire through hinges to frame.

WOOD FACE TYPES

Standard thickness face veneers range from $^1/_{16}$ in. to $^1/_{32}$ in.; they are bonded to hardwood with a crossband ($^1/_{10}$ in. to $^1/_{16}$ in.) and are the most economical and widely used veneer type. Face veneers inhibit checking in the finish but are difficult to refinish or repair. They can be used on all cores.

Bonded to a crossband, $^1/_8$ in. sawn veneers are easily refinished and repaired.

Staved-block and stile-and-rail solid cores take $^1/_4$ in. sawn veneers. These are the same as $^1/_8$ in. sawn veneers but do not have a crossband on stile-and-rail solid cores with horizontal blocks. Faces can be cut with decorative grooves.

LIGHT AND LOUVER OPENINGS

Custom made to specifications, this type of door has wood beads and slats that match the face veneer. Space between the opening in the door and the edge of the door can be no less than 5 in.

In hollow-core doors, the cutout area can be at most half the height of the door. Doors with openings greater than 40% are not guaranteed. Weatherproofing of exterior doors is required to prevent moisture from leaking into the core.

FACTORY FINISHING

Partial finishing is available, with sealing coats in place but the final finish applied on the job. Complete factory finishing requires the door to be prefit and premachined.

SPECIAL FACING

For opaque finishes only, high or medium-low density overlay faces of phenolic resins and cellulose fibers can be fused to the inner faces of a hardwood door to serve as a base for the final finish.

Laminated plastic ($^1/_{16}$ in. thick, minimum) can be bonded to a wood back of two or more plies ($^1/_{16}$ in., minimum).

Hardboard, $^1/_8$ in. thick and smooth on one or both sides, can be used as a facing.

GENERAL NOTES: WOOD DOORS

1. Kiln-dried wood: moisture content at 6–12%.
2. Type I doors: fully waterproof bond, exterior and interior.
3. Type II doors: water-resistant bond, interior only.

Daniel F. C. Hayes, AIA; Washington, D.C.

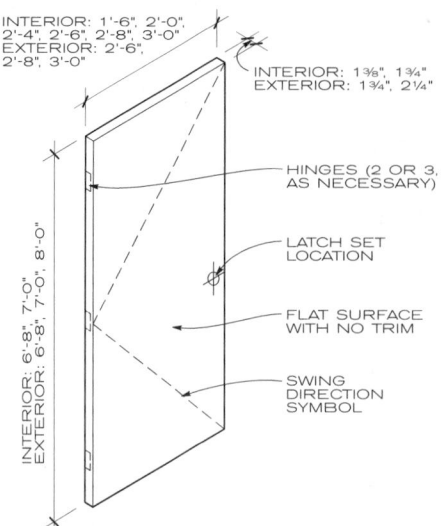

INTERIOR: 1'-6", 2'-0", 2'-4", 2'-6", 2'-8", 3'-0"
EXTERIOR: 2'-6", 2'-8", 3'-0"

INTERIOR: 1⅜", 1¾"
EXTERIOR: 1¾", 2¼"

HINGES (2 OR 3, AS NECESSARY)

LATCH SET LOCATION

FLAT SURFACE WITH NO TRIM

SWING DIRECTION SYMBOL

INTERIOR: 6'-8", 7'-0", 8'-0"
EXTERIOR: 6'-8", 7'-0", 8'-0"

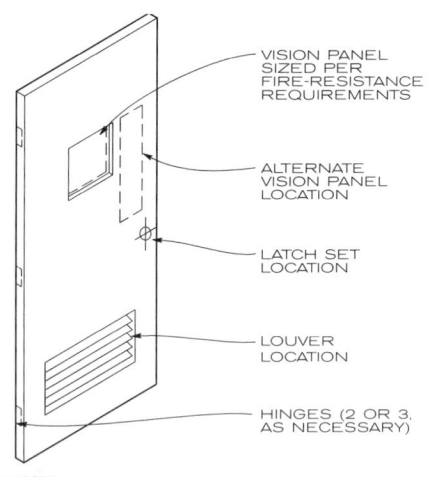

VISION PANEL SIZED PER FIRE-RESISTANCE REQUIREMENTS

ALTERNATE VISION PANEL LOCATION

LATCH SET LOCATION

LOUVER LOCATION

HINGES (2 OR 3, AS NECESSARY)

NOTE

Louvers are sized per mechanical requirements. Fire-resistance regulations require closable louvers or preclude installation in smoke-barrier doors and certain fire-rated doors.

VISION OR LOUVERED DOOR

TYPICAL FLUSH DOOR SIZES AND CHARACTERISTICS

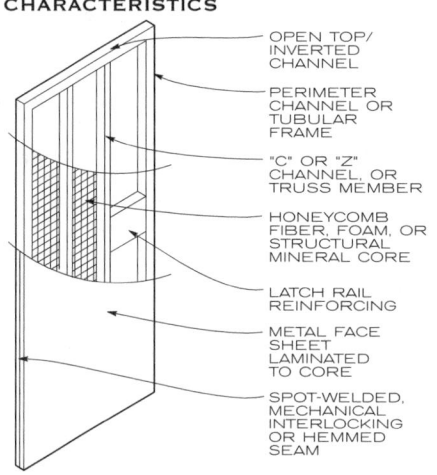

OPEN TOP/INVERTED CHANNEL

PERIMETER CHANNEL OR TUBULAR FRAME

"C" OR "Z" CHANNEL, OR TRUSS MEMBER

HONEYCOMB FIBER, FOAM, OR STRUCTURAL MINERAL CORE

LATCH RAIL REINFORCING

METAL FACE SHEET LAMINATED TO CORE

SPOT-WELDED, MECHANICAL INTERLOCKING OR HEMMED SEAM

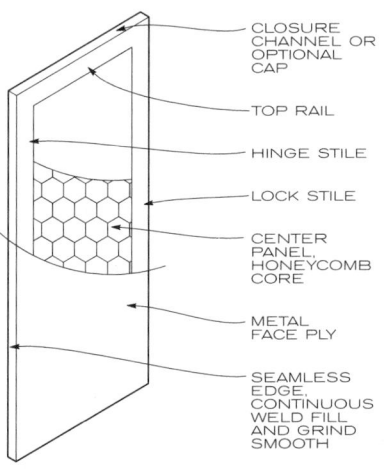

CLOSURE CHANNEL OR OPTIONAL CAP

TOP RAIL

HINGE STILE

LOCK STILE

CENTER PANEL, HONEYCOMB CORE

METAL FACE PLY

SEAMLESS EDGE, CONTINUOUS WELD FILL AND GRIND SMOOTH

HOLLOW METAL DOOR WITH STIFFENED CORE

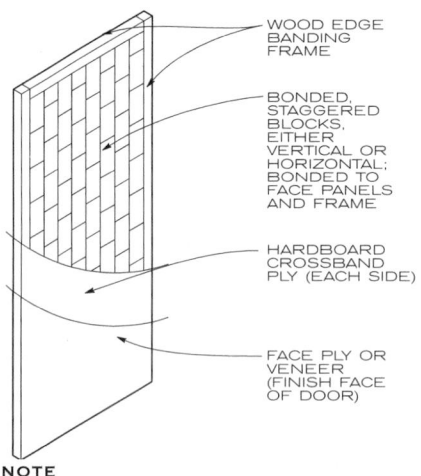

WOOD EDGE BANDING FRAME

BONDED, STAGGERED BLOCKS, EITHER VERTICAL OR HORIZONTAL; BONDED TO FACE PANELS AND FRAME

HARDBOARD CROSSBAND PLY (EACH SIDE)

FACE PLY OR VENEER (FINISH FACE OF DOOR)

NOTE

For bonded blocks, stave core is the most economical and widely used. Other materials include particleboard (heavier, more soundproof, economical) and mineral composition (lighter, difficult cutouts and detailing, lower screw strength).

WOOD SOLID CORE DOOR

4. Tolerances: height, width, thickness, squareness, and warp per NWWDA standards; vary with solid vs. builtup construction.

5. Prefit: doors at $^3/_{16}$ in. less than width and $^1/_8$ in. less in height than nominal size, $\pm^1/_{32}$ in. tolerance, with vertical edges eased.

HOLLOW METAL DOOR WITH STILE AND RAIL

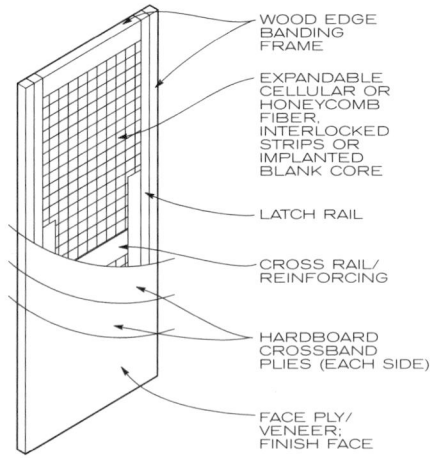

WOOD EDGE BANDING FRAME

EXPANDABLE CELLULAR OR HONEYCOMB FIBER, INTERLOCKED STRIPS OR IMPLANTED BLANK CORE

LATCH RAIL

CROSS RAIL/REINFORCING

HARDBOARD CROSSBAND PLIES (EACH SIDE)

FACE PLY/VENEER; FINISH FACE

NOTE

Acoustical materials may be used to cut sound transmission.

WOOD HOLLOW CORE DOOR

6. Premachining: doors mortised for locks and cut out for hinges when so specified.

7. Premium: for transparent finish; good/custom: for paint or transparent finish; sound: for paint, with two coats completely covering defects.

GENERAL

Panel doors consist of a framework of vertical (stile) and horizontal (rail) members that hold solid wood or plywood panels, glass lights, or louvers in place.

CONSTRUCTION

Doors are made of solid or builtup stiles, rails, and vertical members (muntins), doweled as in NWWDA standards. Stock material includes ponderosa pine or other Western pine, fir, hemlock, or spruce and hardwood veneers. Hardboard, metal, and plastic facings are available in patterns simulating panel doors.

GRADES

Premium (select) grade is used for natural, clear, or stained finishes. Exposed wood is free of defects that affect appearance.

Standard grade is used for opaque finishes. Defects, discoloration, mixed species, and finger joints are permitted if undetectable after finishing.

GLAZING

All glazing in doors must be safety glazing. Insulated glazing is available.

BUILTUP MEMBERS

The core and edge and end strip material is similar to the material used in flush doors. Face veneer is typically hardwood at $1/8$ in. minimum thickness.

STICKING, GLASS STOPS, AND MUNTINS

Typical profiles used are cove, bead, or ovolo.

PANELS

Flat panels are typically 3-ply hardwood or softwood. Raised panels are constructed of solid hardwood or softwood built up of two or more plies. Doors 1 ft 6 in. wide or less are one panel wide.

ADA ACCESSIBILITY GUIDELINES

For opening width compliance, use doors 3 ft 0 in. wide. Door projections, such as Dutch door shelves, may be no more than 4 in. if more than 27 in. above finished floor. Thresholds and saddles must be no higher than $1/2$ in. with beveled edges. Kickplates are recommended outdoors along accessible routes.

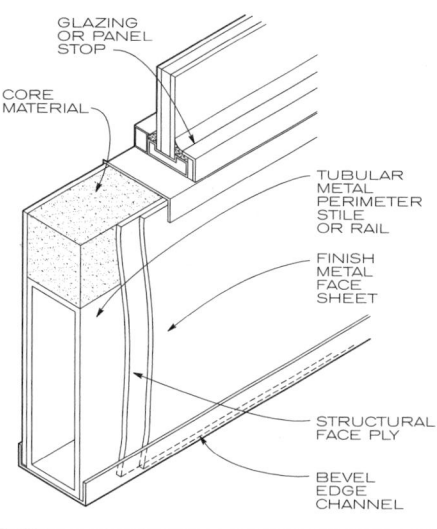

HOLLOW METAL DOOR STILE AND RAIL DETAIL

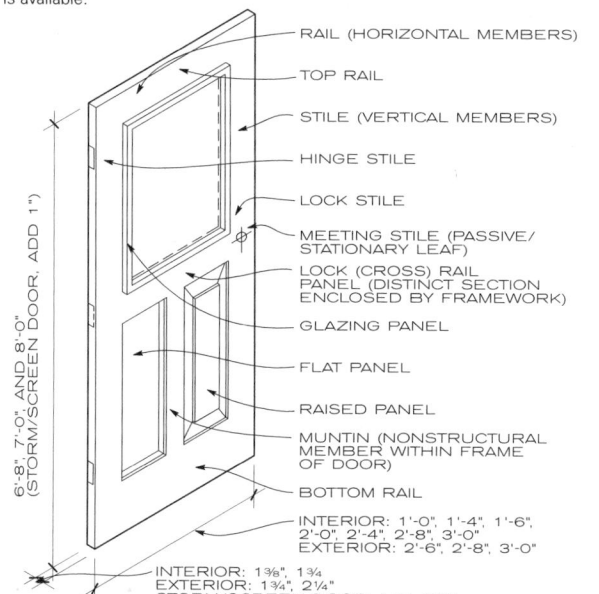

TYPICAL SIZES AND CHARACTERISTICS

STILE AND RAIL DOOR TYPES

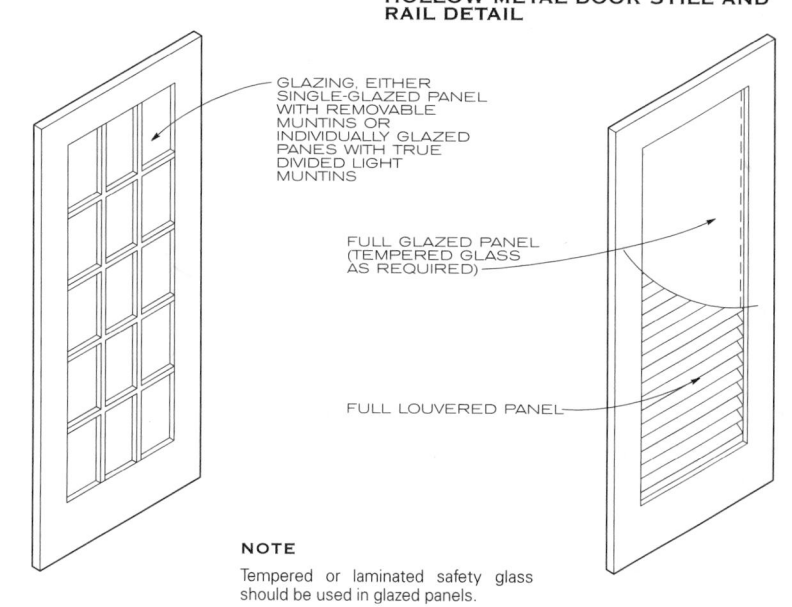

NOTE

Tempered or laminated safety glass should be used in glazed panels.

FRENCH DOOR   GLAZED/LOUVERED DOOR

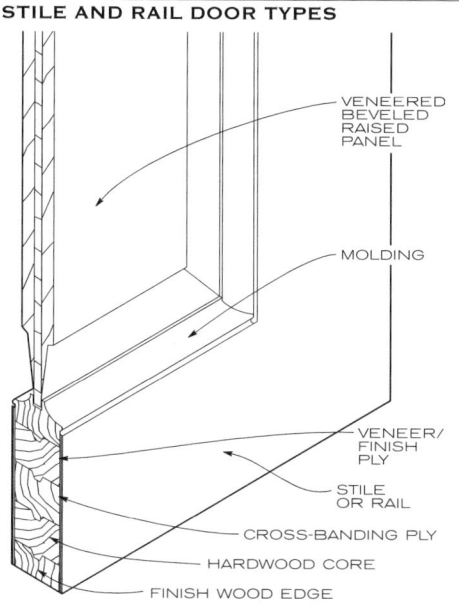

TYPICAL BEVELED RAISED PANEL DOOR

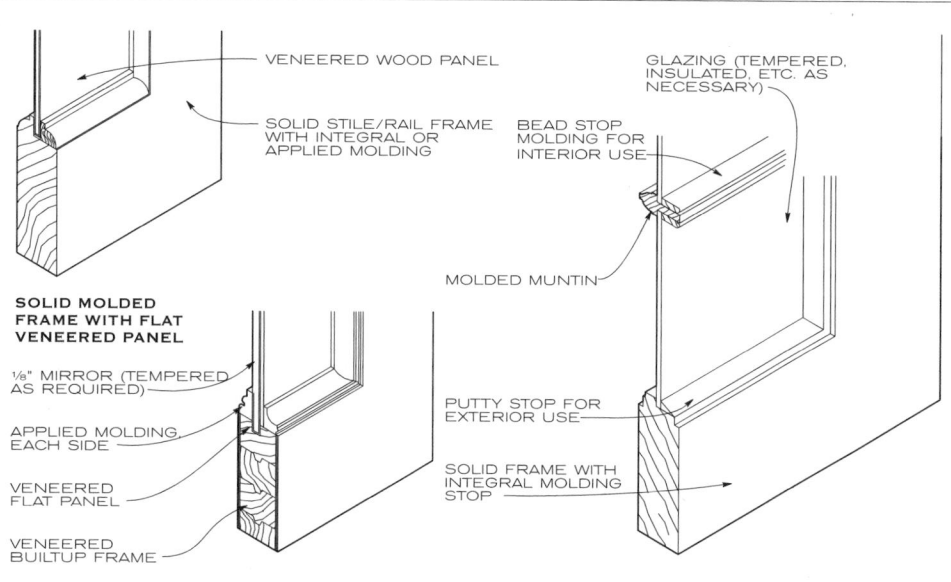

SOLID MOLDED FRAME WITH FLAT VENEERED PANEL

MIRRORED PANEL   GLAZED DOOR

STILE AND RAIL DOOR DETAILS

Jeffrey R. Vandevoort, Talbott Wilson Associates, Inc.; Houston Texas
Daniel F. C. Hayes, AIA; Washington, D.C.

GENERAL

Consider the following when designing a door: aesthetics (the design and look of the door), operation (how the door moves), fire-resistance ratings/egress requirements, accessibility for people with disabilities, size and weight, location, materials/method of construction, glazing requirements, special requirements (sound transmission, containment of harmful material such as x-rays or projectiles), security issues, energy conservation, electrostatic grounding, hardware, and weatherproofing.

Refer to local, state, and federal codes and trade association and manufacturers' specifications and recommendations for additional information and requirements.

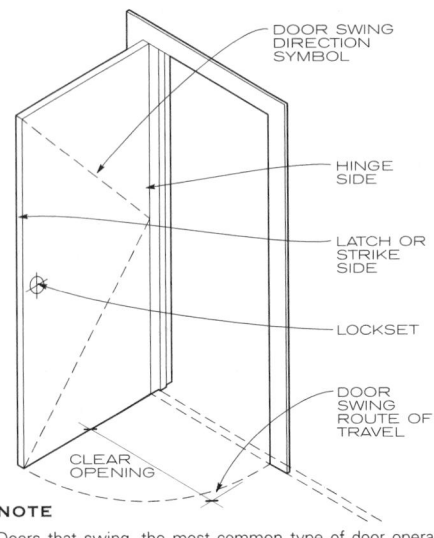

NOTE

Doors that swing, the most common type of door operation, rotate around an axis determined by hinges or pivots.

DOOR AND OPENING CHARACTERISTICS

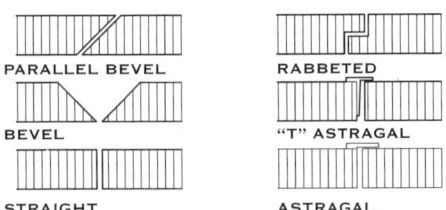

PARALLEL BEVEL

RABBETED

BEVEL

"T" ASTRAGAL

STRAIGHT

ASTRAGAL

MEETING EDGE TYPES FOR DOUBLE DOOR LEAVES

DEFINITIONS

ACTIVE LEAF: the primary operating leaf of a door pair.

AIR CURTAIN: a mechanically produced downward stream of air across a door opening intended to prevent transmission of heat and weather.

AUTOMATIC DOOR: a door fully or partially operated with an external mechanism (door opener) triggered by sensor or switch/button, as opposed to manual operation; refer to accessibility and fire code requirements.

HAND: denotes direction of door movement.

LEAF: a door panel.

LEFT-HINGED DOOR: a door with hinges mounted on the left stile of the active panel.

PASSIVE/INACTIVE DOOR: a door that operates independently of and secondarily to the active leaf of a door pair; normally held closed with floor and head bolts; the strike plate of this door receives the latch of the active leaf.

PREHUNG DOOR: door and frame combination fabricated and assembled by the manufacturer and shipped to the site.

RIGHT-HINGED DOOR: a door with hinges mounted on the right stile of the active panel.

STATIONARY (FIXED) DOOR: a nonoperational leaf.

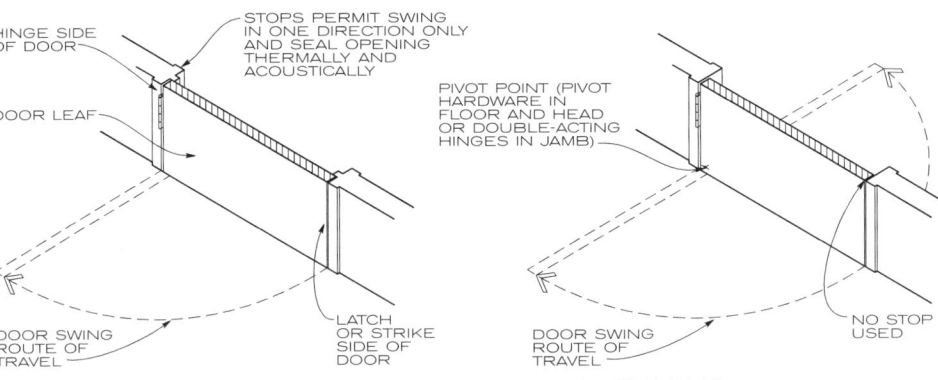

SINGLE-ACTING DOOR

NOTE

The single-acting door, the most common door type, has a leaf that operates in a swinging or sliding motion in only one direction.

DOUBLE-ACTING DOOR

Double-acting doors have a leaf that operates in two directions. There is usually no stop present to restrict the motion of the door, but when the door can be stopped, it can be released mechanically to permit access in an emergency.

SINGLE DOOR LEAF TYPES

SPACE REQUIREMENTS (VARIOUS DOOR WIDTHS—IN.)

	34	36	38	40	42	44
X	21 1/4	23 1/4	25 1/4	23 1/4	25 1/4	27 1/4
Y		12 3/4			16 1/4	
Z		7 1/8			8 7/8	

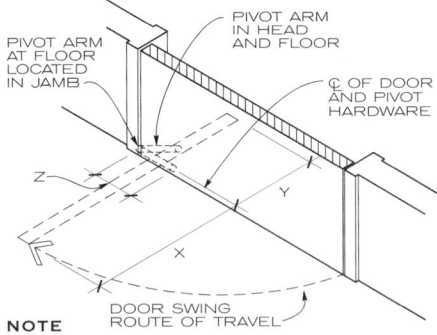

NOTE

A balanced door is a single-action swinging door mounted on offset pivots. The leaf operates independently of the jamb, and the elliptical trajectory of the leaf requires less clear floor space than a conventional swinging door.

BALANCED DOOR

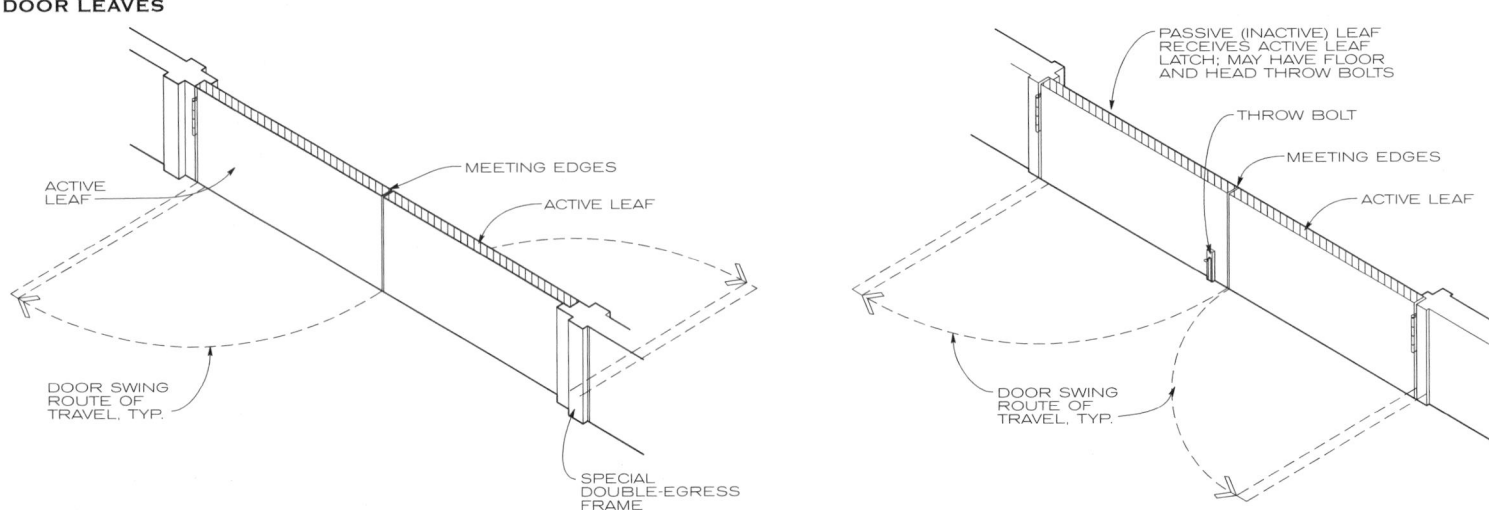

DOUBLE-EGRESS DOORS

DOUBLE OR PAIRED DOORS

NOTE

Double-egress doors have a pair of swinging leaves that operate in opposite directions, permitting equal access to two or more means of passage.

DOUBLE DOOR LEAF TYPES

Double or paired doors have two leaves (of equal or unequal size). that operate either together or independently. They create a doorway with variable widths suitable for differing occupancy/egress requirements.

Richard J. Vitullo, AIA; Oak Leaf Studio; Crownsville, Maryland
Daniel F. C. Hayes, AIA; Washington, D.C.

DOORS

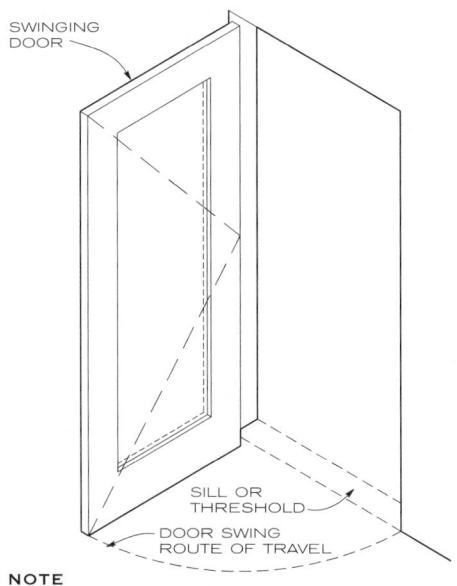

NOTE

Swinging doors rotate on hinges or pivots, require adequate floor space to accommodate outswing, and are used for egress openings. See codes for requirements.

SWINGING DOORS

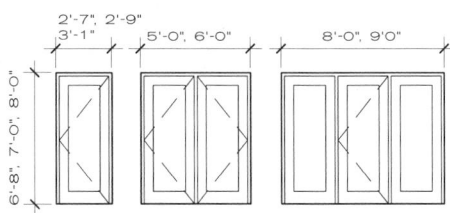

SWINGING DOOR SIZES

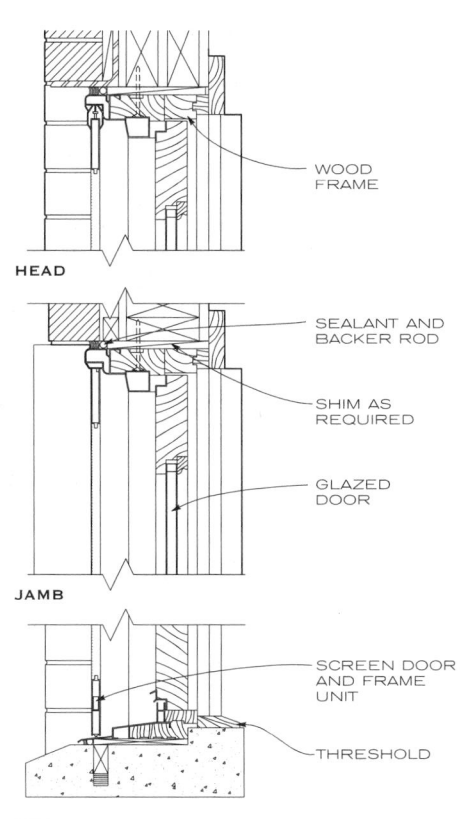

DETAIL—EXTERIOR SWINGING DOOR

Daniel F. C. Hayes, AIA; Washington, D.C.

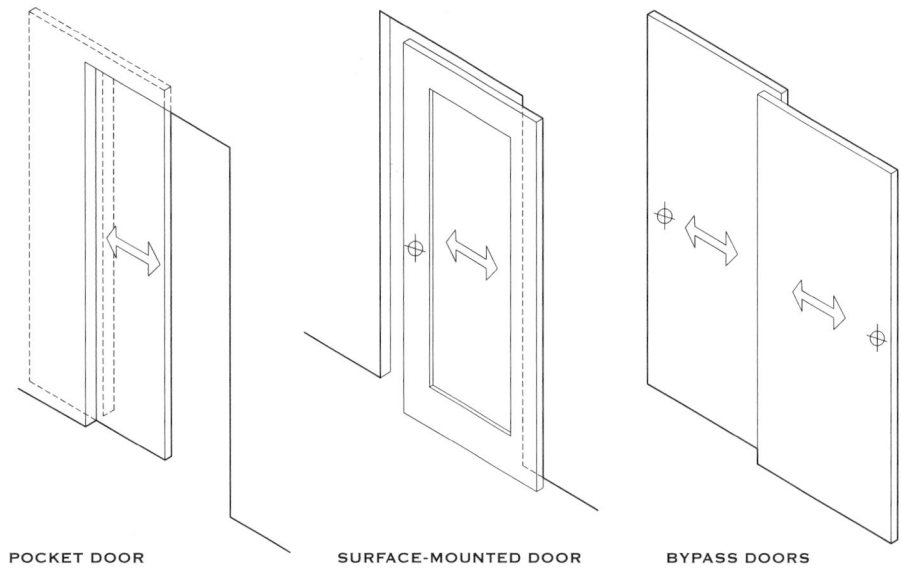

POCKET DOOR   **SURFACE-MOUNTED DOOR**   **BYPASS DOORS**

NOTE

Wood, metal, or glass doors that slide horizontally or vertically on tracks create totally clear openings without the floor space requirements of swinging doors. See codes for egress requirements.

SLIDING DOORS

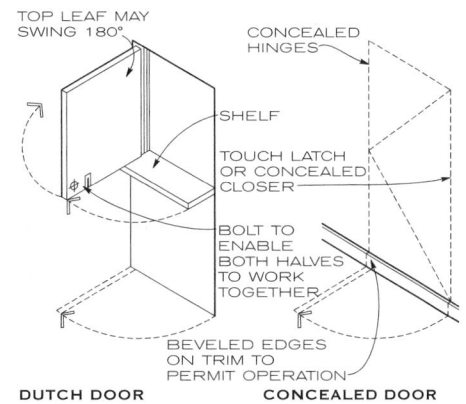

DUTCH DOOR   **CONCEALED DOOR**

SPECIAL SWINGING DOORS

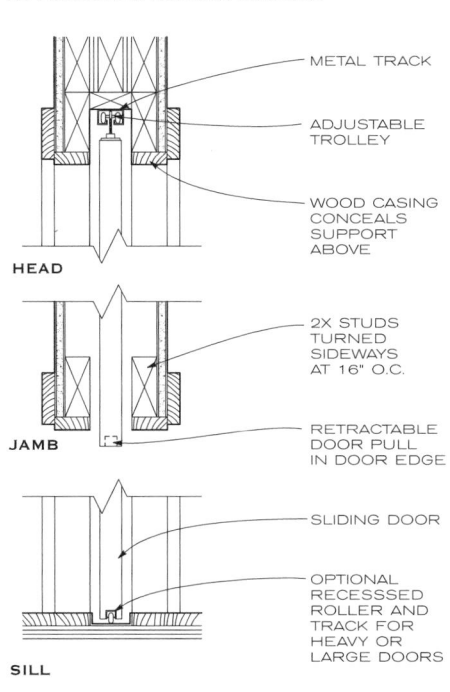

DETAIL—SLIDING POCKET

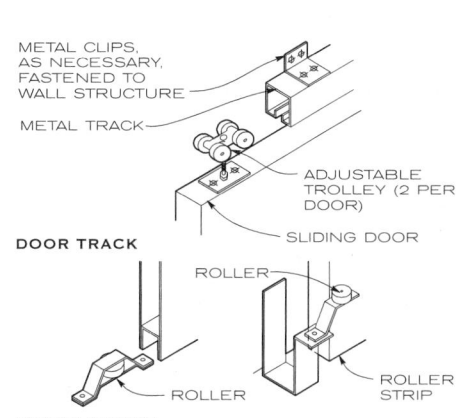

DOOR TRACK

FLOOR GUIDES

HARDWARE FOR BYPASS DOORS

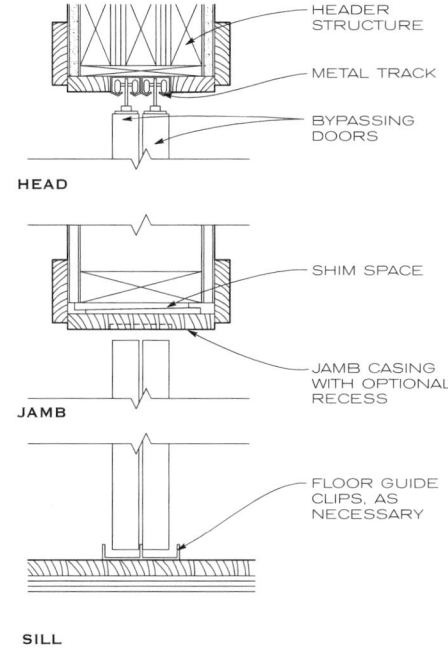

DETAIL—BYPASS DOOR

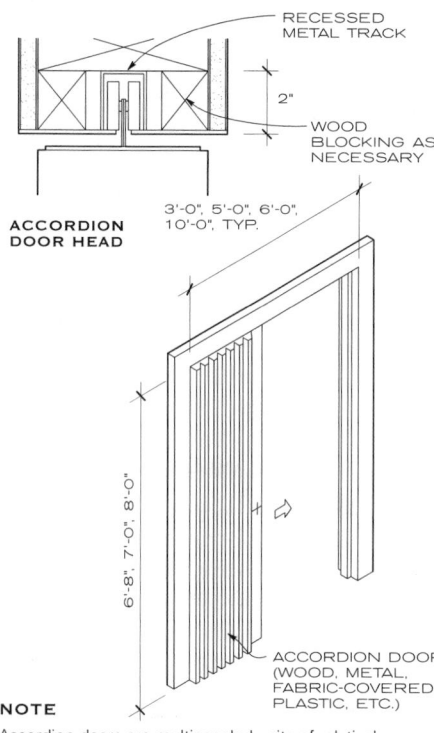

RECESSED METAL TRACK
2"
WOOD BLOCKING AS NECESSARY

ACCORDION DOOR HEAD

3'-0", 5'-0", 6'-0", 10'-0", TYP.

6'-8", 7'-0", 8'-0"

ACCORDION DOOR (WOOD, METAL, FABRIC-COVERED, PLASTIC, ETC.)

NOTE

Accordion doors are multipaneled units of relatively narrow wood or fabric that are hinged together. Track-guided hangers/trolleys and optional jamb-side pivots allow the entire assembly to fold together like an accordion. The stacking distance of the panels when open may encroach upon the clear opening dimension or be concealed in a recessed pocket. Sizes vary from traditional doorways to room dividers. Accordion doors require less floor space than swing doors. Refer to codes for egress requirements.

TYPICAL ACCORDION DOOR

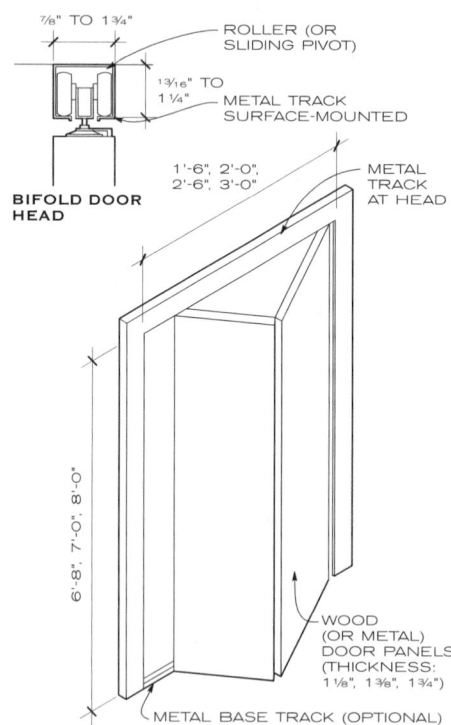

7/8" TO 1 3/4"
ROLLER (OR SLIDING PIVOT)
1 3/16" TO 1 1/4"
METAL TRACK SURFACE-MOUNTED

BIFOLD DOOR HEAD

1'-6", 2'-0", 2'-6", 3'-0"
METAL TRACK AT HEAD

6'-8", 7'-0", 8'-0"

WOOD (OR METAL) DOOR PANELS (THICKNESS: 1 1/8", 1 3/8", 1 3/4")

METAL BASE TRACK (OPTIONAL)

NOTE

Bifold doors are wood or metal door pairs hinged together with pivots at the jamb. Track-guided hangers/trolleys allow the doors to fold against each other when they open. Bifold doors require less floor space than swing doors, but the thickness of the door panels reduces the clear opening.

TYPICAL BIFOLD DOOR

Daniel F. C. Hayes, AIA; Washington, D.C.

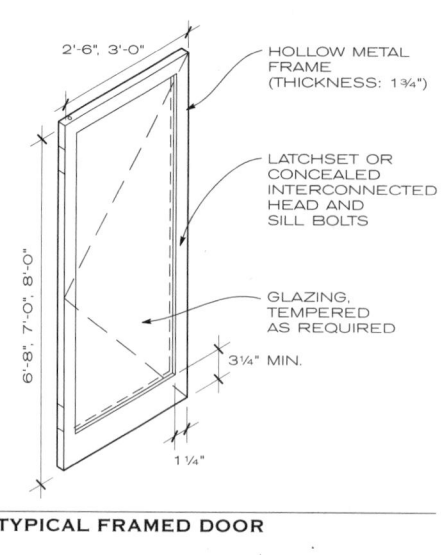

2'-6", 3'-0"
HOLLOW METAL FRAME (THICKNESS: 1 3/4")
LATCHSET OR CONCEALED INTERCONNECTED HEAD AND SILL BOLTS
GLAZING, TEMPERED AS REQUIRED
6'-8", 7'-0", 8'-0"
3 1/4" MIN.
1 1/4"

TYPICAL FRAMED DOOR

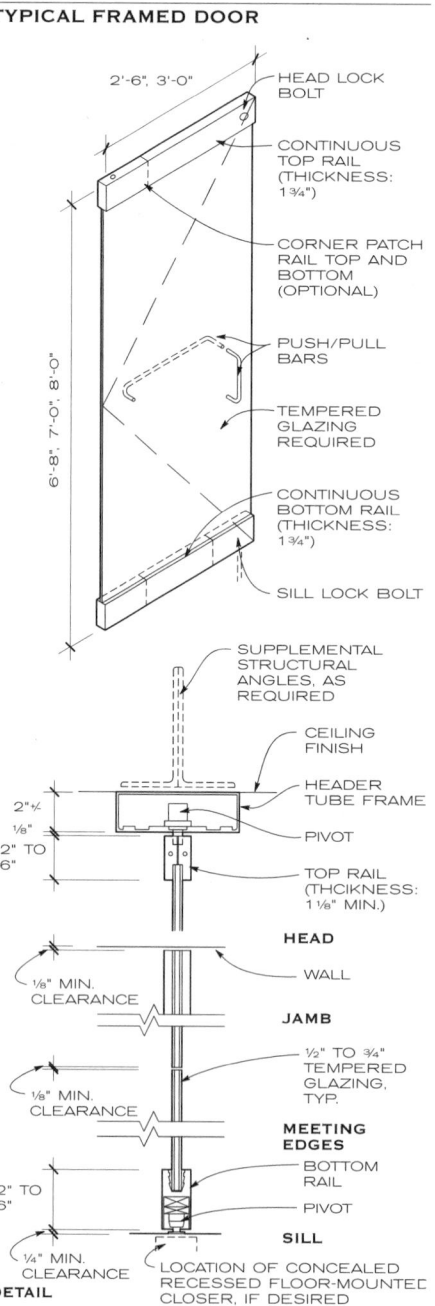

2'-6", 3'-0"
HEAD LOCK BOLT
CONTINUOUS TOP RAIL (THICKNESS: 1 3/4")
CORNER PATCH RAIL TOP AND BOTTOM (OPTIONAL)
PUSH/PULL BARS
6'-8", 7'-0", 8'-0"
TEMPERED GLAZING REQUIRED
CONTINUOUS BOTTOM RAIL (THICKNESS: 1 3/4")
SILL LOCK BOLT

SUPPLEMENTAL STRUCTURAL ANGLES, AS REQUIRED
CEILING FINISH
HEADER TUBE FRAME
PIVOT
2"± 1/8" 2" TO 6"
TOP RAIL (THICKNESS: 1 1/8" MIN.)
HEAD
WALL
JAMB
1/8" MIN. CLEARANCE
1/2" TO 3/4" TEMPERED GLAZING, TYP.
1/8" MIN. CLEARANCE
MEETING EDGES
BOTTOM RAIL
2" TO 6"
PIVOT
SILL
1/4" MIN. CLEARANCE
LOCATION OF CONCEALED RECESSED FLOOR-MOUNTED CLOSER, IF DESIRED
DETAIL

TYPICAL ALL-GLASS DOOR

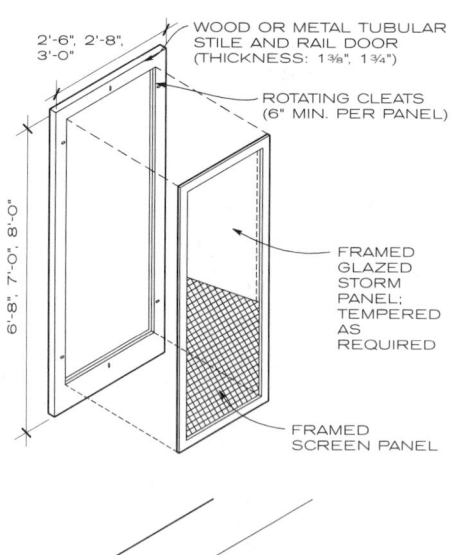

2'-6", 2'-8", 3'-0"
WOOD OR METAL TUBULAR STILE AND RAIL DOOR (THICKNESS: 1 3/8", 1 3/4")
ROTATING CLEATS (6" MIN. PER PANEL)
FRAMED GLAZED STORM PANEL; TEMPERED AS REQUIRED
6'-8", 7'-0", 8'-0"
FRAMED SCREEN PANEL

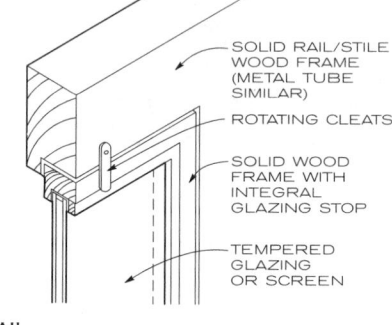

SOLID RAIL/STILE WOOD FRAME (METAL TUBE SIMILAR)
ROTATING CLEATS
SOLID WOOD FRAME WITH INTEGRAL GLAZING STOP
TEMPERED GLAZING OR SCREEN

DETAIL

DOOR WITH REMOVABLE STORM/SCREEN PANEL

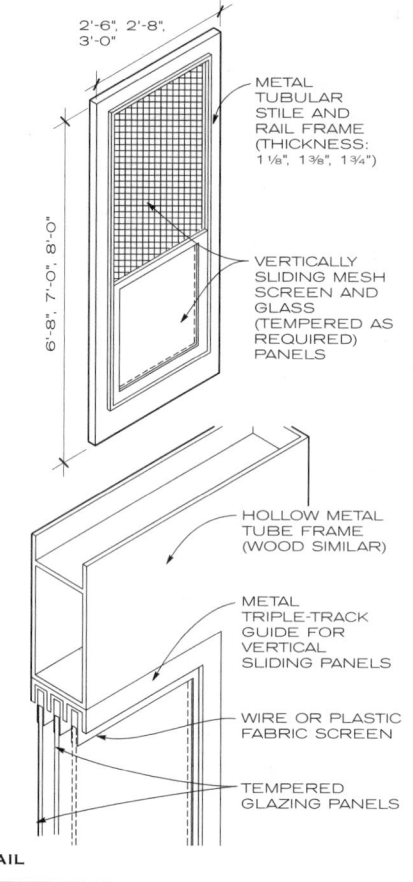

2'-6", 2'-8", 3'-0"
METAL TUBULAR STILE AND RAIL FRAME (THICKNESS: 1 1/8", 1 3/8", 1 3/4")
VERTICALLY SLIDING MESH SCREEN AND GLASS (TEMPERED AS REQUIRED) PANELS
6'-8", 7'-0", 8'-0"
HOLLOW METAL TUBE FRAME (WOOD SIMILAR)
METAL TRIPLE-TRACK GUIDE FOR VERTICAL SLIDING PANELS
WIRE OR PLASTIC FABRIC SCREEN
TEMPERED GLAZING PANELS
DETAIL

COMBINATION STORM/SCREEN DOOR

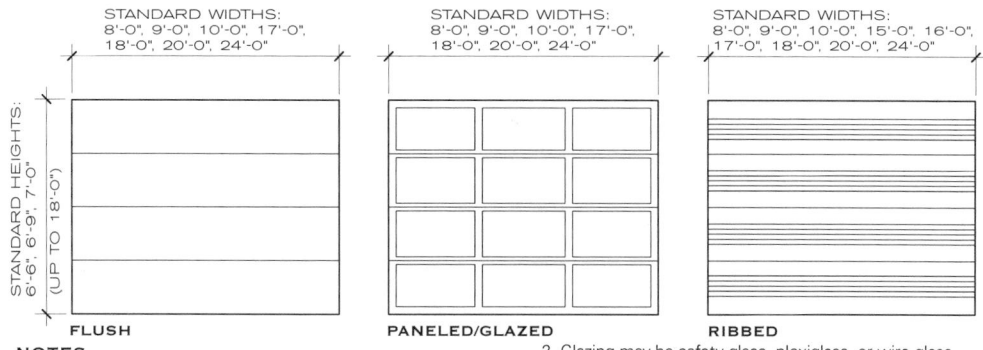

STANDARD WIDTHS:
8'-0", 9'-0", 10'-0", 17'-0", 18'-0", 20'-0", 24'-0"

STANDARD WIDTHS:
8'-0", 9'-0", 10'-0", 17'-0", 18'-0", 20'-0", 24'-0"

STANDARD WIDTHS:
8'-0", 9'-0", 10'-0", 15'-0", 16'-0", 17'-0", 18'-0", 20'-0", 24'-0"

STANDARD HEIGHTS:
6'-6", 6'-9", 7'-0" (UP TO 18'-0")

FLUSH   **PANELED/GLAZED**   **RIBBED**

NOTES

1. Standard commercial doors are designed to wind loads of 20 lb/sq ft.

2. Glazing may be safety glass, plexiglass, or wire glass.

3. Motor operators may be turned on and off by remote electrical switch, radio signal, photoelectrical control, or key lock switch for security.

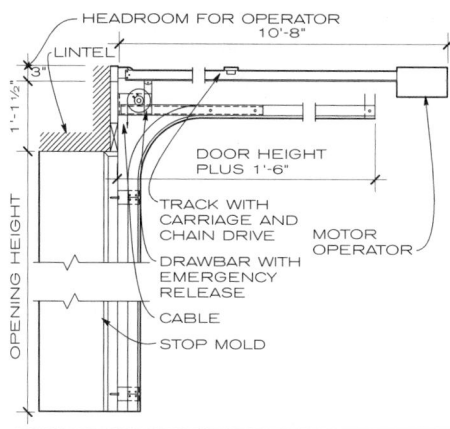

INSTALLATION DETAILS

UPWARD-ACTING SECTIONAL DOORS

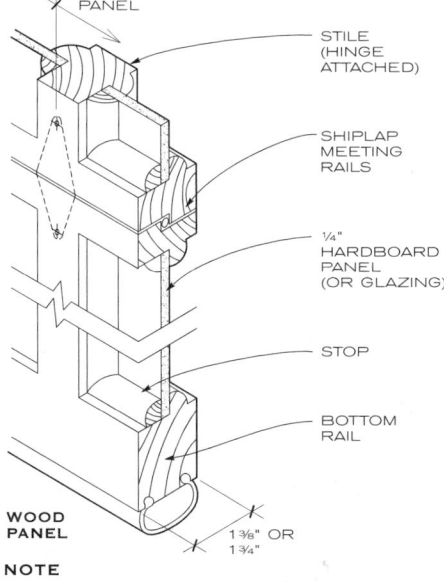

PANEL

STILE (HINGE ATTACHED)

SHIPLAP MEETING RAILS

¼" HARDBOARD PANEL (OR GLAZING)

STOP

BOTTOM RAIL

WOOD PANEL

1 ⅜" OR 1 ¾"

NOTE

Typical maximum width for wood panel sectional doors is 24 ft (6 panels); typical maximum height is 18 ft (9 sections).

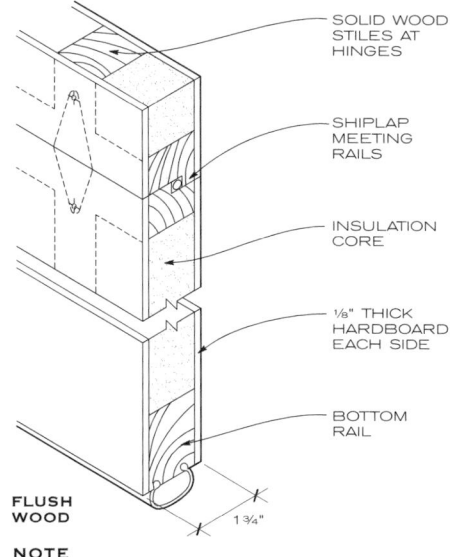

SOLID WOOD STILES AT HINGES

SHIPLAP MEETING RAILS

INSULATION CORE

⅛" THICK HARDBOARD, EACH SIDE

BOTTOM RAIL

FLUSH WOOD

1 ¾"

NOTE

Typical maximum width for flush wood sectional doors is 24 ft (6 panels); typical maximum height is 18 ft (9 sections).

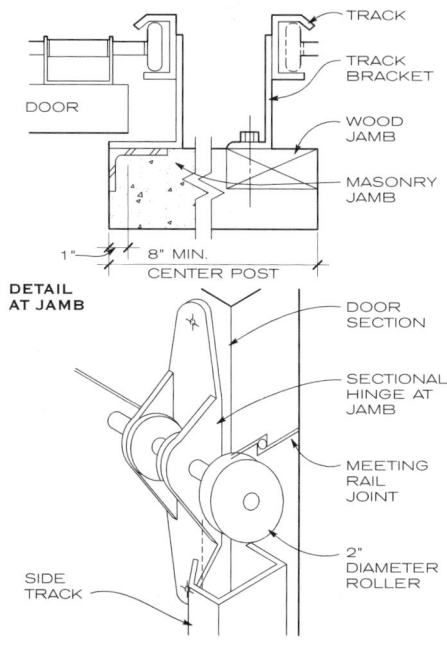

TRACK

TRACK BRACKET

WOOD JAMB

MASONRY JAMB

DOOR

DETAIL AT JAMB

1"   8" MIN.

CENTER POST

DOOR SECTION

SECTIONAL HINGE AT JAMB

MEETING RAIL JOINT

2" DIAMETER ROLLER

SIDE TRACK

HINGE AND ROLLER AT JAMB

WOOD SECTIONAL DOORS

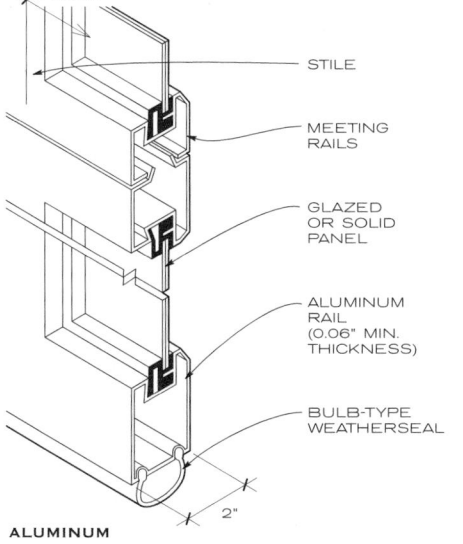

PANEL

STILE

MEETING RAILS

GLAZED OR SOLID PANEL

ALUMINUM RAIL (0.06" MIN. THICKNESS)

BULB-TYPE WEATHERSEAL

ALUMINUM

2"

NOTE

Typical maximum width for aluminum sectional doors is 18 ft (5 panels); typical maximum height is 14 ft (7 sections).

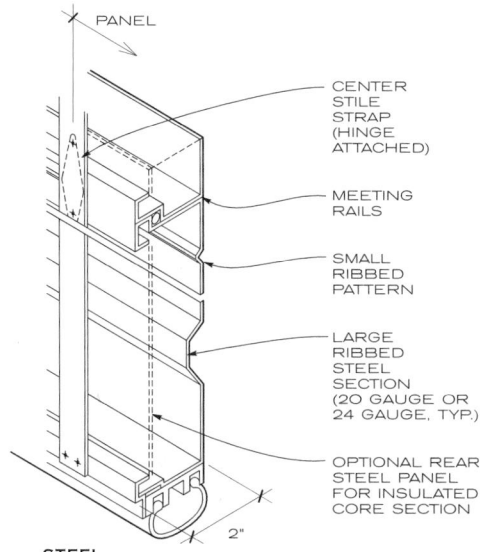

PANEL

CENTER STILE STRAP (HINGE ATTACHED)

MEETING RAILS

SMALL RIBBED PATTERN

LARGE RIBBED STEEL SECTION (20 GAUGE OR 24 GAUGE, TYP.)

OPTIONAL REAR STEEL PANEL FOR INSULATED CORE SECTION

STEEL

2"

NOTE

Typical maximum width for steel sectional doors is 24 ft (7 panels); typical maximum height is 18 ft (9 sections).

SECTIONAL DOOR DETAILS

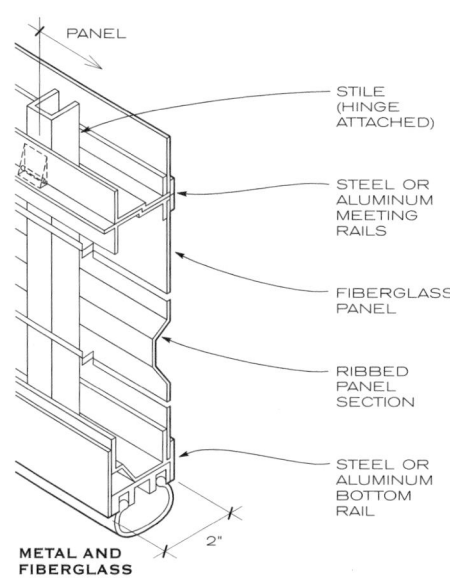

PANEL

STILE (HINGE ATTACHED)

STEEL OR ALUMINUM MEETING RAILS

FIBERGLASS PANEL

RIBBED PANEL SECTION

STEEL OR ALUMINUM BOTTOM RAIL

METAL AND FIBERGLASS

2"

NOTE

Typical maximum width for metal and fiberglass sectional doors is 20 ft (6 panels); typical maximum height is 16 ft (8 sections).

METAL SECTIONAL DOORS

Daniel F. C. Hayes, AIA; Washington, D.C.

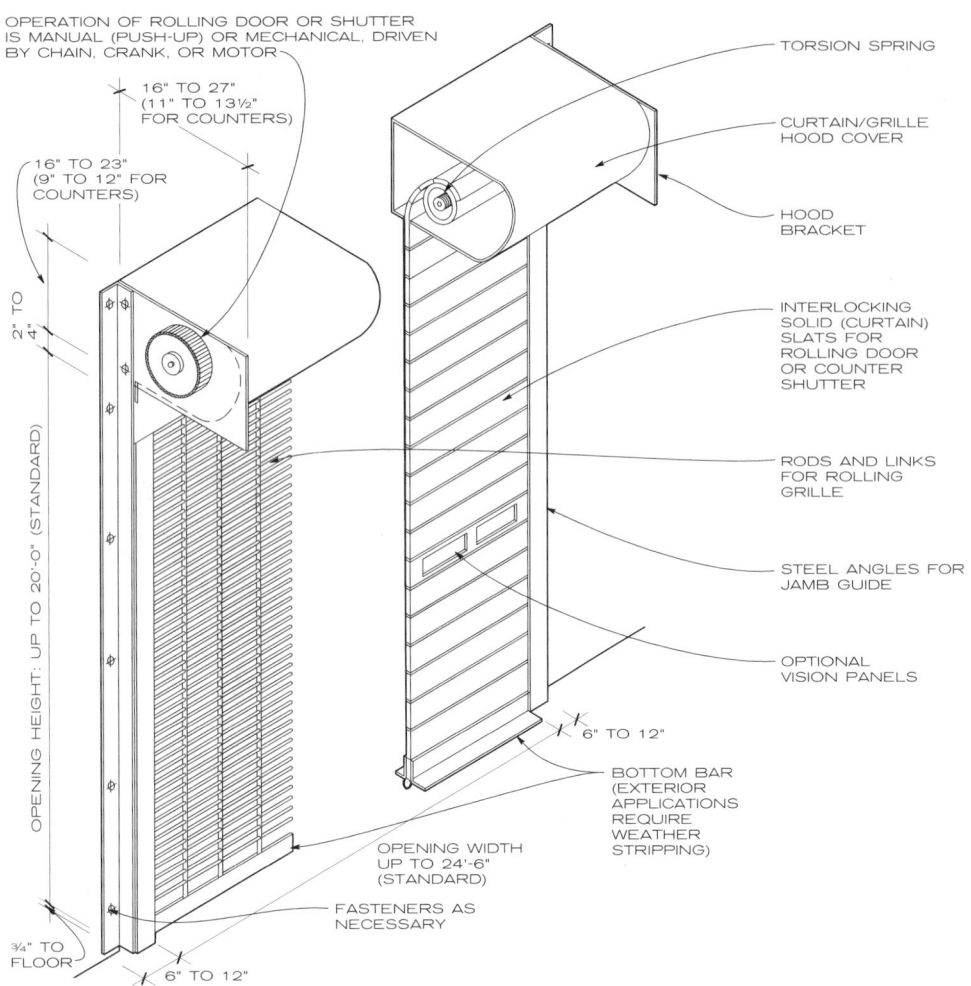

OPERATION OF ROLLING DOOR OR SHUTTER IS MANUAL (PUSH-UP) OR MECHANICAL, DRIVEN BY CHAIN, CRANK, OR MOTOR

16" TO 27" (11" TO 13½" FOR COUNTERS)

16" TO 23" (9" TO 12" FOR COUNTERS)

2" TO 4"

OPENING HEIGHT: UP TO 20'-0" (STANDARD)

¾" TO FLOOR

6" TO 12"

OPENING WIDTH UP TO 24'-6" (STANDARD)

FASTENERS AS NECESSARY

TORSION SPRING

CURTAIN/GRILLE HOOD COVER

HOOD BRACKET

INTERLOCKING SOLID (CURTAIN) SLATS FOR ROLLING DOOR OR COUNTER SHUTTER

RODS AND LINKS FOR ROLLING GRILLE

STEEL ANGLES FOR JAMB GUIDE

OPTIONAL VISION PANELS

6" TO 12"

BOTTOM BAR (EXTERIOR APPLICATIONS REQUIRE WEATHER STRIPPING)

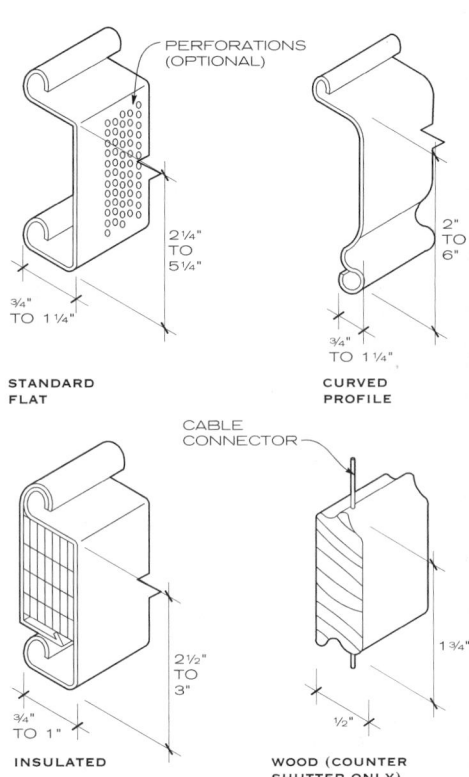

PERFORATIONS (OPTIONAL)

2¼" TO 5¼"

¾" TO 1¼"

STANDARD FLAT

2" TO 6"

¾" TO 1¼"

CURVED PROFILE

CABLE CONNECTOR

2½" TO 3"

¾" TO 1"

INSULATED

1¾"

½"

WOOD (COUNTER SHUTTER ONLY)

NOTES

1. Solid (curtain) slats are made of roll-formed steel (22 to 16 gauge), either prime-painted galvanized or stainless steel or anodized aluminum.

2. Standard flat (nonperforated) and curved slats may be used in fire-rated applications. Other standard or custom slat desings are available; consult manufacturers.

3. Acrylic vision slats may be inserted within standard slats for light transmission and visibility.

4. Counter shutters are available in standard heights up to 7 ft and widths up to 11 ft.

5. Manual, crank, and motor operators are avaliable for counter shutters.

NOTES

1. Motor operators vary from ⅓ HP to 2 HP and may be wall-mounted alongside a curtain hood bracket or bracket-mounted alongside or behind a curtain hood, depending on buliding conditions. Consult manufacturers for all requirements and clearances.

2. Rolling fire doors and counter shutters are typically rated up to UL Class A (3-hr rated). Automatic door closure and hood smoke and flame baffle activation are intiated when fusible link melts or when electromechanical devices are activated by heat detector, smoke detector, or building alarm system.

3. Rolling door jamb guides for fire-rated doors are required to have ¾ in. clearance below bottom of guide to allow for heat expansion in case of fire.

4. Standard curtain doors are designed to withstand a wind load of 20 lb/sq ft.

CURTAIN DOOR AND COUNTER SHUTTER SLAT TYPES

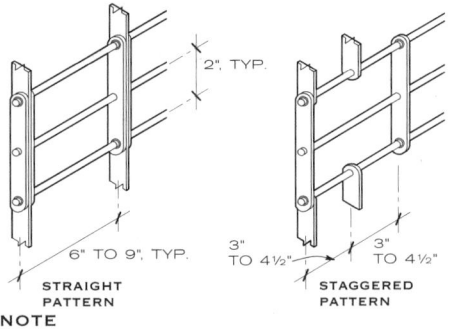

2", TYP.

6" TO 9", TYP.

STRAIGHT PATTERN

3" TO 4½"

3" TO 4½"

STAGGERED PATTERN

NOTE

Grilles are made either from steel or aluminum rods and links. Custom materials are available from manufacturers.

ROLLING GRILLE DOOR TYPES

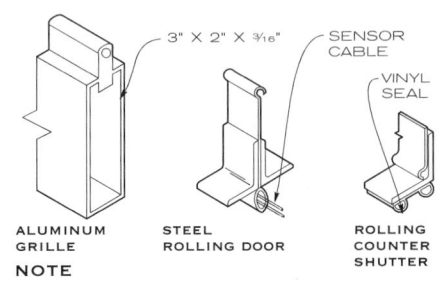

3" X 2" X 3/16"

SENSOR CABLE

VINYL SEAL

ALUMINUM GRILLE

STEEL ROLLING DOOR

ROLLING COUNTER SHUTTER

NOTE

Electric and pneumatic sensor edge types stop or reverse motor-operated doors if they hit something while closing.

BOTTOM BAR TYPES

TYPICAL ROLLING DOOR, COUNTER SHUTTER, AND GRILLE

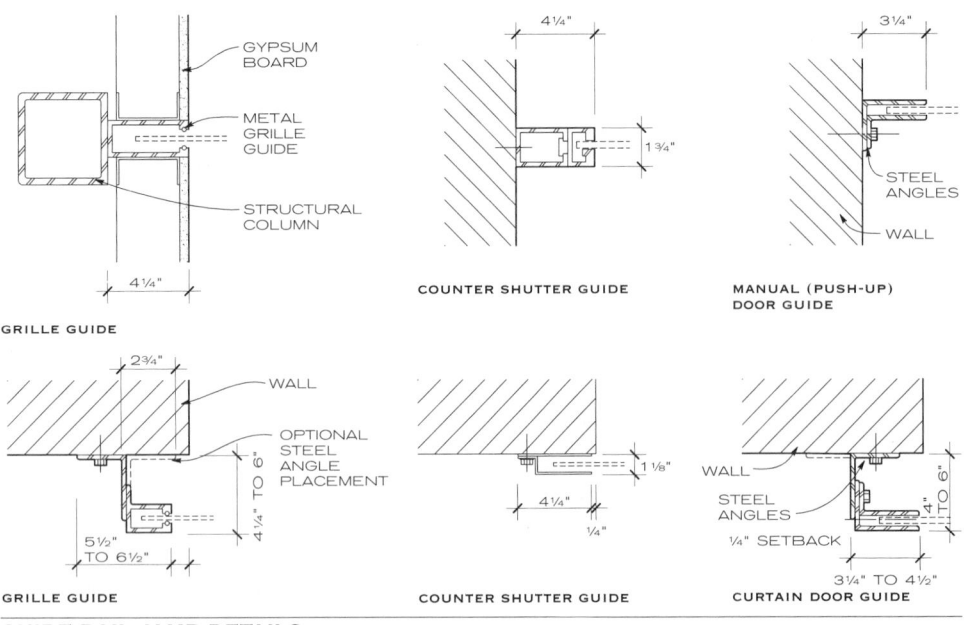

GYPSUM BOARD

METAL GRILLE GUIDE

STRUCTURAL COLUMN

4¼"

4¼"

GRILLE GUIDE

4¼"

1¾"

COUNTER SHUTTER GUIDE

3¼"

STEEL ANGLES

WALL

MANUAL (PUSH-UP) DOOR GUIDE

2¾"

WALL

OPTIONAL STEEL ANGLE PLACEMENT

4¼" TO 6"

5½" TO 6½"

GRILLE GUIDE

1⅛"

4¼"

¼"

COUNTER SHUTTER GUIDE

WALL

STEEL ANGLES

¼" SETBACK

4" TO 6"

3¼" TO 4½"

CURTAIN DOOR GUIDE

GUIDE RAIL JAMB DETAILS

Richard J. Vitullo, AIA, Oak Leaf Studio; Crownsville, Maryland

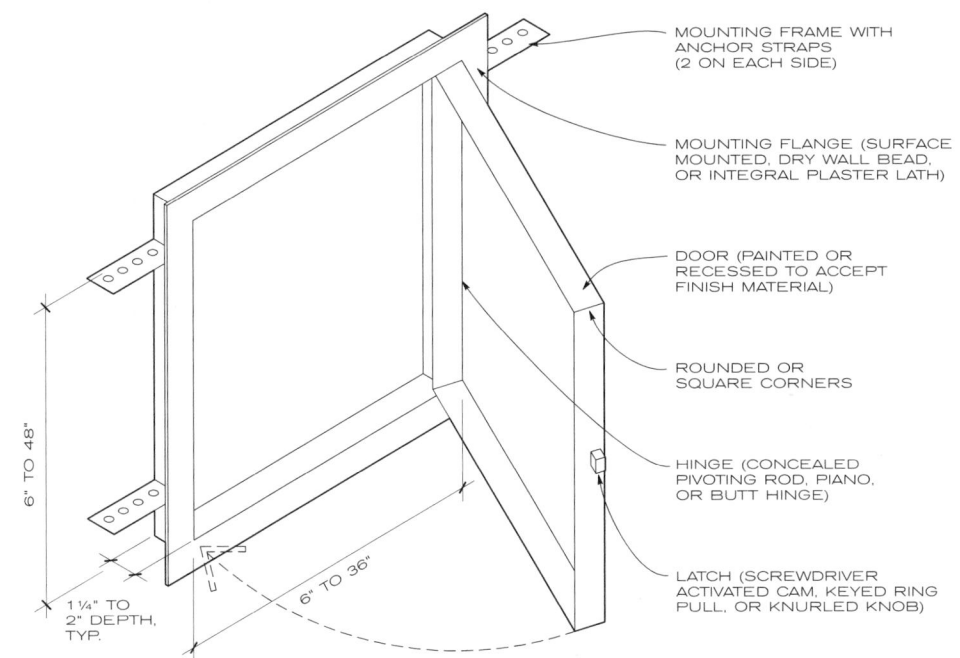

WALL OR CEILING ACCESS DOOR CHARACTERISTICS

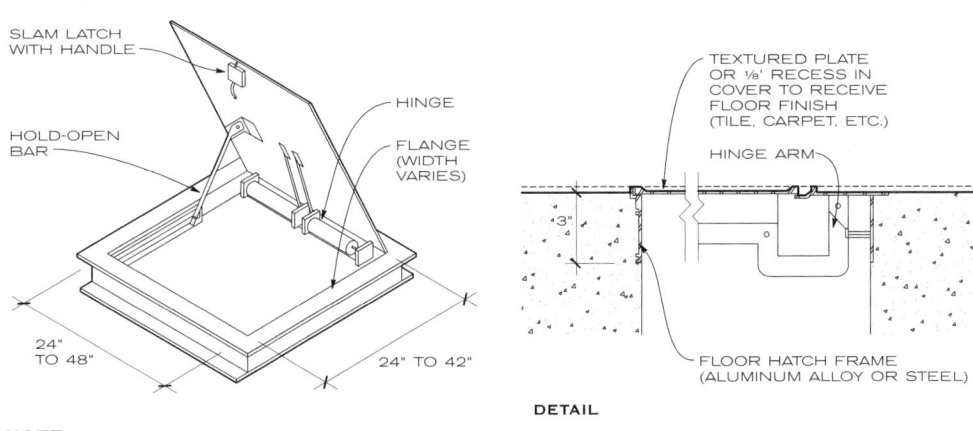

NOTE

Floor hatches usually open to 90° and may be single or double leaf.

DOOR IN FLOOR

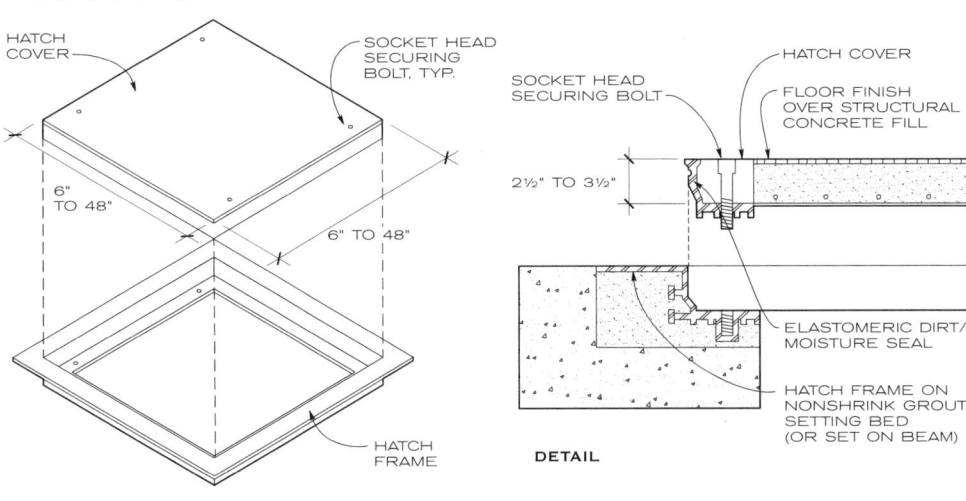

NOTES

1. Hatch cover may be topped with stone, tile, wood, carpet, and the like over a 1½ in. (minimum) layer of concrete, providing a flat, vibration-free surface.
2. Frame and hatch are fabricated from aluminum or steel.

FLOOR ACCESS HATCH

Daniel F. C. Hayes, AIA; Washington, D.C.

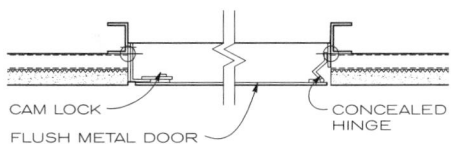

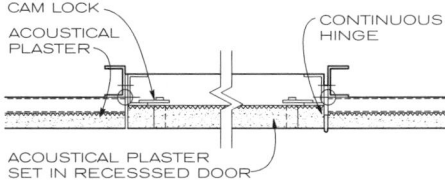

ACOUSTICAL PLASTER

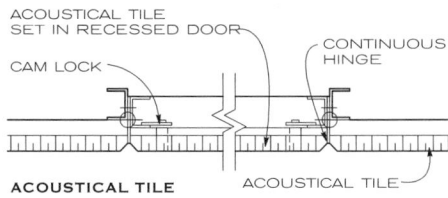

ACOUSTICAL TILE

NOTES

1. Spring-operated, swing-down, and swing-up panels frequently are used for access.
2. Acoustical tile may be fire-rated and recessed in the door.
3. Doors and frames may be galvanized or stainless steel.
4. Other finish ceiling panels are detailed similar to acoustical tiles.

CEILING ACCESS PANELS

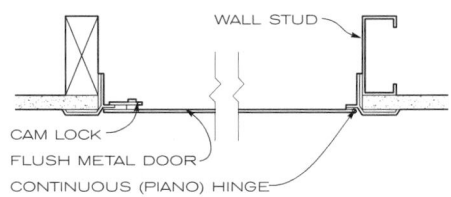

FLUSH DOOR

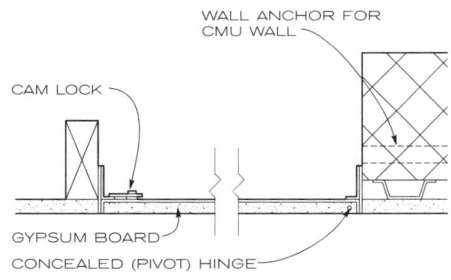

RECESSED DOOR FOR GYPSUM BOARD

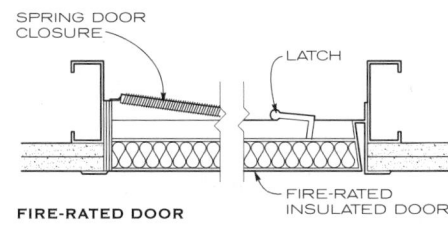

FIRE-RATED DOOR

NOTES

1. Doors may be hinged, set in with clips, or fastened with screws. Hinges may be butt or pivot, separate or continuous, surface or concealed.
2. The fire rating of access panels should be similar to the rating of the wall in which they occur. Access panels larger than 144 sq in. require automatic closers.
3. The minimum size for attic and crawl-space often is specified by building code.

WALL ACCESS DOORS

DEFINITIONS

ABSORPTANCE: the ratio of radiant energy absorbed by a glazing system to the total incident radiant energy in it.

AIR LEAKAGE RATING: a measure of the rate of infiltration around a window or skylight in the presence of a specific air pressure difference. It is expressed in units of cubic feet per minute per square foot of window area (cfm/sq ft) or cubic feet per minute per foot of window perimeter length (cfm/ft). The lower the air leakage rating of a window, the more airtight it is.

COMPOSITE FRAME: a frame made of two or more materials—for example, a frame that is wood on the interior and fiberglass on the exterior.

DOUBLE GLAZING: in general, two thicknesses of glass separated by an air space within an opening intended to improve insulation against heat transfer and/or sound transmission. In factory-made double-glazed units, the air between the glass sheets is thoroughly dried and the space is sealed airtight, eliminating possible condensation and providing superior insulating properties.

EMITTANCE: the ratio of the radiant energy emitted by a surface to that emitted by a blackbody at the same temperature and under the same conditions.

GAS FILL: a gas other than air, usually argon or krypton, placed between window or skylight panes to suppress conduction and convection and thus reduce the U-factor.

LIGHT-TO-SOLAR-GAIN RATIO (LSG): a measure of the ability of glazing to provide light without excessive solar heat gain. It is the ratio between the visible transmittance of a glazing material and its solar heat gain coefficient.

LOW-CONDUCTANCE SPACERS: an assembly of materials designed to reduce heat transfer at the edge of an insulating window. Spacers are placed between the panes of glass in a double- or triple-glazed window.

LOW-EMITTANCE (LOW-E) COATING: microscopically thin, virtually invisible metal or metallic oxide layers deposited on a window or skylight glazing surface primarily intended to reduce the U-factor by suppressing radiative heat flow. A typical type of low-E coating is transparent to the solar spectrum (visible light and short-wave infrared radiation) but reflects long-wave infrared radiation.

REFLECTANCE: the ratio of reflected radiant energy to incident radiant energy.

R-VALUE: a measure of the resistance of a glazing material or fenestration assembly to heat flow. It is the inverse of the U-factor (R = 1/U) and is expressed in units of hr x sq ft x °F/Btu. A high-R-value window has a greater resistance to heat flow and a higher insulating value than one with a low R-value.

SHADING COEFFICIENT (SC): a measure of the ability of a window or skylight to transmit solar heat relative to that ability for $1/8$-in., clear, double-strength, single glass. This measure is being phased out in favor of the solar heat gain coefficient. The SC is approximately equal to the SHGC multiplied by 1.15 and is expressed as a number without units between 0 and 1. The lower a window's solar heat gain coefficient or shading coefficient, the less solar heat it transmits and the greater shading ability it has.

SOLAR HEAT GAIN COEFFICIENT (SHGC): the fraction of incident solar radiation admitted through a window or skylight, including both directly transmitted radiation and that absorbed and subsequently released inward. The SHGC has replaced the shading coefficient as the standard indicator of a window's shading ability. It is expressed as a number between 0 and 1. The lower a window's solar heat gain coefficient, the less solar heat it transmits and the greater its shading ability. The SHGC can be expressed in terms of the glass alone or can refer to the entire window assembly.

SPECTRALLY SELECTIVE GLAZING: a coated or tinted glazing with optical properties that are transparent to some wavelengths of energy and reflective to others. Typical spectrally selective coatings are transparent to visible light and reflect short-wave and long-wave infrared radiation. Usually the term spectrally selective is applied to glazings that reduce heat gain while providing substantial daylight.

SUPERWINDOW: a window with a very low U-factor, typically less than 0.15, achieved through the use of multiple glazings, low-E coatings, and gas fills.

TRANSMITTANCE: the percentage of radiation that can pass through glazing. It can be defined for different types of light or energy, e.g., visible light transmittance, UV transmittance, or total solar energy transmittance.

U-FACTOR (U-VALUE): a measure of the rate of nonsolar heat loss or gain through a material or assembly. It is expressed in units of Btu/hr x sq ft x °F (W/sq m x °C). Values are normally given for NFRC/ASHRAE winter conditions of 0°F (18°C) outdoor temperature, 70°F (21°C) indoor temperature, 15 mph wind, and no solar load. The U-factor may be expressed for the glass alone or the entire window, which includes the effect of the frame and the spacer materials. The lower the U-factor, the greater a window's resistance to heat flow and the better its insulating value.

VISIBLE TRANSMITTANCE (VT): the percentage or fraction of the visible spectrum (380 to 720 nanometers) weighted by the sensitivity of the eye that is transmitted through the glazing.

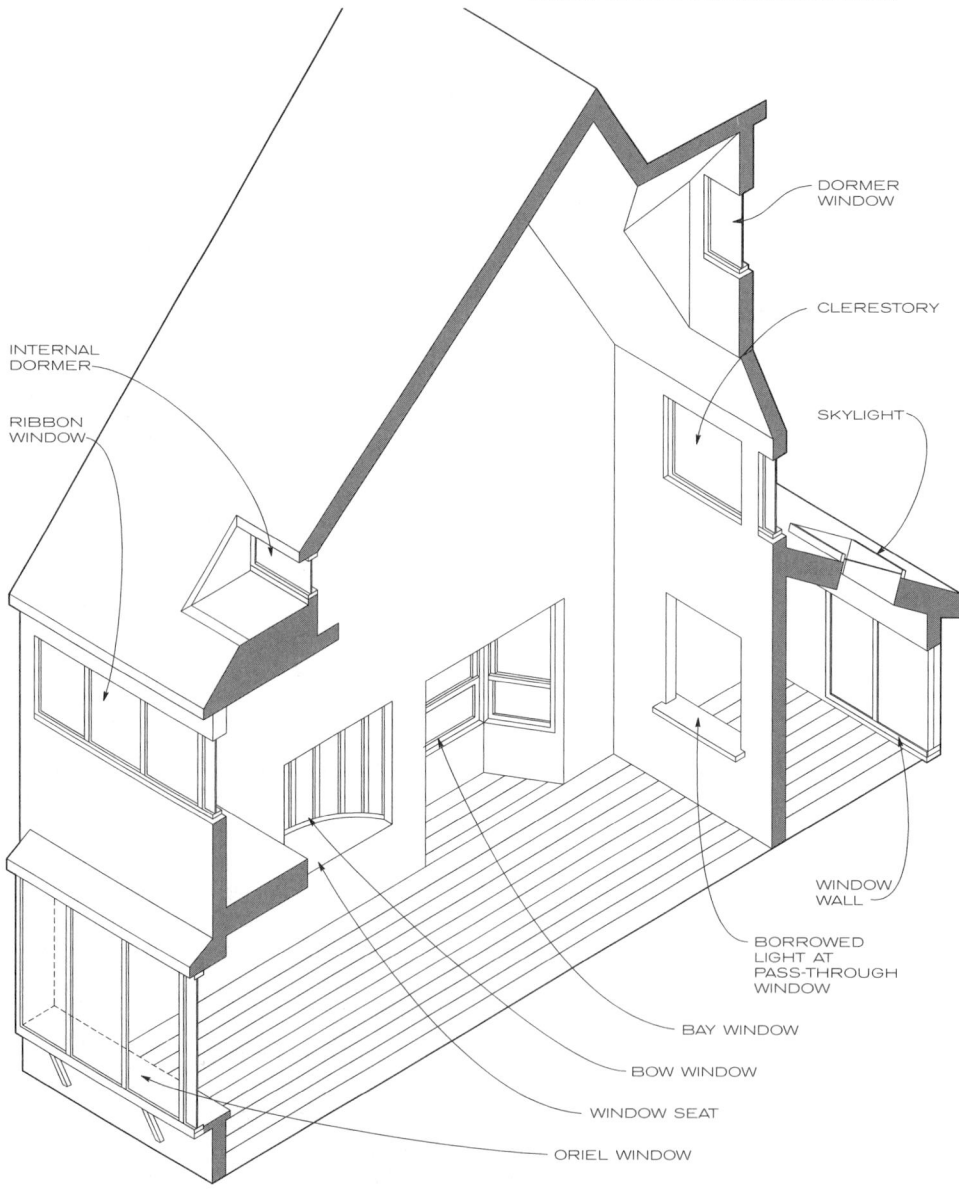

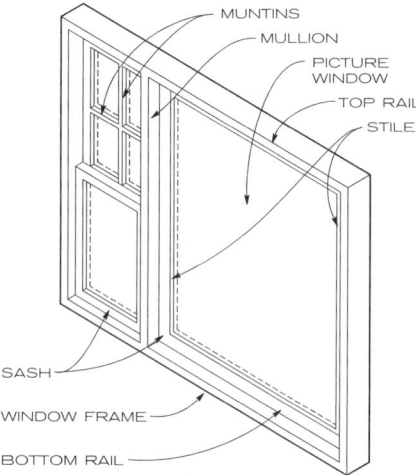

NOTES

1. BORROWED LIGHT: an interior wall opening or window that allows light to be transferred into another space.
2. CLERESTORY: the portion of a wall above an adjacent roof level; a fixed or operable window located in this part of a wall.
3. INTERNAL DORMER: a vertical window set below the line of a sloped roof.
4. ORIEL WINDOW: a bay window supported by brackets, corbeling, or cantilevers.
5. WINDOW WALL: a continuous series of fixed or operable sash, separated by mullions, that form an entire non-load-bearing wall surface.

NOTES

1. MULLION: a slender vertical member separating lights, sashes, windows, or doors.
2. MUNTIN: nonstructural members separating panes within a sash; also called a glazing bar or sash bar.
3. SASH: the basic unit of a window, consisting of frame, glazing, and gasketing; may be stationary or operable.

WINDOW CONFIGURATIONS

PARTS OF A WINDOW

John Carmody, University of Minnesota; Minneapolis, Minnesota
Stephen Selkowitz, Lawrence Berkeley National Laboratory; Berkeley, California

WINDOWS

WINDOW SELECTION

Architects choose fenestration products based on many unique priorities and circumstances. Nonetheless, a number of common considerations apply to most situations. Factors affecting window choice are

APPEARANCE: size and shape, operating type and style, frame materials, glass color and clarity.

FUNCTION: visible light transmittance (provision of daylight), glare control, reduction in fading from ultraviolet radiation, thermal comfort, resistance to condensation, ventilation, sound control, maintenance, and durability.

ENERGY PERFORMANCE: U-value; solar heat gain coefficient (SHGC), which is replacing the shading coefficient; air leakage; annual heating and cooling season performance; and peak load impacts.

COST: initial cost of window units and installation, maintenance and replacement costs, effect on heating and cooling plant costs, and cost of annual heating and cooling energy.

Many designers and homeowners find it difficult to assess the impacts of choosing a more energy-efficient window. Although some basic thermal and optical properties (U-factor, solar heat gain coefficient, and air leakage rate) can be identified if a window is properly labeled (see AGS page that discusses NFRC labels), this information does not tell how these properties influence annual energy use for heating and cooling. This must be determined by using an annual energy rating system or by computer simulation.

MANUFACTURED WINDOW UNITS

The manufactured window units discussed here have a self-contained frame and glazing assembly that can be installed in a wall or roof opening. Used in almost all residential and some nonresidential buildings, manufactured window units are fabricated with a variety of glazing, frame, and operating types.

Technical innovations in glazing and frame design have improved window performance considerably in recent years, and determining window performance regarding heat loss, heat gain, and daylight can be complex. Key window performance characteristics are the U-value, which indicates the rate of heat loss and gain; the solar heat gain coefficient (SHGC), which indicates the rate of heat gain; the air leakage rate; and visible transmittance, which indicates the amount of daylight that passes through the window. The SHGC is gradually replacing the shading coefficient (SC) as an index for measuring heat gain through windows.

When selecting windows, it is important to remember that these characteristics are sometimes given for the glazing alone and sometimes for the whole window unit. To reduce confusion, the National Fenestration Rating Council (NFRC) certifies and labels the performance of manufactured window and skylight units based on whole window values.

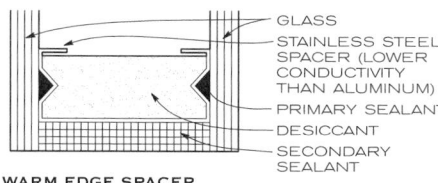

WARM EDGE SPACER

- GLASS
- STAINLESS STEEL SPACER (LOWER CONDUCTIVITY THAN ALUMINUM)
- PRIMARY SEALANT
- DESICCANT
- SECONDARY SEALANT

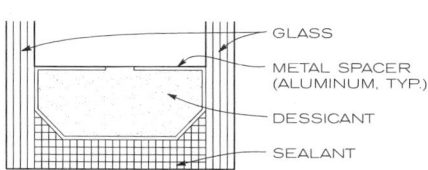

CONVENTIONAL SPACER

- GLASS
- METAL SPACER (ALUMINUM, TYP.)
- DESSICANT
- SEALANT

NOTE

The layers of glazing in an insulating unit must be held apart with spacers. Conventional metal spacers reduce the thermal performance of the glazing unit, but new "warm edge" spacers reduce heat loss and condensation with the use of new designs and materials. The spacer must accommodate stress induced by thermal expansion and pressure differences, provide a moisture barrier that prevents fog in the unit, prevent loss of any low-conductance gas from the air space, and create an insulating barrier that reduces the formation of interior condensation at the edge.

INSULATED GLASS EDGE SPACER

John Carmody, University of Minnesota; Minneapolis, Minnesota
Stephen Selkowitz, Lawrence Berkeley National Laboratories; Berkeley, California

TECHNOLOGICAL IMPROVEMENTS

A series of innovations has resulted in more energy gain and loss control in the window assembly or glass itself. Some technological innovations currently appearing in fenestration products are outlined here:

1. Glazing unit structure: Multiple layers of glass or plastic film improve thermal resistance and reduce heat loss attributed to convection between window layers. Additional layers provide more surfaces for low-E or solar control coatings.

2. Low-emittance coatings: Low-E coatings are highly transparent and virtually invisible but have a high rate of reflectance (low emittance) with long-wavelength infrared radiation. This reduces long-wavelength heat transfer between glazing layers by a factor of 5 to 10, which reduces total heat transfer between the layers. Low-E coatings may be applied directly to glass surfaces or to plastic film, which is then suspended in the air cavity between the interior and exterior glazing layers.

3. Low-conductance gas fills: When a low-E coating is used, heat transfer across a gap is dominated by conduction and natural convection. While air is a relatively good insulator, other gases (such as argon, krypton, and carbon dioxide) have lower thermal conductivities. Using one of these nontoxic gases in an insulating glass unit can reduce heat transfer between glazing layers.

4. Solar control glazings and coatings: To reduce cooling loads, specify new types of tinted glass and new coatings that reduce the effect of the sun's heat without sacrificing views. Spectrally selective glazings and coatings absorb and reflect the infrared portion of sunlight while transmitting visible daylight, thus reducing solar heat gain coefficients and resultant cooling loads. Solar control coatings can also have low-emittance characteristics.

5. Warm edge spacers: Heat transfer through metal spacers used to separate glazing layers can increase heat loss and cause condensation to form at the edge of the window. "Warm edge" spacers use new materials and better design to reduce this effect.

6. Thermally improved sash and frame: Traditional sash and frame designs contribute to heat loss and can represent a large fraction of the total loss when high-performance glass is used. New materials and improved designs can reduce this loss.

7. Improved weatherstripping: Weatherstripping today is made of more durable materials that will provide improved reduction in air leakage over a longer time period than did materials in the past.

STANDARDS

AMERICAN ARCHITECTURAL MANUFACTURERS ASSOCIATION (AAMA)

AAMA 910-93, "Voluntary Life Cycle Specifications and Test Methods for Architectural Grade Windows and Sliding Glass Doors."

AAMA 1503.1-1988, "Voluntary Test Method for Thermal Transmittance and Condensation Resistance of Windows, Doors, and Glazed Wall Sections."

AAMA TIR-A10-1992, "Wind Loads on Components and Cladding for Buildings Less Than 90 Feet Tall."

AAMA CW #2-1979, "The Rain Screen Principle and Pressure-Equalized Wall Design."

AAMA CW #11-1985, "Design Wind Loads for Buildings and Boundary Layer Wind Tunnel Testing."

AAMA/NWWDA, "Voluntary Specifications for Aluminum, Vinyl (PVC), and Wood Windows and Glass Doors—1996."

ANSI/AAMA 101-93, "Voluntary Specifications for Aluminum and Poly (Vinyl Chloride) (PVC) Prime Windows and Glass Doors."

ANSI/AAMA 1002.10-93, "Voluntary Specifications for Insulating Storm Products for Windows and Sliding Glass Doors."

NATIONAL FENESTRATION RATING COUNCIL (NFRC)

NFRC 100-91. "Procedure for Determining Fenestration Product Thermal Properties (Currently Limited to U-values)."

_____. "Attachment A: Interim Standard Test Method for Measuring the Steady-State Thermal Transmittance of Fenestration Systems Using Hot Box Methods."

_____. "Section B: Procedure for Determining Door System Product Thermal Properties (Currently Limited to U-values)."

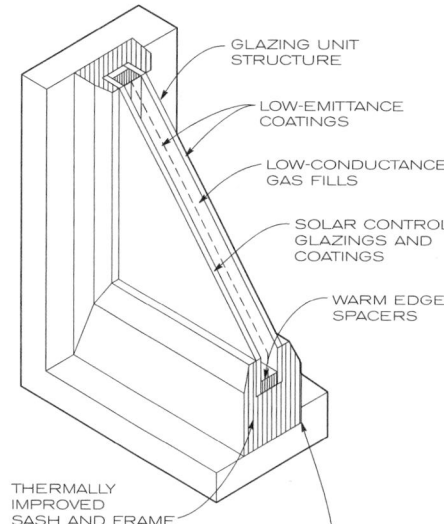

- GLAZING UNIT STRUCTURE
- LOW-EMITTANCE COATINGS
- LOW-CONDUCTANCE GAS FILLS
- SOLAR CONTROL GLAZINGS AND COATINGS
- WARM EDGE SPACERS
- THERMALLY IMPROVED SASH AND FRAME
- IMPROVED WEATHER STRIPPING

MANUFACTURED WINDOW COMPONENTS

NFRC 200-95. "Procedure for Determining Fenestration Product Solar Heat Gain Coefficients at Normal Incidence."

NFRC 300-94. "Procedures for Determining Solar Optical Properties of Simple Fenestration Products."

NFRC 301-93. "Standard Test Method for Emittance of Specular Surfaces Using Spectrometric Measurements."

NFRC 400-95. "Procedure for Determining Fenestration Product Air Leakage."

NFRC 900-95. "Procedure for Determining the Annual Heating and Cooling Energy Ratings of Fenestration Products Used in Residential Dwellings."

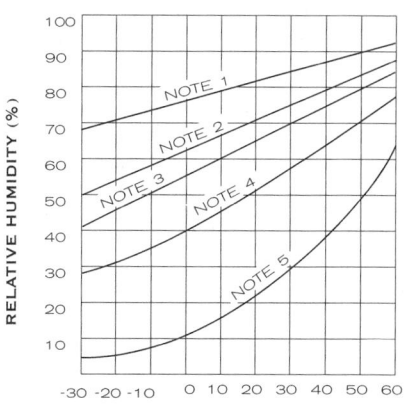

NOTES

1. Triple-glazed windows with two low-E coatings and argon gas fill.
2. Double-glazed windows with a low-E coating and argon gas fill.
3. Double-glazed windows with a low-E coating.
4. Double-glazed windows.
5. Single-glazed windows.

CONDITIONS THAT LEAD TO CONDENSATION ON WINDOWS

CONDENSATION POTENTIAL

The chart above shows the potential for condensation on glazing (at the center of glass) at various outdoor temperature and indoor relative humidity conditions. Condensation can occur at any point on or above the curves. (Note: All air spaces are 1/2 in.; all coatings are E = 0.10.)

EXAMPLE: At 20°F (-7°C) outside, condensation will form on the inner surface of double glazing when the indoor relative humidity is 52 percent or higher. It will form at an indoor relative humidity of 70 percent or higher if a double-pane window with a low-E coating and argon fill is used.

GENERAL

The National Fenestration Rating Council (NFRC) has developed a fenestration energy rating system based on whole product performance. The system accurately accounts for the energy-related effects of all of a product's component parts and prevents misleading comparisons of information about a single component with whole product properties. At this time, NFRC labels on window units give ratings for U-value, solar heat gain coefficient, and visible light transmittance. Soon labels will include air infiltration rates and an annual fenestration heating and cooling rating. The initial development of the NFRC rating system has focused on window units manufactured mainly for residential applications. In the future, the NFRC will adapt the rating system to commercial glazing and curtain wall systems.

Manufacturers of modern fenestration products want to take credit for the technological advances and increasing complexity of their products but these are not easily visually verified. Thus, in 1989, the NFRC was established to develop a fair, accurate, and credible rating system for these products. State energy codes began to incorporate NFRC procedures in 1992, and the National Energy Policy Act provided for the development of a national rating system. The U.S. Department of Energy has certified the NFRC procedures as the national rating system, and they are now referenced in and being incorporated into the Model Energy Code and ASHRAE Standards 90.1 and 90.2.

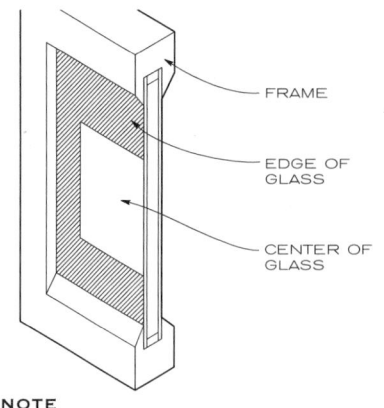

    FRAME

    EDGE OF
    GLASS

    CENTER OF
    GLASS

NOTE

The totat window U-factor takes into account the glass (edge of glass and center of glass) and the frame in a vertical position. Changing the mounting angle can affect the U-factor of a window.

ZONES FOR DETERMINING HEAT LOSS IN WINDOW ASSEMBLY

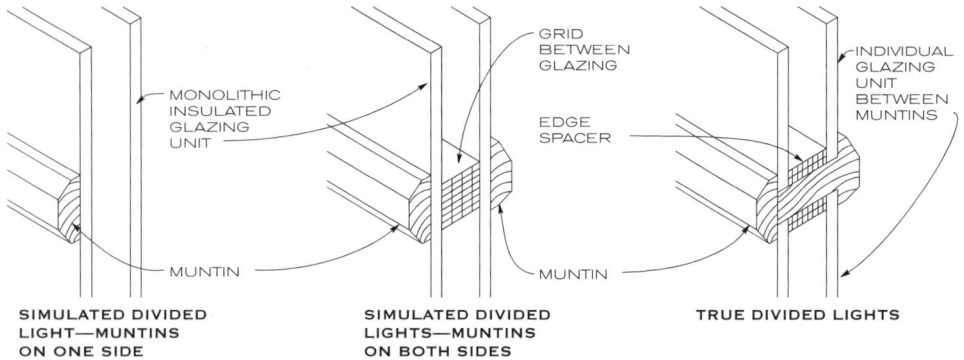

    MONOLITHIC
    INSULATED
    GLAZING
    UNIT

    MUNTIN

    GRID
    BETWEEN
    GLAZING

    EDGE
    SPACER

    MUNTIN

    INDIVIDUAL
    GLAZING
    UNIT
    BETWEEN
    MUNTINS

SIMULATED DIVIDED LIGHT—MUNTINS ON ONE SIDE

SIMULATED DIVIDED LIGHTS—MUNTINS ON BOTH SIDES

TRUE DIVIDED LIGHTS

NOTE

The energy performance of a window unit with muntins on both sides can be comparable to that of a unit with no muntins if the grid set between the lights is at least $1/8$ in. away from both panes of glass.

DIVIDED LIGHT TYPES

National Fenestration Rating Council

Incorporated

AAA WINDOW COMPANY

MANUFACTURER STIPULATES THAT THESE RATINGS WERE DETERMINED IN ACORDANCE WITH APPLICABLE NFRC PROCEDURES

ENERGY RATING FACTORS	RATINGS RESIDENTIAL		PRODUCT DESCRIPTION
U-factor	0.40	0.38	Model 1000 Casement Low-E = 0.2 0.5" gap Argon-filled
Solar heat gain coefficient	0.65	0.66	
Visible light transmittance	0.71	0.71	
Air leakage	0.20	0.20	

NFRC ratings are determined for a fixed set of environmental conditions and specific product sizes and may not be appropriate for directly determining seasonal energy performance.

NOTES

1. Ratings of the basic thermal and optical properties of all fenestration products (windows, doors, skylights) must include the effects of the glass, the sash, and the frame and be in accordance with the appropriate National Fenestration Rating Council (NFRC) standard. Products must be labeled with ratings for these properties, and the manufacturer must certify they are in accordance with the NFRC Product Certification Program.

2. The NFRC standards for the basic thermal and optical properties of fenestration products are as follows: NFRC 100 for the U-factor, NFRC 200 for the solar heat gain coefficient (SHGC), NFRC 300 for visible light transmittance, and NFRC 400 for air leakage.

NFRC WINDOW PRODUCT IDENTIFICATION MARK

CHARACTERISTICS OF SELECTED WINDOW TYPES

CHARACTERISTIC	EXAMPLE 1	EXAMPLE 2	EXAMPLE 3	EXAMPLE 4	EXAMPLE 5	EXAMPLE 6	EXAMPLE 7	EXAMPLE 8
General glazing description	Single-glazed clear	Double-glazed clear	Double-glazed bronze	Double-glazed clear	Double-glazed low-E	Double-glazed spectrally selective	Triple-glazed clear	Triple-glazed low-E superwindow
Layers of glazing and spaces (outside to inside)	$1/8$ in. clear	$1/8$ in. clear	$1/8$ in. bronze	$1/8$ in. clear	$1/8$ in. clear	$1/8$ in. low-E (0.04)	$1/8$ in. clear	low-E (0.08) on $1/8$ in. clear
		$1/2$ in. air	$1/2$ in. air	$1/2$ in. air	$1/2$ in. argon	$1/2$ in. argon	$1/2$ in. air	$1/2$ in. krypton
		$1/8$ in. clear	$1/8$ in. clear	$1/8$ in. clear	low-E (0.20) on $1/8$ in. clear	$1/8$ in. clear	$1/8$ in. clear	$1/8$ in. clear
							$1/2$ in. air	$1/2$ in. krypton
							$1/8$ in. clear	low-E (0.08) on $1/8$ in. clear
Center of glass								
U-factor	1.11	0.49	0.49	0.49	0.30	0.24	0.31	0.11
Solar heat gain coefficient	0.86	0.76	0.62	0.76	0.74	0.41	0.69	0.49
Shading coefficient	1.00	0.89	0.72	0.89	0.86	0.47	0.81	0.57
Visible transmittance	0.90	0.81	0.61	0.81	0.74	0.72	0.75	0.68
Frame								
Type	Aluminum, no thermal break	Aluminum, thermal break	Aluminum, thermal break	Wood or vinyl	Wood or vinyl	Wood or vinyl	Wood or vinyl	Insulated vinyl
U-factor	1.90	1.00	1.00	0.40	0.30	0.30	0.30	0.20
Spacer	—	Aluminum	Aluminum	Aluminum	Stainless	Stainless	Stainless	Insulated
Total window								
U-factor	1.30	0.64	0.64	0.49	0.33	0.29	0.34	0.15
Solar heat gain coefficient	0.79	0.65	0.55	0.58	0.55	0.31	0.52	0.37
Visible transmittance	0.69	0.62	0.47	0.57	0.52	0.51	0.53	0.48
Air leakage								
Cubic ft/min per lin. ft of crack	0.65	0.37	0.37	0.37	0.10	0.10	0.10	0.05
Cubic ft/ min per sq ft of unit	0.98	0.56	0.56	0.56	0.15	0.15	0.15	0.08

Units for all U-factors are Btu/hr-sq ft-F. All values for total window are based on a 2 x 4 foot casement window.

(Source: Carmody, Selkowitz, and Heschong, Residential Windows–New Technologies and Energy Performance, 1996.)

John Carmody, University of Minnesota; Minneapolis, Minnesota
Stephen Selkowitz, Lawrence Berkeley National Laboratories; Berkeley, California

PROPERTIES OF GLAZING MATERIALS USED IN MANUFACTURED WINDOW UNITS

Three things happen to solar radiation as it passes through a glazing material: some is transmitted, some is reflected, and the rest is absorbed. These three components determine many of the other energy-performance properties of a glazing material. Manipulating the proportion of transmittance, reflectance, and absorptance for different wavelengths of solar radiation has been the source of much recent innovation in window energy performance. The four basic properties of glazing that affect radiant energy transfer are transmittance, reflectance, absorptance, and emittance.

Before the recent innovations in the technology of glass, the primary property of glass was its ability to transmit visible light, and its quality was judged by how clear it was. However, as attention focused on improving the total energy performance of glass, it became clear that transparency to visible light is only part of the picture.

Visible light is a small portion of the electromagnetic spectrum. Beyond the blues and purples lie ultraviolet radiation and other higher energy short wavelengths, from X rays to gamma rays. Beyond red light are the near-infrared, given off by very hot objects, the far-infrared, given off by warm room-temperature objects, and the longer microwaves and radio waves.

Glazing types vary in their transparency to different parts of the spectrum. On the simplest level, a glass that appears to be tinted green as you look through it toward the outside will transmit more sunlight from the green portion of the visible spectrum and reflect/absorb more of the other colors. Similarly, bronze-tinted glass will absorb the blues and greens and transmit the warmer colors. Neutral gray tints absorb most colors equally.

This same principle applies outside the visible spectrum. Most glass is partially transparent to at least some ultraviolet radiation, while plastics are commonly more opaque to ultraviolet. Glass is opaque to far-infrared radiation but generally transparent to near-infrared.

With the recent advances in glazing technology, manufacturers can control how glazing materials behave in different areas of the spectrum. The basic properties of the substrate material (glass or plastic) can be altered, and coatings can be added to the surfaces of the substrates. For example, a window optimized for daylighting and for reducing solar heat gain should transmit adequate light in the visible portion of the spectrum but exclude unnecessary heat gain from the near-infrared part of the solar spectrum. On the other hand, a window optimized for collecting solar heat gain in winter should transmit the maximum amount of visible light as well as heat from the near-infrared wavelengths in the solar spectrum, while blocking the lower energy radiant heat in the far-infrared range (an important heat-loss component). These are the strategies of spectrally selective and low-emittance coatings, respectively.

PERFORMANCE OF COMMON GLAZING TYPES

The figures on this page illustrate the solar heat gain and visible light transmittance for common glazing types used in manufactured windows. The figures are for the center of the glass only; the characteristics of the frame must be included to obtain performance information on the whole window unit. The darker arrows indicate the total transmitted and total rejected solar energy. The lighter arrows indicate the amount of transmitted and reflected daylight. Daylight that is neither transmitted nor reflected is absorbed. Not all low-E coatings are the same; use NFRC rated and labeled values.

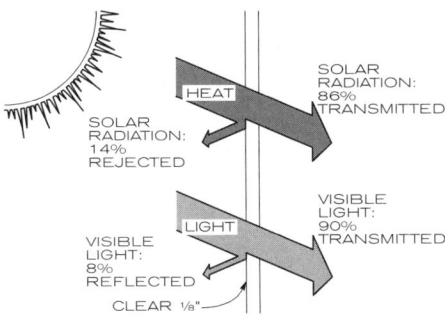

NOTE
U-value=1.11; SHGC=0.86; SC=1.00; VT=0.90

SINGLE GLAZING—CLEAR GLASS

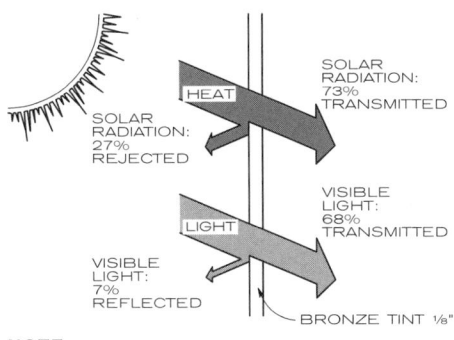

NOTE
U-value=1.11; SHGC=0.73; SC=0.85; VT=0.68

SINGLE GLAZING—BRONZE TINT

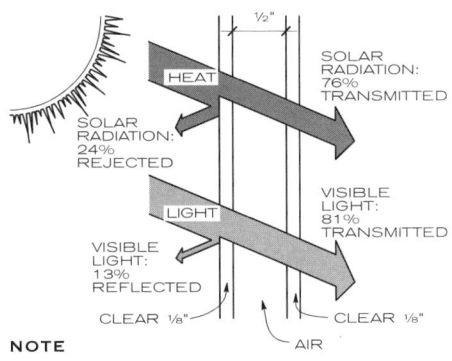

NOTE
U-value=0.49; SHGC=0.76; SC=0.88; VT=0.81

DOUBLE GLAZING—CLEAR GLASS

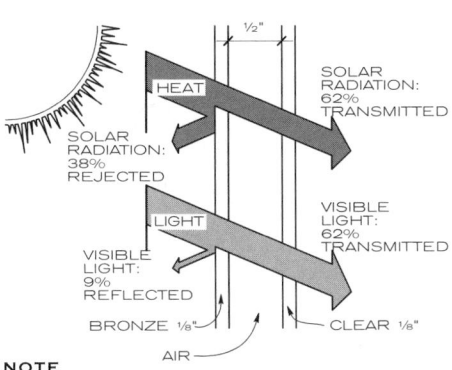

NOTE
U-value=0.49; SHGC=0.62; SC=0.72; VT=0.62

DOUBLE GLAZING—BRONZE TINT

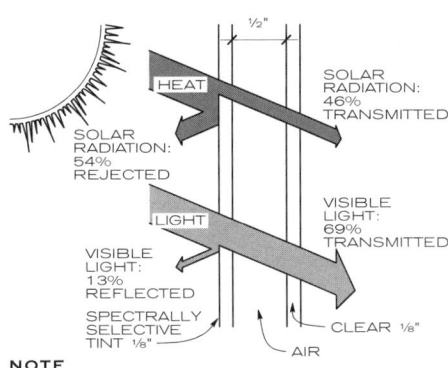

NOTE
U-value=0.49; SHGC=0.46; SC=0.54; VT=0.69

DOUBLE GLAZING—SPECTRALLY SELECTIVE TINT

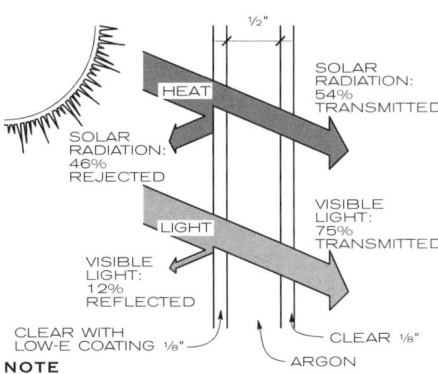

NOTE
U-value=0.26; SHGC=0.54; SC=0.62; VT=0.75

DOUBLE GLAZING—LOW-E COATING

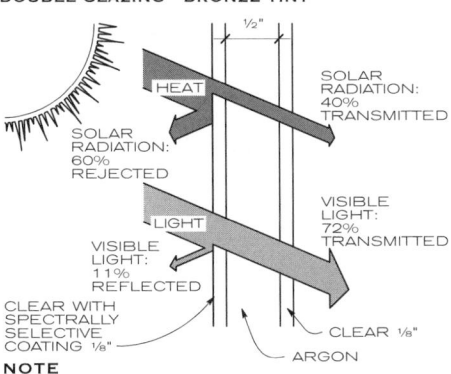

NOTE
U-value=0.24; SHGC=0.40; SC=0.47; VT=0.72

DOUBLE GLAZING—SPECTRALLY SELECTIVE COATING

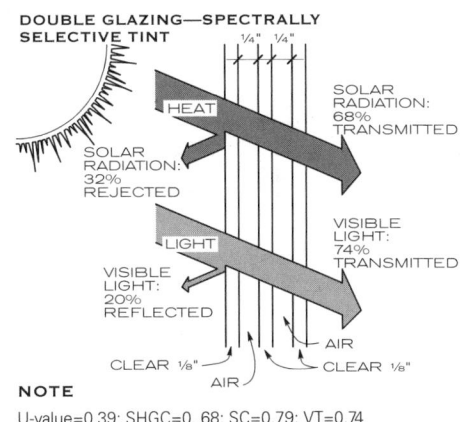

NOTE
U-value=0.39; SHGC=0. 68; SC=0.79; VT=0.74

TRIPLE GLAZING—CLEAR GLASS

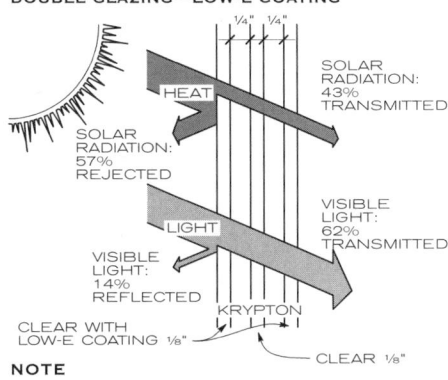

NOTE
U-value=0.14; SHGC=0.43; SC=0.50; VT=0.62

TRIPLE GLAZING—CLEAR AND TWO LOW-E COATINGS

PERFORMANCE OF 1/8-INCH THICK GLASS IN A MANUFACTURED WINDOW ASSEMBLY

John Carmody, University of Minnesota; Minneapolis, Minnesota
Stephen Selkowitz, Lawrence Berkeley National Laboratory; Berkeley, California

PERFORMANCE OF GLAZING

The figures on this page illustrate the solar heat gain and visible light transmittance for common glazing types used in windows and curtain walls in commercial buildings. The figures are for the center of the glass only; the characteristics of the frame must be included to obtain performance information on the whole window assembly. The darker arrows indicate the total admitted and total rejected solar energy. The lighter arrows indicate the amount of transmitted and reflected daylight. Daylight that is neither transmitted nor reflected is absorbed.

ABBREVIATIONS

SHGC: solar heat gain coefficient; SC: shading coefficient; VT: visible transmittance

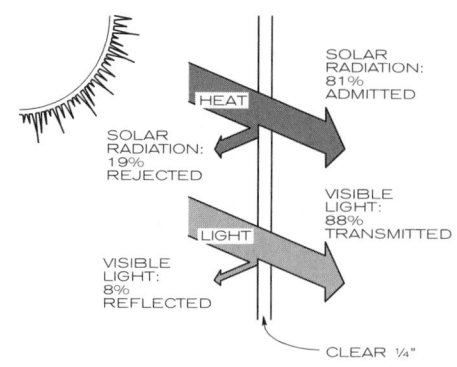

NOTE
U-value=1.09; SHGC=0.81; sc=0.94; VT=0.88

SINGLE GLAZING—CLEAR GLASS

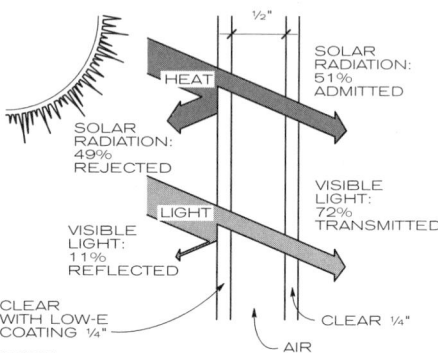

NOTE
U-value=0.45; SHGC=0.70; SC=0.81; VT=0.78

DOUBLE GLAZING—CLEAR GLASS

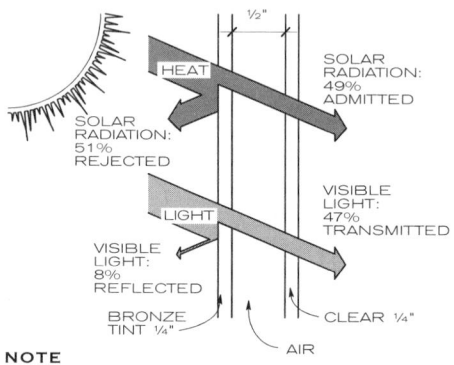

NOTE
U-value=0.48; SHGC=0.49; SC=0.57; VT=0.47

DOUBLE GLAZING—BRONZE TINT

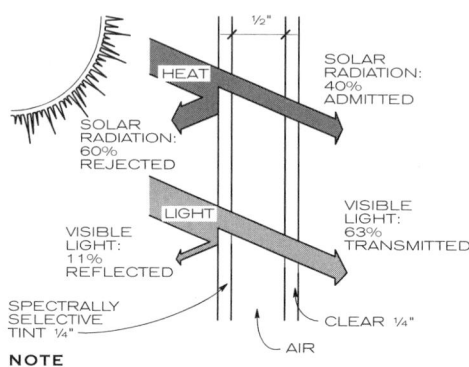

NOTE
U-value=0.48; SHGC=0.40; SC=0.46; VT=0.63

DOUBLE GLAZING—SPECTRALLY SELECTIVE TINT

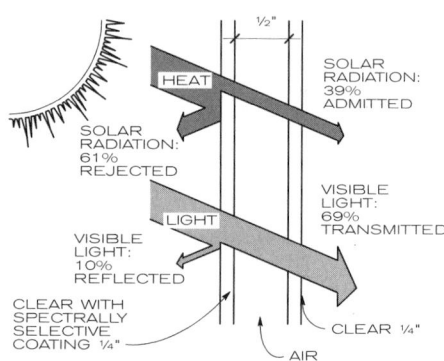

NOTE
U-value=0.31; SHGC=0.51; SC=0.59; VT=0.72

DOUBLE GLAZING—CLEAR GLASS WITH LOW-E COATING

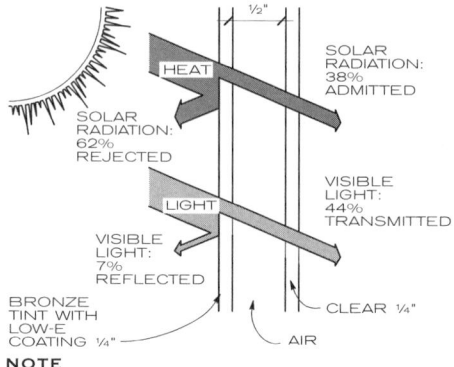

NOTE
U-value=0.31; SHGC=0.38; SC=0.44; VT=0.44

DOUBLE GLAZING—BRONZE TINT WITH LOW-E COATING

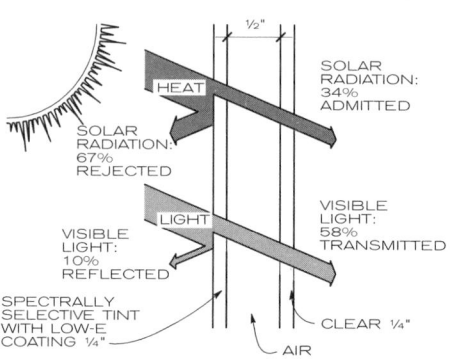

NOTE
U-value=0.31; SHGC=0.34; SC=0.39; VT=0.58

DOUBLE GLAZING—SPECTRALLY SELECTIVE TINT AND LOW-E COATING

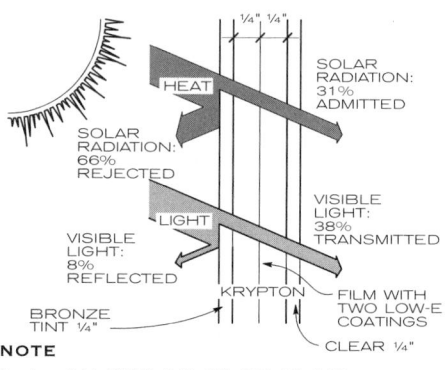

NOTE
U-value=0.29; SHGC=0.39; SC=0.46; VT=0.69

DOUBLE GLAZING—CLEAR GLASS WITH SPECTRALLY SELECTIVE COATING

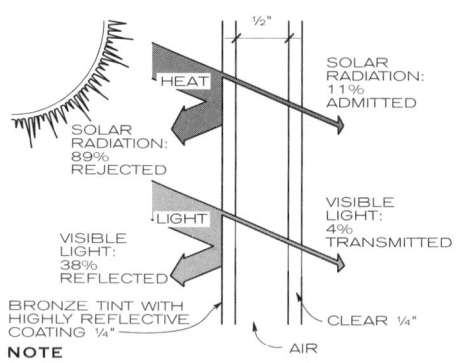

NOTE
U-value=0.48; SHGC=0.11; SC=0.13; VT=0.04

DOUBLE GLAZING—BRONZE TINT WITH HIGHLY REFLECTIVE COATING

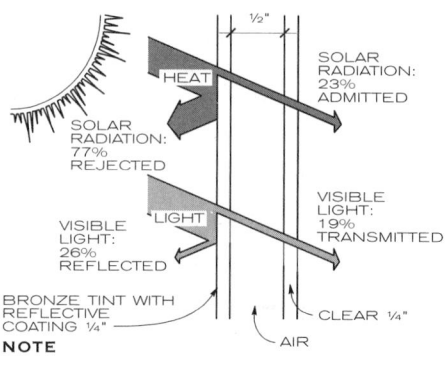

NOTE
U-value=0.48; SHGC=0.23; SC=0.27; VT=0.19

DOUBLE GLAZING—BRONZE TINT WITH REFLECTIVE COATING

NOTE
U-value=0.14; SHGC=0.31; SC=0.36; VT=0.38

TRIPLE GLAZING—BRONZE TINT AND TWO LOW-E COATINGS ON FILM + CLEAR

PERFORMANCE OF 1/4-IN. THICK GLASS IN WINDOWS AND CURTAIN WALLS FOR COMMERCIAL BUILDINGS

John Carmody, University of Minnesota; Minneapolis, Minnesota
Stephen Selkowitz, Lawrence Berkeley National Laboratory; Berkeley, California

WINDOWS

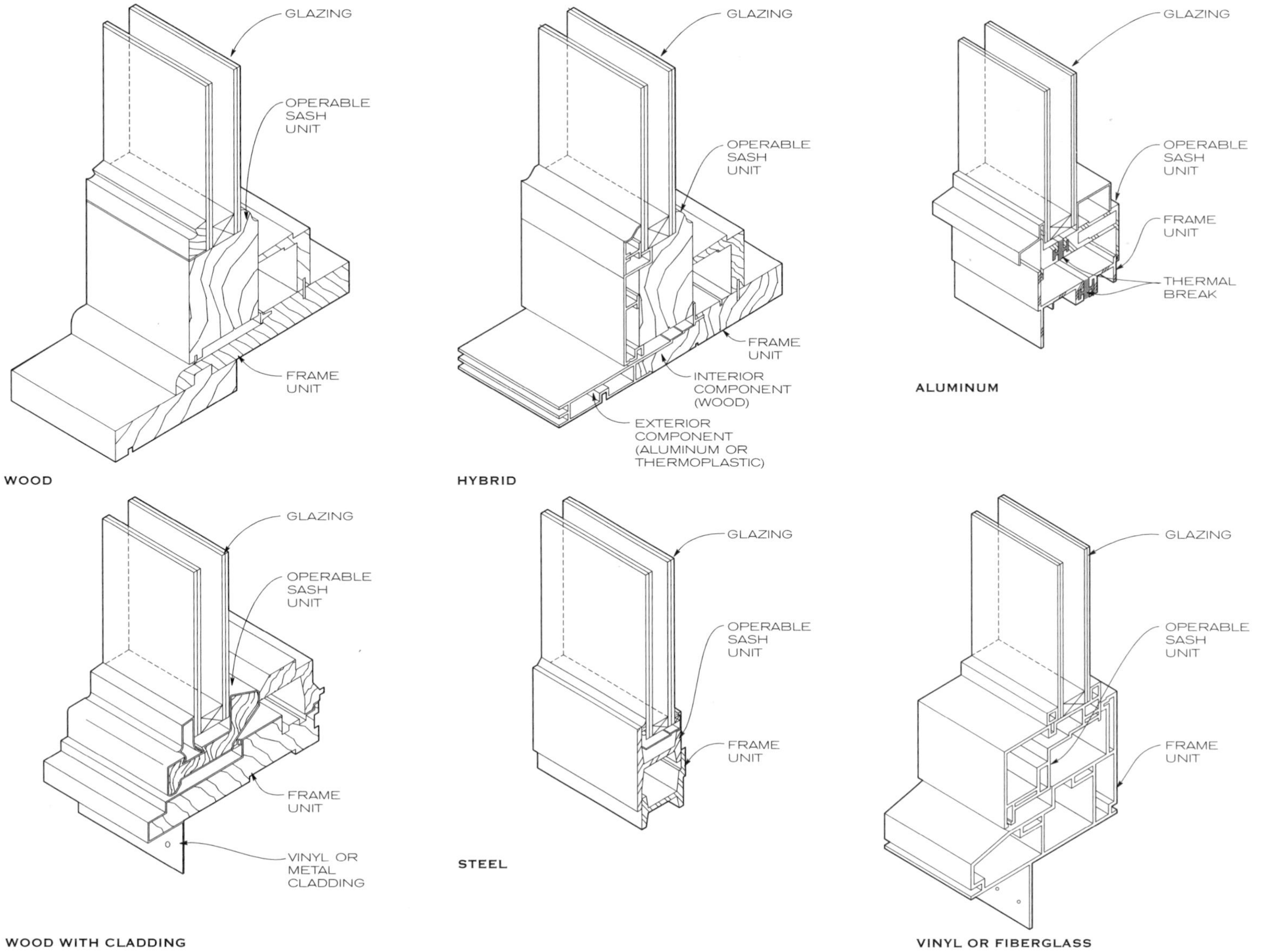

GLAZING

OPERABLE SASH UNIT

FRAME UNIT

WOOD

GLAZING

OPERABLE SASH UNIT

FRAME UNIT

INTERIOR COMPONENT (WOOD)

EXTERIOR COMPONENT (ALUMINUM OR THERMOPLASTIC)

HYBRID

GLAZING

OPERABLE SASH UNIT

FRAME UNIT

THERMAL BREAK

ALUMINUM

GLAZING

OPERABLE SASH UNIT

FRAME UNIT

VINYL OR METAL CLADDING

WOOD WITH CLADDING

GLAZING

OPERABLE SASH UNIT

FRAME UNIT

STEEL

GLAZING

OPERABLE SASH UNIT

FRAME UNIT

VINYL OR FIBERGLASS

WINDOW FRAME DETAILS

WINDOW FRAME TYPES

FRAME TYPE	CHARACTERISTICS	MAINTENANCE	FINISHES	HEAT TRANSFERENCE	SUSTAINABILITY	NOTES
Wood	Solid members; ease of milling into complex shapes; attractive and traditional appearance U-factor: 0.3–0.5	Rot prevention: refinish in 5 to 10-year cycle or permanent finish	Oil or latex paint, stains, oils, or varnishes; preservatives; polyurethane resin coatings; prefinished or site finished	Low	Renewable resource; requires high-quality solid stock	Traditional and typical material; variety of species available; easy repair
Wood with cladding	Metal- or plastic-clad wood U-factor for vinyl clad: 0.3–0.5; for metal clad: 0.4–0.6	Minimal	See metal and plastic frames	Low with vinyl cladding, slightly higher with metal	Use of less desirable wood materials; salvageable cladding	Wood for stability/strength, cladding for maintenance
Hybrids	Wood interior, metal or plastic exterior U-factor for vinyl/wood: 0.3–0.5; for metal/wood: 0.4–0.6	See wood, metal, and plastic categories	See other categories	Low with vinyl/wood hybrid, slightly higher with metal/wood hybrid	Use of lower quantities of any one material	Good interior look with good exterior performance and low maintenance
Steel	Thin bar/ angle steel profiles; cast, extruded, forged U-factor: similar to that of aluminum	Rust prevention: refinish in 5 to 10-year cycle or permanent finish	Galvanizing, zinc-phosphate coatings; primed; painted; factory finishes: baked enamel, fluoropolymer, polyurethane coatings	High, unless thermal break is installed	Non-renewable, salvageable	High strength/smallest frame profiles of all types; stainless steel available but expensive
Aluminum	Box profiles; extrusions; lightweight U-factor: 1.0 (with thermal break), 1.9–2.2 (without thermal break)	Minimal	Natural; factory-applied: baked enamel, epoxy, anodized, electrostatic (powder), fluoropolymer coatings	High unless thermal break is installed	Non-renewable, salvageable	High strength, no maintenance
Vinyl (PVC)	High impact resistance; box profiles; multi-chambered extrusions U-factor for hollow: 0.3–0.5; for insulated: 0.2–0.4	Minimal	Integral when fabricated (limited colors)	Low	Non-renewable, petroleum-based	UV/sun protection from discoloration may be required; salt air and acid resistant
Fiberglass	Box profiles, polymer-based thermoplastic; dimensionally stable U-factor for hollow: 0.3–0.5; for insulated: 0.2–0.4	Minimal	Integral when fabricated	Low	Spun glass in resin binders	More expensive but more structurally stable than vinyl

John Carmody, University of Minnesota; Minneapolis, Minnesota
Stephen Selkowitz, Lawrence Berkeley National Laboratory; Berkeley, California

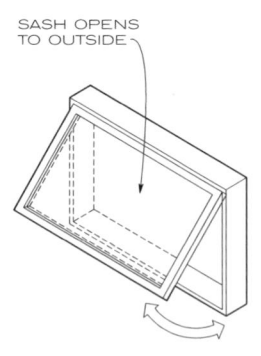

AWNING/PROJECTED

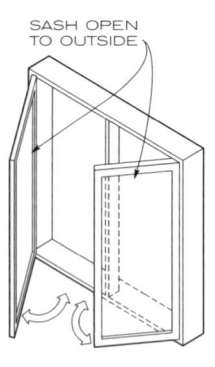

DOUBLE
CASEMENT/PROJECTED

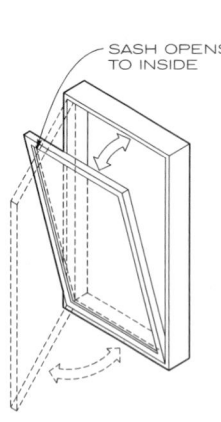

DUAL ACTION

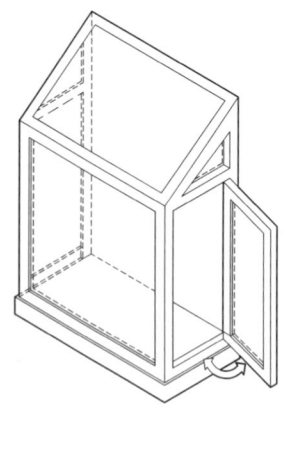

GREENHOUSE

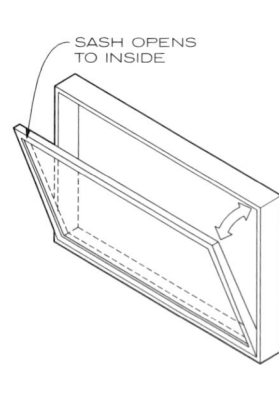

HOPPER

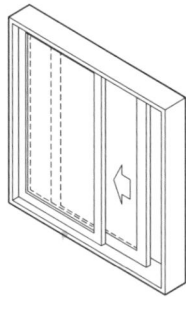

HORIZONTAL SLIDER

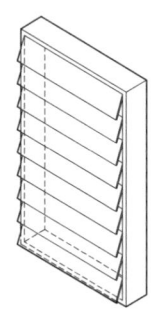

JALOUSIE

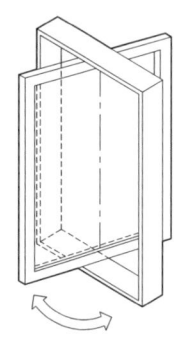

VERTICALLY PIVOTED

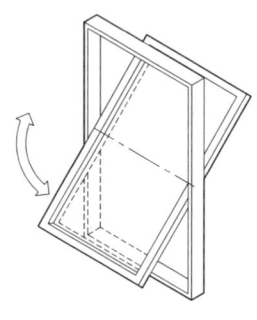

HORIZONTALLY PIVOTED

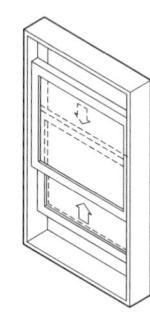

VERTICAL SLIDING
(SINGLE- AND
DOUBLE-HUNG)

WINDOW OPERATION TYPES

CHARACTERISTICS OF WINDOW OPERATION TYPES

OPERATION TYPE	DIRECTION	SCREEN LOCATION	MAXIMUM OPENING (%)	WEATHER PROTECTION (WHEN OPEN)	EGRESS (CLEAR OPENING SIZE GOVERNS)	CLEANABILITY (EXTERIOR FROM INTERIOR)	NOTES
Awning/projected	Swings outward from hinge or pivot at top	Interior	100	Limited	Not possible without special hardware	Difficult	Not for use adjacent to walkways
Casement/projected	Swings outward or inward from a hinge or pivot on the side	Interior or exterior	100	Poor (wind-buffeting)	Good	Single units are difficult, paired windows easier	When outswinging, not suitable for use adjacent to walkways
Dual action	Swings inward from hinge or pivot on bottom (hopper for ventilation, casement for cleaning)	Exterior	10 usually (100 when casement)	Good	Good	Easy	
Greenhouse (may be combined with other operation types)	May swing outward but may not be operable	Depends on window operation type	Depends on window operation type	Good	Poor	Difficult	Unit projects from building; primarily residential use
Hopper/projected	Swings inward with hinge or pivot at bottom	Exterior	100	Good with side vents	Not without special hardware	Easy	
Horizontal sliding	Slides sideways with a guide at top and bottom	Exterior	50, for equal-sized sash	Poor	Good	Difficult (easy with tilt-in feature)	Horizontal or square units operate more easily than tall units
Jalousie	Swings outward from pivots on the side	Interior	100	Limited (interior storm windows available)	Poor	Tedious	Translucent/opaque panes provide additional sun-screening; high air leakage
Pivoted/reversible (horizontally and vertically pivoted)	Swings around vertical or horizontal axis	Rare, but special-shaped screens	100	Poor (wind-buffeting)	Poor (size of clear opening restrictions)	Easy	
Vertical sliding (single- and double-hung)	Slides up and down along guide on the side	Exterior	50, for equal-sized sash	Poor (but good with hospital sills)	Good	Difficult (easy with tilt-in feature)	

John Carmody, University of Minnesota; Minneapolis, Minnesota
Stephen Selkowitz, Lawrence Berkeley National Laboratory; Berkeley, California
Daniel F. C. Hayes, AIA; Washington, D.C.

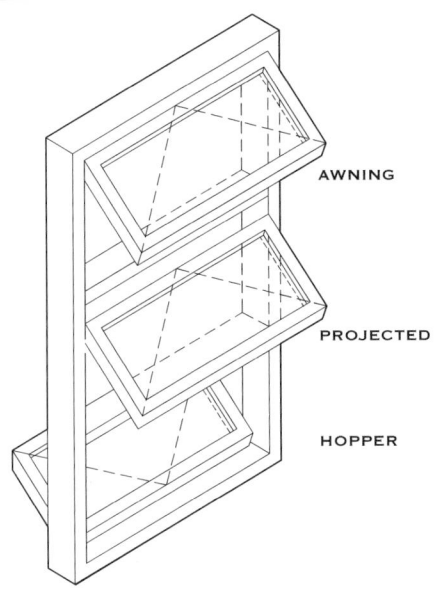

AWNING

PROJECTED

HOPPER

OUTWARD- AND INWARD-SWINGING WINDOW TYPES

DEFINITIONS

AWNING WINDOW: a unit (or series of mechanically interconnected units) that swings outward from top-mounted pivots or hinges.

HOPPER WINDOW: a unit (or series of mechanically interconnected units) that usually swing inward from bottom-mounted pivots or hinges; they may have side-mounted triangular draft barriers.

PROJECTED WINDOW: a window, which operates similarly to awning or hopper windows, in which the hinge or pivot side of the sash frame slides along a track toward the latch side as the window is opened.

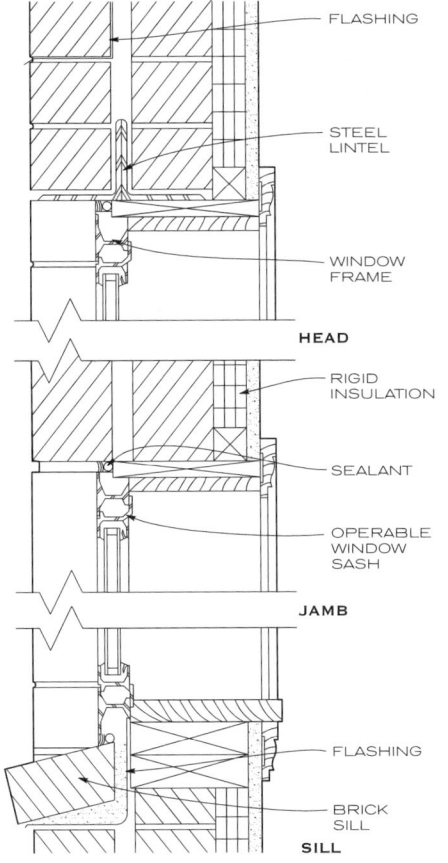

FLASHING

STEEL LINTEL

WINDOW FRAME

HEAD

RIGID INSULATION

SEALANT

OPERABLE WINDOW SASH

JAMB

FLASHING

BRICK SILL

SILL

STEEL PROJECTED WINDOW IN MASONRY CONSTRUCTION

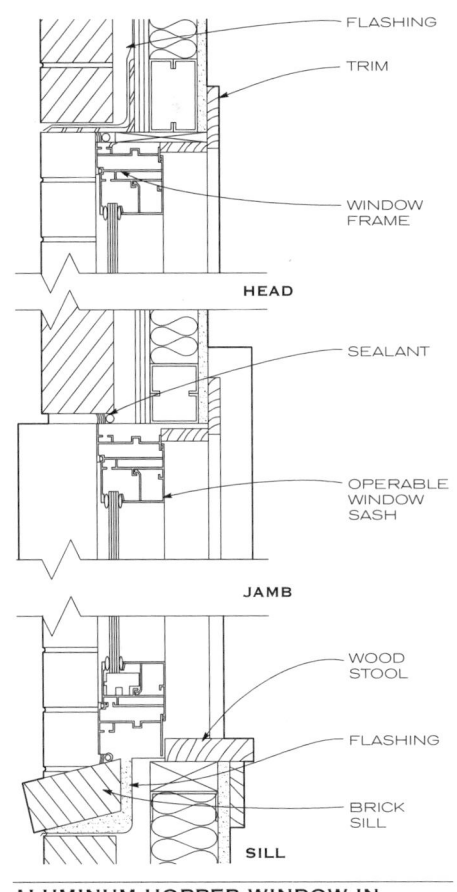

FLASHING

TRIM

WINDOW FRAME

HEAD

SEALANT

OPERABLE WINDOW SASH

JAMB

WOOD STOOL

FLASHING

BRICK SILL

SILL

ALUMINUM HOPPER WINDOW IN BRICK VENEER CONSTRUCTION

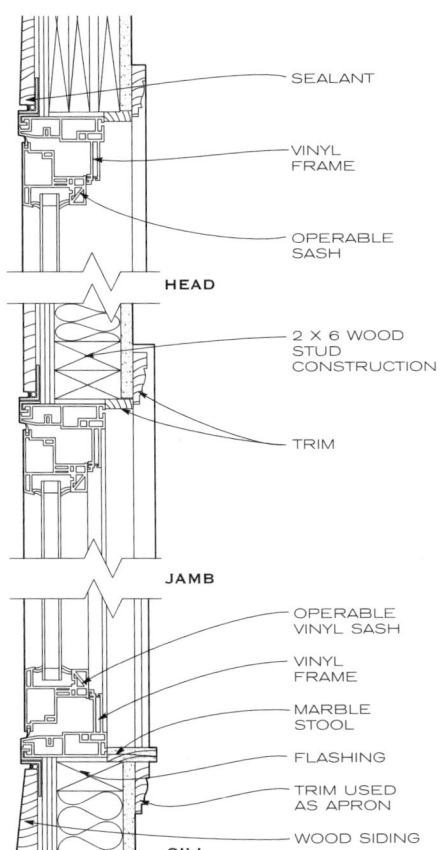

SEALANT

VINYL FRAME

OPERABLE SASH

HEAD

2 X 6 WOOD STUD CONSTRUCTION

TRIM

JAMB

OPERABLE VINYL SASH

VINYL FRAME

MARBLE STOOL

FLASHING

TRIM USED AS APRON

WOOD SIDING

SILL

VINYL WINDOW IN WOOD STUD CONSTRUCTION

AWNING WINDOW INSTALLATION DETAILS

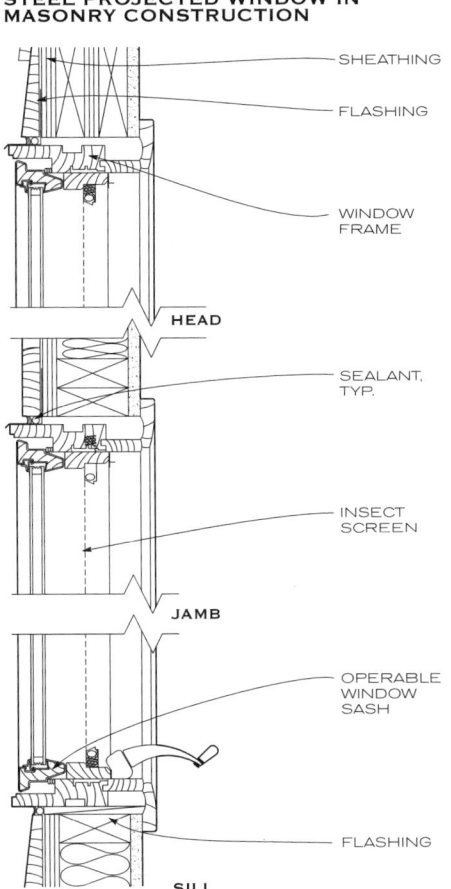

SHEATHING

FLASHING

WINDOW FRAME

HEAD

SEALANT, TYP.

INSECT SCREEN

JAMB

OPERABLE WINDOW SASH

FLASHING

SILL

METAL-CLAD WOOD WINDOW IN WOOD CONSTRUCTION

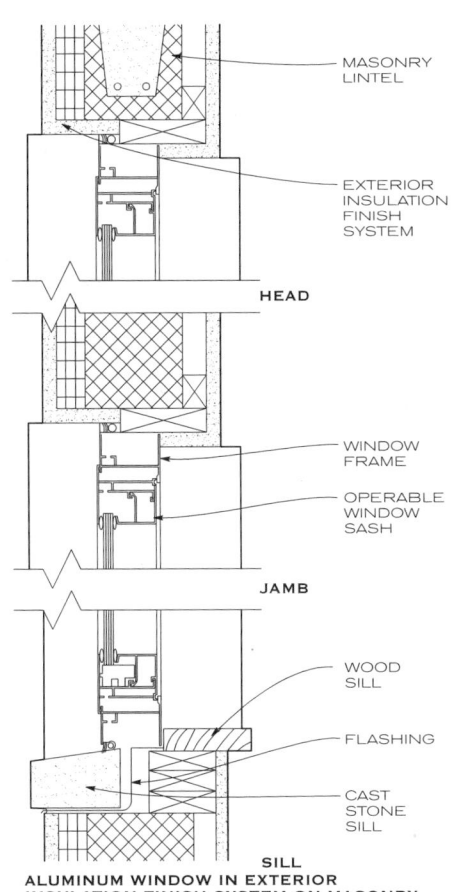

MASONRY LINTEL

EXTERIOR INSULATION FINISH SYSTEM

HEAD

WINDOW FRAME

OPERABLE WINDOW SASH

JAMB

WOOD SILL

FLASHING

CAST STONE SILL

SILL

ALUMINUM WINDOW IN EXTERIOR INSULATION FINISH SYSTEM ON MASONRY

Daniel F. C. Hayes, AIA; Washington, D.C.

DEFINITIONS

CASEMENT WINDOW: a window unit or pair that operates like a door, either on hinges or pivots attached to the jamb or by sliding along tracks at the head and sill.

CREMO(R)NE BOLT: an exposed or concealed fastening mechanism composed of sill and head bolts and strikes connected by rods to a centrally mounted turn-knob device.

FRENCH WINDOW: a pair of tall casements that may serve as a door onto a balcony, porch, or terrace.

LEVER OPERATOR: a gearless mechanism in which a rod sliding through a clasp positions and secures the sash.

OPERATING HARDWARE: hardware used to work a window, including stays, lever operators, roto-operators, and cremo(r)ne bolts.

PIVOT WINDOW: a unit with sash that rotate either vertically or horizontally around center-mounted pivots.

ROTO-OPERATOR: a geared crank-and-worm drive mechanism that positions and secures the sash.

STAY: a bar that holds the sash open in various positions.

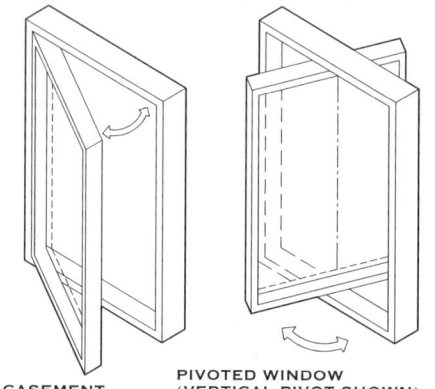

CASEMENT   PIVOTED WINDOW
             (VERTICAL PIVOT SHOWN)

CASEMENT AND PIVOT WINDOWS

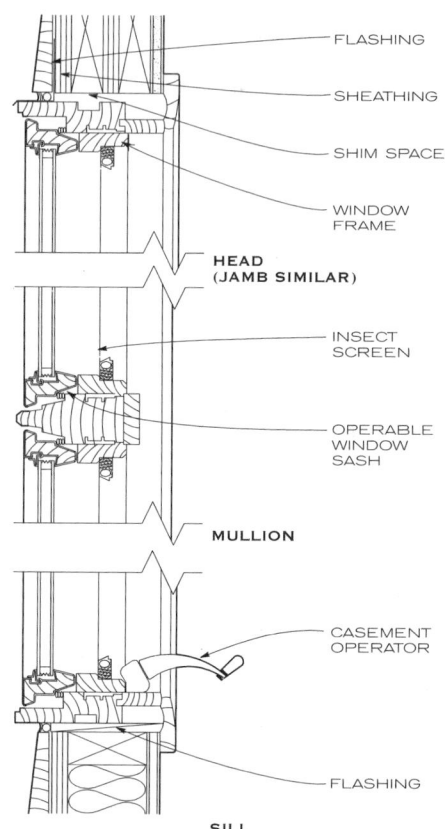

HEAD
(JAMB SIMILAR)

MULLION

SILL

**VINYL-CLAD WOOD IN
WOOD CONSTRUCTION**

CASEMENT WINDOW INSTALLATION DETAILS

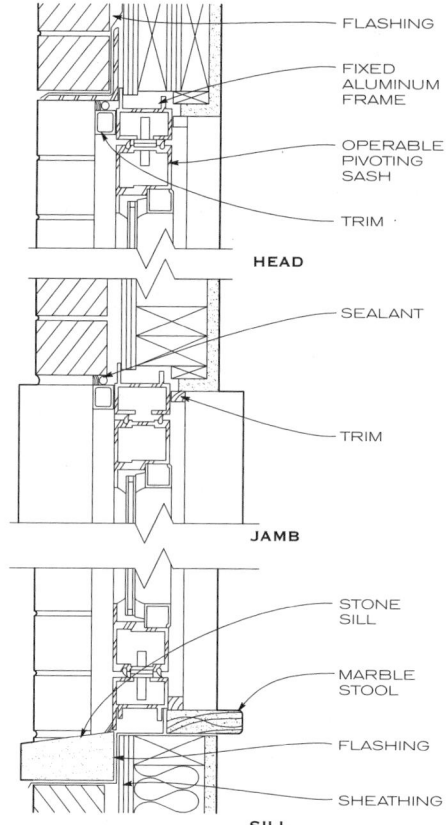

HEAD

JAMB

SILL

**VERTICALLY PIVOTED ALUMINUM WINDOW
IN BRICK VENEER CONSTRUCTION**

PIVOT WINDOW INSTALLATION DETAILS

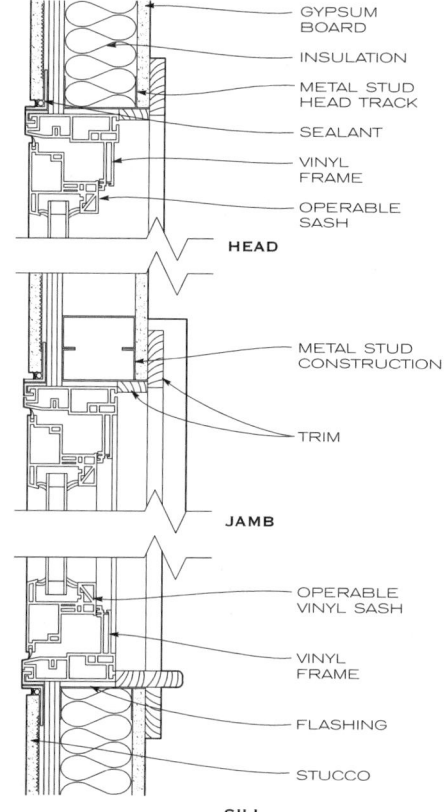

HEAD

JAMB

SILL

**VINYL WINDOW IN STUCCO AND
METAL STUD CONSTRUCTION**

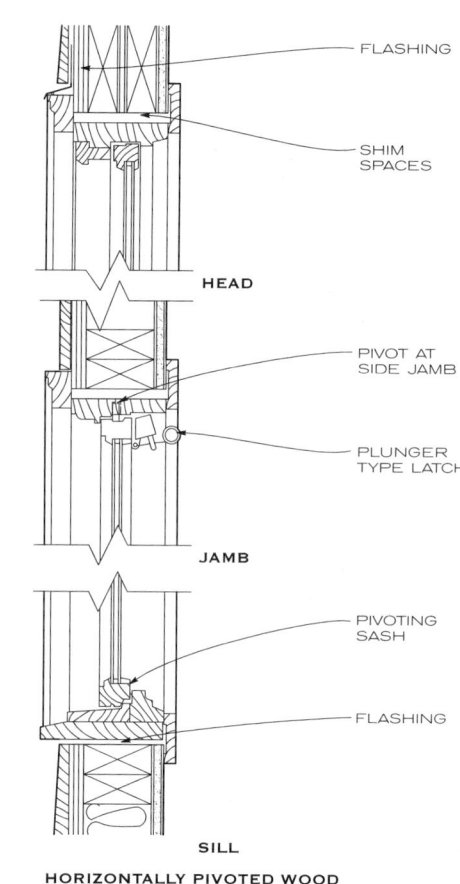

HEAD

JAMB

SILL

**HORIZONTALLY PIVOTED WOOD
WINDOW IN WOOD CONSTRUCTION**

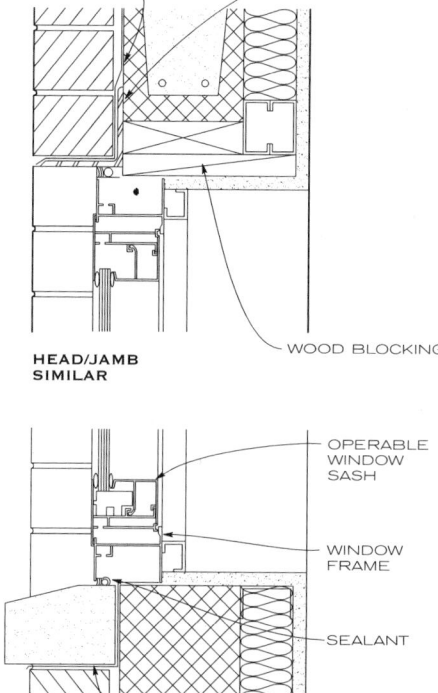

HEAD/JAMB
SIMILAR

SILL

**ALUMINUM WINDOW IN MULTIWYTHE
MASONRY CONSTRUCTION**

Daniel F. C. Hayes, AIA; Washington, D.C.

WINDOWS

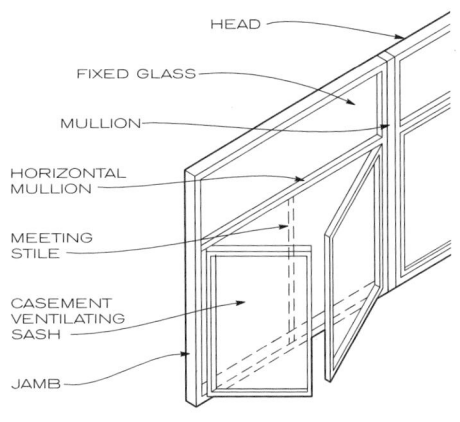

TYPICAL CASEMENT WINDOW

Labels: HEAD, FIXED GLASS, MULLION, HORIZONTAL MULLION, MEETING STILE, CASEMENT VENTILATING SASH, JAMB

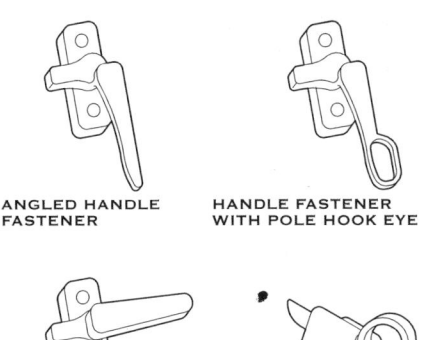

ANGLED HANDLE FASTENER

HANDLE FASTENER WITH POLE HOOK EYE

STRAIGHT HANDLE FASTENER

SPRING CATCH WITH POLE HOOK EYE

FASTENER TYPES

NOTES

1. Window sizes and dimensioning methods are not uniform for all manufacturers. Some manufacturers have no stock sizes, producing only custom work. Check with local suppliers for details.
2. In general, heavier grades of windows offer greater configuration flexibility. Larger operating sash can be produced with heavier members, allowing fixed lights shown for taller steel sash to be avoided, if desired.
3. Insect screens are necessarily installed on the interior and must be taken into account when selecting hardware.
4. The raindrip indicated on the horizontal mullion may be required at ventilating heads if sash are placed flush with the exterior face of the wall.
5. Drawings or specifications must contain the following information: window size and location; installation details for sills, stools, flashing, sealing, and anchors; sash material and finish; glazing material; glazing method (tape, putty, or bead, inside or outside); weatherstripping, insect screen material, and hardware.

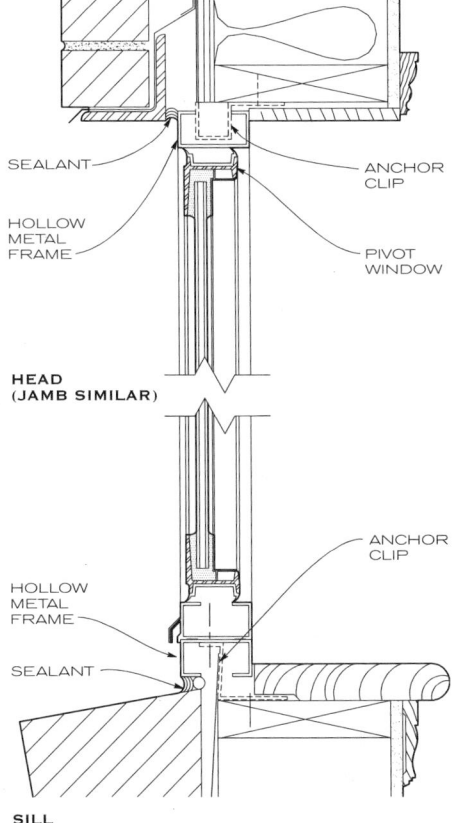

HEAD (JAMB SIMILAR)

Labels: SEALANT, HOLLOW METAL FRAME, ANCHOR CLIP, PIVOT WINDOW, HOLLOW METAL FRAME, ANCHOR CLIP, SEALANT

SILL

REVERSIBLE PIVOT FRAMING SECTION

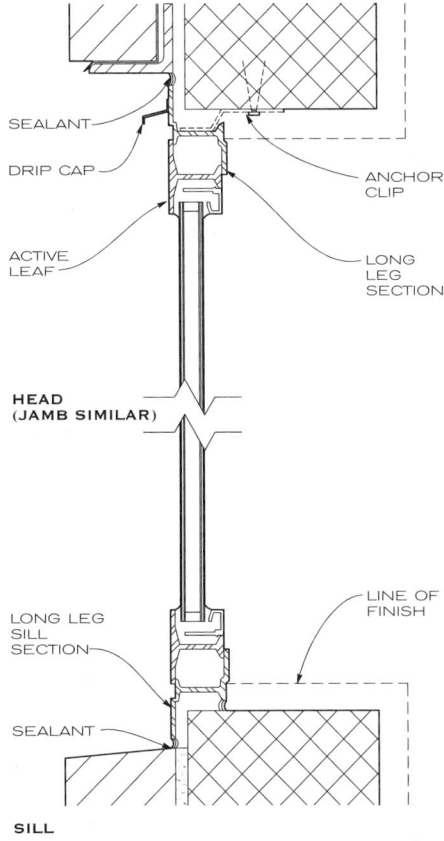

HEAD (JAMB SIMILAR)

Labels: SEALANT, DRIP CAP, ACTIVE LEAF, ANCHOR CLIP, LONG LEG SECTION, LONG LEG SILL SECTION, LINE OF FINISH, SEALANT

SILL

LONG LEG FRAMING SECTION

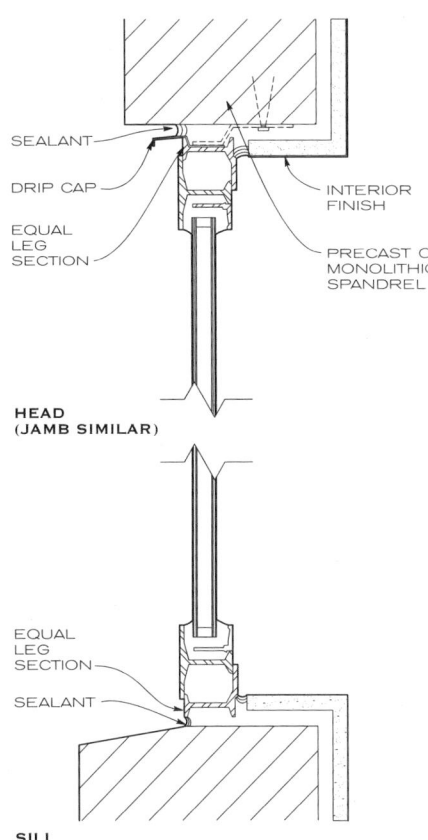

HEAD (JAMB SIMILAR)

Labels: SEALANT, DRIP CAP, EQUAL LEG SECTION, INTERIOR FINISH, PRECAST OR MONOLITHIC SPANDREL, EQUAL LEG SECTION, SEALANT

SILL

EQUAL LEG FRAMING SECTION

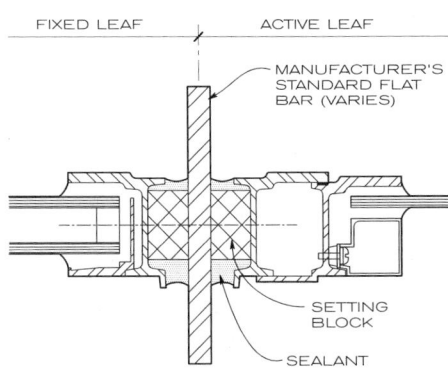

Labels: FIXED LEAF, ACTIVE LEAF, MANUFACTURER'S STANDARD FLAT BAR (VARIES), SETTING BLOCK, SEALANT

NOTE

Alternate glazing types are shown for each leaf.

JAMB REINFORCING: STEEL BAR TYPE

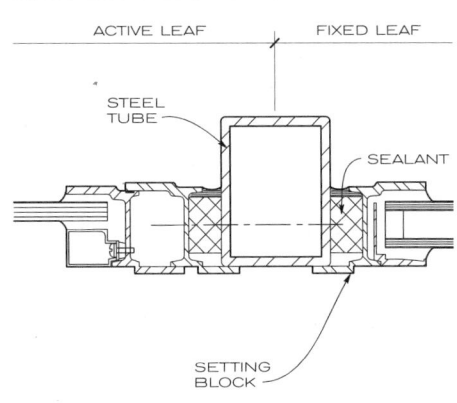

Labels: ACTIVE LEAF, FIXED LEAF, STEEL TUBE, SEALANT, SETTING BLOCK

JAMB REINFORCING: STEEL TUBE TYPE

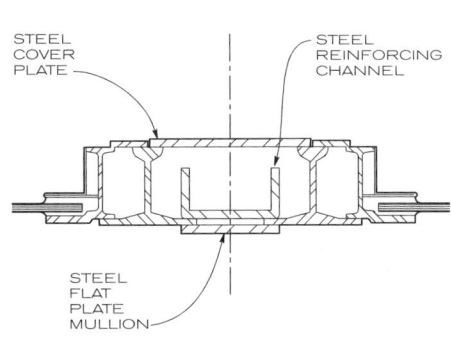

Labels: STEEL COVER PLATE, STEEL REINFORCING CHANNEL, STEEL FLAT PLATE MULLION

TYPICAL MULLION BETWEEN UNITS IN A MULTIPLE RUN

Rippeteau Rollins Architecture + Design; Washington, D.C.

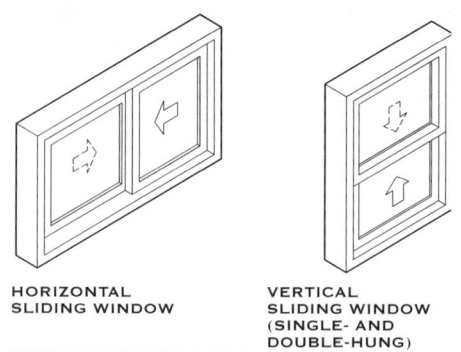

HORIZONTAL SLIDING WINDOW

VERTICAL SLIDING WINDOW (SINGLE- AND DOUBLE-HUNG)

SLIDING WINDOW TYPES

DEFINITIONS

DOUBLE-HUNG WINDOW: multiple operating sash in one unit (also comes as triple-hung).

HOSPITAL SILL: a raised stool that allows the meeting rails to be separated for ventilation while the head and sill rails remain sealed to weather penetration.

HORIZONTAL SLIDING WINDOW: a unit having at least two sash, one or more of which slides along horizontal tracks at the top and bottom of the frame.

POCKET COVER: a part of the jamb casing that can be removed to reach the weights or balances for maintenance.

SASH CORD: a rope or chain that connects the sash weight to the sash.

SASH RIBBON: a metal strip that connects the sash with either weights or spring balances.

SASH WEIGHT: a cast-iron or lead cylindrical counterweight.

SINGLE-HUNG WINDOW: a pair of sash, only one of which operates (by vertically sliding).

SPRING BALANCE: a spring-loaded mechanism used in place of a counterweight.

VERTICAL SLIDING WINDOW: a unit with sash that slide vertically in jamb-mounted tracks. Weights, springs, or friction-resistant jambs counterbalancing gravity or mechanical catches embedded in the jamb hold the sash open. The single-, double-, or triple-operating sash of these windows may stack against each other or, when full ventilation is required, be recessed in pockets above or below the window.

Wood window in brick veneer construction

Labels: PLASTER, FLASHING, SHEATHING, SEALANT, TRIM (VARIES) — **HEAD**

SEALANT, PARTING BEAD, INSULATING GLASS — **JAMB**

WOOD SILL, SHEATHING, INSULATION, BRICK SILL, FLASHING — **SILL**

WOOD WINDOW IN BRICK VENEER CONSTRUCTION

Aluminum window in masonry construction

Labels: CMU, BRICK, FLASHING, ALUMINUM FRAME WITH THERMAL BREAK, EXTERIOR TRIM — **HEAD**

SEALANT AT TRIM (TYP.), DOUBLE-HUNG SASH — **JAMB**

BRICK SILL, WOOD STOOL — **SILL**

ALUMINUM WINDOW IN MASONRY CONSTRUCTION

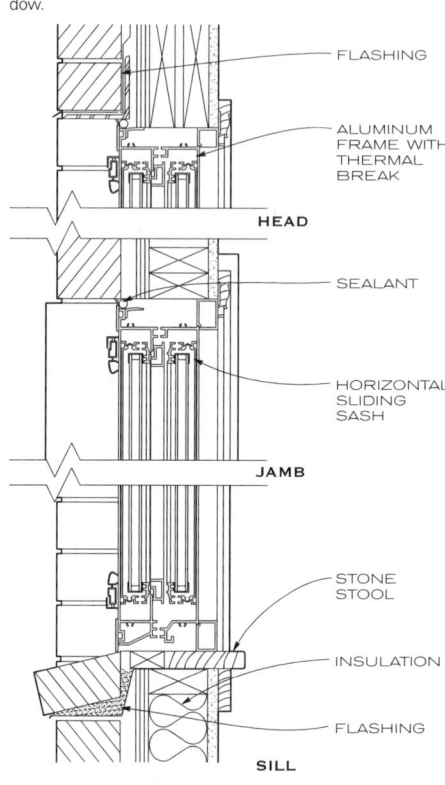

Labels: FLASHING, ALUMINUM FRAME WITH THERMAL BREAK — **HEAD**

SEALANT, HORIZONTAL SLIDING SASH — **JAMB**

STONE STOOL, INSULATION, FLASHING — **SILL**

ALUMINUM WINDOW IN BRICK VENEER CONSTRUCTION

Vinyl window in masonry construction

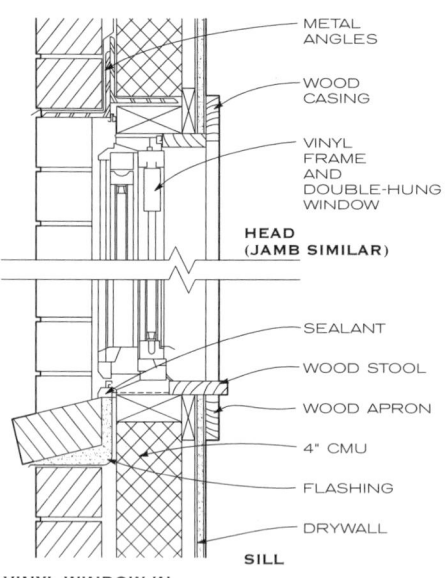

Labels: METAL ANGLES, WOOD CASING, VINYL FRAME AND DOUBLE-HUNG WINDOW — **HEAD (JAMB SIMILAR)**

SEALANT, WOOD STOOL, WOOD APRON, 4" CMU, FLASHING, DRYWALL — **SILL**

VINYL WINDOW IN MASONRY CONTRUCTION

Double-hung vinyl-clad window in wood frame construction

Labels: PLYWOOD SIDING AND SHEATHING, FLASHING (TURN UP 4" MIN. ON INSIDE FACE), TRIM, SHIM SPACE, INSULATING GLASS — **HEAD (JAMB SIMILAR)**

WEATHER STRIPPING, VINYL-CLAD WOOD SILL, FLASHING, INSULATION — **SILL**

DOUBLE-HUNG VINYL-CLAD WINDOW IN WOOD FRAME CONTRUCTION

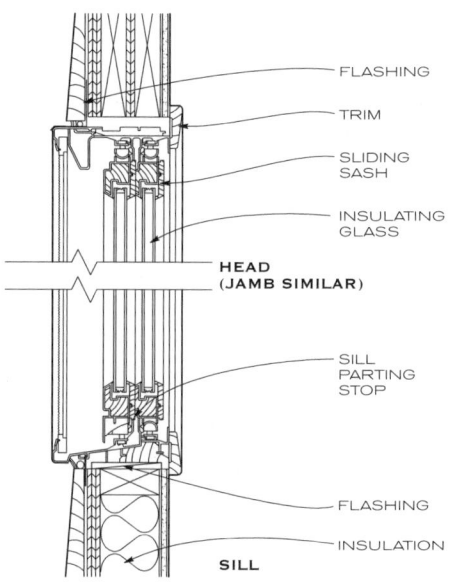

Labels: FLASHING, TRIM, SLIDING SASH, INSULATING GLASS — **HEAD (JAMB SIMILAR)**

SILL PARTING STOP, FLASHING, INSULATION — **SILL**

DOUBLE-HUNG VINYL-CLAD WINDOW IN WOOD FRAME CONTRUCTION

VERTICAL SLIDING (DOUBLE-HUNG) WINDOWS

HORIZONTAL SLIDING WINDOWS

Daniel F. C. Hayes, AIA; Washington, D.C.

  WINDOWS

DEFINITION OF GLASS

Glass is a hard, brittle amorphous substance made by melting silica (sometimes combined with oxides of boron or phosphorus) with certain basic oxides (notably sodium, potassium, calcium, magnesium, and lead) to produce annealed flat glass by a controlled cooling process. Most glasses soften at 932 to 2012°F (500 to 1100°C). The brittleness of glass is such that minute surface scratches in manufacturing greatly reduce its strength.

INDUSTRY QUALITY STANDARDS

ASTM Standard C1036: Specification for Flat Glass.

ASTM Standard C1048: Specification for Heat-treated Flat Glass—Kind HS, Kind FT Coated and Uncoated Glass.

UL Standard 752: Bullet-resistive Material.

UL Standard 972: Burglary-resistive Glazing Material.

AAMA Standard No. 12: Structural Properties of Glass, Aluminum Curtain Wall Series.

ASTM Standard E1300: Practice for Determining the Minimum Thickness of Annealed Glass Required to Resist a Specified Load.

CPSC Standard 16CFR 1201: Standard on Architectural Glazing Materials.

ANSI Z97.1: establishes standards for testing safety glazing material.

ASTM C1172: Specification for Laminated Architectural Flat Glass.

NOTE

Consult glass manufacturers for current information because processes, qualities, finishes, colors, sizes, thickness, and limitations are revised continually. The following information represents one or more manufacturers' guidelines.

BASIC TYPES OF CLEAR GLASS

SHEET GLASS

Sheet glass is manufactured by a horizontal flat or vertical draw process, then annealed slowly to produce a natural flat fired, high gloss surface. It generally is used in residential and industrial applications. Because it is not mechanically polished, inherent surface waves are noticeable in sizes larger than 4 sq ft. For minimum distortion, larger sizes are installed with the wave running horizontally. The width is listed first when specifying.

Sheet glass for architectural applications is either single strength (0.101 in. thick) or double strength (0.134 in. thick). Very little glass is produced in the United States by this process; almost all sheet glass is produced by the float process.

FLOAT GLASS

Generally accepted as the successor to polished plate glass, float glass has become the quality standard of the glass industry. It is manufactured by floating molten glass on a surface of molten tin, then annealing it slowly to produce a transparent flat glass, thus eliminating grinding and polishing.

This process produces a glass with very uniform thickness and flatness, making it suitable for applications requiring excellent optical properties, such as architectural windows, mirrors, and specialty applications. It is available in thicknesses ranging from $1/8$ to $7/8$ in. Float glass is made to the specification requirements of ASTM C1036, and its minimum thickness to resist wind load is established using ASTM E1300.

PLATE GLASS

Transparent flat glass is ground and polished after rolling to make plate glass. Cylindrical and conical shapes can be bent to a desired curvature (within limits). Only glass for specialty applications is produced by this method; it is not produced for widespread use in architectural applications.

VARIATIONS OF BASIC GLASS TYPES

PATTERNED GLASS

Patterned glass is known also as rolled or figured glass. It is made by passing molten glass through rollers that are etched to produce the design. Designs include flutes, ribs, grids, and other regular and random patterns, which provide translucency and a degree of obscurity. Usually only one side of the glass is imprinted with a pattern. Patterned glass is available in thicknesses of $1/8$, $3/16$, and $7/32$ in.

WIRE GLASS

Wire glass is available as clear polished glass or in various patterns such as square welded mesh, diamond welded mesh, and linear parallel wires. Some distortion, wire discoloration, and misalignment are inherent. Some $1/4$ in. wired glass products are recognized as certified safety glazing materials for use in hazardous locations (for example, fire-rated windows, doors, and skylights). For applicable fire and safety codes that govern their use, refer to ANSI Z97.1.

CATHEDRAL GLASS

Cathedral glass is known also as art glass, stained glass, or opalescent glass. It is produced in many colors, textures, and patterns. Cathedral glass is usually $1/8$ in. thick and is used primarily in decorating leaded glass windows. Specialty firms usually contract this type of glass.

OBSCURE GLASS

Obscure glass is used to obscure a view or create a design. The entire surface on one or both sides of the glass can be sandblasted, acid etched, or both. When a glass surface is altered by any of these methods, the glass is weakened and may be difficult to clean.

STRENGTHENED GLASS

Glass can be strengthened by either a controlled heating and cooling process or by immersion in a chemical bath. Both processes have glass thickness, size, and use restrictions that should be verified.

HEAT-TREATED GLASS

Heat-strengthened (Kind HS) and tempered (Kind FT) glass are produced by reheating annealed float glass close to its softening point and then rapidly quenching (cooling) it with high velocity blasts of air. Both types have greatly increased mechanical strength and resistance to thermal stresses. Before it is heat-treated, the glass must be fabricated to its exact size and shape (including any holes), because neither type of glass can be altered after heat treatment.

Most manufacturers heat-treat the glass using a horizontal process that can introduce warpage, kinks, and bowing into the finished product, which may create aesthetic or technical concerns. A vertical process may still be available that produces tong marks or depressions into the glass surface near the suspended edge. The heat treatment quenching pattern on the surface of the glass can become visible as a pattern of light and dark areas at certain oblique viewing angles and with polarized light. This effect can be more pronounced with thicker glass and may be an aesthetic consideration. Refer to ASTM C1048 for allowable tolerances and other properties.

Heat-strengthened glass is generally two to three times stronger than annealed glass. It cannot be cut, drilled, or altered after fabrication. Unlike tempered glass, it breaks into large, sharp shards similar to broken annealed glass. Heat-strengthened glass is not acceptable for safety glazing applications.

TEMPERED GLASS

Tempered glass is generally four to five times stronger than annealed glass. It breaks into innumerable small, cube-shaped fragments. It cannot be cut, drilled, or altered after fabrication; the precise size required and any special features (such as notches, holes, edge treatments, etc.) must be specified when ordering.

Tempered glass can be used as a safety glazing material provided it complies with the ANSI and CPSC references listed on the following "Glass Products" page under the "Laminated Glass" heading. Tempered glass can be used in insulating and laminated assemblies and in wired, patterned, and coated processes. All float and sheet glass $1/8$ in. or thicker may be tempered.

CHEMICALLY TREATED GLASS

Chemically treated glass is produced by submerging annealed float glass in a bath of molten potassium salts. The larger potassium ions in the bath exchange places with the smaller sodium ions in the glass surface, creating a surface compression layer that strengthens the glass. Chemically treated glass breaks into large, sharp shards similar to broken annealed glass. It does not have the visual distortion that can be caused by a heat-treated strengthening process. At present, chemical strengthening is primarily limited to the glass lights of laminated security glass.

HEAT-ABSORBING OR TINTED GLASS

This type of float glass was developed to help control solar heat and glare in large areas of glass. It is available in blue, bronze, gray, or green and in thicknesses ranging from $1/8$ to $1/2$ in. The glass absorbs a portion of the sun's energy because of its admixture contents and thickness (see graphic); it then dissipates the heat to both the exterior and interior. The exterior glass surface rejects some heat, depending on the sun's position. Heat-absorbing glass has a higher temperature when exposed to the sun than does clear glass; thus the central area expands more than the cooler shaded edges, causing edge tensile stress buildup. When designing heat-absorbing or tinted glass windows, consider the following:

1. To minimize shading problems and tensile stress buildup at the edges, provide conditions in which glass edges warm as rapidly as the exposed glass (for example, framing systems with low heat capacity and minimal glass grip or stops). Structural rubber gaskets can be used.
2. The thicker the glass, the greater the solar energy absorption.
3. Indoor shading devices such as blinds and draperies reflect energy back through the glass, thus increasing the temperature of the glass. Spaces between indoor shading devices and the glass, including ceiling pockets, should be vented adequately. Heating elements always should be located on the interior side of shading devices, directing warm air away from the glass.
4. The glass can be heat-treated to increase its strength and resistance to edge tensile stress buildup.

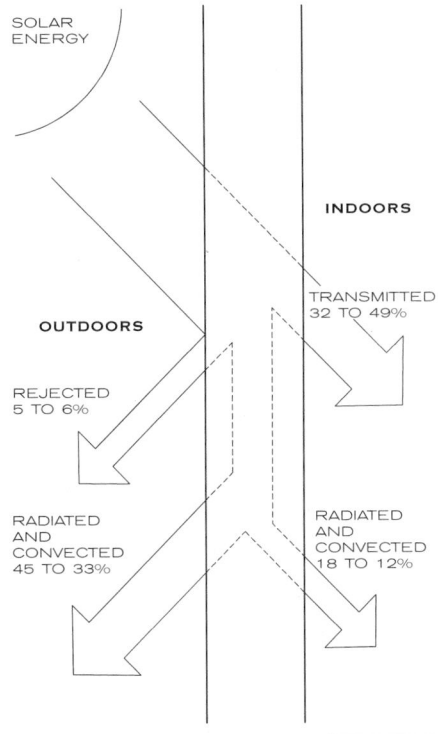

SOLAR PERFORMANCE OF HEAT-ABSORBING OR TINTED GLASS

SPANDREL GLASS

Spandrel glass is available tinted or with reflective, ceramic frit (patterned and solid colors), direct-to-glass polyvinylidene fluoride (Kynar 500 resin) coatings. It can be heat-treated or laminated and is available as insulating glass units. Insulation and vapor retarders can be added to spandrel glass; consult with spandrel glass manufacturers for guidelines.

SOUND CONTROL GLASS

Laminated, insulating, laminated insulating, and double laminated insulating glass products commonly are used for sound control. STC ratings from 31 to 51 are available depending on glass thicknesses, air space size, polyvinyl butyral film thickness, and the number of laminated units used in insulating products.

Thomas F. O'Connor, AIA, FASTM; Smith, Hinchman & Grylls; Detroit, Michigan

GLAZING   ⑧

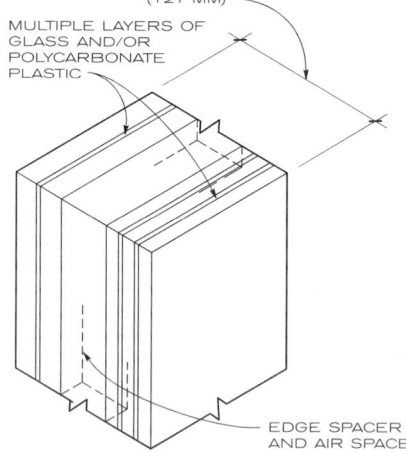

TYPICAL INSULATING OR SPACED CONSTRUCTION SECURITY GLASS PROFILE

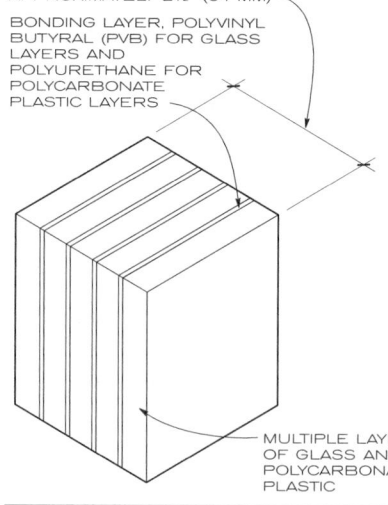

TYPICAL MULTILAYER SECURITY GLASS PROFILE

SECURITY GLASS

Security glass is composed of multiple layers of glass and/or polycarbonate plastic laminated together (under heat and pressure) with a polyvinyl butyral (for glass) or polyurethane plastic (for polycarbonate) film. It is available in multilayer laminated glass, insulating, laminated insulating, and double laminated insulating or spaced configurations, generally in thicknesses from ⅜ in. (10 mm) to 2½ in. (64 mm) as a laminated product and up to about 4¾ in. (121 mm) for insulating and spaced construction products. Bullet-resistant glass should be tested to UL 752 and burglar-resistant to UL 972. Consult manufacturers for blast-resistant glass. Security glass products, depending on type, are subject to size limitations, and some are not recommended for exterior applications; consult with the manufacturer for glazing requirements and restrictions on use.

COATED GLASS

A reflective or low emissivity coating can be applied to the surface of monolithic glass. Generally, only pyrolitically applied "hard" coatings, which have scratch resistance, are used on exposed glass surfaces. During glass manufacture, pyrolitic coatings are sprayed onto the glass before it cools, which integrates them with the glass surface. Magnetically sputtered or "soft" coatings can also be applied to the glass surface but must be protected from the elements as part of an insulating or laminated glass product. The range of coating types, aesthetic appearances, and thermal performance available for pyrolitic coatings is generally less than that available for sputtered coatings.

ULTRACLEAR GLASS

The high clarity and high visible light transmittance that characterize ultraclear glass comes from the special soda lime mixture it is made from, which minimizes the iron content that normally gives a slight greenish color to clear flat glass. Ultraclear glass is generally available in thicknesses from ⅛ in. to ¾ in. (3 mm to 19 mm). It can be heat strengthened, tempered, sand blasted, etched, or assembled into laminated glass. Ultraclear glass is used for commercial display cases, museum cases, display windows, frit-coated spandrel glass, aquariums, mirrors, shelving, security glass, and other uses in which clarity and better color transmittance are required.

LAMINATED GLASS

A tough, clear plastic polyvinyl butyral (PVB) sheet (interlayered), ranging in thickness from 0.015 to 0.090 in. (0.381 to 2.3 mm), is sandwiched, under heat and pressure, between lights of sheet, plate, float, wired, heat-absorbing, tinted, reflective, low emissivity, or heat-treated glass or combinations of each. When laminated glass breaks, the particles tend to adhere to the plastic film. Laminated glass is manufactured to the specification requirements of ASTM C1172. Laminated safety glass should be manufactured to comply with ANSI Z97.1 and CPSC 16CFR 1201.

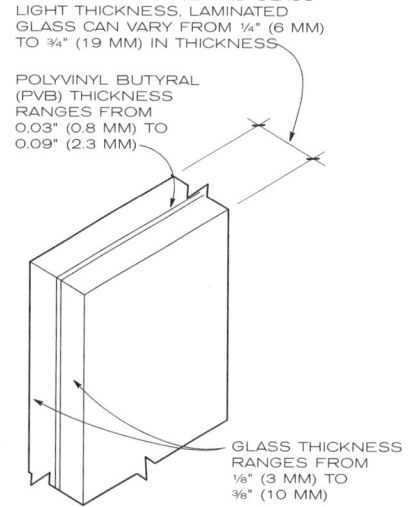

LAMINATED GLASS PROFILE

BENT GLASS

Clear, tinted, ceramic frit-coated spandrel, pyrolitically coated, patterned, laminated, and wire glass are among glass types that can be bent in thicknesses to about 1 in. (25 mm) and to a minimum radius of about 4 in. (102 mm). Sharp angle bends to 90°, edgework, pattern cutting, and tempering (meeting safety glazing standards) and heat-strengthening are also available. Bent glass can be fabricated into insulating glass units. Bent glass tolerances must be compatible with the glazing system. Size, configuration, and product availability vary by fabricator.

PHOTOVOLTAIC GLASS

There are two types of photovoltaic (PV) glass: crystalline silicon sandwiched between two lights of glass and thin-film amorphous silicon applied to an interior facing glass surface. When these arrangements are exposed to sunlight, they generate either DC or AC power, which is transferred by concealed wiring to the building's power system.

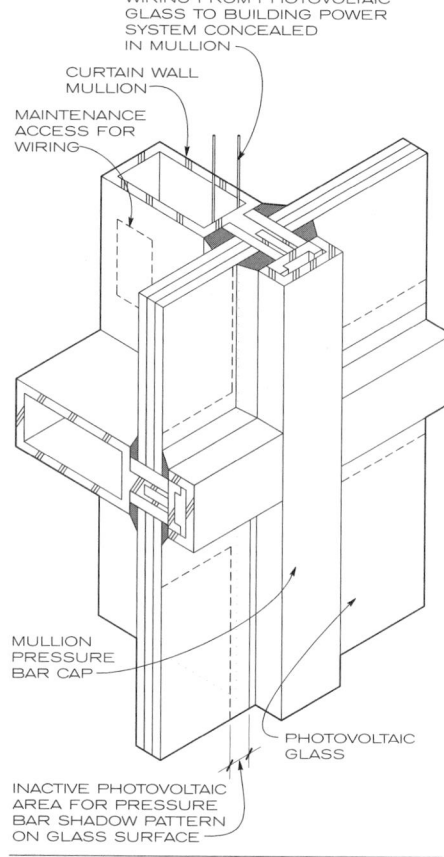

PHOTOVOLTAIC GLASS (IN A PRESSURE BAR FRAMING SYSTEM)

Pressure bar or structural silicone flush glazed curtain walls and skylights, awnings, sunshades, light shelves, and roof panels are some of the systems that can incorporate PV glass. For curtain walls and skylights, the pressure bar type allows easy concealment of the wiring. Shadow patterns from the cap on the PV glass surface must be considered in system design. Flush glazed systems have no shadow patterns, but wiring concealment is more difficult and the PV module on the glass must be kept from reacting with the structural silicone sealant. Both types of PV glass are used for opaque curtain wall spandrel panels and can be used for curtain wall or skylight vision glass if the quality of daylighting and visibility is acceptable. Consult PV glass and metal framing system manufacturers to determine availability, suitability, and cost for a particular application.

DECORATIVE SILK-SCREENED (OR FRIT) GLASS

Annealed clear or tinted glass is washed and ceramic frit paint (in standard or custom color) silk-screened on its surface in a standard or custom pattern or design (such as dots, holes, lines, or a logo) and then dried in an oven. The frit-coated glass is then subjected to very high temperatures in a tempering furnace to fire the ceramic frit permanently to the glass surface. As a result, silk-screened glass will be either heat strengthened or tempered after firing. Reflective and low emissivity coatings can also be applied to the glass surface. Silk-screened glass can be used monolithically or for insulating or laminated glass products.

AVERAGE PERFORMANCE VALUES OF 1/4 IN. (6 MM) UNCOATED GLASS

GLASS TYPE	% TRANSMITTANCE			% REFLECTANCE AVERAGE DAYLIGHT	SHADING COEFFICIENT
	AVERAGE DAYLIGHT	TOTAL SOLAR	ULTRAVIOLET		
Ultraclear	91	89	85	8	1.04
Clear	89–88	78–76	71–62	9–8	0.95–0.94
Clear laminated	86–84	67–64	<1	8–7	0.86–0.83
Green	77–75	42–47	42–30	8–7	0.70–0.67
Blue-green	75–71	49–35	32–28	7	0.72–0.60
Blue	55	47	41	6	0.70
Bronze	55–51	51–48	23–31	6	0.74–0.71
Gray	46–43	49–42	25–32	5–6	0.72–0.66

Thomas F. O'Connor, AIA, FASTM; Smith, Hinchman & Grylls; Detroit, Michigan

GLAZING

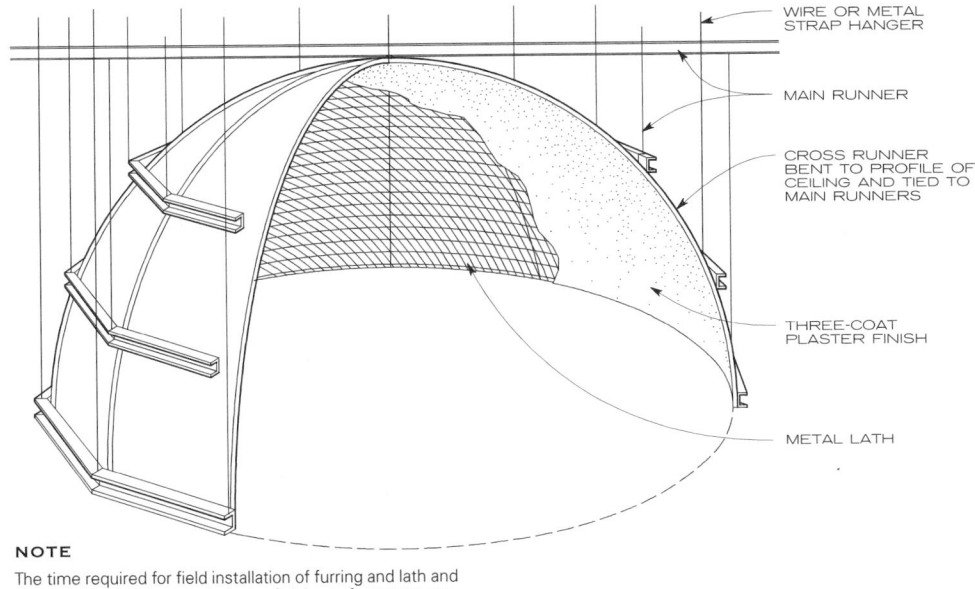

WIRE OR METAL STRAP HANGER

MAIN RUNNER

CROSS RUNNER BENT TO PROFILE OF CEILING AND TIED TO MAIN RUNNERS

THREE-COAT PLASTER FINISH

METAL LATH

NOTE

The time required for field installation of furring and lath and the weight of a three-coat plaster finish are factors to consider when designing this system.

PLASTER DOME BUILT IN PLACE (VAULTS CONSTRUCTED SIMILARLY)

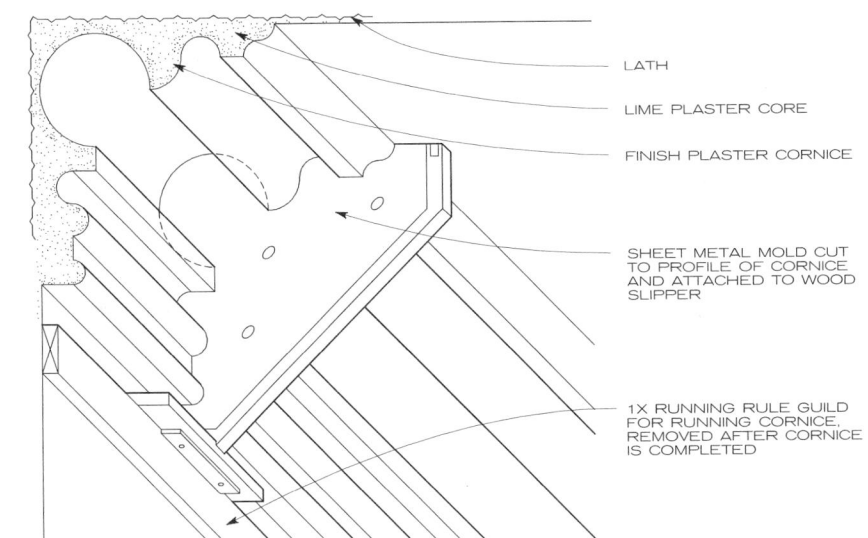

LATH

LIME PLASTER CORE

FINISH PLASTER CORNICE

SHEET METAL MOLD CUT TO PROFILE OF CORNICE AND ATTACHED TO WOOD SLIPPER

1X RUNNING RULE GUILD FOR RUNNING CORNICE, REMOVED AFTER CORNICE IS COMPLETED

RUN-IN-PLACE CORNICE

1X BLOCKING CUT TO PROFILE OF CORNICE AND FASTENED TO FRAMING (ALTERNATE SUPPORT: 1" X ³/₁₆" METAL STRAP BENT TO PROFILE OF CORNICE AND FASTENED TO FRAMING)

METAL LATH

CAST PLASTER ORNAMENT APPLIED WITH PLASTER SLIP

RUN-IN-PLACE PLASTER CORNICE

DENTILS APPLIED TO PLASTER CORNICE WITH PLASTER SLIP

BRACKETED CORNICE RUN IN PLACE WITH STUCK-ON ORNAMENT

Reed A. Black; Oehrlein & Associates; Washington, D.C.

TYPES OF ORNAMENTAL PLASTER

RUN-IN-PLACE: This type of ornament is mounded or applied in its final position while in its plastic state using a three-coat plaster system. This method requires installation of the furring, lath, base plaster coats, and finish plaster ornament and surfaces on site, a time-consuming process that results in relatively heavy assemblies. It is typically used to repair or replace sections of damaged existing and historic plaster ornament.

CAST PLASTER ORNAMENT: This type of ornament, which can be made in panels, is run, cast, or fabricated in a shop and installed after hardening. Joints between sections of ornament are finished in the field. Typically gypsum plaster reinforced with glass fibers, cast plaster is fabricated by laying or spraying the material into a mold. Castings are reinforced with jute rope, burlap, wood lath, or metal framing, depending on the casting size and installation methods. Controlled shop fabrication processes, reduced on-site time, and the ability to fabricate thinner, lighter sections often make this method less costly than run-in-place.

NOTES

MODELS: Models are the "positive" form of the cast ornament and can be fabricated from clay, plaster, or wood as necessary to achieve the desired appearance. When existing ornament is being matched, it can serve as the model.

MOLDS: Typically made of urethane or silicone rubber, molds from which ornament is cast are "negative" forms produced from models. Molds for run-plaster ornament are sheet metal templates cut to the profile of the molding and attached to a wood backing called a "slipper."

ATTACHMENT: Small cast ornament is typically applied using a plaster "slip" made of plaster and water as an adhesive. Large sections of cast plaster ornament are attached with screws or hung with metal hangers.

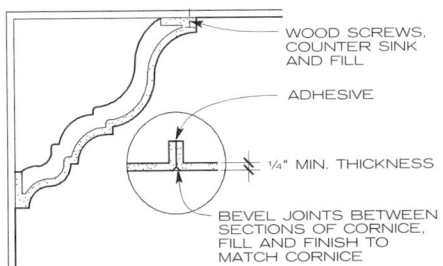

WOOD SCREWS, COUNTER SINK AND FILL

ADHESIVE

¼" MIN. THICKNESS

BEVEL JOINTS BETWEEN SECTIONS OF CORNICE, FILL AND FINISH TO MATCH CORNICE

GLASS FIBER-REINFORCED GYPSUM CORNICE

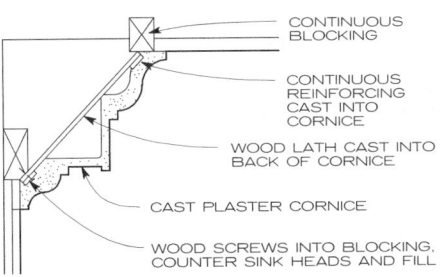

CONTINUOUS BLOCKING

CONTINUOUS REINFORCING CAST INTO CORNICE

WOOD LATH CAST INTO BACK OF CORNICE

CAST PLASTER CORNICE

WOOD SCREWS INTO BLOCKING, COUNTER SINK HEADS AND FILL

CAST PLASTER ORNAMENT ATTACHED WITH SCREWS

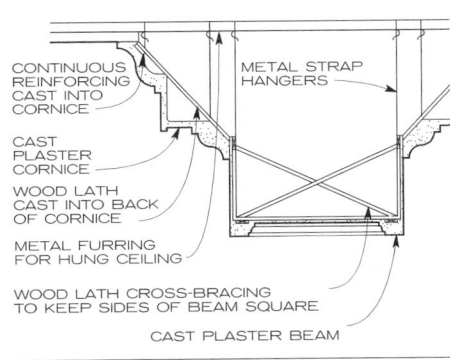

CONTINUOUS REINFORCING CAST INTO CORNICE

CAST PLASTER CORNICE

WOOD LATH CAST INTO BACK OF CORNICE

METAL FURRING FOR HUNG CEILING

WOOD LATH CROSS-BRACING TO KEEP SIDES OF BEAM SQUARE

METAL STRAP HANGERS

CAST PLASTER BEAM

CAST PLASTER CORNICE AND BEAM SCREWED AND HUNG

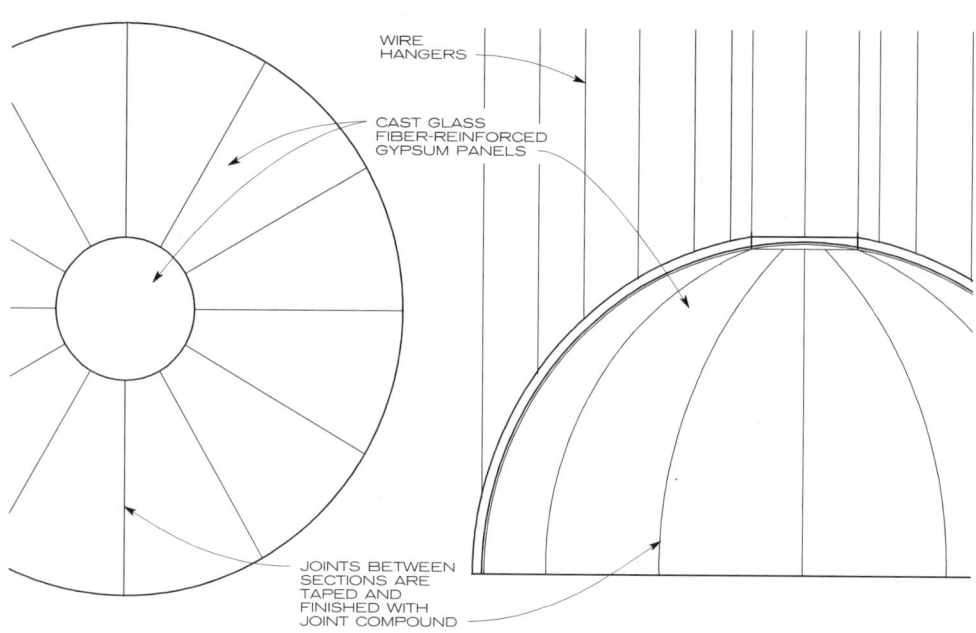

WIRE HANGERS

CAST GLASS FIBER-REINFORCED GYPSUM PANELS

JOINTS BETWEEN SECTIONS ARE TAPED AND FINISHED WITH JOINT COMPOUND

REFLECTED CEILING PLAN   SECTION

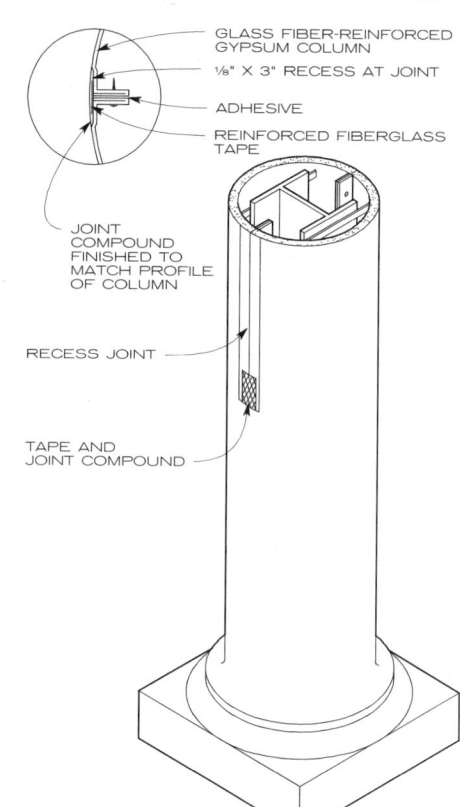

GLASS FIBER-REINFORCED GYPSUM COLUMN

⅛" X 3" RECESS AT JOINT

ADHESIVE

REINFORCED FIBERGLASS TAPE

JOINT COMPOUND FINISHED TO MATCH PROFILE OF COLUMN

RECESS JOINT

TAPE AND JOINT COMPOUND

TWO-PIECE GLASS FIBER-REINFORCED GYPSUM COLUMN

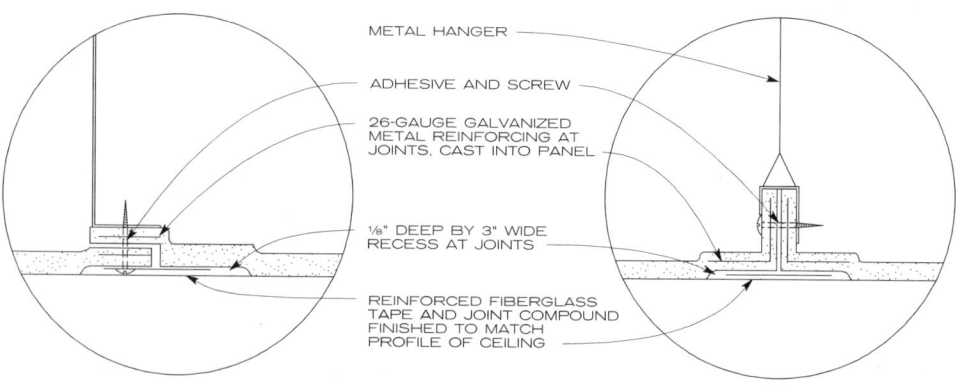

METAL HANGER

ADHESIVE AND SCREW

26-GAUGE GALVANIZED METAL REINFORCING AT JOINTS, CAST INTO PANEL

⅛" DEEP BY 3" WIDE RECESS AT JOINTS

REINFORCED FIBERGLASS TAPE AND JOINT COMPOUND FINISHED TO MATCH PROFILE OF CEILING

ALTERNATE JOINT DETAIL WHEN PANELS ARE NOT ACCESSIBLE FROM THE BACK

JOINT DETAIL

NOTE

Cast fabrications are typically lighter and require less on-site construction time than built-in-place plaster systems. Large cast sections may require structural reinforcing and special cradles for fabrication, shipping, and erection.

CAST GLASS FIBER-REINFORCED GYPSUM DOME (VAULTS ARE SIMILAR)

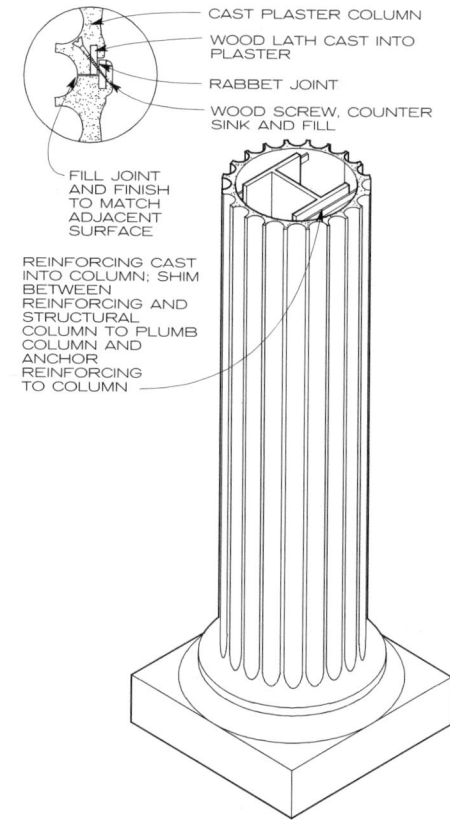

CAST PLASTER COLUMN

WOOD LATH CAST INTO PLASTER

RABBET JOINT

WOOD SCREW, COUNTER SINK AND FILL

FILL JOINT AND FINISH TO MATCH ADJACENT SURFACE

REINFORCING CAST INTO COLUMN; SHIM BETWEEN REINFORCING AND STRUCTURAL COLUMN TO PLUMB COLUMN AND ANCHOR REINFORCING TO COLUMN

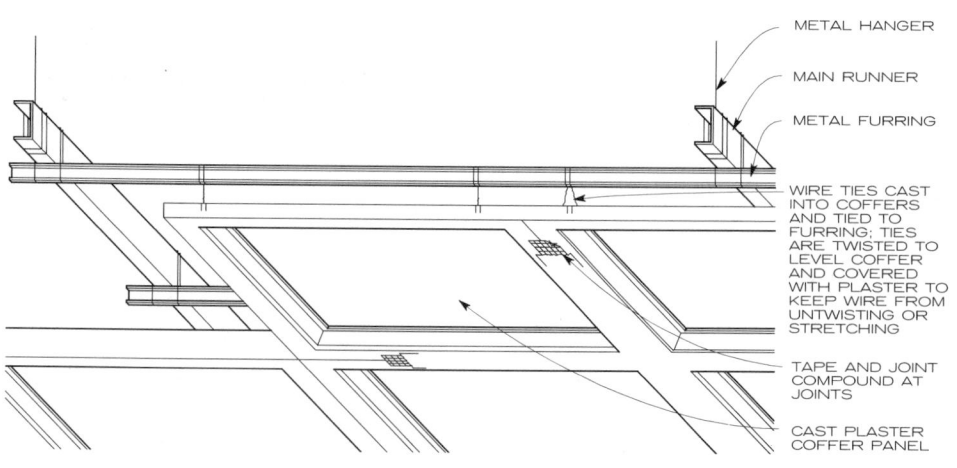

METAL HANGER

MAIN RUNNER

METAL FURRING

WIRE TIES CAST INTO COFFERS AND TIED TO FURRING; TIES ARE TWISTED TO LEVEL COFFER AND COVERED WITH PLASTER TO KEEP WIRE FROM UNTWISTING OR STRETCHING

TAPE AND JOINT COMPOUND AT JOINTS

CAST PLASTER COFFER PANEL

COFFERED CEILING

NOTE

Columns may be fabricated in one piece without joints and seams when they do not have to fit around the building structure.

TWO-PIECE CAST PLASTER COLUMN

Reed A. Black; Oehrlein & Associates; Washington, D.C.

 METAL SUPPORT SYSTEMS

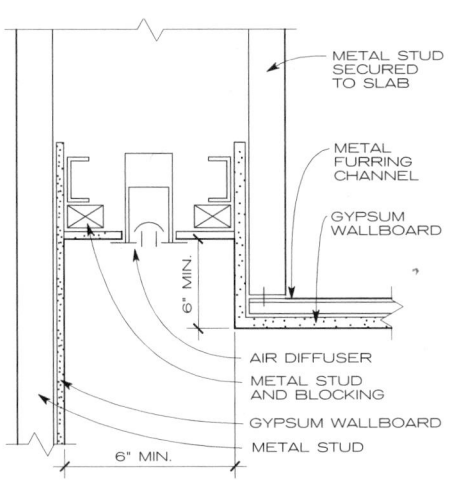

METAL STUD
SECURED
TO SLAB

METAL
FURRING
CHANNEL

GYPSUM
WALLBOARD

6" MIN.

AIR DIFFUSER

METAL STUD
AND BLOCKING

GYPSUM WALLBOARD

METAL STUD

6" MIN.

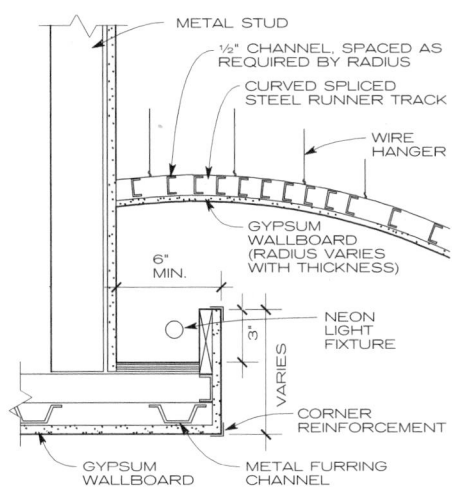

METAL STUD

½" CHANNEL, SPACED AS
REQUIRED BY RADIUS

CURVED SPLICED
STEEL RUNNER TRACK

WIRE
HANGER

GYPSUM
WALLBOARD
(RADIUS VARIES
WITH THICKNESS)

6"
MIN.

NEON
LIGHT
FIXTURE

3"

VARIES

CORNER
REINFORCEMENT

GYPSUM
WALLBOARD

METAL FURRING
CHANNEL

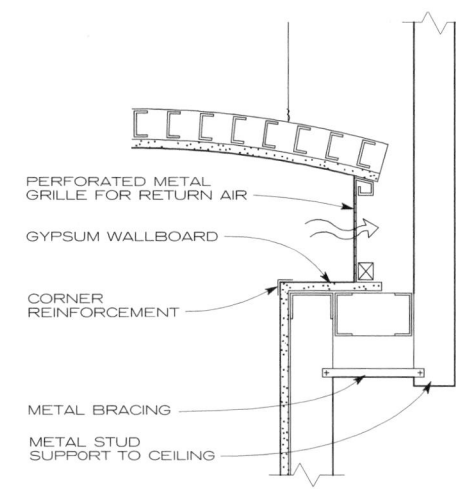

PERFORATED METAL
GRILLE FOR RETURN AIR

GYPSUM WALLBOARD

CORNER
REINFORCEMENT

METAL BRACING

METAL STUD
SUPPORT TO CEILING

CEILING COVES

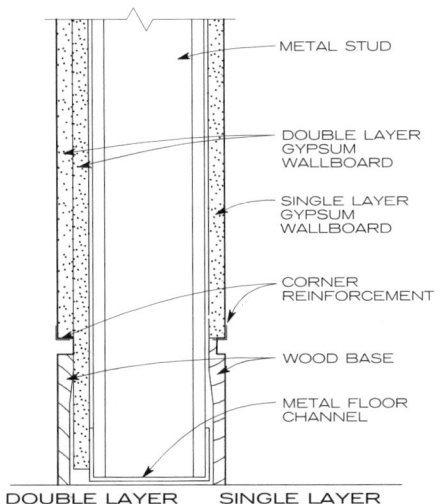

METAL STUD

DOUBLE LAYER
GYPSUM
WALLBOARD

SINGLE LAYER
GYPSUM
WALLBOARD

CORNER
REINFORCEMENT

WOOD BASE

METAL FLOOR
CHANNEL

DOUBLE LAYER   SINGLE LAYER

WALL AT WOOD BASE

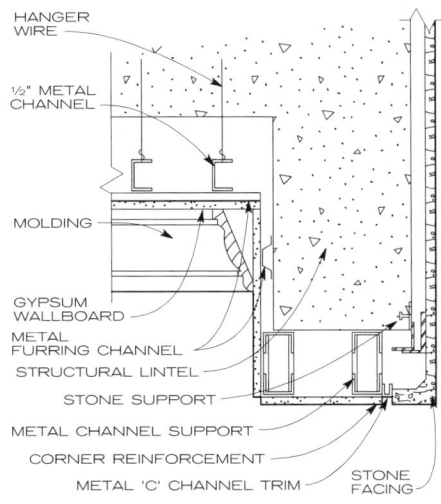

HANGER
WIRE

½" METAL
CHANNEL

MOLDING

GYPSUM
WALLBOARD

METAL
FURRING CHANNEL

STRUCTURAL LINTEL

STONE SUPPORT

METAL CHANNEL SUPPORT

CORNER REINFORCEMENT

METAL 'C' CHANNEL TRIM

STONE
FACING

CEILING SOFFIT AT LINTEL

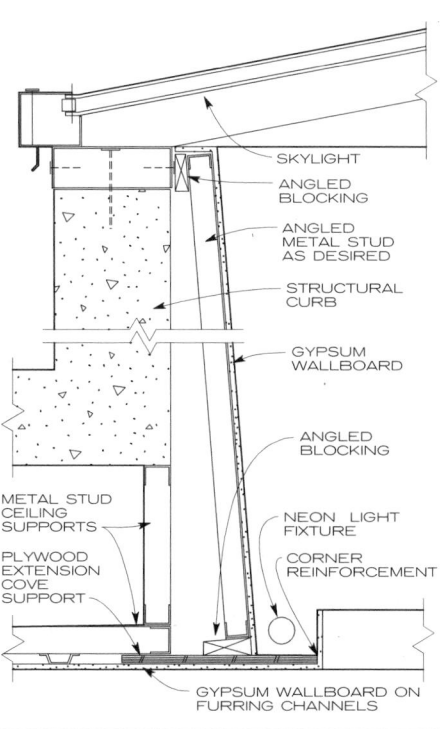

SKYLIGHT

ANGLED
BLOCKING

ANGLED
METAL STUD
AS DESIRED

STRUCTURAL
CURB

GYPSUM
WALLBOARD

ANGLED
BLOCKING

NEON LIGHT
FIXTURE

CORNER
REINFORCEMENT

METAL STUD
CEILING
SUPPORTS

PLYWOOD
EXTENSION
COVE
SUPPORT

GYPSUM WALLBOARD ON
FURRING CHANNELS

SKYLIGHT

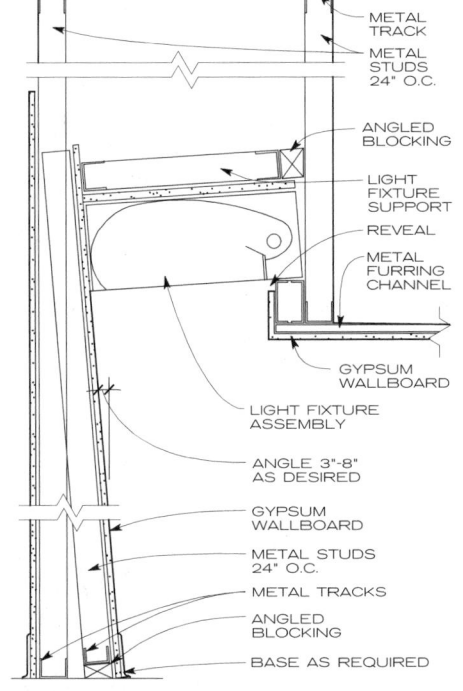

METAL
TRACK

METAL
STUDS
24" O.C.

ANGLED
BLOCKING

LIGHT
FIXTURE
SUPPORT

REVEAL

METAL
FURRING
CHANNEL

GYPSUM
WALLBOARD

LIGHT FIXTURE
ASSEMBLY

ANGLE 3"-8"
AS DESIRED

GYPSUM
WALLBOARD

METAL STUDS
24" O.C.

METAL TRACKS

ANGLED
BLOCKING

BASE AS REQUIRED

CANTED WALL WITH LIGHT COVE

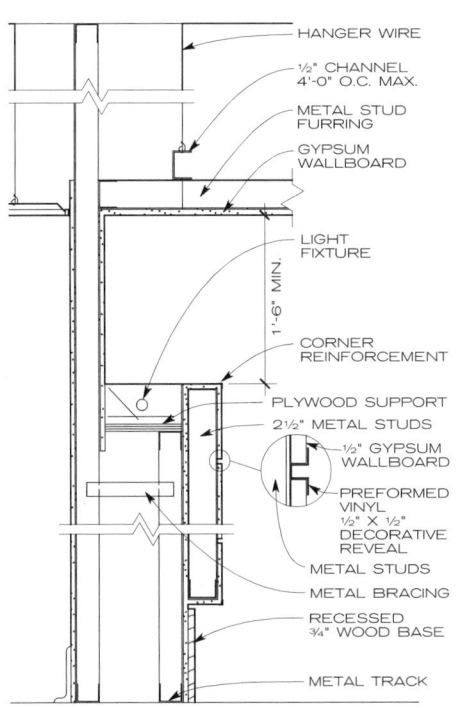

HANGER WIRE

½" CHANNEL
4'-0" O.C. MAX.

METAL STUD
FURRING

GYPSUM
WALLBOARD

LIGHT
FIXTURE

1'-6" MIN.

CORNER
REINFORCEMENT

PLYWOOD SUPPORT

2½" METAL STUDS

½" GYPSUM
WALLBOARD

PREFORMED
VINYL
½" X ½"
DECORATIVE
REVEAL

METAL STUDS

METAL BRACING

RECESSED
¾" WOOD BASE

METAL TRACK

FEATURE WALL WITH LIGHT COVE

PAINT GRADE
WOOD TOPCAP

½" X ½" PREFORMED
VINYL REVEAL

CORNER
REINFORCEMENT

½" BLOCKING

WRAP TOP
WITH GYPSUM
WALLBOARD

UNBRACED HEIGHT

54" MAX.

GYPSUM WALLBOARD
ON STUDS 24" O.C.

PARTITION RETURN
FOR LATERAL
SUPPORT AT END.
3'-0" MAX.
RECOMMENDED AT
UNATTACHED END

BASE AS REQUIRED

PARTIAL HEIGHT PARTITION

Thomas R. Krizmanic, AIA; Studios Architecture; Washington, D.C.

GYPSUM BOARD   9

NEW WALL ASSEMBLIES

FIRE RATING	STC	WALL THICKNESS (IN.)	CONSTRUCTION DESCRIPTION	WALL SECTIONS
1 Hour	40	Varies	EXTERIOR WALL FURRING: One layer $5/8$ in. aluminum foil-backed gypsum wallboard applied to $3/4$ x 1 $1/2$ in. Z furring channel 24 in. o.c., vertically applied with method appropriate to exterior wall. Use 1 in. type S drywall screws 8 in. o.c. to edges and 12 in. o.c. to intermediate Z channel flange. Insulate cavity with 24 x 1 $1/2$ in. rigid foam.	
1 Hour	40	8 $1/8$	SECURITY WALL (15 minute): One base layer of 13-gauge steel expanded metal mesh with nominal 1 x 2 $1/2$ in. grid-spacing under one layer of $3/4$ in. plywood applied to one side of 6 in. metal studs 8 in. o.c. with 1 $1/2$ in. screws. One face layer of $5/8$ in. type X gypsum wallboard applied to each side with 1 in. type S drywall screws 12 in. o.c. Stagger joints 16 in. o.c. each layer and side.	
1 Hour	52	10 $3/4$	CAVITY WALL: One layer $5/8$ in. type X gypsum wallboard applied to outside face of two rows of 1 $5/8$ in. metal studs (air space 9 $1/2$ in. between inside wallboard faces) 24 in. o.c. with 1 in. type S drywall screws 8 in. o.c. to edges and 12 in. o.c. to intermediate studs. Crossbrace at third points vertically with $5/8$ in. wallboard gussets 9 $1/2$ x 12 in. Use 3 $1/2$ in. fiberglass insulation in cavity.	
1 Hour	47	3 $1/2$	PREFINISHED GYPSUM WALL PANELS: One layer, $1/2$ in. type X prefinished vinyl surface gypsum wall panels (prebowed) applied vertically at joints to each side of 2 $1/2$ in. metal studs 24 in. o.c. with 1 in. type S drywall screws 30 in. o.c. Attach to intermediate studs with $3/8$ in. bead of adhesive. Attach at top and bottom with 1 $3/8$ inch matching finish nails 12 in. o.c. Attach aluminum batten retainer to panels at studs with 1 in. type S drywall screws 12 in. o.c. Install matching finish batten over retainers and 2 in. glass fiber insulation in cavity. Stagger joints 24 in. o.c. each side.	
1 Hour	45	5	PREFINISHED GYPSUM WALL PANELS: Base layer $1/4$ in. regular gypsum wallboard nailed to 2 x 4 wood studs 16 in. o.c. with 1 $3/8$ in. 4d coated nails, 12 in. o.c., fire stopped at mid-height. Face layer $1/2$ in. type X prefinished vinyl surface gypsum wall panels (prebowed) applied vertically to each side with laminating compound and $7/8$ in. drywall screws, 12 in. o.c., at top and bottom. Stagger joints 24 in. o.c. each layer and side. Cover exposed fasteners with suitable molding.	
2 Hour	50	5 $3/4$	WATER-RESISTANT WALL (ONE SIDE): One layer $5/8$ in. water-resistant gypsum wallboard applied to wet side of 3 $5/8$ in. 20-gauge metal studs 16 in. o.c. with 1 in. type S drywall screws 12 in. o.c. Opposite side, two layers $5/8$ in. gypsum wallboard installed vertically. Use 3 in. fiber insulation in cavity. Stagger joints 24 in. o.c. each layer and side.	
2 Hour	45	8 $1/4$	BULLET-RESISTANT WALL (ONE SIDE): Base layer of $1/4$ in. steel plate bolted to each side of steel tube framed wall with 4 x $1/4$ in. steel tube at top, bottom, and 4 ft o.c., horizontally. Two layers each side $5/8$ in. type X gypsum wallboard on $7/8$ in. furring channels 24 in. o.c. applied with 1 in. type S drywall screws. Stagger joints 24 in. o.c. each layer and side.	

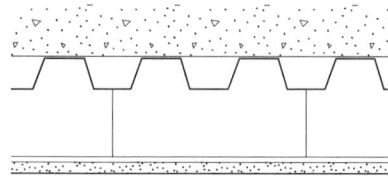

2 HR/STC EST. 50

NOTE

One layer $5/8$ in. type X gypsum wallboard applied with 1 in. type S drywall screws perpendicular to the cross tees of a drywall suspension system suspended from a steel deck. Concrete floors 2 $1/2$ in. thick.

DRYWALL SUSPENSION SYSTEM

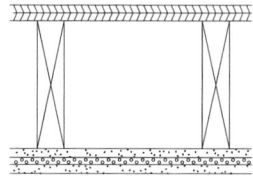

2 HR/STC EST. 45

NOTE

Base layer $5/8$ in. type X gypsum wallboard applied at right angles to 2 x 10 wood joists with 1 in. type S drywall screws 16 in. o.c. Resilient furring channels spaced 24 in. o.c. and nailed through baseboard into and at right angles to joists. Face layer of $5/8$ in. same type wallboard screwed to furring channel with same type screws. Tongue-and-groove sub- and finish floor.

DOUBLE LAYER RESILIENT (WOOD FRAME)

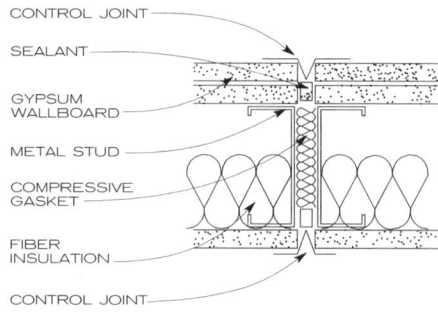

1 $1/2$" CHANNEL
METAL FURRING CHANNEL CLIP
FIBER INSULATION EXTENDED 4'-0" MIN. BEYOND EACH SIDE OF PARTITION
CORNER REINFORCEMENT
SEALANT
PARTITION CEILING RUNNER SCREW ATTACHED TO METAL FURRING CHANNEL
GYPSUM WALLBOARD

SOUND-ISOLATED INTERRUPTED CEILING

CONTROL JOINT
SEALANT
GYPSUM WALLBOARD
METAL STUD
COMPRESSIVE GASKET
FIBER INSULATION
CONTROL JOINT

WALL CONTROL JOINT

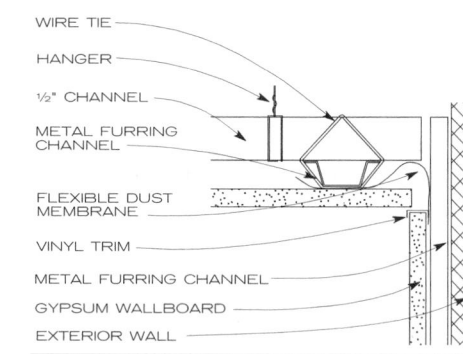

WIRE TIE
HANGER
$1/2$" CHANNEL
METAL FURRING CHANNEL
FLEXIBLE DUST MEMBRANE
VINYL TRIM
METAL FURRING CHANNEL
GYPSUM WALLBOARD
EXTERIOR WALL

EXTERIOR WALL INTERSECTION

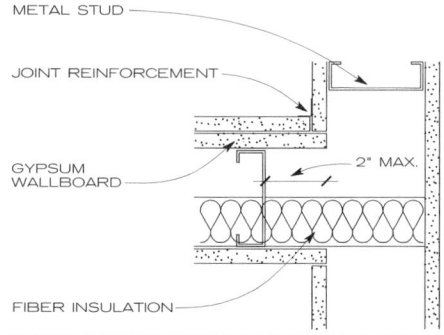

METAL STUD
JOINT REINFORCEMENT
GYPSUM WALLBOARD
2" MAX.
FIBER INSULATION

SOUND-ISOLATED PARTITION INTERSECTION

Thomas R. Krizmanic, AIA; Studios Architecture; Washington, D.C.

 GYPSUM BOARD

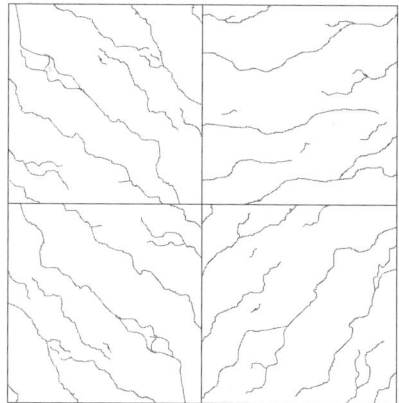

BLEND PATTERN

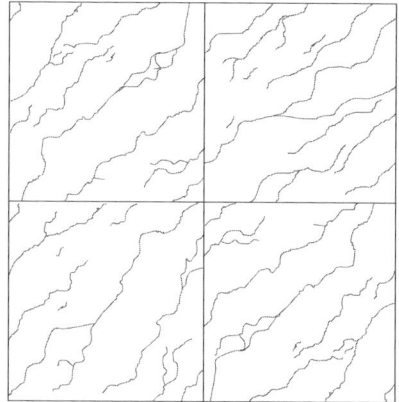

SIDE-SLIP OR END PATTERN

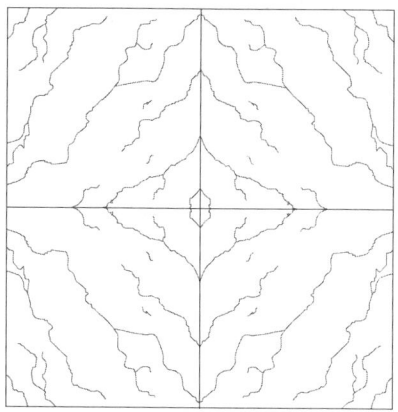

END-MATCH, BOOK-MATCH,
OR QUARTER-MATCH PATTERNS

MARBLE WALL FACING PATTERN

MARBLE WALL FACING PATTERNS

Stone with distinctive texture and markings, such as certain marbles, lends itself to specific pattern arrangements. The markings vary depending on whether the marble veneer is cut with or across its setting bed.

BLEND PATTERN: Panels of the same variety of stone, but not necessarily from the same block, are arranged at random.

SIDE-SLIP OR END-SLIP PATTERN: Panels from the same block are placed side by side or end to end in sequence to give a repetitive pattern and blended color in the horizontal or vertical.

END-MATCH OR BOOK-MATCH PATTERNS: In an end-match pattern, the adjacent faces of panels A and B are finished and panel B is inverted above panel A. In a book-match pattern, panel B is placed next to panel A.

VENEER CUTTING

Quarry blocks are reduced to slabs by a gang saw. The gang saw consists of a series of parallel steel blades in a frame that moves forward and backward. The most productive and precise gang saws use diamond-tipped blades with individual hydraulic blade tensioners; others are fed a cutting abrasive in a stream of water.

Marble blocks can be sawn either parallel or perpendicular to the bedding plane. The perpendicular cut is referred to as an across-the-bed or vein cut. The parallel cut is a with-the-bed or Fleuri cut. Other marbles produce a pleasing surface only when sawn in one direction and are generally available only in that variety.

VENEER PATTERNS

Only certain marbles lend themselves to specific pattern arrangements, such as a side-slip or end-slip pattern, which require a constant natural marking trend throughout the marble block. Formal patterns require selectivity, which usually increases the installed cost of the marble veneer. Usually, material sawn for a vein cut can be matched; Fleuri cuts can only be blended.

NOTE

Although the above arrangements of matched panels indicate an almost perfect match of veining lines, such perfection is impossible because a portion of the marble block is lost during the sawing process and because the vein shifts. Ideally, jointing should be planned for groupings of four panels of equal size.

TYPICAL FINISHES AND COMMON SIZES OF STONE WALL PANELS FOR INTERIOR USE

STONE	GRADE	FINISH	MIN. THICKNESS (IN.)	MAX. FACE DIMENSION (IN.)	NOTES
Granite	Building (exterior) Veneer Masonry	Polished Honed	$^3/_4$ - $1^1/_4$ *	5 x 5	• This very hard and durable surface is not likely to stain. • Many colors and grains are available.
Marble	Group A (exterior) Group B Group C Group D	Polished Honed	$^1/_2$ - $^7/_8$ *	4 x 7	• The most colorful and interesting marbles are in groups B, C, and D; however, some filling of natural voids may be required. • Many colors and patterns are available.
Limestone	Select Standard Rustic Variegated	Smooth Tooled Polished	$^7/_8$ - 3	4 x 9	• Soft and easy to shape, limestone shows wear and may discolor over time. • Colors range in the buffs and grays.
Slate	Ribbon Clear	Natural cleft Sand rubbed Honed	1 - $1^1/_2$	2 - 6 x 5	• Ribbon stock is distinguished by its ornamental, integral bands, which are usually darker than the rest of the stone. • Colors range in the pastel hues.

* $^1/_4$-$^1/_2$ in. tiles (usually a face dimension of 12 in. x 12 in.) available. Tiles can be directly applied to a wall with adhesive or thin-set mortar similar to flooring applications. Tiles are not recommended for walls over 8 ft high.

NOTES

1. Sizes and thicknesses shown are only indicative of some of the common sizes and thicknesses used. Intended use and size generally dictate minimum thickness.

2. Joint width between panels should be specified. Traditionally, it has been $^1/_{16}$ in. minimum.

Mark Forma; Leo A. Daly Company; Washington, D.C.

STONE FACING   ⑨

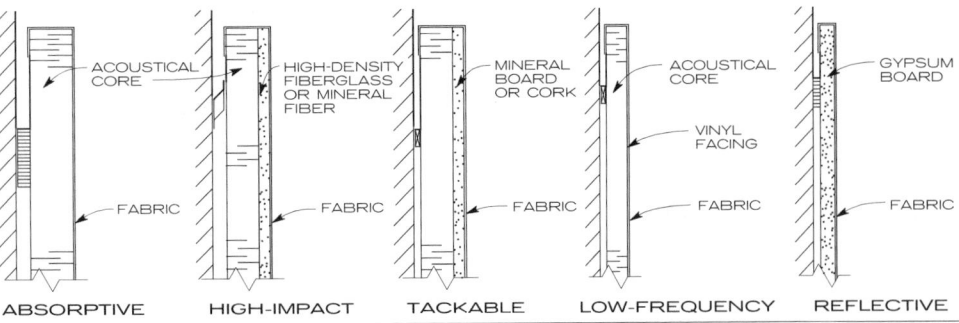

ABSORPTIVE | HIGH-IMPACT | TACKABLE | LOW-FREQUENCY | REFLECTIVE

PANEL TYPES

ABSORPTIVE WALL TREATMENT

1. USE: sound absorption.
2. MATERIALS: factory- or field-assembled fabric wrapped glass fiber or mineral wood panels.
3. NRC: 0.55 to 1.0.
4. THICKNESS: one, two, or four inches.
5. PANEL TYPES: absorptive, high-impact, tackable, and special acoustical characteristics.
6. EDGE PROFILES: square, bevel, radius, and chamfer.
7. EDGE REINFORCEMENT: chemical treatment, metal, plastic, and wood.
8. INSTALLATION HARDWARE: mechanical clips, impaling pins, magnetic fasteners, hook and loop tape, and adhesives (the last two require installation of a metal angle at panel bottom to carry the weight of the panel).

NOTE

Wall panels may be used individually or grouped to form a monolithic wall system. The NRC coefficient varies with the thickness of the material, the acoustical transparency of the fabric, and the installation mounting. Panels are more effective at absorbing mid- and high-frequency sound. Vinyl facing over an acoustical core increases low-frequency absorption and decreases mid- and high-frequency absorption. Panels are not recommended for installation in high abuse areas unless perforated metal or high-density scrim facing protects the acoustical core. Maximum panel size varies with the manufacturer up to 4 x 12 feet.

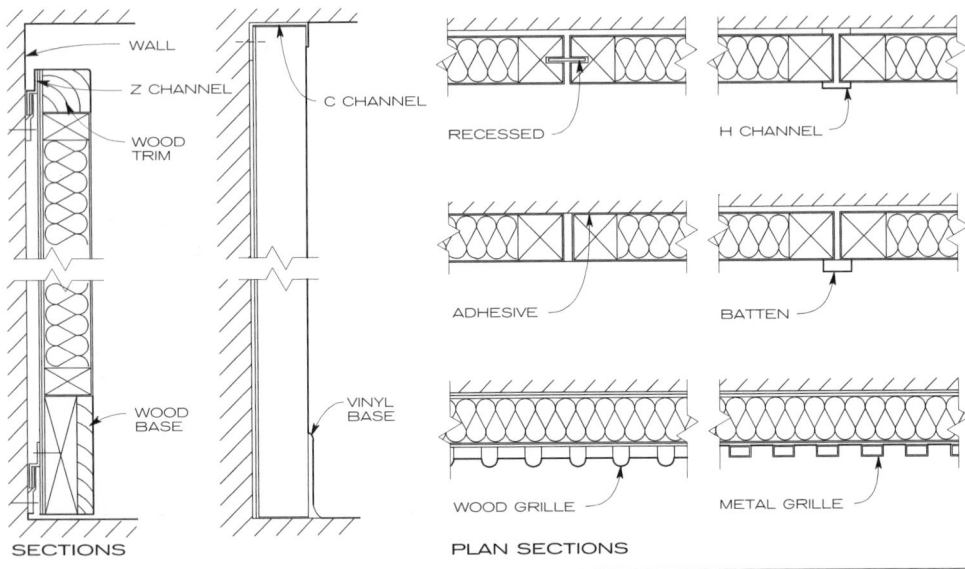

SECTIONS | PLAN SECTIONS

WALL TREATMENT

SPRAY-ON ACOUSTICAL MATERIAL

1. USE: sound absorption.
2. MATERIALS: aerated concrete, mineral, or cellulose fibers spray-applied to metal lath or directly to hard surfaces such as concrete, steel, masonry, or gypsum wallboard.
3. NRC: 0.35 to 1.0.

NOTE

This material is available in thicknesses of $1/2$ to $1^{1}/_2$ in. with abuse-resistant surfaces and fire protection ratings. Applying spray-on acoustical material to lath increases low-frequency sound absorption and makes it possible to accommodate irregular shapes. The NRC rating of this material depends on how it is mounted and the thickness of the material.

ACOUSTICAL MASONRY UNITS

1. USE: sound absorption and diffusion.
2. MATERIALS: concrete masonry units 4, 6, 8, or 12 in. thick, with fiberglass or metal baffle in the slotted area for sound absorption; quadratic residue sequence shaped surface for sound diffusion.
3. NRC: 0.45 to 0.85.

NOTE

Acoustical masonry units are available with glazed, split rib, and ground face masonry finishes. The units offer better sound absorption at low frequencies than at middle to high frequencies and can be used as load-bearing structural walls. Painting slightly reduces the NRC rating of these units.

DIFFUSIVE WALL TREATMENT

1. USE: sound diffusion/scattering.
2. MATERIALS: factory-assembled wood, fiberglass, or fiberglass-reinforced gypsum panels with integrally shaped surfaces.
3. NRC: typically less than 0.30.
4. THICKNESS: up to 18 in. depending on panel shape.

NOTE

Wall panels may be used individually or grouped to form a monolithic wall system. Panels function best if they are installed 4 ft. above the floor surface (ear height) and extend to a minimum of 8 ft. above the floor surface. Maximum panel size varies with the manufacturer up to 4 x 8 ft.

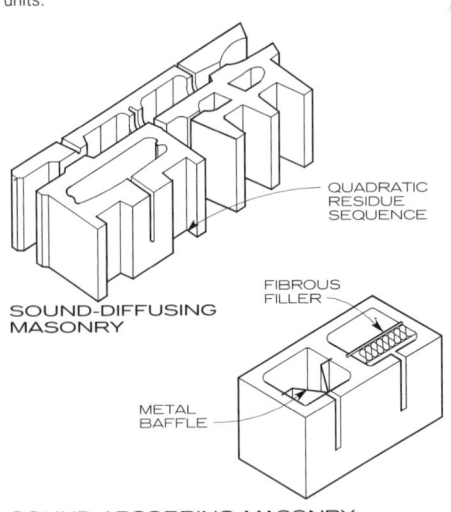

SOUND-DIFFUSING MASONRY

SOUND-ABSORBING MASONRY

ACOUSTICAL MASONRY UNITS

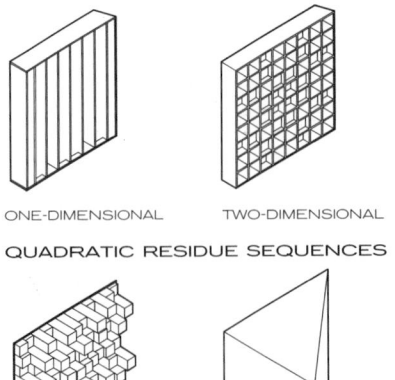

ONE-DIMENSIONAL | TWO-DIMENSIONAL

QUADRATIC RESIDUE SEQUENCES

PRIMITIVE ROOT SEQUENCE | PYRAMID

DIFFUSIVE WALL TREATMENT

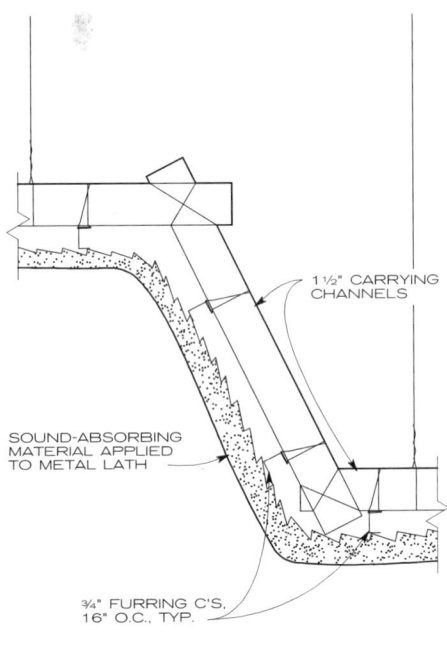

SPRAY-ON ACOUSTICAL MATERIAL

Michael G. Lawrence, AIA; M Lawrence Architects; Washington, D.C.
Neil Thompson Shade; Acoustical Design Collaborative, Ltd.; Falls Church, Virginia

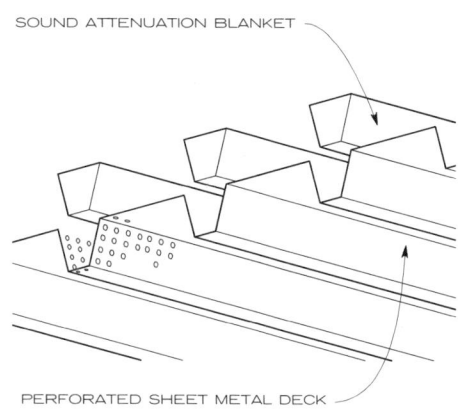

SOUND ATTENUATION BLANKET

PERFORATED SHEET METAL DECK

METAL ACOUSTICAL ROOF DECK

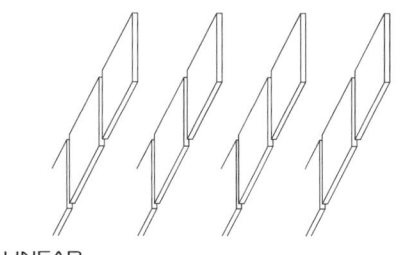

LINEAR

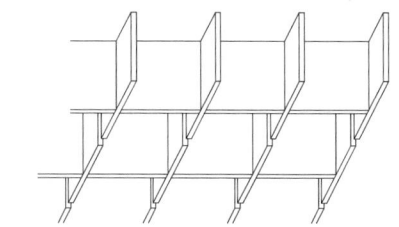

EGGCRATE

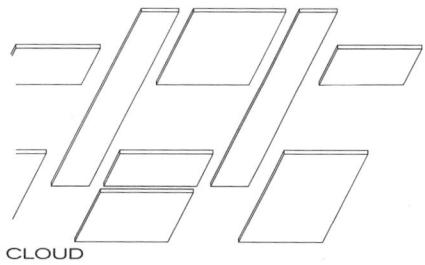

CLOUD

SUSPENDED PANELS

ACOUSTICAL ROOF DECKS

Acoustical roof decks are commonly used in industrial, gymnasium, and similar facilities where the underside of the roof serves as the exposed ceiling surface of the space below. Typically comprised of perforated metal roof deck panels, with fiberglass or mineral fiber infill, acoustical form boards, or structural roof insulation, these decks provide sound absorption and structural support for the exterior roofing material. NRC ratings range from 0.55 to 0.85.

SUSPENDED PANELS

Sound is absorbed through vertical suspension fiberglass blankets wrapped in fabric, vinyl, or perforated metal. Fiberglass or mineral fiber blankets can be used horizontally with perimeter framing. Typically 2 x 4 ft in size, panels can be suspended from the structure or attached directly to the ceiling grid, but installation patterns vary. NRC ratings, often greater than 1.0 due to sound exposure on both sides, depend on panel density and layout geometry. In general, one panel is required per 8 to 10 sq ft of floor area.

Michael G. Lawrence, AIA; M Lawrence Architects; Washington, D.C.
Neil Thompson Shade; Acoustical Design Collaborative, Ltd; Falls Church, Virginia

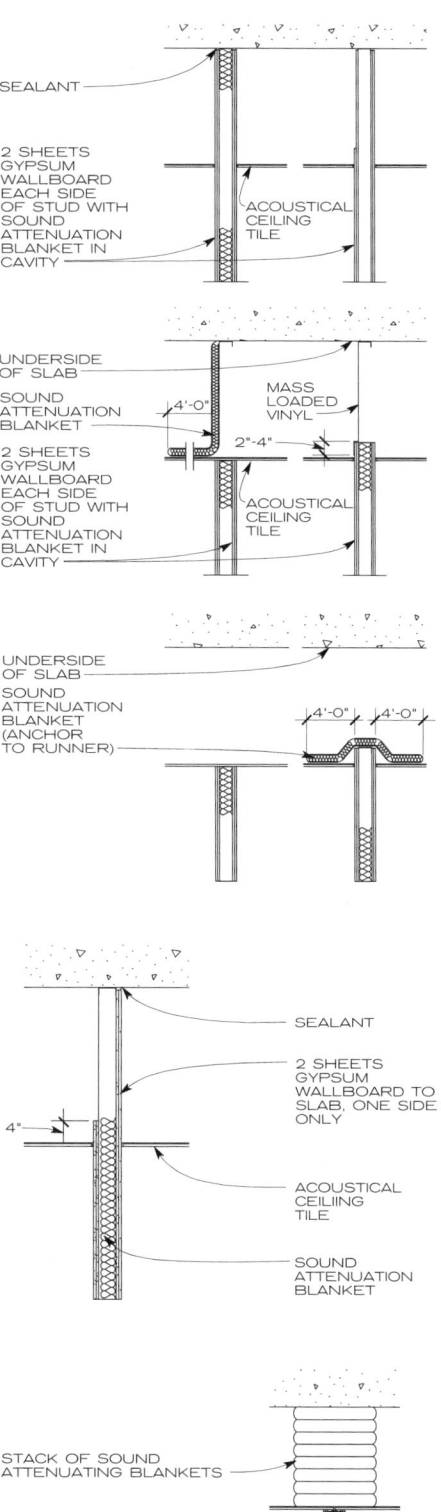

SEALANT

2 SHEETS GYPSUM WALLBOARD EACH SIDE OF STUD WITH SOUND ATTENUATION BLANKET IN CAVITY

ACOUSTICAL TILE

UNDERSIDE OF SLAB

SOUND ATTENUATION BLANKET

4'-0"

MASS LOADED VINYL

2"-4"

2 SHEETS GYPSUM WALLBOARD EACH SIDE OF STUD WITH SOUND ATTENUATION BLANKET IN CAVITY

ACOUSTICAL CEILING TILE

UNDERSIDE OF SLAB

SOUND ATTENUATION BLANKET (ANCHOR TO RUNNER)

4'-0"   4'-0"

SEALANT

2 SHEETS GYPSUM WALLBOARD TO SLAB, ONE SIDE ONLY

4"

ACOUSTICAL CEILIING TILE

SOUND ATTENUATION BLANKET

STACK OF SOUND ATTENUATING BLANKETS

PLENUM BARRIER DETAILS

PLENUM BARRIERS

These products are used to reduce sound transmission through the plenum space above partitions. Materials are mass-loaded vinyl, fiberglass, or mineral fiber batts and gypsum board. All openings through the barrier for pipes, ducts, etc. must be closed off for the barrier to be effective. STC rating is improved from 5 to 40 dB.

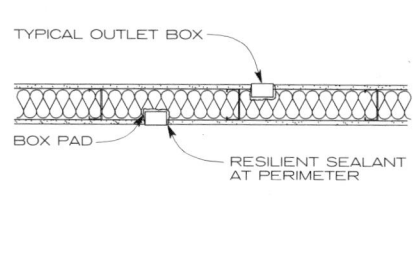

TYPICAL OUTLET BOX

BOX PAD

RESILIENT SEALANT AT PERIMETER

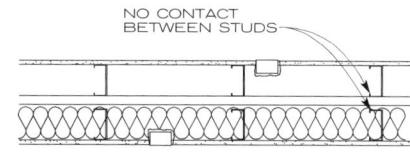

NO CONTACT BETWEEN STUDS

PARTITION PLANS

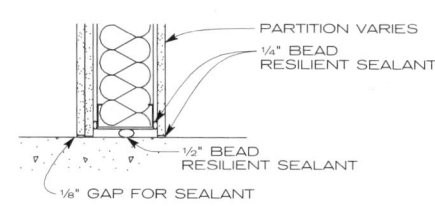

PARTITION VARIES

¼" BEAD RESILIENT SEALANT

½" BEAD RESILIENT SEALANT

⅛" GAP FOR SEALANT

PARTITION SECTION

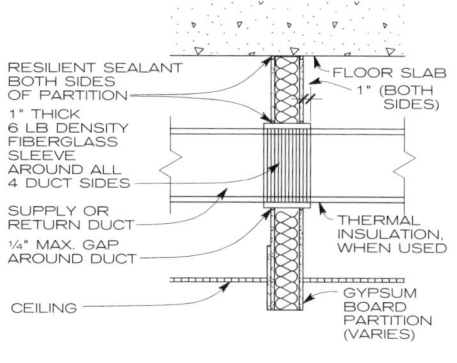

RESILIENT SEALANT BOTH SIDES OF PARTITION

FLOOR SLAB

1" (BOTH SIDES)

1" THICK 6 LB DENSITY FIBERGLASS SLEEVE AROUND ALL 4 DUCT SIDES

SUPPLY OR RETURN DUCT

¼" MAX. GAP AROUND DUCT

THERMAL INSULATION, WHEN USED

CEILING

GYPSUM BOARD PARTITION (VARIES)

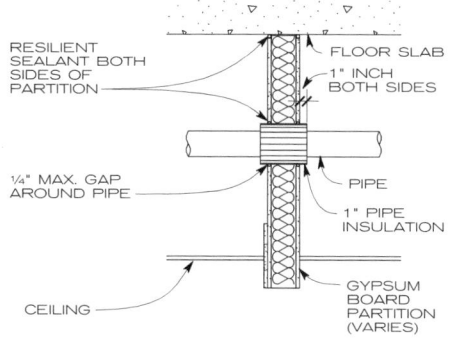

RESILIENT SEALANT BOTH SIDES OF PARTITION

FLOOR SLAB

1" INCH BOTH SIDES

¼" MAX. GAP AROUND PIPE

PIPE

1" PIPE INSULATION

CEILING

GYPSUM BOARD PARTITION (VARIES)

ACOUSTICAL SEALS AND CLOSURES DETAILS

ACOUSTICAL SEALS AND CLOSURES

These seals and closures, usually made of resilient sealant material or fiberglass, are used to close off sound leaks. All penetrations around partitions must be filled with resilient sealant, while pipes and ducts should be isolated from partitions with fiberglass. Use of these materials improves the STC from 5 to 15 dB.

SURFACE CHARACTERISTICS

CHARACTERISTIC	ADVANTAGES
High performance/ durability	Resistant to abuse Abrasion resistant Weather resistant
Nonporous surface	Germ inhibition
Low maintenance	Ease of cleaning
Installation	Lightweight panels Common installation procedures
Versatility	New construction Renovation Demountable Projection/marker surface
Chemical resistance	Resistant to chemical attack*
Fire resistance	Class A fire rating*
Color/texture/pattern availability	Standard/custom color, graphics textures

* Refer to specific manufacturer's literature.

PANEL CONSTRUCTION GUIDE

PANEL COMPO-NENT	MATERIALS	ADVANTAGES
Face	Ceramic on steel Anodized aluminum Painted aluminum Stainless steel Painted steel Fiberglass-reinforced	Variety of finishes Matching adjacent metals Polished finish
Stabilizer panel	Tempered hardboard Asbestos-free board Mineral fiberboard Plywood* Gypsum board* Fire-rated fiberboard Polystyrene foam*	Lower cost, lighter weight Additional fire protection
Back	Ceramic on steel Galvanized sheet steel Aluminum sheet Exposed stabilizer panel	Attractive finished back May be finished in field
Anchors	Screws Concealed trim Exposed trim Plastic/metal rivets* Stainless steel nails*	

* Applicable to fiberglass panels only.

PANEL SIZE LIMITATIONS

PANEL	CERAMIC/ STEEL (IN.)	FIBERGLASS (IN.)
Maximum width	60*	48*
Maximum length	144*	144*

* Custom size, color, and thickness available. Consult manufacturer.

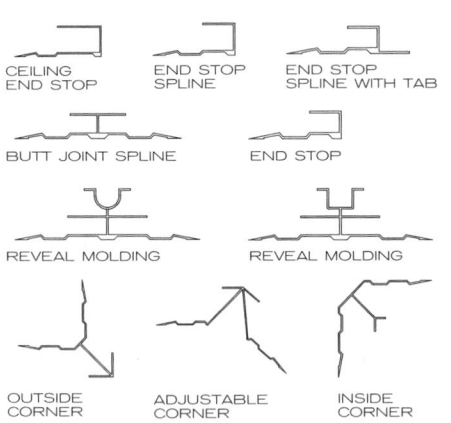

CERAMIC STEEL TRIM COMPONENTS

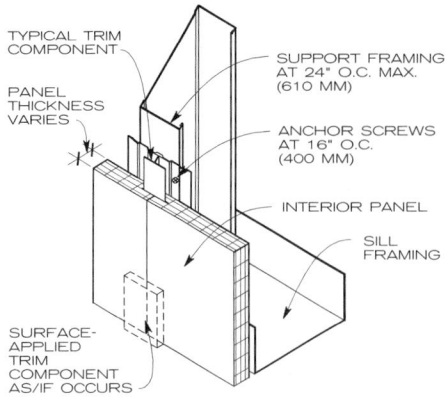

TYPICAL VERTICAL BUTT JOINT

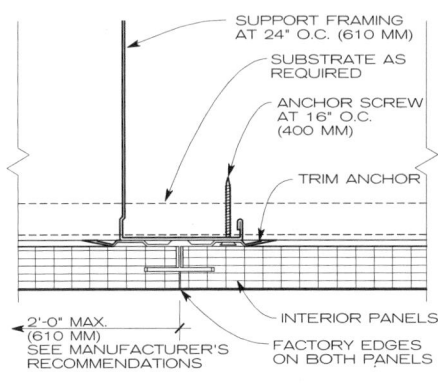

VERTICAL BUTT JOINT WITH CONCEALED TRIM

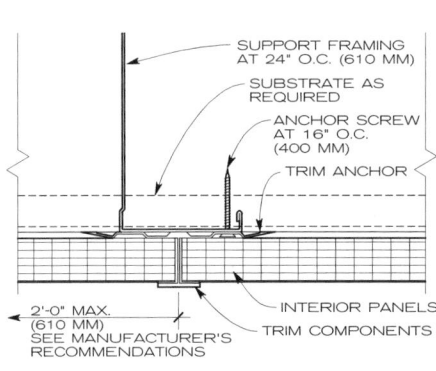

VERTICAL BUTT JOINT WITH EXPOSED TRIM

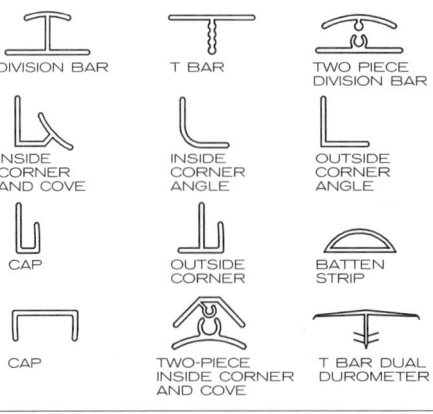

FIBERGLASS/VINYL TRIM COMPONENTS

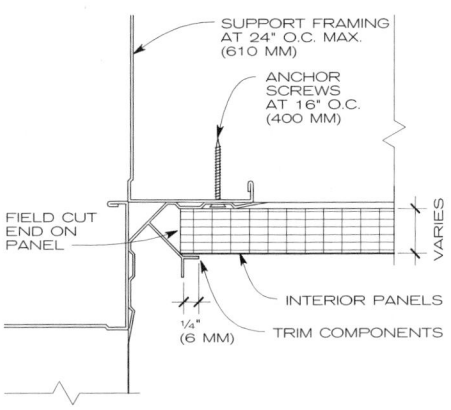

INSIDE CORNER

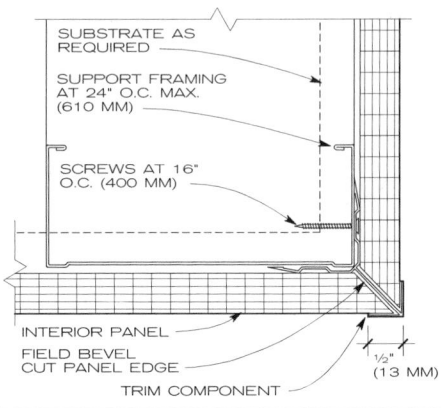

OUTSIDE CORNER DETAIL

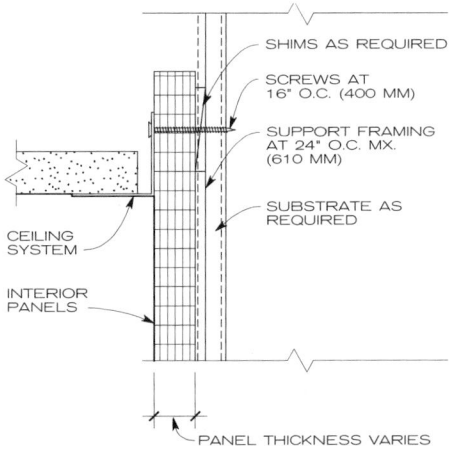

DETAIL AT CEILING

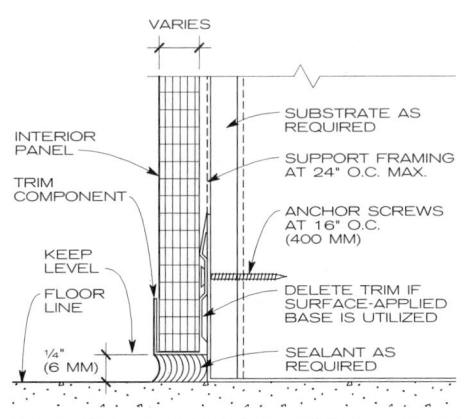

PANEL AT SILL

Kevin R. McDonald, AIA; HNTB Corporation; Alexandria, Virginia
Alliance America; Norcross, Georgia

 SPECIAL WALL SURFACES

LINEAR METAL CEILINGS

PANS

Dimensions: Typical widths range from 4 to 8 inches (100 to 200 mm).

Materials: Roll-formed sheet steel is for interior applications only; roll-formed aluminum can be used for interior or exterior applications.

Surface: Surfaces can be smooth, perforated or unperforated, or textured.

Finish: Baked polyester enamels, metallic coatings, and brushed or polished aluminum with a clear coating are available.

CARRIERS

Material: Roll-formed sheet steel is for interior use only, while roll-formed aluminum is suitable for interior or exterior applications.

Finish: The finish is flat black baked polyester enamel.

ACCESSORIES

Possible accessories include integral light fixtures and air diffusers, trim channels, splices, and end caps.

OPTIONS

Fire-rated and acoustically rated systems are available.

EXTERIOR APPLICATIONS OF LINEAR METAL CEILINGS

Wind loads must be factored in when exterior applications of linear metal ceilings and soffits are planned. Wind loads are determined by geographic conditions and a building's height above the ground. Linear metal systems must be engineered to withstand uplift pressure. Rigid bracing is used instead of suspension wires to support these systems.

LINEAR BAFFLE CEILINGS

Steel or aluminum baffles hung from a suspended ceiling framework mask exposed plenum areas. Baffles are available in a variety of profiles and depths ranging from 4 to 12 inches (100 to 300 mm).

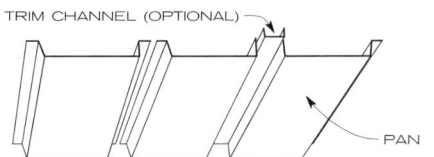

LINEAR METAL CEILING—OPEN REVEAL

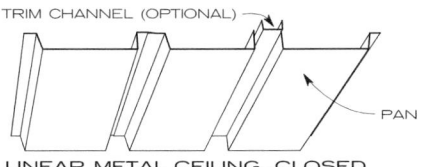

LINEAR METAL CEILING—CLOSED REVEAL

TYPICAL PAN CONFIGURATIONS

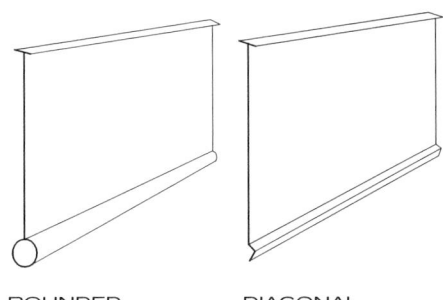

ROUNDED   DIAGONAL

TYPICAL BAFFLE PROFILES

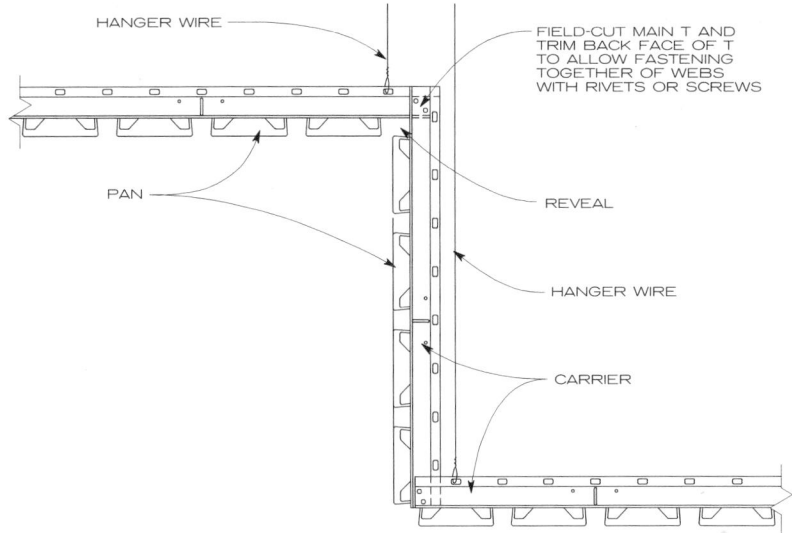

LINEAR METAL CEILING SYSTEM

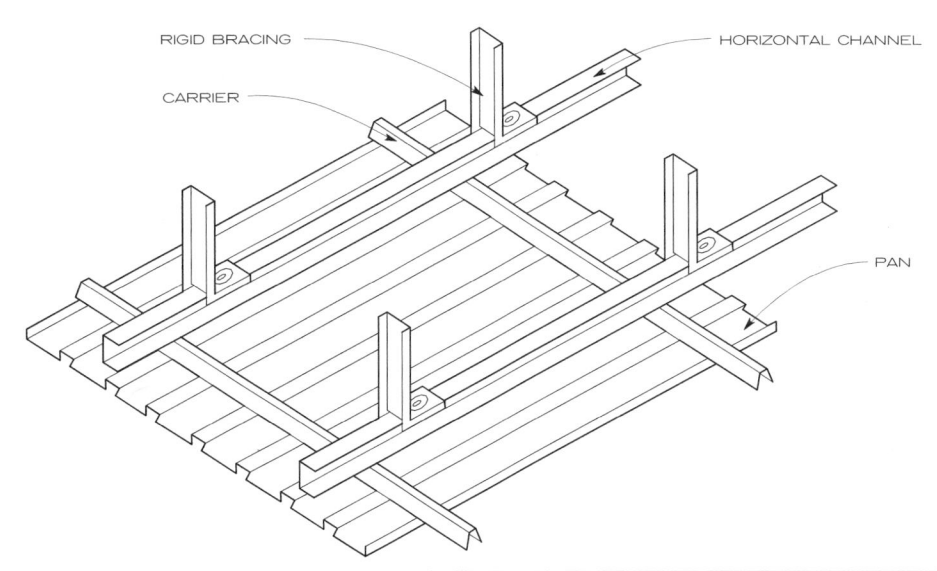

EXTERIOR LINEAR METAL CEILING SYSTEM

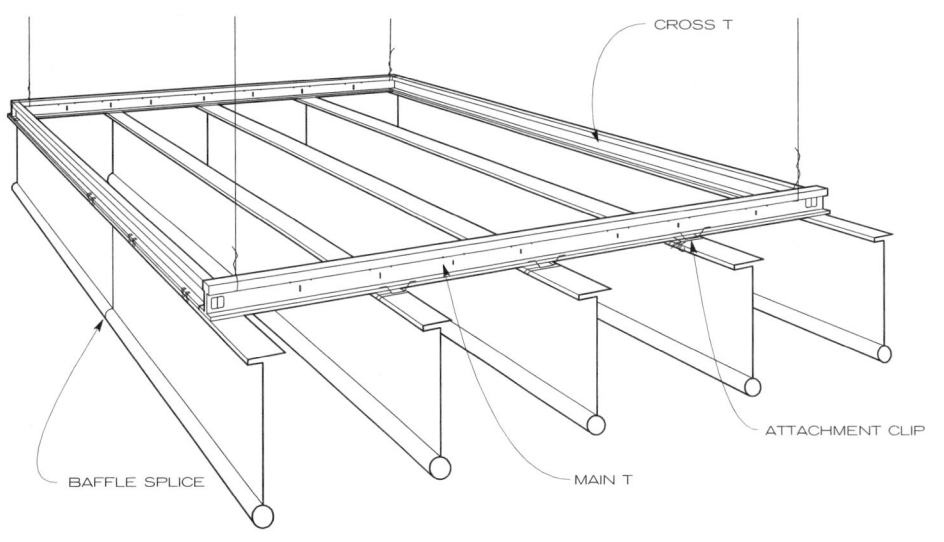

LINEAR BAFFLE CEILING SYSTEM

Keith McCormack, CCS, CSI; RTKL Associates; Baltimore, Maryland
USG Interiors, Inc., Chicago, Illinois

SPECIAL CEILING SURFACES ⑨

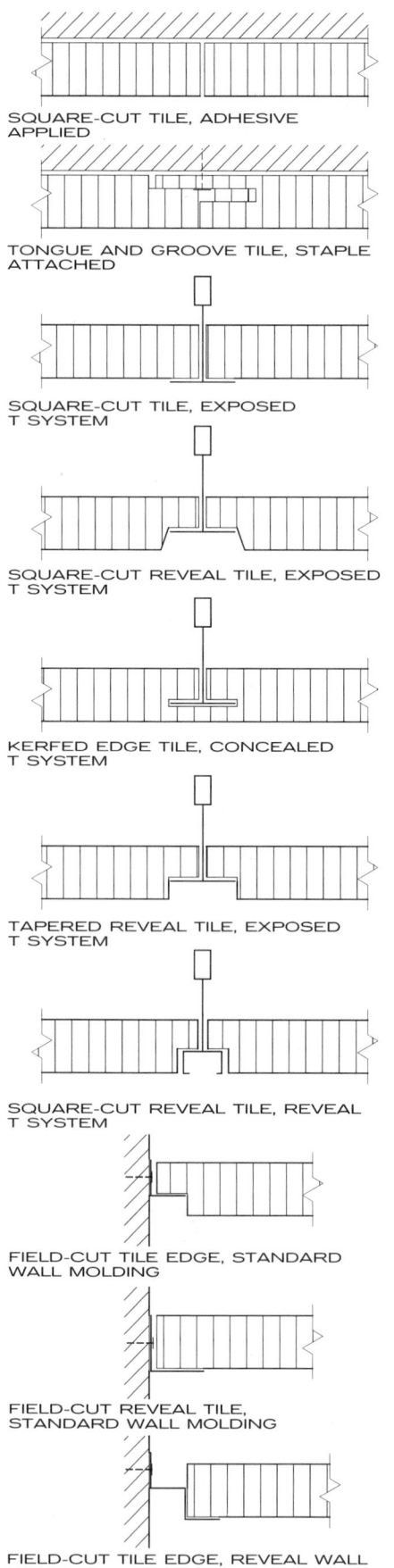

SQUARE-CUT TILE, ADHESIVE APPLIED

TONGUE AND GROOVE TILE, STAPLE ATTACHED

SQUARE-CUT TILE, EXPOSED T SYSTEM

SQUARE-CUT REVEAL TILE, EXPOSED T SYSTEM

KERFED EDGE TILE, CONCEALED T SYSTEM

TAPERED REVEAL TILE, EXPOSED T SYSTEM

SQUARE-CUT REVEAL TILE, REVEAL T SYSTEM

FIELD-CUT TILE EDGE, STANDARD WALL MOLDING

FIELD-CUT REVEAL TILE, STANDARD WALL MOLDING

FIELD-CUT TILE EDGE, REVEAL WALL MOLDING

EDGE CONDITIONS AND SUPPORT SYSTEMS

TYPES OF ACOUSTICAL CEILING UNITS

ACOUSTICAL TILE

These prefabricated, sound-absorbing ceiling units are installed in a concealed suspension system or directly attached to the substrate with adhesive or staples. Typical size is 12 by 12 inches (305 by 305 mm).

ACOUSTICAL PANEL

These prefabricated, sound-absorbing ceiling units are installed in a suspension system. Typical sizes are 24 by 24 inches (610 by 610 mm) and 24 by 48 inches (610 by 1210 mm).

CONSTRUCTION OF ACOUSTICAL CEILING UNITS

CAST (MOLDED)

These ceiling units are composed of mineral fibers, fillers, binders, and water mixed together to form a slurry. The slurry is cast on trays and heat cured. The pattern and sound-absorbing qualities are created by the treatment of the material face in the wet stage. After drying, acoustical units are painted; if color is added to the slurry, the unit will be colored throughout.

NODULAR

Nodular tiles are composed of mineral fibers, perlite, fillers, binders, and water mixed together to form a dry slurry. The slurry is formed into sheets, dried, and cut. The surface is inherently porous and is subsequently textured by mechanical fissuring and embossing; ceiling units are then painted.

WET-FELTED

Wet-felted tiles are composed of mineral fibers, fillers, binders, and water mixed together to form a slurry. The slurry is poured onto felts, drained, compacted, dried, and cut. Textures are created by mechanical perforation, fissuring, and stippling. Surface finishes include paint, fabric, polyester film, and vinyl-coated aluminum.

GLASS FIBER WITH FACING

This type of tile consists of nonwoven fiberglass insulation with a fabric or vinyl film surface finish.

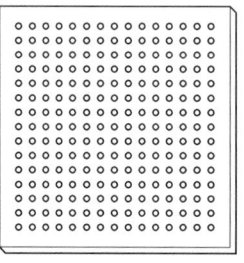

PERFORATED, REGULARLY SPACED HOLES

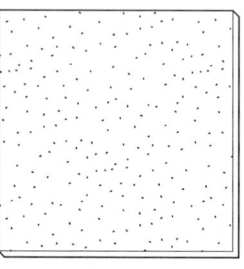

PERFORATEED, RANDOMLY SPACED HOLES

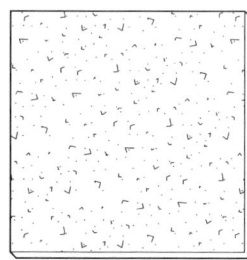

FISSURED

REVEAL EDGE, STIPPLE FINISH

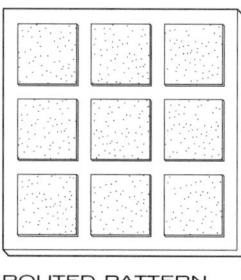

ROUTED PATTERN, PERFORATED FINISH

EMBOSSED DESIGN, STIPPLE FINISH

TWO-SQUARE, STIPPLE FINISH

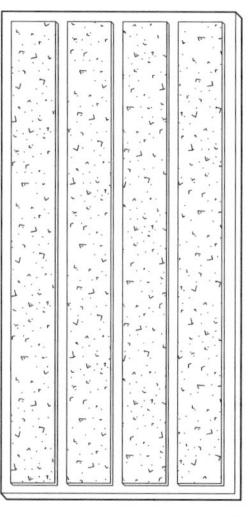

ROUTED LINEAR, FISSURED FINISH

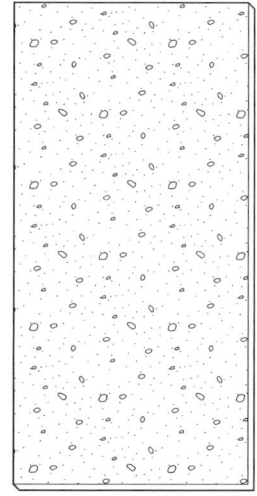

PEBBLE FINISH

ACOUSTICAL CEILING UNIT TEXTURES AND DESIGNS

Keith McCormack, CCS, CSI; RTKL Associates; Baltimore, Maryland

⑨ SPECIAL CEILING SURFACES

GENERAL

The wood flooring types shown on this page are those most commonly used for sports facilities. The specifics of each floor system differ from manufacturer to manufacturer. Some flooring systems are proprietary and protected by patents. Manufacturers can custom configure flooring systems for special uses.

The type of wood sports flooring chosen for a particular situation depends on the following criteria:

1. Cost
2. The performance of the floor
3. Sport(s) to be played on the floor
4. Other uses to which floor will be put
5. Durability
6. The environment in which the floor will be used

GRADES OF WOOD SPORTS FLOORING

Maple is the wood most commonly used for sports flooring in the United States. Maple sports flooring is available in three grades, which designate only the appearance of the floor and not its performance or durability.

FIRST GRADE: nearly free of defects; least color variation, with very little dark hardwood; used in premier sports venues where appearance is of primary concern.

SECOND AND BETTER: may have tight, sound knots and other slight imperfections and some color variation; floor has a generally light appearance.

THIRD GRADE: all defects and color variations permitted; floor is mostly dark heartwood; used when cost is a consideration.

MAPLE FLOOR SYSTEM CHARACTERISTICS

SYSTEM	COST	PERFOR-MANCE	DURA-BILITY	STA-BILITY
Proprietary	High	High	High	High
Sprung	High	High	Medium	High
Sleeper	Medium	Medium	Medium	High
Cushioned	Low	Medium	High	Medium
Channel	Low	Low	High	High
Mastic	Low	Low	High	Medium

FINISHES AND GAME LINES

Wood sports floors are sanded, sealed, and finished with at least two coats of sealer and two coats of finish.

Game lines are painted between the last coat of sealer and the first coat of finish. Game line paint must be compatible with sealer and finish.

REFERENCE

Maple Flooring Manufacturers Association
60 Revere Drive, Suite 500
Northbrook, IL 60062

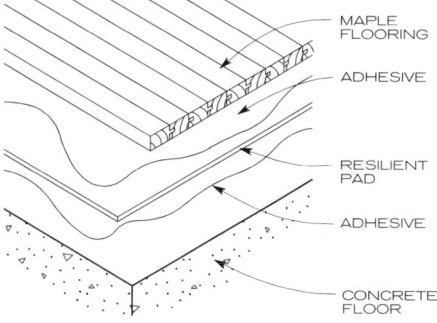

NOTES

1. Lowest cost
2. Easy to install
3. Suitable for multipurpose applications
4. Use where floor performance is not critical

MASTIC APPLIED SYSTEM

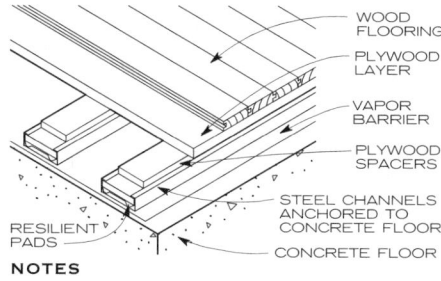

NOTES

1. Good performance characteristics
2. Relatively low cost
3. Susceptible to moisture damage

CUSHIONED SYSTEM

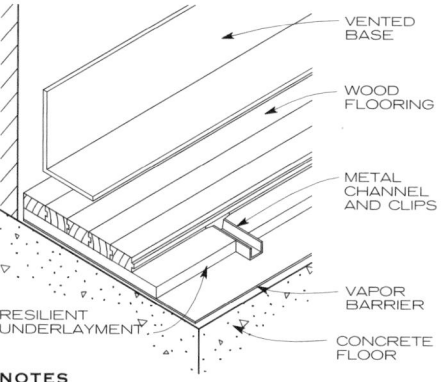

NOTES

1. Good performance
2. Can have dead spots
3. Susceptible to moisture damage
4. More difficult installation

SLEEPER SYSTEM

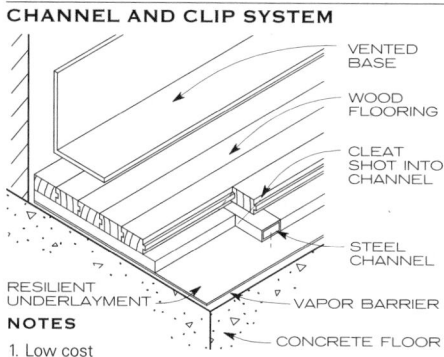

NOTES

1. Superior performance
2. Dimensionally stable
3. Suitable for multipurpose applications
4. A higher cost system

PROPRIETARY FLOATING SYSTEM—ROBBINS BIO-CHANNEL®

NOTES

1. Dimensionally stable in all environments
2. Good multipurpose floor
3. Limited performance characteristics

CHANNEL AND CLIP SYSTEM

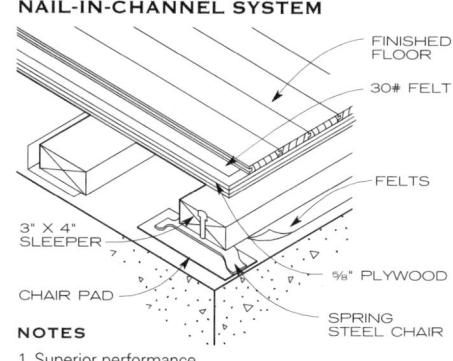

NOTES

1. Low cost
2. Fast installation
3. Dimensionally stable in all environments
4. Good multipurpose floor
5. Limited performance characteristics

NAIL-IN-CHANNEL SYSTEM

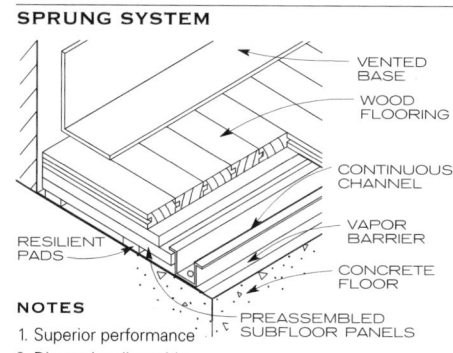

NOTES

1. Superior performance
2. High cost
3. Susceptible to moisture damage
4. More difficult installation

SPRUNG SYSTEM

NOTES

1. Superior performance
2. Dimensionally stable
3. Suitable for multipurpose applications
4. A higher cost system

PROPRIETARY SYSTEM—CONNOR/AGA REZILL CHANNEL®

Jim Swords; HOK Sports Facilities Group; Kansas City, Missouri
Connor/AGA Sports Flooring Corporation; Amasa, Michigan

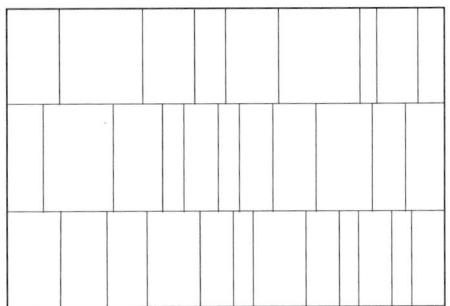

COURSED

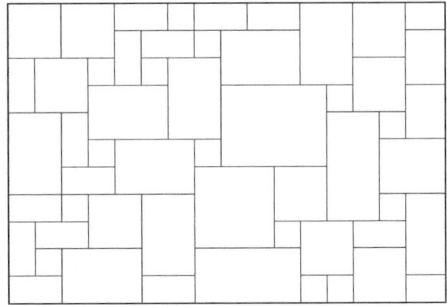

RANDOM RECTANGULAR

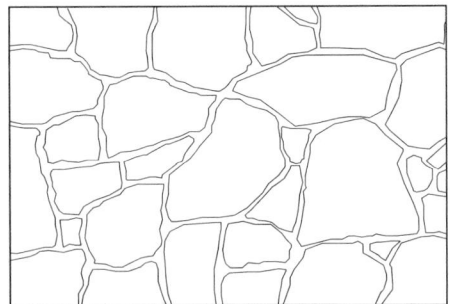

RANDOM IRREGULAR

FLAGSTONE AND SLATE PATTERNS

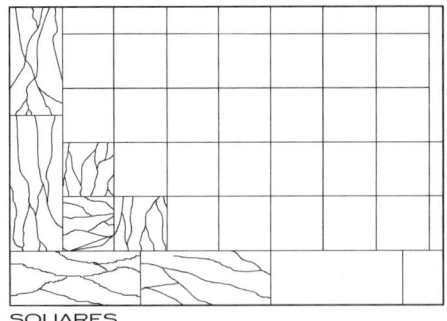

SQUARES

GEOMETRIC

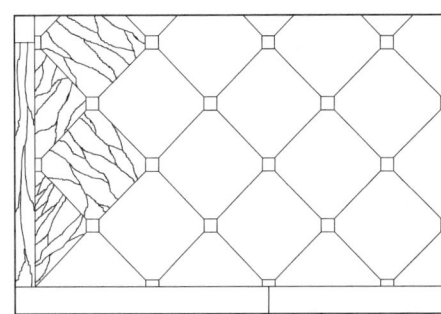

OCTAGON-SQUARE

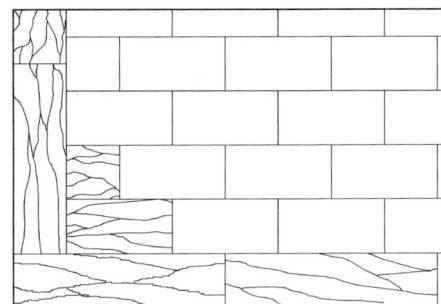

COURSED

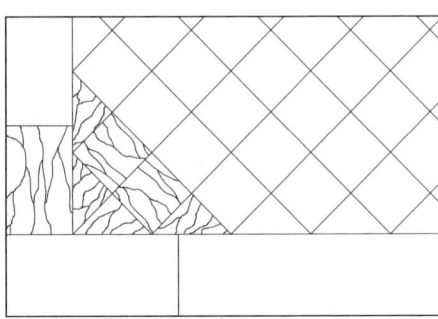

DIAMOND

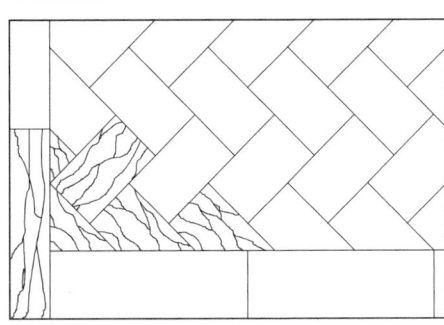

HERRINGBONE

MARBLE AND GRANITE PATTERNS

FINISHES

POLISHED: A glossy surface that brings out the full color of the stone. Generally, polished finishes can only be used on hard, dense material such as granite or marble.

HONED: A satin smooth surface with little or no gloss.

THERMAL: A planar surface with flame finish applied by mechanically controlled means to ensure uniformity. Surface coarseness varies depending on the grain structure of the stone. Generally, thermal finishes are used on granite.

RUBBED: A planar surface with occasional slight scratches.

TYPICAL FINISHES AND COMMON SIZES OF STONE TILES AND PAVERS

STONE	FINISH	THICKNESS (IN.)(MIN.)	FACE DIMENSION (IN.)(MAX.)	HA
Granite	polished honed thermal	$^3/_8$, $^1/_2$ (tiles) $1^1/_4$ - 4 (pavers)	12 x 12 (tiles) 15 x 30 (pavers)	N/A
Marble	polished honed	$^1/_4$ - $^1/_2$ (tiles) $1^1/_4$ (pavers)	12 x 12 (tiles) 24 x 24 (pavers)	10
Limestone	smooth	$1^3/_4$ - $2^1/_2$ (pavers)	24 x 36 (pavers)	10
Slate	natural cleft sand-rubbed	$^1/_4$ - 1	12 x 12 to 24 x 54	8
Flagstone	natural cleft semirubbed	$^1/_2$ - 4	12 x 12 to 24 x 36	8

NOTES

1. *Ha*, the abrasive hardness value, is the reciprocal of the volume of the material abraded multiplied by ten. A minimum value of 10 is recommended for flooring. Stones with a difference of 5 or more in *Ha* value should not be used together because they will wear differently.

2. Joint width should always be specified; $^1/_{16}$ to $^1/_8$ in. is considered standard.

3. Only attempt to set stone flooring over a wood subfloor after the subfloor has been reinforced to ensure against deflection.

4. Lippage is a condition that occurs when tiles are installed with a thin-bed method over an uneven surface. Tiles may "lip," one edge higher than their neighbors, giving the finished surface a ragged appearance. In some conditions, a certain amount of lippage is unavoidable. As a general rule, the recommended maximum variation of the finished surface should be no more than $^3/_{16}$ in. cumulative over a 10 ft. 0 in. lineal measurement, with no more than $^1/_{32}$ in. variation between individual tiles.

Mark Forma; Leo A. Daly Company; Washington, D.C.

STONE FLOORING

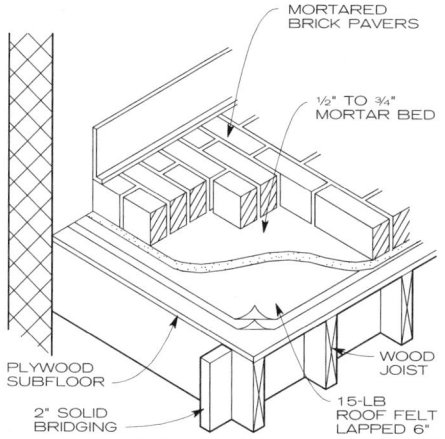

MORTARED BRICK PAVERS ON WOOD FRAMING

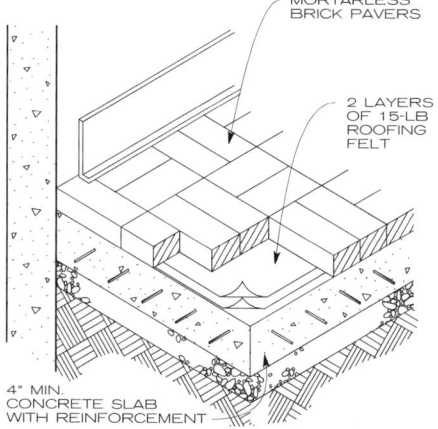

MORTARLESS BRICK PAVERS ON CONCRETE SLAB

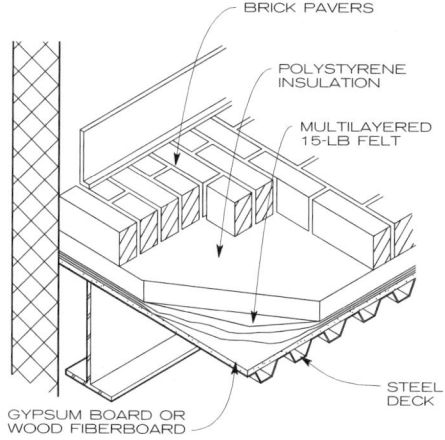

BRICK PAVERS ON STEEL DECK

TYPICAL BRICK AND CONCRETE PAVER TYPE AND NOMINAL SIZE

Brick pavers: 4 x 4 in., 4 x 8 in., 4 x 12 in.; $\frac{1}{2}$ to 2 $\frac{1}{4}$ in. thick. Concrete pavers: 12 x 12 in., 12 x 24 in., 18 x 18 in., 18 x 24 in., 2 $\frac{3}{8}$ to 3 in. thick.

NOTES

1. Brick paving assemblies are classified by type of paving surface and type of base supporting the surface. Interior brick paving may be adapted to suspended diaphragm bases, reinforced brick structural slabs with mortar joints, and conventional concrete slabs on grade.

2. In residential wood joist design, the additional weight of brick pavers must be considered to ensure selection of a suitable grade and joist size. For mortared paving, deflection and diaphragm action must be considered in order to maintain the integrity of the mortar joints.

Mark Forma; Leo A. Daly Company; Washington, D.C.

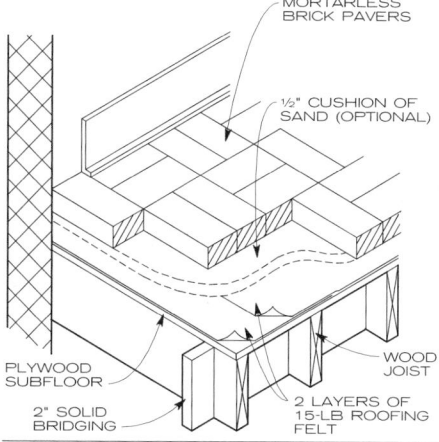

MORTARLESS BRICK PAVERS ON WOOD FRAMING

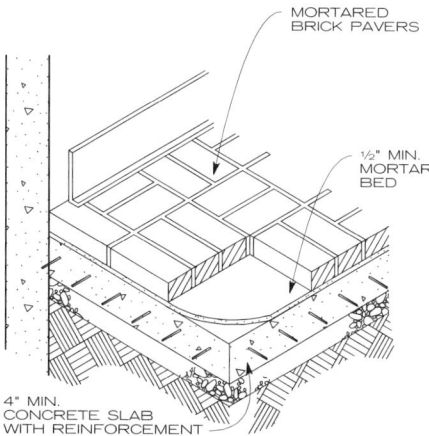

MORTARED BRICK PAVER ON CONCRETE SLAB

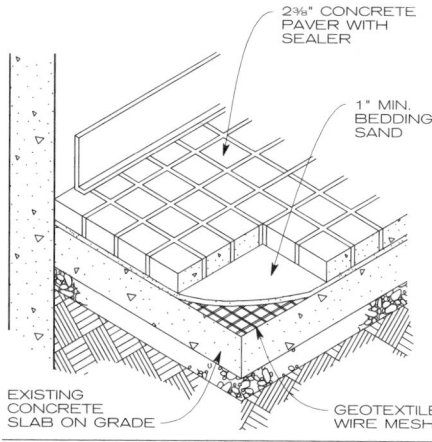

CONCRETE PAVERS ON CONCRETE SLAB

3. Reinforcement of brick masonry paving can eliminate the need for a separate reinforced concrete slab or other rigid base. Reinforced brick paving can be used to span an open space and is a practical system for relatively short spans. For continuous span application, an assembly combining both reinforced brick masonry and steel decking can be used.

4. Maintenance: Brick floors are abrasion resistant and hard-wearing. Coatings and waxes are desirable on interior brick floors, where they enhance appearance and make surfaces easier to clean. Prewaxing brick pavers on the exposed face facilitates cleaning, and applying a sealer locks in loose sand particles and provides an impervious finish.

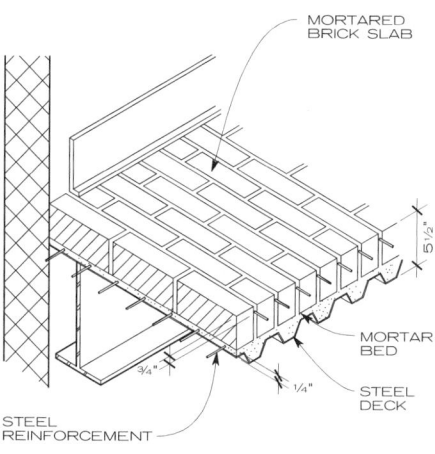

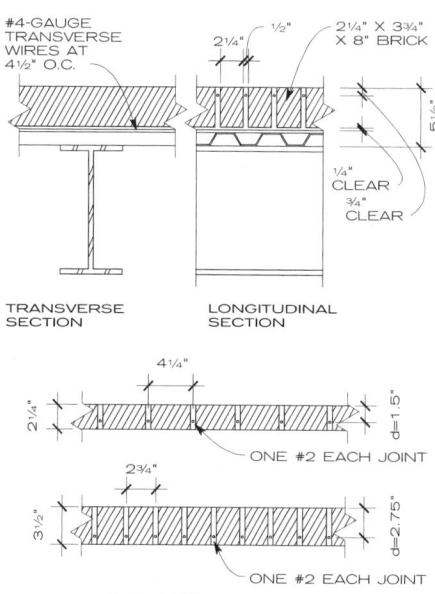

REINFORCED BRICK MASONRY

REINFORCED BRICK MASONRY SLABS

LIVE LOAD (PSF)	MAXIMUM CLEAR SPAN		
	t =2 $\frac{1}{4}$ IN. 1 #2 EACH JOINT	t =3 $\frac{1}{2}$ IN. 1 #2 EACH JOINT	t =6 $\frac{1}{4}$ IN. 1 #3 EVERY 3RD JOINT 1 #2 OTHER JOINTS
30	6'-10"	10'-5"	14'-5"
40	6'-3"	9'-9"	13'-8"
50	5'-10"	9'-2"	13'-1"
100	4'-6"	7'-3"	10'-11"
250	1'-10"	5'-0"	7'-10"

NOTES

1. Design parameters for the table above: The compressive strength average of the brick is 8000 psi. The mortar is type M (1:$\frac{1}{4}$:3), portland cement:lime:sand. Reinforcement steel is ASTM A 82-66, f_s = 20,000 psi. A simple span loading condition was assumed.

$$M = \frac{wl^2}{8}$$

2. All mortar joints are $\frac{1}{2}$ in. thick for the slabs shown, except as noted.

SPECIAL FLOORING

Special flooring manufacture is a constantly changing industry with myriad products and companies. Choose products to meet the requirements of a specific application after consultation with manufacturers. Select a well-established, reputable manufacturer with a tested and proven product. Have the product installed by experienced, factory-trained personnel.

RESINOUS FLOORING

EPOXY RESIN FLOORING: This abrasion- and impact- resistant, broadcast and/or trowel-applied, two-component epoxy resin floor is made of graded aggregates and mineral oxide pigments. Typical thicknesses are $1/8$ and $1/4$ in. Epoxy resin flooring can be applied to a variety of substrates and usually cures overnight, depending on the humidity. It is chemical resistant, fire retardant, and odor free and may be made slip resistant with a satin finish.

ACRYLIC RESIN FLOORING: This two- or three-component system is based on methyl methacrylate acrylic (MMA) resins; it has a low VOC. Four types are available in varying thicknesses: primer/sealers (8-10 mils), coatings ($1/16$ in.), toppings ($1/16$ - $3/16$ in.), and overlays ($3/16$ - $3/8$ in.). The system comprises graded aggregates, mineral oxide pigments, and pigmented topcoats. Typically, a $1/8$ in. thick floor is sufficient for light loads and pedestrian traffic and a $1/4$ in. thick floor is required for normal to heavy loads. Heavy-duty loads require a floor $1/2$ in. thick or thicker. Uses include animal housing/runs, industrial, institutional, coolers/freezers, cafeterias, food preparation, and multipurpose recreational facilities.

LATEX RESIN FLOORING: This trowel-applied, jointless floor offers low absorption and good chemical resistance. Chemical-resistant types are available to handle a variety of anticipated chemical spills. A waterproof membrane may be used to make the floor entirely waterproof, and it may be turned up at the base to form an integral coved base. Uses include showers, laboratories, animal research housing, pharmaceutical plants, and TV studios.

MAGNESIUM OXYCHLORIDE FLOORING

This is a fireproof, trowel-applied, seamless, hard surface floor that is slip resistant in both wet and dry locations. Durable and simple to install, it is used primarily in commercial kitchens and manufacturing locations such as welding shops. Its use is not recommended when standing water or mineral corrosives will be present. The standard color is red, although some earth tones may be available.

EPOXY MARBLE CHIP FLOORING AND SEAMLESS QUARTZ FLOORING

This seamless decorative flooring consists of ceramic-coated quartz or colored quartz aggregates in clear epoxy. It may be broadcast or trowel-applied in thicknesses of $1/16$, $1/8$, or $1/2$ in. Available in a wide range of aggregate colors, it may be slip resistant and is typically installed over concrete substrate. It is used in laboratories, locker rooms, and light manufacturing and institutional locations.

ELASTOMERIC LIQUID FLOORING

Conductive elastomeric liquid flooring—a multiple- or single-part system applied over concrete, metal, or wood substrates—consists of elastomeric resins, nonsparking aggregates, and a carbon or metallic conductive agent. Typically applied in thicknesses of $1/4$ or $1/2$ in., it may be applied to a wide variety of substrates and in a series of coats to achieve a smooth finish. Durable, easy to install, jointless (no divider strips), and waterproof are characteristics of this type of floor.

Elastomeric liquid flooring is designed to provide static control and spark resistance that can prevent electrostatic damage to electronic products as well as the conductivity required to prevent fire or explosions in high-hazard environments. The slab and conductive surface must be grounded and the floor well maintained in order for the floor to keep the required conductivity and static dissipative properties. Typical installations requiring these qualities include clean rooms and electronic manufacturing and assembly facilities. Typical installations requiring the conductive capabilities of elastomeric liquid flooring include arsenals, ammunition plants, chemical processing facilities, and hazardous explosive areas. End user static control and spark resistance must be clearly specified to ensure appropriate levels of resistance. People working in these environments must wear conductive footwear.

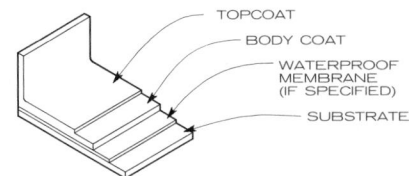

EPOXY RESIN FLOORING

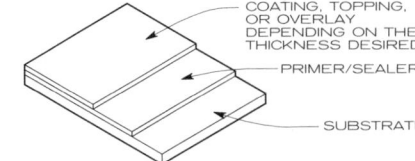

ACRYLIC RESIN FLOORING

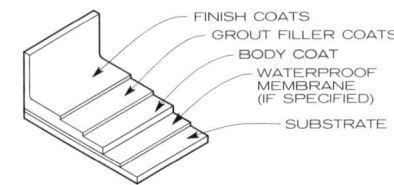

LATEX RESIN FLOORING

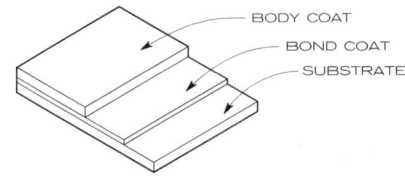

MAGNESIUM OXYCHLORIDE FLOORING

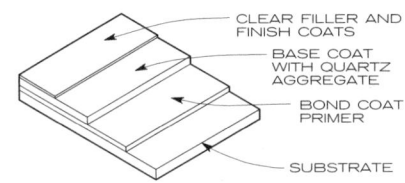

EPOXY MARBLE CHIP/ SEAMLESS QUARTZ FLOORING

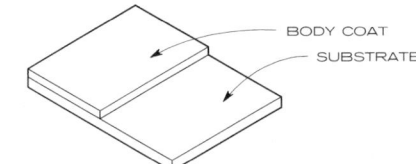

ELASTOMERIC LIQUID FLOORING

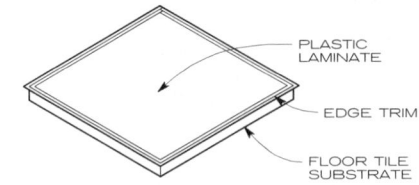

PLASTIC LAMINATE FLOORING

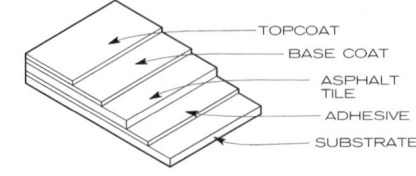

ASPHALT TILE FLOORING
FLOOR COATINGS

PLASTIC LAMINATE FLOORING

Plastic laminate flooring generates and retains low static levels. It has a low sheen, matte finish. Durable, flexible, and easily maintained, it is used exclusively as the top finish surface for access flooring. Applied to access floor substrates of steel, aluminum, wood, or particleboard with moisture-resistant adhesives, this type of flooring consists of a formulated, washable, surface sheet over a melamine-impregnated printed pattern sheet with core layers of phenolic-impregnated kraft paper. Typical tile size is 24 x 24 in., with standard thicknesses of $1/16$, $5/64$, and $1/8$ in., depending on load. Three quality grades are available. Floors must meet or exceed ANSI, NEMA, and NFPA codes and criteria.

ASPHALT PLANK FLOORING

A smooth, heavy-duty, comfortable, long-lasting, low maintenance tile floor, asphalt plank flooring is used in post offices, warehouses, and industrial locations. Tiles are set in adhesive troweled over a concrete substrate. An acrylic protective base coat is applied in two to three layers after the tiles have been set. A topcoat of two to three layers is applied to give the floor a high gloss for easier maintenance. Standard tile size is $1/2$ x 12 x 24 in. Other available thicknesses are $1/4$ - 3 in. Standard available colors are black and red.

MASTIC FILLS

Products described in other categories may also be considered in this one. Examples include self-adhering floor or deck coatings, traffic toppings, and underlayments that also fill cracks or uneven surfaces. Taken literally, this heading can include "mud set" mortar for tile over uneven substrates.

FLOOR TREATMENT

METALLIC-TYPE STATIC-DISSEMINATING AND SPARK-RESISTANT FINISH

This product is designed to provide static-control properties and spark-resistance capabilities that can prevent electrostatic damage to electronic products, as well as the conductivity required to prevent fire or explosions in high-hazard environments. The slab and conductive surface must be grounded. Maintenance of the floor is critical in order to keep the required conductivity and static-dissipative properties. Typical installations requiring static-dissipative products include clean rooms and electronic manufacturing and assembly facilities. Typical installations requiring conductive products include arsenals, ammunition plants, and chemical processing and other explosive hazardous areas. End user static control and spark resistance must be clearly specified to ensure appropriate levels of resistance. People working in these environments must wear conductive footwear.

Dry-shake metallic floor hardener is blended with plasticizing agents and conductive binders. This blend is applied to the surface of plastic concrete and becomes an integral part of the floor surface. It can be applied with a mechanical spreader, by hand, or with a shovel. Concrete admixture, air content, and floor finish requirements are strictly defined by metallic floor hardener manufacturers in terms of compatibility and amount, etc.

SLIP-RESISTANT FLOOR TREATMENT

These cementitious or noncementitious coatings are specifically designed to provide a nonskid finish for interior or exterior floors. Silica or synthetic aggregates provide the nonskid capability. The treatment is formulated for use on concrete or masonry surfaces and may be brushed or rolled on or trowel- or fluid-applied.

Chip Baker; Sverdrup Facilities Inc.; Arlington, Virginia

 SPECIAL FLOORING

DEFINITION

Special coatings are adhesive materials that have been developed for specific purposes such as resisting severe or corrosive environments or other forms of abuse. Special skills and techniques are usually required to mix, handle, and apply these materials.

A "special coating system" includes applied materials used in prime, intermediate, and finish coats. Factors that influence the choice of a system include

1. Substrates
2. Environmental conditions and surroundings
3. Cost

Prime and finish coats should be specified from the same manufacturer to eliminate many compatibility problems.

Proper substrate preparation, priming, and spread rate thickness are important for successful application of special coatings. Application is made by spray, brush, roller, or trowel.

SURFACE PREPARATION

The major reason coatings fail is poor surface preparation, which impairs adhesion. No coating is better than the surface over which it is applied. Surfaces must be prepared by a method suited to how they will be used and the exposure they will receive, in accordance with manufacturers' recommendations and the Steel Structures Painting Council (SSPC).

METAL SURFACES

Before a coating is applied, metal surfaces must be thoroughly cleaned, eliminating all visible deposits of surface dirt, grease, oil, and other deposits. Loose mill scale, rust, paint, and other detrimental foreign matter must also be removed. Grind rough welds and sharp edges, and remove weld spatter.

The SSPC recommends a variety of methods for preparing steel surfaces before application of a coating:

SSPC-SP-1 Solvent Cleaning
SSPC-SP-2 Hand Tool Cleaning
SSPC-SP-3 Power Tool Cleaning
SSPC-SP-5 White Metal Blast Cleaning
SSPC-SP-6 Commercial Blast Cleaning
SSPC-SP-7 Brush-off Blast Cleaning
SSPC-SP-8 Pickling
SSPC-SP-10 Near White Blast Cleaning

CONCRETE AND MASONRY SURFACES

Coatings adhere best to clean and slightly rough substrates. Grease, dirt, oils, efflorescence, laitance, and other surface deposits must be removed before additional surface preparation begins. Cleaning may be achieved by methods such as mechanical abrasion, abrasive blast, high pressure water wash, or acid etching. If cleaning solutions are applied, they must be completely removed before the coating is applied. Surfaces must be dry. If the surface is very smooth, it must be abraded or roughened slightly.

TYPES OF SPECIAL COATINGS

CEMENTITIOUS COATINGS

Polymer-modified, inorganic coatings can be ideal on concrete and masonry substrates. These coatings are primarily used on vertical surfaces above or below grade, on the exterior or interior, and on new construction or restoration and renovation work for aesthetics, permeability, and moisture resistance. They are also useful for walls subject to positive or negative hydrostatic pressure.

ABRASION-RESISTANT COATINGS

Epoxy or elastomeric seamless coating may be used over substrates of brick, stucco, concrete, block, drywall, and plywood in both interior and exterior applications. These coatings may be weatherproof and resist chemicals. Abrasion resistance may be inherent or achieved through an additional topcoat.

ELASTOMERIC COATINGS

Acrylic polymer coatings may be used over exterior concrete, masonry, and stucco surfaces. These thick, dirt-resistant, membranelike coatings are flexible in a range of temperatures, displaying an ability to follow expansion and contraction of surfaces without rupturing or wrinkling. They are very high-build materials that bridge small cracks and protect against deterioration from moisture penetration of the substrate. Like other special coatings, these typically should not be used to bridge building expansion joints. Acrylic polymer coatings are available in smooth and textured finishes.

HIGH-BUILD GLAZED COATINGS

Acrylic resin, elastomeric, or epoxy coatings may be suitable for use over exterior or interior concrete, block, masonry, plaster, stucco, wood, and metal surfaces in vertical or horizontal applications. Applied in multiple coats or thick single coats, these coatings usually provide resistance to chemicals and abrasion. These high-performance coatings provide good adhesion and hardness, producing a tile-like gloss finish. Some systems may be reinforced with fiberglass mesh between base and seal coats to increase maximum impact resistance.

FIRE-RESISTANT PAINTS

Fire-resistant paints are able to withstand fire and protect the substrate for short periods of time, usually less than one hour. They will not support combustion and do not deteriorate readily under fire conditions. They will reduce or prevent the spread of flame over a combustible surface. In some cases they may be used as one component of a fire-rated assembly. The products of such an assembly are non-combustible, and the coating, which prevents oxygen from reaching the substrate, contains chemicals that inhibit the release of volatile gases necessary for combustion.

To be eligible for listing as a fire-retardant paint, a coating must either reduce the flame spread of the surface to which it is applied by at least 30% or have a flame spread rating of 70 or less as tested under current ASTM E-84 guidelines. Manufacturers may recommend a three- to five-year schedule for reapplying the coating in order to maintain its fire-resistant capability. Fire-resistant paints can be used to coat wood, drywall, plaster, and metal.

INTUMESCENT PAINTS

Intumescent paint is a type of fire-resistant paint that behaves differently than typical such products in a fire condition. When subjected to flame or intense heat, intumescent paints liquefy, allowing escaping gases to form an insulating layer of char, which forms a protective layer around the substrate. Fire-resistant designs have been tested by independent laboratories to establish protection requirements and the extent of protection available. Incompatible paints used as a topcoat with intumescent paints may prevent the chemical reactions necessary to form the intumescent char, thereby reducing or negating the fire-resistant property.

GRAFFITI-RESISTANT COATINGS

Graffiti-resistant coatings permit the easy removal of graffiti without damage to the substrate. The system comprises a multicoat base system that increases the hardness of the substrate and a sacrificial, multicoat topcoat system. Cleaners can be nontoxic and do not require sandblasting, solvents, or toxic materials. Additional topcoats can be added after cleaning, if desired, to reinforce the sacrificial protection layer.

COATING SYSTEMS FOR STEEL

Selection of steel coating systems for tanks and piping are primarily governed by substrate and service conditions. Industry specific standards also affect specifications. Water treatment, food processing, energy production, and chemical processing industries have different requirements and standards that should be verified prior to specification. Water tanks in most U.S. jurisdictions must meet very stringent National Sanitary Foundation (NSF) requirements for potable water storage.

EXTERIOR COATING SYSTEM FOR STEEL STORAGE TANKS

Choice of coating for steel storage tank exteriors depends on tank condition and location, the weather during application, and the service conditions. A number of two-part epoxy systems and urethane systems have been formulated to address these concerns. Coatings may possess rust-inhibitive qualities, the ability to cure at low-temperatures, and excellent weathering ability and may offer galvanic protection. Dry-fall ability may be desirable in some instances and is available from alkyd products. Compatible products can be used as metal fillers and to accelerate curing rates. Local regulations regarding the content of volatile organic compounds (VOCs) will influence product selection and application techniques.

INTERIOR COATING SYSTEM FOR STEEL STORAGE TANKS

Choice of coatings for steel storage tank interiors is affected by tank condition and location and service conditions. A number of two-part epoxy systems and phenolic systems have been formulated to address these concerns. These products are designed to provide sustained immersion service in food processing, petrochemical, and water treatment industries for use in freshwater, saltwater, and severe chemical environments. National Sanitation Foundation (NSF) approvals may be necessary in certain applications.

COATING SYSTEM FOR STEEL PIPING

Coatings for steel piping are subject to many of the same conditions as coatings for steel tanks. Coatings for piping used for chemical service must be selected to match the level of chemical exposure expected. Mild exposures may permit the use of an acrylic coating, while aggressive chemical and moisture exposure may require the use of chlorinated rubber coatings. Severe chemical exposures typically require a two-part epoxy system.

The American Society of Mechanical Engineers and ANSI publish standardized color codes for pipe identification. For example, red means fire protection equipment; yellow, dangerous materials; blue, protective materials; green, safe materials; yellow with a black legend or stripe, radioactive materials.

Isabel Ramirez and Ted Hallinan; Sverdrup Facilities Inc.; Arlington, Virginia

CHEMICAL-RESISTANT COATINGS

EXPOSURE	TYPE OF COATING	APPLICATIONS	ALCOHOLS	ALIPHATIC HYDROCARBONS	ALKALI SOLUTIONS	AROMATIC HYDROCARBONS	FRESHWATER	KATONES	MINERAL ACIDS	MINERAL OILS	ORGANIC ACIDS	OXIDIZING AGENTS	SALT SOLUTIONS	VEGETABLE OILS	WASTEWATER	WEATHERING
Rural, urban light industrial	Alkyd primer and alkyd topcoat	Warehouses, manufacturing plants, schools, storage tank exteriors	O	O	N	N	O	N	N	C	N	N	N	N	N	G
Mild chemical	High-build epoxy, polyamide-cured, and urethane topcoat	Wood yards, plywood plants, sawmills	C	C	C	O	C	N	O	C	O	O	C	C	C	E
Fresh and salt water immersion; moderate chemical exposure	Coal tar epoxy, polyamide-cured	Pilings, waste treatment pits, pulp and paper mills, marine structures and barges, cogeneration	C	C	C	C	I	N	O	C	O	O	I	C	I	F
Fresh and potable water immersion	High-build epoxy, amine-cured	Water storage, tank interiors, locks and water control gates	C	C	C	C	I	O	O	C	O	O	I	I	I	F
Severe chemical	High-build epoxy, polyamide-cured, and urethane topcoat	Pulp and paper mills, coal-handling, chemical pits, sour crude refineries, fertilizer plants	C	C	C	O	C	O	O	C	O	O	C	C	C	E
Severe chemical—acid resistance	High-build epoxy, amine-cured	Pulp and paper mills, dockside exposures, fertilizer pits, acid loading docks, dye plants	C	C	C	C	I	O	O	C	C	C	I	I	I	F
Severe chemical—alkali and solvent resistance	Organic zinc-rich epoxy primer and high-build epoxy, polyamide-cured, topcoat	Pulp and paper mills, coal-handling facilities, dockside exposures	C	C	C	C	I	O	O	C	O	O	C	C	I	F
Severe chemical—alkali resistance	Organic zinc-rich epoxy primer and high-build epoxy, polyamide-cured, and urethane topcoat	Capital structures where color and gloss retention are needed	C	C	C	O	C	O	O	C	O	O	C	C	C	E
Severe chemical—solvent and alkali resistance	Inorganic zinc-rich primer and high-build epoxy polyamide-cured topcoat	New construction, pulp and paper mills, power pits, coal liquefaction, cogeneration	C	C	C	C	I	O	O	C	O	O	C	C	I	F
Severe chemical	Zinc-rich primer and urethane topcoat	Where gloss retention and color are important	C	C	C	O	C	C	O	O	C	O	O	C	C	E
High temperature (up to 1200°F)	Heat-resistant silicone aluminum	Stacks, incinerators, super-heated steam lines, boiler casings and drums	O	O	N	N	N	N	N	C	N	N	N	N	N	E
Immersion, severe exposures	Coal tar epoxy polyamide-cured	Waste treatment pits, pulp and paper mills, cogeneration, power pits, sour crude exposures	C	C	C	O	I	N	O	C	O	O	I	C	I	F

I—immersion   C—frequent contact   O—occasional contact   N—not recommended   F—fair   G—good   E—excellent

CHEMICAL-RESISTANT COATINGS

Chemical-resistant coatings are selected according to substrate type and actual chemical exposure. Formulations of this product type vary widely from manufacturer to manufacturer and are subject to changes caused by technological advances and environmental legislation. Dry-film thicknesses, cure rates, and application methods also vary among product types and manufacturers. End user program requirements and consultation with manufacturers is recommended before specifying these products. In-place or laboratory testing may be advisable in critical conditions.

Isabel Ramirez and Ted Hallinan; Sverdrup Facilities Inc.; Arlington, Virginia

SPECIAL COATINGS

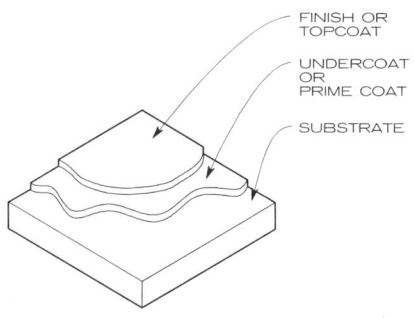

FINISH OR TOPCOAT
UNDERCOAT OR PRIME COAT
SUBSTRATE

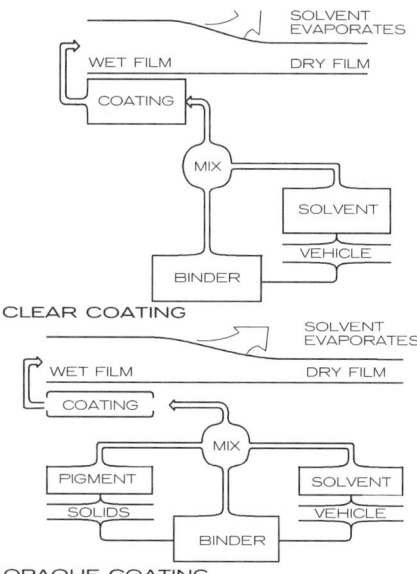

CLEAR COATING

OPAQUE COATING

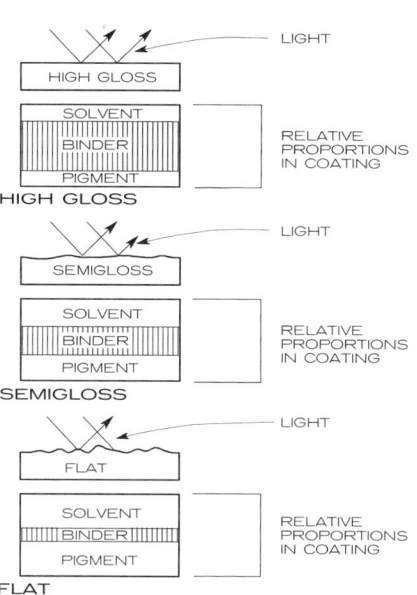

LIGHT
HIGH GLOSS
SOLVENT
BINDER
PIGMENT
RELATIVE PROPORTIONS IN COATING
HIGH GLOSS

LIGHT
SEMIGLOSS
SOLVENT
BINDER
PIGMENT
RELATIVE PROPORTIONS IN COATING
SEMIGLOSS

LIGHT
FLAT
SOLVENT
BINDER
PIGMENT
RELATIVE PROPORTIONS IN COATING
FLAT

COMPOSITION OF COATINGS

GENERAL

Coatings are thin surface facings applied in liquid form which solidify to protect building components from harmful exposure. Appropriate coating selection depends upon performance, appearance, cost, and rate of deterioration of the substrate should the coating fail. Coatings are made up of the prepared substrate, prime coats or undercoats, and finish or topcoats, all of which should be compatible for adhesion and resistance to deterioration.

DESIGN CONSIDERATIONS

Environmental and ambient conditions affect coating performance. Resistance to sun, moisture, pollution, chemicals, extremes of temperature, soiling, and abrasion will determine a set of coatings, from which a selection is made based on remaining criteria. Design considerations should also include:

1. Flow, or ease of application.
2. Leveling or smoothing after application.
3. Drying time, of which two factors are important: (a) set-to-touch or surface drying, when surface resists contaminants, and (b) through-dry, when all layers are dry and ready to recoat.
4. Permeability: moisture migration through coating.
5. Wetting: penetration of coating to a lower level. Lower wetting ability requires greater surface preparation.
6. Film thickness: amount of protection provided by coating.
7. Adhesion between layers.
8. Flexibility: accommodation to changes in moisture and temperature.
9. Abrasion, impact, and stain resistance and ease of cleaning.

TYPES

Coatings are classified by appearance—clear, semitransparent, or opaque, and are water-based or organic solvent-based. Coatings are composed of a vehicle—alone when clear, or with pigments when semitransparent or opaque. The vehicle is in turn composed of binder and solvent. The binder is the nonvolatile part of the vehicle which forms the film of the coating and which bonds pigments when they are used. Additives for special properties, such as driers, stabilizers, plasticizers, and thinners, are included in the binder. The solvent is the volatile part of the vehicle which dissolves the binder to adjust viscosity, and which evaporates as the coating changes from liquid to solid state. Pigment adds opacity and/or color to the vehicle.

Clear coatings only slightly obscure the surface of the substrate. They are used when it is important to preserve appearance, such as the grain of wood or the color of an exposed concrete aggregate. Clear coatings are composed of a vehicle only, solvent and binder, with no pigment added. Sealers, waterproofing, and varnishes are typical examples of clear coatings.

Semitransparent coatings partially obscure the substrate surface. They can modify the appearance of the substrate by changing the color of wood without hiding its grain. Semitransparent coatings are composed of solvent, binder, and limited pigment. Stains are exemplary of this group.

Opaque coatings completely obscure the surface of the substrate. The color and/or texture of the substrate are changed; the original appearance unimportant or undesirable. Opaque coatings are made up of pigment, solvent, and binder. Paints are opaque coatings.

Coating properties are determined by the binder, which forms the surface film and bonds to the substrate. A combination of binders will alter the properties displayed by a coating, as will additives that modify the formation of the

TYPES OF COATINGS

coating. Binders composed of small molecules (e.g., drying oils) penetrate rough surfaces and adhere well but dry slowly and are not chemically resistant. Binders composed of large molecules, built-up or polymerized of smaller molecules, yield strong, chemically resistant films but are susceptible to dissolution in the same solvent when formulated for solvent evaporation only. Large molecules may be formed by reaction between small molecules as in linseed oil; they may be made before application and dissolved in solvent to lower viscosity; or they may be formed by a combination of these two methods.

Pigments hide the substrate by adding opacity and color, but may also increase durability and protective characteristics by screening UV radiation, controlling transmission of moisture and gases, and inhibiting degradation or corrosion of the substrate. Colored pigments absorb some light rays while reflecting others, and white pigments absorb little light, so their hiding efficacy depends on the ability to scatter and reflect incident light. Scattering and reflecting ability in turn depends upon the size, distribution, and refractive index of the pigment particles. Pigment also determines the gloss of the coating finish through its relative proportion to binder and solvent in the vehicle.

Environmental exposure concurrent with or following application of the coating may affect the coating or the substrate. Some types of exposure to consider are atmospheric contamination, such as sulfurous or marine air which may discolor coatings and accelerate chalking and deterioration; mildew in humid environments; and sudden drops or rises in temperature at the time of application, which may flatten or blister a freshly applied coating.

EXTERNAL FACTORS

A number of external factors affect the stability of a coating.

SOLAR RADIATION/UV RADIATION can fade colored pigments, cause chemical reaction in some binders or solvents, and degrade the substrate if the coating is not UV opaque. It may be necessary for the coating to reflect, scatter, or absorb visible light to avoid this problem.

TEMPERATURE: Solar radiation raises the temperature of the coating, causing expansion and accelerating solvent evaporation. Exposure to heat through convection of hot air or other gases, or by conduction through the substrate (as through accidental exposure to fire) may also affect coating performance. Freezing temperatures hinder proper curing of some vehicles.

RAIN: A heated coating can undergo thermal shock when exposed to rain. Rainwater can also be absorbed and cause swelling of the coating or leach pigments from the coating. Rain may also penetrate through cracks or checks and freeze, causing damage to the coating and the substrate.

WATER VAPOR: Vapor may be required to properly cure some coatings. Under some conditions water vapor should be allowed to permeate the coating to prevent condensation, while at other times permeation must be prevented to protect the substrate.

EFFECT OF PIGMENT CONTENT ON GLOSS OF COATING

CHEMICAL FUMES: Generated by chemical processes or by burning fossil fuels, chemical fumes can leave deposits on the coating, by reacting directly with it or by entering solution with rainwater or condensation.

DUST, DIRT: Dust penetrates porous coatings, collects airborne pollutants, and can stain and degrade the coating in reaction with rainwater. Marring of the coating may also be intentional, as with graffiti.

ABRASION, IMPACT: Coatings can be abraded by high-velocity flow of gaseous or liquid substances, by traffic, vandalism, or airborne dust. Impact may be through natural causes such as hailstones, may be accidental, or may be intentional, as with vandalism.

SURFACE WATER: External fresh or sea water can rise and fall, exposing normally submerged portions of the surface to solar radiation and oxygen and subjecting the coating and substrate to differential thermal expansion between the exposed and submerged portions of the surface.

CHEMICAL SOLUTIONS: Coatings may be submerged in chemical solutions such as sea water, sewage, oils, lubricants, or solvents and some of these may react with specific constituent parts of the coating, degrading or dissolving it.

SELECTION CONSIDERATIONS

Coating selection should be based on external or environmental factors (see above), type and degree of exposure to these factors, including an estimate of speed of substrate deterioration should the coating fail. Conditions met by the coating may vary over time, across a surface, or within the substrate, and contingencies should be planned. The possibility of an alkaline substrate such as concrete becoming moist through penetration or condensation should be considered before a non-alkaline-resistant coating is applied. Differential wear on walking or other surfaces should be considered, as well as applications of higher performance coatings.

The in-place cost of a coating accounts for surface preparation and application as well as the coating itself. Failure may result in permanent damage to the substrate, or may require complete removal and preparation for a new coating. The properties of the principal binder should determine the selection of a coating, with modifications and additions to the formulation made for specific job requirements.

SAFETY AND HEALTH CONSIDERATIONS

Hazards associated with coating application and surface preparation include toxic fumes from strong solvents; toxic dust from sandblasting, grinding, or fire; and toxicity of coating solvents when absorbed through skin or inhaled. In addition, use of photochemically reactive solvents may be limited or restricted by air-pollution controlling ordinances.

James W. Laffey; Washington, D.C.

PAINTS AND COATINGS: PROPERTIES

TYPE	PRINCIPAL BINDER	BASE/CURE	TYPICAL USES	COMPARATIVE COST RANGE	IN-SERVICE LIFE RANGE IN YEARS	GLOSS RETENTION	STAIN RESISTANCE	WEATHER RESISTANCE	ABRASION IMPACT RESISTANCE	FLEXIBILITY
Clear	Acrylic, methyl methacrylate copolymer	solvent; water	Waterproofing and surface sealer against dirt retention, graffiti; for vertical surfaces of concrete, masonry, stucco; may be pigmented.	moderate to high	5 to 10	excellent to good	fair	excellent to good	good	good
	Alkyd, spar varnish	solvent	For interior and protected exterior wood surfaces. Also as vehicle for aluminum pigmented coatings.	moderate	up to 1 exterior	fair to good	poor	poor	fair	good
	Phenolic, spar varnish	solvent	Exterior wood surfaces subject to moisture. May be used in marine environments. Also vehicle for aluminum pigment.	moderate to high	up to 2 exterior	fair to good	fair	good	good	good
	Silicone	solvent	Waterproofing and surface sealer against dirt retention for vertical surfaces of concrete, masonry, stucco.	moderate	5 to 7	flat	fair	good	penetrating coating	
	Urethane, one-part	moist cure[1]	Surfaces subject to chemical attack; abrasion, graffiti, heavy or concentrated traffic, such as gymnasium floors.	moderate to high	up to 15	excellent to good	good to excellent	good to excellent	good to excellent	excellent
Stain	Acrylic	solvent; water	Pigmented translucent or semi-opaque exterior surface sealers; solvent based for masonry, concrete; water based for wood.	moderate to low	3 to 5	flat finish	not a factor	good to fair	penetrating coatings—resistance same as for substrate	
	Alkyd	solvent; water	Pigmented exterior or interior surface sealer for wood surfaces such as shingles, does not impart sheen to surface.	moderate	3 to 5	flat finish		fair		
	Oil	solvent	Pigmented exterior or interior surface sealer for wood such as shingles, trim, opaque or semitransparent.	moderate	3 to 5	fair		fair		
Opaque	Acrylic	water	For exterior/interior vertical surfaces of wood, masonry, plaster, gypsum board, metals. Good color retention. Permeable to vapor.	moderate to low	5 to 8	good to fair	fair	good	good to fair	good to excellent
	Acrylic, epoxy modified, two-part	water	High performance coating for interior vertical surfaces subject to graffiti, stains, heavy scrubbing. May be used in food preparation areas.	high	10 to 15	good	good	good to excellent	good to excellent	good to excellent
	Alkyd	solvent; water	For exterior/interior vertical and horizontal surfaces, such as wood, metals, masonry. Poor permeability to vapor.	moderate	5 to 8	good to excellent	fair	fair to good	fair to good	fair to good
	Chlorinated rubber	solvent	Swimming pool coatings. Corrosion protection; isolating dissimilar metals.	high to very high	up to 10	fair	fair	good	fair to good	good
	Chlorosulfonated polyethylene	solvent	Protective coating for tanks, piping, valves, elastomeric roofing membranes.	very high	up to 15	not applicable	fair	excellent	fair to good	excellent
	Epoxy, two-part; epoxy ester, one part	solvent cure; solvent	Moisture/alkali resistant. Two-part for nondecorative interior uses highly resistant to chemicals. Esters in wide choice of colors.	high to very high	15 to 20; up to 10	poor to good	excellent for two-part	good to excellent	excellent	good to excellent
	Phenolic	solvent	Chemical- and moisture-resistant coatings. May be used over alkaline surfaces.	moderate to high	up to 10	fair	fair	good to excellent	good to excellent	good
	Polychloroprene	solvent[2]	Marketed as "Neoprene"; resistant to chemicals, moisture, ultraviolet radiation. Also used as roofing membrane; generally covered with Hypalon.	very high	up to 25	not applicable	good	excellent	excellent	good
	Polyester	solvent	Limited application in field; over cementitious surfaces, metal, plywood for exterior exposures.	high	up to 15	good to excellent	good to excellent	good to excellent	good	good to excellent
	Silicone	solvent	Surfaces with temperatures up to 1200°F. Often with aluminum pigments. Corrosion and solvent resistant.	very high	varies	not applicable, special purpose coating			good	good
	Silicone; modified acrylic, alkyd, epoxy	solvent	High-performance exterior coatings. Industrial siding, curtain walls, when shop-applied baked-on.	high to very high	15 to 20	good to excellent	good	good to excellent	good to excellent	good
	Styrene, butadiene	water	Interior coating for gypsum board, plaster, masonry. Limited exterior use over cementitious substrate, as filler over rough porous surfaces.	moderate to low	4 to 6	poor to fair	fair	poor	fair	good
	Urethane, one or two part	moist or chemical cure[3]	Heavy-duty wall and floor coatings. Resistance to stains, chemicals, graffiti, scrubbing, solvents, impact, abrasion.	high to very high	15 to 20	excellent	good to excellent	good to excellent	good to excellent	excellent
	Vinyl, polyvinyl chloride-acetate	solvent	Residential metal siding and trim, gutters, leaders, baseboard heating covers, when shop-applied, baked-on.	high	up to 15	good	fair	good	good	good to excellent
	Vinyl, polyvinylidene chloride	water	Metal and concrete surfaces in contact with dry and wet food, potable water, wastewater, jet and diesel fuels.	high	up to 10	good	fair	good	good	good
	Vinyl, polyvinyl acetate	water	Exterior and interior vertical surfaces, such as masonry, concrete, wood, plaster, gypsum board, metals. Permeable to vapor.	moderate to low	5 to 8	good to fair	fair	good	good to fair	good
	Bituminous, coal tar pitch, asphalt: emulsions, cutbacks	solvent	Waterproofing of metals, concrete, masonry, portland cement plaster, piping when below grade or immersed.	low	10 to 15 protected	not a factor		good	poor	fair
	Cement	water	Leveling coat over porous masonry or concrete not subject to abrasion or scrubbing. Cement and oil used as primers for metal surfaces.	low	varies	flat finish	poor	poor for color	good	poor

[1] Solvent-based, oil-modified urethane is also available; for use on interior/exterior vertical and horizontal wood surfaces. Cost is moderate.

[2] May be obtained as water-reducible coating; use as field-applied coating very limited; generally used as tank linings.

[3] Solvent base, oil-modified urethane is also available; for use on vertical and horizontal surfaces. Cost is moderate, but durability is lower than for other types.

NOTES

1. Solvent-based acrylic is impermeable to water vapor, high gloss.
2. Water-based acrylic is semigloss, water vapor permeable.
3. Phenolic varnish has a dark tint; will darken with age; may be topcoated with clear alkyd.
4. Clear varnishes are not recommended for exterior wood because of limited durability.
5. Urethane may be formulated to yield hard, glossy surface so that graffiti can be removed with strong solvents.
6. Fillers may be required when using clear coatings over hardwood, such as oak; abraded wood may limit choice; consult manufacturer's literature.
7. Stains may be used as surface sealers to change color of wood and then be topcoated with clear coatings.
8. Stains over exterior wood surfaces generally will provide better protection than clear coatings, but usually will not last as long as opaque coatings.
9. Alkyd may be modified with silicone for better color retention.
10. Epoxy-esters have intermediate properties between two-part epoxies and alkyds and phenolics.
11. Bitumen-epoxy formulations are available for use as heavy-duty waterproofing of underground piping, structural members.
12. Phenolic may chalk upon exterior exposure; high degree of resistance to acids, alkalis, and solvents; some formulations available for surface temperatures of up to 300-350°F.
13. Polyesters available glass fiber reinforced; also used widely for baked-on factory applied finishes for formed metal wall panels.
14. Silicone for high temperature applications generally with aluminum pigment.
15. Polyvinyl chloride film is used for factory-applied finishes for formed metal wall panels.
16. Cement paint will absorb rainwater and will darken until water evaporates; requires moist curing after application; if not properly cured will tend to dust and rub off.
17. For high performance coatings under severe conditions, life expectancy may be less.

James W. Laffey; Washington, D.C.

GENERAL

Paints and coatings are in liquid form before and during application, after which they cure to form a non-self-supporting film. They cannot exist without a solid, generally rigid substrate to receive and support them. Since a coating bonds itself firmly and continuously to the substrate, the exposure, condition, and properties of the substrate, as well as its surface characteristics and defects, directly affect the coating during and after application.

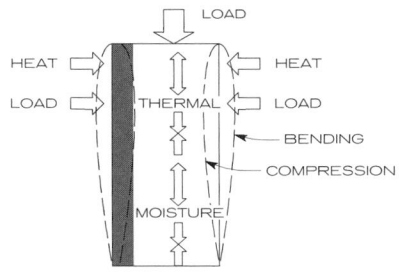

NOTES

Movement in the substrate, which may crack the coating, may result from

1. Thermal expansion/contraction due to exposure to solar radiation; sources of heat outside the substrate, such as heat-generating equipment adjacent to it; and heat-generating processes contained by the substrate.
2. Differential thermal movement between the substrate and the coating it supports, caused by variations in exposure. For example, rain may suddenly cool a coating over a hot substrate or solar radiation may heat a coating over a cold substrate.
3. Shrinking/swelling due to changes in the internal moisture content of the substrate. Under extreme conditions, variations may be as much as 5% or more across the grain in wood.
4. Deflection under load, vertical or horizontal, which induces tensile and compressive stresses in the substrate that may affect the coating.
5. Restrained end conditions of the substrate, which may cause bending stresses. Vibration in the substrate will result in cyclical stress reversals.

SUBSTRATE MOVEMENT

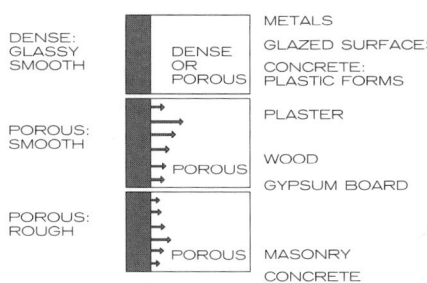

SURFACE	SUBSTRATE	TYPICAL MATERIAL
DENSE: GLASSY SMOOTH	DENSE OR POROUS	METALS, GLAZED SURFACES, CONCRETE: PLASTIC FORMS
POROUS: SMOOTH	POROUS	PLASTER, WOOD, GYPSUM BOARD
POROUS: ROUGH	POROUS	MASONRY, CONCRETE

NOTES

Absorption at the surface of the substrate and that of the substrate itself may vary and affect the choice of coating or its performance characteristics:

1. Glassy dense surfaces, even applied over a porous substrate, will prevent absorption of a coating. Such surfaces may require roughening by sandblasting or acid etching to ensure proper adhesion of most coatings.
2. Porous substrates may have varying degrees of absorption within a continuous surface (for example, different rates of absorption in bands of spring and summer growth of wood). Different rates of absorption will result in different degrees of adhesion and may cause a coating to crack along junction lines between such bands.
3. The rough surface of a porous substrate may cause varying degrees of absorption in an application, even though the absorption of the substrate does not vary significantly. For instance, when the roughness of a surface prevents the application of a film of uniform thickness over it, different rates of absorption may result. This will cause changes in the gloss of the coating, overpigmentation in areas of excessive absorption of the vehicle, and varying degrees of adhesion.

SUBSTRATE ABSORPTION

McCain McMurray; Washington, D.C.

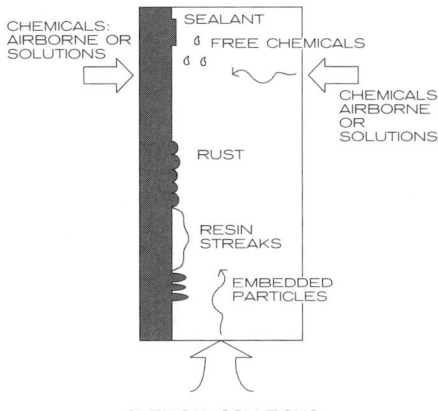

CHEMICAL SOLUTIONS

NOTES

Chemicals may be contained within the substrate or absorbed by it:

1. Soluble alkaline salts in concrete or mortar may be dissolved and crystallize on the surface.
2. Resin streaks in wood may react with the coating and bleed through, or old coatings may react chemically with new ones.
3. Rust deposits may stain some coatings and may impair adhesion.
4. Sealants used in joints may stain the substrate and/or coating.
5. Fasteners may corrode; loose particles of metal may lodge themselves in the substrate and corrode after the coating is applied.
6. Admixtures, form oils, curing agents, and antifreeze solutions used when concrete is cast may prevent proper adhesion of coatings or may react with them.
7. If cleaning solutions used during surface preparation are not completely removed before the coating is applied, they may react with the coating or impair its absorption and/or adhesion.

CHEMICALS IN SUBSTRATE

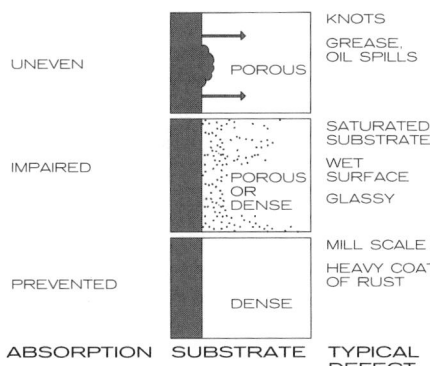

ABSORPTION	SUBSTRATE	TYPICAL DEFECT
UNEVEN	POROUS	KNOTS, GREASE, OIL SPILLS
IMPAIRED	POROUS OR DENSE	SATURATED SUBSTRATE, WET SURFACE, GLASSY
PREVENTED	DENSE	MILL SCALE, HEAVY COAT OF RUST

NOTES

Uneven or impaired adhesion results in coating failure. Adhesion of the coating to the surface of a substrate is affected by

1. Surface defects such as knots, resin streaks in the wood, or surface contaminants such as oil, grease, or salt deposits over any type of substrate. Such defects impair bonding of the coating to the substrate, creating weak spots where vapor may condense. When the vapor expands, it breaks or lifts the film.
2. Moist or wet surfaces. These may impair adhesion of certain coatings. In particular, moisture collection at the bonding surface of coatings may result in blistering or lifting of the film.
3. Use over glassy surfaces. Incomplete adhesion to glassy surfaces may result in flaking and peeling of the film.
4. Deposits of mill scale, heavy coats of rust, and salts. These prevent adhesion.
5. Surface defects and contaminants that have not been corrected or removed before a coating is applied.

ADHESION TO SUBSTRATE

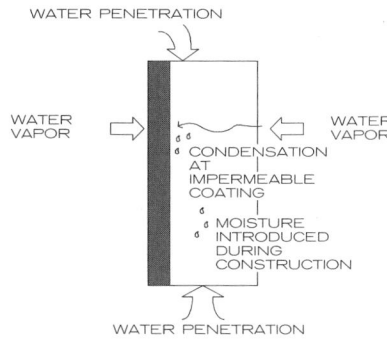

WATER PENETRATION

NOTES

Moisture may penetrate a porous substrate as

1. Water vapor migrating from high vapor pressure areas, such as warm, humid interior spaces, to low vapor pressure areas, such as cold, dry outdoors. If the dew point occurs within the substrate, vapor will condense, especially if the coating is of low permeability and blocks its free passage to the outdoors.
2. Water vapor penetrating a permeable coating to condense on a cold impermeable substrate such as metal
3. Rain penetrating into the substrate through faulty joints, damaged or faulty flashings, or cracks in the coating
4. Water absorbed when the substrate was exposed to rain or ground moisture while improperly stored before or during construction
5. Water that was a constituent part of the substrate during construction and has not yet evaporated. Generally a slow process, this condition often occurs in concrete, mortar, or gypsum plaster since more water is generally used than is required by the hydration process.
6. Moisture in the substrate when the coating is applied, which may prevent proper adhesion
7. Moisture penetrating the substrate after application of a coating, which may destroy the bond between substrate and coating.

MOISTURE IN SUBSTRATE

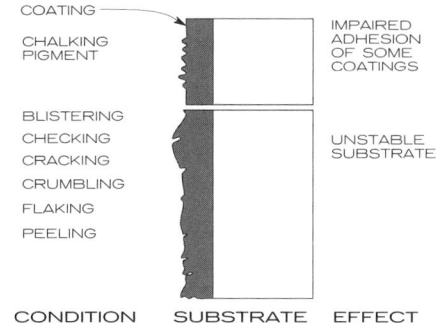

CONDITION	SUBSTRATE	EFFECT
COATING, CHALKING PIGMENT		IMPAIRED ADHESION OF SOME COATINGS
BLISTERING, CHECKING, CRACKING, CRUMBLING, FLAKING, PEELING		UNSTABLE SUBSTRATE

NOTES

When new coatings are applied over previously coated substrate, the surface stability of the old coating may affect the performance of the new coating. All coatings deteriorate over a period of time, and deterioration of a coating may result in

1. Chalking, which leaves behind loose pigment. Chalking occurs when the vehicle is broken down by weathering, particularly solar radiation. Suitable coatings may be applied to surfaces that are chalking with little or no surface preparation, although loose chalk should always be removed as a minimal measure.
2. Checking and cracking. Breaks can develop in coatings as they lose flexibility with age. These occur when stresses imposed on the coating by thermal or moisture movements in the substrate exceed the strength of the coating.
3. Crumbling, flaking, and peeling. Generally caused when moisture and airborne pollutants penetrate the coating, crumbling, flaking, and peeling may follow checking and cracking.

Coatings that have deteriorated until extensive checking is evident generally should not be used as a receiving surface for new coatings. Cracked, crumbling, flaking, or peeling surfaces should never be used, and the old coating must be completely removed from the substrate before application of a new coating.

COATINGS AS SUBSTRATE

EXTERIOR

SUBSTRATE	COATING SYSTEM details	TOPCOAT; TYPE AND BASE	top-coat/primer	PRINCIPAL BINDER	COATING GLOSS	COLOR RETENTION	SUBSTRATE SURFACE CONDITION	NOTES TO DESIGNER OR SPECIFIER
Wood Dry, Vertical	SIDING, vertical/horizontal • recommended moisture content not over 12% • protected from moisture or limited occasional exposure to water Typical components: • veneered plywood siding • MDO plywood siding • hardboard siding • redwood siding • cedar siding, shingles, and shakes	clear; solvent	top-coat	phenolic, tung oil	gloss semigloss	poor	dry only	1. Clear coatings are not recommended for plywood. 2. Light color stains have shorter durability than heavily pigmented ones. 3. PVA is used on yellow pine and red cedar. 4. Acrylic is resistant to ultraviolet rays, thus doesn't become brittle or yellowed. 5. No coating for wet wood has been recommended; wood should be dry before any coating is applied. 6. Opaque stains hide surface imperfections and will last longer but will also hide the wood grain. 7. Wood requires primer to equalize absorption; hardboards require filler to smooth out grain. 8. Always use oil-based primer under any coating on cedar and redwood. 9. Backprime and edge seal wood in locations subject to occasional moisture penetration or to water vapor migration and/or condensation. Unless properly sealed, only permeable coatings such as acrylic should be used; even then, they may peel. 10. Clear phenolic coatings may be protected with alkyd-type clear coatings for better color retention. 11. All knots and pitch streaks should be sealed with shellac and all nails set and nail holes filled. 12. Even galvanized, ferrous metal nails may corrode and stain water-based coatings because such coatings allow water vapor to penetrate to the nails, increasing the possibility of rusting. 13. Alkyds may react with chemicals in previous coatings. 14. Clear finishes for trim and doors may be pigmented to stain the wood, or a staining primer may be used. 15. Extensive surface preparation, when required, applies to both previously coated and uncoated surfaces but principally to previously coated ones.
			primer	self-priming, topcoat, or shellac			dry only	
		stain; water, or solvent	top-coat	alkyd, oil base, self-priming (solvent)	flat	fair	dry only	
		opaque; solvent	top-coat	alkyd	gloss semigloss	good	dry only	
			primer	alkyd, oil base			dry only	
		opaque; water	top-coat	acrylic	semigloss flat	excellent	may be damp	
			primer	alkyd, oil base acrylic, emulsion			dry only	
	TRIM • recommended moisture content not over 12% • occasional exposure to moisture or water Typical components: • shutters • doors • accent areas of limited size • railings	clear; solvent	top-coat	urethane, one part oil modified	gloss semigloss	fair	dry only	
			primer	self-priming			dry only	
		stain; solvent	top-coat	none recommended				
		opaque; water or solvent	top-coat	alkyd, oil base (solvent)	gloss semigloss	good	dry only	
			primer	alkyd, oil base			dry only	
Wood Floors Dry	• recommended moisture content not over 12% • exposed to moisture or water • subject to light to moderate traffic Typical components: • porch decking • exterior stairs	clear; solvent	top-coat	none recommended				1. Clear coatings for exterior floors are not recommended because ultraviolet radiation may degrade not only the coating but the substrate as well. Once the substrate fails, it has to be completely refinished before it can receive another coating; clear coatings may last one to two years and may require yearly maintenance. 2. Pigmented coatings only are recommended for wood exposed to sunlight; pigments used should block penetration of ultraviolet radiation to the substrate. 3. Water-based coatings generally are porous and not sufficiently abrasion resistant for use on surfaces subject to abrasion. 4. Urethane has excellent resistance to abrasion, alkali, acids, solvents, strong detergents, and fuels. Clear urethane is not recommended for exterior exposure due to possible degradation of the substrate by ultraviolet radiation.
			primer	not applicable				
		clear; solvent	top-coat	urethane, one part moist cure	gloss semigloss	fair	dry only	
			primer	self-priming; follow for hardwood recommended			dry only	
		clear; solvent	top-coat	urethane, one part, moisture cure	gloss, semigloss	fair	dry only	
			primer	self-priming			dry only	
Concrete, Masonry, and Stucco Dry, Vertical	• aged over 90 days • no visible signs of efflorescence • protected from moisture entry • limited water vapor diffusion Typical components: • precast concrete panels • concrete, clay masonry • stucco, cement-bound mineral fiber	clear; solvent	top-coat	silicone (min. 5% solution)	flat	N/A	dry only	1. Solvent-based coatings are not recommended for use over exterior concrete or masonry surfaces as such coatings form an impermeable film, preventing the escape of any moisture that may still be present in or may later penetrate the substrate. Condensation at the interface of coating and substrate may also contain soluble alkaline salts; either one or both may cause blistering or peeling. Solvent-based coatings should only be used when the substrate is completely dry and there is no possibility of substantial moisture penetration. 2. Water-based coatings generally allow water vapor to escape to the outside and do not present the same problem as solvent-based coatings. 3. Silicone should be considered more as a water repellent than a coating film. 4. Heavy-bodied, water-based coatings are available as fillers for rough surface masonry units.
		clear; water	top-coat	acrylic, methyl methacrylate	semigloss	good	may be damp	
		opaque; solvent	top-coat	alkyd	gloss semigloss flat	good	dry only	
			primer	styrene-butadiene				
		opaque; water	top-coat	acrylic	semigloss flat	excellent		
			primer	self-priming				

Table continues on following page

McCain McMurray; Washington, D.C.

 PAINTING

EXTERIOR (CONTINUED)

SUBSTRATE	COATING SYSTEM TOPCOAT; TYPE AND BASE		PRINCIPAL BINDER	COATING GLOSS	COLOR RETENTION	SUBSTRATE SURFACE CONDITION	NOTES TO DESIGNER OR SPECIFIER
Concrete floors, Dry	• aged over 90 days • light to moderate traffic • surface intact, dusty	clear; solvent	topcoat	epoxy ester	gloss	fair	dry only	1. Sealers-hardeners are preferably applied to fresh concrete. 2. Epoxy is a high-performance, high-cost coating suitable for floors exposed to heavy wear, chemical spills, and moisture. It may be used to resurface worn floors after proper patching. 3. No coating will perform well over a poor quality substrate. 4. The compatibility of coating with bond breakers, curing agents, and hardeners that may have been used over the substrate should be checked.
			primer	self-priming			dry only	
	• aged over 90 days • light to moderate traffic • surface worn, dusty	opaque; solvent	topcoat	urethane, one-part moisture cure	gloss semigloss	fair	dry only	
			primer	self-priming, substrate to be patched			dry only	
Concrete, Wet	• aged under 30 days or when subject to water penetration or condensation • surfaces cleaned to remove efflorescence Typical components: • concrete walls • concrete floors	clear, or opaque; solvent	topcoat	hardening sealing compounds				1. Epoxy may be used over damp surfaces; it is a high-performance, high-cost coating. 2. Application of coatings should be delayed as long as possible to allow the substrate to dry out. 3. Coatings considered should be water vapor permeable. 4. Bleeding of alkaline salts to the surface may result in brown spots over permeable coatings. If impermeable coatings are used over permeable primer, such coatings are likely to blister and peel.
			primer					
		opaque; water	topcoat	none recommended				
			primer	not applicable				

INTERIOR

SUBSTRATE	COATING SYSTEM TOPCOAT; TYPE AND BASE		PRINCIPAL BINDER	COATING GLOSS	COLOR RETENTION	SUBSTRATE SURFACE CONDITION	NOTES TO DESIGNER OR SPECIFIER
Gypsum Board Walls, Ceilings	Subject to • light scrubbing • mild detergents	opaque; water or solvent	topcoat	alkyd (solvent)	gloss semigloss flat	good	must be dry	1. Epoxy-modified acrylic is suitable for severe exposure in food preparation areas; it is available USDA-approved when required. 2. Solvent-base coatings should not be used directly over gypsum board as they tend to raise the nap of the paper facing. 3. Joints in gypsum board should be taped and spackled; absorption over spackled areas may differ from that of paper facing. 4. When fire resistance is required, intumescent coatings, either solvent or water based, may be selected.
			primer	vinyl, polyvinyl acetate; water			may be damp	
	Subject to • periodic scrubbing • occasional splatter of grease; food stains	opaque; water	topcoat	acrylic	semigloss flat	excellent	may be damp	
			primer	self-priming			may be damp	
Wood Dry, Vertical, Horizontal	Doors, wood veneered Trim Paneling	clear; solvent	topcoat	alkyd; may be over stain	flat	good	dry only	1. Single-component urethane may be applied over stain. 2. Abraded or rough surfaces may restrict use of some coatings; consult manufacturers' literature. 3. Fillers are recommended for open grain wood, such as oak, to smooth out the surface; stain may be added to filler when required. 4. Edges of doors should be sealed to prevent absorption of moisture. 5. Particleboard is generally finished with opaque coatings; for clear use filler and stain; absorption may be uneven. 6. Hardboard is generally finished with opaque coatings only; primers are required. 7. Alkyd for wood veneer and trim may be self-priming.
	Doors, hardboard veneer Doors, wood veneer Trim	opaque; water or solvent	topcoat	alkyd (solvent)	gloss semigloss	good	dry only	
			primer	alkyd (solvent)			dry only	
	Floors, light to moderate use	clear; solvent	topcoat	alkyd, self-priming	gloss semigloss	good	dry only	
	Floors, heavy use	clear; solvent	topcoat	urethane, one part moisture cure	gloss semigloss	good	dry only	
	Floors, moderate to high use	opaque; solvent	topcoat	alkyd, self-priming	gloss	good	dry only	
Concrete, Masonry, Portland Cement Plaster	Dry, not exposed to moisture penetration such as ground moisture Typical components: • concrete and concrete masonry walls and partitions	opaque; water	topcoat	vinyl, polyvinyl acetate	semigloss flat	good	may be damp	1. Cement-water paints may be used in damp areas such as on basement walls; colors generally are limited to light tints; moisture is required during curing period, usually 24 to 48 hours. 2. Use of coatings is not recommended over alkaline substrate; coating of fresh concrete, masonry, or plaster should be delayed for as long as possible. 3. Heavy-bodied primers/fillers are recommended for rough, porous surfaces.
			primer	self-priming or styrene-butadiene			may be damp	
		opaque; solvent	topcoat	alkyd	semigloss flat	good	dry only	
			primer	styrene-butadiene			may be damp	
Concrete floors	Dry, not exposed to ground moisture penetration Light to moderate use	opaque; solvent	topcoat	urethane, one part moisture cure	gloss semigloss	good	dry only	1. Dusting surfaces should be sealed first.
			primer	self-priming			dry only	
Gypsum plaster	Dry, fully cured, no signs of efflorescence, protected from moisture penetration	opaque; water or solvent	topcoat	acrylic (water)	semigloss flat	excellent	may be damp	1. Substrate may be alkaline; therefore, primers/coatings should be alkali resistant. 2. Coating of plaster should be delayed for as long as possible to allow it to dry out.
			primer	self-priming			may be damp	

McCain McMurray; Washington, D.C.

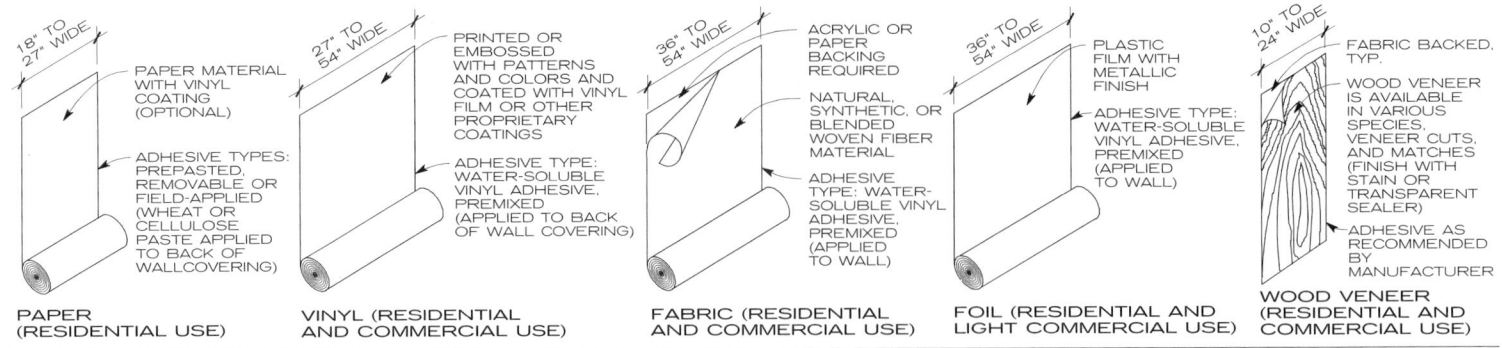

PAPER (RESIDENTIAL USE)

VINYL (RESIDENTIAL AND COMMERCIAL USE)

FABRIC (RESIDENTIAL AND COMMERCIAL USE)

FOIL (RESIDENTIAL AND LIGHT COMMERCIAL USE)

WOOD VENEER (RESIDENTIAL AND COMMERCIAL USE)

WALL-COVERING MATERIALS

NOTES

1. In some installations, fabric-wrapped panel systems have advantages over standard adhesive-applied wall coverings. There is generally less damage to the original wall surface, less surface preparation is needed, and an acoustical or tackable wall panel (which improves the STR or NRC rating of a wall) can be added to a room and concealed behind the fabric wrapping. In addition, the fabric or backing panel can be easily changed.

2. For wrapped panels, fabric or other wall covering should cure to room temperature and humidity conditions before installation.

3. Instruct installer to cut and hang three test panels for architect's inspection and approval before cutting other material from the roll.

4. The following terms apply to wall coverings:

   a. Bolt: typically three continuous rolls of wall covering

   b. Double cutting: trimming method that overlaps edges and forms a butt joint with a single cut

   c. Single roll: from 30 to 36 sq ft wall covering

   d. Double roll: from 60 to 72 sq ft wall covering

   e. Railroading: installing wall covering in horizontal direction

   f. Underlayment: any paper, fabric, or other liner material used to prepare a wall for installation of a wall covering

5. Avoid exposed wall-covering edges. Specify continuous metal or plastic edge trim where required; wrap covering into any reveals that occur.

FIBER CHARACTERISTICS FOR FABRIC WALL COVERINGS (RATING SCALE OF 1–5)

FIBER/ FABRIC	TYPE	DESCRIPTION/SOURCE	GENERAL PROPERTIES							
			DIMENSIONAL STABILITY	RESILIENCY AND ELASTICITY	STRENGTH	ELECTRICAL CONDUCTIVITY	HEAT CONDUCTIVITY	ABSORBENCY	MOISTURE REGAIN	SPECIFIC GRAVITY
Cotton	Natural	Soft, fibrous matter from seed pod of cotton plant	5	2	3	5	5	5	7 to 11%	1.54
Linen	Natural	Strong, lustrous yarn or fabric from the flax plant	5	1	4	5	1	5	8 to 12%	1.52
Wool	Natural	Protein fiber of hair taken from sheep	1	5	1	2	2	5	15%	1.32
Silk	Natural	Single filament protein fiber extruded from silkworm	5	4	4	2	2	4	11%	1.25
Acetate	Man-made	Modified cellulosic fibers	2	1	1	3	3	2	6%	1.32
Viscose rayon	Man-made	Regenerated cellulosic fiber made from wood or other pulp	3	1	1	4	4	5	11 to 14%	1.50 to 1.53
Olefin	Man-made	Synthetic polymers including polypropylene (or polyethylene)	4[f]	5	5	1	1	1[i]	0	0.92
Acrylic	Man-made	Synthetic polymer	5[h]	4	3	1	1	1	1.0 to 2.5%	1.14 to 1.19
Nylon	Man-made	Petroleum-based synthetic polyamide fiber (some natural sources exist)	5[f]	5	5	2	1	1	4.0 to 4.5%	1.14
Polyester	Man-made	Petroleum-based synthetic polymer	5[h]	5	5	1	1	1[i]	0.2 to 0.8%	1.38

NOTES

1. The ratings for these charts use the following numerical system of 1 to 5, "1" meaning the property or resistance level is least applicable and "5" meaning the property or resistance level is most applicable. Also the following notes apply to the charts:

   a. Hydrogen peroxide below 90°F will harm fiber.

   b. Petroleum products safe; acetone harmful to fiber.

   c. Will degrade if wet.

   d. Carpet beetles will attack fabric.

   e. Hydrogen peroxide is not harmful to fiber.

   f. Fabric may shrink at high temperatures.

   g. Long exposure will degrade fabric.

   h. May shrink at high temperatures if not heat set.

   i. Fabric will wick moisture.

   j. Fabric is resistant if behind glass.

   k. Will harm at high temperatures and concentrations.

2. These charts are a general guide to the most significant performance-related properties of common untreated or natural fibers. There are many other properties associated with fibers and, particularly, fabrics, which can have many fiber-blend permutations. Consult the fabric manufacturer for those properties (and ASTM results) relevant to the individual installation.

3. Care must be taken in cleaning any fabric used in an architectural installation. Consult fabric manufacturer for recommended cleaning procedures.

4. The following are definitions of various terms used in the charts:

   Strength—evaluated in terms of breaking, tearing, or bursting strength.

   Electrical conductivity—the ability of a fiber or fabric to carry or transfer electrical charges. Low conductivity fabrics build up static electrical charge.

RESISTANCE LEVELS OF FIBER/FABRIC (RATING SCALE OF 1–5)

FIBER/ FABRIC	RESISTANCE LEVEL OF FIBER/FABRIC TO				
	INSECTS AND MICROORGANISMS	OXIDIZING AGENTS (CHLORINE BLEACHES)	ORGANIC DRY CLEANING SOLVENTS (NAPTHA, ETC.)	SUNLIGHT	AGE
Cotton	5[c]	1	5	2	5
Linen	5[c]	1	5	1	4
Wool	1	1	5	2	5
Silk	5[d]	2[e]	5	1	2
Acetate	4	5[a]	5[b]	2	4
Viscose rayon	not applicable	2	5	2	5
Olefin	5	not applicable	1	2	5
Acrylic	5	5[k]	5	5	5
Nylon	5	not applicable	1	4[g]	5
Polyester	5	5	5	4[j]	5

Heat conductivity—the ability of a fiber or fabric to carry or transfer heat.

Specific gravity—related to the weight of a fiber, expressed as the density of the fiber in relation to the density of an equal volume of water at 4°C.

5. Consult standards developed by the Association for Contract Textiles, the American Society for Testing and Materials, and the American Association of Textile Chemists and Colorists to establish performance guidelines for commercially installed textiles:

   VERTICAL APPLICATION—Direct glue wall coverings

   a. Flammability: ASTM E84 rated (see local code for building occupancy ratings).

   b. Colorfastness to light: AATCC 16A or E/class 4 minimum at 40 hours.

   c. Colorfastness to wet and dry crocking: AATCC 8 class 3 minimum.

   VERTICAL APPLICATION—Panel or upholstered applications

   a. Flammability: ASTM E84 rated (see manufacturer and local code for specific applications).

   b. Breaking/tensile strength: ASTM D3597, 50 pounds minimum/warp and weft directions.

   c. Yarn/seam slippage: ASTM D3597, 25 pounds minimum/warp and weft directions.

   d. Colorfastness to light: AATCC 16A or E/class 4 minimum at 40 hours.

   e. Colorfastness to wet and dry crocking: AATCC 8/class 3 minimum.

Richard J. Vitullo, AIA; Oak Leaf Studio; Crownsville, Maryland
Kristie Strasen; Strasen Frost Associates; New York, New York

 WALL COVERINGS

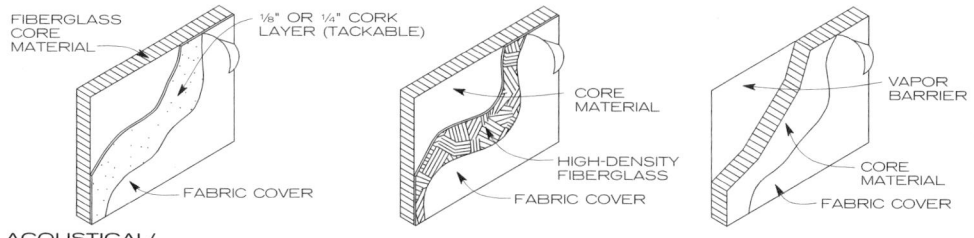

FIBERGLASS CORE MATERIAL — ⅛" OR ¼" CORK LAYER (TACKABLE) — FABRIC COVER

ACOUSTICAL/ TACKABLE PANEL

CORE MATERIAL — HIGH-DENSITY FIBERGLASS — FABRIC COVER

HIGH-IMPACT PANEL

VAPOR BARRIER — CORE MATERIAL — FABRIC COVER

PLENUM PANEL

NOTES

1. In these types of fabric panels the fabric is permanently bonded to the substrate and/or core material. Panels can be manufactured to any size or shape with any corner or edge details; aluminum edge frames can be added for extra stiffness.

2. Panels are fastened to wall surfaces with magnets, foam tape, hook and loop, liquid adhesive, mechanical metal strip, or clip, with optional base support brackets.

PREFABRICATED FABRIC-WRAPPED PANELS

WALL COVERING INSTALLATION

When selecting a wall covering, it is necessary to consider the installation location, traffic patterns, light sources (both natural and man-made), and acoustical requirements. Consider the following when preparing a wall:

1. Wall covering weights vary from 7 to 12 oz per square yard (Type I); 13 oz per square yard (Type II); and 22 or more oz per square yard (Type III). The limited thickness and opacity of Type I and II materials may make wall surface imperfections and colors visible.

2. Before fabrics or other pervious wall coverings are installed, they are usually backed with a paper layer or liquid-applied acrylic coating to prevent seam slippage and adhesive bleed-through, as well as to increase stability and provide a neutral background for light-colored wall coverings. Backings allow the wall covering to be applied with conventional paper-hanging techniques.

3. Wall surfaces should be clean, smooth, dry, and structurally intact. Low spots should be filled and sanded, loose paint and other coverings removed, glossy surfaces sanded to roughen them slightly, and all dust removed.

4. The proper wall primer should be used on wall surfaces, particularly new gypsum wallboard. Not all water-based adhesives can be used over latex paint primer. Consult manufacturers for compatibility of adhesives and primer materials.

5. There are three basic adhesive types: wheat-based (the traditional paste, no longer popular), clay-based (traditionally used for heavy-duty applications), and vinyl (formulated for improperly prepared or problem wall surfaces).

6. When specifying adhesives, ask manufacturers and installers for recommendations to prevent buckling, sagging, delamination, and environmental considerations such as off-gassing.

ESTIMATING WALL COVERING MATERIALS

Wall coverings can be estimated by two methods:

Square Foot Method (no pattern repeat):

1. Measure the length of all walls and calculate the total.

2. Multiply the total combined length of the walls by the greatest wall height rounded up to the nearest foot to determine the total wall area.

3. Add 15% to the total area to account for waste.

4. Find the total area of all doors and windows wider than the width of a strip of wall covering.

5. Subtract total door and window area from total wall area. This will be the approximate square foot amount of wall covering required.

6. Divide the approximate square foot amount of wall covering by the number of square feet in each roll or bolt (refer to manufacturer's literature) to determine the number required for each job.

Panel Method (patterns and materials with highly visible seams):

1. Determine the trimmed width of material (54 in. wide becomes 52 in. wide).

2. On a scaled floor plan, place vertical seams in locations not less than 6 in. from inside and outside corners.

3. Adjust seam locations as necessary for desired seam arrangement, then count the panels. Count partial-width panels as whole widths.

4. Determine the panel height by measuring the floor-to-ceiling height and adding one pattern repeat for vertical patterns.

5. Multiply the number of panels by the adjusted panel height to determine the total material length required.

6. For wall coverings sold by linear yard, divide total length by three to determine the number of yards needed to complete the work. For wall coverings sold by the square foot, convert the total length of material into square feet and divide by the number of square feet in each roll or bolt (check with manufacturer).

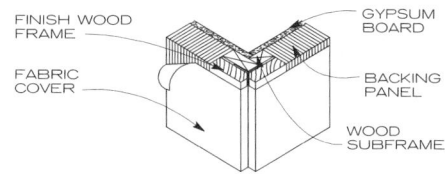

FINISH WOOD FRAME — FABRIC COVER — GYPSUM BOARD — BACKING PANEL — WOOD SUBFRAME

QUIRK MITER CORNER

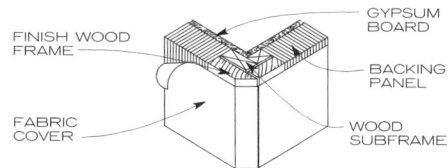

FINISH WOOD FRAME — FABRIC COVER — GYPSUM BOARD — BACKING PANEL — WOOD SUBFRAME

45° BEVELED CORNER

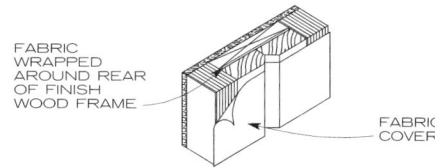

FABRIC WRAPPED AROUND REAR OF FINISH WOOD FRAME — FABRIC COVER

45° BEVELED BUTT JOINT

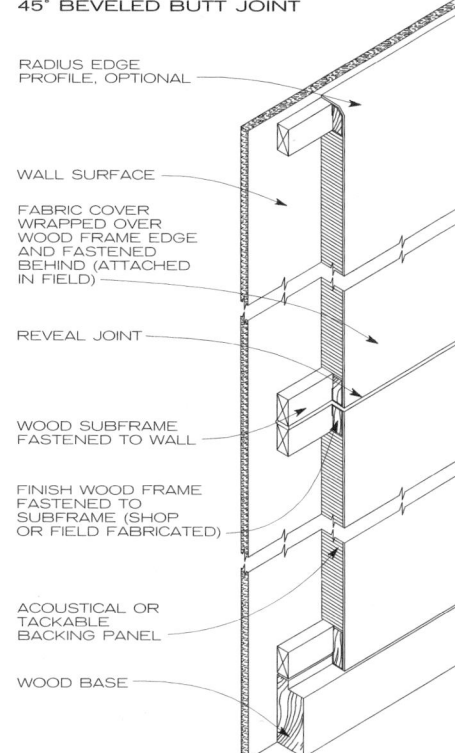

RADIUS EDGE PROFILE, OPTIONAL — WALL SURFACE — FABRIC COVER WRAPPED OVER WOOD FRAME EDGE AND FASTENED BEHIND (ATTACHED IN FIELD) — REVEAL JOINT — WOOD SUBFRAME FASTENED TO WALL — FINISH WOOD FRAME FASTENED TO SUBFRAME (SHOP OR FIELD FABRICATED) — ACOUSTICAL OR TACKABLE BACKING PANEL — WOOD BASE

FABRIC-WRAPPED PANELS—WOOD FRAME SYSTEM

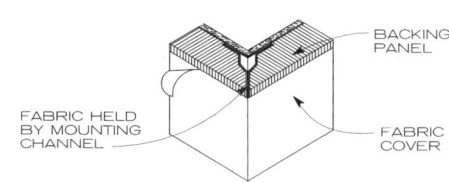

FABRIC HELD BY MOUNTING CHANNEL — BACKING PANEL — FABRIC COVER

OUTSIDE CORNER

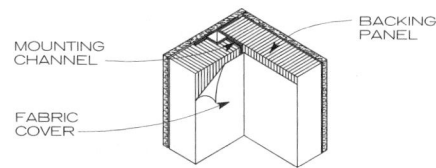

MOUNTING CHANNEL — FABRIC COVER — BACKING PANEL

INSIDE CORNER

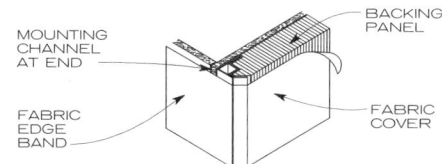

MOUNTING CHANNEL AT END — FABRIC EDGE BAND — BACKING PANEL — FABRIC COVER

45° BEVELED CORNER

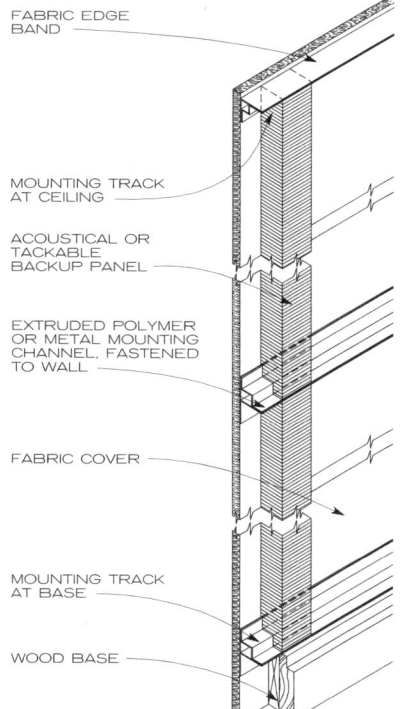

FABRIC EDGE BAND — MOUNTING TRACK AT CEILING — ACOUSTICAL OR TACKABLE BACKUP PANEL — EXTRUDED POLYMER OR METAL MOUNTING CHANNEL, FASTENED TO WALL — FABRIC COVER — MOUNTING TRACK AT BASE — WOOD BASE

FABRIC-WRAPPED PANELS—TRACK SYSTEM

Richard J. Vitullo, AIA; Oak Leaf Studio; Crownsville, Maryland
Kristie Strasen; Strasen Frost Associates; New York, New York

GENERAL NOTES

1. Wall guards, panels, and trim are typically attached to a finished wall surface with adhesive or screws. Panels are typically made of high-density fiberglass and covered with vinyl acrylic claddiing, but they may also have fabric coverings in low impact areas.
2. Most wall and corner guard manufacturers supply inside and outside connector trim pieces, as well as end caps. Consult manufacturers.
3. For all wall and corner guard installations, it is important to provide backup blocking behind areas where fasteners are attached, particularly for handrail-type guards.

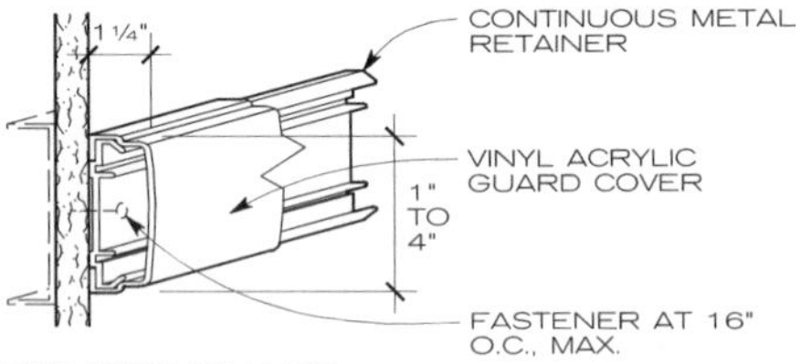
1 1/4"
CONTINUOUS METAL RETAINER
VINYL ACRYLIC GUARD COVER
1" TO 4"
FASTENER AT 16" O.C., MAX.

BUMPER GUARD

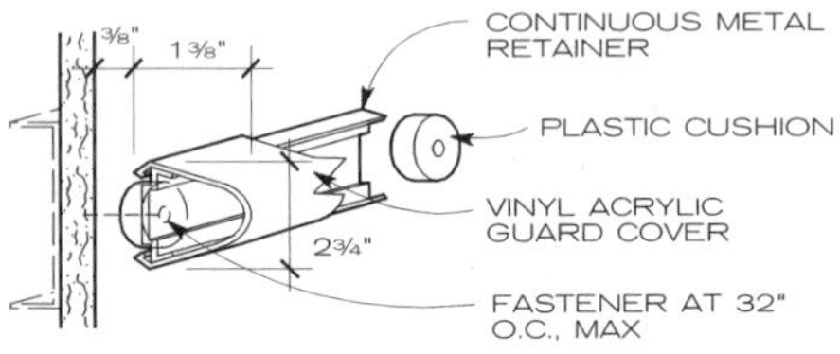
3/8"
1 3/8"
CONTINUOUS METAL RETAINER
PLASTIC CUSHION
VINYL ACRYLIC GUARD COVER
2 3/4"
FASTENER AT 32" O.C., MAX

BUMPER GUARD

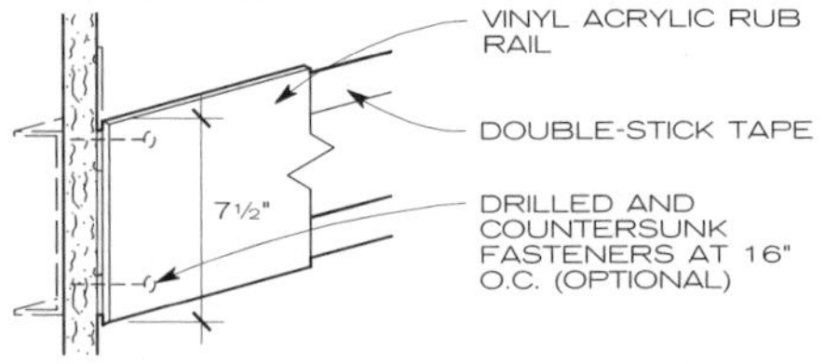
VINYL ACRYLIC RUB RAIL
DOUBLE-STICK TAPE
7 1/2"
DRILLED AND COUNTERSUNK FASTENERS AT 16" O.C. (OPTIONAL)

RUB RAIL GUARD

BUMPER GUARDS

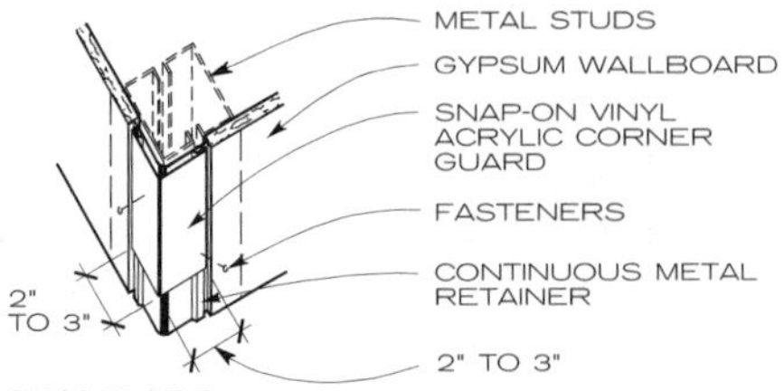
METAL STUDS
GYPSUM WALLBOARD
SNAP-ON VINYL ACRYLIC CORNER GUARD
FASTENERS
CONTINUOUS METAL RETAINER
2" TO 3"
2" TO 3"

STANDARD

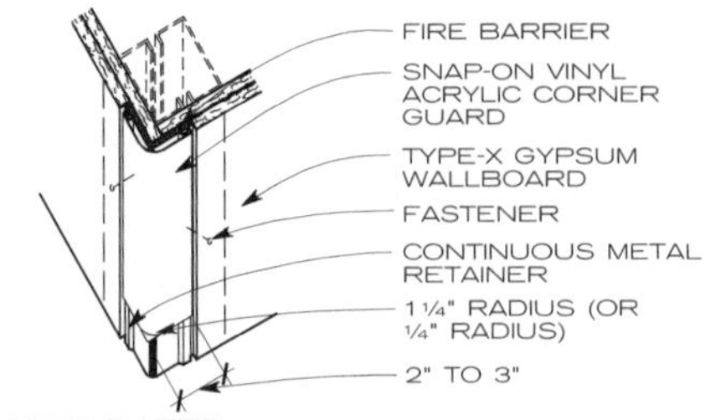
FIRE BARRIER
SNAP-ON VINYL ACRYLIC CORNER GUARD
TYPE-X GYPSUM WALLBOARD
FASTENER
CONTINUOUS METAL RETAINER
1 1/4" RADIUS (OR 1/4" RADIUS)
2" TO 3"

FIRE-RATED

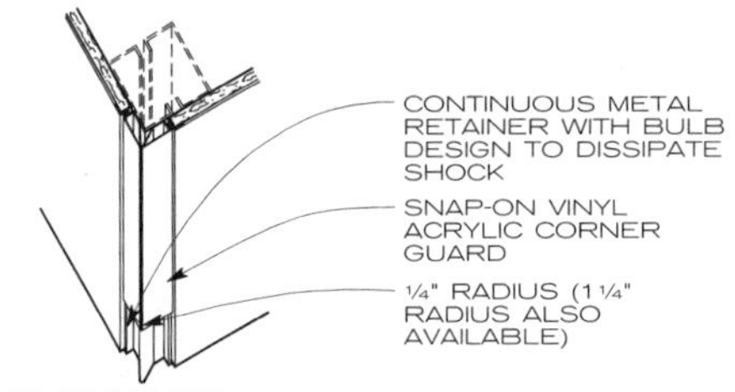
CONTINUOUS METAL RETAINER WITH BULB DESIGN TO DISSIPATE SHOCK
SNAP-ON VINYL ACRYLIC CORNER GUARD
1/4" RADIUS (1 1/4" RADIUS ALSO AVAILABLE)

CUSHIONED

NOTE

Depending on the design of the retainer, corner guards can be mounted to almost any wall angle intersection up to 135 degrees.

FLUSH-MOUNTED CORNER GUARDS

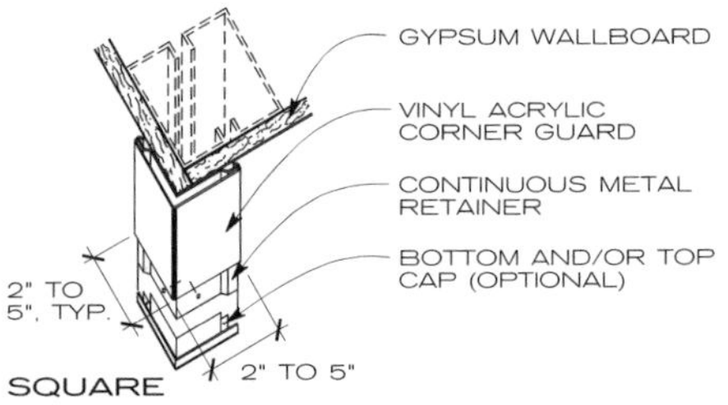
GYPSUM WALLBOARD
VINYL ACRYLIC CORNER GUARD
CONTINUOUS METAL RETAINER
BOTTOM AND/OR TOP CAP (OPTIONAL)
2" TO 5", TYP.
2" TO 5"

SQUARE

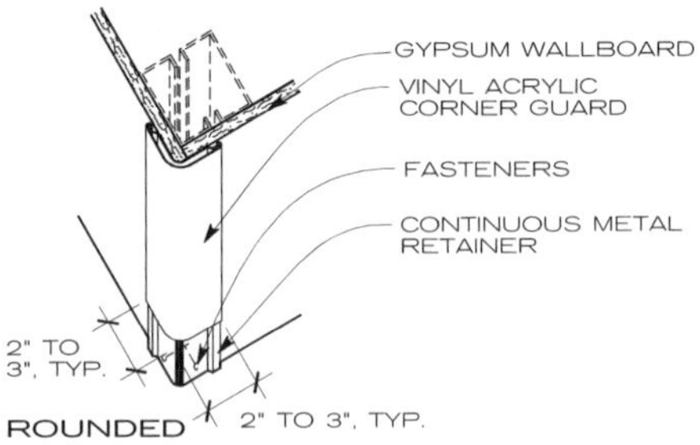
GYPSUM WALLBOARD
VINYL ACRYLIC CORNER GUARD
FASTENERS
CONTINUOUS METAL RETAINER
2" TO 3", TYP.
2" TO 3", TYP.

ROUNDED

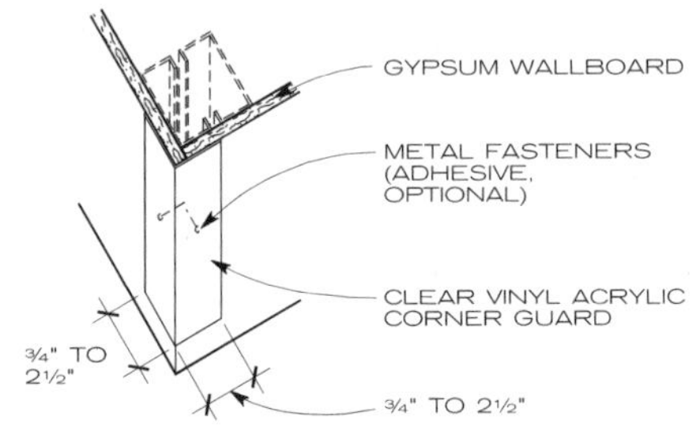
GYPSUM WALLBOARD
METAL FASTENERS (ADHESIVE, OPTIONAL)
CLEAR VINYL ACRYLIC CORNER GUARD
3/4" TO 2 1/2"
3/4" TO 2 1/2"

EXPOSED FASTENER

SURFACE-MOUNTED CORNER GUARDS

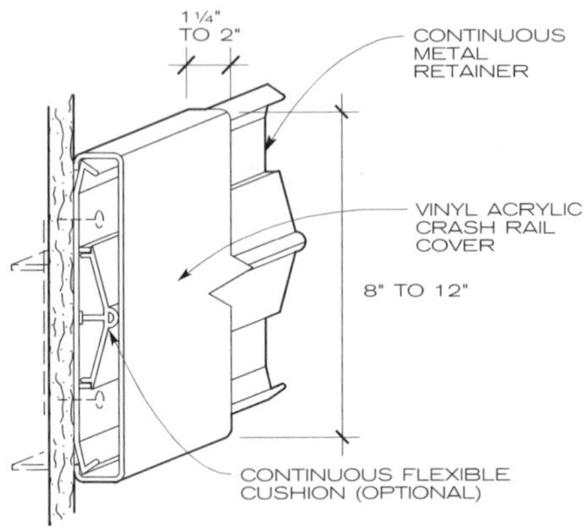
1 1/4" TO 2"
CONTINUOUS METAL RETAINER
VINYL ACRYLIC CRASH RAIL COVER
8" TO 12"
CONTINUOUS FLEXIBLE CUSHION (OPTIONAL)

SURFACE-MOUNTED

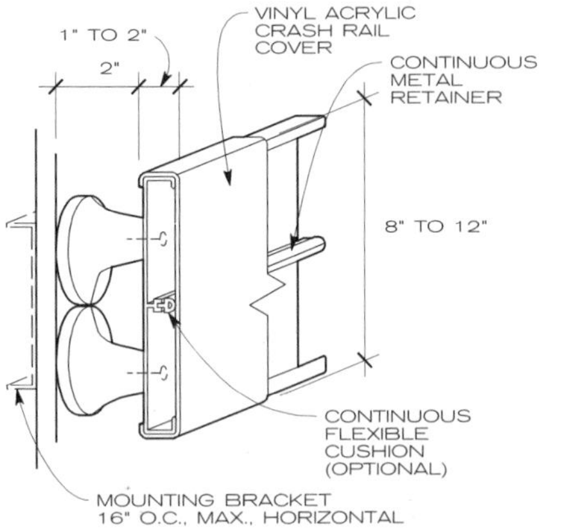
1" TO 2"
2"
VINYL ACRYLIC CRASH RAIL COVER
CONTINUOUS METAL RETAINER
8" TO 12"
CONTINUOUS FLEXIBLE CUSHION (OPTIONAL)
MOUNTING BRACKET 16" O.C., MAX., HORIZONTAL

WALL-HUNG

CRASH RAILS

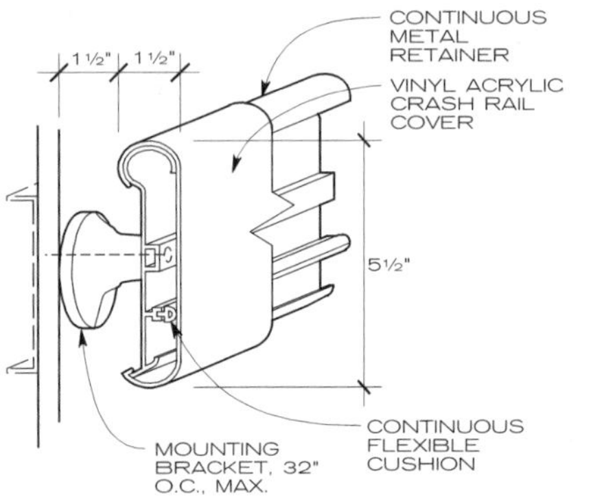
1 1/2" 1 1/2"
CONTINUOUS METAL RETAINER
VINYL ACRYLIC CRASH RAIL COVER
5 1/2"
MOUNTING BRACKET, 32" O.C., MAX.
CONTINUOUS FLEXIBLE CUSHION

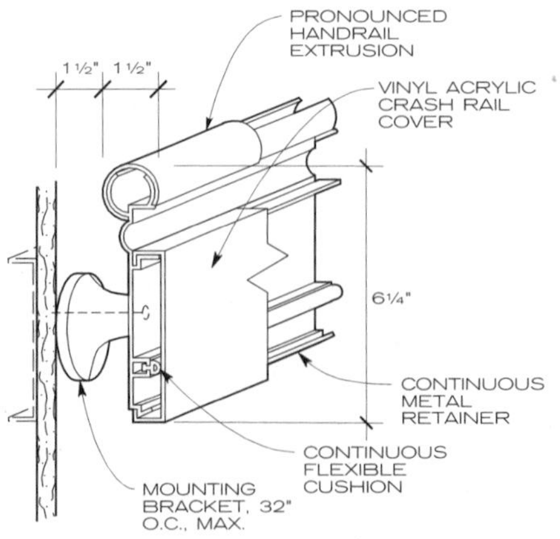
1 1/2" 1 1/2"
PRONOUNCED HANDRAIL EXTRUSION
VINYL ACRYLIC CRASH RAIL COVER
6 1/4"
CONTINUOUS METAL RETAINER
CONTINUOUS FLEXIBLE CUSHION
MOUNTING BRACKET, 32" O.C., MAX.

HANDRAIL WITH BUMPER CUSHION

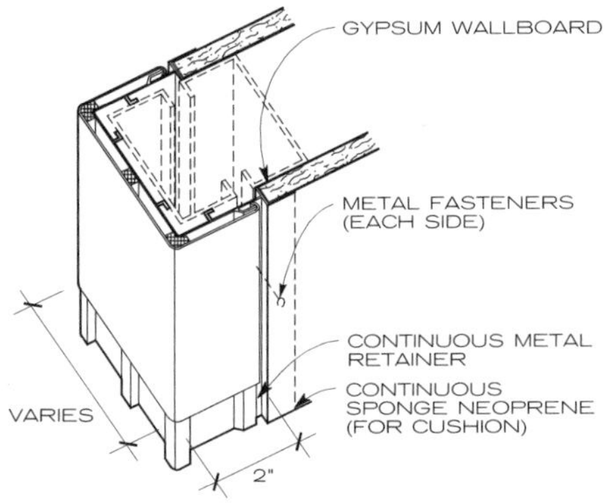
GYPSUM WALLBOARD
METAL FASTENERS (EACH SIDE)
CONTINUOUS METAL RETAINER
CONTINUOUS SPONGE NEOPRENE (FOR CUSHION)
VARIES
2"

WALL-END GUARD

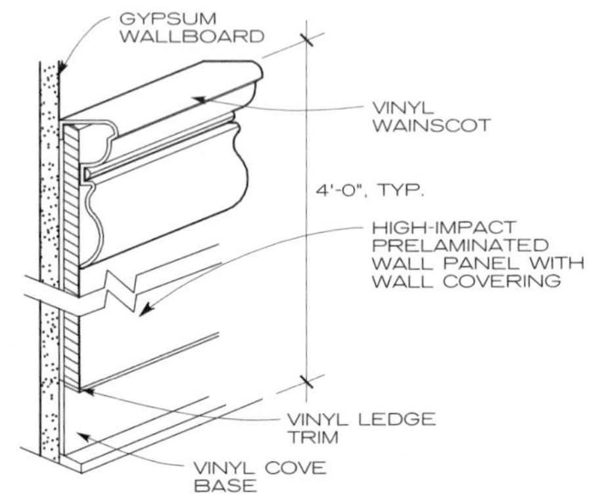
GYPSUM WALLBOARD
VINYL WAINSCOT
4'-0", TYP.
HIGH-IMPACT PRELAMINATED WALL PANEL WITH WALL COVERING
VINYL LEDGE TRIM
VINYL COVE BASE

WAINSCOT PANEL WALL GUARD

Richard J. Vitullo, AIA; Oak Leaf Studio; Crownsville, Maryland

GENERAL NOTES

1. Column and beam covers are designed to conceal and protect structural and mechanical components, although they also have aesthic value. They are installed according to the manufacturers' designs, which may differ from one company to the next. Some are designed with one section of the cover permanently fixed in place and the other section removable. In other designs, more than one section of the cover is removable. Column and beam covers can be used in interior and exterior locations.

2. The most common materials used for the cover super-structure are base metals of extruded aluminum (.063 to .25 in. thick), stainless steel (18 to 11 gauge), and galvanized steel (18-gauge base with finish cover). Factory-applied mechanical finishes include anodized (for aluminum); satin or mirror finish (on brass, aluminum, or stainless steel); Kynar coating (on galvanized steel); and embossed patterns on any base metal. Other factory-applied finishes include baked enamel, powder coat, and primer (for field painting). Clear lacquer coatings are sometimes applied in the field to preserve mirror or other finishes. For high-traffic and highly vulnerable areas where protection from graffiti is also a concern (e.g., mass transit facilities), use of factory-applied ceramic/porcelain veneer on steel is recommended.

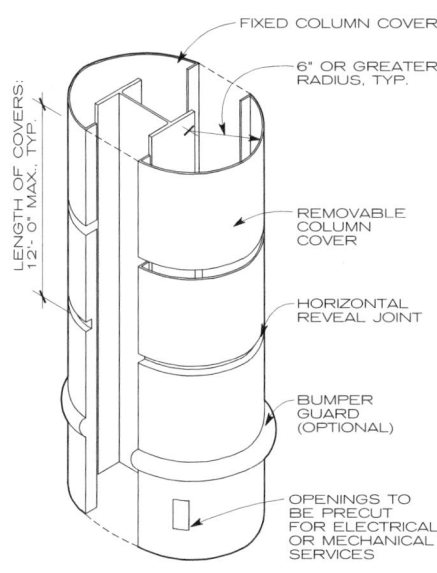

- FIXED COLUMN COVER
- 6" OR GREATER RADIUS, TYP.
- LENGTH OF COVERS: 12'-0" MAX., TYP.
- REMOVABLE COLUMN COVER
- HORIZONTAL REVEAL JOINT
- BUMPER GUARD (OPTIONAL)
- OPENINGS TO BE PRECUT FOR ELECTRICAL OR MECHANICAL SERVICES

TYPICAL FREESTANDING COLUMN COVER

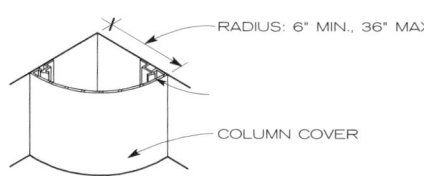

- RADIUS: 6" MIN., 36" MAX.
- COLUMN COVER

QUARTER-ROUND

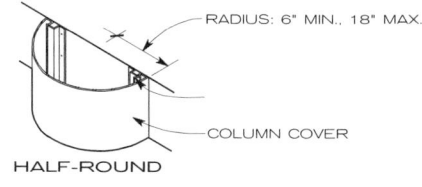

- RADIUS: 6" MIN., 18" MAX.
- COLUMN COVER

HALF-ROUND

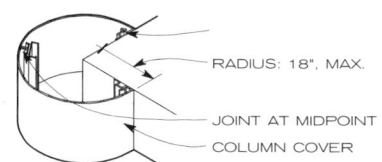

- RADIUS: 18", MAX.
- JOINT AT MIDPOINT
- COLUMN COVER

THREE-QUARTER ROUND

TYPICAL COLUMN COVERS

Richard J. Vitullo, AIA; Oak Leaf Studio; Crownsville, Maryland

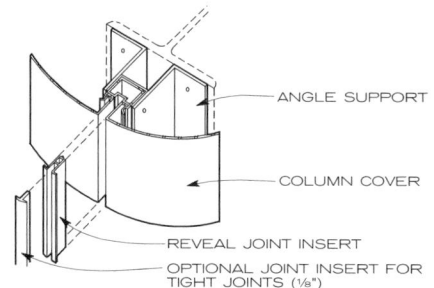

- ANGLE SUPPORT
- COLUMN COVER
- REVEAL JOINT INSERT
- OPTIONAL JOINT INSERT FOR TIGHT JOINTS (⅛")

NOTE

This detail is used to protect joint edges at ceramic-coated steel seams.

COLUMN COVER WITH INSERTS

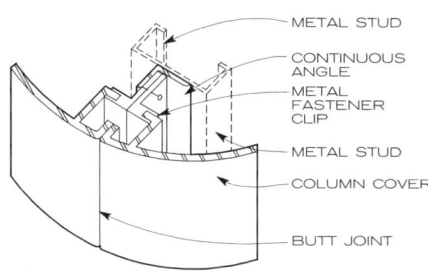

- METAL STUD
- CONTINUOUS ANGLE
- METAL FASTENER CLIP
- METAL STUD
- COLUMN COVER
- BUTT JOINT

BUTT JOINT COLUMN COVER WITH FASTENER CLIP

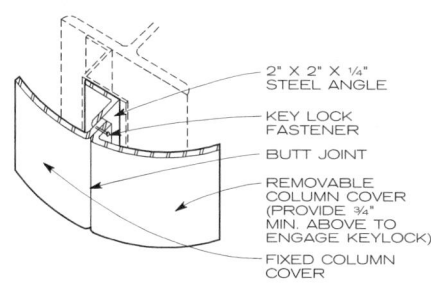

- 2" X 2" X ¼" STEEL ANGLE
- KEY LOCK FASTENER
- BUTT JOINT
- REMOVABLE COLUMN COVER (PROVIDE ¾" MIN. ABOVE TO ENGAGE KEYLOCK)
- FIXED COLUMN COVER

BUTT JOINT COLUMN COVER WITH KEY LOCK

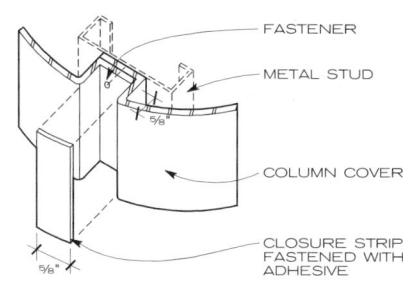

- FASTENER
- METAL STUD
- COLUMN COVER
- CLOSURE STRIP FASTENED WITH ADHESIVE

COLUMN JOINT WITH CLOSURE STRIP

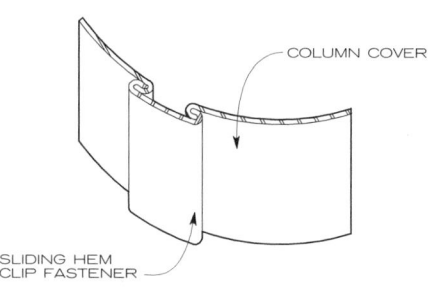

- COLUMN COVER
- SLIDING HEM CLIP FASTENER

SLIDING HEM CLIP

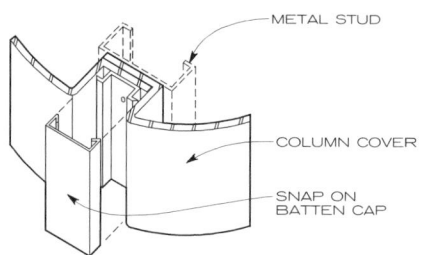

- METAL STUD
- COLUMN COVER
- SNAP ON BATTEN CAP

NOTE

Batten caps are available in a wide variety of sizes, colors, and materials. Consult manufacturers.

COLUMN COVER JOINT WITH BATTEN CAP

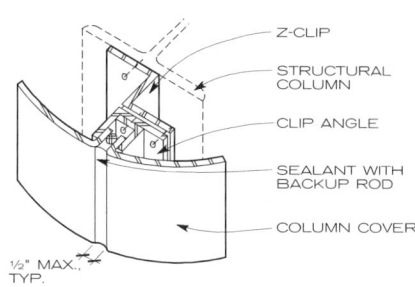

- Z-CLIP
- STRUCTURAL COLUMN
- CLIP ANGLE
- SEALANT WITH BACKUP ROD
- COLUMN COVER
- ½" MAX., TYP.

COLUMN COVER WITH SEALANT JOINT

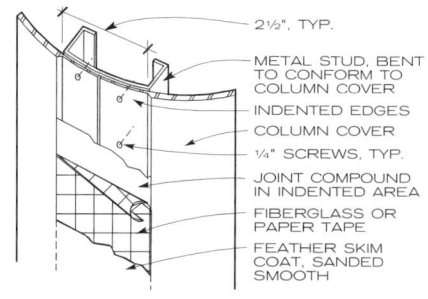

- 2½", TYP.
- METAL STUD, BENT TO CONFORM TO COLUMN COVER
- INDENTED EDGES
- COLUMN COVER
- ¼" SCREWS, TYP.
- JOINT COMPOUND IN INDENTED AREA
- FIBERGLASS OR PAPER TAPE
- FEATHER SKIM COAT, SANDED SMOOTH

COLUMN COVER WITH STANDARD JOINT COMPOUND DETAIL

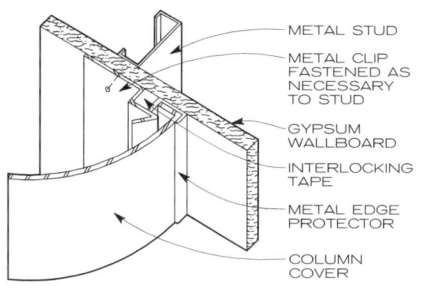

- METAL STUD
- METAL CLIP FASTENED AS NECESSARY TO STUD
- GYPSUM WALLBOARD
- INTERLOCKING TAPE
- METAL EDGE PROTECTOR
- COLUMN COVER

PARTIAL COLUMN COVER—WALL MOUNT DETAIL

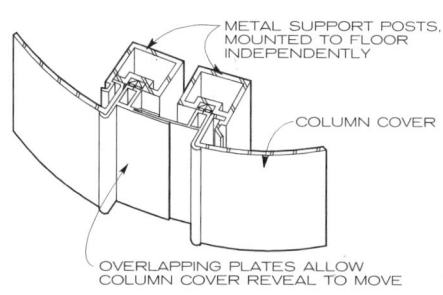

- METAL SUPPORT POSTS, MOUNTED TO FLOOR INDEPENDENTLY
- COLUMN COVER
- OVERLAPPING PLATES ALLOW COLUMN COVER REVEAL TO MOVE

COLUMN COVER AT EXPANSION JOINT

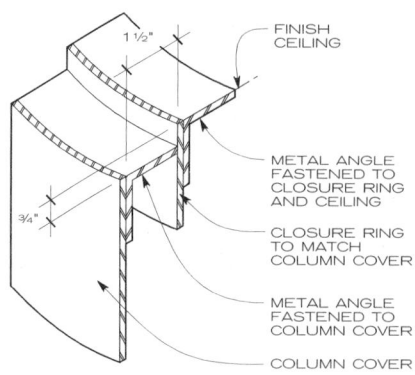

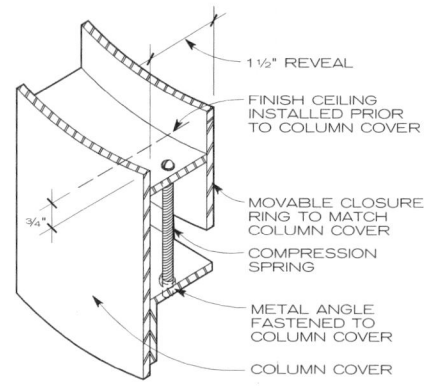

NOTE

This type of column cover can be installed flush with a finished ceiling.

SPRING-ACTIVATED COLUMN COVER CLOSURE

CEILING-FASTENED CLOSURE RING WITH REVEAL

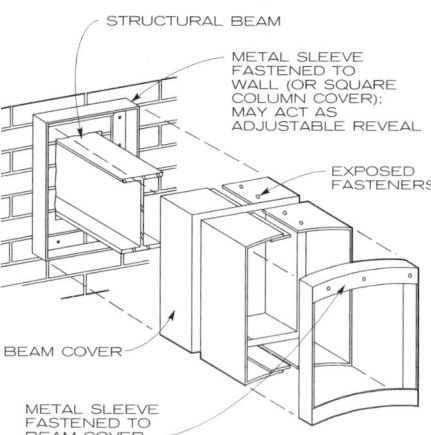

NOTE

Dimensions and joint configurations vary according to design requirements or preference. Consult manufacturers.

BEAM COVER AT WALL

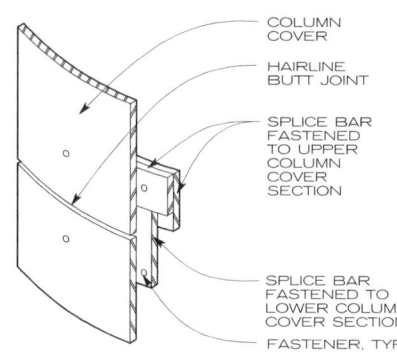

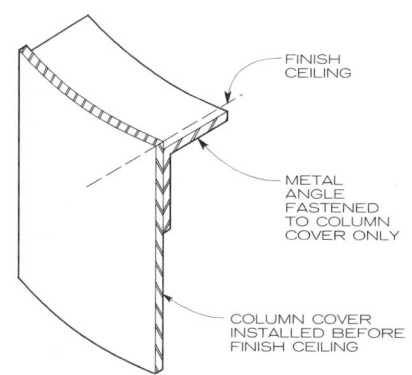

SPRING-ACTIVATED COLUMN COVER CLOSURE WITH REVEAL

CEILING DETAIL WITH FLUSH COLUMN COVER

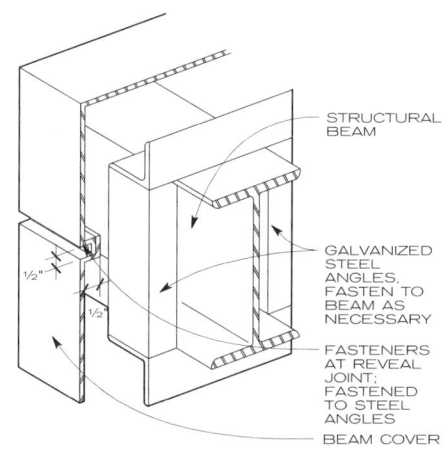

BEAM COVER FASTENING DETAIL

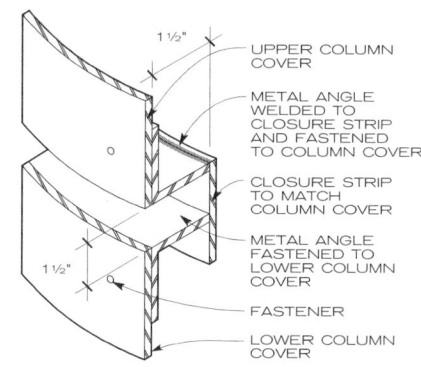

HORIZONTAL SPLICE WITH BUTT JOINT

HORIZONTAL REVEAL JOINT

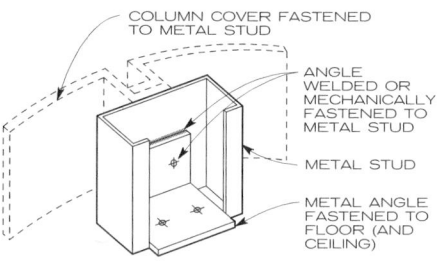

DETAIL AT METAL STUD

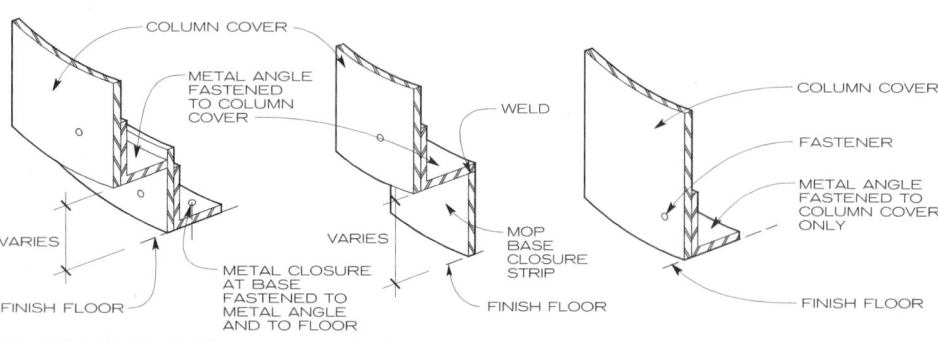

FLOATING MOP BASE   **FIXED MOP BASE**   **FLUSH BASE**

NOTE

Column cover base assemblies are not fastened to floors but only to vertical supports (metal studs, etc.).

COLUMN COVER BASE DETAILS

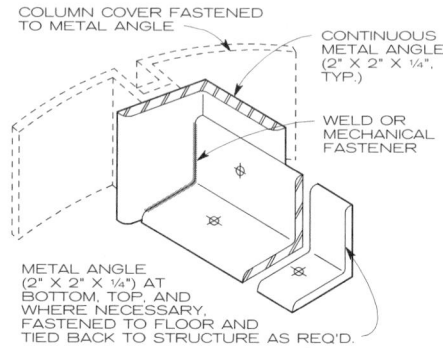

DETAIL AT METAL ANGLE

COLUMN COVER SUBFRAME ATTACHMENTS

Richard J. Vitullo, AIA: Oak Leaf Studio; Crownsville, Maryland

10 WALL AND CORNER GUARDS

GENERAL NOTES

1. APPLIANCE CLASSIFICATIONS: Metal solid-fuel heaters efficiently heat areas ranging in size from a single room to an entire house. They are classified according to the fuel that powers them: woodstoves (cordwood) or pellet stoves (densified biomass). Woodstoves manufactured today burn both softwood and hardwood species of cordwood, which have variable moisture and Btu content but are readily accessible and manually prepared for use.

2. BURNING TECHNOLOGIES: Current EPA regulations for solid-fuel appliances have resulted in woodstoves significantly more efficient than those produced before. The key to efficiency is igniting and burning the smoke and gases released during combustion, particularly during extended and reduced heat burns. Burning smoke and gases reduces fuel consumption, polluting emissions, and the frequency of chimney maintenance. Woodstoves must meet EPA standards for efficiency and cleanliness of burning. EPA standards differ for catalytic and noncatalytic technology, and within the latter category, for wood-burning and pellet-burning stoves.

3. APPLIANCE CONFIGURATIONS: Both woodstoves and pellet stoves can be freestanding, a fireplace insert, or built in. Freestanding appliances are often chosen in new construction or for renovation when no chimney exists. Fireplace inserts are often used to retrofit an open fireplace to increase efficiency and heat output. Built-in heaters are chosen to achieve the look and performance of the fireplace insert without the expense of building a masonry fireplace and chimney. Instead, the built-in uses a high temperature metal chimney, usually concealed in a chase. Noncombustible materials such as brick, stone, or ceramic tile are applied around the appliance face to give the look of a traditional fireplace.

4. HEAT DISTRIBUTION, APPLIANCE PLACEMENT, AND SIZING: The design of an appliance determines how it distributes heat. If the outside walls of the firebox are directly exposed to living space, the appliance is primarily a radiant heater. The heat created when waves of infrared energy from a stove strike solid objects is very comfortable in large open areas but may not be able to reach remote areas of a house.

Convection heaters feature double-wall construction. Radiant energy is converted to currents of warm air in the space between the firebox and the surrounding metal cabinet. Natural convection currents of warm air moving through the house, cooling, and returning to the heater distribute heat gradually or with the assistance of an electric blower.

With the advent of clean glass technology, purely convection heaters completely surrounded by cabinets became rare. Much more common is a third type of heater, which combines the heat distribution qualities of the first two. A combination radiant/convection heater employs a cabinet around part of the heater for convection, but radiant energy is emitted from exposed parts of the firebox wall and the ceramic glass of the loading door. The combination offers even distribution of heat, delivering the radiant energy that heats immediate rooms comfortably and the convection currents that gradually deliver heat to more distant areas. Glass cleaning air wash technology and high-efficiency burning give the user a clear view of the fire and make the stove easier to operate.

Although a central location and open spaces provide optimum heat distribution, both radiant and combination stoves distribute heat satisfactorily if they are placed in a room of adequate size. Placement is often determined by how the living space is used and by the location of the chimney.

The performance of EPA-certified appliances on low burns allows some tolerance for oversizing an appliance for a heating area. However, appliances much too large for the area to be heated makes operation in mild weather difficult. Also important are heating expectations: A stove intended for occasional, recreational, or emergency use can be sized differently from one intended as a primary heat source. Manufacturers' recommendations for heating area capacity may not take into account local climate or the specifics of heat loss; consult a certified dealer.

5. AESTHETICS: The material used to construct a stove has little effect on heating performance. Cast iron offers decorative features such as arches, curves, and relief work unattainable with steel. Steel stoves may come in styles varied through a choice of legs or pedestals, arched door frames, and brass or gold-plated accents. Stoves with soapstone panels are another option. Air wash technology, which keeps the glass clean, is perhaps the most popular design feature in all stoves.

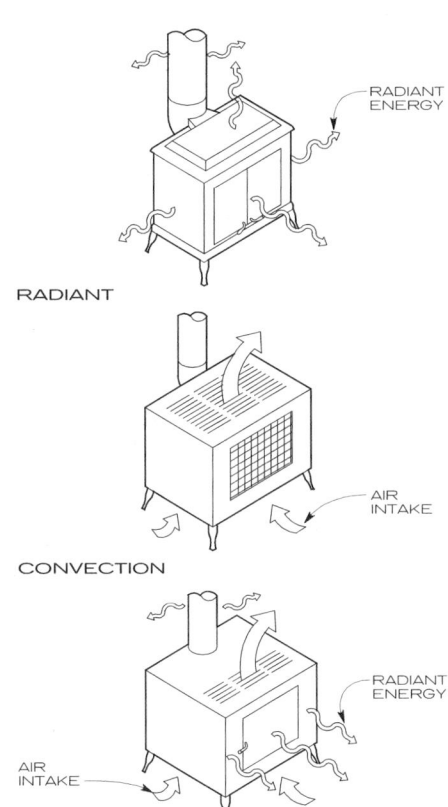

RADIANT

CONVECTION

COMBINATION RADIANT/CONVECTION

HEAT DELIVERY SYSTEMS

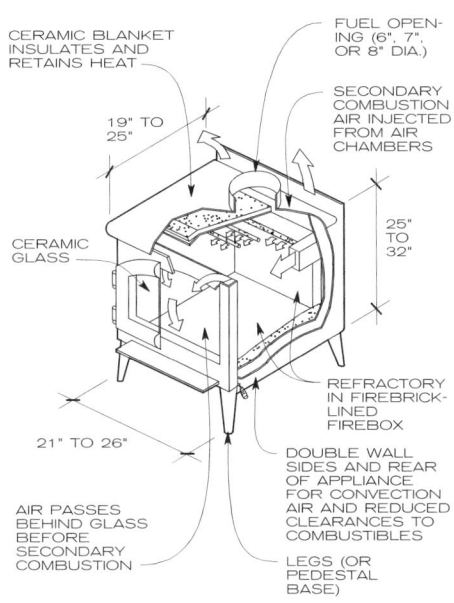

CERAMIC BLANKET INSULATES AND RETAINS HEAT

FUEL OPENING (6", 7", OR 8" DIA.)

SECONDARY COMBUSTION AIR INJECTED FROM AIR CHAMBERS

19" TO 25"

CERAMIC GLASS

25" TO 32"

REFRACTORY IN FIREBRICK-LINED FIREBOX

21" TO 26"

DOUBLE WALL SIDES AND REAR OF APPLIANCE FOR CONVECTION AIR AND REDUCED CLEARANCES TO COMBUSTIBLES

AIR PASSES BEHIND GLASS BEFORE SECONDARY COMBUSTION

LEGS (OR PEDESTAL BASE)

NOTE

Noncatalytic systems create the conditions necessary to burn combustible gases without the use of catalysts. The technology has a number of characteristics: Firebox insulation keeps temperatures high. Devices that reflect heat back into the firebox create the gas turbulence needed for complete combustion and give the gases a long route hot enough for them to burn before being cooled. Heated secondary air supplies ensure that enough oxygen is present. This secondary air is usually fed to the fire above the fuel bed through ducts with small holes.

NONCATALYTIC STOVE SYSTEM

Walter Moberg Design, Inc.; Portland, Oregon
Hearth Education Foundation; Austin, Texas

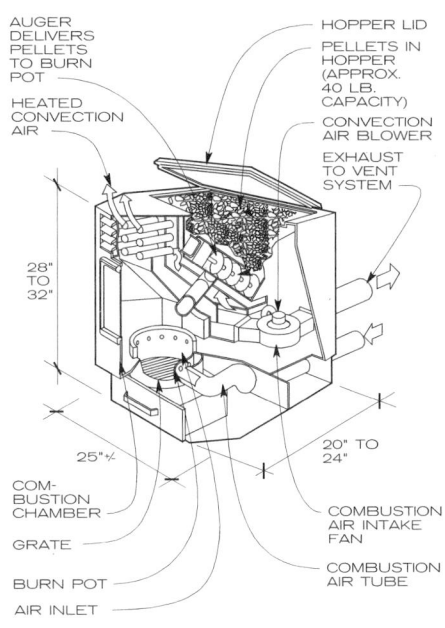

AUGER DELIVERS PELLETS TO BURN POT

HOPPER LID

PELLETS IN HOPPER (APPROX. 40 LB. CAPACITY)

HEATED CONVECTION AIR

CONVECTION AIR BLOWER

EXHAUST TO VENT SYSTEM

28" TO 32"

25"±

20" TO 24"

COMBUSTION CHAMBER

GRATE

BURN POT

AIR INLET

COMBUSTION AIR INTAKE FAN

COMBUSTION AIR TUBE

NOTE

Pellets are a consistently low-moisture fuel made from dried ground wood waste or other biomass waste compressed into small cylinders about 6 mm ($1/4$ in.) in diameter and 25 mm (1 in.) long. The pressure and heat used for their production binds the pellets together without the need for additives. Pellets usually burn cleanly because they are fed to the combustion chamber at a controlled rate and are matched with the right amount of combustion air. Pellet-burning stoves generally can operate at lower emission levels than natural firewood appliances. Some pellet stoves also burn corn.

TYPICAL DENSIFIED PELLET APPLIANCE

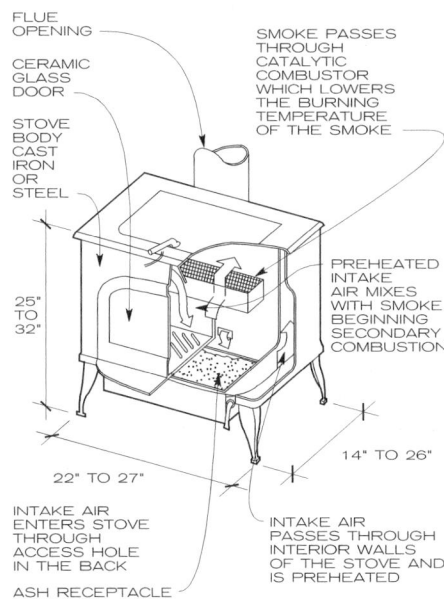

FLUE OPENING

SMOKE PASSES THROUGH CATALYTIC COMBUSTOR WHICH LOWERS THE BURNING TEMPERATURE OF THE SMOKE

CERAMIC GLASS DOOR

STOVE BODY CAST IRON OR STEEL

25" TO 32"

PREHEATED INTAKE AIR MIXES WITH SMOKE, BEGINNING SECONDARY COMBUSTION

22" TO 27"

14" TO 26"

INTAKE AIR ENTERS STOVE THROUGH ACCESS HOLE IN THE BACK

INTAKE AIR PASSES THROUGH INTERIOR WALLS OF THE STOVE AND IS PREHEATED

ASH RECEPTACLE

NOTE

A catalyst is a substance that effects a reaction without being consumed in the process. The catalyst in a catalytic combustion appliance is a coated ceramic honeycomb through which exhaust gas is routed. The catalytic coating, usually palladium and/or platinum, lowers the ignition temperature of the gases from 1000° to 500° F as they pass through, causing them to ignite. This arrangement allows catalytic appliances to operate at low firing rates and still burn cleanly. Because the catalyst restricts gas flow through the appliance, these units always include a bypass damper into the flue. The damper is opened when the appliance is loaded; when a hot fire has been established, it is closed, forcing the gases through the combustor for an extended clean burn.

CATALYTIC SOLID-FUEL APPLIANCE

CHIMNEYS AND DRAFT

The woodstove chimney and pellet stove vent are essential components of the solid-fuel heating system. For wood-stoves, factory-built metal chimneys offer precise sizing (optimum draft is obtained by matching the cross-sectional area of the flue outlet), safety (heat-tested to 2100°F, according to UL 103), and low maintenance (insulation reduces condensation). Masonry chimneys often need to be downsized with a UL 1777-listed stainless steel, poured or factory-built liner that extends from the appliance to the top of the chimney. Liners improve startup and draft, improve safety, and reduce and simplify maintenance.

Follow code or manufacturers' requirements for chimney clearance and height. For safety, follow the 2 ft/10 ft/3 ft rule: The chimney must terminate at least 2 ft higher than anything within 10 ft and extend at least 3 ft above the roof penetration. High-efficiency stoves may need added height to ensure adequate draft; a minimum height of 14 ft from appliance to chimney top is generally recommended.

Pellet appliances often use lower temperature double-wall pellet venting. Mechanical venting for some appliances can be totally horizontal if clearances to adjacent structures and openings are met, but additional vertical venting is recommended in case of unexpected shutdown. Mechanical draft pellet venting that penetrates the roof can terminate as little as 1 ft above the penetration; natural draft venting must be at least 2 ft higher than anything within 10 ft.

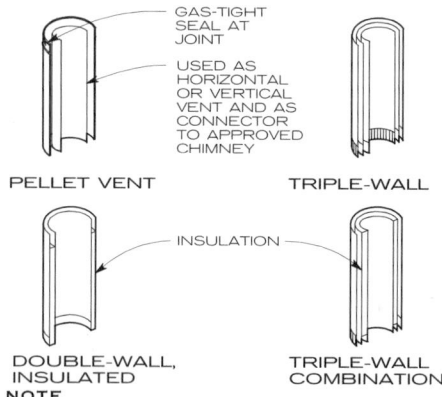

CHIMNEY TYPES FOR WOODSTOVES AND PELLET STOVES

NOTE
Chimneys keep flue gases as warm as possible, keep nearby combustibles at safe temperatures, and exhaust harmful smoke and gases to the outdoors.

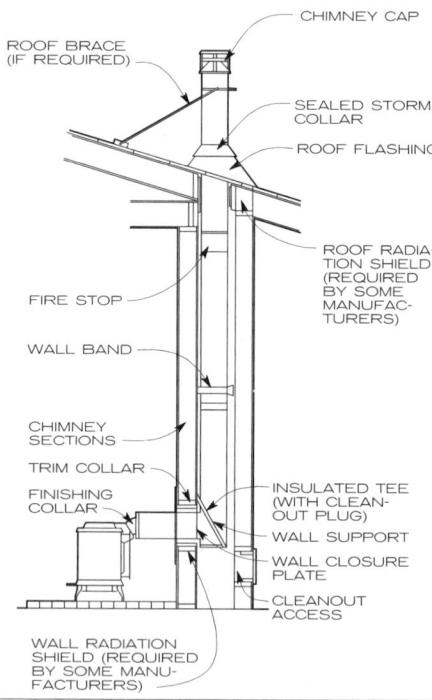

THROUGH-THE-WALL INSTALLATION— FACTORY-BUILT CHIMNEY

Walter Moberg Design, Inc.; Portland, Oregon
Hearth Education Foundation; Austin, Texas

 **FIREPLACES AND STOVES**

INSTALLATION

Underwriters Laboratories tests and lists most woodstoves tested for close clearances to unprotected combustibles. Brick or sheet metal protectors are not usually necessary, and their use in any case cannot reduce required clearance to less than 12 in. Use of double wall connector pipe from the appliance to the chimney may be recommended to reduce clearances for woodstoves, but such pipe must be listed for use with both the appliance and the chimney to which it will be connected.

Pellet appliances are listed by UL (but to a different standard) for very close clearances. They are usually vented with listed pellet venting from the appliance to the outside.

Unlisted appliances should be installed according to the provisions of NFPA 211.

Acceptable floor protection materials and minimum size for these stoves are specified by the manufacturers; if not, follow NFPA 211 or local code requirements.

REFERENCES

HEARTH Education Foundation. *HEARTH Woodstove Specialist Training Manual.* Austin, Tex., 1993.

———. *HEARTH Pellet Appliance Specialist Training Manual.* Austin, Tex., 1995.

National Fire Protection Association. *NFPA 211: Chimneys, Fireplaces, Vent, and Solid-Fuel Burning Appliances.* Quincy, Mass., 1992.

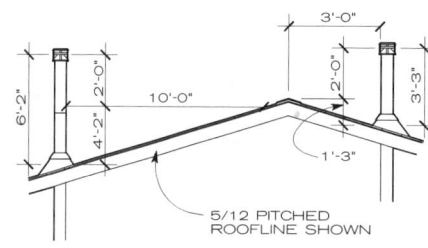

NOTE
Chimney height must meet minimum draft requirements, generally 14 ft from stove to the chimney cap.

CALCULATING CHIMNEY HEIGHTS WITH PITCHED ROOFS

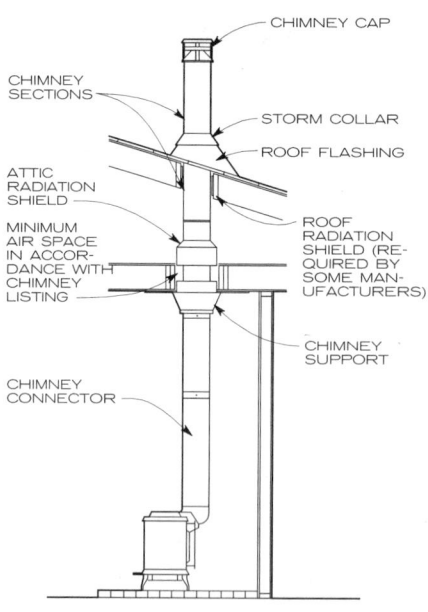

NOTE
Chimney must meet manufacturers' recommendations for minimum height.

STANDARD CEILING INSTALLATION— FACTORY-BUILT CHIMNEY

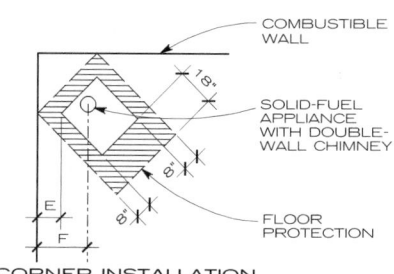

CORNER INSTALLATION

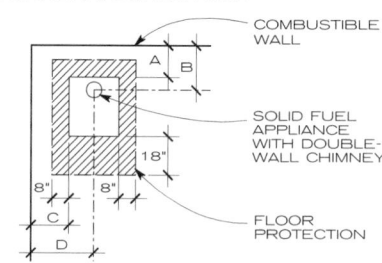

PARALLEL INSTALLATION

NOTE
All clearances shown are subject to change based on manufacturers' specifications, local codes, and any clearance reduction systems used.

MINIMUM CLEARANCES TO COMBUSTIBLES (IN.)

SINGLE WALL CONNECTOR (RESIDENTIAL)

A	B	C	D	E	F
15	21	18	30	11	25

DOUBLE WALL CONNECTOR (LISTED MOBILE HOME OR RESIDENCE, CLOSE CLEARANCE)

A	B	C	D	E	F
8	14	16	28	7	21

NOTE
Floor protection is required as follows: Minimum extension beyond loading door, 18 in.; beyond other sides, 8 in.

TYPICAL LISTED SOLID-FUEL APPLIANCE CLEARANCES

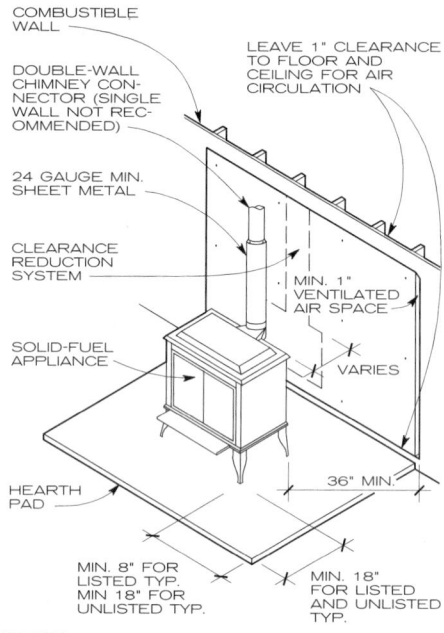

NOTES

1. For stoves with legs 2 to 6 in., hearth pad should be 4-in. hollow masonry with 24-gauge (min.) sheet metal cover.
2. With legs taller than 6 in., hearth pad should be 2-in. solid masonry with 24-gauge (min.) sheet metal cover.
3. Stoves with legs shorter than 2 in. must be installed on a noncombustible floor even if there is a hearth pad.

SOLID-FUEL APPLIANCE WALL CLEARANCE REDUCTION SYSTEM

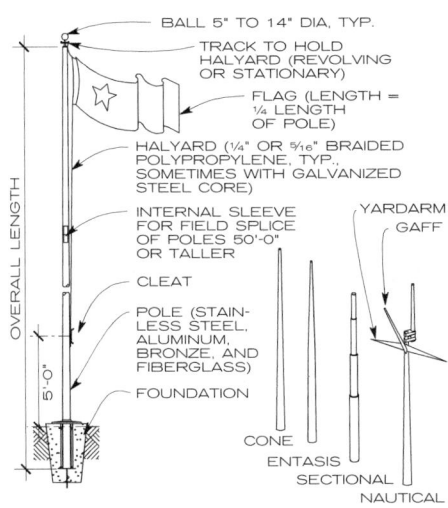

- BALL 5" TO 14" DIA. TYP.
- TRACK TO HOLD HALYARD (REVOLVING OR STATIONARY)
- FLAG (LENGTH = ¼ LENGTH OF POLE)
- HALYARD (¼" OR 5/16" BRAIDED POLYPROPYLENE, TYP., SOMETIMES WITH GALVANIZED STEEL CORE)
- INTERNAL SLEEVE FOR FIELD SPLICE OF POLES 50'-0" OR TALLER
- YARDARM
- GAFF
- CLEAT
- POLE (STAINLESS STEEL, ALUMINUM, BRONZE, AND FIBERGLASS)
- FOUNDATION
- OVERALL LENGTH
- 5'-0"
- CONE
- ENTASIS
- SECTIONAL
- NAUTICAL

NOTE

Flagpoles must withstand wind loads while the flag is flying. The combination wind load on pole and flag should be considered. Refer to wind load tests by the National Association of Architectural Metal Manufacturers (NAAMM).

FLAGPOLE DESIGN

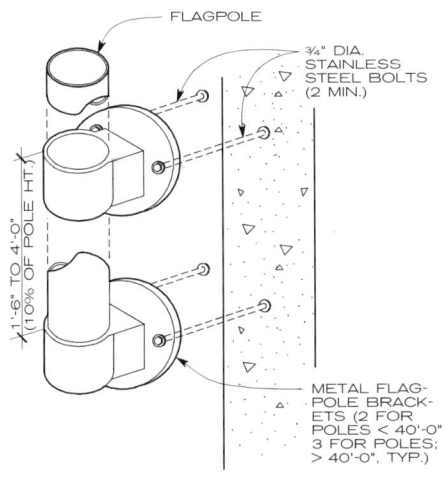

- FLAGPOLE
- ¾" DIA. STAINLESS STEEL BOLTS (2 MIN.)
- 1'-6" TO 4'-0" (10% OF POLE HT.)
- METAL FLAGPOLE BRACKETS (2 FOR POLES < 40'-0" 3 FOR POLES; > 40'-0", TYP.)

NOTE

Brackets are made of cast aluminum, bronze, and stainless steel; designs vary.

VERTICAL WALL-MOUNTED FLAGPOLE

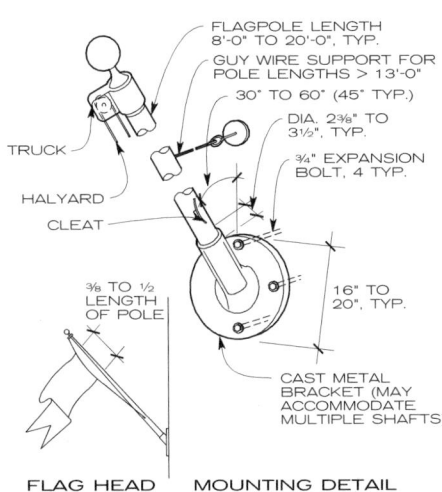

- FLAGPOLE LENGTH 8'-0" TO 20'-0", TYP.
- GUY WIRE SUPPORT FOR POLE LENGTHS > 13'-0"
- 30° TO 60° (45° TYP.)
- DIA. 2⅜" TO 3½", TYP.
- ¾" EXPANSION BOLT, 4 TYP.
- TRUCK
- HALYARD
- CLEAT
- ⅜ TO ½ LENGTH OF POLE
- 16" TO 20", TYP.
- CAST METAL BRACKET (MAY ACCOMMODATE MULTIPLE SHAFTS)
- FLAG HEAD
- MOUNTING DETAIL

OUTRIGGER WALL-MOUNTED FLAGPOLE

Richard J. Vitullo, AIA; Oak Leaf Studio; Crownsville, Maryland

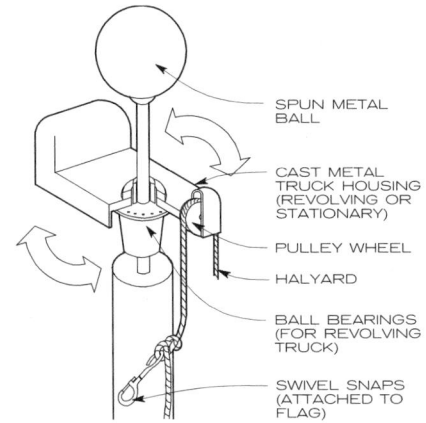

- SPUN METAL BALL
- CAST METAL TRUCK HOUSING (REVOLVING OR STATIONARY)
- PULLEY WHEEL
- HALYARD
- BALL BEARINGS (FOR REVOLVING TRUCK)
- SWIVEL SNAPS (ATTACHED TO FLAG)

NOTE

A revolving truck allows free movement of the flag while flying; a second truck is typically used as backup only, not simultaneously with the first truck.

DOUBLE TRUCK DETAIL

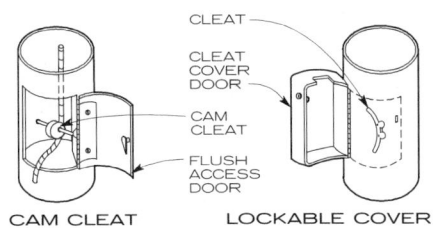

- CLEAT
- CLEAT COVER DOOR
- CAM CLEAT
- FLUSH ACCESS DOOR
- CAM CLEAT
- LOCKABLE COVER

VANDALPROOF CLEAT DETAILS

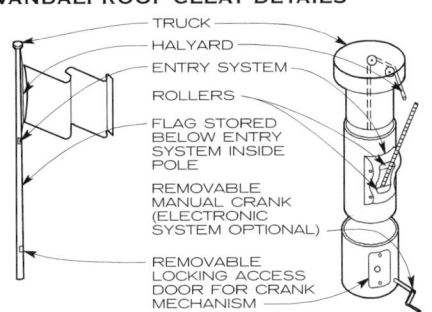

- TRUCK
- HALYARD
- ENTRY SYSTEM
- ROLLERS
- FLAG STORED BELOW ENTRY SYSTEM INSIDE POLE
- REMOVABLE MANUAL CRANK (ELECTRONIC SYSTEM OPTIONAL)
- REMOVABLE LOCKING ACCESS DOOR FOR CRANK MECHANISM
- SELF-STORING FLAGPOLE
- ENTRY SYSTEM DETAIL

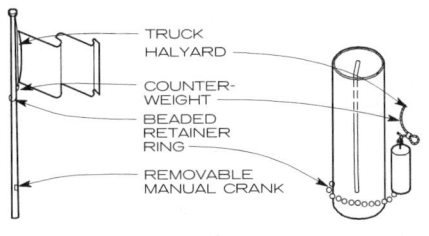

- TRUCK
- HALYARD
- COUNTERWEIGHT
- BEADED RETAINER RING
- REMOVABLE MANUAL CRANK
- CONCEALED HALYARD
- DETAIL

VANDALPROOF FLAGPOLE DESIGN

SUGGESTED FLAG SIZES

FOR GROUND-SET POLES		FOR VERTICAL WALL-SET POLES		FOR ROOF-SET POLES		FOR OUTRIGGER POLES	
EXPOSED POLE HEIGHT (FT)	FLAG SIZE (FT)	EXPOSED POLE HEIGHT (FT)	FLAG SIZE (FT)	EXPOSED POLE HEIGHT (FT)	FLAG SIZE (FT)	POLE LENGTH (FT)	FLAG SIZE (FT)
15	3 x 5	12 to 15	4 x 6	15	4 x 6	8	3 x 5
20 or 25	4 x 6	16 or 30	5 x 8	20 to 30	5 x 8	10 to 12	4 x 6
30 or 35	5 x 8	35 or 40	6 x 10	35 or 40	6 x 10	15 to 16	5 x 8
40 or 45	6 x 10	above top of wall		45 to 50	8 x 12	18 to 23	6 x 10
50, 55, or 60	8 x 12			60 to 65	10 x 15		
65 or 70	10 x 15			70 to 75	10 x 15		
80 or 90	10 x 15						
100	12 x 18						

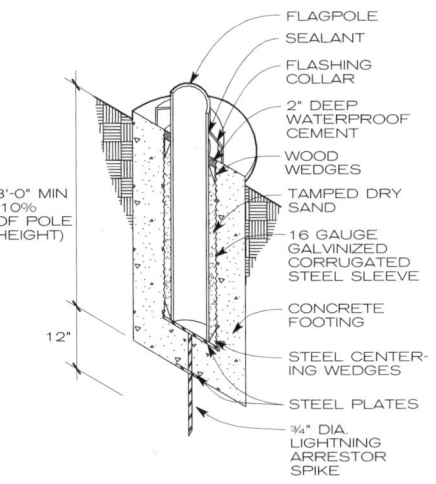

- FLAGPOLE
- SEALANT
- FLASHING COLLAR
- 2" DEEP WATERPROOF CEMENT
- WOOD WEDGES
- TAMPED DRY SAND
- 16 GAUGE GALVINIZED CORRUGATED STEEL SLEEVE
- CONCRETE FOOTING
- STEEL CENTERING WEDGES
- STEEL PLATES
- ¾" DIA. LIGHTNING ARRESTOR SPIKE
- 3'-0" MIN (10% OF POLE HEIGHT)
- 12"

FOUNDATION DETAIL

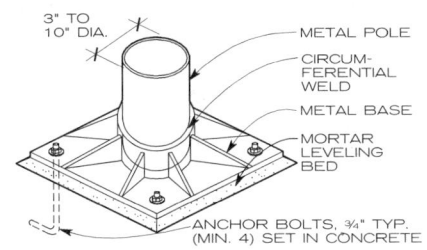

- 3" TO 10" DIA.
- METAL POLE
- CIRCUMFERENTIAL WELD
- METAL BASE
- MORTAR LEVELING BED
- ANCHOR BOLTS, ¾" TYP. (MIN. 4) SET IN CONCRETE

NOTE

Electrical wiring may be threaded through the pole.

SHOE BASE DETAIL

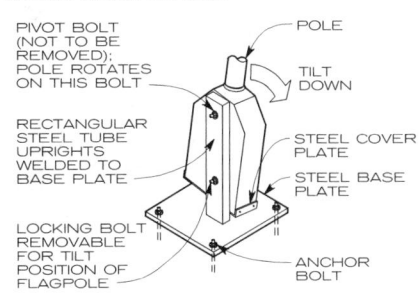

- PIVOT BOLT (NOT TO BE REMOVED); POLE ROTATES ON THIS BOLT
- RECTANGULAR STEEL TUBE UPRIGHTS WELDED TO BASE PLATE
- LOCKING BOLT REMOVABLE FOR TILT POSITION OF FLAGPOLE
- POLE
- TILT DOWN
- STEEL COVER PLATE
- STEEL BASE PLATE
- ANCHOR BOLT

COUNTERBALANCED TILTING POLE

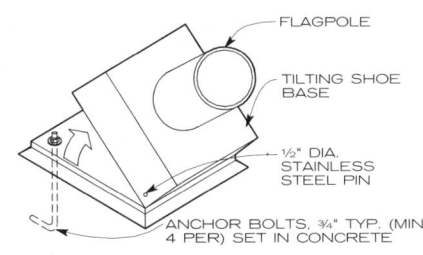

- FLAGPOLE
- TILTING SHOE BASE
- ½" DIA. STAINLESS STEEL PIN
- ANCHOR BOLTS, ¾" TYP. (MIN. 4 PER) SET IN CONCRETE

HINGED TILTING POLE

 TELEPHONE

 MEN'S RESTROOM

 GIFT SHOP

 SMOKING

 WATER WAY

 LOUNGE

 ACCOMMODATION INFORMATION

 LOST AND FOUND

 PARKING

 MAIL

 WOMEN'S RESTROOM

 LUGGAGE

 FIRST AID

 EMERGENCY

 TEXT TELEPHONE

 ACCESSIBLE FOR HEARING LOSS

 VOLUME CONTROL TELEPHONE

 INTERNATIONAL ACCESSIBILITY SYMBOL

 DINING

 RESTROOMS

 LOCKERS

 INFORMATION

 BUS STOP

 CAR RENTAL

 ELEVATOR

 TICKET INFORMATION

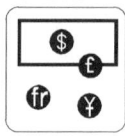 CURRENCY EXCHANGE

 TRAIN STATION

 WOMEN'S RESTROOM

 AIRPORT

 CAFE

 EXIT

 EXIT STAIRS

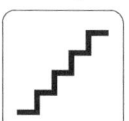 STAIRS

 MEN'S RESTROOM

 RAMP

 DRINKING FOUNTAIN

 WAITING ROOM

 FIRE EXTINGUISHER

 PARKING

 COAT ROOM

 ESCALATOR

 TAXI STAND

 BARBER

 LITTER RECEPTACLE

 CHANGING TABLE

 BANK/CASH MACHINE

 NO PARKING (24" X 24" RECOMMENDED SIZE)

 NO SMOKING

STANDARD PICTOGRAPHS

 EXIT / EXIT

 ACCESSIBLE

 HANDICAPPED PARKING ONLY

 RESERVED PARKING

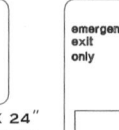 VAN ACCESSIBLE

 ACCESSIBLE ENTRANCE

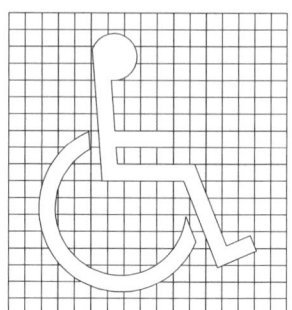

BIOLOGICAL HAZARD   RADIATION HAZARD   HIGH VOLTAGE HAZARD

 EXIT

 RESTROOMS

AREA OF RESCUE ASSISTANCE

IN CASE OF FIRE DO NOT USE ELEVATORS USE STAIRS

FIRE EXIT ONLY ALARM SOUNDS WHEN OPENED

AUTHORIZED VEHICLES ONLY

HAZARD PICTOGRAMS

NO PARKING ANYTIME

RESERVED PARKING

VISITOR PARKING

STOP

STOP (24" X 24" RECOMMENDED SIZE)

emergency exit only

DO NOT ENTER

Proportions of the international symbol of accessibility

EMERGENCY/EGRESS/PROHIBITORY SIGNS

SYMBOL OF ACCESSIBILITY

Mark Knapp Crawfis Association, Inc.; Mansfield, Ohio

10   IDENTIFYING DEVICES

GENERAL

Portable fire extinguishers can serve as a first line of defense against fires of limited size, even property equipped with automatic sprinklers or other fixed protection equipment. The following are criteria for selecting fire extinguishers:

1. Type and severity (size, intensity, and speed of travel) of potential fire hazard.
2. Environmental conditions of potential fire hazard (ambient temperature conditions, presence of fumes, etc.).
3. Effectiveness of extinguisher on potential fire hazard.
4. Ease of use.
5. Suitability for its environment.
6. Any anticipated adverse chemical reactions between the extinguishing agent and the burning materials.
7. Any health and operational safety concerns (exposure of operators during fire control efforts).
8. Training and physical capabilities of available personnel to operate extinguisher.
9. Upkeep and maintenance requirements.

NOTES

1. To comply with the Americans with Disabilities Act of 1990, fire extinguishers that protrude more than 4 in. into walks, halls, corridors, passageways, or aisles must be recessed into the wall.
2. The authority with jurisdiction over the location dictates the number, type, and placement of fire extinguishers and fire extinguisher cabinets.
3. All extinguishers without wheels must be installed on hangers or brackets, mounted in cabinets, or set on shelves. Extinguishers weighing up to 40 lb should be no more than 5 ft above the floor. The top of extinguishers with a gross weight greater than 40 lb should be no more than 3 ft 6 in. above the floor.
4. Halon-type extinguishers are no longer manufactured as a result of an international environmental agreement.
5. These standards and classifications are taken from the National Fire Protection Association Publication 10, *Portable Fire Extinguishers*, 1994 ed. Always check local code requirements before specifying fire extinguishers.

CLASSIFICATION OF OCCUPANCIES BY HAZARD TYPE

1. LIGHT (LOW) HAZARD: Light hazard occupancies have few Class A combustible materials, including furnishings, decorations, and contents. This may include offices, classrooms, churches, or hotels.
2. ORDINARY (MODERATE) HAZARD: Ordinary hazard occupancies have more Class A combustibles and Class B flammables in light hazard occupancies. They include certain dining areas, mercantile shops, and research operations.
3. EXTRA (HIGH) HAZARD: Places with more Class A combustibles and Class B flammables than ordinary hazard occupancies present are extra hazard occupancies. Likely locations include woodworking, vehicle repair, and paint shops and cooking areas.

FIRE EXTINGUISHER SIZE AND PLACEMENT FOR CLASS A HAZARDS

	LIGHT HAZARD OCCUPANCY	ORDINARY HAZARD OCCUPANCY	EXTRA HAZARD OCCUPANCY
Min. rated single extinguisher	2-A[1]	2-A[1]	4-A[2]
Max. floor area per unit of A	3,000 sq ft	1,500 sq ft	1,000 sq ft
Max. floor area for extinguisher	11,250 sq ft	11,250 sq ft	11,250 sq ft
Max. travel distance to extinguisher	75 ft	75 ft	75 ft

[1] Up to two water-type extinguishers with 1-A rating can be used to fulfill the requirements of one 2-A rated extinguisher for light hazard occupancies.

[2] Two $2^1/_2$ gallon (9.45 L) water-type extinguishers can be used to fulfill the requirements of one 4-A rated extinguisher.

MULTIPURPOSE DRY CHEMICAL (CLASS A, B, AND C FIRES)

Capacity (lb)	$2^1/_2$	5	6	10	20
Height (in.)	14	$14^1/_2$	16	20	24
Diameter (in.)	3	$4^1/_4$	5	5	7
Class	1A:10B:C	2A:10B:C;3A:40B:C	3A:40B:C	4A:60B:C	20A:120B:C
Effective range	10 to 20 ft				
Discharge time	5 lb, 10 sec; 10 lb, 11 sec; 20 lb, 15 sec; 30 lb, 15 sec				
Recharge	After use				
Pressure source	Compressed gas				
Temperature effect	Will operate at - 65°F				
Electrical conductivity	Will not conduct				

NOTE: Fluidized and siliconized monoammonium phosphate powder is dispersed, smothers and breaks chain reaction of fire.

CARBON DIOXIDE (CLASS B AND C FIRES ONLY)

Capacity (lb)	5	10	15	20
Height (in.)	$17^3/_4$	24	30	30
Diameter (in.)	$5^1/_4$	7	7	8
Class	5B:C	10B:C	10B:C	10B:C
Effective range	3 to 8 ft			
Discharge time	$2^1/_2$ lb, 12 sec; 5 lb, 22 sec; 10 lb, 23 sec; 15 lb, 26 sec; 20 lb, 25 sec			
Recharge	After use			
Pressure source	Compressed gas			
Temperature effect	Will operate at - 40°F			
Electrical conductivity	Will not conduct			

NOTE: Pressurized liquid carbon dioxide is released, changed into a gas, and appears as a cloud of white "snow," smothering fire.

REGULAR DRY CHEMICAL (CLASS B AND C FIRES)

Capacity (lb)	$2^1/_2$	5	$^1/_2$	6	1O	2O
Height (in.)	$14^3/_8$ to $14^5/_8$	$14^5/_8$ to $15^1/_4$	$14^5/_8$ to $15^1/_4$	$15^1/_2$ to $16^1/_4$	20 to $20^1/_2$	$23^1/_4$ to 24
Diameter (in.)	3	$4^1/_4$	$4^1/_4$	5	5 to 6	7
Class	10B:C	10B:C	40B:C	40B:C	60B:C	120B:C
Effective range	10 to 20 ft					
Discharge time	5 lb, 10 sec; 10 lb, 11 sec; 20 lb, 15 sec; 30 lb, 34 sec					
Recharge	After use					
Pressure source	Compressed gas					
Temperature effect	Will operate at - 40°F					
Electrical conductivity	Will not conduct					

NOTE: A siliconized sodium bicarbonate base (the traditional dry chemical design) extinguishes fire. A base of potassium bicarbonate is also available.

DISTRIBUTION OF FIRE EXTINGUISHERS

The minimum number of fire extinguishers needed to protect a property from Class A fires is determined by the accompanying tables; frequently, additional extinguishers are installed. Fire extinguishers rated for Class B fires are placed a maximum travel distance of 50 ft from the hazard (smaller rated extinguishers are placed no more than 30 ft from the hazard). Fire extinguishers rated for Class C fires shall be required in locations with energized electrical equipment that would require a nonconducting extinguishing medium. For Class D fires, extinguishers are located not more than 75 ft from the Class D hazard.

FIRE CLASSIFICATIONS FOR SELECTING FIRE EXTINGUISHERS

LETTER SYMBOL AND COLOR	PICTURE SYMBOL	DESCRIPTION
Green — A		Class A: Fires involving ordinary combustible materials (such as wood, cloth, paper, rubber, and many plastics) that require the heat-absorbing (cooling) effects of water or water solutions, or the coating effects of certain dry chemicals that retard combustion.
Red — B		Class B: Fires involving flammable or combustible liquids, flammable gases, greases and similar materials that are best extinguished by excluding air (oxygen), inhibiting the release of combustible vapors, or interrupting the combustion chain reaction.
Blue — C		Class C: Fires involving energized electrical equipment where safety to the operator requires the use of electrically nonconductive extinguishing agents.
Yellow — D		Class D: Fires involving combustible metals (such as magnesium, titanium, zirconium, sodium, lithium, and potassium).

PRESSURIZED WATER

Capacity (gal)	$2^1/_2$
Height (in.)	$24^1/_2$
Diameter (in.)	7
Weight (lb)	28
Class	2A
Effective Range	30 ft
Discharge time	50 seconds
Recharge	Weigh cylinder and check annually; in all cases, follow instructions on label
Pressure source	Compressed air
Temperature effect	Will freeze
Electrical conductivity	Will conduct

NOTE

Water quenches fire and cools area.

SODIUM CHLORIDE

Capacity (lb)	30
Height (in.)	$27^3/_4$
Diameter (in.)	7
Class	FM
Effective range	4 to 6 ft
Discharge time	28 seconds
Recharge	After use
Pressure source	Compressed gas
Temperature effect	-40 to +120
Electrical conductivity	Will not conduct

NOTES

1. Sodium chloride dry powder is dispersed over a burning combustible metal or alloy; heat from fire causes dry powder to cake and form exterior crust that excludes air and dissipates heat.
2. For lithium and lithium alloy Class D fires, a copper-based extinguishing agent is used.

Mark Conroy; National Fire Protection Association; Quincy, Massachusetts

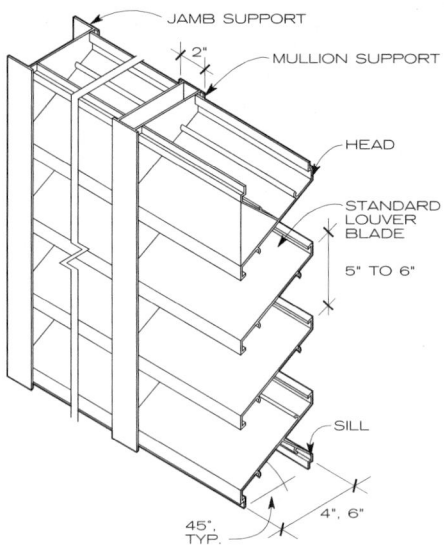

NOTE

Generally, this is the most economical louver type.

EXPOSED MULLION LOUVER

GENERAL NOTES

1. Metal architectural louvers allow airflow through a wall for ventilation, especially of machine exhaust. They protect the interior space from vandalism, weather, insects, or birds and can be used to obscure unsightly views. Louvers can be fabricated in standard rectangles or custom shapes such as circles, triangles, and ellipses. Radiused corners and other details are available from some manufacturers. Penthouses frequently incorporate louvered walls to screen equipment and provide airflow.

2. Standard louver materials are 16-, 18-, or 20-gauge galvanized or cold-rolled steel and 8-, 12-, or 14-gauge extruded aluminum alloy. Other metals can be used for special applications. Translucent fiberglass is a standard blade material when daylighting is desirable. Fasteners are either aluminum or stainless steel. The dimensions shown are the most common; other sizes are available.

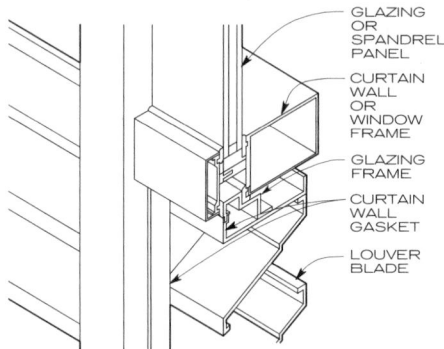

LOUVER INSTALLATION IN CURTAIN WALL

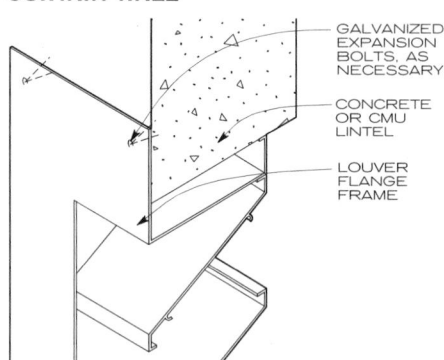

FLANGE MOUNT DETAIL

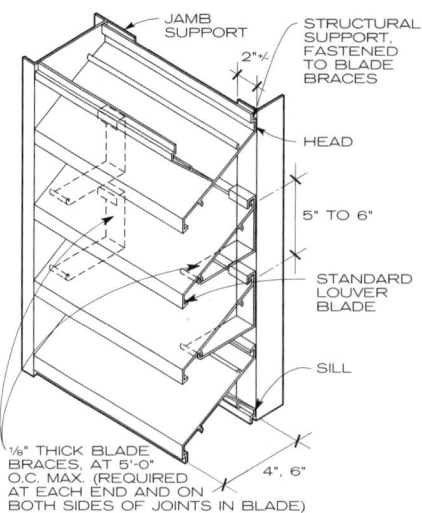

NOTE

This louver type offers a visual line uninterrupted by exposed vertical supports.

CONTINUOUS HORIZONTAL LOUVER

3. Factory finishing is recommended for maximum control of color and durability. The finish for steel louvers is baked enamel, which comes in a variety of colors. Aluminum finishes include mill, clear lacquer, baked enamel, and anodic. Fluorocarbon polymeric finish coatings (kynar), which can be applied to steel or aluminum, resist chalking, ultraviolet deterioration, salts, chemicals, and pollutants.

4. Mechanically assembled extruded aluminum louvers are the most common type of louver assembly on the market. Mechanical fasteners are better than welding in extruded aluminum alloy construction because annealing occurs near the weld, weakening the material along both sides. Also, repairs are easier if mechanical fasteners are used.

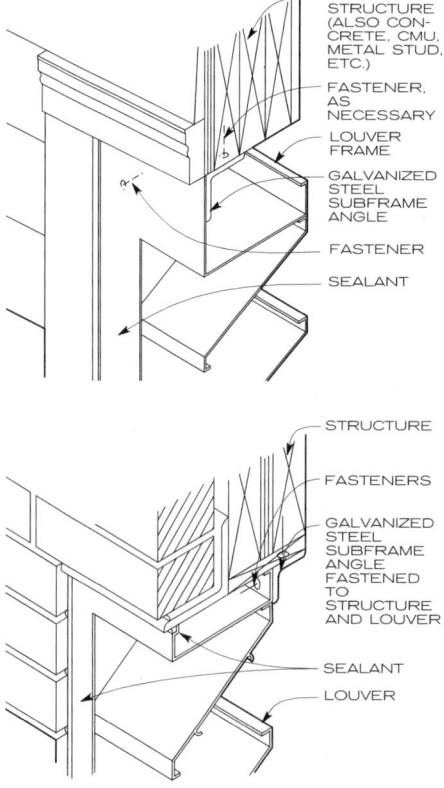

ANGLE SUBFRAME DETAILS

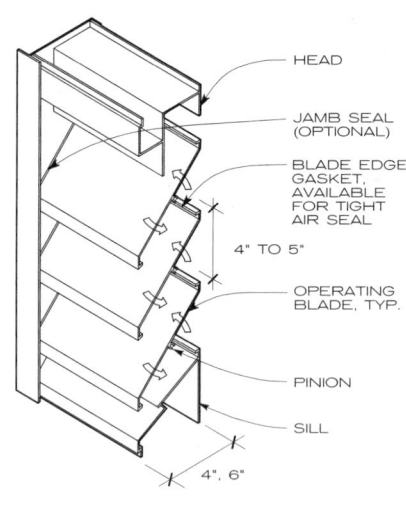

NOTE

Adjustable operating louvers are available with manual, electric, or pneumatic actuators. Free area 38 to 58%.

ADJUSTABLE OPERATING LOUVER

5. With sheet metal, welding an assembly of louvers is easier and less expensive than using clip angles and screws to fasten the blades to the framework.

6. Free area is the net area of free airflow through a louver, generally measured in square feet or as a percentage of the area in the louver type selected. Manufacturers' free area ratings should include the effects of bird or insect screens, which reduce free area.

7. For all louvers servicing mechanical equipment, consult a mechanical engineer for design and specification of the louvers. Louvers are rated for air performance and water penetration and certified through the Air Movement and Control Association. The Building Services Resources and Information Association also rates the performance of metal louvers.

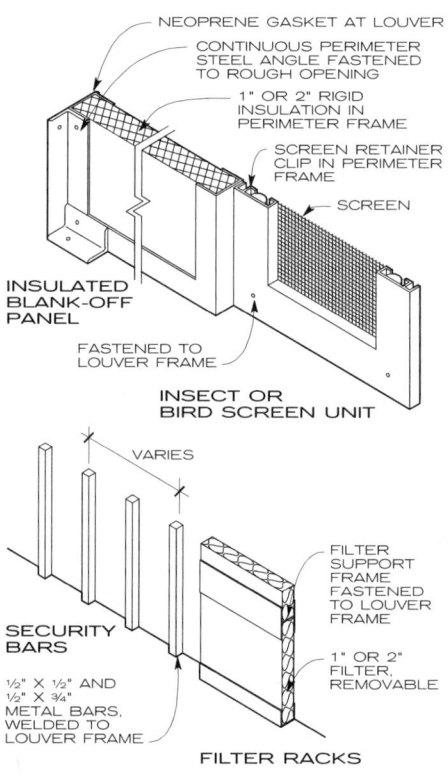

MISCELLANEOUS LOUVER ACCESSORIES

Richard J. Vitullo, AIA; Oak Leaf Studio; Crownsville, Maryland

10 PROTECTIVE COVERS

GENERAL

Louver blades come in many shapes, sizes, and performance types that vary with the manufacturer; the blades illustrated here represent the basic types. Some blades are fixed only; others can be opened and shut. The center-to-center dimensions given are approximate; generally, standard blades (not specialty blades such as acoustic, air-foil, etc.) are designed with minimal overlap so they can obstruct views but maximize the free area.

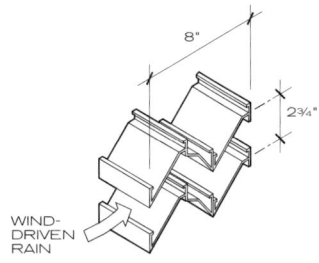

NOTE

Louvers utilizing this blade design completely obscure views and are tamperproof and storm-resistant. This blade prevents nearly 100% of wind-driven rain from entering (generally tested with winds up to 30 mph for one hour).

HORIZONTAL STORM-RESISTANT BLADE

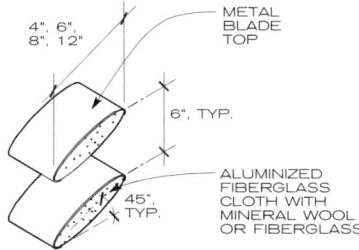

NOTE

Acoustically insulated air-foil blades block sound from inside or out and accommodate high air velocities. Free area is 29%; blades may be fixed or operable.

FIXED AIR-FOIL ACOUSTICAL BLADE

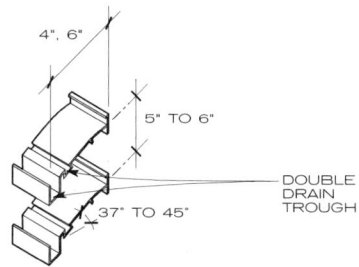

NOTE

This blade type provides high water resistance and a free area of about 50%. Typically employed in louvers with jamb and mullion drains, it is not designed to protect against wind-driven rain.

DOUBLE DRAINABLE LOUVER BLADE

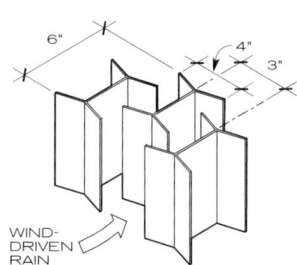

NOTE

Louvers utilizing this blade design completely obscure views and are tamperproof and completely stormproof.

VERTICAL STORM-RESISTANT BLADE

Richard J. Vitullo, AIA; Oak Leaf Studio; Crownsville, Maryland

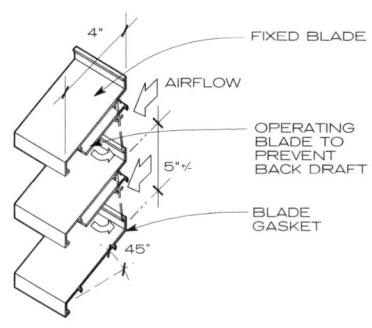

AUTOMATIC EXHAUST DAMPER/LOUVER

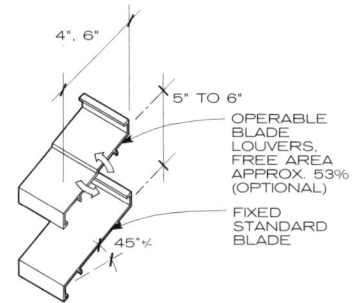

NOTE

Standard blades are suitable for most applications where water infiltration is not a concern. Free area is approximately 48%. Single operating panels should not exceed 48 in. wide x 96 in. high. This blade can be either fixed or operable.

STANDARD BLADE

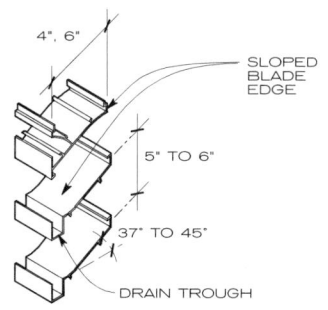

NOTE

Designed to provide high free area (55%) and low water penetration, this blade is not recommended for use with hidden mullions; louvers that employ these blades contain integral drains in their mullions that direct water away from the inside of the louver. All drain troughs must be kept free of debris. Not designed to hinder wind-driven rain.

HIGH-PERFORMANCE DRAINABLE BLADE

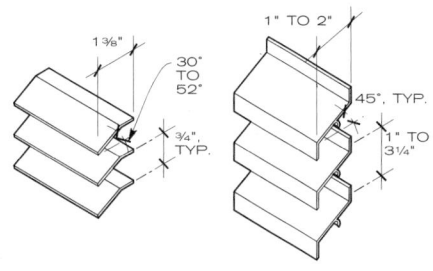

NOTE

These shallow louver blades can allow a very high free area (from 32 to 73%). They are often used when standard-depth louvers are not practical.

SHALLOW AIR CONDITIONING BLADE

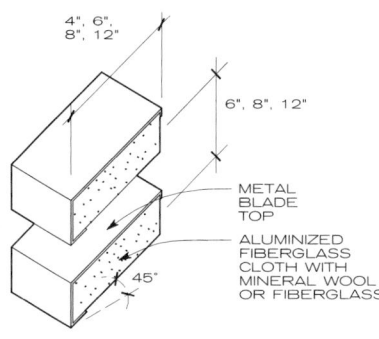

NOTE

Acoustically insulated blades block sound from inside or out and prevent weather infiltration. Free areas range from 21 to 29%. Blades may be fixed or operable.

FIXED ACOUSTICAL LOUVER

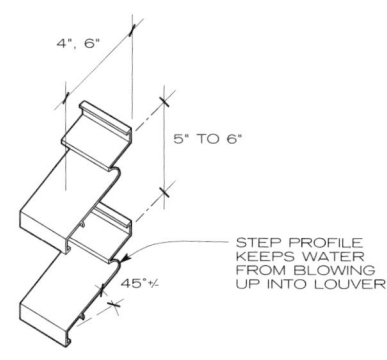

NOTE

Step blades help prevent water infiltration. Free area is approximately 48%.

STEP BLADE PROFILE

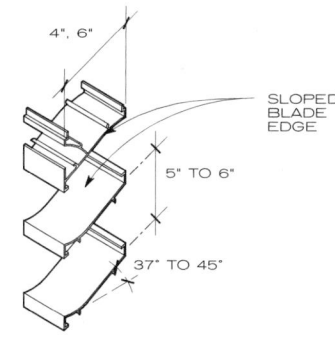

NOTE

Designed to provide a high free area (55%), this blade accommodates high air velocities and protects against wind-blown precipitation.

HIGH-PERFORMANCE STANDARD BLADE

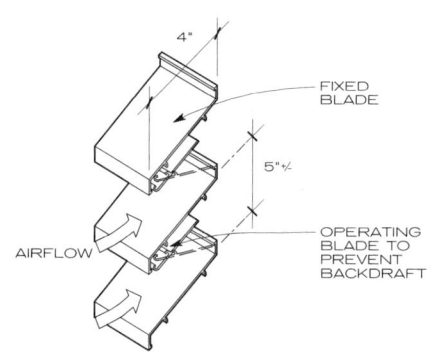

AUTOMATIC INTAKE DAMPER/LOUVER

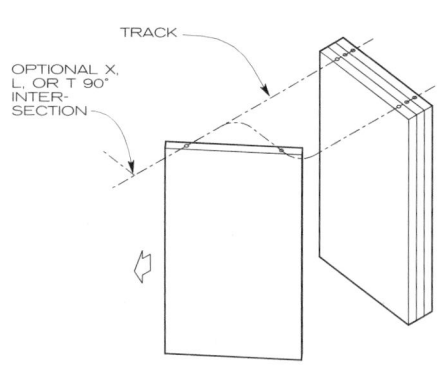

INDIVIDUAL PANELS
NOTE
This manually operated system is for panels more than 16 ft tall (40 ft max. typically), which are supported by two carriers on each panel.

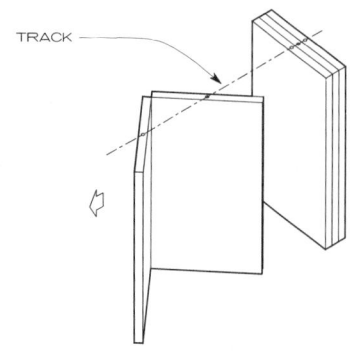

HINGED PAIRS
NOTE
This manually operated system is for panels up to 18 ft in height and typically is used for straight runs only. Each panel has one carrier.

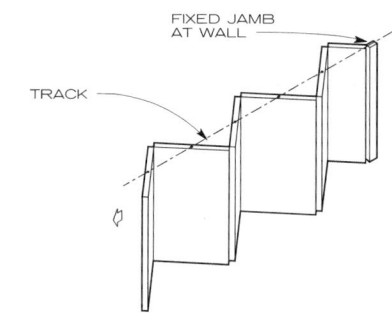

CONTINUOUSLY HINGED
NOTE
Panels are hinged together to form a continuous panel train. This type is manually operated for systems with a total wall weight under 3700 lb and operated with an electric motor for weights exceeding 3700 lb. This type of panel is typically suitable for straight run applications only.

PANEL OPERATION TYPES

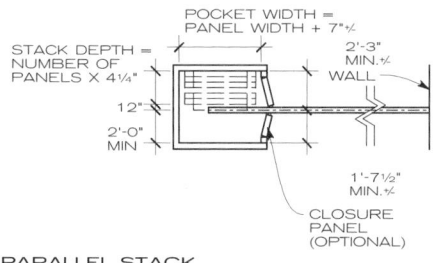

PARALLEL STACK

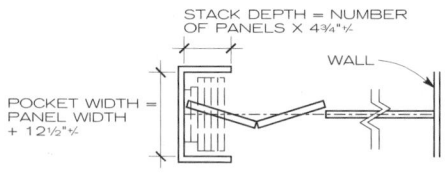

CENTER STACK

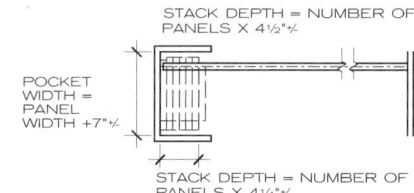

PERPENDICULAR STACK

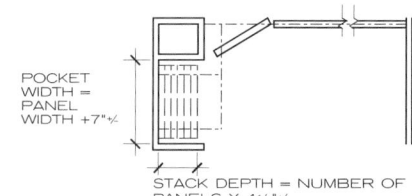

REMOTE STACK

NOTE
Dimensions given are for planning purposes only: consult manufacturer for specifics. Panels with automatic bottom seals require a wider stack storage area; dimensions given are for fixed, adjustable, or operable bottom seals.

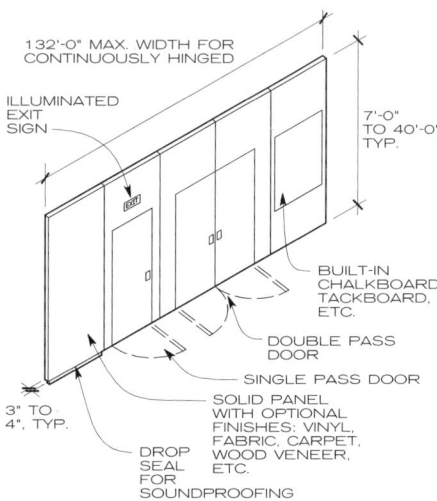

NOTE
Panel wall width for individual and paired panels is unlimited. Sound transmission coefficient ratings for typical panels are available up to 55.

STORAGE ARRANGEMENTS FOR PANEL STACKS

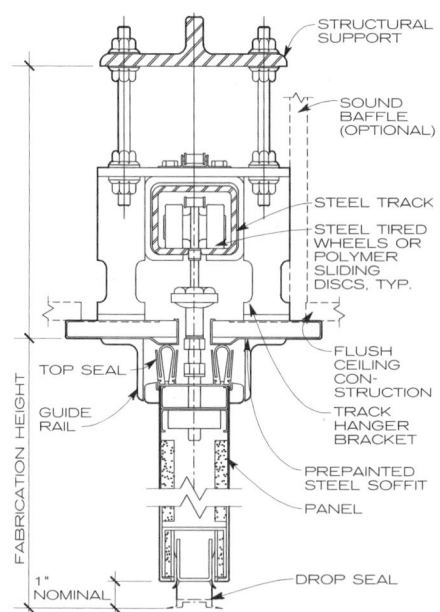

TOP-HUNG FOLDING PARTITION DETAIL

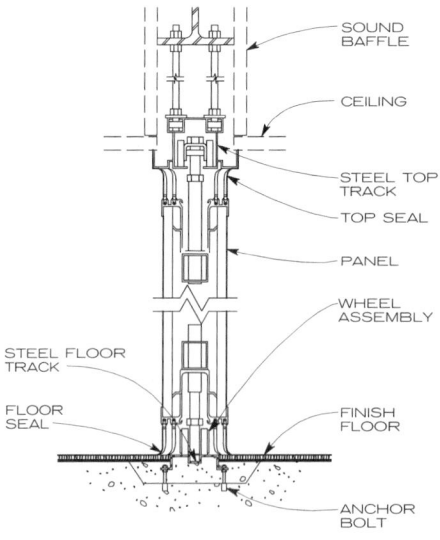

NOTE
The bottom carrier handles about 90% of the panel's weight.

FLOOR-SUPPORTED FOLDING PARTITION DETAIL

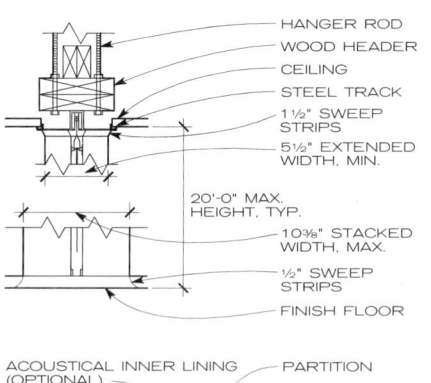

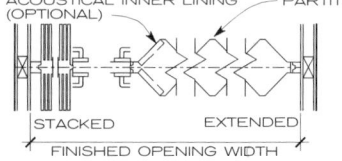

PLAN
NOTE
Acoustical inner liners can be added to these partitions. Typical partitions are either built of laminated panels or individual vinyl-clad steel panels with extruded vinyl hinges.

ACCORDION PARTITIONS

Richard J. Vitullo, AIA; Oak Leaf Studio; Crownsville, Maryland

 PARTITIONS AND OPERABLE PARTITIONS

GENERAL

Movable wall systems of non-load bearing interior partitions offer flexibility for office environments in which functions and layouts may change quickly or repeatedly. Generally, they are manufactured either as one-piece self-contained panels or as two-piece systems in which structure and cladding are independent of each other. In either case, floor and ceiling tracks are installed on finished (carpeted, etc.) floors and fastened to suspended ceiling grids. Height adjustment and leveling are accomplished with components included in a typical panel assembly. Panels may be attached to each other or independently fixed into floor and ceiling channels, offering more flexibility. Typically, movable wall systems delineate space, provide visual and sound privacy, channel power and telecommunications cable, and support storage and work surface components. Various manufacturers offer different features for electric and telecommunications cable raceways and access, opening treatments, connection details, panel/cladding and finish materials, sound transmission coefficient ratings, fire ratings, and demountability/movability options. Consult manufacturers for specific features.

ONE-PIECE PANELS

One-piece panels are composite panels typically made from sheet steel or aluminum with a core of insulation and structural ribs for stiffness. Panels are typically 2 $\frac{3}{8}$ to 3 in. thick, although other thicknesses are available.

TWO-PIECE PANELS

These panels are manufactured as separate structural and cladding systems. The structure is made from steel members that are factory-assembled into panel-sized components and then installed. Panel cladding material varies and may include regular and high-impact vinyl-clad gypsum, insulation-filled sound control panels, or sandwich panels (steel sheets with a honeycomb infill), among others. Panel cladding is typically $\frac{1}{2}$ to $\frac{5}{8}$ in. thick.

GENERAL NOTES

1. Suspended ceilings are usually ineffective as a sound barrier. Consequently, when a series of soundproofed offices are planned under such a ceiling, the chances of sound travel over partitions should be considered. Baffles installed tightly above each run of the slab will eliminate cracks through which sound can easily pass.

2. The perimeter of the partition installation—ceiling, floor, and sides—should be gasketed with a factory-applied sealant. All door frames should be fitted with a factory-applied rubber liner at the head and jambs that compresses when the door is closed.

3. For extra sound control, all doors should have a continuous drop seal and threshold and glazing in doors and partitions should have double lights that are hermetically sealed.

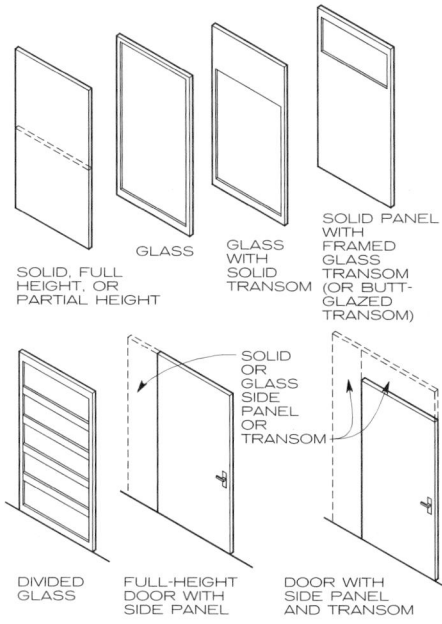

SOLID, FULL HEIGHT, OR PARTIAL HEIGHT

GLASS

GLASS WITH SOLID TRANSOM

SOLID PANEL WITH FRAMED GLASS TRANSOM (OR BUTT-GLAZED TRANSOM)

SOLID OR GLASS SIDE PANEL OR TRANSOM

DIVIDED GLASS

FULL-HEIGHT DOOR WITH SIDE PANEL

DOOR WITH SIDE PANEL AND TRANSOM

NOTE

Wall panel sizes range from 6 to 60 in. wide, up to a single panel height of 1 ft.

PANEL TYPES

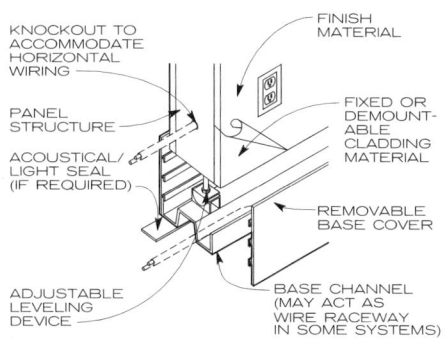

KNOCKOUT TO ACCOMMODATE HORIZONTAL WIRING

PANEL STRUCTURE

ACOUSTICAL/ LIGHT SEAL (IF REQUIRED)

ADJUSTABLE LEVELING DEVICE

FINISH MATERIAL

FIXED OR DEMOUNTABLE CLADDING MATERIAL

REMOVABLE BASE COVER

BASE CHANNEL (MAY ACT AS WIRE RACEWAY IN SOME SYSTEMS)

NOTE

Various locking devices fasten panels to the floor. Consult manufacturers.

BASE DETAIL

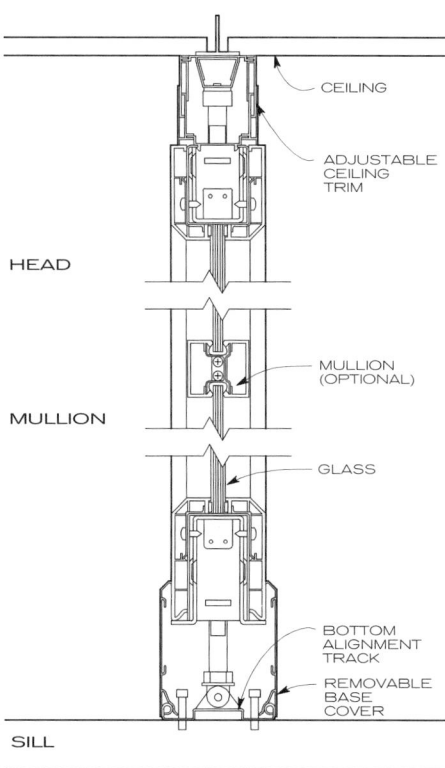

CEILING

ADJUSTABLE CEILING TRIM

HEAD

MULLION (OPTIONAL)

MULLION

GLASS

BOTTOM ALIGNMENT TRACK

REMOVABLE BASE COVER

SILL

GLAZED WALL SECTION DETAIL

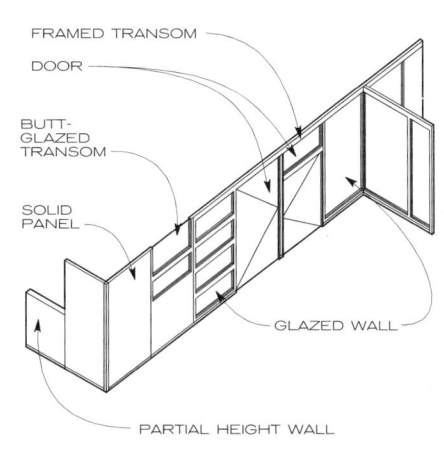

FRAMED TRANSOM

DOOR

BUTT-GLAZED TRANSOM

SOLID PANEL

GLAZED WALL

PARTIAL HEIGHT WALL

WALL CONFIGURATION SHOWING PANEL TYPES

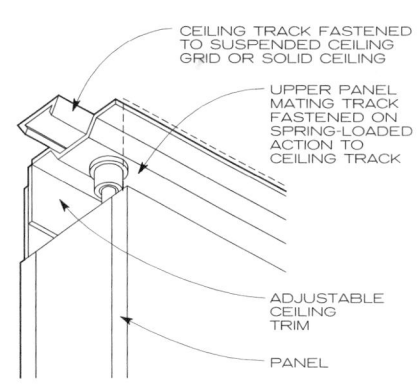

CEILING TRACK FASTENED TO SUSPENDED CEILING GRID OR SOLID CEILING

UPPER PANEL MATING TRACK FASTENED ON SPRING-LOADED ACTION TO CEILING TRACK

ADJUSTABLE CEILING TRIM

PANEL

CEILING DETAIL

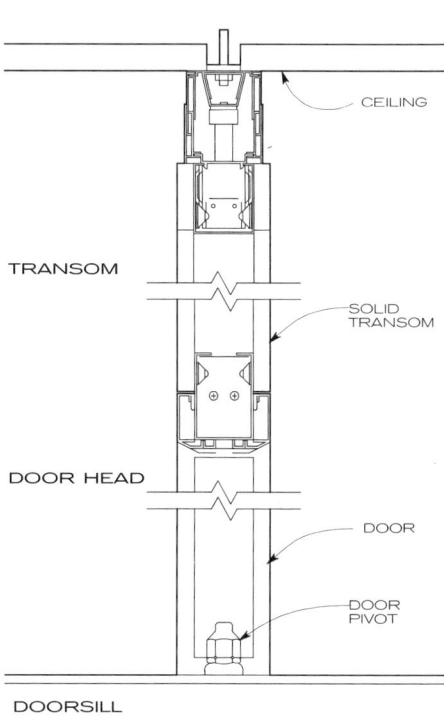

CEILING

TRANSOM

SOLID TRANSOM

DOOR HEAD

DOOR

DOOR PIVOT

DOORSILL

DOOR SECTION DETAIL

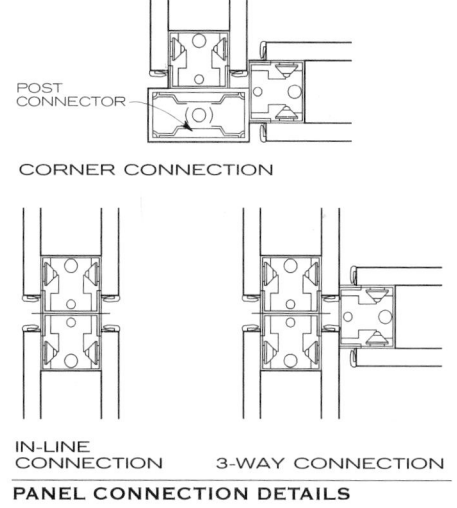

POST CONNECTOR

CORNER CONNECTION

IN-LINE CONNECTION

3-WAY CONNECTION

PANEL CONNECTION DETAILS

Richard J. Vitullo, AIA; Oak Leaf Studio; Crownsville, Maryland

PARTITIONS AND OPERABLE PARTITIONS 10

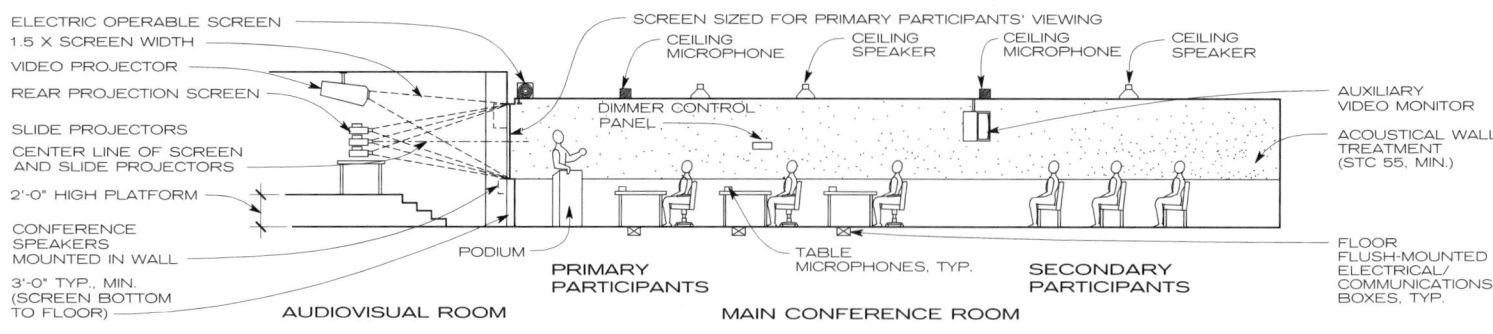

ELECTRIC OPERABLE SCREEN
1.5 X SCREEN WIDTH
VIDEO PROJECTOR
REAR PROJECTION SCREEN
SLIDE PROJECTORS
CENTER LINE OF SCREEN AND SLIDE PROJECTORS
2'-0" HIGH PLATFORM
CONFERENCE SPEAKERS MOUNTED IN WALL
3'-0" TYP., MIN. (SCREEN BOTTOM TO FLOOR)
AUDIOVISUAL ROOM

SCREEN SIZED FOR PRIMARY PARTICIPANTS' VIEWING
CEILING MICROPHONE
CEILING SPEAKER
CEILING MICROPHONE
CEILING SPEAKER
DIMMER CONTROL PANEL
PODIUM
PRIMARY PARTICIPANTS
TABLE MICROPHONES, TYP.
SECONDARY PARTICIPANTS
MAIN CONFERENCE ROOM
AUXILIARY VIDEO MONITOR
ACOUSTICAL WALL TREATMENT (STC 55, MIN.)
FLOOR FLUSH-MOUNTED ELECTRICAL/ COMMUNICATIONS BOXES, TYP.

SECTION—MULTIMEDIA CONFERENCE ROOM

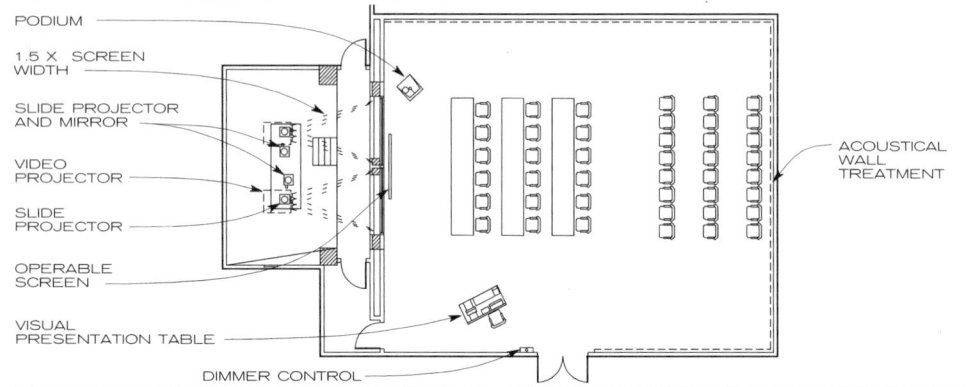

PODIUM
1.5 X SCREEN WIDTH
SLIDE PROJECTOR AND MIRROR
VIDEO PROJECTOR
SLIDE PROJECTOR
OPERABLE SCREEN
VISUAL PRESENTATION TABLE
DIMMER CONTROL
ACOUSTICAL WALL TREATMENT

PLAN—MULTIMEDIA CONFERENCE ROOM

GENERAL

Teleconferencing is voice or data communication between remote locations and the origination site. Videoconferencing is teleconferencing with visual images added to voice and data communications. Generally, a videoconference space includes two video screens (with speaker for each), one screen for a video image from a remote location and another for supplementary images, such as those from a visual presenter, computer, or videocassette recorder.

SCREENS

Rear projection screens or large-screen monitors may be used for videoconferencing. When using a rear projection screen, it is possible to use brighter lights in the conference room during viewing than with a regular video monitor. (The forward projection screen may be perforated for sound. Forward projection systems do not need specially dedicated rooms but are usually mounted in a recess in the ceiling. They are not recommended for videoconference rooms since the high light levels required for video cameras tend to wash out forward projection screens.)

PROJECTORS

Slide, video, and overhead projectors are used in multimedia conference rooms. Video projectors are manufactured in three-lens CRT systems and single-lens LCD "light valve" systems. Three-lens projectors are best for screens up to 10 ft wide, a typical size for conference rooms, and are relatively inexpensive. If an audiovisual room is small, mirrors can be used to increase the image size for rear projection. For extra large conference rooms, with screens typically 15 to 25 ft wide, one-lens projectors can be placed any distance from the screen. This setup offers a bright, sharp image but presently is very expensive compared to the three-lens systems.

SPEAKERS AND MICROPHONES

Speaker placement is very important in a videoconference space. Speaker size usually depends on the size and shape of the space to be served.

There are three main types of speakers: Playback speakers, matched with prerecorded audio and video discs and tapes, are the largest speakers and offer the highest quality sound. Teleconference speakers, located below and near the center of the video screen, bring the audio feed from the remote videoconference space. Voice reinforcement speakers amplify voices from microphones in the same space. Microphones are placed at strategic locations in the videoconference space, including on tables, for primary participant involvement; on a stand, for secondary participant involvement; as a wireless or clip-on feature, for moderator/coordinator; and on the ceiling ("choir" microphones) to pick up specific sounds desired (to minimize feedback, these must be kept as far from the speakers as possible).

Polysonics; Washington, D.C.

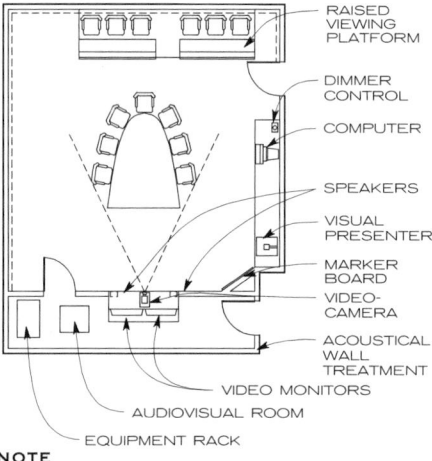

RAISED VIEWING PLATFORM
DIMMER CONTROL
COMPUTER
SPEAKERS
VISUAL PRESENTER
MARKER BOARD
VIDEO CAMERA
ACOUSTICAL WALL TREATMENT
VIDEO MONITORS
AUDIOVISUAL ROOM
EQUIPMENT RACK

NOTE

A rear projection video camera and projection screen may be used with this arrangement; the room size depends on the screen size and video camera distance preferred.

VIDEOCONFERENCE ROOM

AUXILIARY VIDEO MONITORS

Space used by secondary videoconference participants may need auxiliary monitors to display supplementary video images such as charts or graphics that need close scrutiny. The main videoconference screen usually does not require this backup video screen.

MISCELLANEOUS EQUIPMENT

Some videoconference spaces are equipped with remote control systems, which control all electronic functions, including light and sound, from a central control panel. Some spaces are also equipped with special light fixtures that are tilted away from the screen area, shining more light on participants and less on the screen area.

Other equipment typically includes a videocassette player, an amplifier for speakers, an automatic microphone mixer, compact disc player, audiocassette player, matrix switcher, and coder/decoder equipment to convert analog signals to digital signals for fiber-optic transmission.

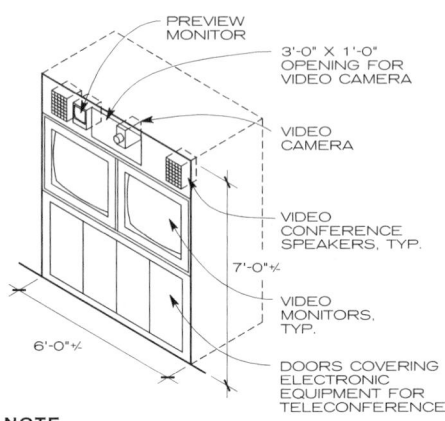

PREVIEW MONITOR
3'-0" X 1'-0" OPENING FOR VIDEO CAMERA
VIDEO CAMERA
VIDEO CONFERENCE SPEAKERS, TYP.
7'-0"±
VIDEO MONITORS, TYP.
DOORS COVERING ELECTRONIC EQUIPMENT FOR TELECONFERENCE
6'-0"±

NOTE

This wall unit may be assembled on a portable console for mobility.

TYPICAL VIDEO MONITOR VIDEOCONFERENCE WALL

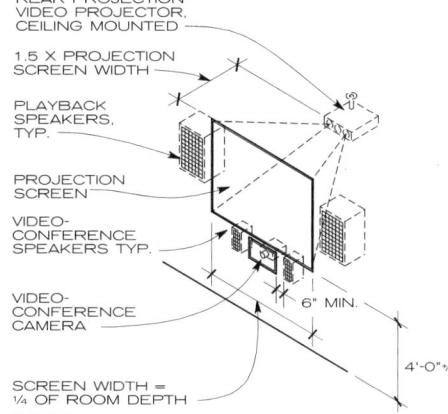

REAR PROJECTION VIDEO PROJECTOR, CEILING MOUNTED
1.5 X PROJECTION SCREEN WIDTH
PLAYBACK SPEAKERS, TYP.
PROJECTION SCREEN
VIDEO-CONFERENCE SPEAKERS TYP.
VIDEO-CONFERENCE CAMERA
SCREEN WIDTH = ¼ OF ROOM DEPTH
6" MIN.
4'-0"±

NOTE

Ratio of screen height to width: video 3:4; HDTV, 9:16.

TYPICAL REAR PROJECTION VIDEOCONFERENCE WALL

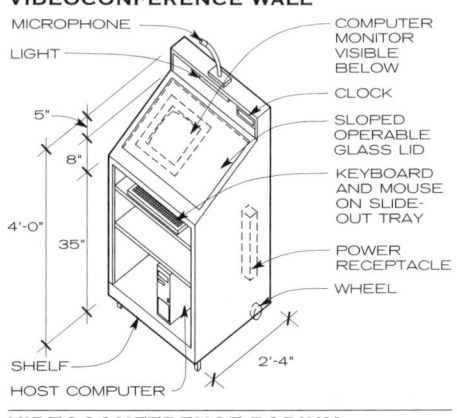

MICROPHONE
LIGHT
5"
8"
4'-0"
35"
SHELF
HOST COMPUTER
COMPUTER MONITOR VISIBLE BELOW
CLOCK
SLOPED OPERABLE GLASS LID
KEYBOARD AND MOUSE ON SLIDE-OUT TRAY
POWER RECEPTACLE
WHEEL
2'-4"

VIDEOCONFERENCE PODIUM

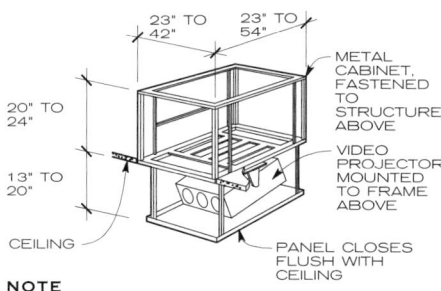

NOTE

This system is typically operated by remote control and may be linked with motorized projection screen operation. Some models are equipped with a trapdoor-type closer.

RETRACTABLE RECESSED VIDEO PROJECTOR MOUNT

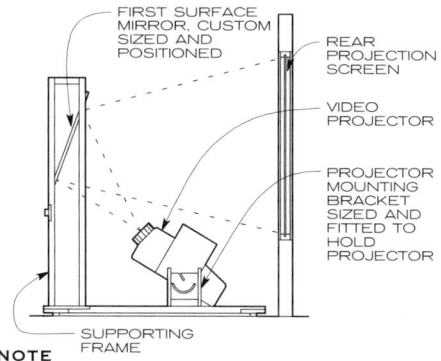

NOTE

This system requires half the space of a direct-projected rear projection system. Rear projection offers the best image quality of all projectors.

REAR PROJECTION VIDEO SCREEN FOR SMALL PROJECTION ROOM

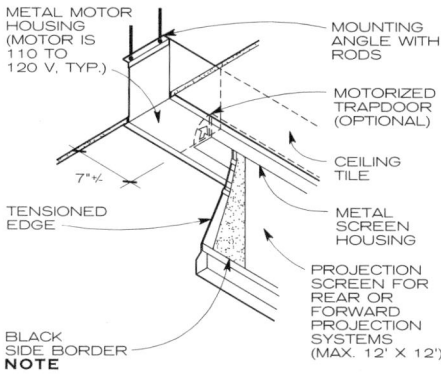

NOTE

Ceiling tile may be installed under the metal housing and cut around a trapdoor with a tile piece attached. The tensioned screen edge keeps it taut, good for three-lens video and data projection, which require perfect convergence.

MOTORIZED RECESSED PROJECTION SCREEN

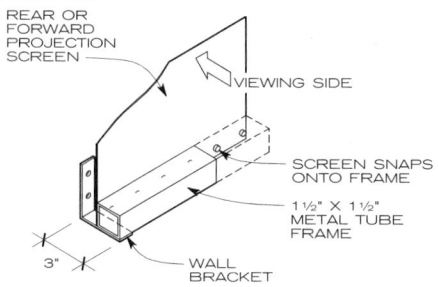

NOTE

This mounting is for forward screens up to 20 ft wide and rear screens up to 12 ft wide.

METAL FRAME SURFACE-MOUNTED PROJECTION SCREEN

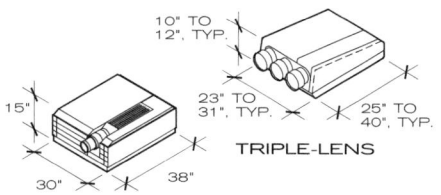

TRIPLE-LENS

SINGLE-LENS

NOTE

Single-lens video projectors do not require a predetermined distance or screen size for placement; they may be placed at any distance and focused like a slide projector. These projectors produce bright, high-resolution images.

VIDEO PROJECTORS

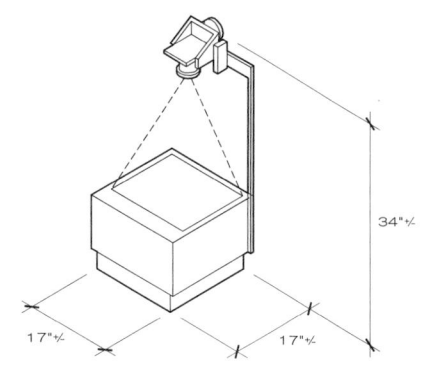

OVERHEAD PROJECTOR

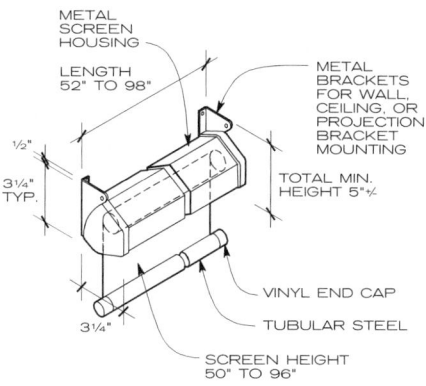

NOTE

This forward projection screen is typically made of silver lenticular fiberglass that is matte white, glass-beaded, and flame and mildew resistant.

SPRING ROLLER-OPERATED PROJECTION SCREEN

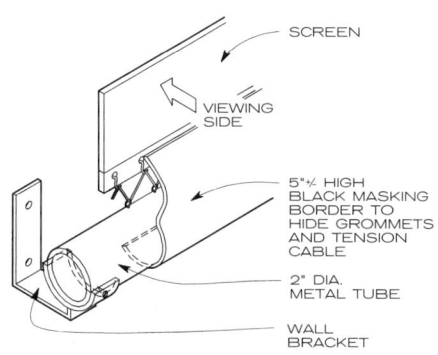

NOTE

This mount is for rear projection screens up to 20 ft wide and forward projection screens up to 30 ft wide.

METAL FRAME/TENSION CABLE PROJECTION SCREEN MOUNT

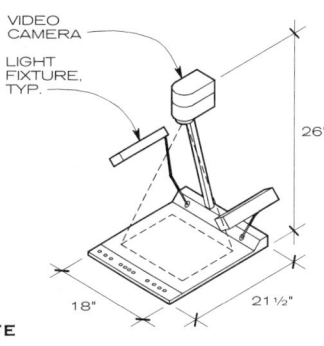

NOTE

The image may be viewed in the room or a remote location.

VISUAL PRESENTER

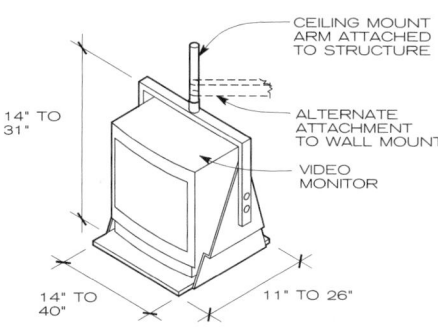

VIDEO MONITOR MOUNTING

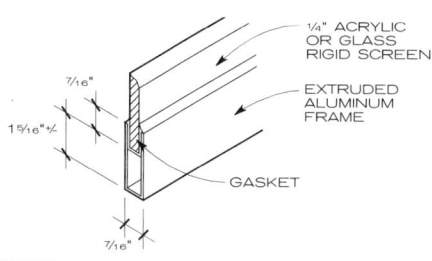

NOTE

This framing detail is for screens approximately 6 ft high by 8 ft wide, maximum.

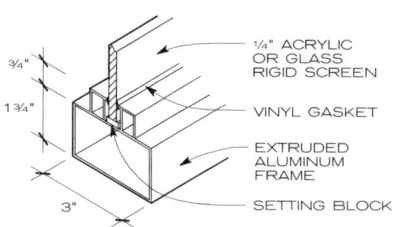

NOTE

This framing detail is for heavy-duty use, for screens up to 10 ft high by 25 ft wide.

REAR PROJECTION SCREEN FRAMING

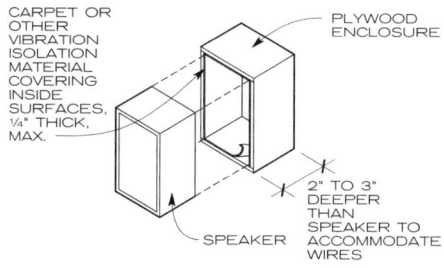

SPEAKER INSTALLATION DETAIL

Polysonics; Washington, D.C.

AUDIOVISUAL EQUIPMENT 11

GENERAL

A typical computer workstation in the office is equipped with a central processing unit (CPU), monitor, keyboard, and mouse. Various peripheral devices to help store, process, and retrieve data (printers, plotters, scanners, tape backup units, etc.) can be attached.

LOCAL AREA NETWORK (LAN)

LANs have changed the layout of computer equipment in the office. In years past, each workstation had its own printer, modem, scanner, etc. With the introduction of networks, these peripheral devices are now shared among a group of users. For example, one printer/modem/scanner can easily service as many as 20 users.

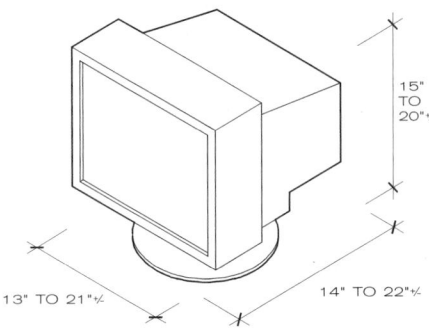

NOTE

Monitors display information to be processed. Available in one of three general types—monochrome, gray-scale, or color—they vary in diagonal screen dimensions from 13 to 21 in. (some are available between 9 and 13 in.).

MONITOR

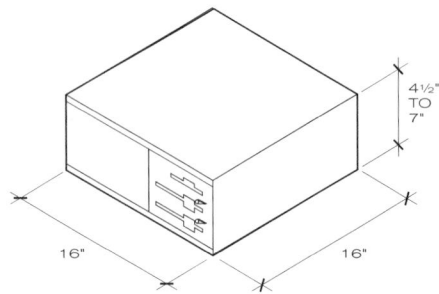

DESK TOP

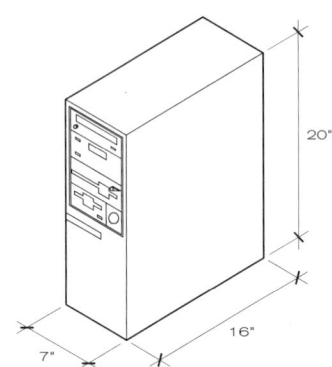

TOWER TYPE
NOTE

The central processing unit (CPU) is where computer data are stored, processed, and retrieved. CPUs are rated by processing speed (megahertz, MHz), hard-disk capacity (megabytes, MB, or gigabytes, GB), and random access memory (RAM).

CENTRAL PROCESSING UNIT (CPU)

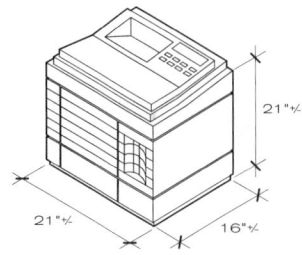

NOTE

Laser printers are typically used in larger business settings where speed, performance, and print quality are important. Most laser printers are rated at 4 to 8 pages per minute (ppm); some may be rated as high as 20 ppm.

LASER PRINTER

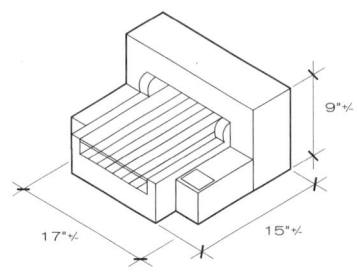

NOTE

Inkjet printers are generally more economical than laser printers. They are typically rated at 2 to 4 pages per minute (some may be as high as 8 ppm) and used in smaller business settings or home offices. The print quality is generally not as crisp as that from a laser printer.

INKJET PRINTER

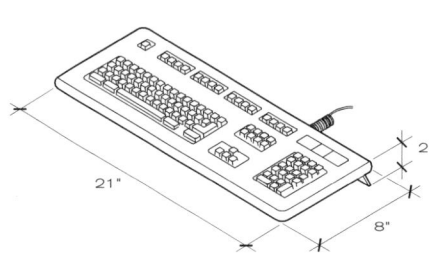

NOTE

The keyboard is a primary computer input device.

KEYBOARD

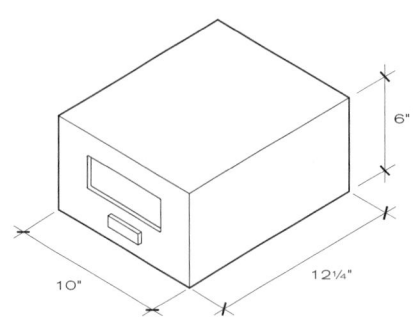

NOTE

A tape backup unit is an external storage device, typically used to copy and save data in case a hard disk crashes.

TAPE BACKUP UNIT

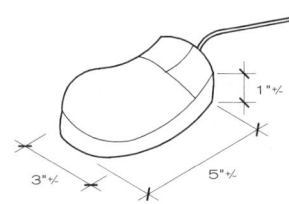

NOTE

A mouse is a pointing device used to move a cursor around a screen. It is helpful in operating a computer with a graphical user interface.

MOUSE

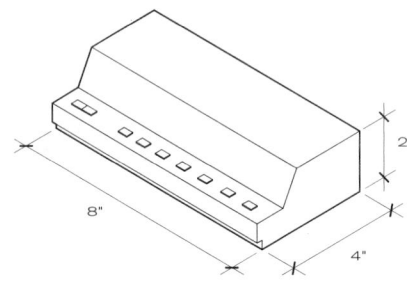

NOTE

A modem is used to transmit data from one computer to another computer or other device, such as a fax machine, via telephone lines.

MODEM

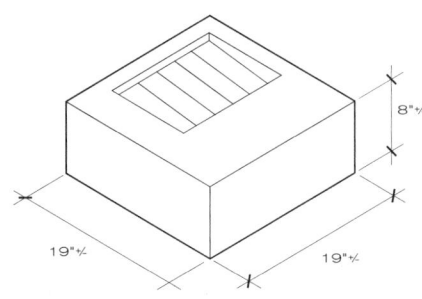

NOTE

Scanners allow a computer to read pictures or words from printed pages. This material is then stored in data files in the computer.

SCANNER

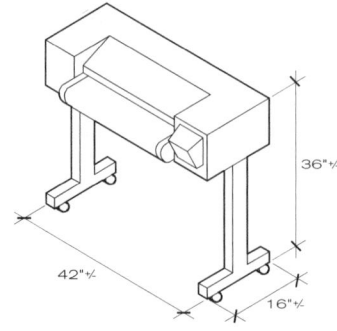

NOTE

A plotter is a device that draws with a plotting pen. It is typically used to plot or print graphics from CAD-type programs.

PLOTTER

Elin Landenburger; Alexandria, Virginia

GENERAL NOTES

1. Food service equipment must meet the sanitation and safety construction standards of the National Sanitation Foundation, an independent nonprofit organization dealing with public health issues. Other organizations involved in standards for food service equipment are Underwriters Laboratories (UL) and the American Society of Mechanical Engineers.

2. Food service equipment is either fabricated from a custom design or selected from a catalog. There are many variations in equipment specifications for such elements as power supply, door swings, finish, metal type, metal gauge, capacity, and accessories. These food service equipment pages show typical layouts and equipment for a mid-sized hotel kitchen that must produce a la carte meals, room service meals, banquets, etc. Equipment size and type will vary according to variables such as dining room size, menu type, and building type.

3. Prefabricated and custom-built walk-in refrigerators and freezers are specified differently. Consult a food service consultant for sizing, since these units can be specified to an infinite variety of sizes and shapes.

4. Food service equipment is primarily gas-powered, unless fumes are a concern, in which case electricity is used. If possible, steam is the preferred energy source because of its economy and efficiency.

5. Confer with a qualified food service consultant to determine the precise equipment and layout for the space to be served.

GAUGE AND USE OF GALVANIZED STEEL

GAUGE	RECOMMENDED USE
12	Support channels and bracing
14	Undershelves and partitions
16	Undershelves and side panels
18	Utensil drawers, hoods, body panels, interior partitions

GAUGE AND USE OF STAINLESS STEEL

GAUGE	TYPICAL USE
8 and 10	Support elements for heavy equiment or at stress points
12	Heavily used tabletops, pot sinks, or other surfaces that will receive a great amount of wear
14	Tabletops, sinks, shelves, and brackets that will be used frequently or that will hold heavy objects
16	Small equipment tops and sides that will carry light objects; shelves under equipment and heavily used side panels
18	Side panels that are not exposed to much wear, equipment doors, hoods, and partitions
20	Covers for supported or insulated panels, such as refrigerators or insulated doors

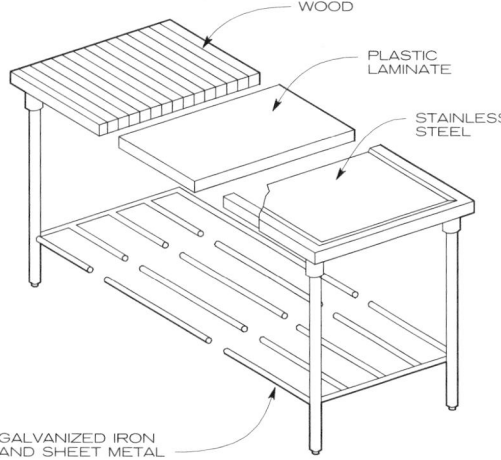

NOTES

1. Wood is used only for dining room or bakery production tables. Hard rock maple and pecan cutting tops are usually specified. Not to be used for nonbakery food production; cracks in wood surface can harbor bacteria.

2. Plastic laminate should not be used where cutting, chopping, or carving will occur. It will not warp or crack; it is an inexpensive substitute for stainless steel for nonfood production or decorative countertops, where codes allow.

3. Stainless steel is the most commonly used material for all areas in a commercial kitchen. Although relatively expensive, it is extremely durable. Cold-rolled steel stock is formed under pressure; welded connections are used only within equipment (bolted connections are used to connect pieces of equipment).

4. Galvanized iron and sheet metal are used as underbracing for equipment and as an inexpensive substitute for stainless steel for legs, tables, and interior shelves.

5. Other materials, including glass, ceramic tile, copper, and brass, may be used for food service equipment, but all surfaces that come into contact with food or the food handler should be smooth and nonporous and resist chipping or wear under frequent use. Surfaces must also resist the corrosive effects of salt, food acids, and oils.

MATERIALS USED IN FOOD SERVICE EQUIPMENT

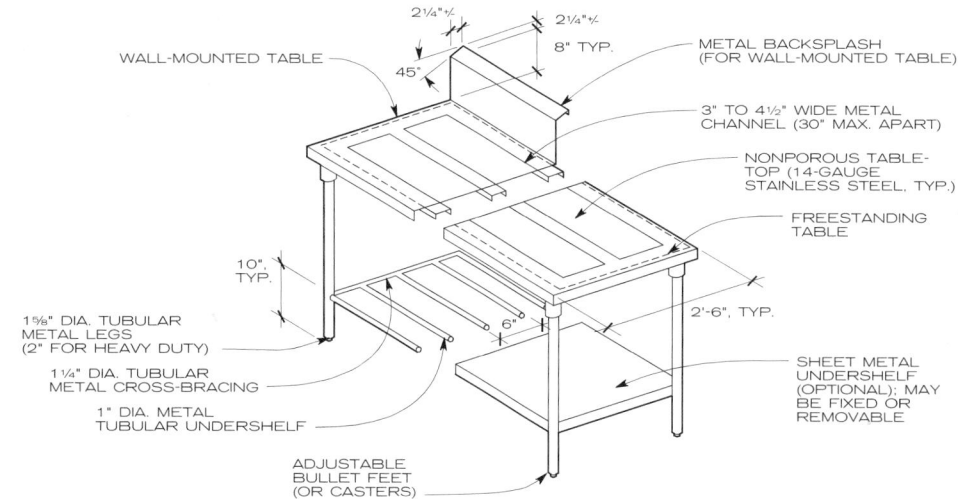

NOTE

Tubular metal pieces should be welded, coved together, and sanded smooth. A layer of cork-based sound-deadening material may be applied to the underside of tabletops and finished with aluminum lacquer. Consult health codes for types of lacquer permitted.

FABRICATED WORKTABLE

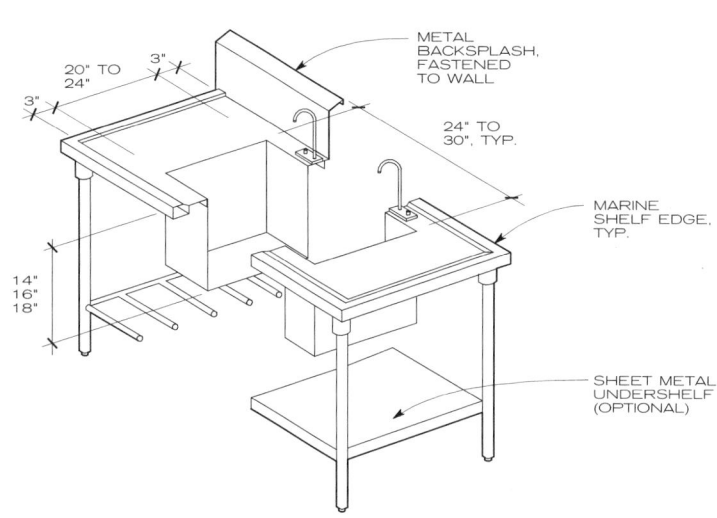

FABRICATED WORKTABLE WITH SINK

John Birchfield; Birchfield Foodsystems, Inc.; Annapolis, Maryland

GENERAL

Exhaust hoods remove air, water vapor, grease, and food odors from the kitchen area and air and water vapor from dish washing areas. Ovens and steam-jacketed kettles only require hoods that remove air, heat, and water vapor, but if large amounts of grease from a broiler, char-broiler, fryer, or grill are present, the hood system must extract this pollutant before the air is drawn outside by fans. This is done with grease "cartridges," or with stainless steel extractors, both of which violently blow the exhausted air around. This flings the grease particles to the sides of the baffles; then they are collected in a trough for easy removal, or run out a drain. The extractors can usually be washed in a standard kitchen dishwasher. Consultation with code officials and food service consultants is of utmost importance when designing exhaust hoods.

NOTES

1. CFM requirements for exhaust hoods are determined by the length of the hood and the equipment types underneath. Typical requirements range from 150 to 450 CFM per linear foot of hood.

2. Some codes may require a higher exhaust rate. To make up this air differential and to prevent more air from being drawn from surrounding areas, introduce air through a supply duct. The supplied air should make up 50 to 85% of the total exhaust.

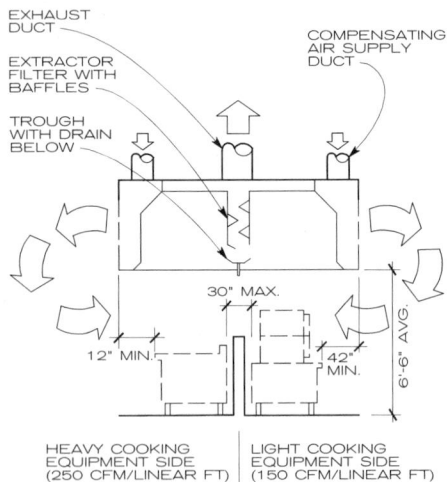

NOTE

Single exhaust hoods are available for single cooking lines. Dimensions and capacities of exhaust hoods vary with particular kitchen cooking requirements.

TYPICAL EXHAUST HOOD REQUIREMENTS

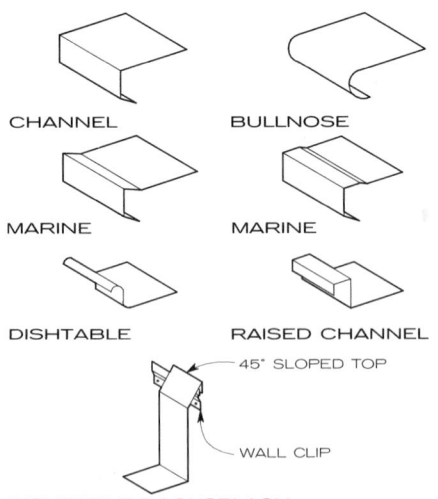

CHANNEL   BULLNOSE

MARINE   MARINE

DISHTABLE   RAISED CHANNEL

DISHTABLE BACKSPLASH

NOTE

Channel edges and bullnose edges are used only when water will not be spilled on the table surface.

TABLE EDGE PROFILES

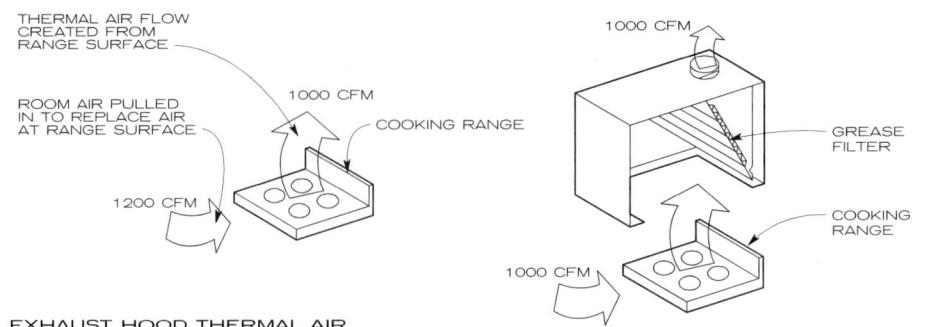

EXHAUST HOOD THERMAL AIR CURRENT PRINCIPLES

HOOD WITH BALANCED AIR CURRENTS

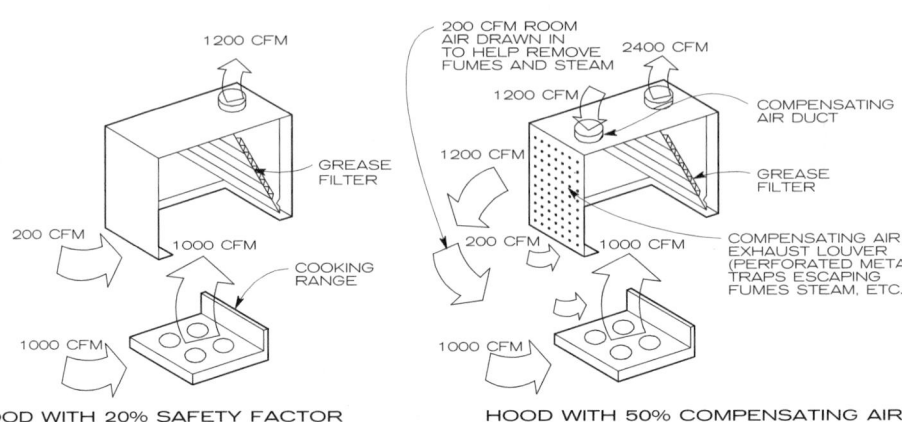

HOOD WITH 20% SAFETY FACTOR

HOOD WITH 50% COMPENSATING AIR

NOTE

Room air drawn in at the front of the hood at the rate of 200 cubic ft per minute (CFM) will create an extra 20% safety margin at the hood to handle thermal surges, crosscurrents, etc.

EXHAUST HOOD CHARACTERISTICS

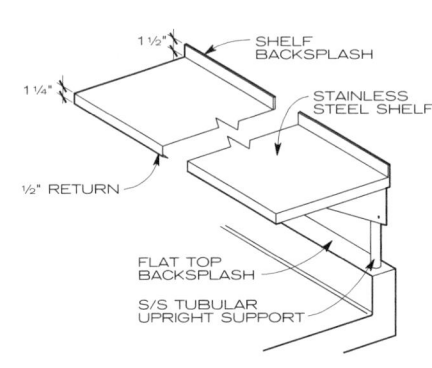

ELEVATED TABLE-MOUNTED SHELF

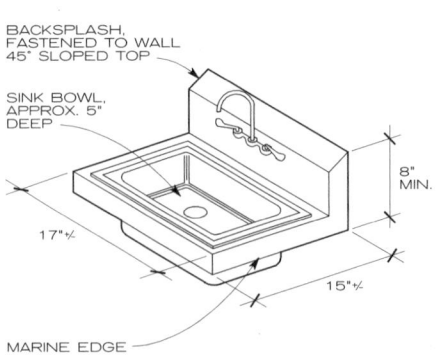

NOTE

Hand sinks are typically required by code near every major work area in the kitchen. Some are equipped with an electronic eye or foot levers to encourage workers to wash their hands.

WALL-MOUNTED HAND SINK

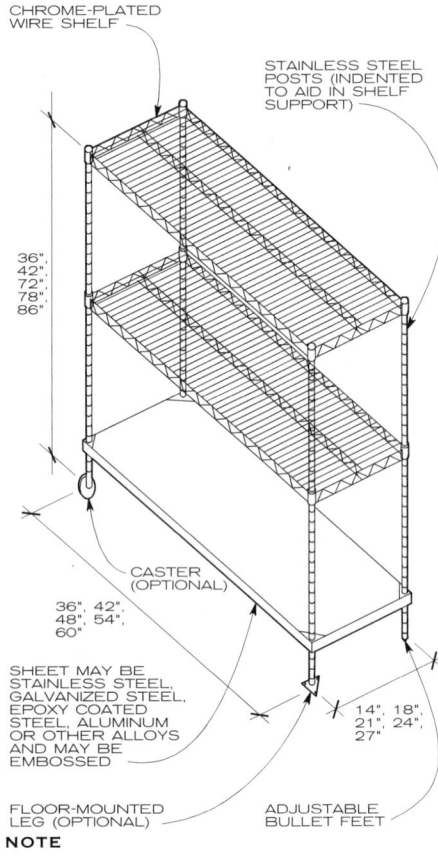

NOTE

This shelf may be used in dry storage rooms and walk-in refrigerators and freezers. Shelving may be mounted to the wall for stability and can be attached to other modular units.

MODULAR WIRE SHELVING UNIT

John Birchfield; Birchfield Foodsystems, Inc.; Annapolis, Maryland

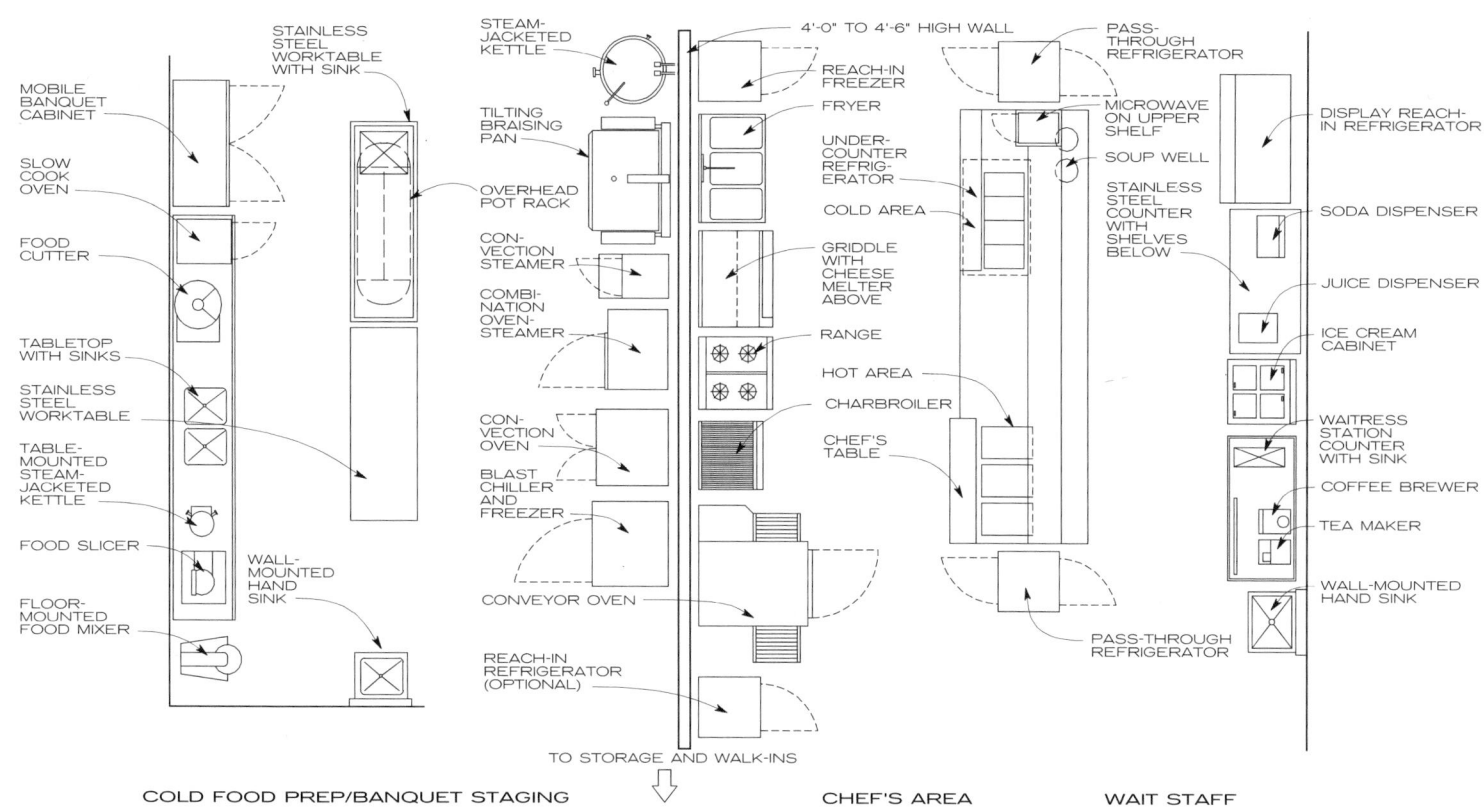

MOBILE BANQUET CABINET

SLOW COOK OVEN

FOOD CUTTER

TABLETOP WITH SINKS

STAINLESS STEEL WORKTABLE

TABLE-MOUNTED STEAM-JACKETED KETTLE

FOOD SLICER

FLOOR-MOUNTED FOOD MIXER

STAINLESS STEEL WORKTABLE WITH SINK

STEAM-JACKETED KETTLE

TILTING BRAISING PAN

OVERHEAD POT RACK

CONVECTION STEAMER

COMBINATION OVEN-STEAMER

CONVECTION OVEN

BLAST CHILLER AND FREEZER

CONVEYOR OVEN

REACH-IN REFRIGERATOR (OPTIONAL)

WALL-MOUNTED HAND SINK

4'-0" TO 4'-6" HIGH WALL

REACH-IN FREEZER

FRYER

UNDER-COUNTER REFRIG-ERATOR

COLD AREA

GRIDDLE WITH CHEESE MELTER ABOVE

RANGE

HOT AREA

CHARBROILER

CHEF'S TABLE

PASS-THROUGH REFRIGERATOR

MICROWAVE ON UPPER SHELF

SOUP WELL

STAINLESS STEEL COUNTER WITH SHELVES BELOW

PASS-THROUGH REFRIGERATOR

DISPLAY REACH-IN REFRIGERATOR

SODA DISPENSER

JUICE DISPENSER

ICE CREAM CABINET

WAITRESS STATION COUNTER WITH SINK

COFFEE BREWER

TEA MAKER

WALL-MOUNTED HAND SINK

TO STORAGE AND WALK-INS

COLD FOOD PREP/BANQUET STAGING   CHEF'S AREA   WAIT STAFF

TYPICAL KITCHEN PLAN

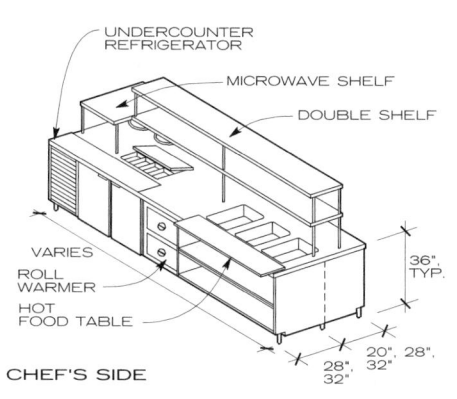

UNDERCOUNTER REFRIGERATOR

MICROWAVE SHELF

DOUBLE SHELF

VARIES

ROLL WARMER

HOT FOOD TABLE

36", TYP.

20", 28", 32"

28", 32"

CHEF'S SIDE

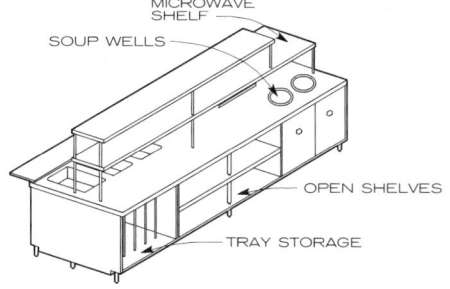

MICROWAVE SHELF

SOUP WELLS

OPEN SHELVES

TRAY STORAGE

WAIT STAFF PICK-UP SIDE

NOTE

The chef's table is the heart of the kitchen operation; it is here the hot and cold food is arranged on plates for pick-up by the wait staff. Since both kitchen and wait staffs need access, the table is usually placed in an island configuration. Usually custom-built to meet the chef's requirements.

CHEF'S TABLE

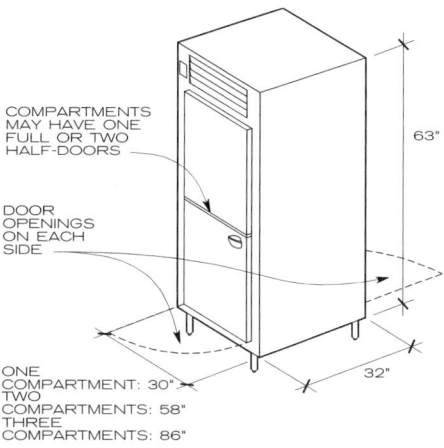

COMPARTMENTS MAY HAVE ONE FULL OR TWO HALF-DOORS

DOOR OPENINGS ON EACH SIDE

63"

32"

ONE COMPARTMENT: 30"
TWO COMPARTMENTS: 58"
THREE COMPARTMENTS: 86"

NOTE

This unit is typically placed either at end of the chef's table or in the wall separating the service area from the kitchen.

PASS-THROUGH REFRIGERATOR

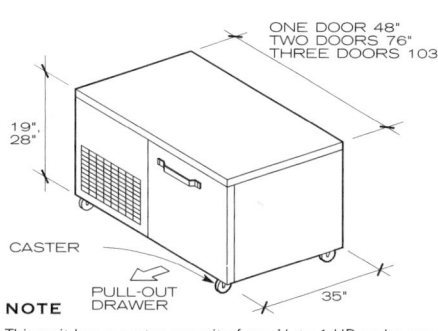

ONE DOOR 48"
TWO DOORS 76"
THREE DOORS 103"

19", 28"

CASTER

PULL-OUT DRAWER

35"

NOTE

This unit has a motor capacity from 1/4 to 1 HP and a maximum load of 500 to 1000 lb.

UNDERCOUNTER REFRIGERATOR FREEZER

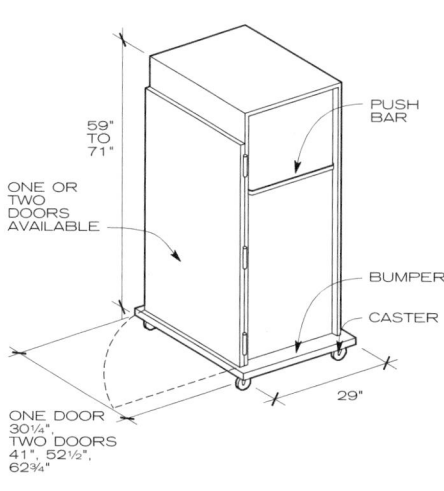

59" TO 71"

ONE OR TWO DOORS AVAILABLE

PUSH BAR

BUMPER

CASTER

ONE DOOR 30¼"
TWO DOORS 41", 52½", 62¾"

29"

NOTE

This cabinet is used to keep preplated meals hot.

MOBILE BANQUET CABINET

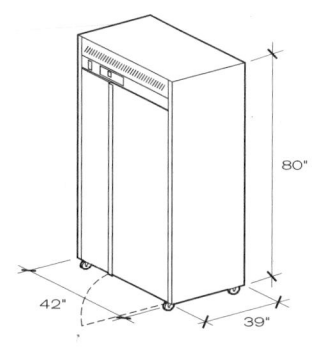

80"

42"

39"

NOTE

This unit provides cook/chill and cook/freeze options.

BLAST CHILLER AND FREEZER

John Birchfield; Birchfield Foodsystems Inc.; Annapolis, Maryland

FOOD SERVICE EQUIPMENT **11**

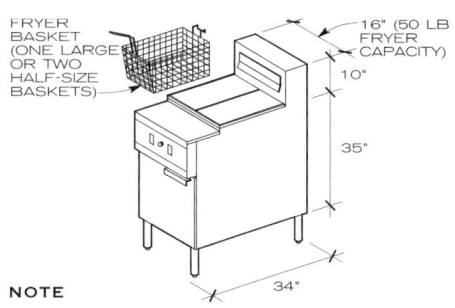

NOTE

Fryers cook food by immersing it in hot fat and are powered by either gas or electricity. Fryers can be either freestanding, table mounted, modular (electric only), or drop-in (electric only). Typical capacities range from 15 to 75 lb of shortening or fat. Two modular units with a filter dump station between them is a common fryer configuration.

FRYER

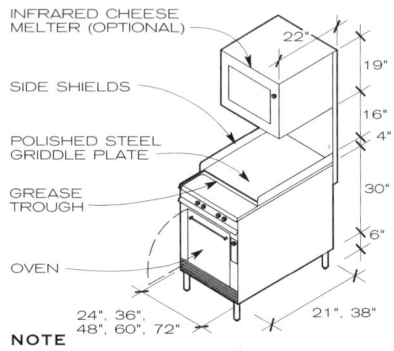

NOTE

Griddles, also called grills, have a flat, heated surface that cooks food quickly. They can be freestanding units, part of a range, table models, or part of a modular unit and are either gas- or electric-powered.

GRIDDLE WITH CHEESE MELTER

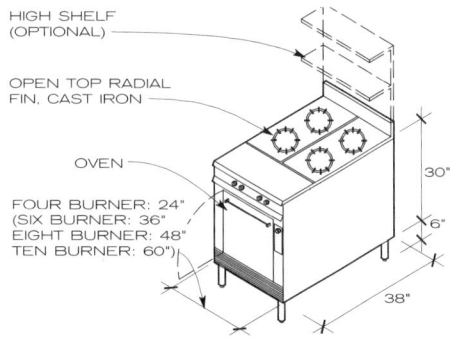

NOTE

The range is often the most heavily used piece of equipment in a food service facility. The open-top gas range is preferred by cooks, especially for sauteing, because the flame is visible and easily adjusted. Electric models are available.

RANGE

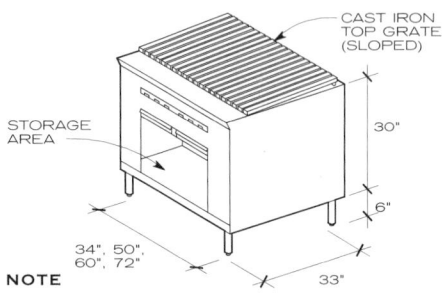

NOTE

A charbroiler cooks food rapidly, one side at a time, usually with radiant heat produced by gas or electricity. There are many types: freestanding top burner broilers, charbroilers, salamanders (small above-the-range broilers for last minute browning), conveyor broilers, and rotisseries.

CHARBROILER

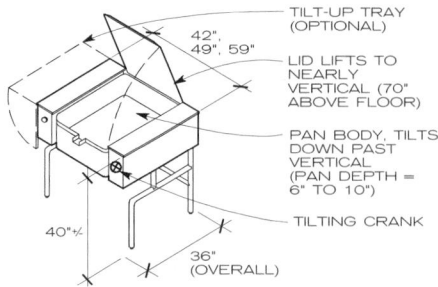

NOTE

Also called a tilting skillet or tilting frying pan, this braising pan can be used for grilling, steaming, braising, sauteing, or stewing. It holds a large volume of food, typically 20 to 40 gallons. The pan body tilts down so that liquids can be poured off, and also to aid in cleaning.

TILTING BRAISING PAN

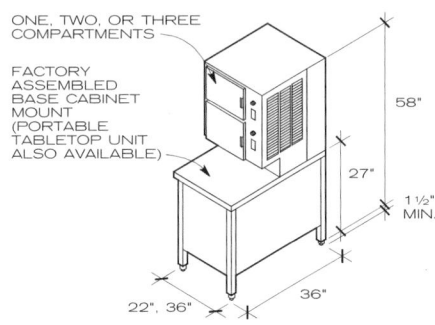

NOTE

Low- (5 lb per sq in.) and no-pressure steamers are used to prepare vegetables, seafood, eggs, rice, and pasta and work very efficiently. They are powered by gas, electricity, direct steam, or a steam coil.

CONVECTION STEAMER

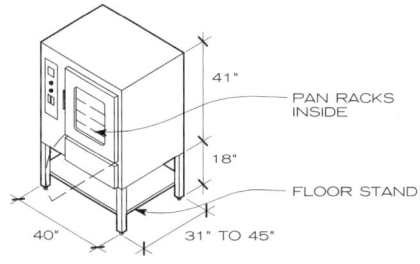

NOTE

Also called a "combi," it combines a convection oven with a steamer in one piece of equipment. It is popular because of its versatility.

COMBINATION OVEN-STEAMER

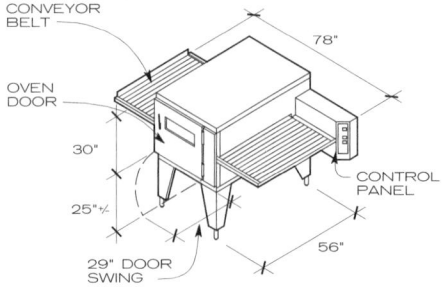

NOTE

A conveyor oven moves food through a heated cavity at a predetermined speed, ensuring even cooking time and allowing high-volume production. Heating is by convection or radiant heat, on one or both sides of the belt. Pizzas, cookies, hamburgers, and seafood all travel this route.

CONVEYOR OVEN

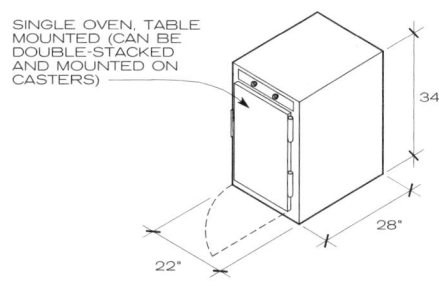

NOTE

Primarily used to roast meats, this oven can also be used to warm hot foods and proof bread or dough. Designed to cook at 200 to 240°F, these ovens reduce shrinkage of roast meats up to 40% and save energy.

SLOW-COOK OVEN

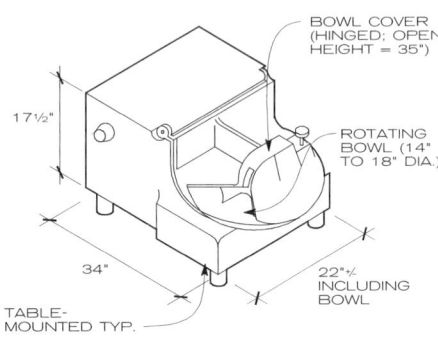

NOTE

Used for chopping meats and vegetables, this machine is similar in function to a food processor. It is also called a "buffalo chopper." Another larger type is a vertical cutter mixer (VCM), with a capacity of 30 to 45 quarts.

FOOD CUTTER

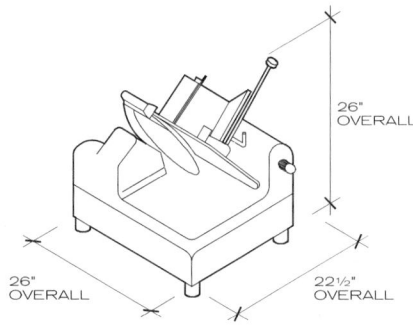

NOTE

Motor capacity varies from $1/5$ to $1/2$ HP.

FOOD SLICER

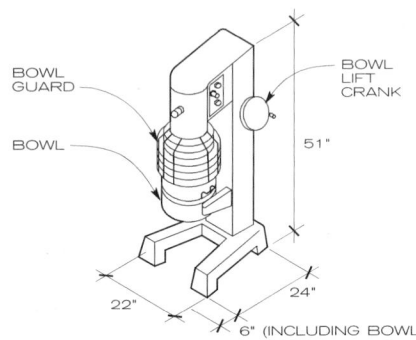

NOTE

This is used to mix/process large quantities of food, especially if a variety of attachments is required.

FOOD MIXER

John Birchfield; Birchfield Foodsystems Inc.; Annapolis, Maryland

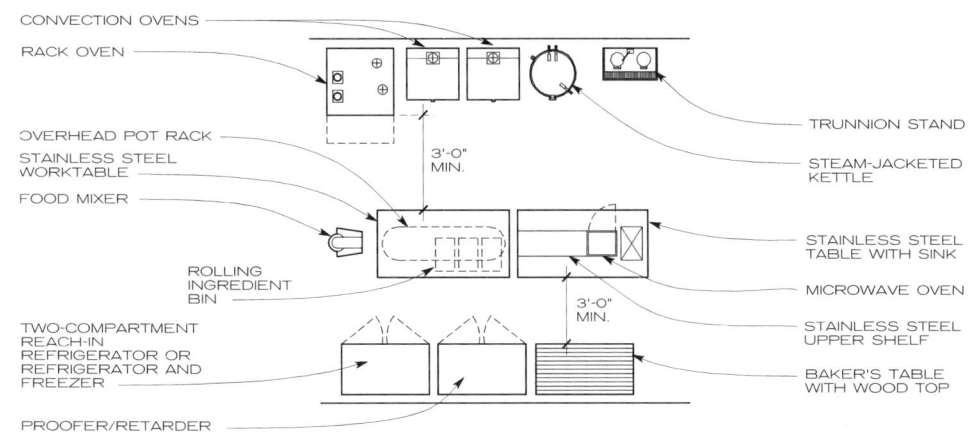

CONVECTION OVENS

RACK OVEN

OVERHEAD POT RACK

STAINLESS STEEL WORKTABLE

FOOD MIXER

ROLLING INGREDIENT BIN

TWO-COMPARTMENT REACH-IN REFRIGERATOR OR REFRIGERATOR AND FREEZER

PROOFER/RETARDER

3'-0" MIN.

3'-0" MIN.

TRUNNION STAND

STEAM-JACKETED KETTLE

STAINLESS STEEL TABLE WITH SINK

MICROWAVE OVEN

STAINLESS STEEL UPPER SHELF

BAKER'S TABLE WITH WOOD TOP

TYPICAL BAKERY AREA PLAN

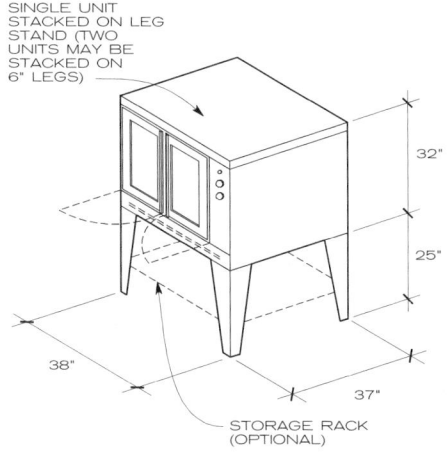

SINGLE UNIT STACKED ON LEG STAND (TWO UNITS MAY BE STACKED ON 6" LEGS)

32"

25"

38"

37"

STORAGE RACK (OPTIONAL)

NOTE

Convection ovens need less energy and less space than other commercial kitchen ovens. A fan circulates heat evenly throughout the oven chamber, and the interior shelves can be stacked very close together.

CONVECTION OVEN

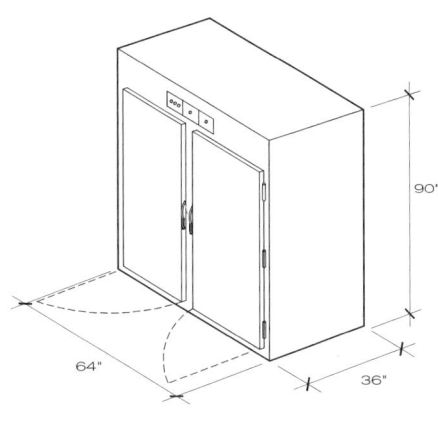

68"

80"

102"

49"

GLASS PANEL IN DOOR

NOTE

The rack is loaded, usually with baked goods, and wheeled into the oven. The rack rotates on a carousel or a ceiling hung bracket, baking food with a steady, even heat. Rack ovens are powered by gas, electricity, or oil.

RACK OVEN

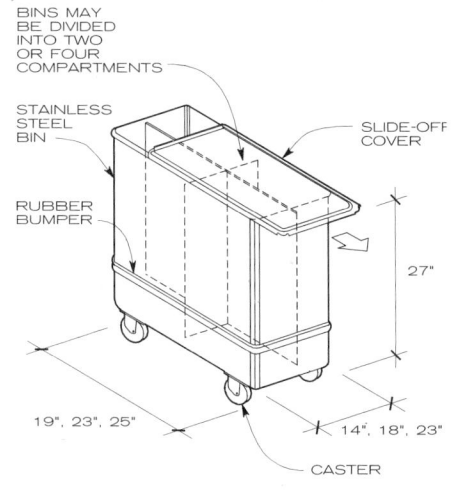

BINS MAY BE DIVIDED INTO TWO OR FOUR COMPARTMENTS

STAINLESS STEEL BIN

SLIDE-OFF COVER

RUBBER BUMPER

27"

19", 23", 25"

14", 18", 23"

CASTER

NOTE

Used for storage of baked goods and ingredients like flour, sugar, and rice. Bin can be stored under open-based tables.

ROLLING INGREDIENT BIN

90"

64"

36"

NOTE

This unit proofs bakery items (emits the moist, low heat that dough needs to rise), then, after a specified amount of time, issues cold air to halt the rising.

RETARDER/PROOFER

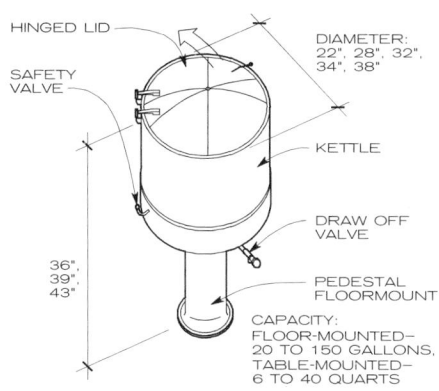

HINGED LID

SAFETY VALVE

DIAMETER: 22", 28", 32", 34", 38"

KETTLE

DRAW OFF VALVE

36", 39", 43"

PEDESTAL FLOORMOUNT

CAPACITY: FLOOR-MOUNTED— 20 TO 150 GALLONS, TABLE-MOUNTED— 6 TO 40 QUARTS

NOTE

A steam-jacketed kettle is used for soups, stews, sauces, boiled meats, etc. The kettle is double-walled; heat comes from an inner jacket that contains the steam. The kettle can be mounted either on a pedestal, on legs, on a yoke (trunnion) for tilting, on the wall, or on a tabletop.

STEAM-JACKETED KETTLE

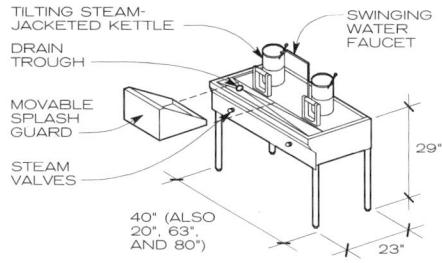

TILTING STEAM-JACKETED KETTLE

SWINGING WATER FAUCET

DRAIN TROUGH

MOVABLE SPLASH GUARD

STEAM VALVES

29"

40" (ALSO 20", 63", AND 80")

23"

NOTE

This stand can hold up to four steam-jacketed kettles on pinions, or trunnions, which enable tilting and pouring.

TRUNNION STAND

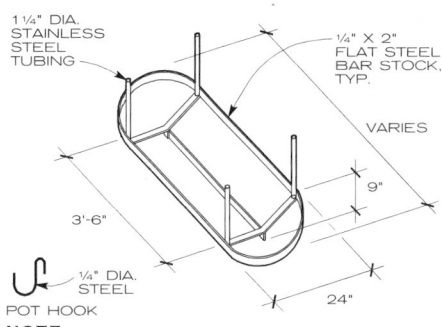

1¼" DIA. STAINLESS STEEL TUBING

¼" X 2" FLAT STEEL BAR STOCK, TYP.

VARIES

9"

3'-6"

24"

¼" DIA. STEEL

POT HOOK

NOTE

Dimensions shown are for medium-use kitchens; review unusual conditions, such as use of extra large pots or need for wider support spans, with a structural engineer.

OVERHEAD POT RACK

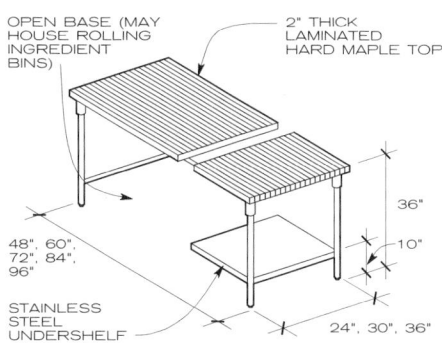

OPEN BASE (MAY HOUSE ROLLING INGREDIENT BINS)

2" THICK LAMINATED HARD MAPLE TOP

48", 60", 72", 84", 96"

STAINLESS STEEL UNDERSHELF

36"

10"

24", 30", 36"

NOTE

Baker's tables are used exclusively for making baked goods. Any other use that could bring bacteria-laden foods into contact with the wood surface is prohibited.

BAKER'S TABLE

John Birchfield; Birchfield Foodsystems Inc.; Annapolis, Maryland

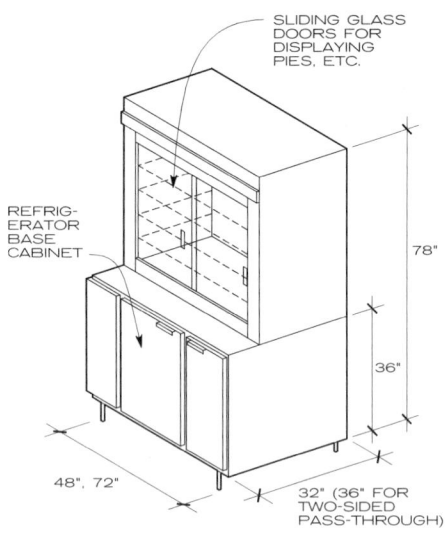

DISPLAY REACH-IN REFRIGERATOR

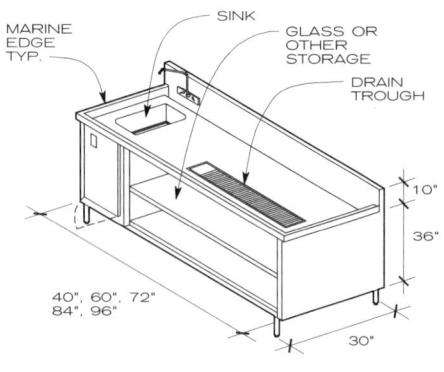

NOTE

Multipurpose table unit used to store cups and glasses and to prepare soft drinks, coffee, tea, and other beverages.

WAITRESS STATION COUNTER

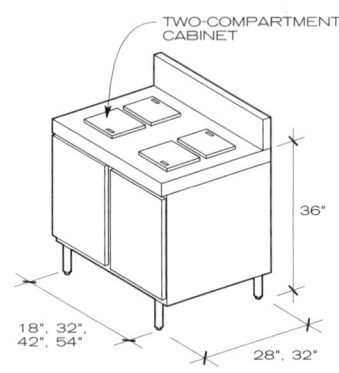

ICE CREAM CABINET

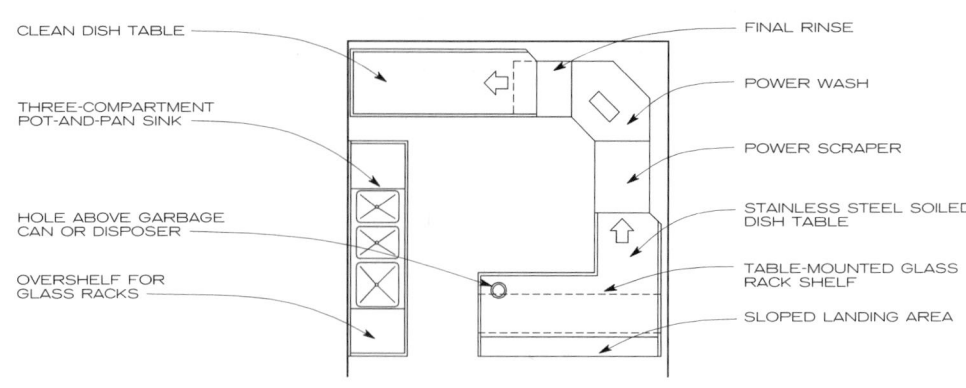

TYPICAL DISHWASHING AREA PLAN

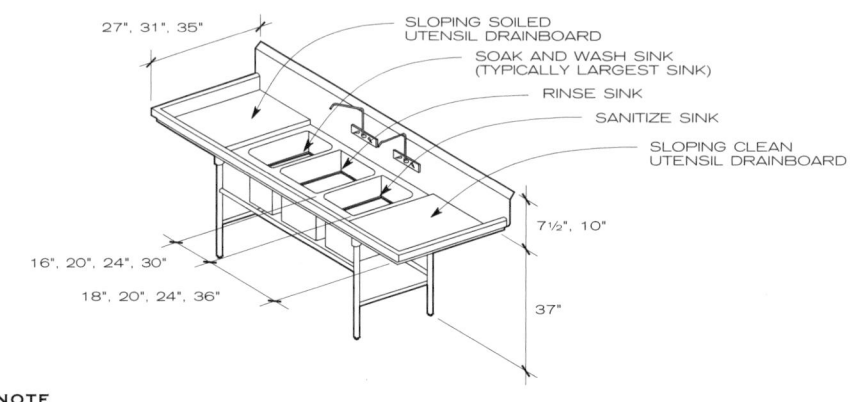

NOTE

The sink illustrated is a fairly common type, but depth of sinks, number of sinks, and size of drainboards can vary.

POT AND PAN SINK

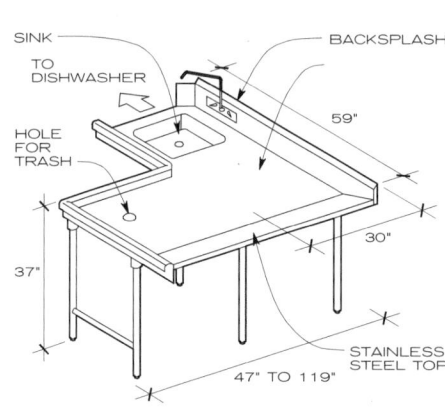

SOILED DISH TABLE

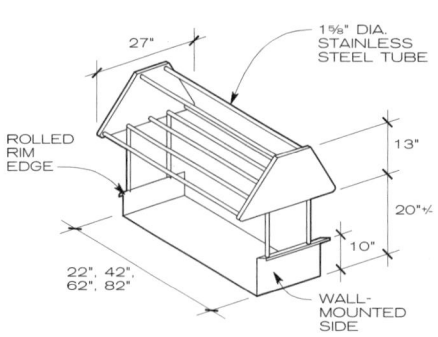

NOTE

Typically this is mounted on the soiled dish table.

TABLE-MOUNTED GLASS RACK SHELF

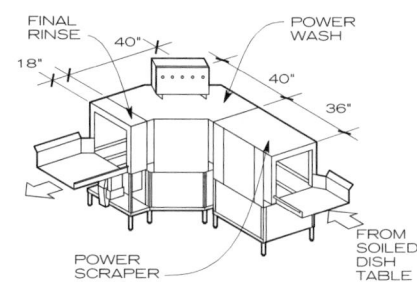

NOTE

A spray of hot water and detergent washes the dishes, followed by a rinse of 180°F water or chemicals to sanitize them. Sometimes an exhaust hood is used; the design of machines varies greatly.

DISHWASHING MACHINE

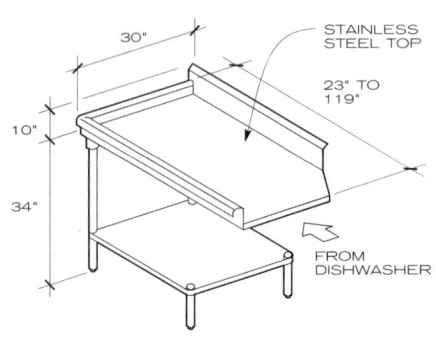

CLEAN DISH TABLE

John Birchfield; Birchfield Foodsystems Inc.; Annapolis, Maryland

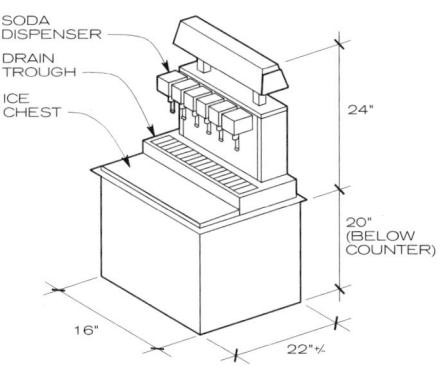

SODA DISPENSER
DRAIN TROUGH
ICE CHEST
24"
20" (BELOW COUNTER)
16"
22"½

NOTE
This drops into a cutout in the wait staff counter.

DROP-IN SODA DISPENSER

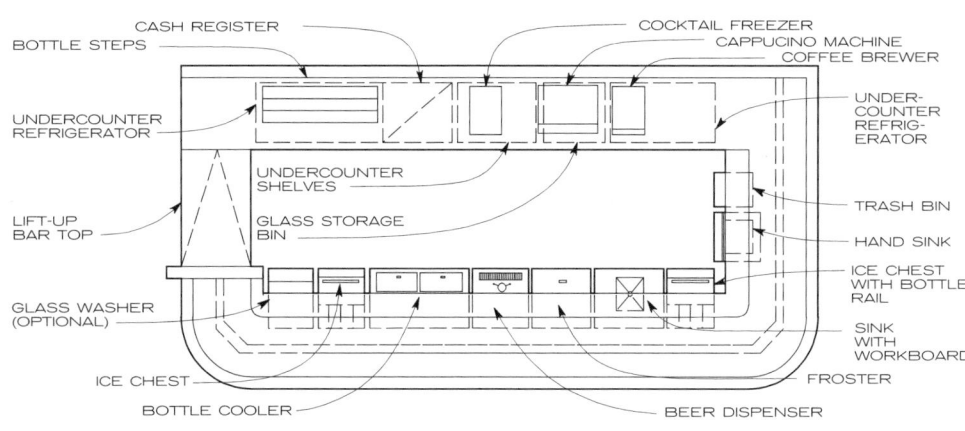

CASH REGISTER
BOTTLE STEPS
COCKTAIL FREEZER
CAPPUCINO MACHINE
COFFEE BREWER
UNDERCOUNTER REFRIGERATOR
UNDER-COUNTER REFRIG-ERATOR
UNDERCOUNTER SHELVES
TRASH BIN
LIFT-UP BAR TOP
GLASS STORAGE BIN
HAND SINK
ICE CHEST WITH BOTTLE RAIL
GLASS WASHER (OPTIONAL)
SINK WITH WORKBOARD
ICE CHEST
FROSTER
BOTTLE COOLER
BEER DISPENSER

TYPICAL BAR EQUIPMENT LAYOUT

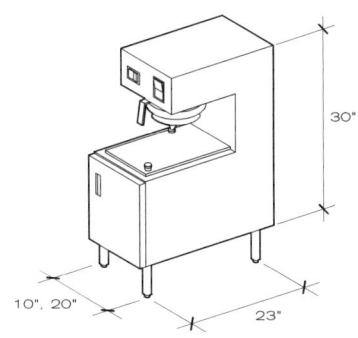

30"
10", 20"
23"

NOTE
Typically tea makers sit on top of the wait staff counter.

TEA MAKER

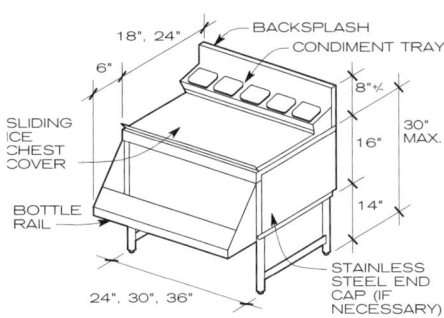

BACKSPLASH
CONDIMENT TRAY
18", 24"
6"
8"½
SLIDING ICE CHEST COVER
16"
30" MAX.
14"
BOTTLE RAIL
24", 30", 36"
STAINLESS STEEL END CAP (IF NECESSARY)

NOTE
These units vary according to use, with different cover opening styles (hinged or sliding), condiment tray configurations, and placement of ice dividers in chest.

ICE CHEST

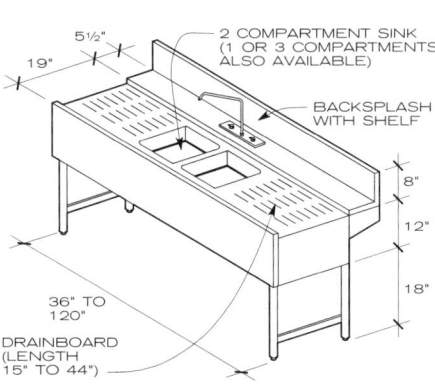

5½"
19"
2 COMPARTMENT SINK (1 OR 3 COMPARTMENTS ALSO AVAILABLE)
BACKSPLASH WITH SHELF
8"
12"
18"
36" TO 120"
DRAINBOARD (LENGTH 15" TO 44")

NOTE
A mechanical glass washer may be substituted for this.

SINK WITH WORKBOARD

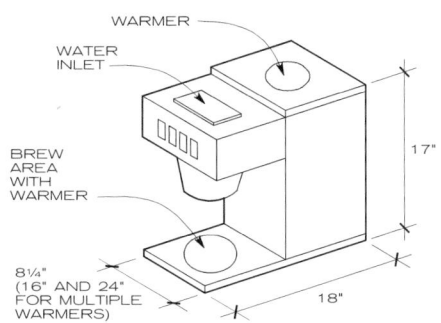

WARMER
WATER INLET
BREW AREA WITH WARMER
17"
8¼" (16" AND 24" FOR MULTIPLE WARMERS)
18"

NOTE
Coffee brewers sit on top of the wait staff counter.

COFFEE BREWER

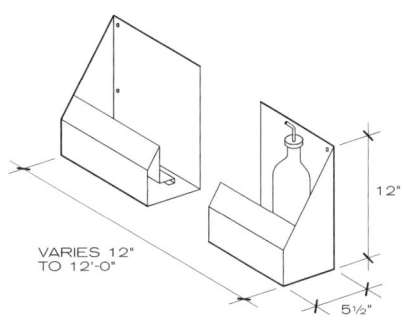

12"
VARIES 12" TO 12'-0"
5½"

NOTE
Bottle rails are attached to the front of sinks, ice chests, or other bar equipment. Lockable models are available.

BOTTLE RAIL

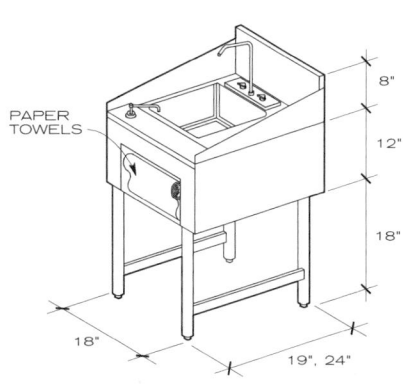

PAPER TOWELS
8"
12"
18"
18"
19", 24"

BAR HAND SINK

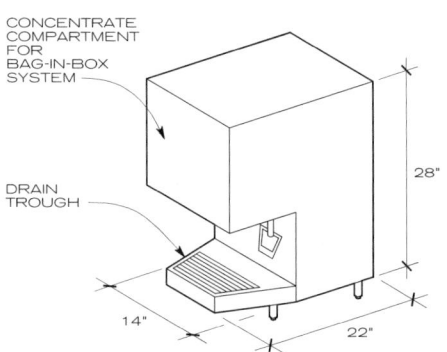

CONCENTRATE COMPARTMENT FOR BAG-IN-BOX SYSTEM
DRAIN TROUGH
28"
14"
22"

NOTE
Juice dispensers sit on top of the wait staff counter.

JUICE DISPENSER

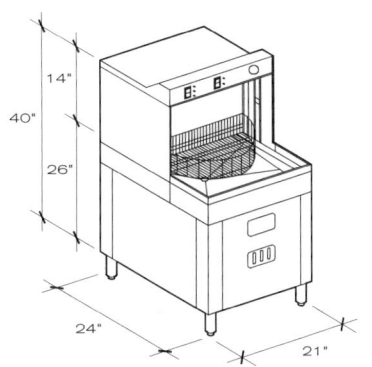

14"
40"
26"
24"
21"

NOTE
A sink with drainboard may be substituted for this.

GLASS WASHER

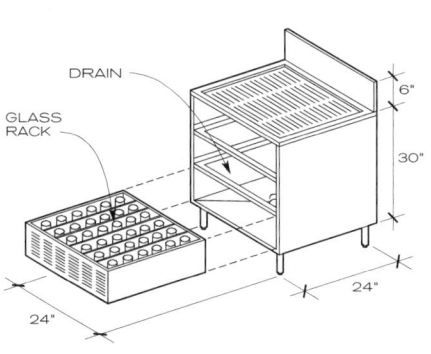

DRAIN
GLASS RACK
6"
30"
24"
24"

GLASS STORAGE BIN

Richard J. Vitullo, AIA; Oak Leaf Studio; Crownsville, Maryland

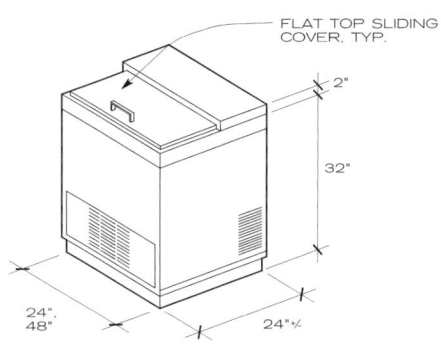

FLAT TOP SLIDING COVER, TYP.

2"

32"

24", 48"

24"±

NOTE

Frosters chill mugs, glasses, and plates to minus 10°F on interior shelves. Usually they are placed under the front bar.

FROSTER

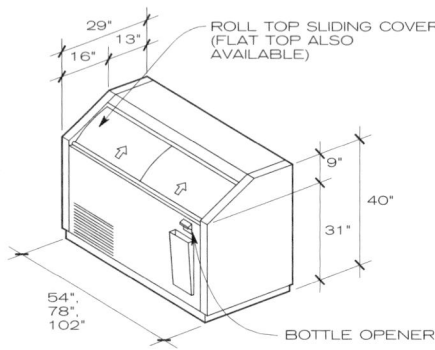

29"
13"
16"

ROLL TOP SLIDING COVER (FLAT TOP ALSO AVAILABLE)

9"
40"
31"

54", 78", 102"

BOTTLE OPENER

NOTE

These are used to cool beverages to between 34° and 40°F.

BOTTLE COOLER

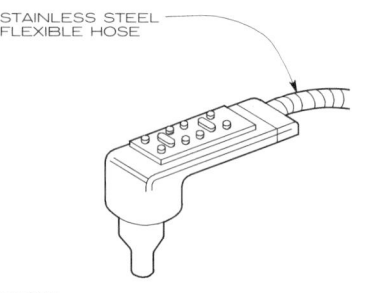

STAINLESS STEEL FLEXIBLE HOSE

NOTE

This dispenses water, soda, wine, and other drinks.

MECHANICAL POSTMIX BAR DISPENSER

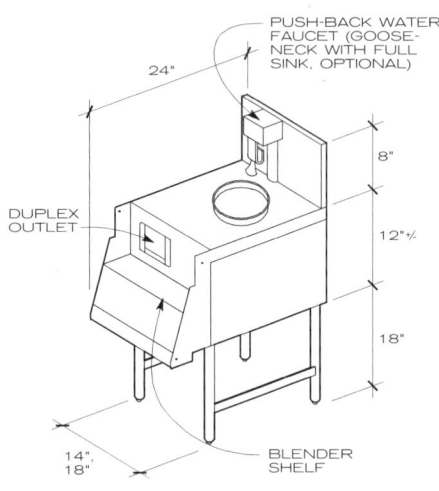

PUSH-BACK WATER FAUCET (GOOSE-NECK WITH FULL SINK, OPTIONAL)

24"

8"

DUPLEX OUTLET

12"±

18"

14", 18"

BLENDER SHELF

BLENDER STATION

DRAUGHT ARM
DRAIN TROUGH
REFRIGERATOR UNIT
BEER KEG

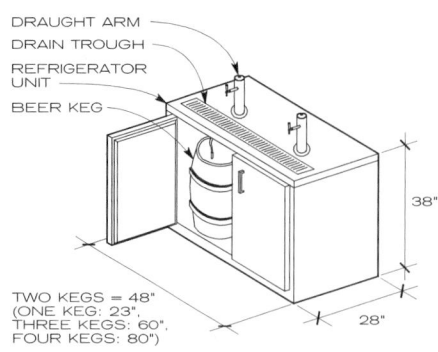

38"

28"

TWO KEGS = 48"
(ONE KEG: 23",
THREE KEGS: 60",
FOUR KEGS: 80")

NOTE

The dispenser shown is a direct draw system. Kegs may be up to 300 ft away from the bar (usually in a walk-in cooler).

BEER DISPENSER

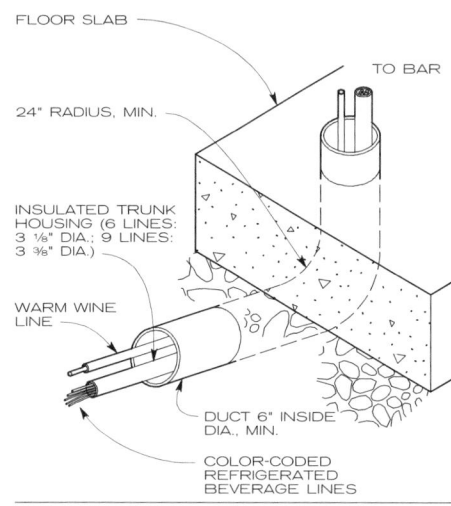

FLOOR SLAB

TO BAR

24" RADIUS, MIN.

INSULATED TRUNK HOUSING (6 LINES: 3 1/8" DIA.; 9 LINES: 3 3/8" DIA.)

WARM WINE LINE

DUCT 6" INSIDE DIA., MIN.

COLOR-CODED REFRIGERATED BEVERAGE LINES

REMOTE BEVERAGE DISPENSER DETAIL

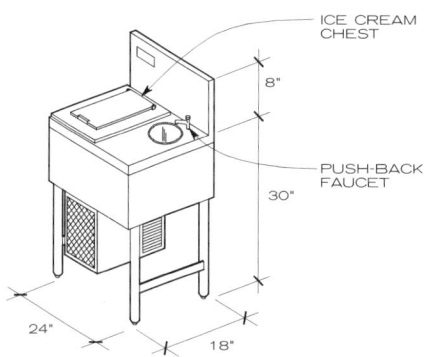

ICE CREAM CHEST

8"

PUSH-BACK FAUCET

30"

24"

18"

ICE CREAM CABINET

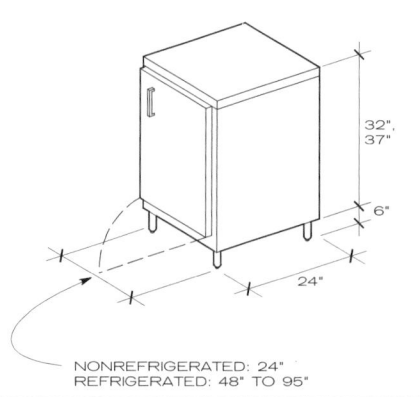

32", 37"

6"

24"

NONREFRIGERATED: 24"
REFRIGERATED: 48" TO 95"

BACK-BAR DRY STORAGE CABINET

FAUCET

VARIES FROM 9" FOR 2 FAUCETS TO 20" FOR 7 FAUCETS

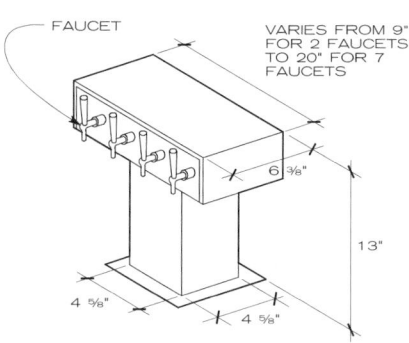

6 3/8"

13"

4 5/8"
4 5/8"

TEE TOWER

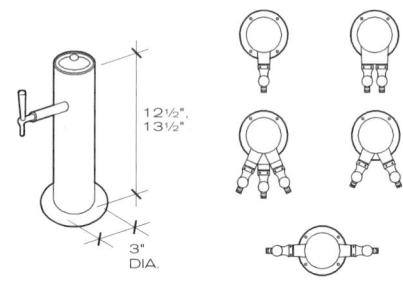

12 1/2", 13 1/2"

3" DIA.

DRAUGHT ARM

DRAUGHT ARM CONFIGURATIONS

BEER DISPENSING FAUCETS

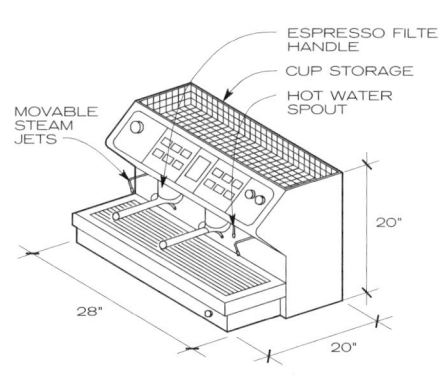

ESPRESSO FILTER HANDLE
CUP STORAGE
HOT WATER SPOUT

MOVABLE STEAM JETS

20"

28"

20"

CAPPUCINO/ESPRESSO MACHINE

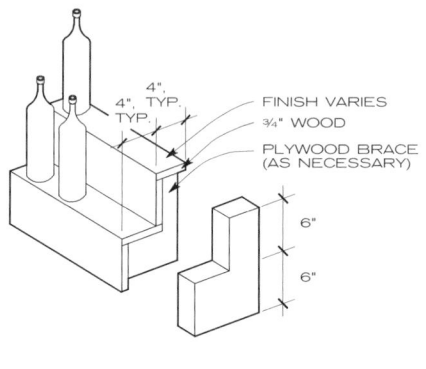

4", TYP.
4", TYP.

FINISH VARIES
3/4" WOOD
PLYWOOD BRACE (AS NECESSARY)

6"

6"

NOTE

These are also called bottle steps.

LIQUOR DISPLAY SHELVES

Richard J. Vitullo, AIA; Oak Leaf Studio; Crownsville, Maryland

11 FOOD SERVICE EQUIPMENT

GENERAL NOTES

1. See kitchen and laundry layout pages for locations of washers, dryers, and dishwashers and their respective wall chases for pipes and vents.

2. Check manufacturers' catalogs for "open-door" dimensions if door clearances may be a problem.

3. All dimensions given are actual ones, but certain variations in body design may affect the actual depth of particular models. Check all units for exact voltage. Some units available with gas.

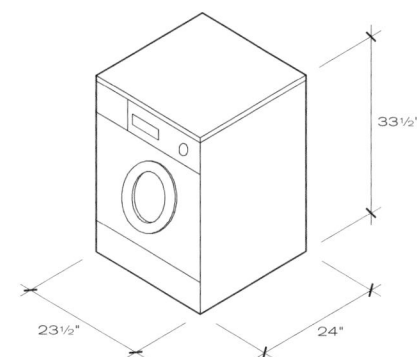

NOTE
Front-loading washers may be equipped with an integral top if not mounted under a counter.

BUILT-IN (UNDERCOUNTER) FRONT-LOADING WASHER

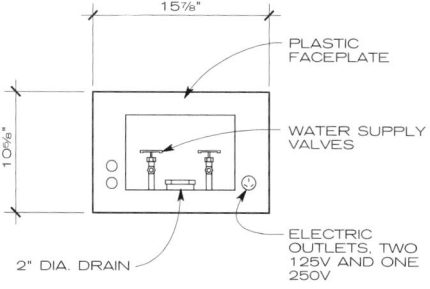

ELEVATION

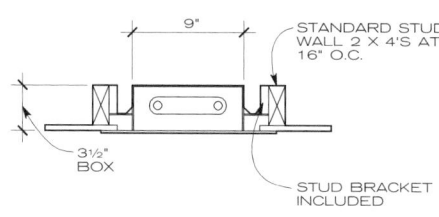

SECTION

UTILITY CONNECTION BOX (RECESSED)

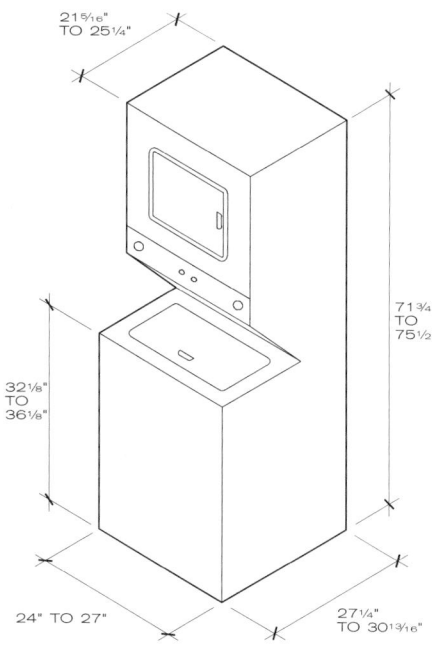

STACKED WASHER-DRYER COMBINATION

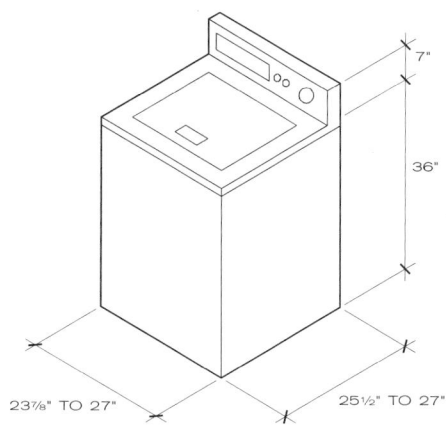

FREESTANDING TOP-LOADING WASHER

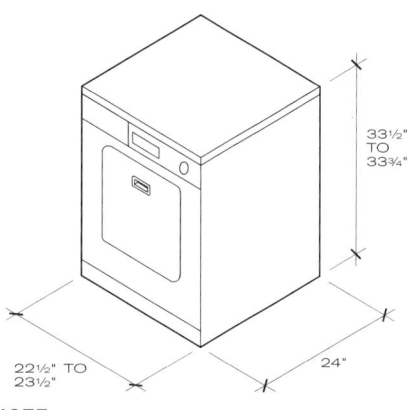

NOTE
Front-loading dryers may be equipped with an integral top if not mounted under a counter.

BUILT-IN (UNDERCOUNTER) FRONT-LOADING DRYER

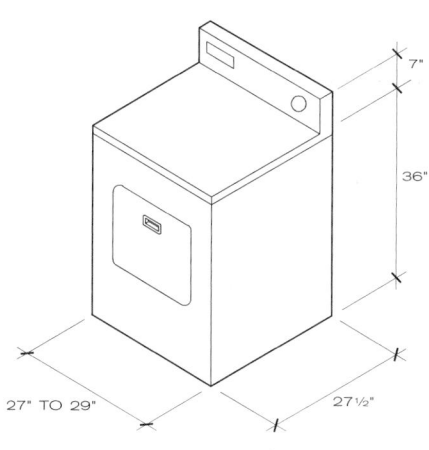

FREESTANDING FRONT-LOADING DRYER

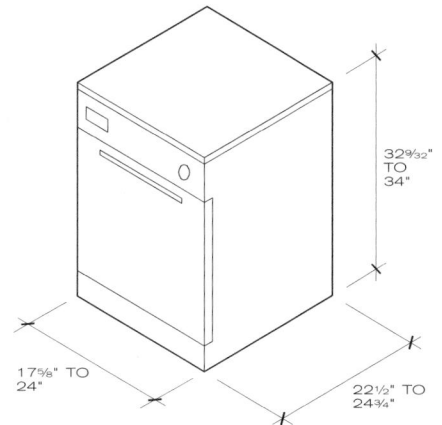

NOTE
Do not place dishwasher farther than 10 ft from sink, typically, for proper drainage.

BUILT-IN DISHWASHER

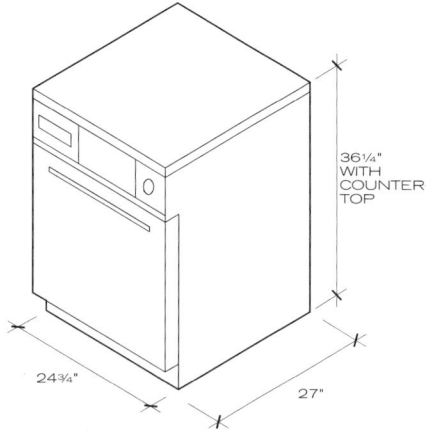

NOTE
Some portable models may be converted to built-in.

PORTABLE DISHWASHER

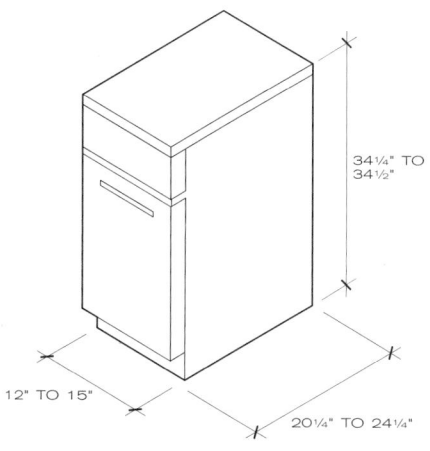

TRASH COMPACTOR

Richard J. Vitullo, AIA; Oak Leaf Studio; Crownsville, Maryland

GENERAL NOTES

1. Electric and gas ranges are available. Smooth surface electric cooktops have radiant and halogen heating elements or an induction coil below a glass-ceramic top. Radiant heating elements (below surface or surface units, plug-in, coil, or solid plate) provide heat directly from resistance elements. Halogen-type elements usually combine radiant elements with a halogen light source, which allows the element to heat up faster than a radiant element alone. Other range options include griddles and charbroilers. Induction elements consist of a high frequency induction coil beneath a glass-ceramic surface. Metal cooking utensils are heated by magnetic friction without directly heating the cooktop surface. Induction elements are considered energy-efficient.

2. Ovens are available in gas or electric, either as conventional, combination radiant/convection, or microwave models. Convection ovens have a dedicated third element (in addition to the top and bottom elements) surrounding the convection fan at the rear of the oven, which circulates heated air evenly throughout the oven, eliminating any unevenness in temperature.

3. All dimensions shown should be used as general guidelines only; consult manufacturers for specific dimensions.

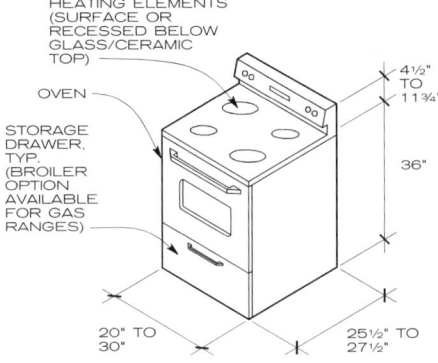

NOTE

Freestanding range/ovens may have front-mounted controls; if so, the backsplash area may be eliminated.

FREESTANDING RANGE/OVEN

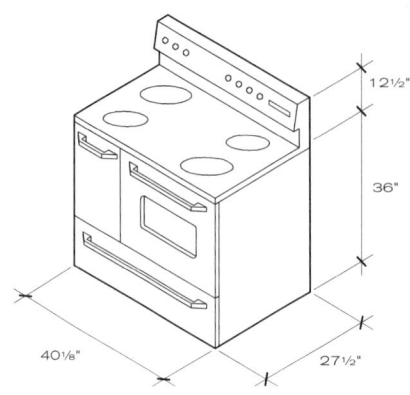

FREESTANDING RANGE WITH LARGE AND SMALL OVENS

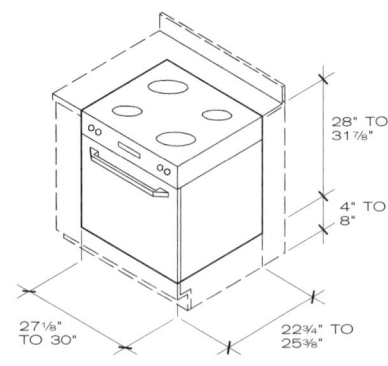

NOTE

Drop-in ranges typically hang from and are supported by the countertop and do not rest on the cabinet or floor below.

DROP-IN RANGE OVEN

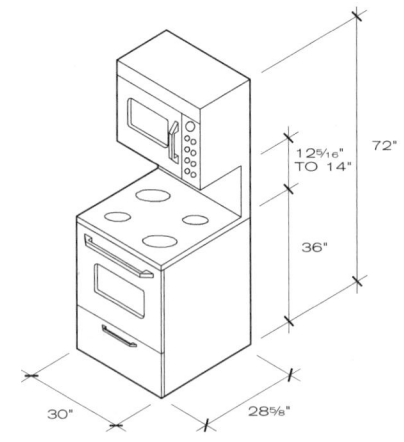

NOTE

Conventional or microwave ovens may be installed above a counter-height range/stove.

FREESTANDING RANGE WITH UPPER AND LOWER OVENS

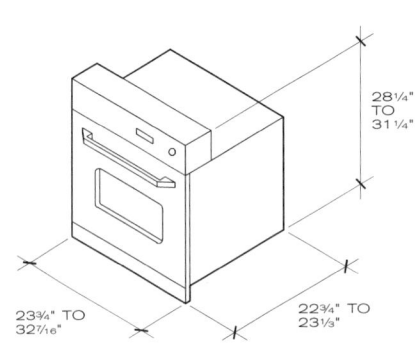

NOTE

Single wall ovens may be installed in a wall cabinet (at eye level) or under the counter in a base cabinet.

BUILT-IN SINGLE WALL OVEN

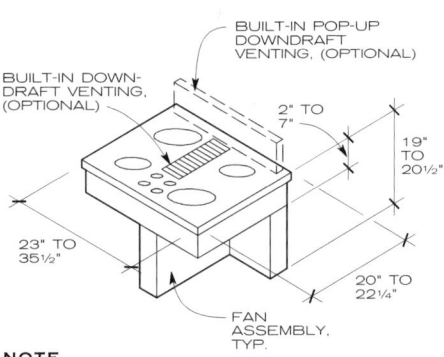

NOTE

Radiant and halogen cooktops typically require a 5 in. min. free area between the countertop and any combustible material below (typically shelving). Downdraft fan assemblies are located directly under a vent (rear pop-up vents offer the best free space under a counter). Available two-element cooktops are approximately 12 in. wide.

DROP-IN RANGE COOKTOP

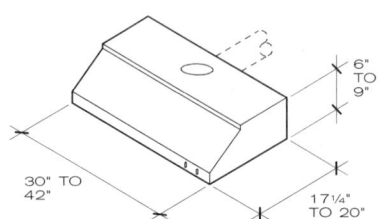

NOTE

Range hoods vent through filters back into the room (self-venting) or through ducts and filters to the outdoors. Accessories such as fans, filters, and lights vary greatly in design configuration. Some ranges and cooktops are equipped with downdraft venting, which may eliminate the need for an overhead range hood. Fans typically vent from 50 to 350 cu ft/min (CFM) of air for standard residential cooktop use. For commercial ranges, consult a design professional for CFM requirements.

RANGE HOOD

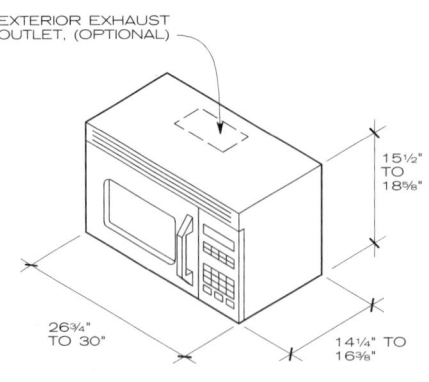

NOTE

Venting may be directed to the outside or recirculated.

BUILT-IN MICROWAVE OVEN

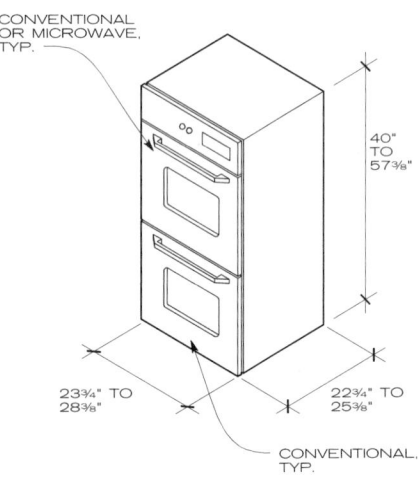

BUILT-IN DOUBLE WALL OVEN

Richard J. Vitullo, AIA; Oak Leaf Studio; Crownsville, Maryland

GENERAL NOTES

1. Ultra energy-efficient refrigerators/freezers are available in AC models for conventional utility power and DC models for alternative (remote) energy applications. Some models use 60 to 90% less energy than standard energy-efficient models. Many standard refrigerator and freezer manufacturers have CFC-free models, which means no CFCs were used in the insulation or in the coolant system. Consult manufacturers.

2. See manufacturers' catalogs for actual dimensions of specific units, which may include the number of burners, refrigerator size, sink size, finish materials, and options such as garbage disposal, range hood, microwave oven, ice maker, dishwasher, or freezer.

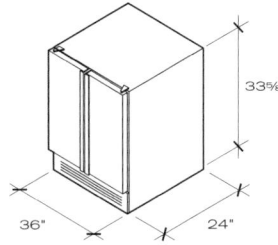

33⅝"
36"   24"

SIDE-BY-SIDE (WITH FREEZER)

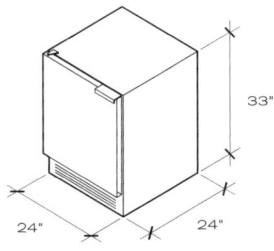

33"
24"   24"

SINGLE DOOR

UNDERCOUNTER REFRIGERATORS

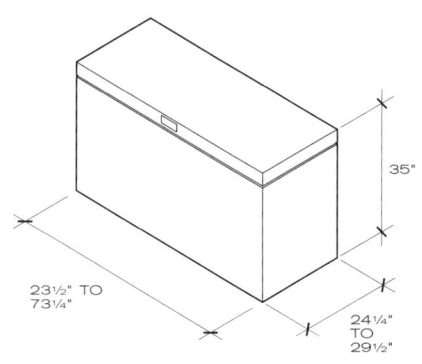

35"
23½" TO 73¼"
24¼" TO 29½"

CHEST FREEZER

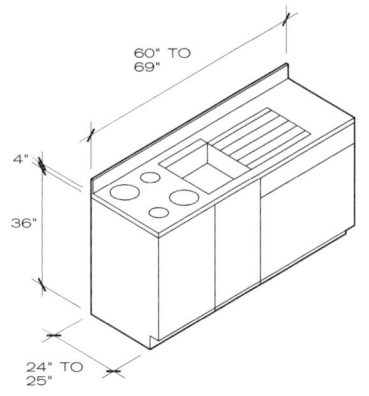   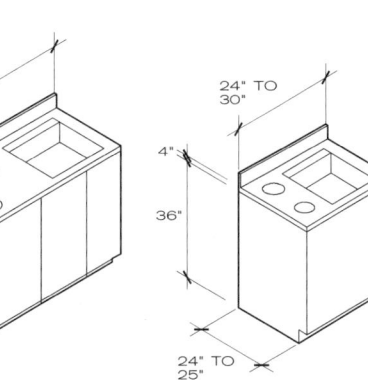

60" TO 69"   48" TO 51"   24" TO 30"
4"   4"   4"
36"   36"   36"
24" TO 25"   24" TO 25"   24" TO 25"

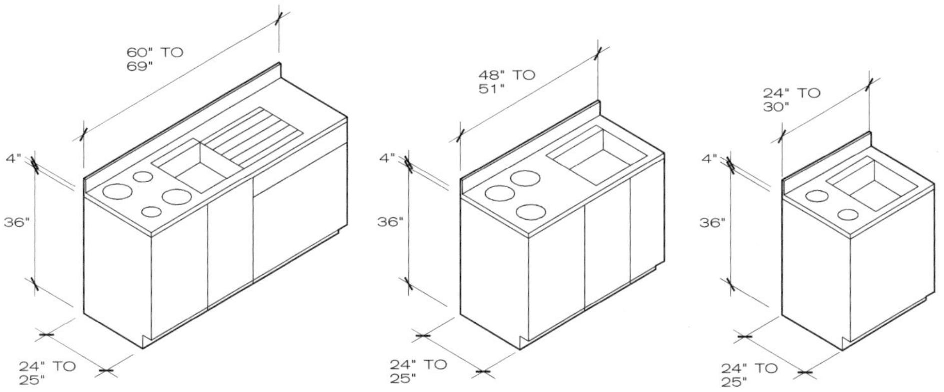

UNIT KITCHENS

Richard J. Vitullo, AIA; Oak Leaf Studio; Crownsville, Maryland

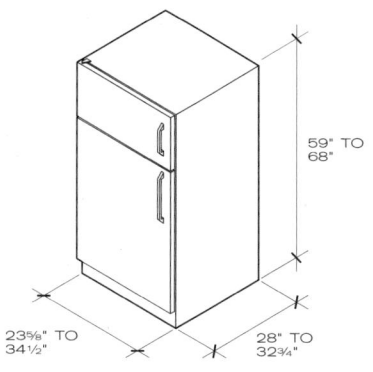

59" TO 68"
23⅝" TO 34½"   28" TO 32¾"

REFRIGERATOR WITH TOP FREEZER

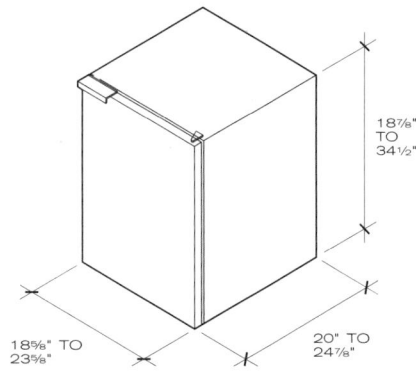

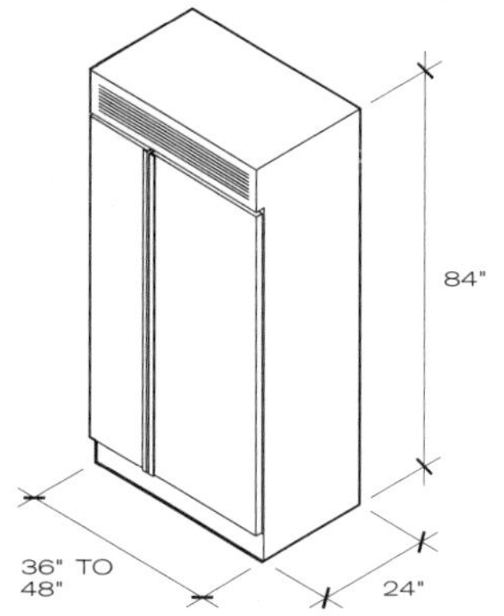

18⅞" TO 34½"
18⅝" TO 23⅝"   20" TO 24⅞"

SMALL CAPACITY FREESTANDING REFRIGERATOR

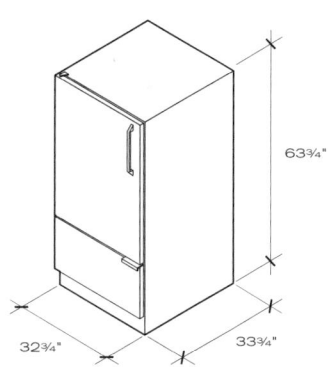

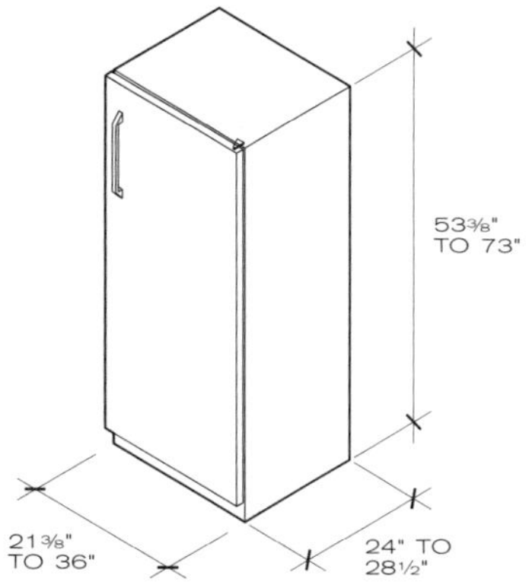

63¾"
32¾"   33¾"

REFRIGERATOR WITH BOTTOM FREEZER

84"
36" TO 48"   24"

BUILT-IN SIDE-BY-SIDE REFRIGERATOR/FREEZER

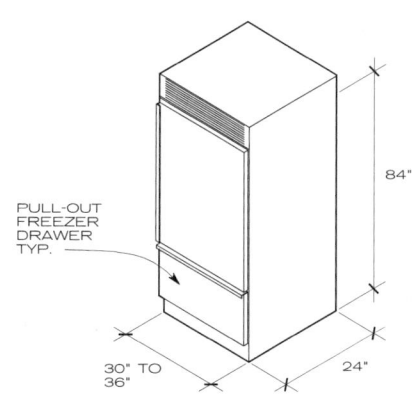

53⅜" TO 73"
21⅜" TO 36"   24" TO 28½"

UPRIGHT FREEZER

84"

PULL-OUT FREEZER DRAWER TYP.

30" TO 36"   24"

BUILT-IN REFRIGERATOR WITH BOTTOM FREEZER

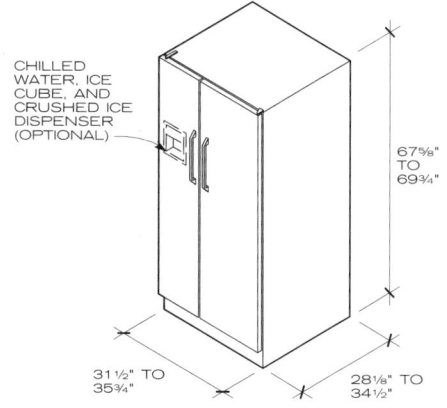

CHILLED WATER, ICE CUBE, AND CRUSHED ICE DISPENSER (OPTIONAL)

67⅝" TO 69¾"
31½" TO 35¾"   28⅛" TO 34½"

SIDE-BY-SIDE REFRIGERATOR

GENERAL

Air-supported structures are lightweight, totally free span structures that maintain stability in space and resist loads with a pressure differential between the interior and exterior. This method of support leaves the interior free of support devices that could interfere with the efficient use of space. The roof and side walls can be a single structural element in pure tension, a fabric envelope. The only compression members are the slightly pressurized air inside and the rigid base of the membrane.

STRUCTURAL MEMBRANE

The structural membrane is usually a nylon, fiberglass, or polyester fabric coated with polyvinyl chloride. Such skins have a life span from 7 to 10 years and offer fire retardation that passes NFPA 701. A urethane topcoat will reduce dirt adhesion and improve service life. Fluorocarbon top finishes further enhance characteristics and can double service life. Teflon-coated fiberglass membranes have a life expectancy of more than 25 years. This material is not combustible, passing ASTM E84, with a flame spread rating of 10, smoke developed < 50, and fuel contributed, 10. An acoustical liner (NRC = 0.65) is also available.

NOTES

1. Most air-supported structures are primarily designed to resist wind loads. Mechanical blowers must maintain 3 to 5 psf pressure inside the structure at all times. Architectural elements of the building must be detailed to avoid loss of air pressure.
2. Consult building codes to determine requirements for all air-supported structures.

GROUND-MOUNTED AIR STRUCTURES

The shape of ground-mounted air structures permits the structure to meet the ground vertically, allowing gravity loads to resist the membrane tension. The semicircular cross-section of the membrane structure has a curvature radius large enough to allow the fabric alone to carry wind forces that may affect the building. If lightweight fabrics are used, catenary cables or webbing may be required as well. Webbing is typically sewn into the fabric seams, forming a one-way system; cables are incorporated into pockets in a one-way system or formed into a cable net harness that is placed over the fabric in a two-way system.

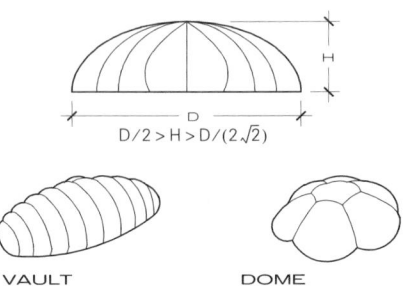

$$D/2 > H > D/(2\sqrt{2})$$

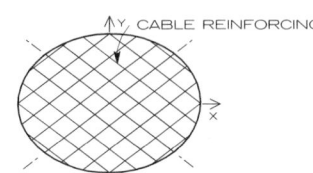

VAULT   DOME

SPAN LIMITATIONS	VAULT	DOME
Without cables	D = 120 ft	D = 150 ft
With cables	D = 400 ft	D = 600 ft

BASIC CONFIGURATION OF GROUND-MOUNTED AIR STRUCTURES

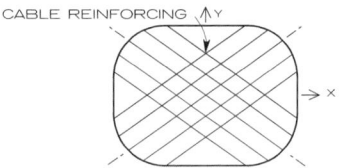

SUPERELLIPSE PLAN

PROGRESSION PLAN

LONG-SPAN DOME STRUCTURE TYPES

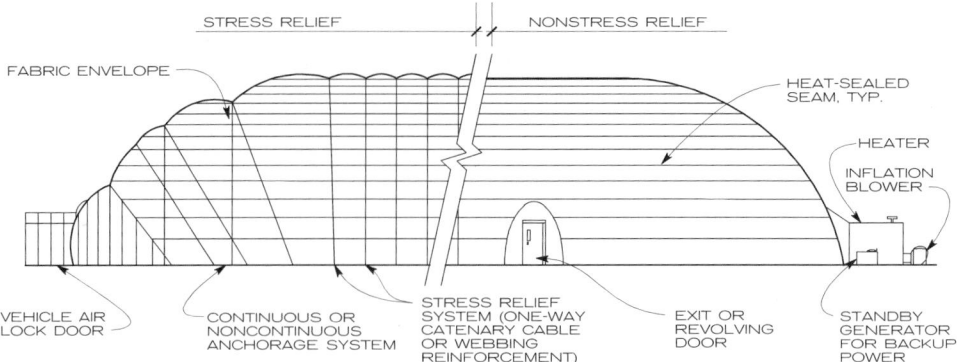

NOTE

For temporary structures, anchorage system may be water tanks, sandbags, earth screw anchors, etc., depending on conditions.

TYPICAL GROUND-MOUNTED AIR-SUPPORTED STRUCTURE

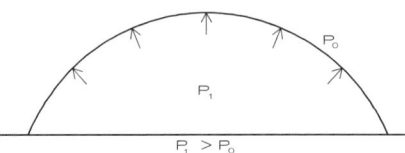

SINGLE MEMBRANE

This is the most common type of air-supported structure. The internal pressure (P_1) is kept approximately 0.03 psi above the external atmospheric pressure (P_0). It is this pressure difference that keeps the dome inflated.

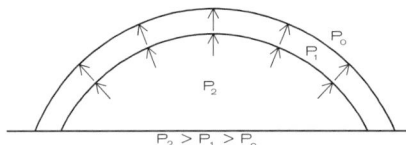

DOUBLE MEMBRANE

The air space between the two membranes is used for insulation and security. If the outer skin is punctured, the inner skin will remain standing. Both single and double membrane air-supported structures require the constant use of blowers to keep them inflated.

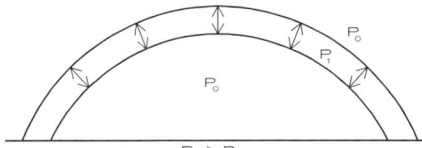

DUAL MEMBRANE

The internal and external pressures are the same in a dual membrane structure. Only the area between the skins is pressurized. This inflated area can be sealed, eliminating the need for constant use of blowers, although blowers are recommended to make up losses from leakage.

AIR-INFLATED STRUCTURES

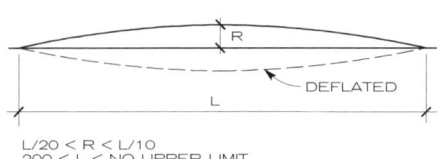

$$L/20 < R < L/10$$
$$200 < L < \text{NO UPPER LIMIT}$$

NOTE

The membrane must be patterned to carry loads without wrinkling. Structural behavior is nonlinear with large displacements. The roof shape must be established so that under maximum loads the horizontal components of the cable forces result in minimum bending moment in the compression ring. Consult an air-supported structures specialist to integrate structural and architectural requirements.

LONG-SPAN DOME STRUCTURE

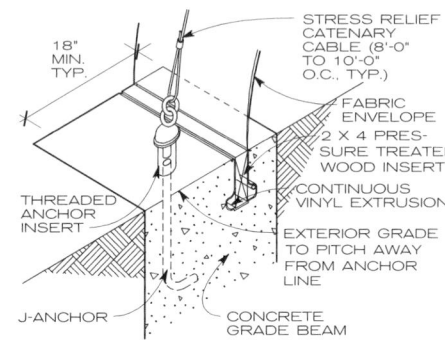

WEDGE INSERT

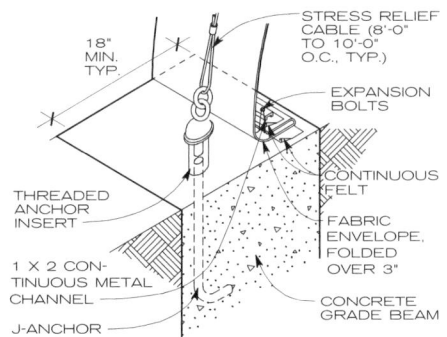

SURFACE-MOUNTED FABRIC ENVELOPE
NOTE

Beam design is based on actual uplift of air structure at the design inflation pressure and wind load.

CONTINUOUS ANCHORAGE DETAILS

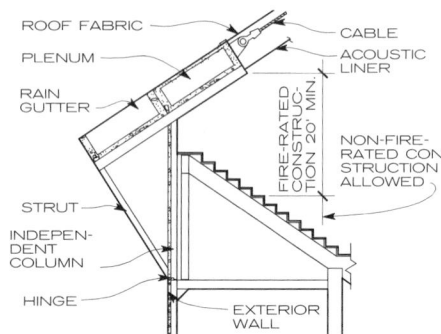

NOTE

The perimeter compression ring must be independent of the support structure to prevent radial restraint.

LONG-SPAN STRUCTURE SUPPORT DETAIL

Paul Gossen, Geiger Engineers, P.C.; Suffern, New York

GENERAL NOTES

1. Doors—standard sizes:

   2 ft 6 in., 3 ft 0 in., 3 ft 6 in., 4 ft 0 in., 5 ft 0 in. wide x 6 ft 6 in. high; 4 ft 0 in. or 5 ft 0 in. wide by 6 ft 6 in. or 7 ft 0 in. high.

   Sliding, double action, and display doors are available. ADA requires a 32-in. clear opening. Doors are manually or electrically operated.

2. Prefabricated insulated panels (nominal size)—standard sizes:

   Thickness: 4 in.

   Width: 11.5 in., 23 in., 46 in.

   Height: 7 ft 6 in., 8 ft 6 in., 10 ft 6 in., 11 ft 6 in.

   Finish material: aluminum, galvanized steel, or stainless steel.

3. Walk-in unit sizes:

   Width: 3 ft 11 in., 5 ft 10 in., 7 ft 9 in., 9 ft 8 in., 11 ft 7 in.

   Length: 5 ft 10 in., 7 ft 9 in., 11 ft 7 in., 13 ft 6 in., 15 ft 5 in., 17 ft 4 in., 19 ft 3 in.

   Height: 7 ft 6 in., 8 ft 6 in., 9 ft 6 in., 10 ft 6 in., 11 ft 6 in.

   Available accessories: stationary or mobile shelf units and adjustable cantilevered shelves, windows, interior partitions, meat rails, floor racks, ramps, and walk-ins.

4. Check local codes for drainage requirements.

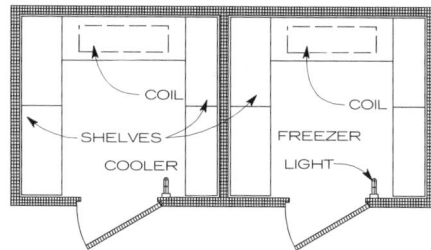

SIDE-BY-SIDE PLAN

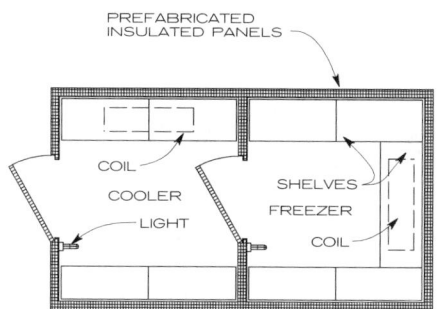

WALK-THROUGH PLAN

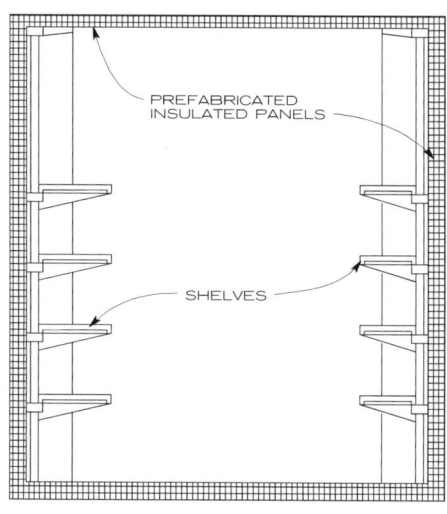

SECTION

TYPICAL WALK-IN UNITS

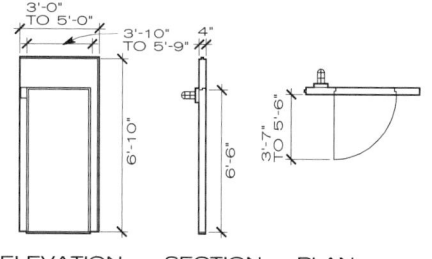

ELEVATION SECTION PLAN

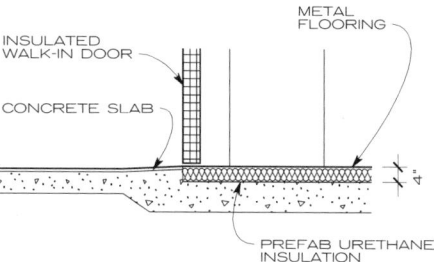

WALK-IN WITH FLUSH METAL FLOOR

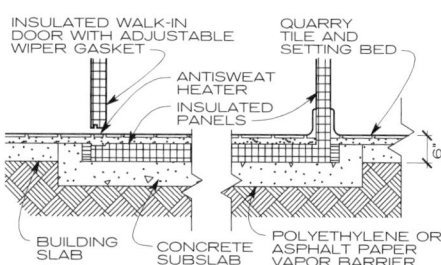

WALK-IN WITH FLUSH TILE

NOTE

Phase service is required for lights and anticondensate heaters on door panels. Connections are made to the junction box at the light, which is always inside the walk-in directly opposite the top hinge.

WALK-IN FLOOR DETAILS IN NEW CONSTRUCTION

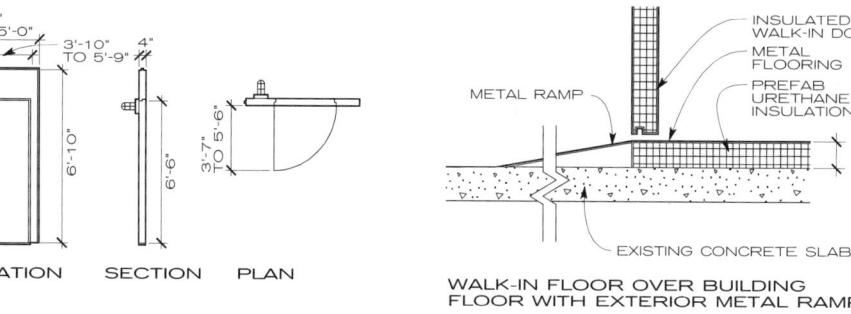

WALK-IN FLOOR OVER BUILDING FLOOR WITH EXTERIOR METAL RAMP

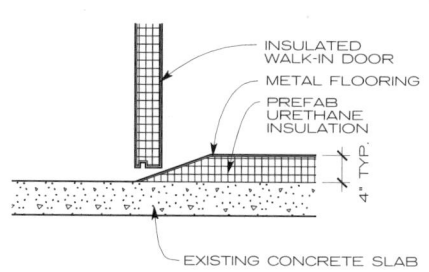

WALK-IN FLOOR OVER BUILDING FLOOR WITH INTERIOR METAL RAMP

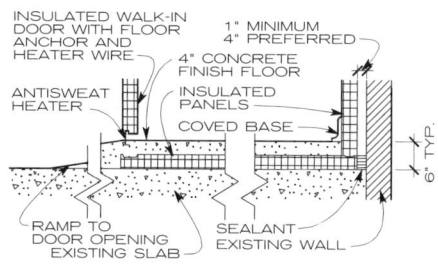

WALK-IN WITH BUILDING FINISH FLOOR AND EXTERIOR RAMP

NOTE

Metal flooring is typically made of galvanized steel, stainless steel, or aluminum grating

WALK-IN DETAILS ON EXISTING SLAB

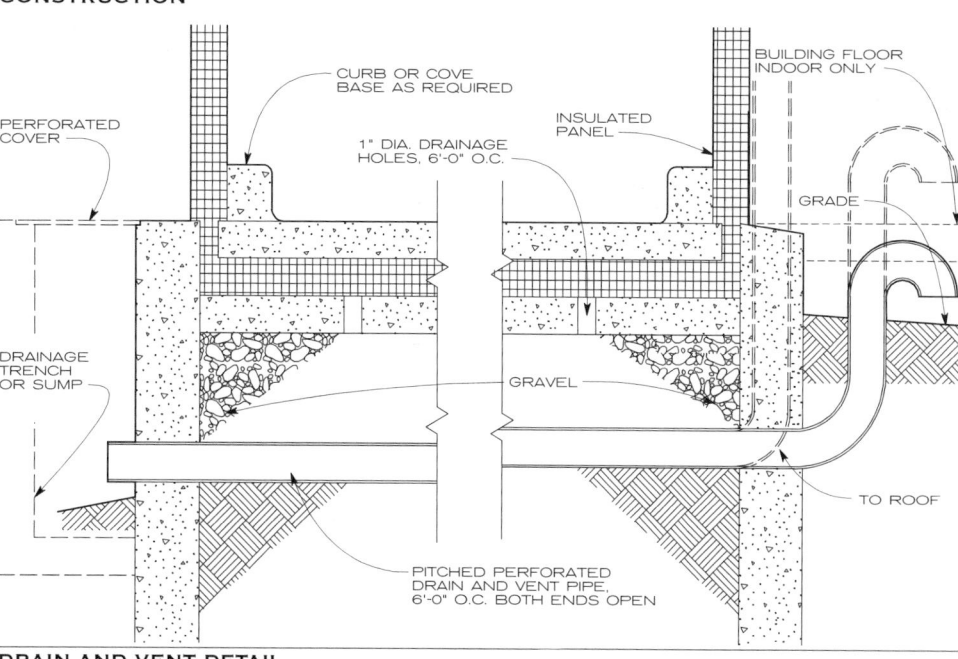

DRAIN AND VENT DETAIL

Cini-Little International, Inc.; Food Service Consultants; Washington, D.C.

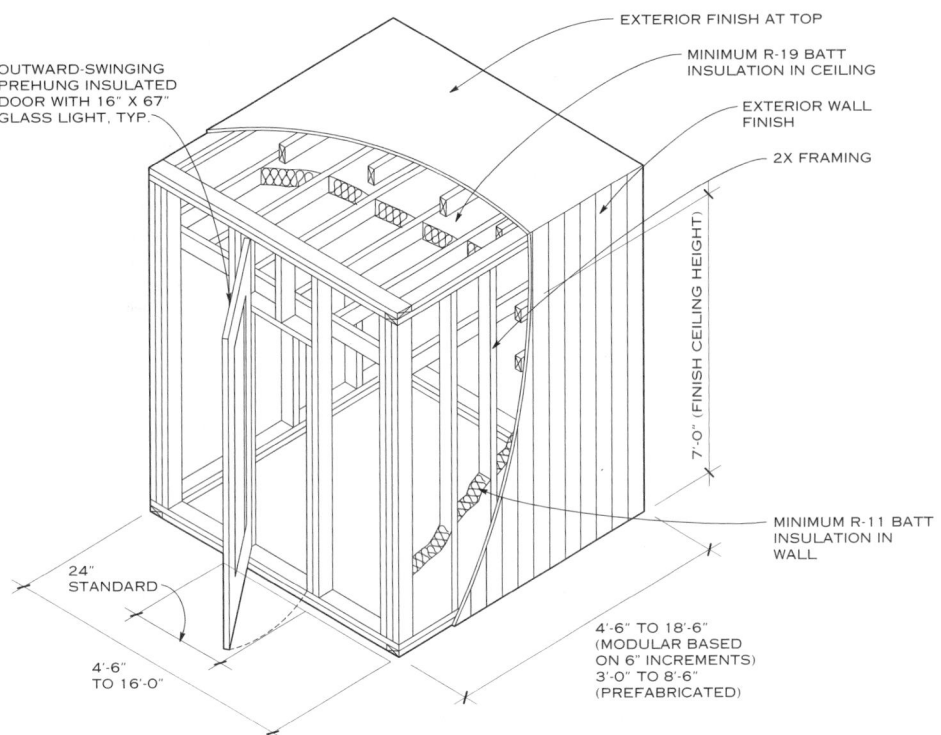

EXTERIOR FINISH AT TOP

MINIMUM R-19 BATT INSULATION IN CEILING

EXTERIOR WALL FINISH

2X FRAMING

OUTWARD-SWINGING PREHUNG INSULATED DOOR WITH 16" X 67" GLASS LIGHT, TYP.

7'-0" (FINISH CEILING HEIGHT)

MINIMUM R-11 BATT INSULATION IN WALL

24" STANDARD

4'-6" TO 16'-0"

4'-6" TO 18'-6" (MODULAR BASED ON 6" INCREMENTS) 3'-0" TO 8'-6" (PREFABRICATED)

SAUNAS

A sauna is a dry heat bath taken in a well-insulated room lined with untreated, kiln-dried softwood and heated by igneous rocks. The purpose of the sauna is to induce perspiration, which cleanses the pores in the skin by removing impurities and lactic acid built up from physical exertion.

Because of the dryness of the air in a sauna (25% humidity, average), the body can accept the higher temperatures a sauna produces (180°F, average). It is usually better to lie down than to sit up in a sauna, for the temperature rises about 18°F for every foot above the floor level. If a bather is lying down, the heat is equally dispensed over the entire body. Saunas should be located near a shower for the cool-down portion of the sauna.

Saunas may be prefabricated (precut pieces assembled on the site), modular (factory-built complete panels joined on the site), or custom built.

NOTES

1. The larger the sauna, the more heat is required; hence, the ceiling should be kept as low as possible within the limits imposed by the benches, which generally require 7 ft clear height.

2. A 24 in. wide, 6 ft 8 in. high, nonlockable door that opens outward is standard in a sauna. This door size maximizes bench space, minimizes heat loss, and provides safe entrance. A 36 in. wide door could make a design compatible with ADA guidelines, but wheelchair access is discouraged to protect the metal and plastic components of a wheelchair from excessive heat. Instead, an attendant can assist wheelchair-bound sauna users (liability and safety issues should be considered).

3. Because of the weight of the door, a pair of 4-in. brass butt hinges with ball bearings is recommended. A heavy ball or roller catch keeps the door closed. Door handles are made of wood.

4. Indirect lighting is recommended in a sauna. The best position for the light is above and slightly behind the bather's normal field of view; the switch is always outside the room.

5. Softwoods like western red cedar and redwood are used in the finish wall surfaces and bench construction of a sauna. Softwoods absorb humidity, keeping the atmosphere dry, and do not absorb heat as readily as hardwoods, keeping the surface comfortable to the touch. Wood should be kiln-dried to a 6 to 11% moisture content.

6. In private saunas, a water bucket and dipper for creating a burst of steam are common accessories. However, these are often not provided in public saunas to prevent misuse by unknowledgeable bathers, as premature or excessive water application can damage heater parts.

NOTES

1. If the sauna framing does not extend to the ceiling of the room outside the sauna, an exterior finish that encloses the top of the sauna is recommended.

2. A 1-in. gap is recommended between the bottom of the door and the threshold for ventilation.

3. Wood-framed baseplates should be made of pressure-treated wood; all other framing may be standard wood framing. Metal framing is not recommended because of its high heat-conductance property.

SAUNA CONSTRUCTION

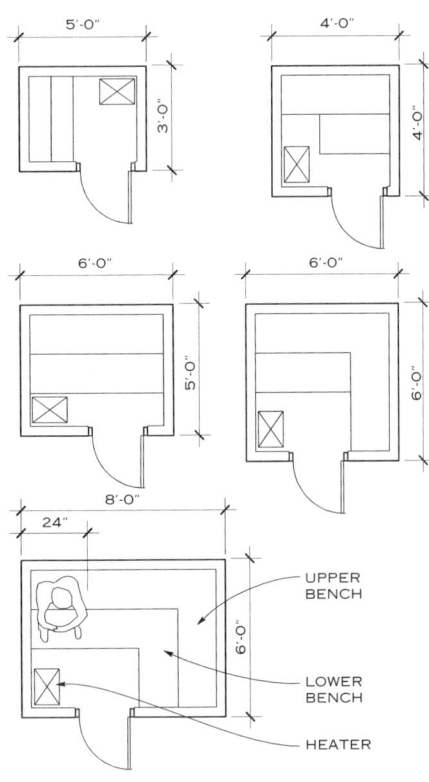

5'-0" · 3'-0"

4'-0" · 4'-0"

6'-0" · 5'-0"

6'-0" · 6'-0"

8'-0" · 6'-0"

24"

UPPER BENCH

LOWER BENCH

HEATER

NOTE

Design benches for a width of 24 in. per person (sitting) and a length of 72 in. per person (reclining).

TYPICAL SAUNA PLAN CONFIGURATIONS

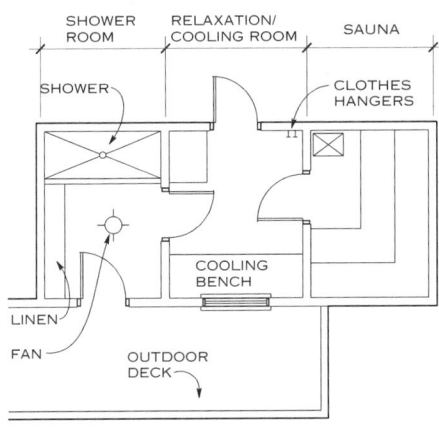

SHOWER ROOM

RELAXATION/ COOLING ROOM

SAUNA

SHOWER

CLOTHES HANGERS

COOLING BENCH

LINEN

FAN

OUTDOOR DECK

NOTE

A sauna suite offers a complete heating and cooling cycle with indoor and outdoor cooling areas.

SAUNA SUITE PLAN

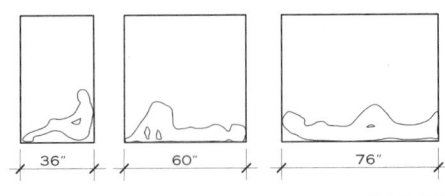

36"   60"   76"

BENCH DIMENSIONS

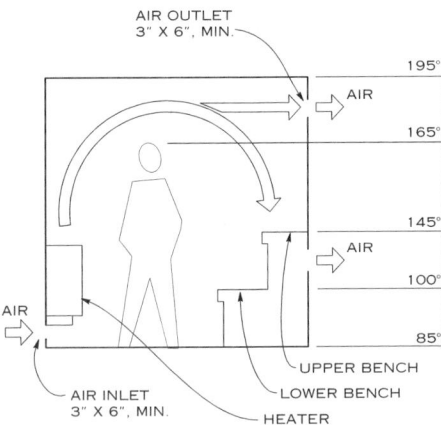

AIR OUTLET 3" X 6", MIN.

AIR

195°

165°

145°

AIR

100°

85°

AIR

AIR INLET 3" X 6", MIN.

UPPER BENCH

LOWER BENCH

HEATER

NOTE

Air must be able to flow freely into and out of a sauna and should be changed 4 to 6 times per hour. Fresh air is provided through updraft action by combining an air inlet in the sauna wall directly below the heater with an air outlet located at least 6 in. from the ceiling and 24 in. higher than the inlet. A vent space below the door may also be used.

AIR VENT AND TEMPERATURE DIAGRAM

Richard J. Vitullo, AIA; Oak Leaf Studio Architects; Crownsville, Maryland

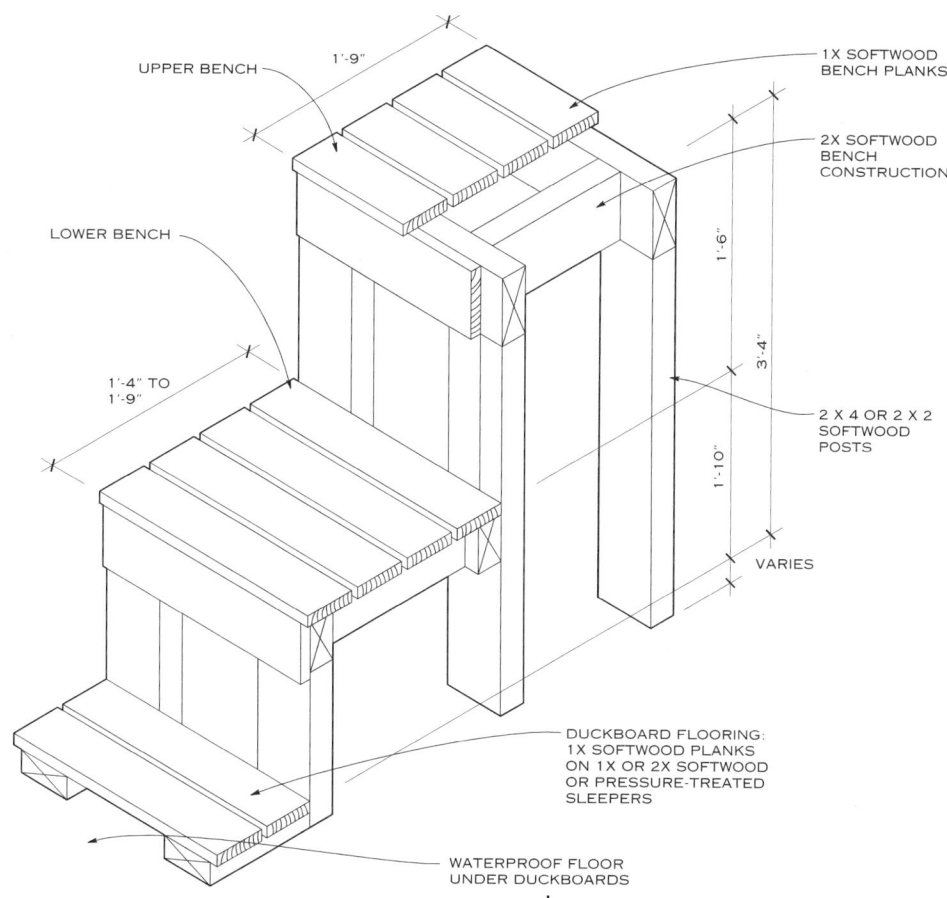

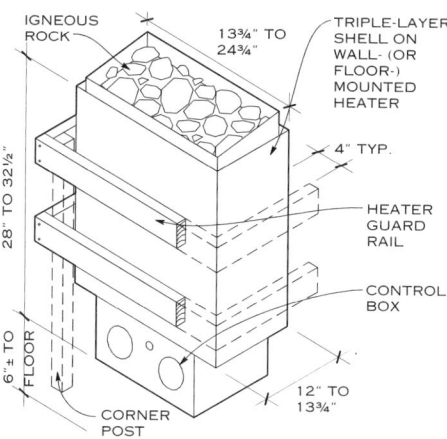

NOTE

The control box may be installed either on the heater (below it, usually) or apart from it but within 6 ft of the heat-sensing device inside the sauna. Controls include a thermostat, heat indicator light, light switch, and timer. The output capacity of the heater depends on the volume of the sauna room, but it generally ranges from 1700 to 15,000 watts. Stones completely cover the electric elements to filter the harsh heat and electromagnetic field.

SAUNA HEATER

STEAM ROOMS

Steam bathing has effects similar to the sauna but in a very different climate. Unlike the dry heat of a sauna, a steam bath (or Roman bath) is taken in a warm, moist atmosphere with temperatures up to 125°F and humidity near 100%. As with the sauna, the critical factor in steam bathing is the bather's interaction between heat and cold.

NOTES

1. Avoid use of exposed, untreated materials that are subject to decay or corrosion.

2. Steam room ceilings should be sloped a minimum of 2 in./ft to prevent condensation from collecting and dripping. Sloping from the middle to the edges reduces the height necessary to accomplish this. The ceiling should be no more than 8 ft high.

3. Use of vents inside the steam room is not recommended, but if they are installed, they must be positive closing with a vaportight seal and waterproof ducts.

4. Flooring should be skid-resistant, with a floor drain for condensation runoff and cleaning.

5. The steam generator must be compatible with the construction materials and the volume of the steam room. Residential steam generators can handle 50 to 500 cu ft, while larger models can service up to 1500 cu ft. Controls for the generator may be located inside or outside the room. The dimensions of the generator range from 13 to 17 in. high, 12 to 16 in. deep, and 7 to 8 in. wide.

NOTE

Floors must be waterproof; cement, tile, and vinyl are appropriate materials. Provide a drain for commercial construction.

Two levels are recommended in a sauna because the top level provides access to higher heat ranges.

SAUNA BENCH AND FLOORING CONSTRUCTION

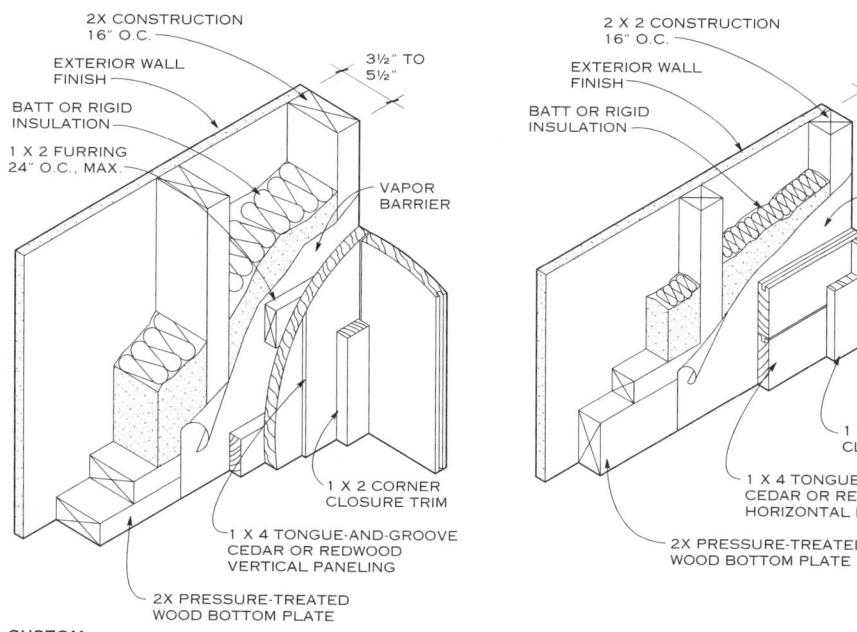

CUSTOM

PREFABRICATED

NOTES

1. The tongue-and-groove boards used for interior finishes should be at least $5/8$ in. thick but no wider than six times their thickness; they are made from softwoods like western red cedar or redwood. Blind nailing with galvanized, aluminum, or stainless steel nails is recommended.

2. Vapor barriers under paneling (whether attached to the insulation or separate) must be vaporproof and heat-resistant and act as a heat reflectant. Foil-backed, mineral-based insulation, R-11 minimum, is recommended.

SAUNA WALL CONSTRUCTION—DETAILS

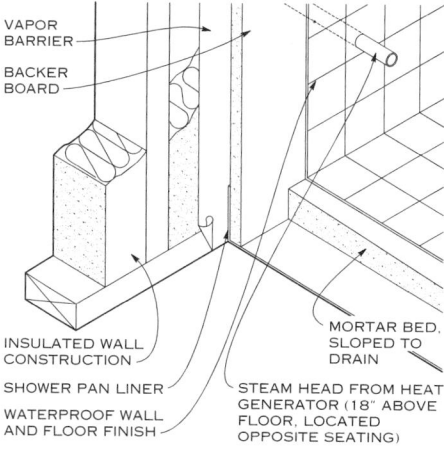

NOTE

1. Walls, ceiling, floor, and benches must be completely covered with a waterproof finish such as tile, marble, or acrylic. Exposed gypsum board or plaster is not recommended.

2. All joints must be filled with waterproof sealant.

STEAM ROOM WALL CONSTRUCTION

Richard J. Vitullo, AIA; Oak Leaf Studio Architects; Crownsville, Maryland

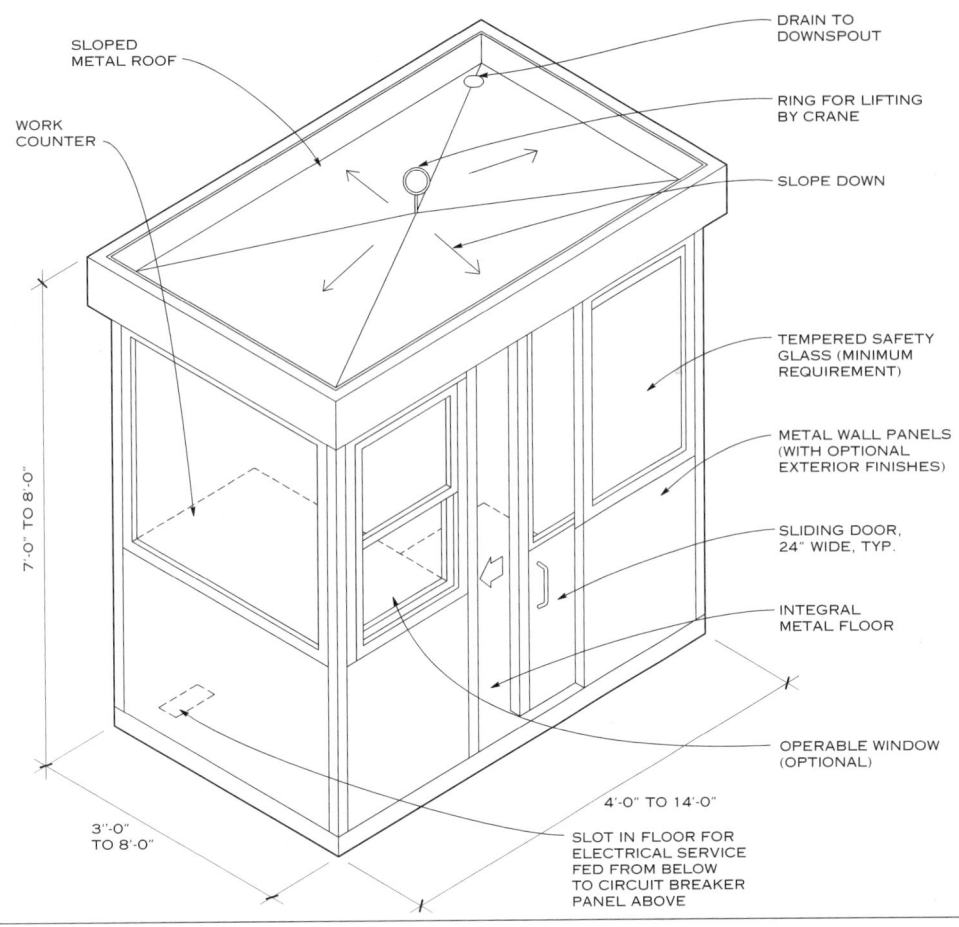

SLOPED METAL ROOF

WORK COUNTER

DRAIN TO DOWNSPOUT

RING FOR LIFTING BY CRANE

SLOPE DOWN

TEMPERED SAFETY GLASS (MINIMUM REQUIREMENT)

METAL WALL PANELS (WITH OPTIONAL EXTERIOR FINISHES)

SLIDING DOOR, 24" WIDE, TYP.

INTEGRAL METAL FLOOR

OPERABLE WINDOW (OPTIONAL)

SLOT IN FLOOR FOR ELECTRICAL SERVICE FED FROM BELOW TO CIRCUIT BREAKER PANEL ABOVE

7'-0" TO 8'-0"

3"-0" TO 8'-0"

4'-0" TO 14'-0"

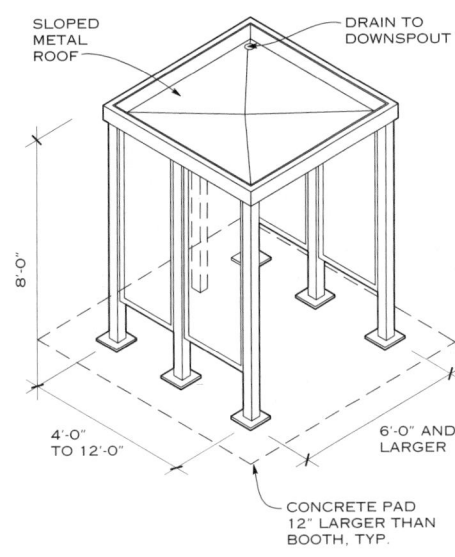

SLOPED METAL ROOF

DRAIN TO DOWNSPOUT

8'-0"

4'-0" TO 12'-0"

6'-0" AND LARGER

CONCRETE PAD 12" LARGER THAN BOOTH, TYP.

PREFABRICATED SHELTER

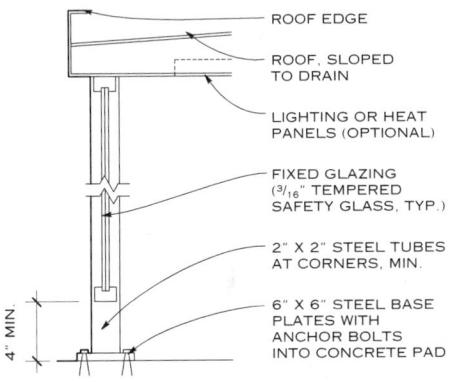

ROOF EDGE

ROOF, SLOPED TO DRAIN

LIGHTING OR HEAT PANELS (OPTIONAL)

FIXED GLAZING ($^{3}/_{16}$" TEMPERED SAFETY GLASS, TYP.)

2" X 2" STEEL TUBES AT CORNERS, MIN.

6" X 6" STEEL BASE PLATES WITH ANCHOR BOLTS INTO CONCRETE PAD

4" MIN.

SHELTER SECTION

NOTES ON SHELTERS

1. Use a switch-operated wall fan to make a smoking shelter. Consult manufacturers for available fan capacities.
2. Benches are typically specified for shelter interiors. Consult manufacturers for sizes and attachment details.

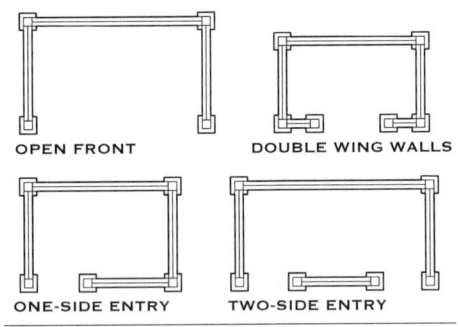

OPEN FRONT   DOUBLE WING WALLS

ONE-SIDE ENTRY   TWO-SIDE ENTRY

SHELTER PLAN TYPES

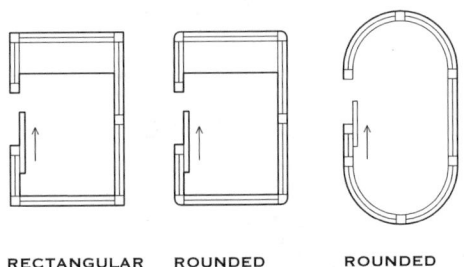

RECTANGULAR   ROUNDED CORNER   ROUNDED END

BOOTH PLAN TYPES

PREFABRICATED BOOTH

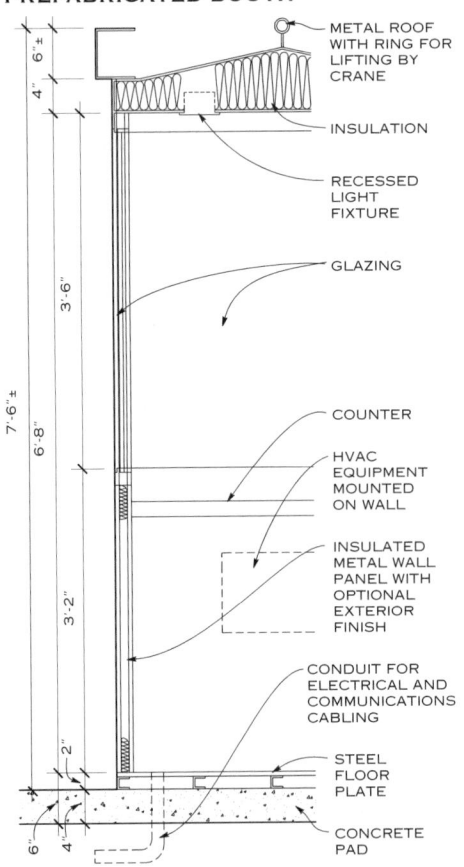

METAL ROOF WITH RING FOR LIFTING BY CRANE

INSULATION

RECESSED LIGHT FIXTURE

GLAZING

COUNTER

HVAC EQUIPMENT MOUNTED ON WALL

INSULATED METAL WALL PANEL WITH OPTIONAL EXTERIOR FINISH

CONDUIT FOR ELECTRICAL AND COMMUNICATIONS CABLING

STEEL FLOOR PLATE

CONCRETE PAD

6" ±   4"   3'-6"   7'-6" ±   6'-8"   3'-2"   2"   6"   4"

BOOTH SECTION

NOTES ON BOOTHS

1. Prefabricated booths are manufactured in a wide variety of designs, shapes, finishes, and sizes. Consult manufacturers for available design options.
2. Exterior finish materials that can be applied to wall panels include brick, cast stone, enameled steel panels, stainless steel, and aluminum.
3. Suitable glazing materials include tempered safety glass, unbreakable polycarbonate and impact-resistant acrylic sheets, and insulated and treated glazing.
4. Manufacturers usually offer bullet-resistant construction as an option for windows, walls, and floors up to Class VII protection. Hardening of HVAC, lighting, and other systems is also available.
5. Consult engineers and manufacturers for wind load design depending on site conditions. Appropriate stiffening and anchorage details may be necessary.
6. Lavatory or storage facilities may be built into booths, usually those 8 x 10 ft or larger.

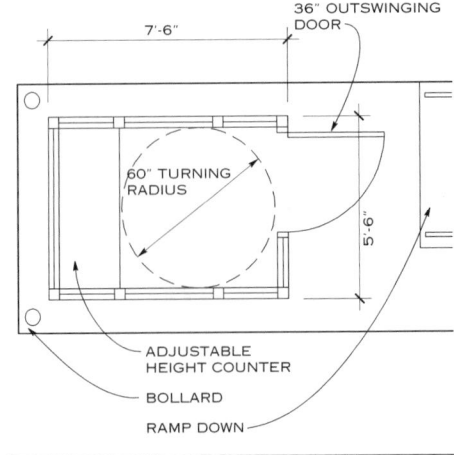

36" OUTSWINGING DOOR

7'-6"

60" TURNING RADIUS

5'-6"

ADJUSTABLE HEIGHT COUNTER

BOLLARD

RAMP DOWN

ADA-COMPLIANT BOOTH

Richard J. Vitullo, AIA; Oak Leaf Studio; Crownsville, Maryland

13   **SPECIAL PURPOSE ROOMS**

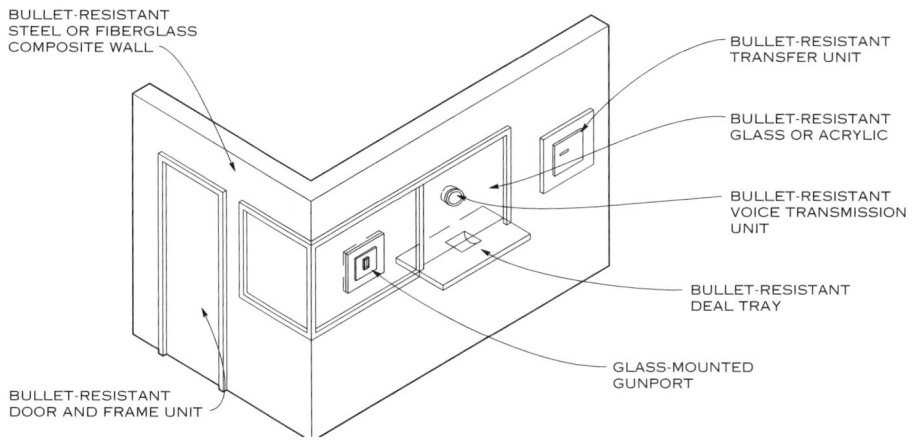

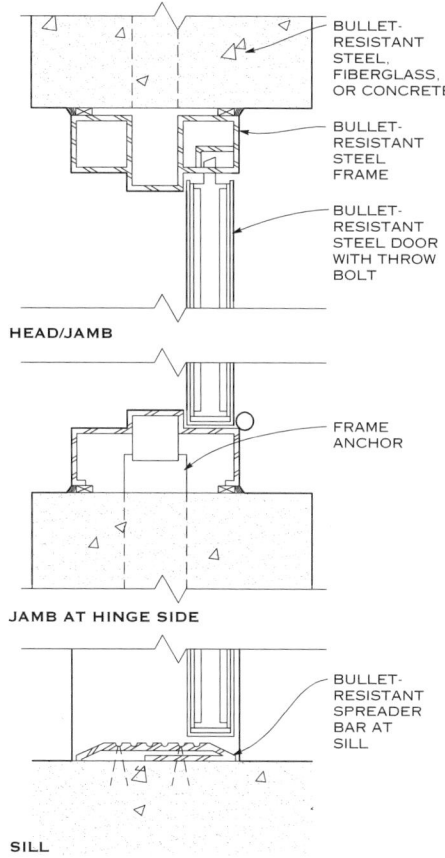

HEAD/JAMB

JAMB AT HINGE SIDE

SILL

BULLET-RESISTANT WALL DETAILS

GENERAL NOTES

1. No construction can be bulletproof, but bullet-resistant construction is possible. Protected areas should be designed to withstand a level of attack based on the threat at that location, in particular the type of arms expected.

2. Each component in a bullet-resistant system must be bullet resistant; there can be no weak links and no gaps.

3. Consult a specialist in bullet-resistant construction.

4. A truly effective protection plan combines a bullet-resistant system with appropriate detection, alarm, communication, escape, and retaliation capabilities.

5. The complete bullet-resistant environment makes it possible for personnel to escape, retaliate against attack, summon help, and defend themselves against the threat of gunfire, flame, and chemical or mechanical attack.

BULLET-RESISTANT DOOR ASSEMBLY NOTES

1. The entire unit should be certified as bullet resistant by an independent testing laboratory.

2. Bullet-resistant doors are heavier than regular doors, so the doorframe and hinges must be properly reinforced and/or of heavy weight.

3. The doorframe must be constructed of bullet-resistant material equivalent to that of the door itself. A proper fit between the door and the frame is required to prevent gaps that could permit ballistic penetration. Ideally, the door and frame should be supplied by the manufacturer as a single unit.

4. Use of appropriate hardware is important. The lockset should be mortised with $5/8$ in. minimum throw on the latch bolt and thoroughly armored to prevent the door from unlatching after assault.

5. The door should be equipped with a heavy-duty closer to ensure it closes completely.

BULLET-RESISTANT WINDOW ASSEMBLY NOTES

1. The entire unit should be certified as bullet resistant by an independent testing laboratory.

2. All elements in a bullet-resistant window assembly must be bullet resistant, including voice communication systems and trays.

3. The window framework must be bullet resistant as well as substantial enough to retain the glazing material under the impact of a projectile.

4. The window should be designed so the bullet-resistant framework and the bullet-resistant glass become an integral unit.

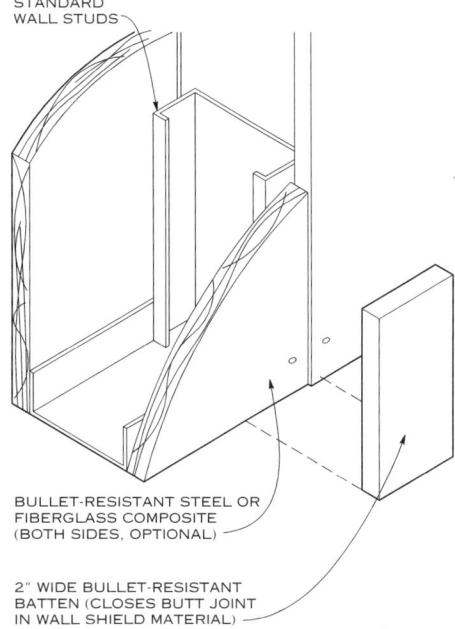

BULLET-RESISTANT COMPOSITE WALL PANEL

BULLET-RESISTANT DOOR IN CONCRETE WALL

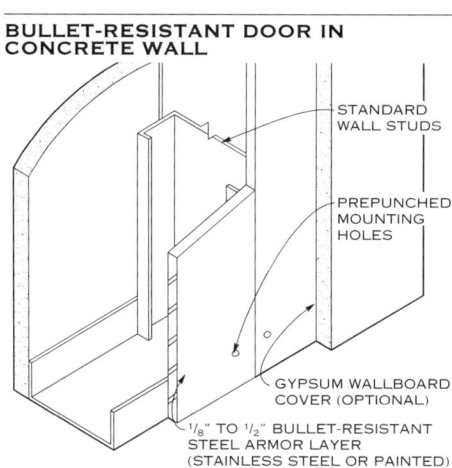

BULLET-RESISTANT STEEL WALL PANEL

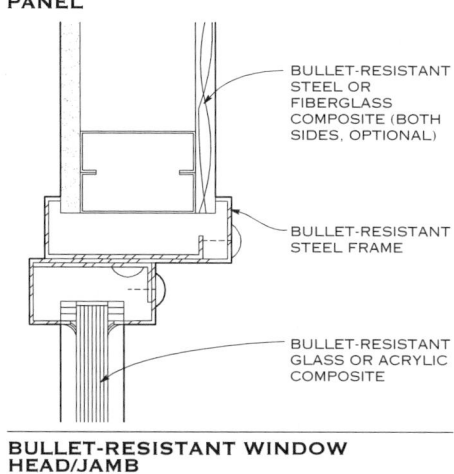

BULLET-RESISTANT WINDOW HEAD/JAMB

TYPICAL BULLET-RESISTANT MATERIALS

MATERIAL	FUNCTIONS AND CHARACTERISTICS	THICKNESS	WEIGHT	REMARKS
Steel	Cost-effective shielding against direct assault Thin Can be fabricated for retrofit Easy installation	$1/8$–1 in.	6–24 psf	—
Glass	Cost-effective vision-panel shield Scratch resistant, chemical resistant Substantial assault can defeat glass	$1 3/16$–2 in.	15–31 psf	One-way security glass is available $5/8$–$1 5/8$ in. thick, weight 7.1–18.2 psf
Plastics (acrylic)	Lighter weight and more impact resistant than glass Spall resistant Relatively high cost Substantial assault can defeat plastic	$1 1/4$ in.	7.8 psf	Glass-clad polycarbonate is available 1–$1 11/16$ in. thick, weight 9.6–17.6 psf
Composites	Can be opaque or transparent Lighter weight alternative for direct assault shielding Composite vision panels can be made stronger than glass Workable, suitable for custom installation Relatively high cost	$1/4$–$1 1/8$ in.	2.5–11.5 psf	Available in 4 x 8 ft sheets

Jessica Powell; Rippeteau Architects, P.C.; Washington, D.C.

SPECIAL PURPOSE ROOMS **13**

GENERAL

Radio frequency (RF) shielding consists of a barrier or shield of electrically conductive materials designed to protect sensitive electronic equipment from the disruptive effects of conducted or radiated electromagnetic interference (EMI).

RF shielding of rooms, large areas, or buildings (called architectural shielding) is designed to contain EMI within a given space (e.g., to protect cardiac pacemakers from EMI generated by magnetic imaging resonance [MRI] equipment) or to protect electronic devices from distortion by outside EMI (e.g., to protect computer data or medical ultrasound images from distortion by radio, television, or cellular phone signals).

Shielding from electromagnetic energy is achieved by metallizing walls, floors, and ceilings in a room or area. Metallizing isolates a space from energy transmitted through the air (radiated) or through a wire (conducted). Typically, RF shielding is created with knockdown galvanized steel modular rooms or architectural shielding achieved with copper paint or sheeting. Proper shielding requires RF treatment of all mechanical and electrical penetrations into an area, which is achieved by using RF-shielded doors and components for plumbing, HVAC systems, and electrical conductors for power, data, and telephone lines.

Rooms or areas may be RF tested to determine the level of shielding achieved, called shielding effectiveness. Shielding effectiveness typically ranges from 40 dB for commercial requirements (99% reduction in radiation) to more than 100 dB (99.999% reduction) for military, government, and hospital MRI enclosures. Shielding effectiveness is always stated in dB of reduction over a frequency range expressed in hertz.

The range of frequency that must be shielded varies from 60 Hz for AC power through the kHz (kilohertz) and MHz (megahertz) range for radio, TV, and cellular phones to the GHz (gigahertz) range for microwave energy such as radar.

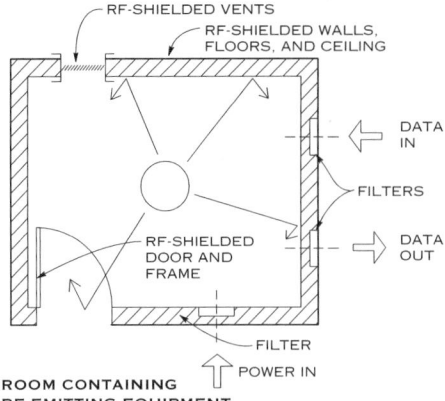

ROOM CONTAINING
RF-EMITTING EQUIPMENT

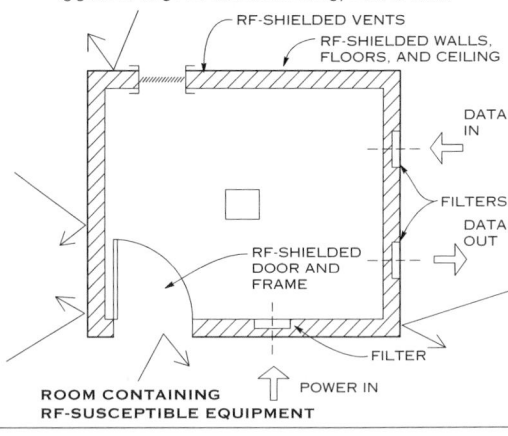

ROOM CONTAINING
RF-SUSCEPTIBLE EQUIPMENT

RF-SHIELDED SPACES

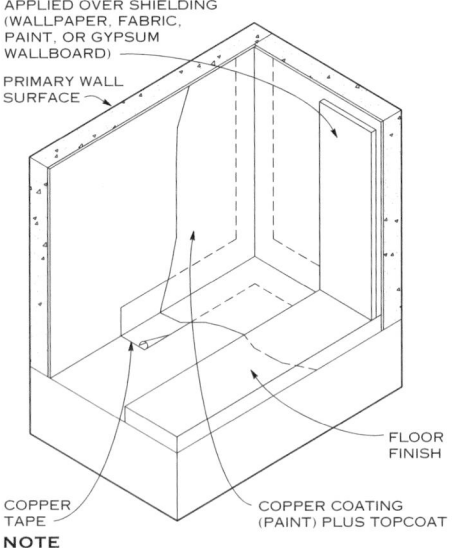

NOTE

When applying wall and floor finishes over shielding, use nonintrusive methods such as adhesive.

COPPER COATING DETAIL FOR WALLS, FLOORS, AND CEILINGS

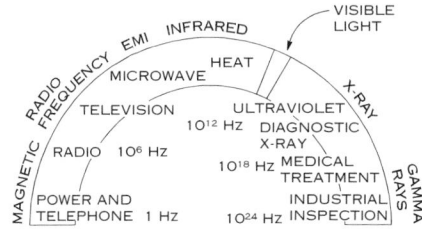

NOTE

Design for shielding against interference from electromagnetic radiation is based on the electromagnetic frequency spectrum. Since all radiated energy occurs in wave form, interference can be identified by its frequency, which is expressed in hertz. The diagram above shows where each type of radiated energy occurs in the electromagnetic spectrum. The lowest frequencies are in the range represented by electrical power and AM radio, the highest in the range represented by gamma rays (used in medical linear accelerators).

Each frequency range in the spectrum may require its own shielding design. In many modern projects, the designer and builder must contend with more than one frequency band at a time. A modern hospital, for instance, may require as many as five different shielding solutions, such as magnetic shielding for a 60 Hz power substation, magnetic and EMI shielding for MRI equipment, RF/EMI shielding for sensitive medical equipment, X-ray shielding for diagnostic X-ray equipment, and gamma ray shielding for a linear accelerator.

ELECTROMAGNETIC SPECTRUM

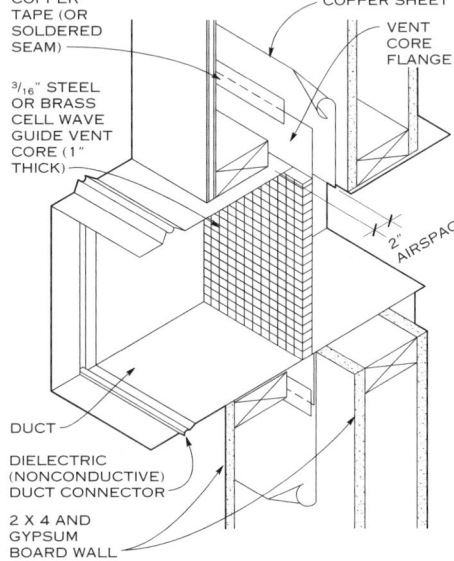

NOTE

Solder seam of vent flange or use copper tape to attach it to copper sheet on all four sides.

RF-SHIELDED DUCT DETAIL

SUMMARY OF SHIELDING SYSTEMS

WELDED STEEL ENCLOSURE	MODULAR PAN ROOM	COPPER SHEET SYSTEM	COPPER COATING SYSTEM
CONSTRUCTION			
Shielding steel min. 28 gauge on structural frame or attached to existing walls	Min. 24-gauge galvanized steel pans	Copper sheets (3–12 oz)	Component system (water-based copper paint, fire-rated doors, vents, laminated windows, power and data filters, copper tape)
JOINING METHODS			
Welded or brazed	Bolted through RF gasketing	Soldered, taped, or stapled	Copper paint on wallboard, wood, and concrete; copper-taped joints
TYPICAL ATTENUATION			
1. Magnetic (H-field) 80 dB @ 14 kHz 110 dB @ 200 kHz	60 dB @ 14 kHz 110 dB @ 200 kHz	90 dB @ 200 MHz	—
2. Electric (E-field) 120 dB @ (20 kHz to 50 MHz)	120 dB (200 kHz to 50 MHz)	100 dB (10–50 MHz)	Minimum + 50 dB (10–50 MHz)
3. Plane wave + 110 dB (50 MHz to 10 GHz)	+ 100 dB (50 MHz to 10 GHz)	100 dB (50 MHz to 10 GHz)	Minimum + 50 dB (10 MHz to 1 GHz)
4. Microwave 100 dB (1–94 GHz)	—	—	—
FEATURES			
Highest attenuation	High attenuation, lightweight, easy to assemble	Nonferrous materials, quick installation	Easy for building trades to install; economical reflective shielding for new and existing construction
INSTALLATION COST			
Highest	Moderate	Low	Lowest
APPLICATIONS			
60-Hz magnetic field shielding, for electrical closets, power substations, UPS systems. Highest possible security projects, research and QC, testing facilities, and MRI rooms	High security areas, government and commercial communication and data processing centers	MRI and EEG rooms, government secure installations, conference rooms or rooms that require architectural finishing	Data processing centers, hospital audiological/neuropsychiatric rooms, radio, TV recording studios, manufacturing facilities for electronic equipment

John Soltis; Tecknit Shielding Systems; Passaic, New Jersey

GENERAL

Radio frequency is abbreviated RF throughout this page.

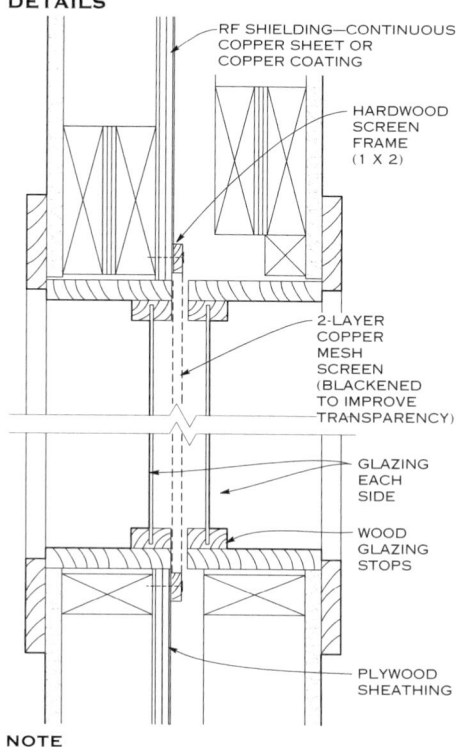

HEAD/JAMB

THRESHOLD

NOTE

This detail is for construction other than modular panel room systems.

RF-SHIELDED INTERIOR DOOR DETAILS

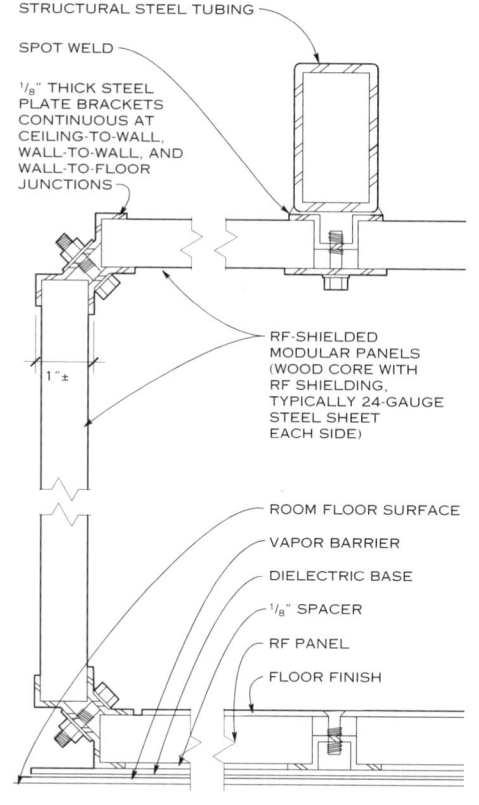

MODULAR ROOM SECTION

NOTE

A dielectric (nonconductive) base electrically isolates an RF-shielded structure from a parent room. Standard panels are

RF-SHIELDED MODULAR PANEL ROOM SYSTEM DETAILS

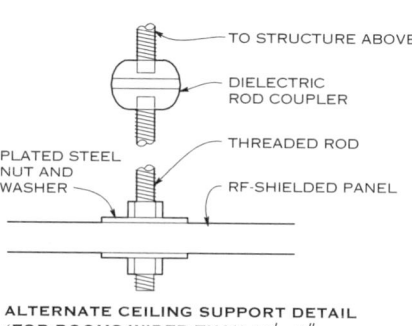

ALTERNATE CEILING SUPPORT DETAIL
(FOR ROOMS WIDER THAN 12' - 0"
IN SHORT DIRECTION)

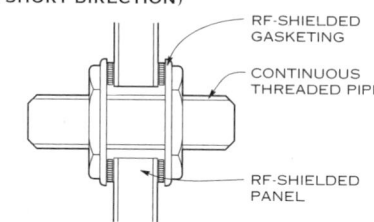

GALVANIZED PIPE PENETRATION

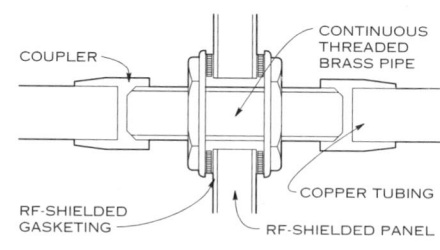

COPPER PIPE PENETRATION

4 x 8 ft and 4 x 10 ft; panels may be custom-cut in field.

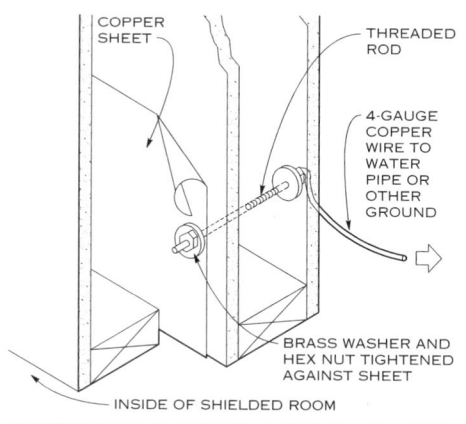

WALL SHIELD GROUNDING DETAIL

POWER AND DATA FILTER DETAIL

NOTE

Solder or use copper tape to fasten the wall shield to the mesh screen on all four sides.

RF-SHIELDED WINDOW DETAIL (INTERIOR)

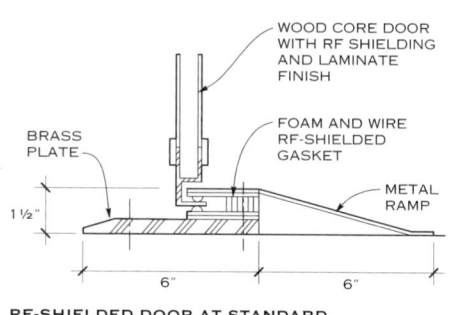

RF-SHIELDED DOOR AT STANDARD
RF-SHIELDED CONSTRUCTION

FLUSH POCKET THRESHOLD DETAILS

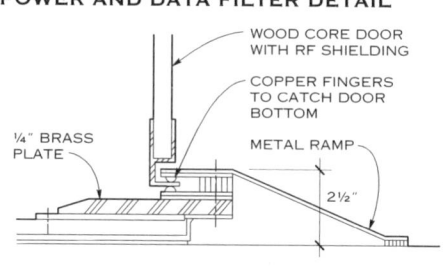

RF-SHIELDED DOOR AT MODULAR
RF-SHIELDED PANEL SYSTEM

John Soltis; Tecknit Shielding Systems; Passaic, New Jersey

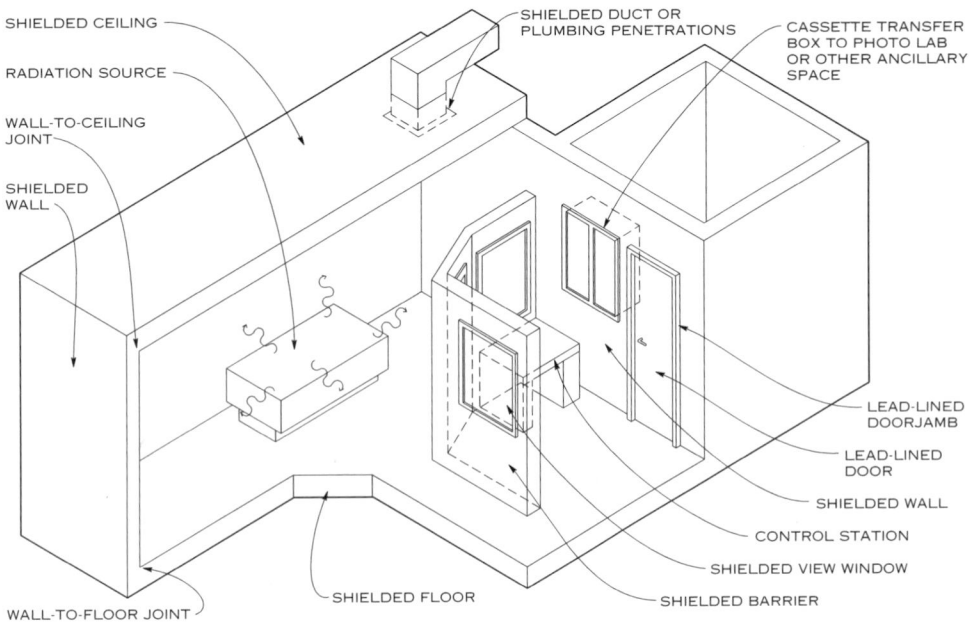

TYPICAL SHIELDED ROOM DESIGN REQUIREMENTS

GENERAL

There are three ways to protect humans from harmful exposure to radiation: Keep people a sufficient distance from the radiation source, limit their time of exposure, and contain the radiation source with a protective shield.

Factors to consider in designing a protective shield are the type, characteristics, and amount of radiation; the type of construction; and the properties of the shielding system. It is important to think of an enclosure for a radiation source as a sealed module. Each component in the system must be lined with lead, and all of the connections must overlap to prevent leaks. Joint details are the most important design element once the shielding system has been selected.

Retain a radiation consultant to analyze project requirements and prescribe the necessary shielding system. The thickness of lead needed is based on the amount of radiation at the site and should be determined by an expert.

NOTES ON LEAD SHIELDING

1. Lead sheets are available in sizes from $1/64$ to 1 in. thick.
2. Specify lead requirements in increments of 0.5 mm, with a minimum thickness of 1 mm ($1/24$ in.).
3. Adequate physical support is required for sheet lead installations.
4. For health and environmental considerations, lead sheet, plate, and brick are designed to be installed behind other materials.
5. Door and window frames must be lined with lead equal to the wall shielding level. Lead glass or lead acrylic glazing must be chosen to match wall and frame shielding levels.
6. Hinges and hardware for lead-lined doors must be designed to carry the weight of the lead.

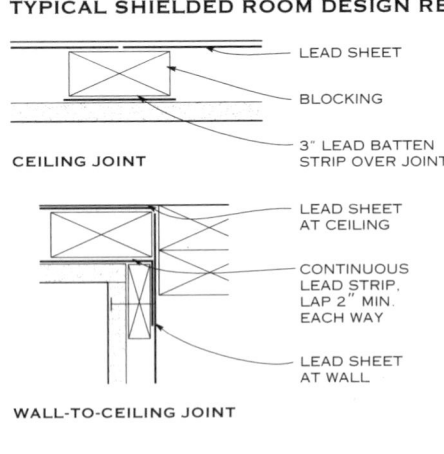

CEILING JOINT

WALL-TO-CEILING JOINT

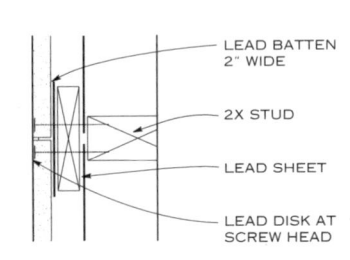

WALL JOINT

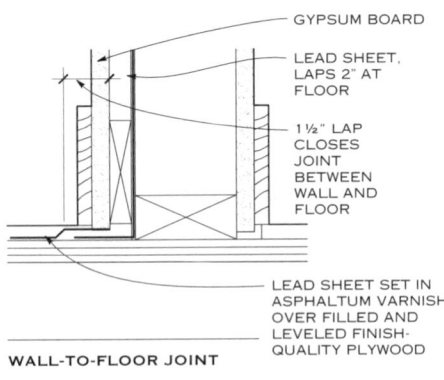

WALL-TO-FLOOR JOINT

LEAD SHEET IN WOOD CONSTRUCTION

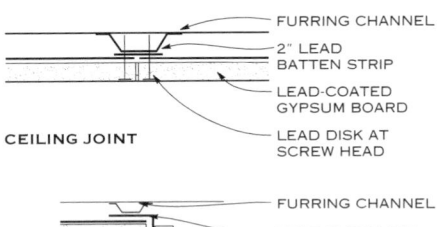

CEILING JOINT

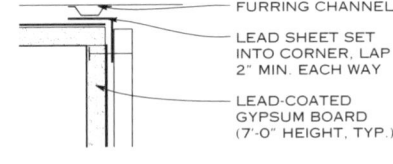

WALL-TO-CEILING JOINT

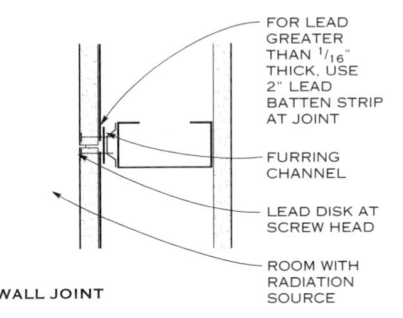

WALL JOINT

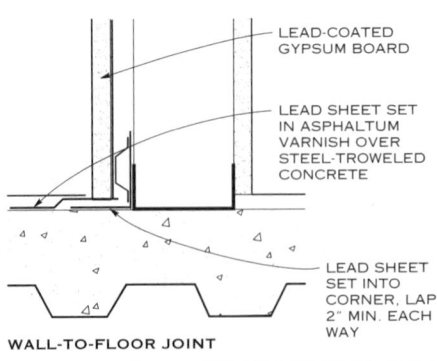

WALL-TO-FLOOR JOINT

STEEL STUD AND LEAD-COATED GYPSUM BOARD

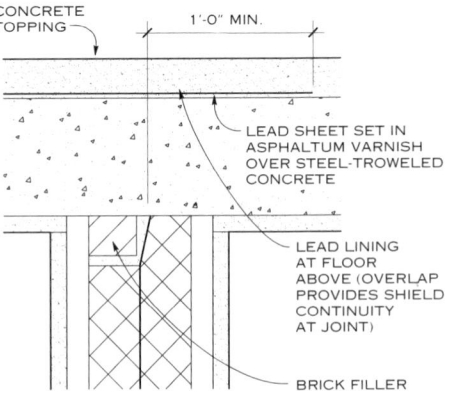

WALL-TO-CEILING JOINT

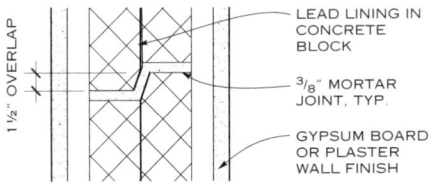

TYPICAL BLOCK JOINT

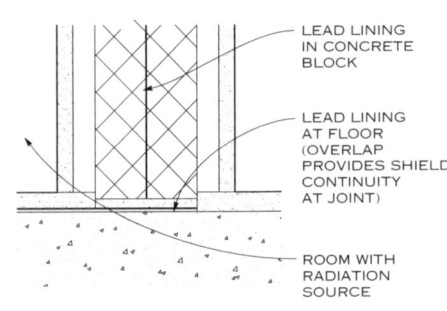

WALL-TO-FLOOR JOINT

LEAD-LINED BLOCK IN CONCRETE FRAME

Jessica Powell; Rippeteau Architects, PC; Washington, D.C.

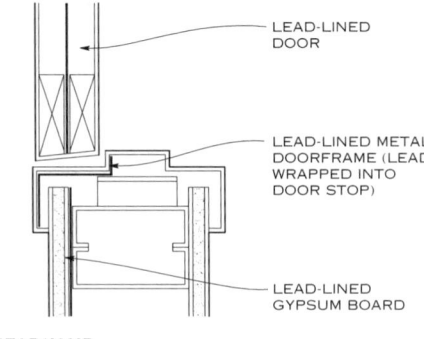

HEAD/JAMB

- LEAD-LINED DOOR
- LEAD-LINED METAL DOORFRAME (LEAD WRAPPED INTO DOOR STOP)
- LEAD-LINED GYPSUM BOARD

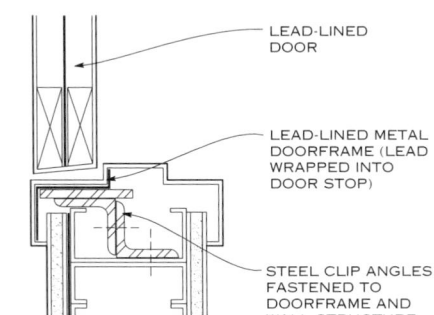

REINFORCED JAMB

- LEAD-LINED DOOR
- LEAD-LINED METAL DOORFRAME (LEAD WRAPPED INTO DOOR STOP)
- STEEL CLIP ANGLES, FASTENED TO DOORFRAME AND WALL STRUCTURE

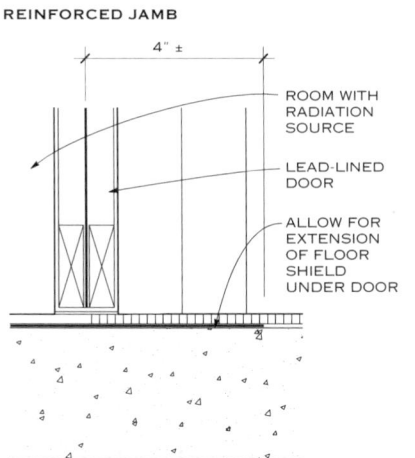

THRESHOLD DETAIL

4" ±

- ROOM WITH RADIATION SOURCE
- LEAD-LINED DOOR
- ALLOW FOR EXTENSION OF FLOOR SHIELD UNDER DOOR

LEAD-LINED DOOR DETAILS

NOTES

1. Lead-lined doors consist of a continuous sheet of lead sandwiched between two wood core panels; they generally measure 1³/₄ in. plus the thickness of the lead, which is specified by the architect or radiation physicist. Typically, the lead sheet is a minimum 1³/₄ in. thick and is covered with a flush-type wood veneer or plastic laminate. For lead thicknesses greater than ³/₁₆ in., consult the manufacturer for door thicknesses. Use pivot or continuous hinges specifically designed to carry the weight of lead-lined doors. Depending on the thickness of the lead and the weight of the door, it may be necessary to reinforce the doorframe. Steel door frames are lined with lead of the same thickness as walls and doors. Lead-lined doors are available with leaded louvers or view windows.

2. For lead-lined wallboard and plywood, an unpierced lead sheet is laminated to a sheet of fire-rated wallboard or plywood. Lead thickness is specified by an architect or radiation physicist. Lead joint strips and screw plugs cover any construction gaps or penetrations.

3. Lead-lined shielding barriers are modular, custom-designed units with clear glazing material on top and a lead-lined opaque panel below. Glazing may be either lead acrylic or lead glass. Check local regulations to ensure that movable radiation shielding is permitted.

4. View windows are formed from telescoping steel frames (for walls 4¹/₂ to 7 in. thick) with lead. These windows may include voice transmission passages and an adjust-

Jessica Powell; Rippeteau Architects, P.C.; Washington, D.C.
John Soltis; Tecknit Shielding Systems; Passaic, New Jersey

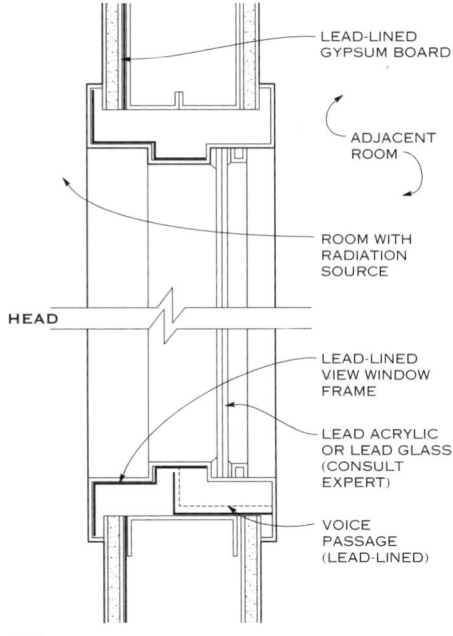

HEAD

- LEAD-LINED GYPSUM BOARD
- ADJACENT ROOM
- ROOM WITH RADIATION SOURCE
- LEAD-LINED VIEW WINDOW FRAME
- LEAD ACRYLIC OR LEAD GLASS (CONSULT EXPERT)
- VOICE PASSAGE (LEAD-LINED)

SILL

FIXED LEAD-LINED HOLLOW METAL VIEW WINDOW

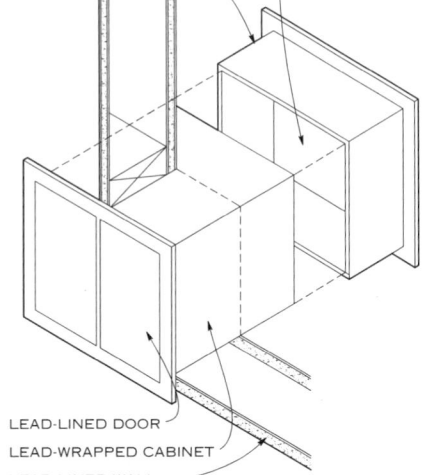

- ROUGH FRAME SLEEVE FITS OVER CABINET TO SECURE TO WALL
- LEAD-LINED DOOR
- LEAD-LINED DOOR
- LEAD-WRAPPED CABINET
- LEAD-LINED WALL

LEAD-LINED PASS-THROUGH CABINET

able glass stop. The stop permits installation of one to eight pieces of lead glass as required for radiation protection. Minimum thickness for the glass is ¹/₄ in., which is equivalent to 2 mm of lead. Windows can be laminated with float glass for increased protection.

5. An X-ray cassette transfer box installed between diagnostic and film processing rooms facilitates quick transfer of developed and undeveloped X rays. These boxes are constructed of steel panels lined with a specified lead thickness.

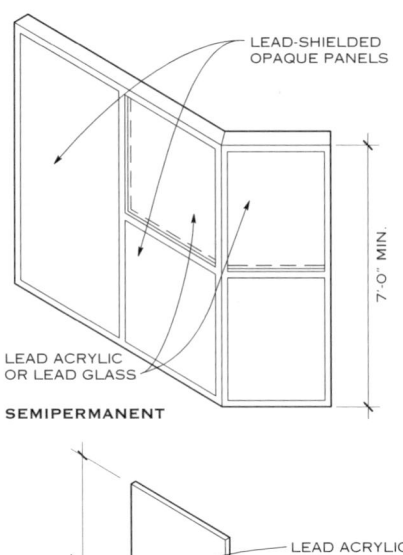

SEMIPERMANENT

- LEAD-SHIELDED OPAQUE PANELS
- LEAD ACRYLIC OR LEAD GLASS
- 7'-0" MIN.

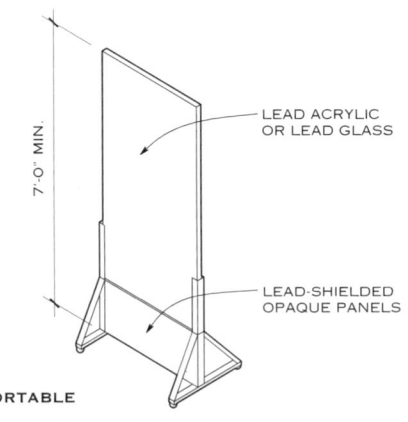

PORTABLE

- LEAD ACRYLIC OR LEAD GLASS
- LEAD-SHIELDED OPAQUE PANELS
- 7'-0" MIN.

RADIATION SHIELDING BARRIERS

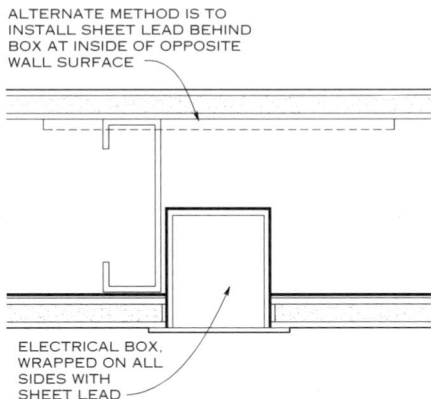

- ALTERNATE METHOD IS TO INSTALL SHEET LEAD BEHIND BOX AT INSIDE OF OPPOSITE WALL SURFACE
- ELECTRICAL BOX, WRAPPED ON ALL SIDES WITH SHEET LEAD

ELECTRICAL, PLUMBING, AND HVAC PENETRATION SHIELDING

6. Leaded X-ray glass is used for all windows in X-ray protection rooms. Typical material uses lead-barium glass with more than 60% heavy metal oxide, including at least 55% lead oxide. Typical glass sizes range from 8 x 10 in. to 48 x 96 in. Glass thickness is 8 mm (lead equivalent 1.8-2.0 mm) to protect against 100 kV X-rays, 11 mm (lead equivalent 2.5-2.7 mm) to protect against 150 kV X-rays, and 14 mm (lead equivalent 3.0-3.2 mm) to protect against 200 kV X-rays.

MEDICAL X-RAY PRODUCT APPLICATION GUIDELINES

APPLICATION	X-RAY COMPONENTS	SHIELDED DOORS	CONTROL WINDOWS
Linear accelerator (LINAC) room	Borated lead walls, lead brick	Borated polyethylene and lead	Telescopic widths 4⁷/₈ to 7 in. (typical), larger widths available
X-ray rooms, dental x-ray	Stationary or mobile control screens, lead-lined wallboard and plywood	Lead-lined in varous lead thicknesses and door sizes	
CAT scan room, PET scan, cardiac catheterization	Lead-lined wallboard and plywood, lead brick (PET scan)	Lead-lined hollow metal and lead-lined solid-core wood doors	
Implant radiology	Interlocking lead brick, lead-lined plywood	Lead-lined doors and frames	

GENERAL

Architectural fabric structures have undergone rapid development since the early 1970s and now can be considered a mature building technology. Due to improvements in materials, structural analysis, and environmental control, these structures can often be considered permanent buildings. This technology, with unique properties that make it useful for certain applications, offers an important alternative to conventional construction.

Fabric structures of a nonpneumatic kind fall into two categories. One type has a fabric membrane with a rigid frame support, usually of metal, and the other is a self-supporting fabric membrane kept in tension with a supporting structure of steel or concrete. The rigid frame structures typically form pyramidal or long, continuous geometric shapes like sheds or barrel vaults. The self-supporting structures rely on opposing curves to distribute the necessary tension and typically form saddle, conical, or hyperboloid (anticlastic) shapes.

The structure that creates and maintains tension on the fabric can consist of cables and masts, a compression ring, trussed gridwork, or tied edges. These mechanisms create pretension in the fabric sufficient to keep it taut at all times. Any compressive loads imposed on the fabric will be balanced or at most reduced by the prestress created by the structure.

MATERIALS

The intended life span of the structure is an important factor in design decisions, fabrication details, and the cost of architectural fabric structures. The life span is most affected by the fabric material or membrane selected. Fabric is a directional material and does not have the same strength or elongation in all directions under a load. Materials with little creep are preferable for tensioned structures, as original prestress can be lost if the fabric stretches or deforms. Details allowing for retensioning must be incorporated if materials with moderate to high creep are used. Generally, the materials used in a membrane are composites consisting of a woven substrate protected with an applied coating.

The membrane is the principal structural component of a self-supporting or tensioned fabric structure. Two materials are generally used for membranes—polyvinyl chloride (PVC)-coated materials and fluorocarbon (Teflon)-coated glass fiber fabric. PVC-coated polyester is a composite material composed of vinyl coating over both faces of a woven polyester fabric. The material is inexpensive, strong, translucent, and easy to fabricate but has a limited life span and is only fire resistant; for these reasons it is only used in temporary or semipermanent structures. Fluorocarbon-coated glass fiber fabric is classified as a noncombustible material. Besides its advantages in fire safety, this fabric is extremely long-lasting, self-cleaning, and translucent and is the accepted material for most permanent installations. Development continues in fabric technology, and new products such as silicon-coated glass fiber may offer an improvement in the range of material characteristics.

DESIGN

In recent years, the structural design of fabric structures has improved due to the increased use of the computer in the engineering process. The first step in the design process aided by computer modeling is the definition of an acceptable surface geometry, such as the hyperboloid. A membrane mesh or network is then developed representing the surface as a grid of lines. This graphic model is "prestressed," and the reactions are analyzed in an iterative, or repetition-based, process. Live loads such as wind, rain, or snow are applied to the model and the stresses calculated in order to select the fabric and design the supporting structure or foundation.

The design, fabrication, and construction of fabric structures require close coordination among the architect, engineer, fabricator, and installer throughout the process to ensure the strict quality control this technology requires. However, since most of the work is completed in the factory, minimizing on-site construction time, it is not unreasonable to maintain tight specifications.

APPLICATIONS

Applications for fabric structures include the semipermanent and temporary fabric-and-frame structures applied to agricultural, greenhouse, and storage uses. Improved materials have allowed use of these structures for waste treatment facilities, tennis courts, and pool facilities. More elaborate configurations, curved in plan and section, serve as outdoor concert halls, enclosed sports facilities, and atrium spaces for larger structures such as office buildings, medical facilities, shopping malls, and airports. Fabric structures are not a substitute for conventional construction, but their unique qualities enable them to perform certain building tasks very efficiently. In general, special performance requirements, such as the need for long spans or for natural lighting, encourage the use of this building system.

ENVIRONMENTAL CONSIDERATIONS

Under certain circumstances, a tensioned fabric structure can reduce energy consumption in a building. The natural light from the translucent surface reduces artificial lighting requirements, the reflectivity of the skin reduces heat gain, and the radiation of waste heat from the warm fabric surface to a cool sky results in an energy-efficient building in warm climates. In cold climates, a second skin or liner is normally used, often with glass fiber insulation in the cavity to further reduce heat loss. These structures can be as energy-efficient as conventional buildings in many applications.

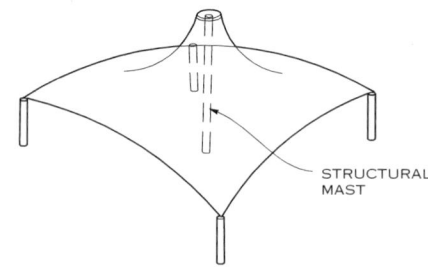

CONICAL-TYPE SURFACE GEOMETRY

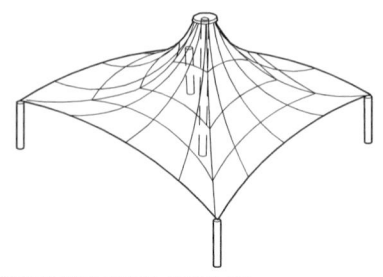

MEMBRANE MESH OVERLAY

STRUCTURAL DESIGN PROCESS

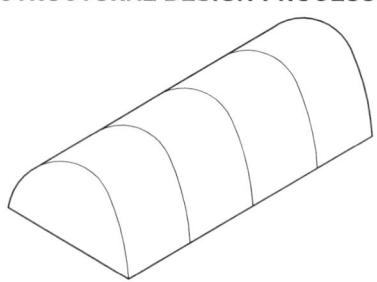

RIGID FRAME BARREL

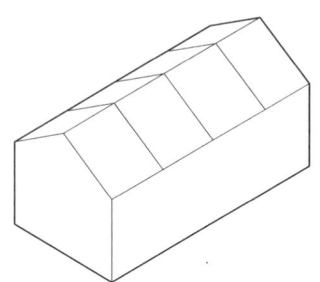

RIGID FRAME GABLE

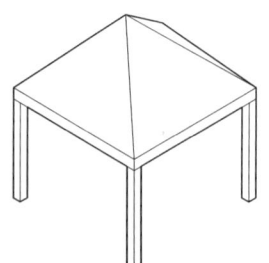

RIGID FRAME PYRAMID

RIGID FRAME MEMBRANE STRUCTURES

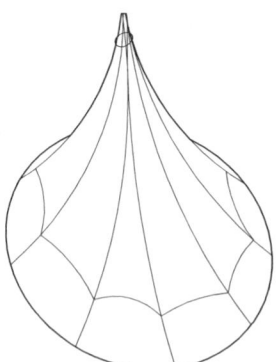

FOLDED PLATE TENSILE

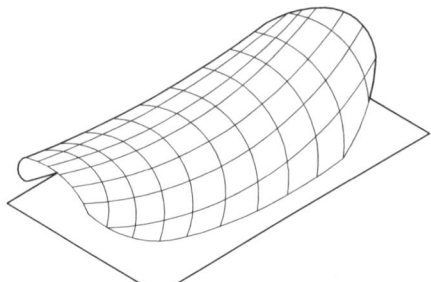

HYPERBOLIC PARABOLOID

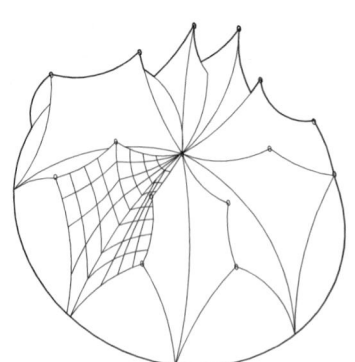

CONE-SHAPED TENSILE

RADIAL FOLDED PLATE

SELF-SUPPORTING MEMBRANE STRUCTURES

Industrial Fabrics Association; Roseville, Minnesota
Adapted with permission from *Architectural Fabric Structures: The Use of Tension Fabric Structures by Federal Agencies* (Washington: National Academy Press, 1985).
Kathleen O'Meara; OM Architecture; Baltimore, Maryland

 PRE-ENGINEERED STRUCTURES

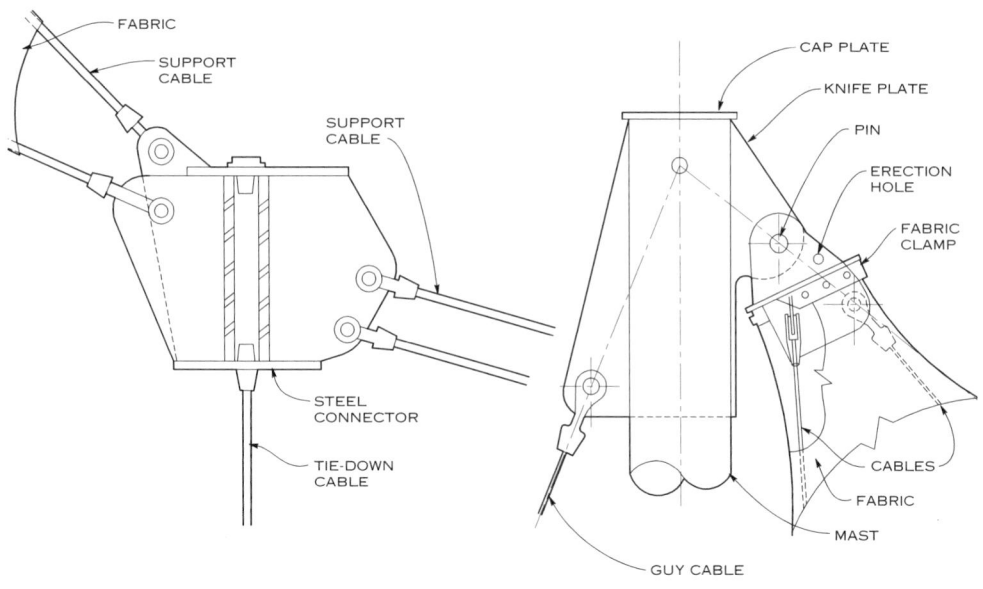

TIE-DOWN SECTION

ALTERNATE EXTERIOR MAST TOP DETAIL

FABRIC STRUCTURE ANCHORAGE DETAILS

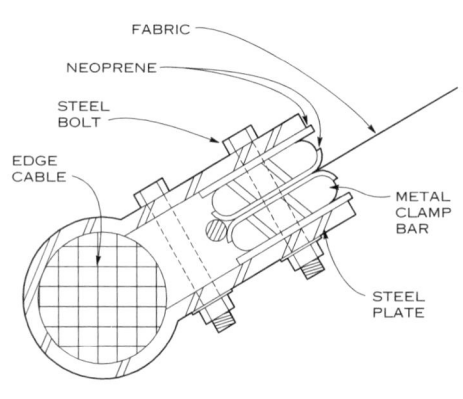

EDGE OR CATENARY CABLE ATTACHMENT DETAIL

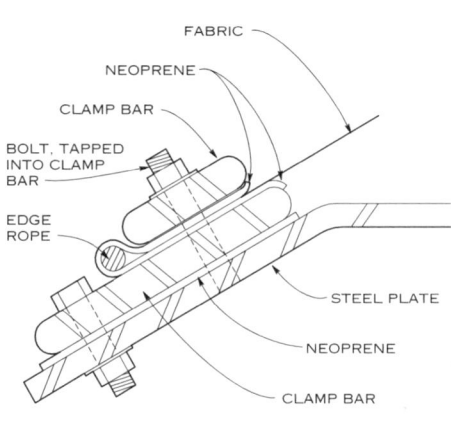

FABRIC EDGE CLAMP ATTACHMENT DETAIL

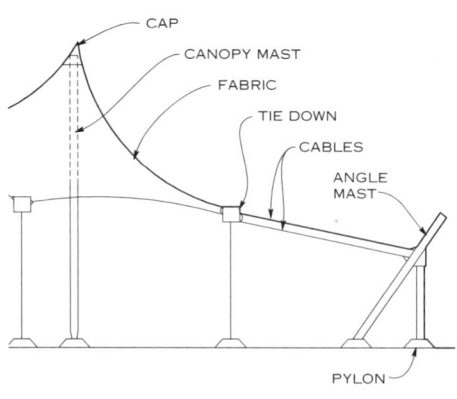

TYPICAL CONE-SHAPED TENSILE FABRIC STRUCTURE

GENERAL

The two primary ways of attaching fabric to anchorages are with edge catenary cables or clamps. Catenaries allow free-form design. When a tighter connection between fabric and building structure is required (e.g., on roofs, skylights, and air structures), a clamp system is used, in which the fabric is sandwiched between clamping bars or plates, which are bolted to the structure. Some membrane structures use both kinds of attachment. Air structures sometimes have sleeves and cables plus a fabric closure panel that extends beyond the cable.

Tensile structures usually are custom designed, and anchoring and connection details are customized also. However, basics, such as clamping systems, have become more standardized. Some frame and connection materials have been adapted from other industries, such as space frames and marine rigging. To determine the appropriate design aesthetic for a project, consider the following aspects:

1. Tensile structures are flexible, and the details must be designed to move under loads.
2. Tensile structures weigh a fraction of the amount of other buildings, and many of the materials are translucent.
3. Lateral forces play a much greater role in tensile structures than in conventional structures.

4. Make sure the physical resolution of each element's force vector (the angle of direction and magnitude) is accurate.
5. Details, material specifications, and reaction forces affecting interfacing structures should be developed with a consulting engineer or a design/build firm with the ability to design such structures.

RELATIVE FABRIC CHARACTERISTICS

FABRIC TYPE	STRENGTH	DIMENSIONAL STABILITY	FIRE RATING	DURABILITY	RESISTANCE TO SOILING	SOLAR TRANSMISSION	COST	TYPICAL USES	LIFE SPAN	REMARKS
PVC-coated polyester	5	3	3	3	3	2	4	Temporary to semipermanent	3–15 years	Large selection of products; top coatings are required for durability, can enhance appearance, and provide improved UV and fire resistance
PVC polyester scrim laminate	2	2	2	1	1	2	5	Temporary	1 year	Limited applications in architecture
PVC-coated fiberglass	4	4	4	3	3	2	3	Temporary to permanent	5–15 years	Limited availability; can be produced to order
PVC-coated Kevlar	5	3	3	3	2	2	2	Semipermanent	5–10 years	Kevlar has strength and durability but is UV sensitive; seams generally hand-sewn
PTFE-coated fiberglass	4	5	5	5	5	4	1	Permanent	25 years or more	Most durable material, now with a 25-year record of use
Silicon-coated fiberglass	3	5	5	4	2	5	2	Semipermanent to permanent	20 years	Seam strength has been a weakness
PTFE fiberglass laminate	3	5	5	5	4	5	1	Semipermanent to permanent	20 years	Relatively new material

Source: Geiger Engineers, Suffern, New York

NOTES

1. Relative comparisons are based on a scale from 0-5, with 0 a poor rating and 5 a very good one. The ratings are intended to provide a general relative comparison of the materials listed.

2. For the cost rating, the least expensive material has the highest rating.
3. All materials listed are composites. Generally, the material strength is provided by a scrim or woven textile that has been sealed and protected with a coating or film.

4. Plastic, PVC, and polyester materials are subject to degradation from ultraviolet (UV) light, while glass fabrics and scrims are degraded by prolonged contact with moisture.

David Campbell; Geiger Engineers; Suffern, New York

BUILDING TYPES AND WIDTHS

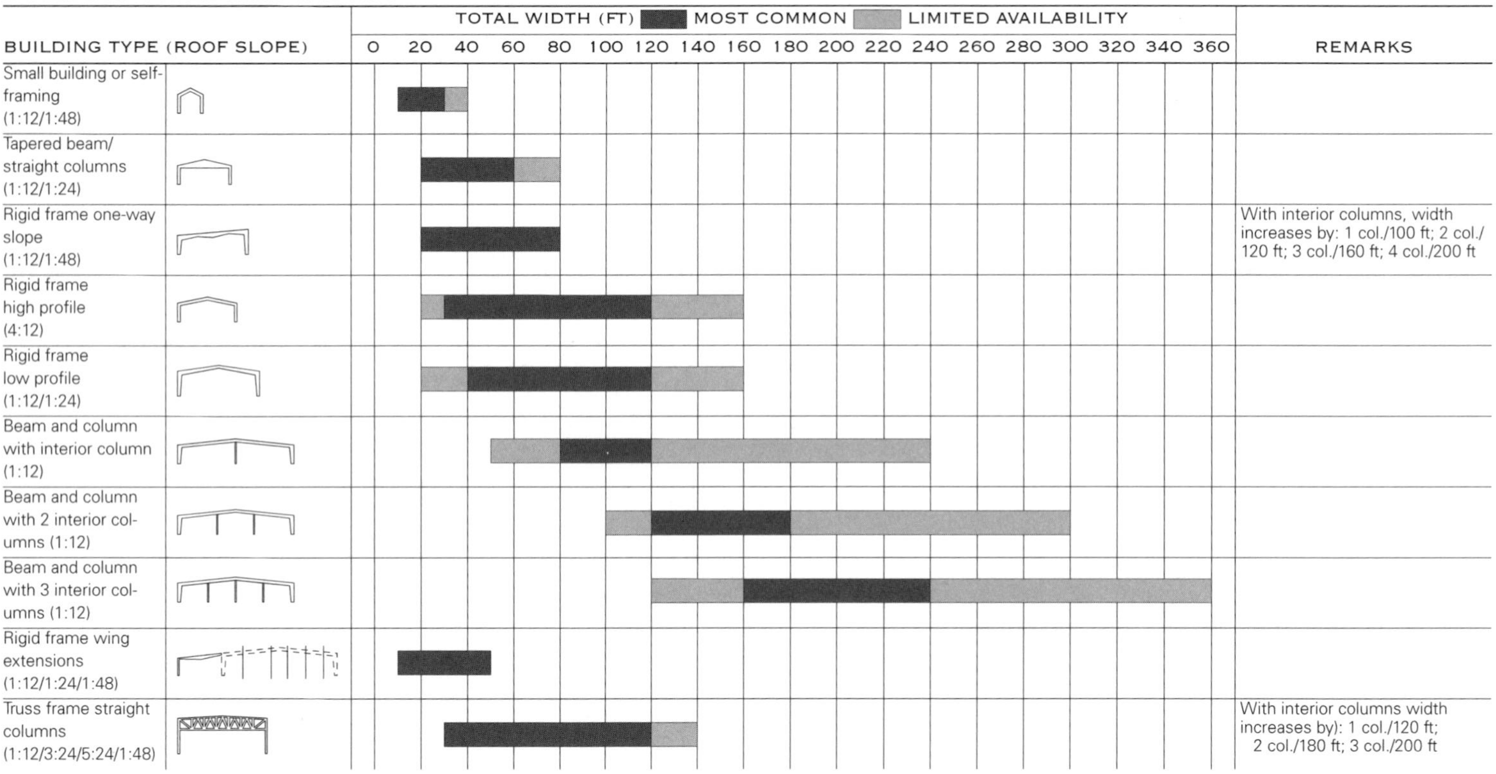

BUILDING TYPE (ROOF SLOPE)	Approx. width range (ft) — ■ MOST COMMON / ▨ LIMITED AVAILABILITY	REMARKS
Small building or self-framing (1:12/1:48)	Most common ~20–40	
Tapered beam/straight columns (1:12/1:24)	Most common ~40–60; limited ~60–80	
Rigid frame one-way slope (1:12/1:48)	Most common ~40–100	With interior columns, width increases by: 1 col./100 ft; 2 col./120 ft; 3 col./160 ft; 4 col./200 ft
Rigid frame high profile (4:12)	Limited ~30–40; most common ~40–120; limited ~120–160	
Rigid frame low profile (1:12/1:24)	Limited ~40–60; most common ~60–120; limited ~120–160	
Beam and column with interior column (1:12)	Limited ~60–100; most common ~100–120; limited ~120–220	
Beam and column with 2 interior columns (1:12)	Limited ~120–140; most common ~140–180; limited ~180–300	
Beam and column with 3 interior columns (1:12)	Limited ~160–220; most common ~220–260; limited ~260–360	
Rigid frame wing extensions (1:12/1:24/1:48)	Most common ~20–60	
Truss frame straight columns (1:12/3:24/5:24/1:48)	Most common ~60–140; limited ~140–160	With interior columns width increases by): 1 col./120 ft; 2 col./180 ft; 3 col./200 ft

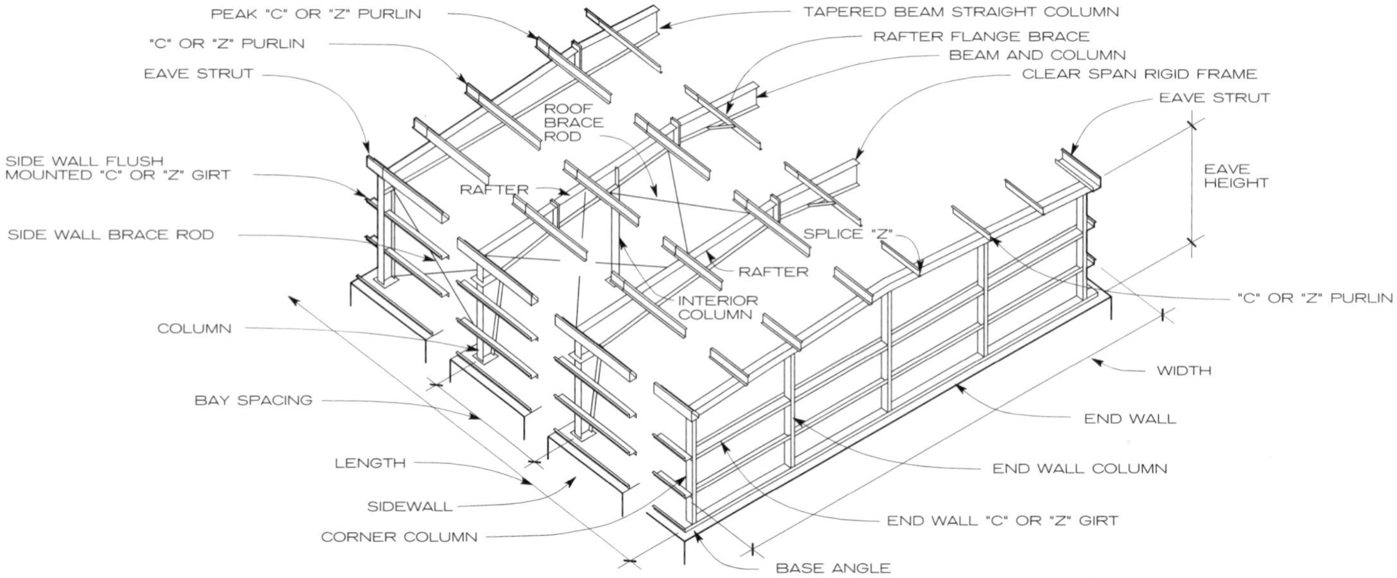

Width scale markers: 0, 20, 40, 60, 80, 100, 120, 140, 160, 180, 200, 220, 240, 260, 280, 300, 320, 340, 360

Framing isometric diagram labels:
PEAK "C" OR "Z" PURLIN · "C" OR "Z" PURLIN · EAVE STRUT · SIDE WALL FLUSH MOUNTED "C" OR "Z" GIRT · SIDE WALL BRACE ROD · COLUMN · BAY SPACING · LENGTH · SIDEWALL · CORNER COLUMN · ROOF BRACE ROD · RAFTER · INTERIOR COLUMN · RAFTER · BASE ANGLE · TAPERED BEAM STRAIGHT COLUMN · RAFTER FLANGE BRACE · BEAM AND COLUMN · CLEAR SPAN RIGID FRAME · EAVE STRUT · EAVE HEIGHT · SPLICE "Z" · "C" OR "Z" PURLIN · WIDTH · END WALL · END WALL COLUMN · END WALL "C" OR "Z" GIRT

FRAMING SYSTEMS COMPONENTS

DEFINITIONS

Pre-engineered metal buildings are available in standard framing sizes and types from various manufacturers. The following definitions are those used by the metal building industry:

BAY refers to the dimension along a wall between the centerlines of wall columns and the dimension from the outside of an end wall corner column to the centerline of the first adjacent wall column. Spacings range from 18 to 30 ft, with 20 to 25 ft most common.

WIDTH is measured from the surface of the outside wall girts. Inside clearance varies.

EAVE HEIGHT is measured from the bottom of a wall column to the top of an eave strut. Nominal 2-ft increments vary from 10 to 30 ft.

LOADS, other than those provided by the manufacturer, should be specified during the structural design phase.

Future additional loads also should be considered. Roof live loads are those loads, including snow load, exerted on a roof except dead, wind, and lateral loads. Commonly available in 12, 20, or 40 psf. Dead load is the weight of all permanent roof framing and covering materials only and varies with the manufacturer.

LATERAL LOADS are dead loads other than the metal building framing, such as sprinklers, mechanical and electrical systems, and ceilings. They are commonly available in 15, 20, or 25 psf.

WIND LOAD is loading caused by the wind blowing from any horizontal direction. Site and atmospheric conditions needing special consideration should be specified.

SEISMIC LOAD is required for earthquake zones and must be specified for individual designs.

AUXILIARY LOADS are dynamic live loads other than basic design loads, such as cranes, materials handling systems, and impact loads.

DIAGONAL BRACING normally is required in the plane of the columns and beams in one or more bays to prevent racking and to resist lateral loading perpendicular to the span of the frames.

GIRTS are horizontal structural members that transmit lateral loads (pressure and suction) from the exterior walls to the columns. Sag rods may be needed to support the girts about the weak axis and to achieve design economy.

ANCHOR BOLTS are necessary to resist reactions at column bases. Foundations must be designed for reactions transmitted by the column bases and anchor bolts.

NOTE

The user should verify that individual manufacturer's standard practice and any special design considerations meet or exceed established engineering principles, local practice, and applicable building codes.

Robert P. Burns, AIA; Burns and Burns, Architects; Iowa City, Iowa

 PRE-ENGINEERED STRUCTURES

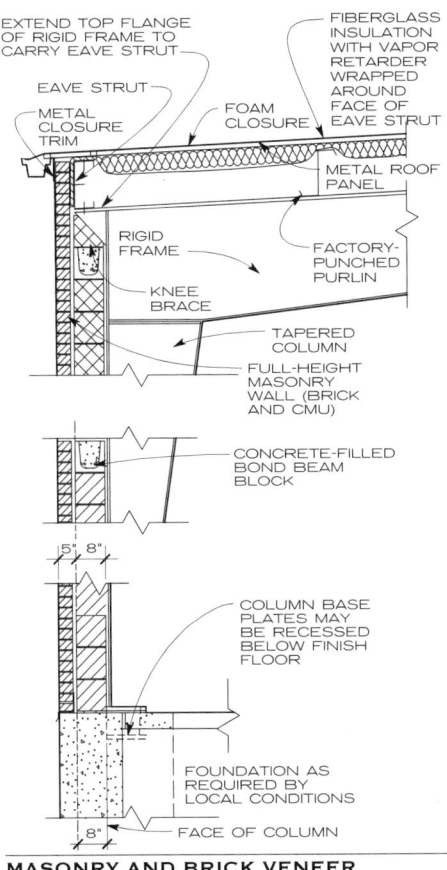

EXTEND TOP FLANGE OF RIGID FRAME TO CARRY EAVE STRUT

EAVE STRUT

METAL CLOSURE TRIM

FOAM CLOSURE

FIBERGLASS INSULATION WITH VAPOR RETARDER WRAPPED AROUND FACE OF EAVE STRUT

METAL ROOF PANEL

RIGID FRAME

KNEE BRACE

FACTORY-PUNCHED PURLIN

TAPERED COLUMN

FULL-HEIGHT MASONRY WALL (BRICK AND CMU)

CONCRETE-FILLED BOND BEAM BLOCK

5" 8"

COLUMN BASE PLATES MAY BE RECESSED BELOW FINISH FLOOR

FOUNDATION AS REQUIRED BY LOCAL CONDITIONS

8"

FACE OF COLUMN

MASONRY AND BRICK VENEER WALL SECTION

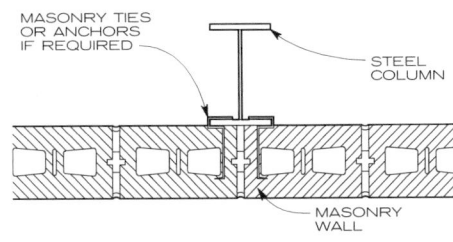

MASONRY TIES OR ANCHORS IF REQUIRED

STEEL COLUMN

MASONRY WALL

BOND-BEAM BLOCK TO COLUMN CONNECTION

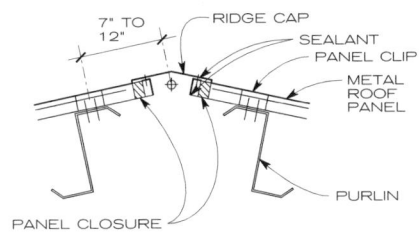

7" TO 12"

RIDGE CAP

SEALANT

PANEL CLIP

METAL ROOF PANEL

PANEL CLOSURE

PURLIN

RIDGE DETAIL

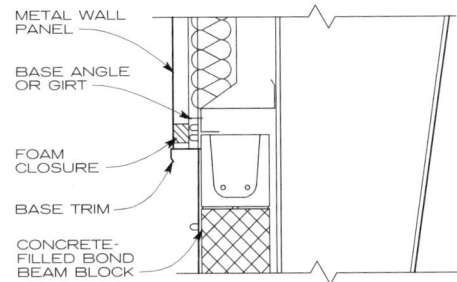

METAL WALL PANEL

BASE ANGLE OR GIRT

FOAM CLOSURE

BASE TRIM

CONCRETE-FILLED BOND BEAM BLOCK

MASONRY WALL AND METAL PANEL CONNECTION

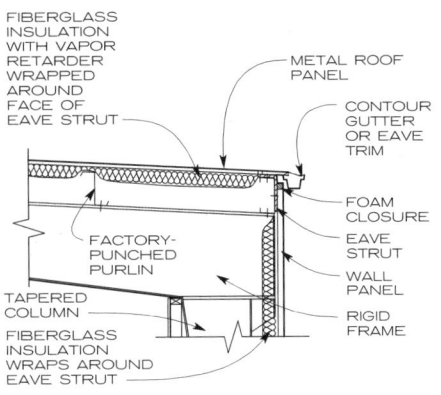

FIBERGLASS INSULATION WITH VAPOR RETARDER WRAPPED AROUND FACE OF EAVE STRUT

METAL ROOF PANEL

CONTOUR GUTTER OR EAVE TRIM

FOAM CLOSURE

EAVE STRUT

WALL PANEL

RIGID FRAME

FACTORY-PUNCHED PURLIN

TAPERED COLUMN

FIBERGLASS INSULATION WRAPS AROUND EAVE STRUT

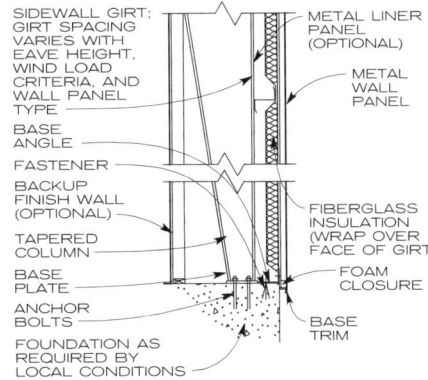

SIDEWALL GIRT; GIRT SPACING VARIES WITH EAVE HEIGHT, WIND LOAD CRITERIA, AND WALL PANEL TYPE

BASE ANGLE

FASTENER

BACKUP FINISH WALL (OPTIONAL)

TAPERED COLUMN

BASE PLATE

ANCHOR BOLTS

FOUNDATION AS REQUIRED BY LOCAL CONDITIONS

METAL LINER PANEL (OPTIONAL)

METAL WALL PANEL

FIBERGLASS INSULATION (WRAP OVER FACE OF GIRT)

FOAM CLOSURE

BASE TRIM

NOTE

A sidewall girt may be inset between columns, attached by clip angles to the steel frame.

METAL WALL PANEL SECTION

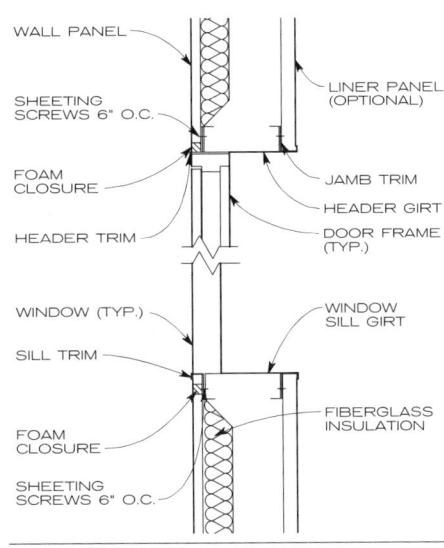

WALL PANEL

SHEETING SCREWS 6" O.C.

FOAM CLOSURE

HEADER TRIM

WINDOW (TYP.)

SILL TRIM

FOAM CLOSURE

SHEETING SCREWS 6" O.C.

LINER PANEL (OPTIONAL)

JAMB TRIM

HEADER GIRT

DOOR FRAME (TYP.)

WINDOW SILL GIRT

FIBERGLASS INSULATION

DOOR/WINDOW HEAD AND SILL DETAIL

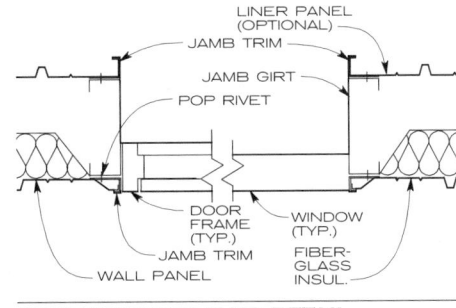

LINER PANEL (OPTIONAL)

JAMB TRIM

JAMB GIRT

POP RIVET

DOOR FRAME (TYP.)

JAMB TRIM

WALL PANEL

WINDOW (TYP.)

FIBER-GLASS INSUL.

DOOR/WINDOW JAMB DETAIL

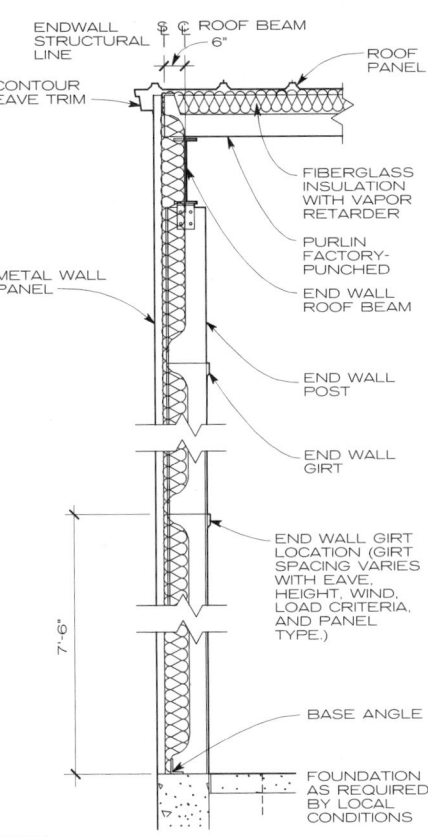

ENDWALL STRUCTURAL LINE

$ $ C ROOF BEAM

6"

ROOF PANEL

CONTOUR EAVE TRIM

METAL WALL PANEL

FIBERGLASS INSULATION WITH VAPOR RETARDER

PURLIN FACTORY-PUNCHED

END WALL ROOF BEAM

END WALL POST

END WALL GIRT

END WALL GIRT LOCATION (GIRT SPACING VARIES WITH EAVE, HEIGHT, WIND, LOAD CRITERIA, AND PANEL TYPE.)

BASE ANGLE

7'-6"

FOUNDATION AS REQUIRED BY LOCAL CONDITIONS

NOTE

Column face is approximately 1 in. inside the structural line.

END WALL CONDITION SECTION

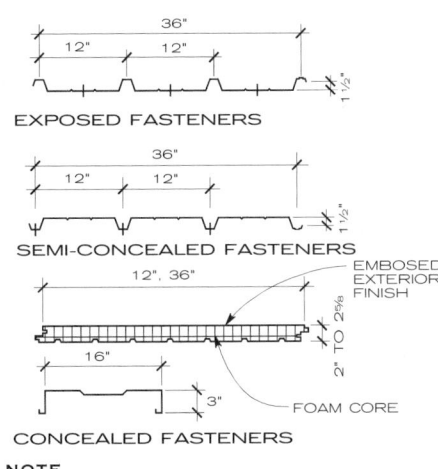

36"

12"   12"

EXPOSED FASTENERS

1½"

36"

12"   12"

SEMI-CONCEALED FASTENERS

1½"

12", 36"

EMBOSED EXTERIOR FINISH

16"

2" TO 2⅝"

3"

FOAM CORE

CONCEALED FASTENERS

NOTE

Wall panels are installed vertically, in lengths, typically up to 40 ft. Finishes include painted metal with smooth or textured finish.

WALL PANEL TYPES

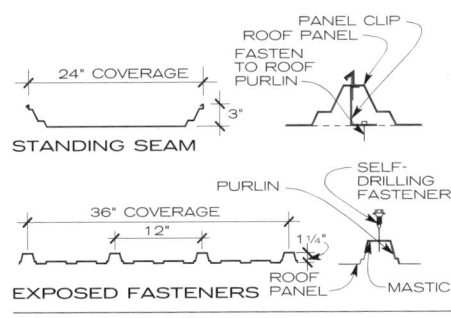

24" COVERAGE

3"

STANDING SEAM

PANEL CLIP ROOF PANEL

FASTEN TO ROOF PURLIN

36" COVERAGE

12"

1¼"

PURLIN

SELF-DRILLING FASTENER

ROOF PANEL

MASTIC

EXPOSED FASTENERS

ROOF PANEL TYPES

Robert P. Burns, AIA; Burns & Burns, Architects; Iowa City, Iowa

PRE-ENGINEERED STRUCTURES 13

EXPLOSION PREVENTION

Accidental ignition of flammable solids, liquids, and gases can best be prevented by eliminating potential flammable materials and sparks or flames. Use hard-finish surfaces of inert, spark-resistant, nonflammable materials. Dust and debris constitute a hazard: Hooded dust-collection systems and sloping horizontal surfaces, coved bases, and coved indoor corners can help.

Provisions should be made for containing spilled liquids and solids. For flammable gases, provide ventilation for health safety and prevention of concentrated vapors. Provide explosion-proof electrical devices and grounding systems in accordance with the NEC, NFPA, and insurance underwriters' requirements.

EXPLOSION SUPPRESSION

Explosion suppression is a specialized application in which an extinguishing agent snuffs out an explosion in its developing stages. Explosion detection systems detect the pressure rise associated with an explosion and immediately discharge extinguishing or suppression agents.

From start to finish, the entire detection/extinguishing process may take only 65/1000 of a second, which limits application to very small confined areas. Ideal applications include the interiors of tanks, hoppers, ductwork, or other equipment containing explosive concentrations of vapors, dust, and powders. Refer to NFPA 69.

SPECIAL EXTINGUISHING SYSTEMS

Automatic fire suppression and extinguishing systems are permanent building installations that protect a structure, its contents, and its occupants against the hazards of fire and explosion. The nature and magnitude of the hazard dictate the extinguishing agent and system configuration to be used. Extinguishing agents include water, clean agent, carbon dioxide, foam, and dry chemicals. Systems may be either total flooding or local application types.

Total flooding systems consist of an extinguishing agent, distribution piping, discharge nozzles, detection devices, alarms, and controls in sufficient supply to reach a mandated concentration of agent within an enclosed space.

Local application systems consist of those components listed above but are designed to direct extinguishing agents to achieve calculated surface coverages of hazardous areas.

CLEAN AGENT SYSTEMS

Clean agent refers to EPA-approved, electrically nonconducting, volatile, or gaseous fire extinguishment that does not leave a residue upon evaporation.

Clean agent systems extinguish a fire by lowering oxygen content. Since such systems cause no water damage and leave no residue, they are ideal for protecting valuable records and electronic equipment. Clean agent systems can be discharged in occupied areas, allowing time for orderly shutdown of equipment and evacuation.

The relatively high cost of clean agent systems mandates their use to protect confined areas such as storage vaults, tape libraries or computer rooms, and spaces under floors.

A typical total-flooding clean agent installation consists of storage cylinders, distribution piping, discharge nozzles, detectors (heat, smoke, UV), and alarms. Interfaces among the clean agent extinguishing system, HVAC equipment, and electrical equipment are required to ensure adequate shutdown during alarm conditions. Special construction of doors, door closers, partitions, and ceilings is necessary to make space as airtight as possible.

Because clean agent systems are depleted totally upon discharge, backup or redundant storage cylinders may be required while the system is being serviced and recharged. Local codes or underwriting agencies may require sprinkler backup in areas protected by clean agent within sprinklered buildings. Refer to NFPA 2001.

DRY CHEMICAL SYSTEMS

Dry chemical, powderlike products are available for use as extinguishing agents. Although effective against flammable liquid fires and electrical fires, dry chemical systems can cause extensive cleanup problems and may damage sensitive electronic components or equipment. For these reasons, the most common use of dry chemical systems is for local applications over relatively small areas such as cooking surfaces, dip tanks, and spray booths.

CARBON DIOXIDE SYSTEMS

Carbon dioxide (CO_2) is suitable for extinguishing flammable liquid fires and fires involving energized electrical equipment. CO_2 systems extinguish fire by reducing the concentrations of oxygen in the air, the vapor phase of the fuel, or both to the point where combustion stops. These systems are generally used in unoccupied areas or places where an electrically nonconductive medium is essential: electrical equipment rooms, transformers, vaults, or areas containing rotating equipment or flammable liquids. Types include local flooding, local application, hand hose line, and standpipe systems.

Personnel hazards such as suffocation and reduced visibility due to fogging during and after discharge must be considered in the application of total flooding CO_2 systems. Such systems must allow for total evacuation of the area prior to discharge and incorporate audible predischarge alarms. Local application systems usually are installed in confined areas such as restaurant range hoods, open top tanks, and printing presses. Activation of CO_2 systems may be automatic or manual.

In general, large systems requiring a lot of CO_2 use low-pressure storage systems for outside installation, while systems requiring small CO_2 quantities can use high-pressure storage cylinders inside the building.

Natural leakage occurring around doors, windows, and dampers generally provides sufficient venting of CO_2 from rooms, ductwork, and equipment enclosures after discharge; therefore, special venting considerations are required only in gas-tight enclosures. Refer to NFPA 12.

FOAM SYSTEMS

Foaming agents used for fire protection fall into one of three major classes: low-, medium-, and high-expansion foams, as determined by foam-to-solution volume ratios.

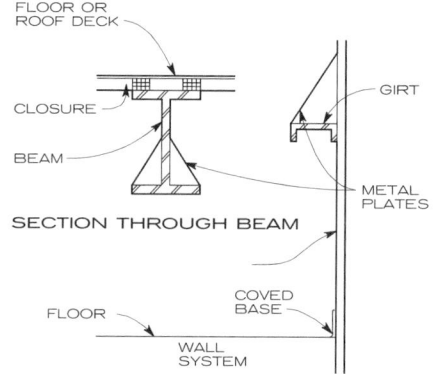

SECTION THROUGH BEAM

SECTION THROUGH WALL

MINIMIZING ACCUMULATION OF FLAMMABLE SOLIDS

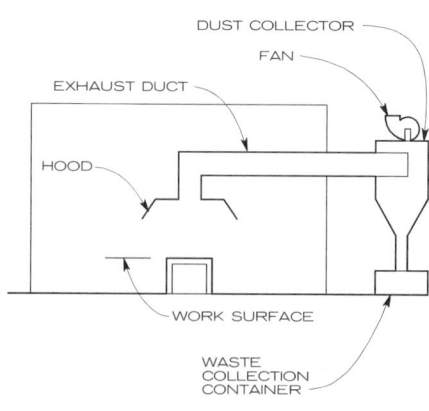

LOCALIZED DUST COLLECTION

Foam provides a unique agent for total flooding of confined spaces, transporting water to otherwise inaccessible places, and for volumetric displacement of vapor, heat, and smoke.

Foam is used principally to form a floating blanket on flammable or combustible liquids, preventing or extinguishing fire by excluding air and cooling the fuel. It also prevents reignition by suppressing formation of flammable vapors. Film coating characteristics of fire-fighting foams also provide a measure of protection from adjacent fires.

Foam-type fire suppression systems may consist of portable foam-generating equipment with hand-held nozzles or may involve fixed applications for the protection of entire facilities. Liquid fuel storage and unloading facilities and aircraft hangars and fueling areas often employ foam systems. High-expansion foams have proved effective in high-rack storage areas. Refer to NFPA Chapters 11 and 11A.

EXPLOSION VENTING

Explosion venting, required in many high-hazard occupancies, provides a relief area to the building exterior, thereby controlling the direction of a blast. The vent relief area is governed by the pressure resistance of the non-relieving portions of the building.

The relief area may be walls of lightweight material, lightly fastened hatch covers, lightly fastened outward swinging doors in exterior walls, and lightly fastened walls or roofs. Venting devices are normally designed to release at a maximum internal pressure of 20 psf, and the remaining walls, roof, and floors are designed to withstand a minimum internal pressure of 100 psf. Refer to building codes, NFPA 68, and insurance underwriters' guidelines for specific requirements and design guidelines.

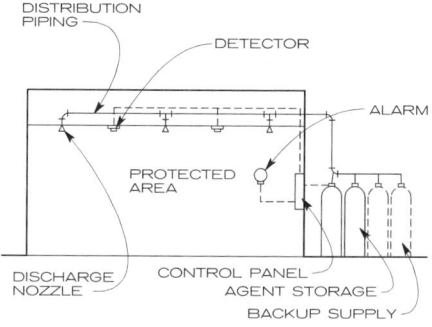

TOTAL FLOODING EXTINGUISHING SYSTEM

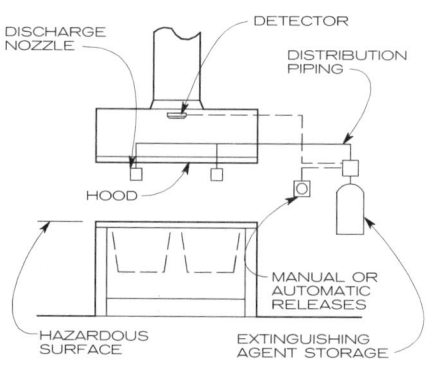

LOCAL APPLICATION EXTINGUISHING SYSTEM

Lockwood Greene; Atlanta, Georgia

FIRE SUPPRESSION AND SUPERVISORY SYSTEMS

GENERAL

An elevator system is a major building component and as such must be carefully considered throughout the design process. Decisions about the number, size, speed, and type of elevators for an installation are based on a number of factors, including the handling capacity and quality of service desired. Proper selection also depends on the type of tenancy, number of occupants, and building design (number of floors, floor heights, building circulation, and other factors). In addition, passenger elevators on accessible routes should comply with the requirements of the Americans with Disabilities Act Accessibility Guidelines (ADAAG).

Consult representatives of the elevator industry or elevator engineers during the decision-making process to ensure selection of the most suitable elevator system for an application. Because elevator installation is highly regulated, it is advisable to consult local code officials.

Elevators should be located where they can provide efficient, easily reached service. As well, the operational systems (hoistway pit and machine room) and passenger spaces (lobby and elevator car) must be accommodated.

ELEVATOR SYSTEMS

An elevator system includes a hoistway, machine room, elevator car, and waiting lobbies.

HOISTWAY

The hoistway is a vertical shaft for the travel of one or more elevators. It includes a pit and usually terminates at the underside of the machine room in a traction system and at the underside of the roof over the hoistway in a hydraulic system. Access to the elevator car and hoistway is normally through hoistway doors at each floor serviced by the elevator system. Hoistway design is determined by the characteristics of the elevator system selected and by applicable code requirements for fire separation, ventilation, soundproofing, and nonstructural elements.

MACHINE ROOM FOR TRACTION ELEVATOR

The machine room for a traction elevator is usually located directly above the hoistway but could also be situated below, to the side, or to the rear of it. The machine room contains elevator hoisting machinery and electronic control equipment. Adequate ventilation, soundproofing, and structural support for the elevator must be supplied. Also, the machine room must have a self-closing, self-locking access door. Local codes may forbid placement of electrical or mechanical equipment not associated with the elevator in the machine room.

MACHINE ROOM FOR HYDRAULIC ELEVATOR

Normally located near the base of the hoistway, a machine room for hydraulic elevators contains a hydraulic pump unit

and electronic controls. Provisions should be made for adequate ventilation and soundproofing, and the room must have a self-closing, self-locking access door. Local codes may forbid placement of electrical or mechanical equipment not associated with the elevator in the machine room.

ELEVATOR CAR

Guided by vertical rails on each side, the elevator car conveys passengers or freight between floors. It is constructed within a supporting platform and frame. Design of the car focuses on ceiling, wall, floor, and door finishes and accompanying lighting, ventilation, and elevator signal equipment.

The car and frame of a hydraulic elevator system are supported by a piston or cylinder.

The car and frame of a traction elevator system are supported by the hoist machine. The elevator and its counterweight are connected with steel ropes.

LOBBIES

Elevator waiting areas are designed to allow free circulation of passengers, rapid access to elevator cars, and clearly visible elevator signals. All elevator lobbies must be enclosed with the exception of that at the entry level of the main building.

ELEVATOR TYPES

HYDRAULIC ELEVATORS use an oil hydraulic driving machine to raise and lower the elevator car and its load. Lower speeds and the piston length restrict the use of this system to heights of approximately 55 ft. Although it generally requires the least initial installation expense, this elevator type requires more power to operate.

TRACTION ELEVATORS are power elevators in which the energy is applied by means of an electric driving machine. Medium to high speeds and virtually limitless rise allow this elevator type to serve high-rise, medium-rise, and low-rise buildings.

GEARED TRACTION ELEVATOR SYSTEMS are designed to operate within the range of 100 to 450 ft/min, restricting their use to medium-rise buildings.

GEARLESS TRACTION ELEVATOR SYSTEMS are available in preengineered units with speeds of 500 to 1200 ft/min. They offer the advantages of a long life and a smooth ride.

SERVICE ELEVATORS in industrial, residential, and commercial buildings are often standard passenger elevator packages modified for service use.

FREIGHT ELEVATORS are usually classed as general freight loading, motor vehicle loading, industrial truck, or concentrated loading elevators. General freight loading elevators may be electric drum type or traction or hydraulic elevators.

PRIVATE RESIDENTIAL ELEVATORS may be installed only in a private residence or to serve a single unit in a building with multiple dwelling units. By code, elevators in private residences are limited in size, capacity, rise, and speed.

BUILDING CHARACTERISTICS

Physical building characteristics (such as building height and hoistway location) are considered with population characteristics to determine the size, speed, type, and location of elevator systems. Characteristics that particularly affect the elevator systems are

1. Height: Determine the distance of elevator travel from lowest terminal to top terminal, the number of floors, and the floor height.
2. Building use: Identify the location of heavily used building entrance areas, such as those leading to cafeterias, restaurants, auditoriums, and service areas. Typically, plan a building so that no prospective passengers must walk more than 200 ft to reach an elevator.

The elevator selection process must begin with a thorough analysis of how people will occupy the building. Four issues are pertinent:

1. Total population and density: Determine this figure for each floor.
2. Peak loading: Identify the periods when elevators will carry the highest traffic loads.
3. Waiting time: This is the length of time a passenger is expected to wait for the next elevator to arrive.
4. Demand for quality: Smooth operation may be as important as fancy finishes.

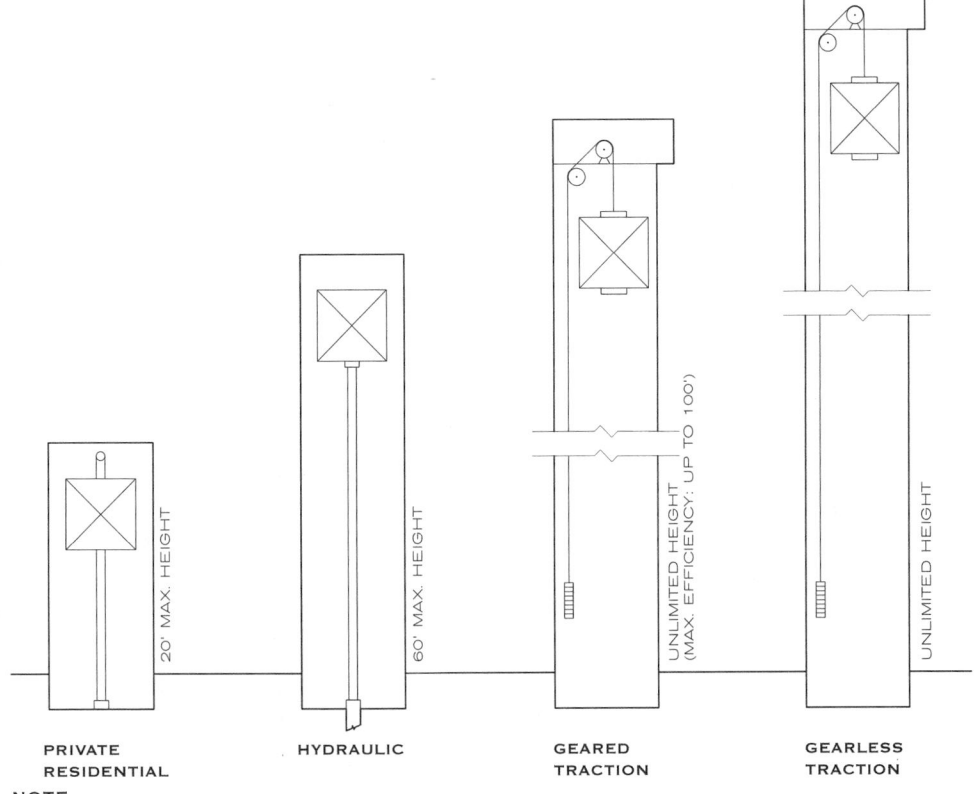

| | PRIVATE RESIDENTIAL | HYDRAULIC | GEARED TRACTION | GEARLESS TRACTION |

NOTE

These dimensions are general guidelines for selecting an elevator using height as a criterion.

ELEVATOR TYPES

ELEVATOR TYPES BY USE

| NEED/USE | ELEVATOR TYPE | | | |
	PRIVATE RESIDENTIAL	HYDRAULIC	GEARED TRACTION	GEARLESS TRACTION
Private houses	X			
Low-rise, low speed		X		
Medium-rise, moderate speed			X	
High-rise, high speed				X
Low initial cost		X		
No penthouse, lightweight construction		X		
Freight, low-rise		X	X	
Freight, high-rise			X	

Rippeteau Rollins Architecture + Design; Washington, D.C.

GENERAL

Guidelines for selecting an elevator for a private residence can be simplified to a few parameters. By code, residential elevators are limited in size, capacity, rise, and speed and can be installed only in a private residence or in a multiple dwelling as a means of access to a single residence. Preengineered systems generally offer only a few options for speed, capacity, aesthetic design, and electronic controls.

BUILDING POPULATION analysis involves identifying the needs of prospective users. Relevant information includes the type of expected occupancy (mixed or single occupancy and whether the elevator must accommodate an unassisted wheelchair user), the number of passengers expected to occupy the elevator in one trip, and elevator service in a given time period.

BUILDING CHARACTERISTICS affect elevator selection by establishing the building height (distance of elevator travel) and hoistway location. In private residences, the elevator may occupy a tier of closets, an exterior shaft, a room corner, or a stairwell.

ELEVATOR SYSTEMS FOR PRIVATE RESIDENTIAL USE

Two types of elevator systems are commonly used in private residences:

WINDING-DRUM MACHINE

This type of traction elevator employs a grooved drum around which the hoisting cable wraps as it operates. This elevator type does not require a counterweight or a machine room above the hoistway, making it more practical for small places than a standard traction system.

HYDRAULIC ELEVATOR

Hydraulic elevators in private residential use employ either a standard hole-less arrangement or a roped hydraulic machine. Both types eliminate major construction and drilling, making the system economical and an excellent selection for retrofit applications.

NOTES

1. DIMENSIONS: Dimensions may vary among manufacturers and according to the elevator system. Elevators carrying greater loads or operating at higher speeds require more clearance overhead and in pit areas. Elevator cars with higher interior clearances also require more overhead clearance in the hoistway.

   The dimensions given here are appropriate for most applications. For exact dimensions required in specific circumstances, consult manufacturers.

2. ELEVATOR CARS: Typical car sizes, A x B, are 36 x 36 in., 42 x 42 in., and 36 x 48 in. The maximum platform size allowed by the National Elevator Code for residential elevators, ANSI A17.1, is 12 sq ft; however, this platform size does not meet the National Handicapped Access Code, ANSI A117.1, for use by an unassisted wheelchair-bound person.

3. LOAD CAPACITY: The load capacity of drum-type machines is 500 lb; speed is 30 ft/min. The load capacity of traction and hydraulic machines is 750 lb; speed is 36 ft/min.

4. POWER SUPPLY: Elevators operate on a 220/230 volt, single-phase power supply. A disconnect switch must be provided within sight of the machine. A 110V, single-phase power supply is required to light the machine area of the hoistway.

5. HOISTWAY ENCLOSURES: Enclosures are recommended for all hoistways. The fire rating of these enclosures and the access doors must be consistent with the fire rating of the building. See local codes.

6. GUIDE RAILS: Manufacturers usually provide guide rails in 5-ft sections, although some manufacturers offer rails that can span the distance from floor structure to floor structure. If a third guide rail is required, it is supplied in 3 ft 4 in. sections.

   If an existing structure cannot support guide rails, manufacturers can provide a self-supporting elevator tower that transmits the load to its base. This tower requires increased horizontal clearance in the hoistway.

   Elevator cars can be provided with openings on two sides; when this option is employed, guide rails must be located accordingly. Consult manufacturers.

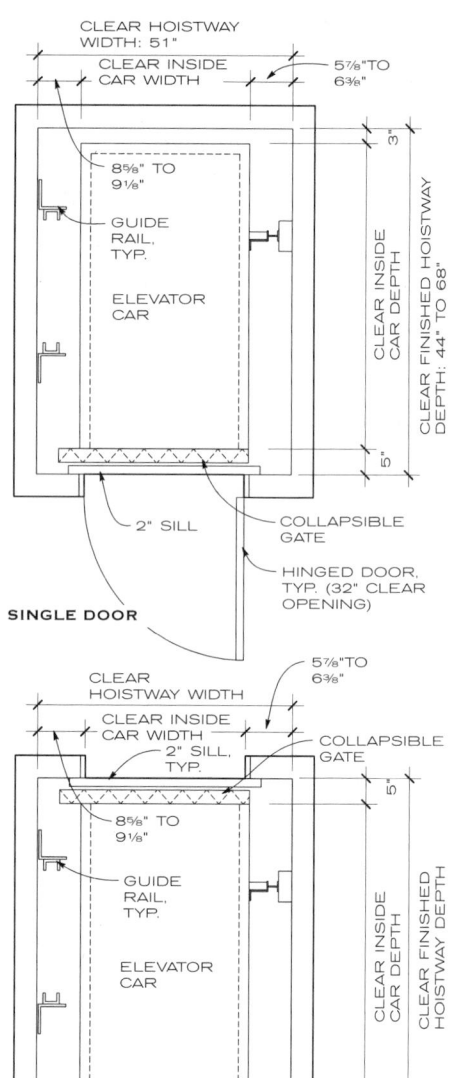

SINGLE DOOR

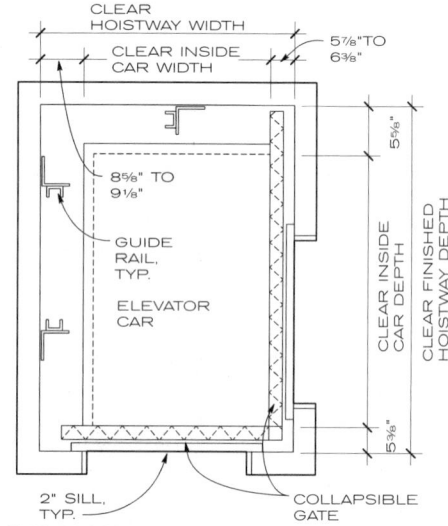

TWO DOORS—OPPOSITE SIDES

TWO DOORS—ADJACENT SIDES

NOTE

Standard car size is 36 in. wide x 48 in. deep x 80 in. high. Other car depths available are 36 in. and 60 in.

RESIDENTIAL ELEVATOR PLANS

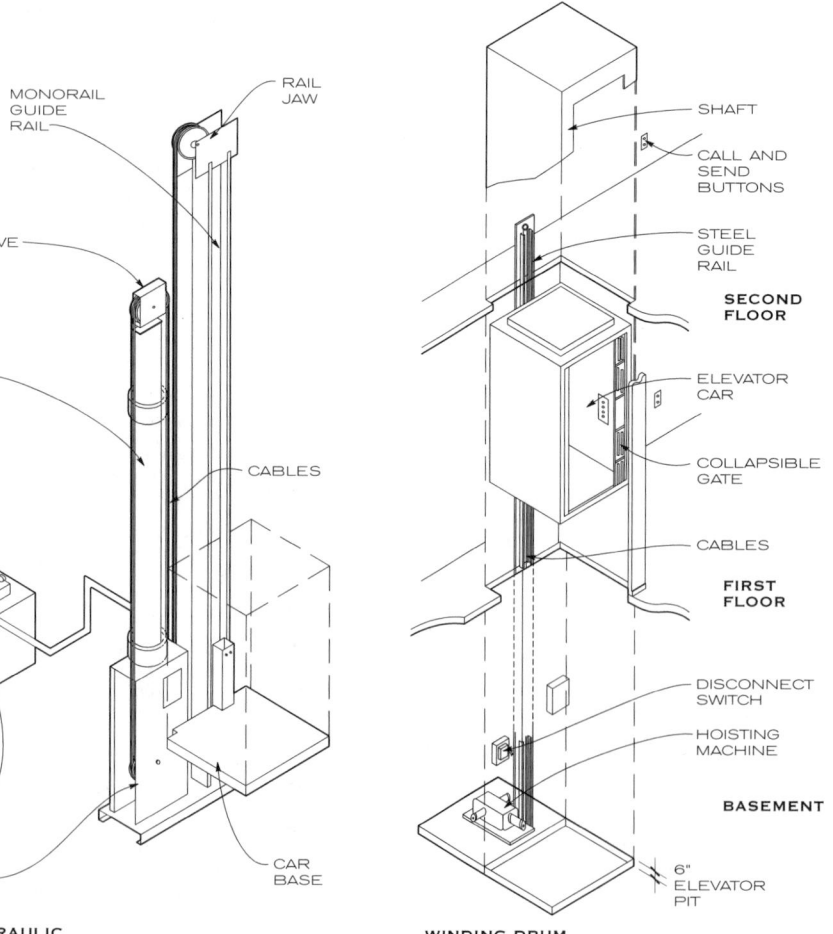

ROPED HYDRAULIC

WINDING-DRUM

ELEVATOR TYPES

Rippeteau Rollins Architecture + Design; Washington, D.C.

GENERAL

Medium- and high-rise buildings require geared traction and gearless traction elevator systems. The main difference between the two systems lies in travel speed. General design considerations involving hoistway, machine room, and elevator planning are similar.

Both geared and gearless drive units are governed by electronic controls, which coordinate car leveling, passenger calls, collective operation of elevators, door operation, car acceleration and deceleration, and safety applications. A broad range of control systems is available to meet individual building requirements.

Structural requirements call for the total weight of the elevator system to be supported by the machine beams and transmitted to the building (or hoistway) structure. Consult with elevator consultants and structural engineers.

NOTES

1. Pit depths, overhead clearances, and penthouse sizes should be in accordance with ASME requirements. Local codes may vary from these requirements.
2. All overhead dimensions for passenger elevators are based on standard 8-ft-high cabs.
3. Layout dimensions of the passenger elevator are based on center-opening entrances. Other types are available.
4. The machine room for traction elevators is usually located directly above the hoistway. Space must be provided for the elevator drive, electronic control equipment, and governor; provide sufficient clearance for equipment installation, repair, and removal. Adequate lighting and ventilation (temperature maintained between 65 and 100°F or 18 and 38°C are required by codes, and sound insulation should be provided. Machine room sizes may vary depending on number of cars, type of control, etc. Check with elevator consultant for requirements.
5. Check local codes for required fire enclosures.

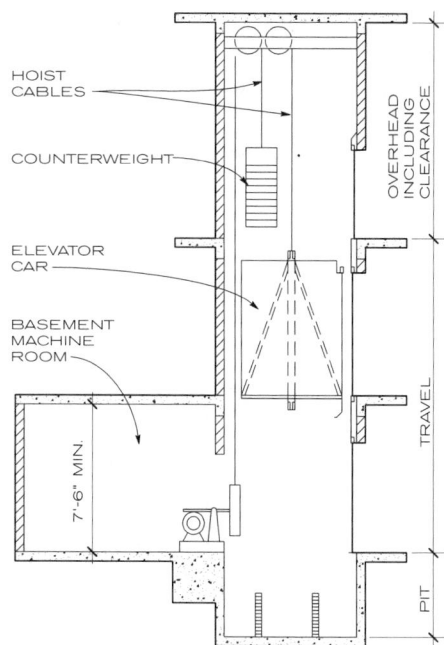

NOTE

This is a very specialized application, and consultation with experts is advised. Traction elevators with basement machine rooms are used in new and existing buildings where overhead clearance is limited.

TRACTION ELEVATOR WITH BASEMENT MACHINE ROOM

Rippeteau Rollins Architecture + Design; Washington, D.C.

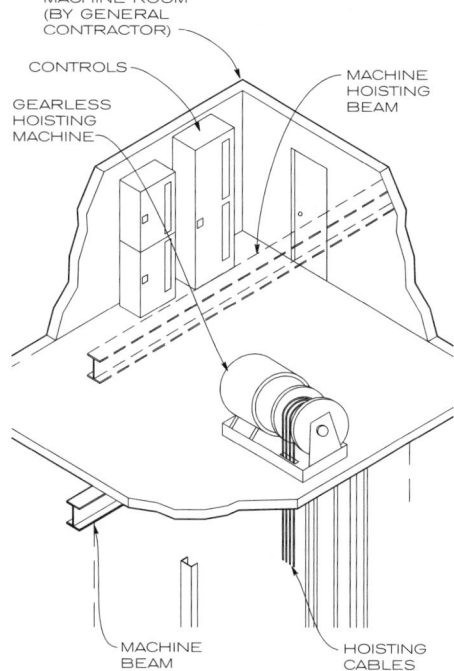

GEARLESS ELEVATOR MACHINE ROOM

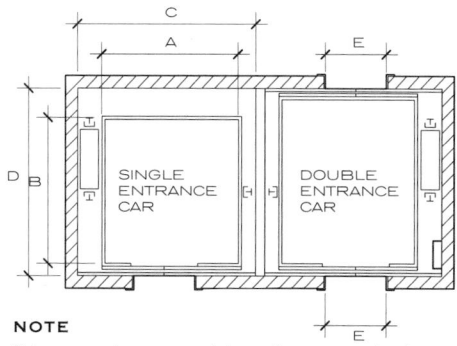

NOTE

Side-mounted counterweights allow an optional rear entrance door.

SIDE-MOUNTED COUNTERWEIGHT

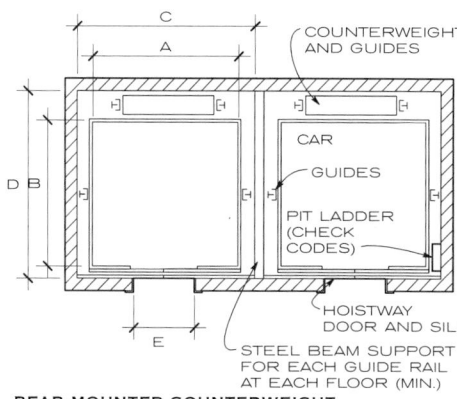

REAR-MOUNTED COUNTERWEIGHT
ELEVATOR HOISTWAY TYPES

TRACTION ELEVATOR DIMENSIONS (FT-IN)

RATED LOAD (LB)	A	B	C	D	E
2000	5-8	4-3	7-4	6-11	3-0
2500	6-8	4-3	8-4	6-11	3-6
3000	6-8	4-7	8-4	7-5	3-6
3500	6-8	5-3	8-4	8-1	3-6
4500	5-8	7-10	8-2	10-5	4-0

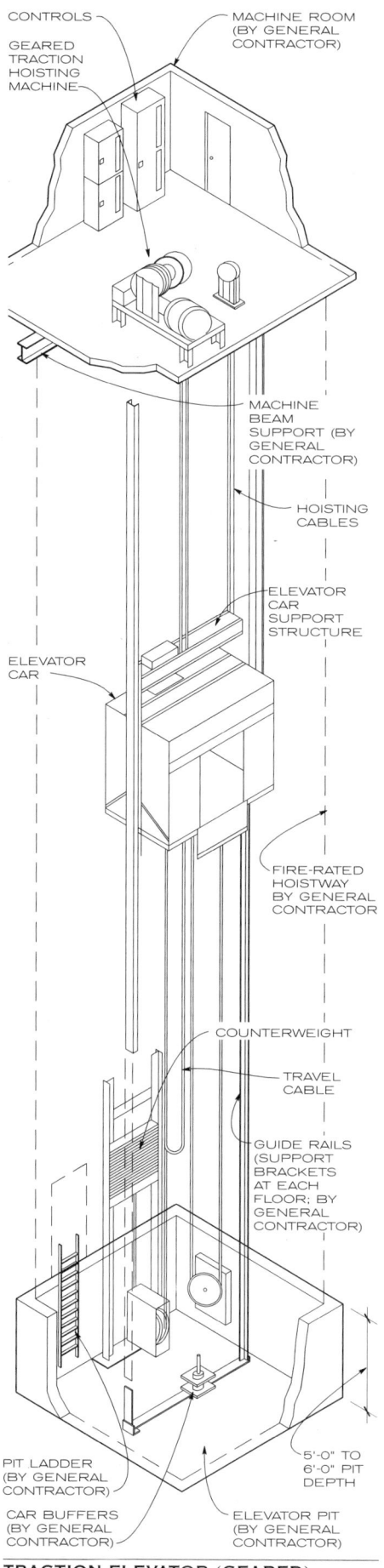

TRACTION ELEVATOR (GEARED)

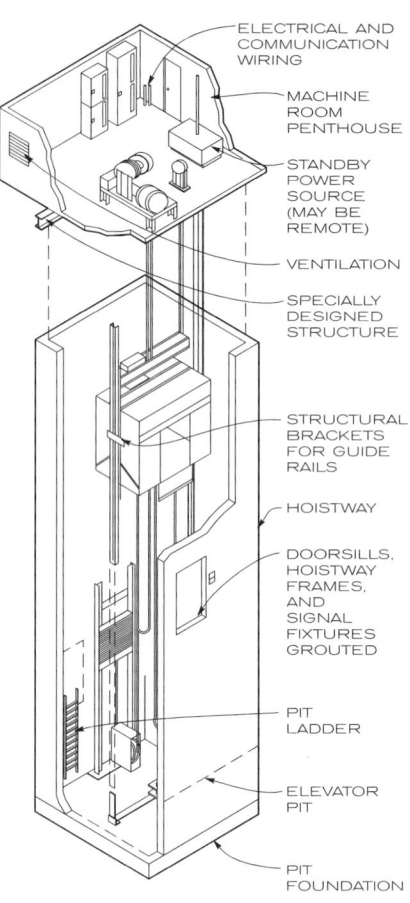

ELECTRICAL AND COMMUNICATION WIRING

MACHINE ROOM PENTHOUSE

STANDBY POWER SOURCE (MAY BE REMOTE)

VENTILATION

SPECIALLY DESIGNED STRUCTURE

STRUCTURAL BRACKETS FOR GUIDE RAILS

HOISTWAY

DOORSILLS, HOISTWAY FRAMES, AND SIGNAL FIXTURES GROUTED

PIT LADDER

ELEVATOR PIT

PIT FOUNDATION

ELEVATOR PLANNING DETAILS

BUILDING PREPARATION FOR ELEVATOR INSTALLATION

The following base building preparatory work is required in order to install elevator equipment properly:

1. An enclosed elevator equipment room with electrical outlets, adequate lighting, and heating and ventilation sufficient to maintain the room at a temperature between 50°F (minimum) and 100°F (maximum).

2. Adequate supports and foundations to carry the loads of all equipment, including supports for guide rail brackets.

3. Complete connections from the electric power mains to each controller, including necessary circuit breakers and fused main line disconnect switches.

4. Electric power of the same characteristics as the permanent supply for construction, testing, and adjusting.

5. Trenching and backfilling for any underground piping or conduit.

6. Divider beams for rail bracket support as required.

7. Cutting of walls, floor, etc. and removal of any obstructions; setting of anchors and sleeves.

8. Grouting of doorsills, hoistway frames, and signal fixtures after installation of elevator equipment.

9. All painting, except as otherwise specified.

10. Temporary enclosures, barricades, or other protection from open hoistways and elevator work areas while the elevator is being installed.

11. Temporary elevator service prior to completion.

12. Heat and smoke sensors as required by NFPA.

13. All telephone wiring to machine room control panel, and installation of telephone instruments.

14. A standby power source when elevator operation from an alternate power supply is required.

15. Adequate storage facilities for elevator equipment before and during installation.

16. A means to disconnect the elevator's main line power supply automatically to protect the machine room equipment from water damage.

17. A plumb and legal hoistway; a pit of proper depth with a pit ladder for each elevator; drains, lights, access doors, waterproofing, and hoistway ventilation, as required.

Rippeteau Rollins Architecture + Design; Washington, D.C.

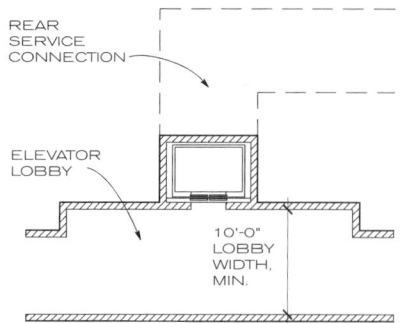

REAR SERVICE CONNECTION

ELEVATOR LOBBY

10'-0" LOBBY WIDTH, MIN.

SINGLE CAR

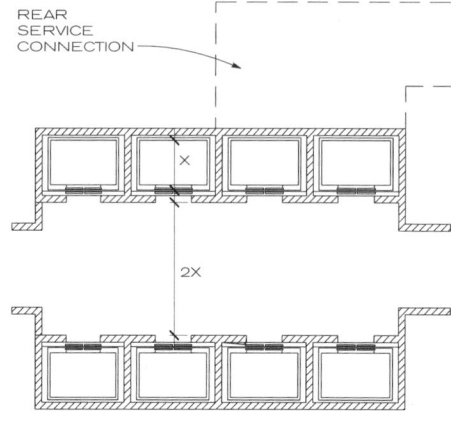

REAR SERVICE CONNECTION

2X

FOUR-EIGHT CAR ARRANGEMENT

NOTES

1. Elevators should be centrally located, near the main entrance, and easily accessible on all floors. Groups of elevators should be arranged to minimize walking distance between cars. Lobby space must be sufficient to accommodate group movement. Elevators may not open into a corridor.

2. The largest practical grouping of elevators in a building is eight cars. One row of more than four cars is generally unacceptable. With groupings of four or six cars, waiting

ELEVATOR LOBBY PLANNING

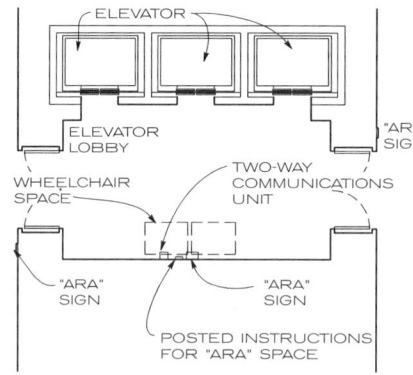

ELEVATOR

ELEVATOR LOBBY

"ARA" SIGN

WHEELCHAIR SPACE

TWO-WAY COMMUNICATIONS UNIT

"ARA" SIGN

"ARA" SIGN

POSTED INSTRUCTIONS FOR "ARA" SPACE

NOTE

An Area of Rescue Assistance is defined in the Americans with Disabilities Act Accessibility Guidelines as "an area, which has direct access to an exit, where people who are unable to use stairs may remain temporarily in safety to await further instructions or assistance during emergency evacuation."

The elevator lobby and shaft must be pressurized for smokeproof enclosure as required by the local building official. The pressurization system must be activated by smoke detectors in locations approved by the local building official. The system's equipment and ducts must be of 2-hour fire-resistant construction.

ELEVATOR LOBBY DESIGNED AS AREA OF RESCUE ASSISTANCE (ARA)

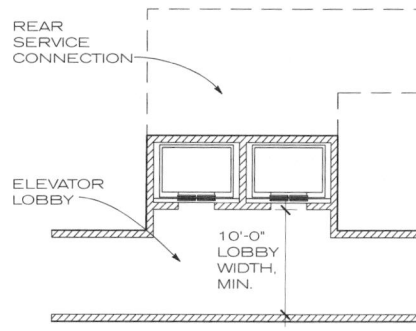

REAR SERVICE CONNECTION

ELEVATOR LOBBY

10'-0" LOBBY WIDTH, MIN.

PAIRED CARS

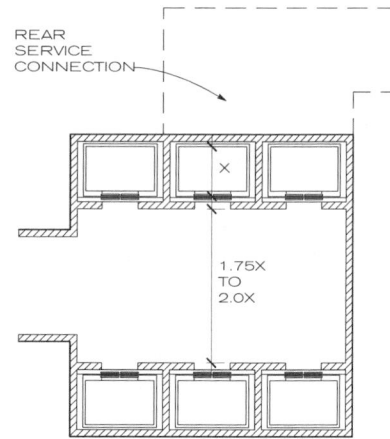

REAR SERVICE CONNECTION

1.75X TO 2.0X

THREE-SIX CAR ARRANGEMENT

lobbies may be closed at one end, forming an alcove, or open at both ends.

3. In buildings with several elevator groupings, one group may serve lower floors, while others serve as express elevators to upper floors.

4. When four or more elevators serve all or the same part of a building, they must be located in no fewer than two hoistways, but no more than four elevators can be located in any one hoistway.

5. Consider the option of rear access for trash removal.

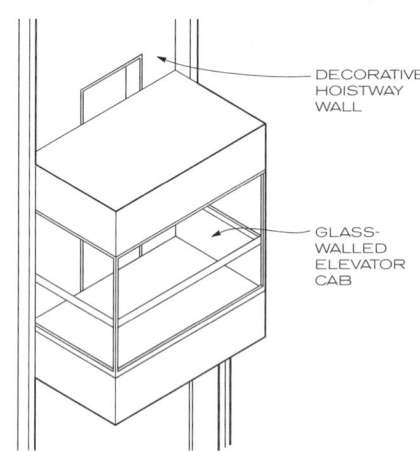

DECORATIVE HOISTWAY WALL

GLASS-WALLED ELEVATOR CAB

NOTE

Observation and glassback elevators travel outside of a hoistway or in a hoistway open on one side. Machinery is concealed or designed to be inconspicuous. Elevators may be engineered for hydraulic, geared, or gearless use. Cabs can be custom designed with more than 75% of wall area as glass. Only the rear panel is glass in glassback cabs. Safety barriers must be provided at floor penetrations and the ground floor, completely surrounding that part of the elevator not enclosed by the hoistway. This is a very specialized application; consultation is advised.

GLASS-WALLED ELEVATOR CARS

GENERAL

Hydraulic elevator systems are used primarily in low-rise installations, where moderate car speed (up to 150 ft per minute) is required. A car is connected to the top of a long piston that moves up and down in a cylinder. The car moves up when hydraulic fluid is pumped into the cylinder from a reservoir, raising the piston. The car is lowered when the hydraulic fluid returns to the reservoir. The up and down motions of the elevator car are controlled by the hydraulic valve.

The main space planning elements of a hydraulic elevator system are the machine room, usually located at the base, and the hoistway, which serves as a fire-protected, ventilated passageway for the elevator car. Adequate structure must be provided at the base of the hoistway to bear the load of the elevator car and its supporting piston or cylinder.

NOTES

1. The elevator pit should be reinforced to sustain the vertical forces generated by the system configuration. Consult manufacturer's representatives. All pit depths and overhead clearances should be in accordance with ASME requirements. Local codes may vary from these requirements.

2. Car and hoistway dimensions of preengineered units are for reference purposes only. A variety of units is available. Consult manufacturers for dimensions of specific systems.

3. Hoistway walls usually serve primarily as fireproof enclosures. Check local codes for required fire ratings.

4. Guide rails extend from the floor of the pit to the underside of the overhead (top of hoistway). Consult the elevator manufacturer for the special requirements of excessive floor heights.

5. Rail brackets typically are at each floor level. A bracket is required at the top of the hoistway, and an intermediate bracket may be required for certain floor-to-floor heights. Consult manufacturer.

6. Some hydraulic applications may require jack hole blockouts in the floor of the pit.

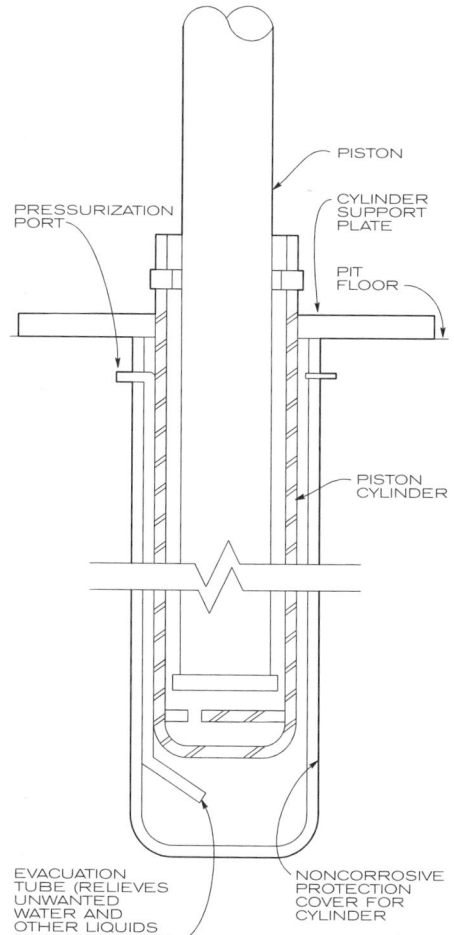

PISTON AND CYLINDER DETAIL

Rippeteau Rollins Architecture + Design; Washington, D.C.

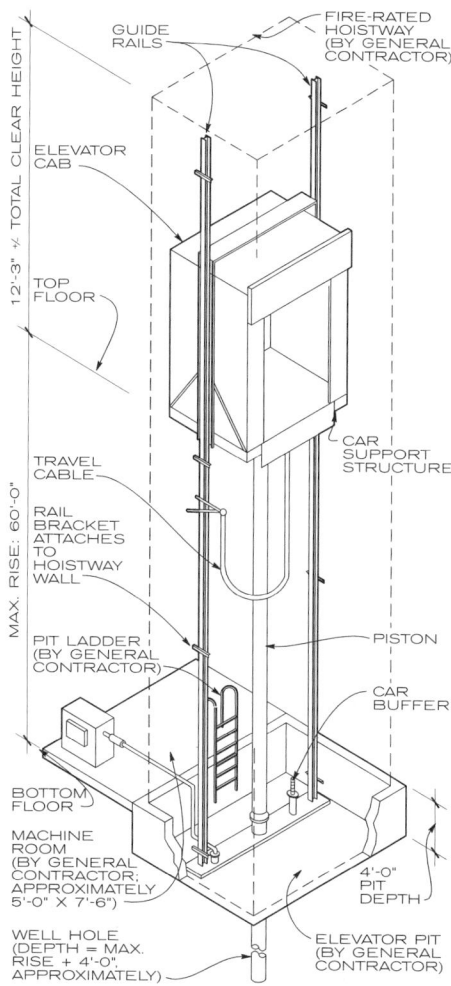

HOLED HYDRAULIC ELEVATOR

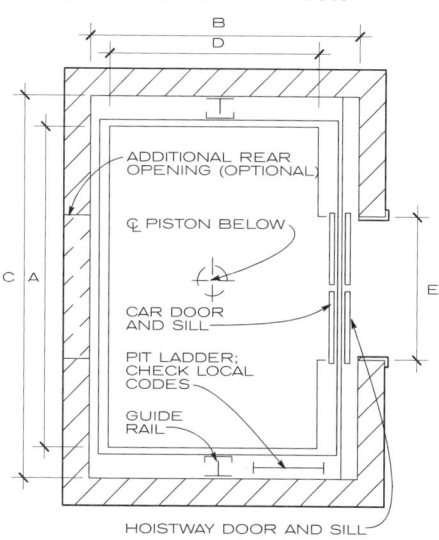

HYDRAULIC ELEVATOR DIMENSIONS (FT-IN.)

RATED LOAD (LB)	A	B	C	D	E
2000	5–8	4–3	7–4	5–11	3–0
2500	6–8	4–3	8–4	5–11	3–6
3000	6–8	4–7	8–4	6–3	3–6
3500	6–8	5–3	8–4	6–11	3–6
4500	5–8	7–10	7–5	10–0	4–0

NOTE

"A" and "B" dimensions are "clear inside." Rated speeds are 75 to 200 ft/min.

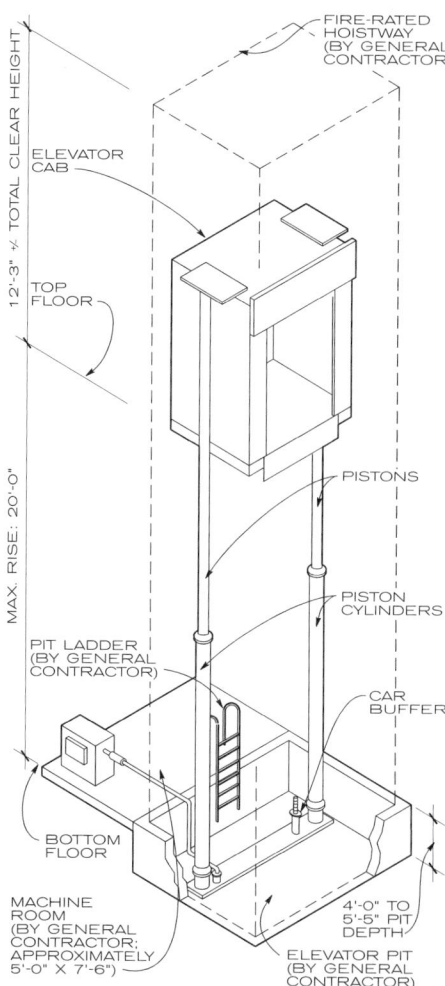

HOLELESS HYDRAULIC ELEVATOR

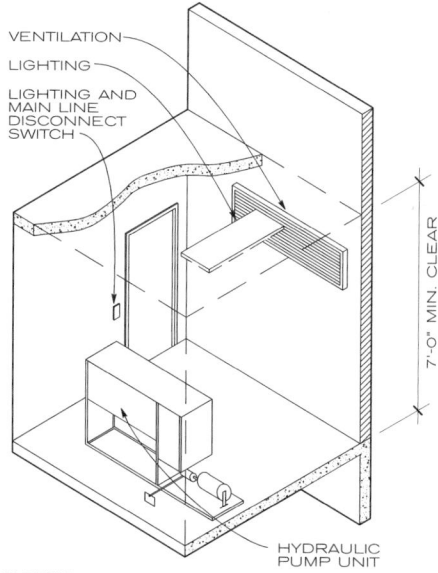

NOTES

1. A machine room, meeting code requirements and ventilated for temperatures between 65° and 100°F (18° and 38°C), must be provided for all elevators. It is usually located next to the hoistway at or near the bottom terminal landing. Room size may vary depending on the number of cars, capacity, and speed.

2. Machinery consists of a pump and motor drive unit, hydraulic fluid storage tank, and electronic control panel. Adequate ventilation, lighting, and entrance access (usually 3 ft 6 in x 7 ft) should be provided.

MACHINE ROOM

GENERAL

General freight elevators with capacities of 2000 to 8000 lb satisfy a variety of material-handling requirements. Industrial truck freight elevators require special design considerations to handle truckloads of 10,000 to 20,000 lb or more.

General freight or industrial truck elevators may have either hydraulic or traction drive systems similar to those of other elevator systems. However, the units are usually custom-designed with vertical bipart doors and special structural support to accommodate heavy loads and eccentric loading conditions. Freight elevators usually have simple control systems and operate at slower speeds than other elevators. Their capacity must be sized for the largest expected load.

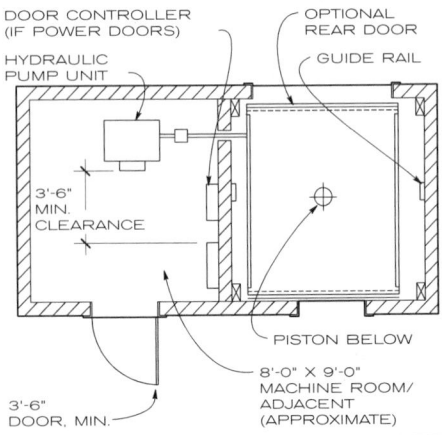

HYDRAULIC FREIGHT ELEVATOR

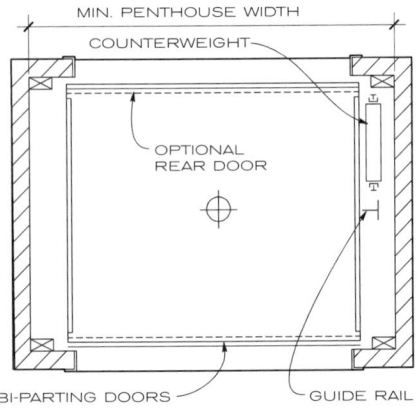

TRACTION FREIGHT ELEVATOR

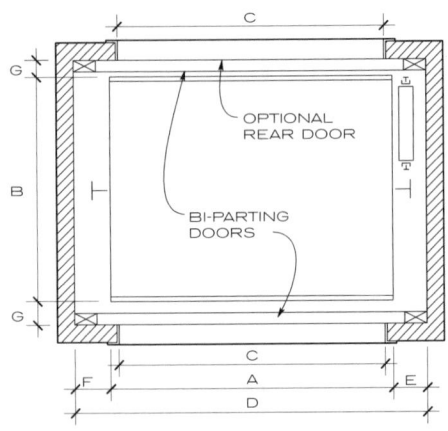

NOTE

G = 5 in. (127 mm) for regular counterbalanced hoistway doors and 6 3/4 in. (172 mm) for pass-type counterbalanced hoistway doors. Pass-type doors are required when floor heights are less than 11 ft (3350 mm) for 7-ft (2134 mm) openings and less than 12 ft 6 in. (3810 mm) for 8-ft (2458 mm) openings.

KEY PLAN

Rippeteau Rollins Architecture + Design; Washington, D.C.

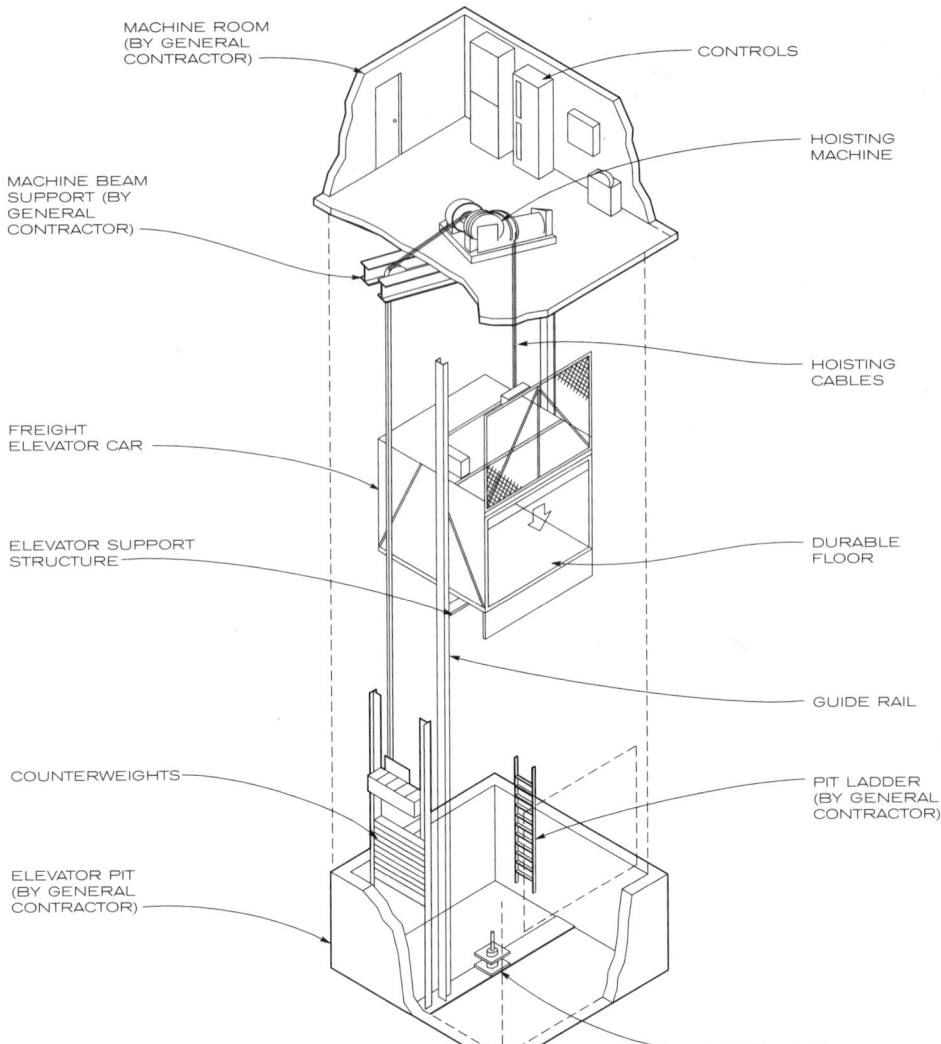

NOTES

1. Hoistway walls: Local building codes govern design characteristics; consult with appropiate agencies to determine requirements such as fire rating.

2. Traction elevators: The hoisting machine may be mounted directly overhead or at the side of the hoistway at any level, including the lowest landing. Special structural design considerations are necessary based on forces created by the use of traction equipment.

3. Guide rail bracket support: Freight elevators create horizontal forces greater than those created by passenger elevators. Vertical steel is installed within the hoistway to provide bracket support at elevations with bracket locations.

4. Truckable sills: At the edge of the building floor (leading into the elevator hoistway), a structural steel angle must be in place to avoid deterioration of the building floor through continued use of hand trucks, battery-operated pallet lifts, forklifts, etc.

5. Flooring: A variety of materials may be used for flooring in a freight elevator, including checkered steel plate, nonskid materials, galvanized steel, or high-density wood.

FREIGHT ELEVATOR

TRACTION FREIGHT ELEVATORS

CAPACITY IN LB (KG)	LIGHT- AND MEDIUM-DUTY			HEAVY-DUTY POWER TRUCK LOADING		
	DIMENSIONS IN FT-IN. (MM)					
	A	B	C	D	E	F
2500 (1134)	5–4 (1626)	7–0 (2134)	5–0 (1524)	7–10 (3150)	1–7 (483)	0–11 (279)
4000 (1814)	6–4 (1930)	8–0 (2438)	6–0 (1829)	8–10 (2692)	1–7 (483)	0–11 (279)
8000 (3629)	8–4 (2540)	10–0 (3048)	8–0 (2438)	10–10 (3302)	1–7 (483)	0–11 (279)
12,000 (6443)	10–4 (3150)	14–0 (4267)	10–0 (3048)	13–6 (4115)	1–7 (483)	0–11 (279)
20,000 (9072)	12–4 (3759)	20–4 (6196)	12–0 (3658)	16–6 (5029)	1–7 (483)	0–11 (279)

HYDRAULIC FREIGHT ELEVATORS

CAPACITY IN LB (KG)	LIGHT- AND MEDIUM-DUTY			HEAVY-DUTY POWER TRUCK LOADING	
	DIMENSIONS IN FT-IN. (MM)				
	A	B	C	D (MANUAL DOORS)	E (POWER DOORS)
2000 (967)	5–0 (1524)	6–0 (1829)	4–8 (1422)	6–4 (1930)	6–10 (2083)
4000 (1814)	6–6 (1981)	8–0 (2438)	6–2 (1880)	7–10 (2388)	8–4 (2540)
8000 (3629)	8–6 (2591)	12–0 (3658)	8–2 (2490)	10–6 (3200)	10–6 (3200)
12,000 (5443)	10–6 (3200)	14–0 (4267)	10–2 (3098)	12–6 (3810)	12–6 (3810)
20,000 (9072)	12–6 (3810)	20–0 (6096)	12–2 (3708)	14–6 (4420)	14–6 (4420)

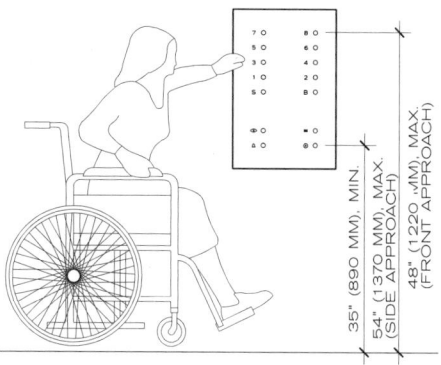

CONTROL PANEL HEIGHT

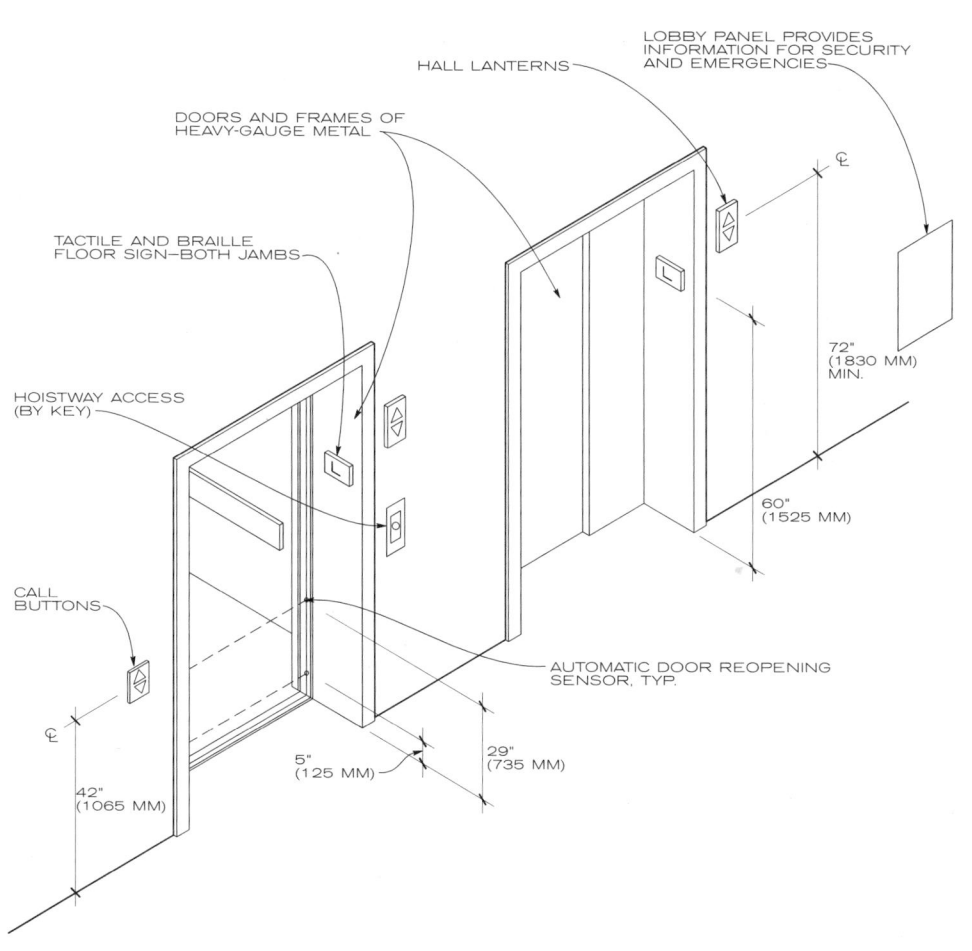

LOBBY PANEL PROVIDES INFORMATION FOR SECURITY AND EMERGENCIES

HALL LANTERNS

DOORS AND FRAMES OF HEAVY-GAUGE METAL

TACTILE AND BRAILLE FLOOR SIGN—BOTH JAMBS

HOISTWAY ACCESS (BY KEY)

CALL BUTTONS

AUTOMATIC DOOR REOPENING SENSOR, TYP.

72" (1830 MM) MIN.

60" (1525 MM)

5" (125 MM)

29" (735 MM)

42" (1065 MM)

ELEVATOR LOBBY

GENERAL NOTES

1. Floor designations should be indicated in 2-in. high letters, including braille.

2. Hall lanterns sound once for up, twice for down; minimum 2 1/2 in. smallest dimension.

3. Use a car position indicator that is both visual and audible.

4. See Americans with Disabilities Act Accessibility Guidelines (ADAAG) for mechanical requirements.

5. Elevator doors must open and close automatically and have a reopening device that will stop the elevator and reopen car and hoistway doors automatically if the doors are obstructed by an object or person. The reopening device must not require physical contact for activation; typically a light or other type of sensor is used. Door reopening devices must remain effective for at least 20 seconds.

6. The control panel inside the elevator car is designed to accommodate all required emergency devices, including the alarm button and keyed emergency stop.

7. The elevator telephone should comply with ADA and be accessible to individuals with all types of disabilities.

ELEVATOR CAR INTERIOR FINISHES

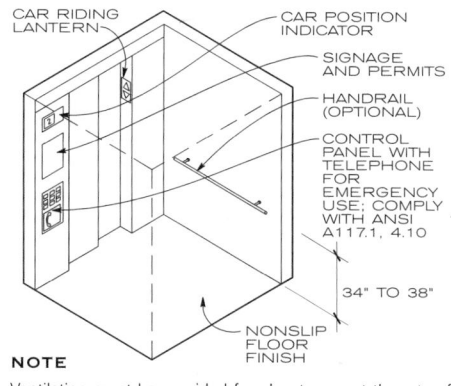

CAR RIDING LANTERN

CAR POSITION INDICATOR

SIGNAGE AND PERMITS

HANDRAIL (OPTIONAL)

CONTROL PANEL WITH TELEPHONE FOR EMERGENCY USE; COMPLY WITH ANSI A117.1, 4.10

34" TO 38"

NONSLIP FLOOR FINISH

NOTE

Ventilation must be provided for elevator car at the rate of two air changes per minute, minimum. Five footcandles of glarefree light, minimum, should be provided at the car sill.

ELEVATOR CAR INTERIOR

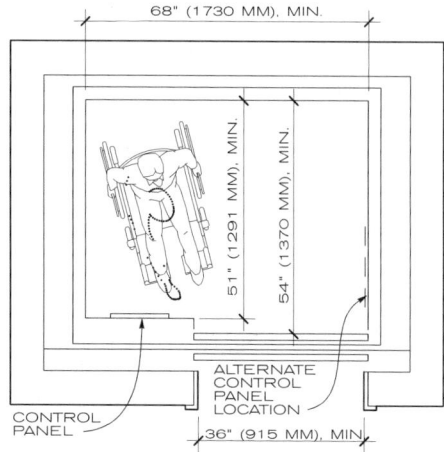

CAR WITH SIDE OPENING DOORS

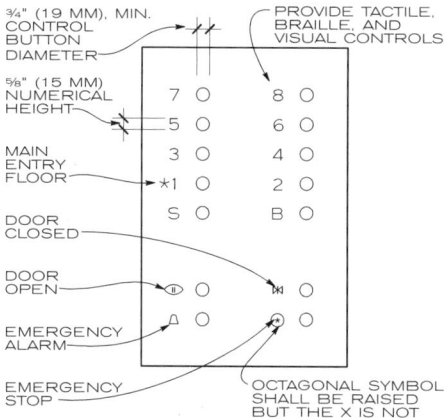

CONTROL PANEL DETAIL

BUILDING TYPE	FLOORS	WALLS	DOORS	CEILING	CONTROL PANEL
Apartment					
Basic	Level loop carpet	Plastic laminate	Plastic laminate	Acrylic panel	Metal
Luxury	Pile carpet	Wood	Decorative metal	Suspended decorative	Metal
Office					
Basic	Pile carpet	Plastic laminate	Plastic laminate	Acrylic panel	Metal
Medium traffic	Ceramic tile	Woven wire or plastic fabric	Brushed metal	Suspended decorative	Metal
High traffic	Granite tile	Marble or wood	Decorative metal	Decorative with cove lighting	Metal
Hospital	Vinyl tile	Plastic laminate	Plastic laminate	Acrylic panel	Metal
Courthouse	Carpet or tile	Woven wire or plastic	Metal	Integral metal	Metal
Government	Granite tile	Plastic laminate/stone	Metal	Suspended decorative	Metal

Rippeteau Rollins Architecture + Design; Washington, D.C.

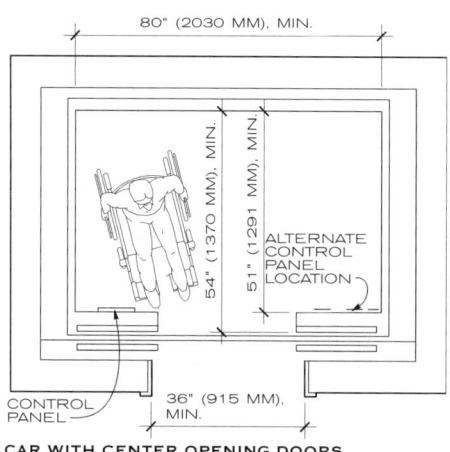

CAR WITH CENTER OPENING DOORS

ACCESSIBILITY FOR ELEVATORS

GENERAL

The lifts presented illustrate systems and equipment available to move loads vertically. Specific sizes and capacity should be obtained from lift manufacturers.

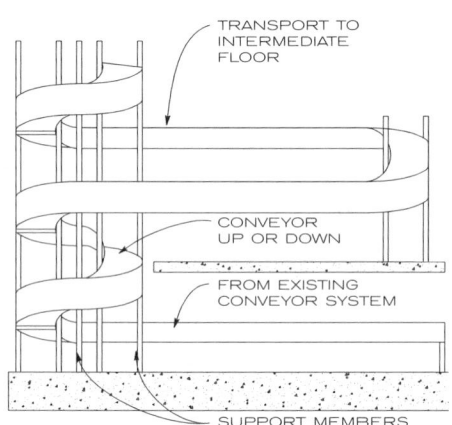

NOTES

1. Circular conveyor lifts are used to transport cartons between operating levels and between workstations within a level. They are useful when vertical distance is great but horizontal distance is limited.
2. Lift height: 45 to 144 in. vertical lift per 360° unit (lift height is relative to radius of unit); load sizes: width is 6 to 48 in., length is relative to width and radius of conveyor; installation: depends on height of feed and exit conveyors, system requires shaft through floor as deep as the operating depth (OD) of the conveyor plus 12 in.

CIRCULAR CONVEYOR LIFT

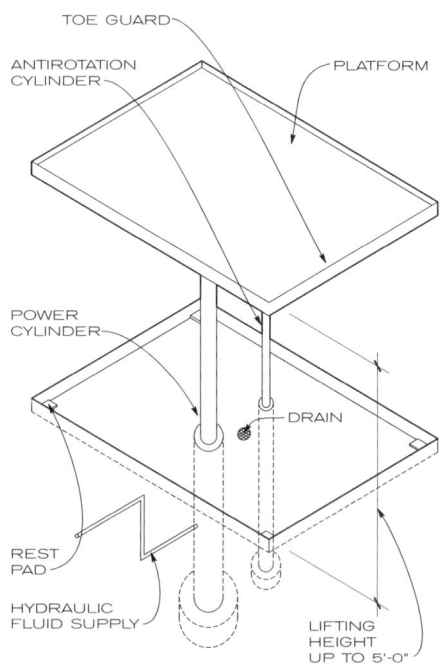

NOTES

1. Cylinder platform lifts are used to move unitized loads from floor or ground to delivery vehicle level to facilitate loading/unloading operations. They are also used for machine loading/unloading of heavy/bulky materials.
2. Load capacity: 2000 to 30,000 lb; platform sizes: typically 5 x 5 ft to 8 x 15 ft, but other sizes can be specified; lift rate: cycle rate is manually controlled by loading/unloading rate (up cycle of lift ranges up to 12 fpm); installation: pit used to allow platform to be flush with floor or ground for loading/unloading, cylinder shaft is centered under the platform with an antirotational shaft at one end (both shafts recessed in ground).

CYLINDER PLATFORM LIFT

St. Onge, Ruff and Associates, Inc., York, Pennsylvania

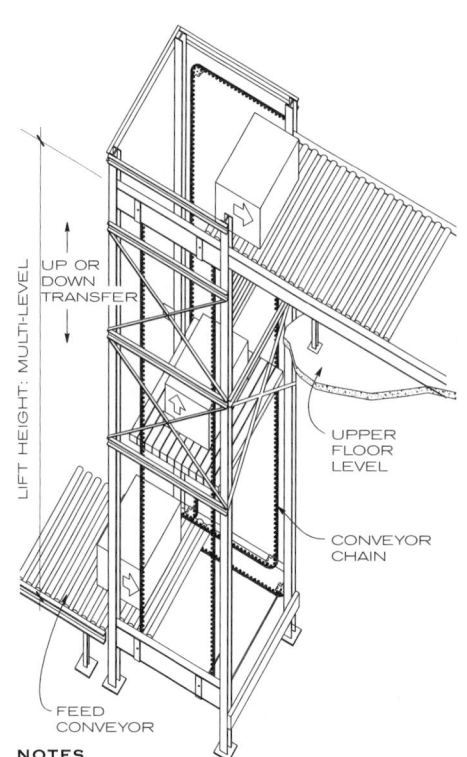

NOTES

1. Continuous vertical pallet lifts are used to transport unit loads between operating levels in multiple level or multiple floor buildings. They are typically used when vertical lift is great and a continuous conveyor system is used to load/unload the lift.
2. Capacity: up to 20,000 lb; load sizes: typically 48 x 40 x 72 in., but other sizes can be specified; lift speed: 60 ft/min.; installation: typically installed floor to floor, with shaft through each floor.

CONTINUOUS VERTICAL PALLET LIFT

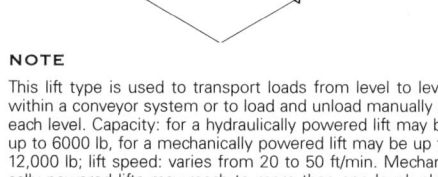
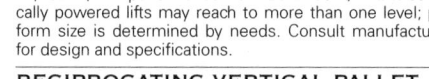

NOTE

This lift type is used to transport loads from level to level within a conveyor system or to load and unload manually at each level. Capacity: for a hydraulically powered lift may be up to 6000 lb, for a mechanically powered lift may be up to 12,000 lb; lift speed: varies from 20 to 50 ft/min. Mechanically powered lifts may reach to more than one level; platform size is determined by needs. Consult manufacturers for design and specifications.

RECIPROCATING VERTICAL PALLET LIFT

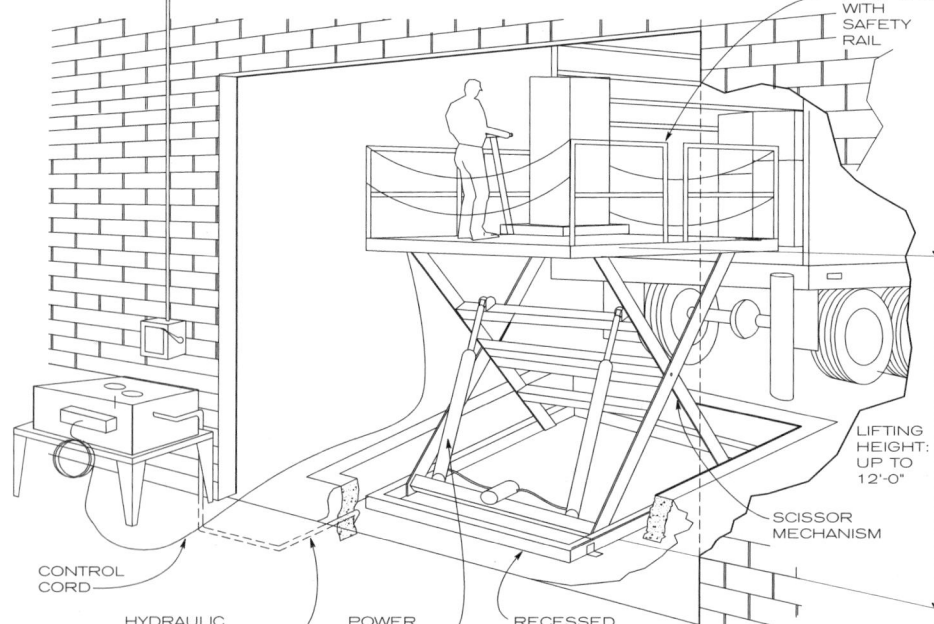

NOTES

1. Scissor lifts are used to raise and lower unit loads to delivery vehicles from ground or floor levels that do not align with vehicles.
2. Load capacity: 2500 to 30,000 lb; platform sizes: typically 5 x 7 ft to 8 x 12 ft, but other sizes can be specified; lift rate: cycle rate is manually controlled by loading/unloading rate (up cycle of lift ranges from 40 to 100 sec depending on lift size); installation: available in permanent pit installation or portable aboveground units (limiting factor is electric power source for hydraulic pump and reservoir).

SCISSOR LIFT

GENERAL

Material-conveying systems are designed to carry either bulk material or unit items. Bulk materials include agricultural and food products, chemicals, solid fuels, pastes, and powders. Unit materials include luggage, envelopes, cases, parts, part bins, pallets, bags, and cans.

Conveyors are usually designed as complete systems by engineers who specialize in such systems. The choice and design of a conveying system should include consideration of material properties, containment, damage, capacity, speed, loading and unloading, control, reliability, safety, and maintainability.

Access to conveyors must be provided for equipment maintenance, clearing of load jams, and loading and unloading. Because mechanical conveyors have inherent safety hazards, guards and emergency stop controls are required to reduce the chance of injuries. Most conveyors are used in a controlled access environment such as a security area or industrial plant. Equipment accessed or used by the public must be specifically designed for safety.

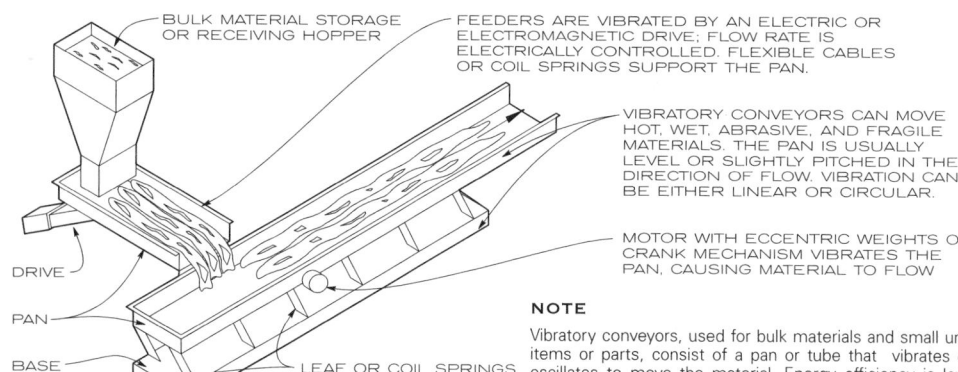

BULK MATERIAL STORAGE OR RECEIVING HOPPER

FEEDERS ARE VIBRATED BY AN ELECTRIC OR ELECTROMAGNETIC DRIVE; FLOW RATE IS ELECTRICALLY CONTROLLED. FLEXIBLE CABLES OR COIL SPRINGS SUPPORT THE PAN.

VIBRATORY CONVEYORS CAN MOVE HOT, WET, ABRASIVE, AND FRAGILE MATERIALS. THE PAN IS USUALLY LEVEL OR SLIGHTLY PITCHED IN THE DIRECTION OF FLOW. VIBRATION CAN BE EITHER LINEAR OR CIRCULAR.

MOTOR WITH ECCENTRIC WEIGHTS OR CRANK MECHANISM VIBRATES THE PAN, CAUSING MATERIAL TO FLOW

DRIVE
PAN
BASE
LEAF OR COIL SPRINGS SUPPORT PAN AND CONTROL ITS MOTION

NOTE

Vibratory conveyors, used for bulk materials and small unit items or parts, consist of a pan or tube that vibrates or oscillates to move the material. Energy efficiency is low. Most uses involve flow control or material alignment in processing applications.

VIBRATORY CONVEYORS

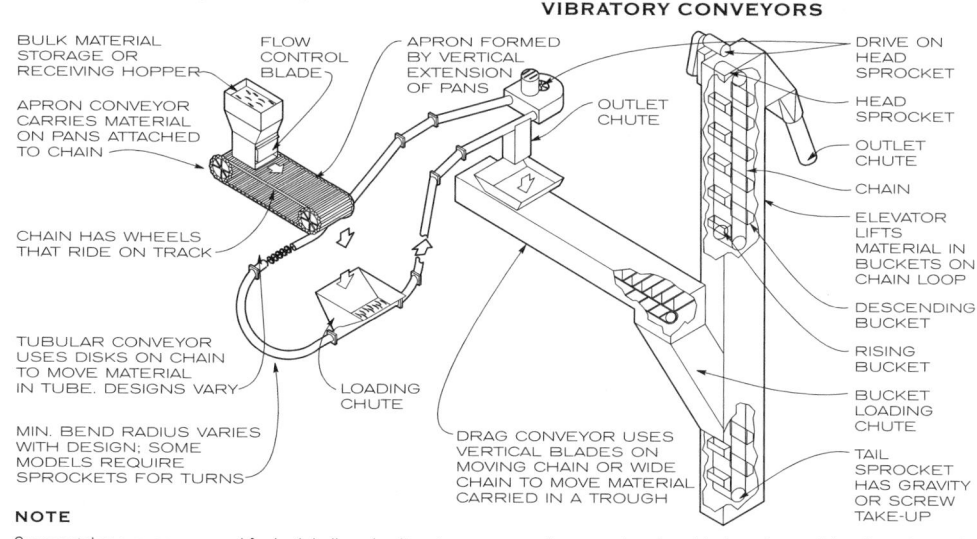

BULK MATERIAL STORAGE OR RECEIVING HOPPER

FLOW CONTROL BLADE

APRON FORMED BY VERTICAL EXTENSION OF PANS

APRON CONVEYOR CARRIES MATERIAL ON PANS ATTACHED TO CHAIN

OUTLET CHUTE

DRIVE ON HEAD SPROCKET
HEAD SPROCKET
OUTLET CHUTE
CHAIN
ELEVATOR LIFTS MATERIAL IN BUCKETS ON CHAIN LOOP
DESCENDING BUCKET
RISING BUCKET
BUCKET LOADING CHUTE
TAIL SPROCKET HAS GRAVITY OR SCREW TAKE-UP

CHAIN HAS WHEELS THAT RIDE ON TRACK

TUBULAR CONVEYOR USES DISKS ON CHAIN TO MOVE MATERIAL IN TUBE. DESIGNS VARY

LOADING CHUTE

MIN. BEND RADIUS VARIES WITH DESIGN; SOME MODELS REQUIRE SPROCKETS FOR TURNS

DRAG CONVEYOR USES VERTICAL BLADES ON MOVING CHAIN OR WIDE CHAIN TO MOVE MATERIAL CARRIED IN A TROUGH

NOTE

Segmental conveyors are used for both bulk and unit materials. Although slow and not energy-efficient, they have durable carrying surfaces and can handle heavy loads and materials that are hot, abrasive, or fragile. They allow precise control and positioning of material and can be configured in complex and multiple curves. They are expensive and used for specialty applications.

SEGMENTAL CONVEYORS

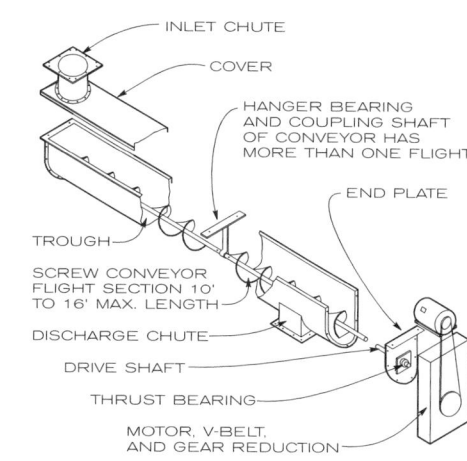

INLET CHUTE
COVER
HANGER BEARING AND COUPLING SHAFT OF CONVEYOR HAS MORE THAN ONE FLIGHT
END PLATE
TROUGH
SCREW CONVEYOR FLIGHT SECTION 10' TO 16' MAX. LENGTH
DISCHARGE CHUTE
DRIVE SHAFT
THRUST BEARING
MOTOR, V-BELT, AND GEAR REDUCTION

NOTE

Screw conveyors are only used for bulk materials. They can convey hot, wet, or dusty materials but become plugged by sticky or stringy material; they are not suitable for fragile materials. They can have multiple inlets and discharges and are often used for mixing and flow control.

SCREW CONVEYORS

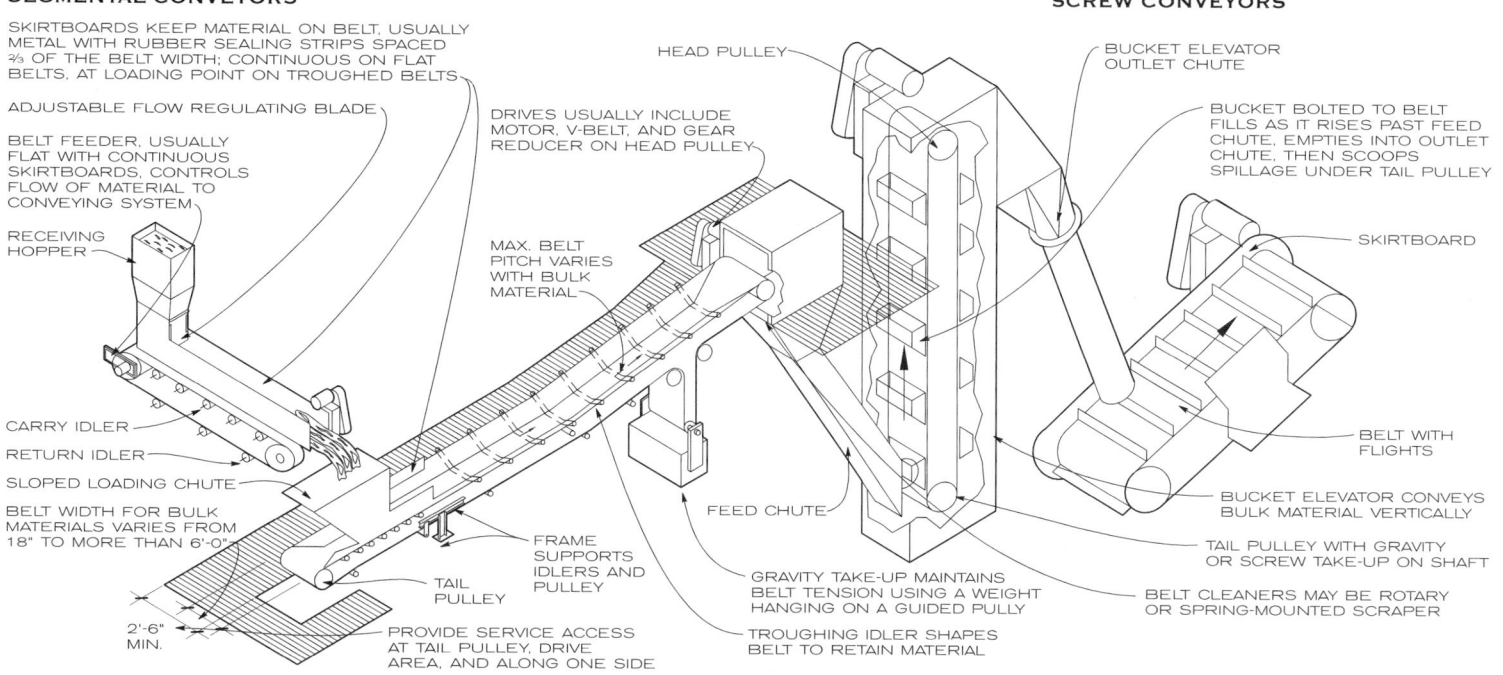

SKIRTBOARDS KEEP MATERIAL ON BELT, USUALLY METAL WITH RUBBER SEALING STRIPS SPACED ⅔ OF THE BELT WIDTH; CONTINUOUS ON FLAT BELTS, AT LOADING POINT ON TROUGHED BELTS

ADJUSTABLE FLOW REGULATING BLADE

BELT FEEDER, USUALLY FLAT WITH CONTINUOUS SKIRTBOARDS, CONTROLS FLOW OF MATERIAL TO CONVEYING SYSTEM

RECEIVING HOPPER

HEAD PULLEY

DRIVES USUALLY INCLUDE MOTOR, V-BELT, AND GEAR REDUCER ON HEAD PULLEY

MAX. BELT PITCH VARIES WITH BULK MATERIAL

BUCKET ELEVATOR OUTLET CHUTE

BUCKET BOLTED TO BELT FILLS AS IT RISES PAST FEED CHUTE, EMPTIES INTO OUTLET CHUTE, THEN SCOOPS SPILLAGE UNDER TAIL PULLEY

SKIRTBOARD

CARRY IDLER
RETURN IDLER
SLOPED LOADING CHUTE
BELT WIDTH FOR BULK MATERIALS VARIES FROM 18" TO MORE THAN 6'-0"

2'-6" MIN.

TAIL PULLEY

FRAME SUPPORTS IDLERS AND PULLEY

PROVIDE SERVICE ACCESS AT TAIL PULLEY, DRIVE AREA, AND ALONG ONE SIDE

FEED CHUTE

GRAVITY TAKE-UP MAINTAINS BELT TENSION USING A WEIGHT HANGING ON A GUIDED PULLY

TROUGHING IDLER SHAPES BELT TO RETAIN MATERIAL

BELT WITH FLIGHTS

BUCKET ELEVATOR CONVEYS BULK MATERIAL VERTICALLY

TAIL PULLEY WITH GRAVITY OR SCREW TAKE-UP ON SHAFT

BELT CLEANERS MAY BE ROTARY OR SPRING-MOUNTED SCRAPER

NOTE

Belt conveyors, used for both bulk and unit materials, are often chosen for superior speed, capacity, length, energy efficiency, and economy. They vary in width from one inch to more than 8 feet and in length from less than a foot to more than a mile. At steeper angles, belts must have skirtboards to retain material and roughened surfaces or flights to keep it from sliding. Belts typically are made of rubber-covered fabric; belt slippage and alignment can be a problem.

BELT CONVEYORS

Alpha Engineers, Inc.; Pocatello, Idaho

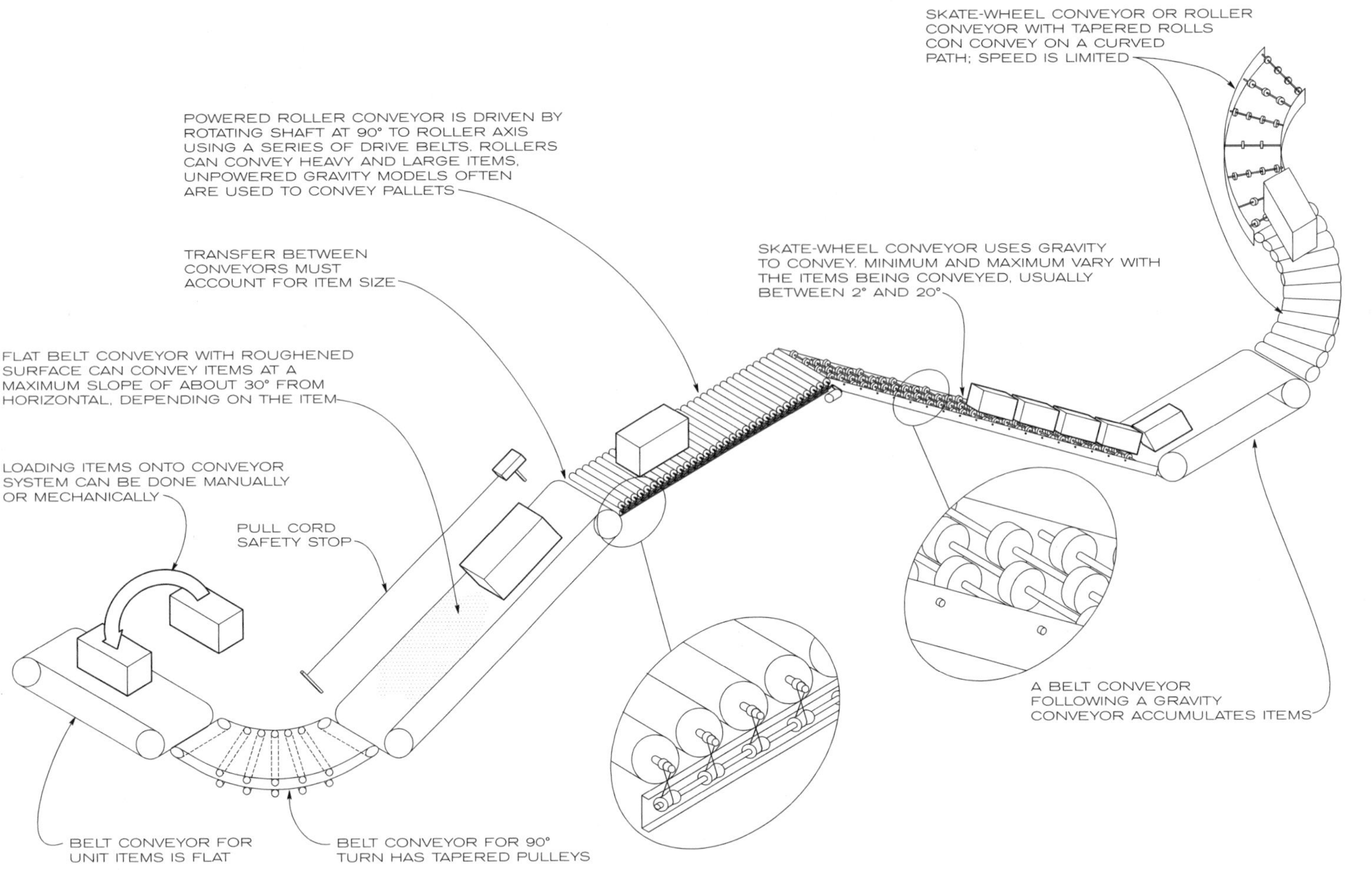

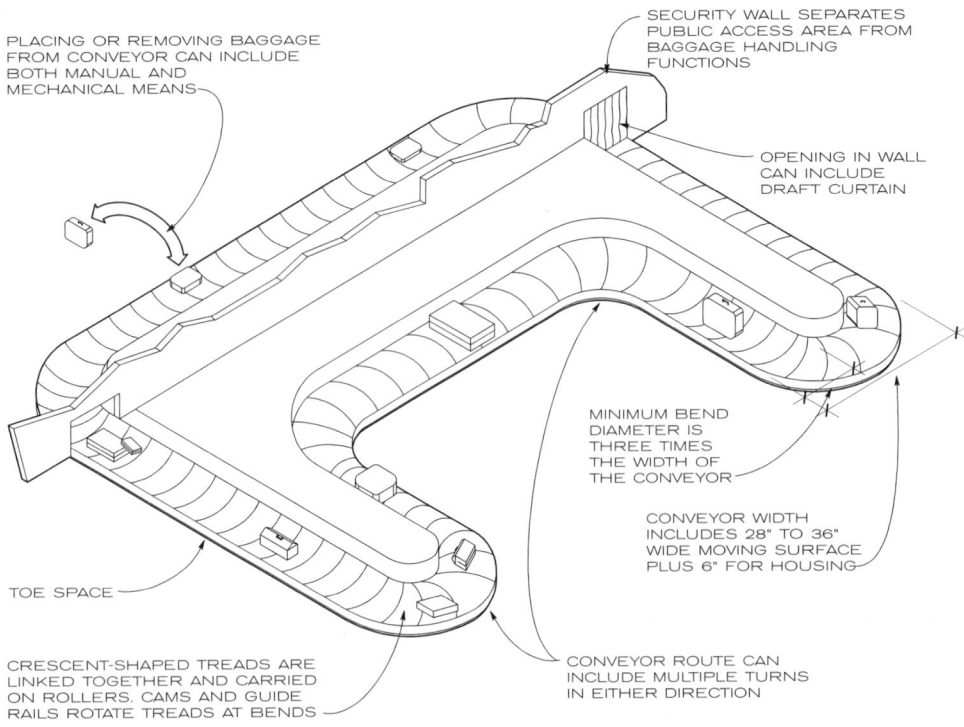

SKATE-WHEEL CONVEYOR OR ROLLER CONVEYOR WITH TAPERED ROLLS CON CONVEY ON A CURVED PATH; SPEED IS LIMITED

POWERED ROLLER CONVEYOR IS DRIVEN BY ROTATING SHAFT AT 90° TO ROLLER AXIS USING A SERIES OF DRIVE BELTS. ROLLERS CAN CONVEY HEAVY AND LARGE ITEMS. UNPOWERED GRAVITY MODELS OFTEN ARE USED TO CONVEY PALLETS

TRANSFER BETWEEN CONVEYORS MUST ACCOUNT FOR ITEM SIZE

SKATE-WHEEL CONVEYOR USES GRAVITY TO CONVEY. MINIMUM AND MAXIMUM VARY WITH THE ITEMS BEING CONVEYED, USUALLY BETWEEN 2° AND 20°

FLAT BELT CONVEYOR WITH ROUGHENED SURFACE CAN CONVEY ITEMS AT A MAXIMUM SLOPE OF ABOUT 30° FROM HORIZONTAL, DEPENDING ON THE ITEM

LOADING ITEMS ONTO CONVEYOR SYSTEM CAN BE DONE MANUALLY OR MECHANICALLY

PULL CORD SAFETY STOP

A BELT CONVEYOR FOLLOWING A GRAVITY CONVEYOR ACCUMULATES ITEMS

BELT CONVEYOR FOR UNIT ITEMS IS FLAT

BELT CONVEYOR FOR 90° TURN HAS TAPERED PULLEYS

NOTE

Unit conveyors use rollers or wheels on stationary shafts to carry items that must have a flat bottom surface. Rollers may be gravity or power driven. Gravity units are economical and often portable. Items move independently on rollers, allowing materials to be paused or accumulated.

Systems often use sensors and automated diverters to sort and direct items to different destinations.

UNIT CONVEYORS

PLACING OR REMOVING BAGGAGE FROM CONVEYOR CAN INCLUDE BOTH MANUAL AND MECHANICAL MEANS

SECURITY WALL SEPARATES PUBLIC ACCESS AREA FROM BAGGAGE HANDLING FUNCTIONS

OPENING IN WALL CAN INCLUDE DRAFT CURTAIN

RUBBER BUMPER TRAVELS ON LOWER END OF CONVEYOR SURFACE TO CUSHION AND RETAIN BAGGAGE

BAGGAGE DELIVERY CONVEYOR MAY SLOPE FROM A FLOOR BELOW (AS SHOWN) OR ABOVE

25'-0" MINIMUM LENGTH TO ALLOW FOR SLOPE OF DELIVERY CONVEYOR

MINIMUM BEND DIAMETER IS THREE TIMES THE WIDTH OF THE CONVEYOR

CONVEYOR WIDTH INCLUDES 28" TO 36" WIDE MOVING SURFACE PLUS 6" FOR HOUSING

16'-0" MIN.

5'-0" MIN.

TOE SPACE

CRESCENT-SHAPED TREADS ARE LINKED TOGETHER AND CARRIED ON ROLLERS. CAMS AND GUIDE RAILS ROTATE TREADS AT BENDS

CONVEYOR ROUTE CAN INCLUDE MULTIPLE TURNS IN EITHER DIRECTION

OVERLAPPING PLATES AT A 20° SLOPE FORM CONVEYING SURFACE. PLATES ARE LINKED AND DRIVEN BY A ROLLER CHAIN. EACH PLATE IS CARRIED BY WHEELS ON TRACKS UNDER THE CONVEYING SURFACE

CRESENT BAGGAGE CONVEYOR

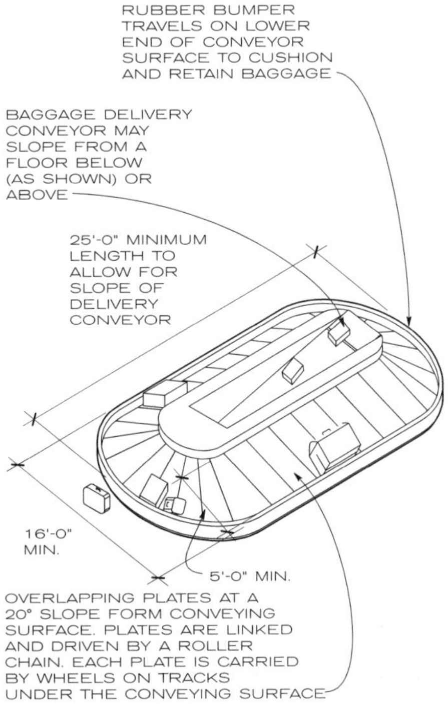

BAGGAGE CLAIM CONVEYOR

Alpha Engineers, Inc.; Pocatello, Idaho

14 MATERIAL-HANDLING SYSTEMS

CAST-IRON PIPE

Cast-iron (CI) pipe and fittings are manufactured in two weight classes, standard and extra heavy. Each class is available either with hub and spigot ends (ASTM A-74) or hubless (CISPI 301 pipe and CISPI 310 fittings).

High-silicon (acid-resistant ASTM A-861) hub-and-spigot cast-iron pipe and fittings are manufactured for laboratory drainage service. Hub-and-spigot pipes are joined with caulked or compression gasket joints and hubless pipe with compression couplings.

Cast-iron pipe is used for nonpressure, sanitary and storm water gravity drainage service above and below grade. The most commonly used pipe above grade is hubless, service-weight cast-iron; below grade it is serviceweight, hub-and-spigot pipe with compression gaskets. High-silicon pipe uses caulked joints aboveground and sealing sleeves below grade. Some codes require extra heavy class pipe below grade.

STEEL PIPE

Carbon steel (CS) pipe is available in a variety of alloys, the most common being ASTM A-53 for general service and ASTM A-106 for high pressure, high temperature service. Stainless steel (SS) pipe encompasses a variety of alloys and is widely used in the chemical, pharmaceutical, and food processing industries; the most commonly used materials are type 304 and 316.

Steel pipe is manufactured either seamless (extruded) or welded. Wall thickness, known as "schedule," ranges from schedule 5 (thinnest) to schedule 160 (thickest). Steel pipe can be joined by welding or with flanges or threaded joints.

COPPER TUBE

Available as either hard (annealed) or drawn (soft) temper, seamless copper (CU) tube can be joined by soldering, brazing, flared joints, and flanges. It is manufactured for specific applications in the following types:

ASTM B-88. Types K, L, and M (thickest to thinnest wall) are used primarily for potable water service and noncritical laboratory gases. Type L hard temper is often used aboveground and type K soft temper underground.

ASTM B-819. Similar to B-88, this tubing is cleaned for laboratory and health care facilities and available only in types K and L hard temper. It is joined mostly by brazing.

ASTM B-75. Termed capillary tubing, this is available only in small diameters and soft temper and is generally used to connect instruments in laboratory service. It is joined with flare joints and by soldering.

ASTM B-280. Type ACR is available only in small diameters and soft temper and is generally used for air conditioning and refrigeration service. It can be joined with flared fittings or by soldering.

ASTM B-306. Known as DWV for drainage, waste, and vent, this tubing is used for drainage service and is joined by soldering. It has the thinnest wall of any copper product.

ASTM B-837. Type G is primarily used for fuel gas service. It is joined by using soldering and flare fittings.

BRASS PIPE

Brass pipes (BR) are made of an alloy of copper and zinc that conforms to ASTM B-43. The proportion of copper varies from 85% (in red brass) to 67% (in yellow brass). Brass pipe is joined by threading, soldering, brazing, or using flanged fittings.

Larger brass pipes are used for potable water and sometimes for branch drainage lines. Fittings and castings made from an alloy different than the pipe may not be suitable for potable water service.

GLASS PIPE

Glass pipe (GL) is made from a low expansion borosilicate glass with a low alkali content. It is used for laboratory gravity waste service and is available in sizes up to 6 inches in diameter. Glass pipe must conform to ASTM C-599.

PLASTIC PIPE

Plastic (PL) has become the material of choice for piping systems used to convey a variety of liquids, including chemical drainage, pharmaceuticals, sewage, water, liquid fuel, and fuel gases. To convey potable water, plastic pipe must be listed by NSF International.

Plastic materials used for pipe are either thermoplastic or thermosetting. Thermoplastics, the most commonly used pipe materials, soften when heat is applied and reharden when cool so the pipe can be extruded or molded into shapes. Thermosetting plastics must be cured by heating or with a curing chemical to achieve permanent shapes; once shaped, they cannot be reformed.

Subclassifications of plastic pipe are based on the pipe material; the two most common are polyolefins and fluoroplastics.

Following is an explanation of the terms used in various consensus standards for plastic pipe:

1. SDR means standard dimensional ratio. The SDR is found by dividing the average outside diameter of a pipe by the wall thickness. This designation has yielded a series of preferred industry standard numbers that are constant for all sizes of pipe.
2. DR means dimensional ratio and is often incorrectly used interchangeably with SDR. The DR is found in the same way as the SDR and means the same thing but is used when a product does not have the preferred SDR number established by prevailing standards.
3. OD Controlled is the designation used when the outside diameter of a pipe is the controlling factor in its selection.
4. ID Controlled is the designation used when the inside diameter of a pipe is the controlling factor in its selection.
5. PR is a designation used when the pressure rating is the controlling factor in the selection of a pipe.
6. Schedule is a designation used to match the standard dimensions for metallic pipe sizes. The pressure rating of the pipe varies with pipe size. Some standards use iron pipe size (IPS) in lieu of schedule to keep a wall thickness consistent with iron pipe.
7. Plastic pipe can be joined with heat fusion (either butt or socket fusion), flanged joints, solvent cement, or threaded pipe of schedule 80 wall thickness or greater. Consult manufacturers for specific recommendations.

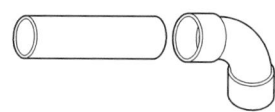

SOLDERED OR BRAZED (COPPER AND BRASS)

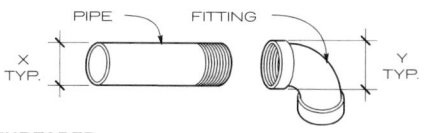

THREADED (FERROUS AND BRASS)

PIPE CONNECTION TYPES

PROPERTIES OF PIPE

NOMINAL PIPE SIZE	O.D. PIPE (DIMENSION X)				O.D. FITTINGS (DIMENSION Y)								WEIGHT OF PIPE (LB/LINEAR FT)					
	STANDARD WEIGHT CAST-IRON	TYPES L AND DWV COPPER	GLASS	SCHEDULE 40 STEEL, BRASS, PLASTIC	CAULKED ELASTOMERIC GASKET	THREADED	FLANGED (150 LB)	BRAZED SOLDERED	COMPRESSION COUPLING	SPLIT COUPLING (GROOVED)	FLARED	SOCKET	STANDARD WEIGHT CAST-IRON	SCHEDULE 40 STEEL	TYPE L COPPER	BRASS	PLASTIC	GLASS
1/4		0.37		0.54				0.43			0.61	0.84		0.42	0.12	0.45	0.05	
5/16		0.43						0.49			0.68				0.15			
3/8		0.50						0.56			0.76			0.57	0.19	0.62	0.12	
1/2		0.62		0.84		1.30	3.90	0.70			1.00	1.30		0.85	0.28	0.93	0.18	
3/4		0.87		1.00		1.50	4.00	1.00			1.20	1.50		1.10	0.45	1.30	0.22	
1		1.13		1.30		1.80	4.30	1.40		4.20	1.70	1.80		1.70	0.65	1.80	0.34	
1 1/4		1.34		1.70		2.30	4.60	1.50		4.50	2.10	2.40		2.30	0.88	2.60	0.46	
1 1/2	1.90	1.62	1.90	1.90	3.00	2.50	5.00	1.80	2.80	4.80	2.50	2.70	2.50	2.70	1.10	3.10	0.54	0.87
2	2.40	2.10	2.40	2.40	4.00	3.00	6.00	2.30	3.30	5.50	3.30	3.20	4.00	3.70		4.10	0.74	1.10
2 1/2		2.60		2.80		3.50	7.00	2.80		6.10	3.90			5.80		6.00	1.20	
3	3.50	3.10	3.40	3.50	5.30	4.30	7.50	3.40	4.30	6.80		4.60	6.20	7.60		8.60	1.50	2.00
4	4.50	4.10	4.60	4.50	6.30	5.40	9.00	4.30	5.30	8.30		5.80	8.40	10.90		12.70	2.00	3.40
5	5.50	5.10		5.50	7.30	6.60	10.00	5.40	6.30	9.80		7.00	10.10	14.80		15.80	2.80	
6	6.50	6.10	6.70	6.60	8.30	8.00	11.00	6.30	7.30	10.80		8.00	12.40	19.10		19.00	3.50	6.30
8	8.80	8.10		8.60	11.00	10.60	13.50	8.50	9.30	13.50		9.40	20.00	25.50			5.10	
10	10.80			10.70	13.30	13.10	16.00		11.30	16.80		11.50	30.00	35.70			6.10	
12	12.80			12.70	15.30	15.50	19.00			18.50		13.50	36.00	44.50			8.20	
14				14.70						19.80				46.00			8.70	
15	15.90				18.80								52.00					

1. All dimensions are in inches.

2. O.D.—outside dimension, I.D.—inside dimension; refer to illustration of pipe connection types for X and Y dimensions.

American Society of Plumbing Engineers; Westlake, California
Michael Frankel, CIPE, Utility Systems Consultants; Somerset, New Jersey

PIPE FITTINGS

Fittings are used to connect pipes to one another, to change the direction of flow of fluids within a pipe, and to change the size of a pipe run. Often one fitting is used to provide all these features. An alternative to changing direction with fittings is to bend the pipe itself, but this method is rarely used except for soft temper copper tubing.

Drainage pipe requires special long radius Y-type fittings to achieve the best flow characteristics. These fittings are called sanitary or drainage-type fittings. In addition to the common fittings illustrated, manufacturers make many specialty combination drainage fittings, primarily for multiple-dwelling construction.

In general, fittings are made of the same material as the pipe to which they are attached, with the following exceptions: Fittings for copper tubing are either of a cast copper alloy that conforms to ANSI B16.18 or wrought copper that conforms to ANSI 16.22.4. Threaded fittings for steel pipe are generally cast-iron pressure fittings that conform to ANSI B-16.4 or malleable iron-banded fittings that conform to ANSI B-16.3.

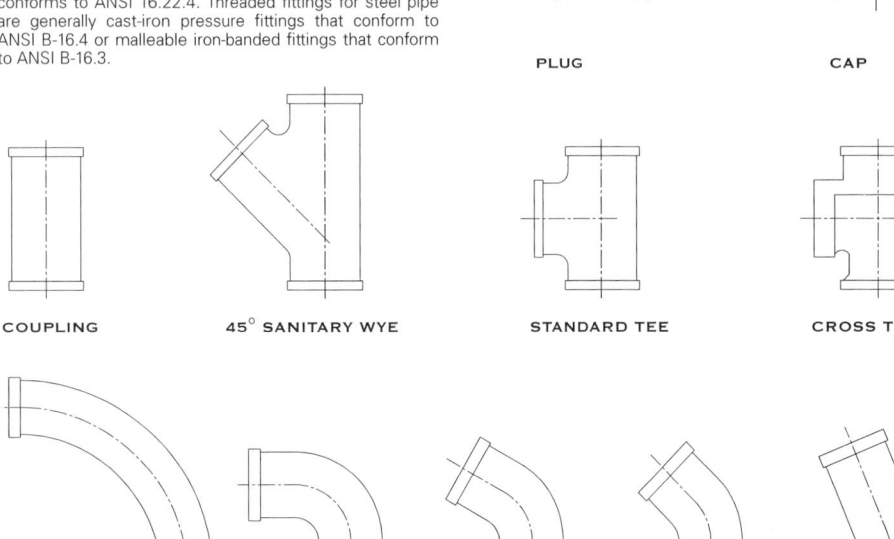

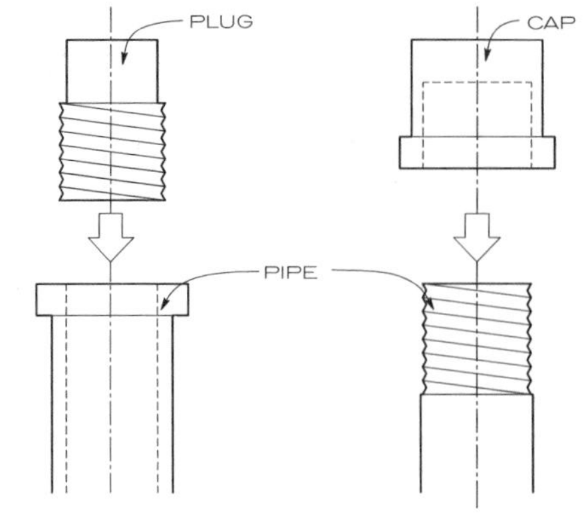

PLUG

CAP

PIPE FITTINGS

COUPLING 45° SANITARY WYE STANDARD TEE CROSS TEE

90° SWEEP 90° ELBOW 60° BEND 45° BEND 22½° BEND

FIXTURES AND TRAPS

Plumbing codes establish a minimum acceptable standard for the design, materials, and installation of plumbing systems. Some aspects of these systems may be subject to other regulations as well. For example, health department requirements and utility company rules regulate the public supply of water and gas and the disposal of storm water and sanitary drainage effluent. The information that appears here is general and not meant for design purposes.

A PLUMBING FIXTURE is any approved receptacle specifically designed and manufactured to receive human (sanitary) or other waterborne effluent (waste) that discharges directly into the sanitary drainage system.

A FIXTURE UNIT is a dimensionless, arbitrary, and comparative value assigned to a plumbing fixture to represent the probable flow of water into the fixture or the effluent it discharges into the drainage system as compared to the function of other fixtures. The effluent discharged is different from the water input so they are separated into drainage fixture units (DFU) and water fixture units (WFU).

A FIXTURE TRAP is a U-shaped section of pipe deep enough to prevent the passage of sewer gas into a fixture. Traps must be self-cleaning, provide a liquid seal of at least 2 in. (larger when required), conform to local code requirements regarding minimum size, have an accessible cleanout, and be able to drain a fixture rapidly. All traps must be vented, unless waived by local codes. All fixtures directly connected to the sanitary drainage system must be trapped and vented.

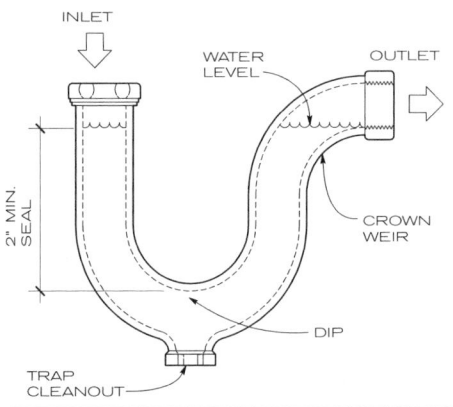

TYPICAL PLUMBING FIXTURE TRAP

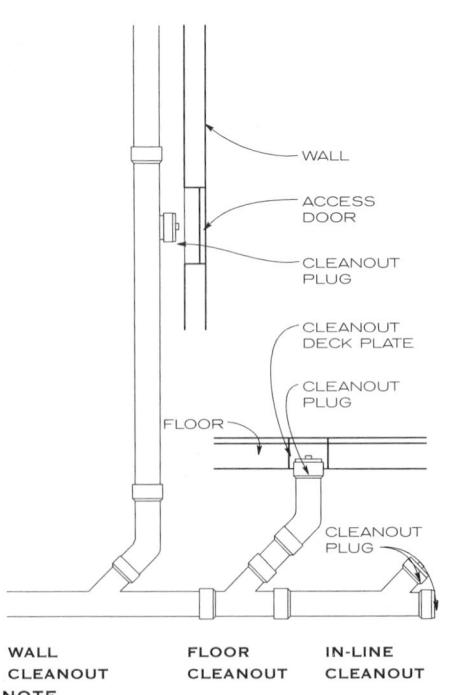

WALL CLEANOUT   FLOOR CLEANOUT   IN-LINE CLEANOUT

NOTE

Cleanouts are typically used for ferrrous or plastic drainage pipe only.

TYPICAL CLEANOUT INSTALLATION

TYPICAL PLUMBING FIXTURE/PIPE SIZE SCHEDULE

PLUMBING FIXTURE	DRAINAGE			WATER			
	DFU[1]	SIZE (IN.)		WFU[2]	SIZE (IN.)		FLOW (GPM)
		TRAP	VENT		COLD	HOT	
Automatic clothes washer	3	2	1½	2	½	½	5
Bathroom group (WC, LAV, SH/BT) FV	8			8			
Bathroom group (WC, LAV, SH/BT) tank	6			6			
Bathtub (BT), with or without SH	2	1½	1½	2	½	½	5
Dishwasher, domestic	2	1½	1½	1	½	½	3
Drinking fountain (DF, EWC)	½	1¼	1¼	½	½		1½
Floor drain (FD)	5	3	1½				
Kitchen sink and tray, single 1.5 trap (KS)	2	1½	1½	2	½	½	3
Kitchen sink and tray, multiple 1.5 traps	3	1½	1½	2	½	½	3
Lavatory, private (LAV)	1	1¼	1¼	1	⅜	⅜	2
Lavatory, public (LAV)	2	1¼	1¼	2	⅜	⅜	2
Laundry tray, 1 or 2 compartments	2	1½	1½	2	½	½	5
Shower (SH) per head or stall	2	2	1½	2	½	½	3
Service sink (SS)	3	3	1½	3	¾	¾	4
Sink, pot and scullery (SK)	2	1½	2	2	½	½	4½
Sink, wash fountain, per faucet	2	1½	1½	2	½	½	2½
Urinal (UR)	4	2	1½	5	¾		10–20
Water closet private flush valve (WC)	6	3	1½	10	1		15–40
Water closet private tank type	4	3	1½	5	½		3–5
Water closet private pressure tank	4	3	1½	4	½		3–5
Water closet public flush valve	6	3	1½	10	1		15–40
Water closet public tank type	4	3	1½	5	½		3–5
Water closet public pressure tank	4	3	1½	4	½		3–5
Wall hydrant, hose bibb					¾		3

[1] DFU—drainage fixture units

[2] WFU—water fixture units

American Society of Plumbing Engineers; Westlake, California
Michael Frankel, CIPE, Utility Systems Consultants; Somerset, New Jersey

GENERAL

A joint is required to connect pipe to itself, a fitting, or a piece of equipment. The joint type selected for a particular application depends on the pipe material and wall thickness, pipe contents, system pressure, system temperature, disassembly requirements, and the applicable plumbing code.

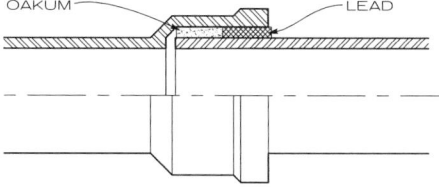

NOTE

Caulked joints are only used to connect metal hub-and-spigot end pipes. Suitable for above- or belowground installation, this labor-intensive, rigid, nonpressure joint has largely been replaced with no-hub compression couplings aboveground and compression gaskets belowground.

CAULKED JOINT

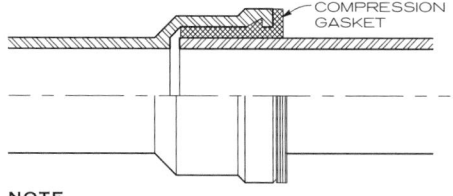

NOTE

Compression gasket joints, used only with hub-and-plain end pipes, are flexible pressure joints suitable for gravity drainage and pressurized liquid systems compatible with the pipe and gasket.

COMPRESSION GASKET JOINT

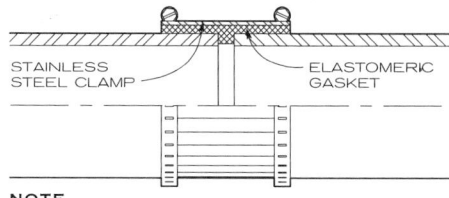

NOTE

Compression coupling joints are rigid nonpressure joints used to join plain end drainage pipes. They are suitable for gravity drainage systems.

COMPRESSION COUPLING

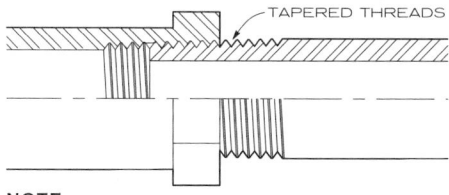

NOTE

Threaded joints can be used for any pipe with walls thick enough to have threads cut. This rigid pressure joint is generally limited to 4-in. pipe as it is difficult to turn larger pipe. Threaded ends come tapered (for plumbing and utility pipe per ANSI B-2.1) and standard (for process pipe systems).

THREADED JOINT

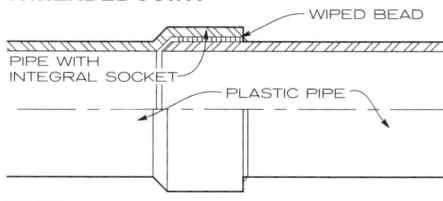

NOTE

Solvent cement joints are rigid pressure joints used only with plastic pipe. Each plastic requires a specific solvent/cement combination recommended by the manufacturer. A joint created with solvent cement looks like a soldered joint, but the cement is used to soften and dissolve the plastic, after which it hardens into a homogeneous joint.

SOLVENT CEMENT JOINT

American Society of Plumbing Engineers; Westlake, California
Michael Frankel, CIPE, Utility Systems Consultants; Somerset, New Jersey

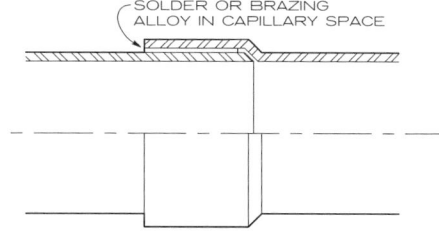

NOTE

Soldered and brazed joints, used to join copper and copper alloy pipe and fittings, are rigid pressure-type joints. The distinction between soldering and brazing is the temperature required to melt the filler metal that enters the joint by capillary action. Solder requires a temperature of 950°F or less, while brazing uses a higher temperature.

Flux is required for solder and some types of brazing filler metal but is prohibited for use with gases installed in health care facilities. Filler metal for soldering consists of 50% tin and 50% lead. No lead is permitted for potable water systems, where an alloy of 95% tin and 5% antimony or a proprietary solder is used.

Soldered joints are used for relatively low pressure applications. Brazing filler metal is of two types: those containing 30-60% silver constitute the BAG class, while those with copper and phosphorus are known as BCuP type. Brazing produces joints stronger than the pipe itself. When used in health care facilities, no flux is permitted.

SOLDERED AND BRAZED JOINT

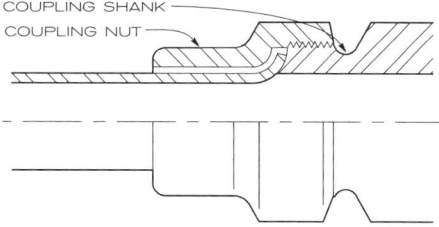

NOTE

Flared joints are rigid pressure joints used for relatively low pressure applications on small diameter pipes made of soft copper or other metals. They are commonly used with capillary piping in laboratories and small diameter underground water piping. Proprietary types of flared fittings are available for high-pressure applications.

FLARED JOINT

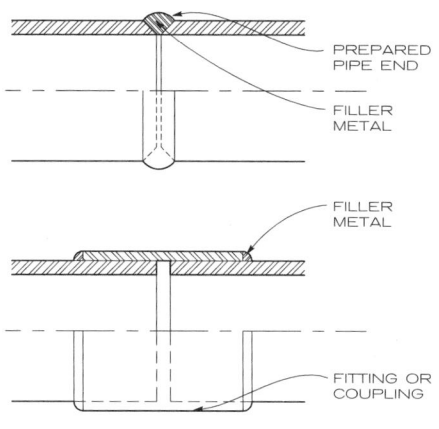

SOCKET WELD

NOTE

Welded joints are rigid pressure joints formed as butt-fused joints or socket welds. Butt-fused joints are created by melting prepared end metal pipes or square end plastic pipes then butting them together and fusing them, which forms a homogeneous joint upon hardening. Metal pipe ends are externally heated and melted with an electric arc or flame and filler metal added to form the joint. For plastic pipe, the ends are melted separately and brought together to form the joint with the use of a special machine. For a socket weld, a plain pipe end is placed inside a socket and the end of the socket fitting is welded to the exterior of the pipe to form a rigid joint.

WELDED JOINTS

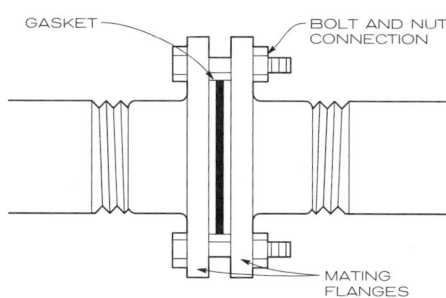

NOTE

Flanged joints are rigid pressure-type joints that use bolts to connect the mating pipe ends, with or without an additional gasket between the ends. Flanges can be installed on the pipe end by welding, threading, or brazing.

FLANGED JOINT

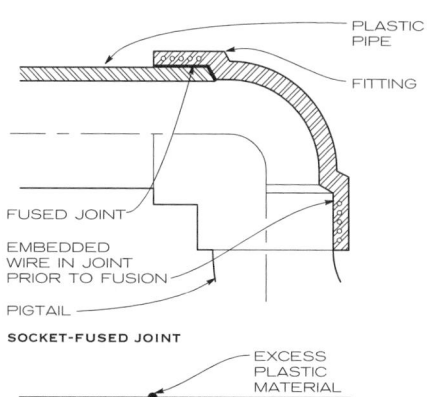

SOCKET-FUSED JOINT

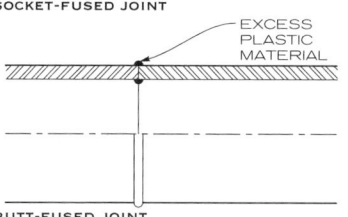

BUTT-FUSED JOINT

NOTE

Heat-fused joints, used only for thermoplastic pipe, are rigid pressure joints. A special socket fitting has resistance heating wire embedded near the outer edge facing the pipe to be joined, complete with pigtails extended outside the fitting. An external electrical power source is connected to the wire pigtails to generate the heat to melt both the inside of the socket and the outside of the pipe in the area where the wire is embedded. When the material is cool, a rigid joint has been formed and the pigtails are cut off.

HEAT-FUSED JOINTS

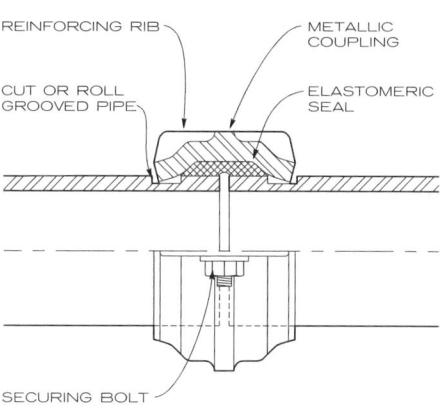

NOTE

Split coupling (grooved) joints require two types of pipe end preparation, roll grooving (shoulder) and cut grooving. The latter method is stronger, but roll grooves must be used when the pipe is too thin for a groove. Couplings must conform to AWWA C606. These rigid pressure-type joints are well-suited for both pressure and nonpressure lines.

SPLIT COUPLING JOINT

ROOF AND FLOOR DRAINS

A floor drain removes liquids from interior, normally occupied areas of a building and discharges them into either the sanitary or an industrial waste drainage system. A commonly cited standard for floor drains is ANSI A-112.21.

A roof drain removes rainwater from roofs and other areas exposed to the weather (such as balconies or canopies) and discharges the effluent into the storm water drainage system. Specialized drain types are available for installation in specific exposed or interior locations; consult drain manufacturers for details.

Major components of drains are outlined below:

The GRATE or DOME is the component that allows liquid into a drain body while excluding larger solids. Grates are available in a wide variety of shapes, slot configurations, materials, and load-bearing capability from light to extra heavy. The high dome on the roof drain allows storm water to enter the drain if some debris accumulates at the bottom. A generally accepted practice has the open area of a grate twice that of the discharge pipe. Generally, an adjustable grate allows the grate top to be adjusted to the finished floor level.

A SEDIMENT TRAP or BUCKET is installed inside a floor drain to trap solids not eliminated by the grate. When space is not available for a sediment bucket, another method is to install a secondary grate.

A FLANGE is the part of the drain body that anchors the drain into a slab.

A FLASHING RING is provided to secure any flashing directly to the drain body to prevent leakage around the drain. Often, roof drains are provided with an integral gravel stop to keep gravel from built-up roofing from entering the drain.

An UNDER-DECK CLAMP is used to secure the drain body to a slab through an opening prior to the installation of any roof, slab finish, or piping.

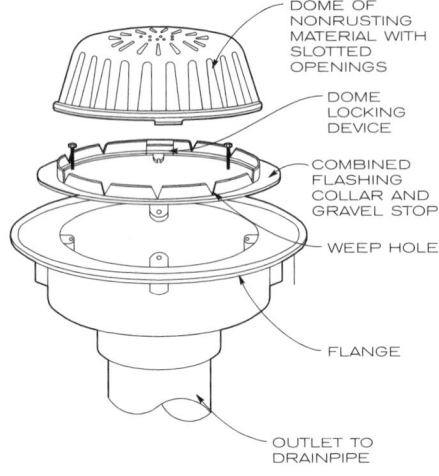

ROOF DRAIN

INTERIOR STORM WATER DRAINAGE PIPE SIZING

The size of storm water lines is based on the area (in sq ft) of the roof to be drained, the pitch of the pipe, and the rate of rainfall in inches per hour (obtained from the authority having jurisdiction).

To design a drainage system for a project, begin by locating the roof drains and designing the piping network. Next, establish the rainfall rate, and calculate the area contributing rain to each roof drain, including the side wall area (half of the area, in sq ft, of any two adjacent vertical walls).

At each design point add all of the area (in sq ft) for all drains together. In the table sizing horizontal drains, look under the pitch established for the piping in a project and find the figure that equals or exceeds the drainage area calculated. Find the applicable pipe size in the column labeled "diameter of drain."

For vertical drain lines, use the table for sizing vertical lines. Use the table for gutters and leaders to find the pipe size for gutters and leaders draining small areas of roof.

American Society of Plumbing Engineers; Westlake, California
Michael Frankel, CIPE, Utility Systems Consultants; Somerset, New Jersey

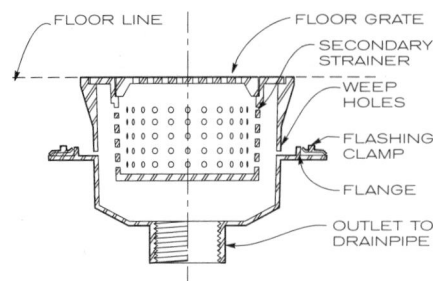

FLOOR DRAIN (BOTTOM OUTLET)

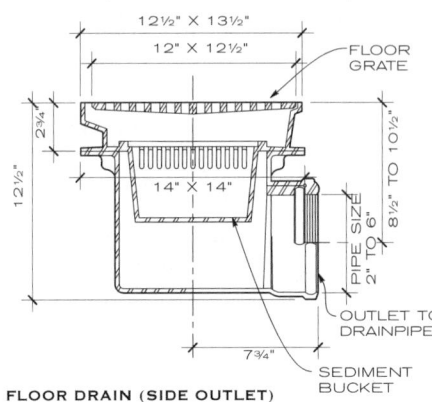

FLOOR DRAIN (SIDE OUTLET)

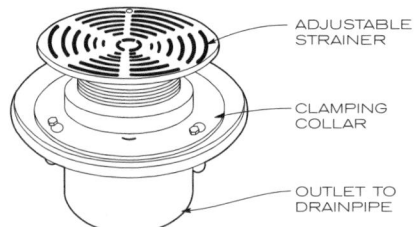

SHOWER DRAIN ISOMETRIC

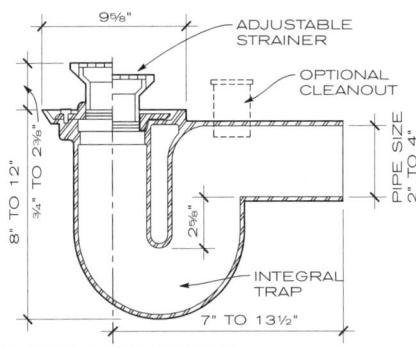

SHOWER DRAIN SECTION

FLOOR AND SHOWER DRAINS

SIZE OF VERTICAL CONDUCTORS AND LEADERS[1]

DIAMETER OF LEADER OR CONDUCTOR (IN.)[2]	MAXIMUM PROJECTED ROOF AREA	
	SQ FT	GPM
2	544	23
2 1/2	987	41
3	1,610	67
4	3,460	144
5	6,280	261
6	10,200	424
8	22,000	913

[1] Based on a maximum rate of rainfall of 4 in./hr and on the hydraulic capacities of vertical circular pipes flowing between a third and a half full at terminal velocity, computed by the method of NBS Mono. 31. Where maximum rates are not 4 in./hr, adjust the figures for drainage area by multiplying by 4 and dividing by the local rate in in./hr.

[2] The area of rectangular leaders should be equivalent to that of the circular leader or conductor required, while the ratio of width to depth of rectangular leaders should not exceed 3 to 1.

SIZE OF ROOF GUTTERS[1]

DIAMETER OF GUTTER (IN.)[2]	MAXIMUM PROJECTED ROOF AREA FOR GUTTERS OF VARIOUS SLOPES (SQ FT)			
	1/16 IN.	1/8 IN.	1/4 IN.	1/2 IN. AND VERTICAL
3	170	240	340	480
4	360	510	720	1,020
5	625	880	1,250	1,770
6	960	1,360	1,950	2,770
7	1,380	1,920	2,760	3,900
8	1,990	2,800	3,980	5,600
10	3,600	5,100	7,200	10,000

[1] Sizes shown are based on a 4 in./hr rainfall.

[2] Gutters other than semicircular ones must have an equivalent cross-sectional area.

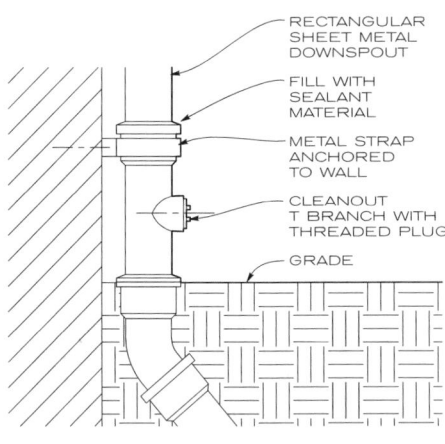

LEADER BOOT DETAIL

SIZE OF HORIZONTAL STORM DRAINS, SINGLE RAINFALL RATE*

DIAMETER OF DRAIN (IN.)	MAXIMUM PROJECTED ROOF AREA FOR GUTTERS OF VARIOUS SLOPES (SQ FT)					
	1/8-IN. SLOPE		1/4-IN. SLOPE		1/2-IN. SLOPE	
	SQ FT	GPM	SQ FT	GPM	SQ FT	GPM
3	822	34	1,160	48	1,644	68
4	1,880	78	2,650	110	3,760	156
5	3,340	139	4,720	196	6,680	278
6	5,350	222	7,550	314	10,700	445
8	11,500	478	16,300	677	23,000	956
10	20,700	860	29,200	1,214	41,400	1,721
12	33,300	1,384	47,000	1,953	66,600	2,768
15	59,500	2,473	84,000	3,491	119,000	4,946

*The figures in this chart are based on a maximum rate of rainfall of 4 in./hr. Where maximum rates are more or less than 4 in./hr, adjust the figures for drainage by multiplying by 4 and dividing by the local rate in inches per hour.

DRAINAGE AND WASTE PIPE SIZING

The sizing of drainage and waste lines from fixtures is based on total DFUs, the pitch of the drainage pipe, and the classification of the line as a branch, stack, or building drain.

The fixture schedule shows the minimum size line permitted from a fixture. At each design point, add all DFUs together. Enter the chart based on line classification and the pitch of the pipe, and find a figure equal to or greater than the DFUs calculated. Read horizontally to find the pipe size.

The minimum pitch for branches 3 in. and smaller is $1/4$ in./ft. For lines 4 in. and larger, it is $1/8$ in./ft. A branch interval is the rough equivalent of one floor level. The minimum pitch for building drains (main lines inside the building) and building sewers (main lines outside the building that connect with the public sewer) is $1/16$ in./ft.

BUILDING DRAINS AND SEWERS[1]

MAXIMUM NUMBER OF FIXTURE UNITS THAT MAY BE CONNECTED TO ANY PORTION OF BUILDING DRAIN OR BUILDING SEWER[2]

DIAMETER OF PIPE (IN.)	SLOPE PER FOOT			
	1/16 IN.	1/8 IN.	1/4 IN.	1/2 IN.
2			21	26
$1^1/_2$			24	31
3			42[3]	50[3]
4		180	216	250
5		390	480	575
6		700	840	1000
8	1400	1600	1920	2300
10	2500	2900	3500	4200
12	2900	4600	5600	6700
15	7000	8300	10000	12000

[1] On-site sewers that serve more than one building may be sized according to current standards and specifications of the administrative authority for public sewers.

[2] Consult local building codes for exact requirements.

[3] No more than 2 water closets or 2 bathroom groups (except in single-family dwellings, no more than 3 water closets or 3 bathroom groups) may be installed.

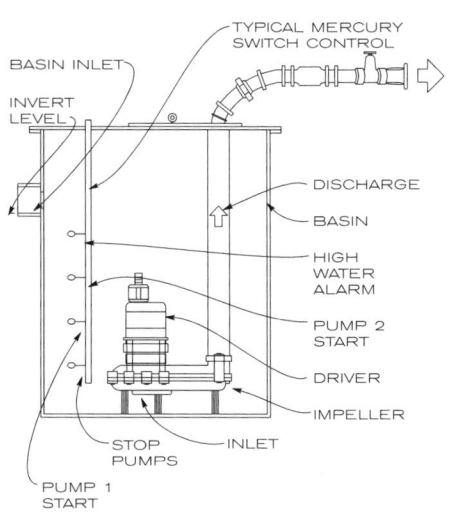

EJECTOR PUMP FOR SUBMERSIBLE PUMP SYSTEM

PUMP SYSTEMS

Ejector pumps are intended to transport sanitary waste with large suspended solids. Sump pumps transport turbid, nonsanitary effluent with small suspended solids. They use different impellers. Minimum recommended pump running time is one minute for optimum reliability.

To find the basin depth, use the following approximate dimensions as a guide, assuming duplex pumps and starting from the invert of the inlet pipe.

1. From the invert of the inlet pipe, allow 6 in. to the high water alarm.

2. From the high water alarm, allow 6 in. to pump 2 start in a duplex installation.

American Society of Plumbing Engineers; Westlake, California
Michael Frankel, CIPE, Utility Systems Consultants; Somerset, New Jersey

DRAINAGE BRANCHES AND STACKS

MAXIMUM NUMBER OF FIXTURE UNITS THAT MAY BE CONNECTED TO VARIOUS BRANCHES[1]

DIAMETER OF PIPE (IN.)	ANY HORIZONTAL FIXTURE BRANCH[2] (DFU)	ONE STACK OF THREE OR FEWER BRANCH INTERVALS (DFU)	STACKS WITH MORE THAN THREE BRANCH INTERVALS	
			TOTAL FOR STACK[3] (DFU)	TOTAL AT ONE BRANCH INTERVAL (DFU)
$1^1/_2$	3	4	8	2
2	6	10	24	6
$2^1/_2$	12	20	42	9
3	20[4]	48[4]	72[4]	20[4]
4	160	240	500	90
5	360	540	1100	200
6	620	960	1900	350
8	1400	2200	3600	600
10	2500	3800	5600	1000
12	3900	6000	8400	1500
15	7000			

[1] Consult local building codes for exact requirements.

[2] Does not include branches of the building drain.

[3] Size stacks according to the total accumulated connected load at each story or branch interval. Stacks may be reduced in size as this load decreases, to a minimum diameter of half the largest size required.

[4] No more than 2 water closets or bathroom groups within each branch interval and no more than 6 water closets or bathroom groups on the stack.

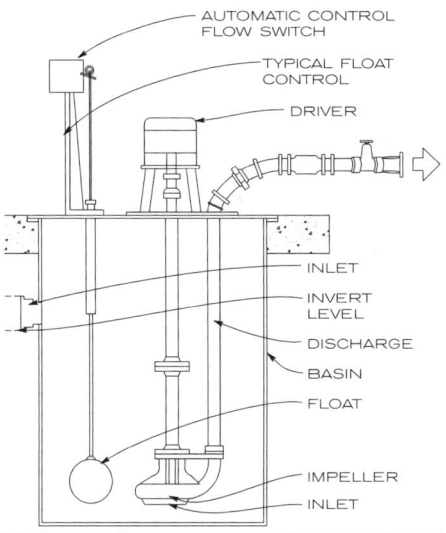

SUMP OR EJECTOR FOR VERTICAL LIFT SUBMERGED PUMP SYSTEM

CAPACITY OF SUMP AND EJECTOR BASINS (GAL/FT DEPTH)

CIRCULAR		SQUARE	
DIAMETER (FT)	GALLONS	SIDE (FT)	GALLONS
2.0	23.50	2.0	30.00
2.5	36.72	2.5	45.00
3.0	52.88	3.0	67.50
3.5	71.91	3.5	90.00
4.0	94.00	4.0	120.00
4.5	110.32	4.5	149.60
5.0	146.89	5.0	187.00
6.0	158.64	6.0	270.00
7.0	170.00	7.0	365.50
8.0	181.00		
9.0	193.00		
10.0	204.00		

3. From pump 2 start, allow 6 in. to pump 1 start.

4. Below pump 1 start, the dimension of the liquid capacity depends on a 1- to 5-min. operating period of the selected pump. The lower level of the storage portion is pump(s) stop. The table on capacity of sump and ejector basins gives the storage capacity of different size basins.

5. Allow 6 in. from pump stop to the inlet of the pump.

6. Allow 1 ft to the basin bottom from the inlet of the pump. This dimension varies according to manufacturer.

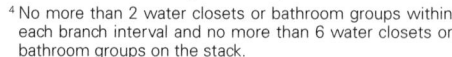

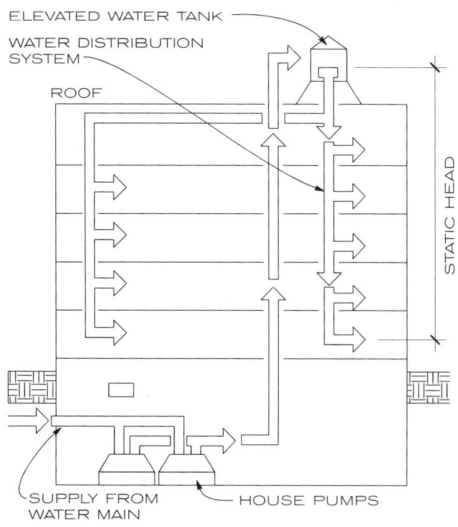

DOWNFEED WATER SUPPLY SYSTEM

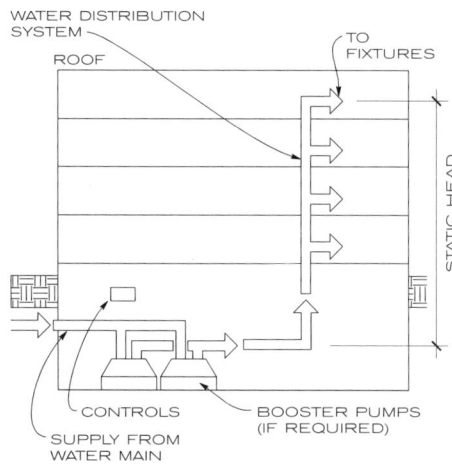

UPFEED WATER SUPPLY SYSTEM

7. Sewage and waste effluents have the same hydraulic characteristics as water. Ejector discharge lines should be a minimum of 3 in. and sump discharge lines should be a minimum of 2 in. to prevent stoppages. The pump head is found by adding the distance from the bottom of the basin to one foot higher than the point of discharge and the friction loss of water through the discharge pipe.

8. Duplex pumps generally require a minimum diameter of 4 ft.

SIZING POTABLE WATER LINES

Water lines are sized according to flow rate in gallons per minute (GPM), the allowable pressure loss of water flowing through the pipe, and the velocity of the flowing water that has been calculated for each specific project. The GPM is found using "Hunters Curve," which converts water fixture units (WFUs) into GPM. This information is available in the ASPE (American Society of Plumbing Engineers) Data Book. A simplified general procedure for sizing potable water lines is outlined here.

Obtain the elevation and location of the water main and the lowest residual water pressure from the utility company. Also determine the requirements regarding the need for and location of the water meter, backflow preventer (BFP), and shutoff valves. Run the piping from the source into the building on the plans.

When the water source is a well, design the service using good engineering practice. Choose the well location in conjunction with the authority having jurisdiction.

Calculate the available water pressure to a point just inside the building. First, add together all the service losses, such as that caused by the difference in elevation between the main and the point of entry, the water meter, the backflow preventer (if any), valves, and the friction loss of water in the building service. Subtract that figure from the residual pressure in the main.

Calculate the required water pressure for the building by determining the operating pressure for the most remote fixture (ask the manufacturer), the height from the point of entry to the highest fixture, and an estimated friction loss through the water distribution system. If the figure determined is equal to or less than the available pressure, no booster pressure system will be required. If the pressure required is greater than that available, a booster pressure system must be provided.

The friction loss of water flowing through pipes can be obtained from the ASPE Data Book or Cameron's Hydraulic Data (Ingersol Rand). The decision to use an upfeed or downfeed distribution system and the choice of method used to boost the water pressure are based on cost, available space conditions, and aesthetic considerations.

Generally available methods for boosting water pressure include an elevated tank, constant running of booster pumps, and a hydropneumatic system similar to those used for well pump systems. A generally accepted maximum water pressure is 80 psig. Pressures above that require a pressure regulating valve (PRV).

FUEL GAS LINE SIZING

Fuel gases are natural gas (mostly methane) and liquefied petroleum gas (LPG), mostly propane. Natural gas has a heating value of about 1,000 British thermal units per cubic foot, although this value varies in different parts of the country.

LPG has a heating value of about 2,500 Btu/cu ft. Most installations require a meter and a regulator to reduce the pressure to about 7 to 10 in. water column pressure at the building, referred to as low pressure. Higher pressures are common, particularly to supply boilers. All pressure requirements are obtained from the utility company. The applicable code is NFPA-54 (the sizing table is used with permission from the National Fire Protection Association, Quincy, Mass.).

Gas lines are sized according to the cubic feet per hour (cfh) flow, allowable friction loss for the piping distribution network, and a diversity factor if applicable. A conservative method of sizing is described here:

1. First, establish the location of equipment using gas, then ask the manufacturer for the cfh flow for each piece of equipment. With the piping network drawn on plans, measure the total horizontal and vertical run, in feet, from the meter to the most remote device. (Vertical runs are ignored for natural gas only.) Next, establish a friction loss for the system. It is common practice to use a loss of 0.3 in. of water column in low pressure systems.
2. At each design point add the cfh flows for all the equipment. Be sure to apply any applicable diversity factors to allow for the possibility that not all devices will be used at once.
3. To determine what size gas line is needed, look in the table called "Low-Pressure Gas Pipe Sizing Schedule." First, find the column showing the length of the total pipe run for the application (this is the only distance used). Find the required pipe size in the column on the left at the intersection of the distance column that equals or exceeds the measured distance of the pipe in the project and the row showing the cfh value that meets or exceeds the cfh value calculated for that project.

The table has been prepared for use with natural gas at a specific gravity of 0.60. To use it for LPG at a specific gravity of 1.50, multiply the cfh figure by 0.63.

VENT PIPE SIZING

The purpose of a vent system is to limit the pneumatic pressure in a drainage system to plus or minus one inch of water column. Vent systems terminate in the outside air and connect directly to every fixture trap.

Vent lines are sized using three factors: drainage fixture units (DFUs), the size of the drainage line (or stack) to which the fixtures are connected, and the length of the vent line from the fixture to the vent stack.

The drainage and vent system is assumed to be drawn on the plans and the drainage system sized. At each design point, enter the chart horizontally with the size of the drainage line and the total DFUs. Using the measured length of the vent from the fixture to the vent stack, select a figure equal to or greater than that length. Read vertically up to find the vent line size. The minimum size vent for fixtures is found in the fixture schedule.

MAXIMUM LENGTH OF TRAP ARM

DIAMETER OF TRAP ARM (IN.)	DISTANCE FROM TRAP TO VENT (FT)
1 1/4	3 1/2
1 1/2	5
2	8
3	10
4	12

SIZE AND LENGTH OF VENTS

SIZE OF SOIL OR WASTE STACK (IN.)	FIXTURE UNITS CONNECTED	DIAMETER OF VENT REQUIRED (IN.)					
		1 1/4	1 1/2	2	2 1/2	3	4
		MAXIMUM LENGTH OF VENT (FT)					
1.5	8	50	150				
2.0	12	30	75	200			
2.0	20	26	50	150			
2.5	42		30	100	300		
3.0	10		30	100	100	600	
3.0	30			60	200	500	
3.0	60			50	80	400	
4.0	100			35	100	260	1000
4.0	200			30	90	250	900
4.0	500			20	70	180	700
5.0	200				35	80	350
5.0	500				30	70	300
5.0	1100				20	50	200
6.0	350				25	50	200
6.0	620				15	30	125
6.0	960					24	100
6.0	1900					20	70
8.0	600						50
8.0	1400						40
8.0	2200						30
8.0	3600						25
10.0	1000						
10.0	2500						
10.0	3800						
10.0	5600						

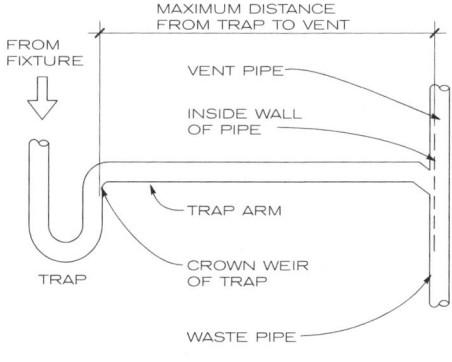

TRAP ARM

LOW-PRESSURE GAS PIPE SIZING SCHEDULE*

NOMINAL IRON PIPE SIZE (IN.)	INTERNAL DIAMETER (IN.)	LENGTH OF PIPE (FT)													
		10	20	30	40	50	60	70	80	90	100	125	150	175	200
1/4	0.364	32	22	18	15	14	12	11	11	10	9	8	8	7	6
3/8	0.493	72	49	40	34	30	27	25	23	22	21	18	17	15	14
1/2	0.622	132	92	73	63	56	50	46	43	40	38	34	31	28	26
3/4	0.824	278	190	152	130	115	105	96	90	84	79	72	64	59	55
1	1.049	520	350	285	245	215	195	180	170	160	150	130	120	110	100
1 1/4	1.380	1,050	730	590	500	440	400	370	350	320	305	275	250	225	210
1 1/2	1.610	1,600	1,100	890	760	670	610	560	530	490	460	410	380	350	320
2	2.067	3,050	2,100	1,650	1,450	1,270	1,150	1,050	990	930	870	780	710	650	610
2 1/2	2.469	4,800	3,300	2,700	2,300	2,000	1,850	1,700	1,600	1,500	1,400	1,250	1,130	1,050	980
3	3.068	8,500	5,900	4,700	4,100	3,600	3,250	3,000	2,800	2,600	2,500	2,200	2,000	1,850	1,700
4	4.026	17,500	12,000	9,700	8,300	7,400	6,800	6,200	5,800	5,400	5,100	4,500	4,100	3,800	3,500

*Maximum capacity of pipe in cu ft of gas per hour for gas pressure of 0.5 psig or less and a pressure drop of 0.3 in water column, based on a 0.60 specific gravity gas
(Chart courtesy National Fire Protection Association)

American Society of Plumbing Engineers; Westlake, California
Michael Frankel, CIPE, Utility Systems Consultants; Somerset, New Jersey

GENERAL

Valves are used to turn on or off, control the flow of, prevent the reverse flow of, and adjust the pressure of fluids in a piping system. Operation can be linear (straight up and down) or rotary (multiturn or quarter turn). Valves are classified by the shape of their closure member. Plastic valves are suitable for use in most utility services and are rapidly replacing metallic valves due to their increased corrosion resistance and lower cost. Valves are selected according to resistance to flow; throttling ability; system working pressure; intended service, such as WOG (water, oil, gas), WWP (water working pressure), or WSP (working steam pressure); and jointing method.

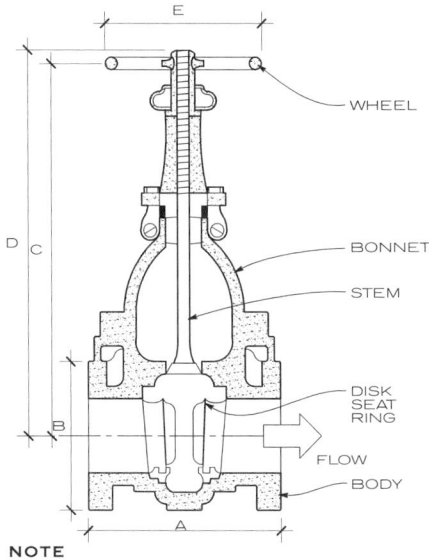

NOTE

Gate valves have a wedge-shaped closure member seated into a metal recess. Used for on-and-off control, generally for liquids, they are available in a wide variety of sizes, body shapes, stem configurations, body and internal materials, and pressure ranges. They are not recommended for throttling service, and they have low resistance to flow.

GATE VALVE

TYPICAL GATE VALVE DIMENSIONS (IN.)

NOMINAL SIZE	A	B	C	D	E
2	7	6	11 3/4	14 3/8	6
2 1/2	7 1/2	7	12 3/4	16 1/16	6
3	8	7 1/2	14 1/16	18 1/8	8
3 1/2	8 1/2	8 1/2	15 1/4	19 7/8	8
4	9	9	16 7/8	21 3/4	10
5	10	10	20 3/4	26 7/8	12
6	10 1/2	11	23 1/2	30 9/16	12
8	11 1/2	13 1/2	29 3/4	39	14
10	13	16	35 3/4	46 7/8	16
12	14	19	41 1/4	55	18

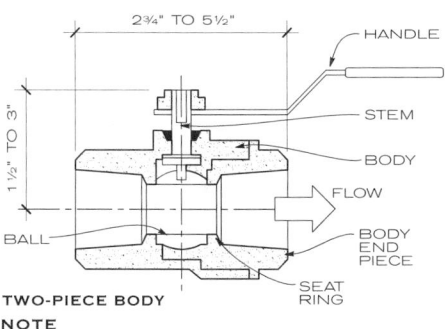

TWO-PIECE BODY

NOTE

Ball valves are named for the round closure member that consists of a round port drilled through the valve and sealed tightly on a resilient seat when turned. Classified as a quarter turn valve, the body is available in one-, two-, or three-

BALL VALVE

American Society of Plumbing Engineers; Westlake, California
Michael Frankel, CIPE, Utility Systems Consultants; Somerset, New Jersey

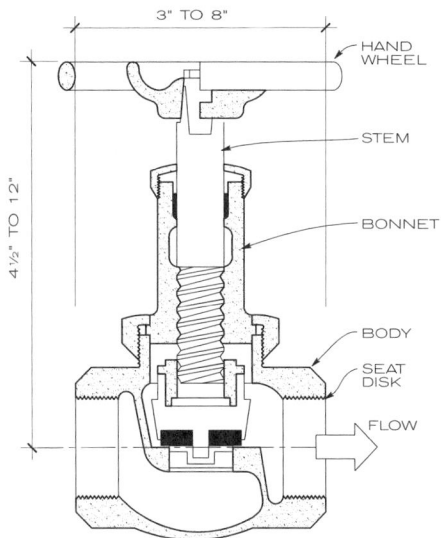

NOTE

Globe valves, named for the round shape of the body, have a closure member that is generally a disc sealed on a resilient seat. Body types include straight through and angle configurations. Used primarily for throttling service, they have a high resistance to flow because of the diverted passage of fluid around the seat.

GLOBE VALVE

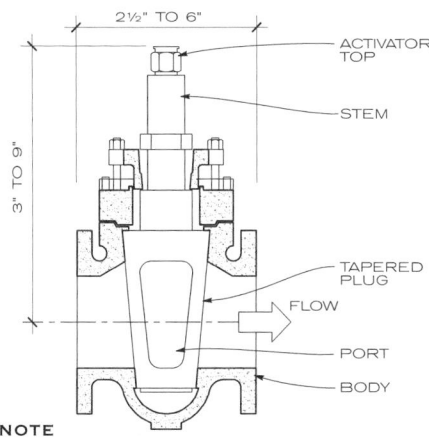

NOTE

Plug valves are named for the tapered, cylindrical closure member, which has a port through it that seals tightly on a resilient seat when turned. Classified as a quarter turn valve, they are available either lubricated (larger sizes) or nonlubricated. They are used primarily for fuel gas service but also for both throttling and shutoff service. They have low resistance to flow and are well-suited for power actuation.

PLUG VALVE

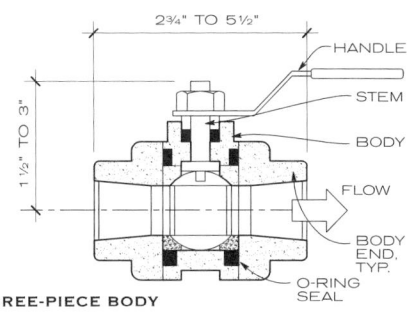

THREE-PIECE BODY

piece construction. Used for throttling and shutoff service, ball valves are suitable for liquids and gases. They are well-suited for power actuation and have low resistance to flow. They are often used for medical gas service when specifically cleaned and packaged for health care facilities.

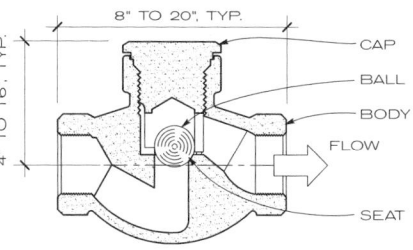

BALL CHECK

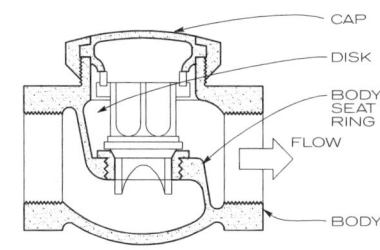

LIFT CHECK

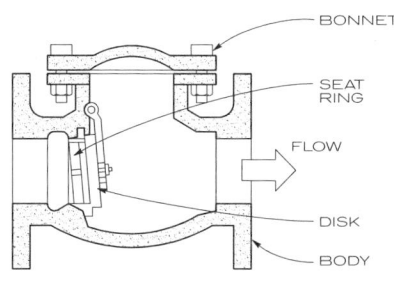

SWING CHECK

NOTE

Check valves prevent the reverse flow of fluids. The most commonly used valves are lift and swing types, although ball closures are also available. When used for sanitary drainage service, check valves are referred to as backwater valves.

CHECK VALVES

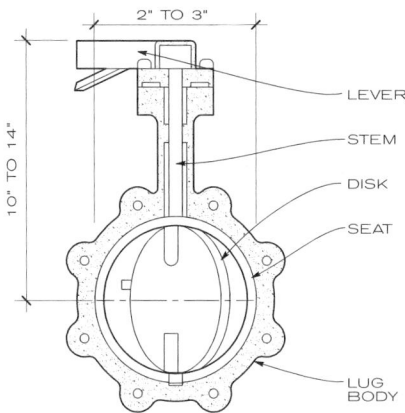

NOTE

Butterfly valves use a thin, rotating disk in the flow path as the closure member, seating on a resilient seal at the perimeter of the valve body. Classified as a quarter turn valve, they are used for both throttling and shutoff service. When no leakage is desired, a "bubble tight" seat is used. Butterfly valves have low resistance to flow and are well-suited for power actuation.

BUTTERFLY VALVE

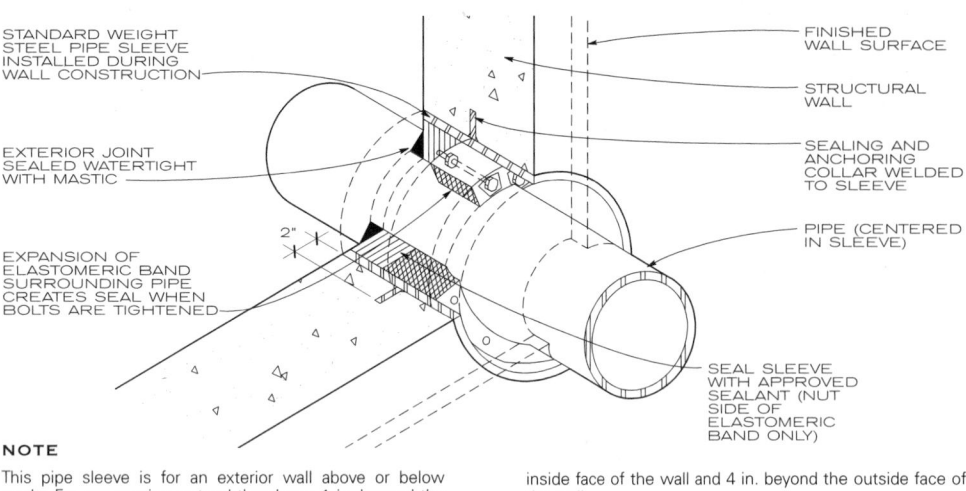

STANDARD WEIGHT STEEL PIPE SLEEVE INSTALLED DURING WALL CONSTRUCTION

FINISHED WALL SURFACE

STRUCTURAL WALL

EXTERIOR JOINT SEALED WATERTIGHT WITH MASTIC

SEALING AND ANCHORING COLLAR WELDED TO SLEEVE

PIPE (CENTERED IN SLEEVE)

EXPANSION OF ELASTOMERIC BAND SURROUNDING PIPE CREATES SEAL WHEN BOLTS ARE TIGHTENED

2"

SEAL SLEEVE WITH APPROVED SEALANT (NUT SIDE OF ELASTOMERIC BAND ONLY)

NOTE

This pipe sleeve is for an exterior wall above or below grade. For gas service, extend the sleeve 1 in. beyond the inside face of the wall and 4 in. beyond the outside face of the wall.

PIPE SLEEVE IN EXTERIOR WALL

SEAL OR CAULK SLEEVE

FINISHED WALL SURFACE

STANDARD WEIGHT STEEL PIPE SLEEVE OF SIZE TO PASS PIPE (WITH INSULATION, IF USED)

TERMINATE SLEEVE FLUSH WITH FINISHED WALL SURFACE

PIPE (AND INSULATION) TO BE CENTERED IN SLEEVE (DO NOT SUPPORT PIPE FROM SLEEVE)

FINISHED ESCUTCHEON PLATE FLUSH AGAINST WALL AND SIZED TO COMPLETELY COVER OPENING

NOTE

Pipe sleeve is typically two pipe sizes larger than the outside diameter of the pipe or insulation.

PIPE SLEEVE IN INTERIOR WALL

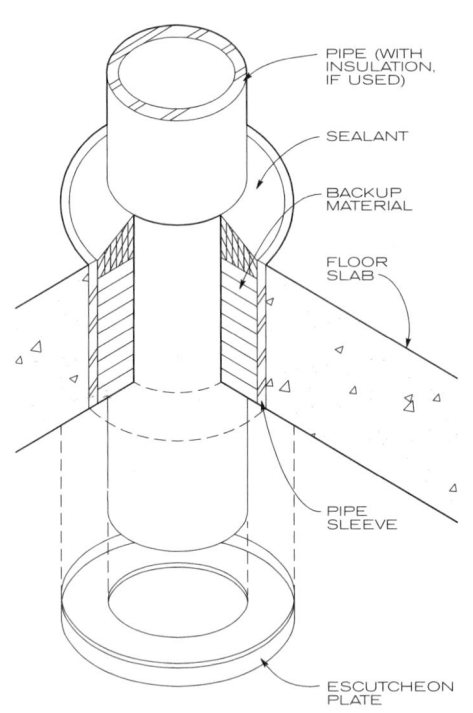

PIPE (WITH INSULATION, IF USED)

SEALANT

BACKUP MATERIAL

FLOOR SLAB

PIPE SLEEVE

ESCUTCHEON PLATE

PIPE SLEEVE IN FLOOR SLAB

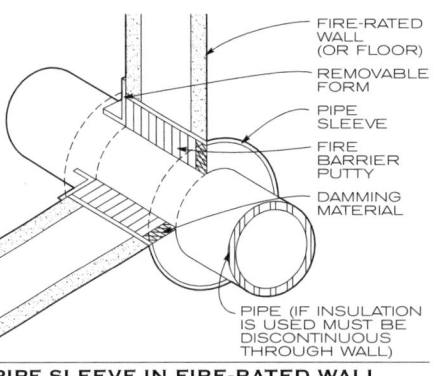

FIRE-RATED WALL (OR FLOOR)

REMOVABLE FORM

PIPE SLEEVE

FIRE BARRIER PUTTY

DAMMING MATERIAL

PIPE (IF INSULATION IS USED MUST BE DISCONTINUOUS THROUGH WALL)

PIPE SLEEVE IN FIRE-RATED WALL

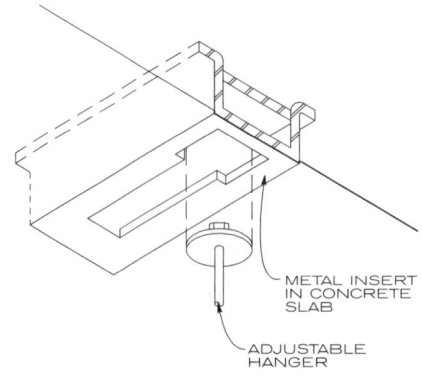

METAL INSERT IN CONCRETE SLAB

ADJUSTABLE HANGER

PIPE HANGER FROM CONCRETE SLAB

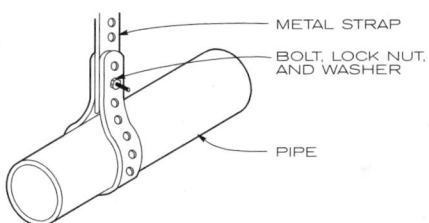

METAL STRAP

BOLT, LOCK NUT, AND WASHER

PIPE

STRAP HANGER

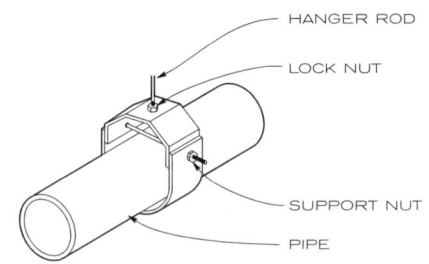

HANGER ROD

LOCK NUT

SUPPORT NUT

PIPE

CLEVIS HANGER

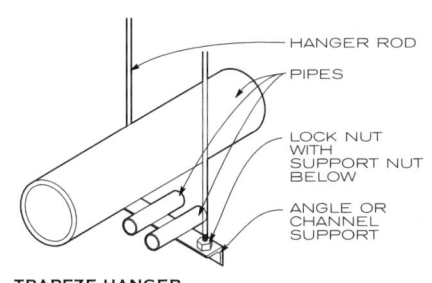

HANGER ROD

PIPES

LOCK NUT WITH SUPPORT NUT BELOW

ANGLE OR CHANNEL SUPPORT

TRAPEZE HANGER

NOTE

Hangers are required at all turns and junctions; spacing is determined by pipe size.

TYPICAL PIPE HANGERS

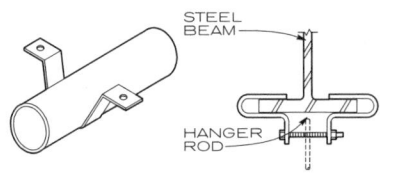

STEEL BEAM

HANGER ROD

PIPE CLIP   **CENTER BEAM CLAMP**

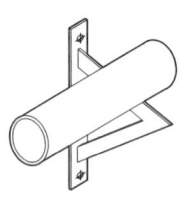

STEEL BRACKET   **C-CLAMP**

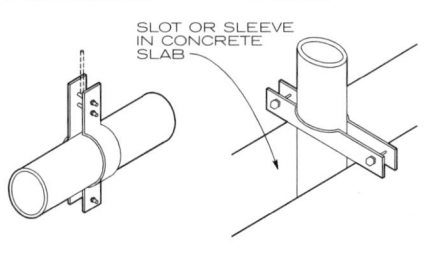

SLOT OR SLEEVE IN CONCRETE SLAB

PIPE CLAMP   **VERTICAL RISER CLAMP**

MISCELLANEOUS PIPE HANGERS AND CLAMPS

American Society of Plumbing Engineers; Westlake, California
Michael Frankel, CIPE, Utility Systems Consultants; Somerset, New Jersey

GENERAL

The primary purpose of insulation is to retard the flow of heat and water vapor from pipes, ducts, and equipment. An insulation system consists of the insulation itself; a jacket to cover it; and, if needed, an additional jacket to provide specific characteristics such as weather protection or the ability to be repeatedly cleaned. Code limitations for flame spread and amount of smoke developed established for components in fireproof and noncombustible buildings apply to these insulation system elements.

COMMON INSULATION TYPES

The insulation materials described here are identified by generic names rather than manufacturers' trade names.

FIBERGLASS INSULATION (ASTM C 547) is fibrous glass made plain or with a heat-resistant binder to help the fiberglass hold its shape. Material with a density of 3 to 5 lb/cu ft typically has an R value of 3.8 to 4.5.

Felted glass fiber without any binder is available in rolls. With a thermosetting resin binder, it is available in varying degrees of stiffness. The form most commonly used for pipe is molded and shaped into semicircular sections. A cover is needed to protect this type of insulation from physical damage, permit it to be firmly attached to the pipe, and prevent penetration of water vapor. Fiberglass insulation, recommended for temperatures from 35° to 800°F, is available in thicknesses from $1/2$ to 5 in. for $1/2$-in. to 33-in. pipe.

CELLULAR GLASS INSULATION (ASTM C 552) is pure glass with closed-cell air spaces. It offers a flame spread of 5, smoke developed rate of 0, and 0 perm rating; typical R value is 2.6. Form-fitting covers are used for standard components. The type of jacket used for abrasion resistance depends on the severity of service. Recommended applications include temperatures ranging from -450° to +450°F (adhesive type varies with the temperature). Cellular glass insulation, impervious to common acids and corrosive environments and hard enough to cut with a saw, is used when an extremely strong, impermeable material is required.

ELASTOMERIC PLASTIC INSULATION (ASTM C 534) is an expanded foam, closed-cell material made from nitrile rubber and polyvinyl chloride resin. Typical R value is 3.6, and the perm rating is only 0.17. This material does not require a jacket except for appearance. The flame rating of 50 is valid for all thicknesses. For material $3/4$ in. thick and less, a smoked-developed rating of 50 has been established; with 1-in. thickness, the rating is close to 150. Because of the high rating, building codes do not allow use of this type of insulation in all types of construction.

Commonly called "rubber," elastomeric plastic insulation is available in $1/2$ and $3/4$ in. thicknesses for pipe sizes up to 5 in. in diameter (iron pipe size). Recommended applications for pipe include temperatures from 35° to 220°F, except for sheets, which can be used only up to 180°F because of the adhesive used to apply them to a tank. This flexible insulation is used in pipe spaces and boiler and mechanical equipment rooms, where code requirements may be relaxed and the ease of application could make it the most cost-effective material.

FOAMED PLASTIC INSULATION is a continuously molded, closed-cell rigid product made from foaming plastic resin. Plastic materials typically are polyurethane (C 591), polystrene (C 578), and polyethylene. A factory-applied jacket is usually provided. Typical R value is 6.7. The fire rating varies by manufacturer because of the wide variety in composition of materials in this category of insulation. Although the materials are combustible, they can be made self-extinguishing. Foamed plastic is recommended for low temperatures, including cryogenic applications, and for moderate temperatures, generally up to 220°F.

CALCIUM SILICATE (ASTM C 533) insulation is a rigid material compounded from silica, asbestos-free reinforcing fibers, and lime. At 500°F, it has an R value of 2.0. A field-applied jacket is required.

MINERAL FIBER (ASTM C 553) insulation is a rigid material composed of rock and slag made into fibers and bound together with a heat-resistant inorganic binder; typical R value is 4.9. This material is good for high temperature work.

JACKETS

A jacket is any material (excluding cement and paint) that can be directly applied to insulation on a pipe, duct, or vessel in order to cover or protect the insulation. The type of jacket chosen depends on the application. Jackets come in various forms and types, which can be divided into three general categories: rigid (plastic, aluminum, or stainless steel), membrane (glass cloth, coated papers, treated papers, and foil- or cloth-laminated papers), and mastic. The most common jacket for fiberglass insulation is an all-service jacket or ASJ, which comprises laminated kraft paper, fiberglass cloth (skrim), and either aluminum foil or metalized film as a vapor barrier. This jacket type is sometimes called an FSK (foil, skrim, and kraft) jacket.

INSTALLATION

Proper installation of insulation on a pipe or duct is critical to the longevity of an insulation system. Typical installations of insulation on the outside of a duct, elastomeric insulation around a pipe, insulation with a nonmetallic jacket, and insulation with a metallic jacket are illustrated on this page.

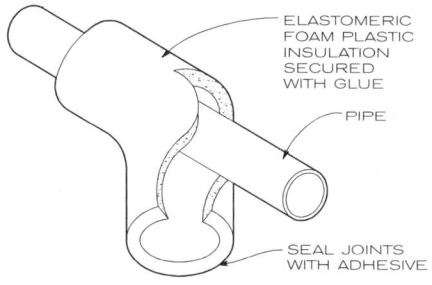

ELASTOMERIC PLASTIC INSULATION

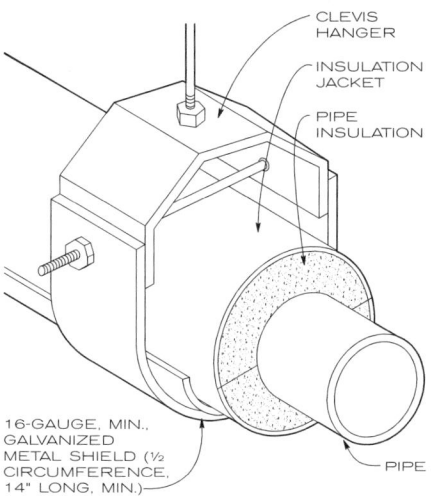

METAL SHIELD SUPPORT

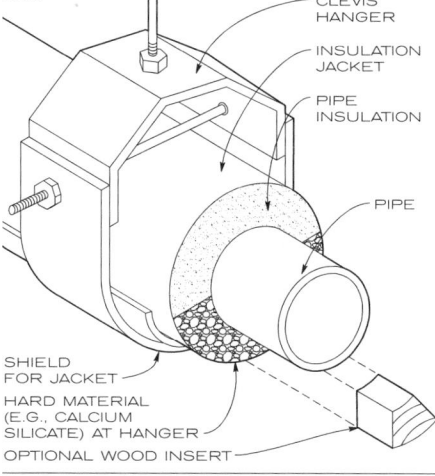

HARD MATERIAL SUPPORT

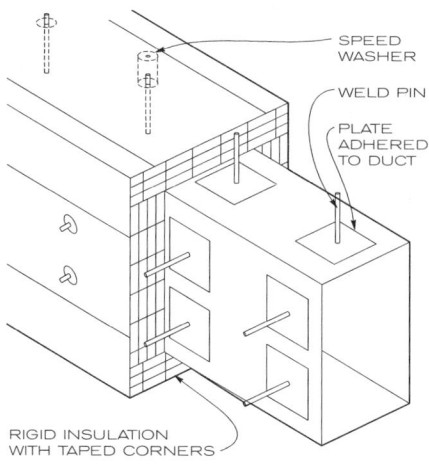

DUCT INSULATION INSTALLED ON OUTSIDE

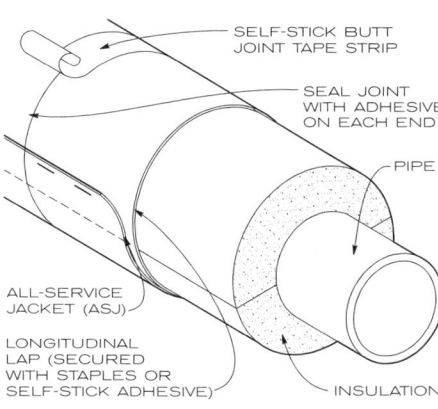

PIPE INSULATION WITH NONMETALLIC JACKET

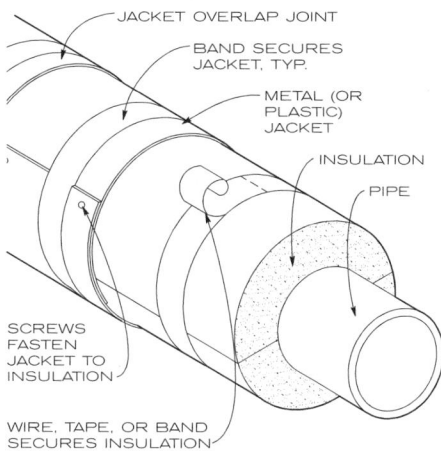

PIPE INSULATION WITH METALLIC JACKET

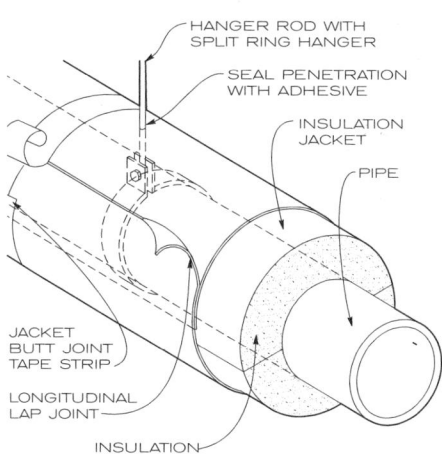

PIPE INSULATION WITH SPLIT-RING HANGER

American Society of Plumbing Engineers; Westlake, California
Michael Frankel, CIPE, Utility Systems Consultants; Somerset, New Jersey

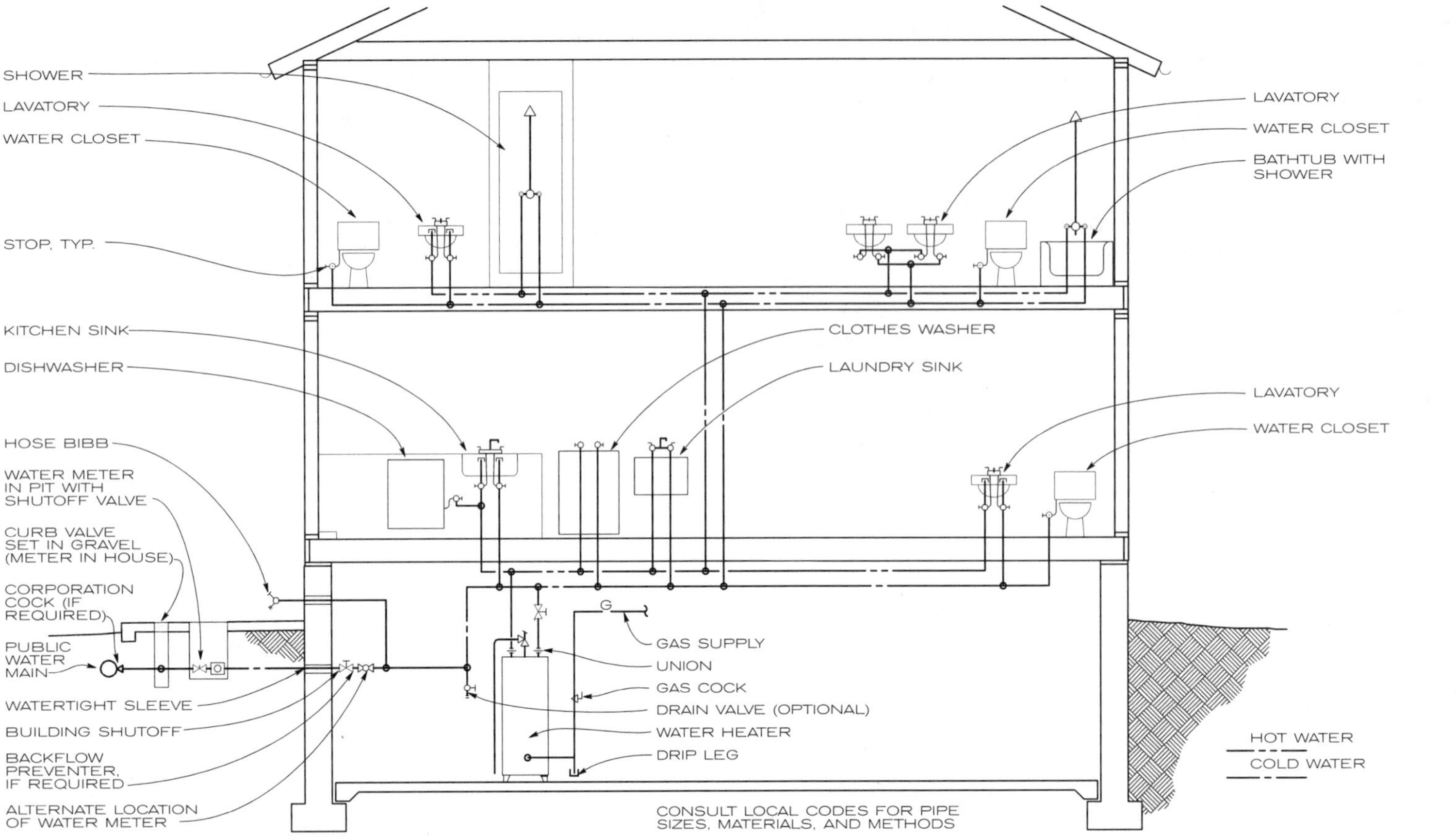

SHOWER

LAVATORY

WATER CLOSET

STOP, TYP.

KITCHEN SINK

DISHWASHER

HOSE BIBB

WATER METER
IN PIT WITH
SHUTOFF VALVE

CURB VALVE
SET IN GRAVEL
(METER IN HOUSE)

CORPORATION
COCK (IF
REQUIRED)

PUBLIC
WATER
MAIN

WATERTIGHT SLEEVE

BUILDING SHUTOFF

BACKFLOW
PREVENTER,
IF REQUIRED

ALTERNATE LOCATION
OF WATER METER

LAVATORY

WATER CLOSET

BATHTUB WITH
SHOWER

CLOTHES WASHER

LAUNDRY SINK

LAVATORY

WATER CLOSET

GAS SUPPLY

UNION

GAS COCK

DRAIN VALVE (OPTIONAL)

WATER HEATER

DRIP LEG

HOT WATER

COLD WATER

CONSULT LOCAL CODES FOR PIPE
SIZES, MATERIALS, AND METHODS

WATER SUPPLY PIPING

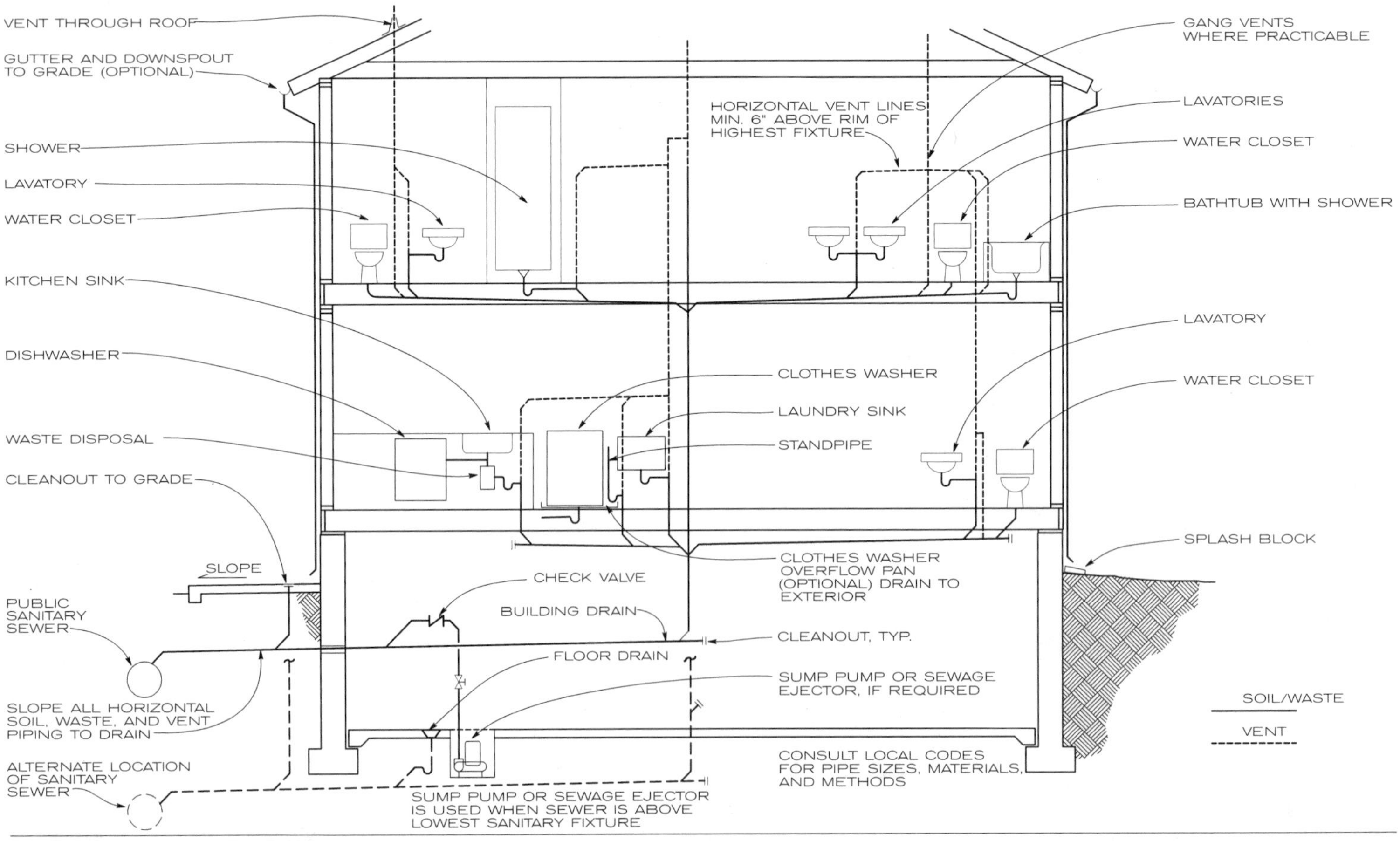

VENT THROUGH ROOF

GUTTER AND DOWNSPOUT
TO GRADE (OPTIONAL)

SHOWER

LAVATORY

WATER CLOSET

KITCHEN SINK

DISHWASHER

WASTE DISPOSAL

CLEANOUT TO GRADE

SLOPE

PUBLIC
SANITARY
SEWER

SLOPE ALL HORIZONTAL
SOIL, WASTE, AND VENT
PIPING TO DRAIN

ALTERNATE LOCATION
OF SANITARY
SEWER

GANG VENTS
WHERE PRACTICABLE

HORIZONTAL VENT LINES
MIN. 6" ABOVE RIM OF
HIGHEST FIXTURE

LAVATORIES

WATER CLOSET

BATHTUB WITH SHOWER

LAVATORY

WATER CLOSET

CLOTHES WASHER

LAUNDRY SINK

STANDPIPE

CLOTHES WASHER
OVERFLOW PAN
(OPTIONAL) DRAIN TO
EXTERIOR

SPLASH BLOCK

CHECK VALVE

BUILDING DRAIN

CLEANOUT, TYP.

FLOOR DRAIN

SUMP PUMP OR SEWAGE
EJECTOR, IF REQUIRED

SOIL/WASTE

VENT

SUMP PUMP OR SEWAGE EJECTOR
IS USED WHEN SEWER IS ABOVE
LOWEST SANITARY FIXTURE

CONSULT LOCAL CODES
FOR PIPE SIZES, MATERIALS,
AND METHODS

DRAINAGE AND VENT PIPING

Brent Dickens, AIA, Architecture & Planning; San Rafael, California
Michael Frankel. CIPE, Utility Systems Consultants; Somerset, New Jersey
American Society of Plumbing Engineers; Westlake, California

15   PLUMBING RISER DIAGRAMS

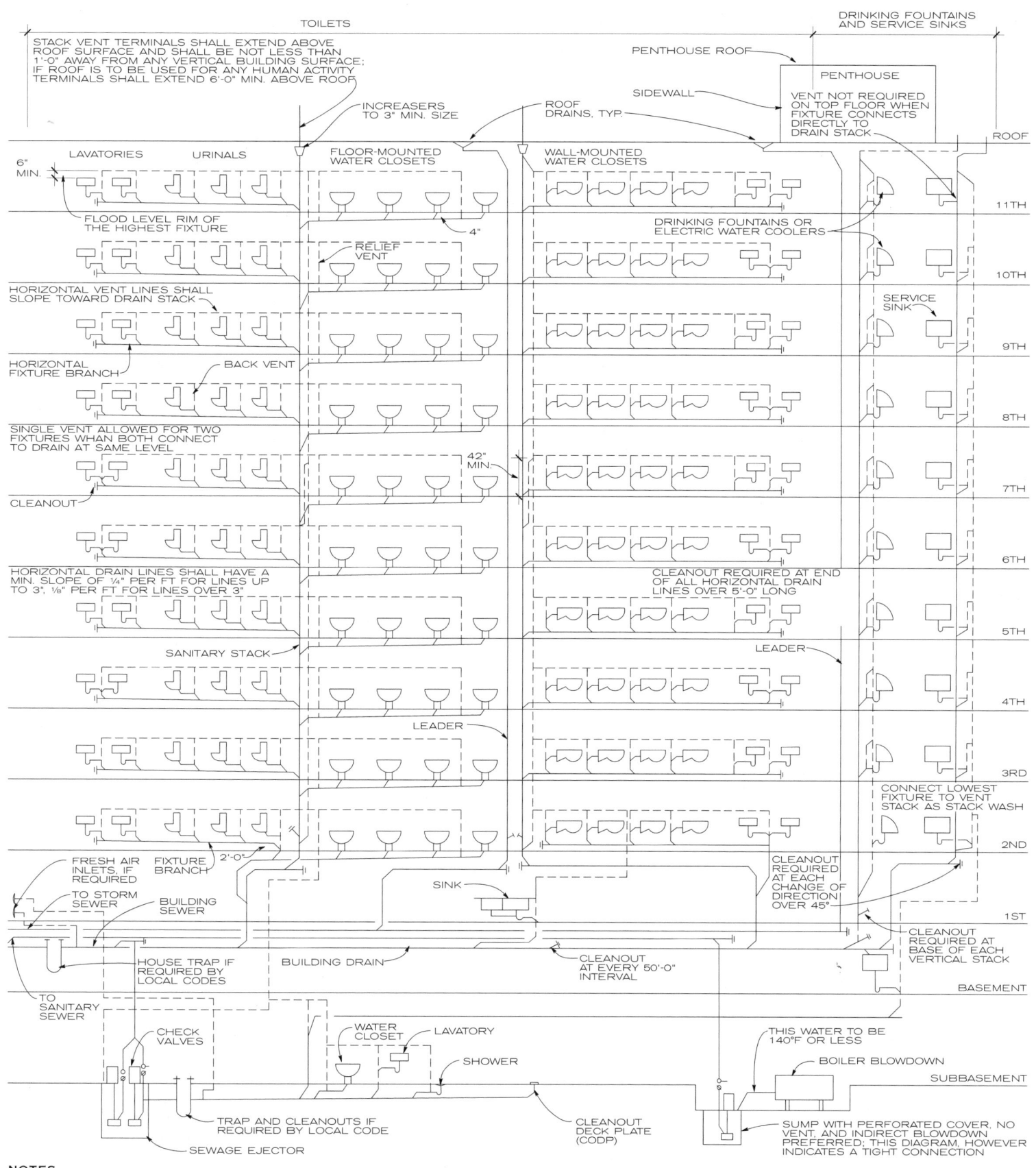

TOILETS

DRINKING FOUNTAINS
AND SERVICE SINKS

STACK VENT TERMINALS SHALL EXTEND ABOVE
ROOF SURFACE AND SHALL BE NOT LESS THAN
1'-0" AWAY FROM ANY VERTICAL BUILDING SURFACE;
IF ROOF IS TO BE USED FOR ANY HUMAN ACTIVITY
TERMINALS SHALL EXTEND 6'-0" MIN. ABOVE ROOF

PENTHOUSE ROOF

PENTHOUSE

SIDEWALL

VENT NOT REQUIRED
ON TOP FLOOR WHEN
FIXTURE CONNECTS
DIRECTLY TO
DRAIN STACK

INCREASERS
TO 3" MIN. SIZE

ROOF
DRAINS, TYP.

ROOF

LAVATORIES   URINALS

FLOOR-MOUNTED
WATER CLOSETS

WALL-MOUNTED
WATER CLOSETS

6"
MIN.

11TH

FLOOD LEVEL RIM OF
THE HIGHEST FIXTURE

4"

DRINKING FOUNTAINS OR
ELECTRIC WATER COOLERS

RELIEF
VENT

10TH

HORIZONTAL VENT LINES SHALL
SLOPE TOWARD DRAIN STACK

SERVICE
SINK

9TH

HORIZONTAL
FIXTURE BRANCH

BACK VENT

8TH

SINGLE VENT ALLOWED FOR TWO
FIXTURES WHEN BOTH CONNECT
TO DRAIN AT SAME LEVEL

42"
MIN.

7TH

CLEANOUT

6TH

HORIZONTAL DRAIN LINES SHALL HAVE A
MIN. SLOPE OF ¼" PER FT FOR LINES UP
TO 3", ⅛" PER FT FOR LINES OVER 3"

CLEANOUT REQUIRED AT END
OF ALL HORIZONTAL DRAIN
LINES OVER 5'-0" LONG

5TH

SANITARY STACK

LEADER

4TH

LEADER

3RD

CONNECT LOWEST
FIXTURE TO VENT
STACK AS STACK WASH

2ND

FRESH AIR
INLETS, IF
REQUIRED

FIXTURE
BRANCH

2'-0"

SINK

CLEANOUT
REQUIRED
AT EACH
CHANGE OF
DIRECTION
OVER 45°

1ST

TO STORM
SEWER

BUILDING
SEWER

CLEANOUT
REQUIRED AT
BASE OF EACH
VERTICAL STACK

HOUSE TRAP IF
REQUIRED BY
LOCAL CODES

BUILDING DRAIN

CLEANOUT
AT EVERY 50'-0"
INTERVAL

BASEMENT

TO
SANITARY
SEWER

CHECK
VALVES

WATER
CLOSET

LAVATORY

SHOWER

THIS WATER TO BE
140°F OR LESS

BOILER BLOWDOWN

SUBBASEMENT

TRAP AND CLEANOUTS IF
REQUIRED BY LOCAL CODE

CLEANOUT
DECK PLATE
(CODP)

SUMP WITH PERFORATED COVER, NO
VENT, AND INDIRECT BLOWDOWN
PREFERRED; THIS DIAGRAM, HOWEVER
INDICATES A TIGHT CONNECTION

SEWAGE EJECTOR

NOTES

1. This diagram generally illustrates plumbing drainage solutions that constitute good plumbing practice. Because of variations in local code, some of the items shown may be prohibited in some areas, while others may far exceed the minimum requirements of a local code.

2. Always consult local codes for exact requirements and for such items as fixture unit values, pipe sizing, pipe materials, general regulations, and special conditions.

3. Forty-five degrees or less from vertical may be considered as straight stock in sizing, except that no fixtures or branches may be connected within 2 ft of offset.

Killebrew/Rucker/Associates, Inc., Architects/Planners/Engineers; Wichita Falls, Texas
Michael Frankel, CIPE; American Society of Plumbing Engineers, Somerset, New Jersey

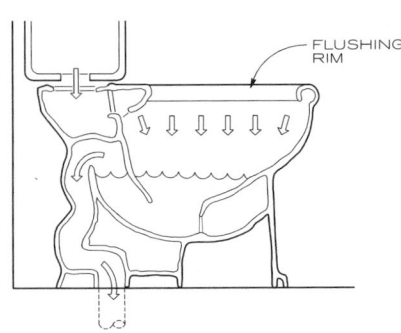

REVERSE TRAP
NOTE

Water is introduced into the fixture only through the rim by a gravity flush tank. This action is low cost and used mostly for residential projects. Reverse traps may be used with flush tanks or valves.

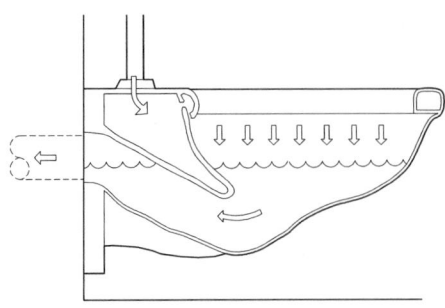

BLOWOUT
NOTE

Water is introduced at high velocity through jets at the bottom of the waterway in blowout action. This action is used for public facilities and industrial projects because of its ability to remove larger objects thrown into the fixture. Blowouts are used with flush valve water supply only.

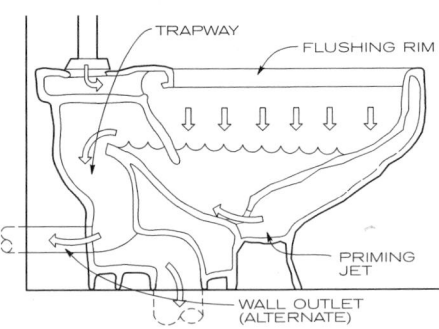

SIPHON JET
NOTE

Water is introduced into the fixture both through the rim and by a jet at the bottom of the waterway. Quiet flushing and moderate cost make this the most commonly used flushing action. Less costly variations include "washout" and "washdown" actions that do not use the jet. The siphon jet can be used with flush valves or tanks.

FIXTURE FLUSHING ACTION TYPES

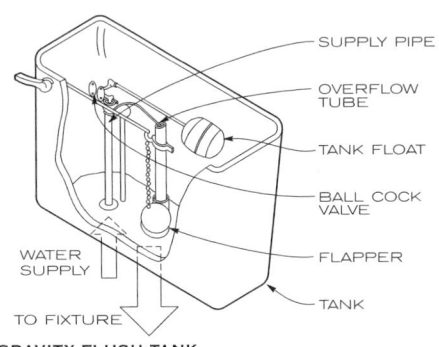

GRAVITY FLUSH TANK
NOTE

Water enters the tank through a ball cock and is stopped when the float valve reaches a predetermined level. The handle raises the flapper to release all the water in the tank into the fixture and stops when the flapper closes. Gravity flush tanks require 10 psi water pressure.

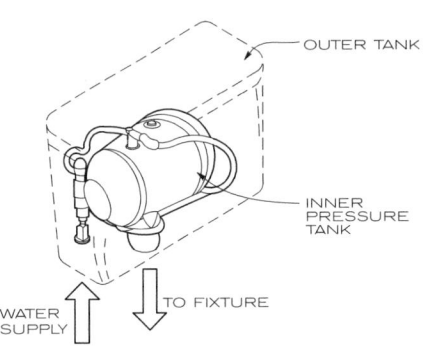

PRESSURE-ASSISTED FLUSH TANK
NOTE

Water enters a pressure tank installed inside an outer tank, partially filling the tank and compressing the air inside. When flushing is started, the air pressure causes the quick release of water into the fixture. Pressure-assisted flush tanks require 30 psi water pressure.

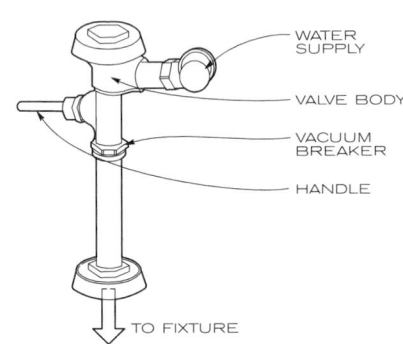

FLUSH VALVE
NOTE

Flush valves are available in a wide variety of manual and automatic operation fixtures, some with infrared and other proximity sensors. Once flushing has started, a measured quantity of water is quickly introduced into the fixture. Flush valves require 25 psi water pressure.

FIXTURE WATER SUPPLY TYPES

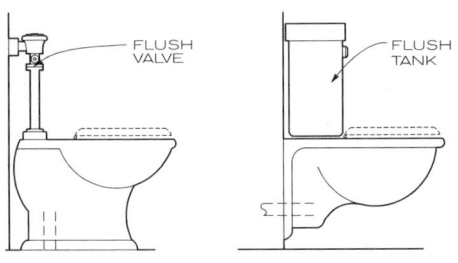

NOTES

1. Flush valves and tanks can be installed on either floor-mounted or wall-mounted water closets.

2. ADA 4.16 (Water Closets) describes grab bar requirements for water closets. ADA 4.17 (Toilet Stalls) describes approach, floor space, and grab bar require-

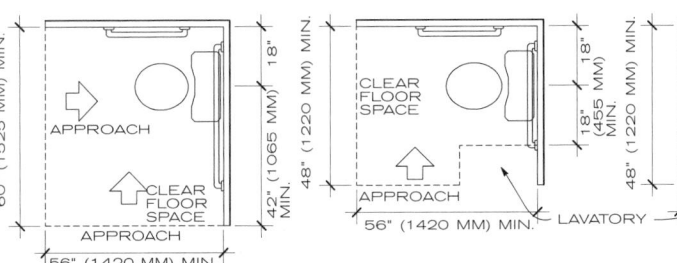

FRONT AND SIDE APPROACH   **SIDE APPROACH**   **FRONT APPROACH**

ments for water closets within toilet stalls (see AGS ninth edition page on "Accessible Water Closets, Stalls, Urinals, and Lavatories"). Water closet height should be 17–19 in. to the top of the toilet seat. Seats should not spring up. The force required to activate controls should be a maximum of 5 lbf. Mount controls on the wide side of the toilet no more than 44 in. above the floor.

3. For rough-in dimensions, refer to manufacturers' manuals.

4. Special toilet types are sometimes used, such as vacuum-vented toilets, composting toilets, and chemical toilets.

5. Current code requires that water closet flush valves and tanks be limited to 1.6 gal. maximum per flush of water.

WATER CLOSET MOUNTING TYPES AND CLEARANCES

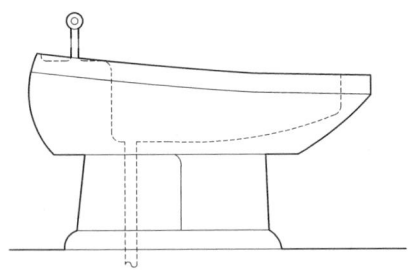

NOTE

This low, basinlike plumbing fixture is designed to be straddled for bathing the posterior parts of the body.

BIDET

URINALS

NOTES

1. Urinals require flush valves as source of water supply.

2. ADA 4.18 (Urinals) requires 30 x 48 in. clear floor space in front of urinals to allow a forward approach. Urinals should be stall type or wall-hung with an elongated rim a maximum of 17 in. above the floor. Shields, if provided, should not extend beyond the front of the urinal rim and must have a clearance of 29 in. Flush controls should be accessible and no more than 44 in. above the floor.

3. If used, urinal tanks should be 92–94 in. above the floor.

4. Battery stalls, except accessible ones, should be installed 21–24 in. on center.

5. For styles and rough-in dimensions, refer to manufacturers' manuals.

American Society of Plumbing Engineers; Westlake, California
Michael Frankel, CIPE, Utility Systems Consultants; Somerset, New Jersey
Jacqueline Jones (American Standard) and Philip Kenyon (Kohler)

15   PLUMBING FIXTURES

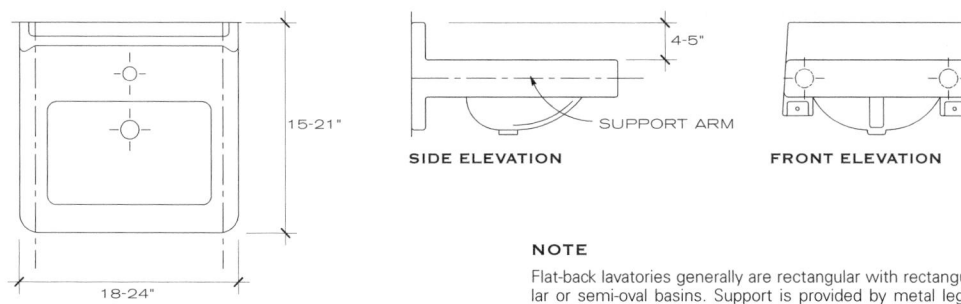

PLAN

SLAB LAVATORY

NOTE

Slab lavatories typically are rectangular with rectangular basins and are spaced from the finish wall with 2-in. escutcheons. A vitreous china leg with brackets can serve as an alternate means of support. A lavatory may be ADA compliant when installed with an offset drain.

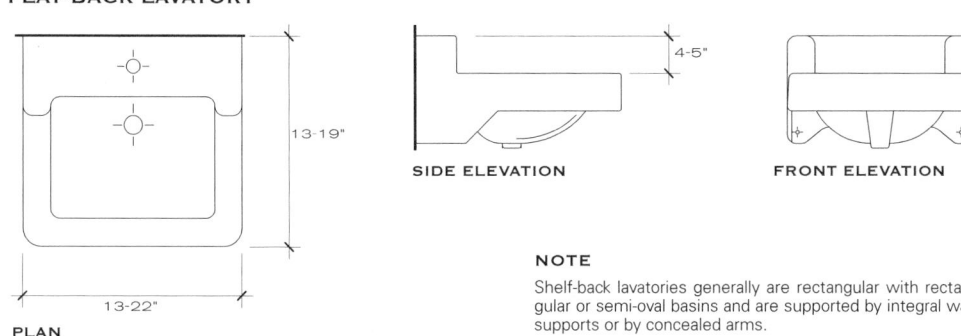

PLAN

FLAT-BACK LAVATORY

NOTE

Flat-back lavatories generally are rectangular with rectangular or semi-oval basins. Support is provided by metal legs with brackets or by concealed arms.

PLAN

SHELF-BACK LAVATORY

NOTE

Shelf-back lavatories generally are rectangular with rectangular or semi-oval basins and are supported by integral wall supports or by concealed arms.

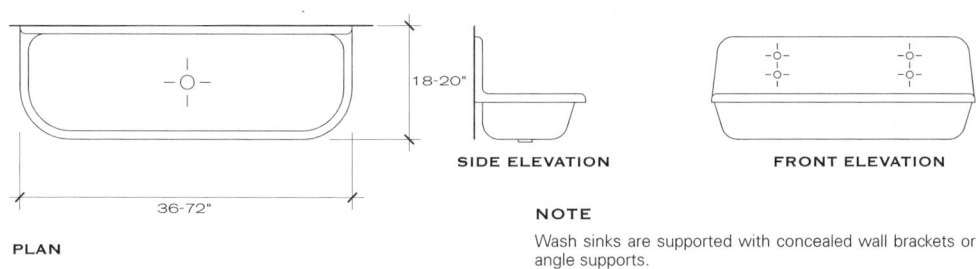

PLAN

WHEELCHAIR ACCESSIBLE LAVATORY

NOTE

Wheelchair accessible lavatories must be supported with a concealed arm carrier. Pipes should be covered and cannot obstruct access. Faucet levers should be accessible or photoelectric.

PLAN

WALL-MOUNTED WASH SINK

NOTE

Wash sinks are supported with concealed wall brackets or angle supports.

American Society of Plumbing Engineers; Westlake, California
Michael Frankel, CIPE, Utility Systems Consultants; Somerset, New Jersey

GENERAL

Lavatories are available in vitreous china, cast acrylic resin, enameled cast iron, enameled steel, and stainless steel. The most commonly used means of support is the chair or wall carrier with concealed arms. Consult manufacturers' data for specific fixture design and support recommendations.

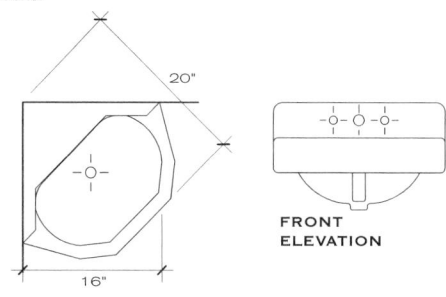

PLAN

NOTE

Corner lavatories are available angled with an oval basin or rectangular with an offset rectangular basin. They are supported with wall brackets or concealed arms.

CORNER LAVATORY

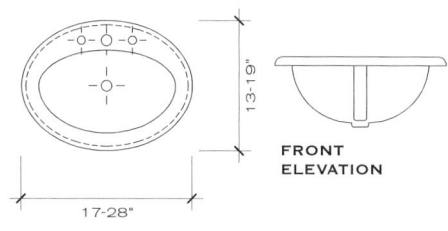

PLAN

NOTE

Built-in (or drop-in) lavatories come in oval, rectangular, and circular shapes. Typically self-rimming, they are also available with metal rims or rimless for undercounter installations. They may meet ADA requirements if placed in an accessible counter.

BUILT-IN LAVATORY

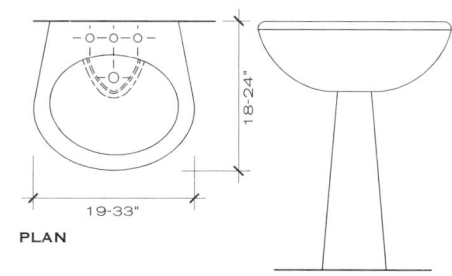

PLAN

NOTE

Pedestal lavatories may be either wall-mounted or free-standing. Consult manufacturers for specific designs, forms, and dimensions.

PEDESTAL LAVATORY

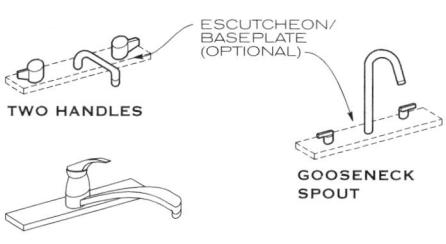

TYPICAL LAVATORY AND SINK FAUCETS

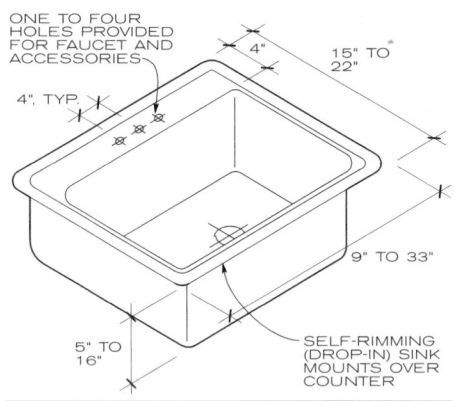

SINGLE BOWL AND BAR SINK

ONE TO FOUR HOLES PROVIDED FOR FAUCET AND ACCESSORIES

4", TYP.

4"

15" TO 22"

9" TO 33"

5" TO 16"

SELF-RIMMING (DROP-IN) SINK MOUNTS OVER COUNTER

NOTES

1. Sink materials include stainless steel, enameled iron or steel, and cast resin.
2. The underside of stainless steel sinks typically is coated with a sound-deadening material.
3. Sink accessories include pull-out faucets, instant hot or chilled water dispensers, and soap dispensers.
4. Consult manufacturers for available stainless steel finishes.

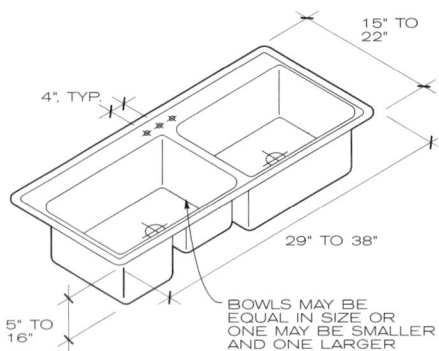

DOUBLE BOWL SINK

15" TO 22"

4", TYP.

29" TO 38"

5" TO 16"

BOWLS MAY BE EQUAL IN SIZE OR ONE MAY BE SMALLER AND ONE LARGER

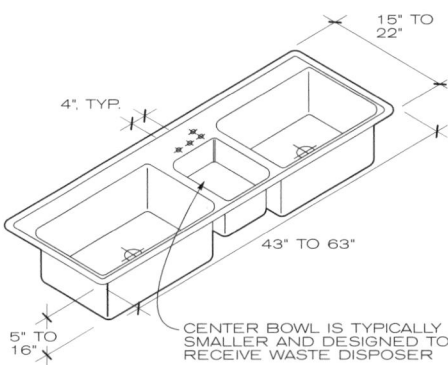

TRIPLE BOWL SINK

15" TO 22"

4", TYP.

43" TO 63"

5" TO 16"

CENTER BOWL IS TYPICALLY SMALLER AND DESIGNED TO RECEIVE WASTE DISPOSER

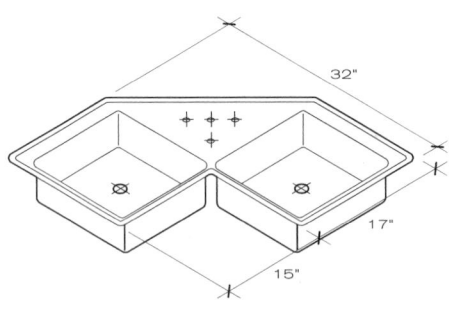

CORNER BOWL SINK

32"

17"

15"

American Society of Plumbing Engineers; Westlake, California
Michael Frankel, CIPE, Utility Systems Consultants; Somerset, New Jersey

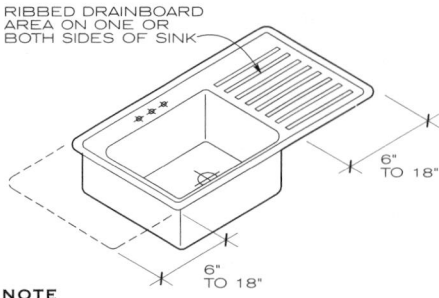

RIBBED DRAINBOARD AREA ON ONE OR BOTH SIDES OF SINK

6" TO 18"

6" TO 18"

NOTE

Drainboard area may be used with single-, double-, and triple-bowl sinks. Institutional kitchen sinks may have longer drainboards. Consult manufacturer.

SINK WITH DRAINBOARD AREA

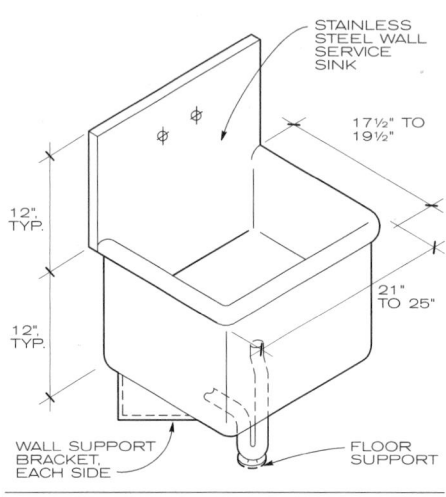

STAINLESS STEEL WALL SERVICE SINK

17½" TO 19½"

12" TYP.

21" TO 25"

12" TYP.

WALL SUPPORT BRACKET, EACH SIDE

FLOOR SUPPORT

WALL SERVICE SINK

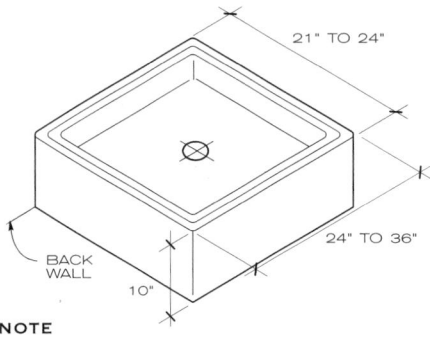

21" TO 24"

BACK WALL

24" TO 36"

10"

NOTE

Available in stainless steel and terrazzo.

FLOOR SERVICE SINK

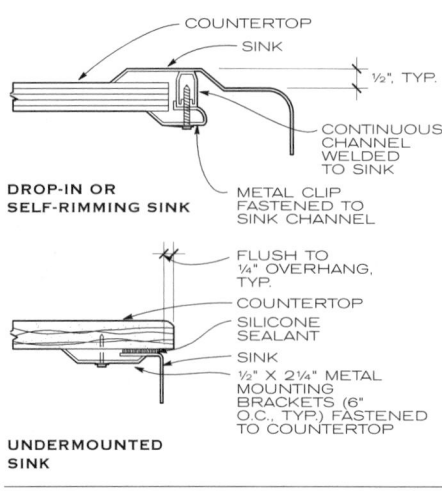

COUNTERTOP

SINK

½", TYP.

CONTINUOUS CHANNEL WELDED TO SINK

DROP-IN OR SELF-RIMMING SINK

METAL CLIP FASTENED TO SINK CHANNEL

FLUSH TO ¼" OVERHANG, TYP.

COUNTERTOP

SILICONE SEALANT

SINK

½" X 2¼" METAL MOUNTING BRACKETS (6" O.C., TYP.) FASTENED TO COUNTERTOP

UNDERMOUNTED SINK

SINK MOUNTING DETAILS

2'-0", TYP.

1¼" SUPPLY, MIN.

SHOWER HEAD (16" MIN. RADIUS UNOBSTRUCTED)

PULL CHAIN FOR SHOWER

HAND CONTROL FOR EYEWASH

¾" SUPPLY LINE, MIN.

EYEWASH OR FACEWASH

DRAIN

FOOT CONTROL FOR EYEWASH

FLOOR SUPPORT

COMBINATION EMERGENCY SHOWER AND EYEWASH

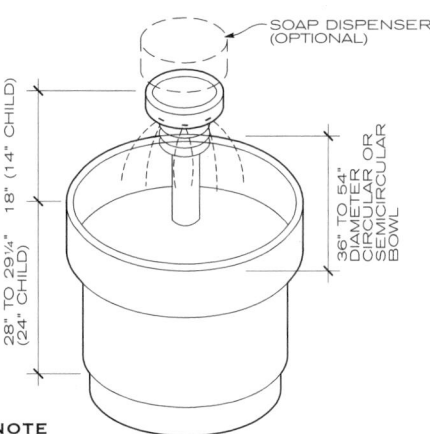

SOAP DISPENSER, (OPTIONAL)

18" (14" CHILD)

36" TO 54" DIAMETER CIRCULAR OR SEMICIRCULAR BOWL

28" TO 29¼" (24" CHILD)

NOTE

Materials include stainless steel, terrazzo, and cast resin. Most sinks have foot controls; some have hand controls or sensors. Supply from above, below, or through the wall.

WASH SINK

SINK DRAIN

6", MIN.

OUTLET

TRAP

8"

10" DIAMETER

NOTE

Disposers are available in ½, ¾, and 1 horsepower units.

GARBAGE DISPOSER

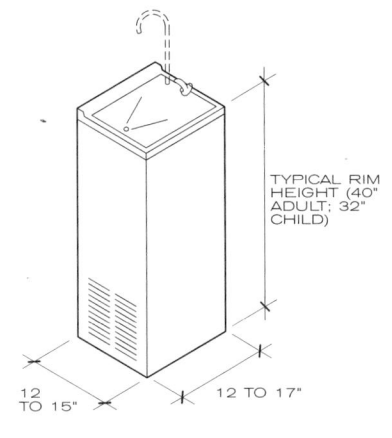

TYPICAL RIM HEIGHT (40" ADULT; 32" CHILD)

12 TO 15"   12 TO 17"

FLOOR MOUNTED

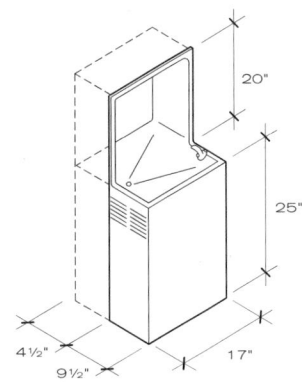

20"

25"

4½"   9½"   17"

SEMIRECESSED

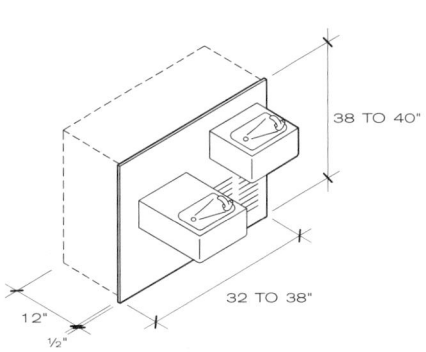

38 TO 40"

32 TO 38"

12"   ½"

BI-LEVEL

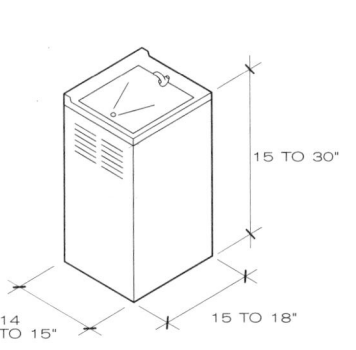

15 TO 30"

14 TO 15"   15 TO 18"

WALL MOUNTED

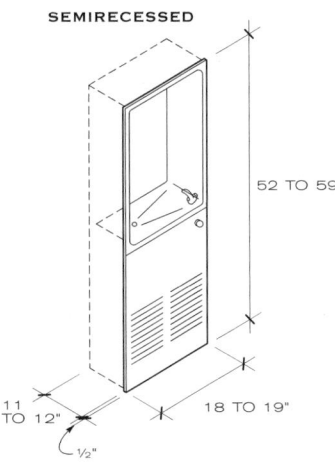

52 TO 59"

11 TO 12"   ½"   18 TO 19"

FULLY RECESSED

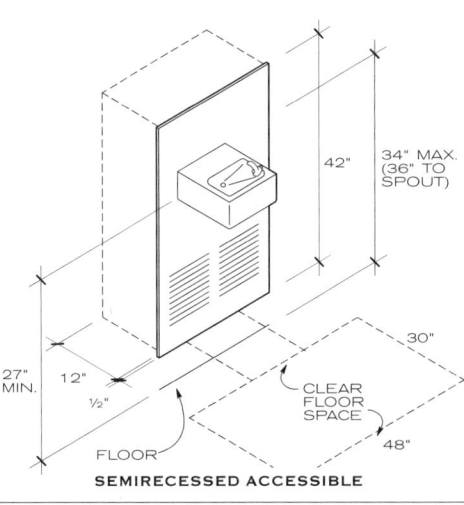

42"   34" MAX. (36" TO SPOUT)

27" MIN.   12"   ½"

FLOOR   CLEAR FLOOR SPACE   30"   48"

SEMIRECESSED ACCESSIBLE

TYPICAL INTERIOR ELECTRIC WATER COOLERS

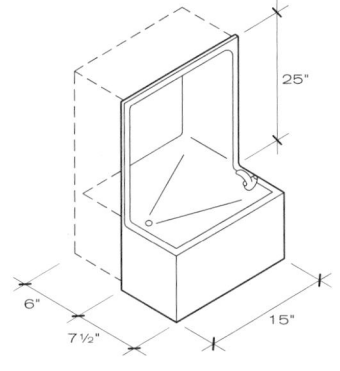

25"

6"   7½"   15"

SEMIRECESSED

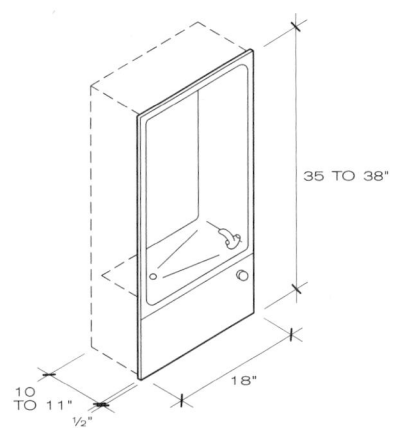

35 TO 38"

10 TO 11"   ½"   18"

FULLY RECESSED

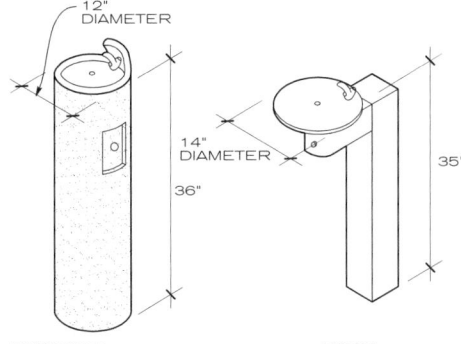

12" DIAMETER

14" DIAMETER

36"

35"

EXTERIOR CONCRETE PEDESTAL   **METAL PEDESTAL**

TYPICAL EXTERIOR DRINKING FOUNTAINS

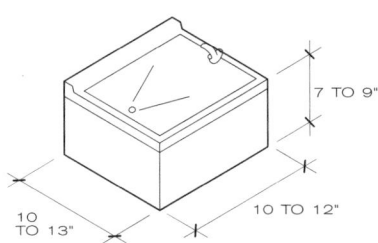

7 TO 9"

10 TO 13"   10 TO 12"

WALL MOUNTED

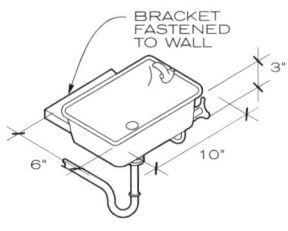

BRACKET FASTENED TO WALL

3"

6"   10"

BRACKET FOUNTAIN

TYPICAL INTERIOR DRINKING FOUNTAINS

American Society of Plumbing Engineers; Westlake, California
Michael Frankel, CIPE, Utility Systems Consultants; Somerset, New Jersey

NOTES

1. Drinking fountains (DF) use only water at ambient temperatures; electric water coolers (EWC) use an integral or remote chiller to cool water for drinking.

2. Use air-cooled condensers for normal room temperatures and water-cooled units for high room temperatures and larger capacities. Many models are available with hot and cold water supply, a cup-filling spout, or refrigerated compartments.

3. Install half of required fountains as accessible, but design the layout so accessible fountains do not obstruct movement of the visually impaired.

4. Special explosion-proof fountains are recommended for use in hazardous atmospheres. Corrosion-resistant fountains are available for harsh environments.

5. Consult local building codes for the minimum number of drinking fountains required.

GENERAL

When a floor-mounted support cannot be installed, wall-mounted supports can be used if the wall structure is strong enough to support the entire weight of the fixture. In such installations, the support arms are attached to a plate bolted directly into the wall structure.

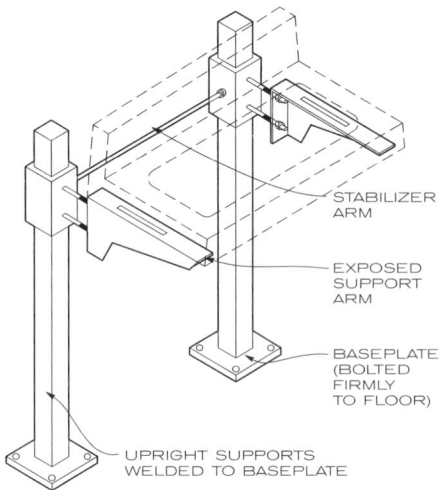

NOTE

This support typically is used with a vitreous china lavatory.

EXPOSED ARM FIXTURE SUPPORT

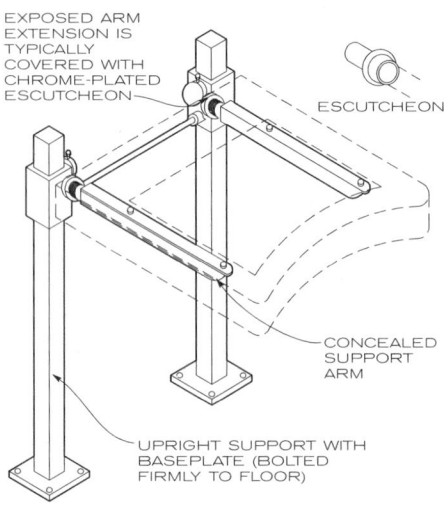

NOTE

When using lavatories of the flat slab type (that is, without a backsplash), manufacturers typically require a 2 to 6 in. space between the wall finish and the rear of the lavatory to prevent water accumulation.

CONCEALED ARM FIXTURE SUPPORT

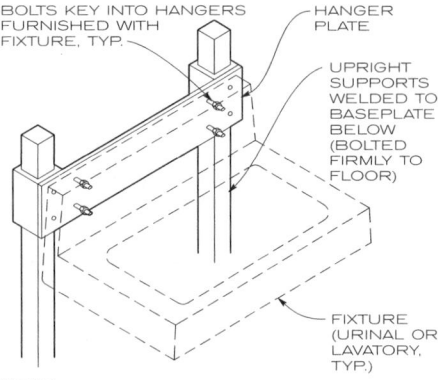

NOTE

An enameled cast-iron high-back lavatory is supported on a hanger-type support.

HANGER-TYPE FIXTURE SUPPORT

American Society of Plumbing Engineers; Westlake, California
Michael Frankel, CIPE, Utility Systems Consultants; Somerset, New Jersey

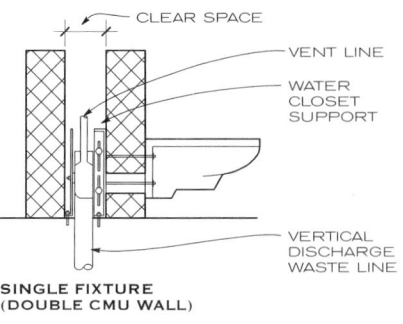

SINGLE FIXTURE (DOUBLE CMU WALL)

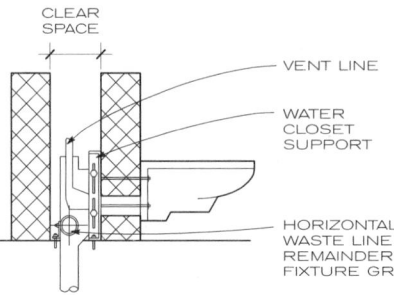

SINGLE FIXTURE IN FIXTURE GROUP (DOUBLE CMU WALL)

SINGLE FIXTURE WATER CLOSET SUPPORTS

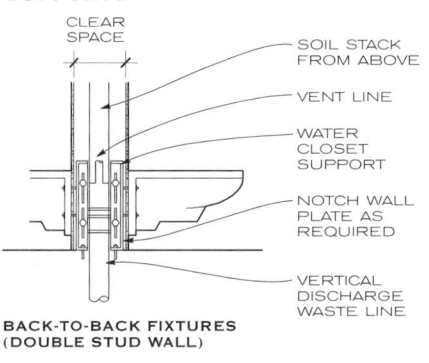

BACK-TO-BACK FIXTURES (DOUBLE STUD WALL)

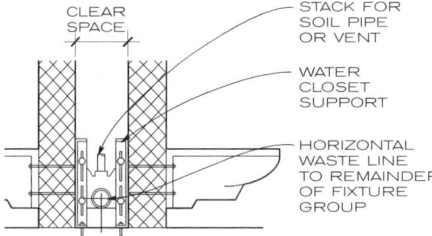

BACK-TO-BACK FIXTURES IN FIXTURE GROUP (DOUBLE CMU WALL)

SUPPORTS FOR WATER CLOSET

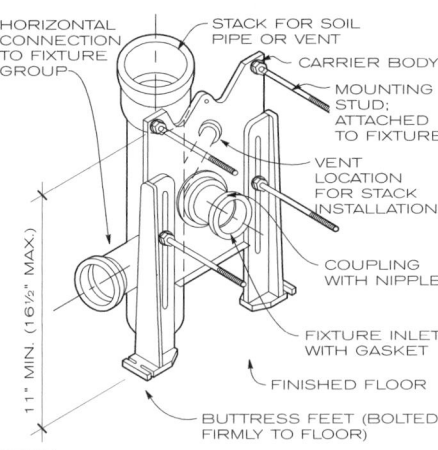

NOTE

Cast-iron supports with chrome-plated trim are typically used with blowout and siphon jet water closets.

ADJUSTABLE WALL-HUNG WATER CLOSET SUPPORT

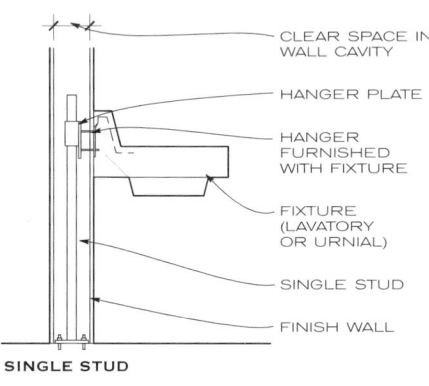

SINGLE STUD

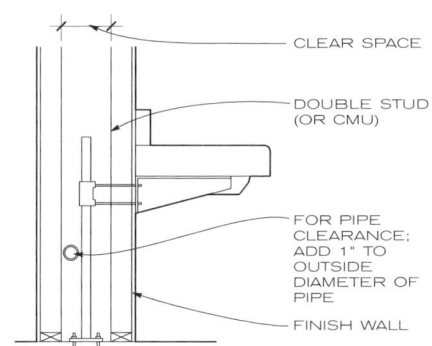

DOUBLE STUD OR CMU

CLEAR SPACE IN WALL FOR LAVATORY AND URINAL SUPPORTS

FIXTURE SUPPORT AND MINIMUM PIPE SPACE REQUIREMENTS

FIXTURE (ABBREVIATION)	ARRANGEMENT	MINIMUM CLEAR SPACE			MINIMUM WALL THICKNESS (INCLUDES FINISH)
		DOUBLE BLOCK	DOUBLE STUD	SINGLE STUD	
Water closet (WC)	S, V	10	4		4
Water closet (WC)	BB, V	10	5		4
Water closet (WC)	S, FG, V	10	9		4
Water closet (WC)	BB, FG, V	10	11		4
Urinal (WC)	S. BB, FG, V, HP			5	$1/2$
Lavatory (LAV)	S, BB, FG, V, A			6	$1/2$
Lavatory (LAV)	S, BB, FG, V, HP			5	$1/2$
Urinal stall (UR)				4	
Shower (SH)				4	
Sink (SK)				5	
Service sink (SS)				6	
Drinking fountain (DF)				3	

S—single fixture; BB—back to back; FG—fixture group (a battery of two or more fixtures along one wall); V—vertical discharge; A—arm support (concealed or exposed); HP—hanger plate

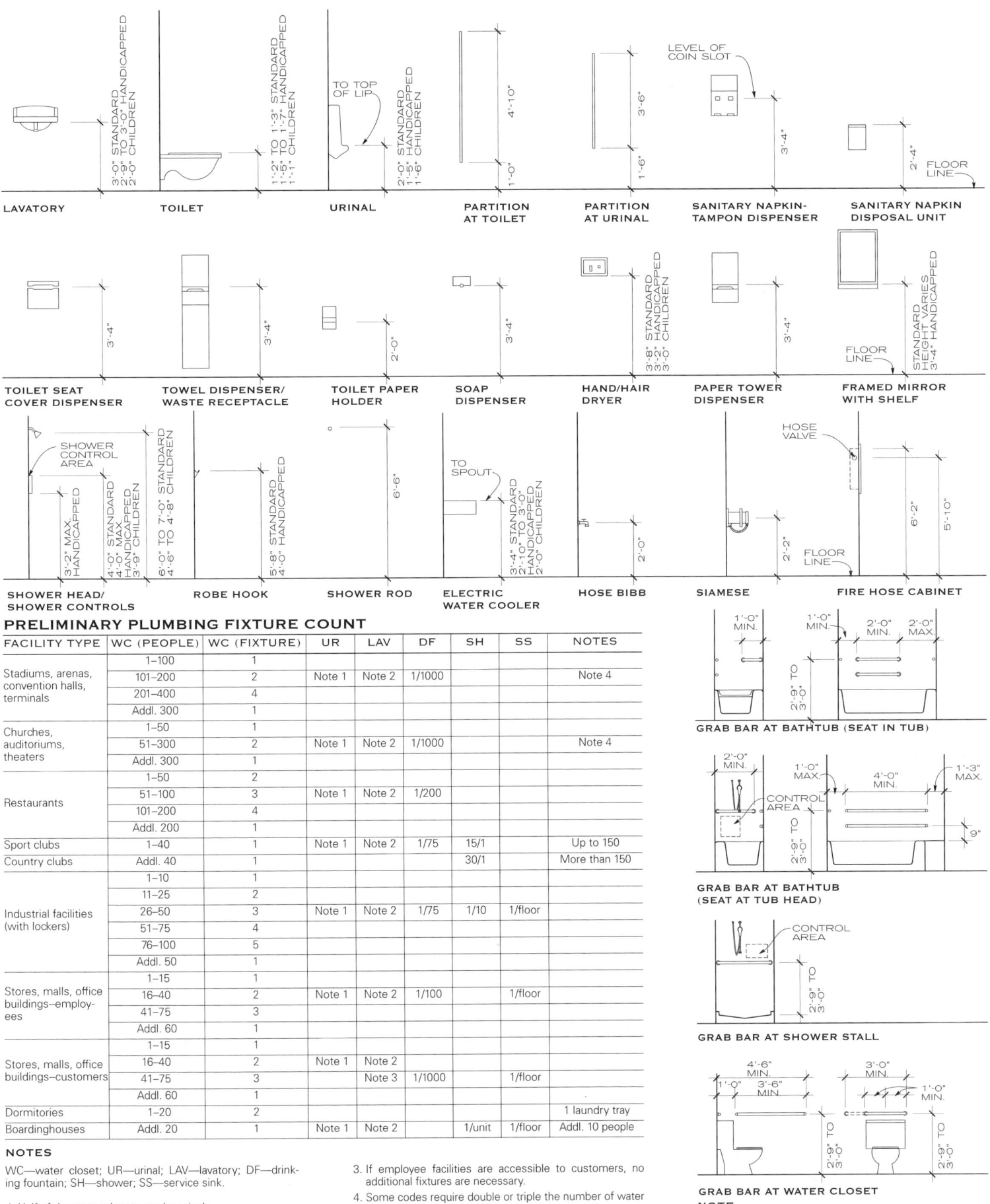

LAVATORY — 3'-0" STANDARD / 2'-9" TO 3'-0" HANDICAPPED / 2'-0" CHILDREN

TOILET — 1'-2" TO 1'-3" STANDARD / 1'-5" TO 1'-7" HANDICAPPED / 1'-1" CHILDREN

URINAL — TO TOP OF LIP / 2'-0" STANDARD / 1'-5" HANDICAPPED / 1'-6" CHILDREN / 1'-0"

PARTITION AT TOILET — 4'-10"

PARTITION AT URINAL — 3'-6" / 1'-6"

SANITARY NAPKIN-TAMPON DISPENSER — LEVEL OF COIN SLOT / 3'-4"

SANITARY NAPKIN DISPOSAL UNIT — 2'-4" / FLOOR LINE

TOILET SEAT COVER DISPENSER — 3'-4"

TOWEL DISPENSER/ WASTE RECEPTACLE — 3'-4"

TOILET PAPER HOLDER — 2'-0"

SOAP DISPENSER — 3'-4"

HAND/HAIR DRYER — 3'-8" STANDARD / 3'-2" HANDICAPPED / 3'-0" CHILDREN

PAPER TOWER DISPENSER — 3'-4"

FRAMED MIRROR WITH SHELF — FLOOR LINE / STANDARD HEIGHT VARIES / 3'-4" HANDICAPPED

SHOWER HEAD/ SHOWER CONTROLS — SHOWER CONTROL AREA / 3'-2" MAX. HANDICAPPED / 4'-0" STANDARD / 4'-0" MAX. HANDICAPPED / 3'-9" CHILDREN

ROBE HOOK — 6'-0" TO 7'-0" STANDARD / 4'-6" TO 4'-8" CHILDREN

SHOWER ROD — 5'-8" STANDARD / 4'-0" HANDICAPPED / 6'-6"

ELECTRIC WATER COOLER — TO SPOUT / 3'-4" STANDARD / 2'-10" TO 3'-0" HANDICAPPED / 2'-0" CHILDREN

HOSE BIBB — 2'-0"

SIAMESE — HOSE VALVE / 2'-2" / FLOOR LINE

FIRE HOSE CABINET — 6'-2" / 5'-10"

PRELIMINARY PLUMBING FIXTURE COUNT

FACILITY TYPE	WC (PEOPLE)	WC (FIXTURE)	UR	LAV	DF	SH	SS	NOTES
Stadiums, arenas, convention halls, terminals	1–100	1						
	101–200	2	Note 1	Note 2	1/1000			Note 4
	201–400	4						
	Addl. 300	1						
Churches, auditoriums, theaters	1–50	1						
	51–300	2	Note 1	Note 2	1/1000			Note 4
	Addl. 300	1						
Restaurants	1–50	2						
	51–100	3	Note 1	Note 2	1/200			
	101–200	4						
	Addl. 200	1						
Sport clubs Country clubs	1–40	1	Note 1	Note 2	1/75	15/1		Up to 150
	Addl. 40	1				30/1		More than 150
Industrial facilities (with lockers)	1–10	1						
	11–25	2						
	26–50	3	Note 1	Note 2	1/75	1/10	1/floor	
	51–75	4						
	76–100	5						
	Addl. 50	1						
Stores, malls, office buildings--employees	1–15	1						
	16–40	2	Note 1	Note 2	1/100		1/floor	
	41–75	3						
	Addl. 60	1						
Stores, malls, office buildings--customers	1–15	1						
	16–40	2	Note 1	Note 2				
	41–75	3		Note 3	1/1000		1/floor	
	Addl. 60	1						
Dormitories	1–20	2						1 laundry tray
Boardinghouses	Addl. 20	1	Note 1	Note 2		1/unit	1/floor	Addl. 10 people

NOTES

WC—water closet; UR—urinal; LAV—lavatory; DF—drinking fountain; SH—shower; SS—service sink.

1. Half of the water closets can be urinals.

2. Half of the lavatories can be water closets.

3. If employee facilities are accessible to customers, no additional fixtures are necessary.

4. Some codes require double or triple the number of water closets for women.

5. Consult local plumbing codes for exact requirements.

GRAB BAR AT BATHTUB (SEAT IN TUB) — 1'-0" MIN. / 1'-0" MIN. / 2'-0" MIN. / 2'-0" MAX. / 2'-9" TO 3'-0"

GRAB BAR AT BATHTUB (SEAT AT TUB HEAD) — 2'-0" MIN. / 1'-0" MAX. / 4'-0" MIN. / 1'-3" MAX. / CONTROL AREA / 2'-9" TO 3'-0" / 9"

GRAB BAR AT SHOWER STALL — CONTROL AREA / 2'-9" TO 3'-0"

GRAB BAR AT WATER CLOSET — 4'-6" MIN. / 1'-0" / 3'-6" MIN. / 3'-0" MIN. / 1'-0" MIN. / 2'-9" TO 3'-0" / 2'-9" TO 3'-0"

NOTE
For grab bars at toilet stalls, consult ANSI A117.1.

American Society of Plumbing Engineers; Westlake, California
Michael Frankel, CIPE, Utility Systems Consultants; Somerset, New Jersey

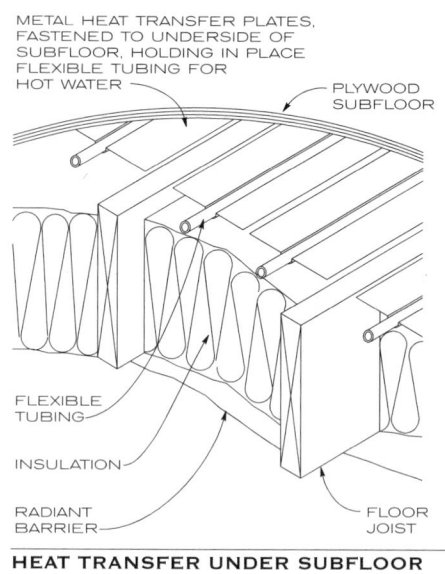

METAL HEAT TRANSFER PLATES, FASTENED TO UNDERSIDE OF SUBFLOOR, HOLDING IN PLACE FLEXIBLE TUBING FOR HOT WATER

PLYWOOD SUBFLOOR

FLEXIBLE TUBING

INSULATION

RADIANT BARRIER

FLOOR JOIST

HEAT TRANSFER UNDER SUBFLOOR

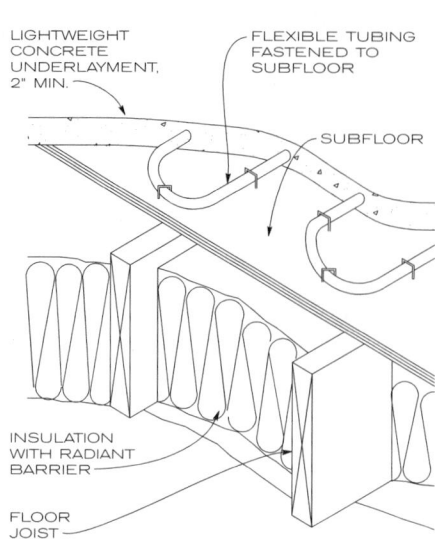

LIGHTWEIGHT CONCRETE UNDERLAYMENT, 2" MIN.

FLEXIBLE TUBING FASTENED TO SUBFLOOR

SUBFLOOR

INSULATION WITH RADIANT BARRIER

FLOOR JOIST

HEAT TRANSFER THROUGH CONCRETE UNDERLAYMENT

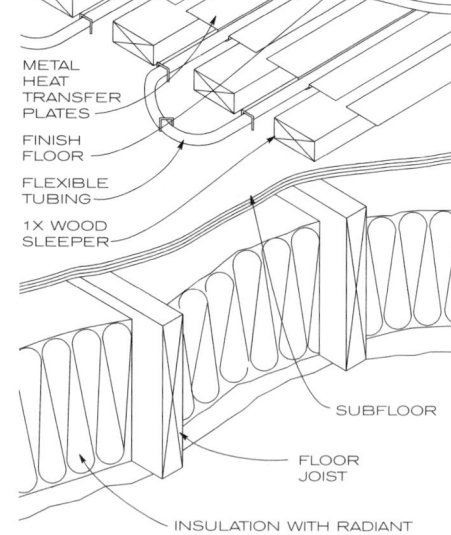

METAL HEAT TRANSFER PLATES

FINISH FLOOR

FLEXIBLE TUBING

1X WOOD SLEEPER

SUBFLOOR

FLOOR JOIST

INSULATION WITH RADIANT BARRIER AT BOTTOM

HEAT TRANSFER AT SUSPENDED FLOOR

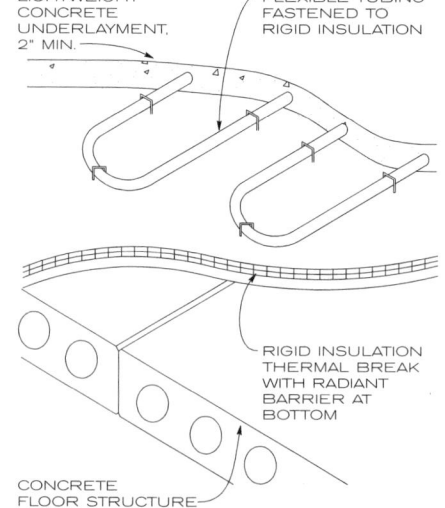

LIGHTWEIGHT CONCRETE UNDERLAYMENT, 2" MIN.

FLEXIBLE TUBING FASTENED TO RIGID INSULATION

RIGID INSULATION THERMAL BREAK WITH RADIANT BARRIER AT BOTTOM

CONCRETE FLOOR STRUCTURE

HEAT TRANSFER IN CONCRETE TOPPING SLAB

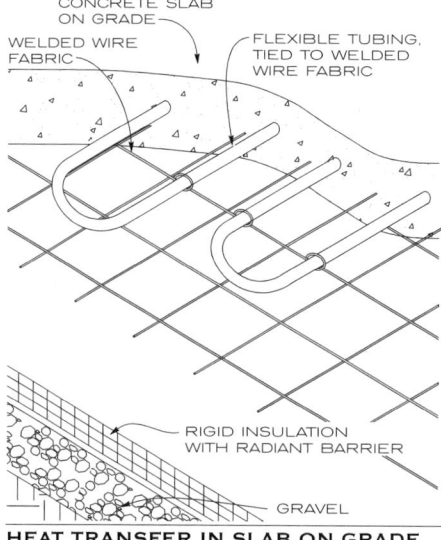

CONCRETE SLAB ON GRADE

WELDED WIRE FABRIC

FLEXIBLE TUBING, TIED TO WELDED WIRE FABRIC

RIGID INSULATION WITH RADIANT BARRIER

GRAVEL

HEAT TRANSFER IN SLAB ON GRADE

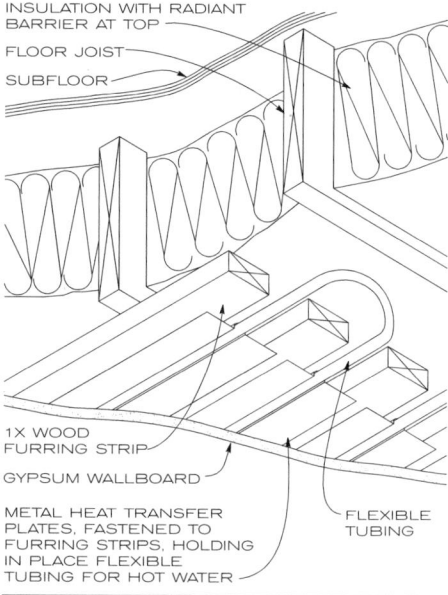

INSULATION WITH RADIANT BARRIER AT TOP

FLOOR JOIST

SUBFLOOR

1X WOOD FURRING STRIP

GYPSUM WALLBOARD

METAL HEAT TRANSFER PLATES, FASTENED TO FURRING STRIPS, HOLDING IN PLACE FLEXIBLE TUBING FOR HOT WATER

FLEXIBLE TUBING

HEAT TRANSFER THROUGH CEILING

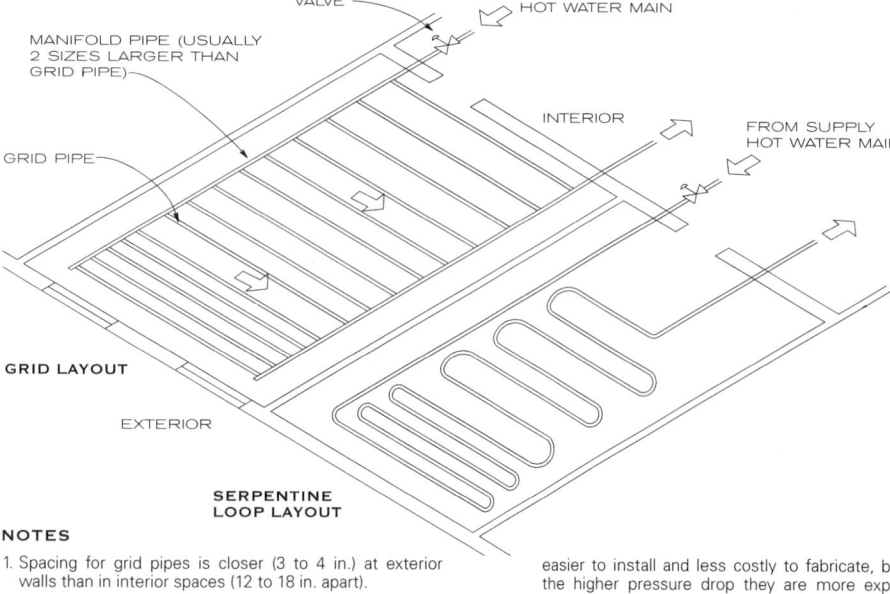

VALVE

FROM SUPPLY HOT WATER MAIN

MANIFOLD PIPE (USUALLY 2 SIZES LARGER THAN GRID PIPE)

INTERIOR

FROM SUPPLY HOT WATER MAIN

GRID PIPE

GRID LAYOUT

EXTERIOR

SERPENTINE LOOP LAYOUT

NOTES

1. Spacing for grid pipes is closer (3 to 4 in.) at exterior walls than in interior spaces (12 to 18 in. apart).
2. Grid pipe layouts have a lower pressure drop than serpentine pipe layouts. Serpentine layouts are generally easier to install and less costly to fabricate, but due to the higher pressure drop they are more expensive to operate.

RADIANT HEATING LAYOUTS

Alfred Greenberg, P.E., C.E.M.; Murray Hill, New Jersey

GENERAL

Radiant heating systems transfer heat from hot water tubing (or electric cables) embedded in the floor or ceiling to a medium that will distribute heat to the specified space. The tubing or cables are laid out to maximize heat distribution to the areas of greatest heat loss. The choice of hot water or electric cable heat is made based on installation, energy, and total life-cycle costs and code constraints. Consult a mechanical engineer.

For appropriate applications, properly designed and operated radiant heating systems will provide greater comfort at lower operating costs than other heating systems because of the inherent nature of the human body's thermal functions. About 70% of the body's heat is transferred by radiation (via electromagnetic waves, like light), 25% by convection (via air or water), and 5% by conduction (via physical contact).

In terms of overall system configuration, a radiant floor, wall, or ceiling is equivalent to a radiator, convector, or any other terminal heating element. The primary caveat is that a suitable control system must be provided to ensure that floor surface temperatures do not rise above 75° F or, if ceiling systems are used, above 120° F. Thermostats for radiant systems can generally be set several degrees lower for heating than thermostats for other types of systems. Finish floor should not be of a thermal insulating material; ceramic tile or wood flooring would be suitable.

HVAC SYSTEM FUNDAMENTALS

In the broadest sense, the term "air conditioning" means that, to the extent required for a particular space condition, a quantity of air must be

1. Mixed with the required amount of outside (fresh) air.
2. Filtered to remove specified amounts of particulate and/ or gaseous elements.
3. Heated and/or cooled as conditions dictate and as directed by an appropriate temperature control system.
4. Humidified or dehumidified to meet space requirements.
5. Under certain conditions, ionized, ozonated, or otherwise treated to provide specific space conditions.
6. Delivered to the air-conditioned spaces and distributed in a quiet, draft-free manner.

Conditioning of the air is basically performed within an enclosure called an air-handling unit (shown in its most generalized form). The components need not be located within the central air-handling unit to perform their functions effectively. Space limitations, the operating and control results desired, and energy optimization considerations may affect where the components are situated.

Sources of electric power, heating and cooling media, water, steam, natural gas, etc. are often remote from the air-handling unit. However, in packaged air-conditioning equipment such as air heating units, room air conditioners, and many rooftop units, the heating and/or cooling "plant" is part of the package.

To the extent that an air-conditioning system does not provide all of the functions described above, it may not be furnishing the total space air conditioning required for optimum comfort and health. The tendency to use the term "air conditioning" synonymously with "cooling" should be altogether discouraged. It falsely implies that the other functions of air conditioning, such as proper filtration and humidification, are less important to total health and comfort and may be eliminated.

The types of air-conditioning systems used and the selection and organization of their components are the most critical and complex elements in the proper design of an HVAC system. For the optimum health, safety, and comfort of occupants and materials within the air-conditioned spaces, and to ensure the optimum life-cycle economics for a particular installation, this process should be entrusted only to experienced and knowledgeable engineers.

ALL-AIR SYSTEMS

In an all-air system, the heating and refrigerating plants may be located in a central mechanical room some distance from the conditioned space or may be contained within the all-air system as packaged units in the air-conditioned spaces or on the roof. The air-handling unit is designed to mix outside and return air as desired, then to filter, heat, cool, and humidify the air before it is delivered to conditioned spaces. It may also exhaust portions of the return air based on how much return air is brought in.

Air-conditioning functions do not necessarily occur within the air-handling unit. Depending on the specific design criteria and space conditions, some air-conditioning elements may be remote from the air-handling unit.

Some common all-air systems are single-duct, constant or variable volume airflow; dual duct (rarely used); multizone; single-duct with powered terminal and either constant or variable volume airflow; and a single-duct system with self-contained airflow volume controls and thermostats in each diffuser in the conditioned space.

SPATIAL REQUIREMENTS

The dimensions between system components shown in the accompanying illustration are the minimum required for proper inspection and maintenance of walk-in units (units with air quantities of 15,000 cu ft/min. or more). Spacing for smaller units may be somewhat less but must allow adequate access for inspection and maintenance.

All spaces between unit components should have hinged access doors designed to prevent air leakage when the doors are closed. For smaller units, the entire panel between components should open. For walk-in units, access doors should be a minimum of 30 x 60 in. Access doors should be designed to open from the inside.

The floors of the sections between components should be pitched to facilitate drainage of liquids that may form. Light switches and electronic controls should be located on the outside of the unit enclosures. If a fan is situated on the inside of a unit enclosure, the return air inlets must have safety screens. Walk-in unit interiors should have permanent vapor-proof and explosion-proof lighting.

Alfred Greenberg, P.E., C.E.M.; Murray Hill, New Jersey

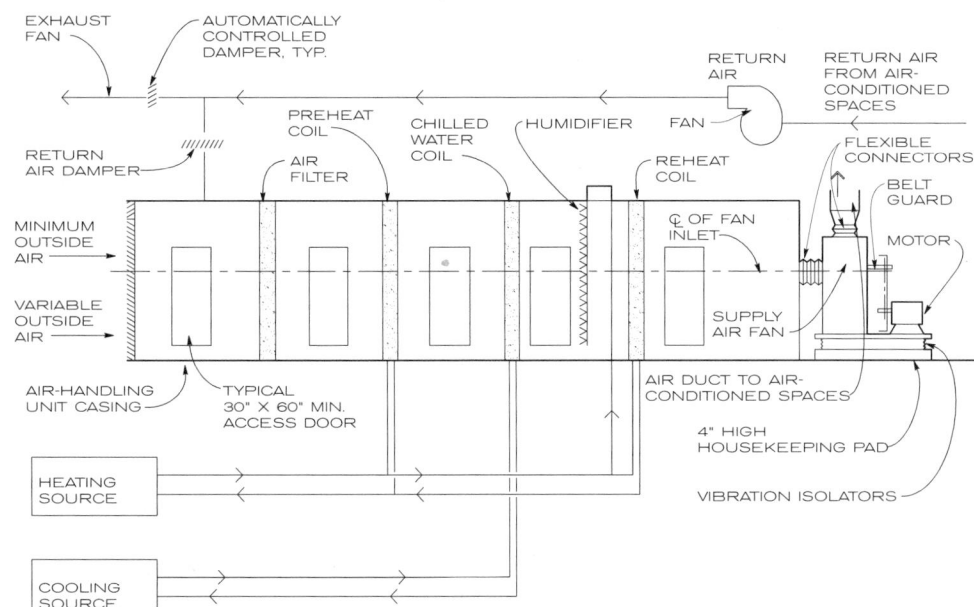

NOTES

1. Minimum outside air damper: usually two positions.
2. Variable outside air damper: closed when only minimum outside air is desired (for example, when outside air temperature is extremely high or low). Designed to open in response to the capability of outside air to contribute to a building's heating or cooling needs. Exhaust and return air dampers are controlled to operate in accordance with the setting of the variable outside air damper.
3. Preheat coil (PHC): required only if the temperature and distribution of the return air mixture could cause freezing temperatures within the casing.
4. Air-handling unit (AHU): may be field- or factory-fabricated. Pitch the floor of the AHU casing between components as required and provide piped floor drains to remove any moisture that develops.
5. Direct expansion coil (DXC): cooling coil may be a DXC if refrigerant is used instead of chilled water.
6. Humidifier (H): may use steam or water as the humidification medium.
7. Reheat coil (RHC): used in the air-handling unit only when a fixed discharge air temperature is to be supplied to all areas served by the duct system. If different spaces require varying temperatures, a separate reheat coil may be placed in each duct serving a different temperature zone.

COMPONENTS OF A BASIC ALL-AIR SYSTEM

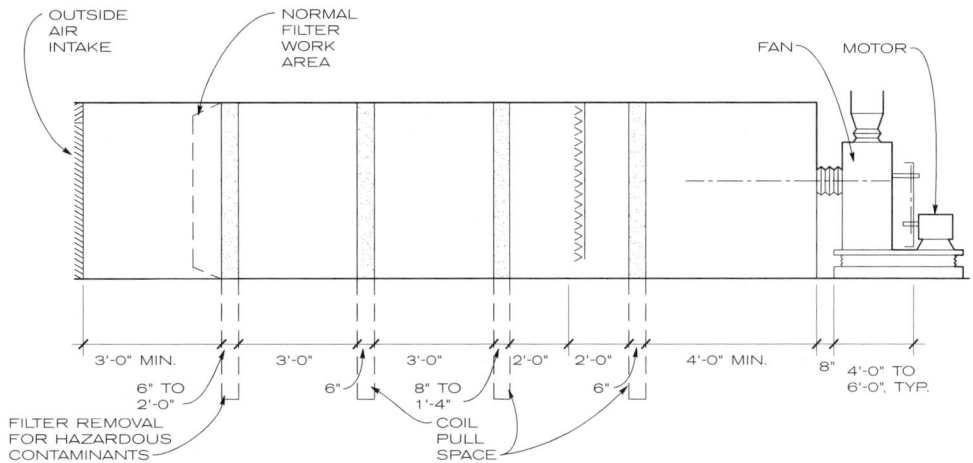

NOTES

1. The primary factors in determining spatial requirements for a basic HVAC system are space for proper air flow, thermodynamic heat transfer, and service and maintenance.
2. The net cross-sectional area (in sq ft) of the interior of an air-handling unit should be at least equal to the total air supply (measured in cu ft/min) divided by 500.
3. The aspect ratio of the casing of the air-handling unit should fit the space available, considering maintenance requirements and the ability of personnel to enter the unit to perform required tasks.
4. A single-width single-inlet (SWSI) fan is shown. If a double-width, double-inlet (DWDI) fan is used, it may be incorporated into the air-handling unit casing. This arrangement generally decreases the overall length of the system and the height required at the fan; however, the required width at the fan will increase.

GENERAL SPATIAL REQUIREMENTS FOR ALL-AIR SYSTEMS

Air-handling units may be located anywhere that suits building space conditions and offers proximity to the conditioned spaces. However, careful consideration must be given to the outside air duct location and the noise and vibration that will emanate from the fans.

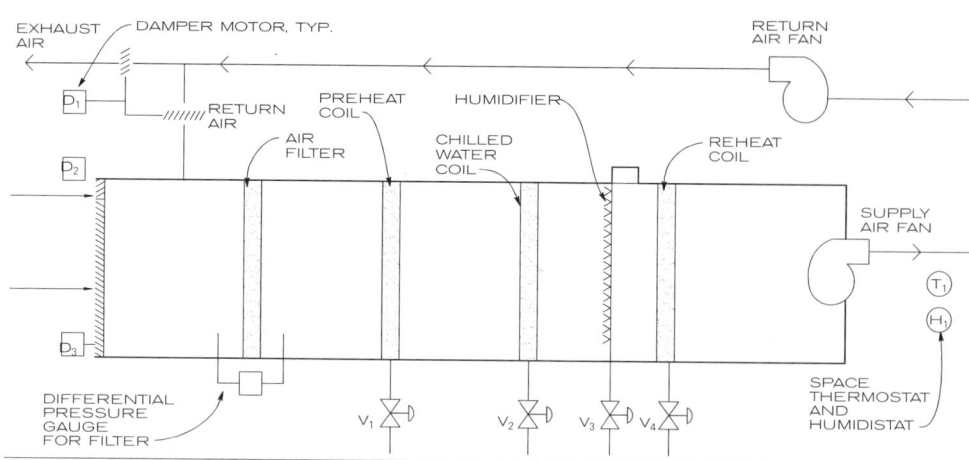

TEMPERATURE AND HUMIDITY CONTROLS FOR ALL-AIR SYSTEMS

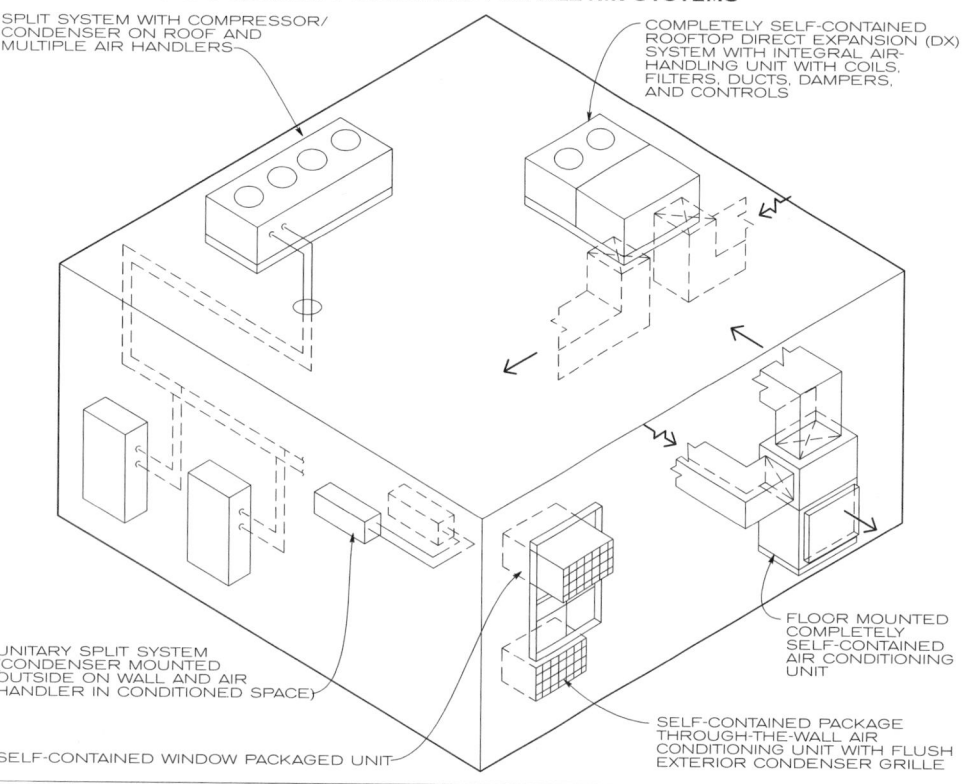

DIRECT-EXPANSION SYSTEM

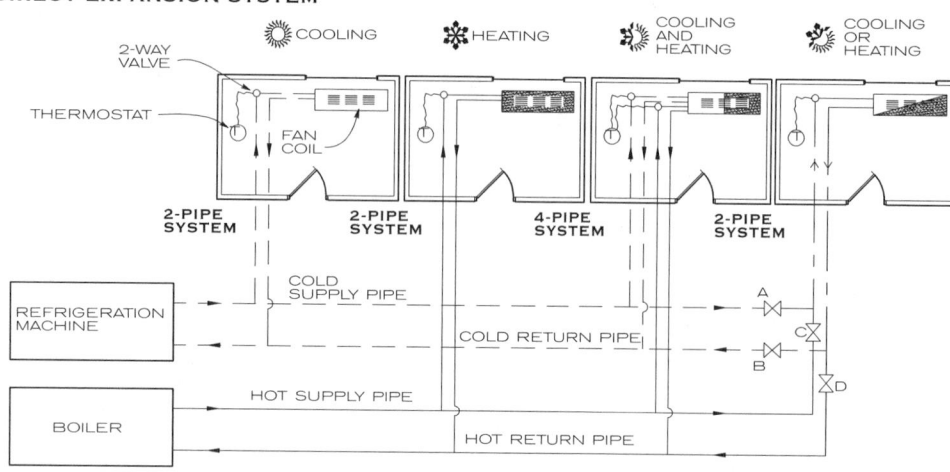

NOTES

1. Valves A and B are closed during the heating season.

2. Valves C and D are closed during the cooling season.

3. A majority of existing buildings with central heating and cooling use the two-pipe distribution system.

ALL-WATER SYSTEM

Alfred Greenberg, P.E., C.E.M.; Murray Hill, New Jersey

CONTROLS FOR ALL-AIR SYSTEMS

The typical sequence of operation for an air-handling system is outlined here:

1. When the supply air fan has been turned on but the motor is not yet turning, minimum outside air damper D_2 and exhaust air damper D_1 open, the latter to its minimum position to match the amount of incoming air. The exhaust air and return air dampers are interlocked: When the exhaust air damper is shut, the return air damper is fully open; when the exhaust air damper is fully open, the return air damper is minimally open.

2. When dampers are in proper open positions, the supply air fan starts running and the return air fan is turned on, either manually or electrically. This sequence is necessary to prevent the supply air fan from sucking air out of the air-handling unit and collapsing the casing and to keep the return air fan from blowing excess air into the casing and "bursting the bubble."

3. Space thermostat T_1 and humidistat H_1 take control of the system. If humidification is required, H_1 controls the operation of control valve V_3 at the humidifier in the air-handling unit. If heating is required, T_1 controls the operation of reheat coil control valve V_4. If cooling is needed, T_1 controls the cooling coil control valve V_2. At this time, control valves V_1, V_3, and V_4 are closed. Control valve V_1 for the preheat coil is controlled by a thermostat on the discharge side of the coil.

4. Many control system variations are possible to improve comfort and conserve energy. In one commonly used variation, an "economizer cycle" is established in which an outdoor thermostat is added to the control system. This permits the system to decide whether T_1 should open the heating or cooling coil control valve damper to initiate heating or cooling, depending on the season, or whether heating or cooling can be accomplished by opening variable outside air damper D_3 proportionally.

5. On a balmy spring or autumn day, it may be possible for total space conditioning needs to be supplied by fully open outdoor air dampers. In this case, damper D_1 would be fully open for exhaust air and fully closed for return air. D_2 and D_3 would be fully open, and V_1 through V_4 fully closed.

DIRECT-EXPANSION SYSTEMS

The term "direct expansion" means that a chemical refrigerant is used in the refrigeration circuit to remove heat and reject it, usually to the outdoors. Direct-expansion systems come in "cooling only" mode or in specially designed heat pumps, which can furnish either heating or cooling.

The most common direct-expansion system is the packaged unit installed through the wall or in a window. These can also be floor-mounted in or out of the air-conditioned space or located on the roof. Another type of direct-expansion system is the "split" system, in which the heat rejection components of the condenser and compressor are packaged separately and can be located remotely from the evaporator and fan, which must be in the air-conditioned space. The two subassemblies, which are attached to the system with refrigerant piping, may be as close as on opposite sides of a wall or up to 100 ft away.

ALL-WATER SYSTEMS

The term "all-water system" is a misnomer, since all air-conditioning systems furnish conditioned "fresh" air to the air-conditioned spaces. All-water systems may have fan coil or radiant panel terminal units with separate all-air systems to supply the "fresh" air. "Fresh" air furnished through openings in the walls behind the fan coil units is not considered properly conditioned because most fan coil units are not designed to provide satisfactory filtering and humidity control or to prohibit the entry of outdoor noise.

In the vast majority of all-water systems, water is used to provide either heating or cooling through a two-pipe distribution system. A freeze protection chemical can be added to some systems when needed. When clients demand simultaneous heating or cooling everywhere, the piping will be either a three- or four-pipe distribution system and the heating and cooling plants must be able to run at all times. The three-pipe system is seldom used because it is difficult to operate properly and to run efficiently.

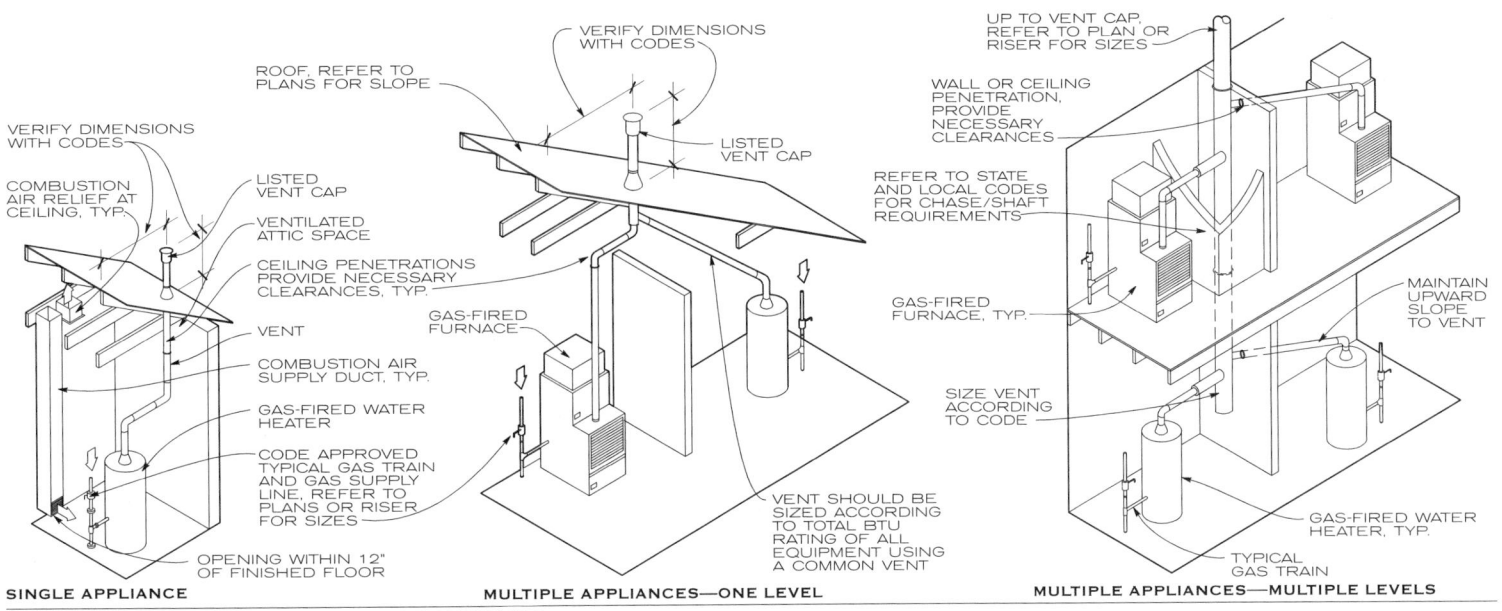

GAS APPLIANCES WITH VENT ARRANGEMENTS

SINGLE APPLIANCE

MULTIPLE APPLIANCES—ONE LEVEL

MULTIPLE APPLIANCES—MULTIPLE LEVELS

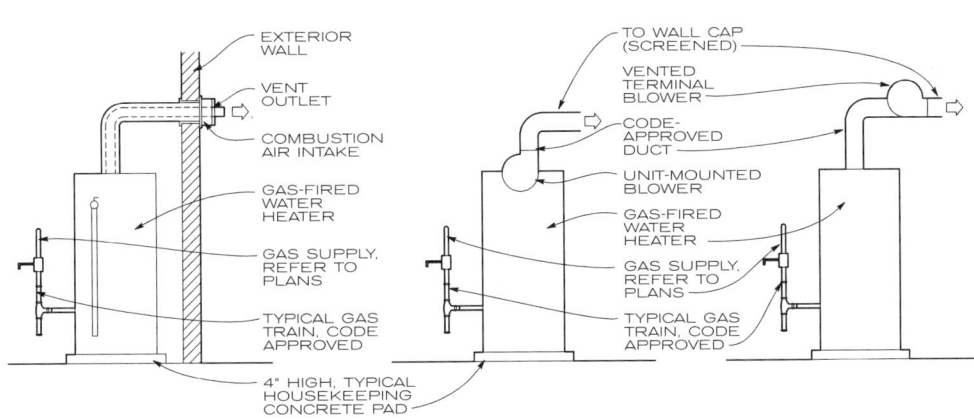

DIRECT VENT

POWER VENT

POWER VENT

SIDEWALL VENTED GAS-FIRED WATER HEATERS

TYPICAL GAS TRAIN

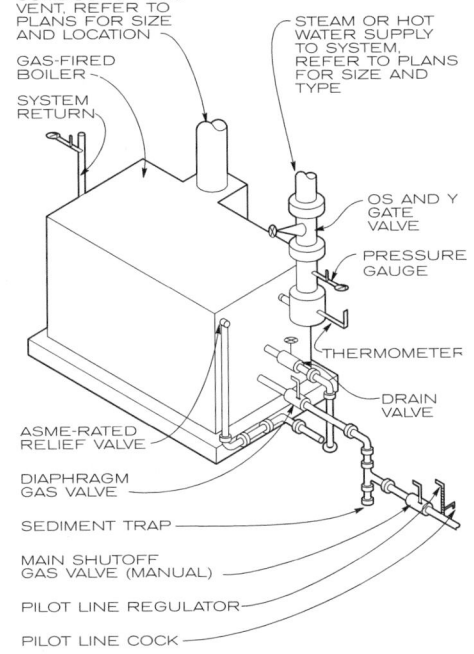

TYPICAL GAS-FIRED BOILER

TYPICAL GAS-FIRED HIGH-EFFICIENCY FURNACE

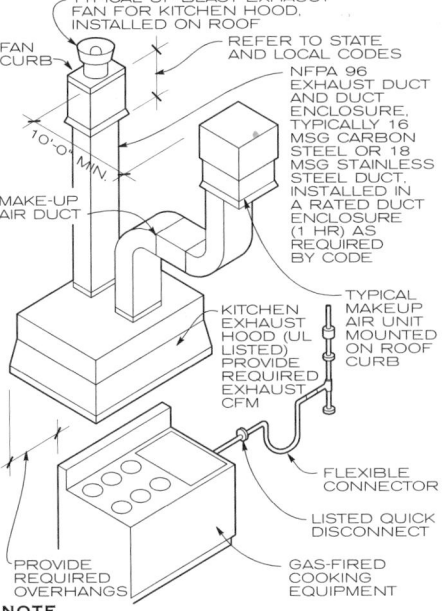

NOTE

MSG: manufacturer's standard gauge thickness.

TYPICAL KITCHEN HOOD INSTALLATION

NOTES

1. For high-efficiency furnaces, contractors have the option of using a combination vent/intake air kit (with either wall or roof installation) when allowed by code.

2. Code requires fire extinguishing systems in kitchen hood installations in commercial facilities.

3. Drawings on this page are for reference only. Refer to state and local codes/ordinances and manufacturers' installation instructions for requirements governing maintenance, clearances, gas piping, combustion air, and venting in specific situations.

Alfred Greenberg, PE, CEM; Murray Hill, New Jersey
American Gas Association; Washington, D.C.

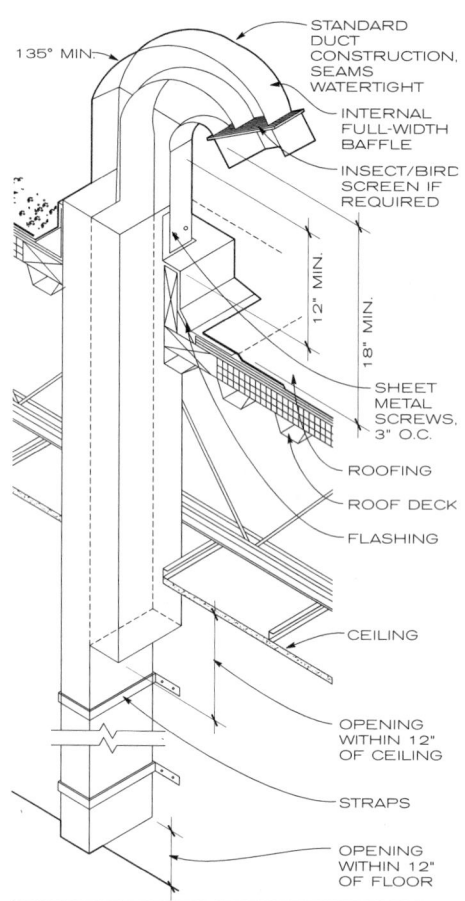

135° MIN.

STANDARD DUCT CONSTRUCTION, SEAMS WATERTIGHT

INTERNAL FULL-WIDTH BAFFLE

INSECT/BIRD SCREEN IF REQUIRED

12" MIN.

18" MIN.

SHEET METAL SCREWS, 3" O.C.

ROOFING

ROOF DECK

FLASHING

CEILING

OPENING WITHIN 12" OF CEILING

STRAPS

OPENING WITHIN 12" OF FLOOR

TYPICAL COMBUSTION AIR GOOSENECK

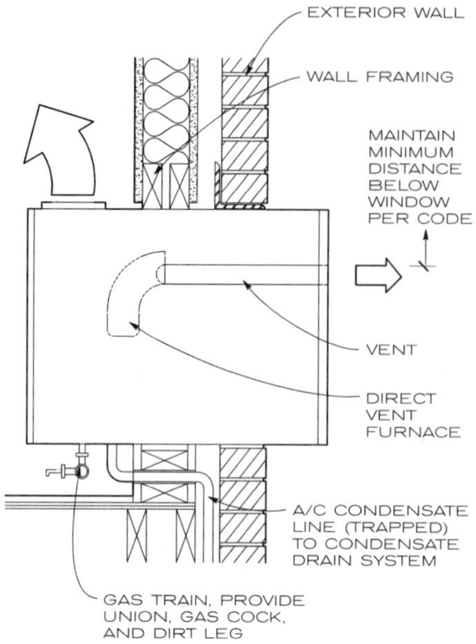

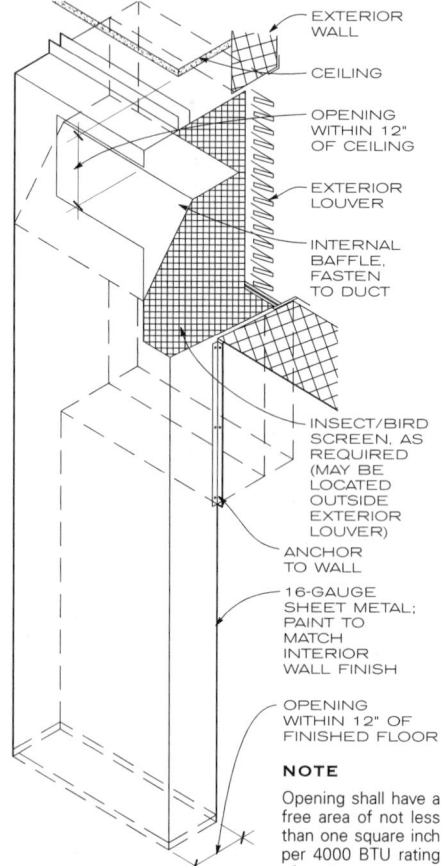

EXTERIOR WALL

CEILING

OPENING WITHIN 12" OF CEILING

EXTERIOR LOUVER

INTERNAL BAFFLE, FASTEN TO DUCT

INSECT/BIRD SCREEN, AS REQUIRED (MAY BE LOCATED OUTSIDE EXTERIOR LOUVER)

ANCHOR TO WALL

16-GAUGE SHEET METAL; PAINT TO MATCH INTERIOR WALL FINISH

OPENING WITHIN 12" OF FINISHED FLOOR

NOTE

Opening shall have a free area of not less than one square inch per 4000 BTU rating of equipment.

TYPICAL COMBUSTION AIR LOUVER

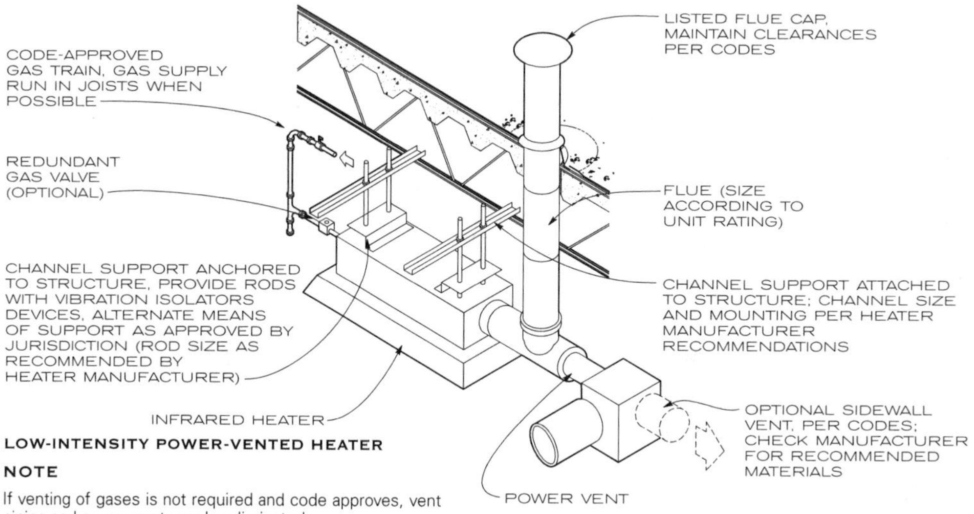

Alfred Greenberg, PE, CEM; Murray Hill, New Jersey
American Gas Association; Washington, D.C.

EXTERIOR WALL

WALL FRAMING

MAINTAIN MINIMUM DISTANCE BELOW WINDOW PER CODE

VENT

DIRECT VENT FURNACE

A/C CONDENSATE LINE (TRAPPED) TO CONDENSATE DRAIN SYSTEM

GAS TRAIN, PROVIDE UNION, GAS COCK, AND DIRT LEG

NOTE

Weatherproof these through-wall units at the wall.

TYPICAL GAS HEATING/ELECTRIC COOLING THROUGH-WALL UNIT

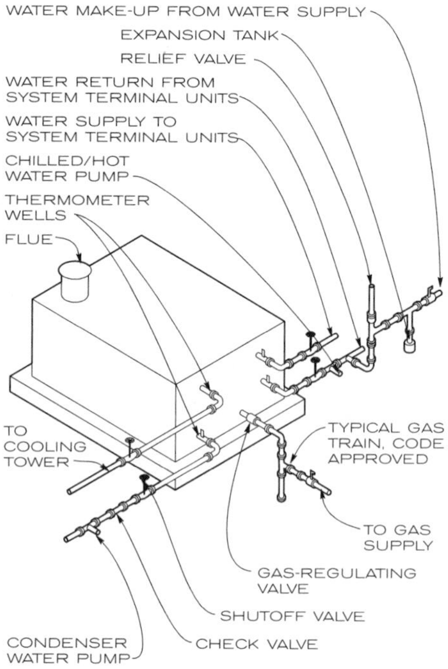

CODE-APPROVED GAS TRAIN, GAS SUPPLY RUN IN JOISTS WHEN POSSIBLE

REDUNDANT GAS VALVE (OPTIONAL)

CHANNEL SUPPORT ANCHORED TO STRUCTURE, PROVIDE RODS WITH VIBRATION ISOLATORS DEVICES, ALTERNATE MEANS OF SUPPORT AS APPROVED BY JURISDICTION (ROD SIZE AS RECOMMENDED BY HEATER MANUFACTURER)

INFRARED HEATER

LOW-INTENSITY POWER-VENTED HEATER

NOTE

If venting of gases is not required and code approves, vent piping and power vent may be eliminated.

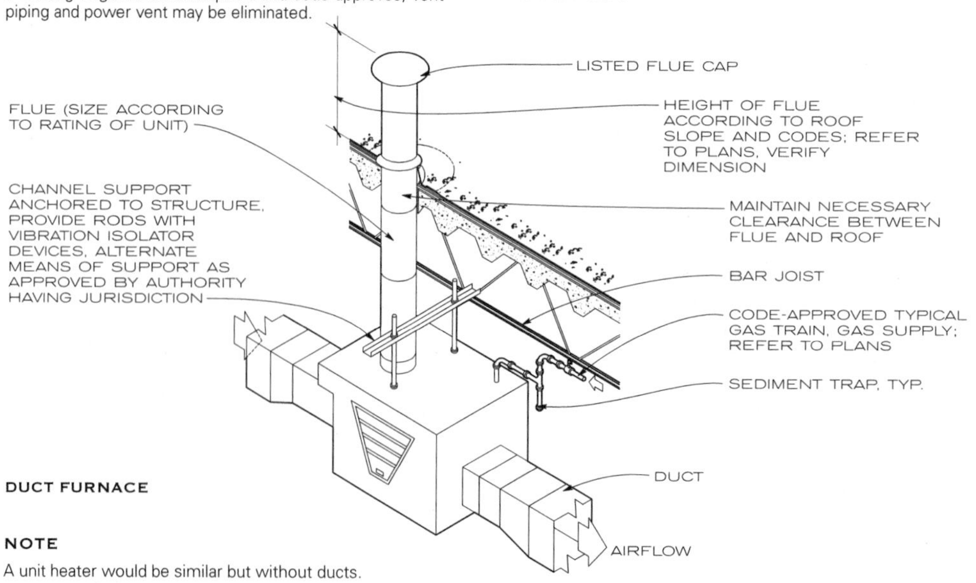

LISTED FLUE CAP, MAINTAIN CLEARANCES PER CODES

FLUE (SIZE ACCORDING TO UNIT RATING)

CHANNEL SUPPORT ATTACHED TO STRUCTURE; CHANNEL SIZE AND MOUNTING PER HEATER MANUFACTURER RECOMMENDATIONS

OPTIONAL SIDEWALL VENT, PER CODES; CHECK MANUFACTURER FOR RECOMMENDED MATERIALS

POWER VENT

WATER MAKE-UP FROM WATER SUPPLY

EXPANSION TANK

RELIEF VALVE

WATER RETURN FROM SYSTEM TERMINAL UNITS

WATER SUPPLY TO SYSTEM TERMINAL UNITS

CHILLED/HOT WATER PUMP

THERMOMETER WELLS

FLUE

TO COOLING TOWER

TYPICAL GAS TRAIN, CODE APPROVED

TO GAS SUPPLY

GAS-REGULATING VALVE

SHUTOFF VALVE

CHECK VALVE

CONDENSER WATER PUMP

DIRECT GAS-FIRED CHILLER/HEATER

FLUE (SIZE ACCORDING TO RATING OF UNIT)

CHANNEL SUPPORT ANCHORED TO STRUCTURE, PROVIDE RODS WITH VIBRATION ISOLATOR DEVICES, ALTERNATE MEANS OF SUPPORT AS APPROVED BY AUTHORITY HAVING JURISDICTION

LISTED FLUE CAP

HEIGHT OF FLUE ACCORDING TO ROOF SLOPE AND CODES; REFER TO PLANS, VERIFY DIMENSION

MAINTAIN NECESSARY CLEARANCE BETWEEN FLUE AND ROOF

BAR JOIST

CODE-APPROVED TYPICAL GAS TRAIN, GAS SUPPLY; REFER TO PLANS

SEDIMENT TRAP, TYP.

DUCT

AIRFLOW

DUCT FURNACE

NOTE

A unit heater would be similar but without ducts.

GAS-FIRED HEATERS

GENERAL

This and the accompanying page describe several HVAC systems commonly used in medium to large buildings. Systems covered are single duct with terminal reheat, single duct with variable volume, dual duct, and multizone.

CONSTANT VOLUME SINGLE-DUCT WITH TERMINAL REHEAT

This system provides a constant flow of air to the zone(s) served by the HVAC system. Zone temperature is maintained by changing the temperature of the constant airflow. Dehumidification is provided by the combination of a cooling coil and a reheat coil in the terminal mixing box in each zone. Cooling is provided by a cooling coil that uses either direct expansion of the refrigerant or chilled water provided by a central plant. Heating is provided in the outside air preheat coil and in the reheat coil using hot water from a boiler. Normally, the amount of outside air provided corresponds with the amount of ventilation appropriate for anticipated occupancy levels.

Winter and summer operation of the system is best understood by tracing the system state points on a psychrometric

chart. The state points for summer conditions of 95°F, 50% RH outdoor conditions, zonal conditions of 78°F and 50% RH, and system set points of 10% outside air, cooling coil set point of 55°F, and a maximum reheat coil set point of 110°F. The preheat coil is assumed inactive in the summer and the cooling coil is inactive in the winter when the mixed air is less than 55°F.

During summer conditions, the mixed airstream (point C, 80°F, 50% RH), which consists of 10% outside air (points B and B', 95°F, 50% RH) and 90% return air (point A, 78°F, 50% RH), is cooled to 55°F and 90–100% RH as it passes through the cooling coil (point D). This 55°F air is then provided to the terminal box in each zone, where it is reheated to meet the zonal cooling load; in this case, the 55°F, 90–100% RH air is reheated to 65°F and 70% RH in the terminal mixing box before it enters the zone.

During the winter, the preheat coil heats outside air to 45°F. The mixed airstream (point C, 69°F, 50% RH), which consists of 10% outside air (point B, 35°F, 50% RH) that has been preheated to 45°F and 35% RH (point B') and 90% return air (point A, 72°F, 50% RH), passes through the cooling coil where it is cooled to 55°F and 80% RH and is heated in the terminal box to 90°F and 25% RH.

ADVANTAGES

1. Can provide heating and cooling as needed.
2. Good dehumidification.
3. Boiler and chiller can be installed at central plant.
4. Air-handling unit runs continuously, providing good ventilation.
5. Long equipment life.
6. An economizer can be added to take advantage of free cooling during appropriate conditions.

DISADVANTAGES

1. No humidification, so this type of system may produce very dry conditions indoors during winter.
2. Requires distribution ductwork to each zone.
3. Air-handling unit runs continuously, which can cause excessive electricity consumption.
4. Reheat coils require plumbing run to each zone or electric resistance heating.
5. Use of reheat during dehumidification uses unnecessary heating in the summer.
6. Chiller and boiler both must operate except in extreme winter conditions.

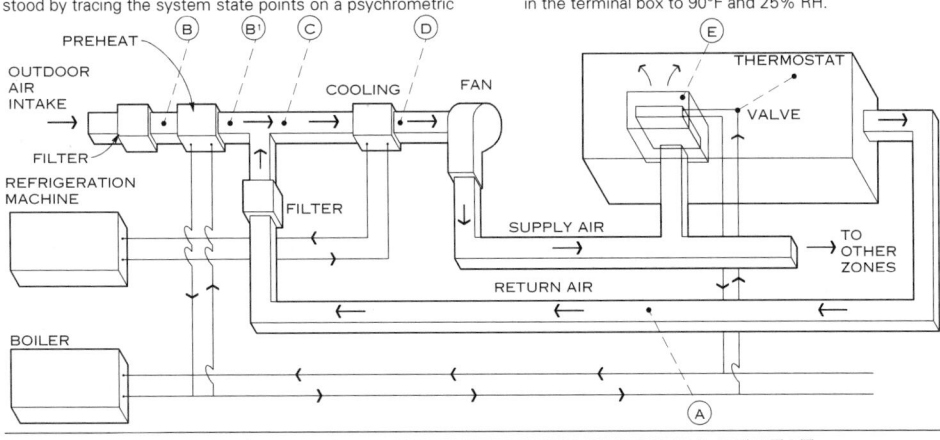
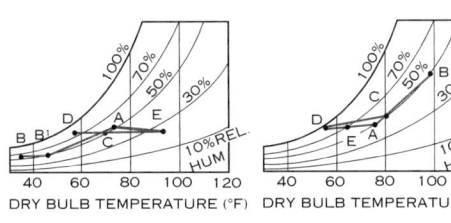

PSYCHROMETRIC CHART—WINTER

PSYCHROMETRIC CHART—SUMMER

CONSTANT VOLUME SINGLE-DUCT SYSTEM WITH TERMINAL REHEAT

VARIABLE VOLUME SINGLE-DUCT WITH REHEAT

This system provides a variable flow of air to the zone or zones served by the HVAC system. The amount of air is regulated by opening and closing individual terminal mixing boxes in each zone. Static pressure is maintained by varying the fan speed. During cooling, the temperature in each zone is maintained by changing the flow rate of the air. During heating, the cooling coil is inactive and the heating coil heats the main supply air to the minimum temperature necessary to meet the maximum load of any zone served. In the winter a thermostat in each zone regulates the heated airflow to meet the zone load. Dehumidification is provided by the combination of a cooling coil and a reheat coil. Humidification is not provided but can be added by inserting a humidification device immediately after the fan. Cooling is provided by a cooling coil that uses either direct expansion of the refrigerant or chilled water provided by a central plant. Hot water from a boiler provides heating in the outside air preheat coil and in the main reheat coil. Normally, a fixed amount of outside air is provided, corresponding to the amount of ventilation appropriate for anticipated occupancy levels.

Winter and summer operation of the system is best understood by tracing the system state points on a psychrometric

chart. The state points for summer conditions of 95°F and 50% RH outdoors, zonal conditions of 78°F and 50% RH, and system set points of 10% outside air, cooling coil set point of 55°F, and a maximum reheat coil set point of 110°F. The preheat coil is assumed to be inactive in the summer; the cooling coil is inactive in the winter when the mixed air is less than 55°F.

In summer conditions the mixed airstream (point C, 80°F, 50% RH), which consists of 10% outside air (points B and B', 95°F, 50% RH) and 90% return air (point A, 78°F, 50% RH), is cooled to 55°F and 90–100% RH as it passes through the cooling coil (point D). This 55°F air is then reheated to 65°F and 70% RH in the main reheat coil. Reheating must be controlled to maintain RH at or below 60% in all zones served in summer conditions. The amount of air entering each zone is then modulated to meet the cooling load.

During the winter the preheat coil heats outside air to 45°F; the cooling coil is inactive. The mixed airstream (point C, 69°F, 50% RH), which consists of 10% outside air (point B, 35°F, 50% RH) that has been preheated to 45°F and 35% RH (point B') and 90% return air (point A, 72°F, 50% RH), passes through the cooling coil unaffected and is heated in the main reheat coil to 110°F, 15% RH.

ADVANTAGES

1. Can provide heating and cooling as needed.
2. Average dehumidification.
3. Boiler and chiller can be installed at central plant.
4. Air-handling unit runs continuously at variable volume, which provides adequate ventilation.
5. Long equipment life.
6. An economizer can be added to take advantage of free cooling during appropriate ambient conditions.
7. Does not require piping into individual zones.

DISADVANTAGES

1. No humidification, so this type of system may produce very dry conditions indoors during winter.
2. Requires distribution ductwork to each zone.
3. Volume of air provided to air-handling units varies, which can result in inadequate ventilation if not properly balanced.
4. One main reheat coil for the entire system can result in a very cold building in extremely humid climates. Could require humidity sensor to moderate supply air temperature to maintain humidity at or below 60% RH.
5. Use of reheat during dehumidification uses unnecessary heating in the summer.
6. One main heating coil may cause hot interior zones when internal loads require year-round cooling.

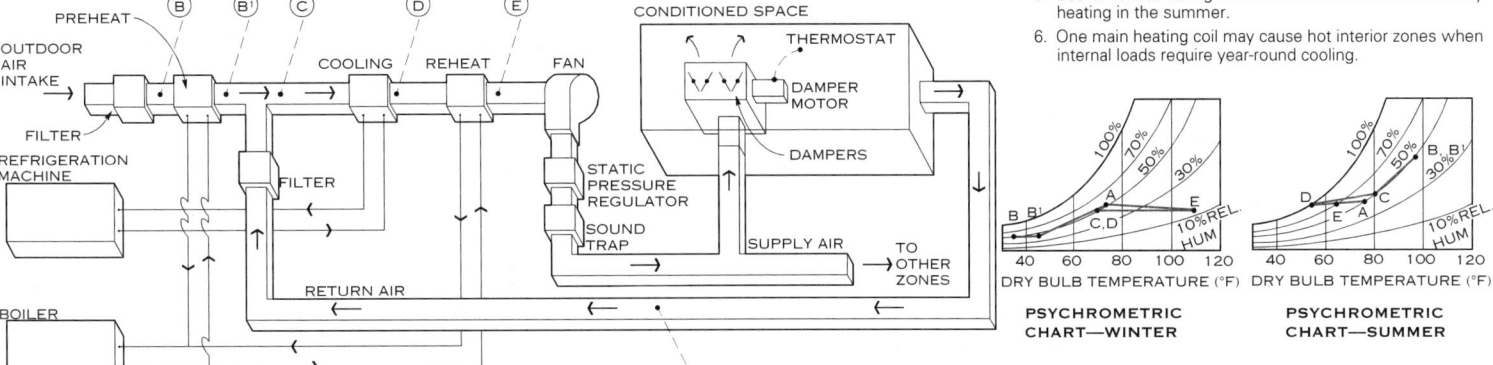

PSYCHROMETRIC CHART—WINTER

PSYCHROMETRIC CHART—SUMMER

VARIABLE VOLUME SINGLE-DUCT SYSTEM WITH REHEAT

Jeff Haberl, Ph.D, PE; Texas A&M University; College Station, Texas

CONSTANT VOLUME DUAL-DUCT

A constant volume dual-duct system provides a constant flow of air to zone(s) served by the HVAC system. Zone temperature is maintained by changing the temperature of the constant airflow that leaves the terminal mixing box in each zone. Dehumidification is provided by the cooling coil and any remixing of air in the terminal mixing boxes. Humidification is not provided in the system shown but can be added by inserting a humidification device immediately after the main cooling coil. Cooling is provided by a cooling coil that uses either direct expansion of the refrigerant or chilled water provided by a central plant. Heating is provided in the outside air preheat coil and in the main heating coil using hot water from a boiler. Normally, the fixed amount of outside air provided corresponds to the appropriate amount of ventilation for anticipated occupancy levels. However, in a dual-duct system both hot and cold airstreams are always available to each terminal mixing box. The temperature of the air leaving the cooling coil is always between 45°F (winter) and 55°F (summer). Air leaving the heating coil is either fixed at 110°F or can be moderated by an outside reset thermostat. Varying amounts of hot and cold air are mixed in the terminal boxes to achieve the required cooling or heating load.

Winter and summer operation of the system is best understood by tracing system state points on a psychrometric chart. The state points for summer and winter are the same as those indicated for the constant volume single-duct system with reheat (see the AGS page on this system).

In summer conditions the mixed airstream (point C, 80°F, 50% RH), which consists of 10% outside air (points B and B', 95°F, 50% RH) and 90% return air (point A, 78°F, 50% RH), is either cooled to 55°F and 90–100% RH as it passes through the cooling coil (point D) or heated to 110°F and 20% RH as it passes through the main heating coil. Both the 55°F cold air and 110°F hot air are then made available to the terminal mixing box, where the two airstreams are mixed to produce a constant flow, variable temperature airstream to meet the cooling and dehumidification load (point F).

During winter conditions the preheat coil heats outside air to 45°F. The mixed airstream (point C, 69°F, 50% RH), which consists of 10% outside air (point B, 35°F, 50% RH) that has been preheated to 45°F and 35% RH (point B') and 90% return air (point A, 72°F, 50% RH), passes through the cooling coil where it is cooled to 55°F and 82% RH or is heated in the main heating coil to 110°F and about 15% RH. Both

the 45°F cold air and 110°F hot air are then made available to the terminal mixing box, which mixes the two to produce a constant flow, variable temperature airstream to meet the heating load (point F). This type of system does not provide humidification so may produce extremely dry conditions indoors during the winter.

ADVANTAGES

Constant volume dual-duct systems have the same advantages as those listed in numbers 1–5 on the AGS page on constant volume single-duct systems with reheat. An economizer can be added to reduce the mixed air to 55°F so the cooling load can be reduced.

DISADVANTAGES

Constant volume dual-duct systems have the same disadvantages as those listed in numbers 1–3 and 5–6 on the AGS page on constant volume single-duct systems with reheat.

NOTE

This system can easily be modified to make a variable volume dual-duct system. Install a variable speed controller on the main fan and modify the terminal mixing boxes to allow for varying airflow rates. An economizer can also be added to reduce winter cooling loads.

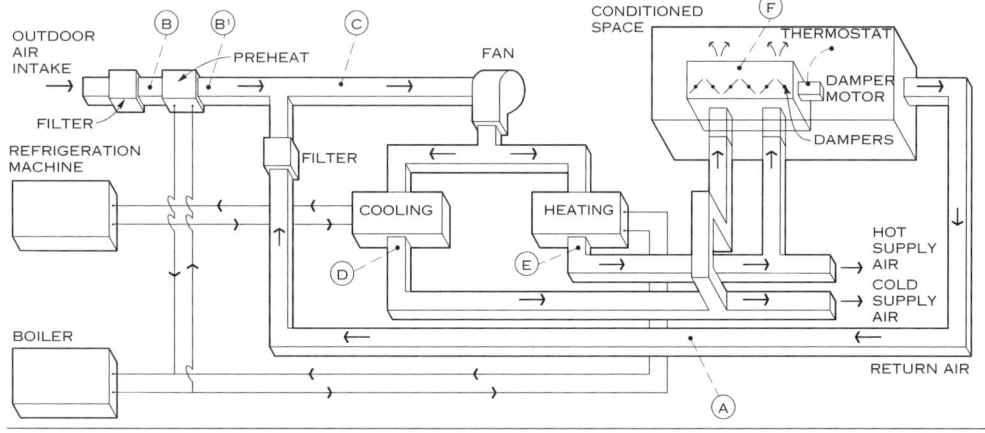

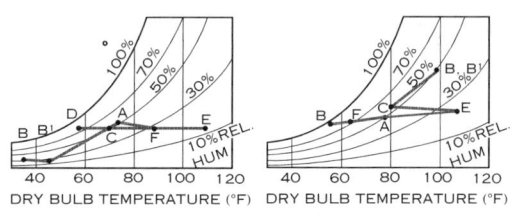

PSYCHROMETRIC CHART—WINTER   **PSYCHROMETRIC CHART—SUMMER**

CONSTANT VOLUME DUAL-DUCT SYSTEM

CONSTANT VOLUME MULTIZONE

A constant volume multizone system provides a constant flow of air to the zones served by the system. Zone temperature is maintained by changing the temperature of the constant airflow that leaves the multizone unit. Dehumidification is provided by the cooling coil and any remixing of air from the heating coil before it enters a zone. The system shown does not provide humidification, but a dehumidification device can be added just after the main heating coil for each zone. Cooling is provided by a cooling coil that uses either direct expansion of the refrigerant or chilled water provided by a central plant. Heating is provided in the outside air preheat coil and in the main heating coil using hot water from a boiler. Normally, a fixed amount of outside air corresponds to the amount of ventilation appropriate for the occupancy level. In a multizone system both hot and cold airstreams are always available to each zone. The temperature of the air leaving the cooling coil is always between 45°F (winter) and 55°F (summer). Air leaving the heating coil is fixed at 110°F

or can be moderated by an outside reset thermostat. Varying amounts of hot and cold air are mixed according to the required cooling or heating load in each zone.

Summer and winter operation of the system is best understood by tracing system state points on a psychrometric chart. The state points for summer and winter conditions are the same as those indicated for the constant volume single-duct system with reheat (see the AGS page on this system).

During summer conditions the mixed airstream (point C, 80°F, 50% RH), which consists of 10% outside air (points B and B', 95°F, 50% RH) and 90% return air (point A, 78°F, 50% RH), is either cooled to 55°F and 90-100% RH as it passes through the cooling coil (point D) or is heated to 110°F and 20% RH as it passes through the main heating coil. Both the 55°F cold air and 110°F hot air are then made available to each zone to meet the cooling and dehumidification load.

During winter conditions the preheat coil heats outside air to 45°F. The mixed airstream (point C, 69°F, 50% RH), which consists of 10% outside air (point B, 35°F, 50% RH) that has been preheated to 45°F and 35% RH (point B') and 90% return air (point A, 72°F, 50% RH) passes through the cooling coil where it is cooled to 55°F and 80% RH or is heated in the main heating coil to 110°F and about 15% RH. Both the 55°F cold air and 110°F hot air are then made available to the individual zones to meet the heating load (point F). This type of system does not provide humidification and so may produce extremely dry conditions indoors in the winter.

ADVANTAGES

Constant volume multizone systems have the same advantages as those listed in numbers 1–6 on the AGS page on constant volume single-duct systems with reheat. An economizer can also be added to reduce winter cooling loads.

DISADVANTAGES

Constant volume multizone systems have the same disadvantages as those listed in numbers 1–3 and 5–6 on the AGS page on constant volume single-duct systems with reheat.

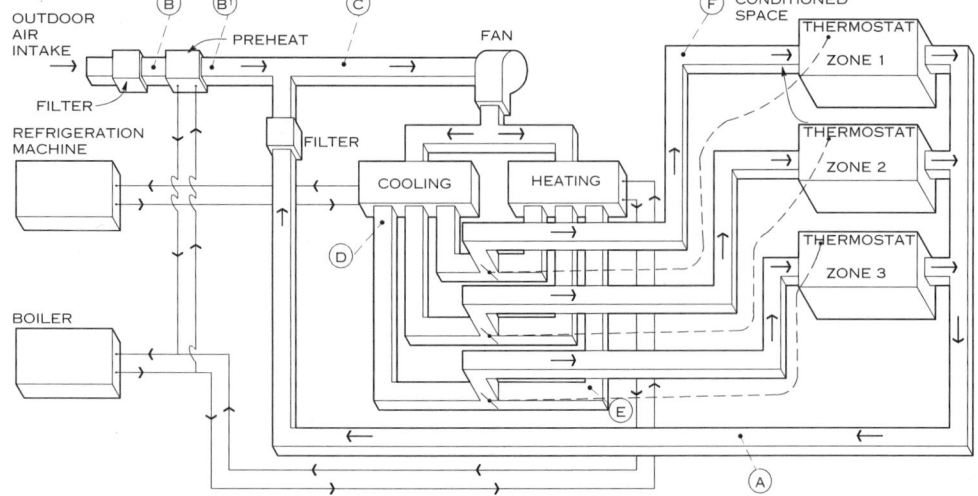

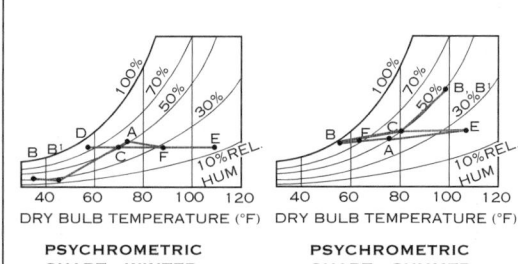

PSYCHROMETRIC CHART—WINTER   **PSYCHROMETRIC CHART—SUMMER**

CONSTANT VOLUME MULTIZONE SYSTEM

Jeff Haberl, Ph.D, P.E.; Texas A&M University; College Station, Texas

15 AIR DISTRIBUTION

GENERAL

The six diagrams on the AGS pages on multiple interior zone HVAC systems describe systems found in K–12 schools and small commercial office buildings.

FOUR-PIPE, SINGLE-ZONE AIR-HANDLING UNIT

Zonal air-handling units (AHUs) in this system provide heating and cooling for specific zones. Each AHU has a blower, filter, and heating and cooling coils. A fixed amount of fresh air to the units is pretempered to 55°F in a preconditioning unit. Both chilled and hot water are simultaneously provided to zonal and preconditioning units to carry the loads on the cooling and heating coils. Chilled water is provided by a chiller located in a central mechanical room (which contains a heat-rejecting condensing unit), and hot water is provided by a boiler, often located in the same mechanical room. Some single-zone AHUs run continuously. Newer units may

have a variable volume fan that regulates airflow according to zone loads. The chiller or boiler must operate when any single zonal unit requires cooling or heating.

Each unit is controlled by a zone thermostat that adjusts the supply-air temperature to meet heating or cooling loads. The preconditioning unit is controlled to maintain 55°F by preheating air in winter and precooling it in the summer. The temperatures of the chilled water and hot water supplied to the units may be controlled with an outside reset thermostat.

ADVANTAGES

1. This system can provide heating and cooling as needed.
2. The system offers good dehumidification.
3. The boiler and chiller are installed at a central location.
4. The system operates with minimal distribution ductwork.
5. Zonal air-handling units can be shut down without affecting adjacent areas.

6. Chiller efficiency is higher than for individual heat pumps.
7. The boiler and chiller have a long life (25 years).

DISADVANTAGES

1. A four-pipe system is slightly more expensve than a two-pipe system.
2. The hot water and chiller water loop must run even if only one zone needs heating or cooling.
3. The entire system is shut down when the loop fails.
4. The water-cooled condenser tower needs frequent service and water quality checks.
5. The temperature is higher in an air-cooled condenser than a water-cooled condenser, making chillers less efficient.
6. This system may require more energy than others because of the energy needed to run a four-pipe central loop.
7. The system has no humidification.

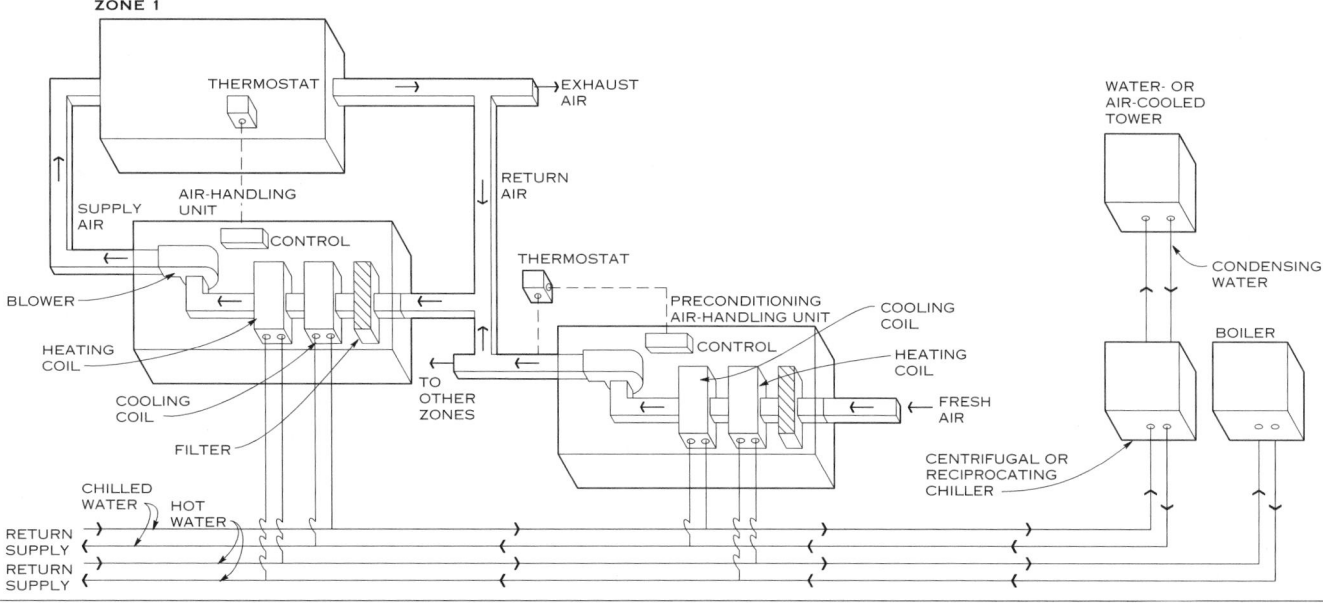

FOUR-PIPE, SINGLE-ZONE AIR-HANDLING UNIT

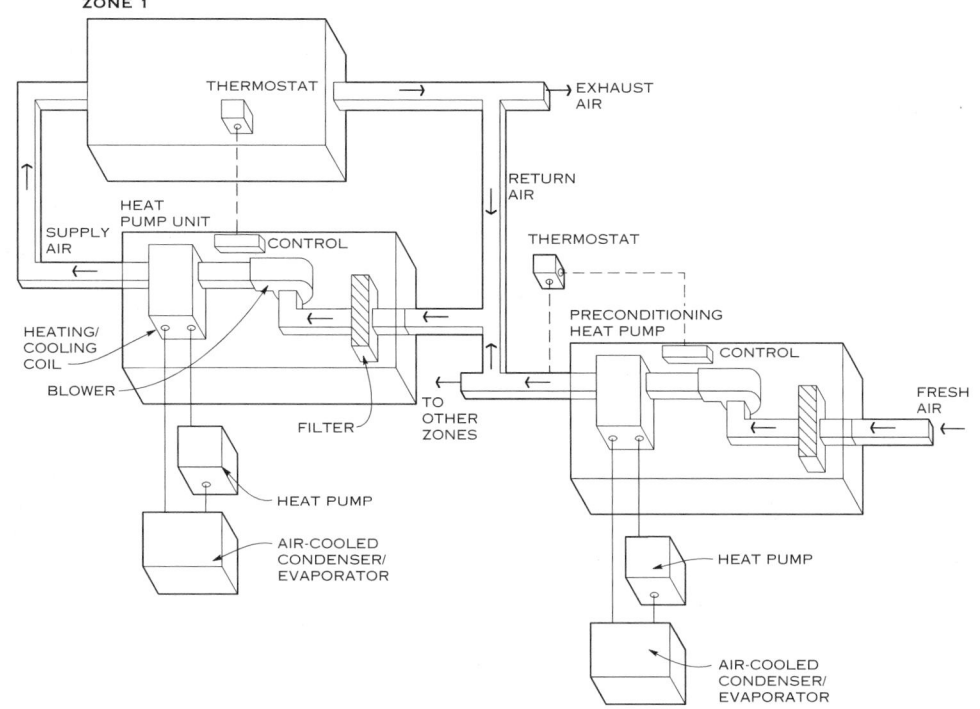

PACKAGED SPLIT SYSTEM WITH INDIVIDUAL HEAT PUMPS

PACKAGED SPLIT SYSTEM WITH INDIVIDUAL HEAT PUMPS

This system provides heating and cooling for individual zones with zonal heat pumps. Each heat pump unit contains a blower, filter, and heating/cooling coil. A fixed amount of fresh air to the units is pretempered to 55°F in a preconditioning heat pump unit. Each heat pump has its own heat rejection (or ambient heat source during cold weather). Emergency electric resistance heating is often provided for severe conditions.

The zonal heat pumps cycle on and off when the zone thermostat calls for heating or cooling. Airflow to the zones also cycles on and off according to zone demand. In general, the heat pump that preconditions outside air must run continuously to provide adequate preconditioned fresh air.

ADVANTAGES

1. Installation, system operation, and maintenance are simple.
2. No mechanical room is required.
3. Ductwork is only required for fresh air.
4. The initial cost is low.
5. This system is well-suited to spaces that require many zones of individual temperature control.

DISADVANTAGES

1. The noise level of this system is generally high.
2. Maintenance costs are high.
3. Overall efficiencies of individual heat pumps are less than that of one large chiller.
4. The system needs electric resistance heating when the outside air temperature is below 35°F.
5. Humidity control can be problematic if there is no preconditioning unit and zonal heat pumps are oversized.
6. Wall penetration is required for refrigerant lines to and from the condenser/evaporator.
7. Equipment life may be relatively short (typically 10 years).
8. The system has no humidification.

Jeff Haberl, Ph.D, P.E.; Texas A&M University; College Station, Texas

TWO-PIPE WATER LOOP HEAT PUMP WITH PACKAGED SPLIT SYSTEM

In this system, zonal heat pumps provide heating and cooling for individual zones. Each heat pump unit has a blower, filter, and heating/cooling coil. A fixed amount of fresh air to the units is pretempered to 55°F in a preconditioning heat pump unit. The system has a heat rejection loop, and each heat pump is connected to it with a heat exchanger. The heat rejection loop is maintained within a preset temperature range (e.g., 40–100°F) using a central boiler in the winter and one or more heat rejecting cooling towers in the summer. Usually, this type of system does not need emergency electric resistance heating for severe conditions. The

heat rejection loop must operate when one or more heat pumps are running. In some cases, a variable speed loop can be used, although care must be taken to provide adequate flow to keep the heat pump heat exchangers from freezing up and/or to avoid heat transfer problems in the boiler caused by low flow.

The zonal heat pumps cycle on and off when the zone thermostat calls for heating or cooling. Air flow to the zones also cycles on and off according to zone demand. In general, to provide an adequate source of preconditioned fresh air, the outside air preconditioning heat pump must run continuously. An air-cooled condenser can be provided for the preconditioning units to allow for the main loop to be shut down.

TWO-PIPE, GROUND-COUPLED WATER LOOP HEAT PUMP WITH PACKAGED SPLIT SYSTEM

This system has zonal air-handling units (AHUs) that provide heating and cooling for individual zones. Each zonal heat pump contains a blower, filter, and heating/cooling coil. A fixed amount of fresh air to the units is pretempered to 55°F in a preconditioning heat pump unit. Each heat pump is connected to the system heat rejection loop with a heat exchanger. However, in contrast to the water loop system that has an auxiliary boiler and heat rejection tower, this water loop rejects heat in a series of wells or trenches that put it in direct contact with the earth. This heat rejection loop is also maintained within a preset temperature range (e.g., 40–100°F) using the thermal mass of the earth it contacts. This type of system does not need emergency electric resistance heating for severe conditions. The ground-coupled heat rejection loop must operate when one or more heat pumps are running. A variable speed heat rejection loop can be used, although care must be taken to provide adequate flow to avoid freeze-up of the heat pump heat exchangers.

Zonal heat pumps cycle on and off whenever the zone thermostat calls for heating or cooling. Airflow to the zones also cycles on and off according to zone demand. In most cases, the outside air preconditioning heat pump runs continuously to provide an adequate source of preconditioned fresh air.

EVALUATION OF SYSTEM FEATURES

The following advantages/disadvantages apply to both systems described on this page, unless otherwise noted.

ADVANTAGES

1. The systems conserve energy by recovering heat from interior zones and/or waste heat.
2. The systems do not require wall penetrations to provide for the rejection of heat from air-cooled condensers.
3. Air-cooled preconditioning allows fresh air to be supplied without running the main loop.
4. The noise level can be lower than that of air-cooled equipment because individual condenser fans are eliminated and the compression ratio is lower.
5. The systems can be maintained locally, as no special chiller repairmen are required for the heat pumps (a special repairman is needed for the boiler in the system without ground coupling).
6. Units have a longer service life than air-cooled heat pumps.
7. The entire system does not shut down when a zonal unit fails.
8. Ground-coupled systems normally do not need a boiler and cooling tower. The mechanical room to house the loop pumps can be minimized.
9. The life-cycle cost of the two-pipe water loop heat pump with packaged split system (without ground coupling) compares favorably with that of central systems when installation costs, operating costs, and system life are considered.

DISADVANTAGES

1. The initial cost for these systems may be higher than for systems that use multiple unitary HVAC equipment.
2. Cleanliness of the piping loop must be maintained.
3. The water-cooled tower needs frequent service and water quality checks (this does not usually apply to the ground-coupled system).
4. If air-cooled preconditioning is not used, the loop must run 24 hr/day when any zone needs cooling or heating.
5. The entire system shuts down when the loop fails.
6. More maintenance will be required than for some other systems since the heat-pump equipment and air-handling units are decentralized.
7. These systems have no humidification.
8. In the ground-coupled system, soil type, moisture content, composition, density, and uniformity affect the success of this method of heat exchange.
9. In the ground-coupled system, the pipe material and the corrosiveness of the local soil and groundwater may affect heat transfer and service life.
10. In the ground-coupled system, a large area is needed in which to drill wells.

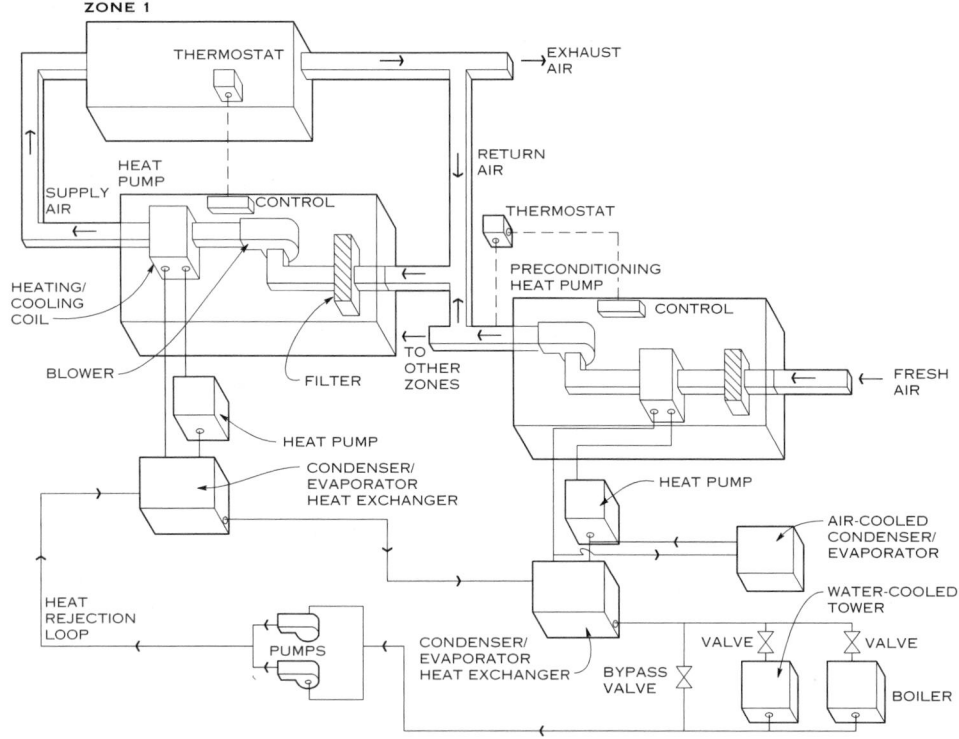

TWO-PIPE WATER LOOP HEAT PUMP WITH PACKAGED SPLIT SYSTEM

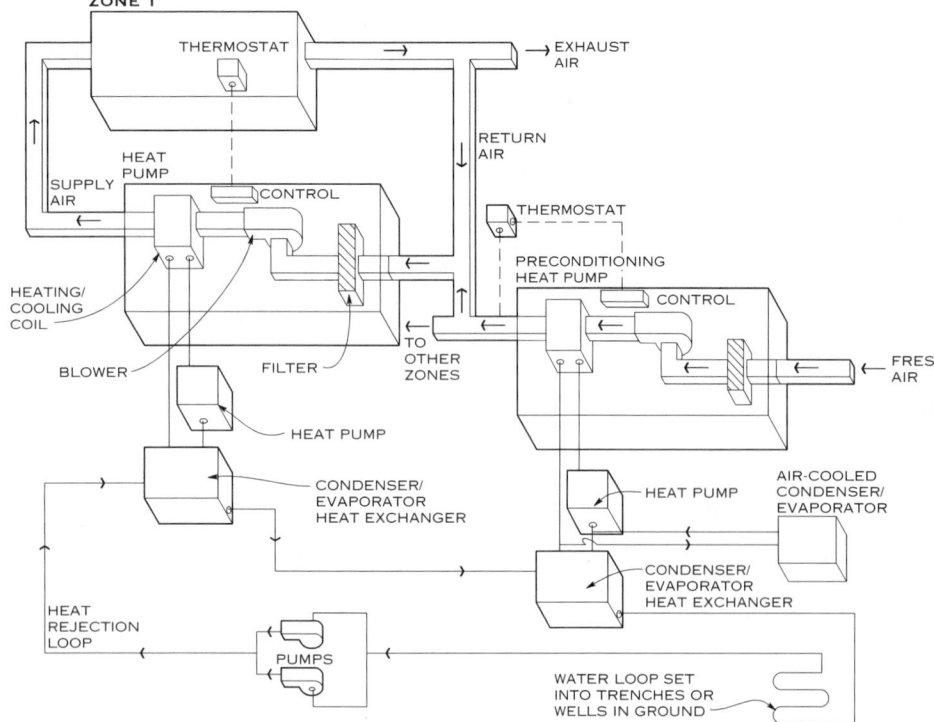

TWO-PIPE, GROUND-COUPLED WATER LOOP HEAT PUMP WITH PACKAGED SPLIT SYSTEM

Jeff Haberl, Ph.D, P.E.; Texas A&M University; College Station, Texas

15 **AIR DISTRIBUTION**

FOUR-PIPE MULTIZONE SYSTEM WITH COLD DECK BYPASS

Multizone air-handling units (AHUs) provide heating and cooling for several zones (typically 4 to 10). Each multizone unit contains a blower, filter, heating coils, cooling coils, and bypass dampers. Chilled water and hot water are simultaneously provided to the zonal units to carry loads on the cooling and heating coils respectively. Chilled water is provided by a chiller located in a central mechanical room (which contains a heat-rejecting condensing unit) and hot water is provided by a boiler, often located in the same mechanical room. The multizone units run continuously. The chiller or boiler must operate when any multizone unit or pre-conditioning unit requires heating or cooling. Newer units may contain a variable volume fan that regulates the airflow according to the zone loads.

Each zone is controlled by a zone thermostat that changes the temperature of the supply air to meet heating or cooling loads. The supply air is conditioned by an arrangement of dampers that allows the correct portion of air either to flow across or to bypass the cold deck. A reheat coil can be provided for locations with extremely humid conditions. A pre-heat coil can be provided for extreme winter conditions. The temperature of the chilled water and hot water supplied to the units may be controlled with an outside reset thermostat.

ADVANTAGES

1. The system supplies several zones from centrally located AHUs.
2. No pipes are required that could leak in occupied areas.
3. The system can provide heating and cooling as needed.
4. The boiler and the chiller are centrally located.
5. Chiller efficiency is often higher than that of individual heat pumps.
6. The system offers good dehumidification.

DISADVANTAGES

1. The hot water and chiller water loop must run when only one zone needs heating or cooling.
2. The chiller and boiler require service by specially trained repairmen.
3. A water-cooled condenser tower needs frequent service and water quality checks.
4. Additional space is required for distribution ductwork.
5. The air-cooled condenser temperature is higher than that of a water-cooled condenser, making the chiller less efficient.
6. The central system may use more energy because the loop has to run more often.
7. The system has no humidification.

FOUR-PIPE FAN COIL UNITS

In this system, fan coil units in each zone provide heating or cooling for that zone. Each fan coil unit contains a blower, filter, and heating-cooling coil. A fixed amount of fresh air to the units is pretempered to 55°F in a preconditioning unit that serves a number of zones. Chilled water and hot water are simultaneously provided to the zonal units and the pre-conditioning units to carry loads on the cooling and heating coils respectively. Chilled water is provided by a chiller located in a central mechanical room (which contains a heat-rejecting condensing unit) and hot water is provided by a boiler, which is often located in the same mechanical room. The zonal fans can either run continuously and modulate temperature or turn on and off as needed to satisfy the zone thermostat. Newer units may contain a variable volume fan that regulates the airflow depending upon zone loads.

Each zonal fan coil unit is controlled by a zone thermostat, which changes the temperature of the supply air to meet heating or cooling loads. The preconditioning maintains a temperature of 55°F by preheating the air in the winter and precooling it in the summer. The temperature of the chilled water and hot water supplied to the units may be controlled with an outside reset thermostat.

ADVANTAGES

1. The system provides all-season heating and cooling at each unit.
2. The boiler and chiller are installed at a central location.
3. The only ductwork needed is for preconditioned air (about 10–20% of fan coil air).
4. Chiller efficiency is higher than that of individual heat pumps.
5. The zonal fan coil unit can be shut down for maintenance without affecting adjacent areas.
6. No summer/winter changeover is required.
7. This system operates more simply than the others described in this AGS section on multiple interior zone HVAC systems.
8. Cooling of preconditioned air may not be required in northern climates with hot, dry summers.

DISADVANTAGES

1. Four-pipe systems are slightly more expensive to install than two-pipe systems.
2. The hot water and chilled water loop must run when only one zone needs heating or cooling.
3. The chiller and boiler need servicing by specially trained repairmen.
4. Noise from individual units may be a problem.
5. The water-cooled condenser tower needs frequent service and water quality checks.
6. The air-cooled condenser temperature is higher than that of a water-cooled condenser, making the chiller less efficient.
7. This central system may use more energy because of the frequent running of the loop.
8. Decentralized maintenance of zonal units can require additional maintenance time.
9. Zonal units need a sanitary sewer connection to drain condensate. These drains can be a maintenance concern.
10. The system has no humidification.

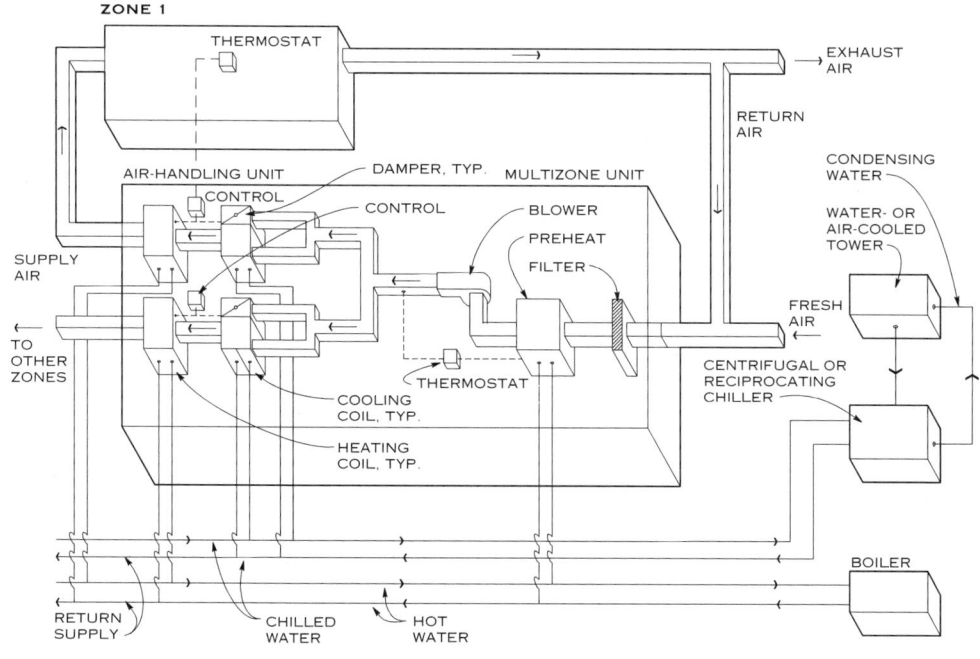

FOUR-PIPE MULTIZONE SYSTEM WITH COLD DECK BYPASS

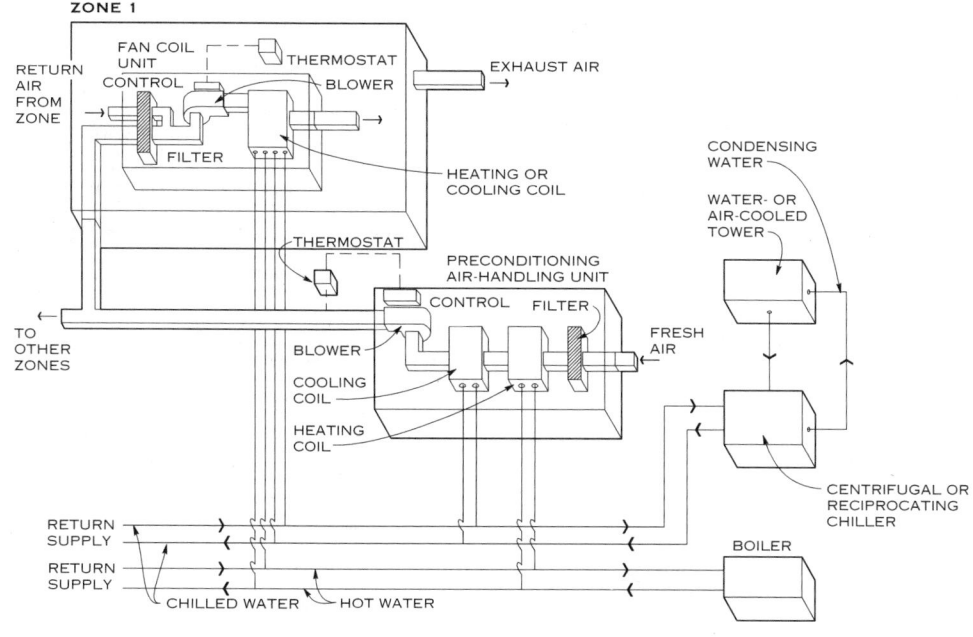

FOUR-PIPE FAN COIL UNITS

Jeff Haberl, Ph.D, P.E.; Texas A&M University; College Station, Texas

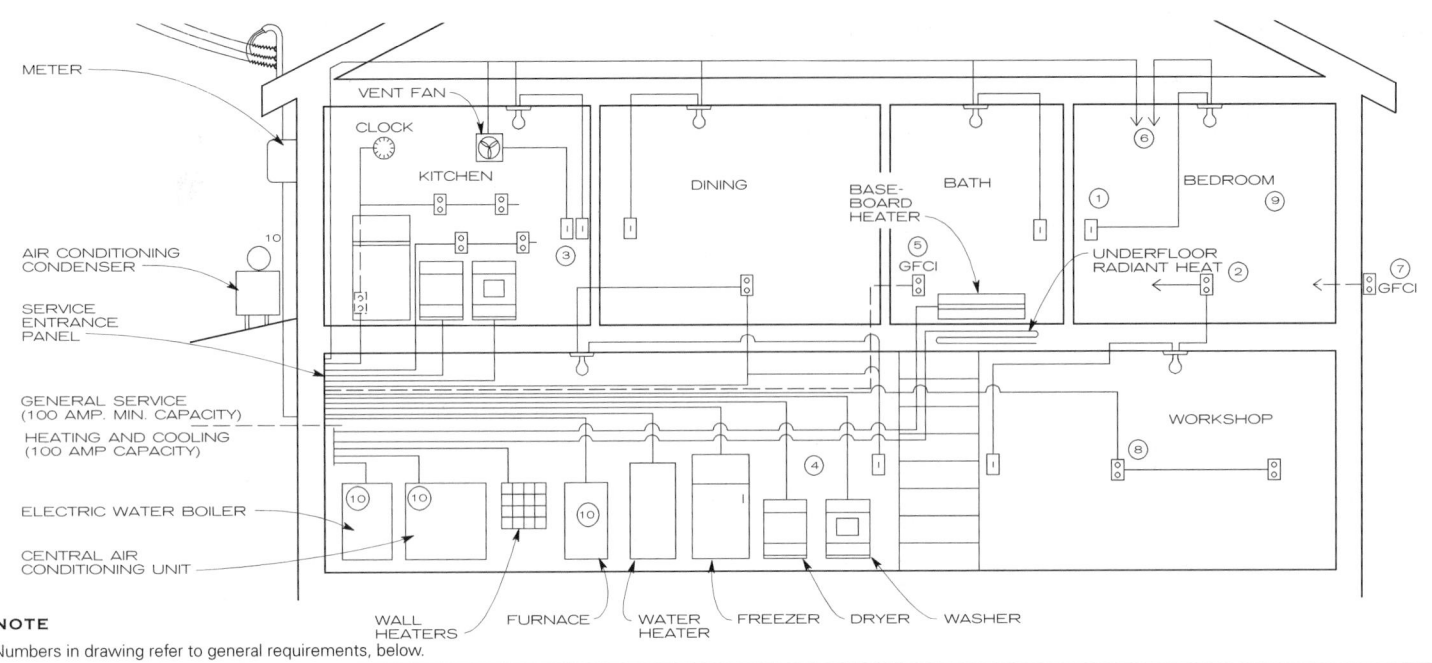

NOTE

Numbers in drawing refer to general requirements, below.

SCHEMATIC DIAGRAM OF TYPICAL RESIDENTIAL ELECTRICAL LAYOUT

GENERAL REQUIREMENTS

1. A minimum of one wall-switch-controlled lighting outlet is required in every habitable room, hallway, stairway, attached garage, and outdoor entrance. Exception: In habitable rooms other than kitchens and bathrooms one or more receptacles controlled by a wall switch are permitted in lieu of lighting outlets.

2. In every kitchen, family room, dining room, den, breakfast room, living room, parlor, sunroom, bedroom, recreation room, and similar rooms, receptacle outlets must be installed so that no point along the floor line is farther than 12 ft, measured horizontally, from an outlet, including any wall space 2 ft or more wide and the wall space occupied by sliding panels in exterior walls.

3. A minimum of two #12 wire 20-A small appliance circuits are required to serve only small appliance outlets, including refrigeration equipment, in the kitchen, pantry, dining room, breakfast room, and family room. Both circuits must extend to the kitchen; the other rooms may be served by one or both of them. No other outlets may be connected to these circuits, except a receptacle installed solely for an electric clock. In kitchen and dining areas, receptacle outlets must be installed at each and every counter space wider than 12 in.

4. A minimum of one #12 wire 20-A circuit must be provided to supply the laundry receptacle(s), and it may have no other outlets.

5. At least one receptacle outlet must be installed in the bathroom near the basin and must be provided with ground fault circuit interrupter protection.

6. Code requires sufficient 15- and 20-A circuits to supply three watts of power for every square foot of floor space, not including garage and open porch areas. Minimum code suggestion is one circuit per 600 sq ft; one circuit per 500 sq ft is desirable.

7. A minimum of one exterior receptacle outlet is required (two are desirable) and must be provided with ground fault circuit interrupter protection.

8. A minimum of one receptacle outlet is required in basement and garage, in addition to the one in the laundry. In attached garages it must be provided with ground fault circuit interrupter protection.

9. Many building codes require a smoke detector in the hallway outside bedrooms or above the stairway leading to upper floor bedrooms.

10. Disconnect switches are required.

NOTE

Refer to the National Electrical Code (NEC) for further information on residential requirements.

LEGEND FOR FIRST FLOOR AND BASEMENT PLANS

A = Mount receptacles at countertop locations 2 in. above backsplash.

B = Mount receptacle 48 in. above finish floor (AFF).

C = Range and oven outlet boxes should be wall mounted, 36 in. AFF. Use flexible connections to units.

D = Switch and outlet for exhaust fan. The switch should be wall mounted above the sink backsplash and the outlet blank cover mounted adjacent to the fan wall opening. A separate switch may be omitted if the fan is supplied with an integral switch.

E = Dishwasher receptacle is wall mounted behind unit, 6 in. AFF.

F = Equipped with self-closing gasketed waterproof cover.

G = Mount 42 in. AFF.

NOTES

1. Wiring shown as exposed indicates absence of finished ceiling in basement level. All BX cable run through framing members. Attachment below ceiling joists is not permitted.

2. Connect to two incandescent porcelain lamp holders with pull chain. Mount two evenly spaced ceiling fixtures in crawl space.

3. Connect to shutdown switch at top of stairs.

4. Boiler wiring safety disconnect switch should have red wall plate, clearly marked "BOILER ON-OFF."

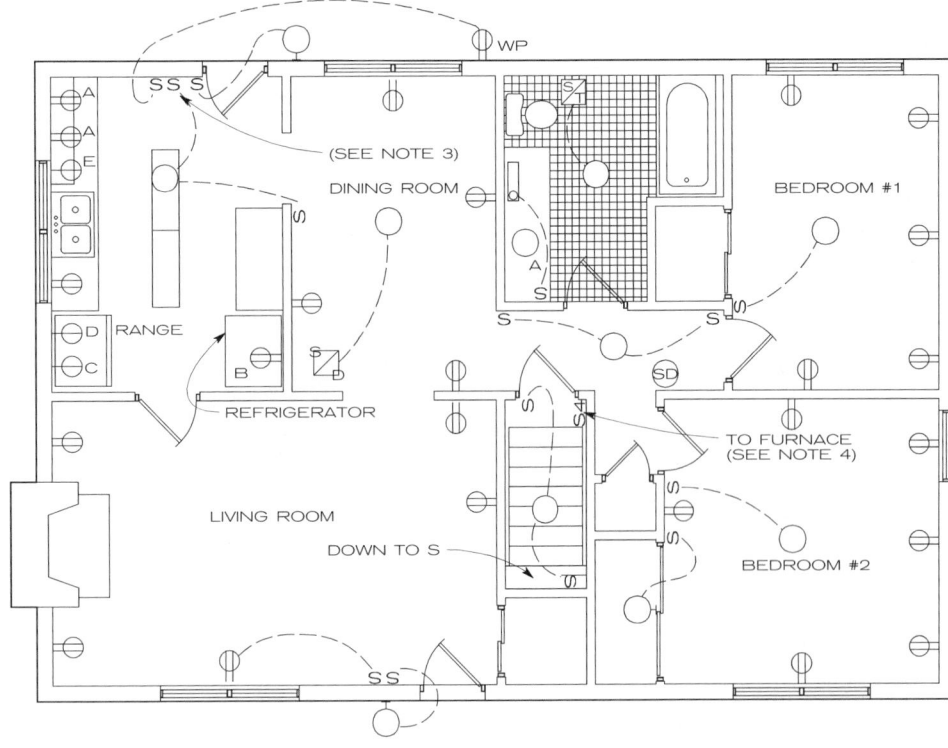

FIRST FLOOR PLAN OF ELECTRICAL EQUIPMENT AND DEVICES

Charles B. Towles, P.E.; TEI Consulting Engineers; Washington, D.C.

 **WIRING AND RELATED MATERIALS**

AVERAGE WATTAGES OF COMMON ELECTRICAL DEVICES

TYPE	WATTS
Air conditioner, central	2500§–6000
Air conditioner, room type	800–2500
Blanket, electric	150–200
Clock	2–3
Clothes dryer	4000–6000
Dishwasher	1000–1500
Fan, portable	50–200
Food blender	500–1000
Freezer	300–500
Frying pan, electric	1000–1200
Furnace blower	380–670
Garbage disposal	500–900
Hair dryer	350–1200
Heater, portable	1000–1500
Heating pad	50–75
Heat lamp (infrared)	250
Iron, hand	600–1200
Lamp, incandescent	10 upward
Lamp, fluorescent	15–16
Lights, Christmas tree	30–150
Microwave oven	1000–1500
Mixer	120–250
Power tools	up to 1000
Projector, slide or movie	300–500
Radio	40–150
Range (all burners and oven)	8000–14000
Range top (separate)	4000–8000
Range oven (separate)	4000–5000
Refrigerator	150–300
Refrigerator, frostless	400–600
Sewing machine	60–90
Stereo (solid-state)	30–100
Television	50–450
Vacuum cleaner	250–1200
Washer, automatic	500–800
Water heater	2000–5000

BRANCH CIRCUIT PROTECTION

Lighting (general purpose)	#14 wires	15 A
Small appliances	#12 wires	20 A
Individual appliances	#12 wires	20 A
	#10 wires	30 A
	#8 wires	40 A
	#6 wires	50 A

LOADS, CIRCUITS AND RECEPTACLES FOR RESIDENTIAL ELECTRICAL EQUIPMENT

APPLIANCE	TYPICAL CONNECTED VOLT-AMPERES[1]	VOLTS	WIRES[2]	CIRCUIT BREAKER OR FUSE[3]	OUTLETS ON CIRCUIT	NEMA[11] DEVICE[4] AND CONFIGURATION
KITCHEN						
Range[5]	12000	115/230	3 # 6	60 A	1	14-60R
Oven (built-in)[3]	4500	115/230	3 # 10	30 A	1	14-30R
Range top[3]	6000	115/230	3 # 10	30 A	1	14-30R
Dishwasher[3]	1200	115	2 # 12	20 A	1	5-20R
Waste disposer[3]	300	115	2 # 12	20 A	1	5-20R
Broiler[5]	1500	115	2 # 12	20 A	1 or more	5-20R
Refrigerator[6]	300	115	2 # 12	20 A	1 or more	5-20R
Freezer[6]	350	115	2 # 12	20 A	1 or more	5-20R
LAUNDRY						
Washing machine	1200	115	2 # 12	20 A	1 or more	5-20R
Dryer[3]	5000	115/230	3 # 10	30 A	1	14-30R
Hand iron; ironer	1650	115	2 # 12	20 A	1 or more	5-20R
LIVING AREAS						
Workshop	1500	115	2 # 12	20 A	1 or more	5-20R
Portable heater[7]	1300	115	2 # 12	20 A	1	5-20R
Television[7]	300	115	2 # 12	20 A	1 or more	5-20R
FIXED UTILITIES						
Fixed lighting	1200	115	2 # 12	20 A	1 or more	5-20R
Air conditioner 3/4 hp[8]	1200	115	2 # 12	20 A or 30 A	1	5-20R
Central air conditioner[9]	5000	115/230	3 # 10	40 A	1	
Sump pump[9]	300	115	2 # 12	20 A	1 or more	5-20 R
Heating plant, i.e., forced-air furnace[8 10]	600	115	2 # 12	20 A	1	
Attic fan[9]	300	115	2 # 12	20 A	1 or more	5-20R

[1] Wherever possible, use actual equipment rating.

[2] Number of wires does not include equipment grounding wires. Ground wire is No. 12 AWG for 20-A circuit and No. 10 AWG for 30-A and 50-A circuits.

[3] May be direct connected. For a discussion of disconnect requirements, see NEC Article 422.

[4] Equipment ground is provided in each receptacle.

[5] Heavy-duty appliances regularly used at one location should have separate circuits. Only one such unit should be attached to a single circuit.

[6] Separate circuit serving only one other outlet is recommended.

[7] Should not be connected to a circuit with appliances or other heavy loads

[8] Separate circuit recommended.

[9] Recommended that all motor-driven devices be protected by a local motor-protection element unless motor protection is built into the device.

[10] Connect through disconnect switch equipped with motor-protection element.

[11] National Electrical Manufacturers Association (NEMA).

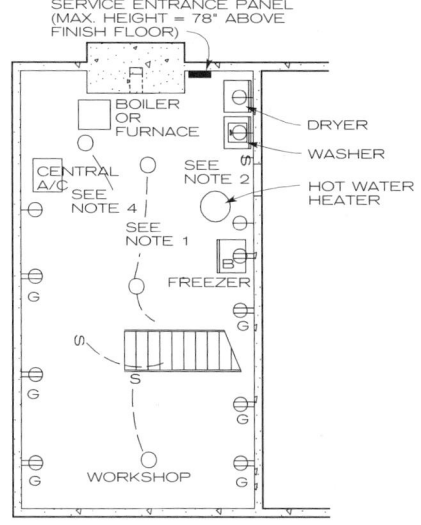

NOTE

See legend on previous page.

BASEMENT PLAN OF ELECTRICAL EQUIPMENT

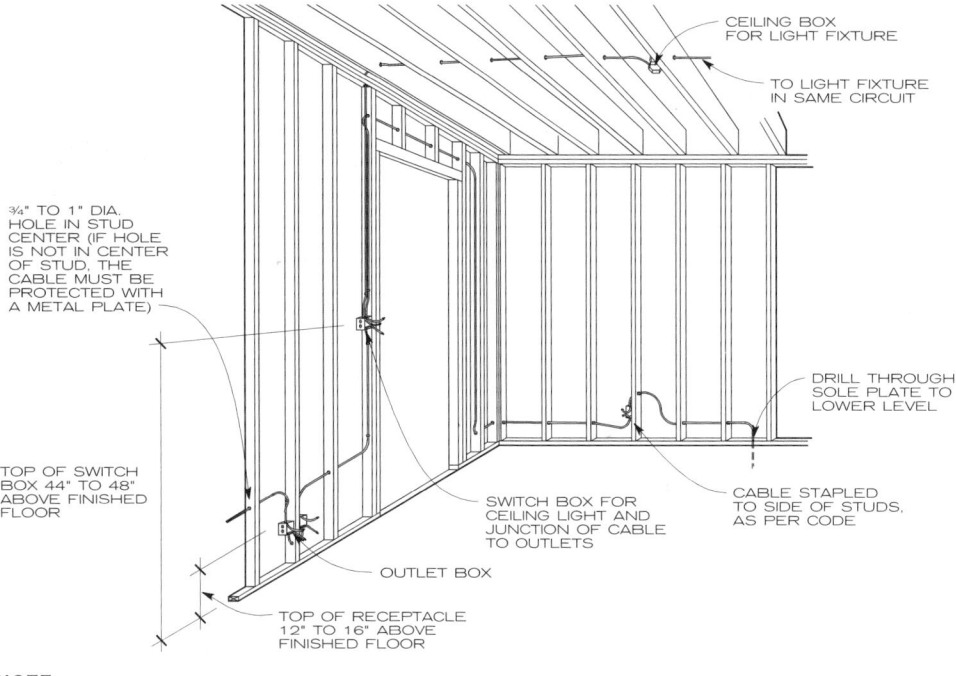

NOTE

In metal stud construction, cables are passed through pre-cut openings in place of field-drilled holes.

TYPICAL WIRING IN WOOD CONSTRUCTION

Charles B. Towles, P.E.; TEI Consulting Engineers; Washington, D.C.

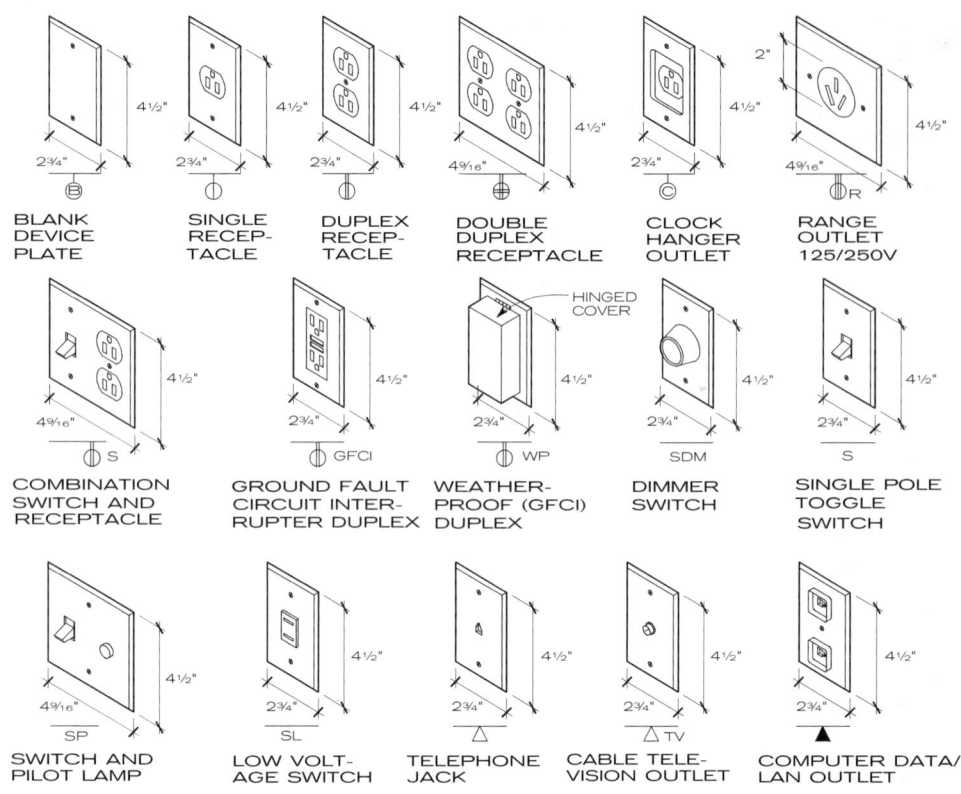

BLANK DEVICE PLATE

SINGLE RECEP-TACLE

DUPLEX RECEP-TACLE

DOUBLE DUPLEX RECEPTACLE

CLOCK HANGER OUTLET

RANGE OUTLET 125/250V

COMBINATION SWITCH AND RECEPTACLE

GROUND FAULT CIRCUIT INTER-RUPTER DUPLEX

WEATHER-PROOF (GFCI) DUPLEX

DIMMER SWITCH

SINGLE POLE TOGGLE SWITCH

SWITCH AND PILOT LAMP

LOW VOLT-AGE SWITCH

TELEPHONE JACK

CABLE TELE-VISION OUTLET

COMPUTER DATA/ LAN OUTLET

RECEPTACLES AND SWITCHES

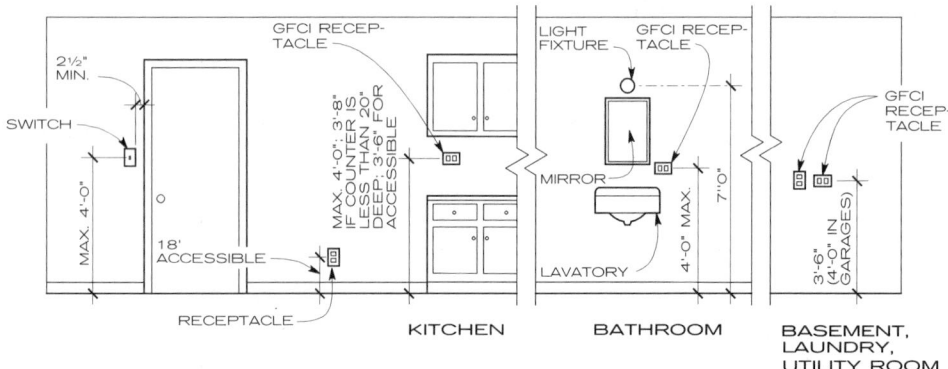

KITCHEN

BATHROOM

BASEMENT, LAUNDRY, UTILITY ROOM

NOTES

1. Outlets and switches shown are those most generally used. Number of gangs behind one wall plate depends on the type of devices used.

2. Symbols used are ASA standard.

3. Interchangeable devices (miniature devices) available in various combinations using any of the following—switch, convenience outlet, radio outlet, pilot light, bell button—in one gang. Combined gangs are available.

SWITCH AND OUTLET LOCATIONS

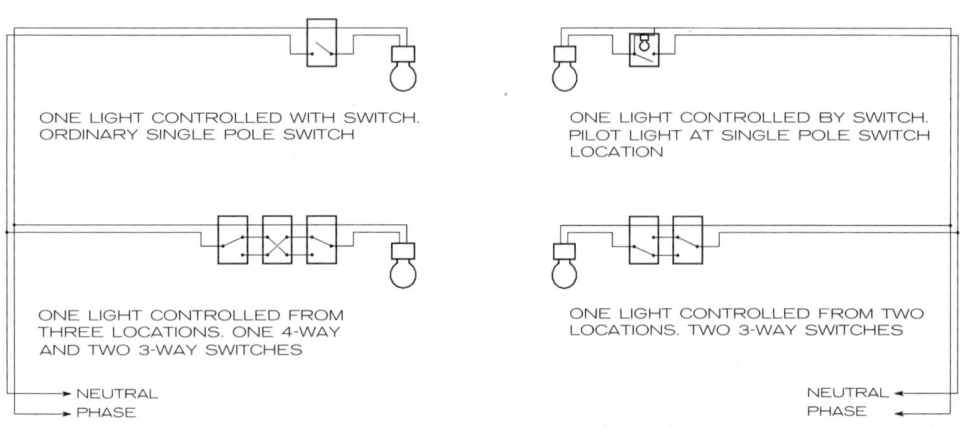

ONE LIGHT CONTROLLED WITH SWITCH. ORDINARY SINGLE POLE SWITCH

ONE LIGHT CONTROLLED BY SWITCH. PILOT LIGHT AT SINGLE POLE SWITCH LOCATION

ONE LIGHT CONTROLLED FROM THREE LOCATIONS. ONE 4-WAY AND TWO 3-WAY SWITCHES

ONE LIGHT CONTROLLED FROM TWO LOCATIONS. TWO 3-WAY SWITCHES

SWITCH WIRING DIAGRAMS

Charles B. Towles, P.E.; TEI Consulting Engineers; Washington, D.C.

GANG SIZE

GANG	HORIZONTAL (IN.)	
	HEIGHT	WIDTH
2	$4^1/_2$	$4^9/_{16}$
3	$4^1/_2$	$6^3/_8$
4	$4^1/_2$	$8^3/_{16}$
5	$4^1/_2$	10
6	$4^1/_2$	$11^{13}/_{16}$

NOTES

1. Add $1^{13}/_{16}$ in. for each added gang. Screws are $1^{13}/_{16}$ in. o.c.

2. Plates are made in plastic, brass (.04 to .06 in. thick), stainless steel, and aluminum.

3. All devices to be approved by Underwriters Laboratories and to comply with the National Electrical Code.

4. All devices to be of NEMA configuration.

5. Ground fault circuit interrupter or circuits are required in baths, garages, unfinished basements, outdoors at grade

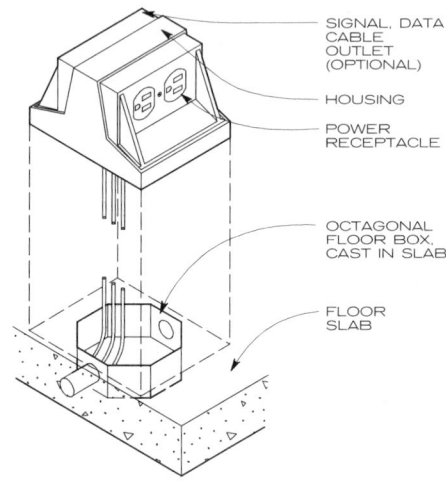

NOTE

Outlets and switches shown are those most generally used. The number of gangs behind one wall plate depends on the type of devices used.

MONUMENT FLOOR OUTLET

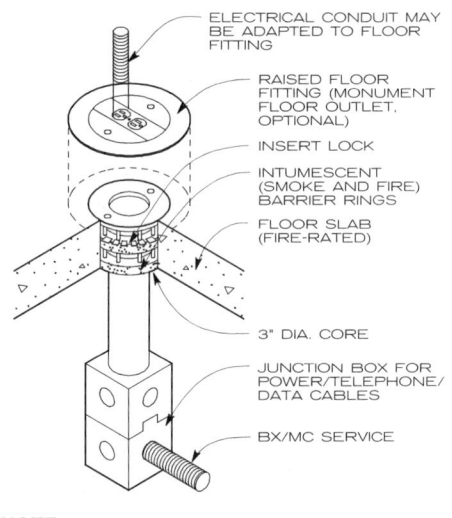

NOTE

Unit is adjustable to accommodate varying floor thicknesses. When abandoned, the floor fitting is replaced with a flat plate.

POKE-THROUGH ELECTRICAL BOX

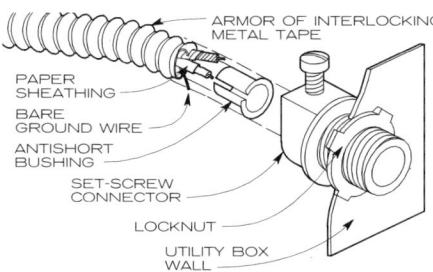

ARMORED (BX)
NOTE

Armored cable is manufactured with 2-, 3-, and 4-conductor insulated wire in sizes 14, 12, 10, 8, 6, 4, 2; its internal bonds help the armor itself serve as a bonding conductor.

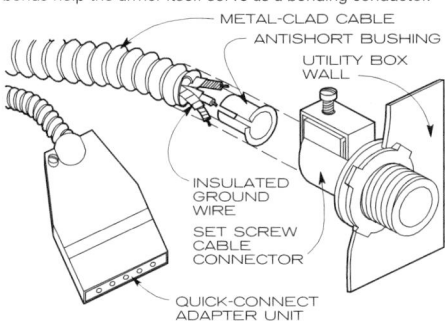

METAL-CLAD (MC)
NOTE

Manufactured in sizes and specs similar to armored cable, metal-clad cable is available with a separate insulated ground conductor and in larger sizes. It may be clad in aluminum or steel, corrugated, smooth, or with metal interlocking tape and may be factory assembled with quick connect adapter units for access floor or ceiling wiring systems. Consult an electrical engineer before installation.

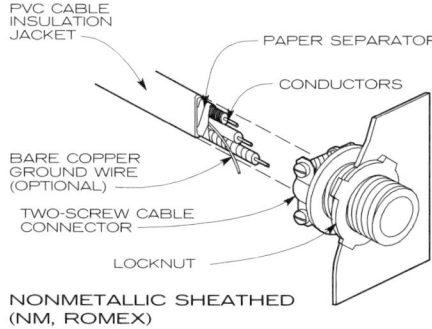

NONMETALLIC SHEATHED
(NM, ROMEX)
NOTE

Manufactured in 2- and 3-conductor PVC insulated wire in sizes 14, 12, 10, 8, 6, and 4 with or without ground wire, nonmetallic sheathed cable is permitted in residential and many other building types up to three stories.

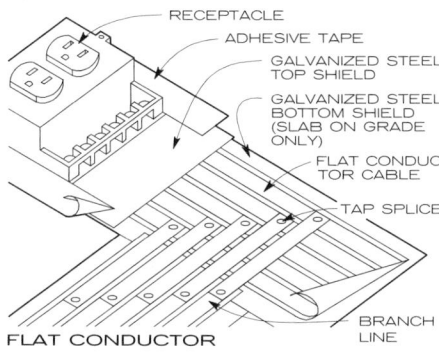

FLAT CONDUCTOR
NOTE

Flat conductor cable has combinations of 3, 4, and 5 conductors for easy access under carpet squares; data, communications, and TV flat cable are available. Consult manufacturers before installation.

CABLES

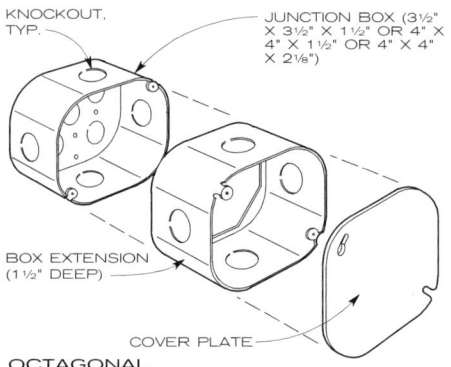

OCTAGONAL
NOTE

Commonly used for flush ceiling outlets, octagonal boxes may also be used as a floor box for monument receptacles.

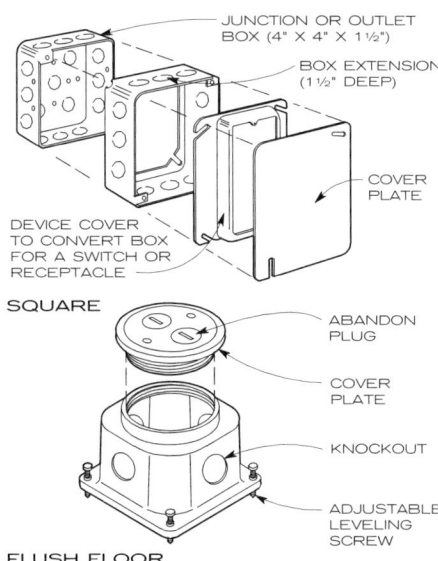

SQUARE

FLUSH FLOOR
NOTE

Boxes are mounted to wood floor structure (nonadjustable) or cast-in-place concrete with leveling screws. Concrete boxes include cast-iron, stamped steel, or nonmetallic materials. This is a heavy-duty box, in comparison to a standard octagonal floor box for monument receptacle.

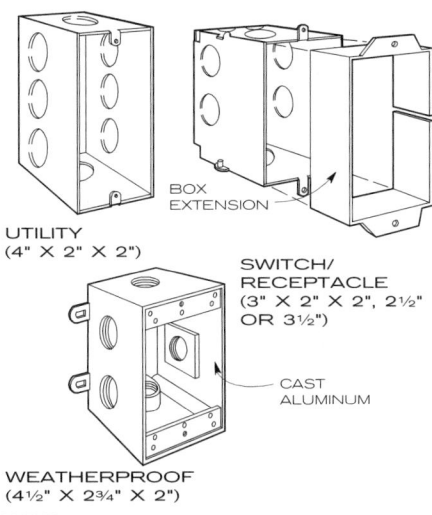

UTILITY
(4" X 2" X 2")

SWITCH/RECEPTACLE
(3" X 2" X 2", 2½" OR 3½")

WEATHERPROOF
(4½" X 2¾" X 2")
NOTE

Metallic and nonmetallic versions; knockout locations vary. Utility and exterior boxes not gangable; switch and masonry boxes may be. Flush mounting in concrete requires a concrete tight box and rigid conduit and tubing; in CMU construction, a raceway or tubing is threaded through the cavities.

ELECTRICAL BOXES

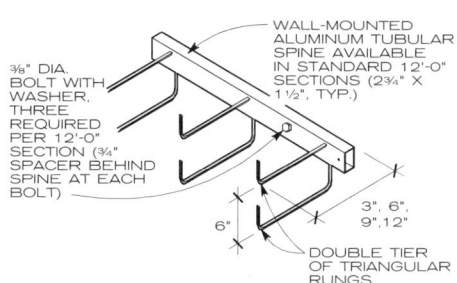

WALL-MOUNT CABLE RACK

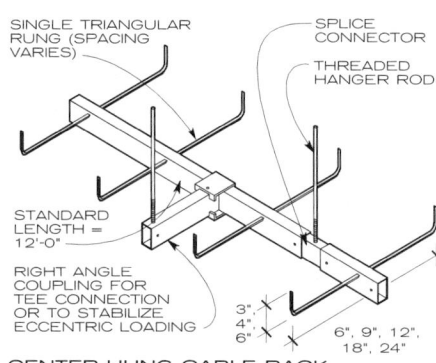

CENTER-HUNG CABLE RACK

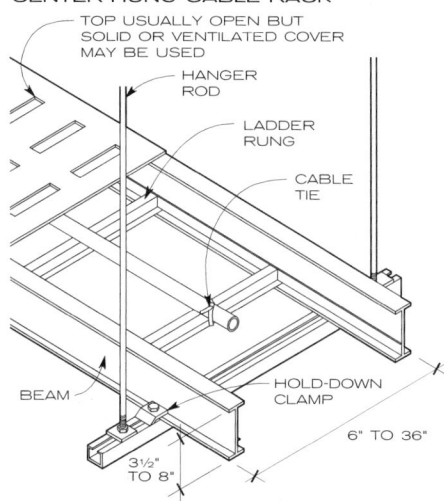

CABLE TRAY SYSTEM
NOTE

Cable trays protect and carry a large number of insulated cables in a limited space. For more protection or where heat buildup is not a problem, perforated or solid bottoms and top covers are available. Many fittings, bends, and tees (horizontal and vertical) are available. Consult manufacturers for materials other than aluminum or steel.

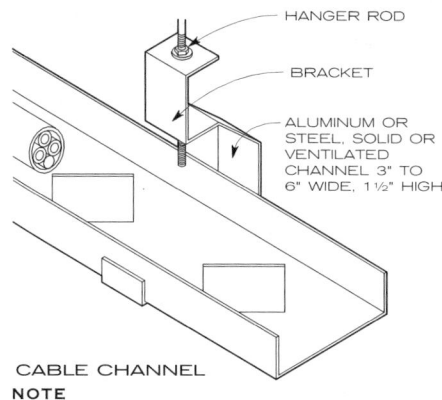

CABLE CHANNEL
NOTE

Cable channel can be used as a branch cable tray to carry a single large cable or conduit or several small ones.

CONDUIT AND CABLE SUPPORTING DEVICES

Charles B. Towles, P.E.; TEI Consulting Engineers; Washington, D.C.

WIRING AND RELATED MATERIALS **16**

POKE THROUGH SYSTEMS

Poke-through systems are used in conjunction with overhead branch distribution systems that run in accessible suspended ceiling cavities to outlets in full-height partitions. When services are required at floor locations without adjacent partitions or columns, as in open office planning, they must either be brought down from a wireway assembly (known as a power pole) or up through a floor penetration containing a fire-rated insert fitting and flush or above-floor outlet assembly. To install a poke-through assembly, the floor slab must either be core drilled or contain preset sleeves arranged in a modular grid. Poke-through assemblies are used in conjunction with cellular deck and underfloor duct systems when the service location required does not fall directly above its associated system raceway.

With one floor penetration, the single poke-through assembly can serve all the power, communications, and computer requirements of a work station. Distribution wiring in the ceiling cavity can be run in raceways. The more cost-effective method is to use armored cable (BX) for power and approved plenum-rated cable for communications and data when the ceiling cavity is used for return air. To minimize disturbance to the office space below when a poke-through assembly must be relocated or added, a modular system of prewired junction boxes for each service can be provided, although it is more common to elect this option for power only. A different type of working system must be selected for a floor slab on grade, above a lobby or retail space, above mechanical equipment space, or above space exposed to the atmosphere.

CELLULAR DECK SYSTEMS

The low initial cost of a poke-through system makes it both viable and attractive for investor-owned buildings when tenants are responsible for future changes and for corporate buildings with limited construction budgets. Poke-through systems are effective when office planning includes interconnecting workstation panels containing provisions (base raceways) to extend wiring above the floor, reducing the number of floor penetrations needed for services.

Based on the projected frequency of changes in office furniture layouts, a corporate or government organization may elect to invest in a permanent raceway system to minimize cost and disturbance to occupants when changes or additions are made. When structural design dictates the use of metal decking, a cellular floor raceway system utilizing trench header ducts is the most likely choice.

Cellular raceways come in a variety of sizes and configurations ranging from $1\frac{1}{2}$ to 3 in. high with cells 8 or 12 in. o.c. and 2 or 3 cells per section. An overall floor deck can be full cellular, where bottom plates are provided throughout, or blended as shown.

Trench header ducts come in various sizes and configurations. The height is adjustable for slab depths above cells of $2\frac{1}{2}$ to 4 in. and widths vary from 9 to 36 in. Cover plates are $\frac{1}{4}$ in. thick, with lengths from 6 to 36 in., and can either be secured with spring clips or flush, flathead bolts. Two versions of trench design are available: One has a compartmental bottom tray with a grommeted access hole for each cell it crosses; the other has a bottomless trench duct consisting of side rails and a separate wireway in the middle, with grommeted access holes only for the power cells.

When service is needed, the floor is core drilled above the desired cell, the cell top is drilled into, and an afterset insert with above-floor fitting is attached. If data and communication wiring can occupy the same cell, with power wiring in an adjacent cell, two separate service fittings are required for each workstation.

When it is necessary to eliminate or minimize core drilling, a modular pattern of preset service flush outlets can be provided along the cellular sections before the floor is poured (as shown). Upon activation, one flush outlet can serve all the power, communication, and data requirements of a workstation.

The modular grid and frequency of preset locations will determine the convenience of service provisions for the workstations.

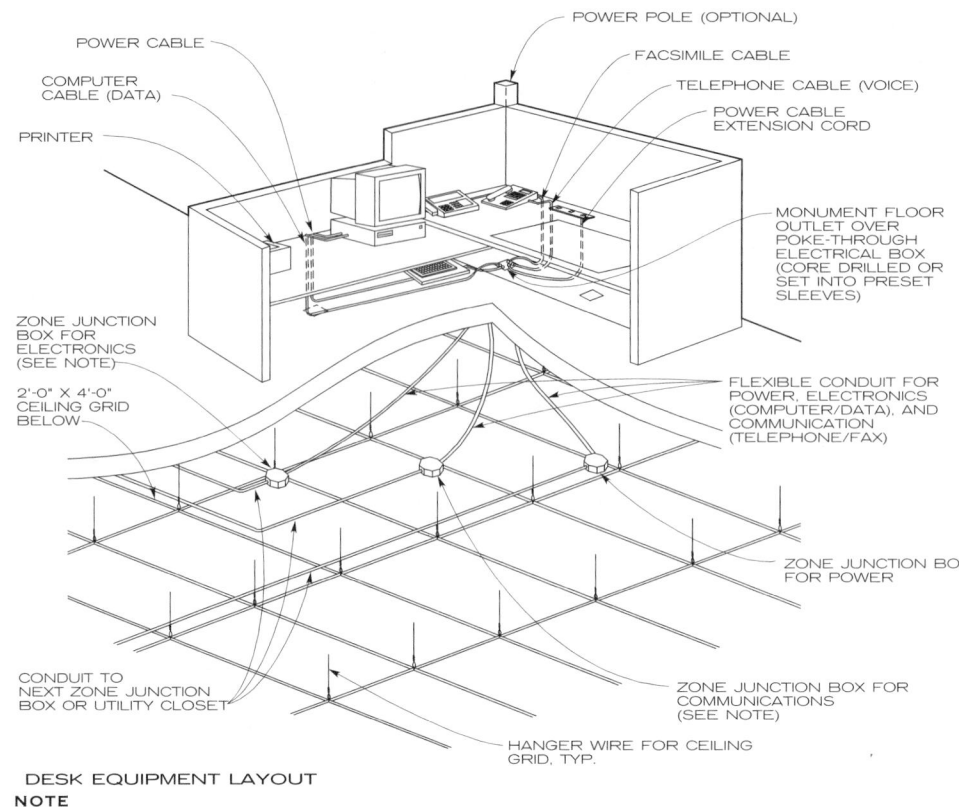

DESK EQUIPMENT LAYOUT

NOTE

Computer and telephone cabling is often combined as an integrated voice/data cabling system, eliminating the need for three raceways except when extra capacity is needed.

POKE-THROUGH HARDWARE SYSTEM/ZONE JUNCTION BOX

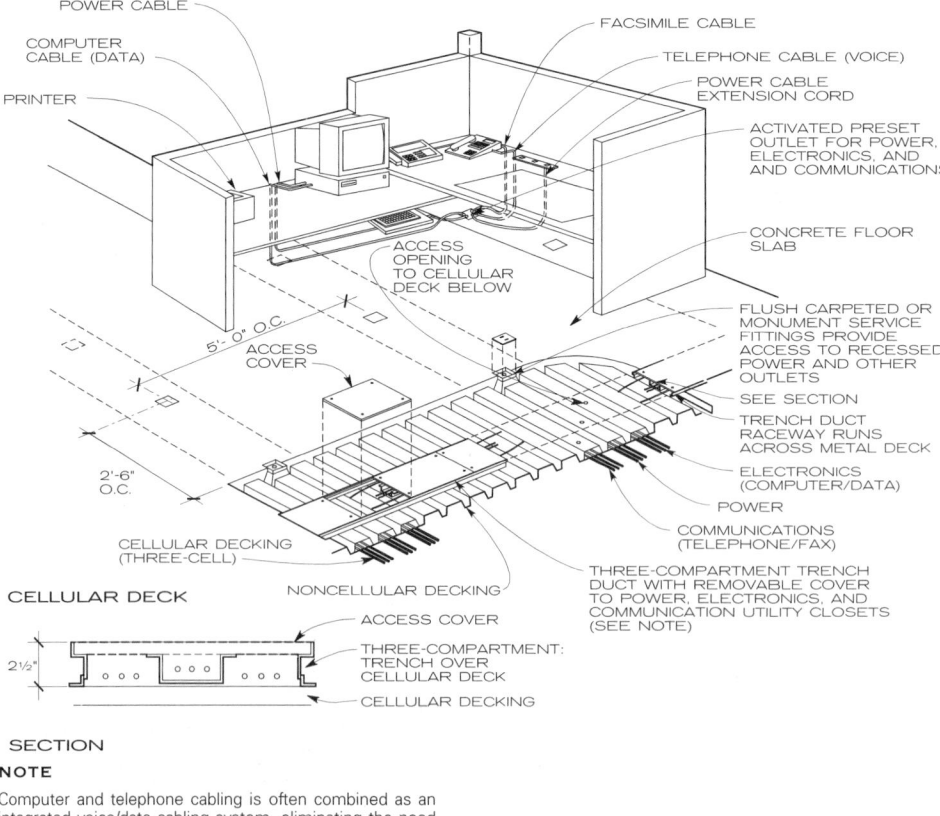

CELLULAR DECK

SECTION

NOTE

Computer and telephone cabling is often combined as an integrated voice/data cabling system, eliminating the need for three raceways except when extra capacity is needed.

CELLULAR DECK SYSTEM WITH TRENCH HEADER DUCTS

Richard F. Humenn, P.E.; Joseph R. Loring & Assoc., Consulting Engineers; New York, New York

 WIRING AND RELATED MATERIALS

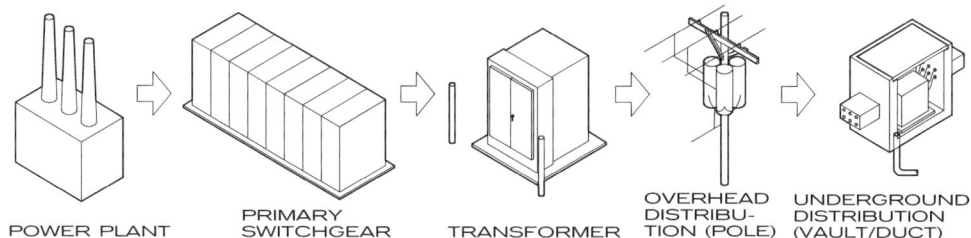

POWER PLANT   PRIMARY SWITCHGEAR   TRANSFORMER   OVERHEAD DISTRIBU-TION (POLE)   UNDERGROUND DISTRIBUTION (VAULT/DUCT)

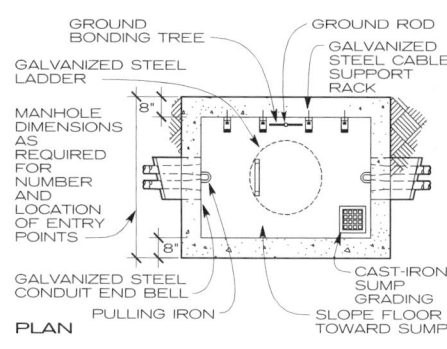

PLAN

GROUND BONDING TREE   GROUND ROD
GALVANIZED STEEL LADDER   GALVANIZED STEEL CABLE SUPPORT RACK
MANHOLE DIMENSIONS AS REQUIRED FOR NUMBER AND LOCATION OF ENTRY POINTS
8"
GALVANIZED STEEL CONDUIT END BELL   CAST-IRON SUMP GRADING
PULLING IRON   SLOPE FLOOR TOWARD SUMP
8"

NOTE

Primary high-voltage service is received at a site via various stages, from the formation of electrical energy (water power, turbines, etc.) to substations that receive the electricity at high voltage and distribute this energy at a lower voltage via conduit to the point of use. At each stage, protective devices (switches or circuit breakers) are installed. Transformers are installed to reduce voltage along the lines for the requirements of the end user.

PRIMARY SERVICE DISTRIBUTION

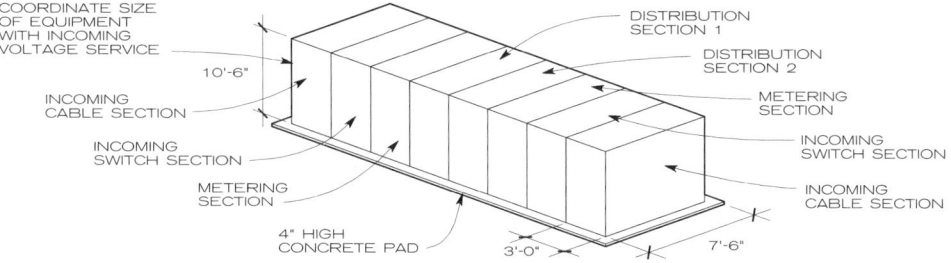

COORDINATE SIZE OF EQUIPMENT WITH INCOMING VOLTAGE SERVICE
10'-6"
INCOMING CABLE SECTION
INCOMING SWITCH SECTION
METERING SECTION
4" HIGH CONCRETE PAD
3'-0"   7'-6"
DISTRIBUTION SECTION 1
DISTRIBUTION SECTION 2
METERING SECTION
INCOMING SWITCH SECTION
INCOMING CABLE SECTION

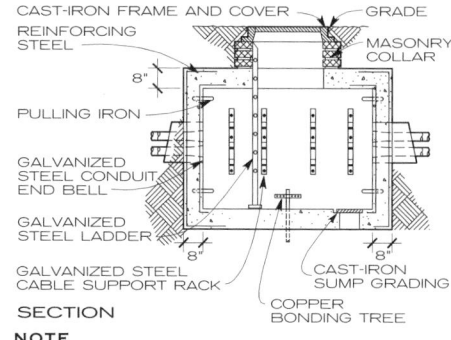

CAST-IRON FRAME AND COVER   GRADE
REINFORCING STEEL   MASONRY COLLAR
8"
PULLING IRON
GALVANIZED STEEL CONDUIT END BELL
GALVANIZED STEEL LADDER
GALVANIZED STEEL CABLE SUPPORT RACK   CAST-IRON SUMP GRADING
8"   COPPER BONDING TREE

SECTION

NOTE

When buildings cover a large area, such as a college campus or medical center, the use of medium voltages of 5 to 34 kV for distribution feeders is usually required. Therefore, the utility company terminates its primary feeders on the owner's metal-clad or metal-enclosed switchgear, which may be inside or of exterior weatherproof construction. Code clearance in front and back of board must be provided in accordance with the National Electrical Code.

NOTE

Manholes are provided for splicing and pulling of electrical cables for underground distribution. Size ductbanks emanating out of the manhole according to the latest edition of the National Electrical Code.

MANHOLE DETAILS

PRIMARY SWITCHGEAR WITH PRIMARY POWER FROM TWO SERVICES

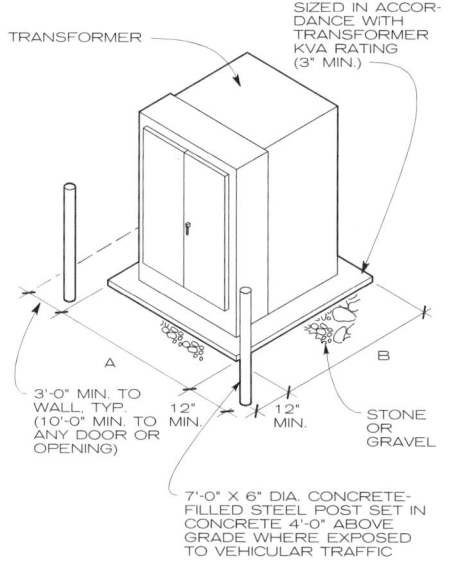

TRANSFORMER
CONCRETE PAD SIZED IN ACCORDANCE WITH TRANSFORMER KVA RATING (3" MIN.)
A
B
3'-0" MIN. TO WALL, TYP. (10'-0" MIN. TO ANY DOOR OR OPENING)
12" MIN.
12" MIN.
STONE OR GRAVEL
7'-0" X 6" DIA. CONCRETE-FILLED STEEL POST SET IN CONCRETE 4'-0" ABOVE GRADE WHERE EXPOSED TO VEHICULAR TRAFFIC

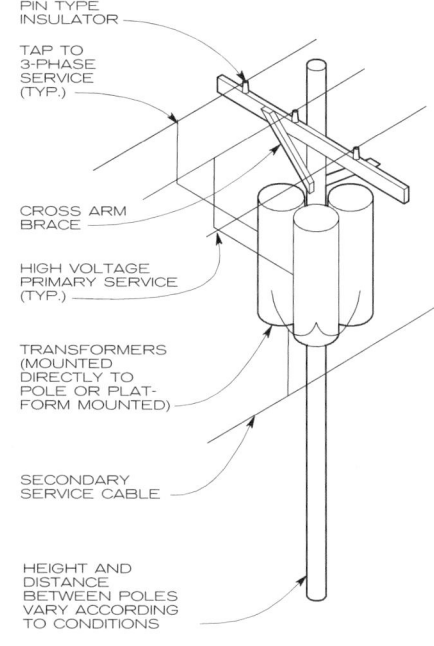

PIN TYPE INSULATOR
TAP TO 3-PHASE SERVICE (TYP.)
CROSS ARM BRACE
HIGH VOLTAGE PRIMARY SERVICE (TYP.)
TRANSFORMERS (MOUNTED DIRECTLY TO POLE OR PLATFORM MOUNTED)
SECONDARY SERVICE CABLE
HEIGHT AND DISTANCE BETWEEN POLES VARY ACCORDING TO CONDITIONS

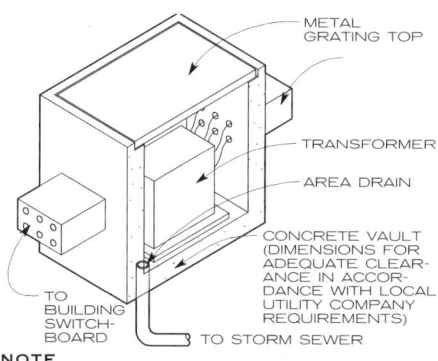

METAL GRATING TOP
TRANSFORMER
AREA DRAIN
CONCRETE VAULT (DIMENSIONS FOR ADEQUATE CLEARANCE IN ACCORDANCE WITH LOCAL UTILITY COMPANY REQUIREMENTS)
TO BUILDING SWITCHBOARD
TO STORM SEWER

NOTE

Underground vaults are generally used for utility company transformers where all distribution feeders are underground. These systems usually constitute a network or spot network. Vaults are often located below the sidewalks and have grating tops. Transformer is usually liquid filled; if an oil-filled transformer is used, an oil interceptor is recommended before discharge to building storm sewer.

UNDERGROUND VAULT

TYPICAL PAD SIZES

POWER	A	B
150 - 300 kVA	75 in.	80 in.
500 - 1500 kVA	84 in.	84 in.

NOTES

1. Pad-mounted transformers with weatherproof, tamperproof enclosures permit installation at ground level without the danger of exposed parts. Three-phase units up to 1500 kVA are normally used with underground primary and secondary feeders. The customer's grounding grids or grounding electrical conductors should not be connected at pad-mounted transformer locations.

2. High voltage compartment requires 10-ft clearance for on-off operation of the insulated stick located on the transformer (known as "hot stick" operation).

PAD-MOUNTED TRANSFORMER

NOTE

Overhead distribution lines are supported by poles from the origin of the electrical service to the termination point. Poles are fabricated out of various kinds of wood (e.g., pine or cedar) or steel, depending on the type of equipment to be supported, weather conditions, and cost of materials. Transformers mounted directly onto the poles or on platforms provide the required low voltage service to the final point. Spacing between the poles, height of the poles, and clearances between electrical lines and the ground depend upon the type of terrain, weather environment, and obstructions (e.g., inhabited area, waterways, railroads, roadways, etc.). See the National Electrical Safety Code for restrictions.

OVERHEAD POLE CONFIGURATION

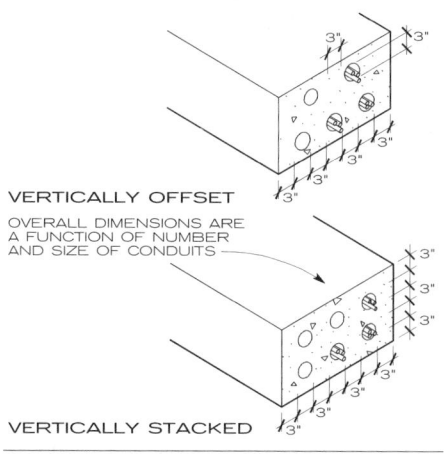

3"   3"
VERTICALLY OFFSET
OVERALL DIMENSIONS ARE A FUNCTION OF NUMBER AND SIZE OF CONDUITS
3"
3"
3"
VERTICALLY STACKED
3"   3"

UNDERGROUND DUCT BANK

Charles B. Towles, P.E.; TEI Consulting Engineers; Washington, D.C.

SERVICE AND DISTRIBUTION   16

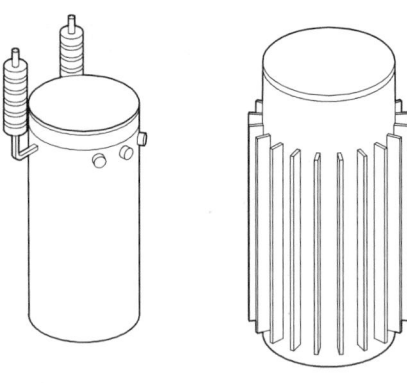

SINGLE-PHASE   THREE-PHASE

NOTE

Rated secondary voltages: 208, 240, or 480. Immersed in oil; self-cooled.

POLE-MOUNTED TRANSFORMERS

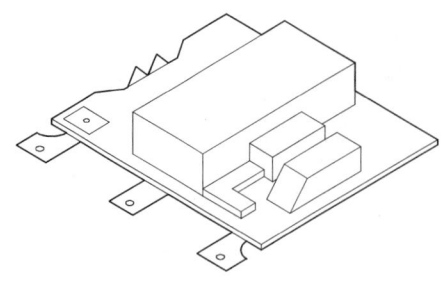

NOTE

Provides convenient control of lighting and power circuits from control stations.

REMOTE CONTROL SWITCH

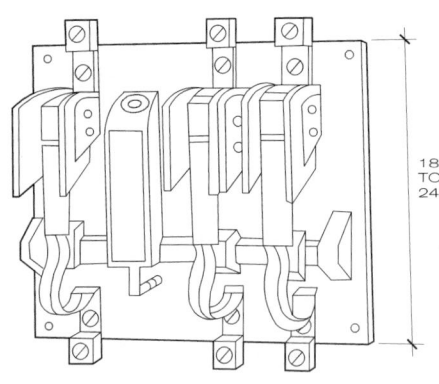

NOTE

Rated voltage: 600 VAC. For circuits that are closed and opened repeatedly, various design combinations are allowed. Used for all classes of magnetically held loads, open or closed.

CONTACTOR

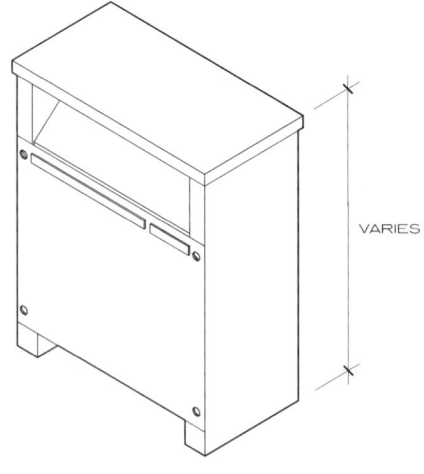

VARIES

NOTE

Rated secondary voltages: 120/208 or 240 volts or three phase. Primarily mounted on indoor floors and walls.

DRY TRANSFORMER

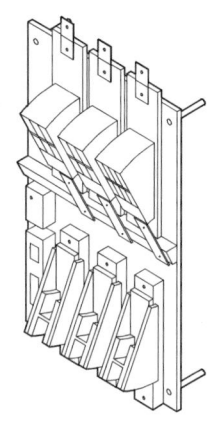

NOTE

Automatically transfers loads from a normal source to the emergency source.

AUTOTRANSFER SWITCH

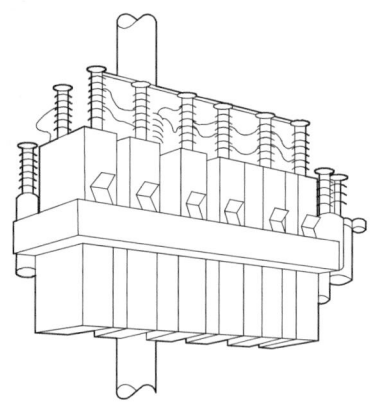

POLE RACK
NOTE

Power factor correction on either low or high voltage systems. Types, indoor or outdoor. Size and voltage as required. Switched or floating.

CAPACITOR

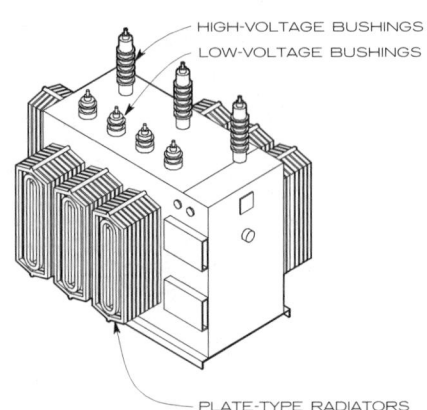

HIGH-VOLTAGE BUSHINGS
LOW-VOLTAGE BUSHINGS

PLATE-TYPE RADIATORS

NOTE

Secondary substation transformer with high to low voltage. Primarily a commercial type for the outdoors. Optional external fan cooling.

LIQUID-FILLED TRANSFORMER

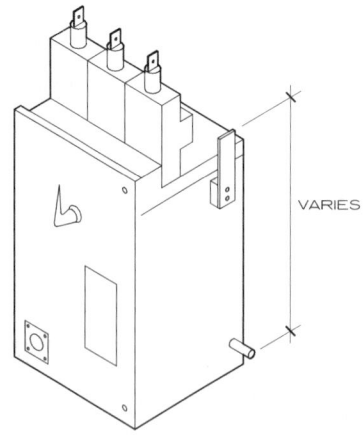

VARIES

NETWORK TYPE
NOTE

Maximum voltage: 125/216 VAC or 277/480 VAC. Interrupting capacity 30,000 and 60,000 A. RMS. SYM. A fault on primary cable or network transformer will open protector to isolate fault from system.

PROTECTOR

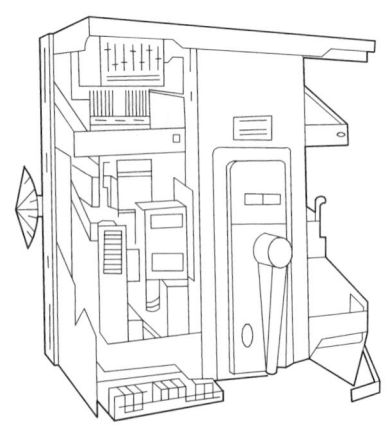

LOW VOLTAGE

NOTE

Rated voltages: 240 VAC, 480 VAC, 600 VAC, and 250 VDC. Manual or electric operation. Electromechanical or solid-state breaker trip devices. Stationary or drawout types.

DISTRIBUTION CIRCUIT BREAKER

Charles B. Towles, P.E.; TEI Consulting Engineers; Washington, D.C.

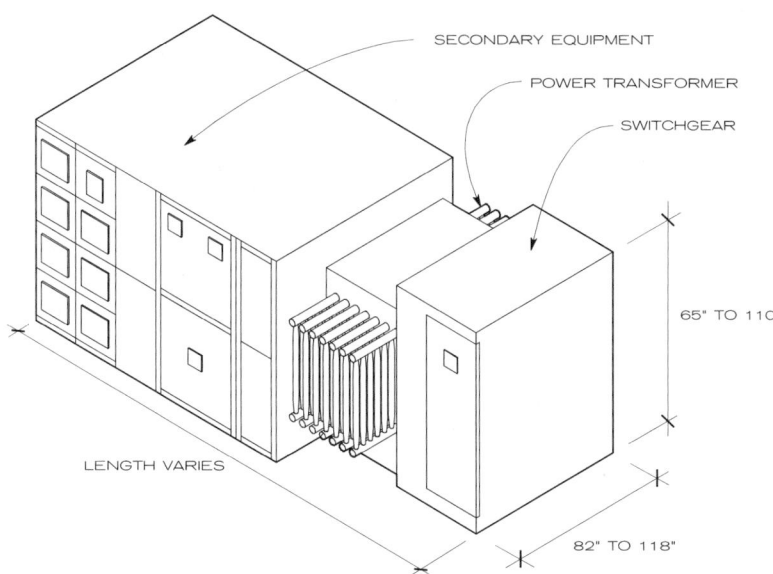

SECONDARY EQUIPMENT

POWER TRANSFORMER

SWITCHGEAR

65" TO 110"

LENGTH VARIES

82" TO 118"

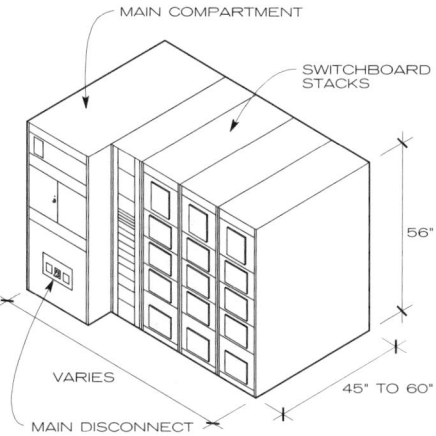

MAIN COMPARTMENT

SWITCHBOARD STACKS

56"

VARIES

MAIN DISCONNECT

45" TO 60"

NOTE

A secondary unit substation, sometimes called a power center, is a close-coupled assembly consisting of three-phase power transformers, enclosed high voltage incoming line sections, and enclosed secondary low voltage outgoing sections encompassing the following electrical ratings:

Transformer kVA: 112.5 through 2500 (self-cooled rating) liquid-filled, dry-type, or cast coil.
Primary voltage: 2.4 kV thru 34.5 kV.
Secondary voltage: 208, 240, 480, or 600 V (max.).

See National Electrical Code for aisle space, ventilation, servicing area, and special building condition requirements.

NOTE

Metering compartment, main disconnect, check meters, and low voltage distribution section. See manufacturer's literature for type, size, and arrangements. See National Electrical Code for required aisle space, servicing area, and room layout.

SECONDARY UNIT SUBSTATION

SWITCHBOARD

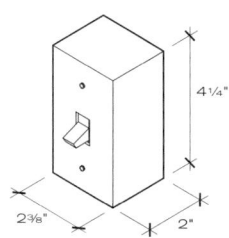

4¼"

2⅜"

2"

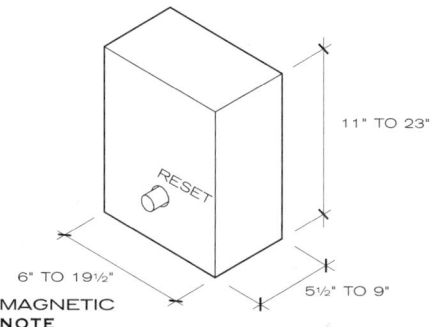

11" TO 23"

RESET

6" TO 19½"

5½" TO 9"

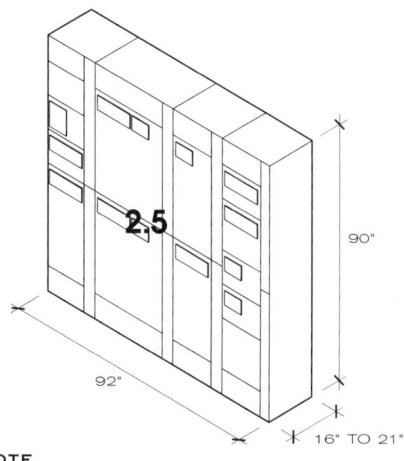

2.5

90"

92"

16" TO 21"

MANUAL
NOTE

Manual single-phase starters are designed to give positive, accurate, trouble-free overload protection to single phase motors rated up to 1 HP. Typical applications are fans, machine tools, motors, HVAC, etc. Maximum voltage is 240 V AC.

MAGNETIC
NOTE

Magnetic motor starters are designed for across-the-line control of squirrel cage motors or as primary control for wound rotor motors. Starters can be furnished for nonreversing, reversing and two-speed applications. Maximum voltage is 600 V AC; maximum horsepower is 200 HP.

NOTE

Motor control centers provide a method for grouping motor control, associated control, and distribution equipment. It is designed to operate machinery, industrial processes, and commercial building systems.

LOW-VOLTAGE MOTOR CONTROL CENTER

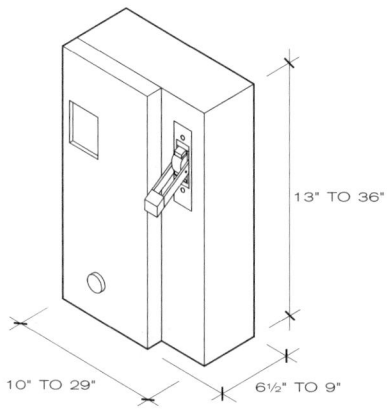

13" TO 36"

10" TO 29"

6½" TO 9"

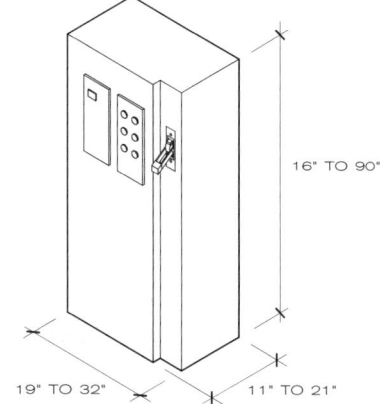

16" TO 90"

19" TO 32"

11" TO 21"

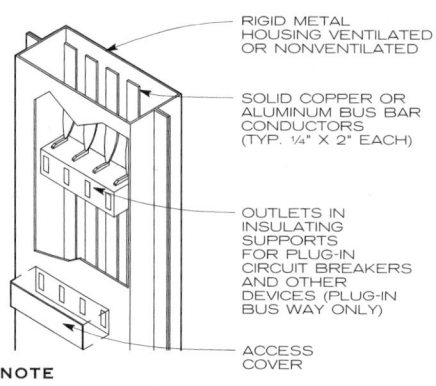

RIGID METAL HOUSING VENTILATED OR NONVENTILATED

SOLID COPPER OR ALUMINUM BUS BAR CONDUCTORS (TYP. ¼" X 2" EACH)

OUTLETS IN INSULATING SUPPORTS FOR PLUG-IN CIRCUIT BREAKERS AND OTHER DEVICES (PLUG-IN BUS WAY ONLY)

ACCESS COVER

COMBINATION
NOTE

Magnetic combination starters are designed for across-the-line control of squirrel cage motors or as primary control for wound rotor motors. In addition, they provide a disconnect means and short-circuit protection. They are available for nonreversing or reversing applications.

SOLID-STATE
NOTE

This unit is a reduced voltage motor starter, used to reduce starting current and high starting torque. Typical applications for controllers are in motors used in cranes, belt-driven equipment, conveyors, material handling facilities, compressors, and woodworking equipment. Available for AC motors 5 to 900 HP.

NOTE

Plug-in and feeder busways carry current from 50 to 5000 amps. They are utilized when large blocks of low voltage power (up to 600 V) must be transmitted over long distances or when taps must be made at various points, as in vertical risers in office buildings. Codes limit locations in buildings where different types of busways may be installed. Consult an electrical engineer before using this system. Busway housing may be hung from an overhead support, mounted to a wall, or braced to the structure in vertical riser installation.

MOTOR STARTERS

BUSWAY SYSTEM

Charles B. Towles, P.E.; TEI Consulting Engineers; Washington, D.C.

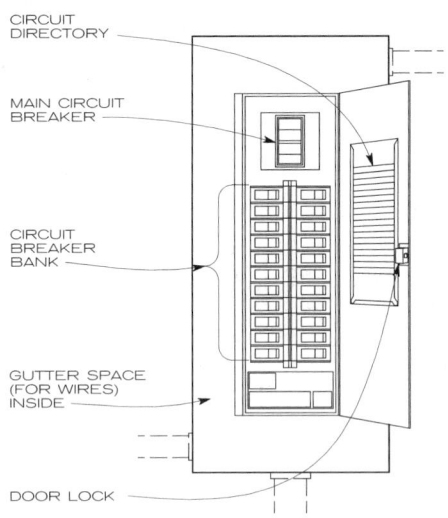

NOTE

Knockout holes allow conduit connections from all sides.

PANELBOARD DIMENSIONS

MAXIMUM NUMBER OF CIRCUITS	BOX DIMENSIONS (IN.)		
	WIDTH	HEIGHT	DEPTH
12	9–15	13–20	$3\frac{3}{4}$–$4\frac{5}{8}$
20	9–15	$20\frac{1}{4}$–24	$3\frac{3}{4}$–$4\frac{5}{8}$
30	12–15	30–33	$3\frac{3}{4}$–$4\frac{5}{8}$
40	14–15	34–39	4–$4\frac{5}{8}$

RESIDENTIAL AND COMMERCIAL PANELBOARD

PLUG FUSE

1. Rated voltage: 125
2. Ampere rating: 1-30
3. Fuse types: S, T

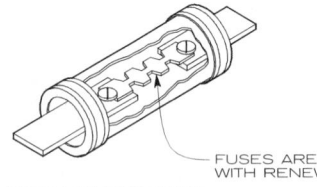

KNIFE BLADE FUSE

1. Rated voltage: 250 and 600
2. Ampere ratings: 70-6000
3. Fuse types: K1, RK1, K5, RK5, J, H, G, and L

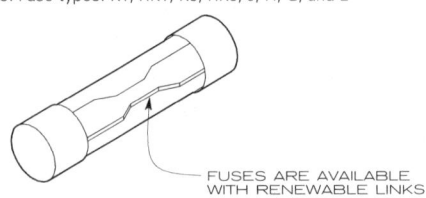

CARTRIDGE FUSE

1. Rated voltage: 250 and 600
2. Ampere rating: $\frac{1}{10}$-60
3. Fuse types: K1, RK1, K5, RK5, J, H, and G

NOTE

Cartridge and knife blade fuses are available for short circuit protection up to 200,000 A (Rms).

FUSES

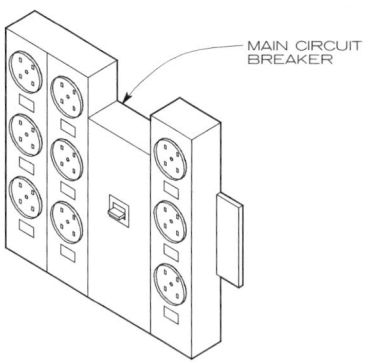

MULTIPLE METER BANK WITH MAIN CIRCUIT BREAKER

1. Rated voltages: 120/240 V, 3-wire, single-phase or 208/120 V, 4-wire, three-phase.
2. Either indoor or outdoor construction.
3. Number of sockets as required by application.

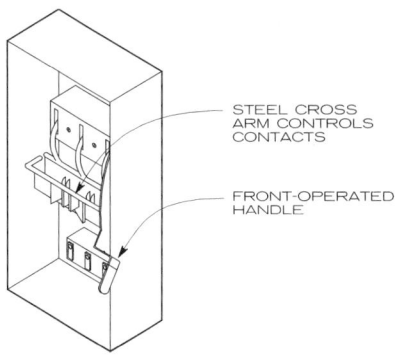

FUSED SAFETY

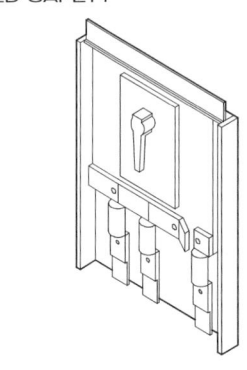

HIGH-PRESSURE CONTACT

NOTE

High-pressure contact switches may be top or bottom feed; 600 V AC max; 800–4000 A.

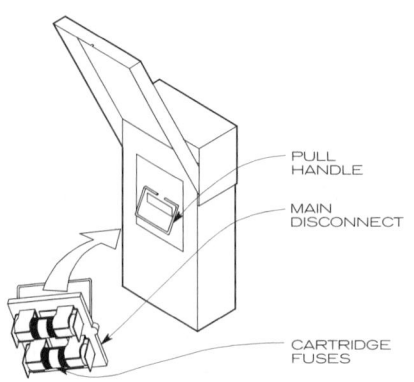

FUSE BOX

DISCONNECT SWITCHES

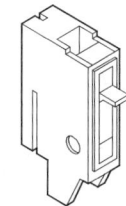

MOLDED CASE

1. Rated voltages: 120 VAC, 240 VAC, 600 VAC, 125 VDC, and 250 VDC.
2. Frame sizes: 100, 150, 225, 400, 600, 800, 1200 A poles, 2 or 3 above 100 A.
3. Current limiting types with fuses.

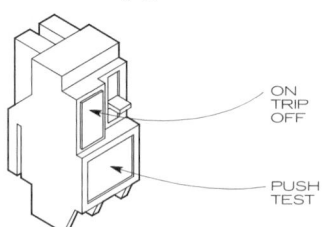

MOLDED CASE WITH GROUND FAULT

1. Rated voltages: 120 VAC or 120/240 VAC.
2. Frame size: 100 A ratings, 15-30 A poles, 1 or 2.

CIRCUIT BREAKERS

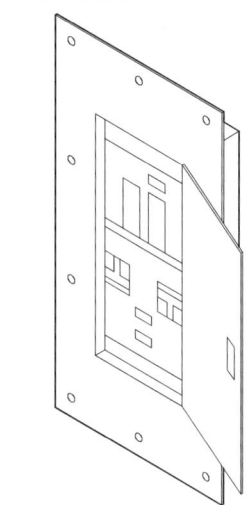

CIRCUIT BREAKER

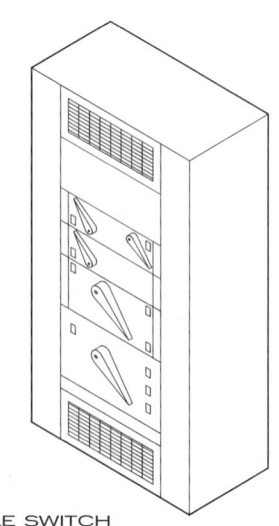

FUSIBLE SWITCH

DISTRIBUTION PANEL BOARDS

Charles B. Towles, P.E.; TEI Consulting Engineers; Washington, D.C.

16 SERVICE AND DISTRIBUTION

LAMPS IN THE DESIGN PROCESS

The goal of lighting design is to supply appropriate lighting characteristics to a given environment in an efficient manner. Characteristics such as quality of light, quantity of light, and spatial distribution are dictated by the needs of the users and the requirements of the space.

A lighting system primarily consists of lamps (which supply and regulate the lighting), ballasts, and luminaires. However, other aspects of the design with which the lighting system interacts, such as fenestration, surface treatments, and control systems, are also considered part of the lighting system.

A lamp, commonly known as a lightbulb, is the artificial light source that changes electrical energy into light energy. A ballast supplies the proper electrical characteristics to start and operate a lamp. Ballasts are not needed for lamps that operate directly on line power, such as most incandescent types. A luminaire, commonly known as a fixture, distributes and modifies the light from a lightbulb.

The lighting characteristics required in a space are primarily supplied by the lamp but may be modified by other elements. For instance, the type of ballast dictates flicker, and the luminaire may modify light distribution and color.

COLOR TEMPERATURE

Color temperature is a measure of the color of the light source itself. It is indicated in degrees Kelvin. Some light sources (incandescent and the sun) operate essentially as black-body radiators. Others (fluorescent and high-intensity discharge) must be referred to by their correlated color temperatures (CCT). Lamps with low Kelvin temperatures are "warm" or reddish light sources and emphasize reds, oranges, and yellows. Those with high color temperatures are "cool" or bluish in appearance and emphasize blues and greens. A wide range of color temperatures encompasses "white light" and, without a visual comparison, the human eye sees all of these as white.

COLOR RENDERING

Color rendering refers to how objects appear when illuminated by a light source. It is usually measured by a color rendering index (CRI) with a scale of zero to 100. The higher the CRI, the better a source makes objects appear. At the bottom of the scale, there is no ability to discern colors. At 100, colors are rendered exactly as they appear under a given reference light source, which is the black-body radiator for the same or correlated color temperature. For this reason, color rendering can only be compared among light sources of the same color temperature.

Lamps with good color rendering require a lower illuminance (the amount of light reaching a surface) to achieve judgments of equivalent brightness, visual clarity, and visual satisfaction. Therefore, higher-CRI lamps require fewer lumens, and fewer watts, than lower-CRI lamps.

COLOR TEMPERATURES OF SELECTED LIGHT SOURCES*

DAYLIGHT

Blue sky	10,000 to 30,000
Overcast sky	7000
Noon sunlight	5250

FLUORESCENT LAMPS

RE 50 very cool tri-phosphor	5000
Cool white halophosphate	4100
RE 41 cool tri-phosphor	4100
RE 30 warm tri-phosphor	3000
Compact fluorescent (most screw-in types)	2700 or 2800

INCANDESCENT LAMPS

Halogen low-voltage MR16	3100
Halogen reflector PAR	2800 to 2925
General service 60W-200W	2790 to 2980
CANDLE FLAME	1800

* Degrees Kelvin; approximate, correlated values

ECONOMICS OF ENERGY SAVINGS

SUBSTITUTION		WATTS SAVED	RATED LIFE (HOURS)	DOLLARS SAVED OVER LIFE*	SIMPLE RETURN ON INVESTMENT
FROM	TO				
90W A19 (incandescent)	23W compact fluorescent	67	10,000	$67	335%
4-34W T12 fluorescent, 2 magnetic ballasts	4-32W T8 fluorescent, 1 electronic ballast	15	20,000	$30	300%
200W A23 incandescent	70W metal halide with fixture	111	6,000	$67	33%

* Figured at 10 cents per kilowatt hour.

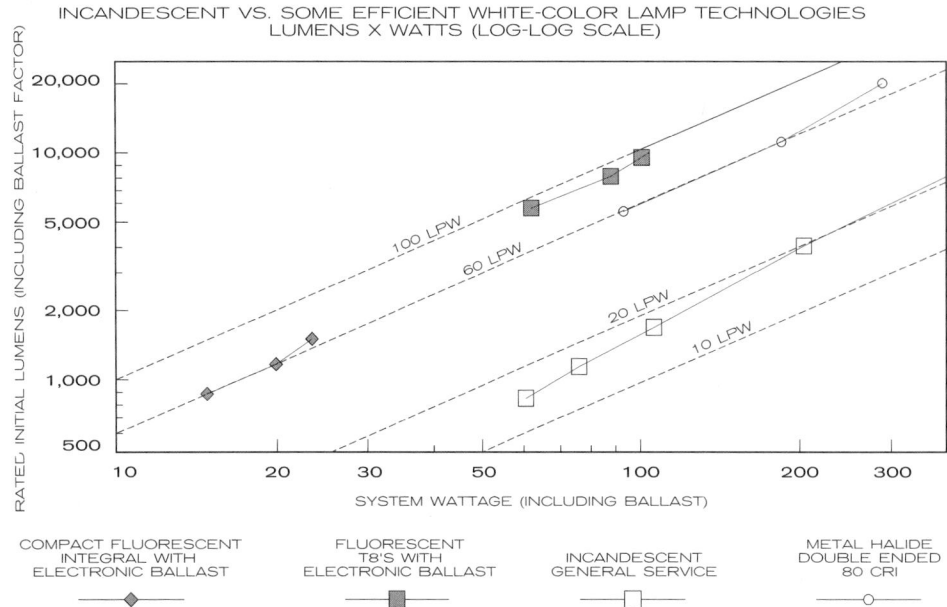

INCANDESCENT VS. SOME EFFICIENT WHITE-COLOR LAMP TECHNOLOGIES
LUMENS X WATTS (LOG-LOG SCALE)

COMPACT FLUORESCENT INTEGRAL WITH ELECTRONIC BALLAST	FLUORESCENT T8'S WITH ELECTRONIC BALLAST	INCANDESCENT GENERAL SERVICE	METAL HALIDE DOUBLE ENDED 80 CRI

RELATIVE EFFICACIES OF LAMP TECHNOLOGIES

LIGHT OUTPUT

Visible light power radiated in all directions from a lamp is measured in lumens. Rated lumen output for fluorescent lamps should be modified according to the ballast factor of the ballast used. Light emitted by a lamp will be diminished by the reflectance and geometry of the luminaire, dust, age, and other factors. Mean lumens or design lumens take into account the depreciation of light as a result of lamp aging. Further, since light does its useful work only when appropriately reflected off surfaces into the eye, the light output of different lamps cannot be fully compared independent of the rest of the lighting design.

In some specialized situations the lamp itself is the design—for instance, in marquee lighting and some LED signs. The brightness at the surface of a lamp is measured in candle units. This measure of brightness is important in lamps used for directional lighting, such as reflector lamps.

ELECTRICAL INPUT

Electrical power is measured in watts. For ballasted lamps, rated wattage is nominal—it is the power drawn by the lamp alone from a standardized reference ballast. Real input is the combined lamp and ballast wattage of the system.

Power accumulated yields energy, which is measured in watt-hours or kilowatt-hours. For most situations, this can be calculated if it is known how much time the lighting system is on. Some systems, including low-pressure sodium and any one offering dimming, have variable wattage.

EFFICACY

The energy efficiency of a lamp is measured as light output divided by power input, or lumens per watt, or efficacy. For lamps that have ballasts, the wattage of the complete system should be considered. Efficacy is generally determined by technology type: Incandescent is the least efficient electric source type; low-pressure sodium is the most efficient. Subfamilies within technology types may be further differentiated by efficacy. For instance, krypton-fill, halogen, and infrared reflector are all technological improvements within the incandescent category. Among lamps of a given technology type, efficacy increases as input increases. Therefore, two 60-watt incandescent lamps provide about as much light as one 100-watt incandescent.

As shown in the graph below. Lamps vary significantly in their efficacy. At relatively low lumen levels, compact fluorescent technology can provide lumens approximately equivalent to that provided by incandescent technology with approximately four times better efficacy. Among white-color, higher-lumen sources, double-ended metal halide lamps achieve approximately 60 lumens per watt, and T8 fluorescents with electronic ballasts provide almost 100 lumens per watt. High-intensity discharge lamps can achieve even higher efficacies and are appropriate if color quality is not critical.

ENERGY AND ECONOMICS

By incorporating efficiency when appropriate into lamps, ballasts, luminaires, controls, and overall design, lighting systems can consume dramatically less energy. Compared to standard design, decreases in overall energy consumed can be anywhere from 20 to 50% or more. Depending on local electrical rates, an efficient lighting design can save the end user a significant amount in reduced electrical rates. The extra cost of purchasing and installing efficient devices is usually very small compared with the savings that can be achieved.

Fred Davis, C.L.E.P.; Fred Davis Corp., Energy and Lighting; Medfield, Massachusetts

LIFETIME

Lamps are rated according to the number of hours burned after which half the lamps will no longer light in test conditions with a burn cycle of 3 hours. Since the actual life of a lamp is determined by actual burn cycles and other factors such as temperature and vibration, the actual life of a lamp may not equal its rated life. Generally, the longer the burn cycle, the longer the life of a lamp.

Lamps may be expected to last longer than their rated life if burned on longer cycles; conversely, a shorter life is likely for burn cycles shorter than 3 hours. A rapid-start fluorescent lamp may last 160% of its rated life if burned continuously.

FLICKER

All discharge lamps (fluorescent and HID) flicker, i.e., they turn on and off many times per second. Generally, this is imperceptible except to a small percentage of the population. Caution must be taken, however, to avoid a stroboscopic effect in the presence of moving machinery, which may appear motionless if it is moving in a rhythm synchronous with the lighting flicker. High-frequency electronic ballasts generally eliminate any perceptible flicker.

TEMPERATURE CONDITIONS

The lifetime and light output of a lamp can be affected by temperature. Incandescent and high-intensity discharge (HID) lamps generally perform well in cold outdoor conditions; special jacketed versions of fluorescent lamps are also suited to outdoor use.

SHIELDING

Most lamp types should be shielded from direct precipitation; incandescent PAR lamps are one exception. Some metal halide lamps must be enclosed in fixtures to protect users from ultraviolet radiation or "nonpassive" failures. Electrodeless lamps generally operate at radio frequencies, and shielding users from radiation is essential.

BASE TYPES

The medium screw-base, the most well-known base type for electric lamps, is used with many lamp types. Interchangeability among lamp types is an important feature in many luminaires with this socket.

Most other base types are specific to certain lamp types to ensure correct electrical and positional matches. For example, recessed double contact (RDC) sockets are used with high output and very high output fluorescents, which have RDC bases and require ballasts to supply the proper voltage; many high-wattage incandescents (300-1000W) have mogul screw-bases and will not fit into medium screw sockets; many HID and specialized incandescent lamps have base-socket arrangements that ensure the light center is positioned correctly in a directional luminaire.

There are important exceptions to lamp-base-socket matching. For instance, both T8 and T12 four-foot fluorescent lamps have medium bipin sockets, even though they require different ballast types. Because of this, it is important to avoid an electrical mismatch in a fixture with medium bi-pin bases.

BALLASTED AND SELF-BALLASTED LAMPS

Incandescent lamps generally operate at line voltages, but all other lamp types require ballasts to supply the proper electrical characteristics. Many types of compact fluorescent, and a few high-pressure sodium and mercury vapor lamps, are available in self-ballasted, screw-in versions. Some of these use kits, which consist of a separate screw-in ballast and lamp.

NOMENCLATURE

Lamp designations incorporate references to the shape and size of the lamp. The shape is described with one or more capital letters, for instance "G" stands for globe, "ER" stands for ellipsoidal reflector, and "T" stands for tubular. The size of the lamp is denoted as the diameter in $1/8$ inches. Thus, a G40 lamp has a globe shape and is $40/8$ (or 5) inches in diameter; a T12 lamp is tubular and $12/8$ (or $1 1/2$) inches in diameter.

Fluorescent lamp designations begin with "F." "FB" is used for U-bent lamps and "FO" for T8 (optic) fluorescents. The next number is either the nominal wattage, for preheat and rapid-start lamps, or the length, for slimline and HO lamps. Therefore, F40 is a fluorescent lamp of 40 watts, and F96 is a fluorescent lamp 96 inches long.

MERCURY CONTENT AND DISPOSAL

Almost all non-incandescent lamps contain small quantities of mercury, which becomes an environmental pollutant upon disposal. Nonetheless, using incandescents is actually worse for the environment, given the pollution generated by the power plants producing the much higher quantities of electricity consumed. Given the mix of power plants in the United States in the early 1990s, the net contribution of pollutants to the environment—from disposal and power production—is much less for fluorescent than for incandescent lamps. This is true for each pollutant.

Sgnificant strides have been taken in the 1990s to reduce the mercury content of lamps. In 1995 a mercury-free high-pressure sodium lamp and fluorescents with a very low mercury content were introduced.

Disposal of lamps containing mercury has been a subject of regulatory concern. This is not because a typical disposal causes significant pollution—spent fluorescent lamps, in particular, contain small quantities of mercury, which are quite stabilized at the end of the tube's life. However, regulations may require that spent lamps, especially in large quantities, be treated as hazardous waste.

Consult current state and federal regulations, and consider commercial services for proper disposal. Disposal services available include pickup, reclamation of the mercury, recycling of other lamp components, and proper disposal.

ENERGY POLICY ACT

The U.S. Energy Policy Act of 1992, public law 102-486 (EPAct), was signed into law on October 24, 1992. It outlines energy-efficient standards and other regulations that preclude the manufacture or importation of certain lamps in the United States after certain dates. To comply with the act, lamps must meet minimum efficacy and color rendering requirements. Lamps not intended for general service, such as traffic signal, decorative, and plant-growth lamps, are exempt from the act.

LAMPS AFFECTED BY THE U.S. ENERGY POLICY ACT OF 1992

COMPLIANCE DATE	LAMPS AFFECTED	STANDARDS TO BE DEVELOPED BY
April 1994	8 ft fluorescent	
October 1995	4 ft fluorescent	
October 1995	2 ft. U-bent fluorescent	
October 1995	PAR, R incandescent	
October 1999	High-intensity discharge	October 1996
October 2001	General service fluorescent and incandescent	October 1998
October 2005	General service fluorescent and reflector incandescent	October 2002

IMPACT OF ENERGY POLICY REPRESENTATIVE REPLACEMENT OPTIONS

LAMP TYPE MADE OBSOLETE (AS OF OCT. 1995)	BEST EFFICIENCY SYSTEM SOLUTION 36-73% ENERGY SAVINGS	GOOD EFFICIENCY SUBSTITUTION 12-60% ENERGY SAVINGS
LINEAR FLUORESCENT		
F40T12/CW	FO32T8/RE841	F40T12/RE741/34W
F40T12/WW	FO32T8/RE830	F40T12/RE730/34W
F40T12/D	FO32T8/RE850	F40T12/RE765/34W
FB40/6"/CW	FBO32T8/6"/RE841	FB40T12/RE741/6"/34W
F96T12/CW	FO96T8/RE841	F96T12/RE741/60W
F96T12/CW/HO	FO96T8/HO/RE841	F96T12/HO/RE741/95W
INCANDESCENT REFLECTOR		
75WR30/FL,SP	Triple 18W compact fluorescent in reflector fixture	50WPAR30/FL,SP/HCAP
75WPAR38/FL,SP		45WPAR38/FL,SP/HCAP
150WPAR38/FL	60WPAR38/FL/HCAP IR	90WPAR38/FL/HCAP
150WR40/FL	35W M/PAR30 metal halide fixture	

LAMPS BY FORM AND FUNCTION

Lamps illuminate by radiating light. The geometric form of this radiation and its interaction with surrounding surfaces determine how a space is illuminated. Light sources may be classified by their geometry: area, reflector, linear, and planar. The geometry of light distribution, or photometry, is usually determined, or at least modified, by the luminaire. "Distributed light" systems redirect the output of a lamp in a more radical manner, and source technology no longer limits the geometry of lamps.

AREA LIGHT SOURCES

Area light sources distribute light more or less symmetrical in all directions. A theoretical "point source" would illuminate the interior of a sphere equally at all points. The sun, in space, because of its distance, might be considered a point source, as might a candle. Typically in most modern spaces, light sources are not in the center, and illumination is not desired equally at all points.

The smaller the light source, the greater the brightness and, ability to achieve qualities such as brilliance and sparkle. The common A-19 incandescent is a fairly good approximation of a point source, as the size of its filament, and thus its light center, is fairly small. Incandescent halogen types have even smaller filaments and thus provide greater brightness for a given wattage. Most HID lamps are also area light sources; typically, their brightness is very high for the area they illuminate.

As the components have shrunk, compact fluorescents have come closer to matching the outside shape of an A19 incandescent lamp. Because light is diffused over the surface, compact fluorescents are not able to achieve qualities such as brilliance and sparkle; however, they are very efficient as area lighting sources.

REFLECTOR LIGHT SOURCES

Light distributed from reflector sources is directed and confined, more or less, within a cone. "Flood" and "spot" types are examples, but these terms may be obsolete considering the wide range of beams now available. Limiting light to directional distribution is performed by the lamp, by the luminaire, or by a combination of the two. Optical control is determined by the geometry and reflectivity of the reflector and interactions with the photometry of the light source itself.

Center beam candlepower (CBCP) is the maximum output in the center of the beam, measured in candelas. The size of the cone of light is most often designated as "beam spread," the conical angle at which light output is 50% of the CBCP. How evenly the light is distributed might also be described, as smooth, ringed, etc.

Optical control of a beam is better with smaller light sources. Since a halogen burner is the closest to a true point source, it is often used in reflector applications. Generally, the narrower the beam spread, the more advantageous a small source is. Halogen reflectors are thus more efficient than compact fluorescents for narrow beam spreads. Some HID types are also available in lamp shapes that serve as reflectors.

LINEAR LIGHT SOURCES

The most common linear light source is the straight-tube fluorescent, usually used in ceiling applications, which essentially demand a planar source. To translate the linear source into a planar one requires a combination of longitudinal reflectors behind and flat diffusers in front. Light output is fairly even radially along the length of the tube. Strategies to increase overall efficiency have taken advantage of customized-bend, high-reflectivity retrofit reflectors.

Incandescent lamps are also available in a few linear shapes, such as single-end 20W T-6 1/2 for exit signs and double-end 60W T8 for vanity fixtures. However, much more efficient alternatives are available for most such applications.

PLANAR LIGHT SOURCES

Fluorescent lights are available now in many planar shapes: the U-bent, the circline, the long compact fluorescent, the square, and the flat compact fluorescent.

DISTRIBUTED LIGHT

Recent developments in optical reflector and transmissive materials have made it possible to separate light sources physically from their applications. Fiber optics and light pipes have been used for displays, signs, and theatrical effects. Larger cables and more efficient couplings between source and cable provide opportunities for architectural lighting that is reasonably efficient. Lamps that provide efficient input for such systems include a specialized metal halide whose light is very narrowly focused.

Fred Davis, C.L.E.P.; Fred Davis Corp., Energy and Lighting; Medfield, Massachusetts

GENERAL

Fluorescent technology offers among the highest efficacies of all lamps for high color quality white light and is three to five times more efficient than incandescent technology. Fluorescent lamps, as well as high-intensity discharge (HID) lamps, work on an electric-discharge principle and require a ballast. Light in a fluorescent lamp is produced when fluorescent powders are activated by ultraviolet energy generated by a mercury arc.

Fluorescent lamps are available in many types. Variations in phosphor chemistry, gas fill, size, and electrical input make possible many colors, efficiencies, sizes, and light outputs.

PHOSPHORS

Phosphors are the chemical powders that line the inside of a fluorescent tube. Their composition is responsible for the color, quality, and efficiency of light emanating from a fluorescent lamp. Among "white" sources, halophosphate phosphors such as cool white and warm white were the most popular types from the 1950s through the 1970s. In the 1980s trichromatic rare earth (RE) phosphors were developed, which offered greater efficiency and improved color rendering. These are now the predominant phosphors available in T10, T8, and compact fluorescent lamps; they are also available in most T12 sizes.

Trichromatic phosphors are available in two grades on the color rendering index (CRI) and a number of color temperatures. So-called "thin-coat" trichromatic phosphors have a CRI in the low to mid 70s; "thick-coat" phosphors have a CRI in the low 80s. By comparison, cool white halophosphate lamps had a CRI of 62. Both triphosphor series are available in a number of color temperatures, including warm–3000K, neutral–3500K, and cool–4100K. Very cool–5000K and 6500K–colors are available in some types.

Other, specialized phosphors are available in some straight-tube fluorescents, although these are usually much less efficient. Some high-CRI white lamps, with CRIs over 90, are available for applications that demand color matching; the lamps highest on the CRI are available at the highest Kelvin temperatures, up to 7500K. Colors, particularly red, blue, and gold, are used for special effects.

FLUORESCENT STRAIGHT TUBES

Fluorescent straight-tube lamps are the predominant lamp type in indoor commercial lighting. Because of their widespread use, much attention has been focused on developing a wide variety and more efficacious versions.

The T12 (1½-in. diameter) was the predominant shape for decades, and by far the most popular of these was the F40T12, rapid-start, 40W, cool white (CW) four-footer. As a requirement of the Energy Policy Act of 1992, manufacturers stopped making this lamp for U.S. use in October 1995.

"Energy-saver" lamps, with krypton added to the gas fill, are direct substitutes for most "standard" or full-wattage lamps. The light output in these lamps is reduced along with the reduction in power input. A 34W lamp is the energy-saver version of the standard 40W F40T12. It is intended for use in environments of 60°F or warmer.

TUBE DIAMETER

Among straight-tube fluorescents, tube diameter is an important determinant of efficacy: Generally, the narrower the tube, the higher the efficacy. In the 1980s lamps of smaller diameter and thus of higher efficacy were devel-

STRAIGHT TUBE FLUORESCENT SHAPES AND TYPICAL NOMINAL LENGTHS

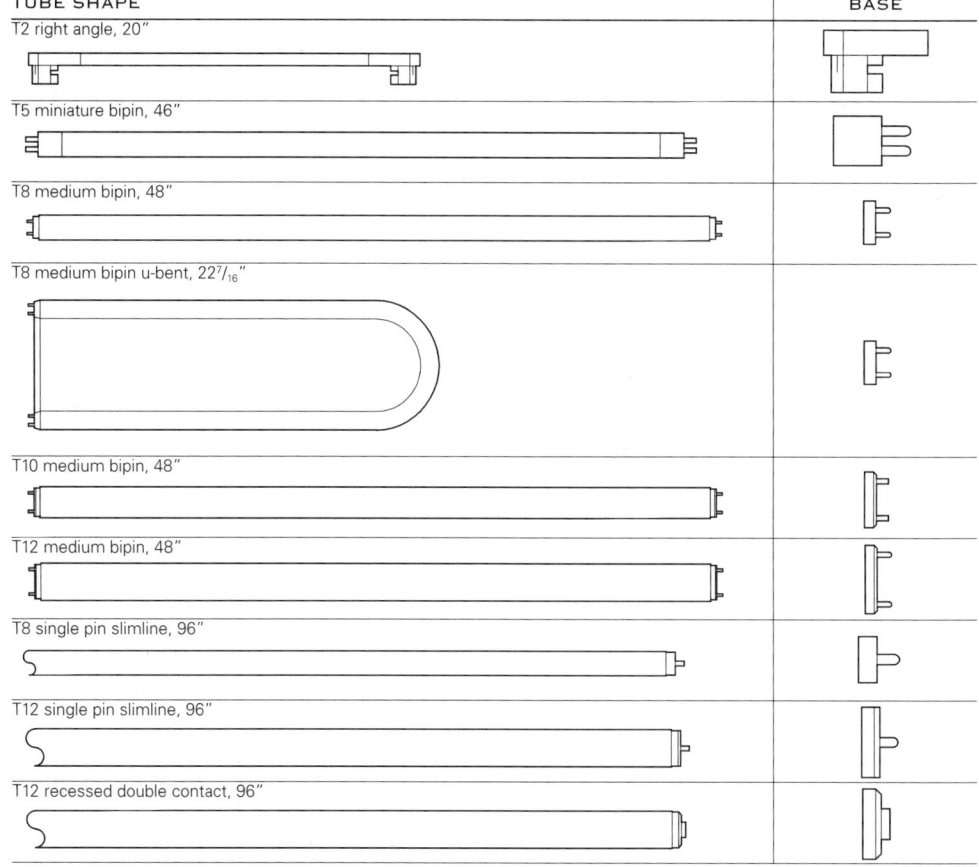

TUBE SHAPE	BASE
T2 right angle, 20"	
T5 miniature bipin, 46"	
T8 medium bipin, 48"	
T8 medium bipin u-bent, 22⁷⁄₁₆"	
T10 medium bipin, 48"	
T12 medium bipin, 48"	
T8 single pin slimline, 96"	
T12 single pin slimline, 96"	
T12 recessed double contact, 96"	

NOTE

Lamps are not to scale; nominal length is from back of socket to back of socket.

oped. Compared to the "standard" F40 CW, the T10 lamp provides increased light output and improved color, with a slight increase in electrical input. The thick-coat triphosphor T8 lamp provides the same light output, improved color, and a significant decrease in electrical input.

T8 lamps use 20% fewer watts than standard F40s and operate even more efficiently when used on electronic ballasts. In 1995 efficient indoor lighting design generally uses a combination of T8 series lamps with electronic ballasts.

The next straight-tube development is the T5 shape, introduced in Europe in 1995. These lamps, which use miniature bi-pin bases, offer further efficacy gains but are manufactured in lengths compatible with European building module dimensions of 600 mm and 1200 mm rather than the 2-ft and 4-ft dimensions standard in the United States. Therefore, T5 lamps need their own, dedicated luminaires.

LENGTH AND SHAPE

Straight-tube fluorescents are available in a wide range of lengths, from 6 to 96 in. In general, the longer the tube, the higher the efficacy.

A number of variants of the straight-tube shape are available. The U-shaped lamp is essentially a straight-tube lamp bent in half. It comes with center-to-center leg-spacings of 1⅝ in. (16, 24, 31W T8), 3⅝ in. (35, 40W T12), or 6 in. (32W T8; 34, 40W T12). Circular fluorescents basically are straight tubes bent in a circle. They are available in outside diameters of 6½ in. (20W), 8¼ in. (22W), 12 in. (32W), and 16 in. (40W) T9 shapes. Straight tubes with outer glass jackets are designed for locations outdoors or in other sub-zero temperatures.

REPRESENTATIVE 4-FT AND 8-FT LAMPS AND LAMP/BALLAST COMBINATIONS

	NOMINAL LAMP RATINGS						ACTUAL LAMP/BALLAST COMBINATION			
WATTAGE	LENGTH (IN.)	SHAPE	PHOSPHOR TYPE	START MODE	INITIAL LUMENS	LAMP EFFICACY (LPW)	NUMBER OF LAMPS; BALLAST TYPE: ELECTRONIC/MAGNETIC	BALLAST FACTOR	SYSTEM WATTS	SYSTEM EFFICACY (LPW)
40*	48	T12	Cool White	Rapid	3,050	76	2-L M	0.94	88	65
32	48	T12	RE700	Rapid (Cathode cutout)	2,650	83	2-L M	0.87	67	69
34	48	T12	RE800	Rapid	2,850	84	2-L E	0.88	62	81
42	48	T10	RE800	Rapid	3,700	88	2-L E	0.85	74	85
32	48	T8	RE700	Instant	2,900	91	2-L E	0.95	65	87
32	48	T8	RE800	Instant	3,050	95	2-L E	0.95	63	92
32	48	T8	RE700	Instant	2,900	91	3-L E	0.91	87	91
32	48	T8	RE700	Instant	2,900	91	4-L E	0.89	111	93
75*	96	T12	Cool White	Instant (Slimline)	6,150	82	2-L M	0.94	158	73
59	96	T8	RE800	Instant	6,000	102	2-L E	0.85	105	97

* These lamps are no longer manufactured; shown as base-case reference only.

Fred Davis, C.L.E.P; Fred Davis Corp., Energy and Lighting; Medfield, Massachusetts

BALLASTS AND STARTING MODES

The ballast provides the proper electrical characteristics to start and operate a fluorescent lamp. The starting process occurs in two stages: First, a sufficient voltage between an electrode and ground ionizes the gas (mercury plus an inert gas) in the lamp. Next, a voltage must develop across the lamp sufficient to extend the ionization throughout the lamp and to develop an arc.

The three starting modes for ballasts for fluorescent lamps are preheat, instant-start, and rapid-start. Each ballast type is used only with compatible lamps. Electronic ballasts are available in both instant-start and rapid-start designs.

For the preheat mode, a separate starter button is often used to heat the electrodes before high voltage is applied across the lamp. The instant-start mode applies a high voltage (400 to 1000 V) across the lamp to ionize the gas and initiate arc discharge. This design provides the lowest energy consumption, sometimes at the expense of lamp life. In the rapid-start mode, electrodes (cathodes) are heated continuously by means of low voltage windings built into the ballast, allowing a gentle start. A variation cuts power to the cathodes after the arc is struck. Ballast factor is the percentage of a lamp's rated lumens produced when operated on a specific commercial ballast.

ELECTRONIC BALLASTS

Electronic ballasts improve the efficacy of lamps by driving them at high frequencies, above 15 kHz. Such ballasts eliminate flicker and are much lighter than electromagnetic ballasts. The improvement in efficacy made possible by electronic ballasts alone is approximately 10-12% for 4-ft lamps and 5% for 8-ft lamps, compared to operation at 60 Hz. Electronic ballasts are available that operate one, two, three, or four 4-ft T8 lamps at once.

Like magnetic ballasts, most electronic ballasts are designed so actual lumen output is as close to the rated lumens as possible. However, some electronic ballasts have been designed to deliberately provide higher than rated lumens (ballast factor > 1.0), while others have been designed for lower than rated lumens (ballast factor < 0.9). The ballast factor should be consulted carefully to ensure that the lighting design meets the desired light output.

FLUORESCENT FAMILIES

Fluorescent lamp families differ from each other in base type, starting characteristics, and "loading" (the amount of electrical energy applied per length of lamp). Generally, the most efficacious lamp family is the T8, and it should be used where appropriate. Applications requiring high output may call for multiple fluorescent lamps, efficient high-intensity discharge, or one of the higher loading families. For low light levels, any fluorescents are more efficacious than incandescent lamps.

Subminiature lamps use a T2 bulb with a "right-angle" base. They are available in 8-in. 6W, 12-in. 8W, and 20-in. 13W sizes.

Preheat fluorescent lamps utilize separate starters. These T5, T8, T12, and T17 lamps range in length from 6 to 60 in. The smallest of these uses a miniature bipin base. Lamp lifetime is 6000 to 7500 hours for T5s and T8s, 9000 for T12 and T17. These lamps are not commonly used in commercial general lighting.

The rapid-start T12 lamp, which operates at 430 mA with a medium bipin base, was formerly the mainstay of commercial lighting, even though it is available in only F30 36-in. and F40 48-in. sizes. The Energy Policy Act of 1992 eliminated inefficient halophosphate 4-ft full-wattage (40W) versions, leaving trichromatic phosphor types available for full wattage. Energy savers of all phosphors are available in 25W and 34W. 32W cathode-cutout 4-ft lamps cut electrical input to the cathode after starting, but they should not be used in situations with frequent on and off switching.

T8 lamps, operating at 265 mA, are the lamps of choice for energy-efficiency. They are available in 2-ft 17W, 3-ft 25W, 4-ft 32W, 5-ft 40W, and 8-ft 59W sizes. The 8-ft lamp has single-pin bases, for instant start only. The remainder have medium bipin bases and can operate on instant-start or rapid-start ballasts as long as they are specific to the T8 lamp. Rated life on instant-start ballasts is 15,000 hours, as opposed to 20,000 hours on rapid-start ballasts; however, in typical use, with 8- to 12-hr burn cycles on electronic ballasts, actual life difference is minimal.

Slimline lamps are single-pin based and range from 2 to 8 ft. They operate on instant-start ballasts. The F96 T12 lamp was the standard lamp in 8-ft luminaires.

High output lamps operate at 800 mA and produce approximately 45% more light than slimlines of the same length, although at lower efficacy. They have recessed double con-

tact (RDC) bases and rated life ranges from 9000 to 12000 hours. Very high output lamps operate at 1500 mA and range as high as 215 watts.

COMPACT FLUORESCENTS

Compact fluorescents were developed in the early 20th century to put the efficiency of fluorescent technology into a package small enough to compete with incandescent lamps in some application niches. Technological improvements have provided several generations of ever smaller, brighter glass shapes.

These glass shapes are fitted to either plug-in pin bases, which need a separate ballast, or to screw-in bases with ballasts built in. Compact fluorescents are used in a variety of luminaires, including most types that were historically designed for incandescent. For best efficiency, fixtures should be designed around the photometrics particular to the compact fluorescent.

Lamps with plug-in pin bases are dedicated for a ballast type. Two-pin lamps are preheat types that contain a glow starter in the lamp base, whereas four-pin lamps work with electronic ballasts that incorporate the starting function. As with straight-tubes, when compared to magnetic ballasts, electronic ballasts for compact fluorescents are lighter and more efficacious and eliminate flicker. Base-down operation of some compact fluorescents yields fewer than rated lumens; others have amalgam chemistry that offsets this phenomenon. Optimum output is close to horizontal.

REPRESENTATIVE COMPACT FLUORESCENT CHARACTERISTICS

LAMP	WATTS*	INITIAL LUMENS	MAX. OVERALL LENGTH (IN.)
Tube integral screw-in	18	1100	7.19
Twin lamp alone	13	900	7.50
Quad modular side-mount	22	1200	7.75
Triple integral screw-In	15	900	4.94
Triple integral screw-in	25	1750	6.20
Triple lamp alone	32	2200	5.80
Circline lamp alone	22	1100	8.25 O.D.
Flat lamp alone	36	2800	8.50
Reflector modular screw-in	13	860	6.38
Long CFL lamp alone	18	1250	8.94
Long CFL lamp alone	40	1550	6.95

* Watts exclude ballasts, except for integral units, which use electronic ballasts. All lamps listed have thick-coat trichromatic phosphors.

REPRESENTATIVE COMPACT FLUORESCENT SHAPES

GLASS SHAPES	PLUG-IN VERSION (FOR BALLASTED FIXTURE)			SCREW-IN VERSION (FOR USE IN MEDIUM SOCKET)	
	LAMP ALONE	BASE 2-PIN	BASE 4-PIN	MODULAR ASSEMBLY (LAMP AND BALLAST)	INTEGRAL (ONE-PIECE)
Globe, tube	—	—	—		
Twin					
Quad					
Triple					
Octic	—	—	—		
Helical					
Circline					
2-D			—		—
Flat				—	—
Reflector	—	—	—		
Long CFL					

Fred Davis, C.L.E.P.; Fred Davis Corp., Energy and Lighting; Medfield, Massachusetts

GENERAL

Incandescent lamps are the least efficient electric lighting sources, converting only 7–12% of electrical input to visible light. They operate on the principle of electric resistance: As electric current flows through a filament, resistance causes it to heat to a temperature high enough to glow, or incandesce.

Despite the many efficient alternatives to incandescents, they remain popular in certain applications because they can be dimmed easily and inexpensively and because they sparkle the most brilliantly. Incandescents have traditionally worked best for low-lumen applications, but LED and electroluminescent technologies now offer low-wattage alternatives. Switching on instantly and interchangeability among a variety of wattages are other advantages of incandescents. Most important, the small filament size of halogen reflector lamps makes them the most efficient type in narrow-beam applications.

The low initial price of incandescent lamps and luminaires can be misleading because their operating costs are relatively high: Such costs include not only electricity, but also the cost of replacing lamps. Another factor to consider is lamp life: As a rule, light output decreases over time. Therefore, if a lower lumen level is acceptable, a lower wattage lamp should be considered.

INCANDESCENT TECHNOLOGY IMPROVEMENTS

Incandescent technology has improved over the years, but the efficacy of the most efficient incandescents—more than 30 lumens per watt for infrared reflecting halogen—is still far lower than that of the least efficient fluorescents.

Early improvements in incandescent technology included the coiled-coil filament and the use of inert gases as fill material in the lamp. For greater efficacy still, krypton gas is used: It is less conductive than the standard argon-nitrogen mixture but more expensive.

Tungsten-halogen lamps use a halogen regenerative cycle to keep the filament from evaporating. A halogen additive in the fill gas, usually iodine or bromine, reacts chemically with tungsten molecules that have evaporated off the filament. The tungsten is then redeposited onto the filament instead of on the bulb wall. The lamp operates at an extremely high temperature, which necessitates that a special glass envelope, usually quartz, surround the filament.

The high temperature of tungsten-halogen lamps also gives them greater efficacy than standard incandescents—their color temperature is 200 to 300° K higher. The small, vertical filaments in tungsten-halogen lamps allow for very efficient reflectors. As a result, some low-wattage halogen reflectors are more energy-efficient than some compact fluorescent types for relatively narrow-beam applications.

A further improvement in halogen lamps involves infrared-reflective (IR) film. A very thin dichroic coating applied to the halogen lamp or capsule reflects infrared (heat) energy back onto the filament, allowing visible light to pass through. The hotter filament increases lumen output, thus improving efficacy.

Lamps whose outside bulb walls are made of quartz require special handling, as oils from bare hands can damage them. Many manufacturers now enclose the halogen capsule in an outer glass envelope, eliminating this problem.

AREA SOURCES

General service area lamps range from a 15-watt A15 to a 1500-watt PS52. They are designed for 120/, 125/, and 130/ volt circuits. Besides the most popular A, or arbitrary, shape, other shapes include PS, or pear straight. Halogen capsule versions of A-type shapes provide slightly better efficacy than standard incandescents.

Decorative shapes include FL (flame), B (bulbular), and G (globe). These are usually less efficient than standard incandescents, and efficient design will use low-wattage versions if necessary. The T (tubular shape) has been used in exit signs and for illuminating mirrors and pictures, which can also use linear and compact fluorescents if color is appropriate.

Tungsten halogen lamps are also available in noncapsule versions. Single-ended T3 and T4 tungsten halogen lamps range from 75 to 1500 watts, with the mini-candelabra screw base being the most common base. Double-ended tungsten halogens are linear shapes ranging up to 1500 watts. Small, low-voltage halogen type lamps are often used in reflectorized luminaires; usually under 2 in. in length, they use bipin bases, and range from 5 to 150 watts. IR versions of some linear halogen wattages provide substantial energy savings.

REFLECTOR SOURCES

The most popular flood and spot lamps were R (reflector) shapes, both R30 and R40 sizes. Flood R30 lamps had a beam spread of 130 degrees and much of the light in the outer part of the beam was often trapped in luminaires, especially recessed luminaires. Most are no longer manufactured. The newer ER (ellipsoidal reflector) and BR (bulged reflector) shapes maintain more lumens in the center of the beam than the R design.

PAR (parabolic reflector) lamps use a hard glass outside lens and are available in both "spot" (smooth glass len)/ and "flood" (stippled lens) versions. Halogen versions range from 35 to 120 watts, in PAR16, 20, 30, and 38 shapes, all of which use a medium screw socket. Beam spread ranges from 8 to 50 degrees. Other designations such as FL (flood), SP (spot), V (very), N (narrow), and W (wide) may not be standardized, and rated beam spreads should be verified. Halogen infrared technology is available in some PAR38 versions and affords the highest efficacy among incandescent reflectors.

Small, low-voltage halogen reflector lamps, usually 12 volts, are used in luminaires with transformers for the purpose. MR11 and MR16 shapes, originally used in slide projectors, became popular in display and other accent lighting applications. Wattages range from 20 to 75. Like line-voltage halogen PARs, MRs come in a very wide range of beam spreads.

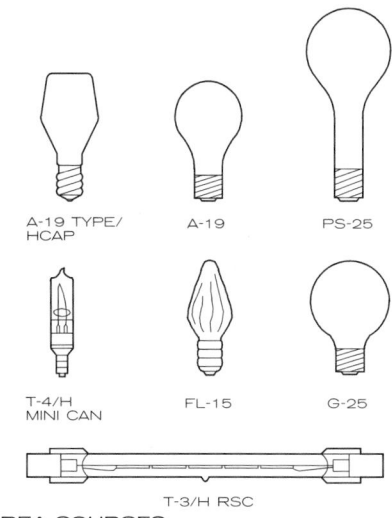

A-19 TYPE/HCAP   A-19   PS-25

T-4/H MINI CAN   FL-15   G-25

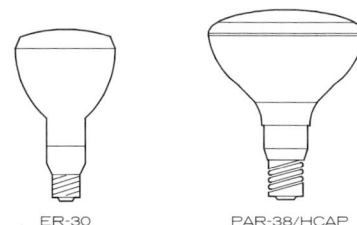

T-3/H RSC

AREA SOURCES

ER-30   PAR-38/HCAP

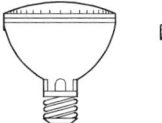  

PAR-30/HCAP   PAR-20/HCAP   PAR-16/HCAP

REFLECTOR SOURCES

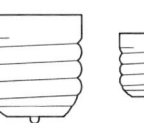 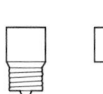 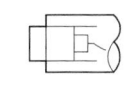

MOGUL   MEDIUM   MINIATURE CANDELABRA   RECESSED SINGLE CONTACT RSC

BASES

REPRESENTATIVE INCANDESCENT SHAPES

REFLECTOR INCANDESCENT LAMPS
REPRESENTATIVE LAMP RATINGS

SHAPE/BEAM/HALOGEN	WATTS	CENTER BEAM CANDLE POWER	BEAM SPREAD TO 50% OF MAX.	HOURS LIFE	MAXIMUM OVERALL LENGTH (IN.)
MR16/NSP/H 12V	20	5000	8	2000	1.75
PAR20/ NFL/HCAP	35	900	30	2500	3.25
PAR38/SP/HCAP	45	5500	12	2500	5.31
PAR20/NFL/HCAP	50	1250	30	2500	3.25
PAR30/WFL/HCAP (long-neck)	50	500	50	2500	4.69
PAR38/FL/HCAP IR	60	3650	30	3000	5.31
R30/FL*	75	470	130	2000	5.38
ER30	75	1500	36	2000	6.38
PAR30/FL/HCAP	75	2000	40	2500	3.63
PAR38/FL/HCAP	90	3750	30	2500	5.31
R40/FL*	100	900	120	2000	6.50
PAR38/FL*	150	4000	30	2000	5.31

* These lamps no longer manufactured, shown as reference.

NOTE

All with medium base except MR.

AREA INCANDESCENT LAMPS
REPRESENTATIVE LAMP RATINGS

SHAPE/HALOGEN/BASE	WATTS	INITIAL LUMENS	HOURS LIFE	MAXIMUM OVERALL LENGTH (IN.)
A15/medium	15	115	2500	3.50
G25/medium	40	410	1500	4.50
A19 type/HCAP/med.	52	770	3500	4.38
A19/medium	60	860	1000	4.44
A-19/medium	75	1180	750	4.44
A21/medium	100	1690	750	5.25
PS25/medium	150	2650	750	6.94
T4/H/mini-can	150	2800	2000	3.00
T4/H/mini-can	250	5000	2000	3.16
T3 linear/HIR/RSC	350	10,000	2000	4.69
T3 linear/H/RSC	500	11,100	2000	4.69
PS40/mogul	500	9100	1000	9.75

H=halogen; CAP=capsule; IR=infrared reflective film

Fred Davis, C.L.E.P.; Fred Davis Corp., Energy and Lighting; Medfield, Massachusetts

HIGH-INTENSITY DISCHARGE

High-intensity discharge (HID) lamps are the most common electric lights other than incandescent and fluorescent. In rough order of increasing efficacy, the categories of HID lamps include mercury vapor, metal halide, high-pressure sodium, and low-pressure sodium. The highest efficacies among them, however, have the poorest color qualities.

Like fluorescents, HID lamps use a ballast to provide proper starting and operating voltages. Light is produced by an electric arc discharging through a mixture of gases. Unlike fluorescents, HID lamps use a fairly compact arc tube that operates under very high temperature and pressure. The small point source makes HID lamps and luminaires compact and powerful. Most are particularly suited to outdoor applications or large rooms with high ceilings, as long as frequent switching is not needed. Clear lamps offer best optical control; coated lamps offer more diffuse light.

Unlike incandescents and fluorescents, HID lamps require a warmup period to reach full light output. After power is applied, temperature and pressure in the mixture of gases and metals gradually builds, forcing vapors into the arc and releasing light. Depending on lamp type, warmup, ranges from 2 to 15 minutes. If power is extinguished, HID lamps must cool before the arc can restrike. Restrike time lasts from 1 to 15 minutes, depending on lamp type. A few "instant restrike" types are available.

Over time, HID lamps may shift in color and the lumen output of some may drop substantially. For these, lamp change-outs should be planned well before the end of rated life. Rating the life of HID lamps is based on 10-hour cycles, as opposed to the three hours for rating incandescents and fluorescents. As with fluorescents, strobe effects with moving machinery should be avoided. HID lamps may have medium, mogul, or numerous other base types. A very few specialized types may be interchanged with metal halide, high-pressure sodium, and mercury vapor lamps.

METAL HALIDE

Originally developed in 1965, metal halide technology has continually improved. Today, its high efficacy and good color qualities make metal halide the best choice for many indoor and outdoor applications.

Common metal halide lamps have a color temperature of around 3500–4300K, and a CRI of 65–70. In addition, there are warm color lamps, 2700–3200K. In the early 1990s, some metal halide lamps were developed with very high CRIs, up to 93. Wattages range from 32 to 1500 watts, with a large variety of lamp and base configurations.

Metal halide lamps contain various metal halides and mercury. When the halide vapor approaches the high temperature in the central core of the arc, it disassociates into the halogen and the metal, with the metals radiating the appropriate spectra. Most metal halide lamps must be used in luminaires made to withstand an explosive rupture of the arc tube. Many should be used in luminaires that include a device to automatically turn the lamp off if the fixture is opened or broken. Most lamps should be turned off for a minimum of 15 minutes at least once per week.

Varieties of metal halide lamps include universal position burning, lamps optimized for burning in specific positions, cool or warm color temperatures in clear or phosphor coatings, safety lamps that extinguish if the outer envelope breaks, lamps with internal shielding that can withstand a rupture of the arc tube for use in open luminaires, and compact lamps that produce a high CRI in a small arc tube.

Electronic ballasts available for some metal halide types offer lighter weight, increased efficacy of 4–10%, less flicker, improved color and lumen maintenance, and increased life. Metal halide lamps with ceramic arc tubes have recently been introduced. These provide improved color control, more than 80 CRI, and higher efficacy.

HIGH-PRESSURE SODIUM

High-pressure sodium (HPS) lamps are highly efficacious, ranging from 65 to 125 lumens per watt (including ballast losses). They have a gold-pink color, 1900–2100K. CRI is poor, under 25. They are used where color rendering is not critical—in street, security, and industrial lighting.

Using xenon gas as an aid in starting, HPS lamps produce light by electric current passing through vaporized sodium. HPS lamps do not need enclosure (except from precipitation), and are fairly insensitive to operating position. So-called "deluxe" HPS have a CRI of 65. "White" HPS lamps of 2500–2800K have a CRI over 75. These improvements in color quality come at the cost of efficacy.

ALL LAMPS—COMPARISON OF GENERAL CHARACTERISTICS

LAMP TYPE	LAMP LUMENS PER WATT	HOURS LIFE	COLOR RENDITION	RELIGHT TIME
Incandescent	10 – 30	750 – 4000	Excellent	Immediate
Fluorescent	55 – 100	7500 – 24000	Good to excellent	Immediate
Metal halide	80 – 125	3000 – 20000	Good to excellent	10–15 min.
High-pressure sodium	65 – 140	16000 – 24000	Fair	Less than 1 minute
Low-pressure sodium	up to 180	18,000	Nonexistent	0–5 minutes
Mercury vapor	30 – 63	16000 – 24000	Fair to good	3–5 minutes

HID LAMPS—REPRESENTATIVE LAMP RATINGS

HID/SHAPE/BASE*	WATTS	INITIAL LUMENS	HOURS LIFE	CRI	MAX. OVERALL LENGTH (IN.)
M / ED-17 / medium	70	5,200	15000	65	5.44
M / ED-17 / medium	70	6,200	10000	85	5.44
M / T-6 1/2 / RSC	70	5,000	10000	85	—
M / ED-17 / medium	100	8,500	15000	65	5.44
M / ED-17 / medium	100	9,200	10000	85	5.44
M / ED-17 / medium	150	10,800	15000	65	5.44
M / BT-28 / mogul	175	11,600	15000	65	5.44
M / BT-28 / mogul	250	22,000	10000	65	8.31
M / BT-37 / mogul	400	36,000	12000	65	8.31
M / BT-37 / mogul	1000	110,000	12000	65	11.50
S / ED-17 / medium	70	6,300	24000	21	5.44
S / ED-17 / medium	100	9,500	24000	21	5.44
S / ET-23 1/2 / mogul	150	16,000	24000	21	5.44
S / ET-18 / mogul	250	24,000	24000	21	9.75
S / ET-18 / mogul	400	50,000	24000	21	11.50
S / E-25 / mogul	1000	140,000	24000	21	15.06
L / T-17 / BY22d	35	4,800	18000	NA	12.19
L / T-21 / BY22d	90	13,500	18000	NA	20.75
H / A-23 / medium	100	4,300	24000	45	5.44
H / ED-28 / mogul	250	12,100	24000	45	8.31

*M = metal halides; S = high-pressure sodium; L = low pressure sodium; H = mercury.

LOW-PRESSURE SODIUM

Low-pressure sodium (LPS) lamps were first introduced in 1932 and have the highest efficacy of any light source available. However, the most important characteristic of LPS lamps is that they are monochromatic. The starting gas is neon, which emits a reddish glow as the lamp heats up. At full output, light from LPS is monochromatic yellow, and there is no color rendering ability. LPS comes in tubular lamps, from 18 to 180 watts, and is used for security and some roadway lighting.

MERCURY VAPOR

Developed in the early 1900s, mercury vapor is the least efficient of the HID sources. The technology involves excitation of mercury in a vaporized state. It is available in clear or phosphor coatings. The phosphors work much as they do in fluorescents, to convert ultraviolet light to visible light and to improve color rendering. Because efficacy and color quality is so much better, metal halide is preferred over mercury vapor in most situations.

OTHER LAMP TYPES

Electrodeless lamps first appeared commercially in the 1990s. These are sources excited by electromagnetic energy passing through the glass lamp without using an electrode. Coupling energy into a lamp at high frequencies forms plasma conditions that allow long life and fairly high efficacies. However, these high-frequency and microwave-powered sources must contain radiation within the lamp. The first products range from 23 to 85 watts, with efficacies from 48 to 70. Prototypes of a high-wattage sulfur lamp have shown the potential for high efficacy.

Other efficient lamp types are used in applications requiring low lumen levels, such as in exit signs. Energy consumption in exit signs is important because they are on continuously. Very low wattages allow an exit sign to use under 2 watts, compared to 20–50 watts with incandescent lamps.

Small light-emitting diodes (LEDs) are p-n junction semiconductor lamps. First used as indicator lights, they are now available in exit sign strips. Electroluminescent lamps are thin, flat area sources in which light is produced by a phosphor excited by a pulsating electric field. Typically, green panels are used in LED exit signs. Radioactive tritium tubes are self-contained sources requiring no power supply.

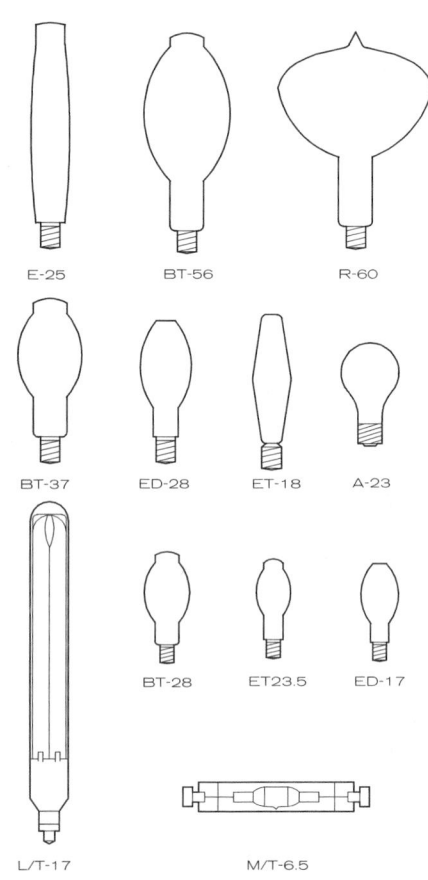

E-25   BT-56   R-60

BT-37   ED-28   ET-18   A-23

BT-28   ET23.5   ED-17

L/T-17   M/T-6.5

REPRESENTATIVE HID SHAPES

Fred Davis, C.L.E.P.; Fred Davis Corp., Energy and Lighting; Medfield, Massachusetts

GENERAL

UPS (uninterruptible power supply) is designed to provide continuous power with specific electrical characteristics by conditioning utility company power, battery power, or generator-supplied power.

Uninterruptible power supply (UPS) systems closely control the power supply voltage and frequency to critical equipment such as computers, communications systems, and medical instrumentation.

UPS systems are either on line, with power routing through them continuously, or off line, with power routed through them only when the incoming power is interrupted or departs from the design characteristics. The time required for an off-line, solid-state UPS to automatically switch on varies with the type of switch selected: The quicker the switch, the more expensive the switching equipment in general. The time needs to be matched to the tolerances of the critical equipment being supplied by the UPS to prevent loss of data or other problems.

Battery backup time is selected to allow a controlled shutdown of equipment or to allow a backup generator to be started and stabilize at full power.

Redundant UPS systems may be required if UPS power loss cannot be tolerated for system maintenance or equipment breakdown.

Some equipment can produce electrical disturbances that are fed back into the electrical circuit. This must be prevented through filtering in order to maintain clean power to the other equipment being supplied by the UPS.

The UPS unit and battery should be placed close together. Some UPS cabinets contain sealed batteries; others require separate batteries.

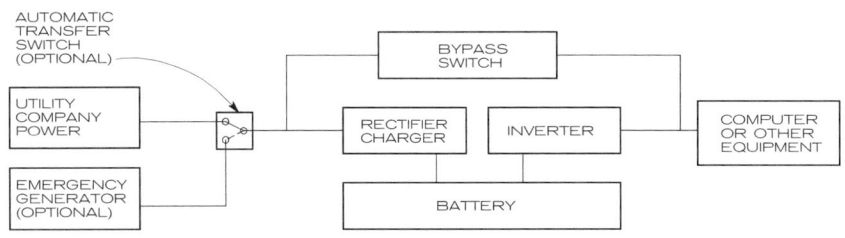

TYPICAL UNINTERUPTIBLE POWER SUPPLY SYSTEM DIAGRAM

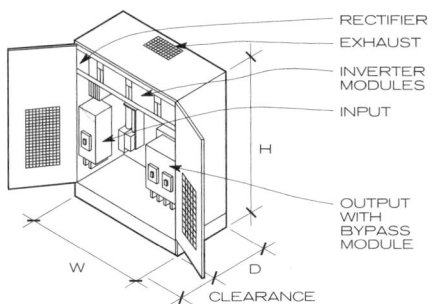

SOLID-STATE UPS

SOLID-STATE UPS SIZES

KVA	W (IN.)	D (IN.)	H (IN.)	WEIGHT (LB)
25	28	32	70	1400
50	72	36	72	4000
125	72	36	72	5600
200	72	36	72	6000
350	168	32	76	12,700
500	168	40	76	14,600

NOTE

Sound level approximately 65–70 dB. Heat rejection approximately 450–700 Btu/hr/kVA at 50 kVA to 250 Btu/hr/kVA at 500 kVA. Maintain room temperature at 70–80°F. Some units require clearance for access.

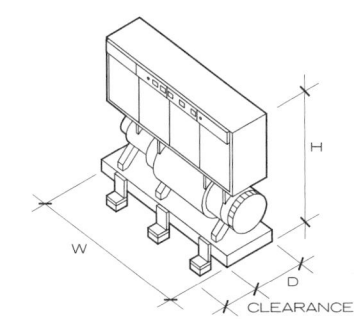

ROTARY UPS

ROTARY UPS SIZES

KVA	W (IN.)	D (IN.)	H (IN.)	WEIGHT (LB)
25	80	24	62	2600
50	80	24	62	3400
125	125	32	74	7000
250	140	32	80	10,000
500	164	60	84	15,000
1000	173	64	98	32,200

NOTE

Sound level approximately 60 to 80 dB. Heat rejection approximately 400 Btu/hr/kVA at 50 kVA to 250 Btu/hr/kVA at 500 kVA. Maintain room temperature at 70–80°F. Some units require front and rear clearance for access.

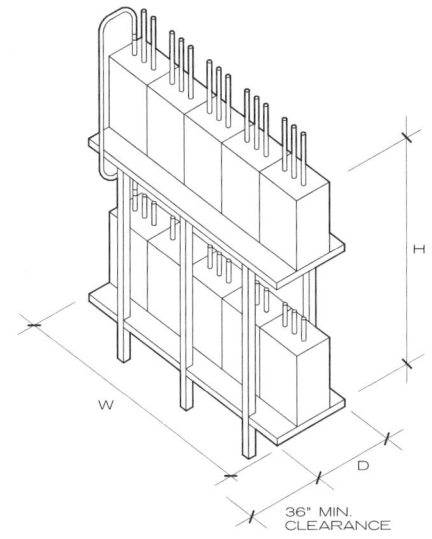

BATTERY RACKS

BATTERY CABINET SIZES

KVA	TIME (MIN)	W (IN.)	D (IN.)	H (IN.)	WGT. (LB)	NUMBER REQUIRED
75	15	40	32	76	2300	2
100	15	40	32	76	2300	3
200	15	48	32	76	2300	4
400	10	40	32	76	2300	8
500	7.5	40	32	76	2300	4

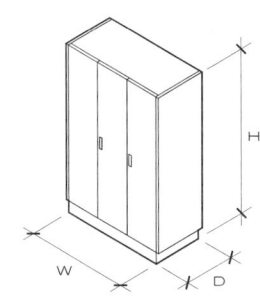

BATTERY CABINET

TWO-TIER RACK SIZES

KVA	TIME (MIN.)	W (IN.)	D (IN.)	H (IN.)	WGT. (LB)	NUMBER REQUIRED
15	30	96	16	54	3100	2
100	15	168	18	52	1000	4
250	15	108	18	52	20,500	6
500	15	156	18	52	34,600	6

THREE-TIER RACK SIZES

25	15	108	18	79	4300	1
50	15	108	18	79	5000	1
100	15	108	18	79	10,000	2
250	15	144	18	79	20,500	3
500	15	108	18	79	34,600	6

NOTE

Racks can be placed back to back. Provide shower and eyewash station and ventilation, and maintain approximately 77°F room temperature. Place battery racks close to UPS units. Providing seismic bracing required by code.

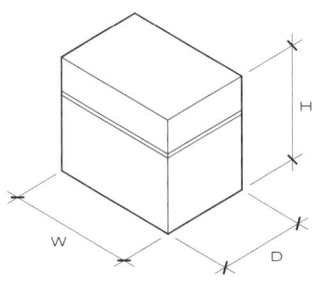

UPS UNDER 10 KVA

UPS UNDER 10 KVA SIZES

WATTS	W (IN.)	D (IN.)	H (IN.)	TIME (MIN.)
200	8	15	6	15–20
800	22	16	9	15–20
1500	22	16	18	15–20
KVA				
3.0	26	19	52	10
5.0	36	19	52	10
10.0	36	19	52	10

NOTE

A wide variety of UPS systems is available for smaller applications, ranging from desktop models for single microcomputers to floor models that can supply several computers or other equipment.

Charles B. Towles, P.E.: TEI Consulting Engineers; Washington, D.C.

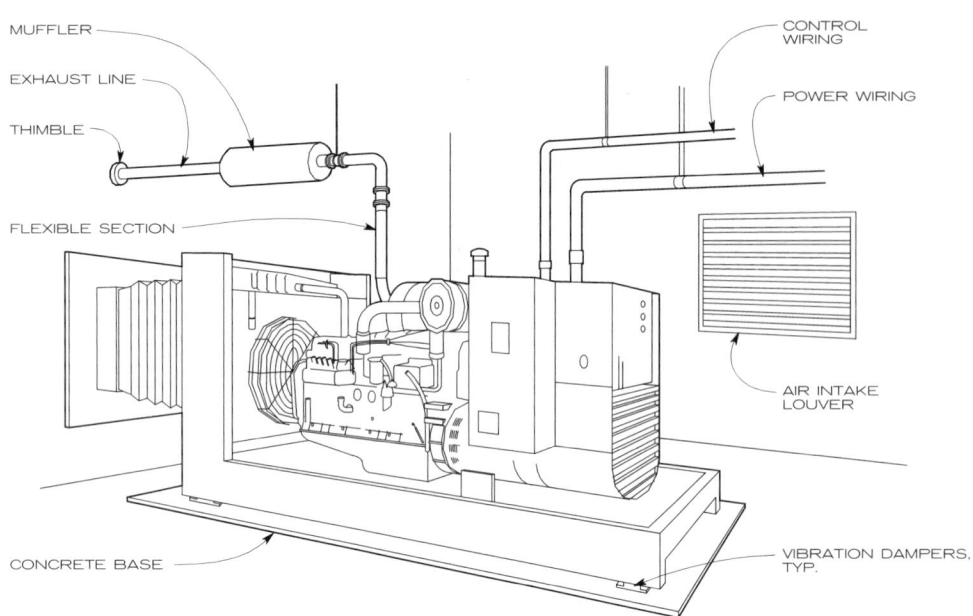

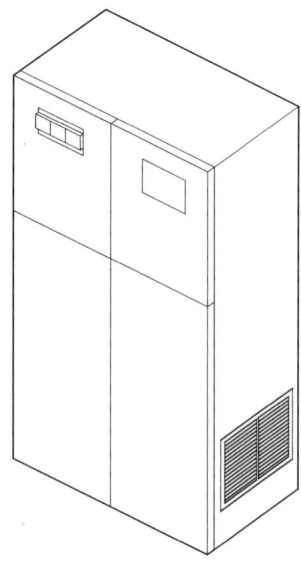

NOTE

Standby generators provide emergency power during power outages, when life safety lighting and/or critical equipment power requirements are beyond the capacity of battery units or when required by code (as in hospitals or high-rise buildings). Engines should be located away from main electrical switchgear. Engine rooms must have adequate ventilation for engine- and generator-radiated heat and must be protected against extreme environments under all conditions of airflow.

There must be enough room around a power generating unit to service it and to remove the unit. Standby generators require frequent inspections, tests under load conditions, and maintenance. Provisions must be made to prevent vibration transmission to nearby occupied areas. In addition to the cooling methods illustrated, cooling by remote radiator, heat exchanger, submerged pipe, cooling tower, and evaporative cooler should be considered. See National Electric Code for working space requirements and proper application.

NOTE

Battery-powered lighting equipment provides the minimal emergency illumination required for personnel safety and evacuation in buildings not requiring standby generator power. It is also used in buildings requiring standby generator power for the central control, telephone switchboard, generator, and electrical switchgear rooms to provide lighting for critical operations and troubleshooting if the generator fails to start. The batteries, which require frequent inspection, tests, and maintenance, are available in lead calcium, nickel cadmium, and wet lead acid.

EMERGENCY ENGINE GENERATOR WITH CONTROL PANEL

EMERGENCY LIGHTING BATTERY SYSTEMS

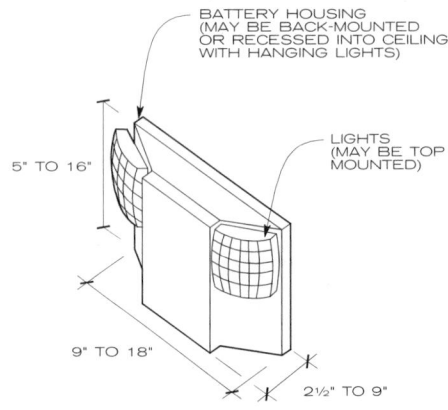

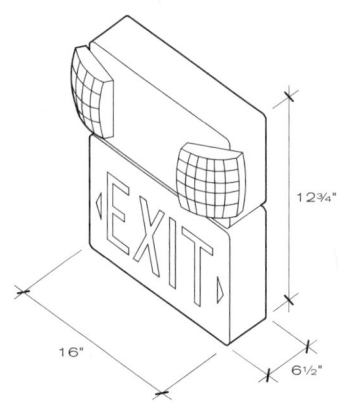

WITH EMERGENCY LIGHTING

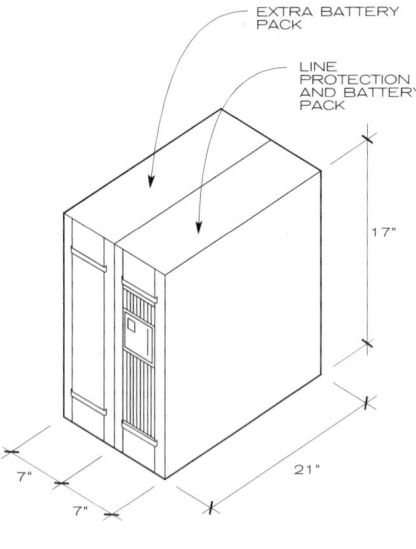

NOTE

Used to light exit passageways during power outages. Typically powered by lead calcium or nickel cadmium batteries.

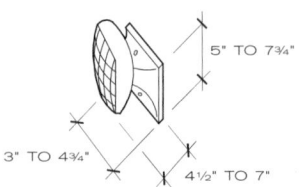

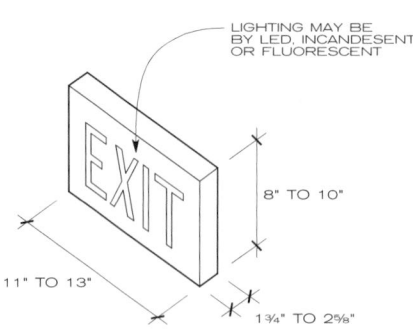

NOTE

Available in solid acrylic, cast aluminum with acrylic letters, steel, or polycarbonate housing, these signs may be side-, top-, or back-mounted or recessed. They can be powered by standard AC or battery pack.

NOTE

This unit protects network data and telecommunications equipment and eliminates a wide range of potential power problems: spikes, surges and extended overvoltage conditions, noise, sags, extended brownouts, and harmonics and frequency variations common with standby generator operation. Power rating ranges from 1000 to 3000 V.

REMOTE FIXTURE

NOTE

Used with an emergency lighting battery system, this remote fixture may have one or two heads.

EXIT AND EMERGENCY LIGHTING

EXIT SIGNS

DATA AND TELECOMMUNICATIONS PROTECTION

Charles B. Towles, P.E.; TEI Consulting Engineers; Washington, D.C.

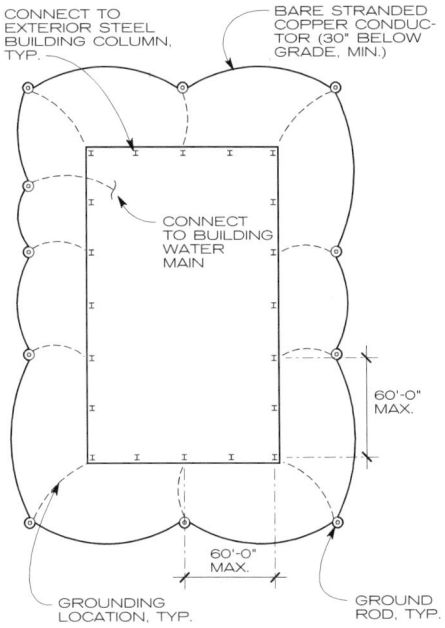

CONNECT TO EXTERIOR STEEL BUILDING COLUMN, TYP.

BARE STRANDED COPPER CONDUCTOR (30" BELOW GRADE, MIN.)

CONNECT TO BUILDING WATER MAIN

60'-0" MAX.

60'-0" MAX.

GROUNDING LOCATION, TYP.

GROUND ROD, TYP.

NOTE

All buildings and equipment should be grounded to protect people and equipment from fault currents. A complete interconnected system should be installed according to the requirements of the National Electrical Code and the National Electrical Safety Code. The structural steel of the building is connected to a buried "ground grid" to provide this requirement. All electrical equipment is connected with this system to provide a direct path to earth. Specify the number of ground rods and conductor size according to National Electrical Code requirements.

BUILDING GROUND GRID

4'-0" MAX.

SMALL EQUIPMENT

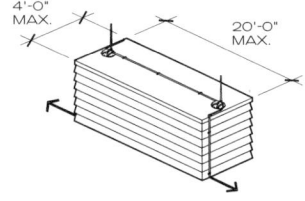

4'-0" MAX.

20'-0" MAX.

MEDIUM EQUIPMENT

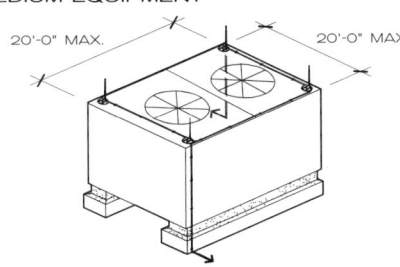

20'-0" MAX.

20'-0" MAX.

LARGE EQUIPMENT

NOTE

Codes vary slightly regarding bonding requirements for metal bodies on rooftops. Generally, if a metal body is in a zone of protection (lower than adjacent air terminals) and within 6 ft or a calculated bonding distance, it should be bonded to the lightning protection system. Smaller, secondary size materials may be used for these connections. Metal bodies taller than the air terminals and less than $3/16$ in. thick require air terminal protection. Those greater than $3/16$ in. thick are protected if adequately bonded.

ROOFTOP EQUIPMENT BONDING AND PROTECTION

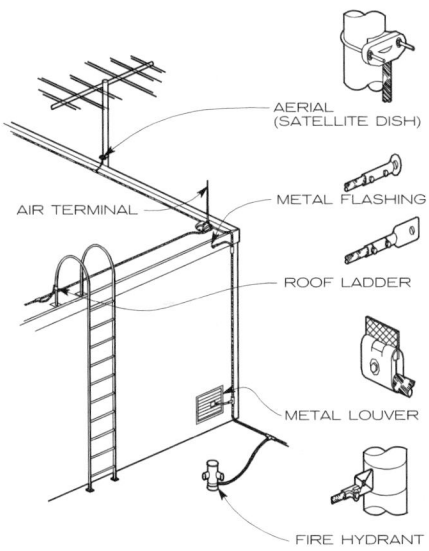

AERIAL (SATELLITE DISH)

AIR TERMINAL

METAL FLASHING

ROOF LADDER

METAL LOUVER

FIRE HYDRANT

FASTENER TYPES

MISCELLANEOUS ROOFTOP EQUIPMENT

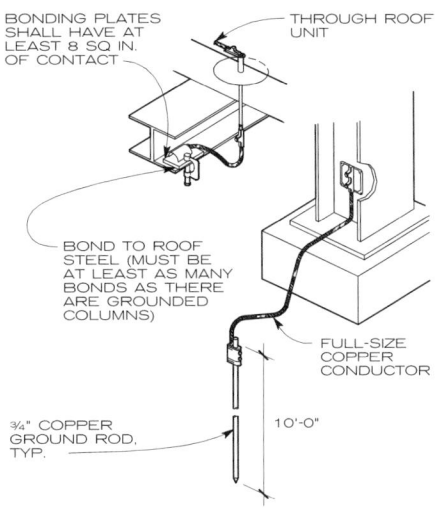

BONDING PLATES SHALL HAVE AT LEAST 8 SQ IN. OF CONTACT

THROUGH ROOF UNIT

BOND TO ROOF STEEL (MUST BE AT LEAST AS MANY BONDS AS THERE ARE GROUNDED COLUMNS)

FULL-SIZE COPPER CONDUCTOR

$3/4$" COPPER GROUND ROD, TYP.

10'-0"

NOTE

In some cases, especially on tall structures, it may be advantageous to substitute the steel frame of a structure for portions of the usual conductor system, normally the downleads. Connections are made to cleaned areas of the building steel, at grade and at roof level, and the columns serve to connect the roof and ground systems.

STEEL FRAME AS CONDUCTOR

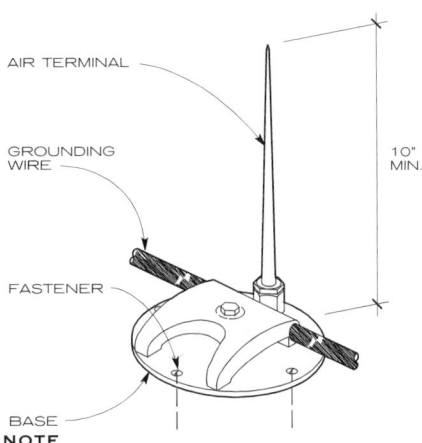

AIR TERMINAL

GROUNDING WIRE

FASTENER

BASE

10" MIN.

NOTE

Adhesives are typically used for flat roof installation.

TOP-MOUNTED AIR TERMINAL (LIGHTNING ROD) DETAIL

GENERAL

A lightning protection system is an integrated arrangement of air terminals, bonding connections, arresters, splicers, and other fittings installed on a structure in order to safely conduct to ground any lightning discharge to the structure.

Lightning protection systems and components are grouped into three categories (U.L. classes) based on building height and intended applications. Class I equipment and systems are for ordinary buildings under 75 ft in height, Class II is for those over 75 ft in height, and Class II Modified is a special group covering only large, heavy-duty stacks and chimneys similar to those used at power plants. Each of these system types comprises five or six major groups of components:

1. Air terminals (lightning rods) located on the roof and building projections.
2. Main conductors that tie the air terminals together and connect them with the grounding systems.
3. Bonds to metal roof structures and equipment.
4. Arresters to prevent power line surge damage.
5. Ground terminals, typically rods or plates driven or buried in the earth.
6. Tree protection (usually applicable only to residential work).

Each of these types of equipment and the methods for their installation is covered in the accompanying drawings.

Beyond these material requirements, other factors to be considered relative to lightning protection systems include selection of codes for compliance, inspection criteria (again based on code), criteria to evaluate competence of installing personnel, and requirements for annual inspection and maintenance.

OVERALL SYSTEMS DESIGN NOTES

1. Air terminals should be located around the perimeter of flat roof buildings and along the ridge of pitched roof buildings spaced at 20 ft on center maximum and located not more than 2 ft from ridge ends, outside corners, and edges of building walls.
2. Full-size main conductors should connect all air terminals.
3. Additional air terminals should be located in the center of large open flat spacings not to exceed 50 ft.
4. Cable runs connecting these center roof air terminals should be no longer than 150 ft without a lead back to the perimeter cable.
5. Gently sloping roofs are classed as flat under the rules shown above.
6. Download cables to ground should be connected to the roof perimeter cable at a maximum spacing of 100 ft on center. Buildings with a perimeter of 250 to 300 ft should have three downloads. For each additional 100 ft or fraction thereof add one download.
7. No building or structure should have fewer than two downloads.
8. Arresters should be installed on the electric and telephone services and on all radio and television lead-ins to a structure. Responsibility and jurisdiction for the installation of these devices can vary with locality, so special consideration may have to be given to these items.
9. Trees adjacent to residences pose a special hazard. It is recommended that all trees larger than an adjacent structure and within 10 ft of it be fully protected. Consult codes or manufacturer for recommendations on materials and installation requirements.
10. On-site inspections and certification of completed systems, installer competency certification, and guaranteed inspection/maintenance options are all available under existing standards. Consult codes and standards for specifics.

REFERENCES

The following codes, technical sources, and quality control procedures are standards for lightning protection systems.

Lightning Protection Institute, "Installation Code LPI–175."

National Fire Protection Association, "Lightning Protection Code NFPA 780."

Underwriters Laboratories, master labeled program under "U.L. Installation Requirements 96A."

Douglas J. Franklin; Thompson Lightning Protection, Inc.; St. Paul, Minnesota

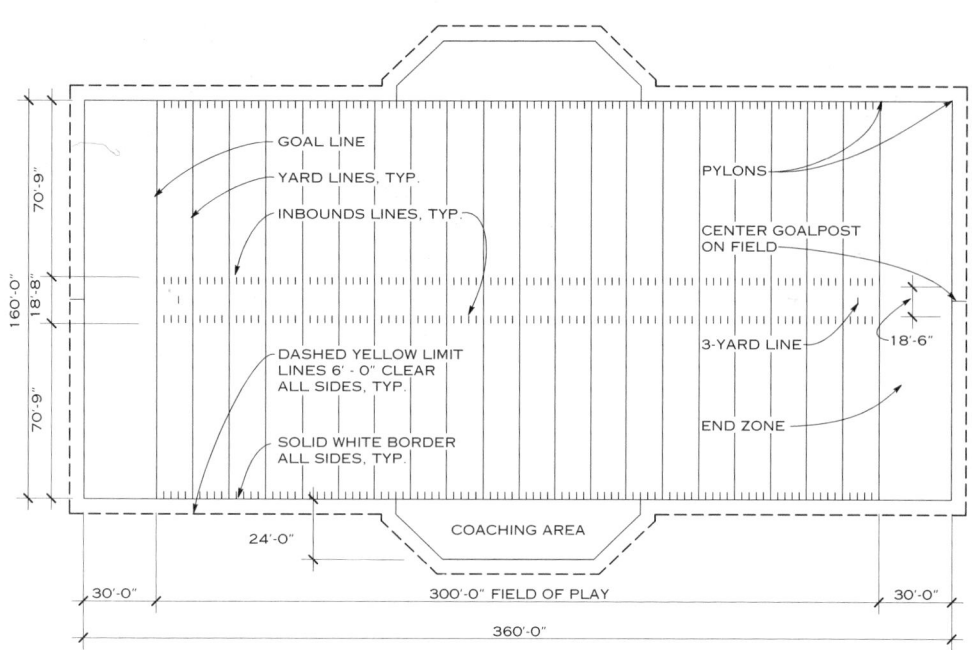

NATIONAL FOOTBALL LEAGUE FIELD

NOTES

1. In the National Football League (NFL), the playing field is 360 ft long by 160 ft wide. The preferred orientation of the field is with the long axis stretching northwest to southeast; there is no recommended slope. (For further information, contact the NFL in New York City.)
2. All lines are 4 in. wide, except the goal lines and yellow lines, which are 8 in. wide. All lines are marked with a nontoxic material.
3. The goalpost must be padded as prescribed by the NFL.

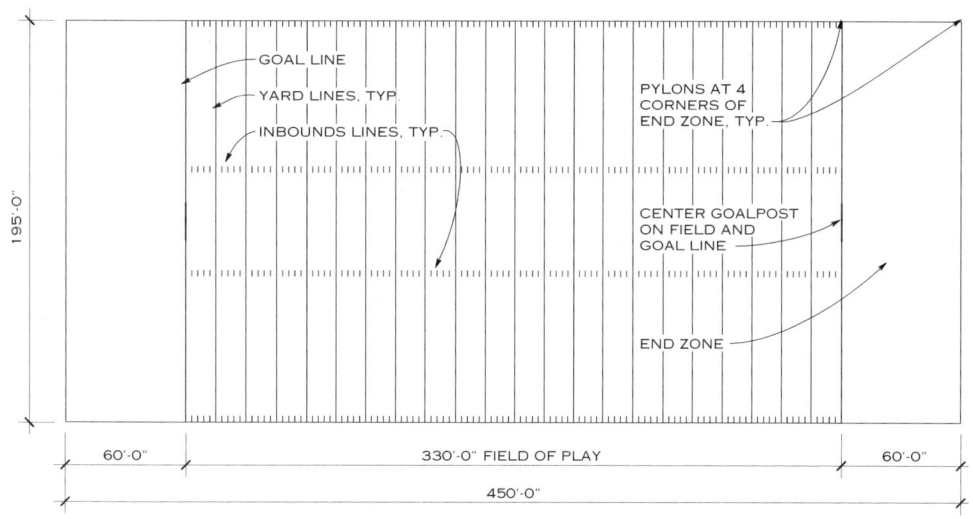

CANADIAN FOOTBALL LEAGUE FIELD

NOTES

1. In the Canadian Football League (CFL), the playing field is 450 ft long by 195 ft wide. The preferred orientation is with the long axis running northwest to southeast; there is no recommended slope. (For further information, contact the CFL in Toronto.)
2. All lines are 4 in. wide except the goal lines and yellow lines, which are 8 in. wide. All lines are marked with a nontoxic material.
3. The goalpost must be padded as prescribed by the CFL.

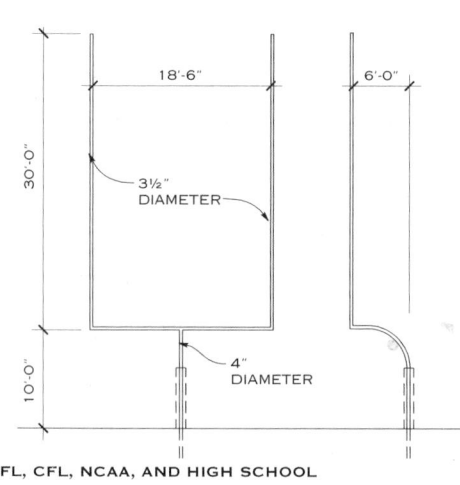

NFL, CFL, NCAA, AND HIGH SCHOOL

GOALPOSTS

NOTE

Goalposts should be padded to 6 ft or as prescribed by the NFL or CFL. They should be yellow or white.

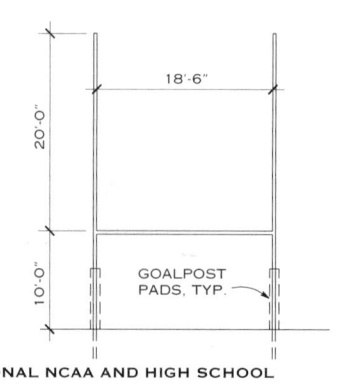

OPTIONAL NCAA AND HIGH SCHOOL

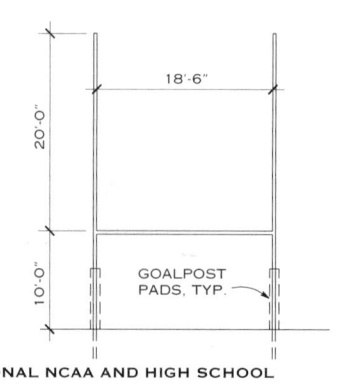

NOTE

The football is a prolate spheroid with a long axis of 11 to 11 1/4 in.; it weighs 14 to 15 oz.

FOOTBALL

Dean Cox, AIA; Collins Rimer Gordon Architects; Cleveland, Ohio

17 **FIELD SPORTS**

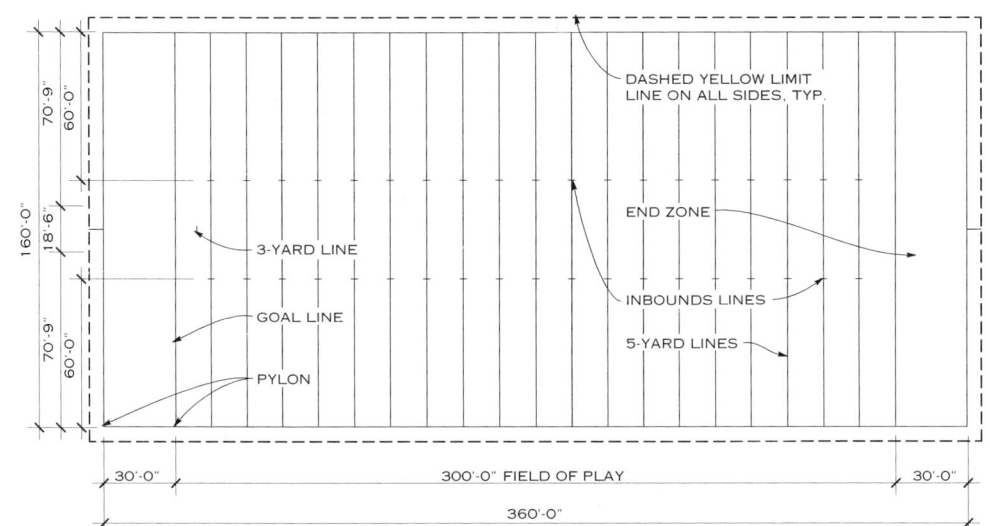

NATIONAL COLLEGIATE ATHLETIC ASSOCIATION FIELD

NOTES

1. In the National Collegiate Athletic Association (NCAA), the playing field is 360 ft long by 160 ft wide, with an additional 12 ft recommended (6 ft minimum required) on all sides. The preferred orientation of the field is with the long axis stretching northwest to southeast. The field should be graded away from the centerline; subsoil drainage may be necessary.

2. All field dimension lines are 4 in. wide and should be marked with a white, nontoxic material. All measurements are from the edge of the line closest to the center of the playing field.

3. End zone marking should not overlap goal lines, sidelines, and end lines.

4. Inbounds lines are located 60 ft from the sidelines for college football (53 ft 4 in. for high school). Marks should be 4 in. wide by 2 ft long.

5. Goalposts should be padded to a height of 6 ft. The color of the posts should be yellow or white.

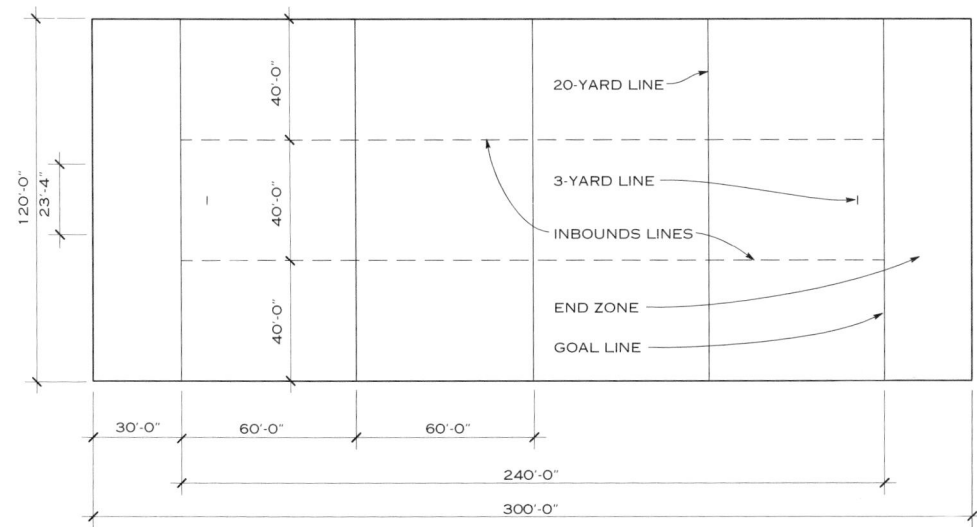

TOUCH FOOTBALL FIELD

NOTES

1. In touch football, the playing field is 300 ft long by 120 ft wide, with an additional 6 ft allowed on all sides. The preferred orientation is with the long axis running northwest to southeast; the recommended slope for proper drainage is 1%, which should run away from each side of the long-axis centerline.

2. All measurements are from the inside edge of the lines, which are 4 in. wide and marked with a white, nontoxic material.

3. The goalposts are similar to those used in college football.

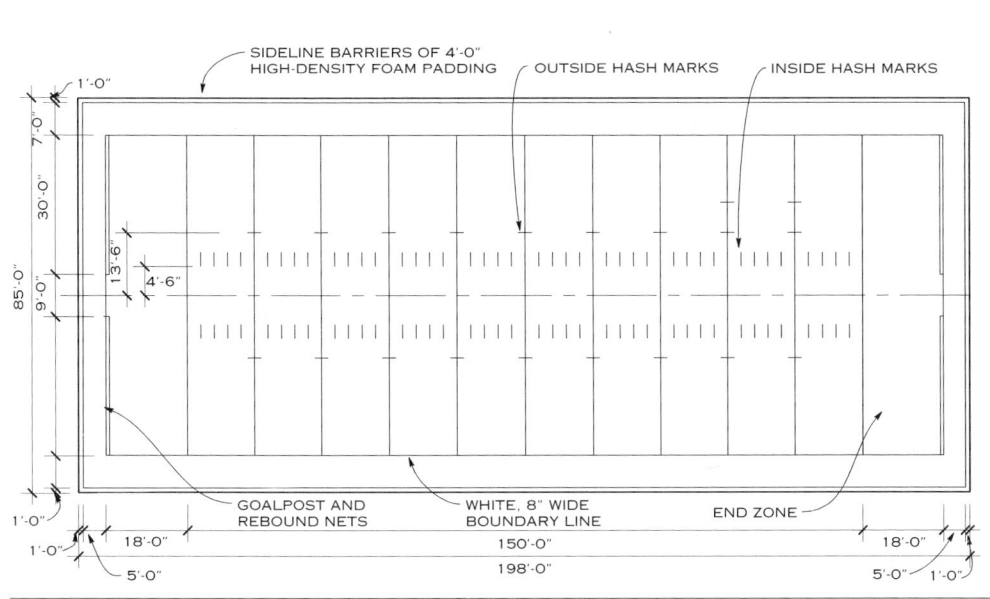

ARENA FOOTBALL FIELD

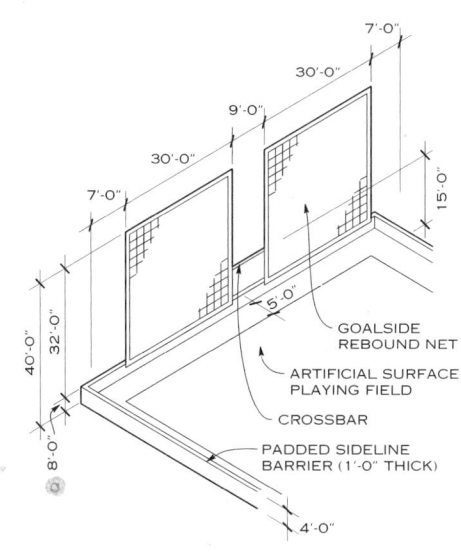

NOTE

The playing field is made of padded artificial turf. For more information, contact Gridiron Enterprises in Chicago.

Dean Cox, AIA; Collins Rimer Gordon Architects; Cleveland, Ohio

FIELD SPORTS **17**

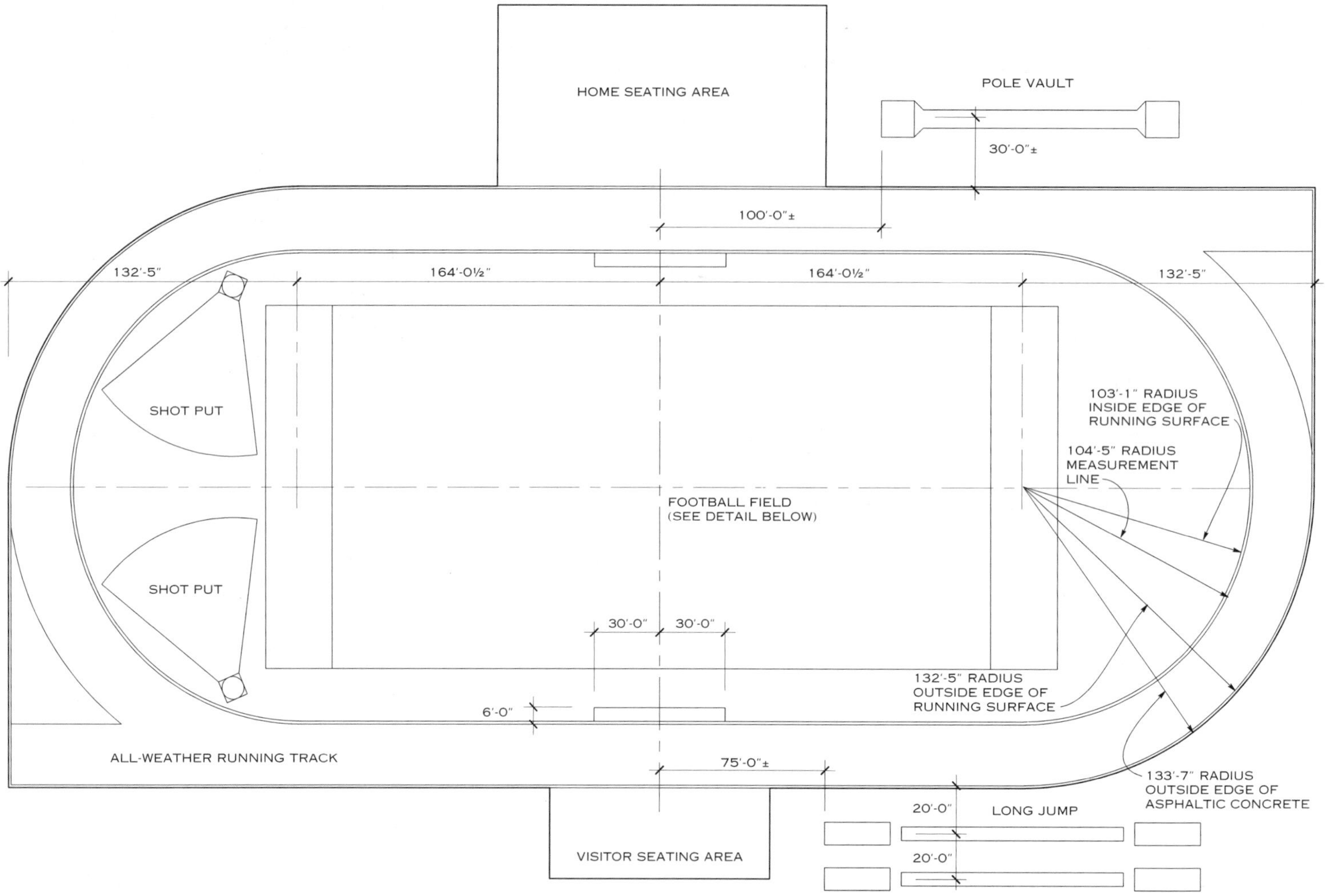

HOME SEATING AREA

POLE VAULT

30'-0"±

100'-0"±

132'-5"   164'-0½"   164'-0½"   132'-5"

SHOT PUT

103'-1" RADIUS
INSIDE EDGE OF
RUNNING SURFACE

104'-5" RADIUS
MEASUREMENT
LINE

SHOT PUT

FOOTBALL FIELD
(SEE DETAIL BELOW)

30'-0"   30'-0"

132'-5" RADIUS
OUTSIDE EDGE OF
RUNNING SURFACE

6'-0"

ALL-WEATHER RUNNING TRACK

75'-0"±

133'-7" RADIUS
OUTSIDE EDGE OF
ASPHALTIC CONCRETE

20'-0"   LONG JUMP

20'-0"

VISITOR SEATING AREA

NOTES

1. The stadium layout shown is generic and should be modified to suit the needs of a particular project.

2. Lighting, drainage, and fencing systems are not shown on the layout illustrated, but they must be considered when applicable to a project.

3. Refer to other Architectural Graphic Standards sports pages for information regarding individual events that might be held in a multipurpose high school stadium.

4. Seating is shown here schematically; actual sizes should be based on the requirements of a project. It is recommended that the seating assembly be placed over concrete paved areas.

5. A chain-link fence, 4 ft high, is usually located outside the track area and extended around the remaining track and field events.

6. Striping is usually provided on the track to allow for measured lanes for running events.

7. Other support facilities include locker areas, restrooms, concession stands, and additional field equipment storage space.

MULTIPURPOSE HIGH SCHOOL STADIUM

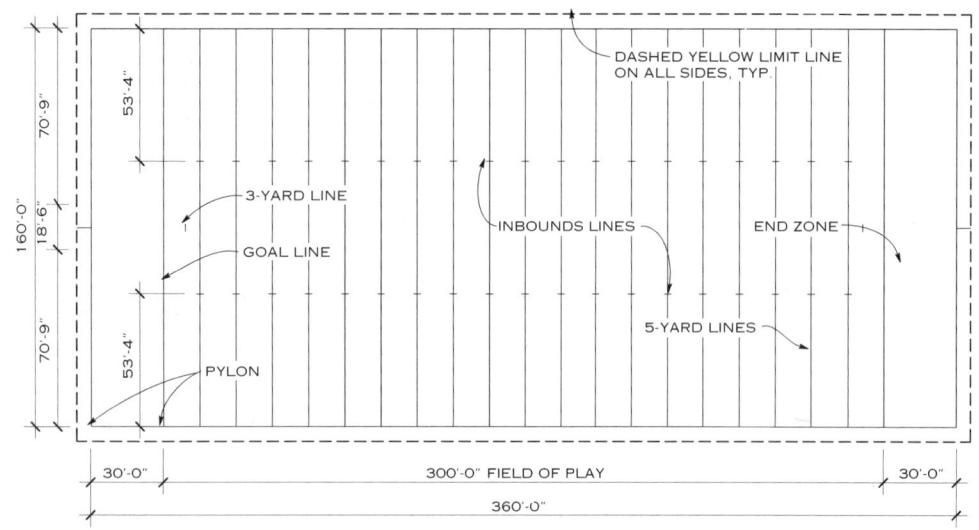

53'-4"

70'-9"

DASHED YELLOW LIMIT LINE
ON ALL SIDES, TYP.

18'-6"

3-YARD LINE

160'-0"

GOAL LINE

INBOUNDS LINES   END ZONE

70'-9"

53'-4"

5-YARD LINES

PYLON

30'-0"   300'-0" FIELD OF PLAY   30'-0"

360'-0"

NOTES

1. In high school football, the field is 360 ft long x 160 ft wide, with an additional 12 ft recommended (6 ft minimum required) on all sides. The preferred orientation of the field is with the long axis stretching northwest to southeast. The field should be graded away from the centerline; subsoil drainage may be necessary.

2. All field dimension lines are 4 in. wide and should be marked with a white, nontoxic material. All measurements are from the edge of the line closest to the center of the playing field.

3. End zone marking should not overlap goal lines, sidelines, and end lines.

4. Inbounds lines are located 53 ft 4 in. from the sidelines for high school football (as compared to 60 ft for college football). Marks should be 4 in. wide x 2 ft long.

5. Goalposts should be padded to a height of 6 ft. The color of the posts should be yellow or white.

HIGH SCHOOL FOOTBALL FIELD

Dean Cox, AIA; Collins Rimer Gordon Architects; Cleveland, Ohio
Behnke Associates, Inc. Landscape Architects/Planners; Cleveland, Ohio

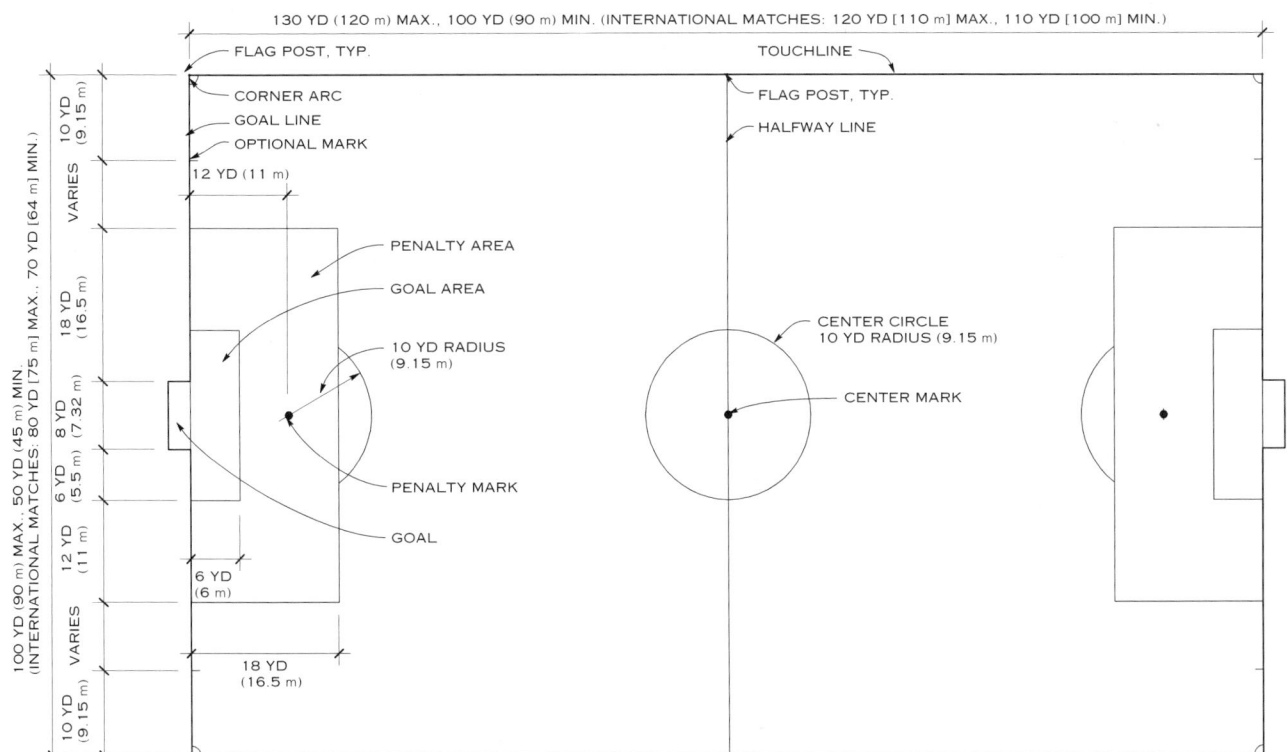

130 YD (120 m) MAX., 100 YD (90 m) MIN. (INTERNATIONAL MATCHES: 120 YD [110 m] MAX., 110 YD [100 m] MIN.)

FLAG POST, TYP.
TOUCHLINE
CORNER ARC
FLAG POST, TYP.
GOAL LINE
OPTIONAL MARK
HALFWAY LINE
12 YD (11 m)

10 YD (9.15 m)
VARIES
18 YD (16.5 m)
8 YD (7.32 m)
6 YD (5.5 m)
12 YD (11 m)
VARIES
10 YD (9.15 m)

100 YD (90 m) MAX., 50 YD (45 m) MIN
(INTERNATIONAL MATCHES: 80 YD [75 m] MAX., 70 YD [64 m] MIN.)

PENALTY AREA
GOAL AREA
10 YD RADIUS (9.15 m)
CENTER CIRCLE 10 YD RADIUS (9.15 m)
CENTER MARK
PENALTY MARK
GOAL
6 YD (6 m)
18 YD (16.5 m)

NOTE

The dimensions given are in accordance with regulations of the United States Soccer Federation (USSF) and the Federation Internationale de Football Association (FIFA). All field marking lines should be no more than 5 in. (12 cm) wide.

PROFESSIONAL SOCCER

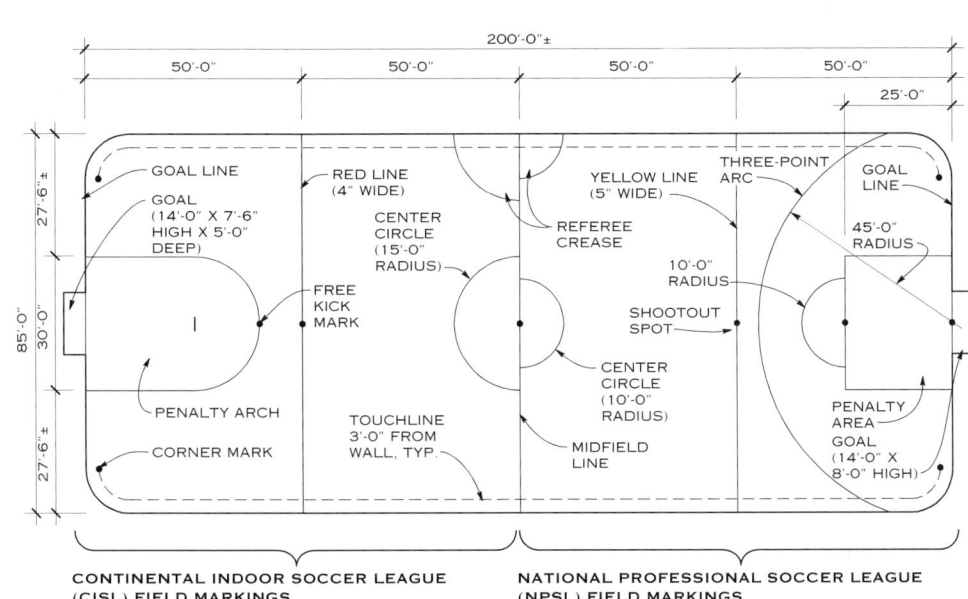

200'-0"±
50'-0" 50'-0" 50'-0" 50'-0"
25'-0"

GOAL LINE
RED LINE (4" WIDE)
YELLOW LINE (5" WIDE)
THREE-POINT ARC
GOAL LINE
GOAL (14'-0" X 7'-6" HIGH X 5'-0" DEEP)
CENTER CIRCLE (15'-0" RADIUS)
REFEREE CREASE
45'-0" RADIUS
27'-6" ±
30'-0"
85'-0"
FREE KICK MARK
10'-0" RADIUS
SHOOTOUT SPOT
CENTER CIRCLE (10'-0" RADIUS)
PENALTY ARCH
TOUCHLINE 3'-0" FROM WALL, TYP.
MIDFIELD LINE
PENALTY AREA GOAL (14'-0" X 8'-0" HIGH)
27'-6" ±
CORNER MARK

CONTINENTAL INDOOR SOCCER LEAGUE (CISL) FIELD MARKINGS

NATIONAL PROFESSIONAL SOCCER LEAGUE (NPSL) FIELD MARKINGS

NOTE

Indoor soccer, in both the USSF or the FIFA, is typically played in hockey arenas within the existing rink walls on an artificial playing surface affixed to the rink surface.

INDOOR SOCCER

NOTES

1. Professional soccer balls are 27 in. (68.58 cm) in circumference and weigh 14-16 oz (396–453 grams).
2. In the northern hemisphere, the length of the field should be oriented northwest-southeast for the best sun angle during the fall playing season.
3. The preferred drainage on a field is a longitudinal crown with a 1% slope from the center to each side.
4. In addition to the architectural differences between them, indoor and outdoor soccer are very different in nature. Refer to the appropriate governing bodies for details.

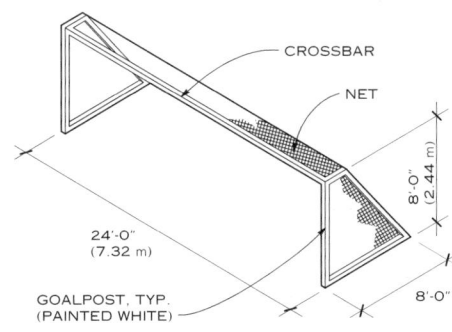

CROSSBAR
NET
8'-0" (2.44 m)
24'-0" (7.32 m)
GOALPOST, TYP. (PAINTED WHITE)
8'-0"

NOTES

1. The goalposts and crossbar must not be wider than 5 in. or narrower than 4 in. and must present a flat surface to the playing field. The net must be attached to the ground, the goalposts, and the crossbar, and it must extend back from and level with the crossbar for 2 ft (.61 m).
2. Indoor soccer goals measure 14 ft wide (inside the posts) and 7 ft 6 in. from the playing surface to the underside of the crossbar.

SOCCER GOAL

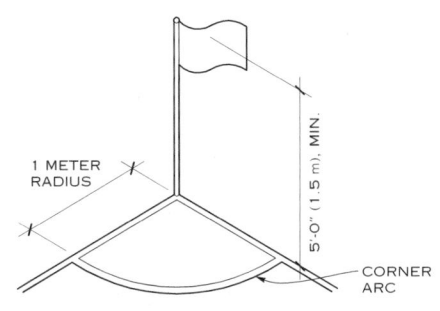

1 METER RADIUS
5'-0" (1.5 m). MIN.
CORNER ARC

NOTE

Use of a corner flag post is compulsory.

CORNER FLAG POST

U.S. Soccer Federation; Chicago, Illinois

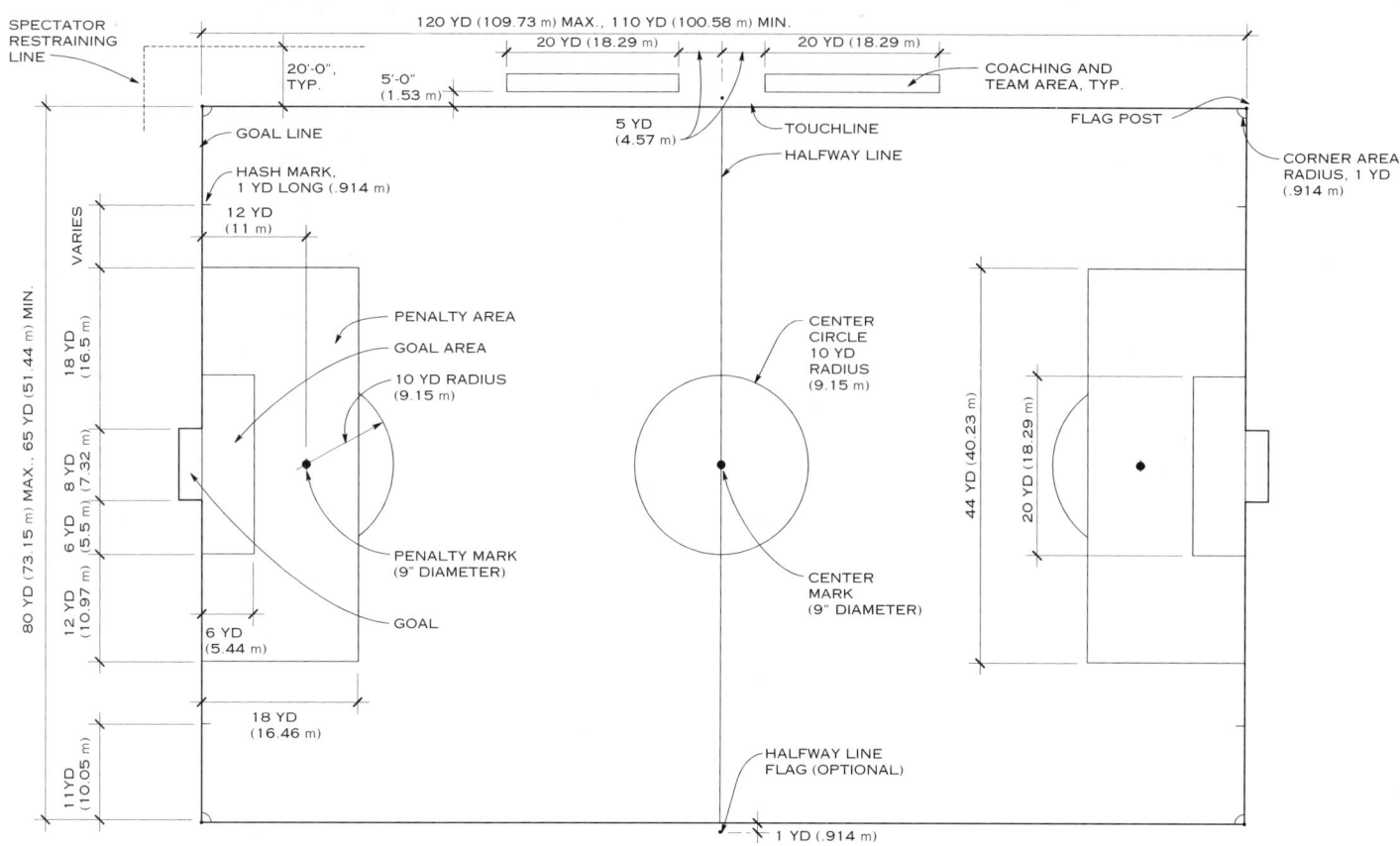

NOTE

For new facilities, the minimum width of the field should be 70 yd (64.01 m) and the minimum length 115 yd (105.15 m).

Recommended field dimensions are 75 yd (68.58 m) wide x 120 yd (109.73 m) long.

NCAA SOCCER

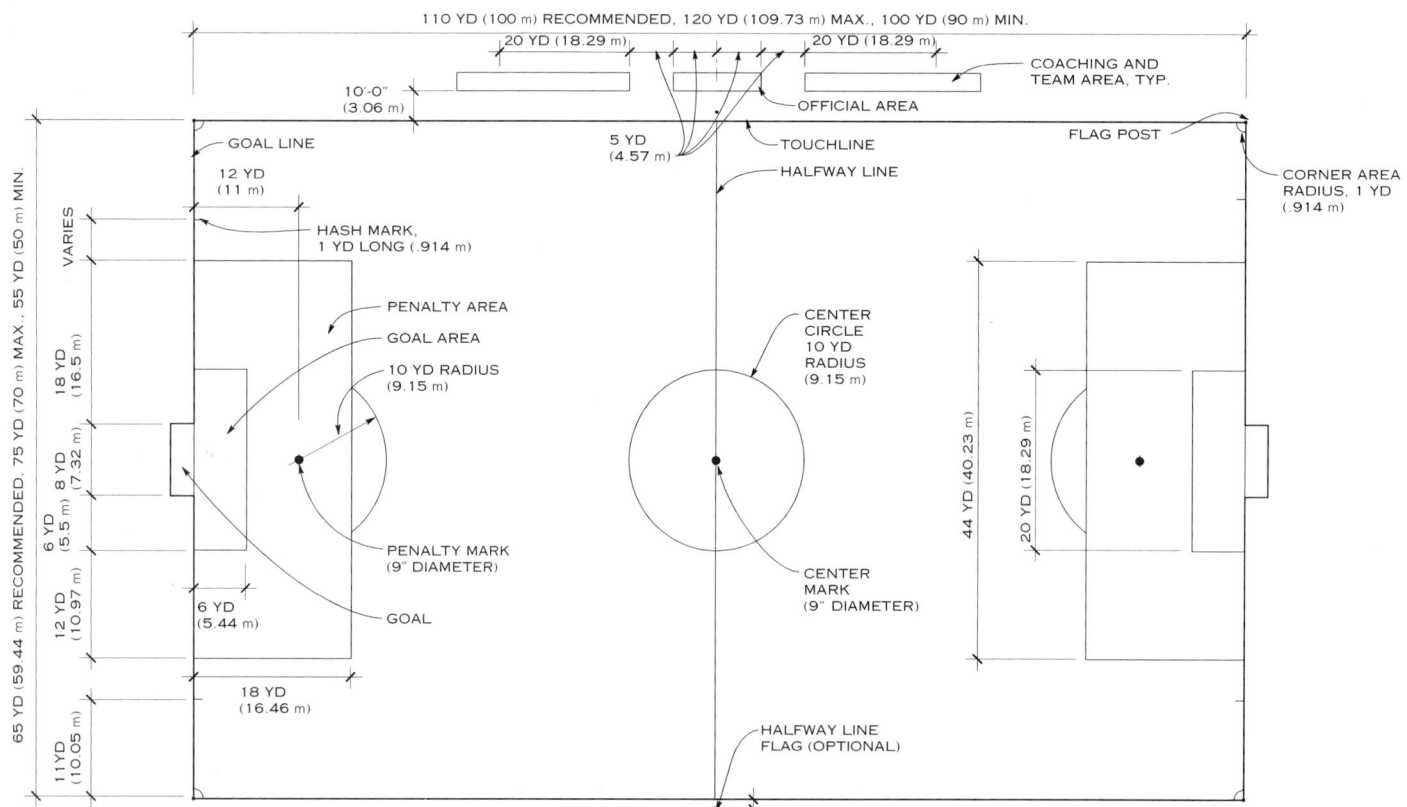

NOTE

Recommended field dimensions for middle school soccer are 55 yd (50 m) wide x 100 yd (90 m) long. Field marking lines should be 4 in. (0.10 m) wide.

HIGH SCHOOL SOCCER

U.S. Soccer Federation; Chicago, Illinois

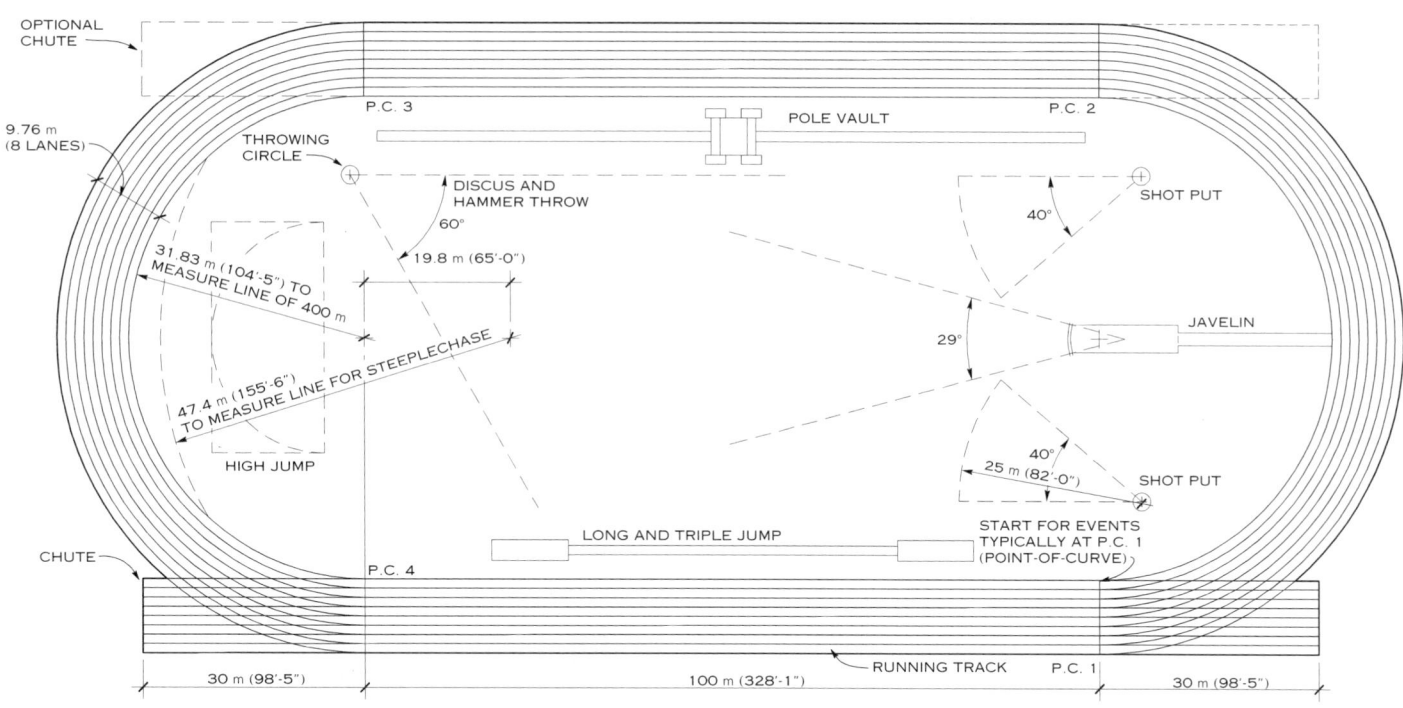

400-METER EQUAL QUADRANT TRACK WITH LAYOUT GUIDE FOR TRACK AND FIELD EVENTS

TRACK SPECIFICATIONS

GOVERNING BODY	LENGTH OF TRACK	WIDTH OF TRACK	RADIUS REQUIREMENTS	INCLINATION	LANE WIDTH	CURB DIMENSIONS AND MATERIAL
International Amateur Athletic Foundation (IAAF)	Not less than 400 m	Minimum 7.32 m (6 lanes), but 8 lanes, each 1.22 m wide, recommended	World records cannot be set on a track when outside lane has a curve radius greater than 50 m	Maximum lateral inclination 1:100; maximum downward inclination in the running direction 1:1000 (lateral inclination down toward inside lane)	Minimum width of 1.22 m (48 in.); the 5 cm wide right lane line is included in the width of the lane	Should be 5 cm x 5 cm, concrete or other material; if curb is raised to allow drainage under it, maximum height is 6.5 cm
National Collegiate Athletic Association (NCAA)	No specified length	6.40 m minimum (6 lanes)	No recommendation	Same as IAAF	Same as IAAF but will permit lanes of at least 91.4 cm (3 ft) if track is not wide enough to accommodate at least 8 wider lanes	Minimum height is 5.08 cm (2 in.) and maximum width is 10.16 cm (4 in.); use concrete, wood, or other suitable material with edges rounded
National Federation of State High School Associations (NFHS)	400 m is standard	No minimum width	No recommendation	Maximum lateral inclination is 2:100; maximum inclination in the running direction is 1:1000	Recommended width 1.07 m (42 in.) ; the 5 cm wide right lane line is included in the width of the lane	Curb will be 5 cm (2 in.) high with a rounded top of solid material
USA Track and Field (USAT&F)	No specified length	No specified width	Same as IAAF	Same as IAAF	Same as NFHS	Same as IAAF, except must be unbroken on curves and straightaways

NOTE

Information in the chart comes from current rules of the governing bodies of track and field and is subject to change. For a specific rules determination, contact the appropriate governing body.

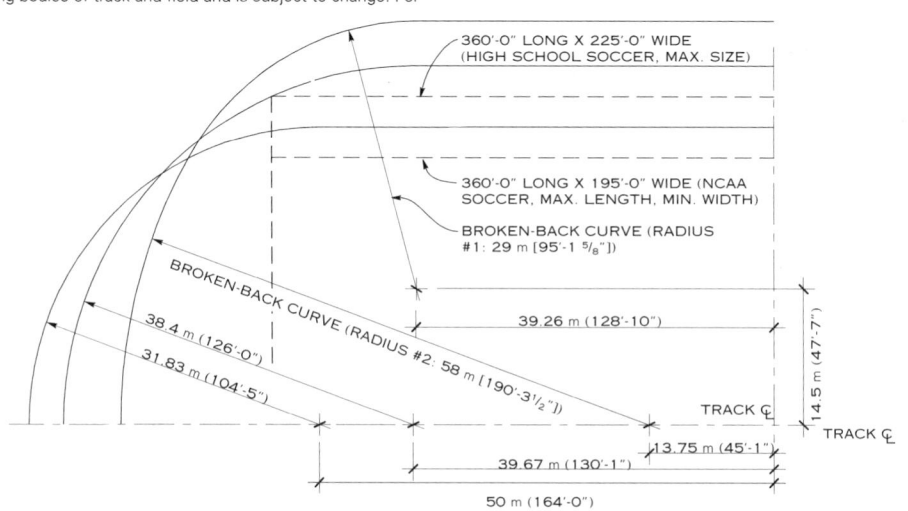

NOTE

When designing a track, consider the official sizes and needs of the interior playing fields and the location and layout of field events. Necessary radii dimensions for several different types of playing field are shown above. Be sure to allow the necessary sideline area for safety and comfort. Use of the International Broken-Back Curve design can permit a wider facility with a layout that still meets all rules.

TRACK AND PLAYING FIELD CONFIGURATION

Kathleen O'Meara; OM Architecture; Baltimore, Maryland
U.S. Tennis Court and Track Builders Association; Ellicott City, Maryland
National Federation of State High School Associations; Kansas City, Missouri

ORIENTATION

It is often difficult in siting a track/playing field to reconcile the requirements regarding wind direction and facing the setting sun. Thus, when possible, it is common to provide alternative directions for running, jumping, and throwing.

SURFACE

Synthetic materials provide a consistently good track surface capable of continuous and unlimited use in most weather conditions. Maintenance is minimal, consisting of periodic cleaning with hose or brush, repainting line markings when necessary, and making an occasional repair.

Cinder surfaces require considerable maintenance by a skilled groundsman every time a track is used. They are not suitable for all-weather use and seldom provide a consistently good running surface. They are, however, much cheaper to construct and are suitable for club use and training.

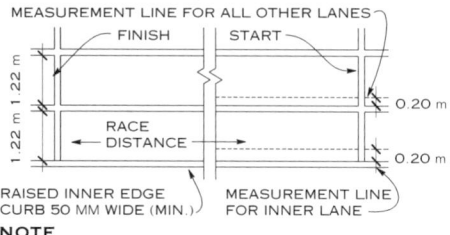

NOTE

All white lines are 55 mm wide.

METHOD OF MARKING LANES

SITE ISSUES FOR OUTDOOR TENNIS COURTS

The overall area required for an individual tennis court is at least 60 x 120 ft. The outside dimensions of the playing lines are 36 x 78 ft for doubles.

Consider the position of the sun when deciding how to orient the court. In particular, plan around the extreme sun angles of late afternoon and early morning so players do not have to look directly into the sun when serving or tracking the ball.

Design the area surrounding the court to minimize distractions. A solid, dark background is desirable. White backgrounds and any movement such as pedestrians or traffic, particularly at the ends of the court, can be distracting. Landscaping or background curtains can be used as screens; however, the space directly over the court must be free from overhanging limbs or other obstructions and the minimum clear height at the fence should be 18 ft. When selecting vegetation, avoid species that would distract with irregular shadow patterns, stain the court surface, or require constant maintenance to clean up fallen leaves, needles, or fruit.

If outdoor lighting is used, locate fixtures outside the playing lines, preferably parallel to the alley lines, and outside the fence. Placement is especially important with fast-dry surfaces that can be damaged by rain dripping off the fixtures.

A high, dry site with well-drained, compacted soil is preferable. Ensure proper drainage of the court surface and the subsurface, and redirect any water from the surrounding area. Water under the court is a prime cause of surface cracking, heaving of fence posts, and undulating pavement. Employ open swales, closed drains, or a combination of the two systems to drain water from the area.

NOTE

The Americans with Disabilities Act requires that tennis courts be accessible to both players and spectators in wheelchairs. At least one court must be fully accessible in a small facility; more may be required in a large facility. Curb cuts, walkways to and from the courts, gateways, drinking fountains, restrooms, locker rooms, and other spectator or player amenities must comply with federal, state, and local codes on accessibility. As well, adequate parking for persons with disabilities must be provided.

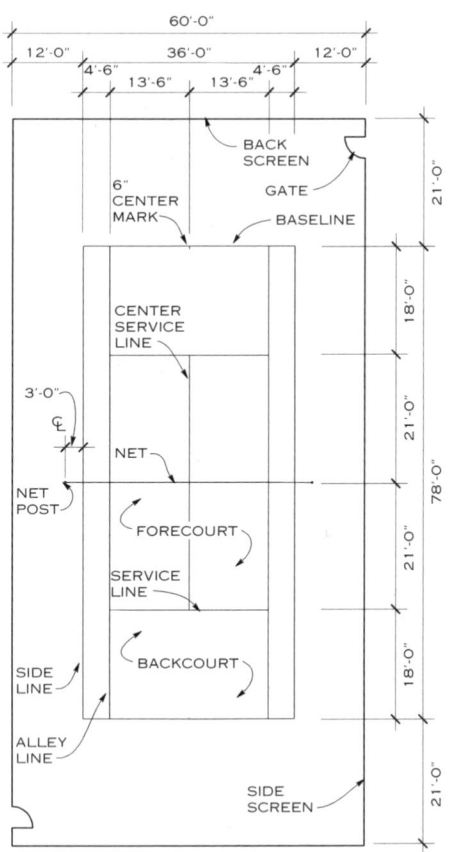

TYPICAL INDIVIDUAL TENNIS COURT

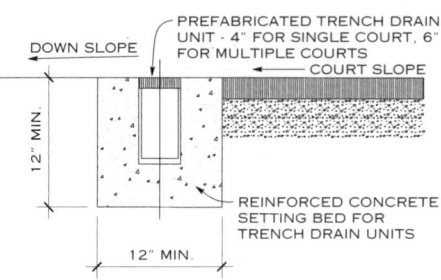

GRATED TRENCH DRAIN

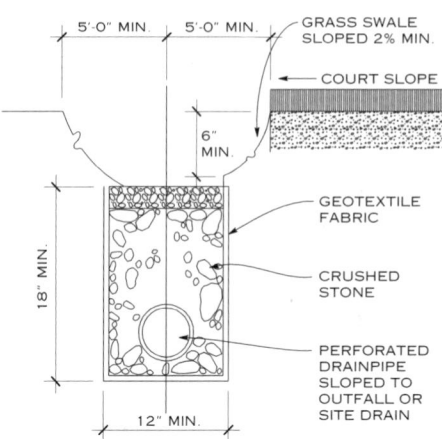

SWALE WITH GRAVEL TRENCH DRAIN

SITE DRAINAGE

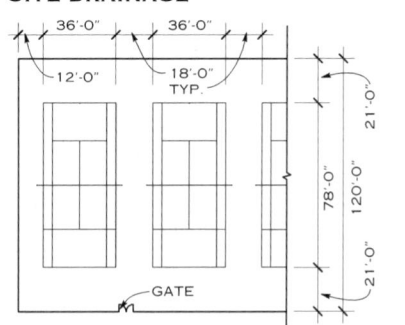

NOTE

Provide at least one gate for every two tennis courts.

TYPICAL MULTIPLE TENNIS COURT LAYOUT

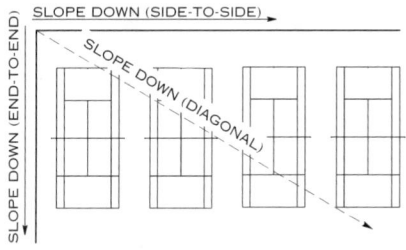

SURFACE TYPE	% SLOPE	RATIO OF SLOPE
Hard surface	0.833% to 1%	1:120 to 1:100
Grass surface	1%	1:100
Soft surface	0.28% to 0.35%	1:360 to 1:288

NOTES

1. Courts must slope as one true plane, with no more than three courts sloped together in the same direction. A slope from side to side is best, followed by an end-to-end slope; diagonally sloped courts are the least satisfactory.
2. Never slope a court to or from the net or to or from the centerline.

COURT SURFACE SLOPE

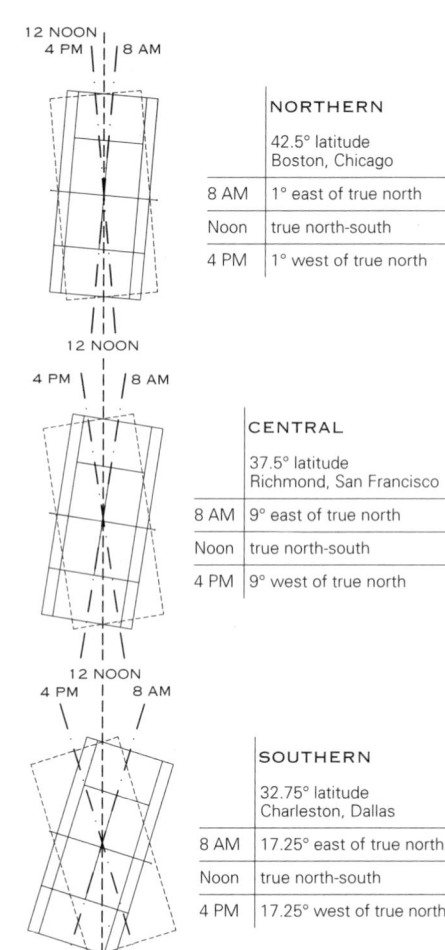

NORTHERN	
42.5° latitude Boston, Chicago	
8 AM	1° east of true north
Noon	true north-south
4 PM	1° west of true north

CENTRAL	
37.5° latitude Richmond, San Francisco	
8 AM	9° east of true north
Noon	true north-south
4 PM	9° west of true north

SOUTHERN	
32.75° latitude Charleston, Dallas	
8 AM	17.25° east of true north
Noon	true north-south
4 PM	17.25° west of true north

NOTE

Base the orientation of a tennis court on the latitude in which it is built, the season(s) it will be used, and the time of day it will be used. It may be necessary to compromise the three factors. A critical determining factor will be the solar orientation of the court during early morning (8 AM) and late afternoon (4 PM) hours, since the angle of the sun is at its most distracting to players and spectators at those times. It is best to locate the longitudinal axis of the court perpendicular to the azimuth of the sun between 8 AM and 4 PM.

COURT ORIENTATION

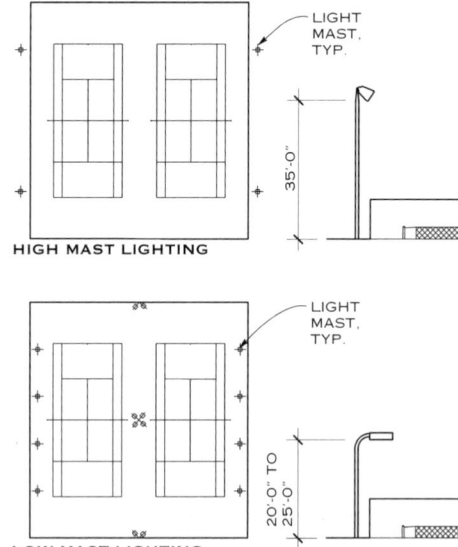

HIGH MAST LIGHTING

LOW MAST LIGHTING

OUTDOOR LIGHTING FOR TENNIS COURTS

Kathleen O'Meara; OM Architecture; Baltimore, Maryland
U.S. Tennis Court and Track Builders Association; Ellicott City, Maryland

OUTDOOR PLAYING SURFACES

Tennis playing surfaces are categorized as porous or nonporous. Geographic location is a key factor in the selection of playing surface for a site. The northeastern United States has numerous freeze-thaw cycles per year, which affect maintenance and the useful life of tennis courts. In the western states, the sun bleaches the color out of hard courts and dries out clay or fast-dry courts. Mildew or algae may be problems at courts in southern states like Florida.

Intended use and player preference are considerations in choosing a court surface. Tennis players commonly classify courts as soft- or hard-surfaced.

Soft courts include clay, fast-dry, and sand-filled synthetic turf. Soft courts are easy on a player's feet and legs and provide cool, glare-free surfaces. They are less expensive to construct than hard surfaces but may require annual resurfacing or repair and the daily maintenance of watering, brooming, and rolling the surface.

Hard courts include asphalt and concrete with acrylic coatings or roll or sheet goods coverings. They are generally more durable, require less maintenance, and offer longer playing seasons in cold climates than soft courts. A resilient layer or layers can be incorporated in a hard surface, providing a cushioned, nonporous, all-weather surface that softens the impact on a player's legs and back. Hard surfaces are generally more expensive to construct than soft surfaces and are easily damaged by street shoes and play equipment such as skateboards or in-line skates.

VISIBILITY IN INDOOR COURTS

A highly reflective ceiling surface and indirect lighting reduce shadows and provide the most even lighting conditions.

For optimum color contrast between the court, background, and ball, medium dark colors are best up to 8 ft along the sides of the court and 12 to 14 ft high behind the court area. Above these zones, white or light matte finish is best.

Perimeter curtains and dividing nets can also be used to provide a background that reduces distractions and keeps the ball from going into adjacent courts. These are generally black or green and are hung so the top of the divider is 12 ft above the floor, stopping 1/2 to 2 in. above the court surface.

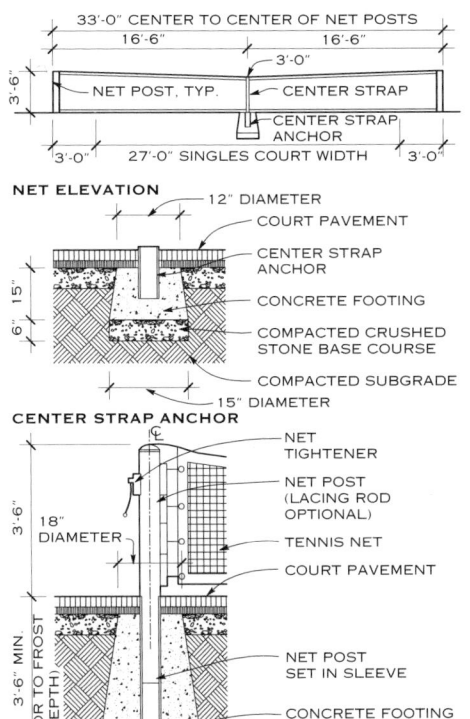

NET ELEVATION

CENTER STRAP ANCHOR

NET POST

NOTE

The net should be installed with the recommended tension of 500 to 550 lb.

NET

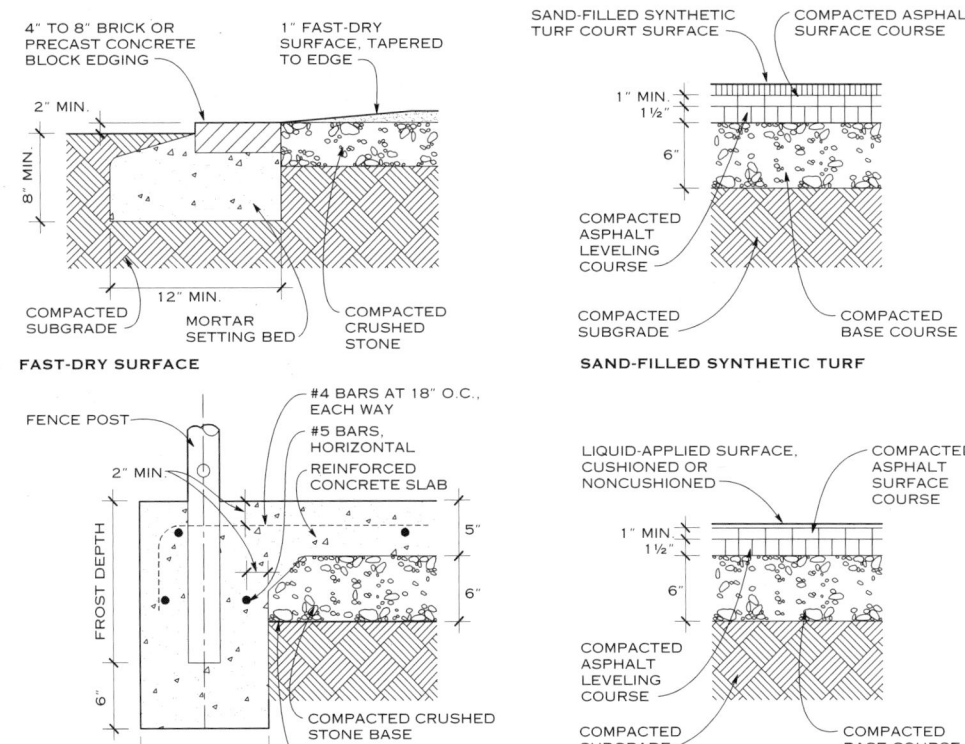

FAST-DRY SURFACE

SAND-FILLED SYNTHETIC TURF

REINFORCED CONCRETE WITH FENCE POST

ASPHALT—FOR FREEZE/THAW

OUTDOOR PLAYING SURFACES

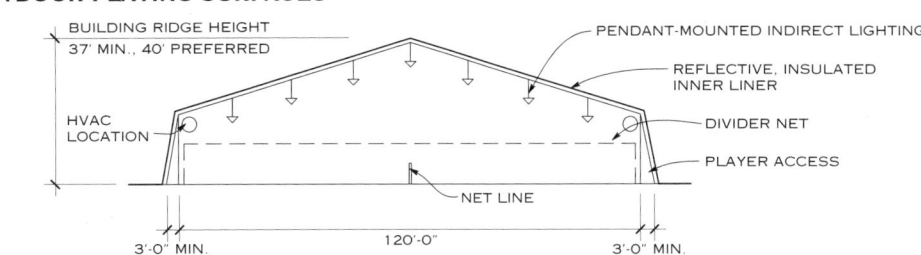

FABRIC FRAME COURT BUILDING—SECTION

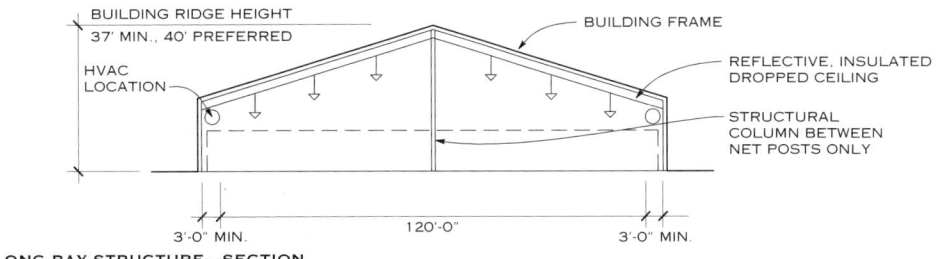

LONG-BAY STRUCTURE—SECTION

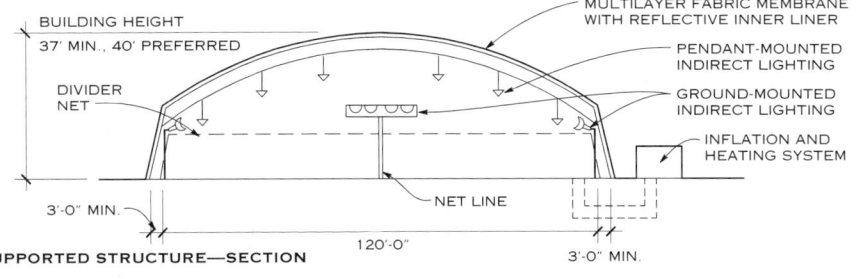

AIR-SUPPORTED STRUCTURE—SECTION

NOTE

Enclosures for tennis courts can be either temporary or permanent structures. They are generally constructed of fabric over a rigid frame, air-supported fabric, or wide-span or long-bay steel structures.

INDOOR COURT BUILDING ENCLOSURES

Kathleen O'Meara; OM Architecture; Baltimore, Maryland
U.S. Tennis Court and Track Builders Association; Ellicott City, Maryland

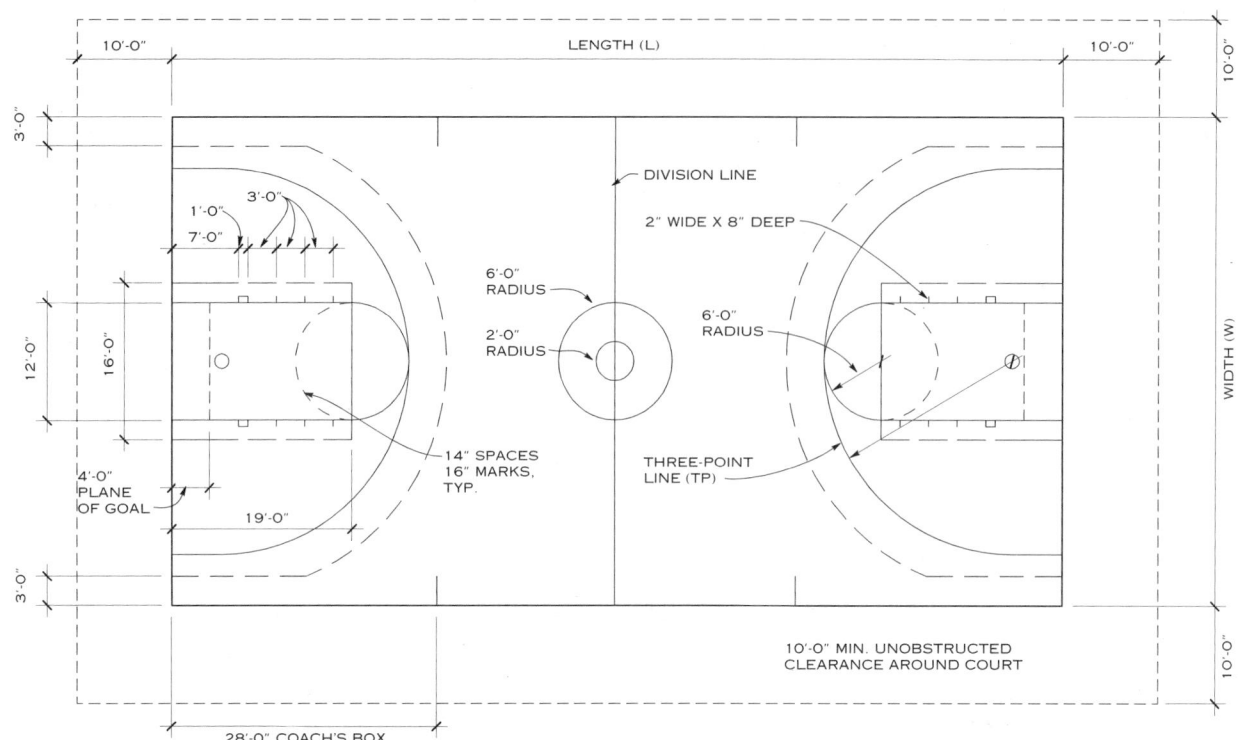

BASKETBALL COURT AND BALL DIMENSIONS

COURT				BASKETBALL				
TYPE	L (FT)	W (FT)	TP (FT-IN.)	TYPE	MAX. DIAMETER (IN.)	MIN. DIAMETER (IN.)	MAX. WEIGHT (OZ)	MIN. WEIGHT (OZ)
NBA	94	50	23-9 R	NBA	30	29.5	22	20
International	94	50	20.61 R	International	30	29.5	22	20
NCAA (men)	94	50	19-9 R	NCAA (men)	30	29.5	22	20
WNBA, NCAA (women)	94	50	19-9 R	WNBA, NCAA (women)	29	28.5	20	18
High school (men)	84	50	19-9 R	High school (men)	30	29.5	22	20
High school (women)	84	50	19-9 R	High school (women)	29	28.5	20	18

L–length   W–width   TP–three-point line

BASKETBALL COURTS

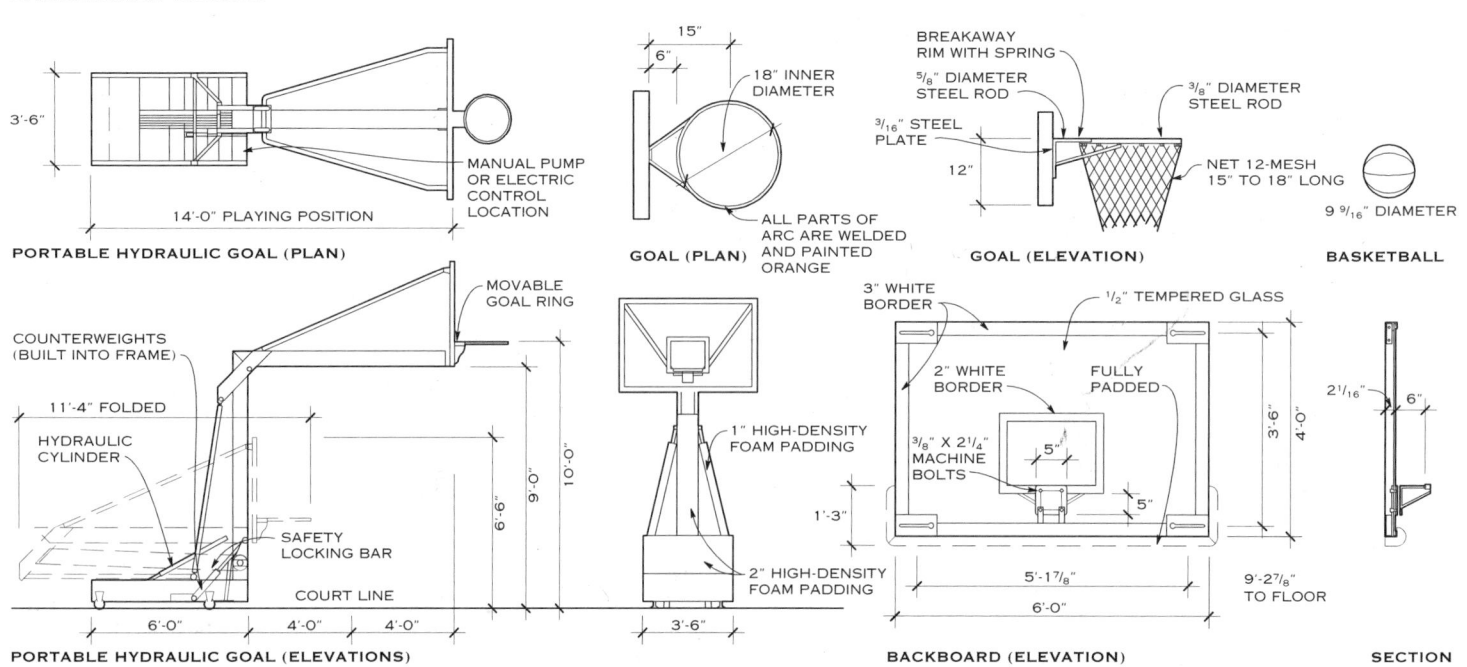

BASKETBALL BACKBOARD AND GOAL

Dean Cox, AIA; Collins Rimer Gordon Architects; Cleveland, Ohio

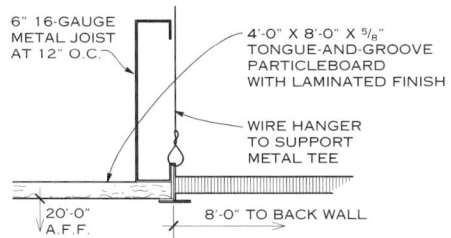

CEILING CONDITION—DETAIL

6" 16-GAUGE METAL JOIST AT 12" O.C.

4'-0" X 8'-0" X ⁵/₈" TONGUE-AND-GROOVE PARTICLEBOARD WITH LAMINATED FINISH

WIRE HANGER TO SUPPORT METAL TEE

20'-0" A.F.F.

8'-0" TO BACK WALL

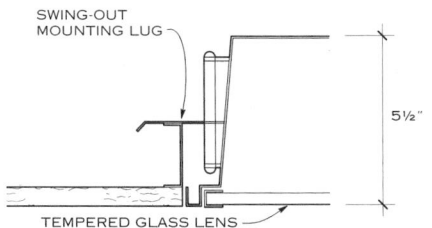

LIGHT FIXTURE—DETAIL

SWING-OUT MOUNTING LUG

5½"

TEMPERED GLASS LENS

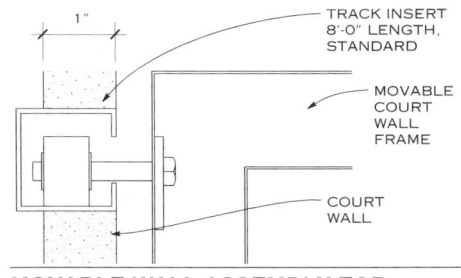

MOVABLE WALL ASSEMBLY FOR COURT CONVERSION—DETAIL

1"

TRACK INSERT 8'-0" LENGTH, STANDARD

MOVABLE COURT WALL FRAME

COURT WALL

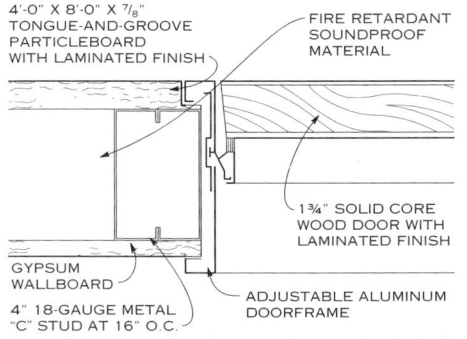

DOOR AT JAMB—DETAIL

4'-0" X 8'-0" X ⁷/₈" TONGUE-AND-GROOVE PARTICLEBOARD WITH LAMINATED FINISH

FIRE RETARDANT SOUNDPROOF MATERIAL

1¾" SOLID CORE WOOD DOOR WITH LAMINATED FINISH

GYPSUM WALLBOARD

4" 18-GAUGE METAL "C" STUD AT 16" O.C.

ADJUSTABLE ALUMINUM DOORFRAME

NOTES

1. Racquetball and handball use essentially the same size court; however, handball may be played on courts with one, three, or four walls, indoors or outdoors. For a standard one-wall handball court, the wall should be 20 ft from the outside edge of one sideline to the outside edge of the other sideline and 16 ft high, including any top line. For three-wall handball, the side walls should be 44 ft long but the court marked for 40 ft long.

2. Temperature and humidity requirements for racquetball courts must be maintained during storage, installation, and operation. The range for temperature is 65 to 78°F and for humidity is 40 to 60%.

3. All lines should be 1¹/₂ in. (38 mm) wide, painted red. Racquetballs are 2 in. in diameter; handballs are 1⁷/₈ in. in diameter.

4. Materials and installation of glass wall systems must comply with the safety and performance standards for walls established by the appropriate court sport association, the manufacturer, and local building codes. For this and other guidelines, contact the U.S. Handball Association or the U.S. Racquetball Association.

5. A movable rear wall unit may be specified to convert a racquetball court that is 40-ft long into a 32-ft long squash court. The World Squash Federation sanctions the use of a 20-ft wide racquetball court for squash, which normally has a court 21 ft wide.

U.S. Racquetball Association; Colorado Springs, Colorado
U.S. Handball Association; Tucson, Arizona

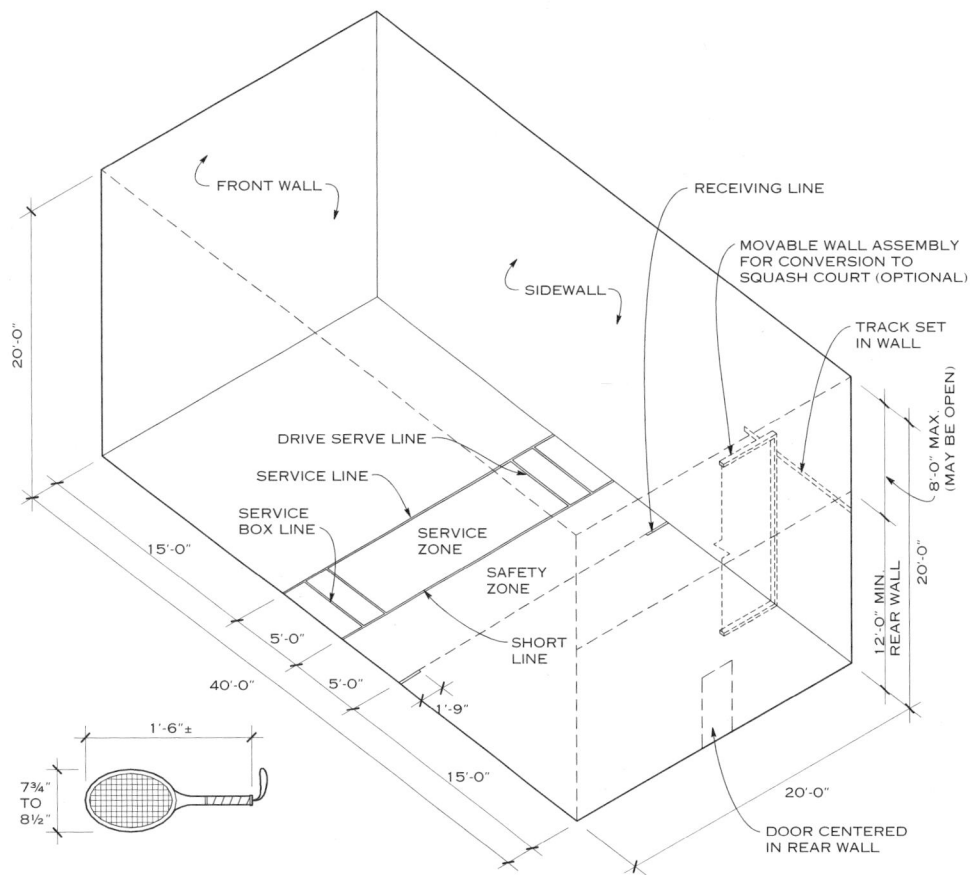

FRONT WALL

RECEIVING LINE

SIDEWALL

MOVABLE WALL ASSEMBLY FOR CONVERSION TO SQUASH COURT (OPTIONAL)

TRACK SET IN WALL

8'-0" MAX (MAY BE OPEN)

20'-0"

DRIVE SERVE LINE

SERVICE LINE

SERVICE BOX LINE

SERVICE ZONE

SAFETY ZONE

SHORT LINE

12'-0" MIN REAR WALL

20'-0"

15'-0"

5'-0"

40'-0"

5'-0"

1'-9"

15'-0"

20'-0"

DOOR CENTERED IN REAR WALL

1'-6"±

7¾" TO 8½"

RACQUETBALL COURT

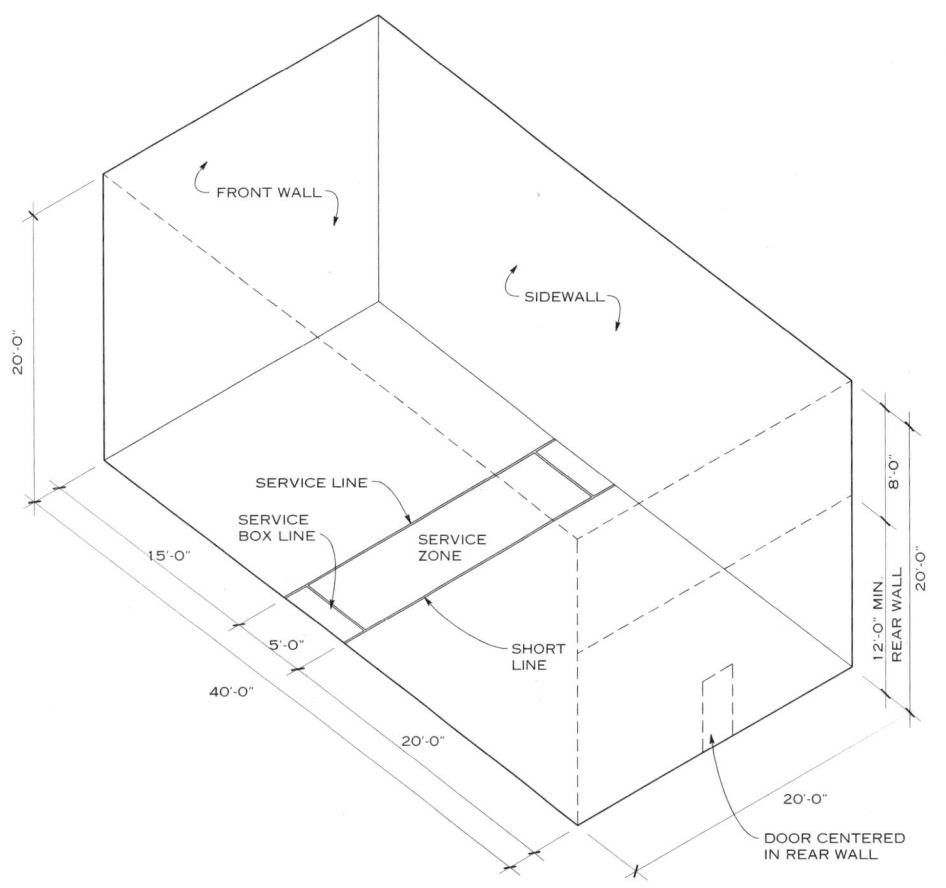

FRONT WALL

SIDEWALL

20'-0"

SERVICE LINE

SERVICE BOX LINE

SERVICE ZONE

SHORT LINE

8'-0"

20'-0"

12'-0" MIN REAR WALL

15'-0"

5'-0"

40'-0"

20'-0"

20'-0"

DOOR CENTERED IN REAR WALL

HANDBALL COURT

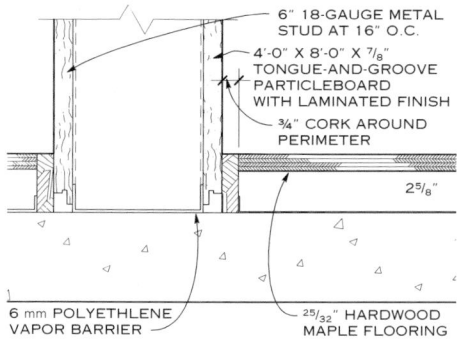

6" 18-GAUGE METAL STUD AT 16" O.C.

4'-0" X 8'-0" X 7/8" TONGUE-AND-GROOVE PARTICLEBOARD WITH LAMINATED FINISH

3/4" CORK AROUND PERIMETER

2 5/8"

6 mm POLYETHLENE VAPOR BARRIER

25/32" HARDWOOD MAPLE FLOORING

SECTION AT COMMON SIDEWALL

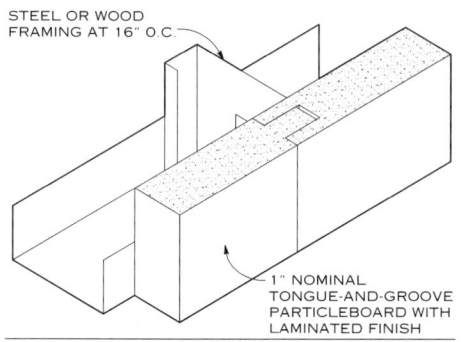

STEEL OR WOOD FRAMING AT 16" O.C.

1" NOMINAL TONGUE-AND-GROOVE PARTICLEBOARD WITH LAMINATED FINISH

COURT WALL—DETAIL

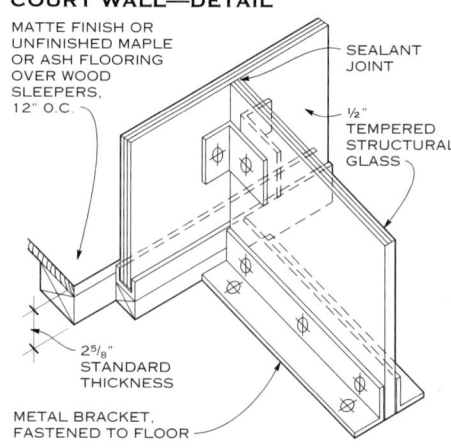

MATTE FINISH OR UNFINISHED MAPLE OR ASH FLOORING OVER WOOD SLEEPERS, 12" O.C.

SEALANT JOINT

1/2" TEMPERED STRUCTURAL GLASS

2 5/8" STANDARD THICKNESS

METAL BRACKET, FASTENED TO FLOOR

GLASS WALL SYSTEM—DETAIL

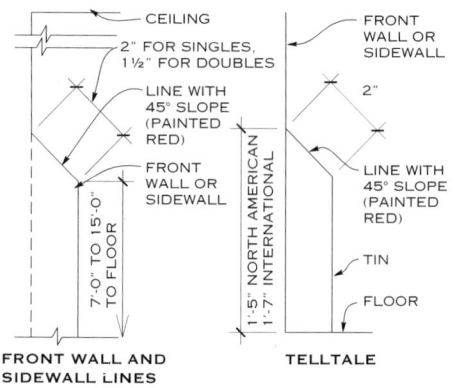

CEILING

2" FOR SINGLES, 1 1/2" FOR DOUBLES

LINE WITH 45° SLOPE (PAINTED RED)

FRONT WALL OR SIDEWALL

7'-0" TO 15'-0" TO FLOOR

FRONT WALL OR SIDEWALL

2"

LINE WITH 45° SLOPE (PAINTED RED)

TIN

FLOOR

1'-5" NORTH AMERICAN 1'-7" INTERNATIONAL

FRONT WALL AND SIDEWALL LINES

TELLTALE

COURT MARKINGS

NOTES

1. All playing walls of the court should be constructed of the same materials, with a hard, smooth finish and strength and deflection characteristics as defined by the World Squash Federation or the United States Squash Racquets Association.

2. A squash court may be constructed from a number of materials, providing they have suitable ball rebound characteristics and are safe for play as recommended by the governing squash association.

Kenneth D. Jaffe; U.S. Squash Racquets Association; Bala-Cynwyd, Pennsylvania

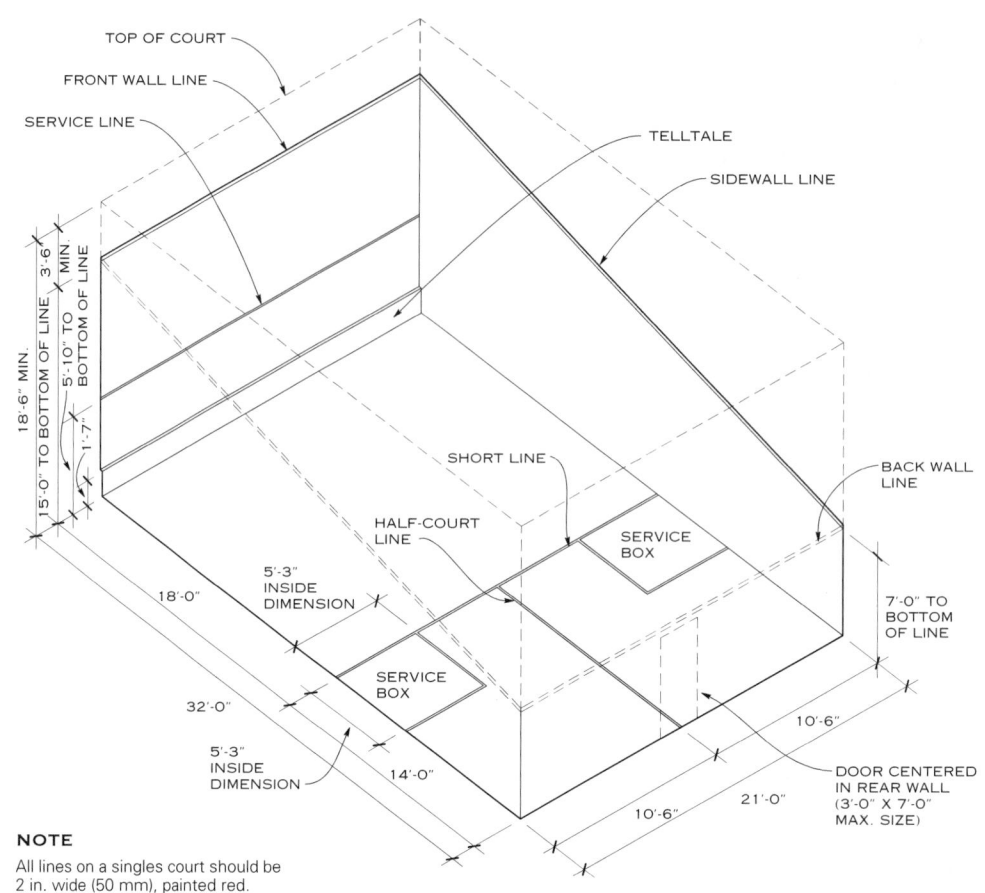

TOP OF COURT

FRONT WALL LINE

SERVICE LINE

TELLTALE

SIDEWALL LINE

SHORT LINE

BACK WALL LINE

HALF-COURT LINE

SERVICE BOX

SERVICE BOX

7'-0" TO BOTTOM OF LINE

18'-6" MIN.

15'-0" TO BOTTOM OF LINE

3'-6" MIN

5'-10" TO BOTTOM OF LINE

1'-7"

18'-0"

5'-3" INSIDE DIMENSION

32'-0"

5'-3" INSIDE DIMENSION

14'-0"

10'-6"

10'-6"

21'-0"

DOOR CENTERED IN REAR WALL (3'-0" X 7'-0" MAX. SIZE)

NOTE

All lines on a singles court should be 2 in. wide (50 mm), painted red.

INTERNATIONAL SINGLES SQUASH COURT (SOFT BALL)

TOP OF COURT

SERVICE LINE

TELLTALE

FRONT WALL

31'-0"

SIDEWALL

14'-0"

20'-0"

8'-2" TO TOP OF LINE

1'-5"

SERVICE QUARTER-CIRCLE

HALF-COURT LINE

SHORT LINE

30'-0"

4'-6" RADIUS

45'-0"

15'-0"

7'-0" REAR WALL

15'-0"

5'-0"

12'-6"

12'-6"

25'-0"

DOOR CENTERED IN REAR WALL (3'-0" X 7'-0" MAX. SIZE)

NOTES

1. Lines on a doubles court should be 1 in. wide, except the upper game line, which should be a 1 1/2 in. wide bevel.

2. The ceiling height of the doubles court should be a minimum of 24 ft high, with the lighting at that height.

NORTH AMERICAN DOUBLES SQUASH COURT (HARD BALL)

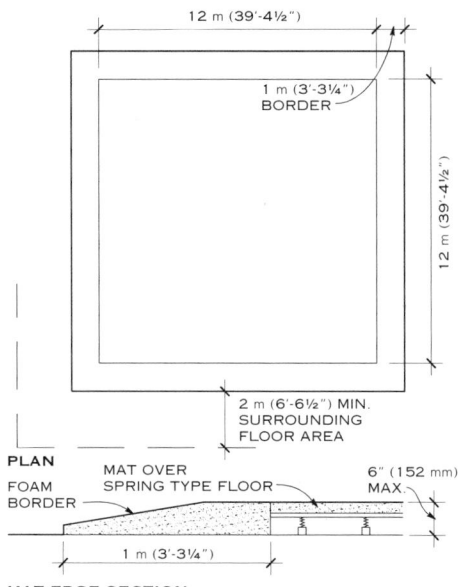

12 m (39'-4½")

1 m (3'-3¼")
BORDER

12 m (39'-4½")

2 m (6'-6½") MIN.
SURROUNDING
FLOOR AREA

PLAN

MAT OVER
SPRING TYPE FLOOR
FOAM
BORDER

6" (152 mm)
MAX.

1 m (3'-3¼")

MAT EDGE SECTION

FLOOR EXERCISE MAT

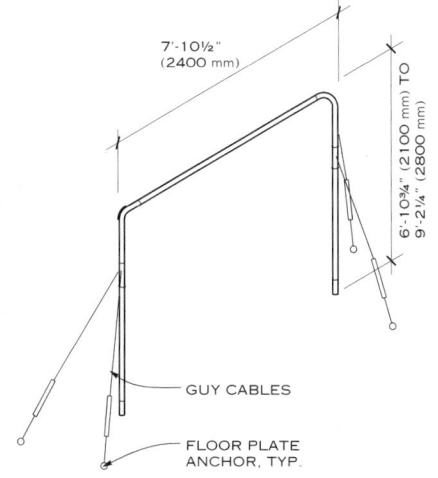

7'-10½"
(2400 mm)

6'-10¾" (2100 mm) TO
9'-2¼" (2800 mm)

GUY CABLES

FLOOR PLATE
ANCHOR, TYP.

NOTE

Bar height typically adjusts in 50 mm increments.

HORIZONTAL BAR

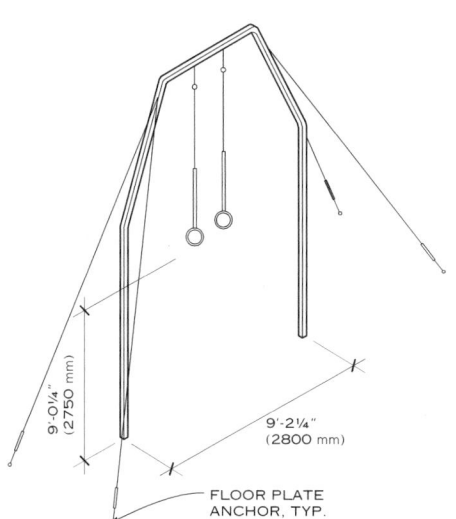

9'-0¼"
(2750 mm)

9'-2¼"
(2800 mm)

FLOOR PLATE
ANCHOR, TYP.

RINGS AND RING FRAME

Richard J. Vitullo, AIA; Oak Leaf Studio; Crownsville, Maryland

---

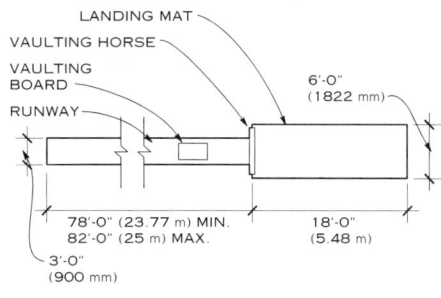

LANDING MAT
VAULTING HORSE
VAULTING
BOARD
RUNWAY

6'-0"
(1822 mm)

78'-0" (23.77 m) MIN.
82'-0" (25 m) MAX.

18'-0"
(5.48 m)

3'-0"
(900 mm)

VAULTING RUNWAY

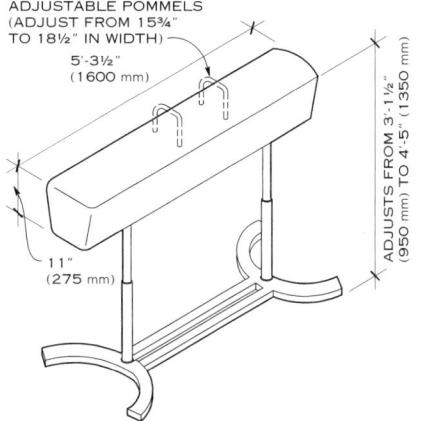

ADJUSTABLE POMMELS
(ADJUST FROM 15¾"
TO 18½" IN WIDTH)

5'-3½"
(1600 mm)

ADJUSTS FROM 3'-1½"
(950 mm) TO 4'-5" (1350 mm)

11"
(275 mm)

NOTE

A practice vaulting buck is similar to a vaulting horse but is only 2 ft 9 in. (825 mm) long.

VAULTING AND POMMEL HORSE

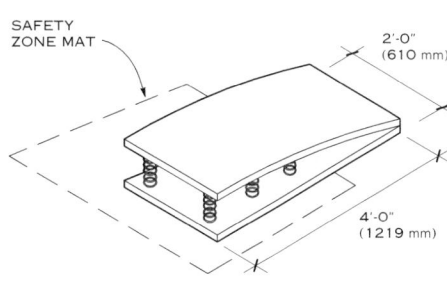

SAFETY
ZONE MAT

2'-0"
(610 mm)

4'-0"
(1219 mm)

NOTE

A safety zone mat is placed snugly around the board for all round-off entry vaults.

VAULTING BOARD

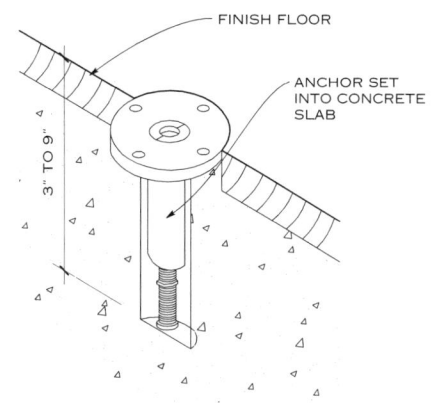

FINISH FLOOR

ANCHOR SET
INTO CONCRETE
SLAB

3' TO 9'

NOTE

Floor plates, installed flush with the top of the floor finish, are used to anchor horizontal bars, ring frames, etc., to the floor. Plates must be used with eye screw attachments.

FLOOR PLATE DETAIL

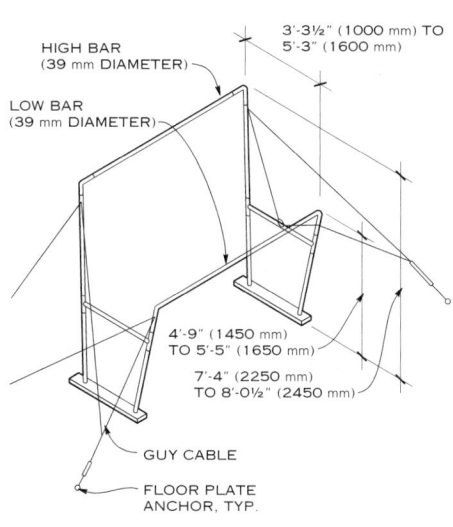

HIGH BAR
(39 mm DIAMETER)

LOW BAR
(39 mm DIAMETER)

3'-3½" (1000 mm) TO
5'-3" (1600 mm)

4'-9" (1450 mm)
TO 5'-5" (1650 mm)

7'-4" (2250 mm)
TO 8'-0½" (2450 mm)

GUY CABLE

FLOOR PLATE
ANCHOR, TYP.

NOTE

Bar height typically adjusts in 50 mm increments.

UNEVEN BARS

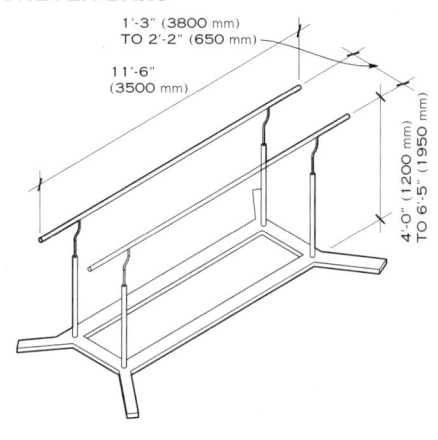

1'-3" (3800 mm)
TO 2'-2" (650 mm)

11'-6"
(3500 mm)

4'-0" (1200 mm)
TO 6'-5 (1950 mm)

PARALLEL BARS

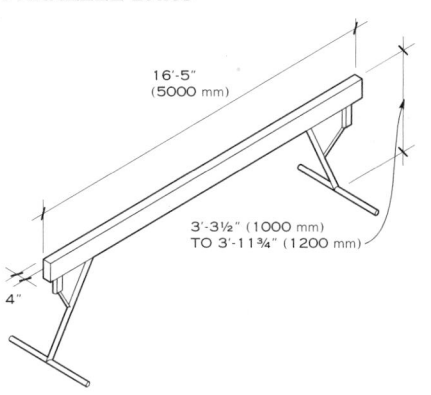

16'-5"
(5000 mm)

3'-3½" (1000 mm)
TO 3'-11¾" (1200 mm)

4"

BALANCE BEAM

NOTES

1. The dimensions and specifications on this page are for general reference only. Refer to the appropriate safety manual for specific requirements for recreational or training gymnastics or for state, regional, national, and international competitions: Federation Internationale de Gymnastique (FIG); U.S.A. Gymnastics (USAG); National Collegiate Athletic Association (NCAA); and National Federation of State High School Associations (NFSH).

2. A clearance of 5 to 6 ft is recommended from one apparatus to another, including corresponding mat area or obstructions such as other apparatus, walls, or columns. Each competitive area must have its own physical space, which may not overlap another competitive area. The floor exercise area must be free of obstructions. Leave room for mounting, dismounting, and vaulting areas.

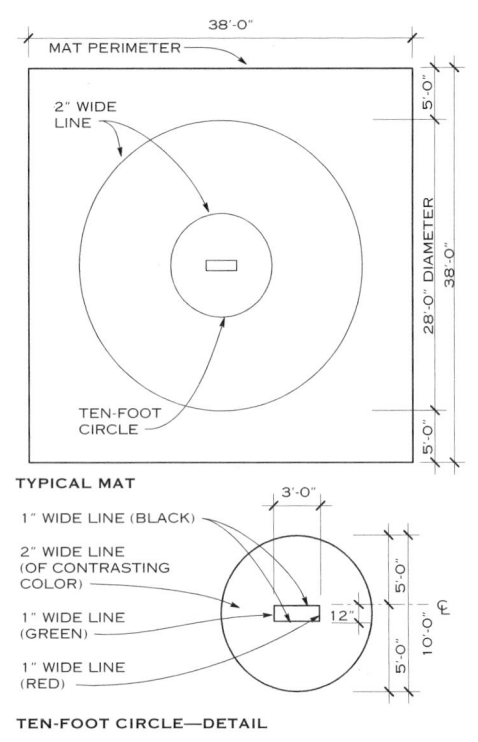

TYPICAL MAT

1" WIDE LINE (BLACK)
2" WIDE LINE (OF CONTRASTING COLOR)
1" WIDE LINE (GREEN)
1" WIDE LINE (RED)

TEN-FOOT CIRCLE—DETAIL

WRESTLING

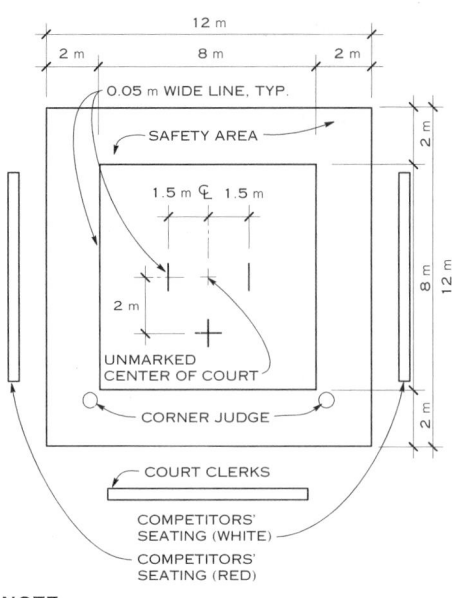

NOTE

Ceilings should be a minimum of 10 ft high to accommodate the swinging of swords and bows. Structural support is needed in the ceiling for the heavy bags used in karate. Eight 100-lb bags are located approximately 4 ft on center. Doors should not open into the mat area, and no mirrors or windows should be nearby.

KARATE

PLAN

2 LAYERS OF ¾" PLYWOOD SCREWED INTO BASE
2 LAYERS OF ¾" RUBBER INSERTED INTO PLYWOOD
THREADED STEEL ROD (3 PER PLATFORM, TYP.)
4 X 4 WOOD PIECES IN SERIES, FASTENED TOGETHER WITH THREADED RODS, TYP.

PLATFORM DETAIL

NOTE

Platform is required to be between 5 and 15 cm high (2 to 6 in.), constructed of materials that can absorb the shock caused by normally returned weights.

WEIGHT LIFTING

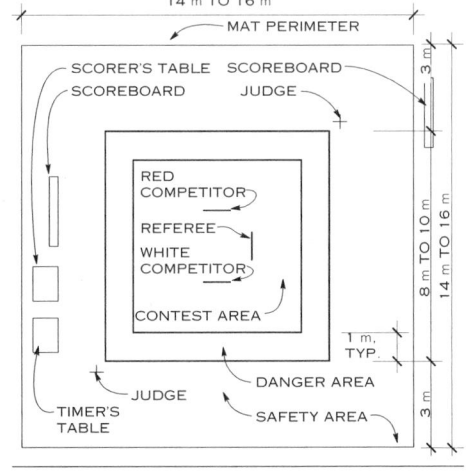

AMATEUR BOXING

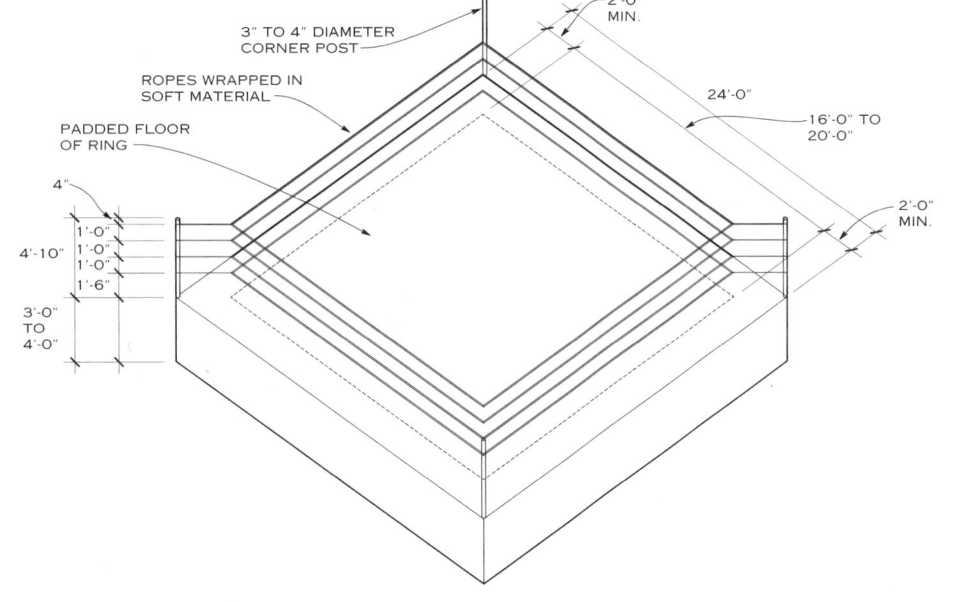

JUDO

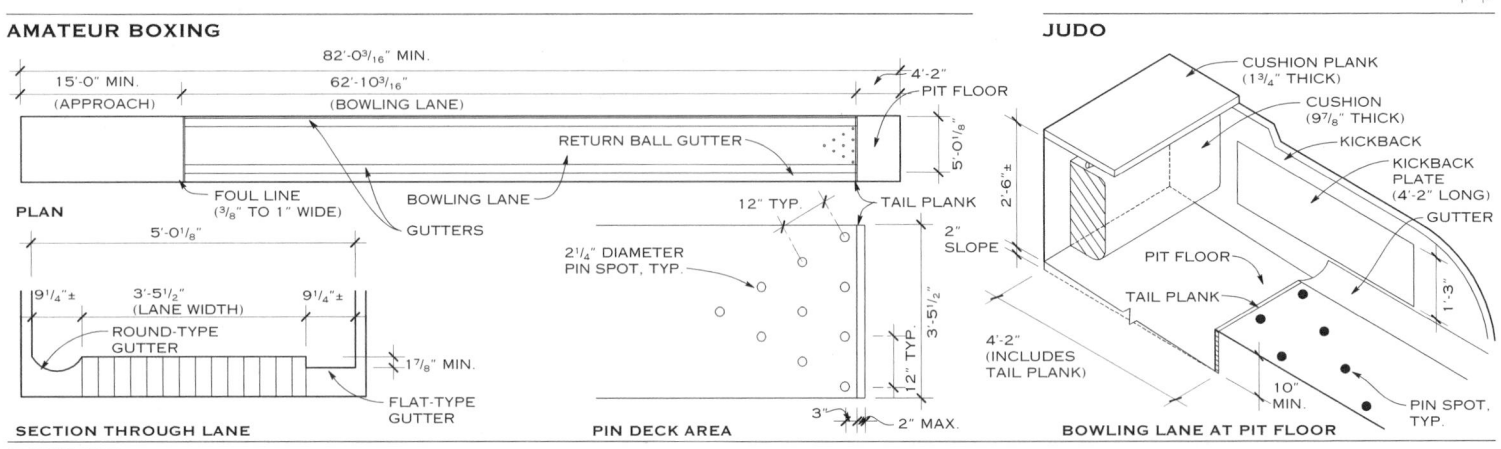

PLAN

SECTION THROUGH LANE

PIN DECK AREA

BOWLING LANE AT PIT FLOOR

BOWLING

Richard J. Vitullo, AIA; Oak Leaf Studio Architects; Crownsville, Maryland

17 COURT SPORTS

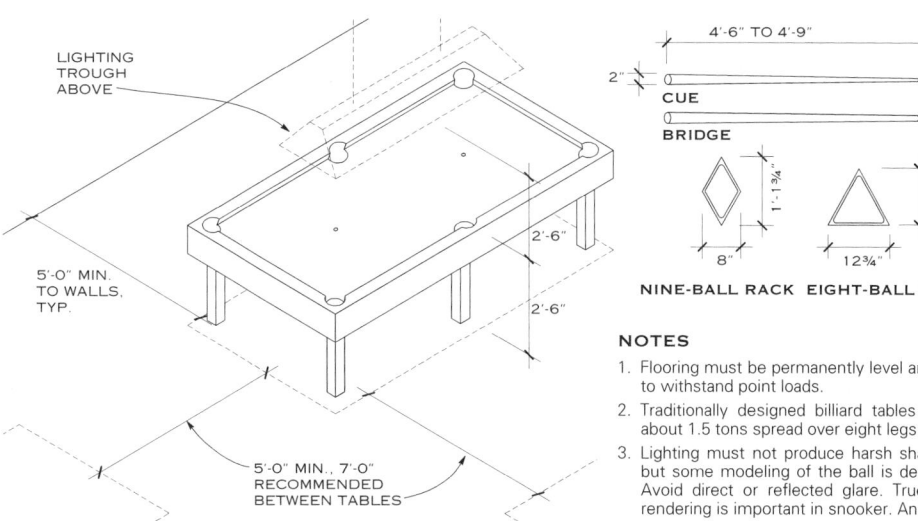

NINE-BALL RACK   EIGHT-BALL RACK

TABLE DIMENSIONS (FT-IN.)

TYPE OF TABLE	PLAYING SURFACE		TABLE SIZE	
	W	L	W	L
English (Snooker)	7-2	14-4	8-2	15-4
Standard 9 ft	4-2	8-4	5-2	9-4
Standard 8 ft	3-8	7-4	4-8	8-4
Standard 7 ft	3-2	6-4	4-2	7-4
Oversized 8 ft	3-10	7-8	4-10	8-8

NOTES

1. Flooring must be permanently level and able to withstand point loads.
2. Traditionally designed billiard tables weigh about 1.5 tons spread over eight legs.
3. Lighting must not produce harsh shadows, but some modeling of the ball is desirable. Avoid direct or reflected glare. True color rendering is important in snooker. An overall bright light is needed for each table; natural lighting is not essential. Lighting at the table surface should be approximately 375 lumens, which can be achieved with three 150-watt tungsten filament lamps suspended in a lighting trough. Fluorescent lamps are unacceptable.
4. Some sound insulation is required to prevent distractions from outside the playing area.

BILLIARDS, POCKET BILLIARDS, AND SNOOKER

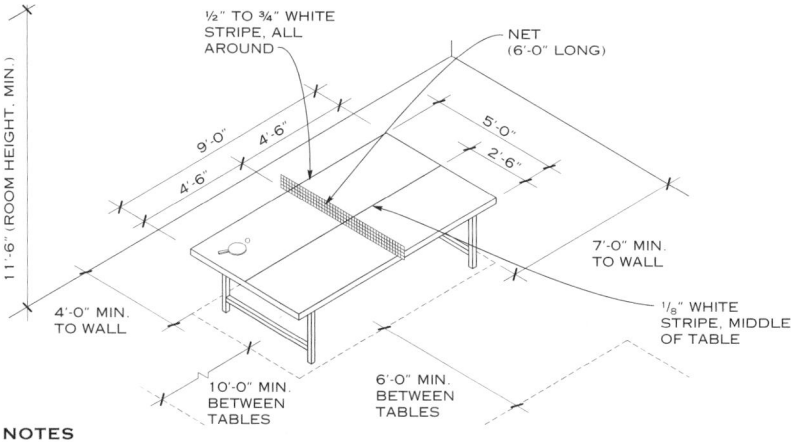

NOTES

1. Flooring should be level and slightly resilient; do not use nonskid material.
2. Walls should provide a uniformly dark, matte background with enough contrast to help players follow the ball.
3. Lighting often varies for different standards of play, but 150 to 500 lumens at table height is the acceptable range. Do not use fluorescent or natural lighting; tungsten halogen lighting is preferable.
4. Sectional tables are stored upright when not in use.

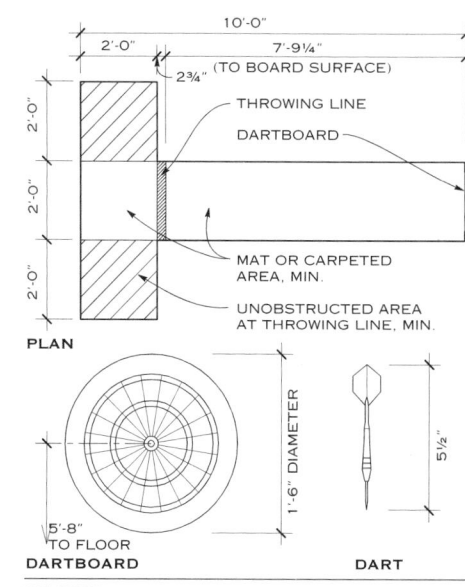

PLAN

DARTBOARD   **DART**

DARTS

TABLE TENNIS

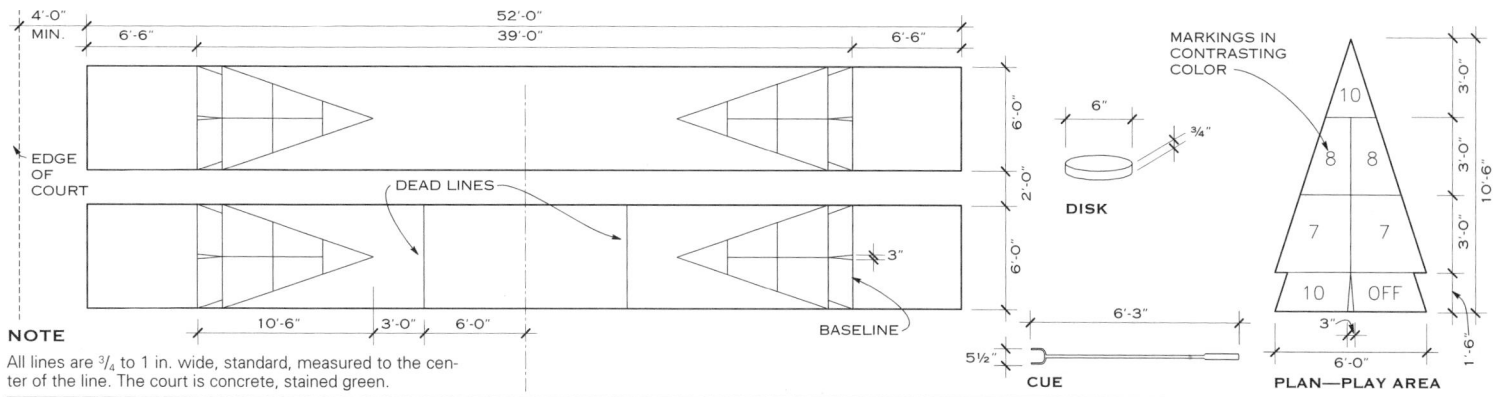

NOTE

All lines are 3/4 to 1 in. wide, standard, measured to the center of the line. The court is concrete, stained green.

DISK

CUE

PLAN—PLAY AREA

SHUFFLEBOARD

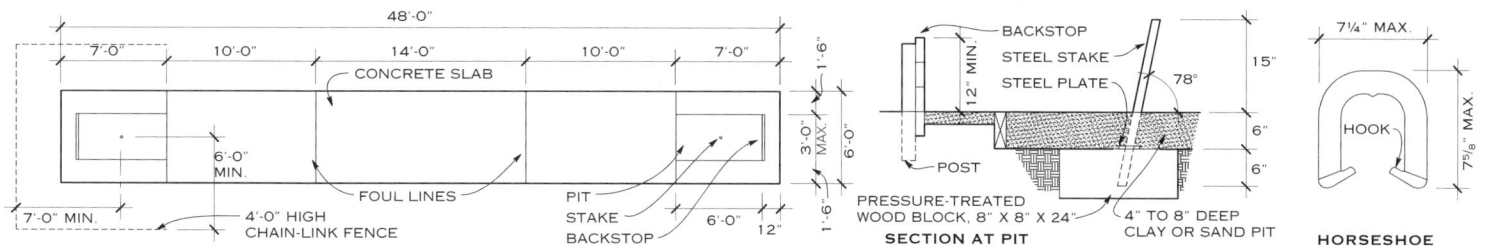

SECTION AT PIT

HORSESHOE

HORSESHOES

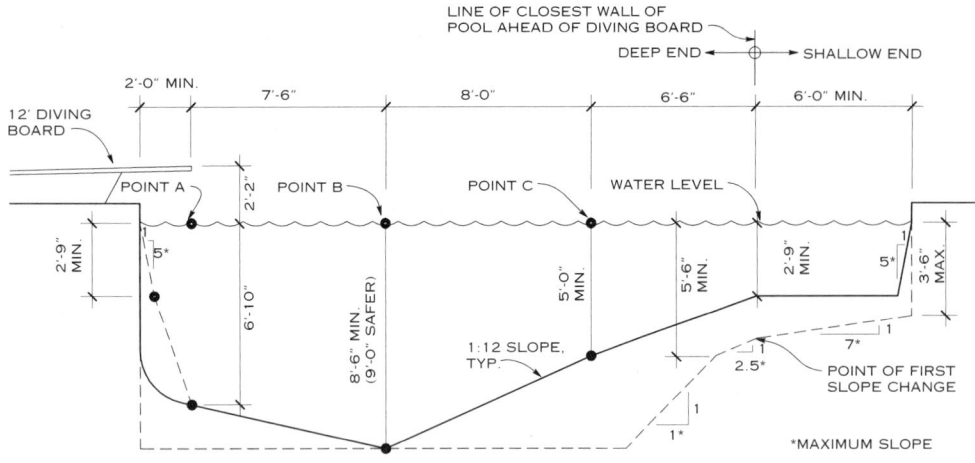

NOTE

For a 10-ft board, Point B must be 8 ft 0 in. (8 ft 6 in. is safer).

LONGITUDINAL SECTION AT CENTERLINE (TYPE III POOL)

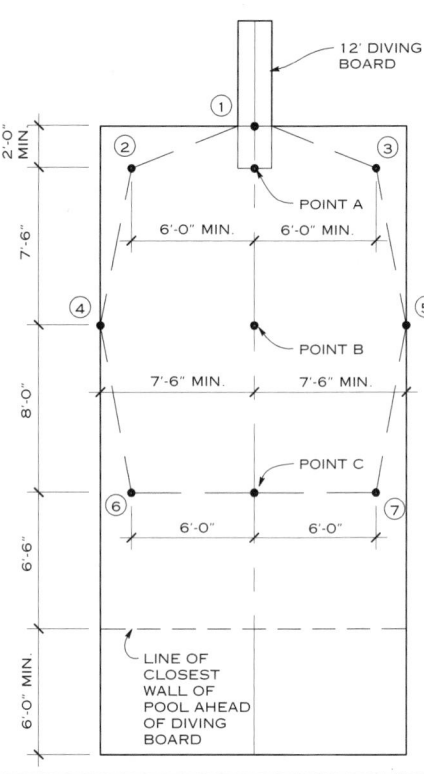

7-POINT GRID DIMENSION PLAN

PERMITS AND RESTRICTIONS

In most areas, permits are required from building, health, plumbing, and electrical departments and zoning boards. Check for setback restrictions and easements covering power and telephone lines, sewers, and storm drains.

CONSTRUCTION AND SHAPES

Residential pools are generally made of gunite (a mixture of pea stone, sand, cement, fly ash, and water sprayed on a steel reinforcement rod framework), a vinyl liner with a structural wall backup and formed floor (steel or thermoplastic vertical wall sections and lightweight concrete or sand base), or a prefabricated fiberglass shell (used primarily where high water tables and nonfrost penetrating conditions exist). Shapes are virtually unlimited within limitations for safety and minimum dimensions.

FILTERING

Filtration is the mechanical process of removing insoluble matter from swimming pool water. Pool water carrying particulate matter, solids, and debris is passed through filtering media and returned to the pool.

Pool water flows through the filters by pressure or vacuum. As water passes through the filter, particulate matter and solids collect on the surface of the filter medium. The ability to hold and screen fine particles varies according to filter type. Three basic media are used for swimming pool filtration—diatomaceous earth, sand, and cartridge filters.

Filters are sized by dividing the pool volume by the required turnover time (established by the local board of health), then dividing that figure by 60 min/hr, which equals the flow rate in GPM. Divide the flow rate in GPM by the filtration rate (established by the board of health), which is in GPM/sq ft. The result is the required filter area in sq ft.

HEATERS AND PUMPS

Pool heaters have become a necessity for user comfort and maintenance of proper chemical balance. Heater size is determined by the frequency of pool use, the size of the pool, and the average outside air temperature. Use a pool cover to minimize evaporation. A solar cover can add heat to a pool.

The size of a pool pump establishes the limit of the volume of water that can be recirculated. The pump causes water to flow and determines the direction of flow. Pump capacity is measured in GPM for flow and in feet of head for pressure.

In most swimming pools, filtered pool water is returned below the water surface; thus, after the pump has been primed and all air expelled, the pump need only overcome the friction in the piping system and the pressure drop across the filter to maintain consistent circulation.

WATER TREATMENT

Pool water must be disinfected and recirculated. Seven principal factors are balanced by basic chemically treated water: total alkalinity, pH balance, calcium hardness, free available disinfectant, total disinfectant, total dissolved solids, temperature.

Many alternative combinations of chemicals are available for water treatment, but growing concern over using chemical treatment alone has led to the development of ozone-based systems. Ozone generators are used to disinfect and oxidize the water, making it more easily filtered and decreasing the amount of sanitizer needed.

NOTES

1. The drawings above illustrate the use of a 7-point dimension grid that expresses the minimum desirable dimensions to be used when specifying or designing a rectangular pool for residential use.

2. Width, length, and depth dimensions may apply to residential pools of any shape.

3. The minimum length with diving board and wading area is 32 ft. The average length of a residential pool is 32–40 ft.

4. Standards for residential swimming pools have been published by the National Spa and Pool Institute (1989).

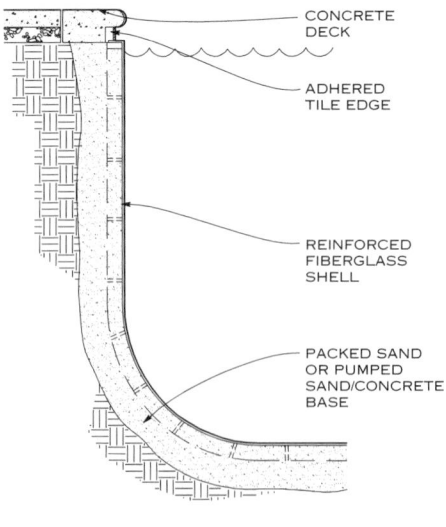

VINYL POOL LINER OVER STRUCTURAL POLYMER WALL

FIBERGLASS SHELL POOL

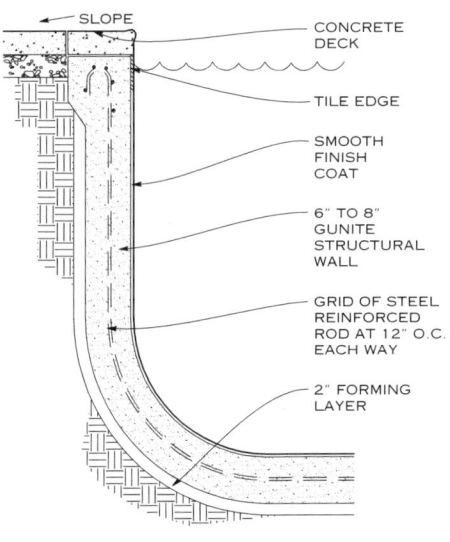

FORMED CONCRETE (GUNITE) WALL AND DECK

Robert D. Buckley, AIA; robert d. buckley * architect; Kalamazoo, Michigan
D. J. Hunsaker; Counsilman/Hunsaker & Associates; St. Louis, Missouri
National Swimming Pool Foundation; Merrick, New York

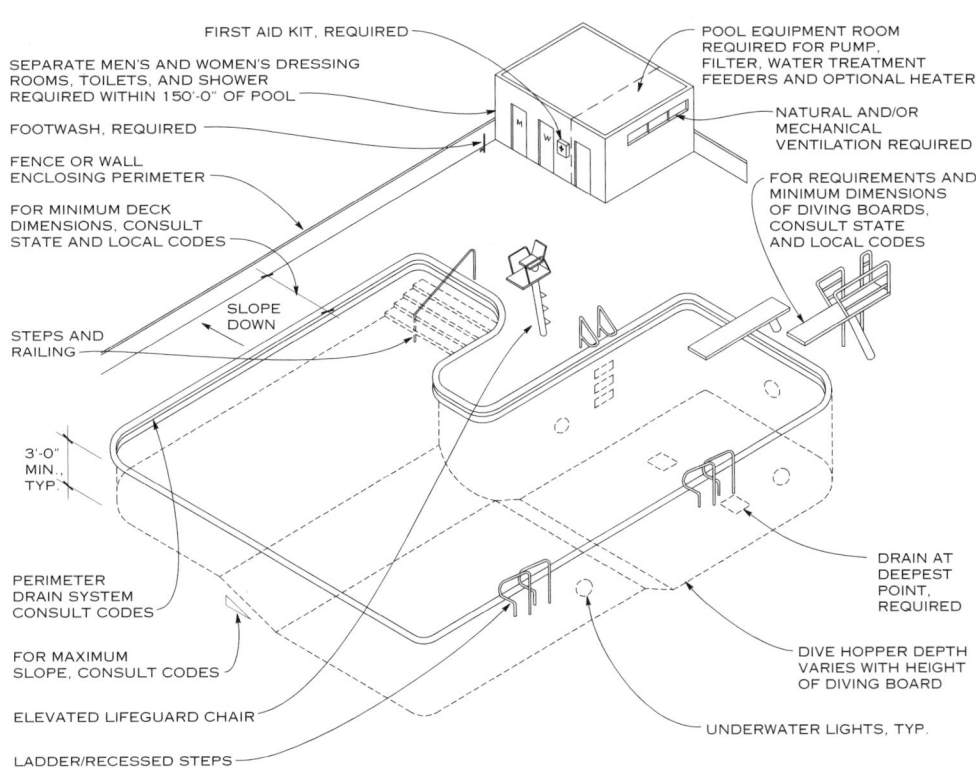

FIRST AID KIT, REQUIRED

SEPARATE MEN'S AND WOMEN'S DRESSING ROOMS, TOILETS, AND SHOWER REQUIRED WITHIN 150'-0" OF POOL

FOOTWASH, REQUIRED

FENCE OR WALL ENCLOSING PERIMETER

FOR MINIMUM DECK DIMENSIONS, CONSULT STATE AND LOCAL CODES

STEPS AND RAILING

SLOPE DOWN

3'-0" MIN., TYP.

PERIMETER DRAIN SYSTEM CONSULT CODES

FOR MAXIMUM SLOPE, CONSULT CODES

ELEVATED LIFEGUARD CHAIR

LADDER/RECESSED STEPS

POOL EQUIPMENT ROOM REQUIRED FOR PUMP, FILTER, WATER TREATMENT FEEDERS AND OPTIONAL HEATER

NATURAL AND/OR MECHANICAL VENTILATION REQUIRED

FOR REQUIREMENTS AND MINIMUM DIMENSIONS OF DIVING BOARDS, CONSULT STATE AND LOCAL CODES

DRAIN AT DEEPEST POINT, REQUIRED

DIVE HOPPER DEPTH VARIES WITH HEIGHT OF DIVING BOARD

UNDERWATER LIGHTS, TYP.

NOTES

1. All swimming pools must be equipped with a filtration system for clarifying the water; the system must be an integral part of the circulation system and consist of one or more filter units, either sand, diatomaceous earth, or cartridge type.

2. Every swimming pool must be equipped with a disinfectant feeder as required to keep the microbiological, chemical, and physical characteristics of the pool water within prescribed limits.

3. All swimming pools must have the water depth marked plainly at or above the waterline on the vertical wall where possible and on the edge of the deck next to the pool; depth markers must be 25 ft or less on center.

4. When visitor or spectator areas are provided at swimming pools, there must be an absolute separation between those areas and the pool area. Provide separate toilets for visitors and spectators.

5. Every public pool must have a readily accessible room or area designated and equipped for emergency care.

TYPICAL PUBLIC SWIMMING AND DIVING POOL REQUIREMENTS

STANDARD DIMENSIONS FOR PUBLIC SWIMMING POOLS IN FT-IN. (M)[1]

| POOL TYPE | DIVING EQUIPMENT | | MINIMUM DIMENSIONS[2] | | | | | | | | MINIMUM WIDTH OF POOL AT POINTS | | |
	MAX. BOARD LENGTH	MAX. HEIGHT OVER WATER	D_1	D_2	R	L_1	L_2	L_3	L_4	L_5	A	B	C
VI	10-0 —	0-26 (2/3)	7-0 (2.13)	8-6 (2.59)	5-6 (1.68)	2-6 (0.76)	8-0 (2.44)	10-6 (3.20)	7-0 (2.13)	28-0 (8.53)	16-0 (4.88)	18-0 (5.49)	18-0 (5.49)
VII	12-0 —	0-30 (3/4)	7-6 (2.29)	9-0 (2.74)	6-0 (1.83)	3-0 (0.91)	9-0 (2.74)	12-0 (3.66)	4-0 (1.22)	28-0 (8.53)	18-0 (5.49)	20-0 (6.10)	20-0 (6.10)
VIII	16-0 —	— (1)	8-6 (2.59)	10-0 (3.05)	7-0 (2.13)	4-0 (1.22)	10-0 (3.05)	15-0 (4.57)	2-0 (0.61)	31-0 (9.45)	20-0 (6.10)	22-0 (6.71)	22-0 (6.71)
IX	16-0 —	— (3)	11-0 (3.35)	12-0 (3.66)	8-6 (2.59)	6-0 (1.83)	10-6 (3.20)	21-0 (6.40)	—	37-6 (11.43)	22-0 (6.71)	24-0 (7.32)	24-0 (7.32)

Source: National Spa and Pool Institute (NSPI), Alexandria, Virginia

[1]The dimensions given are the currently recommended standards for public swimming pools and are not designed for sanctioned competition.

[2]L_2, L_3, and L_4 combined represent the minimum distance from the tip of a board to the pool wall opposite the diving equipment.

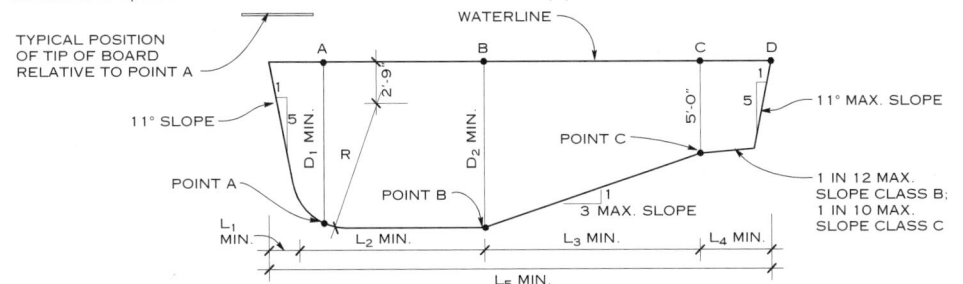

TYPICAL POSITION OF TIP OF BOARD RELATIVE TO POINT A

WATERLINE

11° SLOPE

D_1 MIN.

R

POINT A

POINT B

L_1 MIN.

L_2 MIN.

D_2 MIN.

L_3 MIN.

L_4 MIN.

POINT C

5'-0"

11° MAX. SLOPE

1 IN 12 MAX. SLOPE CLASS B; 1 IN 10 MAX. SLOPE CLASS C

$\frac{1}{3}$ MAX. SLOPE

L_5 MIN.

STANDARD DIMENSIONS KEY

Robert D. Buckley, AIA; robert d. buckley * architect; Kalamazoo, Michigan
D. J. Hunsaker; Counsilman/Hunsaker & Associates; St. Louis, Missouri
National Swimming Pool Foundation; Merrick, New York

GENERAL NOTES

1. Public pools are those operated and intended for the collective use of unrelated persons, whether or not a fee is charged. Semipublic pools are those intended for use by housing facility occupants and their invited guests. Private residential pools are those located on private property for use by the owner's family and/or invited guests.

2. Special purpose pools are those designed for specific uses and not defined as public, semipublic, or private residential.

3. A spa is defined as a special facility that is not drained, cleaned, or refilled after each individual use and may include hydrojet circulation, hot water, cold water, mineral bath, air induction bubbles, or any combination of these.

4. The water supply serving a public swimming pool and all plumbing fixtures, including drinking fountains, lavatories, toilets, and showers, must meet all applicable requirements for potable water. All portions of the water distribution system serving the swimming pool and auxiliary facilities must be protected against backflow.

5. Swimming pools must be designed and constructed to withstand all anticipated loadings for both empty and full conditions.

6. A hydrostatic relief valve must be provided for in-ground swimming pools in areas with a high water table.

7. Provisions must be made for complete, continuous circulation of water through all areas of the swimming pool.

8. The shape of any swimming pool must not impair swimmer safety or the circulation of water through all areas of the pool.

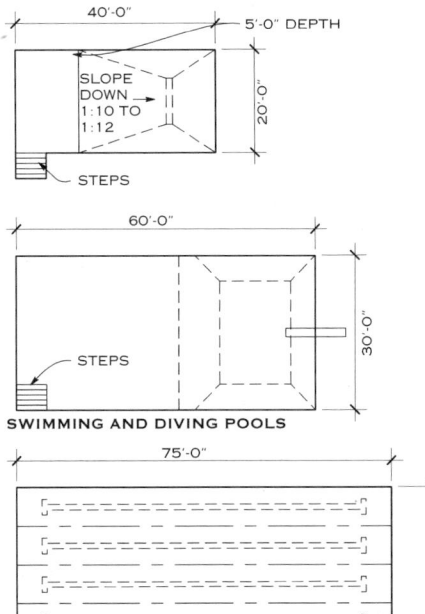

40'-0"

5'-0" DEPTH

SLOPE DOWN 1:10 TO 1:12

20'-0"

STEPS

60'-0"

30'-0"

STEPS

SWIMMING AND DIVING POOLS

75'-0"

45'-0"

6-LANE LAP POOL

TYPICAL PUBLIC POOL SHAPES

DIVING BOARD DIMENSIONS

There must be a completely unobstructed, clear vertical distance of 13 ft above any diving board, measured from the center of the front end of the board. This area must extend horizontally at least 8 ft behind, 8 ft to each side, and 16 ft ahead of point A (see key).

For diving board placement, observe these minimum distances from the pool edge or adjacent boards:

Deck-level board to pool side:	8 ft
1-meter board to pool side:	10 ft
3-meter board to pool side:	11 ft
1-meter or deck-level board to 3-meter board:	10 ft
1-meter or deck-level board to another 1-meter or deck-level board:	8 ft
3-meter board to another 3-meter board:	10 ft

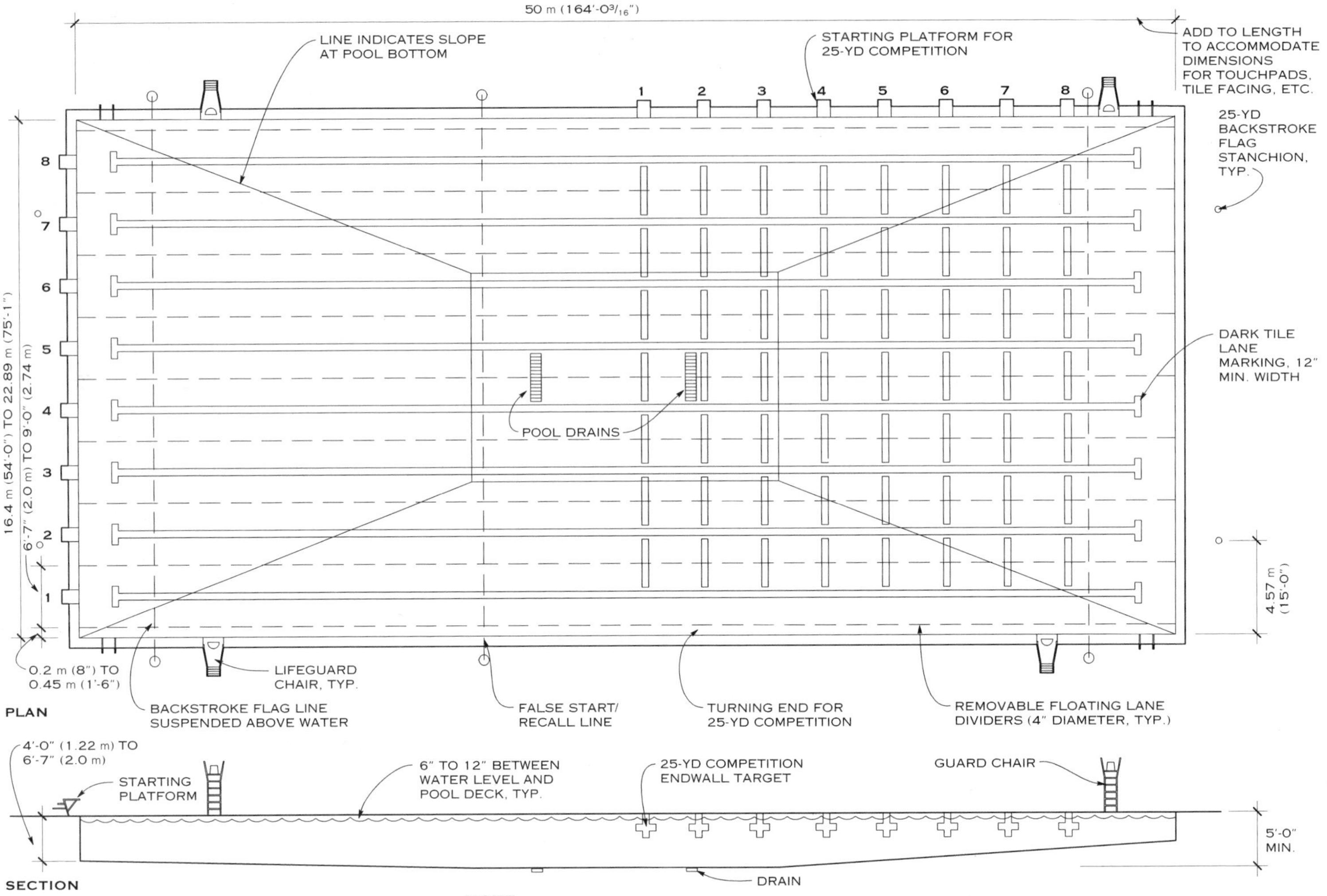

50 m (164'-0³/₁₆")

LINE INDICATES SLOPE AT POOL BOTTOM

STARTING PLATFORM FOR 25-YD COMPETITION

ADD TO LENGTH TO ACCOMMODATE DIMENSIONS FOR TOUCHPADS, TILE FACING, ETC.

25-YD BACKSTROKE FLAG STANCHION, TYP.

DARK TILE LANE MARKING, 12" MIN. WIDTH

POOL DRAINS

16.4 m (54'-0") TO 22.89 m (75'-1")

6'-7" (2.0 m) TO 9'-0" (2.74 m)

4.57 m (15'-0")

0.2 m (8") TO 0.45 m (1'-6")

PLAN

LIFEGUARD CHAIR, TYP.

BACKSTROKE FLAG LINE SUSPENDED ABOVE WATER

FALSE START/ RECALL LINE

TURNING END FOR 25-YD COMPETITION

REMOVABLE FLOATING LANE DIVIDERS (4" DIAMETER, TYP.)

4'-0" (1.22 m) TO 6'-7" (2.0 m)

STARTING PLATFORM

6" TO 12" BETWEEN WATER LEVEL AND POOL DECK, TYP.

25-YD COMPETITION ENDWALL TARGET

GUARD CHAIR

5'-0" MIN.

SECTION

DRAIN

NOTE

A 25-meter pool width will provide 10 lanes for training or competition and accommodate international meets of any distance. An economical alternative for pool length is 70 meters with at least one bulkhead to separate training and competition areas.

50-METER COMPETITION SWIMMING POOL

NOTES ON POOL DESIGN

1. The information on this page is based on current standards and rules for swimming races, competition diving, and other aquatic competitions stipulated by the following aquatic sport organizations:

   FINA (Federation Internationale de Natation Amateur) governs international competition, including the Olympic Games.

   US Swimming (United States Swimming, Inc.) governs open and age group levels in the United States.

   US Diving (United States Diving, Inc.) governs open and age group levels in the United States.

   NCAA (National Collegiate Athletic Association) governs all collegiate competition.

   NFHS (National Federation of State High School Associations) governs all high school competition.

2. Because they represent different groups and/or skill levels within a sport, the regulatory organizations do not always agree on the dimensions and features required for a pool facility. In addition to complying with the rules of pertinent organizations, the engineering of a swimming pool must follow the design regulations of any local, state, or federal agency that has jurisdiction over the facility. Sanitary and structural considerations vary almost as much between agencies as competitive guidelines do.

3. Consult the *Official Swimming Pool Design Compendium* (Merrick, N.Y.: National Swimming Pool Foundation, rev. ed. 1997) for specific rules of all the governing bodies.

4. Swimming pool dimensions shall be measured from the inside walls or from the tile or timing devices attached to the walls. Touchpads for automatic timing may be used if they do not shorten the race course beyond minimum specifications. Markings on the finish pad and bulkheads must conform to required markings on the endwalls. Visible numbers identifying lanes must be provided.

5. Endwalls and movable bulkheads serving as endwalls must be parallel and vertical for a distance of 3 ft 6 in. (1.0668 m) below the overflow level of the water. No protrusions are permitted below the surface. Endwalls should be finished with a nonslip surface.

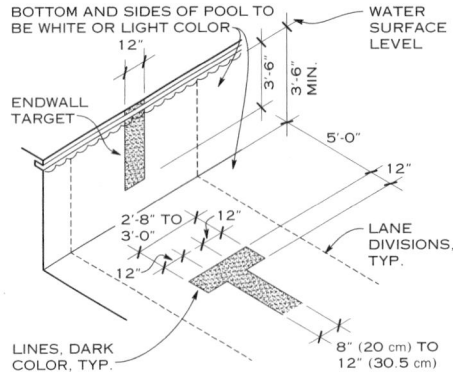

BOTTOM AND SIDES OF POOL TO BE WHITE OR LIGHT COLOR

WATER SURFACE LEVEL

12"

3'-6" MIN.

ENDWALL TARGET

5'-0"

12"

2'-8" TO 3'-0"

12"

12"

LANE DIVISIONS, TYP.

LINES, DARK COLOR, TYP.

8" (20 cm) TO 12" (30.5 cm)

NOTE

For endwall target design, see the rules of the appropriate governing organization.

LANE END MARKINGS

6. All ladders, steps, or stairs must be recessed into side walls or easily removed for competition.

7. Lighting at water level should be 100 footcandles. (FINA standards dictate 600 lux at water level.)

8. Lane markers must be continuous, clearly visible floats that indicate the lateral limits of each lane. They must be attached to and stretched between the endwalls and anchored at surface water level in a recessed receptacle. Solid color floats are recommended within 15 ft 0 in. (4.572 m) of both endwalls in contrast with the center portion of the lane markers.

9. Backstroke flag lines are required for all events in which the backstroke is swum. At least three 12-18 in. long pennants of two or more alternating colors must hang from the line.

NOTES ON POOL DIMENSIONS

1. When a range of dimensions is given, consult the appropriate governing organization (FINA, USS, NCAA, or NFHS) for specific dimensions.

2. Depending on the governing organization, pool size, and competition type, the following information applies for dimensions from the starting platform end of the pool:

   To the backstroke flag line, the dimension ranges from 15 ft 0 in. (4.57 m) to 16 ft 4.

   For 50-m pools, the dimension to the false start/recall stanchion ranges from 42 ft 0 in. (10.973 m) to 65 ft 7 in. (20.0 m).

   For 25-yd and 25-m pools, the dimension to the false start/recall stanchion ranges from 33 ft 1 in. (10.08 m) to 60 ft 1 in. (18.31 m).

Robert D. Buckley, AIA; robert d. buckley * architect; Kalamazoo, Michigan
D. J. Hunsaker; Counsilman/Hunsaker & Associates; St. Louis, Missouri
National Swimming Pool Foundation; Merrick, New York

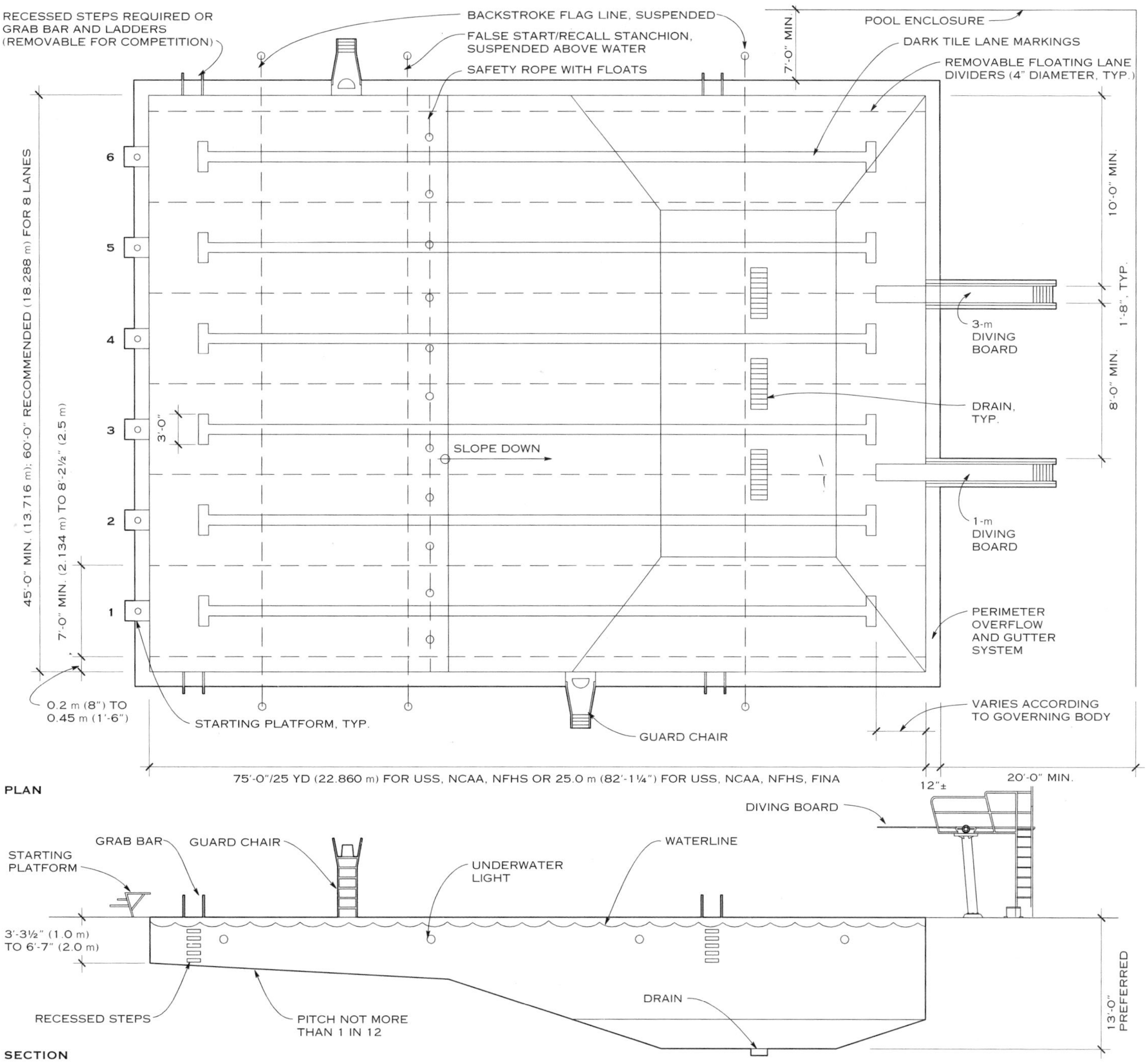

RECESSED STEPS REQUIRED OR GRAB BAR AND LADDERS (REMOVABLE FOR COMPETITION)

BACKSTROKE FLAG LINE, SUSPENDED

FALSE START/RECALL STANCHION, SUSPENDED ABOVE WATER

SAFETY ROPE WITH FLOATS

POOL ENCLOSURE

DARK TILE LANE MARKINGS

REMOVABLE FLOATING LANE DIVIDERS (4" DIAMETER, TYP.)

7'-0" MIN.

10'-0" MIN.

1'-8", TYP.

8'-0" MIN.

3-m DIVING BOARD

DRAIN, TYP.

1-m DIVING BOARD

45'-0" MIN. (13.716 m); 60'-0" RECOMMENDED (18.288 m) FOR 8 LANES

7'-0" MIN. (2.134 m) TO 8'-2½" (2.5 m)

3'-0"

SLOPE DOWN

PERIMETER OVERFLOW AND GUTTER SYSTEM

0.2 m (8") TO 0.45 m (1'-6")

STARTING PLATFORM, TYP.

GUARD CHAIR

VARIES ACCORDING TO GOVERNING BODY

PLAN

75'-0"/25 YD (22.860 m) FOR USS, NCAA, NFHS OR 25.0 m (82'-1¼") FOR USS, NCAA, NFHS, FINA

12"±

20'-0" MIN.

DIVING BOARD

WATERLINE

STARTING PLATFORM

GRAB BAR

GUARD CHAIR

UNDERWATER LIGHT

3'-3½" (1.0 m) TO 6'-7" (2.0 m)

13'-0" PREFERRED

RECESSED STEPS

PITCH NOT MORE THAN 1 IN 12

DRAIN

SECTION

25-METER AND 25-YARD COMPETITION SWIMMING AND DIVING POOL

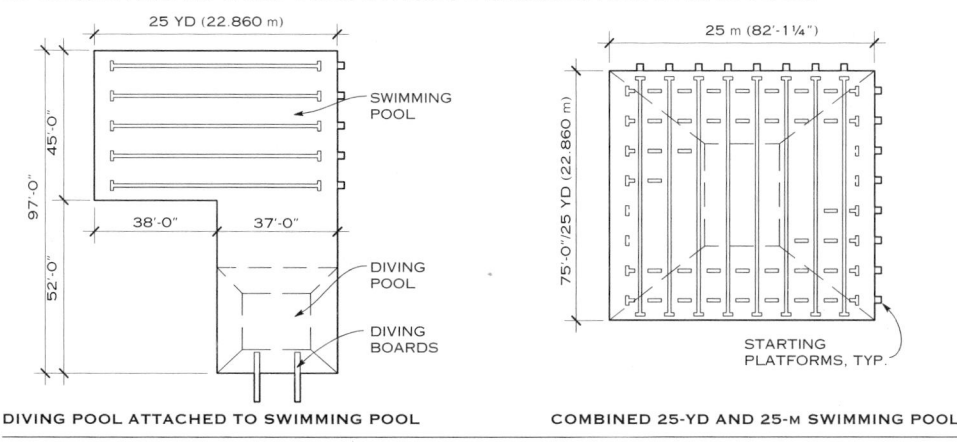

25 YD (22.860 m)

SWIMMING POOL

97'-0"

45'-0"

52'-0"

38'-0"

37'-0"

DIVING POOL

DIVING BOARDS

DIVING POOL ATTACHED TO SWIMMING POOL

25 m (82'-1¼")

75'-0"/25 YD (22.860 m)

STARTING PLATFORMS, TYP.

COMBINED 25-YD AND 25-m SWIMMING POOL

NOTES ON POOL DIMENSIONS

1. When a range of dimensions is given, consult the appropriate governing organization (FINA, USS, NCAA, or NFHS) for specific dimensions.

2. Depending on the governing organization, pool size, and competition type, the following information applies for dimensions from the starting platform end of the pool:

   To the backstroke flag line, the dimension ranges from 15 ft 0 in. (4.57 m) to 16 ft 4¾ in. (5.0 m).

   To the false start/recall stanchion, the dimension ranges from 33 ft 1 in. (10.08 m) to 60 ft 1 in. (18.31 m).

ALTERNATE POOL LAYOUTS

Robert D. Buckley, AIA; robert d. buckley * architect; Kalamazoo, Michigan
D. J. Hunsaker; Counsilman/Hunsaker & Associates; St. Louis, Missouri
National Swimming Pool Foundation; Merrick, New York

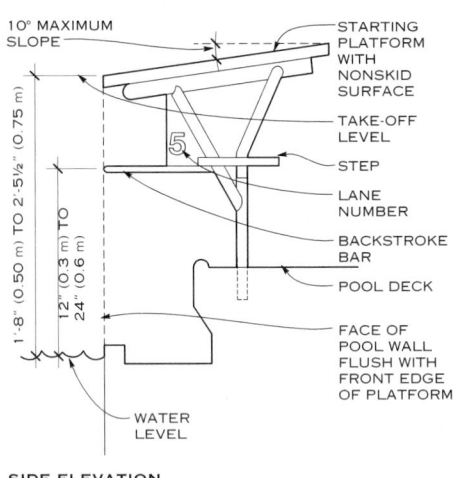

SIDE ELEVATION

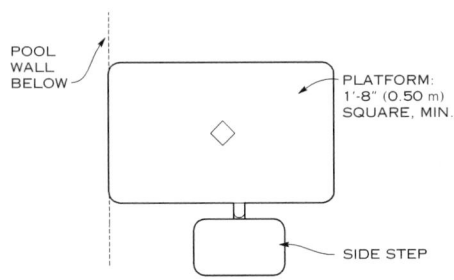

PLAN

NOTES

1. In pools with a water depth of 3 ft 6 in. to 4 ft at the starting end (measured at the end wall or any point within 12 in. of the end wall), starting platforms shall be no more than 18 in. above the water surface; otherwise, the swimmers must start from the deck or in the water.

2. In pools with a water depth less than 3 ft 6 in. in the starting end, the swimmers must start in the water.

STARTING PLATFORM REQUIREMENTS

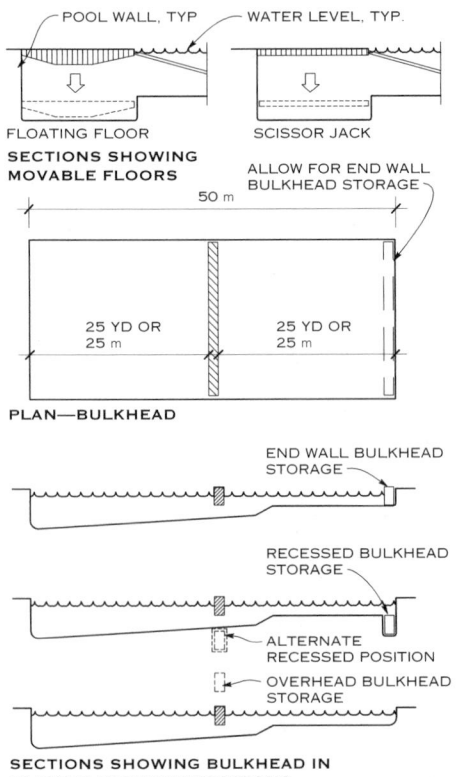

SECTIONS SHOWING MOVABLE FLOORS

PLAN—BULKHEAD

SECTIONS SHOWING BULKHEAD IN VARIOUS STORAGE POSITIONS

BULKHEADS AND MOVABLE FLOORS

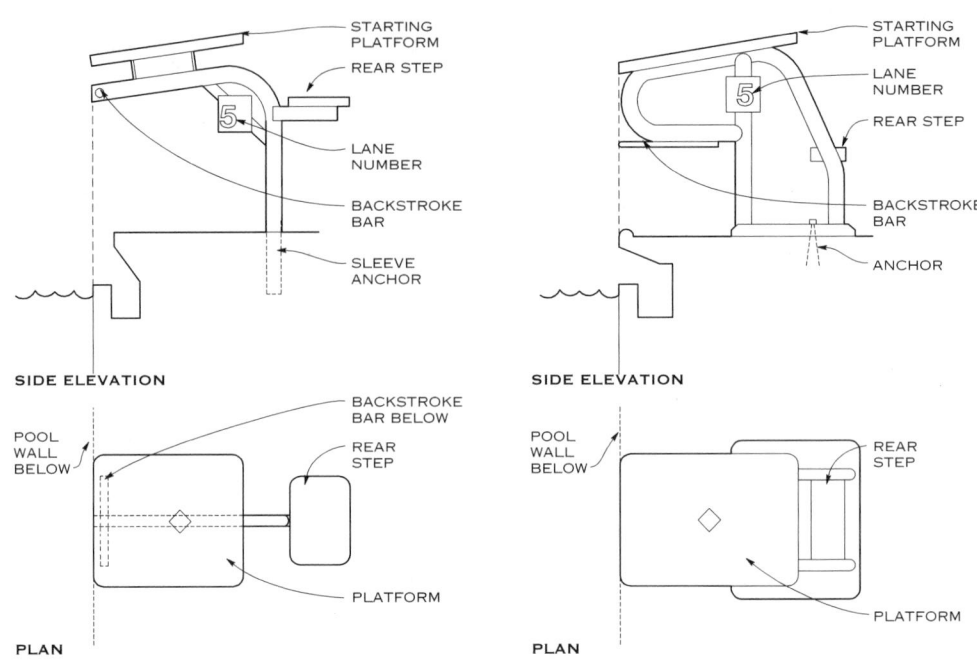

SIDE ELEVATION

PLAN

ALTERNATE STARTING PLATFORMS

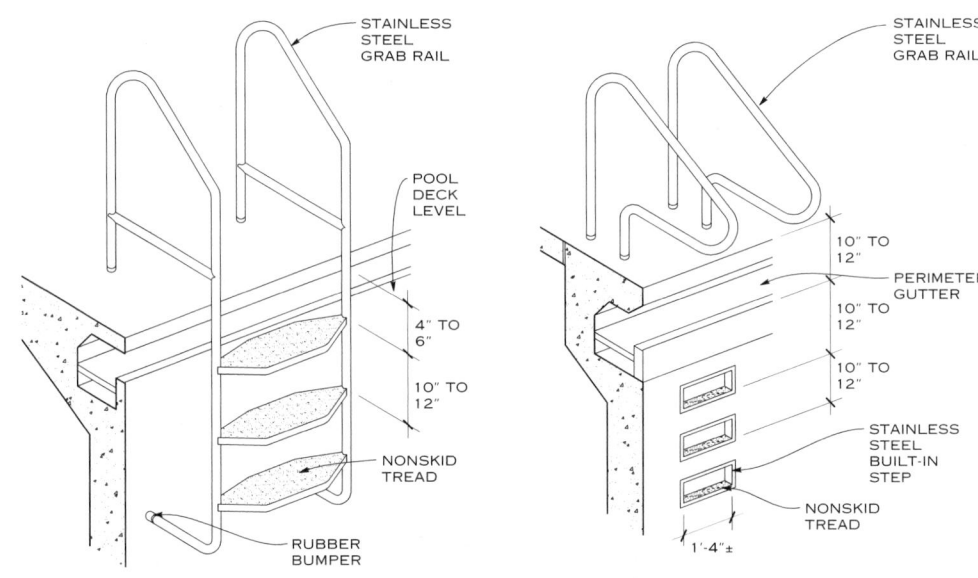

POOL LADDER

BUILT-IN STEPS WITH GRAB RAILS

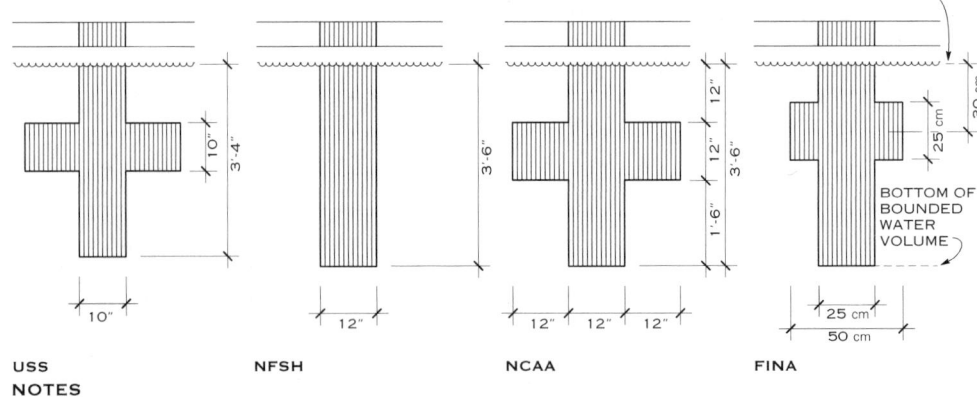

USS   NFSH   NCAA   FINA

NOTES

For placement and dimensions of touch pads specified by the various governing agencies, refer to the section on electronic starting, timing, and judging devices in National Swimming Pool Foundation, *Official Swimming Pool Design Compendium*, updated 5th ed. (1997).

END WALL TARGETS

Robert D. Buckley, AIA; robert d. buckley * architect; Kalamazoo, Michigan
D. J. Hunsaker; Counsilman/Hunsaker; St. Louis, Missouri

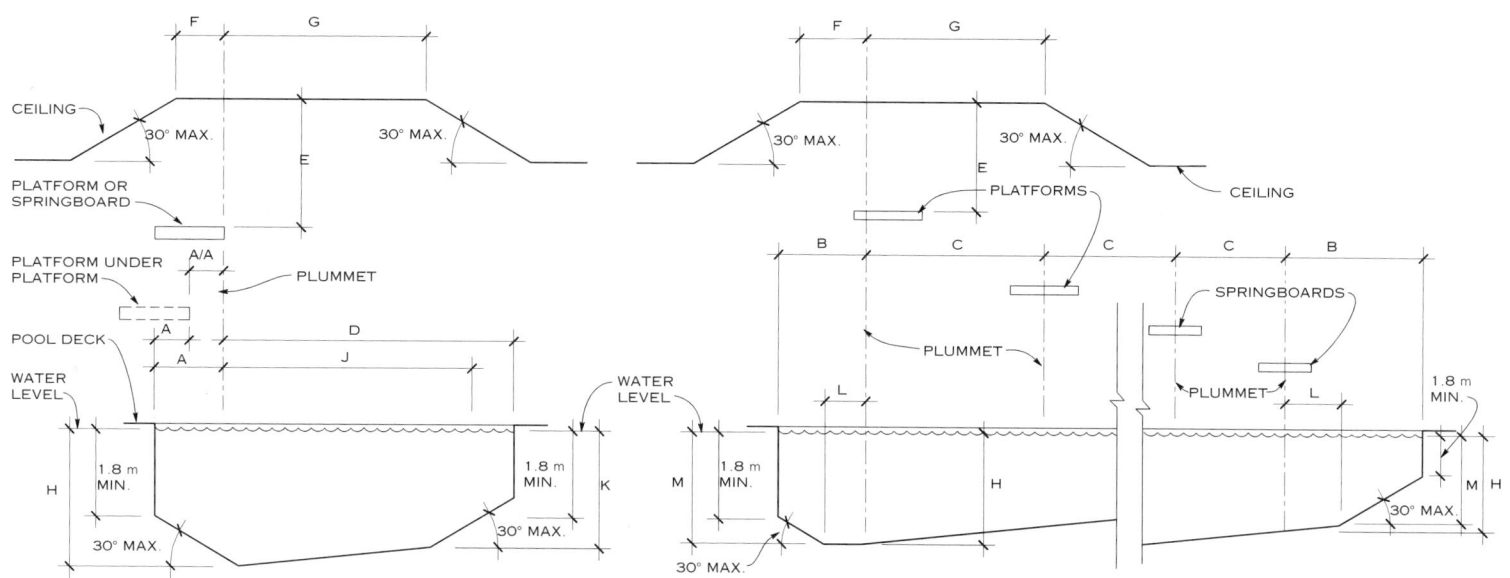

LONGITUDINAL SECTION   TRANSVERSE CROSS-SECTION

DIAGRAM OF RECOMMENDED DIMENSIONS FOR FINA, US DIVING, NCAA, AND NFHS DIVING FACILITIES

DIMENSIONS FOR DIVING FACILITIES

	Design Criteria		FINA (IN M) SPRINGBOARD 1 meter Horiz.	Vert.	3 meter Horiz.	Vert.	PLATFORM 1 meter Horiz.	Vert.	3 meter Horiz.	Vert.	5 meter Horiz.	Vert.	7.5 meter Horiz.	Vert.	10 meter Horiz.	Vert.	U.S. DIVING AND NCAA (IN FT-IN.)[1] SPRINGBOARD 1 meter Horiz.	Vert.	3 meter Horiz.	Vert.	PLATFORM 5 meter Horiz.	Vert.	7.5 meter Horiz.	Vert.	10 meter Horiz.	Vert.
	Length		4.80		4.80		5.00		5.00		6.00		6.00		6.00		16'-0"		16'-0"		20'-0"		20'-0"		20'-0"	
	Width		0.50		0.50		0.60		0.60 min. (1.50 pref)		1.50		1.50		2.00		1'-8"		1'-8"		5'-0"		5'-0"		6'-7"	
	Height		1.00		3.00		0.60-1.00		2.60-3.00		5.00		5.00		10.00		3'-4"		10'-0"		16'-5"		24'-8"		32'-10"	
A	From plummet back to pool wall	Desig.	A-1		A-3		A-1PL		A-3PL		A-5		A-7.5		A-10		A-1		A-3		A-5		A-7.5		A-10	
		Min.	1.50		1.50		0.75		1.25		1.25		1.50		1.50		5-0		5-0		4-2		5-0		5-0	
		Pref.	1.80		1.80		0.75		1.25		1.25		1.50		1.50		6-1		6-1		4-2		5-0		5-0	
A/A	From plummet back to platform (plummet directly below)	Desig.									A/A5/1		A/A7.5/3, 1		A/A10/5, 3, 1						A/A5		A/A7.5		A/A10	
		Min.																			2-6		2-6		2-6	
		Pref.																			4-2		4-2		4-2	
B	From plummet to pool wall at side	Desig.	B-1		B-3		B-1PL		B-3PL		B-5		B-7.5		B-10		B-1		B-3		B-5		B-7.5		B-10	
		Min.	2.50		3.50		2.30		2.80		3.25		4.25		5.25		8-3		11-6		10-8		14-0		17-3	
		Pref.	2.50		3.50		2.30		2.90		3.75		4.50		5.25		8-3		11-6		12-4		14-10		17-3	
C[2]	From plummet to adjacent plummet	Desig.	C1-1		C3-3, 3-1		C1-1PL		C3-3PL, 1PL		C5-3, 5-1		C7.5-5, 3, 1		C10-7.5, 5, 3, 1		C-11		C-331		C-531		C-7.5531		C-107.55531	
		Min.	2.00		2.20		1.65		2.00		2.25		2.50		2.75		6-7		7-3		7-5		8-3		9-1	
		Pref.	2.40		2.60		1.95		2.10		2.50		2.50		2.75		7-1		8-3		8-3		8-3		9-1	
D	From plummet to pool wall ahead	Desig.	D-1		D-3		D-1PL		D-3PL		D-5		D-7.5		D-10		D-1		D-3		D-5		D-7.5		D-10	
		Min.	9.00		10.25		8.00		9.50		10.25		11.0		13.50		29-7		33-8		33-8		36-2		44-4	
		Pref.	9.00		10.25		8.00		9.50		10.25		11.0		13.50		29-7		33-8		33-8		36-2		44-4	
E	On plummet, from board to ceiling	Desig.		E-1		E-3		E-1PL		E-3PL		E-5		E-7.5		E-10		E-1		E-3		E-5		E-7.5		E-10
		Min.		5.00		5.00		3.25		3.25		3.25		3.25		4.00		16-5		16-5		10-8		10-8		13-2
		Pref.		5.00		5.00		3.50		3.50		3.50		3.50		5.00		16-5		16-5		11-6		11-6		16-5
F	Clear overhead behind and each side of plummet	Desig.	F-1	E-1	F-3	E-3	F-1PL	E-1PL	F-3PL	E-3PL	F-5	E-5	F-7.5	E-7.5	F-10	E-10	F-1	E-1	F-3	E-3	F-5	E-5	F-7.5	E-7.5	F-10	E-10
		Min.	2.50	5.00	2.50	5.00	2.75	3.25	2.75	3.25	2.75	3.25	2.75	3.25	2.75	4.00	8-3	16-5	8-3	16-5	9-1	10-8	9-1	10-9	9-1	13-2
		Pref.	2.50	5.00	2.50	5.00	2.75	3.50	2.75	3.50	2.75	3.50	2.75	3.50	2.75	5.00	8-3	16-5	8-3	16-5	9-1	11-6	9-1	11-6	9-1	16-5
G	Clear overhead ahead of plummet	Desig.	G-1	E-1	G-3	E-3	G-1PL	E-1PL	G-3PL	E-3PL	G-5	E-5	G-7.5	E-7.5	G-10	E-10	G-1	E-1	G-3	E-3	G-5	E-5	G-7.5	E-7.5	G-10	E-10
		Min.	5.00	5.00	5.00	5.00	5.00	3.25	5.00	3.25	5.00	3.25	5.00	3.25	6.00	4.00	16-5	16-5	16-5	16-5	16-5	10-8	16-5	10-8	19-9	13-2
		Pref.	5.00	5.00	5.00	5.00	5.00	3.50	5.00	3.50	5.00	3.50	5.00	3.50	6.00	5.00	16-5	16-5	16-5	16-5	16-5	11-6	16-5	11-6	19-9	16-5
H	Depth of water at plummet	Desig.		H-1		H-3		H-1PL		H-3PL		H-6		H-7.5		H-10		H-1		H-3		H-5		H-7.5		H-10
		Min.		3.40		3.70		3.20		3.50		3.70		4.10		4.50		11-0		12-0		12-2		13-6		14-10
		Pref.		3.50		3.80		3.30		3.60		3.80		4.50		5.00		11-6		12-6		12-6		14-10		16-5
J/K	Distance and depth ahead of plummet	Desig.	J-1	K-1	J-3	K-3	J-1PL	K-1PL	J-3PL	K-3PL	J-5	K-5	J-7.5	K-7.5	J-10	K-10	J-1	K-1	J-3	K-3	J-5	K-5	J-7.5	K-7.5	J-10	K-10
		Min.	5.00	3.30	6.00	3.60	4.50	3.10	5.50	3.40	6.00	3.60	8.00	4.00	11.00	4.25	16-5	10-10	16-5	11-10	19-9	11-10	26-3	13-2	36-2	14-0
		Pref.	5.00	3.40	6.00	3.70	4.50	3.20	5.50	3.50	6.00	3.70	8.00	4.40	11.00	4.75	16-5	11-2	19-9	12-2	19-9	12-2	26-3	14-6	36-2	15-7
L/M	Distance and depth each side of plummet	Desig.	L-1	M-1	L-3	M-3	L-1PL	M-1PL	L-3PL	M-3PL	L-5	M-5	L-7.5	M-7.5	L-10	M-10	L-1	M-1	L-3	M-3	L-5	M-5	L-7.5	M-7.5	L-10	M-10
		Min.	1.50	3.30	2.00	3.60	1.40	3.10	1.80	3.40	3.00	3.60	3.75	4.00	4.50	4.25	5-0	10-10	6-7	11-10	19-11	11-10	12-4	13-2	14-10	14-0
		Pref.	2.00	3.40	2.50	3.70	1.90	3.20	2.30	3.50	3.50	3.70	4.50	4.40	5.25	4.75	9-11	11-2	8-3	12-2	11-6	12-2	14-10	14-6	17-3	15-7
N	Maximum slope to reduce dimensions beyond full requirements is 30 degrees for both pool depth and ceiling height																									

[1] All dimensions in the US Diving and NCAA section of this chart are rounded up, even when the dimension is only fractionally greater than the next lowest inch.

[2] Dimension C (plummet to adjacent plummet) applies to platforms with widths as specified in this chart. If platform widths are increased, dimension C must be increased by half the additional width(s).

Robert D. Buckley, AIA; robert d. buckley * architect; Kalamazoo, Michigan
D. J. Hunsaker; Counsilman/Hunsaker & Associates; St. Louis, Missouri
National Swimming Pool Foundation; Merrick, New York

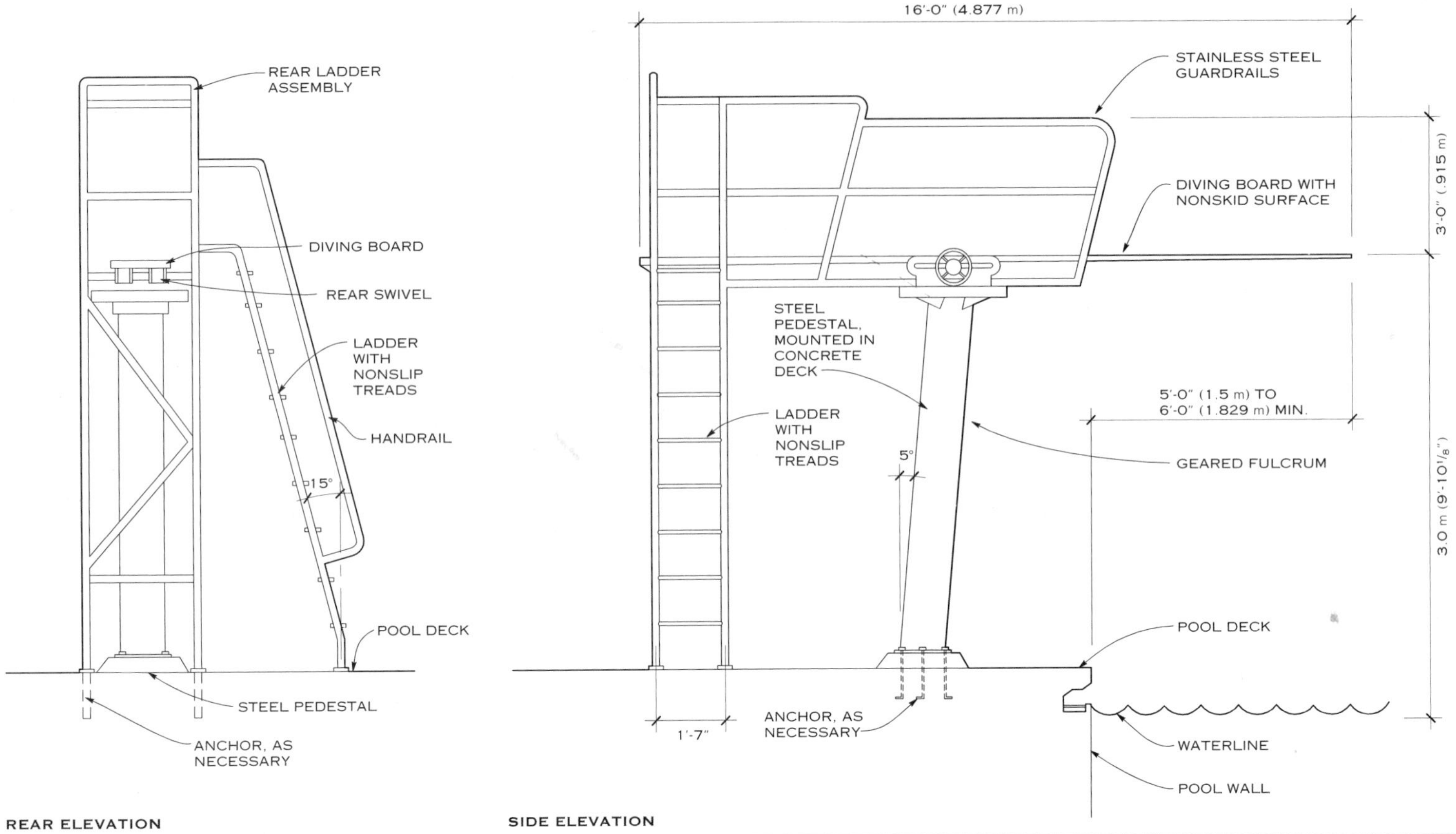

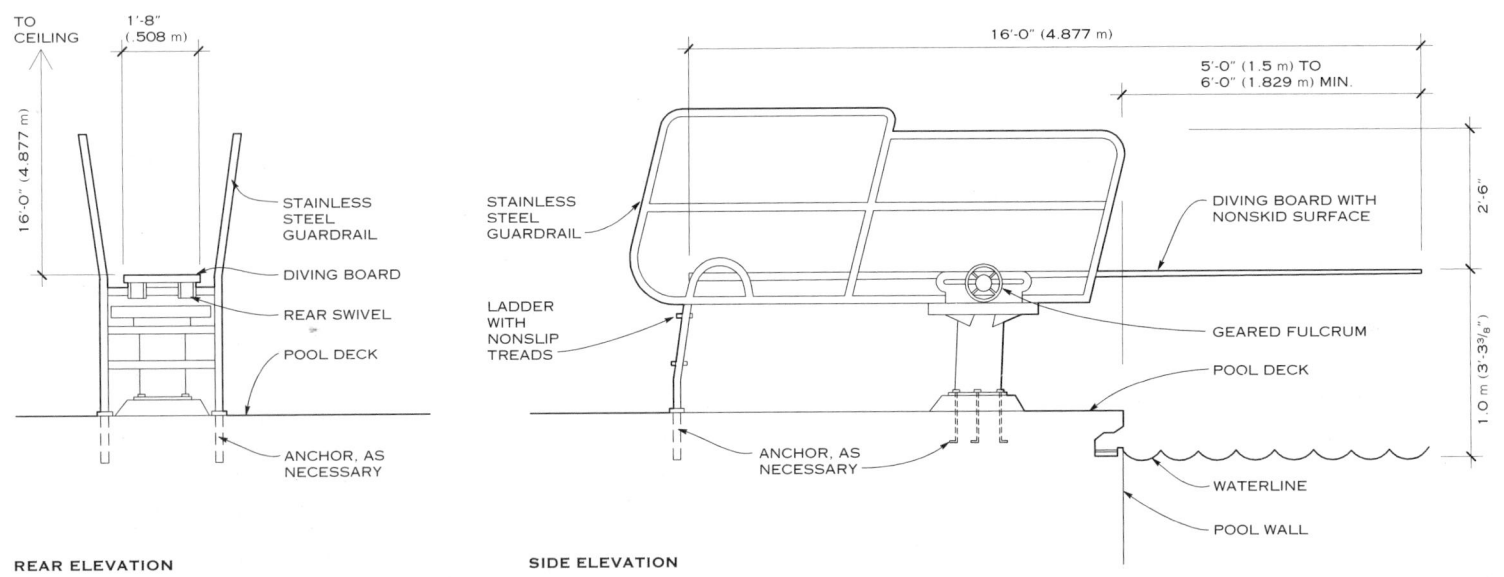

REAR ELEVATION

SIDE ELEVATION

3-METER DIVING BOARD

REAR ELEVATION

SIDE ELEVATION

1-METER DIVING BOARD

NOTES

1. Both 1- and 3-meter boards are required for amateur, collegiate, and international meets. Consult the *Official Swimming Pool Design Compendium* (Merrick, N.Y.: National Swimming Pool Foundation, rev. ed. 1997) for specific FINA, US Diving, NCAA, and NFHS details and specifications.

2. When a range of dimensions is given, consult the appropriate governing organization for specific dimensions.

3. When selecting a 1- or 3-meter diving tower, pay special attention to the materials it is made of. Differences in wall tubing thickness, anchorage, and fulcrum materials influence the flexibility and spring from the tower.

4. A fulcrum, which can be moved and set at varying positions between 5 ft 6 in. (1.676 m) and 7 ft 6 in. (2.286 m) from the rear of the diving board, is required. The board must remain horizontal with the fulcrum in any position. The range of movement of the fulcrum may be limited under certain conditions. Consult with the appropriate governing body for diving competition regulations.

5. A water agitation system is recommended that produces water surface agitation extending 5 ft (1.524 m) beyond the end of the board with a width of 2 ft (.6096 m).

6. The maximum depth reduction rate of diving pools that do not exceed minimum depth requirements shall be 6.25% for a distance of 20 ft (6.096 m) forward and 6 ft (1.829 m) back and to the sides. Deeper pools may have proportionally steeper depth reduction rates.

7. Three choices are available for diving board supports for 1- and 3-meter boards: a manufactured cantilevered steel stand; a manufactured cast aluminum stand; and a cast-in-place concrete platform with a fulcrum assembly mounted directly to the top of the slab.

Robert D. Buckley, AIA; robert d. buckley * architect; Kalamazoo, Michigan
D. J. Hunsaker; Counsilman/Hunsaker & Associates; St. Louis, Missouri
National Swimming Pool Foundation; Merrick, New York

NOTE

In these drawings, S/S stands for stainless steel.

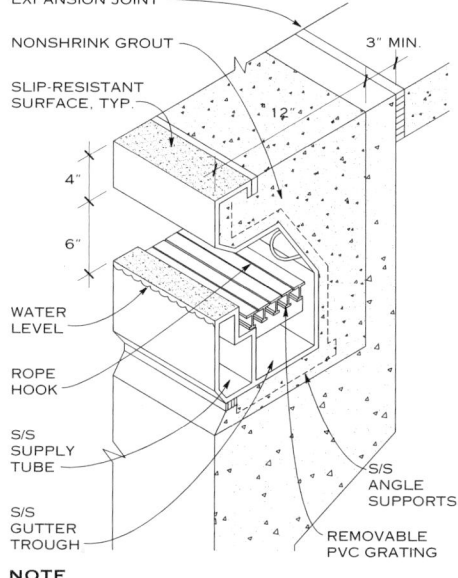

ROLLOUT GUTTER SYSTEM

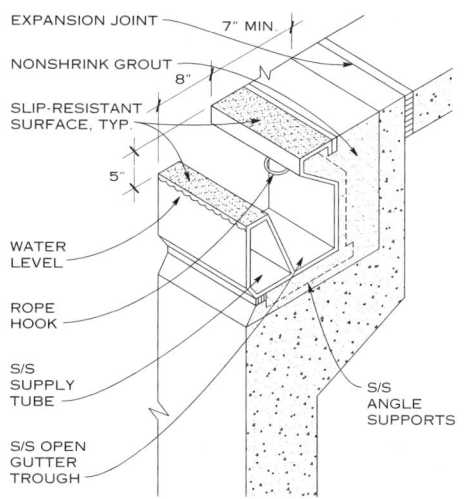

SEMIRECESSED OPEN GUTTER SYSTEM

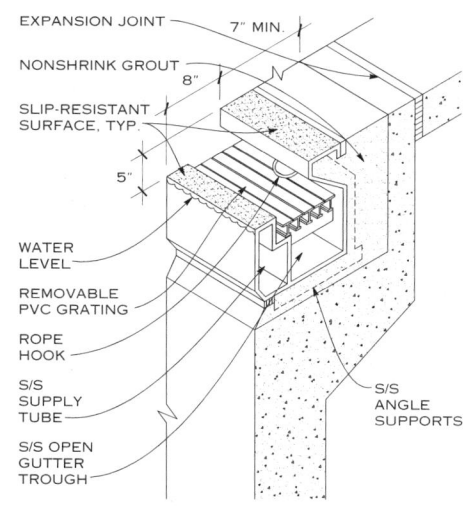

SEMIRECESSED GUTTER SYSTEM

FULLY RECESSED GUTTER SYSTEM

NOTE

In addition to the stainless steel system shown, gutters may be designed as an integral part of the concrete deck edge.

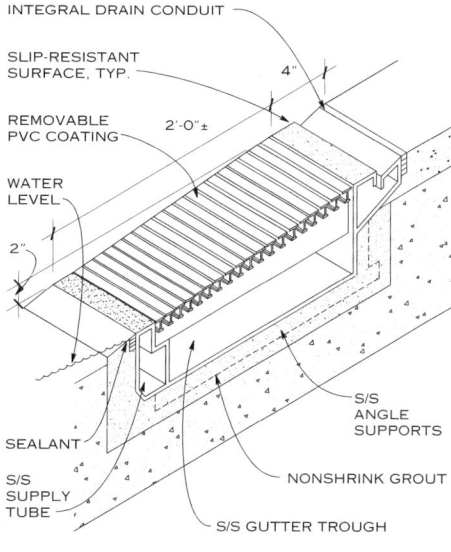

NOTE

The zero depth gutter system is typically used for walk-in or leisure-type pools only, if necessary.

ZERO DEPTH GUTTER SYSTEM

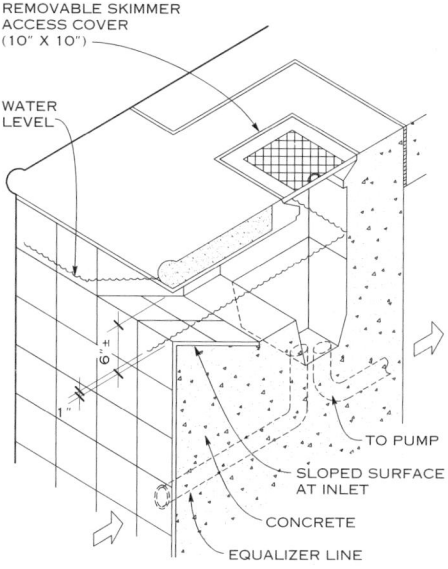

NOTE

Surface skimmers are not recommended for use in competitive pools.

SKIMMER DETAIL

NOTES ON PERIMETER OVERFLOW

1. A perimeter overflow system must be provided on all public swimming pools. The system must be designed and constructed to maintain the water level of the pool at the operating level of the overflow rim or weir device. Applicable codes determine the dimension from the deck to the water level.

2. When used as the only overflow system on a pool, a perimeter overflow system must extend around a minimum of half the swimming pool perimeter. Perimeter overflow systems must be connected to the circulation system with a system surge capacity of not less than 1 gal/sq ft of pool surface.

3. The perimeter overflow system in combination with the upper rim of the pool must constitute a handhold. It must be designed to prevent entrapment of a swimmer's arms, legs, or feet and to permit inspection and cleaning.

4. In some states, the hydraulic capacity of the overflow system must be sufficient to handle 100% of the circulation flow.

5. Rollout and/or zero depth flush perimeter overflow systems are most commonly used in recreational pools and walk-in shallow areas. Competitive pools that have semirecessed gutters along their length to trap wave surge and prevent reflected waves must have fully recessed gutters at the ends or provide a visual barrier that can be seen by competing swimmers.

6. Perimeter overflows are commonly used on public swimming pools. Some state health departments do not approve skimmers on public swimming pools that exceed a certain surface area. Check current state codes or swimming pool regulations to determine limits of use, minimum dimensions, and other factors regarding overflow design.

7. Metal swimming pool systems with built-in perimeter overflow are available. In addition to the overflow channel, the metal liner may contain the return waterline from the filtration system. A metal liner that incorporates a cove between wall and floor is desirable to facilitate cleaning.

8. Deck areas adjoining an overflow system are generally required to slope away from it to separate drains. When a deck is sloped to the pool overflow, provide for diverting the overflow to waste during deck cleaning.

9. A stainless steel perimeter system may combine the supply and return functions of the swimming pool recirculation system around the pool perimeter to optimize surge control and provide water supply, return conduit, and continuous surface skimming.

10. Return water may enter the gutter through a series of skimming weirs spaced around the pool perimeter or by overflow into the gutter. For normal recreational use, the water level is kept at the center of the skimmer face, allowing the pool to act as a surge chamber and absorb water displacement caused by swimmers. For competitive use the water level is raised to the gutter lip. Waves then flow over the lip and are returned through the surge tank without rebound.

SURFACE SKIMMERS

If surface skimmers are used, provide one for each 500 sq ft or fraction thereof of the pool surface. When two or more skimmers are used, they must be located so they maintain effective skimming action over the entire surface of the pool. To obtain the most effective skimming action, locate the skimmers with regard to the prevailing wind and drift, shape of the pool, and water circulation pattern. Use of directional inlet fittings will help ensure a proper circulation pattern.

Skimmers may not be permitted in larger pools; see local health department codes for limitations on public pool use. Skimmers are not recommended for use in competitive pools.

Surface skimmers are available from many swimming pool suppliers. Metal or plastic units come in various capacities. An access cover in the deck provides for removal and cleaning of the strainer. Surface skimmers should comply with the joint National Swimming Pool Institute–National Sanitation Foundation performance standards

Robert D. Buckley, AIA; robert d. buckley * architect; Kalamazoo, Michigan
D. J. Hunsaker; Counsilman/Hunsaker & Associates; St. Louis, Missouri
National Swimming Pool Foundation; Merrick, New York

PLAN

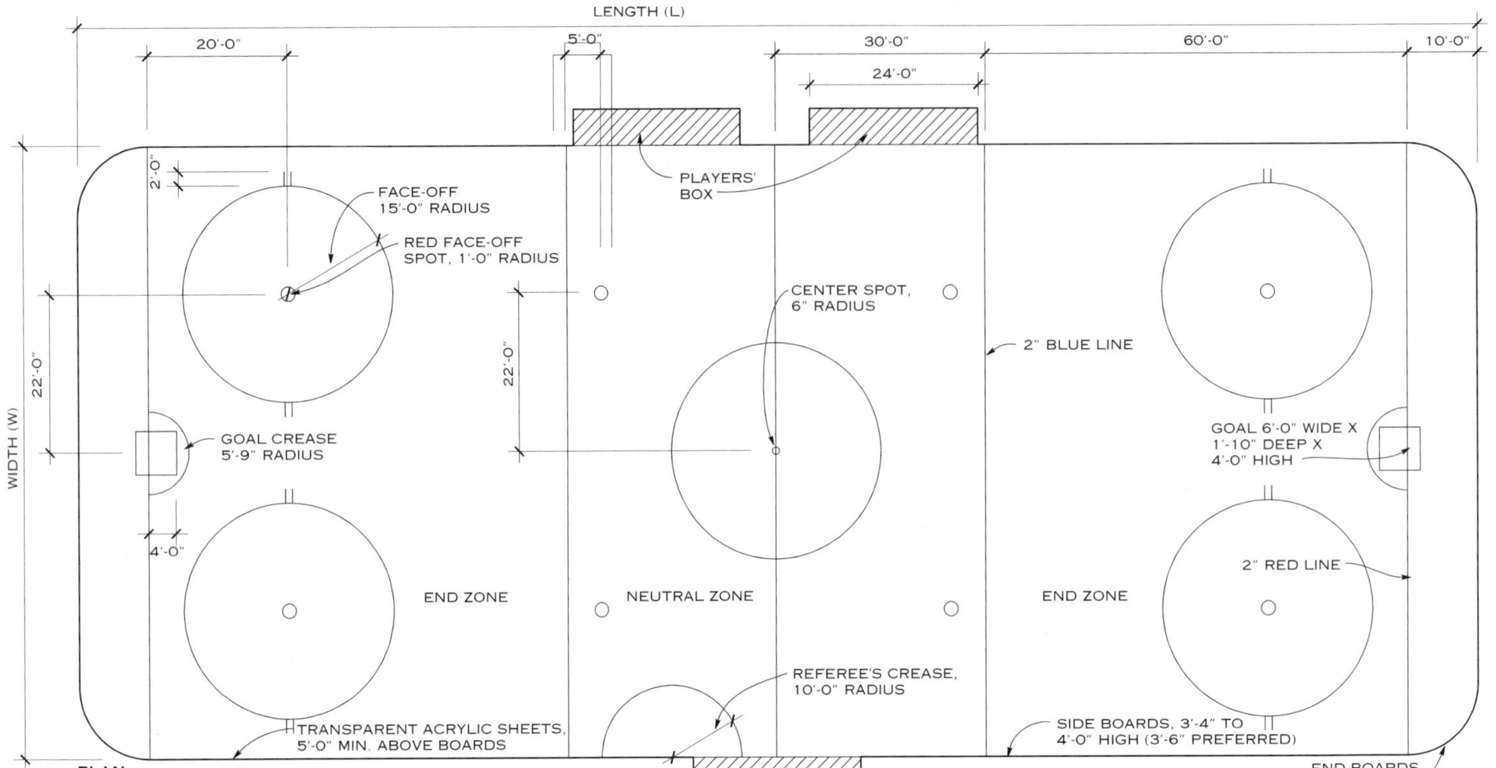

ICE HOCKEY RINK SIZE

RINK TYPE	L (FT)	W (FT)
NHL	200	85
Olympic	200	100
NCAA	200	85
High School	200	85

HOCKEY PUCK

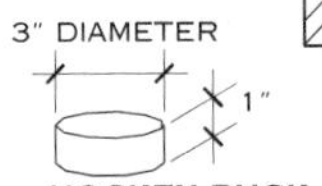

NOTE

For year-round rinks, provide a heating system below the ice surface to prevent permafrost and movement in the subsurface soil.

STICKS

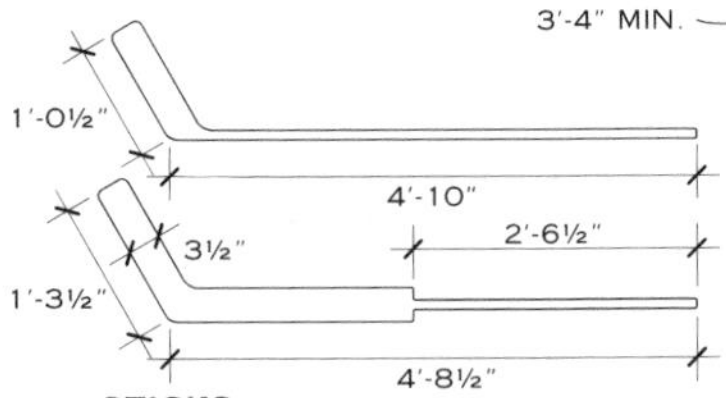

ICE HOCKEY RINKS

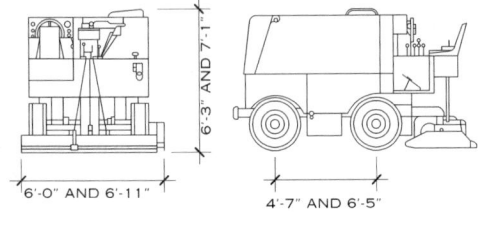

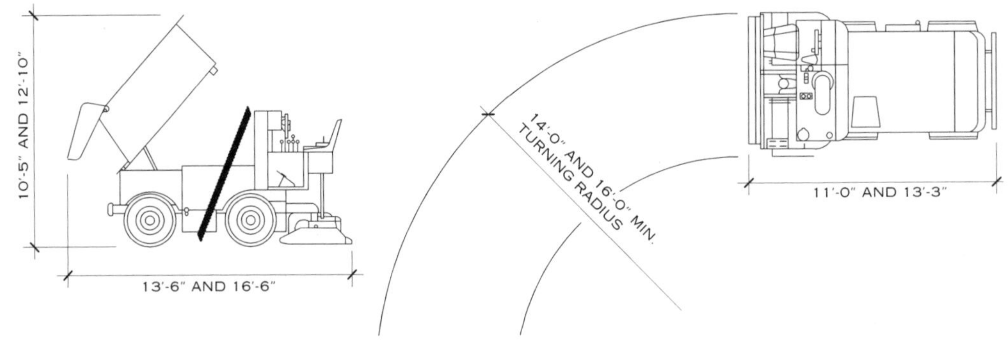

NOTE

The vehicle dimensions shown represent two of the available models. Consult the manufacturer for additional information.

ZAMBONI ICE RESURFACER

CURLING STONE

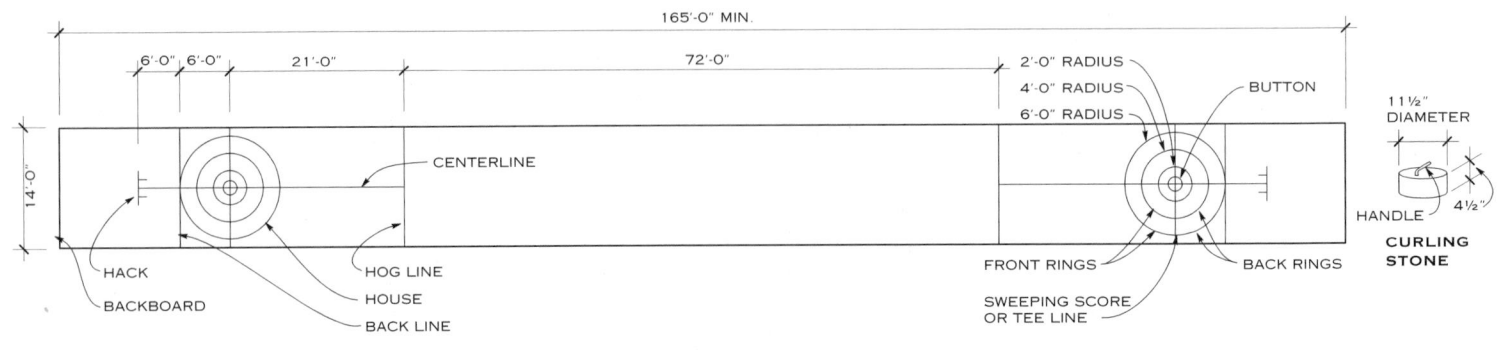

CURLING

Dean Cox, AIA; Collins Rimer Gordon Architects; Cleveland, Ohio

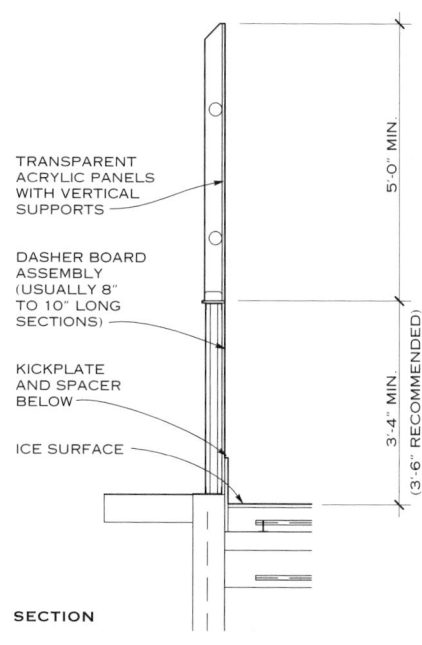

SECTION

- TRANSPARENT ACRYLIC PANELS WITH VERTICAL SUPPORTS
- DASHER BOARD ASSEMBLY (USUALLY 8" TO 10" LONG SECTIONS)
- KICKPLATE AND SPACER BELOW
- ICE SURFACE

5'-0" MIN

3'-4" MIN (3'-6" RECOMMENDED)

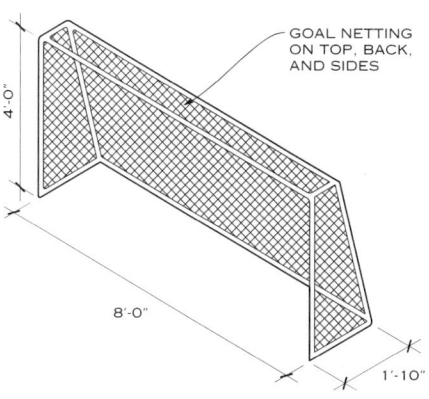

- GOAL NETTING ON TOP, BACK, AND SIDES

4'-0"

8'-0"

1'-10"

ICE HOCKEY GOAL

ANCILLARY SPACES AT ICE RINKS

The design of an ice rink must include planning for the ancillary space requirements described here:

1. Large hinged swing gates that open into the ice rink, usually at one end, are needed to accommodate the Zamboni, a machine used for resurfacing the ice.
2. An area is needed outside the main ice rink for disposal of ice removed by the Zamboni. This space customarily is large enough to allow $1/2$ to 1 cu yd of ice to melt into a drainage sump. However, some smaller indoor facilities simply remove the scraped ice to the exterior of the building.
3. A header trench 3 ft wide x 3 ft deep should be located at one side of the ice rink to accommodate piping connections to underfloor systems.
4. Floor surfaces where access to the rink is required for skaters and a Zamboni normally consist of a rubber belting assembly or similar material.

GENERAL NOTES

1. The details shown on this page represent typical systems. Acutal details must be modified as appropriate for individual projects.
2. The details shown indicate options for seasonal and year-round operations. Which design, detailing, underfloor heating, insulation, and other features are chosen depends on the anticipated operation of a particular rink.
3. Considerations affecting ice rink design and planning include requirements for underfloor drainage, ventilation, and humidity control; subsoil conditions at the site; the requirements of refrigeration plants, the ice-making system, and lighting and other electrical features; and maintenance and operational needs.
4. It is recommended that a qualified consultant be involved in the design and planning of ice rink systems.

Dean Cox, AIA; Collins Rimer Gordon Architects; Cleveland, Ohio

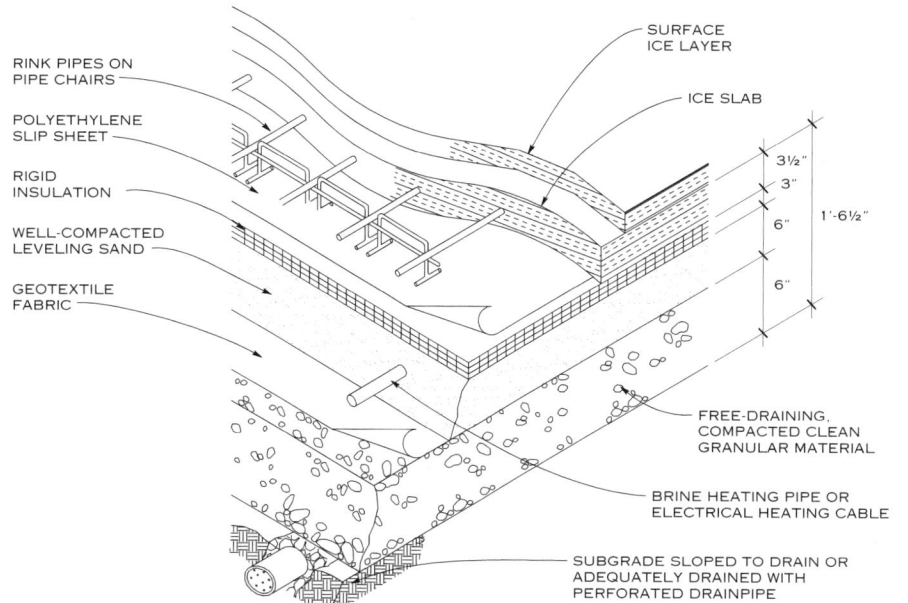

- RINK PIPES ON PIPE CHAIRS
- POLYETHYLENE SLIP SHEET
- RIGID INSULATION
- WELL-COMPACTED LEVELING SAND
- GEOTEXTILE FABRIC
- SURFACE ICE LAYER
- ICE SLAB
- FREE-DRAINING, COMPACTED CLEAN GRANULAR MATERIAL
- BRINE HEATING PIPE OR ELECTRICAL HEATING CABLE
- SUBGRADE SLOPED TO DRAIN OR ADEQUATELY DRAINED WITH PERFORATED DRAINPIPE

3½" 3" 6" 6" 1'-6½"

YEAR-ROUND RINK (NATURAL SAND FLOOR WITH INSULATION)

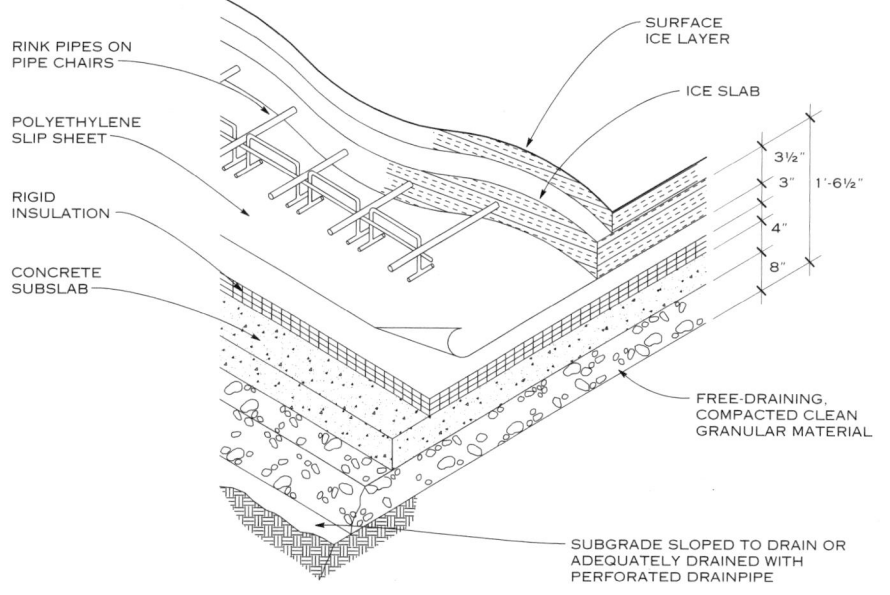

- RINK PIPES ON PIPE CHAIRS
- POLYETHYLENE SLIP SHEET
- RIGID INSULATION
- CONCRETE SUBSLAB
- SURFACE ICE LAYER
- ICE SLAB
- FREE-DRAINING, COMPACTED CLEAN GRANULAR MATERIAL
- SUBGRADE SLOPED TO DRAIN OR ADEQUATELY DRAINED WITH PERFORATED DRAINPIPE

3½" 3" 4" 8" 1'-6½"

SEASONAL ARENA OR CURLING RINK (CONCRETE FLOOR WITH INSULATION)

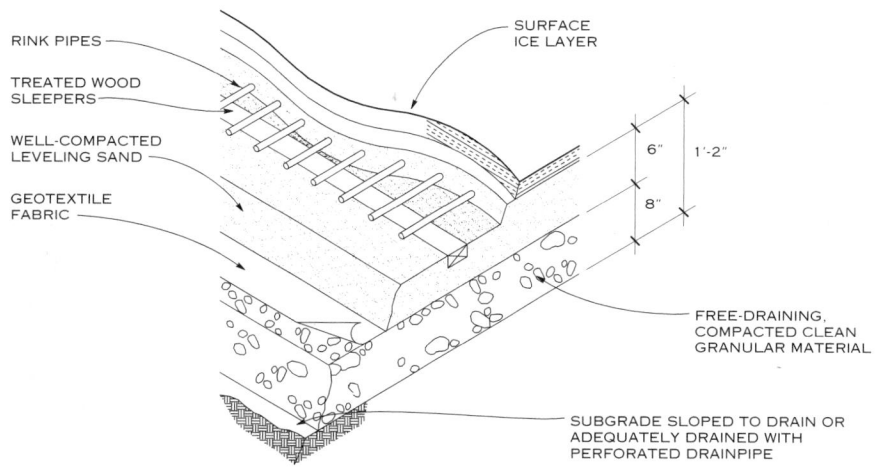

- RINK PIPES
- TREATED WOOD SLEEPERS
- WELL-COMPACTED LEVELING SAND
- GEOTEXTILE FABRIC
- SURFACE ICE LAYER
- FREE-DRAINING, COMPACTED CLEAN GRANULAR MATERIAL
- SUBGRADE SLOPED TO DRAIN OR ADEQUATELY DRAINED WITH PERFORATED DRAINPIPE

6" 8" 1'-2"

SEASONAL HOCKEY OR CURLING RINK (SAND FLOOR WITH NO INSULATION)

ICE AND SNOW SPORTS 17

TYPES OF COURTS

There are many different types of courts in the United States, each with its own characteristics and requirements. Federal courts have several levels of jurisdiction, beginning with the magistrate courts and the U.S. district courts. Courts of appeals hear appeals from the district courts, and the U.S. Supreme Court—the court of last resort—hears appeals from the appeals courts. Tax and bankruptcy courts are also part of the federal judiciary.

Each state has its own judicial system. Some states have special jurisdiction courts, such as juvenile or traffic courts. A good source for information on each state's court system is the National Center for State Courts.

Limited jurisdiction courts can be part of a state system or of a smaller municipal entity. They hear only such matters as misdemeanors and traffic offenses. General jurisdiction courts have trial jurisdiction over all matters and may have some authority to renew appeals from limited jurisdiction courts.

SYMBOLISM AND IMAGE

Historically, the American courthouse has been characterized by its size, siting, and specific architectural elements such as columns, domes, clock towers, and grand entrances. The architectural elements of a courthouse should reflect the dignity of the judiciary and its importance in the community.

PLANNING COURTROOM SPACES

The spaces required in a typical trial courthouse vary considerably from state to state and by level of court. Most contain courtrooms, judicial chambers (offices), jury assembly and deliberation rooms (for courts with jury trials), clerks' offices, records rooms, and prisoner holding cells (in criminal courts). Court clerks, law clerks, court reporters, and administrators need offices, and witness waiting rooms and attorney-client conference rooms are needed. Other offices might include those for the prosecutor (district attorney), public defender, and parole officers. Some courts require special courtrooms, or hearing rooms, for arbitration, mediation, high security criminal cases, and juvenile, family, and traffic cases.

The courthouse must be designed with its special circulation patterns in mind. Separate and distinct circulation paths for the public, judges and their staff, and in-custody defendants help ensure efficiency, safety, and security and are a distinctive feature of modern courthouses.

The public circulation area includes all areas used by the public, attorneys, clients, witnesses, and jurors (before selection), such as the main lobby, corridors, public elevators, public restrooms, waiting areas, and clerk of court counters.

The private circulation area allows judges and trial-related court personnel to move between chambers and courtrooms and jurors to move between courtrooms and jury deliberation rooms. Private circulation usually connects secured, private parking facilities for judges to private elevators and corridors leading to courtrooms and chambers.

Secure circulation provides a path for in-custody defendants, who enter the courthouse through a secure vehicular sally port and are taken to a secure central holding and staging area. A secure prisoner elevator serving holding units between two courtrooms is an easy way to move prisoners to courtrooms without crossing private judicial/juror/staff corridors.

INTERNAL LOCATION OF COURT FUNCTIONS

Clerks' offices, windows for paying fines, and other offices that attract heavy visitor traffic should be located near the main entrance. Courtrooms should be located away from the entrance to minimize noise and distractions. Chambers should also be located away from high-volume public areas. Busier traffic, misdemeanor, and other limited jurisdiction courts belong closer to public entrances, while general jurisdiction courtrooms should be less accessible, perhaps on an upper floor. Jury deliberation rooms, courtroom holding facilities, attorney-client conference rooms, witness waiting rooms, and security officers' stations should be near courtrooms.

LEGEND

OVERVIEW OF COURT TYPES

	FEDERAL	STATE	LOCAL
Appellate	Supreme Court, Court of appeals	Supreme Court, intermediate, and appellate court	
General jurisdiction	District courts	Circuit Superior District	
Limited jurisdiction	Magistrate courts	Justice, district, and county courts	Municipal, city, and town courts
Special courts (examples)	Bankruptcy, tax	Juvenile, traffic, and small claims	
Administrative law courts (examples)	Hearing officers, U.S. Atomic Energy Comm., Federal Maritime Comm.	Workers' comp., public utility commissions, admin. law judges	

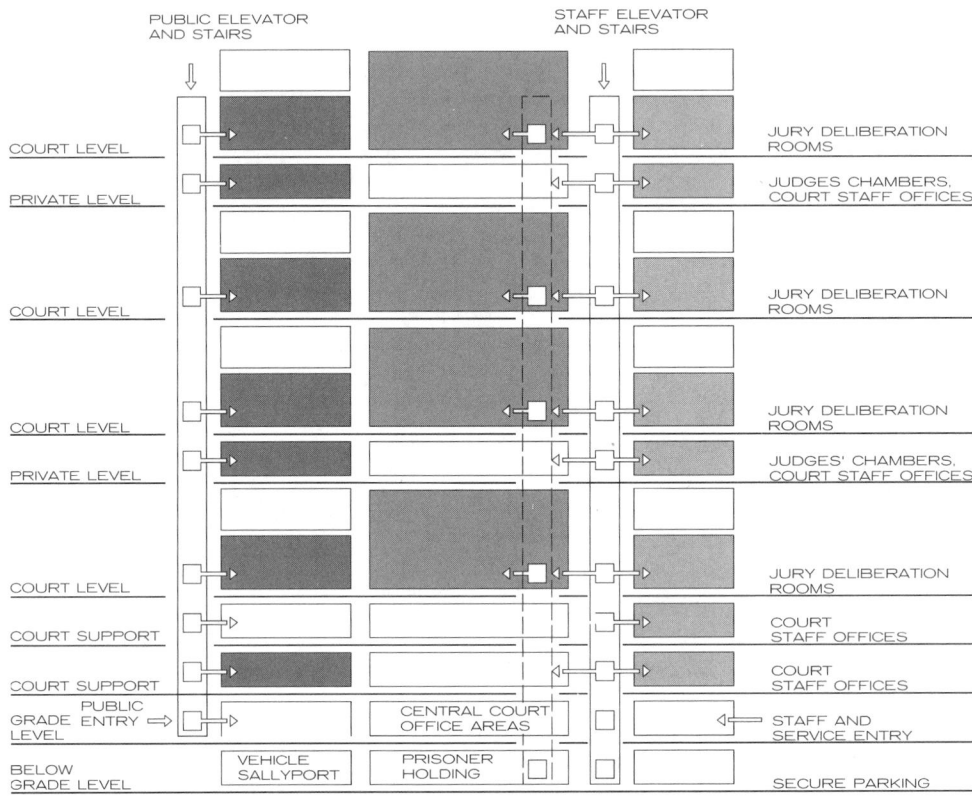

TYPICAL COURTHOUSE STACKING

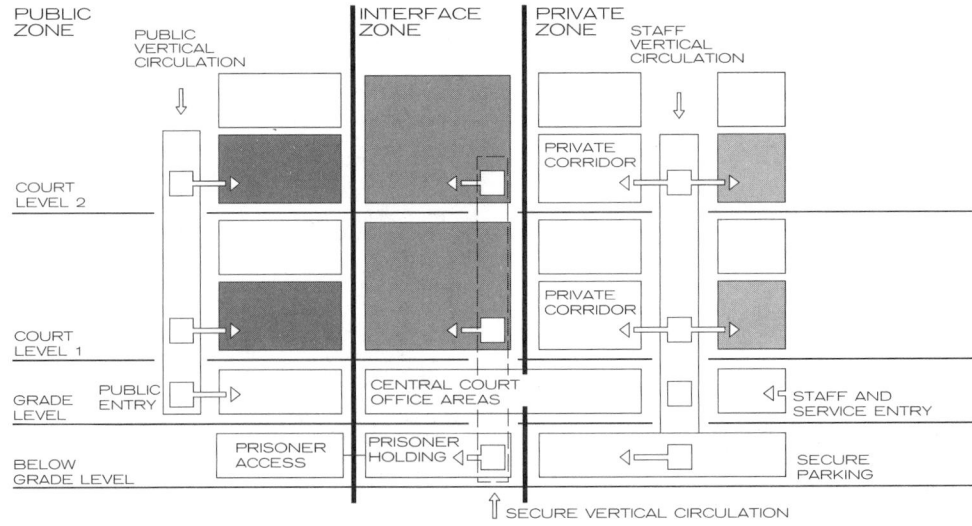

COURTHOUSE CIRCULATION AND ZONING SECTION

Don Hardenbergh; Courtworks; Williamsburg, Virginia

 **JUSTICE FACILITY PLANNING**

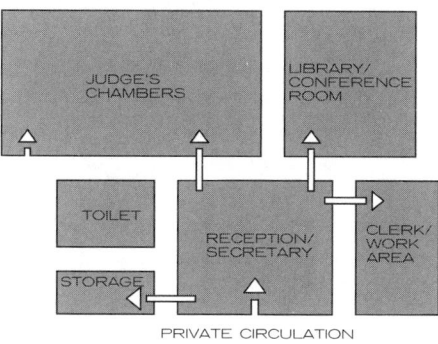

TYPICAL CHAMBER DIAGRAM

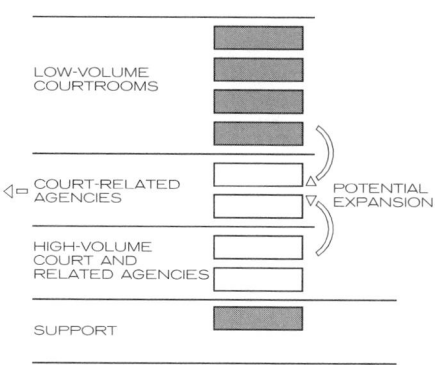

PROVISION FOR FUTURE VERTICAL EXPANSION

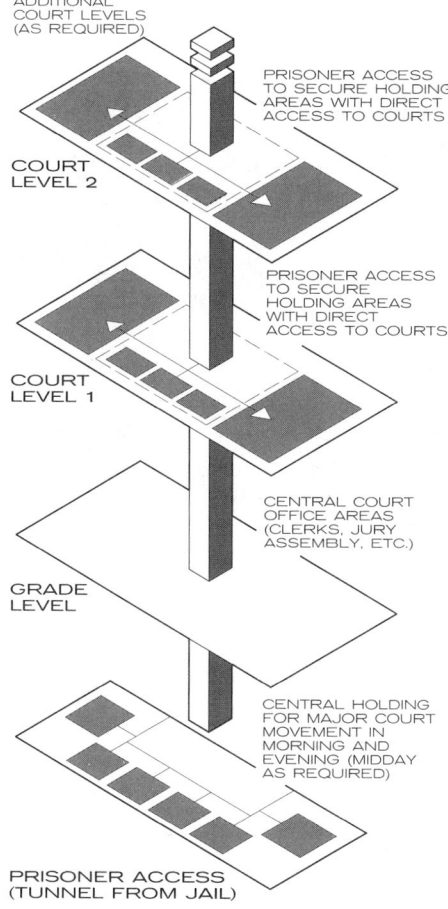

VERTICAL SECURITY CIRCULATION

COURTROOMS

Courtrooms should be easily accessible to the public. In large multistory facilities, they may be on an upper floor, but in small rural courthouses they may be located near the main entrance. Staff and judges should be able to enter the courtroom through a private corridor, and prisoners should enter directly from a secure holding area adjacent to the courtroom. Prisoners and defendants should not enter the courtroom near the public, jurors, or witnesses. Jurors should not pass near the defendant or the public on their way into the courtroom and should be able to move directly from the courtroom to the deliberation room.

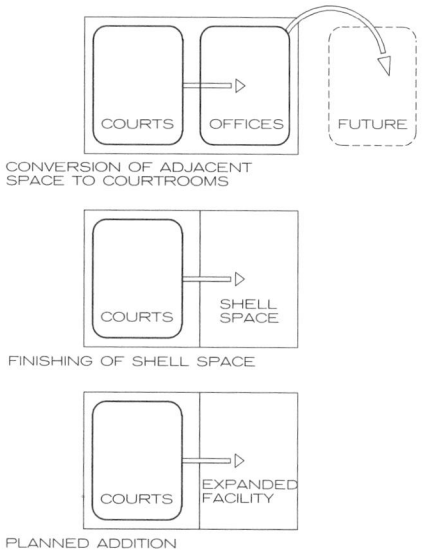

PROVISIONS FOR FUTURE HORIZONTAL EXPANSION

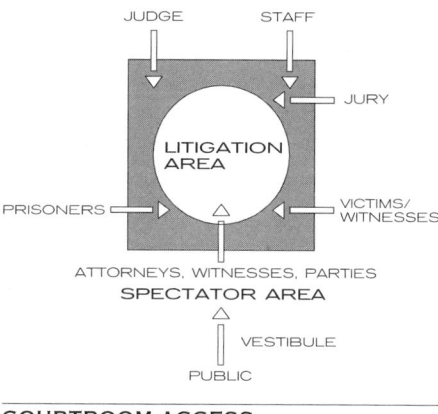

COURTROOM ACCESS

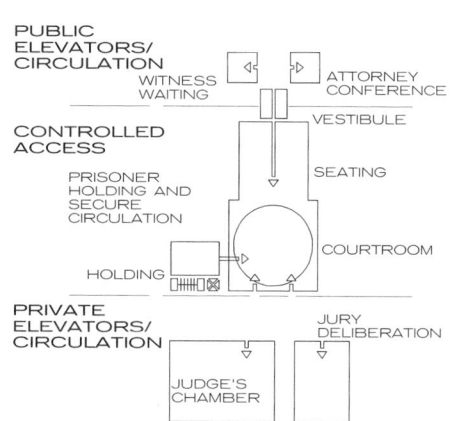

COURT FLOOR ZONING

Judicial chambers contain the judges' private offices and space for judicial staff such as a secretary, court clerk, and law clerk. Chambers may include a conference room and law library. They should be in a private, quiet, and safe area of the courthouse, usually away from the main entrance or on an upper floor. Judges should have quick and easy access to the courtrooms, while persons meeting with them should pass through a reception or screening area.

Traditionally, judicial chambers are adjacent to the judge's courtroom. While this is convenient for the judge, it makes future organizational changes more difficult. In larger courthouses, it is becoming popular to separate judges' chambers from the courtrooms; sometimes they are even on different floors. Such separation permits sharing of common resources such as the law library, conference areas, and court staff rooms; enhances security; and provides flexibility for later adjustments.

GROSSING AND EFFICIENCY FACTORS

Functional courthouses require more space for circulation and building support functions than most other building types. The departmental gross square footage (DGSF) needed for administrative purposes is reasonably consistent with similar requirements in commercial office or government administration buildings. But highly specialized areas such as courtrooms and holding facilities require considerably more internal circulation.

Basic core functions include major public corridors linking departments; private corridors linking courtrooms, judges' chambers, jury deliberation rooms, and other dedicated support spaces; secure corridors linking courtrooms with prisoner detention facilities; public elevators and elevator lobbies; private and secure elevators; stairs; mechanical, electrical, and plumbing chases; public toilet facilities; and the exterior walls of the building.

Because courthouses have unique security and circulation requirements, individual functional areas must be larger than in an office building. To handle the crowds of disparate people, courthouse lobbies, elevator cores and elevator lobbies, and public corridors must be larger than in a typical office building. An appropriate building gross square foot (BGSF) multiplier for courthouses is typically 1.20 to 1.25 of the DGSF.

TYPICAL COURTHOUSE EFFICIENCY FACTORS

Net area	57 to 65%
Departmental gross area	75 to 85%
Building gross area	100%

SECURITY

Effective courthouse security is maintained by combining structural elements, traffic pattern control, security devices, specific security policies, and security staff. The danger of armed violence requires controlled courthouse access; walk-through metal detectors and X-ray devices at the entrance are necessary in larger urban courthouses. The number of public entrances should be limited and lobbies sized and configured to permit queuing at security checkpoints without making people wait outside.

General court floor security should be controlled by a bailiff station in the public area, with access to private corridors restricted by a proximity card access system. Access to private corridors serving judges' chambers, staff, and jury deliberation rooms may be regulated by closed-circuit television (CCTV) and intercom systems or by a receptionist.

Prisoners should move from a secure sally port into a central holding area. Good sight lines in the courtroom are vital to effective control. Bullet-resistant materials should surround the judge's bench, and duress alarms (linked to a CCTV system) are essential for rapid emergency response. Fine and fee payment windows should have security glazing and duress alarms.

FLEXIBILITY AND EXPANSION

Several measures can prolong the operational life of a courthouse. Floor-to-floor heights and bay sizes may be standardized throughout the building to permit future conversion of noncourtroom space into courtrooms. Locating low-to-medium volume office functions on middle floors makes future modifications easier: As these offices outgrow their space they can be moved to adjacent buildings, allowing court functions to expand upward from the high-volume public floors and downward from the trial courtroom floors. Another strategy is to build shell space (an empty floor or room), which can be fitted out and occupied when needed.

Don Hardenbergh; Courtworks; Williamsburg, Virginia

FUNCTION VS. OPERATION

Courthouses can be organized by function or by type of court. All courtrooms, all chambers, and all clerks' offices are grouped together in a functional organization. An operational arrangement separates different types of courts or departments, such as criminal courts, general jurisdiction trial courts, traffic courts, or family courts. Judges for each court are housed with their clerks and courtrooms on separate floors, or in separate areas, of the building.

COURTROOM DESIGN

Image, symbolism, and functionality are important in courthouse design. The arrangement of the participants and furniture reflects society's view of the relationships between the defendant and judicial authority or, in a civil case, of the relationship between the parties. Furnishings and finishes should reflect the seriousness of the proceedings, yet not be too dark and overbearing.

Courtroom space is needed for the judge, court reporter, clerk, bailiff (security officer); prosecutor or plaintiff and attorney; defendant and attorney; witnesses, jury, and spectators. Other participants include social workers, probation officers, interpreters, police officers, and the press.

The traditional courtroom is rectangular and deeper than it is wide, although some modern courtrooms are round or square. The shape of the courtroom must allow all participants to see and hear one another clearly without having to look back and forth too much.

Functionally, courtrooms are divided into a litigation (well) area and a public (spectator) area, separated by a bar or low railing. The litigation area may be rectangular, with the judge's bench located along the front wall or in the corner of the room.

The depth of the litigation area is determined by whether a jury box is included and the distance needed to separate the judge's bench and attorneys' tables. This separation is necessary both to provide adequate circulation within the litigation area and to give prominence to the judge.

The spectator area in most types of courtrooms should have a minimum seating capacity of 75. Traffic or misdemeanor courts, however, may require a minimum seating of 100 or more depending upon the court's workload.

The height of the courtroom should be proportional to the size of the room and should provide appropriate distance from the ceiling for a judge standing at the bench. The ceiling height over the litigation area may be higher than that over the spectator area.

Acoustics should allow no reverberations or echoes, so that participants are able to hear the proceedings clearly. A public address system is generally recommended.

Soundproofing between courtrooms and surrounding spaces (particularly holding cells), double-door vestibules between the public corridors and courtrooms, and carpeting all reduce noise in the courtroom. Generally, the front wall of the courtroom may be constructed of reflective materials to enhance the sound from the litigation area, while the back wall should be covered with sound-absorptive materials to reduce noise.

Courtrooms with exterior windows can suffer from sunlight shadowing and dappling effects, heating and cooling complications, reduced security, exterior noise, and visual distractions. If the location permits, skylights are an excellent source of natural light without the problems presented by windows.

ACCESS FOR PERSONS WITH DISABILITIES

All courtrooms should comply with the Americans with Disabilities Act Accessibility Guidelines for Buildings and Facilities (ADAAG). Areas of the courtroom that need to be accessible are spectator seating, the witness stand, counsel tables, and the jury box. Space should be provided so that all other workstations can be made accessible in the future. The first tier of the jury box may be at floor level, and so may the witness box (the witness box and first tier of the jury box should be the same height).

Allow 48-in.-wide spaces for wheelchairs in the spectator area. The number of wheelchair accessible spaces must meet the seating requirements for assembly areas. All courtrooms with public seating of 51 or more (to a maximum of 300) require four wheelchair locations.

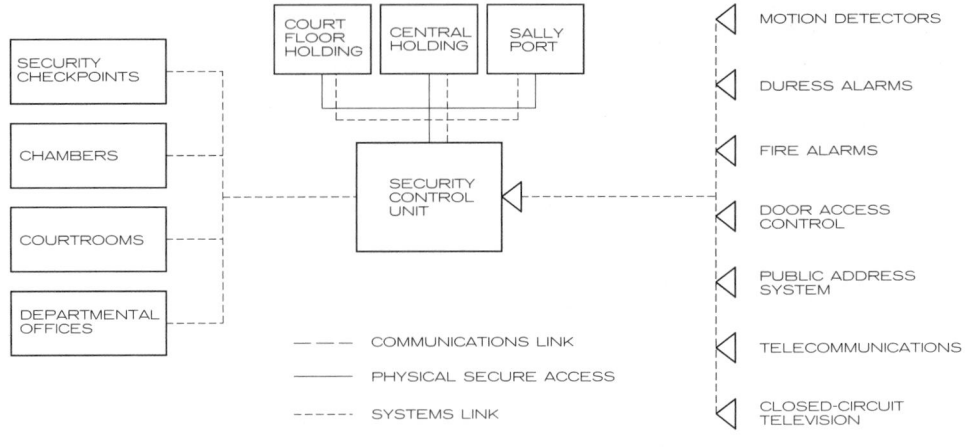

SECURITY CONTROL DIAGRAM

ORGANIZATIONAL STACKING	FUNCTIONAL STACKING
CIRCUIT COURT	COURTROOMS
DISTRICT COURT	CHAMBERS
JUVENILE COURT	COURT-RELATED OFFICES
PROSECUTOR LOBBY/SECURITY	LOBBY/CLERKS/SECURITY

STACKING DIAGRAMS

TYPICAL DIMENSIONS FOR LITIGATION AREAS

TYPE OF COURTROOM	WIDTH (FT)	DEPTH (FT)	TOTAL AREA (SQ FT)
Formal nonjury hearing room	28	30	840
Jury courtroom (1-tier jury box)	32	32	1024
Jury courtroom (2-tier jury box)	36	32	1152
Jury courtroom (3-tier jury box)	38	32	1216
Ceremonial/large courtroom	40	34	1360

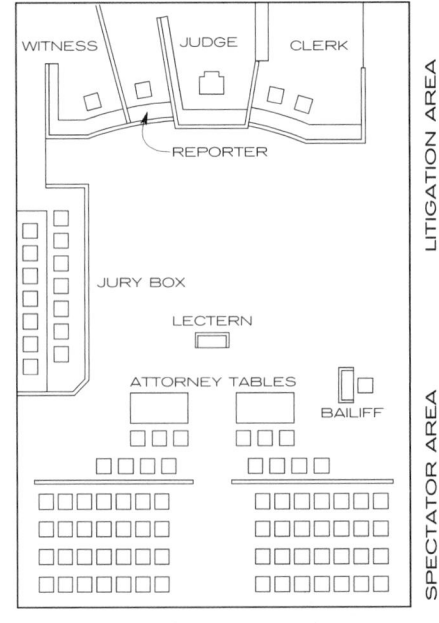

TYPICAL COURTROOM WITH WITNESS ADJACENT TO JURY

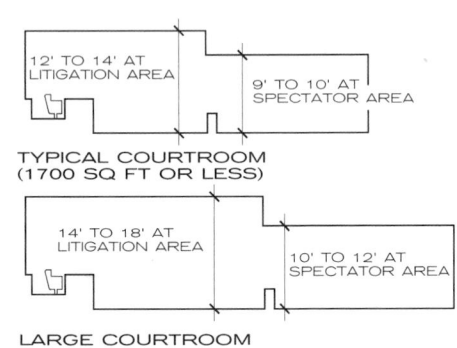

COURTROOM CEILING HEIGHT

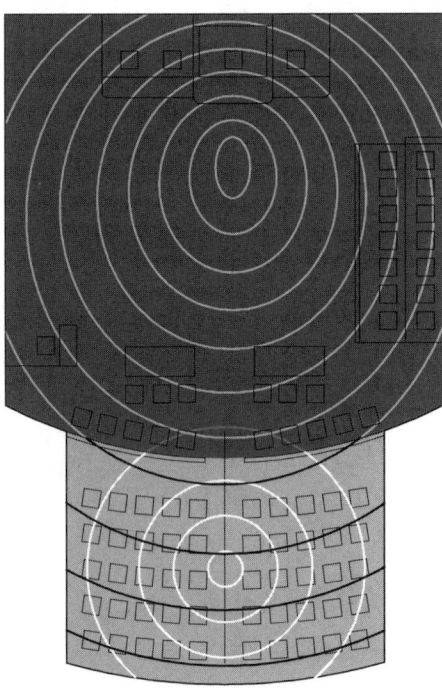

COURTROOM ACOUSTICS

Don Hardenbergh; Courtworks; Williamsburg, Virgina

Sound amplification for the hearing impaired must be installed and available. At least half of each type of courtroom, hearing room, jury deliberation room, and jury assembly room should have an assistive listening (either FM, audio loop, or infrared) device.

SECURITY

Circulation routes for courtroom participants should be clearly separated, and there should be no spaces where a weapon or bomb might be placed or posts or pillars in the courtroom behind which someone might hide. The judge's bench should be shielded with bullet-absorptive material and equipped with duress alarms connected to the central security station.

FURNISHINGS AND FINISHES

The colors and tones of the walls and ceilings should project dignity and calm. Furnishings and finishes should be comfortable, sturdy, durable, vandal-resistant, and easy to clean. Draperies or other window coverings should be used if the courtroom has windows. Seats, benches, and chairs should be comfortable and easy to maintain.

TECHNOLOGICAL APPLICATIONS

Judges, court staff, and attorneys increasingly need access to audiovisual and video equipment, computer terminals, and information databases. While live court reporters will continue taking the record in the immediate future, electronic sound and video recording and playback equipment is becoming more popular and should be available in courtrooms, both for recording the trial and for videoconferencing and hearing remote testimony.

SOUND AND VIDEO EQUIPMENT

Microphones should be located at the bench, clerk's workstation, witness stand, lectern, jury box, and attorneys' tables. Allow space for video display monitors to be installed at the attorneys' tables, lectern, witness stand, and jury box. Camera locations for potential video court reporting, video arraignment, media coverage, or courtroom security surveillance should be identified. Camera coverage of the court proceedings should avoid coverage of the jurors.

SOUND AMPLIFICATION SYSTEMS

All courtrooms should be equipped with sound amplification equipment for assisting the hearing-impaired and for playing back audio exhibits. The master controls should be located at the bench or clerk's station.

COMPUTER TERMINALS AND OTHER EQUIPMENT

Plan on future installation of computer terminals and monitors for the bench, court clerk's station, and court reporter's station in all courtrooms. If possible, recess the clerk's and judge's monitor into the millwork.

Allow for installation of additional electrical outlets at the attorneys' tables, jury box, clerk's station, bench, and public seating area.

THE COURT

CLERK'S WORKSTATION

The court clerk checks case files and records appropriate case dispositions. The clerk frequently passes files to and from the judge and must be close enough to do so easily. The clerk should generally be elevated on one riser so he or she can see the whole courtroom.

The court clerk's work surface should be approximately 30 to 36 in. deep and 4 ft long in order to accommodate case files and computer equipment. The workstation requires the same task lighting as the judge's bench and the clerk's station may have the same duress alarm/intercom link with the central security station as the judge. There should be desk drawers or pigeonholes for paperwork and an inconspicuous, lockable storage area where evidence and trial materials may be stored during recesses.

The court clerk's station should have flush, floor-mounted electrical receptacles, a telephone jack, and cable conduits for computer terminals and a built-in computer monitor. The computer terminal should be equipped with a silent keyboard and laser printer. The control console for the sound amplification system may be located at the court clerk's station, along with a microphone for the clerk.

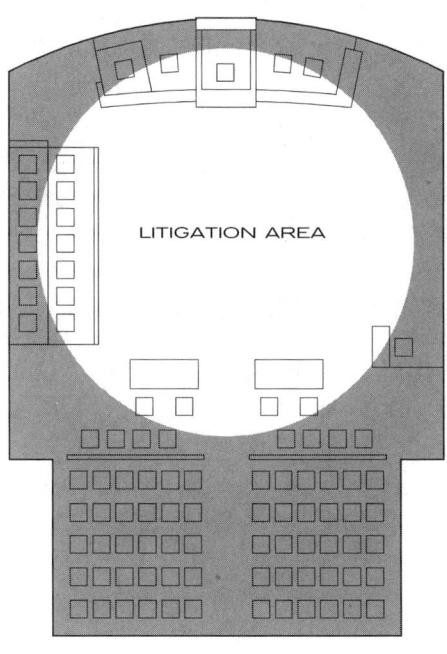

70 FOOTCANDLES

30 FOOTCANDLES

MINIMUM COURTROOM LIGHTING LEVELS

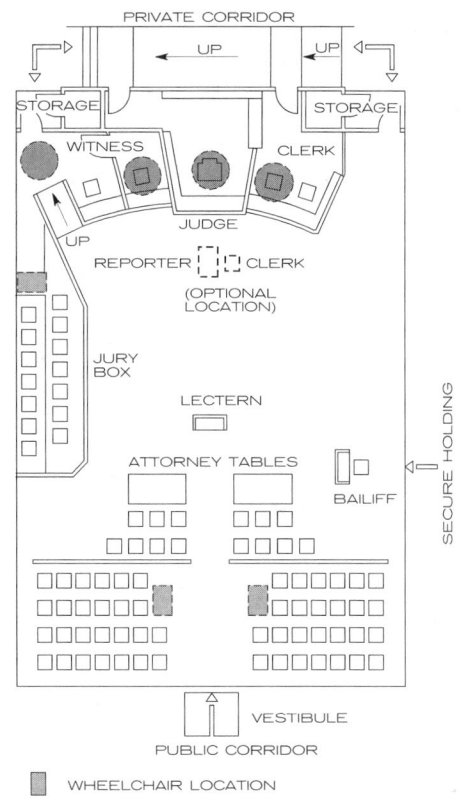

WHEELCHAIR LOCATION

WHEELCHAIR TURNING CIRCLE

WHEELCHAIR ACCESSIBLE COURTROOM

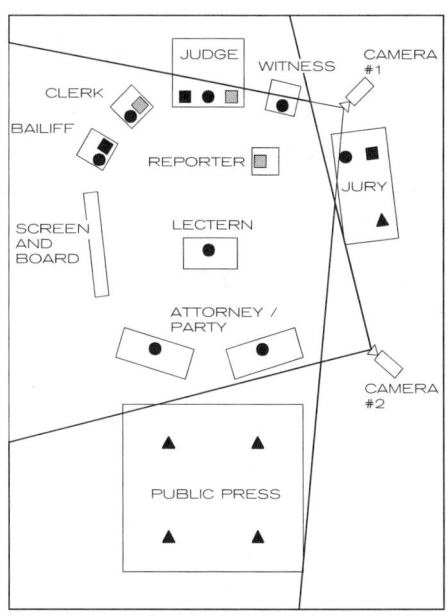

■ DURESS ALARM

▲ SPEAKER

● MICROPHONE

▪ COMPUTER

AUDIOVISUAL EQUIPMENT LOCATIONS

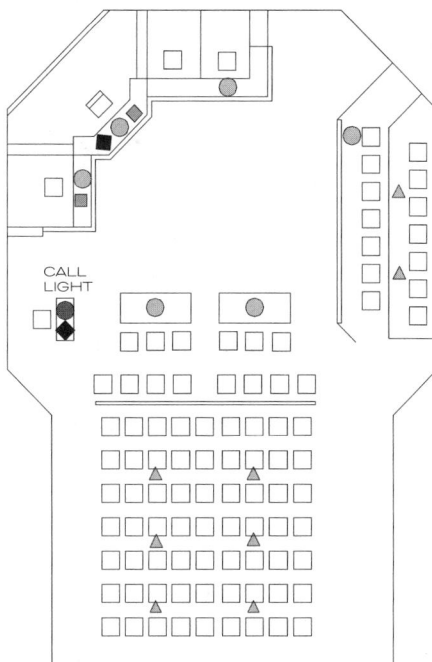

■ COMPUTER TERMINAL

● MICROPHONE

◆ ALARM BUTTON

▲ CEILING-MOUNTED LOUDSPEAKERS

SYSTEM CONTROL LOCATIONS

Don Hardenbergh; Courtworks; Williamsburg, Virginia

JUDGE'S BENCH

The judge's bench should convey dignity and authority. From the bench, the judge should be able to see and hear all courtroom participants, exercise a protective influence over witnesses, address all persons in the courtroom, and pass and receive documents from attorneys, the court clerk, and the court reporter.

The size of the judge's bench should be proportionate to the size of the courtroom. There should be at least 4 ft behind the judge's desk so the judge can move freely for sidebar conferences, reach for reference books, and easily enter and exit the bench.

The bench should include several drawers for supplies and personal items, as well as a bookcase at least six ft wide for legal reference books.

The eye level of the judge should be higher than that of a standing person of average height. Generally, the judge's bench should be elevated 21 in. or at least three risers. A barrier such as an ornamental rail along the front of the bench prevents individuals from approaching too close to the bench or reading documents or notes that are on the judge's bench.

Room lighting should be augmented by task lighting directly above the bench. Lighting controls for the entire courtroom should be located at or near the bench or the clerk's station.

Electrical receptacles flush-mounted in the floor and cable conduits for a built-in video display and computer terminal should be installed. The bench should be equipped with a telephone and a microphone connected to an amplifier controlled by the judge or the clerk.

COURT REPORTER

The court reporter's station should be adjacent to the witness stand so the reporter can clearly view and hear voice testimony. The court reporter should also have an unobstructed view of the entire litigation area, including the judge, witness box, jury box, and attorneys' tables.

The court reporter's station is generally at floor level, which accentuates the prominence of the judge's bench and keeps clear the judge's and attorneys' view of the witness. It should have space and comfortable seating appropriate to the recording methods being used. The workstation should have several electrical outlets and enough space for electronic recording equipment and sound reinforcement equipment should be provided. It also should be made ready for computer equipment and video recording technology. A silent printer in the courtroom may be needed for producing transcripts.

WITNESS STAND

All courtroom participants must be able clearly to hear and see the witness. In addition, because many witnesses testify at a personal sacrifice of time, money, and sometimes safety, they deserve the court's courtesy and protection.

The witness stand is traditionally placed between the jury and the judge, but many courts now use a movable witness box that can face the jury box. The witness stand should be no closer than 4 ft to the jury box so the nearest juror is 7 to 8 ft away. There should be a physical barrier between the witness stand and the judge to prevent the witness from seizing objects from the bench.

The witness stand should be 3$\frac{1}{2}$ to 4 ft wide and approximately 5 ft deep to allow for easy entry and exit. Witnesses must frequently receive, examine, and return exhibits; a desk area approximately 15 to 18 in. deep for resting files or evidence may extend from the front or side of the stand.

The exhibit area for screens, chalkboards, and computer and video monitors should be close to the witness stand and visible to jurors and witnesses. The exhibit area could be placed between the witness stand and the jury box.

There should be electrical receptacles and cable conduits for built-in video display of recorded evidence and taped depositions and for review of automated case transcripts. A movable microphone should be mounted in the witness stand so that it is both unobtrusive and able to pick up the testimony of children and soft-spoken witnesses.

JURY BOX

Jurors are temporary "officers of the court" and should be afforded the comfort and courtesies appropriate to their role. The front of the jury box should be shielded with a modesty panel. A 9- or 10-in. shelf should be installed as part of the rail around the jury box, both to allow jurors to examine documents and exhibits and to prevent attorneys from getting too close to the jurors. The first row of seating may be at floor level to permit wheelchair access, with the second tier elevated on one riser. The jury box should accommodate 14 jurors (12 jurors and 2 alternates).

Jurors must be able to hear the judge, witnesses, and attorneys clearly, and they should have unobstructed sight lines to the judge, witness, attorneys, and exhibit area.

The jury box should allow 10 to 12 sq ft per juror. A 14-person jury box needs to be 19 to 21 ft long and approximately 8 ft deep. The jury box should be large enough to accommodate a wheelchair. Audio jacks for earphones for the hearing impaired may be installed at one or two positions. Seats should be fastened to the floor and should swivel and have armrests. Many jury boxes have a footrail.

The jury box should be at least 4 ft from the nearest attorneys' table and 6 ft from the nearest attorney's chair. In addition it should be far enough from the spectator area to inhibit any physical or verbal contact. A bailiff's station may be located between the jurors and the spectators to prevent such communication.

The entrance to the jury box should be near the exit to the jury deliberation rooms. Jurors should not have to cross the courtroom or move through the spectator seating area.

The jury box may be equipped with electrical receptacles, cable conduits, and computer and video terminals for display of recorded and automated evidence, taped depositions, and case transcripts. A microphone may be placed near the jury box.

ATTORNEYS' TABLES

Each table should be at least 7 ft long and should seat up to four people. The tabletop should be 3 to 4 ft wide to accommodate books, documents, and other work materials. The area of each attorneys' table, including chairs and 2-ft circulation space behind the chairs, should be approximately 64 sq ft to allow the parties to move freely around the table. The tables should not have drawers or concealed recesses where a weapon or bomb may be placed.

Attorneys should be able to see and hear all courtroom participants clearly. The litigation area lighting above the attorneys' tables may be augmented with direct task lighting if necessary.

Attorneys and litigants should be able to confer in private. To prevent conversations from being overheard, or documents from being read, attorneys' tables should be 4 ft apart and about 6 ft from the nearest juror or spectator.

The front of the judge's bench should be at least 10 ft from the front of the attorneys' tables. This distance conveys judicial objectivity and dignity.

Electrical receptacles and cable conduits for built-in computer display terminals may be provided for accessing legal databases, reviewing taped depositions, and video display of evidence, exhibits, and transcripts. There should be flush floor-mounted electrical outlets, microphones, and a telephone line so that attorneys may be connected to their office computers by modem.

BAILIFF'S STATION

The bailiff, or deputy sheriff, is responsible for the security of the courtroom and all participants. He or she must have access to an alarm connected to the main security office.

The bailiff generally moves about the courtroom but should be provided with a small table and movable swivel chair, which should occupy no more than 15 sq ft. The area surrounding the bailiff's station should be free of obstacles.

The bailiff should be able to see all areas of the courtroom clearly. The bailiff's station should be located near the defendant's table or by the jury box.

SPECTATOR SEATING

Public bench-type seating at floor level allows access by disabled persons and accentuates the raised litigation area and judge's bench. Aisles should be wide enough to allow wheelchair access.

Public entry into the courtroom should be through a vestibule for security purposes and for noise control. The floor should be carpeted and the surrounding walls acoustically treated.

EVIDENCE DISPLAY AND STORAGE

After exhibits are introduced into evidence and marked, they should be displayed in full view of the court. Hazardous exhibits, such as firearms and other objects that could be used as weapons, drugs, and toxic substances should be placed away from the witness, jury box, and defendant's table. Usually, the clerk's station is the most suitable location. Charts and displays are best presented either between the witness box and the jury box, so the witness may point to them, or across from the jury box if their detail is large enough to be seen at a distance. Increasingly, evidence, including videotapes, physical evidence, computer animations, X-rays, and documents, will be displayed on video monitors.

The courtroom should have an inconspicuous evidence closet where the clerk may secure items during recess. In addition, approximately 40 sq ft should be provided for storing such items as projectors, television monitors, chart boards, easel pads, tripods, chalk and markers, cleaning cloths, pins and tape, and pointers. These may be stored behind the courtroom.

ADDITIONAL SOURCES OF INFORMATION

American Bar Association. *Twenty Years of Courthouse Design Revisited, Supplement to the American Courthouse.* Chicago, 1993.

American Institute of Architects. *Justice Facilities Review.* Washington, D.C. (published annually).

Don Hardenbergh. *The Courthouse, A Planning and Design Guide for Courthouse Facilities.* Williamsburg, Va., 1991.

Hunter Hurst. *Shaping a New Order in the Court: Sourcebook for Juvenile and Family Court Design.* Pittsburgh, Pa., 1992.

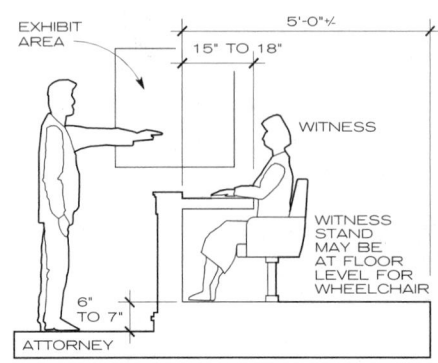

JUDGE'S BENCH

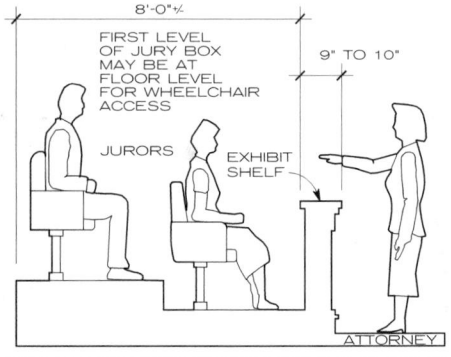

WITNESS STAND

TWO-TIER JURY BOX

Don Hardenbergh; Courtworks; Williamsburg, Virginia

GENERAL

The regional enclosed mall is suburbia's answer to the small town main street. Tenants of all types offer a comprehensive and diverse range of products that fit all budgets, attracting many types of shoppers to this type of facility. In fact, in sparsely populated areas, a regional enclosed mall can draw from a radius of 200 miles.

LOCATION

The success of a regional enclosed shopping mall depends on its accessibility to the consumer. Convenient, efficient, and easily recognized access to a facility is essential. Therefore, malls must be located adjacent to several major vehicular routes and within the reach of public transportation. The site must be able to accommodate not only the mall structure itself, but convenient parking for thousands of cars. If a site does not have enough space to meet the parking requirements set forth by the local government, a parking garage may be considered. However, the cost of a garage is enormous and should be avoided if possible.

PARKING

The number of parking spaces required for a regional enclosed mall is generally determined in relation to the area of the anchor store at a typical rate of 5-6 cars per 1000 sq ft. Delineation, organization, and facilitation of vehicular distribution among thousands of parking spaces is accomplished with inner and outer ring roads. The inner ring typically follows the contours of the mall, separating the structure from the parking area, while the outer ring (perimeter road) follows the perimeter of the parking area, property line, or site constraints, connecting adjacent roadways to the parking area.

Between the ring roads the parking spaces are oriented in a fan pattern with each row perpendicular to the mall structure. Orientation in this fashion eliminates the hierarchical pitfalls that result from parking rows situated parallel to the mall. When rows are parallel, shoppers often wait for someone to pull out of the rows they consider more desirable, causing traffic jams near mall entrances.

In a warm or moderate climate, long rows of parking should be interrupted by tree islands to provide shade. However, in a climate where snow is a factor, parking lot segmentation should be avoided. Cost-effective, efficient snow removal requires large unobstructed areas.

Regardless of climate, parking lot drainage is a factor and should be considered. Low points should be located so a shopper's path will not cross a wet or icy drainage area en route from car to mall or vice versa.

ENTRANCES AND EXITS

Opportunities for shoppers to enter the mall must be provided at regular intervals to limit ambulatory travel distance. Anchor stores often furnish several entrances that allow shoppers to enter the store directly. In fact, 40% of all mall shoppers choose to enter malls in this manner, while the remainder use entrances into the mall.

Mall entrances are typically located at the midpoint between anchor stores. However, if anchor stores are particularly far apart, additional mall entrances should be furnished. Keep both horizontal and vertical travel distances between the mall entrance and the parking area to a minimum. Straight pedestrian sidewalks with few steps and/or ramps are appreciated by both the handicapped and other, package-laden shoppers. Ramps and curb-cuts are required for handicapped access.

Because of the relative size of the mall structure and the number of entrances, it is imperative that each mall entrance be creatively and independently designated with correlating signage. This practice allows shoppers to easily recall which entrance they used to enter the mall.

While all mall and anchor store entrances double as egress locations, most local building codes require interstitial exits. Typically, an exit is required every 400 ft, so that shoppers need not traverse more than 200 ft to reach the nearest exit. Often, emergency exits from the primary and secondary concourses are permitted to connect to delivery halls behind the tenant spaces, which lead to an exterior door. For required door quantities and travel distance limitations, check local codes.

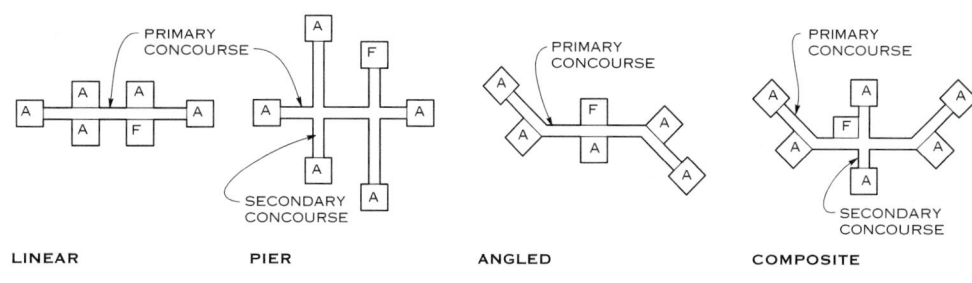

A—anchor store; F—food court

MALL CONFIGURATION TYPES

LINEAR PIER ANGLED COMPOSITE

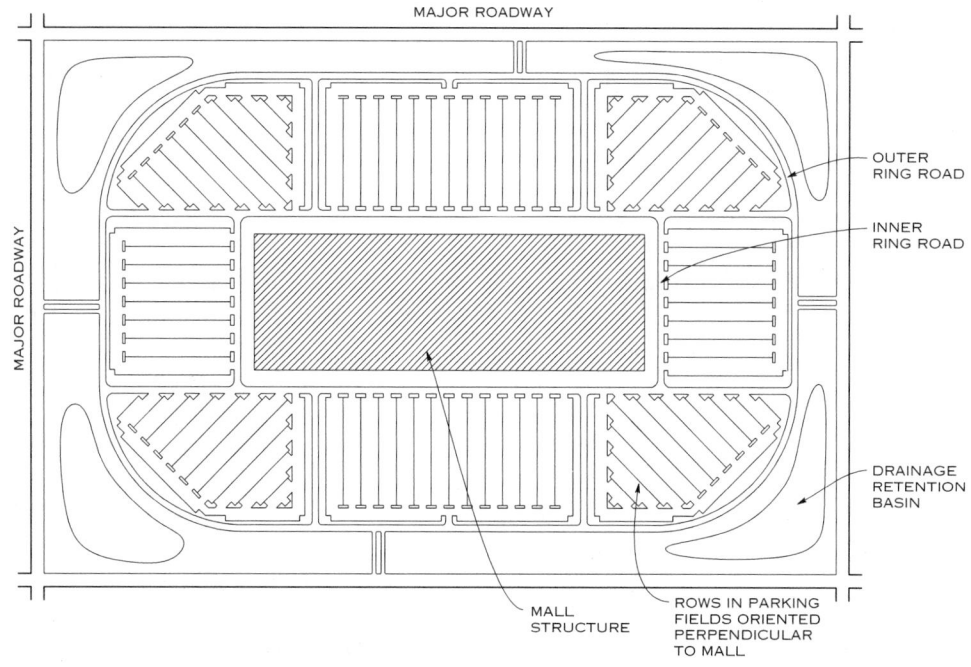

SHOPPING MALL SITING/PARKING

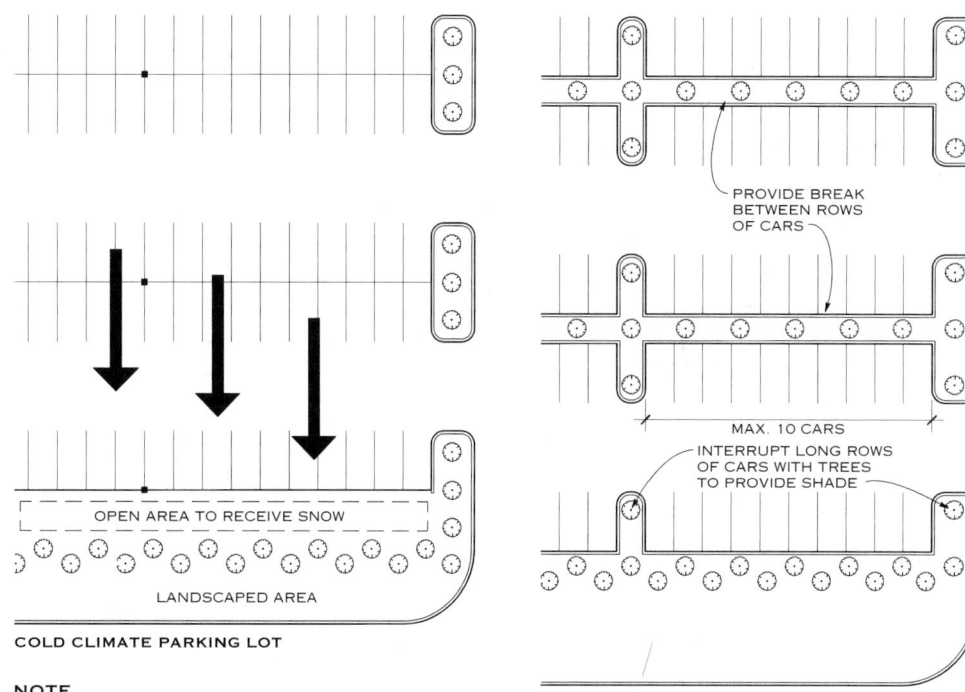

COLD CLIMATE PARKING LOT

WARM CLIMATE PARKING LOT

NOTE

Parking lots in cold climates must be obstruction free; snowplows should be able to clear long swaths easily.

SHOPPING MALL PARKING LAYOUTS

Richard M. Roberts, AIA; Omega Design Architects, P.C.; Syracuse, New York

CONCOURSES

Regional enclosed malls must be designed in a way that will draw visitors through the massive space, past the attractions of storefront display windows. The design feature used to accomplish this is the node, a point element with gravitational qualities. Careful placement of nodes throughout the common areas of a mall will encourage mall visitors to travel to areas beyond the limit of their view. Since this limit at any given moment in a mall is about 300 ft, it is essential to place a magnetic draw—a node—every 300 ft or less. Concourse intersections, mall entrances, and anchor store en-trances constitute nodes.

Nodes at concourse intersections offer opportunities to break up long linear spaces and provide soothing features such as landscaping, fountains, and furniture. Nodes also serve as log-ical pivot points around which to bend mall concourses should that be necessary or desired. Tenant spaces adjacent to concourse intersections command high lease rates, making it desirable to maximize this type of space in a mall.

A typical regional enclosed mall consists of a primary concourse transected by several secondary concourses. The primary concourse is terminated at both ends with an anchor store. These stores and accompanying signage provide focal points that conduct shoppers through the mall space. Secondary concourses end at anchor stores or mall entrances.

A typical concourse should be between 25 and 80 ft wide, and up to 80% of this width should be effective pedestrian traffic area. The concourse ceiling height should be 60-100% of the concourse width. Ceiling heights outside this range result in spatial proportions that discomfort shoppers, resulting in decreased shopper traffic.

In multiple level malls, floor/ceiling penetrations within concourses are essential to allow shoppers to see what is on other levels. These penetrations, which entice shoppers from one level to another, should be placed and sized so a shopper on one level can see the signage of a store above or below on the opposite side of the concourse.

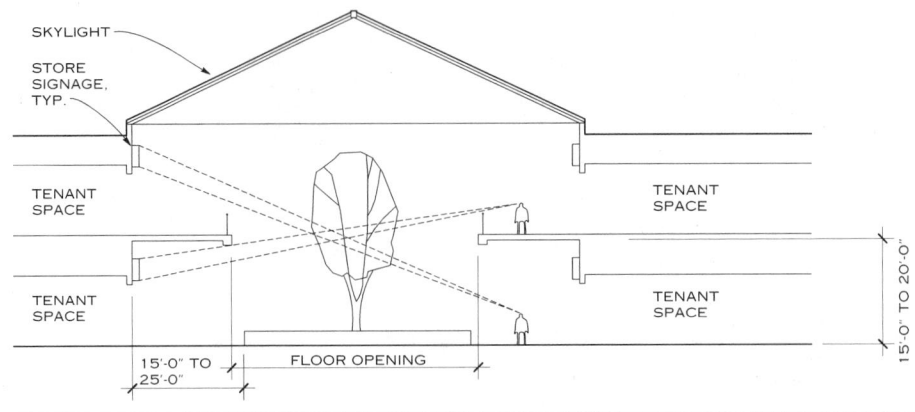

SIGHT LINES WITHIN MALL CONCOURSE

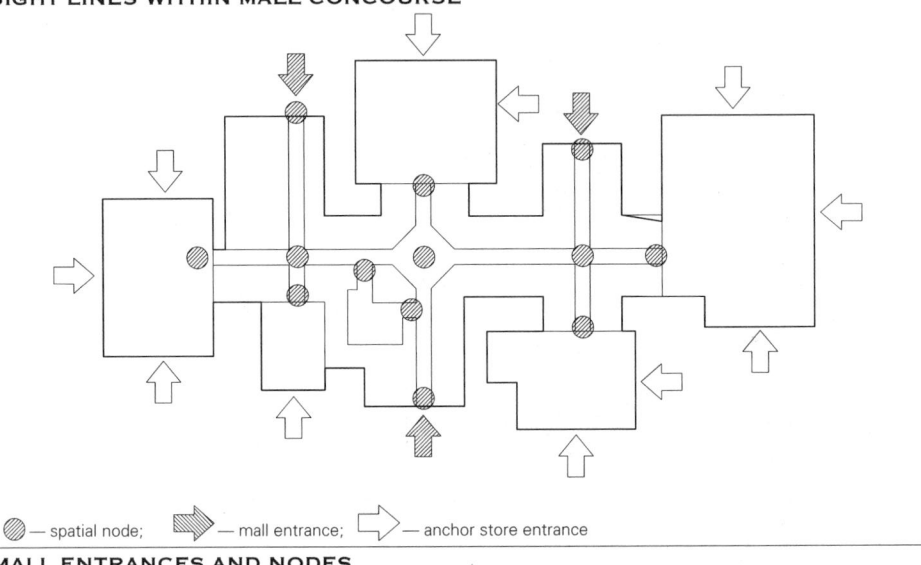

— spatial node;　— mall entrance;　— anchor store entrance

MALL ENTRANCES AND NODES

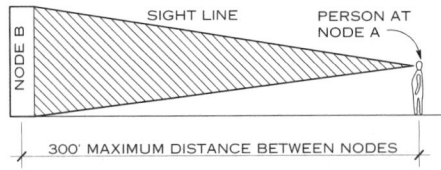

HORIZONTAL PERCEPTION LIMIT

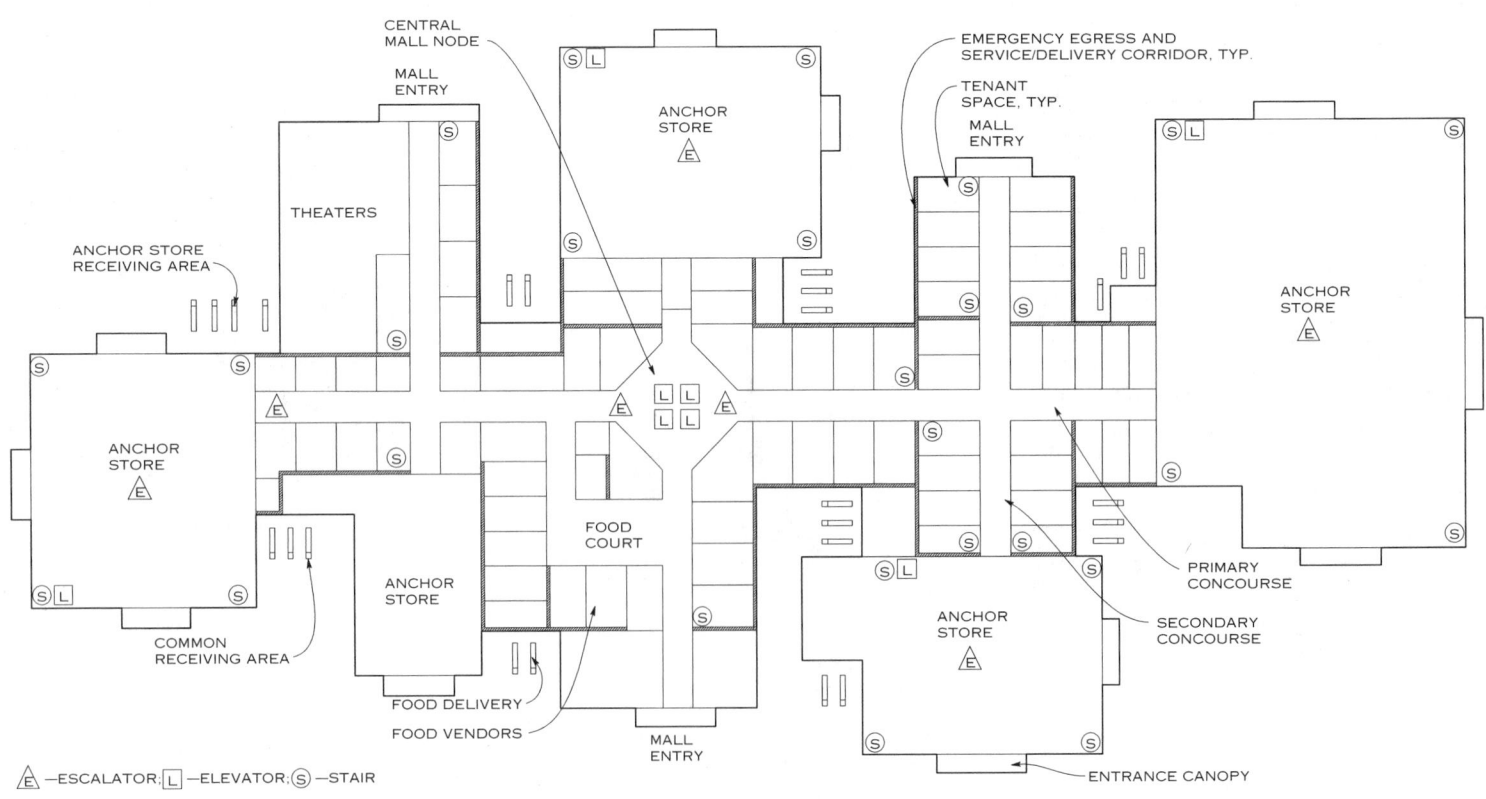

 —ESCALATOR; L —ELEVATOR; S —STAIR

TYPICAL MALL LAYOUT

Richard M. Roberts, AIA; Omega Design Architects, P.C.; Syracuse, New York

VERTICAL TRANSPORTATION

In multiple story malls it is necessary to provide escalators, stairs, and elevators to accommodate hundreds or thousands of visitors with varying degrees of mobility.

Escalators are the primary mode of interlevel transport in shopping malls as they can handle the greatest volume of people in a given unit of time and can function as stairs in the event of a power outage. Locate escalators in pairs (up and down) in several convenient locations within the primary concourse and in lengthy secondary concourses. Shoppers should be able to see both the point of departure and the destination before committing to the interlevel travel.

Stairs are the secondary mode of interlevel transport in shopping malls. Locate several stairways in the primary and secondary concourses in much the same manner as the escalators. In addition, provide stairs in accordance with local codes to accommodate exiting shoppers in the event of a fire. Fire stairs are typically located every 400 ft, so the maximum travel distance from any point to a fire stairwell is 200 ft. Check local codes to confirm this distance.

Elevators, the tertiary mode of vertical transportation, are required to accommodate shoppers with limited mobility or a handicap, carrying heavy packages, or pushing strollers. Elevators should be clearly identified and located near both a concourse intersection and a mall entrance.

THEATERS

Regional enclosed malls often include a theater complex with 6 to 24 screens. Generally, the number of screens is based on the market demand as determined by the theater company. Theaters draw large numbers of visitors in hours that do not coincide with the hours of operation of most stores in the mall. As a result, a dead space in front of the theater entrance is often created. For this reason, a theater complex entrance is often located close to a mall entrance in an area that does not command prime lease rates and does not interrupt pedestrian flow.

Theaters require multiple exits that deposit viewers from the screen area to the exterior of the mall. These exits often open into parking or landscaped areas, so it is necessary to plan landscaping, lighting, and connections to the parking areas to provide adequate security.

FOOD COURTS/RESTAURANTS

Food courts draw tremendous numbers of mall visitors. For this reason adjacent tenant spaces are extremely desirable and command prime lease rates. Locate food courts in conjunction with a mall entrance or concourse intersection and

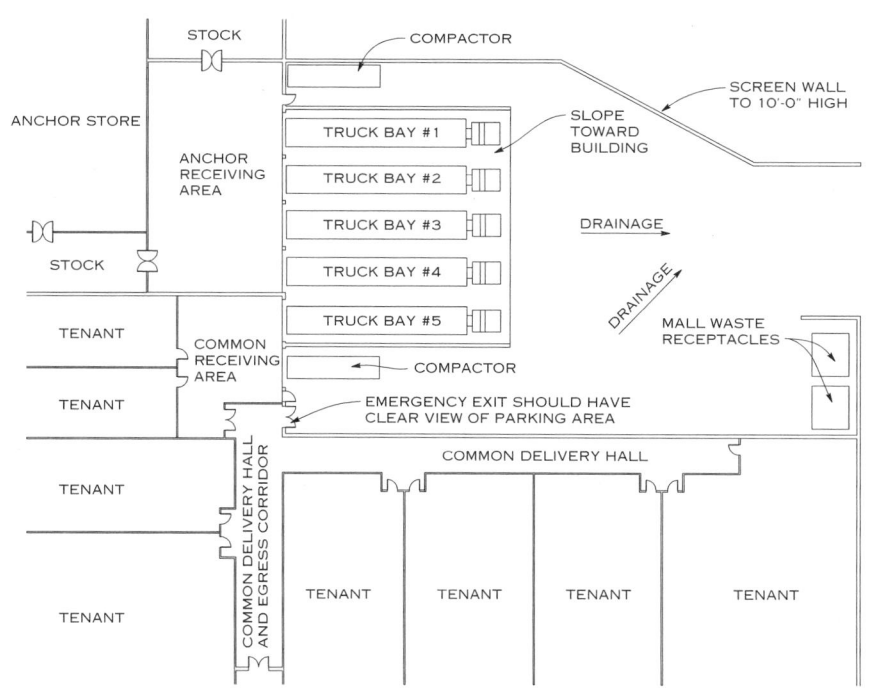

NOTES

1. Each anchor store will have its own receiving area comprising three or more truck bays and a compactor.
2. Interstitial tenants do not occupy enough space or move enough product to warrant individual receiving areas. Instead, several tenants (as many as 25) utilize a common receiving area and loading dock, which usually comprises two truck bays and a compactor. Bay depth should be great enough to allow a delivery vehicle to remain parked without interrupting vehicular traffic in the parking lot.
3. A network of halls behind individual tenant spaces connects stores to the shared receiving area, and each tenant space has one or more doors that access a support hall. Waste collection is performed through this hall.

TYPICAL MALL DELIVERY AREA

provide direct access to a service hall for food delivery and garbage removal.

The size of a food court and the number of food vendors depends on the size of the mall, the number of out-parcel restaurants nearby, and the developer's vision.

In addition to the many food vendors in the food court, it is typical to see several sit-down restaurants in a regional shopping mall. These restaurants are usually located along exterior walls of the mall near mall entrances and often have their own entrances from the outdoors. A location along outside walls allows these establishments to have windows.

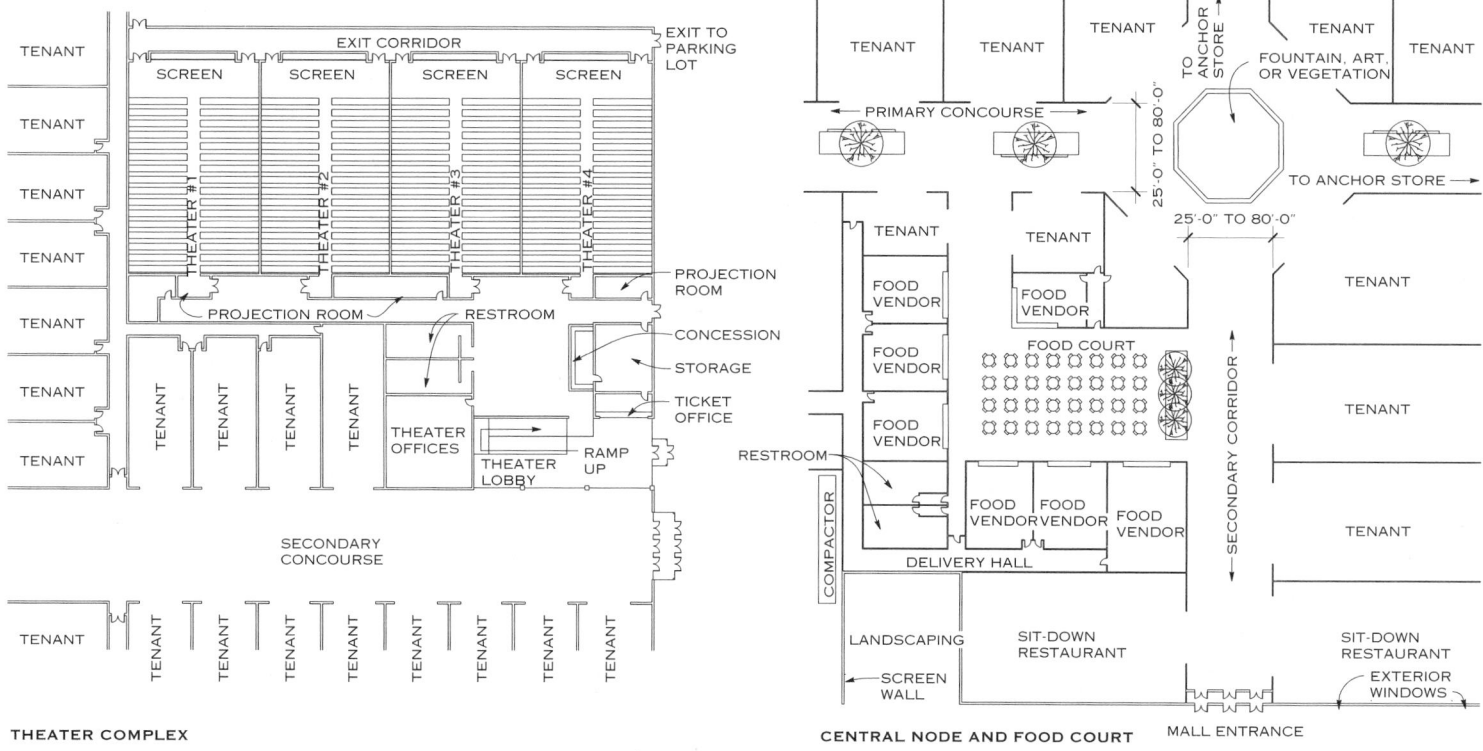

THEATER COMPLEX   **CENTRAL NODE AND FOOD COURT**

TYPICAL MALL COMMERCIAL AMENITIES

Richard M. Roberts, AIA; Omega Design Architects, P.C.; Syracuse, New York

MALL GENERAL OFFICES

All regional enclosed malls have general mall offices located somewhere in the building. Generally included are offices for leasing officers, the mall manager, and the operations manager. Because this office space generates no rent, it is commonly situated in an obscure, although not inaccessible, location far from the typical path of a mall visitor. It is common to see community rooms and space available to the public for rent near mall offices.

SECURITY OFFICES

A mall employs several security officers who monitor cameras, traverse the concourses, respond to security emergencies, and provide other security services. These individuals have offices in areas of security risks or low rent generation but not inaccessible to mall visitors. Often security offices are located next to restrooms or adjacent to the mall general offices.

PUBLIC RESTROOMS

Restrooms are equally distributed throughout a mall, generally off a secondary concourse. It is essential, however, not to place the restrooms in a remote location where security could be a problem. It is good practice to locate mall restrooms adjacent to mall offices, security offices, community rooms, and information areas, as these elements offer some security. A struggle or scream from an individual in the restroom should be audible in these adjacent spaces. A large restroom must be located adjacent to the food court.

All mall restrooms must be accessible to the handicapped with proper fixtures, partitions, and doors. All materials used in restrooms should be made of vandal-resistant materials.

ANCHOR STORES

A mall's success relies heavily on the presence of anchor stores, so much so that mall development proceeds only after anchor store leases have been secured. Anchor stores reside at the prime locations in a mall—the termini of primary and secondary concourses. Store signage is located on all visible exterior faces and above the interior mall entrance. Anchor stores generally comprise as much as 60% of the total gross lease area (GLA) of the mall.

Typically an anchor store is between 50,000 and 150,000 sq ft and has one or more levels. If a store has multiple levels, it will have internal vertical transportation via escalators, stairs, and elevators. An anchor store generally incorporates the following spaces:

The SALES FLOOR occupies 70-80% of the total floor area of a store. The floor, which incorporates shopper circulation paths, is divided into departments with stud walls, fixtures, and material variation.

FITTING ROOMS are provided in departments selling wearable items. They are usually built without a ceiling and with walls that end below the ceiling of the store to prevent shoplifters from concealing items in the ceiling.

STOCK/STORAGE AREAS occupy 5-15% of the total floor area of a store. They have no wall, floor, or ceiling finishes and are adjacent to the receiving area.

The RECEIVING AREA/LOADING DOCK is located on an exterior wall adjacent to the stock/storage area.

STORE OFFICES occupy 3-5% of the total floor area of a store. They are usually grouped in a cluster, often adjacent to the restrooms, but several may be scattered around the sales floor, where they are more accessible to the public.

RESTROOMS are often located near store offices and vertical transportation. Multiple restrooms are provided for shoppers, while separate facilities for employees may be placed elsewhere in the store. Restrooms are built with gypsum wallboard ceilings to prevent shoplifters from concealing items.

TENANT SPACES

Mall tenants and their requirements differ so greatly it is difficult to typify tenant space. Occupied area can be as small as 500 sq ft (jewelry or specialty stores) or as large as 40,000 sq ft (book or large chain clothing stores). Generally, tenant space is on a single level, but many larger tenants spread their space between levels, with a vertical transportation connection in the space.

Tenant space generally includes the following:

The SALES FLOOR occupies 80-90% of the total floor area of a tenant space. Most have few, if any, integrated aisles (created with display cases or floor materials), although especially large tenants may use the space more like an anchor store.

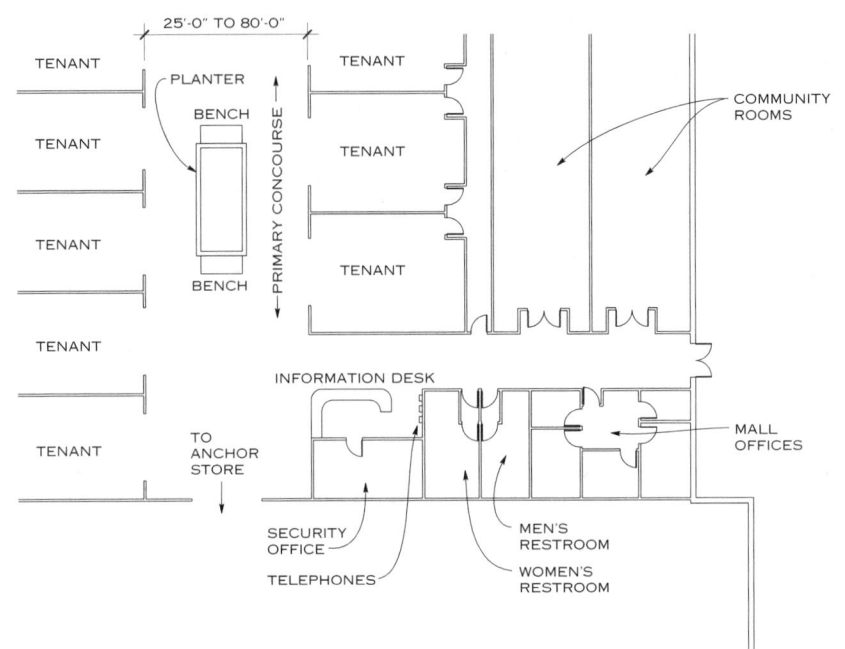

TYPICAL MALL OFFICES, COMMUNITY ROOMS, AND RESTROOMS

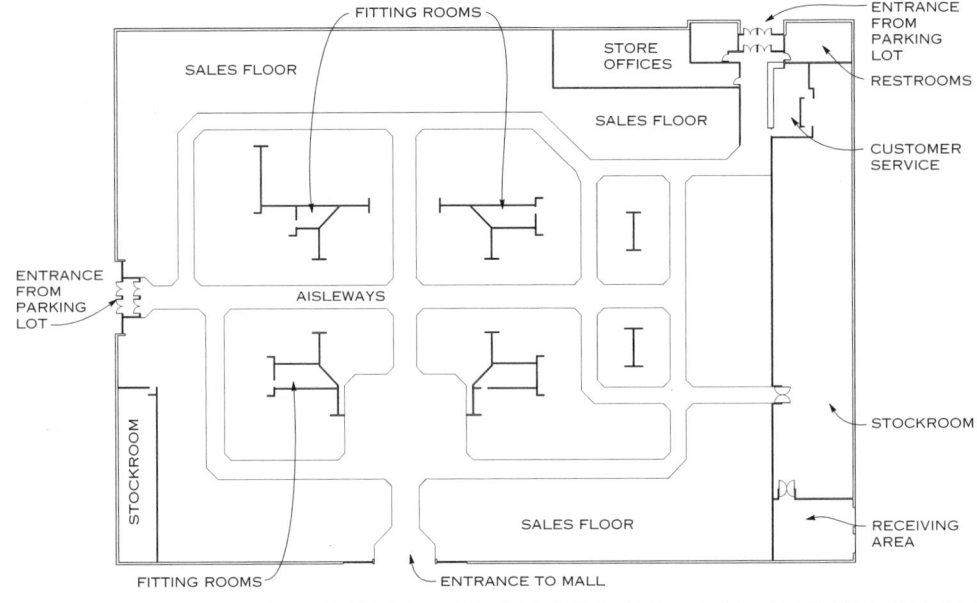

TYPICAL ANCHOR STORE

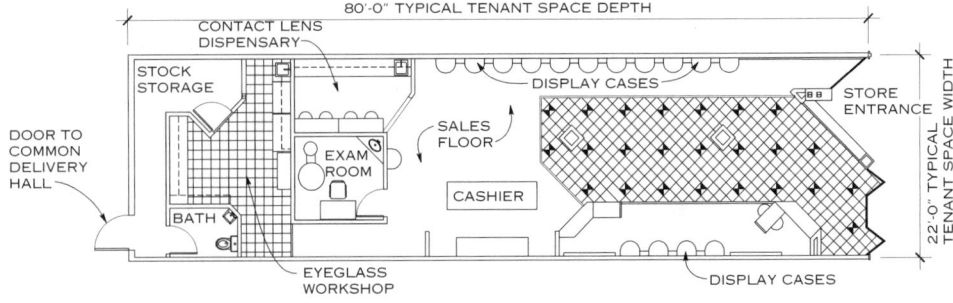

TYPICAL TENANT SPACE (SPECIALTY EYEGLASS SHOP SHOWN)

FITTING ROOMS are often located along rear or side walls of a store and are built without a ceiling and with walls below the ceiling of the store to prevent shoplifters from concealing items in the ceiling.

The STOCK/STORAGE AREA occupies 10-20% of the total floor area in tenant spaces. Located in the rear of the store, it has access to shared receiving areas and delivery halls.

The STORE OFFICE is typically in the rear of the store, where it is used by the store manager. It is not meant to be accessible to the public.

RESTROOMS are provided for employee use only in the stock/storage area. Small stores typically have one unisex restroom, while larger stores have multiple restrooms.

Richard M. Roberts, AIA; Omega Design Architects, P.C.; Syracuse, New York

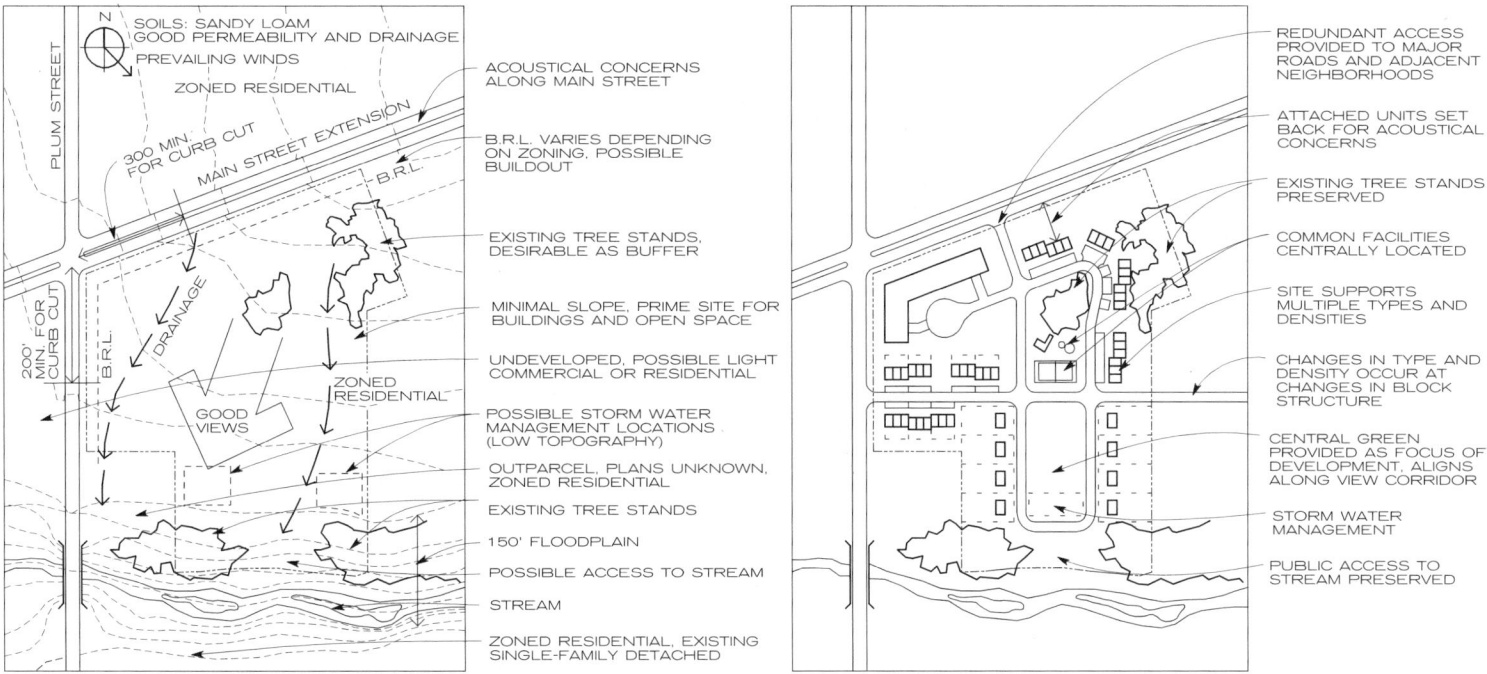

SITE ANALYSIS AND SCHEMATIC SITE PLAN

GENERAL

Residential site planning requires balance among a large number of complex and often competing priorities.

ORIENTATION

No unit should be without sun for at least part of a winter day; south-facing units are premium. Prevailing winds, both regional and local, should be studied so that no building is entirely masked. At the same time, harsh winds should be buffered by plantings, and if buildings are differentiated by side, bedroom and service sides should face the harsh wind.

USE AND ENHANCEMENT OF NATURAL AMENITIES

Too frequently, housing projects are named for amenities that are destroyed during development. Promontories, mature trees, and water features should be incorporated into the design and, if possible, enhanced.

PROVISION FOR VIEWS

Spectacular views can drive the design of a housing project, but every project should strive to provide reasonable views from all units. Although no unit should have a parking area as its only view, many people enjoy views of streets and roadways. Views of green space are important, especially in urban projects.

CONTEXT

The designer must strive to identify valuable off-site resources and influences so that they are recognized in the design.

Such resources include the following:

1. Geometries and alignments
2. Slopes and soils
3. Views of singular objects and natural amenities
4. Recreational facilities
5. Topography and drainage
6. Surrounding and adjoining uses
7. Available infrastructure
8. Market and location

CLEAR DELINEATION OF PRIVATE AND PUBLIC AREAS

Beyond unit design considerations, the site should be organized so that all territory can be clearly allocated to either private custody or public care and maintenance. It is frequently desirable for each unit to control some private open space. However, in higher density developments such space is often limited or filled in unique ways.

REGULATORY REQUIREMENTS

Land available for housing and related uses may face restrictions, including the following:

1. Rights of way for future uses
2. Area required for storm water management and sediment control
3. Mandated unusable areas between projects (called buffers)
4. Building restriction lines: setbacks, build-to lines, height limits, viewsheds, watersheds, separations, rights of way, easements
5. Roadways and parking areas
6. Protection of environmentally sensitive and natural resource areas such as forests, streams, and animal habitats

DENSITY AND BUILDING TYPES

These factors are the most critical to the developed character of the site and are prescribed by zoning and by developer preference—as informed by the architect and others. Zoning density is expressed numerically along with limitations that are often intended to suggest unit type. But any prescribed density can be reached by combining building types with associated parking arrangements. The permitted density may ultimately be reduced through restrictions of various sorts and is rarely achievable on small or irregular sites.

UNITY AND VARIETY

In site design, monotony and excessive repetition are as undesirable as meaningless variation, which can be disorienting and appear chaotic.

EMERGENCY ACCESS

Size and turning radius of emergency equipment, especially fire engines, can mandate street width, turning radius, and access patterns. Access to buildings becomes an issue at higher densities; installation of sprinkler systems can often balance equipment access around buildings. Always consult the fire marshal in the early stages of design.

SECURITY

Because projects are produced and marketed as discrete places, security considerations can reinforce their hermetic character and prevent integration into the larger community. At higher densities, this phenomenon can produce gated communities with limited or single access, card-accessed parking areas, and private police.

Conventional urban patterns can replace costly and artificial surveillance systems: building placement, window location, and resident awareness, together with architectural limitations on free circulation, can enhance neighborhood security.

ACCESS

Although singular access is frequently desired for marketing and control, redundant access from existing automotive and pedestrian networks provides choice and convenience while reducing concentrations of traffic.

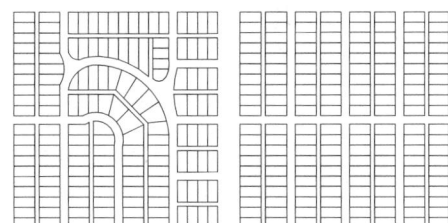

ARBITRARY VARIATION AND MONOTONOUS REPETITION

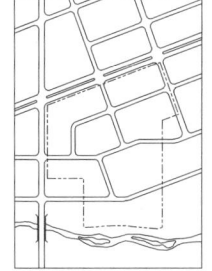

MULTIPLE ACCESS AND SINGLE ACCESS

Ralph Bennett; Bennett Frank McCarthy Architects, Inc.; Silver Spring, Maryland

GENERAL

Numerical definition of density is the most important planning index in housing but it can also be the most misleading. Density numbers frequently become inflammatory in planning debates, so it is important that the architect provide specific images of the actual appearance of planned settlements.

Density appears in two forms: gross and net. Gross density is the index applied to large areas—15 to 20 acres or more—and includes private as well as public improvements such as roads, schools, parks, and residentially oriented retail uses.

Net density is used in relation to project-sized areas—smaller than 15 to 20 acres—and consists of the number of proposed dwelling units divided by the site area. Net density is usually expressed in acres and includes access drives, parking areas, common and buffer areas, and community facilities.

FACTORS AFFECTING DENSITY

1. Dwelling unit size and arrangement.
2. Parking: on grade, in garages, in units, structured in large groups.
3. Passive and active open space.
4. Land use restrictions such as buffers, easements, and setbacks.
5. Land price: the owner's objectives are ultimately formed by this factor, in conjunction with market projections.

TYPICAL DENSITIES

1. SINGLE-FAMILY DETACHED HOUSES: The density in developments of this type is generally 6 dwelling units or fewer per acre. In the example illustrated, the density is 4.5 dwelling units per acre, with on-site parking but no garages and 7,500-sq-ft lots.
2. SINGLE-FAMILY ATTACHED TOWN HOUSES (parking on grade): The density in a development of this type is up to 14 dwelling units per acre.
3. SINGLE-FAMILY ATTACHED TOWN HOUSES WITH GARAGE: Up to 20 dwelling units per acre will fit in a development of this sort.
4. TWO-STORY ATTACHED HOUSES: With carports, these houses are designed at a density of around 10 units per acre.
5. GARDEN APARTMENTS: Parking on grade is provided in a garden apartment complex, which contains up to 18 dwelling units per acre. In the example shown, each apartment building has 36 units, for a density of 18 units per acre.
6. WALK-UP APARTMENTS: Built over one parking level, a walk-up apartment complex could accommodate up to 30 dwelling units per acre.
7. ELEVATOR BUILDINGS: Elevator buildings with structured parking can be built at a density of up to 100 dwelling units per acre. The example shown is a double-loaded corridor slab building with 200 units. With surface parking, it offers a density of 45 units per acre.
8. MIXED NEIGHBORHOODS: A mixed neighborhood encompasses a variety of dwelling types and, correspondingly, a variety of housing unit densities. The example shown includes an 8-unit walk-up apartment building on a 16,000-sq-ft lot, with a density of 16 units per acre, and single-family detached houses with garages on 8,000-sq-ft lots, with a density of 4 units per acre. The overall density in this example is 6.4 units per acre.

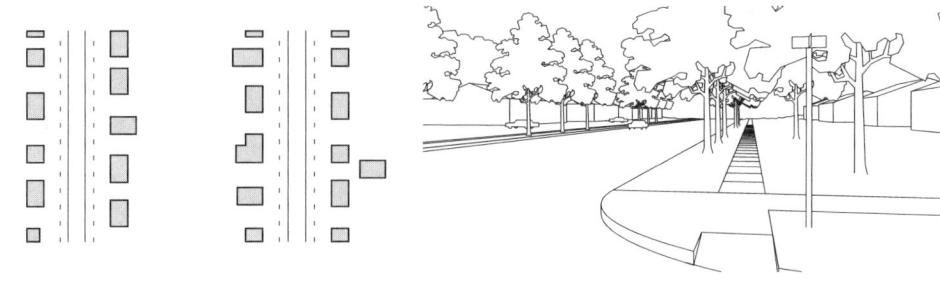

SINGLE-FAMILY DETACHED HOUSES

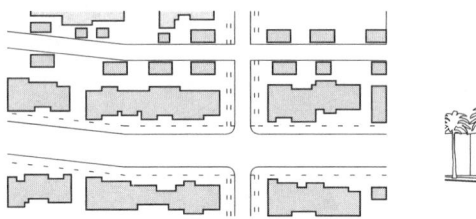

TWO-STORY ATTACHED HOUSES

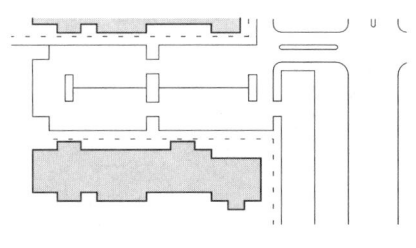

GARDEN APARTMENTS (THREE-STORY WALK-UP BACK-TO-BACK)

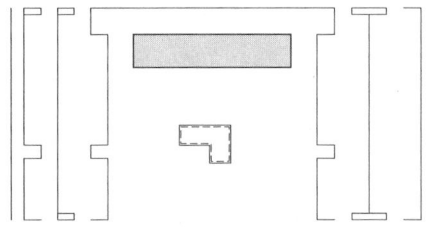

ELEVATOR BUILDING

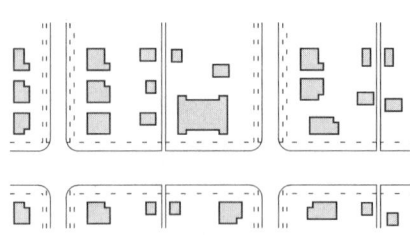
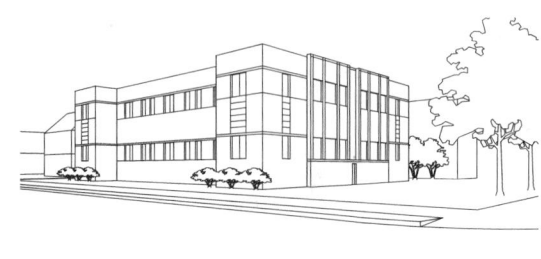

MIXED NEIGHBORHOOD

Ralph Bennett; Bennett Frank McCarthy Architects, Inc.; Silver Spring, Maryland

SITE PLAN CONSIDERATIONS

ACCESS

1. Where possible, access should connect and align with existing systems.
2. Marketing and security considerations frequently dictate single access, but redundant circulation gives choice and improved service.

PEDESTRIAN CIRCULATION

1. Rarely provided at lower densities, pedestrian access is essential at higher densities.
2. Pedestrian walkways usually parallel streets.
3. Connections to mass transit are appropriate.

PARKING

1. Parking arrangements have a significant impact on density and appearance.
2. On-street parking for guests is desirable at lower densities and essential at higher densities.

RELATION TO TOPOGRAPHY

1. ADA and subdivision regulations dictate street and walk grades and mandate site reformation at all but the lowest densities.

SERVICE

1. Trash pickup, mail service, and deliveries depend on street access to individual units.
2. Fire apparatus usually dictates road standards.

STREET ACCESS

TECHNOLOGY

STRUCTURE

1. Typically wood frame.
2. Fire separation is required for incorporated parking (garage).

MECHANICAL

1. Air, water.
2. Oil, gas heat, or heat pump.
3. Compression refrigeration or heat pump cooling.
4. Exterior condenser for heat pump or air-conditioning. This type has greatest flexibility for solar and other alternative energy systems.
5. Sprinklers are required in some jurisdictions.

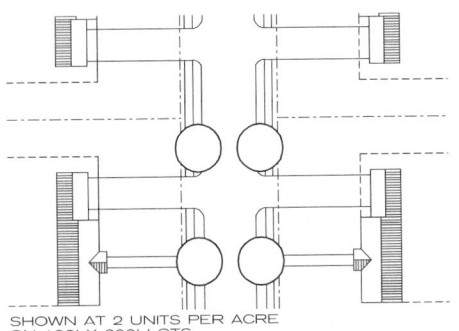
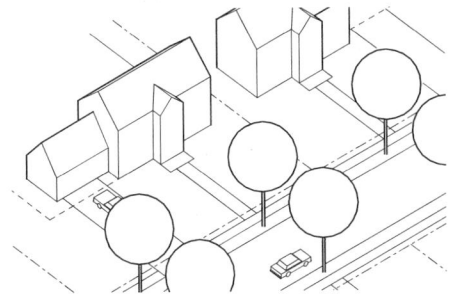

SHOWN AT 2 UNITS PER ACRE ON 100' X 200' LOTS
LARGE LOT SINGLE-FAMILY HOUSES

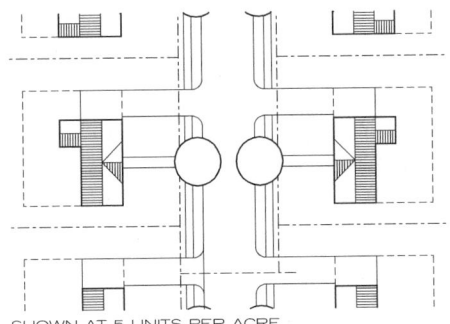
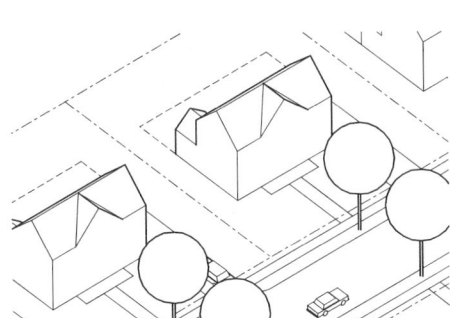

SHOWN AT 5 UNITS PER ACRE ON 75' X 100' LOTS
SMALL LOT SINGLE-FAMILY HOUSES

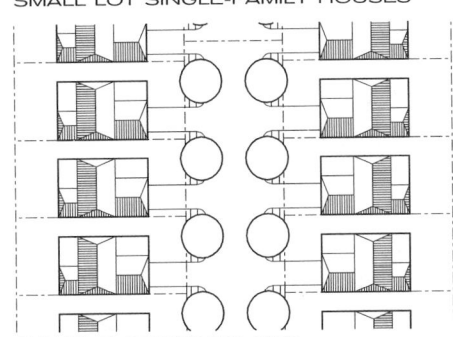
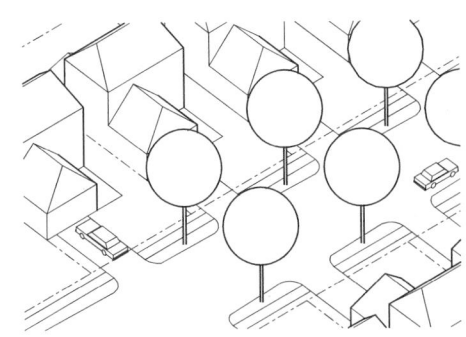

SHOWN AT 10 UNITS PER ACRE ON 40' X 90' LOTS
ZERO LOT SINGLE-FAMILY HOUSES

DENSITY CONFIGURATIONS

DETACHED HOUSING CHARACTERISTICS

TYPE	LOT SIZE (SQ FT)	DENSITY RANGE (D.U./ACRE)*	CHARACTERISTICS
Large lot	20,000 and up	0.5 - 5	Flexibility in orientation. Building restriction lines not significant. Expansion simple. Site character can be exploited.
Small lot	5000 - 10,000	4 - 8	Aggregation becomes important. Community planning important. Services important (fire, mail, rubbish). Pedestrian circulation possible and required. Urban design principles apply. Building restriction lines become important. Public sewer and water needed. Clear delineation between public and private space needed.
Zero lot	3000 - 5000	8 - 11.5	Eliminates one sidelot setback. Shallower lots possible. Other side yard usable as private space. Windows on property line reduced or eliminated.
Z-lot	3000 - 5000	8 - 13	Similar to zero lot. Allows more flexible allocation of land. Lot line views over neighboring ownership must be avoided.
Alternating-width lots	3000 - 5000	8 - 11.5	Gives variety along street.

* D.U.—Dwelling units

Ralph Bennett; Bennett Frank McCarthy Architects, Inc.; Silver Spring, Maryland

SITE PLAN CONSIDERATIONS

ACCESS

1. Where possible, should connect and align with existing systems.
2. Many arrangements are possible, including alleys, on-site parking, pooled parking and on-street parking.

PEDESTRIAN CIRCULATION

1. Necessary to connect dwellings to common facilities and off-site facilities.
2. Usually parallels streets.

PARKING

1. Has significant impact on density and appearance.
2. If not pooled, on-street essential for guests and over-flow.

RELATION TO TOPOGRAPHY

1. ADA, Fair Housing, and subdivision regulations dictate street and walk grades and mandate site reformation at all but the lowest densities.

SERVICE

1. Trash pickup, mail service, and deliveries rely on access from street to individual units.
2. Fire apparatus usually dictates road standards.

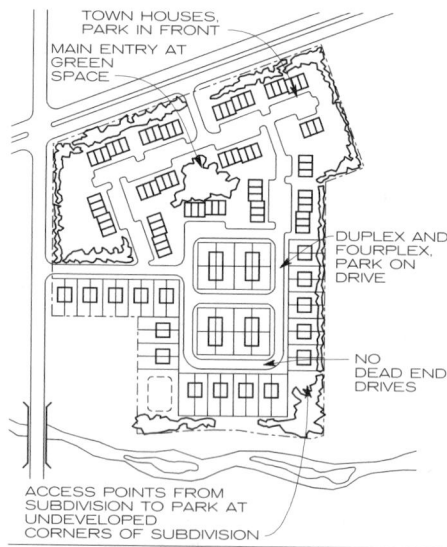

TOWN HOUSES, PARK IN FRONT
MAIN ENTRY AT GREEN SPACE
DUPLEX AND FOURPLEX, PARK ON DRIVE
NO DEAD END DRIVES
ACCESS POINTS FROM SUBDIVISION TO PARK AT UNDEVELOPED CORNERS OF SUBDIVISION

STREET ACCESS

MASSING

Variety and richness can be achieved by massing buildings so that individual units are not diagrammatically identifiable. Scale is given by secondary elements, room sized or smaller. Basic combinations are manipulated to produce complex unit configurations; the resulting composition is very different from basic types.

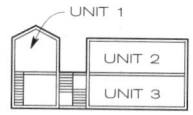

UNIT 1
UNIT 2
UNIT 3

THREE-UNIT BUILDING OF COMBINED TYPES (MANOR)

TECHNOLOGY

STRUCTURE

1. Typically wood frame.
2. Gypsum board walls between units (party walls), 2-hour rating. Some jurisdictions require masonry.
3. Parking must have rated separation if sharing wall or ceiling with unit.

MECHANICAL

1. Air, gas heat, electric baseboard heat, or heat pump.
2. Compression refrigeration or heat pump cooling.
3. Exterior condenser for heat pump or air-conditioning.
4. Sprinklers required in many jurisdictions.

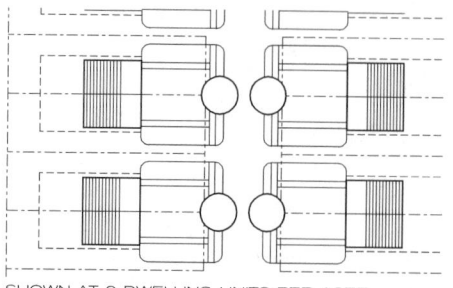

SHOWN AT 9 DWELLING UNITS PER ACRE
DUPLEX HOUSES

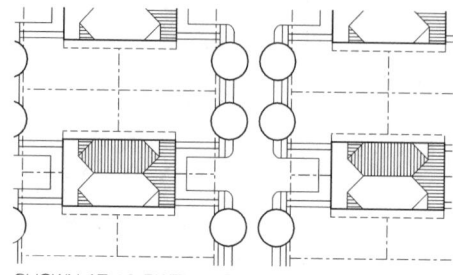

SHOWN AT 10 DWELLING UNITS PER ACRE
FOURPLEX HOUSES

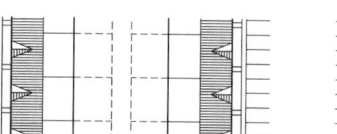
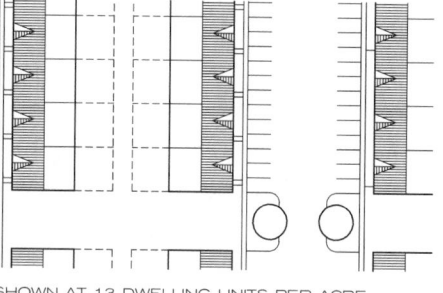

SHOWN AT 13 DWELLING UNITS PER ACRE
ATTACHED HOUSES (TOWN HOUSES)

DENSITY CONFIGURATIONS

ATTACHED HOUSING CHARACTERISTICS

TYPE	LOT SIZE (SQ FT)	DENSITY RANGE (D.U./ACRE)*	CHARACTERISTICS
Duplex	3000 - 5000	8 - 10	Allows grouping of parking, access. Side yard can be used. Houses have three exposures.
Fourplex	2000 - 3000	10 - 15	Houses have two exposures. High level of privacy possible. Masses as larger building.
Townhouse	1000 - 1500	12 - 22	Urban type exported. Public/private clearly delineated. Maximum flexibility for minimum surface. Makes satisfactory streets.

* D.U. = Dwelling units

GARAGE UNDER HOUSE—FRONT ENTRY

GARAGE UNDER HOUSE—REAR ENTRY

GARAGE IN FRONT OF HOUSE

GARAGE BEHIND HOUSE

NOTE

Attached houses achieve the highest density possible with individual structured parking (garages). Combining this housing type with parking produces many rich variations.

PARKING

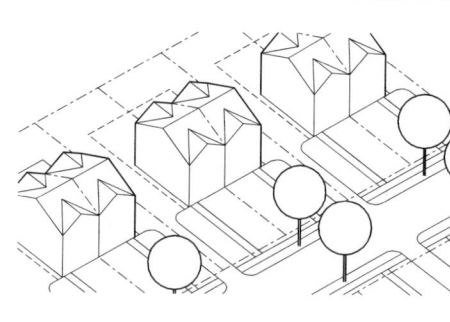

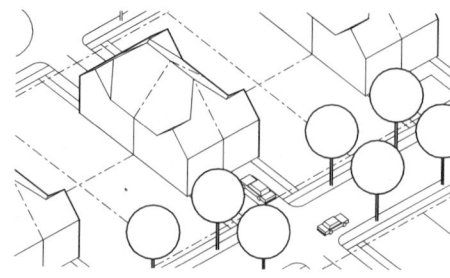

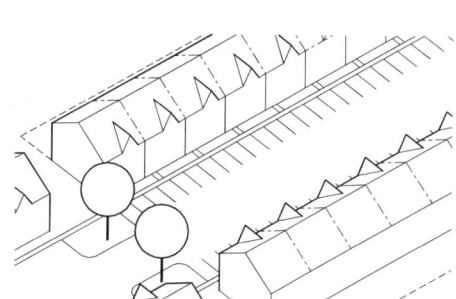

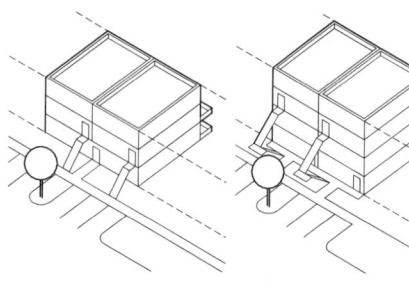

TOWN HOUSES OVER FLATS
TOWN HOUSES OVER TOWN HOUSES

NOTE

Town houses can be stacked upon themselves or on one-story units (flats). Density is increased and fire separations are required horizontally as well as vertically. Individual entries are usually provided.

MULTISTORY VARIANTS

Ralph Bennett; Bennett Frank McCarthy Architects, Inc.; Silver Spring, Maryland

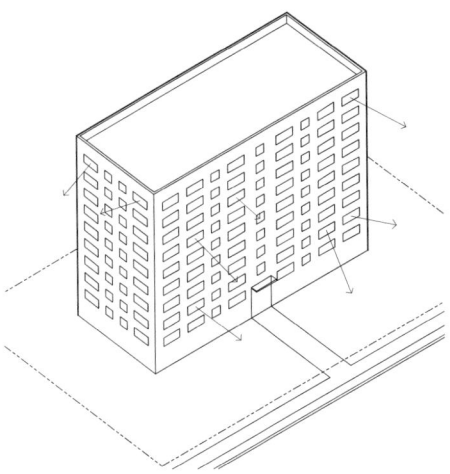

HIGH-RISE BUILDING

NOTES

1. In high-rise, single-entry buildings, the views of most residents are distant from public areas.

SUPERVISION OF PUBLIC AREAS

GENERAL

Clear delineation of usable exterior space is essential to the success of any housing design. Proper planning of exterior space improves security, reduces maintenance, enhances appearance, and permits residents to act as responsible citizens.

DESIGN

On traditional city streets, public and private realms are clearly defined.

The street is in the public realm. Semipublic areas—the entry and foyer—open onto the street from a short distance. The semiprivate areas of the house—living, dining, and/or cooking areas—look out onto the public realm but are screened. The private areas of the house—the bedrooms—are a floor or more above the street, looking out but secluded from view. Semiprivate outdoor areas are at the back of the house, visible to neighbors but secluded from the street.

In multifamily buildings, the provision of a supervised public realm is more complicated than in the attached house. In this case, buildings need to be arranged so that unit windows and common circulation space overlook the public areas of the project. This can be accomplished by

1. Keeping buildings in the two- to six-story height range
2. Clustering the dwelling units so their entrances are distributed rather than concentrated
3. Arranging unit windows so no portion of the ground surface is invisible to dwelling units

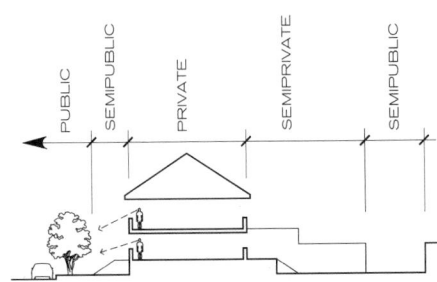

PUBLIC AND PRIVATE ZONES IN A ROW HOUSE

LOW-RISE BUILDING

2. Low-rise, multiple-entry buildings facilitate close supervision of public areas.

BUILDING LOCATION

Separation of buildings from parking and minimum distances between buildings are often mandated by zoning and by building codes.

To avoid involuntary eye contact, vertical walls containing windows and balconies should be at least 60 ft apart. This dimension is often reduced; if so, attention must be paid to elements that can provide elective privacy, such as

1. Curtains and blinds
2. Balcony walls with adjustable opacity
3. Deformation of the wall to provide bays and oblique, rather than frontal, views

ADJACENT USES

Location of certain site activities near unit windows can cause conflict. Although common practice often places back-to-back garden apartments overlooking parking, this setup is not optimum. This arrangement can be improved if the parking area is planted, illumination is at a low level, and the building design provides other views.

Recreational uses such as basketball, tennis, and other noisy, large-muscle activities should be kept away from unit windows and balconies.

Play areas for small children ideally are located where they can be seen from dwelling unit windows.

LANDSCAPE DESIGN

The provision of green space is essential for housing, even in intensely urban areas. Street trees and planted courtyards add value to the densest housing site.

Where space permits, passive green space without specific programmatic purpose can be an attractive addition. Such space should not be so large as to be unsupervisable from the dwellings, and dwellings should be located to take advantage of the amenity it provides.

NOTE

Architectural and landscape devices help demarcate private and public spaces between a house front and the street.

DIVISION OF PUBLIC AND PRIVATE SPACE

COMMUNITY FACILITIES

Two houses make a community and offer opportunities for elective socialization and joint use.

In small developments, the ordinary activities of daily life offer opportunities for community focus. These activities include picking up mail, putting out trash, doing laundry, and working on cars.

In larger projects, the following activities may provide opportunity for community activity and physical focus:

1. Marketing and management
2. Activities requiring shelter, such as meeting, fitness, day care, and convenience retail
3. Outdoor recreation, such as swimming, tennis, handball, and racquetball

DETAILS

Architectural devices mark and enhance the public and private realms. These devices include fences; walls; changes of level provided by stairs and ramps; zones of planting; and porches, stoops, and terraces.

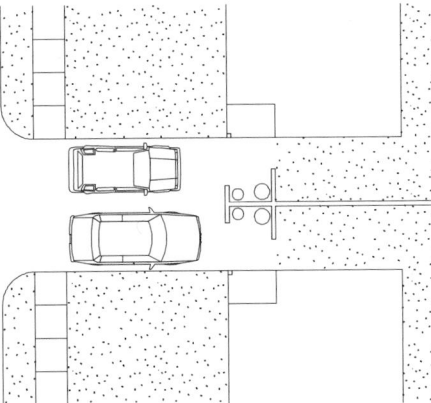

ADJACENT HOUSE ENTRANCES

Ralph Bennett; Bennett Frank McCarthy Architects, Inc.; Silver Spring, Maryland

GENERAL

The regulatory climate for housing is complex and ever-changing. Therefore, designers should consult regulatory agencies at all levels of government before initiating planning or detailed design of any housing project.

Information on this page is related to site design, building arrangement, and design of the exterior path to the dwelling unit and other common facilities. Further information related to housing can be found in Chapters 1, 11, and 20 of the ninth edition of *Architectural Graphic Standards.*

FAIR HOUSING AMENDMENTS ACT

The Fair Housing Amendments Act (FHAA) was passed in 1988 and applies to all housing scheduled for first occupancy after March 13, 1991. The act is unusual in that it is a civil rights law, not a building code or standard. Although the U.S. Department of Housing and Urban Development (HUD) developed and promulgates the guidelines, HUD has no plans to review its role and will enforce FHAA primarily based on complaints. Compliance will be achieved through complaints by affected individuals and by professional testers.

FAIR HOUSING ACCESSIBILITY GUIDELINES

The most comprehensive instructions for compliance with the construction provisions of the FHAA are provided by the Fair Housing Accessibility Guidelines (FHAG), which were released in their final form in March 1991.

WHAT PROJECTS ARE COVERED

Any multifamily project with four or more dwelling units is covered by the legislation, but not all parts of all dwelling units in all covered projects must be accessible.

Other standards that supplement or supersede the FHAG are the following:

1. SPACES FOR COMMON USE: ANSI standard A117.1-1986
2. SPACES FOR PUBLIC USE (if any): Americans with Disabilities Act (ADA) Guidelines
3. ANY SPACE: Any local building code standard that HUD deems more restrictive

In buildings equipped with passenger elevators, all units must be accessible. Multistory dwelling units (except loft units) not located in elevator buildings are exempt from this requirement.

In walk-up multistory buildings, FHAA requires all ground floor units to be accessible where practical, based on site considerations. A minimum of 20% of the units must be accessible. FHAA definition of the ground floor in walk-up buildings is unclear, but the intention of the legislation was to avoid the installation of elevators in buildings not otherwise needing them. Because interpretations of the law vary, guidance should be sought.

NOTE

The FHAA does not clearly define "ground floor" in requiring that all ground floor units be accessible when practical. For situations such as that shown here, it may be wise to seek guidance regarding accessibility requirements for ground floor units on the lowest level.

GROUND FLOOR UNIT ACCESSIBILITY

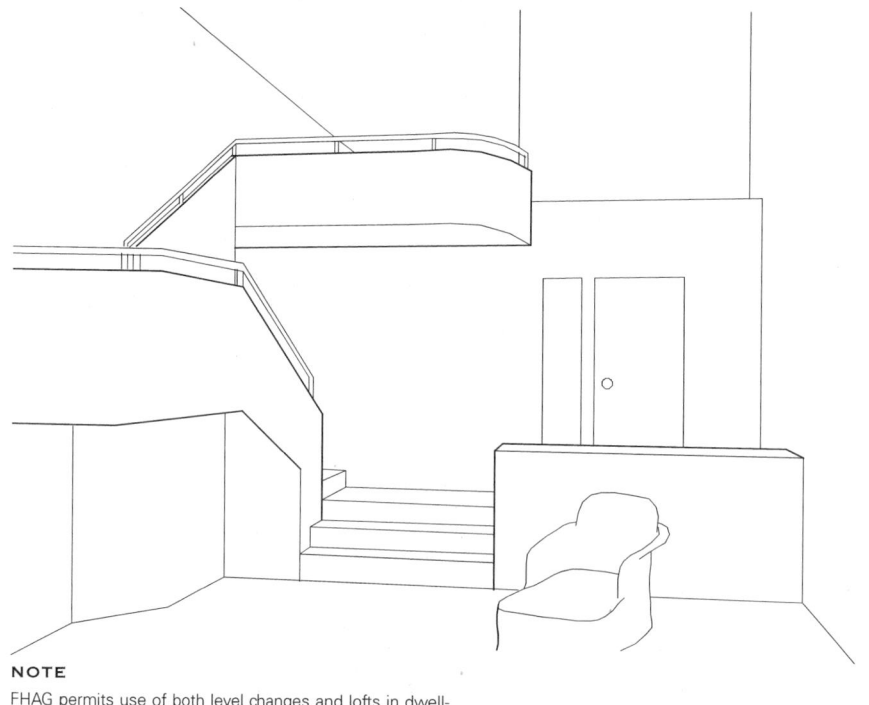

NOTE

FHAG permits use of both level changes and lofts in dwelling units as long as common areas are accessible.

DESIGN FEATURES PERMITTED IN ACCESSIBLE UNITS

SITE PLANNING ISSUES

Site accessibility for housing is defined as the existence of a continuous accessible route of travel from a suitable automobile or transit drop-off point (called the arrival point) to the dwelling unit. Such a route may include parking access aisles, curb ramps, walks, ramps, and lifts and must meet the requirements of ANSI A117.1-1986.

Sloped walkways, when included, are defined as being no steeper than 5%. Steeper walkways are defined as ramps and must have a maximum slope of 8.5%; ramps require handrails.

All community facilities must be connected to all covered dwelling units by an accessible route. In certain circumstances, use of a private automobile may be considered part of such a route.

SITE PRACTICALITY TESTS

The designer may use either of two tests to determine whether accessibility is practical at a particular site:

1. INDIVIDUAL BUILDING TEST: Locate an arrival point and entrance for each building or entry, and estimate the slope between them. If a line connecting these two points is steeper than 10%, access is deemed impractical. This test must be conducted both before and after regrading.
2. SLOPE ANALYSIS TEST: Calculate the percentage of the site sloped at grades steeper than 10%. This percentage is the percentage of ground floor units (with a minimum of 20%) that must be accessible.

DWELLING UNIT DESIGN

Dwelling units covered by the FHAA must be designed according to the FHAG. The difference between these requirements and the ANSI A117.1-1986 standard is substantial. Under the FHAG, the unit must be usable and include adaptable features but does not have to be fully accessible according to the ANSI standard. Planning decisions such as door and corridor widths and bathroom and kitchen layouts must meet certain standards, some not as restrictive as the ANSI standard. Items such as accessible plumbing fixtures and counters can be provided as required by specific owners and users.

Units covered by the law must have the following characteristics:

1. Usable doors to enter all rooms
2. An accessible route into and throughout the dwelling unit
3. Switches and controls mounted in accessible locations
4. Usable bathrooms with concealed reinforcing installed in the walls
5. Usable kitchens that permit wheelchair access

Certain design features, including level changes, are permitted. Intermediate levels (lofts) are permitted, although they are not precisely defined. In buildings equipped with elevators, multistory units must include a toilet on the accessible (ground) floor.

Changes in floor level are permitted if they can be defined as "design features" that do not interrupt the accessible route through the remainder of the dwelling.

ITEMS THAT TYPICALLY ARE NOT AFFECTED BY FHAG

1. Windows
2. Interior door hardware
3. Doors not used for passage
4. Fireplaces
5. Stairs
6. Upper floor levels
7. Lower floor levels
8. Closet shelving
9. Circuit breakers
10. Mechanical equipment
11. Individual garages
12. Lofts
13. Basements

Ralph Bennett, Bennett Frank McCarthy Architects, Inc.; Silver Spring, Maryland
Thomas Davies, Jr., AIA; Kim A. Beasley, AIA; Paradigm Design Group; Washington, D.C.

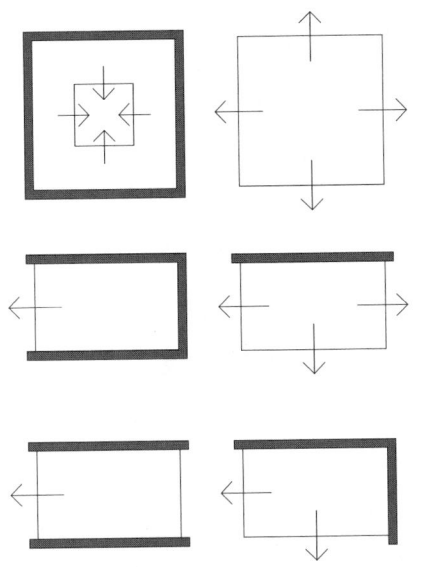

NOTE

The number of sides exposed to light and air and whether they are adjacent can be used to describe all dwelling units.

UNIT DESIGN—POSSIBLE EXPOSURES

GENERAL

Before design of a housing project begins, a unit density and mix of types that suit the site must be determined. Units composing the mix are designed according to standards related to the sales price or monthly rental of the dwelling unit. Unit characteristics can be summarized as follows:

MINIMAL HOUSING: No foyer; combined living and dining; small bedrooms (80 sq ft); one bath.

AFFORDABLE HOUSING: Small foyer; combined living and dining; large bedroom may have private bath; other bedrooms share bath with common rooms; minimal storage.

LUXURY HOUSING: Foyer; living, dining, and family (or great) rooms; circulation in hall, some semiprivate rooms (study/sitting); ample to lavish master bedroom suite; other bedrooms share one or two baths; two- or three-car garage.

CUSTOM HOUSING: Large foyer; separate living, dining, and family rooms; porch; large kitchen and pantry; grand circulation; frequent redundant circulation (H&V); many semiprivate rooms; large bedrooms; multiple bathrooms; ample storage; staff service space.

IDENTITY FROM EXTERIOR

With the possible exception of deeply subsidized housing, all housing must survive in the market. This means the project must not deviate greatly from the demonstrated preferences of its market, although it must also offer an identifiable image or appearance.

This image, often called "curb appeal," is frequently defined for the architect by advertising and marketing specialists. In single-family houses, the house itself constitutes a statement. Attached houses also make individual statements, as well as developing community imagery for the potential tenant or buyer. In multifamily housing, the identity of the dwelling is submerged within the group and the individual unit is distinguished by its internal arrangement. Thus, group and individual identity must be defined and developed.

SIDEDNESS

Dwelling units always benefit when buildings are designed with a clear front or public side and a back or semiprivate side. Sidedness enables the cultivation of other contrasting characteristics such as ceremonial/intimate, open/closed, noisy/quiet, ornamented/plain, and urban/pastoral.

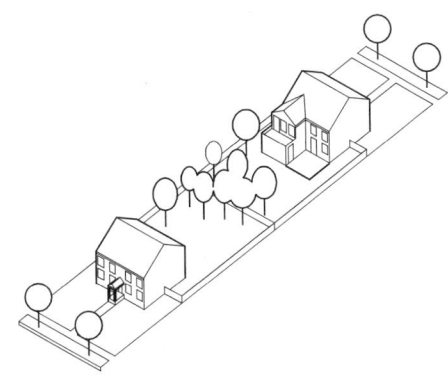

NOTE

Housing design should distinguish between public and semiprivate sides of the dwelling unit.

SIDEDNESS

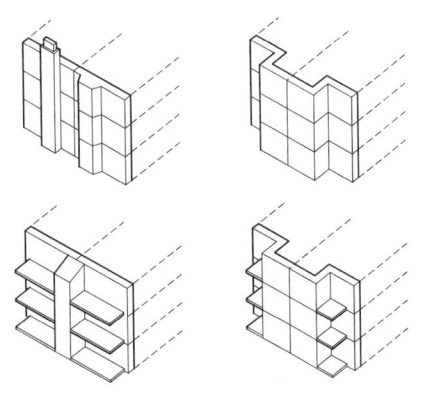

BUILDING MASSING

DWELLING UNIT PLANNING

Dwellings of all sizes have common elements and sequences that must be identifiable.

ENTRANCE

Marketing concerns usually demand a dramatic spatial event at the moment of entry, whether a double-height foyer in a luxury house or a sweep of the living and dining areas in an apartment. However, the architectural organization of this event may require a transitional space, perhaps somewhat enclosed, as compression before expansion into the major semipublic areas of the unit.

CIRCULATION AND ROOMS

In large houses it is possible to separate circulation from the rooms served using devices such as corridors, passageways, foyers, vestibules, and the like. Circulation in smaller units occurs through rooms, most often living and dining rooms.

PLAN BALANCE

In dwelling unit design, all aspects of the plan must be proportional and consistent. A many-bedroom dwelling with living areas too small to accommodate all the occupants is problematic. So is the house with enormous living and dining areas but too few or too small bedrooms. Kitchens, general storage, and circulation must also be sized according to the number of occupants.

FOCUS

All good dwellings offer a hierarchy of experience culminating in a focus, which is commonly the living or living/dining area or family room/kitchen. This spatial focus is often enhanced by spatial definition and/or greater height and by features such as fireplaces (the hearth, of course, is the traditional center of the house), stairs, or access to outdoors.

NOTE

In small plans, circulation should occur through no more than two adjacent corners of living and dining rooms. After accounting for circulation, sufficient space should remain for reasonable furniture arrangements.

CIRCULATION

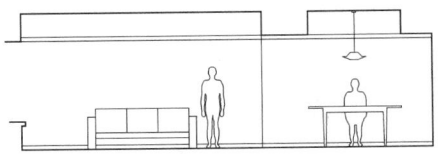

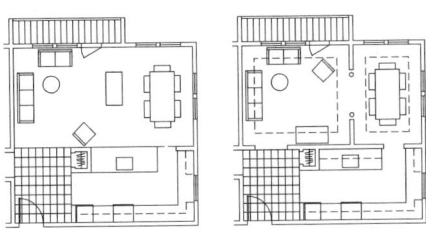

NOTE

Spaces defined by walls can be reinforced by articulation of the ceiling. Even in small units, ceiling drops and soffits can provide reinforcement of activity areas and spaces.

ARTICULATION OF SPACE

ACCESS TO EXTERIOR

Contemporary living requires connection to outdoor space by circulation where possible or at least by view. In apartments, where this connection may take the form of a balcony, it is usually made at the living room. But since a balcony reduces view and light, it may be placed at the bedroom instead, with access from the living room. Bedroom balconies are a luxury amenity.

UNIT PLAN AND BUILDING MASSING

Plan arrangement is related to building massing; by projecting and recessing adjacent rooms or parts of rooms, building mass can be broken down. Similarly, continuous alignment of exterior walls leads to large-scale massing and elevations in which surface elements such as windows and textured and colored surface areas can be used to compose and adjust scale.

Components such as balconies, storage closets, and fireplaces are often useful for composing elevations and massing, particularly when simplified plan geometries produce large, basic massing.

Ralph Bennett; Bennett Frank McCarthy Architects, Inc.; Silver Spring, Maryland

SITE PLAN CONSIDERATIONS

ACCESS

1. Where possible, points of access should connect and align with existing systems.
2. Many arrangements are possible with streets, courts, and freestanding buildings

PEDESTRIAN CIRCULATION

1. Pedestrian connections are necessary between apartments and common facilities and off-site facilities.
2. Usually parallels streets except where site plan offers rustic walks.

PARKING

1. Parking sites must be pooled or in structures.

RELATION TO TOPOGRAPHY

1. ADA and subdivision regulations dictate street and walk grades and mandate site reformation at all but the lowest densities.
2. Breaks between stairwell groups allow adjustment to the terrain.

COMMON FACILITIES

1. Rental and management offices are common for 50 units or more.
2. Pools and recreation facilities are common in complexes of more than 100 units.
3. Maintenance and storage facilities are common in larger projects.
4. Tot lots and play areas are required for complexes of 20 units or more in many jurisdictions.
5. RV and boat storage are offered in some areas.

SERVICE

1. Mail service and deliveries to stairwells or larger group boxes; trash to Dumpsters distributed in parking lots or other central locations.
2. Fire apparatus usually dictates road standards; sprinklers may permit reduced equipment access.

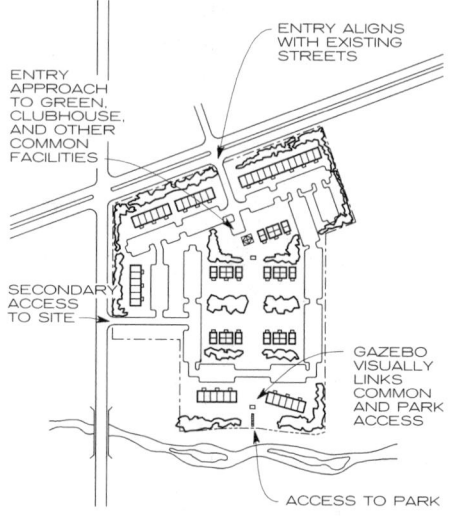

ENTRY ALIGNS WITH EXISTING STREETS

ENTRY APPROACH TO GREEN, CLUBHOUSE, AND OTHER COMMON FACILITIES

SECONDARY ACCESS TO SITE

GAZEBO VISUALLY LINKS COMMON AND PARK ACCESS

ACCESS TO PARK

SITE PLAN

TECHNOLOGY

STRUCTURE

1. Wood frame.
2. Walls between stairwell groups must be masonry or heavy gypsum (2-hr rating).
3. Unit wall must be gypsum board on wood or steel studs (1-hr rating).
4. Second stair must be in rated enclosure.

MECHANICAL

1. Forced air, gas heat, or heat pump.
2. Compression refrigeration or heat pump cooling.
3. Larger units (two bedrooms or more) have centrally located furnaces with ducts and exterior condensers for heat pumps and refrigeration; smaller units may have through-the-wall units with no exterior condenser.
4. Sprinklers required in many jurisdictions.

WALK-UP HOUSING CHARACTERISTICS

TYPE	DENSITY RANGE (D.U./ACRE)*	CHARACTERISTICS
Through unit	Up to 17 (including off-street parking)	Permits sided site planning. Two exposures for each unit. Bedrooms or living areas can be oriented toward parking or view.
Back-to-back unit	Up to 20 (including off-street parking)	Efficient: 4 units per floor. As usually deployed, 50% of units face parking, 50% face view and green.

* D.U. = Dwelling units

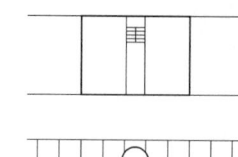

THROUGH UNIT

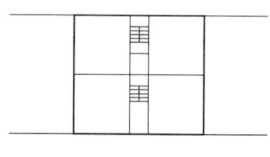

BACK-TO-BACK UNIT

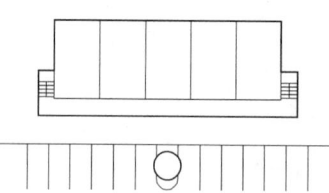

SINGLE-LOADED GALLERY ACCESS

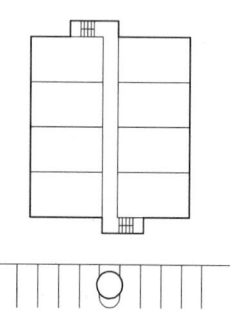

DOUBLE-LOADED GALLERY ACCESS

WALK-UP APARTMENT CONFIGURATIONS

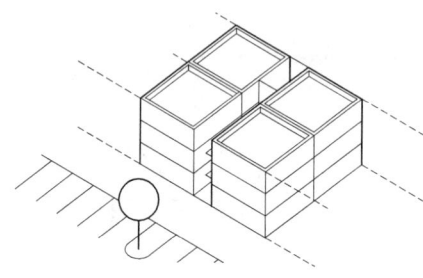

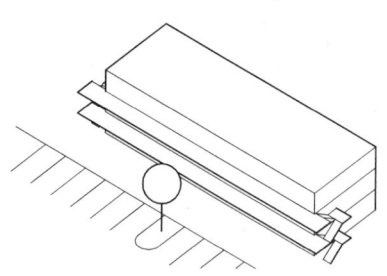

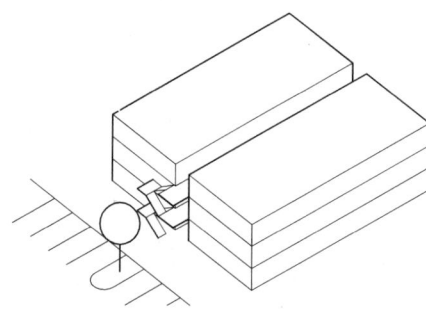

CONFIGURATION

Walk-up apartments are ubiquitous in the United States and come in many varieties. Their appeal lies in the great efficiency of their circulation. Two-story buildings are common and generally require only one stair. Three-story buildings generally require two stairs, one of which must be rated. Buildings higher than three stories present market problems but do exist. Combination walk-up buildings, with elevators going to higher stories, are common in Europe but are uncommon in the United States due to the higher proportional cost of elevators.

Ralph Bennett; Bennett Frank McCarthy Architects, Inc.; Silver Spring, Maryland

SITE PLAN CONSIDERATIONS

ACCESS

1. Entrances should, where possible, connect and align with existing systems.
2. Many arrangements are possible, including alleys, on-site parking, pooled parking, and on-street parking.

PEDESTRIAN CIRCULATION

1. Necessary to connect dwellings to common facilities and off-site facilities.
2. Usually parallels streets.

PARKING

1. Has significant impact on density and appearance.
2. If not pooled, on-street essential for guests, overflow.

RELATION TO TOPOGRAPHY

1. ADA and subdivision regulations dictate street and walk grades, and mandate site reformation at all but the lowest densities.

SERVICE

1. Trash through chutes to compactor in trash room in basement or ground floor; mail to mail room on ground floor; delivery to units or security guard.
2. Fire marshal may request access around building depending on building height and sprinkler system.

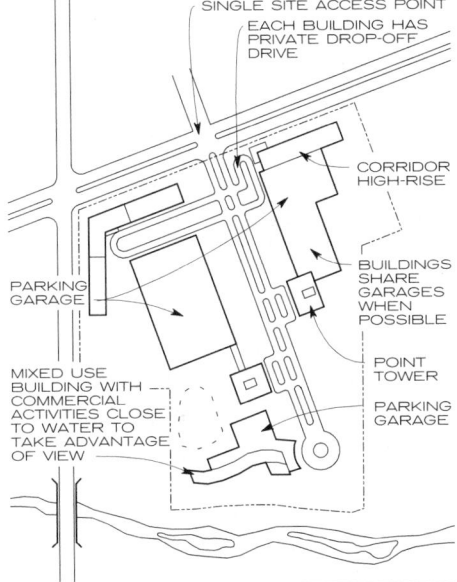

SITE PLAN

TECHNOLOGY

STRUCTURE

1. Masonry or concrete, occasionally fire-protected steel.
2. A full range of high-rise building safety measures are required, especially for structures taller than nine stories, which is generally the maximum reach for rescue equipment.

MECHANICAL

1. Decentralized air, gas heat, or heat pump.
2. Compression refrigeration or heat pump cooling.
3. Larger units (two bedrooms or more) have centrally located furnaces with ducts and exterior condensers for heat pumps and refrigeration; smaller units may have through-the-wall units with no exterior condenser.
4. Large and/or luxury buildings may have central systems with boilers, central chillers, and a condenser and two- or four-pipe systems.
5. Sprinklers are required in many jurisdictions.

GROUND FLOOR PLANNING

Ground floors in elevator buildings are significantly different from ground floors in other housing structures because larger numbers of people pass through on the way to their dwellings and because the ground floor is a smaller proportion of the area of the building. Urban versions of the type offer opportunities for retail and commercial uses that can be accessed directly from the street.

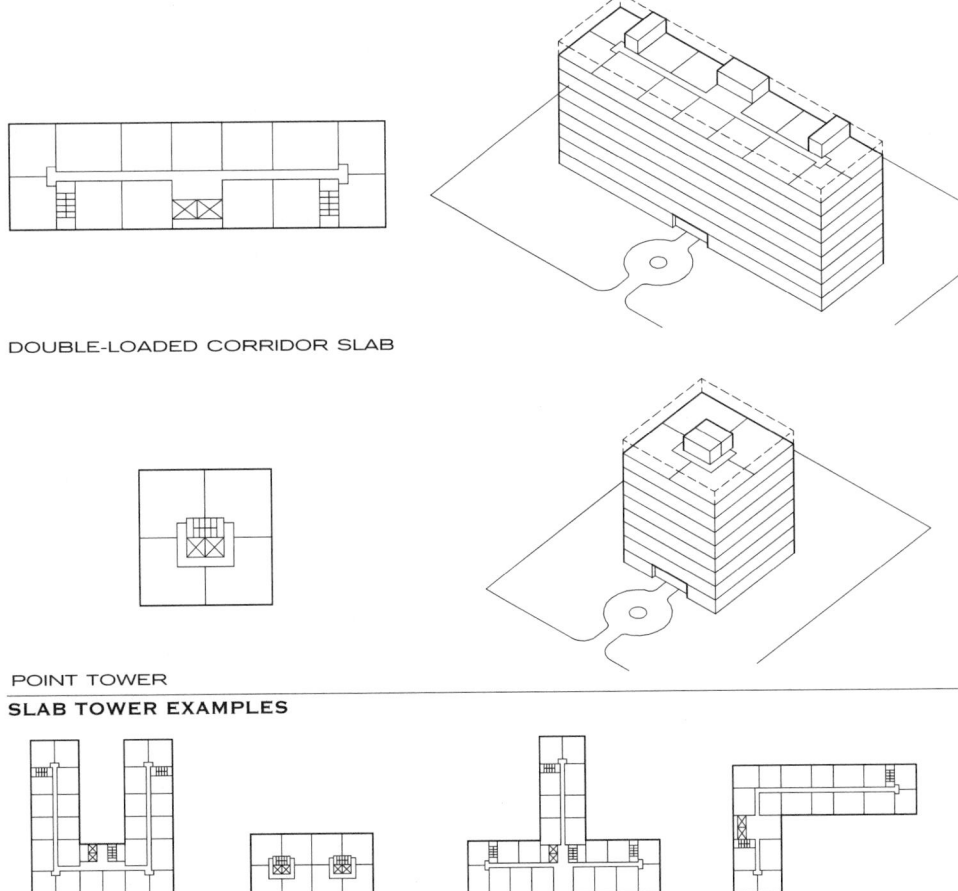

DOUBLE-LOADED CORRIDOR SLAB

POINT TOWER

SLAB TOWER EXAMPLES

U-SHAPED PLAN WITH SINGLE CORE | SLAB COMPOSED OF TWO TOWERS JOINED | T-SHAPED PLAN WITH SINGLE CORE | L-SHAPED PLAN WITH SINGLE CORE

SLAB TOWER PLAN VARIATIONS

ELEVATOR APARTMENT CHARACTERISTICS

TYPE	CHARACTERISTICS
Double-loaded corridor (slab)	Units have only one exposure. Corridors are interior spaces. Units can be shallow and wide (lengthening corridors, but bringing much light into unit) or narrow and deep (shortening corridors but making a dark zone on the interior). Stairs are required at ends of corridors (limited dead ends allowed).
Single-loaded corridor (slab)	Less efficient than double-loaded corridor. Useful when oriented east-west because all units can face south. Corridor can be naturally illuminated.
Point tower	Efficient circulation because of small number of units/floor; scissors egress stairs can make circulation more efficient. Units can have two exposures. Casts minimal shadow on lower buildings.

Frequently, therefore, the ground floor of elevator buildings is set aside for common spaces and uses. Lobby and security; mail; meeting space; management offices; trash; and mechanical, electrical, and fire equipment frequently are located at grade. In urban situations, retail and commercial uses are appropriate.

If dwelling units are located on the ground floor, they can offer direct access to outdoors.

CIRCULATION VARIATIONS

In the great majority of elevator buildings, the double-loaded corridor is used, which produces a corridor on each floor. By using multifloor units, or by adding stairwell circulation up and down from elevator landings, the number of floors with corridors can be reduced by two-thirds and up to two-thirds of units can have two exposures. Fair Housing Accessibility Guidelines may prohibit some of these variations, especially the skip-stop.

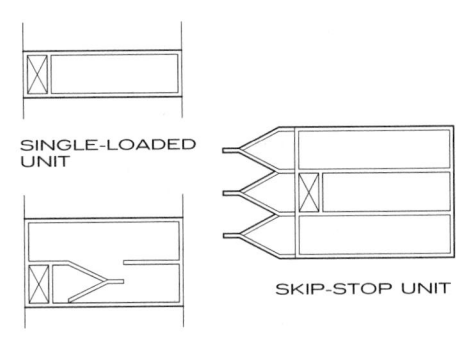

SINGLE-LOADED UNIT

SKIP-STOP UNIT

TWO-STORY UNIT

CROSS-SECTION OF VARIATIONS IN CIRCULATION

Ralph Bennett; Bennett Frank McCarthy Architects, Inc.; Silver Spring, Maryland

GENERAL

Special populations require housing forms suited to their needs. Most significantly, small groups of people with special requirements tend to live together so that their needs can be met in a concentrated and efficient way. Facility size is often dictated by financial and operating considerations; the larger the facility, the more difficulty the designer has in making a residentially scaled environment.

Group residences are available for elderly persons, for persons in transition from addiction and psychiatric programs and from incarceration, for persons with terminal illnesses (hospices), and for those who may share another kind of common need.

These facilities typically provide a number of small, simple rooms along with common spaces that include living, dining, and food preparation areas, as well as recreational and administrative facilities.

A more complex group-housing arrangement recently imported from Scandinavia is co-housing—a form of group living that usually features more elaborate individual accommodations along with the common areas found in group homes.

SITE CONSIDERATIONS

1. Direct but controlled access is required from parking and transit facilities to a clearly identifiable entrance.
2. Views from unit windows become especially important in developments where residents spend considerable time in their unit.
3. A variety of views is desirable, from active streets to quiet landscapes. This gives tenants choice in otherwise uniform accommodations.
4. Solar orientation becomes important for such facilities: no unit should be without direct sun at some time during a winter day.
5. Since direct access to outdoors is rarely practical in such housing, exterior access from common spaces becomes more important. Such space should be agreeable for sedentary occupation—sunny but with shade and sheltered from the wind.

TECHNOLOGY

STRUCTURE

1. Single-story buildings can be wood frame in most jurisdictions if properly protected. Two-story or higher buildings must be masonry or protected steel in most jurisdictions.

MECHANICAL

1. Decentralized air, gas heat, or heat pump.
2. Compression refrigeration or heat pump cooling incorporated into through-the-wall units is often used.
3. Common areas have centrally located furnaces with ducts and exterior condensers for heat pumps and refrigeration.
4. Buildings such as hospices, where temperature and humidity control are crucial, use central systems with boilers, central chillers and condenser, and two- or four-pipe systems.
5. Buildings serving persons with special medical needs may require specialized HVAC systems for isolations.
6. Sprinklers are required in most jurisdictions.

SAFETY

1. Systems to announce and report emergencies as well as accommodations for egress are strongly related to the level of assistance required to allow residents to exit the building. The more assistance required, the more extensive the measures required.
2. Building code and fire safety requirements for special needs housing are complex and changing. Protected construction, sprinklers, and supervised fire and smoke alarm systems are generally required.
3. Precautions above this level are dictated by the occupants' ability to perceive danger and act to remove themselves from it. Corridor widths, exit requirements including horizontal exits, separations between dwelling and corridor, and resident staff requirements are all subject to negotiation with local authorities, using model codes as the basis.
4. Local building code authorities should be consulted early in the design process.

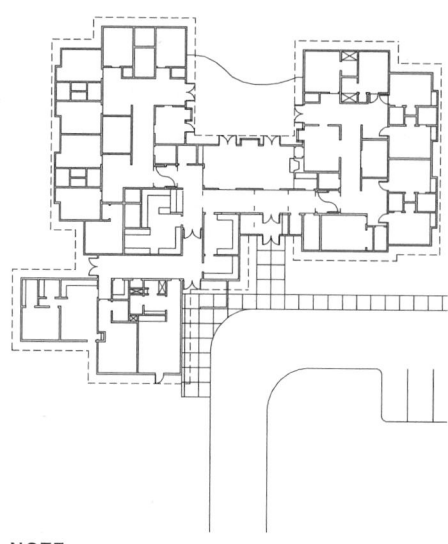

NOTE

This 14-unit facility is divided into two clusters of seven rooms, each cluster is served by a lounge and a spa (a room for bathing and personal care). Common facilities include a large living room, kitchen with snack bar, and administration and staff facilities including a residence for the manager. Rooms offer varying aspects from a busy road to a semi-enclosed garden off the common living room to distant landscape views.

HOSPICE RESIDENCE; MONTGOMERY HOSPICE, INC.; OLNEY, MARYLAND BENNETT FRANK MCCARTHY ARCHITECTS.

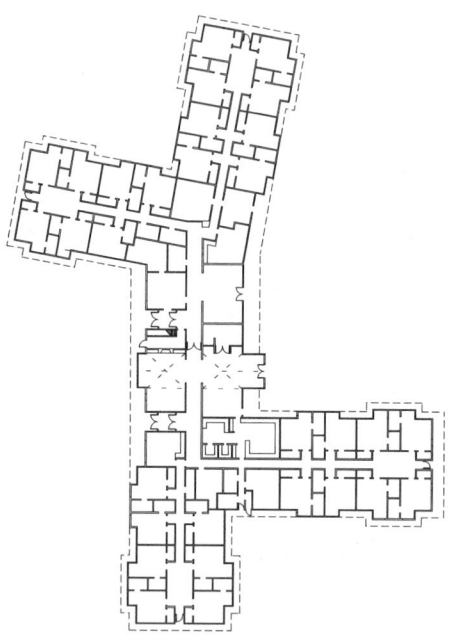

NOTE

This 30-unit group assisted-living facility is divided into two fire-separated buildings to meet subsidy requirements that limit facilities to 15 units. Common areas are linked with openings protected by smoke-actuated doors. Common areas include living room, dining room, institutional kitchen, and laundry.

RAPHAEL HOUSE, VICTORY HOUSING; ROCKVILLE, MARYLAND BENNETT FRANK MCCARTHY ARCHITECTS, INC.

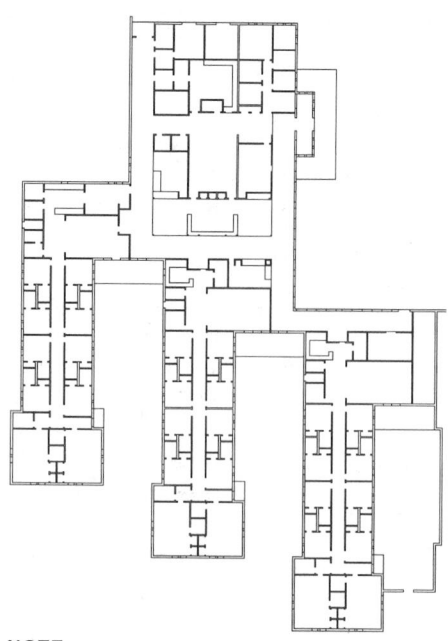

NOTE

This 36-room group home is designed for elderly persons suffering from Alzheimer's disease and dementia. Each group and subgroup of units has its own vivid and distinct visual identity. Easily accessed outdoor space is controlled to limit wandering. The plan is organized to permit supervision by limited staff.

WOODSIDE PLACE AT PRESBYTERIAN MEDICAL CENTER; OAKMONT, PENNSYLVANIA PERKINS EASTMAN & PARTNERS

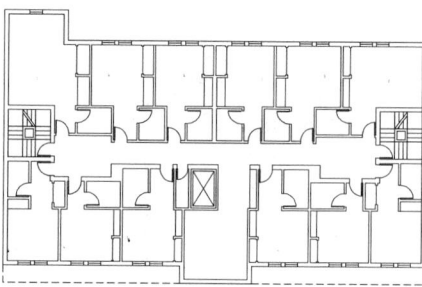

TYPICAL FLOOR

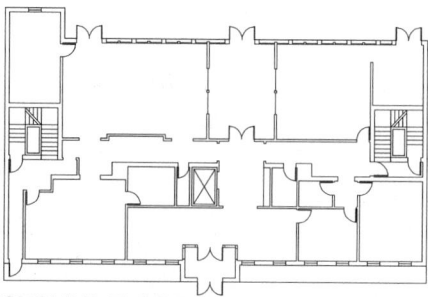

GROUND FLOOR

NOTE

This 36-room single-room-occupancy hotel is designed for emotionally disturbed homeless persons. Social services are offered on the ground floor. Bedrooms are enriched with private bathrooms and mini-kitchens. A private garden for the residents is provided at the rear of the building.

NEW YORK SRO; BROOKLYN, NEW YORK ARCHITROPE

EXAMPLES OF SPECIAL NEEDS HOUSING

Ralph Bennett; Bennett Frank McCarthy Architects, Inc.; Silver Spring, Maryland

GENERAL

Distribution facilities are highly efficient operations in which products are stored and from which orders are filled and shipped to meet customer demand. Distribution facilities house raw materials, parts, or finished products, most commonly at the manufacturing or distribution level. This storage, all along the supply chain, from raw material to product delivery, adds cost, which can be reduced by efficient distribution practices and facilities.

Distribution facilities are designed from the inside out. That is, the size and shape of the product determines how the facility will be operated and what form the building will take. Storage volume can be increased much more cheaply by increasing the height of a building than by increasing its footprint. Column layouts must accommodate a combination of rack types and allow for changes in rack type. Mixed rack types may be placed together in one storage area.

In addition to storage areas, distribution facilities require a battery charging area, a maintenance area, shipping and receiving offices, other business offices, utility equipment spaces, and truck and rail docks.

Truck loading docks are high traffic areas and should be segregated from pedestrian traffic. Railroad access is less commonly required than in previous decades, but when rail sidings are included, the track elevation and geometry control the warehouse location and elevation of the floor.

Most new facilities are built so it will be easy to double the storage area at a later date. Expansion requirements usually direct the organization of storage areas, as it is difficult to expand through a loading dock and disruptive and expensive to expand through utility spaces or offices.

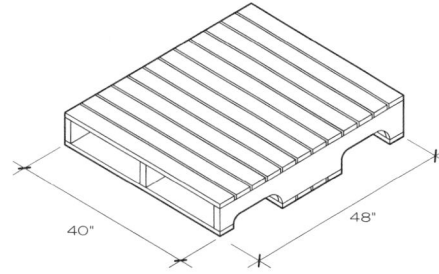

40" 48"

NOTE

Identical items are usually packed together to form a case. Typically, cases of only one SKU are stored on a pallet to make a unit load. Heights vary according to gross weight, product durability, and manageable size. The pallet illustrated is used by the Grocery Manufacturers Association.

TYPICAL GMA PALLET

STORAGE BASICS

The stored product is the module that determines an efficient warehouse size. To provide uniformity in the industry, a common unit load format has developed using a pallet as the tool for shipping, storing, and receiving product. The palletized unit load is now the modular building block from which 90 percent of warehouse dimensions are derived.

The most common method of handling products uses a standardized Grocery Manufacturers Association pallet. Different product combinations can be packed on a single pallet. For identification, each product is called a stock keeping unit (SKU), although the same product in different packaging, or with different cost structures, can be identified as a distinct SKU.

When a unit load is stackable and large amounts of the same SKU are stored in one place (typical at a manufacturing facility), unit loads can be stacked on the floor. Typically, these stacks are no higher than 3 ft in lanes no deeper than 12 unit loads from front to back. Unit loads are also stored in pallet racks. Typically made of steel (cold-rolled or formed), racks are available in numerous types. The type of pallet rack appropriate for any application depends on the variety, quantity, and movement (velocity) of the unit loads being stored and retrieved.

In a typical distribution facility, the contents are rotated ten to twenty times a year. However, depending on many factors, this "inventory turn" number may vary from two turns to 52 turns for perishable products (52 turns means an average product storage time of about a week).

Distribution center management seeks to minimize construction costs by increasing product movement (turns) and choosing storage layouts that minimize the building footprint. It is less expensive to build taller buildings for vertical storage than to increase the building footprint; however, it may be more labor intensive to access very high storage areas. Moving unit loads in and out of pallet racking is very different from selecting cases or individual items from unit loads.

Most distribution centers receive product in full unit loads. Some ship full unit loads, while others ship smaller numbers of cases or less than case quantities. Most distribution centers ship a combination of full unit loads and smaller quantities.

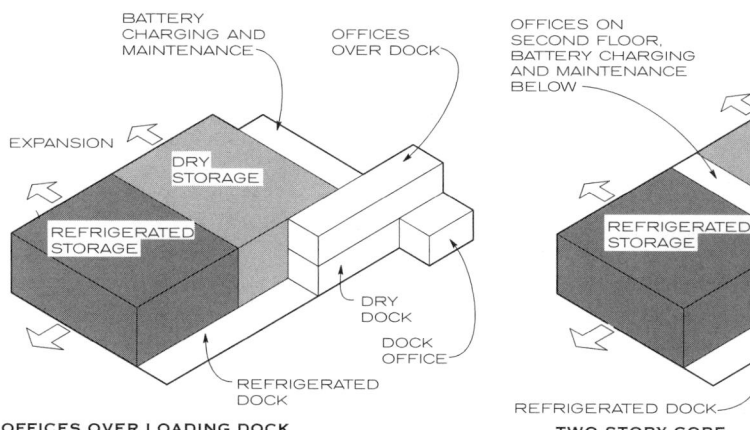

OFFICES OVER LOADING DOCK

TWO-STORY CORE

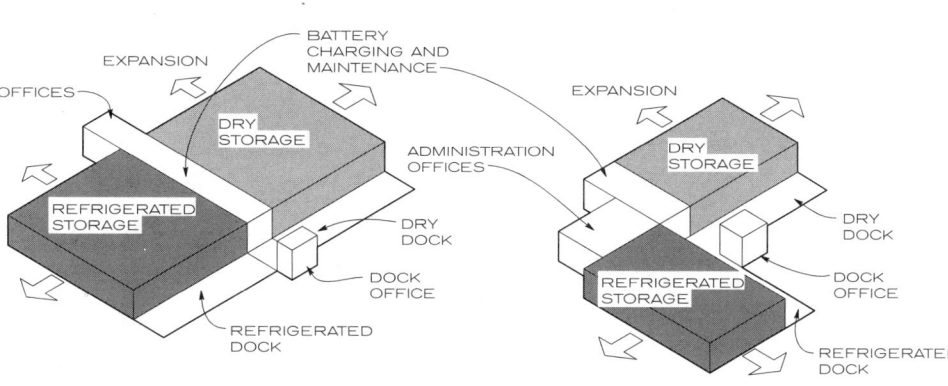

ONE-STORY CORE

STORAGE WAREHOUSES ROTATED ABOUT ADMINISTRATION AREA

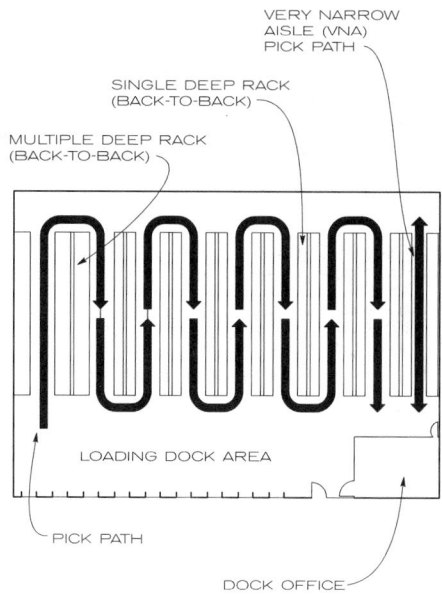

NOTE

Grocery distribution facilities exemplify distribution to retail outlets, demonstrating the complexity involved in storing products with varying requirements. Grocery facilities often require five or more coolers with different temperatures, a freezer, and an ice cream freezer, as well as a heated storage area and special fruit-ripening rooms. The building configuration is determined by the temperature-conditioned space requirements.

Illustrated are four configurations for a grocery distribution facility. In each, the architectural plan has been designed around the facility operation. The storage rooms, with their varying conditions, complicate the space layout. Also, because each space may expand independently, planning for future expansion must consider each space individually.

Refrigerated space is a specialized single use space and, as such, can double the cost of constructing warehouse space. Refrigerated rooms, particularly freezers, should not open directly into unconditioned environments. Typically a refrigerated dock serves as a buffer between these rooms and nonrefrigerated spaces.

NOTES

1. The rack layout used determines the building column spacing. Often, the column layout accommodates combinations of different rack types.
2. An even number of selection aisles is preferable so the selection path begins and ends on the dock or at the order assembly area.

TYPICAL GROCERY DISTRIBUTION FACILITIES

St. Onge, Ruff and Associates, Inc.; York, Pennsylvania

TYPICAL WAREHOUSE PLAN

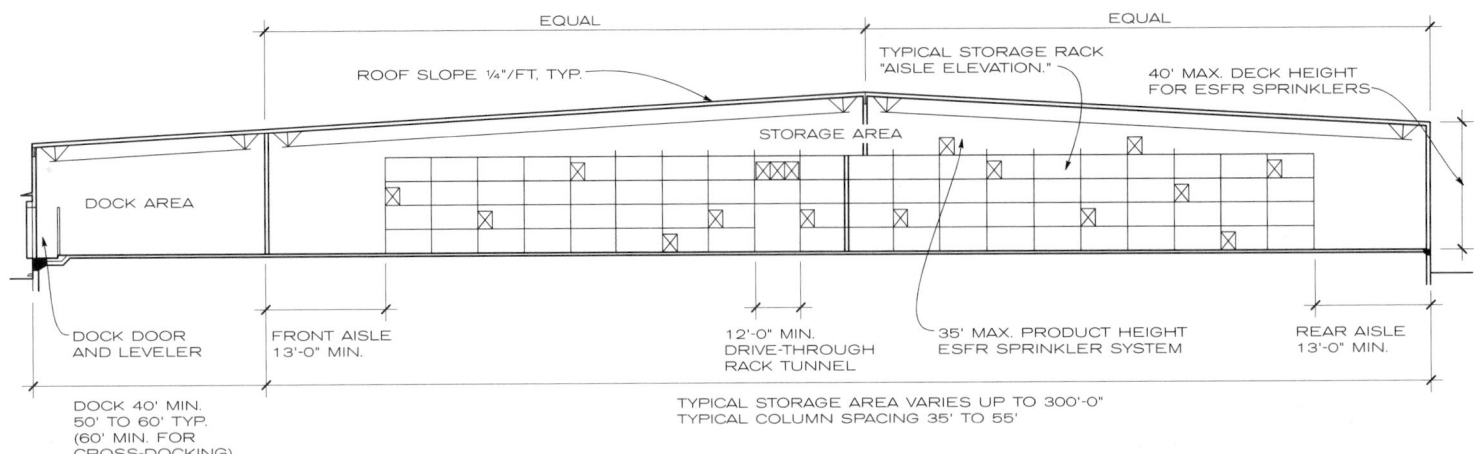

EQUAL | EQUAL

ROOF SLOPE ¼"/FT, TYP.

TYPICAL STORAGE RACK "AISLE ELEVATION."

40' MAX. DECK HEIGHT FOR ESFR SPRINKLERS

STORAGE AREA

DOCK AREA

DOCK DOOR AND LEVELER

FRONT AISLE 13'-0" MIN.

12'-0" MIN. DRIVE-THROUGH RACK TUNNEL

35' MAX. PRODUCT HEIGHT ESFR SPRINKLER SYSTEM

REAR AISLE 13'-0" MIN.

DOCK 40' MIN. 50' TO 60' TYP. (60' MIN. FOR CROSS-DOCKING)

TYPICAL STORAGE AREA VARIES UP TO 300'-0" TYPICAL COLUMN SPACING 35' TO 55'

TYPICAL DISTRIBUTION FACILITY CROSS-SECTION

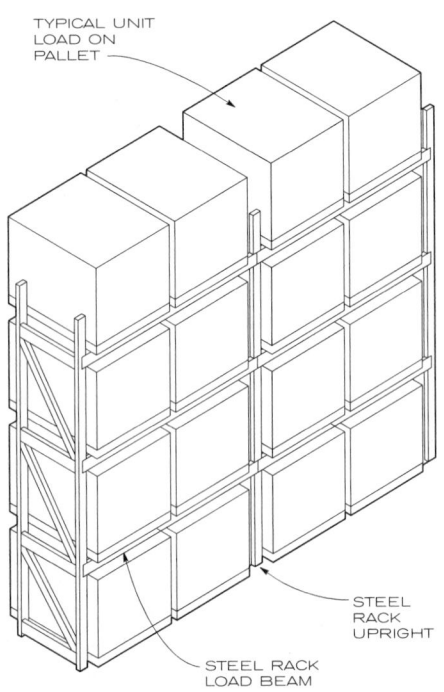

TYPICAL UNIT LOAD ON PALLET

STEEL RACK UPRIGHT

STEEL RACK LOAD BEAM

TYPICAL PALLET STORAGE RACK

TYPICAL DISTRIBUTION FACILITY CROSS-SECTION

The cross-section of a distribution facility is determined by the storage height requirement and the roof slope. Some building codes require a minimum roof slope of $1/4$ in./ft; a roof slope of $1/8$ in./ft is the minimum for most roof systems.

Because internal roof drainage is expensive, it is preferable to drain the roof using downspouts at the building perimeter.

Depending on the combustibility of the stored product, in-rack sprinklers are required for most storage rack systems. Except in refrigerated spaces, ESFR (early suppression fast response) sprinklers installed at the ceiling can be used in lieu of in-rack sprinklers.

ESFR sprinklers impose a height limitation on warehouses where they are used. They limit the roof height to 40 ft and the top of the stored product to 35 ft.

TYPICAL PALLET STORAGE RACK

Although pallet racking design often depends on the height and footprint of a building, it is preferable for this relationship to be the other way around. Distribution centers should be designed "inside out" so the warehousing and material handling needs are free of external constraints. In any case, applicable building codes and fire protection guidelines (NFPA standard 231C) must be followed. Building clearances must allow for lights, steel, etc. but should not be excessive to avoid wasting storage space (measured in cubic volume).

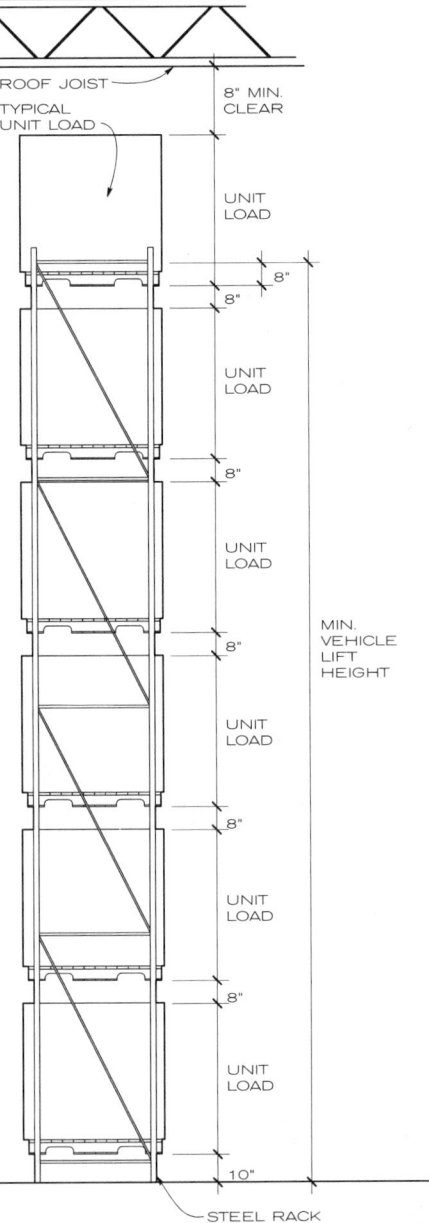

ROOF JOIST

TYPICAL UNIT LOAD

8" MIN. CLEAR

UNIT LOAD

8"

8"

UNIT LOAD

8"

UNIT LOAD

8"

UNIT LOAD

8"

UNIT LOAD

8"

UNIT LOAD

8"

UNIT LOAD

10"

STEEL RACK

MIN. VEHICLE LIFT HEIGHT

PALLET STORAGE HEIGHT REQUIREMENT

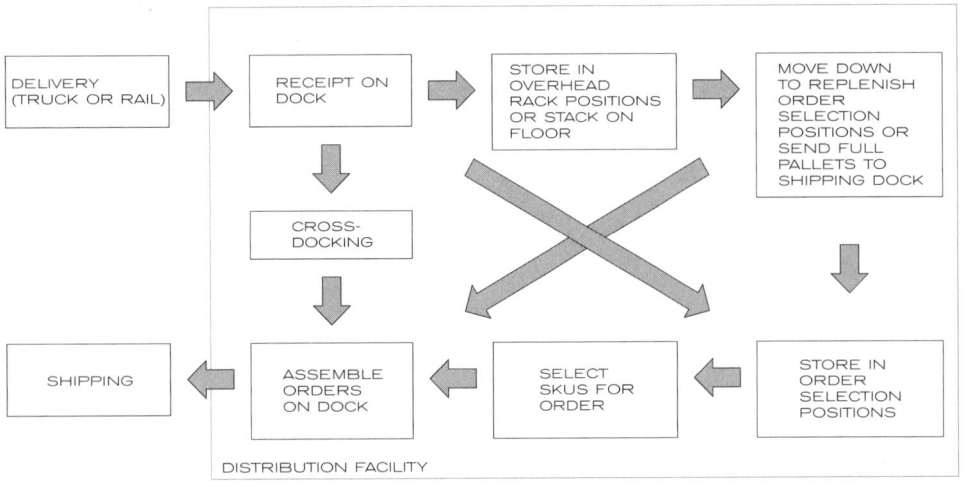

DELIVERY (TRUCK OR RAIL) → RECEIPT ON DOCK → STORE IN OVERHEAD RACK POSITIONS OR STACK ON FLOOR → MOVE DOWN TO REPLENISH ORDER SELECTION POSITIONS OR SEND FULL PALLETS TO SHIPPING DOCK

CROSS-DOCKING

SHIPPING ← ASSEMBLE ORDERS ON DOCK ← SELECT SKUS FOR ORDER ← STORE IN ORDER SELECTION POSITIONS

DISTRIBUTION FACILITY

TYPICAL DISTRIBUTION CENTER FLOW CHART

St. Onge, Ruff and Associates, Inc.; York, Pennsylvania

TYPICAL STORAGE ARRANGEMENT TYPES

The storage modes illustrated accommodate a wide range of uses. Floor stacking unit loads is the simplest method because it involves no special equipment except the device used to transport the loads. The unit load racking illustrations demonstrate a gradual increase in storage and move-

ment philosophy. Rack systems require specialized equipment that can access all levels of storage and work efficiently in the aisles. Building columns, in-rack fire protection, and utility lines must be considered when laying out a storage system. When racking is placed back-to-back in a warehouse, a minimum space of 6 in. may be required between racks for in-rack sprinkler system piping or 18 in. for building columns.

BUILDING AREA (SQ FT) PER PALLET POSITION*

TYPE OF STORAGE	STORAGE HEIGHT BY UNIT LOAD					
	2	3	4	6	8	12
4 deep floor stack	11.5	7.6	-	-	-	-
6 deep floor stack	10.4	7.0	-	-	-	-
Single deep	18.9	12.6	9.5	6.3	-	-
2 deep (MDR)	15.6	10.4	7.8	5.2	-	-
3 deep (MDR)	13.9	9.3	6.9	4.6	-	-
2 deep push back	14.4	9.6	7.2	4.8	-	-
Double deep	14.4	9.6	7.2	4.8	-	-
VNA (turret truck)	-	-	-	5.2	3.9	-
AS/RS (single deep)	-	-	-	-	2.1	1.4

*Storage area only, does not include end aisles or intermediate cross aisles.

NOTE

The square footage in a building footprint occupied by each unit load decreases as stacking height increases, since a vertical stack of unit loads occupies the same floor space as a single load of the same dimension. A reduction in aisle width from the combination of rack usage and equipment type could also reduce building square footage.

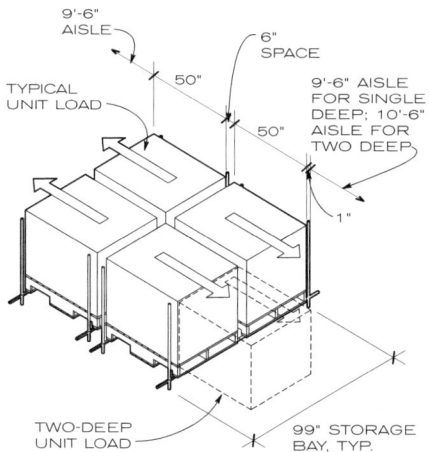

NOTE

One-deep (single) or selective racks are the most commonly used. They are typically constructed with two unit loads per storage bay (the space between uprights). When this rack is used, one unit load sits on each side of the aisle.

For product in large groups or lots, two-deep racks may be used to allow for more product in the building footprint. Two deep racks require the use of a vehicle capable of reaching into the rack for the inner unit load. Push-back-racks are an alternative arrangement that is similar in plan.

ONE- AND TWO-DEEP LOAD RACK LAYOUTS

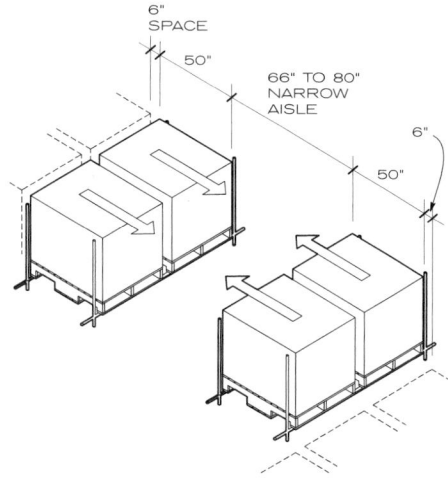

NOTE

VNA rack layout is similar to one-deep racks except the aisle is narrower, which both saves space and places opposite sides of the aisle within reach of a specialized order picker. An employee riding the vehicle can select cases from unit loads on the floor and from each of the overhead storage positions. The narrow aisle also requires special equipment for loading. Allow 16 ft clear at the front of the aisle and 12 ft at the rear for VNA vehicle access.

VERY NARROW AISLE (VNA) RACK LAYOUT

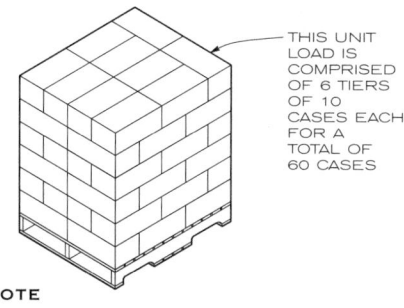

NOTE

Unit loads are assembled (or palletized) either manually through case stacking or with an automatic palletizing machine. The tiers of cases in the unit load illustrated are rotated 180 degrees from the adjacent tiers; the interlocked cases stabilize the load.

TYPICAL UNIT LOAD

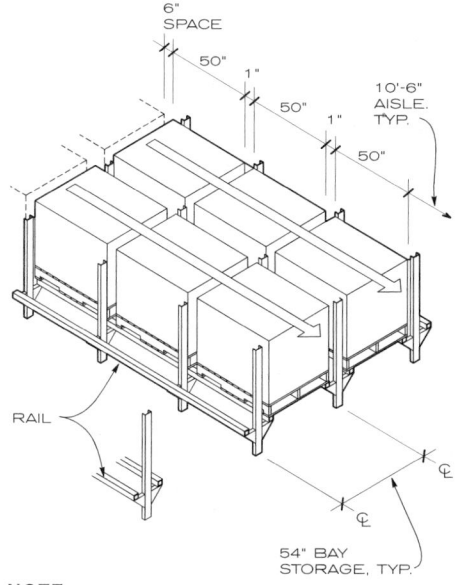

NOTE

Drive-in racks, which are one unit load wide, are used to store large quantities of the same unit load. The unit load rests on rails that extend the depth of the rack. Drive-in racks have unit load depths of two or more (3 units are illustrated). To access inner loads, a fork truck must be driven into the rack between the rails that support the unit load.

DRIVE-IN UNIT LOAD RACK LAYOUT

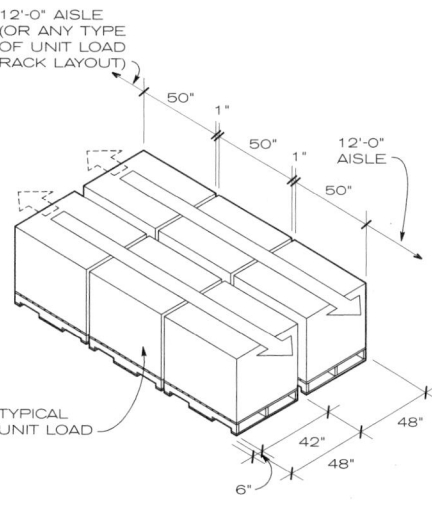

NOTE

Floor stacking of unit loads does not require racks, which can save capital costs. However, floor-stacked product is not easily selected as the stacks can only be reached from the top tier. Unit load characterisitcs usually limit stacking heights to three high. Floor stacking is most often used when large quantities of the same unit are stored.

THREE-DEEP UNIT LOAD FLOOR STACK LAYOUT

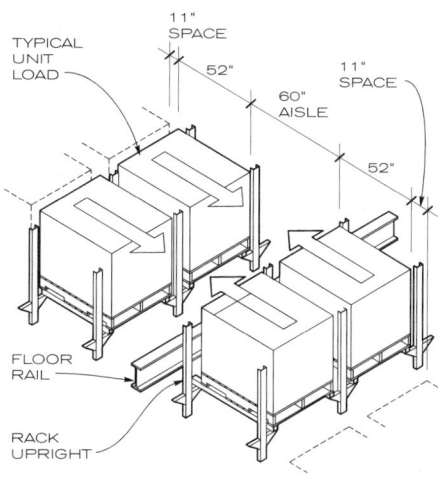

NOTE

Automated storage and retrieval systems (AS/RS) incorporate an unmanned storage and retrieval machine or SRM (described in AGS chapter 14). Allow 15 ft minimum clear space at the front runout and 25 ft minimum at the rear for crane access. AS/RS systems, which are often 80 ft tall, automate the distribution operation and can store more unit loads in a smaller space than other rack systems. Often, the AS/RS rack system serves as the building structure as well.

AS/RS RACK LAYOUT

St. Onge, Ruff and Associates, Inc.; York, Pennsylvania

GENERAL

Cold storage distribution facilities are differentiated from other distribution facilities because they are refrigerated. In addition to the requirement for mechanical refrigeration to provide a cold environment, the construction of these buildings is very different. The cooler or freezer rooms must be well-insulated to reduce energy costs; gaps in the thermal envelope are not acceptable. The low temperatures also cause a vapor drive toward the refrigerated space, which requires that the thermal envelope have a continuous vapor barrier to prevent condensation or frost in the cold space. Specialized materials and details are needed to construct a hermetically sealed vapor envelope.

NOTES

1. Small coolers and freezers may be constructed with insulated panels inside a weatherproof building shell. Often these are prefabricated units.

2. The least costly way to build coolers and freezers is to use the walls, roof, and floors of the building as the thermal envelope. This envelope must be vapor-tight and have continuous insulation, particularly at the corners and across penetrations of the envelope. To achieve this requires an extensive amount of specialized detailing and craftsmanship.

3. For rooms with temperatures below 32°F, insulation and subfloor heating must be considered.

4. Refrigeration evaporators must be placed with consideration for maintenance access, effective air circulation, noise, and protection from vehicle or product damage.

5. Air units and piping must be protected from damage, especially when ammonia refrigeration is used. The ammonia hazard inside a building can be reduced by locating the ammonia piping and valves above the roof.

6. Dock areas are subject to a great deal of air infiltration because of the openings for trucks. Select dock equipment that will minimize this infiltration. Refrigerating the dock reduces the amount of moisture vapor that reaches the interior freezer.

7. Dock temperatures below 32°F require features that prevent frost accumulation at truck openings. In cold climates, refrigerated docks may also require heating.

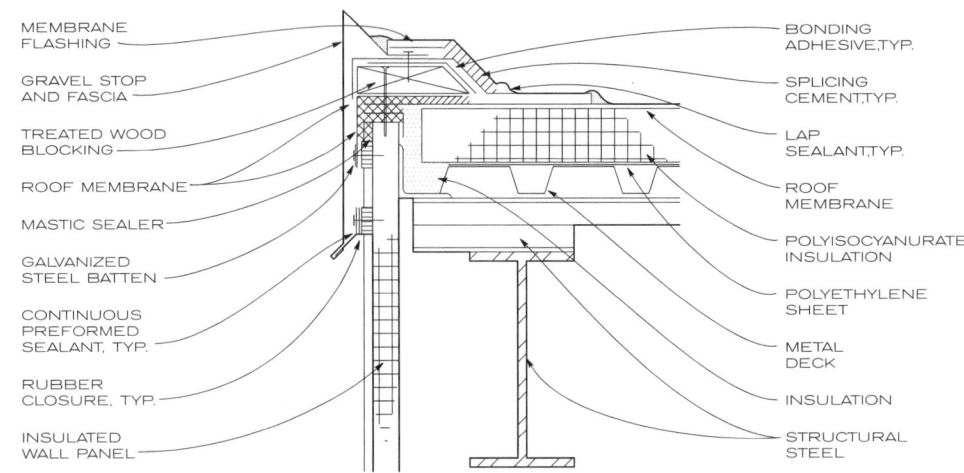

TYPICAL COLD STORAGE EAVE DETAIL

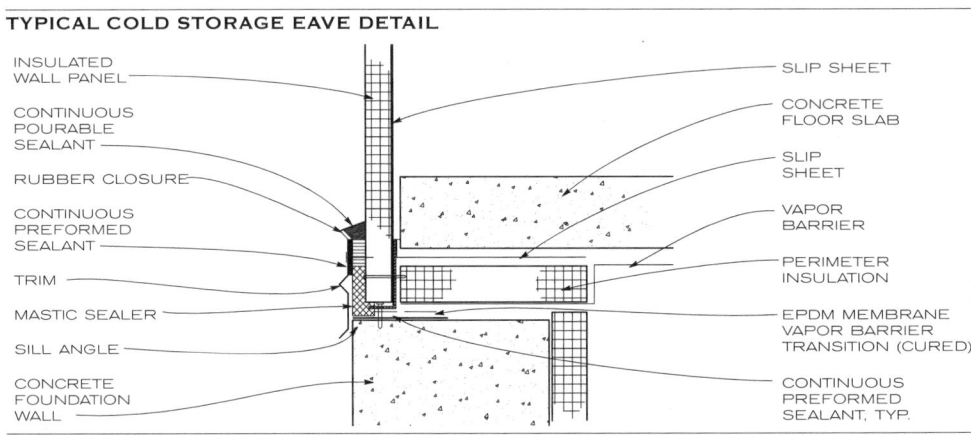

TYPICAL COLD STORAGE SILL DETAIL

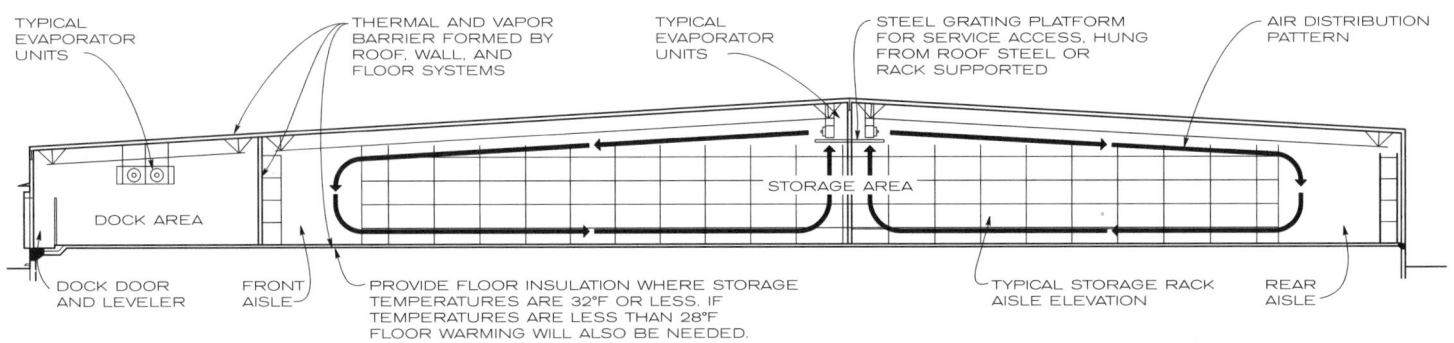

SECTION—CONVENTIONAL INTERIOR EVAPORATOR PLACEMENT

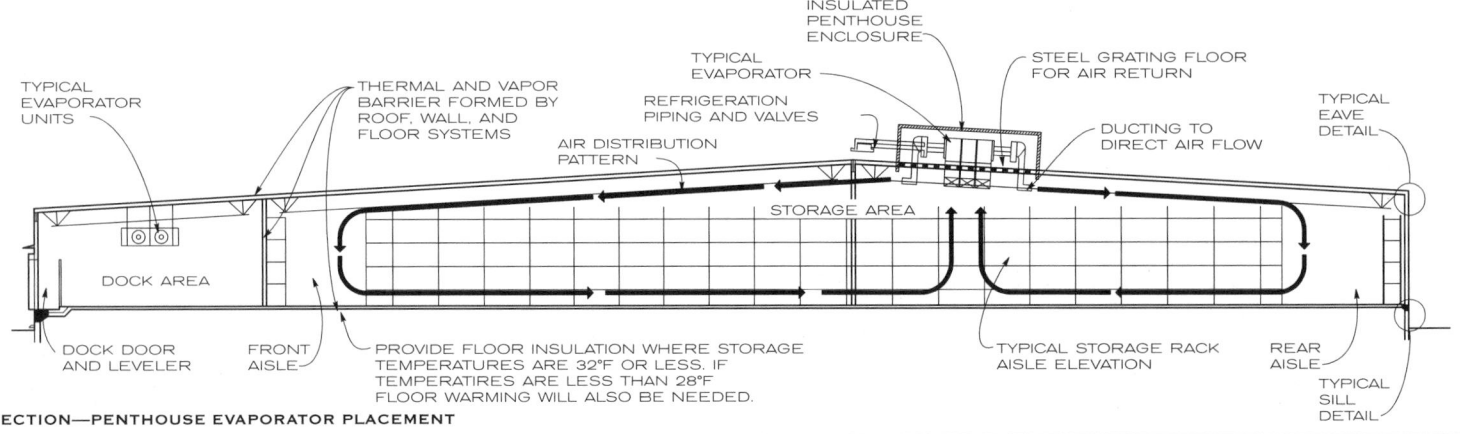

SECTION—PENTHOUSE EVAPORATOR PLACEMENT

COLD STORAGE AIR DISTRIBUTION BUILDING TYPES

St. Onge, Ruff and Associates, Inc.; York, Pennsylvania

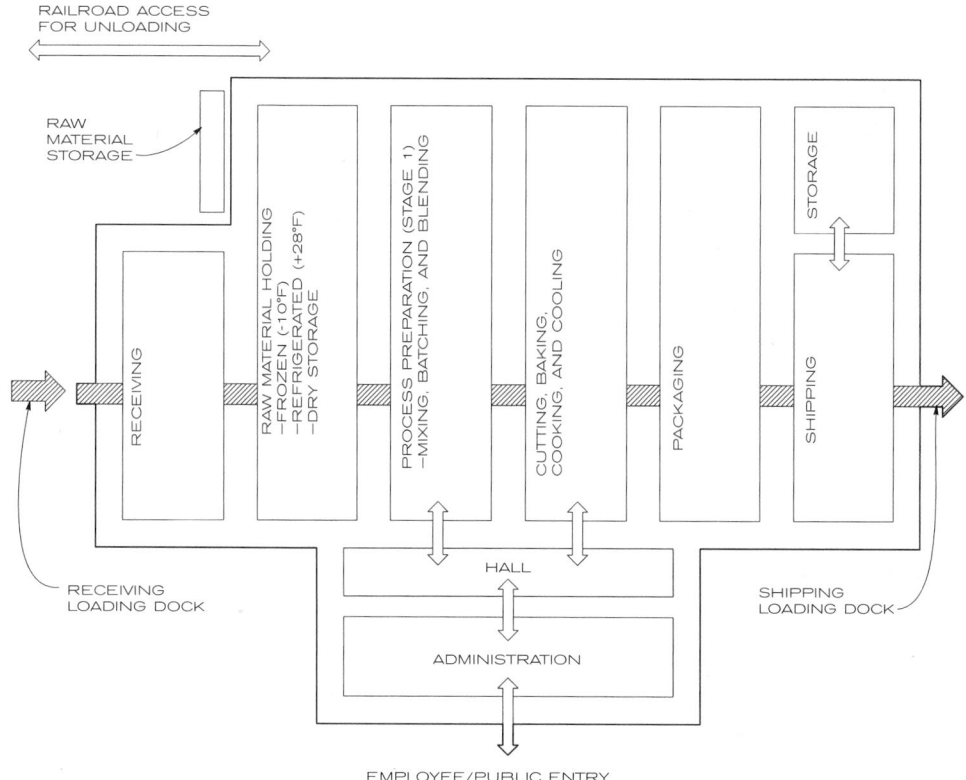

RAILROAD ACCESS FOR UNLOADING

RAW MATERIAL STORAGE

RECEIVING

RAW MATERIAL HOLDING
-FROZEN (-10°F)
-REFRIGERATED (+28°F)
-DRY STORAGE

PROCESS PREPARATION (STAGE 1)
-MIXING, BATCHING, AND BLENDING

CUTTING, BAKING, COOKING, AND COOLING

PACKAGING

SHIPPING

STORAGE

RECEIVING LOADING DOCK

SHIPPING LOADING DOCK

HALL

ADMINISTRATION

EMPLOYEE/PUBLIC ENTRY

SPACE RELATIONSHIPS

GENERAL

Food processing facilities process raw materials into either a single food product or a common line of food products, each processed according to its own specifications. Several types of process facilities are described on this page:

1. Fluid processing of products such as milk, beverages, or concentrates
2. Meat, poultry, and fish processing, ranging from slaughter operations to packing individual meat portions for retail sale
3. Fresh or frozen baked goods
4. Cereals and other grain products
5. Fresh, canned, and frozen vegetables
6. Snack foods and sugar and confectionery products
7. Specialty items and food additives

TYPES OF FOOD PROCESSES

Each food product can be handled and processed in a variety of ways to produce various end products. For example, fresh vegetables can be canned or frozen for easier distribution and longer shelf life. Food processing facilities can be designed to handle each process in several ways:

1. Batch: In a batch operation the product flows through the process in distinct steps or stages. For example, soups may be cooked in a kettle or juice may be mixed in a large tank before it is packaged.
2. Continuous flow: In this operation the product flows through the process in a continuous stream. For example, milk is produced in a continuous fashion from pasteurization to bottling.
3. Combination of batch processing and continuous flow: A product may begin in a batch form and be finished in a continuous flow. For example, cake batters can be mixed as a batch and then transferred to an oven for continuous baking.

Many products can be processed either in a batch or in a continuous flow mode. For example, juice can be produced from concentrate by mixing a batch in a tank or by mixing it with water in a continuous stream. Higher production runs usually can justify the additional expense of complex equipment needed to run a continuous process.

St. Onge, Ruff and Associates, Inc.; York, Pennsylvania

TYPICAL PROCESS FACILITY AREAS

Depending on the food processed and the way it is processed, a typical food manufacturing facility may contain several or all of the following functions:

RECEIVING

1. Raw materials such as milk, flour, and granular or liquid sugars can be received in large quantities, either by truck or rail car, and placed in bulk storage tanks.
2. Raw materials are also received on pallets delivered by trucks to loading docks.
3. Materials can also be received in reusable totes and bulk containers. Packaging supplies usually are received on pallets delivered by truck.

STORAGE

1. Storage of finished products should be minimized to achieve maximum shelf life in retail stores. Many products are processed and loaded directly onto trucks without being stored in the plant.
2. Many food products must be stored frozen to gain maximum shelf life. Ice cream products are usually stored at -20°F. Some finished products, such as milk, must be tested before distribution to confirm regulation compliance.

SHIPPING

Trucks can be loaded with fork trucks or pallet jacks. Some processes lend themselves to staging an entire truckload on the dock and automatically transferring it to the truck.

ADMINISTRATIVE AREAS AND EMPLOYEE AMENITIES

Administrative offices support the operations of the plant. Lockers and toilets should be provided so that workers can properly prepare themselves before entering the processing areas. An access hallway is sometimes required to limit entry to sensitive processing areas. Additional sanitary measures may be required in some process spaces.

Lunchrooms, computer rooms, quality control, research and development, and maintenance are other functions typically located in these areas.

RAW MATERIAL HOLDING

1. Some raw materials need to be quarantined before they are released for processing. This holding period allows the product to be tested for bacteria or impurities before processing.
2. Dry storage areas are provided for packaging goods and raw materials that do not need to be kept cool or frozen.
3. Refrigerated storage areas can be for fresh or frozen products that would spoil if not refrigerated. Refrigerated rooms may need to be divided to prevent cross-contamination of raw materials. For example, raw meat species need to be separated.
4. Tempering rooms are provided to thaw frozen materials before they are sent to production. Some raw materials requiring tempering include meats and frozen fruits.

PROCESS PREPARATION, MIXING, BATCHING, AND BLENDING

1. Most raw materials that are prepared for use in recipes or food processes need to be unboxed, debagged, sorted, weighed, and measured. Raw vegetables must be cleaned and washed. A convenient location needs to be provided to remove trash.
2. To make a food product, several raw ingredients may need to be mixed together. Ingredients such as preservatives and artificial colors and flavors may be weighed separately in a prebatching room.

CUTTING, BAKING, COOKING, AND COOLING

Examples of these functions include:

1. cutting steaks and roasts from larger beef portions.
2. baking cake products in continuous ovens.
3. cooking soups and sauces in batches in large kettles.

PACKAGING

Finish goods can be packaged manually into boxes or be handled by automatic packing equipment.

PROCESS FLOW

A well-designed food processing facility will aid in maintaining sanitary conditions and ensuring production of a safe food product. Typically the facility is wrapped around process functions. The ideal process facility would consist of a process flow that proceeds in linear fashion straight through the facility as shown in the accompanying plans.

A straight-through facility:

1. minimizes cross-traffic.
2. minimizes the potential for cross-contamination of raw and cooked products.
3. eliminates confusion between receiving and shipping functions.

Not all sites lend themselves to a straight-through flow. A U-shaped plan, for example, means the product is received and shipped from the same side of the building.

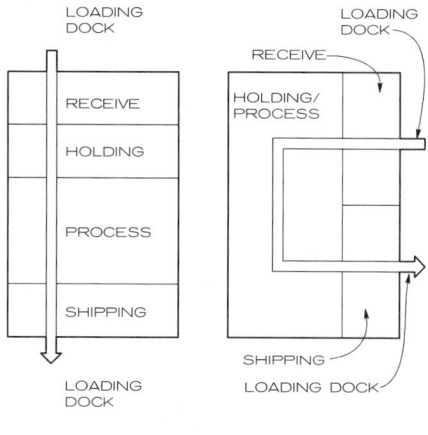

LOADING DOCK

RECEIVE

HOLDING

PROCESS

SHIPPING

LOADING DOCK

STRAIGHT-THROUGH FLOW

LOADING DOCK

RECEIVE

HOLDING/PROCESS

SHIPPING

LOADING DOCK

U-SHAPED FLOW

PROCESS FLOW LAYOUT TYPES

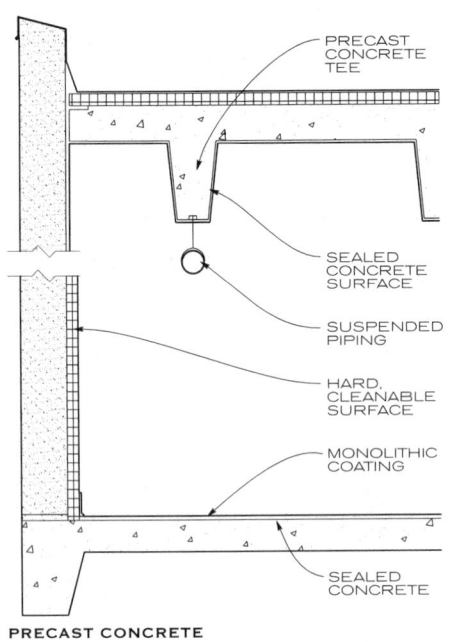

PRECAST CONCRETE TEE

SEALED CONCRETE SURFACE

SUSPENDED PIPING

HARD, CLEANABLE SURFACE

MONOLITHIC COATING

SEALED CONCRETE

PRECAST CONCRETE

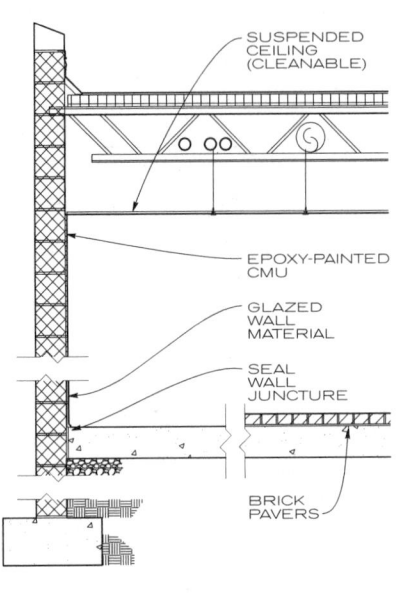

SUSPENDED CEILING (CLEANABLE)

EPOXY-PAINTED CMU

GLAZED WALL MATERIAL

SEAL WALL JUNCTURE

BRICK PAVERS

CMU WALL AND STEEL JOIST WITH SUSPENDED CEILING

SANITARY FINISHES ON BUILDING MATERIALS

NOTES

1. In general, sanitary finishes must be hard, durable, smooth, and easy to clean. Food processing rooms should be free of any hidden areas or ledges that may hinder cleaning and sanitizing.

2. Precast concrete tees are often used on process rooms. One disadvantage is that all piping and utilities are exposed and must be cleaned regularly.

3. Precast concrete with a smooth, void-free surface provides a hard surface and is usually sealed to provide good chemical resistance.

4. Monolithic coatings of epoxy and other types of materials are trowel applied in $1/8$ to $1/4$ in. thickness to provide better resistance to harsh process environments.

5. Fiberglass-reinforced panels or galvanized metal wall panels provide a hard, cleanable surface.

6. Sealed concrete provides minimum protection from processes and clean-up chemicals.

7. Suspended ceilings composed of stainless steel grids and panels provide a cleanable surface. One disadvantage of this type of finish is that the space above must be properly ventilated.

8. Epoxy-painted concrete masonry units (CMUs) provide a resistant surface if "pinholes" are filled to prevent places where bacteria can grow.

9. Ceramic tile or glazed CMU with epoxy joints provides the most durable and long-lasting process room finish.

10. Brick pavers generally provide the best resistance to harsh process and cleanup chemicals. Fill joints with cementitious material or a more chemical and heat resistant material like Furan (a specialized concrete mix).

SANITARY DESIGN

Various government organizations regulate food processing facilities, including the U.S. Department of Agriculture (USDA), the Food and Drug Administration (FDA), and state and local health departments. These organizations attempt to curtail three potential food hazards:

1. Bacteria: Many food products are susceptible to environmental or in-plant contamination. Bacterial cross-contamination of a product can occur when raw products and cooked products are in close proximity. Food processing plants should be arranged to eliminate this possibility.

2. Physical: Process lines should generally be positioned away from overhead piping, walkways, and other features from which contaminants can fall into the product. Metal particles from process pumps and other equipment can also be a physical hazard.

3. Chemical: Pesticides and other chemicals used for rodent control can contaminate processed products. Preservatives and other food additives should be added in proper quantities. Boiler water chemicals and equipment lubricants should be used appropriately.

General sanitary considerations begin with proper landscaping and lighting on the building exterior. Landscape stones placed around the building perimeter help prevent vermin from nesting close to the building. Exterior lights should be located away from doorways because they attract insects at night. On the interior, specify no glass in the process area; unprotected light bulbs could break and fall into the product. There should not be painted surfaces in process rooms; paint can chip and fall into the product.

FACILITY CLEANING

Use a dry process to clean up as much as possible to prevent process wastes from entering the sewer. Provide hose stations and high-pressure, low-flow wash stations.

Some process equipment can be left in place for cleaning. Cleaning and sanitizing solutions are circulated through the process lines. Some equipment should be disassembled and cleaned at a remote site. Foam cleaners, which mix air and foaming chemicals, can be sprayed on processing equipment, tanks, and vessels to help hold detergent on the surface.

PIPING AND UTILITIES

As far as possible, keep utilities and piping to a minimum. Piping runs should not be located over process equipment because pipes can leak and drip condensate into the product. Locate piping away from walls or tight to the wall or other surface and caulk it on both sides. Provide proper insulation and jacketing of all piping.

Typical process utilities include steam and condensate return; process water; hot water; chilled water for cooling jackets; compressed air and control air; gas ovens or hot water heaters; hydraulics for hydraulically operated motors; refrigeration for process or space cooling; electrical; plumbing (no standing water on floors; 400 sq ft/drain); hand-washing and cleanup stations.

PIPING LOCATIONS

Within the processing space, piping should be on pipe racks. To make changes or repairs to piping, the food processing line usually must be shut down to avoid product contamination. An alternative is to locate piping in a crawl space above the process room. This utility service area allows utility drops to occur at the connection point to the processing equipment. Changes and repairs to piping and utilities in the utility service space can usually be made while the food processing line is running.

TEMPERATURE AND LIGHTING OF PROCESS AREAS

Keep temperatures to USDA-specified levels or lower to slow growth of bacteria. Refer to ASHRAE guide for manufacture of particular products. Lighting considerations include proper lighting levels and good color rendition for inspection of products. All fixtures should be enclosed and, possibly, gasketed for wash-down service.

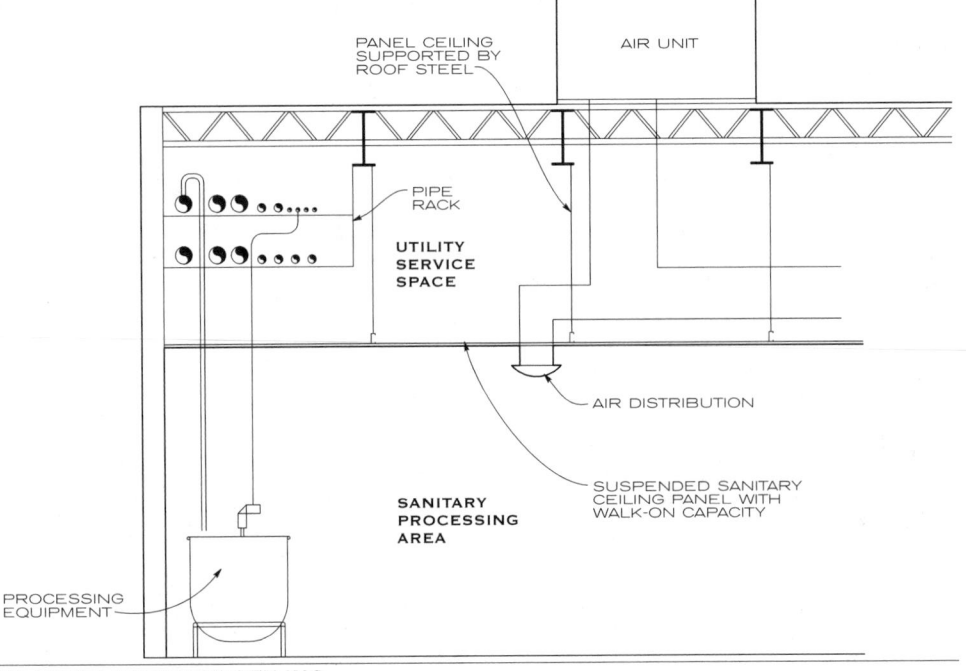

PANEL CEILING SUPPORTED BY ROOF STEEL

AIR UNIT

PIPE RACK

UTILITY SERVICE SPACE

AIR DISTRIBUTION

SUSPENDED SANITARY CEILING PANEL WITH WALK-ON CAPACITY

SANITARY PROCESSING AREA

PROCESSING EQUIPMENT

WALK-ON SANITARY CEILING

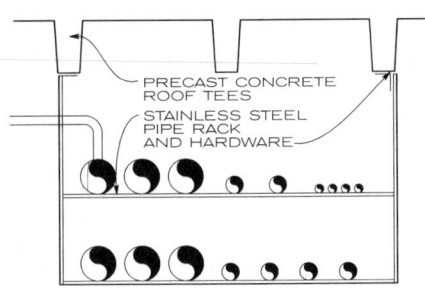

PRECAST CONCRETE ROOF TEES

STAINLESS STEEL PIPE RACK AND HARDWARE

NOTE

Pipe rack may include food processing piping, utility piping, electrical wiring, and control circuits.

PIPE RACK DETAIL

St. Onge, Ruff and Associates, Inc.; York, Pennsylvania

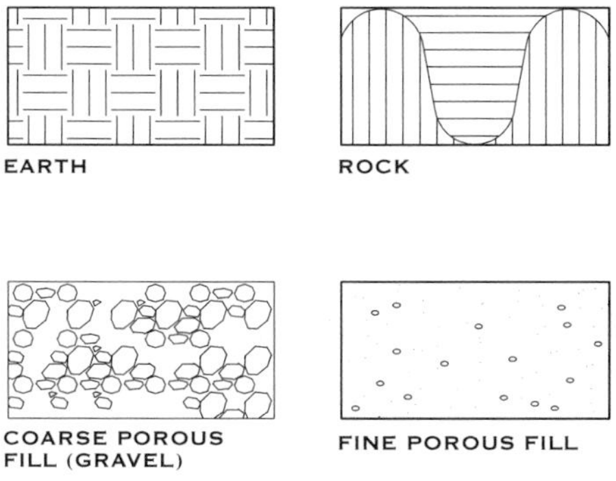

EARTH

ROCK

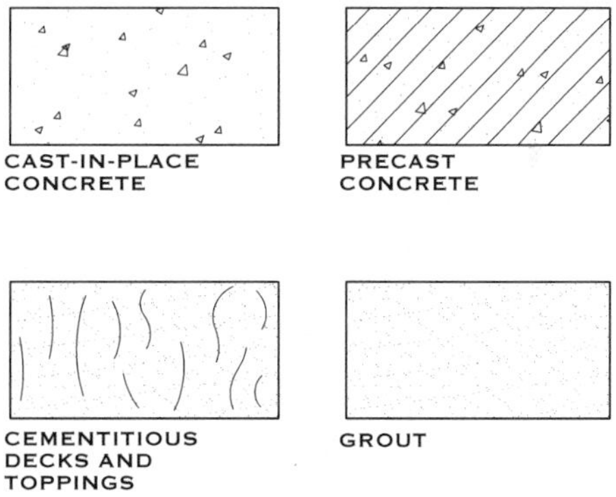

CAST-IN-PLACE CONCRETE

PRECAST CONCRETE

CONTINUOUS ROUGH WOOD FRAMING

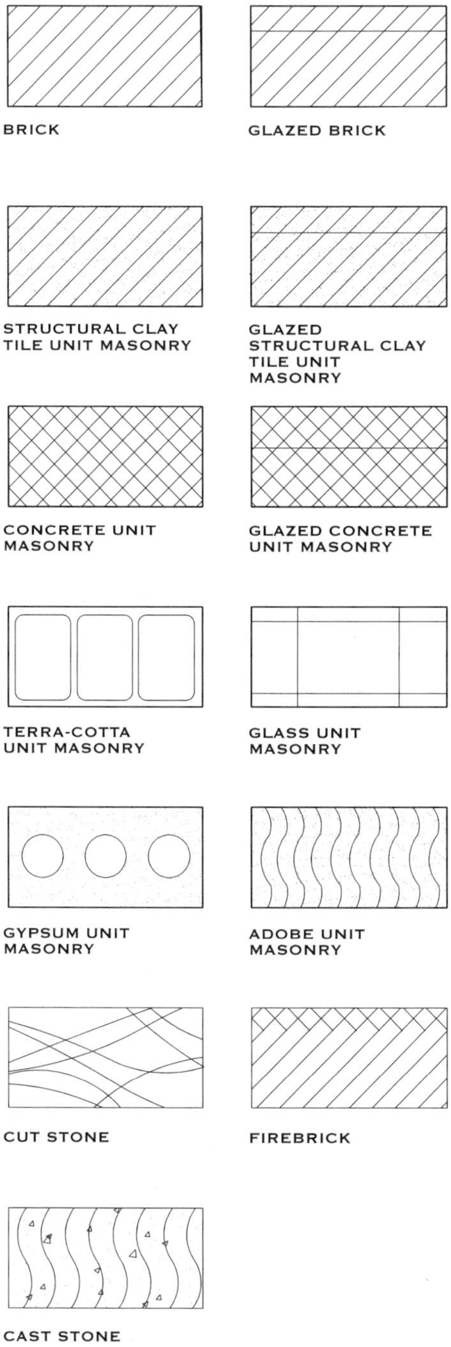

WOOD BLOCKING

COARSE POROUS FILL (GRAVEL)

FINE POROUS FILL

CEMENTITIOUS DECKS AND TOPPINGS

GROUT

PLYWOOD (ROUGH)

PLYWOOD FOR ARCHITECTURAL WOODWORK

SITEWORK

CONCRETE

PARTICLEBOARD (ROUGH)

PARTICLEBOARD FOR ARCHITECTURAL WOODWORK

BRICK

GLAZED BRICK

BATT/FIBROUS INSULATION

FOAM INSULATION

ORIENTED STRAND BOARD (OSB)

FINISH WOOD FOR ARCHITECTURAL WOODWORK

STRUCTURAL CLAY TILE UNIT MASONRY

GLAZED STRUCTURAL CLAY TILE UNIT MASONRY

RIGID INSULATION BOARD

LOOSE FILL INSULATION

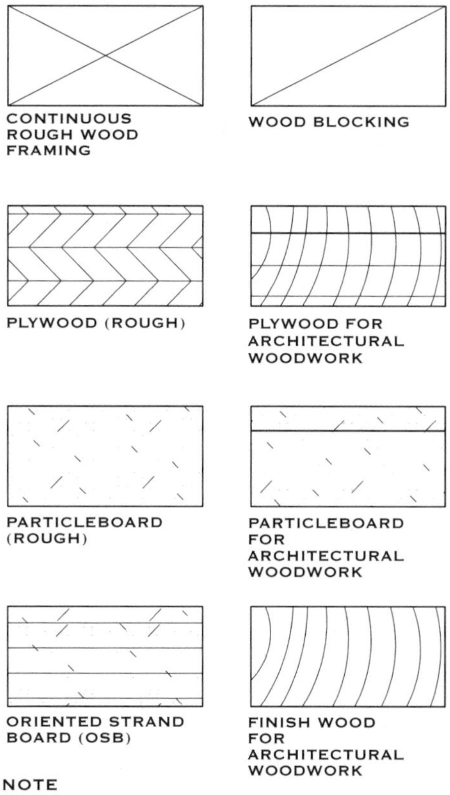

NOTE

Indicate laminate material used for architectural woodwork.

WOOD

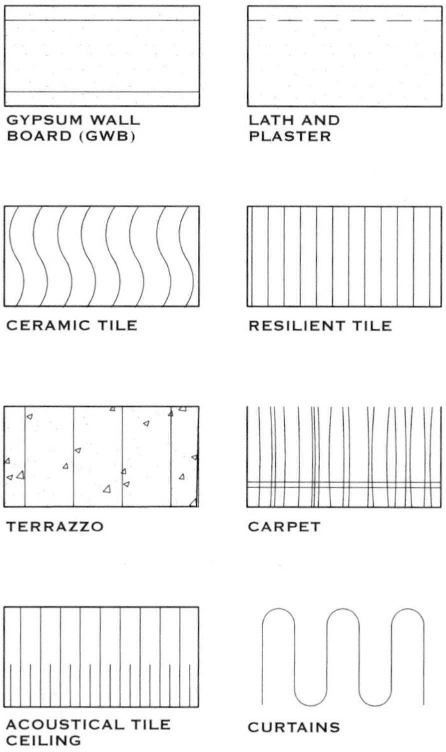

CONCRETE UNIT MASONRY

GLAZED CONCRETE UNIT MASONRY

EXTERIOR INSULATION AND FINISH SYSTEM (EIFS)

FIBROUS FIRE SAFING

GYPSUM WALL BOARD (GWB)

LATH AND PLASTER

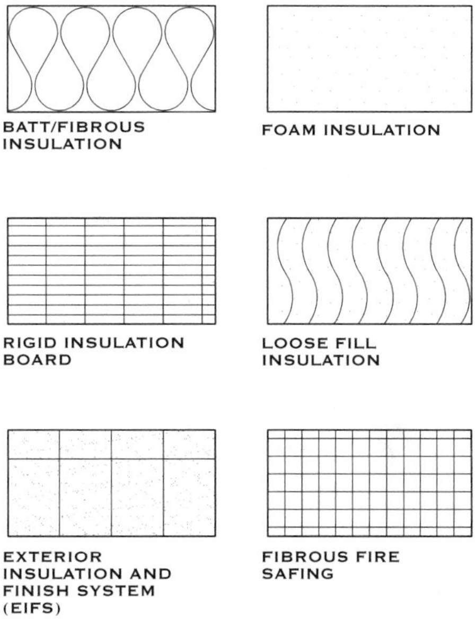

THERMAL AND MOISTURE PROTECTION

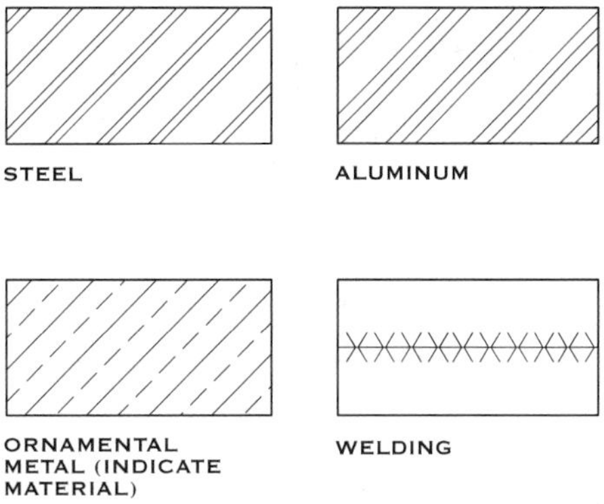

TERRA-COTTA UNIT MASONRY

GLASS UNIT MASONRY

CERAMIC TILE

RESILIENT TILE

STEEL

ALUMINUM

GYPSUM UNIT MASONRY

ADOBE UNIT MASONRY

TERRAZZO

CARPET

CUT STONE

FIREBRICK

ORNAMENTAL METAL (INDICATE MATERIAL)

WELDING

ACOUSTICAL TILE CEILING

CURTAINS

METAL

CAST STONE

MASONRY

GLASS

PLASTIC

FINISHES AND FURNISHINGS

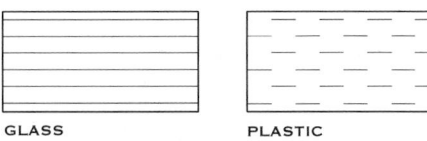

CENTERLINE OF FASTENER (INDICATE TYPE)

WOOD OR METAL FASTENER

GLAZING

FASTENERS

Keith McCormack, AIA; RTKL, Inc.; Baltimore, Maryland

GRAPHIC SYMBOLS A

GRAPHIC SYMBOLS

The following symbols are commonly used by architecture firms.

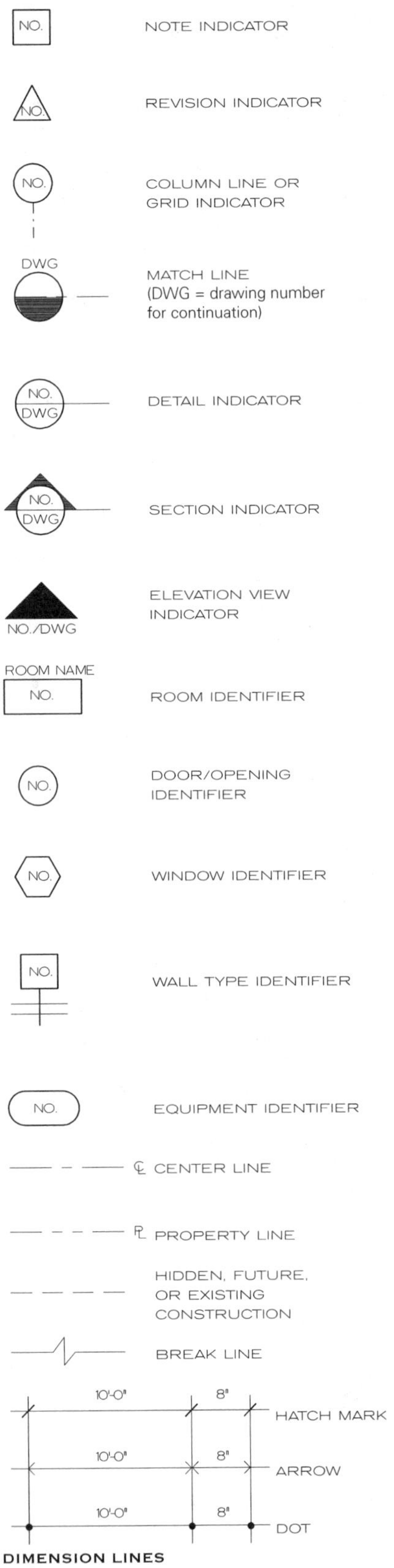

NOTE INDICATOR

REVISION INDICATOR

COLUMN LINE OR GRID INDICATOR

MATCH LINE
(DWG = drawing number for continuation)

DETAIL INDICATOR

SECTION INDICATOR

ELEVATION VIEW INDICATOR

ROOM IDENTIFIER

DOOR/OPENING IDENTIFIER

WINDOW IDENTIFIER

WALL TYPE IDENTIFIER

EQUIPMENT IDENTIFIER

CENTER LINE

PROPERTY LINE

HIDDEN, FUTURE, OR EXISTING CONSTRUCTION

BREAK LINE

HATCH MARK

ARROW

DOT

DIMENSION LINES

NOTE

In the symbols above: NO.—sequential alphanumeric designation; DWG—drawing number.

GENERAL SYMBOLS AND CONVENTIONS

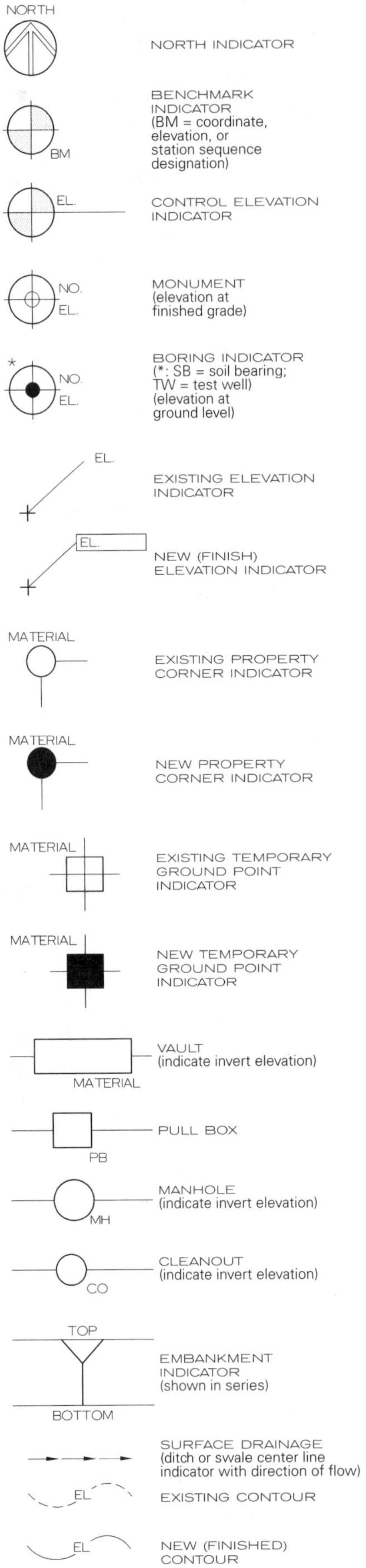

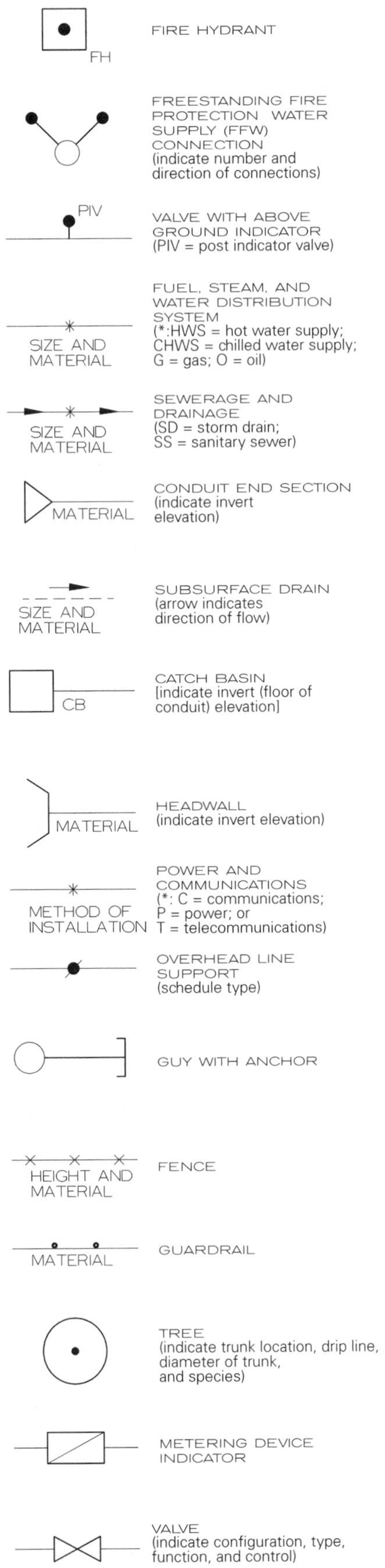

Keith McCormack, AIA; RTKL Associates, Inc; Baltimore, Maryland

NORTH INDICATOR

BENCHMARK INDICATOR
(BM = coordinate, elevation, or station sequence designation)

CONTROL ELEVATION INDICATOR

MONUMENT
(elevation at finished grade)

BORING INDICATOR
(*: SB = soil bearing; TW = test well)
(elevation at ground level)

EXISTING ELEVATION INDICATOR

NEW (FINISH) ELEVATION INDICATOR

EXISTING PROPERTY CORNER INDICATOR

NEW PROPERTY CORNER INDICATOR

EXISTING TEMPORARY GROUND POINT INDICATOR

NEW TEMPORARY GROUND POINT INDICATOR

VAULT
(indicate invert elevation)

PULL BOX

MANHOLE
(indicate invert elevation)

CLEANOUT
(indicate invert elevation)

EMBANKMENT INDICATOR
(shown in series)

SURFACE DRAINAGE
(ditch or swale center line indicator with direction of flow)

EXISTING CONTOUR

NEW (FINISHED) CONTOUR

SITEWORK SYMBOLS

FIRE HYDRANT

FREESTANDING FIRE PROTECTION WATER SUPPLY (FFW) CONNECTION
(indicate number and direction of connections)

VALVE WITH ABOVE GROUND INDICATOR
(PIV = post indicator valve)

FUEL, STEAM, AND WATER DISTRIBUTION SYSTEM
(*:HWS = hot water supply; CHWS = chilled water supply; G = gas; O = oil)

SEWERAGE AND DRAINAGE
(SD = storm drain; SS = sanitary sewer)

CONDUIT END SECTION
(indicate invert elevation)

SUBSURFACE DRAIN
(arrow indicates direction of flow)

CATCH BASIN
[indicate invert (floor of conduit) elevation]

HEADWALL
(indicate invert elevation)

POWER AND COMMUNICATIONS
(*: C = communications; P = power; or T = telecommunications)

OVERHEAD LINE SUPPORT
(schedule type)

GUY WITH ANCHOR

FENCE

GUARDRAIL

TREE
(indicate trunk location, drip line, diameter of trunk, and species)

METERING DEVICE INDICATOR

VALVE
(indicate configuration, type, function, and control)

NOTE

In the symbols above: EL.—elevation; NO.—sequential alphanumeric designation.

 GRAPHIC SYMBOLS

RIGID CONDUIT
(indicate size and
material, if required)

FLEXIBLE CONDUIT
(indicate size and
material, if required)

HOMERUN TO PANELBOARD
(indicate circuit and
panel)

WIRING, NEUTRAL

WIRING, HOT

WIRING GROUND

WIRING, SWITCH LEG

JUNCTION BOX
(indicate size and type, if required)

FLOOR JUNCTION BOX
(indicate size and type, if required)

SINGLE RECEPTACLE
(indicate nonstandard
mounting height;
* = GFI—ground fault
interrupt; IG—isolated
ground; S—integral
switch; WP—weatherproof;
XP—explosionproof)

DUPLEX RECEPTACLE
(indicate nonstandard
mounting height; * = same
as above for single
receptacle)

QUADRAPLEX RECEPTACLE
(indicate nonstandard
mounting height; * = same
as above for single
receptacle)

SPECIAL PURPOSE
RECEPTACLE
(indicate nonstandard
mounting height)

CLOCK RECEPTACLE
(indicate nonstandard
mounting height)

DATA COMMUNICATIONS
OUTLET
(indicate nonstandard
mounting height)

TELEPHONE OUTLET
(indicate nonstandard
mounting height)

SINGLE FLOOR RECEPTACLE
(indicate nonstandard
mounting height;
* = GFI—ground fault interrupt;
IG—isolated ground;
S—integral switch;
WP—weatherproof;
XP—explosionproof)

DUPLEX FLOOR RECEPTACLE
(indicate nonstandard
mounting height; * = same
as above for single
floor receptacle)

**CONDUIT, WIRING, AND OUTLET
SYMBOLS**

FLOOR SPECIAL
PURPOSE RECEPTACLE
(indicate configuration)

FLOOR TELEPHONE OUTLET

FLOOR DATA
COMMUNICATIONS OUTLET

RANGE OUTLET

SPLIT-WIRED DUPLEX
RECEPTACLE OUTLET

FAN HANGER RECEPTACLE

TELEVISION OUTLET
(indicate nonstandard
mounting height)

SWITCH
(* = [none]—single pole; 2—two-pole;
3—three-way; 4—four-way;
D—door; K—key operated;
LV—low voltage;
M—momentary contact;
P—pilot light)

DIMMER SWITCH
(indicate nonstandard
mounting height)

CEILING PULL SWITCH

SWITCH AND SINGLE
RECEPTACLE

SWITCH AND DOUBLE
RECEPTACLE

PLUGMOLD
(indicate spacing and
nonstandard mounting height)

SWITCH AND OUTLET SYMBOLS

GENERATOR

Y-CONNECTION, LOW OR
MEDIUM VOLTAGE

DELTA CONNECTION, LOW OR
MEDIUM VOLTAGE

CIRCUIT BREAKER, MEDIUM
VOLTAGE

DISCONNECT/INTERRUPTER
SWITCH, MEDIUM VOLTAGE
(indicate size)

**MISCELLANEOUS ELECTRICAL
DEVICE SYMBOLS**

CONTROL POWER
TRANSFORMER

POTENTIAL
TRANSFORMER

CURRENT TRANSFORMER

CABLE POT HEAD
(may be used for
overhead or
underground)

BUS DUCT
(indicate size)

CIRCUIT BREAKER

GROUND FAULT RELAY

FUSE, LOW OR MEDIUM
VOLTAGE

FUSED CUTOUT

MOTOR STARTER

COMBINATION MOTOR
STARTER

MANUAL MOTOR
STARTER

MAGNETIC ONLY
CIRCUIT BREAKER

MOTOR
(* = horsepower)

CONTACTOR, NORMALLY
CLOSED

CONTACTOR, NORMALLY
OPEN

TRANSFER SWITCH
(* = A—automatic;
M—manual; #P—no. of
poles; #—amp rating)

WALL BRACKET
(for wall-mounted
electrical items)

**MISCELLANEOUS ELECTRICAL
DEVICE SYMBOLS**

GRAPHIC SYMBOLS

F — PULL STATION, FIRE ALARM

F◁ — FIRE ALARM HORN AND/OR STROBE

◁ F — FIREFIGHTERS' PHONE

F◖ — FIRE ALARM BELL

M — MAGNETIC HOLD-OPEN DEVICE

Ⓢ* — SPEAKER (F—fire; NC—nurse call; PA—public address)

🕐 HEIGHT — CLOCK

▱ — ELECTRIC RESISTANCE HEATER

◿ — BUZZER

◿ — BUZZER AND BELL COMBINATION

▭ — BELL

▫* — PUSH-BUTTON SWITCH (indicate emergency power off [EPO], if required)

— SWITCH

PE — PHOTOELECTRIC CELL

Ⓣ* — PNEUMATIC THERMOSTAT (* = A—aspirating; C—cooling; D—day; D/N—day/night; H—heating; H/C— heating/cooling; N—night)

T* — ELECTRIC THERMOSTAT (* = same as above for pneumatic thermostat)

Ⓗ — HUMIDISTAT

Ⓢ* — SENSOR (* = H—humidity; P—pressure; T—temperature)

┤⊏ — CAPACITOR

◁ — SERVICE WEATHERHEAD

Ⓧ — METER (* = A—ammeter; KW—kilowatt meter; KWD—kilowatt demand meter; KWH—kilowatt hour meter; M—meter; PF—power factor meter; V—voltmeter; VAR—VAR meter)

┤├ — BATTERY

— LIGHTNING ARRESTER

⇑ — DRAWOUT CONNECTION

Ⓐ — FLAME DETECTOR

Ⓘ — HEAT DETECTOR (indicate type)

Ⓢ* — SMOKE DETECTOR (* = I—ionization; P—photoelectric)

● — GAS DETECTOR (Indicate type)

▣* — DETECTOR OR SELECTOR SWITCH (* = FS—flow switch; LS—level switch; PS—pressure switch; TS—tamper switch; AS—ammeter; VS—voltmeter)

/ — DISCONNECT/INTERRUPTER SWITCH, LOW VOLTAGE (indicate size)

▱ — DISCONNECT SWITCH (indicate size)

▱ — FUSED DISCONNECT (indicate size)

⏚ — GROUND CONNECTION

⎨ — TRANSFORMER, LOW VOLTAGE (for use on single line diagrams)

▱ — FLUSH-MOUNTED PANELBOARD AND CABINET

▭ — SURFACE-MOUNTED PANELBOARD AND CABINET

ELECTRICAL DEVICES, SWITCHES, AND PANELBOARD SYMBOLS

○ — CEILING-MOUNTED LIGHT FIXTURE (indicate type)

⊗ — EXIT LIGHT (indicate type; shading indicates lighted face)

◐ — WALL WASHER (indicate type; shading indicates lighted face)

○→ — SPOTLIGHT (indicate type; arrow indicates direction of focus)

▭ — FLUORESCENT FIXTURE (indicate type; draw to scale)

▣ ▣ — SURFACE-MOUNTED FLUORESCENT

▨ — EMERGENCY FLUORESCENT FIXTURE (indicate type; draw to scale)

▷ — FLUORESCENT STRIP LIGHT (indicate type; draw to scale)

△ △ △ — LIGHT TRACK (indicate type; show number of fixtures required)

Ⓓ — DROP CORD

⊓ — EMERGENCY BATTERY-POWERED LIGHT (indicate single or double lamp)

▽ — EMERGENCY BATTERY-POWERED LIGHT, REMOTE (indicate single or double lamp)

○—● —○ — ARM-MOUNTED OUTDOOR POLE FIXTURE

◖ —◗ — REMOTE EMERGENCY SEALED BEAM HEAD WITH OUTLET BOX

Ⓛ —Ⓛ — OUTLET CONTROLLED BY LOW VOLTAGE SWITCHING WHEN RELAY IS INSTALLED IN OUTLET BOX

Ⓛ PS —Ⓛ PS — LAMP HOLDER WITH PULL SWITCH

Ⓑ —Ⓑ — BLANKED OUTLET

LIGHTING SYMBOLS

 GRAPHIC SYMBOLS

DESCRIPTION GOES HERE

VALVES

DESCRIPTION

Configuration	Function
3-way	Balancing
4-way	Pneumatic
Angle	Pressure relief
In-line	Shutoff
Type	**Control**
Ball	Differential pressure
Butterfly	Manual
Gate	Pressure regulator
Globe	Pneumatic
	Self-activating
	Solenoid
	Thermostatic

NOTE

Combine modifiers as required.

AUTOMATIC 2-WAY VALVE

AUTOMATIC 3-WAY VALVE

AIR LINE VALVE

AIR ELIMINATOR VALVE

LOCK SHIELD VALVE

PIPING

* DESCRIPTION			
A	alkali	N	nitrogen
AW	acid waste	NG	natural gas
C	condensate	NO	nitrous oxide
CA	compressed air	NTW	nontoxic industrial waste
CHW	chilled water		
CO2	carbon dioxide	O	oxygen
CRW	chome waste	RFGT	refrigerant
CW	cold water (domestic)	STM	steam
		SW	sea water
CYW	cyanide waste	TW	toxic industrial waste
D	diesel fuel		
DIW	deionized water	W	water
DSP	dry standpipe	WO	waste oil
FO	fuel oil	WST	wet standpipe
GAS	gasoline	* FUNCTION	
H	hydrogen	DR	drain
HAL	halon	DWV	drain, waste, and vent
HG	hot gas		
HW	hot water	FP	fire protection
LO	lubricating oil	HY	hydronic
LPG	liquefied propane gas	R	return
		RWL	rainwater leader
MUW	makeup water	S	supply
		SUCT	suction

NOTE

Combine modifiers as required.

VENT PIPING
(* = AWV—acid waste vent; V—vent)

FLOW DIRECTION

REDUCER OR INCREASER

UNION

PIPE ANCHOR

FLANGES

ALIGNMENT

STEAM TRAP
(* = B—bucket; F—float; T—thermostatic)

HOSE BIBB HYDRANT
(schedule types)

COCK OR PLUG

CHECK VALVE

DRIP POCKET

STRAINER

TEMPERATURE GAUGE

PRESSURE GAUGE

THERMOMETER

SPRINKLER HEAD
(schedule types)

SIDEWALL SPRINKLER HEAD
(schedule types)

CLEANOUT AT END OF PIPE

CEANOUT AT WALL

DRAIN
(* = AD—area drain; FD—floor drain; FS—floor sink; RD—roof drain)

EXPANSION JOINT

FLEXIBLE PIPE CONNECTION

PIPE FLANGE, BLIND

PIPE ELBOW, DOWN

PIPE ELBOW, UP

PIPE TEE, DOWN

PIPE TEE, UP

DUCTWORK, SINGLE LINE
(indicate size, shape, and type)

SUPPLY DUCTWORK
(indicate size, shape, and type)

RETURN, RELIEF, OR EXHAUST DUCTWORK
(indicate size, shape, and type)

FLEXIBLE DUCTWORK
(indicate size, shape, and type)

DAMPER
(* = AD—automatic damper; BD—backdraft damper; FD—fire damper; MD—motorized damper; SD—smoke damper; VD—volume damper)

RECTANGULAR DIFFUSER
(schedule size, indicate cu ft/min. and directions of throw)

ROUND DIFFUSER
(schedule size, indicate cu ft/min. and directions of throw)

LINEAR DIFFUSER
(schedule size, indicate cu ft/min. and directions of throw)

RETURN, RELIEF, OR EXHAUST REGISTER
(schedule size)

SIDEWALL DIFFUSER
(schedule size, indicate cu ft/min. and direction of flow)

RETURN, RELIEF, OR EXHAUST REGISTER
(schedule size)

FLOOR REGISTER

10 X 20   DUCT
(width X depth)

DIRECTION OF FLOW

DUCTWORK WITH ACOUSTICAL LINING

FLEXIBLE CONNECTION

INCLINED AIRFLOW
(* = R—rise, D—drop)

LOUVER OPENING
(schedule size; indicate cu ft/min. and direction of flow)

PLUMBING AND PIPING SYMBOLS

Keith McCormack, AIA; RTKL, Inc.; Baltimore, Maryland

HVAC SYMBOLS

GRAPHIC SYMBOLS

GENERAL

Virtually all computer-aided design (CAD) systems support the concept of layers, which allow grouping of graphic information for display or plotting. Intelligent use of layers can reduce drawing time and improve drawing coordination. For example, a single CAD file can be used to produce a floor plan, a reflected ceiling plan, a power plan, and a lighting plan. In addition to increased drawing productivity, use of standardized CAD layers provides these other benefits:

1. Improved coordination between architects, engineers, and consultants
2. Efficient creation of facility management record drawings from construction documents
3. Symbols and details that can be reused without conversion of layers

In 1990 the first industry standard for the use of CAD layers in architecture, engineering, and facility management was introduced with the publication of *CAD Layer Guidelines*. In 1997 the second edition of *CAD Layer Guidelines* was published, expanding the work begun in the first edition in the following ways:

1. Adds discipline designations for interior design, telecommunications, and other fields
2. Expands layer designations for remodeling projects
3. Designates the "long format" as the single approved layer name format
4. Coordinates with the Construction Specification Institute's Uniform Drafting System
5. Defines a standard for naming and organizing CAD files

CONVENTIONS FOR NAMING LAYERS

The CAD layer guidelines are organized using a hierarchical structure that provides for flexibility and expandability. The first level of the hierarchy is the discipline code. Discipline codes follow traditional sheet numbering conventions as shown here:

A	Architectural
C	Civil
E	Electrical
F	Fire protection
G	General
H	Hazardous materials
I	Interiors
L	Landscape
M	Mechanical
P	Plumbing
Q	Equipment
R	Resource
S	Structural
T	Telecommunications
X	Other disciplines
Z	Contractor/shop drawings

Discipline codes are followed by either a hyphen or another letter that designates a specialized discipline. For example, AG is used for architectural graphics.

The second level of the hierarchy is the major group code. This is used to designate a construction system or type of information. For example, a drawing might contain layers with the following discipline and major group codes:

A-WALL	Walls
A-DOOR	Doors
A-GLAZ	Glazing
A-EQPM	Equipment
A-CLNG	Ceiling information
A-ROOF	Roof
E-POWR	Power
S-COLS	Structural columns

Layer names can be further extended with a minor group code and a status code. The minor group is an optional, four-character field used to define subcategories of information. For example, A-WALL-PART indicates architecture, new, wall, partial height. IDEN for identification and PATT for pattern are two commonly used modifiers in the minor group field.

Status codes are four-character designators used to differentiate new construction from demolition, remodeling, and construction that is "existing to remain." They are only needed when a project has phases of work that must be differentiated. Defined values for this field are shown on this page under the heading "Status Field Modifiers."

Layers representing the dominant phase of a project can be named without using a status field. For example, in a small remodeling project, NEWW would indicate new construction, while layers without status fields would indicate parts

of the existing building that will remain. For example, a remodeling plan might contain the following layers:

A-WALL-NEWW	New walls
A-DOOR-NEWW	New doors
A-WALL-DEMO	Walls to be demolished
A-DOOR-DEMO	Doors to be demolished
A-WALL	Existing walls to remain
A-DOOR	Existing doors to remain

Conversely, a remodeling project consisting of mostly new construction might use EXST to indicate layers referring to "existing to remain" construction and layers without status fields to represent new construction.

The status field is always placed as the last field of the layer name. In a simple layer name such as A-WALL, the status field would be the third field (A-WALL-DEMO). In a more detailed layer name, the status field would be the fourth field (A-WALL-FULL-DEMO).

MASTER LAYER LIST

The master layer list identifies all defined layers in the CAD layer guidelines. Users are free to add their own layers, but should identify them as "user-defined." The use of an asterisk (*) indicates a place holder for the discipline code, major group, or minor group. Some layers included in the following list are new or have been revised since the first edition of *CAD Layer Guidelines*.

This list is arranged alphabetically by discipline. Layers within each discipline are arranged by construction system.

ANNOTATION LAYERS

*-ANNO-TEXT	Text
*-ANNO-REDL	Redline
*-ANNO-SYMB	Symbols
*-ANNO-LEGN	Legends and schedules
*-ANNO-DIMS	Dimensions
*-ANNO-TTLB	Border and title block
*-ANNO-NOTE	Notes
*-ANNO-NPLT infor-	Construction lines, nonplotting
	mation
*-ANNO-KEYN	Key notes
*-ANNO-REVS	Revisions

NOTE

Annotation layer names may be appended with a four-character sheet name designator when needed.

COMMON MODIFIERS

*-****-PATT	Cross-hatching, poché
*-****-IDEN	Identification tags
*-****-ELEV	Elevation (vertical surfaces in 3D)
X-RDME	Read-me layer, not to be plotted

STATUS FIELD MODIFIERS

*-****-NEWW	New work
*-****-EXST	Existing to remain
*-****-DEMO	Demolition
*-****-FUTR	Future work
*-****-TEMP	Temporary work
*-****-MOVE	Items to be moved
*-****-RELO	Relocated items
*-****-NICN	Not in contract
*-****-PHS1-9	Phase numbers (1-9)

NOTE

The status field may also occur as the fourth field, following a minor group.

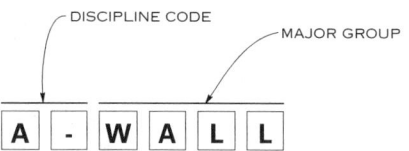

SIMPLE LAYER NAME WITH ONLY MAJOR GROUP

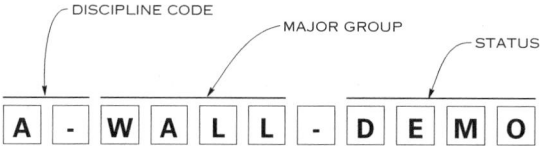

LAYER NAME WITH MAJOR GROUP AND STATUS FIELD

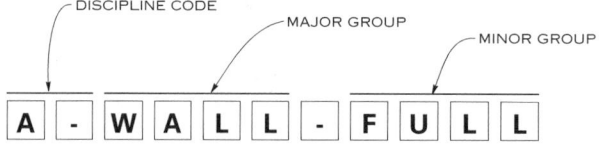

LAYER NAME WITH MAJOR GROUP AND MINOR GROUP

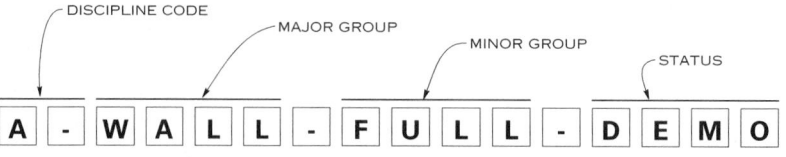

LAYER NAME WITH MAJOR GROUP, MINOR GROUP, AND STATUS FIELD

_____

OPTIONS FOR LAYER NAME FORMATS

Michael K. Schley, AIA, ed., *CAD Layer Guidelines*, 2d ed. (Washington: The American Institute of Architects Press, 1997)

ARCHITECTURAL LAYERS

A-WALL-FULL	Full-height walls, stair and shaft walls, walls to structure
A-WALL-PRHT	Partial-height walls (do not appear on reflected ceiling plans)
A-WALL-MOVE	Movable partitions
A-WALL-HEAD	Door and window headers (appear on reflected ceiling plans)
A-WALL-JAMB	Door and window jambs (do not appear on reflected ceiling plans)
A-WALL-PATT	Wall insulation, hatching and fill
A-WALL-ELEV	Wall surfaces: 3D views
A-WALL-FIRE	Fire wall patterning
A-DOOR	Doors
A-DOOR-FULL	Full-height (to ceiling) door: swing and leaf
A-DOOR-PRHT	Partial-height door: swing and leaf
A-DOOR-IDEN	Door number, hardware group, etc.
A-DOOR-ELEV	Doors: 3D views
A-GLAZ	Windows, window walls, curtain walls, glazed partitions
A-GLAZ-FULL	Full-height glazed walls and partitions
A-GLAZ-PRHT	Windows and partial-height glazed partitions
A-GLAZ-SILL	Windowsills
A-GLAZ-IDEN	Window number
A-GLAZ-ELEV	Glazing and mullions--elevation views
A-FLOR	Floor information
A-FLOR-OTLN	Floor or building outline
A-FLOR-LEVL	Level changes, ramps, pits, depressions
A-FLOR-STRS	Stair treads, escalators, ladders
A-FLOR-RISR	Stair risers
A-FLOR-HRAL	Stair and balcony handrails, guardrails
A-FLOR-EVTR	Elevator cars and equipment
A-FLOR-TPTN	Toilet partitions
A-FLOR-SPCL	Architectural specialties (toilet room accessories, display cases)
A-FLOR-WDWK	Architectural woodwork (field-built cabinets and counters)
A-FLOR-CASE	Casework (manufactured cabinets)
A-FLOR-OVHD	Overhead items (skylights, overhangs—usually dashed line)
A-FLOR-RAIS	Raised floors
A-FLOR-IDEN	Room numbers, names, targets, etc.
A-FLOR-PATT	Paving, tile, carpet patterns
A-FLOR-PFIX	Plumbing fixtures
A-FLOR-FIXT	Miscellaneous fixtures
A-FLOR-SIGN	Signage
A-EQPM	Equipment
A-EQPM-FIXD	Fixed equipment
A-EQPM-MOVE	Movable equipment
A-EQPM-NICN	Equipment not in contract
A-EQPM-ACCS	Equipment access
A-EQPM-IDEN	Equipment identification numbers
A-EQPM-ELEV	Equipment surfaces: 3D views
A-EQPM-CLNG	Ceiling-mounted or suspended equipment
A-FURN	Furniture
A-FURN-FREE	Furniture: freestanding (desks, credenzas, etc.)
A-FURN-CHAR	Chairs and other seating
A-FURN-FILE	File cabinets
A-FURN-PNLS	Furniture system panels
A-FURN-WKSF	Furniture system work surface components
A-FURN-STOR	Furniture system storage components
A-FURN-POWR	Furniture system—power designations
A-FURN-IDEN	Furniture numbers
A-FURN-PLNT	Plants
A-FURN-PATT	Finish patterns
A-FURN-ELEV	Furniture: 3D views
A-CLNG	Ceiling information
A-CLNG-GRID	Ceiling grid
A-CLNG-OPEN	Ceiling/roof penetrations
A-CLNG-TEES	Main tees
A-CLNG-SUSP	Suspended elements
A-CLNG-PATT	Ceiling patterns
A-CLNG-ACCS	Ceiling access
A-LITE	Light fixtures
A-COLS	Columns
A-HVAC-SDFF	Supply diffusers
A-HVAC-RDFF	Return air diffusers
A-GRID	Planning grid or column grid
A-ROOF	Roof
A-ROOF-OTLN	Roof outline
A-ROOF-LEVL	Level changes
A-ROOF-STRS	Stair treads, ladders
A-ROOF-RISR	Stair risers
A-ROOF-HRAL	Stair handrails, nosings, guardrails
A-ROOF-PATT	Roof surface patterns, hatching
A-ROOF-ELEV	Roof surfaces: 3D views
A-AREA	Area calculation boundary lines
A-AREA-PATT	Area cross hatching
A-AREA-IDEN	Room numbers, tenant identifications, area calculation
A-AREA-OCCP	Occupant or employee names
A-ELEV	Interior and exterior elevations
A-ELEV-OTLN	Building outlines
A-ELEV-FNSH	Finishes, woodwork, trim
A-ELEV-CASE	Wall-mounted casework
A-ELEV-FIXT	Miscellaneous fixtures
A-ELEV-PFIXT	Plumbing fixtures in elevation
A-ELEV-SIGN	Signage
A-ELEV-PATT	Textures and hatch patterns
A-ELEV-IDEN	Component identification numbers
A-SECT	Sections
A-SECT-MCUT	Material cut by section
A-SECT-MBND	Material beyond section cut
A-SECT-PATT	Textures and hatch patterns
A-SECT-IDEN	Component identification numbers
A-DETL	Details
A-DETL-MCUT	Material cut by section
A-DETL-MBND	Material beyond section cut
A-DETL-PATT	Textures and hatch patterns
A-DETL-IDEN	Component identification numbers

CIVIL LAYERS

C-PROP	Property lines, survey benchmarks
C-PROP-ESMT	Easements, rights-of-way, setback lines
C-PROP-BRNG	Bearings and distance labels
C-PROP-CONS	Construction controls
C-TOPO	Proposed contour lines and elevations
C-TOPO-SPOT	Spot elevations
C-TOPO-BORE	Test borings
C-TOPO-RTWL	Retaining wall
C-BLDG	Proposed building footprints
C-PKNG	Parking lots
C-PKNG-STRP	Parking lot striping, handicapped symbol
C-PKNG-CARS	Graphic illustration of cars
C-PKNG-ISLD	Parking islands
C-PKNG-DRAN	Parking lot drainage slope indications
C-ROAD	Roadways
C-ROAD-CNTR	Center lines
C-ROAD-CURB	Curbs
C-STRM	Storm drainage catch basins, manholes
C-STRM-UNDR	Storm drainage pipe—underground
C-COMM	Site communication/telephone poles, boxes, towers
C-COMM-UNDR	Underground communication lines
C-COMM-OVHD	Overhead communication lines
C-WATR	Domestic water—manholes, pumping stations, storage tanks
C-WATR-UNDR	Domestic water—underground lines
C-FIRE	Fire protection—hydrants, connections
C-FIRE-UNDR	Fire protection—underground lines
C-NGAS	Natural gas—manholes, meters, storage tanks
C-NGAS-UNDR	Natural gas—underground lines
C-SSWR	Sanitary sewer—manholes, pumping stations
C-SSWR-UNDR	Sanitary sewer—underground lines

ELECTRICAL LAYERS

E-LITE	Lighting
E-LITE-SPCL	Special lighting
E-LITE-EMER	Emergency lighting
E-LITE-EXIT	Exit lighting
E-LITE-CLNG	Ceiling-mounted lighting
E-LITE-WALL	Wall-mounted lighting
E-LITE-FLOR	Floor-mounted lighting
E-LITE-OTLN	Lighting outline for background (optional)
E-LITE-NUMB	Lighting circuit numbers
E-LITE-ROOF	Roof lighting
E-LITE-SITE	Site lighting (see also civil group)
E-LITE-SWCH	Lighting—switches
E-LITE-CIRC	Lighting circuits
E-LITE-IDEN	Luminaire identification and text
E-LITE-JBOX	Junction box

E-POWR	Power
E-POWR-WALL	Power wall outlets and receptacles
E-POWR-CLNG	Power—ceiling receptacles and devices
E-POWR-PANL	Power panels
E-POWR-EQPM	Power equipment
E-POWR-SWBD	Power switchboards
E-POWR-CIRC	Power circuits
E-POWR-URAC	Underfloor raceways
E-POWR-UCPT	Under-carpet wiring
E-POWR-CABL	Cable trays
E-POWR-FEED	Feeders
E-POWR-BUSW	Busways
E-POWR-NUMB	Power circuit numbers
E-POWR-IDEN	Power identification, text
E-POWR-SITE	Site power (see also civil group)
E-POWR-ROOF	Roof power
E-POWR-OTLN	Power outline for backgrounds
E-POWR-JBOX	Junction box
E-CTRL	Electric control systems
E-CTRL-DEVC	Control system devices
E-CTRL-WIRE	Control system wiring
E-GRND	Ground system
E-GRND-CIRC	Ground system circuits
E-GRND-REFR	Reference ground system
E-GRND-EQUI	Equipotential ground system
E-GRND-DIAG	Ground system diagram
E-AUXL	Auxiliary systems
E-LTNG	Lightning protection system
E-FIRE	Fire alarm, fire extinguishers
E-COMM	Telephone, communication outlets
E-DATA	Data outlets
E-SOUN	Sound/PA system
E-TVAN	TV antenna system
E-CCTV	Closed-circuit TV
E-NURS	Nurse call system
E-SERT	Security
E-PGNG	Paging system
E-DICT	Central dictation system
E-BELL	Bell system
E-CLOK	Clock system
E-ALRM	Miscellaneous alarm system
E-INTC	Intercom system
E-LEGN	Legend of symbols
E-1LIN	One-line diagrams
E-RISR	Riser diagram
E-SITE	Site electrical substations, poles
E-SITE-LITE	Site lighting
E-SITE-UNDR	Underground electrical lines
E-SITE-POLE	Electric poles
E-SITE-OVHD	Overhead lines

FIRE PROTECTION LAYERS

F-CO2S	CO_2 system
F-CO2S-PIPE	CO_2 sprinkler piping
F-CO2S-EQPM	CO_2 equipment
F-HALN	Halon
F-HALN-EQPM	Halon equipment
F-HALN-PIPE	Halon piping
F-IGAS	Inert gas
F-IGAS-EQPM	Inert gas equipment
F-IGAS-PIPE	Inert gas piping
F-SPRN	Fire protection sprinkler system
F-SPRN-CLHD	Sprinkler head—ceiling
F-SPRN-OTHD	Sprinkler head—other
F-SPRN-PIPE	Sprinkler piping
F-SPRN-STAN	Sprinkler system standpipe
F-STAN	Fire protection standpipe system
F-PROT	Fire protection systems
F-PROT-EQPM	Fire system equipment (fire hose cabinet extinguishers)
F-PROT-ALRM	Fire alarm
F-PROT-SMOK	Smoke detectors/heat sensors

GENERAL LAYERS

G-PLAN	Floor plan—key plan
G-SITE	Site plan—key map
G-ACCS	Access plan
G-FIRE	Fire protection plan
G-EVAC	Evacuation plan
G-CODE	Code compliance plan

HAZARDOUS LAYERS

H-PLAN	Floor plan
H-SITE	Site plan

Michael K. Schley, AIA, ed., *CAD Layer Guidelines*, 2d ed. (Washington: The American Institute of Architects Press, 1997).

INTERIOR LAYERS

I-WALL-FULL	Full-height walls, stair and shaft walls, walls to structure
I-WALL-PRHT	Partial-height walls (do not appear on reflected ceiling plans)
I-WALL-MOVE	Movable partitions
I-WALL-HEAD	Door and window headers (appear on reflected ceiling plan)
I-WALL-JAMB	Door and window jambs (do not appear on reflected ceiling plans)
I-WALL-PATT	Wall insulation, hatching and fill
I-WALL-ELEV	Wall surfaces: 3D views
I-WALL-FIRE	Fire wall patterning
I-DOOR	Doors
I-DOOR-FULL	Full-height (to ceiling) door: swing and leaf
I-DOOR-PRHT	Partial height door: swing and leaf
I-DOOR-IDEN	Door number, hardware group, etc.
I-DOOR-ELEV	Doors: 3D views
I-GLAZ	Glazing
I-GLAZ-FULL	Full-height glazed walls and partitions
I-GLAZ-PRHT	Windows and partial-height glazed partitions
I-GLAZ-SILL	Windowsills
I-GLAZ-IDEN	Window number
I-GLAZ-ELEV	Glazing and mullions—elevation views
I-FLOR	Floor information
I-FLOR-OTLN	Floor or building outline
I-FLOR-LEVL	Level changes, ramps, pits, depressions
I-FLOR-STRS	Stair treads, escalators, ladders
I-FLOR-RISR	Stair risers
I-FLOR-HRAL	Stair and balcony handrails, guardrails
I-FLOR-EVTR	Elevator cars and equipment
I-FLOR-TPTN	Toilet partitions
I-FLOR-SPCL	Architectural specialties (toilet room accessories, display cases)
I-FLOR-WDWK	Architectural woodwork (field-built cabinets and counters)
I-FLOR-CASE	Casework (manufactured cabinets)
I-FLOR-OVHD	Overhead items (skylights, overhangs—usually dashed lines)
I-FLOR-RAIS	Raised floors
I-FLOR-IDEN	Room numbers, names, targets, etc.
I-FLOR-PATT	Paving, tile, carpet patterns
I-FLOR-PFIX	Plumbing fixtures
I-FLOR-FIXT	Miscellaneous fixtures
I-FLOR-SIGN	Signage
I-EQPM	Equipment
I-EQPM-FIXD	Fixed equipment
I-EQPM-MOVE	Movable equipment
I-EQPM-NICN	Equipment not in contract
I-EQPM-ACCS	Equipment access
I-EQPM-IDEN	Equipment identification numbers
I-EQPM-ELEV	Equipment surfaces: 3D views
I-EQPM-CLNG	Ceiling-mounted or suspended equipment
I-FURN	Furniture
I-FURN-FREE	Furniture: freestanding (desks, credenzas, etc.)
I-FURN-CHAR	Chairs and other seating
I-FURN-FILE	File cabinets
I-FURN-PNLS	Furniture system panels
I-FURN-WKSF	Furniture system work surface components
I-FURN-STOR	Furniture system storage components
I-FURN-POWR	Furniture system—power designations
I-FURN-IDEN	Furniture numbers
I-FURN-PLNT	Plants
I-FURN-PATT	Finish patterns
I-FURN-ELEV	Furniture: 3D views
I-CLNG	Ceiling information
I-CLNG-GRID	Ceiling grid
I-CLNG-OPEN	Ceiling/roof penetrations
I-CLNG-TEES	Main tees
I-CLNG-SUSP	Suspended elements
I-CLNG-PATT	Ceiling patterns
I-CLNG-ACCS	Ceiling access
I-LITE	Light fixtures
I-COLS	Columns
I-HVAC-SDFF	Supply diffusers
I-HVAC-RDFF	Return air diffusers
I-GRID	Planning grid or column grid
I-AREA	Area calculation lines
I-AREA-PATT	Area cross hatching
I-AREA-IDEN	Room numbers, tenant identifications, area calculation
I-AREA-OCCP	Occupant or employee names
I-ELEV	Interior and exterior elevations
I-ELEV-FNSH	Finishes, woodwork, trim
I-ELEV-CASE	Wall-mounted casework
I-ELEV-FIXT	Miscellaneous fixtures
I-ELEV-PFIXT	Plumbing fixtures in elevation
I-ELEV-SIGN	Signage
I-ELEV-PATT	Textures and hatch patterns
I-ELEV-IDEN	Component identification numbers
I-SECT	Sections
I-SECT-MCUT	Material cut by section
I-SECT-MBND	Material beyond section cut
I-SECT-PATT	Textures and hatch patterns
I-SECT-IDEN	Component identification numbers
I-DETL	Details
I-DETL-MCUT	Material cut by section
I-DETL-MBND	Material beyond section cut
I-DETL-PATT	Textures and hatch patterns
I-DETL-IDEN	Component identification numbers

LANDSCAPE LAYERS

L-PLNT	Plant and landscape materials
L-PLNT-TREE	Trees
L-PLNT-GRND	Ground covers and vines
L-PLNT-BEDS	Rock, bark, and other landscaping beds
L-PLNT-TURF	Lawn areas
L-PLNT-PLAN	Planting plants
L-IRRG	Irrigation system
L-IRRG-SPKL	Irrigation sprinklers
L-IRRG-PIPE	Irrigation piping
L-IRRG-EQPT	Irrigation equipment
L-IRRG-COVR	Irrigation coverage
L-WALK	Walks and steps
L-WALK-PATT	Walks and steps—cross-hatch patterns
L-SITE	Site improvements
L-SITE-FENC	Fencing
L-SITE-WALL	Walls
L-SITE-STEP	Steps
L-SITE-DECK	Decks
L-SITE-BRDG	Bridges
L-SITE-POOL	Pools and spas
L-SITE-SPRT	Sports fields
L-SITE-PLAY	Play structures
L-SITE-FURN	Site furnishings

MECHANICAL LAYERS

M-BRIN	Brine systems
M-BRIN-EQPM	Brine system equipment
M-BRIN-PIPE	Brine system piping
M-CHIM	Prefabricated chimneys
M-CMPA	Compressed air systems
M-CMPA-CEQP	Compressed air equipment
M-CMPA-CPIP	Compressed air piping
M-CMPA-PEQP	Process air equipment
M-CMPA-PPIP	Process air piping
M-CONT	Controls and instrumentation
M-CONT-THER	Thermostats
M-CONT-WIRE	Low voltage wiring
M-DUST	Dust and fume collection system
M-DUST-EQPM	Dust and fume collection equipment
M-DUST-DUCT	Dust and fume ductwork
M-ELHT-EQPM	Electric heat equipment
M-ENER	Energy management system
M-ENER-EQPM	Energy management equipment
M-ENER-WIRE	Energy management wiring
M-RCOV	Energy recovery
M-RCOV-EQPM	Energy recovery equipment
M-RCOV-PIPE	Energy recovery piping
M-FUME-EXHS	Fume hood exhaust system
M-FUME-EQPM	Fume hoods
M-EXHS	Exhaust system
M-EXHS-EQPM	Exhaust system equipment
M-EXHS-DUCT	Exhaust system ductwork
M-EXHS-RFEQ	Rooftop exhaust equipment
M-FUEL	Fuel system piping
M-FUEL-GPRP	Fuel gas process piping
M-FUEL-GGEP	Fuel gas general piping
M-FUEL-OPRP	Fuel oil process piping
M-FUEL-OGEP	Fuel oil general piping
M-HVAC	HVAC system
M-HVAC-CDFF	HVAC ceiling diffusers
M-HVAC-ODFF	HVAC other diffusers
M-HVAC-DUCT	HVAC ductwork
M-HVAC-EQPM	HVAC equipment
M-HVAC-SDFF	Supply diffusers
M-HVAC-RDFF	Return air diffusers
M-HOTW	Hot water heating system
M-HOTW-EQPM	Hot water equipment
M-HOTW-PIPE	Hot water piping
M-CWTR	Chilled water systems
M-CWTR-PIPE	Chilled water piping
M-CWTR-EQPM	Chilled water equipment
M-MACH	Machine shop equipment
M-MDGS	Medical gas systems
M-MDGS-EQPM	Medical gas equipment
M-MDGS-PIPE	Medical gas piping
M-LGAS	Laboratory gas systems
M-LGAS-EQPM	Laboratory gas equipment
M-LGAS-PIPE	Laboratory gas piping
M-NGAS	Natural gas systems
M-NGAS-EQPM	Natural gas equipment
M-NGAS-PIPE	Natural gas piping
M-PROC	Process systems
M-PROC-EQPM	Process equipment
M-PROC-PIPE	Process piping
M-REFG	Refrigeration systems
M-REFG-EQPM	Refrigeration equipment
M-REFG-PIPE	Refrigeration piping
M-SPCL	Special systems
M-SPCL-EQPM	Special systems equipment
M-SPCL-PIPE	Special systems piping
M-STEM	Steam systems
M-STEM-CONP	Steam systems condensate piping
M-STEM-EQPM	Steam systems equipment
M-STEM-LPIP	Low pressure steam piping
M-STEM-HPIP	High pressure steam piping
M-STEM-MPIP	Medium pressure steam piping
M-TEST-EQPM	Test equipment

PLUMBING LAYERS

P-ACID	Acid, alkaline, oil waste systems
P-ACID-PIPE	Acid, alkaline, oil waste piping
P-DOMW	Domestic hot and cold water systems
P-DOMW-EQPM	Domestic hot and cold water equipment
P-DOMW-HPIP	Domestic hot water piping
P-DOMW-CPIP	Domestic cold water piping
P-DOMW-RISR	Domestic hot and cold water risers
P-SANR	Sanitary drainage
P-SANR-PIPE	Sanitary piping
P-SANR-FIXT	Plumbing fixtures
P-SANR-FLDR	Floor drains
P-SANR-RISR	Sanitary risers
P-SANR-EQPM	Sanitary equipment
P-STRM	Storm drainage system
P-STRM-PIPE	Storm drain piping
P-STRM-RISR	Storm drain risers
P-STRM-RFDR	Roof drains
P-EQPM	Plumbing—miscellaneous equipment
P-FIXT	Plumbing fixtures

EQUIPMENT LAYERS

Q-OTLN	Equipment outlines
Q-POWR	Power information
Q-PIPE	Piping information

RESOURCE LAYERS

(information provided by product manufacturers)

R-****-OTLN	Outline or profile graphics
R-****-DETL	Additional detail graphics
R-****-PATT	Textures and hatch patterns
R-****-ANNO	Annotation

STRUCTURAL LAYERS

S-GRID	Column grid
S-GRID-EXTR	Column grid outside building
S-GRID-INTR	Column grid inside building
S-GRID-DIMS	Column grid dimensions
S-GRID-IDEN	Column grid tags
S-FNDN	Foundation
S-FNDN-PILE	Piles, drilled piers
S-FNDN-RBAR	Foundation reinforcing
S-SLAB	Slab
S-SLAB-EDGE	Edge of slab
S-SLAB-RBAR	Slab reinforcing
S-SLAB-JOIN	Slab control joints
S-ABLT	Anchor bolts
S-COLS	Columns
S-WALL	Structural bearing or shear walls
S-METL	Miscellaneous metal
S-BEAM	Beams
S-JOIS	Joists
S-DECK	Structural floor deck

TELECOMMUNICATION LAYERS

T-CABL	Cable plan
T-EQPM	Equipment plan
T-JACK	Data/telephone jacks
T-DIAG	Diagram

Michael K. Schley, AIA, ed., *CAD Layer Guidelines*, 2d ed. (Washington: The American Institute of Architects Press, 1997)

INDEX

This is a cumulative index for the ninth edition of *Architectural Graphic Standards* and the *1998 Supplement*. Page references in **boldface** preceded by **S** indicate *Supplement* pages.

NOTE: Page references in **boldface** preceded by **S** indicate *Supplement* pages.

NOTE: Page references in **boldface** preceded by **S** indicate *Supplement* pages.

NOTE: Page references in **boldface** preceded by **S** indicate *Supplement* pages.

NOTE: Page references in **boldface** preceded by **S** indicate *Supplement* pages.

NOTE: Page references in **boldface** preceded by **S** indicate *Supplement* pages.

NOTE: Page references in **boldface** preceded by **S** indicate *Supplement* pages.

NOTE: Page references in **boldface** preceded by **S** indicate *Supplement* pages.

NOTE: Page references in **boldface** preceded by **S** indicate *Supplement* pages.

NOTE: Page references in **boldface** preceded by **S** indicate *Supplement* pages.

NOTE: Page references in **boldface** preceded by **S** indicate *Supplement* pages.

NOTE: Page references in **boldface** preceded by **S** indicate *Supplement* pages.

NOTE: Page references in **boldface** preceded by S indicate *Supplement* pages.

NOTE: Page references in **boldface** preceded by **S** indicate *Supplement* pages.

NOTE: Page references in **boldface** preceded by **S** indicate *Supplement* pages.

NOTE: Page references in **boldface** preceded by **S** indicate *Supplement* pages.

NOTE: Page references in **boldface** preceded by **S** indicate *Supplement* pages.

NOTE: Page references in **boldface** preceded by **S** indicate *Supplement* pages.

NOTE: Page references in **boldface** preceded by **S** indicate *Supplement* pages.

NOTE: Page references in **boldface** preceded by **S** indicate *Supplement* pages.